Presented to

by

on

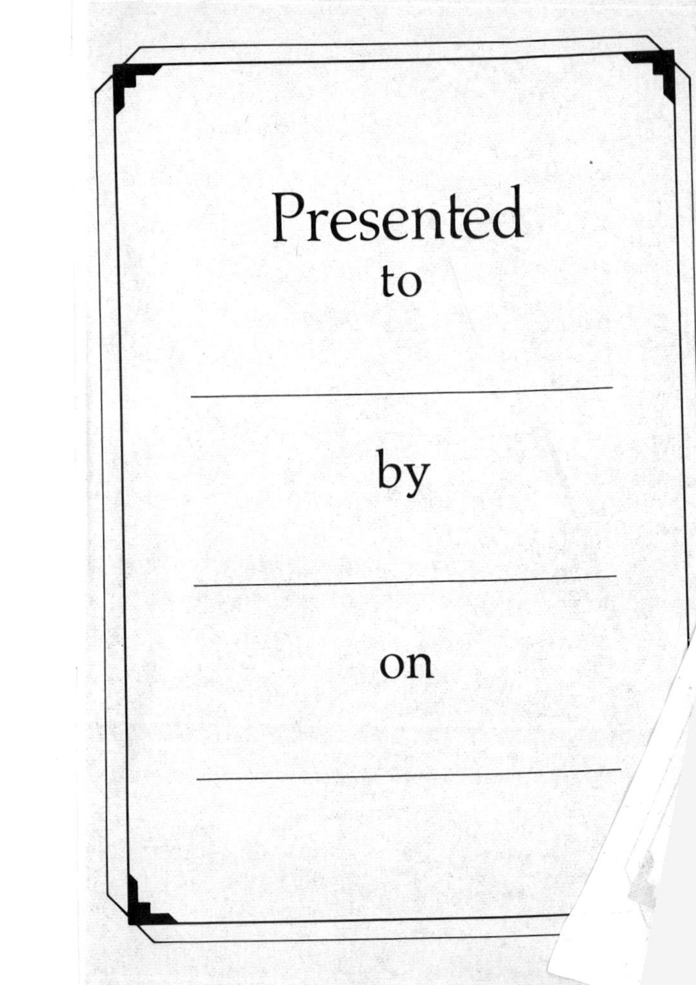
Presented
to
by
on

The HOLY BIBLE

NEW INTERNATIONAL VERSION

Containing The Old Testament and The New Testament

GRAND RAPIDS, MICHIGAN 49530

ZONDERVAN™

NIV Compact Reference

Published by Zondervan
Grand Rapids, Michigan 49530, U.S.A.

www.zondervan.com

Library of Congress Catalog Card Number 73-174297

Printed in China

02 03 04 / TS / 24 23 22 21 20

> You will be pleased to know that a portion o the purchase price of your new NIV Bible has been provided to International Bible Society to help spread the gospel of Jesus Christ around the world!

Contents

THE BOOKS OF *The Old Testament*

THE BOOKS OF *The New Testament*

Maps and Charts

Introduction to the Cross-Reference System

The New International Version has one of the most thorough, accurate and best organized cross-reference systems available. It began with the vision of one individual more than a decade ago and by the time it was completed involved more than forty people and a half-dozen computers.

The cross references link words or phrases in the NIV text with counterpart Biblical references listed in a center column on each page. The raised letters indicating these cross references are set in a light italic typeface to distinguish them from the NIV text note letters, which use a roman typeface. When a single word is addressed by both, the roman NIV text note comes first, as in Matthew 1:21, "Jesus[c] [*i*]."

The lists of references are in Biblical order with one exception: If reference is made to a verse within the same chapter, that verse (indicated by "ver") is listed first.

In the Old Testament some references are marked with an asterisk (*), which means that the Old Testament verse or phrase is quoted in the New Testament (see, for example, Genesis 1:3). The corresponding information is provided in the New Testament by the NIV text note (see 2 Corinthians 4:6).

An important feature of this cross-reference system is in its notation of parallel and reference passages. When two or more sections of Scripture are nearly identical or deal with the same event, "parallel passage" ("pp") is noted at the sectional heading (see Matthew 21:33-46). These parallel passages are especially common in the Gospels and in Samuel, Kings, and Chronicles. When the passages are similar but do not deal with the same event, they are noted with "Ref" at the sectional headings (see Matthew 22:2-14).

To conserve space and avoid repetition, parallel passages or references that are noted at sectional headings are not repeated in the reference column.

Preface

THE NEW INTERNATIONAL VERSION is a completely new translation of the Holy Bible made by over a hundred scholars working directly from the best available Hebrew, Aramaic and Greek texts. It had its beginning in 1965 when, after several years of exploratory study by committees from the Christian Reformed Church and the National Association of Evangelicals, a group of scholars met at Palos Heights, Illinois, and concurred in the need for a new translation of the Bible in contemporary English. This group, though not made up of official church representatives, was transdenominational. Its conclusion was endorsed by a large number of leaders from many denominations who met in Chicago in 1966.

Responsibility for the new version was delegated by the Palos Heights group to a self-governing body of fifteen, the Committee on Bible Translation, composed for the most part of biblical scholars from colleges, universities and seminaries. In 1967 the New York Bible Society (now the International Bible Society) generously undertook the financial sponsorship of the project—a sponsorship that made it possible to enlist the help of many distinguished scholars. The fact that participants from the United States, Great Britain, Canada, Australia and New Zealand worked together gave the project its international scope. That they were from many denominations—including Anglican, Assemblies of God, Baptist, Brethren, Christian Reformed, Church of Christ, Evangelical Free, Lutheran, Mennonite, Methodist, Nazarene, Presbyterian, Wesleyan and other churches—helped to safeguard the translation from sectarian bias.

How it was made helps to give the New International Version its distinctiveness. The translation of each book was assigned to a team of scholars. Next, one of the Intermediate Editorial Committees revised the initial translation, with constant reference to the Hebrew, Aramaic or Greek. Their work then went to one of the General Editorial Committees, which checked it in detail and made another thorough revision. This revision in turn was carefully reviewed by the Committee on Bible Translation, which made further changes and then released the final version for publication. In this way the entire Bible underwent three revisions, during each of which the translation was examined for its faithfulness to the original languages and for its English style.

All this involved many thousands of hours of research and discussion regarding the meaning of the texts and the precise way of putting them into English. It may well be that no other translation has been made by a more thorough process of review and revision from committee to committee than this one.

From the beginning of the project, the Committee on Bible Translation held to certain goals for the New International Version: that it would be an accurate translation and one that would have clarity and literary quality and so prove suitable for public and private reading, teaching, preaching, memorizing and liturgical use. The Committee also sought to preserve some measure of continuity with the long tradition of translating the Scriptures into English.

In working toward these goals, the translators were united in their commitment to the authority and infallibility of the Bible as God's Word in written form. They believe that it contains the divine answer to the deepest needs of humanity, that it sheds unique light on our path in a dark world, and that it sets forth the way to our eternal well-being.

The first concern of the translators has been the accuracy of the translation and its fidelity to the thought of the biblical writers. They have weighed the significance of the lexical and grammatical details of the Hebrew, Aramaic and Greek texts. At the same time, they have striven for more than a word-for-word translation. Because thought patterns and syntax differ from language to language, faithful communication of the meaning of the writers of the Bible demands frequent modifications in sentence structure and constant regard for the contextual meanings of words.

A sensitive feeling for style does not always accompany scholarship. Accordingly the Committee on Bible Translation submitted the developing version to a number of stylistic consultants. Two of them read every book of both Old and New Testaments twice—once before and once after the last major revision—and made invaluable suggestions. Samples of the translation were tested for clarity and ease of reading by various kinds of people—young and old, highly educated and less well educated, ministers and laymen.

Concern for clear and natural English—that the New International Version should be idiomatic but not idiosyncratic, contemporary but not dated—motivated the translators and consultants. At the same time, they tried to reflect the differing styles of the biblical writers. In view of the international use of English, the translators sought to avoid obvious Americanisms on the one hand and obvious Anglicisms on the other. A British edition reflects the comparatively few differences of significant idiom and of spelling.

As for the traditional pronouns "thou," "thee" and "thine" in reference to the Deity, the translators judged that to use these archaisms (along with the old verb forms such as "doest," "wouldest" and "hadst") would violate accuracy in translation. Neither Hebrew, Aramaic nor Greek uses special pronouns for the persons of the Godhead. A present-day translation is not enhanced by forms that in the time of the King James Version were used in everyday speech, whether referring to God or man.

For the Old Testament the standard Hebrew text, the Masoretic Text as published in the latest editions of *Biblia Hebraica,* was used throughout. The Dead Sea Scrolls contain material bearing on an earlier stage of the Hebrew text. They were consulted, as were the Samaritan Pentateuch and the ancient scribal traditions relating to textual changes. Sometimes a variant Hebrew reading in the margin of the Masoretic Text was followed instead of the text itself. Such instances, being variants within the Masoretic tradition, are not specified by footnotes. In rare cases, words in the consonantal text were divided differently from the way they appear in the Masoretic Text. Footnotes indicate this. The translators also consulted the more important early versions—the Septuagint; Aquila, Symmachus and Theodotion; the Vulgate; the Syriac Peshitta; the Targums; and for the Psalms the *Juxta Hebraica* of Jerome. Readings from these versions were occasionally followed where the Masoretic Text seemed doubtful and where accepted principles of textual criticism showed that one or more of these textual witnesses appeared to provide the correct reading. Such instances are footnoted. Sometimes vowel letters and vowel signs did not, in the judgment of the translators, represent the correct vowels for the original consonantal text. Accordingly some words were read with a different set of vowels. These instances are usually not indicated by footnotes.

The Greek text used in translating the New Testament was an eclectic one. No other piece of ancient literature has such an abundance of manuscript witnesses as does the New Testament. Where existing manuscripts differ, the translators made their choice of readings according to accepted principles of New Testament textual criticism. Footnotes call attention to places where there was uncertainty about what the original text was. The best current printed texts of the Greek New Testament were used.

There is a sense in which the work of translation is never wholly finished. This applies to all great literature and uniquely so to the Bible. In 1973 the New Testament in the New International Version was published. Since then, suggestions for corrections and revisions have been received from various sources. The Committee on Bible Translation carefully considered the suggestions and adopted a number of them. These were incorporated in the first printing of the entire Bible in 1978. Additional revisions were made by the Committee on Bible Translation in 1983 and appear in printings after that date.

As in other ancient documents, the precise meaning of the biblical texts is sometimes uncertain. This is more often the case with the Hebrew and Aramaic texts than with the Greek text. Although archaeological and linguistic discoveries in this century aid in understanding difficult passages, some uncertainties remain. The more significant of these have been called to the reader's attention in the footnotes.

In regard to the divine name *YHWH,* commonly referred to as the *Tetragrammaton,* the translators adopted the device used in most English versions of rendering that name as "LORD" in capital letters to distinguish it from *Adonai,* another Hebrew word rendered "Lord," for which small letters are used. Wherever the two names stand together in the Old Testament as a compound name of God, they are rendered "Sovereign LORD."

Because for most readers today the phrases "the LORD of hosts" and "God of hosts" have little meaning, this version renders them "the LORD Almighty" and "God Almighty." These renderings convey the sense of the Hebrew, namely, "he who is sovereign over all the 'hosts' (powers) in heaven and on earth, especially over the 'hosts' (armies) of Israel." For readers unacquainted with Hebrew this does not make clear the distinction between *Sabaoth* ("hosts" or "Almighty") and *Shaddai* (which can also be translated "Almighty"), but the latter occurs infrequently and is always footnoted. When *Adonai* and *YHWH Sabaoth* occur together, they are rendered "the Lord, the LORD Almighty."

As for other proper nouns, the familiar spellings of the King James Version are generally retained. Names traditionally spelled with "ch," except where it is final, are usually spelled in this translation with "k" or "c," since the biblical languages do not have the sound that "ch" frequently indicates in English—for example, in *chant*. For well-known names such as Zechariah, however, the traditional spelling has been retained. Variation in the spelling of names in the original languages has usually not been indicated. Where a person or place has two or more different names in the Hebrew, Aramaic or Greek texts, the more familiar one has generally been used, with footnotes where needed.

To achieve clarity the translators sometimes supplied words not in the original texts but required by the context. If there was uncertainty about such material, it is enclosed in brackets. Also for the sake of clarity or style, nouns, including some proper nouns, are sometimes substituted for pronouns, and vice versa. And though the Hebrew writers often shifted back and forth between first, second and third personal pronouns without change of antecedent, this translation often makes them uniform, in accordance with English style and without the use of footnotes.

Poetical passages are printed as poetry, that is, with indentation of lines and with separate stanzas. These are generally designed to reflect the structure of Hebrew poetry. This poetry is normally characterized by parallelism in balanced lines. Most of the poetry in the Bible is in the Old Testament, and scholars differ regarding the scansion of Hebrew lines. The translators determined the stanza divisions for the most part by analysis of the subject matter. The stanzas therefore serve as poetic paragraphs.

As an aid to the reader, italicized sectional headings are inserted in most of the books. They are not to be regarded as part of the NIV text, are not for oral reading, and are not intended to dictate the interpretation of the sections they head.

The footnotes in this version are of several kinds, most of which need no explanation. Those giving alternative translations begin with "Or" and generally introduce the alternative with the last word preceding it in the text, except when it is a single-word alternative; in poetry quoted in a footnote a slant mark indicates a line division. Footnotes introduced by "Or" do not have uniform significance. In some cases two possible translations were considered to have about equal validity. In other cases, though the translators were convinced that the translation in the text was correct, they judged that another interpretation was possible and of sufficient importance to be represented in a footnote.

In the New Testament, footnotes that refer to uncertainty regarding the original text are introduced by "Some manuscripts" or similar expressions. In the Old Testament, evidence for the reading chosen is given first and evidence for the alternative is added after a semicolon (for example: Septuagint; Hebrew *father*). In such notes the term "Hebrew" refers to the Masoretic Text.

It should be noted that minerals, flora and fauna, architectural details, articles of clothing and jewelry, musical instruments and other articles cannot always be identified with precision. Also measures of capacity in the biblical period are particularly uncertain (see the table of weights and measures following the text).

Like all translations of the Bible, made as they are by imperfect man, this one undoubtedly falls short of its goals. Yet we are grateful to God for the extent to which he has enabled us to realize these goals and for the strength he has given us and our colleagues to complete our task. We offer this version of the Bible to him in whose name and for whose glory it has been made. We pray that it will lead many into a better understanding of the Holy Scriptures and a fuller knowledge of Jesus Christ the incarnate Word, of whom the Scriptures so faithfully testify.

The Committee on Bible Translation

June 1978
(Revised August 1983)

Names of the translators and editors may be secured from the International Bible Society, translation sponsors of the New International Version, 1820 Jet Stream Drive, Colorado Springs, Colorado, 80921-3696 U.S.A.

The Old Testament

Genesis

Title and Background

The first phrase in the Hebrew text of Genesis 1:1 means "In the beginning." The book of Genesis is about many beginnings—the beginning of the universe, the beginning of man and woman, the beginning of human sin, and the beginning of God's promises and plans for salvation.

Author and Date of Writing

Jews and Christians alike hold that Moses was the author/compiler of Genesis, the first of the five books of the Old Testament known as the Pentateuch (meaning "five-volumed book").

The historical period during which Moses lived is most likely the one referred to in 1 Kings 6:1, which states that "the fourth year of Solomon's reign over Israel" was the same as "the four hundred and eightieth year after the Israelites had come out of Egypt." Since the former was about 966 B.C., the latter—and thus the date of the exodus—was about 1446 B.C. The forty-year period of Israel's wanderings in the desert, which lasted from about 1446 to about 1406 B.C., would have been the most likely time for Moses to write Genesis.

Theme and Message

The message of Genesis is rich and complex, but it is mainly a book of relationships, highlighting those between God and nature, God and man, and man and man. It stresses the fact that the one true God is sovereign over all that exists, whether good or evil. It introduces us to the way in which God initiates and enters into covenants with his chosen people, pledging his love and faithfulness to them.

Outline

- I. Primeval History: Four Great Events (1:1-11:32)
  - A. The Creation of the Universe, Adam and Eve (1:1-2:25)
  - B. Man's Fall and the Results of Sin (3:1-5:32)
  - C. The Flood (6:1-9:29)
  - D. The Scattering of the Nations (10:1-11:32)
- II. Patriarchal History: Four Great Characters (12:1-50:26)
  - A. Abraham (12:1-20:18)
  - B. Isaac (21:1-26:35)
  - C. Jacob (27:1-37:1)
  - D. Joseph (37:2-50:26)

The Beginning

1 In the beginning[a] God created the heavens and the
earth.[b] 2Now the earth was[a]
formless and empty,[c] darkness was over the surface of
the deep, and the Spirit of
God[d] was hovering over the
waters.
3And God said,[e] "Let there be
light," and there was light.[f]
4God saw that the light was
good, and he separated the
light from the darkness. 5God
called the light "day," and the
darkness he called "night."[g]

1:1 [a]Jn 1:1-2 [b]Ps 90:2; Isa 42:5; Ac 17:24 Rev 4:11 **1:2** [c]Jer 4:23 [d]Ps 104:30 **1:3** [e]Ps 33:6,9; [f]2Co 4:6* **1:5** [g]Ps 74:16

[a]2 Or possibly *became*

And there was evening, and
there was morning—the first
day.
6And God said, "Let there be an
expanse[a] between the waters
to separate water from water."
7So God made the expanse
and separated the water under the expanse from the water above it.[b] And it was so.
8God called the expanse
"sky." And there was evening,
and there was morning—the
second day.
9And God said, "Let the water under the sky be gathered to one
place,[c] and let dry ground appear." And it was so. **10**God
called the dry ground "land,"
and the gathered waters he
called "seas." And God saw
that it was good.
11Then God said, "Let the
land produce vegetation:[d]
seed-bearing plants and trees
on the land that bear fruit
with seed in it, according to
their various kinds." And it
was so. **12**The land produced
vegetation: plants bearing
seed according to their kinds
and trees bearing fruit with
seed in it according to their
kinds. And God saw that it
was good. **13**And there was
evening, and there was morning—the third day.
14And God said, "Let there be
lights[e] in the expanse of the
sky to separate the day from
the night, and let them serve
as signs[f] to mark seasons[g]
and days and years, **15**and let
them be lights in the expanse
of the sky to give light on the
earth." And it was so. **16**God
made two great lights—the
greater light to govern[h] the
day and the lesser light to govern[i] the night. He also made
the stars.[j] **17**God set them in
the expanse of the sky to give
light on the earth, **18**to govern
the day and the night,[k] and to
separate light from darkness.
And God saw that it was good.
19And there was evening, and

1:6 [a] Jer 10:12
1:7 [b] Job 38:8-11, 16; Ps 148:4
1:9 [c] Job 38:8-11; Ps 104:6-9; Pr 8:29; Jer 5:22; 2Pe 3:5
1:11 [d] Ps 65:9-13; 104:14
1:14 [e] Ps 74:16 [f] Jer 10:2 [g] Ps 104:19
1:16 [h] Ps 136:8 [i] Ps 136:9 [j] Job 38:7, 31-32; Ps 8:3; Isa 40:26
1:18 [k] Jer 33:20,25
1:21 [l] Ps 104:25-26
1:22 [m] ver 28; Ge 8:17
1:25 [n] Jer 27:5
1:26 [o] Ps 100:3 [p] Ge 9:6; Jas 3:9 [q] Ps 8:6-8
1:27 [r] 1Co 11:7 [s] Ge 5:2; Mt 19:4*; Mk 10:6*
1:28 [t] Ge 9:1,7; Lev 26:9

there was morning—the
fourth day.
20And God said, "Let the water
teem with living creatures,
and let birds fly above the
earth across the expanse of
the sky." **21**So God created
the great creatures of the sea
and every living and moving
thing with which the water
teems,[l] according to their
kinds, and every winged bird
according to its kind. And
God saw that it was good.
22God blessed them and said,
"Be fruitful and increase in
number and fill the water in
the seas, and let the birds increase on the earth."[m] **23**And
there was evening, and there
was morning—the fifth day.
24And God said, "Let the land
produce living creatures according to their kinds: livestock, creatures that move
along the ground, and wild
animals, each according to its
kind." And it was so. **25**God
made the wild animals[n] according to their kinds, the
livestock according to their
kinds, and all the creatures
that move along the ground
according to their kinds. And
God saw that it was good.
26Then God said, "Let us[o]
make man in our image,[p] in
our likeness, and let them
rule[q] over the fish of the sea
and the birds of the air, over
the livestock, over all the
earth,[b] and over all the creatures that move along the
ground."

27So God created man in his own
image,[r]
in the image of God he
created him;
male and female[s] he created
them.

28God blessed them and
said to them, "Be fruitful and
increase in number; fill the
earth[t] and subdue it. Rule

[b]26 Hebrew; Syriac *all the wild animals*

over the fish of the sea and the
birds of the air and over every
living creature that moves on
the ground."
29Then God said, "I give you
every seed-bearing plant on
the face of the whole earth
and every tree that has fruit
with seed in it. They will be
yours for food.[a] 30And to all
the beasts of the earth and all
the birds of the air and all the
creatures that move on the
ground—everything that has
the breath of life in it—I give
every green plant for food.[b]"
And it was so.
31God saw all that he had
made,[c] and it was very
good.[d] And there was evening, and there was morning
—the sixth day.

2 Thus the heavens and the
earth were completed in all
their vast array.

2By the seventh day God had finished the work he had been
doing; so on the seventh day
he rested[c] from all his work.[e]
3And God blessed the seventh
day and made it holy,[f] because on it he rested from all
the work of creating that he
had done.

Adam and Eve

4This is the account of the heavens and the earth when they were
created.

When the LORD God made the
earth and the heavens— 5and no
shrub of the field had yet appeared
on the earth[d] and no plant of the
field had yet sprung up,[g] for the
LORD God had not sent rain on the
earth[d][h] and there was no man to
work the ground, 6but streams[e]
came up from the earth and watered the whole surface of the
ground— 7the LORD God formed
the man[f] from the dust[i] of the
ground[j] and breathed into his
nostrils the breath[k] of life,[l] and
the man became a living being.[m]
8Now the LORD God had planted
a garden in the east, in Eden;[n] and
there he put the man he had
formed. 9And the LORD God made
all kinds of trees grow out of the
ground—trees that were pleasing
to the eye and good for food. In the
middle of the garden were the tree
of life[o] and the tree of the knowledge of good and evil.[p]

10A river watering the garden
flowed from Eden; from there it
was separated into four headwa-
ters. 11The name of the first is the
Pishon; it winds through the entire
land of Havilah, where there is
gold. 12(The gold of that land is
good; aromatic resin[g] and onyx are
also there.) 13The name of the second river is the Gihon; it winds
through the entire land of Cush.[h]
14The name of the third river is the
Tigris;[q] it runs along the east side
of Asshur. And the fourth river is
the Euphrates.

15The LORD God took the man
and put him in the Garden of Eden
to work it and take care of it. 16And
the LORD God commanded the
man, "You are free to eat from any
tree in the garden; 17but you must
not eat from the tree of the knowledge of good and evil, for when you
eat of it you will surely die."[r]

18The LORD God said, "It is not
good for the man to be alone. I will
make a helper suitable for him."[s]

19Now the LORD God had formed
out of the ground all the beasts of
the field[t] and all the birds of the
air. He brought them to the man to
see what he would name them; and
whatever the man called each living creature,[u] that was its name.
20So the man gave names to all the
livestock, the birds of the air and
all the beasts of the field.

But for Adam[i] no suitable helper was found. 21So the LORD God
caused the man to fall into a deep
sleep; and while he was sleeping,

1:29 [a]Ps 104:14
1:30 [b]Ps 104:14, 27; 145:15
1:31 [c]Ps 104:24 [d]1Ti 4:4
2:2 [e]Ex 20:11; 31:17; Heb 4:4*
2:3 [f]Lev 23:3; Isa 58:13
2:5 [g]Ge 1:11 [h]Ps 65:9-10
2:7 [i]Ge 3:19 [j]Ps 103:14 [k]Job 33:4 [l]Ac 17:25 [m]1Co 15:45*
2:8 [n]Ge 3:23,24; Isa 51:3
2:9 [o]Ge 3:22,24; Rev 2:7; 22:2, 14,19 [p]Eze 47:12
2:14 [q]Da 10:4
2:17 [r]Dt 30:15,19; Ro 5:12; 6:23; Jas 1:15
2:18 [s]1Co 11:9
2:19 [t]Ps 8:7 [u]Ge 1:24

[c]*2* Or *ceased*; also in verse 3 [d]*5* Or *land*; also in verse 6 [e]*6* Or *mist* [f]*7* The Hebrew for *man (adam)* sounds like and may be related to the Hebrew for *ground (adamah)*; it is also the name *Adam* (see Gen. 2:20). [g]*12* Or *good; pearls* [h]*13* Possibly southeast Mesopotamia [i]*20* Or *the man*

he took one of the man's ribs[j] and closed up the place with flesh. 22Then the LORD God made a woman from the rib[k][a] he had taken out of the man, and he brought her to the man.

23The man said,

"This is now bone of my bones
and flesh of my flesh;[b]
she shall be called 'woman,[l]'
for she was taken out of man."

24For this reason a man will leave his father and mother and be united[c] to his wife, and they will become one flesh.[d]

25The man and his wife were both naked,[e] and they felt no shame.

The Fall of Man

3 Now the serpent[f] was more crafty than any of the wild animals the LORD God had made. He said to the woman, "Did God really say, 'You must not eat from any tree in the garden'?"

2The woman said to the serpent, "We may eat fruit from the trees in the garden, 3but God did say, 'You must not eat fruit from the tree that is in the middle of the garden, and you must not touch it, or you will die.' "

4"You will not surely die," the serpent said to the woman.[g] 5"For God knows that when you eat of it your eyes will be opened, and you will be like God,[h] knowing good and evil."

6When the woman saw that the fruit of the tree was good for food and pleasing to the eye, and also desirable[i] for gaining wisdom, she took some and ate it. She also gave some to her husband, who was with her, and he ate it.[j] 7Then the eyes of both of them were opened, and they realized they were naked; so they sewed fig leaves together and made coverings for themselves.

8Then the man and his wife heard the sound of the LORD God as he was walking[k] in the garden in the cool of the day, and they hid[l] from the LORD God among the trees of the garden. 9But the LORD God called to the man, "Where are you?"

10He answered, "I heard you in the garden, and I was afraid because I was naked; so I hid."

11And he said, "Who told you that you were naked? Have you eaten from the tree that I commanded you not to eat from?"

12The man said, "The woman you put here with me—she gave me some fruit from the tree, and I ate it."

13Then the LORD God said to the woman, "What is this you have done?"

The woman said, "The serpent deceived me,[m] and I ate."

14So the LORD God said to the serpent, "Because you have done this,

"Cursed[n] are you above all the livestock
and all the wild animals!
You will crawl on your belly
and you will eat dust[o]
all the days of your life.
15And I will put enmity
between you and the woman,
and between your
offspring[m][p] and hers;[q]
he will crush[n] your head,[r]
and you will strike his heel."

16To the woman he said,

"I will greatly increase your
pains in childbearing;
with pain you will give birth
to children.
Your desire will be for your
husband,
and he will rule over you.[s]"

17To Adam he said, "Because you listened to your wife and ate from the tree about which I commanded you, 'You must not eat of it,'

"Cursed[t] is the ground
because of you;

2:22 [a] 1Co 11:8,9, 12
2:23 [b] Ge 29:14; Eph 5:28-30
2:24 [c] Mal 2:15 [d] Mt 19:5*; Mk 10:7-8*; 1Co 6:16*; Eph 5:31*
2:25 [e] Ge 3:7,10-11
3:1 [f] 2Co 11:3; Rev 12:9; 20:2
3:4 [g] Jn 8:44; 2Co 11:3
3:5 [h] Isa 14:14; Eze 28:2
3:6 [i] Jas 1:14-15; 1Jn 2:16 [j] 1Ti 2:14
3:8 [k] Dt 23:14 [l] Job 31:33; Ps 139:7-12; Jer 23:24
3:13 [m] 2Co 11:3; 1Ti 2:14
3:14 [n] Dt 28:15-20 [o] Isa 65:25; Mic 7:17
3:15 [p] Jn 8:44; Ac 13:10; 1Jn 3:8 [q] Isa 7:14; Mt 1:23; Rev 12:17 [r] Ro 16:20; Heb 2:14
3:16 [s] 1Co 11:3; Eph 5:22
3:17 [t] Ge 5:29; Ro 8:20-22

[j] *21* Or *took part of the man's side* [k] *22* Or *part* [l] *23* The Hebrew for *woman* sounds like the Hebrew for *man.* [m] *15* Or *seed* [n] *15* Or *strike*

through painful toil you will
eat of it
all the days of your life.[a]
18It will produce thorns and
thistles for you,
and you will eat the plants of
the field.[b]
19By the sweat of your brow
you will eat your food[c]
until you return to the ground,
since from it you were taken;
for dust you are
and to dust you will
return."[d]

20Adam[o] named his wife Eve,[p]
because she would become the
mother of all the living.
21The LORD God made garments
of skin for Adam and his wife and
clothed them. **22**And the LORD God
said, "The man has now become
like one of us, knowing good and
evil. He must not be allowed to
reach out his hand and take also
from the tree of life[e] and eat, and
live forever." **23**So the LORD God
banished him from the Garden of
Eden[f] to work the ground[g] from
which he had been taken. **24**After
he drove the man out, he placed on
the east side[q] of the Garden of
Eden cherubim[h] and a flaming
sword[i] flashing back and forth to
guard the way to the tree of life.[j]

Cain and Abel

4 Adam[o] lay with his wife Eve,
and she became pregnant and
gave birth to Cain.[r] She said,
"With the help of the LORD I have
brought forth[s] a man." **2**Later she
gave birth to his brother Abel.[k]
Now Abel kept flocks, and Cain
worked the soil. **3**In the course of
time Cain brought some of the
fruits of the soil as an offering to
the LORD.[l] **4**But Abel brought fat
portions[m] from some of the firstborn of his flock.[n] The LORD looked
with favor on Abel and his offering,[o] **5**but on Cain and his offering
he did not look with favor. So Cain
was very angry, and his face was
downcast.
6Then the LORD said to Cain,
"Why are you angry? Why is your
face downcast? **7**If you do what is
right, will you not be accepted? But
if you do not do what is right, sin is
crouching at your door;[p] it desires
to have you, but you must master
it.[q]"
8Now Cain said to his brother
Abel, "Let's go out to the field."[t]
And while they were in the field,
Cain attacked his brother Abel and
killed him.[r]
9Then the LORD said to Cain,
"Where is your brother Abel?"
"I don't know," he replied. "Am I
my brother's keeper?"
10The LORD said, "What have you
done? Listen! Your brother's blood
cries out to me from the ground.[s]
11Now you are under a curse and
driven from the ground, which
opened its mouth to receive your
brother's blood from your hand.
12When you work the ground, it
will no longer yield its crops for
you. You will be a restless wanderer
on the earth."
13Cain said to the LORD, "My
punishment is more than I can
bear. **14**Today you are driving me
from the land, and I will be hidden
from your presence;[t] I will be a
restless wanderer on the earth, and
whoever finds me will kill me."[u]
15But the LORD said to him, "Not
so[u]; if anyone kills Cain[v], he will
suffer vengeance seven times
over.[w]" Then the LORD put a mark
on Cain so that no one who found
him would kill him. **16**So Cain went
out from the LORD's presence and
lived in the land of Nod,[v] east of
Eden.[x]
17Cain lay with his wife, and she
became pregnant and gave birth to
Enoch. Cain was then building a
city, and he named it after his son[y]
Enoch. **18**To Enoch was born Irad,
and Irad was the father of Mehuja-

3:17 [a]Job 5:7; 14:1; Ecc 2:23
3:18 [b]Ps 104:14
3:19 [c]2Th 3:10 [d]Ge 2:7; Ps 90:3; 104:29; Ecc 12:7
3:22 [e]Rev 22:14
3:23 [f]Ge 2:8 [g]Ge 4:2
3:24 [h]Ex 25:18-22 [i]Ps 104:4 [j]Ge 2:9
4:2 [k]Lk 11:51
4:3 [l]Nu 18:12
4:4 [m]Lev 3:16 [n]Ex 13:2,12 [o]Heb 11:4
4:7 [p]Nu 32:23 [q]Ro 6:16
4:8 [r]Mt 23:35; 1Jn 3:12
4:10 [s]Ge 9:5; Nu 35:33; Heb 12:24; Rev 6:9-10
4:14 [t]2Ki 17:18; Ps 51:11; 139:7-12; Jer 7:15; 52:3 [u]Ge 9:6; Nu 35:19,21, 27,33
4:15 [v]Eze 9:4,6 [w]ver 24; Ps 79:12
4:16 [x]Ge 2:8
4:17 [y]Ps 49:11

[o]*20,1* Or *The man* [p]*20* *Eve* probably means *living.* [q]*24* Or *placed in front* [r]*1* *Cain* sounds like the Hebrew for *brought forth* or *acquired.* [s]*1* Or *have acquired*
[t]*8* Samaritan Pentateuch, Septuagint, Vulgate and Syriac; Masoretic Text does not have *"Let's go out to the field."* [u]*15* Septuagint, Vulgate and Syriac; Hebrew *Very well*
[v]*16* *Nod* means *wandering* (see verses 12 and 14).

el, and Mehujael was the father of Methushael, and Methushael was the father of Lamech.

[19]Lamech married two women, one named Adah and the other Zillah. [20]Adah gave birth to Jabal; he was the father of those who live in tents and raise livestock. [21]His brother's name was Jubal; he was the father of all who play the harp and flute. [22]Zillah also had a son, Tubal-Cain, who forged all kinds of tools out of[w] bronze and iron. Tubal-Cain's sister was Naamah.

[23]Lamech said to his wives,

"Adah and Zillah, listen to me;
wives of Lamech, hear my words.
I have killed[x][a] a man for wounding me,
a young man for injuring me.
[24]If Cain is avenged[b] seven times,[c]
then Lamech seventy-seven times."

[25]Adam lay with his wife again, and she gave birth to a son and named him Seth,[y][d] saying, "God has granted me another child in place of Abel, since Cain killed him."[e] [26]Seth also had a son, and he named him Enosh.

At that time men began to call on[z] the name of the LORD.[f]

From Adam to Noah

5 This is the written account of Adam's line.

When God created man, he made him in the likeness of God.[g] [2]He created them male and female[h] and blessed them. And when they were created, he called them "man.[a]"

[3]When Adam had lived 130 years, he had a son in his own likeness, in his own image;[i] and he named him Seth. [4]After Seth was born, Adam lived 800 years and had other sons and daughters. [5]Altogether, Adam lived 930 years, and then he died.[j]

[6]When Seth had lived 105 years, he became the father[b] of Enosh. [7]And after he became the father of Enosh, Seth lived 807 years and had other sons and daughters. [8]Altogether, Seth lived 912 years, and then he died.

[9]When Enosh had lived 90 years, he became the father of Kenan. [10]And after he became the father of Kenan, Enosh lived 815 years and had other sons and daughters. [11]Altogether, Enosh lived 905 years, and then he died.

[12]When Kenan had lived 70 years, he became the father of Mahalalel. [13]And after he became the father of Mahalalel, Kenan lived 840 years and had other sons and daughters. [14]Altogether, Kenan lived 910 years, and then he died.

[15]When Mahalalel had lived 65 years, he became the father of Jared. [16]And after he became the father of Jared, Mahalalel lived 830 years and had other sons and daughters. [17]Altogether, Mahalalel lived 895 years, and then he died.

[18]When Jared had lived 162 years, he became the father of Enoch.[k] [19]And after he became the father of Enoch, Jared lived 800 years and had other sons and daughters. [20]Altogether, Jared lived 962 years, and then he died.

[21]When Enoch had lived 65 years, he became the father of Methuselah. [22]And after he became the father of Methuselah, Enoch walked with God[l] 300 years and had other sons and daughters. [23]Altogether, Enoch lived 365 years. [24]Enoch walked with God;[m] then he was no more, because God took him away.[n]

[25]When Methuselah had lived 187 years, he became the father of Lamech. [26]And after he became the father of Lamech, Methuselah lived 782 years and had other sons and daughters. [27]Altogether, Methuselah lived 969 years, and then he died.

[28]When Lamech had lived 182 years, he had a son. [29]He named

4:23 [a]Ex 20:13; Lev 19:18
4:24 [b]Dt 32:35 [c]ver 15
4:25 [d]Ge 5:3 [e]ver 8
4:26 [f]Ge 12:8; 1Ki 18:24; Ps 116:17; Joel 2:32; Zep 3:9; Ac 2:21; 1Co 1:2
5:1 [g]Ge 1:27; Eph 4:24; Col 3:10
5:2 [h]Ge 1:27; Mt 19:4; Mk 10:6; Gal 3:28
5:3 [i]Ge 1:26; 1Co 15:49
5:5 [j]Ge 3:19
5:18 [k]Jude 1:14
5:22 [l]ver 24; Ge 6:9; 17:1; 48:15; Mic 6:8; Mal 2:6
5:24 [m]ver 22 [n]2Ki 2:1,11; Heb 11:5

[w]*22* Or *who instructed all who work in* [x]*23* Or *I will kill* [y]*25* *Seth* probably means *granted.* [z]*26* Or *to proclaim* [a]*2* Hebrew *adam* [b]*6* *Father* may mean *ancestor;* also in verses 7-26.

him Noah[c] and said, "He will comfort us in the labor and painful toil
of our hands caused by the ground
the LORD has cursed.[a]" **30**After
Noah was born, Lamech lived 595
years and had other sons and
daughters. **31**Altogether, Lamech
lived 777 years, and then he died.
32After Noah was 500 years old,
he became the father of Shem,
Ham and Japheth.

The Flood

6 When men began to increase
in number on the earth[b] and
daughters were born to them, **2**the
sons of God saw that the daughters
of men were beautiful, and they
married any of them they chose.
3Then the LORD said, "My Spirit will
not contend with[d] man forever,[c]
for he is mortal[e];[d] his days will be
a hundred and twenty years."
4The Nephilim[e] were on the
earth in those days—and also afterward—when the sons of God
went to the daughters of men and
had children by them. They were
the heroes of old, men of renown.
5The LORD saw how great man's
wickedness on the earth had become, and that every inclination of
the thoughts of his heart was only
evil all the time.[f] **6**The LORD was
grieved[g] that he had made man on
the earth, and his heart was filled
with pain. **7**So the LORD said, "I will
wipe mankind, whom I have created, from the face of the earth—
men and animals, and creatures
that move along the ground, and
birds of the air—for I am grieved
that I have made them." **8**But Noah
found favor in the eyes of the
LORD.[h]

9This is the account of Noah.

Noah was a righteous man,
blameless among the people of his
time,[i] and he walked with God.[j]
10Noah had three sons: Shem,
Ham and Japheth.[k]
11Now the earth was corrupt in
God's sight and was full of violence.[l] **12**God saw how corrupt the
earth had become, for all the people on earth had corrupted their
ways.[m] **13**So God said to Noah, "I
am going to put an end to all people, for the earth is filled with violence because of them. I am surely
going to destroy both them and the
earth.[n] **14**So make yourself an ark
of cypress[f] wood;[o] make rooms in
it and coat it with pitch[p] inside
and out. **15**This is how you are to
build it: The ark is to be 450 feet
long, 75 feet wide and 45 feet
high.[g] **16**Make a roof for it and finish[h] the ark to within 18 inches[i]
of the top. Put a door in the side of
the ark and make lower, middle
and upper decks. **17**I am going to
bring floodwaters on the earth to
destroy all life under the heavens,
every creature that has the breath
of life in it. Everything on earth will
perish.[q] **18**But I will establish my
covenant with you,[r] and you will
enter the ark[s]—you and your sons
and your wife and your sons' wives
with you. **19**You are to bring into
the ark two of all living creatures,
male and female, to keep them
alive with you. **20**Two[t] of every
kind of bird, of every kind of animal
and of every kind of creature that
moves along the ground will come
to you to be kept alive. **21**You are to
take every kind of food that is to be
eaten and store it away as food for
you and for them."
22Noah did everything just as
God commanded him.[u]

7 The LORD then said to Noah,
"Go into the ark, you and your
whole family,[v] because I have
found you righteous[w] in this generation. **2**Take with you seven[j] of every kind of clean[x] animal, a male
and its mate, and two of every kind
of unclean animal, a male and its
mate, **3**and also seven of every kind
of bird, male and female, to keep
their various kinds alive through-

5:29 [a]Ge 3:17; Ro 8:20
6:1 [b]Ge 1:28
6:3 [c]Isa 57:16 [d]Ps 78:39
6:4 [e]Nu 13:33
6:5 [f]Ge 8:21; Ps 14:1-3
6:6 [g]1Sa 15:11, 35; Isa 63:10
6:8 [h]Ge 19:19; Ex 33:12,13, 17; Lk 1:30; Ac 7:46
6:9 [i]Ge 7:1; Eze 14:14,20; Heb 11:7; 2Pe 2:5 [j]Ge 5:22
6:10 [k]Ge 5:32
6:11 [l]Eze 7:23; 8:17
6:12 [m]Ps 14:1-3
6:13 [n]ver 17; Eze 7:2-3
6:14 [o]Heb 11:7; 1Pe 3:20 [p]Ex 2:3
6:17 [q]Ge 7:4, 21-23; 2Pe 2:5
6:18 [r]Ge 9:9-16 [s]Ge 7:1,7,13
6:20 [t]Ge 7:15
6:22 [u]Ge 7:5,9,16
7:1 [v]Mt 24:38 [w]Ge 6:9; Eze 14:14
7:2 [x]ver 8; Ge 8:20; Lev 10:10; 11:1-47

[c]29 *Noah* sounds like the Hebrew for *comfort.* [d]3 Or *My spirit will not remain in* [e]3 Or *corrupt* [f]14 The meaning of the Hebrew for this word is uncertain. [g]15 Hebrew *300 cubits long, 50 cubits wide and 30 cubits high* (about 140 meters long, 23 meters wide and 13.5 meters high) [h]16 Or *Make an opening for light by finishing* [i]16 Hebrew *a cubit* (about 0.5 meter) [j]2 Or *seven pairs*; also in verse 3

out the earth. 4 Seven days from
now I will send rain on the earth for
forty days and forty nights, and
I will wipe from the face of the
earth every living creature I have
made."
5 And Noah did all that the LORD
commanded him.[a]
6 Noah was six hundred years old
when the floodwaters came on the
earth. 7 And Noah and his sons and
his wife and his sons' wives entered
the ark to escape the waters of the
flood. 8 Pairs of clean and unclean
animals, of birds and of all creatures that move along the ground,
9 male and female, came to Noah
and entered the ark, as God had
commanded Noah. 10 And after the
seven days the floodwaters came
on the earth.
11 In the six hundredth year of
Noah's life, on the seventeenth day
of the second month—on that day
all the springs of the great deep[b]
burst forth, and the floodgates of
the heavens[c] were opened. 12 And
rain fell on the earth forty days and
forty nights.[d]
13 On that very day Noah and his
sons, Shem, Ham and Japheth, together with his wife and the wives
of his three sons, entered the ark.
14 They had with them every wild
animal according to its kind, all
livestock according to their kinds,
every creature that moves along the
ground according to its kind and
every bird according to its kind, everything with wings. 15 Pairs of all
creatures that have the breath of
life in them came to Noah and entered the ark.[e] 16 The animals going in were male and female of every living thing, as God had commanded Noah. Then the LORD shut
him in.
17 For forty days[f] the flood kept
coming on the earth, and as the waters increased they lifted the ark
high above the earth. 18 The waters
rose and increased greatly on the
earth, and the ark floated on the
surface of the water. 19 They rose
greatly on the earth, and all the
high mountains under the entire
heavens were covered.[g] 20 The waters rose and covered the mountains to a depth of more than twenty feet.[k,l] 21 Every living thing
that moved on the earth perished
—birds, livestock, wild animals, all
the creatures that swarm over the
earth, and all mankind.[h] 22 Everything on dry land that had the
breath of life[i] in its nostrils died.
23 Every living thing on the face of
the earth was wiped out; men and
animals and the creatures that
move along the ground and the
birds of the air were wiped from the
earth.[j] Only Noah was left, and
those with him in the ark.[k]
24 The waters flooded the earth
for a hundred and fifty days.[l]

8 But God remembered[m] Noah
and all the wild animals and
the livestock that were with him in
the ark, and he sent a wind over the
earth,[n] and the waters receded.
2 Now the springs of the deep and
the floodgates of the heavens[o] had
been closed, and the rain had
stopped falling from the sky. 3 The
water receded steadily from the
earth. At the end of the hundred
and fifty days the water had gone
down, 4 and on the seventeenth day
of the seventh month the ark came
to rest on the mountains of Ararat.
5 The waters continued to recede
until the tenth month, and on the
first day of the tenth month the
tops of the mountains became visible.
6 After forty days Noah opened
the window he had made in the ark
7 and sent out a raven, and it kept
flying back and forth until the water had dried up from the earth.
8 Then he sent out a dove to see if
the water had receded from the
surface of the ground. 9 But the
dove could find no place to set its
feet because there was water over
all the surface of the earth; so it returned to Noah in the ark. He
reached out his hand and took the
dove and brought it back to himself
in the ark. 10 He waited seven more

7:5 [a]Ge 6:22
7:11 [b]Eze 26:19 [c]Ge 8:2
7:12 [d]ver 4
7:15 [e]Ge 6:19
7:17 [f]ver 4
7:19 [g]Ps 104:6
7:21 [h]Ge 6:7,13
7:22 [i]Ge 1:30
7:23 [j]Mt 24:39; Lk 17:27; 1Pe 3:20; 2Pe 2:5 [k]Heb 11:7
7:24 [l]Ge 8:3
8:1 [m]Ge 9:15; 19:29; Ex 2:24; 1Sa 1:11,19 [n]Ex 14:21
8:2 [o]Ge 7:11

[k]20 Hebrew *fifteen cubits* (about 6.9 meters)
[l]20 Or *rose more than twenty feet, and the mountains were covered*

days and again sent out the dove
from the ark. 11When the dove returned to him in the evening, there
in its beak was a freshly plucked
olive leaf! Then Noah knew that
the water had receded from the
earth. 12He waited seven more
days and sent the dove out again,
but this time it did not return to
him.

13By the first day of the first
month of Noah's six hundred and
first year, the water had dried up
from the earth. Noah then removed
the covering from the ark and saw
that the surface of the ground was
dry. 14By the twenty-seventh day of
the second month the earth was
completely dry.

15Then God said to Noah,
16"Come out of the ark, you and
your wife and your sons and their
wives.[a] 17Bring out every kind of
living creature that is with you—
the birds, the animals, and all the
creatures that move along the
ground—so they can multiply on
the earth and be fruitful and increase in number upon it."[b]

18So Noah came out, together
with his sons and his wife and his
sons' wives. 19All the animals and
all the creatures that move along
the ground and all the birds—everything that moves on the earth
—came out of the ark, one kind after another.

20Then Noah built an altar to the
Lord[c] and, taking some of all the
clean animals and clean[d] birds, he
sacrificed burnt offerings[e] on it.
21The Lord smelled the pleasing
aroma[f] and said in his heart:
"Never again will I curse the
ground[g] because of man, even
though[m] every inclination of his
heart is evil from childhood.[h] And
never again will I destroy all living
creatures,[i] as I have done.

22"As long as the earth endures,
seedtime and harvest,
cold and heat,
summer and winter,
day and night
will never cease."[j]

8:16 [a]Ge 7:13
8:17 [b]Ge 1:22
8:20 [c]Ge 12:7-8; 13:18; 22:9 [d]Ge 7:8; Lev 11:1-47 [e]Ge 22:2,13; Ex 10:25
8:21 [f]Lev 1:9,13; 2Co 2:15 [g]Ge 3:17 [h]Ge 6:5; Ps 51:5; Jer 17:9 [i]Ge 9:11,15; Isa 54:9
8:22 [j]Ge 1:14; Jer 33:20,25
9:1 [k]Ge 1:22
9:3 [l]Ge 1:29
9:4 [m]Lev 3:17; 17:10-14; Dt 12:16, 23-25; 1Sa 14:33
9:5 [n]Ex 21:28-32 [o]Ge 4:10
9:6 [p]Ge 4:14; Ex 21:12,14; Lev 24:17; Mt 26:52 [q]Ge 1:26
9:7 [r]Ge 1:22
9:9 [s]Ge 6:18
9:11 [t]ver 16; Isa 24:5 [u]Ge 8:21; Isa 54:9
9:12 [v]ver 17; Ge 17:11

God's Covenant With Noah

9 Then God blessed Noah and
his sons, saying to them, "Be
fruitful and increase in number
and fill the earth.[k] 2The fear and
dread of you will fall upon all the
beasts of the earth and all the birds
of the air, upon every creature that
moves along the ground, and upon
all the fish of the sea; they are given
into your hands. 3Everything that
lives and moves will be food for
you.[l] Just as I gave you the green
plants, I now give you everything.

4"But you must not eat meat
that has its lifeblood still in it.[m]
5And for your lifeblood I will surely
demand an accounting. I will demand an accounting from every animal.[n] And from each man, too, I
will demand an accounting for the
life of his fellow man.[o]

6"Whoever sheds the blood of
man,
by man shall his blood be
shed;[p]
for in the image of God[q]
has God made man.

7As for you, be fruitful and increase
in number; multiply on the earth
and increase upon it."[r]

8Then God said to Noah and to
his sons with him: 9"I now establish my covenant with you[s] and
with your descendants after you
10and with every living creature
that was with you—the birds, the
livestock and all the wild animals,
all those that came out of the ark
with you—every living creature on
earth. 11I establish my covenant[t]
with you: Never again will all life be
cut off by the waters of a flood; never again will there be a flood to destroy the earth.[u]"

12And God said, "This is the sign
of the covenant[v] I am making between me and you and every living
creature with you, a covenant for
all generations to come: 13I have
set my rainbow in the clouds, and
it will be the sign of the covenant
between me and the earth.
14Whenever I bring clouds over the

[m]*21* Or *man, for*

earth and the rainbow appears in
the clouds, **15**I will remember my
covenant[a] between me and you
and all living creatures of every
kind. Never again will the waters
become a flood to destroy all life.
16Whenever the rainbow appears in
the clouds, I will see it and remember the everlasting covenant[b] between God and all living creatures
of every kind on the earth."
17So God said to Noah, "This is
the sign of the covenant[c] I have established between me and all life
on the earth."

The Sons of Noah

18The sons of Noah who came
out of the ark were Shem, Ham and
Japheth. (Ham was the father of
Canaan.)[d] **19**These were the three
sons of Noah, and from them came
the people who were scattered over
the earth.[e]
20Noah, a man of the soil, proceeded[n] to plant a vineyard.
21When he drank some of its wine,
he became drunk and lay uncovered inside his tent. **22**Ham, the father of Canaan, saw his father's nakedness and told his two brothers
outside. **23**But Shem and Japheth
took a garment and laid it across
their shoulders; then they walked
in backward and covered their father's nakedness. Their faces were
turned the other way so that they
would not see their father's nakedness.
24When Noah awoke from his
wine and found out what his youngest son had done to him, **25**he
said,

"Cursed be Canaan![f]
The lowest of slaves
will he be to his brothers.[g]"

26He also said,

"Blessed be the LORD, the God
of Shem!
May Canaan be the slave of
Shem.[o]
27May God extend the territory of
Japheth[p];
may Japheth live in the tents
of Shem,

9:15 [a]Ex 2:24; Lev 26:42,45; Dt 7:9; Eze 16:60
9:16 [b]ver 11; Ge 17:7,13,19; 2Sa 7:13; 23:5
9:17 [c]ver 12; Ge 17:11
9:18 [d]ver 25-27; Ge 10:6,15
9:19 [e]Ge 10:32
9:25 [f]ver 18 [g]Ge 25:23; Jos 9:23
10:1 [h] Ge 2:4
10:2 [i]Eze 38:6 [j]Eze 38:2; Rev 20:8 [k]Isa 66:19
10:3 [l]Jer 51:27 [m]Eze 27:14; 38:6
10:4 [n]Eze 27:12,25; Jnh 1:3
10:6 [o]ver 15; Ge 9:18

and may Canaan be his[q]
slave."

28After the flood Noah lived 350
years. **29**Altogether, Noah lived 950
years, and then he died.

The Table of Nations

10 This is the account[h] of
Shem, Ham and Japheth,
Noah's sons, who themselves had
sons after the flood.

The Japhethites

10:2-5pp — 1Ch 1:5-7

2The sons[r] of Japheth:
Gomer,[i] Magog,[j] Madai,
Javan, Tubal,[k] Meshech
and Tiras.
3The sons of Gomer:
Ashkenaz,[l] Riphath and
Togarmah.[m]
4The sons of Javan:
Elishah, Tarshish,[n] the Kittim and the Rodanim.[s]
5(From these the maritime
peoples spread out into
their territories by their
clans within their nations,
each with its own lan-
guage.)

The Hamites

10:6-20pp — 1Ch 1:8-16

6The sons of Ham:
Cush, Mizraim,[t] Put and
Canaan.[o]
7The sons of Cush:
Seba, Havilah, Sabtah, Raa-
mah and Sabteca.
The sons of Raamah:
Sheba and Dedan.

8Cush was the father[u] of Nimrod, who grew to be a mighty warrior on the earth. **9**He was a mighty
hunter before the LORD; that is why

[n]20 Or *soil, was the first* [o]26 Or *be his slave* [p]27 *Japheth* sounds like the Hebrew for *extend.* [q]27 Or *their* [r]2 *Sons* may mean *descendants* or *successors* or *nations;* also in verses 3, 4, 6, 7, 20-23, 29 and 31. [s]4 Some manuscripts of the Masoretic Text and Samaritan Pentateuch (see also Septuagint and 1 Chron. 1:7); most manuscripts of the Masoretic Text *Dodanim* [t]6 That is, Egypt; also in verse 13 [u]8 *Father* may mean *ancestor* or *predecessor* or *founder;* also in verses 13, 15, 24 and 26.

it is said, "Like Nimrod, a mighty
hunter before the LORD." **10**The first
centers of his kingdom were Babylon,[a] Erech, Akkad and Calneh,
in[v] Shinar.[w][b] **11**From that land he
went to Assyria,[c] where he built
Nineveh,[d] Rehoboth Ir,[x] Calah
12and Resen, which is between
Nineveh and Calah; that is the
great city.

13Mizraim was the father of
the Ludites, Anamites,
Lehabites, Naphtuhites,
14Pathrusites, Casluhites
(from whom the Philis-
tines[e] came) and Caphtorites.
15Canaan[f] was the father of
Sidon[g] his firstborn,[y] and
of the Hittites,[h] **16**Jebusites,[i] Amorites, Girgashites, **17**Hivites, Arkites,
Sinites, **18**Arvadites, Zemarites and Hamathites.

Later the Canaanite[j] clans scattered **19**and the borders of Canaan[k] reached from Sidon[l] toward Gerar as far as Gaza, and then
toward Sodom, Gomorrah, Admah
and Zeboiim, as far as Lasha.
20These are the sons of Ham by
their clans and languages, in their
territories and nations.

The Semites

10:21-31pp — Ge 11:10-27; 1Ch 1:17-27

21Sons were also born to Shem,
whose older brother was[z] Japheth;
Shem was the ancestor of all the
sons of Eber.[m]
22The sons of Shem:
Elam,[n] Asshur, Arphax-
ad,[o] Lud and Aram.
23The sons of Aram:
Uz,[p] Hul, Gether and Meshech.[a]
24Arphaxad was the father of[b]
Shelah,
and Shelah the father of
Eber.[q]
25Two sons were born to Eber:
One was named Peleg,[c] because in his time the earth
was divided; his brother was
named Joktan.
26Joktan was the father of
Almodad, Sheleph, Hazar-
maveth, Jerah, **27**Hadoram,
Uzal, Diklah, **28**Obal, Abimael, Sheba, **29**Ophir, Havilah and Jobab. All these
were sons of Joktan.

30The region where they lived
stretched from Mesha toward Se-
phar, in the eastern hill country.
31These are the sons of Shem by
their clans and languages, in their
territories and nations.
32These are the clans of Noah's
sons,[r] according to their lines of
descent, within their nations.
From these the nations spread out
over the earth[s] after the flood.

The Tower of Babel

11 Now the whole world had
one language and a com-
mon speech. **2**As men moved eastward,[d] they found a plain in Shinar[w][t] and settled there.
3They said to each other, "Come,
let's make bricks[u] and bake them
thoroughly." They used brick instead of stone, and tar[v] for mortar.
4Then they said, "Come, let us
build ourselves a city, with a tower
that reaches to the heavens,[w] so
that we may make a name[x] for ourselves and not be scattered over the
face of the whole earth."[y]
5But the LORD came down[z] to
see the city and the tower that the
men were building. **6**The LORD said,
"If as one people speaking the
same language they have begun to
do this, then nothing they plan to
do will be impossible for them.
7Come, let us[a] go down and con-
fuse their language so they will not
understand each other."[b]
8So the LORD scattered them
from there over all the earth,[c] and
they stopped building the city.

10:10 [a]Ge 11:9 [b]Ge 11:2
10:11 [c]Ps 83:8; Mic 5:6 [d]Jnh 1:2; 4:11; Na 1:1
10:14 [e]Ge 21:32,34; 26:1,8
10:15 [f]ver 6; Ge 9:18 [g]Eze 28:21 [h]Ge 23:3,20
10:16 [i]1Ch 11:4
10:18 [j]Ge 12:6; Ex 13:11
10:19 [k]Ge 11:31; 13:12; 17:8 [l]ver 15
10:21 [m]ver 24; Nu 24:24
10:22 [n]Jer 49:34 [o]Lk 3:36
10:23 [p]Job 1:1
10:24 [q]ver 21
10:32 [r]ver 1 [s]Ge 9:19
11:2 [t]Ge 10:10
11:3 [u]Ex 1:14 [v]Ge 14:10
11:4 [w]Dt 1:28; 9:1 [x]Ge 6:4 [y]Dt 4:27
11:5 [z]ver 7; Ge 18:21; Ex 3:8; 19:11,18,20
11:7 [a]Ge 1:26 [b]Ge 42:23
11:8 [c]Ge 9:19; Lk 1:51

[v]*10* Or *Erech and Akkad—all of them in* [w]*10,2* That is, Babylonia [x]*11* Or *Nineveh with its city squares* [y]*15* Or *of the Sidonians, the foremost* [z]*21* Or *Shem, the older brother of* [a]*23* See Septuagint and 1 Chron. 1:17; Hebrew *Mash* [b]*24* Hebrew; Septuagint *father of Cainan, and Cainan was the father of* [c]*25* *Peleg* means *division.* [d]*2* Or *from the east*; or *in the east*

9 That is why it was called Babel[e][a]—because there the LORD confused the language of the whole world. From there the LORD scattered them over the face of the whole earth.

From Shem to Abram

11:10–27pp — Ge 10:21–31; 1Ch 1:17–27

10 This is the account of Shem.

Two years after the flood, when Shem was 100 years old, he became the father[f] of Arphaxad. 11 And after he became the father of Arphaxad, Shem lived 500 years and had other sons and daughters.

12 When Arphaxad had lived 35 years, he became the father of Shelah.[b] 13 And after he became the father of Shelah, Arphaxad lived 403 years and had other sons and daughters.[g]

14 When Shelah had lived 30 years, he became the father of Eber. 15 And after he became the father of Eber, Shelah lived 403 years and had other sons and daughters.

16 When Eber had lived 34 years, he became the father of Peleg. 17 And after he became the father of Peleg, Eber lived 430 years and had other sons and daughters.

18 When Peleg had lived 30 years, he became the father of Reu. 19 And after he became the father of Reu, Peleg lived 209 years and had other sons and daughters.

20 When Reu had lived 32 years, he became the father of Serug.[c] 21 And after he became the father of Serug, Reu lived 207 years and had other sons and daughters.

22 When Serug had lived 30 years, he became the father of Nahor. 23 And after he became the father of Nahor, Serug lived 200 years and had other sons and daughters.

24 When Nahor had lived 29 years, he became the father of Terah.[d] 25 And after he became the father of Terah, Nahor lived 119 years and had other sons and daughters.

26 After Terah had lived 70 years, he became the father of Abram,[e] Nahor[f] and Haran.

27 This is the account of Terah.

Terah became the father of Abram, Nahor and Haran. And Haran became the father of Lot.[g] 28 While his father Terah was still alive, Haran died in Ur of the Chaldeans,[h] in the land of his birth. 29 Abram and Nahor both married. The name of Abram's wife was Sarai,[i] and the name of Nahor's wife was Milcah;[j] she was the daughter of Haran, the father of both Milcah and Iscah. 30 Now Sarai was barren; she had no children.[k]

31 Terah took his son Abram, his grandson Lot son of Haran, and his daughter-in-law Sarai, the wife of his son Abram, and together they set out from Ur of the Chaldeans[l] to go to Canaan.[m] But when they came to Haran, they settled there.

32 Terah lived 205 years, and he died in Haran.

The Call of Abram

12 The LORD had said to Abram, "Leave your country, your people and your father's household and go to the land I will show you.[n]

2 "I will make you into a great
nation[o]
and I will bless you;[p]
I will make your name great,
and you will be a blessing.
3 I will bless those who bless
you,
and whoever curses you I will
curse;[q]
and all peoples on earth
will be blessed through
you.[r]"

4 So Abram left, as the LORD had

11:9 [a]Ge 10:10
11:12 [b]Lk 3:35
11:20 [c]Lk 3:35
11:24 [d]Lk 3:34
11:26 [e]Lk 3:34 [f]Jos 24:2
11:27 [g]ver 31; Ge 12:4; 14:12; 19:1; 2Pe 2:7
11:28 [h]ver 31; Ge 15:7
11:29 [i]Ge 17:15 [j]Ge 22:20
11:30 [k]Ge 16:1; 18:11
11:31 [l]Ge 15:7; Ne 9:7; Ac 7:4 [m]Ge 10:19
12:1 [n]Ac 7:3*; Heb 11:8
12:2 [o]Ge 15:5; 17:2,4; 18:18; 22:17; Dt 26:5 [p]Ge 24:1,35
12:3 [q]Ge 27:29; Ex 23:22; Nu 24:9 [r]Ge 18:18; 22:18; 26:4; Ac 3:25; Gal 3:8*

[e]9 That is, Babylon; *Babel* sounds like the Hebrew for *confused.* [f]10 *Father* may mean *ancestor;* also in verses 11-25.
[g]*12,13* Hebrew; Septuagint (see also Luke 3:35, 36 and note at Gen. 10:24) *35 years, he became the father of Cainan. 13 And after he became the father of Cainan, Arphaxad lived 430 years and had other sons and daughters, and then he died. When Cainan had lived 130 years, he became the father of Shelah. And after he became the father of Shelah, Cainan lived 330 years and had other sons and daughters*

told him; and Lot went with him.
Abram was seventy-five years old
when he set out from Haran.[a] 5He
took his wife Sarai, his nephew Lot,
all the possessions they had accumulated and the people[b] they had
acquired in Haran, and they set out
for the land of Canaan, and they arrived there.

6Abram traveled through the
land[c] as far as the site of the great
tree of Moreh[d] at Shechem. At
that time the Canaanites[e] were in
the land. 7The LORD appeared to
Abram[f] and said, "To your offspring[h] I will give this land."[g] So
he built an altar there to the LORD,[h]
who had appeared to him.

8From there he went on toward
the hills east of Bethel[i] and
pitched his tent, with Bethel on the
west and Ai on the east. There he
built an altar to the LORD and called
on the name of the LORD. 9Then
Abram set out and continued toward the Negev.[j]

Abram in Egypt

12:10–20Ref – Ge 20:1–18; 26:1–11

10Now there was a famine in the
land, and Abram went down to
Egypt to live there for a while because the famine was severe. 11As
he was about to enter Egypt, he
said to his wife Sarai, "I know what
a beautiful woman you are.
12When the Egyptians see you,
they will say, 'This is his wife.'
Then they will kill me but will let
you live. 13Say you are my sister,[k]
so that I will be treated well for
your sake and my life will be spared
because of you."

14When Abram came to Egypt,
the Egyptians saw that she was a
very beautiful woman. 15And when
Pharaoh's officials saw her, they
praised her to Pharaoh, and she
was taken into his palace. 16He
treated Abram well for her sake,
and Abram acquired sheep and cattle, male and female donkeys,
menservants and maidservants,
and camels.

17But the LORD inflicted serious
diseases on Pharaoh and his
household[l] because of Abram's
wife Sarai. 18So Pharaoh summoned Abram. "What have you
done to me?"[m] he said. "Why
didn't you tell me she was your
wife? 19Why did you say, 'She is my
sister,' so that I took her to be my
wife? Now then, here is your wife.
Take her and go!" 20Then Pharaoh
gave orders about Abram to his
men, and they sent him on his way,
with his wife and everything he
had.

Abram and Lot Separate

13 So Abram went up from
Egypt to the Negev,[n] with
his wife and everything he had, and
Lot went with him. 2Abram had become very wealthy in livestock and
in silver and gold.

3From the Negev he went from
place to place until he came to
Bethel,[o] to the place between
Bethel and Ai where his tent had
been earlier 4and where he had
first built an altar.[p] There Abram
called on the name of the LORD.

5Now Lot, who was moving
about with Abram, also had flocks
and herds and tents. 6But the land
could not support them while they
stayed together, for their possessions were so great that they
were not able to stay together.[q]
7And quarreling[r] arose between
Abram's herdsmen and the herdsmen of Lot. The Canaanites and
Perizzites were also living in the
land[s] at that time.

8So Abram said to Lot, "Let's not
have any quarreling between you
and me,[t] or between your herdsmen and mine, for we are brothers.[u] 9Is not the whole land before
you? Let's part company. If you go
to the left, I'll go to the right; if you
go to the right, I'll go to the left."

10Lot looked up and saw that the
whole plain of the Jordan was well
watered, like the garden of the
LORD,[v] like the land of Egypt, toward Zoar.[w] (This was before the
LORD destroyed Sodom and Gomorrah.)[x] 11So Lot chose for himself

12:4 [a]Ge 11:31
12:5 [b]Ge 14:14; 17:23
12:6 [c]Heb 11:9 [d]Ge 35:4; Dt 11:30 [e]Ge 10:18
12:7 [f]Ge 17:1; 18:1; Ex 6:3 [g]Ge 13:15,17; 15:18; 17:8; Ps 105:9-11 [h]Ge 13:4
12:8 [i]Ge 13:3
12:9 [j]Ge 13:1,3
12:13 [k]Ge 20:2; 26:7
12:17 [l]1Ch 16:21
12:18 [m]Ge 20:9; 26:10
13:1 [n]Ge 12:9
13:3 [o]Ge 12:8
13:4 [p]Ge 12:7
13:6 [q]Ge 36:7
13:7 [r]Ge 26:20,21 [s]Ge 12:6
13:8 [t]Pr 15:18; 20:3 [u]Ps 133:1
13:10 [v]Ge 2:8-10; Isa 51:3 [w]Ge 19:22,30 [x]Ge 14:8; 19:17-29

h7 Or *seed*

the whole plain of the Jordan and
set out toward the east. The two
men parted company: **12**Abram
lived in the land of Canaan, while
Lot lived among the cities of the
plain[a] and pitched his tents near
Sodom.[b] **13**Now the men of Sodom
were wicked and were sinning
greatly against the LORD.[c]

14The LORD said to Abram after
Lot had parted from him, "Lift up
your eyes from where you are and
look north and south, east and
west.[d] **15**All the land that you see
I will give to you and your offspring[i] forever.[e] **16**I will make
your offspring like the dust of the
earth, so that if anyone could count
the dust, then your offspring could
be counted. **17**Go, walk through
the length and breadth of the
land,[f] for I am giving it to you."

18So Abram moved his tents and
went to live near the great trees of
Mamre[g] at Hebron,[h] where he
built an altar to the LORD.[i]

Abram Rescues Lot

14 At this time Amraphel king
of Shinar,[i][j] Arioch king of
Ellasar, Kedorlaomer king of Elam
and Tidal king of Goiim **2**went to
war against Bera king of Sodom,
Birsha king of Gomorrah, Shinab
king of Admah, Shemeber king of
Zeboiim,[k] and the king of Bela
(that is, Zoar).[l] **3**All these latter
kings joined forces in the Valley of
Siddim (the Salt Sea[k][m]). **4**For
twelve years they had been subject
to Kedorlaomer, but in the thirteenth year they rebelled.

5In the fourteenth year, Kedorlaomer and the kings allied with him
went out and defeated the Rephaites[n] in Ashteroth Karnaim, the
Zuzites in Ham, the Emites[o] in
Shaveh Kiriathaim **6**and the Horites[p] in the hill country of Seir,[q]
as far as El Paran[r] near the desert.
7Then they turned back and went
to En Mishpat (that is, Kadesh),
and they conquered the whole territory of the Amalekites, as well as
the Amorites who were living in
Hazazon Tamar.[s]

8Then the king of Sodom, the
king of Gomorrah,[t] the king of Admah, the king of Zeboiim[u] and the
king of Bela (that is, Zoar) marched
out and drew up their battle lines
in the Valley of Siddim **9**against
Kedorlaomer king of Elam, Tidal
king of Goiim, Amraphel king of
Shinar and Arioch king of Ellasar
—four kings against five. **10**Now
the Valley of Siddim was full of tar
pits, and when the kings of Sodom
and Gomorrah fled, some of the
men fell into them and the rest fled
to the hills.[v] **11**The four kings
seized all the goods of Sodom and
Gomorrah and all their food; then
they went away. **12**They also carried off Abram's nephew Lot and
his possessions, since he was living
in Sodom.

13One who had escaped came
and reported this to Abram the Hebrew. Now Abram was living near
the great trees of Mamre[w] the Amorite, a brother[l] of Eshcol and
Aner, all of whom were allied with
Abram. **14**When Abram heard that
his relative had been taken captive,
he called out the 318 trained men
born in his household[x] and went
in pursuit as far as Dan.[y] **15**During
the night Abram divided his men to
attack them and he routed them,
pursuing them as far as Hobah,
north of Damascus. **16**He recovered
all the goods and brought back his
relative Lot and his possessions,
together with the women and the
other people.

17After Abram returned from defeating Kedorlaomer and the kings
allied with him, the king of Sodom
came out to meet him in the Valley
of Shaveh (that is, the King's Valley).[z]

18Then Melchizedek[a] king of
Salem[m][b] brought out bread and
wine. He was priest of God Most
High, **19**and he blessed Abram,[c]
saying,

13:12 [a]Ge 19:17,25,29 [b]Ge 14:12
13:13 [c]Ge 18:20; Eze 16:49-50; 2Pe 2:8
13:14 [d]Ge 28:14; Dt 3:27
13:15 [e]Ge 12:7; Gal 3:16*
13:17 [f]ver 15; Nu 13:17-25
13:18 [g]Ge 14:13,24; 18:1 [h]Ge 35:27 [i]Ge 8:20
14:1 [j]Ge 10:10
14:2 [k]Ge 10:19 [l]Ge 13:10
14:3 [m]Nu 34:3,12; Dt 3:17; Jos 3:16; 15:2,5
14:5 [n]Ge 15:20; Dt 2:11,20 [o]Dt 2:10
14:6 [p]Dt 2:12,22 [q]Dt 2:1,5,22 [r]Ge 21:21; Nu 10:12
14:7 [s]2Ch 20:2
14:8 [t]Ge 13:10; 19:17-29 [u]Dt 29:23
14:10 [v]Ge 19:17,30
14:13 [w]ver 24; Ge 13:18
14:14 [x]Ge 15:3 [y]Dt 34:1; Jdg 18:29
14:17 [z]2Sa 18:18
14:18 [a]Ps 110:4; Heb 5:6 [b]Ps 76:2; Heb 7:2
14:19 [c]Heb 7:6

[i] *15* Or *seed*; also in verse 16 [j] *1* That is, Babylonia; also in verse 9 [k] *3* That is, the Dead Sea [l] *13* Or *a relative*; or *an ally* [m] *18* That is, Jerusalem

"Blessed be Abram by God
Most High,
Creator[n] of heaven and
earth.[a]
20And blessed be[o] God Most
High,[b]
who delivered your enemies
into your hand."

Then Abram gave him a tenth of everything.[c]
21The king of Sodom said to
Abram, "Give me the people and
keep the goods for yourself."
22But Abram said to the king of
Sodom, "I have raised my hand[d] to
the LORD, God Most High, Creator
of heaven and earth,[e] and have
taken an oath **23**that I will accept
nothing belonging to you,[f] not
even a thread or the thong of a sandal, so that you will never be able
to say, 'I made Abram rich.' **24**I will
accept nothing but what my men
have eaten and the share that belongs to the men who went with
me—to Aner, Eshcol and Mamre.
Let them have their share."

God's Covenant With Abram

15 After this, the word of the
LORD came to Abram[g] in a
vision:

"Do not be afraid,[h] Abram.
I am your shield,[p][i]
your very great reward.[q]"

2But Abram said, "O Sovereign
LORD, what can you give me since I
remain childless[j] and the one who
will inherit[r] my estate is Eliezer of
Damascus?" **3**And Abram said,
"You have given me no children; so
a servant[k] in my household will be
my heir."
4Then the word of the LORD came
to him: "This man will not be your
heir, but a son coming from your
own body will be your heir.[l]" **5**He
took him outside and said, "Look
up at the heavens and count the
stars[m]—if indeed you can count
them." Then he said to him, "So
shall your offspring be."[n]
6Abram believed the LORD, and
he credited it to him as righteousness.[o]
7He also said to him, "I am the
LORD, who brought you out of Ur of
the Chaldeans to give you this land
to take possession of it."
8But Abram said, "O Sovereign
LORD, how can I know[p] that I will
gain possession of it?"
9So the LORD said to him, "Bring
me a heifer, a goat and a ram, each
three years old, along with a dove
and a young pigeon."
10Abram brought all these to
him, cut them in two and arranged
the halves opposite each other;[q]
the birds, however, he did not cut
in half.[r] **11**Then birds of prey came
down on the carcasses, but Abram
drove them away.
12As the sun was setting, Abram
fell into a deep sleep,[s] and a thick
and dreadful darkness came over
him. **13**Then the LORD said to him,
"Know for certain that your
descendants will be strangers in a
country not their own, and they
will be enslaved[t] and mistreated
four hundred years.[u] **14**But I will
punish the nation they serve as
slaves, and afterward they will
come out[v] with great possessions.[w] **15**You, however, will go to
your fathers in peace and be buried
at a good old age.[x] **16**In the fourth
generation your descendants will
come back here, for the sin of the
Amorites[y] has not yet reached its
full measure."
17When the sun had set and
darkness had fallen, a smoking
firepot with a blazing torch appeared and passed between the
pieces.[z] **18**On that day the LORD
made a covenant with Abram and
said, "To your descendants I give
this land,[a] from the river[s] of
Egypt[b] to the great river, the Euphrates— **19**the land of the Kenites, Kenizzites, Kadmonites,
20Hittites, Perizzites, Rephaites,
21Amorites, Canaanites, Girgashites and Jebusites."

14:19 [a]ver 22
14:20 [b]Ge 24:27 [c]Ge 28:22; Dt 26:12; Heb 7:4
14:22 [d]Ex 6:8; Da 12:7; Rev 10:5-6 [e]ver 19
14:23 [f]2Ki 5:16
15:1 [g]Da 10:1 [h]Ge 21:17; 26:24; 46:3; 2Ki 6:16; Ps 27:1; Isa 41:10, 13-14 [i]Dt 33:29; 2Sa 22:3,31; Ps 3:3
15:2 [j]Ac 7:5
15:3 [k]Ge 24:2,34
15:4 [l]Gal 4:28
15:5 [m]Ps 147:4; Jer 33:22 [n]Ge 12:2; 22:17; Ex 32:13; Ro 4:18*; Heb 11:12
15:6 [o]Ps 106:31; Ro 4:3*, 20-24*; Gal 3:6*; Jas 2:23*
15:8 [p]Lk 1:18
15:10 [q]ver 17; Jer 34:18 [r]Lev 1:17
15:12 [s]Ge 2:21
15:13 [t]Ex 1:11 [u]ver 16; Ex 12:40; Ac 7:6,17
15:14 [v]Ac 7:7* [w]Ex 12:32-38
15:15 [x]Ge 25:8
15:16 [y]1Ki 21:26
15:17 [z]ver 10
15:18 [a]Ge 12:7 [b]Nu 34:5

[n]*19* Or *Possessor,* also in verse 22 [o]*20* Or *And praise be to* [p]*1* Or *sovereign* [q]*1* Or *shield; / your reward will be very great* [r]*2* The meaning of the Hebrew for this phrase is uncertain. [s]*18* Or *Wadi*

Hagar and Ishmael

16 Now Sarai, Abram's wife, had borne him no children.[a] But she had an Egyptian maidservant[b] named Hagar; **2**so she said to Abram, "The LORD has kept me from having children. Go, sleep with my maidservant; perhaps I can build a family through her."[c]

Abram agreed to what Sarai said. **3**So after Abram had been living in Canaan[d] ten years, Sarai his wife took her Egyptian maidservant Hagar and gave her to her husband to be his wife. **4**He slept with Hagar, and she conceived.

When she knew she was pregnant, she began to despise her mistress. **5**Then Sarai said to Abram, "You are responsible for the wrong I am suffering. I put my servant in your arms, and now that she knows she is pregnant, she despises me. May the LORD judge between you and me."[e]

6"Your servant is in your hands," Abram said. "Do with her whatever you think best." Then Sarai mistreated Hagar; so she fled from her.

7The angel of the LORD[f] found Hagar near a spring in the desert; it was the spring that is beside the road to Shur.[g] **8**And he said, "Hagar, servant of Sarai, where have you come from, and where are you going?"

"I'm running away from my mistress Sarai," she answered.

9Then the angel of the LORD told her, "Go back to your mistress and submit to her." **10**The angel added, "I will so increase your descendants that they will be too numerous to count."[h]

11The angel of the LORD also said to her:

"You are now with child
and you will have a son.
You shall name him Ishmael,[t]
for the LORD has heard of
your misery.[i]
12He will be a wild donkey of a
man;
his hand will be against
everyone
and everyone's hand against
him,
and he will live in hostility
toward[u] all his brothers.[j]"

13She gave this name to the LORD who spoke to her: "You are the God who sees me," for she said, "I have now seen[v] the One who sees me."[k] **14**That is why the well was called Beer Lahai Roi[w]; it is still there, between Kadesh and Bered.

15So Hagar bore Abram a son,[l] and Abram gave the name Ishmael to the son she had borne. **16**Abram was eighty-six years old when Hagar bore him Ishmael.

The Covenant of Circumcision

17 When Abram was ninety-nine years old, the LORD appeared to him and said, "I am God Almighty[x];[m] walk before me and be blameless.[n] **2**I will confirm my covenant between me and you[o] and will greatly increase your numbers."

3Abram fell facedown, and God said to him, **4**"As for me, this is my covenant with you:[p] You will be the father of many nations.[q] **5**No longer will you be called Abram[y]; your name will be Abraham,[z][r] for I have made you a father of many nations.[s] **6**I will make you very fruitful;[t] I will make nations of you, and kings will come from you.[u] **7**I will establish my covenant as an everlasting covenant between me and you and your descendants after you for the generations to come, to be your God[v] and the God of your descendants after you.[w] **8**The whole land of Canaan,[x] where you are now an alien,[y] I will give as an everlasting possession to you and your descendants after you;[z] and I will be their God."

9Then God said to Abraham, "As for you, you must keep my covenant, you and your descendants

16:1 [a]Ge 11:30; Gal 4:24-25 [b]Ge 21:9
16:2 [c]Ge 30:3-4, 9-10
16:3 [d]Ge 12:5
16:5 [e]Ge 31:53
16:7 [f]Ge 21:17; 22:11,15; 31:11 [g]Ge 20:1
16:10 [h]Ge 13:16; 17:20
16:11 [i]Ex 2:24; 3:7, 9
16:12 [j]Ge 25:18
16:13 [k]Ge 32:30
16:15 [l]Gal 4:22
17:1 [m]Ge 28:3; Ex 6:3 [n]Dt 18:13
17:2 [o]Ge 15:18
17:4 [p]Ge 15:18 [q]ver 16; Ge 12:2; 35:11; 48:19
17:5 [r]ver 15; Ne 9:7 [s]Ro 4:17*
17:6 [t]Ge 35:11 [u]Mt 1:6
17:7 [v]Ex 29:45,46 [w]Ro 9:8; Gal 3:16
17:8 [x]Ps 105:9,11 [y]Ge 23:4; 28:4; Ex 6:4 [z]Ge 12:7

[t]11 *Ishmael* means *God hears.* [u]12 Or *live to the east of* [v]13 Or *seen the back of* [w]14 *Beer Lahai Roi* means *well of the Living One who sees me.* [x]1 Hebrew *El-Shaddai* [y]5 *Abram* means *exalted father.* [z]5 *Abraham* means *father of many.*

after you for the generations to
come. **10**This is my covenant with
you and your descendants after
you, the covenant you are to keep:
Every male among you shall be circumcised.[a] **11**You are to undergo
circumcision,[b] and it will be the
sign of the covenant[c] between me
and you. **12**For the generations to
come every male among you who is
eight days old must be circumcised,[d] including those born in
your household or bought with
money from a foreigner—those
who are not your offspring.
13Whether born in your household
or bought with your money, they
must be circumcised. My covenant
in your flesh is to be an everlasting
covenant. **14**Any uncircumcised
male, who has not been circumcised in the flesh, will be cut off
from his people;[e] he has broken
my covenant."

15God also said to Abraham, "As
for Sarai your wife, you are no longer to call her Sarai; her name will
be Sarah. **16**I will bless her and will
surely give you a son by her.[f] I will
bless her so that she will be the
mother of nations;[g] kings of peoples will come from her."

17Abraham fell facedown; he
laughed[h] and said to himself,
"Will a son be born to a man a hundred years old? Will Sarah bear a
child at the age of ninety?" **18**And
Abraham said to God, "If only Ishmael might live under your blessing!"

19Then God said, "Yes, but your
wife Sarah will bear you a son,[i]
and you will call him Isaac.[a] I will
establish my covenant with him[j]
as an everlasting covenant for his
descendants after him. **20**And as
for Ishmael, I have heard you: I will
surely bless him; I will make him
fruitful and will greatly increase his
numbers.[k] He will be the father of
twelve rulers,[l] and I will make him
into a great nation.[m] **21**But my covenant I will establish with Isaac,
whom Sarah will bear to you by this
time next year."[n] **22**When he had
finished speaking with Abraham,
God went up from him.

17:10 [a] ver 23; Ge 21:4; Jn 7:22; Ac 7:8; Ro 4:11
17:11 [b] Ex 12:48; Dt 10:16 [c] Ro 4:11
17:12 [d] Lev 12:3; Lk 2:21
17:14 [e] Ex 4:24-26
17:16 [f] Ge 18:10 [g] Ge 35:11; Gal 4:31
17:17 [h] Ge 18:12; 21:6
17:19 [i] Ge 18:14; 21:2 [j] Ge 26:3
17:20 [k] Ge 16:10 [l] Ge 25:12-16 [m] Ge 21:18
17:21 [n] Ge 21:2
17:24 [o] Ro 4:11
18:1 [p] Ge 13:18; 14:13
18:2 [q] ver 16,22; Ge 32:24; Jos 5:13; Jdg 13:6-11; Heb 13:2
18:4 [r] Ge 19:2; 43:24
18:5 [s] Jdg 13:15
18:8 [t] Ge 19:3

23On that very day Abraham took
his son Ishmael and all those born
in his household or bought with his
money, every male in his household, and circumcised them, as
God told him. **24**Abraham was
ninety-nine years old when he was
circumcised,[o] **25**and his son Ishmael was thirteen; **26**Abraham and
his son Ishmael were both circumcised on that same day. **27**And every male in Abraham's household,
including those born in his household or bought from a foreigner,
was circumcised with him.

The Three Visitors

18 The LORD appeared to Abraham near the great trees of
Mamre[p] while he was sitting at the
entrance to his tent in the heat of
the day. **2**Abraham looked up and
saw three men[q] standing nearby.
When he saw them, he hurried
from the entrance of his tent to
meet them and bowed low to the
ground.

3He said, "If I have found favor in
your eyes, my lord,[b] do not pass
your servant by. **4**Let a little water
be brought, and then you may all
wash your feet[r] and rest under this
tree. **5**Let me get you something to
eat,[s] so you can be refreshed and
then go on your way—now that you
have come to your servant."

"Very well," they answered, "do
as you say."

6So Abraham hurried into the
tent to Sarah. "Quick," he said,
"get three seahs[c] of fine flour and
knead it and bake some bread."

7Then he ran to the herd and selected a choice, tender calf and
gave it to a servant, who hurried to
prepare it. **8**He then brought some
curds and milk and the calf that
had been prepared, and set these
before them.[t] While they ate, he
stood near them under a tree.

9"Where is your wife Sarah?"
they asked him.

"There, in the tent," he said.

[a] *19 Isaac* means *he laughs.* [b] *3* Or *O Lord*
[c] *6* That is, probably about 20 quarts (about 22 liters)

10Then the LORD[d] said, "I will surely return to you about this time next year, and Sarah your wife will have a son."[a]

Now Sarah was listening at the entrance to the tent, which was behind him. **11**Abraham and Sarah were already old and well advanced in years,[b] and Sarah was past the age of childbearing.[c] **12**So Sarah laughed[d] to herself as she thought, "After I am worn out and my master[e][e] is old, will I now have this pleasure?"

13Then the LORD said to Abraham, "Why did Sarah laugh and say, 'Will I really have a child, now that I am old?' **14**Is anything too hard for the LORD?[f] I will return to you at the appointed time next year and Sarah will have a son."

15Sarah was afraid, so she lied and said, "I did not laugh."

But he said, "Yes, you did laugh."

Abraham Pleads for Sodom

16When the men got up to leave, they looked down toward Sodom, and Abraham walked along with them to see them on their way. **17**Then the LORD said, "Shall I hide from Abraham[g] what I am about to do?[h] **18**Abraham will surely become a great and powerful nation,[i] and all nations on earth will be blessed through him. **19**For I have chosen him, so that he will direct his children[j] and his household after him to keep the way of the LORD[k] by doing what is right and just, so that the LORD will bring about for Abraham what he has promised him."

20Then the LORD said, "The outcry against Sodom and Gomorrah is so great and their sin so grievous **21**that I will go down[l] and see if what they have done is as bad as the outcry that has reached me. If not, I will know."

22The men turned away and went toward Sodom,[m] but Abraham remained standing before the LORD.[f] **23**Then Abraham approached him and said: "Will you sweep away the righteous with the wicked?[n] **24**What if there are fifty righteous people in the city? Will you really sweep it away and not spare[g] the place for the sake of the fifty righteous people in it?[o] **25**Far be it from you to do such a thing—to kill the righteous with the wicked, treating the righteous and the wicked alike. Far be it from you! Will not the Judge[h] of all the earth do right?"[p]

26The LORD said, "If I find fifty righteous people in the city of Sodom, I will spare the whole place for their sake.[q]"

27Then Abraham spoke up again: "Now that I have been so bold as to speak to the Lord, though I am nothing but dust and ashes,[r] **28**what if the number of the righteous is five less than fifty? Will you destroy the whole city because of five people?"

"If I find forty-five there," he said, "I will not destroy it."

29Once again he spoke to him, "What if only forty are found there?"

He said, "For the sake of forty, I will not do it."

30Then he said, "May the Lord not be angry, but let me speak. What if only thirty can be found there?"

He answered, "I will not do it if I find thirty there."

31Abraham said, "Now that I have been so bold as to speak to the Lord, what if only twenty can be found there?"

He said, "For the sake of twenty, I will not destroy it."

32Then he said, "May the Lord not be angry, but let me speak just once more.[s] What if only ten can be found there?"

He answered, "For the sake of ten,[t] I will not destroy it."

33When the LORD had finished speaking with Abraham, he left, and Abraham returned home.

18:10 [a]Ro 9:9*
18:11 [b]Ge 17:17 [c]Ro 4:19
18:12 [d]Ge 17:17; 21:6 [e]1Pe 3:6
18:14 [f]Jer 32:17,27; Zec 8:6; Mt 19:26; Lk 1:37; Ro 4:21
18:17 [g]Am 3:7 [h]Ge 19:24
18:18 [i]Gal 3:8*
18:19 [j]Dt 4:9-10; 6:7 [k]Jos 24:15; Eph 6:4
18:21 [l]Ge 11:5
18:22 [m]Ge 19:1
18:23 [n]Nu 16:22
18:24 [o]Jer 5:1
18:25 [p]Job 8:3,20; Ps 58:11; 94:2; Isa 3:10-11; Ro 3:6
18:26 [q]Jer 5:1
18:27 [r]Ge 2:7; 3:19; Job 30:19; 42:6
18:32 [s]Jdg 6:39 [t]Jer 5:1

[d]*10* Hebrew *Then he* [e]*12* Or *husband*
[f]*22* Masoretic Text; an ancient Hebrew scribal tradition *but the LORD remained standing before Abraham* [g]*24* Or *forgive*; also in verse 26
[h]*25* Or *Ruler*

Sodom and Gomorrah Destroyed

19 The two angels arrived at
Sodom[a] in the evening,
and Lot was sitting in the gateway
of the city.[b] When he saw them, he
got up to meet them and bowed
down with his face to the ground.
2"My lords," he said, "please turn
aside to your servant's house. You
can wash your feet[c] and spend the
night and then go on your way early
in the morning."

"No," they answered, "we will
spend the night in the square."

3But he insisted so strongly that
they did go with him and entered
his house. He prepared a meal for
them, baking bread without yeast,
and they ate.[d] **4**Before they had
gone to bed, all the men from every
part of the city of Sodom—both
young and old—surrounded the
house. **5**They called to Lot, "Where
are the men who came to you tonight? Bring them out to us so that
we can have sex with them."[e]

6Lot went outside to meet
them[f] and shut the door behind
him **7**and said, "No, my friends.
Don't do this wicked thing. **8**Look,
I have two daughters who have never slept with a man. Let me bring
them out to you, and you can do
what you like with them. But don't
do anything to these men, for they
have come under the protection of
my roof."[g]

9"Get out of our way," they replied. And they said, "This fellow
came here as an alien, and now he
wants to play the judge![h] We'll
treat you worse than them." They
kept bringing pressure on Lot and
moved forward to break down the
door.

10But the men inside reached
out and pulled Lot back into the
house and shut the door. **11**Then
they struck the men who were at
the door of the house, young and
old, with blindness[i] so that they
could not find the door.

12The two men said to Lot, "Do
you have anyone else here—sons-
in-law, sons or daughters, or anyone else in the city who belongs to
you?[j] Get them out of here, **13**because we are going to destroy this
place. The outcry to the LORD
against its people is so great that
he has sent us to destroy it."[k]

14So Lot went out and spoke to
his sons-in-law, who were pledged
to marry[i] his daughters. He said,
"Hurry and get out of this place,
because the LORD is about to destroy the city![l]" But his sons-in-
law thought he was joking.[m]

15With the coming of dawn, the
angels urged Lot, saying, "Hurry!
Take your wife and your two
daughters who are here, or you will
be swept away[n] when the city is
punished.[o]"

16When he hesitated, the men
grasped his hand and the hands of
his wife and of his two daughters
and led them safely out of the city,
for the LORD was merciful to them.
17As soon as they had brought
them out, one of them said, "Flee
for your lives![p] Don't look back,[q]
and don't stop anywhere in the
plain! Flee to the mountains or you
will be swept away!"

18But Lot said to them, "No, my
lords,[j] please! **19**Your[k] servant
has found favor in your[k] eyes, and
you[k] have shown great kindness to
me in sparing my life. But I can't
flee to the mountains; this disaster
will overtake me, and I'll die.
20Look, here is a town near enough
to run to, and it is small. Let me
flee to it—it is very small, isn't it?
Then my life will be spared."

21He said to him, "Very well, I
will grant this request too; I will not
overthrow the town you speak of.
22But flee there quickly, because I
cannot do anything until you reach
it." (That is why the town was
called Zoar.[l])

23By the time Lot reached Zoar,
the sun had risen over the land.
24Then the LORD rained down burning sulfur on Sodom and Gomorrah[r]—from the LORD out of the

19:1 [a]Ge 18:22 [b]Ge 18:1
19:2 [c]Ge 18:4; Lk 7:44
19:3 [d]Ge 18:6
19:5 [e]Jdg 19:22; Isa 3:9; Ro 1:24-27
19:6 [f]Jdg 19:23
19:8 [g]Jdg 19:24
19:9 [h]Ex 2:14; Ac 7:27
19:11 [i]Dt 28:28-29; 2Ki 6:18; Ac 13:11
19:12 [j]Ge 7:1
19:13 [k]1Ch 21:15
19:14 [l]Nu 16:21 [m]Ex 9:21; Lk 17:28
19:15 [n]Nu 16:26 [o]Rev 18:4
19:17 [p]Jer 48:6 [q]ver 26
19:24 [r]Dt 29:23; Isa 1:9; 13:19

[i]*14* Or *were married to* [j]*18* Or *No, Lord*; or *No, my lord* [k]*19* The Hebrew is singular. [l]*22* *Zoar* means *small.*

heavens.[a] 25Thus he overthrew
those cities and the entire plain,
including all those living in the cities—and also the vegetation in the
land.[b] 26But Lot's wife looked
back,[c] and she became a pillar of
salt.[d]

27Early the next morning Abraham got up and returned to the
place where he had stood before
the LORD.[e] 28He looked down toward Sodom and Gomorrah, toward all the land of the plain, and
he saw dense smoke rising from the
land, like smoke from a furnace.[f]

29So when God destroyed the
cities of the plain, he remembered
Abraham, and he brought Lot out
of the catastrophe[g] that overthrew
the cities where Lot had lived.

Lot and His Daughters

30Lot and his two daughters left
Zoar and settled in the mountains,[h] for he was afraid to stay in
Zoar. He and his two daughters
lived in a cave. 31One day the older
daughter said to the younger, "Our
father is old, and there is no man
around here to lie with us, as is the
custom all over the earth. 32Let's
get our father to drink wine and
then lie with him and preserve our
family line through our father."

33That night they got their father
to drink wine, and the older daughter went in and lay with him. He
was not aware of it when she lay
down or when she got up.

34The next day the older daughter said to the younger, "Last night
I lay with my father. Let's get him
to drink wine again tonight, and
you go in and lie with him so we
can preserve our family line
through our father." 35So they got
their father to drink wine that night
also, and the younger daughter
went and lay with him. Again he
was not aware of it when she lay
down or when she got up.

36So both of Lot's daughters became pregnant by their father.
37The older daughter had a son,
and she named him Moab[m]; he is
the father of the Moabites[i] of today. 38The younger daughter also
had a son, and she named him
Ben-Ammi[n]; he is the father of the
Ammonites[j] of today.

Abraham and Abimelech

20:1–18Ref — Ge 12:10–20; 26:1–11

20 Now Abraham moved on
from there[k] into the region
of the Negev and lived between Kadesh and Shur. For a while he
stayed in Gerar,[l] 2and there Abraham said of his wife Sarah, "She is
my sister.[m]" Then Abimelech king
of Gerar sent for Sarah and took
her.[n]

3But God came to Abimelech in
a dream[o] one night and said to
him, "You are as good as dead because of the woman you have tak-
en; she is a married woman."[p]

4Now Abimelech had not gone
near her, so he said, "Lord, will you
destroy an innocent nation?[q] 5Did
he not say to me, 'She is my sister,'
and didn't she also say, 'He is my
brother'? I have done this with a
clear conscience and clean hands."

6Then God said to him in the
dream, "Yes, I know you did this
with a clear conscience, and so I
have kept[r] you from sinning
against me. That is why I did not let
you touch her. 7Now return the
man's wife, for he is a prophet, and
he will pray for you[s] and you will
live. But if you do not return her,
you may be sure that you and all
yours will die."

8Early the next morning Abimelech summoned all his officials,
and when he told them all that had
happened, they were very much
afraid. 9Then Abimelech called
Abraham in and said, "What have
you done to us? How have I
wronged you that you have brought
such great guilt upon me and my
kingdom? You have done things to
me that should not be done.[t]"
10And Abimelech asked Abraham,
"What was your reason for doing
this?"

11Abraham replied, "I said to

19:24 [a]Lk 17:29; 2Pe 2:6; Jude 7
19:25 [b]Ps 107:34; Eze 16:48
19:26 [c]ver 17 [d]Lk 17:32
19:27 [e]Ge 18:22
19:28 [f]Rev 9:2; 18:9
19:29 [g]2Pe 2:7
19:30 [h]ver 19
19:37 [i]Dt 2:9
19:38 [j]Dt 2:19
20:1 [k]Ge 18:1 [l]Ge 26:1,6,17
20:2 [m]ver 12; Ge 12:13; 26:7 [n]Ge 12:15
20:3 [o]Job 33:15; Mt 27:19 [p]Ps 105:14
20:4 [q]Ge 18:25
20:6 [r]1Sa 25:26,34
20:7 [s]ver 17; 1Sa 7:5; Job 42:8
20:9 [t]Ge 12:18; 26:10; 34:7

[m]37 *Moab* sounds like the Hebrew for *from father.* [n]38 *Ben-Ammi* means *son of my people.*

myself, 'There is surely no fear of God[a] in this place, and they will kill me because of my wife.'[b] **12**Besides, she really is my sister, the daughter of my father though not of my mother; and she became my wife. **13**And when God had me wander from my father's household, I said to her, 'This is how you can show your love to me: Everywhere we go, say of me, "He is my brother." ' "

14Then Abimelech brought sheep and cattle and male and female slaves and gave them to Abraham,[c] and he returned Sarah his wife to him. **15**And Abimelech said, "My land is before you; live wherever you like."[d]

16To Sarah he said, "I am giving your brother a thousand shekels[o] of silver. This is to cover the offense against you before all who are with you; you are completely vindicated."

17Then Abraham prayed to God,[e] and God healed Abimelech, his wife and his slave girls so they could have children again, **18**for the LORD had closed up every womb in Abimelech's household because of Abraham's wife Sarah.[f]

The Birth of Isaac

21 Now the LORD was gracious to Sarah[g] as he had said, and the LORD did for Sarah what he had promised.[h] **2**Sarah became pregnant and bore a son[i] to Abraham in his old age,[j] at the very time God had promised him. **3**Abraham gave the name Isaac[p][k] to the son Sarah bore him. **4**When his son Isaac was eight days old, Abraham circumcised him,[l] as God commanded him. **5**Abraham was a hundred years old when his son Isaac was born to him.

6Sarah said, "God has brought me laughter,[m] and everyone who hears about this will laugh with me." **7**And she added, "Who would have said to Abraham that Sarah would nurse children? Yet I have borne him a son in his old age."

Hagar and Ishmael Sent Away

8The child grew and was weaned, and on the day Isaac was weaned Abraham held a great feast. **9**But Sarah saw that the son whom Hagar the Egyptian had borne to Abraham[n] was mocking,[o] **10**and she said to Abraham, "Get rid of that slave woman and her son, for that slave woman's son will never share in the inheritance with my son Isaac."[p]

11The matter distressed Abraham greatly because it concerned his son.[q] **12**But God said to him, "Do not be so distressed about the boy and your maidservant. Listen to whatever Sarah tells you, because it is through Isaac that your offspring[q] will be reckoned.[r] **13**I will make the son of the maidservant into a nation[s] also, because he is your offspring."

14Early the next morning Abraham took some food and a skin of water and gave them to Hagar. He set them on her shoulders and then sent her off with the boy. She went on her way and wandered in the desert of Beersheba.[t]

15When the water in the skin was gone, she put the boy under one of the bushes. **16**Then she went off and sat down nearby, about a bowshot away, for she thought, "I cannot watch the boy die." And as she sat there nearby, she[r] began to sob.

17God heard the boy crying,[u] and the angel of God called to Hagar from heaven and said to her, "What is the matter, Hagar? Do not be afraid; God has heard the boy crying as he lies there. **18**Lift the boy up and take him by the hand, for I will make him into a great nation.[v]"

19Then God opened her eyes[w] and she saw a well of water. So she went and filled the skin with water and gave the boy a drink.

20God was with the boy[x] as he

20:11 [a] Ge 42:18; Ps 36:1 [b] Ge 12:12; 26:7
20:14 [c] Ge 12:16
20:15 [d] Ge 13:9
20:17 [e] Job 42:9
20:18 [f] Ge 12:17
21:1 [g] 1Sa 2:21 [h] Ge 8:1; 17:16,21; Gal 4:23
21:2 [i] Ge 17:19 [j] Gal 4:22; Heb 11:11
21:3 [k] Ge 17:19
21:4 [l] Ge 17:10,12; Ac 7:8
21:6 [m] Ge 17:17; Isa 54:1
21:9 [n] Ge 16:15 [o] Gal 4:29
21:10 [p] Gal 4:30*
21:11 [q] Ge 17:18
21:12 [r] Ro 9:7*; Heb 11:18*
21:13 [s] ver 18
21:14 [t] ver 31,32
21:17 [u] Ex 3:7
21:18 [v] ver 13
21:19 [w] Nu 22:31
21:20 [x] Ge 26:3,24; 28:15; 39:2, 21,23

[o] 16 That is, about 25 pounds (about 11.5 kilograms) [p] 3 *Isaac* means *he laughs.* [q] 12 Or *seed* [r] 16 Hebrew; Septuagint *the child*

grew up. He lived in the desert and
became an archer. 21While he was
living in the Desert of Paran, his
mother got a wife for him[a] from
Egypt.

The Treaty at Beersheba

22At that time Abimelech and
Phicol the commander of his forces
said to Abraham, "God is with you
in everything you do. 23Now
swear[b] to me here before God
that you will not deal falsely with
me or my children or my descendants. Show to me and the country
where you are living as an alien the
same kindness I have shown to
you."

24Abraham said, "I swear it."

25Then Abraham complained to
Abimelech about a well of water
that Abimelech's servants had
seized.[c] 26But Abimelech said, "I
don't know who has done this. You
did not tell me, and I heard about
it only today."

27So Abraham brought sheep
and cattle and gave them to Abimelech, and the two men made a treaty.[d] 28Abraham set apart seven
ewe lambs from the flock, 29and
Abimelech asked Abraham, "What
is the meaning of these seven ewe
lambs you have set apart by themselves?"

30He replied, "Accept these sev-
en lambs from my hand as a witness[e] that I dug this well."

31So that place was called Beersheba,[s][f] because the two men
swore an oath there.

32After the treaty had been made
at Beersheba, Abimelech and Phicol the commander of his forces returned to the land of the Philistines. 33Abraham planted a tamarisk tree in Beersheba, and there he
called upon the name of the LORD,[g]
the Eternal God.[h] 34And Abraham
stayed in the land of the Philistines
for a long time.

Abraham Tested

22 Some time later God tested[i] Abraham. He said to
him, "Abraham!"

"Here I am," he replied.

2Then God said, "Take your
son[j], your only son, Isaac, whom
you love, and go to the region of
Moriah.[k] Sacrifice him there as a
burnt offering on one of the mountains I will tell you about."

3Early the next morning Abraham got up and saddled his donkey. He took with him two of his
servants and his son Isaac. When
he had cut enough wood for the
burnt offering, he set out for the
place God had told him about. 4On
the third day Abraham looked up
and saw the place in the distance.
5He said to his servants, "Stay here
with the donkey while I and the boy
go over there. We will worship and
then we will come back to you."

6Abraham took the wood for the
burnt offering and placed it on his
son Isaac,[l] and he himself carried
the fire and the knife. As the two of
them went on together, 7Isaac
spoke up and said to his father
Abraham, "Father?"

"Yes, my son?" Abraham replied.

"The fire and wood are here,"
Isaac said, "but where is the lamb[m]
for the burnt offering?"

8Abraham answered, "God himself will provide the lamb for the
burnt offering, my son." And the
two of them went on together.

9When they reached the place
God had told him about, Abraham
built an altar there and arranged
the wood on it. He bound his son
Isaac and laid him on the altar,[n]
on top of the wood. 10Then he
reached out his hand and took the
knife to slay his son. 11But the angel of the LORD called out to him
from heaven, "Abraham! Abraham!"

"Here I am," he replied.

12"Do not lay a hand on the
boy," he said. "Do not do anything
to him. Now I know that you fear
God,[o] because you have not withheld from me your son, your only
son.[p]"

13Abraham looked up and there

21:21 [a]Ge 24:4,38
21:23 [b]ver 31; Jos 2:12
21:25 [c]Ge 26:15,18, 20-22
21:27 [d]Ge 26:28,31
21:30 [e]Ge 31:44,47, 48,50,52
21:31 [f]Ge 26:33
21:33 [g]Ge 4:26 [h]Dt 33:27
22:1 [i]Dt 8:2,16; Heb 11:17; Jas 1:12-13
22:2 [j]ver 12,16; Jn 3:16; Heb 11:17; 1Jn 4:9 [k]2Ch 3:1
22:6 [l]Jn 19:17
22:7 [m]Lev 1:10
22:9 [n]Heb 11:17-19; Jas 2:21
22:12 [o]1Sa 15:22; Jas 2:21-22 [p]ver 2; Jn 3:16

[s]31 *Beersheba* can mean *well of seven* or *well of the oath.*

in a thicket he saw a ram[t] caught
by its horns. He went over and took
the ram and sacrificed it as a burnt
offering instead of his son.[a] 14So
Abraham called that place The
LORD Will Provide. And to this day
it is said, "On the mountain of the
LORD it will be provided.[b]"
15The angel of the LORD called to
Abraham from heaven a second
time 16and said, "I swear by myself,[c] declares the LORD, that because you have done this and have
not withheld your son, your only
son, 17I will surely bless you and
make your descendants[d] as numerous as the stars in the sky[e] and
as the sand on the seashore.[f] Your
descendants will take possession
of the cities of their enemies,[g]
18and through your offspring[u] all
nations on earth will be blessed,[h]
because you have obeyed me."[i]
19Then Abraham returned to his
servants, and they set off together
for Beersheba. And Abraham
stayed in Beersheba.

Nahor's Sons

20Some time later Abraham was
told, "Milcah is also a mother; she
has borne sons to your brother Nahor:[j] 21Uz the firstborn, Buz his
brother, Kemuel (the father of
Aram), 22Kesed, Hazo, Pildash,
Jidlaph and Bethuel." 23Bethuel
became the father of Rebekah.[k]
Milcah bore these eight sons to
Abraham's brother Nahor. 24His
concubine, whose name was Reu-
mah, also had sons: Tebah, Ga-
ham, Tahash and Maacah.

The Death of Sarah

23 Sarah lived to be a hundred
and twenty-seven years old.
2She died at Kiriath Arba[l] (that is,
Hebron)[m] in the land of Canaan,
and Abraham went to mourn for
Sarah and to weep over her.
3Then Abraham rose from beside
his dead wife and spoke to the Hittites.[v] He said, 4"I am an alien and
a stranger[n] among you. Sell me
some property for a burial site here
so I can bury my dead."
5The Hittites replied to Abraham, 6"Sir, listen to us. You are a
mighty prince[o] among us. Bury
your dead in the choicest of our
tombs. None of us will refuse you
his tomb for burying your dead."
7Then Abraham rose and bowed
down before the people of the land,
the Hittites. 8He said to them, "If
you are willing to let me bury my
dead, then listen to me and intercede with Ephron son of Zohar[p] on
my behalf 9so he will sell me the
cave of Machpelah, which belongs
to him and is at the end of his field.
Ask him to sell it to me for the full
price as a burial site among you."
10Ephron the Hittite was sitting
among his people and he replied to
Abraham in the hearing of all the
Hittites who had come to the gate[q]
of his city. 11"No, my lord," he
said. "Listen to me; I give[w][r] you
the field, and I give[w] you the cave
that is in it. I give[w] it to you in the
presence of my people. Bury your
dead."
12Again Abraham bowed down
before the people of the land 13and
he said to Ephron in their hearing,
"Listen to me, if you will. I will pay
the price of the field. Accept it from
me so I can bury my dead there."
14Ephron answered Abraham,
15"Listen to me, my lord; the land
is worth four hundred shekels[x] of
silver,[s] but what is that between
me and you? Bury your dead."
16Abraham agreed to Ephron's
terms and weighed out for him the
price he had named in the hearing
of the Hittites: four hundred shekels of silver,[t] according to the
weight current among the merchants.
17So Ephron's field in Machpelah near Mamre[u]—both the field
and the cave in it, and all the trees
within the borders of the field—
was deeded 18to Abraham as his
property in the presence of all the
Hittites who had come to the gate

22:13 [a] Ro 8:32
22:14 [b] ver 8
22:16 [c] Lk 1:73; Heb 6:13
22:17 [d] Heb 6:14* [e] Ge 15:5 [f] Ge 26:24; 32:12 [g] Ge 24:60
22:18 [h] Ge 12:2,3; Ac 3:25*; Gal 3:8* [i] ver 10
22:20 [j] Ge 11:29
22:23 [k] Ge 24:15
23:2 [l] Jos 14:15 [m] ver 19; Ge 13:18
23:4 [n] Ge 17:8; 1Ch 29:15; Ps 105:12; Heb 11:9,13
23:6 [o] Ge 14:14-16; 24:35
23:8 [p] Ge 25:9
23:10 [q] Ge 34:20-24; Ru 4:4
23:11 [r] 2Sa 24:23
23:15 [s] Eze 45:12
23:16 [t] Jer 32:9; Zec 11:12
23:17 [u] Ge 25:9; 49:30-32; 50:13; Ac 7:16

[t] *13* Many manuscripts of the Masoretic Text, Samaritan Pentateuch, Septuagint and Syriac; most manuscripts of the Masoretic Text *a ram behind him* [u] *18* Or *seed* [v] *3* Or *the sons of Heth*; also in verses 5, 7, 10, 16, 18 and 20 [w] *11* Or *sell* [x] *15* That is, about 10 pounds (about 4.5 kilograms)

of the city. 19Afterward Abraham
buried his wife Sarah in the cave in
the field of Machpelah near Mamre
(which is at Hebron) in the land of
Canaan. 20So the field and the cave
in it were deeded[a] to Abraham by
the Hittites as a burial site.

Isaac and Rebekah

24 Abraham was now old and
well advanced in years, and
the LORD had blessed him in every
way.[b] 2He said to the chief[y] servant in his household, the one in
charge of all that he had,[c] "Put
your hand under my thigh.[d] 3I
want you to swear by the LORD, the
God of heaven and the God of
earth,[e] that you will not get a wife
for my son[f] from the daughters of
the Canaanites,[g] among whom I
am living, 4but will go to my country and my own relatives[h] and get
a wife for my son Isaac."

5The servant asked him, "What if
the woman is unwilling to come
back with me to this land? Shall I
then take your son back to the
country you came from?"

6"Make sure that you do not take
my son back there," Abraham said.
7"The LORD, the God of heaven,
who brought me out of my father's
household and my native land and
who spoke to me and promised me
on oath, saying, 'To your offspring[z][i] I will give this land'[j]—
he will send his angel before you[k]
so that you can get a wife for my
son from there. 8If the woman is
unwilling to come back with you,
then you will be released from this
oath of mine. Only do not take my
son back there." 9So the servant
put his hand under the thigh[l] of
his master Abraham and swore an
oath to him concerning this matter.

10Then the servant took ten of
his master's camels and left, taking
with him all kinds of good things
from his master. He set out for
Aram Naharaim[a] and made his
way to the town of Nahor. 11He had
the camels kneel down near the
well[m] outside the town; it was toward evening, the time the women
go out to draw water.[n]

12Then he prayed, "O LORD, God
of my master Abraham,[o] give me
success today, and show kindness
to my master Abraham. 13See, I am
standing beside this spring, and
the daughters of the townspeople
are coming out to draw water.
14May it be that when I say to a girl,
'Please let down your jar that I may
have a drink,' and she says, 'Drink,
and I'll water your camels too'—let
her be the one you have chosen for
your servant Isaac. By this I will
know[p] that you have shown kindness to my master."

15Before he had finished praying,[q] Rebekah[r] came out with her
jar on her shoulder. She was the
daughter of Bethuel son of Milcah,[s] who was the wife of Abraham's brother Nahor.[t] 16The girl
was very beautiful,[u] a virgin; no
man had ever lain with her. She
went down to the spring, filled her
jar and came up again.

17The servant hurried to meet
her and said, "Please give me a little water from your jar."

18"Drink,[v] my lord," she said,
and quickly lowered the jar to her
hands and gave him a drink.

19After she had given him a
drink, she said, "I'll draw water for
your camels too,[w] until they have
finished drinking." 20So she quickly emptied her jar into the trough,
ran back to the well to draw more
water, and drew enough for all his
camels. 21Without saying a word,
the man watched her closely to
learn whether or not the LORD had
made his journey successful.[x]

22When the camels had finished
drinking, the man took out a gold
nose ring[y] weighing a beka[b] and
two gold bracelets weighing ten
shekels.[c] 23Then he asked,
"Whose daughter are you? Please
tell me, is there room in your father's house for us to spend the
night?"

23:20 [a] Jer 32:10
24:1 [b] ver 35
24:2 [c] Ge 39:4-6 [d] ver 9; Ge 47:29
24:3 [e] Ge 14:19 [f] Ge 28:1; Dt 7:3 [g] Ge 10:15-19
24:4 [h] Ge 12:1; 28:2
24:7 [i] Gal 3:16* [j] Ge 12:7; 13:15 [k] Ex 23:20,23
24:9 [l] ver 2
24:11 [m] Ex 2:15 [n] ver 13; 1Sa 9:11
24:12 [o] ver 27,42,48; Ge 26:24; Ex 3:6,15,16
24:14 [p] Jdg 6:17,37
24:15 [q] ver 45 [r] Ge 22:23 [s] Ge 22:20 [t] Ge 11:29
24:16 [u] Ge 26:7
24:18 [v] ver 14
24:19 [w] ver 14
24:21 [x] ver 12
24:22 [y] ver 47

[y] 2 Or *oldest* [z] 7 Or *seed* [a] 10 That is, Northwest Mesopotamia [b] 22 That is, about 1/5 ounce (about 5.5 grams) [c] 23 That is, about 4 ounces (about 110 grams)

24She answered him, "I am the
daughter of Bethuel, the son that
Milcah bore to Nahor.[a]" 25And she
added, "We have plenty of straw
and fodder, as well as room for you
to spend the night."
26Then the man bowed down
and worshiped the LORD,[b] 27saying,
"Praise be to the LORD,[c] the
God of my master Abraham, who
has not abandoned his kindness
and faithfulness[d] to my master. As
for me, the LORD has led me on the
journey[e] to the house of my master's
relatives."[f]
28The girl ran and told her mother's
household about these things.
29Now Rebekah had a brother
named Laban,[g] and he hurried out
to the man at the spring. 30As soon
as he had seen the nose ring, and
the bracelets on his sister's arms,
and had heard Rebekah tell what
the man said to her, he went out to
the man and found him standing by
the camels near the spring.
31"Come, you who are blessed by
the LORD,"[h] he said. "Why are you
standing out here? I have prepared
the house and a place for the camels."
32So the man went to the house,
and the camels were unloaded.
Straw and fodder were brought for
the camels, and water for him and
his men to wash their feet.[i]
33Then food was set before him,
but he said, "I will not eat until I
have told you what I have to say."
"Then tell us," Laban said.
34So he said, "I am Abraham's
servant. 35The LORD has blessed my
master abundantly,[j] and he has
become wealthy. He has given him
sheep and cattle, silver and gold,
menservants and maidservants,
and camels and donkeys.[k] 36My
master's wife Sarah has borne him
a son in her[d] old age,[l] and he has
given him everything he owns.[m]
37And my master made me swear
an oath, and said, 'You must not
get a wife for my son from the
daughters of the Canaanites, in
whose land I live,[n] 38but go to my
father's family and to my own clan,
and get a wife for my son.'[o]

24:24 [a] ver 15
24:26 [b] ver 48,52; Ex 4:31
24:27 [c] Ex 18:10; Ru 4:14; 1Sa 25:32 [d] ver 49; Ge 32:10; Ps 98:3 [e] ver 21 [f] ver 12,48
24:29 [g] ver 4; Ge 29:5,12,13
24:31 [h] Ge 26:29; Ru 3:10; Ps 115:15
24:32 [i] Ge 43:24; Jdg 19:21
24:35 [j] ver 1 [k] Ge 13:2
24:36 [l] Ge 21:2,10 [m] Ge 25:5
24:37 [n] ver 3
24:38 [o] ver 4
24:39 [p] ver 5
24:40 [q] ver 7
24:41 [r] ver 8
24:42 [s] ver 12
24:43 [t] ver 13 [u] ver 14
24:45 [v] 1Sa 1:13 [w] ver 15 [x] ver 17
24:46 [y] ver 18-19
24:47 [z] ver 23 [a] ver 24 [b] Eze 16:11-12
24:48 [c] ver 26 [d] ver 27
24:49 [e] Ge 47:29; Jos 2:14

39"Then I asked my master,
'What if the woman will not come
back with me?'[p]
40"He replied, 'The LORD, before
whom I have walked, will send his
angel with you[q] and make your
journey a success, so that you can
get a wife for my son from my own
clan and from my father's family.
41Then, when you go to my clan,
you will be released from my oath
even if they refuse to give her to
you—you will be released from my
oath.'[r]
42"When I came to the spring today,
I said, 'O LORD, God of my master
Abraham, if you will, please
grant success[s] to the journey on
which I have come. 43See, I am
standing beside this spring;[t] if a
maiden comes out to draw water
and I say to her, "Please let me
drink a little water from your jar,"[u]
44and if she says to me, "Drink, and
I'll draw water for your camels
too," let her be the one the LORD
has chosen for my master's son.'
45"Before I finished praying in
my heart,[v] Rebekah came out,
with her jar on her shoulder.[w] She
went down to the spring and drew
water, and I said to her, 'Please give
me a drink.'[x]
46"She quickly lowered her jar
from her shoulder and said, 'Drink,
and I'll water your camels too.'[y] So
I drank, and she watered the camels
also.
47"I asked her, 'Whose daughter
are you?'[z]
"She said, 'The daughter of Bethuel
son of Nahor, whom Milcah
bore to him.'[a]
"Then I put the ring in her nose
and the bracelets on her arms,[b]
48and I bowed down and worshiped
the LORD.[c] I praised the LORD, the
God of my master Abraham, who
had led me on the right road to get
the granddaughter of my master's
brother for his son.[d] 49Now if you
will show kindness and faithfulness[e]
to my master, tell me; and if
not, tell me, so I may know which
way to turn."

[d]36 Or *his*

50Laban and Bethuel answered,
"This is from the LORD;[a] we can say
nothing to you one way or the other.[b] **51**Here is Rebekah; take her
and go, and let her become the wife
of your master's son, as the LORD
has directed."
52When Abraham's servant
heard what they said, he bowed
down to the ground before the
LORD.[c] **53**Then the servant brought
out gold and silver jewelry and articles of clothing and gave them to
Rebekah; he also gave costly gifts[d]
to her brother and to her mother.
54Then he and the men who were
with him ate and drank and spent
the night there.
When they got up the next morning, he said, "Send me on my way[e]
to my master."
55But her brother and her mother replied, "Let the girl remain with
us ten days or so; then you[e] may
go."
56But he said to them, "Do not
detain me, now that the LORD has
granted success to my journey.
Send me on my way so I may go to
my master."
57Then they said, "Let's call the
girl and ask her about it." **58**So they
called Rebekah and asked her,
"Will you go with this man?"
"I will go," she said.
59So they sent their sister Rebekah on her way, along with her
nurse[f] and Abraham's servant and
his men. **60**And they blessed Rebekah and said to her,

"Our sister, may you increase
to thousands upon
thousands;[g]
may your offspring possess
the gates of their enemies."[h]

61Then Rebekah and her maids
got ready and mounted their camels and went back with the man.
So the servant took Rebekah and
left.
62Now Isaac had come from Beer
Lahai Roi,[i] for he was living in the
Negev.[j] **63**He went out to the field
one evening to meditate,[f][k] and as
he looked up, he saw camels approaching. **64**Rebekah also looked
up and saw Isaac. She got down
from her camel **65**and asked the
servant, "Who is that man in the
field coming to meet us?"
"He is my master," the servant
answered. So she took her veil and
covered herself.
66Then the servant told Isaac all
he had done. **67**Isaac brought her
into the tent of his mother Sarah,
and he married Rebekah.[l] So she
became his wife, and he loved
her;[m] and Isaac was comforted after his mother's death.[n]

The Death of Abraham

25:1–4pp — 1Ch 1:32–33

25 Abraham took[g] another
wife, whose name was Ke-
turah. **2**She bore him Zimran, Jokshan, Medan, Midian, Ishbak and
Shuah.[o] **3**Jokshan was the father
of Sheba and Dedan; the descendants of Dedan were the Asshu-
rites, the Letushites and the Leum-
mites. **4**The sons of Midian were
Ephah, Epher, Hanoch, Abida and
Eldaah. All these were descendants of Keturah.
5Abraham left everything he
owned to Isaac.[p] **6**But while he
was still living, he gave gifts to the
sons of his concubines[q] and sent
them away from his son Isaac[r] to
the land of the east.
7Altogether, Abraham lived a
hundred and seventy-five years.
8Then Abraham breathed his last
and died at a good old age,[s] an old
man and full of years; and he was
gathered to his people.[t] **9**His sons
Isaac and Ishmael buried him[u] in
the cave of Machpelah near Mamre, in the field of Ephron son of Zohar the Hittite,[v] **10**the field Abraham had bought from the Hit-
tites.[h][w] There Abraham was
buried with his wife Sarah. **11**After
Abraham's death, God blessed his
son Isaac, who then lived near Beer
Lahai Roi.[x]

24:50 [a]Ps 118:23 [b]Ge 31:7,24,29,42
24:52 [c]ver 26
24:53 [d]ver 10,22
24:54 [e]ver 56,59
24:59 [f]Ge 35:8
24:60 [g]Ge 17:16 [h]Ge 22:17
24:62 [i]Ge 16:14; 25:11 [j]Ge 20:1
24:63 [k]Ps 1:2; 77:12; 119:15,27,48,97,148; 143:5; 145:5
24:67 [l]Ge 25:20 [m]Ge 29:18,20 [n]Ge 23:1-2
25:2 [o]1Ch 1:32,33
25:5 [p]Ge 24:36
25:6 [q]Ge 22:24 [r]Ge 21:10,14
25:8 [s]Ge 15:15 [t]ver 17; Ge 35:29; 49:29,33
25:9 [u]Ge 35:29 [v]Ge 50:13
25:10 [w]Ge 23:16
25:11 [x]Ge 16:14

[e]55 Or *she* [f]63 The meaning of the Hebrew for this word is uncertain. [g]1 Or *had taken* [h]10 Or *the sons of Heth*

Ishmael's Sons

25:12–16pp – 1Ch 1:29–31

12This is the account of Abraham's son Ishmael, whom Sarah's
maidservant, Hagar[a] the Egyptian,
bore to Abraham.[b]

13These are the names of the
sons of Ishmael, listed in the order
of their birth: Nebaioth the firstborn of Ishmael, Kedar, Adbeel,
Mibsam, 14Mishma, Dumah, Massa, 15Hadad, Tema, Jetur, Naphish
and Kedemah. 16These were the
sons of Ishmael, and these are the
names of the twelve tribal rulers[c]
according to their settlements and
camps. 17Altogether, Ishmael lived
a hundred and thirty-seven years.
He breathed his last and died, and
he was gathered to his people.[d]
18His descendants settled in the
area from Havilah to Shur, near the
border of Egypt, as you go toward
Asshur. And they lived in hostility
toward[i] all their brothers.[e]

Jacob and Esau

19This is the account of Abraham's son Isaac.

Abraham became the father of
Isaac, 20and Isaac was forty years
old[f] when he married Rebekah[g]
daughter of Bethuel the Aramean
from Paddan Aram[j] and sister of
Laban[h] the Aramean.

21Isaac prayed to the LORD on behalf of his wife, because she was
barren. The LORD answered his
prayer,[i] and his wife Rebekah became pregnant. 22The babies jos-
tled each other within her, and she
said, "Why is this happening to
me?" So she went to inquire of the
LORD.[j]

23The LORD said to her,

"Two nations[k] are in your
womb,
and two peoples from within
you will be separated;
one people will be stronger
than the other,
and the older will serve the
younger.[l]"

24When the time came for her to
give birth, there were twin boys in
her womb. 25The first to come out
was red, and his whole body was
like a hairy garment;[m] so they
named him Esau.[k] 26After this, his
brother came out, with his hand
grasping Esau's heel;[n] so he was
named Jacob.[l][o] Isaac was sixty
years old when Rebekah gave birth
to them.

27The boys grew up, and Esau
became a skillful hunter, a man of
the open country,[p] while Jacob
was a quiet man, staying among
the tents. 28Isaac, who had a taste
for wild game,[q] loved Esau, but
Rebekah loved Jacob.[r]

29Once when Jacob was cooking
some stew, Esau came in from the
open country, famished. 30He said
to Jacob, "Quick, let me have some
of that red stew! I'm famished!"
(That is why he was also called
Edom.[m])

31Jacob replied, "First sell me
your birthright."

32"Look, I am about to die,"
Esau said. "What good is the birthright to me?"

33But Jacob said, "Swear to me
first." So he swore an oath to him,
selling his birthright[s] to Jacob.

34Then Jacob gave Esau some
bread and some lentil stew. He ate
and drank, and then got up and
left.

So Esau despised his birthright.

Isaac and Abimelech

26:1–11Ref – Ge 12:10–20; 20:1–18

26 Now there was a famine in
the land[t]—besides the
earlier famine of Abraham's time
—and Isaac went to Abimelech
king of the Philistines in Gerar.[u]
2The LORD appeared[v] to Isaac and
said, "Do not go down to Egypt; live
in the land where I tell you to live.[w]
3Stay in this land for a while,[x] and
I will be with you and will bless
you.[y] For to you and your descen-

25:12 [a]Ge 16:1 [b]Ge 16:15
25:16 [c]Ge 17:20
25:17 [d]ver 8
25:18 [e]Ge 16:12
25:20 [f]ver 26; Ge 26:34 [g]Ge 24:67 [h]Ge 24:29
25:21 [i]1Ch 5:20; 2Ch 33:13; Ezr 8:23; Ps 127:3; Ro 9:10
25:22 [j]1Sa 9:9; 10:22
25:23 [k]Ge 17:4 [l]Ge 27:29,40; Mal 1:3; Ro 9:11-12*
25:25 [m]Ge 27:11
25:26 [n]Hos 12:3 [o]Ge 27:36
25:27 [p]Ge 27:3,5
25:28 [q]Ge 27: 19 [r]Ge 27:6
25:33 [s]Ge 27:36; Heb 12:16
26:1 [t]Ge 12:10 [u]Ge 20:1
26:2 [v]Ge 12:7; 17:1; 18:1 [w]Ge 12:1
26:3 [x]Ge 20:1; 28:15 [y]Ge 12:2; 22:16-18

[i]18 *Or lived to the east of* [j]20 That is, Northwest Mesopotamia [k]25 *Esau* may mean *hairy*; he was also called Edom, which means *red.* [l]26 *Jacob* means *he grasps the heel* (figuratively, *he deceives*). [m]30 *Edom* means *red.*

dants I will give all these lands[a] and will confirm the oath I swore to your father Abraham. 4I will make your descendants as numerous as the stars in the sky[b] and will give them all these lands, and through your offspring[n] all nations on earth will be blessed,[c] 5because Abraham obeyed me[d] and kept my requirements, my commands, my decrees and my laws." 6So Isaac stayed in Gerar.

7When the men of that place asked him about his wife, he said, "She is my sister,[e]" because he was afraid to say, "She is my wife." He thought, "The men of this place might kill me on account of Rebekah, because she is beautiful."

8When Isaac had been there a long time, Abimelech king of the Philistines looked down from a window and saw Isaac caressing his wife Rebekah. 9So Abimelech summoned Isaac and said, "She is really your wife! Why did you say, 'She is my sister'?"

Isaac answered him, "Because I thought I might lose my life on account of her."

10Then Abimelech said, "What is this you have done to us?[f] One of the men might well have slept with your wife, and you would have brought guilt upon us."

11So Abimelech gave orders to all the people: "Anyone who molests[g] this man or his wife shall surely be put to death."

12Isaac planted crops in that land and the same year reaped a hundredfold, because the LORD blessed him.[h] 13The man became rich, and his wealth continued to grow until he became very wealthy.[i] 14He had so many flocks and herds and servants[j] that the Philistines envied him.[k] 15So all the wells[l] that his father's servants had dug in the time of his father Abraham, the Philistines stopped up,[m] filling them with earth.

16Then Abimelech said to Isaac, "Move away from us; you have become too powerful for us.[n]"

17So Isaac moved away from there and encamped in the Valley of Gerar and settled there. 18Isaac reopened the wells[o] that had been dug in the time of his father Abraham, which the Philistines had stopped up after Abraham died, and he gave them the same names his father had given them.

19Isaac's servants dug in the valley and discovered a well of fresh water there. 20But the herdsmen of Gerar quarreled with Isaac's herdsmen and said, "The water is ours!"[p] So he named the well Esek,[o] because they disputed with him. 21Then they dug another well, but they quarreled over that one also; so he named it Sitnah.[p] 22He moved on from there and dug another well, and no one quarreled over it. He named it Rehoboth,[q] saying, "Now the LORD has given us room and we will flourish[q] in the land."

23From there he went up to Beersheba. 24That night the LORD appeared to him and said, "I am the God of your father Abraham.[r] Do not be afraid,[s] for I am with you; I will bless you and will increase the number of your descendants[t] for the sake of my servant Abraham."[u]

25Isaac built an altar[v] there and called on the name of the LORD. There he pitched his tent, and there his servants dug a well.

26Meanwhile, Abimelech had come to him from Gerar, with Ahuzzath his personal adviser and Phicol the commander of his forces.[w] 27Isaac asked them, "Why have you come to me, since you were hostile to me and sent me away?[x]"

28They answered, "We saw clearly that the LORD was with you;[y] so we said, 'There ought to be a sworn agreement between us'—between us and you. Let us make a treaty with you 29that you will do us no harm, just as we did not molest you but always treated you well and

26:3 [a]Ge 12:7; 13:15; 15:18
26:4 [b]Ge 15:5; 22:17; Ex 32:13 [c]Ge 12:3; 22:18; Gal 3:8
26:5 [d]Ge 22:16
26:7 [e]Ge 12:13; 20:2,12; Pr 29:25
26:10 [f]Ge 20:9
26:11 [g]Ps 105:15
26:12 [h]ver 3; Job 42:12
26:13 [i]Pr 10:22
26:14 [j]Ge 24:36 [k]Ge 37:11
26:15 [l]Ge 21:30 [m]Ge 21:25
26:16 [n]Ex 1:9
26:18 [o]Ge 21:30
26:20 [p]Ge 21:25
26:22 [q]Ge 17:6; Ex 1:7
26:24 [r]Ge 24:12; Ex 3:6 [s]Ge 15:1 [t]ver 4 [u]Ge 17:7
26:25 [v]Ge 12:7,8; 13:4,18; Ps 116:17
26:26 [w]Ge 21:22
26:27 [x]ver 16
26:28 [y]Ge 21:22

[n]4 Or *seed* [o]20 *Esek* means *dispute.*
[p]21 *Sitnah* means *opposition.*
[q]22 *Rehoboth* means *room.*

sent you away in peace. And now
you are blessed by the LORD."[a]
30 Isaac then made a feast[b] for
them, and they ate and drank.
31 Early the next morning the men
swore an oath[c] to each other.
Then Isaac sent them on their way,
and they left him in peace.
32 That day Isaac's servants came
and told him about the well they
had dug. They said, "We've found
water!" 33 He called it Shibah,[r] and
to this day the name of the town
has been Beersheba.[s][d]
34 When Esau was forty years
old,[e] he married Judith daughter
of Beeri the Hittite, and also Basemath daughter of Elon the Hittite.[f] 35 They were a source of grief
to Isaac and Rebekah.[g]

Jacob Gets Isaac's Blessing

27 When Isaac was old and his
eyes were so weak that he
could no longer see,[h] he called for
Esau his older son[i] and said to
him, "My son."
"Here I am," he answered.
2 Isaac said, "I am now an old
man and don't know the day of my
death.[j] 3 Now then, get your weapons—your quiver and bow—and go
out to the open country[k] to hunt
some wild game for me. 4 Prepare
me the kind of tasty food I like and
bring it to me to eat, so that I may
give you my blessing[l] before I
die."
5 Now Rebekah was listening as
Isaac spoke to his son Esau. When
Esau left for the open country to
hunt game and bring it back, 6 Rebekah said to her son Jacob,[m]
"Look, I overheard your father say
to your brother Esau, 7 'Bring me
some game and prepare me some
tasty food to eat, so that I may give
you my blessing in the presence of
the LORD before I die.' 8 Now, my
son, listen carefully and do what I
tell you:[n] 9 Go out to the flock and
bring me two choice young goats,
so I can prepare some tasty food for
your father, just the way he likes it.
10 Then take it to your father to eat,
so that he may give you his blessing
before he dies."
11 Jacob said to Rebekah his
mother, "But my brother Esau is a
hairy man,[o] and I'm a man with
smooth skin. 12 What if my father
touches me?[p] I would appear to be
tricking him and would bring down
a curse on myself rather than a
blessing."
13 His mother said to him, "My
son, let the curse fall on me.[q] Just
do what I say;[r] go and get them for
me."
14 So he went and got them and
brought them to his mother, and
she prepared some tasty food, just
the way his father liked it. 15 Then
Rebekah took the best clothes[s] of
Esau her older son, which she had
in the house, and put them on her
younger son Jacob. 16 She also covered his hands and the smooth part
of his neck with the goatskins.
17 Then she handed to her son Jacob the tasty food and the bread
she had made.
18 He went to his father and said,
"My father."
"Yes, my son," he answered.
"Who is it?"
19 Jacob said to his father, "I am
Esau your firstborn. I have done as
you told me. Please sit up and eat
some of my game so that you may
give me your blessing."[t]
20 Isaac asked his son, "How did
you find it so quickly, my son?"
"The LORD your God gave me success,[u]" he replied.
21 Then Isaac said to Jacob,
"Come near so I can touch you,[v]
my son, to know whether you really
are my son Esau or not."
22 Jacob went close to his father
Isaac, who touched him and said,
"The voice is the voice of Jacob,
but the hands are the hands of
Esau." 23 He did not recognize him,
for his hands were hairy like those
of his brother Esau;[w] so he blessed
him. 24 "Are you really my son
Esau?" he asked.
"I am," he replied.
25 Then he said, "My son, bring

26:29 [a] Ge 24:31; Ps 115:15
26:30 [b] Ge 19:3
26:31 [c] Ge 21:31
26:33 [d] Ge 21:14
26:34 [e] Ge 25:20 [f] Ge 28:9; 36:2
26:35 [g] Ge 27:46
27:1 [h] Ge 48:10; 1Sa 3:2 [i] Ge 25:25
27:2 [j] Ge 47:29
27:3 [k] Ge 25:27
27:4 [l] ver 10,25,31; Ge 49:28; Dt 33:1; Heb 11:20
27:6 [m] Ge 25:28
27:8 [n] ver 13,43
27:11 [o] Ge 25:25
27:12 [p] ver 22
27:13 [q] Mt 27:25 [r] ver 8
27:15 [s] ver 27
27:19 [t] ver 4
27:20 [u] Ge 24:12
27:21 [v] ver 12
27:23 [w] ver 16

[r]33 *Shibah* can mean *oath* or *seven.*
[s]33 *Beersheba* can mean *well of the oath* or *well of seven.*

me some of your game to eat, so
that I may give you my blessing."[a]
Jacob brought it to him and he
ate; and he brought some wine and
he drank. 26Then his father Isaac
said to him, "Come here, my son,
and kiss me."
27So he went to him and kissed
him[b]. When Isaac caught the
smell of his clothes,[c] he blessed
him and said,

"Ah, the smell of my son
  is like the smell of a field
  that the LORD has blessed.[d]
28May God give you of heaven's
    dew[e]
  and of earth's richness[f]—
  an abundance of grain and
    new wine.[g]
29May nations serve you
  and peoples bow down to
    you.[h]
Be lord over your brothers,
  and may the sons of your
    mother bow down to
    you.[i]
May those who curse you be
    cursed
  and those who bless you be
    blessed.[j]"

30After Isaac finished blessing
him and Jacob had scarcely left his
father's presence, his brother Esau
came in from hunting. 31He too
prepared some tasty food and
brought it to his father. Then he
said to him, "My father, sit up and
eat some of my game, so that you
may give me your blessing."[k]
32His father Isaac asked him,
"Who are you?"[l]
"I am your son," he answered,
"your firstborn, Esau."
33Isaac trembled violently and
said, "Who was it, then, that hunted game and brought it to me? I ate
it just before you came and I
blessed him—and indeed he will
be blessed![m]"
34When Esau heard his father's
words, he burst out with a loud and
bitter cry[n] and said to his father,
"Bless me—me too, my father!"
35But he said, "Your brother
came deceitfully[o] and took your
blessing."

27:25 [a]ver 4
27:27 [b]Heb 11:20 [c]SS 4:11 [d]Ps 65:9-13
27:28 [e]Dt 33:13 [f]ver 39 [g]Ge 45:18; Nu 18:12; Dt 33:28
27:29 [h]Isa 45:14,23; 49:7,23 [i]Ge 9:25; 25:23; 37:7 [j]Ge 12:3; Nu 24:9; Zep 2:8
27:31 [k]ver 4
27:32 [l]ver 18
27:33 [m]ver 29; Ge 28:3,4; Ro 11:29
27:34 [n]Heb 12:17
27:35 [o]Jer 9:4; 12:6
27:36 [p]Ge 25:26 [q]Ge 25:33
27:37 [r]ver 28
27:38 [s]Heb 12:17
27:39 [t]ver 28
27:40 [u]2Sa 8:14 [v]Ge 25:23 [w]2Ki 8:20-22
27:41 [x]Ge 37:4 [y]Ge 32:11 [z]Ge 50:4,10 [a]Ob 1:10
27:43 [b]ver 8 [c]Ge 24:29 [d]Ge 11:31
27:44 [e]Ge 31:38,41
27:45 [f]ver 35

36Esau said, "Isn't he rightly
named Jacob[t]?[p] He has deceived
me these two times: He took my
birthright,[q] and now he's taken my
blessing!" Then he asked, "Haven't
you reserved any blessing for me?"
37Isaac answered Esau, "I have
made him lord over you and have
made all his relatives his servants,
and I have sustained him with grain
and new wine.[r] So what can I possibly do for you, my son?"
38Esau said to his father, "Do
you have only one blessing, my father? Bless me too, my father!"
Then Esau wept aloud.[s]
39His father Isaac answered him,

"Your dwelling will be
  away from the earth's
    richness,
  away from the dew[t] of
    heaven above.
40You will live by the sword
  and you will serve[u] your
    brother.[v]
But when you grow restless,
  you will throw his yoke
  from off your neck.[w]"

Jacob Flees to Laban

41Esau held a grudge[x] against
Jacob[y] because of the blessing his
father had given him. He said to
himself, "The days of mourning[z]
for my father are near; then I will
kill my brother Jacob."[a]
42When Rebekah was told what
her older son Esau had said, she
sent for her younger son Jacob and
said to him, "Your brother Esau is
consoling himself with the thought
of killing you. 43Now then, my son,
do what I say:[b] Flee at once to my
brother Laban[c] in Haran.[d] 44Stay
with him for a while[e] until your
brother's fury subsides. 45When
your brother is no longer angry with
you and forgets what you did to
him,[f] I'll send word for you to
come back from there. Why should
I lose both of you in one day?"
46Then Rebekah said to Isaac,
"I'm disgusted with living because

[t]36 *Jacob* means *he grasps the heel* (figuratively, *he deceives*).

of these Hittite women. If Jacob takes a wife from among the women of this land, from Hittite women like these, my life will not be worth living."[a]

28 So Isaac called for Jacob and blessed[u] him and commanded him: "Do not marry a Canaanite woman.[b] **2**Go at once to Paddan Aram,[v] to the house of your mother's father Bethuel.[c] Take a wife for yourself there, from among the daughters of Laban, your mother's brother. **3**May God Almighty[w][d] bless you and make you fruitful[e] and increase your numbers until you become a community of peoples. **4**May he give you and your descendants the blessing given to Abraham,[f] so that you may take possession of the land where you now live as an alien,[g] the land God gave to Abraham." **5**Then Isaac sent Jacob on his way, and he went to Paddan Aram,[h] to Laban son of Bethuel the Aramean, the brother of Rebekah,[i] who was the mother of Jacob and Esau.

6Now Esau learned that Isaac had blessed Jacob and had sent him to Paddan Aram to take a wife from there, and that when he blessed him he commanded him, "Do not marry a Canaanite woman,"[j] **7**and that Jacob had obeyed his father and mother and had gone to Paddan Aram. **8**Esau then realized how displeasing the Canaanite women[k] were to his father Isaac;[l] **9**so he went to Ishmael and married Mahalath, the sister of Nebaioth[m] and daughter of Ishmael son of Abraham, in addition to the wives he already had.[n]

Jacob's Dream at Bethel

10Jacob left Beersheba and set out for Haran.[o] **11**When he reached a certain place, he stopped for the night because the sun had set. Taking one of the stones there, he put it under his head and lay down to sleep. **12**He had a dream[p] in which he saw a stairway[x] resting on the earth, with its top reaching to heaven, and the angels of God were ascending and descending on it.[q] **13**There above it[y] stood the LORD,[r] and he said: "I am the LORD, the God of your father Abraham and the God of Isaac.[s] I will give you and your descendants the land[t] on which you are lying. **14**Your descendants will be like the dust of the earth, and you[u] will spread out to the west and to the east, to the north and to the south.[v] All peoples on earth will be blessed through you and your offspring.[w] **15**I am with you[x] and will watch over you[y] wherever you go, and I will bring you back to this land. I will not leave you[z] until I have done what I have promised you."[a]

16When Jacob awoke from his sleep, he thought, "Surely the LORD is in this place, and I was not aware of it." **17**He was afraid and said, "How awesome is this place![b] This is none other than the house of God; this is the gate of heaven."

18Early the next morning Jacob took the stone he had placed under his head and set it up as a pillar[c] and poured oil on top of it.[d] **19**He called that place Bethel,[z] though the city used to be called Luz.[e]

20Then Jacob made a vow,[f] saying, "If God will be with me and will watch over me[g] on this journey I am taking and will give me food to eat and clothes to wear **21**so that I return safely[h] to my father's house, then the LORD[a] will be my God[i] **22**and[b] this stone that I have set up as a pillar will be God's house,[j] and of all that you give me I will give you a tenth.[k]"

Jacob Arrives in Paddan Aram

29 Then Jacob continued on his journey and came to the land of the eastern peoples.[l] **2**There he saw a well in the field, with three flocks of sheep lying

27:46 [a]Ge 26:35
28:1 [b]Ge 24:3
28:2 [c]Ge 25:20
28:3 [d]Ge 17:1 [e]Ge 17:6
28:4 [f]Ge 12:2,3 [g]Ge 17:8
28:5 [h]Hos 12:12 [i]Ge 24:29
28:6 [j]ver 1
28:8 [k]Ge 24:3 [l]Ge 26:35
28:9 [m]Ge 25:13 [n]Ge 26:34
28:10 [o]Ge 11:31
28:12 [p]Ge 20:3 [q]Jn 1:51
28:13 [r]Ge 12:7; 35:7,9; 48:3 [s]Ge 26:24 [t]Ge 13:15; 35:12
28:14 [u]Ge 26:4 [v]Ge 13:14 [w]Ge 12:3; 18:18; 22:18; Gal 3:8
28:15 [x]Ge 26:3; 48:21 [y]Nu 6:24; Ps 121:5,7-8 [z]Dt 31:6,8 [a]Nu 23:19
28:17 [b]Ex 3:5; Jos 5:15
28:18 [c]Ge 35:14 [d]Lev 8:11
28:19 [e]Jdg 1:23,26
28:20 [f]Ge 31:13; Jdg 11:30; 2Sa 15:8 [g]ver 15
28:21 [h]Jdg 11:31 [i]Dt 26:17
28:22 [j]Ge 35:7,14 [k]Ge 14:20; Lev 27:30
29:1 [l]Jdg 6:3,33

[u]*1* Or *greeted* [v]*2* That is, Northwest Mesopotamia; also in verses 5, 6 and 7 [w]*3* Hebrew *El-Shaddai* [x]*12* Or *ladder* [y]*13* Or *There beside him* [z]*19* *Bethel* means *house of God.* [a]*20,21* Or *Since God . . . father's house, the LORD* [b]*21,22* Or *house, and the LORD will be my God, 22then*

near it because the flocks were watered from that well. The stone over the mouth of the well was large. 3When all the flocks were gathered there, the shepherds would roll the stone away from the well's mouth and water the sheep. Then they would return the stone to its place over the mouth of the well.

4Jacob asked the shepherds, "My brothers, where are you from?"

"We're from Haran,[a]" they replied.

5He said to them, "Do you know Laban, Nahor's grandson?"

"Yes, we know him," they answered.

6Then Jacob asked them, "Is he well?"

"Yes, he is," they said, "and here comes his daughter Rachel with the sheep."

7"Look," he said, "the sun is still high; it is not time for the flocks to be gathered. Water the sheep and take them back to pasture."

8"We can't," they replied, "until all the flocks are gathered and the stone has been rolled away from the mouth of the well. Then we will water the sheep."

9While he was still talking with them, Rachel came with her father's sheep,[b] for she was a shepherdess. 10When Jacob saw Rachel daughter of Laban, his mother's brother, and Laban's sheep, he went over and rolled the stone away from the mouth of the well and watered his uncle's sheep.[c] 11Then Jacob kissed Rachel and began to weep aloud.[d] 12He had told Rachel that he was a relative[e] of her father and a son of Rebekah. So she ran and told her father.[f]

13As soon as Laban[g] heard the news about Jacob, his sister's son, he hurried to meet him. He embraced him and kissed him and brought him to his home, and there Jacob told him all these things. 14Then Laban said to him, "You are my own flesh and blood."[h]

29:4 [a]Ge 28:10
29:9 [b]Ex 2:16
29:10 [c]Ex 2:17
29:11 [d]Ge 33:4
29:12 [e]Ge 13:8; 14:14,16 [f]Ge 24:28
29:13 [g]Ge 24:29
29:14 [h]Ge 2:23; Jdg 9:2; 2Sa 19:12-13
29:18 [i]Hos 12:12
29:20 [j]SS 8:7; Hos 12:12
29:21 [k]Jdg 15:1
29:22 [l]Jdg 14:10; Jn 2:1-2
29:25 [m]Ge 12:18 [n]Ge 27:36
29:27 [o]Jdg 14:12
29:29 [p]Ge 30:3

Jacob Marries Leah and Rachel

After Jacob had stayed with him for a whole month, 15Laban said to him, "Just because you are a relative of mine, should you work for me for nothing? Tell me what your wages should be."

16Now Laban had two daughters; the name of the older was Leah, and the name of the younger was Rachel. 17Leah had weak[c] eyes, but Rachel was lovely in form, and beautiful. 18Jacob was in love with Rachel and said, "I'll work for you seven years in return for your younger daughter Rachel."[i]

19Laban said, "It's better that I give her to you than to some other man. Stay here with me." 20So Jacob served seven years to get Rachel, but they seemed like only a few days to him because of his love for her.[j]

21Then Jacob said to Laban, "Give me my wife. My time is completed, and I want to lie with her.[k]"

22So Laban brought together all the people of the place and gave a feast.[l] 23But when evening came, he took his daughter Leah and gave her to Jacob, and Jacob lay with her. 24And Laban gave his servant girl Zilpah to his daughter as her maidservant.

25When morning came, there was Leah! So Jacob said to Laban, "What is this you have done to me?[m] I served you for Rachel, didn't I? Why have you deceived me?[n]"

26Laban replied, "It is not our custom here to give the younger daughter in marriage before the older one. 27Finish this daughter's bridal week;[o] then we will give you the younger one also, in return for another seven years of work."

28And Jacob did so. He finished the week with Leah, and then Laban gave him his daughter Rachel to be his wife. 29Laban gave his servant girl Bilhah[p] to his daughter

[c]17 Or *delicate*

Rachel as her maidservant.[a] 30Jacob lay with Rachel also, and he loved Rachel more than Leah.[b] And he worked for Laban another seven years.[c]

Jacob's Children

31When the LORD saw that Leah was not loved,[d] he opened her womb,[e] but Rachel was barren. 32Leah became pregnant and gave birth to a son. She named him Reuben,[d] for she said, "It is because the LORD has seen my misery.[f] Surely my husband will love me now."

33She conceived again, and when she gave birth to a son she said, "Because the LORD heard that I am not loved, he gave me this one too." So she named him Simeon.[e][g]

34Again she conceived, and when she gave birth to a son she said, "Now at last my husband will become attached to me,[h] because I have borne him three sons." So he was named Levi.[f][i]

35She conceived again, and when she gave birth to a son she said, "This time I will praise the LORD." So she named him Judah.[g][j] Then she stopped having children.

30 When Rachel saw that she was not bearing Jacob any children,[k] she became jealous of her sister.[l] So she said to Jacob, "Give me children, or I'll die!"

2Jacob became angry with her and said, "Am I in the place of God, who has kept you from having children?"[m]

3Then she said, "Here is Bilhah, my maidservant. Sleep with her so that she can bear children for me and that through her I too can build a family."[n]

4So she gave him her servant Bilhah as a wife.[o] Jacob slept with her,[p] 5and she became pregnant and bore him a son. 6Then Rachel said, "God has vindicated me;[q] he has listened to my plea and given me a son." Because of this she named him Dan.[h][r]

7Rachel's servant Bilhah conceived again and bore Jacob a second son. 8Then Rachel said, "I have had a great struggle with my sister, and I have won."[s] So she named him Naphtali.[i][t]

9When Leah saw that she had stopped having children, she took her maidservant Zilpah and gave her to Jacob as a wife.[u] 10Leah's servant Zilpah bore Jacob a son. 11Then Leah said, "What good fortune!"[j] So she named him Gad.[k][v]

12Leah's servant Zilpah bore Jacob a second son. 13Then Leah said, "How happy I am! The women will call me[w] happy."[x] So she named him Asher.[l][y]

14During wheat harvest, Reuben went out into the fields and found some mandrake plants,[z] which he brought to his mother Leah. Rachel said to Leah, "Please give me some of your son's mandrakes."

15But she said to her, "Wasn't it enough[a] that you took away my husband? Will you take my son's mandrakes too?"

"Very well," Rachel said, "he can sleep with you tonight in return for your son's mandrakes."

16So when Jacob came in from the fields that evening, Leah went out to meet him. "You must sleep with me," she said. "I have hired you with my son's mandrakes." So he slept with her that night.

17God listened to Leah,[b] and she became pregnant and bore Jacob a fifth son. 18Then Leah said, "God has rewarded me for giving my maidservant to my husband." So she named him Issachar.[m][c]

19Leah conceived again and bore Jacob a sixth son. 20Then Leah said, "God has presented me with a precious gift. This time my husband will treat me with honor, be-

29:29 [a]Ge 16:1
29:30 [b]ver 16 [c]Ge 31:41
29:31 [d]Dt 21:15-17 [e]Ge 11:30; 30:1; Ps 127:3
29:32 [f]Ge 16:11; 31:42; Ex 4:31; Dt 26:7; Ps 25:18
29:33 [g]Ge 34:25; 49:5
29:34 [h]Ge 30:20; 1Sa 1:2-4 [i]Ge 49:5-7
29:35 [j]Ge 49:8; Mt 1:2-3
30:1 [k]Ge 29:31; 1Sa 1:5-6 [l]Lev 18:18
30:2 [m]Ge 16:2; 20:18; 29:31
30:3 [n]Ge 16:2
30:4 [o]ver 9,18 [p]Ge 16:3-4
30:6 [q]Ps 35:24; 43:1; La 3:59 [r]Ge 49:16-17
30:8 [s]Hos 12:3-4 [t]Ge 49:21
30:9 [u]ver 4
30:11 [v]Ge 49:19
30:13 [w]Ps 127:3 [x]Pr 31:28; Lk 1:48 [y]Ge 49:20
30:14 [z]SS 7:13
30:15 [a]Nu 16:9,13
30:17 [b]Ge 25:21
30:18 [c]Ge 49:14

[d]32 *Reuben* sounds like the Hebrew for *he has seen my misery;* the name means *see, a son.* [e]33 *Simeon* probably means *one who hears.* [f]34 *Levi* sounds like and may be derived from the Hebrew for *attached.* [g]35 *Judah* sounds like and may be derived from the Hebrew for *praise.* [h]6 *Dan* here means *he has vindicated.* [i]8 *Naphtali* means *my struggle.* [j]11 Or *"A troop is coming!"* [k]11 *Gad* can mean *good fortune* or *a troop.* [l]13 *Asher* means *happy.* [m]18 *Issachar* sounds like the Hebrew for *reward.*

cause I have borne him six sons." So she named him Zebulun.[n][a]

21 Some time later she gave birth to a daughter and named her Dinah.

22 Then God remembered Rachel;[b] he listened to her and opened her womb.[c] 23 She became pregnant and gave birth to a son[d] and said, "God has taken away my disgrace."[e] 24 She named him Joseph,[o][f] and said, "May the LORD add to me another son."[g]

Jacob's Flocks Increase

25 After Rachel gave birth to Joseph, Jacob said to Laban, "Send me on my way[h] so I can go back to my own homeland. 26 Give me my wives and children, for whom I have served you,[i] and I will be on my way. You know how much work I've done for you."

27 But Laban said to him, "If I have found favor in your eyes, please stay. I have learned by divination that[p] the LORD has blessed me because of you."[j] 28 He added, "Name your wages,[k] and I will pay them."

29 Jacob said to him, "You know how I have worked for you[l] and how your livestock has fared under my care.[m] 30 The little you had before I came has increased greatly, and the LORD has blessed you wherever I have been. But now, when may I do something for my own household?[n]"

31 "What shall I give you?" he asked.

"Don't give me anything," Jacob replied. "But if you will do this one thing for me, I will go on tending your flocks and watching over them: 32 Let me go through all your flocks today and remove from them every speckled or spotted sheep, every dark-colored lamb and every spotted or speckled goat.[o] They will be my wages. 33 And my honesty will testify for me in the future, whenever you check on the wages you have paid me. Any goat in my possession that is not speckled or spotted, or any lamb that is not dark-colored, will be considered stolen."

34 "Agreed," said Laban. "Let it be as you have said." 35 That same day he removed all the male goats that were streaked or spotted, and all the speckled or spotted female goats (all that had white on them) and all the dark-colored lambs, and he placed them in the care of his sons.[p] 36 Then he put a three-day journey between himself and Jacob, while Jacob continued to tend the rest of Laban's flocks.

37 Jacob, however, took fresh-cut branches from poplar, almond and plane trees and made white stripes on them by peeling the bark and exposing the white inner wood of the branches. 38 Then he placed the peeled branches in all the watering troughs, so that they would be directly in front of the flocks when they came to drink. When the flocks were in heat and came to drink, 39 they mated in front of the branches. And they bore young that were streaked or speckled or spotted. 40 Jacob set apart the young of the flock by themselves, but made the rest face the streaked and dark-colored animals that belonged to Laban. Thus he made separate flocks for himself and did not put them with Laban's animals. 41 Whenever the stronger females were in heat, Jacob would place the branches in the troughs in front of the animals so they would mate near the branches, 42 but if the animals were weak, he would not place them there. So the weak animals went to Laban and the strong ones to Jacob. 43 In this way the man grew exceedingly prosperous and came to own large flocks, and maidservants and menservants, and camels and donkeys.[q]

Jacob Flees From Laban

31 Jacob heard that Laban's sons were saying, "Jacob

30:20 [a] Ge 35:23; 49:13; Mt 4:13
30:22 [b] Ge 8:1; 1Sa 1:19-20 [c] Ge 29:31
30:23 [d] ver 6 [e] Isa 4:1; Lk 1:25
30:24 [f] Ge 35:24; 37:2; 39:1; 49:22-26 [g] Ge 35:17
30:25 [h] Ge 24:54
30:26 [i] Ge 29:20,30; Hos 12:12
30:27 [j] Ge 26:24; 39:3,5
30:28 [k] Ge 29:15
30:29 [l] Ge 31:6 [m] Ge 31:38-40
30:30 [n] 1Ti 5:8
30:32 [o] Ge 31:8,12
30:35 [p] Ge 31:1
30:43 [q] ver 30; Ge 12:16; 13:2; 24:35; 26:13-14

[n] 20 *Zebulun* probably means *honor.*
[o] 24 *Joseph* means *may he add.*
[p] 27 Or possibly *have become rich and*

has taken everything our father
owned and has gained all this
wealth from what belonged to our
father." **2**And Jacob noticed that
Laban's attitude toward him was
not what it had been.

3Then the LORD said to Jacob,
"Go back[a] to the land of your fathers and to your relatives, and I
will be with you."[b]

4So Jacob sent word to Rachel
and Leah to come out to the fields
where his flocks were. **5**He said to
them, "I see that your father's attitude toward me is not what it was
before, but the God of my father
has been with me.[c] **6**You know
that I've worked for your father
with all my strength,[d] **7**yet your father has cheated me by changing
my wages ten times.[e] However,
God has not allowed him to harm
me.[f] **8**If he said, 'The speckled
ones will be your wages,' then all
the flocks gave birth to speckled
young; and if he said, 'The streaked
ones will be your wages,'[g] then all
the flocks bore streaked young. **9**So
God has taken away your father's
livestock and has given them to
me.[h]

10"In breeding season I once had
a dream in which I looked up and
saw that the male goats mating
with the flock were streaked,
speckled or spotted. **11**The angel of
God[i] said to me in the dream, 'Jacob.' I answered, 'Here I am.'
12And he said, 'Look up and see
that all the male goats mating with
the flock are streaked, speckled or
spotted, for I have seen all that Laban has been doing to you.[j] **13**I am
the God of Bethel,[k] where you
anointed a pillar and where you
made a vow to me. Now leave this
land at once and go back to your
native land.[l]' "

14Then Rachel and Leah replied,
"Do we still have any share in the
inheritance of our father's estate?
15Does he not regard us as foreigners? Not only has he sold us, but he
has used up what was paid for us.[m]
16Surely all the wealth that God
took away from our father belongs
to us and our children. So do whatever God has told you."

17Then Jacob put his children
and his wives on camels, **18**and he
drove all his livestock ahead of
him, along with all the goods he
had accumulated in Paddan
Aram,[q] to go to his father Isaac[n] in
the land of Canaan.[o]

19When Laban had gone to shear
his sheep, Rachel stole her father's
household gods.[p] **20**Moreover, Jacob deceived[q] Laban the Aramean
by not telling him he was running
away.[r] **21**So he fled with all he
had, and crossing the River,[r] he
headed for the hill country of
Gilead.[s]

Laban Pursues Jacob

22On the third day Laban was
told that Jacob had fled. **23**Taking
his relatives with him, he pursued
Jacob for seven days and caught up
with him in the hill country of Gilead. **24**Then God came to Laban the
Aramean in a dream at night and
said to him,[t] "Be careful not to say
anything to Jacob, either good or
bad."[u]

25Jacob had pitched his tent in
the hill country of Gilead when Laban overtook him, and Laban and
his relatives camped there too.
26Then Laban said to Jacob, "What
have you done? You've deceived
me,[v] and you've carried off my
daughters like captives in war.[w]
27Why did you run off secretly and
deceive me? Why didn't you tell
me, so I could send you away with
joy and singing to the music of
tambourines[x] and harps?[y] **28**You
didn't even let me kiss my grandchildren and my daughters good-
by.[z] You have done a foolish thing.
29I have the power to harm you;[a]
but last night the God of your father[b] said to me, 'Be careful not to
say anything to Jacob, either good
or bad.' **30**Now you have gone off
because you longed to return to
your father's house. But why did
you steal my gods?[c]"

31:3 [a]ver 13; Ge 32:9 [b]Ge 21:22; 26:3; 28:15
31:5 [c]Ge 21:22; 26:3
31:6 [d]Ge 30:29
31:7 [e]ver 41; Job 19:3 [f]ver 52; Ps 37:28; 105:14
31:8 [g]Ge 30:32
31:9 [h]ver 1,16; Ge 30:42
31:11 [i]Ge 16:7; 48:16
31:12 [j]Ex 3:7
31:13 [k]Ge 28:10-22 [l]ver 3; Ge 32:9
31:15 [m]Ge 29:20
31:18 [n]Ge 35:27 [o]Ge 10:19
31:19 [p]ver 30,32, 34-35; Ge 35:2; Jdg 17:5; 1Sa 19:13; Hos 3:4
31:20 [q]Ge 27:36 [r]ver 27
31:21 [s]Ge 37:25
31:24 [t]Ge 20:3; Job 33:15 [u]Ge 24:50
31:26 [v]Ge 27:36 [w]1Sa 30:2-3
31:27 [x]Ex 15:20 [y]Ge 4:21
31:28 [z]ver 55
31:29 [a]ver 7 [b]ver 53
31:30 [c]ver 19; Jdg 18:24

[q]*18* That is, Northwest Mesopotamia
[r]*21* That is, the Euphrates

31Jacob answered Laban, "I was afraid, because I thought you would take your daughters away from me by force. **32**But if you find anyone who has your gods, he shall not live.[a] In the presence of our relatives, see for yourself whether there is anything of yours here with me; and if so, take it." Now Jacob did not know that Rachel had stolen the gods.

33So Laban went into Jacob's tent and into Leah's tent and into the tent of the two maidservants, but he found nothing. After he came out of Leah's tent, he entered Rachel's tent. **34**Now Rachel had taken the household gods and put them inside her camel's saddle and was sitting on them. Laban searched[b] through everything in the tent but found nothing.

35Rachel said to her father, "Don't be angry, my lord, that I cannot stand up in your presence;[c] I'm having my period." So he searched but could not find the household gods.

36Jacob was angry and took Laban to task. "What is my crime?" he asked Laban. "What sin have I committed that you hunt me down? **37**Now that you have searched through all my goods, what have you found that belongs to your household? Put it here in front of your relatives[d] and mine, and let them judge between the two of us.

38"I have been with you for twenty years now. Your sheep and goats have not miscarried, nor have I eaten rams from your flocks. **39**I did not bring you animals torn by wild beasts; I bore the loss myself. And you demanded payment from me for whatever was stolen by day or night.[e] **40**This was my situation: The heat consumed me in the daytime and the cold at night, and sleep fled from my eyes. **41**It was like this for the twenty years I was in your household. I worked for you fourteen years for your two daughters[f] and six years for your flocks, and you changed my wages ten times.[g] **42**If the God of my father,[h] the God of Abraham and the Fear of Isaac,[i] had not been with me,[j] you would surely have sent me away empty-handed. But God has seen my hardship and the toil of my hands,[k] and last night he rebuked you."

43Laban answered Jacob, "The women are my daughters, the children are my children, and the flocks are my flocks. All you see is mine. Yet what can I do today about these daughters of mine, or about the children they have borne? **44**Come now, let's make a covenant,[l] you and I, and let it serve as a witness between us."[m]

45So Jacob took a stone and set it up as a pillar.[n] **46**He said to his relatives, "Gather some stones." So they took stones and piled them in a heap, and they ate there by the heap. **47**Laban called it Jegar Sahadutha,[s] and Jacob called it Galeed.[t]

48Laban said, "This heap is a witness between you and me today." That is why it was called Galeed. **49**It was also called Mizpah,[u][o] because he said, "May the LORD keep watch between you and me when we are away from each other. **50**If you mistreat my daughters or if you take any wives besides my daughters, even though no one is with us, remember that God is a witness[p] between you and me."

51Laban also said to Jacob, "Here is this heap, and here is this pillar[q] I have set up between you and me. **52**This heap is a witness, and this pillar is a witness,[r] that I will not go past this heap to your side to harm you and that you will not go past this heap and pillar to my side to harm me.[s] **53**May the God of Abraham[t] and the God of Nahor, the God of their father, judge between us."[u]

So Jacob took an oath[v] in the name of the Fear of his father Isaac.[w] **54**He offered a sacrifice there in the hill country and invited

31:32 [a]Ge 44:9
31:34 [b]ver 37; Ge 44:12
31:35 [c]Ex 20:12; Lev 19:3,32
31:37 [d]ver 23
31:39 [e]Ex 22:13
31:41 [f]Ge 29:30 [g]ver 7
31:42 [h]ver 5; Ex 3:15; 1Ch 12:17 [i]ver 53; Isa 8:13 [j]Ps 124:1-2 [k]Ge 29:32
31:44 [l]Ge 21:27; 26:28 [m]Jos 24:27
31:45 [n]Ge 28:18
31:49 [o]Jdg 11:29; 1Sa 7:5-6
31:50 [p]Jer 29:23; 42:5
31:51 [q]Ge 28:18
31:52 [r]Ge 21:30 [s]ver 7; Ge 26:29
31:53 [t]Ge 28:13 [u]Ge 16:5 [v]Ge 21:23,27 [w]ver 42

[s]47 The Aramaic *Jegar Sahadutha* means *witness heap.* [t]47 The Hebrew *Galeed* means *witness heap.* [u]49 *Mizpah* means *watchtower.*

his relatives to a meal. After they had eaten, they spent the night there.

55Early the next morning Laban kissed his grandchildren and his daughters[a] and blessed them. Then he left and returned home.[b]

Jacob Prepares to Meet Esau

32 Jacob also went on his way, and the angels of God[c] met him. **2**When Jacob saw them, he said, "This is the camp of God!"[d] So he named that place Mahanaim.[v][e]

3Jacob sent messengers ahead of him to his brother Esau[f] in the land of Seir, the country of Edom.[g] **4**He instructed them: "This is what you are to say to my master Esau: 'Your servant Jacob says, I have been staying with Laban and have remained there till now. **5**I have cattle and donkeys, sheep and goats, menservants and maidservants.[h] Now I am sending this message to my lord, that I may find favor in your eyes.[i]' "

6When the messengers returned to Jacob, they said, "We went to your brother Esau, and now he is coming to meet you, and four hundred men are with him."[j]

7In great fear[k] and distress Jacob divided the people who were with him into two groups,[w] and the flocks and herds and camels as well. **8**He thought, "If Esau comes and attacks one group,[x] the group[x] that is left may escape."

9Then Jacob prayed, "O God of my father Abraham, God of my father Isaac,[l] O LORD, who said to me, 'Go back to your country and your relatives, and I will make you prosper,'[m] **10**I am unworthy of all the kindness and faithfulness[n] you have shown your servant. I had only my staff when I crossed this Jordan, but now I have become two groups. **11**Save me, I pray, from the hand of my brother Esau, for I am afraid he will come and attack me,[o] and also the mothers with their children.[p] **12**But you have said, 'I will surely make you prosper and will make your descendants like the sand[q] of the sea, which cannot be counted.[r]' "

13He spent the night there, and from what he had with him he selected a gift[s] for his brother Esau: **14**two hundred female goats and twenty male goats, two hundred ewes and twenty rams, **15**thirty female camels with their young, forty cows and ten bulls, and twenty female donkeys and ten male donkeys. **16**He put them in the care of his servants, each herd by itself, and said to his servants, "Go ahead of me, and keep some space between the herds."

17He instructed the one in the lead: "When my brother Esau meets you and asks, 'To whom do you belong, and where are you going, and who owns all these animals in front of you?' **18**then you are to say, 'They belong to your servant[t] Jacob. They are a gift sent to my lord Esau, and he is coming behind us.' "

19He also instructed the second, the third and all the others who followed the herds: "You are to say the same thing to Esau when you meet him. **20**And be sure to say, 'Your servant Jacob is coming behind us.' " For he thought, "I will pacify him with these gifts I am sending on ahead; later, when I see him, perhaps he will receive me."[u] **21**So Jacob's gifts went on ahead of him, but he himself spent the night in the camp.

Jacob Wrestles With God

22That night Jacob got up and took his two wives, his two maidservants and his eleven sons and crossed the ford of the Jabbok.[v] **23**After he had sent them across the stream, he sent over all his possessions. **24**So Jacob was left alone, and a man[w] wrestled with him till daybreak. **25**When the man saw that he could not overpower him, he touched the socket of Jacob's hip[x] so that his hip was wrenched as he wrestled with the man.

31:55 [a]ver 28 [b]Ge 18:33; 30:25
32:1 [c]Ge 16:11; 2Ki 6:16-17; Ps 34:7; 91:11; Heb 1:14
32:2 [d]Ge 28:17 [e]2Sa 2:8,29
32:3 [f]Ge 27:41-42 [g]Ge 25:30; 36:8,9
32:5 [h]Ge 12:16; 30:43 [i]Ge 33:8,10, 15
32:6 [j]Ge 33:1
32:7 [k]ver 11
32:9 [l]Ge 28:13; 31:42 [m]Ge 31:13
32:10 [n]Ge 24:27
32:11 [o]Ps 59:2 [p]Ge 27:41
32:12 [q]Ge 22:17 [r]Ge 28:13-15; Hos 1:10; Ro 9:27
32:13 [s]Ge 43:11,15, 25,26; Pr 18:16
32:18 [t]Ge 18:3
32:20 [u]Ge 33:10; Pr 21:14
32:22 [v]Dt 2:37; 3:16; Jos 12:2
32:24 [w]Ge 18:2
32:25 [x]ver 32

[v]2 *Mahanaim* means *two camps.* [w]7 Or *camps*; also in verse 10 [x]8 Or *camp*

JACOB'S JOURNEYS

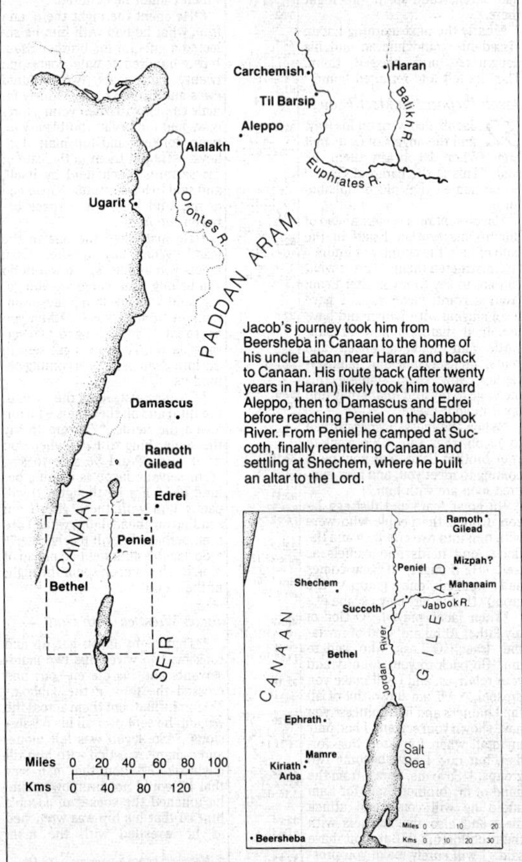

Jacob's journey took him from Beersheba in Canaan to the home of his uncle Laban near Haran and back to Canaan. His route back (after twenty years in Haran) likely took him toward Aleppo, then to Damascus and Edrei before reaching Peniel on the Jabbok River. From Peniel he camped at Succoth, finally reentering Canaan and settling at Shechem, where he built an altar to the Lord.

26Then the man said, "Let me go, for it is daybreak."

But Jacob replied, "I will not let you go unless you bless me."[a]

27The man asked him, "What is your name?"

"Jacob," he answered.

28Then the man said, "Your name will no longer be Jacob, but Israel,[y][b] because you have struggled with God and with men and have overcome."

29Jacob said, "Please tell me your name."[c]

But he replied, "Why do you ask my name?"[d] Then he blessed[e] him there.

30So Jacob called the place Peniel,[z] saying, "It is because I saw God face to face,[f] and yet my life was spared."

31The sun rose above him as he passed Peniel,[a] and he was limping because of his hip. 32Therefore to this day the Israelites do not eat the tendon attached to the socket of the hip, because the socket of Jacob's hip was touched near the tendon.

Jacob Meets Esau

33 Jacob looked up and there was Esau, coming with his four hundred men;[g] so he divided the children among Leah, Rachel and the two maidservants. 2He put the maidservants and their children in front, Leah and her children next, and Rachel and Joseph in the rear. 3He himself went on ahead and bowed down to the ground[h] seven times as he approached his brother.

4But Esau ran to meet Jacob and embraced him; he threw his arms around his neck and kissed him. And they wept.[i] 5Then Esau looked up and saw the women and children. "Who are these with you?" he asked.

Jacob answered, "They are the children God has graciously given your servant.[j]"

6Then the maidservants and their children approached and bowed down. 7Next, Leah and her children came and bowed down. Last of all came Joseph and Rachel, and they too bowed down.

8Esau asked, "What do you mean by all these droves I met?"[k]

"To find favor in your eyes, my lord,"[l] he said.

9But Esau said, "I already have plenty, my brother. Keep what you have for yourself."

10"No, please!" said Jacob. "If I have found favor in your eyes, accept this gift from me. For to see your face is like seeing the face of God,[m] now that you have received me favorably.[n] 11Please accept the present[o] that was brought to you, for God has been gracious to me[p] and I have all I need." And because Jacob insisted, Esau accepted it.

12Then Esau said, "Let us be on our way; I'll accompany you."

13But Jacob said to him, "My lord knows that the children are tender and that I must care for the ewes and cows that are nursing their young. If they are driven hard just one day, all the animals will die. 14So let my lord go on ahead of his servant, while I move along slowly at the pace of the droves before me and that of the children, until I come to my lord in Seir.[q]"

15Esau said, "Then let me leave some of my men with you."

"But why do that?" Jacob asked. "Just let me find favor in the eyes of my lord."[r]

16So that day Esau started on his way back to Seir. 17Jacob, however, went to Succoth,[s] where he built a place for himself and made shelters for his livestock. That is why the place is called Succoth.[b]

18After Jacob came from Paddan Aram,[c][t] he arrived safely at the[d] city of Shechem[u] in Canaan and camped within sight of the city. 19For a hundred pieces of silver,[e] he bought from the sons of Hamor, the father of Shechem,[v] the plot of ground[w] where he pitched his tent.

32:26 [a]Hos 12:4
32:28 [b]Ge 17:5; 35:10; 1Ki 18:31
32:29 [c]Jdg 13:17 [d]Jdg 13:18 [e]Ge 35:9
32:30 [f]Ge 16:13; Ex 24:11; Nu 12:8; Jdg 6:22; 13:22
33:1 [g]Ge 32:6
33:3 [h]Ge 18:2; 42:6
33:4 [i]Ge 45:14-15
33:5 [j]Ge 48:9; Ps 127:3; Isa 8:18
33:8 [k]Ge 32:14-16 [l]Ge 24:9; 32:5
33:10 [m]Ge 16:13 [n]Ge 32:20
33:11 [o]1Sa 25:27 [p]Ge 30:43
33:14 [q]Ge 32:3
33:15 [r]Ge 34:11; 47:25; Ru 2:13
33:17 [s]Jos 13:27; Jdg 8:5,6,8, 14,14-16,15, 16; Ps 60:6
33:18 [t]Ge 25:20; 28:2 [u]Jos 24:1; Jdg 9:1
33:19 [v]Jos 24:32 [w]Jn 4:5

[y]28 *Israel* means *he struggles with God.*
[z]30 *Peniel* means *face of God.*
[a]31 Hebrew *Penuel,* a variant of *Peniel*
[b]17 *Succoth* means *shelters.*
[c]18 That is, Northwest Mesopotamia
[d]18 Or *arrived at Shalem, a*
[e]19 Hebrew *hundred kesitahs;* a kesitah was a unit of money of unknown weight and value.

20There he set up an altar and
called it El Elohe Israel.[f]

Dinah and the Shechemites

34 Now Dinah,[a] the daughter
Leah had borne to Jacob,
went out to visit the women of the
land. **2**When Shechem son of Hamor the Hivite, the ruler of that
area, saw her, he took her and violated her. **3**His heart was drawn to
Dinah daughter of Jacob, and he
loved the girl and spoke tenderly to
her. **4**And Shechem said to his father Hamor, "Get me this girl as my
wife."
5When Jacob heard that his
daughter Dinah had been defiled,
his sons were in the fields with his
livestock; so he kept quiet about it
until they came home.
6Then Shechem's father Hamor
went out to talk with Jacob.[b]
7Now Jacob's sons had come in
from the fields as soon as they
heard what had happened. They
were filled with grief and fury, because Shechem had done a disgraceful thing in[g] Israel[c] by lying
with Jacob's daughter—a thing
that should not be done.[d]
8But Hamor said to them, "My
son Shechem has his heart set on
your daughter. Please give her to
him as his wife. **9**Intermarry with
us; give us your daughters and take
our daughters for yourselves. **10**You
can settle among us;[e] the land is
open to you.[f] Live in it, trade[h] in
it,[g] and acquire property in it."
11Then Shechem said to Dinah's
father and brothers, "Let me find
favor in your eyes, and I will give
you whatever you ask. **12**Make the
price for the bride[h] and the gift I
am to bring as great as you like, and
I'll pay whatever you ask me. Only
give me the girl as my wife."
13Because their sister Dinah had
been defiled, Jacob's sons replied
deceitfully as they spoke to Shechem and his father Hamor.
14They said to them, "We can't do
such a thing; we can't give our sister to a man who is not circumcised.[i] That would be a disgrace to
us. **15**We will give our consent to
you on one condition only: that you
become like us by circumcising all
your males.[j] **16**Then we will give
you our daughters and take your
daughters for ourselves. We'll settle among you and become one
people with you. **17**But if you will
not agree to be circumcised, we'll
take our sister[i] and go."
18Their proposal seemed good to
Hamor and his son Shechem.
19The young man, who was the
most honored of all his father's
household, lost no time in doing
what they said, because he was delighted with Jacob's daughter.[k]
20So Hamor and his son Shechem
went to the gate of their city[l] to
speak to their fellow townsmen.
21"These men are friendly toward
us," they said. "Let them live in our
land and trade in it; the land has
plenty of room for them. We can
marry their daughters and they can
marry ours. **22**But the men will consent to live with us as one people
only on the condition that our
males be circumcised, as they
themselves are. **23**Won't their livestock, their property and all their
other animals become ours? So let
us give our consent to them, and
they will settle among us."
24All the men who went out of
the city gate[m] agreed with Hamor
and his son Shechem, and every
male in the city was circumcised.
25Three days later, while all of
them were still in pain, two of Jacob's sons, Simeon and Levi, Dinah's brothers, took their swords[n]
and attacked the unsuspecting
city, killing every male.[o] **26**They
put Hamor and his son Shechem to
the sword and took Dinah from
Shechem's house and left. **27**The
sons of Jacob came upon the dead
bodies and looted the city where[j]
their sister had been defiled.
28They seized their flocks and
herds and donkeys and everything
else of theirs in the city and out in

34:1 [a] Ge 30:21
34:6 [b] Jdg 14:2-5
34:7 [c] Dt 22:21; Jdg 20:6; 2Sa 13:12 [d] Jos 7:15
34:10 [e] Ge 47:6,27 [f] Ge 13:9; 20:15 [g] Ge 42:34
34:12 [h] Ex 22:16; Dt 22:29; 1Sa 18:25
34:14 [i] Ge 17:14; Jdg 14:3
34:15 [j] Ex 12:48
34:19 [k] ver 3
34:20 [l] Ru 4:1; 2Sa 15:2
34:24 [m] Ge 23:10
34:25 [n] Ge 49:5 [o] Ge 49:7

[f] *20 El Elohe Israel* can mean *God, the God of Israel* or *mighty is the God of Israel.* [g] *7* Or *against* [h] *10* Or *move about freely;* also in verse 21 [i] *17* Hebrew *daughter* [j] *27* Or *because*

the fields. 29They carried off all their wealth and all their women and children, taking as plunder everything in the houses.

30Then Jacob said to Simeon and Levi, "You have brought trouble on me by making me a stench[a] to the Canaanites and Perizzites, the people living in this land.[b] We are few in number,[c] and if they join forces against me and attack me, I and my household will be destroyed."

31But they replied, "Should he have treated our sister like a prostitute?"

Jacob Returns to Bethel

35 Then God said to Jacob, "Go up to Bethel[d] and settle there, and build an altar there to God, who appeared to you when you were fleeing from your brother Esau."[e]

2So Jacob said to his household[f] and to all who were with him, "Get rid of the foreign gods[g] you have with you, and purify yourselves and change your clothes.[h] 3Then come, let us go up to Bethel, where I will build an altar to God, who answered me in the day of my distress[i] and who has been with me wherever I have gone.[j]" 4So they gave Jacob all the foreign gods they had and the rings in their ears, and Jacob buried them under the oak at Shechem.[k] 5Then they set out, and the terror of God[l] fell upon the towns all around them so that no one pursued them.

6Jacob and all the people with him came to Luz[m] (that is, Bethel) in the land of Canaan. 7There he built an altar, and he called the place El Bethel,[k] because it was there that God revealed himself to him[n] when he was fleeing from his brother.

8Now Deborah, Rebekah's nurse,[o] died and was buried under the oak below Bethel. So it was named Allon Bacuth.[l]

9After Jacob returned from Paddan Aram,[m] God appeared to him again and blessed him.[p] 10God said to him, "Your name is Jacob,[n] but you will no longer be called Jacob; your name will be Israel.[o]"[q] So he named him Israel.

11And God said to him, "I am God Almighty[p];[r] be fruitful and increase in number. A nation[s] and a community of nations will come from you, and kings will come from your body.[t] 12The land I gave to Abraham and Isaac I also give to you, and I will give this land to your descendants after you.[u]"[v] 13Then God went up from him[w] at the place where he had talked with him.

14Jacob set up a stone pillar at the place where God had talked with him, and he poured out a drink offering on it; he also poured oil on it.[x] 15Jacob called the place where God had talked with him Bethel.[q][y]

The Deaths of Rachel and Isaac

35:23-26pp — 1Ch 2:1-2

16Then they moved on from Bethel. While they were still some distance from Ephrath, Rachel began to give birth and had great difficulty. 17And as she was having great difficulty in childbirth, the midwife said to her, "Don't be afraid, for you have another son."[z] 18As she breathed her last—for she was dying—she named her son Ben-Oni.[r] But his father named him Benjamin.[s]

19So Rachel died and was buried on the way to Ephrath (that is, Bethlehem[a]). 20Over her tomb Jacob set up a pillar, and to this day that pillar marks Rachel's tomb.[b]

21Israel moved on again and pitched his tent beyond Migdal Eder. 22While Israel was living in that region, Reuben went in and slept with his father's concubine[c] Bilhah,[d] and Israel heard of it.

34:30 [a]Ex 5:21; 1Sa 13:4 [b]Ge 13:7 [c]Ge 46:27; 1Ch 16:19; Ps 105:12
35:1 [d]Ge 28:19 [e]Ge 27:43
35:2 [f]Ge 18:19; Jos 24:15 [g]Ge 31:19 [h]Ex 19:10,14
35:3 [i]Ge 32:7 [j]Ge 28:15, 20-22; 31:3, 42
35:4 [k]Jos 24:25-26
35:5 [l]Ex 15:16; 23:27; Jos 2:9
35:6 [m]Ge 28:19; 48:3
35:7 [n]Ge 28:13
35:8 [o]Ge 24:59
35:9 [p]Ge 32:29
35:10 [q]Ge 17:5
35:11 [r]Ge 17:1; Ex 6:3 [s]Ge 28:3; 48:4 [t]Ge 17:6
35:12 [u]Ge 13:15; 28:13 [v]Ge 12:7; 26:3
35:13 [w]Ge 17:22
35:14 [x]Ge 28:18
35:15 [y]Ge 28:19
35:17 [z]Ge 30:24
35:19 [a]Ge 48:7; Ru 1:1,19; Mic 5:2; Mt 2:16
35:20 [b]1Sa 10:2
35:22 [c]Ge 49:4; 1Ch 5:1 [d]Ge 29:29; Lev 18:8

[k]7 *El Bethel* means *God of Bethel.* [l]8 *Allon Bacuth* means *oak of weeping.* [m]9 That is, Northwest Mesopotamia; also in verse 26 [n]10 *Jacob* means *he grasps the heel* (figuratively, *he deceives*). [o]10 *Israel* means *he struggles with God.* [p]11 Hebrew *El-Shaddai* [q]15 *Bethel* means *house of God.* [r]18 *Ben-Oni* means *son of my trouble.* [s]18 *Benjamin* means *son of my right hand.*

Jacob had twelve sons:
23The sons of Leah:
Reuben the firstborn[a] of Jacob,
Simeon, Levi, Judah,[b] Issachar and Zebulun.[c]
24The sons of Rachel:
Joseph[d] and Benjamin.[e]
25The sons of Rachel's maidservant Bilhah:
Dan and Naphtali.[f]
26The sons of Leah's maidservant Zilpah:
Gad[g] and Asher.[h]
These were the sons of Jacob,
who were born to him in Paddan
Aram.

27Jacob came home to his father
Isaac in Mamre,[i] near Kiriath
Arba[j] (that is, Hebron), where
Abraham and Isaac had stayed.
28Isaac lived a hundred and eighty
years.[k] 29Then he breathed his last
and died and was gathered to his
people,[l] old and full of years.[m]
And his sons Esau and Jacob buried him.[n]

Esau's Descendants

36:10–14pp — 1Ch 1:35–37
36:20–28pp — 1Ch 1:38–42

36 This is the account of Esau (that is, Edom).[o]

2Esau took his wives from
the women of Canaan:[p] Adah
daughter of Elon the Hittite,[q]
and Oholibamah daughter of
Anah[r] and granddaughter of
Zibeon the Hivite— 3also Basemath daughter of Ishmael
and sister of Nebaioth.
4Adah bore Eliphaz to Esau,
Basemath bore Reuel,[s] 5and
Oholibamah bore Jeush, Jalam and Korah. These were
the sons of Esau, who were
born to him in Canaan.
6Esau took his wives and
sons and daughters and all the
members of his household, as
well as his livestock and all his
other animals and all the
goods he had acquired in Canaan,[t] and moved to a land
some distance from his brother Jacob. 7Their possessions
were too great for them to remain together; the land where
they were staying could not
support them both because of
their livestock.[u] 8So Esau[v]
(that is, Edom) settled in the
hill country of Seir.[w]

9This is the account of Esau the
father of the Edomites in the hill
country of Seir.

10These are the names of Esau's sons:
Eliphaz, the son of Esau's wife Adah, and Reuel, the son of Esau's wife Basemath.
11The sons of Eliphaz:[x]
Teman,[y] Omar, Zepho, Gatam and Kenaz.
12Esau's son Eliphaz also had a concubine named Timna, who bore him Amalek.[z] These were grandsons of Esau's wife Adah.[a]
13The sons of Reuel:
Nahath, Zerah, Shammah and Mizzah. These were grandsons of Esau's wife Basemath.
14The sons of Esau's wife Oholibamah daughter of Anah and granddaughter of Zibeon, whom she bore to Esau:
Jeush, Jalam and Korah.

15These were the chiefs[b] among
Esau's descendants:
The sons of Eliphaz the firstborn of Esau:
Chiefs Teman,[c] Omar, Ze-
pho, Kenaz, 16Korah,[t] Ga-
tam and Amalek. These were the chiefs descended from Eliphaz in Edom; they were grandsons of Adah.[d]
17The sons of Esau's son Reuel:[e]
Chiefs Nahath, Zerah, Shammah and Mizzah. These were the chiefs descended from Reuel in Edom; they were grandsons of Esau's wife Basemath.

35:23 [a]Ge 46:8 [b]Ge 29:35 [c]Ge 30:20
35:24 [d]Ge 30:24 [e]ver 18
35:25 [f]Ge 30:8
35:26 [g]Ge 30:11 [h]Ge 30:13
35:27 [i]Ge 13:18; 18:1 [j]Jos 14:15
35:28 [k]Ge 25:7,20
35:29 [l]Ge 25:8; 49:33 [m]Ge 15:15 [n]Ge 25:9
36:1 [o]Ge 25:30
36:2 [p]Ge 28:8-9 [q]Ge 26:34 [r]ver 25
36:4 [s]1Ch 1:35
36:6 [t]Ge 12:5
36:7 [u]Ge 13:6; 17:8; 28:4
36:8 [v]Dt 2:4 [w]Ge 32:3
36:11 [x]ver 15-16; Job 2:11 [y]Am 1:12; Hab 3:3
36:12 [z]Ex 17:8,16; Nu 24:20; 1Sa 15:2 [a]ver 16
36:15 [b]Ex 15:15 [c]Job 2:11
36:16 [d]ver 12
36:17 [e]1Ch 1:37

[t]*16* Masoretic Text; Samaritan Pentateuch (see also Gen. 36:11 and 1 Chron. 1:36) does not have *Korah*.

18 The sons of Esau's wife Oholibamah:
Chiefs Jeush, Jalam and Korah. These were the chiefs descended from Esau's wife Oholibamah daughter of Anah.
19 These were the sons of Esau
(that is, Edom),[a] and these were
their chiefs.

20 These were the sons of Seir the
Horite,[b] who were living in the region:
Lotan, Shobal, Zibeon,
Anah, 21 Dishon, Ezer and
Dishan. These sons of Seir in Edom were Horite chiefs.
22 The sons of Lotan:
Hori and Homam.[u] Timna was Lotan's sister.
23 The sons of Shobal:
Alvan, Manahath, Ebal, Shepho and Onam.
24 The sons of Zibeon:
Aiah and Anah. This is the Anah who discovered the hot springs[v] in the desert while he was grazing the donkeys of his father Zibeon.
25 The children of Anah:
Dishon and Oholibamah daughter of Anah.
26 The sons of Dishon[w]:
Hemdan, Eshban, Ithran and Keran.
27 The sons of Ezer:
Bilhan, Zaavan and Akan.
28 The sons of Dishan:
Uz and Aran.
29 These were the Horite chiefs:
Lotan, Shobal, Zibeon,
Anah, 30 Dishon, Ezer and
Dishan. These were the Horite chiefs, according to their divisions, in the land of Seir.

The Rulers of Edom

36:31–43pp — 1Ch 1:43–54

31 These were the kings who
reigned in Edom before any Israelite king[c] reigned[x]:
32 Bela son of Beor became king of Edom. His city was named Dinhabah.
33 When Bela died, Jobab son of Zerah from Bozrah[d] succeeded him as king.
34 When Jobab died, Husham from the land of the Temanites[e] succeeded him as king.
35 When Husham died, Hadad son of Bedad, who defeated Midian in the country of Moab,[f] succeeded him as king. His city was named Avith.
36 When Hadad died, Samlah from Masrekah succeeded him as king.
37 When Samlah died, Shaul from Rehoboth on the river[y] succeeded him as king.
38 When Shaul died, Baal-Hanan son of Acbor succeeded him as king.
39 When Baal-Hanan son of Acbor died, Hadad[z] succeeded him as king. His city was named Pau, and his wife's name was Mehetabel daughter of Matred, the daughter of Me-Zahab.

40 These were the chiefs descended from Esau, by name, according to their clans and regions:
Timna, Alvah, Jetheth,
41 Oholibamah, Elah, Pi-
non, 42 Kenaz, Teman, Mibzar, 43 Magdiel and Iram.
These were the chiefs of Edom, according to their settlements in the land they occupied.

This was Esau the father of the Edomites.

Joseph's Dreams

37 Jacob lived in the land where his father had stayed,[g] the land of Canaan.[h]

36:19 [a] Ge 25:30
36:20 [b] Ge 14:6; Dt 2:12,22; 1Ch 1:38
36:31 [c] Ge 17:6; 1Ch 1:43
36:33 [d] Jer 49:13,22
36:34 [e] Eze 25:13
36:35 [f] Ge 19:37; Nu 22:1; Dt 1:5; Ru 1:1,6
37:1 [g] Ge 17:8 [h] Ge 10:19

[u] *22* Hebrew *Hemam,* a variant of *Homam* (see 1 Chron. 1:39) [v] *24* Vulgate; Syriac *discovered water;* the meaning of the Hebrew for this word is uncertain. [w] *26* Hebrew *Dishan,* a variant of *Dishon* [x] *31* Or *before an Israelite king reigned over them* [y] *37* Possibly the Euphrates [z] *39* Many manuscripts of the Masoretic Text, Samaritan Pentateuch and Syriac (see also 1 Chron. 1:50); most manuscripts of the Masoretic Text *Hadar*

2This is the account of Jacob.

Joseph, a young man of seventeen, was tending the flocks[a] with his brothers, the sons of Bilhah[b] and the sons of Zilpah,[c] his father's wives, and he brought their father a bad report[d] about them.

3Now Israel loved Joseph more than any of his other sons,[e] because he had been born to him in his old age;[f] and he made a richly ornamented[a] robe[g] for him. 4When his brothers saw that their father loved him more than any of them, they hated him[h] and could not speak a kind word to him.

5Joseph had a dream,[i] and when he told it to his brothers, they hated him all the more. 6He said to them, "Listen to this dream I had: 7We were binding sheaves of grain out in the field when suddenly my sheaf rose and stood upright, while your sheaves gathered around mine and bowed down to it."[j]

8His brothers said to him, "Do you intend to reign over us? Will you actually rule us?"[k] And they hated him all the more because of his dream and what he had said.

9Then he had another dream, and he told it to his brothers. "Listen," he said, "I had another dream, and this time the sun and moon and eleven stars were bowing down to me."

10When he told his father as well as his brothers,[l] his father rebuked him and said, "What is this dream you had? Will your mother and I and your brothers actually come and bow down to the ground before you?"[m] 11His brothers were jealous of him,[n] but his father kept the matter in mind.[o]

Joseph Sold by His Brothers

12Now his brothers had gone to graze their father's flocks near Shechem, 13and Israel said to Joseph, "As you know, your brothers are grazing the flocks near Shechem. Come, I am going to send you to them."

"Very well," he replied.

14So he said to him, "Go and see if all is well with your brothers and with the flocks, and bring word back to me." Then he sent him off from the Valley of Hebron.[p]

When Joseph arrived at Shechem, 15a man found him wandering around in the fields and asked him, "What are you looking for?"

16He replied, "I'm looking for my brothers. Can you tell me where they are grazing their flocks?"

17"They have moved on from here," the man answered. "I heard them say, 'Let's go to Dothan.[q]' "

So Joseph went after his brothers and found them near Dothan. 18But they saw him in the distance, and before he reached them, they plotted to kill him.[r]

19"Here comes that dreamer!" they said to each other. 20"Come now, let's kill him and throw him into one of these cisterns[s] and say that a ferocious animal devoured him. Then we'll see what comes of his dreams."[t]

21When Reuben heard this, he tried to rescue him from their hands. "Let's not take his life," he said.[u] 22"Don't shed any blood. Throw him into this cistern here in the desert, but don't lay a hand on him." Reuben said this to rescue him from them and take him back to his father.

23So when Joseph came to his brothers, they stripped him of his robe—the richly ornamented robe he was wearing— 24and they took him and threw him into the cistern.[v] Now the cistern was empty; there was no water in it.

25As they sat down to eat their meal, they looked up and saw a caravan of Ishmaelites coming from Gilead. Their camels were loaded with spices, balm and myrrh,[w] and they were on their way to take them down to Egypt.[x]

26Judah said to his brothers, "What will we gain if we kill our brother and cover up his blood?[y] 27Come, let's sell him to the Ish-

37:2 [a] Ps 78:71 [b] Ge 35:25 [c] Ge 35:26 [d] 1Sa 2:24
37:3 [e] Ge 25:28 [f] Ge 44:20 [g] 2Sa 13:18-19
37:4 [h] Ge 27:41; 49:22-23; Ac 7:9
37:5 [i] Ge 20:3; 28:12
37:7 [j] Ge 42:6,9; 43:26,28; 44:14; 50:18
37:8 [k] Ge 49:26
37:10 [l] ver 5 [m] ver 7; Ge 27:29
37:11 [n] Ac 7:9 [o] Lk 2:19,51
37:14 [p] Ge 13:18; 35:27
37:17 [q] 2Ki 6:13
37:18 [r] 1Sa 19:1; Mk 14:1; Ac 23:12
37:20 [s] Jer 38:6,9 [t] Ge 50:20
37:21 [u] Ge 42:22
37:24 [v] Jer 41:7
37:25 [w] Ge 43:11 [x] ver 28
37:26 [y] ver 20; Ge 4:10

[a]3 The meaning of the Hebrew for *richly ornamented* is uncertain; also in verses 23 and 32.

maelites and not lay our hands on him; after all, he is our brother,[a] our own flesh and blood." His brothers agreed.

28So when the Midianite[b] merchants came by, his brothers pulled Joseph up out of the cistern and sold him for twenty shekels[b] of silver to the Ishmaelites, who took him to Egypt.[c]

29When Reuben returned to the cistern and saw that Joseph was not there, he tore his clothes.[d] 30He went back to his brothers and said, "The boy isn't there! Where can I turn now?"[e]

31Then they got Joseph's robe,[f] slaughtered a goat and dipped the robe in the blood. 32They took the ornamented robe back to their father and said, "We found this. Examine it to see whether it is your son's robe."

33He recognized it and said, "It is my son's robe! Some ferocious animal[g] has devoured him. Joseph has surely been torn to pieces."[h]

34Then Jacob tore his clothes,[i] put on sackcloth[j] and mourned for his son many days.[k] 35All his sons and daughters came to comfort him, but he refused to be comforted. "No," he said, "in mourning will I go down to the grave[c][l] to my son." So his father wept for him.

36Meanwhile, the Midianites[d] sold Joseph in Egypt to Potiphar, one of Pharaoh's officials, the captain of the guard.[m]

Judah and Tamar

38 At that time, Judah left his brothers and went down to stay with a man of Adullam named Hirah. 2There Judah met the daughter of a Canaanite man named Shua.[n] He married her and lay with her; 3she became pregnant and gave birth to a son, who was named Er.[o] 4She conceived again and gave birth to a son and named him Onan. 5She gave birth to still another son and named him Shelah. It was at Kezib that she gave birth to him.

6Judah got a wife for Er, his firstborn, and her name was Tamar. 7But Er, Judah's firstborn, was wicked in the LORD's sight; so the LORD put him to death.[p]

8Then Judah said to Onan, "Lie with your brother's wife and fulfill your duty to her as a brother-in-law to produce offspring for your brother."[q] 9But Onan knew that the offspring would not be his; so whenever he lay with his brother's wife, he spilled his semen on the ground to keep from producing offspring for his brother. 10What he did was wicked in the LORD's sight; so he put him to death also.[r]

11Judah then said to his daughter-in-law Tamar, "Live as a widow in your father's house until my son Shelah grows up."[s] For he thought, "He may die too, just like his brothers." So Tamar went to live in her father's house.

12After a long time Judah's wife, the daughter of Shua, died. When Judah had recovered from his grief, he went up to Timnah,[t] to the men who were shearing his sheep, and his friend Hirah the Adullamite went with him.

13When Tamar was told, "Your father-in-law is on his way to Timnah to shear his sheep," 14she took off her widow's clothes, covered herself with a veil to disguise herself, and then sat down at the entrance to Enaim, which is on the road to Timnah. For she saw that, though Shelah[u] had now grown up, she had not been given to him as his wife.

15When Judah saw her, he thought she was a prostitute, for she had covered her face. 16Not realizing that she was his daughter-in-law,[v] he went over to her by the roadside and said, "Come now, let me sleep with you."

"And what will you give me to sleep with you?" she asked.

17"I'll send you a young goat[w] from my flock," he said.

"Will you give me something as a

37:27 [a]Ge 42:21
37:28 [b]Ge 25:2; Jdg 6:1-3 [c]Ge 45:4-5; Ps 105:17; Ac 7:9
37:29 [d]ver 34; Ge 44:13; Job 1:20
37:30 [e]ver 22; Ge 42:13,36
37:31 [f]ver 3,23
37:33 [g]ver 20 [h]Ge 44:20,28
37:34 [i]ver 29 [j]2Sa 3:31 [k]Ge 50:3,10, 11
37:35 [l]Ge 42:38; 44:22,29,31
37:36 [m]Ge 39:1
38:2 [n]1Ch 2:3
38:3 [o]ver 6; Ge 46:12; Nu 26:19
38:7 [p]ver 10; Ge 46:12; 1Ch 2:3
38:8 [q]Dt 25:5-6; Mt 22:24-28
38:10 [r]Ge 46:12; Dt 25:7-10
38:11 [s]Ru 1:13
38:12 [t]ver 14; Jos 15:10,57
38:14 [u]ver 11
38:16 [v]Lev 18:15; 20:12
38:17 [w]Eze 16:33

[b]*28* That is, about 8 ounces (about 0.2 kilogram) [c]*35* Hebrew *Sheol* [d]*36* Samaritan Pentateuch, Septuagint, Vulgate and Syriac (see also verse 28); Masoretic Text *Medanites*

pledge[a] until you send it?" she
asked.
18He said, "What pledge should I
give you?"
"Your seal[b] and its cord, and the
staff in your hand," she answered.
So he gave them to her and slept
with her, and she became pregnant
by him. 19After she left, she took
off her veil and put on her widow's
clothes[c] again.
20Meanwhile Judah sent the
young goat by his friend the Adullamite in order to get his pledge
back from the woman, but he did
not find her. 21He asked the men
who lived there, "Where is the
shrine prostitute[d] who was beside
the road at Enaim?"
"There hasn't been any shrine
prostitute here," they said.
22So he went back to Judah and
said, "I didn't find her. Besides, the
men who lived there said, 'There
hasn't been any shrine prostitute
here.' "
23Then Judah said, "Let her
keep what she has, or we will become a laughingstock. After all, I
did send her this young goat, but
you didn't find her."
24About three months later Judah was told, "Your daughter-in-
law Tamar is guilty of prostitution,
and as a result she is now pregnant."
Judah said, "Bring her out and
have her burned to death!"[e]
25As she was being brought out,
she sent a message to her father-
in-law. "I am pregnant by the man
who owns these," she said. And she
added, "See if you recognize whose
seal and cord and staff these are."[f]
26Judah recognized them and
said, "She is more righteous than
I,[g] since I wouldn't give her to my
son Shelah.[h]" And he did not sleep
with her again.
27When the time came for her to
give birth, there were twin boys in
her womb.[i] 28As she was giving
birth, one of them put out his
hand; so the midwife took a scarlet
thread and tied it on his wrist and
said, "This one came out first."
29But when he drew back his hand,

38:17 [a]ver 20
38:18 [b]ver 25
38:19 [c]ver 14
38:21 [d]Lev 19:29; Hos 4:14
38:24 [e]Lev 21:9; Dt 22:21,22
38:25 [f]ver 18
38:26 [g]1Sa 24:17 [h]ver 11
38:27 [i]Ge 25:24
38:29 [j]Ge 46:12; Nu 26:20,21; Ru 4:12,18; 1Ch 2:4; Mt 1:3
38:30 [k]1Ch 2:4
39:1 [l]Ge 37:36 [m]Ge 37:25; Ps 105:17
39:2 [n]Ge 21:20,22; Ac 7:9
39:3 [o]Ge 21:22; 26:28 [p]Ps 1:3
39:4 [q]ver 8,22; Ge 24:2
39:5 [r]Ge 26:24; 30:27
39:6 [s]1Sa 16:12
39:7 [t]2Sa 13:11; Pr 7:15-18
39:8 [u]Pr 6:23-24
39:9 [v]Ge 41:33,40 [w]Ge 20:6; 42:18; 2Sa 12:13

his brother came out, and she said,
"So this is how you have broken
out!" And he was named Perez.[e][j]
30Then his brother, who had the
scarlet thread on his wrist, came
out and he was given the name Zerah.[f][k]

Joseph and Potiphar's Wife

39 Now Joseph had been tak-
en down to Egypt. Potiphar,
an Egyptian who was one of Pharaoh's officials, the captain of the
guard,[l] bought him from the Ishmaelites who had taken him
there.[m]
2The LORD was with Joseph[n] and
he prospered, and he lived in the
house of his Egyptian master.
3When his master saw that the
LORD was with him[o] and that the
LORD gave him success in everything he did,[p] 4Joseph found favor
in his eyes and became his attendant. Potiphar put him in charge of
his household, and he entrusted to
his care everything he owned.[q]
5From the time he put him in
charge of his household and of all
that he owned, the LORD blessed
the household of the Egyptian because of Joseph.[r] The blessing of
the LORD was on everything Potiphar had, both in the house and in
the field. 6So he left in Joseph's
care everything he had; with Joseph in charge, he did not concern
himself with anything except the
food he ate.
Now Joseph was well-built and
handsome,[s] 7and after a while his
master's wife took notice of Joseph
and said, "Come to bed with me!"[t]
8But he refused.[u] "With me in
charge," he told her, "my master
does not concern himself with anything in the house; everything he
owns he has entrusted to my care.
9No one is greater in this house
than I am.[v] My master has withheld nothing from me except you,
because you are his wife. How then
could I do such a wicked thing and
sin against God?"[w] 10And though

[e]29 *Perez* means *breaking out.* [f]30 *Zerah* can mean *scarlet* or *brightness.*

she spoke to Joseph day after day, he refused to go to bed with her or even be with her.

11One day he went into the house to attend to his duties, and none of the household servants was inside. 12She caught him by his cloak[a] and said, "Come to bed with me!" But he left his cloak in her hand and ran out of the house.

13When she saw that he had left his cloak in her hand and had run out of the house, 14she called her household servants. "Look," she said to them, "this Hebrew has been brought to us to make sport of us! He came in here to sleep with me, but I screamed.[b] 15When he heard me scream for help, he left his cloak beside me and ran out of the house."

16She kept his cloak beside her until his master came home. 17Then she told him this story:[c] "That Hebrew slave you brought us came to me to make sport of me. 18But as soon as I screamed for help, he left his cloak beside me and ran out of the house."

19When his master heard the story his wife told him, saying, "This is how your slave treated me," he burned with anger.[d] 20Joseph's master took him and put him in prison,[e] the place where the king's prisoners were confined.

But while Joseph was there in the prison, 21the LORD was with him; he showed him kindness and granted him favor in the eyes of the prison warden.[f] 22So the warden put Joseph in charge of all those held in the prison, and he was made responsible for all that was done there.[g] 23The warden paid no attention to anything under Joseph's care, because the LORD was with Joseph and gave him success in whatever he did.[h]

The Cupbearer and the Baker

40 Some time later, the cupbearer[i] and the baker of the king of Egypt offended their master, the king of Egypt. 2Pharaoh was angry[j] with his two officials, the chief cupbearer and the chief baker, 3and put them in custody in the house of the captain of the guard,[k] in the same prison where Joseph was confined. 4The captain of the guard assigned them to Joseph,[l] and he attended them.

After they had been in custody for some time, 5each of the two men—the cupbearer and the baker of the king of Egypt, who were being held in prison—had a dream the same night, and each dream had a meaning of its own.[m]

6When Joseph came to them the next morning, he saw that they were dejected. 7So he asked Pharaoh's officials who were in custody with him in his master's house, "Why are your faces so sad today?"[n]

8"We both had dreams," they answered, "but there is no one to interpret them."[o]

Then Joseph said to them, "Do not interpretations belong to God?[p] Tell me your dreams."

9So the chief cupbearer told Joseph his dream. He said to him, "In my dream I saw a vine in front of me, 10and on the vine were three branches. As soon as it budded, it blossomed, and its clusters ripened into grapes. 11Pharaoh's cup was in my hand, and I took the grapes, squeezed them into Pharaoh's cup and put the cup in his hand."

12"This is what it means,[q]" Joseph said to him. "The three branches are three days. 13Within three days Pharaoh will lift up your head and restore you to your position, and you will put Pharaoh's cup in his hand, just as you used to do when you were his cupbearer. 14But when all goes well with you, remember me[r] and show me kindness;[s] mention me to Pharaoh and get me out of this prison. 15For I was forcibly carried off from the land of the Hebrews,[t] and even here I have done nothing to deserve being put in a dungeon."

16When the chief baker saw that Joseph had given a favorable interpretation, he said to Joseph, "I too had a dream: On my head were

39:12 [a] Pr 7:13
39:14 [b] Dt 22:24,27
39:17 [c] Ex 23:1,7; Ps 101:5
39:19 [d] Pr 6:34
39:20 [e] Ge 40:3; Ps 105:18
39:21 [f] Ex 3:21
39:22 [g] ver 4
39:23 [h] ver 3
40:1 [i] Ne 1:11
40:2 [j] Pr 16:14,15
40:3 [k] Ge 39:20
40:4 [l] Ge 39:4
40:5 [m] Ge 41:11
40:7 [n] Ne 2:2
40:8 [o] Ge 41:8,15 [p] Ge 41:16; Da 2:22,28,47
40:12 [q] Ge 41:12,15, 25; Da 2:36; 4:19
40:14 [r] Lk 23:42 [s] Jos 2:12; 1Sa 20:14,42; 1Ki 2:7
40:15 [t] Ge 37:26-28

three baskets of bread.[g] **17**In the top basket were all kinds of baked goods for Pharaoh, but the birds were eating them out of the basket on my head."

18"This is what it means," Joseph said. "The three baskets are three days.[a] **19**Within three days Pharaoh will lift off your head[b] and hang you on a tree.[h] And the birds will eat away your flesh."

20Now the third day was Pharaoh's birthday,[c] and he gave a feast for all his officials.[d] He lifted up the heads of the chief cupbearer and the chief baker in the presence of his officials: **21**He restored the chief cupbearer to his position, so that he once again put the cup into Pharaoh's hand,[e] **22**but he hanged[i] the chief baker,[f] just as Joseph had said to them in his interpretation.[g]

23The chief cupbearer, however, did not remember Joseph; he forgot him.[h]

Pharaoh's Dreams

41 When two full years had passed, Pharaoh had a dream:[i] He was standing by the Nile, **2**when out of the river there came up seven cows, sleek and fat,[j] and they grazed among the reeds.[k] **3**After them, seven other cows, ugly and gaunt, came up out of the Nile and stood beside those on the riverbank. **4**And the cows that were ugly and gaunt ate up the seven sleek, fat cows. Then Pharaoh woke up.

5He fell asleep again and had a second dream: Seven heads of grain, healthy and good, were growing on a single stalk. **6**After them, seven other heads of grain sprouted—thin and scorched by the east wind. **7**The thin heads of grain swallowed up the seven healthy, full heads. Then Pharaoh woke up; it had been a dream.

8In the morning his mind was troubled,[l] so he sent for all the magicians[m] and wise men of Egypt. Pharaoh told them his dreams, but no one could interpret them for him.

9Then the chief cupbearer said to Pharaoh, "Today I am reminded of my shortcomings. **10**Pharaoh was once angry with his servants,[n] and he imprisoned me and the chief baker in the house of the captain of the guard.[o] **11**Each of us had a dream the same night, and each dream had a meaning of its own.[p] **12**Now a young Hebrew was there with us, a servant of the captain of the guard. We told him our dreams, and he interpreted them for us, giving each man the interpretation of his dream.[q] **13**And things turned out exactly as he interpreted them to us: I was restored to my position, and the other man was hanged.[i][r]"

14So Pharaoh sent for Joseph, and he was quickly brought from the dungeon.[s] When he had shaved and changed his clothes, he came before Pharaoh.

15Pharaoh said to Joseph, "I had a dream, and no one can interpret it. But I have heard it said of you that when you hear a dream you can interpret it."[t]

16"I cannot do it," Joseph replied to Pharaoh, "but God will give Pharaoh the answer he desires."[u]

17Then Pharaoh said to Joseph, "In my dream I was standing on the bank of the Nile, **18**when out of the river there came up seven cows, fat and sleek, and they grazed among the reeds. **19**After them, seven other cows came up—scrawny and very ugly and lean. I had never seen such ugly cows in all the land of Egypt. **20**The lean, ugly cows ate up the seven fat cows that came up first. **21**But even after they ate them, no one could tell that they had done so; they looked just as ugly as before. Then I woke up.

22"In my dreams I also saw seven heads of grain, full and good, growing on a single stalk. **23**After them, seven other heads sprouted—withered and thin and scorched by the east wind. **24**The thin heads of

40:18 [a]ver 12
40:19 [b]ver 13
40:20 [c]Mt 14:6-10 [d]Mk 6:21
40:21 [e]ver 13
40:22 [f]ver 19 [g]Ps 105:19
40:23 [h]Job 19:14; Ecc 9:15
41:1 [i]Ge 20:3
41:2 [j]ver 26 [k]Isa 19:6
41:8 [l]Da 2:1,3; 4:5, 19 [m]Ex 7:11, 22; Da 1:20; 2:2,27; 4:7
41:10 [n]Ge 40:2 [o]Ge 39:20
41:11 [p]Ge 40:5
41:12 [q]Ge 40:12
41:13 [r]Ge 40:22
41:14 [s]Ps 105:20; Da 2:25
41:15 [t]Da 5:16
41:16 [u]Ge 40:8; Da 2:30; Ac 3:12; 2Co 3:5

[g]*16* Or *three wicker baskets* [h]*19* Or *and impale you on a pole* [i]*22,13* Or *impaled*

grain swallowed up the seven good
heads. I told this to the magicians,
but none could explain it to me.[a]"
25Then Joseph said to Pharaoh,
"The dreams of Pharaoh are one
and the same. God has revealed to
Pharaoh what he is about to do.[b]
26The seven good cows[c] are seven
years, and the seven good heads of
grain are seven years; it is one and
the same dream. **27**The seven lean,
ugly cows that came up afterward
are seven years, and so are the sev-
en worthless heads of grain
scorched by the east wind: They are
seven years of famine.[d]
28"It is just as I said to Pharaoh:
God has shown Pharaoh what he is
about to do. **29**Seven years of great
abundance[e] are coming throughout the land of Egypt, **30**but seven
years of famine[f] will follow them.
Then all the abundance in Egypt
will be forgotten, and the famine
will ravage the land.[g] **31**The abundance in the land will not be remembered, because the famine
that follows it will be so severe.
32The reason the dream was given
to Pharaoh in two forms is that the
matter has been firmly decided[h]
by God, and God will do it soon.
33"And now let Pharaoh look for
a discerning and wise man[i] and
put him in charge of the land of
Egypt. **34**Let Pharaoh appoint commissioners over the land to take a
fifth[j] of the harvest of Egypt during the seven years of abundance.[k]
35They should collect all the food
of these good years that are coming
and store up the grain under the
authority of Pharaoh, to be kept in
the cities for food.[l] **36**This food
should be held in reserve for the
country, to be used during the sev-
en years of famine that will come
upon Egypt,[m] so that the country
may not be ruined by the famine."
37The plan seemed good to Pharaoh and to all his officials.[n] **38**So
Pharaoh asked them, "Can we find
anyone like this man, one in whom
is the spirit of God[i]?"[o]
39Then Pharaoh said to Joseph,
"Since God has made all this
known to you, there is no one so
discerning and wise as you. **40**You
shall be in charge of my palace, and
all my people are to submit to your
orders.[p] Only with respect to the
throne will I be greater than you."

Joseph in Charge of Egypt

41So Pharaoh said to Joseph, "I
hereby put you in charge of the
whole land of Egypt."[q] **42**Then
Pharaoh took his signet ring[r] from
his finger and put it on Joseph's
finger. He dressed him in robes of
fine linen and put a gold chain
around his neck.[s] **43**He had him
ride in a chariot as his second-in-
command,[k] and men shouted before him, "Make way[l]!"[t] Thus he
put him in charge of the whole land
of Egypt.
44Then Pharaoh said to Joseph,
"I am Pharaoh, but without your
word no one will lift hand or foot in
all Egypt."[u] **45**Pharaoh gave Joseph the name Zaphenath-Paneah
and gave him Asenath daughter of
Potiphera, priest of On,[m] to be his
wife.[v] And Joseph went throughout the land of Egypt.
46Joseph was thirty years old[w]
when he entered the service[x] of
Pharaoh king of Egypt. And Joseph
went out from Pharaoh's presence
and traveled throughout Egypt.
47During the seven years of abundance the land produced plentiful-
ly. **48**Joseph collected all the food
produced in those seven years of
abundance in Egypt and stored it
in the cities. In each city he put the
food grown in the fields surrounding it. **49**Joseph stored up huge
quantities of grain, like the sand of
the sea; it was so much that he
stopped keeping records because it
was beyond measure.
50Before the years of famine
came, two sons were born to Joseph by Asenath daughter of Potiphera, priest of On.[y] **51**Joseph
named his firstborn[z] Manasseh[n]

[i]38 Or *of the gods* [k]43 Or *in the chariot of his second-in-command*; or *in his second chariot* [l]43 Or *Bow down* [m]45 That is, Heliopolis; also in verse 50 [n]51 *Manasseh* sounds like and may be derived from the Hebrew for *forget*.

41:24 [a]ver 8
41:25 [b]Da 2:45
41:26 [c]ver 2
41:27 [d]Ge 12:10; 2Ki 8:1
41:29 [e]ver 47
41:30 [f]ver 54; Ge 47:13 [g]ver 56
41:32 [h]Nu 23:19; Isa 46:10-11
41:33 [i]ver 39
41:34 [j]1Sa 8:15 [k]ver 48
41:35 [l]ver 48
41:36 [m]ver 56
41:37 [n]Ge 45:16
41:38 [o]Nu 27:18; Job 32:8; Da 4:8,8-9,18; 5:11,14
41:40 [p]Ps 105:21-22; Ac 7:10
41:41 [q]Ge 42:6; Da 6:3
41:42 [r]Est 3:10 [s]Da 5:7,16,29
41:43 [t]Est 6:9
41:44 [u]Ps 105:22
41:45 [v]ver 50; Ge 46:20,27
41:46 [w]Ge 37:2 [x]1Sa 16:21; Da 1:19
41:50 [y]Ge 46:20; 48:5
41:51 [z]Ge 48:14,18, 20

and said, "It is because God has
made me forget all my trouble and
all my father's household." 52The
second son he named Ephraim[o][a]
and said, "It is because God has
made me fruitful[b] in the land of
my suffering."
53The seven years of abundance
in Egypt came to an end, 54and the
seven years of famine began,[c] just
as Joseph had said. There was famine in all the other lands, but in the
whole land of Egypt there was food.
55When all Egypt began to feel the
famine,[d] the people cried to Pharaoh for food. Then Pharaoh told all
the Egyptians, "Go to Joseph and
do what he tells you."[e]
56When the famine had spread
over the whole country, Joseph
opened the storehouses and sold
grain to the Egyptians, for the famine[f] was severe throughout Egypt.
57And all the countries came to
Egypt to buy grain from Joseph,[g]
because the famine was severe in
all the world.

Joseph's Brothers Go to Egypt

42 When Jacob learned that
there was grain in Egypt,[h]
he said to his sons, "Why do you
just keep looking at each other?"
2He continued, "I have heard that
there is grain in Egypt. Go down
there and buy some for us, so that
we may live and not die."[i]
3Then ten of Joseph's brothers
went down to buy grain from Egypt.
4But Jacob did not send Benjamin,
Joseph's brother, with the others,
because he was afraid that harm
might come to him.[j] 5So Israel's
sons were among those who went
to buy grain,[k] for the famine was in
the land of Canaan also.[l]
6Now Joseph was the governor of
the land,[m] the one who sold grain
to all its people. So when Joseph's
brothers arrived, they bowed down
to him with their faces to the
ground.[n] 7As soon as Joseph saw
his brothers, he recognized them,
but he pretended to be a stranger
and spoke harshly to them.[o]
"Where do you come from?" he
asked.

"From the land of Canaan," they
replied, "to buy food."
8Although Joseph recognized his
brothers, they did not recognize
him.[p] 9Then he remembered his
dreams[q] about them and said to
them, "You are spies! You have
come to see where our land is unprotected."
10"No, my lord," they answered.
"Your servants have come to buy
food. 11We are all the sons of one
man. Your servants are honest
men, not spies."
12"No!" he said to them. "You
have come to see where our land is
unprotected."
13But they replied, "Your servants were twelve brothers, the
sons of one man, who lives in the
land of Canaan. The youngest is
now with our father, and one is no
more."[r]
14Joseph said to them, "It is just
as I told you: You are spies! 15And
this is how you will be tested: As
surely as Pharaoh lives,[s] you will
not leave this place unless your
youngest brother comes here.
16Send one of your number to get
your brother; the rest of you will be
kept in prison, so that your words
may be tested to see if you are telling the truth.[t] If you are not, then
as surely as Pharaoh lives, you are
spies!" 17And he put them all in
custody[u] for three days.
18On the third day, Joseph said
to them, "Do this and you will live,
for I fear God:[v] 19If you are honest
men, let one of your brothers stay
here in prison, while the rest of you
go and take grain back for your
starving households. 20But you
must bring your youngest brother
to me,[w] so that your words may be
verified and that you may not die."
This they proceeded to do.
21They said to one another,
"Surely we are being punished because of our brother.[x] We saw how
distressed he was when he pleaded
with us for his life, but we would

41:52 [a]Ge 48:1,5; 50:23 [b]Ge 17:6; 28:3; 49:22
41:54 [c]ver 30; Ps 105:11; Ac 7:11
41:55 [d]Dt 32:24 [e]ver 41
41:56 [f]Ge 12:10
41:57 [g]Ge 42:5; 47:15
42:1 [h]Ac 7:12
42:2 [i]Ge 43:8
42:4 [j]ver 38
42:5 [k]Ge 41:57 [l]Ge 12:10; Ac 7:11
42:6 [m]Ge 41:41 [n]Ge 37:7-10
42:7 [o]ver 30
42:8 [p]Ge 37:2
42:9 [q]Ge 37:7
42:13 [r]Ge 37:30,33; 44:20
42:15 [s]1Sa 17:55
42:16 [t]ver 11
42:17 [u]Ge 40:4
42:18 [v]Ge 20:11; Lev 25:43
42:20 [w]ver 15,34; Ge 43:5; 44:23
42:21 [x]Ge 37:26-28

[o]52 *Ephraim* sounds like the Hebrew for *twice fruitful.*

not listen; that's why this distress[a]
has come upon us."
22Reuben replied, "Didn't I tell
you not to sin against the boy?[b]
But you wouldn't listen! Now we
must give an accounting[c] for his
blood."[d] 23They did not realize
that Joseph could understand
them, since he was using an inter-
preter.
24He turned away from them and
began to weep, but then turned
back and spoke to them again. He
had Simeon taken from them and
bound before their eyes.[e]
25Joseph gave orders to fill their
bags with grain,[f] to put each
man's silver back in his sack,[g] and
to give them provisions for their
journey.[h] After this was done for
them, 26they loaded their grain on
their donkeys and left.
27At the place where they
stopped for the night one of them
opened his sack to get feed for his
donkey, and he saw his silver in the
mouth of his sack.[i] 28"My silver
has been returned," he said to his
brothers. "Here it is in my sack."
Their hearts sank and they
turned to each other trembling and
said, "What is this that God has
done to us?"[j]
29When they came to their father
Jacob in the land of Canaan, they
told him all that had happened to
them. They said, 30"The man who
is lord over the land spoke harshly
to us[k] and treated us as though we
were spying on the land. 31But we
said to him, 'We are honest men;
we are not spies.[l] 32We were
twelve brothers, sons of one father.
One is no more, and the youngest
is now with our father in Canaan.'
33"Then the man who is lord
over the land said to us, 'This is
how I will know whether you are
honest men: Leave one of your
brothers here with me, and take
food for your starving households
and go.[m] 34But bring your youngest
brother to me so I will know that
you are not spies but honest men.
Then I will give your brother back
to you, and you can trade[p] in the
land.[n]' "

42:21 [a]Hos 5:15
42:22 [b]Ge 37:21-22 [c]Ge 9:5 [d]1Ki 2:32; 2Ch 24:22; Ps 9:12
42:24 [e]ver 13; Ge 43:14,23; 45:14-15
42:25 [f]Ge 43:2 [g]Ge 44:1,8 [h]Ro 12:17, 20-21
42:27 [i]Ge 43:21-22
42:28 [j]Ge 43:23
42:30 [k]ver 7
42:31 [l]ver 11
42:33 [m]ver 19,20
42:34 [n]Ge 34:10
42:35 [o]Ge 43:12,15, 18
42:36 [p]Ge 43:14
42:38 [q]Ge 37:33 [r]ver 4 [s]Ge 37:35 [t]Ge 44:29,34
43:1 [u]Ge 12:10; 41:56-57
43:3 [v]Ge 42:15; 44:23
43:5 [w]Ge 42:15; 2Sa 3:13
43:7 [x]ver 27 [y]Ge 42:13

35As they were emptying their
sacks, there in each man's sack
was his pouch of silver! When they
and their father saw the money
pouches, they were frightened.[o]
36Their father Jacob said to them,
"You have deprived me of my children. Joseph is no more and Simeon is no more, and now you want to
take Benjamin.[p] Everything is
against me!"
37Then Reuben said to his father, "You may put both of my sons
to death if I do not bring him back
to you. Entrust him to my care, and
I will bring him back."
38But Jacob said, "My son will
not go down there with you; his
brother is dead[q] and he is the only
one left. If harm comes to him[r] on
the journey you are taking, you will
bring my gray head down to the
grave[q][s] in sorrow.[t]"

The Second Journey to Egypt

43 Now the famine was still severe in the land.[u] 2So when
they had eaten all the grain they
had brought from Egypt, their father said to them, "Go back and
buy us a little more food."
3But Judah said to him, "The
man warned us solemnly, 'You will
not see my face again unless your
brother is with you.'[v] 4If you will
send our brother along with us, we
will go down and buy food for you.
5But if you will not send him, we
will not go down, because the man
said to us, 'You will not see my face
again unless your brother is with
you.[w]' "
6Israel asked, "Why did you
bring this trouble on me by telling
the man you had another brother?"
7They replied, "The man questioned us closely about ourselves
and our family. 'Is your father still
living?'[x] he asked us. 'Do you have
another brother?'[y] We simply answered his questions. How were we
to know he would say, 'Bring your
brother down here'?"
8Then Judah said to Israel his fa-

p34 *Or move about freely* q38 Hebrew *Sheol*

ther, "Send the boy along with me
and we will go at once, so that we
and you and our children may live
and not die.[a] **9**I myself will guarantee his safety; you can hold me personally responsible for him. If I do
not bring him back to you and set
him here before you, I will bear the
blame before you all my life.[b] **10**As
it is, if we had not delayed, we
could have gone and returned
twice."

11Then their father Israel said to
them, "If it must be, then do this:
Put some of the best products of
the land in your bags and take
them down to the man as a gift[c]
—a little balm[d] and a little honey,
some spices[e] and myrrh, some pis-
tachio nuts and almonds. **12**Take
double the amount of silver with
you, for you must return the silver
that was put back into the mouths
of your sacks.[f] Perhaps it was a
mistake. **13**Take your brother also
and go back to the man at once.
14And may God Almighty[r][g] grant
you mercy before the man so that
he will let your other brother and
Benjamin come back with you.[h]
As for me, if I am bereaved, I am
bereaved."[i]

15So the men took the gifts and
double the amount of silver, and
Benjamin also. They hurried[j]
down to Egypt and presented
themselves[k] to Joseph. **16**When
Joseph saw Benjamin with them,
he said to the steward of his
house,[l] "Take these men to my
house, slaughter an animal and
prepare dinner;[m] they are to eat
with me at noon."

17The man did as Joseph told
him and took the men to Joseph's
house. **18**Now the men were frightened[n] when they were taken to his
house. They thought, "We were
brought here because of the silver
that was put back into our sacks
the first time. He wants to attack
us and overpower us and seize us as
slaves and take our donkeys."

19So they went up to Joseph's
steward and spoke to him at the
entrance to the house. **20**"Please,
sir," they said, "we came down
here the first time to buy food.[o]
21But at the place where we
stopped for the night we opened
our sacks and each of us found his
silver—the exact weight—in the
mouth of his sack. So we have
brought it back with us.[p] **22**We
have also brought additional silver
with us to buy food. We don't know
who put our silver in our sacks."

23"It's all right," he said. "Don't
be afraid. Your God, the God of
your father, has given you treasure
in your sacks;[q] I received your silver." Then he brought Simeon out
to them.[r]

24The steward took the men into
Joseph's house,[s] gave them water
to wash their feet[t] and provided
fodder for their donkeys. **25**They
prepared their gifts for Joseph's arrival at noon, because they had
heard that they were to eat there.

26When Joseph came home,
they presented to him the gifts[u]
they had brought into the house,
and they bowed down before him
to the ground.[v] **27**He asked them
how they were, and then he said,
"How is your aged father you told
me about? Is he still living?"[w]

28They replied, "Your servant
our father is still alive and well."
And they bowed low to pay him
honor.[x]

29As he looked about and saw
his brother Benjamin, his own
mother's son, he asked, "Is this
your youngest brother, the one you
told me about?"[y] And he said,
"God be gracious to you,[z] my son."
30Deeply moved[a] at the sight of
his brother, Joseph hurried out and
looked for a place to weep. He went
into his private room and wept[b]
there.

31After he had washed his face,
he came out and, controlling himself,[c] said, "Serve the food."

32They served him by himself,
the brothers by themselves, and
the Egyptians who ate with him by
themselves, because Egyptians
could not eat with Hebrews,[d] for
that is detestable to Egyptians.[e]

43:8 [a] Ge 42:2; Ps 33:18-19
43:9 [b] Ge 42:37; 44:32; Phm 1:18-19
43:11 [c] Ge 32:20; Pr 18:16 [d] Ge 37:25; Jer 8:22 [e] 1Ki 10:2
43:12 [f] Ge 42:25
43:14 [g] Ge 17:1; 28:3; 35:11 [h] Ge 42:24 [i] Est 4:16
43:15 [j] Ge 45:9,13 [k] Ge 47:2,7
43:16 [l] Ge 44:1,4,12 [m] ver 31; Lk 15:23
43:18 [n] Ge 42:35
43:20 [o] Ge 42:3
43:21 [p] ver 15; Ge 42:27,35
43:23 [q] Ge 42:28 [r] Ge 42:24
43:24 [s] ver 16 [t] Ge 18:4; 24:32
43:26 [u] Mt 2:11 [v] Ge 37:7,10
43:27 [w] ver 7
43:28 [x] Ge 37:7
43:29 [y] Ge 42:13 [z] Nu 6:25; Ps 67:1
43:30 [a] Jn 11:33,38 [b] Ge 42:24; 45:2,14,15; 46:29
43:31 [c] Ge 45:1
43:32 [d] Gal 2:12 [e] Ge 46:34; Ex 8:26

[r]14 Hebrew *El-Shaddai*

33The men had been seated before
him in the order of their ages, from
the firstborn to the youngest; and
they looked at each other in aston-
ishment. 34When portions were
served to them from Joseph's table, Benjamin's portion was five
times as much as anyone else's.[a]
So they feasted and drank freely
with him.

A Silver Cup in a Sack

44 Now Joseph gave these instructions to the steward of
his house: "Fill the men's sacks
with as much food as they can carry, and put each man's silver in the
mouth of his sack.[b] 2Then put my
cup, the silver one, in the mouth of
the youngest one's sack, along with
the silver for his grain." And he did
as Joseph said.
3As morning dawned, the men
were sent on their way with their
donkeys. 4They had not gone far
from the city when Joseph said to
his steward, "Go after those men at
once, and when you catch up with
them, say to them, 'Why have you
repaid good with evil?[c] 5Isn't this
the cup my master drinks from and
also uses for divination?[d] This is a
wicked thing you have done.' "
6When he caught up with them,
he repeated these words to them.
7But they said to him, "Why does
my lord say such things? Far be it
from your servants to do anything
like that! 8We even brought back to
you from the land of Canaan the
silver we found inside the mouths
of our sacks.[e] So why would we
steal silver or gold from your master's house? 9If any of your servants
is found to have it, he will die;[f]
and the rest of us will become my
lord's slaves."
10"Very well, then," he said, "let
it be as you say. Whoever is found
to have it will become my slave; the
rest of you will be free from
blame."
11Each of them quickly lowered
his sack to the ground and opened
it. 12Then the steward proceeded
to search, beginning with the oldest and ending with the youngest.
And the cup was found in Benjamin's sack.[g] 13At this, they tore
their clothes.[h] Then they all loaded their donkeys and returned to
the city.
14Joseph was still in the house
when Judah and his brothers came
in, and they threw themselves to
the ground before him.[i] 15Joseph
said to them, "What is this you
have done? Don't you know that a
man like me can find things out by
divination?[j]"
16"What can we say to my lord?"
Judah replied. "What can we say?
How can we prove our innocence?
God has uncovered your servants'
guilt. We are now my lord's
slaves[k]—we ourselves and the one
who was found to have the cup.[l]"
17But Joseph said, "Far be it
from me to do such a thing! Only
the man who was found to have the
cup will become my slave. The rest
of you, go back to your father in
peace."
18Then Judah went up to him
and said: "Please, my lord, let your
servant speak a word to my lord. Do
not be angry[m] with your servant,
though you are equal to Pharaoh
himself. 19My lord asked his servants, 'Do you have a father or a
brother?'[n] 20And we answered,
'We have an aged father, and there
is a young son born to him in his
old age.[o] His brother is dead,[p] and
he is the only one of his mother's
sons left, and his father loves
him.'[q]
21"Then you said to your servants, 'Bring him down to me so I
can see him for myself.'[r] 22And we
said to my lord, 'The boy cannot
leave his father; if he leaves him,
his father will die.'[s] 23But you told
your servants, 'Unless your youngest brother comes down with you,
you will not see my face again.'[t]
24When we went back to your servant my father, we told him what
my lord had said.
25"Then our father said, 'Go
back and buy a little more food.'[u]
26But we said, 'We cannot go
down. Only if our youngest brother
is with us will we go. We cannot see

43:34 [a]Ge 37:3; 45:22
44:1 [b]Ge 42:25
44:4 [c]Ps 35:12
44:5 [d]Ge 30:27; Dt 18:10-14
44:8 [e]Ge 42:25; 43:21
44:9 [f]Ge 31:32
44:12 [g]ver 2
44:13 [h]Ge 37:29; Nu 14:6; 2Sa 1:11
44:14 [i]Ge 37:7,10
44:15 [j]ver 5; Ge 30:27
44:16 [k]ver 9; Ge 43:18 [l]ver 2
44:18 [m]Ge 18:30; Ex 32:22
44:19 [n]Ge 43:7
44:20 [o]Ge 37:3 [p]Ge 37:33 [q]Ge 42:13
44:21 [r]Ge 42:15
44:22 [s]Ge 37:35
44:23 [t]Ge 43:5
44:25 [u]Ge 43:2

the man's face unless our youngest brother is with us.'

27"Your servant my father said to us, 'You know that my wife bore me two sons.[a] 28One of them went away from me, and I said, "He has surely been torn to pieces."[b] And I have not seen him since. 29If you take this one from me too and harm comes to him, you will bring my gray head down to the grave[s] in misery.'[c]

30"So now, if the boy is not with us when I go back to your servant my father and if my father, whose life is closely bound up with the boy's life,[d] 31sees that the boy isn't there, he will die. Your servants will bring the gray head of our father down to the grave in sorrow. 32Your servant guaranteed the boy's safety to my father. I said, 'If I do not bring him back to you, I will bear the blame before you, my father, all my life!'[e]

33"Now then, please let your servant remain here as my lord's slave[f] in place of the boy,[g] and let the boy return with his brothers. 34How can I go back to my father if the boy is not with me? No! Do not let me see the misery that would come upon my father."[h]

Joseph Makes Himself Known

45 Then Joseph could no longer control himself[i] before all his attendants, and he cried out, "Have everyone leave my presence!" So there was no one with Joseph when he made himself known to his brothers. 2And he wept[j] so loudly that the Egyptians heard him, and Pharaoh's household heard about it.[k]

3Joseph said to his brothers, "I am Joseph! Is my father still living?"[l] But his brothers were not able to answer him,[m] because they were terrified at his presence.

4Then Joseph said to his brothers, "Come close to me." When they had done so, he said, "I am your brother Joseph, the one you sold into Egypt![n] 5And now, do not be distressed[o] and do not be angry with yourselves for selling me here,[p] because it was to save lives that God sent me ahead of you.[q] 6For two years now there has been famine in the land, and for the next five years there will not be plowing and reaping. 7But God sent me ahead of you to preserve for you a remnant[r] on earth and to save your lives by a great deliverance.[t][s]

8"So then, it was not you who sent me here, but God. He made me father[t] to Pharaoh, lord of his entire household and ruler of all Egypt.[u] 9Now hurry back to my father and say to him, 'This is what your son Joseph says: God has made me lord of all Egypt. Come down to me; don't delay.[v] 10You shall live in the region of Goshen[w] and be near me—you, your children and grandchildren, your flocks and herds, and all you have. 11I will provide for you there,[x] because five years of famine are still to come. Otherwise you and your household and all who belong to you will become destitute.'

12"You can see for yourselves, and so can my brother Benjamin, that it is really I who am speaking to you. 13Tell my father about all the honor accorded me in Egypt and about everything you have seen. And bring my father down here quickly.[y]"

14Then he threw his arms around his brother Benjamin and wept, and Benjamin embraced him, weeping. 15And he kissed[z] all his brothers and wept over them. Afterward his brothers talked with him.[a]

16When the news reached Pharaoh's palace that Joseph's brothers had come,[b] Pharaoh and all his officials were pleased. 17Pharaoh said to Joseph, "Tell your brothers, 'Do this: Load your animals and return to the land of Canaan, 18and bring your father and your families back to me. I will give you the best of the land of Egypt[c] and you can enjoy the fat of the land.'[d]

44:27 [a]Ge 46:19
44:28 [b]Ge 37:33
44:29 [c]Ge 42:38
44:30 [d]1Sa 18:1
44:32 [e]Ge 43:9
44:33 [f]Ge 43:18 [g]Jn 15:13
44:34 [h]Est 8:6
45:1 [i]Ge 43:31
45:2 [j]Ge 29:11 [k]ver 16; Ge 46:29
45:3 [l]Ac 7:13 [m]ver 15
45:4 [n]Ge 37:28
45:5 [o]Ge 42:21 [p]Ge 42:22 [q]ver 7-8; Ge 50:20; Ps 105:17
45:7 [r]2Ki 19:4,30, 31; Isa 10:20, 21; Mic 4:7; Zep 2:7 [s]Ex 15:2; Est 4:14; Isa 25:9
45:8 [t]Jdg 17:10 [u]Ge 41:41
45:9 [v]Ge 43:10
45:10 [w]Ge 46:28,34; 47:1
45:11 [x]Ge 47:12
45:13 [y]Ac 7:14
45:15 [z]Lk 15:20 [a]ver 3
45:16 [b]Ac 7:13
45:18 [c]Ge 27:28; 46:34; 47:6, 11,27; Nu 18:12,29 [d]Ps 37:19

[s]29 Hebrew *Sheol*; also in verse 31 [t]7 Or *save you as a great band of survivors*

19"You are also directed to tell
them, 'Do this: Take some carts[a]
from Egypt for your children and
your wives, and get your father and
come. 20Never mind about your belongings, because the best of all
Egypt will be yours.' "
21So the sons of Israel did this.
Joseph gave them carts, as Pharaoh
had commanded, and he also gave
them provisions for their journey.[b]
22To each of them he gave new
clothing, but to Benjamin he gave
three hundred shekels[u] of silver
and five sets of clothes.[c] 23And
this is what he sent to his father:
ten donkeys loaded with the best
things of Egypt, and ten female
donkeys loaded with grain and
bread and other provisions for his
journey. 24Then he sent his brothers away, and as they were leaving
he said to them, "Don't quarrel on
the way!"[d]
25So they went up out of Egypt
and came to their father Jacob in
the land of Canaan. 26They told
him, "Joseph is still alive! In fact,
he is ruler of all Egypt." Jacob was
stunned; he did not believe them.[e]
27But when they told him everything Joseph had said to them, and
when he saw the carts[f] Joseph had
sent to carry him back, the spirit of
their father Jacob revived. 28And
Israel said, "I'm convinced! My son
Joseph is still alive. I will go and
see him before I die."

Jacob Goes to Egypt

46 So Israel set out with all
that was his, and when he
reached Beersheba,[g] he offered
sacrifices to the God of his father
Isaac.[h]
2And God spoke to Israel in a vision at night[i] and said, "Jacob! Jacob!"
"Here I am,"[j] he replied.
3"I am God, the God of your father,"[k] he said. "Do not be afraid
to go down to Egypt, for I will make
you into a great nation[l] there.[m] 4I
will go down to Egypt with you, and
I will surely bring you back again.[n]
And Joseph's own hand will close
your eyes.[o]"

5Then Jacob left Beersheba, and
Israel's sons took their father Jacob and their children and their
wives in the carts[p] that Pharaoh
had sent to transport him. 6They
also took with them their livestock
and the possessions they had acquired in Canaan, and Jacob and
all his offspring went to Egypt.[q]
7He took with him to Egypt his
sons and grandsons and his daughters and granddaughters—all his
offspring.[r]

8These are the names of the sons
of Israel[s] (Jacob and his descendants) who went to Egypt:

Reuben the firstborn of Jacob.
9The sons of Reuben:[t]
Hanoch, Pallu, Hezron and
Carmi.
10The sons of Simeon:[u]
Jemuel,[v] Jamin, Ohad, Jakin, Zohar and Shaul the
son of a Canaanite woman.
11The sons of Levi:[w]
Gershon, Kohath and Mera-
ri.
12The sons of Judah:[x]
Er, Onan, Shelah, Perez and
Zerah (but Er and Onan had
died in the land of Canaan).
The sons of Perez:[y]
Hezron and Hamul.
13The sons of Issachar:[z]
Tola, Puah,[v][a] Jashub[w]
and Shimron.
14The sons of Zebulun:[b]
Sered, Elon and Jahleel.
15These were the sons Leah bore
to Jacob in Paddan Aram,[x] besides
his daughter Dinah. These sons
and daughters of his were thirty-
three in all.

16The sons of Gad:[c]
Zephon,[y][d] Haggi, Shuni,
Ezbon, Eri, Arodi and Areli.
17The sons of Asher:[e]

45:19 [a]Ge 46:5
45:21 [b]Ge 42:25
45:22 [c]Ge 37:3; 43:34
45:24 [d]Ge 42:21-22
45:26 [e]Ge 44:28
45:27 [f]ver 19
46:1 [g]Ge 21:14; 28:10 [h]Ge 26:24; 28:13; 31:42
46:2 [i]Ge 15:1; Job 33:14-15 [j]Ge 22:1; 31:11
46:3 [k]Ge 28:13 [l]Ge 12:2; Dt 26:5 [m]Ex 1:7
46:4 [n]Ge 28:15; 48:21; Ex 3:8 [o]Ge 50:1,24
46:5 [p]Ge 45:19
46:6 [q]Dt 26:5; Jos 24:4; Ps 105:23; Isa 52:4; Ac 7:15
46:7 [r]Ge 45:10
46:8 [s]Ex 1:1; Nu 26:4
46:9 [t]1Ch 5:3
46:10 [u]Ge 29:33; Nu 26:14 [v]Ex 6:15
46:11 [w]Ge 29:34; Nu 3:17
46:12 [x]Ge 29:35 [y]1Ch 2:5; Mt 1:3
46:13 [z]Ge 30:18 [a]1Ch 7:1
46:14 [b]Ge 30:20
46:16 [c]Ge 30:11 [d]Nu 26:15
46:17 [e]Ge 30:13; 1Ch 7:30-31

[u]*22* That is, about 7 1/2 pounds (about 3.5 kilograms) [v]*13* Samaritan Pentateuch and Syriac (see also 1 Chron. 7:1); Masoretic Text *Puvah* [w]*13* Samaritan Pentateuch and some Septuagint manuscripts (see also Num. 26:24 and 1 Chron. 7:1); Masoretic Text *Iob* [x]*15* That is, Northwest Mesopotamia [y]*16* Samaritan Pentateuch and Septuagint (see also Num. 26:15); Masoretic Text *Ziphion*

Imnah, Ishvah, Ishvi and Beriah.
Their sister was Serah.
The sons of Beriah:
Heber and Malkiel.

18 These were the children born to Jacob by Zilpah,[a] whom Laban had given to his daughter Leah[b] —sixteen in all.

19 The sons of Jacob's wife Rachel:
Joseph and Benjamin.[c]
20 In Egypt, Manasseh[d] and Ephraim[e] were born to Joseph by Asenath daughter of Potiphera, priest of On.[z]

21 The sons of Benjamin:[f]
Bela, Beker, Ashbel, Gera, Naaman, Ehi, Rosh, Muppim, Huppim and Ard.

22 These were the sons of Rachel who were born to Jacob—fourteen in all.

23 The son of Dan:
Hushim.

24 The sons of Naphtali:
Jahziel, Guni, Jezer and Shillem.

25 These were the sons born to Jacob by Bilhah,[g] whom Laban had given to his daughter Rachel[h]—seven in all.

26 All those who went to Egypt with Jacob—those who were his direct descendants, not counting his sons' wives—numbered sixty-six persons.[i] 27 With the two sons[a] who had been born to Joseph in Egypt, the members of Jacob's family, which went to Egypt, were seventy[b] in all.[j]

28 Now Jacob sent Judah ahead of him to Joseph to get directions to Goshen.[k] When they arrived in the region of Goshen, 29 Joseph had his chariot made ready and went to Goshen to meet his father Israel. As soon as Joseph appeared before him, he threw his arms around his father[c] and wept for a long time.[l]

30 Israel said to Joseph, "Now I am ready to die, since I have seen for myself that you are still alive."

31 Then Joseph said to his brothers and to his father's household, "I will go up and speak to Pharaoh and will say to him, 'My brothers and my father's household, who were living in the land of Canaan, have come to me.[m] 32 The men are shepherds; they tend livestock, and they have brought along their flocks and herds and everything they own.' 33 When Pharaoh calls you in and asks, 'What is your occupation?'[n] 34 you should answer, 'Your servants have tended livestock from our boyhood on, just as our fathers did.' Then you will be allowed to settle in the region of Goshen,[o] for all shepherds are detestable to the Egyptians.[p]"

47

Joseph went and told Pharaoh, "My father and brothers, with their flocks and herds and everything they own, have come from the land of Canaan and are now in Goshen."[q] 2 He chose five of his brothers and presented them before Pharaoh.

3 Pharaoh asked the brothers, "What is your occupation?"[r]

"Your servants are shepherds," they replied to Pharaoh, "just as our fathers were." 4 They also said to him, "We have come to live here awhile,[s] because the famine is severe in Canaan[t] and your servants' flocks have no pasture. So now, please let your servants settle in Goshen."[u]

5 Pharaoh said to Joseph, "Your father and your brothers have come to you, 6 and the land of Egypt is before you; settle your father and your brothers in the best part of the land.[v] Let them live in Goshen. And if you know of any among them with special ability,[w] put them in charge of my own livestock."

7 Then Joseph brought his father Jacob in and presented him before Pharaoh. After Jacob blessed[d] Pharaoh,[x] 8 Pharaoh asked him, "How old are you?"

9 And Jacob said to Pharaoh,

46:18 [a] Ge 30:10 [b] Ge 29:24
46:19 [c] Ge 44:27
46:20 [d] Ge 41:51 [e] Ge 41:52
46:21 [f] Nu 26:38-41; 1Ch 7:6-12; 8:1
46:25 [g] Ge 30:8 [h] Ge 29:29
46:26 [i] ver 5-7; Ex 1:5; Dt 10:22
46:27 [j] Ac 7:14
46:28 [k] Ge 45:10
46:29 [l] Ge 45:14-15; Lk 15:20
46:31 [m] Ge 47:1
46:33 [n] Ge 47:3
46:34 [o] Ge 45:10 [p] Ge 43:32; Ex 8:26
47:1 [q] Ge 46:31
47:3 [r] Ge 46:33
47:4 [s] Ge 15:13; Dt 26:5 [t] Ge 43:1 [u] Ge 46:34
47:6 [v] Ge 45:18 [w] Ex 18:21,25
47:7 [x] ver 10; 2Sa 14:22

[z] 20 That is, Heliopolis [a] 27 Hebrew; Septuagint *the nine children* [b] 27 Hebrew (see also Exodus 1:5 and footnote); Septuagint (see also Acts 7:14) *seventy-five* [c] 29 Hebrew *around him* [d] 7 Or *greeted*

"The years of my pilgrimage are a
hundred and thirty.[a] My years
have been few and difficult,[b] and
they do not equal the years of the
pilgrimage of my fathers.[c]" **10**Then
Jacob blessed[e] Pharaoh[d] and
went out from his presence.
11So Joseph settled his father
and his brothers in Egypt and gave
them property in the best part of
the land, the district of Rameses,[e]
as Pharaoh directed. **12**Joseph also
provided his father and his brothers and all his father's household
with food, according to the number
of their children.[f]

Joseph and the Famine

13There was no food, however, in
the whole region because the famine was severe; both Egypt and Canaan wasted away because of the
famine.[g] **14**Joseph collected all
the money that was to be found in
Egypt and Canaan in payment for
the grain they were buying, and he
brought it to Pharaoh's palace.[h]
15When the money of the people of
Egypt and Canaan was gone, all
Egypt came to Joseph and said,
"Give us food. Why should we die
before your eyes?[i] Our money is
used up."
16"Then bring your livestock,"
said Joseph. "I will sell you food in
exchange for your livestock, since
your money is gone." **17**So they
brought their livestock to Joseph,
and he gave them food in exchange
for their horses,[j] their sheep and
goats, their cattle and donkeys.
And he brought them through that
year with food in exchange for all
their livestock.
18When that year was over, they
came to him the following year and
said, "We cannot hide from our
lord the fact that since our money
is gone and our livestock belongs to
you, there is nothing left for our
lord except our bodies and our
land. **19**Why should we perish before your eyes—we and our land as
well? Buy us and our land in exchange for food, and we with our
land will be in bondage to Pharaoh.
Give us seed so that we may live
and not die, and that the land may
not become desolate."
20So Joseph bought all the land
in Egypt for Pharaoh. The Egyptians, one and all, sold their fields,
because the famine was too severe
for them. The land became Pharaoh's, **21**and Joseph reduced the
people to servitude,[f] from one end
of Egypt to the other. **22**However,
he did not buy the land of the
priests, because they received a
regular allotment from Pharaoh
and had food enough from the allotment[k] Pharaoh gave them. That
is why they did not sell their land.
23Joseph said to the people,
"Now that I have bought you and
your land today for Pharaoh, here is
seed for you so you can plant the
ground. **24**But when the crop
comes in, give a fifth[l] of it to Pharaoh. The other four-fifths you may
keep as seed for the fields and as
food for yourselves and your households and your children."
25"You have saved our lives,"
they said. "May we find favor in the
eyes of our lord;[m] we will be in
bondage to Pharaoh."
26So Joseph established it as a
law concerning land in Egypt—still
in force today—that a fifth of the
produce belongs to Pharaoh. It was
only the land of the priests that did
not become Pharaoh's.[n]
27Now the Israelites settled in
Egypt in the region of Goshen.
They acquired property there and
were fruitful and increased greatly
in number.[o]
28Jacob lived in Egypt[p] seventeen years, and the years of his life
were a hundred and forty-seven.
29When the time drew near for Israel to die,[q] he called for his son Joseph and said to him, "If I have
found favor in your eyes, put your
hand under my thigh[r] and promise
that you will show me kindness
and faithfulness.[s] Do not bury me
in Egypt, **30**but when I rest with my
fathers, carry me out of Egypt and

47:9 [a]Ge 25:7 [b]Heb 11:9,13 [c]Ge 35:28
47:10 [d]ver 7
47:11 [e]Ex 1:11; 12:37
47:12 [f]Ge 45:11
47:13 [g]Ge 41:30; Ac 7:11
47:14 [h]Ge 41:56
47:15 [i]ver 19; Ex 16:3
47:17 [j]Ex 14:9
47:22 [k]Dt 14:28-29; Ezr 7:24
47:24 [l]Ge 41:34
47:25 [m]Ge 32:5
47:26 [n]ver 22
47:27 [o]Ge 17:6; 46:3; Ex 1:7
47:28 [p]Ps 105:23
47:29 [q]Dt 31:14 [r]Ge 24:2 [s]Ge 24:49

[e]*10* Or *said farewell to* [f]*21* Samaritan Pentateuch and Septuagint (see also Vulgate); Masoretic Text *and he moved the people into the cities*

bury me where they are buried."[a]
"I will do as you say," he said.
31"Swear to me,"[b] he said. Then
Joseph swore to him,[c] and Israel
worshiped as he leaned on the top
of his staff.[g][d]

Manasseh and Ephraim

48 Some time later Joseph was
told, "Your father is ill." So
he took his two sons Manasseh and
Ephraim[e] along with him. 2When
Jacob was told, "Your son Joseph
has come to you," Israel rallied his
strength and sat up on the bed.
3Jacob said to Joseph, "God Almighty[h] appeared to me at Luz[f] in
the land of Canaan, and there he
blessed me[g] 4and said to me, 'I am
going to make you fruitful and will
increase your numbers.[h] I will
make you a community of peoples,
and I will give this land as an everlasting possession to your descendants after you.'
5"Now then, your two sons born
to you in Egypt[i] before I came to
you here will be reckoned as mine;
Ephraim and Manasseh will be
mine,[j] just as Reuben and Simeon
are mine. 6Any children born to
you after them will be yours; in the
territory they inherit they will be
reckoned under the names of their
brothers. 7As I was returning from
Paddan,[i] to my sorrow Rachel
died in the land of Canaan while we
were still on the way, a little distance from Ephrath. So I buried her
there beside the road to Ephrath"
(that is, Bethlehem).[k]
8When Israel saw the sons of Joseph, he asked, "Who are these?"
9"They are the sons God has giv-
en me here,"[l] Joseph said to his
father.
Then Israel said, "Bring them to
me so I may bless[m] them."
10Now Israel's eyes were failing
because of old age, and he could
hardly see.[n] So Joseph brought his
sons close to him, and his father
kissed them[o] and embraced them.
11Israel said to Joseph, "I never
expected to see your face again,
and now God has allowed me to see
your children too."[p]

47:30 [a]Ge 49:29-32; 50:5,13; Ac 7:15-16
47:31 [b]Ge 21:23 [c]Ge 24:3 [d]Heb 11:21 *fn* 1Ki 1:47
48:1 [e]Ge 41:52
48:3 [f]Ge 28:19 [g]Ge 28:13; 35:9-12
48:4 [h]Ge 17:6
48:5 [i]Ge 41:50-52; 46:20 [j]1Ch 5:1; Jos 14:4
48:7 [k]Ge 35:19
48:9 [l]Ge 33:5 [m]Ge 27:4
48:10 [n]Ge 27:1 [o]Ge 27:27
48:11 [p]Ge 50:23; Ps 128:6
48:13 [q]Ps 110:1
48:14 [r]Ge 41:51
48:15 [s]Ge 17:1 [t]Ge 49:24
48:16 [u]Heb 11:21 [v]Ge 28:13
48:17 [w]ver 14
48:19 [x]Ge 17:20 [y]Ge 25:23

12Then Joseph removed them
from Israel's knees and bowed
down with his face to the ground.
13And Joseph took both of them,
Ephraim on his right toward Israel's left hand and Manasseh on his
left toward Israel's right hand,[q]
and brought them close to him.
14But Israel reached out his right
hand and put it on Ephraim's head,
though he was the younger, and
crossing his arms, he put his left
hand on Manasseh's head, even
though Manasseh was the firstborn.[r]
15Then he blessed[s] Joseph and
said,

"May the God before whom my
fathers
Abraham and Isaac walked,
the God who has been my
shepherd[t]
all my life to this day,
16the Angel who has delivered me
from all harm
—may he bless these boys.[u]
May they be called by my name
and the names of my fathers
Abraham and Isaac,[v]
and may they increase greatly
upon the earth."

17When Joseph saw his father
placing his right hand on Ephraim's head[w] he was displeased; so
he took hold of his father's hand to
move it from Ephraim's head to
Manasseh's head. 18Joseph said to
him, "No, my father, this one is the
firstborn; put your right hand on
his head."
19But his father refused and
said, "I know, my son, I know. He
too will become a people, and he
too will become great.[x] Nevertheless, his younger brother will be
greater than he,[y] and his descendants will become a group of nations." 20He blessed them that day
and said,

"In your[j] name will Israel
pronounce this blessing:

[g]31 Or *Israel bowed down at the head of his bed* [h]3 Hebrew *El-Shaddai* [i]7 That is, Northwest Mesopotamia [j]20 The Hebrew is singular.

'May God make you like
Ephraim[a] and
Manasseh.[b]' "

So he put Ephraim ahead of Manasseh.

21Then Israel said to Joseph, "I
am about to die, but God will be
with you[k][c] and take you[k] back to
the land of your[k] fathers.[d] 22And
to you, as one who is over your
brothers,[e] I give the ridge of
land[l][f] I took from the Amorites
with my sword and my bow."

Jacob Blesses His Sons

49:1-28Ref — Dt 33:1-29

49 Then Jacob called for his
sons and said: "Gather
around so I can tell you what will
happen to you in days to come.[g]

2"Assemble and listen, sons of
Jacob;
listen to your father Israel.[h]

3"Reuben, you are my
firstborn,[i]
my might, the first sign of my
strength,[j]
excelling in honor, excelling
in power.
4Turbulent as the waters,[k] you
will no longer excel,
for you went up onto your
father's bed,
onto my couch and defiled
it.[l]

5"Simeon and Levi are
brothers—
their swords[m] are weapons of
violence.[m]
6Let me not enter their council,
let me not join their
assembly,[n]
for they have killed men in
their anger[o]
and hamstrung oxen as they
pleased.
7Cursed be their anger, so fierce,
and their fury, so cruel!
I will scatter them in Jacob
and disperse them in Israel.[p]

8"Judah,[n] your brothers will
praise you;
your hand will be on the
neck of your enemies;
your father's sons will bow
down to you.[q]
9You are a lion's[r] cub,
O Judah;[s]
you return from the prey, my
son.
Like a lion he crouches and
lies down,
like a lioness—who dares to
rouse him?
10The scepter will not depart
from Judah,[t]
nor the ruler's staff from
between his feet,
until he comes to whom it
belongs[o]
and the obedience of the
nations is his.[u]
11He will tether his donkey to a
vine,
his colt to the choicest
branch;
he will wash his garments in
wine,
his robes in the blood of
grapes.
12His eyes will be darker than
wine,
his teeth whiter than milk.[p]

13"Zebulun[v] will live by the
seashore
and become a haven for
ships;
his border will extend toward
Sidon.

14"Issachar[w] is a rawboned[q]
donkey
lying down between two
saddlebags.[r]
15When he sees how good is his
resting place
and how pleasant is his land,
he will bend his shoulder to
the burden
and submit to forced labor.

48:20 [a]Nu 2:18 [b]Nu 2:20; Ru 4:11
48:21 [c]Ge 26:3; 46:4 [d]Ge 28:13; 50:24
48:22 [e]Ge 37:8 [f]Jos 24:32; Jn 4:5
49:1 [g]Nu 24:14; Jer 23:20
49:2 [h]Ps 34:11
49:3 [i]Ge 29:32 [j]Dt 21:17; Ps 78:51
49:4 [k]Isa 57:20 [l]Ge 35:22; Dt 27:20
49:5 [m]Ge 34:25; Pr 4:17
49:6 [n]Pr 1:15; Eph 5:11 [o]Ge 34:26
49:7 [p]Jos 19:1,9; 21:1-42
49:8 [q]Dt 33:7; 1Ch 5:2
49:9 [r]Nu 24:9; Eze 19:5; Mic 5:8 [s]Rev 5:5
49:10 [t]Nu 24:17,19; Ps 60:7 [u]Ps 2:9; Isa 42:1,4
49:13 [v]Ge 30:20; Dt 33:18-19; Jos 19:10-11
49:14 [w]Ge 30:18

[k]*21* The Hebrew is plural. [l]*22* Or *And to you I give one portion more than to your brothers—the portion* [m]*5* The meaning of the Hebrew for this word is uncertain. [n]*8* *Judah* sounds like and may be derived from the Hebrew for *praise.* [o]*10* Or *until Shiloh comes*; or *until he comes to whom tribute belongs* [p]*12* Or *will be dull from wine, / his teeth white from milk* [q]*14* Or *strong* [r]*14* Or *campfires*

16"Dan[s][a] will provide justice for
his people
as one of the tribes of Israel.
17Dan[b] will be a serpent by the
roadside,
a viper along the path,
that bites the horse's heels
so that its rider tumbles
backward.

18"I look for your deliverance,
O LORD.[c]

19"Gad[t][d] will be attacked by a
band of raiders,
but he will attack them at
their heels.

20"Asher's[e] food will be rich;
he will provide delicacies fit
for a king.

21"Naphtali[f] is a doe set free
that bears beautiful fawns.[u]

22"Joseph[g] is a fruitful vine,
a fruitful vine near a spring,
whose branches climb over a
wall.[v]
23With bitterness archers
attacked him;
they shot at him with
hostility.[h]
24But his bow remained steady,
his strong arms[i] stayed[w]
limber,
because of the hand of the
Mighty One of Jacob,[j]
because of the Shepherd, the
Rock of Israel,[k]
25because of your father's God,[l]
who helps you,
because of the Almighty,[x]
who blesses you
with blessings of the heavens
above,
blessings of the deep that
lies below,[m]
blessings of the breast and
womb.
26Your father's blessings are
greater
than the blessings of the
ancient mountains,
than[y] the bounty of the
age-old hills.
Let all these rest on the head
of Joseph,

49:16 [a]Ge 30:6; Dt 33:22; Jdg 18:26-27
49:17 [b]Jdg 18:27
49:18 [c]Ps 119:166, 174
49:19 [d]Ge 30:11; Dt 33:20; 1Ch 5:18
49:20 [e]Ge 30:13; Dt 33:24
49:21 [f]Ge 30:8; Dt 33:23
49:22 [g]Ge 30:24; Dt 33:13-17
49:23 [h]Ge 37:24
49:24 [i]Ps 18:34 [j]Ps 132:2,5; Isa 1:24; 41:10 [k]Isa 28:16
49:25 [l]Ge 28:13 [m]Ge 27:28
49:26 [n]Dt 33:15-16
49:27 [o]Ge 35:18; Jdg 20:12-13
49:29 [p]Ge 50:16 [q]Ge 25:8 [r]Ge 15:15; 47:30; 50:13
49:30 [s]Ge 23:9 [t]Ge 23:20
49:31 [u]Ge 25:9 [v]Ge 23:19 [w]Ge 35:29
49:33 [x]ver 29; Ge 25:8; Ac 7:15
50:1 [y]Ge 46:4
50:2 [z]ver 26; 2Ch 16:14
50:3 [a]Ge 37:34; Nu 20:29; Dt 34:8

on the brow of the prince
among[z] his brothers.[n]

27"Benjamin[o] is a ravenous wolf;
in the morning he devours
the prey,
in the evening he divides the
plunder."

28All these are the twelve tribes
of Israel, and this is what their father said to them when he blessed
them, giving each the blessing appropriate to him.

The Death of Jacob

29Then he gave them these instructions:[p] "I am about to be
gathered to my people.[q] Bury me
with my fathers[r] in the cave in the
field of Ephron the Hittite, 30the
cave in the field of Machpelah,[s]
near Mamre in Canaan, which
Abraham bought as a burial place
from Ephron the Hittite, along with
the field.[t] 31There Abraham[u] and
his wife Sarah[v] were buried, there
Isaac and his wife Rebekah[w] were
buried, and there I buried Leah.
32The field and the cave in it were
bought from the Hittites.[a]"

33When Jacob had finished giving instructions to his sons, he
drew his feet up into the bed,
breathed his last and was gathered
to his people.[x]

50 Joseph threw himself upon
his father and wept over
him and kissed him.[y] 2Then Joseph directed the physicians in his
service to embalm his father Israel.
So the physicians embalmed
him,[z] 3taking a full forty days, for
that was the time required for em-
balming. And the Egyptians
mourned for him seventy days.[a]

4When the days of mourning had
passed, Joseph said to Pharaoh's
court, "If I have found favor in your

[s]16 *Dan* here means *he provides justice.*
[t]19 *Gad* can mean *attack* and *band of raiders.*
[u]21 Or *free; / he utters beautiful words*
[v]22 Or *Joseph is a wild colt, / a wild colt near a spring, / a wild donkey on a terraced hill*
[w]23,24 Or *archers will attack . . . will shoot . . . will remain . . . will stay*
[x]25 Hebrew *Shaddai*
[y]26 Or *of my progenitors, / as great as*
[z]26 Or *the one separated from*
[a]32 Or *the sons of Heth*

eyes, speak to Pharaoh for me. Tell
him, 5'My father made me swear an
oath[a] and said, "I am about to die;
bury me in the tomb I dug for myself[b] in the land of Canaan."[c]
Now let me go up and bury my father; then I will return.' "
6Pharaoh said, "Go up and bury
your father, as he made you swear
to do."
7So Joseph went up to bury his
father. All Pharaoh's officials accompanied him—the dignitaries of
his court and all the dignitaries of
Egypt— 8besides all the members
of Joseph's household and his
brothers and those belonging to his
father's household. Only their children and their flocks and herds
were left in Goshen. 9Chariots and
horsemen[b] also went up with him.
It was a very large company.
10When they reached the threshing floor of Atad, near the Jordan,
they lamented loudly and bitterly;[d] and there Joseph observed a
seven-day period[e] of mourning for
his father. 11When the Canaanites
who lived there saw the mourning
at the threshing floor of Atad, they
said, "The Egyptians are holding a
solemn ceremony of mourning."
That is why that place near the Jordan is called Abel Mizraim.[c]
12So Jacob's sons did as he had
commanded them: 13They carried
him to the land of Canaan and buried him in the cave in the field of
Machpelah, near Mamre, which
Abraham had bought as a burial
place from Ephron the Hittite,
along with the field.[f] 14After burying his father, Joseph returned to
Egypt, together with his brothers
and all the others who had gone
with him to bury his father.

Joseph Reassures His Brothers

15When Joseph's brothers saw
that their father was dead, they
said, "What if Joseph holds a

50:5 [a]Ge 47:31 [b]2Ch 16:14; Isa 22:16 [c]Ge 47:31
50:10 [d]2Sa 1:17; Ac 8:2 [e]1Sa 31:13; Job 2:13
50:13 [f]Ge 23:20; Ac 7:16

[b]9 Or *charioteers* [c]11 *Abel Mizraim* means *mourning of the Egyptians.*

THE TRIBES OF ISRAEL

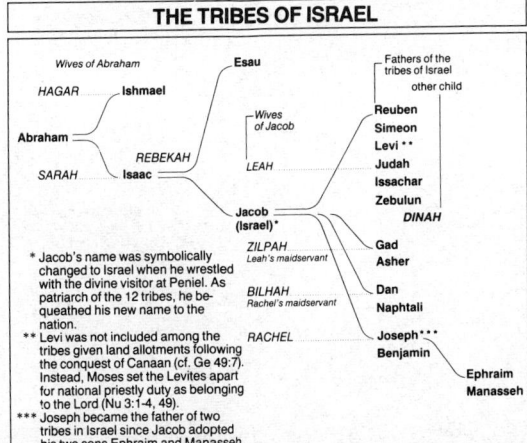

Wives of Abraham

HAGAR — **Ishmael**

Abraham

SARAH — **Isaac**

REBEKAH

Esau

Wives of Jacob

Jacob (Israel)*

LEAH — **Reuben**, **Simeon**, **Levi** **, **Judah**, **Issachar**, **Zebulun**, *DINAH*

ZILPAH *Leah's maidservant* — **Gad**, **Asher**

BILHAH *Rachel's maidservant* — **Dan**, **Naphtali**

RACHEL — **Joseph*****, **Benjamin**

Ephraim, **Manasseh**

Fathers of the tribes of Israel

other child

* Jacob's name was symbolically changed to Israel when he wrestled with the divine visitor at Peniel. As patriarch of the 12 tribes, he bequeathed his new name to the nation.

** Levi was not included among the tribes given land allotments following the conquest of Canaan (cf. Ge 49:7). Instead, Moses set the Levites apart for national priestly duty as belonging to the Lord (Nu 3:1-4, 49).

*** Joseph became the father of two tribes in Israel since Jacob adopted his two sons Ephraim and Manasseh.

grudge against us and pays us back
for all the wrongs we did to him?"[a]
16So they sent word to Joseph, saying, "Your father left these instructions before he died: **17**'This is
what you are to say to Joseph: I ask
you to forgive your brothers the
sins and the wrongs they committed in treating you so badly.' Now
please forgive the sins of the servants of the God of your father."
When their message came to him,
Joseph wept.
18His brothers then came and
threw themselves down before
him.[b] "We are your slaves,"[c] they
said.
19But Joseph said to them,
"Don't be afraid. Am I in the place
of God?[d] **20**You intended to harm
me,[e] but God intended[f] it for
good[g] to accomplish what is now
being done, the saving of many
lives.[h] **21**So then, don't be afraid. I
will provide for you and your children.[i]" And he reassured them
and spoke kindly to them.

50:15 [a]Ge 37:28; 42:21-22
50:18 [b]Ge 37:7 [c]Ge 43:18
50:19 [d]Ro 12:19; Heb 10:30
50:20 [e]Ge 37:20 [f]Mic 4:11-12 [g]Ro 8:28 [h]Ge 45:5
50:21 [i]Ge 45:11; 47:12
50:22 [j]Ge 25:7; Jos 24:29
50:23 [k]Job 42:16 [l]Nu 32:39,40
50:24 [m]Ge 48:21 [n]Ex 3:16-17 [o]Ge 15:14 [p]Ge 12:7; 26:3; 28:13; 35:12
50:25 [q]Ge 47:29-30; Ex 13:19; Jos 24:32; Heb 11:22

The Death of Joseph

22Joseph stayed in Egypt, along
with all his father's family. He lived
a hundred and ten years[j] **23**and
saw the third generation[k] of
Ephraim's children. Also the children of Makir[l] son of Manasseh
were placed at birth on Joseph's
knees.[d]
24Then Joseph said to his brothers, "I am about to die.[m] But God
will surely come to your aid[n] and
take you up out of this land to the
land[o] he promised on oath to
Abraham, Isaac and Jacob."[p]
25And Joseph made the sons of Israel swear an oath and said, "God
will surely come to your aid, and
then you must carry my bones up
from this place."[q]
26So Joseph died at the age of a
hundred and ten. And after they
embalmed him,[r] he was placed in
a coffin in Egypt.

50:26 [r]ver 2

[d]*23* That is, were counted as his

Exodus

Title and Background

"Exodus" is a Latin word (derived from the Greek) that means "exit," "departure," and describes the greatest miracle in the Old Testament record of Israel's history—the "going out" from Egypt and slavery. While the story of the Israelites began with Abraham in Genesis, Exodus is the history of their early years as God's chosen nation, committed to him according to the terms of the Mosaic covenant given at Mount Sinai. The book of Exodus was not intended to exist separately, but was thought of as a continuation of a narrative that began in Genesis and continues through Leviticus, Numbers and Deuteronomy.

Author and Date of Writing

Several statements in Exodus indicate that Moses wrote certain sections of the book (see 17:14; 24:4; 34:27). The New Testament also claims Mosaic authorship for various passages in Exodus (see, for example, Mk 7:10; 12:26; Lk 2:22-23). Taken together, these references strongly suggest that Moses was largely responsible for writing the book of Exodus.

According to 1 Kings 6:1, the exodus took place 480 years before "the fourth year of Solomon's reign over Israel." Since that year was about 966 B.C., the exodus occurred about 1446 B.C. The book of Exodus was most likely written after the exodus from Egypt (about 1446 B.C.) and before the death of Moses (about 1406 B.C.).

Theme and Message

Exodus lays the foundation for a theology of God's revelation of his name, his attributes, his redemption, his law and his worship. It also reports the appointment and work of the first covenant mediator (Moses), describes the beginning of the priesthood, defines the role of the prophet and relates how the ancient covenant relationship between God and his people came under a new administration (the Sinai covenant).

Outline

- I. Preparation for Israel's Deliverance From Bondage (1:1-4:31)
- II. Israel's Deliverance from Egyptian Bondage (5:1-18:27)
  - A. Pharaoh's Resistance and the Lord's Reassurance (5:1-6:27)
  - B. Plagues on Egypt (6:28-12:36)
  - C. The Exodus: From Egypt to Mount Sinai (12:37-18:27)
- III. Covenant at Sinai (19:1-24:18)
- IV. The Tabernacle for Worship (25:1-40:38)

The Israelites Oppressed

1 These are the names of the
sons of Israel[a] who went to
Egypt with Jacob, each with his
family: **2**Reuben, Simeon, Levi and
Judah; **3**Issachar, Zebulun and
Benjamin; **4**Dan and Naphtali; Gad
and Asher. **5**The descendants of Jacob numbered seventy[a] in all;[b]
Joseph was already in Egypt.
6Now Joseph and all his brothers
and all that generation died,[c] **7**but
the Israelites were fruitful and mul-

1:1 [a]Ge 46:8
1:5 [b]Ge 46:26
1:6 [c]Ge 50:26

[a]5 Masoretic Text (see also Gen. 46:27); Dead Sea Scrolls and Septuagint (see also Acts 7:14 and note at Gen. 46:27) *seventy-five*

tiplied greatly and became exceedingly numerous,[a] so that the land
was filled with them.
8Then a new king, who did not
know about Joseph, came to power
in Egypt. **9**"Look," he said to his
people, "the Israelites have become much too numerous[b] for us.
10Come, we must deal shrewdly[c]
with them or they will become even
more numerous and, if war breaks
out, will join our enemies, fight
against us and leave the country."[d]
11So they put slave masters[e]
over them to oppress them with
forced labor,[f] and they built Pi-
thom and Rameses[g] as store cities[h] for Pharaoh. **12**But the more
they were oppressed, the more they
multiplied and spread; so the
Egyptians came to dread the Israelites **13**and worked them ruthlessly.[i] **14**They made their lives bitter
with hard labor in brick and mortar
and with all kinds of work in the
fields; in all their hard labor the
Egyptians used them ruthlessly.[j]
15The king of Egypt said to the
Hebrew midwives, whose names
were Shiphrah and Puah, **16**"When
you help the Hebrew women in
childbirth and observe them on the
delivery stool, if it is a boy, kill him;
but if it is a girl, let her live." **17**The
midwives, however, feared[k] God
and did not do what the king of
Egypt had told them to do;[l] they
let the boys live. **18**Then the king of
Egypt summoned the midwives
and asked them, "Why have you
done this? Why have you let the
boys live?"
19The midwives answered Pharaoh, "Hebrew women are not like
Egyptian women; they are vigorous
and give birth before the midwives
arrive."[m]
20So God was kind to the midwives[n] and the people increased
and became even more numerous.
21And because the midwives
feared God, he gave them families[o] of their own.
22Then Pharaoh gave this order
to all his people: "Every boy that is
born[b] you must throw into the
Nile, but let every girl live."[p]

1:7 [a]Ge 46:3; Dt 26:5; Ac 7:17
1:9 [b]Ps 105:24-25
1:10 [c]Ps 83:3 [d]Ac 7:17-19
1:11 [e]Ex 3:7 [f]Ge 15:13; Ex 2:11; 5:4; 6:6-7 [g]Ge 47:11 [h]1Ki 9:19; 2Ch 8:4
1:13 [i]Dt 4:20
1:14 [j]Ex 2:23; 6:9; Nu 20:15; Ps 81:6; Ac 7:19
1:17 [k]ver 21; Pr 16:6 [l]Da 3:16-18; Ac 4:18-20; 5:29
1:19 [m]Jos 2:4-6; 2Sa 17:20
1:20 [n]ver 12; Pr 11:18; Isa 3:10
1:21 [o]1Sa 2:35; 2Sa 7:11, 27-29; 1Ki 11:38
1:22 [p]Ac 7:19
2:1 [q]Ex 6:20; Nu 26:59
2:2 [r]Ac 7:20; Heb 11:23
2:4 [s]Ex 15:20; Nu 26:59
2:5 [t]Ex 7:15; 8:20
2:11 [u]Ac 7:23; Heb 11:24-26

The Birth of Moses

2 Now a man of the house of Levi
married a Levite woman,[q]
2and she became pregnant and
gave birth to a son. When she saw
that he was a fine child, she hid
him for three months.[r] **3**But when
she could hide him no longer, she
got a papyrus basket for him and
coated it with tar and pitch. Then
she placed the child in it and put it
among the reeds along the bank of
the Nile. **4**His sister[s] stood at a
distance to see what would happen
to him.
5Then Pharaoh's daughter went
down to the Nile to bathe, and her
attendants were walking along the
river bank.[t] She saw the basket
among the reeds and sent her slave
girl to get it. **6**She opened it and
saw the baby. He was crying, and
she felt sorry for him. "This is one
of the Hebrew babies," she said.
7Then his sister asked Pharaoh's
daughter, "Shall I go and get one of
the Hebrew women to nurse the
baby for you?"
8"Yes, go," she answered. And
the girl went and got the baby's
mother. **9**Pharaoh's daughter said
to her, "Take this baby and nurse
him for me, and I will pay you." So
the woman took the baby and
nursed him. **10**When the child grew
older, she took him to Pharaoh's
daughter and he became her son.
She named him Moses,[c] saying, "I
drew him out of the water."

Moses Flees to Midian

11One day, after Moses had
grown up, he went out to where his
own people[u] were and watched
them at their hard labor. He saw an
Egyptian beating a Hebrew, one of
his own people. **12**Glancing this
way and that and seeing no one, he
killed the Egyptian and hid him in
the sand. **13**The next day he went
out and saw two Hebrews fighting.
He asked the one in the wrong,

[b]*22* Masoretic Text; Samaritan Pentateuch, Septuagint and Targums *born to the Hebrews*
[c]*10* *Moses* sounds like the Hebrew for *draw out.*

"Why are you hitting your fellow Hebrew?"[a]

14The man said, "Who made you ruler and judge over us?[b] Are you thinking of killing me as you killed the Egyptian?" Then Moses was afraid and thought, "What I did must have become known."

15When Pharaoh heard of this, he tried to kill Moses, but Moses fled from Pharaoh and went to live in Midian,[c] where he sat down by a well. **16**Now a priest of Midian[d] had seven daughters, and they came to draw water[e] and fill the troughs to water their father's flock. **17**Some shepherds came along and drove them away, but Moses got up and came to their rescue and watered their flock.[f]

18When the girls returned to Reuel[g] their father, he asked them, "Why have you returned so early today?"

19They answered, "An Egyptian rescued us from the shepherds. He even drew water for us and watered the flock."

20"And where is he?" he asked his daughters. "Why did you leave him? Invite him to have something to eat."[h]

21Moses agreed to stay with the man, who gave his daughter Zipporah[i] to Moses in marriage. **22**Zipporah gave birth to a son, and Moses named him Gershom,[d] saying, "I have become an alien[j] in a foreign land."

23During that long period,[k] the king of Egypt died. The Israelites groaned in their slavery and cried out, and their cry[l] for help because of their slavery went up to God. **24**God heard their groaning and he remembered his covenant[m] with Abraham, with Isaac and with Jacob. **25**So God looked on the Israelites and was concerned[n] about them.

Moses and the Burning Bush

3 Now Moses was tending the flock of Jethro[o] his father-in-law, the priest of Midian, and he led the flock to the far side of the desert and came to Horeb,[p] the mountain[q] of God. **2**There the angel of the LORD[r] appeared to him in flames of fire from within a bush.[s] Moses saw that though the bush was on fire it did not burn up. **3**So Moses thought, "I will go over and see this strange sight—why the bush does not burn up."

4When the LORD saw that he had gone over to look, God called to him from within the bush, "Moses! Moses!"

And Moses said, "Here I am."

5"Do not come any closer," God said. "Take off your sandals, for the place where you are standing is holy ground."[t] **6**Then he said, "I am the God of your father, the God of Abraham, the God of Isaac and the God of Jacob."[u] At this, Moses hid his face, because he was afraid to look at God.

7The LORD said, "I have indeed seen the misery of my people in Egypt. I have heard them crying out because of their slave drivers, and I am concerned[v] about their suffering. **8**So I have come down[w] to rescue them from the hand of the Egyptians and to bring them up out of that land into a good and spacious land, a land flowing with milk and honey[x]—the home of the Canaanites, Hittites, Amorites, Perizzites, Hivites and Jebusites.[y] **9**And now the cry of the Israelites has reached me, and I have seen the way the Egyptians are oppressing[z] them. **10**So now, go. I am sending you to Pharaoh to bring my people the Israelites out of Egypt."[a]

11But Moses said to God, "Who am I,[b] that I should go to Pharaoh and bring the Israelites out of Egypt?"

12And God said, "I will be with you.[c] And this will be the sign to you that it is I who have sent you: When you have brought the people out of Egypt, you[e] will worship God on this mountain."

13Moses said to God, "Suppose I go to the Israelites and say to them,

2:13 [a]Ac 7:26
2:14 [b]Ac 7:27*
2:15 [c]Ac 7:29; Heb 11:27
2:16 [d]Ex 3:1 [e]Ge 24:11
2:17 [f]Ge 29:10
2:18 [g]Nu 10:29
2:20 [h]Ge 31:54
2:21 [i]Ex 18:2
2:22 [j]Ex 18:3-4; Heb 11:13
2:23 [k]Ac 7:30 [l]Ex 3:7,9; Dt 26:7; Jas 5:4
2:24 [m]Ex 6:5; Ps 105:10,42
2:25 [n]Ex 3:7; 4:31
3:1 [o]Ex 2:18 [p]1Ki 19:8 [q]Ex 18:5
3:2 [r]Ge 16:7 [s]Dt 33:16; Mk 12:26; Ac 7:30
3:5 [t]Ge 28:17; Jos 5:15; Ac 7:33*
3:6 [u]Ex 4:5; Mt 22:32*; Mk 12:26*; Lk 20:37*; Ac 7:32*
3:7 [v]Ex 2:25
3:8 [w]Ge 50:24 [x]ver 17; Ex 13:5; Dt 1:25 [y]Ge 15:18-21
3:9 [z]Ex 1:14; 2:23
3:10 [a]Mic 6:4
3:11 [b]Ex 6:12,30; 1Sa 18:18
3:12 [c]Ge 31:3; Jos 1:5; Ro 8:31

[d]22 *Gershom* sounds like the Hebrew for *an alien there.* [e]12 The Hebrew is plural.

'The God of your fathers has sent
me to you,' and they ask me, 'What
is his name?' Then what shall I tell
them?"

14God said to Moses, "I AM WHO I
AM.[f] This is what you are to say to
the Israelites: 'I AM[a] has sent me to
you.' "

15God also said to Moses, "Say
to the Israelites, 'The LORD,[g] the
God of your fathers—the God of
Abraham, the God of Isaac and the
God of Jacob—has sent me to you.'
This is my name[b] forever, the
name by which I am to be remembered from generation to generation.

16"Go, assemble the elders[c] of
Israel and say to them, 'The LORD,
the God of your fathers—the God
of Abraham, Isaac and Jacob—appeared to me and said: I have
watched over you and have seen
what has been done to you in
Egypt. **17**And I have promised to
bring you up out of your misery in
Egypt[d] into the land of the Canaanites, Hittites, Amorites, Perizzites, Hivites and Jebusites—a
land flowing with milk and honey.'

18"The elders of Israel will listen[e] to you. Then you and the elders are to go to the king of Egypt
and say to him, 'The LORD, the God
of the Hebrews, has met with us.
Let us take a three-day journey into
the desert to offer sacrifices[f] to
the LORD our God.' **19**But I know
that the king of Egypt will not let
you go unless a mighty hand[g] compels him. **20**So I will stretch out my
hand[h] and strike the Egyptians
with all the wonders[i] that I will
perform among them. After that,
he will let you go.[j]

21"And I will make the Egyptians
favorably disposed[k] toward this
people, so that when you leave you
will not go empty-handed.[l] **22**Every woman is to ask her neighbor
and any woman living in her house
for articles of silver and gold[m]
and for clothing, which you will
put on your sons and daughters. And so you will plunder[n] the
Egyptians."

3:14 [a]Ex 6:2-3; Jn 8:58; Heb 13:8
3:15 [b]Ps 135:13; Hos 12:5
3:16 [c]Ex 4:29
3:17 [d]Ge 15:16; Jos 24:11
3:18 [e]Ex 4:1,8,31 [f]Ex 5:1,3
3:19 [g]Ex 4:21; 5:2
3:20 [h]Ex 6:1,6; 9:15 [i]Dt 6:22; Ne 9:10; Ac 7:36 [j]Ex 12:31-33
3:21 [k]Ex 12:36 [l]Ps 105:37
3:22 [m]Ex 11:2 [n]Eze 39:10
4:1 [o]Ex 3:18; 6:30
4:2 [p]ver 17,20
4:5 [q]Ex 19:9
4:6 [r]Nu 12:10; 2Ki 5:1,27
4:7 [s]Nu 12:13-15; Dt 32:39; 2Ki 5:14; Mt 8:3
4:9 [t]Ex 7:17-21
4:10 [u]Ex 6:12; Jer 1:6

Signs for Moses

4 Moses answered, "What if they
do not believe me or listen[o] to
me and say, 'The LORD did not appear to you'?"

2Then the LORD said to him,
"What is that in your hand?"

"A staff,"[p] he replied.

3The LORD said, "Throw it on the
ground."

Moses threw it on the ground
and it became a snake, and he ran
from it. **4**Then the LORD said to him,
"Reach out your hand and take it
by the tail." So Moses reached out
and took hold of the snake and it
turned back into a staff in his hand.
5"This," said the LORD, "is so that
they may believe[q] that the LORD,
the God of their fathers—the God
of Abraham, the God of Isaac and
the God of Jacob—has appeared to
you."

6Then the LORD said, "Put your
hand inside your cloak." So Moses
put his hand into his cloak, and
when he took it out, it was leprous,[h] like snow.[r]

7"Now put it back into your
cloak," he said. So Moses put his
hand back into his cloak, and when
he took it out, it was restored,[s]
like the rest of his flesh.

8Then the LORD said, "If they do
not believe you or pay attention to
the first miraculous sign, they may
believe the second. **9**But if they do
not believe these two signs or listen
to you, take some water from the
Nile and pour it on the dry ground.
The water you take from the river
will become blood[t] on the
ground."

10Moses said to the LORD, "O
Lord, I have never been eloquent,
neither in the past nor since you
have spoken to your servant. I am
slow of speech and tongue."[u]

11The LORD said to him, "Who
gave man his mouth? Who makes
him deaf or mute? Who gives him

[f]*14* Or *I WILL BE WHAT I WILL BE* [g]*15* The Hebrew for *LORD* sounds like and may be derived from the Hebrew for *I AM* in verse 14. [h]*6* The Hebrew word was used for various diseases affecting the skin—not necessarily leprosy.

sight or makes him blind?[a] Is it
not I, the LORD? **12**Now go; I will
help you speak and will teach you
what to say."[b]
13But Moses said, "O Lord,
please send someone else to do it."
14Then the LORD's anger burned
against Moses and he said, "What
about your brother, Aaron the Levite? I know he can speak well. He
is already on his way to meet[c] you,
and his heart will be glad when he
sees you. **15**You shall speak to him
and put words in his mouth;[d] I will
help both of you speak and will
teach you what to do. **16**He will
speak to the people for you, and it
will be as if he were your mouth[e]
and as if you were God to him.
17But take this staff[f] in your hand
so you can perform miraculous
signs[g] with it."

Moses Returns to Egypt

18Then Moses went back to
Jethro his father-in-law and said to
him, "Let me go back to my own
people in Egypt to see if any of
them are still alive."
Jethro said, "Go, and I wish you
well."
19Now the LORD had said to Moses in Midian, "Go back to Egypt,
for all the men who wanted to kill[h]
you are dead.[i]" **20**So Moses took
his wife and sons, put them on a
donkey and started back to Egypt.
And he took the staff[j] of God in
his hand.
21The LORD said to Moses,
"When you return to Egypt, see
that you perform before Pharaoh
all the wonders[k] I have given you
the power to do. But I will harden
his heart[l] so that he will not let
the people go. **22**Then say to Pharaoh, 'This is what the LORD says: Israel is my firstborn son,[m] **23**and I
told you, "Let my son go,[n] so he
may worship me." But you refused
to let him go; so I will kill your firstborn son.' "[o]
24At a lodging place on the way,
the LORD met ⌊Moses⌋[i] and was
about to kill[p] him. **25**But Zipporah
took a flint knife, cut off her son's
foreskin[q] and touched ⌊Moses'⌋
feet with it.[j] "Surely you are a
bridegroom of blood to me," she
said. **26**So the LORD let him alone.
(At that time she said "bridegroom
of blood," referring to circumcision.)
27The LORD said to Aaron, "Go
into the desert to meet Moses." So
he met Moses at the mountain[r] of
God and kissed[s] him. **28**Then Moses told Aaron everything the LORD
had sent him to say,[t] and also
about all the miraculous signs he
had commanded him to perform.
29Moses and Aaron brought together all the elders[u] of the Israelites, **30**and Aaron told them everything the LORD had said to Moses.
He also performed the signs before
the people, **31**and they believed.[v]
And when they heard that the LORD
was concerned[w] about them and
had seen their misery, they bowed
down and worshiped.

Bricks Without Straw

5 Afterward Moses and Aaron
went to Pharaoh and said,
"This is what the LORD, the God of
Israel, says: 'Let my people go, so
that they may hold a festival[x] to
me in the desert.' "
2Pharaoh said, "Who is the
LORD,[y] that I should obey him and
let Israel go? I do not know the
LORD and I will not let Israel go."[z]
3Then they said, "The God of the
Hebrews has met with us. Now let
us take a three-day journey into the
desert to offer sacrifices to the LORD
our God, or he may strike us with
plagues[a] or with the sword."
4But the king of Egypt said, "Moses and Aaron, why are you taking
the people away from their labor?[b]
Get back to your work!" **5**Then
Pharaoh said, "Look, the people of
the land are now numerous,[c] and
you are stopping them from working."
6That same day Pharaoh gave
this order to the slave drivers and
foremen in charge of the people:
7"You are no longer to supply the

4:11 [a]Ps 94:9; Mt 11:5
4:12 [b]Isa 50:4; Jer 1:9; Mt 10:19-20; Mk 13:11; Lk 12:12; 21:14-15
4:14 [c]ver 27
4:15 [d]Nu 23:5,12, 16
4:16 [e]Ex 7:1-2
4:17 [f]ver 2 [g]Ex 7:9-21
4:19 [h]Ex 2:15 [i]Ex 2:23
4:20 [j]Ex 17:9; Nu 20:8-9,11
4:21 [k]Ex 3:19,20 [l]Ex 7:3,13; 9:12,35; 14:4, 8; Dt 2:30; Isa 63:17; Jn 12:40; Ro 9:18
4:22 [m]Isa 63:16; 64:8; Jer 31:9; Hos 11:1; Ro 9:4
4:23 [n]Ex 5:1; 7:16 [o]Ex 11:5; 12:12,29
4:24 [p]Nu 22:22
4:25 [q]Ge 17:14; Jos 5:2,3
4:27 [r]Ex 3:1 [s]ver 14
4:28 [t]ver 8-9,16
4:29 [u]Ex 3:16
4:31 [v]ver 8; Ex 3:18 [w]Ex 2:25
5:1 [x]Ex 3:18
5:2 [y]2Ki 18:35; Job 21:15 [z]Ex 3:19
5:3 [a]Ex 3:18
5:4 [b]Ex 1:11
5:5 [c]Ex 1:7,9

[i]24 Or *⌊Moses' son⌋*; Hebrew *him* [j]25 Or *and drew near ⌊Moses'⌋ feet*

people with straw for making
bricks; let them go and gather their
own straw. **8**But require them to
make the same number of bricks as
before; don't reduce the quota.
They are lazy; that is why they are
crying out, 'Let us go and sacrifice
to our God.' **9**Make the work harder for the men so that they keep
working and pay no attention to
lies."

10Then the slave drivers and the
foremen went out and said to the
people, "This is what Pharaoh says:
'I will not give you any more straw.
11Go and get your own straw wherever you can find it, but your work
will not be reduced at all.' " **12**So
the people scattered all over Egypt
to gather stubble to use for straw.
13The slave drivers kept pressing
them, saying, "Complete the work
required of you for each day, just as
when you had straw." **14**The Israelite foremen appointed by Pharaoh's slave drivers were beaten[a]
and were asked, "Why didn't you
meet your quota of bricks yesterday or today, as before?"

15Then the Israelite foremen
went and appealed to Pharaoh:
"Why have you treated your servants this way? **16**Your servants are
given no straw, yet we are told,
'Make bricks!' Your servants are
being beaten, but the fault is with
your own people."

17Pharaoh said, "Lazy, that's
what you are—lazy![b] That is why
you keep saying, 'Let us go and sacrifice to the LORD.' **18**Now get to
work. You will not be given any
straw, yet you must produce your
full quota of bricks."

19The Israelite foremen realized
they were in trouble when they
were told, "You are not to reduce
the number of bricks required of
you for each day." **20**When they left
Pharaoh, they found Moses and
Aaron waiting to meet them, **21**and
they said, "May the LORD look upon
you and judge you! You have made
us a stench[c] to Pharaoh and his officials and have put a sword in their
hand to kill us."[d]

5:14 [a]Isa 10:24
5:17 [b]ver 8
5:21 [c]Ge 34:30 [d]Ex 14:11
5:22 [e]Nu 11:11
5:23 [f]Jer 4:10
6:1 [g]Ex 3:19 [h]Ex 3:20 [i]Ex 12:31,33, 39
6:3 [j]Ge 17:1 [k]Ps 68:4; 83:18; Isa 52:6 [l]Ex 3:14
6:4 [m]Ge 15:18 [n]Ge 28:4,13
6:5 [o]Ex 2:23
6:6 [p]Dt 7:8; 1Ch 17:21 [q]Dt 26:8
6:7 [r]Dt 4:20; 2Sa 7:24 [s]Ex 16:12; Isa 41:20
6:8 [t]Ge 15:18; 26:3 [u]Ge 14:22 [v]Ps 136:21-22

God Promises Deliverance

22Moses returned to the LORD
and said, "O Lord, why have you
brought trouble upon this people?[e] Is this why you sent me?
23Ever since I went to Pharaoh to
speak in your name, he has brought
trouble upon this people, and you
have not rescued[f] your people at
all."

6 Then the LORD said to Moses,
"Now you will see what I will
do to Pharaoh: Because of my
mighty hand[g] he will let them
go;[h] because of my mighty hand he
will drive them out of his country."[i]

2God also said to Moses, "I am
the LORD. **3**I appeared to Abraham,
to Isaac and to Jacob as God Almighty,[k][j] but by my name[k] the
LORD[l][l] I did not make myself
known to them.[m] **4**I also established my covenant[m] with them to
give them the land of Canaan,
where they lived as aliens.[n] **5**Moreover, I have heard the groaning[o] of
the Israelites, whom the Egyptians
are enslaving, and I have remembered my covenant.

6"Therefore, say to the Israelites:
'I am the LORD, and I will bring you
out from under the yoke of the
Egyptians. I will free you from being slaves to them, and I will redeem[p] you with an outstretched
arm[q] and with mighty acts of judgment. **7**I will take you as my own
people, and I will be your God.[r]
Then you will know[s] that I am the
LORD your God, who brought you
out from under the yoke of the
Egyptians. **8**And I will bring you to
the land[t] I swore with uplifted
hand[u] to give to Abraham, to Isaac
and to Jacob.[v] I will give it to you
as a possession. I am the LORD.' "

9Moses reported this to the Israelites, but they did not listen to
him because of their discourage-
ment and cruel bondage.

10Then the LORD said to Moses,

[k]3 Hebrew *El-Shaddai* [l]3 See note at Exodus 3:15. [m]3 Or *Almighty, and by my name the LORD did I not let myself be known to them?*

11"Go, tell Pharaoh king of Egypt to let the Israelites go out of his country."

12But Moses said to the Lord, "If the Israelites will not listen to me, why would Pharaoh listen to me, since I speak with faltering lips[n]?"[a]

Family Record of Moses and Aaron

13Now the Lord spoke to Moses and Aaron about the Israelites and Pharaoh king of Egypt, and he commanded them to bring the Israelites out of Egypt.

14These were the heads of their families[o]:[b]

The sons of Reuben the firstborn son of Israel were Hanoch and Pallu, Hezron and Carmi. These were the clans of Reuben.

15The sons of Simeon[c] were Jemuel, Jamin, Ohad, Jakin, Zohar and Shaul the son of a Canaanite woman. These were the clans of Simeon.

16These were the names of the sons of Levi according to their records: Gershon,[d] Kohath and Merari.[e] Levi lived 137 years.

17The sons of Gershon, by clans, were Libni and Shimei.[f]

18The sons of Kohath were Amram, Izhar, Hebron and Uzziel.[g] Kohath lived 133 years.

19The sons of Merari were Mahli and Mushi.[h]

These were the clans of Levi according to their records.

20Amram married his father's sister Jochebed, who bore him Aaron and Moses.[i] Amram lived 137 years.

21The sons of Izhar[j] were Korah, Nepheg and Zicri.

22The sons of Uzziel were Mishael, Elzaphan[k] and Sithri.

23Aaron married Elisheba, daughter of Amminadab[l] and

6:12 [a]ver 30; Ex 4:10; Jer 1:6
6:14 [b]Ge 46:9
6:15 [c]Ge 46:10; 1Ch 4:24
6:16 [d]Ge 46:11 [e]Nu 3:17
6:17 [f]1Ch 6:17
6:18 [g]1Ch 6:2,18
6:19 [h]Nu 1Ch 6:19; 23:21
6:20 [i]Ex 2:1-2; Nu 26:59
6:21 [j]1Ch 6:38
6:22 [k]Lev 10:4; Nu 3:30
6:23 [l]Ru 4:19,20 [m]Lev 10:1 [n]Nu 3:2,32 [o]Nu 26:60
6:24 [p]Nu 26:11
6:25 [q]Nu 25:7,11; Jos 24:33; Ps 106:30
6:26 [r]Ex 7:4; 12:17,41,51
6:29 [s]ver 11; Ex 7:2
6:30 [t]ver 12; Ex 4:10
7:1 [u]Ex 4:16
7:3 [v]Ex 4:21; 11:9
7:4 [w]Ex 11:9 [x]Ex 3:20; 6:6
7:5 [y]ver 17; Ex 8:19,22 [z]Ex 3:20
7:6 [a]ver 2
7:7 [b]Dt 31:2; 34:7; Ac 7:23, 30

sister of Nahshon, and she bore him Nadab and Abihu,[m] Eleazar[n] and Ithamar.[o]

24The sons of Korah[p] were Assir, Elkanah and Abiasaph. These were the Korahite clans.

25Eleazar son of Aaron married one of the daughters of Putiel, and she bore him Phinehas.[q]

These were the heads of the Levite families, clan by clan.

26It was this same Aaron and Moses to whom the Lord said, "Bring the Israelites out of Egypt by their divisions."[r] 27They were the ones who spoke to Pharaoh king of Egypt about bringing the Israelites out of Egypt. It was the same Moses and Aaron.

Aaron to Speak for Moses

28Now when the Lord spoke to Moses in Egypt, 29he said to him, "I am the Lord.[s] Tell Pharaoh king of Egypt everything I tell you."

30But Moses said to the Lord, "Since I speak with faltering lips,[t] why would Pharaoh listen to me?"

7 Then the Lord said to Moses, "See, I have made you like God[u] to Pharaoh, and your brother Aaron will be your prophet. 2You are to say everything I command you, and your brother Aaron is to tell Pharaoh to let the Israelites go out of his country. 3But I will harden Pharaoh's heart,[v] and though I multiply my miraculous signs and wonders in Egypt, 4he will not listen[w] to you. Then I will lay my hand on Egypt and with mighty acts of judgment[x] I will bring out my divisions, my people the Israelites. 5And the Egyptians will know that I am the Lord[y] when I stretch out my hand[z] against Egypt and bring the Israelites out of it."

6Moses and Aaron did just as the Lord commanded[a] them. 7Moses was eighty years old[b] and Aaron

[n]*12* Hebrew *I am uncircumcised of lips*; also in verse 30 [o]*14* The Hebrew for *families* here and in verse 25 refers to units larger than clans.

eighty-three when they spoke to Pharaoh.

Aaron's Staff Becomes a Snake

8The LORD said to Moses and Aaron, **9**"When Pharaoh says to you, 'Perform a miracle,[a]' then say to Aaron, 'Take your staff and throw it down before Pharaoh,' and it will become a snake."[b]

10So Moses and Aaron went to Pharaoh and did just as the LORD commanded. Aaron threw his staff down in front of Pharaoh and his officials, and it became a snake. **11**Pharaoh then summoned wise men and sorcerers, and the Egyptian magicians[c] also did the same things by their secret arts:[d] **12**Each one threw down his staff and it became a snake. But Aaron's staff swallowed up their staffs. **13**Yet Pharaoh's heart[e] became hard and he would not listen to them, just as the LORD had said.

The Plague of Blood

14Then the LORD said to Moses, "Pharaoh's heart is unyielding;[f] he refuses to let the people go. **15**Go to Pharaoh in the morning as he goes out to the water. Wait on the bank of the Nile to meet him, and take in your hand the staff that was changed into a snake. **16**Then say to him, 'The LORD, the God of the Hebrews, has sent me to say to you: Let my people go, so that they may worship[g] me in the desert. But until now you have not listened. **17**This is what the LORD says: By this you will know that I am the LORD:[h] With the staff that is in my hand I will strike the water of the Nile, and it will be changed into blood.[i] **18**The fish in the Nile will die, and the river will stink; the Egyptians will not be able to drink its water.' "[j]

19The LORD said to Moses, "Tell Aaron, 'Take your staff and stretch out your hand[k] over the waters of Egypt—over the streams and canals, over the ponds and all the reservoirs'—and they will turn to blood. Blood will be everywhere in Egypt, even in the wooden buckets and stone jars."

20Moses and Aaron did just as the LORD had commanded. He raised his staff in the presence of Pharaoh and his officials and struck the water of the Nile,[l] and all the water was changed into blood.[m] **21**The fish in the Nile died, and the river smelled so bad that the Egyptians could not drink its water. Blood was everywhere in Egypt.

22But the Egyptian magicians did the same things by their secret arts,[n] and Pharaoh's heart became hard; he would not listen to Moses and Aaron, just as the LORD had said. **23**Instead, he turned and went into his palace, and did not take even this to heart. **24**And all the Egyptians dug along the Nile to get drinking water, because they could not drink the water of the river.

The Plague of Frogs

25Seven days passed after the

8 LORD struck the Nile. **1**Then the LORD said to Moses, "Go to Pharaoh and say to him, 'This is what the LORD says: Let my people go, so that they may worship[o] me. **2**If you refuse to let them go, I will plague your whole country with frogs. **3**The Nile will teem with frogs. They will come up into your palace and your bedroom and onto your bed, into the houses of your officials and on your people,[p] and into your ovens and kneading troughs. **4**The frogs will go up on you and your people and all your officials.' "

5Then the LORD said to Moses, "Tell Aaron, 'Stretch out your hand with your staff[q] over the streams and canals and ponds, and make frogs come up on the land of Egypt.' "

6So Aaron stretched out his hand over the waters of Egypt, and the frogs[r] came up and covered the land. **7**But the magicians did the same things by their secret arts;[s] they also made frogs come up on the land of Egypt.

7:9 [a] Isa 7:11; Jn 2:18 [b] Ex 4:2-5
7:11 [c] Ge 41:8; 2Ti 3:8 [d] ver 22; Ex 8:7,18
7:13 [e] Ex 4:21
7:14 [f] Ex 8:15,32; 10:1,20,27
7:16 [g] Ex 3:18; 5:1,3
7:17 [h] Ex 5:2 [i] Ex 4:9; Rev 11:6; 16:4
7:18 [j] ver 21,24
7:19 [k] Ex 8:5-6,16; 9:22; 10:12,21; 14:21
7:20 [l] Ex 17:5 [m] Ps 78:44; 105:29
7:22 [n] ver 11
8:1 [o] Ex 3:12,18; 4:23
8:3 [p] Ex 10:6
8:5 [q] Ex 7:19
8:6 [r] Ps 78:45; 105:30
8:7 [s] Ex 7:11

8Pharaoh summoned Moses and
Aaron and said, "Pray[a] to the LORD
to take the frogs away from me and
my people, and I will let your people go to offer sacrifices[b] to the
LORD."
9Moses said to Pharaoh, "I leave
to you the honor of setting the time
for me to pray for you and your officials and your people that you and
your houses may be rid of the frogs,
except for those that remain in the
Nile."
10"Tomorrow," Pharaoh said.
Moses replied, "It will be as you
say, so that you may know there is
no one like the LORD our God.[c]
11The frogs will leave you and your
houses, your officials and your people; they will remain only in the
Nile."
12After Moses and Aaron left
Pharaoh, Moses cried out to the
LORD about the frogs he had
brought on Pharaoh. 13And the
LORD did what Moses asked. The
frogs died in the houses, in the
courtyards and in the fields. 14They
were piled into heaps, and the land
reeked of them. 15But when Pharaoh saw that there was relief, he
hardened his heart[d] and would not
listen to Moses and Aaron, just as
the LORD had said.

The Plague of Gnats

16Then the LORD said to Moses,
"Tell Aaron, 'Stretch out your staff
and strike the dust of the ground,'
and throughout the land of Egypt
the dust will become gnats."
17They did this, and when Aaron
stretched out his hand with the
staff and struck the dust of the
ground, gnats[e] came upon men
and animals. All the dust throughout the land of Egypt became
gnats. 18But when the magicians[f]
tried to produce gnats by their secret arts,[g] they could not. And the
gnats were on men and animals.
19The magicians said to Pharaoh, "This is the finger[h] of God."
But Pharaoh's heart was hard and
he would not listen, just as the
LORD had said.

8:8 [a]ver 28; Ex 9:28; 10:17 [b]ver 25
8:10 [c]Ex 9:14; Dt 4:35; 33:26; 2Sa 7:22; 1Ch 17:20; Ps 86:8; Isa 46:9; Jer 10:6
8:15 [d]Ex 7:14
8:17 [e]Ps 105:31
8:18 [f]Ex 9:11; Da 5:8 [g]Ex 7:11
8:19 [h]Ex 7:5; 10:7; Ps 8:3; Lk 11:20
8:20 [i]Ex 7:15; 9:13 [j]ver 1; Ex 3:18
8:22 [k]Ex 9:4,6,26; 10:23; 11:7 [l]Ex 7:5; 9:29
8:24 [m]Ps 78:45; 105:31
8:25 [n]ver 8; Ex 9:27
8:26 [o]Ge 43:32; 46:34
8:27 [p]Ex 3:18
8:28 [q]ver 8; Ex 9:28; 1Ki 13:6
8:29 [r]ver 15

The Plague of Flies

20Then the LORD said to Moses,
"Get up early in the morning[i] and
confront Pharaoh as he goes to the
water and say to him, 'This is what
the LORD says: Let my people go, so
that they may worship[j] me. 21If
you do not let my people go, I will
send swarms of flies on you and
your officials, on your people and
into your houses. The houses of the
Egyptians will be full of flies, and
even the ground where they are.
22" 'But on that day I will deal
differently with the land of Goshen, where my people live;[k] no
swarms of flies will be there, so
that you will know[l] that I, the
LORD, am in this land. 23I will make
a distinction[p] between my people
and your people. This miraculous
sign will occur tomorrow.' "
24And the LORD did this. Dense
swarms of flies poured into Pharaoh's palace and into the houses of
his officials, and throughout Egypt
the land was ruined by the flies.[m]
25Then Pharaoh summoned[n]
Moses and Aaron and said, "Go,
sacrifice to your God here in the
land."
26But Moses said, "That would
not be right. The sacrifices we offer
the LORD our God would be detestable to the Egyptians.[o] And if we
offer sacrifices that are detestable
in their eyes, will they not stone
us? 27We must take a three-day
journey into the desert to offer sacrifices[p] to the LORD our God, as he
commands us."
28Pharaoh said, "I will let you go
to offer sacrifices to the LORD your
God in the desert, but you must not
go very far. Now pray[q] for me."
29Moses answered, "As soon as I
leave you, I will pray to the LORD,
and tomorrow the flies will leave
Pharaoh and his officials and his
people. Only be sure that Pharaoh
does not act deceitfully[r] again by
not letting the people go to offer
sacrifices to the LORD."
30Then Moses left Pharaoh and

[p]23 Septuagint and Vulgate; Hebrew *will put a deliverance*

prayed to the LORD,[a] **31**and the LORD did what Moses asked: The flies left Pharaoh and his officials and his people; not a fly remained. **32**But this time also Pharaoh hardened his heart[b] and would not let the people go.

The Plague on Livestock

9 Then the LORD said to Moses, "Go to Pharaoh and say to him, 'This is what the LORD, the God of the Hebrews, says: "Let my people go, so that they may worship[c] me." **2**If you refuse to let them go and continue to hold them back, **3**the hand[d] of the LORD will bring a terrible plague on your livestock in the field—on your horses and donkeys and camels and on your cattle and sheep and goats. **4**But the LORD will make a distinction between the livestock of Israel and that of Egypt,[e] so that no animal belonging to the Israelites will die." ' "

5The LORD set a time and said, "Tomorrow the LORD will do this in the land." **6**And the next day the LORD did it: All the livestock[f] of the Egyptians died,[g] but not one animal belonging to the Israelites died. **7**Pharaoh sent men to investigate and found that not even one of the animals of the Israelites had died. Yet his heart was unyielding and he would not let the people go.[h]

The Plague of Boils

8Then the LORD said to Moses and Aaron, "Take handfuls of soot from a furnace and have Moses toss it into the air in the presence of Pharaoh. **9**It will become fine dust over the whole land of Egypt, and festering boils[i] will break out on men and animals throughout the land."

10So they took soot from a furnace and stood before Pharaoh. Moses tossed it into the air, and festering boils broke out on men and animals. **11**The magicians[j] could not stand before Moses because of the boils that were on them and on all the Egyptians. **12**But the LORD hardened Pharaoh's heart[k] and he would not listen to Moses and Aaron, just as the LORD had said to Moses.

The Plague of Hail

13Then the LORD said to Moses, "Get up early in the morning, confront Pharaoh and say to him, 'This is what the LORD, the God of the Hebrews, says: Let my people go, so that they may worship[l] me, **14**or this time I will send the full force of my plagues against you and against your officials and your people, so you may know[m] that there is no one like[n] me in all the earth. **15**For by now I could have stretched out my hand and struck you and your people[o] with a plague that would have wiped you off the earth. **16**But I have raised you up[q] for this very purpose,[p] that I might show you my power[q] and that my name might be proclaimed in all the earth. **17**You still set yourself against my people and will not let them go. **18**Therefore, at this time tomorrow I will send the worst hailstorm[r] that has ever fallen on Egypt, from the day it was founded till now.[s] **19**Give an order now to bring your livestock and everything you have in the field to a place of shelter, because the hail will fall on every man and animal that has not been brought in and is still out in the field, and they will die.' "

20Those officials of Pharaoh who feared[t] the word of the LORD hurried to bring their slaves and their livestock inside. **21**But those who ignored the word of the LORD left their slaves and livestock in the field.

22Then the LORD said to Moses, "Stretch out your hand toward the sky so that hail will fall all over Egypt—on men and animals and on everything growing in the fields of Egypt." **23**When Moses stretched out his staff toward the sky, the LORD sent thunder[u] and hail,[v] and lightning flashed down to the ground. So the LORD rained hail on the land of Egypt; **24**hail fell and

8:30 [a]ver 12
8:32 [b]ver 8,15; Ex 4:21
9:1 [c]Ex 8:1
9:3 [d]Ex 7:4
9:4 [e]ver 26; Ex 8:22
9:6 [f]ver 19-21; Ex 11:5 [g]Ps 78:48-50
9:7 [h]Ex 7:14; 8:32
9:9 [i]Dt 28:27,35; Rev 16:2
9:11 [j]Ex 8:18
9:12 [k]Ex 4:21
9:13 [l]Ex 8:20
9:14 [m]Ex 8:10 [n]2Sa 7:22; 1Ch 17:20; Ps 86:8; Isa 46:9; Jer 10:6
9:15 [o]Ex 3:20
9:16 [p]Pr 16:4 [q]Ro 9:17*
9:18 [r]ver 23 [s]ver 24
9:20 [t]Pr 13:13
9:23 [u]Ps 18:13 [v]Jos 10:11; Ps 78:47; 105:32; Isa 30:30; Eze 38:22; Rev 8:7; 16:21

[q]16 Or *have spared you*

lightning flashed back and forth. It was the worst storm in all the land of Egypt since it had become a nation. **25**Throughout Egypt hail struck everything in the fields—both men and animals; it beat down everything growing in the fields and stripped every tree.[a] **26**The only place it did not hail was the land of Goshen,[b] where the Israelites were.[c]

27Then Pharaoh summoned Moses and Aaron. "This time I have sinned,"[d] he said to them. "The LORD is in the right,[e] and I and my people are in the wrong. **28**Pray[f] to the LORD, for we have had enough thunder and hail. I will let you go;[g] you don't have to stay any longer."

29Moses replied, "When I have gone out of the city, I will spread out my hands[h] in prayer to the LORD. The thunder will stop and there will be no more hail, so you may know that the earth[i] is the LORD's. **30**But I know that you and your officials still do not fear the LORD God."

31(The flax and barley[j] were destroyed, since the barley had headed and the flax was in bloom. **32**The wheat and spelt, however, were not destroyed, because they ripen later.)

33Then Moses left Pharaoh and went out of the city. He spread out his hands toward the LORD; the thunder and hail stopped, and the rain no longer poured down on the land. **34**When Pharaoh saw that the rain and hail and thunder had stopped, he sinned again: He and his officials hardened their hearts. **35**So Pharaoh's heart[k] was hard and he would not let the Israelites go, just as the LORD had said through Moses.

The Plague of Locusts

10 Then the LORD said to Moses, "Go to Pharaoh, for I have hardened his heart[l] and the hearts of his officials so that I may perform these miraculous signs[m] of mine among them **2**that you may tell your children[n] and grandchildren how I dealt harshly with the Egyptians and how I performed my signs among them, and that you may know that I am the LORD."

3So Moses and Aaron went to Pharaoh and said to him, "This is what the LORD, the God of the Hebrews, says: 'How long will you refuse to humble[o] yourself before me? Let my people go, so that they may worship me. **4**If you refuse to let them go, I will bring locusts[p] into your country tomorrow. **5**They will cover the face of the ground so that it cannot be seen. They will devour what little you have left[q] after the hail, including every tree that is growing in your fields. **6**They will fill your houses and those of all your officials and all the Egyptians—something neither your fathers nor your forefathers have ever seen from the day they settled in this land till now.'" Then Moses turned and left Pharaoh.

7Pharaoh's officials said to him, "How long will this man be a snare[r] to us? Let the people go, so that they may worship the LORD their God. Do you not yet realize that Egypt is ruined?"[s]

8Then Moses and Aaron were brought back to Pharaoh. "Go, worship[t] the LORD your God," he said. "But just who will be going?"

9Moses answered, "We will go with our young and old, with our sons and daughters, and with our flocks and herds, because we are to celebrate a festival to the LORD."

10Pharaoh said, "The LORD be with you—if I let you go, along with your women and children! Clearly you are bent on evil.[1] **11**No! Have only the men go; and worship the LORD, since that's what you have been asking for." Then Moses and Aaron were driven out of Pharaoh's presence.

12And the LORD said to Moses, "Stretch out your hand[u] over Egypt so that locusts will swarm over the land and devour everything growing in the fields, everything left by the hail."

13So Moses stretched out his

9:25 [a] Ps 105:32-33
9:26 [b] ver 4 [c] Ex 8:22; 10:23; 11:7; 12:13
9:27 [d] Ex 10:16 [e] 2Ch 12:6; Ps 129:4; La 1:18
9:28 [f] Ex 10:17 [g] Ex 8:8
9:29 [h] 1Ki 8:22,38; Ps 143:6; Isa 1:15 [i] Ex 19:5; Ps 24:1; 1Co 10:26
9:31 [j] Ru 1:22; 2:23
9:35 [k] Ex 4:21
10:1 [l] Ex 4:21 [m] Ex 7:3
10:2 [n] Ex 12:26-27; 13:8,14; Dt 4:9; Ps 44:1; 78:4,5; Joel 1:3
10:3 [o] 1Ki 21:29; Jas 4:10; 1Pe 5:6
10:4 [p] Rev 9:3
10:5 [q] Ex 9:32; Joel 1:4
10:7 [r] Ex 23:33; Jos 23:7-13; 1Sa 18:21; Ecc 7:26 [s] Ex 8:19
10:8 [t] Ex 8:8
10:12 [u] Ex 7:19

[1] 10 Or *Be careful, trouble is in store for you!*

staff over Egypt, and the LORD made
an east wind blow across the land
all that day and all that night. By
morning the wind had brought the
locusts;[a] 14they invaded all Egypt
and settled down in every area of
the country in great numbers. Never before had there been such a
plague of locusts,[b] nor will there
ever be again. 15They covered all
the ground until it was black. They
devoured[c] all that was left after
the hail—everything growing in the
fields and the fruit on the trees.
Nothing green remained on tree or
plant in all the land of Egypt.
16Pharaoh quickly summoned
Moses and Aaron and said, "I have
sinned[d] against the LORD your God
and against you. 17Now forgive my
sin once more and pray[e] to the
LORD your God to take this deadly
plague away from me."
18Moses then left Pharaoh and
prayed to the LORD.[f] 19And the
LORD changed the wind to a very
strong west wind, which caught up
the locusts and carried them into
the Red Sea.[s] Not a locust was left
anywhere in Egypt. 20But the LORD
hardened Pharaoh's heart,[g] and
he would not let the Israelites go.

The Plague of Darkness

21Then the LORD said to Moses,
"Stretch out your hand toward the
sky so that darkness[h] will spread
over Egypt—darkness that can be
felt." 22So Moses stretched out his
hand toward the sky, and total
darkness[i] covered all Egypt for
three days. 23No one could see anyone else or leave his place for three
days. Yet all the Israelites had light
in the places where they lived.[j]
24Then Pharaoh summoned Moses and said, "Go, worship the
LORD. Even your women and children[k] may go with you; only leave
your flocks and herds behind."
25But Moses said, "You must allow us to have sacrifices and burnt
offerings to present to the LORD our
God. 26Our livestock too must go
with us; not a hoof is to be left behind. We have to use some of them
in worshiping the LORD our God,

10:13 [a]Ps 105:34
10:14 [b]Ps 78:46; Joel 2:1-11,25
10:15 [c]ver 5; Ps 105:34-35
10:16 [d]Ex 9:27
10:17 [e]Ex 8:8
10:18 [f]Ex 8:30
10:20 [g]Ex 4:21; 11:10
10:21 [h]Dt 28:29
10:22 [i]Ps 105:28; Rev 16:10
10:23 [j]Ex 8:22
10:24 [k]ver 8-10
10:27 [l]ver 20; Ex 4:21
10:29 [m]Heb 11:27
11:2 [n]Ex 3:21,22
11:3 [o]Dt 34:11
11:4 [p]Ex 12:29
11:5 [q]Ex 4:23; Ps 78:51
11:6 [r]Ex 12:30
11:7 [s]Ex 8:22
11:8 [t]Ex 12:31-33
11:9 [u]Ex 7:4

and until we get there we will not
know what we are to use to worship
the LORD."
27But the LORD hardened Pharaoh's heart,[l] and he was not willing to let them go. 28Pharaoh said
to Moses, "Get out of my sight!
Make sure you do not appear before me again! The day you see my
face you will die."
29"Just as you say," Moses replied, "I will never appear[m] before
you again."

The Plague on the Firstborn

11 Now the LORD had said to
Moses, "I will bring one
more plague on Pharaoh and on
Egypt. After that, he will let you go
from here, and when he does, he
will drive you out completely. 2Tell
the people that men and women
alike are to ask their neighbors for
articles of silver and gold."[n] 3(The
LORD made the Egyptians favorably
disposed toward the people, and
Moses himself was highly regarded[o] in Egypt by Pharaoh's officials
and by the people.)
4So Moses said, "This is what the
LORD says: 'About midnight[p] I will
go throughout Egypt. 5Every firstborn[q] son in Egypt will die, from
the firstborn son of Pharaoh, who
sits on the throne, to the firstborn
son of the slave girl, who is at her
hand mill, and all the firstborn of
the cattle as well. 6There will be
loud wailing[r] throughout Egypt
—worse than there has ever been
or ever will be again. 7But among
the Israelites not a dog will bark at
any man or animal.' Then you will
know that the LORD makes a distinction[s] between Egypt and Israel. 8All these officials of yours will
come to me, bowing down before
me and saying, 'Go,[t] you and all
the people who follow you!' After
that I will leave." Then Moses, hot
with anger, left Pharaoh.
9The LORD had said to Moses,
"Pharaoh will refuse to listen[u] to
you—so that my wonders may be
multiplied in Egypt." 10Moses and

[s]19 Hebrew *Yam Suph*; that is, Sea of Reeds

Aaron performed all these wonders
before Pharaoh, but the LORD hardened Pharaoh's heart,[a] and he
would not let the Israelites go out
of his country.

The Passover

12:14–20pp — Lev 23:4–8; Nu 28:16–25; Dt 16:1–8

12 The LORD said to Moses and
Aaron in Egypt, 2"This
month is to be for you the first
month,[b] the first month of your
year. 3Tell the whole community of
Israel that on the tenth day of this
month each man is to take a lamb[t]
for his family, one for each household. 4If any household is too small
for a whole lamb, they must share
one with their nearest neighbor,
having taken into account the
number of people there are. You
are to determine the amount of
lamb needed in accordance with
what each person will eat. 5The animals you choose must be year-old
males without defect,[c] and you
may take them from the sheep or
the goats. 6Take care of them until
the fourteenth day of the month,[d]
when all the people of the community of Israel must slaughter them
at twilight.[e] 7Then they are to take
some of the blood and put it on the
sides and tops of the doorframes of
the houses where they eat the
lambs. 8That same night[f] they are
to eat the meat roasted[g] over the
fire, along with bitter herbs,[h] and
bread made without yeast.[i] 9Do
not eat the meat raw or cooked in
water, but roast it over the fire—
head, legs and inner parts. 10Do
not leave any of it till morning;[j] if
some is left till morning, you must
burn it. 11This is how you are to eat
it: with your cloak tucked into your
belt, your sandals on your feet and
your staff in your hand. Eat it in
haste;[k] it is the LORD's Passover.[l]
12"On that same night I will pass
through[m] Egypt and strike down
every firstborn—both men and animals—and I will bring judgment on
all the gods[n] of Egypt. I am the
LORD.[o] 13The blood will be a sign
for you on the houses where you
are; and when I see the blood, I will
pass over you. No destructive
plague will touch you when I strike
Egypt.
14"This is a day you are to commemorate;[p] for the generations to
come you shall celebrate it as a festival to the LORD—a lasting ordinance.[q] 15For seven days you are
to eat bread made without yeast.[r]
On the first day remove the yeast
from your houses, for whoever eats
anything with yeast in it from the
first day through the seventh must
be cut off[s] from Israel. 16On the
first day hold a sacred assembly,
and another one on the seventh
day. Do no work at all on these
days, except to prepare food for everyone to eat—that is all you may
do.
17"Celebrate the Feast of Unleavened Bread, because it was on
this very day that I brought your divisions out of Egypt.[t] Celebrate
this day as a lasting ordinance for
the generations to come. 18In the
first month[u] you are to eat bread
made without yeast, from the evening of the fourteenth day until the
evening of the twenty-first day.
19For seven days no yeast is to be
found in your houses. And whoever
eats anything with yeast in it must
be cut off from the community of
Israel, whether he is an alien or native-born. 20Eat nothing made with
yeast. Wherever you live, you must
eat unleavened bread."
21Then Moses summoned all the
elders of Israel and said to them,
"Go at once and select the animals
for your families and slaughter the
Passover[v] lamb. 22Take a bunch of
hyssop, dip it into the blood in the
basin and put some of the blood[w]
on the top and on both sides of the
doorframe. Not one of you shall go
out the door of his house until
morning. 23When the LORD goes
through the land to strike down the
Egyptians, he will see the blood[x]
on the top and sides of the doorframe and will pass over[y] that

11:10 [a]Ex 4:21; 10:20,27
12:2 [b]Ex 13:4; Dt 16:1
12:5 [c]Lev 22:18-21; Heb 9:14
12:6 [d]Lev 23:5; Nu 9:1-3,5,11 [e]Ex 16:12; Dt 16:4,6
12:8 [f]Ex 34:25; Nu 9:12 [g]Dt 16:7 [h]Nu 9:11 [i]Dt 16:3-4; 1Co 5:8
12:10 [j]Ex 23:18; 34:25
12:11 [k]Dt 16:3 [l]ver 13,21,27, 43; Dt 16:1
12:12 [m]Ex 11:4; Am 5:17 [n]Nu 33:4 [o]Ex 6:2
12:14 [p]Ex 13:9 [q]ver 17,24; Ex 13:5,10; 2Ki 23:21
12:15 [r]Ex 13:6-7; 23:15; 34:18; Lev 23:6; Dt 16:3 [s]Ge 17:14; Nu 9:13
12:17 [t]ver 41; Ex 13:3
12:18 [u]ver 2; Lev 23:5-8; Nu 28:16-25
12:21 [v]ver 11; Mk 14:12-16
12:22 [w]ver 7; Heb 11:28
12:23 [x]Rev 7:3 [y]ver 13

t3 The Hebrew word can mean *lamb* or *kid*; also in verse 4.

HEBREW CALENDAR AND SELECTED EVENTS

Sacred Sequence Begins	Hebrew Name	Modern Equivalent	Biblical References	Agriculture	Feasts
1	**Abib; Nisan**	March-April	Ex 12:2; 13:4; 23:15; 34:18; Dt 16:1; Ne 2:1; Est 3:7	Spring (later) rains; barley and flax harvest begins	Passover; Unleavened Bread; Firstfruits
2	**Ziv (Iyyar)***	April-May	1 Ki 6:1,37	Barley havest; dry season begins	
3	**Sivan**	May-June	Est 8:9	Wheat harvest	Pentecost (Weeks)
4	**(Tammuz)***	June-July		Tending vines	
5	**(Ab)***	July-August		Ripening of grapes, figs and olives	
6	**Elul**	August-September	Ne 6:15	Processing grapes, figs and olives	
7	**Ethanim (Tishri)***	September-October	1 Ki 8:2	Autumn (early) rains begin; plowing	Trumpets; Atonement; Tabernacles (Booths)
8	**Bul (Marcheshvan)***	October-November	1 Ki 6:38	Sowing of wheat and barley	
9	**Kislev**	November-December	Ne 1:1, Zec 7:1	Winter rains begin (snow in some areas)	Hanukkah ("Dedication")
10	**Tebeth**	December-January	Est 2:16		
11	**Shebat**	January-February	Zec 1:7		
12	**Adar**	February-March	Ezr 6:15; Est 3:7,13; 8:12; 9:1,15,17,19,21	Almond trees bloom; citrus fruit harvest	Purim
		(Adar Sheni)* **Second Adar**	This intercalary month was added about every three years so the lunar calendar would correspond to the solar year.		

* Names in parentheses are not in the Bible

doorway, and he will not permit the destroyer[a] to enter your houses and strike you down.

24“Obey these instructions as a lasting ordinance for you and your descendants. 25When you enter the land that the LORD will give you as he promised, observe this ceremony. 26And when your children[b] ask you, ‘What does this ceremony mean to you?’ 27then tell them, ‘It is the Passover[c] sacrifice to the LORD, who passed over the houses of the Israelites in Egypt and spared our homes when he struck down the Egyptians.’ ” Then the people bowed down and worshiped.[d] 28The Israelites did just what the LORD commanded Moses and Aaron.

29At midnight[e] the LORD struck down all the firstborn[f] in Egypt, from the firstborn of Pharaoh, who sat on the throne, to the firstborn of the prisoner, who was in the dungeon, and the firstborn of all the livestock[g] as well. 30Pharaoh and all his officials and all the Egyptians got up during the night, and there was loud wailing[h] in Egypt, for there was not a house without someone dead.

The Exodus

31During the night Pharaoh summoned Moses and Aaron and said, “Up! Leave my people, you and the Israelites! Go, worship[i] the LORD as you have requested. 32Take your flocks and herds,[j] as you have said, and go. And also bless me.”

33The Egyptians urged the people to hurry and leave[k] the country. “For otherwise,” they said, “we will all die!” 34So the people took their dough before the yeast was added, and carried it on their shoulders in kneading troughs wrapped in clothing. 35The Israelites did as Moses instructed and asked the Egyptians for articles of silver and gold[l] and for clothing. 36The LORD had made the Egyptians favorably disposed toward the people, and they gave them what they asked for; so they plundered[m] the Egyptians.

37The Israelites journeyed from Rameses to Succoth.[n] There were about six hundred thousand men[o] on foot, besides women and children. 38Many other people[p] went up with them, as well as large droves of livestock, both flocks and herds. 39With the dough they had brought from Egypt, they baked cakes of unleavened bread. The dough was without yeast because they had been driven out[q] of Egypt and did not have time to prepare food for themselves.

40Now the length of time the Israelite people lived in Egypt[u] was 430 years.[r] 41At the end of the 430 years, to the very day, all the LORD’s divisions[s] left Egypt.[t] 42Because the LORD kept vigil that night to bring them out of Egypt, on this night all the Israelites are to keep vigil to honor the LORD for the generations to come.[u]

Passover Restrictions

43The LORD said to Moses and Aaron, “These are the regulations for the Passover:[v]

“No foreigner[w] is to eat of it. 44Any slave you have bought may eat of it after you have circumcised[x] him, 45but a temporary resident and a hired worker[y] may not eat of it.

46“It must be eaten inside one house; take none of the meat outside the house. Do not break any of the bones.[z] 47The whole community of Israel must celebrate it.

48“An alien living among you who wants to celebrate the LORD’s Passover must have all the males in his household circumcised; then he may take part like one born in the land.[a] No uncircumcised male may eat of it. 49The same law applies to the native-born and to the alien[b] living among you.”

50All the Israelites did just what the LORD had commanded Moses and Aaron. 51And on that very day the LORD brought the Israelites out of Egypt by their divisions.[c]

12:23 [a] 1Co 10:10; Heb 11:28
12:26 [b] Ex 10:2; 13:8,14-15; Jos 4:6
12:27 [c] ver 11 [d] Ex 4:31
12:29 [e] Ex 11:4 [f] Ex 4:23; Ps 78:51 [g] Ex 9:6
12:30 [h] Ex 11:6
12:31 [i] Ex 8:8
12:32 [j] Ex 10:9,26
12:33 [k] Ps 105:38
12:35 [l] Ex 3:22
12:36 [m] Ex 3:22
12:37 [n] Nu 33:3-5 [o] Ex 38:26; Nu 1:46; 11:13,21
12:38 [p] Nu 11:4
12:39 [q] ver 31-33; Ex 6:1; 11:1
12:40 [r] Ge 15:13; Ac 7:6; Gal 3:17
12:41 [s] ver 17; Ex 6:26 [t] Ex 3:10
12:42 [u] Ex 13:10; Dt 16:1,6
12:43 [v] ver 11 [w] ver 48; Nu 9:14
12:44 [x] Ge 17:12-13
12:45 [y] Lev 22:10
12:46 [z] Nu 9:12; Jn 19:36*
12:48 [a] Nu 9:14
12:49 [b] Nu 15:15-16, 29; Gal 3:28
12:51 [c] ver 41; Ex 6:26

[u] *40* Masoretic Text; Samaritan Pentateuch and Septuagint *Egypt and Canaan*

Consecration of the Firstborn

13 The LORD said to Moses,
2"Consecrate to me every
firstborn male.[a] The first offspring
of every womb among the Israelites
belongs to me, whether man or animal."

3Then Moses said to the people,
"Commemorate this day, the day
you came out of Egypt, out of the
land of slavery, because the LORD
brought you out of it with a mighty
hand.[b] Eat nothing containing
yeast.[c] 4Today, in the month of
Abib,[d] you are leaving. 5When the
LORD brings you into the land of the
Canaanites, Hittites, Amorites, Hivites and Jebusites[e]—the land he
swore to your forefathers to give
you, a land flowing with milk and
honey—you are to observe this ceremony[f] in this month: 6For seven
days eat bread made without yeast
and on the seventh day hold a festival[g] to the LORD. 7Eat unleavened
bread during those seven days;
nothing with yeast in it is to be
seen among you, nor shall any
yeast be seen anywhere within your
borders. 8On that day tell your
son,[h] 'I do this because of what the
LORD did for me when I came out of
Egypt.' 9This observance will be for
you like a sign on your hand and a
reminder on your forehead[i] that
the law of the LORD is to be on your
lips. For the LORD brought you out
of Egypt with his mighty hand.
10You must keep this ordinance[j]
at the appointed time year after
year.

11"After the LORD brings you into
the land of the Canaanites and
gives it to you, as he promised on
oath to you and your forefathers,
12you are to give over to the LORD
the first offspring of every womb.
All the firstborn males of your livestock belong to the LORD.[k] 13Re-
deem with a lamb every firstborn
donkey, but if you do not redeem it,
break its neck.[l] Redeem every
firstborn among your sons.[m]

14"In days to come, when your
son[n] asks you, 'What does this
mean?' say to him, 'With a mighty
hand the LORD brought us out of
Egypt, out of the land of slavery.[o]
15When Pharaoh stubbornly refused to let us go, the LORD killed
every firstborn in Egypt, both man
and animal. This is why I sacrifice
to the LORD the first male offspring
of every womb and redeem each of
my firstborn sons.'[p] 16And it will
be like a sign on your hand and a
symbol on your forehead[q] that the
LORD brought us out of Egypt with
his mighty hand."

Crossing the Sea

17When Pharaoh let the people
go, God did not lead them on the
road through the Philistine country, though that was shorter. For
God said, "If they face war, they
might change their minds and return to Egypt."[r] 18So God led[s] the
people around by the desert road
toward the Red Sea.[v] The Israelites went up out of Egypt armed for
battle.[t]

19Moses took the bones of Joseph[u] with him because Joseph
had made the sons of Israel swear
an oath. He had said, "God will
surely come to your aid, and then
you must carry my bones up with
you from this place."[w][v]

20After leaving Succoth they
camped at Etham on the edge of
the desert.[w] 21By day the LORD
went ahead of them in a pillar of
cloud[x] to guide them on their way
and by night in a pillar of fire to
give them light, so that they could
travel by day or night. 22Neither
the pillar of cloud by day nor the
pillar of fire by night left its place in
front of the people.

14 Then the LORD said to Moses, 2"Tell the Israelites to
turn back and encamp near Pi Hahiroth, between Migdol[y] and the
sea. They are to encamp by the sea,
directly opposite Baal Zephon.
3Pharaoh will think, 'The Israelites
are wandering around the land in
confusion, hemmed in by the
desert.' 4And I will harden Phar-

13:2 [a] ver 12,13,15; Ex 22:29; Nu 3:13; Dt 15:19; Lk 2:23*
13:3 [b] Ex 3:20; 6:1 [c] Ex 12:19
13:4 [d] Ex 12:2
13:5 [e] Ex 3:8 [f] Ex 12:25-26
13:6 [g] Ex 12:15-20
13:8 [h] ver 14; Ex 10:2; Ps 78:5-6
13:9 [i] ver 16; Dt 6:8; 11:18
13:10 [j] Ex 12:24-25
13:12 [k] Lev 27:26; Lk 2:23*
13:13 [l] Ex 34:20 [m] Nu 18:15
13:14 [n] Ex 10:2; 12:26-27; Dt 6:20 [o] ver 3,9
13:15 [p] Ex 12:29
13:16 [q] ver 9
13:17 [r] Ex 14:11; Nu 14:1-4; Dt 17:16
13:18 [s] Ps 136:16 [t] Jos 1:14
13:19 [u] Jos 24:32; Ac 7:16 [v] Ge 50:24-25
13:20 [w] Nu 33:6
13:21 [x] Ex 14:19,24; 33:9-10; Nu 9:16; Dt 1:33; Ne 9:12,19; Ps 78:14; 99:7; 105:39; Isa 4:5; 1Co 10:1
14:2 [y] Nu 33:7; Jer 44:1

[v] *18* Hebrew *Yam Suph*; that is, Sea of Reeds
[w] *19* See Gen. 50:25.

aoh's heart,[a] and he will pursue
them. But I will gain glory[b] for myself through Pharaoh and all his
army, and the Egyptians will know
that I am the LORD."[c] So the Israelites did this.
5When the king of Egypt was told
that the people had fled, Pharaoh
and his officials changed their
minds about them and said, "What
have we done? We have let the Israelites go and have lost their services!" **6**So he had his chariot made
ready and took his army with him.
7He took six hundred of the best
chariots, along with all the other
chariots of Egypt, with officers over
all of them. **8**The LORD hardened
the heart[d] of Pharaoh king of
Egypt, so that he pursued the Israelites, who were marching
out boldly.[e] **9**The Egyptians—all
Pharaoh's horses and chariots,
horsemen[x] and troops—pursued
the Israelites and overtook[f] them
as they camped by the sea near Pi
Hahiroth, opposite Baal Zephon.
10As Pharaoh approached, the
Israelites looked up, and there
were the Egyptians, marching after
them. They were terrified and
cried[g] out to the LORD. **11**They said
to Moses, "Was it because there
were no graves in Egypt that you
brought us to the desert to die?[h]
What have you done to us by bringing us out of Egypt? **12**Didn't we
say to you in Egypt, 'Leave us
alone; let us serve the Egyptians'?
It would have been better for us to
serve the Egyptians than to die in
the desert!"
13Moses answered the people,
"Do not be afraid.[i] Stand firm and
you will see[j] the deliverance the
LORD will bring you today. The
Egyptians you see today you will
never see[k] again. **14**The LORD will
fight[l] for you; you need only to be
still."[m]
15Then the LORD said to Moses,
"Why are you crying out to me? Tell
the Israelites to move on. **16**Raise
your staff[n] and stretch out your
hand over the sea to divide the water[o] so that the Israelites can go
through the sea on dry ground. **17**I
will harden the hearts of the Egyptians so that they will go in after
them.[p] And I will gain glory
through Pharaoh and all his army,
through his chariots and his horsemen. **18**The Egyptians will know
that I am the LORD when I gain glory
through Pharaoh, his chariots and
his horsemen."
19Then the angel of God, who
had been traveling in front of Israel's army, withdrew and went behind them. The pillar of cloud[q]
also moved from in front and stood
behind them, **20**coming between
the armies of Egypt and Israel.
Throughout the night the cloud
brought darkness to the one side
and light to the other side; so neither went near the other all night
long.
21Then Moses stretched out his
hand over the sea, and all that
night the LORD drove the sea back
with a strong east wind[r] and
turned it into dry land. The waters
were divided,[s] **22**and the Israelites
went through the sea on dry
ground,[t] with a wall of water on
their right and on their left.
23The Egyptians pursued them,
and all Pharaoh's horses and chariots and horsemen followed them
into the sea. **24**During the last
watch of the night the LORD looked
down from the pillar of fire and
cloud[u] at the Egyptian army and
threw it into confusion. **25**He made
the wheels of their chariots come
off[y] so that they had difficulty driving. And the Egyptians said, "Let's
get away from the Israelites! The
LORD is fighting[v] for them against
Egypt."
26Then the LORD said to Moses,
"Stretch out your hand over the sea
so that the waters may flow back
over the Egyptians and their chariots and horsemen." **27**Moses
stretched out his hand over the sea,
and at daybreak the sea went back
to its place.[w] The Egyptians were
fleeing toward[z] it, and the LORD

14:4 [a]Ex 4:21 [b]Ro 9:17, 22-23 [c]Ex 7:5
14:8 [d]ver 4; Ex 11:10 [e]Nu 33:3; Ac 13:17
14:9 [f]Ex 15:9
14:10 [g]Jos 24:7; Ne 9:9; Ps 34:17
14:11 [h]Ps 106:7-8
14:13 [i]Ge 15:1 [j]2Ch 20:17; Isa 41:10, 13-14 [k]ver 30
14:14 [l]ver 25; Ex 15:3; Dt 1:30; 3:22; 2Ch 20:29 [m]Ps 37:7; 46:10; Isa 30:15
14:16 [n]Ex 4:17; Nu 20:8-9,11 [o]Isa 10:26
14:17 [p]ver 4
14:19 [q]Ex 13:21
14:21 [r]Ex 15:8 [s]Ps 74:13; 114:5; Isa 63:12
14:22 [t]Ex 15:19; Ne 9:11; Ps 66:6; Heb 11:29
14:24 [u]Ex 13:21
14:25 [v]ver 14
14:27 [w]Jos 4:18

[x]9 Or *charioteers*; also in verses 17, 18, 23, 26 and 28 [y]25 Or *He jammed the wheels of their chariots* (see Samaritan Pentateuch, Septuagint and Syriac) [z]27 Or *from*

swept them into the sea.[a] 28The
water flowed back and covered the
chariots and horsemen—the entire
army of Pharaoh that had followed
the Israelites into the sea. Not one
of them survived.

29But the Israelites went
through the sea on dry ground,[b]
with a wall of water on their right
and on their left. 30That day the
LORD saved[c] Israel from the hands
of the Egyptians, and Israel saw the
Egyptians lying dead on the shore.
31And when the Israelites saw the
great power the LORD displayed
against the Egyptians, the people
feared the LORD and put their
trust[d] in him and in Moses his servant.

The Song of Moses and Miriam

15 Then Moses and the Israelites sang this song[e] to the
LORD:

"I will sing[f] to the LORD,
for he is highly exalted.
The horse and its rider
he has hurled into the sea.
2The LORD is my strength[g] and
my song;
he has become my
salvation.[h]
He is my God,[i] and I will
praise him,
my father's God, and I will
exalt[j] him.
3The LORD is a warrior;[k]
the LORD is his name.[l]
4Pharaoh's chariots and his
army[m]
he has hurled into the sea.
The best of Pharaoh's officers
are drowned in the Red
Sea.[a]
5The deep waters have covered
them;
they sank to the depths like
a stone.[n]
6"Your right hand,[o] O LORD,
was majestic in power.
Your right hand, O LORD,
shattered the enemy.
7In the greatness of your majesty
you threw down those who
opposed you.
You unleashed your burning
anger;[p]
it consumed them like
stubble.
8By the blast of your nostrils[q]
the waters piled up.[r]
The surging waters stood firm
like a wall;[s]
the deep waters congealed in
the heart of the sea.
9"The enemy boasted,
'I will pursue,[t] I will
overtake them.
I will divide the spoils;[u]
I will gorge myself on them.
I will draw my sword
and my hand will destroy
them.'
10But you blew with your breath,
and the sea covered them.
They sank like lead
in the mighty waters.[v]
11"Who among the gods is like
you,[w] O LORD?
Who is like you—
majestic in holiness,[x]
awesome in glory,[y]
working wonders?
12You stretched out your right
hand
and the earth swallowed
them.
13"In your unfailing love you will
lead[z]
the people you have
redeemed.
In your strength you will guide
them
to your holy dwelling.[a]
14The nations will hear and
tremble;[b]
anguish will grip the people
of Philistia.
15The chiefs[c] of Edom will be
terrified,
the leaders of Moab will be
seized with trembling,[d]
the people[b] of Canaan will
melt[e] away;
16 terror[f] and dread will fall
upon them.
By the power of your arm

14:27 [a]Ex 15:1,21; Ps 78:53; 106:11
14:29 [b]ver 22
14:30 [c]Ps 106:8,10,21
14:31 [d]Ps 106:12; Jn 2:11
15:1 [e]Rev 15:3 [f]Ps 106:12
15:2 [g]Ps 59:17 [h]Ps 18:2,46; Isa 12:2; Hab 3:18 [i]Ge 28:21 [j]Ex 3:6,15-16; Isa 25:1
15:3 [k]Ex 14:14; Ps 24:8; Rev 19:11 [l]Ex 6:2-3,7-8; Ps 83:18
15:4 [m]Ex 14:6-7
15:5 [n]ver 10; Ne 9:11
15:6 [o]Ps 118:15
15:7 [p]Ps 78:49-50
15:8 [q]Ex 14:21 [r]Ps 78:13 [s]Ex 14:22
15:9 [t]Ex 14:5-9 [u]Jdg 5:30; Isa 53:12
15:10 [v]ver 5; Ex 14:27-28
15:11 [w]Ex 8:10; Dt 3:24; Ps 77:13 [x]Isa 6:3; Rev 4:8 [y]Ps 8:1
15:13 [z]Ne 9:12; Ps 77:20 [a]Ps 78:54
15:14 [b]Dt 2:25
15:15 [c]Ge 36:15 [d]Nu 22:3 [e]Jos 5:1
15:16 [f]Ex 23:27; Jos 2:9

[a]4 Hebrew *Yam Suph*; that is, Sea of Reeds; also in verse 22 [b]15 Or *rulers*

they will be as still as a
stone[a]—
until your people pass by,
O LORD,
until the people you
bought[c][b] pass by.
17You will bring them in and
plant[c] them
on the mountain[d] of your
inheritance—
the place, O LORD, you made
for your dwelling,
the sanctuary, O Lord, your
hands established.
18The LORD will reign
for ever and ever."

19When Pharaoh's horses, chariots and horsemen[d] went into the
sea,[e] the LORD brought the waters
of the sea back over them, but the
Israelites walked through the sea
on dry ground.[f] 20Then Miriam[g]
the prophetess,[h] Aaron's sister,
took a tambourine in her hand, and
all the women followed her, with
tambourines and dancing.[i] 21Mir-
iam sang to them:

"Sing to the LORD,
for he is highly exalted.
The horse and its rider
he has hurled into the sea."[j]

The Waters of Marah and Elim

22Then Moses led Israel from the
Red Sea and they went into the
Desert of Shur. For three days they
traveled in the desert without finding water. 23When they came to
Marah, they could not drink its water because it was bitter. (That is
why the place is called Marah.[e][k])
24So the people grumbled[l] against
Moses, saying, "What are we to
drink?"
25Then Moses cried out[m] to the
LORD, and the LORD showed him a
piece of wood. He threw it into the
water, and the water became
sweet.
There the LORD made a decree
and a law for them, and there he
tested[n] them. 26He said, "If you
listen carefully to the voice of the
LORD your God and do what is right
in his eyes, if you pay attention to
his commands and keep all his de-

15:16 [a]1Sa 25:37 [b]Ps 74:2
15:17 [c]Ps 44:2 [d]Ps 78:54,68
15:19 [e]Ex 14:28 [f]Ex 14:22
15:20 [g]Nu 26:59 [h]Jdg 4:4 [i]Jdg 11:34; 1Sa 18:6; Ps 30:11; 150:4
15:21 [j]ver 1; Ex 14:27
15:23 [k]Nu 33:8
15:24 [l]Ex 14:12; 16:2
15:25 [m]Ex 14:10 [n]Jdg 3:4
15:26 [o]Dt 7:12 [p]Dt 28:27, 58-60 [q]Ex 23:25-26
15:27 [r]Nu 33:9
16:1 [s]Nu 33:11,12
16:2 [t]Ex 14:11; 15:24; 1Co 10:10
16:3 [u]Ex 17:3 [v]Nu 11:4,34
16:4 [w]Dt 8:3; Jn 6:31*
16:5 [x]ver 22
16:6 [y]Ex 6:6
16:7 [z]ver 10; Isa 35:2; 40:5 [a]ver 12; Nu 14:2,27,28 [b]Nu 16:11
16:8 [c]1Sa 8:7; Ro 13:2

crees,[o] I will not bring on you any
of the diseases[p] I brought on the
Egyptians, for I am the LORD, who
heals[q] you."
27Then they came to Elim,
where there were twelve springs
and seventy palm trees, and they
camped[r] there near the water.

Manna and Quail

16 The whole Israelite community set out from Elim
and came to the Desert of Sin,[s]
which is between Elim and Sinai,
on the fifteenth day of the second
month after they had come out of
Egypt. 2In the desert the whole
community grumbled[t] against
Moses and Aaron. 3The Israelites
said to them, "If only we had died
by the LORD's hand in Egypt![u]
There we sat around pots of meat
and ate all the food[v] we wanted,
but you have brought us out into
this desert to starve this entire assembly to death."
4Then the LORD said to Moses, "I
will rain down bread from heaven[w]
for you. The people are to go out
each day and gather enough for
that day. In this way I will test them
and see whether they will follow
my instructions. 5On the sixth day
they are to prepare what they bring
in, and that is to be twice[x] as
much as they gather on the other
days."
6So Moses and Aaron said to all
the Israelites, "In the evening you
will know that it was the LORD who
brought you out of Egypt,[y] 7and in
the morning you will see the glory[z]
of the LORD, because he has heard
your grumbling[a] against him. Who
are we, that you should grumble
against us?"[b] 8Moses also said,
"You will know that it was the LORD
when he gives you meat to eat in
the evening and all the bread you
want in the morning, because he
has heard your grumbling against
him. Who are we? You are not
grumbling against us, but against
the LORD."[c]

[c]16 Or *created* [d]19 Or *charioteers*
[e]23 *Marah* means *bitter.*

9Then Moses told Aaron, "Say to
the entire Israelite community,
'Come before the LORD, for he has
heard your grumbling.' "
10While Aaron was speaking to
the whole Israelite community,
they looked toward the desert, and
there was the glory[a] of the LORD
appearing in the cloud.[b]
11The LORD said to Moses, **12**"I
have heard the grumbling[c] of the
Israelites. Tell them, 'At twilight
you will eat meat, and in the morning you will be filled with bread.
Then you will know that I am the
LORD your God.' "
13That evening quail[d] came and
covered the camp, and in the morning there was a layer of dew[e]
around the camp. **14**When the dew
was gone, thin flakes like frost[f] on
the ground appeared on the desert
floor. **15**When the Israelites saw it,
they said to each other, "What is
it?" For they did not know what it
was.
Moses said to them, "It is the
bread[g] the LORD has given you to
eat. **16**This is what the LORD has
commanded: 'Each one is to gather
as much as he needs. Take an
omer[f][h] for each person you have
in your tent.' "
17The Israelites did as they were
told; some gathered much, some
little. **18**And when they measured it
by the omer, he who gathered
much did not have too much, and
he who gathered little did not have
too little.[i] Each one gathered as
much as he needed.
19Then Moses said to them, "No
one is to keep any of it until morning."[j]
20However, some of them paid
no attention to Moses; they kept
part of it until morning, but it was
full of maggots and began to smell.
So Moses was angry with them.
21Each morning everyone gathered as much as he needed, and
when the sun grew hot, it melted
away. **22**On the sixth day, they
gathered twice[k] as much—two
omers[g] for each person—and the
leaders of the community[l] came
and reported this to Moses. **23**He
said to them, "This is what the
LORD commanded: 'Tomorrow is to
be a day of rest, a holy Sabbath[m] to
the LORD. So bake what you want
to bake and boil what you want
to boil. Save whatever is left and
keep it until morning.' "
24So they saved it until morning,
as Moses commanded, and it did
not stink or get maggots in it.
25"Eat it today," Moses said, "because today is a Sabbath to the
LORD. You will not find any of it on
the ground today. **26**Six days you
are to gather it, but on the seventh
day, the Sabbath,[n] there will not
be any."
27Nevertheless, some of the people went out on the seventh day to
gather it, but they found none.
28Then the LORD said to Moses,
"How long will you[h] refuse to keep
my commands[o] and my instructions? **29**Bear in mind that the LORD
has given you the Sabbath; that is
why on the sixth day he gives you
bread for two days. Everyone is to
stay where he is on the seventh
day; no one is to go out." **30**So the
people rested on the seventh day.
31The people of Israel called the
bread manna.[i][p] It was white like
coriander seed and tasted like wafers made with honey. **32**Moses
said, "This is what the LORD has
commanded: 'Take an omer of
manna and keep it for the generations to come, so they can see the
bread I gave you to eat in the desert
when I brought you out of Egypt.' "
33So Moses said to Aaron, "Take
a jar and put an omer of manna[q] in
it. Then place it before the LORD to
be kept for the generations to
come."
34As the LORD commanded Moses, Aaron put the manna in front
of the Testimony,[r] that it might be
kept. **35**The Israelites ate manna[s]
forty years,[t] until they came to a
land that was settled; they ate

16:10 [a]ver 7; Nu 16:19 [b]Ex 13:21; 1Ki 8:10
16:12 [c]ver 7
16:13 [d]Nu 11:31; Ps 78:27-28; 105:40 [e]Nu 11:9
16:14 [f]ver 31; Nu 11:7-9; Ps 105:40
16:15 [g]ver 4; Jn 6:31
16:16 [h]ver 32,36
16:18 [i]2Co 8:15*
16:19 [j]ver 23; Ex 12:10; 23:18
16:22 [k]ver 5 [l]Ex 34:31
16:23 [m]Ge 2:3; Ex 20:8; 23:12; Lev 23:3
16:26 [n]Ex 20:9-10
16:28 [o]2Ki 17:14; Ps 78:10; 106:13
16:31 [p]Nu 11:7-9
16:33 [q]Heb 9:4
16:34 [r]Ex 25:16,21,22; 40:20; Nu 17:4,10
16:35 [s]Jn 6:31,49 [t]Ne 9:21

[f]*16* That is, probably about 2 quarts (about 2 liters); also in verses 18, 32, 33 and 36
[g]*22* That is, probably about 4 quarts (about 4.5 liters)
[h]*28* The Hebrew is plural.
[i]*31* *Manna* means *What is it?* (see verse 15).

manna until they reached the border of Canaan.[a]

[36](An omer is one tenth of an ephah.)

Water From the Rock

17 The whole Israelite community set out from the Desert of Sin,[b] traveling from place to place as the LORD commanded. They camped at Rephidim, but there was no water[c] for the people to drink. [2]So they quarreled with Moses and said, "Give us water[d] to drink."

Moses replied, "Why do you quarrel with me? Why do you put the LORD to the test?"[e]

[3]But the people were thirsty for water there, and they grumbled[f] against Moses. They said, "Why did you bring us up out of Egypt to make us and our children and livestock die of thirst?"

[4]Then Moses cried out to the LORD, "What am I to do with these people? They are almost ready to stone[g] me."

[5]The LORD answered Moses, "Walk on ahead of the people. Take with you some of the elders of Israel and take in your hand the staff with which you struck the Nile,[h] and go. [6]I will stand there before you by the rock at Horeb. Strike the rock, and water[i] will come out of it for the people to drink." So Moses did this in the sight of the elders of Israel. [7]And he called the place Massah[i] and Meribah[k][j] because the Israelites quarreled and because they tested the LORD saying, "Is the LORD among us or not?"

The Amalekites Defeated

[8]The Amalekites[k] came and attacked the Israelites at Rephidim. [9]Moses said to Joshua, "Choose some of our men and go out to fight the Amalekites. Tomorrow I will stand on top of the hill with the staff[l] of God in my hands."

[10]So Joshua fought the Amalekites as Moses had ordered, and Moses, Aaron and Hur[m] went to the top of the hill. [11]As long as Moses held up his hands, the Israelites were winning,[n] but whenever he lowered his hands, the Amalekites were winning. [12]When Moses' hands grew tired, they took a stone and put it under him and he sat on it. Aaron and Hur held his hands up—one on one side, one on the other—so that his hands remained steady till sunset. [13]So Joshua overcame the Amalekite army with the sword.

[14]Then the LORD said to Moses, "Write[o] this on a scroll as something to be remembered and make sure that Joshua hears it, because I will completely blot out the memory of Amalek[p] from under heaven."

[15]Moses built an altar and called it The LORD is my Banner. [16]He said, "For hands were lifted up to the throne of the LORD. The[l] LORD will be at war against the Amalekites from generation to generation."

Jethro Visits Moses

18 Now Jethro, the priest of Midian[q] and father-in-law of Moses, heard of everything God had done for Moses and for his people Israel, and how the LORD had brought Israel out of Egypt.

[2]After Moses had sent away his wife Zipporah,[r] his father-in-law Jethro received her [3]and her two sons.[s] One son was named Gershom,[m] for Moses said, "I have become an alien in a foreign land";[t] [4]and the other was named Eliezer,[n][u] for he said, "My father's God was my helper; he saved me from the sword of Pharaoh."

[5]Jethro, Moses' father-in-law, together with Moses' sons and wife, came to him in the desert, where he was camped near the mountain[v] of God. [6]Jethro had sent word to him, "I, your father-in-law Jethro, am coming to you

16:35 [a]Jos 5:12
17:1 [b]Ex 16:1 [c]Nu 33:14
17:2 [d]Nu 20:2 [e]Dt 6:16; Ps 78:18,41; 1Co 10:9
17:3 [f]Ex 15:24; 16:2-3
17:4 [g]Nu 14:10; 1Sa 30:6
17:5 [h]Ex 7:20
17:6 [i]Nu 20:11; Ps 114:8; 1Co 10:4
17:7 [j]Nu 20:13,24; Ps 81:7
17:8 [k]Ge 36:12; Dt 25:17-19
17:9 [l]Ex 4:17
17:10 [m]Ex 24:14
17:11 [n]Jas 5:16
17:14 [o]Ex 24:4; 34:27; Nu 33:2 [p]1Sa 15:3; 30:17-18
18:1 [q]Ex 2:16; 3:1
18:2 [r]Ex 2:21; 4:25
18:3 [s]Ex 4:20; Ac 7:29 [t]Ex 2:22
18:4 [u]1Ch 23:15
18:5 [v]Ex 3:1

[i]7 *Massah* means *testing.* [k]7 *Meribah* means *quarreling.* [l]16 Or *"Because a hand was against the throne of the LORD, the* [m]3 *Gershom* sounds like the Hebrew for *an alien there.* [n]4 *Eliezer* means *my God is helper.*

with your wife and her two sons."
7So Moses went out to meet his
father-in-law and bowed down[a]
and kissed[b] him. They greeted
each other and then went into the
tent. 8Moses told his father-in-law
about everything the LORD had
done to Pharaoh and the Egyptians
for Israel's sake and about all the
hardships they had met along the
way and how the LORD had saved[c]
them.
9Jethro was delighted to hear
about all the good things the LORD
had done for Israel in rescuing
them from the hand of the Egyptians. 10He said, "Praise be to the
LORD,[d] who rescued you from the
hand of the Egyptians and of Pharaoh, and who rescued the people
from the hand of the Egyptians.
11Now I know that the LORD is
greater than all other gods,[e] for he
did this to those who had treated
Israel arrogantly."[f] 12Then Jethro,
Moses' father-in-law, brought a
burnt offering and other sacrifices
to God, and Aaron came with all
the elders of Israel to eat bread
with Moses' father-in-law in the
presence[g] of God.
13The next day Moses took his
seat to serve as judge for the people, and they stood around him
from morning till evening. 14When
his father-in-law saw all that Moses
was doing for the people, he said,
"What is this you are doing for the
people? Why do you alone sit as
judge, while all these people stand
around you from morning till evening?"
15Moses answered him, "Because the people come to me to
seek God's will.[h] 16Whenever they
have a dispute, it is brought to me,
and I decide between the parties
and inform them of God's decrees
and laws."[i]
17Moses' father-in-law replied,
"What you are doing is not good.
18You and these people who come
to you will only wear yourselves
out. The work is too heavy for you;
you cannot handle it alone.[j] 19Lis-
ten now to me and I will give you
some advice, and may God be with
you.[k] You must be the people's
representative before God and
bring their disputes[l] to him.
20Teach them the decrees and
laws,[m] and show them the way to
live[n] and the duties they are to
perform.[o] 21But select capable
men[p] from all the people—men
who fear God, trustworthy men
who hate dishonest gain[q]—and
appoint them as officials[r] over
thousands, hundreds, fifties and
tens. 22Have them serve as judges
for the people at all times, but have
them bring every difficult case[s] to
you; the simple cases they can decide themselves. That will make
your load lighter, because they will
share[t] it with you. 23If you do this
and God so commands, you will be
able to stand the strain, and all
these people will go home satisfied."
24Moses listened to his father-
in-law and did everything he said.
25He chose capable men from all
Israel and made them leaders of
the people, officials over thousands, hundreds, fifties and tens.[u]
26They served as judges for the
people at all times. The difficult
cases they brought to Moses, but
the simple ones they decided
themselves.[v]
27Then Moses sent his father-
in-law on his way, and Jethro returned to his own country.[w]

At Mount Sinai

19 In the third month after the
Israelites left Egypt—on
the very day—they came to the
Desert of Sinai. 2After they set out
from Rephidim,[x] they entered the
Desert of Sinai, and Israel camped
there in the desert in front of the
mountain.[y]
3Then Moses went up to God,
and the LORD called[z] to him from
the mountain and said, "This is
what you are to say to the house of
Jacob and what you are to tell the
people of Israel: 4'You yourselves
have seen what I did to Egypt,[a]
and how I carried you on eagles'
wings[b] and brought you to myself.
5Now if you obey me fully[c] and

18:7 [a]Ge 43:28 [b]Ge 29:13
18:8 [c]Ex 15:6,16; Ps 81:7
18:10 [d]Ge 14:20; Ps 68:19-20
18:11 [e]Ex 12:12; 15:11; 2Ch 2:5 [f]Lk 1:51
18:12 [g]Dt 12:7
18:15 [h]Nu 9:6,8; Dt 17:8-13
18:16 [i]Lev 24:12
18:18 [j]Nu 11:11,14, 17
18:19 [k]Ex 3:12 [l]Nu 27:5
18:20 [m]Dt 5:1 [n]Ps 143:8 [o]Dt 1:18
18:21 [p]Ac 6:3 [q]Dt 16:19; Ps 15:5; Eze 18:8 [r]Dt 1:13,15; 2Ch 19:5-10
18:22 [s]Dt 1:17-18 [t]Nu 11:17
18:25 [u]Dt 1:13-15
18:26 [v]ver 22
18:27 [w]Nu 10:29-30
19:2 [x]Ex 17:1 [y]Ex 3:1
19:3 [z]Ex 3:4; Ac 7:38
19:4 [a]Dt 29:2 [b]Isa 63:9
19:5 [c]Ex 15:26

keep my covenant,[a] then out of all
nations you will be my treasured
possession.[b] Although the whole
earth[c] is mine, 6you[o] will be for
me a kingdom of priests[d] and a
holy nation.'[e] These are the words
you are to speak to the Israelites."
7So Moses went back and summoned the elders of the people and
set before them all the words the
LORD had commanded him to
speak. 8The people all responded
together, "We will do everything
the LORD has said."[f] So Moses
brought their answer back to the
LORD.
9The LORD said to Moses, "I am
going to come to you in a dense
cloud,[g] so that the people will
hear me speaking[h] with you and
will always put their trust in you."
Then Moses told the LORD what the
people had said.
10And the LORD said to Moses,
"Go to the people and consecrate[i]
them today and tomorrow. Have
them wash their clothes[j] 11and be
ready by the third day,[k] because
on that day the LORD will come
down on Mount Sinai in the sight
of all the people. 12Put limits for
the people around the mountain
and tell them, 'Be careful that you
do not go up the mountain or touch
the foot of it. Whoever touches the
mountain shall surely be put to
death. 13He shall surely be
stoned[l] or shot with arrows; not a
hand is to be laid on him. Whether
man or animal, he shall not be permitted to live.' Only when the
ram's horn sounds a long blast may
they go up to the mountain."
14After Moses had gone down
the mountain to the people, he
consecrated them, and they
washed their clothes. 15Then he
said to the people, "Prepare yourselves for the third day. Abstain
from sexual relations."
16On the morning of the third
day there was thunder and lightning, with a thick cloud over the
mountain, and a very loud trumpet
blast.[m] Everyone in the camp trembled.[n] 17Then Moses led the people out of the camp to meet with
God, and they stood at the foot of
the mountain. 18Mount Sinai was
covered with smoke,[o] because the
LORD descended on it in fire.[p] The
smoke billowed up from it like
smoke from a furnace,[q] the whole
mountain[p] trembled[r] violently,
19and the sound of the trumpet
grew louder and louder. Then Moses spoke and the voice[s] of God
answered[t] him.[q]
20The LORD descended to the top
of Mount Sinai and called Moses to
the top of the mountain. So Moses
went up 21and the LORD said to
him, "Go down and warn the people so they do not force their way
through to see[u] the LORD and many
of them perish. 22Even the priests,
who approach[v] the LORD, must
consecrate themselves, or the LORD
will break out against them."[w]
23Moses said to the LORD, "The
people cannot come up Mount Sinai, because you yourself warned
us, 'Put limits[x] around the mountain and set it apart as holy.' "
24The LORD replied, "Go down
and bring Aaron[y] up with you. But
the priests and the people must not
force their way through to come up
to the LORD, or he will break out
against them."
25So Moses went down to the
people and told them.

The Ten Commandments

20:1–17pp — Dt 5:6–21

20 And God spoke all these
words:

2"I am the LORD your God,
who brought you out of
Egypt, out of the land of
slavery.[z]

3"You shall have no other gods
before[r] me.[a]

4"You shall not make for yourself an idol[b] in the form
of anything in heaven
above or on the earth be-
neath or in the waters be-

19:5 [a]Dt 5:2 [b]Dt 14:2; Ps 135:4 [c]Ex 9:29; Dt 10:14
19:6 [d]1Pe 2:5 [e]Dt 7:6; 26:19; Isa 62:12
19:8 [f]Ex 24:3,7; Dt 5:27
19:9 [g]ver 16; Ex 24:15-16 [h]Dt 4:12,36
19:10 [i]Lev 11:44; Heb 10:22 [j]Ge 35:2
19:11 [k]ver 16
19:13 [l]Heb 12.20*
19:16 [m]Heb 12:18-19; Rev 4:1 [n]Heb 12:21
19:18 [o]Ps 104:32 [p]Ex 3:2; 24:17; Dt 4:11; 2Ch 7:1; Ps 18:8; Heb 12:18 [q]Ge 19:28 [r]Jdg 5:5; Ps 68:8; Jer 4:24
19:19 [s]Ne 9:13 [t]Ps 81:7
19:21 [u]Ex 3:5; 1Sa 6:19
19:22 [v]Lev 10:3 [w]2Sa 6:7
19:23 [x]ver 12
19:24 [y]Ex 24:1,9
20:2 [z]Ex 13:3
20:3 [a]Dt 6:14; Jer 35:15
20:4 [b]Lev 26:1; Dt 4:15-19, 23; 27:15

[o]5,6 Or *possession, for the whole earth is mine.* [6]You [p]18 Most Hebrew manuscripts; a few Hebrew manuscripts and Septuagint *all the people* [q]19 Or *and God answered him with thunder* [r]3 Or *besides*

low. 5You shall not bow
down to them or wor-
ship[a] them; for I, the
LORD your God, am a jeal-
ous God,[b] punishing the
children for the sin of the
fathers to the third and
fourth generation[c] of
those who hate me, 6but
showing love to a thou-
sand[d] ⌊generations⌋ of
those who love me and
keep my command-
ments.
7"You shall not misuse the
name of the LORD your
God, for the LORD will not
hold anyone guiltless
who misuses his name.[e]
8"Remember the Sabbath[f] day
by keeping it holy. 9Six
days you shall labor and
do all your work,[g] 10but
the seventh day is a Sab-
bath to the LORD your
God. On it you shall not
do any work, neither you,
nor your son or daughter,
nor your manservant or
maidservant, nor your an-
imals, nor the alien within your gates. 11For in six
days the LORD made the
heavens and the earth,
the sea, and all that is in
them, but he rested[h] on
the seventh day. There-
fore the LORD blessed the
Sabbath day and made it
holy.
12"Honor your father and your
mother,[i] so that you may
live long in the land the
LORD your God is giving
you.
13"You shall not murder.[j]
14"You shall not commit adultery.[k]
15"You shall not steal.[l]
16"You shall not give false testimony against your neigh-
bor.[m]
17"You shall not covet[n] your
neighbor's house. You
shall not covet your
neighbor's wife, or his
manservant or maidser-

20:5 [a]Isa 44:15,17, 19 [b]Ex 34:14; Dt 4:24 [c]Nu 14:18; Jer 32:18
20:6 [d]Dt 7:9
20:7 [e]Lev 19:12; Mt 5:33
20:8 [f]Ex 31:13-16; Lev 26:2
20:9 [g]Ex 34:21; Lk 13:14
20:11 [h]Ge 2:2
20:12 [i]Mt 15:4*; Mk 7:10*; Eph 6:2
20:13 [j]Mt 5:21*; Ro 13:9*
20:14 [k]Mt 19:18*
20:15 [l]Lev 19:11,13; Mt 19:18*
20:16 [m]Ex 23:1,7; Mt 19:18*
20:17 [n]Ro 7:7*; 13:9*; Eph 5:3
20:18 [o]Ex 19:16-19; Heb 12:18-19
20:19 [p]Dt 5:5, 23-27; Gal 3:19
20:20 [q]Dt 4:10; Isa 8:13 [r]Pr 16:6
20:21 [s]Dt 5:22
20:22 [t]Ne 9:13
20:23 [u]ver 3 [v]Ex 32:4,8,31
20:24 [w]Dt 12:5; 16:6,11; 2Ch 6:6 [x]Ge 12:2
20:25 [y]Dt 27:5-6
21:1 [z]Dt 4:14
21:2 [a]Jer 34:8,14

vant, his ox or donkey, or
anything that belongs to
your neighbor."

18When the people saw the
thunder and lightning and heard
the trumpet[o] and saw the mountain in smoke, they trembled with
fear. They stayed at a distance
19and said to Moses, "Speak to us
yourself and we will listen. But do
not have God speak to us or we will
die."[p]
20Moses said to the people, "Do
not be afraid. God has come to test
you, so that the fear[q] of God will
be with you to keep you from sinning."[r]
21The people remained at a distance, while Moses approached the
thick darkness[s] where God was.

Idols and Altars

22Then the LORD said to Moses,
"Tell the Israelites this: 'You have
seen for yourselves that I have spoken to you from heaven:[t] 23Do not
make any gods to be alongside
me;[u] do not make for yourselves
gods of silver or gods of gold.[v]
24" 'Make an altar of earth for
me and sacrifice on it your burnt
offerings and fellowship offerings,[s] your sheep and goats and
your cattle. Wherever I cause my
name[w] to be honored, I will come
to you and bless[x] you. 25If you
make an altar of stones for me, do
not build it with dressed stones, for
you will defile it if you use a tool[y]
on it. 26And do not go up to my altar on steps, lest your nakedness be
exposed on it.'

21 "These are the laws[z] you
are to set before them:

Hebrew Servants

21:2-6pp — Dt 15:12-18
21:2-11Ref — Lev 25:39-55

2"If you buy a Hebrew servant,
he is to serve you for six years. But
in the seventh year, he shall go
free,[a] without paying anything. 3If
he comes alone, he is to go free
alone; but if he has a wife when he

[s]24 Traditionally *peace offerings*

comes, she is to go with him. 4If his
master gives him a wife and she
bears him sons or daughters, the
woman and her children shall belong to her master, and only the
man shall go free.
5"But if the servant declares, 'I
love my master and my wife and
children and do not want to go
free,'[a] 6then his master must take
him before the judges.[t][b] He shall
take him to the door or the door-
post and pierce his ear with an awl.
Then he will be his servant for
life.[c]
7"If a man sells his daughter as a
servant, she is not to go free as
menservants do. 8If she does not
please the master who has selected
her for himself,[u] he must let her be
redeemed. He has no right to sell
her to foreigners, because he has
broken faith with her. 9If he selects
her for his son, he must grant her
the rights of a daughter. 10If he
marries another woman, he must
not deprive the first one of her
food, clothing and marital rights.[d]
11If he does not provide her with
these three things, she is to go free,
without any payment of money.

Personal Injuries

12"Anyone who strikes a man
and kills him shall surely be put to
death.[e] 13However, if he does not
do it intentionally, but God lets it
happen, he is to flee to a place[f] I
will designate. 14But if a man
schemes and kills another man deliberately,[g] take him away from
my altar and put him to death.[h]
15"Anyone who attacks[v] his father or his mother must be put to
death.
16"Anyone who kidnaps another
and either sells[i] him or still has
him when he is caught must be put
to death.[j]
17"Anyone who curses his father
or mother must be put to death.[k]
18"If men quarrel and one hits
the other with a stone or with his
fist[w] and he does not die but is
confined to bed, 19the one who
struck the blow will not be held responsible if the other gets up and
walks around outside with his staff;
however, he must pay the injured
man for the loss of his time and see
that he is completely healed.
20"If a man beats his male or female slave with a rod and the slave
dies as a direct result, he must be
punished, 21but he is not to be
punished if the slave gets up after
a day or two, since the slave is his
property.[l]
22"If men who are fighting hit a
pregnant woman and she gives
birth prematurely[x] but there is no
serious injury, the offender must
be fined whatever the woman's
husband demands[m] and the court
allows. 23But if there is serious injury, you are to take life for life,[n]
24eye for eye, tooth for tooth,[o]
hand for hand, foot for foot, 25burn
for burn, wound for wound, bruise
for bruise.
26"If a man hits a manservant or
maidservant in the eye and destroys it, he must let the servant go
free to compensate for the eye.
27And if he knocks out the tooth of
a manservant or maidservant, he
must let the servant go free to compensate for the tooth.
28"If a bull gores a man or a
woman to death, the bull must be
stoned to death,[p] and its meat
must not be eaten. But the owner
of the bull will not be held responsible. 29If, however, the bull has
had the habit of goring and the
owner has been warned but has not
kept it penned up and it kills a man
or woman, the bull must be stoned
and the owner also must be put to
death. 30However, if payment is
demanded of him, he may redeem
his life by paying whatever is demanded.[q] 31This law also applies
if the bull gores a son or daughter.
32If the bull gores a male or female
slave, the owner must pay thirty
shekels[y][r] of silver to the master of
the slave, and the bull must be
stoned.

21:5 [a]Dt 15:16
21:6 [b]Ex 22:8-9 [c]Ne 5:5
21:10 [d]1Co 7:3-5
21:12 [e]Ge 9:6; Mt 26:52
21:13 [f]Nu 35:10-34; Dt 19:2-13; Jos 20:9; 1Sa 24:4,10, 18
21:14 [g]Heb 10:26 [h]Dt 19:11-12; 1Ki 2:28-34
21:16 [i]Ge 37:28 [j]Ex 22:4; Dt 24:7
21:17 [k]Lev 20:9-10; Mt 15:4*; Mk 7:10*
21:21 [l]Lev 25:44-46
21:22 [m]ver 30; Dt 22:18-19
21:23 [n]Lev 24:19; Dt 19:21
21:24 [o]Mt 5:38*
21:28 [p]ver 32; Ge 9:5
21:30 [q]ver 22; Nu 35:31
21:32 [r]Zec 11:12-13; Mt 26:15; 27:3,9

[t]6 Or *before God* [u]8 Or *master so that he does not choose her* [v]15 Or *kills* [w]18 Or *with a tool* [x]22 Or *she has a miscarriage* [y]32 That is, about 12 ounces (about 0.3 kilogram)

33"If a man uncovers a pit or digs
one and fails to cover it and an ox
or a donkey falls into it, 34the owner of the pit must pay for the loss;
he must pay its owner, and the
dead animal will be his.
35"If a man's bull injures the bull
of another and it dies, they are to
sell the live one and divide both the
money and the dead animal equally. 36However, if it was known that
the bull had the habit of goring, yet
the owner did not keep it penned
up, the owner must pay, animal for
animal, and the dead animal will
be his.

Protection of Property

22 "If a man steals an ox or a
sheep and slaughters it or
sells it, he must pay back[a] five
head of cattle for the ox and four
sheep for the sheep.
2"If a thief is caught breaking
in[b] and is struck so that he dies,
the defender is not guilty of bloodshed;[c] 3but if it happens[z] after
sunrise, he is guilty of bloodshed.
"A thief must certainly make restitution, but if he has nothing, he
must be sold[d] to pay for his theft.
4"If the stolen animal is found
alive in his possession—whether
ox or donkey or sheep—he must
pay back double.[e]
5"If a man grazes his livestock in
a field or vineyard and lets them
stray and they graze in another
man's field, he must make restitution from the best of his own field
or vineyard.
6"If a fire breaks out and spreads
into thornbushes so that it burns
shocks of grain or standing grain or
the whole field, the one who started the fire must make restitution.
7"If a man gives his neighbor silver or goods for safekeeping and
they are stolen from the neighbor's
house, the thief, if he is caught,
must pay back double.[f] 8But if the
thief is not found, the owner of the
house must appear before the
judges[a][g] to determine whether he
has laid his hands on the other
man's property. 9In all cases of illegal possession of an ox, a donkey,
a sheep, a garment, or any other
lost property about which somebody says, 'This is mine,' both parties are to bring their cases before
the judges.[h] The one whom the
judges declare[b] guilty must pay
back double to his neighbor.
10"If a man gives a donkey, an
ox, a sheep or any other animal to
his neighbor for safekeeping and it
dies or is injured or is taken away
while no one is looking, 11the issue
between them will be settled by the
taking of an oath[i] before the LORD
that the neighbor did not lay hands
on the other person's property. The
owner is to accept this, and no restitution is required. 12But if the animal was stolen from the neighbor,
he must make restitution to the
owner. 13If it was torn to pieces by
a wild animal, he shall bring in the
remains as evidence and he will not
be required to pay for the torn animal.[j]
14"If a man borrows an animal
from his neighbor and it is injured
or dies while the owner is not
present, he must make restitution.
15But if the owner is with the animal, the borrower will not have to
pay. If the animal was hired, the
money paid for the hire covers the
loss.

Social Responsibility

16"If a man seduces a virgin[k]
who is not pledged to be married
and sleeps with her, he must pay
the bride-price, and she shall be
his wife. 17If her father absolutely
refuses to give her to him, he must
still pay the bride-price for virgins.
18"Do not allow a sorceress[l] to
live.
19"Anyone who has sexual relations with an animal[m] must be put
to death.
20"Whoever sacrifices to any god
other than the LORD must be destroyed.[c][n]
21"Do not mistreat an alien[o] or

22:1 [a]2Sa 12:6; Pr 6:31; Lk 19:8
22:2 [b]Mt 6:19-20; 24:43 [c]Nu 35:27
22:3 [d]Ex 21:2; Mt 18:25
22:4 [e]Ge 43:12
22:7 [f]ver 4
22:8 [g]Ex 21:6; Dt 17:8-9; 19:17
22:9 [h]ver 28; Dt 25:1
22:11 [i]Heb 6:16
22:13 [j]Ge 31:39
22:16 [k]Dt 22:28
22:18 [l]Lev 20:27; Dt 18:11; 1Sa 28:3
22:19 [m]Lev 18:23; Dt 27:21
22:20 [n]Dt 17:2-5
22:21 [o]Lev 19:33

[z]3 Or *if he strikes him* [a]8 Or *before God*; also in verse 9 [b]9 Or *whom God declares* [c]20 The Hebrew term refers to the irrevocable giving over of things or persons to the LORD, often by totally destroying them.

oppress him, for you were aliens[a]
in Egypt.
22"Do not take advantage of a
widow or an orphan.[b] **23**If you do
and they cry out[c] to me, I will certainly hear their cry.[d] **24**My anger
will be aroused, and I will kill you
with the sword; your wives will become widows and your children fatherless.[e]
25"If you lend money to one of
my people among you who is
needy, do not be like a moneylender; charge him no interest.[d][f] **26**If
you take your neighbor's cloak as a
pledge,[g] return it to him by sunset,
27because his cloak is the only covering he has for his body. What else
will he sleep in? When he cries out
to me, I will hear, for I am compassionate.[h]
28"Do not blaspheme God[e][i] or
curse the ruler of your people.[j]
29"Do not hold back offerings[k]
from your granaries or your vats.[f]
"You must give me the firstborn
of your sons.[l] **30**Do the same with
your cattle and your sheep.[m] Let
them stay with their mothers for
seven days, but give them to me on
the eighth day.[n]
31"You are to be my holy people.[o] So do not eat the meat of an
animal torn by wild beasts;[p] throw
it to the dogs.

Laws of Justice and Mercy

23 "Do not spread false reports.[q] Do not help a wicked man by being a malicious witness.[r]
2"Do not follow the crowd in doing wrong. When you give testimony in a lawsuit, do not pervert justice[s] by siding with the crowd,
3and do not show favoritism to a
poor man in his lawsuit.
4"If you come across your enemy's ox or donkey wandering off,
be sure to take it back to him.[t] **5**If
you see the donkey[u] of someone
who hates you fallen down under
its load, do not leave it there; be
sure you help him with it.
6"Do not deny justice[v] to your
poor people in their lawsuits.
7Have nothing to do with a false
charge[w] and do not put an innocent or honest person to death, for
I will not acquit the guilty.
8"Do not accept a bribe,[x] for a
bribe blinds those who see and
twists the words of the righteous.
9"Do not oppress an alien;[y] you
yourselves know how it feels to be
aliens, because you were aliens in
Egypt.

Sabbath Laws

10"For six years you are to sow
your fields and harvest the crops,
11but during the seventh year let
the land lie unplowed and unused.
Then the poor among your people
may get food from it, and the wild
animals may eat what they leave.
Do the same with your vineyard
and your olive grove.
12"Six days do your work,[z] but
on the seventh day do not work, so
that your ox and your donkey may
rest and the slave born in your
household, and the alien as well,
may be refreshed.
13"Be careful[a] to do everything I
have said to you. Do not invoke the
names of other gods; do not let
them be heard on your lips.

The Three Annual Festivals

14"Three times[b] a year you are
to celebrate a festival to me.
15"Celebrate the Feast of Unleavened Bread;[c] for seven days
eat bread made without yeast, as I
commanded you. Do this at the appointed time in the month of Abib,
for in that month you came out of
Egypt.
"No one is to appear before me
empty-handed.[d]
16"Celebrate the Feast of Harvest with the firstfruits[e] of the
crops you sow in your field.
"Celebrate the Feast of Ingather-
ing at the end of the year, when you
gather in your crops from the
field.[f]
17"Three times[g] a year all the

22:21 [a]Dt 10:19
22:22 [b]Dt 24:6,10,12,17
22:23 [c]Lk 18:7 [d]Dt 15:9; Ps 18:6
22:24 [e]Ps 69:24; 109:9
22:25 [f]Lev 25:35-37; Dt 23:20; Ps 15:5
22:26 [g]Dt 24:6
22:27 [h]Ex 34:6
22:28 [i]Lev 24:11,16 [j]Ecc 10:20; Ac 23:5*
22:29 [k]Ex 23:15,16,19 [l]Ex 13:2
22:30 [m]Ex 13:12; Dt 15:19 [n]Lev 22:27
22:31 [o]Lev 19:2 [p]Eze 4:14
23:1 [q]Ex 20:16; Ps 101:5 [r]Ps 35:11; Ac 6:11
23:2 [s]Dt 16:19
23:4 [t]Dt 22:1-3
23:5 [u]Dt 22:4
23:6 [v]ver 2
23:7 [w]Eph 4:25
23:8 [x]Dt 10:17; 16:19; Pr 15:27
23:9 [y]Ex 22:21
23:12 [z]Ex 20:9
23:13 [a]1Ti 4:16
23:14 [b]Ex 34:23,24
23:15 [c]Ex 12:17 [d]Ex 34:20
23:16 [e]Ex 34:22 [f]Dt 16:13
23:17 [g]Dt 16:16

[d]25 Or *excessive interest* [e]28 Or *Do not revile the judges* [f]29 The meaning of the Hebrew for this phrase is uncertain.

men are to appear before the Sovereign LORD.

18"Do not offer the blood of a sacrifice to me along with anything containing yeast.[a]

"The fat of my festival offerings must not be kept until morning.[b]

19"Bring the best of the firstfruits[c] of your soil to the house of the LORD your God.

"Do not cook a young goat in its mother's milk.[d]

God's Angel to Prepare the Way

20"See, I am sending an angel[e] ahead of you to guard you along the way and to bring you to the place I have prepared.[f] 21Pay attention to him and listen[g] to what he says. Do not rebel against him; he will not forgive your rebellion,[h] since my Name is in him. 22If you listen carefully to what he says and do all that I say, I will be an enemy[i] to your enemies and will oppose those who oppose you. 23My angel will go ahead of you and bring you into the land of the Amorites, Hittites, Perizzites, Canaanites, Hivites and Jebusites,[j] and I will wipe them out. 24Do not bow down before their gods or worship[k] them or follow their practices.[l] You must demolish[m] them and break their sacred stones to pieces. 25Worship the LORD your God,[n] and his blessing[o] will be on your food and water. I will take away sickness[p] from among you, 26and none will miscarry or be barren[q] in your land. I will give you a full life span.[r]

27"I will send my terror[s] ahead of you and throw into confusion[t] every nation you encounter. I will make all your enemies turn their backs and run. 28I will send the hornet[u] ahead of you to drive the Hivites, Canaanites and Hittites out of your way. 29But I will not drive them out in a single year, because the land would become desolate and the wild animals[v] too numerous for you. 30Little by little I will drive them out before you, until you have increased enough to take possession of the land.

31"I will establish your borders from the Red Sea[g] to the Sea of the Philistines,[h] and from the desert to the River.[i w] I will hand over to you the people who live in the land and you will drive them out[x] before you. 32Do not make a covenant[y] with them or with their gods. 33Do not let them live in your land, or they will cause you to sin against me, because the worship of their gods will certainly be a snare[z] to you."

The Covenant Confirmed

24 Then he said to Moses, "Come up to the LORD, you and Aaron, Nadab and Abihu,[a] and seventy of the elders[b] of Israel. You are to worship at a distance, 2but Moses alone is to approach the LORD; the others must not come near. And the people may not come up with him."

3When Moses went and told the people all the LORD's words and laws, they responded with one voice, "Everything the LORD has said we will do."[c] 4Moses then wrote[d] down everything the LORD had said.

He got up early the next morning and built an altar at the foot of the mountain and set up twelve stone pillars[e] representing the twelve tribes of Israel. 5Then he sent young Israelite men, and they offered burnt offerings and sacrificed young bulls as fellowship offerings[j] to the LORD. 6Moses took half of the blood[f] and put it in bowls, and the other half he sprinkled on the altar. 7Then he took the Book of the Covenant[g] and read it to the people. They responded, "We will do everything the LORD has said; we will obey."

8Moses then took the blood, sprinkled it on the people and said, "This is the blood of the covenant[h] that the LORD has made with you in

23:18 [a]Ex 34:25 [b]Dt 16:4
23:19 [c]Ex 22:29; Dt 26:2,10 [d]Dt 14:21
23:20 [e]Ex 14:19; 32:34 [f]Ex 15:17
23:21 [g]Nu 14:11; Dt 18:19 [h]Ps 78:8,40, 56
23:22 [i]Ge 12:3; Dt 30:7
23:23 [j]ver 20; Jos 24:8,11
23:24 [k]Ex 20:5 [l]Dt 12:30-31 [m]Ex 34:13; Nu 33:52
23:25 [n]Dt 6:13; Mt 4:10 [o]Dt 7:12-15; 28:1-14 [p]Ex 15:26
23:26 [q]Dt 7:14; Mal 3:11 [r]Job 5:26
23:27 [s]Ex 15:14; Dt 2:25 [t]Dt 7:23
23:28 [u]Dt 7:20; Jos 24:12
23:29 [v]Dt 7:22
23:31 [w]Ge 15:18 [x]Jos 21:44; 24:12,18
23:32 [y]Ex 34:12; Dt 7:2
23:33 [z]Dt 7:16; Ps 106:36
24:1 [a]Ex 6:23; Lev 10:1-2 [b]Nu 11:16
24:3 [c]Ex 19:8; Dt 5:27
24:4 [d]Dt 31:9 [e]Ge 28:18
24:6 [f]Heb 9:18
24:7 [g]Heb 9:19
24:8 [h]Heb 9:20*; 1Pe 1:2

[g]31 Hebrew *Yam Suph*; that is, Sea of Reeds [h]31 That is, the Mediterranean [i]31 That is, the Euphrates [j]5 Traditionally *peace offerings*

accordance with all these words."
9Moses and Aaron, Nadab and
Abihu, and the seventy elders[a] of
Israel went up 10and saw[b] the God
of Israel. Under his feet was something like a pavement made of sapphire,[k][c] clear as the sky[d] itself.
11But God did not raise his hand
against these leaders of the Israelites; they saw[e] God, and they ate
and drank.
12The LORD said to Moses,
"Come up to me on the mountain
and stay here, and I will give you
the tablets of stone,[f] with the law
and commands I have written for
their instruction."
13Then Moses set out with Joshua[g] his aide, and Moses went up
on the mountain[h] of God. 14He
said to the elders, "Wait here for us
until we come back to you. Aaron
and Hur are with you, and anyone
involved in a dispute can go to
them."
15When Moses went up on the
mountain, the cloud[i] covered it,
16and the glory[j] of the LORD settled on Mount Sinai. For six days
the cloud covered the mountain,
and on the seventh day the LORD
called to Moses from within the
cloud.[k] 17To the Israelites the glory of the LORD looked like a consuming fire[l] on top of the mountain. 18Then Moses entered the
cloud as he went on up the mountain. And he stayed on the mountain forty[m] days and forty nights.[n]

Offerings for the Tabernacle

25:1–7pp — Ex 35:4–9

25 The LORD said to Moses,
2"Tell the Israelites to bring
me an offering. You are to receive
the offering for me from each man
whose heart prompts[o] him to give.
3These are the offerings you are to
receive from them: gold, silver and
bronze; 4blue, purple and scarlet
yarn and fine linen; goat hair; 5ram
skins dyed red and hides of sea
cows[l]; acacia wood; 6olive oil[p] for
the light; spices for the anointing
oil and for the fragrant incense;
7and onyx stones and other gems
to be mounted on the ephod[q] and
breastpiece.[r]
8"Then have them make a sanctuary[s] for me, and I will dwell[t]
among them. 9Make this tabernacle and all its furnishings exactly
like the pattern[u] I will show you.

The Ark

25:10–20pp — Ex 37:1–9

10"Have them make a chest[v] of
acacia wood—two and a half cubits
long, a cubit and a half wide, and a
cubit and a half high.[m] 11Overlay it
with pure gold, both inside and
out, and make a gold molding
around it. 12Cast four gold rings for
it and fasten them to its four feet,
with two rings on one side and two
rings on the other. 13Then make
poles of acacia wood and overlay
them with gold. 14Insert the poles
into the rings on the sides of the
chest to carry it. 15The poles are to
remain in the rings of this ark; they
are not to be removed.[w] 16Then
put in the ark the Testimony,[x]
which I will give you.
17"Make an atonement cover[n][y]
of pure gold—two and a half cubits
long and a cubit and a half wide.[o]
18And make two cherubim out of
hammered gold at the ends of the
cover. 19Make one cherub on one
end and the second cherub on the
other; make the cherubim of one
piece with the cover, at the two
ends. 20The cherubim are to have
their wings spread upward, overshadowing[z] the cover with them.
The cherubim are to face each other, looking toward the cover.
21Place the cover on top of the
ark[a] and put in the ark the Testimony,[b] which I will give you.
22There, above the cover between
the two cherubim[c] that are over
the ark of the Testimony, I will
meet[d] with you and give you all my
commands for the Israelites.

24:9 [a]ver 1 **24:10** [b]Mt 17:2; Jn 1:18; 6:46 [c]Eze 1:26 [d]Rev 4:3 **24:11** [e]Ge 32:30; Ex 19:21 **24:12** [f]Ex 32:15-16 **24:13** [g]Ex 17:9 [h]Ex 3:1 **24:15** [i]Ex 19:9 **24:16** [j]Ex 16:10 [k]Ps 99:7 **24:17** [l]Ex 3:2; Dt 4:36; Heb 12:18,29 **24:18** [m]Dt 9:9 [n]Ex 34:28 **25:2** [o]Ex 35:21; 1Ch 29:5,7,9; Ezr 2:68; 2Co 8:11-12; 9:7 **25:6** [p]Ex 27:20; 30:22-32 **25:7** [q]Ex 28:4,6-14 [r]Ex 28:15-30 **25:8** [s]Ex 36:1-5; Heb 9:1-2 [t]Ex 29:45; 1Ki 6:13; 2Co 6:16; Rev 21:3 **25:9** [u]ver 40; Ac 7:44; Heb 8:5 **25:10** [v]Dt 10:1-5; Heb 9:4 **25:15** [w]1Ki 8:8 **25:16** [x]Dt 31:26; Heb 9:4 **25:17** [y]Ro 3:25 **25:20** [z]1Ki 8:7; 1Ch 28:18; Heb 9:5 **25:21** [a]Ex 26:34 [b]ver 16 **25:22** [c]Nu 7:89; 1Sa 4:4; 2Sa 6:2; 2Ki 19:15; Ps 80:1; Isa 37:16 [d]Ex 29:42-43

[k]*10* Or *lapis lazuli* [l]*5* That is, dugongs [m]*10* That is, about 3 3/4 feet (about 1.1 meters) long and 2 1/4 feet (about 0.7 meter) wide and high [n]*17* Traditionally *a mercy seat* [o]*17* That is, about 3 3/4 feet (about 1.1 meters) long and 2 1/4 feet (about 0.7 meter) wide

The Table

25:23–29pp — Ex 37:10–16

23"Make a table[a] of acacia wood—two cubits long, a cubit wide and a cubit and a half high.[p] 24Overlay it with pure gold and make a gold molding around it. 25Also make around it a rim a handbreadth[q] wide and put a gold molding on the rim. 26Make four gold rings for the table and fasten them to the four corners, where the four legs are. 27The rings are to be close to the rim to hold the poles used in carrying the table. 28Make the poles of acacia wood, overlay them with gold and carry the table with them. 29And make its plates and dishes of pure gold, as well as its pitchers and bowls for the pouring out of offerings.[b] 30Put the bread of the Presence[c] on this table to be before me at all times.

The Lampstand

25:31–39pp — Ex 37:17–24

31"Make a lampstand[d] of pure gold and hammer it out, base and shaft; its flowerlike cups, buds and blossoms shall be of one piece with it. 32Six branches are to extend from the sides of the lampstand—three on one side and three on the other. 33Three cups shaped like almond flowers with buds and blossoms are to be on one branch, three on the next branch, and the same for all six branches extending from the lampstand. 34And on the lampstand there are to be four cups shaped like almond flowers with buds and blossoms. 35One bud shall be under the first pair of branches extending from the lampstand, a second bud under the second pair, and a third bud under the third pair—six branches in all. 36The buds and branches shall all be of one piece with the lampstand, hammered out of pure gold.

37"Then make its seven lamps[e] and set them up on it so that they light the space in front of it. 38Its wick trimmers and trays are to be of pure gold. 39A talent[r] of pure gold is to be used for the lampstand and all these accessories. 40See that you make them according to the pattern[f] shown you on the mountain.

25:23 [a]Heb 9:2
25:29 [b]Nu 4:7
25:30 [c]Lev 24:5-9
25:31 [d]1Ki 7:49; Zec 4:2; Heb 9:2; Rev 1:12
25:37 [e]Ex 27:21; Lev 24:3-4; Nu 8:2
25:40 [f]Ex 26:30; Nu 8:4; Ac 7:44; Heb 8:5*

The Tabernacle

26:1–37pp — Ex 36:8–38

26 "Make the tabernacle with ten curtains of finely twisted linen and blue, purple and scarlet yarn, with cherubim worked into them by a skilled craftsman. 2All the curtains are to be the same size—twenty-eight cubits long and four cubits wide.[s] 3Join five of the curtains together, and do the same with the other five. 4Make loops of blue material along the edge of the end curtain in one set, and do the same with the end curtain in the other set. 5Make fifty loops on one curtain and fifty loops on the end curtain of the other set, with the loops opposite each other. 6Then make fifty gold clasps and use them to fasten the curtains together so that the tabernacle is a unit.

7"Make curtains of goat hair for the tent over the tabernacle—eleven altogether. 8All eleven curtains are to be the same size—thirty cubits long and four cubits wide.[t] 9Join five of the curtains together into one set and the other six into another set. Fold the sixth curtain double at the front of the tent. 10Make fifty loops along the edge of the end curtain in one set and also along the edge of the end curtain in the other set. 11Then make fifty bronze clasps and put them in the loops to fasten the tent together as a unit. 12As for the additional length of the tent curtains, the half curtain that is left over is to hang down at the rear of the tabernacle. 13The tent curtains will be a cubit[u]

[p]*23* That is, about 3 feet (about 0.9 meter) long and 1 1/2 feet (about 0.5 meter) wide and 2 1/4 feet (about 0.7 meter) high [q]*25* That is, about 3 inches (about 8 centimeters) [r]*39* That is, about 75 pounds (about 34 kilograms) [s]*2* That is, about 42 feet (about 12.5 meters) long and 6 feet (about 1.8 meters) wide [t]*8* That is, about 45 feet (about 13.5 meters) long and 6 feet (about 1.8 meters) wide [u]*13* That is, about 1 1/2 feet (about 0.5 meter)

longer on both sides; what is left
will hang over the sides of the tabernacle so as to cover it. **14**Make for
the tent a covering of ram skins
dyed red, and over that a covering
of hides of sea cows.[v][a]
15"Make upright frames of acacia wood for the tabernacle. **16**Each
frame is to be ten cubits long and a
cubit and a half wide,[w] **17**with two
projections set parallel to each other. Make all the frames of the tabernacle in this way. **18**Make twenty
frames for the south side of the tabernacle **19**and make forty silver
bases to go under them—two bases
for each frame, one under each
projection. **20**For the other side,
the north side of the tabernacle,
make twenty frames **21**and forty silver bases—two under each frame.
22Make six frames for the far end,
that is, the west end of the tabernacle, **23**and make two frames for the
corners at the far end. **24**At these
two corners they must be double
from the bottom all the way to the
top, and fitted into a single ring;
both shall be like that. **25**So there
will be eight frames and sixteen silver bases—two under each frame.
26"Also make crossbars of acacia
wood: five for the frames on one
side of the tabernacle, **27**five for
those on the other side, and five for
the frames on the west, at the far
end of the tabernacle. **28**The center
crossbar is to extend from end to
end at the middle of the frames.
29Overlay the frames with gold and
make gold rings to hold the crossbars. Also overlay the crossbars
with gold.
30"Set up the tabernacle according to the plan[b] shown you on the
mountain.
31"Make a curtain[c] of blue, purple and scarlet yarn and finely
twisted linen, with cherubim[d]
worked into it by a skilled craftsman. **32**Hang it with gold hooks on
four posts of acacia wood overlaid
with gold and standing on four silver bases. **33**Hang the curtain from
the clasps and place the ark of the
Testimony behind the curtain.[e]
The curtain will separate the Holy
Place from the Most Holy Place.[f]
34Put the atonement cover[g] on the
ark of the Testimony in the Most
Holy Place. **35**Place the table[h] outside the curtain on the north side
of the tabernacle and put the lampstand[i] opposite it on the south
side.
36"For the entrance to the tent
make a curtain of blue, purple and
scarlet yarn and finely twisted lin-
en—the work of an embroiderer.
37Make gold hooks for this curtain
and five posts of acacia wood overlaid with gold. And cast five bronze
bases for them.

The Altar of Burnt Offering

27:1–8pp — Ex 38:1–7

27 "Build an altar[j] of acacia
wood, three cubits[x] high; it
is to be square, five cubits long and
five cubits wide.[y] **2**Make a horn[k]
at each of the four corners, so that
the horns and the altar are of one
piece, and overlay the altar with
bronze. **3**Make all its utensils of
bronze—its pots to remove the
ashes, and its shovels, sprinkling
bowls, meat forks and firepans.
4Make a grating for it, a bronze network, and make a bronze ring at
each of the four corners of the network. **5**Put it under the ledge of the
altar so that it is halfway up the altar. **6**Make poles of acacia wood for
the altar and overlay them with
bronze. **7**The poles are to be inserted into the rings so they will be on
two sides of the altar when it is carried. **8**Make the altar hollow, out of
boards. It is to be made just as you
were shown[l] on the mountain.

The Courtyard

27:9–19pp — Ex 38:9–20

9"Make a courtyard for the tabernacle. The south side shall be a
hundred cubits[z] long and is to

26:14 [a]Ex 36:19; Nu 4:25
26:30 [b]Ex 25:9,40; Ac 7:44; Heb 8:5
26:31 [c]2Ch 3:14; Mt 27:51; Heb 9:3 [d]Ex 36:35
26:33 [e]Ex 40:3,21; Lev 16:2 [f]Heb 9:2-3
26:34 [g]Ex 25:21; 40:20; Heb 9:5
26:35 [h]Heb 9:2 [i]Ex 40:22,24
27:1 [j]Eze 43:13
27:2 [k]Ps 118:27
27:8 [l]Ex 25:9,40

[v]*14* That is, dugongs [w]*16* That is, about 15 feet (about 4.5 meters) long and 2 1/4 feet (about 0.7 meter) wide [x]*1* That is, about 4 1/2 feet (about 1.3 meters) [y]*1* That is, about 7 1/2 feet (about 2.3 meters) long and wide [z]*9* That is, about 150 feet (about 46 meters); also in verse 11

have curtains of finely twisted lin-
en, **10**with twenty posts and twenty
bronze bases and with silver hooks
and bands on the posts. **11**The
north side shall also be a hundred
cubits long and is to have curtains,
with twenty posts and twenty
bronze bases and with silver hooks
and bands on the posts.

12"The west end of the courtyard
shall be fifty cubits[a] wide and have
curtains, with ten posts and ten
bases. **13**On the east end, toward
the sunrise, the courtyard shall
also be fifty cubits wide. **14**Curtains
fifteen cubits[b] long are to be on
one side of the entrance, with three
posts and three bases, **15**and curtains fifteen cubits long are to be
on the other side, with three posts
and three bases.

16"For the entrance to the courtyard, provide a curtain twenty cubits[c] long, of blue, purple and
scarlet yarn and finely twisted lin-
en—the work of an embroiderer
—with four posts and four bases.
17All the posts around the courtyard are to have silver bands and
hooks, and bronze bases. **18**The
courtyard shall be a hundred cubits
long and fifty cubits wide,[d] with
curtains of finely twisted linen five
cubits[e] high, and with bronze bases. **19**All the other articles used
in the service of the tabernacle,
whatever their function, including
all the tent pegs for it and those
for the courtyard, are to be of
bronze.

Oil for the Lampstand

27:20–21pp — Lev 24:1–3

20"Command the Israelites to
bring you clear oil of pressed olives
for the light so that the lamps may
be kept burning. **21**In the Tent of
Meeting,[a] outside the curtain that
is in front of the Testimony,[b] Aaron and his sons are to keep the
lamps[c] burning before the LORD
from evening till morning. This is
to be a lasting ordinance[d] among
the Israelites for the generations to
come.

The Priestly Garments

28 "Have Aaron[e] your brother
brought to you from among
the Israelites, along with his sons
Nadab and Abihu, Eleazar and Ithamar, so they may serve me as
priests.[f] **2**Make sacred garments[g]
for your brother Aaron, to give him
dignity and honor. **3**Tell all the
skilled men[h] to whom I have given
wisdom[i] in such matters that they
are to make garments for Aaron, for
his consecration, so he may serve
me as priest. **4**These are the garments they are to make: a breastpiece,[j] an ephod, a robe,[k] a woven tunic,[l] a turban and a sash.
They are to make these sacred garments for your brother Aaron and
his sons, so they may serve me as
priests. **5**Have them use gold, and
blue, purple and scarlet yarn, and
fine linen.

The Ephod

28:6–14pp — Ex 39:2–7

6"Make the ephod of gold, and of
blue, purple and scarlet yarn, and
of finely twisted linen—the work of
a skilled craftsman. **7**It is to have
two shoulder pieces attached to
two of its corners, so it can be fastened. **8**Its skillfully woven waistband is to be like it—of one piece
with the ephod and made with
gold, and with blue, purple and
scarlet yarn, and with finely twisted linen.

9"Take two onyx stones and engrave on them the names of the
sons of Israel **10**in the order of their
birth—six names on one stone and
the remaining six on the other.
11Engrave the names of the sons of
Israel on the two stones the way a
gem cutter engraves a seal. Then
mount the stones in gold filigree
settings **12**and fasten them on the
shoulder pieces of the ephod as

27:21 [a]Ex 28:43 [b]Ex 26:31,33 [c]Ex 25:37; 30:8; 1Sa 3:3; 2Ch 13:11 [d]Ex 29:9; Lev 3:17; 16:34; Nu 18:23; 19:21

28:1 [e]Heb 5:4 [f]Nu 18:1-7; Heb 5:1

28:2 [g]Ex 29:5,29; 31:10; 39:1; Lev 8:7-9,30

28:3 [h]Ex 31:6; 36:1 [i]Ex 31:3

28:4 [j]ver 15-30 [k]ver 31-35 [l]ver 39

[a]*12* That is, about 75 feet (about 23 meters); also in verse 13 [b]*14* That is, about 22 1/2 feet (about 6.9 meters); also in verse 15
[c]*16* That is, about 30 feet (about 9 meters)
[d]*18* That is, about 150 feet (about 46 meters) long and 75 feet (about 23 meters) wide
[e]*18* That is, about 7 1/2 feet (about 2.3 meters)

memorial stones for the sons of Israel. Aaron is to bear the names on his shoulders as a memorial before the LORD. 13Make gold filigree settings 14and two braided chains of pure gold, like a rope, and attach the chains to the settings.

The Breastpiece

28:15–28pp — Ex 39:8–21

15"Fashion a breastpiece for making decisions—the work of a skilled craftsman. Make it like the ephod: of gold, and of blue, purple and scarlet yarn, and of finely twisted linen. 16It is to be square —a span[f] long and a span wide —and folded double. 17Then mount four rows of precious stones on it. In the first row there shall be a ruby, a topaz and a beryl; 18in the second row a turquoise, a sapphire[g] and an emerald; 19in the third row a jacinth, an agate and an amethyst; 20in the fourth row a chrysolite, an onyx and a jasper.[h] Mount them in gold filigree settings. 21There are to be twelve stones, one for each of the names of the sons of Israel, each engraved like a seal with the name of one of the twelve tribes.

22"For the breastpiece make braided chains of pure gold, like a rope. 23Make two gold rings for it and fasten them to two corners of the breastpiece. 24Fasten the two gold chains to the rings at the corners of the breastpiece, 25and the other ends of the chains to the two settings, attaching them to the shoulder pieces of the ephod at the front. 26Make two gold rings and attach them to the other two corners of the breastpiece on the inside edge next to the ephod. 27Make two more gold rings and attach them to the bottom of the shoulder pieces on the front of the ephod, close to the seam just above the waistband of the ephod. 28The rings of the breastpiece are to be tied to the rings of the ephod with blue cord, connecting it to the waistband, so that the breastpiece will not swing out from the ephod.

28:29 [a]ver 12

28:30 [b]Lev 8:8; Nu 27:21; Dt 33:8; Ezr 2:63; Ne 7:65

28:36 [c]Zec 14:20

28:38 [d]Lev 10:17; 22:9,16; Nu 18:1; Heb 9:28; 1Pe 2:24

28:40 [e]ver 4; Ex 39:41

29"Whenever Aaron enters the Holy Place,[a] he will bear the names of the sons of Israel over his heart on the breastpiece of decision as a continuing memorial before the LORD. 30Also put the Urim and the Thummim[b] in the breastpiece, so they may be over Aaron's heart whenever he enters the presence of the LORD. Thus Aaron will always bear the means of making decisions for the Israelites over his heart before the LORD.

Other Priestly Garments

28:31–43pp — Ex 39:22–31

31"Make the robe of the ephod entirely of blue cloth, 32with an opening for the head in its center. There shall be a woven edge like a collar[i] around this opening, so that it will not tear. 33Make pomegranates of blue, purple and scarlet yarn around the hem of the robe, with gold bells between them. 34The gold bells and the pomegranates are to alternate around the hem of the robe. 35Aaron must wear it when he ministers. The sound of the bells will be heard when he enters the Holy Place before the LORD and when he comes out, so that he will not die.

36"Make a plate of pure gold and engrave on it as on a seal: HOLY TO THE LORD.[c] 37Fasten a blue cord to it to attach it to the turban; it is to be on the front of the turban. 38It will be on Aaron's forehead, and he will bear the guilt[d] involved in the sacred gifts the Israelites consecrate, whatever their gifts may be. It will be on Aaron's forehead continually so that they will be acceptable to the LORD.

39"Weave the tunic of fine linen and make the turban of fine linen. The sash is to be the work of an embroiderer. 40Make tunics, sashes and headbands for Aaron's sons,[e] to give them dignity and

[f]*16* That is, about 9 inches (about 22 centimeters) [g]*18* Or *lapis lazuli* [h]*20* The precise identification of some of these precious stones is uncertain. [i]*32* The meaning of the Hebrew for this word is uncertain.

honor. 41After you put these clothes on your brother Aaron and his sons, anoint[a] and ordain them. Consecrate them so they may serve me as priests.[b]

42"Make linen undergarments[c] as a covering for the body, reaching from the waist to the thigh. 43Aaron and his sons must wear them whenever they enter the Tent of Meeting[d] or approach the altar to minister in the Holy Place, so that they will not incur guilt and die.[e]

"This is to be a lasting ordinance[f] for Aaron and his descendants.

Consecration of the Priests

29:1–37pp — Lev 8:1–36

29 "This is what you are to do to consecrate them, so they may serve me as priests: Take a young bull and two rams without defect. 2And from fine wheat flour, without yeast, make bread, and cakes mixed with oil, and wafers spread with oil.[g] 3Put them in a basket and present them in it—along with the bull and the two rams. 4Then bring Aaron and his sons to the entrance to the Tent of Meeting and wash them with water.[h] 5Take the garments[i] and dress Aaron with the tunic, the robe of the ephod, the ephod itself and the breastpiece. Fasten the ephod on him by its skillfully woven waistband.[j] 6Put the turban on his head and attach the sacred diadem[k] to the turban. 7Take the anointing oil[l] and anoint him by pouring it on his head. 8Bring his sons and dress them in tunics 9and put headbands on them. Then tie sashes on Aaron and his sons.[i][m] The priesthood is theirs by a lasting ordinance.[n] In this way you shall ordain Aaron and his sons.

10"Bring the bull to the front of the Tent of Meeting, and Aaron and his sons shall lay their hands on its head. 11Slaughter it in the LORD's presence at the entrance to the Tent of Meeting. 12Take some of the bull's blood and put it on the horns[o] of the altar with your finger, and pour out the rest of it at the base of the altar. 13Then take all the fat[p] around the inner parts, the covering of the liver, and both kidneys with the fat on them, and burn them on the altar. 14But burn the bull's flesh and its hide and its offal outside the camp.[q] It is a sin offering.

15"Take one of the rams, and Aaron and his sons shall lay their hands on its head. 16Slaughter it and take the blood and sprinkle it against the altar on all sides. 17Cut the ram into pieces and wash the inner parts and the legs, putting them with the head and the other pieces. 18Then burn the entire ram on the altar. It is a burnt offering to the LORD, a pleasing aroma,[r] an offering made to the LORD by fire.

19"Take the other ram,[s] and Aaron and his sons shall lay their hands on its head. 20Slaughter it, take some of its blood and put it on the lobes of the right ears of Aaron and his sons, on the thumbs of their right hands, and on the big toes of their right feet. Then sprinkle blood against the altar on all sides. 21And take some of the blood[t] on the altar and some of the anointing oil[u] and sprinkle it on Aaron and his garments and on his sons and their garments. Then he and his sons and their garments will be consecrated.[v]

22"Take from this ram the fat, the fat tail, the fat around the inner parts, the covering of the liver, both kidneys with the fat on them, and the right thigh. (This is the ram for the ordination.) 23From the basket of bread made without yeast, which is before the LORD, take a loaf, and a cake made with oil, and a wafer. 24Put all these in the hands of Aaron and his sons and wave them before the LORD as a wave offering.[w] 25Then take them from their hands and burn them on the altar along with the burnt offering for a pleasing aroma to the LORD, an offering made to the LORD by fire. 26After you take the breast

28:41 [a] Ex 29:7; Lev 10:7 [b] Ex 29:7-9; 30:30; 40:15; Lev 8:1-36; Heb 7:28
28:42 [c] Lev 6:10; 16:4,23; Eze 44:18
28:43 [d] Ex 27:21 [e] Ex 20:26 [f] Lev 17:7
29:2 [g] Lev 2:1,4; 6:19-23
29:4 [h] Ex 40:12; Heb 10:22
29:5 [i] Ex 28:2; Lev 8:7 [j] Ex 28:8
29:6 [k] Lev 8:9
29:7 [l] Ex 30:25,30, 31; Lev 8:12; 21:10; Nu 35:25; Ps 133:2
29:9 [m] Ex 28:40 [n] Ex 40:15; Nu 3:10; 18:7; 25:13; Dt 18:5
29:12 [o] Ex 27:2
29:13 [p] Lev 3:3,5,9
29:14 [q] Lev 4:11-12, 21; Heb 13:11
29:18 [r] Ge 8:21
29:19 [s] ver 3
29:21 [t] Heb 9:22 [u] Ex 30:25,31 [v] ver 1
29:24 [w] Lev 7:30

i9 Hebrew; Septuagint *on them*

of the ram for Aaron's ordination, wave it before the LORD as a wave offering, and it will be your share.[a]

27"Consecrate those parts of the ordination ram that belong to Aaron and his sons:[b] the breast that was waved and the thigh that was presented. **28**This is always to be the regular share from the Israelites for Aaron and his sons. It is the contribution the Israelites are to make to the LORD from their fellowship offerings.[k][c]

29"Aaron's sacred garments will belong to his descendants so that they can be anointed and ordained in them.[d] **30**The son[e] who succeeds him as priest and comes to the Tent of Meeting to minister in the Holy Place is to wear them seven days.

31"Take the ram for the ordination and cook the meat in a sacred place. **32**At the entrance to the Tent of Meeting, Aaron and his sons are to eat the meat of the ram and the bread[f] that is in the basket. **33**They are to eat these offerings by which atonement was made for their ordination and consecration. But no one else may eat[g] them, because they are sacred. **34**And if any of the meat of the ordination ram or any bread is left over till morning,[h] burn it up. It must not be eaten, because it is sacred.

35"Do for Aaron and his sons everything I have commanded you, taking seven days to ordain them. **36**Sacrifice a bull each day[i] as a sin offering to make atonement. Purify the altar by making atonement for it, and anoint it to consecrate[j] it. **37**For seven days make atonement for the altar and consecrate it. Then the altar will be most holy, and whatever touches it will be holy.[k]

38"This is what you are to offer on the altar regularly each day:[l] two lambs a year old. **39**Offer one in the morning and the other at twilight.[m] **40**With the first lamb offer a tenth of an ephah[l] of fine flour mixed with a quarter of a hin[m] of oil from pressed olives, and a quarter of a hin of wine as a drink offering. **41**Sacrifice the other lamb at twilight with the same grain offering and its drink offering as in the morning—a pleasing aroma, an offering made to the LORD by fire.

42"For the generations to come[n] this burnt offering is to be made regularly at the entrance to the Tent of Meeting before the LORD. There I will meet you and speak to you;[o] **43**there also I will meet with the Israelites, and the place will be consecrated by my glory.[p]

44"So I will consecrate the Tent of Meeting and the altar and will consecrate Aaron and his sons to serve me as priests.[q] **45**Then I will dwell[r] among the Israelites and be their God.[s] **46**They will know that I am the LORD their God, who brought them out of Egypt so that I might dwell among them. I am the LORD their God.[t]

The Altar of Incense

30:1–5pp — Ex 37:25–28

30 "Make an altar[u] of acacia wood for burning incense.[v] **2**It is to be square, a cubit long and a cubit wide, and two cubits high[n]—its horns[w] of one piece with it. **3**Overlay the top and all the sides and the horns with pure gold, and make a gold molding around it. **4**Make two gold rings for the altar below the molding—two on opposite sides—to hold the poles used to carry it. **5**Make the poles of acacia wood and overlay them with gold. **6**Put the altar in front of the curtain that is before the ark of the Testimony—before the atonement cover[x] that is over the Testimony—where I will meet with you.

7"Aaron must burn fragrant incense[y] on the altar every morning when he tends the lamps. **8**He must burn incense again when he lights the lamps at twilight so incense will burn regularly before the LORD for the generations to come.

29:26 [a]Lev 7:31-34
29:27 [b]Lev 7:31,34; Dt 18:3
29:28 [c]Lev 10:15
29:29 [d]Nu 20:26,28
29:30 [e]Nu 20:28
29:32 [f]Mt 12:4
29:33 [g]Lev 10:14; 22:10,13
29:34 [h]Ex 12:10
29:36 [i]Heb 10:11 [j]Ex 40:10
29:37 [k]Ex 30:28-29; 40:10; Mt 23:19
29:38 [l]Nu 28:3-8; 1Ch 16:40; Da 12:11
29:39 [m]Eze 46:13-15
29:42 [n]Ex 30:8 [o]Ex 25:22
29:43 [p]1Ki 8:11
29:44 [q]Lev 21:15
29:45 [r]Ex 25:8; Lev 26:12; Zec 2:10; Jn 14:17 [s]2Co 6:16; Rev 21:3
29:46 [t]Ex 20:2
30:1 [u]Ex 37:25 [v]Rev 8:3
30:2 [w]Ex 27:2
30:6 [x]Ex 25:22; 26:34
30:7 [y]ver 34-35; Ex 27:21; 1Sa 2:28

[k]*28* Traditionally *peace offerings* [l]*40* That is, probably about 2 quarts (about 2 liters) [m]*40* That is, probably about 1 quart (about 1 liter) [n]*2* That is, about 1 1/2 feet (about 0.5 meter) long and wide and about 3 feet (about 0.9 meter) high

9Do not offer on this altar any other
incense[a] or any burnt offering or
grain offering, and do not pour a
drink offering on it. **10**Once a year
Aaron shall make atonement[b] on
its horns. This annual atonement
must be made with the blood of the
atoning sin offering for the generations to come. It is most holy to the
LORD."

Atonement Money

11Then the LORD said to Moses,
12"When you take a census[c] of the
Israelites to count them, each one
must pay the LORD a ransom[d] for
his life at the time he is counted.
Then no plague[e] will come on
them when you number them.
13Each one who crosses over to
those already counted is to give a
half shekel,[o] according to the
sanctuary shekel,[f] which weighs
twenty gerahs. This half shekel is
an offering to the LORD. **14**All who
cross over, those twenty years old
or more, are to give an offering to
the LORD. **15**The rich are not to give
more than a half shekel and the
poor are not to give less[g] when you
make the offering to the LORD to
atone for your lives. **16**Receive the
atonement money from the Israelites and use it for the service of the
Tent of Meeting.[h] It will be a memorial for the Israelites before the
LORD, making atonement for your
lives."

Basin for Washing

17Then the LORD said to Moses,
18"Make a bronze basin,[i] with its
bronze stand, for washing. Place it
between the Tent of Meeting and
the altar, and put water in it. **19**Aaron and his sons are to wash their
hands and feet[j] with water[k] from
it. **20**Whenever they enter the Tent
of Meeting, they shall wash with
water so that they will not die.
Also, when they approach the altar
to minister by presenting an offering made to the LORD by fire, **21**they
shall wash their hands and feet so
that they will not die. This is to be
a lasting ordinance[l] for Aaron and
his descendants for the generations to come."

Anointing Oil

22Then the LORD said to Moses,
23"Take the following fine spices:
500 shekels[p] of liquid myrrh,[m]
half as much (that is, 250 shekels)
of fragrant cinnamon, 250 shekels
of fragrant cane, **24**500 shekels of
cassia[n]—all according to the sanctuary shekel—and a hin[q] of olive
oil. **25**Make these into a sacred
anointing oil, a fragrant blend, the
work of a perfumer.[o] It will be the
sacred anointing oil.[p] **26**Then use
it to anoint[q] the Tent of Meeting,
the ark of the Testimony, **27**the table and all its articles, the lampstand and its accessories, the altar
of incense, **28**the altar of burnt offering and all its utensils, and the
basin with its stand. **29**You shall
consecrate them so they will be
most holy, and whatever touches
them will be holy.[r]
30"Anoint Aaron and his sons
and consecrate[s] them so they may
serve me as priests. **31**Say to the Israelites, 'This is to be my sacred
anointing oil for the generations to
come. **32**Do not pour it on men's
bodies and do not make any oil
with the same formula. It is sacred,
and you are to consider it sacred.[t]
33Whoever makes perfume like it
and whoever puts it on anyone other than a priest must be cut off[u]
from his people.' "

Incense

34Then the LORD said to Moses,
"Take fragrant spices—gum resin,
onycha and galbanum—and pure
frankincense, all in equal amounts,
35and make a fragrant blend of incense, the work of a perfumer.[v] It
is to be salted and pure and sacred.
36Grind some of it to powder and
place it in front of the Testimony in
the Tent of Meeting, where I will
meet with you. It shall be most
holy[w] to you. **37**Do not make any

30:9 [a]Lev 10:1
30:10 [b]Lev 16:18-19, 30
30:12 [c]Ex 38:25; Nu 1:2,49; 2Sa 24:1 [d]Nu 31:50; Mt 20:28 [e]2Sa 24:13
30:13 [f]Nu 3:47; Mt 17:24
30:15 [g]Pr 22:2; Eph 6:9
30:16 [h]Ex 38:25-28
30:18 [i]Ex 38:8; 40:7,30
30:19 [j]Ex 40:31-32; Isa 52:11 [k]Ps 26:6
30:21 [l]Ex 27:21; 28:43
30:23 [m]Ge 37:25
30:24 [n]Ps 45:8
30:25 [o]Ex 37:29 [p]Ex 40:9
30:26 [q]Ex 40:9; Lev 8:10; Nu 7:1
30:29 [r]Ex 29:37
30:30 [s]Ex 29:7; Lev 8:2,12,30
30:32 [t]ver 25,37
30:33 [u]ver 38; Ge 17:14
30:35 [v]ver 25
30:36 [w]ver 32; Ex 29:37; Lev 2:3

[o]*13* That is, about 1/5 ounce (about 6 grams); also in verse 15 [p]*23* That is, about 12 1/2 pounds (about 6 kilograms) [q]*24* That is, probably about 4 quarts (about 4 liters)

incense with this formula for yourselves; consider it holy[a] to the
LORD. **38**Whoever makes any like it
to enjoy its fragrance must be cut
off[b] from his people."

Bezalel and Oholiab

31:2–6pp — Ex 35:30–35

31 Then the LORD said to Moses, **2**"See, I have chosen
Bezalel[c] son of Uri, the son of Hur,
of the tribe of Judah, **3**and I have
filled him with the Spirit of God,
with skill, ability and knowledge in
all kinds of crafts[d]— **4**to make artistic designs for work in gold, silver and bronze, **5**to cut and set
stones, to work in wood, and to engage in all kinds of craftsmanship.
6Moreover, I have appointed Oholiab son of Ahisamach, of the tribe of
Dan, to help him. Also I have given
skill to all the craftsmen to make
everything I have commanded you:
7the Tent of Meeting,[e] the ark of
the Testimony[f] with the atonement cover[g] on it, and all the other
furnishings of the tent— **8**the table[h] and its articles, the pure gold
lampstand[i] and all its accessories,
the altar of incense, **9**the altar of
burnt offering and all its utensils,
the basin with its stand— **10**and
also the woven garments[j], both
the sacred garments for Aaron the
priest and the garments for his sons
when they serve as priests, **11**and
the anointing oil[k] and fragrant incense for the Holy Place. They are
to make them just as I commanded
you."

The Sabbath

12Then the LORD said to Moses,
13"Say to the Israelites, 'You must
observe my Sabbaths.[l] This will be
a sign[m] between me and you for
the generations to come, so you
may know that I am the LORD, who
makes you holy.[r][n]

14" 'Observe the Sabbath, because it is holy to you. Anyone who
desecrates it must be put to
death;[o] whoever does any work on
that day must be cut off from his
people. **15**For six days, work[p] is to
be done, but the seventh day is a
Sabbath of rest,[q] holy to the LORD.
Whoever does any work on the Sabbath day must be put to death.
16The Israelites are to observe the
Sabbath, celebrating it for the generations to come as a lasting covenant. **17**It will be a sign[r] between
me and the Israelites forever, for in
six days the LORD made the heavens
and the earth, and on the seventh
day he abstained from work and
rested.[s]' "

18When the LORD finished speaking to Moses on Mount Sinai, he
gave him the two tablets of the Testimony, the tablets of stone[t] inscribed by the finger of God.[u]

The Golden Calf

32 When the people saw that
Moses was so long in com-
ing down from the mountain,[v]
they gathered around Aaron and
said, "Come, make us gods[s] who
will go before us. As for this fellow
Moses who brought us up out of
Egypt, we don't know what has
happened to him."[w]

2Aaron answered them, "Take
off the gold earrings[x] that your
wives, your sons and your daughters are wearing, and bring them to
me." **3**So all the people took off
their earrings and brought them to
Aaron. **4**He took what they handed
him and made it into an idol cast in
the shape of a calf,[y] fashioning it
with a tool. Then they said, "These
are your gods,[t] O Israel, who
brought you up out of Egypt."

5When Aaron saw this, he built
an altar in front of the calf and announced, "Tomorrow there will be
a festival[z] to the LORD." **6**So the
next day the people rose early and
sacrificed burnt offerings and presented fellowship offerings.[u][a] Afterward they sat down to eat and
drink and got up to indulge in revelry.[b]

7Then the LORD said to Moses,
"Go down, because your people,

30:37 [a]ver 32
30:38 [b]ver 33
31:2 [c]Ex 36:1,2; 1Ch 2:20
31:3 [d]1Ki 7:14
31:7 [e]Ex 36:8-38 [f]Ex 37:1-5 [g]Ex 37:6
31:8 [h]Ex 37:10-16 [i]Ex 37:17-24
31:10 [j]Ex 28:2; 39:1,41
31:11 [k]Ex 30:22-32
31:13 [l]Ex 20:8; Lev 19:3,30 [m]Eze 20:12, 20 [n]Lev 11:44
31:14 [o]Nu 15:32-36
31:15 [p]Ex 20:8-11 [q]Ge 2:3; Ex 16:23
31:17 [r]ver 13 [s]Ge 2:2-3
31:18 [t]Ex 24:12 [u]Ex 32:15-16; 34:1,28; Dt 4:13; 5:22
32:1 [v]Ex 24:18; Dt 9:9-12 [w]Ac 7:40*
32:2 [x]Ex 35:22
32:4 [y]Dt 9:16; Ne 9:18; Ps 106:19; Ac 7:41
32:5 [z]Lev 23:2,37; 2Ki 10:20
32:6 [a]Nu 25:2; Ac 7:41 [b]ver 17-19; 1Co 10:7*

[r]13 Or *who sanctifies you*; or *who sets you apart as holy* [s]1 Or *a god*; also in verses 23 and 31 [t]4 Or *This is your god*; also in verse 8 [u]6 Traditionally *peace offerings*

whom you brought up out of
Egypt,[a] have become corrupt.[b]
8They have been quick to turn
away from what I commanded
them and have made themselves
an idol[c] cast in the shape of a calf.
They have bowed down to it and
sacrificed[d] to it and have said,
'These are your gods, O Israel, who
brought you up out of Egypt.'[e]
9"I have seen these people," the
LORD said to Moses, "and they are a
stiff-necked[f] people. 10Now leave
me alone so that my anger may
burn against them and that I may
destroy them. Then I will make you
into a great nation."[g]
11But Moses sought the favor[h]
of the LORD his God. "O LORD," he
said, "why should your anger burn
against your people, whom you
brought out of Egypt with great
power and a mighty hand?[i] 12Why
should the Egyptians say, 'It was
with evil intent that he brought
them out, to kill them in the mountains and to wipe them off the face
of the earth'?[j] Turn from your
fierce anger; relent and do not
bring disaster on your people.
13Remember[k] your servants Abraham, Isaac and Israel, to whom you
swore by your own self:[l] 'I will
make your descendants as numerous as the stars[m] in the sky and I
will give your descendants all this
land[n] I promised them, and it will
be their inheritance forever.' "
14Then the LORD relented[o] and did
not bring on his people the disaster
he had threatened.
15Moses turned and went down
the mountain with the two tablets
of the Testimony[p] in his hands.[q]
They were inscribed on both sides,
front and back. 16The tablets were
the work of God; the writing was
the writing of God, engraved on the
tablets.[r]
17When Joshua heard the noise
of the people shouting, he said to
Moses, "There is the sound of war
in the camp."
18Moses replied:

"It is not the sound of victory,
it is not the sound of defeat;
it is the sound of singing that
I hear."

19When Moses approached the
camp and saw the calf[s] and the
dancing, his anger burned and he
threw the tablets out of his hands,
breaking them to pieces[t] at the
foot of the mountain. 20And he
took the calf they had made and
burned it in the fire; then he
ground it to powder, scattered it on
the water[u] and made the Israelites
drink it.
21He said to Aaron, "What did
these people do to you, that you led
them into such great sin?"
22"Do not be angry, my lord,"
Aaron answered. "You know how
prone these people are to evil.[v]
23They said to me, 'Make us gods
who will go before us. As for this
fellow Moses who brought us up
out of Egypt, we don't know what
has happened to him.'[w] 24So I told
them, 'Whoever has any gold jewelry, take it off.' Then they gave me
the gold, and I threw it into the fire,
and out came this calf!"[x]
25Moses saw that the people
were running wild and that Aaron
had let them get out of control and
so become a laughingstock to their
enemies. 26So he stood at the entrance to the camp and said, "Whoever is for the LORD, come to me."
And all the Levites rallied to him.
27Then he said to them, "This is
what the LORD, the God of Israel,
says: 'Each man strap a sword to
his side. Go back and forth through
the camp from one end to the other, each killing his brother and
friend and neighbor.' "[y] 28The Levites did as Moses commanded,
and that day about three thousand
of the people died. 29Then Moses
said, "You have been set apart to
the LORD today, for you were
against your own sons and brothers, and he has blessed you this
day."
30The next day Moses said to the
people, "You have committed a
great sin.[z] But now I will go up to
the LORD; perhaps I can make
atonement[a] for your sin."

32:7 [a]ver 4,11 [b]Ge 6:11-12; Dt 9:12
32:8 [c]Ex 20:4 [d]Ex 22:20 [e]1Ki 12:28
32:9 [f]Ex 33:3,5; 34:9; Isa 48:4; Ac 7:51
32:10 [g]Nu 14:12; Dt 9:14
32:11 [h]Dt 9:18 [i]Dt 9:26
32:12 [j]Nu 14:13-16; Dt 9:28
32:13 [k]Ex 2:24 [l]Ge 22:16; Heb 6:13 [m]Ge 15:5; 26:4 [n]Ge 12:7
32:14 [o]2Sa 24:16; Ps 106:45
32:15 [p]Ex 31:18 [q]Dt 9:15
32:16 [r]Ex 31:18
32:19 [s]Dt 9:16 [t]Dt 9:17
32:20 [u]Dt 9:21
32:22 [v]Dt 9:24
32:23 [w]ver 1
32:24 [x]ver 4
32:27 [y]Nu 25:3,5; Dt 33:9
32:30 [z]1Sa 12:20 [a]Lev 1:4; Nu 25:13

31So Moses went back to the
LORD and said, "Oh, what a great
sin these people have committed![a]
They have made themselves gods
of gold.[b] 32But now, please forgive
their sin—but if not, then blot
me[c] out of the book[d] you have
written."
33The LORD replied to Moses,
"Whoever has sinned against me I
will blot out[e] of my book. 34Now
go, lead the people to the place[f] I
spoke of, and my angel[g] will go before you. However, when the time
comes for me to punish,[h] I will
punish them for their sin."
35And the LORD struck the people
with a plague because of what they
did with the calf[i] Aaron had made.
33 Then the LORD said to Moses, "Leave this place, you
and the people you brought up out
of Egypt, and go up to the land I
promised on oath to Abraham,
Isaac and Jacob, saying, 'I will give
it to your descendants.'[j] 2I will
send an angel[k] before you and
drive out the Canaanites, Amorites, Hittites, Perizzites, Hivites
and Jebusites.[l] 3Go up to the land
flowing with milk and honey.[m] But
I will not go with you, because you
are a stiff-necked[n] people and I
might destroy[o] you on the way."
4When the people heard these
distressing words, they began to
mourn[p] and no one put on any ornaments. 5For the LORD had said to
Moses, "Tell the Israelites, 'You are
a stiff-necked people. If I were to go
with you even for a moment, I
might destroy you. Now take off
your ornaments and I will decide
what to do with you.'" 6So the Israelites stripped off their ornaments
at Mount Horeb.

The Tent of Meeting

7Now Moses used to take a tent
and pitch it outside the camp some
distance away, calling it the "tent
of meeting."[q] Anyone inquiring of
the LORD would go to the tent of
meeting outside the camp. 8And
whenever Moses went out to the
tent, all the people rose and stood
at the entrances to their tents,[r]

32:31 [a]Dt 9:18 [b]Ex 20:23
32:32 [c]Ro 9:3 [d]Ps 69:28; Da 12:1; Php 4:3; Rev 3:5; 21:27
32:33 [e]Dt 29:20; Ps 9:5
32:34 [f]Ex 3:17 [g]Ex 23:20 [h]Dt 32:35; Ps 99:8; Ro 2:5-6
32:35 [i]ver 4
33:1 [j]Ge 12:7
33:2 [k]Ex 32:34 [l]Ex 23:27-31; Jos 24:11
33:3 [m]Ex 3:8 [n]Ex 32:9 [o]Ex 32:10
33:4 [p]Nu 14:39
33:7 [q]Ex 29:42-43
33:8 [r]Nu 16:27
33:9 [s]Ex 13:21 [t]Ex 31:18; Ps 99:7
33:11 [u]Nu 12:8; Dt 34:10
33:12 [v]Ex 3:10 [w]ver 17; Jn 10:14-15; 2Ti 2:19
33:13 [x]Ps 25:4; 86:11; 119:33 [y]Ex 34:9; Dt 9:26,29
33:14 [z]Isa 63:9 [a]Jos 21:44; 22:4
33:16 [b]Nu 14:14 [c]Ex 34:10
33:19 [d]Ro 9:15*

watching Moses until he entered
the tent. 9As Moses went into the
tent, the pillar of cloud[s] would
come down and stay at the entrance, while the LORD spoke[t] with
Moses. 10Whenever the people saw
the pillar of cloud standing at the
entrance to the tent, they all stood
and worshiped, each at the entrance to his tent. 11The LORD
would speak to Moses face to
face,[u] as a man speaks with his
friend. Then Moses would return to
the camp, but his young aide Joshua son of Nun did not leave the
tent.

Moses and the Glory of the LORD

12Moses said to the LORD, "You
have been telling me, 'Lead these
people,'[v] but you have not let me
know whom you will send with me.
You have said, 'I know you by
name[w] and you have found favor
with me.' 13If you are pleased with
me, teach me your ways[x] so I may
know you and continue to find favor with you. Remember that this
nation is your people."[y]
14The LORD replied, "My Presence[z] will go with you, and I will
give you rest."[a]
15Then Moses said to him, "If
your Presence does not go with us,
do not send us up from here.
16How will anyone know that you
are pleased with me and with your
people unless you go with us?[b]
What else will distinguish me and
your people from all the other people on the face of the earth?"[c]
17And the LORD said to Moses, "I
will do the very thing you have
asked, because I am pleased with
you and I know you by name."
18Then Moses said, "Now show
me your glory."
19And the LORD said, "I will
cause all my goodness to pass in
front of you, and I will proclaim my
name, the LORD, in your presence. I
will have mercy on whom I will
have mercy, and I will have compassion on whom I will have compassion.[d] 20But," he said, "you

cannot see my face, for no one may see[a] me and live."

21Then the LORD said, "There is a place near me where you may stand on a rock. 22When my glory passes by, I will put you in a cleft in the rock and cover you with my hand[b] until I have passed by. 23Then I will remove my hand and you will see my back; but my face must not be seen."

The New Stone Tablets

34 The LORD said to Moses, "Chisel out two stone tablets like the first ones, and I will write on them the words that were on the first tablets,[c] which you broke.[d] 2Be ready in the morning, and then come up on Mount Sinai.[e] Present yourself to me there on top of the mountain. 3No one is to come with you or be seen anywhere on the mountain;[f] not even the flocks and herds may graze in front of the mountain."

4So Moses chiseled out two stone tablets like the first ones and went up Mount Sinai early in the morning, as the LORD had commanded him; and he carried the two stone tablets in his hands. 5Then the LORD came down in the cloud and stood there with him and proclaimed his name, the LORD.[g] 6And he passed in front of Moses, proclaiming, "The LORD, the LORD, the compassionate[h] and gracious God, slow to anger,[i] abounding in love[j] and faithfulness,[k] 7maintaining love to thousands,[l] and forgiving wickedness, rebellion and sin.[m] Yet he does not leave the guilty unpunished;[n] he punishes the children and their children for the sin of the fathers to the third and fourth generation."

8Moses bowed to the ground at once and worshiped. 9"O Lord, if I have found favor in your eyes," he said, "then let the Lord go with us.[o] Although this is a stiff-necked people, forgive our wickedness and our sin, and take us as your inheritance."[p]

10Then the LORD said: "I am making a covenant[q] with you. Before all your people I will do wonders never before done in any nation in all the world.[r] The people you live among will see how awesome is the work that I, the LORD, will do for you. 11Obey what I command you today. I will drive out before you the Amorites, Canaanites, Hittites, Perizzites, Hivites and Jebusites.[s] 12Be careful not to make a treaty with those who live in the land where you are going, or they will be a snare[t] among you. 13Break down their altars, smash their sacred stones and cut down their Asherah poles.[v][u] 14Do not worship any other god,[v] for the LORD, whose name is Jealous, is a jealous God.[w]

15"Be careful not to make a treaty with those who live in the land; for when they prostitute[x] themselves to their gods and sacrifice to them, they will invite you and you will eat their sacrifices.[y] 16And when you choose some of their daughters as wives[z] for your sons and those daughters prostitute themselves to their gods,[a] they will lead your sons to do the same.

17"Do not make cast idols.[b]

18"Celebrate the Feast of Unleavened Bread.[c] For seven days eat bread made without yeast,[d] as I commanded you. Do this at the appointed time in the month of Abib,[e] for in that month you came out of Egypt.

19"The first offspring[f] of every womb belongs to me, including all the firstborn males of your livestock, whether from herd or flock. 20Redeem the firstborn donkey with a lamb, but if you do not redeem it, break its neck.[g] Redeem all your firstborn sons.

"No one is to appear before me empty-handed.[h]

21"Six days you shall labor, but on the seventh day you shall rest;[i] even during the plowing season and harvest you must rest.

22"Celebrate the Feast of Weeks with the firstfruits of the wheat harvest, and the Feast of Ingather-

33:20 [a]Ge 32:30; Isa 6:5
33:22 [b]Ps 91:4
34:1 [c]Dt 10:2,4 [d]Ex 32:19
34:2 [e]Ex 19:11
34:3 [f]Ex 19:12-13, 21
34:5 [g]Ex 33:19
34:6 [h]Ps 86:15 [i]Nu 14:18; Ro 2:4 [j]Ne 9:17; Ps 103:8; Joel 2:13 [k]Ps 108:4
34:7 [l]Ex 20:6 [m]Ps 103:3; 130:4,8; Da 9:9; 1Jn 1:9 [n]Job 10:14; Na 1:3
34:9 [o]Ex 33:15 [p]Ps 33:12
34:10 [q]Dt 5:2-3 [r]Ex 33:16; Dt 4:32
34:11 [s]Ex 33:2
34:12 [t]Ex 23:32-33
34:13 [u]Ex 23:24; Dt 12:3; 2Ki 18:4
34:14 [v]Ex 20:3 [w]Ex 20:5; Dt 4:24
34:15 [x]Jdg 2:17 [y]Nu 25:2; 1Co 8:4
34:16 [z]Dt 7:3 [a]1Ki 11:4
34:17 [b]Ex 32:8
34:18 [c]Ex 12:17 [d]Ex 12:15 [e]Ex 12:2
34:19 [f]Ex 13:2
34:20 [g]Ex 13:13,15 [h]Ex 23:15; Dt 16:16
34:21 [i]Ex 20:9; Lk 13:14

[v]*13* That is, symbols of the goddess Asherah

ing[a] at the turn of the year.[w] **23**Three times[b] a year all your men are to appear before the Sovereign LORD, the God of Israel. **24**I will drive out nations[c] before you and enlarge your territory, and no one will covet your land when you go up three times each year to appear before the LORD your God.

25"Do not offer the blood of a sacrifice to me along with anything containing yeast,[d] and do not let any of the sacrifice from the Passover Feast remain until morning.[e]

26"Bring the best of the firstfruits of your soil to the house of the LORD your God.

"Do not cook a young goat in its mother's milk."[f]

27Then the LORD said to Moses, "Write[g] down these words, for in accordance with these words I have made a covenant with you and with Israel." **28**Moses was there with the LORD forty days and forty nights[h] without eating bread or drinking water. And he wrote on the tablets[i] the words of the covenant —the Ten Commandments.[j]

The Radiant Face of Moses

29When Moses came down from Mount Sinai with the two tablets of the Testimony in his hands,[k] he was not aware that his face was radiant[l] because he had spoken with the LORD. **30**When Aaron and all the Israelites saw Moses, his face was radiant, and they were afraid to come near him. **31**But Moses called to them; so Aaron and all the leaders of the community came back to him, and he spoke to them. **32**Afterward all the Israelites came near him, and he gave them all the commands[m] the LORD had given him on Mount Sinai.

33When Moses finished speaking to them, he put a veil[n] over his face. **34**But whenever he entered the LORD's presence to speak with him, he removed the veil until he came out. And when he came out and told the Israelites what he had been commanded, **35**they saw that his face was radiant. Then Moses would put the veil back over his face until he went in to speak with the LORD.

Sabbath Regulations

35 Moses assembled the whole Israelite community and said to them, "These are the things the LORD has commanded[o] you to do: **2**For six days, work is to be done, but the seventh day shall be your holy day, a Sabbath[p] of rest to the LORD. Whoever does any work on it must be put to death. **3**Do not light a fire in any of your dwellings on the Sabbath day.[q]"

Materials for the Tabernacle

35:4–9pp — Ex 25:1–7
35:10–19pp — Ex 39:32–41

4Moses said to the whole Israelite community, "This is what the LORD has commanded: **5**From what you have, take an offering for the LORD. Everyone who is willing is to bring to the LORD an offering of gold, silver and bronze; **6**blue, purple and scarlet yarn and fine linen; goat hair; **7**ram skins dyed red and hides of sea cows[x]; acacia wood; **8**olive oil for the light; spices for the anointing oil and for the fragrant incense; **9**and onyx stones and other gems to be mounted on the ephod and breastpiece.

10"All who are skilled among you are to come and make everything the LORD has commanded:[r] **11**the tabernacle[s] with its tent and its covering, clasps, frames, crossbars, posts and bases; **12**the ark[t] with its poles and the atonement cover and the curtain that shields it; **13**the table[u] with its poles and all its articles and the bread of the Presence; **14**the lampstand[v] that is for light with its accessories, lamps and oil for the light; **15**the altar[w] of incense with its poles, the anointing oil[x] and the fragrant incense;[y] the curtain for the doorway at the entrance to the tabernacle; **16**the altar[z] of burnt offering with its bronze grating, its poles and all its utensils; the bronze basin with its

34:22 [a]Ex 23:16
34:23 [b]Ex 23:14
34:24 [c]Ex 23:28; 33:2; Ps 78:55
34:25 [d]Ex 23:18 [e]Ex 12:8,10
34:26 [f]Ex 23:19
34:27 [g]Ex 17:14; 24:4
34:28 [h]Ge 7:4; Ex 24:18; Mt 4:2 [i]ver 1; Ex 31:18 [j]Dt 4:13; 10:4
34:29 [k]Ex 32:15 [l]Ps 34:5; Mt 17:2; 2Co 3:7,13
34:32 [m]Ex 24:3
34:33 [n]2Co 3:13
35:1 [o]Ex 34:32
35:2 [p]Ex 20:9-10; 34:21; Lev 23:3
35:3 [q]Ex 16:23
35:10 [r]Ex 31:6
35:11 [s]Ex 26:1-37
35:12 [t]Ex 25:10-22
35:13 [u]Ex 25:23-30; Lev 24:5-6
35:14 [v]Ex 25:31
35:15 [w]Ex 30:1-6 [x]Ex 30:25 [y]Ex 30:34-38
35:16 [z]Ex 27:1-8

[w]*22* That is, in the fall [x]*7* That is, dugongs; also in verse 23

stand; 17the curtains of the courtyard with its posts and bases, and the curtain for the entrance to the courtyard;[a] 18the tent pegs for the tabernacle and for the courtyard, and their ropes; 19the woven garments worn for ministering in the sanctuary—both the sacred garments[b] for Aaron the priest and the garments for his sons when they serve as priests."

20Then the whole Israelite community withdrew from Moses' presence, 21and everyone who was willing and whose heart moved him came and brought an offering to the LORD for the work on the Tent of Meeting, for all its service, and for the sacred garments. 22All who were willing, men and women alike, came and brought gold jewelry of all kinds: brooches, earrings, rings and ornaments. They all presented their gold as a wave offering to the LORD. 23Everyone who had blue, purple or scarlet yarn[c] or fine linen, or goat hair, ram skins dyed red or hides of sea cows brought them. 24Those presenting an offering of silver or bronze brought it as an offering to the LORD, and everyone who had acacia wood for any part of the work brought it. 25Every skilled woman[d] spun with her hands and brought what she had spun—blue, purple or scarlet yarn or fine linen. 26And all the women who were willing and had the skill spun the goat hair. 27The leaders[e] brought onyx stones and other gems to be mounted on the ephod and breastpiece. 28They also brought spices and olive oil for the light and for the anointing oil and for the fragrant incense.[f] 29All the Israelite men and women who were willing[g] brought to the LORD freewill offerings[h] for all the work the LORD through Moses had commanded them to do.

Bezalel and Oholiab

35:30–35pp — Ex 31:2–6

30Then Moses said to the Israelites, "See, the LORD has chosen Bezalel son of Uri, the son of Hur, of the tribe of Judah, 31and he has filled him with the Spirit of God, with skill, ability and knowledge in all kinds of crafts[i]— 32to make artistic designs for work in gold, silver and bronze, 33to cut and set stones, to work in wood and to engage in all kinds of artistic craftsmanship. 34And he has given both him and Oholiab[j] son of Ahisamach, of the tribe of Dan, the ability to teach[k] others. 35He has filled them with skill to do all kinds of work[l] as craftsmen, designers, embroiderers in blue, purple and scarlet yarn and fine linen, and weavers—all of them master craftsmen and designers.

36 1So Bezalel, Oholiab and every skilled person[m] to whom the LORD has given skill and ability to know how to carry out all the work of constructing the sanctuary[n] are to do the work just as the Lord has commanded."

2Then Moses summoned Bezalel[o] and Oholiab[p] and every skilled person to whom the LORD had given ability and who was willing[q] to come and do the work. 3They received from Moses all the offerings[r] the Israelites had brought to carry out the work of constructing the sanctuary. And the people continued to bring freewill offerings morning after morning. 4So all the skilled craftsmen who were doing all the work on the sanctuary left their work 5and said to Moses, "The people are bringing more than enough[s] for doing the work the LORD commanded to be done."

6Then Moses gave an order and they sent this word throughout the camp: "No man or woman is to make anything else as an offering for the sanctuary." And so the people were restrained from bringing more, 7because what they already had was more[t] than enough to do all the work.

The Tabernacle

36:8–38pp — Ex 26:1–37

8All the skilled men among the

35:17 [a]Ex 27:9
35:19 [b]Ex 28:2; 31:10; 39:1
35:23 [c]1Ch 29:8
35:25 [d]Ex 28:3
35:27 [e]1Ch 29:6; Ezr 2:68
35:28 [f]Ex 25:6
35:29 [g]ver 21; 1Ch 29:9 [h]ver 4-9; Ex 25:1-7; 36:3; 2Ki 12:4
35:31 [i]ver 35; 2Ch 2:7,14
35:34 [j]Ex 31:6 [k]2Ch 2:14
35:35 [l]ver 31; Ex 31:3,6; 1Ki 7:14
36:1 [m]Ex 28:3 [n]Ex 25:8
36:2 [o]Ex 31:2 [p]Ex 31:6 [q]Ex 25:2; 35:21,26; 1Ch 29:5
36:3 [r]Ex 35:29
36:5 [s]2Ch 24:14; 31:10; 2Co 8:2-3
36:7 [t]1Ki 7:47

workmen made the tabernacle with ten curtains of finely twisted linen and blue, purple and scarlet yarn, with cherubim worked into them by a skilled craftsman. 9All the curtains were the same size—twenty-eight cubits long and four cubits wide.[y] 10They joined five of the curtains together and did the same with the other five. 11Then they made loops of blue material along the edge of the end curtain in one set, and the same was done with the end curtain in the other set. 12They also made fifty loops on one curtain and fifty loops on the end curtain of the other set, with the loops opposite each other. 13Then they made fifty gold clasps and used them to fasten the two sets of curtains together so that the tabernacle was a unit.[a]

14They made curtains of goat hair for the tent over the tabernacle—eleven altogether. 15All eleven curtains were the same size—thirty cubits long and four cubits wide.[z] 16They joined five of the curtains into one set and the other six into another set. 17Then they made fifty loops along the edge of the end curtain in one set and also along the edge of the end curtain in the other set. 18They made fifty bronze clasps to fasten the tent together as a unit.[b] 19Then they made for the tent a covering of ram skins dyed red, and over that a covering of hides of sea cows.[a]

20They made upright frames of acacia wood for the tabernacle. 21Each frame was ten cubits long and a cubit and a half wide,[b] 22with two projections set parallel to each other. They made all the frames of the tabernacle in this way. 23They made twenty frames for the south side of the tabernacle 24and made forty silver bases to go under them—two bases for each frame, one under each projection. 25For the other side, the north side of the tabernacle, they made twenty frames 26and forty silver bases—two under each frame. 27They made six frames for the far end, that is, the west end of the tabernacle, 28and two frames were made for the corners of the tabernacle at the far end. 29At these two corners the frames were double from the bottom all the way to the top and fitted into a single ring; both were made alike. 30So there were eight frames and sixteen silver bases—two under each frame.

31They also made crossbars of acacia wood: five for the frames on one side of the tabernacle, 32five for those on the other side, and five for the frames on the west, at the far end of the tabernacle. 33They made the center crossbar so that it extended from end to end at the middle of the frames. 34They overlaid the frames with gold and made gold rings to hold the crossbars. They also overlaid the crossbars with gold.

35They made the curtain[c] of blue, purple and scarlet yarn and finely twisted linen, with cherubim worked into it by a skilled craftsman. 36They made four posts of acacia wood for it and overlaid them with gold. They made gold hooks for them and cast their four silver bases. 37For the entrance to the tent they made a curtain of blue, purple and scarlet yarn and finely twisted linen—the work of an embroiderer;[d] 38and they made five posts with hooks for them. They overlaid the tops of the posts and their bands with gold and made their five bases of bronze.

The Ark

37:1–9pp — Ex 25:10–20

37 Bezalel[e] made the ark[f] of acacia wood—two and a half cubits long, a cubit and a half wide, and a cubit and a half high.[c] 2He overlaid it with pure gold,[g] both inside and out, and made a gold molding around it. 3He cast

36:13 [a]ver 18
36:18 [b]ver 13
36:35 [c]Ex 39:38; Mt 27:51; Lk 23:45; Heb 9:3
36:37 [d]Ex 27:16
37:1 [e]Ex 31:2 [f]Ex 30:6; 39:35; Dt 10:3
37:2 [g]ver 11,26

[y]9 That is, about 42 feet (about 12.5 meters) long and 6 feet (about 1.8 meters) wide
[z]15 That is, about 45 feet (about 13.5 meters) long and 6 feet (about 1.8 meters) wide
[a]19 That is, dugongs
[b]21 That is, about 15 feet (about 4.5 meters) long and 2 1/4 feet (about 0.7 meter) wide
[c]1 That is, about 3 3/4 feet (about 1.1 meters) long and 2 1/4 feet (about 0.7 meter) wide and high

four gold rings for it and fastened
them to its four feet, with two rings
on one side and two rings on the
other. **4**Then he made poles of acacia wood and overlaid them with
gold. **5**And he inserted the poles
into the rings on the sides of the
ark to carry it.

6He made the atonement cover[a]
of pure gold—two and a half cubits
long and a cubit and a half wide.[d]
7Then he made two cherubim[b] out
of hammered gold at the ends of
the cover. **8**He made one cherub on
one end and the second cherub on
the other; at the two ends he made
them of one piece with the cover.
9The cherubim had their wings
spread upward, overshadowing[c]
the cover with them. The cherubim
faced each other, looking toward
the cover.[d]

The Table

37:10–16pp — Ex 25:23–29

10They[e] made the table[e] of acacia wood—two cubits long, a cubit
wide, and a cubit and a half high.[f]
11Then they overlaid it with pure
gold[f] and made a gold molding
around it. **12**They also made
around it a rim a handbreadth[g]
wide and put a gold molding on the
rim. **13**They cast four gold rings for
the table and fastened them to the
four corners, where the four legs
were. **14**The rings[g] were put close
to the rim to hold the poles used in
carrying the table. **15**The poles for
carrying the table were made of
acacia wood and were overlaid with
gold. **16**And they made from pure
gold the articles for the table—its
plates and dishes and bowls and its
pitchers for the pouring out of
drink offerings.

The Lampstand

37:17–24pp — Ex 25:31–39

17They made the lampstand[h] of
pure gold and hammered it out,
base and shaft; its flowerlike cups,
buds and blossoms were of one
piece with it. **18**Six branches extended from the sides of the lampstand—three on one side and three
on the other. **19**Three cups shaped
like almond flowers with buds and
blossoms were on one branch,
three on the next branch and the
same for all six branches extending
from the lampstand. **20**And on the
lampstand were four cups shaped
like almond flowers with buds and
blossoms. **21**One bud was under
the first pair of branches extending
from the lampstand, a second bud
under the second pair, and a third
bud under the third pair—six
branches in all. **22**The buds and the
branches were all of one piece with
the lampstand, hammered out of
pure gold.[i]

23They made its seven lamps,[j]
as well as its wick trimmers
and trays, of pure gold. **24**They
made the lampstand and all its accessories from one talent[h] of pure
gold.

The Altar of Incense

37:25–28pp — Ex 30:1–5

25They made the altar of incense[k] out of acacia wood. It was
square, a cubit long and a cubit
wide, and two cubits high[i]—its
horns[l] of one piece with it. **26**They
overlaid the top and all the sides
and the horns with pure gold, and
made a gold molding around it.
27They made two gold rings[m] below the molding—two on opposite
sides—to hold the poles used to
carry it. **28**They made the poles of
acacia wood and overlaid them
with gold.[n]

29They also made the sacred
anointing oil[o] and the pure, fragrant incense[p]—the work of a perfumer.

37:6 [a]Ex 26:34; 31:7; Heb 9:5
37:7 [b]Eze 41:18
37:9 [c]Heb 9:5 [d]Dt 10:3
37:10 [e]Heb 9:2
37:11 [f]ver 2
37:14 [g]ver 27
37:17 [h]Heb 9:2; Rev 1:12
37:22 [i]ver 17; Nu 8:4
37:23 [j]Ex 40:4,25
37:25 [k]Ex 30:34-36; Lk 1:11; Heb 9:4; Rev 8:3 [l]Ex 27:2; Rev 9:13
37:27 [m]ver 14
37:28 [n]Ex 25:13
37:29 [o]Ex 31:11 [p]Ex 30:1,25; 39:38

[d]6 That is, about 3 3/4 feet (about 1.1 meters) long and 2 1/4 feet (about 0.7 meter) wide
[e]10 Or *He;* also in verses 11-29
[f]10 That is, about 3 feet (about 0.9 meter) long, 1 1/2 feet (about 0.5 meter) wide, and 2 1/4 feet (about 0.7 meter) high
[g]12 That is, about 3 inches (about 8 centimeters)
[h]24 That is, about 75 pounds (about 34 kilograms)
[i]25 That is, about 1 1/2 feet (about 0.5 meter) long and wide, and about 3 feet (about 0.9 meter) high

The Altar of Burnt Offering

38:1–7pp — Ex 27:1–8

38 They[j] built the altar of burnt offering of acacia wood, three cubits[k] high; it was square, five cubits long and five cubits wide.[l] **2**They made a horn at each of the four corners, so that the horns and the altar were of one piece, and they overlaid the altar with bronze.[a] **3**They made all its utensils[b] of bronze—its pots, shovels, sprinkling bowls, meat forks and firepans. **4**They made a grating for the altar, a bronze network, to be under its ledge, halfway up the altar. **5**They cast bronze rings to hold the poles for the four corners of the bronze grating. **6**They made the poles of acacia wood and overlaid them with bronze. **7**They inserted the poles into the rings so they would be on the sides of the altar for carrying it. They made it hollow, out of boards.

Basin for Washing

8They made the bronze basin[c] and its bronze stand from the mirrors of the women[d] who served at the entrance to the Tent of Meeting.

The Courtyard

38:9–20pp — Ex 27:9–19

9Next they made the courtyard. The south side was a hundred cubits[m] long and had curtains of finely twisted linen, **10**with twenty posts and twenty bronze bases, and with silver hooks and bands on the posts. **11**The north side was also a hundred cubits long and had twenty posts and twenty bronze bases, with silver hooks and bands on the posts.

12The west end was fifty cubits[n] wide and had curtains, with ten posts and ten bases, with silver hooks and bands on the posts. **13**The east end, toward the sunrise, was also fifty cubits wide. **14**Curtains fifteen cubits[o] long were on one side of the entrance, with three posts and three bases, **15**and curtains fifteen cubits long were on the other side of the entrance to the courtyard, with three posts and three bases. **16**All the curtains around the courtyard were of finely twisted linen. **17**The bases for the posts were bronze. The hooks and bands on the posts were silver, and their tops were overlaid with silver; so all the posts of the courtyard had silver bands.

18The curtain for the entrance to the courtyard was of blue, purple and scarlet yarn and finely twisted linen—the work of an embroiderer. It was twenty cubits[p] long and, like the curtains of the courtyard, five cubits[q] high, **19**with four posts and four bronze bases. Their hooks and bands were silver, and their tops were overlaid with silver. **20**All the tent pegs[e] of the tabernacle and of the surrounding courtyard were bronze.

The Materials Used

21These are the amounts of the materials used for the tabernacle, the tabernacle of the Testimony,[f] which were recorded at Moses' command by the Levites under the direction of Ithamar[g] son of Aaron, the priest. **22**(Bezalel[h] son of Uri, the son of Hur, of the tribe of Judah, made everything the LORD commanded Moses; **23**with him was Oholiab[i] son of Ahisamach, of the tribe of Dan—a craftsman and designer, and an embroiderer in blue, purple and scarlet yarn and fine linen.) **24**The total amount of the gold from the wave offering used for all the work on the sanctuary[j] was 29 talents and 730 shekels,[r] according to the sanctuary shekel.[k]

25The silver obtained from those of the community who were counted in the census[l] was 100 talents

38:2 [a]2Ch 1:5
38:3 [b]Ex 31:9
38:8 [c]Ex 30:18; 40:7 [d]Dt 23:17; 1Sa 2:22; 1Ki 14:24
38:20 [e]Ex 35:18
38:21 [f]Nu 1:50,53; 8:24; 9:15; 10:11; 17:7; 1Ch 23:32; 2Ch 24:6; Ac 7:44; Rev 15:5 [g]Nu 4:28,33
38:22 [h]Ex 31:2
38:23 [i]Ex 31:6
38:24 [j]Ex 30:16 [k]Ex 30:13; Lev 27:25; Nu 3:47; 18:16
38:25 [l]Ex 30:12

[j]*1* Or *He*; also in verses 2-9 [k]*1* That is, about 4 1/2 feet (about 1.3 meters) [l]*1* That is, about 7 1/2 feet (about 2.3 meters) long and wide [m]*9* That is, about 150 feet (about 46 meters) [n]*12* That is, about 75 feet (about 23 meters) [o]*14* That is, about 22 1/2 feet (about 6.9 meters) [p]*18* That is, about 30 feet (about 9 meters) [q]*18* That is, about 7 1/2 feet (about 2.3 meters) [r]*24* The weight of the gold was a little over one ton (about 1 metric ton).

and 1,775 shekels,[s] according to
the sanctuary shekel— **26**one beka
per person,[a] that is, half a shekel,[t] according to the sanctuary
shekel,[b] from everyone who had
crossed over to those counted,
twenty years old or more,[c] a total
of 603,550 men.[d] **27**The 100 talents[u] of silver were used to cast
the bases[e] for the sanctuary and
for the curtain—100 bases from
the 100 talents, one talent for each
base. **28**They used the 1,775 shekels[v] to make the hooks for the
posts, to overlay the tops of the
posts, and to make their bands.
29The bronze from the wave offering was 70 talents and 2,400
shekels.[w] **30**They used it to make
the bases for the entrance to the
Tent of Meeting, the bronze altar
with its bronze grating and all its
utensils, **31**the bases for the surrounding courtyard and those for
its entrance and all the tent pegs
for the tabernacle and those for the
surrounding courtyard.

The Priestly Garments

39 From the blue, purple and
scarlet yarn[f] they made
woven garments for ministering in
the sanctuary.[g] They also made sacred garments[h] for Aaron, as the
LORD commanded Moses.

The Ephod

39:2–7pp — Ex 28:6–14

2They[x] made the ephod of gold,
and of blue, purple and scarlet
yarn, and of finely twisted linen.
3They hammered out thin sheets of
gold and cut strands to be worked
into the blue, purple and scarlet
yarn and fine linen—the work of a
skilled craftsman. **4**They made
shoulder pieces for the ephod,
which were attached to two of its
corners, so it could be fastened.
5Its skillfully woven waistband was
like it—of one piece with the
ephod and made with gold, and
with blue, purple and scarlet yarn,
and with finely twisted linen, as
the LORD commanded Moses.
6They mounted the onyx stones
in gold filigree settings and engraved them like a seal with the
names of the sons of Israel. **7**Then
they fastened them on the shoulder pieces of the ephod as memorial[i] stones for the sons of Israel, as
the LORD commanded Moses.

The Breastpiece

39:8–21pp — Ex 28:15–28

8They fashioned the breastpiece[j]—the work of a skilled
craftsman. They made it like the
ephod: of gold, and of blue, purple
and scarlet yarn, and of finely
twisted linen. **9**It was square—a
span[y] long and a span wide—and
folded double. **10**Then they mounted four rows of precious stones on
it. In the first row there was a ruby,
a topaz and a beryl; **11**in the second
row a turquoise, a sapphire[z] and
an emerald; **12**in the third row a jacinth, an agate and an amethyst;
13in the fourth row a chrysolite, an
onyx and a jasper.[a] They were
mounted in gold filigree settings.
14There were twelve stones, one for
each of the names of the sons of
Israel, each engraved like a seal
with the name of one of the twelve
tribes.[k]
15For the breastpiece they made
braided chains of pure gold, like a
rope. **16**They made two gold filigree
settings and two gold rings, and
fastened the rings to two of the corners of the breastpiece. **17**They fastened the two gold chains to the
rings at the corners of the breastpiece, **18**and the other ends of the
chains to the two settings, attaching them to the shoulder pieces of
the ephod at the front. **19**They
made two gold rings and attached
them to the other two corners of
the breastpiece on the inside edge

38:26 [a]Ex 30:12 [b]Ex 30:13 [c]Ex 30:14 [d]Ex 12:37; Nu 1:46
38:27 [e]Ex 26:19
39:1 [f]Ex 35:23 [g]Ex 35:19 [h]ver 41; Ex 28:2
39:7 [i]Lev 24:7; Jos 4:7
39:8 [j]Lev 8:8
39:14 [k]Rev 21:12

[s]*25* The weight of the silver was a little over 3 3/4 tons (about 3.4 metric tons).
[t]*26* That is, about 1/5 ounce (about 5.5 grams)
[u]*27* That is, about 3 3/4 tons (about 3.4 metric tons)
[v]*28* That is, about 45 pounds (about 20 kilograms)
[w]*29* The weight of the bronze was about 2 1/2 tons (about 2.4 metric tons).
[x]*2* Or *He;* also in verses 7, 8 and 22
[y]*9* That is, about 9 inches (about 22 centimeters)
[z]*11* Or *lapis lazuli*
[a]*13* The precise identification of some of these precious stones is uncertain.

next to the ephod. 20Then they made two more gold rings and attached them to the bottom of the shoulder pieces on the front of the ephod, close to the seam just above the waistband of the ephod. 21They tied the rings of the breastpiece to the rings of the ephod with blue cord, connecting it to the waistband so that the breastpiece would not swing out from the ephod—as the LORD commanded Moses.

Other Priestly Garments

39:22–31pp — Ex 28:31–43

22They made the robe of the ephod entirely of blue cloth—the work of a weaver— 23with an opening in the center of the robe like the opening of a collar,[b] and a band around this opening, so that it would not tear. 24They made pomegranates of blue, purple and scarlet yarn and finely twisted linen around the hem of the robe. 25And they made bells of pure gold and attached them around the hem between the pomegranates. 26The bells and pomegranates alternated around the hem of the robe to be worn for ministering, as the LORD commanded Moses.

27For Aaron and his sons, they made tunics of fine linen[a]—the work of a weaver— 28and the turban[b] of fine linen, the linen headbands and the undergarments of finely twisted linen. 29The sash was of finely twisted linen and blue, purple and scarlet yarn—the work of an embroiderer—as the LORD commanded Moses.

30They made the plate, the sacred diadem, out of pure gold and engraved on it, like an inscription on a seal: HOLY TO THE LORD. 31Then they fastened a blue cord to it to attach it to the turban, as the LORD commanded Moses.

Moses Inspects the Tabernacle

39:32–41pp — Ex 35:10–19

32So all the work on the tabernacle, the Tent of Meeting, was completed. The Israelites did everything just as the LORD commanded Moses.[c] 33Then they brought the tabernacle to Moses: the tent and all its furnishings, its clasps, frames, crossbars, posts and bases; 34the covering of ram skins dyed red, the covering of hides of sea cows[c] and the shielding curtain; 35the ark of the Testimony[d] with its poles and the atonement cover; 36the table with all its articles and the bread of the Presence; 37the pure gold lampstand[e] with its row of lamps and all its accessories, and the oil for the light; 38the gold altar,[f] the anointing oil, the fragrant incense, and the curtain[g] for the entrance to the tent; 39the bronze altar with its bronze grating, its poles and all its utensils; the basin with its stand; 40the curtains of the courtyard with its posts and bases, and the curtain for the entrance to the courtyard;[h] the ropes and tent pegs for the courtyard; all the furnishings for the tabernacle, the Tent of Meeting; 41and the woven garments worn for ministering in the sanctuary, both the sacred garments for Aaron the priest and the garments for his sons when serving as priests.

42The Israelites had done all the work just as the LORD had commanded Moses.[i] 43Moses inspected the work and saw that they had done it just as the LORD had commanded. So Moses blessed[j] them.

Setting Up the Tabernacle

40 Then the LORD said to Moses: 2"Set up the tabernacle, the Tent of Meeting,[k] on the first day of the first month.[l] 3Place the ark[m] of the Testimony in it and shield the ark with the curtain. 4Bring in the table and set out what belongs on it.[n] Then bring in the lampstand[o] and set up its lamps. 5Place the gold altar[p] of incense in front of the ark of the Testimony and put the curtain at the entrance to the tabernacle.

6"Place the altar of burnt offering in front of the entrance to the

39:27 [a]Lev 6:10
39:28 [b]Ex 28:4
39:32 [c]ver 42-43; Ex 25:9
39:35 [d]Ex 30:6
39:37 [e]Ex 25:31
39:38 [f]Ex 30:1-10 [g]Ex 36:35
39:40 [h]Ex 27:9-19
39:42 [i]Ex 25:9
39:43 [j]Lev 9:22,23; Nu 6:23-27; 2Sa 6:18; 1Ki 8:14,55; 2Ch 30:27
40:2 [k]Nu 1:1 [l]ver 17; Ex 12:2
40:3 [m]ver 21; Nu 4:5; Ex 26:33
40:4 [n]Ex 25:30 [o]ver 22-25; Ex 26:35
40:5 [p]ver 26; Ex 30:1

b23 The meaning of the Hebrew for this word is uncertain. c34 That is, dugongs

tabernacle, the Tent of Meeting;
7place the basin[a] between the
Tent of Meeting and the altar and
put water in it. **8**Set up the courtyard around it and put the curtain
at the entrance to the courtyard.

9"Take the anointing oil and
anoint[b] the tabernacle and everything in it; consecrate it and all its
furnishings, and it will be holy.
10Then anoint the altar of burnt offering and all its utensils; consecrate[c] the altar, and it will be most
holy. **11**Anoint the basin and its
stand and consecrate them.

12"Bring Aaron and his sons to
the entrance to the Tent of Meeting and wash them with water.[d]
13Then dress Aaron in the sacred
garments,[e] anoint him and consecrate[f] him so he may serve me as
priest. **14**Bring his sons and dress
them in tunics. **15**Anoint them just
as you anointed their father, so
they may serve me as priests. Their
anointing will be to a priesthood
that will continue for all generations to come.[g]" **16**Moses did everything just as the LORD commanded him.

17So the tabernacle[h] was set up
on the first day of the first month[i]
in the second year. **18**When Moses
set up the tabernacle, he put the
bases in place, erected the frames,
inserted the crossbars and set up
the posts. **19**Then he spread the
tent over the tabernacle and put
the covering over the tent, as the
LORD commanded him.

20He took the Testimony[j] and
placed it in the ark, attached the
poles to the ark and put the atonement cover over it. **21**Then he
brought the ark into the tabernacle
and hung the shielding curtain[k]
and shielded the ark of the Testimony, as the LORD commanded
him.

22Moses placed the table[l] in the
Tent of Meeting on the north side
of the tabernacle outside the curtain **23**and set out the bread[m] on it
before the LORD, as the LORD commanded him.

24He placed the lampstand[n] in
the Tent of Meeting opposite the
table on the south side of the tabernacle **25**and set up the lamps[o] before the LORD, as the LORD commanded him.

26Moses placed the gold altar[p]
in the Tent of Meeting in front of
the curtain **27**and burned fragrant
incense on it, as the LORD commanded[q] him. **28**Then he put up
the curtain[r] at the entrance to the
tabernacle.

29He set the altar of burnt offering near the entrance to the tabernacle, the Tent of Meeting, and offered on it burnt offerings and grain
offerings,[s] as the LORD commanded him.

30He placed the basin[t] between
the Tent of Meeting and the altar
and put water in it for washing,
31and Moses and Aaron and his
sons used it to wash their hands
and feet. **32**They washed whenever
they entered the Tent of Meeting or
approached the altar,[u] as the LORD
commanded Moses.

33Then Moses set up the courtyard[v] around the tabernacle and
altar and put up the curtain[w] at the
entrance to the courtyard. And so
Moses finished the work.

The Glory of the LORD

34Then the cloud[x] covered the
Tent of Meeting, and the glory of
the LORD filled the tabernacle.
35Moses could not enter the Tent
of Meeting because the cloud had
settled upon it, and the glory of the
LORD filled the tabernacle.[y]

36In all the travels of the Israelites, whenever the cloud lifted
from above the tabernacle, they
would set out;[z] **37**but if the cloud
did not lift, they did not set out
—until the day it lifted. **38**So the
cloud[a] of the LORD was over the
tabernacle by day, and fire was in
the cloud by night, in the sight of
all the house of Israel during all
their travels.

40:7 [a] ver 30; Ex 30:18
40:9 [b] Ex 30:26; Lev 8:10
40:10 [c] Ex 29:36
40:12 [d] Lev 8:1-13
40:13 [e] Ex 28:41 [f] Lev 8:12
40:15 [g] Ex 29:9; Nu 25:13
40:17 [h] Nu 7:1 [i] ver 2
40:20 [j] Ex 16:34; 25:16; Dt 10:5; 1Ki 8:9; Heb 9:4
40:21 [k] Ex 26:33
40:22 [l] Ex 26:35
40:23 [m] ver 4
40:24 [n] Ex 26:35
40:25 [o] ver 4; Ex 25:37
40:26 [p] ver 5; Ex 30:6
40:27 [q] Ex 30:7
40:28 [r] Ex 26:36
40:29 [s] ver 6; Ex 29:38-42
40:30 [t] ver 7
40:32 [u] Ex 30:20
40:33 [v] Ex 27:9 [w] ver 8
40:34 [x] Nu 9:15-23; 1Ki 8:12
40:35 [y] 1Ki 8:11; 2Ch 5:13-14
40:36 [z] Nu 9:17-23; 10:13; Ne 9:19
40:38 [a] Ex 13:21; Nu 9:15; 1Co 10:1

Leviticus

Title and Background

Leviticus receives its name from the Septuagint (the Greek translation of the Old Testament) and means "relating to the Levites." Although Leviticus does not deal only with the special duties of the Levites, it is so named because it is concerned mainly with the service of worship at the tabernacle. Exodus had given the directions for building the tabernacle. Leviticus gives the laws and regulations for worship at the tabernacle, along with instructions on ceremonial cleanness, moral laws, holy days, the sabbath year, and the Year of Jubilee.

Author and Date of Writing

Leviticus 1:1 states that the contents of Leviticus were given to Moses by God. In more than fifty places in the book it is said that the Lord spoke to Moses. The date for the writing of the book by Moses would appear to be between about 1446 and about 1406 B.C.

Theme and Message

The key thought of Leviticus is holiness—the holiness of God and of man. The command to be holy is stated in 11:45—"be holy, because I am holy." The instructions or laws in the book were given to help the Israelites worship and live as God's holy people. Some of the instructions deal with such things as offering sacrifices, handling everyday problems concerning cleanliness, and observing special holidays. The Levitical priests are also given special instructions for making sacrifices and carrying out God's commands.

Outline

I. Laws and Instructions for Offerings (1:1-7:38)
II. Appointment of Aaron and His Sons as God's Priests (8:1-10:20)
III. Rules for Holy Living (11:1-15:33)
IV. The Day of Atonement (16:1-34)
V. Practical Holiness (17:1-22:33)
VI. The Sabbath, Feasts and Seasons (23:1-25:55)
VII. Conditions for God's Blessings (26:1-27:34)

The Burnt Offering

1 The LORD called to Moses[a] and spoke to him from the Tent of Meeting.[b] He said, **2**"Speak to the Israelites and say to them: 'When any of you brings an offering to the LORD, bring as your offering an animal from either the herd or the flock.[c]

3" 'If the offering is a burnt offering from the herd, he is to offer a male without defect.[d] He must present it at the entrance to the Tent[e] of Meeting so that it[a] will be acceptable to the LORD. **4**He is to lay his hand on the head[f] of the burnt offering, and it will be accepted on his behalf to make atonement[g] for him. **5**He is to slaughter[h] the young bull before the LORD, and then Aaron's sons the priests shall bring the blood and sprinkle it against the altar on all sides[i] at the entrance to the Tent of Meeting. **6**He is to skin[j]

1:1 [a]Ex 19:3; 25:22 [b]Nu 7:89
1:2 [c]Lev 22:18-19
1:3 [d]Ex 12:5; Dt 15:21; Heb 9:14; 1Pe 1:19 [e]Lev 17:9
1:4 [f]Ex 29:10,15; Lev 3:2 [g]2Ch 29:23-24
1:5 [h]Lev 3:2,8 [i]Heb 12:24; 1Pe 1:2 **1:6** [j]Lev 7:8

[a]3 Or *he*

the burnt offering and cut it into
pieces. **7**The sons of Aaron the
priest are to put fire on the altar
and arrange wood[a] on the fire.
8Then Aaron's sons the priests
shall arrange the pieces, including
the head and the fat,[b] on the burning wood that is on the altar. **9**He is
to wash the inner parts and the legs
with water, and the priest is to burn
all of it on the altar.[c] It is a burnt
offering, an offering made by fire,
an aroma pleasing to the LORD.[d]
10" 'If the offering is a burnt offering from the flock, from either
the sheep or the goats,[e] he is to
offer a male without defect. **11**He is
to slaughter it at the north side of
the altar before the LORD, and Aaron's sons the priests shall sprinkle
its blood against the altar on all
sides.[f] **12**He is to cut it into pieces,
and the priest shall arrange them,
including the head and the fat, on
the burning wood that is on the altar. **13**He is to wash the inner parts
and the legs with water, and the
priest is to bring all of it and burn
it on the altar. It is a burnt offering,
an offering made by fire, an aroma
pleasing to the LORD.
14" 'If the offering to the LORD is
a burnt offering of birds, he is to
offer a dove or a young pigeon.[g]
15The priest shall bring it to the altar, wring off the head and burn it
on the altar; its blood shall be
drained out on the side of the altar.[h] **16**He is to remove the crop
with its contents[b] and throw it to
the east side of the altar, where the
ashes[i] are. **17**He shall tear it open
by the wings, not severing it completely,[j] and then the priest shall
burn it on the wood[k] that is on the
fire on the altar. It is a burnt offering, an offering made by fire, an
aroma pleasing to the LORD.

The Grain Offering

2 " 'When someone brings a
grain offering[l] to the LORD, his
offering is to be of fine flour. He is
to pour oil[m] on it, put incense on it
2and take it to Aaron's sons the
priests. The priest shall take a
handful of the fine flour[n] and oil,
together with all the incense,[o] and
burn this as a memorial portion[p]
on the altar, an offering made by
fire, an aroma pleasing to the LORD.
3The rest of the grain offering belongs to Aaron and his sons;[q] it is
a most holy part of the offerings
made to the LORD by fire.
4" 'If you bring a grain offering
baked in an oven, it is to consist of
fine flour: cakes made without
yeast and mixed with oil, or[c] wafers made without yeast and spread
with oil.[r] **5**If your grain offering is
prepared on a griddle, it is to be
made of fine flour mixed with oil,
and without yeast. **6**Crumble it and
pour oil on it; it is a grain offering.
7If your grain offering is cooked in
a pan,[s] it is to be made of fine flour
and oil. **8**Bring the grain offering
made of these things to the LORD;
present it to the priest, who shall
take it to the altar. **9**He shall take
out the memorial portion[t] from
the grain offering and burn it on
the altar as an offering made by
fire, an aroma pleasing to the
LORD.[u] **10**The rest of the grain offering belongs to Aaron and his
sons;[v] it is a most holy part of the
offerings made to the LORD by fire.
11" 'Every grain offering you
bring to the LORD must be made
without yeast,[w] for you are not to
burn any yeast or honey in an offering made to the LORD by fire. **12**You
may bring them to the LORD as an
offering of the firstfruits,[x] but they
are not to be offered on the altar as
a pleasing aroma. **13**Season all your
grain offerings with salt. Do not
leave the salt of the covenant[y] of
your God out of your grain offerings; add salt to all your offerings.
14" 'If you bring a grain offering
of firstfruits[z] to the LORD, offer
crushed heads of new grain roasted
in the fire. **15**Put oil and incense on
it; it is a grain offering. **16**The priest
shall burn the memorial portion[a]
of the crushed grain and the oil, together with all the incense, as an

1:7 [a]Lev 6:12
1:8 [b]ver 12
1:9 [c]Ex 29:18 [d]ver 13; Ge 8:21; Nu 15:8-10; Eph 5:2
1:10 [e]ver 3; Ex 12:5
1:11 [f]ver 5
1:14 [g]Ge 15:9; Lev 5:7; Lk 2:24
1:15 [h]Lev 5:9
1:16 [i]Lev 6:10
1:17 [j]Ge 15:10 [k]Lev 5:8
2:1 [l]Lev 6:14-18 [m]Nu 15:4
2:2 [n]Lev 5:11 [o]Lev 6:15; Isa 66:3 [p]ver 9,16; Lev 5:12; 6:15; 24:7; Ac 10:4
2:3 [q]ver 10; Lev 6:16; 10:12,13
2:4 [r]Ex 29:2
2:7 [s]Lev 7:9
2:9 [t]ver 2 [u]Ex 29:18; Lev 6:15
2:10 [v]ver 3
2:11 [w]Ex 23:18; 34:25; Lev 6:16
2:12 [x]Lev 7:13; 23:10
2:13 [y]Nu 18:19; Eze 43:24
2:14 [z]Lev 23:10
2:16 [a]ver 2

[b]*16* Or *crop and the feathers*; the meaning of the Hebrew for this word is uncertain.
[c]*4* Or *and*

offering made to the LORD by fire.

The Fellowship Offering

3 " 'If someone's offering is a fellowship offering,[d][a] and he offers an animal from the herd, whether male or female, he is to present before the LORD an animal without defect.[b] **2**He is to lay his hand on the head[c] of his offering and slaughter it[d] at the entrance to the Tent of Meeting. Then Aaron's sons the priests shall sprinkle the blood against the altar on all sides. **3**From the fellowship offering he is to bring a sacrifice made to the LORD by fire: all the fat[e] that covers the inner parts or is connected to them, **4**both kidneys with the fat on them near the loins, and the covering of the liver, which he will remove with the kidneys. **5**Then Aaron's sons[f] are to burn it on the altar on top of the burnt offering[g] that is on the burning wood, as an offering made by fire, an aroma pleasing to the LORD.

6" 'If he offers an animal from the flock as a fellowship offering[h] to the LORD, he is to offer a male or female without defect. **7**If he offers a lamb, he is to present it before the LORD.[i] **8**He is to lay his hand on the head of his offering and slaughter it[j] in front of the Tent of Meeting. Then Aaron's sons shall sprinkle its blood against the altar on all sides. **9**From the fellowship offering he is to bring a sacrifice made to the LORD by fire: its fat, the entire fat tail cut off close to the backbone, all the fat that covers the inner parts or is connected to them, **10**both kidneys with the fat on them near the loins, and the covering of the liver, which he will remove with the kidneys. **11**The priest shall burn them on the altar[k] as food,[l] an offering made to the LORD by fire.

12" 'If his offering is a goat, he is to present it before the LORD. **13**He is to lay his hand on its head and slaughter it in front of the Tent of Meeting. Then Aaron's sons shall sprinkle[m] its blood against the altar on all sides. **14**From what he offers he is to make this offering to the LORD by fire: all the fat that covers the inner parts or is connected to them, **15**both kidneys with the fat on them near the loins, and the covering of the liver, which he will remove with the kidneys. **16**The priest shall burn them on the altar as food, an offering made by fire, a pleasing aroma. All the fat is the LORD's.[n]

17" 'This is a lasting ordinance for the generations to come,[o] wherever you live: You must not eat any fat or any blood.[p]' "

The Sin Offering

4 The LORD said to Moses, **2**"Say to the Israelites: 'When anyone sins unintentionally[q] and does what is forbidden in any of the LORD's commands—

3" 'If the anointed priest sins, bringing guilt on the people, he must bring to the LORD a young bull[r] without defect as a sin offering[s] for the sin he has committed. **4**He is to present the bull at the entrance to the Tent of Meeting before the LORD.[t] He is to lay his hand on its head and slaughter it before the LORD. **5**Then the anointed priest shall take some of the bull's blood[u] and carry it into the Tent of Meeting. **6**He is to dip his finger into the blood and sprinkle some of it seven times before the LORD, in front of the curtain of the sanctuary. **7**The priest shall then put some of the blood on the horns of the altar of fragrant incense that is before the LORD in the Tent of Meeting. The rest of the bull's blood he shall pour out at the base of the altar[v] of burnt offering[w] at the entrance to the Tent of Meeting. **8**He shall remove all the fat[x] from the bull of the sin offering—the fat that covers the inner parts or is connected to them, **9**both kidneys with the fat on them near the loins, and the covering of the liver, which he will remove with the kidneys[y]— **10**just as the fat is

[d]*1* Traditionally *peace offering*; also in verses 3, 6 and 9

3:1 [a]Lev 7:11-34 [b]Lev 1:3; 22:21
3:2 [c]Ex 29:10,15 [d]Lev 1:5
3:3 [e]Ex 29:13
3:5 [f]Lev 7:29-34 [g]Ex 29:13, 38-42
3:6 [h]ver 1
3:7 [i]Lev 17:8-9
3:8 [j]ver 2; Lev 1:5
3:11 [k]ver 5 [l]ver 16; Lev 21:6,17
3:13 [m]Ex 24:6
3:16 [n]1Sa 2:16
3:17 [o]Lev 6:18; 17:7 [p]Ge 9:4; Lev 7:25-26; 17:10-16; Dt 12:16; Ac 15:20
4:2 [q]Lev 5:15-18; Ps 19:12; Heb 9:7
4:3 [r]ver 14; Ps 66:15 [s]Lev 9:2-22; Heb 9:13-14
4:4 [t]Lev 1:3
4:5 [u]Lev 16:14
4:7 [v]ver 34; Lev 8:15 [w]ver 18,30; Lev 5:9; 9:9; 16:18
4:8 [x]Lev 3:3-5
4:9 [y]Lev 3:4

OLD TESTAMENT SACRIFICES

Sacrifice	OT References	Elements	Purpose
BURNT OFFERING	Lev 1; 6:8-13; 8:18-21; 16:24	Bull, ram or male bird (dove or young pigeon for poor); wholly consumed; no defect	Voluntary act of worship; atonement for unintentional sin in general; expression of devotion, commitment and complete surrender to God
GRAIN OFFERING	Lev 2; 6:14-23	Grain, fine flour, olive oil, incense, baked bread (cakes or wafers), salt; no yeast or honey; accompanied burnt offering and fellowship offering (along with drink offering)	Voluntary act of worship; recognition of God's goodness and provisions; devotion to God
FELLOWSHIP OFFERING	Lev 3; 7:11-34	Any animal without defect from herd or flock; variety of breads	Voluntary act of worship; thanksgiving and fellowship (it included a communal meal)
SIN OFFERING	Lev 4:1-5:13; 6:24-30; 8:14-17; 16:3-22	1. Young bull: for high priest and congregation 2. Male goat: for leader 3. Female goat or lamb: for common person 4. Dove or pigeon: for the poor 5. Tenth of an ephah of fine flour: for the very poor	Mandatory atonement for specific unintentional sin; confession of sin; forgiveness of sin; cleansing from defilement
GUILT OFFERING	Lev 5:14-6:7; 7:1-6	Ram or lamb	Mandatory atonement for unintentional sin requiring restitution; cleansing from defilement; make restitution; pay 20% fine

When more than one kind of offering was presented (as in Nu 7:16, 17), the procedure was usually as follows: (1) sin offering or guilt offering, (2) burnt offering, (3) fellowship offering and grain offering (along with a drink offering). This sequence furnishes part of the spiritual significance of the sacrificial system. First, sin had to be dealt with (sin offering or guilt offering). Second, the worshiper committed himself completely to God (burnt offering and grain offering). Third, fellowship or communion between the Lord, the priest and the worshiper (fellowship offering) was established.

removed from the ox[e] sacrificed as a fellowship offering.[f] Then the priest shall burn them on the altar of burnt offering. **11**But the hide of the bull and all its flesh, as well as the head and legs, the inner parts and offal[a]— **12**that is, all the rest of the bull—he must take outside the camp[b] to a place ceremonially clean,[c] where the ashes are thrown, and burn it in a wood fire on the ash heap.

13" 'If the whole Israelite community sins unintentionally[d] and does what is forbidden in any of the LORD's commands, even though the community is unaware of the matter, they are guilty. **14**When they become aware of the sin they committed, the assembly must bring a young bull[e] as a sin offering[f] and present it before the Tent of Meeting. **15**The elders of the community are to lay their hands on the bull's head[g] before the LORD, and the bull shall be slaughtered before the LORD. **16**Then the anointed priest is to take some of the bull's blood[h] into the Tent of Meeting. **17**He shall dip his finger into the blood and sprinkle it before the LORD[i] seven times in front of the curtain. **18**He is to put some of the blood on the horns of the altar that is before the LORD[j] in the Tent of Meeting. The rest of the blood he shall pour out at the base of the altar of burnt offering at the entrance to the Tent of Meeting. **19**He shall remove all the fat[k] from it and burn it on the altar, **20**and do with this bull just as he did with the bull for the sin offering. In this way the priest will make atonement[l] for them, and they will be forgiven.[m] **21**Then he shall take the bull outside the camp and burn it as he burned the first bull. This is the sin offering for the community.[n]

22" 'When a leader[o] sins unintentionally[p] and does what is forbidden in any of the commands of the LORD his God, he is guilty. **23**When he is made aware of the sin he committed, he must bring as his offering a male goat without defect. **24**He is to lay his hand on the goat's head and slaughter it at the place where the burnt offering is slaughtered before the LORD. It is a sin offering. **25**Then the priest shall take some of the blood of the sin offering with his finger and put it on the horns of the altar of burnt offering and pour out the rest of the blood at the base of the altar.[q] **26**He shall burn all the fat on the altar as he burned the fat of the fellowship offering. In this way the priest will make atonement for the man's sin, and he will be forgiven.[r]

27" 'If a member of the community sins unintentionally[s] and does what is forbidden in any of the LORD's commands, he is guilty. **28**When he is made aware of the sin he committed, he must bring as his offering[t] for the sin he committed a female goat[u] without defect. **29**He is to lay his hand on the head[v] of the sin offering[w] and slaughter it at the place of the burnt offering. **30**Then the priest is to take some of the blood with his finger and put it on the horns of the altar of burnt offering[x] and pour out the rest of the blood at the base of the altar. **31**He shall remove all the fat, just as the fat is removed from the fellowship offering, and the priest shall burn it on the altar as an aroma pleasing to the LORD.[y] In this way the priest will make atonement for him, and he will be forgiven.

32" 'If he brings a lamb as his sin offering, he is to bring a female without defect.[z] **33**He is to lay his hand on its head and slaughter it for a sin offering at the place where the burnt offering is slaughtered.[a] **34**Then the priest shall take some of the blood of the sin offering with his finger and put it on the horns of the altar of burnt offering and pour out the rest of the blood at the base of the altar.[b] **35**He shall remove all the fat, just as the fat is removed

4:11 [a]Ex 29:14; Lev 9:11; Nu 19:5
4:12 [b]Heb 13:11 [c]Lev 6:11
4:13 [d]ver 2; Lev 5:2-4,17; Nu 15:24-26
4:14 [e]ver 3 [f]ver 23, 28
4:15 [g]Lev 1:4; 8:14,22; Nu 8:10
4:16 [h]ver 5
4:17 [i]ver 6
4:18 [j]ver 7
4:19 [k]ver 8
4:20 [l]Heb 10:10-12 [m]Nu 15:25
4:21 [n]Lev 16:5,15
4:22 [o]Nu 31:13 [p]ver 2
4:25 [q]ver 7,18,30, 34; Lev 9:9
4:26 [r]Lev 5:10
4:27 [s]ver 2; Nu 15:27
4:28 [t]ver 23 [u]ver 3
4:29 [v]ver 4,24 [w]Lev 1:4
4:30 [x]ver 7
4:31 [y]Ge 8:21
4:32 [z]ver 28
4:33 [a]ver 29
4:34 [b]ver 7

[e]*10* The Hebrew word can include both male and female. [f]*10* Traditionally *peace offering*; also in verses 26, 31 and 35

from the lamb of the fellowship offering, and the priest shall burn it on the altar[a] on top of the offerings made to the LORD by fire. In this way the priest will make atonement for him for the sin he has committed, and he will be forgiven.

5 " 'If a person sins because he does not speak up when he hears a public charge to testify[b] regarding something he has seen or learned about, he will be held responsible.[c]

2" 'Or if a person touches anything ceremonially unclean—whether the carcasses of unclean wild animals or of unclean livestock or of unclean creatures that move along the ground[d]—even though he is unaware of it, he has become unclean and is guilty.

3" 'Or if he touches human uncleanness[e]—anything that would make him unclean—even though he is unaware of it, when he learns of it he will be guilty.

4" 'Or if a person thoughtlessly takes an oath[f] to do anything, whether good or evil—in any matter one might carelessly swear about—even though he is unaware of it, in any case when he learns of it he will be guilty.

5" 'When anyone is guilty in any of these ways, he must confess[g] in what way he has sinned 6and, as a penalty for the sin he has committed, he must bring to the LORD a female lamb or goat from the flock as a sin offering;[h] and the priest shall make atonement for him for his sin.

7" 'If he cannot afford[i] a lamb, he is to bring two doves or two young pigeons to the LORD as a penalty for his sin—one for a sin offering and the other for a burnt offering. 8He is to bring them to the priest, who shall first offer the one for the sin offering. He is to wring its head from its neck,[j] not severing it completely,[k] 9and is to sprinkle some of the blood of the sin offering against the side of the altar; the rest of the blood must be drained out at the base of the altar.[l] It is a sin offering. 10The priest shall then offer the other as a burnt offering in the prescribed way[m] and make atonement for him for the sin he has committed, and he will be forgiven.[n]

11" 'If, however, he cannot afford two doves or two young pigeons, he is to bring as an offering for his sin a tenth of an ephah[g] of fine flour[o] for a sin offering. He must not put oil or incense on it, because it is a sin offering. 12He is to bring it to the priest, who shall take a handful of it as a memorial portion and burn it on the altar on top of the offerings made to the LORD by fire. It is a sin offering. 13In this way the priest will make atonement[p] for him for any of these sins he has committed, and he will be forgiven. The rest of the offering will belong to the priest,[q] as in the case of the grain offering.' "

The Guilt Offering

14The LORD said to Moses: 15"When a person commits a violation and sins unintentionally in regard to any of the LORD's holy things, he is to bring to the LORD as a penalty[r] a ram[s] from the flock, one without defect and of the proper value in silver, according to the sanctuary shekel.[h][t] It is a guilt offering. 16He must make restitution[u] for what he has failed to do in regard to the holy things, add a fifth of the value[v] to that and give it all to the priest, who will make atonement for him with the ram as a guilt offering, and he will be forgiven.

17"If a person sins and does what is forbidden in any of the LORD's commands, even though he does not know it,[w] he is guilty and will be held responsible. 18He is to bring to the priest as a guilt offering a ram from the flock, one without defect and of the proper value. In this way the priest will make atonement for him for the wrong he has

4:35 [a]ver 26,31
5:1 [b]Pr 29:24 [c]ver 17
5:2 [d]Lev 11:11, 24-40; Dt 14:8
5:3 [e]Nu 19:11-16
5:4 [f]Nu 30:6,8
5:5 [g]Lev 16:21; 26:40; Nu 5:7; Pr 28:13
5:6 [h]Lev 4:28
5:7 [i]Lev 12:8; 14:21
5:8 [j]Lev 1:15 [k]Lev 1:17
5:9 [l]Lev 4:7,18
5:10 [m]Lev 1:14-17 [n]Lev 4:26
5:11 [o]Lev 2:1
5:13 [p]Lev 4:26 [q]Lev 2:3
5:15 [r]Lev 22:14 [s]Nu 5:8 [t]Ex 30:13
5:16 [u]Lev 6:4 [v]Lev 22:14; Nu 5:7
5:17 [w]ver 15; Lev 4:2

g11 That is, probably about 2 quarts (about 2 liters) h15 That is, about 2/5 ounce (about 11.5 grams)

committed unintentionally, and he
will be forgiven.[a] **19**It is a guilt offering; he has been guilty of[i]
wrongdoing against the LORD."

6 The LORD said to Moses: **2**"If
anyone sins and is unfaithful
to the LORD[b] by deceiving his
neighbor[c] about something entrusted to him or left in his care[d]
or stolen, or if he cheats him, **3**or if
he finds lost property and lies
about it,[e] or if he swears falsely, or
if he commits any such sin that
people may do— **4**when he thus
sins and becomes guilty, he must
return[f] what he has stolen or tak-
en by extortion, or what was entrusted to him, or the lost property
he found, **5**or whatever it was he
swore falsely about. He must make
restitution[g] in full, add a fifth of
the value to it and give it all to the
owner on the day he presents his
guilt offering.[h] **6**And as a penalty
he must bring to the priest, that is,
to the LORD, his guilt offering,[i] a
ram from the flock, one without defect and of the proper value. **7**In
this way the priest will make atonement[j] for him before the LORD,
and he will be forgiven for any of
these things he did that made him
guilty."

The Burnt Offering

8The LORD said to Moses: **9**"Give
Aaron and his sons this command:
'These are the regulations for the
burnt offering: The burnt offering
is to remain on the altar hearth
throughout the night, till morning,
and the fire must be kept burning
on the altar. **10**The priest shall then
put on his linen clothes, with linen
undergarments next to his body,[k]
and shall remove the ashes of the
burnt offering that the fire has consumed on the altar and place them
beside the altar. **11**Then he is to
take off these clothes and put on
others, and carry the ashes outside
the camp to a place that is ceremonially clean.[l] **12**The fire on the
altar must be kept burning; it must
not go out. Every morning the
priest is to add firewood and arrange the burnt offering on the fire
and burn the fat of the fellowship
offerings[j] on it. **13**The fire must be
kept burning on the altar continu-
ously; it must not go out.

The Grain Offering

14" 'These are the regulations for
the grain offering:[m] Aaron's sons
are to bring it before the LORD, in
front of the altar. **15**The priest is to
take a handful of fine flour and oil,
together with all the incense on the
grain offering,[n] and burn the memorial portion[o] on the altar as an
aroma pleasing to the LORD. **16**Aaron and his sons[p] shall eat the
rest[q] of it, but it is to be eaten
without yeast[r] in a holy place;[s]
they are to eat it in the courtyard of
the Tent of Meeting. **17**It must not
be baked with yeast; I have given it
as their share of the offerings made
to me by fire. Like the sin offering
and the guilt offering, it is most
holy.[t] **18**Any male descendant of
Aaron may eat it.[u] It is his regular
share of the offerings made to the
LORD by fire for the generations to
come. Whatever touches them will
become holy.[k,v] "

19The LORD also said to Moses,
20"This is the offering Aaron and
his sons are to bring to the LORD on
the day he[l] is anointed: a tenth of
an ephah[m,w] of fine flour as a regular grain offering,[x] half of it in the
morning and half in the evening.
21Prepare it with oil on a griddle;[y]
bring it well-mixed and present the
grain offering broken[n] in pieces as
an aroma pleasing to the LORD.
22The son who is to succeed him as
anointed priest shall prepare it. It
is the LORD's regular share and is to
be burned completely. **23**Every
grain offering of a priest shall be
burned completely; it must not be
eaten."

The Sin Offering

24The LORD said to Moses, **25**"Say

5:18 [a]ver 15
6:2 [b]Nu 5:6; Ac 5:4; Col 3:9 [c]Pr 24:28 [d]Ex 22:7
6:3 [e]Dt 22:1-3
6:4 [f]Lk 19:8
6:5 [g]Nu 5:7 [h]Lev 5:15
6:6 [i]Lev 5:15
6:7 [j]Lev 4:26
6:10 [k]Ex 28:39-42, 43; 39:28
6:11 [l]Lev 4:12
6:14 [m]Lev 2:1; 15:4
6:15 [n]Lev 2:9 [o]Lev 2:2
6:16 [p]Lev 2:3 [q]Eze 44:29 [r]Lev 2:11 [s]Lev 10:13
6:17 [t]ver 29; Ex 40:10; Nu 18:9,10
6:18 [u]ver 29; Nu 18:9-10 [v]ver 27
6:20 [w]Ex 16:36 [x]Ex 29:2
6:21 [y]Lev 2:5

[i]*19* Or *has made full expiation for his*
[j]*12* Traditionally *peace offerings* [k]*18* Or *Whoever touches them must be holy*; similarly in verse 27 [l]*20* Or *each* [m]*20* That is, probably about 2 quarts (about 2 liters)
[n]*21* The meaning of the Hebrew for this word is uncertain.

to Aaron and his sons: 'These are the regulations for the sin offering: The sin offering is to be slaughtered before the LORD[a] in the place[b] the burnt offering is slaughtered; it is most holy. **26**The priest who offers it shall eat it; it is to be eaten in a holy place,[c] in the courtyard[d] of the Tent of Meeting. **27**Whatever touches any of the flesh will become holy,[e] and if any of the blood is spattered on a garment, you must wash it in a holy place. **28**The clay pot[f] the meat is cooked in must be broken; but if it is cooked in a bronze pot, the pot is to be scoured and rinsed with water. **29**Any male in a priest's family may eat it;[g] it is most holy.[h] **30**But any sin offering whose blood is brought into the Tent of Meeting to make atonement in the Holy Place[i] must not be eaten; it must be burned.[j]

The Guilt Offering

7 " 'These are the regulations for the guilt offering,[k] which is most holy: **2**The guilt offering is to be slaughtered in the place where the burnt offering is slaughtered, and its blood is to be sprinkled against the altar on all sides. **3**All its fat[l] shall be offered: the fat tail and the fat that covers the inner parts, **4**both kidneys with the fat on them near the loins, and the covering of the liver, which is to be removed with the kidneys. **5**The priest shall burn them on the altar as an offering made to the LORD by fire. It is a guilt offering. **6**Any male in a priest's family may eat it,[m] but it must be eaten in a holy place; it is most holy.[n]

7" 'The same law applies to both the sin offering and the guilt offering: They belong to the priest[o] who makes atonement with them. **8**The priest who offers a burnt offering for anyone may keep its hide for himself. **9**Every grain offering baked in an oven or cooked in a pan or on a griddle[p] belongs to the priest who offers it, **10**and every grain offering, whether mixed with oil or dry, belongs equally to all the sons of Aaron.

The Fellowship Offering

11" 'These are the regulations for the fellowship offering[o] a person may present to the LORD:

12" 'If he offers it as an expression of thankfulness, then along with this thank offering[q] he is to offer cakes of bread made without yeast and mixed with oil, wafers[r] made without yeast and spread with oil, and cakes of fine flour well-kneaded and mixed with oil. **13**Along with his fellowship offering of thanksgiving he is to present an offering with cakes of bread made with yeast.[s] **14**He is to bring one of each kind as an offering, a contribution to the LORD; it belongs to the priest who sprinkles the blood of the fellowship offerings. **15**The meat of his fellowship offering of thanksgiving must be eaten on the day it is offered; he must leave none of it till morning.[t]

16" 'If, however, his offering is the result of a vow or is a freewill offering, the sacrifice shall be eaten on the day he offers it, but anything left over may be eaten on the next day.[u] **17**Any meat of the sacrifice left over till the third day must be burned up. **18**If any meat of the fellowship offering is eaten on the third day, it will not be accepted.[v] It will not be credited[w] to the one who offered it, for it is impure; the person who eats any of it will be held responsible.

19" 'Meat that touches anything ceremonially unclean must not be eaten; it must be burned up. As for other meat, anyone ceremonially clean may eat it. **20**But if anyone who is unclean eats any meat of the fellowship offering belonging to the LORD, that person must be cut off from his people.[x] **21**If anyone touches something unclean[y]—whether human uncleanness or an unclean animal or any unclean, detestable thing—and then eats any

6:25 [a] Lev 1:3 [b] Lev 1:5,11
6:26 [c] ver 16 [d] Lev 10:17-18
6:27 [e] Ex 29:37
6:28 [f] Lev 11:33; 15:12
6:29 [g] ver 18 [h] ver 17
6:30 [i] Lev 4:18 [j] Lev 4:12
7:1 [k] Lev 5:14-6:7
7:3 [l] Ex 29:13; Lev 3:4,9
7:6 [m] Lev 6:18; Nu 18:9-10 [n] Lev 2:3
7:7 [o] Lev 6:17,26; 1Co 9:13
7:9 [p] Lev 2:5
7:12 [q] ver 13,15 [r] Lev 2:4; Nu 6:15
7:13 [s] Lev 23:17; Am 4:5
7:15 [t] Lev 22:30
7:16 [u] Lev 19:5-8
7:18 [v] Lev 19:7 [w] Nu 18:27
7:20 [x] Lev 22:3-7
7:21 [y] Lev 5:2; 11:24,28

[o] *11* Traditionally *peace offering;* also in verses 13-37

of the meat of the fellowship offering belonging to the LORD, that person must be cut off from his people.' "

Eating Fat and Blood Forbidden

22The LORD said to Moses, 23"Say to the Israelites: 'Do not eat any of the fat of cattle, sheep or goats.[a] 24The fat of an animal found dead or torn by wild animals[b] may be used for any other purpose, but you must not eat it. 25Anyone who eats the fat of an animal from which an offering by fire may be[p] made to the LORD must be cut off from his people. 26And wherever you live, you must not eat the blood[c] of any bird or animal. 27If anyone eats blood,[d] that person must be cut off from his people.' "

The Priests' Share

28The LORD said to Moses, 29"Say to the Israelites: 'Anyone who brings a fellowship offering to the LORD is to bring part of it as his sacrifice to the LORD. 30With his own hands he is to bring the offering made to the LORD by fire; he is to bring the fat, together with the breast, and wave the breast before the LORD as a wave offering.[e] 31The priest shall burn the fat on the altar, but the breast belongs to Aaron and his sons.[f] 32You are to give the right thigh of your fellowship offerings to the priest as a contribution.[g] 33The son of Aaron who offers the blood and the fat of the fellowship offering shall have the right thigh as his share. 34From the fellowship offerings of the Israelites, I have taken the breast that is waved and the thigh[h] that is presented and have given them to Aaron the priest and his sons[i] as their regular share from the Israelites.' "

35This is the portion of the offerings made to the LORD by fire that were allotted to Aaron and his sons on the day they were presented to serve the LORD as priests. 36On the day they were anointed,[j] the LORD commanded that the Israelites give this to them as their regular share for the generations to come.

37These, then, are the regulations for the burnt offering,[k] the grain offering,[l] the sin offering, the guilt offering, the ordination offering[m] and the fellowship offering, 38which the LORD gave Moses on Mount Sinai on the day he commanded the Israelites to bring their offerings to the LORD,[n] in the Desert of Sinai.

The Ordination of Aaron and His Sons

8:1-36pp — Ex 29:1-37

8 The LORD said to Moses, 2"Bring Aaron and his sons, their garments, the anointing oil,[o] the bull for the sin offering, the two rams and the basket containing bread made without yeast,[p] 3and gather the entire assembly[q] at the entrance to the Tent of Meeting." 4Moses did as the LORD commanded him, and the assembly gathered at the entrance to the Tent of Meeting.

5Moses said to the assembly, "This is what the LORD has commanded to be done." 6Then Moses brought Aaron and his sons forward and washed them with water.[r] 7He put the tunic on Aaron, tied the sash around him, clothed him with the robe and put the ephod on him. He also tied the ephod to him by its skillfully woven waistband; so it was fastened on him.[s] 8He placed the breastpiece on him and put the Urim and Thummim[t] in the breastpiece. 9Then he placed the turban on Aaron's head and set the gold plate, the sacred diadem,[u] on the front of it, as the LORD commanded Moses.

10Then Moses took the anointing oil[v] and anointed[w] the tabernacle and everything in it, and so consecrated them. 11He sprinkled some of the oil on the altar seven times, anointing the altar and all its utensils and the basin with its stand, to consecrate them.[x] 12He

p25 Or *fire is*

7:23 [a]Lev 3:17; 17:13-14
7:24 [b]Ex 22:31
7:26 [c]Ge 9:4
7:27 [d]Lev 17:10-24; Ac 15:20,29
7:30 [e]Ex 29:24; Nu 6:20
7:31 [f]ver 34
7:32 [g]ver 34; Lev 9:21; Nu 6:20
7:34 [h]Lev 10:15 [i]Ex 29:27; Nu 18:18-19
7:36 [j]Ex 40:13,15; Lev 8:12,30
7:37 [k]Lev 6:9 [l]Lev 6:14 [m]ver 1,11
7:38 [n]Lev 1:2
8:2 [o]Ex 30:23-25, 30 [p]Ex 29:2-3
8:3 [q]Nu 8:9
8:6 [r]Ex 29:4; 30:19; Ps 26:6; Ac 22:16; 1Co 6:11; Eph 5:26
8:7 [s]Ex 28:4
8:8 [t]Ex 28:30
8:9 [u]Ex 28:36
8:10 [v]ver 2 [w]Ex 30:26
8:11 [x]Ex 30:29

poured some of the anointing oil on Aaron's head and anointed[a] him to consecrate him.[b] **13**Then he brought Aaron's sons forward, put tunics on them, tied sashes around them and put headbands on them, as the LORD commanded Moses.

14He then presented the bull[c] for the sin offering,[d] and Aaron and his sons laid their hands on its head. **15**Moses slaughtered the bull and took some of the blood, and with his finger he put it on all the horns of the altar[e] to purify the altar.[f] He poured out the rest of the blood at the base of the altar. So he consecrated it to make atonement for it.[g] **16**Moses also took all the fat around the inner parts, the covering of the liver, and both kidneys and their fat, and burned it on the altar. **17**But the bull with its hide and its flesh and its offal[h] he burned up outside the camp,[i] as the LORD commanded Moses.

18He then presented the ram[j] for the burnt offering, and Aaron and his sons laid their hands on its head. **19**Then Moses slaughtered the ram and sprinkled the blood against the altar on all sides. **20**He cut the ram into pieces and burned the head, the pieces and the fat. **21**He washed the inner parts and the legs with water and burned the whole ram on the altar as a burnt offering, a pleasing aroma, an offering made to the LORD by fire, as the LORD commanded Moses.

22He then presented the other ram, the ram for the ordination,[k] and Aaron and his sons laid their hands on its head. **23**Moses slaughtered the ram and took some of its blood and put it on the lobe of Aaron's right ear, on the thumb of his right hand and on the big toe of his right foot. **24**Moses also brought Aaron's sons forward and put some of the blood on the lobes of their right ears, on the thumbs of their right hands and on the big toes of their right feet. Then he sprinkled blood against the altar on all sides.[l] **25**He took the fat, the fat tail, all the fat around the inner parts, the covering of the liver, both kidneys and their fat and the right thigh. **26**Then from the basket of bread made without yeast, which was before the LORD, he took a cake of bread, and one made with oil, and a wafer; he put these on the fat portions and on the right thigh. **27**He put all these in the hands of Aaron and his sons and waved them before the LORD as a wave offering. **28**Then Moses took them from their hands and burned them on the altar on top of the burnt offering as an ordination offering, a pleasing aroma, an offering made to the LORD by fire. **29**He also took the breast—Moses' share of the ordination ram[m]—and waved it before the LORD as a wave offering, as the LORD commanded Moses.

30Then Moses took some of the anointing oil and some of the blood from the altar and sprinkled them on Aaron and his garments[n] and on his sons and their garments. So he consecrated[o] Aaron and his garments and his sons and their garments.

31Moses then said to Aaron and his sons, "Cook the meat at the entrance to the Tent of Meeting and eat it there with the bread from the basket of ordination offerings, as I commanded, saying,[q] 'Aaron and his sons are to eat it.' **32**Then burn up the rest of the meat and the bread. **33**Do not leave the entrance to the Tent of Meeting for seven days, until the days of your ordination are completed, for your ordination will last seven days. **34**What has been done today was commanded by the LORD[p] to make atonement for you. **35**You must stay at the entrance to the Tent of Meeting day and night for seven days and do what the LORD requires,[q] so you will not die; for that is what I have been commanded." **36**So Aaron and his sons did everything the LORD commanded through Moses.

8:12 [a]Lev 21:10,12 [b]Ex 30:30
8:14 [c]Lev 4:3 [d]Ps 66:15; Eze 43:19
8:15 [e]Lev 4:7 [f]Heb 9:22 [g]Eze 43:20
8:17 [h]Lev 4:11 [i]Lev 4:12
8:18 [j]ver 2
8:22 [k]ver 2
8:24 [l]Heb 9:18-22
8:29 [m]Lev 7:31-34
8:30 [n]Ex 28:2 [o]Nu 3:3
8:34 [p]Heb 7:16
8:35 [q]Nu 3:7; 9:19; Dt 11:1; 1Ki 2:3; Eze 48:11

[q]*31* Or *I was commanded:*

The Priests Begin Their Ministry

9 On the eighth day[a] Moses
summoned Aaron and his sons
and the elders of Israel. **2**He said to
Aaron, "Take a bull calf for your sin
offering and a ram for your burnt
offering, both without defect, and
present them before the LORD.
3Then say to the Israelites: 'Take a
male goat for a sin offering, a calf
and a lamb—both a year old and
without defect—for a burnt offering, **4**and an ox[r] and a ram for a
fellowship offering[s] to sacrifice
before the LORD, together with a
grain offering mixed with oil. For
today the LORD will appear to
you.[b]' "

5They took the things Moses
commanded to the front of the
Tent of Meeting, and the entire assembly came near and stood before
the LORD. **6**Then Moses said, "This
is what the LORD has commanded
you to do, so that the glory of the
LORD[c] may appear to you."

7Moses said to Aaron, "Come to
the altar and sacrifice your sin offering and your burnt offering and
make atonement for yourself and
the people; sacrifice the offering
that is for the people and make
atonement for them, as the LORD
has commanded.[d]"

8So Aaron came to the altar and
slaughtered the calf as a sin offering[e] for himself. **9**His sons brought
the blood to him,[f] and he dipped
his finger into the blood and put it
on the horns of the altar; the rest of
the blood he poured out at the base
of the altar.[g] **10**On the altar he
burned the fat, the kidneys and the
covering of the liver from the sin
offering, as the LORD commanded
Moses; **11**the flesh and the hide[h]
he burned up outside the camp.[i]

12Then he slaughtered the burnt
offering. His sons handed him the
blood, and he sprinkled it against
the altar on all sides. **13**They handed him the burnt offering piece by
piece, including the head, and he
burned them on the altar.[j] **14**He
washed the inner parts and the legs
and burned them on top of the
burnt offering on the altar.

15Aaron then brought the offering that was for the people.[k] He
took the goat for the people's sin
offering and slaughtered it and offered it for a sin offering as he did
with the first one.

16He brought the burnt offering
and offered it in the prescribed
way.[l] **17**He also brought the grain
offering, took a handful of it and
burned it on the altar in addition to
the morning's burnt offering.[m]

18He slaughtered the ox and the
ram as the fellowship offering for
the people.[n] His sons handed him
the blood, and he sprinkled it
against the altar on all sides. **19**But
the fat portions of the ox and the
ram—the fat tail, the layer of fat,
the kidneys and the covering of the
liver— **20**these they laid on the
breasts, and then Aaron burned the
fat on the altar. **21**Aaron waved the
breasts and the right thigh before
the LORD as a wave offering,[o] as
Moses commanded.

22Then Aaron lifted his hands toward the people and blessed
them.[p] And having sacrificed the
sin offering, the burnt offering and
the fellowship offering, he stepped
down.

23Moses and Aaron then went
into the Tent of Meeting. When
they came out, they blessed the
people; and the glory of the LORD[q]
appeared to all the people. **24**Fire[r]
came out from the presence of the
LORD and consumed the burnt offering and the fat portions on the
altar. And when all the people saw
it, they shouted for joy and fell
facedown.[s]

The Death of Nadab and Abihu

10 Aaron's sons Nadab and
Abihu[t] took their censers,
put fire in them[u] and added incense; and they offered unauthorized fire before the LORD, contrary

9:1 [a]Eze 43:27
9:4 [b]Ex 29:43
9:6 [c]ver 23; Ex 24:16
9:7 [d]Heb 5:1,3; 7:27
9:8 [e]Lev 4:1-12
9:9 [f]ver 12,18 [g]Lev 4:7
9:11 [h]Lev 4:11 [i]Lev 4:12; 8:17
9:13 [j]Lev 1:8
9:15 [k]Lev 4:27-31
9:16 [l]Lev 1:1-13
9:17 [m]Lev 2:1-2; 3:5
9:18 [n]Lev 3:1-11
9:21 [o]Ex 29:24,26; Lev 7:30-34
9:22 [p]Nu 6:23; Dt 21:5; Lk 24:50
9:23 [q]ver 6
9:24 [r]Jdg 6:21; 2Ch 7:1 [s]1Ki 18:39
10:1 [t]Ex 24:1; Nu 3:2-4; 26:61 [u]Lev 16:12

[r]4 The Hebrew word can include both male and female; also in verses 18 and 19.
[s]4 Traditionally *peace offering*; also in verses 18 and 22

to his command.[a] 2So fire came out from the presence of the LORD and consumed them,[b] and they died before the LORD. 3Moses then said to Aaron, "This is what the LORD spoke of when he said:

" 'Among those who approach me[c]
I will show myself holy;[d]
in the sight of all the people
I will be honored.[e]' "

Aaron remained silent.

4Moses summoned Mishael and Elzaphan,[f] sons of Aaron's uncle Uzziel,[g] and said to them, "Come here; carry your cousins outside the camp,[h] away from the front of the sanctuary." 5So they came and carried them, still in their tunics,[i] outside the camp, as Moses ordered.

6Then Moses said to Aaron and his sons Eleazar and Ithamar, "Do not let your hair become unkempt,[t][j] and do not tear your clothes, or you will die and the LORD will be angry with the whole community.[k] But your relatives, all the house of Israel, may mourn for those the LORD has destroyed by fire. 7Do not leave the entrance to the Tent of Meeting or you will die, because the LORD's anointing oil[l] is on you." So they did as Moses said.

8Then the LORD said to Aaron, 9"You and your sons are not to drink wine[m] or other fermented drink[n] whenever you go into the Tent of Meeting, or you will die. This is a lasting ordinance for the generations to come. 10You must distinguish between the holy and the common, between the unclean and the clean,[o] 11and you must teach[p] the Israelites all the decrees the LORD has given them through Moses.[q]"

12Moses said to Aaron and his remaining sons, Eleazar and Ithamar, "Take the grain offering left over from the offerings made to the LORD by fire and eat it prepared without yeast beside the altar,[r] for it is most holy. 13Eat it in a holy place, because it is your share and

10:1 [a]Ex 30:9
10:2 [b]Nu 3:4; 16:35; 26:61
10:3 [c]Ex 19:22 [d]Ex 30:29; Lev 21:6; Eze 28:22 [e]Ex Isa 49:3
10:4 [f]Ex 6:22 [g]Ex 6:18 [h]Ac 5:6,9,10
10:5 [i]Lev 8:13
10:6 [j]Lev 21:10 [k]Nu 1:53; 16:22; Jos 7:1; 22:18; 2Sa 24:1
10:7 [l]Ex 28:41; Lev 21:12
10:9 [m]Hos 4:11 [n]Pr 20:1; Isa 28:7; Eze 44:21; Lk 1:15; Eph 5:18; 1Ti 3:3; Tit 1:7
10:10 [o]Lev 11:47; 20:25; Eze 22:26
10:11 [p]Mal 2:7 [q]Dt 24:8
10:12 [r]Lev 6:14-18; 21:22
10:14 [s]Ex 29:24, 26-27; Lev 7:31,34; Nu 18:11
10:15 [t]Lev 7:34
10:16 [u]Lev 9:3
10:17 [v]Lev 6:24-30
10:18 [w]Lev 6:26,30
10:19 [x]Lev 9:12
11:2 [y]Ac 10:12-14

your sons' share of the offerings made to the LORD by fire; for so I have been commanded. 14But you and your sons and your daughters may eat the breast that was waved and the thigh that was presented. Eat them in a ceremonially clean place;[s] they have been given to you and your children as your share of the Israelites' fellowship offerings.[u] 15The thigh[t] that was presented and the breast that was waved must be brought with the fat portions of the offerings made by fire, to be waved before the LORD as a wave offering. This will be the regular share for you and your children, as the LORD has commanded."

16When Moses inquired about the goat of the sin offering[u] and found that it had been burned up, he was angry with Eleazar and Ithamar, Aaron's remaining sons, and asked, 17"Why didn't you eat the sin offering[v] in the sanctuary area? It is most holy; it was given to you to take away the guilt of the community by making atonement for them before the LORD. 18Since its blood was not taken into the Holy Place,[w] you should have eaten the goat in the sanctuary area, as I commanded."

19Aaron replied to Moses, "Today they sacrificed their sin offering and their burnt offering[x] before the LORD, but such things as this have happened to me. Would the LORD have been pleased if I had eaten the sin offering today?" 20When Moses heard this, he was satisfied.

Clean and Unclean Food

11:1–23pp — Dt 14:3–20

11 The LORD said to Moses and Aaron, 2"Say to the Israelites: 'Of all the animals that live on land, these are the ones you may eat:[y] 3You may eat any animal that has a split hoof completely divided and that chews the cud.

4" 'There are some that only

[t]6 Or *Do not uncover your heads*
[u]14 Traditionally *peace offerings*

chew the cud or only have a split
hoof, but you must not eat them.
The camel, though it chews the
cud, does not have a split hoof; it is
ceremonially unclean for you. **5**The
coney,[v] though it chews the cud,
does not have a split hoof; it is unclean for you. **6**The rabbit, though
it chews the cud, does not have a
split hoof; it is unclean for you.
7And the pig,[a] though it has a split
hoof completely divided, does not
chew the cud; it is unclean for you.
8You must not eat their meat or
touch their carcasses; they are unclean for you.[b]
9" 'Of all the creatures living in
the water of the seas and the
streams, you may eat any that have
fins and scales. **10**But all creatures
in the seas or streams that do not
have fins and scales—whether
among all the swarming things or
among all the other living creatures
in the water—you are to detest.[c]
11And since you are to detest them,
you must not eat their meat and
you must detest their carcasses.
12Anything living in the water that
does not have fins and scales is to
be detestable to you.
13" 'These are the birds you are
to detest and not eat because they
are detestable: the eagle, the vulture, the black vulture, **14**the red
kite, any kind of black kite, **15**any
kind of raven, **16**the horned owl,
the screech owl, the gull, any kind
of hawk, **17**the little owl, the cor-
morant, the great owl, **18**the white
owl, the desert owl, the osprey,
19the stork, any kind of heron, the
hoopoe and the bat.[w]
20" 'All flying insects that walk
on all fours are to be detestable to
you.[d] **21**There are, however, some
winged creatures that walk on all
fours that you may eat: those that
have jointed legs for hopping on
the ground. **22**Of these you may eat
any kind of locust,[e] katydid, crick-
et or grasshopper. **23**But all other
winged creatures that have four
legs you are to detest.
24" 'You will make yourselves
unclean by these; whoever touches
their carcasses will be unclean till
evening. **25**Whoever picks up one of
their carcasses must wash his
clothes,[f] and he will be unclean
till evening.[g]
26" 'Every animal that has a split
hoof not completely divided or that
does not chew the cud is unclean
for you; whoever touches ⌞the carcass of⌟ any of them will be unclean. **27**Of all the animals that
walk on all fours, those that walk
on their paws are unclean for you;
whoever touches their carcasses
will be unclean till evening. **28**Anyone who picks up their carcasses
must wash his clothes, and he will
be unclean till evening. They are
unclean for you.
29" 'Of the animals that move
about on the ground, these are unclean for you: the weasel, the rat,[h]
any kind of great lizard, **30**the
gecko, the monitor lizard, the wall
lizard, the skink and the chame-
leon. **31**Of all those that move
along the ground, these are unclean for you. Whoever touches
them when they are dead will be
unclean till evening. **32**When one
of them dies and falls on something, that article, whatever its use,
will be unclean, whether it is made
of wood, cloth, hide or sackcloth.[i]
Put it in water; it will be unclean
till evening, and then it will be
clean. **33**If one of them falls into a
clay pot, everything in it will be unclean, and you must break the
pot.[j] **34**Any food that could be eat-
en but has water on it from such a
pot is unclean, and any liquid that
could be drunk from it is unclean.
35Anything that one of their carcasses falls on becomes unclean;
an oven or cooking pot must be
broken up. They are unclean, and
you are to regard them as unclean.
36A spring, however, or a cistern for
collecting water remains clean, but
anyone who touches one of these
carcasses is unclean. **37**If a carcass
falls on any seeds that are to be
planted, they remain clean. **38**But

11:7 [a]Isa 65:4; 66:3,17
11:8 [b]Isa 52:11; Heb 9:10
11:10 [c]Lev 7:18
11:20 [d]Ac 10:14
11:22 [e]Mt 3:4; Mk 1:6
11:25 [f]Lev 14:8,47; 15:5 [g]ver 40; Nu 31:24
11:29 [h]Isa 66:17
11:32 [i]Lev 15:12
11:33 [j]Lev 6:28; 15:12

[v]*5* That is, the hyrax or rock badger
[w]*19* The precise identification of some of the birds, insects and animals in this chapter is uncertain.

if water has been put on the seed
and a carcass falls on it, it is unclean for you.
39" 'If an animal that you are allowed to eat dies, anyone who
touches the carcass will be unclean
till evening. 40Anyone who eats
some of the carcass must wash his
clothes, and he will be unclean till
evening.[a] Anyone who picks up
the carcass must wash his clothes,
and he will be unclean till evening.
41" 'Every creature that moves
about on the ground is detestable;
it is not to be eaten. 42You are not
to eat any creature that moves
about on the ground, whether it
moves on its belly or walks on all
fours or on many feet; it is detestable. 43Do not defile yourselves by
any of these creatures.[b] Do not
make yourselves unclean by means
of them or be made unclean by
them. 44I am the LORD your God;[c]
consecrate yourselves[d] and be
holy,[e] because I am holy.[f] Do not
make yourselves unclean by any
creature that moves about on the
ground. 45I am the LORD who
brought you up out of Egypt[g] to be
your God;[h] therefore be holy, because I am holy.[i]
46" 'These are the regulations
concerning animals, birds, every
living thing that moves in the water
and every creature that moves
about on the ground. 47You must
distinguish between the unclean
and the clean, between living creatures that may be eaten and those
that may not be eaten.[j]' "

Purification After Childbirth

12 The LORD said to Moses,
2"Say to the Israelites: 'A
woman who becomes pregnant and
gives birth to a son will be ceremonially unclean for seven days,
just as she is unclean during her
monthly period.[k] 3On the eighth
day the boy is to be circumcised.[l]
4Then the woman must wait thirty-three days to be purified from
her bleeding. She must not touch
anything sacred or go to the sanctuary until the days of her purification are over. 5If she gives birth to
a daughter, for two weeks the woman will be unclean, as during her
period. Then she must wait sixty-
six days to be purified from her
bleeding.
6" 'When the days of her purification for a son or daughter are
over,[m] she is to bring to the priest
at the entrance to the Tent of
Meeting a year-old lamb[n] for a
burnt offering and a young pigeon
or a dove for a sin offering.[o] 7He
shall offer them before the LORD to
make atonement for her, and then
she will be ceremonially clean from
her flow of blood.
" 'These are the regulations for
the woman who gives birth to a boy
or a girl. 8If she cannot afford a
lamb, she is to bring two doves or
two young pigeons,[p] one for a
burnt offering and the other for a
sin offering.[q] In this way the priest
will make atonement for her, and
she will be clean.[r]' "

Regulations About Infectious Skin Diseases

13 The LORD said to Moses and
Aaron, 2"When anyone has
a swelling[s] or a rash or a bright
spot[t] on his skin that may become
an infectious skin disease,[x][u] he
must be brought to Aaron the
priest[v] or to one of his sons[y] who
is a priest. 3The priest is to examine the sore on his skin, and if the
hair in the sore has turned white
and the sore appears to be more
than skin deep,[z] it is an infectious
skin disease. When the priest examines him, he shall pronounce
him ceremonially unclean.[w] 4If the
spot[x] on his skin is white but does
not appear to be more than skin
deep and the hair in it has not
turned white, the priest is to put
the infected person in isolation for
seven days.[y] 5On the seventh day[z]
the priest is to examine him,[a] and
if he sees that the sore is un-

11:40 [a]Lev 17:15; 22:8; Eze 44:31
11:43 [b]Lev 20:25
11:44 [c]Ex 6:2,7; Isa 43:3; 51:15 [d]Lev 20:7 [e]Ex 19:6 [f]Lev 19:2; Ps 99:3; Eph 1:4; 1Th 4:7; 1Pe 1:15,16*
11:45 [g]Lev 25:38, 55; Ex 6:7; 20:2 [h]Ge 17:7 [i]Ex 19:6; 1Pe 1:16*
11:47 [j]Lev 10:10
12:2 [k]Lev 15:19; 18:19
12:3 [l]Ge 17:12; Lk 1:59; 2:21
12:6 [m]Lk 2:22 [n]Ex 29:38; Lev 23:12; Nu 6:12,14; 7:15 [o]Lev 5:7
12:8 [p]Ge 15:9; Lev 14:22 [q]Lev 5:7; Lk 2:22-24* [r]Lev 4:26
13:2 [s]ver 10,19,28, 43 [t]ver 4,38, 39; Lev 14:56 [u]ver 3,9,15; Ex 4:6; Lev 14:3,32; Nu 5:2; Dt 24:8 [v]Dt 24:8
13:3 [w]ver 8,11,20, 30; Lev 21:1; Nu 9:6
13:4 [x]ver 2 [y]ver 5, 21,26,33,46; Lev 14:38; Nu 12:14,15; Dt 24:9
13:5 [z]Lev 14:9 [a]ver 27,32,34, 51

[x]2 Traditionally *leprosy*; the Hebrew word was used for various diseases affecting the skin—not necessarily leprosy; also elsewhere in this chapter. [y]2 Or *descendants*
[z]3 Or *be lower than the rest of the skin*; also elsewhere in this chapter

changed and has not spread in the
skin, he is to keep him in isolation
another seven days. 6On the seventh day the priest is to examine
him again, and if the sore has faded
and has not spread in the skin, the
priest shall pronounce him clean;[a]
it is only a rash. The man must
wash his clothes,[b] and he will be
clean.[c] 7But if the rash does
spread in his skin after he has
shown himself to the priest to be
pronounced clean, he must appear
before the priest again.[d] 8The
priest is to examine him, and if the
rash has spread in the skin, he shall
pronounce him unclean; it is an infectious disease.

9"When anyone has an infectious skin disease, he must be
brought to the priest. 10The priest
is to examine him, and if there is a
white swelling in the skin that has
turned the hair white and if there is
raw flesh in the swelling, 11it is a
chronic skin disease[e] and the
priest shall pronounce him unclean. He is not to put him in isolation, because he is already unclean.

12"If the disease breaks out all
over his skin and, so far as the
priest can see, it covers all the skin
of the infected person from head to
foot, 13the priest is to examine
him, and if the disease has covered
his whole body, he shall pronounce
that person clean. Since it has all
turned white, he is clean. 14But
whenever raw flesh appears on
him, he will be unclean. 15When
the priest sees the raw flesh, he
shall pronounce him unclean. The
raw flesh is unclean; he has an infectious disease.[f] 16Should the
raw flesh change and turn white, he
must go to the priest. 17The priest
is to examine him, and if the sores
have turned white, the priest shall
pronounce the infected person
clean;[g] then he will be clean.

18"When someone has a boil[h]
on his skin and it heals, 19and in
the place where the boil was, a
white swelling or reddish-white[i]
spot[j] appears, he must present
himself to the priest. 20The priest
is to examine it, and if it appears to
be more than skin deep and the
hair in it has turned white, the
priest shall pronounce him unclean. It is an infectious skin disease[k] that has broken out where
the boil was. 21But if, when the
priest examines it, there is no
white hair in it and it is not more
than skin deep and has faded, then
the priest is to put him in isolation
for seven days. 22If it is spreading
in the skin, the priest shall pronounce him unclean; it is infectious. 23But if the spot is unchanged and has not spread, it is
only a scar from the boil, and the
priest shall pronounce him clean.[l]

24"When someone has a burn on
his skin and a reddish-white or
white spot appears in the raw flesh
of the burn, 25the priest is to examine the spot, and if the hair in it has
turned white, and it appears to be
more than skin deep, it is an infectious disease that has broken out
in the burn. The priest shall pronounce him unclean; it is an infectious skin disease.[m] 26But if the
priest examines it and there is no
white hair in the spot and if it is not
more than skin deep and has faded,
then the priest is to put him in isolation for seven days.[n] 27On the
seventh day the priest is to examine him,[o] and if it is spreading in
the skin, the priest shall pronounce
him unclean; it is an infectious
skin disease. 28If, however, the
spot is unchanged and has not
spread in the skin but has faded, it
is a swelling from the burn, and the
priest shall pronounce him clean;
it is only a scar from the burn.[p]

29"If a man or woman has a sore
on the head[q] or on the chin, 30the
priest is to examine the sore, and if
it appears to be more than skin
deep and the hair in it is yellow and
thin, the priest shall pronounce
that person unclean; it is an itch,
an infectious disease of the head or
chin. 31But if, when the priest examines this kind of sore, it does not
seem to be more than skin deep
and there is no black hair in it, then
the priest is to put the infected per-

13:6 [a]ver 13,17,23,28,34; Mt 8:3; Lk 5:12-14 [b]Lev 11:25 [c]Lev 11:25; 14:8,9,20,48; 15:8; Nu 8:7
13:7 [d]Lk 5:14
13:11 [e]Ex 4:6; Lev 14:8; Nu 12:10; Mt 8:2
13:15 [f]ver 2
13:17 [g]ver 6
13:18 [h]Ex 9:9
13:19 [i]ver 24,42; Lev 14:37 [j]ver 2
13:20 [k]ver 2
13:23 [l]ver 6
13:25 [m]ver 11
13:26 [n]ver 4
13:27 [o]ver 5
13:28 [p]ver 2
13:29 [q]ver 43,44

son in isolation for seven days.[a]
32On the seventh day the priest is
to examine the sore,[b] and if the
itch has not spread and there is no
yellow hair in it and it does not appear to be more than skin deep,
33he must be shaved except for the
diseased area, and the priest is to
keep him in isolation another sev-
en days. **34**On the seventh day the
priest is to examine the itch,[c] and
if it has not spread in the skin and
appears to be no more than skin
deep, the priest shall pronounce
him clean. He must wash his
clothes, and he will be clean.[d]
35But if the itch does spread in the
skin after he is pronounced clean,
36the priest is to examine him, and
if the itch has spread in the skin,
the priest does not need to look for
yellow hair; the person is unclean.[e] **37**If, however, in his judgment it is unchanged and black
hair has grown in it, the itch is
healed. He is clean, and the priest
shall pronounce him clean.

38"When a man or woman has
white spots on the skin, **39**the
priest is to examine them, and if
the spots are dull white, it is a
harmless rash that has broken
out on the skin; that person is
clean.

40"When a man has lost his hair
and is bald,[f] he is clean. **41**If he
has lost his hair from the front of
his scalp and has a bald forehead,
he is clean. **42**But if he has a reddish-white sore on his bald head or
forehead, it is an infectious disease
breaking out on his head or forehead. **43**The priest is to examine
him, and if the swollen sore on his
head or forehead is reddish-white
like an infectious skin disease,
44the man is diseased and is unclean. The priest shall pronounce
him unclean because of the sore on
his head.

45"The person with such an infectious disease must wear torn
clothes,[g] let his hair be unkempt,[a] cover the lower part of his
face[h] and cry out, 'Unclean! Unclean!'[i] **46**As long as he has the in-
fection he remains unclean. He
must live alone; he must live outside the camp.[j]

Regulations About Mildew

47"If any clothing is contaminated with mildew—any woolen or
linen clothing, **48**any woven or
knitted material of linen or wool,
any leather or anything made of
leather— **49**and if the contamination in the clothing, or leather, or
woven or knitted material, or any
leather article, is greenish or reddish, it is a spreading mildew and
must be shown to the priest.[k]
50The priest is to examine the mildew[l] and isolate the affected article for seven days. **51**On the seventh day he is to examine it,[m] and
if the mildew has spread in the
clothing, or the woven or knitted
material, or the leather, whatever
its use, it is a destructive mildew;
the article is unclean.[n] **52**He must
burn up the clothing, or the woven
or knitted material of wool or linen,
or any leather article that has the
contamination in it, because the
mildew is destructive; the article
must be burned up.[o]

53"But if, when the priest examines it, the mildew has not spread
in the clothing, or the woven or
knitted material, or the leather article, **54**he shall order that the contaminated article be washed. Then
he is to isolate it for another seven
days. **55**After the affected article
has been washed, the priest is to
examine it, and if the mildew has
not changed its appearance, even
though it has not spread, it is unclean. Burn it with fire, whether
the mildew has affected one side or
the other. **56**If, when the priest examines it, the mildew has faded after the article has been washed, he
is to tear the contaminated part out
of the clothing, or the leather, or
the woven or knitted material.
57But if it reappears in the clothing, or in the woven or knitted material, or in the leather article, it is
spreading, and whatever has the
mildew must be burned with fire.

13:31 [a]ver 4
13:32 [b]ver 5
13:34 [c]ver 5 [d]Lev 11:25
13:36 [e]ver 30
13:40 [f]Lev 21:5; 2Ki 2:23; Isa 3:24; 15:2; 22:12; Eze 27:31; 29:18; Am 8:10; Mic 1:16
13:45 [g]Lev 10:6 [h]Eze 24:17, 22; Mic 3:7 [i]Lev 5:2; La 4:15; Lk 17:12
13:46 [j]Nu 5:1-4, 12:14; 2Ki 7:3; 15:5; Lk 17:12
13:49 [k]Mk 1:44
13:50 [l]Eze 44:23
13:51 [m]ver 5 [n]Lev 14:44
13:52 [o]ver 55,57

[a]45 *Or clothes, uncover his head*

58The clothing, or the woven or knitted material, or any leather article that has been washed and is rid of the mildew, must be washed again, and it will be clean."

59These are the regulations concerning contamination by mildew in woolen or linen clothing, woven or knitted material, or any leather article, for pronouncing them clean or unclean.

Cleansing From Infectious Skin Diseases

14 The LORD said to Moses, 2"These are the regulations for the diseased person at the time of his ceremonial cleansing, when he is brought to the priest:[a] 3The priest is to go outside the camp and examine him.[b] If the person has been healed of his infectious skin disease,[b] 4the priest shall order that two live clean birds and some cedar wood, scarlet yarn and hyssop be brought for the one to be cleansed.[c] 5Then the priest shall order that one of the birds be killed over fresh water in a clay pot. 6He is then to take the live bird and dip it, together with the cedar wood, the scarlet yarn and the hyssop, into the blood of the bird that was killed over the fresh water.[d] 7Seven times he shall sprinkle[e] the one to be cleansed of the infectious disease and pronounce him clean. Then he is to release the live bird in the open fields.

8"The person to be cleansed must wash his clothes,[f] shave off all his hair and bathe with water;[g] then he will be ceremonially clean.[h] After this he may come into the camp,[i] but he must stay outside his tent for seven days. 9On the seventh day he must shave off all his hair; he must shave his head, his beard, his eyebrows and the rest of his hair. He must wash his clothes and bathe himself with water, and he will be clean.

10"On the eighth day[j] he must bring two male lambs and one ewe lamb a year old, each without defect, along with three-tenths of an ephah[c] of fine flour mixed with oil for a grain offering,[k] and one log[d] of oil.[l] 11The priest who pronounces him clean shall present both the one to be cleansed and his offerings before the LORD at the entrance to the Tent of Meeting.

12"Then the priest is to take one of the male lambs and offer it as a guilt offering,[m] along with the log of oil; he shall wave them before the LORD as a wave offering.[n] 13He is to slaughter the lamb in the holy place[o] where the sin offering and the burnt offering are slaughtered. Like the sin offering, the guilt offering belongs to the priest;[p] it is most holy. 14The priest is to take some of the blood of the guilt offering and put it on the lobe of the right ear of the one to be cleansed, on the thumb of his right hand and on the big toe of his right foot.[q] 15The priest shall then take some of the log of oil, pour it in the palm of his own left hand, 16dip his right forefinger into the oil in his palm, and with his finger sprinkle some of it before the LORD seven times. 17The priest is to put some of the oil remaining in his palm on the lobe of the right ear of the one to be cleansed, on the thumb of his right hand and on the big toe of his right foot, on top of the blood of the guilt offering. 18The rest of the oil in his palm the priest shall put on the head of the one to be cleansed and make atonement for him before the LORD.

19"Then the priest is to sacrifice the sin offering and make atonement for the one to be cleansed from his uncleanness. After that, the priest shall slaughter the burnt offering 20and offer it on the altar, together with the grain offering, and make atonement for him, and he will be clean.[r]

21"If, however, he is poor[s] and cannot afford these,[t] he must take

14:2 [a] Mt 8:2-4; Mk 1:40-44; Lk 5:12-14; 17:14
14:3 [b] Lev 13:46
14:4 [c] ver 6,49,51, 52; Nu 19:6; Ps 51:7
14:6 [d] ver 4
14:7 [e] 2Ki 5:10,14; Isa 52:15; Eze 36:25
14:8 [f] Lev 11:25; 13:6 [g] ver 9 [h] ver 20 [i] Nu 5:2,3; 12:14,15; 2Ch 26:21
14:10 [j] Mt 8:4; Mk 1:44; Lk 5:14 [k] Lev 2:1 [l] ver 12,15,21, 24
14:12 [m] Lev 5:18; 6:6-7 [n] Ex 29:24
14:13 [o] Ex 29:11 [p] Lev 6:24-30; 7:7
14:14 [q] Ex 29:20; Lev 8:23
14:20 [r] ver 8
14:21 [s] Lev 5:7; 12:8 [t] ver 22,32

[b]3 Traditionally *leprosy;* the Hebrew word was used for various diseases affecting the skin—not necessarily leprosy; also elsewhere in this chapter. [c]*10* That is, probably about 6 quarts (about 6.5 liters) [d]*10* That is, probably about 2/3 pint (about 0.3 liter); also in verses 12, 15, 21 and 24

one male lamb as a guilt offering to
be waved to make atonement for
him, together with a tenth of an
ephah[e] of fine flour mixed with oil
for a grain offering, a log of oil,
22and two doves or two young pigeons,[a] which he can afford, one
for a sin offering and the other for
a burnt offering.

23"On the eighth day he must
bring them for his cleansing to the
priest at the entrance to the Tent of
Meeting, before the LORD.[b] **24**The
priest is to take the lamb for the
guilt offering,[c] together with the
log of oil,[d] and wave them before
the LORD as a wave offering.[e] **25**He
shall slaughter the lamb for the
guilt offering and take some of its
blood and put it on the lobe of the
right ear of the one to be cleansed,
on the thumb of his right hand and
on the big toe of his right foot.[f]
26The priest is to pour some of the
oil into the palm of his own left
hand,[g] **27**and with his right forefinger sprinkle some of the oil from
his palm seven times before the
LORD. **28**Some of the oil in his palm
he is to put on the same places he
put the blood of the guilt offering
—on the lobe of the right ear of the
one to be cleansed, on the thumb
of his right hand and on the big toe
of his right foot. **29**The rest of the
oil in his palm the priest shall put
on the head of the one to be
cleansed, to make atonement for
him before the LORD.[h] **30**Then he
shall sacrifice the doves or the
young pigeons, which the person
can afford,[i] **31**one[f] as a sin offering and the other as a burnt offering,[j] together with the grain offering. In this way the priest will make
atonement before the LORD on behalf of the one to be cleansed.[k]"

32These are the regulations for
anyone who has an infectious skin
disease[l] and who cannot afford
the regular offerings[m] for his
cleansing.

Cleansing From Mildew

33The LORD said to Moses and
Aaron, **34**"When you enter the land
of Canaan,[n] which I am giving you
as your possession,[o] and I put a
spreading mildew in a house in
that land, **35**the owner of the house
must go and tell the priest, 'I have
seen something that looks like mildew in my house.' **36**The priest is to
order the house to be emptied before he goes in to examine the mildew, so that nothing in the house
will be pronounced unclean. After
this the priest is to go in and inspect the house. **37**He is to examine the mildew on the walls, and if
it has greenish or reddish[p] depres-
sions that appear to be deeper than
the surface of the wall, **38**the priest
shall go out the doorway of the
house and close it up for seven
days.[q] **39**On the seventh day[r] the
priest shall return to inspect the
house. If the mildew has spread on
the walls, **40**he is to order that the
contaminated stones be torn out
and thrown into an unclean place
outside the town.[s] **41**He must have
all the inside walls of the house
scraped and the material that is
scraped off dumped into an unclean place outside the town.
42Then they are to take other
stones to replace these and take
new clay and plaster the house.

43"If the mildew reappears in the
house after the stones have been
torn out and the house scraped and
plastered, **44**the priest is to go and
examine it and, if the mildew has
spread in the house, it is a destructive mildew; the house is unclean.[t] **45**It must be torn down—
its stones, timbers and all the plaster—and taken out of the town to
an unclean place.

46"Anyone who goes into the
house while it is closed up will be
unclean till evening.[u] **47**Anyone
who sleeps or eats in the house
must wash his clothes.[v]

48"But if the priest comes to examine it and the mildew has not
spread after the house has been
plastered, he shall pronounce the
house clean,[w] because the mildew

14:22 [a] Lev 5:7
14:23 [b] ver 10,11
14:24 [c] Nu 6:14 [d] ver 10 [e] ver 12
14:25 [f] ver 14; Ex 29:20
14:26 [g] ver 15
14:29 [h] ver 18
14:30 [i] Lev 5:7
14:31 [j] ver 22; Lev 5:7; 15:15,30 [k] ver 18,19
14:32 [l] Lev 13:2 [m] ver 21
14:34 [n] Ge 12:5; Ex 6:4; Nu 13:2 [o] Ge 17:8; 48:4; Nu 27:12; 32:22; Dt 3:27; 7:1; 32:49
14:37 [p] Lev 13:19
14:38 [q] Lev 13:4
14:39 [r] Lev 13:5
14:40 [s] ver 45
14:44 [t] Lev 13:51
14:46 [u] Lev 11:24
14:47 [v] Lev 11:25
14:48 [w] Lev 13:6

[e] *21* That is, probably about 2 quarts (about 2 liters) [f] *31* Septuagint and Syriac; Hebrew *31such as the person can afford, one*

is gone. **49**To purify the house he is
to take two birds and some cedar
wood, scarlet yarn and hyssop.[a]
50He shall kill one of the birds over
fresh water in a clay pot.[b] **51**Then
he is to take the cedar wood, the
hyssop,[c] the scarlet yarn and the
live bird, dip them into the blood of
the dead bird and the fresh water,
and sprinkle the house seven
times.[d] **52**He shall purify the
house with the bird's blood, the
fresh water, the live bird, the cedar
wood, the hyssop and the scarlet
yarn. **53**Then he is to release the
live bird in the open fields[e] outside the town. In this way he will
make atonement for the house,
and it will be clean.[f]"

54These are the regulations for
any infectious skin disease,[g] for an
itch, **55**for mildew[h] in clothing or
in a house, **56**and for a swelling, a
rash or a bright spot,[i] **57**to determine when something is clean or
unclean.

These are the regulations for infectious skin diseases and mildew.[j]

Discharges Causing Uncleanness

15 The LORD said to Moses and
Aaron, **2**"Speak to the Israelites and say to them: 'When any
man has a bodily discharge,[k] the
discharge is unclean. **3**Whether it
continues flowing from his body or
is blocked, it will make him unclean. This is how his discharge
will bring about uncleanness:

4" 'Any bed the man with a discharge lies on will be unclean, and
anything he sits on will be unclean.
5Anyone who touches his bed must
wash his clothes[l] and bathe with
water,[m] and he will be unclean till
evening.[n] **6**Whoever sits on anything that the man with a discharge
sat on must wash his clothes and
bathe with water, and he will be
unclean till evening.

7" 'Whoever touches the man[o]
who has a discharge[p] must wash
his clothes and bathe with water,
and he will be unclean till evening.

8" 'If the man with the discharge
spits[q] on someone who is clean,
that person must wash his clothes
and bathe with water, and he will
be unclean till evening.

9" 'Everything the man sits on
when riding will be unclean, **10**and
whoever touches any of the things
that were under him will be unclean till evening; whoever picks
up those things[r] must wash his
clothes and bathe with water, and
he will be unclean till evening.

11" 'Anyone the man with a discharge touches without rinsing his
hands with water must wash his
clothes and bathe with water, and
he will be unclean till evening.

12" 'A clay pot[s] that the man
touches must be broken, and any
wooden article[t] is to be rinsed
with water.

13" 'When a man is cleansed
from his discharge, he is to count
off seven days[u] for his ceremonial
cleansing; he must wash his
clothes and bathe himself with
fresh water, and he will be clean.[v]
14On the eighth day he must take
two doves or two young pigeons[w]
and come before the LORD to the
entrance to the Tent of Meeting
and give them to the priest. **15**The
priest is to sacrifice them, the one
for a sin offering[x] and the other for
a burnt offering.[y] In this way he
will make atonement before the
LORD for the man because of his
discharge.[z]

16" 'When a man has an emission of semen,[a] he must bathe his
whole body with water, and he will
be unclean till evening.[b] **17**Any
clothing or leather that has semen
on it must be washed with water,
and it will be unclean till evening.
18When a man lies with a woman
and there is an emission of semen,[c] both must bathe with water, and they will be unclean till
evening.

19" 'When a woman has her regular flow of blood, the impurity of
her monthly period[d] will last seven
days, and anyone who touches her
will be unclean till evening.

20" 'Anything she lies on during

14:49 [a]ver 4; 1Ki 4:33; ver 4
14:50 [b]ver 5
14:51 [c]ver 6; Ps 51:7 [d]ver 4,7
14:53 [e]ver 7 [f]ver 20
14:54 [g]Lev 13:2,30
14:55 [h]Lev 13:47-52
14:56 [i]Lev 13:2
14:57 [j]Lev 10:10
15:2 [k]ver 16,32; Lev 22:4; Nu 5:2; 2Sa 3:29; Mt 9:20
15:5 [l]Lev 11:25 [m]Lev 14:8 [n]Lev 11:24
15:7 [o]ver 19; Lev 22:5 [p]ver 16; Lev 22:4
15:8 [q]Nu 12:14
15:10 [r]Nu 19:10
15:12 [s]Lev 6:28 [t]Lev 11:32
15:13 [u]Lev 8:33 [v]ver 5
15:14 [w]Lev 14:22
15:15 [x]Lev 5:7 [y]Lev 14:31 [z]Lev 14:18,19
15:16 [a]ver 2; Lev 22:4; Dt 23:10 [b]ver 5; Dt 23:11
15:18 [c]1Sa 21:4
15:19 [d]ver 24; Lev 12:2

her period will be unclean, and
anything she sits on will be unclean. **21**Whoever touches her bed
must wash his clothes and bathe
with water, and he will be unclean
till evening.[a] **22**Whoever touches
anything she sits on must wash his
clothes and bathe with water, and
he will be unclean till evening.
23Whether it is the bed or anything
she was sitting on, when anyone
touches it, he will be unclean till
evening.

24" 'If a man lies with her and
her monthly flow[b] touches him, he
will be unclean for seven days; any
bed he lies on will be unclean.

25" 'When a woman has a discharge of blood for many days at a
time other than her monthly period[c] or has a discharge that continues beyond her period, she will be
unclean as long as she has the discharge, just as in the days of her
period. **26**Any bed she lies on while
her discharge continues will be unclean, as is her bed during her
monthly period, and anything she
sits on will be unclean, as during
her period. **27**Whoever touches
them will be unclean; he must
wash his clothes and bathe with
water, and he will be unclean till
evening.

28" 'When she is cleansed from
her discharge, she must count off
seven days, and after that she will
be ceremonially clean. **29**On the
eighth day she must take two doves
or two young pigeons[d] and bring
them to the priest at the entrance
to the Tent of Meeting. **30**The
priest is to sacrifice one for a sin
offering and the other for a burnt
offering. In this way he will make
atonement for her before the LORD
for the uncleanness of her discharge.[e]

31" 'You must keep the Israelites
separate from things that make
them unclean, so they will not die
in their uncleanness for defiling my
dwelling place,[g][f] which is among
them.' "

32These are the regulations for a
man with a discharge, for anyone
made unclean by an emission of semen,[g] **33**for a woman in her
monthly period, for a man or a
woman with a discharge, and for a
man who lies with a woman who is
ceremonially unclean.[h]

15:21 [a]ver 27
15:24 [b]ver 19; Lev 12:2; 18:19; 20:18; Eze 18:6
15:25 [c]Mt 9:20; Mk 5:25; Lk 8:43
15:29 [d]Lev 14:22
15:30 [e]Lev 5:10; 14:20,31; 18:19; 2Sa 11:4; Mk 5:25; Lk 8:43
15:31 [f]Lev 20:3; Nu 5:3; 19:13,20; 2Sa 15:25; 2Ki 21:7; Ps 33:14; 74:7; 76:2; Eze 5:11; 23:38
15:32 [g]ver 2
15:33 [h]ver 19,24,25
16:1 [i]Lev 10:1
16:2 [j]Ex 30:10; Heb 9:7 [k]Heb 9:25; 10:19 [l]Ex 25:22 [m]Ex 40:34
16:3 [n]Heb 9:24,25
16:4 [o]Ex 28:39 [p]Ex 28:42 [q]ver 24; Heb 10:22
16:5 [r]Lev 4:13-21 [s]2Ch 29:23
16:6 [t]Lev 9:7; Heb 5:3; 7:27; 9:7,12
16:10 [u]Isa 53:4-10; Ro 3:25; 1Jn 2:2

The Day of Atonement

16:2–34pp — Lev 23:26–32; Nu 29:7–11

16 The LORD spoke to Moses
after the death of the two
sons of Aaron who died when they
approached the LORD.[i] **2**The LORD
said to Moses: "Tell your brother
Aaron not to come whenever he
chooses[j] into the Most Holy
Place[k] behind the curtain in front
of the atonement cover on the ark,
or else he will die, because I appear[l] in the cloud[m] over the
atonement cover.

3"This is how Aaron is to enter
the sanctuary area:[n] with a young
bull for a sin offering and a ram for
a burnt offering. **4**He is to put on
the sacred linen tunic, with linen
undergarments next to his body; he
is to tie the linen sash around him
and put on the linen turban.[o]
These are sacred garments;[p] so he
must bathe himself with water[q]
before he puts them on. **5**From the
Israelite community[r] he is to take
two male goats[s] for a sin offering
and a ram for a burnt offering.

6"Aaron is to offer the bull for his
own sin offering to make atonement for himself and his household.[t] **7**Then he is to take the two
goats and present them before the
LORD at the entrance to the Tent of
Meeting. **8**He is to cast lots for the
two goats—one lot for the LORD and
the other for the scapegoat.[h] **9**Aaron shall bring the goat whose lot
falls to the LORD and sacrifice it for
a sin offering. **10**But the goat chosen by lot as the scapegoat shall be
presented alive before the LORD to
be used for making atonement[u] by
sending it into the desert as a
scapegoat.

11"Aaron shall bring the bull for
his own sin offering to make atone-

[g]*31* Or *my tabernacle* [h]*8* That is, the goat of removal; Hebrew *azazel*; also in verses 10 and 26

ment for himself and his household,[a] and he is to slaughter the bull for his own sin offering. 12He is to take a censer full of burning coals[b] from the altar before the LORD and two handfuls of finely ground fragrant incense[c] and take them behind the curtain. 13He is to put the incense on the fire before the LORD, and the smoke of the incense will conceal the atonement cover above the Testimony, so that he will not die.[d] 14He is to take some of the bull's blood[e] and with his finger sprinkle it on the front of the atonement cover; then he shall sprinkle some of it with his finger seven times before the atonement cover.[f]

15"He shall then slaughter the goat for the sin offering for the people[g] and take its blood behind the curtain[h] and do with it as he did with the bull's blood: He shall sprinkle it on the atonement cover and in front of it. 16In this way he will make atonement[i] for the Most Holy Place because of the uncleanness and rebellion of the Israelites, whatever their sins have been. He is to do the same for the Tent of Meeting, which is among them in the midst of their uncleanness. 17No one is to be in the Tent of Meeting from the time Aaron goes in to make atonement in the Most Holy Place until he comes out, having made atonement for himself, his household and the whole community of Israel.

18"Then he shall come out to the altar[j] that is before the LORD and make atonement for it. He shall take some of the bull's blood and some of the goat's blood and put it on all the horns of the altar.[k] 19He shall sprinkle some of the blood on it with his finger seven times to cleanse it and to consecrate it from the uncleanness of the Israelites.[l]

20"When Aaron has finished making atonement for the Most Holy Place, the Tent of Meeting and the altar, he shall bring forward the live goat. 21He is to lay both hands on the head of the live goat and confess[m] over it all the wickedness and rebellion of the Israelites—all their sins—and put them on the goat's head. He shall send the goat away into the desert in the care of a man appointed for the task. 22The goat will carry on itself all their sins[n] to a solitary place; and the man shall release it in the desert.

23"Then Aaron is to go into the Tent of Meeting and take off the linen garments he put on before he entered the Most Holy Place, and he is to leave them there.[o] 24He shall bathe himself with water in a holy place and put on his regular garments.[p] Then he shall come out and sacrifice the burnt offering for himself and the burnt offering for the people, to make atonement for himself and for the people. 25He shall also burn the fat of the sin offering on the altar.

26"The man who releases the goat as a scapegoat must wash his clothes[q] and bathe himself with water; afterward he may come into the camp. 27The bull and the goat for the sin offerings, whose blood was brought into the Most Holy Place to make atonement, must be taken outside the camp;[r] their hides, flesh and offal are to be burned up. 28The man who burns them must wash his clothes and bathe himself with water; afterward he may come into the camp.

29"This is to be a lasting ordinance for you: On the tenth day of the seventh month you must deny yourselves[i][s] and not do any work—whether native-born or an alien living among you— 30because on this day atonement will be made for you, to cleanse you. Then, before the LORD, you will be clean from all your sins.[t] 31It is a sabbath of rest, and you must deny yourselves;[u] it is a lasting ordinance. 32The priest who is anointed and ordained to succeed his father as high priest is to make atonement. He is to put on the sacred linen garments[v] 33and make atonement for the Most Holy

16:11 [a] Heb 7:27; 9:7
16:12 [b] Lev 10:1 [c] Ex 30:34-38
16:13 [d] Ex 28:43; Lev 22:9
16:14 [e] Lev 4:5; Heb 9:7,13,25 [f] Lev 4:6
16:15 [g] Heb 9:7,12 [h] Heb 9:3
16:16 [i] Ex 29:36
16:18 [j] Lev 4:7 [k] Lev 4:25
16:19 [l] Eze 43:20
16:21 [m] Lev 5:5
16:22 [n] Isa 53:12
16:23 [o] Eze 42:14; 44:19
16:24 [p] ver 3-5
16:26 [q] Lev 11:25
16:27 [r] Lev 4:12,21; Heb 13:11
16:29 [s] Lev 23:27,32; Nu 29:7; Isa 58:3
16:30 [t] Jer 33:8; Eph 5:26
16:31 [u] Isa 58:3,5
16:32 [v] ver 4; Nu 20:26,28

[i]29 Or *must fast*; also in verse 31

Place, for the Tent of Meeting and
the altar, and for the priests and all
the people of the community.[a]
34"This is to be a lasting ordinance for you: Atonement is to be
made once a year[b] for all the sins
of the Israelites."

And it was done, as the LORD
commanded Moses.

Eating Blood Forbidden

17 The LORD said to Moses,
2"Speak to Aaron and his
sons and to all the Israelites and
say to them: 'This is what the LORD
has commanded: **3**Any Israelite
who sacrifices an ox,[j] a lamb or a
goat in the camp or outside of it
4instead of bringing it to the entrance to the Tent of Meeting to
present it as an offering to the LORD
in front of the tabernacle of the
LORD[c]—that man shall be considered guilty of bloodshed; he has
shed blood and must be cut off
from his people.[d] **5**This is so the
Israelites will bring to the LORD the
sacrifices they are now making in
the open fields. They must bring
them to the priest, that is, to the
LORD, at the entrance to the Tent of
Meeting and sacrifice them as fellowship offerings.[k] **6**The priest is
to sprinkle the blood against the altar of the LORD[e] at the entrance to
the Tent of Meeting and burn the
fat as an aroma pleasing to the
LORD.[f] **7**They must no longer offer
any of their sacrifices to the goat
idols[l][g] to whom they prostitute
themselves.[h] This is to be a lasting
ordinance for them and for the generations to come.'

8"Say to them: 'Any Israelite or
any alien living among them who
offers a burnt offering or sacrifice
9and does not bring it to the entrance to the Tent of Meeting[i] to
sacrifice it to the LORD—that man
must be cut off from his people.

10" 'Any Israelite or any alien living among them who eats any
blood—I will set my face against
that person who eats blood[j] and
will cut him off from his people.
11For the life of a creature is in the
blood,[k] and I have given it to you
to make atonement for yourselves
on the altar; it is the blood that
makes atonement for one's life.[l]
12Therefore I say to the Israelites,
"None of you may eat blood, nor
may an alien living among you eat
blood."

13" 'Any Israelite or any alien living among you who hunts any animal or bird that may be eaten must
drain out the blood and cover it
with earth,[m] **14**because the life of
every creature is its blood. That is
why I have said to the Israelites,
"You must not eat the blood of any
creature, because the life of every
creature is its blood; anyone who
eats it must be cut off."[n]

15" 'Anyone, whether native-
born or alien, who eats anything
found dead or torn by wild animals[o] must wash his clothes and
bathe with water, and he will be
ceremonially unclean till evening;
then he will be clean. **16**But if he
does not wash his clothes and
bathe himself, he will be held responsible.' "

Unlawful Sexual Relations

18 The LORD said to Moses,
2"Speak to the Israelites
and say to them: 'I am the LORD
your God.[p] **3**You must not do as
they do in Egypt, where you used to
live, and you must not do as they
do in the land of Canaan, where I
am bringing you. Do not follow
their practices.[q] **4**You must obey
my laws and be careful to follow my
decrees. I am the LORD your God.[r]
5Keep my decrees and laws, for the
man who obeys them will live by
them.[s] I am the LORD.

6" 'No one is to approach any
close relative to have sexual relations. I am the LORD.

7" 'Do not dishonor your father[t]
by having sexual relations with
your mother.[u] She is your mother;
do not have relations with her.

8" 'Do not have sexual relations

16:33 [a]ver 11,16-18
16:34 [b]Heb 9:7,25
17:4 [c]Dt 12:5-21 [d]Ge 17:14
17:6 [e]Lev 3:2 [f]Nu 18:17
17:7 [g]Ex 22:20; 2Ch 11:15 [h]Ex 32:8; 34:15; Dt 32:17; 1Co 10:20
17:9 [i]ver 4
17:10 [j]Ge 9:4; Lev 3:17; Dt 12:16,23; 1Sa 14:33
17:11 [k]ver 14; Ge 9:4 [l]Heb 9:22
17:13 [m]Lev 7:26; Dt 12:16
17:14 [n]ver 11; Ge 9:4
17:15 [o]Ex 22:31; Dt 14:21
18:2 [p]Ex 6:7; Lev 11:44; Eze 20:5
18:3 [q]ver 24-30; Ex 23:24; Lev 20:23
18:4 [r]ver 2
18:5 [s]Eze 20:11; Ro 10:5*; Gal 3:12*
18:7 [t]Lev 20:11 [u]Eze 22:10

j3 The Hebrew word can include both male and female. k5 Traditionally *peace offerings* l7 Or *demons*

with your father's wife;[a] that
would dishonor your father.[b]
9" 'Do not have sexual relations
with your sister,[c] either your father's daughter or your mother's
daughter, whether she was born in
the same home or elsewhere.
10" 'Do not have sexual relations
with your son's daughter or your
daughter's daughter; that would
dishonor you.
11" 'Do not have sexual relations
with the daughter of your father's
wife, born to your father; she is
your sister.
12" 'Do not have sexual relations
with your father's sister;[d] she is
your father's close relative.
13" 'Do not have sexual relations
with your mother's sister, because
she is your mother's close relative.
14" 'Do not dishonor your father's brother by approaching his
wife to have sexual relations; she is
your aunt.[e]
15" 'Do not have sexual relations
with your daughter-in-law.[f] She is
your son's wife; do not have relations with her.
16" 'Do not have sexual relations
with your brother's wife;[g] that
would dishonor your brother.
17" 'Do not have sexual relations
with both a woman and her daughter.[h] Do not have sexual relations
with either her son's daughter or
her daughter's daughter; they are
her close relatives. That is wickedness.
18" 'Do not take your wife's sister as a rival wife and have sexual
relations with her while your wife is
living.
19" 'Do not approach a woman to
have sexual relations during the
uncleanness of her monthly period.[i]
20" 'Do not have sexual relations
with your neighbor's wife[j] and defile yourself with her.
21" 'Do not give any of your children[k] to be sacrificed[m] to Molech,[l] for you must not profane
the name of your God.[m] I am the
LORD.
22" 'Do not lie with a man as one
lies with a woman;[n] that is detestable.
23" 'Do not have sexual relations
with an animal and defile yourself
with it. A woman must not present
herself to an animal to have sexual
relations with it; that is a perversion.[o]
24" 'Do not defile yourselves in
any of these ways, because this is
how the nations that I am going to
drive out before you[p] became defiled.[q] 25Even the land was defiled; so I punished it for its sin,[r]
and the land vomited out its inhabitants.[s] 26But you must keep my
decrees and my laws. The native-
born and the aliens living among
you must not do any of these detestable things, 27for all these
things were done by the people
who lived in the land before you,
and the land became defiled.
28And if you defile the land, it will
vomit you out as it vomited out the
nations that were before you.
29" 'Everyone who does any of
these detestable things—such persons must be cut off from their people. 30Keep my requirements[t] and
do not follow any of the detestable
customs that were practiced before
you came and do not defile yourselves with them. I am the LORD
your God.[u]' "

Various Laws

19 The LORD said to Moses,
2"Speak to the entire as-
sembly of Israel and say to them:
'Be holy because I, the LORD your
God, am holy.[v]
3" 'Each of you must respect his
mother and father,[w] and you must
observe my Sabbaths. I am the
LORD your God.[x]
4" 'Do not turn to idols or make
gods of cast metal for yourselves.[y]
I am the LORD your God.
5" 'When you sacrifice a fellowship offering[n] to the LORD, sacrifice
it in such a way that it will be accepted on your behalf. 6It shall be
eaten on the day you sacrifice it or

18:8 [a] 1Co 5:1 [b] Lev 20:11
18:9 [c] Lev 20:17
18:12 [d] Lev 20:19
18:14 [e] Lev 20:20
18:15 [f] Lev 20:12
18:16 [g] Lev 20:21
18:17 [h] Lev 20:14
18:19 [i] Lev 15:24; 20:18
18:20 [j] Ex 20:14; Lev 20:10; Mt 5:27,28; 1Co 6:9; Heb 13:4
18:21 [k] Dt 12:31 [l] Lev 20:2-5 [m] Lev 19:12; 21:6; Eze 36:20
18:22 [n] Lev 20:13; Dt 23:18; Ro 1:27
18:23 [o] Ex 22:19; Lev 20:15; Dt 27:21
18:24 [p] ver 3,27,30 [q] Dt 18:12
18:25 [r] Lev 20:23; Dt 9:5; 18:12 [s] ver 28; Lev 20:22
18:30 [t] Dt 11:1 [u] ver 2
19:2 [v] 1Pe 1:16*; Lev 11:44
19:3 [w] Ex 20:12 [x] Lev 11:44
19:4 [y] Ex 20:4,23; 34:17; Lev 26:1; Ps 96:5; 115:4-7

m21 Or *to be passed through the fire,*
n5 Traditionally *peace offering*

on the next day; anything left over
until the third day must be burned
up. **7**If any of it is eaten on the third
day, it is impure and will not be accepted. **8**Whoever eats it will be
held responsible because he has
desecrated what is holy to the
LORD; that person must be cut off
from his people.

9" 'When you reap the harvest of
your land, do not reap to the very
edges of your field or gather the
gleanings of your harvest.[a] **10**Do
not go over your vineyard a second
time or pick up the grapes that
have fallen. Leave them for the
poor and the alien. I am the LORD
your God.

11" 'Do not steal.[b]

" 'Do not lie.[c]

" 'Do not deceive one another.

12" 'Do not swear falsely by my
name[d] and so profane the name of
your God. I am the LORD.

13" 'Do not defraud your neighbor or rob him.[e]

" 'Do not hold back the wages of
a hired man overnight.[f]

14" 'Do not curse the deaf or put
a stumbling block in front of the
blind,[g] but fear your God. I am the
LORD.

15" 'Do not pervert justice;[h] do
not show partiality[i] to the poor or
favoritism to the great, but judge
your neighbor fairly.

16" 'Do not go about spreading
slander[j] among your people.

" 'Do not do anything that en-
dangers your neighbor's life.[k] I am
the LORD.

17" 'Do not hate your brother in
your heart.[l] Rebuke your neighbor
frankly[m] so you will not share in
his guilt.

18" 'Do not seek revenge[n] or
bear a grudge[o] against one of your
people, but love your neighbor as
yourself.[p] I am the LORD.

19" 'Keep my decrees.

" 'Do not mate different kinds of
animals.

" 'Do not plant your field with
two kinds of seed.[q]

" 'Do not wear clothing woven of
two kinds of material.[r]

20" 'If a man sleeps with a woman who is a slave girl promised to
another man but who has not been
ransomed or given her freedom,
there must be due punishment. Yet
they are not to be put to death, because she had not been freed.
21The man, however, must bring a
ram to the entrance to the Tent of
Meeting for a guilt offering to the
LORD.[s] **22**With the ram of the guilt
offering the priest is to make
atonement for him before the LORD
for the sin he has committed, and
his sin will be forgiven.

23" 'When you enter the land and
plant any kind of fruit tree, regard
its fruit as forbidden.[o] For three
years you are to consider it forbidden[o]; it must not be eaten. **24**In
the fourth year all its fruit will be
holy,[t] an offering of praise to the
LORD. **25**But in the fifth year you
may eat its fruit. In this way your
harvest will be increased. I am the
LORD your God.

26" 'Do not eat any meat with the
blood still in it.[u]

" 'Do not practice divination or
sorcery.[v]

27" 'Do not cut the hair at the
sides of your head or clip off the
edges of your beard.[w]

28" 'Do not cut your bodies for
the dead or put tattoo marks on
yourselves. I am the LORD.

29" 'Do not degrade your daughter by making her a prostitute,[x] or
the land will turn to prostitution
and be filled with wickedness.

30" 'Observe my Sabbaths and
have reverence for my sanctuary. I
am the LORD.[y]

31" 'Do not turn to mediums or
seek out spiritists,[z] for you will be
defiled by them. I am the LORD your
God.

32" 'Rise in the presence of the
aged, show respect for the elderly[a]
and revere your God. I am the LORD.

33" 'When an alien lives with you
in your land, do not mistreat him.
34The alien living with you must be
treated as one of your native-
born.[b] Love him as yourself, for

o23 Hebrew *uncircumcised*

19:9 [a]Lev 23:10, 22; Dt 24:19-22
19:11 [b]Ex 20:15 [c]Eph 4:25
19:12 [d]Ex 20:7; Mt 5:33
19:13 [e]Ex 22:15, 25-27 [f]Dt 24:15; Jas 5:4
19:14 [g]Dt 27:18
19:15 [h]Ex 23:2,6 [i]Dt 1:17
19:16 [j]Ps 15:3; Eze 22:9 [k]Ex 23:7
19:17 [l]1Jn 2:9; 3:15 [m]Mt 18:15; Lk 17:3
19:18 [n]Ro 12:19 [o]Ps 103:9 [p]Mt 5:43*; 19:16*; 22:39*; Mk 12:31*; Lk 10:27*; Jn 13:34; Ro 13:9*; Gal 5:14*; Jas 2:8*
19:19 [q]Dt 22:9 [r]Dt 22:11
19:21 [s]Lev 5:15
19:24 [t]Pr 3:9
19:26 [u]Lev 17:10 [v]Dt 18:10
19:27 [w]Lev 21:5
19:29 [x]Dt 23:18
19:30 [y]Lev 26:2
19:31 [z]Lev 20:6; Isa 8:19
19:32 [a]1Ti 5:1
19:34 [b]Ex 12:48

you were aliens in Egypt.[a] I am the LORD your God.

[35]" 'Do not use dishonest standards when measuring length, weight or quantity. [36]Use honest scales and honest weights, an honest ephah[p] and an honest hin.[q][b] I am the LORD your God, who brought you out of Egypt.

[37]" 'Keep all my decrees and all my laws and follow them. I am the LORD.' "

Punishments for Sin

20 The LORD said to Moses, [2]"Say to the Israelites: 'Any Israelite or any alien living in Israel who gives[r] any of his children to Molech must be put to death. The people of the community are to stone him. [3]I will set my face against that man and I will cut him off from his people; for by giving his children to Molech, he has defiled my sanctuary[c] and profaned my holy name.[d] [4]If the people of the community close their eyes when that man gives one of his children to Molech and they fail to put him to death,[e] [5]I will set my face against that man and his family and will cut off from their people both him and all who follow him in prostituting themselves to Molech.

[6]" 'I will set my face against the person who turns to mediums and spiritists to prostitute himself by following them, and I will cut him off from his people.[f]

[7]" 'Consecrate yourselves and be holy,[g] because I am the LORD your God. [8]Keep my decrees and follow them. I am the LORD, who makes you holy.[s][h]

[9]" 'If anyone curses his father or mother,[i] he must be put to death.[j] He has cursed his father or his mother, and his blood will be on his own head.[k]

[10]" 'If a man commits adultery with another man's wife[l]—with the wife of his neighbor—both the adulterer and the adulteress must be put to death.

[11]" 'If a man sleeps with his father's wife, he has dishonored his father.[m] Both the man and the woman must be put to death; their blood will be on their own heads.

[12]" 'If a man sleeps with his daughter-in-law,[n] both of them must be put to death. What they have done is a perversion; their blood will be on their own heads.

[13]" 'If a man lies with a man as one lies with a woman, both of them have done what is detestable.[o] They must be put to death; their blood will be on their own heads.

[14]" 'If a man marries both a woman and her mother,[p] it is wicked. Both he and they must be burned in the fire, so that no wickedness will be among you.[q]

[15]" 'If a man has sexual relations with an animal,[r] he must be put to death, and you must kill the animal.

[16]" 'If a woman approaches an animal to have sexual relations with it, kill both the woman and the animal. They must be put to death; their blood will be on their own heads.

[17]" 'If a man marries his sister[s], the daughter of either his father or his mother, and they have sexual relations, it is a disgrace. They must be cut off before the eyes of their people. He has dishonored his sister and will be held responsible.

[18]" 'If a man lies with a woman during her monthly period[t] and has sexual relations with her, he has exposed the source of her flow, and she has also uncovered it. Both of them must be cut off from their people.

[19]" 'Do not have sexual relations with the sister of either your mother or your father,[u] for that would dishonor a close relative; both of you would be held responsible.

[20]" 'If a man sleeps with his aunt,[v] he has dishonored his uncle. They will be held responsible; they will die childless.

[21]" 'If a man marries his broth-

19:34 [a]Dt 10:19
19:36 [b]Dt 25:13-15
20:3 [c]Lev 15:31 [d]Lev 18:21
20:4 [e]Dt 17:2-5
20:6 [f]Lev 19:31
20:7 [g]Eph 1:4; 1Pe 1:16*
20:8 [h]Ex 31:13
20:9 [i]Dt 27:16 [j]Ex 21:17; Mt 15:4*; Mk 7:10* [k]ver 11; 2Sa 1:16
20:10 [l]Ex 20:14; Dt 5:18; 22:22
20:11 [m]Lev 18:7; Dt 27:23
20:12 [n]Lev 18:15
20:13 [o]Lev 18:22
20:14 [p]Lev 18:17 [q]Dt 27:23
20:15 [r]Lev 18:23
20:17 [s]Lev 18:9
20:18 [t]Lev 15:24; 18:19
20:19 [u]Lev 18:12-13
20:20 [v]Lev 18:14

[p]36 An ephah was a dry measure. [q]36 A hin was a liquid measure. [r]2 Or *sacrifices;* also in verses 3 and 4 [s]8 Or *who sanctifies you;* or *who sets you apart as holy*

er's wife,[a] it is an act of impurity;
he has dishonored his brother.
They will be childless.

22" 'Keep all my decrees and
laws and follow them, so that the
land[b] where I am bringing you to
live may not vomit you out. **23**You
must not live according to the customs of the nations[c] I am going to
drive out before you.[d] Because
they did all these things, I abhorred
them. **24**But I said to you, "You will
possess their land; I will give it to
you as an inheritance, a land flowing with milk and honey."[e] I am
the LORD your God, who has set you
apart from the nations.[f]

25" 'You must therefore make a
distinction between clean and unclean animals and between unclean and clean birds.[g] Do not defile yourselves by any animal or
bird or anything that moves along
the ground—those which I have set
apart as unclean for you. **26**You are
to be holy to me[t] because I, the
LORD, am holy,[h] and I have set you
apart from the nations to be my
own.

27" 'A man or woman who is a
medium or spiritist among you
must be put to death.[i] You are to
stone them; their blood will be on
their own heads.' "

Rules for Priests

21 The LORD said to Moses,
"Speak to the priests, the
sons of Aaron, and say to them: 'A
priest must not make himself ceremonially unclean for any of his
people who die,[j] **2**except for a
close relative, such as his mother
or father, his son or daughter, his
brother, **3**or an unmarried sister
who is dependent on him since she
has no husband—for her he may
make himself unclean. **4**He must
not make himself unclean for people related to him by marriage,[u]
and so defile himself.

5" 'Priests must not shave their
heads or shave off the edges of
their beards[k] or cut their bodies.[l]
6They must be holy to their God
and must not profane the name of
their God.[m] Because they present
the offerings made to the LORD by
fire,[n] the food of their God, they
are to be holy.

7" 'They must not marry women
defiled by prostitution or divorced
from their husbands,[o] because
priests are holy to their God.[p] **8**Regard them as holy,[q] because they
offer up the food of your God. Consider them holy, because I the LORD
am holy—I who make you holy.[v]

9" 'If a priest's daughter defiles
herself by becoming a prostitute,
she disgraces her father; she must
be burned in the fire.[r]

10" 'The high priest, the one
among his brothers who has had
the anointing oil poured on his
head and who has been ordained to
wear the priestly garments,[s] must
not let his hair become unkempt[w]
or tear his clothes.[t] **11**He must not
enter a place where there is a dead
body.[u] He must not make himself
unclean,[v] even for his father or
mother, **12**nor leave the sanctuary
of his God or desecrate it, because
he has been dedicated by the
anointing oil[w] of his God. I am the
LORD.

13" 'The woman he marries must
be a virgin.[x] **14**He must not marry
a widow, a divorced woman, or a
woman defiled by prostitution, but
only a virgin from his own people,
15so he will not defile his offspring
among his people. I am the LORD,
who makes him holy.[x]' "

16The LORD said to Moses, **17**"Say
to Aaron: 'For the generations to
come none of your descendants
who has a defect may come near to
offer the food of his God.[y] **18**No
man who has any defect[z] may
come near: no man who is blind or
lame, disfigured or deformed; **19**no
man with a crippled foot or hand,
20or who is hunchbacked or
dwarfed, or who has any eye defect,
or who has festering or running
sores or damaged testicles.[a] **21**No

20:21 [a]Lev 18:16
20:22 [b]Lev 18:25-28
20:23 [c]Lev 18:3 [d]Lev 18:24, 27,30
20:24 [e]Ex 3:8; 13:5; 33:3 [f]Ex 33:16
20:25 [g]Lev 11:1-47; Dt 14:3-21
20:26 [h]Lev 19:2
20:27 [i]Lev 19:31
21:1 [j]Eze 44:25
21:5 [k]Eze 44:20 [l]Lev 19:28; Dt 14:1
21:6 [m]Lev 18:21 [n]Lev 3:11
21:7 [o]ver 13,14 [p]Eze 44:22
21:8 [q]ver 6
21:9 [r]Ge 38:24; Lev 19:29
21:10 [s]Lev 16:32 [t]Lev 10:6
21:11 [u]Nu 19:11,13, 14 [v]Lev 19:28
21:12 [w]Ex 29:6-7; Lev 10:7
21:13 [x]Eze 44:22
21:17 [y]ver 6
21:18 [z]Lev 22:19-25
21:20 [a]Dt 23:1; Isa 56:3

[t]26 Or *be my holy ones* [u]4 Or *unclean as a leader among his people* [v]8 Or *who sanctify you; or who set you apart as holy* [w]10 Or *not uncover his head* [x]15 Or *who sanctifies him; or who sets him apart as holy*

descendant of Aaron the priest who
has any defect is to come near to
present the offerings made to the
LORD by fire. He has a defect; he
must not come near to offer the
food of his God. **22**He may eat the
most holy food of his God,[a] as well
as the holy food; **23**yet because of
his defect, he must not go near the
curtain or approach the altar, and
so desecrate my sanctuary. I am
the LORD, who makes them
holy.[y]' "

24So Moses told this to Aaron
and his sons and to all the Israelites.

22 The LORD said to Moses,
2"Tell Aaron and his sons to
treat with respect the sacred offerings the Israelites consecrate to
me, so they will not profane my
holy name. I am the LORD.

3"Say to them: 'For the generations to come, if any of your
descendants is ceremonially unclean and yet comes near the sacred offerings that the Israelites
consecrate to the LORD, that person
must be cut off from my presence.[b] I am the LORD.

4" 'If a descendant of Aaron has
an infectious skin disease[z] or a
bodily discharge,[c] he may not eat
the sacred offerings until he is
cleansed. He will also be unclean if
he touches something defiled by a
corpse[d] or by anyone who has an
emission of semen, **5**or if he
touches any crawling thing[e] that
makes him unclean, or any person[f] who makes him unclean,
whatever the uncleanness may be.
6The one who touches any such
thing will be unclean till evening.
He must not eat any of the sacred
offerings unless he has bathed
himself with water. **7**When the sun
goes down, he will be clean, and after that he may eat the sacred offerings, for they are his food.[g] **8**He
must not eat anything found dead[h]
or torn by wild animals,[i] and so
become unclean[j] through it. I am
the LORD.

9" 'The priests are to keep my requirements so that they do not become guilty and die[k] for treating
them with contempt. I am the
LORD, who makes them holy.[a]

10" 'No one outside a priest's
family may eat the sacred offering,
nor may the guest of a priest or his
hired worker eat it. **11**But if a priest
buys a slave with money, or if a
slave is born in his household, that
slave may eat his food.[l] **12**If a
priest's daughter marries anyone
other than a priest, she may not eat
any of the sacred contributions.
13But if a priest's daughter becomes a widow or is divorced, yet
has no children, and she returns to
live in her father's house as in her
youth, she may eat of her father's
food. No unauthorized person,
however, may eat any of it.

14" 'If anyone eats a sacred offering by mistake, he must make restitution to the priest for the offering
and add a fifth of the value[m] to it.
15The priests must not desecrate
the sacred offerings the Israelites
present to the LORD[n] **16**by allowing
them to eat the sacred offerings
and so bring upon them guilt re-
quiring payment.[o] I am the LORD,
who makes them holy.' "

Unacceptable Sacrifices

17The LORD said to Moses,
18"Speak to Aaron and his sons and
to all the Israelites and say to them:
'If any of you—either an Israelite or
an alien living in Israel—presents a
gift[p] for a burnt offering to the
LORD, either to fulfill a vow or as a
freewill offering, **19**you must
present a male without defect[q]
from the cattle, sheep or goats in
order that it may be accepted on
your behalf. **20**Do not bring anything with a defect,[r] because it
will not be accepted on your behalf. **21**When anyone brings from
the herd or flock a fellowship offering[b][s] to the LORD to fulfill a special vow or as a freewill offering, it

21:22 [a] 1Co 9:13
22:3 [b] Lev 7:20,21; Nu 19:13
22:4 [c] Lev 14:1-32; 15:2-15 [d] Lev 11:24-28, 39
22:5 [e] Lev 11:24-28, 43 [f] Lev 15:7
22:7 [g] Nu 18:11
22:8 [h] Lev 11:39 [i] Ex 22:31; Lev 17:15 [j] Lev 11:40
22:9 [k] ver 16; Ex 28:43
22:11 [l] Ge 17:13; Ex 12:44
22:14 [m] Lev 5:15
22:15 [n] Nu 18:32
22:16 [o] ver 9
22:18 [p] Lev 1:2
22:19 [q] Lev 1:3
22:20 [r] Dt 15:21; 17:1; Mal 1:8, 14; Heb 9:14; 1Pe 1:19
22:21 [s] Lev 3:6; Nu 15:3,8

[y]23 Or *who sanctifies them*; or *who sets them apart as holy* [z]4 Traditionally *leprosy*; the Hebrew word was used for various diseases affecting the skin—not necessarily leprosy.
[a]9 Or *who sanctifies them*; or *who sets them apart as holy*; also in verse 16
[b]21 Traditionally *peace offering*

must be without defect or blemish
to be acceptable. **22**Do not offer to
the LORD the blind, the injured or
the maimed, or anything with warts
or festering or running sores. Do
not place any of these on the altar
as an offering made to the LORD by
fire. **23**You may, however, present
as a freewill offering an ox[c] or a
sheep that is deformed or stunted,
but it will not be accepted in fulfillment of a vow. **24**You must not offer
to the LORD an animal whose testicles are bruised, crushed, torn or
cut.[a] You must not do this in your
own land, **25**and you must not accept such animals from the hand of
a foreigner and offer them as the
food of your God.[b] They will not be
accepted on your behalf, because
they are deformed and have de-
fects.' "
26The LORD said to Moses,
27"When a calf, a lamb or a goat is
born, it is to remain with its mother
for seven days.[c] From the eighth
day on, it will be acceptable as an
offering made to the LORD by fire.
28Do not slaughter a cow or a
sheep and its young on the same
day.[d]

29"When you sacrifice a thank
offering[e] to the LORD, sacrifice it in
such a way that it will be accepted
on your behalf. **30**It must be eaten
that same day; leave none of it till
morning.[f] I am the LORD.

31"Keep[g] my commands and
follow them. I am the LORD. **32**Do
not profane my holy name.[h] I must
be acknowledged as holy by the Israelites.[i] I am the LORD, who
makes[d] you holy[e] **33**and who
brought you out of Egypt to be your
God.[j] I am the LORD."

23 The LORD said to Moses,
2"Speak to the Israelites
and say to them: 'These are my appointed feasts,[k] the appointed
feasts of the LORD, which you are to
proclaim as sacred assemblies.[l]

The Sabbath

3" 'There are six days when you
may work,[m] but the seventh day is

22:24 [a]Lev 21:20
22:25 [b]Lev 21:6
22:27 [c]Ex 22:30
22:28 [d]Dt 22:6,7
22:29 [e]Lev 7:12; Ps 107:22
22:30 [f]Lev 7:15
22:31 [g]Dt 4:2,40; Ps 105:45
22:32 [h]Lev 18:21 [i]Lev 10:3
22:33 [j]Lev 11:45
23:2 [k]ver 4,37,44; Nu 29:39 [l]ver 21,27
23:3 [m]Ex 20:9 [n]Ex 20:10; 31:13-17; Lev 19:3; Dt 5:13; Heb 4:9,10
23:5 [o]Ex 12:18-19; Nu 28:16-17; Dt 16:1-8
23:7 [p]ver 3,8
23:10 [q]Ex 23:16,19; 34:26
23:11 [r]Ex 29:24
23:13 [s]Lev 2:14-16; 6:20
23:14 [t]Ex 34:26

a Sabbath of rest,[n] a day of sacred
assembly. You are not to do any
work; wherever you live, it is a Sabbath to the LORD.

The Passover and Unleavened Bread

23:4–8pp — Ex 12:14–20; Nu 28:16–25; Dt 16:1–8

4" 'These are the LORD's appointed feasts, the sacred assemblies
you are to proclaim at their appointed times: **5**The LORD's Passover begins at twilight on the fourteenth day of the first month.[o]
6On the fifteenth day of that month
the LORD's Feast of Unleavened
Bread begins; for seven days you
must eat bread made without
yeast. **7**On the first day hold a sacred assembly[p] and do no regular
work. **8**For seven days present an
offering made to the LORD by fire.
And on the seventh day hold a sacred assembly and do no regular
work.' "

Firstfruits

9The LORD said to Moses,
10"Speak to the Israelites and say
to them: 'When you enter the land
I am going to give you and you reap
its harvest, bring to the priest a
sheaf[q] of the first grain you harvest. **11**He is to wave the sheaf before the LORD[r] so it will be accepted on your behalf; the priest is to
wave it on the day after the Sabbath. **12**On the day you wave the
sheaf, you must sacrifice as a burnt
offering to the LORD a lamb a year
old without defect, **13**together with
its grain offerings[s] of two-tenths of
an ephah[f] of fine flour mixed with
oil—an offering made to the LORD
by fire, a pleasing aroma—and its
drink offering of a quarter of a hin[g]
of wine. **14**You must not eat any
bread, or roasted or new grain, until the very day you bring this offering to your God.[t] This is to be a

[c]23 The Hebrew word can include both male and female. [d]32 Or *made* [e]32 Or *who sanctifies you*; or *who sets you apart as holy* [f]13 That is, probably about 4 quarts (about 4.5 liters); also in verse 17 [g]13 That is, probably about 1 quart (about 1 liter)

lasting ordinance for the generations to come, wherever you live.

Feast of Weeks

23:15–22pp — Nu 28:26–31; Dt 16:9–12

15" 'From the day after the Sabbath, the day you brought the sheaf of the wave offering, count off seven full weeks. **16**Count off fifty days up to the day after the seventh Sabbath,[a] and then present an offering of new grain to the LORD. **17**From wherever you live, bring two loaves made of two-tenths of an ephah of fine flour, baked with yeast, as a wave offering of firstfruits[b] to the LORD. **18**Present with this bread seven male lambs, each a year old and without defect, one young bull and two rams. They will be a burnt offering to the LORD, together with their grain offerings and drink offerings—an offering made by fire, an aroma pleasing to the LORD. **19**Then sacrifice one male goat for a sin offering and two lambs, each a year old, for a fellowship offering.[h] **20**The priest is to wave the two lambs before the LORD as a wave offering, together with the bread of the firstfruits. They are a sacred offering to the LORD for the priest. **21**On that same day you are to proclaim a sacred assembly[c] and do no regular work.[d] This is to be a lasting ordinance for the generations to come, wherever you live.

22" 'When you reap the harvest[e] of your land, do not reap to the very edges of your field or gather the gleanings of your harvest.[f] Leave them for the poor and the alien. I am the LORD your God.' "

Feast of Trumpets

23:23–25pp — Nu 29:1–6

23The LORD said to Moses, **24**"Say to the Israelites: 'On the first day of the seventh month you are to have a day of rest, a sacred assembly commemorated with trumpet blasts.[g] **25**Do no regular work,[h] but present an offering made to the LORD by fire.' "

Day of Atonement

23:26–32pp — Lev 16:2–34; Nu 29:7–11

26The LORD said to Moses, **27**"The tenth day of this seventh month[i] is the Day of Atonement.[j] Hold a sacred assembly[k] and deny yourselves,[i] and present an offering made to the LORD by fire. **28**Do no work on that day, because it is the Day of Atonement, when atonement is made for you before the LORD your God. **29**Anyone who does not deny himself on that day must be cut off from his people.[l] **30**I will destroy from among his people[m] anyone who does any work on that day. **31**You shall do no work at all. This is to be a lasting ordinance for the generations to come, wherever you live. **32**It is a sabbath of rest for you, and you must deny yourselves. From the evening of the ninth day of the month until the following evening you are to observe your sabbath."

Feast of Tabernacles

23:33–43pp — Nu 29:12–39; Dt 16:13–17

33The LORD said to Moses, **34**"Say to the Israelites: 'On the fifteenth day of the seventh month the LORD's Feast of Tabernacles[n] begins, and it lasts for seven days. **35**The first day is a sacred assembly; do no regular work. **36**For seven days present offerings made to the LORD by fire, and on the eighth day hold a sacred assembly[o] and present an offering made to the LORD by fire. It is the closing assembly; do no regular work.

37(" 'These are the LORD's appointed feasts, which you are to proclaim as sacred assemblies for bringing offerings made to the LORD by fire—the burnt offerings and grain offerings, sacrifices and drink offerings[p] required for each day. **38**These offerings are in addition to those for the LORD's Sabbaths[q] and[i] in addition to your gifts and whatever you have vowed and all

23:16 [a]Nu 28:26; Ac 2:1
23:17 [b]Ex 34:22; Lev 2:12
23:21 [c]ver 2 [d]ver 3
23:22 [e]Lev 19:9 [f]Lev 19:10; Dt 24:19-21; Ru 2:15
23:24 [g]Lev 25:9; Nu 10:9,10; 29:1
23:25 [h]ver 21
23:27 [i]Lev 16:29 [j]Ex 30:10 [k]Nu 29:7
23:29 [l]Ge 17:14; Nu 5:2
23:30 [m]Lev 20:3
23:34 [n]Ex 23:16; Dt 16:13; Ezr 3:4; Ne 8:14; Zec 14:16; Jn 7:2
23:36 [o]2Ch 7:9; Ne 8:18; Jn 7:37
23:37 [p]ver 2,4
23:38 [q]Eze 45:17

[h]19 Traditionally *peace offering* [i]27 Or *and fast*; also in verses 29 and 32 [i]38 Or *These feasts are in addition to the LORD's Sabbaths, and these offerings are*

the freewill offerings you give to
the LORD.)
39" 'So beginning with the fifteenth day of the seventh month,
after you have gathered the crops
of the land, celebrate the festival to
the LORD for seven days;[a] the first
day is a day of rest, and the eighth
day also is a day of rest. 40On the
first day you are to take choice fruit
from the trees, and palm fronds,
leafy branches and poplars,[b] and
rejoice before the LORD your God
for seven days. 41Celebrate this as
a festival to the LORD for seven days
each year. This is to be a lasting ordinance for the generations to
come; celebrate it in the seventh
month. 42Live in booths[c] for seven
days: All native-born Israelites are
to live in booths 43so your descendants will know[d] that I had the Israelites live in booths when I
brought them out of Egypt. I am
the LORD your God.' "
44So Moses announced to the Israelites the appointed feasts of the
LORD.

Oil and Bread Set Before the LORD

24:1-3pp — Ex 27:20-21

24 The LORD said to Moses,
2"Command the Israelites
to bring you clear oil of pressed olives for the light so that the lamps
may be kept burning continually.
3Outside the curtain of the Testimony in the Tent of Meeting, Aaron is to tend the lamps before the
LORD from evening till morning,
continually. This is to be a lasting
ordinance for the generations to
come. 4The lamps on the pure gold
lampstand[e] before the LORD must
be tended continually.
5"Take fine flour and bake
twelve loaves of bread,[f] using
two-tenths of an ephah[k] for each
loaf. 6Set them in two rows, six in
each row, on the table of pure
gold[g] before the LORD. 7Along each
row put some pure incense as a memorial portion[h] to represent the
bread and to be an offering made to
the LORD by fire. 8This bread is to
be set out before the LORD regularly,[i] Sabbath after Sabbath,[j] on
behalf of the Israelites, as a lasting
covenant. 9It belongs to Aaron and
his sons,[k] who are to eat it in a
holy place, because it is a most
holy part of their regular share of
the offerings made to the LORD by
fire."

A Blasphemer Stoned

10Now the son of an Israelite
mother and an Egyptian father
went out among the Israelites, and
a fight broke out in the camp between him and an Israelite. 11The
son of the Israelite woman blasphemed the Name[l] with a curse;
so they brought him to Moses. (His
mother's name was Shelomith, the
daughter of Dibri the Danite.)
12They put him in custody until the
will of the LORD should be made
clear to them.[m]
13Then the LORD said to Moses:
14"Take the blasphemer outside
the camp. All those who heard him
are to lay their hands on his head,
and the entire assembly is to stone
him.[n] 15Say to the Israelites: 'If
anyone curses his God,[o] he will be
held responsible; 16anyone who
blasphemes the name of the LORD
must be put to death.[p] The entire
assembly must stone him. Whether
an alien or native-born, when he
blasphemes the Name, he must be
put to death.
17" 'If anyone takes the life of a
human being, he must be put to
death.[q] 18Anyone who takes the
life of someone's animal must
make restitution[r]—life for life.
19If anyone injures his neighbor,
whatever he has done must be
done to him: 20fracture for frac-
ture, eye for eye, tooth for tooth.[s]
As he has injured the other, so he
is to be injured. 21Whoever kills an
animal must make restitution, but
whoever kills a man must be put to
death.[t] 22You are to have the same
law for the alien[u] and the native-
born.[v] I am the LORD your God.' "

23:39 [a] Ex 23:16; Dt 16:13
23:40 [b] Ne 8:14-17
23:42 [c] Ne 8:14-16
23:43 [d] Dt 31:13; Ps 78:5
24:4 [e] Ex 25:31; 31:8
24:5 [f] Ex 25:30
24:6 [g] Ex 25:23-30; 1Ki 7:48
24:7 [h] Lev 2:2
24:8 [i] Nu 4:7; 1Ch 9:32; 2Ch 2:4 [j] Mt 12:5
24:9 [k] Lev 8:31; Mt 12:4; Mk 2:26; Lk 6:4
24:11 [l] Ex 3:15
24:12 [m] Ex 18:16; Nu 15:34
24:14 [n] Lev 20:27; Dt 13:9; 17:5, 7; 21:21
24:15 [o] Ex 22:28
24:16 [p] 1Ki 21:10, 13; Mt 26:66
24:17 [q] Ge 9:6; Ex 21:12; Nu 35:30-31; Dt 27:24
24:18 [r] ver 21
24:20 [s] Ex 21:24; Mt 5:38*
24:21 [t] ver 17
24:22 [u] Ex 12:49 [v] Nu 9:14; 15:16

k5 That is, probably about 4 quarts (about 4.5 liters)

23Then Moses spoke to the Israelites, and they took the blasphemer outside the camp and stoned
him. The Israelites did as the LORD
commanded Moses.

The Sabbath Year

25 The LORD said to Moses on
Mount Sinai, 2"Speak to
the Israelites and say to them:
'When you enter the land I am going to give you, the land itself must
observe a sabbath to the LORD. 3For
six years sow your fields, and for six
years prune your vineyards and
gather their crops.[a] 4But in the
seventh year the land is to have a
sabbath of rest, a sabbath to the
LORD. Do not sow your fields or
prune your vineyards. 5Do not reap
what grows of itself or harvest the
grapes of your untended vines. The
land is to have a year of rest.
6Whatever the land yields during
the sabbath year[b] will be food for
you—for yourself, your manservant
and maidservant, and the hired
worker and temporary resident
who live among you, 7as well as for
your livestock and the wild animals
in your land. Whatever the land
produces may be eaten.

The Year of Jubilee

25:8–38Ref — Dt 15:1–11
25:39–55Ref — Ex 21:2–11; Dt 15:12–18

8" 'Count off seven sabbaths of
years—seven times seven years—
so that the seven sabbaths of years
amount to a period of forty-nine
years. 9Then have the trumpet[c]
sounded everywhere on the tenth
day of the seventh month; on the
Day of Atonement sound the trumpet throughout your land. 10Conse-
crate the fiftieth year and proclaim
liberty[d] throughout the land to all
its inhabitants. It shall be a jubilee[e] for you; each one of you is to
return to his family property and
each to his own clan. 11The fiftieth
year shall be a jubilee for you; do
not sow and do not reap what grows
of itself or harvest the untended
vines. 12For it is a jubilee and is to
be holy for you; eat only what is
taken directly from the fields.

13" 'In this Year of Jubilee[f] everyone is to return to his own property.

14" 'If you sell land to one of your
countrymen or buy any from him,
do not take advantage of each other.[g] 15You are to buy from your
countryman on the basis of the
number of years[h] since the Jubilee. And he is to sell to you on the
basis of the number of years left for
harvesting crops. 16When the years
are many, you are to increase the
price, and when the years are few,
you are to decrease the price,[i] because what he is really selling you
is the number of crops. 17Do not
take advantage of each other,[j] but
fear your God.[k] I am the LORD your
God.[l]

18" 'Follow my decrees and be
careful to obey my laws, and you
will live safely in the land.[m] 19Then
the land will yield its fruit,[n] and
you will eat your fill and live there
in safety. 20You may ask, "What
will we eat in the seventh year[o] if
we do not plant or harvest our
crops?" 21I will send you such a
blessing[p] in the sixth year that the
land will yield enough for three
years. 22While you plant during the
eighth year, you will eat from the
old crop and will continue to eat
from it until the harvest of the
ninth year comes in.[q]

23" 'The land must not be sold
permanently, because the land is
mine[r] and you are but aliens[s] and
my tenants. 24Throughout the
country that you hold as a possession, you must provide for the redemption of the land.

25" 'If one of your countrymen
becomes poor and sells some of his
property, his nearest relative[t] is to
come and redeem[u] what his countryman has sold. 26If, however, a
man has no one to redeem it for
him but he himself prospers and
acquires sufficient means to redeem it, 27he is to determine the
value for the years since he sold it
and refund the balance to the man
to whom he sold it; he can then go
back to his own property. 28But if
he does not acquire the means to

25:3 [a]Ex 23:10
25:6 [b]ver 20
25:9 [c]Lev 23:24
25:10 [d]Isa 61:1; Jer 34:8,15, 17; Lk 4:19 [e]Nu 36:4
25:13 [f]ver 10
25:14 [g]Lev 19:13; 1Sa 12:3,4
25:15 [h]Lev 27:18,23
25:16 [i]ver 27,51,52
25:17 [j]Pr 22:22; Jer 7:5,6; 1Th 4:6 [k]Lev 19:14 [l]Lev 19:32
25:18 [m]Lev 26:4,5; Dt 12:10; Ps 4:8; Jer 23:6
25:19 [n]Lev 26:4
25:20 [o]ver 4
25:21 [p]Dt 28:8,12; Hag 2:19; Mal 3:10
25:22 [q]Lev 26:10
25:23 [r]Ex 19:5 [s]Ge 23:4; 1Ch 29:15; Ps 39:12; Heb 11:13; 1Pe 2:11
25:25 [t]Ru 2:20; Jer 32:7 [u]Lev 27:13, 19,31; Ru 4:4

repay him, what he sold will remain in the possession of the buyer
until the Year of Jubilee. It will be
returned in the Jubilee, and he can
then go back to his property.[a]
29" 'If a man sells a house in a
walled city, he retains the right of
redemption a full year after its sale.
During that time he may redeem it.
30If it is not redeemed before a full
year has passed, the house in the
walled city shall belong permanently to the buyer and his descendants. It is not to be returned in the
Jubilee. 31But houses in villages
without walls around them are to
be considered as open country.
They can be redeemed, and they
are to be returned in the Jubilee.
32" 'The Levites always have the
right to redeem their houses in the
Levitical towns,[b] which they possess. 33So the property of the Levites is redeemable—that is, a
house sold in any town they hold
—and is to be returned in the Jubilee, because the houses in the
towns of the Levites are their property among the Israelites. 34But the
pastureland belonging to their
towns must not be sold; it is their
permanent possession.[c]
35" 'If one of your countrymen
becomes poor[d] and is unable to
support himself among you, help
him[e] as you would an alien or a
temporary resident, so he can continue to live among you. 36Do not
take interest[f] of any kind[1] from
him, but fear your God, so that your
countryman may continue to live
among you. 37You must not lend
him money at interest or sell him
food at a profit. 38I am the LORD
your God, who brought you out of
Egypt to give you the land of Canaan and to be your God.[g]
39" 'If one of your countrymen
becomes poor among you and sells
himself to you, do not make him
work as a slave.[h] 40He is to be
treated as a hired worker or a temporary resident among you; he is to
work for you until the Year of Jubilee. 41Then he and his children are
to be released, and he will go back
to his own clan and to the property[i] of his forefathers. 42Because
the Israelites are my servants,
whom I brought out of Egypt, they
must not be sold as slaves. 43Do
not rule over them ruthlessly,[j] but
fear your God.
44" 'Your male and female slaves
are to come from the nations
around you; from them you may
buy slaves. 45You may also buy
some of the temporary residents
living among you and members of
their clans born in your country,
and they will become your property. 46You can will them to your
children as inherited property and
can make them slaves for life, but
you must not rule over your fellow
Israelites ruthlessly.
47" 'If an alien or a temporary
resident among you becomes rich
and one of your countrymen becomes poor and sells himself to the
alien living among you or to a
member of the alien's clan, 48he retains the right of redemption after
he has sold himself. One of his relatives[k] may redeem him: 49An uncle or a cousin or any blood relative
in his clan may redeem him. Or if
he prospers,[l] he may redeem himself. 50He and his buyer are to
count the time from the year he
sold himself up to the Year of Jubilee. The price for his release is to
be based on the rate paid to a hired
man[m] for that number of years. 51If
many years remain, he must pay for
his redemption a larger share of the
price paid for him. 52If only a few
years remain until the Year of Jubilee, he is to compute that and pay
for his redemption accordingly.
53He is to be treated as a man hired
from year to year; you must see to
it that his owner does not rule over
him ruthlessly.
54" 'Even if he is not redeemed
in any of these ways, he and his
children are to be released in the
Year of Jubilee, 55for the Israelites
belong to me as servants. They are
my servants, whom I brought out of
Egypt. I am the LORD your God.

25:28 [a]ver 10
25:32 [b]Nu 35:1-8; Jos 21:2
25:34 [c]Nu 35:2-5
25:35 [d]Dt 24:14,15 [e]Dt 15:8; Ps 37:21,26; Lk 6:35
25:36 [f]Ex 22:25; Dt 23:19-20
25:38 [g]Ge 17:7; Lev 11:45
25:39 [h]Ex 21:2; Dt 15:12; 1Ki 9:22
25:41 [i]ver 28
25:43 [j]Ex 1:13; Eze 34:4; Col 4:1
25:48 [k]Ne 5:5
25:49 [l]ver 26
25:50 [m]Job 7:1; Isa 16:14; 21:16

[1]36 Or *take excessive interest*; similarly in verse 37

Reward for Obedience

26 "'Do not make idols[a] or set up an image or a sacred stone[b] for yourselves, and do not place a carved stone[c] in your land to bow down before it. I am the LORD your God.

2 "'Observe my Sabbaths and have reverence for my sanctuary.[d] I am the LORD.

3 "'If you follow my decrees and are careful to obey[e] my commands, 4 I will send you rain[f] in its season, and the ground will yield its crops and the trees of the field their fruit.[g] 5 Your threshing will continue until grape harvest and the grape harvest will continue until planting, and you will eat all the food you want[h] and live in safety in your land.[i]

6 "'I will grant peace in the land,[j] and you will lie down[k] and no one will make you afraid.[l] I will remove savage beasts[m] from the land, and the sword will not pass through your country. 7 You will pursue your enemies, and they will fall by the sword before you. 8 Five of you will chase a hundred, and a hundred of you will chase ten thousand, and your enemies will fall by the sword before you.[n]

9 "'I will look on you with favor and make you fruitful and increase your numbers,[o] and I will keep my covenant[p] with you. 10 You will still be eating last year's harvest when you will have to move it out to make room for the new.[q] 11 I will put my dwelling place[m][r] among you, and I will not abhor you. 12 I will walk[s] among you and be your God, and you will be my people.[t] 13 I am the LORD your God, who brought you out of Egypt so that you would no longer be slaves to the Egyptians; I broke the bars of your yoke[u] and enabled you to walk with heads held high.

Punishment for Disobedience

14 "'But if you will not listen to me and carry out all these commands,[v] 15 and if you reject my decrees and abhor my laws and fail to carry out all my commands and so violate my covenant, 16 then I will do this to you: I will bring upon you sudden terror, wasting diseases and fever[w] that will destroy your sight and drain away your life.[x] You will plant seed in vain, because your enemies will eat it.[y] 17 I will set my face[z] against you so that you will be defeated by your enemies; those who hate you will rule over you,[a] and you will flee even when no one is pursuing you.[b]

18 "'If after all this you will not listen to me, I will punish you for your sins seven times over.[c] 19 I will break down your stubborn pride[d] and make the sky above you like iron and the ground beneath you like bronze.[e] 20 Your strength will be spent in vain,[f] because your soil will not yield its crops, nor will the trees of the land yield their fruit.[g]

21 "'If you remain hostile toward me and refuse to listen to me, I will multiply your afflictions seven times over,[h] as your sins deserve. 22 I will send wild animals[i] against you, and they will rob you of your children, destroy your cattle and make you so few in number that your roads will be deserted.

23 "'If in spite of these things you do not accept my correction[j] but continue to be hostile toward me, 24 I myself will be hostile toward you and will afflict you for your sins seven times over. 25 And I will bring the sword upon you to avenge the breaking of the covenant. When you withdraw into your cities, I will send a plague[k] among you, and you will be given into enemy hands. 26 When I cut off your supply of bread,[l] ten women will be able to bake your bread in one oven, and they will dole out the bread by weight. You will eat, but you will not be satisfied.

27 "'If in spite of this you still do not listen to me but continue to be hostile toward me, 28 then in my

26:1 [a] Ex 20:4; Lev 19:4; Dt 5:8 [b] Ex 23:24 [c] Nu 33:52
26:2 [d] Lev 19:30
26:3 [e] Dt 7:12; 11:13,22; 28:1,9
26:4 [f] Dt 11:14 [g] Ps 67:6
26:5 [h] Dt 11:15; Joel 2:19,26; Am 9:13 [i] Lev 25:18
26:6 [j] Ps 29:11; 85:8; 147:14 [k] Ps 4:8 [l] Zep 3:13 [m] ver 22
26:8 [n] Dt 32:30; Jos 23:10
26:9 [o] Ge 17:6; Ne 9:23 [p] Ge 17:7
26:10 [q] Lev 25:22
26:11 [r] Ex 25:8; Ps 76:2; Eze 37:27
26:12 [s] Ge 3:8 [t] 2Co 6:16*
26:13 [u] Eze 34:27
26:14 [v] Dt 28:15-68; Mal 2:2
26:16 [w] Dt 28:22,35 [x] 1Sa 2:33 [y] Job 31:8
26:17 [z] Lev 17:10 [a] Ps 106:41 [b] ver 36,37; Dt 28:7,25; Ps 53:5
26:18 [c] ver 21
26:19 [d] Isa 25:11 [e] Dt 28:23
26:20 [f] Ps 127:1; Isa 17:11 [g] Dt 11:17
26:21 [h] ver 18
26:22 [i] Dt 32:24
26:23 [j] Jer 2:30; 5:3
26:25 [k] Nu 14:12; Eze 5:17
26:26 [l] Ps 105:16; Isa 3:1; Mic 6:14

[m] 11 Or *my tabernacle*

anger I will be hostile toward you,
and I myself will punish you for
your sins seven times over. 29You
will eat the flesh of your sons and
the flesh of your daughters.[a] 30I
will destroy your high places,[b] cut
down your incense altars[c] and pile
your dead bodies on the lifeless
forms of your idols,[d] and I will abhor you. 31I will turn your cities
into ruins and lay waste your sanctuaries,[e] and I will take no delight
in the pleasing aroma of your offerings. 32I will lay waste the land,[f]
so that your enemies who live there
will be appalled. 33I will scatter you
among the nations[g] and will draw
out my sword and pursue you. Your
land will be laid waste, and your
cities will lie in ruins. 34Then the
land will enjoy its sabbath years all
the time that it lies desolate and
you are in the country of your enemies;[h] then the land will rest and
enjoy its sabbaths. 35All the time
that it lies desolate, the land will
have the rest it did not have during
the sabbaths you lived in it.

36" 'As for those of you who are
left, I will make their hearts so fearful in the lands of their enemies
that the sound of a windblown leaf
will put them to flight.[i] They will
run as though fleeing from the
sword, and they will fall, even
though no one is pursuing them.
37They will stumble over one another as though fleeing from the
sword, even though no one is pursuing them. So you will not be able
to stand before your enemies.[j]
38You will perish among the nations; the land of your enemies will
devour you.[k] 39Those of you who
are left will waste away in the lands
of their enemies because of their
sins; also because of their fathers'
sins they will waste away.[l]

40" 'But if they will confess their
sins and the sins of their fathers[m]—their treachery against me
and their hostility toward me,
41which made me hostile toward
them so that I sent them into the
land of their enemies—then when
their uncircumcised hearts[n] are
humbled and they pay for their sin,

26:29 [a]Dt 28:53
26:30 [b]2Ch 34:3; Eze 6:3 [c]Eze 6:6 [d]Eze 6:13
26:31 [e]Ps 74:3-7
26:32 [f]Jer 9:11
26:33 [g]Dt 4:27; Eze 12:15; 20:23; Zec 7:14
26:34 [h]ver 43; 2Ch 36:21
26:36 [i]Eze 21:7
26:37 [j]Jos 7:12
26:38 [k]Dt 4:26
26:39 [l]Eze 4:17
26:40 [m]Jer 3:12-15; Lk 15:18; 1Jn 1:9
26:41 [n]Eze 44:7,9; Ac 7:51
26:42 [o]Ge 22:15-18; 28:15 [p]Ge 26:5
26:44 [q]Ro 11:2 [r]Dt 4:31; Jer 30:11 [s]Jer 33:26
26:45 [t]Ge 17:7 [u]Ex 6:8; Lev 25:38
26:46 [v]Lev 7:38; 27:34
27:2 [w]Nu 6:2
27:3 [x]Ex 30:13; Nu 3:47; 18:16
27:6 [y]Nu 18:16

42I will remember my covenant
with Jacob[o] and my covenant with
Isaac[p] and my covenant with Abraham, and I will remember the land.
43For the land will be deserted by
them and will enjoy its sabbaths
while it lies desolate without them.
They will pay for their sins because
they rejected my laws and abhorred
my decrees. 44Yet in spite of this,
when they are in the land of their
enemies, I will not reject them or
abhor[q] them so as to destroy them
completely,[r] breaking my covenant[s] with them. I am the LORD
their God. 45But for their sake I will
remember[t] the covenant with
their ancestors whom I brought out
of Egypt[u] in the sight of the nations to be their God. I am the
LORD.' "

46These are the decrees, the laws
and the regulations that the LORD
established on Mount Sinai between himself and the Israelites
through Moses.[v]

Redeeming What Is the LORD's

27 The LORD said to Moses,
2"Speak to the Israelites
and say to them: 'If anyone makes
a special vow[w] to dedicate persons
to the LORD by giving equivalent
values, 3set the value of a male between the ages of twenty and sixty
at fifty shekels[n] of silver, according to the sanctuary shekel[o];[x]
4and if it is a female, set her value
at thirty shekels.[p] 5If it is a person
between the ages of five and twenty, set the value of a male at twenty
shekels[q] and of a female at ten
shekels.[r] 6If it is a person between
one month and five years, set the
value of a male at five shekels[s][y] of
silver and that of a female at three
shekels[t] of silver. 7If it is a person
sixty years old or more, set the val-

[n]3 That is, about 1 1/4 pounds (about 0.6 kilogram); also in verse 16 [o]3 That is, about 2/5 ounce (about 11.5 grams); also in verse 25 [p]4 That is, about 12 ounces (about 0.3 kilogram) [q]5 That is, about 8 ounces (about 0.2 kilogram) [r]5 That is, about 4 ounces (about 110 grams); also in verse 7 [s]6 That is, about 2 ounces (about 55 grams) [t]6 That is, about 1 1/4 ounces (about 35 grams)

ue of a male at fifteen shekels[u] and
of a female at ten shekels. **8**If anyone making the vow is too poor to
pay[a] the specified amount, he is to
present the person to the priest,
who will set the value[b] for him according to what the man making
the vow can afford.
9" 'If what he vowed is an animal
that is acceptable as an offering to
the LORD, such an animal given to
the LORD becomes holy. **10**He must
not exchange it or substitute a
good one for a bad one, or a bad
one for a good one;[c] if he should
substitute one animal for another,
both it and the substitute become
holy. **11**If what he vowed is a ceremonially unclean animal—one that
is not acceptable as an offering to
the LORD—the animal must be presented to the priest, **12**who will
judge its quality as good or bad.
Whatever value the priest then sets,
that is what it will be. **13**If the owner wishes to redeem[d] the animal,
he must add a fifth to its value.
14" 'If a man dedicates his house
as something holy to the LORD, the
priest will judge its quality as good
or bad. Whatever value the priest
then sets, so it will remain. **15**If the
man who dedicates his house redeems it,[e] he must add a fifth to
its value, and the house will again
become his.
16" 'If a man dedicates to the
LORD part of his family land, its value is to be set according to the
amount of seed required for it—fifty shekels of silver to a homer[v] of
barley seed. **17**If he dedicates his
field during the Year of Jubilee, the
value that has been set remains.
18But if he dedicates his field after
the Jubilee, the priest will determine the value according to the
number of years that remain[f] until
the next Year of Jubilee, and its set
value will be reduced. **19**If the man
who dedicates the field wishes to
redeem it, he must add a fifth to its
value, and the field will again become his. **20**If, however, he does
not redeem the field, or if he has
sold it to someone else, it can never
be redeemed. **21**When the field is
released in the Jubilee,[g] it will become holy, like a field devoted to
the LORD;[h] it will become the property of the priests.[w]
22" 'If a man dedicates to the
LORD a field he has bought, which is
not part of his family land, **23**the
priest will determine its value up to
the Year of Jubilee, and the man
must pay its value on that day as
something holy to the LORD. **24**In
the Year of Jubilee the field will revert to the person from whom he
bought it,[i] the one whose land it
was. **25**Every value is to be set according to the sanctuary shekel,[j]
twenty gerahs[k] to the shekel.
26" 'No one, however, may dedicate the firstborn of an animal,
since the firstborn already belongs
to the LORD;[l] whether an ox[x] or a
sheep, it is the LORD's. **27**If it is one
of the unclean animals,[m] he may
buy it back at its set value, adding
a fifth of the value to it. If he does
not redeem it, it is to be sold at its
set value.
28" 'But nothing that a man
owns and devotes[y][n] to the LORD
—whether man or animal or family
land—may be sold or redeemed;
everything so devoted is most holy
to the LORD.
29" 'No person devoted to destruction[z] may be ransomed; he
must be put to death.
30" 'A tithe[o] of everything from
the land, whether grain from the
soil or fruit from the trees, belongs
to the LORD; it is holy to the LORD.
31If a man redeems any of his tithe,
he must add a fifth of the value to
it. **32**The entire tithe of the herd
and flock—every tenth animal that
passes under the shepherd's rod[p]
—will be holy to the LORD. **33**He
must not pick out the good from
the bad or make any substitution.[q]
If he does make a substitution,

27:8 [a]Lev 5:11 [b]ver 12,14
27:10 [c]ver 33
27:13 [d]ver 15,19; Lev 25:25
27:15 [e]ver 13,20
27:18 [f]Lev 25:15
27:21 [g]Lev 25:10 [h]ver 28; Nu 18:14; Eze 44:29
27:24 [i]Lev 25:28
27:25 [j]Ex 30:13; Nu 18:16 [k]Nu 3:47; Eze 45:12
27:26 [l]Ex 13:2,12
27:27 [m]ver 11
27:28 [n]Nu 18:14; Jos 6:17-19
27:30 [o]Ge 28:22; 2Ch 31:6; Mal 3:8
27:32 [p]Jer 33:13; Eze 20:37
27:33 [q]ver 10

[u]7 That is, about 6 ounces (about 170 grams) [v]*16* That is, probably about 6 bushels (about 220 liters) [w]*21* Or *priest* [x]*26* The Hebrew word can include both male and female. [y]*28* The Hebrew term refers to the irrevocable giving over of things or persons to the LORD. [z]*29* The Hebrew term refers to the irrevocable giving over of things or persons to the LORD, often by totally destroying them.

both the animal and its substitute
become holy and cannot be redeemed.' "

[34]These are the commands the
LORD gave Moses on Mount Sinai
for the Israelites.[a]

27:34
[a] Lev 26:46; Dt 4:5

Numbers

Title and Background

The book of Numbers gets its name from the two numberings or countings of the Israelites during their 38 years of wandering in the wilderness. These countings are found in chapters 1 and 26. Numbers presents an account of that wandering in the desert following the establishment of the covenant at Sinai.

Author and Date of Writing

Numbers has been traditionally ascribed to Moses. This assignment is based on: (1) the statements concerning Moses' writing activity (e.g., 33:1-2; Ex 17:14; 24:4; 34:27); (2) the assumption that the Pentateuch is a unity and comes from one great author; and (3) the New Testament's ascription of quotations from the Pentateuch to Moses (e.g., Mt 19:8; Jn 5:46-47; Ro 10:5). Numbers was written by Moses shortly before his death in 1406 B.C.

Theme and Message

Numbers relates the story of Israel's journey from Mount Sinai to the plains of Moab on the border of Canaan. It tells of the murmuring and rebellion of God's people and of their subsequent judgment. They were condemned to live out their lives in the desert; only their children would enjoy the fulfillment of the promise that had originally been theirs. Throughout the years in the desert, one thing became clear to Israel—God's constant care for them. Not only did he meet their needs, but he also loved and forgave his people continually.

Outline

I. Israel at Sinai, Preparing to Go to Canaan (1:1-10:10)
II. From Sinai to Kadesh Barnea (10:11-12:16)
III. Israel at Kadesh, the Delay Resulting From Rebellion (13:1-20:13)
IV. From Kadesh to the Plains of Moab (20:14-22:1)
V. Israel on the Plains of Moab, Anticipating the Taking of Canaan (22:2-32:42)
VI. Supplements Dealing With Various Matters (33:1-36:13)

The Census

1 The LORD spoke to Moses in
the Tent of Meeting[a] in the
Desert of Sinai[b] on the first day of
the second month[c] of the second
year after the Israelites came out of
Egypt. He said: **2**"Take a census[d]
of the whole Israelite community
by their clans and families, listing
every man by name, one by one.
3You and Aaron are to number by
their divisions all the men in Israel
twenty years old or more[e] who are
able to serve in the army. **4**One
man from each tribe, each the head
of his family,[f] is to help you.[g]
5These are the names of the men
who are to assist you:

from Reuben,[h] Elizur son of Shedeur;
6from Simeon, Shelumiel son of Zurishaddai;
7from Judah,[i] Nahshon son of Amminadab;[j]
8from Issachar,[k] Nethanel son of Zuar;
9from Zebulun,[l] Eliab son of Helon;
10from the sons of Joseph:

1:1 [a]Ex 40:2 [b]Ex 19:1 [c]Ex 40:17 **1:2** [d]Ex 30:11-16; Nu 26:2 **1:3** [e]Ex 30:14 **1:4** [f]ver 16 [g]Ex 18:21; Dt 1:15 **1:5** [h]Ge 29:32; Dt 33:6; Rev 7:5 **1:7** [i]Ge 29:35; Ps 78:68 [j]Ru 4:20; 1Ch 2:10; Lk 3:32 **1:8** [k]Ge 30:18 **1:9** [l]ver 30

from Ephraim,[a] Elishama
son of Ammihud;
from Manasseh, Gamaliel
son of Pedahzur;
11from Benjamin, Abidan son of
Gideoni;
12from Dan,[b] Ahiezer son of
Ammishaddai;
13from Asher,[c] Pagiel son of Ocran;
14from Gad, Eliasaph son of
Deuel;[d]
15from Naphtali,[e] Ahira son of
Enan."

16These were the men appointed
from the community, the leaders[f]
of their ancestral tribes. They were
the heads of the clans of Israel.[g]
17Moses and Aaron took these
men whose names had been given,
18and they called the whole community together on the first day of
the second month.[h] The people indicated their ancestry[i] by their
clans and families, and the men
twenty years old or more were listed by name, one by one, **19**as the
LORD commanded Moses. And so
he counted them in the Desert of
Sinai:

20From the descendants of Reuben[j] the firstborn son of Israel:
All the men twenty years
old or more who were able
to serve in the army were
listed by name, one by one,
according to the records of
their clans and families.
21The number from the
tribe of Reuben was 46,500.

22From the descendants of Simeon:[k]
All the men twenty years
old or more who were able
to serve in the army were
counted and listed by
name, one by one, according to the records of their
clans and families. **23**The
number from the tribe of
Simeon was 59,300.

24From the descendants of Gad:[l]
All the men twenty years
old or more who were able
to serve in the army were
listed by name, according to
the records of their clans
and families. **25**The number
from the tribe of Gad was
45,650.

26From the descendants of Judah:[m]
All the men twenty years
old or more who were able
to serve in the army were
listed by name, according to
the records of their clans
and families. **27**The number
from the tribe of Judah was
74,600.

28From the descendants of Issachar:[n]
All the men twenty years
old or more who were able
to serve in the army were
listed by name, according to
the records of their clans
and families. **29**The number
from the tribe of Issachar
was 54,400.

30From the descendants of Zebulun:[o]
All the men twenty years
old or more who were able
to serve in the army were
listed by name, according to
the records of their clans
and families. **31**The number
from the tribe of Zebulun
was 57,400.

32From the sons of Joseph:
From the descendants of Ephraim:[p]
All the men twenty years
old or more who were able
to serve in the army were
listed by name, according to
the records of their clans
and families. **33**The number
from the tribe of Ephraim
was 40,500.

34From the descendants of Manasseh:[q]
All the men twenty years
old or more who were able
to serve in the army were
listed by name, according to
the records of their clans
and families. **35**The number

1:10 [a] ver 32
1:12 [b] ver 38
1:13 [c] ver 40
1:14 [d] Nu 2:14
1:15 [e] ver 42
1:16 [f] Ex 18:25 [g] ver 4; Ex 18:21; Nu 7:2
1:18 [h] ver 1 [i] Ezr 2:59; Heb 7:3
1:20 [j] Nu 26:5-11; Rev 7:5
1:22 [k] Nu 26:12-14; Rev 7:7
1:24 [l] Ge 30:11; Nu 26:15-18; Rev 7:5
1:26 [m] Ge 29:35; Nu 26:19-22; Mt 1:2; Rev 7:5
1:28 [n] Nu 26:23-25; Rev 7:7
1:30 [o] Nu 26:26-27; Rev 7:8
1:32 [p] Nu 26:35-37
1:34 [q] Nu 26:28-34; Rev 7:6

from the tribe of Manasseh
was 32,200.

36From the descendants of Benjamin:[a]

All the men twenty years
old or more who were able
to serve in the army were
listed by name, according to
the records of their clans
and families. **37**The number
from the tribe of Benjamin
was 35,400.

38From the descendants of Dan:[b]
All the men twenty years
old or more who were able
to serve in the army were
listed by name, according to
the records of their clans
and families. **39**The number
from the tribe of Dan was
62,700.

40From the descendants of Asher:[c]

All the men twenty years
old or more who were able
to serve in the army were
listed by name, according to
the records of their clans
and families. **41**The number
from the tribe of Asher was
41,500.

42From the descendants of Naphtali:[d]

All the men twenty years
old or more who were able
to serve in the army were
listed by name, according to
the records of their clans
and families. **43**The number
from the tribe of Naphtali
was 53,400.

44These were the men counted
by Moses and Aaron[e] and the
twelve leaders of Israel, each one
representing his family. **45**All the
Israelites twenty years old or more
who were able to serve in Israel's
army were counted according to
their families. **46**The total number
was 603,550.[f]

47The families of the tribe of
Levi,[g] however, were not counted[h] along with the others. **48**The
LORD had said to Moses: **49**"You
must not count the tribe of Levi or
include them in the census of the
other Israelites. **50**Instead, appoint
the Levites to be in charge of the
tabernacle of the Testimony[i]—
over all its furnishings and everything belonging to it. They are to
carry the tabernacle and all its furnishings; they are to take care of it
and encamp around it. **51**Whenever
the tabernacle is to move, the Levites are to take it down, and whenever the tabernacle is to be set up,
the Levites shall do it.[j] Anyone
else who goes near it shall be put to
death. **52**The Israelites are to set up
their tents by divisions, each man
in his own camp under his own
standard.[k] **53**The Levites, however, are to set up their tents around
the tabernacle of the Testimony so
that wrath will not fall[l] on the Israelite community. The Levites are
to be responsible for the care of the
tabernacle of the Testimony.[m]"

54The Israelites did all this just
as the LORD commanded Moses.

The Arrangement of the Tribal Camps

2 The LORD said to Moses and
Aaron: **2**"The Israelites are to
camp around the Tent of Meeting
some distance from it, each man
under his standard[n] with the banners of his family."

3On the east, toward the
sunrise, the divisions of the
camp of Judah are to encamp
under their standard. The
leader of the people of Judah
is Nahshon son of Ammina-
dab.[o] **4**His division numbers
74,600.

5The tribe of Issachar will
camp next to them. The leader
of the people of Issachar is Nethanel son of Zuar.[p] **6**His division numbers 54,400.

7The tribe of Zebulun will
be next. The leader of the people of Zebulun is Eliab son of
Helon.[q] **8**His division numbers 57,400.

9All the men assigned to the
camp of Judah, according to

1:36 [a] Nu 26:38-41; 2Ch 17:17; Rev 7:8
1:38 [b] Ge 30:6; Nu 26:42-43
1:40 [c] Nu 26:44-47; Rev 7:6
1:42 [d] Nu 26:48-50; Rev 7:6
1:44 [e] Nu 26:64
1:46 [f] Ex 12:37; 38:26; Nu 2:32; 26:51
1:47 [g] Nu 2:33; 26:57 [h] Nu 4:3,49
1:50 [i] Ex 38:21; Ac 7:44
1:51 [j] Nu 3:38; 4:1-33
1:52 [k] Nu 2:2; Ps 20:5
1:53 [l] Lev 10:6; Nu 16:46; 18:5 [m] Nu 18:2-4
2:2 [n] Nu 1:52; Ps 74:4; Isa 31:9
2:3 [o] Nu 10:14; Ru 4:20; 1Ch 2:10
2:5 [p] Nu 1:8
2:7 [q] Nu 1:9

their divisions, number 186,400. They will set out first.[a]

10 On the south will be the divisions of the camp of Reuben under their standard. The leader of the people of Reuben is Elizur son of Shedeur.[b] 11 His division numbers 46,500.

12 The tribe of Simeon will camp next to them. The leader of the people of Simeon is Shelumiel son of Zurishaddai.[c] 13 His division numbers 59,300.

14 The tribe of Gad will be next. The leader of the people of Gad is Eliasaph son of Deuel.[a][d] 15 His division numbers 45,650.

16 All the men assigned to the camp of Reuben,[e] according to their divisions, number 151,450. They will set out second.

17 Then the Tent of Meeting and the camp of the Levites[f] will set out in the middle of the camps. They will set out in the same order as they encamp, each in his own place under his standard.

18 On the west will be the divisions of the camp of Ephraim[g] under their standard. The leader of the people of Ephraim is Elishama son of Ammihud.[h] 19 His division numbers 40,500.

20 The tribe of Manasseh will be next to them. The leader of the people of Manasseh is Gamaliel son of Pedahzur.[i] 21 His division numbers 32,200.

22 The tribe of Benjamin will be next. The leader of the people of Benjamin is Abidan son of Gideoni.[j] 23 His division numbers 35,400.

24 All the men assigned to the camp of Ephraim,[k] according to their divisions, number 108,100. They will set out third.[l]

25 On the north will be the divisions of the camp of Dan, under their standard. The leader of the people of Dan is Ahiezer son of Ammishaddai.[m] 26 His division numbers 62,700.

27 The tribe of Asher will camp next to them. The leader of the people of Asher is Pagiel son of Ocran.[n] 28 His division numbers 41,500.

29 The tribe of Naphtali will be next. The leader of the people of Naphtali is Ahira son of Enan.[o] 30 His division numbers 53,400.

31 All the men assigned to the camp of Dan number 157,600. They will set out last,[p] under their standards.

32 These are the Israelites, counted according to their families. All those in the camps, by their divisions, number 603,550.[q] 33 The Levites, however, were not counted[r] along with the other Israelites, as the LORD commanded Moses.

34 So the Israelites did everything the LORD commanded Moses; that is the way they encamped under their standards, and that is the way they set out, each with his clan and family.

The Levites

3 This is the account of the family of Aaron and Moses[s] at the time the LORD talked with Moses on Mount Sinai.

2 The names of the sons of Aaron were Nadab the firstborn and Abihu, Eleazar and Ithamar.[t] 3 Those were the names of Aaron's sons, the anointed priests,[u] who were ordained to serve as priests. 4 Nadab and Abihu, however, fell dead before the LORD[v] when they made an offering with unauthorized fire before him in the Desert of Sinai.[w]

2:9 [a] Nu 10:14
2:10 [b] Nu 1:5
2:12 [c] Nu 1:6
2:14 [d] Nu 1:14
2:16 [e] Nu 10:18
2:17 [f] Nu 1:53; 10:21
2:18 [g] Ge 48:20; Jer 31:18-20 [h] Nu 1:10
2:20 [i] Nu 1:10
2:22 [j] Nu 1:11; Ps 68:27
2:24 [k] Nu 10:22 [l] Ps 80:2
2:25 [m] Nu 1:12
2:27 [n] Nu 1:13
2:29 [o] Nu 1:15
2:31 [p] Nu 10:25
2:32 [q] Ex 38:26; Nu 1:46
2:33 [r] Nu 1:47; 26:57-62
3:1 [s] Ex 6:27
3:2 [t] Ex 6:23; Nu 26:60
3:3 [u] Ex 28:41
3:4 [v] Lev 10:2 [w] Lev 10:1

[a] *14* Many manuscripts of the Masoretic Text, Samaritan Pentateuch and Vulgate (see also Num. 1:14); most manuscripts of the Masoretic Text *Reuel*

They had no sons; so only Eleazar
and Ithamar served as priests during the lifetime of their father Aaron.[a]
5 The LORD said to Moses, 6 "Bring
the tribe of Levi[b] and present
them to Aaron the priest to assist
him.[c] 7 They are to perform duties
for him and for the whole community at the Tent of Meeting by doing the work[d] of the tabernacle.
8 They are to take care of all the furnishings of the Tent of Meeting,
fulfilling the obligations of the Israelites by doing the work of the
tabernacle. 9 Give the Levites to
Aaron and his sons;[e] they are the
Israelites who are to be given wholly to him.[b] 10 Appoint Aaron and
his sons to serve as priests;[f] anyone else who approaches the sanctuary must be put to death."[g]
11 The LORD also said to Moses,
12 "I have taken the Levites[h] from
among the Israelites in place of the
first male offspring[i] of every Israelite woman. The Levites are
mine,[j] 13 for all the firstborn are
mine.[k] When I struck down all the
firstborn in Egypt, I set apart for
myself every firstborn in Israel,
whether man or animal. They are
to be mine. I am the LORD."
14 The LORD said to Moses in the
Desert of Sinai, 15 "Count[l] the Levites by their families and clans.
Count every male a month old or
more."[m] 16 So Moses counted
them, as he was commanded by the
word of the LORD.
17 These were the names of the
sons of Levi:[n]
Gershon, Kohath and Mera-
ri.[o]
18 These were the names of the
Gershonite clans:
Libni and Shimei.[p]
19 The Kohathite clans:
Amram, Izhar, Hebron and
Uzziel.[q]
20 The Merarite clans:[r]
Mahli and Mushi.[s]
These were the Levite clans, according to their families.

21 To Gershon belonged the
clans of the Libnites and Shime-
ites;[t] these were the Gershonite
clans. 22 The number of all the
males a month old or more who
were counted was 7,500. 23 The
Gershonite clans were to camp on
the west, behind the tabernacle.
24 The leader of the families of the
Gershonites was Eliasaph son of
Lael. 25 At the Tent of Meeting the
Gershonites were responsible for
the care of the tabernacle[u] and
tent, its coverings,[v] the curtain at
the entrance[w] to the Tent of Meeting, 26 the curtains of the courtyard[x], the curtain at the entrance
to the courtyard surrounding the
tabernacle and altar, and the
ropes[y]—and everything related to
their use.

27 To Kohath belonged the clans
of the Amramites, Izharites, Hebronites and Uzzielites;[z] these
were the Kohathite clans. 28 The
number of all the males a month
old or more was 8,600.[c] The Kohathites were responsible for the
care of the sanctuary. 29 The Kohathite clans were to camp on the
south side[a] of the tabernacle.
30 The leader of the families of the
Kohathite clans was Elizaphan son
of Uzziel. 31 They were responsible
for the care of the ark,[b] the table,[c]
the lampstand,[d] the altars,[e] the
articles of the sanctuary used in
ministering, the curtain,[f] and everything related to their use.[g]
32 The chief leader of the Levites
was Eleazar son of Aaron, the
priest. He was appointed over
those who were responsible for the
care of the sanctuary.

33 To Merari belonged the clans
of the Mahlites and the Mushites;[h]
these were the Merarite clans.
34 The number of all the males a
month old or more who were
counted was 6,200. 35 The leader of
the families of the Merarite clans
was Zuriel son of Abihail; they were

3:4 [a] 1Ch 24:1
3:6 [b] Dt 10:8; 31:9; 1Ch 15:2 [c] Nu 8:6-22; 18:1-7; 2Ch 29:11
3:7 [d] Lev 8:35; Nu 1:50
3:9 [e] Nu 8:19; 18:6
3:10 [f] Ex 29:9 [g] Nu 1:51
3:12 [h] Mal 2:4 [i] ver 41; Nu 8:16,18 [j] Ex 13:2
3:13 [k] Ex 13:12
3:15 [l] ver 39 [m] Nu 26:62
3:17 [n] Ge 46:11 [o] Ex 6:16
3:18 [p] Ex 6:17
3:19 [q] Ex 6:18
3:20 [r] Ge 46:11 [s] Ex 6:19
3:21 [t] Ex 6:17
3:25 [u] Ex 25:9 [v] Ex 26:14 [w] Ex 26:36; Nu 4:25
3:26 [x] Ex 27:9 [y] Ex 35:18
3:27 [z] 1Ch 26:23
3:29 [a] Nu 1:53
3:31 [b] Ex 25:10-22 [c] Ex 25:23 [d] Ex 25:31 [e] Ex 27:1; 30:1 [f] Ex 26:33 [g] Nu 4:15
3:33 [h] Ex 6:19

b9 Most manuscripts of the Masoretic Text; some manuscripts of the Masoretic Text, Samaritan Pentateuch and Septuagint (see also Num. 8:16) *to me* c28 Hebrew; some Septuagint manuscripts *8,300*

to camp on the north side of the tabernacle.[a] 36The Merarites were appointed[b] to take care of the frames of the tabernacle, its crossbars, posts, bases, all its equipment, and everything related to their use, 37as well as the posts of the surrounding courtyard with their bases, tent pegs and ropes.

38Moses and Aaron and his sons were to camp to the east[c] of the tabernacle, toward the sunrise, in front of the Tent of Meeting.[d] They were responsible for the care of the sanctuary[e] on behalf of the Israelites. Anyone else who approached the sanctuary was to be put to death.[f]

39The total number of Levites counted at the LORD's command by Moses and Aaron according to their clans, including every male a month old or more, was 22,000.[g]

40The LORD said to Moses, "Count all the firstborn Israelite males who are a month old or more[h] and make a list of their names. 41Take the Levites for me in place of all the firstborn of the Israelites,[i] and the livestock of the Levites in place of all the firstborn of the livestock of the Israelites. I am the LORD."

42So Moses counted all the firstborn of the Israelites, as the LORD commanded him. 43The total number of firstborn males a month old or more, listed by name, was 22,273.[j]

44The LORD also said to Moses, 45"Take the Levites in place of all the firstborn of Israel, and the livestock of the Levites in place of their livestock. The Levites are to be mine. I am the LORD. 46To redeem[k] the 273 firstborn Israelites who exceed the number of the Levites, 47collect five shekels[d][l] for each one, according to the sanctuary shekel,[m] which weighs twenty gerahs.[n] 48Give the money for the redemption of the additional Israelites to Aaron and his sons."

49So Moses collected the redemption money from those who exceeded the number redeemed by the Levites. 50From the firstborn of the Israelites he collected silver weighing 1,365 shekels,[e][o] according to the sanctuary shekel. 51Moses gave the redemption money to Aaron and his sons, as he was commanded by the word of the LORD.

The Kohathites

4 The LORD said to Moses and Aaron: 2"Take a census[p] of the Kohathite branch of the Levites by their clans and families. 3Count all the men from thirty to fifty years of age[q] who come to serve in the work in the Tent of Meeting.

4"This is the work of the Kohathites in the Tent of Meeting: the care of the most holy things.[r] 5When the camp is to move, Aaron and his sons are to go in and take down the shielding curtain[s] and cover the ark of the Testimony with it.[t] 6Then they are to cover this with hides of sea cows,[f] spread a cloth of solid blue over that and put the poles[u] in place.

7"Over the table of the Presence[v] they are to spread a blue cloth and put on it the plates, dishes and bowls, and the jars for drink offerings; the bread that is continually there[w] is to remain on it. 8Over these they are to spread a scarlet cloth, cover that with hides of sea cows and put its poles in place.

9"They are to take a blue cloth and cover the lampstand that is for light, together with its lamps, its wick trimmers and trays,[x] and all its jars for the oil used to supply it. 10Then they are to wrap it and all its accessories in a covering of hides of sea cows and put it on a carrying frame.

11"Over the gold altar[y] they are to spread a blue cloth and cover that with hides of sea cows and put its poles in place.

3:35 [a]Nu 1:53; 2:25
3:36 [b]Nu 4:32
3:38 [c]Nu 2:3 [d]Nu 1:53 [e]ver 7; Nu 18:5 [f]ver 10; Nu 1:51
3:39 [g]Nu 26:62
3:40 [h]ver 15
3:41 [i]ver 12
3:43 [j]ver 39
3:46 [k]Ex 13:13; Nu 18:15
3:47 [l]Lev 27:6 [m]Ex 30:13 [n]Lev 27:25
3:50 [o]ver 46-48
4:2 [p]Ex 30:12
4:3 [q]ver 23; Nu 8:25; 1Ch 23:3,24, 27; Ezr 3:8
4:4 [r]ver 19
4:5 [s]Ex 26:31,33 [t]Ex 25:10,16
4:6 [u]Ex 25:13-15; 1Ki 8:7; 2Ch 5:8
4:7 [v]Ex 25:23,29; Lev 24:6 [w]Ex 25:30
4:9 [x]Ex 25:31,37, 38
4:11 [y]Ex 30:1

[d]47 That is, about 2 ounces (about 55 grams)
[e]50 That is, about 35 pounds (about 15.5 kilograms)
[f]6 That is, dugongs; also in verses 8, 10, 11, 13, 14 and 25

12"They are to take all the articles used for ministering in the
sanctuary, wrap them in a blue
cloth, cover that with hides of sea
cows and put them on a carrying
frame.
13"They are to remove the ashes
from the bronze altar[a] and spread
a purple cloth over it. 14Then they
are to place on it all the utensils
used for ministering at the altar, including the firepans, meat forks,[b]
shovels and sprinkling bowls.[c]
Over it they are to spread a covering of hides of sea cows and put its
poles[d] in place.
15"After Aaron and his sons have
finished covering the holy furnishings and all the holy articles, and
when the camp is ready to move,
the Kohathites are to come to do
the carrying.[e] But they must not
touch the holy things or they will
die.[f] The Kohathites are to carry
those things that are in the Tent of
Meeting.
16"Eleazar[g] son of Aaron, the
priest, is to have charge of the oil
for the light,[h] the fragrant incense,
the regular grain offering[i] and the
anointing oil. He is to be in charge
of the entire tabernacle and everything in it, including its holy furnishings and articles."
17The LORD said to Moses and
Aaron, 18"See that the Kohathite
tribal clans are not cut off from the
Levites. 19So that they may live and
not die when they come near the
most holy things,[j] do this for
them: Aaron and his sons are to go
into the sanctuary and assign to
each man his work and what he is
to carry. 20But the Kohathites must
not go in to look[k] at the holy
things, even for a moment, or they
will die."

The Gershonites

21The LORD said to Moses,
22"Take a census also of the Gershonites by their families and
clans. 23Count all the men from
thirty to fifty years of age[l] who
come to serve in the work at the
Tent of Meeting.
24"This is the service of the Gershonite clans as they work and carry burdens: 25They are to carry the
curtains of the tabernacle,[m] the
Tent of Meeting,[n] its covering[o]
and the outer covering of hides of
sea cows, the curtains for the entrance to the Tent of Meeting,
26the curtains of the courtyard surrounding the tabernacle and altar,
the curtain for the entrance, the
ropes and all the equipment used
in its service. The Gershonites are
to do all that needs to be done with
these things. 27All their service,
whether carrying or doing other
work, is to be done under the direction of Aaron and his sons. You
shall assign to them as their responsibility all they are to carry.
28This is the service of the Gershonite clans[p] at the Tent of Meeting. Their duties are to be under
the direction of Ithamar son of Aaron, the priest.

The Merarites

29"Count the Merarites by their
clans and families.[q] 30Count all
the men from thirty to fifty years of
age who come to serve in the work
at the Tent of Meeting. 31This is
their duty as they perform service
at the Tent of Meeting: to carry the
frames of the tabernacle, its crossbars, posts and bases,[r] 32as well as
the posts of the surrounding courtyard with their bases, tent pegs,
ropes, all their equipment and everything related to their use. Assign to each man the specific
things he is to carry. 33This is the
service of the Merarite clans as
they work at the Tent of Meeting
under the direction of Ithamar son
of Aaron, the priest."

The Numbering of the Levite Clans

34Moses, Aaron and the leaders
of the community counted the Kohathites[s] by their clans and families. 35All the men from thirty to
fifty years of age who came to serve
in the work in the Tent of Meeting,
36counted by clans, were 2,750.
37This was the total of all those in

4:13 [a]Ex 27:1-8
4:14 [b]2Ch 4:16 [c]Jer 52:18 [d]Ex 27:6
4:15 [e]Nu 7:9 [f]Nu 1:51; 2Sa 6:6,7
4:16 [g]Lev 10:6 [h]Ex 25:6 [i]Ex 29:41; Lev 6:14-23
4:19 [j]ver 15
4:20 [k]Ex 19:21; 1Sa 6:19
4:23 [l]ver 3; 1Ch 23:3,24, 27
4:25 [m]Ex 27:10-18; Nu 3:26 [n]Nu 3:25 [o]Ex 26:14
4:28 [p]Nu 7:7
4:29 [q]Ge 46:11
4:31 [r]Nu 3:36
4:34 [s]ver 2

the Kohathite clans[a] who served in the Tent of Meeting. Moses and Aaron counted them according to the LORD's command through Moses.

38 The Gershonites[b] were counted by their clans and families. 39 All the men from thirty to fifty years of age who came to serve in the work at the Tent of Meeting, 40 counted by their clans and families, were 2,630. 41 This was the total of those in the Gershonite clans who served at the Tent of Meeting. Moses and Aaron counted them according to the LORD's command.

42 The Merarites were counted by their clans and families. 43 All the men from thirty to fifty years of age who came to serve in the work at the Tent of Meeting, 44 counted by their clans, were 3,200. 45 This was the total of those in the Merarite clans.[c] Moses and Aaron counted them according to the LORD's command through Moses.

46 So Moses, Aaron and the leaders of Israel counted all the Levites by their clans and families. 47 All the men from thirty to fifty years of age[d] who came to do the work of serving and carrying the Tent of Meeting 48 numbered 8,580.[e] 49 At the LORD's command through Moses, each was assigned his work and told what to carry.

Thus they were counted,[f] as the LORD commanded Moses.

The Purity of the Camp

5 The LORD said to Moses, 2 "Command the Israelites to send away from the camp anyone who has an infectious skin disease[g][g] or a discharge[h] of any kind, or who is ceremonially unclean[i] because of a dead body. 3 Send away male and female alike; send them outside the camp so they will not defile their camp, where I dwell among them.[j]" 4 The Israelites did this; they sent them outside the camp. They did just as the LORD had instructed Moses.

Restitution for Wrongs

5 The LORD said to Moses, 6 "Say to the Israelites: 'When a man or woman wrongs another in any way[h] and so is unfaithful[k] to the LORD, that person is guilty[l] 7 and must confess[m] the sin he has committed. He must make full restitution[n] for his wrong, add one fifth to it and give it all to the person he has wronged. 8 But if that person has no close relative to whom restitution can be made for the wrong, the restitution belongs to the LORD and must be given to the priest, along with the ram with which atonement is made for him.[o] 9 All the sacred contributions the Israelites bring to a priest will belong to him.[p] 10 Each man's sacred gifts are his own, but what he gives to the priest will belong to the priest.[q]' "

The Test for an Unfaithful Wife

11 Then the LORD said to Moses, 12 "Speak to the Israelites and say to them: 'If a man's wife goes astray[r] and is unfaithful to him 13 by sleeping with another man,[s] and this is hidden from her husband and her impurity is undetected (since there is no witness against her and she has not been caught in the act), 14 and if feelings of jealousy[t] come over her husband and he suspects his wife and she is impure—or if he is jealous and suspects her even though she is not impure— 15 then he is to take his wife to the priest. He must also take an offering of a tenth of an ephah[i][u] of barley flour[v] on her behalf. He must not pour oil on it or put incense on it, because it is a grain offering for jealousy, a reminder[w] offering to draw attention to guilt.

16 " 'The priest shall bring her and have her stand before the LORD. 17 Then he shall take some holy water in a clay jar and put some dust from the tabernacle floor into the

4:37 [a] Nu 3:27
4:38 [b] Ge 46:11
4:45 [c] ver 29
4:47 [d] ver 3
4:48 [e] Nu 3:39
4:49 [f] Nu 1:47
5:2 [g] Lev 13:46 [h] Lev 15:2; Mt 9:20 [i] Lev 13:3; Nu 9:6-10
5:3 [j] Lev 26:12; Nu 35:34; 2Co 6:16
5:6 [k] Lev 6:2 [l] Lev 5:14-6:7
5:7 [m] Lev 5:5; 26:40; Jos 7:19; Lk 19:8 [n] Lev 6:5
5:8 [o] Lev 6:6,7; 7:7
5:9 [p] Lev 6:17; 7:6-14
5:10 [q] Lev 10:13
5:12 [r] Ex 20:14
5:13 [s] Lev 18:20; 20:10
5:14 [t] Pr 6:34; SS 8:6
5:15 [u] Ex 16:36 [v] Lev 6:20 [w] Eze 29:16

g2 Traditionally *leprosy*; the Hebrew word was used for various diseases affecting the skin—not necessarily leprosy. h6 Or *woman commits any wrong common to mankind* i15 That is, probably about 2 quarts (about 2 liters)

water. **18**After the priest has had the woman stand before the LORD, he shall loosen her hair[a] and place in her hands the reminder offering, the grain offering for jealousy, while he himself holds the bitter water that brings a curse. **19**Then the priest shall put the woman under oath and say to her, "If no other man has slept with you and you have not gone astray[b] and become impure while married to your husband, may this bitter water that brings a curse not harm you. **20**But if you have gone astray[c] while married to your husband and you have defiled yourself by sleeping with a man other than your husband"— **21**here the priest is to put the woman under this curse of the oath[d] —"may the LORD cause your people to curse and denounce you when he causes your thigh to waste away and your abdomen to swell.[i] **22**May this water[e] that brings a curse[f] enter your body so that your abdomen swells and your thigh wastes away.[k]"

" 'Then the woman is to say, "Amen. So be it.[g]"

23" 'The priest is to write these curses on a scroll[h] and then wash them off into the bitter water. **24**He shall have the woman drink the bitter water that brings a curse, and this water will enter her and cause bitter suffering. **25**The priest is to take from her hands the grain offering for jealousy, wave it before the LORD[i] and bring it to the altar. **26**The priest is then to take a handful of the grain offering as a memorial offering and burn it on the altar; after that, he is to have the woman drink the water. **27**If she has defiled herself and been unfaithful to her husband, then when she is made to drink the water that brings a curse, it will go into her and cause bitter suffering; her abdomen will swell and her thigh waste away,[l] and she will become accursed[j] among her people. **28**If, however, the woman has not defiled herself and is free from impurity, she will be cleared of guilt and will be able to have children.

5:18 [a] Lev 10:6; 1Co 11:6
5:19 [b] ver 12,29
5:20 [c] ver 12
5:21 [d] Jos 6:26; 1Sa 14:24; Ne 10:29
5:22 [e] Ps 109:18 [f] ver 18 [g] Dt 27:15
5:23 [h] Jer 45:1
5:25 [i] Lev 8:27
5:27 [j] Isa 43:28; 65:15; Jer 26:6; 29:18; 42:18; 44:12,22; Zec 8:13
5:29 [k] ver 19
5:31 [l] Lev 5:1; 20:17
6:2 [m] Ge 28:20; Ac 21:23 [n] Jdg 13:5; 16:17; Am 2:11,12
6:3 [o] Lk 1:15 [p] Ru 2:14; Ps 69:21; Pr 10:26
6:5 [q] Ps 52:2; 57:4; 59:7; Isa 7:20; Eze 5:1 [r] 1Sa 1:11
6:6 [s] Lev 21:1-3; Nu 19:11-22
6:7 [t] Nu 9:6
6:9 [u] ver 18 [v] Lev 14:9

29" 'This, then, is the law of jealousy when a woman goes astray[k] and defiles herself while married to her husband, **30**or when feelings of jealousy come over a man because he suspects his wife. The priest is to have her stand before the LORD and is to apply this entire law to her. **31**The husband will be innocent of any wrongdoing, but the woman will bear the consequences[l] of her sin.' "

The Nazirite

6 The LORD said to Moses, **2**"Speak to the Israelites and say to them: 'If a man or woman wants to make a special vow[m], a vow of separation to the LORD as a Nazirite,[n] **3**he must abstain from wine[o] and other fermented drink and must not drink vinegar[p] made from wine or from other fermented drink. He must not drink grape juice or eat grapes or raisins. **4**As long as he is a Nazirite, he must not eat anything that comes from the grapevine, not even the seeds or skins.

5" 'During the entire period of his vow of separation no razor[q] may be used on his head.[r] He must be holy until the period of his separation to the LORD is over; he must let the hair of his head grow long. **6**Throughout the period of his separation to the LORD he must not go near a dead body.[s] **7**Even if his own father or mother or brother or sister dies, he must not make himself ceremonially unclean[t] on account of them, because the symbol of his separation to God is on his head. **8**Throughout the period of his separation he is consecrated to the LORD.

9" 'If someone dies suddenly in his presence, thus defiling the hair he has dedicated,[u] he must shave his head on the day of his cleansing[v]—the seventh day. **10**Then on

[i]21 *Or causes you to have a miscarrying womb and barrenness* [k]22 *Or body and cause you to be barren and have a miscarrying womb* [l]27 *Or suffering; she will have barrenness and a miscarrying womb*

the eighth day he must bring two
doves or two young pigeons[a] to the
priest at the entrance to the Tent of
Meeting. **11**The priest is to offer
one as a sin offering and the other
as a burnt offering[b] to make atonement[c] for him because he sinned
by being in the presence of the
dead body. That same day he is to
consecrate his head. **12**He must
dedicate himself to the LORD for the
period of his separation and must
bring a year-old male lamb as a
guilt offering. The previous days do
not count, because he became defiled during his separation.

13" 'Now this is the law for the
Nazirite when the period of his separation is over.[d] He is to be
brought to the entrance to the Tent
of Meeting. **14**There he is to
present his offerings to the LORD: a
year-old male lamb without defect
for a burnt offering, a year-old ewe
lamb without defect for a sin offering,[e] a ram without defect for a fellowship offering,[m] **15**together with
their grain offerings and drink offerings,[f] and a basket of bread
made without yeast—cakes made
of fine flour mixed with oil, and wafers spread with oil.[g]

16" 'The priest is to present them
before the LORD and make the sin
offering and the burnt offering.
17He is to present the basket of unleavened bread and is to sacrifice
the ram as a fellowship offering to
the LORD, together with its grain offering and drink offering.

18" 'Then at the entrance to the
Tent of Meeting, the Nazirite must
shave off the hair that he dedicated.[h] He is to take the hair and put
it in the fire that is under the sacrifice of the fellowship offering.

19" 'After the Nazirite has
shaved off the hair of his dedication, the priest is to place in his
hands a boiled shoulder of the ram,
and a cake and a wafer from the
basket, both made without yeast.
20The priest shall then wave them
before the LORD as a wave offering;
they are holy and belong to the
priest, together with the breast that
was waved and the thigh that was
presented. After that, the Nazirite
may drink wine.[i]

21" 'This is the law of the Nazirite who vows his offering to the
LORD in accordance with his separation, in addition to whatever else
he can afford. He must fulfill the
vow he has made, according to the
law of the Nazirite.' "

The Priestly Blessing

22The LORD said to Moses,
23"Tell Aaron and his sons, 'This is
how you are to bless[j] the Israelites. Say to them:

24" ' "The LORD bless you[k]
and keep you;[l]
25the LORD make his face shine
upon you[m]
and be gracious to you;[n]
26the LORD turn his face[o] toward
you
and give you peace.[p]" '

27"So they will put my name[q] on
the Israelites, and I will bless
them."

Offerings at the Dedication of the Tabernacle

7 When Moses finished setting
up the tabernacle,[r] he anointed it and consecrated it and all its
furnishings.[s] He also anointed
and consecrated the altar and all
its utensils.[t] **2**Then the leaders of
Israel,[u] the heads of families who
were the tribal leaders in charge of
those who were counted, made offerings. **3**They brought as their gifts
before the LORD six covered carts
and twelve oxen—an ox from each
leader and a cart from every two.
These they presented before the
tabernacle.

4The LORD said to Moses, **5**"Accept these from them, that they
may be used in the work at the Tent
of Meeting. Give them to the Levites as each man's work requires."

6So Moses took the carts and
oxen and gave them to the Levites.
7He gave two carts and four oxen to
the Gershonites,[v] as their work re-

6:10 [a] Lev 5:7; 14:22
6:11 [b] Ge 8:20 [c] Ex 29:36
6:13 [d] Ac 21:26
6:14 [e] Lev 14:10; Nu 15:27
6:15 [f] Nu 15:1-7 [g] Ex 29:2; Lev 2:4
6:18 [h] ver 9; Ac 21:24
6:20 [i] Ecc 9:7
6:23 [j] Dt 21:5; 1Ch 23:13
6:24 [k] Dt 28:3-6; Ps 28:9 [l] 1Sa 2:9; Ps 17:8
6:25 [m] Job 29:24; Ps 31:16; 80:3; 119:135 [n] Ge 43:29; Ps 25:16; 86:16
6:26 [o] Ps 4:6; 44:3 [p] Ps 29:11; 37:11,37; Jn 14:27
6:27 [q] Dt 28:10; 2Sa 7:23; 2Ch 7:14; Ne 9:10; Jer 25:29
7:1 [r] Ex 40:17 [s] Ex 40:9 [t] ver 84,88; Ex 40:10
7:2 [u] Nu 1:5-16
7:7 [v] Nu 4:24-26, 28

[m]*14* Traditionally *peace offering*; also in verses 17 and 18

quired, **8**and he gave four carts and
eight oxen to the Merarites,[a] as
their work required. They were all
under the direction of Ithamar son
of Aaron, the priest. **9**But Moses
did not give any to the Kohathites,
because they were to carry on their
shoulders[b] the holy things, for
which they were responsible.
10When the altar was anointed,[c]
the leaders brought their offerings
for its dedication[d] and presented
them before the altar. **11**For the
LORD had said to Moses, "Each day
one leader is to bring his offering
for the dedication of the altar."

12The one who brought his offering
on the first day was Nahshon son of
Amminadab of the tribe of Judah.
13His offering was one silver
plate weighing a hundred and
thirty shekels,[n] and one silver
sprinkling bowl weighing seventy shekels,[o] both according
to the sanctuary shekel,[e]
each filled with fine flour
mixed with oil as a grain offering;[f] **14**one gold dish weighing ten shekels,[p] filled with
incense;[g] **15**one young bull,[h]
one ram and one male lamb a
year old, for a burnt offering;[i]
16one male goat for a sin offering;[j] **17**and two oxen, five
rams, five male goats and five
male lambs a year old, to be
sacrificed as a fellowship offering.[q][k] This was the offering of Nahshon son of Amminadab.[l]

18On the second day Nethanel son
of Zuar,[m] the leader of Issachar,
brought his offering.
19The offering he brought was
one silver plate weighing a
hundred and thirty shekels,
and one silver sprinkling bowl
weighing seventy shekels,
both according to the sanctuary shekel, each filled with
fine flour mixed with oil as a
grain offering; **20**one gold
dish[n] weighing ten shekels,
filled with incense; **21**one
young bull, one ram and one
male lamb a year old, for a
burnt offering; **22**one male
goat for a sin offering; **23**and
two oxen, five rams, five male
goats and five male lambs a
year old, to be sacrificed as a
fellowship offering. This was
the offering of Nethanel son of
Zuar.

24On the third day, Eliab son of Helon,[o] the leader of the people of
Zebulun, brought his offering.
25His offering was one silver
plate weighing a hundred and
thirty shekels, and one silver
sprinkling bowl weighing seventy shekels, both according
to the sanctuary shekel, each
filled with fine flour mixed
with oil as a grain offering;
26one gold dish weighing ten
shekels, filled with incense;
27one young bull, one ram and
one male lamb a year old, for a
burnt offering; **28**one male
goat for a sin offering; **29**and
two oxen, five rams, five male
goats and five male lambs a
year old, to be sacrificed as a
fellowship offering. This was
the offering of Eliab son of Helon.

30On the fourth day Elizur son of
Shedeur,[p] the leader of the people
of Reuben, brought his offering.
31His offering was one silver
plate weighing a hundred and
thirty shekels, and one silver
sprinkling bowl weighing seventy shekels, both according
to the sanctuary shekel, each
filled with fine flour mixed
with oil as a grain offering;
32one gold dish weighing ten
shekels, filled with incense;
33one young bull, one ram and
one male lamb a year old, for a
burnt offering; **34**one male
goat for a sin offering; **35**and
two oxen, five rams, five male

7:8 [a]Nu 4:31-33
7:9 [b]Nu 4:15
7:10 [c]ver 1 [d]2Ch 7:9
7:13 [e]Ex 30:13; Nu 3:47 [f]Lev 2:1
7:14 [g]Ex 30:34
7:15 [h]Ex 24:5; 29:3; Nu 28:11 [i]Lev 1:3
7:16 [j]Lev 4:3,23
7:17 [k]Lev 3:1 [l]Nu 1:7
7:18 [m]Nu 1:8
7:20 [n]ver 14
7:24 [o]Nu 1:9
7:30 [p]Nu 1:5

[n]*13* That is, about 3 1/4 pounds (about 1.5 kilograms); also elsewhere in this chapter
[o]*13* That is, about 1 3/4 pounds (about 0.8 kilogram); also elsewhere in this chapter
[p]*14* That is, about 4 ounces (about 110 grams); also elsewhere in this chapter
[q]*17* Traditionally *peace offering*; also elsewhere in this chapter

goats and five male lambs a
year old, to be sacrificed as a
fellowship offering. This was
the offering of Elizur son of
Shedeur.

36 On the fifth day Shelumiel son of
Zurishaddai,[a] the leader of the
people of Simeon, brought his offering.

37 His offering was one silver
plate weighing a hundred and
thirty shekels, and one silver
sprinkling bowl weighing seventy shekels, both according
to the sanctuary shekel, each
filled with fine flour mixed
with oil as a grain offering;
38 one gold dish weighing ten
shekels, filled with incense;
39 one young bull, one ram and
one male lamb a year old, for a
burnt offering; 40 one male
goat for a sin offering; 41 and
two oxen, five rams, five male
goats and five male lambs a
year old, to be sacrificed as a
fellowship offering. This was
the offering of Shelumiel son
of Zurishaddai.

42 On the sixth day Eliasaph son of
Deuel,[b] the leader of the people of
Gad, brought his offering.

43 His offering was one silver
plate weighing a hundred and
thirty shekels, and one silver
sprinkling bowl weighing seventy shekels, both according
to the sanctuary shekel, each
filled with fine flour mixed
with oil as a grain offering;
44 one gold dish weighing ten
shekels, filled with incense;
45 one young bull, one ram and
one male lamb a year old, for a
burnt offering; 46 one male
goat for a sin offering; 47 and
two oxen, five rams, five male
goats and five male lambs a
year old, to be sacrificed as a
fellowship offering. This was
the offering of Eliasaph son of
Deuel.

48 On the seventh day Elishama son
of Ammihud,[c] the leader of the
people of Ephraim, brought his offering.

49 His offering was one silver
plate weighing a hundred and
thirty shekels, and one silver
sprinkling bowl weighing seventy shekels, both according
to the sanctuary shekel, each
filled with fine flour mixed
with oil as a grain offering;
50 one gold dish weighing ten
shekels, filled with incense;
51 one young bull, one ram and
one male lamb a year old, for a
burnt offering; 52 one male
goat for a sin offering; 53 and
two oxen, five rams, five male
goats and five male lambs a
year old, to be sacrificed as a
fellowship offering. This was
the offering of Elishama son of
Ammihud.[d]

54 On the eighth day Gamaliel son
of Pedahzur,[e] the leader of the
people of Manasseh, brought his
offering.

55 His offering was one silver
plate weighing a hundred and
thirty shekels, and one silver
sprinkling bowl weighing seventy shekels, both according
to the sanctuary shekel, each
filled with fine flour mixed
with oil as a grain offering;
56 one gold dish weighing ten
shekels, filled with incense;
57 one young bull, one ram and
one male lamb a year old, for a
burnt offering; 58 one male
goat for a sin offering; 59 and
two oxen, five rams, five male
goats and five male lambs a
year old, to be sacrificed as a
fellowship offering. This was
the offering of Gamaliel son of
Pedahzur.

60 On the ninth day Abidan son of
Gideoni,[f] the leader of the people
of Benjamin, brought his offering.

61 His offering was one silver
plate weighing a hundred and
thirty shekels, and one silver
sprinkling bowl weighing seventy shekels, both according
to the sanctuary shekel, each
filled with fine flour mixed

7:36 [a] Nu 1:6
7:42 [b] Nu 1:14
7:48 [c] Nu 1:10
7:53 [d] Nu 1:10
7:54 [e] Nu 1:10; 2:20
7:60 [f] Nu 1:11

with oil as a grain offering;
62 one gold dish weighing ten
shekels, filled with incense;
63 one young bull, one ram and
one male lamb a year old, for a
burnt offering; **64** one male
goat for a sin offering; **65** and
two oxen, five rams, five male
goats and five male lambs a
year old, to be sacrificed as a
fellowship offering. This was
the offering of Abidan son of
Gideoni.

66 On the tenth day Ahiezer son of
Ammishaddai,[a] the leader of the
people of Dan, brought his offering.
67 His offering was one silver
plate weighing a hundred and
thirty shekels, and one silver
sprinkling bowl weighing seventy shekels, both according
to the sanctuary shekel, each
filled with fine flour mixed
with oil as a grain offering;
68 one gold dish weighing ten
shekels, filled with incense;
69 one young bull, one ram and
one male lamb a year old, for a
burnt offering; **70** one male
goat for a sin offering; **71** and
two oxen, five rams, five male
goats and five male lambs a
year old, to be sacrificed as a
fellowship offering. This was
the offering of Ahiezer son of
Ammishaddai.

72 On the eleventh day Pagiel son of
Ocran,[b] the leader of the people of
Asher, brought his offering.
73 His offering was one silver
plate weighing a hundred and
thirty shekels, and one silver
sprinkling bowl weighing seventy shekels, both according
to the sanctuary shekel, each
filled with fine flour mixed
with oil as a grain offering;
74 one gold dish weighing ten
shekels, filled with incense;
75 one young bull, one ram and
one male lamb a year old, for a
burnt offering; **76** one male
goat for a sin offering; **77** and
two oxen, five rams, five male
goats and five male lambs a
year old, to be sacrificed as a
fellowship offering. This was
the offering of Pagiel son of
Ocran.

78 On the twelfth day Ahira son of
Enan,[c] the leader of the people of
Naphtali, brought his offering.
79 His offering was one silver
plate weighing a hundred and
thirty shekels, and one silver
sprinkling bowl weighing seventy shekels, both according
to the sanctuary shekel, each
filled with fine flour mixed
with oil as a grain offering;
80 one gold dish weighing ten
shekels, filled with incense;
81 one young bull, one ram and
one male lamb a year old, for a
burnt offering; **82** one male
goat for a sin offering; **83** and
two oxen, five rams, five male
goats and five male lambs a
year old, to be sacrificed as a
fellowship offering. This was
the offering of Ahira son of
Enan.

84 These were the offerings of the
Israelite leaders for the dedication
of the altar when it was anointed:[d]
twelve silver plates, twelve silver
sprinkling bowls[e] and twelve gold
dishes.[f] **85** Each silver plate
weighed a hundred and thirty shekels, and each sprinkling bowl seventy shekels. Altogether, the silver
dishes weighed two thousand four
hundred shekels,[r] according to
the sanctuary shekel. **86** The twelve
gold dishes filled with incense
weighed ten shekels each, according to the sanctuary shekel. Altogether, the gold dishes weighed a
hundred and twenty shekels.[s]
87 The total number of animals for
the burnt offering came to twelve
young bulls, twelve rams and
twelve male lambs a year old, together with their grain offering.
Twelve male goats were used for
the sin offering. **88** The total number of animals for the sacrifice of
the fellowship offering came to

7:66 [a] Nu 1:12; 2:25
7:72 [b] Nu 1:13
7:78 [c] Nu 1:15; 2:29
7:84 [d] ver 1,10 [e] Nu 4:14 [f] ver 14

[r] *85* That is, about 60 pounds (about 28 kilograms) [s] *86* That is, about 3 pounds (about 1.4 kilograms)

twenty-four oxen, sixty rams, sixty male goats and sixty male lambs a year old. These were the offerings for the dedication of the altar after it was anointed.[a]

89 When Moses entered the Tent of Meeting to speak with the LORD,[b] he heard the voice speaking to him from between the two cherubim above the atonement cover[c] on the ark of the Testimony. And he spoke with him.

Setting Up the Lamps

8 The LORD said to Moses, 2 "Speak to Aaron and say to him, 'When you set up the seven lamps, they are to light the area in front of the lampstand.[d] ' "

3 Aaron did so; he set up the lamps so that they faced forward on the lampstand, just as the LORD commanded Moses. 4 This is how the lampstand was made: It was made of hammered gold[e]—from its base to its blossoms. The lampstand was made exactly like the pattern[f] the LORD had shown Moses.

The Setting Apart of the Levites

5 The LORD said to Moses: 6 "Take the Levites from among the other Israelites and make them ceremonially clean.[g] 7 To purify them, do this: Sprinkle the water of cleansing[h] on them; then have them shave their whole bodies[i] and wash their clothes,[j] and so purify themselves. 8 Have them take a young bull with its grain offering of fine flour mixed with oil;[k] then you are to take a second young bull for a sin offering. 9 Bring the Levites to the front of the Tent of Meeting[l] and assemble the whole Israelite community.[m] 10 You are to bring the Levites before the LORD, and the Israelites are to lay their hands on them.[n] 11 Aaron is to present the Levites before the LORD as a wave offering[o] from the Israelites, so that they may be ready to do the work of the LORD.

12 "After the Levites lay their hands on the heads of the bulls,[p] use the one for a sin offering to the LORD and the other for a burnt offering, to make atonement[q] for the Levites. 13 Have the Levites stand in front of Aaron and his sons and then present them as a wave offering to the LORD. 14 In this way you are to set the Levites apart from the other Israelites, and the Levites will be mine.[r]

15 "After you have purified the Levites and presented them as a wave offering,[s] they are to come to do their work at the Tent of Meeting. 16 They are the Israelites who are to be given wholly to me. I have taken them as my own in place of the firstborn, the first male offspring[t] from every Israelite woman. 17 Every firstborn male in Israel, whether man or animal,[u] is mine. When I struck down all the firstborn in Egypt, I set them apart for myself.[v] 18 And I have taken the Levites in place of all the firstborn sons in Israel.[w] 19 Of all the Israelites, I have given the Levites as gifts to Aaron and his sons[x] to do the work at the Tent of Meeting on behalf of the Israelites[y] and to make atonement for them[z] so that no plague will strike the Israelites when they go near the sanctuary."

20 Moses, Aaron and the whole Israelite community did with the Levites just as the LORD commanded Moses. 21 The Levites purified themselves and washed their clothes.[a] Then Aaron presented them as a wave offering before the LORD and made atonement for them to purify them.[b] 22 After that, the Levites came to do their work at the Tent of Meeting under the supervision of Aaron and his sons. They did with the Levites just as the LORD commanded Moses.

23 The LORD said to Moses, 24 "This applies to the Levites: Men twenty-five years old or more[c] shall come to take part in the work at the Tent of Meeting,[d] 25 but at the age of fifty, they must retire from their regular service and work no longer. 26 They may assist their brothers in performing their duties

7:88 [a] ver 1,10
7:89 [b] Ex 25:21,22; 33:9,11 [c] Ps 80:1; 99:1
8:2 [d] Ex 25:37; Lev 24:2,4
8:4 [e] Ex 25:18,36; 25:18 [f] Ex 25:9
8:6 [g] Lev 22:2; Isa 1:16; 52:11
8:7 [h] Nu 19:9,17 [i] Lev 14:9; Dt 21:12 [j] Lev 14:8
8:8 [k] Lev 2:1; Nu 15:8-10
8:9 [l] Ex 40:12 [m] Lev 8:3
8:10 [n] Ac 6:6
8:11 [o] Lev 7:30
8:12 [p] Ex 29:10 [q] Ex 29:36
8:14 [r] Nu 3:12
8:15 [s] Ex 29:24
8:16 [t] Nu 3:12
8:17 [u] Ex 4:23 [v] Ex 13:2; Lk 2:23
8:18 [w] Nu 3:12
8:19 [x] Nu 3:9 [y] Nu 1:53 [z] Nu 16:46
8:21 [a] ver 7 [b] ver 12
8:24 [c] 1Ch 23:3 [d] Ex 38:21; Nu 4:3

at the Tent of Meeting, but they
themselves must not do the work.
This, then, is how you are to assign
the responsibilities of the Levites."

The Passover

9 The LORD spoke to Moses in
the Desert of Sinai in the first
month[a] of the second year after
they came out of Egypt.[b] He said,
2"Have the Israelites celebrate the
Passover at the appointed time.
3Celebrate it at the appointed
time, at twilight on the fourteenth
day of this month, in accordance
with all its rules and regulations.[c]"
4So Moses told the Israelites to
celebrate the Passover, 5and they
did so in the Desert of Sinai at twilight on the fourteenth day of the
first month.[d] The Israelites did everything just as the LORD commanded Moses.
6But some of them could not celebrate the Passover on that day because they were ceremonially unclean[e] on account of a dead body.
So they came to Moses and Aaron[f]
that same day 7and said to Moses,
"We have become unclean because
of a dead body, but why should we
be kept from presenting the LORD's
offering with the other Israelites at
the appointed time?"
8Moses answered them, "Wait
until I find out what the LORD commands concerning you."[g]
9Then the LORD said to Moses,
10"Tell the Israelites: 'When any of
you or your descendants are unclean because of a dead body or are
away on a journey, they may still
celebrate[h] the LORD's Passover.
11They are to celebrate it on the
fourteenth day of the second
month at twilight. They are to eat
the lamb, together with unleavened bread and bitter herbs.[i]
12They must not leave any of it till
morning[j] or break any of its
bones.[k] When they celebrate the
Passover, they must follow all the
regulations. 13But if a man who is
ceremonially clean and not on a
journey fails to celebrate the Passover, that person must be cut off
from his people[l] because he did
not present the LORD's offering at
the appointed time. That man will
bear the consequences of his sin.
14" 'An alien[m] living among you
who wants to celebrate the LORD's
Passover must do so in accordance
with its rules and regulations. You
must have the same regulations for
the alien and the native-born.' "

The Cloud Above the Tabernacle

15On the day the tabernacle, the
Tent of the Testimony, was set up,
the cloud[n] covered it. From evening till morning the cloud above
the tabernacle looked like fire.[o]
16That is how it continued to be;
the cloud covered it, and at night it
looked like fire. 17Whenever the
cloud lifted from above the Tent,
the Israelites set out; wherever the
cloud settled, the Israelites encamped.[p] 18At the LORD's command the Israelites set out, and at
his command they encamped. As
long as the cloud stayed over the
tabernacle, they remained in
camp. 19When the cloud remained
over the tabernacle a long time, the
Israelites obeyed the LORD's order
and did not set out. 20Sometimes
the cloud was over the tabernacle
only a few days; at the LORD's command they would encamp, and
then at his command they would
set out. 21Sometimes the cloud
stayed only from evening till morning, and when it lifted in the morning, they set out. Whether by day or
by night, whenever the cloud lifted,
they set out. 22Whether the cloud
stayed over the tabernacle for two
days or a month or a year, the Israelites would remain in camp and
not set out; but when it lifted, they
would set out. 23At the LORD's command they encamped, and at the
LORD's command they set out. They
obeyed the LORD's order, in accordance with his command through
Moses.

The Silver Trumpets

10 The LORD said to Moses:
2"Make two trumpets[q] of

9:1 [a]Ex 40:2 [b]Nu 1:1
9:3 [c]Ex 12:2-11, 43-49; Lev 23:5-8; Dt 16:1-8
9:5 [d]Ex 12:1-13; Jos 5:10
9:6 [e]Lev 5:3 [f]Ex 18:15; Nu 27:2
9:8 [g]Ex 18:15; Nu 27:5,21; Ps 85:8
9:10 [h]2Ch 30:2
9:11 [i]Ex 12:8
9:12 [j]Ex 12:10,43 [k]Ex 12:46; Jn 19:36*
9:13 [l]Ge 17:14; Ex 12:15
9:14 [m]Ex 12:48,49
9:15 [n]Ex 40:34 [o]Ex 13:21
9:17 [p]Ex 40:36-38; Nu 10:11,12; 1Co 10:1
10:2 [q]Ne 12:35; Ps 47:5

hammered silver, and use them for calling the community[a] together and for having the camps set out. **3**When both are sounded, the whole community is to assemble before you at the entrance to the Tent of Meeting. **4**If only one is sounded, the leaders[b]—the heads of the clans of Israel—are to assemble before you. **5**When a trumpet blast is sounded, the tribes camping on the east are to set out.[c] **6**At the sounding of a second blast, the camps on the south are to set out.[d] The blast will be the signal for setting out. **7**To gather the assembly, blow the trumpets,[e] but not with the same signal.[f]

8"The sons of Aaron, the priests, are to blow the trumpets. This is to be a lasting ordinance for you and the generations to come.[g] **9**When you go into battle in your own land against an enemy who is oppressing you,[h] sound a blast on the trumpets. Then you will be remembered[i] by the LORD your God and rescued from your enemies.[j] **10**Also at your times of rejoicing—your appointed feasts and New Moon festivals[k]—you are to sound the trumpets[l] over your burnt offerings and fellowship offerings,[†] and they will be a memorial for you before your God. I am the LORD your God."

The Israelites Leave Sinai

11On the twentieth day of the second month of the second year,[m] the cloud lifted[n] from above the tabernacle of the Testimony. **12**Then the Israelites set out from the Desert of Sinai and traveled from place to place until the cloud came to rest in the Desert of Paran. **13**They set out, this first time, at the LORD's command through Moses.[o]

14The divisions of the camp of Judah went first, under their standard.[p] Nahshon son of Amminadab[q] was in command. **15**Nethanel son of Zuar was over the division of the tribe of Issachar, **16**and Eliab son of Helon was over the division of the tribe of Zebulun. **17**Then the tabernacle was taken down, and the Gershonites and Merarites, who carried it, set out.[r]

18The divisions of the camp of Reuben went next, under their standard.[s] Elizur son of Shedeur was in command. **19**Shelumiel son of Zurishaddai was over the division of the tribe of Simeon, **20**and Eliasaph son of Deuel was over the division of the tribe of Gad. **21**Then the Kohathites set out, carrying the holy things.[t] The tabernacle was to be set up before they arrived.[u]

22The divisions of the camp of Ephraim[v] went next, under their standard. Elishama son of Ammihud was in command. **23**Gamaliel son of Pedahzur was over the division of the tribe of Manasseh, **24**and Abidan son of Gideoni was over the division of the tribe of Benjamin.

25Finally, as the rear guard[w] for all the units, the divisions of the camp of Dan set out, under their standard. Ahiezer son of Ammishaddai was in command. **26**Pagiel son of Ocran was over the division of the tribe of Asher, **27**and Ahira son of Enan was over the division of the tribe of Naphtali. **28**This was the order of march for the Israelite divisions as they set out.

29Now Moses said to Hobab[x] son of Reuel[y] the Midianite, Moses' father-in-law,[z] "We are setting out for the place about which the LORD said, 'I will give it to you.'[a] Come with us and we will treat you well, for the LORD has promised good things to Israel."

30He answered, "No, I will not go;[b] I am going back to my own land and my own people."

31But Moses said, "Please do not leave us. You know where we should camp in the desert, and you can be our eyes.[c] **32**If you come with us, we will share with you[d] whatever good things the LORD gives us.[e]"

33So they set out[f] from the mountain of the LORD and traveled for three days. The ark of the cov-

†*10* Traditionally *peace offerings*

10:2 [a]Jer 4:5,19; 6:1; Hos 5:8; Joel 2:1,15; Am 3:6
10:4 [b]Ex 18:21; Nu 1:16; 7:2
10:5 [c]ver 14
10:6 [d]ver 18
10:7 [e]Eze 33:3; Joel 2:1 [f]1Co 14:8
10:8 [g]Nu 31:6
10:9 [h]Jdg 2:18; 6:9; 1Sa 10:18; Ps 106:42 [i]Ge 8:1 [j]Ps 106:4
10:10 [k]Ps 81:3 [l]Lev 23:24
10:11 [m]Ex 40:17 [n]Nu 9:17
10:13 [o]Dt 1:6
10:14 [p]Nu 2:3-9 [q]Nu 1:7
10:17 [r]Nu 4:21-32
10:18 [s]Nu 2:10-16
10:21 [t]Nu 4:20 [u]ver 17
10:22 [v]Nu 2:24
10:25 [w]Nu 2:31; Jos 6:9
10:29 [x]Jdg 4:11 [y]Ex 2:18 [z]Ex 3:1 [a]Ge 12:7
10:30 [b]Mt 21:29
10:31 [c]Job 29:15
10:32 [d]Dt 10:18 [e]Ps 22:27-31; 67:5-7
10:33 [f]ver 12; Dt 1:33

enant of the LORD[a] went before them during those three days to find them a place to rest. 34The cloud of the LORD was over them by day when they set out from the camp.[b]

35Whenever the ark set out, Moses said,

"Rise up, O LORD!
  May your enemies be
    scattered;[c]
  may your foes flee before
    you.[d]"

36Whenever it came to rest, he said,

"Return,[e] O LORD,
  to the countless thousands of
    Israel.[f]"

Fire From the LORD

11 Now the people complained about their hardships in the hearing of the LORD, and when he heard them his anger was aroused. Then fire from the LORD burned among them[g] and consumed some of the outskirts of the camp. 2When the people cried out to Moses, he prayed to the LORD[h] and the fire died down. 3So that place was called Taberah,[u][i] because fire from the LORD had burned among them.

Quail From the LORD

4The rabble with them began to crave other food,[j] and again the Israelites started wailing[k] and said, "If only we had meat to eat! 5We remember the fish we ate in Egypt at no cost—also the cucumbers, melons, leeks, onions and garlic.[l] 6But now we have lost our appetite; we never see anything but this manna!"

7The manna was like coriander seed[m] and looked like resin.[n] 8The people went around gathering it, and then ground it in a handmill or crushed it in a mortar. They cooked it in a pot or made it into cakes. And it tasted like something made with olive oil. 9When the dew[o] settled on the camp at night, the manna also came down.

10Moses heard the people of every family wailing, each at the entrance to his tent. The LORD became exceedingly angry, and Moses was troubled. 11He asked the LORD, "Why have you brought this trouble on your servant? What have I done to displease you that you put the burden of all these people on me?[p] 12Did I conceive all these people? Did I give them birth? Why do you tell me to carry them in my arms, as a nurse carries an infant,[q] to the land you promised on oath to their forefathers?[r] 13Where can I get meat for all these people?[s] They keep wailing to me, 'Give us meat to eat!' 14I cannot carry all these people by myself; the burden is too heavy for me.[t] 15If this is how you are going to treat me, put me to death[u] right now[v]—if I have found favor in your eyes—and do not let me face my own ruin."

16The LORD said to Moses: "Bring me seventy of Israel's elders who are known to you as leaders and officials among the people. Have them come to the Tent of Meeting, that they may stand there with you. 17I will come down and speak with you there, and I will take of the Spirit that is on you and put the Spirit on them.[w] They will help you carry the burden of the people so that you will not have to carry it alone.[x]

18"Tell the people: 'Consecrate yourselves[y] in preparation for tomorrow, when you will eat meat. The LORD heard you when you wailed,[z] "If only we had meat to eat! We were better off in Egypt!"[a] Now the LORD will give you meat, and you will eat it. 19You will not eat it for just one day, or two days, or five, ten or twenty days, 20but for a whole month—until it comes out of your nostrils and you loathe it[b]—because you have rejected the LORD,[c] who is among you, and have wailed before him, saying, "Why did we ever leave Egypt?"' "

21But Moses said, "Here I am among six hundred thousand

10:33 [a]Jos 3:3
10:34 [b]Nu 9:15-23
10:35 [c]Ps 68:1 [d]Dt 7:10; 32:41; Ps 68:2; Isa 17:12-14
10:36 [e]Isa 63:17 [f]Dt 1:10
11:1 [g]Lev 10:2
11:2 [h]Nu 21:7
11:3 [i]Dt 9:22
11:4 [j]Ex 12:38 [k]Ps 78:18; 1Co 10:6
11:5 [l]Ex 16:3
11:7 [m]Ex 16:31 [n]Ge 2:12
11:9 [o]Ex 16:13
11:11 [p]Ex 5:22
11:12 [q]Isa 40:11; 49:23 [r]Ex 13:5
11:13 [s]Jn 6:5-9
11:14 [t]Ex 18:18
11:15 [u]Ex 32:32 [v]1Ki 19:4; Jnh 4:3
11:17 [w]ver 25,29; 1Sa 10:6; 2Ki 2:9,15; Joel 2:28 [x]Ex 18:18
11:18 [y]Ex 19:10 [z]Ex 16:7 [a]ver 5; Ac 7:39
11:20 [b]Ps 78:29; 106:14,15 [c]Jos 24:27; 1Sa 10:19

[u]3 *Taberah* means *burning*.

men[a] on foot, and you say, 'I will
give them meat to eat for a whole
month!' **22**Would they have enough
if flocks and herds were slaughtered for them? Would they have
enough if all the fish in the sea
were caught for them?"[b]
23The LORD answered Moses, "Is
the LORD's arm too short?[c] You will
now see whether or not what I say
will come true for you.[d]"
24So Moses went out and told
the people what the LORD had said.
He brought together seventy of
their elders and had them stand
around the Tent. **25**Then the LORD
came down in the cloud[e] and
spoke with him,[f] and he took of
the Spirit[g] that was on him and
put the Spirit on the seventy elders.[h] When the Spirit rested on
them, they prophesied,[i] but they
did not do so again.[v]
26However, two men, whose
names were Eldad and Medad, had
remained in the camp. They were
listed among the elders, but did
not go out to the Tent. Yet the Spirit also rested on them, and they
prophesied in the camp. **27**A young
man ran and told Moses, "Eldad
and Medad are prophesying in the
camp."
28Joshua son of Nun, who had
been Moses' aide[j] since youth,
spoke up and said, "Moses, my
lord, stop them!"[k]
29But Moses replied, "Are you
jealous for my sake? I wish that all
the LORD's people were prophets[l]
and that the LORD would put his
Spirit on them!" **30**Then Moses and
the elders of Israel returned to the
camp.
31Now a wind went out from the
LORD and drove quail[m] in from the
sea. It brought them[w] down all
around the camp to about three
feet[x] above the ground, as far as a
day's walk in any direction. **32**All
that day and night and all the next
day the people went out and gathered quail. No one gathered less
than ten homers.[y] Then they
spread them out all around the
camp. **33**But while the meat was
still between their teeth[n] and before it could be consumed, the anger of the LORD burned against the
people, and he struck them with a
severe plague.[o] **34**Therefore the
place was named Kibroth Hattaavah,[z][p] because there they buried
the people who had craved other
food.
35From Kibroth Hattaavah the
people traveled to Hazeroth[q] and
stayed there.

Miriam and Aaron Oppose Moses

12 Miriam and Aaron began to
talk against Moses because
of his Cushite wife,[r] for he had
married a Cushite. **2**"Has the LORD
spoken only through Moses?" they
asked. "Hasn't he also spoken
through us?"[s] And the LORD heard
this.[t]
3(Now Moses was a very humble
man,[u] more humble than anyone
else on the face of the earth.)
4At once the LORD said to Moses,
Aaron and Miriam, "Come out to
the Tent of Meeting, all three of
you." So the three of them came
out. **5**Then the LORD came down in
a pillar of cloud;[v] he stood at the
entrance to the Tent and summoned Aaron and Miriam. When
both of them stepped forward, **6**he
said, "Listen to my words:

"When a prophet of the LORD is
among you,
I reveal myself to him in
visions,[w]
I speak to him in dreams.[x]
7But this is not true of my
servant Moses;[y]
he is faithful in all my
house.[z]
8With him I speak face to face,
clearly and not in riddles;[a]
he sees the form of the
LORD.[b]
Why then were you not afraid
to speak against my servant
Moses?"

11:21 [a]Ex 12:37
11:22 [b]Mt 15:33
11:23 [c]Isa 50:2; 59:1 [d]Nu 23:19; Eze 12:25; 24:14
11:25 [e]Nu 12:5 [f]ver 17 [g]1Sa 10:6 [h]Ac 2:17 [i]1Sa 10:10
11:28 [j]Ex 33:11; Jos 1:1 [k]Mk 9:38-40
11:29 [l]1Co 14:5
11:31 [m]Ex 16:13; Ps 78:26-28
11:33 [n]Ps 78:30 [o]Ps 106:15
11:34 [p]Dt 9:22
11:35 [q]Nu 33:17
12:1 [r]Ex 2:21
12:2 [s]Nu 16:3 [t]Nu 11:1
12:3 [u]Mt 11:29
12:5 [v]Nu 11:25
12:6 [w]Ge 15:1; 46:2 [x]Ge 31:10; 1Ki 3:5; Heb 1:1
12:7 [y]Jos 1:1-2; Ps 105:26 [z]Heb 3:2,5
12:8 [a]Dt 34:10 [b]Ex 20:4; Ps 17:15

[v]25 Or *prophesied and continued to do so*
[w]31 Or *They flew*
[x]31 Hebrew *two cubits* (about 1 meter)
[y]32 That is, probably about 60 bushels (about 2.2 kiloliters)
[z]34 *Kibroth Hattaavah* means *graves of craving.*

9 The anger of the LORD burned
against them, and he left them.[a]
10 When the cloud lifted from
above the Tent, there stood Miriam—leprous,[a] like snow.[b] Aaron
turned toward her and saw that she
had leprosy;[c] 11 and he said to Moses, "Please, my lord, do not hold
against us the sin we have so foolishly committed.[d] 12 Do not let her
be like a stillborn infant coming
from its mother's womb with its
flesh half eaten away."
13 So Moses cried out to the LORD,
"O God, please heal her![e]"
14 The LORD replied to Moses, "If
her father had spit in her face,[f]
would she not have been in disgrace for seven days? Confine her
outside the camp[g] for seven days;
after that she can be brought
back." 15 So Miriam was confined
outside the camp for seven days,
and the people did not move on till
she was brought back.
16 After that, the people left Hazeroth[h] and encamped in the
Desert of Paran.

Exploring Canaan

13 The LORD said to Moses,
2 "Send some men to ex-
plore[i] the land of Canaan, which I
am giving to the Israelites. From
each ancestral tribe send one of its
leaders."
3 So at the LORD's command Moses sent them out from the Desert
of Paran. All of them were leaders
of the Israelites. 4 These are their
names:

from the tribe of Reuben,
Shammua son of Zaccur;
5 from the tribe of Simeon, Shaphat son of Hori;
6 from the tribe of Judah, Caleb
son of Jephunneh;[j]
7 from the tribe of Issachar, Igal
son of Joseph;
8 from the tribe of Ephraim, Hoshea son of Nun;
9 from the tribe of Benjamin,
Palti son of Raphu;
10 from the tribe of Zebulun,
Gaddiel son of Sodi;
11 from the tribe of Manasseh (a
tribe of Joseph), Gaddi son
of Susi;
12 from the tribe of Dan, Ammiel
son of Gemalli;
13 from the tribe of Asher, Sethur
son of Michael;
14 from the tribe of Naphtali,
Nahbi son of Vophsi;
15 from the tribe of Gad, Geuel
son of Maki.

16 These are the names of the men
Moses sent to explore the land.
(Moses gave Hoshea son of Nun[k]
the name Joshua.)[l]
17 When Moses sent them to explore Canaan, he said, "Go up
through the Negev[m] and on into
the hill country.[n] 18 See what the
land is like and whether the people
who live there are strong or weak,
few or many. 19 What kind of land
do they live in? Is it good or bad?
What kind of towns do they live in?
Are they unwalled or fortified?
20 How is the soil? Is it fertile or
poor? Are there trees on it or not?
Do your best to bring back some of
the fruit of the land.[o]" (It was the
season for the first ripe grapes.)
21 So they went up and explored
the land from the Desert of Zin[p] as
far as Rehob,[q] toward Lebo[b] Hamath.[r] 22 They went up through
the Negev and came to Hebron,
where Ahiman, Sheshai and Talmai,[s] the descendants of Anak,[t]
lived. (Hebron had been built sev-
en years before Zoan in Egypt.)[u]
23 When they reached the Valley of
Eshcol,[c] they cut off a branch
bearing a single cluster of grapes.
Two of them carried it on a pole
between them, along with some
pomegranates and figs. 24 That
place was called the Valley of Eshcol because of the cluster of grapes
the Israelites cut off there. 25 At the
end of forty days they returned
from exploring the land.

Report on the Exploration

26 They came back to Moses and

12:9 [a] Ge 17:22
12:10 [b] Ex 4:6; Dt 24:9 [c] 2Ki 5:1,27
12:11 [d] 2Sa 19:19; 24:10
12:13 [e] Isa 30:26; Jer 17:14
12:14 [f] Dt 25:9; Job 17:6; 30:9-10; Isa 50:6 [g] Lev 13:46; Nu 5:2-3
12:16 [h] Nu 11:35
13:2 [i] Dt 1:22
13:6 [j] ver 30; Nu 14:6,24; 34:19; Jdg 1:12-15
13:16 [k] ver 8 [l] Dt 32:44
13:17 [m] Ge 12:9 [n] Jdg 1:9
13:20 [o] Dt 1:25
13:21 [p] Nu 20:1; 27:14; 33:36; Jos 15:1 [q] Jos 19:28 [r] Jos 13:5
13:22 [s] Jos 15:14 [t] Jos 15:13 [u] Ps 78:12,43; Isa 19:11,13

[a] *10* The Hebrew word was used for various diseases affecting the skin—not necessarily leprosy. [b] *21* Or *toward the entrance to* [c] *23* *Eshcol* means *cluster*, also in verse 24.

Aaron and the whole Israelite community at Kadesh in the Desert of Paran. There they reported to them[a] and to the whole assembly and showed them the fruit of the land. 27They gave Moses this account: "We went into the land to which you sent us, and it does flow with milk and honey![b] Here is its fruit.[c] 28But the people who live there are powerful, and the cities are fortified and very large.[d] We even saw descendants of Anak there. 29The Amalekites live in the Negev; the Hittites, Jebusites and Amorites live in the hill country; and the Canaanites live near the sea and along the Jordan."

30Then Caleb silenced the people before Moses and said, "We should go up and take possession of the land, for we can certainly do it."

31But the men who had gone up with him said, "We can't attack those people; they are stronger than we are."[e] 32And they spread among the Israelites a bad report[f] about the land they had explored. They said, "The land we explored devours[g] those living in it. All the people we saw there are of great size.[h] 33We saw the Nephilim[i] there (the descendants of Anak[j] come from the Nephilim). We seemed like grasshoppers in our own eyes, and we looked the same to them."

The People Rebel

14 That night all the people of the community raised their voices and wept aloud. 2All the Israelites grumbled against Moses and Aaron, and the whole assembly said to them, "If only we had died in Egypt! Or in this desert![k] 3Why is the LORD bringing us to this land only to let us fall by the sword? Our wives and children will be taken as plunder. Wouldn't it be better for us to go back to Egypt?" 4And they said to each other, "We should choose a leader and go back to Egypt.[l]"

5Then Moses and Aaron fell facedown[m] in front of the whole Israelite assembly gathered there. 6Joshua son of Nun and Caleb son of Jephunneh, who were among those who had explored the land, tore their clothes 7and said to the entire Israelite assembly, "The land we passed through and explored is exceedingly good.[n] 8If the LORD is pleased with us,[o] he will lead us into that land, a land flowing with milk and honey,[p] and will give it to us. 9Only do not rebel[q] against the LORD. And do not be afraid of the people of the land,[r] because we will swallow them up. Their protection is gone, but the LORD is with us. Do not be afraid of them."

10But the whole assembly talked about stoning[s] them. Then the glory of the LORD[t] appeared at the Tent of Meeting to all the Israelites. 11The LORD said to Moses, "How long will these people treat me with contempt? How long will they refuse to believe in me,[u] in spite of all the miraculous signs I have performed among them? 12I will strike them down with a plague and destroy them, but I will make you into a nation[v] greater and stronger than they."

13Moses said to the LORD, "Then the Egyptians will hear about it! By your power you brought these people up from among them.[w] 14And they will tell the inhabitants of this land about it. They have already heard[x] that you, O LORD, are with these people and that you, O LORD, have been seen face to face, that your cloud stays over them, and that you go before them in a pillar of cloud by day and a pillar of fire by night.[y] 15If you put these people to death all at one time, the nations who have heard this report about you will say, 16'The LORD was not able to bring these people into the land he promised them on oath; so he slaughtered them in the desert.'[z]

17"Now may the Lord's strength be displayed, just as you have declared: 18'The LORD is slow to anger, abounding in love and forgiving sin and rebellion.[a] Yet he does

13:26 [a] Nu 32:8
13:27 [b] Ex 3:8 [c] Dt 1:25
13:28 [d] Dt 1:28; 9:1, 2
13:31 [e] Dt 1:28; 9:1; Jos 14:8
13:32 [f] Nu 14:36,37 [g] Eze 36:13,14 [h] Am 2:9
13:33 [i] Ge 6:4 [j] Dt 1:28
14:2 [k] Nu 11:1
14:4 [l] Ne 9:17
14:5 [m] Nu 16:4,22, 45
14:7 [n] Nu 13:27; Dt 1:25
14:8 [o] Dt 10:15 [p] Nu 13:27
14:9 [q] Dt 1:26; 9:7, 23,24 [r] Dt 1:21; 7:18; 20:1
14:10 [s] Ex 17:4 [t] Lev 9:23
14:11 [u] Ps 78:22; 106:24
14:12 [v] Ex 32:10
14:13 [w] Ex 32:11-14; Ps 106:23
14:14 [x] Ex 15:14 [y] Ex 13:21
14:16 [z] Jos 7:7
14:18 [a] Ex 34:6; Ps 145:8; Jnh 4:2

not leave the guilty unpunished; he
punishes the children for the sin of
the fathers to the third and fourth
generation.'[a] 19In accordance
with your great love, forgive[b] the
sin of these people,[c] just as you
have pardoned them from the time
they left Egypt until now."[d]

20The LORD replied, "I have forgiven them,[e] as you asked. 21Nev-
ertheless, as surely as I live[f] and as
surely as the glory of the LORD fills
the whole earth,[g] 22not one of the
men who saw my glory and the miraculous signs I performed in Egypt
and in the desert but who disobeyed me and tested me ten
times[h]— 23not one of them will
ever see the land I promised on
oath[i] to their forefathers. No one
who has treated me with contempt
will ever see it.[j] 24But because my
servant Caleb has a different spirit
and follows me wholeheartedly,[k] I
will bring him into the land he
went to, and his descendants will
inherit it.[l] 25Since the Amalekites
and Canaanites are living in the
valleys, turn[m] back tomorrow and
set out toward the desert along the
route to the Red Sea.[d]"

26The LORD said to Moses and
Aaron: 27"How long will this wicked community grumble against
me? I have heard the complaints of
these grumbling Israelites.[n] 28So
tell them, 'As surely as I live,[o] declares the LORD, I will do to you the
very things I heard you say: 29In
this desert your bodies will fall[p]
—every one of you twenty years old
or more[q] who was counted in the
census and who has grumbled
against me. 30Not one of you will
enter the land I swore with uplifted
hand to make your home, except
Caleb son of Jephunneh and Joshua son of Nun. 31As for your children that you said would be taken
as plunder, I will bring them in to
enjoy the land you have rejected.[r]
32But you—your bodies will fall[s]
in this desert. 33Your children will
be shepherds here for forty years,
suffering for your unfaithfulness,
until the last of your bodies lies in
the desert. 34For forty years—one
year for each of the forty days you
explored the land[t]—you will suffer for your sins and know what it is
like to have me against you.' 35I,
the LORD, have spoken, and I will
surely do these things[u] to this
whole wicked community, which
has banded together against me.
They will meet their end in this
desert; here they will die."

36So the men Moses had sent[v]
to explore the land, who returned
and made the whole community
grumble against him by spreading a
bad report[w] about it— 37these
men responsible for spreading the
bad report[x] about the land were
struck down and died of a plague[y]
before the LORD. 38Of the men who
went to explore the land, only
Joshua son of Nun and Caleb son
of Jephunneh survived.[z]

39When Moses reported this to
all the Israelites, they mourned[a]
bitterly. 40Early the next morning
they went up toward the high hill
country. "We have sinned[b]," they
said. "We will go up to the place
the LORD promised."

41But Moses said, "Why are you
disobeying the LORD's command?
This will not succeed![c] 42Do not
go up, because the LORD is not with
you. You will be defeated by your
enemies,[d] 43for the Amalekites
and Canaanites will face you there.
Because you have turned away
from the LORD, he will not be with
you and you will fall by the sword."

44Nevertheless, in their pre-
sumption they went up[e] toward
the high hill country, though neither Moses nor the ark of the LORD's
covenant moved from the camp.[f]
45Then the Amalekites and Canaanites who lived in that hill
country came down and attacked
them and beat them down all the
way to Hormah.[g]

Supplementary Offerings

15 The LORD said to Moses,
2"Speak to the Israelites
and say to them: 'After you enter
the land I am giving you[h] as a

14:18 [a]Ex 20:5
14:19 [b]Ex 34:9 [c]Ps 106:45 [d]Ps 78:38
14:20 [e]Ps 106:23; Mic 7:18-20
14:21 [f]Dt 32:40; Isa 49:18 [g]Ps 72:19; Isa 6:3; Hab 2:14
14:22 [h]Ex 14:11; 32:1; 1Co 10:5
14:23 [i]Nu 32:11 [j]Heb 3:18
14:24 [k]ver 6-9; Jos 14:8,14 [l]Nu 32:12
14:25 [m]Dt 1:40
14:27 [n]Ex 16:12
14:28 [o]ver 21
14:29 [p]Nu 26:65 [q]Nu 1:45
14:31 [r]Ps 106:24
14:32 [s]1Co 10:5
14:34 [t]Nu 13:25
14:35 [u]Nu 23:19
14:36 [v]Nu 13:4-16 [w]Nu 13:32
14:37 [x]1Co 10:10 [y]Nu 16:49
14:38 [z]Jos 14:6
14:39 [a]Ex 33:4
14:40 [b]Dt 1:41
14:41 [c]2Ch 24:20
14:42 [d]Dt 1:42
14:44 [e]Dt 1:43 [f]Nu 31:6
14:45 [g]Nu 21:3; Dt 1:44; Jdg 1:17
15:2 [h]Lev 23:10

[d]25 Hebrew *Yam Suph*; that is, Sea of Reeds

home **3**and you present to the LORD
offerings made by fire, from the
herd or the flock,[a] as an aroma
pleasing to the LORD[b]—whether
burnt offerings[c] or sacrifices, for
special vows or freewill offerings[d]
or festival offerings[e]— **4**then the
one who brings his offering shall
present to the LORD a grain offering[f] of a tenth of an ephah[e] of fine
flour mixed with a quarter of a
hin[f] of oil. **5**With each lamb for the
burnt offering or the sacrifice, prepare a quarter of a hin of wine[g] as
a drink offering.
6" 'With a ram[h] prepare a grain
offering[i] of two-tenths of an
ephah[g] of fine flour mixed with a
third of a hin[h] of oil,[j] **7**and a third
of a hin of wine as a drink offering.
Offer it as an aroma pleasing to the
LORD.
8" 'When you prepare a young
bull as a burnt offering or sacrifice,
for a special vow or a fellowship offering[i][k] to the LORD, **9**bring with
the bull a grain offering of three-
tenths of an ephah[j][l] of fine flour
mixed with half a hin[k] of oil.
10Also bring half a hin of wine as a
drink offering. It will be an offering
made by fire, an aroma pleasing to
the LORD. **11**Each bull or ram, each
lamb or young goat, is to be prepared in this manner. **12**Do this for
each one, for as many as you prepare.
13" 'Everyone who is native-
born[m] must do these things in this
way when he brings an offering
made by fire as an aroma pleasing
to the LORD. **14**For the generations
to come, whenever an alien or anyone else living among you presents
an offering made by fire as an aroma pleasing to the LORD, he must
do exactly as you do. **15**The community is to have the same rules for
you and for the alien living among
you; this is a lasting ordinance for
the generations to come.[n] You and
the alien shall be the same before
the LORD: **16**The same laws and regulations will apply both to you and
to the alien living among you.[o]' "
17The LORD said to Moses,
18"Speak to the Israelites and say
to them: 'When you enter the land
to which I am taking you **19**and you
eat the food of the land,[p] present
a portion as an offering to the LORD.
20Present a cake from the first of
your ground meal[q] and present it
as an offering from the threshing
floor.[r] **21**Throughout the generations to come you are to give this
offering to the LORD from the first of
your ground meal.[s]

Offerings for Unintentional Sins

22" 'Now if you unintentionally
fail to keep any of these commands
the LORD gave Moses[t]— **23**any of
the LORD's commands to you
through him, from the day the LORD
gave them and continuing through
the generations to come— **24**and if
this is done unintentionally without the community being aware of
it,[u] then the whole community is
to offer a young bull for a burnt offering[v] as an aroma pleasing to the
LORD, along with its prescribed
grain offering and drink offering,
and a male goat for a sin offering.[w]
25The priest is to make atonement
for the whole Israelite community,
and they will be forgiven,[x] for it
was not intentional and they have
brought to the LORD for their wrong
an offering made by fire and a sin
offering. **26**The whole Israelite
community and the aliens living
among them will be forgiven, because all the people were involved
in the unintentional wrong.[y]
27" 'But if just one person sins
unintentionally,[z] he must bring a
year-old female goat for a sin offering. **28**The priest is to make atonement before the LORD for the one
who erred by sinning unintentionally, and when atonement has been
made for him, he will be forgiven.[a]

15:3 [a]Lev 1:2 [b]ver 24; Ge 8:21; Ex 29:18 [c]Nu 28:19,27 [d]Lev 22:18, 21; Ezr 1:4 [e]Lev 23:1-44
15:4 [f]Lev 2:1; 6:14
15:5 [g]Nu 28:7,14
15:6 [h]Lev 5:15 [i]Nu 28:12 [j]Eze 46:14
15:8 [k]Lev 1:3; 3:1
15:9 [l]Lev 14:10
15:13 [m]Lev 16:29
15:15 [n]ver 29; Nu 9:14
15:16 [o]Nu 9:14
15:19 [p]Jos 5:11,12
15:20 [q]Ex 34:26; Lev 23:14; Dt 26:2,10 [r]Lev 2:14
15:21 [s]Ro 11:16
15:22 [t]Lev 4:2
15:24 [u]Lev 5:15 [v]Lev 4:14 [w]Lev 4:3
15:25 [x]Lev 4:20; Ro 3:25; Heb 2:17
15:26 [y]ver 24
15:27 [z]Lev 4:27
15:28 [a]Lev 4:35

[e]4 That is, probably about 2 quarts (about 2 liters) [f]4 That is, probably about 1 quart (about 1 liter); also in verse 5 [g]6 That is, probably about 4 quarts (about 4.5 liters) [h]6 That is, probably about 1 1/4 quarts (about 1.2 liters); also in verse 7 [i]8 Traditionally *peace offering* [j]9 That is, probably about 6 quarts (about 6.5 liters) [k]9 That is, probably about 2 quarts (about 2 liters); also in verse 10

29One and the same law applies to
everyone who sins unintentionally,
whether he is a native-born Israelite or an alien.
30" 'But anyone who sins defiantly,[a] whether native-born or
alien,[b] blasphemes the LORD, and
that person must be cut off from
his people. 31Because he has despised the LORD's word and broken
his commands,[c] that person must
surely be cut off; his guilt remains
on him.[d] ' "

The Sabbath-Breaker Put to Death

32While the Israelites were in the
desert, a man was found gathering wood on the Sabbath day.[e]
33Those who found him gathering
wood brought him to Moses and
Aaron and the whole assembly,
34and they kept him in custody, because it was not clear what should
be done to him.[f] 35Then the LORD
said to Moses, "The man must
die.[g] The whole assembly must
stone him outside the camp.[h]"
36So the assembly took him outside the camp and stoned him to
death, as the LORD commanded
Moses.

Tassels on Garments

37The LORD said to Moses,
38"Speak to the Israelites and say
to them: 'Throughout the generations to come you are to make tassels on the corners of your garments,[i] with a blue cord on each
tassel. 39You will have these tassels to look at and so you will remember[j] all the commands of the
LORD, that you may obey them and
not prostitute yourselves by going
after the lusts of your own hearts
and eyes. 40Then you will remember to obey all my commands and
will be consecrated to your God.[k]
41I am the LORD your God, who
brought you out of Egypt to be your
God. I am the LORD your God.' "

Korah, Dathan and Abiram

16 Korah[l] son of Izhar, the
son of Kohath, the son of

15:30 [a]Nu 14:40-44; Dt 1:43; 17:13; Ps 19:13 [b]ver 14
15:31 [c]2Sa 12:9; Ps 119:126; Pr 13:13 [d]Lev 5:1; Eze 18:20
15:32 [e]Ex 31:14,15; 35:2,3
15:34 [f]Nu 9:8
15:35 [g]Ex 31:14,15; Dt 21:21 [h]Lev 20:2; 24:14; Ac 7:58
15:38 [i]Dt 22:12; Mt 23:5
15:39 [j]Dt 4:23; 6:12; Ps 73:27
15:40 [k]Lev 11:44; Ro 12:1; Col 1:22; 1Pe 1:15
16:1 [l]Jude 1:11 [m]Nu 26:8; Dt 11:6
16:2 [n]Nu 1:16; 26:9
16:3 [o]ver 7; Ps 106:16 [p]Ex 19:6 [q]Nu 14:14 [r]Nu 12:2
16:4 [s]Nu 14:5
16:5 [t]Lev 10:3; 2Ti 2:19* [u]Nu 17:5; Ps 65:4
16:9 [v]Nu 3:6; Dt 10:8
16:10 [w]Nu 3:10; 18:7
16:11 [x]1Co 10:10 [y]Ex 16:7
16:13 [z]Nu 14:2 [a]Ac 7:27,35
16:14 [b]Lev 20:24

Levi, and certain Reubenites—Dathan and Abiram, sons of Eliab,[m]
and On son of Peleth—became insolent[1] 2and rose up against Moses. With them were 250 Israelite
men, well-known community leaders who had been appointed members of the council.[n] 3They came
as a group to oppose Moses and
Aaron[o] and said to them, "You
have gone too far! The whole community is holy,[p] every one of them,
and the LORD is with them.[q] Why
then do you set yourselves above
the LORD's assembly?"[r]
4When Moses heard this, he fell
facedown.[s] 5Then he said to Korah and all his followers: "In the
morning the LORD will show who
belongs to him and who is holy,[t]
and he will have that person come
near him. The man he chooses[u] he
will cause to come near him. 6You,
Korah, and all your followers are to
do this: Take censers 7and tomorrow put fire and incense in them
before the LORD. The man the LORD
chooses will be the one who is holy.
You Levites have gone too far!"
8Moses also said to Korah, "Now
listen, you Levites! 9Isn't it enough
for you that the God of Israel has
separated you from the rest of the
Israelite community and brought
you near himself to do the work at
the LORD's tabernacle and to stand
before the community and minister to them?[v] 10He has brought
you and all your fellow Levites near
himself, but now you are trying to
get the priesthood too.[w] 11It is
against the LORD that you and all
your followers have banded together. Who is Aaron that you should
grumble[x] against him?[y]"
12Then Moses summoned Da-
than and Abiram, the sons of Eliab.
But they said, "We will not come!
13Isn't it enough that you have
brought us up out of a land flowing
with milk and honey to kill us in
the desert?[z] And now you also
want to lord it over us?[a] 14More-
over, you haven't brought us into a
land flowing with milk and honey[b]

[1]1 Or *Peleth—took* ⌞*men*⌟

or given us an inheritance of fields and vineyards.[a] Will you gouge out the eyes of[m] these men?[b] No, we will not come!"

15Then Moses became very angry and said to the LORD, "Do not accept their offering. I have not taken so much as a donkey[c] from them, nor have I wronged any of them."

16Moses said to Korah, "You and all your followers are to appear before the LORD tomorrow—you and they and Aaron.[d] **17**Each man is to take his censer and put incense in it—250 censers in all—and present it before the LORD. You and Aaron are to present your censers also." **18**So each man took his censer, put fire and incense in it, and stood with Moses and Aaron at the entrance to the Tent of Meeting. **19**When Korah had gathered all his followers in opposition to them[e] at the entrance to the Tent of Meeting, the glory of the LORD[f] appeared to the entire assembly. **20**The LORD said to Moses and Aaron, **21**"Separate yourselves from this assembly so I can put an end to them at once."[g]

22But Moses and Aaron fell facedown[h] and cried out, "O God, God of the spirits of all mankind,[i] will you be angry with the entire assembly when only one man sins?"[j]

23Then the LORD said to Moses, **24**"Say to the assembly, 'Move away from the tents of Korah, Dathan and Abiram.' "

25Moses got up and went to Dathan and Abiram, and the elders of Israel followed him. **26**He warned the assembly, "Move back from the tents of these wicked men![k] Do not touch anything belonging to them, or you will be swept away[l] because of all their sins." **27**So they moved away from the tents of Korah, Dathan and Abiram. Dathan and Abiram had come out and were standing with their wives, children and little ones at the entrances to their tents.

28Then Moses said, "This is how you will know that the LORD has sent me[m] to do all these things and that it was not my idea: **29**If these men die a natural death and experience only what usually happens to men, then the LORD has not sent me.[n] **30**But if the LORD brings about something totally new, and the earth opens its mouth and swallows them, with everything that belongs to them, and they go down alive into the grave,[n][o] then you will know that these men have treated the LORD with contempt."

31As soon as he finished saying all this, the ground under them split apart[p] **32**and the earth opened its mouth and swallowed them,[q] with their households and all Korah's men and all their possessions. **33**They went down alive into the grave, with everything they owned; the earth closed over them, and they perished and were gone from the community. **34**At their cries, all the Israelites around them fled, shouting, "The earth is going to swallow us too!"

35And fire came out from the LORD[r] and consumed[s] the 250 men who were offering the incense.

36The LORD said to Moses, **37**"Tell Eleazar son of Aaron, the priest, to take the censers out of the smoldering remains and scatter the coals some distance away, for the censers are holy— **38**the censers of the men who sinned at the cost of their lives.[t] Hammer the censers into sheets to overlay the altar, for they were presented before the LORD and have become holy. Let them be a sign[u] to the Israelites."

39So Eleazar the priest collected the bronze censers brought by those who had been burned up, and he had them hammered out to overlay the altar, **40**as the LORD directed him through Moses. This was to remind the Israelites that no one except a descendant of Aaron should come to burn incense[v] before the LORD,[w] or he would become like Korah and his followers.[x]

16:14 [a]Ex 22:5; 23:11; Nu 20:5 [b]Jdg 16:21; 1Sa 11:2
16:15 [c]1Sa 12:3
16:16 [d]ver 6
16:19 [e]ver 42 [f]Ex 16:7; Nu 14:10; 20:6
16:21 [g]Ex 32:10
16:22 [h]Nu 14:5 [i]Nu 27:16; Job 12:10; Heb 12:9 [j]Ge 18:23
16:26 [k]Isa 52:11 [l]Ge 19:15
16:28 [m]Ex 3:12; Jn 5:36; 6:38
16:29 [n]Ecc 3:19
16:30 [o]ver 33; Ps 55:15
16:31 [p]Mic 1:3-4
16:32 [q]Nu 26:11; Dt 11:6; Ps 106:17
16:35 [r]Nu 11:1-3; 26:10 [s]Lev 10:2
16:38 [t]Pr 20:2 [u]Nu 26:10; Eze 14:8; 2Pe 2:6
16:40 [v]Ex 30:7-10; Nu 1:51 [w]2Ch 26:18 [x]Nu 3:10

[m]*14* Or *you make slaves of*; or *you deceive*
[n]*30* Hebrew *Sheol*; also in verse 33

41The next day the whole Israelite community grumbled against Moses and Aaron. "You have killed the LORD's people," they said.

42But when the assembly gathered in opposition[a] to Moses and Aaron and turned toward the Tent of Meeting, suddenly the cloud covered it and the glory of the LORD appeared. **43**Then Moses and Aaron went to the front of the Tent of Meeting, **44**and the LORD said to Moses, **45**"Get away from this assembly so I can put an end to them at once." And they fell facedown.

46Then Moses said to Aaron, "Take your censer and put incense in it, along with fire from the altar, and hurry to the assembly[b] to make atonement[c] for them. Wrath has come out from the LORD; the plague[d] has started." **47**So Aaron did as Moses said, and ran into the midst of the assembly. The plague had already started among the people,[e] but Aaron offered the incense and made atonement for them. **48**He stood between the living and the dead, and the plague stopped.[f] **49**But 14,700 people died from the plague, in addition to those who had died because of Korah.[g] **50**Then Aaron returned to Moses at the entrance to the Tent of Meeting, for the plague had stopped.

The Budding of Aaron's Staff

17 The LORD said to Moses, **2**"Speak to the Israelites and get twelve staffs from them, one from the leader of each of their ancestral tribes. Write the name of each man on his staff. **3**On the staff of Levi write Aaron's name,[h] for there must be one staff for the head of each ancestral tribe. **4**Place them in the Tent of Meeting in front of the Testimony,[i] where I meet with you.[j] **5**The staff belonging to the man I choose[k] will sprout, and I will rid myself of this constant grumbling against you by the Israelites."

6So Moses spoke to the Israelites, and their leaders gave him twelve staffs, one for the leader of each of their ancestral tribes, and Aaron's staff was among them. **7**Moses placed the staffs before the LORD in the Tent of the Testimony.[l]

8The next day Moses entered the Tent of the Testimony and saw that Aaron's staff, which represented the house of Levi, had not only sprouted but had budded, blossomed and produced almonds.[m] **9**Then Moses brought out all the staffs from the LORD's presence to all the Israelites. They looked at them, and each man took his own staff.

10The LORD said to Moses, "Put back Aaron's staff in front of the Testimony, to be kept as a sign to the rebellious.[n] This will put an end to their grumbling against me, so that they will not die." **11**Moses did just as the LORD commanded him.

12The Israelites said to Moses, "We will die! We are lost, we are all lost![o] **13**Anyone who even comes near the tabernacle of the LORD will die.[p] Are we all going to die?"

Duties of Priests and Levites

18 The LORD said to Aaron, "You, your sons and your father's family are to bear the responsibility for offenses against the sanctuary,[q] and you and your sons alone are to bear the responsibility for offenses against the priesthood. **2**Bring your fellow Levites from your ancestral tribe to join you and assist you when you and your sons minister[r] before the Tent of the Testimony. **3**They are to be responsible to you and are to perform all the duties of the Tent,[s] but they must not go near the furnishings of the sanctuary or the altar, or both they and you will die.[t] **4**They are to join you and be responsible for the care of the Tent of Meeting—all the work at the Tent—and no one else may come near where you are.

5"You are to be responsible for the care of the sanctuary and the altar,[u] so that wrath will not fall on the Israelites again. **6**I myself have

16:42 [a]ver 19; Nu 20:6
16:46 [b]Lev 10:6 [c]Nu 18:5; 25:13; Dt 9:22 [d]Nu 8:19; Ps 106:29
16:47 [e]Nu 25:6-8
16:48 [f]Nu 25:8; Ps 106:30
16:49 [g]ver 32
17:3 [h]Nu 1:3
17:4 [i]ver 7 [j]Ex 25:22
17:5 [k]Nu 16:5
17:7 [l]Ex 38:21; Ac 7:44
17:8 [m]Eze 17:24; Heb 9:4
17:10 [n]Dt 9:24
17:12 [o]Isa 6:5
17:13 [p]Nu 1:51
18:1 [q]Ex 28:38
18:2 [r]Nu 3:10
18:3 [s]Nu 1:51 [t]ver 7; Nu 4:15
18:5 [u]Nu 16:46

selected your fellow Levites from
among the Israelites as a gift to
you,[a] dedicated to the LORD to do
the work at the Tent of Meeting.
7But only you and your sons may
serve as priests in connection with
everything at the altar and inside
the curtain.[b] I am giving you the
service of the priesthood as a
gift.[c] Anyone else who comes near
the sanctuary must be put to
death.[d]"

Offerings for Priests and Levites

8Then the LORD said to Aaron, "I
myself have put you in charge of
the offerings presented to me; all
the holy offerings the Israelites give
me I give to you and your sons as
your portion and regular share.[e]
9You are to have the part of the
most holy offerings that is kept
from the fire. From all the gifts they
bring me as most holy offerings,
whether grain[f] or sin[g] or guilt offerings,[h] that part belongs to you
and your sons. **10**Eat it as something most holy; every male shall
eat it.[i] You must regard it as holy.
11"This also is yours: whatever is
set aside from the gifts of all the
wave offerings[j] of the Israelites. I
give this to you and your sons and
daughters as your regular share.
Everyone in your household who is
ceremonially clean[k] may eat it.
12"I give you all the finest olive
oil and all the finest new wine and
grain they give the LORD as the firstfruits of their harvest.[l] **13**All the
land's firstfruits that they bring to
the LORD will be yours.[m] Everyone
in your household who is ceremonially clean may eat it.
14"Everything in Israel that is devoted[o] to the LORD[n] is yours.
15The first offspring of every womb,
both man and animal, that is offered to the LORD is yours.[o] But you
must redeem[p] every firstborn son
and every firstborn male of unclean
animals.[q] **16**When they are a
month old, you must redeem them
at the redemption price set at five
shekels[p][r] of silver, according to
the sanctuary shekel,[s] which
weighs twenty gerahs.
17"But you must not redeem the
firstborn of an ox, a sheep or a goat;
they are holy.[t] Sprinkle their
blood[u] on the altar and burn their
fat as an offering made by fire, an
aroma pleasing to the LORD. **18**Their
meat is to be yours, just as the
breast of the wave offering[v] and
the right thigh are yours. **19**Whatever is set aside from the holy offerings the Israelites present to the
LORD I give to you and your sons
and daughters as your regular
share. It is an everlasting covenant
of salt[w] before the LORD for both
you and your offspring."
20The LORD said to Aaron, "You
will have no inheritance in their
land, nor will you have any share
among them;[x] I am your share and
your inheritance[y] among the Israelites.
21"I give to the Levites all the
tithes[z] in Israel as their inheritance[a] in return for the work they
do while serving at the Tent of
Meeting. **22**From now on the Israelites must not go near the Tent of
Meeting, or they will bear the consequences of their sin and will
die.[b] **23**It is the Levites who are to
do the work at the Tent of Meeting
and bear the responsibility for offenses against it. This is a lasting
ordinance for the generations to
come. They will receive no inheritance[c] among the Israelites. **24**Instead, I give to the Levites as their
inheritance the tithes that the Israelites present as an offering to the
LORD. That is why I said concerning
them: 'They will have no inheritance among the Israelites.' "
25The LORD said to Moses,
26"Speak to the Levites and say to
them: 'When you receive from the
Israelites the tithe I give you[d] as
your inheritance, you must present
a tenth of that tithe as the LORD's
offering.[e] **27**Your offering will be
reckoned to you as grain from the

18:6 [a]Nu 3:9
18:7 [b]Heb 9:3,6 [c]ver 20; Ex 29:9 [d]Nu 3:10
18:8 [e]Lev 6:16; 7:6,31-34,36
18:9 [f]Lev 2:1 [g]Lev 6:25 [h]Lev 5:15; 7:7
18:10 [i]Lev 6:16
18:11 [j]Ex 29:26 [k]Lev 22:1-16
18:12 [l]Ex 23:19; Ne 10:35
18:13 [m]Ex 22:29; 23:19
18:14 [n]Lev 27:28
18:15 [o]Ex 13:2 [p]Nu 3:46 [q]Ex 13:13
18:16 [r]Lev 27:6 [s]Ex 30:13
18:17 [t]Dt 15:19 [u]Lev 3:2
18:18 [v]Lev 7:30
18:19 [w]Lev 2:13; 2Ch 13:5
18:20 [x]Dt 12:12 [y]Dt 10:9; 14:27; 18:1-2; Jos 13:33; Eze 44:28
18:21 [z]Dt 14:22; Mal 3:8 [a]Lev 27:30-33; Heb 7:5
18:22 [b]Lev 22:9; Nu 1:51
18:23 [c]ver 20
18:26 [d]ver 21 [e]Ne 10:38

[o]*14* The Hebrew term refers to the irrevocable giving over of things or persons to the LORD.
[p]*16* That is, about 2 ounces (about 55 grams)

threshing floor or juice from the winepress. **28**In this way you also will present an offering to the LORD from all the tithes[a] you receive from the Israelites. From these tithes you must give the LORD's portion to Aaron the priest. **29**You must present as the LORD's portion the best and holiest part of everything given to you.'

30"Say to the Levites: 'When you present the best part, it will be reckoned to you as the product of the threshing floor or the winepress.[b] **31**You and your households may eat the rest of it anywhere, for it is your wages for your work at the Tent of Meeting. **32**By presenting the best part[c] of it you will not be guilty in this matter; then you will not defile the holy offerings[d] of the Israelites, and you will not die.' "

The Water of Cleansing

19 The LORD said to Moses and Aaron: **2**"This is a requirement of the law that the LORD has commanded: Tell the Israelites to bring you a red heifer[e] without defect or blemish[f] and that has never been under a yoke.[g] **3**Give it to Eleazar[h] the priest; it is to be taken outside the camp[i] and slaughtered in his presence. **4**Then Eleazar the priest is to take some of its blood on his finger and sprinkle[j] it seven times toward the front of the Tent of Meeting. **5**While he watches, the heifer is to be burned—its hide, flesh, blood and offal.[k] **6**The priest is to take some cedar wood, hyssop[l] and scarlet wool[m] and throw them onto the burning heifer. **7**After that, the priest must wash his clothes and bathe himself with water.[n] He may then come into the camp, but he will be ceremonially unclean till evening. **8**The man who burns it must also wash his clothes and bathe with water, and he too will be unclean till evening.

9"A man who is clean shall gather up the ashes of the heifer[o] and put them in a ceremonially clean place outside the camp. They shall be kept by the Israelite community for use in the water of cleansing;[p] it is for purification from sin. **10**The man who gathers up the ashes of the heifer must also wash his clothes, and he too will be unclean till evening. This will be a lasting ordinance both for the Israelites and for the aliens living among them.

11"Whoever touches the dead body[q] of anyone will be unclean for seven days.[r] **12**He must purify himself with the water on the third day and on the seventh day;[s] then he will be clean. But if he does not purify himself on the third and seventh days, he will not be clean. **13**Whoever touches the dead body[t] of anyone and fails to purify himself defiles the LORD's tabernacle.[u] That person must be cut off from Israel.[v] Because the water of cleansing has not been sprinkled on him, he is unclean;[w] his uncleanness remains on him.

14"This is the law that applies when a person dies in a tent: Anyone who enters the tent and anyone who is in it will be unclean for seven days, **15**and every open container without a lid fastened on it will be unclean.

16"Anyone out in the open who touches someone who has been killed with a sword or someone who has died a natural death,[x] or anyone who touches a human bone or a grave,[y] will be unclean for seven days.

17"For the unclean person, put some ashes[z] from the burned purification offering into a jar and pour fresh water over them. **18**Then a man who is ceremonially clean is to take some hyssop,[a] dip it in the water and sprinkle the tent and all the furnishings and the people who were there. He must also sprinkle anyone who has touched a human bone or a grave or someone who has been killed or someone who has died a natural death. **19**The man who is clean is to sprinkle the unclean person on the third and seventh days, and on the seventh day he is to purify him.[b] The person being cleansed must wash his

18:28 [a]Mal 3:8
18:30 [b]ver 27
18:32 [c]Lev 22:15 [d]Lev 19:8
19:2 [e]Ge 15:9; Heb 9:13 [f]Lev 22:19-25 [g]Dt 21:3; 1Sa 6:7
19:3 [h]Nu 3:4 [i]Lev 4:12,21; Heb 13:11
19:4 [j]Lev 4:17
19:5 [k]Ex 29:14
19:6 [l]ver 18; Ps 51:7 [m]Lev 14:4
19:7 [n]Lev 11:25; 16:26,28; 22:6
19:9 [o]Heb 9:13 [p]ver 13; Nu 8:7
19:11 [q]Lev 21:1; Nu 5:2 [r]Nu 31:19
19:12 [s]ver 19; Nu 31:19
19:13 [t]Lev 20:3 [u]Lev 15:31; 2Ch 36:14 [v]Lev 7:20; 22:3 [w]Hag 2:13
19:16 [x]Nu 31:19 [y]Mt 23:27
19:17 [z]ver 9
19:18 [a]ver 6
19:19 [b]Eze 36:25; Heb 10:22

clothes and bathe with water, and that evening he will be clean. **20**But if a person who is unclean does not purify himself, he must be cut off from the community, because he has defiled the sanctuary of the LORD. The water of cleansing has not been sprinkled on him, and he is unclean. **21**This is a lasting ordinance for them.

"The man who sprinkles the water of cleansing must also wash his clothes, and anyone who touches the water of cleansing will be unclean till evening. **22**Anything that an unclean[a] person touches becomes unclean, and anyone who touches it becomes unclean till evening."

Water From the Rock

20 In the first month the whole Israelite community arrived at the Desert of Zin,[b] and they stayed at Kadesh.[c] There Miriam[d] died and was buried.

2Now there was no water for the community,[e] and the people gathered in opposition[f] to Moses and Aaron. **3**They quarreled[g] with Moses and said, "If only we had died when our brothers fell dead before the LORD![h] **4**Why did you bring the LORD's community into this desert, that we and our livestock should die here?[i] **5**Why did you bring us up out of Egypt to this terrible place? It has no grain or figs, grapevines or pomegranates.[j] And there is no water to drink!"

6Moses and Aaron went from the assembly to the entrance to the Tent of Meeting and fell facedown,[k] and the glory of the LORD[l] appeared to them. **7**The LORD said to Moses, **8**"Take the staff,[m] and you and your brother Aaron gather the assembly together. Speak to that rock before their eyes and it will pour out its water.[n] You will bring water out of the rock for the community so they and their livestock can drink."

9So Moses took the staff from the LORD's presence,[o] just as he commanded him. **10**He and Aaron gathered the assembly together in front of the rock and Moses said to them, "Listen, you rebels, must we bring you water out of this rock?"[p] **11**Then Moses raised his arm and struck the rock twice with his staff. Water[q] gushed out, and the community and their livestock drank.

12But the LORD said to Moses and Aaron, "Because you did not trust in me enough to honor me as holy[r] in the sight of the Israelites, you will not bring this community into the land I give them."[s]

13These were the waters of Meribah,[q][t] where the Israelites quarreled[u] with the LORD and where he showed himself holy among them.

Edom Denies Israel Passage

14Moses sent messengers from Kadesh[v] to the king of Edom,[w] saying:

"This is what your brother Israel says: You know[x] about all the hardships that have come upon us. **15**Our forefathers went down into Egypt,[y] and we lived there many years.[z] The Egyptians mistreated[a] us and our fathers, **16**but when we cried out to the LORD, he heard our cry[b] and sent an angel[c] and brought us out of Egypt.

"Now we are here at Kadesh, a town on the edge of your territory. **17**Please let us pass through your country. We will not go through any field or vineyard, or drink water from any well. We will travel along the king's highway and not turn to the right or to the left until we have passed through your territory.[d]"

18But Edom answered:

"You may not pass through here; if you try, we will march out and attack you with the sword."

19The Israelites replied:

"We will go along the main road, and if we or our live-

19:22 [a]Lev 5:2; Hag 2:13,14
20:1 [b]Nu 13:21 [c]Nu 33:36 [d]Ex 15:20
20:2 [e]Ex 17:1 [f]Nu 16:19
20:3 [g]Ex 17:2 [h]Nu 14:2; 16:31-35
20:4 [i]Ex 14:11; 17:3; Nu 14:3; 16:13
20:5 [j]Nu 16:14
20:6 [k]Nu 14:5 [l]Nu 16:19
20:8 [m]Ex 4:17,20 [n]Ex 17:6; Isa 43:20
20:9 [o]Nu 17:10
20:10 [p]Ps 106:32,33
20:11 [q]Ex 17:6; Dt 8:15; Ps 78:16; Isa 48:2; 1Co 10:4
20:12 [r]Nu 27:14 [s]ver 24; Dt 1:37; 3:27
20:13 [t]Ex 17:7 [u]Dt 33:8; Ps 95:8; 106:32
20:14 [v]Jdg 11:16-17 [w]Dt 2:4 [x]Jos 2:11; 9:9
20:15 [y]Ge 46:6 [z]Ge 15:13; Ex 12:40 [a]Ex 1:11; Dt 26:6
20:16 [b]Ex 2:23; 3:7 [c]Ex 14:19
20:17 [d]Nu 21:22

[q]13 *Meribah* means *quarreling.*

stock[a] drink any of your water, we will pay for it.[b] We
only want to pass through on
foot—nothing else."

20Again they answered:

"You may not pass through."

Then Edom came out against
them with a large and powerful
army. **21**Since Edom refused to let
them go through their territory, Israel turned away from them.[c]

The Death of Aaron

22The whole Israelite community set out from Kadesh and came to
Mount Hor.[d] **23**At Mount Hor,
near the border of Edom,[e] the
LORD said to Moses and Aaron,
24"Aaron will be gathered to his
people.[f] He will not enter the land
I give the Israelites, because both
of you rebelled against my command[g] at the waters of Meribah.
25Get Aaron and his son Eleazar
and take them up Mount Hor.[h]
26Remove Aaron's garments and
put them on his son Eleazar, for
Aaron will be gathered to his people;[i] he will die there."
27Moses did as the LORD commanded: They went up Mount Hor
in the sight of the whole community. **28**Moses removed Aaron's garments and put them on his son Eleazar.[j] And Aaron died there[k] on
top of the mountain. Then Moses
and Eleazar came down from the
mountain, **29**and when the whole
community learned that Aaron had
died, the entire house of Israel
mourned for him[l] thirty days.

Arad Destroyed

21 When the Canaanite king of
Arad,[m] who lived in the
Negev,[n] heard that Israel was coming along the road to Atharim, he
attacked the Israelites and captured some of them. **2**Then Israel
made this vow to the LORD: "If you
will deliver these people into our
hands, we will totally destroy[r]
their cities." **3**The LORD listened to
Israel's plea and gave the Canaanites over to them. They completely
destroyed them and their towns; so
the place was named Hormah.[s]

The Bronze Snake

4They traveled from Mount
Hor[o] along the route to the Red
Sea,[t] to go around Edom. But the
people grew impatient on the
way;[p] **5**they spoke against God[q]
and against Moses, and said, "Why
have you brought us up out of
Egypt to die in the desert?[r] There
is no bread! There is no water! And
we detest this miserable food!"[s]

6Then the LORD sent venomous
snakes[t] among them; they bit the
people and many Israelites died.[u]
7The people came to Moses[v] and
said, "We sinned when we spoke
against the LORD and against you.
Pray that the LORD[w] will take the
snakes away from us." So Moses
prayed[x] for the people.

8The LORD said to Moses, "Make
a snake and put it up on a pole;[y]
anyone who is bitten can look at it
and live." **9**So Moses made a
bronze snake[z] and put it up on a
pole. Then when anyone was bitten
by a snake and looked at the
bronze snake, he lived.[a]

The Journey to Moab

10The Israelites moved on and
camped at Oboth.[b] **11**Then they
set out from Oboth and camped in
Iye Abarim, in the desert that faces
Moab[c] toward the sunrise. **12**From
there they moved on and camped
in the Zered Valley.[d] **13**They set
out from there and camped alongside the Arnon[e], which is in the
desert extending into Amorite territory. The Arnon is the border of
Moab, between Moab and the Amorites. **14**That is why the Book of
the Wars of the LORD says:

"... Waheb in Suphah[u] and
the ravines,

r2 The Hebrew term refers to the irrevocable giving over of things or persons to the LORD, often by totally destroying them; also in verse 3. s3 *Hormah* means *destruction.*
t4 Hebrew *Yam Suph;* that is, Sea of Reeds
u14 The meaning of the Hebrew for this phrase is uncertain.

20:19 [a]Ex 12:38 [b]Dt 2:6,28
20:21 [c]Dt 2:8; Jdg 11:18
20:22 [d]Nu 33:37
20:23 [e]Nu 33:37
20:24 [f]Ge 25:8 [g]ver 10
20:25 [h]Nu 33:38
20:26 [i]ver 24
20:28 [j]Ex 29:29 [k]Nu 33:38; Dt 10:6; 32:50
20:29 [l]Dt 34:8
21:1 [m]Nu 33:40; Jos 12:14 [n]Jdg 1:9,16
21:4 [o]Nu 20:22 [p]Dt 2:8; Jdg 11:18
21:5 [q]Ps 78:19 [r]Nu 14:2,3 [s]Nu 11:6
21:6 [t]Dt 8:15; Jer 8:17 [u]1Co 10:9
21:7 [v]Ps 78:34; Hos 5:15 [w]Ex 8:8; Ac 8:24 [x]Nu 11:2
21:8 [y]Jn 3:14
21:9 [z]2Ki 18:4 [a]Jn 3:14-15
21:10 [b]Nu 33:43
21:11 [c]Nu 33:44
21:12 [d]Dt 2:13,14
21:13 [e]Nu 22:36; Jdg 11:13,18

the Arnon 15and[v] the slopes
of the ravines
that lead to the site of Ar[a]
and lie along the border of
Moab."

16From there they continued on to
Beer,[b] the well where the LORD
said to Moses, "Gather the people
together and I will give them water."
17Then Israel sang this song:[c]

"Spring up, O well!
Sing about it,
18about the well that the princes
dug,
that the nobles of the people
sank—
the nobles with scepters and
staffs."

Then they went from the desert to
Mattanah, 19from Mattanah to Nahaliel, from Nahaliel to Bamoth,
20and from Bamoth to the valley in
Moab where the top of Pisgah overlooks the wasteland.

Defeat of Sihon and Og

21Israel sent messengers to say
to Sihon[d] king of the Amorites:

22"Let us pass through your
country. We will not turn aside
into any field or vineyard, or
drink water from any well. We
will travel along the king's
highway until we have passed
through your territory.[e]"

23But Sihon would not let Israel
pass through his territory.[f] He
mustered his entire army and
marched out into the desert
against Israel. When he reached Jahaz,[g] he fought with Israel. 24Isra-
el, however, put him to the sword[h]
and took over his land from the Arnon to the Jabbok, but only as far
as the Ammonites,[i] because their
border was fortified. 25Israel captured all the cities of the Amorites[j] and occupied them, including Heshbon and all its surrounding settlements. 26Heshbon was
the city of Sihon[k] king of the Amorites, who had fought against the
former king of Moab and had taken
from him all his land as far as the
Arnon.
27That is why the poets say:

"Come to Heshbon and let it
be rebuilt;
let Sihon's city be restored.

28"Fire went out from Heshbon,
a blaze from the city of
Sihon.[l]
It consumed Ar[m] of Moab,
the citizens of Arnon's
heights.[n]
29Woe to you, O Moab![o]
You are destroyed, O people
of Chemosh![p]
He has given up his sons as
fugitives[q]
and his daughters as
captives[r]
to Sihon king of the
Amorites.

30"But we have overthrown them;
Heshbon is destroyed all the
way to Dibon.[s]
We have demolished them as
far as Nophah,
which extends to Medeba."

31So Israel settled in the land of
the Amorites.
32After Moses had sent spies to
Jazer,[t] the Israelites captured its
surrounding settlements and drove
out the Amorites who were there.
33Then they turned and went up
along the road toward Bashan,[u],[v]
and Og king of Bashan and his
whole army marched out to meet
them in battle at Edrei.[w]
34The LORD said to Moses, "Do
not be afraid of him, for I have
handed him over to you, with his
whole army and his land. Do to him
what you did to Sihon king of the
Amorites, who reigned in Heshbon.[x]"
35So they struck him down, together with his sons and his whole
army, leaving them no survivors.
And they took possession of his
land.

21:15 [a]ver 28; Dt 2:9,18
21:16 [b]Jdg 9:21
21:17 [c]Ex 15:1
21:21 [d]Dt 1:4; 2:26-27; Jdg 11:19-21
21:22 [e]Nu 20:17
21:23 [f]Nu 20:21 [g]Dt 2:32; Jdg 11:20
21:24 [h]Dt 2:33; Ps 135:10-11; Am 2:9 [i]Dt 2:37
21:25 [j]Nu 13:29; Jdg 10:11; Am 2:10
21:26 [k]Dt 29:7; Ps 135:11
21:28 [l]Jer 48:45 [m]ver 15 [n]Nu 22:41; Isa 15:2
21:29 [o]Isa 25:10; Jer 48:46 [p]Jdg 11:24; 1Ki 11:7,33; 2Ki 23:13; Jer 48:7,46 [q]Isa 15:5 [r]Isa 16:2
21:30 [s]Nu 32:3; Isa 15:2; Jer 48:18,22
21:32 [t]Nu 32:1,3, 35; Jer 48:32
21:33 [u]Dt 3:3 [v]Dt 3:4 [w]Dt 1:4; 3:1, 10; Jos 13:12, 31
21:34 [x]Dt 3:2

[v]*14,15* Or *"I have been given from Suphah and the ravines / of the Arnon* [15]*to*

Balak Summons Balaam

22 Then the Israelites traveled
to the plains of Moab and
camped along the Jordan across
from Jericho.[w][a]

2Now Balak son of Zippor[b] saw
all that Israel had done to the Amorites, 3and Moab was terrified because there were so many people.
Indeed, Moab was filled with
dread[c] because of the Israelites.

4The Moabites said to the elders
of Midian, "This horde is going to
lick up everything around us, as an
ox licks up the grass of the field."

So Balak son of Zippor, who was
king of Moab at that time, 5sent
messengers to summon Balaam
son of Beor,[d] who was at Pethor,
near the River,[x] in his native land.
Balak said:

> "A people has come out of
> Egypt; they cover the face of
> the land and have settled next
> to me. 6Now come and put a
> curse[e] on these people, be-
> cause they are too powerful for
> me. Perhaps then I will be able
> to defeat them and drive them
> out of the country. For I know
> that those you bless are
> blessed, and those you curse
> are cursed."

7The elders of Moab and Midian
left, taking with them the fee for
divination.[f] When they came to
Balaam, they told him what Balak
had said.

8"Spend the night here," Balaam
said to them, "and I will bring you
back the answer the LORD gives
me.[g]" So the Moabite princes
stayed with him.

9God came to Balaam[h] and
asked,[i] "Who are these men with
you?"

10Balaam said to God, "Balak
son of Zippor, king of Moab, sent
me this message: 11'A people that
has come out of Egypt covers the
face of the land. Now come and put
a curse on them for me. Perhaps
then I will be able to fight them and
drive them away.' "

12But God said to Balaam, "Do
not go with them. You must not put
a curse on those people, because
they are blessed.[j]"

13The next morning Balaam got
up and said to Balak's princes, "Go
back to your own country, for the
LORD has refused to let me go with
you."

14So the Moabite princes returned to Balak and said, "Balaam
refused to come with us."

15Then Balak sent other princes,
more numerous and more distinguished than the first. 16They came
to Balaam and said:

> "This is what Balak son of
> Zippor says: Do not let any-
> thing keep you from coming to
> me, 17because I will reward
> you handsomely[k] and do
> whatever you say. Come and
> put a curse[l] on these people
> for me."

18But Balaam answered them,
"Even if Balak gave me his palace
filled with silver and gold, I could
not do anything great or small to go
beyond the command of the LORD
my God.[m] 19Now stay here tonight
as the others did, and I will find out
what else the LORD will tell me.[n]"

20That night God came to Balaam[o] and said, "Since these men
have come to summon you, go with
them, but do only what I tell
you."[p]

Balaam's Donkey

21Balaam got up in the morning,
saddled his donkey and went with
the princes of Moab. 22But God
was very angry[q] when he went, and
the angel of the LORD[r] stood in the
road to oppose him. Balaam was
riding on his donkey, and his two
servants were with him. 23When
the donkey saw the angel of the
LORD standing in the road with a
drawn sword[s] in his hand, she
turned off the road into a field. Balaam beat her[t] to get her back on
the road.

24Then the angel of the LORD

22:1 [a]Nu 33:48
22:2 [b]Jdg 11:25
22:3 [c]Ex 15:15
22:5 [d]Dt 23:4; Jos 13:22; 24:9; Ne 13:2; Mic 6:5; 2Pe 2:15
22:6 [e]ver 12,17; Nu 23:7,11,13
22:7 [f]Nu 23:23; 24:1
22:8 [g]ver 19
22:9 [h]Ge 20:3 [i]ver 20
22:12 [j]Ge 12:2; 22:17; Nu 23:20
22:17 [k]ver 37; Nu 24:11 [l]ver 6
22:18 [m]ver 38; Nu 23:12,26; 24:13; 1Ki 22:14; 2Ch 18:13; Jer 42:4
22:19 [n]ver 8
22:20 [o]Ge 20:3 [p]ver 35,38; Nu 23:5,12, 16,26; 24:13; 2Ch 18:13
22:22 [q]Ex 4:14 [r]Ge 16:7; Ex 23:20; Jdg 13:3,6,13
22:23 [s]Jos 5:13 [t]ver 25,27

[w]*1* Hebrew *Jordan of Jericho*; possibly an ancient name for the Jordan River [x]*5* That is, the Euphrates

stood in a narrow path between
two vineyards, with walls on both
sides. **25**When the donkey saw the
angel of the LORD, she pressed close
to the wall, crushing Balaam's foot
against it. So he beat her again.
26Then the angel of the LORD
moved on ahead and stood in a narrow place where there was no room
to turn, either to the right or to the
left. **27**When the donkey saw the
angel of the LORD, she lay down under Balaam, and he was angry[a] and
beat her with his staff. **28**Then
the LORD opened the donkey's
mouth,[b] and she said to Balaam,
"What have I done to you to make
you beat me these three times?[c]"
29Balaam answered the donkey,
"You have made a fool of me! If I
had a sword in my hand, I would
kill you right now.[d]"
30The donkey said to Balaam,
"Am I not your own donkey, which
you have always ridden, to this
day? Have I been in the habit of doing this to you?"
"No," he said.
31Then the LORD opened Balaam's eyes,[e] and he saw the angel
of the LORD standing in the road
with his sword drawn. So he bowed
low and fell facedown.
32The angel of the LORD asked
him, "Why have you beaten your
donkey these three times? I have
come here to oppose you because
your path is a reckless one before
me.[y] **33**The donkey saw me and
turned away from me these three
times. If she had not turned away,
I would certainly have killed you by
now,[f] but I would have spared
her."
34Balaam said to the angel of the
LORD, "I have sinned.[g] I did not realize you were standing in the road
to oppose me. Now if you are displeased, I will go back."
35The angel of the LORD said to
Balaam, "Go with the men, but
speak only what I tell you." So Balaam went with the princes of Balak.
36When Balak heard that Balaam was coming, he went out to
meet him at the Moabite town on
the Arnon[h] border, at the edge of
his territory. **37**Balak said to Balaam, "Did I not send you an urgent
summons? Why didn't you come to
me? Am I really not able to reward
you?"
38"Well, I have come to you
now," Balaam replied. "But can I
say just anything? I must speak
only what God puts in my
mouth."[i]
39Then Balaam went with Balak
to Kiriath Huzoth. **40**Balak sacrificed cattle and sheep,[j] and gave
some to Balaam and the princes
who were with him. **41**The next
morning Balak took Balaam up to
Bamoth Baal,[k] and from there he
saw part of the people.[l]

Balaam's First Oracle

23 Balaam said, "Build me seven altars here, and prepare
seven bulls and seven rams[m] for
me." **2**Balak did as Balaam said,
and the two of them offered a bull
and a ram on each altar.[n]
3Then Balaam said to Balak,
"Stay here beside your offering
while I go aside. Perhaps the LORD
will come to meet with me.[o] Whatever he reveals to me I will tell
you." Then he went off to a barren
height.
4God met with him,[p] and Balaam said, "I have prepared seven
altars, and on each altar I have offered a bull and a ram."
5The LORD put a message in Balaam's mouth[q] and said, "Go back
to Balak and give him this message."[r]
6So he went back to him and
found him standing beside his offering, with all the princes of
Moab.[s] **7**Then Balaam[t] uttered
his oracle:[u]

"Balak brought me from Aram,
the king of Moab from the
eastern mountains.
'Come,' he said, 'curse Jacob
for me;
come, denounce Israel.'[v]
8How can I curse

22:27 [a]Nu 11:1; Jas 1:19
22:28 [b]2Pe 2:16 [c]ver 32
22:29 [d]Dt 25:4; Pr 12:10; 27:23-27; Mt 15:19
22:31 [e]Ge 21:19
22:33 [f]ver 29
22:34 [g]Ge 39:9; Nu 14:40; 1Sa 15:24,30; 2Sa 12:13; 24:10; Job 33:27; Ps 51:4
22:36 [h]Nu 21:13
22:38 [i]Nu 23:5,16, 26
22:40 [j]Nu 23:1,14, 29; Eze 45:23
22:41 [k]Nu 21:28 [l]Nu 23:13
23:1 [m]Nu 22:40
23:2 [n]ver 14,30
23:3 [o]ver 15
23:4 [p]ver 16
23:5 [q]Dt 18:18; Jer 1:9 [r]Nu 22:20
23:6 [s]ver 17
23:7 [t]Nu 22:5 [u]ver 18; Nu 24:3,21 [v]Nu 22:6; Dt 23:4

[y]32 The meaning of the Hebrew for this clause is uncertain.

those whom God has not
cursed?[a]
How can I denounce
those whom the LORD has not
denounced?
9From the rocky peaks I see
them,
from the heights I view them.
I see a people who live apart
and do not consider
themselves one of the
nations.[b]
10Who can count the dust of
Jacob[c]
or number the fourth part of
Israel?
Let me die the death of the
righteous,[d]
and may my end be like
theirs![e]"

11Balak said to Balaam, "What
have you done to me? I brought you
to curse my enemies, but you have
done nothing but bless them!"[f]
12He answered, "Must I not
speak what the LORD puts in my
mouth?"[g]

Balaam's Second Oracle

13Then Balak said to him,
"Come with me to another place
where you can see them; you will
see only a part but not all of them.
And from there, curse them for
me." 14So he took him to the field
of Zophim on the top of Pisgah, and
there he built seven altars and offered a bull and a ram on each altar.[h]
15Balaam said to Balak, "Stay
here beside your offering while I
meet with him over there."
16The LORD met with Balaam and
put a message in his mouth[i] and
said, "Go back to Balak and give
him this message."
17So he went to him and found
him standing beside his offering,
with the princes of Moab. Balak
asked him, "What did the LORD
say?"
18Then he uttered his oracle:

"Arise, Balak, and listen;
hear me, son of Zippor.
19God is not a man,[j] that he
should lie,

23:8 [a]Nu 22:12
23:9 [b]Ex 33:16; Dt 32:8; 33:28
23:10 [c]Ge 13:16 [d]Ps 116:15; Isa 57:1 [e]Ps 37:37
23:11 [f]Nu 24:10; Ne 13:2
23:12 [g]Nu 22:20,38
23:14 [h]ver 2
23:16 [i]Nu 22:38
23:19 [j]Isa 55:9; Hos 11:9 [k]1Sa 15:29; Mal 3:6; Tit 1:2; Jas 1:17
23:20 [l]Ge 22:17; Nu 22:12 [m]Isa 43:13
23:21 [n]Ps 32:2,5; Ro 4:7-8 [o]Isa 40:2; Jer 50:20 [p]Ex 29:45,46; Ps 145:18 [q]Dt 33:5; Ps 89:15-18
23:22 [r]Nu 24:8 [s]Dt 33:17; Job 39:9
23:23 [t]Nu 24:1; Jos 13:22
23:24 [u]Na 2:11 [v]Ge 49:9
23:27 [w]ver 13
23:28 [x]Ps 106:28

nor a son of man, that he
should change his
mind.[k]
Does he speak and then not
act?
Does he promise and not
fulfill?
20I have received a command to
bless;
he has blessed,[l] and I
cannot change it.[m]

21"No misfortune is seen in
Jacob,[n]
no misery observed in
Israel.[z][o]
The LORD their God is with
them;[p]
the shout of the King[q] is
among them.
22God brought them out of
Egypt;[r]
they have the strength of a
wild ox.[s]
23There is no sorcery against
Jacob,
no divination[t] against Israel.
It will now be said of Jacob
and of Israel, 'See what God
has done!'
24The people rise like a lioness;[u]
they rouse themselves like a
lion[v]
that does not rest till he
devours his prey
and drinks the blood of his
victims."

25Then Balak said to Balaam,
"Neither curse them at all nor bless
them at all!"
26Balaam answered, "Did I not
tell you I must do whatever the
LORD says?"

Balaam's Third Oracle

27Then Balak said to Balaam,
"Come, let me take you to another
place.[w] Perhaps it will please God
to let you curse them for me from
there." 28And Balak took Balaam
to the top of Peor,[x] overlooking
the wasteland.
29Balaam said, "Build me seven
altars here, and prepare seven bulls

[z]21 Or *He has not looked on Jacob's offenses / or on the wrongs found in Israel.*

and seven rams for me." 30Balak
did as Balaam had said, and offered
a bull and a ram on each altar.

24 Now when Balaam saw that
it pleased the LORD to bless
Israel, he did not resort to sorcery[a]
as at other times, but turned his
face toward the desert.[b] 2When
Balaam looked out and saw Israel
encamped tribe by tribe, the Spirit
of God came upon him[c] 3and he
uttered his oracle:

"The oracle of Balaam son of
Beor,
the oracle of one whose eye
sees clearly,
4the oracle of one who hears the
words of God,[d]
who sees a vision from the
Almighty,[a][e]
who falls prostrate, and
whose eyes are opened:

5"How beautiful are your tents,
O Jacob,
your dwelling places,
O Israel!

6"Like valleys they spread out,
like gardens beside a river,
like aloes[f] planted by the
LORD,
like cedars beside the
waters.[g]
7Water will flow from their
buckets;
their seed will have abundant
water.

"Their king will be greater than
Agag;[h]
their kingdom will be
exalted.[i]

8"God brought them out of
Egypt;
they have the strength of a
wild ox.
They devour hostile nations
and break their bones in
pieces;[j]
with their arrows they pierce
them.[k]
9Like a lion they crouch and lie
down,
like a lioness[l]—who dares
to rouse them?

"May those who bless you be
blessed
and those who curse you be
cursed!"[m]

10Then Balak's anger burned
against Balaam. He struck his
hands together[n] and said to him,
"I summoned you to curse my enemies, but you have blessed them[o]
these three times.[p] 11Now leave at
once and go home! I said I would
reward you handsomely,[q] but the
LORD has kept you from being rewarded."
12Balaam answered Balak, "Did
I not tell the messengers you sent
me,[r] 13'Even if Balak gave me his
palace filled with silver and gold, I
could not do anything of my own
accord, good or bad, to go beyond
the command of the LORD[s]—and I
must say only what the LORD
says'?[t] 14Now I am going back to
my people, but come, let me warn
you of what this people will do to
your people in days to come."[u]

Balaam's Fourth Oracle

15Then he uttered his oracle:

"The oracle of Balaam son of
Beor,
the oracle of one whose eye
sees clearly,
16the oracle of one who hears the
words of God,
who has knowledge from the
Most High,
who sees a vision from the
Almighty,
who falls prostrate, and
whose eyes are opened:

17"I see him, but not now;
I behold him, but not near.[v]
A star will come out of Jacob;[w]
a scepter will rise out of
Israel.[x]
He will crush the foreheads of
Moab,[y]
the skulls[b] of[c] all the sons
of Sheth.[d]

24:1 [a]Nu 23:23 [b]Nu 23:28
24:2 [c]Nu 11:25,26; 1Sa 10:10; 19:20; 2Ch 15:1
24:4 [d]Nu 22:20 [e]Ge 15:1
24:6 [f]Ps 45:8 [g]Ps 1:3; 104:16
24:7 [h]2Sa 15:8 [i]2Sa 5:12; 1Ch 14:2; Ps 145:11-13
24:8 [j]Ps 2:9; Jer 50:17 [k]Ps 45:5
24:9 [l]Ge 49:9; Nu 23:24 [m]Ge 12:3
24:10 [n]Eze 21:14 [o]Nu 23:11 [p]Ne 13:2
24:11 [q]Nu 22:17
24:12 [r]Nu 22:18
24:13 [s]Nu 22:18 [t]Nu 22:20
24:14 [u]Ge 49:1; Nu 31:8,16; Da 2:28; Mic 6:5
24:17 [v]Rev 1:7 [w]Mt 2:2 [x]Ge 49:10 [y]Nu 21:29; Isa 15:1-16:14

[a]4 Hebrew *Shaddai*; also in verse 16 [b]17 Samaritan Pentateuch (see also Jer. 48:45); the meaning of the word in the Masoretic Text is uncertain. [c]17 Or possibly *Moab, / batter* [d]17 Or *all the noisy boasters*

18Edom[a] will be conquered;
Seir, his enemy, will be
conquered,
but Israel will grow strong.
19A ruler will come out of Jacob[b]
and destroy the survivors of
the city."

Balaam's Final Oracles

20Then Balaam saw Amalek[c]
and uttered his oracle:

"Amalek was first among the
nations,
but he will come to ruin at
last."

21Then he saw the Kenites[d] and
uttered his oracle:

"Your dwelling place is secure,
your nest is set in a rock;
22yet you Kenites will be
destroyed
when Asshur[e] takes you
captive."

23Then he uttered his oracle:

"Ah, who can live when God
does this?[e]
24 Ships will come from the
shores of Kittim;[f]
they will subdue Asshur and
Eber,[g]
but they too will come to
ruin.[h]"

25Then Balaam[i] got up and returned home and Balak went his
own way.

Moab Seduces Israel

25 While Israel was staying in
Shittim,[j] the men began to
indulge in sexual immorality[k] with
Moabite women,[l] 2who invited
them to the sacrifices[m] to their
gods.[n] The people ate and bowed
down before these gods. 3So Israel
joined in worshiping the Baal of
Peor.[o] And the LORD's anger
burned against them.
4The LORD said to Moses, "Take
all the leaders of these people, kill
them and expose them in broad
daylight before the LORD,[p] so that
the LORD's fierce anger[q] may turn
away from Israel."
5So Moses said to Israel's judges,
"Each of you must put to death[r]
those of your men who have joined
in worshiping the Baal of Peor."
6Then an Israelite man brought
to his family a Midianite woman
right before the eyes of Moses and
the whole assembly of Israel while
they were weeping at the entrance
to the Tent of Meeting. 7When
Phinehas son of Eleazar, the son of
Aaron, the priest, saw this, he left
the assembly, took a spear in his
hand 8and followed the Israelite
into the tent. He drove the spear
through both of them—through
the Israelite and into the woman's
body. Then the plague against the
Israelites was stopped;[s] 9but those
who died in the plague[t] numbered
24,000.[u]
10The LORD said to Moses,
11"Phinehas son of Eleazar, the
son of Aaron, the priest, has turned
my anger away from the Israelites;[v] for he was as zealous as I am
for my honor[w] among them, so
that in my zeal I did not put an end
to them. 12Therefore tell him I am
making my covenant of peace[x]
with him. 13He and his descendants will have a covenant of a lasting priesthood,[y] because he was
zealous for the honor of his God
and made atonement[z] for the Israelites."
14The name of the Israelite who
was killed with the Midianite woman was Zimri son of Salu, the leader
of a Simeonite family. 15And the
name of the Midianite woman who
was put to death was Cozbi[a]
daughter of Zur, a tribal chief of a
Midianite family.[b]
16The LORD said to Moses,
17"Treat the Midianites[c] as enemies and kill them, 18because they
treated you as enemies when they
deceived you in the affair of Peor[d]
and their sister Cozbi, the daughter
of a Midianite leader, the woman
who was killed when the plague
came as a result of Peor."

24:18 [a]Am 9:12
24:19 [b]Ge 49:10; Mic 5:2
24:20 [c]Ex 17:14
24:21 [d]Ge 15:19
24:22 [e]Ge 10:22
24:24 [f]Ge 10:4 [g]Ge 10:21 [h]ver 20
24:25 [i]Nu 31:8
25:1 [j]Jos 2:1; Mic 6:5 [k]1Co 10:8; Rev 2:14 [l]Nu 31:16
25:2 [m]Ex 34:15 [n]Ex 20:5; Dt 32:38; 1Co 10:20
25:3 [o]Ps 106:28; Hos 9:10
25:4 [p]Dt 4:3 [q]Dt 13:17
25:5 [r]Ex 32:27
25:8 [s]Nu 16:46-48; Ps 106:30
25:9 [t]Nu 14:37; 1Co 10:8 [u]Nu 31:16
25:11 [v]Ps 106:30 [w]Ex 20:5; Dt 32:16,21; Ps 78:58
25:12 [x]Isa 54:10; Eze 34:25; Mal 2:4,5
25:13 [y]Ex 29:9 [z]Nu 16:46
25:15 [a]ver 18 [b]Nu 31:8; Jos 13:21
25:17 [c]Nu 31:1-3
25:18 [d]Nu 31:16

[e]23 Masoretic Text; with a different word division of the Hebrew *A people will gather from the north.*

The Second Census

26 After the plague the LORD
said to Moses and Eleazar
son of Aaron, the priest, 2"Take a
census[a] of the whole Israelite
community by families—all those
twenty years old or more who are
able to serve in the army[b] of Israel." 3So on the plains of Moab[c] by
the Jordan across from Jericho,[fd]
Moses and Eleazar the priest spoke
with them and said, 4"Take a census of the men twenty years old or
more, as the LORD commanded Moses."

These were the Israelites who
came out of Egypt:

5The descendants of Reuben, the
firstborn son of Israel, were:
through Hanoch,[e] the Ha-
nochite clan;
through Pallu,[f] the Palluite
clan;
6through Hezron, the Hezronite
clan;
through Carmi, the Carmite
clan.
7These were the clans of Reuben;
those numbered were 43,730.
8The son of Pallu was Eliab,
9and the sons of Eliab[g] were Nemuel, Dathan and Abiram. The same
Dathan and Abiram were the community[h] officials who rebelled
against Moses and Aaron and were
among Korah's followers when
they rebelled against the LORD.[i]
10The earth opened its mouth and
swallowed them along with Korah,
whose followers died when the fire
devoured the 250 men. And they
served as a warning sign.[j] 11The
line of Korah,[k] however, did not
die out.[l]

12The descendants of Simeon by
their clans were:
through Nemuel, the Nemuel-
ite clan;
through Jamin,[m] the Jaminite
clan;
through Jakin, the Jakinite
clan;
13through Zerah,[n] the Zerahite
clan;

26:2 [a]Ex 30:11-16; 38:25-26; Nu 1:2 [b]Nu 1:3
26:3 [c]Nu 33:48 [d]Nu 22:1
26:5 [e]Ge 46:9 [f]1Ch 5:3
26:9 [g]Nu 16:1 [h]Nu 1:16 [i]Nu 16:2
26:10 [j]Nu 16:35,38
26:11 [k]Ex 6:24 [l]Nu 16:33; Dt 24:16
26:12 [m]1Ch 4:24
26:13 [n]Ge 46:10
26:14 [o]Nu 1:23
26:15 [p]Ge 46:16
26:18 [q]Nu 1:25; Jos 13:24-28
26:19 [r]Ge 38:2-10; 46:12
26:20 [s]1Ch 2:3 [t]Jos 7:17
26:21 [u]Ru 4:19; 1Ch 2:9
26:22 [v]Nu 1:27
26:23 [w]Ge 46:13; 1Ch 7:1
26:24 [x]Ge 46:13

through Shaul, the Shaulite
clan.
14These were the clans of Simeon;
there were 22,200 men.[o]

15The descendants of Gad by their
clans were:
through Zephon,[p] the Zeph-
onite clan;
through Haggi, the Haggite
clan;
through Shuni, the Shunite
clan;
16through Ozni, the Oznite clan;
through Eri, the Erite clan;
17through Arodi,[g] the Arodite
clan;
through Areli, the Arelite clan.
18These were the clans of Gad;[q]
those numbered were 40,500.

19Er and Onan were sons of Judah,
but they died[r] in Canaan.
20The descendants of Judah by
their clans were:
through Shelah,[s] the Shelan-
ite clan;
through Perez, the Perezite
clan;
through Zerah, the Zerahite
clan.[t]
21The descendants of Perez
were:
through Hezron,[u] the Hezronite clan;
through Hamul, the Hamul-
ite clan.
22These were the clans of Judah;[v]
those numbered were 76,500.

23The descendants of Issachar by
their clans were:
through Tola,[w] the Tolaite
clan;
through Puah, the Puite[h]
clan;
24through Jashub,[x] the Jashub-
ite clan;
through Shimron, the Shim-
ronite clan.
25These were the clans of Issa-

[f]3 Hebrew *Jordan of Jericho*; possibly an ancient name for the Jordan River; also in verse 63 [g]17 Samaritan Pentateuch and Syriac (see also Gen. 46:16); Masoretic Text *Arod* [h]23 Samaritan Pentateuch, Septuagint, Vulgate and Syriac (see also 1 Chron. 7:1); Masoretic Text *through Puvah, the Punite*

char;[a] those numbered were 64,-
300.

26The descendants of Zebulun by
their clans were:
through Sered, the Seredite
clan;
through Elon, the Elonite
clan;
through Jahleel, the Jahleelite
clan.
27These were the clans of Zebulun;[b] those numbered were 60,-
500.

28The descendants of Joseph by
their clans through Manasseh and
Ephraim were:

29The descendants of Manasseh:
through Makir,[c] the Makirite
clan (Makir was the father
of Gilead[d]);
through Gilead, the Gileadite
clan.
30These were the descendants of
Gilead:
through Iezer,[e] the Iezerite
clan;
through Helek, the Helekite
clan;
31through Asriel, the Asrielite
clan;
through Shechem, the She-
chemite clan;
32through Shemida, the She-
midaite clan;
through Hepher, the He-
pherite clan.
33(Zelophehad[f] son of Hepher had no sons; he had
only daughters, whose
names were Mahlah, Noah,
Hoglah, Milcah and Tir-
zah.)[g]
34These were the clans of Manasseh; those numbered were 52,-
700.[h]

35These were the descendants of
Ephraim by their clans:
through Shuthelah, the Shu-
thelahite clan;
through Beker, the Bekerite
clan;
through Tahan, the Tahanite
clan.
36These were the descendants of
Shuthelah:
through Eran, the Eranite
clan.
37These were the clans of Ephraim;[i] those numbered were 32,500.

These were the descendants of Joseph by their clans.

38The descendants of Benjamin[j]
by their clans were:
through Bela, the Belaite clan;
through Ashbel, the Ashbelite
clan;
through Ahiram, the Ahiram-
ite clan;
39through Shupham,[i] the Shu-
phamite clan;
through Hupham, the Hu-
phamite clan.
40The descendants of Bela
through Ard[k] and Naaman
were:
through Ard,[j] the Ardite
clan;
through Naaman, the Naa-
mite clan.
41These were the clans of Benjamin;[l] those numbered were 45,-
600.

42These were the descendants of
Dan by their clans:
through Shuham,[m] the Shuhamite clan.
These were the clans of Dan: 43All
of them were Shuhamite clans; and
those numbered were 64,400.

44The descendants of Asher by
their clans were:
through Imnah, the Imnite
clan;
through Ishvi, the Ishvite clan;
through Beriah, the Beriite
clan;
45and through the descendants
of Beriah:
through Heber, the Heber-
ite clan;
through Malkiel, the Malki-
elite clan.
46(Asher had a daughter named
Serah.)

26:25 [a]Nu 1:29
26:27 [b]Nu 1:31
26:29 [c]Jos 17:1 [d]Jdg 11:1
26:30 [e]Jos 17:2; Jdg 6:11
26:33 [f]Nu 27:1 [g]Nu 36:11
26:34 [h]Nu 1:35
26:37 [i]Nu 1:33
26:38 [j]Ge 46:21; 1Ch 7:6
26:40 [k]Ge 46:21; 1Ch 8:3
26:41 [l]Nu 1:37
26:42 [m]Ge 46:23

i39 A few manuscripts of the Masoretic Text, Samaritan Pentateuch, Vulgate and Syriac (see also Septuagint); most manuscripts of the Masoretic Text *Shephupham* j40 Samaritan Pentateuch and Vulgate (see also Septuagint); Masoretic Text does not have *through Ard*.

47These were the clans of Asher;[a]
those numbered were 53,400.

48The descendants of Naphtali[b]
by their clans were:
through Jahzeel, the Jahzeel-
ite clan;
through Guni, the Gunite
clan;
49through Jezer, the Jezerite
clan;
through Shillem, the Shillem-
ite clan.
50These were the clans of Naphtali;[c] those numbered were 45,400.

51The total number of the men of
Israel was 601,730.[d]

52The LORD said to Moses,
53"The land is to be allotted to
them as an inheritance based on
the number of names.[e] 54To a larger group give a larger inheritance,
and to a smaller group a smaller
one; each is to receive its inheritance according to the number[f] of
those listed. 55Be sure that the
land is distributed by lot.[g] What
each group inherits will be according to the names for its ancestral
tribe. 56Each inheritance is to be
distributed by lot among the larger
and smaller groups."

57These were the Levites[h] who
were counted by their clans:
through Gershon, the Ger-
shonite clan;
through Kohath, the Kohathite clan;
through Merari, the Merarite
clan.
58These also were Levite clans:
the Libnite clan,
the Hebronite clan,
the Mahlite clan,
the Mushite clan,
the Korahite clan.
(Kohath was the forefather of
Amram;[i] 59the name of Amram's wife was Jochebed,[j] a
descendant of Levi, who was
born to the Levites[k] in Egypt.
To Amram she bore Aaron,
Moses[k] and their sister Miriam. 60Aaron was the father of
Nadab and Abihu, Eleazar and

26:47 [a]Nu 1:41
26:48 [b]Ge 46:24; 1Ch 7:13
26:50 [c]Nu 1:43
26:51 [d]Ex 12:37; 38:26; Nu 1:46; 11:21
26:53 [e]Jos 11:23; 14:1; Eze 45:8
26:54 [f]Nu 33:54
26:55 [g]Nu 34:14
26:57 [h]Ge 46:11; Ex 6:16-19
26:58 [i]Ex 6:20
26:59 [j]Ex 2:1 [k]Ex 6:20
26:60 [l]Nu 3:2
26:61 [m]Lev 10:1-2 [n]Nu 3:4
26:62 [o]Nu 3:39 [p]Nu 1:47 [q]Nu 18:23 [r]Nu 2:33; Dt 10:9
26:63 [s]ver 3
26:64 [t]Nu 14:29; Dt 2:14-15; Heb 3:17
26:65 [u]Nu 14:28; 1Co 10:5 [v]Jos 14:6-10
27:1 [w]Nu 26:33 [x]Jos 17:2,3 [y]Nu 36:1
27:3 [z]Nu 26:65 [a]Nu 16:2 [b]Nu 26:33
27:5 [c]Ex 18:19 [d]Nu 9:8

Ithamar.[l] 61But Nadab and
Abihu[m] died when they made
an offering before the LORD
with unauthorized fire.)[n]

62All the male Levites a month old
or more numbered 23,000.[o] They
were not counted[p] along with the
other Israelites because they received no inheritance[q] among
them.[r]

63These are the ones counted by
Moses and Eleazar the priest when
they counted the Israelites on the
plains of Moab[s] by the Jordan
across from Jericho. 64Not one of
them was among those counted[t]
by Moses and Aaron the priest
when they counted the Israelites in
the Desert of Sinai. 65For the LORD
had told those Israelites they
would surely die in the desert,[u]
and not one of them was left except
Caleb son of Jephunneh and Joshua son of Nun.[v]

Zelophehad's Daughters

27:1–11pp — Nu 36:1-12

27 The daughters of Zelophehad[w] son of Hepher,[x] the
son of Gilead, the son of Makir,[y]
the son of Manasseh, belonged to
the clans of Manasseh son of Joseph. The names of the daughters
were Mahlah, Noah, Hoglah, Milcah and Tirzah. They approached
2the entrance to the Tent of Meeting and stood before Moses, Eleazar the priest, the leaders and the
whole assembly, and said, 3"Our
father died in the desert.[z] He was
not among Korah's followers, who
banded together against the
LORD,[a] but he died for his own sin
and left no sons.[b] 4Why should our
father's name disappear from his
clan because he had no son? Give
us property among our father's relatives."

5So Moses brought their case[c]
before the LORD[d] 6and the LORD
said to him, 7"What Zelophehad's
daughters are saying is right. You
must certainly give them property

[k]59 Or *Jochebed, a daughter of Levi, who was born to Levi*

as an inheritance[a] among their father's relatives and turn their father's inheritance over to them.[b]
8"Say to the Israelites, 'If a man
dies and leaves no son, turn his inheritance over to his daughter. 9If
he has no daughter, give his inheritance to his brothers. 10If he has no
brothers, give his inheritance to his
father's brothers. 11If his father
had no brothers, give his inheritance to the nearest relative in his
clan, that he may possess it. This is
to be a legal requirement[c] for the
Israelites, as the LORD commanded
Moses.' "

Joshua to Succeed Moses

12Then the LORD said to Moses,
"Go up this mountain in the Abarim range[d] and see the land[e] I
have given the Israelites. 13After
you have seen it, you too will be
gathered to your people,[f] as your
brother Aaron[g] was, 14for when
the community rebelled at the waters in the Desert of Zin, both of
you disobeyed my command to
honor me as holy[h] before their
eyes." (These were the waters of
Meribah[i] Kadesh, in the Desert of
Zin.)
15Moses said to the LORD,
16"May the LORD, the God of the
spirits of all mankind,[j] appoint a
man over this community 17to go
out and come in before them, one
who will lead them out and bring
them in, so the LORD's people will
not be like sheep without a shepherd."[k]
18So the LORD said to Moses,
"Take Joshua son of Nun, a man in
whom is the spirit,[l][l] and lay your
hand on him.[m] 19Have him stand
before Eleazar the priest and the
entire assembly and commission
him[n] in their presence.[o] 20Give
him some of your authority so the
whole Israelite community will
obey him.[p] 21He is to stand before
Eleazar the priest, who will obtain
decisions for him by inquiring[q] of
the Urim[r] before the LORD. At his
command he and the entire community of the Israelites will go out,
and at his command they will come
in."
22Moses did as the LORD commanded him. He took Joshua and
had him stand before Eleazar the
priest and the whole assembly.
23Then he laid his hands on him
and commissioned him, as the
LORD instructed through Moses.

Daily Offerings

28 The LORD said to Moses,
2"Give this command to the
Israelites and say to them: 'See
that you present to me at the appointed time the food[s] for my offerings made by fire, as an aroma
pleasing to me.' 3Say to them: 'This
is the offering made by fire that you
are to present to the LORD: two
lambs a year old without defect, as
a regular burnt offering each day.[t]
4Prepare one lamb in the morning
and the other at twilight, 5together
with a grain offering of a tenth of an
ephah[m] of fine flour mixed with a
quarter of a hin[n] of oil[u] from
pressed olives. 6This is the regular
burnt offering instituted at Mount
Sinai[v] as a pleasing aroma, an offering made to the LORD by fire.
7The accompanying drink offering[w] is to be a quarter of a hin of
fermented drink with each lamb.
Pour out the drink offering to the
LORD at the sanctuary.[x] 8Prepare
the second lamb at twilight, along
with the same kind of grain offering
and drink offering that you prepare
in the morning. This is an offering
made by fire, an aroma pleasing to
the LORD.[y]

Sabbath Offerings

9" 'On the Sabbath[z] day, make
an offering of two lambs a year old
without defect, together with its
drink offering and a grain offering
of two-tenths of an ephah[o][a] of
fine flour mixed with oil. 10This is
the burnt offering for every Sab-

[l]18 Or *Spirit* [m]5 That is, probably about 2 quarts (about 2 liters); also in verses 13, 21 and 29 [n]5 That is, probably about 1 quart (about 1 liter); also in verses 7 and 14
[o]9 That is, probably about 4 quarts (about 4.5 liters); also in verses 12, 20 and 28

27:7 [a]Job 42:15 [b]Jos 17:4
27:11 [c]Nu 35:29
27:12 [d]Nu 33:47; Jer 22:20 [e]Dt 3:23-27; 32:48-52
27:13 [f]Nu 31:2 [g]Nu 20:28
27:14 [h]Nu 20:12 [i]Ex 17:7; Dt 32:51; Ps 106:32
27:16 [j]Nu 16:22
27:17 [k]Dt 31:2; 1Ki 22:17; Eze 34:5; Zec 10:2; Mt 9:36; Mk 6:34
27:18 [l]Ge 41:38; Nu 11:25-29 [m]ver 23; Dt 34:9
27:19 [n]Dt 3:28; 31:14,23 [o]Dt 31:7
27:20 [p]Jos 1:16,17
27:21 [q]Jos 9:14 [r]Ex 28:30
28:2 [s]Lev 3:11
28:3 [t]Ex 29:38
28:5 [u]Lev 2:1; Nu 15:4
28:6 [v]Ex 19:3
28:7 [w]Ex 29:41 [x]Lev 3:7
28:8 [y]Lev 1:9
28:9 [z]Ex 20:10 [a]Lev 23:13

bath, in addition to the regular
burnt offering[a] and its drink offering.

Monthly Offerings

11" 'On the first of every
month,[b] present to the LORD a
burnt offering of two young bulls,
one ram and seven male lambs a
year old, all without defect.[c]
12With each bull there is to be a
grain offering[d] of three-tenths of
an ephah[p][e] of fine flour mixed
with oil; with the ram, a grain offering of two-tenths of an ephah of
fine flour mixed with oil; 13and
with each lamb, a grain offering[f]
of a tenth of an ephah of fine flour
mixed with oil. This is for a burnt
offering, a pleasing aroma, an offering made to the LORD by fire. 14With
each bull there is to be a drink offering[g] of half a hin[q] of wine; with
the ram, a third of a hin[r]; and with
each lamb, a quarter of a hin. This
is the monthly burnt offering to be
made at each new moon[h] during
the year. 15Besides the regular
burnt offering[i] with its drink offering, one male goat is to be presented to the LORD as a sin offering.[j]

The Passover

28:16–25pp — Ex 12:14–20; Lev 23:4–8; Dt 16:1–8

16" 'On the fourteenth day of the
first month the LORD's Passover[k] is
to be held. 17On the fifteenth day
of this month there is to be a festival; for seven days[l] eat bread
made without yeast.[m] 18On the
first day hold a sacred assembly
and do no regular work.[n] 19Present
to the LORD an offering made by
fire, a burnt offering of two young
bulls, one ram and seven male
lambs a year old, all without defect. 20With each bull prepare a
grain offering of three-tenths of an
ephah[o] of fine flour mixed with
oil; with the ram, two-tenths;
21and with each of the seven
lambs, one-tenth. 22Include one
male goat as a sin offering[p] to
make atonement for you.[q] 23Pre-
pare these in addition to the regular morning burnt offering. 24In

28:10 [a]ver 3
28:11 [b]Nu 10:10 [c]Lev 1:3
28:12 [d]Nu 15:6 [e]Nu 15:9
28:13 [f]Lev 6:14
28:14 [g]Nu 15:7 [h]Ezr 3:5
28:15 [i]ver 3,23,24 [j]Lev 4:3
28:16 [k]Ex 12:6,18; Lev 23:5; Dt 16:1
28:17 [l]Ex 12:19 [m]Ex 23:15; 34:18; Lev 23:6; Dt 16:3-8
28:18 [n]Ex 12:16; Lev 23:7
28:20 [o]Lev 14:10
28:22 [p]Ro 8:3 [q]Nu 15:28
28:26 [r]Ex 34:22 [s]Ex 23:16 [t]ver 18; Dt 16:10
28:29 [u]ver 13
28:31 [v]ver 3,19
29:1 [w]Lev 23:24
29:2 [x]Nu 28:2 [y]Nu 28:3

this way prepare the food for the
offering made by fire every day for
seven days as an aroma pleasing to
the LORD; it is to be prepared in addition to the regular burnt offering
and its drink offering. 25On the seventh day hold a sacred assembly
and do no regular work.

Feast of Weeks

28:26–31pp — Lev 23:15–22; Dt 16:9–12

26" 'On the day of firstfruits,[r]
when you present to the LORD an
offering of new grain during the
Feast of Weeks,[s] hold a sacred assembly and do no regular work.[t]
27Present a burnt offering of two
young bulls, one ram and seven
male lambs a year old as an aroma
pleasing to the LORD. 28With each
bull there is to be a grain offering of
three-tenths of an ephah of fine
flour mixed with oil; with the ram,
two-tenths; 29and with each of the
seven lambs, one-tenth.[u] 30In-
clude one male goat to make
atonement for you. 31Prepare these
together with their drink offerings,
in addition to the regular burnt offering[v] and its grain offering. Be
sure the animals are without defect.

Feast of Trumpets

29:1–6pp — Lev 23:23–25

29 " 'On the first day of the
seventh month hold a sa-
cred assembly and do no regular
work.[w] It is a day for you to sound
the trumpets. 2As an aroma pleasing to the LORD,[x] prepare a burnt
offering of one young bull, one ram
and seven male lambs a year old,
all without defect.[y] 3With the bull
prepare a grain offering of three-
tenths of an ephah[s] of fine flour
mixed with oil; with the ram,
two-tenths[t]; 4and with each of the

[p]*12* That is, probably about 6 quarts (about 6.5 liters); also in verses 20 and 28 [q]*14* That is, probably about 2 quarts (about 2 liters) [r]*14* That is, probably about 1 1/4 quarts (about 1.2 liters) [s]*3* That is, probably about 6 quarts (about 6.5 liters); also in verses 9 and 14 [t]*3* That is, probably about 4 quarts (about 4.5 liters); also in verses 9 and 14

seven lambs, one-tenth.[u] **5**Include one male goat[a] as a sin offering to make atonement for you. **6**These are in addition to the monthly[b] and daily burnt offerings[c] with their grain offerings and drink offerings as specified. They are offerings made to the LORD by fire—a pleasing aroma.

Day of Atonement

29:7–11pp — Lev 16:2–34; 23:26–32

7" 'On the tenth day of this seventh month hold a sacred assembly. You must deny yourselves[v][d] and do no work.[e] **8**Present as an aroma pleasing to the LORD a burnt offering of one young bull, one ram and seven male lambs a year old, all without defect. **9**With the bull prepare a grain offering[f] of three-tenths of an ephah of fine flour mixed with oil; with the ram, two-tenths; **10**and with each of the seven lambs, one-tenth.[g] **11**Include one male goat as a sin offering, in addition to the sin offering for atonement and the regular burnt offering[h] with its grain offering, and their drink offerings.

Feast of Tabernacles

29:12–39pp — Lev 23:33–43; Dt 16:13–17

12" 'On the fifteenth day of the seventh[i] month,[j] hold a sacred assembly and do no regular work. Celebrate a festival to the LORD for seven days. **13**Present an offering made by fire as an aroma pleasing to the LORD, a burnt offering of thirteen young bulls, two rams and fourteen male lambs a year old, all without defect. **14**With each of the thirteen bulls prepare a grain offering[k] of three-tenths of an ephah of fine flour mixed with oil; with each of the two rams, two-tenths; **15**and with each of the fourteen lambs, one-tenth. **16**Include one male goat as a sin offering, in addition to the regular burnt offering with its grain offering and drink offering.[l]

17" 'On the second day[m] prepare twelve young bulls, two rams and fourteen male lambs a year old, all without defect.[n] **18**With the bulls, rams and lambs, prepare their grain offerings[o] and drink offerings[p] according to the number specified.[q] **19**Include one male goat as a sin offering,[r] in addition to the regular burnt offering with its grain offering, and their drink offerings.

20" 'On the third day prepare eleven bulls, two rams and fourteen male lambs a year old, all without defect.[s] **21**With the bulls, rams and lambs, prepare their grain offerings and drink offerings according to the number specified.[t] **22**Include one male goat as a sin offering, in addition to the regular burnt offering with its grain offering and drink offering.

23" 'On the fourth day prepare ten bulls, two rams and fourteen male lambs a year old, all without defect. **24**With the bulls, rams and lambs, prepare their grain offerings and drink offerings according to the number specified. **25**Include one male goat as a sin offering, in addition to the regular burnt offering with its grain offering and drink offering.

26" 'On the fifth day prepare nine bulls, two rams and fourteen male lambs a year old, all without defect. **27**With the bulls, rams and lambs, prepare their grain offerings and drink offerings according to the number specified. **28**Include one male goat as a sin offering, in addition to the regular burnt offering with its grain offering and drink offering.

29" 'On the sixth day prepare eight bulls, two rams and fourteen male lambs a year old, all without defect. **30**With the bulls, rams and lambs, prepare their grain offerings and drink offerings according to the number specified. **31**Include one male goat as a sin offering, in addition to the regular burnt offering with its grain offering and drink offering.

32" 'On the seventh day prepare

29:5 [a]Nu 28:15
29:6 [b]Nu 28:11 [c]Nu 28:3
29:7 [d]Ac 27:9 [e]Ex 31:15; Lev 16:29; 23:26-32
29:9 [f]ver 3,18
29:10 [g]Nu 28:13
29:11 [h]Lev 16:3; Nu 28:3
29:12 [i]1Ki 8:2 [j]Lev 23:24
29:14 [k]ver 3
29:16 [l]ver 6
29:17 [m]Lev 23:36 [n]Nu 28:3
29:18 [o]ver 9 [p]Nu 28:7 [q]Nu 15:4-12
29:19 [r]Nu 28:15
29:20 [s]ver 17
29:21 [t]ver 18

[u]4 That is, probably about 2 quarts (about 2 liters); also in verses 10 and 15 [v]7 Or *must fast*

seven bulls, two rams and fourteen
male lambs a year old, all without
defect. 33With the bulls, rams and
lambs, prepare their grain offerings
and drink offerings according to
the number specified. 34Include
one male goat as a sin offering, in
addition to the regular burnt offering with its grain offering and drink
offering.

35" 'On the eighth day hold an
assembly[a] and do no regular work.
36Present an offering made by fire
as an aroma pleasing to the LORD,[b]
a burnt offering of one bull, one
ram and seven male lambs a year
old,[c] all without defect. 37With
the bull, the ram and the lambs,
prepare their grain offerings and
drink offerings according to the
number specified. 38Include one
male goat as a sin offering, in addition to the regular burnt offering
with its grain offering and drink offering.

39" 'In addition to what you
vow[d] and your freewill offerings,
prepare these for the LORD at your
appointed feasts:[e] your burnt offerings,[f] grain offerings, drink offerings and fellowship offerings.[w] ' "

40Moses told the Israelites all
that the LORD commanded him.

Vows

30 Moses said to the heads of
the tribes of Israel:[g] "This
is what the LORD commands:
2When a man makes a vow to the
LORD or takes an oath to obligate
himself by a pledge, he must not
break his word but must do everything he said.[h]

3"When a young woman still living in her father's house makes a
vow to the LORD or obligates herself
by a pledge 4and her father hears
about her vow or pledge but says
nothing to her, then all her vows
and every pledge by which she obligated herself will stand.[i] 5But if
her father forbids her when he
hears about it, none of her vows or
the pledges by which she obligated
herself will stand; the LORD will release her because her father has
forbidden her.

6"If she marries after she makes
a vow[j] or after her lips utter a rash
promise by which she obligates
herself 7and her husband hears
about it but says nothing to her,
then her vows or the pledges by
which she obligated herself will
stand. 8But if her husband[k] forbids her when he hears about it, he
nullifies the vow that obligates her
or the rash promise by which she
obligates herself, and the LORD will
release her.

9"Any vow or obligation taken by
a widow or divorced woman will be
binding on her.

10"If a woman living with her
husband makes a vow or obligates
herself by a pledge under oath
11and her husband hears about it
but says nothing to her and does
not forbid her, then all her vows or
the pledges by which she obligated
herself will stand. 12But if her husband nullifies them when he hears
about them, then none of the vows
or pledges that came from her lips
will stand.[l] Her husband has nul-
lified them, and the LORD will release her. 13Her husband may confirm or nullify any vow she makes
or any sworn pledge to deny herself. 14But if her husband says
nothing to her about it from day to
day, then he confirms all her vows
or the pledges binding on her. He
confirms them by saying nothing to
her when he hears about them.
15If, however, he nullifies them
some time after he hears about
them, then he is responsible for her
guilt."

16These are the regulations the
LORD gave Moses concerning relationships between a man and his
wife, and between a father and his
young daughter still living in his
house.

Vengeance on the Midianites

31 The LORD said to Moses,
2"Take vengeance on the
Midianites[m] for the Israelites. Af-

29:35 [a] Lev 23:36
29:36 [b] Lev 1:9 [c] ver 2
29:39 [d] Nu 6:2 [e] Lev 23:2 [f] Lev 1:3; 1Ch 23:31; 2Ch 31:3
30:1 [g] Nu 1:4
30:2 [h] Dt 23:21-23; Jdg 11:35; Job 22:27; Ps 22:25; 50:14; 116:14; Pr 20:25; Ecc 5:4,5; Jnh 1:16
30:4 [i] ver 7
30:6 [j] Lev 5:4
30:8 [k] Ge 3:16
30:12 [l] Eph 5:22; Col 3:18
31:2 [m] Ge 25:2

[w]39 Traditionally *peace offerings*

ter that, you will be gathered to your people.[a]"

3So Moses said to the people, "Arm some of your men to go to war against the Midianites and to carry out the LORD's vengeance[b] on them. 4Send into battle a thousand men from each of the tribes of Israel." 5So twelve thousand men armed for battle, a thousand from each tribe, were supplied from the clans of Israel. 6Moses sent them into battle, a thousand from each tribe, along with Phinehas son of Eleazar, the priest, who took with him articles from the sanctuary[c] and the trumpets[d] for signaling.

7They fought against Midian, as the LORD commanded Moses, and killed every man.[e] 8Among their victims were Evi, Rekem, Zur, Hur and Reba[f]—the five kings of Midian.[g] They also killed Balaam son of Beor with the sword.[h] 9The Israelites captured the Midianite women and children and took all the Midianite herds, flocks and goods as plunder. 10They burned all the towns where the Midianites had settled, as well as all their camps.[i] 11They took all the plunder and spoils, including the people and animals,[j] 12and brought the captives, spoils and plunder to Moses and Eleazar the priest and the Israelite assembly[k] at their camp on the plains of Moab, by the Jordan across from Jericho.[x]

13Moses, Eleazar the priest and all the leaders of the community went to meet them outside the camp. 14Moses was angry with the officers of the army[l]—the commanders of thousands and commanders of hundreds—who returned from the battle.

15"Have you allowed all the women to live?" he asked them. 16"They were the ones who followed Balaam's advice[m] and were the means of turning the Israelites away from the LORD in what happened at Peor,[n] so that a plague struck the LORD's people. 17Now kill all the boys. And kill every woman who has slept with a man,[o] 18but save for yourselves every girl who has never slept with a man.

19"All of you who have killed anyone or touched anyone who was killed[p] must stay outside the camp seven days. On the third and seventh days you must purify yourselves[q] and your captives. 20Purify every garment[r] as well as everything made of leather, goat hair or wood."

21Then Eleazar the priest said to the soldiers who had gone into battle, "This is the requirement of the law that the LORD gave Moses: 22Gold, silver, bronze, iron,[s] tin, lead 23and anything else that can withstand fire must be put through the fire,[t] and then it will be clean. But it must also be purified with the water of cleansing.[u] And whatever cannot withstand fire must be put through that water. 24On the seventh day wash your clothes and you will be clean.[v] Then you may come into the camp."

Dividing the Spoils

25The LORD said to Moses, 26"You and Eleazar the priest and the family heads of the community are to count all the people[w] and animals that were captured. 27Divide[x] the spoils between the soldiers who took part in the battle and the rest of the community. 28From the soldiers who fought in the battle, set apart as tribute for the LORD[y] one out of every five hundred, whether persons, cattle, donkeys, sheep or goats. 29Take this tribute from their half share and give it to Eleazar the priest as the LORD's part. 30From the Israelites' half, select one out of every fifty, whether persons, cattle, donkeys, sheep, goats or other animals. Give them to the Levites, who are responsible for the care of the LORD's tabernacle.[z]" 31So Moses and Eleazar the priest did as the LORD commanded Moses.

32The plunder remaining from the spoils that the soldiers took

31:2 [a]Nu 20:26; 27:13
31:3 [b]Jdg 11:36; 1Sa 24:12; 2Sa 4:8; 22:48; Ps 94:1; 149:7
31:6 [c]Nu 14:44 [d]Nu 10:9
31:7 [e]Dt 20:13; Jdg 21:11; 1Ki 11:15,16
31:8 [f]Jos 13:21 [g]Nu 25:15 [h]Jos 13:22
31:10 [i]Ge 25:16; 1Ch 6:54; Ps 69:25; Eze 25:4
31:11 [j]Dt 20:14
31:12 [k]Nu 27:2
31:14 [l]ver 48; Ex 18:21; Dt 1:15
31:16 [m]2Pe 2:15; Rev 2:14 [n]Nu 25:1-9
31:17 [o]Dt 7:2; 20:16-18; Jdg 21:11
31:19 [p]Nu 19:16 [q]Nu 19:12
31:20 [r]Nu 19:19
31:22 [s]Jos 6:19; 22:8
31:23 [t]1Co 3:13 [u]Nu 19:9,17
31:24 [v]Lev 11:25
31:26 [w]Nu 1:19
31:27 [x]Jos 22:8; 1Sa 30:24
31:28 [y]Nu 18:21
31:30 [z]Nu 3:7; 18:3

[x]12 Hebrew *Jordan of Jericho*; possibly an ancient name for the Jordan River

was 675,000 sheep, **33**72,000 cattle, **34**61,000 donkeys **35**and 32,-
000 women who had never slept
with a man.
36The half share of those who
fought in the battle was:

337,500 sheep, **37**of which the
tribute for the LORD[a] was
675;
3836,000 cattle, of which the
tribute for the LORD was
72;
3930,500 donkeys, of which the
tribute for the LORD was
61;
4016,000 people, of which the
tribute for the LORD was
32.

41Moses gave the tribute to Eleazar the priest as the LORD's part,[b]
as the LORD commanded Moses.
42The half belonging to the Israelites, which Moses set apart from
that of the fighting men— **43**the
community's half—was 337,500
sheep, **44**36,000 cattle, **45**30,500
donkeys **46**and 16,000 people.
47From the Israelites' half, Moses
selected one out of every fifty persons and animals, as the LORD commanded him, and gave them to the
Levites, who were responsible for
the care of the LORD's tabernacle.
48Then the officers who were
over the units of the army—the
commanders of thousands and
commanders of hundreds—went
to Moses **49**and said to him, "Your
servants have counted the soldiers
under our command, and not one
is missing.[c] **50**So we have brought
as an offering to the LORD the gold
articles each of us acquired—arm-
lets, bracelets, signet rings, earrings and necklaces—to make
atonement for ourselves[d] before
the LORD."
51Moses and Eleazar the priest
accepted from them the gold—all
the crafted articles. **52**All the gold
from the commanders of thousands and commanders of hundreds that Moses and Eleazar presented as a gift to the LORD weighed
16,750 shekels.[y] **53**Each soldier
had taken plunder[e] for himself.
54Moses and Eleazar the priest accepted the gold from the commanders of thousands and commanders of hundreds and brought
it into the Tent of Meeting as a memorial[f] for the Israelites before
the LORD.

The Transjordan Tribes

32 The Reubenites and Gadites, who had very large
herds and flocks, saw that the
lands of Jazer[g] and Gilead were
suitable for livestock.[h] **2**So they
came to Moses and Eleazar the
priest and to the leaders of the
community, and said, **3**"Ataroth,[i]
Dibon, Jazer, Nimrah,[j] Heshbon,
Elealeh,[k] Sebam, Nebo and
Beon[l]— **4**the land the LORD subdued[m] before the people of Israel
—are suitable for livestock,[n] and
your servants have livestock. **5**If we
have found favor in your eyes," they
said, "let this land be given to your
servants as our possession. Do not
make us cross the Jordan."
6Moses said to the Gadites and
Reubenites, "Shall your countrymen go to war while you sit here?
7Why do you discourage the Israelites from going over into the land
the LORD has given them?[o] **8**This is
what your fathers did when I sent
them from Kadesh Barnea to look
over the land.[p] **9**After they went up
to the Valley of Eshcol[q] and
viewed the land, they discouraged
the Israelites from entering the
land the LORD had given them.
10The LORD's anger was aroused[r]
that day and he swore this oath:
11'Because they have not followed
me wholeheartedly, not one of the
men twenty years old or more[s]
who came up out of Egypt will see
the land I promised on oath[t] to
Abraham, Isaac and Jacob[u]—
12not one except Caleb son of Jephunneh the Kenizzite and Joshua
son of Nun, for they followed the
LORD wholeheartedly.'[v] **13**The
LORD's anger burned against Israel[w] and he made them wander in

31:37 [a]ver 38-41
31:41 [b]Nu 5:9; 18:8
31:49 [c]Jer 23:4
31:50 [d]Ex 30:16
31:53 [e]Dt 20:14
31:54 [f]Ex 28:12
32:1 [g]Nu 21:32 [h]Ex 12:38
32:3 [i]ver 34 [j]ver 36 [k]ver 37; Isa 15:4; 16:9; Jer 48:34 [l]ver 38; Jos 13:17; Eze 25:9
32:4 [m]Nu 21:34 [n]Ex 12:38
32:7 [o]Nu 13:27-14:4
32:8 [p]Nu 13:3,26; Dt 1:19-25
32:9 [q]Nu 13:23; Dt 1:24
32:10 [r]Nu 11:1
32:11 [s]Ex 30:14 [t]Nu 14:23 [u]Nu 14:28-30
32:12 [v]Nu 14:24,30; Dt 1:36; Ps 63:8
32:13 [w]Ex 4:14

[y]*52* That is, about 420 pounds (about 190 kilograms)

the desert forty years, until the whole generation of those who had done evil in his sight was gone.[a]

14"And here you are, a brood of sinners, standing in the place of your fathers and making the LORD even more angry with Israel.[b] **15**If you turn away from following him, he will again leave all this people in the desert, and you will be the cause of their destruction.[c]"

16Then they came up to him and said, "We would like to build pens here for our livestock[d] and cities for our women and children. **17**But we are ready to arm ourselves and go ahead of the Israelites[e] until we have brought them to their place.[f] Meanwhile our women and children will live in fortified cities, for protection from the inhabitants of the land. **18**We will not return to our homes until every Israelite has received his inheritance.[g] **19**We will not receive any inheritance with them on the other side of the Jordan, because our inheritance has come to us on the east side of the Jordan."[h]

20Then Moses said to them, "If you will do this—if you will arm yourselves before the LORD for battle,[i] **21**and if all of you will go armed over the Jordan before the LORD until he has driven his enemies out before him— **22**then when the land is subdued before the LORD, you may return[j] and be free from your obligation to the LORD and to Israel. And this land will be your possession before the LORD.[k]

23"But if you fail to do this, you will be sinning against the LORD; and you may be sure that your sin will find you out.[l] **24**Build cities for your women and children, and pens for your flocks,[m] but do what you have promised.[n]"

25The Gadites and Reubenites said to Moses, "We your servants will do as our lord commands. **26**Our children and wives, our flocks and herds will remain here in the cities of Gilead.[o] **27**But your servants, every man armed for battle, will cross over to fight before the LORD, just as our lord says."

28Then Moses gave orders about them[p] to Eleazar the priest and Joshua son of Nun and to the family heads of the Israelite tribes. **29**He said to them, "If the Gadites and Reubenites, every man armed for battle, cross over the Jordan with you before the LORD, then when the land is subdued before you, give them the land of Gilead as their possession. **30**But if they do not cross over with you armed, they must accept their possession with you in Canaan."

31The Gadites and Reubenites answered, "Your servants will do what the LORD has said.[q] **32**We will cross over before the LORD into Canaan armed, but the property we inherit will be on this side of the Jordan."

33Then Moses gave to the Gadites,[r] the Reubenites and the half-tribe of Manasseh son of Joseph the kingdom of Sihon king of the Amorites[s] and the kingdom of Og king of Bashan—the whole land with its cities and the territory around them.[t]

34The Gadites built up Dibon, Ataroth, Aroer,[u] **35**Atroth Shophan, Jazer,[v] Jogbehah, **36**Beth Nimrah[w] and Beth Haran as fortified cities, and built pens for their flocks. **37**And the Reubenites rebuilt Heshbon, Elealeh and Kiriathaim, **38**as well as Nebo[x] and Baal Meon (these names were changed) and Sibmah. They gave names to the cities they rebuilt.

39The descendants of Makir[y] son of Manasseh went to Gilead, captured it and drove out the Amorites who were there. **40**So Moses gave Gilead to the Makirites,[z] the descendants of Manasseh, and they settled there. **41**Jair, a descendant of Manasseh, captured their settlements and called them Havvoth Jair.[z][a] **42**And Nobah captured Kenath and its surrounding settlements and called it Nobah after himself.[b]

32:13 [a]Nu 14:28-35; 26:64,65
32:14 [b]ver 10; Dt 1:34; Ps 78:59
32:15 [c]Dt 30:17-18; 2Ch 7:20
32:16 [d]Ex 12:38; Dt 3:19
32:17 [e]Jos 4:12,13 [f]Nu 22:4; Dt 3:20
32:18 [g]Jos 22:1-4
32:19 [h]Jos 12:1
32:20 [i]Dt 3:18
32:22 [j]Jos 22:4 [k]Dt 3:18-20
32:23 [l]Ge 4:7; 44:16; Isa 59:12
32:24 [m]ver 1,16 [n]Nu 30:2
32:26 [o]Jos 1:14
32:28 [p]Dt 3:18-20; Jos 1:13
32:31 [q]ver 29
32:33 [r]Jos 13:24-28; 1Sa 13:7 [s]Dt 2:26 [t]Nu 21:24; Jos 12:6
32:34 [u]Dt 2:36; Jdg 11:26
32:35 [v]ver 3
32:36 [w]ver 3
32:38 [x]ver 3; Isa 15:2; Jer 48:1,22
32:39 [y]Ge 50:23
32:40 [z]Dt 3:15; Jos 17:1
32:41 [a]Dt 3:14; Jos 13:30; Jdg 10:4; 1Ch 2:23
32:42 [b]2Sa 18:18; Ps 49:11

[z]41 *Or them the settlements of Jair*

Stages in Israel's Journey

33 Here are the stages in the
journey of the Israelites
when they came out of Egypt[a] by
divisions under the leadership of
Moses and Aaron.[b] 2 At the LORD's
command Moses recorded the
stages in their journey. This is their
journey by stages:

3 The Israelites set out from
Rameses on the fifteenth day
of the first month, the day after the Passover.[c] They
marched out boldly[d] in full
view of all the Egyptians, 4 who
were burying all their firstborn, whom the LORD had
struck down among them; for
the LORD had brought judgment on their gods.[e]
5 The Israelites left Rameses
and camped at Succoth.[f]
6 They left Succoth and
camped at Etham, on the edge
of the desert.[g]
7 They left Etham, turned
back to Pi Hahiroth, to the
east of Baal Zephon,[h] and
camped near Migdol.[i]
8 They left Pi Hahiroth[a] and
passed through the sea[j] into
the desert, and when they had
traveled for three days in the
Desert of Etham, they camped
at Marah.[k]
9 They left Marah and went
to Elim, where there were
twelve springs and seventy
palm trees, and they camped[l]
there.
10 They left Elim and
camped by the Red Sea.[b]
11 They left the Red Sea and
camped in the Desert of Sin.[m]
12 They left the Desert of Sin
and camped at Dophkah.
13 They left Dophkah and
camped at Alush.
14 They left Alush and
camped at Rephidim, where
there was no water for the people to drink.
15 They left Rephidim[n] and
camped in the Desert of Sinai.[o]
16 They left the Desert of Sinai and camped at Kibroth
Hattaavah.[p]
17 They left Kibroth Hattaavah and camped at Haze-
roth.[q]
18 They left Hazeroth and
camped at Rithmah.
19 They left Rithmah and
camped at Rimmon Perez.
20 They left Rimmon Perez
and camped at Libnah.[r]
21 They left Libnah and
camped at Rissah.
22 They left Rissah and
camped at Kehelathah.
23 They left Kehelathah and
camped at Mount Shepher.
24 They left Mount Shepher
and camped at Haradah.
25 They left Haradah and
camped at Makheloth.
26 They left Makheloth and
camped at Tahath.
27 They left Tahath and
camped at Terah.
28 They left Terah and
camped at Mithcah.
29 They left Mithcah and
camped at Hashmonah.
30 They left Hashmonah and
camped at Moseroth.[s]
31 They left Moseroth and
camped at Bene Jaakan.
32 They left Bene Jaakan
and camped at Hor Haggid-
gad.
33 They left Hor Haggidgad
and camped at Jotbathah.[t]
34 They left Jotbathah and
camped at Abronah.
35 They left Abronah and
camped at Ezion Geber.[u]
36 They left Ezion Geber and
camped at Kadesh, in the
Desert of Zin.[v]
37 They left Kadesh and
camped at Mount Hor,[w] on
the border of Edom.[x] 38 At the
LORD's command Aaron the
priest went up Mount Hor,
where he died[y] on the first
day of the fifth month of the

33:1 [a]Mic 6:4 [b]Ps 77:20
33:3 [c]Ex 13:4 [d]Ex 14:8
33:4 [e]Ex 12:12
33:5 [f]Ex 12:37
33:6 [g]Ex 13:20
33:7 [h]Ex 14:9 [i]Ex 14:2
33:8 [j]Ex 14:22 [k]Ex 15:23
33:9 [l]Ex 15:27
33:11 [m]Ex 16:1
33:15 [n]Ex 17:1 [o]Ex 19:1
33:16 [p]Nu 11:34
33:17 [q]Nu 11:35
33:20 [r]Jos 10:29
33:30 [s]Dt 10:6
33:33 [t]Dt 10:7
33:35 [u]Dt 2:8; 1Ki 9:26; 22:48
33:36 [v]Nu 20:1
33:37 [w]Nu 20:22 [x]Nu 20:16; 21:4
33:38 [y]Dt 10:6

[a]*8* Many manuscripts of the Masoretic Text, Samaritan Pentateuch and Vulgate; most manuscripts of the Masoretic Text *left from before Hahiroth* [b]*10* Hebrew *Yam Suph*; that is, Sea of Reeds, also in verse 11

fortieth year after the Israelites came out of Egypt.[a]
39Aaron was a hundred and
twenty-three years old when
he died on Mount Hor.
40The Canaanite king of
Arad,[b] who lived in the Negev
of Canaan, heard that the Israelites were coming.
41They left Mount Hor and
camped at Zalmonah.
42They left Zalmonah and
camped at Punon.
43They left Punon and
camped at Oboth.[c]
44They left Oboth and
camped at Iye Abarim, on the
border of Moab.[d]
45They left Iyim[c] and
camped at Dibon Gad.
46They left Dibon Gad and
camped at Almon Diblathaim.
47They left Almon Diblathaim and camped in the mountains of Abarim,[e] near Nebo.
48They left the mountains
of Abarim and camped on the
plains of Moab by the Jordan
across from Jericho.[d][f]
49There on the plains of Moab
they camped along the Jordan
from Beth Jeshimoth to Abel
Shittim.[g]

50On the plains of Moab by the
Jordan across from Jericho the
LORD said to Moses, 51"Speak to
the Israelites and say to them:
'When you cross the Jordan into
Canaan,[h] 52drive out all the inhabitants of the land before you. Destroy all their carved images and
their cast idols, and demolish all
their high places.[i] 53Take possession of the land and settle in it, for
I have given you the land to possess.[j] 54Distribute the land by lot,
according to your clans.[k] To a larger group give a larger inheritance,
and to a smaller group a smaller
one. Whatever falls to them by lot
will be theirs. Distribute it according to your ancestral tribes.
55" 'But if you do not drive out
the inhabitants of the land, those
you allow to remain will become
barbs in your eyes and thorns[l] in

33:38 [a]Nu 20:25-28
33:40 [b]Nu 21:1
33:43 [c]Nu 21:10
33:44 [d]Nu 21:11
33:47 [e]Nu 27:12
33:48 [f]Nu 22:1
33:49 [g]Nu 25:1
33:51 [h]Jos 3:17
33:52 [i]Ex 23:24; 34:13; Lev 26:1; Dt 7:2,5; 12:3; Jos 11:12; Ps 106:34-36
33:53 [j]Dt 11:31; Jos 21:43
33:54 [k]Nu 26:54
33:55 [l]Jos 23:13; Jdg 2:3; Ps 106:36
34:2 [m]Ge 17:8; Dt 1:7-8; Ps 78:54-55 [n]Eze 47:15
34:3 [o]Jos 15:1-3 [p]Ge 14:3
34:4 [q]Jos 15:3 [r]Nu 32:8
34:5 [s]Ge 15:18; Jos 15:4
34:7 [t]Eze 47:15-17
34:8 [u]Nu 13:21; Jos 13:5
34:11 [v]2Ki 23:33; Jer 39:5 [w]Dt 3:17; Jos 11:2; 13:27
34:13 [x]Jos 14:1-5

your sides. They will give you trouble in the land where you will live.
56And then I will do to you what I
plan to do to them.' "

Boundaries of Canaan

34 The LORD said to Moses,
2"Command the Israelites
and say to them: 'When you enter
Canaan, the land that will be allotted to you as an inheritance[m] will
have these boundaries:[n]

3" 'Your southern side will include some of the Desert of Zin[o]
along the border of Edom. On the
east, your southern boundary will
start from the end of the Salt
Sea,[e][p] 4cross south of Scorpion[f]
Pass,[q] continue on to Zin and go
south of Kadesh Barnea.[r] Then it
will go to Hazar Addar and over to
Azmon, 5where it will turn, join the
Wadi of Egypt[s] and end at the
Sea.[g]

6" 'Your western boundary will
be the coast of the Great Sea. This
will be your boundary on the west.
7" 'For your northern boundary,[t] run a line from the Great Sea
to Mount Hor 8and from Mount
Hor to Lebo[h] Hamath.[u] Then the
boundary will go to Zedad, 9contin-
ue to Ziphron and end at Hazar
Enan. This will be your boundary
on the north.
10" 'For your eastern boundary,
run a line from Hazar Enan to Shepham. 11The boundary will go
down from Shepham to Riblah[v] on
the east side of Ain and continue
along the slopes east of the Sea of
Kinnereth.[i][w] 12Then the boundary will go down along the Jordan
and end at the Salt Sea.
" 'This will be your land, with its
boundaries on every side.' "
13Moses commanded the Israelites: "Assign this land by lot as an
inheritance.[x] The LORD has or-

[c]*45* That is, Iye Abarim [d]*48* Hebrew *Jordan of Jericho*; possibly an ancient name for the Jordan River; also in verse 50
[e]*3* That is, the Dead Sea; also in verse 12
[f]*4* Hebrew *Akrabbim* [g]*5* That is, the Mediterranean; also in verses 6 and 7
[h]*8* Or *to the entrance to* [i]*11* That is, Galilee

dered that it be given to the nine and a half tribes, 14because the families of the tribe of Reuben, the tribe of Gad and the half-tribe of Manasseh have received their inheritance.[a] 15These two and a half tribes have received their inheritance on the east side of the Jordan of Jericho,[i] toward the sunrise."

16The LORD said to Moses, 17"These are the names of the men who are to assign the land for you as an inheritance: Eleazar the priest and Joshua[b] son of Nun. 18And appoint one leader from each tribe to help[c] assign the land. 19These are their names:

Caleb[d] son of Jephunneh,
from the tribe of Judah;[e]
20Shemuel son of Ammihud,
from the tribe of Simeon;[f]
21Elidad son of Kislon,
from the tribe of Benjamin;[g]
22Bukki son of Jogli,
the leader from the tribe of Dan;
23Hanniel son of Ephod,
the leader from the tribe of Manasseh son of Joseph;
24Kemuel son of Shiphtan,
the leader from the tribe of Ephraim son of Joseph;
25Elizaphan son of Parnach,
the leader from the tribe of Zebulun;
26Paltiel son of Azzan,
the leader from the tribe of Issachar;
27Ahihud son of Shelomi,
the leader from the tribe of Asher;[h]
28Pedahel son of Ammihud,
the leader from the tribe of Naphtali."

29These are the men the LORD commanded to assign the inheritance to the Israelites in the land of Canaan.

Towns for the Levites

35 On the plains of Moab by the Jordan across from Jericho,[k] the LORD said to Moses, 2"Command the Israelites to give the Levites towns to live in[i] from the inheritance the Israelites will possess. And give them pasturelands around the towns. 3Then they will have towns to live in and pasturelands for their cattle, flocks and all their other livestock.

4"The pasturelands around the towns that you give the Levites will extend out fifteen hundred feet[l] from the town wall. 5Outside the town, measure three thousand feet[m] on the east side, three thousand on the south side, three thousand on the west and three thousand on the north, with the town in the center. They will have this area as pastureland for the towns.

Cities of Refuge

35:6-34Ref – Dt 4:41-43; 19:1-14; Jos 20:1-9

6"Six of the towns you give the Levites will be cities of refuge, to which a person who has killed someone may flee.[j] In addition, give them forty-two other towns. 7In all you must give the Levites forty-eight towns, together with their pasturelands. 8The towns you give the Levites from the land the Israelites possess are to be given in proportion to the inheritance of each tribe: Take many towns from a tribe that has many, but few from one that has few."[k]

9Then the LORD said to Moses: 10"Speak to the Israelites and say to them: 'When you cross the Jordan into Canaan,[l] 11select some towns to be your cities of refuge, to which a person who has killed someone[m] accidentally[n] may flee. 12They will be places of refuge from the avenger,[o] so that a person accused of murder may not die before he stands trial before the assembly. 13These six towns you give will be your cities of refuge. 14Give three on this side of the Jordan and three in Canaan as cities of refuge. 15These six towns will be a place of refuge for Israelites, aliens and any

34:14 [a]Nu 32:33; Jos 14:3
34:17 [b]Jos 14:1
34:18 [c]Nu 1:4,16
34:19 [d]Nu 26:65 [e]Ge 29:35; Dt 33:7
34:20 [f]Ge 49:5
34:21 [g]Ge 49:27; Ps 68:27
34:27 [h]Nu 1:40
35:2 [i]Lev 25:32-34; Jos 14:3,4
35:6 [j]Jos 20:7-9; 21:3,13
35:8 [k]Nu 26:54; 33:54; Jos 21:1-42
35:10 [l]Jos 20:2
35:11 [m]ver 22-25 [n]Ex 21:13; Dt 19:1-13
35:12 [o]Dt 19:6; Jos 20:3

i15 *Jordan of Jericho* was possibly an ancient name for the Jordan River. k1 Hebrew *Jordan of Jericho*; possibly an ancient name for the Jordan River l4 Hebrew *a thousand cubits* (about 450 meters) m5 Hebrew *two thousand cubits* (about 900 meters)

other people living among them, so
that anyone who has killed another
accidentally can flee there.
16" 'If a man strikes someone
with an iron object so that he dies,
he is a murderer; the murderer
shall be put to death.[a] 17Or if anyone has a stone in his hand that
could kill, and he strikes someone
so that he dies, he is a murderer;
the murderer shall be put to death.
18Or if anyone has a wooden object
in his hand that could kill, and he
hits someone so that he dies, he is
a murderer; the murderer shall be
put to death. 19The avenger of
blood shall put the murderer to
death; when he meets him, he shall
put him to death.[b] 20If anyone
with malice aforethought shoves
another or throws something at
him intentionally[c] so that he dies
21or if in hostility he hits him with
his fist so that he dies, that person
shall be put to death; he is a murderer. The avenger of blood shall
put the murderer to death when he
meets him.
22" 'But if without hostility
someone suddenly shoves another
or throws something at him unintentionally[d] 23or, without seeing
him, drops a stone on him that
could kill him, and he dies, then
since he was not his enemy and he
did not intend to harm him, 24the
assembly[e] must judge between
him and the avenger of blood according to these regulations. 25The
assembly must protect the one accused of murder from the avenger
of blood and send him back to the
city of refuge to which he fled. He
must stay there until the death of
the high priest, who was anointed
with the holy oil.[f]
26" 'But if the accused ever goes
outside the limits of the city of refuge to which he has fled 27and the
avenger of blood finds him outside
the city, the avenger of blood may
kill the accused without being
guilty of murder. 28The accused
must stay in his city of refuge until
the death of the high priest; only
after the death of the high priest
may he return to his own property.

29" 'These are to be legal requirements[g] for you throughout
the generations to come, wherever
you live.
30" 'Anyone who kills a person is
to be put to death as a murderer
only on the testimony of witnesses.
But no one is to be put to death on
the testimony of only one witness.[h]
31" 'Do not accept a ransom for
the life of a murderer, who deserves
to die. He must surely be put to
death.
32" 'Do not accept a ransom for
anyone who has fled to a city of refuge and so allow him to go back
and live on his own land before the
death of the high priest.
33" 'Do not pollute the land
where you are. Bloodshed pollutes
the land,[i] and atonement cannot
be made for the land on which
blood has been shed, except by the
blood of the one who shed it. 34Do
not defile the land[j] where you live
and where I dwell,[k] for I, the LORD,
dwell among the Israelites.' "

Inheritance of Zelophehad's Daughters

36:1-12pp — Nu 27:1-11

36 The family heads of the
clan of Gilead[l] son of Makir, the son of Manasseh, who were
from the clans of the descendants
of Joseph, came and spoke before
Moses and the leaders,[m] the heads
of the Israelite families. 2They
said, "When the LORD commanded
my lord to give the land as an inheritance to the Israelites by lot, he ordered you to give the inheritance of
our brother Zelophehad[n] to his
daughters. 3Now suppose they
marry men from other Israelite
tribes; then their inheritance will
be taken from our ancestral inheritance and added to that of the tribe
they marry into. And so part of the
inheritance allotted to us will be
taken away. 4When the Year of Jubilee[o] for the Israelites comes,
their inheritance will be added to
that of the tribe into which they

35:16 [a] Ex 21:12; Lev 24:17
35:19 [b] ver 21
35:20 [c] Ge 4:8; Ex 21:14; Dt 19:11; 2Sa 3:27; 20:10
35:22 [d] ver 11; Ex 21:13
35:24 [e] ver 12; Jos 20:6
35:25 [f] Ex 29:7
35:29 [g] Nu 27:11
35:30 [h] ver 16; Dt 17:6; 19:15; Mt 18:16; Jn 7:51; 2Co 13:1; Heb 10:28
35:33 [i] Ge 9:6; Ps 106:38; Mic 4:11
35:34 [j] Lev 18:24,25 [k] Ex 29:45
36:1 [l] Nu 26:29 [m] Nu 27:2
36:2 [n] Nu 26:33; 27:1,7
36:4 [o] Lev 25:10

marry, and their property will be
taken from the tribal inheritance of
our forefathers."

5 Then at the LORD's command
Moses gave this order to the Israelites: "What the tribe of the descendants of Joseph is saying is right.
6 This is what the LORD commands
for Zelophehad's daughters: They
may marry anyone they please as
long as they marry within the tribal
clan of their father. 7 No inheritance[a] in Israel is to pass from
tribe to tribe, for every Israelite
shall keep the tribal land inherited
from his forefathers. 8 Every daughter who inherits land in any Israelite tribe must marry someone in
her father's tribal clan,[b] so that every Israelite will possess the inheritance of his fathers. 9 No inheritance may pass from tribe to tribe,
for each Israelite tribe is to keep
the land it inherits."

10 So Zelophehad's daughters did
as the LORD commanded Moses.
11 Zelophehad's daughters—Mahlah, Tirzah, Hoglah, Milcah and
Noah[c]—married their cousins on
their father's side. 12 They married
within the clans of the descendants
of Manasseh son of Joseph, and
their inheritance remained in their
father's clan and tribe.

13 These are the commands and
regulations the LORD gave through
Moses[d] to the Israelites on the
plains of Moab by the Jordan
across from Jericho.[n][e]

36:7 [a] 1Ki 21:3
36:8 [b] 1Ch 23:22
36:11 [c] Nu 26:33; 27:1
36:13 [d] Lev 26:46; 27:34 [e] Nu 22:1

[n] *13* Hebrew *Jordan of Jericho*; possibly an ancient name for the Jordan River

CITIES OF REFUGE

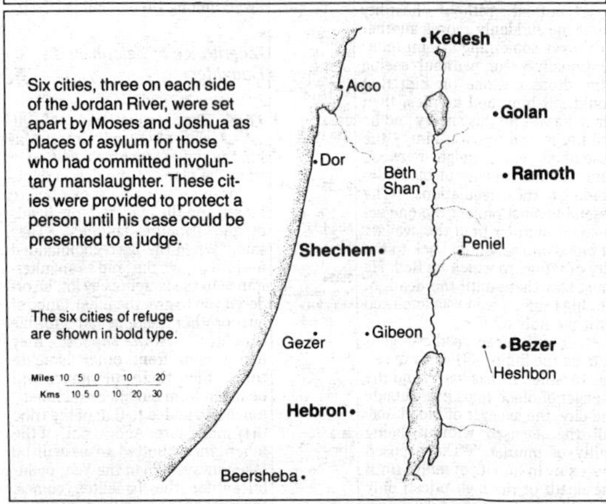

Six cities, three on each side of the Jordan River, were set apart by Moses and Joshua as places of asylum for those who had committed involuntary manslaughter. These cities were provided to protect a person until his case could be presented to a judge.
The six cities of refuge are shown in bold type.
Miles 10 5 0 10 20
Kms 10 5 0 10 20 30
Kedesh
Acco
Golan
Dor
Beth Shan
Ramoth
Shechem
Peniel
Gibeon
Gezer
Bezer
Heshbon
Hebron
Beersheba

Deuteronomy

Title and Background

The word "Deuteronomy" means "repetition of the law." After forty years the Israelites were about to enter Canaan. But before they did, Moses wanted to remind them of their history, all that God had done for them, and the laws they had to continue to obey as God's chosen people.

Author and Date of Writing

The book itself testifies that, for the most part, Moses wrote it (1:5; 31:9,22,24) as other Old Testament books agree (1Ki 2:3; 8:53; 2Ki 14:6; 18:12). Jesus bears the same testimony (Mt 19:7-8; Mk 10:3-5; Jn 5:45-47), and so do other New Testament writers (Ac 3:22-23; 7:37-38; Ro 10:19). Moreover, Jesus quotes Deuteronomy as authoritative (Mt 4:4,7,10). The book was written shortly before Moses' death in about 1406 B.C.

Theme and Message

Moses reminded the people of God's goodness to them throughout their journey and of his giving to them the land of Canaan. He also summarized God's laws, including the Ten Commandments. One subject that pervades the whole book is the love relationship of the Lord to his people and that of the people to the Lord as their sovereign God.

Outline

I. Preamble (1:1-5)
II. Historical Prologue (1:6-4:43)
III. Stipulations of the Covenant (4:44-26:19)
  A. Primary Demands (4:44-11:32)
  B. Supplementary Requirements (12:1-26:19)
IV. Ratification, and Curses and Blessings (27:1-30:20)
V. Succession Under the Covenant (31:1-34:12)

The Command to Leave Horeb

1 These are the words Moses
spoke to all Israel in the desert
east of the Jordan—that is, in the
Arabah—opposite Suph, between
Paran and Tophel, Laban, Hazeroth and Dizahab. 2(It takes eleven
days to go from Horeb[a] to Kadesh
Barnea[b] by the Mount Seir road.)
3In the fortieth year,[c] on the
first day of the eleventh month,
Moses proclaimed[d] to the Israelites all that the LORD had commanded him concerning them.
4This was after he had defeated Sihon[e] king of the Amorites, who
reigned in Heshbon,[f] and at Edrei
had defeated Og[g] king of Bashan,
who reigned in Ashtaroth.
5East of the Jordan in the territory of Moab, Moses began to expound this law, saying:

6The LORD our God said to us[h] at
Horeb,[i] "You have stayed long
enough at this mountain. 7Break
camp and advance into the hill
country of the Amorites; go to all
the neighboring peoples in the Arabah, in the mountains, in the western foothills, in the Negev[j] and
along the coast, to the land of the
Canaanites and to Lebanon,[k] as
far as the great river, the Euphrates. 8See, I have given you this

1:2 [a]Ex 3:1 [b]Nu 13:26; Dt 9:23
1:3 [c]Nu 33:38 [d]Dt 4:1-2
1:4 [e]Nu 21:21-26 [f]Nu 21:25 [g]Nu 21:33-35; Jos 13:12
1:6 [h]Nu 10:13 [i]Ex 3:1
1:7 [j]Jos 10:40 [k]Dt 11:24

land. Go in and take possession of the land that the LORD swore[a] he would give to your fathers—to Abraham, Isaac and Jacob—and to their descendants after them."

The Appointment of Leaders

9At that time I said to you, "You are too heavy a burden for me to carry alone.[b] **10**The LORD your God has increased your numbers so that today you are as many[c] as the stars in the sky.[d] **11**May the LORD, the God of your fathers, increase you a thousand times and bless you as he has promised![e] **12**But how can I bear your problems and your burdens and your disputes all by myself? **13**Choose some wise, understanding and respected men[f] from each of your tribes, and I will set them over you."

14You answered me, "What you propose to do is good."

15So I took[g] the leading men of your tribes, wise and respected men, and appointed them to have authority over you—as commanders of thousands, of hundreds, of fifties and of tens and as tribal officials. **16**And I charged your judges at that time: Hear the disputes between your brothers and judge fairly,[h] whether the case is between brother Israelites or between one of them and an alien.[i] **17**Do not show partiality[j] in judging; hear both small and great alike. Do not be afraid of any man,[k] for judgment belongs to God. Bring me any case too hard for you, and I will hear it.[l] **18**And at that time I told you everything you were to do.

Spies Sent Out

19Then, as the LORD our God commanded us, we set out from Horeb and went toward the hill country of the Amorites through all that vast and dreadful desert[m] that you have seen, and so we reached Kadesh Barnea.[n] **20**Then I said to you, "You have reached the hill country of the Amorites, which the LORD our God is giving us. **21**See, the LORD your God has given you the land. Go up and take possession of it as the LORD, the God of your fathers, told you. Do not be afraid;[o] do not be discouraged."

22Then all of you came to me and said, "Let us send men ahead to spy out the land for us and bring back a report about the route we are to take and the towns we will come to."

23The idea seemed good to me; so I selected[p] twelve of you, one man from each tribe. **24**They left and went up into the hill country, and came to the Valley of Eshcol[q] and explored it. **25**Taking with them some of the fruit of the land, they brought it down to us and reported,[r] "It is a good land that the LORD our God is giving us."

Rebellion Against the LORD

26But you were unwilling to go up;[s] you rebelled against the command of the LORD your God. **27**You grumbled[t] in your tents and said, "The LORD hates us; so he brought us out of Egypt to deliver us into the hands of the Amorites to destroy us. **28**Where can we go? Our brothers have made us lose heart. They say, 'The people are stronger and taller[u] than we are; the cities are large, with walls up to the sky. We even saw the Anakites[v] there.' "

29Then I said to you, "Do not be terrified; do not be afraid of them. **30**The LORD your God, who is going before you, will fight[w] for you, as he did for you in Egypt, before your very eyes, **31**and in the desert. There you saw how the LORD your God carried[x] you, as a father carries his son, all the way you went until you reached this place."

32In spite of this, you did not trust[y] in the LORD your God, **33**who went ahead of you on your journey, in fire by night and in a cloud by day,[z] to search[a] out places for you to camp and to show you the way you should go.

34When the LORD heard what you said, he was angry and solemnly swore:[b] **35**"Not a man of this evil generation shall see the good land[c] I swore to give your forefa-

1:8 [a]Ge 12:7; 15:18; 17:7-8; 26:4; 28:13
1:9 [b]Ex 18:18
1:10 [c]Ge 15:5 [d]Dt 10:22; 28:62
1:11 [e]Ge 22:17; Ex 32:13
1:13 [f]Ex 18:21
1:15 [g]Ex 18:25
1:16 [h]Dt 16:18; Jn 7:24 [i]Lev 24:22
1:17 [j]Lev 19:15; Dt 16:19; Pr 24:23; Jas 2:1 [k]2Ch 19:6 [l]Ex 18:26
1:19 [m]Dt 8:15; Jer 2:2,6 [n]ver 2; Nu 13:26
1:21 [o]Jos 1:6,9,18
1:23 [p]Nu 13:1-3
1:24 [q]Nu 13:21-25
1:25 [r]Nu 13:27
1:26 [s]Nu 14:1-4
1:27 [t]Dt 9:28; Ps 106:25
1:28 [u]Nu 13:32 [v]Nu 13:33; Dt 9:1-3
1:30 [w]Ex 14:14; Dt 3:22; Ne 4:20
1:31 [x]Dt 32:10-12; Isa 46:3-4; 63:9; Hos 11:3; Ac 13:18
1:32 [y]Ps 106:24; Jude 1:5
1:33 [z]Ex 13:21; Ps 78:14 [a]Nu 10:33
1:34 [b]Nu 14:23, 28-30
1:35 [c]Ps 95:11

thers, 36except Caleb son of Jephunneh. He will see it, and I will
give him and his descendants the
land he set his feet on, because he
followed the LORD wholeheartedly.[a]"

37Because of you the LORD became angry[b] with me also and
said, "You shall not enter[c] it, either. 38But your assistant, Joshua[d]
son of Nun, will enter it. Encourage[e] him, because he will lead[f]
Israel to inherit it. 39And the little
ones that you said would be taken
captive,[g] your children who do not
yet know[h] good from bad—they
will enter the land. I will give it to
them and they will take possession
of it. 40But as for you, turn around
and set out toward the desert along
the route to the Red Sea.[a][i]"

41Then you replied, "We have
sinned against the LORD. We will go
up and fight, as the LORD our God
commanded us." So every one of
you put on his weapons, thinking it
easy to go up into the hill country.
42But the LORD said to me, "Tell
them, 'Do not go up and fight, because I will not be with you. You
will be defeated by your enemies.' "[j]

43So I told you, but you would
not listen. You rebelled against the
LORD's command and in your arrogance you marched up into the hill
country. 44The Amorites who lived
in those hills came out against you;
they chased you like a swarm of
bees[k] and beat you down from Seir
all the way to Hormah. 45You came
back and wept before the LORD, but
he paid no attention to your weeping and turned a deaf ear to you.
46And so you stayed in Kadesh[l]
many days—all the time you spent
there.

Wanderings in the Desert

2 Then we turned back and set
out toward the desert along the
route to the Red Sea,[a][m] as the
LORD had directed me. For a long
time we made our way around the
hill country of Seir.
2Then the LORD said to me,
3"You have made your way around
this hill country long enough; now
turn north. 4Give the people these
orders:[n] 'You are about to pass
through the territory of your brothers the descendants of Esau, who
live in Seir. They will be afraid of
you, but be very careful. 5Do not
provoke them to war, for I will not
give you any of their land, not even
enough to put your foot on. I have
given Esau the hill country of Seir
as his own.[o] 6You are to pay them
in silver for the food you eat and
the water you drink.' "

7The LORD your God has blessed
you in all the work of your hands.
He has watched[p] over your journey
through this vast desert. These forty years the LORD your God has
been with you, and you have not
lacked anything.

8So we went on past our brothers
the descendants of Esau, who live
in Seir. We turned from the Arabah
road, which comes up from Elath
and Ezion Geber,[q] and traveled
along the desert road of Moab.[r]

9Then the LORD said to me, "Do
not harass the Moabites or provoke
them to war, for I will not give you
any part of their land. I have given
Ar[s] to the descendants of Lot[t] as
a possession."

10(The Emites[u] used to live
there—a people strong and numerous, and as tall as the Anakites.[v]
11Like the Anakites, they too were
considered Rephaites, but the Moabites called them Emites. 12Ho-
rites used to live in Seir, but the
descendants of Esau drove them
out. They destroyed the Horites
from before them and settled in
their place, just as Israel did[w] in
the land the LORD gave them as
their possession.)

13And the LORD said, "Now get
up and cross the Zered Valley." So
we crossed the valley.

14Thirty-eight years passed from
the time we left Kadesh Barnea[x]
until we crossed the Zered Valley.
By then, that entire generation[y] of
fighting men had perished from the
camp, as the LORD had sworn to

1:36 [a]Nu 14:24; Jos 14:9
1:37 [b]Dt 3:26; 4:21 [c]Nu 20:12
1:38 [d]Nu 14:30 [e]Dt 31:7 [f]Dt 3:28
1:39 [g]Nu 14:3 [h]Isa 7:15-16
1:40 [i]Nu 14:25
1:42 [j]Nu 14:41-43
1:44 [k]Ps 118:12
1:46 [l]Nu 20:1; Jdg 11:17
2:1 [m]Nu 21:4
2:4 [n]Nu 20:14-21
2:5 [o]Ge 36:8; Jos 24:4
2:7 [p]Dt 8:2-4
2:8 [q]1Ki 9:26 [r]Jdg 11:18
2:9 [s]Nu 21:15 [t]Ge 19:36-38
2:10 [u]Ge 14:5 [v]Nu 13:22,33
2:12 [w]ver 22
2:14 [x]Nu 13:26 [y]Nu 14:29-35

[a]40,1 Hebrew *Yam Suph*; that is, Sea of Reeds

them.[a] **15**The LORD's hand was
against them until he had completely eliminated[b] them from the
camp.
16Now when the last of these
fighting men among the people
had died, **17**the LORD said to me,
18"Today you are to pass by the region of Moab at Ar. **19**When you
come to the Ammonites,[c] do not
harass them or provoke them to
war, for I will not give you possession of any land belonging to the
Ammonites. I have given it as a
possession to the descendants of
Lot.[d]"
20(That too was considered a
land of the Rephaites, who used to
live there; but the Ammonites
called them Zamzummites. **21**They
were a people strong and numerous, and as tall as the Anakites.[e]
The LORD destroyed them from before the Ammonites, who drove
them out and settled in their place.
22The LORD had done the same for
the descendants of Esau, who lived
in Seir,[f] when he destroyed the
Horites from before them. They
drove them out and have lived in
their place to this day. **23**And as for
the Avvites[g] who lived in villages
as far as Gaza, the Caphtorites[h]
coming out from Caphtor[b][i] destroyed them and settled in their
place.)

Defeat of Sihon King of Heshbon

24"Set out now and cross the Arnon Gorge.[j] See, I have given into
your hand Sihon the Amorite, king
of Heshbon, and his country. Begin
to take possession of it and engage
him in battle. **25**This very day I will
begin to put the terror[k] and fear[l]
of you on all the nations under
heaven. They will hear reports of
you and will tremble[m] and be in
anguish because of you."
26From the desert of Kedemoth I
sent messengers to Sihon king of
Heshbon offering peace and saying, **27**"Let us pass through your
country. We will stay on the main
road; we will not turn aside to the

2:14 [a]Dt 1:34-35
2:15 [b]Ps 106:26
2:19 [c]Ge 19:38 [d]ver 9
2:21 [e]ver 10
2:22 [f]Ge 36:8
2:23 [g]Jos 13:3 [h]Ge 10:14 [i]Am 9:7
2:24 [j]Nu 21:13-14; Jdg 11:13,18
2:25 [k]Dt 11:25 [l]Jos 2:9,11 [m]Ex 15:14-16
2:27 [n]Nu 21:21-22
2:28 [o]Nu 20:19
2:30 [p]Jos 11:20 [q]Ex 4:21; Nu 21:23; Ro 9:18
2:31 [r]Dt 1:8
2:32 [s]Nu 21:23
2:33 [t]Dt 29:7
2:34 [u]Dt 3:6; 7:2
2:36 [v]Dt 3:12; 4:48; Jos 13:9 [w]Ps 44:3
2:37 [x]ver 18-19 [y]Nu 21:24 [z]Ge 32:22; Dt 3:16
3:1 [a]Nu 21:33
3:2 [b]Nu 21:34

right or to the left.[n] **28**Sell us food
to eat and water to drink for their
price in silver. Only let us pass
through on foot[o]— **29**as the
descendants of Esau, who live in
Seir, and the Moabites, who live in
Ar, did for us—until we cross the
Jordan into the land the LORD our
God is giving us." **30**But Sihon king
of Heshbon refused to let us pass
through. For the LORD[p] your God
had made his spirit stubborn[q] and
his heart obstinate in order to give
him into your hands, as he has now
done.
31The LORD said to me, "See, I
have begun to deliver Sihon and his
country over to you. Now begin to
conquer and possess his land."[r]
32When Sihon and all his army
came out to meet us in battle[s] at
Jahaz, **33**the LORD our God delivered him over to us and we struck
him down,[t] together with his sons
and his whole army. **34**At that time
we took all his towns and completely destroyed[c][u] them—men,
women and children. We left no
survivors. **35**But the livestock and
the plunder from the towns we had
captured we carried off for ourselves. **36**From Aroer[v] on the rim
of the Arnon Gorge, and from the
town in the gorge, even as far as
Gilead, not one town was too
strong for us. The LORD our God
gave[w] us all of them. **37**But in accordance with the command of the
LORD our God,[x] you did not encroach on any of the land of the
Ammonites,[y] neither the land
along the course of the Jabbok[z]
nor that around the towns in the
hills.

Defeat of Og King of Bashan

3 Next we turned and went up
along the road toward Bashan,
and Og king of Bashan with his
whole army marched out to meet
us in battle at Edrei.[a] **2**The LORD
said to me, "Do not be afraid[b] of
him, for I have handed him over to

[b]23 That is, Crete [c]34 The Hebrew term refers to the irrevocable giving over of things or persons to the LORD, often by totally destroying them.

you with his whole army and his land. Do to him what you did to Sihon king of the Amorites, who reigned in Heshbon."

3So the LORD our God also gave into our hands Og king of Bashan and all his army. We struck them down, leaving no survivors.[a] 4At that time we took all his cities. There was not one of the sixty cities that we did not take from them—the whole region of Argob, Og's kingdom in Bashan.[b] 5All these cities were fortified with high walls and with gates and bars, and there were also a great many unwalled villages. 6We completely destroyed[d] them, as we had done with Sihon king of Heshbon, destroying[d][c] every city—men, women and children. 7But all the livestock and the plunder from their cities we carried off for ourselves.

8So at that time we took from these two kings of the Amorites the territory east of the Jordan, from the Arnon Gorge as far as Mount Hermon. 9(Hermon is called Sirion[d] by the Sidonians; the Amorites call it Senir.)[e] 10We took all the towns on the plateau, and all Gilead, and all Bashan as far as Salecah[f] and Edrei, towns of Og's kingdom in Bashan. 11(Only Og king of Bashan was left of the remnant of the Rephaites.[g] His bed[e] was made of iron and was more than thirteen feet long and six feet wide.[f] It is still in Rabbah[h] of the Ammonites.)

Division of the Land

12Of the land that we took over at that time, I gave the Reubenites and the Gadites the territory north of Aroer[i] by the Arnon Gorge, including half the hill country of Gilead, together with its towns. 13The rest of Gilead and also all of Bashan, the kingdom of Og, I gave to the half tribe of Manasseh. (The whole region of Argob in Bashan used to be known as a land of the Rephaites. 14Jair,[j] a descendant of Manasseh, took the whole region of Argob as far as the border of the Geshurites and the Maacathites; it was named after him, so that to this day Bashan is called Havvoth Jair.[g]) 15And I gave Gilead to Makir.[k] 16But to the Reubenites and the Gadites I gave the territory extending from Gilead down to the Arnon Gorge (the middle of the gorge being the border) and out to the Jabbok River,[l] which is the border of the Ammonites. 17Its western border was the Jordan in the Arabah, from Kinnereth[m] to the Sea of the Arabah (the Salt Sea[h][n]), below the slopes of Pisgah.

18I commanded you at that time: "The LORD your God has given you this land to take possession of it. But all your able-bodied men, armed for battle, must cross over ahead of your brother Israelites.[o] 19However, your wives, your children and your livestock (I know you have much livestock) may stay in the towns I have given you, 20until the LORD gives rest to your brothers as he has to you, and they too have taken over the land that the LORD your God is giving them, across the Jordan. After that, each of you may go back to the possession I have given you."

Moses Forbidden to Cross the Jordan

21At that time I commanded Joshua: "You have seen with your own eyes all that the LORD your God has done to these two kings. The LORD will do the same to all the kingdoms over there where you are going. 22Do not be afraid[p] of them; the LORD your God himself will fight[q] for you."

23At that time I pleaded with the LORD: 24"O Sovereign LORD, you have begun to show to your servant your greatness[r] and your strong hand. For what god[s] is there in heaven or on earth who can do the

3:3 [a]Nu 21:35
3:4 [b]1Ki 4:13
3:6 [c]Dt 2:24,34
3:9 [d]Dt 4:48; Ps 29:6 [e]1Ch 5:23
3:10 [f]Jos 13:11
3:11 [g]Ge 14:5 [h]2Sa 12:26; Jer 49:2
3:12 [i]Nu 32:32-38; Dt 2:36; Jos 13:8-13
3:14 [j]Nu 32:41; 1Ch 2:22
3:15 [k]Nu 32:39-40
3:16 [l]Nu 21:24
3:17 [m]Nu 34:11; Jos 13:27 [n]Ge 14:3; Jos 12:3
3:18 [o]Nu 32:17
3:22 [p]Dt 1:29 [q]Ex 14:14; Dt 20:4
3:24 [r]Dt 11:2 [s]Ex 15:11; Ps 86:8

[d]6 The Hebrew term refers to the irrevocable giving over of things or persons to the LORD, often by totally destroying them. [e]11 Or *sarcophagus* [f]11 Hebrew *nine cubits long and four cubits wide* (about 4 meters long and 1.8 meters wide) [g]14 Or *called the settlements of Jair* [h]17 That is, the Dead Sea

deeds and mighty works[a] you do?[b] 25Let me go over and see the good land[c] beyond the Jordan—that fine hill country and Lebanon."

26But because of you the LORD was angry[d] with me and would not listen to me. "That is enough," the LORD said. "Do not speak to me anymore about this matter. 27Go up to the top of Pisgah and look west and north and south and east. Look at the land with your own eyes, since you are not going to cross this Jordan.[e] 28But commission[f] Joshua, and encourage and strengthen him, for he will lead this people across[g] and will cause them to inherit the land that you will see." 29So we stayed in the valley near Beth Peor.[h]

Obedience Commanded

4 Hear now, O Israel, the decrees and laws I am about to teach you. Follow them so that you may live[i] and may go in and take possession of the land that the LORD, the God of your fathers, is giving you. 2Do not add[j] to what I command you and do not subtract from it, but keep the commands of the LORD your God that I give you.

3You saw with your own eyes what the LORD did at Baal Peor.[k] The LORD your God destroyed from among you everyone who followed the Baal of Peor, 4but all of you who held fast to the LORD your God are still alive today.

5See, I have taught you decrees and laws as the LORD my God commanded me, so that you may follow them in the land you are entering to take possession of it. 6Observe them carefully, for this will show your wisdom[l] and understanding to the nations, who will hear about all these decrees and say, "Surely this great nation is a wise and understanding people."[m] 7What other nation is so great[n] as to have their gods near[o] them the way the LORD our God is near us whenever we pray to him? 8And what other nation is so great as to have such righteous decrees and laws as this body of laws I am setting before you today?

9Only be careful,[p] and watch yourselves closely so that you do not forget the things your eyes have seen or let them slip from your heart as long as you live. Teach[q] them to your children[r] and to their children after them. 10Remember the day you stood before the LORD your God at Horeb,[s] when he said to me, "Assemble the people before me to hear my words so that they may learn to revere me as long as they live in the land and may teach them to their children." 11You came near and stood at the foot of the mountain while it blazed with fire[t] to the very heavens, with black clouds and deep darkness. 12Then the LORD spoke[u] to you out of the fire. You heard the sound of words but saw no form; there was only a voice. 13He declared to you his covenant,[v] the Ten Commandments,[w] which he commanded you to follow and then wrote them on two stone tablets. 14And the LORD directed me at that time to teach you the decrees and laws you are to follow in the land that you are crossing the Jordan to possess.

Idolatry Forbidden

15You saw no form[x] of any kind the day the LORD spoke to you at Horeb out of the fire. Therefore watch yourselves very carefully,[y] 16so that you do not become corrupt and make for yourselves an idol,[z] an image of any shape, whether formed like a man or a woman, 17or like any animal on earth or any bird that flies in the air, 18or like any creature that moves along the ground or any fish in the waters below. 19And when you look up to the sky and see the sun,[a] the moon and the stars—all the heavenly array[b]—do not be enticed into bowing down to them and worshiping things the LORD your God has apportioned to all the nations under heaven. 20But as for you, the LORD took you and brought you out of the iron-smelting fur-

3:24 [a] Ps 71:16,19 [b] 2Sa 7:22
3:25 [c] Dt 4:22
3:26 [d] Dt 1:37; 31:2
3:27 [e] Nu 27:12
3:28 [f] Nu 27:18-23 [g] Dt 31:3,23
3:29 [h] Dt 4:46; 34:6
4:1 [i] Dt 5:33; 8:1; 16:20; 30:15-20; Eze 20:11; Ro 10:5
4:2 [j] Dt 12:32; Jos 1:7; Rev 22:18-19
4:3 [k] Nu 25:1-9; Ps 106:28
4:6 [l] Dt 30:19-20; Ps 19:7; Pr 1:7 [m] Job 28:28
4:7 [n] 2Sa 7:23 [o] Ps 46:1; Isa 55:6
4:9 [p] Pr 4:23 [q] Ge 18:19; Eph 6:4 [r] Ps 78:5-6
4:10 [s] Ex 19:9,16
4:11 [t] Ex 19:18; Heb 12:18-19
4:12 [u] Ex 20:22; Dt 5:4,22
4:13 [v] Dt 9:9,11 [w] Ex 24:12; 31:18; 34:28
4:15 [x] Isa 40:18 [y] Jos 23:11
4:16 [z] Ex 20:4-5; 32:7; Dt 5:8; Ro 1:23
4:19 [a] Dt 17:3; Job 31:26 [b] 2Ki 17:16; 21:3; Ro 1:25

nace,[a] out of Egypt, to be the people of his inheritance,[b] as you now are.

21 The LORD was angry with me[c] because of you, and he solemnly swore that I would not cross the Jordan and enter the good land the LORD your God is giving you as your inheritance. 22 I will die in this land; I will not cross the Jordan; but you are about to cross over and take possession of that good land.[d] 23 Be careful not to forget the covenant[e] of the LORD your God that he made with you; do not make for yourselves an idol[f] in the form of anything the LORD your God has forbidden. 24 For the LORD your God is a consuming fire,[g] a jealous God.

25 After you have had children and grandchildren and have lived in the land a long time—if you then become corrupt and make any kind of idol, doing evil[h] in the eyes of the LORD your God and provoking him to anger, 26 I call heaven and earth as witnesses against you[i] this day that you will quickly perish from the land that you are crossing the Jordan to possess. You will not live there long but will certainly be destroyed. 27 The LORD will scatter[j] you among the peoples, and only a few of you will survive among the nations to which the LORD will drive you. 28 There you will worship man-made gods[k] of wood and stone, which cannot see or hear or eat or smell.[l] 29 But if from there you seek[m] the LORD your God, you will find him if you look for him with all your heart[n] and with all your soul.[o] 30 When you are in distress and all these things have happened to you, then in later days[p] you will return to the LORD your God and obey him. 31 For the LORD your God is a merciful[q] God; he will not abandon or destroy you or forget the covenant with your forefathers, which he confirmed to them by oath.

The LORD Is God

32 Ask[r] now about the former days, long before your time, from the day God created man on the earth;[s] ask from one end of the heavens to the other.[t] Has anything so great as this ever happened, or has anything like it ever been heard of? 33 Has any other people heard the voice of God[i] speaking out of fire, as you have, and lived?[u] 34 Has any god ever tried to take for himself one nation out of another nation,[v] by testings, by miraculous signs[w] and wonders,[x] by war, by a mighty hand and an outstretched arm,[y] or by great and awesome deeds,[z] like all the things the LORD your God did for you in Egypt before your very eyes?

35 You were shown these things so that you might know that the LORD is God; besides him there is no other.[a] 36 From heaven he made you hear his voice[b] to discipline you. On earth he showed you his great fire, and you heard his words from out of the fire. 37 Because he loved[c] your forefathers and chose their descendants after them, he brought you out of Egypt by his Presence and his great strength,[d] 38 to drive out before you nations greater and stronger than you and to bring you into their land to give it to you for your inheritance,[e] as it is today.

39 Acknowledge and take to heart this day that the LORD is God in heaven above and on the earth below. There is no other.[f] 40 Keep[g] his decrees and commands, which I am giving you today, so that it may go well[h] with you and your children after you and that you may live long[i] in the land the LORD your God gives you for all time.

Cities of Refuge

4:41–43Ref – Nu 35:6–34; Dt 19:1–14; Jos 20:1–9

41 Then Moses set aside three cities east of the Jordan, 42 to which anyone who had killed a person could flee if he had unintentionally killed his neighbor without malice

4:20 [a] 1Ki 8:51; Jer 11:4 [b] Ex 19:5; Dt 9:29 **4:21** [c] Nu 20:12; Dt 1:37 **4:22** [d] Dt 3:25 **4:23** [e] ver 9,16 [f] Ex 20:4 **4:24** [g] Ex 24:17; Dt 9:3; Heb 12:29 **4:25** [h] 2Ki 17:2,17 **4:26** [i] Dt 30:18-19; Isa 1:2; Mic 6:2 **4:27** [j] Lev 26:33; Dt 28:36,64; Ne 1:8 **4:28** [k] Dt 28:36,64; 1Sa 26:19; Jer 16:13 [l] Ps 115:4-8; 135:15-18 **4:29** [m] 2Ch 15:4; Isa 55:6 [n] Jer 29:13 [o] Dt 30:1-3,10 **4:30** [p] Dt 31:29; Jer 23:20; Hos 3:5 **4:31** [q] 2Ch 30:9; Ne 9:31; Ps 116:5; Jnh 4:2 **4:32** [r] Dt 32:7; Job 8:8 [s] Ge 1:27 [t] Mt 24:31 **4:33** [u] Ex 20:22; Dt 5:24-26 **4:34** [v] Ex 6:6 [w] Ex 7:3 [x] Dt 7:19; 26:8 [y] Ex 13:3 [z] Dt 34:12 **4:35** [a] Dt 32:39; 1Sa 2:2; Isa 45:5,18 **4:36** [b] Ex 19:9,19 **4:37** [c] Dt 10:15 [d] Ex 13:3,9,14 **4:38** [e] Dt 7:1; 9:5 **4:39** [f] ver 35; Jos 2:11 **4:40** [g] Lev 22:31; Dt 5:33 [h] Dt 5:16 [i] Dt 6:3,18; Eph 6:2-3

[i] 33 Or *of a god*

aforethought. He could flee into
one of these cities and save his life.
43The cities were these: Bezer in
the desert plateau, for the Reubenites; Ramoth in Gilead, for the
Gadites; and Golan in Bashan, for
the Manassites.

Introduction to the Law

44This is the law Moses set before the Israelites. **45**These are the
stipulations, decrees and laws Moses gave them when they came out
of Egypt **46**and were in the valley
near Beth Peor east of the Jordan,
in the land of Sihon[a] king of the
Amorites, who reigned in Heshbon
and was defeated by Moses and the
Israelites as they came out of
Egypt. **47**They took possession of
his land and the land of Og king of
Bashan, the two Amorite kings east
of the Jordan. **48**This land extended from Aroer[b] on the rim of the
Arnon Gorge to Mount Siyon[i][c]
(that is, Hermon), **49**and included
all the Arabah east of the Jordan,
as far as the Sea of the Arabah,[k]
below the slopes of Pisgah.

The Ten Commandments

5:6–21pp — Ex 20:1–17

5 Moses summoned all Israel
and said:

Hear, O Israel, the decrees and
laws I declare in your hearing today. Learn them and be sure to follow them. **2**The LORD our God made
a covenant[d] with us at Horeb. **3**It
was not with our fathers that the
LORD made this covenant, but with
us, with all of us who are alive here
today.[e] **4**The LORD spoke[f] to you
face to face out of the fire on the
mountain. **5**(At that time I stood
between[g] the LORD and you to declare to you the word of the LORD,
because you were afraid[h] of the
fire and did not go up the mountain.) And he said:

6"I am the LORD your God,
who brought you out of
Egypt, out of the land of
slavery.

7"You shall have no other gods
before[l] me.

4:46 [a]Nu 21:26; Dt 3:29
4:48 [b]Dt 2:36 [c]Dt 3:9
5:2 [d]Ex 19:5
5:3 [e]Heb 8:9
5:4 [f]Dt 4:12,33, 36
5:5 [g]Gal 3:19 [h]Ex 20:18,21
5:9 [i]Ex 34:7
5:10 [j]Jer 32:18
5:11 [k]Lev 19:12; Mt 5:33-37
5:12 [l]Ex 20:8
5:14 [m]Ge 2:2; Heb 4:4
5:15 [n]Dt 4:34
5:16 [o]Ex 20:12; Lev 19:3; Dt 27:16; Eph 6:2-3*; Col 3:20

8"You shall not make for yourself an idol in the form of
anything in heaven above
or on the earth beneath
or in the waters below.
9You shall not bow down
to them or worship them;
for I, the LORD your God,
am a jealous God, pun-
ishing the children for
the sin of the fathers to
the third and fourth gen-
eration of those who hate
me,[i] **10**but showing love
to a thousand ⌊genera-
tions⌋ of those who love
me and keep my com-
mandments.[j]

11"You shall not misuse the
name of the LORD your
God, for the LORD will not
hold anyone guiltless
who misuses his name.[k]

12"Observe the Sabbath day by
keeping it holy,[l] as the
LORD your God has com-
manded you. **13**Six days
you shall labor and do all
your work, **14**but the seventh day[m] is a Sabbath to
the LORD your God. On it
you shall not do any
work, neither you, nor
your son or daughter, nor
your manservant or maid-
servant, nor your ox, your
donkey or any of your animals, nor the alien within
your gates, so that your
manservant and maidser-
vant may rest, as you do.
15Remember that you
were slaves in Egypt and
that the LORD your God
brought you out of there
with a mighty hand and
an outstretched arm.[n]
Therefore the LORD your
God has commanded you
to observe the Sabbath
day.

16"Honor your father and your
mother,[o] as the LORD
your God has command-

i48 Hebrew; Syriac (see also Deut. 3:9) *Sirion*
k49 That is, the Dead Sea
l7 Or *besides*

ed you, so that you may
live long[a] and that it may
go well with you in the
land the LORD your God is
giving you.

17"You shall not murder.[b]

18"You shall not commit adultery.[c]

19"You shall not steal.

20"You shall not give false testimony against your neigh-
bor.

21"You shall not covet your
neighbor's wife. You shall
not set your desire on
your neighbor's house or
land, his manservant or
maidservant, his ox or
donkey, or anything that
belongs to your neigh-
bor."[d]

22These are the commandments
the LORD proclaimed in a loud voice
to your whole assembly there on
the mountain from out of the fire,
the cloud and the deep darkness;
and he added nothing more. Then
he wrote them on two stone tablets[e] and gave them to me.

23When you heard the voice out
of the darkness, while the mountain was ablaze with fire, all the
leading men of your tribes and your
elders came to me. 24And you said,
"The LORD our God has shown us
his glory and his majesty, and we
have heard his voice from the fire.
Today we have seen that a man can
live even if God speaks with him.[f]
25But now, why should we die?
This great fire will consume us, and
we will die if we hear the voice of
the LORD our God any longer.[g]
26For what mortal man has ever
heard the voice of the living God
speaking out of fire, as we have,
and survived?[h] 27Go near and listen to all that the LORD our God
says. Then tell us whatever the
LORD our God tells you. We will listen and obey."

28The LORD heard you when you
spoke to me and the LORD said to
me, "I have heard what this people
said to you. Everything they said
was good.[i] 29Oh, that their hearts
would be inclined to fear me[j] and
keep all my commands[k] always, so
that it might go well with them and
their children forever![l]

30"Go, tell them to return to
their tents. 31But you stay here[m]
with me so that I may give you all
the commands, decrees and laws
you are to teach them to follow in
the land I am giving them to possess."

32So be careful to do what the
LORD your God has commanded
you; do not turn aside to the right
or to the left.[n] 33Walk in all the
way that the LORD your God has
commanded you,[o] so that you may
live and prosper and prolong your
days[p] in the land that you will possess.

Love the LORD Your God

6 These are the commands, decrees and laws the LORD your
God directed me to teach you to
observe in the land that you are
crossing the Jordan to possess, 2so
that you, your children and their
children after them may fear[q] the
LORD your God as long as you live by
keeping all his decrees and commands that I give you, and so that
you may enjoy long life. 3Hear, O
Israel, and be careful to obey so
that it may go well with you and
that you may increase greatly[r] in a
land flowing with milk and honey,[s] just as the LORD, the God of
your fathers, promised you.

4Hear, O Israel: The LORD our
God, the LORD is one.[m][t] 5Love[u]
the LORD your God with all your
heart and with all your soul and
with all your strength.[v] 6These
commandments that I give you today are to be upon your hearts.[w]
7Impress them on your children.
Talk about them when you sit at
home and when you walk along the
road, when you lie down and when
you get up.[x] 8Tie them as symbols
on your hands and bind them on
your foreheads.[y] 9Write them on

5:16 [a]Dt 4:40
5:17 [b]Mt 5:21-22*
5:18 [c]Mt 5:27-30; Lk 18:20*; Jas 2:11*
5:21 [d]Ro 7:7*; 13:9*
5:22 [e]Ex 24:12; 31:18; Dt 4:13
5:24 [f]Ex 19:19
5:25 [g]Dt 18:16
5:26 [h]Dt 4:33
5:28 [i]Dt 18:17
5:29 [j]Ps 81:8,13 [k]Dt 11:1; Isa 48:18 [l]Dt 4:1,40
5:31 [m]Ex 24:12
5:32 [n]Dt 17:11,20; 28:14; Jos 1:7; 23:6; Pr 4:27
5:33 [o]Jer 7:23 [p]Dt 4:40
6:2 [q]Ex 20:20; Dt 10:12-13
6:3 [r]Dt 5:33 [s]Ex 3:8
6:4 [t]Mk 12:29*; 1Co 8:4
6:5 [u]Mt 22:37*; Mk 12:30*; Lk 10:27* [v]Dt 10:12
6:6 [w]Dt 11:18
6:7 [x]Dt 4:9; 11:19; Eph 6:4
6:8 [y]Ex 13:9,16; Dt 11:18

m4 Or *The LORD our God is one LORD*; or *The LORD is our God, the LORD is one*; or *The LORD is our God, the LORD alone*

the doorframes of your houses and
on your gates.[a]
10When the LORD your God
brings you into the land he swore to
your fathers, to Abraham, Isaac
and Jacob, to give you—a land with
large, flourishing cities you did not
build,[b] 11houses filled with all
kinds of good things you did not
provide, wells you did not dig, and
vineyards and olive groves you did
not plant—then when you eat and
are satisfied,[c] 12be careful that
you do not forget the LORD, who
brought you out of Egypt, out of the
land of slavery.
13Fear the LORD[d] your God,
serve him only[e] and take your
oaths in his name. 14Do not follow
other gods, the gods of the peoples
around you; 15for the LORD your
God[f], who is among you, is a jealous God and his anger will burn
against you, and he will destroy you
from the face of the land. 16Do not
test the LORD your God[g] as you did
at Massah. 17Be sure to keep the
commands of the LORD your God
and the stipulations and decrees
he has given you.[h] 18Do what is
right and good in the LORD's sight,
so that it may go well[i] with you
and you may go in and take over
the good land that the LORD promised on oath to your forefathers,
19thrusting out all your enemies
before you, as the LORD said.
20In the future, when your son
asks you,[j] "What is the meaning of
the stipulations, decrees and laws
the LORD our God has commanded
you?" 21tell him: "We were slaves
of Pharaoh in Egypt, but the LORD
brought us out of Egypt with a
mighty hand. 22Before our eyes the
LORD sent miraculous signs and
wonders—great and terrible—
upon Egypt and Pharaoh and his
whole household. 23But he
brought us out from there to bring
us in and give us the land that he
promised on oath to our forefathers. 24The LORD commanded us
to obey all these decrees and to
fear the LORD our God,[k] so that we
might always prosper and be kept
alive, as is the case today.[l] 25And
if we are careful to obey all this law
before the LORD our God, as he has
commanded us, that will be our
righteousness.[m]"

Driving Out the Nations

7 When the LORD your God brings
you into the land you are entering to possess and drives out before
you many nations[n]—the Hittites,
Girgashites, Amorites, Canaanites,
Perizzites, Hivites and Jebusites,
seven nations larger and stronger
than you— 2and when the LORD
your God has delivered them over
to you and you have defeated them,
then you must destroy them totally.[n] Make no treaty[o] with them,
and show them no mercy.[p] 3Do
not intermarry with them.[q] Do not
give your daughters to their sons or
take their daughters for your sons,
4for they will turn your sons away
from following me to serve other
gods, and the LORD's anger will
burn against you and will quickly
destroy[r] you. 5This is what you are
to do to them: Break down their altars, smash their sacred stones, cut
down their Asherah poles[o] and
burn their idols in the fire.[s] 6For
you are a people holy[t] to the LORD
your God.[u] The LORD your God has
chosen[v] you out of all the peoples
on the face of the earth to be his
people, his treasured possession.
7The LORD did not set his affection on you and choose you because you were more numerous
than other peoples, for you were
the fewest of all peoples.[w] 8But it
was because the LORD loved[x] you
and kept the oath he swore[y] to
your forefathers that he brought
you out with a mighty hand and redeemed you from the land of slavery,[z] from the power of Pharaoh
king of Egypt. 9Know therefore
that the LORD your God is God;[a] he
is the faithful God,[b] keeping his
covenant of love[c] to a thousand

6:9 [a] Dt 11:20
6:10 [b] Jos 24:13
6:11 [c] Dt 8:10
6:13 [d] Dt 10:20 [e] Mt 4:10*; Lk 4:8*
6:15 [f] Dt 4:24
6:16 [g] Ex 17:7; Mt 4:7*; Lk 4:12*
6:17 [h] Dt 11:22; Ps 119:4
6:18 [i] Dt 4:40
6:20 [j] Ex 13:14
6:24 [k] Dt 10:12; Jer 32:39 [l] Ps 41:2
6:25 [m] Dt 24:13; Ro 10:3,5
7:1 [n] Dt 31:3; Ac 13:19
7:2 [o] Ex 23:32 [p] Dt 13:8
7:3 [q] Ex 34:15-16; Ezr 9:2
7:4 [r] Dt 6:15
7:5 [s] Ex 23:24; Dt 12:2-3
7:6 [t] Ex 19:5-6; 1Pe 2:9 [u] Ps 50:5; Jer 2:3 [v] Dt 14:2
7:7 [w] Dt 10:22
7:8 [x] Dt 10:15 [y] Ex 32:13 [z] Ex 13:14
7:9 [a] Dt 4:35 [b] 1Co 1:9; 2Ti 2:13 [c] Ne 1:5; Da 9:4

n2 The Hebrew term refers to the irrevocable giving over of things or persons to the LORD, often by totally destroying them; also in verse 26. o5 That is, symbols of the goddess Asherah; here and elsewhere in Deuteronomy

generations of those who love him and keep his commands. 10But

those who hate him he will
  repay to their face by
  destruction;
he will not be slow to repay
  to their face those who
  hate him.

11Therefore, take care to follow the commands, decrees and laws I give you today.

12If you pay attention to these laws and are careful to follow them, then the LORD your God will keep his covenant of love with you, as he swore to your forefathers.[a] 13He will love you and bless you[b] and increase your numbers. He will bless the fruit of your womb, the crops of your land—your grain, new wine and oil—the calves of your herds and the lambs of your flocks in the land that he swore to your forefathers to give you.[c] 14You will be blessed more than any other people; none of your men or women will be childless, nor any of your livestock without young.[d] 15The LORD will keep you free from every disease.[e] He will not inflict on you the horrible diseases you knew in Egypt, but he will inflict them on all who hate you. 16You must destroy all the peoples the LORD your God gives over to you. Do not look on them with pity[f] and do not serve their gods, for that will be a snare[g] to you.

17You may say to yourselves, "These nations are stronger than we are. How can we drive them out?[h]" 18But do not be afraid[i] of them; remember well what the LORD your God did to Pharaoh and to all Egypt.[j] 19You saw with your own eyes the great trials, the miraculous signs and wonders, the mighty hand and outstretched arm, with which the LORD your God brought you out. The LORD your God will do the same to all the peoples you now fear.[k] 20Moreover, the LORD your God will send the hornet[l] among them until even the survivors who hide from you have perished. 21Do not be terrified by them, for the LORD your God, who is among you,[m] is a great and awesome God.[n] 22The LORD your God will drive out those nations before you, little by little.[o] You will not be allowed to eliminate them all at once, or the wild animals will multiply around you. 23But the LORD your God will deliver them over to you, throwing them into great confusion until they are destroyed. 24He will give their kings into your hand, and you will wipe out their names from under heaven. No one will be able to stand up against you;[p] you will destroy them. 25The images of their gods you are to burn[q] in the fire. Do not covet[r] the silver and gold on them, and do not take it for yourselves, or you will be ensnared[s] by it, for it is detestable[t] to the LORD your God. 26Do not bring a detestable thing into your house or you, like it, will be set apart for destruction.[u] Utterly abhor and detest it, for it is set apart for destruction.

Do Not Forget the LORD

8 Be careful to follow every command I am giving you today, so that you may live[v] and increase and may enter and possess the land that the LORD promised on oath to your forefathers. 2Remember how the LORD your God led[w] you all the way in the desert these forty years, to humble you and to test you in order to know what was in your heart, whether or not you would keep his commands. 3He humbled you, causing you to hunger and then feeding you with manna,[x] which neither you nor your fathers had known, to teach you that man does not live on bread alone but on every word that comes from the mouth of the LORD.[y] 4Your clothes did not wear out and your feet did not swell during these forty years.[z] 5Know then in your heart that as a man disciplines his son, so the LORD your God disciplines you.[a]

6Observe the commands of the LORD your God, walking in his ways

7:12 [a]Lev 26:3-13; Dt 28:1-14; Ps 105:8-9
7:13 [b]Jn 14:21 [c]Dt 28:4
7:14 [d]Ex 23:26
7:15 [e]Ex 15:26
7:16 [f]ver 2; Ex 23:33 [g]Jdg 8:27
7:17 [h]Nu 33:53
7:18 [i]Dt 31:6 [j]Ps 105:5
7:19 [k]Dt 4:34
7:20 [l]Ex 23:28; Jos 24:12
7:21 [m]Jos 3:10 [n]Dt 10:17; Ne 9:32
7:22 [o]Ex 23:28-30
7:24 [p]Jos 23:9
7:25 [q]Ex 32:20; 1Ch 14:12 [r]Jos 7:21 [s]Jdg 8:27 [t]Dt 17:1
7:26 [u]Lev 27:28-29
8:1 [v]Dt 4:1
8:2 [w]Am 2:10
8:3 [x]Ex 16:12,14,35 [y]Ex 16:2-3; Mt 4:4*; Lk 4:4*
8:4 [z]Dt 29:5; Ne 9:21
8:5 [a]2Sa 7:14; Pr 3:11-12; Heb 12:5-11; Rev 3:19

and revering him. 7For the LORD
your God is bringing you into a
good land—a land with streams
and pools of water, with springs
flowing in the valleys and hills;[a] 8a
land with wheat and barley, vines
and fig trees, pomegranates, olive
oil and honey; 9a land where bread
will not be scarce and you will lack
nothing; a land where the rocks are
iron and you can dig copper out of
the hills.
10When you have eaten and are
satisfied,[b] praise the LORD your
God for the good land he has given
you. 11Be careful that you do not
forget the LORD your God, failing to
observe his commands, his laws
and his decrees that I am giving you
this day. 12Otherwise, when you
eat and are satisfied, when you
build fine houses and settle
down,[c] 13and when your herds and
flocks grow large and your silver
and gold increase and all you have
is multiplied, 14then your heart
will become proud and you will forget[d] the LORD your God, who
brought you out of Egypt, out of the
land of slavery. 15He led you
through the vast and dreadful
desert,[e] that thirsty and waterless
land, with its venomous snakes[f]
and scorpions. He brought you water out of hard rock.[g] 16He gave
you manna to eat in the desert,
something your fathers had never
known,[h] to humble and to test you
so that in the end it might go well
with you. 17You may say to yourself,[i] "My power and the strength
of my hands have produced this
wealth for me." 18But remember
the LORD your God, for it is he who
gives you the ability to produce
wealth,[j] and so confirms his covenant, which he swore to your forefathers, as it is today.
19If you ever forget the LORD your
God and follow other gods and worship and bow down to them, I testify against you today that you
will surely be destroyed.[k] 20Like
the nations the LORD destroyed
before you, so you will be destroyed for not obeying the LORD
your God.

Not Because of Israel's Righteousness

9 Hear, O Israel. You are now
about to cross the Jordan to go
in and dispossess nations greater
and stronger than you,[l] with large
cities that have walls up to the
sky.[m] 2The people are strong and
tall—Anakites! You know about
them and have heard it said: "Who
can stand up against the Anakites?"[n] 3But be assured today
that the LORD your God is the one
who goes across ahead of you[o] like
a devouring fire.[p] He will destroy
them; he will subdue them before
you. And you will drive them out
and annihilate them quickly,[q] as
the LORD has promised you.
4After the LORD your God has
driven them out before you, do not
say to yourself,[r] "The LORD has
brought me here to take possession
of this land because of my righteousness." No, it is on account of
the wickedness of these nations[s]
that the LORD is going to drive them
out before you. 5It is not because of
your righteousness or your integrity[t] that you are going in to take
possession of their land; but on account of the wickedness of these
nations, the LORD your God will
drive them out before you, to accomplish what he swore[u] to your
fathers, to Abraham, Isaac and Jacob. 6Understand, then, that it is
not because of your righteousness
that the LORD your God is giving you
this good land to possess, for you
are a stiff-necked people.[v]

The Golden Calf

7Remember this and never forget
how you provoked the LORD your
God to anger in the desert. From
the day you left Egypt until you arrived here, you have been rebellious against the LORD. 8At Horeb
you aroused the LORD's wrath so
that he was angry enough to destroy you.[w] 9When I went up on the
mountain to receive the tablets of
stone, the tablets of the covenant
that the LORD had made with you, I
stayed on the mountain forty days

8:7 [a] Dt 11:9-12
8:10 [b] Dt 6:10-12
8:12 [c] Hos 13:6
8:14 [d] Ps 106:21
8:15 [e] Jer 2:6 [f] Nu 21:6 [g] Nu 20:11; Ps 78:15; 114:8
8:16 [h] Ex 16:15
8:17 [i] Dt 9:4,7,24
8:18 [j] Pr 10:22; Hos 2:8
8:19 [k] Dt 4:26; 30:18
9:1 [l] Dt 4:38; 11:23,31 [m] Dt 1:28
9:2 [n] Nu 13:22,28, 32-33
9:3 [o] Dt 31:3; Jos 3:11 [p] Dt 4:24; Heb 12:29 [q] Ex 23:31; Dt 7:23-24
9:4 [r] Dt 8:17 [s] Lev 18:21, 24-30; Dt 18:9-14
9:5 [t] Tit 3:5 [u] Ge 12:7; 13:15; 15:7; 17:8; 26:4
9:6 [v] ver 13; Ex 32:9; Dt 31:27
9:8 [w] Ex 32:7-10; Ps 106:19

and forty nights; I ate no bread and
drank no water.[a] 10The LORD gave
me two stone tablets inscribed by
the finger of God.[b] On them were
all the commandments the LORD
proclaimed to you on the mountain
out of the fire, on the day of the
assembly.
11At the end of the forty days and
forty nights, the LORD gave me the
two stone tablets, the tablets of the
covenant. 12Then the LORD told me,
"Go down from here at once, because your people whom you
brought out of Egypt have become
corrupt.[c] They have turned away
quickly[d] from what I commanded
them and have made a cast idol for
themselves."
13And the LORD said to me, "I
have seen this people[e], and they
are a stiff-necked people indeed!
14Let me alone,[f] so that I may destroy them and blot out[g] their
name from under heaven. And I
will make you into a nation stronger and more numerous than they."
15So I turned and went down
from the mountain while it was
ablaze with fire. And the two tablets of the covenant were in my
hands.[p][h] 16When I looked, I saw
that you had sinned against the
LORD your God; you had made for
yourselves an idol cast in the shape
of a calf.[i] You had turned aside
quickly from the way that the LORD
had commanded you. 17So I took
the two tablets and threw them out
of my hands, breaking them to
pieces before your eyes.
18Then once again I fell[j] prostrate before the LORD for forty days
and forty nights; I ate no bread and
drank no water, because of all the
sin you had committed, doing what
was evil in the LORD's sight and so
provoking him to anger. 19I feared
the anger and wrath of the LORD, for
he was angry enough with you to
destroy you.[k] But again the LORD
listened to me.[l] 20And the LORD
was angry enough with Aaron to
destroy him, but at that time I
prayed for Aaron too. 21Also I took
that sinful thing of yours, the calf
you had made, and burned it in the
fire. Then I crushed it and ground it
to powder as fine as dust and threw
the dust into a stream that flowed
down the mountain.[m]
22You also made the LORD angry
at Taberah,[n] at Massah[o] and at
Kibroth Hattaavah.[p]
23And when the LORD sent you
out from Kadesh Barnea, he said,
"Go up and take possession of the
land I have given you." But you rebelled against the command of the
LORD your God. You did not trust[q]
him or obey him. 24You have been
rebellious against the LORD ever
since I have known you.[r]
25I lay prostrate before the LORD
those forty days and forty nights
because the LORD had said he
would destroy you.[s] 26I prayed to
the LORD and said, "O Sovereign
LORD, do not destroy your people,
your own inheritance that you redeemed by your great power and
brought out of Egypt with a mighty
hand.[t] 27Remember your servants
Abraham, Isaac and Jacob. Overlook the stubbornness of this people, their wickedness and their sin.
28Otherwise, the country from
which you brought us will say, 'Because the LORD was not able to take
them into the land he had promised them, and because he hated
them, he brought them out to put
them to death in the desert.'[u]
29But they are your people, your inheritance[v] that you brought out by
your great power and your outstretched arm.[w]"

Tablets Like the First Ones

10 At that time the LORD said
to me, "Chisel out two
stone tablets[x] like the first ones
and come up to me on the mountain. Also make a wooden chest.[q]
2I will write on the tablets the
words that were on the first tablets,
which you broke. Then you are to
put them in the chest."[y]
3So I made the ark out of acacia
wood[z] and chiseled[a] out two

9:9 [a]Ex 24:12,15, 18; 34:28
9:10 [b]Ex 31:18; Dt 4:13
9:12 [c]Ex 32:7-8; Dt 31:29 [d]Jdg 2:17
9:13 [e]ver 6; Ex 32:9; Dt 10:16
9:14 [f]Ex 32:10 [g]Nu 14:12; Dt 29:20
9:15 [h]Ex 19:18; 32:15
9:16 [i]Ex 32:19
9:18 [j]Ex 34:28
9:19 [k]Ex 32:10-11, 14 [l]Dt 10:10
9:21 [m]Ex 32:20
9:22 [n]Nu 11:3 [o]Ex 17:7 [p]Nu 11:34
9:23 [q]Ps 106:24
9:24 [r]ver 7; Dt 31:27
9:25 [s]ver 18
9:26 [t]Ex 32:11
9:28 [u]Ex 32:12; Nu 14:16
9:29 [v]Dt 4:20; 1Ki 8:51 [w]Dt 4:34; Ne 1:10
10:1 [x]Ex 25:10; 34:1-2
10:2 [y]Ex 25:16,21; Dt 4:13
10:3 [z]Ex 25:5,10; 37:1-9 [a]Ex 34:4

p15 Or *And I had the two tablets of the covenant with me, one in each hand*
q1 That is, an ark

stone tablets like the first ones,
and I went up on the mountain
with the two tablets in my hands.
4The LORD wrote on these tablets
what he had written before, the
Ten Commandments he had proclaimed[a] to you on the mountain,
out of the fire, on the day of the
assembly. And the LORD gave them
to me. 5Then I came back down the
mountain[b] and put the tablets in
the ark[c] I had made, as the LORD
commanded me, and they are there
now.[d]

6(The Israelites traveled from
the wells of the Jaakanites to Mo-
serah.[e] There Aaron died and was
buried, and Eleazar his son succeeded him as priest.[f] 7From
there they traveled to Gudgodah
and on to Jotbathah, a land with
streams of water.[g] 8At that time
the LORD set apart the tribe of
Levi[h] to carry the ark of the covenant of the LORD, to stand before
the LORD to minister[i] and to pronounce blessings[j] in his name, as
they still do today. 9That is why the
Levites have no share or inheritance among their brothers; the
LORD is their inheritance,[k] as the
LORD your God told them.)

10Now I had stayed on the
mountain forty days and nights, as
I did the first time, and the LORD
listened to me at this time also. It
was not his will to destroy you.[l]
11"Go," the LORD said to me, "and
lead the people on their way, so
that they may enter and possess
the land that I swore to their fathers to give them."

Fear the LORD

12And now, O Israel, what does
the LORD your God ask of you[m] but
to fear the LORD your God, to walk
in all his ways, to love him,[n] to
serve the LORD your God with all
your heart[o] and with all your soul,
13and to observe the LORD's commands and decrees that I am giving
you today for your own good?

14To the LORD your God belong
the heavens, even the highest heavens,[p] the earth and everything in
it.[q] 15Yet the LORD set his affection
on your forefathers and loved[r]
them, and he chose you, their
descendants, above all the nations,
as it is today. 16Circumcise[s] your
hearts, therefore, and do not be
stiff-necked[t] any longer. 17For the
LORD your God is God of gods[u] and
Lord of lords, the great God,
mighty and awesome, who shows
no partiality[v] and accepts no
bribes. 18He defends the cause of
the fatherless and the widow,[w] and
loves the alien, giving him food and
clothing. 19And you are to love
those who are aliens, for you yourselves were aliens in Egypt.[x]
20Fear the LORD your God and serve
him.[y] Hold fast[z] to him and take
your oaths in his name.[a] 21He is
your praise;[b] he is your God, who
performed for you those great and
awesome wonders[c] you saw with
your own eyes. 22Your forefathers
who went down into Egypt were
seventy in all,[d] and now the LORD
your God has made you as numerous as the stars in the sky.[e]

Love and Obey the LORD

11 Love[f] the LORD your God
and keep his requirements,
his decrees, his laws and his commands always.[g] 2Remember today
that your children were not the
ones who saw and experienced the
discipline of the LORD your God:[h]
his majesty, his mighty hand, his
outstretched arm; 3the signs he
performed and the things he did in
the heart of Egypt, both to Pharaoh
king of Egypt and to his whole
country; 4what he did to the Egyptian army, to its horses and chariots, how he overwhelmed them
with the waters of the Red Sea[r][i]
as they were pursuing you, and how
the LORD brought lasting ruin on
them. 5It was not your children
who saw what he did for you in the
desert until you arrived at this
place, 6and what he did[j] to Dathan and Abiram, sons of Eliab the
Reubenite, when the earth opened
its mouth right in the middle of all
Israel and swallowed them up with

10:4 [a]Ex 20:1
10:5 [b]Ex 34:29 [c]Ex 40:20 [d]1Ki 8:9
10:6 [e]Nu 33:30-31, 38 [f]Nu 20:25-28
10:7 [g]Nu 33:32-34
10:8 [h]Nu 3:6 [i]Dt 18:5 [j]Dt 21:5
10:9 [k]Nu 18:20; Dt 18:1-2; Eze 44:28
10:10 [l]Ex 33:17; 34:28; Dt 9:18-19,25
10:12 [m]Mic 6:8 [n]Dt 5:33; 6:13; Mt 22:37 [o]Dt 6:5
10:14 [p]1Ki 8:27 [q]Ex 19:5
10:15 [r]Dt 4:37
10:16 [s]Jer 4:4 [t]Dt 9:6
10:17 [u]Jos 22:22; Da 2:47 [v]Ac 10:34; Ro 2:11; Eph 6:9
10:18 [w]Ps 68:5
10:19 [x]Lev 19:34
10:20 [y]Mt 4:10 [z]Dt 11:22 [a]Ps 63:11
10:21 [b]Ex 15:2; Jer 17:14 [c]Ps 106:21-22
10:22 [d]Ge 46:26-27 [e]Ge 15:5; Dt 1:10
11:1 [f]Dt 10:12 [g]Zec 3:7
11:2 [h]Dt 5:24; 8:5
11:4 [i]Ex 14:27
11:6 [j]Nu 16:1-35

[r]4 Hebrew *Yam Suph*; that is, Sea of Reeds

their households, their tents and
every living thing that belonged to
them. 7But it was your own eyes
that saw all these great things the
LORD has done.
8Observe therefore all the commands I am giving you today, so
that you may have the strength to
go in and take over the land that
you are crossing the Jordan to possess,[a] 9and so that you may live
long[b] in the land that the LORD
swore[c] to your forefathers to give
to them and their descendants, a
land flowing with milk and honey.[d] 10The land you are entering to
take over is not like the land of
Egypt, from which you have come,
where you planted your seed and
irrigated it by foot as in a vegetable
garden. 11But the land you are
crossing the Jordan to take possession of is a land of mountains and
valleys that drinks rain from heav-
en.[e] 12It is a land the LORD your
God cares for; the eyes[f] of the
LORD your God are continually on it
from the beginning of the year to
its end.
13So if you faithfully obey[g] the
commands I am giving you today
—to love[h] the LORD your God and
to serve him with all your heart and
with all your soul— 14then I will
send rain[i] on your land in its season, both autumn and spring
rains,[j] so that you may gather in
your grain, new wine and oil. 15I
will provide grass[k] in the fields for
your cattle, and you will eat and be
satisfied.[l]
16Be careful, or you will be enticed to turn away and worship other gods and bow down to them.[m]
17Then the LORD's anger[n] will burn
against you, and he will shut[o] the
heavens so that it will not rain and
the ground will yield no produce,
and you will soon perish[p] from the
good land the LORD is giving you.
18Fix these words of mine in your
hearts and minds; tie them as symbols on your hands and bind them
on your foreheads.[q] 19Teach them
to your children,[r] talking about
them when you sit at home and
when you walk along the road,
when you lie down and when you
get up.[s] 20Write them on the doorframes of your houses and on your
gates,[t] 21so that your days and the
days of your children may be
many[u] in the land that the LORD
swore to give your forefathers, as
many as the days that the heavens
are above the earth.[v]
22If you carefully observe[w] all
these commands I am giving you to
follow—to love the LORD your God,
to walk in all his ways and to hold
fast[x] to him— 23then the LORD will
drive out all these nations before
you, and you will dispossess nations larger and stronger than
you.[y] 24Every place where you set
your foot will be yours:[z] Your territory will extend from the desert to
Lebanon, and from the Euphrates
River to the western sea.[s] 25No
man will be able to stand against
you. The LORD your God, as he
promised you, will put the terror
and fear of you on the whole land,
wherever you go.[a]
26See, I am setting before you today a blessing and a curse[b]—
27the blessing[c] if you obey the
commands of the LORD your God
that I am giving you today; 28the
curse if you disobey[d] the commands of the LORD your God and
turn from the way that I command
you today by following other gods,
which you have not known.
29When the LORD your God has
brought you into the land you are
entering to possess, you are to proclaim on Mount Gerizim the blessings, and on Mount Ebal the
curses.[e] 30As you know, these
mountains are across the Jordan,
west of the road,[t] toward the setting sun, near the great trees of Moreh,[f] in the territory of those Canaanites living in the Arabah in the
vicinity of Gilgal.[g] 31You are about
to cross the Jordan to enter and
take possession[h] of the land the
LORD your God is giving you. When
you have taken it over and are living there, 32be sure that you obey

11:8 [a]Jos 1:7
11:9 [b]Dt 4:40; Pr 10:27 [c]Dt 9:5 [d]Ex 3:8
11:11 [e]Dt 8:7
11:12 [f]1Ki 9:3
11:13 [g]Dt 6:17 [h]Dt 10:12
11:14 [i]Lev 26:4; Dt 28:12 [j]Joel 2:23; Jas 5:7
11:15 [k]Ps 104:14 [l]Dt 6:11
11:16 [m]Dt 8:19, 29:18; Job 31:9,27
11:17 [n]Dt 6:15 [o]1Ki 8:35; 2Ch 6:26 [p]Dt 4:26
11:18 [q]Dt 6:6-8
11:19 [r]Dt 6:7 [s]Dt 4:9-10
11:20 [t]Dt 6:9
11:21 [u]Pr 3:2; 4:10 [v]Ps 72:5
11:22 [w]Dt 6:17 [x]Dt 10:20
11:23 [y]Dt 4:38; 9:1
11:24 [z]Ge 15:18; Ex 23:31; Jos 1:3; 14:9
11:25 [a]Ex 23:27; Dt 7:24
11:26 [b]Dt 30:1,15, 19
11:27 [c]Dt 28:1-14
11:28 [d]Dt 28:15
11:29 [e]Dt 27:12-13; Jos 8:33
11:30 [f]Ge 12:6 [g]Jos 4:19
11:31 [h]Dt 9:1; Jos 1:11

[s]24 That is, the Mediterranean [t]30 Or *Jordan, westward*

all the decrees and laws I am setting before you today.

The One Place of Worship

12 These are the decrees and
laws you must be careful to
follow in the land that the LORD, the
God of your fathers, has given you
to possess—as long as you live in
the land.[a] **2**Destroy completely all
the places on the high mountains
and on the hills and under every
spreading tree[b] where the nations
you are dispossessing worship their
gods. **3**Break down their altars,
smash[c] their sacred stones and
burn their Asherah poles in the
fire; cut down the idols of their
gods and wipe out their names
from those places.
4You must not worship the LORD
your God in their way. **5**But you are
to seek the place the LORD your God
will choose from among all your
tribes to put his Name there for his
dwelling.[d] To that place you must
go; **6**there bring your burnt offerings and sacrifices, your tithes[e]
and special gifts, what you have
vowed to give and your freewill offerings, and the firstborn of your
herds and flocks. **7**There, in the
presence of the LORD your God, you
and your families shall eat and
shall rejoice[f] in everything you
have put your hand to, because the
LORD your God has blessed you.
8You are not to do as we do here
today, everyone as he sees fit,
9since you have not yet reached the
resting place and the inheritance
the LORD your God is giving you.
10But you will cross the Jordan and
settle in the land the LORD your God
is giving[g] you as an inheritance,
and he will give you rest from all
your enemies around you so that
you will live in safety. **11**Then to
the place the LORD your God will
choose as a dwelling for his
Name[h]—there you are to bring everything I command you: your
burnt offerings and sacrifices, your
tithes and special gifts, and all the
choice possessions you have vowed
to the LORD. **12**And there rejoice[i]
before the LORD your God, you, your
sons and daughters, your menservants and maidservants, and the
Levites from your towns, who have
no allotment or inheritance[j] of
their own. **13**Be careful not to sacrifice your burnt offerings anywhere
you please. **14**Offer them only at
the place the LORD will choose[k] in
one of your tribes, and there observe everything I command you.
15Nevertheless, you may slaughter your animals in any of your
towns and eat as much of the meat
as you want, as if it were gazelle or
deer,[l] according to the blessing
the LORD your God gives you. Both
the ceremonially unclean and the
clean may eat it. **16**But you must
not eat the blood;[m] pour it out on
the ground like water.[n] **17**You
must not eat in your own towns the
tithe of your grain and new wine
and oil, or the firstborn of your
herds and flocks, or whatever you
have vowed to give, or your freewill
offerings or special gifts. **18**Instead,
you are to eat[o] them in the presence of the LORD your God at the
place the LORD your God will
choose[p]—you, your sons and
daughters, your menservants and
maidservants, and the Levites from
your towns—and you are to rejoice[q] before the LORD your God in
everything you put your hand to.
19Be careful not to neglect the Levites[r] as long as you live in your
land.
20When the LORD your God has
enlarged your territory[s] as he
promised[t] you, and you crave
meat and say, "I would like some
meat," then you may eat as much
of it as you want. **21**If the place
where the LORD your God chooses
to put his Name is too far away
from you, you may slaughter animals from the herds and flocks the
LORD has given you, as I have commanded you, and in your own
towns you may eat as much of
them as you want. **22**Eat them as
you would gazelle or deer.[u] Both
the ceremonially unclean and the
clean may eat. **23**But be sure you do
not eat the blood,[v] because the
blood is the life, and you must not

12:1 [a]Dt 4:9-10; 1Ki 8:40
12:2 [b]2Ki 16:4; 17:10
12:3 [c]Nu 33:52; Dt 7:5; Jdg 2:2
12:5 [d]ver 11,13; 2Ch 7:12,16
12:6 [e]Dt 14:22-23
12:7 [f]ver 12,18; Lev 23:40; Dt 14:26
12:10 [g]Dt 11:31
12:11 [h]ver 5; Dt 15:20; 16:2
12:12 [i]ver 7 [j]Dt 10:9; 14:29
12:14 [k]ver 11
12:15 [l]ver 20-23; Dt 14:5; 15:22
12:16 [m]Ge 9:4; Lev 7:26; 17:10-12 [n]Dt 15:23
12:18 [o]Dt 14:23 [p]ver 5 [q]ver 7, 12
12:19 [r]Dt 14:27
12:20 [s]Dt 19:8 [t]Ge 15:18; Dt 11:24
12:22 [u]ver 15
12:23 [v]ver 16; Ge 9:4; Lev 17:11,14

the Levites[a] living in your towns,
for they have no allotment or inheritance of their own.[b]

28At the end of every three years,
bring all the tithes of that year's
produce and store it in your
towns,[c] 29so that the Levites (who
have no allotment[d] or inheritance
of their own) and the aliens,[e] the
fatherless and the widows who live
in your towns may come and eat
and be satisfied, and so that the
LORD your God may bless[f] you in
all the work of your hands.

The Year for Canceling Debts

15:1–11Ref – Lev 25:8–38

15 At the end of every seven
years you must cancel
debts.[g] 2This is how it is to be
done: Every creditor shall cancel
the loan he has made to his fellow
Israelite. He shall not require payment from his fellow Israelite or
brother, because the LORD's time
for canceling debts has been proclaimed. 3You may require payment from a foreigner,[h] but you
must cancel any debt your brother
owes you. 4However, there should
be no poor among you, for in the
land the LORD your God is giving
you to possess as your inheritance,
he will richly bless[i] you, 5if only
you fully obey the LORD your God
and are careful to follow[j] all these
commands I am giving you today.
6For the LORD your God will bless
you as he has promised, and you
will lend to many nations but will
borrow from none. You will rule
over many nations but none will
rule over you.[k]

7If there is a poor man among
your brothers in any of the towns of
the land that the LORD your God is
giving you, do not be hardhearted
or tightfisted[l] toward your poor
brother. 8Rather be openhanded[m]
and freely lend him whatever he
needs. 9Be careful not to harbor
this wicked thought: "The seventh
year, the year for canceling debts,"[n]
is near," so that you do not show ill
will[o] toward your needy brother
and give him nothing. He may then

14:27 [a]Dt 12:19 [b]Nu 18:20
14:28 [c]Dt 26:12
14:29 [d]ver 27 [e]Dt 26:12 [f]Dt 15:10; Mal 3:10
15:1 [g]Dt 31:10
15:3 [h]Dt 23:20
15:4 [i]Dt 28:8
15:5 [j]Dt 28:1
15:6 [k]Dt 28:12-13, 44
15:7 [l]1Jn 3:17
15:8 [m]Mt 5:42; Lk 6:34
15:9 [n]ver 1 [o]Mt 20:15 [p]Dt 24:15
15:10 [q]2Co 9:5 [r]Dt 14:29; 24:19
15:11 [s]Mt 26:11; Mk 14:7; Jn 12:8
15:12 [t]Ex 21:2; Lev 25:39; Jer 34:14
15:15 [u]Dt 5:15 [v]Dt 16:12
15:19 [w]Ex 13:2
15:20 [x]Dt 12:5-7,17, 18; 14:23

appeal to the LORD against you, and
you will be found guilty of sin.[p]
10Give generously to him and do so
without a grudging heart;[q] then
because of this the LORD your God
will bless[r] you in all your work and
in everything you put your hand to.
11There will always be poor people
in the land. Therefore I command
you to be openhanded toward your
brothers and toward the poor and
needy in your land.[s]

Freeing Servants

15:12–18pp – Ex 21:2–6
15:12–18Ref – Lev 25:38–55

12If a fellow Hebrew, a man or a
woman, sells himself to you and
serves you six years, in the seventh
year you must let him go free.[t]
13And when you release him, do
not send him away empty-handed.
14Supply him liberally from your
flock, your threshing floor and your
winepress. Give to him as the LORD
your God has blessed you. 15Re-
member that you were slaves[u] in
Egypt and the LORD your God redeemed you.[v] That is why I give
you this command today.

16But if your servant says to you,
"I do not want to leave you," because he loves you and your family
and is well off with you, 17then
take an awl and push it through his
ear lobe into the door, and he will
become your servant for life. Do
the same for your maidservant.

18Do not consider it a hardship
to set your servant free, because his
service to you these six years has
been worth twice as much as that
of a hired hand. And the LORD your
God will bless you in everything
you do.

The Firstborn Animals

19Set apart for the LORD your God
every firstborn male[w] of your herds
and flocks. Do not put the firstborn
of your oxen to work, and do not
shear the firstborn of your sheep.
20Each year you and your family
are to eat them in the presence of
the LORD your God at the place he
will choose.[x] 21If an animal has a
defect, is lame or blind, or has any

serious flaw, you must not sacrifice
it to the LORD your God.[a] **22**You are
to eat it in your own towns. Both
the ceremonially unclean and the
clean may eat it, as if it were gazelle or deer.[b] **23**But you must not
eat the blood; pour it out on the
ground like water.[c]

Passover

16:1–8pp — Ex 12:14–20; Lev 23:4–8; Nu 28:16–25

16 Observe the month of
Abib[d] and celebrate the
Passover of the LORD your God, because in the month of Abib he
brought you out of Egypt by night.
2Sacrifice as the Passover to the
LORD your God an animal from your
flock or herd at the place the LORD
will choose as a dwelling for his
Name.[e] **3**Do not eat it with bread
made with yeast, but for seven days
eat unleavened bread, the bread of
affliction,[f] because you left Egypt
in haste[g]—so that all the days of
your life you may remember the
time of your departure from
Egypt.[h] **4**Let no yeast be found in
your possession in all your land for
seven days. Do not let any of the
meat you sacrifice on the evening
of the first day remain until morning.[i]
5You must not sacrifice the Passover in any town the LORD your God
gives you **6**except in the place he
will choose as a dwelling for his
Name. There you must sacrifice
the Passover in the evening, when
the sun goes down, on the anniver-
sary[x][j] of your departure from
Egypt. **7**Roast[k] it and eat it at the
place the LORD your God will
choose. Then in the morning return to your tents. **8**For six days eat
unleavened bread and on the seventh day hold an assembly[l] to the
LORD your God and do no work.

Feast of Weeks

16:9–12pp — Lev 23:15–22; Nu 28:26–31

9Count off seven weeks[m] from
the time you begin to put the sickle
to the standing grain.[n] **10**Then celebrate the Feast of Weeks to the
LORD your God by giving a freewill
offering in proportion to the blessings the LORD your God has given
you. **11**And rejoice[o] before the
LORD your God at the place he will
choose as a dwelling for his
Name—you, your sons and daughters, your menservants and maidservants, the Levites[p] in your
towns, and the aliens, the fatherless and the widows living among
you. **12**Remember that you were
slaves in Egypt,[q] and follow carefully these decrees.

Feast of Tabernacles

16:13–17pp — Lev 23:33–43; Nu 29:12–39

13Celebrate the Feast of Tabernacles for seven days after you have
gathered the produce of your
threshing floor[r] and your winepress.[s] **14**Be joyful[t] at your
Feast—you, your sons and daughters, your menservants and maidservants, and the Levites, the
aliens, the fatherless and the widows who live in your towns. **15**For
seven days celebrate the Feast to
the LORD your God at the place the
LORD will choose. For the LORD your
God will bless you in all your harvest and in all the work of your
hands, and your joy[u] will be complete.
16Three times a year all your
men must appear before the LORD
your God at the place he will
choose: at the Feast of Unleavened
Bread, the Feast of Weeks and the
Feast of Tabernacles.[v] No man
should appear before the LORD
empty-handed:[w] **17**Each of you
must bring a gift in proportion to
the way the LORD your God has
blessed you.

Judges

18Appoint judges[x] and officials
for each of your tribes in every town
the LORD your God is giving you,
and they shall judge the people
fairly. **19**Do not pervert justice[y] or
show partiality.[z] Do not accept a
bribe,[a] for a bribe blinds the eyes
of the wise and twists the words of

15:21 [a] Lev 22:19-25
15:22 [b] Dt 12:15,22
15:23 [c] Dt 12:16
16:1 [d] Ex 12:2; 13:4
16:2 [e] Dt 12:5,26
16:3 [f] Ex 12:8,39; 34:18 [g] Ex 12:11,15, 19 [h] Ex 13:3, 6-7
16:4 [i] Ex 12:10; 34:25
16:6 [j] Ex 12:6; Dt 12:5
16:7 [k] Ex 12:8; 2Ch 35:13
16:8 [l] Ex 12:16; 13:6; Lev 23:8
16:9 [m] Ex 34:22; Lev 23:15 [n] Ex 23:16; Nu 28:26
16:11 [o] Dt 12:7 [p] Dt 12:12
16:12 [q] Dt 15:15
16:13 [r] Lev 23:34 [s] Ex 23:16
16:14 [t] ver 11
16:15 [u] Lev 23:39
16:16 [v] Ex 23:14,16 [w] Ex 34:20
16:18 [x] Dt 1:16
16:19 [y] Ex 23:2,8 [z] Lev 19:15; Dt 1:17 [a] Ecc 7:7

[x]6 Or *down, at the time of day*

the righteous. 20 Follow justice and
justice alone, so that you may live
and possess the land the LORD your
God is giving you.

Worshiping Other Gods

21 Do not set up any wood-
en Asherah pole[y][a] beside the altar you build to the LORD your
God,[b] 22 and do not erect a sacred
stone,[c] for these the LORD your
God hates.

17 Do not sacrifice to the LORD
your God an ox or a sheep
that has any defect[d] or flaw in it,
for that would be detestable to
him.[e]

2 If a man or woman living among
you in one of the towns the LORD
gives you is found doing evil in the
eyes of the LORD your God in violation of his covenant,[f] 3 and contrary to my command[g] has worshiped other gods, bowing down to
them or to the sun[h] or the moon or
the stars of the sky, 4 and this has
been brought to your attention,
then you must investigate it thoroughly. If it is true and it has been
proved that this detestable thing
has been done in Israel,[i] 5 take the
man or woman who has done this
evil deed to your city gate and
stone that person to death.[j] 6 On
the testimony of two or three witnesses a man shall be put to death,
but no one shall be put to death on
the testimony of only one witness.[k] 7 The hands of the witnesses
must be the first in putting him to
death, and then the hands of all the
people. You must purge the evil[l]
from among you.

Law Courts

8 If cases come before your courts
that are too difficult for you to
judge—whether bloodshed, lawsuits or assaults[m]—take them to
the place the LORD your God will
choose.[n] 9 Go to the priests, who
are Levites, and to the judge who is
in office at that time. Inquire of
them and they will give you the verdict.[o] 10 You must act according to
the decisions they give you at the
place the LORD will choose. Be careful to do everything they direct you
to do. 11 Act according to the law
they teach you and the decisions
they give you. Do not turn aside
from what they tell you, to the right
or to the left.[p] 12 The man who
shows contempt[q] for the judge or
for the priest who stands ministering there to the LORD your God
must be put to death. You must
purge the evil from Israel. 13 All
the people will hear and be afraid,
and will not be contemptuous
again.[r]

The King

14 When you enter the land the
LORD your God is giving you and
have taken possession of it and settled in it, and you say, "Let us set
a king over us like all the nations
around us,"[s] 15 be sure to appoint
over you the king the LORD your
God chooses. He must be from
among your own brothers.[t] Do not
place a foreigner over you, one who
is not a brother Israelite. 16 The
king, moreover, must not acquire
great numbers of horses for himself[u] or make the people return to
Egypt[v] to get more of them,[w] for
the LORD has told you, "You are not
to go back that way again."[x] 17 He
must not take many wives,[y] or his
heart will be led astray. He must
not accumulate large amounts of
silver and gold.

18 When he takes the throne of
his kingdom, he is to write[z] for
himself on a scroll a copy of this
law, taken from that of the priests,
who are Levites. 19 It is to be with
him, and he is to read it all the days
of his life[a] so that he may learn to
revere the LORD his God and follow
carefully all the words of this law
and these decrees 20 and not consider himself better than his brothers and turn from the law[b] to the
right or to the left.[c] Then he and
his descendants will reign a long
time over his kingdom in Israel.

16:21 [a] Dt 7:5 [b] Ex 34:13; 2Ki 17:16; 21:3; 2Ch 33:3
16:22 [c] Lev 26:1
17:1 [d] Mal 1:8,13 [e] Dt 15:21
17:2 [f] Dt 13:6-11
17:3 [g] Jer 7:22-23 [h] Job 31:26
17:4 [i] Dt 13:12-14
17:5 [j] Lev 24:14
17:6 [k] Nu 35:30; Dt 19:15; Jos 7:25; Mt 18:16; Jn 8:17; 2Co 13:1; 1Ti 5:19; Heb 10:28
17:7 [l] Dt 13:5,9
17:8 [m] 2Ch 19:10 [n] Dt 12:5; Hag 2:11
17:9 [o] Dt 19:17; Eze 44:24
17:11 [p] Dt 25:1
17:12 [q] Nu 15:30
17:13 [r] Dt 13:11; 19:20
17:14 [s] Dt 11:31; 1Sa 8:5,19-20
17:15 [t] Jer 30:21
17:16 [u] 1Ki 4:26; 10:26 [v] Isa 31:1; Hos 11:5 [w] 1Ki 10:28; Eze 17:15 [x] Ex 13:17
17:17 [y] 1Ki 11:3
17:18 [z] Dt 31:22,24
17:19 [a] Jos 1:8
17:20 [b] 1Ki 15:5 [c] Dt 5:32

y21 Or *Do not plant any tree dedicated to Asherah*

Offerings for Priests and Levites

18 The priests, who are Levites—indeed the whole
tribe of Levi—are to have no allotment or inheritance with Israel.
They shall live on the offerings
made to the LORD by fire, for that is
their inheritance.[a] **2**They shall
have no inheritance among their
brothers; the LORD is their inheritance, as he promised them.

3This is the share due the priests
from the people who sacrifice a
bull or a sheep: the shoulder, the
jowls and the inner parts.[b] **4**You
are to give them the firstfruits of
your grain, new wine and oil, and
the first wool from the shearing of
your sheep,[c] **5**for the LORD your
God has chosen them[d] and their
descendants out of all your tribes
to stand and minister[e] in the
LORD's name always.

6If a Levite moves from one of
your towns anywhere in Israel
where he is living, and comes in all
earnestness to the place the LORD
will choose,[f] **7**he may minister in
the name of the LORD his God like
all his fellow Levites who serve
there in the presence of the LORD.
8He is to share equally in their benefits, even though he has received
money from the sale of family possessions.[g]

Detestable Practices

9When you enter the land the
LORD your God is giving you, do not
learn to imitate[h] the detestable
ways of the nations there. **10**Let no
one be found among you who sacrifices his son or daughter in[z] the
fire, who practices divination[i] or
sorcery, interprets omens, engages
in witchcraft,[j] **11**or casts spells, or
who is a medium or spiritist or who
consults the dead. **12**Anyone who
does these things is detestable to
the LORD, and because of these detestable practices the LORD your
God will drive out those nations
before you.[k] **13**You must be blameless before the LORD your God.

The Prophet

14The nations you will dispossess listen to those who practice
sorcery or divination. But as for
you, the LORD your God has not permitted you to do so. **15**The LORD
your God will raise up for you a
prophet like me from among your
own brothers.[l] You must listen to
him. **16**For this is what you asked of
the LORD your God at Horeb on the
day of the assembly when you said,
"Let us not hear the voice of the
LORD our God nor see this great fire
anymore, or we will die."[m]

17The LORD said to me: "What
they say is good. **18**I will raise up for
them a prophet like you from
among their brothers; I will put my
words[n] in his mouth, and he will
tell them everything I command
him.[o] **19**If anyone does not listen
to my words that the prophet
speaks in my name, I myself will
call him to account.[p] **20**But a
prophet who presumes to speak in
my name anything I have not commanded him to say, or a prophet
who speaks in the name of other
gods,[q] must be put to death."[r]

21You may say to yourselves,
"How can we know when a message has not been spoken by the
LORD?" **22**If what a prophet proclaims in the name of the LORD
does not take place or come true,
that is a message the LORD has not
spoken.[s] That prophet has spoken
presumptuously.[t] Do not be afraid
of him.

Cities of Refuge

19:1–14Ref — Nu 35:6–34; Dt 4:41–43; Jos 20:1–9

19 When the LORD your God
has destroyed the nations
whose land he is giving you, and
when you have driven them out and
settled in their towns and houses,[u]
2then set aside for yourselves three
cities centrally located in the land
the LORD your God is giving you to
possess. **3**Build roads to them and

18:1 [a]Dt 10:9; 1Co 9:13
18:3 [b]Lev 7:28-34
18:4 [c]Ex 22:29; Nu 18:12
18:5 [d]Ex 28:1 [e]Dt 10:8
18:6 [f]Nu 35:2-3
18:8 [g]2Ch 31:4; Ne 12:44,47
18:9 [h]Dt 12:29-31
18:10 [i]Dt 12:31 [j]Lev 19:31
18:12 [k]Lev 18:24; Dt 9:4
18:15 [l]Jn 1:21; Ac 3:22*; 7:37*
18:16 [m]Ex 20:19; Dt 5:23-27
18:18 [n]Isa 51:16; Jn 17:8 [o]Jn 4:25-26; 8:28; 12:49-50
18:19 [p]Ac 3:23*
18:20 [q]Jer 14:14 [r]Dt 13:1-5
18:22 [s]Jer 28:9 [t]ver 20
19:1 [u]Dt 12:29

[z]10 *Or who makes his son or daughter pass through*

divide into three parts the land the LORD your God is giving you as an inheritance, so that anyone who kills a man may flee there.

4This is the rule concerning the man who kills another and flees there to save his life—one who kills his neighbor unintentionally, without malice aforethought. 5For instance, a man may go into the forest with his neighbor to cut wood, and as he swings his ax to fell a tree, the head may fly off and hit his neighbor and kill him. That man may flee to one of these cities and save his life. 6Otherwise, the avenger of blood[a] might pursue him in a rage, overtake him if the distance is too great, and kill him even though he is not deserving of death, since he did it to his neighbor without malice aforethought. 7This is why I command you to set aside for yourselves three cities.

8If the LORD your God enlarges your territory, as he promised on oath to your forefathers, and gives you the whole land he promised them, 9because you carefully follow all these laws I command you today—to love the LORD your God and to walk always in his ways[b]—then you are to set aside three more cities. 10Do this so that innocent blood will not be shed in your land, which the LORD your God is giving you as your inheritance, and so that you will not be guilty of bloodshed.[c]

11But if a man hates his neighbor and lies in wait for him, assaults and kills him,[d] and then flees to one of these cities, 12the elders of his town shall send for him, bring him back from the city, and hand him over to the avenger of blood to die. 13Show him no pity.[e] You must purge from Israel the guilt of shedding innocent blood,[f] so that it may go well with you.

14Do not move your neighbor's boundary stone set up by your predecessors in the inheritance you receive in the land the LORD your God is giving you to possess.[g]

19:6 [a]Nu 35:12
19:9 [b]Jos 20:7-8
19:10 [c]Nu 35:33; Dt 21:1-9
19:11 [d]Nu 35:16
19:13 [e]Dt 7:2 [f]1Ki 2:31
19:14 [g]Dt 27:17; Pr 22:28; Hos 5:10
19:15 [h]Nu 35:30; Dt 17:6; Mt 18:16*; Jn 8:17; 2Co 13:1*; 1Ti 5:19; Heb 10:28
19:16 [i]Ex 23:1; Ps 27:12
19:17 [j]Dt 17:9
19:19 [k]Pr 19:5,9
19:20 [l]Dt 17:13; 21:21
19:21 [m]ver 13 [n]Ex 21:24; Lev 24:20; Mt 5:38*
20:1 [o]Ps 20:7; Isa 31:1 [p]Dt 31:6,8 [q]2Ch 32:7-8
20:3 [r]Jos 23:10
20:4 [s]Dt 1:30; 3:22; Jos 23:10
20:5 [t]Ne 12:27

Witnesses

15One witness is not enough to convict a man accused of any crime or offense he may have committed. A matter must be established by the testimony of two or three witnesses.[h]

16If a malicious witness[i] takes the stand to accuse a man of a crime, 17the two men involved in the dispute must stand in the presence of the LORD before the priests and the judges[j] who are in office at the time. 18The judges must make a thorough investigation, and if the witness proves to be a liar, giving false testimony against his brother, 19then do to him as he intended to do to his brother.[k] You must purge the evil from among you. 20The rest of the people will hear of this and be afraid,[l] and never again will such an evil thing be done among you. 21Show no pity:[m] life for life, eye for eye, tooth for tooth, hand for hand, foot for foot.[n]

Going to War

20 When you go to war against your enemies and see horses and chariots and an army greater than yours,[o] do not be afraid[p] of them,[q] because the LORD your God, who brought you up out of Egypt, will be with you. 2When you are about to go into battle, the priest shall come forward and address the army. 3He shall say: "Hear, O Israel, today you are going into battle against your enemies. Do not be fainthearted[r] or afraid; do not be terrified or give way to panic before them. 4For the LORD your God is the one who goes with you to fight[s] for you against your enemies to give you victory."

5The officers shall say to the army: "Has anyone built a new house and not dedicated[t] it? Let him go home, or he may die in battle and someone else may dedicate it. 6Has anyone planted a vineyard and not begun to enjoy it? Let him go home, or he may die in battle and someone else enjoy it. 7Has

anyone become pledged to a woman and not married her? Let him go
home, or he may die in battle and
someone else marry her.[a]" **8**Then
the officers shall add, "Is any man
afraid or fainthearted? Let him
go home so that his brothers will
not become disheartened too."[b]
9When the officers have finished
speaking to the army, they shall appoint commanders over it.
10When you march up to attack a
city, make its people an offer of
peace.[c] **11**If they accept and open
their gates, all the people in it shall
be subject to forced labor[d] and
shall work for you. **12**If they refuse
to make peace and they engage you
in battle, lay siege to that city.
13When the LORD your God delivers
it into your hand, put to the sword
all the men in it.[e] **14**As for the
women, the children, the livestock[f] and everything else in the
city, you may take these as plunder
for yourselves. And you may use
the plunder the LORD your God
gives you from your enemies.
15This is how you are to treat all
the cities that are at a distance
from you and do not belong to the
nations nearby.
16However, in the cities of the
nations the LORD your God is giving
you as an inheritance, do not leave
alive anything that breathes.[g]
17Completely destroy[a] them—the
Hittites, Amorites, Canaanites,
Perizzites, Hivites and Jebusites
—as the LORD your God has commanded you. **18**Otherwise, they
will teach you to follow all the detestable things they do in worshiping their gods,[h] and you will sin[i]
against the LORD your God.
19When you lay siege to a city for
a long time, fighting against it to
capture it, do not destroy its trees
by putting an ax to them, because
you can eat their fruit. Do not cut
them down. Are the trees of the
field people, that you should besiege them?[b] **20**However, you may
cut down trees that you know are
not fruit trees and use them to
build siege works until the city at
war with you falls.

20:7 [a]Dt 24:5
20:8 [b]Jdg 7:3
20:10 [c]Lk 14:31-32
20:11 [d]1Ki 9:21
20:13 [e]Nu 31:7
20:14 [f]Jos 8:2; 22:8
20:16 [g]Ex 23:31-33; Nu 21:2-3; Dt 7:2; Jos 11:14
20:18 [h]Ex 34:16; Dt 7:4; 12:30-31 [i]Ex 23:33
21:5 [j]1Ch 23:13 [k]Dt 17:8-11
21:6 [l]Mt 27:24
21:8 [m]Nu 35:33-34
21:9 [n]Dt 19:13
21:10 [o]Jos 21:44
21:12 [p]Lev 14:9; Nu 6:9

Atonement for an Unsolved Murder

21 If a man is found slain, lying
in a field in the land the
LORD your God is giving you to possess, and it is not known who killed
him, **2**your elders and judges shall
go out and measure the distance
from the body to the neighboring
towns. **3**Then the elders of the
town nearest the body shall take a
heifer that has never been worked
and has never worn a yoke **4**and
lead her down to a valley that has
not been plowed or planted and
where there is a flowing stream.
There in the valley they are to
break the heifer's neck. **5**The
priests, the sons of Levi, shall step
forward, for the LORD your God has
chosen them to minister and to
pronounce blessings[j] in the name
of the LORD and to decide all cases
of dispute and assault.[k] **6**Then all
the elders of the town nearest the
body shall wash their hands[l] over
the heifer whose neck was broken
in the valley, **7**and they shall declare: "Our hands did not shed this
blood, nor did our eyes see it done.
8Accept this atonement for your
people Israel, whom you have redeemed, O LORD, and do not hold
your people guilty of the blood of
an innocent man." And the bloodshed will be atoned for.[m] **9**So you
will purge[n] from yourselves the
guilt of shedding innocent blood,
since you have done what is right in
the eyes of the LORD.

Marrying a Captive Woman

10When you go to war against
your enemies and the LORD your
God delivers them into your
hands[o] and you take captives, **11**if
you notice among the captives a
beautiful woman and are attracted
to her, you may take her as your
wife. **12**Bring her into your home
and have her shave her head,[p] trim

[a]*17* The Hebrew term refers to the irrevocable giving over of things or persons to the LORD, often by totally destroying them. [b]*19* Or *down to use in the siege, for the fruit trees are for the benefit of man.*

her nails **13**and put aside the
clothes she was wearing when captured. After she has lived in your
house and mourned her father and
mother for a full month,[a] then you
may go to her and be her husband
and she shall be your wife. **14**If you
are not pleased with her, let her go
wherever she wishes. You must not
sell her or treat her as a slave, since
you have dishonored her.[b]

The Right of the Firstborn

15If a man has two wives, and he
loves one but not the other, and
both bear him sons but the firstborn is the son of the wife he does
not love,[c] **16**when he wills his
property to his sons, he must not
give the rights of the firstborn to
the son of the wife he loves in pref-
erence to his actual firstborn, the
son of the wife he does not love.[d]
17He must acknowledge the son of
his unloved wife as the firstborn by
giving him a double share of all he
has. That son is the first sign of his
father's strength.[e] The right of the
firstborn belongs to him.[f]

A Rebellious Son

18If a man has a stubborn and rebellious son who does not obey his
father and mother[g] and will not
listen to them when they discipline
him, **19**his father and mother shall
take hold of him and bring him to
the elders at the gate of his town.
20They shall say to the elders,
"This son of ours is stubborn and
rebellious. He will not obey us. He
is a profligate and a drunkard."
21Then all the men of his town
shall stone him to death. You must
purge the evil[h] from among you.
All Israel will hear of it and be
afraid.[i]

Various Laws

22If a man guilty of a capital offense[j] is put to death and his body
is hung on a tree, **23**you must not
leave his body on the tree overnight.[k] Be sure to bury him that
same day, because anyone who is
hung on a tree is under God's
curse.[l] You must not desecrate[m]
the land the LORD your God is giving
you as an inheritance.

22 If you see your brother's ox
or sheep straying, do not ignore it but be sure to take it back
to him.[n] **2**If the brother does not
live near you or if you do not know
who he is, take it home with you
and keep it until he comes looking
for it. Then give it back to him. **3**Do
the same if you find your brother's
donkey or his cloak or anything he
loses. Do not ignore it.

4If you see your brother's donkey[o] or his ox fallen on the road,
do not ignore it. Help him get it to
its feet.

5A woman must not wear men's
clothing, nor a man wear women's
clothing, for the LORD your God detests anyone who does this.

6If you come across a bird's nest
beside the road, either in a tree or
on the ground, and the mother is
sitting on the young or on the eggs,
do not take the mother with the
young.[p] **7**You may take the young,
but be sure to let the mother go, so
that it may go well with you and
you may have a long life.[q]

8When you build a new house,
make a parapet around your roof so
that you may not bring the guilt of
bloodshed on your house if someone falls from the roof.

9Do not plant two kinds of seed
in your vineyard;[r] if you do, not
only the crops you plant but also
the fruit of the vineyard will be defiled.[c]

10Do not plow with an ox and a
donkey yoked together.[s]

11Do not wear clothes of wool
and linen woven together.[t]

12Make tassels on the four corners of the cloak you wear.[u]

Marriage Violations

13If a man takes a wife and, after
lying with her[v], dislikes her **14**and
slanders her and gives her a bad
name, saying, "I married this woman, but when I approached her, I
did not find proof of her virginity,"
15then the girl's father and mother

21:13 [a] Ps 45:10
21:14 [b] Ge 34:2
21:15 [c] Ge 29:33
21:16 [d] 1Ch 26:10
21:17 [e] Ge 49:3 [f] Ge 25:31
21:18 [g] Pr 1:8; Isa 30:1; Eph 6:1-3
21:21 [h] Dt 19:19 [i] Dt 13:11
21:22 [j] Dt 22:26; Mk 14:64; Ac 23:29
21:23 [k] Jos 8:29; 10:27; Jn 19:31 [l] Gal 3:13* [m] Lev 18:25; Nu 35:34
22:1 [n] Ex 23:4-5
22:4 [o] Ex 23:5
22:6 [p] Lev 22:28
22:7 [q] Dt 4:40
22:9 [r] Lev 19:19
22:10 [s] 2Co 6:14
22:11 [t] Lev 19:19
22:12 [u] Nu 15:37-41; Mt 23:5
22:13 [v] Dt 24:1

c9 *Or be forfeited to the sanctuary*

shall bring proof that she was a virgin to the town elders at the gate.
16The girl's father will say to the
elders, "I gave my daughter in marriage to this man, but he dislikes
her. **17**Now he has slandered her
and said, 'I did not find your daughter to be a virgin.' But here is the
proof of my daughter's virginity."
Then her parents shall display the
cloth before the elders of the town,
18and the elders[a] shall take the
man and punish him. **19**They shall
fine him a hundred shekels of silver[d] and give them to the girl's father, because this man has given an
Israelite virgin a bad name. She
shall continue to be his wife; he
must not divorce her as long as he
lives.
20If, however, the charge is true
and no proof of the girl's virginity
can be found, **21**she shall be
brought to the door of her father's
house and there the men of her
town shall stone her to death. She
has done a disgraceful thing[b] in Israel by being promiscuous while
still in her father's house. You must
purge the evil from among you.
22If a man is found sleeping with
another man's wife, both the man
who slept with her and the woman
must die.[c] You must purge the evil
from Israel.
23If a man happens to meet in a
town a virgin pledged to be married
and he sleeps with her, **24**you shall
take both of them to the gate of
that town and stone them to
death—the girl because she was in
a town and did not scream for help,
and the man because he violated
another man's wife. You must
purge the evil from among you.[d]
25But if out in the country a man
happens to meet a girl pledged to
be married and rapes her, only the
man who has done this shall die.
26Do nothing to the girl; she has
committed no sin deserving death.
This case is like that of someone
who attacks and murders his
neighbor, **27**for the man found the
girl out in the country, and though
the betrothed girl screamed, there
was no one to rescue her.

22:18 [a]Ex 18:21
22:21 [b]Ge 34:7; Dt 13:5; 23:17-18; Jdg 20:6; 2Sa 13:12
22:22 [c]Lev 20:10; Jn 8:5
22:24 [d]ver 21-22; 1Co 5:13*
22:28 [e]Ex 22:16
22:30 [f]Lev 18:8; 20:11; 18:8; Dt 27:20; 1Co 5:1
23:3 [g]Ne 13:2
23:4 [h]Nu 22:5-6; 23:7; 2Pe 2:15
23:5 [i]Pr 26:2
23:6 [j]Ezr 9:12
23:7 [k]Ge 25:26; Ob 1:10,12 [l]Ex 22:21; 23:9; Lev 19:34; Dt 10:19

28If a man happens to meet a virgin who is not pledged to be married and rapes her and they are discovered,[e] **29**he shall pay the girl's
father fifty shekels of silver.[e] He
must marry the girl, for he has violated her. He can never divorce her
as long as he lives.
30A man is not to marry his father's wife; he must not dishonor
his father's bed.[f]

Exclusion From the Assembly

23 No one who has been emas-
culated by crushing or cutting may enter the assembly of the
LORD.
2No one born of a forbidden marriage[f] nor any of his descendants
may enter the assembly of the
LORD, even down to the tenth generation.
3No Ammonite or Moabite or
any of his descendants may enter
the assembly of the LORD, even
down to the tenth generation.[g]
4For they did not come to meet you
with bread and water on your way
when you came out of Egypt, and
they hired Balaam[h] son of Beor
from Pethor in Aram Naharaim[g] to
pronounce a curse on you. **5**However, the LORD your God would not listen to Balaam but turned the
curse[i] into a blessing for you, because the LORD your God loves you.
6Do not seek a treaty of friendship
with them as long as you live.[j]
7Do not abhor an Edomite, for
he is your brother.[k] Do not abhor
an Egyptian, because you lived as
an alien in his country.[l] **8**The third
generation of children born to
them may enter the assembly of
the LORD.

Uncleanness in the Camp

9When you are encamped
against your enemies, keep away
from everything impure. **10**If one of
your men is unclean because of a
nocturnal emission, he is to go out-

[d]19 That is, about 2 1/2 pounds (about 1 kilogram) [e]29 That is, about 1 1/4 pounds (about 0.6 kilogram) [f]2 Or *one of illegitimate birth* [g]4 That is, Northwest Mesopotamia

MAJOR SOCIAL CONCERNS IN THE COVENANT

1. PERSONHOOD
Everyone's person is to be secure (Ex 20:13; Dt 5:17; Ex 21:16-21, 26-31; Lev 19:14; Dt 24:7; 27:18).

2. FALSE ACCUSATION
Everyone is to be secure against slander and false accusation (Ex 20:16; Dt 5:20; Ex 23:1-3; Lev 19:16; Dt 19:15-21).

3. WOMAN
No woman is to be taken advantage of within her subordinate status in society (Ex 21:7-11, 20, 26-32; 22:16-17; Dt. 21:10-14; 22:13-30; 24:1-5).

4. PUNISHMENT
Punishment for wrongdoing shall not be excessive so that the culprit is dehumanized (Dt 25:1-5).

5. DIGNITY
Every Israelite's dignity and right to be God's freedman and servant are to be honored and safeguarded (Ex 21:2, 5-6; Lev 25; Dt 15:12-18).

6. INHERITANCE
Every Israelite's inheritance in the promised land is to be secure (Lev 25; Nu 27:5-7; 36:1-9; Dt 25:5-10).

7. PROPERTY
Everyone's property is to be secure (Ex 20:15; Dt 5:19; Ex 21:33-36; 22:1-15; 23:4-5; Lev 19:35-36; Dt 22:1-4; 25:13-15).

8. FRUIT OF LABOR
Everyone is to receive the fruit of his labors (Lev 19:13; Dt 24:14; 25:4).

9. FRUIT OF THE GROUND
Everyone is to share the fruit of the ground (Ex 23:10-11; Lev 19:9-10; 23:22; 25:3-55; Dt. 14:28-29; 24:19-21).

10. REST ON SABBATH
Everyone, down to the humblest servant and the resident alien, is to share in the weekly rest of God's Sabbath (Ex 20:8-11; Dt 5:12-15; Ex 23:12).

11. MARRIAGE
The marriage relationship is to be kept inviolate (Ex 20:14; Dt 5:18; see also Lev 18:6-23; 20:10-21; Dt 22:13-30).

12. EXPLOITATION
No one, however disabled, impoverished or powerless, is to be oppressed or exploited (Ex 22:21-27; Lev 19:14, 33-34; 25:35-36; Dt 23:19; 24:6, 12-15, 17; 27:18).

13. FAIR TRIAL
Everyone is to have free access to the courts and is to be afforded a fair trial (Ex 23:6,8; Lev 19:15; Dt 1:17; 10:17-18; 16:18-20; 17:8-13; 19:15-21).

14. SOCIAL ORDER
Every person's God-given place in the social order is to be honored (Ex 20:12; Dt 5:16; Ex 21:15, 17; 22:28; Lev 19:3, 32; 20:9; Dt 17:8-13; 21:15-21; 27:16).

15. LAW
No one shall be above the law, not even the king (Dt 17:18-20).

16. ANIMALS
Concern for the welfare of other creatures is to be extended to the animal world (Ex 23:5, 11; Lev 25:7, Dt 22:4, 6-7; 25:4).

side the camp and stay there.[a] 11But as evening approaches he is to wash himself, and at sunset he may return to the camp.

12Designate a place outside the camp where you can go to relieve yourself. 13As part of your equipment have something to dig with, and when you relieve yourself, dig a hole and cover up your excrement. 14For the LORD your God moves[b] about in your camp to protect you and to deliver your enemies to you. Your camp must be holy,[c] so that he will not see among you anything indecent and turn away from you.

Miscellaneous Laws

15If a slave has taken refuge with you, do not hand him over to his master.[d] 16Let him live among you wherever he likes and in whatever town he chooses. Do not oppress[e] him.

17No Israelite man[f] or woman is to become a shrine prostitute.[g] 18You must not bring the earnings of a female prostitute or of a male prostitute[h] into the house of the LORD your God to pay any vow, because the LORD your God detests them both.

19Do not charge your brother interest, whether on money or food or anything else that may earn interest.[h] 20You may charge a foreigner interest, but not a brother Israelite, so that the LORD your God may bless[i] you in everything you put your hand to in the land you are entering to possess.

21If you make a vow to the LORD your God, do not be slow to pay it, for the LORD your God will certainly demand it of you and you will be guilty of sin.[j] 22But if you refrain from making a vow, you will not be guilty. 23Whatever your lips utter you must be sure to do, because you made your vow freely to the LORD your God with your own mouth.

24If you enter your neighbor's vineyard, you may eat all the grapes you want, but do not put any in your basket. 25If you enter your neighbor's grainfield, you may pick kernels with your hands, but you must not put a sickle to his standing grain.[k]

24 If a man marries a woman who becomes displeasing to him[l] because he finds something indecent about her, and he writes her a certificate of divorce,[m] gives it to her and sends her from his house, 2and if after she leaves his house she becomes the wife of another man, 3and her second husband dislikes her and writes her a certificate of divorce, gives it to her and sends her from his house, or if he dies, 4then her first husband, who divorced her, is not allowed to marry her again after she has been defiled. That would be detestable in the eyes of the LORD. Do not bring sin upon the land the LORD[n] your God is giving you as an inheritance.

5If a man has recently married, he must not be sent to war or have any other duty laid on him. For one year he is to be free to stay at home and bring happiness to the wife he has married.[o]

6Do not take a pair of millstones—not even the upper one—as security for a debt, because that would be taking a man's livelihood as security.

7If a man is caught kidnapping one of his brother Israelites and treats him as a slave or sells him, the kidnapper must die.[p] You must purge the evil from among you.

8In cases of leprous[i] diseases be very careful to do exactly as the priests, who are Levites, instruct you. You must follow carefully what I have commanded them.[q] 9Remember what the LORD your God did to Miriam along the way after you came out of Egypt.[r]

10When you make a loan of any kind to your neighbor, do not go into his house to get what he is offering as a pledge. 11Stay outside

23:10 [a]Lev 15:16
23:14 [b]Lev 26:12 [c]Ex 3:5
23:15 [d]1Sa 30:15
23:16 [e]Ex 22:21
23:17 [f]Ge 19:25; 2Ki 23:7 [g]Lev 19:29; Dt 22:21
23:19 [h]Ex 22:25; Lev 25:35-37
23:20 [i]Dt 15:10; 28:12
23:21 [j]Nu 30:1-2; Ecc 5:4-5; Mt 5:33
23:25 [k]Mt 12:1; Mk 2:23; Lk 6:1
24:1 [l]Dt 22:13 [m]Mt 5:31*; 19:7-9; Mk 10:4-5
24:4 [n]Jer 3:1
24:5 [o]Dt 20:7
24:7 [p]Ex 21:16
24:8 [q]Lev 13:1-46; 14:2
24:9 [r]Nu 12:10

[h]*18* Hebrew *of a dog* [i]*8* The Hebrew word was used for various diseases affecting the skin—not necessarily leprosy.

and let the man to whom you are
making the loan bring the pledge
out to you. 12If the man is poor, do
not go to sleep with his pledge in
your possession. 13Return his
cloak to him by sunset[a] so that he
may sleep in it. Then he will thank
you, and it will be regarded as a
righteous act in the sight of the
LORD your God.[b]

14Do not take advantage of a
hired man who is poor and needy,
whether he is a brother Israelite or
an alien living in one of your
towns.[c] 15Pay him his wages each
day before sunset, because he is
poor[d] and is counting on it.[e] Otherwise he may cry to the LORD
against you, and you will be guilty
of sin.[f]

16Fathers shall not be put to
death for their children, nor children put to death for their fathers;
each is to die for his own sin.[g]

17Do not deprive the alien or the
fatherless of justice,[h] or take the
cloak of the widow as a pledge.
18Remember that you were slaves
in Egypt and the LORD your God redeemed you from there. That is
why I command you to do this.

19When you are harvesting in
your field and you overlook a sheaf,
do not go back to get it.[i] Leave it
for the alien, the fatherless and the
widow, so that the LORD your God
may bless[j] you in all the work of
your hands. 20When you beat the
olives from your trees, do not go
over the branches a second time.[k]
Leave what remains for the alien,
the fatherless and the widow.
21When you harvest the grapes in
your vineyard, do not go over the
vines again. Leave what remains
for the alien, the fatherless and the
widow. 22Remember that you were
slaves in Egypt. That is why I command you to do this.[l]

25 When men have a dispute,
they are to take it to court
and the judges will decide the
case,[m] acquitting the innocent and
condemning the guilty.[n] 2If the
guilty man deserves to be beaten,[o]
the judge shall make him lie down
and have him flogged in his presence with the number of lashes his
crime deserves, 3but he must not
give him more than forty lashes.[p]
If he is flogged more than that, your
brother will be degraded in your
eyes.[q]

4Do not muzzle an ox while it is
treading out the grain.[r]

5If brothers are living together
and one of them dies without a son,
his widow must not marry outside
the family. Her husband's brother
shall take her and marry her and
fulfill the duty of a brother-in-law
to her.[s] 6The first son she bears
shall carry on the name of the dead
brother so that his name will not be
blotted out from Israel.[t]

7However, if a man does not
want to marry his brother's wife,
she shall go to the elders at the
town gate and say, "My husband's
brother refuses to carry on his
brother's name in Israel. He will
not fulfill the duty of a brother-
in-law to me."[u] 8Then the elders of
his town shall summon him and
talk to him. If he persists in saying,
"I do not want to marry her," 9his
brother's widow shall go up to him
in the presence of the elders, take
off one of his sandals,[v] spit in his
face and say, "This is what is done
to the man who will not build up
his brother's family line." 10That
man's line shall be known in Israel as The Family of the Unsan-
daled.

11If two men are fighting and the
wife of one of them comes to rescue her husband from his assail-
ant, and she reaches out and seizes
him by his private parts, 12you
shall cut off her hand. Show her no
pity.[w]

13Do not have two differing
weights in your bag—one heavy,
one light.[x] 14Do not have two differing measures in your house—
one large, one small. 15You must
have accurate and honest weights
and measures, so that you may live
long[y] in the land the LORD your
God is giving you. 16For the LORD
your God detests anyone who does
these things, anyone who deals dis-
honestly.[z]

24:13 [a] Ex 22:26 [b] Dt 6:25; Da 4:27
24:14 [c] Lev 25:35-43; Dt 15:12-18
24:15 [d] Jer 22:13 [e] Lev 19:13 [f] Dt 15:9; Jas 5:4
24:16 [g] 2Ki 14:6; 2Ch 25:4; Jer 31:29-30; Eze 18:20
24:17 [h] Dt 1:17; 10:17-18; 16:19
24:19 [i] Lev 19:9; 23:22 [j] Pr 19:17
24:20 [k] Lev 19:10
24:22 [l] ver 18
25:1 [m] Dt 19:17 [n] Dt 1:16-17
25:2 [o] Lk 12:47-48
25:3 [p] 2Co 11:24 [q] Job 18:3
25:4 [r] Pr 12:10; 1Co 9:9*; 1Ti 5:18*
25:5 [s] Mt 22:24; Mk 12:19; Lk 20:28
25:6 [t] Ge 38:9; Ru 4:5,10
25:7 [u] Ru 4:1-2,5-6
25:9 [v] Ru 4:7-8,11
25:12 [w] Dt 19:13
25:13 [x] Lev 19:35-37; Pr 11:1; Eze 45:10; Mic 6:11
25:15 [y] Ex 20:12
25:16 [z] Pr 11:1

17Remember what the Amalekites[a] did to you along the way when you came out of Egypt. **18**When you were weary and worn out, they met you on your journey and cut off all who were lagging behind; they had no fear of God.[b] **19**When the LORD your God gives you rest from all the enemies around you in the land he is giving you to possess as an inheritance, you shall blot out the memory of Amalek[c] from under heaven. Do not forget!

Firstfruits and Tithes

26 When you have entered the land the LORD your God is giving you as an inheritance and have taken possession of it and settled in it, **2**take some of the firstfruits[d] of all that you produce from the soil of the land the LORD your God is giving you and put them in a basket. Then go to the place the LORD your God will choose as a dwelling for his Name[e] **3**and say to the priest in office at the time, "I declare today to the LORD your God that I have come to the land the LORD swore to our forefathers to give us." **4**The priest shall take the basket from your hands and set it down in front of the altar of the LORD your God. **5**Then you shall declare before the LORD your God: "My father was a wandering Aramean,[f] and he went down into Egypt with a few people[g] and lived there and became a great nation, powerful and numerous. **6**But the Egyptians mistreated us and made us suffer,[h] putting us to hard labor. **7**Then we cried out to the LORD, the God of our fathers, and the LORD heard our voice[i] and saw[j] our misery, toil and oppression. **8**So the LORD brought us out of Egypt with a mighty hand and an outstretched arm, with great terror and with miraculous signs and wonders.[k] **9**He brought us to this place and gave us this land, a land flowing with milk and honey;[l] **10**and now I bring the firstfruits of the soil that you, O LORD, have given me." Place the basket before the LORD your God and bow down before him. **11**And you and the Levites[m] and the aliens among you shall rejoice[n] in all the good things the LORD your God has given to you and your household.

12When you have finished setting aside a tenth[o] of all your produce in the third year, the year of the tithe,[p] you shall give it to the Levite, the alien, the fatherless and the widow, so that they may eat in your towns and be satisfied. **13**Then say to the LORD your God: "I have removed from my house the sacred portion and have given it to the Levite, the alien, the fatherless and the widow, according to all you commanded. I have not turned aside from your commands nor have I forgotten any of them.[q] **14**I have not eaten any of the sacred portion while I was in mourning, nor have I removed any of it while I was unclean,[r] nor have I offered any of it to the dead. I have obeyed the LORD my God; I have done everything you commanded me. **15**Look down from heaven,[s] your holy dwelling place, and bless your people Israel and the land you have given us as you promised on oath to our forefathers, a land flowing with milk and honey."

Follow the LORD's Commands

16The LORD your God commands you this day to follow these decrees and laws; carefully observe them with all your heart and with all your soul.[t] **17**You have declared this day that the LORD is your God and that you will walk in his ways, that you will keep his decrees, commands and laws, and that you will obey him. **18**And the LORD has declared this day that you are his people, his treasured possession[u] as he promised, and that you are to keep all his commands. **19**He has declared that he will set you in praise, fame and honor high above all the nations[v] he has made and that you will be a people holy[w] to the LORD your God, as he promised.

25:17 [a] Ex 17:8
25:18 [b] Ps 36:1; Ro 3:18
25:19 [c] 1Sa 15:2-3
26:2 [d] Ex 22:29; 23:16,19; Nu 18:13; Pr 3:9 [e] Dt 12:5
26:5 [f] Hos 12:12 [g] Ge 43:1-2; 45:7,11; 46:27; Dt 10:22
26:6 [h] Ex 1:11,14
26:7 [i] Ex 2:23-25 [j] Ex 3:9
26:8 [k] Dt 4:34
26:9 [l] Ex 3:8
26:11 [m] Dt 12:7 [n] Dt 16:11
26:12 [o] Lev 27:30 [p] Nu 18:24; Dt 14:28-29; Heb 7:5,9
26:13 [q] Ps 119:141, 153,176
26:14 [r] Lev 7:20; Hos 9:4
26:15 [s] Isa 63:15; Zec 2:13
26:16 [t] Dt 4:29
26:18 [u] Ex 6:7; 19:5; Dt 7:6; 14:2; 28:9
26:19 [v] Dt 4:7-8; 28:1,13,44 [w] Ex 19:6; Dt 7:6; 1Pe 2:9

The Altar on Mount Ebal

27 Moses and the elders of Israel commanded the people: "Keep all these commands that I give you today. 2When you have crossed the Jordan into the land the LORD your God is giving you, set up some large stones and coat them with plaster.[a] 3Write on them all the words of this law when you have crossed over to enter the land the LORD your God is giving you, a land flowing with milk and honey,[b] just as the LORD, the God of your fathers, promised you. 4And when you have crossed the Jordan, set up these stones on Mount Ebal,[c] as I command you today, and coat them with plaster. 5Build there an altar[d] to the LORD your God, an altar of stones. Do not use any iron tool[e] upon them. 6Build the altar of the LORD your God with fieldstones and offer burnt offerings on it to the LORD your God. 7Sacrifice fellowship offerings[i] there, eating them and rejoicing in the presence of the LORD your God. 8And you shall write very clearly all the words of this law on these stones you have set up."

Curses From Mount Ebal

9Then Moses and the priests, who are Levites, said to all Israel, "Be silent, O Israel, and listen! You have now become the people of the LORD your God.[f] 10Obey the LORD your God and follow his commands and decrees that I give you today."

11On the same day Moses commanded the people:

12When you have crossed the Jordan, these tribes shall stand on Mount Gerizim[g] to bless the people: Simeon, Levi, Judah, Issachar, Joseph and Benjamin.[h] 13And these tribes shall stand on Mount Ebal to pronounce curses: Reuben, Gad, Asher, Zebulun, Dan and Naphtali.

14The Levites shall recite to all the people of Israel in a loud voice:

15"Cursed is the man who carves an image or casts an idol[i]—a thing detestable to the LORD, the work of the craftsman's hands—and sets it up in secret."
Then all the people shall say,
"Amen!"

16"Cursed is the man who dishonors his father or his mother."[j]
Then all the people shall say,
"Amen!"

17"Cursed is the man who moves his neighbor's boundary stone."[k]
Then all the people shall say,
"Amen!"

18"Cursed is the man who leads the blind astray on the road."[l]
Then all the people shall say,
"Amen!"

19"Cursed is the man who withholds justice from the alien,[m] the fatherless or the widow."[n]
Then all the people shall say,
"Amen!"

20"Cursed is the man who sleeps with his father's wife, for he dishonors his father's bed."[o]
Then all the people shall say,
"Amen!"

21"Cursed is the man who has sexual relations with any animal."[p]
Then all the people shall say,
"Amen!"

22"Cursed is the man who sleeps with his sister, the daughter of his father or the daughter of his mother."[q]
Then all the people shall say,
"Amen!"

23"Cursed is the man who sleeps with his mother-in-law."[r]
Then all the people shall say,
"Amen!"

24"Cursed is the man who kills[s] his neighbor secretly."
Then all the people shall say,
"Amen!"

25"Cursed is the man who accepts a bribe to kill an innocent person."[t]

27:2 [a]Jos 8:31
27:3 [b]Dt 26:9
27:4 [c]Dt 11:29
27:5 [d]Jos 8:31 [e]Ex 20:25
27:9 [f]Dt 26:18
27:12 [g]Dt 11:29 [h]Jos 8:35
27:15 [i]Ex 20:4; 34:17; Lev 19:4; 26:1; Dt 4:16, 23; 5:8; Isa 44:9
27:16 [j]Ex 20:12; 21:17; Lev 19:3; 20:9
27:17 [k]Dt 19:14; Pr 22:28
27:18 [l]Lev 19:14
27:19 [m]Ex 22:21; Dt 24:19 [n]Dt 10:18
27:20 [o]Lev 18:7; Dt 22:30
27:21 [p]Lev 18:23
27:22 [q]Lev 18:9; 20:17
27:23 [r]Lev 20:14
27:24 [s]Lev 24:17; Nu 35:31
27:25 [t]Ex 23:7-8; Dt 10:17; Eze 22:12

i7 Traditionally *peace offerings*

Then all the people shall say,
"Amen!"

26"Cursed is the man who does not uphold the words of this law by carrying them out."[a]
Then all the people shall say,
"Amen!"

Blessings for Obedience

28 If you fully obey the LORD your God and carefully follow all his commands[b] I give you today, the LORD your God will set you high above all the nations on earth.[c] 2All these blessings will come upon you[d] and accompany you if you obey the LORD your God:

3You will be blessed[e] in the city and blessed in the country.[f]
4The fruit of your womb will be blessed, and the crops of your land and the young of your livestock—the calves of your herds and the lambs of your flocks.[g]
5Your basket and your kneading trough will be blessed.
6You will be blessed when you come in and blessed when you go out.[h]

7The LORD will grant that the enemies who rise up against you will be defeated before you. They will come at you from one direction but flee from you in seven.[i]

8The LORD will send a blessing on your barns and on everything you put your hand to. The LORD your God will bless you in the land he is giving you.

9The LORD will establish you as his holy people,[j] as he promised you on oath, if you keep the commands of the LORD your God and walk in his ways. 10Then all the peoples on earth will see that you are called by the name[k] of the LORD, and they will fear you. 11The LORD will grant you abundant prosperity—in the fruit of your womb, the young of your livestock and the crops of your ground—in the land he swore to your forefathers to give you.[l]

12The LORD will open the heavens, the storehouse of his bounty, to send rain[m] on your land in season and to bless all the work of your hands. You will lend to many nations but will borrow from none.[n] 13The LORD will make you the head, not the tail. If you pay attention to the commands of the LORD your God that I give you this day and carefully follow them, you will always be at the top, never at the bottom. 14Do not turn aside from any of the commands I give you today, to the right or to the left,[o] following other gods and serving them.

Curses for Disobedience

15However, if you do not obey[p] the LORD your God and do not carefully follow all his commands and decrees I am giving you today, all these curses will come upon you and overtake you:[q]

16You will be cursed in the city and cursed in the country.
17Your basket and your kneading trough will be cursed.
18The fruit of your womb will be cursed, and the crops of your land, and the calves of your herds and the lambs of your flocks.
19You will be cursed when you come in and cursed when you go out.

20The LORD will send on you curses,[r] confusion and rebuke[s] in everything you put your hand to, until you are destroyed and come to sudden ruin[t] because of the evil you have done in forsaking him.[k] 21The LORD will plague you with diseases until he has destroyed you from the land you are entering to possess.[u] 22The LORD will strike you with wasting disease, with fever and inflammation, with scorching heat and drought,[v] with blight and mildew, which will plague you

27:26 [a]Jer 11:3; Gal 3:10*
28:1 [b]Ex 15:26; Lev 26:3; Dt 7:12-26 [c]Dt 26:19
28:2 [d]Zec 1:6
28:3 [e]Ps 128:1,4 [f]Ge 39:5
28:4 [g]Ge 49:25; Pr 10:22
28:6 [h]Ps 121:8
28:7 [i]Lev 26:8,17
28:9 [j]Ex 19:6; Dt 7:6
28:10 [k]2Ch 7:14
28:11 [l]Dt 30:9; Pr 10:22
28:12 [m]Lev 26:4 [n]Dt 15:3,6
28:14 [o]Dt 5:32
28:15 [p]Lev 26:14 [q]Jos 23:15; Da 9:11; Mal 2:2
28:20 [r]Mal 2:2 [s]Isa 51:20; 66:15 [t]Dt 4:26
28:21 [u]Lev 26:25; Jer 24:10
28:22 [v]Lev 26:16

[k]20 Hebrew *me*

until you perish.[a] **23**The sky over your head will be bronze, the ground beneath you iron.[b] **24**The LORD will turn the rain of your country into dust and powder; it will come down from the skies until you are destroyed.

25The LORD will cause you to be defeated before your enemies. You will come at them from one direction but flee from them in seven,[c] and you will become a thing of horror to all the kingdoms on earth.[d] **26**Your carcasses will be food for all the birds of the air and the beasts of the earth, and there will be no one to frighten them away.[e] **27**The LORD will afflict you with the boils of Egypt[f] and with tumors, festering sores and the itch, from which you cannot be cured. **28**The LORD will afflict you with madness, blindness and confusion of mind. **29**At midday you will grope[g] about like a blind man in the dark. You will be unsuccessful in everything you do; day after day you will be oppressed and robbed, with no one to rescue you.

30You will be pledged to be married to a woman, but another will take her and ravish her.[h] You will build a house, but you will not live in it.[i] You will plant a vineyard, but you will not even begin to enjoy its fruit.[j] **31**Your ox will be slaughtered before your eyes, but you will eat none of it. Your donkey will be forcibly taken from you and will not be returned. Your sheep will be given to your enemies, and no one will rescue them. **32**Your sons and daughters will be given to another nation,[k] and you will wear out your eyes watching for them day after day, powerless to lift a hand. **33**A people that you do not know will eat what your land and labor produce, and you will have nothing but cruel oppression all your days.[l] **34**The sights you see will drive you mad. **35**The LORD will afflict your knees and legs with painful boils[m] that cannot be cured, spreading from the soles of your feet to the top of your head.

36The LORD will drive you and the king[n] you set over you to a nation unknown to you or your fathers.[o] There you will worship other gods, gods of wood and stone.[p] **37**You will become a thing of horror and an object of scorn and ridicule to all the nations where the LORD will drive you.[q]

38You will sow much seed in the field but you will harvest little,[r] because locusts will devour[s] it. **39**You will plant vineyards and cultivate them but you will not drink the wine or gather the grapes, because worms will eat them.[t] **40**You will have olive trees throughout your country but you will not use the oil, because the olives will drop off.[u] **41**You will have sons and daughters but you will not keep them, because they will go into captivity.[v] **42**Swarms of locusts will take over all your trees and the crops of your land.

43The alien who lives among you will rise above you higher and higher, but you will sink lower and lower.[w] **44**He will lend to you, but you will not lend to him.[x] He will be the head, but you will be the tail.[y]

45All these curses will come upon you. They will pursue you and overtake you until you are destroyed,[z] because you did not obey the LORD your God and observe the commands and decrees he gave you. **46**They will be a sign and a wonder to you and your descendants forever.[a] **47**Because you did not serve[b] the LORD your God joyfully and gladly[c] in the time of prosperity, **48**therefore in hunger and thirst, in nakedness and dire poverty, you will serve the enemies the LORD sends against you. He will put an iron yoke[d] on your neck until he has destroyed you.

49The LORD will bring a nation against you from far away, from the ends of the earth,[e] like an eagle[f] swooping down, a nation whose language you will not understand, **50**a fierce-looking nation without respect for the old[g] or pity for the young. **51**They will devour the young of your livestock and the crops of your land until you are de-

28:22 [a]Am 4:9
28:23 [b]Lev 26:19
28:25 [c]Isa 30:17 [d]Jer 15:4; 24:9; Eze 23:46
28:26 [e]Jer 7:33; 16:4; 34:20
28:27 [f]ver 60-61; 1Sa 5:6
28:29 [g]Job 5:14; Isa 59:10
28:30 [h]Job 31:10; Jer 8:10 [i]Am 5:11 [j]Jer 12:13
28:32 [k]ver 41
28:33 [l]Jer 5:15-17
28:35 [m]ver 27
28:36 [n]2Ki 17:4,6; 24:12,14; 25:7,11 [o]Jer 16:13 [p]Dt 4:28
28:37 [q]Jer 24:9
28:38 [r]Mic 6:15; Hag 1:6,9 [s]Joel 1:4
28:39 [t]Isa 5:10; 17:10-11
28:40 [u]Mic 6:15
28:41 [v]ver 32
28:43 [w]ver 13
28:44 [x]ver 12 [y]ver 13
28:45 [z]ver 15
28:46 [a]Isa 8:18; Eze 14:8
28:47 [b]Dt 32:15 [c]Ne 9:35
28:48 [d]Jer 28:13-14
28:49 [e]Jer 5:15; 6:22 [f]La 4:19; Hos 8:1
28:50 [g]Isa 47:6

stroyed. They will leave you no
grain, new wine or oil, nor any
calves of your herds or lambs of
your flocks until you are ruined.[a]
52They will lay siege to all the cities
throughout your land until the high
fortified walls in which you trust
fall down. They will besiege all the
cities throughout the land the LORD
your God is giving you.[b]
53Because of the suffering that
your enemy will inflict on you during the siege, you will eat the fruit
of the womb, the flesh of the sons
and daughters the LORD your God
has given you.[c] **54**Even the most
gentle and sensitive man among
you will have no compassion on his
own brother or the wife he loves or
his surviving children, **55**and he
will not give to one of them any of
the flesh of his children that he is
eating. It will be all he has left because of the suffering your enemy
will inflict on you during the siege
of all your cities. **56**The most gentle
and sensitive[d] woman among
you—so sensitive and gentle that
she would not venture to touch the
ground with the sole of her foot
—will begrudge the husband she
loves and her own son or daughter
57the afterbirth from her womb and
the children she bears. For she intends to eat them secretly during
the siege and in the distress that
your enemy will inflict on you in
your cities.
58If you do not carefully follow
all the words of this law, which are
written in this book, and do not revere[e] this glorious and awesome
name[f]—the LORD your God—
59the LORD will send fearful plagues
on you and your descendants,
harsh and prolonged disasters, and
severe and lingering illnesses. **60**He
will bring upon you all the diseases
of Egypt[g] that you dreaded, and
they will cling to you. **61**The LORD
will also bring on you every kind of
sickness and disaster not recorded
in this Book of the Law, until you
are destroyed.[h] **62**You who were as
numerous as the stars in the sky[i]
will be left but few in number, because you did not obey the LORD

28:51 [a]ver 33
28:52 [b]Jer 10:18; Zep 1:14-16, 17
28:53 [c]Lev 26:29; 2Ki 6:28-29; Jer 19:9; La 2:20; 4:10
28:56 [d]ver 54
28:58 [e]Mal 1:14 [f]Ex 6:3
28:60 [g]ver 27
28:61 [h]Dt 4:25-26
28:62 [i]Dt 4:27; 10:22; Ne 9:23
28:63 [j]Jer 32:41 [k]Pr 1:26 [l]Jer 12:14; 45:4
28:64 [m]Lev 26:33; Dt 4:27 [n]Ne 1:8
28:65 [o]Lev 26:16,36
28:67 [p]ver 34; Job 7:4
29:1 [q]Dt 5:2-3
29:2 [r]Ex 19:4
29:3 [s]Dt 4:34; 7:19
29:4 [t]Isa 6:10; Ac 28:26-27; Ro 11:8*; Eph 4:18

your God. **63**Just as it pleased[j] the
LORD to make you prosper and increase in number, so it will please[k]
him to ruin and destroy you. You
will be uprooted[l] from the land
you are entering to possess.
64Then the LORD will scatter[m]
you among all nations,[n] from one
end of the earth to the other. There
you will worship other gods—gods
of wood and stone, which neither
you nor your fathers have known.
65Among those nations you will
find no repose, no resting place for
the sole of your foot. There the
LORD will give you an anxious mind,
eyes weary with longing, and a despairing heart.[o] **66**You will live in
constant suspense, filled with
dread both night and day, never
sure of your life. **67**In the morning
you will say, "If only it were evening!" and in the evening, "If only
it were morning!"—because of the
terror that will fill your hearts and
the sights that your eyes will see.[p]
68The LORD will send you back in
ships to Egypt on a journey I said
you should never make again.
There you will offer yourselves for
sale to your enemies as male and
female slaves, but no one will buy
you.

Renewal of the Covenant

29 These are the terms of the
covenant the LORD com-
manded Moses to make with the Israelites in Moab, in addition to the
covenant he had made with them
at Horeb.[q]
2Moses summoned all the Israelites and said to them:

Your eyes have seen all that the
LORD did in Egypt to Pharaoh, to all
his officials and to all his land.[r]
3With your own eyes you saw those
great trials, those miraculous signs
and great wonders.[s] **4**But to this
day the LORD has not given you a
mind that understands or eyes that
see or ears that hear.[t] **5**During the
forty years that I led you through
the desert, your clothes did not
wear out, nor did the sandals on

your feet. 6You ate no bread and
drank no wine or other fermented
drink. I did this so that you might
know that I am the LORD your
God.[a]

7When you reached this place,
Sihon[b] king of Heshbon and Og
king of Bashan came out to fight
against us, but we defeated them.[c]
8We took their land and gave it as
an inheritance to the Reubenites,
the Gadites and the half-tribe of
Manasseh.[d]

9Carefully follow[e] the terms of
this covenant, so that you may
prosper in everything you do.[f]
10All of you are standing today in
the presence of the LORD your
God—your leaders and chief men,
your elders and officials, and all
the other men of Israel, 11together
with your children and your wives,
and the aliens living in your camps
who chop your wood and carry your
water.[g] 12You are standing here in
order to enter into a covenant with
the LORD your God, a covenant the
LORD is making with you this day
and sealing with an oath, 13to confirm you this day as his people,[h]
that he may be your God[i] as he
promised you and as he swore to
your fathers, Abraham, Isaac and
Jacob. 14I am making this covenant,[j] with its oath, not only with
you 15who are standing here with
us today in the presence of the
LORD our God but also with those
who are not here today.[k]

16You yourselves know how we
lived in Egypt and how we passed
through the countries on the way
here. 17You saw among them their
detestable images and idols of
wood and stone, of silver and
gold.[l] 18Make sure there is no
man or woman, clan or tribe among
you today whose heart turns away
from the LORD our God to go and
worship the gods of those nations;
make sure there is no root among
you that produces such bitter poison.[m]

19When such a person hears the
words of this oath, he invokes a
blessing on himself and therefore
thinks, "I will be safe, even though
I persist in going my own way."
This will bring disaster on the watered land as well as the dry.[1]
20The LORD will never be willing to
forgive him; his wrath and zeal[n]
will burn[o] against that man. All
the curses written in this book will
fall upon him, and the LORD will
blot[p] out his name from under
heaven. 21The LORD will single him
out from all the tribes of Israel for
disaster, according to all the curses
of the covenant written in this
Book of the Law.

22Your children who follow you
in later generations and foreigners
who come from distant lands will
see the calamities that have fallen
on the land and the diseases with
which the LORD has afflicted it.[q]
23The whole land will be a burning
waste[r] of salt[s] and sulfur—nothing planted, nothing sprouting, no
vegetation growing on it. It will be
like the destruction of Sodom and
Gomorrah,[t] Admah and Zeboiim,
which the LORD overthrew in fierce
anger. 24All the nations will ask:
"Why has the LORD done this to this
land?[u] Why this fierce, burning anger?"

25And the answer will be: "It is
because this people abandoned the
covenant of the LORD, the God of
their fathers, the covenant he
made with them when he brought
them out of Egypt. 26They went off
and worshiped other gods and
bowed down to them, gods they did
not know, gods he had not given
them. 27Therefore the LORD's anger
burned against this land, so that he
brought on it all the curses written
in this book.[v] 28In furious anger
and in great wrath the LORD uprooted[w] them from their land and
thrust them into another land, as it
is now."

29The secret things belong to the
LORD our God, but the things revealed belong to us and to our children forever, that we may follow all
the words of this law.

29:6 [a] Dt 8:3
29:7 [b] Dt 2:32; 3:1 [c] Nu 21:21-24, 33-35
29:8 [d] Nu 32:33; Dt 3:12-13
29:9 [e] Dt 4:6; Jos 1:7 [f] 1Ki 2:3
29:11 [g] Jos 9:21,23, 27
29:13 [h] Dt 28:9 [i] Ge 17:7; Ex 6:7
29:14 [j] Jer 31:31
29:15 [k] Ac 2:39
29:17 [l] Dt 28:36
29:18 [m] Dt 11:16; Heb 12:15
29:20 [n] Eze 23:25 [o] Ps 74:1; 79:5 [p] Ex 32:33; Dt 9:14
29:22 [q] Jer 19:8
29:23 [r] Isa 34:9 [s] Jer 17:6 [t] Ge 19:24,25; Zep 2:9
29:24 [u] 1Ki 9:8; Jer 22:8-9
29:27 [v] Da 9:11,13, 14
29:28 [w] 1Ki 14:15; 2Ch 7:20; Ps 52:5; Pr 2:22

[1] 19 Or *way, in order to add drunkenness to thirst."*

Prosperity After Turning to the Lord

30 When all these blessings and curses[a] I have set before you come upon you and you take them to heart wherever the LORD your God disperses you among the nations,[b] **2**and when you and your children return[c] to the LORD your God and obey him with all your heart and with all your soul according to everything I command you today, **3**then the LORD your God will restore your fortunes[m][d] and have compassion on you and gather[e] you again from all the nations where he scattered you.[f] **4**Even if you have been banished to the most distant land under the heavens, from there the LORD your God will gather you and bring you back.[g] **5**He will bring[h] you to the land that belonged to your fathers, and you will take possession of it. He will make you more prosperous and numerous than your fathers. **6**The LORD your God will circumcise your hearts and the hearts of your descendants,[i] so that you may love him with all your heart and with all your soul, and live. **7**The LORD your God will put all these curses on your enemies who hate and persecute you.[j] **8**You will again obey the LORD and follow all his commands I am giving you today. **9**Then the LORD your God will make you most prosperous in all the work of your hands and in the fruit of your womb, the young of your livestock and the crops of your land.[k] The LORD will again delight in you and make you prosperous, just as he delighted in your fathers, **10**if you obey the LORD your God and keep his commands and decrees that are written in this Book of the Law and turn to the LORD your God with all your heart and with all your soul.[l]

The Offer of Life or Death

11Now what I am commanding you today is not too difficult for you or beyond your reach.[m] **12**It is not up in heaven, so that you have to ask, "Who will ascend into heaven to get it and proclaim it to us so we may obey it?"[n] **13**Nor is it beyond the sea, so that you have to ask, "Who will cross the sea to get it and proclaim it to us so we may obey it?" **14**No, the word is very near you; it is in your mouth and in your heart so you may obey it.

15See, I set before you today life and prosperity, death and destruction.[o] **16**For I command you today to love the LORD your God, to walk in his ways, and to keep his commands, decrees and laws; then you will live and increase, and the LORD your God will bless you in the land you are entering to possess.

17But if your heart turns away and you are not obedient, and if you are drawn away to bow down to other gods and worship them, **18**I declare to you this day that you will certainly be destroyed.[p] You will not live long in the land you are crossing the Jordan to enter and possess.

19This day I call heaven and earth as witnesses against you[q] that I have set before you life and death, blessings and curses.[r] Now choose life, so that you and your children may live **20**and that you may love[s] the LORD your God, listen to his voice, and hold fast to him. For the LORD is your life,[t] and he will give you many years in the land he swore to give to your fathers, Abraham, Isaac and Jacob.

Joshua to Succeed Moses

31 Then Moses went out and spoke these words to all Israel: **2**"I am now a hundred and twenty years old[u] and I am no longer able to lead you.[v] The LORD has said to me, 'You shall not cross the Jordan.'[w] **3**The LORD your God himself will cross[x] over ahead of you.[y] He will destroy these nations before you, and you will take possession of their land. Joshua also will cross[z] over ahead of you, as the LORD said. **4**And the LORD will do to them what he did to Sihon

30:1 [a]ver 15,19; Dt 11:26 [b]Lev 26:40-45; Dt 28:64; 29:28; 1Ki 8:47
30:2 [c]Dt 4:30; Ne 1:9
30:3 [d]Ps 126:4 [e]Ps 147:2; Jer 32:37; Eze 34:13 [f]Jer 29:14
30:4 [g]Ne 1:8-9; Isa 43:6
30:5 [h]Jer 29:14
30:6 [i]Dt 10:16; Jer 32:39
30:7 [j]Dt 7:15
30:9 [k]Dt 28:11; Jer 31:28; 32:41
30:10 [l]Dt 4:29
30:11 [m]Isa 45:19,23
30:12 [n]Ro 10:6*
30:15 [o]Dt 11:26
30:18 [p]Dt 8:19
30:19 [q]Dt 4:26 [r]ver 1
30:20 [s]Dt 6:5; 10:20 [t]Ps 27:1; Jn 11:25
31:2 [u]Dt 34:7 [v]Nu 27:17; 1Ki 3:7 [w]Dt 3:23,26
31:3 [x]Nu 27:18 [y]Dt 9:3 [z]Dt 3:28

m3 Or *will bring you back from captivity*

and Og, the kings of the Amorites,
whom he destroyed along with
their land. **5**The LORD will deliver[a]
them to you, and you must do to
them all that I have commanded
you. **6**Be strong and courageous.[b]
Do not be afraid or terrified[c] because of them, for the LORD your
God goes with you;[d] he will never
leave you[e] nor forsake[f] you."
7Then Moses summoned Joshua
and said[g] to him in the presence of
all Israel, "Be strong and courageous, for you must go with this
people into the land that the LORD
swore to their forefathers to give
them, and you must divide it
among them as their inheritance.
8The LORD himself goes before you
and will be with you;[h] he will never
leave you nor forsake you. Do not
be afraid; do not be discouraged."

The Reading of the Law

9So Moses wrote down this law
and gave it to the priests, the sons
of Levi, who carried[i] the ark of the
covenant of the LORD, and to all the
elders of Israel. **10**Then Moses
commanded them: "At the end of
every seven years, in the year for
canceling debts,[j] during the Feast
of Tabernacles,[k] **11**when all Israel
comes to appear[l] before the LORD
your God at the place he will
choose, you shall read this law[m]
before them in their hearing. **12**Assemble the people—men, women
and children, and the aliens living
in your towns—so they can listen
and learn[n] to fear the LORD your
God and follow carefully all the
words of this law. **13**Their children,[o] who do not know this law,
must hear it and learn to fear the
LORD your God as long as you live in
the land you are crossing the Jordan to possess."

Israel's Rebellion Predicted

14The LORD said to Moses, "Now
the day of your death[p] is near. Call
Joshua and present yourselves at
the Tent of Meeting, where I will
commission him." So Moses and
Joshua came and presented themselves at the Tent of Meeting.
15Then the LORD appeared at the
Tent in a pillar of cloud, and the
cloud stood over the entrance to
the Tent.[q] **16**And the LORD said to
Moses: "You are going to rest with
your fathers, and these people will
soon prostitute[r] themselves to the
foreign gods of the land they are
entering. They will forsake[s] me
and break the covenant I made
with them. **17**On that day I will become angry[t] with them and forsake[u] them; I will hide[v] my face
from them, and they will be destroyed. Many disasters and difficulties will come upon them, and
on that day they will ask, 'Have not
these disasters come upon us because our God is not with us?'[w]
18And I will certainly hide my face
on that day because of all their
wickedness in turning to other
gods.
19"Now write down for yourselves this song and teach it to the
Israelites and have them sing it, so
that it may be a witness for me
against them. **20**When I have
brought them into the land flowing
with milk and honey, the land I
promised on oath to their forefathers,[x] and when they eat their fill
and thrive, they will turn to other
gods[y] and worship them, rejecting
me and breaking my covenant.[z]
21And when many disasters and
difficulties come upon them,[a] this
song will testify against them, because it will not be forgotten by
their descendants. I know what
they are disposed to do,[b] even before I bring them into the land I
promised them on oath." **22**So Moses wrote[c] down this song that day
and taught it to the Israelites.
23The LORD gave this command[d]
to Joshua son of Nun: "Be strong
and courageous,[e] for you will bring
the Israelites into the land I promised them on oath, and I myself will
be with you."
24After Moses finished writing in
a book the words of this law from
beginning to end, **25**he gave this
command to the Levites who carried the ark of the covenant of the
LORD: **26**"Take this Book of the Law

31:5 [a]Dt 7:2
31:6 [b]Jos 10:25; 1Ch 22:13 [c]Dt 7:18 [d]Dt 1:29; 20:4 [e]Jos 1:5 [f]Heb 13:5*
31:7 [g]Dt 1:38; 3:28
31:8 [h]Ex 13:21; 33:14
31:9 [i]ver 25; Nu 4:15; Jos 3:3
31:10 [j]Dt 15:1 [k]Lev 23:34
31:11 [l]Dt 16:16 [m]Jos 8:34-35; 2Ki 23:2
31:12 [n]Dt 4:10
31:13 [o]Dt 11:2; Ps 78:6-7
31:14 [p]Nu 27:13; Dt 32:49-50
31:15 [q]Ex 33:9
31:16 [r]Jdg 2:12 [s]Jdg 10:6,13
31:17 [t]Jdg 2:14,20 [u]Jdg 6:13; 2Ch 15:2 [v]Dt 32:20; Isa 1:15; 8:17 [w]Nu 14:42
31:20 [x]Dt 6:10-12 [y]Dt 32:15-17 [z]ver 16
31:21 [a]ver 17 [b]Hos 5:3
31:22 [c]ver 19
31:23 [d]ver 7 [e]Jos 1:6

and place it beside the ark of the
covenant of the LORD your God.
There it will remain as a witness
against you.[a] 27For I know how rebellious and stiff-necked[b] you are.
If you have been rebellious against
the LORD while I am still alive and
with you, how much more will you
rebel after I die! 28Assemble before
me all the elders of your tribes and
all your officials, so that I can
speak these words in their hearing
and call heaven and earth to testify
against them.[c] 29For I know that
after my death you are sure to become utterly corrupt[d] and to turn
from the way I have commanded
you. In days to come, disaster[e] will
fall upon you because you will do
evil in the sight of the LORD and
provoke him to anger by what your
hands have made."

The Song of Moses

30And Moses recited the words
of this song from beginning to end
in the hearing of the whole assembly of Israel:

32

Listen, O heavens,[f] and I
will speak;
hear, O earth, the words of
my mouth.
2Let my teaching fall like rain
and my words descend like
dew,[g]
like showers[h] on new grass,
like abundant rain on tender
plants.

3I will proclaim the name of the
LORD.[i]
Oh, praise the greatness[j] of
our God!
4He is the Rock,[k] his works are
perfect,[l]
and all his ways are just.
A faithful God[m] who does no
wrong,
upright and just is he.

5They have acted corruptly
toward him;
to their shame they are no
longer his children,
but a warped and crooked
generation.[n][n]

31:26 [a]ver 19
31:27 [b]Ex 32:9; Dt 9:6,24
31:28 [c]Dt 4:26; 30:19; 32:1
31:29 [d]Dt 32:5; Jdg 2:19 [e]Dt 28:15
32:1 [f]Isa 1:2
32:2 [g]Isa 55:11 [h]Ps 72:6
32:3 [i]Ex 33:19 [j]Dt 3:24
32:4 [k]ver 15,18,30 [l]2Sa 22:31 [m]Dt 7:9
32:5 [n]Dt 31:29
32:6 [o]Ps 116:12 [p]Ps 74:2 [q]Dt 1:31; Isa 63:16 [r]ver 15
32:7 [s]Ex 13:14
32:8 [t]Ge 11:8; Ac 17:26
32:9 [u]Jer 10:16 [v]1Ki 8:51,53
32:10 [w]Jer 2:6 [x]Ps 17:8; Zec 2:8
32:11 [y]Ex 19:4
32:12 [z]ver 39
32:13 [a]Isa 58:14

6Is this the way you repay[o] the
LORD,
O foolish and unwise
people?[p]
Is he not your Father,[q] your
Creator,[o]
who made you and formed
you?[r]

7Remember the days of old;
consider the generations long
past.
Ask your father and he will tell
you,
your elders, and they will
explain to you.[s]
8When the Most High gave the
nations their
inheritance,
when he divided all
mankind,[t]
he set up boundaries for the
peoples
according to the number of
the sons of Israel.[p]
9For the LORD's portion[u] is his
people,
Jacob his allotted
inheritance.[v]

10In a desert[w] land he found
him,
in a barren and howling
waste.
He shielded him and cared for
him;
he guarded him as the apple
of his eye,[x]
11like an eagle that stirs up its
nest
and hovers over its young,[y]
that spreads its wings to catch
them
and carries them on its
pinions.
12The LORD alone led him;
no foreign god was with
him.[z]

13He made him ride on the
heights[a] of the land
and fed him with the fruit of
the fields.

[n]5 Or *Corrupt are they and not his children, / a generation warped and twisted to their shame*
[o]6 Or *Father, who bought you*
[p]8 Masoretic Text; Dead Sea Scrolls (see also Septuagint) *sons of God*

He nourished him with honey
from the rock,
and with oil[a] from the flinty
crag,
14with curds and milk from herd
and flock
and with fattened lambs and
goats,
with choice rams of Bashan
and the finest kernels of
wheat.[b]
You drank the foaming blood
of the grape.[c]

15Jeshurun[q] grew fat[d] and
kicked;
filled with food, he became
heavy and sleek.
He abandoned[e] the God who
made him
and rejected the Rock[f] his
Savior.
16They made him jealous[g] with
their foreign gods
and angered[h] him with their
detestable idols.
17They sacrificed to demons,
which are not God—
gods they had not known,[i]
gods that recently
appeared,[j]
gods your fathers did not
fear.
18You deserted the Rock, who
fathered you;
you forgot[k] the God who
gave you birth.

19The LORD saw this and rejected
them[l]
because he was angered
by his sons and
daughters.[m]
20"I will hide my face[n] from
them," he said,
"and see what their end will
be;
for they are a perverse
generation,[o]
children who are unfaithful.
21They made me jealous[p] by
what is no god
and angered me with their
worthless idols.[q]
I will make them envious by
those who are not a
people;
I will make them angry by a
nation that has no
understanding.[r]
22For a fire has been kindled by
my wrath,
one that burns to the realm
of death[r] below.[s]
It will devour the earth and its
harvests
and set afire the foundations
of the mountains.

23"I will heap calamities[t] upon
them
and spend my arrows[u]
against them.
24I will send wasting famine
against them,
consuming pestilence[v] and
deadly plague;[w]
I will send against them the
fangs of wild beasts,[x]
the venom of vipers[y] that
glide in the dust.
25In the street the sword will
make them childless;
in their homes terror will
reign.[z]
Young men and young women
will perish,
infants and gray-haired
men.[a]
26I said I would scatter[b] them
and blot out their memory
from mankind,[c]
27but I dreaded the taunt of the
enemy,
lest the adversary
misunderstand
and say, 'Our hand has
triumphed;
the LORD has not done all
this.' "[d]

28They are a nation without
sense,
there is no discernment in
them.
29If only they were wise and
would understand this[e]
and discern what their end
will be!
30How could one man chase a
thousand,
or two put ten thousand to
flight,[f]

32:13 [a]Job 29:6
32:14 [b]Ps 81:16; 147:14 [c]Ge 49:11
32:15 [d]Dt 31:20 [e]ver 6; Isa 1:4,28 [f]ver 4
32:16 [g]1Co 10:22 [h]Ps 78:58
32:17 [i]Dt 28:64 [j]Jdg 5:8
32:18 [k]Isa 17:10
32:19 [l]Jer 44:21-23 [m]Ps 106:40
32:20 [n]Dt 31:17,29 [o]ver 5
32:21 [p]1Co 10:22 [q]1Ki 16:13,26 [r]Ro 10:19*
32:22 [s]Ps 18:7-8; Jer 15:14; La 4:11
32:23 [t]Dt 29:21 [u]Ps 7:13; Eze 5:16
32:24 [v]Dt 28:22 [w]Ps 91:6 [x]Lev 26:22 [y]Am 5:18-19
32:25 [z]Eze 7:15 [a]2Ch 36:17; La 2:21
32:26 [b]Dt 4:27 [c]Ps 34:16
32:27 [d]Isa 10:13
32:29 [e]Dt 5:29; Ps 81:13
32:30 [f]Lev 26:8

[q]*15 Jeshurun* means *the upright one,* that is, Israel. [r]*22* Hebrew *to Sheol*

unless their Rock had sold
them,
unless the LORD had given
them up?[a]
31For their rock is not like our
Rock,
as even our enemies
concede.
32Their vine comes from the
vine of Sodom
and from the fields of
Gomorrah.
Their grapes are filled with
poison,
and their clusters with
bitterness.
33Their wine is the venom
of serpents,
the deadly poison of
cobras.[b]

34"Have I not kept this in reserve
and sealed it in my vaults?[c]
35It is mine to avenge; I will
repay.[d]
In due time their foot will
slip;[e]
their day of disaster is near
and their doom rushes upon
them.[f]"

36The LORD will judge his people
and have compassion on his
servants[g]
when he sees their strength is
gone
and no one is left, slave or
free.
37He will say: "Now where are
their gods,
the rock they took refuge
in,[h]
38the gods who ate the fat of
their sacrifices
and drank the wine of their
drink offerings?
Let them rise up to help you!
Let them give you shelter!

39"See now that I myself am
He![i]
There is no god besides me.[j]
I put to death and I bring to
life,[k]
I have wounded and I will
heal,[l]
and no one can deliver out of
my hand.[m]

32:30 [a]Ps 44:12
32:33 [b]Ps 58:4
32:34 [c]Jer 2:22; Hos 13:12
32:35 [d]Ro 12:19*; Heb 10:30* [e]Jer 23:12 [f]Eze 7:8-9
32:36 [g]Dt 30:1-3; Ps 135:14; Joel 2:14
32:37 [h]Jdg 10:14; Jer 2:28
32:39 [i]Isa 41:4 [j]Isa 45:5 [k]1Sa 2:6; Ps 68:20 [l]Hos 6:1 [m]Ps 50:22
32:41 [n]Isa 34:6; 66:16; Eze 21:9-10 [o]Jer 50:29
32:42 [p]ver 23 [q]Jer 46:10,14
32:43 [r]Ro 15:10* [s]2Ki 9:7 [t]Ps 65:3; 85:1; Rev 19:2
32:44 [u]Nu 13:8,16
32:46 [v]Eze 40:4
32:47 [w]Dt 30:20
32:49 [x]Nu 27:12

40I lift my hand to heaven and
declare:
As surely as I live forever,
41when I sharpen my flashing
sword[n]
and my hand grasps it in
judgment,
I will take vengeance on my
adversaries
and repay those who hate
me.[o]
42I will make my arrows drunk
with blood,[p]
while my sword devours
flesh:[q]
the blood of the slain and the
captives,
the heads of the enemy
leaders."

43Rejoice,[r] O nations, with his
people,[s,t]
for he will avenge the blood
of his servants;[s]
he will take vengeance on his
enemies
and make atonement for his
land and people.[t]

44Moses came with Joshua[u][u]
son of Nun and spoke all the words
of this song in the hearing of the
people. 45When Moses finished re-
citing all these words to all Israel,
46he said to them, "Take to heart
all the words I have solemnly declared to you this day,[v] so that you
may command your children to
obey carefully all the words of this
law. 47They are not just idle words
for you—they are your life.[w] By
them you will live long in the land
you are crossing the Jordan to possess."

Moses to Die on Mount Nebo

48On that same day the LORD told
Moses, 49"Go up into the Abarim[x]
Range to Mount Nebo in Moab,
across from Jericho, and view Canaan, the land I am giving the Israelites as their own possession.
50There on the mountain that you

[s]43 Or *Make his people rejoice, O nations*
[t]43 Masoretic Text; Dead Sea Scrolls (see also Septuagint) *people, / and let all the angels worship him /*
[u]44 Hebrew *Hoshea*, a variant of *Joshua*

have climbed you will die[a] and be
gathered to your people, just as
your brother Aaron died on Mount
Hor and was gathered to his people. 51This is because both of you
broke faith with me in the presence
of the Israelites at the waters of
Meribah Kadesh in the Desert of
Zin[b] and because you did not uphold my holiness among the Israelites.[c] 52Therefore, you will see the
land only from a distance;[d] you
will not enter[e] the land I am giving
to the people of Israel."

Moses Blesses the Tribes

33:1–29Ref — Ge 49:1–28

33 This is the blessing that
Moses the man of God[f]
pronounced on the Israelites before his death. 2He said:

"The LORD came from Sinai[g]
and dawned over them from
Seir;[h]
he shone forth from Mount
Paran.[i]
He came with[v] myriads of holy
ones[j]
from the south, from his
mountain slopes.[w]
3Surely it is you who love[k] the
people;
all the holy ones are in your
hand.[l]
At your feet they all bow
down,[m]
and from you receive
instruction,
4the law that Moses gave us,[n]
the possession of the
assembly of Jacob.[o]
5He was king over Jeshurun[x]
when the leaders of the
people assembled,
along with the tribes of
Israel.

6"Let Reuben live and not die,
nor[y] his men be few."

7And this he said about Judah:[p]

"Hear, O LORD, the cry of
Judah;
bring him to his people.
With his own hands he defends
his cause.
Oh, be his help against his
foes!"

8About Levi he said:

"Your Thummim and Urim[q]
belong
to the man you favored.
You tested him at Massah;
you contended with him at
the waters of Meribah.[r]
9He said of his father and
mother,[s]
'I have no regard for them.'
He did not recognize his
brothers
or acknowledge his own
children,
but he watched over your word
and guarded your covenant.[t]
10He teaches your precepts to
Jacob
and your law to Israel.[u]
He offers incense before you
and whole burnt offerings on
your altar.[v]
11Bless all his skills, O LORD,
and be pleased with the work
of his hands.[w]
Smite the loins of those who
rise up against him;
strike his foes till they rise
no more."

12About Benjamin he said:

"Let the beloved of the LORD
rest secure in him,[x]
for he shields him all day
long,
and the one the LORD loves
rests between his
shoulders.[y]"

13About Joseph[z] he said:

"May the LORD bless his land
with the precious dew from
heaven above
and with the deep waters
that lie below;[a]
14with the best the sun brings
forth
and the finest the moon can
yield;

32:50 [a] Ge 25:8
32:51 [b] Nu 20:11-13 [c] Nu 27:14
32:52 [d] Dt 34:1-3 [e] Dt 1:37
33:1 [f] Jos 14:6
33:2 [g] Ex 19:18; Ps 68:8 [h] Jdg 5:4 [i] Hab 3:3 [j] Da 7:10; Ac 7:53; Rev 5:11
33:3 [k] Hos 11:1 [l] Dt 14:2 [m] Lk 10:39
33:4 [n] Jn 1:17 [o] Ps 119:111
33:7 [p] Ge 49:10
33:8 [q] Ex 28:30 [r] Ex 17:7
33:9 [s] Ex 32:26-29 [t] Mal 2:5
33:10 [u] Lev 10:11; Dt 31:9-13 [v] Ps 51:19
33:11 [w] 2Sa 24:23
33:12 [x] Dt 12:10 [y] Ex 28:12
33:13 [z] Ge 49:25 [a] Ge 27:28

[v]2 Or *from* [w]2 The meaning of the Hebrew for this phrase is uncertain. [x]5 *Jeshurun* means *the upright one,* that is, Israel; also in verse 26. [y]6 Or *but let*

15with the choicest gifts of the ancient mountains[a]
and the fruitfulness of the everlasting hills;
16with the best gifts of the earth and its fullness
and the favor of him who dwelt in the burning bush.[b]
Let all these rest on the head of Joseph,
on the brow of the prince among[z] his brothers.
17In majesty he is like a firstborn bull;
his horns are the horns of a wild ox.[c]
With them he will gore[d] the nations,
even those at the ends of the earth.
Such are the ten thousands of Ephraim;
such are the thousands of Manasseh."

18About Zebulun[e] he said:

"Rejoice, Zebulun, in your going out,
and you, Issachar, in your tents.
19They will summon peoples to the mountain[f]
and there offer sacrifices of righteousness;[g]
they will feast on the abundance of the seas,[h]
on the treasures hidden in the sand."

20About Gad[i] he said:

"Blessed is he who enlarges Gad's domain!
Gad lives there like a lion,
tearing at arm or head.
21He chose the best land for himself;[j]
the leader's portion was kept for him.
When the heads of the people assembled,
he carried out the LORD's righteous will,[k]
and his judgments concerning Israel."

22About Dan[l] he said:

"Dan is a lion's cub,
springing out of Bashan."

23About Naphtali he said:

"Naphtali is abounding with the favor of the LORD
and is full of his blessing;
he will inherit southward to the lake."

24About Asher[m] he said:

"Most blessed of sons is Asher;
let him be favored by his brothers,
and let him bathe his feet in oil.[n]
25The bolts of your gates will be iron and bronze,
and your strength will equal your days.[o]
26"There is no one like the God of Jeshurun,[p]
who rides on the heavens to help you[q]
and on the clouds in his majesty.
27The eternal God is your refuge,[r]
and underneath are the everlasting arms.
He will drive out your enemy before you,[s]
saying, 'Destroy him!'[t]
28So Israel will live in safety alone;[u]
Jacob's spring is secure
in a land of grain and new wine,
where the heavens drop dew.[v]
29Blessed are you, O Israel![w]
Who is like you,[x]
a people saved by the LORD?[y]
He is your shield and helper[z]
and your glorious sword.
Your enemies will cower before you,
and you will trample down their high places.[a][a]"

The Death of Moses

34 Then Moses climbed Mount Nebo from the plains of Moab to the top of Pisgah,

33:15 [a]Hab 3:6
33:16 [b]Ex 3:2
33:17 [c]Nu 23:22 [d]1Ki 22:11; Ps 44:5
33:18 [e]Ge 49:13-15
33:19 [f]Ex 15:17; Isa 2:3 [g]Ps 4:5 [h]Isa 60:5,11
33:20 [i]Ge 49:19
33:21 [j]Nu 32:1-5, 31-32 [k]Jos 4:12; 22:1-3
33:22 [l]Ge 49:16
33:24 [m]Ge 49:21 [n]Ge 49:20; Job 29:6
33:25 [o]Dt 4:40; 32:47
33:26 [p]Ex 15:11 [q]Ps 104:3
33:27 [r]Ps 90:1 [s]Jos 24:18 [t]Dt 7:2
33:28 [u]Nu 23:9; Jer 23:6 [v]Ge 27:28
33:29 [w]Ps 144:15 [x]Ps 18:44 [y]2Sa 7:23 [z]Ps 115:9-11 [a]Dt 32:13

[z]16 Or *of the one separated from* [a]29 Or *will tread upon their bodies*

across from Jericho.[a] There the
LORD showed[b] him the whole
land—from Gilead to Dan, 2all of
Naphtali, the territory of Ephraim
and Manasseh, all the land of Judah as far as the western sea,[b][c]
3the Negev and the whole region
from the Valley of Jericho, the City
of Palms,[d] as far as Zoar. 4Then
the LORD said to him, "This is the
land I promised on oath[e] to Abraham, Isaac and Jacob when I said,
'I will give it[f] to your descendants.' I have let you see it with
your eyes, but you will not cross[g]
over into it."

5And Moses the servant of the
LORD[h] died[i] there in Moab, as the
LORD had said. 6He buried him[c] in
Moab, in the valley opposite Beth
Peor,[j] but to this day no one
knows where his grave is.[k] 7Moses
was a hundred and twenty years
old[l] when he died, yet his eyes
were not weak[m] nor his strength
gone. 8The Israelites grieved for
Moses in the plains of Moab thirty
days, until the time of weeping and
mourning[n] was over.

9Now Joshua son of Nun was
filled with the spirit[d] of wisdom[o]
because Moses had laid his hands
on him.[p] So the Israelites listened
to him and did what the LORD had
commanded Moses.

10Since then, no prophet has ris-
en in Israel like Moses,[q] whom the
LORD knew face to face,[r] 11who did
all those miraculous signs and
wonders[s] the LORD sent him to do
in Egypt—to Pharaoh and to all his
officials[t] and to his whole land.
12For no one has ever shown the
mighty power or performed the
awesome deeds that Moses did in
the sight of all Israel.

34:1 [a]Dt 32:49 [b]Dt 32:52 **34:2** [c]Dt 11:24 **34:3** [d]Jdg 1:16; 3:13; 2Ch 28:15 **34:4** [e]Ge 28:13 [f]Ge 12:7 [g]Dt 3:27 **34:5** [h]Nu 12:7 [i]Dt 32:50; Jos 1:1-2 **34:6** [j]Dt 3:29 [k]Jude 1:9 **34:7** [l]Dt 31:2 [m]Ge 27:1 **34:8** [n]Ge 50:3,10; 2Sa 11:27 **34:9** [o]Ge 41:38; Isa 11:2; Da 6:3 [p]Nu 27:18,23 **34:10** [q]Dt 18:15,18 [r]Ex 33:11; Nu 12:6,8; Dt 5:4 **34:11** [s]Dt 4:34 [t]Dt 7:19

[b]2 That is, the Mediterranean [c]6 Or *He was buried* [d]9 Or *Spirit*

Joshua

Title and Background

This book is named after its leading character, Joshua, whom God named as Israel's leader before Moses' death. Where Deuteronomy ends, the book of Joshua begins—with the tribes still camped on the east side of the Jordan River.

Author and Date of Writing

The earliest Jewish traditions (Talmud) claim that Joshua wrote his own book except for the final section about his funeral, which is assigned to Eleazar son of Aaron. Others think that Samuel may have shaped or compiled the materials of the book. However, we have no sure knowledge of who the author was. The book of Joshua was written sometime before 1000 B.C.

Theme and Message

The theme of the book is the establishment of Israel in the promised land. With God's help the people crossed the Jordan River and took possession of all the main areas of Canaan. Toward the end of the book Joshua reminded the people of God's covenant promises to them and instructed them to keep on loving and obeying God.

Outline

I. Preparation for Possession of Canaan (1:1-5:12)
II. The Conquest of Canaan (5:13-12:24)
III. The Division of Land by Tribes (13:1-21:45)
IV. Farewell and Death of Joshua (22:1-24:33)

The LORD Commands Joshua

1 After the death of Moses the
servant of the LORD,[a] the LORD
said to Joshua[b] son of Nun, Moses' aide: **2**"Moses my servant is
dead. Now then, you and all these
people, get ready to cross the Jordan River[c] into the land I am
about to give to them—to the Israelites. **3**I will give you every place
where you set your foot,[d] as I
promised Moses. **4**Your territory
will extend from the desert to Lebanon, and from the great river, the
Euphrates[e]—all the Hittite country—to the Great Sea[a] on the
west.[f] **5**No one will be able to
stand up against you[g] all the days
of your life. As I was with[h] Moses,
so I will be with you; I will never
leave you nor forsake[i] you.
6"Be strong and courageous, because you will lead these people to
inherit the land I swore to their
forefathers[j] to give them. **7**Be
strong and very courageous. Be
careful to obey all the law my servant Moses gave you; do not turn
from it to the right or to the left,[k]
that you may be successful wherever you go.[l] **8**Do not let this Book
of the Law depart from your mouth;
meditate on it day and night, so
that you may be careful to do everything written in it. Then you will be
prosperous and successful.[m] **9**Have
I not commanded you? Be strong
and courageous. Do not be terrified;[n] do not be discouraged, for
the LORD your God will be with you
wherever you go."[o]
10So Joshua ordered the officers
of the people: **11**"Go through the
camp and tell the people, 'Get your

1:1 [a]Nu 12:7; Dt 34:5 [b]Ex 24:13; Dt 1:38
1:2 [c]ver 11
1:3 [d]Dt 11:24
1:4 [e]Ge 15:18 [f]Nu 34:2-12
1:5 [g]Dt 7:24 [h]Jos 3:7; 6:27 [i]Dt 31:6-8
1:6 [j]Dt 31:23
1:7 [k]Dt 5:32; 28:14 [l]Jos 11:15
1:8 [m]Dt 29:9; Ps 1:1-3
1:9 [n]Ps 27:1 [o]ver 7; Dt 31:7-8; Jer 1:8

[a]4 That is, the Mediterranean

supplies ready. Three days from now you will cross the Jordan here to go in and take possession[a] of the land the LORD your God is giving you for your own.' "

12But to the Reubenites, the Gadites and the half-tribe of Manasseh,[b] Joshua said, 13"Remember the command that Moses the servant of the LORD gave you: 'The LORD your God is giving you rest[c] and has granted you this land.' 14Your wives, your children and your livestock may stay in the land that Moses gave you east of the Jordan, but all your fighting men, fully armed, must cross over ahead of your brothers. You are to help your brothers 15until the LORD gives them rest, as he has done for you, and until they too have taken possession of the land that the LORD your God is giving them. After that, you may go back and occupy your own land, which Moses the servant of the LORD gave you east of the Jordan toward the sunrise."[d]

16Then they answered Joshua, "Whatever you have commanded us we will do, and wherever you send us we will go. 17Just as we fully obeyed Moses, so we will obey you.[e] Only may the LORD your God be with you as he was with Moses. 18Whoever rebels against your word and does not obey your words, whatever you may command them, will be put to death. Only be strong and courageous!"

Rahab and the Spies

2 Then Joshua son of Nun secretly sent two spies[f] from Shittim.[g] "Go, look over the land," he said, "especially Jericho." So they went and entered the house of a prostitute[b] named Rahab[h] and stayed there.

2The king of Jericho was told, "Look! Some of the Israelites have come here tonight to spy out the land." 3So the king of Jericho sent this message to Rahab: "Bring out the men who came to you and entered your house, because they have come to spy out the whole land."

4But the woman had taken the two men and hidden them.[i] She said, "Yes, the men came to me, but I did not know where they had come from. 5At dusk, when it was time to close the city gate, the men left. I don't know which way they went. Go after them quickly. You may catch up with them." 6(But she had taken them up to the roof and hidden them under the stalks of flax[j] she had laid out on the roof.)[k] 7So the men set out in pursuit of the spies on the road that leads to the fords of the Jordan, and as soon as the pursuers had gone out, the gate was shut.

8Before the spies lay down for the night, she went up on the roof 9and said to them, "I know that the LORD has given this land to you and that a great fear[l] of you has fallen on us, so that all who live in this country are melting in fear because of you. 10We have heard how the LORD dried up[m] the water of the Red Sea[c] for you when you came out of Egypt,[n] and what you did to Sihon and Og,[o] the two kings of the Amorites east of the Jordan, whom you completely destroyed.[d] 11When we heard of it, our hearts melted and everyone's courage failed because of you,[p] for the LORD your God is God in heaven above and on the earth[q] below. 12Now then, please swear to me by the LORD that you will show kindness to my family, because I have shown kindness to you. Give me a sure sign[r] 13that you will spare the lives of my father and mother, my brothers and sisters, and all who belong to them, and that you will save us from death."

14"Our lives for your lives!" the men assured her. "If you don't tell what we are doing, we will treat you kindly and faithfully[s] when the LORD gives us the land."

15So she let them down by a rope through the window,[t] for the

1:11 [a]Joel 3:2
1:12 [b]Nu 32:20-22
1:13 [c]Dt 3:18-20
1:15 [d]Jos 22:1-4
1:17 [e]ver 5,9
2:1 [f]Jas 2:25 [g]Nu 25:1; Jos 3:1 [h]Heb 11:31
2:4 [i]2Sa 17:19-20
2:6 [j]Jas 2:25 [k]Ex 1:17,19; 2Sa 17:19
2:9 [l]Ge 35:5; Ex 23:27; Dt 2:25
2:10 [m]Ex 14:21 [n]Nu 23:22 [o]Nu 21:21,24, 34-35
2:11 [p]Ex 15:14; Jos 5:1; 7:5; Ps 22:14; Isa 13:7 [q]Dt 4:39
2:12 [r]ver 18
2:14 [s]Jdg 1:24; Mt 5:7
2:15 [t]Ac 9:25

[b]*1* Or possibly *an innkeeper* [c]*10* Hebrew *Yam Suph*; that is, Sea of Reeds [d]*10* The Hebrew term refers to the irrevocable giving over of things or persons to the LORD, often by totally destroying them.

house she lived in was part of the
city wall. **16**Now she had said to
them, "Go to the hills so the pursuers will not find you. Hide yourselves there three days[a] until they
return, and then go on your way."[b]

17The men said to her, "This
oath[c] you made us swear will not
be binding on us **18**unless, when we
enter the land, you have tied this
scarlet cord in the window through
which you let us down, and unless
you have brought your father and
mother, your brothers and all your
family[d] into your house. **19**If anyone goes outside your house into
the street, his blood will be on his
own head;[e] we will not be responsible. As for anyone who is in the
house with you, his blood will be
on our head[f] if a hand is laid on
him. **20**But if you tell what we are
doing, we will be released from the
oath you made us swear."

21"Agreed," she replied. "Let it
be as you say." So she sent them
away and they departed. And she
tied the scarlet cord in the window.

22When they left, they went into
the hills and stayed there three
days, until the pursuers had
searched all along the road and returned without finding them.
23Then the two men started back.
They went down out of the hills,
forded the river and came to Joshua son of Nun and told him everything that had happened to them.
24They said to Joshua, "The LORD
has surely given the whole land
into our hands;[g] all the people are
melting in fear because of us."

Crossing the Jordan

3 Early in the morning Joshua
and all the Israelites set out
from Shittim[h] and went to the Jordan, where they camped before
crossing over. **2**After three days the
officers went throughout the
camp,[i] **3**giving orders to the people: "When you see the ark of the
covenant[j] of the LORD your God,
and the priests,[k] who are Levites,
carrying it, you are to move out
from your positions and follow it.
4Then you will know which way to
go, since you have never been this
way before. But keep a distance of
about a thousand yards[e] between
you and the ark; do not go near it."

5Joshua told the people, "Consecrate yourselves,[l] for tomorrow
the LORD will do amazing things
among you."

6Joshua said to the priests,
"Take up the ark of the covenant
and pass on ahead of the people."
So they took it up and went ahead
of them.

7And the LORD said to Joshua,
"Today I will begin to exalt you[m] in
the eyes of all Israel, so they may
know that I am with you as I was
with Moses.[n] **8**Tell the priests[o]
who carry the ark of the covenant:
'When you reach the edge of the
Jordan's waters, go and stand in
the river.' "

9Joshua said to the Israelites,
"Come here and listen to the words
of the LORD your God. **10**This is how
you will know that the living God[p]
is among you and that he will certainly drive out before you the Canaanites, Hittites, Hivites, Perizzites, Girgashites, Amorites and
Jebusites.[q] **11**See, the ark of the
covenant of the Lord of all the
earth[r] will go into the Jordan
ahead of you. **12**Now then, choose
twelve men[s] from the tribes of Israel, one from each tribe. **13**And as
soon as the priests who carry the
ark of the LORD—the Lord of all the
earth[t]—set foot in the Jordan, its
waters flowing downstream[u] will
be cut off and stand up in a
heap.[v]"

14So when the people broke
camp to cross the Jordan, the
priests carrying the ark of the covenant[w] went ahead[x] of them.
15Now the Jordan is at flood
stage[y] all during harvest. Yet as
soon as the priests who carried the
ark reached the Jordan and their
feet touched the water's edge,
16the water from upstream stopped
flowing.[z] It piled up in a heap a
great distance away, at a town

2:16 [a]Jas 2:25 [b]Heb 11:31
2:17 [c]Ge 24:8
2:18 [d]ver 12; Jos 6:23
2:19 [e]Eze 33:4 [f]Mt 27:25
2:24 [g]ver 9; Jos 6:2
3:1 [h]Jos 2:1
3:2 [i]Jos 1:11
3:3 [j]Nu 10:33 [k]Dt 31:9
3:5 [l]Ex 19:10,14; Lev 20:7; Jos 7:13; 1Sa 16:5; Joel 2:16
3:7 [m]Jos 4:14; 1Ch 29:25 [n]Jos 1:5
3:8 [o]ver 3
3:10 [p]Dt 5:26; 1Sa 17:26,36; 2Ki 19:4,16; Hos 1:10; Mt 16:16; 1Th 1:9 [q]Ex 33:2; Dt 7:1
3:11 [r]ver 13; Job 41:11; Zec 6:5
3:12 [s]Jos 4:2,4
3:13 [t]ver 11 [u]ver 16 [v]Ex 15:8; Ps 78:13
3:14 [w]Ps 132:8 [x]Ac 7:44-45
3:15 [y]Jos 4:18; 1Ch 12:15
3:16 [z]Ps 66:6; 74:15

e4 Hebrew *about two thousand cubits* (about 900 meters)

called Adam in the vicinity of Zarethan,[a] while the water flowing
down[b] to the Sea of the Arabah[c]
(the Salt Sea [f][d]) was completely
cut off. So the people crossed over
opposite Jericho. **17**The priests
who carried the ark of the covenant
of the LORD stood firm on dry
ground in the middle of the Jordan,
while all Israel passed by until the
whole nation had completed the
crossing on dry ground.[e]

4 When the whole nation had
finished crossing the Jordan,[f]
the LORD said to Joshua, **2**"Choose
twelve men[g] from among the people, one from each tribe, **3**and tell
them to take up twelve stones[h]
from the middle of the Jordan from
right where the priests stood and to
carry them over with you and put
them down at the place where you
stay tonight.[i]"

4So Joshua called together the
twelve men he had appointed from
the Israelites, one from each tribe,
5and said to them, "Go over before
the ark of the LORD your God into
the middle of the Jordan. Each of
you is to take up a stone on his
shoulder, according to the number
of the tribes of the Israelites, **6**to
serve as a sign among you. In the
future, when your children ask you,
'What do these stones mean?'[j]
7tell them that the flow of the Jordan was cut off[k] before the ark of
the covenant of the LORD. When it
crossed the Jordan, the waters of
the Jordan were cut off. These
stones are to be a memorial[l] to the
people of Israel forever."

8So the Israelites did as Joshua
commanded them. They took
twelve stones from the middle of
the Jordan, according to the number of the tribes of the Israelites, as
the LORD had told Joshua;[m] and
they carried them over with them
to their camp, where they put them
down. **9**Joshua set up the twelve
stones[n] that had been[g] in the
middle of the Jordan at the spot
where the priests who carried the
ark of the covenant had stood. And
they are there to this day.

10Now the priests who carried
the ark remained standing in the
middle of the Jordan until everything the LORD had commanded
Joshua was done by the people,
just as Moses had directed Joshua.
The people hurried over, **11**and as
soon as all of them had crossed, the
ark of the LORD and the priests
came to the other side while the
people watched. **12**The men of
Reuben, Gad and the half-tribe of
Manasseh crossed over, armed, in
front of the Israelites,[o] as Moses
had directed them. **13**About forty
thousand armed for battle crossed
over before the LORD to the plains
of Jericho for war.

14That day the LORD exalted[p]
Joshua in the sight of all Israel; and
they revered him all the days of his
life, just as they had revered Moses.

15Then the LORD said to Joshua,
16"Command the priests carrying
the ark of the Testimony[q] to come
up out of the Jordan."

17So Joshua commanded the
priests, "Come up out of the Jordan."

18And the priests came up out of
the river carrying the ark of the covenant of the LORD. No sooner had
they set their feet on the dry
ground than the waters of the Jordan returned to their place and ran
at flood stage[r] as before.

19On the tenth day of the first
month the people went up from the
Jordan and camped at Gilgal[s] on
the eastern border of Jericho.
20And Joshua set up at Gilgal the
twelve stones[t] they had taken out
of the Jordan. **21**He said to the Israelites, "In the future when your
descendants ask their fathers,
'What do these stones mean?'[u]
22tell them, 'Israel crossed the Jordan on dry ground.'[v] **23**For the
LORD your God dried up the Jordan
before you until you had crossed
over. The LORD your God did to the
Jordan just what he had done to
the Red Sea[h] when he dried it up
before us until we had crossed

3:16 [a] 1Ki 4:12; 7:46 [b] ver 13 [c] Dt 1:1 [d] Ge 14:3
3:17 [e] Ex 14:22,29
4:1 [f] Dt 27:2
4:2 [g] Jos 3:12
4:3 [h] ver 20 [i] ver 19
4:6 [j] ver 21; Ex 12:26; 13:14
4:7 [k] Jos 3:13 [l] Ex 12:14
4:8 [m] ver 20
4:9 [n] Ge 28:18; Jos 24:26; 1Sa 7:12
4:12 [o] Nu 32:27
4:14 [p] Jos 3:7
4:16 [q] Ex 25:22
4:18 [r] Jos 3:15
4:19 [s] Jos 5:9
4:20 [t] ver 3,8
4:21 [u] ver 6
4:22 [v] Jos 3:17

[f]16 That is, the Dead Sea [g]9 Or *Joshua also set up twelve stones* [h]23 Hebrew *Yam Suph*; that is, Sea of Reeds

over.[a] **24**He did this so that all the peoples of the earth might know[b] that the hand of the LORD is powerful[c] and so that you might always fear the LORD your God.[d]"

Circumcision at Gilgal

5 Now when all the Amorite kings west of the Jordan and all the Canaanite kings along the coast[e] heard how the LORD had dried up the Jordan before the Israelites until we had crossed over, their hearts melted[f] and they no longer had the courage to face the Israelites.

2At that time the LORD said to Joshua, "Make flint knives[g] and circumcise the Israelites again." **3**So Joshua made flint knives and circumcised the Israelites at Gibeath Haaraloth.[i]

4Now this is why he did so: All those who came out of Egypt—all the men of military age—died in the desert on the way after leaving Egypt.[h] **5**All the people that came out had been circumcised, but all the people born in the desert during the journey from Egypt had not. **6**The Israelites had moved about in the desert forty years[i] until all the men who were of military age when they left Egypt had died, since they had not obeyed the LORD. For the LORD had sworn to them that they would not see the land that he had solemnly promised their fathers to give us,[j] a land flowing with milk and honey.[k] **7**So he raised up their sons in their place, and these were the ones Joshua circumcised. They were still uncircumcised because they had not been circumcised on the way. **8**And after the whole nation had been circumcised, they remained where they were in camp until they were healed.[l]

9Then the LORD said to Joshua, "Today I have rolled away the reproach of Egypt from you." So the place has been called Gilgal[j] to this day.

10On the evening of the fourteenth day of the month,[m] while camped at Gilgal on the plains of Jericho, the Israelites celebrated the Passover. **11**The day after the Passover, that very day, they ate some of the produce of the land:[n] unleavened bread and roasted grain.[o] **12**The manna stopped the day after[k] they ate this food from the land; there was no longer any manna for the Israelites, but that year they ate of the produce of Canaan.[p]

The Fall of Jericho

13Now when Joshua was near Jericho, he looked up and saw a man[q] standing in front of him with a drawn sword[r] in his hand. Joshua went up to him and asked, "Are you for us or for our enemies?"

14"Neither," he replied, "but as commander of the army of the LORD I have now come." Then Joshua fell facedown[s] to the ground in reverence, and asked him, "What message does my Lord[l] have for his servant?"

15The commander of the LORD's army replied, "Take off your sandals, for the place where you are standing is holy."[t] And Joshua did so.

6 Now Jericho[u] was tightly shut up because of the Israelites. No one went out and no one came in.

2Then the LORD said to Joshua, "See, I have delivered[v] Jericho into your hands, along with its king and its fighting men. **3**March around the city once with all the armed men. Do this for six days. **4**Have seven priests carry trumpets of rams' horns in front of the ark. On the seventh day, march around the city seven times, with the priests blowing the trumpets.[w] **5**When you hear them sound a long blast[x] on the trumpets, have all the people give a loud shout;[y] then the wall of the city will collapse and the people will go up, every man straight in."

6So Joshua son of Nun called the priests and said to them, "Take up

4:23 [a]Ex 14:21
4:24 [b]1Ki 8:42-43; 2Ki 19:19; Ps 106:8; Jer 10:7 [c]Ex 15:16; 1Ch 29:12; Ps 89:13 [d]Ex 14:31
5:1 [e]Nu 13:29 [f]Jos 2:9-11
5:2 [g]Ex 4:25
5:4 [h]Dt 2:14
5:6 [i]Dt 2:7 [j]Nu 14:23, 29-35; Dt 2:14 [k]Ex 3:8
5:8 [l]Ge 34:25
5:10 [m]Ex 12:6
5:11 [n]Nu 15:19 [o]Lev 23:14
5:12 [p]Ex 16:35
5:13 [q]Ge 18:2; 32:24 [r]Nu 22:23
5:14 [s]Ge 17:3
5:15 [t]Ex 3:5; Ac 7:33
6:1 [u]Jos 24:11
6:2 [v]Dt 7:24; Jos 2:9,24; 8:1
6:4 [w]Lev 25:9; Nu 10:8
6:5 [x]Ex 19:13 [y]ver 20; 1Sa 4:5; Ps 42:4; Isa 42:13

[i]3 *Gibeath Haaraloth* means *hill of foreskins.*
[j]9 *Gilgal* sounds like the Hebrew for *roll.*
[k]12 Or *the day* [l]14 Or *lord*

the ark of the covenant of the LORD
and have seven priests carry trumpets in front of it." 7And he ordered
the people, "Advance[a]! March
around the city, with the armed
guard going ahead of the ark of the
LORD."
8When Joshua had spoken to the
people, the seven priests carrying
the seven trumpets before the LORD
went forward, blowing their trumpets, and the ark of the LORD's covenant followed them. 9The armed
guard marched ahead of the priests
who blew the trumpets, and the
rear guard[b] followed the ark. All
this time the trumpets were sounding. 10But Joshua had commanded
the people, "Do not give a war cry,
do not raise your voices, do not say
a word until the day I tell you to
shout. Then shout![c]" 11So he had
the ark of the LORD carried around
the city, circling it once. Then the
people returned to camp and spent
the night there.
12Joshua got up early the next
morning and the priests took up
the ark of the LORD. 13The seven
priests carrying the seven trumpets
went forward, marching before the
ark of the LORD and blowing the
trumpets. The armed men went
ahead of them and the rear guard
followed the ark of the LORD, while
the trumpets kept sounding. 14So
on the second day they marched
around the city once and returned
to the camp. They did this for six
days.
15On the seventh day, they got
up at daybreak and marched
around the city seven times in the
same manner, except that on that
day they circled the city seven
times.[d] 16The seventh time
around, when the priests sounded
the trumpet blast, Joshua commanded the people, "Shout! For
the LORD has given you the city!
17The city and all that is in it are to
be devoted[m][e] to the LORD. Only
Rahab the prostitute[n] and all who
are with her in her house shall be
spared, because she hid[f] the spies
we sent. 18But keep away from the
devoted things,[g] so that you will
not bring about your own destruction by taking any of them. Otherwise you will make the camp of Israel liable to destruction[h] and
bring trouble[i] on it. 19All the silver and gold and the articles of
bronze and iron[j] are sacred to the
LORD and must go into his treasury."
20When the trumpets sounded,[k]
the people shouted, and at the
sound of the trumpet, when the
people gave a loud shout,[l] the wall
collapsed; so every man charged
straight in, and they took the city.[m]
21They devoted the city to the LORD
and destroyed[n] with the sword every living thing in it—men and
women, young and old, cattle,
sheep and donkeys.
22Joshua said to the two men
who had spied out the land, "Go
into the prostitute's house and
bring her out and all who belong to
her, in accordance with your oath
to her.[o]" 23So the young men who
had done the spying went in and
brought out Rahab, her father and
mother and brothers and all who
belonged to her.[p] They brought
out her entire family and put them
in a place outside the camp of Israel.
24Then they burned the whole
city and everything in it, but they
put the silver and gold and the articles of bronze and iron[q] into the
treasury of the LORD's house. 25But
Joshua spared Rahab the prostitute,[r] with her family and all who
belonged to her, because she hid
the men Joshua had sent as spies
to Jericho[s]—and she lives among
the Israelites to this day.
26At that time Joshua pronounced this solemn oath: "Cursed
before the LORD is the man who un-
dertakes to rebuild this city, Jericho:

"At the cost of his firstborn son
 will he lay its foundations;
at the cost of his youngest

6:7 [a]Ex 14:15
6:9 [b]ver 13; Isa 52:12
6:10 [c]ver 20
6:15 [d]1Ki 18:44
6:17 [e]Lev 27:28; Dt 20:17 [f]Jos 2:4
6:18 [g]Jos 7:1 [h]Jos 7:12 [i]Jos 7:25,26
6:19 [j]ver 24; Nu 31:22
6:20 [k]Jdg 6:34; Jer 4:21; Am 2:2 [l]ver 5 [m]Heb 11:30
6:21 [n]Dt 20:16
6:22 [o]Jos 2:14; Heb 11:31
6:23 [p]Jos 2:13
6:24 [q]ver 19
6:25 [r]Heb 11:31 [s]Jos 2:6

[m]*17* The Hebrew term refers to the irrevocable giving over of things or persons to the LORD, often by totally destroying them; also in verses 18 and 21. [n]*17* Or possibly *innkeeper*; also in verses 22 and 25

will he set up its gates."[a]
27So the LORD was with Joshua,[b]
and his fame spread[c] throughout
the land.

Achan's Sin

7 But the Israelites acted unfaithfully in regard to the devoted things[o];[d] Achan son of Carmi, the son of Zimri,[p] the son of
Zerah,[e] of the tribe of Judah, took
some of them..So the LORD's anger
burned against Israel.
2Now Joshua sent men from Jericho to Ai, which is near Beth
Aven[f] to the east of Bethel, and
told them, "Go up and spy out the
region." So the men went up and
spied out Ai.
3When they returned to Joshua,
they said, "Not all the people will
have to go up against Ai. Send two
or three thousand men to take it
and do not weary all the people, for
only a few men are there." 4So
about three thousand men went
up; but they were routed by the
men of Ai,[g] 5who killed about thirty-six of them. They chased the Israelites from the city gate as far as
the stone quarries[q] and struck
them down on the slopes. At this
the hearts of the people melted[h]
and became like water.
6Then Joshua tore his clothes[i]
and fell facedown to the ground before the ark of the LORD, remaining
there till evening. The elders of Israel did the same, and sprinkled
dust[j] on their heads. 7And Joshua
said, "Ah, Sovereign LORD, why did
you ever bring this people across
the Jordan to deliver us into the
hands of the Amorites to destroy
us?[k] If only we had been content
to stay on the other side of the Jordan! 8O Lord, what can I say, now
that Israel has been routed by its
enemies? 9The Canaanites and the
other people of the country will
hear about this and they will surround us and wipe out our name
from the earth.[l] What then will
you do for your own great name?"
10The LORD said to Joshua,
"Stand up! What are you doing
down on your face? 11Israel has
sinned; they have violated my covenant,[m] which I commanded them
to keep. They have taken some of
the devoted things; they have stolen, they have lied,[n] they have put
them with their own possessions.
12That is why the Israelites cannot
stand against their enemies;[o] they
turn their backs and run because
they have been made liable to destruction.[p] I will not be with you
anymore unless you destroy whatever among you is devoted to destruction.
13"Go, consecrate the people.
Tell them, 'Consecrate yourselves[q] in preparation for tomorrow; for this is what the LORD, the
God of Israel, says: That which is
devoted is among you, O Israel.
You cannot stand against your enemies until you remove it.
14" 'In the morning, present
yourselves tribe by tribe. The tribe
that the LORD takes[r] shall come
forward clan by clan; the clan that
the LORD takes shall come forward
family by family; and the family
that the LORD takes shall come forward man by man. 15He who is
caught with the devoted things
shall be destroyed by fire, along
with all that belongs to him.[s] He
has violated the covenant[t] of the
LORD and has done a disgraceful
thing in Israel!' "[u]
16Early the next morning Joshua
had Israel come forward by tribes,
and Judah was taken. 17The clans
of Judah came forward, and he
took the Zerahites.[v] He had the
clan of the Zerahites come forward
by families, and Zimri was taken.
18Joshua had his family come forward man by man, and Achan son
of Carmi, the son of Zimri, the son
of Zerah, of the tribe of Judah, was
taken.
19Then Joshua said to Achan,
"My son, give glory[w] to the LORD,[r]

6:26 [a] 1Ki 16:34
6:27 [b] Ge 39:2; Jos 1:5 [c] Jos 9:1
7:1 [d] Jos 6:18 [e] Jos 22:20
7:2 [f] Jos 18:12; 1Sa 13:5; 14:23
7:4 [g] Lev 26:17; Dt 28:25
7:5 [h] Lev 26:36; Jos 2:9,11; Eze 21:7; Na 2:10
7:6 [i] Ge 37:29 [j] 1Sa 4:12; 2Sa 13:19; Ne 9:1; Job 2:12; La 2:10; Rev 18:19
7:7 [k] Ex 5:22
7:9 [l] Ex 32:12; Dt 9:28
7:11 [m] Jos 6:17-19 [n] Ac 5:1-2
7:12 [o] Nu 14:45; Jdg 2:14 [p] Jos 6:18
7:13 [q] Jos 3:5; 6:18
7:14 [r] Pr 16:33
7:15 [s] 1Sa 14:39 [t] ver 11 [u] Ge 34:7
7:17 [v] Nu 26:20
7:19 [w] 1Sa 6:5; Jer 13:16; Jn 9:24*

[o] *1* The Hebrew term refers to the irrevocable giving over of things or persons to the LORD, often by totally destroying them; also in verses 11, 12, 13 and 15. [p] *1* See Septuagint and 1 Chron. 2:6; Hebrew *Zabdi*; also in verses 17 and 18. [q] *5* Or *as far as Shebarim* [r] *19* A solemn charge to tell the truth

the God of Israel, and give him the
praise.[s] Tell[a] me what you have
done; do not hide it from me."
20Achan replied, "It is true! I
have sinned against the LORD, the
God of Israel. This is what I have
done: 21When I saw in the plunder
a beautiful robe from Babylonia,[t]
two hundred shekels[u] of silver and
a wedge of gold weighing fifty shekels,[v] I coveted[b] them and took
them. They are hidden in the
ground inside my tent, with the silver underneath."
22So Joshua sent messengers,
and they ran to the tent, and there
it was, hidden in his tent, with the
silver underneath. 23They took the
things from the tent, brought them
to Joshua and all the Israelites and
spread them out before the LORD.
24Then Joshua, together with all
Israel, took Achan son of Zerah, the
silver, the robe, the gold wedge, his
sons and daughters, his cattle,
donkeys and sheep, his tent and all
that he had, to the Valley of
Achor.[c] 25Joshua said, "Why have
you brought this trouble[d] on us?
The LORD will bring trouble on you
today."
Then all Israel stoned him,[e] and
after they had stoned the rest, they
burned them. 26Over Achan they
heaped up a large pile of rocks,
which remains to this day. Then
the LORD turned from his fierce anger.[f] Therefore that place has
been called the Valley of Achor[w][g]
ever since.

Ai Destroyed

8 Then the LORD said to Joshua,
"Do not be afraid;[h] do not be
discouraged.[i] Take the whole
army[j] with you, and go up and attack Ai. For I have delivered[k] into
your hands the king of Ai, his people, his city and his land. 2You
shall do to Ai and its king as you
did to Jericho and its king, except
that you may carry off their plunder
and livestock for yourselves.[l] Set
an ambush behind the city."
3So Joshua and the whole army
moved out to attack Ai. He chose
thirty thousand of his best fighting
men and sent them out at night
4with these orders: "Listen carefully. You are to set an ambush behind
the city. Don't go very far from it.
All of you be on the alert. 5I and all
those with me will advance on the
city, and when the men come out
against us, as they did before, we
will flee from them. 6They will pursue us until we have lured them
away from the city, for they will
say, 'They are running away from
us as they did before.' So when we
flee from them, 7you are to rise up
from ambush and take the city. The
LORD your God will give it into your
hand.[m] 8When you have taken the
city, set it on fire.[n] Do what the
LORD has commanded.[o] See to it;
you have my orders."
9Then Joshua sent them off, and
they went to the place of ambush[p]
and lay in wait between Bethel and
Ai, to the west of Ai—but Joshua
spent that night with the people.
10Early the next morning[q] Joshua mustered his men, and he and
the leaders of Israel[r] marched before them to Ai. 11The entire force
that was with him marched up and
approached the city and arrived in
front of it. They set up camp north
of Ai, with the valley between them
and the city. 12Joshua had taken
about five thousand men and set
them in ambush between Bethel
and Ai, to the west of the city.
13They had the soldiers take up
their positions—all those in the
camp to the north of the city and
the ambush to the west of it. That
night Joshua went into the valley.
14When the king of Ai saw this,
he and all the men of the city hurried out early in the morning to
meet Israel in battle at a certain
place overlooking the Arabah.[s]
But he did not know[t] that an ambush had been set against him behind the city. 15Joshua and all Israel let themselves be driven back[u]
before them, and they fled toward

7:19 [a] 1Sa 14:43
7:21 [b] Dt 7:25; Eph 5:5; 1Ti 6:10
7:24 [c] ver 26; Jos 15:7
7:25 [d] Jos 6:18 [e] Dt 17:5
7:26 [f] Nu 25:4; Dt 13:17 [g] ver 24; Isa 65:10; Hos 2:15
8:1 [h] Dt 31:6 [i] Dt 1:21; 7:18; Jos 1:9 [j] Jos 10:7 [k] Jos 6:2
8:2 [l] ver 27; Dt 20:14
8:7 [m] Jdg 7:7; 1Sa 23:4
8:8 [n] Jdg 20:29-38 [o] ver 19
8:9 [p] 2Ch 13:13
8:10 [q] Ge 22:3 [r] Jos 7:6
8:14 [s] Dt 1:1 [t] Jdg 20:34
8:15 [u] Jdg 20:36

[s] *19* Or *and confess to him* [t] *21* Hebrew *Shinar* [u] *21* That is, about 5 pounds (about 2.3 kilograms) [v] *21* That is, about 1 1/4 pounds (about 0.6 kilogram) [w] *26* *Achor* means *trouble.*

the desert.[a] **16**All the men of Ai
were called to pursue them, and
they pursued Joshua and were
lured away[b] from the city. **17**Not a
man remained in Ai or Bethel who
did not go after Israel. They left the
city open and went in pursuit of Israel.
18Then the LORD said to Joshua,
"Hold out toward Ai the javelin[c]
that is in your hand,[d] for into your
hand I will deliver the city." So
Joshua held out his javelin[e] toward Ai. **19**As soon as he did this,
the men in the ambush rose quickly[f] from their position and rushed
forward. They entered the city and
captured it and quickly set it on
fire.[g]
20The men of Ai looked back and
saw the smoke of the city rising
against the sky,[h] but they had no
chance to escape in any direction,
for the Israelites who had been
fleeing toward the desert had
turned back against their pursuers.
21For when Joshua and all Israel
saw that the ambush had taken the
city and that smoke was going up
from the city, they turned around
and attacked the men of Ai. **22**The
men of the ambush also came out
of the city against them, so that
they were caught in the middle,
with Israelites on both sides. Israel
cut them down, leaving them neither survivors nor fugitives.[i] **23**But
they took the king of Ai alive[j] and
brought him to Joshua.
24When Israel had finished killing all the men of Ai in the fields
and in the desert where they had
chased them, and when every one
of them had been put to the sword,
all the Israelites returned to Ai and
killed those who were in it.
25Twelve thousand men and wom-
en fell that day—all the people of
Ai.[k] **26**For Joshua did not draw
back the hand that held out his javelin until he had destroyed[x][l] all
who lived in Ai.[m] **27**But Israel did
carry off for themselves the livestock and plunder of this city, as
the LORD had instructed Joshua.[n]
28So Joshua burned[o] Ai[p] and
made it a permanent heap of ruins,[q] a desolate place to this day.[r]
29He hung the king of Ai on a tree
and left him there until evening. At
sunset,[s] Joshua ordered them to
take his body from the tree and
throw it down at the entrance of
the city gate. And they raised a
large pile of rocks[t] over it, which
remains to this day.

The Covenant Renewed at Mount Ebal

30Then Joshua built on Mount
Ebal[u] an altar[v] to the LORD, the
God of Israel, **31**as Moses the servant of the LORD had commanded
the Israelites. He built it according
to what is written in the Book of
the Law of Moses—an altar of uncut stones, on which no iron tool[w]
had been used. On it they offered
to the LORD burnt offerings and sacrificed fellowship offerings.[y][x]
32There, in the presence of the Israelites, Joshua copied on stones
the law of Moses, which he had
written.[y] **33**All Israel, aliens and
citizens[z] alike, with their elders,
officials and judges, were standing
on both sides of the ark of the covenant of the LORD, facing those who
carried it—the priests, who were
Levites.[a] Half of the people stood
in front of Mount Gerizim and half
of them in front of Mount Ebal,[b] as
Moses the servant of the LORD had
formerly commanded when he
gave instructions to bless the people of Israel.
34Afterward, Joshua read all the
words of the law—the blessings
and the curses—just as it is written
in the Book of the Law.[c] **35**There
was not a word of all that Moses
had commanded that Joshua did
not read to the whole assembly of
Israel, including the women and
children, and the aliens who lived
among them.[d]

The Gibeonite Deception

9 Now when all the kings west of
the Jordan heard about these

8:15 [a]Jos 15:61; 16:1; 18:12
8:16 [b]Jdg 20:31
8:18 [c]Job 41:26; Ps 35:3 [d]Ex 4:2; 14:16; 17:9-12 [e]ver 26
8:19 [f]Jdg 20:33 [g]ver 8
8:20 [h]Jdg 20:40
8:22 [i]Dt 7:2; Jos 10:1
8:23 [j]1Sa 15:8
8:25 [k]Dt 20:16-18
8:26 [l]Nu 21:2 [m]Ex 17:12
8:27 [n]ver 2
8:28 [o]Nu 31:10 [p]Jos 7:2; Jer 49:3 [q]Dt 13:16; Jos 10:1 [r]Ge 35:20
8:29 [s]Dt 21:23; Jn 19:31 [t]2Sa 18:17
8:30 [u]Dt 11:29 [v]Ex 20:24
8:31 [w]Ex 20:25 [x]Dt 27:6-7
8:32 [y]Dt 27:8
8:33 [z]Lev 16:29 [a]Dt 31:12 [b]Dt 11:29; 27:11-14
8:34 [c]Dt 28:61; 31:11; Jos 1:8
8:35 [d]Ex 12:38; Dt 31:12

[x]*26* The Hebrew term refers to the irrevocable giving over of things or persons to the LORD, often by totally destroying them.
[y]*31* Traditionally *peace offerings*

were left reached their fortified cities. **21**The whole army then returned safely to Joshua in the camp at Makkedah, and no one uttered a word against the Israelites.

22Joshua said, "Open the mouth of the cave and bring those five kings out to me." **23**So they brought the five kings out of the cave—the kings of Jerusalem, Hebron, Jarmuth, Lachish and Eglon. **24**When they had brought these kings to Joshua, he summoned all the men of Israel and said to the army commanders who had come with him, "Come here and put your feet[a] on the necks of these kings." So they came forward and placed their feet[b] on their necks.

25Joshua said to them, "Do not be afraid; do not be discouraged. Be strong and courageous.[c] This is what the LORD will do to all the enemies you are going to fight." **26**Then Joshua struck and killed the kings and hung them on five trees, and they were left hanging on the trees until evening.

27At sunset[d] Joshua gave the order and they took them down from the trees and threw them into the cave where they had been hiding. At the mouth of the cave they placed large rocks, which are there to this day.

28That day Joshua took Makkedah. He put the city and its king to the sword and totally destroyed everyone in it. He left no survivors.[e] And he did to the king of Makkedah as he had done to the king of Jericho.[f]

Southern Cities Conquered

29Then Joshua and all Israel with him moved on from Makkedah to Libnah and attacked it. **30**The LORD also gave that city and its king into Israel's hand. The city and everyone in it Joshua put to the sword. He left no survivors there. And he did to its king as he had done to the king of Jericho.

31Then Joshua and all Israel with him moved on from Libnah to Lachish; he took up positions against it and attacked it. **32**The LORD handed Lachish over to Israel, and Joshua took it on the second day. The city and everyone in it he put to the sword, just as he had done to Libnah. **33**Meanwhile, Horam king of Gezer[g] had come up to help Lachish, but Joshua defeated him and his army—until no survivors were left.

34Then Joshua and all Israel with him moved on from Lachish to Eglon; they took up positions against it and attacked it. **35**They captured it that same day and put it to the sword and totally destroyed everyone in it, just as they had done to Lachish.

36Then Joshua and all Israel with him went up from Eglon to Hebron[h] and attacked it. **37**They took the city and put it to the sword, together with its king, its villages and everyone in it. They left no survivors. Just as at Eglon, they totally destroyed it and everyone in it.

38Then Joshua and all Israel with him turned around and attacked Debir.[i] **39**They took the city, its king and its villages, and put them to the sword. Everyone in it they totally destroyed. They left no survivors. They did to Debir and its king as they had done to Libnah and its king and to Hebron.

40So Joshua subdued the whole region, including the hill country, the Negev,[j] the western foothills and the mountain slopes,[k] together with all their kings.[l] He left no survivors. He totally destroyed all who breathed, just as the LORD, the God of Israel, had commanded.[m] **41**Joshua subdued them from Kadesh Barnea[n] to Gaza[o] and from the whole region of Goshen[p] to Gibeon. **42**All these kings and their lands Joshua conquered in one campaign, because the LORD, the God of Israel, fought[q] for Israel.

43Then Joshua returned with all Israel to the camp at Gilgal.[r]

Northern Kings Defeated

11 When Jabin[s] king of Hazor[t] heard of this, he sent word to Jobab king of Madon, to

10:24 [a]Mal 4:3 [b]Ps 110:1
10:25 [c]Dt 31:6
10:27 [d]Dt 21:23; Jos 8:9,29
10:28 [e]Dt 20:16 [f]Jos 6:21
10:33 [g]Jos 16:3,10; Jdg 1:29; 1Ki 9:15
10:36 [h]Jos 14:13; 15:13; Jdg 1:10
10:38 [i]Jos 15:15; Jdg 1:11
10:40 [j]Ge 12:9; Jos 12:8 [k]Dt 1:7 [l]Dt 7:24 [m]Dt 20:16-17
10:41 [n]Ge 14:7 [o]Ge 10:19 [p]Jos 11:16; 15:51
10:42 [q]ver 14
10:43 [r]ver 15; Jos 5:9
11:1 [s]Jdg 4:2,7,23 [t]ver 10; 1Sa 12:9

the kings of Shimron[a] and Acshaph, **2**and to the northern kings who were in the mountains, in the Arabah[b] south of Kinnereth,[c] in the western foothills and in Naphoth Dor[d][d] on the west; **3**to the Canaanites in the east and west; to the Amorites, Hittites, Perizzites and Jebusites in the hill country; and to the Hivites[e] below Hermon in the region of Mizpah.[f] **4**They came out with all their troops and a large number of horses and chariots—a huge army, as numerous as the sand on the seashore.[g] **5**All these kings joined forces[h] and made camp together at the Waters of Merom, to fight against Israel.

6The LORD said to Joshua, "Do not be afraid of them, because by this time tomorrow I will hand all of them over[i] to Israel, slain. You are to hamstring[j] their horses and burn their chariots."

7So Joshua and his whole army came against them suddenly at the Waters of Merom and attacked them, **8**and the LORD gave them into the hand of Israel. They defeated them and pursued them all the way to Greater Sidon, to Misrephoth Maim,[k] and to the Valley of Mizpah on the east, until no survivors were left. **9**Joshua did to them as the LORD had directed: He hamstrung their horses and burned their chariots.

10At that time Joshua turned back and captured Hazor and put its king to the sword. (Hazor had been the head of all these kingdoms.) **11**Everyone in it they put to the sword. They totally destroyed[e] them, not sparing anything that breathed,[l] and he burned up Hazor itself.

12Joshua took all these royal cities and their kings and put them to the sword. He totally destroyed them, as Moses the servant of the LORD had commanded.[m] **13**Yet Israel did not burn any of the cities built on their mounds—except Hazor, which Joshua burned. **14**The Israelites carried off for themselves all the plunder and livestock of these cities, but all the people they put to the sword until they completely destroyed them, not sparing anyone that breathed.[n] **15**As the LORD commanded his servant Moses, so Moses commanded Joshua, and Joshua did it; he left nothing undone of all that the LORD commanded Moses.[o]

16So Joshua took this entire land: the hill country, all the Negev, the whole region of Goshen, the western foothills,[p] the Arabah and the mountains of Israel with their foothills, **17**from Mount Halak, which rises toward Seir, to Baal Gad in the Valley of Lebanon[q] below Mount Hermon. He captured all their kings and struck them down, putting them to death.[r] **18**Joshua waged war against all these kings for a long time. **19**Except for the Hivites living in Gibeon,[s] not one city made a treaty of peace with the Israelites, who took them all in battle. **20**For it was the LORD himself who hardened their hearts[t] to wage war against Israel, so that he might destroy them totally, exterminating them without mercy, as the LORD had commanded Moses.[u]

21At that time Joshua went and destroyed the Anakites[v] from the hill country: from Hebron, Debir and Anab, from all the hill country of Judah, and from all the hill country of Israel. Joshua totally destroyed them and their towns. **22**No Anakites were left in Israelite territory; only in Gaza, Gath[w] and Ashdod[x] did any survive. **23**So Joshua took the entire land,[y] just as the LORD had directed Moses, and he gave it as an inheritance[z] to Israel according to their tribal divisions.[a]

Then the land had rest from war.[b]

List of Defeated Kings

12 These are the kings of the land whom the Israelites

11:1 [a]Jos 19:15
11:2 [b]Jos 12:3 [c]Nu 34:11 [d]Jos 17:11; Jdg 1:27; 1Ki 4:11
11:3 [e]Dt 7:1; Jdg 3:3,5; 1Ki 9:20 [f]Ge 31:49; Jos 15:38; 18:26
11:4 [g]Jdg 7:12; 1Sa 13:5
11:5 [h]Jdg 5:19
11:6 [i]Jos 10:8 [j]2Sa 8:4
11:8 [k]Jos 13:6
11:11 [l]Dt 20:16-17
11:12 [m]Nu 33:50-52; Dt 7:2
11:14 [n]Nu 31:11-12
11:15 [o]Ex 34:11; Jos 1:7
11:16 [p]Jos 10:41
11:17 [q]Jos 12:7 [r]Dt 7:24
11:19 [s]Jos 9:3
11:20 [t]Ex 14:17; Ro 9:18 [u]Dt 7:16; Jdg 14:4
11:21 [v]Nu 13:22,33; Dt 9:2
11:22 [w]1Sa 17:4; 1Ki 2:39; 1Ch 8:13 [x]1Sa 5:1; Isa 20:1
11:23 [y]Jos 21:43-45 [z]Dt 1:38; 12:9-10; 25:19 [a]Nu 26:53 [b]Jos 14:15

[d]2 Or *in the heights of Dor* [e]11 The Hebrew term refers to the irrevocable giving over of things or persons to the LORD, often by totally destroying them; also in verses 12, 20 and 21.

had defeated and whose territory
they took over east of the Jordan,
from the Arnon Gorge to Mount
Hermon,[a] including all the eastern side of the Arabah:

[2]Sihon king of the Amorites,
who reigned in Heshbon. He
ruled from Aroer on the rim of
the Arnon Gorge—from the
middle of the gorge—to the
Jabbok River, which is the border of the Ammonites. This included half of Gilead.[b] [3]He
also ruled over the eastern Arabah from the Sea of Kinnereth[f][c] to the Sea of the Arabah (the Salt Sea[g]), to Beth
Jeshimoth,[d] and then southward below the slopes of Pisgah.

[4]And the territory of Og king of Bashan,[e]
one of the last of the Rephaites, who reigned in Ashtaroth[f] and Edrei. [5]He ruled
over Mount Hermon, Sale-
cah,[g] all of Bashan to the border of the people of Geshur[h]
and Maacah,[i] and half of Gilead to the border of Sihon king
of Heshbon.

[6]Moses, the servant of the LORD,
and the Israelites conquered them.
And Moses the servant of the LORD
gave their land to the Reubenites,
the Gadites and the half-tribe of
Manasseh to be their possession.[j]

[7]These are the kings of the land
that Joshua and the Israelites conquered on the west side of the Jordan, from Baal Gad in the Valley of
Lebanon[k] to Mount Halak, which
rises toward Seir (their lands Joshua gave as an inheritance to the
tribes of Israel according to their
tribal divisions— [8]the hill country,
the western foothills, the Arabah,
the mountain slopes, the desert
and the Negev[l]—the lands of the
Hittites, Amorites, Canaanites,
Perizzites, Hivites and Jebusites):

[9]the king of Jericho[m] one
the king of Ai[n] (near
Bethel) one
[10]the king of Jerusalem[o] one
the king of Hebron one
[11]the king of Jarmuth one
the king of Lachish one
[12]the king of Eglon one
the king of Gezer[p] one
[13]the king of Debir one
the king of Geder one
[14]the king of Hormah one
the king of Arad[q] one
[15]the king of Libnah one
the king of Adullam one
[16]the king of Makkedah one
the king of Bethel[r] one
[17]the king of Tappuah one
the king of Hepher[s] one
[18]the king of Aphek[t] one
the king of Lasharon one
[19]the king of Madon one
the king of Hazor one
[20]the king of Shimron
Meron one
the king of Acshaph[u] one
[21]the king of Taanach one
the king of Megiddo one
[22]the king of Kedesh[v] one
the king of Jokneam in
Carmel[w] one
[23]the king of Dor (in
Naphoth Dor[h][x]) one
the king of Goyim in
Gilgal one
[24]the king of Tirzah one
thirty-one kings in all.[y]

Land Still to Be Taken

13 When Joshua was old and
well advanced in years,[z]
the LORD said to him, "You are very
old, and there are still very large areas of land to be taken over.

[2]"This is the land that remains: all the regions of the
Philistines and Geshurites:
[3]from the Shihor River[a] on
the east of Egypt to the territory of Ekron[b] on the north, all
of it counted as Canaanite (the
territory of the five Philistine
rulers[c] in Gaza, Ashdod, Ashkelon, Gath and Ekron—that
of the Avvites);[d] [4]from the
south, all the land of the Canaanites, from Arah of the Sidonians as far as Aphek,[e] the

12:1 [a]Dt 3:8
12:2 [b]Dt 2:36
12:3 [c]Jos 11:2 [d]Jos 13:20
12:4 [e]Nu 21:21,33; Dt 3:11 [f]Dt 1:4
12:5 [g]Dt 3:10 [h]1Sa 27:8 [i]Dt 3:14
12:6 [j]Nu 32:29,33; Jos 13:8
12:7 [k]Jos 11:17
12:8 [l]Jos 11:16
12:9 [m]Jos 6:2 [n]Jos 8:29
12:10 [o]Jos 10:23
12:12 [p]Jos 10:33
12:14 [q]Nu 21:1
12:16 [r]Jos 7:2
12:17 [s]1Ki 4:10
12:18 [t]Jos 13:4
12:20 [u]Jos 11:1
12:22 [v]Jos 19:37; 20:7; 21:32 [w]1Sa 15:12
12:23 [x]Jos 11:2
12:24 [y]Ps 135:11; Dt 7:24
13:1 [z]Ge 24:1; Jos 14:10
13:3 [a]Jer 2:18 [b]Jdg 1:18 [c]Jdg 3:3 [d]Dt 2:23
13:4 [e]Jos 12:18; 19:30

[f]3 That is, Galilee [g]3 That is, the Dead Sea [h]23 Or *in the heights of Dor*

region of the Amorites,[a] **5**the
area of the Gebalites[i];[b] and
all Lebanon[c] to the east, from
Baal Gad below Mount Her-
mon to Lebo[j] Hamath.

6"As for all the inhabitants of the
mountain regions from Lebanon to
Misrephoth Maim,[d] that is, all the
Sidonians, I myself will drive them
out before the Israelites. Be sure to
allocate this land to Israel for an
inheritance, as I have instructed
you,[e] **7**and divide it as an inheritance[f] among the nine tribes and
half of the tribe of Manasseh."

Division of the Land East of the Jordan

8The other half of Manasseh,[k] the
Reubenites and the Gadites had received the inheritance that Moses
had given them east of the Jordan,
as he, the servant of the LORD, had
assigned[g] it to them.

9It extended from Aroer[h] on
the rim of the Arnon Gorge,
and from the town in the middle of the gorge, and included
the whole plateau[i] of Medeba
as far as Dibon,[j] **10**and all the
towns of Sihon king of the Amorites, who ruled in Heshbon,
out to the border of the Ammonites.[k] **11**It also included
Gilead, the territory of the
people of Geshur and Maacah,
all of Mount Hermon and all
Bashan as far as Salecah[l]—
12that is, the whole kingdom
of Og in Bashan,[m] who had
reigned in Ashtaroth[n] and Edrei and had survived as one of
the last of the Rephaites.[o]
Moses had defeated them and
taken over their land. **13**But
the Israelites did not drive out
the people of Geshur[p] and
Maacah,[q] so they continue to
live among the Israelites to
this day.

14But to the tribe of Levi he gave
no inheritance, since the offerings
made by fire to the LORD, the God of
Israel, are their inheritance, as he
promised them.[r]

15This is what Moses had given to
the tribe of Reuben, clan by clan:

16The territory from Aroer[s] on
the rim of the Arnon Gorge,
and from the town in the middle of the gorge, and the whole
plateau past Medeba[t] **17**to
Heshbon and all its towns on
the plateau, including Dibon,[u] Bamoth Baal, Beth Baal
Meon,[v] **18**Jahaz,[w] Kedemoth,
Mephaath,[x] **19**Kiriathaim,[y]
Sibmah, Zereth Shahar on the
hill in the valley, **20**Beth
Peor,[z] the slopes of Pisgah,
and Beth Jeshimoth **21**—all
the towns on the plateau and
the entire realm of Sihon king
of the Amorites, who ruled at
Heshbon. Moses had defeated
him and the Midianite
chiefs,[a] Evi, Rekem, Zur, Hur
and Reba[b]—princes allied
with Sihon—who lived in that
country. **22**In addition to those
slain in battle, the Israelites
had put to the sword Balaam
son of Beor,[c] who practiced
divination. **23**The boundary of
the Reubenites was the bank
of the Jordan. These towns
and their villages were the inheritance of the Reubenites,
clan by clan.

24This is what Moses had given to
the tribe of Gad, clan by clan:

25The territory of Jazer,[d] all
the towns of Gilead and half
the Ammonite country as far
as Aroer, near Rabbah; **26**and
from Heshbon[e] to Ramath
Mizpah and Betonim, and
from Mahanaim to the territory of Debir;[f] **27**and in the valley, Beth Haram, Beth Nim-
rah, Succoth[g] and Zaphon
with the rest of the realm of
Sihon king of Heshbon (the
east side of the Jordan, the
territory up to the end of the
Sea of Kinnereth[l][h]). **28**These

13:4 [a]Am 2:10
13:5 [b]1Ki 5:18; Ps 83:7; Eze 27:9 [c]Jos 12:7
13:6 [d]Jos 11:8 [e]Nu 33:54
13:7 [f]Jos 11:23; Ps 78:55
13:8 [g]Jos 12:6
13:9 [h]ver 16; Jdg 11:26 [i]Jer 48:8,21 [j]Nu 21:30
13:10 [k]Nu 21:24
13:11 [l]Jos 12:5
13:12 [m]Dt 3:11 [n]Jos 12:4 [o]Ge 14:5
13:13 [p]Jos 12:5 [q]Dt 3:14
13:14 [r]ver 33; Dt 18:1-2
13:16 [s]ver 9; Jos 12:2 [t]Nu 21:30
13:17 [u]Nu 32:3 [v]1Ch 5:8
13:18 [w]Nu 21:23 [x]Jer 48:21
13:19 [y]Nu 32:37
13:20 [z]Dt 3:29
13:21 [a]Nu 25:15 [b]Nu 31:8
13:22 [c]Nu 22:5; 31:8
13:25 [d]Nu 21:32; Jos 21:39
13:26 [e]Nu 21:25; Jer 49:3 [f]Jos 10:3
13:27 [g]Ge 33:17 [h]Nu 34:11

[i]5 That is, the area of Byblos [j]5 Or *to the entrance to* [k]8 Hebrew *With it* (that is, with the other half of Manasseh) [l]27 That is, Galilee

towns and their villages were the inheritance of the Gadites,[a] clan by clan.

29 This is what Moses had given to the half-tribe of Manasseh, that is, to half the family of the descendants of Manasseh, clan by clan:

30 The territory extending from Mahanaim[b] and including all of Bashan, the entire realm of Og king of Bashan—all the settlements of Jair[c] in Bashan, sixty towns, 31 half of Gilead, and Ashtaroth and Edrei (the royal cities of Og in Bashan). This was for the descendants of Makir[d] son of Manasseh—for half of the sons of Makir, clan by clan.

32 This is the inheritance Moses had given when he was in the plains of Moab across the Jordan east of Jericho. 33 But to the tribe of Levi, Moses had given no inheritance; the LORD, the God of Israel, is their inheritance,[e] as he promised them.[f]

Division of the Land West of the Jordan

14 Now these are the areas the Israelites received as an inheritance in the land of Canaan, which Eleazar the priest, Joshua son of Nun and the heads of the tribal clans of Israel allotted to them.[g] 2 Their inheritances were assigned by lot[h] to the nine-and-a-half tribes, as the LORD had commanded through Moses. 3 Moses had granted the two-and-a-half tribes their inheritance east of the Jordan[i] but had not granted the Levites an inheritance among the rest,[j] 4 for the sons of Joseph had become two tribes—Manasseh and Ephraim.[k] The Levites received no share of the land but only towns to live in, with pasturelands for their flocks and herds. 5 So the Israelites divided the land, just as the LORD had commanded Moses.[l]

Hebron Given to Caleb

6 Now the men of Judah approached Joshua at Gilgal, and Caleb son of Jephunneh[m] the Kenizzite said to him, "You know what the LORD said to Moses the man of God at Kadesh Barnea[n] about you and me. 7 I was forty years old when Moses the servant of the LORD sent me from Kadesh Barnea to explore the land.[o] And I brought him back a report according to my convictions,[p] 8 but my brothers who went up with me made the hearts of the people melt with fear.[q] I, however, followed the LORD my God wholeheartedly.[r] 9 So on that day Moses swore to me, 'The land on which your feet have walked will be your inheritance and that of your children[s] forever, because you have followed the LORD my God wholeheartedly.'[m]

10 "Now then, just as the LORD promised,[t] he has kept me alive for forty-five years since the time he said this to Moses, while Israel moved about in the desert. So here I am today, eighty-five years old! 11 I am still as strong[u] today as the day Moses sent me out; I'm just as vigorous to go out to battle now as I was then. 12 Now give me this hill country that the LORD promised me that day. You yourself heard then that the Anakites[v] were there and their cities were large and fortified,[w] but, the LORD helping me, I will drive them out just as he said."

13 Then Joshua blessed[x] Caleb son of Jephunneh and gave him Hebron[y] as his inheritance.[z] 14 So Hebron has belonged to Caleb son of Jephunneh the Kenizzite ever since, because he followed the LORD, the God of Israel, wholeheartedly. 15 (Hebron used to be called Kiriath Arba[a] after Arba,[b] who was the greatest man among the Anakites.)

Then the land had rest[c] from war.

Allotment for Judah

15:15–19pp — Jdg 1:11–15

15 The allotment for the tribe of Judah, clan by clan, ex-

13:28 [a] Nu 32:33
13:30 [b] Ge 32:2 [c] Nu 32:41
13:31 [d] Ge 50:23
13:33 [e] Nu 18:20 [f] ver 14; Jos 18:7
14:1 [g] Nu 34:17-18
14:2 [h] Nu 26:55
14:3 [i] Nu 32:33 [j] Jos 13:14
14:4 [k] Ge 41:52; 48:5
14:5 [l] Nu 34:13; 35:2; Jos 21:2
14:6 [m] Nu 13:6; 14:30 [n] Nu 13:26
14:7 [o] Nu 13:17 [p] Nu 13:30; 14:6-9
14:8 [q] Nu 13:31 [r] Nu 14:24
14:9 [s] Nu 14:24; Dt 1:36
14:10 [t] Nu 14:30
14:11 [u] Dt 34:7
14:12 [v] Nu 13:33 [w] Nu 13:28
14:13 [x] Jos 22:6,7 [y] Jos 10:36 [z] Jdg 1:20; 1Ch 6:56
14:15 [a] Ge 23:2 [b] Jos 15:13 [c] Jos 11:23

m9 Deut. 1:36

tended down to the territory of
Edom,[a] to the Desert of Zin[b] in
the extreme south.
2Their southern boundary
started from the bay at the
southern end of the Salt Sea,[n]
3crossed south of Scorpion[o]
Pass,[c] continued on to Zin
and went over to the south of
Kadesh Barnea. Then it ran
past Hezron up to Addar and
curved around to Karka. **4**It
then passed along to Azmon[d]
and joined the Wadi of
Egypt,[e] ending at the sea.
This is their[p] southern boundary.
5The eastern boundary[f] is
the Salt Sea as far as the
mouth of the Jordan.
The northern boundary[g]
started from the bay of the sea
at the mouth of the Jordan,
6went up to Beth Hoglah[h] and
continued north of Beth Arabah to the Stone of Bohan[i]
son of Reuben. **7**The boundary
then went up to Debir from
the Valley of Achor[j] and
turned north to Gilgal, which
faces the Pass of Adummim
south of the gorge. It continued along to the waters of En
Shemesh and came out at En
Rogel.[k] **8**Then it ran up the
Valley of Ben Hinnom along
the southern slope of the Jebusite[l] city (that is, Jerusalem). From there it climbed to
the top of the hill west of the
Hinnom Valley at the northern
end of the Valley of Rephaim.
9From the hilltop the boundary headed toward the spring
of the waters of Nephtoah,[m]
came out at the towns of
Mount Ephron and went down
toward Baalah[n] (that is, Kiriath Jearim). **10**Then it curved
westward from Baalah to
Mount Seir, ran along the
northern slope of Mount Jearim (that is, Kesalon), continued down to Beth Shemesh
and crossed to Timnah.[o] **11**It
went to the northern slope of
Ekron, turned toward Shikke-
ron, passed along to Mount
Baalah and reached Jabneel.[p]
The boundary ended at the
sea.
12The western boundary is
the coastline of the Great
Sea.[q][q]
These are the boundaries around
the people of Judah by their clans.

13In accordance with the LORD's
command to him, Joshua gave to
Caleb son of Jephunneh a portion
in Judah—Kiriath Arba, that is,
Hebron. (Arba was the forefather of
Anak.)[r] **14**From Hebron Caleb
drove out the three Anakites[s]—
Sheshai, Ahiman and Talmai[t]—
descendants of Anak.[u] **15**From
there he marched against the people living in Debir (formerly called
Kiriath Sepher). **16**And Caleb said,
"I will give my daughter Acsah[v] in
marriage to the man who attacks
and captures Kiriath Sepher."
17Othniel[w] son of Kenaz, Caleb's
brother, took it; so Caleb gave his
daughter Acsah to him in marriage.
18One day when she came to
Othniel, she urged him[r] to ask her
father for a field. When she got off
her donkey, Caleb asked her,
"What can I do for you?"
19She replied, "Do me a special
favor. Since you have given me land
in the Negev, give me also springs
of water." So Caleb gave her the upper and lower springs.

20This is the inheritance of the
tribe of Judah, clan by clan:

21The southernmost towns of the
tribe of Judah in the Negev toward
the boundary of Edom were:
Kabzeel, Eder,[x] Jagur,
22Kinah, Dimonah, Adadah,
23Kedesh, Hazor, Ithnan,
24Ziph,[y] Telem, Bealoth,
25Hazor Hadattah, Kerioth
Hezron (that is, Hazor),
26Amam, Shema, Moladah,[z]

15:1 [a]Nu 34:3 [b]Nu 33:36
15:3 [c]Nu 34:4
15:4 [d]Nu 34:5 [e]Ge 15:18
15:5 [f]Nu 34:10 [g]Jos 18:15-19
15:6 [h]Jos 18:19,21 [i]Jos 18:17
15:7 [j]Jos 7:24 [k]2Sa 17:17; 1Ki 1:9
15:8 [l]ver 63; Jos 18:16,28; Jdg 1:21; 19:10
15:9 [m]Jos 18:15 [n]1Ch 13:6
15:10 [o]Ge 38:12; Jdg 14:1
15:11 [p]Jos 19:33
15:12 [q]Nu 34:6
15:13 [r]Jos 14:13-15
15:14 [s]Nu 13:33 [t]Nu 13:22 [u]Jdg 1:10,20
15:16 [v]Jdg 1:12
15:17 [w]Jdg 3:9,11
15:21 [x]Ge 35:21
15:24 [y]1Sa 23:14
15:26 [z]1Ch 4:28

[n]*2* That is, the Dead Sea; also in verse 5 [o]*3* Hebrew *Akrabbim* [p]*4* Hebrew *your* [q]*12* That is, the Mediterranean; also in verse 47 [r]*18* Hebrew and some Septuagint manuscripts; other Septuagint manuscripts (see also note at Judges 1:14) *Othniel, he urged her*

27 Hazar Gaddah, Heshmon,
Beth Pelet, 28 Hazar Shual, Beersheba,[a] Biziothiah, 29 Baalah,[b] Iim, Ezem, 30 Eltolad,[c]
Kesil, Hormah, 31 Ziklag,[d]
Madmannah, Sansannah,
32 Lebaoth, Shilhim, Ain and
Rimmon[e]—a total of twenty-nine towns and their villages.

33 In the western foothills:
Eshtaol,[f] Zorah, Ashnah,
34 Zanoah,[g] En Gannim, Tappuah, Enam, 35 Jarmuth,[h]
Adullam,[i] Socoh, Azekah,
36 Shaaraim, Adithaim and Gederah[j] (or Gederothaim)[s]—
fourteen towns and their villages.
37 Zenan, Hadashah, Migdal
Gad, 38 Dilean, Mizpah, Joktheel,[k] 39 Lachish,[l] Bozkath,[m] Eglon, 40 Cabbon, Lah-
mas, Kitlish, 41 Gederoth,
Beth Dagon, Naamah and
Makkedah[n]—sixteen towns
and their villages.
42 Libnah, Ether, Ashan,[o]
43 Iphtah, Ashnah, Nezib,
44 Keilah, Aczib[p] and Mareshah[q]—nine towns and their
villages.
45 Ekron, with its surrounding settlements and villages;
46 west of Ekron, all that were
in the vicinity of Ashdod, together with their villages;
47 Ashdod,[r] its surrounding
settlements and villages; and
Gaza, its settlements and villages, as far as the Wadi of
Egypt[s] and the coastline of
the Great Sea.[t]

48 In the hill country:
Shamir, Jattir,[u] Socoh,
49 Dannah, Kiriath Sannah
(that is, Debir[v]), 50 Anab, Esh-
temoh,[w] Anim, 51 Goshen,[x]
Holon and Giloh—eleven
towns and their villages.
52 Arab, Dumah,[y] Eshan,
53 Janim, Beth Tappuah,
Aphekah, 54 Humtah, Kiriath
Arba (that is, Hebron) and
Zior—nine towns and their villages.
55 Maon, Carmel,[z] Ziph,
Juttah, 56 Jezreel,[a] Jokdeam,
Zanoah, 57 Kain, Gibeah[b] and
Timnah—ten towns and their
villages.
58 Halhul, Beth Zur,[c] Gedor, 59 Maarath, Beth Anoth
and Eltekon—six towns and
their villages.
60 Kiriath Baal (that is, Kiriath Jearim[d]) and Rabbah[e]
—two towns and their vil-
lages.

61 In the desert:
Beth Arabah, Middin, Seca-
cah, 62 Nibshan, the City of
Salt and En Gedi[f]—six towns
and their villages.
63 Judah could not[g] dislodge the
Jebusites[h], who were living in Jerusalem; to this day the Jebusites
live there with the people of Judah.

Allotment for Ephraim and Manasseh

16 The allotment for Jo-
seph began at the Jor-
dan of Jericho,[t] east of the
waters of Jericho, and went up
from there through the
desert[i] into the hill country
of Bethel. 2 It went on from
Bethel (that is, Luz[j]),[u]
crossed over to the territory of
the Arkites in Ataroth, 3 descended westward to the territory of the Japhletites as far as
the region of Lower Beth Horon[k] and on to Gezer,[l] ending at the sea.
4 So Manasseh and Ephraim, the
descendants of Joseph, received
their inheritance.[m]

5 This was the territory of Ephraim,
clan by clan:
The boundary of their inheritance went from Ataroth Addar[n] in the east to Upper Beth
Horon 6 and continued to the
sea. From Micmethath[o] on

15:28 a Ge 21:31
15:29 b ver 9
15:30 c Jos 19:4
15:31 d 1Sa 27:6
15:32 e Jdg 20:45
15:33 f Jdg 13:25; 16:31
15:34 g 1Ch 4:18; Ne 3:13
15:35 h Jos 10:3 i 1Sa 22:1
15:36 j 1Ch 12:4
15:38 k 2Ki 14:7
15:39 l Jos 10:3; 2Ki 14:19 m 2Ki 22:1
15:41 n Jos 10:10
15:42 o 1Sa 30:30
15:44 p Jdg 1:31 q Mic 1:15
15:47 r Jos 11:22 s ver 4 t Nu 34:6
15:48 u 1Sa 30:27
15:49 v Jos 10:3
15:50 w Jos 21:14
15:51 x Jos 10:41; 11:16
15:52 y Ge 25:14
15:55 z Jos 12:22
15:56 a Jos 17:16
15:57 b Jos 18:28; Jdg 19:12
15:58 c 1Ch 2:45
15:60 d Jos 18:14 e Dt 3:11
15:62 f 1Sa 23:29
15:63 g Jdg 1:21 h 2Sa 5:6
16:1 i Jos 8:15; 18:12
16:2 j Jos 18:13
16:3 k 2Ch 8:5 l Jos 10:33; 1Ki 9:15
16:4 m Jos 17:14
16:5 n Jos 18:13 **16:6** o Jos 17:7

s36 Or *Gederah and Gederothaim* t1 *Jordan of Jericho* was possibly an ancient name for the Jordan River. u2 Septuagint; Hebrew *Bethel to Luz*

the north it curved eastward to
Taanath Shiloh, passing by it
to Janoah on the east. 7Then it
went down from Janoah to Ataroth[a] and Naarah, touched
Jericho and came out at the
Jordan. 8From Tappuah the
border went west to the Kanah
Ravine[b] and ended at the sea.
This was the inheritance of
the tribe of the Ephraimites,
clan by clan. 9It also included
all the towns and their villages
that were set aside for the
Ephraimites within the inheritance of the Manassites.
10They did not dislodge the Canaanites living in Gezer; to this day
the Canaanites live among the people of Ephraim but are required to
do forced labor.[c]

17 This was the allotment for
the tribe of Manasseh as Joseph's firstborn,[d] that is, for Makir,[e] Manasseh's firstborn. Makir
was the ancestor of the Gileadites,
who had received Gilead and Bashan because the Makirites were
great soldiers. 2So this allotment
was for the rest of the people of
Manasseh—the clans of Abiezer,[f]
Helek, Asriel, Shechem, Hepher
and Shemida. These are the other
male descendants of Manasseh son
of Joseph by their clans.

3Now Zelophehad son of He-
pher,[g] the son of Gilead, the son of
Makir, the son of Manasseh, had
no sons but only daughters,[h]
whose names were Mahlah, Noah,
Hoglah, Milcah and Tirzah. 4They
went to Eleazar the priest, Joshua
son of Nun, and the leaders and
said, "The LORD commanded Moses to give us an inheritance among
our brothers." So Joshua gave them
an inheritance along with the
brothers of their father, according
to the LORD's command.[i] 5Manas-
seh's share consisted of ten tracts
of land besides Gilead and Bashan
east of the Jordan, 6because the
daughters of the tribe of Manasseh
received an inheritance among the
sons. The land of Gilead belonged
to the rest of the descendants of
Manasseh.

16:7 [a] 1Ch 7:28
16:8 [b] Jos 17:9
16:10 [c] Jos 17:13; Jdg 1:28-29; 1Ki 9:16
17:1 [d] Ge 41:51 [e] Ge 50:23
17:2 [f] Nu 26:30; 1Ch 7:18
17:3 [g] Nu 27:1 [h] Nu 26:33
17:4 [i] Nu 27:5-7
17:7 [j] Jos 16:6 [k] Ge 12:6; Jos 21:21
17:8 [l] Jos 16:8
17:9 [m] Jos 16:8
17:10 [n] Ge 30:18
17:11 [o] 1Sa 31:10; 1Ki 4:12; 1Ch 7:29 [p] Jos 11:2 [q] 1Sa 28:7; Ps 83:10 [r] 1Ki 9:15
17:12 [s] Jdg 1:27
17:13 [t] Jos 16:10
17:14 [u] Nu 26:28-37
17:15 [v] Ge 14:5

7The territory of Manasseh
extended from Asher to Micmethath[j] east of Shechem.[k]
The boundary ran southward
from there to include the people living at En Tappuah.
8(Manasseh had the land of
Tappuah, but Tappuah[l] itself, on the boundary of Manasseh, belonged to the
Ephraimites.) 9Then the
boundary continued south to
the Kanah Ravine.[m] There
were towns belonging to
Ephraim lying among the
towns of Manasseh, but the
boundary of Manasseh was the
northern side of the ravine and
ended at the sea. 10On the
south the land belonged to
Ephraim, on the north to Manasseh. The territory of Manasseh reached the sea and
bordered Asher on the north
and Issachar[n] on the east.

11Within Issachar and Asher, Manasseh also had Beth
Shan,[o] Ibleam and the people
of Dor,[p] Endor,[q] Taanach
and Megiddo,[r] together with
their surrounding settlements
(the third in the list is Naphoth[v]).
12Yet the Manassites were not
able[s] to occupy these towns, for
the Canaanites were determined to
live in that region. 13However,
when the Israelites grew stronger,
they subjected the Canaanites to
forced labor but did not drive them
out completely.[t]

14The people of Joseph said to
Joshua, "Why have you given us
only one allotment and one portion
for an inheritance? We are a numerous people and the LORD has
blessed us abundantly."[u]

15"If you are so numerous,"
Joshua answered, "and if the hill
country of Ephraim is too small for
you, go up into the forest and clear
land for yourselves there in the
land of the Perizzites and Rephaites.[v]"

16The people of Joseph replied,

[v] 11 That is, Naphoth Dor

"The hill country is not enough for
us, and all the Canaanites who live
in the plain have iron chariots,[a]
both those in Beth Shan and its
settlements and those in the Valley
of Jezreel."
17But Joshua said to the house
of Joseph—to Ephraim and Manasseh—"You are numerous and
very powerful. You will have not
only one allotment 18but the for-
ested hill country as well. Clear it,
and its farthest limits will be yours;
though the Canaanites have iron
chariots[b] and though they are
strong, you can drive them out."

Division of the Rest of the Land

18 The whole assembly of the
Israelites gathered at Shiloh[c] and set up the Tent of Meeting[d] there. The country was
brought under their control, 2but
there were still seven Israelite
tribes who had not yet received
their inheritance.
3So Joshua said to the Israelites:
"How long will you wait before you
begin to take possession of the
land that the LORD, the God of your
fathers, has given you? 4Appoint
three men from each tribe. I will
send them out to make a survey of
the land and to write a description
of it, according to the inheritance
of each.[e] Then they will return to
me. 5You are to divide the land into
seven parts. Judah is to remain in
its territory on the south[f] and the
house of Joseph in its territory on
the north.[g] 6After you have written
descriptions of the seven parts of
the land, bring them here to me
and I will cast lots[h] for you in the
presence of the LORD our God. 7The
Levites, however, do not get a portion among you, because the
priestly service of the LORD is their
inheritance.[i] And Gad, Reuben
and the half-tribe of Manasseh
have already received their inheritance on the east side of the Jordan. Moses the servant of the LORD
gave it to them.[j]"
8As the men started on their way

17:16 [a]Jdg 1:19; 4:3,13
17:18 [b]ver 16
18:1 [c]Jos 19:51; 21:2; Jdg 18:31; 21:12,19; 1Sa 1:3; 4:3; Jer 7:12; 26:6 [d]Ex 27:21
18:4 [e]Mic 2:5
18:5 [f]Jos 15:1 [g]Jos 16:1-4
18:6 [h]Jos 14:2
18:7 [i]Jos 13:33 [j]Jos 13:8
18:8 [k]ver 1
18:10 [l]Nu 34:13 [m]ver 1; Jer 7:12 [n]Nu 33:54; Jos 19:51
18:12 [o]Jos 16:1 [p]Jos 7:2
18:13 [q]Ge 28:19 [r]Jdg 1:23 [s]Jos 16:5
18:14 [t]Jos 10:10
18:15 [u]Jos 15:9
18:16 [v]Jos 15:8; 2Ki 23:10 [w]Jos 15:7

to map out the land, Joshua instructed them, "Go and make a
survey of the land and write a description of it. Then return to me,
and I will cast lots for you here at
Shiloh[k] in the presence of the
LORD." 9So the men left and went
through the land. They wrote its
description on a scroll, town by
town, in seven parts, and returned
to Joshua in the camp at Shiloh.
10Joshua then cast lots[l] for them
in Shiloh in the presence[m] of the
LORD, and there he distributed the
land to the Israelites according to
their tribal divisions.[n]

Allotment for Benjamin

11The lot came up for the tribe of
Benjamin, clan by clan. Their allotted territory lay between the tribes
of Judah and Joseph:
12On the north side their
boundary began at the Jordan,
passed the northern slope of
Jericho and headed west into
the hill country, coming out at
the desert[o] of Beth Aven.[p]
13From there it crossed to the
south slope of Luz[q] (that is,
Bethel[r]) and went down to
Ataroth Addar[s] on the hill
south of Lower Beth Horon.
14From the hill facing Beth
Horon[t] on the south the
boundary turned south along
the western side and came out
at Kiriath Baal (that is, Kiriath
Jearim), a town of the people
of Judah. This was the western
side.
15The southern side began
at the outskirts of Kiriath Jearim on the west, and the
boundary came out at the
spring of the waters of Nephtoah.[u] 16The boundary went
down to the foot of the hill facing the Valley of Ben Hinnom,
north of the Valley of Rephaim. It continued down the
Hinnom Valley[v] along the
southern slope of the Jebusite
city and so to En Rogel.[w] 17It
then curved north, went to En
Shemesh, continued to Geliloth, which faces the Pass of

Adummim, and ran down to
the Stone of Bohan[a] son of
Reuben. **18**It continued to the
northern slope of Beth Arabah[w b] and on down into the
Arabah. **19**It then went to the
northern slope of Beth Hoglah
and came out at the northern
bay of the Salt Sea,[x c] at the
mouth of the Jordan in the
south. This was the southern
boundary.
20The Jordan formed the
boundary on the eastern side.
These were the boundaries that
marked out the inheritance of the
clans of Benjamin on all sides.[d]

21The tribe of Benjamin, clan by
clan, had the following cities:
Jericho, Beth Hoglah, Emek
Keziz, **22**Beth Arabah, Zemara-
im, Bethel,[e] **23**Avvim, Parah,
Ophrah, **24**Kephar Ammoni,
Ophni and Geba[f]—twelve
towns and their villages.
25Gibeon,[g] Ramah,[h] Beeroth,[i] **26**Mizpah,[j] Kephirah,
Mozah, **27**Rekem, Irpeel, Tara-
lah, **28**Zelah,[k] Haeleph, the
Jebusite city[l] (that is, Jerusalem[m]), Gibeah[n] and Kiriath
—fourteen towns and their villages.
This was the inheritance of Benjamin for its clans.

Allotment for Simeon

19:2–10pp — 1Ch 4:28–33

19 The second lot came out for
the tribe of Simeon, clan by
clan. Their inheritance lay within
the territory of Judah.[o] **2**It included:
Beersheba[p] (or Sheba),[y]
Moladah, **3**Hazar Shual, Ba-
lah, Ezem, **4**Eltolad, Bethul,
Hormah, **5**Ziklag, Beth Marcaboth, Hazar Susah, **6**Beth Lebaoth and Sharuhen—thir-
teen towns and their villages;
7Ain, Rimmon, Ether and
Ashan[q]—four towns and their
villages— **8**and all the villages
around these towns as far as
Baalath Beer (Ramah in the
Negev).[r]

18:17 [a]Jos 15:6
18:18 [b]Jos 15:6
18:19 [c]Ge 14:3
18:20 [d]Jos 21:4,17; 1Sa 9:1
18:22 [e]Jos 16:1
18:24 [f]Isa 10:29
18:25 [g]Jos 9:3 [h]Jdg 4:5 [i]Jos 9:17
18:26 [j]Jos 11:3
18:28 [k]2Sa 21:14 [l]Jos 15:8 [m]Jos 10:1 [n]Jos 15:57
19:1 [o]ver 9; Ge 49:7
19:2 [p]Ge 21:14; 1Ki 19:3
19:7 [q]Jos 15:42
19:8 [r]Jos 10:40
19:9 [s]Ge 49:7 [t]Eze 48:24
19:10 [u]Jos 21:7,34
19:11 [v]Jos 12:22
19:13 [w]Jos 15:32
19:15 [x]Ge 35:19
19:16 [y]ver 10; Jos 21:7 [z]Eze 48:26
19:17 [a]Ge 30:18
19:18 [b]Jos 15:56 [c]1Sa 28:4; 2Ki 4:8
19:22 [d]Jdg 4:6,12; Ps 89:12 [e]Jos 15:10

This was the inheritance of the
tribe of the Simeonites, clan by
clan. **9**The inheritance of the Simeonites was taken from the share of
Judah,[s] because Judah's portion
was more than they needed. So the
Simeonites received their inheritance within the territory of Judah.[t]

Allotment for Zebulun

10The third lot came up for Zebulun,[u] clan by clan:
The boundary of their inheritance went as far as Sarid.
11Going west it ran to Mara-
lah, touched Dabbesheth, and
extended to the ravine near
Jokneam.[v] **12**It turned east
from Sarid toward the sunrise
to the territory of Kisloth Tabor and went on to Daberath
and up to Japhia. **13**Then it
continued eastward to Gath
Hepher and Eth Kazin; it came
out at Rimmon[w] and turned
toward Neah. **14**There the
boundary went around on the
north to Hannathon and ended at the Valley of Iphtah El.
15Included were Kattath, Nahalal, Shimron, Idalah and
Bethlehem.[x] There were
twelve towns and their villages.
16These towns and their villages
were the inheritance of Zebulun,[y]
clan by clan.[z]

Allotment for Issachar

17The fourth lot came out for Issachar,[a] clan by clan. **18**Their territory included:
Jezreel,[b] Kesulloth, Shunem,[c] **19**Hapharaim, Shion,
Anaharath, **20**Rabbith, Kishion, Ebez, **21**Remeth, En Gannim, En Haddah and Beth Paz-
zez. **22**The boundary touched
Tabor,[d] Shahazumah and
Beth Shemesh,[e] and ended at
the Jordan. There were sixteen towns and their villages.

[w]*18* Septuagint; Hebrew *slope facing the Arabah* [x]*19* That is, the Dead Sea
[y]*2* Or *Beersheba, Sheba*; 1 Chron. 4:28 does not have *Sheba*.

23 These towns and their villages
were the inheritance of the tribe of
Issachar,[a] clan by clan.[b]

Allotment for Asher

24 The fifth lot came out for the
tribe of Asher,[c] clan by clan.
25 Their territory included:

Helkath, Hali, Beten, Ac-
shaph, 26 Allammelech, Amad
and Mishal. On the west the
boundary touched Carmel[d]
and Shihor Libnath. 27 It then
turned east toward Beth Dagon, touched Zebulun[e] and
the Valley of Iphtah El, and
went north to Beth Emek and
Neiel, passing Cabul[f] on the
left. 28 It went to Abdon,[z] Rehob,[g] Hammon[h] and Kanah,
as far as Greater Sidon.[i]
29 The boundary then turned
back toward Ramah[j] and
went to the fortified city of
Tyre,[k] turned toward Hosah
and came out at the sea in the
region of Aczib,[l] 30 Ummah,
Aphek and Rehob. There were
twenty-two towns and their
villages.

31 These towns and their villages
were the inheritance of the tribe of
Asher,[m] clan by clan.

Allotment for Naphtali

32 The sixth lot came out for Naphtali, clan by clan:

33 Their boundary went from
Heleph and the large tree in
Zaanannim, passing Adami
Nekeb and Jabneel to Lakkum
and ending at the Jordan.
34 The boundary ran west
through Aznoth Tabor and
came out at Hukkok. It
touched Zebulun on the
south, Asher on the west and
the Jordan[a] on the east.
35 The fortified cities were Zid-
dim, Zer, Hammath, Rakkath,
Kinnereth,[n] 36 Adamah, Ramah,[o] Hazor,[p] 37 Kedesh, Edrei,[q] En Hazor, 38 Iron, Migdal
El, Horem, Beth Anath and
Beth Shemesh. There were
nineteen towns and their villages.

19:23 [a] Jos 17:10 [b] Ge 49:15; Eze 48:25
19:24 [c] Jos 17:7
19:26 [d] Jos 12:22
19:27 [e] ver 10 [f] 1Ki 9:13
19:28 [g] Jdg 1:31 [h] 1Ch 6:76 [i] Ge 10:19; Jos 11:8
19:29 [j] Jos 18:25 [k] 2Sa 5:11; 24:7; Isa 23:1; Jer 25:22; Eze 26:2 [l] Jdg 1:31
19:31 [m] Ge 30:13; Eze 48:2
19:35 [n] Jos 11:2
19:36 [o] Jos 18:25 [p] Jos 11:1
19:37 [q] Nu 21:33
19:39 [r] Dt 33:23; Eze 48:3
19:42 [s] Jdg 1:35
19:43 [t] Ge 38:12
19:45 [u] Jos 21:24; 1Ch 6:69
19:46 [v] 2Ch 2:16; Jnh 1:3
19:47 [w] Jdg 18:1 [x] Jdg 18:7,14 [y] Jdg 18:27,29
19:48 [z] Ge 30:6
19:50 [a] Jos 24:30
19:51 [b] Jos 14:1; 18:10; Ac 13:19

39 These towns and their villages
were the inheritance of the tribe of
Naphtali, clan by clan.[r]

Allotment for Dan

40 The seventh lot came out for the
tribe of Dan, clan by clan. 41 The
territory of their inheritance included:

Zorah, Eshtaol, Ir Shemesh,
42 Shaalabbin, Aijalon,[s] Ith-
lah, 43 Elon, Timnah,[t] Ekron,
44 Eltekeh, Gibbethon, Baalath, 45 Jehud, Bene Berak,
Gath Rimmon,[u] 46 Me Jarkon
and Rakkon, with the area facing Joppa.[v]

47 (But the Danites had difficulty
taking possession of their territory,[w] so they went up and attacked
Leshem[x], took it, put it to the
sword and occupied it. They settled in Leshem and named it Dan
after their forefather.)[y]
48 These towns and their villages
were the inheritance of the tribe of
Dan,[z] clan by clan.

Allotment for Joshua

49 When they had finished dividing the land into its allotted portions, the Israelites gave Joshua
son of Nun an inheritance among
them, 50 as the LORD had commanded. They gave him the town he
asked for—Timnath Serah[b][a] in
the hill country of Ephraim. And he
built up the town and settled there.

51 These are the territories that
Eleazar the priest, Joshua son of
Nun and the heads of the tribal
clans of Israel assigned by lot at
Shiloh in the presence of the LORD
at the entrance to the Tent of
Meeting. And so they finished di-
viding the land.[b]

Cities of Refuge

20:1-9Ref — Nu 35:9-34; Dt 4:41-43; 19:1-14

20 Then the LORD said to Joshua: 2 "Tell the Israelites to

[z] *28* Some Hebrew manuscripts (see also Joshua 21:30); most Hebrew manuscripts *Ebron* [a] *34* Septuagint; Hebrew *west, and Judah, the Jordan,* [b] *50* Also known as *Timnath Heres* (see Judges 2:9)

designate the cities of refuge, as I instructed you through Moses, **3**so that anyone who kills a person accidentally and unintentionally[a] may flee there and find protection from the avenger of blood.[b]

4"When he flees to one of these cities, he is to stand in the entrance of the city gate[c] and state his case before the elders[d] of that city. Then they are to admit him into their city and give him a place to live with them. **5**If the avenger of blood pursues him, they must not surrender the one accused, because he killed his neighbor unintentionally and without malice aforethought. **6**He is to stay in that city until he has stood trial before the assembly[e] and until the death of the high priest who is serving at that time. Then he may go back to his own home in the town from which he fled."

7So they set apart Kedesh[f] in Galilee in the hill country of Naphtali, Shechem[g] in the hill country of Ephraim, and Kiriath Arba (that is, Hebron[h]) in the hill country of Judah.[i] **8**On the east side of the Jordan of Jericho[c] they designated Bezer[j] in the desert on the plateau in the tribe of Reuben, Ramoth in Gilead[k] in the tribe of Gad, and Golan in Bashan in the tribe of Manasseh. **9**Any of the Israelites or any alien living among them who killed someone accidentally could flee to these designated cities and not be killed by the avenger of blood prior to standing trial before the assembly.[l]

Towns for the Levites

21:4–39pp — 1Ch 6:54–80

21 Now the family heads of the Levites approached Eleazar the priest, Joshua son of Nun, and the heads of the other tribal families of Israel[m] **2**at Shiloh[n] in Canaan and said to them, "The LORD commanded through Moses that you give us towns to live in, with pasturelands for our livestock."[o] **3**So, as the LORD had commanded, the Israelites gave the Levites the following towns and pasturelands out of their own inheritance:

4The first lot came out for the Kohathites, clan by clan. The Levites who were descendants of Aaron the priest were allotted thirteen towns from the tribes of Judah, Simeon and Benjamin.[p] **5**The rest of Kohath's descendants were allotted ten towns from the clans of the tribes of Ephraim, Dan and half of Manasseh.[q]

6The descendants of Gershon were allotted thirteen towns from the clans of the tribes of Issachar,[r] Asher, Naphtali and the half-tribe of Manasseh in Bashan.

7The descendants of Merari,[s] clan by clan, received twelve towns from the tribes of Reuben, Gad and Zebulun.[t]

8So the Israelites allotted to the Levites these towns and their pasturelands, as the LORD had commanded through Moses.

9From the tribes of Judah and Simeon they allotted the following towns by name **10**(these towns were assigned to the descendants of Aaron who were from the Kohathite clans of the Levites, because the first lot fell to them):

11They gave them Kiriath Arba (that is, Hebron[u]), with its surrounding pastureland, in the hill country of Judah. (Arba was the forefather of Anak.) **12**But the fields and villages around the city they had given to Caleb son of Jephunneh as his possession.

13So to the descendants of Aaron the priest they gave Hebron (a city of refuge for one accused of murder), Libnah,[v] **14**Jattir,[w] Eshtemoa,[x] **15**Holon,[y] Debir, **16**Ain, Juttah[z] and Beth Shemesh,[a] together with their pasturelands—nine towns from these two tribes.

17And from the tribe of Benjamin they gave them Gibeon, Geba,[b] **18**Anathoth and Al-

20:3 [a]Lev 4:2 [b]Nu 35:12
20:4 [c]Ru 4:1; Jer 38:7 [d]Jos 7:6
20:6 [e]Nu 35:12
20:7 [f]Jos 21:32; 1Ch 6:76 [g]Ge 12:6 [h]Jos 10:36; 21:11 [i]Lk 1:39
20:8 [j]Jos 21:36; 1Ch 6:78 [k]Jos 12:2
20:9 [l]Ex 21:13; Nu 35:15
21:1 [m]Jos 14:1
21:2 [n]Jos 18:1 [o]Nu 35:2-3
21:4 [p]ver 19
21:5 [q]ver 26
21:6 [r]Ge 30:18
21:7 [s]Ex 6:16 [t]Jos 19:10
21:11 [u]Jos 15:13; 1Ch 6:55
21:13 [v]Jos 15:42; 1Ch 6:57
21:14 [w]Jos 15:48 [x]Jos 15:50
21:15 [y]Jos 15:51
21:16 [z]Jos 15:55 [a]Jos 15:10
21:17 [b]Jos 18:24

[c]8 *Jordan of Jericho* was possibly an ancient name for the Jordan River.

mon, together with their pasturelands—four towns.
19All the towns for the priests, the
descendants of Aaron, were thirteen, together with their pasturelands.

20The rest of the Kohathite clans of
the Levites were allotted towns
from the tribe of Ephraim:
21In the hill country of
Ephraim they were given Shechem[a] (a city of refuge for one
accused of murder) and Gezer,
22Kibzaim and Beth Horon,[b]
together with their pasturelands—four towns.[c]
23Also from the tribe of Dan
they received Eltekeh, Gibbethon, **24**Aijalon and Gath Rimmon,[d] together with their
pasturelands—four towns.
25From half the tribe of Manasseh they received Taanach
and Gath Rimmon, together
with their pasturelands—two
towns.
26All these ten towns and their pasturelands were given to the rest of
the Kohathite clans.

27The Levite clans of the Gershonites were given:
from the half-tribe of Manasseh,
Golan in Bashan[e] (a city of
refuge for one accused of murder[f]) and Be Eshtarah, together with their pasturelands—two towns;
28from the tribe of Issachar,[g]
Kishion, Daberath, **29**Jarmuth
and En Gannim, together
with their pasturelands—four
towns;
30from the tribe of Asher,[h]
Mishal, Abdon, **31**Helkath and
Rehob, together with their
pasturelands—four towns;
32from the tribe of Naphtali,
Kedesh[i] in Galilee (a city of
refuge for one accused of murder[j]), Hammoth Dor and Kar-
tan, together with their pasturelands—three towns.
33All the towns of the Gershonite[k]
clans were thirteen, together with
their pasturelands.

34The Merarite clans (the rest of
the Levites) were given:
from the tribe of Zebulun,[l]
Jokneam, Kartah, **35**Dimnah
and Nahalal, together
with their pasturelands—four
towns;
36from the tribe of Reuben,
Bezer,[m] Jahaz, **37**Kedemoth
and Mephaath, together with
their pasturelands—four
towns;
38from the tribe of Gad,
Ramoth[n] in Gilead (a city of
refuge for one accused of murder), Mahanaim,[o] **39**Heshbon
and Jazer, together with their
pasturelands—four towns in
all.
40All the towns allotted to the Merarite clans, who were the rest of
the Levites, were twelve.
41The towns of the Levites in the
territory held by the Israelites were
forty-eight in all, together with
their pasturelands.[p] **42**Each of
these towns had pasturelands surrounding it; this was true for all
these towns.

43So the LORD gave Israel all the
land he had sworn to give their
forefathers,[q] and they took possession[r] of it and settled there.[s]
44The LORD gave them rest[t] on every side, just as he had sworn to
their forefathers. Not one of their
enemies[u] withstood them; the
LORD handed all their enemies[v]
over to them.[w] **45**Not one of all the
LORD's good promises[x] to the
house of Israel failed; every one
was fulfilled.

Eastern Tribes Return Home

22 Then Joshua summoned
the Reubenites, the Gadites
and the half-tribe of Manasseh
2and said to them, "You have done
all that Moses the servant of the
LORD commanded,[y] and you have
obeyed me in everything I commanded. **3**For a long time now—to
this very day—you have not deserted your brothers but have carried
out the mission the LORD your God
gave you. **4**Now that the LORD your

21:21 [a]Jos 17:7; 20:7
21:22 [b]Jos 10:10 [c]1Sa 1:1
21:24 [d]Jos 19:45
21:27 [e]Jos 12:5 [f]Nu 35:6
21:28 [g]Ge 30:18
21:30 [h]Jos 17:7
21:32 [i]Jos 12:22 [j]Nu 35:6; Jos 20:7
21:33 [k]ver 6
21:34 [l]Jos 19:10; 1Ch 6:77
21:36 [m]Jos 20:8
21:38 [n]Dt 4:43 [o]Ge 32:2
21:41 [p]Nu 35:7
21:43 [q]Dt 34:4 [r]Dt 11:31 [s]Dt 17:14
21:44 [t]Ex 33:14; Jos 1:13 [u]Dt 6:19 [v]Ex 23:31 [w]Dt 7:24; 21:10
21:45 [x]Jos 23:14; Ne 9:8
22:2 [y]Nu 32:25

God has given your brothers rest as
he promised, return to your
homes[a] in the land that Moses the
servant of the LORD gave you on the
other side of the Jordan.[b] **5**But be
very careful to keep the commandment[c] and the law that Moses the
servant of the LORD gave you: to
love the LORD your God, to walk in
all his ways, to obey his commands,[d] to hold fast to him and to
serve him with all your heart and
all your soul.[e]"
6Then Joshua blessed[f] them
and sent them away, and they went
to their homes. **7**(To the half-tribe
of Manasseh Moses had given land
in Bashan,[g] and to the other half
of the tribe Joshua gave land on the
west side[h] of the Jordan with their
brothers.) When Joshua sent them
home, he blessed them, **8**saying,
"Return to your homes with your
great wealth—with large herds of
livestock,[i] with silver, gold,
bronze and iron, and a great quantity of clothing—and divide[j] with
your brothers the plunder[k] from
your enemies."
9So the Reubenites, the Gadites
and the half-tribe of Manasseh left
the Israelites at Shiloh in Canaan
to return to Gilead,[l] their own
land, which they had acquired in
accordance with the command of
the LORD through Moses.
10When they came to Geliloth
near the Jordan in the land of Canaan, the Reubenites, the Gadites
and the half-tribe of Manasseh
built an imposing altar there by the
Jordan. **11**And when the Israelites
heard that they had built the altar
on the border of Canaan at Geliloth
near the Jordan on the Israelite
side, **12**the whole assembly of Israel gathered at Shiloh[m] to go to war
against them.
13So the Israelites sent Phinehas[n] son of Eleazar,[o] the priest, to
the land of Gilead—to Reuben,
Gad and the half-tribe of Manasseh. **14**With him they sent ten of
the chief men, one for each of the
tribes of Israel, each the head of a
family division among the Israelite
clans.[p]

15When they went to Gilead—to
Reuben, Gad and the half-tribe of
Manasseh—they said to them:
16"The whole assembly of the LORD
says: 'How could you break faith[q]
with the God of Israel like this?
How could you turn away from the
LORD and build yourselves an altar
in rebellion[r] against him now?
17Was not the sin of Peor[s] enough
for us? Up to this very day we have
not cleansed ourselves from that
sin, even though a plague fell on
the community of the LORD! **18**And
are you now turning away from the
LORD?
" 'If you rebel against the LORD
today, tomorrow he will be angry
with the whole community[t] of Israel. **19**If the land you possess is defiled, come over to the LORD's land,
where the LORD's tabernacle
stands, and share the land with us.
But do not rebel against the LORD or
against us by building an altar for
yourselves, other than the altar of
the LORD our God. **20**When Achan
son of Zerah acted unfaithfully regarding the devoted things,[d][u] did
not wrath[v] come upon the whole
community of Israel? He was not
the only one who died for his
sin.' "[w]
21Then Reuben, Gad and the
half-tribe of Manasseh replied to
the heads of the clans of Israel:
22"The Mighty One, God, the LORD!
The Mighty One, God,[x] the LORD![y]
He knows![z] And let Israel know! If
this has been in rebellion or disobedience to the LORD, do not spare
us this day. **23**If we have built our
own altar to turn away from the
LORD and to offer burnt offerings
and grain offerings,[a] or to sacrifice
fellowship offerings[e] on it, may
the LORD himself call us to account.[b]
24"No! We did it for fear that
some day your descendants might
say to ours, 'What do you have to
do with the LORD, the God of Israel?

22:4 [a]Nu 32:22; Dt 3:20 [b]Nu 32:18; Jos 1:13-15
22:5 [c]Isa 43:22 [d]Dt 5:29 [e]Dt 6:6,17
22:6 [f]Ex 39:43
22:7 [g]Nu 32:33; Jos 12:5 [h]Jos 17:2,5
22:8 [i]Dt 20:14 [j]Nu 31:27 [k]Ge 49:27; 1Sa 30:16; Isa 9:3
22:9 [l]Nu 32:26,29
22:12 [m]Jos 18:1
22:13 [n]Nu 25:7 [o]Nu 3:32; Jos 24:33
22:14 [p]Nu 1:4
22:16 [q]Dt 13:14 [r]Dt 12:13-14
22:17 [s]Nu 25:1-9
22:18 [t]Lev 10:6; Nu 16:22
22:20 [u]Jos 7:1 [v]Ps 7:11 [w]Jos 7:5
22:22 [x]Dt 10:17 [y]Ps 50:1 [z]1Ki 8:39; Job 10:7; Ps 44:21; Jer 17:10
22:23 [a]Jer 41:5 [b]Dt 12:11; 18:19; 1Sa 20:16

[d]*20* The Hebrew term refers to the irrevocable giving over of things or persons to the LORD, often by totally destroying them.
[e]*23* Traditionally *peace offerings*; also in verse 27

25The LORD has made the Jordan a
boundary between us and you—
you Reubenites and Gadites! You
have no share in the LORD.' So your
descendants might cause ours to
stop fearing the LORD.
26"That is why we said, 'Let us
get ready and build an altar—but
not for burnt offerings or sacrifices.' 27On the contrary, it is to be
a witness[a] between us and you and
the generations that follow, that
we will worship the LORD at his
sanctuary with our burnt offerings,
sacrifices and fellowship offerings.[b] Then in the future your
descendants will not be able to say
to ours, 'You have no share in the
LORD.'
28"And we said, 'If they ever say
this to us, or to our descendants,
we will answer: Look at the replica
of the LORD's altar, which our fathers built, not for burnt offerings
and sacrifices, but as a witness between us and you.'
29"Far be it from us to rebel[c]
against the LORD and turn away
from him today by building an altar
for burnt offerings, grain offerings
and sacrifices, other than the altar
of the LORD our God that stands before his tabernacle.[d]"
30When Phinehas the priest and
the leaders of the community—the
heads of the clans of the Israelites—heard what Reuben, Gad and
Manasseh had to say, they were
pleased. 31And Phinehas son of Eleazar, the priest, said to Reuben,
Gad and Manasseh, "Today we
know that the LORD is with us,[e] because you have not acted unfaithfully toward the LORD in this matter. Now you have rescued the Israelites from the LORD's hand."
32Then Phinehas son of Eleazar,
the priest, and the leaders returned
to Canaan from their meeting with
the Reubenites and Gadites in Gilead and reported to the Israelites.
33They were glad to hear the report
and praised God.[f] And they talked
no more about going to war against
them to devastate the country
where the Reubenites and the Gadites lived.

22:27 [a]Ge 21:30; Jos 24:27 [b]Dt 12:6
22:29 [c]Jos 24:16 [d]Dt 12:13-14
22:31 [e]Lev 26:11-12; 2Ch 15:2
22:33 [f]1Ch 29:20; Da 2:19; Lk 2:28
22:34 [g]Ge 21:30
23:1 [h]Dt 12:9; Jos 21:44 [i]Jos 13:1
23:2 [j]Jos 7:6 [k]Jos 24:1
23:3 [l]Ex 14:14
23:4 [m]Jos 19:51 [n]Nu 34:6
23:5 [o]Ex 23:30; Nu 33:53
23:6 [p]Dt 5:32; Jos 1:7
23:7 [q]Ex 23:13; Ps 16:4; Jer 5:7 [r]Ex 20:5
23:8 [s]Dt 10:20
23:9 [t]Dt 11:23 [u]Dt 7:24
23:10 [v]Lev 26:8 [w]Ex 14:14; Dt 3:22
23:11 [x]Jos 22:5

34And the Reubenites and the
Gadites gave the altar this name: A
Witness[g] Between Us that the
LORD is God.

Joshua's Farewell to the Leaders

23 After a long time had
passed and the LORD had
given Israel rest[h] from all their enemies around them, Joshua, by
then old and well advanced in
years,[i] 2summoned all Israel—
their elders,[j] leaders, judges and
officials[k]—and said to them: "I am
old and well advanced in years.
3You yourselves have seen everything the LORD your God has done
to all these nations for your sake; it
was the LORD your God who fought
for you.[l] 4Remember how I have
allotted[m] as an inheritance for
your tribes all the land of the nations that remain—the nations I
conquered—between the Jordan
and the Great Sea[fn] in the west.
5The LORD your God himself will
drive them out of your way. He will
push them out before you, and you
will take possession of their land,
as the LORD your God promised
you.[o]
6"Be very strong; be careful to
obey all that is written in the Book
of the Law of Moses, without turning aside to the right or to the left.[p]
7Do not associate with these nations that remain among you; do
not invoke the names of their gods
or swear[q] by them. You must not
serve them or bow down[r] to them.
8But you are to hold fast to the
LORD[s] your God, as you have until
now.
9"The LORD has driven out before
you great and powerful nations;[t]
to this day no one has been able to
withstand you.[u] 10One of you
routs a thousand,[v] because the
LORD your God fights for you,[w] just
as he promised. 11So be very careful to love the LORD[x] your God.
12"But if you turn away and ally
yourselves with the survivors of
these nations that remain among

[t4] That is, the Mediterranean

you and if you intermarry with them[a] and associate with them,[b] 13then you may be sure that the LORD your God will no longer drive out these nations before you. Instead, they will become snares[c] and traps for you, whips on your backs and thorns in your eyes,[d] until you perish from this good land, which the LORD your God has given you.

14"Now I am about to go the way of all the earth.[e] You know with all your heart and soul that not one of all the good promises the LORD your God gave you has failed. Every promise has been fulfilled; not one has failed.[f] 15But just as every good promise of the LORD your God has come true, so the LORD will bring on you all the evil he has threatened, until he has destroyed you from this good land he has given you.[g] 16If you violate the covenant of the LORD your God, which he commanded you, and go and serve other gods and bow down to them, the LORD's anger will burn against you, and you will quickly perish from the good land he has given you.[h]"

The Covenant Renewed at Shechem

24 Then Joshua assembled all the tribes of Israel at Shechem. He summoned the elders, leaders, judges and officials of Israel,[i] and they presented themselves before God.

2Joshua said to all the people, "This is what the LORD, the God of Israel, says: 'Long ago your forefathers, including Terah the father of Abraham and Nahor, lived beyond the River[g] and worshiped other gods.[j] 3But I took your father Abraham from the land beyond the River and led him throughout Canaan[k] and gave him many descendants.[l] I gave him Isaac,[m] 4and to Isaac I gave Jacob and Esau.[n] I assigned the hill country of Seir[o] to Esau, but Jacob and his sons went down to Egypt.[p]

5" 'Then I sent Moses and Aaron,[q] and I afflicted the Egyptians by what I did there, and I brought you out. 6When I brought your fathers out of Egypt, you came to the sea, and the Egyptians pursued them with chariots and horsemen[h][r] as far as the Red Sea.[i] 7But they cried to the LORD for help, and he put darkness[s] between you and the Egyptians; he brought the sea over them and covered them.[t] You saw with your own eyes what I did to the Egyptians. Then you lived in the desert for a long time.[u]

8" 'I brought you to the land of the Amorites who lived east of the Jordan. They fought against you, but I gave them into your hands. I destroyed them from before you, and you took possession of their land.[v] 9When Balak son of Zippor,[w] the king of Moab, prepared to fight against Israel, he sent for Balaam son of Beor to put a curse on you.[x] 10But I would not listen to Balaam, so he blessed you[y] again and again, and I delivered you out of his hand.

11" 'Then you crossed the Jordan[z] and came to Jericho.[a] The citizens of Jericho fought against you, as did also the Amorites, Perizzites, Canaanites, Hittites, Girgashites, Hivites and Jebusites, but I gave them into your hands.[b] 12I sent the hornet[c] ahead of you, which drove them out before you—also the two Amorite kings. You did not do it with your own sword and bow. 13So I gave you a land on which you did not toil and cities you did not build; and you live in them and eat from vineyards and olive groves that you did not plant.'[d]

14"Now fear the LORD and serve him with all faithfulness.[e] Throw away the gods[f] your forefathers worshiped beyond the River and in Egypt,[g] and serve the LORD. 15But if serving the LORD seems undesirable to you, then choose for yourselves this day whom you will

23:12 [a]Dt 7:3 [b]Ex 34:16; Ps 106:34-35
23:13 [c]Ex 23:33 [d]Nu 33:55
23:14 [e]1Ki 2:2 [f]Jos 21:45
23:15 [g]Lev 26:17; Dt 28:15
23:16 [h]Dt 4:25-26
24:1 [i]Jos 23:2
24:2 [j]Ge 11:32
24:3 [k]Ge 12:1 [l]Ge 15:5 [m]Ge 21:3
24:4 [n]Ge 25:26 [o]Dt 2:5 [p]Ge 46:5-6
24:5 [q]Ex 3:10
24:6 [r]Ex 14:9
24:7 [s]Ex 14:20 [t]Ex 14:28 [u]Dt 1:46
24:8 [v]Nu 21:31
24:9 [w]Nu 22:2 [x]Nu 22:6
24:10 [y]Nu 23:11; Dt 23:5
24:11 [z]Jos 3:16-17 [a]Jos 6:1 [b]Ex 23:23; Dt 7:1
24:12 [c]Ex 23:28; Dt 7:20; Ps 44:3,6-7
24:13 [d]Dt 6:10-11
24:14 [e]Dt 10:12; 18:13; 1Sa 12:24; 2Co 1:12 [f]ver 23 [g]Eze 23:3

[g]2 That is, the Euphrates; also in verses 3, 14 and 15 [h]6 Or *charioteers* [i]6 Hebrew *Yam Suph*; that is, Sea of Reeds

serve, whether the gods your forefathers served beyond the River, or
the gods of the Amorites,[a] in
whose land you are living. But as
for me and my household, we will
serve the LORD."[b]
16Then the people answered,
"Far be it from us to forsake the
LORD to serve other gods! **17**It was
the LORD our God himself who
brought us and our fathers up out
of Egypt, from that land of slavery,
and performed those great signs
before our eyes. He protected us on
our entire journey and among all
the nations through which we traveled. **18**And the LORD drove out before us all the nations, including
the Amorites, who lived in the
land. We too will serve the LORD,
because he is our God."
19Joshua said to the people,
"You are not able to serve the LORD.
He is a holy God;[c] he is a jealous
God.[d] He will not forgive your rebellion[e] and your sins. **20**If you forsake the LORD[f] and serve foreign
gods, he will turn[g] and bring disaster on you and make an end of
you,[h] after he has been good to
you."
21But the people said to Joshua,
"No! We will serve the LORD."
22Then Joshua said, "You are
witnesses against yourselves that
you have chosen[i] to serve the
LORD."
"Yes, we are witnesses," they replied.
23"Now then," said Joshua,
"throw away the foreign gods[j] that
are among you and yield your
hearts[k] to the LORD, the God of Israel."
24And the people said to Joshua,
"We will serve the LORD our God
and obey him."[l]
25On that day Joshua made a
covenant[m] for the people, and

24:15 [a]Jdg 6:10; Ru 1:15 [b]Ru 1:16; 1Ki 18:21
24:19 [c]Lev 19:2; 20:26 [d]Ex 20:5 [e]Ex 23:21
24:20 [f]1Ch 28:9,20 [g]Ac 7:42 [h]Jos 23:15
24:22 [i]Ps 119:30, 173
24:23 [j]ver 14 [k]1Ki 8:58; Ps 119:36; 141:4
24:24 [l]Ex 19:8; 24:3,7; Dt 5:27
24:25 [m]Ex 24:8 [n]Ex 15:25
24:26 [o]Dt 31:24 [p]Ge 28:18
24:27 [q]Jos 22:27
24:29 [r]Jdg 2:8
24:30 [s]Jos 19:50
24:31 [t]Jdg 2:7
24:32 [u]Ge 50:25; Ex 13:19 [v]Ge 33:19; Jn 4:5; Ac 7:16
24:33 [w]Jos 22:13 [x]Ex 6:25

there at Shechem he drew up for
them decrees and laws.[n] **26**And
Joshua recorded these things in
the Book of the Law of God.[o] Then
he took a large stone[p] and set it up
there under the oak near the holy
place of the LORD.
27"See!" he said to all the people. "This stone will be a witness[q]
against us. It has heard all the
words the LORD has said to us. It
will be a witness against you if you
are untrue to your God."

Buried in the Promised Land

24:29–31pp — Jdg 2:6–9

28Then Joshua sent the people
away, each to his own inheritance.
29After these things, Joshua son
of Nun, the servant of the LORD,
died at the age of a hundred and
ten.[r] **30**And they buried him in the
land of his inheritance, at Timnath
Serah[i][s] in the hill country of
Ephraim, north of Mount Gaash.
31Israel served the LORD throughout the lifetime of Joshua and of
the elders[t] who outlived him and
who had experienced everything
the LORD had done for Israel.
32And Joseph's bones, which the
Israelites had brought up from
Egypt,[u] were buried at Shechem in
the tract of land[v] that Jacob
bought for a hundred pieces of silver[k] from the sons of Hamor, the
father of Shechem. This became
the inheritance of Joseph's descendants.
33And Eleazar son of Aaron[w]
died and was buried at Gibeah,
which had been allotted to his son
Phinehas[x] in the hill country of
Ephraim.

[i]*30* Also known as *Timnath Heres* (see Judges 2:9) [k]*32* Hebrew *hundred kesitahs*; a kesitah was a unit of money of unknown weight and value.

Judges

Title and Background

The title describes the type of leaders Israel had from the time of the elders who outlived Joshua until the time of the monarchy. Their principal purpose for having these leaders is best expressed in 2:16: "Then the LORD raised up judges, who saved them out of the hands of these raiders." The book tells of Israel's history for the period between the death of Joshua and the ministry of Samuel.

Author and Date of Writing

According to tradition, Samuel wrote the book, but actual authorship is uncertain. It is possible that Samuel assembled some of the accounts from the period of the judges and that some of the prophets had a hand in shaping and editing the material (see 1Ch 29:29). The date of composition was undoubtedly sometime after 1000 B.C.

Theme and Message

On the one hand, the book of Judges is an account of frequent apostasy, provoking divine chastening. On the other hand, it tells of urgent appeals to God in times of crisis, moving the Lord to raise up leaders (judges) through whom he throws off foreign oppressors and restores the land to peace. It is a number of accounts of recurring cycles (apostasy, oppression, distress and deliverance). Judges reveals an age when "Israel had no king; everyone did as he saw fit" (17:6).

Outline

I. Introduction: Incomplete Conquest and Apostasy (1:1-3:6)
   A. First Episode (1:1-2:5)
   B. Second Episode (2:6-3:6)
II. Oppression by Nations and Deliverance by Judges (3:7-16:31)
III. Epilogue: Religious and Moral Disorder (17:1-21:25)
   A. First Episode (17:1-18:31)
   B. Second Episode (19:1-21:25)

Israel Fights the Remaining Canaanites

1:11–15pp — Jos 15:15–19

1 After the death[a] of Joshua,
the Israelites asked the LORD,
"Who will be the first[b] to go up and
fight for us against the Canaanites?[c]"
²The LORD answered, "Judah[d] is
to go; I have given the land into
their hands.[e]"
³Then the men of Judah said to
the Simeonites their brothers,
"Come up with us into the territory
allotted to us, to fight against the
Canaanites. We in turn will go with
you into yours." So the Simeonites[f] went with them.
⁴When Judah attacked, the LORD
gave the Canaanites and Perizzites[g] into their hands and they
struck down ten thousand men at
Bezek.[h] ⁵It was there that they
found Adoni-Bezek and fought
against him, putting to rout the Canaanites and Perizzites. ⁶Adoni-
Bezek fled, but they chased him
and caught him, and cut off his
thumbs and big toes.
⁷Then Adoni-Bezek said, "Seventy kings with their thumbs and

1:1 [a] Jos 24:29 [b] Nu 27:21 [c] ver 27; Jdg 3:1-6
1:2 [d] Ge 49:8 [e] ver 4; Jdg 3:28
1:3 [f] ver 17
1:4 [g] Ge 13:7; Jos 3:10 [h] 1Sa 11:8

big toes cut off have picked up
scraps under my table. Now God
has paid me back[a] for what I did to
them." They brought him to Jerusalem, and he died there.
8The men of Judah attacked Jerusalem[b] also and took it. They
put the city to the sword and set it
on fire.
9After that, the men of Judah
went down to fight against the Canaanites living in the hill country,[c]
the Negev[d] and the western foothills. 10They advanced against the
Canaanites living in Hebron[e] (formerly called Kiriath Arba[f]) and
defeated Sheshai, Ahiman and Talmai.[g]
11From there they advanced
against the people living in Debir[h]
(formerly called Kiriath Sepher).
12And Caleb said, "I will give my
daughter Acsah in marriage to the
man who attacks and captures Kiriath Sepher." 13Othniel son of Kenaz, Caleb's younger brother, took
it; so Caleb gave his daughter Acsah to him in marriage.
14One day when she came to
Othniel, she urged him[a] to ask her
father for a field. When she got off
her donkey, Caleb asked her,
"What can I do for you?"
15She replied, "Do me a special
favor. Since you have given me land
in the Negev, give me also springs
of water." Then Caleb gave her the
upper and lower springs.
16The descendants of Moses' father-in-law,[i] the Kenite,[j] went
up from the City of Palms[b][k] with
the men of Judah to live among the
people of the Desert of Judah in
the Negev near Arad.[l]
17Then the men of Judah went
with the Simeonites[m] their brothers and attacked the Canaanites
living in Zephath, and they totally
destroyed[c] the city. Therefore it
was called Hormah.[d][n] 18The men
of Judah also took[e] Gaza,[o] Ashkelon and Ekron—each city with its
territory.
19The LORD was with[p] the men
of Judah. They took possession of
the hill country, but they were unable to drive the people from the
plains, because they had iron chariots.[q] 20As Moses had promised,
Hebron[r] was given to Caleb, who
drove from it the three sons of
Anak.[s] 21The Benjamites, however, failed[t] to dislodge the Jebusites, who were living in Jerusalem;[u] to this day the Jebusites live
there with the Benjamites.
22Now the house of Joseph attacked Bethel, and the LORD was
with them. 23When they sent men
to spy out Bethel (formerly called
Luz),[v] 24the spies saw a man coming out of the city and they said to
him, "Show us how to get into the
city and we will see that you are
treated well.[w]" 25So he showed
them, and they put the city to the
sword but spared[x] the man and his
whole family. 26He then went to
the land of the Hittites, where he
built a city and called it Luz, which
is its name to this day.
27But Manasseh did not drive
out the people of Beth Shan or Taanach or Dor or Ibleam[y] or Megiddo
and their surrounding settlements,
for the Canaanites[z] were determined to live in that land. 28When
Israel became strong, they pressed
the Canaanites into forced labor
but never drove them out completely. 29Nor did Ephraim drive
out the Canaanites living in Gezer,[a] but the Canaanites continued to live there among them.[b]
30Neither did Zebulun drive out
the Canaanites living in Kitron or
Nahalol, who remained among
them; but they did subject them to
forced labor. 31Nor did Asher drive
out those living in Acco or Sidon or
Ahlab or Aczib[c] or Helbah or
Aphek or Rehob, 32and because of
this the people of Asher lived
among the Canaanite inhabitants
of the land. 33Neither did Naphtali
drive out those living in Beth Shemesh or Beth Anath[d]; but the
Naphtalites too lived among the

1:7 [a]Lev 24:19
1:8 [b]ver 21; Jos 15:63
1:9 [c]Nu 13:17 [d]Nu 21:1
1:10 [e]Ge 13:18 [f]Ge 35:27 [g]Jos 15:14
1:11 [h]Jos 15:15
1:16 [i]Nu 10:29 [j]Ge 15:19; Jdg 4:11 [k]Dt 34:3; Jdg 3:13 [l]Nu 21:1
1:17 [m]ver 3 [n]Nu 21:3
1:18 [o]Jos 11:22
1:19 [p]ver 2 [q]Jos 17:16
1:20 [r]Jos 14:9; 15:13-14 [s]ver 10; Jos 14:13
1:21 [t]Jos 15:63 [u]ver 8
1:23 [v]Ge 28:19
1:24 [w]Jos 2:12,14
1:25 [x]Jos 6:25
1:27 [y]Jos 17:11 [z]ver 1
1:29 [a]1Ki 9:16 [b]Jos 16:10
1:31 [c]Jdg 10:6
1:33 [d]Jos 19:38

[a]*14* Hebrew; Septuagint and Vulgate *Othniel, he urged her* [b]*16* That is, Jericho
[c]*17* The Hebrew term refers to the irrevocable giving over of things or persons to the LORD, often by totally destroying them.
[d]*17* *Hormah* means *destruction.*
[e]*18* Hebrew; Septuagint *Judah did not take*

Canaanite inhabitants of the land,
and those living in Beth Shemesh
and Beth Anath became forced laborers for them. 34 The Amorites[a]
confined the Danites to the hill
country, not allowing them to
come down into the plain. 35 And
the Amorites were determined also
to hold out in Mount Heres, Aijalon[b] and Shaalbim, but when the
power of the house of Joseph increased, they too were pressed into
forced labor. 36 The boundary of the
Amorites was from Scorpion[f]
Pass[c] to Sela and beyond.

The Angel of the LORD at Bokim

2 The angel of the LORD[d] went
up from Gilgal to Bokim[e] and
said, "I brought you up out of
Egypt[f] and led you into the land
that I swore to give to your forefathers.[g] I said, 'I will never break
my covenant with you,[h] 2 and you
shall not make a covenant with the
people of this land,[i] but you shall
break down their altars.[j]' Yet you
have disobeyed me. Why have you
done this? 3 Now therefore I tell you
that I will not drive them out before
you;[k] they will be ⌞thorns⌟[l] in your
sides and their gods will be a
snare[m] to you."

4 When the angel of the LORD had
spoken these things to all the Israelites, the people wept aloud, 5 and
they called that place Bokim.[g]
There they offered sacrifices to the
LORD.

Disobedience and Defeat

2:6–9pp — Jos 24:29–31

6 After Joshua had dismissed the
Israelites, they went to take possession of the land, each to his own
inheritance. 7 The people served
the LORD throughout the lifetime of
Joshua and of the elders who outlived him and who had seen all the
great things the LORD had done for
Israel.

8 Joshua son of Nun, the servant
of the LORD, died at the age of a
hundred and ten. 9 And they buried
him in the land of his inheritance,
at Timnath Heres[h][n] in the hill
country of Ephraim, north of
Mount Gaash.

10 After that whole generation
had been gathered to their fathers,
another generation grew up, who
knew neither the LORD nor what he
had done for Israel.[o] 11 Then the
Israelites did evil in the eyes of the
LORD[p] and served the Baals.[q]
12 They forsook the LORD, the God
of their fathers, who had brought
them out of Egypt. They followed
and worshiped various gods[r] of
the peoples around them.[s] They
provoked the LORD to anger 13 because they forsook him and served
Baal and the Ashtoreths.[t] 14 In his
anger[u] against Israel the LORD
handed them over[v] to raiders who
plundered them. He sold them[w] to
their enemies all around, whom
they were no longer able to resist.[x]
15 Whenever Israel went out to
fight, the hand of the LORD was
against them to defeat them, just
as he had sworn to them. They
were in great distress.

16 Then the LORD raised up
judges,[i][y] who saved[z] them out of
the hands of these raiders. 17 Yet
they would not listen to their
judges but prostituted[a] themselves to other gods and worshiped
them. Unlike their fathers, they
quickly turned from the way in
which their fathers had walked, the
way of obedience to the LORD's
commands.[b] 18 Whenever the LORD
raised up a judge for them, he was
with the judge and saved them out
of the hands of their enemies as
long as the judge lived; for the LORD
had compassion[c] on them as they
groaned[d] under those who oppressed and afflicted them. 19 But
when the judge died, the people returned to ways even more corrupt[e]
than those of their fathers, following other gods and serving and worshiping them.[f] They refused to
give up their evil practices and
stubborn ways.

1:34 [a] Ex 3:17
1:35 [b] Jos 19:42
1:36 [c] Jos 15:3
2:1 [d] Jdg 6:11 [e] ver 5 [f] Ex 20:2 [g] Ge 17:8 [h] Lev 26:42-44; Dt 7:9
2:2 [i] Ex 23:32; 34:12; Dt 7:2 [j] Ex 34:13
2:3 [k] Jos 23:13 [l] Nu 33:55 [m] Dt 7:16; Jdg 3:6; Ps 106:36
2:9 [n] Jos 19:50
2:10 [o] Ex 5:2; 1Sa 2:12; 1Ch 28:9; Gal 4:8
2:11 [p] Jdg 3:12; 4:1; 6:1; 10:6 [q] Jdg 3:7; 8:33
2:12 [r] Ps 106:36 [s] Dt 31:16; Jdg 10:6
2:13 [t] Jdg 10:6
2:14 [u] Dt 31:17 [v] Ps 106:41 [w] Dt 32:30; Jdg 3:8 [x] Dt 28:25
2:16 [y] Ac 13:20 [z] Ps 106:43
2:17 [a] Ex 34:15 [b] ver 7
2:18 [c] Dt 32:36; Jos 1:5 [d] Ps 106:44
2:19 [e] Jdg 3:12 [f] Jdg 4:1; 8:33

f36 Hebrew *Akrabbim* g5 *Bokim* means *weepers.* h9 Also known as *Timnath Serah* (see Joshua 19:50 and 24:30) i16 Or *leaders*; similarly in verses 17-19

20Therefore the LORD was very
angry[a] with Israel and said, "Because this nation has violated the
covenant that I laid down for their
forefathers and has not listened to
me, 21I will no longer drive out[b]
before them any of the nations
Joshua left when he died. 22I will
use them to test[c] Israel and see
whether they will keep the way of
the LORD and walk in it as their
forefathers did." 23The LORD had
allowed those nations to remain;
he did not drive them out at once
by giving them into the hands of
Joshua.

3 These are the nations the LORD
left to test[d] all those Israelites
who had not experienced any of
the wars in Canaan 2(he did this
only to teach warfare to the
descendants of the Israelites who
had not had previous battle experience): 3the five[e] rulers of the Philistines, all the Canaanites, the Sidonians, and the Hivites living in
the Lebanon mountains from
Mount Baal Hermon to Lebo[i] Hamath. 4They were left to test[f] the
Israelites to see whether they
would obey the LORD's commands,
which he had given their forefathers through Moses.

5The Israelites lived[g] among the
Canaanites, Hittites, Amorites,
Perizzites, Hivites and Jebusites.
6They took their daughters in marriage and gave their own daughters
to their sons, and served their
gods.[h]

Othniel

7The Israelites did evil in the
eyes of the LORD; they forgot the
LORD[i] their God and served the Baals and the Asherahs.[j] 8The anger
of the LORD burned against Israel so
that he sold[k] them into the hands
of Cushan-Rishathaim king of
Aram Naharaim,[k] to whom the Israelites were subject for eight
years. 9But when they cried out[l] to
the LORD, he raised up for them a
deliverer, Othniel[m] son of Kenaz,
Caleb's younger brother, who
saved them. 10The Spirit of the
LORD came upon him,[n] so that he
became Israel's judge[l] and went to
war. The LORD gave Cushan-Rishathaim king of Aram into the hands
of Othniel, who overpowered him.
11So the land had peace for forty
years, until Othniel son of Kenaz
died.

Ehud

12Once again the Israelites did
evil in the eyes of the LORD,[o] and
because they did this evil the LORD
gave Eglon king of Moab[p] power
over Israel. 13Getting the Ammonites and Amalekites to join him,
Eglon came and attacked Israel,
and they took possession of the
City of Palms.[m][q] 14The Israelites
were subject to Eglon king of Moab
for eighteen years.

15Again the Israelites cried out
to the LORD, and he gave them a deliverer[r]—Ehud, a left-handed
man, the son of Gera the Benjamite. The Israelites sent him with
tribute to Eglon king of Moab.
16Now Ehud had made a double-
edged sword about a foot and a
half[n] long, which he strapped to
his right thigh under his clothing.
17He presented the tribute to Eglon king of Moab, who was a very
fat man.[s] 18After Ehud had presented the tribute, he sent on their
way the men who had carried it.
19At the idols[o] near Gilgal he himself turned back and said, "I have a
secret message for you, O king."

The king said, "Quiet!" And all
his attendants left him.

20Ehud then approached him
while he was sitting alone in the
upper room of his summer palace[p]
and said, "I have a message from
God for you." As the king rose from
his seat, 21Ehud reached with his
left hand, drew the sword from his
right thigh and plunged it into the
king's belly. 22Even the handle
sank in after the blade, which came
out his back. Ehud did not pull the

2:20 [a]ver 14; Jos 23:16
2:21 [b]Jos 23:13
2:22 [c]Dt 8:2,16; Jdg 3:1,14
3:1 [d]Jdg 2:21-22
3:3 [e]Jos 13:3
3:4 [f]Dt 8:2; Jdg 2:22
3:5 [g]Ps 106:35
3:6 [h]Ex 34:16; Dt 7:3-4
3:7 [i]Dt 4:9 [j]Ex 34:13; Jdg 2:11,13
3:8 [k]Jdg 2:14
3:9 [l]ver 15; Jdg 6:6,7; 10:10; Ps 106:44 [m]Jdg 1:13
3:10 [n]Nu 11:25,29; 24:2; Jdg 6:34; 11:29; 13:25; 14:6,19; 1Sa 11:6
3:12 [o]Jdg 2:11,14 [p]1Sa 12:9
3:13 [q]Jdg 1:16
3:15 [r]ver 9; Ps 78:34; 107:13
3:17 [s]ver 12

[i]*3* Or *to the entrance to* [k]*8* That is, Northwest Mesopotamia [l]*10* Or *leader* [m]*13* That is, Jericho [n]*16* Hebrew *a cubit* (about 0.5 meter) [o]*19* Or *the stone quarries*; also in verse 26 [p]*20* The meaning of the Hebrew for this phrase is uncertain.

sword out, and the fat closed in over it. **23**Then Ehud went out to the porch[q]; he shut the doors of the upper room behind him and locked them.

24After he had gone, the servants came and found the doors of the upper room locked. They said, "He must be relieving himself[a] in the inner room of the house." **25**They waited to the point of embarrassment,[b] but when he did not open the doors of the room, they took a key and unlocked them. There they saw their lord fallen to the floor, dead.

26While they waited, Ehud got away. He passed by the idols and escaped to Seirah. **27**When he arrived there, he blew a trumpet[c] in the hill country of Ephraim, and the Israelites went down with him from the hills, with him leading them.

28"Follow me," he ordered, "for the LORD has given Moab, your enemy, into your hands.[d]" So they followed him down and, taking possession of the fords of the Jordan[e] that led to Moab, they allowed no one to cross over. **29**At that time they struck down about ten thousand Moabites, all vigorous and strong; not a man escaped. **30**That day Moab was made subject to Israel, and the land had peace[f] for eighty years.

Shamgar

31After Ehud came Shamgar son of Anath,[g] who struck down six hundred[h] Philistines with an oxgoad. He too saved Israel.

Deborah

4 After Ehud died, the Israelites once again did evil[i] in the eyes of the LORD. **2**So the LORD sold them into the hands of Jabin, a king of Canaan, who reigned in Hazor.[j] The commander of his army was Sisera,[k] who lived in Harosheth Haggoyim. **3**Because he had nine hundred iron chariots[l] and had cruelly oppressed[m] the Israelites for twenty years, they cried to the LORD for help.

4Deborah, a prophetess, the wife of Lappidoth, was leading[r] Israel at that time. **5**She held court under the Palm of Deborah between Ramah and Bethel[n] in the hill country of Ephraim, and the Israelites came to her to have their disputes decided. **6**She sent for Barak son of Abinoam[o] from Kedesh in Naphtali and said to him, "The LORD, the God of Israel, commands you: 'Go, take with you ten thousand men of Naphtali and Zebulun and lead the way to Mount Tabor. **7**I will lure Sisera, the commander of Jabin's army, with his chariots and his troops to the Kishon River[p] and give him into your hands.' "

8Barak said to her, "If you go with me, I will go; but if you don't go with me, I won't go."

9"Very well," Deborah said, "I will go with you. But because of the way you are going about this,[s] the honor will not be yours, for the LORD will hand Sisera over to a woman." So Deborah went with Barak to Kedesh,[q] **10**where he summoned[r] Zebulun and Naphtali. Ten thousand men followed him, and Deborah also went with him.

11Now Heber the Kenite had left the other Kenites,[s] the descendants of Hobab,[t] Moses' brother-in-law,[t] and pitched his tent by the great tree in Zaanannim[u] near Kedesh.

12When they told Sisera that Barak son of Abinoam had gone up to Mount Tabor, **13**Sisera gathered together his nine hundred iron chariots[v] and all the men with him, from Harosheth Haggoyim to the Kishon River.

14Then Deborah said to Barak, "Go! This is the day the LORD has given Sisera into your hands. Has not the LORD gone ahead[w] of you?" So Barak went down Mount Tabor, followed by ten thousand men. **15**At Barak's advance, the LORD routed[x] Sisera and all his chariots

3:24 [a] 1Sa 24:3
3:25 [b] 2Ki 2:17; 8:11
3:27 [c] Jdg 6:34; 1Sa 13:3
3:28 [d] Jdg 7:9,15 [e] Jos 2:7; Jdg 7:24; 12:5
3:30 [f] ver 11
3:31 [g] Jdg 5:6 [h] Jos 23:10
4:1 [i] Jdg 2:19
4:2 [j] Jos 11:1 [k] ver 13,16; 1Sa 12:9; Ps 83:9
4:3 [l] Jdg 1:19 [m] Ps 106:42
4:5 [n] Ge 35:8
4:6 [o] Heb 11:32
4:7 [p] Ps 83:9
4:9 [q] ver 21; Jdg 2:14
4:10 [r] ver 14; Jdg 5:15,18
4:11 [s] Jdg 1:16 [t] Nu 10:29 [u] Jos 19:33
4:13 [v] ver 3
4:14 [w] Dt 9:3; 2Sa 5:24; Ps 68:7
4:15 [x] Jos 10:10; Ps 83:9-10

[q]23 The meaning of the Hebrew for this word is uncertain. [r]4 Traditionally *judging*
[s]9 Or *But on the expedition you are undertaking* [t]11 Or *father-in-law*

and army by the sword, and Sisera
abandoned his chariot and fled on
foot. 16But Barak pursued the chariots and army as far as Harosheth
Haggoyim. All the troops of Sisera
fell by the sword; not a man was
left.[a]

17Sisera, however, fled on foot to
the tent of Jael, the wife of Heber
the Kenite, because there were
friendly relations between Jabin
king of Hazor and the clan of Heber
the Kenite.

18Jael went out to meet Sisera
and said to him, "Come, my lord,
come right in. Don't be afraid." So
he entered her tent, and she put a
covering over him.

19"I'm thirsty," he said. "Please
give me some water." She opened a
skin of milk,[b] gave him a drink,
and covered him up.

20"Stand in the doorway of the
tent," he told her. "If someone
comes by and asks you, 'Is anyone
here?' say 'No.' "

21But Jael, Heber's wife, picked
up a tent peg and a hammer and
went quietly to him while he lay
fast asleep, exhausted. She drove
the peg through his temple into the
ground, and he died.[c]

22Barak came by in pursuit of
Sisera, and Jael went out to meet
him. "Come," she said, "I will show
you the man you're looking for." So
he went in with her, and there lay
Sisera with the tent peg through his
temple—dead.

23On that day God subdued[d] Jabin, the Canaanite king, before the
Israelites. 24And the hand of the Israelites grew stronger and stronger
against Jabin, the Canaanite king,
until they destroyed him.

The Song of Deborah

5 On that day Deborah and Barak son of Abinoam sang this
song:[e]

2"When the princes in Israel
take the lead,
when the people willingly
offer[f] themselves—
praise the LORD![g]

3"Hear this, you kings! Listen,
you rulers!
I will sing to[u] the LORD, I
will sing;
I will make music to[v] the
LORD, the God of Israel.[h]

4"O LORD, when you went out
from Seir,[i]
when you marched from the
land of Edom,
the earth shook, the heavens
poured,
the clouds poured down
water.[j]
5The mountains quaked[k] before
the LORD, the One of
Sinai,
before the LORD, the God of
Israel.

6"In the days of Shamgar son of
Anath,[l]
in the days of Jael,[m] the
roads[n] were abandoned;
travelers took to winding
paths.
7Village life[w] in Israel ceased,
ceased until I,[x] Deborah,
arose,
arose a mother in Israel.
8When they chose new gods,[o]
war came to the city gates,
and not a shield or spear was
seen
among forty thousand in
Israel.
9My heart is with Israel's
princes,
with the willing volunteers[p]
among the people.
Praise the LORD!

10"You who ride on white
donkeys,[q]
sitting on your saddle
blankets,
and you who walk along the
road,
consider 11the voice of the
singers[y] at the watering
places.
They recite the righteous
acts[r] of the LORD,

4:16 [a]Ex 14:28; Ps 83:9
4:19 [b]Jdg 5:25
4:21 [c]Jdg 5:26
4:23 [d]Ne 9:24; Ps 18:47
5:1 [e]Ex 15:1
5:2 [f]2Ch 17:16; Ps 110:3 [g]ver 9
5:3 [h]Ps 27:6
5:4 [i]Dt 33:2 [j]Ps 68:8
5:5 [k]Ex 19:18; Ps 68:8; 97:5; Isa 64:3
5:6 [l]Jdg 3:31 [m]Jdg 4:17 [n]Isa 33:8
5:8 [o]Dt 32:17
5:9 [p]ver 2
5:10 [q]Jdg 10:4; 12:14
5:11 [r]1Sa 12:7; Mic 6:5

[u]3 Or *of* [v]3 Or / *with song I will praise* [w]7 Or *Warriors* [x]7 Or *you* [y]11 Or *archers*; the meaning of the Hebrew for this word is uncertain.

the righteous acts of his warriors[z] in Israel.

"Then the people of the LORD went down to the city gates.[a]
12'Wake up,[b] wake up, Deborah! Wake up, wake up, break out in song!
Arise, O Barak! Take captive your captives,[c] O son of Abinoam.'

13"Then the men who were left came down to the nobles;
the people of the LORD came to me with the mighty.
14Some came from Ephraim, whose roots were in Amalek;[d]
Benjamin was with the people who followed you.
From Makir captains came down,
from Zebulun those who bear a commander's staff.
15The princes of Issachar were with Deborah;[e]
yes, Issachar was with Barak, rushing after him into the valley.
In the districts of Reuben there was much searching of heart.
16Why did you stay among the campfires[a]
to hear the whistling for the flocks?[f]
In the districts of Reuben there was much searching of heart.
17Gilead stayed beyond the Jordan.
And Dan, why did he linger by the ships?
Asher remained on the coast[g] and stayed in his coves.
18The people of Zebulun risked their very lives;
so did Naphtali on the heights of the field.[h]

19"Kings came[i], they fought;
the kings of Canaan fought
at Taanach by the waters of Megiddo,[j]
but they carried off no silver, no plunder.[k]
20From the heavens[l] the stars fought,
from their courses they fought against Sisera.
21The river Kishon[m] swept them away,
the age-old river, the river Kishon.
March on, my soul; be strong!
22Then thundered the horses' hoofs—
galloping, galloping go his mighty steeds.
23'Curse Meroz,' said the angel of the LORD.
'Curse its people bitterly,
because they did not come to help the LORD,
to help the LORD against the mighty.'

24"Most blessed of women be Jael,[n]
the wife of Heber the Kenite,
most blessed of tent-dwelling women.
25He asked for water, and she gave him milk;[o]
in a bowl fit for nobles she brought him curdled milk.
26Her hand reached for the tent peg,
her right hand for the workman's hammer.
She struck Sisera, she crushed his head,
she shattered and pierced his temple.[p]
27At her feet he sank,
he fell; there he lay.
At her feet he sank, he fell;
where he sank, there he fell—dead.

28"Through the window peered Sisera's mother;
behind the lattice she cried out,[q]
'Why is his chariot so long in coming?

5:11 [a]ver 8
5:12 [b]Ps 57:8 [c]Ps 68:18; Eph 4:8
5:14 [d]Jdg 3:13
5:15 [e]Jdg 4:10
5:16 [f]Nu 32:1
5:17 [g]Jos 19:29
5:18 [h]Jdg 4:6,10
5:19 [i]Jos 11:5; Jdg 4:13 [j]Jdg 1:27 [k]ver 30
5:20 [l]Jos 10:11
5:21 [m]Jdg 4:7
5:24 [n]Jdg 4:17
5:25 [o]Jdg 4:19
5:26 [p]Jdg 4:21
5:28 [q]Pr 7:6

[z]11 Or *villagers* [a]16 Or *saddlebags*

Why is the clatter of his
chariots delayed?'
29The wisest of her ladies answer
her;
indeed, she keeps saying to
herself,
30'Are they not finding and
dividing the spoils:[a]
a girl or two for each man,
colorful garments as plunder
for Sisera,
colorful garments
embroidered,
highly embroidered garments
for my neck—
all this as plunder?'

31"So may all your enemies
perish, O LORD!
But may they who love you
be like the sun[b]
when it rises in its strength."

Then the land had peace[c] forty years.

Gideon

6 Again the Israelites did evil in the eyes of the LORD,[d] and for seven years he gave them into the hands of the Midianites.[e] **2**Because the power of Midian was so oppressive,[f] the Israelites prepared shelters for themselves in mountain clefts, caves and strongholds.[g] **3**Whenever the Israelites planted their crops, the Midianites, Amalekites[h] and other eastern peoples invaded the country. **4**They camped on the land and ruined the crops[i] all the way to Gaza and did not spare a living thing for Israel, neither sheep nor cattle nor donkeys. **5**They came up with their livestock and their tents like swarms of locusts.[j] It was impossible to count the men and their camels;[k] they invaded the land to ravage it. **6**Midian so impoverished the Israelites that they cried out[l] to the LORD for help.

7When the Israelites cried to the LORD because of Midian, **8**he sent them a prophet, who said, "This is what the LORD, the God of Israel, says: I brought you up out of Egypt,[m] out of the land of slavery. **9**I snatched you from the power of Egypt and from the hand of all your oppressors. I drove them from before you and gave you their land.[n] **10**I said to you, 'I am the LORD your God; do not worship[o] the gods of the Amorites,[p] in whose land you live.' But you have not listened to me."

11The angel of the LORD[q] came and sat down under the oak in Ophrah that belonged to Joash the Abiezrite,[r] where his son Gideon[s] was threshing wheat in a winepress to keep it from the Midianites. **12**When the angel of the LORD appeared to Gideon, he said, "The LORD is with you,[t] mighty warrior."

13"But sir," Gideon replied, "if the LORD is with us, why has all this happened to us? Where are all his wonders that our fathers told[u] us about when they said, 'Did not the LORD bring us up out of Egypt?' But now the LORD has abandoned[v] us and put us into the hand of Midian."

14The LORD turned to him and said, "Go in the strength you have[w] and save Israel out of Midian's hand. Am I not sending you?"

15"But Lord,[b]" Gideon asked, "how can I save Israel? My clan is the weakest in Manasseh, and I am the least in my family.[x]"

16The LORD answered, "I will be with you[y], and you will strike down all the Midianites together."

17Gideon replied, "If now I have found favor in your eyes, give me a sign[z] that it is really you talking to me. **18**Please do not go away until I come back and bring my offering and set it before you."

And the LORD said, "I will wait until you return."

19Gideon went in, prepared a young goat, and from an ephah[c] of flour he made bread without yeast. Putting the meat in a basket and its broth in a pot, he brought them out and offered them to him under the oak.[a]

20The angel of God said to him,

5:30 [a]Ex 15:9; 1Sa 30:24
5:31 [b]2Sa 23:4; Ps 19:4; 89:36 [c]Jdg 3:11
6:1 [d]Jdg 2:11 [e]Nu 25:15-18; 31:1-3
6:2 [f]1Sa 13:6; Isa 8:21 [g]Heb 11:38
6:3 [h]Jdg 3:13
6:4 [i]Lev 26:16; Dt 28:30,51
6:5 [j]Jdg 7:12 [k]Jdg 8:10
6:6 [l]Jdg 3:9
6:8 [m]Jdg 2:1
6:9 [n]Ps 44:2
6:10 [o]2Ki 17:35 [p]Jer 10:2
6:11 [q]Ge 16:7 [r]Jos 17:2 [s]Heb 11:32
6:12 [t]Jos 1:5; Jdg 13:3; Lk 1:11,28
6:13 [u]Ps 44:1 [v]2Ch 15:2
6:14 [w]Heb 11:34
6:15 [x]Ex 3:11; 1Sa 9:21
6:16 [y]Ex 3:12; Jos 1:5
6:17 [z]ver 36-37; Ge 24:14; Isa 38:7-8
6:19 [a]Ge 18:7-8

[b]*15* Or *sir* [c]*19* That is, probably about 3/5 bushel (about 22 liters)

"Take the meat and the unleavened bread, place them on this
rock,[a] and pour out the broth."
And Gideon did so. 21With the tip
of the staff that was in his hand, the
angel of the LORD touched the meat
and the unleavened bread.[b] Fire
flared from the rock, consuming
the meat and the bread. And the
angel of the LORD disappeared.
22When Gideon realized[c] that it
was the angel of the LORD, he exclaimed, "Ah, Sovereign LORD! I
have seen the angel of the LORD
face to face!"[d]

23But the LORD said to him,
"Peace! Do not be afraid.[e] You are
not going to die."

24So Gideon built an altar to the
LORD there and called[f] it The LORD
is Peace. To this day it stands in
Ophrah[g] of the Abiezrites.

25That same night the LORD said
to him, "Take the second bull from
your father's herd, the one seven
years old.[d] Tear down your father's
altar to Baal and cut down the
Asherah pole[e][h] beside it. 26Then
build a proper kind of[f] altar to the
LORD your God on the top of this
height. Using the wood of the
Asherah pole that you cut down,
offer the second[g] bull as a burnt
offering."

27So Gideon took ten of his servants and did as the LORD told him.
But because he was afraid of his
family and the men of the town, he
did it at night rather than in the
daytime.

28In the morning when the men
of the town got up, there was Baal's
altar,[i] demolished, with the Asherah pole beside it cut down and the
second bull sacrificed on the newly
built altar!

29They asked each other, "Who
did this?"

When they carefully investigated, they were told, "Gideon son of
Joash did it."

30The men of the town demanded of Joash, "Bring out your son.
He must die, because he has broken down Baal's altar and cut down
the Asherah pole beside it."

31But Joash replied to the hostile crowd around him, "Are you
going to plead Baal's cause? Are
you trying to save him? Whoever
fights for him shall be put to death
by morning! If Baal really is a god,
he can defend himself when someone breaks down his altar." 32So
that day they called Gideon "Jerub-Baal,[h][j]" saying, "Let Baal contend with him," because he broke
down Baal's altar.

33Now all the Midianites, Amalekites and other eastern peoples[k]
joined forces and crossed over the
Jordan and camped in the Valley of
Jezreel.[l] 34Then the Spirit of the
LORD came upon[m] Gideon, and he
blew a trumpet,[n] summoning the
Abiezrites to follow him. 35He sent
messengers throughout Manasseh,
calling them to arms, and also into
Asher, Zebulun and Naphtali,[o] so
that they too went up to meet
them.

36Gideon said to God, "If you
will save[p] Israel by my hand as you
have promised— 37look, I will
place a wool fleece on the threshing floor.[q] If there is dew only on
the fleece and all the ground is dry,
then I will know[r] that you will save
Israel by my hand, as you said."
38And that is what happened. Gideon rose early the next day; he
squeezed the fleece and wrung out
the dew—a bowlful of water.

39Then Gideon said to God, "Do
not be angry with me. Let me make
just one more request.[s] Allow me
one more test with the fleece. This
time make the fleece dry and the
ground covered with dew." 40That
night God did so. Only the fleece
was dry; all the ground was covered
with dew.

Gideon Defeats the Midianites

7 Early in the morning, Jerub-
Baal[t] (that is, Gideon) and all
his men camped at the spring of
Harod. The camp of Midian was

6:20 [a]Jdg 13:19
6:21 [b]Lev 9:24
6:22 [c]Jdg 13:16,21 [d]Ge 32:30; Ex 33:20; Jdg 13:22
6:23 [e]Da 10:19
6:24 [f]Ge 22:14 [g]Jdg 8:32
6:25 [h]Ex 34:13; Dt 7:5
6:28 [i]1Ki 16:32
6:32 [j]Jdg 7:1; 8:29, 35; 1Sa 12:11
6:33 [k]ver 3 [l]Jos 17:16
6:34 [m]Jdg 3:10; 1Ch 12:18; 2Ch 24:20 [n]Jdg 3:27
6:35 [o]Jdg 4:6
6:36 [p]ver 14
6:37 [q]Ex 4:3-7 [r]Ge 24:14
6:39 [s]Ge 18:32
7:1 [t]Jdg 6:32

[d]25 Or *Take a full-grown, mature bull from your father's herd* [e]25 That is, a symbol of the goddess Asherah; here and elsewhere in Judges [f]26 Or *build with layers of stone an* [g]26 Or *full-grown*; also in verse 28 [h]32 *Jerub-Baal* means *let Baal contend.*

north of them in the valley near the hill of Moreh.[a] 2The LORD said to Gideon, "You have too many men for me to deliver Midian into their hands. In order that Israel may not boast against me that her own strength[b] has saved her, 3announce now to the people, 'Anyone who trembles with fear may turn back and leave Mount Gilead.[c]' " So twenty-two thousand men left, while ten thousand remained.

4But the LORD said to Gideon, "There are still too many[d] men. Take them down to the water, and I will sift them for you there. If I say, 'This one shall go with you,' he shall go; but if I say, 'This one shall not go with you,' he shall not go."

5So Gideon took the men down to the water. There the LORD told him, "Separate those who lap the water with their tongues like a dog from those who kneel down to drink." 6Three hundred men lapped with their hands to their mouths. All the rest got down on their knees to drink.

7The LORD said to Gideon, "With the three hundred men that lapped I will save you and give the Midianites into your hands. Let all the other men go, each to his own place."[e] 8So Gideon sent the rest of the Israelites to their tents but kept the three hundred, who took over the provisions and trumpets of the others.

Now the camp of Midian lay below him in the valley. 9During that night the LORD said to Gideon, "Get up, go down against the camp, because I am going to give it into your hands.[f] 10If you are afraid to attack, go down to the camp with your servant Purah 11and listen to what they are saying. Afterward, you will be encouraged to attack the camp." So he and Purah his servant went down to the outposts of the camp. 12The Midianites, the Amalekites[g] and all the other eastern peoples had settled in the valley, thick as locusts.[h] Their camels[i] could no more be counted than the sand on the seashore.[j]

13Gideon arrived just as a man was telling a friend his dream. "I had a dream," he was saying. "A round loaf of barley bread came tumbling into the Midianite camp. It struck the tent with such force that the tent overturned and collapsed."

14His friend responded, "This can be nothing other than the sword of Gideon son of Joash, the Israelite. God has given the Midianites and the whole camp into his hands."

15When Gideon heard the dream and its interpretation, he worshiped God.[k] He returned to the camp of Israel and called out, "Get up! The LORD has given the Midianite camp into your hands." 16Dividing the three hundred men[l] into three companies,[m] he placed trumpets and empty jars in the hands of all of them, with torches inside.

17"Watch me," he told them. "Follow my lead. When I get to the edge of the camp, do exactly as I do. 18When I and all who are with me blow our trumpets,[n] then from all around the camp blow yours and shout, 'For the LORD and for Gideon.' "

19Gideon and the hundred men with him reached the edge of the camp at the beginning of the middle watch, just after they had changed the guard. They blew their trumpets and broke the jars that were in their hands. 20The three companies blew the trumpets and smashed the jars. Grasping the torches in their left hands and holding in their right hands the trumpets they were to blow, they shouted, "A sword[o] for the LORD and for Gideon!" 21While each man held his position around the camp, all the Midianites ran, crying out as they fled.[p]

22When the three hundred trumpets sounded,[q] the LORD caused the men throughout the camp to turn on each other[r] with their swords. The army fled to Beth Shittah toward Zererah as far as the border of Abel Meholah[s] near Tabbath. 23Israelites from Naphtali,

7:1 [a] Ge 12:6
7:2 [b] Dt 8:17; 2Co 4:7
7:3 [c] Dt 20:8
7:4 [d] 1Sa 14:6
7:7 [e] 1Sa 14:6
7:9 [f] Jos 2:24; 10:8; 11:6
7:12 [g] Jdg 8:10 [h] Jdg 6:5 [i] Jer 49:29 [j] Jos 11:4
7:15 [k] 1Sa 15:31
7:16 [l] Ge 14:15 [m] 2Sa 18:2
7:18 [n] Jdg 3:27
7:20 [o] ver 14
7:21 [p] 2Ki 7:7
7:22 [q] Jos 6:20 [r] 1Sa 14:20; 2Ch 20:23 [s] 1Ki 4:12; 19:16

Asher and all Manasseh were called out,[a] and they pursued the Midianites. **24**Gideon sent messengers throughout the hill country of Ephraim, saying, "Come down against the Midianites and seize the waters of the Jordan[b] ahead of them as far as Beth Barah."

So all the men of Ephraim were called out and they took the waters of the Jordan as far as Beth Barah. **25**They also captured two of the Midianite leaders, Oreb and Zeeb[c]. They killed Oreb at the rock of Oreb,[d] and Zeeb at the winepress of Zeeb. They pursued the Midianites and brought the heads of Oreb and Zeeb to Gideon, who was by the Jordan.[e]

Zebah and Zalmunna

8 Now the Ephraimites asked Gideon, "Why have you treated us like this? Why didn't you call us when you went to fight Midian?"[f] And they criticized him sharply.[g]

2But he answered them, "What have I accomplished compared to you? Aren't the gleanings of Ephraim's grapes better than the full grape harvest of Abiezer? **3**God gave Oreb and Zeeb,[h] the Midianite leaders, into your hands. What was I able to do compared to you?" At this, their resentment against him subsided.

4Gideon and his three hundred men, exhausted yet keeping up the pursuit, came to the Jordan[i] and crossed it. **5**He said to the men of Succoth,[j] "Give my troops some bread; they are worn out, and I am still pursuing Zebah and Zalmunna,[k] the kings of Midian."

6But the officials of Succoth said, "Do you already have the hands of Zebah and Zalmunna in your possession? Why should we give bread[l] to your troops?"[m]

7Then Gideon replied, "Just for that, when the LORD has given Zebah and Zalmunna[n] into my hand, I will tear your flesh with desert thorns and briers."

8From there he went up to Peniel[i8] and made the same request of them, but they answered as the men of Succoth had. **9**So he said to the men of Peniel, "When I return in triumph, I will tear down this tower."[p]

10Now Zebah and Zalmunna were in Karkor with a force of about fifteen thousand men, all that were left of the armies of the eastern peoples; a hundred and twenty thousand swordsmen had fallen.[q] **11**Gideon went up by the route of the nomads east of Nobah[r] and Jogbehah[s] and fell upon the unsuspecting army. **12**Zebah and Zalmunna, the two kings of Midian, fled, but he pursued them and captured them, routing their entire army.

13Gideon son of Joash then returned from the battle by the Pass of Heres. **14**He caught a young man of Succoth and questioned him, and the young man wrote down for him the names of the seventy-seven officials of Succoth, the elders of the town. **15**Then Gideon came and said to the men of Succoth, "Here are Zebah and Zalmunna, about whom you taunted me by saying, 'Do you already have the hands of Zebah and Zalmunna in your possession? Why should we give bread to your exhausted men?'[t]" **16**He took the elders of the town and taught the men of Succoth a lesson[u] by punishing them with desert thorns and briers. **17**He also pulled down the tower of Peniel and killed the men of the town.[v]

18Then he asked Zebah and Zalmunna, "What kind of men did you kill at Tabor?[w]"

"Men like you," they answered, "each one with the bearing of a prince."

19Gideon replied, "Those were my brothers, the sons of my own mother. As surely as the LORD lives, if you had spared their lives, I would not kill you." **20**Turning to Jether, his oldest son, he said, "Kill them!" But Jether did not draw his

7:23 [a]Jdg 6:35
7:24 [b]Jdg 3:28
7:25 [c]Jdg 8:3; Ps 83:11 [d]Isa 10:26 [e]Jdg 8:4
8:1 [f]Jdg 12:1 [g]2Sa 19:41
8:3 [h]Jdg 7:25; Pr 15:1
8:4 [i]Jdg 7:25
8:5 [j]Ge 33:17 [k]Ps 83:11
8:6 [l]1Sa 25:11 [m]ver 15
8:7 [n]Jdg 7:15
8:8 [o]Ge 32:30; 1Ki 12:25
8:9 [p]ver 17
8:10 [q]Jdg 6:5; 7:12; Isa 9:4
8:11 [r]Nu 32:42 [s]Nu 32:35
8:15 [t]ver 6
8:16 [u]ver 7
8:17 [v]ver 9
8:18 [w]Jos 19:22; Jdg 4:6

i8 Hebrew *Penuel,* a variant of *Peniel;* also in verses 9 and 17

sword, because he was only a boy and was afraid.

21Zebah and Zalmunna said, "Come, do it yourself. 'As is the man, so is his strength.' " So Gideon stepped forward and killed them, and took the ornaments[a] off their camels' necks.

Gideon's Ephod

22The Israelites said to Gideon, "Rule over us—you, your son and your grandson—because you have saved us out of the hand of Midian."

23But Gideon told them, "I will not rule over you, nor will my son rule over you. The LORD will rule[b] over you." 24And he said, "I do have one request, that each of you give me an earring from your share of the plunder." (It was the custom of the Ishmaelites[c] to wear gold earrings.)

25They answered, "We'll be glad to give them." So they spread out a garment, and each man threw a ring from his plunder onto it. 26The weight of the gold rings he asked for came to seventeen hundred shekels,[i] not counting the ornaments, the pendants and the purple garments worn by the kings of Midian or the chains that were on their camels' necks. 27Gideon made the gold into an ephod,[d] which he placed in Ophrah, his town. All Israel prostituted themselves by worshiping it there, and it became a snare[e] to Gideon and his family.

Gideon's Death

28Thus Midian was subdued before the Israelites and did not raise its head again. During Gideon's lifetime, the land enjoyed peace[f] forty years.

29Jerub-Baal[g] son of Joash went back home to live. 30He had seventy sons[h] of his own, for he had many wives. 31His concubine, who lived in Shechem, also bore him a son, whom he named Abimelech.[i] 32Gideon son of Joash died at a good old age[j] and was buried in the tomb of his father Joash in Ophrah of the Abiezrites.

33No sooner had Gideon died than the Israelites again prostituted themselves to the Baals.[k] They set up Baal-Berith[l] as their god[m] and 34did not remember[n] the LORD their God, who had rescued them from the hands of all their enemies on every side. 35They also failed to show kindness to the family of Jerub-Baal (that is, Gideon) for all the good things he had done for them.[o]

Abimelech

9 Abimelech[p] son of Jerub-Baal went to his mother's brothers in Shechem and said to them and to all his mother's clan, 2"Ask all the citizens of Shechem, 'Which is better for you: to have all seventy of Jerub-Baal's sons rule over you, or just one man?' Remember, I am your flesh and blood.[q]"

3When the brothers repeated all this to the citizens of Shechem, they were inclined to follow Abimelech, for they said, "He is our brother." 4They gave him seventy shekels[k] of silver from the temple of Baal-Berith,[r] and Abimelech used it to hire reckless adventurers,[s] who became his followers. 5He went to his father's home in Ophrah and on one stone murdered his seventy brothers,[t] the sons of Jerub-Baal. But Jotham, the youngest son of Jerub-Baal, escaped by hiding.[u] 6Then all the citizens of Shechem and Beth Millo gathered beside the great tree at the pillar in Shechem to crown Abimelech king.

7When Jotham was told about this, he climbed up on the top of Mount Gerizim[v] and shouted to them, "Listen to me, citizens of Shechem, so that God may listen to you. 8One day the trees went out to anoint a king for themselves. They said to the olive tree, 'Be our king.'

9"But the olive tree answered,

8:21 [a]ver 26; Ps 83:11
8:23 [b]Ex 16:8; 1Sa 8:7; 10:19; 12:12
8:24 [c]Ge 25:13
8:27 [d]Jdg 17:5; 18:14 [e]Dt 7:16; Ps 106:39
8:28 [f]Jdg 5:31
8:29 [g]Jdg 7:1
8:30 [h]Jdg 9:2,5,18, 24
8:31 [i]Jdg 9:1
8:32 [j]Ge 25:8
8:33 [k]Jdg 2:11,13, 19 [l]Jdg 9:4 [m]Jdg 9:27,46
8:34 [n]Jdg 3:7; Dt 4:9; Ps 78:11,42
8:35 [o]Jdg 9:16
9:1 [p]Jdg 8:31
9:2 [q]Ge 29:14; Jdg 8:30
9:4 [r]Jdg 8:33 [s]Jdg 11:3; 2Ch 13:7
9:5 [t]ver 2; Jdg 8:30 [u]2Ki 11:2
9:7 [v]Dt 11:29; 27:12; Jn 4:20

i26 That is, about 43 pounds (about 19.5 kilograms) *k4* That is, about 1 3/4 pounds (about 0.8 kilogram)

'Should I give up my oil, by which
both gods and men are honored, to
hold sway over the trees?'
10"Next, the trees said to the fig
tree, 'Come and be our king.'
11"But the fig tree replied,
'Should I give up my fruit, so good
and sweet, to hold sway over the
trees?'
12"Then the trees said to the
vine, 'Come and be our king.'
13"But the vine answered,
'Should I give up my wine,[a] which
cheers both gods and men, to hold
sway over the trees?'
14"Finally all the trees said to
the thornbush, 'Come and be our
king.'
15"The thornbush said to the
trees, 'If you really want to anoint
me king over you, come and take
refuge in my shade;[b] but if not,
then let fire come out[c] of the
thornbush and consume the cedars
of Lebanon!'[d]
16"Now if you have acted honorably and in good faith when you
made Abimelech king, and if you
have been fair to Jerub-Baal and
his family, and if you have treated
him as he deserves— 17and to
think that my father fought for you,
risked his life to rescue you from
the hand of Midian 18(but today
you have revolted against my father's family, murdered his seventy
sons[e] on a single stone, and made
Abimelech, the son of his slave girl,
king over the citizens of Shechem
because he is your brother)— 19if
then you have acted honorably and
in good faith toward Jerub-Baal
and his family today, may Abimelech be your joy, and may you be
his, too! 20But if you have not, let
fire come out[f] from Abimelech
and consume you, citizens of Shechem and Beth Millo, and let fire
come out from you, citizens of Shechem and Beth Millo, and consume Abimelech!"
21Then Jotham fled, escaping to
Beer, and he lived there because he
was afraid of his brother Abimelech.
22After Abimelech had governed
Israel three years, 23God sent an
evil spirit[g] between Abimelech
and the citizens of Shechem, who
acted treacherously against Abimelech. 24God did this in order that
the crime against Jerub-Baal's seventy sons, the shedding[h] of their
blood, might be avenged[i] on their
brother Abimelech and on the citizens of Shechem, who had helped
him[j] murder his brothers. 25In opposition to him these citizens of
Shechem set men on the hilltops to
ambush and rob everyone who
passed by, and this was reported to
Abimelech.
26Now Gaal son of Ebed moved
with his brothers into Shechem,
and its citizens put their confidence in him. 27After they had
gone out into the fields and gathered the grapes and trodden[k]
them, they held a festival in the
temple of their god.[l] While they
were eating and drinking, they
cursed Abimelech. 28Then Gaal
son of Ebed said, "Who[m] is Abimelech, and who is Shechem, that we
should be subject to him? Isn't he
Jerub-Baal's son, and isn't Zebul
his deputy? Serve the men of Hamor,[n] Shechem's father! Why
should we serve Abimelech? 29If
only this people were under my
command![o] Then I would get rid of
him. I would say to Abimelech,
'Call out your whole army!' "[1]
30When Zebul the governor of
the city heard what Gaal son of
Ebed said, he was very angry. 31Un-
der cover he sent messengers to
Abimelech, saying, "Gaal son of
Ebed and his brothers have come
to Shechem and are stirring up the
city against you. 32Now then, during the night you and your men
should come and lie in wait[p] in the
fields. 33In the morning at sunrise,
advance against the city. When
Gaal and his men come out against
you, do whatever your hand finds
to do.[q]"
34So Abimelech and all his
troops set out by night and took up
concealed positions near Shechem

9:13 [a] Ecc 2:3
9:15 [b] Isa 30:2 [c] ver 20 [d] Isa 2:13
9:18 [e] ver 5-6; Jdg 8:30
9:20 [f] ver 15
9:23 [g] 1Sa 16:14, 23; 18:10; 1Ki 22:22; Isa 19:14; 33:1
9:24 [h] Nu 35:33; 1Ki 2:32 [i] ver 56-57 [j] Dt 27:25
9:27 [k] Am 9:13 [l] Jdg 8:33
9:28 [m] 1Sa 25:10; 1Ki 12:16 [n] Ge 34:2,6
9:29 [o] 2Sa 15:4
9:32 [p] Jos 8:2
9:33 [q] 1Sa 10:7

[1]29 Septuagint; Hebrew *him." Then he said to Abimelech, "Call out your whole army!"*

in four companies. **35**Now Gaal son
of Ebed had gone out and was
standing at the entrance to the city
gate just as Abimelech and his soldiers came out from their hiding
place.[a]
36When Gaal saw them, he said
to Zebul, "Look, people are coming
down from the tops of the mountains!"
Zebul replied, "You mistake the
shadows of the mountains for
men."
37But Gaal spoke up again:
"Look, people are coming down
from the center of the land, and a
company is coming from the direction of the soothsayers' tree."
38Then Zebul said to him,
"Where is your big talk now, you
who said, 'Who is Abimelech that
we should be subject to him?'
Aren't these the men you ridiculed?[b] Go out and fight them!"
39So Gaal led out[m] the citizens
of Shechem and fought Abimelech.
40Abimelech chased him, and
many fell wounded in the flight—
all the way to the entrance to the
gate. **41**Abimelech stayed in Aru-
mah, and Zebul drove Gaal and his
brothers out of Shechem.
42The next day the people of
Shechem went out to the fields,
and this was reported to Abimelech. **43**So he took his men, divided
them into three companies[c] and
set an ambush in the fields. When
he saw the people coming out of
the city, he rose to attack them.
44Abimelech and the companies
with him rushed forward to a position at the entrance to the city
gate. Then two companies rushed
upon those in the fields and struck
them down. **45**All that day Abimelech pressed his attack against the
city until he had captured it and
killed its people. Then he destroyed the city[d] and scattered
salt[e] over it.
46On hearing this, the citizens in
the tower of Shechem went into
the stronghold of the temple[f] of
El-Berith. **47**When Abimelech
heard that they had assembled
there, **48**he and all his men went up
Mount Zalmon.[g] He took an ax
and cut off some branches, which
he lifted to his shoulders. He ordered the men with him, "Quick!
Do what you have seen me do!"
49So all the men cut branches and
followed Abimelech. They piled
them against the stronghold and
set it on fire over the people inside.
So all the people in the tower of
Shechem, about a thousand men
and women, also died.
50Next Abimelech went to Thebez[h] and besieged it and captured
it. **51**Inside the city, however, was a
strong tower, to which all the men
and women—all the people of the
city—fled. They locked themselves
in and climbed up on the tower
roof. **52**Abimelech went to the tower and stormed it. But as he approached the entrance to the tower
to set it on fire, **53**a woman dropped
an upper millstone on his head and
cracked his skull.[i]
54Hurriedly he called to his armor-bearer, "Draw your sword and
kill me,[j] so that they can't say, 'A
woman killed him.' " So his servant
ran him through, and he died.
55When the Israelites saw that
Abimelech was dead, they went
home.
56Thus God repaid the wickedness that Abimelech had done to
his father by murdering his seventy
brothers. **57**God also made the men
of Shechem pay for all their wickedness.[k] The curse of Jotham son
of Jerub-Baal came on them.

Tola

10 After the time of Abimelech
a man of Issachar,[l] Tola
son of Puah,[m] the son of Dodo,
rose to save[n] Israel. He lived in
Shamir, in the hill country of
Ephraim. **2**He led[n] Israel twenty-
three years; then he died, and was
buried in Shamir.

Jair

3He was followed by Jair of Gilead, who led Israel twenty-two

[m]39 Or *Gaal went out in the sight of*
[n]2 Traditionally *judged*; also in verse 3

9:35 [a]Ps 32:7; Jer 49:10
9:38 [b]ver 28-29
9:43 [c]Jdg 7:16
9:45 [d]ver 20; 2Ki 3:25 [e]Dt 29:23
9:46 [f]Jdg 8:33
9:48 [g]Ps 68:14
9:50 [h]2Sa 11:21
9:53 [i]2Sa 11:21
9:54 [j]1Sa 31:4; 2Sa 1:9
9:57 [k]ver 20
10:1 [l]Ge 30:18 [m]Ge 46:13 [n]Jdg 2:16; 6:14

years. **4**He had thirty sons, who
rode thirty donkeys. They controlled thirty towns in Gilead,
which to this day are called Havvoth Jair.[o][a] **5**When Jair died, he
was buried in Kamon.

Jephthah

6Again the Israelites did evil in
the eyes of the LORD.[b] They served
the Baals and the Ashtoreths,[c] and
the gods of Aram, the gods of Sidon, the gods of Moab, the gods of
the Ammonites and the gods of the
Philistines.[d] And because the Israelites forsook the LORD[e] and no
longer served him, **7**he became angry[f] with them. He sold them[g]
into the hands of the Philistines
and the Ammonites, **8**who that year
shattered and crushed them. For
eighteen years they oppressed all
the Israelites on the east side of the
Jordan in Gilead, the land of the
Amorites. **9**The Ammonites also
crossed the Jordan to fight against
Judah, Benjamin and the house of
Ephraim; and Israel was in great
distress. **10**Then the Israelites cried
out to the LORD, "We have sinned
against you, forsaking our God and
serving the Baals."[h]

11The LORD replied, "When the
Egyptians,[i] the Amorites, the Ammonites,[j] the Philistines,[k] **12**the
Sidonians, the Amalekites and the
Maonites[p] oppressed you[l] and
you cried to me for help, did I not
save you from their hands? **13**But
you have forsaken me and served
other gods, so I will no longer save
you. **14**Go and cry out to the gods
you have chosen. Let them save
you when you are in trouble![m]"

15But the Israelites said to the
LORD, "We have sinned. Do with us
whatever you think best,[n] but
please rescue us now." **16**Then they
got rid of the foreign gods among
them and served the LORD.[o] And he
could bear Israel's misery[p] no
longer.[q]

17When the Ammonites were
called to arms and camped in Gilead, the Israelites assembled and
camped at Mizpah.[r] **18**The leaders
of the people of Gilead said to each

10:4 [a]Nu 32:41
10:6 [b]Jdg 2:11 [c]Jdg 2:13 [d]Jdg 2:12 [e]Dt 32:15
10:7 [f]Dt 31:17 [g]Dt 32:30; Jdg 2:14; 1Sa 12:9
10:10 [h]1Sa 12:10
10:11 [i]Ex 14:30 [j]Nu 21:21; Jdg 3:13 [k]Jdg 3:31
10:12 [l]Ps 106:42
10:14 [m]Dt 32:37
10:15 [n]1Sa 3:18; 2Sa 15:26
10:16 [o]Jos 24:23; Jer 18:8 [p]Isa 63:9 [q]Dt 32:36; Ps 106:44-45
10:17 [r]Ge 31:49; Jdg 11:29
10:18 [s]Jdg 11:8,9
11:1 [t]Heb 11:32 [u]Jdg 6:12
11:3 [v]2Sa 10:6,8 [w]Jdg 9:4
11:4 [x]Jdg 10:9
11:7 [y]Ge 26:27
11:8 [z]Jdg 10:18
11:10 [a]Ge 31:50; Jer 42:5
11:11 [b]Jos 11:3; Jdg 10:17; 20:1; 1Sa 10:17

other, "Whoever will launch the attack against the Ammonites will be
the head[s] of all those living in Gilead."

11 Jephthah[t] the Gileadite
was a mighty warrior.[u] His
father was Gilead; his mother was a
prostitute. **2**Gilead's wife also bore
him sons, and when they were
grown up, they drove Jephthah
away. "You are not going to get any
inheritance in our family," they
said, "because you are the son of
another woman." **3**So Jephthah
fled from his brothers and settled
in the land of Tob,[v] where a group
of adventurers[w] gathered around
him and followed him.

4Some time later, when the Ammonites[x] made war on Israel, **5**the
elders of Gilead went to get Jephthah from the land of Tob.
6"Come," they said, "be our commander, so we can fight the Ammonites."

7Jephthah said to them, "Didn't
you hate me and drive me from my
father's house?[y] Why do you come
to me now, when you're in trouble?"

8The elders of Gilead said to
him, "Nevertheless, we are turning
to you now; come with us to fight
the Ammonites, and you will be
our head[z] over all who live in Gilead."

9Jephthah answered, "Suppose
you take me back to fight the Ammonites and the LORD gives them to
me—will I really be your head?"

10The elders of Gilead replied,
"The LORD is our witness;[a] we will
certainly do as you say." **11**So Jephthah went with the elders of Gilead, and the people made him head
and commander over them. And he
repeated all his words before the
LORD in Mizpah.[b]

12Then Jephthah sent messengers to the Ammonite king with the
question: "What do you have
against us that you have attacked
our country?"

[o]4 *Or called the settlements of Jair*
[p]12 Hebrew; some Septuagint manuscripts *Midianites*

13The king of the Ammonites answered Jephthah's messengers, "When Israel came up out of Egypt, they took away my land from the Arnon to the Jabbok,[a] all the way to the Jordan. Now give it back peaceably."

14Jephthah sent back messengers to the Ammonite king, **15**saying:

"This is what Jephthah says: Israel did not take the land of Moab[b] or the land of the Ammonites.[c] **16**But when they came up out of Egypt, Israel went through the desert to the Red Sea[q][d] and on to Kadesh.[e] **17**Then Israel sent messengers[f] to the king of Edom, saying, 'Give us permission to go through your country,'[g] but the king of Edom would not listen. They sent also to the king of Moab, and he refused.[h] So Israel stayed at Kadesh.

18"Next they traveled through the desert, skirted the lands of Edom[i] and Moab, passed along the eastern side[j] of the country of Moab, and camped on the other side of the Arnon.[k] They did not enter the territory of Moab, for the Arnon was its border.

19"Then Israel sent messengers to Sihon king of the Amorites, who ruled in Heshbon, and said to him, 'Let us pass through your country to our own place.'[l] **20**Sihon, however, did not trust Israel[r] to pass through his territory. He mustered all his men and encamped at Jahaz and fought with Israel.[m]

21"Then the LORD, the God of Israel, gave Sihon and all his men into Israel's hands, and they defeated them. Israel took over all the land of the Amorites who lived in that country, **22**capturing all of it from the Arnon to the Jabbok and from the desert to the Jordan.[n]

23"Now since the LORD, the God of Israel, has driven the Amorites out before his people Israel, what right have you to take it over? **24**Will you not take what your god Chemosh[o] gives you? Likewise, whatever the LORD our God has given us, we will possess. **25**Are you better than Balak son of Zippor,[p] king of Moab? Did he ever quarrel with Israel or fight with them?[q] **26**For three hundred years Israel occupied[r] Heshbon, Aroer, the surrounding settlements and all the towns along the Arnon. Why didn't you retake them during that time? **27**I have not wronged you, but you are doing me wrong by waging war against me. Let the LORD, the Judge,[s][s] decide[t] the dispute this day between the Israelites and the Ammonites."

28The king of Ammon, however, paid no attention to the message Jephthah sent him.

29Then the Spirit[u] of the LORD came upon Jephthah. He crossed Gilead and Manasseh, passed through Mizpah of Gilead, and from there he advanced against the Ammonites. **30**And Jephthah made a vow[v] to the LORD: "If you give the Ammonites into my hands, **31**whatever comes out of the door of my house to meet me when I return in triumph from the Ammonites will be the LORD's, and I will sacrifice it as a burnt offering."

32Then Jephthah went over to fight the Ammonites, and the LORD gave them into his hands. **33**He devastated twenty towns from Aroer to the vicinity of Minnith,[w] as far as Abel Keramim. Thus Israel subdued Ammon.

34When Jephthah returned to his home in Mizpah, who should come out to meet him but his daughter, dancing to the sound of tambourines![x] She was an only

11:13 [a]Ge 32:22; Nu 21:24
11:15 [b]Dt 2:9 [c]Dt 2:19
11:16 [d]Nu 14:25; Dt 1:40 [e]Nu 20:1
11:17 [f]Nu 20:14 [g]Nu 20:18,21 [h]Jos 24:9
11:18 [i]Nu 21:4 [j]Dt 2:8 [k]Nu 21:13
11:19 [l]Nu 21:21-22; Dt 2:26-27
11:20 [m]Nu 21:23; Dt 2:32
11:22 [n]Dt 2:36
11:24 [o]Nu 21:29; Jos 3:10; 1Ki 11:7
11:25 [p]Nu 22:2 [q]Jos 24:9
11:26 [r]Nu 21:25
11:27 [s]Ge 18:25 [t]Ge 16:5; 31:53; 1Sa 24:12,15
11:29 [u]Nu 11:25; Jdg 3:10; 6:34; 14:6,19; 15:14; 1Sa 11:6; 16:13; Isa 11:2
11:30 [v]Ge 28:20
11:33 [w]Eze 27:17
11:34 [x]Ex 15:20; Jer 31:4

[q]*16* Hebrew *Yam Suph*; that is, Sea of Reeds
[r]*20* Or *however, would not make an agreement for Israel*
[s]*27* Or *Ruler*

child. Except for her he had neither son nor daughter. 35When he saw her, he tore his clothes and cried, "Oh! My daughter! You have made me miserable and wretched, because I have made a vow to the LORD that I cannot break.[a]"

36"My father," she replied, "you have given your word to the LORD. Do to me just as you promised,[b] now that the LORD has avenged you of your enemies,[c] the Ammonites. 37But grant me this one request," she said. "Give me two months to roam the hills and weep with my friends, because I will never marry."

38"You may go," he said. And he let her go for two months. She and the girls went into the hills and wept because she would never marry. 39After the two months, she returned to her father and he did to her as he had vowed. And she was a virgin.

From this comes the Israelite custom 40that each year the young women of Israel go out for four days to commemorate the daughter of Jephthah the Gileadite.

Jephthah and Ephraim

12 The men of Ephraim called out their forces, crossed over to Zaphon and said to Jephthah, "Why did you go to fight the Ammonites without calling us to go with you?[d] We're going to burn down your house over your head."

2Jephthah answered, "I and my people were engaged in a great struggle with the Ammonites, and although I called, you didn't save me out of their hands. 3When I saw that you wouldn't help, I took my life in my hands[e] and crossed over to fight the Ammonites, and the LORD gave me the victory over them. Now why have you come up today to fight me?"

4Jephthah then called together the men of Gilead and fought against Ephraim. The Gileadites struck them down because the Ephraimites had said, "You Gileadites are renegades from Ephraim and Manasseh." 5The Gileadites captured the fords of the Jordan[f] leading to Ephraim, and whenever a survivor of Ephraim said, "Let me cross over," the men of Gilead asked him, "Are you an Ephraimite?" If he replied, "No," 6they said, "All right, say 'Shibboleth.' " If he said, "Sibboleth," because he could not pronounce the word correctly, they seized him and killed him at the fords of the Jordan. Forty-two thousand Ephraimites were killed at that time.

7Jephthah led[t] Israel six years. Then Jephthah the Gileadite died, and was buried in a town in Gilead.

Ibzan, Elon and Abdon

8After him, Ibzan of Bethlehem led Israel. 9He had thirty sons and thirty daughters. He gave his daughters away in marriage to those outside his clan, and for his sons he brought in thirty young women as wives from outside his clan. Ibzan led Israel seven years. 10Then Ibzan died, and was buried in Bethlehem.

11After him, Elon the Zebulunite led Israel ten years. 12Then Elon died, and was buried in Aijalon in the land of Zebulun.

13After him, Abdon son of Hillel, from Pirathon, led Israel. 14He had forty sons and thirty grandsons,[g] who rode on seventy donkeys.[h] He led Israel eight years. 15Then Abdon son of Hillel died, and was buried at Pirathon in Ephraim, in the hill country of the Amalekites.[i]

The Birth of Samson

13 Again the Israelites did evil in the eyes of the LORD, so the LORD delivered them into the hands of the Philistines[j] for forty years.

2A certain man of Zorah,[k] named Manoah, from the clan of the Danites, had a wife who was sterile and remained childless. 3The angel of the LORD[l] appeared to her[m] and said, "You are sterile and childless, but you are going to conceive and have a son.[n] 4Now

11:35 [a]Nu 30:2; Ecc 5:2,4,5
11:36 [b]Lk 1:38 [c]2Sa 18:19
12:1 [d]Jdg 8:1
12:3 [e]1Sa 19:5; 28:21; Job 13:14
12:5 [f]Jos 22:11; Jdg 3:28
12:14 [g]Jdg 10:4 [h]Jdg 5:10
12:15 [i]Jdg 5:14
13:1 [j]Jdg 2:11; 1Sa 12:9
13:2 [k]Jos 15:33; 19:41
13:3 [l]ver 6,8; Jdg 6:12 [m]ver 10 [n]Lk 1:13

[t]7 Traditionally *judged*; also in verses 8-14

see to it that you drink no wine or other fermented drink and that you do not eat anything unclean,[a] 5because you will conceive and give birth to a son. No razor[b] may be used on his head, because the boy is to be a Nazirite,[c] set apart to God from birth, and he will begin[d] the deliverance of Israel from the hands of the Philistines."

6Then the woman went to her husband and told him, "A man of God[e] came to me. He looked like an angel of God,[f] very awesome. I didn't ask him where he came from, and he didn't tell me his name. 7But he said to me, 'You will conceive and give birth to a son. Now then, drink no wine or other fermented drink and do not eat anything unclean, because the boy will be a Nazirite of God from birth until the day of his death.' "

8Then Manoah prayed to the LORD: "O Lord, I beg you, let the man of God you sent to us come again to teach us how to bring up the boy who is to be born."

9God heard Manoah, and the angel of God came again to the woman while she was out in the field; but her husband Manoah was not with her. 10The woman hurried to tell her husband, "He's here! The man who appeared to me the other day!"

11Manoah got up and followed his wife. When he came to the man, he said, "Are you the one who talked to my wife?"

"I am," he said.

12So Manoah asked him, "When your words are fulfilled, what is to be the rule for the boy's life and work?"

13The angel of the LORD answered, "Your wife must do all that I have told her. 14She must not eat anything that comes from the grapevine, nor drink any wine or other fermented drink[g] nor eat anything unclean.[h] She must do everything I have commanded her."

15Manoah said to the angel of the LORD, "We would like you to stay until we prepare a young goat[i] for you."

16The angel of the LORD replied, "Even though you detain me, I will not eat any of your food. But if you prepare a burnt offering,[j] offer it to the LORD." (Manoah did not realize that it was the angel of the LORD.)

17Then Manoah inquired of the angel of the LORD, "What is your name,[k] so that we may honor you when your word comes true?"

18He replied, "Why do you ask my name?[l] It is beyond understanding.[u]" 19Then Manoah took a young goat, together with the grain offering, and sacrificed it on a rock[m] to the LORD. And the LORD did an amazing thing while Manoah and his wife watched: 20As the flame[n] blazed up from the altar toward heaven, the angel of the LORD ascended in the flame. Seeing this, Manoah and his wife fell with their faces to the ground.[o] 21When the angel of the LORD did not show himself again to Manoah and his wife, Manoah realized[p] that it was the angel of the LORD.

22"We are doomed[q] to die!" he said to his wife. "We have seen[r] God!"

23But his wife answered, "If the LORD had meant to kill us, he would not have accepted a burnt offering and grain offering from our hands, nor shown us all these things or now told us this."[s]

24The woman gave birth to a boy and named him Samson.[t] He grew[u] and the LORD blessed him,[v] 25and the Spirit of the LORD began to stir[w] him while he was in Mahaneh Dan,[x] between Zorah and Eshtaol.

Samson's Marriage

14 Samson went down to Timnah[y] and saw there a young Philistine woman. 2When he returned, he said to his father and mother, "I have seen a Philistine woman in Timnah; now get her for me as my wife."[z]

13:4 [a]ver 14; Nu 6:2-4; Lk 1:15
13:5 [b]Nu 6:5; 1Sa 1:11 [c]Nu 6:2,13 [d]1Sa 7:13
13:6 [e]ver 8; 1Sa 2:27; 9:6 [f]ver 17-18; Mt 28:3
13:14 [g]Nu 6:4 [h]ver 4
13:15 [i]ver 3; Jdg 6:19
13:16 [j]Jdg 6:20
13:17 [k]Ge 32:29
13:18 [l]Isa 9:6
13:19 [m]Jdg 6:20
13:20 [n]Lev 9:24 [o]1Ch 21:16; Eze 1:28; Mt 17:6
13:21 [p]ver 16; Jdg 6:22
13:22 [q]Dt 5:26 [r]Ge 32:30; Jdg 6:22
13:23 [s]Ps 25:14
13:24 [t]Heb 11:32 [u]1Sa 3:19 [v]Lk 1:80
13:25 [w]Jdg 3:10 [x]Jdg 18:12
14:1 [y]Ge 38:12
14:2 [z]Ge 21:21; 34:4

[u]18 Or *is wonderful*

3His father and mother replied, "Isn't there an acceptable woman among your relatives or among all our people?[a] Must you go to the uncircumcised[b] Philistines to get a wife?[c]"

But Samson said to his father, "Get her for me. She's the right one for me." 4(His parents did not know that this was from the LORD, who was seeking an occasion to confront the Philistines;[d] for at that time they were ruling over Israel.)[e] 5Samson went down to Timnah together with his father and mother. As they approached the vineyards of Timnah, suddenly a young lion came roaring toward him. 6The Spirit of the LORD came upon him in power[f] so that he tore the lion apart with his bare hands as he might have torn a young goat. But he told neither his father nor his mother what he had done. 7Then he went down and talked with the woman, and he liked her.

8Some time later, when he went back to marry her, he turned aside to look at the lion's carcass. In it was a swarm of bees and some honey, 9which he scooped out with his hands and ate as he went along. When he rejoined his parents, he gave them some, and they too ate it. But he did not tell them that he had taken the honey from the lion's carcass.

10Now his father went down to see the woman. And Samson made a feast there, as was customary for bridegrooms. 11When he appeared, he was given thirty companions.

12"Let me tell you a riddle,[g]" Samson said to them. "If you can give me the answer within the seven days of the feast,[h] I will give you thirty linen garments and thirty sets of clothes.[i] 13If you can't tell me the answer, you must give me thirty linen garments and thirty sets of clothes."

"Tell us your riddle," they said. "Let's hear it."

14He replied,

"Out of the eater, something to eat;
out of the strong, something sweet."

For three days they could not give the answer.

15On the fourth[v] day, they said to Samson's wife, "Coax[j] your husband into explaining the riddle for us, or we will burn you and your father's household to death.[k] Did you invite us here to rob us?"

16Then Samson's wife threw herself on him, sobbing, "You hate me! You don't really love me.[l] You've given my people a riddle, but you haven't told me the answer."

"I haven't even explained it to my father or mother," he replied, "so why should I explain it to you?" 17She cried the whole seven days[m] of the feast. So on the seventh day he finally told her, because she continued to press him. She in turn explained the riddle to her people.

18Before sunset on the seventh day the men of the town said to him,

"What is sweeter than honey?
What is stronger than a lion?"[n]

Samson said to them,

"If you had not plowed with my heifer,
you would not have solved my riddle."

19Then the Spirit of the LORD came upon him in power.[o] He went down to Ashkelon, struck down thirty of their men, stripped them of their belongings and gave their clothes to those who had explained the riddle. Burning with anger,[p] he went up to his father's house. 20And Samson's wife was given to the friend[q] who had attended him at his wedding.

Samson's Vengeance on the Philistines

15 Later on, at the time of wheat harvest, Samson took a young goat[r] and went to vis-

14:3 [a]Ge 24:4 [b]Dt 7:3 [c]Ex 34:16
14:4 [d]Jos 11:20 [e]Jdg 13:1
14:6 [f]Jdg 3:10; 13:25
14:12 [g]1Ki 10:1; Eze 17:2 [h]Ge 29:27 [i]Ge 45:22; 2Ki 5:5
14:15 [j]Jdg 16:5; Ecc 7:26 [k]Jdg 15:6
14:16 [l]Jdg 16:15
14:17 [m]Est 1:5
14:18 [n]ver 14
14:19 [o]Nu 11:25; Jdg 3:10; 6:34; 11:29; 13:25; 15:14; 1Sa 11:6; 16:13; 1Ki 18:46; 2Ch 24:20; Isa 11:2 [p]1Sa 11:6
14:20 [q]Jdg 15:2,6; Jn 3:29
15:1 [r]Ge 38:17

[v]*15* Some Septuagint manuscripts and Syriac; Hebrew *seventh*

it his wife. He said, "I'm going to my wife's room." But her father would not let him go in.

2"I was so sure you thoroughly hated her," he said, "that I gave her to your friend.[a] Isn't her younger sister more attractive? Take her instead."

3Samson said to them, "This time I have a right to get even with the Philistines; I will really harm them." 4So he went out and caught three hundred foxes and tied them tail to tail in pairs. He then fastened a torch to every pair of tails, 5lit the torches and let the foxes loose in the standing grain of the Philistines. He burned up the shocks and standing grain, together with the vineyards and olive groves.

6When the Philistines asked, "Who did this?" they were told, "Samson, the Timnite's son-in-law, because his wife was given to his friend."

So the Philistines went up and burned her and her father to death.[b] 7Samson said to them, "Since you've acted like this, I won't stop until I get my revenge on you." 8He attacked them viciously and slaughtered many of them. Then he went down and stayed in a cave in the rock of Etam.

9The Philistines went up and camped in Judah, spreading out near Lehi.[c] 10The men of Judah asked, "Why have you come to fight us?"

"We have come to take Samson prisoner," they answered, "to do to him as he did to us."

11Then three thousand men from Judah went down to the cave in the rock of Etam and said to Samson, "Don't you realize that the Philistines are rulers over us?[d] What have you done to us?"

He answered, "I merely did to them what they did to me."

12They said to him, "We've come to tie you up and hand you over to the Philistines."

Samson said, "Swear to me that you won't kill me yourselves."

13"Agreed," they answered. "We will only tie you up and hand you over to them. We will not kill you." So they bound him with two new ropes and led him up from the rock. 14As he approached Lehi, the Philistines came toward him shouting. The Spirit of the LORD came upon him in power.[e] The ropes on his arms became like charred flax, and the bindings dropped from his hands. 15Finding a fresh jawbone of a donkey, he grabbed it and struck down a thousand men.[f]

16Then Samson said,

"With a donkey's jawbone
  I have made donkeys of
    them.[w]
With a donkey's jawbone
  I have killed a thousand
    men."

17When he finished speaking, he threw away the jawbone; and the place was called Ramath Lehi.[x]

18Because he was very thirsty, he cried out to the LORD,[g] "You have given your servant this great victory. Must I now die of thirst and fall into the hands of the uncircumcised?" 19Then God opened up the hollow place in Lehi, and water came out of it. When Samson drank, his strength returned and he revived.[h] So the spring was called En Hakkore,[y] and it is still there in Lehi.

20Samson led[z] Israel for twenty years[i] in the days of the Philistines.

Samson and Delilah

16 One day Samson went to Gaza, where he saw a prostitute. He went in to spend the night with her. 2The people of Gaza were told, "Samson is here!" So they surrounded the place and lay in wait for him all night at the city gate.[j] They made no move during the night, saying, "At dawn we'll kill him."

15:2 [a] Jdg 14:20
15:6 [b] Jdg 14:15
15:9 [c] ver 14,17,19
15:11 [d] Jdg 13:1; 14:4; Ps 106:40-42
15:14 [e] Jdg 3:10; 14:19; 1Sa 11:6
15:15 [f] Lev 26:8; Jos 23:10; Jdg 3:31
15:18 [g] Jdg 16:28
15:19 [h] Ge 45:27; Isa 40:29
15:20 [i] Jdg 13:1; 16:31; Heb 11:32
16:2 [j] 1Sa 23:26; Ps 118:10-12; Ac 9:24

[w] *16* Or *made a heap or two*; the Hebrew for *donkey* sounds like the Hebrew for *heap.*
[x] *17 Ramath Lehi* means *jawbone hill.*
[y] *19 En Hakkore* means *caller's spring.*
[z] *20* Traditionally *judged*

3But Samson lay there only until the middle of the night. Then he got up and took hold of the doors of the city gate, together with the two posts, and tore them loose, bar and all. He lifted them to his shoulders and carried them to the top of the hill that faces Hebron.[a]

4Some time later, he fell in love[b] with a woman in the Valley of Sorek whose name was Delilah. 5The rulers of the Philistines[c] went to her and said, "See if you can lure[d] him into showing you the secret of his great strength and how we can overpower him so we may tie him up and subdue him. Each one of us will give you eleven hundred shekels[a] of silver."[e]

6So Delilah said to Samson, "Tell me the secret of your great strength and how you can be tied up and subdued."

7Samson answered her, "If anyone ties me with seven fresh thongs[b] that have not been dried, I'll become as weak as any other man."

8Then the rulers of the Philistines brought her seven fresh thongs that had not been dried, and she tied him with them. 9With men hidden in the room,[f] she called to him, "Samson, the Philistines are upon you!" But he snapped the thongs as easily as a piece of string snaps when it comes close to a flame. So the secret of his strength was not discovered.

10Then Delilah said to Samson, "You have made a fool of me;[g] you lied to me. Come now, tell me how you can be tied."

11He said, "If anyone ties me securely with new ropes[h] that have never been used, I'll become as weak as any other man."

12So Delilah took new ropes and tied him with them. Then, with men hidden in the room, she called to him, "Samson, the Philistines are upon you!" But he snapped the ropes off his arms as if they were threads.

13Delilah then said to Samson, "Until now, you have been making a fool of me and lying to me. Tell me how you can be tied."

He replied, "If you weave the seven braids of my head into the fabric ⌞on the loom⌟ and tighten it with the pin, I'll become as weak as any other man." So while he was sleeping, Delilah took the seven braids of his head, wove them into the fabric 14and[c] tightened it with the pin.

Again she called to him, "Samson, the Philistines are upon you!"[i] He awoke from his sleep and pulled up the pin and the loom, with the fabric.

15Then she said to him, "How can you say, 'I love you,'[j] when you won't confide in me? This is the third time[k] you have made a fool of me and haven't told me the secret of your great strength.[l]" 16With such nagging she prodded him day after day until he was tired to death.

17So he told her everything.[m] "No razor has ever been used on my head," he said, "because I have been a Nazirite[n] set apart to God since birth. If my head were shaved, my strength would leave me, and I would become as weak as any other man."

18When Delilah saw that he had told her everything, she sent word to the rulers of the Philistines[o], "Come back once more; he has told me everything." So the rulers of the Philistines returned with the silver in their hands. 19Having put him to sleep on her lap, she called a man to shave off the seven braids of his hair, and so began to subdue him.[d] And his strength left him.[p]

20Then she called, "Samson, the Philistines are upon you!"

He awoke from his sleep and thought, "I'll go out as before and shake myself free." But he did not know that the LORD had left him.[q]

16:3 [a]Jos 10:36
16:4 [b]Ge 24:67
16:5 [c]Jos 13:3 [d]Ex 10:7; Jdg 14:15 [e]ver 18
16:9 [f]ver 12
16:10 [g]ver 13
16:11 [h]Jdg 15:13
16:14 [i]ver 9,20
16:15 [j]Jdg 14:16 [k]Nu 24:10 [l]ver 5
16:17 [m]Mic 7:5 [n]Nu 6:2,5; Jdg 13:5
16:18 [o]Jos 13:3; 1Sa 5:8
16:19 [p]Pr 7:26-27
16:20 [q]Nu 14:42; Jos 7:12; 1Sa 16:14; 18:12; 28:15

[a]5 That is, about 28 pounds (about 13 kilograms) [b]7 Or *bowstrings*; also in verses 8 and 9 [c]*13,14* Some Septuagint manuscripts; Hebrew *"I can⌞ if you weave the seven braids of my head into the fabric ⌞on the loom⌟." 14So she* [d]*19* Hebrew; some Septuagint manuscripts *and he began to weaken*

21Then the Philistines[a] seized
him, gouged out his eyes[b] and
took him down to Gaza. Binding
him with bronze shackles, they set
him to grinding[c] in the prison.
22But the hair on his head began to
grow again after it had been
shaved.

The Death of Samson

23Now the rulers of the Philistines assembled to offer a great
sacrifice to Dagon[d] their god and
to celebrate, saying, "Our god has
delivered Samson, our enemy, into
our hands."
24When the people saw him,
they praised their god,[e] saying,

"Our god has delivered our
enemy
into our hands,[f]
the one who laid waste our
land
and multiplied our slain."

25While they were in high spirits,[g] they shouted, "Bring out
Samson to entertain us." So they
called Samson out of the prison,
and he performed for them.
When they stood him among the
pillars, **26**Samson said to the servant who held his hand, "Put me
where I can feel the pillars that
support the temple, so that I may
lean against them." **27**Now the
temple was crowded with men and
women; all the rulers of the Philistines were there, and on the roof[h]
were about three thousand men
and women watching Samson perform. **28**Then Samson prayed to the
LORD,[i] "O Sovereign LORD, remember me. O God, please strengthen
me just once more, and let me with
one blow get revenge[j] on the Philistines for my two eyes." **29**Then
Samson reached toward the two
central pillars on which the temple
stood. Bracing himself against
them, his right hand on the one
and his left hand on the other,
30Samson said, "Let me die with
the Philistines!" Then he pushed
with all his might, and down came
the temple on the rulers and all the
people in it. Thus he killed many
more when he died than while he
lived.
31Then his brothers and his father's whole family went down to
get him. They brought him back
and buried him between Zorah and
Eshtaol in the tomb of Manoah[k]
his father. He had led[e][l] Israel
twenty years.[m]

Micah's Idols

17 Now a man named Micah[n]
from the hill country of
Ephraim **2**said to his mother, "The
eleven hundred shekels[f] of silver
that were taken from you and
about which I heard you utter a
curse—I have that silver with me; I
took it."
Then his mother said, "The LORD
bless you,[o] my son!"
3When he returned the eleven
hundred shekels of silver to his
mother, she said, "I solemnly consecrate my silver to the LORD for my
son to make a carved image and a
cast idol.[p] I will give it back to
you."
4So he returned the silver to his
mother, and she took two hundred
shekels[g] of silver and gave them to
a silversmith, who made them into
the image and the idol.[q] And they
were put in Micah's house.
5Now this man Micah had a
shrine,[r] and he made an ephod[s]
and some idols[t] and installed[u]
one of his sons as his priest.[v] **6**In
those days Israel had no king;[w] everyone did as he saw fit.[x]
7A young Levite from Bethlehem
in Judah,[y] who had been living
within the clan of Judah, **8**left that
town in search of some other place
to stay. On his way[h] he came to
Micah's house in the hill country of
Ephraim.
9Micah asked him, "Where are
you from?"
"I'm a Levite from Bethlehem in
Judah," he said, "and I'm looking
for a place to stay."
10Then Micah said to him, "Live

16:21 [a]Jer 47:1 [b]Nu 16:14 [c]Job 31:10; Isa 47:2
16:23 [d]1Sa 5:2; 1Ch 10:10
16:24 [e]Da 5:4 [f]1Sa 31:9; 1Ch 10:9
16:25 [g]Jdg 9:27; Ru 3:7; Est 1:10
16:27 [h]Dt 22:8; Jos 2:8
16:28 [i]Jdg 15:18 [j]Jer 15:15
16:31 [k]Jdg 13:2 [l]Ru 1:1; 1Sa 4:18 [m]Jdg 15:20
17:1 [n]Jdg 18:2,13
17:2 [o]Ru 2:20; 1Sa 15:13; 2Sa 2:5
17:3 [p]Ex 20:4,23; 34:17; Lev 19:4
17:4 [q]Ex 32:4; Isa 17:8
17:5 [r]Isa 44:13; Eze 8:10 [s]Jdg 8:27 [t]Ge 31:19; Jdg 18:14 [u]Nu 16:10 [v]Ex 29:9; Jdg 18:24
17:6 [w]Jdg 18:1; 19:1; 21:25 [x]Dt 12:8
17:7 [y]Jdg 19:1; Ru 1:1-2; Mic 5:2; Mt 2:1

e*31* Traditionally *judged* f*2* That is, about 28 pounds (about 13 kilograms) g*4* That is, about 5 pounds (about 2.3 kilograms)
h*8* Or *To carry on his profession*

with me and be my father and
priest,[a] and I'll give you ten shekels[i] of silver a year, your clothes
and your food." **11**So the Levite
agreed to live with him, and the
young man was to him like one of
his sons. **12**Then Micah installed[b]
the Levite, and the young man became his priest and lived in his
house. **13**And Micah said, "Now I
know that the LORD will be good to
me, since this Levite has become
my priest."

Danites Settle in Laish

18 In those days Israel had no
king.[c]
And in those days the tribe of the
Danites was seeking a place of
their own where they might settle,
because they had not yet come into
an inheritance among the tribes of
Israel.[d] **2**So the Danites[e] sent five
warriors from Zorah and Eshtaol to
spy out the land and explore it.
These men represented all their
clans. They told them, "Go, explore the land."[f]
The men entered the hill country
of Ephraim and came to the house
of Micah,[g] where they spent the
night. **3**When they were near Micah's house, they recognized the
voice of the young Levite; so they
turned in there and asked him,
"Who brought you here? What are
you doing in this place? Why are
you here?"
4He told them what Micah had
done for him, and said, "He has
hired me and I am his priest.[h]"
5Then they said to him, "Please
inquire of God[i] to learn whether
our journey will be successful."
6The priest answered them, "Go
in peace[j]. Your journey has the
LORD's approval."
7So the five men left and came to
Laish,[k] where they saw that the
people were living in safety, like
the Sidonians, unsuspecting and
secure. And since their land lacked
nothing, they were prosperous.[j]
Also, they lived a long way from the
Sidonians[l] and had no relationship with anyone else.[k]
8When they returned to Zorah
and Eshtaol, their brothers asked
them, "How did you find things?"
9They answered, "Come on, let's
attack them! We have seen that the
land is very good. Aren't you going
to do something? Don't hesitate to
go there and take it over.[m] **10**When
you get there, you will find an unsuspecting people and a spacious
land that God has put into your
hands, a land that lacks nothing[n]
whatever.[o]"
11Then six hundred men[p] from
the clan of the Danites,[q] armed for
battle, set out from Zorah and Eshtaol. **12**On their way they set up
camp near Kiriath Jearim in Judah.
This is why the place west of Kiriath Jearim is called Mahaneh
Dan[l][r] to this day. **13**From there
they went on to the hill country of
Ephraim and came to Micah's
house.
14Then the five men who had
spied out the land of Laish said to
their brothers, "Do you know that
one of these houses has an ephod,
other household gods, a carved image and a cast idol?[s] Now you
know what to do." **15**So they turned
in there and went to the house of
the young Levite at Micah's place
and greeted him. **16**The six hundred Danites,[t] armed for battle,
stood at the entrance to the gate.
17The five men who had spied out
the land went inside and took the
carved image, the ephod, the other
household gods[u] and the cast idol
while the priest and the six hundred armed men stood at the entrance to the gate.
18When these men went into Micah's house and took[v] the carved
image, the ephod, the other household gods and the cast idol, the
priest said to them, "What are you
doing?"
19They answered him, "Be quiet![w] Don't say a word. Come with
us, and be our father and priest.[x]
Isn't it better that you serve a tribe

17:10 [a]Jdg 18:19
17:12 [b]Nu 16:10
18:1 [c]Jdg 17:6; 19:1 [d]Jos 19:47
18:2 [e]Jdg 13:25 [f]Jos 2:1 [g]Jdg 17:1
18:4 [h]Jdg 17:12
18:5 [i]1Ki 22:5
18:6 [j]1Ki 22:6
18:7 [k]Jos 19:47 [l]ver 28
18:9 [m]Nu 13:30; 1Ki 22:3
18:10 [n]ver 7,27; Dt 8:9 [o]1Ch 4:40
18:11 [p]ver 16,17 [q]Jdg 13:2
18:12 [r]Jdg 13:25
18:14 [s]Ge 31:19; Jdg 17:5
18:16 [t]ver 11
18:17 [u]Ge 31:19; Mic 5:13
18:18 [v]Isa 46:2; Jer 43:11; Hos 10:5
18:19 [w]Job 21:5; 29:9; 40:4; Mic 7:16 [x]Jdg 17:10

[i]*10* That is, about 4 ounces (about 110 grams)
[j]*7* The meaning of the Hebrew for this clause is uncertain. [k]*7* Hebrew; some Septuagint manuscripts *with the Arameans*
[l]*12* *Mahaneh Dan* means *Dan's camp.*

and clan in Israel as priest rather
than just one man's household?"
20Then the priest was glad. He took
the ephod, the other household
gods and the carved image and
went along with the people. **21**Putting their little children, their livestock and their possessions in front
of them, they turned away and
left.

22When they had gone some distance from Micah's house, the men
who lived near Micah were called
together and overtook the Danites.
23As they shouted after them, the
Danites turned and said to Micah,
"What's the matter with you that
you called out your men to fight?"

24He replied, "You took the gods
I made, and my priest, and went
away. What else do I have? How
can you ask, 'What's the matter
with you?' "

25The Danites answered, "Don't
argue with us, or some hot-tempered men will attack you, and you
and your family will lose your
lives." **26**So the Danites went their
way, and Micah, seeing that they
were too strong for him,[a] turned
around and went back home.

27Then they took what Micah
had made, and his priest, and went
on to Laish, against a peaceful and
unsuspecting people.[b] They attacked them with the sword and
burned down their city.[c] **28**There
was no one to rescue them because
they lived a long way from Sidon[d]
and had no relationship with anyone else. The city was in a valley
near Beth Rehob.[e]

The Danites rebuilt the city and
settled there. **29**They named it
Dan[f] after their forefather Dan,
who was born to Israel—though
the city used to be called Laish.[g]
30There the Danites set up for
themselves the idols, and Jonathan
son of Gershom,[h] the son of Moses,[m] and his sons were priests for
the tribe of Dan until the time of
the captivity of the land. **31**They
continued to use the idols Micah
had made, all the time the house of
God[i] was in Shiloh.[j]

18:26 [a]Ps 18:17; 35:10
18:27 [b]ver 7,10 [c]Ge 49:17; Jos 19:47
18:28 [d]ver 7 [e]Nu 13:21; 2Sa 10:6
18:29 [f]Ge 14:14 [g]Jos 19:47; 1Ki 15:20
18:30 [h]Ex 2:22; Jdg 17:3,5
18:31 [i]Jdg 19:18 [j]Jos 18:1; Jer 7:14
19:1 [k]Jdg 18:1 [l]Ru 1:1
19:4 [m]Ex 32:6
19:5 [n]ver 8; Ge 18:5
19:6 [o]ver 9,22; Jdg 16:25
19:10 [p]Ge 10:16; Jos 15:8; 1Ch 11:4-5

A Levite and His Concubine

19 In those days Israel had no
king.

Now a Levite who lived in a remote area in the hill country of
Ephraim[k] took a concubine from
Bethlehem in Judah.[l] **2**But she
was unfaithful to him. She left him
and went back to her father's
house in Bethlehem, Judah. After
she had been there four months,
3her husband went to her to persuade her to return. He had with
him his servant and two donkeys.
She took him into her father's
house, and when her father saw
him, he gladly welcomed him. **4**His
father-in-law, the girl's father, prevailed upon him to stay; so he remained with him three days, eating
and drinking,[m] and sleeping there.

5On the fourth day they got up
early and he prepared to leave, but
the girl's father said to his son-
in-law, "Refresh yourself[n] with
something to eat; then you can go."
6So the two of them sat down to eat
and drink together. Afterward the
girl's father said, "Please stay tonight and enjoy yourself.[o]" **7**And
when the man got up to go, his father-in-law persuaded him, so he
stayed there that night. **8**On the
morning of the fifth day, when he
rose to go, the girl's father said,
"Refresh yourself. Wait till afternoon!" So the two of them ate together.

9Then when the man, with his
concubine and his servant, got up
to leave, his father-in-law, the girl's
father, said, "Now look, it's almost
evening. Spend the night here; the
day is nearly over. Stay and enjoy
yourself. Early tomorrow morning
you can get up and be on your way
home." **10**But, unwilling to stay another night, the man left and went
toward Jebus[p] (that is, Jerusalem), with his two saddled donkeys
and his concubine.

11When they were near Jebus
and the day was almost gone, the

[m]*30* An ancient Hebrew scribal tradition, some Septuagint manuscripts and Vulgate; Masoretic Text *Manasseh*

servant said to his master, "Come, let's stop at this city of the Jebusites[a] and spend the night."

12His master replied, "No. We won't go into an alien city, whose people are not Israelites. We will go on to Gibeah." 13He added, "Come, let's try to reach Gibeah or Ramah[b] and spend the night in one of those places." 14So they went on, and the sun set as they neared Gibeah in Benjamin.[c] 15There they stopped to spend the night. They went and sat in the city square,[d] but no one took them into his home for the night.

16That evening[e] an old man from the hill country of Ephraim,[f] who was living in Gibeah (the men of the place were Benjamites), came in from his work in the fields. 17When he looked and saw the traveler in the city square, the old man asked, "Where are you going? Where did you come from?"[g]

18He answered, "We are on our way from Bethlehem in Judah to a remote area in the hill country of Ephraim where I live. I have been to Bethlehem in Judah and now I am going to the house of the LORD.[h] No one has taken me into his house. 19We have both straw and fodder[i] for our donkeys and bread and wine[j] for ourselves your servants—me, your maidservant, and the young man with us. We don't need anything."

20"You are welcome at my house," the old man said. "Let me supply whatever you need. Only don't spend the night in the square." 21So he took him into his house and fed his donkeys. After they had washed their feet, they had something to eat and drink.[k]

22While they were enjoying themselves,[l] some of the wicked men[m] of the city surrounded the house. Pounding on the door, they shouted to the old man who owned the house, "Bring out the man who came to your house so we can have sex with him.[n]"

23The owner of the house went outside[o] and said to them, "No, my friends, don't be so vile. Since this man is my guest, don't do this disgraceful thing.[p] 24Look, here is my virgin daughter,[q] and his concubine. I will bring them out to you now, and you can use them and do to them whatever you wish. But to this man, don't do such a disgraceful thing."

25But the men would not listen to him. So the man took his concubine and sent her outside to them, and they raped her and abused her[r] throughout the night, and at dawn they let her go. 26At daybreak the woman went back to the house where her master was staying, fell down at the door and lay there until daylight.

27When her master got up in the morning and opened the door of the house and stepped out to continue on his way, there lay his concubine, fallen in the doorway of the house, with her hands on the threshold. 28He said to her, "Get up; let's go." But there was no answer. Then the man put her on his donkey and set out for home.

29When he reached home, he took a knife[s] and cut up his concubine, limb by limb, into twelve parts and sent them into all the areas of Israel.[t] 30Everyone who saw it said, "Such a thing has never been seen or done, not since the day the Israelites came up out of Egypt.[u] Think about it! Consider it! Tell us what to do![v]"

Israelites Fight the Benjamites

20 Then all the Israelites[w] from Dan to Beersheba[x] and from the land of Gilead came out as one man[y] and assembled[z] before the LORD in Mizpah. 2The leaders of all the people of the tribes of Israel took their places in the assembly of the people of God, four hundred thousand soldiers[a] armed with swords. 3(The Benjamites heard that the Israelites had gone up to Mizpah.) Then the Israelites said, "Tell us how this awful thing happened."

4So the Levite, the husband of the murdered woman, said, "I and my concubine came to Gibeah[b] in

19:11 [a]Jos 3:10
19:13 [b]Jos 18:25
19:14 [c]1Sa 10:26; Isa 10:29
19:15 [d]Ge 19:2
19:16 [e]Ps 104:23 [f]ver 1
19:17 [g]Ge 29:4
19:18 [h]Jdg 18:31
19:19 [i]Ge 24:25 [j]Ge 14:18
19:21 [k]Ge 24:32-33; Lk 7:44
19:22 [l]Jdg 16:25 [m]Dt 13:13 [n]Ge 19:4-5; Jdg 20:5; Ro 1:26-27
19:23 [o]Ge 19:6 [p]Ge 34:7; Lev 19:29; Dt 22:21; Jdg 20:6; 2Sa 13:12; Ro 1:27
19:24 [q]Ge 19:8; Dt 21:14
19:25 [r]1Sa 31:4
19:29 [s]Ge 22:6 [t]Jdg 20:6; 1Sa 11:7
19:30 [u]Hos 9:9 [v]Jdg 20:7; Pr 13:10
20:1 [w]Jdg 21:5 [x]1Sa 3:20; 2Sa 3:10; 1Ki 4:25 [y]1Sa 11:7 [z]1Sa 7:5
20:2 [a]Jdg 8:10
20:4 [b]Jos 15:57

Benjamin to spend the night.[a]
5During the night the men of Gibeah came after me and surrounded
the house, intending to kill me.[b]
They raped my concubine, and she
died.[c] **6**I took my concubine, cut
her into pieces and sent one piece
to each region of Israel's inheritance,[d] because they committed
this lewd and disgraceful act[e] in
Israel. **7**Now, all you Israelites,
speak up and give your verdict.[f]"

8All the people rose as one man,
saying, "None of us will go home.
No, not one of us will return to his
house. **9**But now this is what we'll
do to Gibeah: We'll go up against it
as the lot directs.[g] **10**We'll take ten
men out of every hundred from all
the tribes of Israel, and a hundred
from a thousand, and a thousand
from ten thousand, to get provisions for the army. Then, when the
army arrives at Gibeah[n] in Benjamin, it can give them what they deserve for all this vileness done in
Israel." **11**So all the men of Israel
got together and united as one
man[h] against the city.

12The tribes of Israel sent men
throughout the tribe of Benjamin,
saying, "What about this awful
crime that was committed among
you? **13**Now surrender those wicked men[i] of Gibeah so that we may
put them to death and purge the
evil from Israel.[j]"

But the Benjamites would not
listen to their fellow Israelites.
14From their towns they came together at Gibeah to fight against
the Israelites. **15**At once the Benjamites mobilized twenty-six thousand swordsmen from their towns,
in addition to seven hundred chosen men from those living in Gibeah. **16**Among all these soldiers
there were seven hundred chosen
men who were left-handed,[k] each
of whom could sling a stone at a
hair and not miss.

17Israel, apart from Benjamin,
mustered four hundred thousand
swordsmen, all of them fighting
men.

18The Israelites went up to Bethel[o] and inquired of God.[l] They
said, "Who of us shall go first to
fight[m] against the Benjamites?"

The LORD replied, "Judah shall
go first."

19The next morning the Israelites got up and pitched camp near
Gibeah. **20**The men of Israel went
out to fight the Benjamites and
took up battle positions against
them at Gibeah. **21**The Benjamites
came out of Gibeah and cut down
twenty-two thousand Israelites[n]
on the battlefield that day. **22**But
the men of Israel encouraged one
another and again took up their positions where they had stationed
themselves the first day. **23**The Israelites went up and wept before
the LORD until evening,[o] and they
inquired of the LORD. They said,
"Shall we go up again to battle[p]
against the Benjamites, our brothers?"

The LORD answered, "Go up
against them."

24Then the Israelites drew near
to Benjamin the second day. **25**This
time, when the Benjamites came
out from Gibeah to oppose them,
they cut down another eighteen
thousand Israelites,[q] all of them
armed with swords.

26Then the Israelites, all the
people, went up to Bethel, and
there they sat weeping before the
LORD.[r] They fasted that day until
evening and presented burnt offerings and fellowship offerings[p] to
the LORD.[s] **27**And the Israelites inquired of the LORD. (In those days
the ark of the covenant of God[t]
was there, **28**with Phinehas son of
Eleazar,[u] the son of Aaron, ministering before it.)[v] They asked,
"Shall we go up again to battle with
Benjamin our brother, or not?"

The LORD responded, "Go, for tomorrow I will give them into your
hands.[w]"

29Then Israel set an ambush[x]
around Gibeah. **30**They went up
against the Benjamites on the third
day and took up positions against

20:4 [a]Jdg 19:15
20:5 [b]Jdg 19:22 [c]Jdg 19:25-26
20:6 [d]Jdg 19:29 [e]Jos 7:15; Jdg 19:23
20:7 [f]Jdg 19:30
20:9 [g]Lev 16:8
20:11 [h]ver 1
20:13 [i]Dt 13:13; Jdg 19:22 [j]Dt 17:12
20:16 [k]Jdg 3:15; 1Ch 12:2
20:18 [l]ver 26-27; Nu 27:21 [m]ver 23,28
20:21 [n]ver 25
20:23 [o]Jos 7:6 [p]ver 18
20:25 [q]ver 21
20:26 [r]ver 23 [s]Jdg 21:4
20:27 [t]Jos 18:1
20:28 [u]Jos 24:33 [v]Dt 18:5 [w]Jdg 7:9
20:29 [x]Jos 8:2,4

[n]*10* One Hebrew manuscript; most Hebrew manuscripts *Geba,* a variant of *Gibeah*
[o]*18* Or *to the house of God*; also in verse 26
[p]*26* Traditionally *peace offerings*

Gibeah as they had done before. 31The Benjamites came out to meet them and were drawn away[a] from the city. They began to inflict casualties on the Israelites as before, so that about thirty men fell in the open field and on the roads—the one leading to Bethel and the other to Gibeah.

32While the Benjamites were saying, "We are defeating them as before,"[b] the Israelites were saying, "Let's retreat and draw them away from the city to the roads."

33All the men of Israel moved from their places and took up positions at Baal Tamar, and the Israelite ambush charged out of its place[c] on the west[q] of Gibeah.[r] 34Then ten thousand of Israel's finest men made a frontal attack on Gibeah. The fighting was so heavy that the Benjamites did not realize[d] how near disaster was.[e] 35The LORD defeated Benjamin[f] before Israel, and on that day the Israelites struck down 25,100 Benjamites, all armed with swords. 36Then the Benjamites saw that they were beaten.

Now the men of Israel had given way[g] before Benjamin, because they relied on the ambush they had set near Gibeah. 37The men who had been in ambush made a sudden dash into Gibeah, spread out and put the whole city to the sword.[h] 38The men of Israel had arranged with the ambush that they should send up a great cloud of smoke[i] from the city, 39and then the men of Israel would turn in the battle.

The Benjamites had begun to inflict casualties on the men of Israel (about thirty), and they said, "We are defeating them as in the first battle."[j] 40But when the column of smoke began to rise from the city, the Benjamites turned and saw the smoke of the whole city going up into the sky.[k] 41Then the men of Israel turned on them, and the men of Benjamin were terrified, because they realized that disaster had come upon them. 42So they fled before the Israelites in the direction of the desert, but they could not escape the battle. And the men of Israel who came out of the towns cut them down there. 43They surrounded the Benjamites, chased them and easily[s] overran them in the vicinity of Gibeah on the east. 44Eighteen thousand Benjamites fell, all of them valiant fighters.[l] 45As they turned and fled toward the desert to the rock of Rimmon,[m] the Israelites cut down five thousand men along the roads. They kept pressing after the Benjamites as far as Gidom and struck down two thousand more.

46On that day twenty-five thousand Benjamite swordsmen fell, all of them valiant fighters. 47But six hundred men turned and fled into the desert to the rock of Rimmon, where they stayed four months. 48The men of Israel went back to Benjamin and put all the towns to the sword, including the animals and everything else they found. All the towns they came across they set on fire.[n]

Wives for the Benjamites

21 The men of Israel had taken an oath[o] at Mizpah:[p] "Not one of us will give[q] his daughter in marriage to a Benjamite."

2The people went to Bethel,[t] where they sat before God until evening, raising their voices and weeping bitterly. 3"O LORD, the God of Israel," they cried, "why has this happened to Israel? Why should one tribe be missing from Israel today?"

4Early the next day the people built an altar and presented burnt offerings and fellowship offerings.[u][r]

5Then the Israelites asked, "Who from all the tribes of Israel[s] has failed to assemble before the LORD?" For they had taken a solemn oath that anyone who failed to

20:31 [a]Jos 8:16
20:32 [b]ver 39
20:33 [c]Jos 8:19
20:34 [d]Jos 8:14 [e]Isa 47:11
20:35 [f]1Sa 9:21
20:36 [g]Jos 8:15
20:37 [h]Jos 8:19
20:38 [i]Jos 8:20
20:39 [j]ver 32
20:40 [k]Jos 8:20
20:44 [l]Ps 76:5
20:45 [m]Jos 15:32; Jdg 21:13
20:48 [n]Jdg 21:23
21:1 [o]Jos 9:18 [p]Jdg 20:1 [q]ver 7,18
21:4 [r]Jdg 20:26; 2Sa 24:25
21:5 [s]Jdg 5:23; 20:1

[q]33 Some Septuagint manuscripts and Vulgate; the meaning of the Hebrew for this word is uncertain. [r]33 Hebrew *Geba,* a variant of *Gibeah* [s]43 The meaning of the Hebrew for this word is uncertain. [t]2 Or *to the house of God* [u]4 Traditionally *peace offerings*

assemble before the LORD at Mizpah should certainly be put to death.

6Now the Israelites grieved for their brothers, the Benjamites. "Today one tribe is cut off from Israel," they said. 7"How can we provide wives for those who are left, since we have taken an oath[a] by the LORD not to give them any of our daughters in marriage?" 8Then they asked, "Which one of the tribes of Israel failed to assemble before the LORD at Mizpah?" They discovered that no one from Jabesh Gilead[b] had come to the camp for the assembly. 9For when they counted the people, they found that none of the people of Jabesh Gilead were there.

10So the assembly sent twelve thousand fighting men with instructions to go to Jabesh Gilead and put to the sword those living there, including the women and children. 11"This is what you are to do," they said. "Kill every male and every woman who is not a virgin.[c]" 12They found among the people living in Jabesh Gilead four hundred young women who had never slept with a man, and they took them to the camp at Shiloh[d] in Canaan.

13Then the whole assembly sent an offer of peace[e] to the Benjamites at the rock of Rimmon.[f] 14So the Benjamites returned at that time and were given the women of Jabesh Gilead who had been spared. But there were not enough for all of them.

15The people grieved for Benjamin,[g] because the LORD had made a gap in the tribes of Israel. 16And the elders of the assembly said, "With the women of Benjamin destroyed, how shall we provide wives for the men who are left? 17The Benjamite survivors must have heirs," they said, "so that a tribe of Israel will not be wiped out. 18We can't give them our daughters as wives, since we Israelites have taken this oath: 'Cursed be anyone who gives[h] a wife to a Benjamite.' 19But look, there is the annual festival of the LORD in Shiloh,[i] to the north of Bethel, and east of the road that goes from Bethel to Shechem, and to the south of Lebonah."

20So they instructed the Benjamites, saying, "Go and hide in the vineyards 21and watch. When the girls of Shiloh come out to join in the dancing,[j] then rush from the vineyards and each of you seize a wife from the girls of Shiloh and go to the land of Benjamin. 22When their fathers or brothers complain to us, we will say to them, 'Do us a kindness by helping them, because we did not get wives for them during the war, and you are innocent, since you did not give[k] your daughters to them.' "

23So that is what the Benjamites did. While the girls were dancing, each man caught one and carried her off to be his wife. Then they returned to their inheritance and rebuilt the towns and settled in them.[l]

24At that time the Israelites left that place and went home to their tribes and clans, each to his own inheritance.

25In those days Israel had no king; everyone did as he saw fit.[m]

21:7 [a] ver 1
21:8 [b] 1Sa 11:1; 31:11
21:11 [c] Nu 31:17-18
21:12 [d] Jos 18:1
21:13 [e] Dt 20:10 [f] Jdg 20:47
21:15 [g] ver 6
21:18 [h] ver 1
21:19 [i] Jos 18:1; Jdg 18:31; 1Sa 1:3
21:21 [j] Ex 15:20; Jdg 11:34
21:22 [k] ver 1,18
21:23 [l] Jdg 20:48
21:25 [m] Dt 12:8; Jdg 17:6; 18:1; 19:1

Ruth

Title and Background

This book is named after the leading character whose story is told here. Ruth was the great-grandmother of David and an ancestress of Jesus (Mt 1:1,5). The story is set in the time of the judges and reflects a temporary time of peace between Israel and Moab. It gives a series of intimate glances into the private lives of the members of an Israelite family and presents a delightful account of the remnant of true faith and piety during this period.

Author and Date of Writing

The author is unknown, although Jewish tradition points to Samuel. This is unlikely because the mention of David (4:17,22) implies a later date. The literary style of Hebrew used suggests that it was written during the monarchy, probably sometime after 1000 B.C.

Theme and Message

Redemption is a key concept throughout the book; the Hebrew word in its various forms occurs twenty-three times. The word shows how God is working out his plan for salvation. The book of Ruth also illustrates love and devotion—self-giving love that fulfills God's law, and God's love in blessing the lives of his children.

Outline

I. Introduction: Naomi Emptied (1:1-5)
II. Naomi Returns From Moab (1:6-22)
III. Ruth and Boaz Meet in the Harvest Fields (2:1-23)
IV. Ruth Goes to Boaz at the Threshing Floor (3:1-18)
V. Boaz Arranges to Marry Ruth (4:1-12)
VI. Conclusion: Naomi Filled (4:13-17)
VII. Epilogue: Genealogy of David (4:18-22)

Naomi and Ruth

1 In the days when the judges
ruled,[a][a] there was a famine in
the land,[b] and a man from Bethlehem in Judah, together with his
wife and two sons, went to live for
a while in the country of Moab.[c]
2The man's name was Elimelech,
his wife's name Naomi, and the
names of his two sons were Mahlon
and Kilion. They were Ephrathites
from Bethlehem,[d] Judah. And
they went to Moab and lived there.
3Now Elimelech, Naomi's husband, died, and she was left with
her two sons. 4They married Moabite women, one named Orpah and
the other Ruth.[e] After they had
lived there about ten years, 5both
Mahlon and Kilion also died, and
Naomi was left without her two
sons and her husband.
6When she heard in Moab that
the LORD had come to the aid of his
people[f] by providing food[g] for
them, Naomi and her daughters-
in-law prepared to return home
from there. 7With her two daughters-in-law she left the place where
she had been living and set out on
the road that would take them
back to the land of Judah.
8Then Naomi said to her two

1:1 [a]Jdg 2:16-18 [b]Ge 12:10; Ps 105:16 [c]Jdg 3:30
1:2 [d]Ge 35:19
1:4 [e]Mt 1:5
1:6 [f]Ex 4:31; Jer 29:10; Zep 2:7 [g]Ps 132:15; Mt 6:11

[a]*1* Traditionally *judged*

daughters-in-law, "Go back, each of you, to your mother's home. May the LORD show kindness[a] to you, as you have shown to your dead[b] and to me. 9May the LORD grant that each of you will find rest[c] in the home of another husband."

Then she kissed them and they wept aloud 10and said to her, "We will go back with you to your people."

11But Naomi said, "Return home, my daughters. Why would you come with me? Am I going to have any more sons, who could become your husbands?[d] 12Return home, my daughters; I am too old to have another husband. Even if I thought there was still hope for me—even if I had a husband tonight and then gave birth to sons— 13would you wait until they grew up? Would you remain unmarried for them? No, my daughters. It is more bitter for me than for you, because the LORD's hand has gone out against me![e]"

14At this they wept again. Then Orpah kissed her mother-in-law[f] good-by, but Ruth clung to her.[g]

15"Look," said Naomi, "your sister-in-law is going back to her people and her gods.[h] Go back with her."

16But Ruth replied, "Don't urge me to leave you[i] or to turn back from you. Where you go I will go, and where you stay I will stay. Your people will be my people and your God my God.[j] 17Where you die I will die, and there I will be buried. May the LORD deal with me, be it ever so severely,[k] if anything but death separates you and me." 18When Naomi realized that Ruth was determined to go with her, she stopped urging her.[l]

19So the two women went on until they came to Bethlehem. When they arrived in Bethlehem, the whole town was stirred[m] because of them, and the women exclaimed, "Can this be Naomi?"

20"Don't call me Naomi,[b]" she told them. "Call me Mara,[c] because the Almighty[d][n] has made my life very bitter.[o] 21I went away full, but the LORD has brought me back empty.[p] Why call me Naomi? The LORD has afflicted[e] me; the Almighty has brought misfortune upon me."

22So Naomi returned from Moab accompanied by Ruth the Moabitess, her daughter-in-law, arriving in Bethlehem as the barley harvest[q] was beginning.[r]

Ruth Meets Boaz

2 Now Naomi had a relative[s] on her husband's side, from the clan of Elimelech,[t] a man of standing, whose name was Boaz.[u]

2And Ruth the Moabitess said to Naomi, "Let me go to the fields and pick up the leftover grain[v] behind anyone in whose eyes I find favor."

Naomi said to her, "Go ahead, my daughter." 3So she went out and began to glean in the fields behind the harvesters. As it turned out, she found herself working in a field belonging to Boaz, who was from the clan of Elimelech.

4Just then Boaz arrived from Bethlehem and greeted the harvesters, "The LORD be with you![w]"

"The LORD bless you![x]" they called back.

5Boaz asked the foreman of his harvesters, "Whose young woman is that?"

6The foreman replied, "She is the Moabitess[y] who came back from Moab with Naomi. 7She said, 'Please let me glean and gather among the sheaves behind the harvesters.' She went into the field and has worked steadily from morning till now, except for a short rest in the shelter."

8So Boaz said to Ruth, "My daughter, listen to me. Don't go and glean in another field and don't go away from here. Stay here with my servant girls. 9Watch the field where the men are harvesting, and follow along after the girls. I have told the men not to touch you. And whenever you are thirsty, go

1:8 [a]Ru 2:20; 2Ti 1:16 [b]ver 5
1:9 [c]Ru 3:1
1:11 [d]Ge 38:11; Dt 25:5
1:13 [e]Jdg 2:15; Job 4:5; 19:21; Ps 32:4
1:14 [f]Ru 2:11 [g]Pr 17:17; 18:24
1:15 [h]Jos 24:14; Jdg 11:24
1:16 [i]2Ki 2:2 [j]Ru 2:11,12
1:17 [k]1Sa 3:17; 25:22; 2Sa 19:13; 2Ki 6:31
1:18 [l]Ac 21:14
1:19 [m]Mt 21:10
1:20 [n]Ex 6:3 [o]ver 13; Job 6:4
1:21 [p]Job 1:21
1:22 [q]Ex 9:31; Ru 2:23 [r]2Sa 21:9
2:1 [s]Ru 3:2,12 [t]Ru 1:2 [u]Ru 4:21
2:2 [v]ver 7; Lev 19:9; 23:22; Dt 24:19
2:4 [w]Jdg 6:12; Lk 1:28; 2Th 3:16 [x]Ps 129:7-8
2:6 [y]Ru 1:22

[b]20 *Naomi* means *pleasant*; also in verse 21. [c]20 *Mara* means *bitter.* [d]20 Hebrew *Shaddai*; also in verse 21 [e]21 Or *has testified against*

and get a drink from the water jars
the men have filled."
10At this, she bowed down with
her face to the ground.[a] She exclaimed, "Why have I found such
favor in your eyes that you notice
me[b]—a foreigner?[c]"
11Boaz replied, "I've been told
all about what you have done for
your mother-in-law[d] since the
death of your husband—how you
left your father and mother and
your homeland and came to live
with a people you did not know before.[e] **12**May the LORD repay you
for what you have done. May you be
richly rewarded by the LORD,[f] the
God of Israel, under whose wings[g]
you have come to take refuge.[h]"
13"May I continue to find favor
in your eyes, my lord," she said.
"You have given me comfort and
have spoken kindly to your servant—though I do not have the
standing of one of your servant
girls."
14At mealtime Boaz said to her,
"Come over here. Have some bread
and dip it in the wine vinegar."
When she sat down with the harvesters, he offered her some roasted grain. She ate all she wanted
and had some left over.[i] **15**As she
got up to glean, Boaz gave orders to
his men, "Even if she gathers
among the sheaves, don't embar-
rass her. **16**Rather, pull out some
stalks for her from the bundles and
leave them for her to pick up, and
don't rebuke her."
17So Ruth gleaned in the field
until evening. Then she threshed
the barley she had gathered, and it
amounted to about an ephah.[f]
18She carried it back to town, and
her mother-in-law saw how much
she had gathered. Ruth also
brought out and gave her what she
had left over[j] after she had eaten
enough.
19Her mother-in-law asked her,
"Where did you glean today?
Where did you work? Blessed be
the man who took notice of you![k]"
Then Ruth told her mother-in-
law about the one at whose place
she had been working. "The name

2:10 [a]1Sa 25:23 [b]Ps 41:1 [c]Dt 15:3
2:11 [d]Ru 1:14 [e]Ru 1:16-17
2:12 [f]1Sa 24:19 [g]Ps 17:8; 36:7; 57:1; 61:4; 63:7; 91:4 [h]Ru 1:16
2:14 [i]ver 18
2:18 [j]ver 14
2:19 [k]ver 10; Ps 41:1
2:20 [l]Ru 3:10; 2Sa 2:5; Pr 17:17 [m]Ru 3:9,12; 4:1,14
2:23 [n]Dt 16:9
3:1 [o]Ru 1:9
3:2 [p]Dt 25:5-10; Ru 2:1
3:3 [q]2Sa 14:2
3:5 [r]Eph 6:1; Col 3:20
3:7 [s]Jdg 19:6,9, 22; 2Sa 13:28; 1Ki 21:7; Est 1:10

of the man I worked with today is
Boaz," she said.
20"The LORD bless him!" Naomi
said to her daughter-in-law. "He
has not stopped showing his kindness[l] to the living and the dead."
She added, "That man is our close
relative; he is one of our kins-
man-redeemers.[m]"
21Then Ruth the Moabitess said,
"He even said to me, 'Stay with my
workers until they finish harvesting
all my grain.' "
22Naomi said to Ruth her daughter-in-law, "It will be good for you,
my daughter, to go with his girls,
because in someone else's field
you might be harmed."
23So Ruth stayed close to the
servant girls of Boaz to glean until
the barley and wheat harvests[n]
were finished. And she lived with
her mother-in-law.

Ruth and Boaz at the Threshing Floor

3 One day Naomi her mother-
in-law said to her, "My daughter, should I not try to find a
home[g][o] for you, where you will be
well provided for? **2**Is not Boaz,
with whose servant girls you have
been, a kinsman[p] of ours? Tonight
he will be winnowing barley on the
threshing floor. **3**Wash and perfume yourself,[q] and put on your
best clothes. Then go down to the
threshing floor, but don't let him
know you are there until he has finished eating and drinking. **4**When
he lies down, note the place where
he is lying. Then go and uncover his
feet and lie down. He will tell you
what to do."
5"I will do whatever you say,"[r]
Ruth answered. **6**So she went down
to the threshing floor and did everything her mother-in-law told her
to do.
7When Boaz had finished eating
and drinking and was in good spirits,[s] he went over to lie down at
the far end of the grain pile. Ruth

[f]*17* That is, probably about 3/5 bushel (about 22 liters) [g]*1* Hebrew *find rest* (see Ruth 1:9)

approached quietly, uncovered his
feet and lay down. **8**In the middle
of the night something startled the
man, and he turned and discovered
a woman lying at his feet.
9"Who are you?" he asked.
"I am your servant Ruth," she
said. "Spread the corner of your
garment[a] over me, since you are a
kinsman-redeemer.[b]"
10"The LORD bless you, my
daughter," he replied. "This kindness is greater than that which you
showed earlier: You have not run
after the younger men, whether
rich or poor. **11**And now, my daughter, don't be afraid. I will do for you
all you ask. All my fellow townsmen know that you are a woman of
noble character.[c] **12**Although it is
true that I am near of kin, there
is a kinsman-redeemer[d] nearer
than[e] I. **13**Stay here for the night,
and in the morning if he wants to
redeem,[f] good; let him redeem.
But if he is not willing, as surely as
the LORD lives[g] I will do it. Lie here
until morning."
14So she lay at his feet until
morning, but got up before anyone
could be recognized; and he said,
"Don't let it be known that a woman came to the threshing floor."[h]
15He also said, "Bring me the
shawl you are wearing and hold it
out." When she did so, he poured
into it six measures of barley and
put it on her. Then he[h] went back
to town.
16When Ruth came to her mother-in-law, Naomi asked, "How did
it go, my daughter?"
Then she told her everything
Boaz had done for her **17**and added,
"He gave me these six measures of
barley, saying, 'Don't go back to
your mother-in-law empty-handed.' "
18Then Naomi said, "Wait, my
daughter, until you find out what
happens. For the man will not rest
until the matter is settled today."[i]

Boaz Marries Ruth

4 Meanwhile Boaz went up to
the town gate and sat there.
When the kinsman-redeemer he
had mentioned[j] came along, Boaz
said, "Come over here, my friend,
and sit down." So he went over and
sat down.
2Boaz took ten of the elders[k] of
the town and said, "Sit here," and
they did so. **3**Then he said to the
kinsman-redeemer, "Naomi, who
has come back from Moab, is selling the piece of land that belonged
to our brother Elimelech. **4**I
thought I should bring the matter
to your attention and suggest that
you buy it in the presence of these
seated here and in the presence of
the elders of my people. If you will
redeem it, do so. But if you[i] will
not, tell me, so I will know. For no
one has the right to do it except
you,[l] and I am next in line."
"I will redeem it," he said.
5Then Boaz said, "On the day
you buy the land from Naomi and
from Ruth the Moabitess, you acquire[j] the dead man's widow, in
order to maintain the name of the
dead with his property."[m]
6At this, the kinsman-redeemer
said, "Then I cannot redeem[n] it
because I might endanger my own
estate. You redeem it yourself. I
cannot do it."
7(Now in earlier times in Israel,
for the redemption and transfer of
property to become final, one party
took off his sandal and gave it to
the other. This was the method of
legalizing transactions in Israel.)[o]
8So the kinsman-redeemer said
to Boaz, "Buy it yourself." And he
removed his sandal.
9Then Boaz announced to the elders and all the people, "Today you
are witnesses that I have bought
from Naomi all the property of
Elimelech, Kilion and Mahlon. **10**I
have also acquired Ruth the Moabitess, Mahlon's widow, as my wife,
in order to maintain the name of
the dead with his property, so that
his name will not disappear from

3:9 [a] Eze 16:8 [b] ver 12; Ru 2:20
3:11 [c] Pr 12:4; 31:10
3:12 [d] ver 9 [e] Ru 4:1
3:13 [f] Dt 25:5; Ru 4:5; Mt 22:24 [g] Jdg 8:19; Jer 4:2
3:14 [h] Ro 14:16; 2Co 8:21
3:18 [i] Ps 37:3-5
4:1 [j] Ru 3:12
4:2 [k] 1Ki 21:8; Pr 31:23
4:4 [l] Lev 25:25; Jer 32:7-8
4:5 [m] Ge 38:8; Dt 25:5-6; Ru 3:13; Mt 22:24
4:6 [n] Lev 25:25; Ru 3:13
4:7 [o] Dt 25:7-9

[h] *15* Most Hebrew manuscripts; many Hebrew manuscripts, Vulgate and Syriac *she*
[i] *4* Many Hebrew manuscripts, Septuagint, Vulgate and Syriac; most Hebrew manuscripts *he*
[j] *5* Hebrew; Vulgate and Syriac *Naomi, you acquire Ruth the Moabitess,*

among his family or from the town
records.[a] Today you are witnesses!"

11Then the elders and all those
at the gate said, "We are witnesses.[b] May the LORD make the
woman who is coming into your
home like Rachel and Leah,[c] who
together built up the house of Israel. May you have standing in Ephrathah[d] and be famous in Bethlehem. **12**Through the offspring the
LORD gives you by this young woman, may your family be like that of
Perez,[e] whom Tamar bore to Judah."

The Genealogy of David

4:18–22pp — 1Ch 2:5–15; Mt 1:3–6; Lk 3:31–33

13So Boaz took Ruth and she became his wife. Then he went to her,
and the LORD enabled her to conceive,[f] and she gave birth to a son.
14The women[g] said to Naomi:
"Praise be to the LORD, who this day
has not left you without a kinsman-redeemer. May he become famous throughout Israel! **15**He will
renew your life and sustain you in
your old age. For your daughter-
in-law, who loves you and who is
better to you than seven sons,[h] has
given him birth."

16Then Naomi took the child,
laid him in her lap and cared for
him. **17**The women living there
said, "Naomi has a son." And they
named him Obed. He was the father of Jesse,[i] the father of David.

18This, then, is the family line of
Perez[j]:

Perez was the father of Hezron,
19Hezron the father of Ram,
Ram the father of Ammina-
dab,[k]
20Amminadab the father of Nahshon,
Nahshon the father of Salmon,[k]
21Salmon the father of Boaz,[l]
Boaz the father of Obed,
22Obed the father of Jesse,
and Jesse the father of David.

4:10 [a] Dt 25:6
4:11 [b] Dt 25:9 [c] Ps 127:3; 128:3 [d] Ge 35:16
4:12 [e] ver 18; Ge 38:29
4:13 [f] Ge 29:31; 33:5; Ru 3:11
4:14 [g] Lk 1:58
4:15 [h] Ru 1:16-17; 2:11-12; 1Sa 1:8
4:17 [i] ver 22; 1Sa 16:1,18; 1Ch 2:12,13
4:18 [j] Mt 1:3-6
4:19 [k] Ex 6:23
4:21 [l] Ru 2:1

[k]*20* A few Hebrew manuscripts, some Septuagint manuscripts and Vulgate (see also verse 21 and Septuagint of 1 Chron. 2:11); most Hebrew manuscripts *Salma*

1 Samuel

Title and Background

1 and 2 Samuel are named after the individual whom God used to establish kingship in Israel. These two books were originally one book, but it was divided into two parts by the translators of the Septuagint (the Greek translation of the Old Testament). The book of 1 Samuel records the lives of Samuel and Saul, and much of the life of David.

Author and Date of Writing

Who the author was is uncertain because the book itself gives no indication as to his identity. The author probably wrote shortly after the division of the kingdom that followed upon the death of Solomon in 930 B.C.

Theme and Message

1 Samuel portrays the establishment of kingship in Israel. When the people demanded a king, Samuel, by God's leading, anointed Saul to be the first king of Israel. But Saul was disobedient to God, and God rejected him as king. Then Samuel secretly anointed David to take Saul's place. The struggles between Saul and David make up the rest of the book. The weaknesses and sins of these men are shown, as well as the goodness of Samuel and David and their obedience to God.

Outline

I. Background for the Establishment of Kingship in Israel (1:1-7:17)
II. Establishment of Kingship in Israel (8:1-12:25)
III. Failure of Saul's Kingship (13:1-15:35)
IV. David and Saul (16:1-30:31)
V. Death of Saul (31:1-13)

The Birth of Samuel

1 There was a certain man from
Ramathaim, a Zuphite[a] from
the hill country[a] of Ephraim,
whose name was Elkanah[b] son of
Jeroham, the son of Elihu, the son
of Tohu, the son of Zuph, an Ephraimite. 2He had two wives;[c] one
was called Hannah and the other
Peninnah. Peninnah had children,
but Hannah had none.
3Year after year[d] this man went
up from his town to worship[e] and
sacrifice to the LORD Almighty at
Shiloh,[f] where Hophni and Phinehas, the two sons of Eli, were
priests of the LORD. 4Whenever the
day came for Elkanah to sacrifice,[g]
he would give portions of the meat
to his wife Peninnah and to all her
sons and daughters. 5But to Hannah he gave a double portion because he loved her, and the LORD
had closed her womb.[h] 6And because the LORD had closed her
womb, her rival kept provoking her
in order to irritate her.[i] 7This went
on year after year. Whenever Hannah went up to the house of the
LORD, her rival provoked her till she
wept and would not eat. 8Elkanah
her husband would say to her,
"Hannah, why are you weeping?
Why don't you eat? Why are you
downhearted? Don't I mean more
to you than ten sons?[j]"
9Once when they had finished
eating and drinking in Shiloh, Han-

1:1 *a* Jos 17:17-18 *b* 1Ch 6:27,34
1:2 *c* Dt 21:15-17; Lk 2:36
1:3 *d* ver 21; Ex 23:14; 34:23; Lk 2:41 *e* Dt 12:5-7 *f* Jos 18:1
1:4 *g* Dt 12:17-18
1:5 *h* Ge 16:1; 30:2
1:6 *i* Job 24:21
1:8 *j* Ru 4:15

a*1* Or *from Ramathaim Zuphim*

nah stood up. Now Eli the priest
was sitting on a chair by the door-
post of the LORD's temple.[b][a] **10**In
bitterness of soul[b] Hannah wept
much and prayed to the LORD.
11And she made a vow, saying, "O
LORD Almighty, if you will only look
upon your servant's misery and remember[c] me, and not forget your
servant but give her a son, then I
will give him to the LORD for all the
days of his life, and no razor[d] will
ever be used on his head."

12As she kept on praying to the
LORD, Eli observed her mouth.
13Hannah was praying in her heart,
and her lips were moving but her
voice was not heard. Eli thought
she was drunk **14**and said to her,
"How long will you keep on getting
drunk? Get rid of your wine."

15"Not so, my lord," Hannah replied, "I am a woman who is deeply
troubled. I have not been drinking
wine or beer; I was pouring[e] out
my soul to the LORD. **16**Do not take
your servant for a wicked woman; I
have been praying here out of my
great anguish and grief."

17Eli answered, "Go in peace,[f]
and may the God of Israel grant you
what you have asked of him.[g]"

18She said, "May your servant
find favor in your eyes.[h]" Then she
went her way and ate something,
and her face was no longer downcast.[i]

19Early the next morning they
arose and worshiped before the
LORD and then went back to their
home at Ramah. Elkanah lay with
Hannah his wife, and the LORD remembered[j] her. **20**So in the
course of time Hannah conceived
and gave birth to a son. She
named[k] him Samuel,[c] saying,
"Because I asked the LORD for
him."

Hannah Dedicates Samuel

21When the man Elkanah went
up with all his family to offer the
annual[l] sacrifice to the LORD and
to fulfill his vow,[m] **22**Hannah did
not go. She said to her husband,
"After the boy is weaned, I will take
him and present[n] him before the
LORD, and he will live there always."

23"Do what seems best to you,"
Elkanah her husband told her.
"Stay here until you have weaned
him; only may the LORD make
good[o] his[d] word." So the woman
stayed at home and nursed her son
until she had weaned him.

24After he was weaned, she took
the boy with her, young as he was,
along with a three-year-old bull,[e][p]
an ephah[f] of flour and a skin of
wine, and brought him to the
house of the LORD at Shiloh.
25When they had slaughtered the
bull, they brought the boy to Eli,
26and she said to him, "As surely as
you live, my lord, I am the woman
who stood here beside you praying
to the LORD. **27**I prayed[q] for this
child, and the LORD has granted me
what I asked of him. **28**So now I
give him to the LORD. For his whole
life[r] he will be given over to the
LORD." And he worshiped the LORD
there.

Hannah's Prayer

2 Then Hannah prayed and
said:[s]

"My heart rejoices[t] in the
LORD;
in the LORD my horn[g][u] is
lifted high.
My mouth boasts over my
enemies,
for I delight in your
deliverance.

2"There is no one holy[h][v] like
the LORD;
there is no one besides you;
there is no Rock[w] like our
God.

3"Do not keep talking so
proudly
or let your mouth speak such
arrogance,[x]

1:9 [a]1Sa 3:3
1:10 [b]Job 7:11
1:11 [c]Ge 8:1; 28:20; 29:32 [d]Nu 6:1-21; Jdg 13:5
1:15 [e]Ps 42:4; 62:8; La 2:19
1:17 [f]Jdg 18:6; 1Sa 25:35; 2Ki 5:19; Mk 5:34 [g]Ps 20:3-5
1:18 [h]Ru 2:13 [i]Ecc 9:7; Ro 15:13
1:19 [j]Ge 4:1; 30:22
1:20 [k]Ge 41:51-52; Ex 2:10,22; Mt 1:21
1:21 [l]ver 3 [m]Dt 12:11
1:22 [n]ver 11,28; Lk 2:22
1:23 [o]ver 17; Nu 30:7
1:24 [p]Nu 15:8-10; Dt 12:5; Jos 18:1
1:27 [q]ver 11-13; Ps 66:19-20
1:28 [r]ver 11,22; Ge 24:26,52
2:1 [s]Lk 1:46-55 [t]Ps 9:14; 13:5 [u]Ps 89:17,24; 92:10; Isa 12:2-3
2:2 [v]Ex 15:11; Lev 19:2 [w]Dt 32:30-31; 2Sa 22:2,32
2:3 [x]Pr 8:13

[b]9 That is, tabernacle [c]20 *Samuel* sounds like the Hebrew for *heard of God.* [d]23 Masoretic Text; Dead Sea Scrolls, Septuagint and Syriac *your* [e]24 Dead Sea Scrolls, Septuagint and Syriac; Masoretic Text *with three bulls* [f]24 That is, probably about 3/5 bushel (about 22 liters) [g]1 *Horn* here symbolizes strength; also in verse 10. [h]2 Or *no Holy One*

for the LORD is a God who
knows,
and by him deeds[a] are
weighed.[b]

4"The bows of the warriors are
broken,[c]
but those who stumbled are
armed with strength.
5Those who were full hire
themselves out for food,
but those who were hungry
hunger no more.
She who was barren[d] has
borne seven children,
but she who has had many
sons pines away.

6"The LORD brings death and
makes alive;[e]
he brings down to the grave[i]
and raises up.[f]
7The LORD sends poverty and
wealth;[g]
he humbles and he exalts.[h]
8He raises[i] the poor from the
dust
and lifts the needy from the
ash heap;
he seats them with princes
and has them inherit a
throne of honor.[j]

"For the foundations[k] of the
earth are the LORD's;
upon them he has set the
world.
9He will guard the feet[l] of his
saints,
but the wicked will be
silenced in darkness.[m]

"It is not by strength[n] that one
prevails;
10 those who oppose the LORD
will be shattered.[o]
He will thunder[p] against them
from heaven;
the LORD will judge[q] the
ends of the earth.

"He will give strength[r] to his
king
and exalt the horn[s] of his
anointed."

11Then Elkanah went home to
Ramah, but the boy ministered[t]
before the LORD under Eli the
priest.

Eli's Wicked Sons

12Eli's sons were wicked men;
they had no regard[u] for the LORD.
13Now it was the practice of the
priests with the people that whenever anyone offered a sacrifice and
while the meat[v] was being boiled,
the servant of the priest would
come with a three-pronged fork in
his hand. 14He would plunge it into
the pan or kettle or caldron or pot,
and the priest would take for himself whatever the fork brought up.
This is how they treated all the Israelites who came to Shiloh. 15But
even before the fat was burned, the
servant of the priest would come
and say to the man who was sacrificing, "Give the priest some meat
to roast; he won't accept boiled
meat from you, but only raw."
16If the man said to him, "Let
the fat be burned up first, and then
take whatever you want," the servant would then answer, "No, hand
it over now; if you don't, I'll take it
by force."
17This sin of the young men was
very great in the LORD's sight, for
they[j] were treating the LORD's offering with contempt.[w]
18But Samuel was ministering[x]
before the LORD—a boy wearing a
linen ephod.[y] 19Each year his
mother made him a little robe and
took it to him when she went up
with her husband to offer the annual[z] sacrifice. 20Eli would bless Elkanah and his wife, saying, "May
the LORD give you children by this
woman to take the place of the one
she prayed[a] for and gave to the
LORD." Then they would go home.
21And the LORD was gracious to
Hannah;[b] she conceived and gave
birth to three sons and two daughters. Meanwhile, the boy Samuel
grew[c] up in the presence of the
LORD.
22Now Eli, who was very old,
heard about everything his sons
were doing to all Israel and how
they slept with the women[d] who
served at the entrance to the Tent
of Meeting. 23So he said to them,

2:3 [a] 1Sa 16:7; 1Ki 8:39 [b] Pr 16:2; 24:11-12
2:4 [c] Ps 37:15
2:5 [d] Ps 113:9; Jer 15:9
2:6 [e] Dt 32:39 [f] Isa 26:19
2:7 [g] Dt 8:18 [h] Job 5:11; Ps 75:7
2:8 [i] Ps 113:7-8 [j] Job 36:7 [k] Job 38:4
2:9 [l] Ps 91:12 [m] Mt 8:12 [n] Ps 33:16-17
2:10 [o] Ps 2:9 [p] Ps 18:13 [q] Ps 96:13 [r] Ps 21:1 [s] Ps 89:24
2:11 [t] ver 18; 1Sa 3:1
2:12 [u] Jer 2:8; 9:6
2:13 [v] Lev 7:29-34
2:17 [w] Mal 2:7-9
2:18 [x] ver 11; 1Sa 3:1 [y] ver 28
2:19 [z] 1Sa 1:3
2:20 [a] 1Sa 1:11, 27-28; Lk 2:34
2:21 [b] Ge 21:1 [c] ver 26; Jdg 13:24; 1Sa 3:19; Lk 2:40
2:22 [d] Ex 38:8

[i]6 Hebrew *Sheol* [j]17 Or *men*

"Why do you do such things? I hear from all the people about these wicked deeds of yours. 24No, my sons; it is not a good report that I hear spreading among the LORD's people. 25If a man sins against another man, God[k] may mediate for him; but if a man sins against the LORD, who will[a] intercede[b] for him?" His sons, however, did not listen to their father's rebuke, for it was the LORD's will to put them to death.

26And the boy Samuel continued to grow[c] in stature and in favor with the LORD and with men.

Prophecy Against the House of Eli

27Now a man of God[d] came to Eli and said to him, "This is what the LORD says: 'Did I not clearly reveal myself to your father's house when they were in Egypt under Pharaoh? 28I chose[e] your father out of all the tribes of Israel to be my priest, to go up to my altar, to burn incense, and to wear an ephod[f] in my presence. I also gave your father's house all the offerings made with fire by the Israelites. 29Why do you[l] scorn my sacrifice and offering[g] that I prescribed for my dwelling?[h] Why do you honor your sons more than me by fattening yourselves on the choice parts of every offering made by my people Israel?'

30"Therefore the LORD, the God of Israel, declares: 'I promised that your house and your father's house would minister before me forever.[i]' But now the LORD declares: 'Far be it from me! Those who honor me I will honor,[j] but those who despise[k] me will be disdained. 31The time is coming when I will cut short your strength and the strength of your father's house, so that there will not be an old man in your family line[l] 32and you will see distress in my dwelling. Although good will be done to Israel, in your family line there will never be an old man.[m] 33Every one of you that I do not cut off from my altar will be spared only to blind your eyes with tears and to grieve your heart, and all your descendants will die in the prime of life.

34" 'And what happens to your two sons, Hophni and Phinehas, will be a sign to you—they will both die[n] on the same day.[o] 35I will raise up for myself a faithful priest,[p] who will do according to what is in my heart and mind. I will firmly establish his house, and he will minister before my anointed[q] one always. 36Then everyone left in your family line will come and bow down before him for a piece of silver and a crust of bread and plead, "Appoint me to some priestly office so I can have food to eat.[r]" ' "

The LORD Calls Samuel

3 The boy Samuel ministered[s] before the LORD under Eli. In those days the word of the LORD was rare;[t] there were not many visions.[u]

2One night Eli, whose eyes[v] were becoming so weak that he could barely see, was lying down in his usual place. 3The lamp[w] of God had not yet gone out, and Samuel was lying down in the temple[m] of the LORD, where the ark of God was. 4Then the LORD called Samuel.

Samuel answered, "Here I am.[x]" 5And he ran to Eli and said, "Here I am; you called me."

But Eli said, "I did not call; go back and lie down." So he went and lay down.

6Again the LORD called, "Samuel!" And Samuel got up and went to Eli and said, "Here I am; you called me."

"My son," Eli said, "I did not call; go back and lie down."

7Now Samuel did not yet know the LORD: The word of the LORD had not yet been revealed[y] to him.

8The LORD called Samuel a third time, and Samuel got up and went to Eli and said, "Here I am; you called me."

Then Eli realized that the LORD

2:25 [a]Nu 15:30; Jos 11:20 [b]Dt 1:17; 1Sa 3:14; Heb 10:26
2:26 [c]ver 21; Lk 2:52
2:27 [d]Ex 4:14-16; 1Ki 13:1
2:28 [e]Ex 28:1 [f]Lev 8:7-8
2:29 [g]ver 12-17 [h]Dt 12:5; Mt 10:37
2:30 [i]Ex 29:9 [j]Ps 50:23; 91:15 [k]Mal 2:9
2:31 [l]1Sa 4:11-18; 22:16-20
2:32 [m]1Ki 2:26-27; Zec 8:4
2:34 [n]1Sa 4:11 [o]1Ki 13:3
2:35 [p]1Sa 12:3; 1Ki 2:35 [q]1Sa 16:13; 2Sa 7:11,27; 1Ki 11:38
2:36 [r]1Ki 2:27
3:1 [s]1Sa 2:11 [t]Ps 74:9 [u]Am 8:11
3:2 [v]1Sa 4:15
3:3 [w]Lev 24:1-4
3:4 [x]Isa 6:8
3:7 [y]Ac 19:12

[k]25 Or *the judges* [l]29 The Hebrew is plural. [m]3 That is, tabernacle

was calling the boy. **9**So Eli told Samuel, "Go and lie down, and if he calls you, say, 'Speak, LORD, for your servant is listening.' " So Samuel went and lay down in his place.

10The LORD came and stood there, calling as at the other times, "Samuel! Samuel!"

Then Samuel said, "Speak, for your servant is listening."

11And the LORD said to Samuel: "See, I am about to do something in Israel that will make the ears of everyone who hears of it tingle.[a] **12**At that time I will carry out against Eli everything[b] I spoke against his family—from beginning to end. **13**For I told him that I would judge his family forever because of the sin he knew about; his sons made themselves contemptible,[n] and he failed to restrain[c] them. **14**Therefore, I swore to the house of Eli, 'The guilt of Eli's house will never be atoned[d] for by sacrifice or offering.' "

15Samuel lay down until morning and then opened the doors of the house of the LORD. He was afraid to tell Eli the vision, **16**but Eli called him and said, "Samuel, my son."

Samuel answered, "Here I am."

17"What was it he said to you?" Eli asked. "Do not hide it from me. May God deal with you, be it ever so severely,[e] if you hide from me anything he told you." **18**So Samuel told him everything, hiding nothing from him. Then Eli said, "He is the LORD; let him do what is good in his eyes."[f]

19The LORD was with[g] Samuel as he grew[h] up, and he let none[i] of his words fall to the ground. **20**And all Israel from Dan to Beersheba[j] recognized that Samuel was attested as a prophet of the LORD. **21**The LORD continued to appear at Shiloh, and there he revealed[k] himself to Samuel through his word.

4 And Samuel's word came to all Israel.

The Philistines Capture the Ark

Now the Israelites went out to fight against the Philistines. The Israelites camped at Ebenezer,[l] and the Philistines at Aphek.[m] **2**The Philistines deployed their forces to meet Israel, and as the battle spread, Israel was defeated by the Philistines, who killed about four thousand of them on the battlefield. **3**When the soldiers returned to camp, the elders of Israel asked, "Why[n] did the LORD bring defeat upon us today before the Philistines? Let us bring the ark[o] of the LORD's covenant from Shiloh, so that it[o] may go with us and save us from the hand of our enemies."

4So the people sent men to Shiloh, and they brought back the ark of the covenant of the LORD Almighty, who is enthroned between the cherubim.[p] And Eli's two sons, Hophni and Phinehas, were there with the ark of the covenant of God.

5When the ark of the LORD's covenant came into the camp, all Israel raised such a great shout[q] that the ground shook. **6**Hearing the uproar, the Philistines asked, "What's all this shouting in the Hebrew camp?"

When they learned that the ark of the LORD had come into the camp, **7**the Philistines were afraid.[r] "A god has come into the camp," they said. "We're in trouble! Nothing like this has happened before. **8**Woe to us! Who will deliver us from the hand of these mighty gods? They are the gods who struck the Egyptians with all kinds of plagues in the desert. **9**Be strong, Philistines! Be men, or you will be subject to the Hebrews, as they[s] have been to you. Be men, and fight!"

10So the Philistines fought, and the Israelites were defeated[t] and every man fled to his tent. The slaughter was very great; Israel lost thirty thousand foot soldiers. **11**The ark of God was captured, and Eli's two sons, Hophni and Phinehas, died.[u]

3:11 [a] 2Ki 21:12; Jer 19:3
3:12 [b] 1Sa 2:27-36
3:13 [c] 1Sa 2:12,17, 22,29-31
3:14 [d] Lev 15:30-31; 1Sa 2:25; Isa 22:14
3:17 [e] Ru 1:17; 2Sa 3:35
3:18 [f] Job 2:10; Isa 39:8
3:19 [g] Ge 21:22; 39:2 [h] 1Sa 2:21 [i] 1Sa 9:6
3:20 [j] Jdg 20:1
3:21 [k] ver 10
4:1 [l] 1Sa 7:12 [m] Jos 12:18; 1Sa 29:1
4:3 [n] Jos 7:7 [o] Nu 10:35; Jos 6:7
4:4 [p] Ex 25:22; 2Sa 6:2
4:5 [q] Jos 6:5,10
4:7 [r] Ex 15:14
4:9 [s] Jdg 13:1; 1Co 16:13
4:10 [t] ver 2; Dt 28:25; 2Sa 18:17; 2Ki 14:12
4:11 [u] 1Sa 2:34; Ps 78:61,64

[n] *13* Masoretic Text; an ancient Hebrew scribal tradition and Septuagint *sons blasphemed God*
[o] *3* Or *he*

Death of Eli

12That same day a Benjamite ran
from the battle line and went to
Shiloh, his clothes torn and dust[a]
on his head. 13When he arrived,
there was Eli[b] sitting on his chair
by the side of the road, watching,
because his heart feared for the ark
of God. When the man entered the
town and told what had happened,
the whole town sent up a cry.
14Eli heard the outcry and asked,
"What is the meaning of this uproar?"
The man hurried over to Eli,
15who was ninety-eight years old
and whose eyes[c] were set so that
he could not see. 16He told Eli, "I
have just come from the battle line;
I fled from it this very day."
Eli asked, "What happened, my
son?"
17The man who brought the
news replied, "Israel fled before
the Philistines, and the army has
suffered heavy losses. Also your
two sons, Hophni and Phinehas,
are dead, and the ark of God has
been captured."
18When he mentioned the ark of
God, Eli fell backward off his chair
by the side of the gate. His neck
was broken and he died, for he was
an old man and heavy. He had
led[p][d] Israel forty years.
19His daughter-in-law, the wife
of Phinehas, was pregnant and
near the time of delivery. When she
heard the news that the ark of God
had been captured and that her father-in-law and her husband were
dead, she went into labor and gave
birth, but was overcome by her labor pains. 20As she was dying, the
women attending her said, "Don't
despair; you have given birth to a
son." But she did not respond or
pay any attention.
21She named the boy Icha-
bod,[q][e] saying, "The glory[f] has departed from Israel"—because of
the capture of the ark of God and
the deaths of her father-in-law and
her husband. 22She said, "The glory has departed from Israel, for the
ark of God has been captured."

4:12 [a]Jos 7:6; 2Sa 1:2; 15:32; Ne 9:1; Job 2:12
4:13 [b]ver 18; 1Sa 1:9
4:15 [c]1Sa 3:2
4:18 [d]ver 13
4:21 [e]Ge 35:18 [f]Ps 26:8; Jer 2:11
5:1 [g]1Sa 4:1; 7:12 [h]Jos 13:3
5:2 [i]Jdg 16:23
5:3 [j]Isa 19:1; 46:7
5:4 [k]Eze 6:6; Mic 1:7
5:5 [l]Zep 1:9
5:6 [m]ver 7; Ex 9:3; Ps 32:4; Ac 13:11 [n]ver 11; Ps 78:66 [o]Dt 28:27; 1Sa 6:5
5:8 [p]ver 11
5:9 [q]ver 6,11; Dt 2:15; 1Sa 7:13; Ps 78:66

The Ark in Ashdod and Ekron

5 After the Philistines had captured the ark of God, they took
it from Ebenezer[g] to Ashdod.[h]
2Then they carried the ark into Dagon's temple and set it beside Dagon.[i] 3When the people of Ashdod
rose early the next day, there was
Dagon, fallen[j] on his face on the
ground before the ark of the LORD!
They took Dagon and put him back
in his place. 4But the following
morning when they rose, there was
Dagon, fallen on his face on the
ground before the ark of the LORD!
His head and hands had been broken[k] off and were lying on the
threshold; only his body remained.
5That is why to this day neither the
priests of Dagon nor any others
who enter Dagon's temple at Ashdod step on the threshold.[l]
6The LORD's hand[m] was heavy
upon the people of Ashdod and its
vicinity; he brought devastation[n]
upon them and afflicted them with
tumors.[r][o] 7When the men of Ashdod saw what was happening, they
said, "The ark of the god of Israel
must not stay here with us, because his hand is heavy upon us
and upon Dagon our god." 8So they
called together all the rulers of the
Philistines and asked them, "What
shall we do with the ark of the god
of Israel?"
They answered, "Have the ark of
the god of Israel moved to Gath.[p]"
So they moved the ark of the God of
Israel.
9But after they had moved it, the
LORD's hand was against that city,
throwing it into a great panic.[q] He
afflicted the people of the city,
both young and old, with an outbreak of tumors.[s] 10So they sent
the ark of God to Ekron.
As the ark of God was entering
Ekron, the people of Ekron cried
out, "They have brought the ark of
the god of Israel around to us to kill

[p]18 Traditionally *judged* [q]21 *Ichabod* means *no glory.* [r]6 Hebrew; Septuagint and Vulgate *tumors. And rats appeared in their land, and death and destruction were throughout the city* [s]9 Or *with tumors in the groin* (see Septuagint)

us and our people." **11**So they called together all the rulers[a] of the Philistines and said, "Send the ark of the god of Israel away; let it go back to its own place, or it[t] will kill us and our people." For death had filled the city with panic; God's hand was very heavy upon it. **12**Those who did not die were afflicted with tumors, and the outcry of the city went up to heaven.

The Ark Returned to Israel

6 When the ark of the LORD had been in Philistine territory seven months, **2**the Philistines called for the priests and the diviners[b] and said, "What shall we do with the ark of the LORD? Tell us how we should send it back to its place."

3They answered, "If you return the ark of the god of Israel, do not send it away empty,[c] but by all means send a guilt offering[d] to him. Then you will be healed, and you will know why his hand[e] has not been lifted from you."

4The Philistines asked, "What guilt offering should we send to him?"

They replied, "Five gold tumors and five gold rats, according to the number[f] of the Philistine rulers, because the same plague has struck both you and your rulers. **5**Make models of the tumors[g] and of the rats that are destroying the country, and pay honor[h] to Israel's god. Perhaps he will lift his hand from you and your gods and your land. **6**Why do you harden[i] your hearts as the Egyptians and Pharaoh did? When he[u] treated them harshly, did they[j] not send the Israelites out so they could go on their way?

7"Now then, get a new cart[k] ready, with two cows that have calved and have never been yoked.[l] Hitch the cows to the cart, but take their calves away and pen them up. **8**Take the ark of the LORD and put it on the cart, and in a chest beside it put the gold objects you are sending back to him as a guilt offering. Send it on its way, **9**but keep watching it. If it goes up to its own territory, toward Beth Shemesh,[m] then the LORD has brought this great disaster on us. But if it does not, then we will know that it was not his hand that struck us and that it happened to us by chance."

10So they did this. They took two such cows and hitched them to the cart and penned up their calves. **11**They placed the ark of the LORD on the cart and along with it the chest containing the gold rats and the models of the tumors. **12**Then the cows went straight up toward Beth Shemesh, keeping on the road and lowing all the way; they did not turn to the right or to the left. The rulers of the Philistines followed them as far as the border of Beth Shemesh.

13Now the people of Beth Shemesh were harvesting their wheat in the valley, and when they looked up and saw the ark, they rejoiced at the sight. **14**The cart came to the field of Joshua of Beth Shemesh, and there it stopped beside a large rock. The people chopped up the wood of the cart and sacrificed the cows as a burnt offering[n] to the LORD. **15**The Levites[o] took down the ark of the LORD, together with the chest containing the gold objects, and placed them on the large rock. On that day the people of Beth Shemesh offered burnt offerings and made sacrifices to the LORD. **16**The five rulers of the Philistines saw all this and then returned that same day to Ekron.

17These are the gold tumors the Philistines sent as a guilt offering to the LORD—one each[p] for Ashdod, Gaza, Ashkelon, Gath and Ekron. **18**And the number of the gold rats was according to the number of Philistine towns belonging to the five rulers—the fortified towns with their country villages. The large rock, on which[v] they set the ark of the LORD, is a witness to this

5:11 [a]ver 6,8-9
6:2 [b]Ge 41:8; Ex 7:11; Isa 2:6
6:3 [c]Ex 23:15; Dt 16:16 [d]Lev 5:15 [e]ver 9
6:4 [f]ver 17-18; Jos 13:3; Jdg 3:3
6:5 [g]1Sa 5:6-11 [h]Jos 7:19; Isa 42:12; Jn 9:24; Rev 14:7
6:6 [i]Ex 7:13; 8:15; 9:34; 14:17 [j]Ex 12:31,33
6:7 [k]2Sa 6:3 [l]Nu 19:2
6:9 [m]ver 3; Jos 15:10; 21:16
6:14 [n]2Sa 24:22; 1Ki 19:21
6:15 [o]Jos 3:3
6:17 [p]ver 4

[t]*11* Or *he* [u]*6* That is, God [v]*18* A few Hebrew manuscripts (see also Septuagint); most Hebrew manuscripts *villages as far as Greater Abel, where*

day in the field of Joshua of Beth
Shemesh.
19But God struck down[a] some
of the men of Beth Shemesh, putting seventy[w] of them to death because they had looked[b] into the
ark of the LORD. The people
mourned because of the heavy
blow the LORD had dealt them,
20and the men of Beth Shemesh
asked, "Who can stand[c] in the
presence of the LORD, this holy[d]
God? To whom will the ark go up
from here?"
21Then they sent messengers to
the people of Kiriath Jearim,[e] saying, "The Philistines have returned
the ark of the LORD. Come down
and take it up to your place."
7 1So the men of Kiriath Jearim
came and took up the ark of the
LORD. They took it to Abinadab's[f]
house on the hill and consecrated
Eleazar his son to guard the ark of
the LORD.

Samuel Subdues the Philistines at Mizpah

2It was a long time, twenty years
in all, that the ark remained at Kiriath Jearim, and all the people of
Israel mourned and sought after
the LORD. 3And Samuel said to the
whole house of Israel, "If you are
returning[g] to the LORD with all
your hearts, then rid[h] yourselves of
the foreign gods and the Ashtoreths[i] and commit[j] yourselves to
the LORD and serve him only,[k] and
he will deliver you out of the hand
of the Philistines." 4So the Israelites put away their Baals and
Ashtoreths, and served the LORD
only.
5Then Samuel said, "Assemble
all Israel at Mizpah[l] and I will intercede with the LORD for you."
6When they had assembled at Mizpah, they drew water and poured[m]
it out before the LORD. On that day
they fasted and there they confessed, "We have sinned against
the LORD." And Samuel was leader[x][n] of Israel at Mizpah.
7When the Philistines heard that
Israel had assembled at Mizpah,
the rulers of the Philistines came
up to attack them. And when the
Israelites heard of it, they were
afraid[o] because of the Philistines.
8They said to Samuel, "Do not stop
crying[p] out to the LORD our God for
us, that he may rescue us from the
hand of the Philistines." 9Then
Samuel[q] took a suckling lamb and
offered it up as a whole burnt offering to the LORD. He cried out to the
LORD on Israel's behalf, and the
LORD answered him.[r]
10While Samuel was sacrificing
the burnt offering, the Philistines
drew near to engage Israel in battle. But that day the LORD thundered[s] with loud thunder against
the Philistines and threw them into
such a panic[t] that they were routed before the Israelites. 11The men
of Israel rushed out of Mizpah and
pursued the Philistines, slaughtering them along the way to a point
below Beth Car.
12Then Samuel took a stone[u]
and set it up between Mizpah and
Shen. He named it Ebenezer,[y] saying, "Thus far has the LORD helped
us." 13So the Philistines were subdued[v] and did not invade Israelite
territory again.
Throughout Samuel's lifetime,
the hand of the LORD was against
the Philistines. 14The towns from
Ekron to Gath that the Philistines
had captured from Israel were restored to her, and Israel delivered
the neighboring territory from the
power of the Philistines. And there
was peace between Israel and the
Amorites.
15Samuel[w] continued as judge
over Israel all the days of his life.
16From year to year he went on a
circuit from Bethel to Gilgal to
Mizpah, judging Israel in all those
places. 17But he always went back
to Ramah,[x] where his home was,
and there he also judged Israel.
And he built an altar[y] there to the
LORD.

6:19 [a] 2Sa 6:7 [b] Ex 19:21; Nu 4:5,15,20
6:20 [c] 2Sa 6:9; Mal 3:2; Rev 6:17 [d] Lev 11:45
6:21 [e] Jos 9:17; 15:9,60; 1Ch 13:5-6
7:1 [f] 2Sa 6:3
7:3 [g] Dt 30:10; Isa 55:7; Hos 6:1 [h] Ge 35:2; Jos 24:14 [i] Jdg 2:12-13; 1Sa 31:10 [j] Joel 2:12 [k] Dt 6:13; Mt 4:10; Lk 4:8
7:5 [l] Jdg 20:1
7:6 [m] Ps 62:8; La 2:19 [n] Jdg 10:10; Ne 9:1; Ps 106:6
7:7 [o] 1Sa 17:11
7:8 [p] 1Sa 12:19, 23; Isa 37:4; Jer 15:1
7:9 [q] Ps 99:6 [r] Jer 15:1
7:10 [s] 1Sa 2:10; 2Sa 22:14-15 [t] Jos 10:10
7:12 [u] Ge 35:14; Jos 4:9
7:13 [v] Jdg 13:1,5; 1Sa 13:5
7:15 [w] ver 6; 1Sa 12:11
7:17 [x] 1Sa 1:19; 8:4 [y] Jdg 21:4

[w] *19* A few Hebrew manuscripts; most Hebrew manuscripts and Septuagint *50,070*
[x] *6* Traditionally *judge*
[y] *12* *Ebenezer* means *stone of help.*

Israel Asks for a King

8 When Samuel grew old, he appointed[a] his sons as judges for
Israel. 2The name of his firstborn
was Joel and the name of his second was Abijah, and they served at
Beersheba.[b] 3But his sons did not
walk in his ways. They turned aside
after dishonest gain and accepted
bribes[c] and perverted justice.

4So all the elders of Israel gathered together and came to Samuel
at Ramah.[d] 5They said to him,
"You are old, and your sons do not
walk in your ways; now appoint a
king[e] to lead[z] us, such as all the
other nations have."

6But when they said, "Give us a
king to lead us," this displeased[f]
Samuel; so he prayed to the LORD.
7And the LORD told him: "Listen to
all that the people are saying to
you; it is not you they have rejected, but they have rejected me as
their king.[g] 8As they have done
from the day I brought them up out
of Egypt until this day, forsaking
me and serving other gods, so they
are doing to you. 9Now listen to
them; but warn them solemnly and
let them know[h] what the king who
will reign over them will do."

10Samuel told all the words of
the LORD to the people who were
asking him for a king. 11He said,
"This is what the king who will
reign over you will do: He will
take[i] your sons and make them
serve with his chariots and horses,
and they will run in front of his
chariots.[j] 12Some he will assign to
be commanders[k] of thousands and
commanders of fifties, and others
to plow his ground and reap his
harvest, and still others to make
weapons of war and equipment for
his chariots. 13He will take your
daughters to be perfumers and
cooks and bakers. 14He will take
the best of your[l] fields and vineyards[m] and olive groves and give
them to his attendants. 15He will
take a tenth of your grain and of
your vintage and give it to his officials and attendants. 16Your menservants and maidservants and the

8:1 [a]Dt 16:18-19
8:2 [b]Ge 22:19; 1Ki 19:3; Am 5:4-5
8:3 [c]Ex 23:8; Dt 16:19; Ps 15:5
8:4 [d]1Sa 7:17
8:5 [e]Dt 17:14-20
8:6 [f]1Sa 15:11
8:7 [g]Ex 16:8; 1Sa 10:19
8:9 [h]ver 11-18; 1Sa 10:25
8:11 [i]1Sa 10:25; 14:52 [j]Dt 17:16; 2Sa 15:1
8:12 [k]1Sa 22:7
8:14 [l]Eze 46:18 [m]1Ki 21:7,15
8:18 [n]Pr 1:28; Isa 1:15; Mic 3:4
8:19 [o]Isa 66:4; Jer 44:16
8:20 [p]ver 5
8:21 [q]Jdg 11:11
8:22 [r]ver 7
9:1 [s]1Sa 14:51; 1Ch 8:33; 9:39
9:2 [t]1Sa 10:24 [u]1Sa 10:23
9:4 [v]Jos 24:33 [w]2Ki 4:42
9:5 [x]1Sa 1:1 [y]1Sa 10:2

best of your cattle[a] and donkeys
he will take for his own use. 17He
will take a tenth of your flocks, and
you yourselves will become his
slaves. 18When that day comes, you
will cry out for relief from the king
you have chosen, and the LORD will
not answer[n] you in that day."

19But the people refused[o] to listen to Samuel. "No!" they said.
"We want a king over us. 20Then we
will be like all the other nations,[p]
with a king to lead us and to go out
before us and fight our battles."

21When Samuel heard all that
the people said, he repeated[q] it
before the LORD. 22The LORD answered, "Listen[r] to them and give
them a king."

Then Samuel said to the men of
Israel, "Everyone go back to his
town."

Samuel Anoints Saul

9 There was a Benjamite, a man
of standing, whose name was
Kish[s] son of Abiel, the son of Ze-
ror, the son of Becorath, the son of
Aphiah of Benjamin. 2He had a son
named Saul, an impressive young
man without equal[t] among the Israelites—a head taller[u] than any
of the others.

3Now the donkeys belonging to
Saul's father Kish were lost, and
Kish said to his son Saul, "Take
one of the servants with you and go
and look for the donkeys." 4So he
passed through the hill[v] country of
Ephraim and through the area
around Shalisha,[w] but they did not
find them. They went on into the
district of Shaalim, but the donkeys were not there. Then he
passed through the territory of
Benjamin, but they did not find
them.

5When they reached the district
of Zuph,[x] Saul said to the servant
who was with him, "Come, let's go
back, or my father will stop thinking about the donkeys and start
worrying[y] about us."

6But the servant replied, "Look,

[z]5 Traditionally *judge*; also in verses 6 and 20
[a]16 Septuagint; Hebrew *young men*

in this town there is a man of God;[a] he is highly respected, and everything[b] he says comes true. Let's go there now. Perhaps he will tell us what way to take."

7Saul said to his servant, "If we go, what can we give the man? The food in our sacks is gone. We have no gift[c] to take to the man of God. What do we have?"

8The servant answered him again. "Look," he said, "I have a quarter of a shekel[b] of silver. I will give it to the man of God so that he will tell us what way to take." 9(Formerly in Israel, if a man went to inquire of God, he would say, "Come, let us go to the seer," because the prophet of today used to be called a seer.)[d]

10"Good," Saul said to his servant. "Come, let's go." So they set out for the town where the man of God was.

11As they were going up the hill to the town, they met some girls coming out to draw[e] water, and they asked them, "Is the seer here?"

12"He is," they answered. "He's ahead of you. Hurry now; he has just come to our town today, for the people have a sacrifice[f] at the high place.[g] 13As soon as you enter the town, you will find him before he goes up to the high place to eat. The people will not begin eating until he comes, because he must bless the sacrifice; afterward, those who are invited will eat. Go up now; you should find him about this time."

14They went up to the town, and as they were entering it, there was Samuel, coming toward them on his way up to the high place.

15Now the day before Saul came, the LORD had revealed this to Samuel: 16"About this time tomorrow I will send you a man from the land of Benjamin. Anoint[h] him leader over my people Israel; he will deliver[i] my people from the hand of the Philistines. I have looked upon my people, for their cry has reached me."

17When Samuel caught sight of Saul, the LORD said to him, "This[j] is the man I spoke to you about; he will govern my people."

18Saul approached Samuel in the gateway and asked, "Would you please tell me where the seer's house is?"

19"I am the seer," Samuel replied. "Go up ahead of me to the high place, for today you are to eat with me, and in the morning I will let you go and will tell you all that is in your heart. 20As for the donkeys[k] you lost three days ago, do not worry about them; they have been found. And to whom is all the desire[l] of Israel turned, if not to you and all your father's family?"

21Saul answered, "But am I not a Benjamite, from the smallest tribe[m] of Israel, and is not my clan the least of all the clans of the tribe of Benjamin?[n] Why do you say such a thing to me?"

22Then Samuel brought Saul and his servant into the hall and seated them at the head of those who were invited—about thirty in number. 23Samuel said to the cook, "Bring the piece of meat I gave you, the one I told you to lay aside."

24So the cook took up the leg[o] with what was on it and set it in front of Saul. Samuel said, "Here is what has been kept for you. Eat, because it was set aside for you for this occasion, from the time I said, 'I have invited guests.' " And Saul dined with Samuel that day.

25After they came down from the high place to the town, Samuel talked with Saul on the roof[p] of his house. 26They rose about daybreak and Samuel called to Saul on the roof, "Get ready, and I will send you on your way." When Saul got ready, he and Samuel went outside together. 27As they were going down to the edge of the town, Samuel said to Saul, "Tell the servant to go on ahead of us"—and the servant did so—"but you stay here awhile, so that I may give you a message from God."

9:6 [a] Dt 33:1; 1Ki 13:1 [b] 1Sa 3:19
9:7 [c] 1Ki 14:3; 2Ki 5:5,15; 8:8
9:9 [d] 2Sa 24:11; 2Ki 17:13; 1Ch 9:22; 26:28; 29:29; Isa 30:10; Am 7:12
9:11 [e] Ge 24:11,13
9:12 [f] Nu 28:11-15; 1Sa 7:17 [g] Ge 31:54; 1Sa 10:5; 1Ki 3:2
9:16 [h] 1Sa 10:1 [i] Ex 3:7-9
9:17 [j] 1Sa 16:12
9:20 [k] ver 3 [l] 1Sa 8:5; 12:13
9:21 [m] 1Sa 15:17 [n] Jdg 20:35,46
9:24 [o] Lev 7:32-34; Nu 18:18
9:25 [p] Dt 22:8; Ac 10:9

b8 That is, about 1/10 ounce (about 3 grams)

10 Then Samuel took a flask[a]
of oil and poured it on
Saul's head and kissed him, saying,
"Has not the LORD anointed[b] you
leader over his inheritance?[c][c]
2When you leave me today, you will
meet two men near Rachel's
tomb,[d] at Zelzah on the border of
Benjamin. They will say to you,
'The donkeys[e] you set out to look
for have been found. And now your
father has stopped thinking about
them and is worried[f] about you.
He is asking, "What shall I do
about my son?"'
3"Then you will go on from there
until you reach the great tree of Tabor. Three men going up to God at
Bethel[g] will meet you there. One
will be carrying three young goats,
another three loaves of bread, and
another a skin of wine. 4They will
greet you and offer you two loaves
of bread, which you will accept
from them.
5"After that you will go to Gibeah of God, where there is a Philistine outpost.[h] As you approach the
town, you will meet a procession of
prophets coming down from the
high place[i] with lyres, tambourines, flutes and harps[j] being
played before them, and they will
be prophesying.[k] 6The Spirit[l] of
the LORD will come upon you in
power, and you will prophesy with
them; and you will be changed into
a different person. 7Once these
signs are fulfilled, do whatever[m]
your hand finds to do, for God is
with[n] you.
8"Go down ahead of me to Gilgal.[o] I will surely come down to
you to sacrifice burnt offerings and
fellowship offerings,[d] but you
must wait seven days until I come
to you and tell you what you are to
do."

Saul Made King

9As Saul turned to leave Samuel,
God changed[p] Saul's heart, and all
these signs were fulfilled that day.
10When they arrived at Gibeah, a
procession of prophets met him;
the Spirit of God came upon him in
power, and he joined in their
prophesying.[q] 11When all those
who had formerly known him saw
him prophesying with the prophets, they asked each other, "What
is this[r] that has happened to the
son of Kish? Is Saul also among the
prophets?"[s]
12A man who lived there answered, "And who is their father?"
So it became a saying: "Is Saul also
among the prophets?" 13After Saul
stopped prophesying, he went to
the high place.
14Now Saul's uncle[t] asked him
and his servant, "Where have you
been?"

"Looking for the donkeys," he
said. "But when we saw they were
not to be found, we went to Samuel."
15Saul's uncle said, "Tell me
what Samuel said to you."
16Saul replied, "He assured us
that the donkeys[u] had been
found." But he did not tell his uncle what Samuel had said about the
kingship.
17Samuel summoned the people
of Israel to the LORD at Mizpah[v]
18and said to them, "This is what
the LORD, the God of Israel, says: 'I
brought Israel up out of Egypt, and
I delivered you from the power of
Egypt and all the kingdoms that
oppressed[w] you.' 19But you have
now rejected your God, who saves
you out of all your calamities and
distresses. And you have said, 'No,
set a king[x] over us.' So now
present[y] yourselves before the
LORD by your tribes and clans."
20When Samuel brought all the
tribes of Israel near, the tribe of
Benjamin was chosen. 21Then he
brought forward the tribe of Benjamin, clan by clan, and Matri's clan
was chosen. Finally Saul son of
Kish was chosen. But when they
looked for him, he was not to be
found. 22So they inquired[z] further

10:1 [a] 1Sa 16:13; 2Ki 9:1,3,6 [b] Ps 2:12 [c] Dt 32:9; Ps 78:62,71
10:2 [d] Ge 35:20 [e] 1Sa 9:4 [f] 1Sa 9:5
10:3 [g] Ge 28:22; 35:7-8
10:5 [h] 1Sa 13:3 [i] 1Sa 9:12 [j] 2Ki 3:15 [k] 1Sa 19:20; 1Co 14:1
10:6 [l] ver 10; Nu 11:25; 1Sa 19:23-24
10:7 [m] Ecc 9:10 [n] Jos 1:5; Jdg 6:12; Heb 13:5
10:8 [o] 1Sa 11:14-15
10:9 [p] ver 6
10:10 [q] ver 5-6; 1Sa 19:20
10:11 [r] Mt 13:54; Jn 7:15 [s] 1Sa 19:24
10:14 [t] 1Sa 14:50
10:16 [u] 1Sa 9:20
10:17 [v] Jdg 20:1; 1Sa 7:5
10:18 [w] Jdg 6:8-9
10:19 [x] 1Sa 8:5-7; 12:12 [y] Jos 7:14; 24:1
10:22 [z] 1Sa 23:2,4, 9-11

[c] *1* Hebrew; Septuagint and Vulgate *over his people Israel? You will reign over the LORD's people and save them from the power of their enemies round about. And this will be a sign to you that the LORD has anointed you leader over his inheritance:* [d] *8* Traditionally *peace offerings*

of the LORD, "Has the man come here yet?"

And the LORD said, "Yes, he has hidden himself among the baggage."

23 They ran and brought him out, and as he stood among the people he was a head taller[a] than any of the others. 24 Samuel said to all the people, "Do you see the man the LORD has chosen?[b] There is no one like him among all the people."

Then the people shouted, "Long live[c] the king!"

25 Samuel explained to the people the regulations[d] of the kingship. He wrote them down on a scroll and deposited it before the LORD. Then Samuel dismissed the people, each to his own home.

26 Saul also went to his home in Gibeah,[e] accompanied by valiant men whose hearts God had touched. 27 But some troublemakers[f] said, "How can this fellow save us?" They despised him and brought him no gifts.[g] But Saul kept silent.

Saul Rescues the City of Jabesh

11 Nahash[h] the Ammonite went up and besieged Jabesh Gilead.[i] And all the men of Jabesh said to him, "Make a treaty[j] with us, and we will be subject to you."

2 But Nahash the Ammonite replied, "I will make a treaty with you only on the condition that I gouge[k] out the right eye of every one of you and so bring disgrace[l] on all Israel."

3 The elders of Jabesh said to him, "Give us seven days so we can send messengers throughout Israel; if no one comes to rescue us, we will surrender to you."

4 When the messengers came to Gibeah[m] of Saul and reported these terms to the people, they all wept[n] aloud. 5 Just then Saul was returning from the fields, behind his oxen, and he asked, "What is wrong with the people? Why are they weeping?" Then they repeated to him what the men of Jabesh had said.

6 When Saul heard their words, the Spirit[o] of God came upon him in power, and he burned with anger. 7 He took a pair of oxen, cut them into pieces, and sent the pieces by messengers throughout Israel,[p] proclaiming, "This is what will be done to the oxen of anyone[q] who does not follow Saul and Samuel." Then the terror of the LORD fell on the people, and they turned out as one man. 8 When Saul mustered[r] them at Bezek,[s] the men of Israel numbered three hundred thousand and the men of Judah thirty thousand.

9 They told the messengers who had come, "Say to the men of Jabesh Gilead, 'By the time the sun is hot tomorrow, you will be delivered.'" When the messengers went and reported this to the men of Jabesh, they were elated. 10 They said to the Ammonites, "Tomorrow we will surrender[t] to you, and you can do to us whatever seems good to you."

11 The next day Saul separated his men into three divisions;[u] during the last watch of the night they broke into the camp of the Ammonites and slaughtered them until the heat of the day. Those who survived were scattered, so that no two of them were left together.

Saul Confirmed as King

12 The people then said to Samuel, "Who[v] was it that asked, 'Shall Saul reign over us?' Bring these men to us and we will put them to death."

13 But Saul said, "No one shall be put to death today,[w] for this day the LORD has rescued[x] Israel."

14 Then Samuel said to the people, "Come, let us go to Gilgal[y] and there reaffirm the kingship.[z]" 15 So all the people went to Gilgal[a] and confirmed Saul as king in the presence of the LORD. There they sacrificed fellowship offerings[e] before the LORD, and Saul and all the

10:23 [a] 1Sa 9:2
10:24 [b] Dt 17:15; 2Sa 21:6 [c] 1Ki 1:25,34, 39
10:25 [d] Dt 17:14-20; 1Sa 8:11-18
10:26 [e] 1Sa 11:4
10:27 [f] Dt 13:13 [g] 1Ki 10:25; 2Ch 17:5
11:1 [h] 1Sa 12:12 [i] Jdg 21:8 [j] 1Ki 20:34; Eze 17:13
11:2 [k] Nu 16:14 [l] 1Sa 17:26
11:4 [m] 1Sa 10:5,26; 15:34 [n] Jdg 2:4; 1Sa 30:4
11:6 [o] Jdg 3:10; 6:34; 13:25; 14:6; 1Sa 10:10; 16:13
11:7 [p] Jdg 19:29 [q] Jdg 21:5
11:8 [r] Jdg 20:2 [s] Jdg 1:4
11:10 [t] ver 3
11:11 [u] Jdg 7:16
11:12 [v] 1Sa 10:27; Lk 19:27
11:13 [w] 2Sa 19:22 [x] Ex 14:13; 1Sa 19:5
11:14 [y] 1Sa 10:8 [z] 1Sa 10:25
11:15 [a] 1Sa 10:8,17

[e] *15* Traditionally *peace offerings*

Israelites held a great celebration.

Samuel's Farewell Speech

12 Samuel said to all Israel, "I
have listened[a] to everything you said to me and have set a
king[b] over you. **2**Now you have a
king as your leader.[c] As for me, I
am old and gray, and my sons are
here with you. I have been your
leader from my youth until this
day. **3**Here I stand. Testify against
me in the presence of the LORD and
his anointed.[d] Whose ox have I
taken? Whose donkey[e] have I tak-
en? Whom have I cheated? Whom
have I oppressed? From whose
hand have I accepted a bribe[f] to
make me shut my eyes? If I have
done[g] any of these, I will make it
right."

4"You have not cheated or oppressed us," they replied. "You
have not taken anything from anyone's hand."

5Samuel said to them, "The LORD
is witness against you, and also his
anointed is witness this day, that
you have not found anything[h] in
my hand.[i]"

"He is witness," they said.

6Then Samuel said to the people, "It is the LORD who appointed
Moses and Aaron and brought[j]
your forefathers up out of Egypt.
7Now then, stand here, because I
am going to confront[k] you with evidence before the LORD as to all the
righteous acts performed by the
LORD for you and your fathers.

8"After Jacob entered Egypt,
they cried[l] to the LORD for help,
and the LORD sent[m] Moses and Aaron, who brought your forefathers
out of Egypt and settled them in
this place.

9"But they forgot[n] the LORD their
God; so he sold them into the hand
of Sisera,[o] the commander of the
army of Hazor, and into the hands
of the Philistines[p] and the king of
Moab,[q] who fought against them.
10They cried out to the LORD and
said, 'We have sinned; we have forsaken[r] the LORD and served the Baals and the Ashtoreths.[s] But now
deliver us from the hands of our enemies, and we will serve you.'
11Then the LORD sent Jerub-
Baal,[f][t] Barak,[g][u] Jephthah[v] and
Samuel,[h] and he delivered you
from the hands of your enemies
on every side, so that you lived securely.

12"But when you saw that Nahash[w] king[x] of the Ammonites
was moving against you, you said to
me, 'No, we want a king to rule[y]
over us'—even though the LORD
your God was your king. **13**Now
here is the king[z] you have chosen,
the one you asked[a] for; see, the
LORD has set a king over you. **14**If
you fear[b] the LORD and serve and
obey him and do not rebel against
his commands, and if both you and
the king who reigns over you follow
the LORD your God—good! **15**But if
you do not obey the LORD, and if
you rebel against[c] his commands,
his hand will be against you, as it
was against your fathers.

16"Now then, stand still and
see[d] this great thing the LORD is
about to do before your eyes! **17**Is it
not wheat harvest[e] now? I will
call[f] upon the LORD to send thunder and rain.[g] And you will realize
what an evil[h] thing you did in the
eyes of the LORD when you asked for
a king."

18Then Samuel called upon the
LORD, and that same day the LORD
sent thunder and rain. So all the
people stood in awe[i] of the LORD
and of Samuel.

19The people all said to Samuel,
"Pray[j] to the LORD your God for
your servants so that we will not
die, for we have added to all our
other sins the evil of asking for a
king."

20"Do not be afraid," Samuel replied. "You have done all this evil;
yet do not turn away from the LORD,
but serve the LORD with all your
heart. **21**Do not turn away after useless[k] idols.[l] They can do you no
good, nor can they rescue you, because they are useless. **22**For the

12:1 [a]1Sa 8:7 [b]1Sa 10:24; 11:15
12:2 [c]1Sa 8:5
12:3 [d]1Sa 10:1; 24:6; 2Sa 1:14 [e]Nu 16:15 [f]Dt 16:19 [g]Ac 20:33
12:5 [h]Ac 23:9; 24:20 [i]Ex 22:4
12:6 [j]Ex 6:26; Mic 6:4
12:7 [k]Isa 1:18; Mic 6:1-5
12:8 [l]Ex 2:23 [m]Ex 3:10; 4:16
12:9 [n]Jdg 3:7 [o]Jdg 4:2 [p]Jdg 10:7; 13:1 [q]Jdg 3:12
12:10 [r]Jdg 10:10,15 [s]Jdg 2:13
12:11 [t]Jdg 6:14,32 [u]Jdg 4:6 [v]Jdg 11:1
12:12 [w]1Sa 11:1 [x]1Sa 8:5 [y]Jdg 8:23; 1Sa 8:6,19
12:13 [z]1Sa 8:5; Hos 13:11 [a]1Sa 10:24
12:14 [b]Jos 24:14
12:15 [c]ver 9; Jos 24:20; Isa 1:20
12:16 [d]Ex 14:13
12:17 [e]1Sa 7:9-10 [f]Jas 5:18 [g]Pr 26:1 [h]1Sa 8:6-7
12:18 [i]Ex 14:31
12:19 [j]ver 23; Ex 9:28; Jas 5:18; 1Jn 5:16
12:21 [k]Isa 41:24,29; Jer 16:19; Hab 2:18 [l]Dt 11:16

[f]*11* Also called *Gideon* [g]*11* Some Septuagint manuscripts and Syriac; Hebrew *Bedan* [h]*11* Hebrew; some Septuagint manuscripts and Syriac *Samson*

sake[a] of his great name[b] the LORD
will not reject[c] his people, because the LORD was pleased to
make[d] you his own. 23As for me,
far be it from me that I should sin
against the LORD by failing to pray[e]
for you. And I will teach[f] you the
way that is good and right. 24But be
sure to fear[g] the LORD and serve
him faithfully with all your heart;
consider[h] what great[i] things he
has done for you. 25Yet if you persist[j] in doing evil, both you and
your king will be swept[k] away."

Samuel Rebukes Saul

13 Saul was ⌊thirty⌋[i] years old
when he became king, and
he reigned over Israel ⌊forty-⌋[j] two
years.
2Saul[k] chose three thousand
men from Israel; two thousand
were with him at Micmash and in
the hill country of Bethel, and a
thousand were with Jonathan at
Gibeah[l] in Benjamin. The rest of
the men he sent back to their
homes.
3Jonathan attacked the Philistine outpost[m] at Geba, and the
Philistines heard about it. Then
Saul had the trumpet blown
throughout the land and said, "Let
the Hebrews hear!" 4So all Israel
heard the news: "Saul has attacked
the Philistine outpost, and now Israel has become a stench[n] to the
Philistines." And the people were
summoned to join Saul at Gilgal.
5The Philistines assembled to
fight Israel, with three thousand[l]
chariots, six thousand charioteers,
and soldiers as numerous as the
sand[o] on the seashore. They went
up and camped at Micmash, east of
Beth Aven. 6When the men of Israel saw that their situation was criti-
cal and that their army was hard
pressed, they hid in caves and
thickets, among the rocks, and in
pits and cisterns.[p] 7Some Hebrews
even crossed the Jordan to the land
of Gad[q] and Gilead.
Saul remained at Gilgal, and all
the troops with him were quaking
with fear. 8He waited seven[r] days,
the time set by Samuel; but Samuel
did not come to Gilgal, and Saul's
men began to scatter. 9So he said,
"Bring me the burnt offering and
the fellowship offerings.[m]" And
Saul offered[s] up the burnt offering. 10Just as he finished making
the offering, Samuel[t] arrived, and
Saul went out to greet him.
11"What have you done?" asked
Samuel.
Saul replied, "When I saw that
the men were scattering, and that
you did not come at the set time,
and that the Philistines were
assembling at Micmash,[u] 12I
thought, 'Now the Philistines will
come down against me at Gilgal,
and I have not sought the LORD's favor.[v]' So I felt compelled to offer
the burnt offering."
13"You acted foolishly,[w]" Samuel said. "You have not kept[x] the
command the LORD your God gave
you; if you had, he would have established your kingdom over Israel
for all time. 14But now your kingdom[y] will not endure; the LORD has
sought out a man after his own
heart[z] and appointed[a] him leader
of his people, because you have not
kept the LORD's command."
15Then Samuel left Gilgal[n] and
went up to Gibeah[b] in Benjamin,
and Saul counted the men who
were with him. They numbered
about six hundred.

Israel Without Weapons

16Saul and his son Jonathan and
the men with them were staying in
Gibeah[o] in Benjamin, while the
Philistines camped at Micmash.
17Raiding[c] parties went out from
the Philistine camp in three de-
tachments. One turned toward
Ophrah[d] in the vicinity of Shual,

12:22 [a] Ps 106:8 [b] Jos 7:9 [c] 1Ki 6:13 [d] Dt 7:7; 1Pe 2:9
12:23 [e] Ro 1:9-10; Col 1:9; 2Ti 1:3 [f] 1Ki 8:36; Ps 34:11; Pr 4:11
12:24 [g] Ecc 12:13 [h] Isa 5:12 [i] Dt 10:21
12:25 [j] 1Sa 31:1-5 [k] Jos 24:20
13:2 [l] 1Sa 10:26
13:3 [m] 1Sa 10:5
13:4 [n] Ge 34:30
13:5 [o] Jos 11:4
13:6 [p] Jdg 6:2
13:7 [q] Nu 32:33
13:8 [r] 1Sa 10:8
13:9 [s] 2Sa 24:25; 1Ki 3:4
13:10 [t] 1Sa 15:13
13:11 [u] ver 2,5,16,23
13:12 [v] Jer 26:19
13:13 [w] 2Ch 16:9 [x] 1Sa 15:23,24
13:14 [y] 1Sa 15:28 [z] Ac 7:46; 13:22 [a] 2Sa 6:21
13:15 [b] 1Sa 14:2
13:17 [c] 1Sa 14:15 [d] Jos 18:23

[i] *1* A few late manuscripts of the Septuagint; Hebrew does not have *thirty.* [j] *1* See the round number in Acts 13:21; Hebrew does not have *forty-.* [k] *1,2* Or *and when he had reigned over Israel two years, [2]he* [l] *5* Some Septuagint manuscripts and Syriac; Hebrew *thirty thousand* [m] *9* Traditionally *peace offerings* [n] *15* Hebrew; Septuagint *Gilgal and went his way; the rest of the people went after Saul to meet the army, and they went out of Gilgal* [o] *16* Two Hebrew manuscripts; most Hebrew manuscripts *Geba,* a variant of *Gibeah*

18another toward Beth Horon,[a]
and the third toward the border-
land overlooking the Valley of Zeboim[b] facing the desert.

19Not a blacksmith[c] could be
found in the whole land of Israel,
because the Philistines had said,
"Otherwise the Hebrews will make
swords or spears!" 20So all Israel
went down to the Philistines to
have their plowshares, mattocks,
axes and sickles[p] sharpened.
21The price was two thirds of a
shekel[q] for sharpening plowshares
and mattocks, and a third of a
shekel[r] for sharpening forks and
axes and for repointing goads.

22So on the day of the battle not
a soldier with Saul and Jonathan[d]
had a sword or spear[e] in his hand;
only Saul and his son Jonathan had
them.

Jonathan Attacks the Philistines

23Now a detachment of Philistines had gone out to the pass[f] at
14 Micmash. 1One day Jonathan son of Saul said to the
young man bearing his armor,
"Come, let's go over to the Philistine outpost on the other side." But
he did not tell his father.

2Saul was staying on the outskirts of Gibeah[g] under a pomegranate tree in Migron.[h] With him
were about six hundred men,
3among whom was Ahijah, who
was wearing an ephod. He was a
son of Ichabod's[i] brother Ahitub[j]
son of Phinehas, the son of Eli,[k]
the LORD's priest in Shiloh. No one
was aware that Jonathan had left.

4On each side of the pass[l] that
Jonathan intended to cross to
reach the Philistine outpost was a
cliff; one was called Bozez, and the
other Seneh. 5One cliff stood to the
north toward Micmash, the other
to the south toward Geba.

6Jonathan said to his young armor-bearer, "Come, let's go over to
the outpost of those uncircumcised[m] fellows. Perhaps the LORD
will act in our behalf. Nothing[n]

13:18 [a]Jos 18:13-14 [b]Ne 11:34
13:19 [c]2Ki 24:14; Jer 24:1
13:22 [d]1Ch 9:39 [e]Jdg 5:8
13:23 [f]1Sa 14:4
14:2 [g]1Sa 13:15 [h]Isa 10:28
14:3 [i]1Sa 4:21 [j]1Sa 22:11,20 [k]1Sa 2:28
14:4 [l]1Sa 13:23
14:6 [m]1Sa 17:26, 36; Jer 9:26 [n]Heb 11:34 [o]Jdg 7:4 [p]1Sa 17:46-47
14:10 [q]Ge 24:14; Jdg 6:36-37
14:11 [r]1Sa 13:6
14:12 [s]1Sa 17:43-44 [t]2Sa 5:24
14:15 [u]Ge 35:5; 2Ki 7:5-7 [v]1Sa 13:17
14:16 [w]2Sa 18:24

can hinder the LORD from saving,
whether by many[o] or by few.[p]"

7"Do all that you have in mind,"
his armor-bearer said. "Go ahead; I
am with you heart and soul."

8Jonathan said, "Come, then; we
will cross over toward the men and
let them see us. 9If they say to us,
'Wait there until we come to you,'
we will stay where we are and not
go up to them. 10But if they say,
'Come up to us,' we will climb up,
because that will be our sign[q] that
the LORD has given them into our
hands."

11So both of them showed themselves to the Philistine outpost.
"Look!" said the Philistines. "The
Hebrews are crawling out of the
holes they were hiding[r] in." 12The
men of the outpost shouted to Jonathan and his armor-bearer, "Come
up to us and we'll teach you a lesson.[s]"

So Jonathan said to his armor-
bearer, "Climb up after me; the
LORD has given them into the
hand[t] of Israel."

13Jonathan climbed up, using
his hands and feet, with his armor-bearer right behind him. The
Philistines fell before Jonathan,
and his armor-bearer followed and
killed behind him. 14In that first attack Jonathan and his armor-bearer killed some twenty men in an
area of about half an acre.[s]

Israel Routs the Philistines

15Then panic[u] struck the whole
army—those in the camp and field,
and those in the outposts and raiding[v] parties—and the ground
shook. It was a panic sent by God.[t]

16Saul's lookouts[w] at Gibeah in
Benjamin saw the army melting
away in all directions. 17Then Saul
said to the men who were with him,
"Muster the forces and see who has
left us." When they did, it was Jon-

[p]*20* Septuagint; Hebrew *plowshares*
[q]*21* Hebrew *pim*; that is, about 1/4 ounce (about 8 grams)
[r]*21* That is, about 1/8 ounce (about 4 grams)
[s]*14* Hebrew *half a yoke*; a "yoke" was the land plowed by a yoke of oxen in one day.
[t]*15* Or *a terrible panic*

athan and his armor-bearer who were not there.

18Saul said to Ahijah, "Bring[a] the ark of God." (At that time it was with the Israelites.)[u] **19**While Saul was talking to the priest, the tumult in the Philistine camp increased more and more. So Saul said to the priest,[b] "Withdraw your hand."

20Then Saul and all his men assembled and went to the battle. They found the Philistines in total confusion, striking[c] each other with their swords. **21**Those Hebrews who had previously been with the Philistines and had gone up with them to their camp went[d] over to the Israelites who were with Saul and Jonathan. **22**When all the Israelites who had hidden[e] in the hill country of Ephraim heard that the Philistines were on the run, they joined the battle in hot pursuit. **23**So the LORD rescued[f] Israel that day, and the battle moved on beyond Beth Aven.[g]

Jonathan Eats Honey

24Now the men of Israel were in distress that day, because Saul had bound the people under an oath,[h] saying, "Cursed be any man who eats food before evening comes, before I have avenged myself on my enemies!" So none of the troops tasted food.

25The entire army[v] entered the woods, and there was honey on the ground. **26**When they went into the woods, they saw the honey oozing out, yet no one put his hand to his mouth, because they feared the oath. **27**But Jonathan had not heard that his father had bound the people with the oath, so he reached out the end of the staff that was in his hand and dipped it into the honeycomb.[i] He raised his hand to his mouth, and his eyes brightened.[w] **28**Then one of the soldiers told him, "Your father bound the army under a strict oath, saying, 'Cursed be any man who eats food today!' That is why the men are faint."

29Jonathan said, "My father has made trouble[j] for the country. See how my eyes brightened[x] when I tasted a little of this honey. **30**How much better it would have been if the men had eaten today some of the plunder they took from their enemies. Would not the slaughter of the Philistines have been even greater?"

31That day, after the Israelites had struck down the Philistines from Micmash to Aijalon,[k] they were exhausted. **32**They pounced on the plunder[l] and, taking sheep, cattle and calves, they butchered them on the ground and ate them, together with the blood.[m] **33**Then someone said to Saul, "Look, the men are sinning against the LORD by eating meat that has blood in it."

"You have broken faith," he said. "Roll a large stone over here at once." **34**Then he said, "Go out among the men and tell them, 'Each of you bring me your cattle and sheep, and slaughter them here and eat them. Do not sin against the LORD by eating meat with blood still in it.' "

So everyone brought his ox that night and slaughtered it there. **35**Then Saul built an altar[n] to the LORD; it was the first time he had done this.

36Saul said, "Let us go down after the Philistines by night and plunder them till dawn, and let us not leave one of them alive."

"Do whatever seems best to you," they replied.

But the priest said, "Let us inquire of God here."

37So Saul asked God, "Shall I go down after the Philistines? Will you give them into Israel's hand?" But God did not answer[o] him that day.

38Saul therefore said, "Come here, all you who are leaders of the army, and let us find out what sin has been committed[p] today. **39**As surely as the LORD who rescues Isra-

14:18 [a] 1Sa 30:7
14:19 [b] Nu 27:21
14:20 [c] Jdg 7:22; 2Ch 20:23
14:21 [d] 1Sa 29:4
14:22 [e] 1Sa 13:6
14:23 [f] Ex 14:30; Ps 44:6-7 [g] 1Sa 13:5
14:24 [h] Jos 6:26
14:27 [i] ver 43; 1Sa 30:12
14:29 [j] Jos 7:25; 1Ki 18:18
14:31 [k] Jos 10:12
14:32 [l] 1Sa 15:19 [m] Ge 9:4; Lev 3:17; 7:26; 17:10-14; 19:26; Dt 12:16, 23-24
14:35 [n] 1Sa 7:17
14:37 [o] 1Sa 10:22; 28:6,15
14:38 [p] Jos 7:11; 1Sa 10:19

[u] *18* Hebrew; Septuagint *"Bring the ephod." (At that time he wore the ephod before the Israelites.)* [v] *25* Or *Now all the people of the land* [w] *27* Or *his strength was renewed* [x] *29* Or *my strength was renewed*

el lives,[a] even if it lies with my son
Jonathan, he must die." But not
one of the men said a word.
40Saul then said to all the Israelites, "You stand over there; I and
Jonathan my son will stand over
here."
"Do what seems best to you," the
men replied.
41Then Saul prayed to the LORD,
the God of Israel, "Give[b] me the
right[c] answer."[y] And Jonathan
and Saul were taken by lot, and the
men were cleared. **42**Saul said,
"Cast the lot between me and Jonathan my son." And Jonathan was
taken.
43Then Saul said to Jonathan,
"Tell me what you have done."[d]
So Jonathan told him, "I merely
tasted a little honey[e] with the end
of my staff. And now must I die?"
44Saul said, "May God deal with
me, be it ever so severely,[f] if you
do not die, Jonathan.[g]"
45But the men said to Saul,
"Should Jonathan die—he who has
brought about this great deliverance in Israel? Never! As surely as
the LORD lives, not a hair[h] of his
head will fall to the ground, for he
did this today with God's help." So
the men rescued[i] Jonathan, and
he was not put to death.
46Then Saul stopped pursuing
the Philistines, and they withdrew
to their own land.
47After Saul had assumed rule
over Israel, he fought against their
enemies on every side: Moab, the
Ammonites,[j] Edom, the kings[z] of
Zobah,[k] and the Philistines. Wherever he turned, he inflicted punishment on them.[a] **48**He fought val-
iantly and defeated the Amalekites,[l] delivering Israel from the
hands of those who had plundered
them.

Saul's Family

49Saul's sons were Jonathan,
Ishvi and Malki-Shua.[m] The name
of his older daughter was Merab,
and that of the younger was Michal.[n] **50**His wife's name was Ahinoam daughter of Ahimaaz. The
name of the commander of Saul's
army was Abner son of Ner, and
Ner was Saul's uncle. **51**Saul's father Kish[o] and Abner's father Ner
were sons of Abiel.
52All the days of Saul there was
bitter war with the Philistines, and
whenever Saul saw a mighty or
brave man, he took[p] him into his
service.

The LORD Rejects Saul as King

15 Samuel said to Saul, "I am
the one the LORD sent to
anoint[q] you king over his people
Israel; so listen now to the message
from the LORD. **2**This is what the
LORD Almighty says: 'I will punish
the Amalekites[r] for what they did
to Israel when they waylaid them
as they came up from Egypt. **3**Now
go, attack the Amalekites and totally[s] destroy[b] everything that belongs to them. Do not spare them;
put to death men and women, children and infants, cattle and sheep,
camels and donkeys.' "
4So Saul summoned the men
and mustered them at Telaim—
two hundred thousand foot soldiers and ten thousand men from
Judah. **5**Saul went to the city of
Amalek and set an ambush in the
ravine. **6**Then he said to the Kenites,[t] "Go away, leave the Amalekites so that I do not destroy you
along with them; for you showed
kindness to all the Israelites when
they came up out of Egypt." So the
Kenites moved away from the Amalekites.
7Then Saul attacked the Amalekites[u] all the way from Havilah
to Shur,[v] to the east of Egypt. **8**He
took Agag king of the Amalekites
alive,[w] and all his people he totally
destroyed with the sword. **9**But
Saul and the army spared[x] Agag
and the best of the sheep and cat-

14:39 [a] 2Sa 12:5
14:41 [b] Ac 1:24 [c] Pr 16:33
14:43 [d] Jos 7:19 [e] ver 27
14:44 [f] Ru 1:17 [g] ver 39
14:45 [h] 1Ki 1:52; Lk 21:18; Ac 27:34 [i] 2Sa 14:11
14:47 [j] 1Sa 11:1-13 [k] ver 52; 2Sa 10:6
14:48 [l] 1Sa 15:2,7
14:49 [m] 1Sa 31:2; 1Ch 8:33 [n] 1Sa 18:17-20
14:51 [o] 1Sa 9:1
14:52 [p] 1Sa 8:11
15:1 [q] 1Sa 9:16
15:2 [r] Ex 17:8-14; Nu 24:20; Dt 25:17-19
15:3 [s] Nu 24:20; Dt 20:16-18; Jos 6:17; 1Sa 22:19
15:6 [t] Ex 18:10,19; Nu 10:29-32; 24:22; Jdg 1:16; 4:1
15:7 [u] 1Sa 14:48 [v] Ge 16:7; 25:17-18; Ex 15:22
15:8 [w] 1Sa 30:1
15:9 [x] ver 3,15

[y]41 Hebrew; Septuagint *"Why have you not answered your servant today? If the fault is in me or my son Jonathan, respond with Urim, but if the men of Israel are at fault, respond with Thummim."* [z]47 Masoretic Text; Dead Sea Scrolls and Septuagint *king* [a]47 Hebrew; Septuagint *he was victorious* [b]3 The Hebrew term refers to the irrevocable giving over of things or persons to the LORD, often by totally destroying them; also in verses 8, 9, 15, 18, 20 and 21.

tle, the fat calves[c] and lambs—everything that was good. These they
were unwilling to destroy completely, but everything that was despised and weak they totally destroyed.
10Then the word of the LORD
came to Samuel: 11"I am grieved[a]
that I have made Saul king, because he has turned[b] away from
me and has not carried out my instructions."[c] Samuel was troubled,[d] and he cried out to the LORD
all that night.
12Early in the morning Samuel
got up and went to meet Saul, but
he was told, "Saul has gone to Carmel.[e] There he has set up a monument in his own honor and has
turned and gone on down to Gilgal."
13When Samuel reached him,
Saul said, "The LORD bless you! I
have carried out the LORD's instructions."
14But Samuel said, "What then
is this bleating of sheep in my ears?
What is this lowing of cattle that I
hear?"
15Saul answered, "The soldiers
brought them from the Amalekites;
they spared the best of the sheep
and cattle to sacrifice to the LORD
your God, but we totally destroyed
the rest."
16"Stop!" Samuel said to Saul.
"Let me tell you what the LORD said
to me last night."
"Tell me," Saul replied.
17Samuel said, "Although you
were once small[f] in your own eyes,
did you not become the head of the
tribes of Israel? The LORD anointed
you king over Israel. 18And he sent
you on a mission, saying, 'Go and
completely destroy those wicked
people, the Amalekites; make war
on them until you have wiped them
out.' 19Why did you not obey the
LORD? Why did you pounce on the
plunder[g] and do evil in the eyes of
the LORD?"
20"But I did obey[h] the LORD,"
Saul said. "I went on the mission
the LORD assigned me. I completely
destroyed the Amalekites and
brought back Agag their king.

15:11 [a] Ge 6:6; 2Sa 24:16 [b] Jos 22:16 [c] 1Sa 13:13; 1Ki 9:6-7 [d] ver 35
15:12 [e] Jos 15:55
15:17 [f] 1Sa 9:21
15:19 [g] 1Sa 14:32
15:20 [h] ver 13
15:22 [i] Ps 40:6-8; 51:16; Isa 1:11-15; Jer 7:22; Hos 6:6; Mic 6:6-8; Mt 12:7; Mk 12:33; Heb 10:6-9
15:23 [j] Dt 18:10 [k] 1Sa 13:13
15:24 [l] 2Sa 12:13 [m] Pr 29:25; Isa 51:12-13
15:25 [n] Ex 10:17
15:26 [o] 1Sa 13:14
15:27 [p] 1Ki 11:11,31
15:28 [q] 1Sa 28:17; 1Ki 11:31
15:29 [r] 1Ch 29:11; Tit 1:2 [s] Nu 23:19; Eze 24:14
15:30 [t] Isa 29:13; Jn 5:44; 12:43

21The soldiers took sheep and cattle from the plunder, the best of
what was devoted to God, in order
to sacrifice them to the LORD your
God at Gilgal."
22But Samuel replied:

"Does the LORD delight in burnt
offerings and sacrifices
as much as in obeying the
voice of the LORD?
To obey is better than
sacrifice,[i]
and to heed is better than
the fat of rams.
23For rebellion is like the sin of
divination,[j]
and arrogance like the evil of
idolatry.
Because you have rejected[k] the
word of the LORD,
he has rejected you as king."

24Then Saul said to Samuel, "I
have sinned.[l] I violated the LORD's
command and your instructions. I
was afraid[m] of the people and so I
gave in to them. 25Now I beg you,
forgive[n] my sin and come back
with me, so that I may worship the
LORD."
26But Samuel said to him, "I will
not go back with you. You have rejected[o] the word of the LORD, and
the LORD has rejected you as king
over Israel!"
27As Samuel turned to leave,
Saul caught hold of the hem of his
robe, and it tore.[p] 28Samuel said
to him, "The LORD has torn[q] the
kingdom of Israel from you today
and has given it to one of your
neighbors—to one better than you.
29He who is the Glory of Israel does
not lie[r] or change[s] his mind; for
he is not a man, that he should
change his mind."
30Saul replied, "I have sinned.
But please honor[t] me before the
elders of my people and before Israel; come back with me, so that I
may worship the LORD your God."
31So Samuel went back with Saul,
and Saul worshiped the LORD.

c9 Or *the grown bulls*; the meaning of the Hebrew for this phrase is uncertain.

32Then Samuel said, "Bring me Agag king of the Amalekites."

Agag came to him confidently,[d] thinking, "Surely the bitterness of death is past."

33But Samuel said,

"As your sword has made
women childless,
so will your mother be
childless among
women."[a]

And Samuel put Agag to death before the LORD at Gilgal.

34Then Samuel left for Ramah,[b] but Saul went up to his home in Gibeah[c] of Saul. **35**Until the day Samuel[d] died, he did not go to see Saul again, though Samuel mourned[e] for him. And the LORD was grieved that he had made Saul king over Israel.

Samuel Anoints David

16 The LORD said to Samuel, "How long will you mourn[f] for Saul, since I have rejected[g] him as king over Israel? Fill your horn with oil[h] and be on your way; I am sending you to Jesse[i] of Bethlehem. I have chosen[j] one of his sons to be king."

2But Samuel said, "How can I go? Saul will hear about it and kill me."

The LORD said, "Take a heifer with you and say, 'I have come to sacrifice to the LORD.' **3**Invite Jesse to the sacrifice, and I will show[k] you what to do. You are to anoint[l] for me the one I indicate."

4Samuel did what the LORD said. When he arrived at Bethlehem,[m] the elders of the town trembled when they met him. They asked, "Do you come in peace?[n]"

5Samuel replied, "Yes, in peace; I have come to sacrifice to the LORD. Consecrate[o] yourselves and come to the sacrifice with me." Then he consecrated Jesse and his sons and invited them to the sacrifice.

6When they arrived, Samuel saw Eliab[p] and thought, "Surely the LORD's anointed stands here before the LORD."

7But the LORD said to Samuel, "Do not consider his appearance or his height, for I have rejected him. The LORD does not look at the things man looks at. Man looks at the outward appearance,[q] but the LORD looks at the heart."[r]

8Then Jesse called Abinadab[s] and had him pass in front of Samuel. But Samuel said, "The LORD has not chosen this one either." **9**Jesse then had Shammah pass by, but Samuel said, "Nor has the LORD chosen this one." **10**Jesse had seven of his sons pass before Samuel, but Samuel said to him, "The LORD has not chosen these." **11**So he asked Jesse, "Are these all[t] the sons you have?"

"There is still the youngest," Jesse answered, "but he is tending the sheep."

Samuel said, "Send for him; we will not sit down[e] until he arrives."

12So he[u] sent and had him brought in. He was ruddy, with a fine appearance and handsome[v] features.

Then the LORD said, "Rise and anoint him; he is the one."

13So Samuel took the horn of oil and anointed him in the presence of his brothers, and from that day on the Spirit of the LORD[w] came upon David in power.[x] Samuel then went to Ramah.

David in Saul's Service

14Now the Spirit of the LORD had departed[y] from Saul, and an evil[f] spirit[z] from the LORD tormented him.

15Saul's attendants said to him, "See, an evil spirit from God is tormenting you. **16**Let our lord command his servants here to search for someone who can play the harp.[a] He will play when the evil spirit from God comes upon you, and you will feel better."

17So Saul said to his attendants, "Find someone who plays well and bring him to me."

15:33 [a]Ge 9:6; Jdg 1:7
15:34 [b]1Sa 7:17 [c]1Sa 11:4
15:35 [d]1Sa 19:24 [e]1Sa 16:1
16:1 [f]1Sa 15:35 [g]1Sa 15:23 [h]2Ki 9:1 [i]Ru 4:17; 1Sa 9:16 [j]Ps 78:70; Ac 13:22
16:3 [k]Ex 4:15 [l]Dt 17:15; 1Sa 9:16
16:4 [m]Ge 48:7; Lk 2:4 [n]1Ki 2:13; 2Ki 9:17
16:5 [o]Ex 19:10,22
16:6 [p]1Sa 17:13
16:7 [q]Ps 147:10 [r]1Ki 8:39; 1Ch 28:9; Isa 55:8
16:8 [s]1Sa 17:13
16:11 [t]1Sa 17:12
16:12 [u]1Sa 9:17 [v]Ge 39:6; 1Sa 17:42
16:13 [w]Nu 27:18; Jdg 11:29 [x]1Sa 10:1,6, 9-10; 11:6
16:14 [y]Jdg 16:20 [z]Jdg 9:23; 1Sa 18:10
16:16 [a]ver 23; 1Sa 18:10; 19:9; 2Ki 3:15

[d]32 Or *him trembling, yet* [e]11 Some Septuagint manuscripts; Hebrew *not gather around* [f]14 Or *injurious*; also in verses 15, 16 and 23

18One of the servants answered, "I have seen a son of Jesse of Bethlehem who knows how to play the harp. He is a brave man and a warrior. He speaks well and is a fine-looking man. And the LORD is with[a] him."

19Then Saul sent messengers to Jesse and said, "Send me your son David, who is with the sheep." 20So Jesse took a donkey loaded with bread,[b] a skin of wine and a young goat and sent them with his son David to Saul.

21David came to Saul and entered his service.[c] Saul liked him very much, and David became one of his armor-bearers. 22Then Saul sent word to Jesse, saying, "Allow David to remain in my service, for I am pleased with him."

23Whenever the spirit from God came upon Saul, David would take his harp and play. Then relief would come to Saul; he would feel better, and the evil spirit[d] would leave him.

David and Goliath

17 Now the Philistines gathered their forces for war and assembled[e] at Socoh in Judah. They pitched camp at Ephes Dammim, between Socoh[f] and Azekah. 2Saul and the Israelites assembled and camped in the Valley of Elah[g] and drew up their battle line to meet the Philistines. 3The Philistines occupied one hill and the Israelites another, with the valley between them.

4A champion named Goliath,[h] who was from Gath, came out of the Philistine camp. He was over nine feet[g] tall. 5He had a bronze helmet on his head and wore a coat of scale armor of bronze weighing five thousand shekels[h]; 6on his legs he wore bronze greaves, and a bronze javelin[i] was slung on his back. 7His spear shaft was like a weaver's rod,[j] and its iron point weighed six hundred shekels.[i] His shield bearer[k] went ahead of him.

8Goliath stood and shouted to the ranks of Israel, "Why do you come out and line up for battle?

16:18 [a] 1Sa 3:19; 17:32-37
16:20 [b] 1Sa 10:27; Pr 18:16
16:21 [c] Ge 41:46; Pr 22:29
16:23 [d] ver 14-16
17:1 [e] 1Sa 13:5 [f] Jos 15:35; 2Ch 28:18
17:2 [g] 1Sa 21:9
17:4 [h] Jos 11:21-22; 2Sa 21:19
17:6 [i] ver 45
17:7 [j] 2Sa 21:19 [k] ver 41
17:8 [l] 1Sa 8:17
17:10 [m] ver 26,45; 2Sa 21:21
17:12 [n] Ru 4:17; 1Ch 2:13-15 [o] Ge 35:19 [p] 1Sa 16:11
17:13 [q] 1Sa 16:6 [r] 1Sa 16:9
17:15 [s] 1Sa 16:19
17:17 [t] 1Sa 25:18
17:18 [u] Ge 37:14

Am I not a Philistine, and are you not the servants of Saul? Choose[l] a man and have him come down to me. 9If he is able to fight and kill me, we will become your subjects; but if I overcome him and kill him, you will become our subjects and serve us." 10Then the Philistine said, "This day I defy[m] the ranks of Israel! Give me a man and let us fight each other." 11On hearing the Philistine's words, Saul and all the Israelites were dismayed and terrified.

12Now David was the son of an Ephrathite named Jesse,[n] who was from Bethlehem[o] in Judah. Jesse had eight[p] sons, and in Saul's time he was old and well advanced in years. 13Jesse's three oldest sons had followed Saul to the war: The firstborn was Eliab;[q] the second, Abinadab; and the third, Shammah.[r] 14David was the youngest. The three oldest followed Saul, 15but David went back and forth from Saul to tend his father's sheep[s] at Bethlehem.

16For forty days the Philistine came forward every morning and evening and took his stand.

17Now Jesse said to his son David, "Take this ephah[j] of roasted grain[t] and these ten loaves of bread for your brothers and hurry to their camp. 18Take along these ten cheeses to the commander of their unit.[k] See how your brothers[u] are and bring back some assurance[l] from them. 19They are with Saul and all the men of Israel in the Valley of Elah, fighting against the Philistines."

20Early in the morning David left the flock with a shepherd, loaded up and set out, as Jesse had directed. He reached the camp as the army was going out to its battle positions, shouting the war cry. 21Israel and the Philistines were drawing up their lines facing each other.

[g]4 Hebrew *was six cubits and a span* (about 3 meters) [h]5 That is, about 125 pounds (about 57 kilograms) [i]7 That is, about 15 pounds (about 7 kilograms) [j]17 That is, probably about 3/5 bushel (about 22 liters) [k]18 Hebrew *thousand* [l]18 Or *some token*; or *some pledge of spoils*

DAVID'S FAMILY TREE

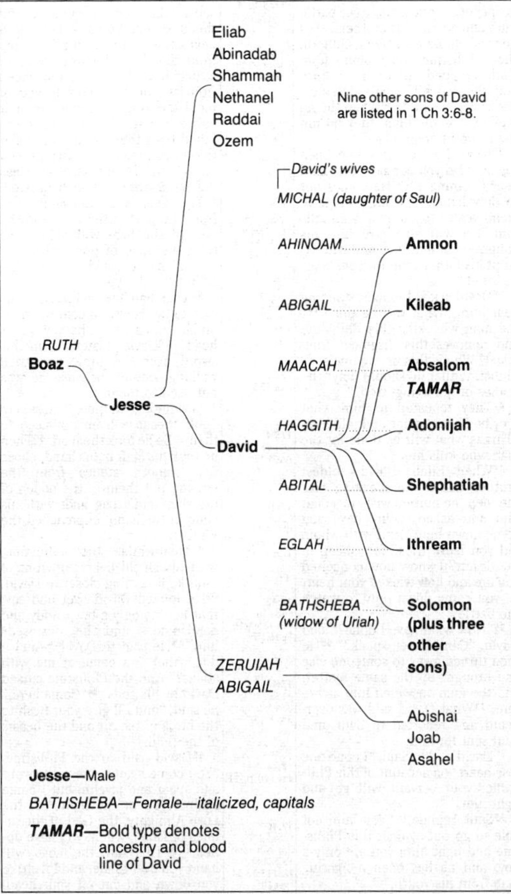
Eliab
Abinadab
Shammah
Nethanel
Raddai
Ozem
Nine other sons of David are listed in 1 Ch 3:6-8.
David's wives
MICHAL (daughter of Saul)
AHINOAM
Amnon
ABIGAIL
Kileab
RUTH
Boaz
MAACAH
Absalom
TAMAR
Jesse
HAGGITH
Adonijah
David
ABITAL
Shephatiah
EGLAH
Ithream
BATHSHEBA (widow of Uriah)
Solomon (plus three other sons)
ZERUIAH
ABIGAIL
Abishai
Joab
Asahel
Jesse—Male
BATHSHEBA—Female—italicized, capitals
TAMAR—Bold type denotes ancestry and blood line of David

22David left his things with the
keeper of supplies, ran to the battle
lines and greeted his brothers. 23As
he was talking with them, Goliath,
the Philistine champion from
Gath, stepped out from his lines
and shouted his usual[a] defiance,
and David heard it. 24When the Israelites saw the man, they all ran
from him in great fear.
25Now the Israelites had been
saying, "Do you see how this man
keeps coming out? He comes out
to defy Israel. The king will give
great wealth to the man who kills
him. He will also give him his
daughter[b] in marriage and will exempt his father's family from taxes
in Israel."
26David asked the men standing
near him, "What will be done for
the man who kills this Philistine
and removes this disgrace[c] from
Israel? Who is this uncircumcised[d]
Philistine that he should defy[e] the
armies of the living[f] God?"
27They repeated to him what
they had been saying and told him,
"This is what will be done for the
man who kills him."
28When Eliab, David's oldest
brother, heard him speaking with
the men, he burned with anger[g] at
him and asked, "Why have you
come down here? And with whom
did you leave those few sheep in
the desert? I know how conceited
you are and how wicked your heart
is; you came down only to watch
the battle."
29"Now what have I done?" said
David. "Can't I even speak?" 30He
then turned away to someone else
and brought up the same matter,
and the men answered him as before. 31What David said was overheard and reported to Saul, and
Saul sent for him.
32David said to Saul, "Let no one
lose heart[h] on account of this Philistine; your servant will go and
fight him."
33Saul replied,[i] "You are not
able to go out against this Philistine and fight him; you are only a
boy, and he has been a fighting
man from his youth."
34But David said to Saul, "Your
servant has been keeping his father's sheep. When a lion[j] or a
bear came and carried off a sheep
from the flock, 35I went after it,
struck it and rescued the sheep
from its mouth. When it turned on
me, I seized it by its hair, struck it
and killed it. 36Your servant has
killed both the lion and the bear;
this uncircumcised Philistine will
be like one of them, because he has
defied the armies of the living God.
37The LORD who delivered[k] me
from the paw of the lion[l] and the
paw of the bear will deliver me
from the hand of this Philistine."
Saul said to David, "Go, and the
LORD be with[m] you."
38Then Saul dressed David in his
own tunic. He put a coat of armor
on him and a bronze helmet on his
head. 39David fastened on his
sword over the tunic and tried
walking around, because he was
not used to them.
"I cannot go in these," he said to
Saul, "because I am not used to
them." So he took them off. 40Then
he took his staff in his hand, chose
five smooth stones from the
stream, put them in the pouch of
his shepherd's bag and, with his
sling in his hand, approached the
Philistine.
41Meanwhile, the Philistine,
with his shield bearer in front of
him, kept coming closer to David.
42He looked David over and saw
that he was only a boy, ruddy and
handsome,[n] and he despised[o]
him. 43He said to David, "Am I a
dog,[p] that you come at me with
sticks?" And the Philistine cursed
David by his gods. 44"Come here,"
he said, "and I'll give your flesh to
the birds of the air and the beasts
of the field![q]"
45David said to the Philistine,
"You come against me with sword
and spear and javelin, but I come
against you in the name[r] of the
LORD Almighty, the God of the armies of Israel, whom you have defied.[s] 46This day the LORD will
hand you over to me, and I'll strike
you down and cut off your head.

17:23 [a]ver 8-10
17:25 [b]Jos 15:16; 1Sa 18:17
17:26 [c]1Sa 11:2 [d]1Sa 14:6 [e]ver 10 [f]Dt 5:26
17:28 [g]Ge 37:4,8, 11; Pr 18:19; Mt 10:36
17:32 [h]Dt 20:3; 1Sa 16:18
17:33 [i]Nu 13:31
17:34 [j]Jer 49:19; Am 3:12
17:37 [k]2Co 1:10 [l]2Ti 4:17 [m]1Sa 20:13; 1Ch 22:11,16
17:42 [n]1Sa 16:12 [o]Ps 123:3-4; Pr 16:18
17:43 [p]1Sa 24:14; 2Sa 3:8; 9:8; 2Ki 8:13
17:44 [q]1Ki 20:10-11
17:45 [r]2Sa 22:33, 35; 2Ch 32:8; Ps 124:8; Heb 11:32-34 [s]ver 10

Today I will give the carcasses[a] of
the Philistine army to the birds of
the air and the beasts of the earth,
and the whole world[b] will know
that there is a God in Israel.[c] 47All
those gathered here will know that
it is not by sword[d] or spear that the
LORD saves;[e] for the battle[f] is the
LORD's, and he will give all of you
into our hands."
48As the Philistine moved closer
to attack him, David ran quickly toward the battle line to meet him.
49Reaching into his bag and taking
out a stone, he slung it and struck
the Philistine on the forehead. The
stone sank into his forehead, and
he fell facedown on the ground.
50So David triumphed over the
Philistine with a sling[g] and a
stone; without a sword in his hand
he struck down the Philistine and
killed him.
51David ran and stood over him.
He took hold of the Philistine's
sword and drew it from the scabbard. After he killed him, he cut[h]
off his head with the sword.[i]
When the Philistines saw that
their hero was dead, they turned
and ran. 52Then the men of Israel
and Judah surged forward with a
shout and pursued the Philistines
to the entrance of Gath[m] and to the
gates of Ekron.[j] Their dead were
strewn along the Shaaraim[k] road
to Gath and Ekron. 53When the Israelites returned from chasing the
Philistines, they plundered their
camp. 54David took the Philistine's
head and brought it to Jerusalem,
and he put the Philistine's weapons in his own tent.
55As Saul watched David[l] going
out to meet the Philistine, he said
to Abner, commander of the army,
"Abner, whose son is that young
man?"
Abner replied, "As surely as you
live, O king, I don't know."
56The king said, "Find out whose
son this young man is."
57As soon as David returned
from killing the Philistine, Abner
took him and brought him before
Saul, with David still holding the
Philistine's head.
58"Whose son are you, young
man?" Saul asked him.
David said, "I am the son of your
servant Jesse[m] of Bethlehem."

Saul's Jealousy of David

18 After David had finished
talking with Saul, Jonathan
became one in spirit with David,
and he loved[n] him as himself.[o]
2From that day Saul kept David
with him and did not let him return
to his father's house. 3And Jonathan made a covenant[p] with David
because he loved him as himself.
4Jonathan took off the robe[q] he
was wearing and gave it to David,
along with his tunic, and even his
sword, his bow and his belt.
5Whatever Saul sent him to do,
David did it so successfully[n] that
Saul gave him a high rank in the
army. This pleased all the people,
and Saul's officers as well.
6When the men were returning
home after David had killed the
Philistine, the women came out
from all the towns of Israel to meet
King Saul with singing and dancing,[r] with joyful songs and with
tambourines[s] and lutes. 7As they
danced, they sang:[t]

"Saul has slain his thousands,
and David his tens[u] of
thousands."

8Saul was very angry; this refrain
galled him. "They have credited
David with tens of thousands," he
thought, "but me with only thousands. What more can he get but
the kingdom?[v]" 9And from that
time on Saul kept a jealous eye on
David.
10The next day an evil[o] spirit[w]
from God came forcefully upon
Saul. He was prophesying in his
house, while David was playing the
harp, as he usually[x] did. Saul had
a spear in his hand 11and he hurled
it, saying to himself,[y] "I'll pin David to the wall." But David eluded[z]
him twice.
12Saul was afraid[a] of David, be-

17:46 [a] Dt 28:26 [b] Jos 4:24; 1Ki 8:43; Isa 52:10 [c] 1Ki 18:36; 2Ki 19:19; Isa 37:20
17:47 [d] Hos 1:7; Zec 4:6 [e] 1Sa 14:6; 2Ch 14:11 [f] 2Ch 20:15; Ps 44:6-7
17:50 [g] 2Sa 23:21
17:51 [h] Heb 11:34 [i] 1Sa 21:9
17:52 [j] Jos 15:11 [k] Jos 15:36
17:55 [l] 1Sa 16:21
17:58 [m] ver 12
18:1 [n] 2Sa 1:26 [o] Ge 44:30
18:3 [p] 1Sa 20:8,16, 17,42
18:4 [q] Ge 41:42
18:6 [r] Ex 15:20 [s] Jdg 11:34; Ps 68:25
18:7 [t] Ex 15:21 [u] 1Sa 21:11; 29:5
18:8 [v] 1Sa 15:8
18:10 [w] 1Sa 16:14 [x] 1Sa 19:7
18:11 [y] 1Sa 20:7,33 [z] 1Sa 19:10
18:12 [a] ver 15,29

[m]52 Some Septuagint manuscripts; Hebrew *a valley* [n]5 Or *wisely* [o]10 Or *injurious*

cause the LORD[a] was with[b] David
but had left Saul. 13So he sent David away from him and gave him
command over a thousand men,
and David led[c] the troops in their
campaigns.[d] 14In everything he
did he had great success,[p][e] because the LORD was with[f] him.
15When Saul saw how successful[q]
he was, he was afraid of him. 16But
all Israel and Judah loved David,
because he led them in their campaigns.[g]
17Saul said to David, "Here is my
older daughter[h] Merab. I will give
her to you in marriage; only serve
me bravely and fight the battles[i]
of the LORD." For Saul said to himself,[j] "I will not raise a hand
against him. Let the Philistines do
that!"
18But David said to Saul, "Who
am I,[k] and what is my family or my
father's clan in Israel, that I should
become the king's son-in-law?[l]"
19So[r] when the time came for Merab,[m] Saul's daughter, to be given
to David, she was given in marriage
to Adriel of Meholah.[n]
20Now Saul's daughter Michal[o]
was in love with David, and when
they told Saul about it, he was
pleased. 21"I will give her to him,"
he thought, "so that she may be a
snare[p] to him and so that the hand
of the Philistines may be against
him." So Saul said to David, "Now
you have a second opportunity to
become my son-in-law."
22Then Saul ordered his attendants: "Speak to David privately
and say, 'Look, the king is pleased
with you, and his attendants all
like you; now become his son-in-
law.' "
23They repeated these words to
David. But David said, "Do you
think it is a small matter to become
the king's son-in-law? I'm only a
poor man and little known."
24When Saul's servants told him
what David had said, 25Saul replied, "Say to David, 'The king
wants no other price[q] for the bride
than a hundred Philistine foreskins, to take revenge on his enemies.' " Saul's plan[r] was to have

18:12 [a] 1Sa 16:13 [b] 1Sa 28:15
18:13 [c] ver 16; Nu 27:17 [d] 2Sa 5:2
18:14 [e] Ge 39:3 [f] Ge 39:2,23; Jos 6:27; 1Sa 16:18
18:16 [g] ver 5
18:17 [h] 1Sa 17:25 [i] Nu 21:14; 1Sa 25:28 [j] ver 25
18:18 [k] 1Sa 9:21; 2Sa 7:18 [l] ver 23
18:19 [m] 2Sa 21:8 [n] Jdg 7:22
18:20 [o] ver 28
18:21 [p] ver 17,26
18:25 [q] Ge 34:12; Ex 22:17; 1Sa 14:24 [r] ver 17
18:27 [s] ver 13; 2Sa 3:14
18:30 [t] ver 5; 2Sa 11:1
19:1 [u] 1Sa 18:1 [v] 1Sa 18:9
19:3 [w] 1Sa 20:12
19:4 [x] 1Sa 20:32; Pr 31:8,9; Jer 18:20 [y] Ge 42:22; Pr 17:13
19:5 [z] 1Sa 11:13; 17:49-50; 1Ch 11:14 [a] Dt 19:10-13; 1Sa 20:32; Mt 27:4

David fall by the hands of the Philistines.
26When the attendants told David these things, he was pleased to
become the king's son-in-law. So
before the allotted time elapsed,
27David and his men went out and
killed two hundred Philistines. He
brought their foreskins and presented the full number to the king
so that he might become the king's
son-in-law. Then Saul gave him his
daughter Michal[s] in marriage.
28When Saul realized that the
LORD was with David and that his
daughter Michal loved David,
29Saul became still more afraid of
him, and he remained his enemy
the rest of his days.
30The Philistine commanders
continued to go out to battle, and
as often as they did, David met with
more success[s][t] than the rest of
Saul's officers, and his name became well known.

Saul Tries to Kill David

19 Saul told his son Jonathan[u] and all the attendants to kill[v] David. But Jonathan
was very fond of David 2and warned
him, "My father Saul is looking for
a chance to kill you. Be on your
guard tomorrow morning; go into
hiding and stay there. 3I will go out
and stand with my father in the
field where you are. I'll speak[w] to
him about you and will tell you
what I find out."
4Jonathan spoke[x] well of David
to Saul his father and said to him,
"Let not the king do wrong[y] to his
servant David; he has not wronged
you, and what he has done has ben-
efited you greatly. 5He took his life
in his hands when he killed the
Philistine. The LORD won a great
victory[z] for all Israel, and you saw
it and were glad. Why then would
you do wrong to an innocent[a] man
like David by killing him for no reason?"
6Saul listened to Jonathan and

[p]14 Or *he was very wise* [q]15 Or *wise*
[r]19 Or *However,* [s]30 Or *David acted more wisely*

took this oath: "As surely as the
LORD lives, David will not be put to
death."
7So Jonathan called David and
told him the whole conversation.
He brought him to Saul, and David
was with Saul as before.[a]
8Once more war broke out, and
David went out and fought the
Philistines. He struck them with
such force that they fled before
him.
9But an evil[t] spirit[b] from the
LORD came upon Saul as he was sitting in his house with his spear in
his hand. While David was playing
the harp, 10Saul tried to pin him to
the wall with his spear, but David
eluded[c] him as Saul drove the
spear into the wall. That night David made good his escape.
11Saul sent men to David's
house to watch[d] it and to kill him
in the morning. But Michal, David's wife, warned him, "If you
don't run for your life tonight, tomorrow you'll be killed." 12So Michal let David down through a window,[e] and he fled and escaped.
13Then Michal took an idol[u] and
laid it on the bed, covering it with
a garment and putting some goats'
hair at the head.
14When Saul sent the men to
capture David, Michal said,[f] "He
is ill."
15Then Saul sent the men back
to see David and told them, "Bring
him up to me in his bed so that I
may kill him." 16But when the men
entered, there was the idol in the
bed, and at the head was some
goats' hair.
17Saul said to Michal, "Why did
you deceive me like this and send
my enemy away so that he escaped?"
Michal told him, "He said to me,
'Let me get away. Why should I kill
you?' "
18When David had fled and
made his escape, he went to Samuel at Ramah[g] and told him all
that Saul had done to him. Then he
and Samuel went to Naioth and
stayed there. 19Word came to Saul:
"David is in Naioth at Ramah";
20so he sent men to capture him.
But when they saw a group of
prophets[h] prophesying, with Samuel standing there as their leader,
the Spirit of God came upon[i]
Saul's men and they also prophesied.[j] 21Saul was told about it, and
he sent more men, and they prophesied too. Saul sent men a third
time, and they also prophesied.
22Finally, he himself left for Ramah and went to the great cistern
at Secu. And he asked, "Where are
Samuel and David?"
"Over in Naioth at Ramah," they
said.
23So Saul went to Naioth at Ramah. But the Spirit of God came
even upon him, and he walked
along prophesying[k] until he came
to Naioth. 24He stripped[l] off his
robes and also prophesied in Samuel's presence. He lay that way all
that day and night. This is why people say, "Is Saul also among the
prophets?"[m]

David and Jonathan

20 Then David fled from Naioth at Ramah and went to
Jonathan and asked, "What have I
done? What is my crime? How have
I wronged[n] your father, that he is
trying to take my life?"
2"Never!" Jonathan replied.
"You are not going to die! Look, my
father doesn't do anything, great or
small, without confiding in me.
Why would he hide this from me?
It's not so!"
3But David took an oath[o] and
said, "Your father knows very well
that I have found favor in your eyes,
and he has said to himself, 'Jonathan must not know this or he will
be grieved.' Yet as surely as the
LORD lives and as you live, there is
only a step between me and
death."
4Jonathan said to David, "Whatever you want me to do, I'll do for
you."
5So David said, "Look, tomorrow
is the New Moon festival,[p] and I

19:7 [a] 1Sa 16:21; 18:2,13
19:9 [b] 1Sa 16:14; 18:10-11
19:10 [c] 1Sa 18:11
19:11 [d] Ps 59 Title
19:12 [e] Jos 2:15; Ac 9:25
19:14 [f] Jos 2:4
19:18 [g] 1Sa 7:17
19:20 [h] ver 11,14; Jn 7:32,45 [i] Nu 11:25 [j] 1Sa 10:5; Joel 2:28
19:23 [k] 1Sa 10:13
19:24 [l] 2Sa 6:20; Isa 20:2; Mic 1:8 [m] 1Sa 10:11
20:1 [n] 1Sa 24:9
20:3 [o] Dt 6:13
20:5 [p] Nu 10:10; 28:11

[t]9 Or *injurious* [u]13 Hebrew *teraphim*; also in verse 16

am supposed to dine with the king; but let me go and hide[a] in the field until the evening of the day after tomorrow. 6If your father misses me at all, tell him, 'David earnestly asked my permission to hurry to Bethlehem,[b] his hometown, because an annual[c] sacrifice is being made there for his whole clan.' 7If he says, 'Very well,' then your servant is safe. But if he loses his temper,[d] you can be sure that he is determined to harm me. 8As for you, show kindness to your servant, for you have brought him into a covenant[e] with you before the LORD. If I am guilty, then kill[f] me yourself! Why hand me over to your father?"

9"Never!" Jonathan said. "If I had the least inkling that my father was determined to harm you, wouldn't I tell you?"

10David asked, "Who will tell me if your father answers you harshly?"

11"Come," Jonathan said, "let's go out into the field." So they went there together.

12Then Jonathan said to David: "By the LORD, the God of Israel, I will surely sound out my father by this time the day after tomorrow! If he is favorably disposed toward you, will I not send you word and let you know? 13But if my father is inclined to harm you, may the LORD deal with me, be it ever so severely,[g] if I do not let you know and send you away safely. May the LORD be with[h] you as he has been with my father. 14But show me unfailing kindness like that of the LORD as long as I live, so that I may not be killed, 15and do not ever cut off your kindness from my family[i]—not even when the LORD has cut off every one of David's enemies from the face of the earth."

16So Jonathan made a covenant[j] with the house of David, saying, "May the LORD call David's enemies to account." 17And Jonathan had David reaffirm his oath[k] out of love for him, because he loved him as he loved himself.

18Then Jonathan said to David: "Tomorrow is the New Moon festival. You will be missed, because your seat will be empty.[l] 19The day after tomorrow, toward evening, go to the place where you hid[m] when this trouble began, and wait by the stone Ezel. 20I will shoot three arrows to the side of it, as though I were shooting at a target. 21Then I will send a boy and say, 'Go, find the arrows.' If I say to him, 'Look, the arrows are on this side of you; bring them here,' then come, because, as surely as the LORD lives, you are safe; there is no danger. 22But if I say to the boy, 'Look, the arrows are beyond[n] you,' then you must go, because the LORD has sent you away. 23And about the matter you and I discussed—remember, the LORD is witness[o] between you and me forever."

24So David hid in the field, and when the New Moon festival came, the king sat down to eat. 25He sat in his customary place by the wall, opposite Jonathan,[v] and Abner sat next to Saul, but David's place was empty.[p] 26Saul said nothing that day, for he thought, "Something must have happened to David to make him ceremonially unclean—surely he is unclean.[q]" 27But the next day, the second day of the month, David's place was empty again. Then Saul said to his son Jonathan, "Why hasn't the son of Jesse come to the meal, either yesterday or today?"

28Jonathan answered, "David earnestly asked me for permission[r] to go to Bethlehem. 29He said, 'Let me go, because our family is observing a sacrifice in the town and my brother has ordered me to be there. If I have found favor in your eyes, let me get away to see my brothers.' That is why he has not come to the king's table."

30Saul's anger flared up at Jonathan and he said to him, "You son of a perverse and rebellious woman! Don't I know that you have sided with the son of Jesse to your own shame and to the shame of the

20:5 [a] 1Sa 19:2
20:6 [b] 1Sa 17:58 [c] Dt 12:5
20:7 [d] 1Sa 25:17
20:8 [e] 1Sa 18:3; 23:18 [f] 2Sa 14:32
20:13 [g] Ru 1:17; 1Sa 3:17 [h] Jos 1:5; 1Sa 17:37; 18:12; 1Ch 22:11,16
20:15 [i] 2Sa 9:7
20:16 [j] 1Sa 25:22
20:17 [k] 1Sa 18:3
20:18 [l] ver 5,25
20:19 [m] 1Sa 19:2
20:22 [n] ver 37
20:23 [o] ver 14-15; Ge 31:50
20:25 [p] ver 18
20:26 [q] Lev 7:20-21; 15:5; 1Sa 16:5
20:28 [r] ver 6

[v]25 Septuagint; Hebrew *wall. Jonathan arose*

mother who bore you? **31**As long as
the son of Jesse lives on this earth,
neither you nor your kingdom will
be established. Now send and
bring him to me, for he must die!"
32"Why[a] should he be put to
death? What[b] has he done?" Jonathan asked his father. **33**But Saul
hurled his spear at him to kill him.
Then Jonathan knew that his father intended[c] to kill David.
34Jonathan got up from the table
in fierce anger; on that second day
of the month he did not eat, because he was grieved at his father's
shameful treatment of David.
35In the morning Jonathan went
out to the field for his meeting with
David. He had a small boy with
him, **36**and he said to the boy, "Run
and find the arrows I shoot." As the
boy ran, he shot an arrow beyond
him. **37**When the boy came to the
place where Jonathan's arrow had
fallen, Jonathan called out after
him, "Isn't the arrow beyond[d]
you?" **38**Then he shouted, "Hurry!
Go quickly! Don't stop!" The boy
picked up the arrow and returned
to his master. **39**(The boy knew
nothing of all this; only Jonathan
and David knew.) **40**Then Jonathan
gave his weapons to the boy and
said, "Go, carry them back to
town."
41After the boy had gone, David
got up from the south side ⌞of the
stone⌟ and bowed down before Jonathan three times, with his face to
the ground. Then they kissed each
other and wept together—but David wept the most.
42Jonathan said to David, "Go in
peace,[e] for we have sworn friendship[f] with each other in the name
of the LORD, saying, 'The LORD is
witness between you and me, and
between your descendants and my
descendants forever.'" Then David
left, and Jonathan went back to the
town.

David at Nob

21 David went to Nob,[g] to
Ahimelech the priest.
Ahimelech trembled[h] when he
met him, and asked, "Why are you
alone? Why is no one with you?"
2David answered Ahimelech the
priest, "The king charged me with
a certain matter and said to me,
'No one is to know anything about
your mission and your instructions.' As for my men, I have told
them to meet me at a certain place.
3Now then, what do you have on
hand? Give me five loaves of bread,
or whatever you can find."
4But the priest answered David,
"I don't have any ordinary bread[i]
on hand; however, there is some
consecrated[j] bread here—provided the men have kept[k] themselves
from women."
5David replied, "Indeed women
have been kept from us, as usual
whenever[w] I set out. The men's
things[x] are holy[l] even on mis-
sions that are not holy. How much
more so today!" **6**So the priest gave
him the consecrated bread,[m] since
there was no bread there except
the bread of the Presence that had
been removed from before the LORD
and replaced by hot bread on the
day it was taken away.
7Now one of Saul's servants was
there that day, detained before the
LORD; he was Doeg[n] the Edomite,[o]
Saul's head shepherd.
8David asked Ahimelech, "Don't
you have a spear or a sword here? I
haven't brought my sword or any
other weapon, because the king's
business was urgent."
9The priest replied, "The sword[p]
of Goliath the Philistine, whom
you killed in the Valley of Elah,[q] is
here; it is wrapped in a cloth behind the ephod. If you want it, take
it; there is no sword here but that
one."
David said, "There is none like it;
give it to me."

David at Gath

10That day David fled from Saul
and went[r] to Achish king of Gath.
11But the servants of Achish said to
him, "Isn't this David, the king of

20:32 [a]1Sa 19:4; Mt 27:23 [b]Ge 31:36; Lk 23:22
20:33 [c]ver 7; 1Sa 18:11,17
20:37 [d]ver 22
20:42 [e]ver 22; 1Sa 1:17 [f]2Sa 1:26; Pr 18:24
21:1 [g]1Sa 14:3; 22:9,19; Ne 11:32; Isa 10:32 [h]1Sa 16:4
21:4 [i]Lev 24:8-9 [j]Ex 25:30; Mt 12:4 [k]Ex 19:15
21:5 [l]1Th 4:4
21:6 [m]Lev 24:8-9; Mt 12:3-4; Mk 2:25-28; Lk 6:1-5
21:7 [n]1Sa 22:9,22 [o]1Sa 14:47; Ps 52 Title
21:9 [p]1Sa 17:51 [q]1Sa 17:2
21:10 [r]1Sa 27:2

[w]5 Or *from us in the past few days since*
[x]5 Or *bodies*

the land? Isn't he the one they sing
about in their dances:

" 'Saul has slain his thousands,
and David his tens of
thousands'?"[a]

12David took these words to
heart and was very much afraid of
Achish king of Gath. 13So he pretended to be insane[b] in their presence; and while he was in their
hands he acted like a madman,
making marks on the doors of the
gate and letting saliva run down his
beard.
14Achish said to his servants,
"Look at the man! He is insane!
Why bring him to me? 15Am I so
short of madmen that you have to
bring this fellow here to carry on
like this in front of me? Must this
man come into my house?"

David at Adullam and Mizpah

22 David left Gath and escaped to the cave[c] of Adullam. When his brothers and his father's household heard about it,
they went down to him there. 2All
those who were in distress or in
debt or discontented gathered[d]
around him, and he became their
leader. About four hundred men
were with him.
3From there David went to Mizpah in Moab and said to the king of
Moab, "Would you let my father
and mother come and stay with you
until I learn what God will do for
me?" 4So he left them with the king
of Moab, and they stayed with him
as long as David was in the stronghold.
5But the prophet Gad[e] said to
David, "Do not stay in the stronghold. Go into the land of Judah."
So David left and went to the forest
of Hereth.

Saul Kills the Priests of Nob

6Now Saul heard that David and
his men had been discovered. And
Saul, spear in hand, was seated[f]
under the tamarisk[g] tree on the
hill at Gibeah, with all his officials
standing around him. 7Saul said to
them, "Listen, men of Benjamin!
Will the son of Jesse give all of you
fields and vineyards? Will he make
all of you commanders[h] of thousands and commanders of hundreds? 8Is that why you have all
conspired against me? No one tells
me when my son makes a covenant[i] with the son of Jesse. None
of you is concerned[j] about me or
tells me that my son has incited my
servant to lie in wait for me, as he
does today."
9But Doeg[k] the Edomite, who
was standing with Saul's officials,
said, "I saw the son of Jesse come
to Ahimelech son of Ahitub at
Nob.[l] 10Ahimelech inquired[m] of
the LORD for him; he also gave him
provisions[n] and the sword of Goliath the Philistine."
11Then the king sent for the
priest Ahimelech son of Ahitub and
his father's whole family, who were
the priests at Nob, and they all
came to the king. 12Saul said, "Listen now, son of Ahitub."
"Yes, my lord," he answered.
13Saul said to him, "Why have
you conspired[o] against me, you
and the son of Jesse, giving him
bread and a sword and inquiring of
God for him, so that he has rebelled against me and lies in wait
for me, as he does today?"
14Ahimelech answered the king,
"Who[p] of all your servants is as
loyal as David, the king's son-in-
law, captain of your bodyguard and
highly respected in your household? 15Was that day the first time
I inquired of God for him? Of
course not! Let not the king accuse
your servant or any of his father's
family, for your servant knows
nothing at all about this whole affair."
16But the king said, "You will
surely die, Ahimelech, you and
your father's whole family."
17Then the king ordered the
guards at his side: "Turn and kill
the priests of the LORD, because
they too have sided with David.
They knew he was fleeing, yet they
did not tell me."
But the king's officials were not

21:11 [a] 1Sa 18:7; 29:5; Ps 56 Title
21:13 [b] Ps 34 Title
22:1 [c] 2Sa 23:13; Ps 57 Title; 142 Title
22:2 [d] 1Sa 23:13; 25:13; 2Sa 15:20
22:5 [e] 2Sa 24:11; 1Ch 21:9; 29:29; 2Ch 29:25
22:6 [f] Jdg 4:5 [g] Ge 21:33
22:7 [h] 1Sa 8:14
22:8 [i] 1Sa 18:3; 20:16 [j] 1Sa 23:21
22:9 [k] 1Sa 21:7; Ps 52 Title [l] 1Sa 21:1
22:10 [m] Nu 27:21; 1Sa 10:22 [n] 1Sa 21:6
22:13 [o] ver 8
22:14 [p] 1Sa 19:4

willing[a] to raise a hand to strike
the priests of the LORD.
18The king then ordered Doeg,
"You turn and strike down the
priests." So Doeg the Edomite
turned and struck them down. That
day he killed eighty-five men who
wore the linen ephod.[b] 19He also
put to the sword[c] Nob, the town of
the priests, with its men and wom-
en, its children and infants, and its
cattle, donkeys and sheep.
20But Abiathar,[d] a son of Ahimelech son of Ahitub, escaped and
fled to join David.[e] 21He told David that Saul had killed the priests
of the LORD. 22Then David said to
Abiathar: "That day, when Doeg[f]
the Edomite was there, I knew he
would be sure to tell Saul. I am responsible for the death of your father's whole family. 23Stay with
me; don't be afraid; the man who is
seeking your life[g] is seeking mine
also. You will be safe with me."

David Saves Keilah

23 When David was told,
"Look, the Philistines are
fighting against Keilah[h] and are
looting the threshing floors," 2he
inquired[i] of the LORD, saying,
"Shall I go and attack these Philistines?"
The LORD answered him, "Go, attack the Philistines and save Keilah."
3But David's men said to him,
"Here in Judah we are afraid. How
much more, then, if we go to Keilah against the Philistine forces!"
4Once again David inquired of
the LORD, and the LORD answered
him, "Go down to Keilah, for I am
going to give the Philistines into
your hand.[j]" 5So David and his
men went to Keilah, fought the
Philistines and carried off their
livestock. He inflicted heavy losses
on the Philistines and saved the
people of Keilah. 6(Now Abiathar[k]
son of Ahimelech had brought the
ephod down with him when he fled
to David at Keilah.)

Saul Pursues David

7Saul was told that David had
gone to Keilah, and he said, "God
has handed him over to me, for David has imprisoned himself by entering a town with gates and bars."
8And Saul called up all his forces
for battle, to go down to Keilah to
besiege David and his men.
9When David learned that Saul
was plotting against him, he said to
Abiathar[l] the priest, "Bring the
ephod." 10David said, "O LORD,
God of Israel, your servant has
heard definitely that Saul plans to
come to Keilah and destroy the
town on account of me. 11Will the
citizens of Keilah surrender me to
him? Will Saul come down, as your
servant has heard? O LORD, God of
Israel, tell your servant."
And the LORD said, "He will."
12Again David asked, "Will the
citizens of Keilah surrender[m] me
and my men to Saul?"
And the LORD said, "They will."
13So David and his men,[n] about
six hundred in number, left Keilah
and kept moving from place to
place. When Saul was told that David had escaped from Keilah, he
did not go there.
14David stayed in the desert
strongholds and in the hills of the
Desert of Ziph.[o] Day after day Saul
searched[p] for him, but God did
not[q] give David into his hands.
15While David was at Horesh in
the Desert of Ziph, he learned that
Saul had come out to take his life.
16And Saul's son Jonathan went to
David at Horesh and helped him
find strength[r] in God. 17"Don't be
afraid," he said. "My father Saul
will not lay a hand on you. You will
be king[s] over Israel, and I will be
second to you. Even my father Saul
knows this." 18The two of them
made a covenant[t] before the LORD.
Then Jonathan went home, but
David remained at Horesh.
19The Ziphites[u] went up to Saul
at Gibeah and said, "Is not David
hiding among us[v] in the strongholds at Horesh, on the hill of Hakilah,[w] south of Jeshimon? 20Now,
O king, come down whenever it
pleases you to do so, and we will be

22:17 [a] Ex 1:17
22:18 [b] 1Sa 2:18,31
22:19 [c] 1Sa 15:3
22:20 [d] 1Sa 23:6,9; 30:7; 1Ki 2:22,26, 27 [e] 1Sa 2:32
22:22 [f] 1Sa 21:7
22:23 [g] 1Ki 2:26
23:1 [h] Jos 15:44
23:2 [i] ver 4,12; 1Sa 30:8; 2Sa 5:19,23
23:4 [j] Jos 8:7; Jdg 7:7
23:6 [k] 1Sa 22:20
23:9 [l] ver 6; 1Sa 22:20; 30:7
23:12 [m] ver 20
23:13 [n] 1Sa 22:2; 25:13
23:14 [o] Jos 15:24,55 [p] Ps 54:3-4 [q] Ps 32:7
23:16 [r] 1Sa 30:6
23:17 [s] 1Sa 20:31; 24:20
23:18 [t] 1Sa 18:3; 20:16,42; 2Sa 9:1; 21:7
23:19 [u] 1Sa 26:1 [v] Ps 54 Title [w] 1Sa 26:3

responsible for handing[a] him over to the king."

21Saul replied, "The LORD bless you for your concern[b] for me. **22**Go and make further preparation. Find out where David usually goes and who has seen him there. They tell me he is very crafty. **23**Find out about all the hiding places he uses and come back to me with definite information.[y] Then I will go with you; if he is in the area, I will track him down among all the clans of Judah."

24So they set out and went to Ziph ahead of Saul. Now David and his men were in the Desert of Maon,[c] in the Arabah south of Jeshimon. **25**Saul and his men began the search, and when David was told about it, he went down to the rock and stayed in the Desert of Maon. When Saul heard this, he went into the Desert of Maon in pursuit of David.

26Saul[d] was going along one side of the mountain, and David and his men were on the other side, hurrying to get away from Saul. As Saul and his forces were closing in on David and his men to capture them, **27**a messenger came to Saul, saying, "Come quickly! The Philistines are raiding the land." **28**Then Saul broke off his pursuit of David and went to meet the Philistines. That is why they call this place Sela Hammahlekoth.[z] **29**And David went up from there and lived in the strongholds of En Gedi.[e]

David Spares Saul's Life

24 After Saul returned from pursuing the Philistines, he was told, "David is in the Desert of En Gedi.[f]" **2**So Saul took three thousand chosen men from all Israel and set out to look[g] for David and his men near the Crags of the Wild Goats.

3He came to the sheep pens along the way; a cave[h] was there, and Saul went in to relieve[i] himself. David and his men were far back in the cave. **4**The men said, "This is the day the LORD spoke[j] of when he said[a] to you, 'I will give your enemy into your hands for you to deal with as you wish.' "[k] Then David crept up unnoticed and cut off a corner of Saul's robe.

5Afterward, David was conscience-stricken[l] for having cut off a corner of his robe. **6**He said to his men, "The LORD forbid that I should do such a thing to my master, the LORD's anointed,[m] or lift my hand against him; for he is the anointed of the LORD." **7**With these words David rebuked his men and did not allow them to attack Saul. And Saul left the cave and went his way.

8Then David went out of the cave and called out to Saul, "My lord the king!" When Saul looked behind him, David bowed down and prostrated himself with his face to the ground.[n] **9**He said to Saul, "Why do you listen when men say, 'David is bent on harming you'? **10**This day you have seen with your own eyes how the LORD delivered you into my hands in the cave. Some urged me to kill you, but I spared you; I said, 'I will not lift my hand against my master, because he is the LORD's anointed.' **11**See, my father, look at this piece of your robe in my hand! I cut off the corner of your robe but did not kill you. Now understand and recognize that I am not guilty[o] of wrongdoing or rebellion. I have not wronged you, but you are hunting[p] me down to take my life. **12**May the LORD judge[q] between you and me. And may the LORD avenge[r] the wrongs you have done to me, but my hand will not touch you. **13**As the old saying goes, 'From evildoers come evil deeds,[s]' so my hand will not touch you.

14"Against whom has the king of Israel come out? Whom are you pursuing? A dead dog?[t] A flea?[u] **15**May the LORD be our judge[v] and decide between us. May he consider my cause and uphold[w] it; may

23:20 [a] ver 12
23:21 [b] 1Sa 22:8
23:24 [c] Jos 15:55; 1Sa 25:2
23:26 [d] Ps 17:9
23:29 [e] 2Ch 20:2
24:1 [f] 1Sa 23:28-29
24:2 [g] 1Sa 26:2
24:3 [h] Ps 57 Title; 142 Title [i] Jdg 3:24
24:4 [j] 1Sa 25:28-30 [k] 1Sa 23:17; 26:8
24:5 [l] 2Sa 24:10
24:6 [m] 1Sa 26:11
24:8 [n] 1Sa 25:23-24
24:11 [o] Ps 7:3 [p] 1Sa 23:14, 23; 1Sa 26:20
24:12 [q] Ge 16:5; 31:53; Job 5:8 [r] Jdg 11:27; 1Sa 26:10
24:13 [s] Mt 7:20
24:14 [t] 1Sa 17:43; 2Sa 9:8 [u] 1Sa 26:20
24:15 [v] ver 12 [w] Ps 35:1,23; Mic 7:9

[y]23 Or *me at Nacon* [z]28 *Sela Hammahlekoth* means *rock of parting.*
[a]4 Or *"Today the LORD is saying*

he vindicate[a] me by delivering[b]
me from your hand."
16When David finished saying
this, Saul asked, "Is that your
voice,[c] David my son?" And he
wept aloud. 17"You are more righteous than I,"[d] he said. "You have
treated me well,[e] but I have treated you badly. 18You have just now
told me of the good you did to me;
the LORD delivered[f] me into your
hands, but you did not kill me.
19When a man finds his enemy,
does he let him get away unharmed? May the LORD reward you
well for the way you treated me today. 20I know that you will surely
be king[g] and that the kingdom[h] of
Israel will be established in your
hands. 21Now swear[i] to me by the
LORD that you will not cut off my
descendants or wipe out my name
from my father's family.[j]"
22So David gave his oath to Saul.
Then Saul returned home, but David and his men went up to the
stronghold.[k]

David, Nabal and Abigail

25 Now Samuel died,[l] and all
Israel assembled and
mourned[m] for him; and they buried
him at his home in Ramah.[n]
Then David moved down into the
Desert of Maon.[b] 2A certain man
in Maon,[o] who had property there
at Carmel, was very wealthy. He
had a thousand goats and three
thousand sheep, which he was
shearing in Carmel. 3His name was
Nabal and his wife's name was Abigail.[p] She was an intelligent and
beautiful woman, but her husband,
a Calebite,[q] was surly and mean in
his dealings.
4While David was in the desert,
he heard that Nabal was shearing
sheep. 5So he sent ten young men
and said to them, "Go up to Nabal
at Carmel and greet him in my
name. 6Say to him: 'Long life to
you! Good health[r] to you and your
household! And good health to all
that is yours![s]
7" 'Now I hear that it is sheep-
shearing time. When your shepherds were with us, we did not mis-

24:15 [a]Ps 43:1 [b]Ps 119:134, 154
24:16 [c]1Sa 26:17
24:17 [d]Ge 38:26; 1Sa 26:21 [e]Mt 5:44
24:18 [f]1Sa 26:23
24:20 [g]1Sa 23:17 [h]1Sa 13:14
24:21 [i]Ge 21:23; 2Sa 21:1-9 [j]1Sa 20:14-15
24:22 [k]1Sa 23:29
25:1 [l]1Sa 28:3 [m]Nu 20:29; Dt 34:8 [n]Ge 21:21; 2Ch 33:20
25:2 [o]Jos 15:55; 1Sa 23:24
25:3 [p]Pr 31:10 [q]Jos 15:13
25:6 [r]Ps 122:7; Lk 10:5 [s]1Ch 12:18
25:7 [t]ver 15
25:8 [u]Ne 8:10
25:10 [v]Jdg 9:28
25:11 [w]Jdg 8:6
25:13 [x]1Sa 23:13 [y]1Sa 30:24
25:14 [z]1Sa 13:10
25:15 [a]ver 7 [b]ver 21
25:16 [c]Ex 14:22; Job 1:10
25:17 [d]1Sa 20:7
25:18 [e]1Ch 12:40

treat[t] them, and the whole time
they were at Carmel nothing of
theirs was missing. 8Ask your own
servants and they will tell you.
Therefore be favorable toward my
young men, since we come at a festive time. Please give your servants
and your son David whatever[u] you
can find for them.' "
9When David's men arrived, they
gave Nabal this message in David's
name. Then they waited.
10Nabal answered David's servants, "Who[v] is this David? Who is
this son of Jesse? Many servants
are breaking away from their masters these days. 11Why should I
take my bread[w] and water, and the
meat I have slaughtered for my
shearers, and give it to men coming
from who knows where?"
12David's men turned around
and went back. When they arrived,
they reported every word. 13David
said to his men, "Put on your
swords!" So they put on their
swords, and David put on his.
About four hundred men went[x] up
with David, while two hundred
stayed with the supplies.[y]
14One of the servants told Nabal's wife Abigail: "David sent messengers from the desert to give our
master his greetings,[z] but he
hurled insults at them. 15Yet these
men were very good to us. They did
not mistreat[a] us, and the whole
time we were out in the fields near
them nothing was missing.[b]
16Night and day they were a wall[c]
around us all the time we were
herding our sheep near them.
17Now think it over and see what
you can do, because disaster is
hanging over our master and his
whole household. He is such a
wicked[d] man that no one can talk
to him."
18Abigail lost no time. She took
two hundred loaves of bread, two
skins of wine, five dressed sheep,
five seahs[c] of roasted grain, a hundred cakes of raisins[e] and two

[b]*1* Some Septuagint manuscripts; Hebrew *Paran* [c]*18* That is, probably about a bushel (about 37 liters)

hundred cakes of pressed figs, and
loaded them on donkeys.[a] 19Then
she told her servants, "Go on
ahead;[b] I'll follow you." But she
did not tell her husband Nabal.
20As she came riding her donkey
into a mountain ravine, there were
David and his men descending toward her, and she met them. 21Da-
vid had just said, "It's been useless—all my watching over this fellow's property in the desert so that
nothing of his was missing. He has
paid[c] me back evil for good. 22May
God deal with David,[d] be it ever so
severely,[d] if by morning I leave
alive one male[e] of all who belong
to him!"
23When Abigail saw David, she
quickly got off her donkey and
bowed down before David with her
face to the ground.[f] 24She fell at
his feet and said: "My lord, let the
blame be on me alone. Please let
your servant speak to you; hear
what your servant has to say. 25May
my lord pay no attention to that
wicked man Nabal. He is just like
his name—his name is Fool,[g] and
folly goes with him. But as for me,
your servant, I did not see the men
my master sent.
26"Now since the LORD has kept
you, my master, from bloodshed[h]
and from avenging[i] yourself with
your own hands, as surely as the
LORD lives and as you live, may your
enemies and all who intend to
harm my master be like Nabal.[j]
27And let this gift,[k] which your
servant has brought to my master,
be given to the men who follow
you. 28Please forgive[l] your servant's offense, for the LORD will certainly make a lasting[m] dynasty for
my master, because he fights the
LORD's battles.[n] Let no wrongdoing[o] be found in you as long as you
live. 29Even though someone is
pursuing you to take your life, the
life of my master will be bound securely in the bundle of the living by
the LORD your God. But the lives of
your enemies he will hurl[p] away as
from the pocket of a sling. 30When
the LORD has done for my master
every good thing he promised concerning him and has appointed
him leader[q] over Israel, 31my master will not have on his conscience
the staggering burden of needless
bloodshed or of having avenged
himself. And when the LORD has
brought my master success, remember[r] your servant."
32David said to Abigail, "Praise[s]
be to the LORD, the God of Israel,
who has sent you today to meet
me. 33May you be blessed for your
good judgment and for keeping me
from bloodshed[t] this day and from
avenging myself with my own
hands. 34Otherwise, as surely as
the LORD, the God of Israel, lives,
who has kept me from harming
you, if you had not come quickly to
meet me, not one male belonging
to Nabal would have been left alive
by daybreak."
35Then David accepted from her
hand what she had brought him
and said, "Go home in peace. I
have heard your words and granted[u] your request."
36When Abigail went to Nabal,
he was in the house holding a banquet like that of a king. He was in
high[v] spirits and very drunk.[w] So
she told[x] him nothing until daybreak. 37Then in the morning,
when Nabal was sober, his wife
told him all these things, and his
heart failed him and he became
like a stone. 38About ten days later,
the LORD struck[y] Nabal and he
died.
39When David heard that Nabal
was dead, he said, "Praise be to the
LORD, who has upheld my cause
against Nabal for treating me with
contempt. He has kept his servant
from doing wrong and has brought
Nabal's wrongdoing down on his
own head."
Then David sent word to Abigail,
asking her to become his wife.
40His servants went to Carmel and
said to Abigail, "David has sent us
to you to take you to become his
wife."
41She bowed down with her face

[d]*22* Some Septuagint manuscripts; Hebrew *with David's enemies*

25:18 [a]2Sa 16:1
25:19 [b]Ge 32:20
25:21 [c]Ps 109:5
25:22 [d]1Sa 3:17; 20:13 [e]1Ki 14:10; 21:21; 2Ki 9:8
25:23 [f]1Sa 20:41
25:25 [g]Pr 14:16
25:26 [h]ver 33 [i]Heb 10:30 [j]2Sa 18:32
25:27 [k]Ge 33:11; 1Sa 30:26
25:28 [l]ver 24 [m]2Sa 7:11,26 [n]1Sa 18:17 [o]1Sa 24:11
25:29 [p]Jer 10:18
25:30 [q]1Sa 13:14
25:31 [r]Ge 40:14
25:32 [s]Ge 24:27; Ex 18:10; Lk 1:68
25:33 [t]ver 26
25:35 [u]Ge 19:21; 1Sa 20:42; 2Ki 5:19
25:36 [v]2Sa 13:23 [w]Pr 20:1; Isa 5:11,22; Hos 4:11 [x]ver 19
25:38 [y]1Sa 26:10; 2Sa 6:7

to the ground and said, "Here is
your maidservant, ready to serve
you and wash the feet of my master's servants." **42**Abigail[a] quickly
got on a donkey and, attended by
her five maids, went with David's
messengers and became his wife.
43David had also married Ahinoam[b] of Jezreel, and they both were
his wives.[c] **44**But Saul had given
his daughter Michal, David's wife,
to Paltiel[e][d] son of Laish, who was
from Gallim.[e]

David Again Spares Saul's Life

26 The Ziphites[f] went to Saul
at Gibeah and said, "Is not
David hiding[g] on the hill of Hakilah, which faces Jeshimon?"
2So Saul went down to the
Desert of Ziph, with his three thousand chosen men of Israel, to
search[h] there for David. **3**Saul
made his camp beside the road on
the hill of Hakilah facing Jeshimon, but David stayed in the
desert. When he saw that Saul had
followed him there, **4**he sent out
scouts and learned that Saul had
definitely arrived.[f]
5Then David set out and went to
the place where Saul had camped.
He saw where Saul and Abner[i] son
of Ner, the commander of the
army, had lain down. Saul was lying inside the camp, with the army
encamped around him.
6David then asked Ahimelech
the Hittite and Abishai son of Zeruiah,[j] Joab's brother, "Who will go
down into the camp with me to
Saul?"
"I'll go with you," said Abishai.
7So David and Abishai went to
the army by night, and there was
Saul, lying asleep inside the camp
with his spear stuck in the ground
near his head. Abner and the soldiers were lying around him.
8Abishai said to David, "Today
God has delivered your enemy into
your hands. Now let me pin him to
the ground with one thrust of my
spear; I won't strike him twice."
9But David said to Abishai,
"Don't destroy him! Who can lay a
hand on the LORD's anointed[k] and
be guiltless?[l] **10**As surely as the
LORD lives," he said, "the LORD himself will strike[m] him; either his
time[n] will come and he will die,[o]
or he will go into battle and perish.
11But the LORD forbid that I should
lay a hand on the LORD's anointed.
Now get the spear and water jug
that are near his head, and let's
go."
12So David took the spear and
water jug near Saul's head, and
they left. No one saw or knew
about it, nor did anyone wake up.
They were all sleeping, because the
LORD had put them into a deep
sleep.[p]
13Then David crossed over to the
other side and stood on top of the
hill some distance away; there was
a wide space between them. **14**He
called out to the army and to Abner
son of Ner, "Aren't you going to answer me, Abner?"
Abner replied, "Who are you who
calls to the king?"
15David said, "You're a man,
aren't you? And who is like you in
Israel? Why didn't you guard your
lord the king? Someone came to
destroy your lord the king. **16**What
you have done is not good. As surely as the LORD lives, you and your
men deserve to die, because you
did not guard your master, the
LORD's anointed. Look around you.
Where are the king's spear and water jug that were near his head?"
17Saul recognized David's voice
and said, "Is that your voice,[q] David my son?"
David replied, "Yes it is, my lord
the king." **18**And he added, "Why is
my lord pursuing his servant? What
have I done, and what wrong[r] am
I guilty of? **19**Now let my lord the
king listen to his servant's words. If
the LORD has incited you against
me, then may he accept an offering.[s] If, however, men have done
it, may they be cursed before the
LORD! They have now driven me
from my share in the LORD's inheritance[t] and have said, 'Go, serve

25:42 [a]Ge 24:61-67
25:43 [b]Jos 15:56 [c]1Sa 27:3; 30:5
25:44 [d]2Sa 3:15 [e]Isa 10:30
26:1 [f]1Sa 23:19 [g]Ps 54 Title
26:2 [h]1Sa 13:2; 24:2
26:5 [i]1Sa 14:50; 17:55
26:6 [j]Jdg 7:10-11; 1Ch 2:16
26:9 [k]2Sa 1:14 [l]1Sa 24:5
26:10 [m]1Sa 25:38; Ro 12:19 [n]Ge 47:29; Dt 31:14; Ps 37:13 [o]1Sa 31:6; 2Sa 1:1
26:12 [p]Ge 2:21; 15:12
26:17 [q]1Sa 24:16
26:18 [r]1Sa 24:9, 11-14
26:19 [s]2Sa 16:11 [t]2Sa 14:16

e44 Hebrew *Palti*, a variant of *Paltiel* f4 Or *had come to Nacon*

other gods.' 20Now do not let my
blood fall to the ground far from
the presence of the LORD. The king
of Israel has come out to look for a
flea[a]—as one hunts a partridge in
the mountains."
21Then Saul said, "I have
sinned.[b] Come back, David my
son. Because you considered my
life precious[c] today, I will not try
to harm you again. Surely I have
acted like a fool and have erred
greatly."
22"Here is the king's spear," David answered. "Let one of your
young men come over and get it.
23The LORD rewards[d] every man for
his righteousness[e] and faithfulness. The LORD delivered you into
my hands today, but I would not lay
a hand on the LORD's anointed.
24As surely as I valued your life today, so may the LORD value my life
and deliver[f] me from all trouble."
25Then Saul said to David, "May
you be blessed, my son David; you
will do great things and surely triumph."
So David went on his way, and
Saul returned home.

David Among the Philistines

27 But David thought to himself, "One of these days I
will be destroyed by the hand of
Saul. The best thing I can do is to
escape to the land of the Philistines. Then Saul will give up
searching for me anywhere in Israel, and I will slip out of his hand."
2So David and the six hundred
men[g] with him left and went[h]
over to Achish[i] son of Maoch king
of Gath. 3David and his men settled in Gath with Achish. Each
man had his family with him, and
David had his two wives:[j] Ahinoam of Jezreel and Abigail of Carmel, the widow of Nabal. 4When
Saul was told that David had fled to
Gath, he no longer searched for
him.
5Then David said to Achish, "If I
have found favor in your eyes, let a
place be assigned to me in one of
the country towns, that I may live
there. Why should your servant live
in the royal city with you?"
6So on that day Achish gave him
Ziklag,[k] and it has belonged to the
kings of Judah ever since. 7David
lived[l] in Philistine territory a year
and four months.
8Now David and his men went
up and raided the Geshurites,[m] the
Girzites and the Amalekites.[n]
(From ancient times these peoples
had lived in the land extending to
Shur[o] and Egypt.) 9Whenever David attacked an area, he did not
leave a man or woman alive,[p] but
took sheep and cattle, donkeys and
camels, and clothes. Then he returned to Achish.
10When Achish asked, "Where
did you go raiding today?" David
would say, "Against the Negev of
Judah" or "Against the Negev of Jerahmeel[q]" or "Against the Negev
of the Kenites.[r]" 11He did not
leave a man or woman alive to be
brought to Gath, for he thought,
"They might inform on us and say,
'This is what David did.' " And
such was his practice as long as he
lived in Philistine territory.
12Achish trusted David and said to
himself, "He has become so odious
to his people, the Israelites, that he
will be my servant forever."

Saul and the Witch of Endor

28 In those days the Philistines gathered[s] their forces
to fight against Israel. Achish said
to David, "You must understand
that you and your men will accompany me in the army."
2David said, "Then you will see
for yourself what your servant can
do."
Achish replied, "Very well, I will
make you my bodyguard for life."
3Now Samuel was dead,[t] and all
Israel had mourned for him and
buried him in his own town of Ramah.[u] Saul had expelled the mediums and spiritists[v] from the land.
4The Philistines assembled and
came and set up camp at Shunem,[w] while Saul gathered all the
Israelites and set up camp at Gilboa.[x] 5When Saul saw the Philis-

26:20 [a] 1Sa 24:14
26:21 [b] Ex 9:27; 1Sa 15:24 [c] 1Sa 24:17
26:23 [d] Ps 62:12 [e] Ps 7:8; 18:20,24
26:24 [f] Ps 54:7
27:2 [g] 1Sa 25:13 [h] 1Sa 21:10 [i] 1Ki 2:39
27:3 [j] 1Sa 25:43; 30:3
27:6 [k] Jos 15:31; 19:5; Ne 11:28
27:7 [l] 1Sa 29:3
27:8 [m] Jos 13:2,13 [n] Ex 17:8; 1Sa 15:7-8 [o] Ex 15:22
27:9 [p] 1Sa 15:3
27:10 [q] 1Sa 30:29; 1Ch 2:9,25 [r] Jdg 1:16
28:1 [s] 1Sa 29:1
28:3 [t] 1Sa 25:1 [u] 1Sa 7:17 [v] Ex 22:18; Lev 19:31; 20:27; Dt 18:10-11; 1Sa 15:23
28:4 [w] Jos 19:18; 2Ki 4:8 [x] 1Sa 31:1,3

tine army, he was afraid; terror
filled his heart. 6He inquired[a] of
the LORD, but the LORD did not answer him by dreams[b] or Urim[c] or
prophets. 7Saul then said to his attendants, "Find me a woman who
is a medium,[d] so I may go and inquire of her."
"There is one in Endor,[e]" they
said.
8So Saul disguised[f] himself,
putting on other clothes, and at
night he and two men went to the
woman. "Consult[g] a spirit for me,"
he said, "and bring up for me the
one I name."
9But the woman said to him,
"Surely you know what Saul has
done. He has cut off[h] the mediums
and spiritists from the land. Why
have you set a trap for my life to
bring about my death?"
10Saul swore to her by the LORD,
"As surely as the LORD lives, you
will not be punished for this."
11Then the woman asked,
"Whom shall I bring up for you?"
"Bring up Samuel," he said.
12When the woman saw Samuel,
she cried out at the top of her voice
and said to Saul, "Why have you deceived me? You are Saul!"
13The king said to her, "Don't be
afraid. What do you see?"
The woman said, "I see a spirit[g]
coming up out of the ground."
14"What does he look like?" he
asked.
"An old man wearing a robe[i] is
coming up," she said.
Then Saul knew it was Samuel,
and he bowed down and prostrated
himself with his face to the ground.
15Samuel said to Saul, "Why
have you disturbed me by bringing
me up?"
"I am in great distress," Saul
said. "The Philistines are fighting
against me, and God has turned[j]
away from me. He no longer answers me, either by prophets or by
dreams. So I have called on you to
tell me what to do."
16Samuel said, "Why do you consult me, now that the LORD has
turned away from you and become
your enemy? 17The LORD has done
what he predicted through me. The
LORD has torn[k] the kingdom out of
your hands and given it to one of
your neighbors—to David. 18Be-
cause you did not obey[l] the LORD
or carry out his fierce wrath[m]
against the Amalekites, the LORD
has done this to you today. 19The
LORD will hand over both Israel and
you to the Philistines, and tomorrow you and your sons[n] will be
with me. The LORD will also hand
over the army of Israel to the Philistines."
20Immediately Saul fell full
length on the ground, filled with
fear because of Samuel's words.
His strength was gone, for he had
eaten nothing all that day and
night.
21When the woman came to Saul
and saw that he was greatly shak-
en, she said, "Look, your maidservant has obeyed you. I took my
life[o] in my hands and did what you
told me to do. 22Now please listen
to your servant and let me give you
some food so you may eat and have
the strength to go on your way."
23He refused[p] and said, "I will
not eat."
But his men joined the woman in
urging him, and he listened to
them. He got up from the ground
and sat on the couch.
24The woman had a fattened calf
at the house, which she butchered
at once. She took some flour,
kneaded it and baked bread without yeast. 25Then she set it before
Saul and his men, and they ate.
That same night they got up and
left.

Achish Sends David Back to Ziklag

29 The Philistines gathered[q]
all their forces at Aphek,[r]
and Israel camped by the spring in
Jezreel.[s] 2As the Philistine rulers
marched with their units of hundreds and thousands, David and
his men were marching at the
rear[t] with Achish. 3The com-

28:6 [a] 1Sa 14:37; 1Ch 10:13-14; Pr 1:28 [b] Nu 12:6 [c] Ex 28:30; Nu 27:21
28:7 [d] Ac 16:16 [e] Jos 17:11
28:8 [f] 2Ch 18:29; 35:22 [g] Dt 18:10-11; 1Ch 10:13; Isa 8:19
28:9 [h] ver 3
28:14 [i] 1Sa 15:27; 24:8
28:15 [j] ver 6; 1Sa 18:12
28:17 [k] 1Sa 15:28
28:18 [l] 1Sa 15:20 [m] 1Ki 20:42
28:19 [n] 1Sa 31:2
28:21 [o] Jdg 12:3; 1Sa 19:5; Job 13:14
28:23 [p] 2Ki 5:13
29:1 [q] 1Sa 28:1 [r] Jos 12:18; 1Sa 4:1 [s] 2Ki 9:30
29:2 [t] 1Sa 28:2

g13 Or *see spirits;* or *see gods*

manders of the Philistines asked,
"What about these Hebrews?"
Achish replied, "Is this not David, who was an officer of Saul king
of Israel? He has already been with
me for over a year,[a] and from the
day he left Saul until now, I have
found no fault in him."
4But the Philistine commanders
were angry with him and said,
"Send[b] the man back, that he may
return to the place you assigned
him. He must not go with us into
battle, or he will turn[c] against us
during the fighting. How better
could he regain his master's favor
than by taking the heads of our
own men? 5Isn't this the David
they sang about in their dances:

" 'Saul has slain his thousands,
and David his tens of
thousands'?"[d]

6So Achish called David and said
to him, "As surely as the LORD lives,
you have been reliable, and I would
be pleased to have you serve with
me in the army. From the day[e] you
came to me until now, I have found
no fault in you, but the rulers[f]
don't approve of you. 7Turn back
and go in peace; do nothing to displease the Philistine rulers."
8"But what have I done?" asked
David. "What have you found
against your servant from the day I
came to you until now? Why can't
I go and fight against the enemies
of my lord the king?"
9Achish answered, "I know that
you have been as pleasing in my
eyes as an angel[g] of God; nevertheless, the Philistine commanders[h]
have said, 'He must not go up with
us into battle.' 10Now get up early,
along with your master's servants
who have come with you, and
leave[i] in the morning as soon as it
is light."
11So David and his men got up
early in the morning to go back to
the land of the Philistines, and the
Philistines went up to Jezreel.

David Destroys the Amalekites

30 David and his men reached
Ziklag[j] on the third day.
Now the Amalekites[k] had raided
the Negev and Ziklag. They had attacked Ziklag and burned it, 2and
had taken captive the women and
all who were in it, both young and
old. They killed none of them, but
carried them off as they went on
their way.
3When David and his men came
to Ziklag, they found it destroyed
by fire and their wives and sons and
daughters taken captive. 4So David
and his men wept aloud until they
had no strength left to weep. 5Da-
vid's two wives[l] had been captured—Ahinoam of Jezreel and Abigail, the widow of Nabal of Carmel. 6David was greatly distressed
because the men were talking of
stoning[m] him; each one was bitter
in spirit because of his sons and
daughters. But David found
strength[n] in the LORD his God.
7Then David said to Abiathar[o]
the priest, the son of Ahimelech,
"Bring me the ephod.[p]" Abiathar
brought it to him, 8and David inquired[q] of the LORD, "Shall I pursue this raiding party? Will I overtake them?"
"Pursue them," he answered.
"You will certainly overtake them
and succeed[r] in the rescue."
9David and the six hundred
men[s] with him came to the Besor
Ravine, where some stayed behind,
10for two hundred men were too
exhausted[t] to cross the ravine.
But David and four hundred men
continued the pursuit.
11They found an Egyptian in a
field and brought him to David.
They gave him water to drink and
food to eat— 12part of a cake of
pressed figs and two cakes of raisins. He ate and was revived,[u] for
he had not eaten any food or drunk
any water for three days and three
nights.
13David asked him, "To whom
do you belong, and where do you
come from?"
He said, "I am an Egyptian, the
slave of an Amalekite. My master
abandoned me when I became ill
three days ago. 14We raided the
Negev of the Kerethites[v] and the

29:3 [a] 1Sa 27:7; Da 6:5
29:4 [b] 1Ch 12:19 [c] 1Sa 14:21
29:5 [d] 1Sa 18:7; 21:11
29:6 [e] 1Sa 27:8-12 [f] ver 3
29:9 [g] 2Sa 14:17, 20; 19:27 [h] ver 4
29:10 [i] 1Ch 12:19
30:1 [j] 1Sa 29:4,11 [k] 1Sa 15:7; 27:8
30:5 [l] 1Sa 25:43; 2Sa 2:2
30:6 [m] Ex 17:4; Jn 8:59 [n] Ps 27:14; 56:3-4,11; Ro 4:20
30:7 [o] 1Sa 22:20 [p] 1Sa 23:9
30:8 [q] 1Sa 23:2 [r] ver 18
30:9 [s] 1Sa 27:2
30:10 [t] ver 9,21
30:12 [u] Jdg 15:19
30:14 [v] 2Sa 8:18; 1Ki 1:38,44; Eze 25:16; Zep 2:5

territory belonging to Judah and the Negev of Caleb.[a] And we burned[b] Ziklag."

15David asked him, "Can you lead me down to this raiding party?"

He answered, "Swear to me before God that you will not kill me or hand me over to my master, and I will take you down to them."

16He led David down, and there they were, scattered over the countryside, eating, drinking and reveling[c] because of the great amount of plunder[d] they had taken from the land of the Philistines and from Judah. **17**David fought[e] them from dusk until the evening of the next day, and none of them got away, except four hundred young men who rode off on camels and fled.[f] **18**David recovered[g] everything the Amalekites had taken, including his two wives. **19**Nothing was missing: young or old, boy or girl, plunder or anything else they had taken. David brought everything back. **20**He took all the flocks and herds, and his men drove them ahead of the other livestock, saying, "This is David's plunder."

21Then David came to the two hundred men who had been too exhausted[h] to follow him and who were left behind at the Besor Ravine. They came out to meet David and the people with him. As David and his men approached, he greeted them. **22**But all the evil men and troublemakers among David's followers said, "Because they did not go out with us, we will not share with them the plunder we recovered. However, each man may take his wife and children and go."

23David replied, "No, my brothers, you must not do that with what the LORD has given us. He has protected us and handed over to us the forces that came against us. **24**Who will listen to what you say? The share of the man who stayed with the supplies is to be the same as that of him who went down to the battle. All will share alike.[i]" **25**David made this a statute and ordinance for Israel from that day to this.

26When David arrived in Ziklag, he sent some of the plunder to the elders of Judah, who were his friends, saying, "Here is a present for you from the plunder of the LORD's enemies."

27He sent it to those who were in Bethel,[j] Ramoth[k] Negev and Jattir;[l] **28**to those in Aroer,[m] Siphmoth, Eshtemoa[n] **29**and Racal; to those in the towns of the Jerahmeelites[o] and the Kenites;[p] **30**to those in Hormah,[q] Bor Ashan,[r] Athach **31**and Hebron;[s] and to those in all the other places where David and his men had roamed.

Saul Takes His Life

31:1–13pp — 2Sa 1:4–12; 1Ch 10:1–12

31 Now the Philistines fought against Israel; the Israelites fled before them, and many fell slain on Mount Gilboa.[t] **2**The Philistines pressed hard after Saul and his sons, and they killed his sons Jonathan, Abinadab and Malki-Shua. **3**The fighting grew fierce around Saul, and when the archers overtook him, they wounded[u] him critically.

4Saul said to his armor-bearer, "Draw your sword and run me through,[v] or these uncircumcised[w] fellows will come and run me through and abuse me."

But his armor-bearer was terrified and would not do it; so Saul took his own sword and fell on it. **5**When the armor-bearer saw that Saul was dead, he too fell on his sword and died with him. **6**So Saul and his three sons and his armor-bearer and all his men died together that same day.

7When the Israelites along the valley and those across the Jordan saw that the Israelite army had fled and that Saul and his sons had died, they abandoned their towns and fled. And the Philistines came and occupied them.

8The next day, when the Philistines came to strip the dead, they found Saul and his three sons fall-

30:14 [a]ver 16; Jos 14:13; 15:13 [b]ver 1
30:16 [c]Lk 12:19 [d]ver 14
30:17 [e]1Sa 11:11 [f]1Sa 15:3
30:18 [g]Ge 14:16
30:21 [h]ver 10
30:24 [i]Nu 31:27; Jos 22:8
30:27 [j]Jos 7:2 [k]Jos 19:8 [l]Jos 15:48
30:28 [m]Jos 13:16 [n]Jos 15:50
30:29 [o]1Sa 27:10 [p]Jdg 1:16; 1Sa 15:6
30:30 [q]Nu 14:45; Jdg 1:17 [r]Jos 15:42
30:31 [s]Jos 14:13; 2Sa 2:1,4
31:1 [t]1Sa 28:4; 1Ch 10:1-12
31:3 [u]2Sa 1:6
31:4 [v]Jdg 9:54; 2Sa 1:6,10 [w]1Sa 14:6

en on Mount Gilboa. 9They cut off
his head and stripped off his armor,
and they sent messengers throughout the land of the Philistines to
proclaim the news[a] in the temple
of their idols and among their people.[b] 10They put his armor in the
temple of the Ashtoreths[c] and fastened his body to the wall of Beth
Shan.[d]
11When the people of Jabesh
Gilead[e] heard of what the Philistines had done to Saul, 12all their
valiant men journeyed through the
night to Beth Shan. They took
down the bodies of Saul and his
sons from the wall of Beth Shan
and went to Jabesh, where they
burned[f] them. 13Then they took
their bones[g] and buried them under a tamarisk[h] tree at Jabesh, and
they fasted[i] seven days.[j]

31:9
[a] 2Sa 1:20
[b] Jdg 16:24
31:10
[c] Jdg 2:12-13; 1Sa 7:3
[d] Jos 17:11; 2Sa 21:12
31:11
[e] 1Sa 11:1
31:12
[f] 2Sa 2:4-7; 2Ch 16:14; Am 6:10
31:13
[g] 2Sa 21:12-14
[h] 1Sa 22:6 [i] 2Sa 1:12 [j] Ge 50:10

2 Samuel

Title and Background

1 and 2 Samuel were originally one book (see Introduction to 1 Samuel).

Author and Date of Writing

See Introduction to 1 Samuel.

Theme and Message

2 Samuel depicts David as a true (though imperfect) representative of the ideal theocratic king. Under David's rule the Lord caused the nation to prosper and to defeat its enemies. In chapter 7 we read of the Lord's promise that David's dynasty would endure forever and of the establishment of the Davidic covenant.

Outline

I. David Becomes King Over Judah (1:1-4:12)
II. David Becomes King Over All Israel (5:1-5)
III. David's Kingship in Its Accomplishments and Glory (5:6-9:12)
IV. David's Kingship in Its Weaknesses and Failures (10:1-20:16)
V. Final Reflections on David's Reign (21:1-24:25)

David Hears of Saul's Death

1:4-12pp — 1Sa 31:1-13; 1Ch 10:1-12

1 After the death[a] of Saul, David returned from defeating[b] the Amalekites and stayed in Ziklag two days. **2**On the third day a man[c] arrived from Saul's camp, with his clothes torn and with dust on his head.[d] When he came to David, he fell to the ground to pay him honor.

3"Where have you come from?" David asked him.

He answered, "I have escaped from the Israelite camp."

4"What happened?" David asked. "Tell me."

He said, "The men fled from the battle. Many of them fell and died. And Saul and his son Jonathan are dead."

5Then David said to the young man who brought him the report, "How do you know that Saul and his son Jonathan are dead?"

6"I happened to be on Mount Gilboa,[e]" the young man said, "and there was Saul, leaning on his spear, with the chariots and riders almost upon him. **7**When he turned around and saw me, he called out to me, and I said, 'What can I do?'

8"He asked me, 'Who are you?'

" 'An Amalekite,[f]' I answered.

9"Then he said to me, 'Stand over me and kill me! I am in the throes of death, but I'm still alive.'

10"So I stood over him and killed him, because I knew that after he had fallen he could not survive. And I took the crown[g] that was on his head and the band on his arm and have brought them here to my lord."

11Then David and all the men with him took hold of their clothes and tore[h] them. **12**They mourned and wept and fasted till evening for Saul and his son Jonathan, and for the army of the LORD and the house of Israel, because they had fallen by the sword.

13David said to the young man who brought him the report, "Where are you from?"

1:1 [a] 1Sa 31:6 [b] 1Sa 30:17
1:2 [c] 2Sa 4:10 [d] 1Sa 4:12
1:6 [e] 1Sa 28:4; 31:2-4
1:8 [f] 1Sa 15:2; 30:13,17
1:10 [g] Jdg 9:54; 2Ki 11:12
1:11 [h] Ge 37:29; 2Sa 3:31; 13:31

"I am the son of an alien, an Amalekite,[a]" he answered.
14David asked him, "Why were
you not afraid to lift your hand to
destroy the LORD's anointed?[b]"
15Then David called one of his
men and said, "Go, strike him
down!"[c] So he struck him down,
and he died.[d] 16For David had said
to him, "Your blood be on your own
head.[e] Your own mouth testified
against you when you said, 'I killed
the LORD's anointed.' "

David's Lament for Saul and Jonathan

17David took up this lament[f]
concerning Saul and his son Jonathan, 18and ordered that the men
of Judah be taught this lament of
the bow (it is written in the Book of
Jashar):[g]

19"Your glory, O Israel, lies slain
on your heights.
How the mighty have
fallen![h]

20"Tell it not in Gath,[i]
proclaim it not in the streets
of Ashkelon,
lest the daughters of the
Philistines[j] be glad,
lest the daughters of the
uncircumcised rejoice.[k]

21"O mountains of Gilboa,[l]
may you have neither dew
nor rain,
nor fields that yield
offerings[m] of grain.
For there the shield of the
mighty was defiled,
the shield of Saul—no longer
rubbed with oil.[n]
22From the blood[o] of the slain,
from the flesh of the mighty,
the bow[p] of Jonathan did not
turn back,
the sword of Saul did not
return unsatisfied.

23"Saul and Jonathan—
in life they were loved and
gracious,
and in death they were not
parted.
They were swifter than eagles,[q]
they were stronger than
lions.[r]

24"O daughters of Israel,
weep for Saul,
who clothed you in scarlet and
finery,
who adorned your garments
with ornaments of gold.

25"How the mighty have fallen in
battle!
Jonathan lies slain on your
heights.
26I grieve for you, Jonathan my
brother;[s]
you were very dear to me.
Your love for me was
wonderful,[t]
more wonderful than that of
women.

27"How the mighty have fallen!
The weapons of war have
perished!"[u]

David Anointed King Over Judah

2 In the course of time, David inquired[v] of the LORD. "Shall I go
up to one of the towns of Judah?"
he asked.
The LORD said, "Go up."
David asked, "Where shall I go?"
"To Hebron,"[w] the LORD answered.
2So David went up there with his
two wives,[x] Ahinoam of Jezreel
and Abigail,[y] the widow of Nabal
of Carmel. 3David also took the
men who were with him,[z] each
with his family, and they settled in
Hebron and its towns. 4Then the
men of Judah came to Hebron[a]
and there they anointed[b] David
king over the house of Judah.
When David was told that it was
the men of Jabesh Gilead[c] who
had buried Saul, 5he sent messengers to the men of Jabesh Gilead to
say to them, "The LORD bless[d] you
for showing this kindness to Saul
your master by burying him. 6May
the LORD now show you kindness
and faithfulness,[e] and I too will
show you the same favor because
you have done this. 7Now then, be
strong and brave, for Saul your

1:13 [a] ver 8
1:14 [b] 1Sa 24:6; 26:9
1:15 [c] 2Sa 4:12 [d] 2Sa 4:10
1:16 [e] Lev 20:9; 2Sa 3:28-29; 1Ki 2:32; Mt 27:24-25; Ac 18:6
1:17 [f] 2Ch 35:25
1:18 [g] Jos 10:13; 1Sa 31:3
1:19 [h] ver 27
1:20 [i] Mic 1:10 [j] 1Sa 31:8 [k] Ex 15:20; 1Sa 18:6
1:21 [l] ver 6; 1Sa 31:1 [m] Eze 31:15 [n] Isa 21:5
1:22 [o] Isa 34:3,7 [p] Dt 32:42; 1Sa 18:4
1:23 [q] Dt 28:49; Jer 4:13 [r] Jdg 14:18
1:26 [s] 1Sa 20:42 [t] 1Sa 18:1
1:27 [u] ver 19,25; 1Sa 2:4
2:1 [v] 1Sa 23:2, 11-12 [w] Ge 13:18; 1Sa 30:31
2:2 [x] 1Sa 25:43; 30:5 [y] 1Sa 25:42
2:3 [z] 1Sa 27:2; 30:9
2:4 [a] 1Sa 30:31 [b] 1Sa 2:35; 2Sa 5:3-5 [c] 1Sa 31:11-13
2:5 [d] 1Sa 23:21
2:6 [e] Ex 34:6; 1Ti 1:16

master is dead, and the house of Judah has anointed me king over them."

War Between the Houses of David and Saul

3:2–5pp — 1Ch 3:1–4

8Meanwhile, Abner[a] son of Ner, the commander of Saul's army, had taken Ish-Bosheth son of Saul and brought him over to Mahanaim.[b]
9He made him king over Gilead,[c] Ashuri[a][d] and Jezreel, and also over Ephraim, Benjamin and all Israel.[e]

10Ish-Bosheth son of Saul was forty years old when he became king over Israel, and he reigned two years. The house of Judah, however, followed David.
11The length of time David was king in Hebron over the house of Judah was seven years and six months.[f]

12Abner son of Ner, together with the men of Ish-Bosheth son of Saul, left Mahanaim and went to Gibeon.[g]
13Joab[h] son of Zeruiah and David's men went out and met them at the pool of Gibeon. One group sat down on one side of the pool and one group on the other side.

14Then Abner said to Joab, "Let's have some of the young men get up and fight hand to hand in front of us."

"All right, let them do it," Joab said.

15So they stood up and were counted off—twelve men for Benjamin and Ish-Bosheth son of Saul, and twelve for David.
16Then each man grabbed his opponent by the head and thrust his dagger into his opponent's side, and they fell down together. So that place in Gibeon was called Helkath Hazzurim.[b]

17The battle that day was very fierce, and Abner and the men of Israel were defeated[i] by David's men.

18The three sons of Zeruiah[j] were there: Joab,[k] Abishai[l] and Asahel.[m] Now Asahel was as fleet-footed as a wild gazelle.[n]
19He chased Abner, turning neither to the right nor to the left as he pursued him.
20Abner looked behind him and asked, "Is that you, Asahel?"

"It is," he answered.

21Then Abner said to him, "Turn aside to the right or to the left; take on one of the young men and strip him of his weapons." But Asahel would not stop chasing him.

22Again Abner warned Asahel, "Stop chasing me! Why should I strike you down? How could I look your brother Joab in the face?"[o]

23But Asahel refused to give up the pursuit; so Abner thrust the butt of his spear into Asahel's stomach,[p] and the spear came out through his back. He fell there and died on the spot. And every man stopped when he came to the place where Asahel had fallen and died.[q]

24But Joab and Abishai pursued Abner, and as the sun was setting, they came to the hill of Ammah, near Giah on the way to the wasteland of Gibeon.
25Then the men of Benjamin rallied behind Abner. They formed themselves into a group and took their stand on top of a hill.

26Abner called out to Joab, "Must the sword devour[r] forever? Don't you realize that this will end in bitterness? How long before you order your men to stop pursuing their brothers?"

27Joab answered, "As surely as God lives, if you had not spoken, the men would have continued the pursuit of their brothers until morning.[c]"

28So Joab[s] blew the trumpet,[t] and all the men came to a halt; they no longer pursued Israel, nor did they fight anymore.

29All that night Abner and his men marched through the Arabah. They crossed the Jordan, contin-

2:8 [a] 1Sa 14:50 [b] Ge 32:2
2:9 [c] Nu 32:26 [d] Jdg 1:32 [e] 1Ch 12:29
2:11 [f] 2Sa 5:5
2:12 [g] Jos 18:25
2:13 [h] 2Sa 8:16; 1Ch 2:16; 11:6
2:17 [i] 2Sa 3:1
2:18 [j] 2Sa 3:39 [k] 2Sa 3:30 [l] 1Sa 26:6 [m] 1Ch 2:16 [n] 1Ch 12:8
2:22 [o] 2Sa 3:27
2:23 [p] 2Sa 3:27; 4:6 [q] 2Sa 20:12
2:26 [r] Dt 32:42; Jer 46:10,14
2:28 [s] 2Sa 18:16 [t] Jdg 3:27

[a]9 Or *Asher* [b]16 *Helkath Hazzurim* means *field of daggers* or *field of hostilities.* [c]27 Or *spoken this morning, the men would not have taken up the pursuit of their brothers;* or *spoken, the men would have given up the pursuit of their brothers by morning*

ued through the whole Bithron[d] and came to Mahanaim.[a]

30Then Joab returned from pursuing Abner and assembled all his men. Besides Asahel, nineteen of David's men were found missing. 31But David's men had killed three hundred and sixty Benjamites who were with Abner. 32They took Asahel and buried him in his father's tomb[b] at Bethlehem. Then Joab and his men marched all night and arrived at Hebron by daybreak.

3 The war between the house of Saul and the house of David lasted a long time.[c] David grew stronger and stronger,[d] while the house of Saul grew weaker and weaker.[e]

2Sons were born to David in Hebron:

His firstborn was Amnon the son of Ahinoam[f] of Jezreel;

3his second, Kileab the son of Abigail[g] the widow of Nabal of Carmel;

the third, Absalom[h] the son of Maacah daughter of Talmai king of Geshur;[i]

4the fourth, Adonijah[j] the son of Haggith;

the fifth, Shephatiah the son of Abital;

5and the sixth, Ithream the son of David's wife Eglah.

These were born to David in Hebron.

Abner Goes Over to David

6During the war between the house of Saul and the house of David, Abner had been strengthening his own position in the house of Saul. 7Now Saul had had a concubine[k] named Rizpah[l] daughter of Aiah. And Ish-Bosheth said to Abner, "Why did you sleep with my father's concubine?"

8Abner was very angry because of what Ish-Bosheth said and he answered, "Am I a dog's head[m]—on Judah's side? This very day I am loyal to the house of your father Saul and to his family and friends. I haven't handed you over to David. Yet now you accuse me of an offense involving this woman! 9May God deal with Abner, be it ever so severely, if I do not do for David what the LORD promised[n] him on oath 10and transfer the kingdom from the house of Saul and establish David's throne over Israel and Judah from Dan to Beersheba."[o] 11Ish-Bosheth did not dare to say another word to Abner, because he was afraid of him.

12Then Abner sent messengers on his behalf to say to David, "Whose land is it? Make an agreement with me, and I will help you bring all Israel over to you."

13"Good," said David. "I will make an agreement with you. But I demand one thing of you: Do not come into my presence unless you bring Michal daughter of Saul when you come to see me."[p] 14Then David sent messengers to Ish-Bosheth son of Saul, demanding, "Give me my wife Michal,[q] whom I betrothed to myself for the price of a hundred Philistine foreskins."

15So Ish-Bosheth gave orders and had her taken away from her husband[r] Paltiel[s] son of Laish. 16Her husband, however, went with her, weeping behind her all the way to Bahurim.[t] Then Abner said to him, "Go back home!" So he went back.

17Abner conferred with the elders[u] of Israel and said, "For some time you have wanted to make David your king. 18Now do it! For the LORD promised David, 'By my servant David I will rescue my people Israel from the hand of the Philistines[v] and from the hand of all their enemies.[w]' "

19Abner also spoke to the Benjamites in person. Then he went to Hebron to tell David everything that Israel and the whole house of Benjamin[x] wanted to do. 20When Abner, who had twenty men with him, came to David at Hebron, David prepared a feast for him and his men. 21Then Abner said to David,

2:29 [a] ver 8
2:32 [b] Ge 49:29
3:1 [c] 1Ki 14:30 [d] 2Sa 5:10 [e] 2Sa 2:17
3:2 [f] 1Sa 25:43; 1Ch 3:1-3
3:3 [g] 1Sa 25:42 [h] 2Sa 13:1,28 [i] 1Sa 27:8; 2Sa 13:37; 14:32; 15:8
3:4 [j] 1Ki 1:5,11
3:7 [k] 2Sa 16:21-22 [l] 2Sa 21:8-11
3:8 [m] 1Sa 24:14; 2Sa 9:8; 16:9
3:9 [n] 1Sa 15:28; 1Ki 19:2
3:10 [o] Jdg 20:1; 1Sa 3:20
3:13 [p] Ge 43:5; 1Sa 18:20
3:14 [q] 1Sa 18:27
3:15 [r] Dt 24:1-4 [s] 1Sa 25:44
3:16 [t] 2Sa 16:5; 19:16
3:17 [u] Jdg 11:11
3:18 [v] 1Sa 9:16 [w] 1Sa 15:28; 2Sa 8:6
3:19 [x] 1Sa 10:20-21; 1Ch 12:2,16, 29

[d]29 Or *morning*; or *ravine*; the meaning of the Hebrew for this word is uncertain.

"Let me go at once and assemble
all Israel for my lord the king, so
that they may make a compact[a]
with you, and that you may rule
over all that your heart desires."[b]
So David sent Abner away, and he
went in peace.

Joab Murders Abner

22Just then David's men and
Joab returned from a raid and
brought with them a great deal of
plunder. But Abner was no longer
with David in Hebron, because David had sent him away, and he had
gone in peace. 23When Joab and all
the soldiers with him arrived, he
was told that Abner son of Ner had
come to the king and that the king
had sent him away and that he had
gone in peace.
24So Joab went to the king and
said, "What have you done? Look,
Abner came to you. Why did you let
him go? Now he is gone! 25You
know Abner son of Ner; he came to
deceive you and observe your
movements and find out everything
you are doing."
26Joab then left David and sent
messengers after Abner, and they
brought him back from the well of
Sirah. But David did not know it.
27Now when Abner[c] returned to
Hebron, Joab took him aside into
the gateway, as though to speak
with him privately. And there, to
avenge the blood of his brother Asahel, Joab stabbed him in the
stomach, and he died.[d]
28Later, when David heard about
this, he said, "I and my kingdom
are forever innocent[e] before the
LORD concerning the blood of Abner son of Ner. 29May his blood[f]
fall upon the head of Joab and
upon all his father's house![g] May
Joab's house never be without
someone who has a running sore[h]
or leprosy[e] or who leans on a
crutch or who falls by the sword or
who lacks food."
30(Joab and his brother Abishai
murdered Abner because he had
killed their brother Asahel in the
battle at Gibeon.)
31Then David said to Joab and
all the people with him, "Tear your
clothes and put on sackcloth[i] and
walk in mourning[j] in front of Abner." King David himself walked
behind the bier. 32They buried Abner in Hebron, and the king wept[k]
aloud at Abner's tomb. All the people wept also.
33The king sang this lament[l] for
Abner:

"Should Abner have died as the
lawless die?
34 Your hands were not bound,
your feet were not fettered.
You fell as one falls before
wicked men."

And all the people wept over him
again.
35Then they all came and urged
David to eat something while it was
still day; but David took an oath,
saying, "May God deal with me, be
it ever so severely,[m] if I taste
bread[n] or anything else before the
sun sets!"
36All the people took note and
were pleased; indeed, everything
the king did pleased them. 37So on
that day all the people and all Israel knew that the king had no part[o]
in the murder of Abner son of Ner.
38Then the king said to his men,
"Do you not realize that a prince
and a great man has fallen[p] in Israel this day? 39And today, though I
am the anointed king, I am weak,
and these sons of Zeruiah[q] are too
strong for me.[r] May the LORD repay[s] the evildoer according to his
evil deeds!"

Ish-Bosheth Murdered

4 When Ish-Bosheth son of Saul
heard that Abner[t] had died in
Hebron, he lost courage, and all Israel became alarmed. 2Now Saul's
son had two men who were leaders
of raiding bands. One was named
Baanah and the other Recab; they
were sons of Rimmon the Beerothite from the tribe of Benjamin—
Beeroth[u] is considered part of
Benjamin, 3because the people of

3:21 [a]ver 10,12 [b]1Ki 11:37
3:27 [c]2Sa 2:8 [d]2Sa 2:22; 20:9-10; 1Ki 2:5
3:28 [e]ver 37; Dt 21:9
3:29 [f]Lev 20:9 [g]1Ki 2:31-33 [h]Lev 15:2
3:31 [i]2Sa 1:2,11; Ps 30:11; Isa 20:2 [j]Ge 37:34
3:32 [k]Nu 14:1; Pr 24:17
3:33 [l]2Sa 1:17
3:35 [m]Ru 1:17; 1Sa 3:17 [n]1Sa 31:13; 2Sa 1:12; 12:17; Jer 16:7
3:37 [o]ver 28
3:38 [p]2Sa 1:19
3:39 [q]2Sa 2:18 [r]2Sa 19:5-7 [s]1Ki 2:5-6, 33-34; Ps 41:10; 101:8
4:1 [t]2Sa 3:27; Ezr 4:4
4:2 [u]Jos 9:17; 18:25

[e]*29* The Hebrew word was used for various diseases affecting the skin—not necessarily leprosy.

Beeroth fled to Gittaim[a] and have lived there as aliens to this day.

4 (Jonathan[b] son of Saul had a son who was lame in both feet. He was five years old when the news[c] about Saul and Jonathan came from Jezreel. His nurse picked him up and fled, but as she hurried to leave, he fell and became crippled.[d] His name was Mephibosheth.)[e]

5 Now Recab and Baanah, the sons of Rimmon the Beerothite, set out for the house of Ish-Bosheth,[f] and they arrived there in the heat of the day while he was taking his noonday rest. 6 They went into the inner part of the house as if to get some wheat, and they stabbed[g] him in the stomach. Then Recab and his brother Baanah slipped away.

7 They had gone into the house while he was lying on the bed in his bedroom. After they stabbed and killed him, they cut off his head. Taking it with them, they traveled all night by way of the Arabah. 8 They brought the head of Ish-Bosheth to David at Hebron and said to the king, "Here is the head of Ish-Bosheth son of Saul,[h] your enemy, who tried to take your life. This day the LORD has avenged my lord the king against Saul and his offspring."

9 David answered Recab and his brother Baanah, the sons of Rimmon the Beerothite, "As surely as the LORD lives, who has delivered[i] me out of all trouble, 10 when a man told me, 'Saul is dead,' and thought he was bringing good news, I seized him and put him to death in Ziklag.[j] That was the reward I gave him for his news! 11 How much more—when wicked men have killed an innocent man in his own house and on his own bed—should I not now demand his blood[k] from your hand and rid the earth of you!"

12 So David gave an order to his men, and they killed them.[l] They cut off their hands and feet and hung the bodies by the pool in Hebron. But they took the head of Ish-Bosheth and buried it in Abner's tomb at Hebron.

David Becomes King Over Israel

5:1–3pp — 1Ch 11:1–3

5 All the tribes of Israel[m] came to David at Hebron and said, "We are your own flesh and blood.[n] 2 In the past, while Saul was king over us, you were the one who led Israel on their military campaigns.[o] And the LORD said to you, 'You will shepherd[p] my people Israel, and you will become their ruler.[q]' "

3 When all the elders of Israel had come to King David at Hebron, the king made a compact[r] with them at Hebron before the LORD, and they anointed[s] David king over Israel.

4 David was thirty years old[t] when he became king, and he reigned[u] forty[v] years. 5 In Hebron he reigned over Judah seven years and six months,[w] and in Jerusalem he reigned over all Israel and Judah thirty-three years.

David Conquers Jerusalem

5:6–10pp — 1Ch 11:4–9
5:11–16pp — 1Ch 3:5–9; 14:1–7

6 The king and his men marched to Jerusalem[x] to attack the Jebusites,[y] who lived there. The Jebusites said to David, "You will not get in here; even the blind and the lame can ward you off." They thought, "David cannot get in here." 7 Nevertheless, David captured the fortress of Zion, the City of David.[z]

8 On that day, David said, "Anyone who conquers the Jebusites will have to use the water shaft[f] to reach those 'lame and blind' who are David's enemies.[g]" That is why they say, "The 'blind and lame' will not enter the palace."

9 David then took up residence in the fortress and called it the City of David. He built up the area around it, from the supporting terraces[h][a]

[f] 8 *Or use scaling hooks* [g] 8 *Or are hated by David* [h] 9 *Or the Millo*

4:3 [a] Ne 11:33
4:4 [b] 1Sa 18:1 [c] 1Sa 31:1-4 [d] Lev 21:18 [e] 2Sa 9:3,6; 1Ch 8:34; 9:40
4:5 [f] 2Sa 2:8
4:6 [g] 2Sa 2:23
4:8 [h] 1Sa 24:4; 25:29
4:9 [i] Ge 48:16; 1Ki 1:29
4:10 [j] 2Sa 1:2-16
4:11 [k] Ge 9:5; Ps 9:12
4:12 [l] 2Sa 1:15
5:1 [m] 2Sa 19:43 [n] 1Ch 11:1
5:2 [o] 1Sa 18:5,13,16 [p] 1Sa 16:1; 2Sa 7:7 [q] 1Sa 25:30
5:3 [r] 2Sa 3:21 [s] 2Sa 2:4
5:4 [t] Lk 3:23 [u] 1Ki 2:11; 1Ch 3:4 [v] 1Ch 26:31; 29:27
5:5 [w] 2Sa 2:11; 1Ch 3:4
5:6 [x] Jdg 1:8 [y] Jos 15:8
5:7 [z] 2Sa 6:12,16; 1Ki 2:10
5:9 [a] ver 7; 1Ki 9:15,24

inward. 10And he became more and more powerful,[a] because the LORD God Almighty was with him.

11Now Hiram[b] king of Tyre sent messengers to David, along with cedar logs and carpenters and stonemasons, and they built a palace for David. 12And David knew that the LORD had established him as king over Israel and had exalted his kingdom for the sake of his people Israel.

13After he left Hebron, David took more concubines and wives[c] in Jerusalem, and more sons and daughters were born to him. 14These are the names of the children born to him there:[d] Shammua, Shobab, Nathan, Solomon, 15Ibhar, Elishua, Nepheg, Japhia, 16Elishama, Eliada and Eliphelet.

David Defeats the Philistines

5:17–25pp — 1Ch 14:8–17

17When the Philistines heard that David had been anointed king over Israel, they went up in full force to search for him, but David heard about it and went down to the stronghold.[e] 18Now the Philistines had come and spread out in the Valley of Rephaim;[f] 19so David inquired[g] of the LORD, "Shall I go and attack the Philistines? Will you hand them over to me?"

The LORD answered him, "Go, for I will surely hand the Philistines over to you."

20So David went to Baal Perazim, and there he defeated them. He said, "As waters break out, the LORD has broken out against my enemies before me." So that place was called Baal Perazim.[i][h] 21The Philistines abandoned their idols there, and David and his men carried them off.[i]

22Once more the Philistines came up and spread out in the Valley of Rephaim; 23so David inquired of the LORD, and he answered, "Do not go straight up, but circle around behind them and attack them in front of the balsam trees. 24As soon as you hear the sound[j] of marching in the tops of the balsam trees, move quickly, because that will mean the LORD has gone out in front[k] of you to strike the Philistine army." 25So David did as the LORD commanded him, and he struck down the Philistines all the way from Gibeon[j][l] to Gezer.[m]

5:10 [a] 2Sa 3:1
5:11 [b] 1Ki 5:1,18; 1Ch 14:1
5:13 [c] Dt 17:17; 1Ch 3:9
5:14 [d] 1Ch 3:5
5:17 [e] 2Sa 23:14; 1Ch 11:16
5:18 [f] Jos 15:8; 17:15; 18:16
5:19 [g] 1Sa 23:2; 2Sa 2:1
5:20 [h] Isa 28:21
5:21 [i] Dt 7:5; 1Ch 14:12; Isa 46:2
5:24 [j] 2Ki 7:6 [k] Jdg 4:14
5:25 [l] Isa 28:21 [m] 1Ch 14:16
6:2 [n] Jos 15:9 [o] 1Sa 4:4; 7:1 [p] Lev 24:16; Isa 63:14 [q] Ps 99:1 [r] Ex 25:22; 1Ch 13:5-6
6:3 [s] Nu 7:4-9; 1Sa 6:7
6:5 [t] 1Sa 18:6-7; Ezr 3:10; Ps 150:5
6:6 [u] Nu 4:15, 19-20; 1Ch 13:9
6:7 [v] 1Ch 15:13-15 [w] Ex 19:22; 1Sa 6:19
6:8 [x] Ps 7:11

The Ark Brought to Jerusalem

6:1–11pp — 1Ch 13:1–14
6:12–19pp — 1Ch 15:25–16:3

6 David again brought together out of Israel chosen men, thirty thousand in all. 2He and all his men set out from Baalah[n] of Judah[k] to bring up from there the ark[o] of God, which is called by the Name,[l][p] the name of the LORD Almighty, who is enthroned[q] between the cherubim[r] that are on the ark. 3They set the ark of God on a new cart[s] and brought it from the house of Abinadab, which was on the hill. Uzzah and Ahio, sons of Abinadab, were guiding the new cart 4with the ark of God on it,[m] and Ahio was walking in front of it. 5David and the whole house of Israel were celebrating with all their might before the LORD, with songs[n] and with harps, lyres, tambourines, sistrums and cymbals.[t]

6When they came to the threshing floor of Nacon, Uzzah reached out and took hold of[u] the ark of God, because the oxen stumbled. 7The LORD's anger burned against Uzzah because of his irreverent act;[v] therefore God struck him down[w] and he died there beside the ark of God.

8Then David was angry because the LORD's wrath[x] had broken out

[i]20 *Baal Perazim* means *the lord who breaks out.* [j]25 Septuagint (see also 1 Chron. 14:16); Hebrew *Geba* [k]2 That is, Kiriath Jearim; Hebrew *Baale Judah,* a variant of *Baalah of Judah* [l]2 Hebrew; Septuagint and Vulgate do not have *the Name.* [m]3,4 Dead Sea Scrolls and some Septuagint manuscripts; Masoretic Text *cart* [4]*and they brought it with the ark of God from the house of Abinadab, which was on the hill* [n]5 See Dead Sea Scrolls, Septuagint and 1 Chronicles 13:8; Masoretic Text *celebrating before the LORD with all kinds of instruments made of pine.*

against Uzzah, and to this day that place is called Perez Uzzah.[o][a]

9 David was afraid of the LORD that day and said, "How[b] can the ark of the LORD ever come to me?" 10 He was not willing to take the ark of the LORD to be with him in the City of David. Instead, he took it aside to the house of Obed-Edom[c] the Gittite. 11 The ark of the LORD remained in the house of Obed-Edom the Gittite for three months, and the LORD blessed him and his entire household.[d]

12 Now King David[e] was told, "The LORD has blessed the household of Obed-Edom and everything he has, because of the ark of God." So David went down and brought up the ark of God from the house of Obed-Edom to the City of David with rejoicing. 13 When those who were carrying the ark of the LORD had taken six steps, he sacrificed[f] a bull and a fattened calf. 14 David, wearing a linen ephod,[g] danced[h] before the LORD with all his might, 15 while he and the entire house of Israel brought up the ark of the LORD with shouts and the sound of trumpets.[i]

16 As the ark of the LORD was entering the City of David,[j] Michal daughter of Saul watched from a window. And when she saw King David leaping and dancing before the LORD, she despised him in her heart.

17 They brought the ark of the LORD and set it in its place inside the tent that David had pitched for it,[k] and David sacrificed burnt offerings[l] and fellowship offerings[p] before the LORD. 18 After he had finished sacrificing[m] the burnt offerings and fellowship offerings, he blessed the people in the name of the LORD Almighty. 19 Then he gave a loaf of bread, a cake of dates and a cake of raisins[n] to each person in the whole crowd of Israelites, both men and women.[o] And all the people went to their homes.

20 When David returned home to bless his household, Michal daughter of Saul came out to meet him and said, "How the king of Israel has distinguished himself today, disrobing[p] in the sight of the slave girls of his servants as any vulgar fellow would!"

21 David said to Michal, "It was before the LORD, who chose me rather than your father or anyone from his house when he appointed[q] me ruler over the LORD's people Israel—I will celebrate before the LORD. 22 I will become even more undignified than this, and I will be humiliated in my own eyes. But by these slave girls you spoke of, I will be held in honor."

23 And Michal daughter of Saul had no children to the day of her death.

God's Promise to David

7:1–17pp — 1Ch 17:1–15

7 After the king was settled in his palace[r] and the LORD had given him rest from all his enemies around him, 2 he said to Nathan the prophet, "Here I am, living in a palace[s] of cedar, while the ark of God remains in a tent."[t]

3 Nathan replied to the king, "Whatever you have in mind, go ahead and do it, for the LORD is with you."

4 That night the word of the LORD came to Nathan, saying:

> 5 "Go and tell my servant David, 'This is what the LORD says: Are you[u] the one to build me a house to dwell in?[v] 6 I have not dwelt in a house from the day I brought the Israelites up out of Egypt to this day. I have been moving from place to place with a tent[w] as my dwelling.[x] 7 Wherever I have moved with all the Israelites,[y] did I ever say to any of their rulers whom I commanded to shepherd[z] my people Israel, "Why have you not built me a house of cedar?[a]" '
>
> 8 "Now then, tell my servant David, 'This is what the LORD Almighty says: I took you from

6:8 [a] Ge 38:29
6:9 [b] Ps 119:120
6:10 [c] 1Ch 13:13; 26:4-5
6:11 [d] Ge 30:27; 39:5
6:12 [e] 1Ki 8:1; 1Ch 15:25
6:13 [f] 1Ki 8:5,62
6:14 [g] Ex 19:6; 1Sa 2:18 [h] Ex 15:20
6:15 [i] Ps 47:5; 98:6
6:16 [j] 2Sa 5:7
6:17 [k] 1Ch 15:1; 2Ch 1:4 [l] Lev 1:1-17; 1Ki 8:62-64
6:18 [m] 1Ki 8:22
6:19 [n] Hos 3:1 [o] Ne 8:10
6:20 [p] ver 14,16
6:21 [q] 1Sa 13:14; 15:28
7:1 [r] 1Ch 17:1
7:2 [s] 2Sa 5:11 [t] Ex 26:1; Ac 7:45-46
7:5 [u] 1Ki 8:19; 1Ch 22:8 [v] 1Ki 5:3-5
7:6 [w] Ex 40:18,34 [x] 1Ki 8:16
7:7 [y] Dt 23:14 [z] 2Sa 5:2 [a] Lev 26:11-12

[o]8 *Perez Uzzah* means *outbreak against Uzzah*
[p]17 Traditionally *peace offerings*; also in verse 18

the pasture and from following the flock[a] to be ruler[b] over my people Israel.[c] **9**I have been with you wherever you have gone,[d] and I have cut off all your enemies from before you.[e] Now I will make your name great, like the names of the greatest men of the earth. **10**And I will provide a place for my people Israel and will plant[f] them so that they can have a home of their own and no longer be disturbed. Wicked[g] people will not oppress them anymore,[h] as they did at the beginning **11**and have done ever since the time I appointed leaders[q][i] over my people Israel. I will also give you rest from all your enemies.[j]

" 'The LORD declares to you that the LORD himself will establish[k] a house[l] for you: **12**When your days are over and you rest[m] with your fathers, I will raise up your offspring to succeed you, who will come from your own body,[n] and I will establish his kingdom. **13**He is the one who will build a house for my Name,[o] and I will establish the throne of his kingdom forever.[p] **14**I will be his father, and he will be my son.[q] When he does wrong, I will punish him with the rod[r] of men, with floggings inflicted by men. **15**But my love will never be taken away from him, as I took it away from Saul,[s] whom I removed from before you. **16**Your house and your kingdom will endure forever before me[r]; your throne[t] will be established forever.[u]' "

17Nathan reported to David all the words of this entire revelation.

David's Prayer

7:18–29pp — 1Ch 17:16–27

18Then King David went in and sat before the LORD, and he said:

"Who am I,[v] O Sovereign LORD, and what is my family, that you have brought me this far? **19**And as if this were not enough in your sight, O Sovereign LORD, you have also spoken about the future of the house of your servant. Is this your usual way of dealing with man,[w] O Sovereign LORD?

20"What more can David say to you? For you know[x] your servant,[y] O Sovereign LORD. **21**For the sake of your word and according to your will, you have done this great thing and made it known to your servant.

22"How great[z] you are,[a] O Sovereign LORD! There is no one like you, and there is no God[b] but you, as we have heard with our own ears.[c] **23**And who is like your people Israel[d]—the one nation on earth that God went out to redeem as a people for himself, and to make a name for himself, and to perform great and awesome wonders[e] by driving out nations and their gods from before your people, whom you redeemed[f] from Egypt?[s] **24**You have established your people Israel as your very own[g] forever, and you, O LORD, have become their God.[h]

25"And now, LORD God, keep forever the promise you have made concerning your servant and his house. Do as you promised, **26**so that your name will be great forever. Then men will say, 'The LORD Almighty is God over Israel!' And the house of your servant David will be established before you.

27"O LORD Almighty, God of Israel, you have revealed this to your servant, saying, 'I will build a house for you.' So your

7:8 [a] 1Sa 16:11 [b] 2Sa 6:21 [c] Ps 78:70-72; 2Co 6:18*
7:9 [d] 2Sa 5:10 [e] Ps 18:37-42
7:10 [f] Ex 15:17; Isa 5:1-7 [g] Ps 89:22-23 [h] Isa 60:18
7:11 [i] Jdg 2:16; 1Sa 12:9-11 [j] ver 1 [k] 1Sa 25:28 [l] ver 27
7:12 [m] 1Ki 2:1 [n] Ps 132:11-12
7:13 [o] 1Ki 5:5; 8:19,29 [p] Isa 9:7
7:14 [q] Ps 89:26; Heb 1:5* [r] Ps 89:30-33
7:15 [s] 1Sa 15:23,28
7:16 [t] Ps 89:36-37 [u] ver 13
7:18 [v] Ex 3:11; 1Sa 18:18
7:19 [w] Isa 55:8-9
7:20 [x] Jn 21:17 [y] 1Sa 16:7
7:22 [z] Ps 48:1; 86:10; Jer 10:6 [a] Dt 3:24 [b] Ex 15:11 [c] Ex 10:2; Ps 44:1
7:23 [d] Dt 4:32-38 [e] Dt 10:21 [f] Dt 9:26; 15:15
7:24 [g] Dt 26:18 [h] Ex 6:6-7; Ps 48:14

[q] *11* Traditionally *judges* [r] *16* Some Hebrew manuscripts and Septuagint; most Hebrew manuscripts *you* [s] *23* See Septuagint and 1 Chron. 17:21; Hebrew *wonders for your land and before your people, whom you redeemed from Egypt, from the nations and their gods.*

servant has found courage to
offer you this prayer. 28O Sovereign LORD, you are God! Your
words are trustworthy,[a] and
you have promised these good
things to your servant. 29Now
be pleased to bless the house
of your servant, that it may
continue forever in your sight;
for you, O Sovereign LORD,
have spoken, and with your
blessing[b] the house of your
servant will be blessed forever."

David's Victories

8:1–14pp — 1Ch 18:1–13

8 In the course of time, David
defeated the Philistines and
subdued them, and he took Me-
theg Ammah from the control of
the Philistines.

2David also defeated the Moabites.[c] He made them lie down on
the ground and measured them off
with a length of cord. Every two
lengths of them were put to death,
and the third length was allowed to
live. So the Moabites became subject to David and brought tribute.

3Moreover, David fought Hadadezer[d] son of Rehob, king of Zobah,[e] when he went to restore his
control along the Euphrates River.
4David captured a thousand of his
chariots, seven thousand charioteers[t] and twenty thousand foot
soldiers. He hamstrung[f] all but a
hundred of the chariot horses.

5When the Arameans of Damascus[g] came to help Hadadezer king
of Zobah, David struck down twenty-two thousand of them. 6He put
garrisons in the Aramean kingdom
of Damascus, and the Arameans
became subject to him and brought
tribute. The LORD gave David victory wherever he went.[h]

7David took the gold shields[i]
that belonged to the officers of
Hadadezer and brought them to Jerusalem. 8From Tebah[u] and Bero-
thai,[j] towns that belonged to Hadadezer, King David took a great
quantity of bronze.

9When Tou[v] king of Hamath[k]
heard that David had defeated the
entire army of Hadadezer, 10he
sent his son Joram[w] to King David
to greet him and congratulate him
on his victory in battle over Hadadezer, who had been at war with
Tou. Joram brought with him articles of silver and gold and bronze.

11King David dedicated[l] these
articles to the LORD, as he had done
with the silver and gold from all the
nations he had subdued: 12Edom[x]
and Moab,[m] the Ammonites[n] and
the Philistines,[o] and Amalek.[p] He
also dedicated the plunder taken
from Hadadezer son of Rehob, king
of Zobah.

13And David became famous[q]
after he returned from striking
down eighteen thousand Edomites[y] in the Valley of Salt.[r]

14He put garrisons throughout
Edom, and all the Edomites[s] became subject to David.[t] The LORD
gave David victory wherever he
went.[u]

David's Officials

8:15–18pp — 1Ch 18:14–17

15David reigned over all Israel,
doing what was just and right for all
his people. 16Joab[v] son of Zeruiah
was over the army; Jehoshaphat[w]
son of Ahilud was recorder; 17Za-
dok[x] son of Ahitub and Ahimelech
son of Abiathar were priests; Seraiah was secretary;[y] 18Benaiah[z]
son of Jehoiada was over the Kerethites[a] and Pelethites; and David's sons were royal advisers.[z]

David and Mephibosheth

9 David asked, "Is there anyone
still left of the house of Saul to

7:28 [a]Ex 34:6; Jn 17:17
7:29 [b]Nu 6:23-27
8:2 [c]Ge 19:37; Nu 24:17
8:3 [d]2Sa 10:16,19 [e]1Sa 14:47
8:4 [f]Jos 11:9
8:5 [g]1Ki 11:24
8:6 [h]ver 14; 2Sa 3:18; 7:9
8:7 [i]1Ki 10:16
8:8 [j]Eze 47:16
8:9 [k]1Ki 8:65; 2Ch 8:4
8:11 [l]1Ki 7:51; 1Ch 26:26
8:12 [m]ver 2 [n]2Sa 10:14 [o]2Sa 5:25 [p]1Sa 27:8
8:13 [q]2Sa 7:9 [r]2Ki 14:7; 1Ch 18:12
8:14 [s]Nu 24:17-18 [t]Ge 27:29, 37-40 [u]ver 6
8:16 [v]2Sa 19:13; 1Ch 11:6 [w]2Sa 20:24; 1Ki 4:3
8:17 [x]2Sa 15:24, 29; 1Ch 16:39; 24:3 [y]1Ki 4:3; 2Ki 12:10
8:18 [z]2Sa 20:23; 1Ki 1:8,38; 1Ch 18:17 [a]1Sa 30:14

t*4* Septuagint (see also Dead Sea Scrolls and 1 Chron. 18:4); Masoretic Text *captured seventeen hundred of his charioteers* u*8* See some Septuagint manuscripts (see also 1 Chron. 18:8); Hebrew *Betah.* v*9* Hebrew *Toi,* a variant of *Tou;* also in verse 10 w*10* A variant of *Hadoram* x*12* Some Hebrew manuscripts, Septuagint and Syriac (see also 1 Chron. 18:11); most Hebrew manuscripts *Aram* y*13* A few Hebrew manuscripts, Septuagint and Syriac (see also 1 Chron. 18:12); most Hebrew manuscripts *Aram* (that is, Arameans) z*18* Or *were priests*

whom I can show kindness for Jonathan's sake?"[a]

2Now there was a servant of Saul's household named Ziba.[b] They called him to appear before David, and the king said to him, "Are you Ziba?"

"Your servant," he replied.

3The king asked, "Is there no one still left of the house of Saul to whom I can show God's kindness?"

Ziba answered the king, "There is still a son of Jonathan;[c] he is crippled[d] in both feet."

4"Where is he?" the king asked.

Ziba answered, "He is at the house of Makir[e] son of Ammiel in Lo Debar."

5So King David had him brought from Lo Debar, from the house of Makir son of Ammiel.

6When Mephibosheth son of Jonathan, the son of Saul, came to David, he bowed down to pay him honor.[f]

David said, "Mephibosheth!"

"Your servant," he replied.

7"Don't be afraid," David said to him, "for I will surely show you kindness for the sake of your father Jonathan. I will restore to you all the land that belonged to your grandfather Saul, and you will always eat at my table.[g]"

8Mephibosheth bowed down and said, "What is your servant, that you should notice a dead dog[h] like me?"

9Then the king summoned Ziba, Saul's servant, and said to him, "I have given your master's grandson everything that belonged to Saul and his family. 10You and your sons and your servants are to farm the land for him and bring in the crops, so that your master's grandson[i] may be provided for. And Mephibosheth, grandson of your master, will always eat at my table." (Now Ziba had fifteen sons and twenty servants.)

11Then Ziba said to the king, "Your servant will do whatever my lord the king commands his servant to do." So Mephibosheth ate at David's[a] table like one of the king's sons.[j]

12Mephibosheth had a young son named Mica, and all the members of Ziba's household were servants of Mephibosheth.[k] 13And Mephibosheth lived in Jerusalem, because he always ate at the king's table, and he was crippled in both feet.

David Defeats the Ammonites

10:1–19pp — 1Ch 19:1–19

10 In the course of time, the king of the Ammonites died, and his son Hanun succeeded him as king. 2David thought, "I will show kindness to Hanun son of Nahash,[l] just as his father showed kindness to me." So David sent a delegation to express his sympathy to Hanun concerning his father.

When David's men came to the land of the Ammonites, 3the Ammonite nobles said to Hanun their lord, "Do you think David is honoring your father by sending men to you to express sympathy? Hasn't David sent them to you to explore the city and spy it out and overthrow it?" 4So Hanun seized David's men, shaved off half of each man's beard,[m] cut off their garments in the middle at the buttocks,[n] and sent them away.

5When David was told about this, he sent messengers to meet the men, for they were greatly humiliated. The king said, "Stay at Jericho till your beards have grown, and then come back."

6When the Ammonites realized that they had become a stench[o] in David's nostrils, they hired twenty thousand Aramean[p] foot soldiers from Beth Rehob[q] and Zobah, as well as the king of Maacah[r] with a thousand men, and also twelve thousand men from Tob.

7On hearing this, David sent Joab out with the entire army of fighting men. 8The Ammonites came out and drew up in battle formation at the entrance to their city gate, while the Arameans of Zobah

9:1 [a] 1Sa 20:14-17, 42
9:2 [b] 2Sa 16:1-4; 19:17,26,29
9:3 [c] 1Sa 20:14 [d] 2Sa 4:4
9:4 [e] 2Sa 17:27-29
9:6 [f] 2Sa 16:4; 19:24-30
9:7 [g] ver 1,3; 2Sa 12:8; 19:28; 1Ki 2:7; 2Ki 25:29
9:8 [h] 2Sa 16:9
9:10 [i] ver 7,11,13; 2Sa 19:28
9:11 [j] Job 36:7; Ps 113:8
9:12 [k] 1Ch 8:34
10:2 [l] 1Sa 11:1
10:4 [m] Lev 19:27; Isa 15:2; Jer 48:37 [n] Isa 20:4
10:6 [o] Ge 34:30 [p] 2Sa 8:5 [q] Jdg 18:28 [r] Dt 3:14

[a] *11* Septuagint; Hebrew *my*

and Rehob and the men of Tob and
Maacah were by themselves in the
open country.

9Joab saw that there were battle
lines in front of him and behind
him; so he selected some of the
best troops in Israel and deployed
them against the Arameans. **10**He
put the rest of the men under the
command of Abishai his brother
and deployed them against the
Ammonites. **11**Joab said, "If the Arameans are too strong for me, then
you are to come to my rescue; but
if the Ammonites are too strong for
you, then I will come to rescue you.
12Be strong[a] and let us fight bravely for our people and the cities of
our God. The LORD will do what is
good in his sight."[b]

13Then Joab and the troops with
him advanced to fight the Arameans, and they fled before him.
14When the Ammonites saw that
the Arameans were fleeing, they
fled before Abishai and went inside
the city. So Joab returned from
fighting the Ammonites and came
to Jerusalem.

15After the Arameans saw that
they had been routed by Israel, they regrouped. **16**Hadadezer
had Arameans brought from beyond the River[b]; they went to Helam, with Shobach the commander of Hadadezer's army leading
them.

17When David was told of this,
he gathered all Israel, crossed the
Jordan and went to Helam. The Arameans formed their battle lines to
meet David and fought against
him. **18**But they fled before Israel,
and David killed seven hundred of
their charioteers and forty thousand of their foot soldiers.[c] He
also struck down Shobach the
commander of their army, and he
died there. **19**When all the kings
who were vassals of Hadadezer saw
that they had been defeated by Israel, they made peace with the Israelites and became subject[c] to
them.

So the Arameans[d] were afraid to
help the Ammonites anymore.

10:12 [a]Dt 31:6; 1Co 16:13; Eph 6:10 [b]Jdg 10:15; 1Sa 3:18; Ne 4:14
10:19 [c]2Sa 8:6 [d]1Ki 11:25; 2Ki 5:1
11:1 [e]1Ki 20:22,26 [f]2Sa 2:18 [g]1Ch 20:1 [h]2Sa 12:26-28
11:2 [i]Dt 22:8; Jos 2:8 [j]Mt 5:28
11:3 [k]1Ch 3:5 [l]2Sa 23:34 [m]2Sa 23:39
11:4 [n]Lev 20:10; Ps 51 Title; Jas 1:14-15 [o]Dt 22:22 [p]Lev 15:25-30; 18:19
11:6 [q]1Ch 11:41
11:8 [r]Ge 18:4; 43:24; Lk 7:44
11:11 [s]2Sa 7:2

David and Bathsheba

11 In the spring,[e] at the time
when kings go off to war,
David sent Joab[f] out with the
king's men and the whole Israelite
army.[g] They destroyed the Ammonites and besieged Rabbah.[h]
But David remained in Jerusalem.

2One evening David got up from
his bed and walked around on the
roof[i] of the palace. From the roof
he saw[j] a woman bathing. The
woman was very beautiful, **3**and
David sent someone to find out
about her. The man said, "Isn't this
Bathsheba,[k] the daughter of Eliam[l] and the wife of Uriah[m] the
Hittite?" **4**Then David sent messengers to get her.[n] She came to
him, and he slept[o] with her. (She
had purified herself from her uncleanness.)[p] Then[d] she went back
home. **5**The woman conceived and
sent word to David, saying, "I am
pregnant."

6So David sent this word to Joab:
"Send me Uriah[q] the Hittite." And
Joab sent him to David. **7**When Uriah came to him, David asked him
how Joab was, how the soldiers
were and how the war was going.
8Then David said to Uriah, "Go
down to your house and wash your
feet."[r] So Uriah left the palace,
and a gift from the king was sent
after him. **9**But Uriah slept at the
entrance to the palace with all his
master's servants and did not go
down to his house.

10When David was told, "Uriah
did not go home," he asked him,
"Haven't you just come from a distance? Why didn't you go home?"

11Uriah said to David, "The ark[s]
and Israel and Judah are staying in
tents, and my master Joab and my
lord's men are camped in the open
fields. How could I go to my house
to eat and drink and lie with my
wife? As surely as you live, I will not
do such a thing!"

12Then David said to him, "Stay

[b]*16* That is, the Euphrates [c]*18* Some Septuagint manuscripts (see also 1 Chron. 19:18); Hebrew *horsemen* [d]*4* Or *with her. When she purified herself from her uncleanness,*

here one more day, and tomorrow I will send you back." So Uriah remained in Jerusalem that day and the next. **13**At David's invitation, he ate and drank with him, and David made him drunk. But in the evening Uriah went out to sleep on his mat among his master's servants; he did not go home.

14In the morning David wrote a letter[a] to Joab and sent it with Uriah. **15**In it he wrote, "Put Uriah in the front line where the fighting is fiercest. Then withdraw from him so he will be struck down[b] and die.[c]"

16So while Joab had the city under siege, he put Uriah at a place where he knew the strongest defenders were. **17**When the men of the city came out and fought against Joab, some of the men in David's army fell; moreover, Uriah the Hittite died.

18Joab sent David a full account of the battle. **19**He instructed the messenger: "When you have finished giving the king this account of the battle, **20**the king's anger may flare up, and he may ask you, 'Why did you get so close to the city to fight? Didn't you know they would shoot arrows from the wall? **21**Who killed Abimelech[d] son of Jerub-Besheth[e]? Didn't a woman throw an upper millstone on him from the wall,[e] so that he died in Thebez? Why did you get so close to the wall?' If he asks you this, then say to him, 'Also, your servant Uriah the Hittite is dead.' "

22The messenger set out, and when he arrived he told David everything Joab had sent him to say. **23**The messenger said to David, "The men overpowered us and came out against us in the open, but we drove them back to the entrance to the city gate. **24**Then the archers shot arrows at your servants from the wall, and some of the king's men died. Moreover, your servant Uriah the Hittite is dead."

25David told the messenger, "Say this to Joab: 'Don't let this upset you; the sword devours one as well as another. Press the attack against the city and destroy it.' Say this to encourage Joab."

26When Uriah's wife heard that her husband was dead, she mourned for him. **27**After the time of mourning was over, David had her brought to his house, and she became his wife and bore him a son. But the thing David had done displeased[f] the LORD.

Nathan Rebukes David

11:1; 12:29–31pp — 1Ch 20:1–3

12 The LORD sent Nathan[g] to David.[h] When he came to him,[i] he said, "There were two men in a certain town, one rich and the other poor. **2**The rich man had a very large number of sheep and cattle, **3**but the poor man had nothing except one little ewe lamb he had bought. He raised it, and it grew up with him and his children. It shared his food, drank from his cup and even slept in his arms. It was like a daughter to him.

4"Now a traveler came to the rich man, but the rich man refrained from taking one of his own sheep or cattle to prepare a meal for the traveler who had come to him. Instead, he took the ewe lamb that belonged to the poor man and prepared it for the one who had come to him."

5David[j] burned with anger against the man and said to Nathan, "As surely as the LORD lives, the man who did this deserves to die! **6**He must pay for that lamb four times over,[k] because he did such a thing and had no pity."

7Then Nathan said to David, "You are the man! This is what the LORD, the God of Israel, says: 'I anointed[l] you[m] king over Israel, and I delivered you from the hand of Saul. **8**I gave your master's house to you,[n] and your master's wives into your arms. I gave you the house of Israel and Judah. And if all this had been too little, I would have given you even more. **9**Why

11:14 [a] 1Ki 21:8
11:15 [b] 2Sa 12:9 [c] 2Sa 12:12
11:21 [d] Jdg 8:31 [e] Jdg 9:50-54
11:27 [f] 2Sa 12:9; Ps 51:4-5
12:1 [g] 2Sa 7:2; 1Ki 20:35-41 [h] Ps 51 Title [i] 2Sa 14:4
12:5 [j] 1Ki 20:40
12:6 [k] Ex 22:1; Lk 19:8
12:7 [l] 1Sa 16:13 [m] 1Ki 20:42
12:8 [n] 2Sa 9:7

[e] *21* Also known as *Jerub-Baal* (that is, Gideon)

did you despise[a] the word of the
LORD by doing what is evil in his
eyes? You struck down[b] Uriah the
Hittite with the sword and took his
wife to be your own. You killed him
with the sword of the Ammonites.
10Now, therefore, the sword[c] will
never depart from your house, because you despised me and took
the wife of Uriah the Hittite to be
your own.'
11"This is what the LORD says:
'Out of your own household I am
going to bring calamity upon you.[d]
Before your very eyes I will take
your wives and give them to one
who is close to you, and he will lie
with your wives in broad daylight.
12You did it in secret,[e] but I will do
this thing in broad daylight[f] before all Israel.' "
13Then David said to Nathan, "I
have sinned[g] against the LORD."
Nathan replied, "The LORD has
taken away[h] your sin.[i] You are
not going to die.[j] **14**But because
by doing this you have made the
enemies of the LORD show utter
contempt,[fk] the son born to you
will die."
15After Nathan had gone home,
the LORD struck[l] the child that Uriah's wife had borne to David, and
he became ill. **16**David pleaded
with God for the child. He fasted
and went into his house and spent
the nights lying[m] on the ground.
17The elders of his household
stood beside him to get him up
from the ground, but he refused,
and he would not eat any food with
them.[n]
18On the seventh day the child
died. David's servants were afraid
to tell him that the child was dead,
for they thought, "While the child
was still living, we spoke to David
but he would not listen to us. How
can we tell him the child is dead?
He may do something desperate."
19David noticed that his servants
were whispering among themselves and he realized the child was
dead. "Is the child dead?" he
asked.
"Yes," they replied, "he is dead."
20Then David got up from the
ground. After he had washed,[o] put
on lotions and changed his
clothes,[p] he went into the house of
the LORD and worshiped. Then he
went to his own house, and at his
request they served him food, and
he ate.
21His servants asked him, "Why
are you acting this way? While the
child was alive, you fasted and
wept,[q] but now that the child is
dead, you get up and eat!"
22He answered, "While the child
was still alive, I fasted and wept. I
thought, 'Who knows?[r] The LORD
may be gracious to me and let the
child live.'[s] **23**But now that he is
dead, why should I fast? Can I bring
him back again? I will go to him,[t]
but he will not return to me."[u]
24Then David comforted his wife
Bathsheba,[v] and he went to her
and lay with her. She gave birth to
a son, and they named him Solomon.[w] The LORD loved him; **25**and
because the LORD loved him, he
sent word through Nathan the
prophet to name him Jedidiah.[gx]
26Meanwhile Joab fought
against Rabbah[y] of the Ammonites and captured the royal citadel.
27Joab then sent messengers to
David, saying, "I have fought
against Rabbah and taken its water
supply. **28**Now muster the rest of
the troops and besiege the city and
capture it. Otherwise I will take the
city, and it will be named after
me."
29So David mustered the entire
army and went to Rabbah, and attacked and captured it. **30**He took
the crown[z] from the head of their
king[h]—its weight was a talent[i] of
gold, and it was set with precious
stones—and it was placed on David's head. He took a great quantity
of plunder from the city **31**and
brought out the people who were
there, consigning them to labor
with saws and with iron picks and

12:9 [a]Nu 15:31; 1Sa 15:19 [b]2Sa 11:15
12:10 [c]2Sa 13:28; 18:14-15; 1Ki 2:25
12:11 [d]Dt 28:30; 2Sa 16:21-22
12:12 [e]2Sa 11:4-15 [f]2Sa 16:22
12:13 [g]Ge 13:13; Nu 22:34; 1Sa 15:24; 2Sa 24:10 [h]Ps 32:1-5; 51:1,9; 103:12; Zec 3:4,9 [i]Pr 28:13; Mic 7:18-19 [j]Lev 20:10; 24:17
12:14 [k]Isa 52:5; Ro 2:24
12:15 [l]1Sa 25:38
12:16 [m]2Sa 13:31; Ps 5:7
12:17 [n]2Sa 3:35
12:20 [o]Mt 6:17 [p]Job 1:20
12:21 [q]Jdg 20:26
12:22 [r]Jnh 3:9 [s]Isa 38:1-5
12:23 [t]Ge 37:35 [u]1Sa 31:13; 2Sa 13:39; Job 7:10; 10:21
12:24 [v]1Ki 1:11 [w]1Ki 1:10; 1Ch 22:9; 28:5; Mt 1:6
12:25 [x]Ne 13:26
12:26 [y]Dt 3:11; 1Ch 20:1-3
12:30 [z]1Ch 20:2; Est 8:15; Ps 21:3; 132:18

[f]*14* Masoretic Text; an ancient Hebrew scribal tradition *this you have shown utter contempt for the LORD* [g]*25* *Jedidiah* means *loved by the LORD.* [h]*30* Or *of Milcom* (that is, Molech) [i]*30* That is, about 75 pounds (about 34 kilograms)

axes, and he made them work at
brickmaking.[j] He did this to all
the Ammonite[a] towns. Then David
and his entire army returned to Jerusalem.

Amnon and Tamar

13 In the course of time, Amnon[b] son of David fell in
love with Tamar,[c] the beautiful
sister of Absalom[d] son of David.
2 Amnon became frustrated to
the point of illness on account of
his sister Tamar, for she was a virgin, and it seemed impossible for
him to do anything to her.
3 Now Amnon had a friend
named Jonadab son of Shimeah,[e]
David's brother. Jonadab was a
very shrewd man. 4 He asked Amnon, "Why do you, the king's son,
look so haggard morning after
morning? Won't you tell me?"
Amnon said to him, "I'm in love
with Tamar, my brother Absalom's
sister."
5 "Go to bed and pretend to be
ill," Jonadab said. "When your father comes to see you, say to him,
'I would like my sister Tamar to
come and give me something to
eat. Let her prepare the food in my
sight so I may watch her and then
eat it from her hand.' "
6 So Amnon lay down and pretended to be ill. When the king
came to see him, Amnon said to
him, "I would like my sister Tamar
to come and make some special
bread in my sight, so I may eat from
her hand."
7 David sent word to Tamar at the
palace: "Go to the house of your
brother Amnon and prepare some
food for him." 8 So Tamar went to
the house of her brother Amnon,
who was lying down. She took
some dough, kneaded it, made the
bread in his sight and baked it.
9 Then she took the pan and served
him the bread, but he refused to
eat.
"Send everyone out of here,"[f]
Amnon said. So everyone left him.
10 Then Amnon said to Tamar,
"Bring the food here into my bedroom so I may eat from your hand."
And Tamar took the bread she had
prepared and brought it to her
brother Amnon in his bedroom.
11 But when she took it to him to
eat, he grabbed[g] her and said,
"Come to bed with me, my sister."[h]
12 "Don't, my brother!" she said
to him. "Don't force me. Such a
thing should not be done in Israel![i] Don't do this wicked thing.[j]
13 What about me?[k] Where could I
get rid of my disgrace? And what
about you? You would be like one
of the wicked fools in Israel. Please
speak to the king; he will not keep
me from being married to you."
14 But he refused to listen to her,
and since he was stronger than she,
he raped her.[l]
15 Then Amnon hated her with
intense hatred. In fact, he hated
her more than he had loved her.
Amnon said to her, "Get up and get
out!"
16 "No!" she said to him. "Sending me away would be a greater
wrong than what you have already
done to me."
But he refused to listen to her.
17 He called his personal servant
and said, "Get this woman out of
here and bolt the door after her."
18 So his servant put her out and
bolted the door after her. She was
wearing a richly ornamented[k]
robe,[m] for this was the kind of garment the virgin daughters of the
king wore. 19 Tamar put ashes[n] on
her head and tore the ornamented[l] robe she was wearing. She put
her hand on her head and went
away, weeping aloud as she went.
20 Her brother Absalom said to
her, "Has that Amnon, your brother, been with you? Be quiet now,
my sister; he is your brother. Don't
take this thing to heart." And Tamar lived in her brother Absalom's
house, a desolate woman.
21 When King David heard all
this, he was furious.[o] 22 Absalom

12:31 [a] 1Sa 14:47
13:1 [b] 2Sa 3:2 [c] 2Sa 14:27; 1Ch 3:9 [d] 2Sa 3:3
13:3 [e] 1Sa 16:9
13:9 [f] Ge 45:1
13:11 [g] Ge 39:12 [h] Ge 38:16
13:12 [i] Lev 20:17; Jdg 20:6 [j] Ge 34:7; Jdg 19:23
13:13 [k] Ge 20:12; Lev 18:9; Dt 22:21, 23-24
13:14 [l] Ge 34:2; Dt 22:25; Eze 22:11
13:18 [m] Ge 37:23; Jdg 5:30
13:19 [n] Jos 7:6; 1Sa 4:12; 2Sa 1:2; Est 4:1; Da 9:3
13:21 [o] Ge 34:7

[j] *31* The meaning of the Hebrew for this clause is uncertain. [k] *18* The meaning of the Hebrew for this phrase is uncertain.
[l] *19* The meaning of the Hebrew for this word is uncertain.

never said a word to Amnon, either
good or bad;[a] he hated[b] Amnon
because he had disgraced his sister
Tamar.

Absalom Kills Amnon

23Two years later, when Absalom's sheepshearers[c] were at Baal
Hazor near the border of Ephraim,
he invited all the king's sons to
come there. 24Absalom went to the
king and said, "Your servant has
had shearers come. Will the king
and his officials please join me?"
25"No, my son," the king replied.
"All of us should not go; we would
only be a burden to you." Although
Absalom urged him, he still refused to go, but gave him his blessing.
26Then Absalom said, "If not,
please let my brother Amnon come
with us."
The king asked him, "Why
should he go with you?" 27But Absalom urged him, so he sent with
him Amnon and the rest of the
king's sons.
28Absalom[d] ordered his men,
"Listen! When Amnon is in high[e]
spirits from drinking wine and I say
to you, 'Strike Amnon down,' then
kill him. Don't be afraid. Have not
I given you this order? Be strong
and brave.[f]" 29So Absalom's men
did to Amnon what Absalom had
ordered. Then all the king's sons
got up, mounted their mules and
fled.
30While they were on their way,
the report came to David: "Absalom has struck down all the king's
sons; not one of them is left."
31The king stood up, tore[g] his
clothes and lay down on the
ground; and all his servants stood
by with their clothes torn.
32But Jonadab son of Shimeah,
David's brother, said, "My lord
should not think that they killed all
the princes; only Amnon is dead.
This has been Absalom's expressed
intention ever since the day Amnon raped his sister Tamar. 33My
lord the king should not be concerned about the report that all the
king's sons are dead. Only Amnon
is dead."
34Meanwhile, Absalom had fled.
Now the man standing watch
looked up and saw many people on
the road west of him, coming down
the side of the hill. The watchman
went and told the king, "I see men
in the direction of Horonaim, on
the side of the hill."[m]
35Jonadab said to the king, "See,
the king's sons are here; it has happened just as your servant said."
36As he finished speaking, the
king's sons came in, wailing loudly.
The king, too, and all his servants
wept very bitterly.
37Absalom fled and went to Talmai[h] son of Ammihud, the king of
Geshur. But King David mourned
for his son every day.
38After Absalom fled and went to
Geshur, he stayed there three
years. 39And the spirit of the king[n]
longed to go to Absalom,[i] for he
was consoled[j] concerning Amnon's death.

Absalom Returns to Jerusalem

14 Joab[k] son of Zeruiah knew
that the king's heart longed
for Absalom. 2So Joab sent someone to Tekoa[l] and had a wise
woman[m] brought from there. He
said to her, "Pretend you are in
mourning. Dress in mourning
clothes, and don't use any cosmet-
ic lotions.[n] Act like a woman who
has spent many days grieving for
the dead. 3Then go to the king and
speak these words to him." And
Joab[o] put the words in her mouth.
4When the woman from Tekoa
went[o] to the king, she fell with her
face to the ground to pay him hon-
or, and she said, "Help me, O
king!"
5The king asked her, "What is
troubling you?"
She said, "I am indeed a widow;
my husband is dead. 6I your servant

13:22 [a]Ge 31:24 [b]Lev 19:17-18; 1Jn 2:9-11
13:23 [c]1Sa 25:7
13:28 [d]2Sa 3:3 [e]Jdg 19:6,9, 22; Ru 3:7; 1Sa 25:36 [f]2Sa 12:10
13:31 [g]Nu 14:6; 2Sa 1:11; 12:16
13:37 [h]ver 34; 2Sa 3:3; 14:23,32
13:39 [i]2Sa 14:13 [j]2Sa 12:19-23
14:1 [k]2Sa 2:18
14:2 [l]2Ch 11:6; Ne 3:5; Jer 6:1; Am 1:1 [m]2Sa 20:16 [n]Ru 3:3; 2Sa 12:20; Isa 1:6
14:3 [o]ver 19

[m]*34* Septuagint; Hebrew does not have this sentence. [n]*39* Dead Sea Scrolls and some Septuagint manuscripts; Masoretic Text *But the spirit of David the king* [o]*4* Many Hebrew manuscripts, Septuagint, Vulgate and Syriac; most Hebrew manuscripts *spoke*

had two sons. They got into a fight with each other in the field, and no one was there to separate them. One struck the other and killed him. **7**Now the whole clan has risen up against your servant; they say, 'Hand over the one who struck his brother down, so that we may put him to death[a] for the life of his brother whom he killed; then we will get rid of the heir[b] as well.' They would put out the only burning coal I have left,[c] leaving my husband neither name nor descendant on the face of the earth."

8The king said to the woman, "Go home,[d] and I will issue an order in your behalf."

9But the woman from Tekoa said to him, "My lord the king, let the blame[e] rest on me and on my father's family,[f] and let the king and his throne be without guilt.[g]"

10The king replied, "If anyone says anything to you, bring him to me, and he will not bother you again."

11She said, "Then let the king invoke the LORD his God to prevent the avenger[h] of blood from adding to the destruction, so that my son will not be destroyed."

"As surely as the LORD lives," he said, "not one hair[i] of your son's head will fall to the ground.[j]"

12Then the woman said, "Let your servant speak a word to my lord the king."

"Speak," he replied.

13The woman said, "Why then have you devised a thing like this against the people of God? When the king says this, does he not convict himself,[k] for the king has not brought back his banished son?[l] **14**Like water[m] spilled on the ground, which cannot be recovered, so we must die.[n] But God does not take away life; instead, he devises ways so that a banished person[o] may not remain estranged from him.

15"And now I have come to say this to my lord the king because the people have made me afraid. Your servant thought, 'I will speak to the king; perhaps he will do what his servant asks. **16**Perhaps the king will agree to deliver his servant from the hand of the man who is trying to cut off both me and my son from the inheritance[p] God gave us.'

17"And now your servant says, 'May the word of my lord the king bring me rest, for my lord the king is like an angel[q] of God in discerning[r] good and evil. May the LORD your God be with you.' "

18Then the king said to the woman, "Do not keep from me the answer to what I am going to ask you."

"Let my lord the king speak," the woman said.

19The king asked, "Isn't the hand of Joab[s] with you in all this?"

The woman answered, "As surely as you live, my lord the king, no one can turn to the right or to the left from anything my lord the king says. Yes, it was your servant Joab who instructed me to do this and who put all these words into the mouth of your servant. **20**Your servant Joab did this to change the present situation. My lord has wisdom[t] like that of an angel of God—he knows everything that happens in the land.[u]"

21The king said to Joab, "Very well, I will do it. Go, bring back the young man Absalom."

22Joab fell with his face to the ground to pay him honor, and he blessed the king.[v] Joab said, "Today your servant knows that he has found favor in your eyes, my lord the king, because the king has granted his servant's request."

23Then Joab went to Geshur and brought Absalom back to Jerusalem. **24**But the king said, "He must go to his own house; he must not see my face." So Absalom went to his own house and did not see the face of the king.

25In all Israel there was not a man so highly praised for his handsome appearance as Absalom. From the top of his head to the sole of his foot there was no blemish in him. **26**Whenever he cut the hair of his head[w]—he used to cut his hair

14:7 [a] Nu 35:19 [b] Mt 21:38 [c] Dt 19:10-13
14:8 [d] 1Sa 25:35
14:9 [e] 1Sa 25:24 [f] Mt 27:25 [g] 1Sa 25:28; 1Ki 2:33
14:11 [h] Nu 35:12,21 [i] Mt 10:30 [j] 1Sa 14:45
14:13 [k] 2Sa 12:7; 1Ki 20:40 [l] 2Sa 13:38-39
14:14 [m] Job 14:11; Ps 58:7; Isa 19:5 [n] Job 10:8; 17:13; 30:23; Ps 22:15; Heb 9:27 [o] Nu 35:15, 25-28; Job 34:15
14:16 [p] Ex 34:9; 1Sa 26:19
14:17 [q] ver 20; 1Sa 29:9; 2Sa 19:27 [r] 1Ki 3:9; Da 2:21
14:19 [s] ver 3
14:20 [t] 1Ki 3:12,28; Isa 28:6 [u] ver 17; 2Sa 18:13; 19:27
14:22 [v] Ge 47:7
14:26 [w] 2Sa 18:9; Eze 44:20

from time to time when it became
too heavy for him—he would weigh
it, and its weight was two hundred
shekels[p] by the royal standard.
27 Three sons[a] and a daughter
were born to Absalom. The daughter's name was Tamar,[b] and she
became a beautiful woman.
28 Absalom lived two years in Jerusalem without seeing the king's
face. 29 Then Absalom sent for Joab
in order to send him to the king,
but Joab refused to come to him.
So he sent a second time, but he
refused to come. 30 Then he said to
his servants, "Look, Joab's field is
next to mine, and he has barley[c]
there. Go and set it on fire." So Absalom's servants set the field on
fire.
31 Then Joab did go to Absalom's
house and he said to him, "Why
have your servants set my field on
fire?[d]"
32 Absalom said to Joab, "Look, I
sent word to you and said, 'Come
here so I can send you to the king
to ask, "Why have I come from Geshur?[e] It would be better for me if
I were still there!" ' Now then, I
want to see the king's face, and if I
am guilty of anything, let him put
me to death."[f]
33 So Joab went to the king and
told him this. Then the king summoned Absalom, and he came in
and bowed down with his face to
the ground before the king. And
the king kissed[g] Absalom.

Absalom's Conspiracy

15 In the course of time,[h] Absalom provided himself
with a chariot[i] and horses and
with fifty men to run ahead of him.
2 He would get up early and stand
by the side of the road leading to
the city gate.[j] Whenever anyone
came with a complaint to be placed
before the king for a decision, Absalom would call out to him, "What
town are you from?" He would answer, "Your servant is from one of
the tribes of Israel." 3 Then Absalom would say to him, "Look, your
claims are valid and proper, but
there is no representative of the
king to hear you."[k] 4 And Absalom
would add, "If only I were appointed judge in the land![l] Then everyone who has a complaint or case
could come to me and I would see
that he gets justice."
5 Also, whenever anyone approached him to bow down before
him, Absalom would reach out his
hand, take hold of him and kiss
him. 6 Absalom behaved in this way
toward all the Israelites who came
to the king asking for justice, and
so he stole the hearts[m] of the men
of Israel.
7 At the end of four[q] years, Absalom said to the king, "Let me go to
Hebron and fulfill a vow I made to
the LORD. 8 While your servant was
living at Geshur[n] in Aram, I made
this vow:[o] 'If the LORD takes me
back to Jerusalem, I will worship
the LORD in Hebron.[r]' "
9 The king said to him, "Go in
peace." So he went to Hebron.
10 Then Absalom sent secret
messengers throughout the tribes
of Israel to say, "As soon as you
hear the sound of the trumpets,[p]
then say, 'Absalom is king in Hebron.' " 11 Two hundred men from
Jerusalem had accompanied Absalom. They had been invited as
guests and went quite innocently,
knowing nothing about the matter.
12 While Absalom was offering sacrifices, he also sent for Ahithophel[q] the Gilonite, David's counselor,[r] to come from Giloh,[s] his
hometown. And so the conspiracy
gained strength, and Absalom's
following kept on increasing.[t]

David Flees

13 A messenger came and told
David, "The hearts of the men of
Israel are with Absalom."
14 Then David said to all his officials who were with him in Jerusalem, "Come! We must flee,[u] or
none of us will escape from Absalom.[v] We must leave immediately,

14:27 [a] 2Sa 18:18 [b] 2Sa 13:1
14:30 [c] Ex 9:31
14:31 [d] Jdg 15:5
14:32 [e] 2Sa 3:3 [f] 1Sa 20:8
14:33 [g] Ge 33:4; Lk 15:20
15:1 [h] 2Sa 12:11 [i] 1Sa 8:11; 1Ki 1:5
15:2 [j] Ge 23:10; 2Sa 19:8
15:3 [k] Pr 12:2
15:4 [l] Jdg 9:29
15:6 [m] Ro 16:18
15:8 [n] 2Sa 3:3; 13:37-38 [o] Ge 28:20
15:10 [p] 1Ki 1:34,39; 2Ki 9:13
15:12 [q] ver 31,34; 2Sa 16:15,23; 1Ch 27:33 [r] Job 19:14; Ps 41:9; 55:13; Jer 9:4 [s] Jos 15:51 [t] Ps 3:1
15:14 [u] 2Sa 12:11; 1Ki 2:26; Ps 132:1; Ps 3 Title [v] 2Sa 19:9

p26 That is, about 5 pounds (about 2.3 kilograms) q7 Some Septuagint manuscripts, Syriac and Josephus; Hebrew *forty* r8 Some Septuagint manuscripts; Hebrew does not have *in Hebron.*

or he will move quickly to overtake
us and bring ruin upon us and put
the city to the sword."
15The king's officials answered
him, "Your servants are ready to do
whatever our lord the king
chooses."
16The king set out, with his entire household following him; but
he left ten concubines[a] to take
care of the palace. 17So the king set
out, with all the people following
him, and they halted at a place
some distance away. 18All his men
marched past him, along with all
the Kerethites[b] and Pelethites;
and all the six hundred Gittites
who had accompanied him from
Gath marched before the king.
19The king said to Ittai[c] the Gittite, "Why should you come along
with us? Go back and stay with
King Absalom. You are a foreigner,[d] an exile from your homeland.
20You came only yesterday. And today shall I make you wander[e]
about with us, when I do not know
where I am going? Go back, and
take your countrymen. May kindness and faithfulness[f] be with
you."
21But Ittai replied to the king,
"As surely as the LORD lives, and as
my lord the king lives, wherever my
lord the king may be, whether it
means life or death, there will your
servant be."[g]
22David said to Ittai, "Go ahead,
march on." So Ittai the Gittite
marched on with all his men and
the families that were with him.
23The whole countryside wept
aloud as all the people passed by.
The king also crossed the Kidron
Valley,[h] and all the people moved
on toward the desert.
24Zadok[i] was there, too, and all
the Levites who were with him
were carrying the ark[j] of the covenant of God. They set down the
ark of God, and Abiathar[k] offered
sacrifices[s] until all the people had
finished leaving the city.
25Then the king said to Zadok,
"Take the ark of God back into the
city. If I find favor in the LORD's
eyes, he will bring me back and let
me see it and his dwelling place[l]
again. 26But if he says, 'I am not
pleased with you,' then I am ready;
let him do to me whatever seems
good to him.[m]"
27The king also said to Zadok the
priest, "Aren't you a seer?[n] Go
back to the city in peace, with your
son Ahimaaz and Jonathan[o] son of
Abiathar. You and Abiathar take
your two sons with you. 28I will
wait at the fords[p] in the desert until word comes from you to inform
me." 29So Zadok and Abiathar took
the ark of God back to Jerusalem
and stayed there.
30But David continued up the
Mount of Olives, weeping[q] as he
went; his head[r] was covered and
he was barefoot. All the people
with him covered their heads too
and were weeping as they went up.
31Now David had been told,
"Ahithophel[s] is among the con-
spirators with Absalom." So David
prayed, "O LORD, turn Ahithophel's
counsel into foolishness."
32When David arrived at the
summit, where people used to worship God, Hushai the Arkite[t] was
there to meet him, his robe torn
and dust[u] on his head. 33David
said to him, "If you go with me, you
will be a burden[v] to me. 34But if
you return to the city and say to Absalom, 'I will be your servant, O
king; I was your father's servant in
the past, but now I will be your servant,'[w] then you can help me by
frustrating Ahithophel's advice.
35Won't the priests Zadok and Abiathar be there with you? Tell them
anything you hear in the king's palace.[x] 36Their two sons, Ahimaaz
son of Zadok and Jonathan[y] son of
Abiathar, are there with them.
Send them to me with anything you
hear."
37So David's friend Hushai[z] arrived at Jerusalem as Absalom[a]
was entering the city.

David and Ziba

16 When David had gone a
short distance beyond the

15:16 [a]2Sa 16:21-22; 20:3
15:18 [b]1Sa 30:14; 2Sa 8:18; 20:7,23; 1Ki 1:38,44; 1Ch 18:17
15:19 [c]2Sa 18:2 [d]Ge 31:15
15:20 [e]1Sa 23:13 [f]2Sa 2:6
15:21 [g]Ru 1:16-17; Pr 17:17
15:23 [h]2Ch 29:16
15:24 [i]2Sa 8:17 [j]Nu 4:15 [k]1Sa 22:20
15:25 [l]Ex 15:13; Ps 43:3; Jer 25:30
15:26 [m]1Sa 3:18; 2Sa 22:20; 1Ki 10:9
15:27 [n]1Sa 9:9 [o]2Sa 17:17
15:28 [p]2Sa 17:16
15:30 [q]2Sa 19:4; Ps 126:6 [r]Est 6:12; Isa 20:2-4
15:31 [s]ver 12; 2Sa 16:23; 17:14,23
15:32 [t]Jos 16:2 [u]2Sa 1:2
15:33 [v]2Sa 19:35
15:34 [w]2Sa 16:19
15:35 [x]2Sa 17:15-16
15:36 [y]ver 27; 2Sa 17:17
15:37 [z]2Sa 16:16-17; 1Ch 27:33 [a]2Sa 16:15

[s]24 Or *Abiathar went up*

summit, there was Ziba,[a] the steward of Mephibosheth, waiting to meet him. He had a string of donkeys saddled and loaded with two hundred loaves of bread, a hundred cakes of raisins, a hundred cakes of figs and a skin of wine.[b]

2The king asked Ziba, "Why have you brought these?"

Ziba answered, "The donkeys are for the king's household to ride on, the bread and fruit are for the men to eat, and the wine is to refresh[c] those who become exhausted in the desert."

3The king then asked, "Where is your master's grandson?"[d]

Ziba said to him, "He is staying in Jerusalem, because he thinks, 'Today the house of Israel will give me back my grandfather's kingdom.' "

4Then the king said to Ziba, "All that belonged to Mephibosheth is now yours."

"I humbly bow," Ziba said. "May I find favor in your eyes, my lord the king."

Shimei Curses David

5As King David approached Bahurim,[e] a man from the same clan as Saul's family came out from there. His name was Shimei[f] son of Gera, and he cursed[g] as he came out. **6**He pelted David and all the king's officials with stones, though all the troops and the special guard were on David's right and left. **7**As he cursed, Shimei said, "Get out, get out, you man of blood, you scoundrel! **8**The LORD has repaid you for all the blood you shed in the household of Saul, in whose place you have reigned.[h] The LORD has handed the kingdom over to your son Absalom. You have come to ruin because you are a man of blood!"

9Then Abishai[i] son of Zeruiah said to the king, "Why should this dead dog curse my lord the king? Let me go over and cut off his head."[j]

10But the king said, "What do you and I have in common, you sons of Zeruiah?[k] If he is cursing because the LORD said to him, 'Curse David,' who can ask, 'Why do you do this?' "[l]

11David then said to Abishai and all his officials, "My son,[m] who is of my own flesh, is trying to take my life. How much more, then, this Benjamite! Leave him alone; let him curse, for the LORD has told him to.[n] **12**It may be that the LORD will see my distress[o] and repay me with good[p] for the cursing I am receiving today.[q]"

13So David and his men continued along the road while Shimei was going along the hillside opposite him, cursing as he went and throwing stones at him and showering him with dirt. **14**The king and all the people with him arrived at their destination exhausted.[r] And there he refreshed himself.

The Advice of Hushai and Ahithophel

15Meanwhile, Absalom[s] and all the men of Israel came to Jerusalem, and Ahithophel[t] was with him. **16**Then Hushai[u] the Arkite, David's friend, went to Absalom and said to him, "Long live the king! Long live the king!"

17Absalom asked Hushai, "Is this the love you show your friend? Why didn't you go with your friend?"[v]

18Hushai said to Absalom, "No, the one chosen by the LORD, by these people, and by all the men of Israel—his I will be, and I will remain with him. **19**Furthermore, whom should I serve? Should I not serve the son? Just as I served your father, so I will serve you."[w]

20Absalom said to Ahithophel, "Give us your advice. What should we do?"

21Ahithophel answered, "Lie with your father's concubines whom he left to take care of the palace. Then all Israel will hear that you have made yourself a stench in your father's nostrils, and the hands of everyone with you will be strengthened." **22**So they pitched a tent for Absalom on the

16:1 [a]2Sa 9:1-13 [b]1Sa 25:18
16:2 [c]2Sa 17:27-29
16:3 [d]2Sa 9:9-10; 19:26-27
16:5 [e]2Sa 3:16 [f]2Sa 19:16-23; 1Ki 2:8-9,36, 44 [g]Ex 22:28
16:8 [h]2Sa 21:9
16:9 [i]2Sa 9:8 [j]Ex 22:28; Lk 9:54
16:10 [k]2Sa 19:22 [l]Ro 9:20
16:11 [m]2Sa 12:11 [n]Ge 45:5
16:12 [o]Ps 4:1; 25:18 [p]Dt 23:5; Ro 8:28 [q]Ps 109:28
16:14 [r]2Sa 17:2
16:15 [s]2Sa 15:37 [t]2Sa 15:12
16:16 [u]2Sa 15:37
16:17 [v]2Sa 19:25
16:19 [w]2Sa 15:34

roof, and he lay with his father's
concubines in the sight of all Israel.[a]
23Now in those days the advice[b]
Ahithophel gave was like that of
one who inquires of God. That was
how both David[c] and Absalom regarded all of Ahithophel's advice.
17 Ahithophel said to Absalom, "I would[t] choose
twelve thousand men and set out
tonight in pursuit of David. 2I
would[u] attack him while he is weary and weak.[d] I would[u] strike him
with terror, and then all the people
with him will flee. I would[u] strike
down only the king[e] 3and bring all
the people back to you. The death
of the man you seek will mean the
return of all; all the people will be
unharmed." 4This plan seemed
good to Absalom and to all the elders of Israel.
5But Absalom said, "Summon
also Hushai[f] the Arkite, so we can
hear what he has to say." 6When
Hushai came to him, Absalom said,
"Ahithophel has given this advice.
Should we do what he says? If not,
give us your opinion."
7Hushai replied to Absalom,
"The advice Ahithophel has given
is not good this time. 8You know
your father and his men; they are
fighters, and as fierce as a wild bear
robbed of her cubs.[g] Besides, your
father is an experienced fighter;[h]
he will not spend the night with the
troops. 9Even now, he is hidden in
a cave or some other place.[i] If he
should attack your troops first,[v]
whoever hears about it will say,
'There has been a slaughter among
the troops who follow Absalom.'
10Then even the bravest soldier,
whose heart is like the heart of a
lion,[j] will melt[k] with fear, for all
Israel knows that your father is a
fighter and that those with him are
brave.[l]
11"So I advise you: Let all Israel,
from Dan to Beersheba[m]—as numerous as the sand[n] on the seashore—be gathered to you, with
you yourself leading them into battle. 12Then we will attack him
wherever he may be found, and we

16:22 [a]2Sa 12:11-12; 15:16
16:23 [b]2Sa 17:14,23 [c]2Sa 15:12
17:2 [d]2Sa 16:14 [e]1Ki 22:31; Zec 13:7
17:5 [f]2Sa 15:32
17:8 [g]Hos 13:8 [h]1Sa 16:18
17:9 [i]Jer 41:9
17:10 [j]1Ch 12:8 [k]Jos 2:9,11; Eze 21:15 [l]2Sa 23:8; 1Ch 11:11
17:11 [m]Jdg 20:1 [n]Ge 12:2; 22:17; Jos 11:4
17:13 [o]Mic 1:6
17:14 [p]2Sa 16:23 [q]2Sa 15:12 [r]2Sa 15:34; Ne 4:15 [s]Ps 9:16 [t]2Ch 10:8
17:16 [u]2Sa 15:28 [v]2Sa 15:35
17:17 [w]2Sa 15:27, 36 [x]Jos 15:7; 18:16
17:18 [y]2Sa 3:16; 16:5
17:19 [z]Jos 2:6
17:20 [a]Ex 1:19; Jos 2:3-5; 1Sa 19:12-17

will fall on him as dew settles on
the ground. Neither he nor any of
his men will be left alive. 13If he
withdraws into a city, then all Israel will bring ropes to that city, and
we will drag it down to the valley[o]
until not even a piece of it can be
found."
14Absalom and all the men of Israel said, "The advice[p] of Hushai
the Arkite is better than that of
Ahithophel."[q] For the LORD had
determined to frustrate[r] the good
advice of Ahithophel in order to
bring disaster[s] on Absalom.[t]
15Hushai told Zadok and Abiathar, the priests, "Ahithophel has
advised Absalom and the elders of
Israel to do such and such, but I
have advised them to do so and so.
16Now send a message immediately and tell David, 'Do not spend the
night at the fords in the desert;[u]
cross over without fail, or the king
and all the people with him will be
swallowed up.[v]' "
17Jonathan[w] and Ahimaaz were
staying at En Rogel.[x] A servant girl
was to go and inform them, and
they were to go and tell King David,
for they could not risk being seen
entering the city. 18But a young
man saw them and told Absalom.
So the two of them left quickly and
went to the house of a man in Bahurim.[y] He had a well in his courtyard, and they climbed down into
it. 19His wife took a covering and
spread it out over the opening of
the well and scattered grain over it.
No one knew anything about it.[z]
20When Absalom's men came to
the woman[a] at the house, they
asked, "Where are Ahimaaz and
Jonathan?"
The woman answered them,
"They crossed over the brook."[w]
The men searched but found no
one, so they returned to Jerusalem.
21After the men had gone, the
two climbed out of the well and
went to inform King David. They
said to him, "Set out and cross the

[t]*1* Or *Let me* [u]*2* Or *will* [v]*9* Or *When some of the men fall at the first attack*
[w]*20* Or *"They passed by the sheep pen toward the water."*

river at once; Ahithophel has advised such and such against you."
22So David and all the people with
him set out and crossed the Jordan. By daybreak, no one was left
who had not crossed the Jordan.
23When Ahithophel saw that his
advice[a] had not been followed, he
saddled his donkey and set out for
his house in his hometown. He put
his house in order[b] and then
hanged himself. So he died and
was buried in his father's tomb.
24David went to Mahanaim,[c]
and Absalom crossed the Jordan
with all the men of Israel. 25Absa-
lom had appointed Amasa[d] over
the army in place of Joab. Amasa
was the son of a man named Jether,[x][e] an Israelite[y] who had
married Abigail,[z] the daughter of
Nahash and sister of Zeruiah the
mother of Joab. 26The Israelites
and Absalom camped in the land of
Gilead.
27When David came to Mahanaim, Shobi son of Nahash[f] from
Rabbah[g] of the Ammonites, and
Makir[h] son of Ammiel from Lo Debar, and Barzillai[i] the Gileadite[j]
from Rogelim 28brought bedding
and bowls and articles of pottery.
They also brought wheat and barley, flour and roasted grain, beans
and lentils,[a] 29honey and curds,
sheep, and cheese from cows' milk
for David and his people to eat.[k]
For they said, "The people have become hungry and tired and thirsty
in the desert.[l]"

Absalom's Death

18 David mustered the men
who were with him and ap-
pointed over them commanders of
thousands and commanders of
hundreds. 2David sent the troops
out[m]—a third under the command
of Joab, a third under Joab's brother Abishai[n] son of Zeruiah, and a
third under Ittai[o] the Gittite. The
king told the troops, "I myself will
surely march out with you."
3But the men said, "You must
not go out; if we are forced to flee,
they won't care about us. Even if
half of us die, they won't care; but

17:23 [a] 2Sa 15:12; 16:23 [b] 2Ki 20:1; Mt 27:5
17:24 [c] Ge 32:2; 2Sa 2:8
17:25 [d] 2Sa 19:13; 20:4,9-12; 1Ki 2:5,32; 1Ch 12:18 [e] 1Ch 2:13-17
17:27 [f] 1Sa 11:1 [g] Dt 3:11; 2Sa 10:1-2; 12:26,29 [h] 2Sa 9:4 [i] 2Sa 19:31-39; 1Ki 2:7 [j] 2Sa 19:31; Ezr 2:61
17:29 [k] 1Ch 12:40 [l] 2Sa 16:2; Ro 12:13
18:2 [m] Jdg 7:16; 1Sa 11:11 [n] 1Sa 26:6 [o] 2Sa 15:19
18:3 [p] 1Sa 18:7 [q] 2Sa 21:17
18:6 [r] Jos 17:18
18:9 [s] 2Sa 14:26
18:11 [t] 2Sa 3:39 [u] 1Sa 18:4

you are worth ten[p] thousand of
us.[b] It would be better now for you
to give us support from the city."[q]
4The king answered, "I will do
whatever seems best to you."
So the king stood beside the gate
while all the men marched out in
units of hundreds and of thousands. 5The king commanded
Joab, Abishai and Ittai, "Be gentle
with the young man Absalom for
my sake." And all the troops heard
the king giving orders concerning
Absalom to each of the commanders.
6The army marched into the
field to fight Israel, and the battle
took place in the forest[r] of Ephraim. 7There the army of Israel was
defeated by David's men, and the
casualties that day were great—
twenty thousand men. 8The battle
spread out over the whole countryside, and the forest claimed more
lives that day than the sword.
9Now Absalom happened to
meet David's men. He was riding
his mule, and as the mule went under the thick branches of a large
oak, Absalom's head[s] got caught
in the tree. He was left hanging in
midair, while the mule he was riding kept on going.
10When one of the men saw this,
he told Joab, "I just saw Absalom
hanging in an oak tree."
11Joab said to the man who had
told him this, "What! You saw him?
Why didn't you strike[t] him to the
ground right there? Then I would
have had to give you ten shekels[c]
of silver and a warrior's belt.[u]"
12But the man replied, "Even if a
thousand shekels[d] were weighed
out into my hands, I would not lift
my hand against the king's son. In

[x]*25* Hebrew *Ithra,* a variant of *Jether*
[y]*25* Hebrew and some Septuagint manuscripts; other Septuagint manuscripts (see also 1 Chron. 2:17) *Ishmaelite* or *Jezreelite*
[z]*25* Hebrew *Abigal,* a variant of *Abigail*
[a]*28* Most Septuagint manuscripts and Syriac; Hebrew *lentils, and roasted grain*
[b]*3* Two Hebrew manuscripts, some Septuagint manuscripts and Vulgate; most Hebrew manuscripts *care; for now there are ten thousand like us*
[c]*11* That is, about 4 ounces (about 115 grams)
[d]*12* That is, about 25 pounds (about 11 kilograms)

our hearing the king commanded you and Abishai and Ittai, 'Protect the young man Absalom for my sake.[e]' 13 And if I had put my life in jeopardy[f]—and nothing is hidden from the king[a]—you would have kept your distance from me."

14 Joab[b] said, "I'm not going to wait like this for you." So he took three javelins in his hand and plunged them into Absalom's heart while Absalom was still alive in the oak tree. 15 And ten of Joab's armor-bearers surrounded Absalom, struck him and killed him.[c]

16 Then Joab[d] sounded the trumpet, and the troops stopped pursuing Israel, for Joab halted them. 17 They took Absalom, threw him into a big pit in the forest and piled up[e] a large heap of rocks[f] over him. Meanwhile, all the Israelites fled to their homes.

18 During his lifetime Absalom had taken a pillar and erected it in the King's Valley[g] as a monument[h] to himself, for he thought, "I have no son[i] to carry on the memory of my name." He named the pillar after himself, and it is called Absalom's Monument to this day.

David Mourns

19 Now Ahimaaz[j] son of Zadok said, "Let me run and take the news to the king that the LORD has delivered him from the hand of his enemies.[k]"

20 "You are not the one to take the news today," Joab told him. "You may take the news another time, but you must not do so today, because the king's son is dead."

21 Then Joab said to a Cushite, "Go, tell the king what you have seen." The Cushite bowed down before Joab and ran off.

22 Ahimaaz son of Zadok again said to Joab, "Come what may, please let me run behind the Cushite."

But Joab replied, "My son, why do you want to go? You don't have any news that will bring you a reward."

23 He said, "Come what may, I want to run."

So Joab said, "Run!" Then Ahimaaz ran by way of the plain[g] and outran the Cushite.

24 While David was sitting between the inner and outer gates, the watchman[l] went up to the roof of the gateway by the wall. As he looked out, he saw a man running alone. 25 The watchman called out to the king and reported it.

The king said, "If he is alone, he must have good news." And the man came closer and closer.

26 Then the watchman saw another man running, and he called down to the gatekeeper, "Look, another man running alone!"

The king said, "He must be bringing good news,[m] too."

27 The watchman said, "It seems to me that the first one runs like[n] Ahimaaz son of Zadok."

"He's a good man," the king said. "He comes with good news."

28 Then Ahimaaz called out to the king, "All is well!" He bowed down before the king with his face to the ground and said, "Praise be to the LORD your God! He has delivered up the men who lifted their hands against my lord the king."

29 The king asked, "Is the young man Absalom safe?"

Ahimaaz answered, "I saw great confusion just as Joab was about to send the king's servant and me, your servant, but I don't know what it was."

30 The king said, "Stand aside and wait here." So he stepped aside and stood there.

31 Then the Cushite arrived and said, "My lord the king, hear the good news! The LORD has delivered you today from all who rose up against you."

32 The king asked the Cushite, "Is the young man Absalom safe?"

The Cushite replied, "May the

18:13 [a] 2Sa 14:19-20
18:14 [b] 2Sa 2:18; 14:30
18:15 [c] 2Sa 12:10
18:16 [d] 2Sa 2:28; 20:22
18:17 [e] Jos 7:26 [f] Jos 8:29
18:18 [g] Ge 14:17 [h] Ge 50:5; Nu 32:42; 1Sa 15:12 [i] 2Sa 14:27
18:19 [j] 2Sa 15:36 [k] ver 31; Jdg 11:36
18:24 [l] 1Sa 14:16; 2Sa 19:8; 2Ki 9:17; Jer 51:12
18:26 [m] 1Ki 1:42; Isa 52:7; 61:1
18:27 [n] 2Ki 9:20

[e] *12* A few Hebrew manuscripts, Septuagint, Vulgate and Syriac; most Hebrew manuscripts may be translated *Absalom, whoever you may be.* [f] *13* Or *Otherwise, if I had acted treacherously toward him* [g] *23* That is, the plain of the Jordan

enemies of my lord the king and all who rise up to harm you be like that young man."[a]

[33]The king was shaken. He went up to the room over the gateway and wept. As he went, he said: "O my son Absalom! My son, my son Absalom! If only I had died[b] instead of you—O Absalom, my son, my son!"[c]

19 Joab was told, "The king is weeping and mourning for Absalom." [2]And for the whole army the victory that day was turned into mourning, because on that day the troops heard it said, "The king is grieving for his son." [3]The men stole into the city that day as men steal in who are ashamed when they flee from battle. [4]The king covered his face and cried aloud, "O my son Absalom! O Absalom, my son, my son!"

[5]Then Joab went into the house to the king and said, "Today you have humiliated all your men, who have just saved your life and the lives of your sons and daughters and the lives of your wives and concubines. [6]You love those who hate you and hate those who love you. You have made it clear today that the commanders and their men mean nothing to you. I see that you would be pleased if Absalom were alive today and all of us were dead. [7]Now go out and encourage your men. I swear by the LORD that if you don't go out, not a man will be left with you by nightfall. This will be worse for you than all the calamities that have come upon you from your youth till now."[d]

[8]So the king got up and took his seat in the gateway. When the men were told, "The king is sitting in the gateway,[e]" they all came before him.

David Returns to Jerusalem

Meanwhile, the Israelites had fled to their homes. [9]Throughout the tribes of Israel, the people were all arguing with each other, saying, "The king delivered us from the hand of our enemies; he is the one who rescued us from the hand of the Philistines.[f] But now he has fled the country because of Absalom;[g] [10]and Absalom, whom we anointed to rule over us, has died in battle. So why do you say nothing about bringing the king back?"

[11]King David sent this message to Zadok[h] and Abiathar, the priests: "Ask the elders of Judah, 'Why should you be the last to bring the king back to his palace, since what is being said throughout Israel has reached the king at his quarters? [12]You are my brothers, my own flesh and blood. So why should you be the last to bring back the king?' [13]And say to Amasa,[i] 'Are you not my own flesh and blood?[j] May God deal with me, be it ever so severely,[k] if from now on you are not the commander of my army in place of Joab.[l]' "

[14]He won over the hearts of all the men of Judah as though they were one man. They sent word to the king, "Return, you and all your men." [15]Then the king returned and went as far as the Jordan.

Now the men of Judah had come to Gilgal[m] to go out and meet the king and bring him across the Jordan. [16]Shimei[n] son of Gera, the Benjamite from Bahurim, hurried down with the men of Judah to meet King David. [17]With him were a thousand Benjamites, along with Ziba,[o] the steward of Saul's household,[p] and his fifteen sons and twenty servants. They rushed to the Jordan, where the king was. [18]They crossed at the ford to take the king's household over and to do whatever he wished.

When Shimei son of Gera crossed the Jordan, he fell prostrate before the king [19]and said to him, "May my lord not hold me guilty. Do not remember how your servant did wrong on the day my lord the king left Jerusalem.[q] May the king put it out of his mind. [20]For I your servant know that I have sinned, but today I have come here as the first of the whole house of Joseph to come down and meet my lord the king."

[21]Then Abishai[r] son of Zeruiah

18:32 [a]Jdg 5:31; 1Sa 25:26
18:33 [b]Ex 32:32 [c]Ge 43:14; 2Sa 19:4; Ro 9:3
19:7 [d]Pr 14:28
19:8 [e]2Sa 15:2
19:9 [f]2Sa 8:1-14 [g]2Sa 15:14
19:11 [h]2Sa 15:24
19:13 [i]2Sa 17:25 [j]Ge 29:14 [k]Ru 1:17; 1Ki 19:2; 8:16 [l]2Sa 2:13
19:15 [m]Jos 5:9; 1Sa 11:15
19:16 [n]2Sa 16:5-13; 1Ki 2:8
19:17 [o]2Sa 9:2; 16:1-2 [p]Ge 43:16
19:19 [q]1Sa 22:15; 2Sa 16:6-8
19:21 [r]1Sa 26:6

said, "Shouldn't Shimei be put to death for this? He cursed[a] the LORD's anointed."[b]

22David replied, "What do you and I have in common, you sons of Zeruiah?[c] This day you have become my adversaries! Should anyone be put to death in Israel today?[d] Do I not know that today I am king over Israel?" **23**So the king said to Shimei, "You shall not die." And the king promised him on oath.[e]

24Mephibosheth,[f] Saul's grandson, also went down to meet the king. He had not taken care of his feet or trimmed his mustache or washed his clothes from the day the king left until the day he returned safely. **25**When he came from Jerusalem to meet the king, the king asked him, "Why didn't you go with me,[g] Mephibosheth?"

26He said, "My lord the king, since I your servant am lame,[h] I said, 'I will have my donkey saddled and will ride on it, so I can go with the king.' But Ziba[i] my servant betrayed me. **27**And he has slandered your servant to my lord the king. My lord the king is like an angel[j] of God; so do whatever pleases you. **28**All my grandfather's descendants deserved nothing but death[k] from my lord the king, but you gave your servant a place among those who eat at your table.[l] So what right do I have to make any more appeals to the king?"

29The king said to him, "Why say more? I order you and Ziba to divide the fields."

30Mephibosheth said to the king, "Let him take everything, now that my lord the king has arrived home safely."

31Barzillai[m] the Gileadite also came down from Rogelim to cross the Jordan with the king and to send him on his way from there. **32**Now Barzillai was a very old man, eighty years of age. He had provided for the king during his stay in Mahanaim, for he was a very wealthy[n] man. **33**The king said to Barzillai, "Cross over with me and stay with me in Jerusalem, and I will provide for you."

34But Barzillai answered the king, "How many more years will I live, that I should go up to Jerusalem with the king? **35**I am now eighty[o] years old. Can I tell the difference between what is good and what is not? Can your servant taste what he eats and drinks? Can I still hear the voices of men and women singers?[p] Why should your servant be an added[q] burden to my lord the king? **36**Your servant will cross over the Jordan with the king for a short distance, but why should the king reward me in this way? **37**Let your servant return, that I may die in my own town near the tomb of my father[r] and mother. But here is your servant Kimham.[s] Let him cross over with my lord the king. Do for him whatever pleases you."

38The king said, "Kimham shall cross over with me, and I will do for him whatever pleases you. And anything you desire from me I will do for you."

39So all the people crossed the Jordan, and then the king crossed over. The king kissed Barzillai and gave him his blessing,[t] and Barzillai returned to his home.

40When the king crossed over to Gilgal, Kimham crossed with him. All the troops of Judah and half the troops of Israel had taken the king over.

41Soon all the men of Israel were coming to the king and saying to him, "Why did our brothers, the men of Judah, steal the king away and bring him and his household across the Jordan, together with all his men?"[u]

42All the men of Judah answered the men of Israel, "We did this because the king is closely related to us. Why are you angry about it? Have we eaten any of the king's provisions? Have we taken anything for ourselves?"

43Then the men of Israel[v] answered the men of Judah, "We have ten shares in the king; and besides, we have a greater claim on David than you have. So why do you treat

19:21 [a] Ex 22:28 [b] 1Sa 12:3; 26:9; 2Sa 16:7-8
19:22 [c] 2Sa 2:18; 16:10 [d] 1Sa 11:13
19:23 [e] 1Ki 2:8,42
19:24 [f] 2Sa 4:4; 9:6-10
19:25 [g] 2Sa 16:17
19:26 [h] Lev 21:18 [i] 2Sa 9:2
19:27 [j] 1Sa 29:9; 2Sa 14:17,20
19:28 [k] 2Sa 16:8; 21:6-9 [l] 2Sa 9:7,13
19:31 [m] 2Sa 17:27-29, 27; 1Ki 2:7
19:32 [n] 1Sa 25:2; 2Sa 17:27
19:35 [o] Ps 90:10 [p] 2Ch 35:25; Ezr 2:65; Ecc 2:8; 12:1; Isa 5:11-12 [q] 2Sa 15:33
19:37 [r] Ge 49:29; 1Ki 2:7 [s] ver 40; Jer 41:17
19:39 [t] Ge 31:55; Ge 47:7
19:41 [u] Jdg 8:1; 12:1
19:43 [v] 2Sa 5:1

us with contempt? Were we not the
first to speak of bringing back our
king?"
But the men of Judah responded
even more harshly than the men of
Israel.

Sheba Rebels Against David

20 Now a troublemaker named
Sheba son of Bicri, a Benjamite, happened to be there. He
sounded the trumpet and shouted,

"We have no share[a] in David,[b]
no part in Jesse's son![c]
Every man to his tent,
O Israel!"

2So all the men of Israel deserted
David to follow Sheba son of Bicri.
But the men of Judah stayed by
their king all the way from the Jordan to Jerusalem.
3When David returned to his palace in Jerusalem, he took the ten
concubines[d] he had left to take
care of the palace and put them in
a house under guard. He provided
for them, but did not lie with them.
They were kept in confinement till
the day of their death, living as widows.
4Then the king said to Amasa,[e]
"Summon the men of Judah to
come to me within three days, and
be here yourself." 5But when Amasa went to summon Judah, he took
longer than the time the king had
set for him.
6David said to Abishai,[f] "Now
Sheba son of Bicri will do us more
harm than Absalom did. Take your
master's men and pursue him, or
he will find fortified cities and escape from us." 7So Joab's men and
the Kerethites[g] and Pelethites and
all the mighty warriors went out
under the command of Abishai.
They marched out from Jerusalem
to pursue Sheba son of Bicri.
8While they were at the great
rock in Gibeon,[h] Amasa came to
meet them. Joab[i] was wearing his
military tunic, and strapped over it
at his waist was a belt with a dagger
in its sheath. As he stepped forward, it dropped out of its sheath.
9Joab said to Amasa, "How are
you, my brother?" Then Joab took
Amasa by the beard with his right
hand to kiss him. 10Amasa was not
on his guard against the dagger[j] in
Joab[k]'s hand, and Joab plunged it
into his belly, and his intestines
spilled out on the ground. Without
being stabbed again, Amasa died.
Then Joab and his brother Abishai
pursued Sheba son of Bicri.
11One of Joab's men stood beside Amasa and said, "Whoever favors Joab, and whoever is for David, let him follow Joab!" 12Amasa
lay wallowing in his blood in the
middle of the road, and the man
saw that all the troops came to a
halt[l] there. When he realized that
everyone who came up to Amasa
stopped, he dragged him from the
road into a field and threw a garment over him. 13After Amasa had
been removed from the road, all
the men went on with Joab to pursue Sheba son of Bicri.
14Sheba passed through all the
tribes of Israel to Abel Beth Maacah[h] and through the entire region
of the Berites,[m] who gathered together and followed him. 15All the
troops with Joab came and besieged Sheba in Abel Beth Maacah.[n] They built a siege ramp[o] up
to the city, and it stood against the
outer fortifications. While they
were battering the wall to bring it
down, 16a wise woman[p] called
from the city, "Listen! Listen! Tell
Joab to come here so I can speak to
him." 17He went toward her, and
she asked, "Are you Joab?"
"I am," he answered.
She said, "Listen to what your
servant has to say."
"I'm listening," he said.
18She continued, "Long ago they
used to say, 'Get your answer at
Abel,' and that settled it. 19We are
the peaceful[q] and faithful in Israel. You are trying to destroy a city
that is a mother in Israel. Why do
you want to swallow up the LORD's
inheritance?"[r]
20"Far be it from me!" Joab re-

20:1 [a]Ge 31:14 [b]Ge 29:14; 1Ki 12:16 [c]1Sa 22:7-8; 2Ch 10:16
20:3 [d]2Sa 15:16; 16:21-22
20:4 [e]2Sa 17:25; 19:13
20:6 [f]2Sa 21:17
20:7 [g]1Sa 30:14; 2Sa 8:18; 15:18; 1Ki 1:38
20:8 [h]Jos 9:3 [i]2Sa 2:18
20:10 [j]Jdg 3:21; 2Sa 2:23; 3:27 [k]1Ki 2:5
20:12 [l]2Sa 2:23
20:14 [m]Nu 21:16
20:15 [n]1Ki 15:20; 2Ki 15:29 [o]2Ki 19:32; Isa 37:33; Jer 6:6; 32:24
20:16 [p]2Sa 14:2
20:19 [q]Dt 2:26 [r]1Sa 26:19; 2Sa 21:3

[h]*14* Or *Abel, even Beth Maacah;* also in verse 15

plied, "Far be it from me to swallow up or destroy! 21That is not the case. A man named Sheba son of Bicri, from the hill country of Ephraim, has lifted up his hand against the king, against David. Hand over this one man, and I'll withdraw from the city."

The woman said to Joab, "His head[a] will be thrown to you from the wall."

22Then the woman went to all the people with her wise advice,[b] and they cut off the head of Sheba son of Bicri and threw it to Joab. So he sounded the trumpet, and his men dispersed from the city, each returning to his home. And Joab went back to the king in Jerusalem.

23Joab[c] was over Israel's entire army; Benaiah son of Jehoiada was over the Kerethites and Pelethites; 24Adoniram[i][d] was in charge of forced labor; Jehoshaphat[e] son of Ahilud was recorder; 25Sheva was secretary; Zadok[f] and Abiathar were priests; 26and Ira the Jairite was David's priest.

The Gibeonites Avenged

21 During the reign of David, there was a famine[g] for three successive years; so David sought[h] the face of the LORD. The LORD said, "It is on account of Saul and his blood-stained house; it is because he put the Gibeonites to death."

2The king summoned the Gibeonites[i] and spoke to them. (Now the Gibeonites were not a part of Israel but were survivors of the Amorites; the Israelites had sworn to spare them, but Saul in his zeal for Israel and Judah had tried to annihilate them.) 3David asked the Gibeonites, "What shall I do for you? How shall I make amends so that you will bless the LORD's inheritance?"[j]

4The Gibeonites answered him, "We have no right to demand silver or gold from Saul or his family, nor do we have the right to put anyone in Israel to death."[k]

"What do you want me to do for you?" David asked.

5They answered the king, "As for the man who destroyed us and plotted against us so that we have been decimated and have no place anywhere in Israel, 6let seven of his male descendants be given to us to be killed and exposed[l] before the LORD at Gibeah of Saul—the LORD's chosen[m] one."

So the king said, "I will give them to you."

7The king spared Mephibosheth[n] son of Jonathan, the son of Saul, because of the oath[o] before the LORD between David and Jonathan son of Saul. 8But the king took Armoni and Mephibosheth, the two sons of Aiah's daughter Rizpah,[p] whom she had borne to Saul, together with the five sons of Saul's daughter Merab,[j] whom she had borne to Adriel son of Barzillai the Meholathite.[q] 9He handed them over to the Gibeonites, who killed and exposed them on a hill before the LORD. All seven of them fell together; they were put to death[r] during the first days of the harvest, just as the barley harvest was beginning.[s]

10Rizpah daughter of Aiah took sackcloth and spread it out for herself on a rock. From the beginning of the harvest till the rain poured down from the heavens on the bodies, she did not let the birds of the air touch them by day or the wild animals by night.[t] 11When David was told what Aiah's daughter Rizpah, Saul's concubine, had done, 12he went and took the bones of Saul[u] and his son Jonathan from the citizens of Jabesh Gilead. (They had taken them secretly from the public square at Beth Shan,[v] where the Philistines had hung[w] them after they struck Saul down on Gilboa.) 13David brought

20:21 [a] 2Sa 4:8
20:22 [b] Ecc 9:13
20:23 [c] 2Sa 2:28; 8:16-18; 24:2
20:24 [d] 1Ki 4:6; 5:14; 12:18; 2Ch 10:18 [e] 2Sa 8:16; 1Ki 4:3
20:25 [f] 1Sa 2:35; 2Sa 8:17
21:1 [g] Ge 12:10; Dt 32:24 [h] Ex 32:11
21:2 [i] Jos 9:15
21:3 [j] 1Sa 26:19; 2Sa 20:19
21:4 [k] Nu 35:33-34
21:6 [l] Nu 25:4 [m] 1Sa 10:24
21:7 [n] 2Sa 4:4 [o] 1Sa 18:3; 20:8,15; 2Sa 9:7
21:8 [p] 2Sa 3:7 [q] 1Sa 18:19
21:9 [r] 2Sa 16:8 [s] Ru 1:22
21:10 [t] ver 8; Dt 21:23; 1Sa 17:44
21:12 [u] 1Sa 31:11-13 [v] Jos 17:11 [w] 1Sa 31:10

i24 Some Septuagint manuscripts (see also 1 Kings 4:6 and 5:14); Hebrew *Adoram*
j8 Two Hebrew manuscripts, some Septuagint manuscripts and Syriac (see also 1 Samuel 18:19); most Hebrew and Septuagint manuscripts *Michal*

the bones of Saul and his son Jonathan from there, and the bones of
those who had been killed and exposed were gathered up.
14They buried the bones of Saul
and his son Jonathan in the tomb
of Saul's father Kish, at Zela[a] in
Benjamin, and did everything the
king commanded. After that,[b] God
answered prayer[c] in behalf of the
land.

Wars Against the Philistines

21:15–22pp — 1Ch 20:4–8

15Once again there was a battle
between the Philistines[d] and Israel. David went down with his men
to fight against the Philistines, and
he became exhausted. **16**And Ish-
bi-Benob, one of the descendants
of Rapha, whose bronze spearhead
weighed three hundred shekels[k]
and who was armed with a new
⌞sword⌟, said he would kill David.
17But Abishai[e] son of Zeruiah
came to David's rescue; he struck
the Philistine down and killed him.
Then David's men swore to him,
saying, "Never again will you go out
with us to battle, so that the lamp[f]
of Israel will not be extinguished.[g]"
18In the course of time, there
was another battle with the Philistines, at Gob. At that time Sibbecai[h] the Hushathite killed Saph,
one of the descendants of Rapha.
19In another battle with the Philistines at Gob, Elhanan son of Jaa-
re-Oregim[l] the Bethlehemite
killed Goliath[m] the Gittite, who
had a spear with a shaft like a weaver's rod.[i]
20In still another battle, which
took place at Gath, there was a
huge man with six fingers on each
hand and six toes on each foot—
twenty-four in all. He also was descended from Rapha. **21**When he
taunted Israel, Jonathan son of
Shimeah,[j] David's brother, killed
him.
22These four were descendants
of Rapha in Gath, and they fell at
the hands of David and his men.

21:14 [a]Jos 18:28 [b]Jos 7:26 [c]2Sa 24:25
21:15 [d]2Sa 5:25
21:17 [e]2Sa 20:6 [f]1Ki 11:36 [g]2Sa 18:3
21:18 [h]1Ch 11:29; 20:4; 27:11
21:19 [i]1Sa 17:7
21:21 [j]1Sa 16:9
22:1 [k]Ex 15:1; Jdg 5:1; Ps 18:2-50
22:2 [l]Dt 32:4; Ps 71:3 [m]Ps 31:3; 91:2 [n]Ps 144:2
22:3 [o]Dt 32:37; Jer 16:19 [p]Ge 15:1 [q]Lk 1:69 [r]Ps 9:9
22:4 [s]Ps 48:1; 96:4
22:5 [t]Ps 69:14-15; 93:4; Jnh 2:3
22:6 [u]Ps 116:3
22:7 [v]Ps 120:1 [w]Ps 34:6,15; 116:4
22:8 [x]Jdg 5:4; Ps 97:4 [y]Ps 77:18 [z]Job 26:11
22:9 [a]Ps 97:3; Heb 12:29

David's Song of Praise

22:1–51pp — Ps 18:1–50

22 David sang[k] to the LORD the
words of this song when the
LORD delivered him from the hand
of all his enemies and from the
hand of Saul. **2**He said:

"The LORD is my rock,[l] my
fortress[m] and my
deliverer;[n]
3 my God is my rock, in whom
I take refuge,[o]
my shield[p] and the horn[n][q]
of my salvation.
He is my stronghold,[r] my
refuge and my savior—
from violent men you save
me.
4I call to the LORD, who is
worthy[s] of praise,
and I am saved from my
enemies.

5"The waves[t] of death swirled
about me;
the torrents of destruction
overwhelmed me.
6The cords of the grave[o][u]
coiled around me;
the snares of death
confronted me.
7In my distress[v] I called[w] to
the LORD;
I called out to my God.
From his temple he heard my
voice;
my cry came to his ears.

8"The earth[x] trembled and
quaked,[y]
the foundations[z] of the
heavens[p] shook;
they trembled because he
was angry.
9Smoke rose from his nostrils;
consuming fire[a] came from
his mouth,
burning coals blazed out of
it.

[k]*16* That is, about 7 1/2 pounds (about 3.5 kilograms) [l]*19* Or *son of Jair the weaver* [m]*19* Hebrew and Septuagint; 1 Chron. 20:5 *son of Jair killed Lahmi the brother of Goliath* [n]*3* *Horn* here symbolizes strength. [o]*6* Hebrew *Sheol* [p]*8* Hebrew; Vulgate and Syriac (see also Psalm 18:7) *mountains*

[10]He parted the heavens and came down;
dark clouds[a] were under his feet.
[11]He mounted the cherubim and flew;
he soared[q] on the wings of the wind.[b]
[12]He made darkness his canopy around him—
the dark[r] rain clouds of the sky.
[13]Out of the brightness of his presence
bolts of lightning[c] blazed forth.
[14]The LORD thundered[d] from heaven;
the voice of the Most High resounded.
[15]He shot arrows[e] and scattered ⌊the enemies⌋,
bolts of lightning and routed them.
[16]The valleys of the sea were exposed
and the foundations of the earth laid bare
at the rebuke[f] of the LORD,
at the blast of breath from his nostrils.

[17]"He reached down from on high[g] and took hold of me;
he drew[h] me out of deep waters.
[18]He rescued me from my powerful enemy,
from my foes, who were too strong for me.
[19]They confronted me in the day of my disaster,
but the LORD was my support.[i]
[20]He brought me out into a spacious[j] place;
he rescued[k] me because he delighted[l] in me.[m]

[21]"The LORD has dealt with me according to my righteousness;[n]
according to the cleanness of my hands[o] he has rewarded me.
[22]For I have kept[p] the ways of the LORD;
I have not done evil by turning from my God.
[23]All his laws are before me;[q]
I have not turned[r] away from his decrees.
[24]I have been blameless[s] before him
and have kept myself from sin.
[25]The LORD has rewarded me according to my righteousness,[t]
according to my cleanness[s] in his sight.

[26]"To the faithful you show yourself faithful,
to the blameless you show yourself blameless,
[27]to the pure[u] you show yourself pure,
but to the crooked you show yourself shrewd.[v]
[28]You save the humble,[w]
but your eyes are on the haughty to bring them low.[x]
[29]You are my lamp,[y] O LORD;
the LORD turns my darkness into light.
[30]With your help I can advance against a troop[t];
with my God I can scale a wall.

[31]"As for God, his way is perfect;[z]
the word of the LORD is flawless.[a]
He is a shield
for all who take refuge in him.
[32]For who is God besides the LORD?
And who is the Rock[b] except our God?
[33]It is God who arms me with strength[u]
and makes my way perfect.

22:10 [a]1Ki 8:12; Na 1:3
22:11 [b]Ps 104:3
22:13 [c]ver 9
22:14 [d]1Sa 2:10
22:15 [e]Dt 32:23
22:16 [f]Na 1:4
22:17 [g]Ps 144:7 [h]Ex 2:10
22:19 [i]Ps 23:4
22:20 [j]Ps 31:8 [k]Ps 118:5 [l]Ps 22:8 [m]2Sa 15:26
22:21 [n]1Sa 26:23 [o]Ps 24:4
22:22 [p]Ge 18:19; Ps 128:1; Pr 8:32
22:23 [q]Dt 6:4-9; Ps 119:30-32 [r]Ps 119:102
22:24 [s]Ge 6:9; Eph 1:4
22:25 [t]ver 21
22:27 [u]Mt 5:8 [v]Lev 26:23-24
22:28 [w]Ex 3:8; Ps 72:12-13 [x]Isa 2:12,17; 5:15
22:29 [y]Ps 27:1
22:31 [z]Dt 32:4; Mt 5:48 [a]Ps 12:6; 119:140; Pr 30:5-6
22:32 [b]1Sa 2:2

[q]*11* Many Hebrew manuscripts (see also Psalm 18:10); most Hebrew manuscripts *appeared* [r]*12* Septuagint and Vulgate (see also Psalm 18:11); Hebrew *massed*
[s]*25* Hebrew; Septuagint and Vulgate (see also Psalm 18:24) *to the cleanness of my hands*
[t]*30* Or *can run through a barricade*
[u]*33* Dead Sea Scrolls, some Septuagint manuscripts, Vulgate and Syriac (see also Psalm 18:32); Masoretic Text *who is my strong refuge*

34He makes my feet like the feet of a deer;[a]
he enables me to stand on the heights.[b]
35He trains my hands[c] for battle;
my arms can bend a bow of bronze.
36You give me your shield[d] of victory;
you stoop down to make me great.
37You broaden the path[e] beneath me,
so that my ankles do not turn.

38"I pursued my enemies and crushed them;
I did not turn back till they were destroyed.
39I crushed[f] them completely,
and they could not rise;
they fell beneath my feet.
40You armed me with strength for battle;
you made my adversaries bow at my feet.[g]
41You made my enemies turn their backs[h] in flight,
and I destroyed my foes.
42They cried for help,[i] but there was no one to save them—[j]
to the LORD, but he did not answer.
43I beat them as fine as the dust of the earth;
I pounded and trampled[k] them like mud[l] in the streets.

44"You have delivered[m] me from the attacks of my people;
you have preserved[n] me as the head of nations.
People[o] I did not know are subject to me,
45 and foreigners come cringing[p] to me;
as soon as they hear me, they obey me.
46They all lose heart;
they come trembling[v][q] from their strongholds.

47"The LORD lives! Praise be to my Rock!
Exalted be God, the Rock, my Savior![r]
48He is the God who avenges me,[s]
who puts the nations under me,
49 who sets me free from my enemies.[t]
You exalted me above my foes;
from violent men you rescued me.
50Therefore I will praise you, O LORD, among the nations;
I will sing praises to your name.[u]
51He gives his king great victories;[v]
he shows unfailing kindness to his anointed,[w]
to David[x] and his descendants forever."[y]

22:34 [a]Hab 3:19 [b]Dt 32:13
22:35 [c]Ps 144:1
22:36 [d]Eph 6:16
22:37 [e]Pr 4:11
22:39 [f]Mal 4:3
22:40 [g]Ps 44:5
22:41 [h]Ex 23:27
22:42 [i]Isa 1:15 [j]Ps 50:22
22:43 [k]Mic 7:10 [l]Isa 10:6; Mic 7:10
22:44 [m]2Sa 3:1 [n]Dt 28:13 [o]2Sa 8:1-14; Isa 55:3-5
22:45 [p]Ps 66:3; 81:15
22:46 [q]Mic 7:17
22:47 [r]Ps 89:26
22:48 [s]Ps 94:1; 144:2; 1Sa 25:39
22:49 [t]Ps 140:1,4
22:50 [u]Ro 15:9*
22:51 [v]Ps 144:9-10 [w]Ps 89:20 [x]2Sa 7:13 [y]Ps 89:24,29
23:1 [z]2Sa 7:8-9; Ps 78:70-71; 89:27 [a]1Sa 16:12-13; Ps 89:20
23:2 [b]Mt 22:43; 2Pe 1:21
23:3 [c]Dt 32:4; 2Sa 22:2,32 [d]Ps 72:2 [e]2Ch 19:7,9; Isa 11:1-5
23:4 [f]Jdg 5:31; Ps 89:36

The Last Words of David

23 These are the last words of David:

"The oracle of David son of Jesse,
the oracle of the man exalted[z] by the Most High,
the man anointed[a] by the God of Jacob,
Israel's singer of songs[w]:

2"The Spirit[b] of the LORD spoke through me;
his word was on my tongue.
3The God of Israel spoke,
the Rock[c] of Israel said to me:
'When one rules over men in righteousness,[d]
when he rules in the fear of God,[e]
4he is like the light of morning at sunrise[f]
on a cloudless morning,
like the brightness after rain
that brings the grass from the earth.'

5"Is not my house right with God?

[v]*46* Some Septuagint manuscripts and Vulgate (see also Psalm 18:45); Masoretic Text *they arm themselves.* [w]*1* Or *Israel's beloved singer*

Has he not made with me an everlasting covenant,[a]
arranged and secured in every part?
Will he not bring to fruition my salvation
and grant me my every desire?
6But evil men are all to be cast aside like thorns,[b]
which are not gathered with the hand.
7Whoever touches thorns
uses a tool of iron or the shaft of a spear;
they are burned up where they lie."

David's Mighty Men

23:8–39pp — 1Ch 11:10–41

8These are the names of David's mighty men:

Josheb-Basshebeth,[x] a Tahkemonite,[y] was chief of the Three; he raised his spear against eight hundred men, whom he killed[z] in one encounter.

9Next to him was Eleazar son of Dodai[c] the Ahohite.[d] As one of the three mighty men, he was with David when they taunted the Philistines gathered ⌞at Pas Dammim⌟[a] for battle. Then the men of Israel retreated, 10but he stood his ground and struck down the Philistines till his hand grew tired and froze to the sword. The LORD brought about a great victory that day. The troops returned to Eleazar, but only to strip the dead.

11Next to him was Shammah son of Agee the Hararite. When the Philistines banded together at a place where there was a field full of lentils, Israel's troops fled from them. 12But Shammah took his stand in the middle of the field. He defended it and struck the Philistines down, and the LORD brought about a great victory.

13During harvest time, three of the thirty chief men came down to David at the cave of Adullam,[e] while a band of Philistines was encamped in the Valley of Rephaim.[f] 14At that time David was in the stronghold,[g] and the Philistine garrison was at Bethlehem.[h] 15David longed for water and said, "Oh, that someone would get me a drink of water from the well near the gate of Bethlehem!" 16So the three mighty men broke through the Philistine lines, drew water from the well near the gate of Bethlehem and carried it back to David. But he refused to drink it; instead, he poured[i] it out before the LORD. 17"Far be it from me, O LORD, to do this!" he said. "Is it not the blood[j] of men who went at the risk of their lives?" And David would not drink it.

Such were the exploits of the three mighty men.

18Abishai[k] the brother of Joab son of Zeruiah was chief of the Three.[b] He raised his spear against three hundred men, whom he killed, and so he became as famous as the Three. 19Was he not held in greater honor than the Three? He became their commander, even though he was not included among them.

20Benaiah[l] son of Jehoiada was a valiant fighter from Kabzeel,[m] who performed great exploits. He struck down two of Moab's best men. He also went down into a pit on a snowy day and killed a lion. 21And he struck down a huge Egyptian. Although the Egyptian had a spear in his hand, Benaiah went against him with a club. He snatched the spear from the Egyptian's hand and killed him with his own spear. 22Such were the exploits of Benaiah son of Jehoiada; he too was as famous as the three mighty men. 23He was held in greater honor than any of the Thirty, but he was not included among

23:5 [a]Ps 89:29; Isa 55:3
23:6 [b]Mt 13:40-41
23:9 [c]1Ch 27:4 [d]1Ch 8:4
23:13 [e]1Sa 22:1 [f]2Sa 5:18
23:14 [g]1Sa 22:4-5 [h]Ru 1:19
23:16 [i]Ge 35:14
23:17 [j]Lev 17:10-12
23:18 [k]2Sa 10:10, 14; 1Ch 11:20
23:20 [l]2Sa 8:18; 20:23 [m]Jos 15:21

[x]*8* Hebrew; some Septuagint manuscripts suggest *Ish-Bosheth,* that is, *Esh-Baal* (see also 1 Chron. 11:11 *Jashobeam*). [y]*8* Probably a variant of *Hacmonite* (see 1 Chron. 11:11) [z]*8* Some Septuagint manuscripts (see also 1 Chron. 11:11); Hebrew and other Septuagint manuscripts *Three; it was Adino the Eznite who killed eight hundred men* [a]*9* See 1 Chron. 11:13; Hebrew *gathered there.* [b]*18* Most Hebrew manuscripts (see also 1 Chron. 11:20); two Hebrew manuscripts and Syriac *Thirty*

the Three. And David put him in
charge of his bodyguard.

[24]Among the Thirty were:
Asahel[a] the brother of Joab,
Elhanan son of Dodo from Bethlehem,
[25]Shammah the Harodite,[b]
Elika the Harodite,
[26]Helez[c] the Paltite,
Ira son of Ikkesh from Tekoa,
[27]Abiezer from Anathoth,[d]
Mebunnai[c] the Hushathite,
[28]Zalmon the Ahohite,
Maharai[e] the Netophathite,[f]
[29]Heled[d] son of Baanah the Netophathite,
Ithai son of Ribai from Gibeah[g] in Benjamin,
[30]Benaiah the Pirathonite,[h]
Hiddai[e] from the ravines of Gaash,[i]
[31]Abi-Albon the Arbathite,
Azmaveth the Barhumite,[j]
[32]Eliahba the Shaalbonite,
the sons of Jashen,
Jonathan [33]son of[f] Shammah the Hararite,
Ahiam son of Sharar[g] the Hararite,
[34]Eliphelet son of Ahasbai the Maacathite,
Eliam[k] son of Ahithophel[l] the Gilonite,
[35]Hezro the Carmelite,[m]
Paarai the Arbite,
[36]Igal son of Nathan from Zobah,[n]
the son of Hagri,[h]
[37]Zelek the Ammonite,
Naharai the Beerothite, the armor-bearer of Joab son of Zeruiah,
[38]Ira the Ithrite,[o]
Gareb the Ithrite
[39]and Uriah[p] the Hittite.
There were thirty-seven in all.

David Counts the Fighting Men

24:1–17pp — 1Ch 21:1–17

24 Again[q] the anger of the
LORD burned against Israel,
and he incited David against them,
saying, "Go and take a census of[r]
Israel and Judah."
[2]So the king said to Joab[s] and
the army commanders[i] with him,
"Go throughout the tribes of Israel
from Dan to Beersheba[t] and enroll
the fighting men, so that I may
know how many there are."
[3]But Joab replied to the king,
"May the LORD your God multiply
the troops a hundred times over,[u]
and may the eyes of my lord the
king see it. But why does my lord
the king want to do such a thing?"
[4]The king's word, however, overruled Joab and the army commanders; so they left the presence
of the king to enroll the fighting
men of Israel.
[5]After crossing the Jordan, they
camped near Aroer,[v] south of the
town in the gorge, and then went
through Gad and on to Jazer.[w]
[6]They went to Gilead and the region of Tahtim Hodshi, and on to
Dan Jaan and around toward Sidon.[x] [7]Then they went toward the
fortress of Tyre[y] and all the towns
of the Hivites and Canaanites. Finally, they went on to Beersheba[z]
in the Negev[a] of Judah.
[8]After they had gone through the
entire land, they came back to Jerusalem at the end of nine months
and twenty days.
[9]Joab reported the number of
the fighting men to the king: In Israel there were eight hundred
thousand able-bodied men who
could handle a sword, and in Judah
five hundred thousand.[b]
[10]David was conscience-strick-
en[c] after he had counted the fighting men, and he said to the LORD, "I
have sinned[d] greatly in what I have

23:24 [a]2Sa 2:18
23:25 [b]Jdg 7:1; 1Ch 11:27
23:26 [c]1Ch 27:10
23:27 [d]Jos 21:18
23:28 [e]1Ch 27:13 [f]2Ki 25:23; Ne 7:26
23:29 [g]Jos 15:57
23:30 [h]Jdg 12:13 [i]Jos 24:30
23:31 [j]2Sa 3:16
23:34 [k]2Sa 11:3 [l]2Sa 15:12
23:35 [m]Jos 12:22
23:36 [n]1Sa 14:47
23:38 [o]2Sa 20:26; 1Ch 2:53
23:39 [p]2Sa 11:3
24:1 [q]Jos 9:15 [r]1Ch 27:23
24:2 [s]2Sa 20:23 [t]Jdg 20:1; 2Sa 3:10
24:3 [u]Dt 1:11
24:5 [v]Dt 2:36; Jos 13:9 [w]Nu 21:32
24:6 [x]Ge 10:19; Jos 19:28; Jdg 1:31
24:7 [y]Jos 19:29 [z]Ge 21:22-33 [a]Dt 1:7; Jos 11:3
24:9 [b]Nu 1:44-46; 1Ch 21:5
24:10 [c]1Sa 24:5 [d]2Sa 12:13

[c]27 Hebrew; some Septuagint manuscripts (see also 1 Chron. 11:29) *Sibbecai* [d]29 Some Hebrew manuscripts and Vulgate (see also 1 Chron. 11:30); most Hebrew manuscripts *Heleb* [e]30 Hebrew; some Septuagint manuscripts (see also 1 Chron. 11:32) *Hurai* [f]33 Some Septuagint manuscripts (see also 1 Chron. 11:34); Hebrew does not have *son of.* [g]33 Hebrew; some Septuagint manuscripts (see also 1 Chron. 11:35) *Sacar* [h]36 Some Septuagint manuscripts (see also 1 Chron. 11:38); Hebrew *Haggadi* [i]2 Septuagint (see also verse 4 and 1 Chron. 21:2); Hebrew *Joab the army commander*

done. Now, O LORD, I beg you,
take away the guilt of your servant. I have done a very foolish
thing.[a]"
11Before David got up the next
morning, the word of the LORD had
come to Gad[b] the prophet, David's
seer:[c] 12"Go and tell David, 'This
is what the LORD says: I am giving
you three options. Choose one of
them for me to carry out against
you.' "
13So Gad went to David and said
to him, "Shall there come upon you
three[i] years of famine[d] in your
land? Or three months of fleeing
from your enemies while they pursue you? Or three days of plague[e]
in your land? Now then, think it
over and decide how I should answer the one who sent me."
14David said to Gad, "I am in
deep distress. Let us fall into the
hands of the LORD, for his mercy[f] is
great; but do not let me fall into the
hands of men."
15So the LORD sent a plague on
Israel from that morning until the
end of the time designated, and
seventy thousand of the people
from Dan to Beersheba died.[g]
16When the angel stretched out his
hand to destroy Jerusalem, the
LORD was grieved[h] because of the
calamity and said to the angel who
was afflicting the people, "Enough!
Withdraw your hand." The angel of
the LORD[i] was then at the threshing floor of Araunah the Jebusite.
17When David saw the angel who
was striking down the people, he
said to the LORD, "I am the one who
has sinned and done wrong. These
are but sheep.[j] What have they
done? Let your hand fall upon me
and my family."[k]

24:10 [a] Nu 12:11; 1Sa 13:13
24:11 [b] 1Sa 22:5 [c] 1Sa 9:9; 1Ch 29:29
24:13 [d] Dt 28:38-42, 48; Eze 14:21 [e] Lev 26:25
24:14 [f] Ne 9:28; Ps 51:1; 103:8,13; 130:4
24:15 [g] 1Ch 27:24
24:16 [h] Ge 6:6; 1Sa 15:11 [i] Ex 12:23; Ac 12:23
24:17 [j] Ps 74:1 [k] Jnh 1:12
24:21 [l] Nu 16:44-50
24:22 [m] 1Sa 6:14; 1Ki 19:21
24:23 [n] Eze 20:40-41
24:24 [o] Mal 1:13-14
24:25 [p] 1Sa 7:17 [q] 2Sa 21:14

David Builds an Altar

24:18–25pp — 1Ch 21:18–26

18On that day Gad went to David
and said to him, "Go up and build
an altar to the LORD on the threshing floor of Araunah the Jebusite."
19So David went up, as the LORD
had commanded through Gad.
20When Araunah looked and saw
the king and his men coming toward him, he went out and bowed
down before the king with his face
to the ground.
21Araunah said, "Why has my
lord the king come to his servant?"
"To buy your threshing floor,"
David answered, "so I can build an
altar to the LORD, that the plague on
the people may be stopped."[l]
22Araunah said to David, "Let
my lord the king take whatever
pleases him and offer it up. Here
are oxen[m] for the burnt offering,
and here are threshing sledges and
ox yokes for the wood. 23O king,
Araunah gives[n] all this to the
king." Araunah also said to him,
"May the LORD your God accept
you."
24But the king replied to Araunah, "No, I insist on paying you for
it. I will not sacrifice to the LORD my
God burnt offerings that cost me
nothing."[o]
So David bought the threshing
floor and the oxen and paid fifty
shekels[k] of silver for them. 25Da-
vid built an altar[p] to the LORD there
and sacrificed burnt offerings and
fellowship offerings.[l] Then the
LORD answered prayer[q] in behalf of
the land, and the plague on Israel
was stopped.

[i] *13* Septuagint (see also 1 Chron. 21:12); Hebrew *seven* [k] *24* That is, about 1 1/4 pounds (about 0.6 kilogram)
[l] *25* Traditionally *peace offerings*

1 Kings

Title and Background

1 and 2 Kings (like 1,2 Samuel and 1,2 Chronicles) are actually one literary work, called in Hebrew tradition simply "Kings." Together Samuel and Kings relate the whole history of the monarchy, from its rise under the ministry of Samuel to its destruction at the hands of the Babylonians. Beginning with Solomon's reign, 1 Kings records the history of Israel through the divided kingdom to the death of Ahab.

Author and Date of Writing

There is little conclusive evidence as to the identity of the author of 1,2 Kings. Whoever the author may have been, it is clear that he was familiar with the book of Deuteronomy—as were many of Israel's prophets. The book was probably written subsequent to Jehoiachin's release from prison (562 B.C.) and prior to the end of the Babylonian exile in 538.

Theme and Message

No explicit statement of purpose or theme is found in 1 or 2 Kings. In general, they described the history of the kings of Israel and Judah in the light of God's covenants. The author was primarily concerned with Israel's faithfulness to the covenants, so he recorded the activities of each ruler as to his/her obedience to the covenant. Obedience to God brought peace and prosperity; disobedience and idol worship resulted in war and disaster.

Outline

I. Solomon's Reign (1:1-12:24)
II. Israel and Judah From Jeroboam/Rehoboam to Ahab/Asa (12:25-16:34)
III. Elijah and King Ahab (17:1-22:40)
IV. Jehoshaphat King of Judah (22:41-50)
V. Ahaziah King of Israel (22:51-53)

Adonijah Sets Himself Up as King

1 When King David was old and
well advanced in years, he
could not keep warm even when
they put covers over him. 2So his
servants said to him, "Let us look
for a young virgin to attend the king
and take care of him. She can lie
beside him so that our lord the king
may keep warm."

3Then they searched throughout
Israel for a beautiful girl and found
Abishag, a Shunammite,[a] and
brought her to the king. 4The girl
was very beautiful; she took care of
the king and waited on him, but
the king had no intimate relations
with her.

5Now Adonijah,[b] whose mother
was Haggith, put himself forward
and said, "I will be king." So he got
chariots[c] and horses[a] ready, with
fifty men to run ahead of him. 6(His
father had never interfered[d] with
him by asking, "Why do you behave
as you do?" He was also very handsome and was born next after Absalom.)

7Adonijah conferred with Joab[e]
son of Zeruiah and with Abiathar[f]
the priest, and they gave him their
support. 8But Zadok[g] the priest,

1:3 [a]Jos 19:18
1:5 [b]2Sa 3:4 [c]2Sa 15:1
1:6 [d]2Sa 3:3-4
1:7 [e]1Ki 2:22,28; 1Ch 11:6 [f]1Sa 22:20; 2Sa 20:25
1:8 [g]2Sa 20:25

a5 Or *charioteers*

Benaiah[a] son of Jehoiada, Nathan[b] the prophet, Shimei[c] and
Rei[b] and David's special guard[d]
did not join Adonijah.
9Adonijah then sacrificed sheep,
cattle and fattened calves at the
Stone of Zoheleth near En Rogel.[e]
He invited all his brothers, the
king's sons, and all the men of Judah who were royal officials, 10but
he did not invite Nathan the prophet or Benaiah or the special guard
or his brother Solomon.[f]
11Then Nathan asked Bathsheba,[g] Solomon's mother, "Have you
not heard that Adonijah,[h] the son
of Haggith, has become king without our lord David's knowing it?
12Now then, let me advise[i] you
how you can save your own life and
the life of your son Solomon. 13Go
in to King David and say to him,
'My lord the king, did you not
swear[j] to me your servant: "Surely
Solomon your son shall be king after me, and he will sit on my
throne"? Why then has Adonijah
become king?' 14While you are still
there talking to the king, I will
come in and confirm what you have
said."
15So Bathsheba went to see the
aged king in his room, where Abishag[k] the Shunammite was attending him. 16Bathsheba bowed
low and knelt before the king.
"What is it you want?" the king
asked.
17She said to him, "My lord, you
yourself swore[l] to me your servant
by the LORD your God: 'Solomon
your son shall be king after me, and
he will sit on my throne.' 18But
now Adonijah has become king,
and you, my lord the king, do not
know about it. 19He has sacrificed[m] great numbers of cattle, fattened calves, and sheep, and has
invited all the king's sons, Abiathar
the priest and Joab the commander
of the army, but he has not invited
Solomon your servant. 20My lord
the king, the eyes of all Israel are
on you, to learn from you who will
sit on the throne of my lord the
king after him. 21Otherwise, as
soon as my lord the king is laid to

1:8 [a]2Sa 8:18 [b]2Sa 12:1 [c]1Ki 4:18 [d]2Sa 23:8
1:9 [e]2Sa 17:17
1:10 [f]2Sa 12:24
1:11 [g]2Sa 12:24 [h]2Sa 3:4
1:12 [i]Pr 15:22
1:13 [j]ver 30; 1Ch 22:9-13
1:15 [k]ver 1
1:17 [l]ver 13,30
1:19 [m]ver 9
1:21 [n]Dt 31:16; 1Ki 2:10
1:26 [o]ver 8,10
1:29 [p]2Sa 4:9
1:30 [q]ver 13,17

rest[n] with his fathers, I and my son
Solomon will be treated as criminals."
22While she was still speaking
with the king, Nathan the prophet
arrived. 23And they told the king,
"Nathan the prophet is here." So
he went before the king and bowed
with his face to the ground.
24Nathan said, "Have you, my
lord the king, declared that Adonijah shall be king after you, and that
he will sit on your throne? 25Today
he has gone down and sacrificed
great numbers of cattle, fattened
calves, and sheep. He has invited
all the king's sons, the commanders of the army and Abiathar the
priest. Right now they are eating
and drinking with him and saying,
'Long live King Adonijah!' 26But
me your servant, and Zadok the
priest, and Benaiah son of Jehoiada, and your servant Solomon he
did not invite.[o] 27Is this something
my lord the king has done without
letting his servants know who
should sit on the throne of my lord
the king after him?"

David Makes Solomon King

1:28–53pp — 1Ch 29:21–25

28Then King David said, "Call in
Bathsheba." So she came into the
king's presence and stood before
him.
29The king then took an oath:
"As surely as the LORD lives, who
has delivered me out of every trouble,[p] 30I will surely carry out today
what I swore[q] to you by the LORD,
the God of Israel: Solomon your
son shall be king after me, and he
will sit on my throne in my place."
31Then Bathsheba bowed low
with her face to the ground and,
kneeling before the king, said,
"May my lord King David live forever!"
32King David said, "Call in Zadok the priest, Nathan the prophet
and Benaiah son of Jehoiada."
When they came before the king,
33he said to them: "Take your
lord's servants with you and set

b8 Or *and his friends*

Solomon my son on my own mule[a]
and take him down to Gihon.[b]
34 There have Zadok the priest and
Nathan the prophet anoint[c] him
king over Israel. Blow the trumpet[d] and shout, 'Long live King
Solomon!' 35 Then you are to go up
with him, and he is to come and sit
on my throne and reign in my
place. I have appointed him ruler
over Israel and Judah."

36 Benaiah son of Jehoiada answered the king, "Amen! May the
LORD, the God of my lord the king,
so declare it. 37 As the LORD was
with my lord the king, so may he be
with[e] Solomon to make his throne
even greater[f] than the throne of
my lord King David!"

38 So Zadok[g] the priest, Nathan
the prophet, Benaiah son of Jehoiada, the Kerethites[h] and the Pelethites went down and put Solomon
on King David's mule and escorted
him to Gihon.[i] 39 Zadok the priest
took the horn of oil[j] from the sacred tent and anointed Solomon.
Then they sounded the trumpet
and all the people shouted,[k]
"Long live King Solomon!" 40 And
all the people went up after him,
playing flutes and rejoicing greatly,
so that the ground shook with the
sound.

41 Adonijah and all the guests
who were with him heard it as they
were finishing their feast. On hearing the sound of the trumpet, Joab
asked, "What's the meaning of all
the noise in the city?"

42 Even as he was speaking, Jonathan[l] son of Abiathar the priest
arrived. Adonijah said, "Come in. A
worthy man like you must be bringing good news."[m]

43 "Not at all!" Jonathan answered. "Our lord King David has
made Solomon king. 44 The king
has sent with him Zadok the priest,
Nathan the prophet, Benaiah son
of Jehoiada, the Kerethites and the
Pelethites, and they have put him
on the king's mule, 45 and Zadok
the priest and Nathan the prophet
have anointed him king at Gihon.
From there they have gone up
cheering, and the city resounds[n]
with it. That's the noise you hear.
46 Moreover, Solomon has taken
his seat on the royal throne. 47 Also,
the royal officials have come to
congratulate our lord King David,
saying, 'May your God make Solomon's name more famous than
yours and his throne greater[o] than
yours!' And the king bowed in worship on his bed 48 and said, 'Praise
be to the LORD, the God of Israel,
who has allowed my eyes to see a
successor[p] on my throne today.'"

49 At this, all Adonijah's guests
rose in alarm and dispersed. 50 But
Adonijah, in fear of Solomon, went
and took hold of the horns[q] of the
altar. 51 Then Solomon was told,
"Adonijah is afraid of King Solomon and is clinging to the horns of
the altar. He says, 'Let King Solomon swear to me today that he will
not put his servant to death with
the sword.'"

52 Solomon replied, "If he shows
himself to be a worthy man, not a
hair[r] of his head will fall to the
ground; but if evil is found in him,
he will die." 53 Then King Solomon
sent men, and they brought him
down from the altar. And Adonijah
came and bowed down to King Solomon, and Solomon said, "Go to
your home."

David's Charge to Solomon

2:10–12pp — 1Ch 29:26–28

2 When the time drew near for
David to die,[s] he gave a charge
to Solomon his son.

2 "I am about to go the way of all
the earth,"[t] he said. "So be
strong,[u] show yourself a man, 3 and
observe[v] what the LORD your God
requires: Walk in his ways, and
keep his decrees and commands,
his laws and requirements, as written in the Law of Moses, so that
you may prosper[w] in all you do and
wherever you go, 4 and that the
LORD may keep his promise[x] to me:
'If your descendants watch how
they live, and if they walk faithfully[y] before me with all their heart
and soul, you will never fail to have
a man on the throne of Israel.'

1:33 [a] 2Sa 20:6-7 [b] 2Ch 32:30; 33:14
1:34 [c] 1Sa 10:1; 16:3,12; 1Ki 19:16; 2Ki 9:3,13 [d] ver 25; 2Sa 5:3; 15:10
1:37 [e] Jos 1:5,17; 1Sa 20:13 [f] ver 47
1:38 [g] ver 8 [h] 2Sa 8:18 [i] ver 33
1:39 [j] Ex 30:23-32; Ps 89:20 [k] ver 34; 1Sa 10:24
1:42 [l] 2Sa 15:27,36 [m] 2Sa 18:26
1:45 [n] ver 40
1:47 [o] ver 37; Ge 47:31
1:48 [p] 2Sa 7:12; 1Ki 3:6
1:50 [q] 1Ki 2:28
1:52 [r] 1Sa 14:45; 2Sa 14:11
2:1 [s] Ge 47:29; Dt 31:14
2:2 [t] Jos 23:14 [u] Dt 31:7,23; Jos 1:6
2:3 [v] Dt 17:14-20; Jos 1:7 [w] 1Ch 22:13
2:4 [x] 2Sa 7:13,25; 1Ki 8:25 [y] 2Ki 20:3; Ps 132:12

5"Now you yourself know what Joab[a] son of Zeruiah did to me—what he did to the two commanders of Israel's armies, Abner[b] son of Ner and Amasa[c] son of Jether. He killed them, shedding their blood in peacetime as if in battle, and with that blood stained the belt around his waist and the sandals on his feet. 6Deal with him according to your wisdom,[d] but do not let his gray head go down to the grave[c] in peace.

7"But show kindness to the sons of Barzillai[e] of Gilead and let them be among those who eat at your table.[f] They stood by me when I fled from your brother Absalom.

8"And remember, you have with you Shimei[g] son of Gera, the Benjamite from Bahurim, who called down bitter curses on me the day I went to Mahanaim. When he came down to meet me at the Jordan, I swore[h] to him by the LORD: 'I will not put you to death by the sword.' 9But now, do not consider him innocent. You are a man of wisdom;[i] you will know what to do to him. Bring his gray head down to the grave in blood."

10Then David rested with his fathers and was buried[j] in the City of David.[k] 11He had reigned[l] forty years over Israel—seven years in Hebron and thirty-three in Jerusalem. 12So Solomon sat on the throne[m] of his father David, and his rule was firmly established.[n]

Solomon's Throne Established

13Now Adonijah, the son of Haggith, went to Bathsheba, Solomon's mother. Bathsheba asked him, "Do you come peacefully?"[o]

He answered, "Yes, peacefully." 14Then he added, "I have something to say to you."

"You may say it," she replied.

15"As you know," he said, "the kingdom was mine. All Israel looked to me as their king. But things changed, and the kingdom has gone to my brother; for it has come to him from the LORD. 16Now I have one request to make of you. Do not refuse me."

"You may make it," she said.

17So he continued, "Please ask King Solomon—he will not refuse you—to give me Abishag[p] the Shunammite as my wife."

18"Very well," Bathsheba replied, "I will speak to the king for you."

19When Bathsheba went to King Solomon to speak to him for Adonijah, the king stood up to meet her, bowed down to her and sat down on his throne. He had a throne brought for the king's mother,[q] and she sat down at his right hand.[r]

20"I have one small request to make of you," she said. "Do not refuse me."

The king replied, "Make it, my mother; I will not refuse you."

21So she said, "Let Abishag[s] the Shunammite be given in marriage to your brother Adonijah."

22King Solomon answered his mother, "Why do you request Abishag[t] the Shunammite for Adonijah? You might as well request the kingdom for him—after all, he is my older brother[u]—yes, for him and for Abiathar the priest and Joab son of Zeruiah!"

23Then King Solomon swore by the LORD: "May God deal with me, be it ever so severely,[v] if Adonijah does not pay with his life for this request! 24And now, as surely as the LORD lives—he who has established me securely on the throne of my father David and has founded a dynasty for me as he promised[w]—Adonijah shall be put to death today!" 25So King Solomon gave orders to Benaiah[x] son of Jehoiada, and he struck down Adonijah and he died.

26To Abiathar[y] the priest the king said, "Go back to your fields in Anathoth.[z] You deserve to die, but I will not put you to death now, because you carried the ark[a] of the Sovereign LORD before my father David and shared all my father's hardships."[b] 27So Solomon removed Abiathar from the priest-

2:5 [a] 2Sa 2:18; 18:5,12,14 [b] 2Sa 3:27 [c] 2Sa 20:10
2:6 [d] ver 9
2:7 [e] 2Sa 17:27; 19:31-39 [f] 2Sa 9:7
2:8 [g] 2Sa 16:5-13 [h] 2Sa 19:18-23
2:9 [i] ver 6
2:10 [j] Ac 2:29; 13:36 [k] 2Sa 5:7
2:11 [l] 2Sa 5:4,5
2:12 [m] 1Ch 29:23 [n] 2Ch 1:1
2:13 [o] 1Sa 16:4
2:17 [p] 1Ki 1:3
2:19 [q] 1Ki 15:13 [r] Ps 45:9
2:21 [s] 1Ki 1:3
2:22 [t] 2Sa 12:8; 1Ki 1:3 [u] 1Ch 3:2
2:23 [v] Ru 1:17
2:24 [w] 2Sa 7:11; 1Ch 22:10
2:25 [x] 2Sa 8:18
2:26 [y] 1Sa 22:20 [z] Jos 21:18 [a] 2Sa 15:24 [b] 1Sa 23:6

c6 Hebrew *Sheol*; also in verse 9

hood of the LORD, fulfilling[a] the
word the LORD had spoken at Shiloh about the house of Eli.
28When the news reached Joab,
who had conspired with Adonijah
though not with Absalom, he fled
to the tent of the LORD and took
hold of the horns[b] of the altar.
29King Solomon was told that Joab
had fled to the tent of the LORD and
was beside the altar. Then Solomon ordered Benaiah[c] son of Jehoiada, "Go, strike him down!"
30So Benaiah entered the tent of
the LORD and said to Joab, "The
king says, 'Come out![d]' "
But he answered, "No, I will die
here."
Benaiah reported to the king,
"This is how Joab answered me."
31Then the king commanded Benaiah, "Do as he says. Strike him
down and bury him, and so clear
me and my father's house of the
guilt of the innocent blood[e] that
Joab shed. **32**The LORD will repay[f]
him for the blood he shed,[g] because without the knowledge of my
father David he attacked two men
and killed them with the sword.
Both of them—Abner son of Ner,
commander of Israel's army, and
Amasa[h] son of Jether, commander
of Judah's army—were better[i]
men and more upright than he.
33May the guilt of their blood rest
on the head of Joab and his
descendants forever. But on David
and his descendants, his house and
his throne, may there be the LORD's
peace forever."
34So Benaiah son of Jehoiada
went up and struck down Joab and
killed him, and he was buried on
his own land[d] in the desert. **35**The
king put Benaiah[j] son of Jehoiada
over the army in Joab's position
and replaced Abiathar with Zadok[k] the priest.
36Then the king sent for Shimei[l] and said to him, "Build yourself a house in Jerusalem and live
there, but do not go anywhere else.
37The day you leave and cross the
Kidron Valley,[m] you can be sure
you will die; your blood will be on
your own head."[n]
38Shimei answered the king,
"What you say is good. Your servant
will do as my lord the king has
said." And Shimei stayed in Jerusalem for a long time.
39But three years later, two of
Shimei's slaves ran off to Achish[o]
son of Maacah, king of Gath, and
Shimei was told, "Your slaves are in
Gath." **40**At this, he saddled his
donkey and went to Achish at Gath
in search of his slaves. So Shimei
went away and brought the slaves
back from Gath.
41When Solomon was told that
Shimei had gone from Jerusalem to
Gath and had returned, **42**the king
summoned Shimei and said to
him, "Did I not make you swear by
the LORD and warn you, 'On the day
you leave to go anywhere else, you
can be sure you will die'? At that
time you said to me, 'What you say
is good. I will obey.' **43**Why then did
you not keep your oath to the LORD
and obey the command I gave
you?"
44The king also said to Shimei,
"You know in your heart all the
wrong[p] you did to my father David.
Now the LORD will repay you for
your wrongdoing. **45**But King Solomon will be blessed, and David's
throne will remain secure[q] before
the LORD forever."
46Then the king gave the order to
Benaiah son of Jehoiada, and he
went out and struck Shimei down
and killed him.
The kingdom was now firmly established[r] in Solomon's hands.

Solomon Asks for Wisdom

3:4-15pp — 2Ch 1:2-13

3 Solomon made an alliance
with Pharaoh king of Egypt
and married[s] his daughter.[t] He
brought her to the City of David[u]
until he finished building his palace[v] and the temple of the LORD,
and the wall around Jerusalem.
2The people, however, were still
sacrificing at the high places,[w] because a temple had not yet been
built for the Name of the LORD.

2:27 [a] 1Sa 2:27-36
2:28 [b] 1Ki 1:7,50
2:29 [c] ver 25
2:30 [d] Ex 21:14
2:31 [e] Nu 35:33; Dt 19:13; 21:8-9
2:32 [f] Jdg 9:57; Ps 7:16 [g] Jdg 9:24 [h] 2Sa 3:27; 20:10 [i] 2Ch 21:13
2:35 [j] 1Ki 4:4 [k] ver 27; 1Ch 29:22
2:36 [l] ver 8; 2Sa 16:5
2:37 [m] 2Sa 15:23 [n] Lev 20:9; Jos 2:19; 2Sa 1:16
2:39 [o] 1Sa 27:2
2:44 [p] 1Sa 25:39; 2Sa 16:5-13; Eze 17:19
2:45 [q] 2Sa 7:13; Pr 25:5
2:46 [r] ver 12; 2Ch 1:1
3:1 [s] 1Ki 7:8 [t] 1Ki 9:24 [u] 2Sa 5:7 [v] 1Ki 7:1; 9:15,19
3:2 [w] Lev 17:3-5; Dt 12:2,4-5; 1Ki 22:43

[d]34 Or *buried in his tomb*

3Solomon showed his love[a] for the
LORD by walking according to the
statutes[b] of his father David, except that he offered sacrifices and
burned incense on the high places.
4The king went to Gibeon[c] to offer sacrifices, for that was the most
important high place, and Solomon offered a thousand burnt offerings on that altar. **5**At Gibeon
the LORD appeared[d] to Solomon
during the night in a dream,[e] and
God said, "Ask for whatever you
want me to give you."
6Solomon answered, "You have
shown great kindness to your servant, my father David, because he
was faithful[f] to you and righteous
and upright in heart. You have continued this great kindness to him
and have given him a son[g] to sit on
his throne this very day.
7"Now, O LORD my God, you have
made your servant king in place of
my father David. But I am only a
little child[h] and do not know how
to carry out my duties. **8**Your servant is here among the people you
have chosen,[i] a great people, too
numerous to count or number.[j]
9So give your servant a discerning[k]
heart to govern your people and to
distinguish[l] between right and
wrong. For who is able[m] to govern
this great people of yours?"
10The Lord was pleased that Solomon had asked for this. **11**So God
said to him, "Since you have
asked[n] for this and not for long life
or wealth for yourself, nor have
asked for the death of your enemies but for discernment in administering justice, **12**I will do what
you have asked.[o] I will give you a
wise[p] and discerning heart, so that
there will never have been anyone
like you, nor will there ever be.
13Moreover, I will give you what
you have not[q] asked for—both
riches and honor[r]—so that in your
lifetime you will have no equal[s]
among kings. **14**And if you walk[t] in
my ways and obey my statutes and
commands as David your father
did, I will give you a long life."[u]
15Then Solomon awoke[v]—and he
realized it had been a dream.

3:3 [a]Dt 6:5; Ps 31:23; 1Co 8:3 [b]1Ki 2:3; 9:4; 11:4,6,38
3:4 [c]1Ch 16:39
3:5 [d]1Ki 9:2 [e]Nu 12:6; Mt 1:20
3:6 [f]1Ki 2:4; 9:4 [g]1Ki 1:48
3:7 [h]Nu 27:17; 1Ch 29:1
3:8 [i]Dt 7:6 [j]Ge 15:5
3:9 [k]2Sa 14:17; Jas 1:5 [l]Pr 2:3-9; Heb 5:14 [m]Ps 72:1-2
3:11 [n]Jas 4:3
3:12 [o]1Jn 5:14-15 [p]1Ki 4:29,30, 31; 5:12; 10:23; Ecc 1:16
3:13 [q]Mt 6:33; Eph 3:20 [r]1Ki 4:21-24; Pr 3:1-2,16 [s]1Ki 10:23
3:14 [t]ver 6; Pr 3:1-2,16 [u]Ps 61:6; 91:16
3:15 [v]Ge 41:7 [w]1Ki 8:65 [x]Mk 6:21 [y]Est 1:3,9; Da 5:1
3:26 [z]Ge 43:30; Isa 49:15; Jer 31:20; Hos 11:8

He returned to Jerusalem, stood before the ark of the Lord's covenant and sacrificed burnt offerings[w] and fellowship offerings.[e][x] Then he gave a feast[y] for all his court.

A Wise Ruling

16Now two prostitutes came to
the king and stood before him.
17One of them said, "My lord, this
woman and I live in the same
house. I had a baby while she was
there with me. **18**The third day after my child was born, this woman
also had a baby. We were alone;
there was no one in the house but
the two of us.
19"During the night this woman's son died because she lay on
him. **20**So she got up in the middle
of the night and took my son from
my side while I your servant was
asleep. She put him by her breast
and put her dead son by my breast.
21The next morning, I got up to
nurse my son—and he was dead!
But when I looked at him closely in
the morning light, I saw that it
wasn't the son I had borne."
22The other woman said, "No!
The living one is my son; the dead
one is yours."
But the first one insisted, "No!
The dead one is yours; the living
one is mine." And so they argued
before the king.
23The king said, "This one says,
'My son is alive and your son is
dead,' while that one says, 'No!
Your son is dead and mine is
alive.' "
24Then the king said, "Bring me
a sword." So they brought a sword
for the king. **25**He then gave an order: "Cut the living child in two and
give half to one and half to the other."
26The woman whose son was
alive was filled with compassion[z]
for her son and said to the king,
"Please, my lord, give her the living
baby! Don't kill him!"
But the other said, "Neither I nor

[e]*15* Traditionally *peace offerings*

you shall have him. Cut him in two!"

27Then the king gave his ruling: "Give the living baby to the first woman. Do not kill him; she is his mother."

28When all Israel heard the verdict the king had given, they held the king in awe, because they saw that he had wisdom[a] from God to administer justice.

Solomon's Officials and Governors

4 So King Solomon ruled over all Israel. **2**And these were his chief officials:

Azariah[b] son of Zadok—the priest;
3Elihoreph and Ahijah, sons of Shisha—secretaries;
Jehoshaphat[c] son of Ahilud—recorder;
4Benaiah[d] son of Jehoiada—commander in chief;
Zadok[e] and Abiathar—priests;
5Azariah son of Nathan—in charge of the district officers;
Zabud son of Nathan—a priest and personal adviser to the king;
6Ahishar—in charge of the palace;
Adoniram son of Abda—in charge of forced labor.

7Solomon also had twelve district governors over all Israel, who supplied provisions for the king and the royal household. Each one had to provide supplies for one month in the year. **8**These are their names:

Ben-Hur—in the hill country[f] of Ephraim;
9Ben-Deker—in Makaz, Shaalbim,[g] Beth Shemesh[h] and Elon Bethhanan;
10Ben-Hesed—in Arubboth (Socoh[i] and all the land of Hepher[j] were his);
11Ben-Abinadab—in Naphoth Dor[f][k] (he was married to Taphath daughter of Solomon);
12Baana son of Ahilud—in Taanach and Megiddo, and in all of Beth Shan[l] next to Zarethan[m] below Jezreel, from Beth Shan to Abel Meholah[n] across to Jokmeam;[o]
13Ben-Geber—in Ramoth Gilead (the settlements of Jair[p] son of Manasseh in Gilead were his, as well as the district of Argob in Bashan and its sixty large walled cities[q] with bronze gate bars);
14Ahinadab son of Iddo—in Mahanaim;[r]
15Ahimaaz[s]—in Naphtali (he had married Basemath daughter of Solomon);
16Baana son of Hushai[t]—in Asher and in Aloth;
17Jehoshaphat son of Paruah—in Issachar;
18Shimei[u] son of Ela—in Benjamin;
19Geber son of Uri—in Gilead (the country of Sihon king of the Amorites and the country of Og[v] king of Bashan). He was the only governor over the district.

Solomon's Daily Provisions

20The people of Judah and Israel were as numerous as the sand[w] on the seashore; they ate, they drank and they were happy. **21**And Solomon ruled[x] over all the kingdoms from the River[g][y] to the land of the Philistines, as far as the border of Egypt.[z] These countries brought tribute[a] and were Solomon's subjects all his life.

22Solomon's daily provisions were thirty cors[h] of fine flour and sixty cors[i] of meal, **23**ten head of stall-fed cattle, twenty of pasture-fed cattle and a hundred sheep and goats, as well as deer, gazelles, roebucks and choice fowl. **24**For he

3:28 [a]ver 9,11-12; Col 2:3
4:2 [b]1Ch 6:10
4:3 [c]2Sa 8:16
4:4 [d]1Ki 2:35 [e]1Ki 2:27
4:8 [f]Jos 24:33
4:9 [g]Jdg 1:35 [h]Jos 21:16
4:10 [i]Jos 15:35 [j]Jos 12:17
4:11 [k]Jos 11:2
4:12 [l]Jos 17:11; Jdg 5:19 [m]Jos 3:16 [n]1Ki 19:16 [o]1Ch 6:68
4:13 [p]Nu 32:41 [q]Dt 3:4
4:14 [r]Jos 13:26
4:15 [s]2Sa 15:27
4:16 [t]2Sa 15:32
4:18 [u]1Ki 1:8
4:19 [v]Dt 3:8-10
4:20 [w]Ge 22:17; 32:12; 1Ki 3:8
4:21 [x]2Ch 9:26; Ps 72:11 [y]Jos 1:4; Ps 72:8 [z]Ge 15:18 [a]Ps 68:29

[f]*11* Or *in the heights of Dor* [g]*21* That is, the Euphrates; also in verse 24 [h]*22* That is, probably about 185 bushels (about 6.6 kiloliters) [i]*22* That is, probably about 375 bushels (about 13.2 kiloliters)

temple an inner sanctuary, the Most Holy Place.[a] **17**The main hall in front of this room was forty cubits[y] long. **18**The inside of the temple was cedar,[b] carved with gourds and open flowers. Everything was cedar; no stone was to be seen.

19He prepared the inner sanctuary[c] within the temple to set the ark of the covenant[d] of the LORD there. **20**The inner sanctuary[e] was twenty cubits long, twenty wide and twenty high.[z] He overlaid the inside with pure gold, and he also overlaid the altar of cedar. **21**Solomon covered the inside of the temple with pure gold, and he extended gold chains across the front of the inner sanctuary, which was overlaid with gold. **22**So he overlaid the whole interior with gold. He also overlaid with gold the altar that belonged to the inner sanctuary.

23In the inner sanctuary he made a pair of cherubim[f] of olive wood, each ten cubits[a] high. **24**One wing of the first cherub was five cubits long, and the other wing five cubits—ten cubits from wing tip to wing tip. **25**The second cherub also measured ten cubits, for the two cherubim were identical in size and shape. **26**The height of each cherub was ten cubits. **27**He placed the cherubim[g] inside the innermost room of the temple, with their wings spread out. The wing of one cherub touched one wall, while the wing of the other touched the other wall, and their wings touched each other in the middle of the room. **28**He overlaid the cherubim with gold.

29On the walls all around the temple, in both the inner and outer rooms, he carved cherubim,[h] palm trees and open flowers. **30**He also covered the floors of both the inner and outer rooms of the temple with gold.

31For the entrance of the inner sanctuary he made doors of olive wood with five-sided jambs. **32**And on the two olive wood doors he carved cherubim, palm trees and open flowers, and overlaid the cherubim and palm trees with beaten gold. **33**In the same way he made four-sided jambs of olive wood for the entrance to the main hall. **34**He also made two pine doors, each having two leaves that turned in sockets. **35**He carved cherubim, palm trees and open flowers on them and overlaid them with gold hammered evenly over the carvings.

36And he built the inner courtyard of three courses[i] of dressed stone and one course of trimmed cedar beams.

37The foundation of the temple of the LORD was laid in the fourth year, in the month of Ziv. **38**In the eleventh year in the month of Bul, the eighth month, the temple was finished in all its details according to its specifications.[j] He had spent seven years building it.

Solomon Builds His Palace

7 It took Solomon thirteen years, however, to complete the construction of his palace.[k] **2**He built the Palace[l] of the Forest of Lebanon[m] a hundred cubits long, fifty wide and thirty high,[b] with four rows of cedar columns supporting trimmed cedar beams. **3**It was roofed with cedar above the beams that rested on the columns—forty-five beams, fifteen to a row. **4**Its windows were placed high in sets of three, facing each other. **5**All the doorways had rectangular frames; they were in the front part in sets of three, facing each other.[c]

6He made a colonnade fifty cubits long and thirty wide.[d] In front of it was a portico, and in front of that were pillars and an overhanging roof.

7He built the throne hall, the Hall of Justice, where he was to

6:16 [a] Ex 26:33; Lev 16:2; 1Ki 8:6
6:18 [b] 1Ki 7:24; Ps 74:6
6:19 [c] 1Ki 8:6 [d] 1Sa 3:3
6:20 [e] Eze 41:3-4
6:23 [f] Ex 37:1-9
6:27 [g] Ex 25:20; 37:9; 1Ki 8:7; 2Ch 5:8
6:29 [h] ver 32,35
6:36 [i] 1Ki 7:12; Ezr 6:4
6:38 [j] Heb 8:5
7:1 [k] 1Ki 9:10; 2Ch 8:1
7:2 [l] 2Sa 7:2 [m] 1Ki 10:17; 2Ch 9:16

[y] *17* That is, about 60 feet (about 18 meters) [z] *20* That is, about 30 feet (about 9 meters) long, wide and high [a] *23* That is, about 15 feet (about 4.5 meters) [b] *2* That is, about 150 feet (about 46 meters) long, 75 feet (about 23 meters) wide and 45 feet (about 13.5 meters) high [c] *5* The meaning of the Hebrew for this verse is uncertain. [d] *6* That is, about 75 feet (about 23 meters) long and 45 feet (about 13.5 meters) wide

judge,[a] and he covered it with cedar from floor to ceiling.[e][b] 8And
the palace in which he was to live,
set farther back, was similar in design. Solomon also made a palace
like this hall for Pharaoh's daughter, whom he had married.[c]
9All these structures, from the
outside to the great courtyard and
from foundation to eaves, were
made of blocks of high-grade stone
cut to size and trimmed with a saw
on their inner and outer faces.
10The foundations were laid with
large stones of good quality, some
measuring ten cubits[f] and some
eight.[g] 11Above were high-grade
stones, cut to size, and cedar
beams. 12The great courtyard was
surrounded by a wall of three
courses[d] of dressed stone and one
course of trimmed cedar beams, as
was the inner courtyard of the temple of the LORD with its portico.

The Temple's Furnishings

7:23–26pp — 2Ch 4:2–5
7:38–51pp — 2Ch 4:6,10–5:1

13King Solomon sent to Tyre and
brought Huram,[h][e] 14whose mother was a widow from the tribe of
Naphtali and whose father was a
man of Tyre and a craftsman in
bronze. Huram was highly skilled[f]
and experienced in all kinds of
bronze work. He came to King Solomon and did all[g] the work assigned to him.
15He cast two bronze pillars,[h]
each eighteen cubits high and
twelve cubits around,[i] by line.
16He also made two capitals[i] of
cast bronze to set on the tops of the
pillars; each capital was five cubits[j] high. 17A network of interwoven chains festooned the capitals
on top of the pillars, seven for each
capital. 18He made pomegranates
in two rows[k] encircling each network to decorate the capitals on
top of the pillars.[l] He did the same
for each capital. 19The capitals on
top of the pillars in the portico
were in the shape of lilies, four cubits[m] high. 20On the capitals of
both pillars, above the bowl-
shaped part next to the network,
were the two hundred pomegranates[j] in rows all around. 21He
erected the pillars at the portico of
the temple. The pillar to the south
he named Jakin[n] and the one to
the north Boaz.[o][k] 22The capitals
on top were in the shape of lilies.
And so the work on the pillars was
completed.
23He made the Sea[l] of cast metal, circular in shape, measuring ten
cubits[f] from rim to rim and five
cubits high. It took a line of thirty
cubits[p] to measure around it.
24Below the rim, gourds encircled
it—ten to a cubit. The gourds were
cast in two rows in one piece with
the Sea.
25The Sea stood on twelve
bulls,[m] three facing north, three
facing west, three facing south and
three facing east. The Sea rested on
top of them, and their hindquarters
were toward the center. 26It was a
handbreadth[q] in thickness, and its
rim was like the rim of a cup, like
a lily blossom. It held two thousand baths.[r]
27He also made ten movable
stands[n] of bronze; each was four
cubits long, four wide and three
high.[s] 28This is how the stands
were made: They had side panels
attached to uprights. 29On the panels between the uprights were lions, bulls and cherubim—and on
the uprights as well. Above and be-

7:7 [a]Ps 122:5; Pr 20:8 [b]1Ki 6:15
7:8 [c]1Ki 3:1; 2Ch 8:11
7:12 [d]1Ki 6:36
7:13 [e]2Ch 2:13
7:14 [f]Ex 31:2-5; 35:31; 36:1; 2Ch 2:14 [g]2Ch 4:11,16
7:15 [h]2Ki 25:17; 2Ch 3:15; 4:12; 52:17, 21
7:16 [i]2Ki 25:17
7:20 [j]2Ch 3:16; 4:13; Jer 52:23
7:21 [k]1Ki 6:3; 2Ch 3:17
7:23 [l]2Ki 25:13; 1Ch 18:8; Jer 52:17
7:25 [m]2Ch 4:4-5; Jer 52:20
7:27 [n]ver 38; 2Ch 4:14

[e]7 Vulgate and Syriac; Hebrew *floor*
[f]*10,23* That is, about 15 feet (about 4.5 meters)
[g]*10* That is, about 12 feet (about 3.6 meters)
[h]*13* Hebrew *Hiram,* a variant of *Huram*; also in verses 40 and 45
[i]*15* That is, about 27 feet (about 8.1 meters) high and 18 feet (about 5.4 meters) around
[j]*16* That is, about 7 1/2 feet (about 2.3 meters); also in verse 23
[k]*18* Two Hebrew manuscripts and Septuagint; most Hebrew manuscripts *made the pillars, and there were two rows*
[l]*18* Many Hebrew manuscripts and Syriac; most Hebrew manuscripts *pomegranates*
[m]*19* That is, about 6 feet (about 1.8 meters); also in verse 38
[n]*21* *Jakin* probably means *he establishes.*
[o]*21* *Boaz* probably means *in him is strength.*
[p]*23* That is, about 45 feet (about 13.5 meters)
[q]*26* That is, about 3 inches (about 8 centimeters)
[r]*26* That is, probably about 11,500 gallons (about 44 kiloliters); the Septuagint does not have this sentence.
[s]*27* That is, about 6 feet (about 1.8 meters) long and wide and about 4 1/2 feet (about 1.3 meters) high

low the lions and bulls were
wreaths of hammered work.
30Each stand[a] had four bronze
wheels with bronze axles, and each
had a basin resting on four supports, cast with wreaths on each
side. 31On the inside of the stand
there was an opening that had a
circular frame one cubit[t] deep.
This opening was round, and with
its basework it measured a cubit
and a half.[u] Around its opening
there was engraving. The panels of
the stands were square, not round.
32The four wheels were under the
panels, and the axles of the wheels
were attached to the stand. The di-
ameter of each wheel was a cubit
and a half. 33The wheels were
made like chariot wheels; the axles, rims, spokes and hubs were all
of cast metal.

34Each stand had four handles,
one on each corner, projecting
from the stand. 35At the top of the
stand there was a circular band half
a cubit[v] deep. The supports and
panels were attached to the top of
the stand. 36He engraved cherubim, lions and palm trees on the
surfaces of the supports and on the
panels, in every available space,
with wreaths all around. 37This is
the way he made the ten stands.
They were all cast in the same
molds and were identical in size
and shape.

38He then made ten bronze basins,[b] each holding forty baths[w]
and measuring four cubits across,
one basin to go on each of the ten
stands. 39He placed five of the
stands on the south side of the
temple and five on the north. He
placed the Sea on the south side, at
the southeast corner of the temple.
40He also made the basins and
shovels and sprinkling bowls.

So Huram finished all the work
he had undertaken for King Solomon in the temple of the LORD:

41the two pillars;
the two bowl-shaped capitals
on top of the pillars;
the two sets of network decorating the two bowl-shaped
capitals on top of the pillars;
42the four hundred pomegranates for the two sets of network (two rows of pome-
granates for each network,
decorating the bowl-shaped
capitals[c] on top of the pillars);
43the ten stands with their ten
basins;
44the Sea and the twelve bulls
under it;
45the pots, shovels and sprinkling bowls.[d]

All these objects that Huram
made for King Solomon for the
temple of the LORD were of burnished bronze. 46The king had
them cast in clay molds in the
plain[e] of the Jordan between Succoth[f] and Zarethan.[g] 47Solomon
left all these things unweighed,[h]
because there were so many; the
weight of the bronze was not determined.

48Solomon also made all the furnishings that were in the LORD's
temple:

the golden altar;
the golden table[i] on which
was the bread of the Presence;[j]
49the lampstands[k] of pure gold
(five on the right and five on
the left, in front of the inner
sanctuary);
the gold floral work and lamps
and tongs;
50the pure gold basins, wick
trimmers, sprinkling bowls,
dishes and censers;[l]
and the gold sockets for the
doors of the innermost
room, the Most Holy Place,
and also for the doors of the
main hall of the temple.

51When all the work King Solomon had done for the temple of the
LORD was finished, he brought in
the things his father David had

7:30 [a] 2Ki 16:17
7:38 [b] Ex 30:18; 2Ch 4:6
7:42 [c] ver 20
7:45 [d] Ex 27:3
7:46 [e] 2Ch 4:17 [f] Ge 33:17; Jos 13:27 [g] Jos 3:16
7:47 [h] 1Ch 22:3
7:48 [i] Ex 37:10 [j] Ex 25:30
7:49 [k] Ex 25:31-38
7:50 [l] 2Ki 25:13

[t] *31* That is, about 1 1/2 feet (about 0.5 meter) [u] *31* That is, about 2 1/4 feet (about 0.7 meter); also in verse 32 [v] *35* That is, about 3/4 foot (about 0.2 meter) [w] *38* That is, about 230 gallons (about 880 liters)

dedicated[a]—the silver and gold
and the furnishings—and he
placed them in the treasuries of the
LORD's temple.

The Ark Brought to the Temple

8:1–21pp — 2Ch 5:2–6:11

8 Then King Solomon summoned into his presence at Jerusalem the elders of Israel, all the
heads of the tribes and the chiefs[b]
of the Israelite families, to bring up
the ark[c] of the LORD's covenant
from Zion, the City of David.[d] 2All
the men of Israel came together to
King Solomon at the time of the
festival[e] in the month of Ethanim,
the seventh month.[f]

3When all the elders of Israel had
arrived, the priests[g] took up the
ark, 4and they brought up the ark of
the LORD and the Tent of Meeting[h]
and all the sacred furnishings in it.
The priests and Levites carried
them up, 5and King Solomon and
the entire assembly of Israel that
had gathered about him were before the ark, sacrificing[i] so many
sheep and cattle that they could
not be recorded or counted.

6The priests then brought the
ark of the LORD's covenant[j] to its
place in the inner sanctuary of the
temple, the Most Holy Place, and
put it beneath the wings of the
cherubim.[k] 7The cherubim spread
their wings over the place of the ark
and overshadowed the ark and its
carrying poles. 8These poles were
so long that their ends could be
seen from the Holy Place in front of
the inner sanctuary, but not from
outside the Holy Place; and they
are still there today.[l] 9There was
nothing in the ark except the two
stone tablets[m] that Moses had
placed in it at Horeb, where the
LORD made a covenant with the Israelites after they came out of
Egypt.

10When the priests withdrew
from the Holy Place, the cloud[n]
filled the temple of the LORD. 11And
the priests could not perform their
service because of the cloud, for

7:51 [a]2Sa 8:11
8:1 [b]Nu 7:2 [c]2Sa 6:17 [d]2Sa 5:7
8:2 [e]2Ch 7:8 [f]Lev 23:34
8:3 [g]Nu 7:9; Jos 3:3
8:4 [h]1Ki 3:4; 2Ch 1:3
8:5 [i]2Sa 6:13
8:6 [j]2Sa 6:17 [k]1Ki 6:19,27
8:8 [l]Ex 25:13-15
8:9 [m]Ex 24:7-8; 25:21; 40:20; Dt 10:2-5; Heb 9:4
8:10 [n]Ex 40:34-35; 2Ch 7:1-2
8:12 [o]Ps 18:11; 97:2
8:13 [p]Ex 15:17; 2Sa 7:13; Ps 132:13
8:14 [q]2Sa 6:18
8:15 [r]2Sa 7:12-13; 1Ch 29:10, 20; Ne 9:5; Lk 1:68
8:16 [s]Dt 12:5 [t]1Sa 16:1 [u]2Sa 7:4-6,8
8:17 [v]2Sa 7:2; 1Ch 17:1
8:19 [w]2Sa 7:5 [x]2Sa 7:13; 1Ki 5:3,5
8:20 [y]1Ch 28:6

the glory of the LORD filled his temple.

12Then Solomon said, "The LORD
has said that he would dwell in a
dark cloud;[o] 13I have indeed built
a magnificent temple for you, a
place for you to dwell[p] forever."

14While the whole assembly of
Israel was standing there, the king
turned around and blessed[q] them.
15Then he said:

> "Praise be to the LORD,[r] the
> God of Israel, who with his
> own hand has fulfilled what he
> promised with his own mouth
> to my father David. For he
> said, 16'Since the day I
> brought my people Israel out
> of Egypt, I have not chosen a
> city in any tribe of Israel to
> have a temple built for my
> Name[s] to be there, but I have
> chosen[t] David[u] to rule my
> people Israel.'
>
> 17"My father David had it in
> his heart to build a temple[v]
> for the Name of the LORD, the
> God of Israel. 18But the LORD
> said to my father David, 'Because it was in your heart to
> build a temple for my Name,
> you did well to have this in
> your heart. 19Nevertheless,
> you[w] are not the one to build
> the temple, but your son, who
> is your own flesh and blood
> —he is the one who will build
> the temple for my Name.'[x]
>
> 20"The LORD has kept the
> promise he made: I have succeeded David my father and
> now I sit on the throne of Israel, just as the LORD promised,
> and I have built[y] the temple
> for the Name of the LORD, the
> God of Israel. 21I have provided a place there for the ark, in
> which is the covenant of the
> LORD that he made with our fathers when he brought them
> out of Egypt."

Solomon's Prayer of Dedication

8:22–53pp — 2Ch 6:12–40

22Then Solomon stood before
the altar of the LORD in front of the

whole assembly of Israel, spread
out his hands[a] toward heaven
23and said:

"O LORD, God of Israel, there
is no God like[b] you in heaven
above or on earth below—you
who keep your covenant of
love[c] with your servants who
continue wholeheartedly in
your way. 24You have kept
your promise to your servant
David my father; with your
mouth you have promised and
with your hand you have fulfilled it—as it is today.

25"Now LORD, God of Israel,
keep for your servant David my
father the promises[d] you
made to him when you said,
'You shall never fail to have a
man to sit before me on the
throne of Israel, if only your
sons are careful in all they do
to walk before me as you have
done.' 26And now, O God of Israel, let your word that you
promised[e] your servant David
my father come true.

27"But will God really
dwell[f] on earth? The heavens,
even the highest heaven, cannot contain[g] you. How much
less this temple I have built!
28Yet give attention to your
servant's prayer and his plea
for mercy, O LORD my God.
Hear the cry and the prayer
that your servant is praying in
your presence this day. 29May
your eyes be open[h] toward[i]
this temple night and day, this
place of which you said, 'My
Name[j] shall be there,' so that
you will hear the prayer your
servant prays toward this
place. 30Hear the supplication
of your servant and of your
people Israel when they pray
toward this place. Hear from
heaven, your dwelling place,
and when you hear, forgive.[k]

31"When a man wrongs his
neighbor and is required to
take an oath and he comes
and swears the oath[l] before
your altar in this temple,
32then hear from heaven and
act. Judge between your servants, condemning the guilty
and bringing down on his own
head what he has done. Declare the innocent not guilty,
and so establish his innocence.[m]

33"When your people Israel
have been defeated[n] by an enemy because they have
sinned[o] against you, and
when they turn back to you
and confess your name, praying and making supplication
to you in this temple, 34then
hear from heaven and forgive
the sin of your people Israel
and bring them back to the
land you gave to their fathers.

35"When the heavens are
shut up and there is no rain[p]
because your people have
sinned against you, and when
they pray toward this place
and confess your name and
turn from their sin because
you have afflicted them,
36then hear from heaven and
forgive the sin of your servants, your people Israel.
Teach[q] them the right way[r]
to live, and send rain on the
land you gave your people for
an inheritance.

37"When famine[s] or plague
comes to the land, or blight[t]
or mildew, locusts or grasshoppers, or when an enemy
besieges them in any of their
cities, whatever disaster or
disease may come, 38and
when a prayer or plea is made
by any of your people Israel
—each one aware of the afflictions of his own heart, and
spreading out his hands toward this temple— 39then
hear from heaven, your dwelling place. Forgive and act;
deal with each man according
to all he does, since you
know[u] his heart (for you alone
know the hearts of all men),
40so that they will fear[v] you
all the time they live in the
land you gave our fathers.

8:22 [a]Ex 9:29; Ezr 9:5
8:23 [b]1Sa 2:2; 2Sa 7:22 [c]Dt 7:9,12; Ne 1:5; 9:32; Da 9:4
8:25 [d]1Ki 2:4
8:26 [e]2Sa 7:25
8:27 [f]Ac 7:48 [g]2Ch 2:6; Ps 139:7-16; Isa 66:1; Jer 23:24
8:29 [h]2Ch 7:15; Ne 1:6 [i]Da 6:10 [j]Dt 12:11
8:30 [k]Ps 85:2
8:31 [l]Ex 22:11
8:32 [m]Dt 25:1
8:33 [n]Lev 26:17; Dt 28:25 [o]Lev 26:39
8:35 [p]Lev 26:19; Dt 28:24
8:36 [q]1Sa 12:23; Ps 25:4; 94:12 [r]Ps 5:8; 27:11; Jer 6:16
8:37 [s]Lev 26:26 [t]Dt 28:22
8:39 [u]1Sa 16:7; 1Ch 28:9; Ps 11:4; Jer 17:10; Jn 2:24; Ac 1:24
8:40 [v]Ps 130:4

41"As for the foreigner who
does not belong to your people
Israel but has come from a distant land because of your
name— 42for men will hear of
your great name and your
mighty hand[a] and your outstretched arm—when he
comes and prays toward this
temple, 43then hear from
heaven, your dwelling place,
and do whatever the foreigner
asks of you, so that all the peoples of the earth may know[b]
your name and fear[c] you, as
do your own people Israel, and
may know that this house I
have built bears your Name.
44"When your people go to
war against their enemies,
wherever you send them, and
when they pray to the LORD toward the city you have chosen
and the temple I have built for
your Name, 45then hear from
heaven their prayer and their
plea, and uphold their cause.
46"When they sin against
you—for there is no one who
does not sin[d]—and you become angry with them and
give them over to the enemy,
who takes them captive[e] to
his own land, far away or near;
47and if they have a change of
heart in the land where they
are held captive, and repent
and plead[f] with you in the
land of their conquerors and
say, 'We have sinned, we have
done wrong, we have acted
wickedly';[g] 48and if they turn
back to you with all their
heart[h] and soul in the land of
their enemies who took them
captive, and pray[i] to you toward the land you gave their
fathers, toward the city you
have chosen and the temple[j]
I have built for your Name;
49then from heaven, your
dwelling place, hear their
prayer and their plea, and uphold their cause. 50And forgive
your people, who have sinned
against you; forgive all the offenses they have committed
against you, and cause their
conquerors to show them mercy;[k] 51for they are your people
and your inheritance,[l] whom
you brought out of Egypt, out
of that iron-smelting furnace.[m]
52"May your eyes be open to
your servant's plea and to the
plea of your people Israel, and
may you listen to them whenever they cry out to you. 53For
you singled them out from all
the nations of the world to be
your own inheritance,[n] just as
you declared through your servant Moses when you, O Sovereign LORD, brought our fathers out of Egypt."

54When Solomon had finished
all these prayers and supplications
to the LORD, he rose from before the
altar of the LORD, where he had
been kneeling with his hands
spread out toward heaven. 55He
stood and blessed[o] the whole assembly of Israel in a loud voice,
saying:

56"Praise be to the LORD,
who has given rest[p] to his
people Israel just as he promised. Not one word has failed
of all the good promises[q] he
gave through his servant Moses. 57May the LORD our God
be with us as he was with our
fathers; may he never leave us
nor forsake[r] us. 58May he
turn our hearts[s] to him, to
walk in all his ways and to
keep the commands, decrees
and regulations he gave our fathers. 59And may these words
of mine, which I have prayed
before the LORD, be near to the
LORD our God day and night,
that he may uphold the cause
of his servant and the cause of
his people Israel according to
each day's need, 60so that all
the peoples[t] of the earth may
know that the LORD is God and
that there is no other.[u] 61But
your hearts must be fully committed[v] to the LORD our God,
to live by his decrees and obey

8:42 [a]Dt 3:24
8:43 [b]1Sa 17:46; 2Ki 19:19 [c]Ps 102:15
8:46 [d]Pr 20:9; Ecc 7:20; Ro 3:9; 1Jn 1:8-10 [e]Lev 26:33-39; Dt 28:64
8:47 [f]Lev 26:40; Ne 1:6 [g]Ps 106:6; Da 9:5
8:48 [h]Dt 4:29; Jer 29:12-14 [i]Da 6:10 [j]Jnh 2:4
8:50 [k]2Ch 30:9; Ps 106:46
8:51 [l]Dt 4:20; 9:29; Ne 1:10 [m]Jer 11:4
8:53 [n]Ex 19:5; Dt 9:26-29
8:55 [o]ver 14; 2Sa 6:18
8:56 [p]Dt 12:10 [q]Jos 21:45; 23:15
8:57 [r]Dt 31:6; Jos 1:5; Heb 13:5
8:58 [s]Ps 119:36
8:60 [t]Jos 4:24; 1Sa 17:46 [u]Dt 4:35; 1Ki 18:39; Jer 10:10-12
8:61 [v]1Ki 11:4; 15:3,14; 2Ki 20:3

his commands, as at this time."

The Dedication of the Temple

8:62–66pp — 2Ch 7:1–10

62Then the king and all Israel with him offered sacrifices before the LORD. **63**Solomon offered a sacrifice of fellowship offerings[x] to the LORD: twenty-two thousand cattle and a hundred and twenty thousand sheep and goats. So the king and all the Israelites dedicated the temple of the LORD.

64On that same day the king consecrated the middle part of the courtyard in front of the temple of the LORD, and there he offered burnt offerings, grain offerings and the fat of the fellowship offerings, because the bronze altar[a] before the LORD was too small to hold the burnt offerings, the grain offerings and the fat of the fellowship offerings.

65So Solomon observed the festival[b] at that time, and all Israel with him—a vast assembly, people from Lebo[y] Hamath[c] to the Wadi of Egypt.[d] They celebrated it before the LORD our God for seven days and seven days more, fourteen days in all. **66**On the following day he sent the people away. They blessed the king and then went home, joyful and glad in heart for all the good things the LORD had done for his servant David and his people Israel.

The LORD Appears to Solomon

9:1–9pp — 2Ch 7:11–22

9 When Solomon had finished[e] building the temple of the LORD and the royal palace, and had achieved all he had desired to do, **2**the LORD appeared[f] to him a second time, as he had appeared to him at Gibeon. **3**The LORD said to him:

"I have heard[g] the prayer and plea you have made before me; I have consecrated this temple, which you have built, by putting my Name there forever. My eyes[h] and my heart will always be there.

4"As for you, if you walk before me in integrity of heart[i] and uprightness, as David[j] your father did, and do all I command and observe my decrees and laws, **5**I will establish[k] your royal throne over Israel forever, as I promised David your father when I said, 'You shall never fail[l] to have a man on the throne of Israel.'

6"But if you[z] or your sons turn away[m] from me and do not observe the commands and decrees I have given you[z] and go off to serve other gods and worship them, **7**then I will cut off Israel from the land[n] I have given them and will reject this temple I have consecrated for my Name.[o] Israel will then become a byword[p] and an object of ridicule[q] among all peoples. **8**And though this temple is now imposing, all who pass by will be appalled and will scoff and say, 'Why has the LORD done such a thing to this land and to this temple?'[r] **9**People will answer, 'Because they have forsaken the LORD their God, who brought their fathers out of Egypt, and have embraced other gods, worshiping and serving them—that is why the LORD brought all this disaster on them.' "

Solomon's Other Activities

9:10–28pp — 2Ch 8:1–18

10At the end of twenty years, during which Solomon built these two buildings—the temple of the LORD and the royal palace— **11**King Solomon gave twenty towns in Galilee to Hiram king of Tyre, because Hiram had supplied him with all the cedar and pine and gold[s] he wanted. **12**But when Hiram went from Tyre to see the towns that Solomon had given him, he was not

8:64 [a]2Ch 4:1
8:65 [b]ver 2; Lev 23:34 [c]Nu 34:8; Jos 13:5; Jdg 3:3; 2Ki 14:25 [d]Ge 15:18
9:1 [e]1Ki 7:1; 2Ch 8:6
9:2 [f]1Ki 3:5
9:3 [g]2Ki 20:5; Ps 10:17 [h]Dt 11:12; 1Ki 8:29
9:4 [i]Ge 17:1 [j]1Ki 15:5
9:5 [k]1Ch 22:10 [l]2Sa 7:15; 1Ki 2:4
9:6 [m]2Sa 7:14
9:7 [n]2Ki 17:23; 25:21 [o]Jer 7:14 [p]Ps 44:14 [q]Dt 28:37
9:8 [r]Dt 29:24; Jer 22:8-9
9:11 [s]2Ch 8:2

[x]63 Traditionally *peace offerings*; also in verse 64 [y]65 Or *from the entrance to* [z]6 The Hebrew is plural.

pleased with them. **13**"What kind of towns are these you have given me, my brother?" he asked. And he called them the Land of Cabul,[a][a] a name they have to this day. **14**Now Hiram had sent to the king 120 talents[b] of gold.

15Here is the account of the forced labor King Solomon conscripted[b] to build the LORD's temple, his own palace, the supporting terraces,[c][c] the wall of Jerusalem, and Hazor,[d] Megiddo and Gezer.[e] **16**(Pharaoh king of Egypt had attacked and captured Gezer. He had set it on fire. He killed its Canaanite inhabitants and then gave it as a wedding gift to his daughter, Solomon's wife. **17**And Solomon rebuilt Gezer.) He built up Lower Beth Horon,[f] **18**Baalath,[g] and Tadmor[d] in the desert, within his land, **19**as well as all his store cities[h] and the towns for his chariots[i] and for his horses[e]—whatever he desired to build in Jerusalem, in Lebanon and throughout all the territory he ruled.

20All the people left from the Amorites, Hittites, Perizzites, Hivites and Jebusites (these peoples were not Israelites), **21**that is, their descendants[j] remaining in the land, whom the Israelites could not exterminate[f][k]—these Solomon conscripted for his slave labor force,[l] as it is to this day. **22**But Solomon did not make slaves[m] of any of the Israelites; they were his fighting men, his government officials, his officers, his captains, and the commanders of his chariots and charioteers. **23**They were also the chief officials[n] in charge of Solomon's projects—550 officials supervising the men who did the work.

24After Pharaoh's daughter[o] had come up from the City of David to the palace Solomon had built for her, he constructed the supporting terraces.[p]

25Three[q] times a year Solomon sacrificed burnt offerings and fellowship offerings[g] on the altar he had built for the LORD, burning incense before the LORD along with them, and so fulfilled the temple obligations.

26King Solomon also built ships[r] at Ezion Geber,[s] which is near Elath in Edom, on the shore of the Red Sea.[h] **27**And Hiram sent his men—sailors[t] who knew the sea—to serve in the fleet with Solomon's men. **28**They sailed to Ophir[u] and brought back 420 talents[i] of gold, which they delivered to King Solomon.

The Queen of Sheba Visits Solomon

10:1–13pp — 2Ch 9:1–12

10 When the queen of Sheba[v] heard about the fame of Solomon and his relation to the name of the LORD, she came to test him with hard questions.[w] **2**Arriving at Jerusalem with a very great caravan—with camels carrying spices, large quantities of gold, and precious stones—she came to Solomon and talked with him about all that she had on her mind. **3**Solomon answered all her questions; nothing was too hard for the king to explain to her. **4**When the queen of Sheba saw all the wisdom of Solomon and the palace he had built, **5**the food on his table,[x] the seating of his officials, the attending servants in their robes, his cupbearers, and the burnt offerings he made at[j] the temple of the LORD, she was overwhelmed.

6She said to the king, "The report I heard in my own country about your achievements and your wisdom is true. **7**But I did not believe these things until I came and saw with my own eyes. Indeed, not even half was told me; in wisdom and wealth[y] you have far exceeded

9:13 [a]Jos 19:27
9:15 [b]Jos 16:10; 1Ki 5:13 [c]ver 24; 2Sa 5:9 [d]Jos 19:36 [e]Jos 17:11
9:17 [f]Jos 16:3; 2Ch 8:5
9:18 [g]Jos 19:44
9:19 [h]ver 1 [i]1Ki 4:26
9:21 [j]Ge 9:25-26 [k]Jos 15:63; 17:12; Jdg 1:21,27, 29 [l]Ezr 2:55, 58
9:22 [m]Lev 25:39
9:23 [n]1Ki 5:16
9:24 [o]1Ki 3:1; 7:8 [p]2Sa 5:9; 1Ki 11:27; 2Ch 32:5
9:25 [q]Ex 23:14; 2Ch 8:12-13, 16
9:26 [r]1Ki 22:48 [s]Nu 33:35; Dt 2:8
9:27 [t]1Ki 10:11; Eze 27:8
9:28 [u]1Ch 29:4
10:1 [v]Ge 10:7,28; Mt 12:42; Lk 11:31 [w]Jdg 14:12
10:5 [x]1Ch 26:16
10:7 [y]1Ch 29:25

[a]*13* *Cabul* sounds like the Hebrew for *good-for-nothing.* [b]*14* That is, about 4 1/2 tons (about 4 metric tons) [c]*15* Or *the Millo*; also in verse 24 [d]*18* The Hebrew may also be read *Tamar.* [e]*19* Or *charioteers* [f]*21* The Hebrew term refers to the irrevocable giving over of things or persons to the LORD, often by totally destroying them. [g]*25* Traditionally *peace offerings* [h]*26* Hebrew *Yam Suph*; that is, Sea of Reeds [i]*28* That is, about 16 tons (about 14.5 metric tons) [j]*5* Or *the ascent by which he went up to*

the report I heard. 8How happy
your men must be! How happy your
officials, who continually stand before you and hear[a] your wisdom!
9Praise[b] be to the LORD your God,
who has delighted in you and
placed you on the throne of Israel.
Because of the LORD's eternal love
for Israel, he has made you king, to
maintain justice[c] and righteousness."

10And she gave the king 120 talents[k] of gold,[d] large quantities of
spices, and precious stones. Never
again were so many spices brought
in as those the queen of Sheba gave
to King Solomon.

11(Hiram's ships brought gold
from Ophir;[e] and from there they
brought great cargoes of almugwood[l] and precious stones. 12The
king used the almugwood to make
supports for the temple of the LORD
and for the royal palace, and to
make harps and lyres for the musicians. So much almugwood has
never been imported or seen since
that day.)

13King Solomon gave the queen
of Sheba all she desired and asked
for, besides what he had given her
out of his royal bounty. Then she
left and returned with her retinue
to her own country.

Solomon's Splendor

10:14-29pp — 2Ch 1:14-17; 9:13-28

14The weight of the gold[f] that
Solomon received yearly was 666
talents,[m] 15not including the revenues from merchants and traders
and from all the Arabian kings and
the governors of the land.

16King Solomon made two hundred large shields[g] of hammered
gold; six hundred bekas[n] of gold
went into each shield. 17He also
made three hundred small shields
of hammered gold, with three minas[o] of gold in each shield. The
king put them in the Palace of the
Forest of Lebanon.[h]

18Then the king made a great
throne inlaid with ivory and overlaid with fine gold. 19The throne
had six steps, and its back had a
rounded top. On both sides of the
seat were armrests, with a lion
standing beside each of them.
20Twelve lions stood on the six
steps, one at either end of each
step. Nothing like it had ever been
made for any other kingdom. 21All
King Solomon's goblets were gold,
and all the household articles in
the Palace of the Forest of Lebanon
were pure gold. Nothing was made
of silver, because silver was considered of little value in Solomon's
days. 22The king had a fleet of trading ships[p][i] at sea along with the
ships of Hiram. Once every three
years it returned, carrying gold, silver and ivory, and apes and baboons.

23King Solomon was greater in
riches[j] and wisdom[k] than all the
other kings of the earth. 24The
whole world sought audience with
Solomon to hear the wisdom[l] God
had put in his heart. 25Year after
year, everyone who came brought a
gift—articles of silver and gold,
robes, weapons and spices, and
horses and mules.

26Solomon accumulated chariots and horses;[m] he had fourteen
hundred chariots and twelve thousand horses,[q] which he kept in the
chariot cities and also with him in
Jerusalem. 27The king made silver
as common[n] in Jerusalem as
stones, and cedar as plentiful as
sycamore-fig trees in the foothills.
28Solomon's horses were imported
from Egypt[r] and from Kue[s]—the
royal merchants purchased them
from Kue. 29They imported a chariot from Egypt for six hundred shekels[t] of silver, and a horse for a hundred and fifty.[u] They also exported
them to all the kings of the Hittites[o] and of the Arameans.

10:8 [a] Pr 8:34
10:9 [b] 1Ki 5:7 [c] 2Sa 8:15; Ps 33:5; 72:2
10:10 [d] ver 2
10:11 [e] Ge 10:29; 1Ki 9:27-28
10:14 [f] 1Ki 9:28
10:16 [g] 1Ki 14:26-28
10:17 [h] 1Ki 7:2
10:22 [i] 1Ki 9:26
10:23 [j] 1Ki 3:13 [k] 1Ki 4:30
10:24 [l] 1Ki 3:9,12,28
10:26 [m] Dt 17:16; 1Ki 4:26; 9:19; 2Ch 1:14; 9:25
10:27 [n] Dt 17:17
10:29 [o] 2Ki 7:6-7

[k] *10* That is, about 4 1/2 tons (about 4 metric tons) [l] *11* Probably a variant of *algumwood*; also in verse 12 [m] *14* That is, about 25 tons (about 23 metric tons) [n] *16* That is, about 7 1/2 pounds (about 3.5 kilograms) [o] *17* That is, about 3 3/4 pounds (about 1.7 kilograms) [p] *22* Hebrew *of ships of Tarshish* [q] *26* Or *charioteers* [r] *28* Or possibly *Muzur*, a region in Cilicia; also in verse 29 [s] *28* Probably *Cilicia* [t] *29* That is, about 15 pounds (about 7 kilograms) [u] *29* That is, about 3 3/4 pounds (about 1.7 kilograms)

Solomon's Wives

11 King Solomon, however, loved many foreign women[a] besides Pharaoh's daughter—Moabites, Ammonites, Edomites, Sidonians and Hittites. **2**They were from nations about which the LORD had told the Israelites, "You must not intermarry[b] with them, because they will surely turn your hearts after their gods." Nevertheless, Solomon held fast to them in love. **3**He had seven hundred wives of royal birth and three hundred concubines, and his wives led him astray. **4**As Solomon grew old, his wives turned his heart after other gods, and his heart was not fully devoted[c] to the LORD his God, as the heart of David his father had been. **5**He followed Ashtoreth[d] the goddess of the Sidonians, and Molech[v][e] the detestable god of the Ammonites. **6**So Solomon did evil in the eyes of the LORD; he did not follow the LORD completely, as David his father had done.

7On a hill east[f] of Jerusalem, Solomon built a high place for Chemosh[g] the detestable god of Moab, and for Molech[h] the detestable god of the Ammonites. **8**He did the same for all his foreign wives, who burned incense and offered sacrifices to their gods.

9The LORD became angry with Solomon because his heart had turned away from the LORD, the God of Israel, who had appeared[i] to him twice. **10**Although he had forbidden Solomon to follow other gods,[j] Solomon did not keep the LORD's command.[k] **11**So the LORD said to Solomon, "Since this is your attitude and you have not kept my covenant and my decrees, which I commanded you, I will most certainly tear[l] the kingdom away from you and give it to one of your subordinates. **12**Nevertheless, for the sake of David your father, I will not do it during your lifetime. I will tear it out of the hand of your son. **13**Yet I will not tear the whole kingdom from him, but will give him one tribe[m] for the sake[n] of David my servant and for the sake of Jerusalem, which I have chosen."[o]

Solomon's Adversaries

14Then the LORD raised up against Solomon an adversary, Hadad the Edomite, from the royal line of Edom. **15**Earlier when David was fighting with Edom, Joab the commander of the army, who had gone up to bury the dead, had struck down all the men in Edom.[p] **16**Joab and all the Israelites stayed there for six months, until they had destroyed all the men in Edom. **17**But Hadad, still only a boy, fled to Egypt with some Edomite officials who had served his father. **18**They set out from Midian and went to Paran.[q] Then taking men from Paran with them, they went to Egypt, to Pharaoh king of Egypt, who gave Hadad a house and land and provided him with food.

19Pharaoh was so pleased with Hadad that he gave him a sister of his own wife, Queen Tahpenes, in marriage. **20**The sister of Tahpenes bore him a son named Genubath, whom Tahpenes brought up in the royal palace. There Genubath lived with Pharaoh's own children.

21While he was in Egypt, Hadad heard that David rested with his fathers and that Joab the commander of the army was also dead. Then Hadad said to Pharaoh, "Let me go, that I may return to my own country."

22"What have you lacked here that you want to go back to your own country?" Pharaoh asked.

"Nothing," Hadad replied, "but do let me go!"

23And God raised up against Solomon another adversary,[r] Rezon son of Eliada, who had fled from his master, Hadadezer[s] king of Zobah. **24**He gathered men around him and became the leader of a band of rebels when David destroyed the forces[w] ⌞of Zobah⌟; the rebels went to Damascus,[t] where they settled and took control.

11:1 [a]Dt 17:17; Ne 13:26
11:2 [b]Ex 34:16; Dt 7:3-4
11:4 [c]1Ki 8:61; 9:4
11:5 [d]ver 33; Jdg 2:13; 2Ki 23:13 [e]ver 7
11:7 [f]2Ki 23:13 [g]Nu 21:29; Jdg 11:24 [h]Lev 20:2-5; Ac 7:43
11:9 [i]ver 2-3; 1Ki 3:5; 9:2
11:10 [j]1Ki 9:6 [k]1Ki 6:12
11:11 [l]ver 31; 1Ki 12:15-16; 2Ki 17:21
11:13 [m]1Ki 12:20 [n]2Sa 7:15 [o]Dt 12:11
11:15 [p]Dt 20:13; 2Sa 8:14; 1Ch 18:12
11:18 [q]Nu 10:12
11:23 [r]ver 14 [s]2Sa 8:3
11:24 [t]2Sa 8:5; 10:8,18

[v]*5* Hebrew *Milcom*; also in verse 33
[w]*24* Hebrew *destroyed them*

25Rezon was Israel's adversary as
long as Solomon lived, adding to
the trouble caused by Hadad. So
Rezon ruled in Aram[a] and was hostile toward Israel.

Jeroboam Rebels Against Solomon

26Also, Jeroboam son of Nebat
rebelled[b] against the king. He was
one of Solomon's officials, an
Ephraimite from Zeredah, and his
mother was a widow named Zeru-
ah.
27Here is the account of how he
rebelled against the king: Solomon
had built the supporting terraces[x][c] and had filled in the gap
in the wall of the city of David his
father. **28**Now Jeroboam was a man
of standing,[d] and when Solomon
saw how well[e] the young man did
his work, he put him in charge of
the whole labor force of the house
of Joseph.
29About that time Jeroboam was
going out of Jerusalem, and Ahijah[f] the prophet of Shiloh met him
on the way, wearing a new cloak.
The two of them were alone out in
the country, **30**and Ahijah took
hold of the new cloak he was wearing and tore[g] it into twelve pieces.
31Then he said to Jeroboam, "Take
ten pieces for yourself, for this is
what the LORD, the God of Israel,
says: 'See, I am going to tear[h] the
kingdom out of Solomon's hand
and give you ten tribes. **32**But for
the sake of my servant David and
the city of Jerusalem, which I have
chosen out of all the tribes of Israel, he will have one tribe. **33**I will do
this because they have[y] forsaken
me and worshiped[i] Ashtoreth the
goddess of the Sidonians, Chemosh the god of the Moabites, and
Molech the god of the Ammonites,
and have not walked in my ways,
nor done what is right in my eyes,
nor kept my statutes[j] and laws as
David, Solomon's father, did.
34" 'But I will not take the whole
kingdom out of Solomon's hand; I
have made him ruler all the days of
his life for the sake of David my servant, whom I chose and who observed my commands and statutes.
35I will take the kingdom from his
son's hands and give you ten tribes.
36I will give one tribe[k] to his son so
that David my servant may always
have a lamp[l] before me in Jerusalem, the city where I chose to put
my Name. **37**However, as for you, I
will take you, and you will rule over
all that your heart desires;[m] you
will be king over Israel. **38**If you do
whatever I command you and walk
in my ways and do what is right in
my eyes by keeping my statutes[n]
and commands, as David my servant did, I will be with you. I will
build you a dynasty[o] as enduring
as the one I built for David and will
give Israel to you. **39**I will humble
David's descendants because of
this, but not forever.' "
40Solomon tried to kill Jeroboam, but Jeroboam fled to Egypt, to
Shishak[p] the king, and stayed
there until Solomon's death.

Solomon's Death

11:41-43pp — 2Ch 9:29-31

41As for the other events of Solomon's reign—all he did and the
wisdom he displayed—are they not
written in the book of the annals of
Solomon? **42**Solomon reigned in
Jerusalem over all Israel forty
years. **43**Then he rested with his fathers and was buried in the city of
David his father. And Rehoboam[q]
his son succeeded him as king.

Israel Rebels Against Rehoboam

12:1-24pp — 2Ch 10:1-11:4

12 Rehoboam went to Shechem, for all the Israelites
had gone there to make him king.
2When Jeroboam son of Nebat
heard this (he was still in Egypt,
where he had fled[r] from King Solomon), he returned from[z] Egypt.
3So they sent for Jeroboam, and he
and the whole assembly of Israel

11:25 [a]2Sa 10:19
11:26 [b]2Sa 20:21; 1Ki 12:2; 2Ch 13:6
11:27 [c]1Ki 9:24
11:28 [d]Ru 2:1 [e]Pr 22:29
11:29 [f]1Ki 12:15; 14:2; 2Ch 9:29
11:30 [g]1Sa 15:27
11:31 [h]ver 11
11:33 [i]ver 5-7 [j]1Ki 3:3
11:36 [k]ver 13; 1Ki 12:17 [l]1Ki 15:4; 2Ki 8:19
11:37 [m]2Sa 3:21
11:38 [n]Dt 17:19 [o]Jos 1:5; 2Sa 7:11,27
11:40 [p]2Ch 12:2
11:43 [q]1Ki 14:21; Mt 1:7
12:2 [r]1Ki 11:40

[x]27 Or *the Millo* [y]33 Hebrew; Septuagint, Vulgate and Syriac *because he has* [z]2 Or *he remained in*

went to Rehoboam and said to him:
4"Your father put a heavy yoke[a] on
us, but now lighten the harsh labor
and the heavy yoke he put on us,
and we will serve you."

5Rehoboam answered, "Go away
for three days and then come back
to me." So the people went
away.

6Then King Rehoboam consulted the elders[b] who had served
his father Solomon during his
lifetime. "How would you advise
me to answer these people?" he
asked.

7They replied, "If today you will
be a servant to these people and
serve them and give them a favorable answer,[c] they will always be
your servants."

8But Rehoboam rejected the advice the elders gave him and consulted the young men who had
grown up with him and were serving him. 9He asked them, "What is
your advice? How should we answer these people who say to me,
'Lighten the yoke your father put
on us'?"

10The young men who had grown
up with him replied, "Tell these
people who have said to you, 'Your
father put a heavy yoke on us, but
make our yoke lighter'—tell them,
'My little finger is thicker than my
father's waist. 11My father laid on
you a heavy yoke; I will make it
even heavier. My father scourged
you with whips; I will scourge you
with scorpions.' "

12Three days later Jeroboam and
all the people returned to Rehoboam, as the king had said, "Come
back to me in three days." 13The
king answered the people harshly.
Rejecting the advice given him by
the elders, 14he followed the advice of the young men and said,
"My father made your yoke heavy;
I will make it even heavier. My father scourged[d] you with whips; I
will scourge you with scorpions."
15So the king did not listen to the
people, for this turn of events was
from the LORD,[e] to fulfill the word
the LORD had spoken to Jeroboam
son of Nebat through Ahijah[f] the
Shilonite.

16When all Israel saw that the
king refused to listen to them, they
answered the king:

"What share do we have in
David,
what part in Jesse's son?
To your tents, O Israel![g]
Look after your own house,
O David!"

So the Israelites went home. 17But
as for the Israelites who were living
in the towns of Judah,[h] Rehoboam
still ruled over them.

18King Rehoboam sent out Adoniram,[a][i] who was in charge of
forced labor, but all Israel stoned
him to death. King Rehoboam,
however, managed to get into his
chariot and escape to Jerusalem.
19So Israel has been in rebellion
against the house of David[j] to this
day.

20When all the Israelites heard
that Jeroboam had returned, they
sent and called him to the assembly and made him king over all Israel. Only the tribe of Judah remained loyal to the house of David.[k]

21When Rehoboam arrived in Jerusalem, he mustered the whole
house of Judah and the tribe of
Benjamin—a hundred and eighty
thousand fighting men—to make
war[l] against the house of Israel
and to regain the kingdom for Rehoboam son of Solomon.

22But this word of God came to
Shemaiah[m] the man of God:
23"Say to Rehoboam son of Solomon king of Judah, to the whole
house of Judah and Benjamin, and
to the rest of the people, 24'This is
what the LORD says: Do not go up to
fight against your brothers, the Israelites. Go home, every one of
you, for this is my doing.' " So they
obeyed the word of the LORD and
went home again, as the LORD had
ordered.

12:4 [a] 1Sa 8:11-18; 1Ki 4:20-28
12:6 [b] 1Ki 4:2
12:7 [c] Pr 15:1
12:14 [d] Ex 1:14; 5:5-9,16-18
12:15 [e] ver 24; Dt 2:30; Jdg 14:4; 2Ch 22:7; 25:20 [f] 1Ki 11:29
12:16 [g] 2Sa 20:1
12:17 [h] 1Ki 11:13,36
12:18 [i] 2Sa 20:24; 1Ki 4:6; 5:14
12:19 [j] 2Ki 17:21
12:20 [k] 1Ki 11:13,32
12:21 [l] 2Ch 11:1
12:22 [m] 2Ch 12:5-7

[a] *18* Some Septuagint manuscripts and Syriac (see also 1 Kings 4:6 and 5:14); Hebrew *Adoram*

Golden Calves at Bethel and Dan

25Then Jeroboam fortified Shechem[a] in the hill country of Ephraim and lived there. From there he went out and built up Peniel.[b][b]

26Jeroboam thought to himself, "The kingdom will now likely revert to the house of David. **27**If these people go up to offer sacrifices at the temple of the LORD in Jerusalem,[c] they will again give their allegiance to their lord, Rehoboam king of Judah. They will kill me and return to King Rehoboam."

28After seeking advice, the king made two golden calves.[d] He said to the people, "It is too much for you to go up to Jerusalem. Here are your gods, O Israel, who brought you up out of Egypt."[e] **29**One he set up in Bethel,[f] and the other in Dan.[g] **30**And this thing became a sin;[h] the people went even as far as Dan to worship the one there.

31Jeroboam built shrines[i] on high places and appointed priests[j] from all sorts of people, even though they were not Levites. **32**He instituted a festival on the fifteenth day of the eighth[k] month, like the festival held in Judah, and offered sacrifices on the altar. This he did in Bethel, sacrificing to the calves he had made. And at Bethel he also installed priests at the high places he had made. **33**On the fifteenth day of the eighth month, a month of his own choosing, he offered sacrifices on the altar he had built at Bethel.[l] So he instituted the festival for the Israelites and went up to the altar to make offerings.

The Man of God From Judah

13 By the word of the LORD a man of God[m] came from Judah to Bethel,[n] as Jeroboam was standing by the altar to make an offering. **2**He cried out against the altar by the word of the LORD: "O altar, altar! This is what the LORD says: 'A son named Josiah[o] will be born to the house of David. On you he will sacrifice the priests of the high places who now make offerings here, and human bones will be burned on you.' " **3**That same day the man of God gave a sign:[p] "This is the sign the LORD has declared: The altar will be split apart and the ashes on it will be poured out."

4When King Jeroboam heard what the man of God cried out against the altar at Bethel, he stretched out his hand from the altar and said, "Seize him!" But the hand he stretched out toward the man shriveled up, so that he could not pull it back. **5**Also, the altar was split apart and its ashes poured out according to the sign given by the man of God by the word of the LORD.

6Then the king said to the man of God, "Intercede[q] with the LORD your God and pray for me that my hand may be restored." So the man of God interceded with the LORD, and the king's hand was restored and became as it was before.

7The king said to the man of God, "Come home with me and have something to eat, and I will give you a gift."[r]

8But the man of God answered the king, "Even if you were to give me half your possessions,[s] I would not go with you, nor would I eat bread[t] or drink water here. **9**For I was commanded by the word of the LORD: 'You must not eat bread or drink water or return by the way you came.' " **10**So he took another road and did not return by the way he had come to Bethel.

11Now there was a certain old prophet living in Bethel, whose sons came and told him all that the man of God had done there that day. They also told their father what he had said to the king. **12**Their father asked them, "Which way did he go?" And his sons showed him which road the man of God from Judah had taken. **13**So he said to his sons, "Saddle the donkey for me." And when they had saddled the donkey for him, he mounted it **14**and rode after the

12:25 [a]Jdg 9:45 [b]Jdg 8:8,17
12:27 [c]Dt 12:5-6
12:28 [d]Ex 32:4; 2Ki 10:29; 17:16 [e]Ex 32:8
12:29 [f]Ge 28:19 [g]Jdg 18:27-31
12:30 [h]1Ki 13:34; 2Ki 17:21
12:31 [i]1Ki 13:32 [j]Nu 3:10; 1Ki 13:33; 2Ki 17:32; 2Ch 11:14-15; 13:9
12:32 [k]Lev 23:33-34; Nu 29:12
12:33 [l]Nu 15:39; 1Ki 13:1; Am 7:13
13:1 [m]2Ki 23:17 [n]1Ki 12:32-33
13:2 [o]2Ki 23:15-16, 20
13:3 [p]Jdg 6:17; Isa 7:14; Jn 2:11; 1Co 1:22
13:6 [q]Ex 8:8; 9:28; 10:17; Lk 6:27-28; Ac 8:24; Jas 5:16
13:7 [r]1Sa 9:7; 2Ki 5:15
13:8 [s]Nu 22:18; 24:13 [t]ver 16

[b]25 Hebrew *Penuel,* a variant of *Peniel*

man of God. He found him sitting
under an oak tree and asked, "Are
you the man of God who came from
Judah?"
"I am," he replied.
15 So the prophet said to him,
"Come home with me and eat."
16 The man of God said, "I cannot
turn back and go with you, nor can
I eat bread[a] or drink water with
you in this place. 17 I have been told
by the word of the LORD: 'You must
not eat bread or drink water there
or return by the way you came.' "
18 The old prophet answered, "I
too am a prophet, as you are. And
an angel said to me by the word of
the LORD: 'Bring him back with you
to your house so that he may eat
bread and drink water.' " (But he
was lying[b] to him.) 19 So the man
of God returned with him and ate
and drank in his house.
20 While they were sitting at the
table, the word of the LORD came to
the old prophet who had brought
him back. 21 He cried out to the
man of God who had come from Judah, "This is what the LORD says:
'You have defied[c] the word of the
LORD and have not kept the command the LORD your God gave you.
22 You came back and ate bread
and drank water in the place where
he told you not to eat or drink.
Therefore your body will not be
buried in the tomb of your fathers.' "
23 When the man of God had finished eating and drinking, the
prophet who had brought him back
saddled his donkey for him. 24 As
he went on his way, a lion[d] met
him on the road and killed him,
and his body was thrown down on
the road, with both the donkey and
the lion standing beside it. 25 Some
people who passed by saw the body
thrown down there, with the lion
standing beside the body, and they
went and reported it in the city
where the old prophet lived.
26 When the prophet who had
brought him back from his journey
heard of it, he said, "It is the man
of God who defied the word of the
LORD. The LORD has given him over
to the lion, which has mauled him
and killed him, as the word of the
LORD had warned him."
27 The prophet said to his sons,
"Saddle the donkey for me," and
they did so. 28 Then he went out
and found the body thrown down
on the road, with the donkey and
the lion standing beside it. The lion
had neither eaten the body nor
mauled the donkey. 29 So the
prophet picked up the body of the
man of God, laid it on the donkey,
and brought it back to his own city
to mourn for him and bury him.
30 Then he laid the body in his own
tomb, and they mourned over him
and said, "Oh, my brother!"[e]
31 After burying him, he said to
his sons, "When I die, bury me in
the grave where the man of God is
buried; lay my bones[f] beside his
bones. 32 For the message he declared by the word of the LORD
against the altar in Bethel and
against all the shrines on the high
places[g] in the towns of Samaria[h]
will certainly come true."[i]
33 Even after this, Jeroboam did
not change his evil ways, but once
more appointed priests for the high
places from all sorts[j] of people.
Anyone who wanted to become a
priest he consecrated for the high
places. 34 This was the sin[k] of the
house of Jeroboam that led to its
downfall and to its destruction[l]
from the face of the earth.

Ahijah's Prophecy Against Jeroboam

14 At that time Abijah son of
Jeroboam became ill, 2 and
Jeroboam said to his wife, "Go, disguise yourself, so you won't be recognized as the wife of Jeroboam.
Then go to Shiloh. Ahijah[m] the
prophet is there—the one who told
me I would be king over this people. 3 Take ten loaves of bread[n]
with you, some cakes and a jar of
honey, and go to him. He will tell
you what will happen to the boy."
4 So Jeroboam's wife did what he
said and went to Ahijah's house in
Shiloh.

13:16 [a] ver 8
13:18 [b] Dt 13:3
13:21 [c] ver 26
13:24 [d] 1Ki 20:36
13:30 [e] Jer 22:18
13:31 [f] 2Ki 23:18
13:32 [g] ver 2; Lev 26:30 [h] 1Ki 16:24,28 [i] 2Ki 23:16
13:33 [j] 1Ki 12:31; 2Ch 11:15; 13:9
13:34 [k] 1Ki 12:30 [l] 1Ki 14:10
14:2 [m] 1Sa 28:8; 2Sa 14:2, 1Ki 11:29
14:3 [n] 1Sa 9:7

Now Ahijah could not see; his
sight was gone because of his age.
5But the LORD had told Ahijah,
"Jeroboam's wife is coming to ask
you about her son, for he is ill, and
you are to give her such and such
an answer. When she arrives, she
will pretend to be someone else."
6So when Ahijah heard the
sound of her footsteps at the door,
he said, "Come in, wife of Jeroboam. Why this pretense? I have been
sent to you with bad news. **7**Go, tell
Jeroboam that this is what the
LORD, the God of Israel, says: 'I
raised you up from among the people and made you a leader[a] over
my people Israel. **8**I tore[b] the kingdom away from the house of David
and gave it to you, but you have not
been like my servant David, who
kept my commands and followed
me with all his heart, doing only
what was right[c] in my eyes. **9**You
have done more evil than all who
lived before you. You have made for
yourself other gods, idols[d] made of
metal; you have provoked me to anger and thrust me behind your
back.[e]
10" 'Because of this, I am going
to bring disaster on the house of
Jeroboam. I will cut off from Jeroboam every last male in Israel—
slave or free.[f] I will burn up the
house of Jeroboam as one burns
dung, until it is all gone.[g] **11**Dogs[h]
will eat those belonging to Jeroboam who die in the city, and the
birds of the air will feed on those
who die in the country. The LORD
has spoken!'
12"As for you, go back home.
When you set foot in your city, the
boy will die. **13**All Israel will mourn
for him and bury him. He is the
only one belonging to Jeroboam
who will be buried, because he is
the only one in the house of Jeroboam in whom the LORD, the God of
Israel, has found anything good.[i]
14"The LORD will raise up for
himself a king over Israel who will
cut off the family of Jeroboam.
This is the day! What? Yes, even
now.[c] **15**And the LORD will strike
Israel, so that it will be like a reed
swaying in the water. He will uproot[j] Israel from this good land
that he gave to their forefathers
and scatter them beyond the River,[d] because they provoked[k] the
LORD to anger by making Asherah[l]
poles.[e] **16**And he will give Israel up
because of the sins[m] Jeroboam has
committed and has caused Israel
to commit."
17Then Jeroboam's wife got up
and left and went to Tirzah.[n] As
soon as she stepped over the
threshold of the house, the boy
died. **18**They buried him, and all Israel mourned for him, as the LORD
had said through his servant the
prophet Ahijah.
19The other events of Jeroboam's reign, his wars and how he
ruled, are written in the book of the
annals of the kings of Israel. **20**He
reigned for twenty-two years and
then rested with his fathers. And
Nadab his son succeeded him as
king.

Rehoboam King of Judah

14:21,25–31pp — 2Ch 12:9–16

21Rehoboam son of Solomon
was king in Judah. He was forty-
one years old when he became
king, and he reigned seventeen
years in Jerusalem, the city the
LORD had chosen out of all the
tribes of Israel in which to put his
Name. His mother's name was Naamah; she was an Ammonite.[o]
22Judah[p] did evil in the eyes of
the LORD. By the sins they committed they stirred up his jealous anger[q] more than their fathers had
done. **23**They also set up for themselves high places, sacred stones[r]
and Asherah poles on every high
hill and under every spreading
tree.[s] **24**There were even male
shrine prostitutes[t] in the land; the
people engaged in all the detestable practices of the nations the
LORD had driven out before the Israelites.

14:7 [a] 2Sa 12:7-8; 1Ki 16:2
14:8 [b] 1Ki 11:31, 33,38 [c] 1Ki 15:5
14:9 [d] Ex 34:17; 1Ki 12:28; 2Ch 11:15 [e] Ne 9:26; Ps 50:17; Eze 23:35
14:10 [f] Dt 32:36; 1Ki 21:21; 2Ki 9:8-9; 14:26 [g] 1Ki 15:29
14:11 [h] 1Ki 16:4; 21:24
14:13 [i] 2Ch 12:12; 19:3
14:15 [j] Dt 29:28; 2Ki 15:29; 17:6; Ps 52:5 [k] Jos 23:15-16 [l] Ex 34:13; Dt 12:3
14:16 [m] 1Ki 12:30; 13:34; 15:30, 34; 16:2
14:17 [n] ver 12; 1Ki 15:33; 16:6-9
14:21 [o] ver 31; 1Ki 11:1; 2Ch 12:13
14:22 [p] 2Ch 12:1 [q] Dt 32:21; Ps 78:58; 1Co 10:22
14:23 [r] Dt 16:22; 2Ki 17:9-10; Eze 16:24-25 [s] Dt 12:2; Isa 57:5
14:24 [t] Dt 23:17; 1Ki 15:12; 2Ki 23:7

[c] *14* The meaning of the Hebrew for this sentence is uncertain. [d] *15* That is, the Euphrates [e] *15* That is, symbols of the goddess Asherah; here and elsewhere in 1 Kings

25In the fifth year of King Rehoboam, Shishak king of Egypt attacked[a] Jerusalem. 26He carried off the treasures of the temple[b] of the LORD and the treasures of the royal palace. He took everything, including all the gold shields[c] Solomon had made. 27So King Rehoboam made bronze shields to replace them and assigned these to the commanders of the guard on duty at the entrance to the royal palace. 28Whenever the king went to the LORD's temple, the guards bore the shields, and afterward they returned them to the guardroom.

29As for the other events of Rehoboam's reign, and all he did, are they not written in the book of the annals of the kings of Judah? 30There was continual warfare[d] between Rehoboam and Jeroboam. 31And Rehoboam rested with his fathers and was buried with them in the City of David. His mother's name was Naamah; she was an Ammonite.[e] And Abijah[f] his son succeeded him as king.

Abijah King of Judah

15:1–2,6–8pp — 2Ch 13:1–2,22–14:1

15 In the eighteenth year of the reign of Jeroboam son of Nebat, Abijah[g] became king of Judah, 2and he reigned in Jerusalem three years. His mother's name was Maacah[f] daughter of Abishalom.[h]

3He committed all the sins his father had done before him; his heart was not fully devoted[g] to the LORD his God, as the heart of David his forefather had been. 4Nevertheless, for David's sake the LORD his God gave him a lamp[h] in Jerusalem by raising up a son to succeed him and by making Jerusalem strong. 5For David had done what was right in the eyes of the LORD and had not failed to keep[i] any of the LORD's commands all the days of his life—except in the case of Uriah[j] the Hittite.

6There was war[k] between Rehoboam[i] and Jeroboam throughout Abijah's lifetime. 7As for the other events of Abijah's reign, and all he did, are they not written in the book of the annals of the kings of Judah? There was war between Abijah and Jeroboam. 8And Abijah rested with his fathers and was buried in the City of David. And Asa his son succeeded him as king.

Asa King of Judah

15:9–22pp — 2Ch 14:2–3; 15:16–16:6
15:23–24pp — 2Ch 16:11–17:1

9In the twentieth year of Jeroboam king of Israel, Asa became king of Judah, 10and he reigned in Jerusalem forty-one years. His grandmother's name was Maacah[l] daughter of Abishalom.

11Asa did what was right in the eyes of the LORD, as his father David had done. 12He expelled the male shrine prostitutes[m] from the land and got rid of all the idols his fathers had made. 13He even deposed his grandmother Maacah from her position as queen mother, because she had made a repulsive Asherah pole. Asa cut the pole down[n] and burned it in the Kidron Valley. 14Although he did not remove the high places, Asa's heart was fully committed[o] to the LORD all his life. 15He brought into the temple of the LORD the silver and gold and the articles that he and his father had dedicated.[p]

16There was war[q] between Asa and Baasha king of Israel throughout their reigns. 17Baasha king of Israel went up against Judah and fortified Ramah[r] to prevent anyone from leaving or entering the territory of Asa king of Judah.

18Asa then took all the silver and gold that was left in the treasuries of the LORD's temple[s] and of his own palace. He entrusted it to his officials and sent[t] them to Ben-

14:25 [a] 1Ki 11:40; 2Ch 12:2
14:26 [b] 1Ki 15:15,18 [c] 1Ki 10:17
14:30 [d] 1Ki 12:21; 15:6
14:31 [e] ver 21; 2Ch 12:16
15:2 [f] 2Ch 11:20; 13:2
15:3 [g] 1Ki 11:4; Ps 119:80
15:4 [h] 2Sa 21:17; 1Ki 11:36; 2Ch 21:7
15:5 [i] 1Ki 9:4; 14:8 [j] 2Sa 11:2-27; 12:9
15:6 [k] 1Ki 14:30
15:10 [l] ver 2
15:12 [m] 1Ki 14:24; 22:46
15:13 [n] Ex 32:20
15:14 [o] ver 3; 1Ki 8:61; 22:43
15:15 [p] 1Ki 7:51
15:16 [q] ver 32
15:17 [r] Jos 18:25; 1Ki 12:27
15:18 [s] ver 15; 1Ki 14:26 [t] 2Ki 12:18

[f] *31* Some Hebrew manuscripts and Septuagint (see also 2 Chron. 12:16); most Hebrew manuscripts *Abijam* [g] *1* Some Hebrew manuscripts and Septuagint (see also 2 Chron. 12:16); most Hebrew manuscripts *Abijam*; also in verses 7 and 8 [h] *2* A variant of *Absalom*; also in verse 10 [i] *6* Most Hebrew manuscripts; some Hebrew manuscripts and Syriac *Abijam* (that is, Abijah)

Hadad[a] son of Tabrimmon, the
son of Hezion, the king of Aram,
who was ruling in Damascus.
19"Let there be a treaty between
me and you," he said, "as there was
between my father and your father.
See, I am sending you a gift of silver
and gold. Now break your treaty
with Baasha king of Israel so he will
withdraw from me."
20Ben-Hadad agreed with King
Asa and sent the commanders of
his forces against the towns of Israel. He conquered[b] Ijon, Dan, Abel
Beth Maacah and all Kinnereth in
addition to Naphtali. **21**When Baasha heard this, he stopped building
Ramah and withdrew to Tirzah.
22Then King Asa issued an order to
all Judah—no one was exempt—
and they carried away from Ramah
the stones and timber Baasha had
been using there. With them King
Asa built up Geba[c] in Benjamin,
and also Mizpah.
23As for all the other events of
Asa's reign, all his achievements,
all he did and the cities he built,
are they not written in the book of
the annals of the kings of Judah? In
his old age, however, his feet became diseased. **24**Then Asa rested
with his fathers and was buried
with them in the city of his father
David. And Jehoshaphat[d] his son
succeeded him as king.

Nadab King of Israel

25Nadab son of Jeroboam became king of Israel in the second
year of Asa king of Judah, and he
reigned over Israel two years. **26**He
did evil in the eyes of the LORD,
walking in the ways of his father[e]
and in his sin, which he had caused
Israel to commit.
27Baasha son of Ahijah of the
house of Issachar plotted against
him, and he struck him down[f] at
Gibbethon,[g] a Philistine town,
while Nadab and all Israel were besieging it. **28**Baasha killed Nadab
in the third year of Asa king of Judah and succeeded him as king.
29As soon as he began to reign,
he killed Jeroboam's whole family.[h] He did not leave Jeroboam
anyone that breathed, but destroyed them all, according to the
word of the LORD given through his
servant Ahijah the Shilonite—
30because of the sins[i] Jeroboam
had committed and had caused Israel to commit, and because he
provoked the LORD, the God of Israel, to anger.
31As for the other events of Nadab's reign, and all he did, are they
not written in the book of the annals of the kings of Israel? **32**There
was war[j] between Asa and Baasha
king of Israel throughout their
reigns.

Baasha King of Israel

33In the third year of Asa king of
Judah, Baasha son of Ahijah became king of all Israel in Tirzah,
and he reigned twenty-four years.
34He did evil[k] in the eyes of the
LORD, walking in the ways of Jeroboam and in his sin, which he had
caused Israel to commit.

16 Then the word of the LORD
came to Jehu[l] son of Ha-
nani[m] against Baasha: **2**"I lifted
you up from the dust[n] and made
you leader[o] of my people Israel,
but you walked in the ways of Jeroboam and caused[p] my people Israel to sin and to provoke me to anger
by their sins. **3**So I am about to consume Baasha and his house,[q] and
I will make your house like that of
Jeroboam son of Nebat. **4**Dogs[r]
will eat those belonging to Baasha
who die in the city, and the birds of
the air will feed on those who die in
the country."
5As for the other events of Baasha's reign, what he did and his
achievements, are they not written
in the book of the annals[s] of the
kings of Israel? **6**Baasha rested with
his fathers and was buried in Tirzah.[t] And Elah his son succeeded
him as king.
7Moreover, the word of the LORD
came[u] through the prophet Jehu[v]
son of Hanani to Baasha and his
house, because of all the evil he
had done in the eyes of the LORD,
provoking him to anger by the
things he did, and becoming like

15:18 [a] 1Ki 11:23-24
15:20 [b] Jdg 18:29; 2Sa 20:14; 2Ki 15:29
15:22 [c] Jos 18:24; 21:17
15:24 [d] Mt 1:8
15:26 [e] 1Ki 12:30; 14:16
15:27 [f] 1Ki 14:14 [g] Jos 19:44; 21:23
15:29 [h] 1Ki 14:10,14
15:30 [i] 1Ki 14:9,16
15:32 [j] ver 16
15:34 [k] ver 26; 1Ki 12:28-29; 13:33; 14:16
16:1 [l] ver 7; 2Ch 19:2; 20:34 [m] 2Ch 16:7
16:2 [n] 1Sa 2:8 [o] 1Ki 14:7-9 [p] 1Ki 15:34
16:3 [q] ver 11; 1Ki 14:10; 15:29; 21:22
16:4 [r] 1Ki 14:11
16:5 [s] 1Ki 14:19; 15:31
16:6 [t] 1Ki 14:17; 15:33
16:7 [u] 1Ki 15:27,29 [v] ver 1

the house of Jeroboam—and also because he destroyed it.

Elah King of Israel

8In the twenty-sixth year of Asa king of Judah, Elah son of Baasha became king of Israel, and he reigned in Tirzah two years.

9Zimri, one of his officials, who had command of half his chariots, plotted against him. Elah was in Tirzah at the time, getting drunk[a] in the home of Arza, the man in charge[b] of the palace at Tirzah. **10**Zimri came in, struck him down and killed him in the twenty-seventh year of Asa king of Judah. Then he succeeded him as king.

11As soon as he began to reign and was seated on the throne, he killed off Baasha's whole family.[c] He did not spare a single male, whether relative or friend. **12**So Zimri destroyed the whole family of Baasha, in accordance with the word of the LORD spoken against Baasha through the prophet Jehu— **13**because of all the sins Baasha and his son Elah had committed and had caused Israel to commit, so that they provoked the LORD, the God of Israel, to anger by their worthless idols.[d]

14As for the other events of Elah's reign, and all he did, are they not written in the book of the annals of the kings of Israel?

Zimri King of Israel

15In the twenty-seventh year of Asa king of Judah, Zimri reigned in Tirzah seven days. The army was encamped near Gibbethon,[e] a Philistine town. **16**When the Israelites in the camp heard that Zimri had plotted against the king and murdered him, they proclaimed Omri, the commander of the army, king over Israel that very day there in the camp. **17**Then Omri and all the Israelites with him withdrew from Gibbethon and laid siege to Tirzah. **18**When Zimri saw that the city was taken, he went into the citadel of the royal palace and set the palace on fire around him. So he died, **19**because of the sins he had committed, doing evil in the eyes of the LORD and walking in the ways of Jeroboam and in the sin he had committed and had caused Israel to commit.

20As for the other events of Zimri's reign, and the rebellion he carried out, are they not written in the book of the annals of the kings of Israel?

Omri King of Israel

21Then the people of Israel were split into two factions; half supported Tibni son of Ginath for king, and the other half supported Omri. **22**But Omri's followers proved stronger than those of Tibni son of Ginath. So Tibni died and Omri became king.

23In the thirty-first year of Asa king of Judah, Omri became king of Israel, and he reigned twelve years, six of them in Tirzah.[f] **24**He bought the hill of Samaria from Shemer for two talents[i] of silver and built a city on the hill, calling it Samaria,[g] after Shemer, the name of the former owner of the hill.

25But Omri did evil[h] in the eyes of the LORD and sinned more than all those before him. **26**He walked in all the ways of Jeroboam son of Nebat and in his sin, which he had caused[i] Israel to commit, so that they provoked the LORD, the God of Israel, to anger by their worthless idols.[j]

27As for the other events of Omri's reign, what he did and the things he achieved, are they not written in the book of the annals of the kings of Israel? **28**Omri rested with his fathers and was buried in Samaria. And Ahab his son succeeded him as king.

Ahab Becomes King of Israel

29In the thirty-eighth year of Asa king of Judah, Ahab son of Omri became king of Israel, and he reigned in Samaria over Israel twenty-two years. **30**Ahab son of

16:9 [a] 2Ki 9:30-33 [b] 1Ki 18:3
16:11 [c] ver 3
16:13 [d] Dt 32:21; 1Sa 12:21; Isa 41:29
16:15 [e] Jos 19:44; 1Ki 15:27
16:23 [f] 1Ki 15:21
16:24 [g] 1Ki 13:32; Jn 4:4
16:25 [h] Dt 4:25; Mic 6:16
16:26 [i] ver 19 [j] Dt 32:21

i24 That is, about 150 pounds (about 70 kilograms)

Omri did more[a] evil in the eyes of
the LORD than any of those before
him. 31He not only considered it
trivial to commit the sins of Jeroboam son of Nebat, but he also
married[b] Jezebel daughter[c] of
Ethbaal king of the Sidonians, and
began to serve Baal[d] and worship
him. 32He set up an altar for Baal in
the temple[e] of Baal that he built in
Samaria. 33Ahab also made an
Asherah pole[f] and did more[g] to
provoke the LORD, the God of Israel,
to anger than did all the kings of
Israel before him.

34In Ahab's time, Hiel of Bethel
rebuilt Jericho. He laid its foundations at the cost of his firstborn son
Abiram, and he set up its gates at
the cost of his youngest son Segub,
in accordance with the word of the
LORD spoken by Joshua son of
Nun.[h]

Elijah Fed by Ravens

17 Now Elijah[i] the Tishbite,
from Tishbe[k] in Gilead,[j]
said to Ahab, "As the LORD, the God
of Israel, lives, whom I serve, there
will be neither dew nor rain[k] in the
next few years except at my word."

2Then the word of the LORD came
to Elijah: 3"Leave here, turn eastward and hide in the Kerith Ravine,
east of the Jordan. 4You will drink
from the brook, and I have ordered
the ravens[l] to feed you there."

5So he did what the LORD had
told him. He went to the Kerith Ravine, east of the Jordan, and stayed
there. 6The ravens brought him
bread and meat in the morning[m]
and bread and meat in the evening,
and he drank from the brook.

The Widow at Zarephath

7Some time later the brook dried
up because there had been no rain
in the land. 8Then the word of the
LORD came to him: 9"Go at once to
Zarephath[n] of Sidon and stay
there. I have commanded a widow[o] in that place to supply you
with food." 10So he went to Zarephath. When he came to the town
gate, a widow was there gathering
sticks. He called to her and asked,

16:30 [a]ver 25; 1Ki 14:9
16:31 [b]Dt 7:3; 1Ki 11:2 [c]Jdg 18:7; 2Ki 9:34 [d]2Ki 10:18; 17:16
16:32 [e]2Ki 10:21, 27; 11:18
16:33 [f]2Ki 13:6 [g]ver 29,30; 1Ki 14:9; 21:25
16:34 [h]Jos 6:26
17:1 [i]Mal 4:5; Jas 5:17 [j]Jdg 12:4 [k]Dt 10:8; 1Ki 18:1; 2Ki 3:14; Lk 4:25
17:4 [l]Ge 8:7
17:6 [m]Ex 16:8
17:9 [n]Ob 1:20 [o]Lk 4:26
17:10 [p]Ge 24:17; Jn 4:7
17:12 [q]ver 1; 2Ki 4:2
17:18 [r]2Ki 3:13; Lk 5:8
17:21 [s]2Ki 4:34; Ac 20:10

"Would you bring me a little water
in a jar so I may have a drink?"[p]
11As she was going to get it, he
called, "And bring me, please, a
piece of bread."

12"As surely as the LORD your
God lives," she replied, "I don't
have any bread—only a handful of
flour in a jar and a little oil[q] in a
jug. I am gathering a few sticks to
take home and make a meal for
myself and my son, that we may eat
it—and die."

13Elijah said to her, "Don't be
afraid. Go home and do as you have
said. But first make a small cake of
bread for me from what you have
and bring it to me, and then make
something for yourself and your
son. 14For this is what the LORD,
the God of Israel, says: 'The jar of
flour will not be used up and the
jug of oil will not run dry until the
day the LORD gives rain on the
land.' "

15She went away and did as Elijah had told her. So there was food
every day for Elijah and for the
woman and her family. 16For the
jar of flour was not used up and the
jug of oil did not run dry, in keeping
with the word of the LORD spoken
by Elijah.

17Some time later the son of the
woman who owned the house became ill. He grew worse and worse,
and finally stopped breathing.
18She said to Elijah, "What do you
have against me, man of God? Did
you come to remind me of my sin[r]
and kill my son?"

19"Give me your son," Elijah replied. He took him from her arms,
carried him to the upper room
where he was staying, and laid him
on his bed. 20Then he cried out to
the LORD, "O LORD my God, have
you brought tragedy also upon this
widow I am staying with, by causing her son to die?" 21Then he
stretched[s] himself out on the boy
three times and cried to the LORD,
"O LORD my God, let this boy's life
return to him!"

22The LORD heard Elijah's cry,

[k]*1* Or *Tishbite, of the settlers*

and the boy's life returned to him,
and he lived. 23Elijah picked up the
child and carried him down from
the room into the house. He gave
him to his mother and said, "Look,
your son is alive!"
24Then the woman said to Elijah, "Now I know[a] that you are a
man of God and that the word of
the LORD from your mouth is the
truth."[b]

Elijah and Obadiah

18 After a long time, in the
third[c] year, the word of the
LORD came to Elijah: "Go and
present yourself to Ahab, and I will
send rain[d] on the land." 2So Elijah
went to present himself to Ahab.
Now the famine was severe in
Samaria, 3and Ahab had summoned Obadiah, who was in
charge[e] of his palace. (Obadiah
was a devout believer[f] in the LORD.
4While Jezebel[g] was killing off the
LORD's prophets, Obadiah had tak-
en a hundred prophets and hidden[h] them in two caves, fifty in
each, and had supplied them with
food and water.) 5Ahab had said to
Obadiah, "Go through the land to
all the springs and valleys. Maybe
we can find some grass to keep the
horses and mules alive so we will
not have to kill any of our animals."
6So they divided the land they were
to cover, Ahab going in one direction and Obadiah in another.
7As Obadiah was walking along,
Elijah met him. Obadiah recognized[i] him, bowed down to the
ground, and said, "Is it really you,
my lord Elijah?"
8"Yes," he replied. "Go tell your
master, 'Elijah is here.' "
9"What have I done wrong,"
asked Obadiah, "that you are
handing your servant over to Ahab
to be put to death? 10As surely as
the LORD your God lives, there is
not a nation or kingdom where my
master has not sent someone to
look[j] for you. And whenever a nation or kingdom claimed you were
not there, he made them swear
they could not find you. 11But now
you tell me to go to my master and
say, 'Elijah is here.' 12I don't know
where the Spirit[k] of the LORD may
carry you when I leave you. If I go
and tell Ahab and he doesn't find
you, he will kill me. Yet I your servant have worshiped the LORD since
my youth. 13Haven't you heard, my
lord, what I did while Jezebel was
killing the prophets of the LORD? I
hid a hundred of the LORD's prophets in two caves, fifty in each, and
supplied them with food and water.
14And now you tell me to go to my
master and say, 'Elijah is here.' He
will kill me!"
15Elijah said, "As the LORD Almighty lives, whom I serve, I will
surely present[l] myself to Ahab today."

Elijah on Mount Carmel

16So Obadiah went to meet Ahab
and told him, and Ahab went to
meet Elijah. 17When he saw Elijah,
he said to him, "Is that you, you
troubler[m] of Israel?"
18"I have not made trouble for Israel," Elijah replied. "But you[n]
and your father's family have. You
have abandoned[o] the LORD's commands and have followed the Baals. 19Now summon the people
from all over Israel to meet me on
Mount Carmel.[p] And bring the
four hundred and fifty prophets of
Baal and the four hundred prophets of Asherah, who eat at Jezebel's
table."
20So Ahab sent word throughout
all Israel and assembled the prophets on Mount Carmel. 21Elijah
went before the people and said,
"How long will you waver[q] between two opinions? If the LORD is
God, follow him; but if Baal is God,
follow him."
But the people said nothing.
22Then Elijah said to them, "I
am the only one of the LORD's
prophets left,[r] but Baal has four
hundred and fifty prophets.[s] 23Get
two bulls for us. Let them choose
one for themselves, and let them
cut it into pieces and put it on the
wood but not set fire to it. I will
prepare the other bull and put it on
the wood but not set fire to it.

17:24 [a] Jn 3:2; 16:30 [b] Ps 119:43; Jn 17:17
18:1 [c] 1Ki 17:1; Lk 4:25; Jas 5:17 [d] Dt 28:12
18:3 [e] 1Ki 16:9 [f] Ne 7:2
18:4 [g] 2Ki 9:7 [h] ver 13; Isa 16:3
18:7 [i] 2Ki 1:8
18:10 [j] 1Ki 17:3
18:12 [k] 2Ki 2:16; Eze 3:14; Ac 8:39
18:15 [l] 1Ki 17:1
18:17 [m] Jos 7:25; 1Ki 21:20; Ac 16:20
18:18 [n] 1Ki 16:31, 33; 21:25 [o] 2Ch 15:2
18:19 [p] Jos 19:26
18:21 [q] Jos 24:15; 2Ki 17:41; Mt 6:24
18:22 [r] 1Ki 19:10 [s] ver 19

24Then you call on the name of
your god, and I will call on the
name of the LORD. The god who answers by fire[a]—he is God."
Then all the people said, "What
you say is good."
25Elijah said to the prophets of
Baal, "Choose one of the bulls and
prepare it first, since there are so
many of you. Call on the name of
your god, but do not light the fire."
26So they took the bull given them
and prepared it.
Then they called on the name of
Baal from morning till noon. "O
Baal, answer us!" they shouted.
But there was no response;[b] no
one answered. And they danced
around the altar they had made.
27At noon Elijah began to taunt
them. "Shout louder!" he said.
"Surely he is a god! Perhaps he is
deep in thought, or busy, or traveling. Maybe he is sleeping and must
be awakened."[c] **28**So they shouted
louder and slashed[d] themselves
with swords and spears, as was
their custom, until their blood
flowed. **29**Midday passed, and they
continued their frantic prophesying until the time for the evening
sacrifice.[e] But there was no response, no one answered, no one
paid attention.[f]
30Then Elijah said to all the people, "Come here to me." They came
to him, and he repaired the altar[g]
of the LORD, which was in ruins.
31Elijah took twelve stones, one for
each of the tribes descended from
Jacob, to whom the word of the
LORD had come, saying, "Your
name shall be Israel."[h] **32**With the
stones he built an altar in the
name[i] of the LORD, and he dug a
trench around it large enough to
hold two seahs[1] of seed. **33**He arranged[j] the wood, cut the bull into
pieces and laid it on the wood.
Then he said to them, "Fill four
large jars with water and pour it on
the offering and on the wood."
34"Do it again," he said, and they
did it again.
"Do it a third time," he ordered,
and they did it the third time.
35The water ran down around the
altar and even filled the trench.
36At the time of sacrifice, the
prophet Elijah stepped forward and
prayed: "O LORD, God of Abraham,[k] Isaac and Israel, let it be
known[l] today that you are God in
Israel and that I am your servant
and have done all these things at
your command.[m] **37**Answer me, O
LORD, answer me, so these people
will know that you, O LORD, are
God, and that you are turning their
hearts back again."
38Then the fire[n] of the LORD fell
and burned up the sacrifice, the
wood, the stones and the soil, and
also licked up the water in the
trench.
39When all the people saw this,
they fell prostrate and cried, "The
LORD—he is God! The LORD—he is
God!"[o]
40Then Elijah commanded
them, "Seize the prophets of Baal.
Don't let anyone get away!" They
seized them, and Elijah had them
brought down to the Kishon Valley[p] and slaughtered[q] there.
41And Elijah said to Ahab, "Go,
eat and drink, for there is the
sound of a heavy rain." **42**So Ahab
went off to eat and drink, but Elijah
climbed to the top of Carmel, bent
down to the ground and put his
face between his knees.[r]
43"Go and look toward the sea,"
he told his servant. And he went up
and looked.
"There is nothing there," he
said.
Seven times Elijah said, "Go
back."
44The seventh time the servant
reported, "A cloud[s] as small as a
man's hand is rising from the sea."
So Elijah said, "Go and tell
Ahab, 'Hitch up your chariot and
go down before the rain stops
you.' "
45Meanwhile, the sky grew black
with clouds, the wind rose, a heavy
rain came on and Ahab rode off to
Jezreel. **46**The power[t] of the LORD

132 That is, probably about 13 quarts (about 15 liters)

18:24 [a]ver 38; 1Ch 21:26
18:26 [b]Ps 115:4-5; Jer 10:5; 1Co 8:4; 12:2
18:27 [c]Hab 2:19
18:28 [d]Lev 19:28; Dt 14:1
18:29 [e]Ex 29:41 [f]ver 26
18:30 [g]1Ki 19:10
18:31 [h]Ge 32:28; 35:10; 2Ki 17:34
18:32 [i]Col 3:17
18:33 [j]Ge 22:9; Lev 1:6-8
18:36 [k]Ex 3:6; Mt 22:32 [l]1Ki 8:43; 2Ki 19:19 [m]Nu 16:28
18:38 [n]Lev 9:24; Jdg 6:21; 1Ch 21:26; 2Ch 7:1; Job 1:16
18:39 [o]ver 24
18:40 [p]Jdg 4:7 [q]Dt 13:5; 18:20; 2Ki 10:24-25
18:42 [r]ver 19-20; Jas 5:18
18:44 [s]Lk 12:54
18:46 [t]2Ki 3:15

came upon Elijah and, tucking his cloak into his belt,[a] he ran ahead of Ahab all the way to Jezreel.

Elijah Flees to Horeb

19 Now Ahab told Jezebel everything Elijah had done and how he had killed[b] all the prophets with the sword. 2So Jezebel sent a messenger to Elijah to say, "May the gods deal with me, be it ever so severely,[c] if by this time tomorrow I do not make your life like that of one of them."

3Elijah was afraid[m] and ran[d] for his life. When he came to Beersheba in Judah, he left his servant there, 4while he himself went a day's journey into the desert. He came to a broom tree, sat down under it and prayed that he might die. "I have had enough, LORD," he said. "Take my life;[e] I am no better than my ancestors." 5Then he lay down under the tree and fell asleep.[f]

All at once an angel touched him and said, "Get up and eat." 6He looked around, and there by his head was a cake of bread baked over hot coals, and a jar of water. He ate and drank and then lay down again.

7The angel of the LORD came back a second time and touched him and said, "Get up and eat, for the journey is too much for you." 8So he got up and ate and drank. Strengthened by that food, he traveled forty[g] days and forty nights until he reached Horeb,[h] the mountain of God. 9There he went into a cave[i] and spent the night.

The LORD Appears to Elijah

And the word of the LORD came to him: "What are you doing here, Elijah?"

10He replied, "I have been very zealous[j] for the LORD God Almighty. The Israelites have rejected your covenant, broken down your altars, and put your prophets to death with the sword. I am the only one left,[k] and now they are trying to kill me too."

11The LORD said, "Go out and stand on the mountain[l] in the presence of the LORD, for the LORD is about to pass by."

Then a great and powerful wind[m] tore the mountains apart and shattered the rocks before the LORD, but the LORD was not in the wind. After the wind there was an earthquake, but the LORD was not in the earthquake. 12After the earthquake came a fire, but the LORD was not in the fire. And after the fire came a gentle whisper.[n] 13When Elijah heard it, he pulled his cloak over his face[o] and went out and stood at the mouth of the cave.

Then a voice said to him, "What are you doing here, Elijah?"

14He replied, "I have been very zealous for the LORD God Almighty. The Israelites have rejected your covenant, broken down your altars, and put your prophets to death with the sword. I am the only one left,[p] and now they are trying to kill me too."

15The LORD said to him, "Go back the way you came, and go to the Desert of Damascus. When you get there, anoint Hazael[q] king over Aram. 16Also, anoint[r] Jehu son of Nimshi king over Israel, and anoint Elisha[s] son of Shaphat from Abel Meholah to succeed you as prophet. 17Jehu will put to death any who escape the sword of Hazael,[t] and Elisha will put to death any who escape the sword of Jehu. 18Yet I reserve[u] seven thousand in Israel—all whose knees have not bowed down to Baal and all whose mouths have not kissed[v] him."

The Call of Elisha

19So Elijah went from there and found Elisha son of Shaphat. He was plowing with twelve yoke of oxen, and he himself was driving the twelfth pair. Elijah went up to him and threw his cloak[w] around him. 20Elisha then left his oxen and ran after Elijah. "Let me kiss my father and mother good-by,"[x] he said, "and then I will come with you."

m3 Or *Elijah saw*

18:46 [a] 2Ki 4:29; 9:1
19:1 [b] 1Ki 18:40
19:2 [c] 1Ki 20:10; 2Ki 6:31; Ru 1:17
19:3 [d] Ge 31:21
19:4 [e] Nu 11:15; Jer 20:18; Jnh 4:8
19:5 [f] Ge 28:11
19:8 [g] Ex 24:18; 34:28; Dt 9:9-11,18; Mt 4:2 [h] Ex 3:1
19:9 [i] Ex 33:22
19:10 [j] Nu 25:13 [k] 1Ki 18:4,22; Ro 11:3*
19:11 [l] Ex 24:12 [m] Eze 1:4; 37:7
19:12 [n] Job 4:16; Zec 4:6
19:13 [o] ver 9; Ex 3:6
19:14 [p] ver 10
19:15 [q] 2Ki 8:7-15
19:16 [r] 2Ki 9:1-3,6 [s] ver 21; 2Ki 2:9,15
19:17 [t] 2Ki 8:12,29; 9:14; 13:3,7, 22
19:18 [u] Ro 11:4* [v] Hos 13:2
19:19 [w] 2Ki 2:8,14
19:20 [x] Mt 8:21-22; Lk 9:61

"Go back," Elijah replied. "What have I done to you?"

21 So Elisha left him and went back. He took his yoke of oxen[a] and slaughtered them. He burned the plowing equipment to cook the meat and gave it to the people, and they ate. Then he set out to follow Elijah and became his attendant.[b]

Ben-Hadad Attacks Samaria

20 Now Ben-Hadad[c] king of Aram mustered his entire army. Accompanied by thirty-two kings with their horses and chariots, he went up and besieged Samaria and attacked it. 2 He sent messengers into the city to Ahab king of Israel, saying, "This is what Ben-Hadad says: 3 'Your silver and gold are mine, and the best of your wives and children are mine.' "

4 The king of Israel answered, "Just as you say, my lord the king. I and all I have are yours."

5 The messengers came again and said, "This is what Ben-Hadad says: 'I sent to demand your silver and gold, your wives and your children. 6 But about this time tomorrow I am going to send my officials to search your palace and the houses of your officials. They will seize everything you value and carry it away.' "

7 The king of Israel summoned all the elders of the land and said to them, "See how this man is looking for trouble![d] When he sent for my wives and my children, my silver and my gold, I did not refuse him."

8 The elders and the people all answered, "Don't listen to him or agree to his demands."

9 So he replied to Ben-Hadad's messengers, "Tell my lord the king, 'Your servant will do all you demanded the first time, but this demand I cannot meet.' " They left and took the answer back to Ben-Hadad.

10 Then Ben-Hadad sent another message to Ahab: "May the gods deal with me, be it ever so severely, if enough dust[e] remains in Samaria to give each of my men a handful."

11 The king of Israel answered, "Tell him: 'One who puts on his armor should not boast[f] like one who takes it off.' "

12 Ben-Hadad heard this message while he and the kings were drinking[g] in their tents,[n] and he ordered his men: "Prepare to attack." So they prepared to attack the city.

Ahab Defeats Ben-Hadad

13 Meanwhile a prophet came to Ahab king of Israel and announced, "This is what the LORD says: 'Do you see this vast army? I will give it into your hand today, and then you will know[h] that I am the LORD.' "

14 "But who will do this?" asked Ahab.

The prophet replied, "This is what the LORD says: 'The young officers of the provincial commanders will do it.' "

"And who will start[i] the battle?" he asked.

The prophet answered, "You will."

15 So Ahab summoned the young officers of the provincial commanders, 232 men. Then he assembled the rest of the Israelites, 7,000 in all. 16 They set out at noon while Ben-Hadad and the 32 kings allied with him were in their tents getting drunk.[j] 17 The young officers of the provincial commanders went out first.

Now Ben-Hadad had dispatched scouts, who reported, "Men are advancing from Samaria."

18 He said, "If they have come out for peace, take them alive; if they have come out for war, take them alive."

19 The young officers of the provincial commanders marched out of the city with the army behind them 20 and each one struck down his opponent. At that, the Arameans fled, with the Israelites in pursuit. But Ben-Hadad king of Aram escaped on horseback with some of his horsemen. 21 The king of Israel advanced and overpowered the

[n] *12* Or *in Succoth*; also in verse 16

19:21 [a] 2Sa 24:22 [b] ver 16
20:1 [c] 1Ki 15:18; 22:31; 2Ki 6:24
20:7 [d] 2Ki 5:7
20:10 [e] 2Sa 22:43; 1Ki 19:2
20:11 [f] Pr 27:1; Jer 9:23
20:12 [g] ver 16; 1Ki 16:9
20:13 [h] ver 28; Ex 6:7
20:14 [i] Jdg 1:1
20:16 [j] ver 12; 1Ki 16:9

horses and chariots and inflicted heavy losses on the Arameans.

[22]Afterward, the prophet[a] came to the king of Israel and said, "Strengthen your position and see what must be done, because next spring[b] the king of Aram will attack you again."

[23]Meanwhile, the officials of the king of Aram advised him, "Their gods are gods[c] of the hills. That is why they were too strong for us. But if we fight them on the plains, surely we will be stronger than they. [24]Do this: Remove all the kings from their commands and replace them with other officers. [25]You must also raise an army like the one you lost—horse for horse and chariot for chariot—so we can fight Israel on the plains. Then surely we will be stronger than they." He agreed with them and acted accordingly.

[26]The next spring[d] Ben-Hadad mustered the Arameans and went up to Aphek[e] to fight against Israel. [27]When the Israelites were also mustered and given provisions, they marched out to meet them. The Israelites camped opposite them like two small flocks of goats, while the Arameans covered the countryside.[f]

[28]The man of God came up and told the king of Israel, "This is what the LORD says: 'Because the Arameans think the LORD is a god of the hills and not a god[g] of the valleys, I will deliver this vast army into your hands, and you will know[h] that I am the LORD.' "

[29]For seven days they camped opposite each other, and on the seventh day the battle was joined. The Israelites inflicted a hundred thousand casualties on the Aramean foot soldiers in one day. [30]The rest of them escaped to the city of Aphek,[i] where the wall collapsed on twenty-seven thousand of them. And Ben-Hadad fled to the city and hid[j] in an inner room.

[31]His officials said to him, "Look, we have heard that the kings of the house of Israel are merciful. Let us go to the king of Israel with sackcloth[k] around our waists and ropes around our heads. Perhaps he will spare your life."

[32]Wearing sackcloth around their waists and ropes around their heads, they went to the king of Israel and said, "Your servant Ben-Hadad says: 'Please let me live.' "

The king answered, "Is he still alive? He is my brother."

[33]The men took this as a good sign and were quick to pick up his word. "Yes, your brother Ben-Hadad!" they said.

"Go and get him," the king said. When Ben-Hadad came out, Ahab had him come up into his chariot.

[34]"I will return the cities[l] my father took from your father," Ben-Hadad offered. "You may set up your own market areas in Damascus,[m] as my father did in Samaria."

Ahab said, "On the basis of a treaty[n] I will set you free." So he made a treaty with him, and let him go.

A Prophet Condemns Ahab

[35]By the word of the LORD one of the sons of the prophets said to his companion, "Strike me with your weapon," but the man refused.[o]

[36]So the prophet said, "Because you have not obeyed the LORD, as soon as you leave me a lion[p] will kill you." And after the man went away, a lion found him and killed him.

[37]The prophet found another man and said, "Strike me, please." So the man struck him and wounded him. [38]Then the prophet went and stood by the road waiting for the king. He disguised himself with his headband down over his eyes. [39]As the king passed by, the prophet called out to him, "Your servant went into the thick of the battle, and someone came to me with a captive and said, 'Guard this man. If he is missing, it will be your life for his life,[q] or you must pay a talent[o] of silver.' [40]While your ser-

20:22 [a]ver 13 [b]ver 26; 2Sa 11:1
20:23 [c]1Ki 14:23; Ro 1:21-23
20:26 [d]ver 22 [e]2Ki 13:17
20:27 [f]Jdg 6:6; 1Sa 13:6
20:28 [g]ver 23 [h]ver 13
20:30 [i]ver 26 [j]1Ki 22:25; 2Ch 18:24
20:31 [k]Ge 37:34
20:34 [l]1Ki 15:20 [m]Jer 49:23-27 [n]Ex 23:32
20:35 [o]1Ki 13:21; 2Ki 2:3-7
20:36 [p]1Ki 13:24
20:39 [q]2Ki 10:24

[o]39 That is, about 75 pounds (about 34 kilograms)

vant was busy here and there, the
man disappeared."
"That is your sentence," the king
of Israel said. "You have pronounced it yourself."
41Then the prophet quickly removed the headband from his eyes,
and the king of Israel recognized
him as one of the prophets. **42**He
said to the king, "This is what the
LORD says: 'You have set free a man
I had determined should die.[p][a]
Therefore it is your life for his life,[b]
your people for his people.' " **43**Sullen and angry,[c] the king of Israel
went to his palace in Samaria.

Naboth's Vineyard

21 Some time later there was
an incident involving a
vineyard belonging to Naboth[d] the
Jezreelite. The vineyard was in Jezreel,[e] close to the palace of Ahab
king of Samaria. **2**Ahab said to Naboth, "Let me have your vineyard
to use for a vegetable garden, since
it is close to my palace. In exchange I will give you a better vineyard or, if you prefer, I will pay you
whatever it is worth."
3But Naboth replied, "The LORD
forbid that I should give you the inheritance[f] of my fathers."
4So Ahab went home, sullen and
angry[g] because Naboth the Jezreelite had said, "I will not give you
the inheritance of my fathers." He
lay on his bed sulking and refused
to eat.
5His wife Jezebel came in and
asked him, "Why are you so sullen?
Why won't you eat?"
6He answered her, "Because I
said to Naboth the Jezreelite, 'Sell
me your vineyard; or if you prefer,
I will give you another vineyard in
its place.' But he said, 'I will not
give you my vineyard.' "
7Jezebel his wife said, "Is this
how you act as king over Israel? Get
up and eat! Cheer up. I'll get you
the vineyard[h] of Naboth the Jezreelite."
8So she wrote letters in Ahab's
name, placed his seal[i] on them,
and sent them to the elders and nobles who lived in Naboth's city
with him. **9**In those letters she
wrote:

"Proclaim a day of fasting
and seat Naboth in a prominent place among the people.
10But seat two scoundrels[j]
opposite him and have them
testify that he has cursed[k]
both God and the king. Then
take him out and stone him to
death."

11So the elders and nobles who
lived in Naboth's city did as Jezebel directed in the letters she had
written to them. **12**They proclaimed a fast[l] and seated Naboth
in a prominent place among the
people. **13**Then two scoundrels
came and sat opposite him and
brought charges against Naboth
before the people, saying, "Naboth
has cursed both God and the king."
So they took him outside the city
and stoned him to death.[m] **14**Then
they sent word to Jezebel: "Naboth
has been stoned and is dead."
15As soon as Jezebel heard that
Naboth had been stoned to death,
she said to Ahab, "Get up and take
possession of the vineyard[n] of Naboth the Jezreelite that he refused
to sell you. He is no longer alive,
but dead." **16**When Ahab heard
that Naboth was dead, he got up
and went down to take possession
of Naboth's vineyard.
17Then the word of the LORD
came to Elijah the Tishbite: **18**"Go
down to meet Ahab king of Israel,
who rules in Samaria. He is now in
Naboth's vineyard, where he has
gone to take possession of it. **19**Say
to him, 'This is what the LORD says:
Have you not murdered a man and
seized his property?' Then say to
him, 'This is what the LORD says: In
the place where dogs licked up Naboth's blood,[o] dogs[p] will lick up
your blood—yes, yours!' "
20Ahab said to Elijah, "So you
have found me, my enemy!"[q]
"I have found you," he answered,
"because you have sold[r] yourself

20:42 [a] Jer 48:10 [b] ver 39; Jos 2:14; 1Ki 22:31-37
20:43 [c] 1Ki 21:4
21:1 [d] 2Ki 9:21 [e] 1Ki 18:45-46
21:3 [f] Lev 25:23; Nu 36:7; Eze 46:18
21:4 [g] 1Ki 20:43
21:7 [h] 1Sa 8:14
21:8 [i] Ge 38:18; Est 3:12; 8:8, 10
21:10 [j] Ac 6:11 [k] Ex 22:28; Lev 24:15-16
21:12 [l] Isa 58:4
21:13 [m] 2Ki 9:26
21:15 [n] 1Sa 8:14
21:19 [o] 2Ki 9:26; Ps 9:12; Isa 14:20 [p] 1Ki 22:38
21:20 [q] 1Ki 18:17 [r] ver 25; 2Ki 17:17; Ro 7:14

p*42* The Hebrew term refers to the irrevocable giving over of things or persons to the LORD, often by totally destroying them.

to do evil in the eyes of the LORD. **21**'I am going to bring disaster on you. I will consume your descendants and cut off from Ahab every last male[a] in Israel—slave or free. **22**I will make your house[b] like that of Jeroboam son of Nebat and that of Baasha son of Ahijah, because you have provoked me to anger and have caused Israel to sin.'[c]

23"And also concerning Jezebel the LORD says: 'Dogs[d] will devour Jezebel by the wall of[q] Jezreel.'

24"Dogs[e] will eat those belonging to Ahab who die in the city, and the birds of the air will feed on those who die in the country."

25(There was never[f] a man like Ahab, who sold himself to do evil in the eyes of the LORD, urged on by Jezebel his wife. **26**He behaved in the vilest manner by going after idols, like the Amorites[g] the LORD drove out before Israel.)

27When Ahab heard these words, he tore his clothes, put on sackcloth[h] and fasted. He lay in sackcloth and went around meekly.

28Then the word of the LORD came to Elijah the Tishbite: **29**"Have you noticed how Ahab has humbled himself before me? Because he has humbled himself, I will not bring this disaster in his day, but I will bring it on his house in the days of his son."[i]

Micaiah Prophesies Against Ahab

22:1-28pp — 2Ch 18:1-27

22 For three years there was no war between Aram and Israel. **2**But in the third year Jehoshaphat king of Judah went down to see the king of Israel. **3**The king of Israel had said to his officials, "Don't you know that Ramoth Gilead[j] belongs to us and yet we are doing nothing to retake it from the king of Aram?"

4So he asked Jehoshaphat, "Will you go with me to fight[k] against Ramoth Gilead?"

Jehoshaphat replied to the king of Israel, "I am as you are, my people as your people, my horses as your horses." **5**But Jehoshaphat also said to the king of Israel, "First seek the counsel[l] of the LORD."

6So the king of Israel brought together the prophets—about four hundred men—and asked them, "Shall I go to war against Ramoth Gilead, or shall I refrain?"

"Go,"[m] they answered, "for the Lord will give it into the king's hand."

7But Jehoshaphat asked, "Is there not a prophet[n] of the LORD here whom we can inquire of?"

8The king of Israel answered Jehoshaphat, "There is still one man through whom we can inquire of the LORD, but I hate[o] him because he never prophesies anything good[p] about me, but always bad. He is Micaiah son of Imlah."

"The king should not say that," Jehoshaphat replied.

9So the king of Israel called one of his officials and said, "Bring Micaiah son of Imlah at once."

10Dressed in their royal robes, the king of Israel and Jehoshaphat king of Judah were sitting on their thrones at the threshing floor[q] by the entrance of the gate of Samaria, with all the prophets prophesying before them. **11**Now Zedekiah son of Kenaanah had made iron horns[r] and he declared, "This is what the LORD says: 'With these you will gore the Arameans until they are destroyed.' "

12All the other prophets were prophesying the same thing. "Attack Ramoth Gilead and be victorious," they said, "for the LORD will give it into the king's hand."

13The messenger who had gone to summon Micaiah said to him, "Look, as one man the other prophets are predicting success for the king. Let your word agree with theirs, and speak favorably."

14But Micaiah said, "As surely as the LORD lives, I can tell him only what the LORD tells me."[s]

15When he arrived, the king

21:21 [a] 1Ki 14:10; 2Ki 9:8
21:22 [b] 1Ki 15:29; 16:3 [c] 1Ki 12:30
21:23 [d] 2Ki 9:10, 34-36
21:24 [e] 1Ki 14:11; 16:4
21:25 [f] ver 20; 1Ki 16:33
21:26 [g] Ge 15:16; Lev 18:25-30; 2Ki 21:11
21:27 [h] Ge 37:34; 2Sa 3:31; 2Ki 6:30
21:29 [i] 2Ki 9:26
22:3 [j] Dt 4:43; Jos 21:38
22:4 [k] 2Ki 3:7
22:5 [l] Ex 33:7; 2Ki 3:11
22:6 [m] 1Ki 18:19
22:7 [n] 2Ki 3:11
22:8 [o] Am 5:10 [p] Isa 5:20
22:10 [q] ver 6
22:11 [r] Dt 33:17; Zec 1:18-21
22:14 [s] Nu 22:18; 24:13; 1Ki 18:10,15

[q]23 Most Hebrew manuscripts; a few Hebrew manuscripts, Vulgate and Syriac (see also 2 Kings 9:26) *the plot of ground at*

asked him, "Micaiah, shall we go to war against Ramoth Gilead, or shall I refrain?"

"Attack and be victorious," he answered, "for the LORD will give it into the king's hand."

16 The king said to him, "How many times must I make you swear to tell me nothing but the truth in the name of the LORD?"

17 Then Micaiah answered, "I saw all Israel scattered on the hills like sheep without a shepherd,[a] and the LORD said, 'These people have no master. Let each one go home in peace.' "

18 The king of Israel said to Jehoshaphat, "Didn't I tell you that he never prophesies anything good about me, but only bad?"

19 Micaiah continued, "Therefore hear the word of the LORD: I saw the LORD sitting on his throne[b] with all the host[c] of heaven standing around him on his right and on his left. 20 And the LORD said, 'Who will entice Ahab into attacking Ramoth Gilead and going to his death there?'

"One suggested this, and another that. 21 Finally, a spirit came forward, stood before the LORD and said, 'I will entice him.'

22 " 'By what means?' the LORD asked.

" 'I will go out and be a lying[d] spirit in the mouths of all his prophets,' he said.

" 'You will succeed in enticing him,' said the LORD. 'Go and do it.'

23 "So now the LORD has put a lying spirit in the mouths of all these prophets[e] of yours. The LORD has decreed disaster for you."

24 Then Zedekiah[f] son of Kenaanah went up and slapped[g] Micaiah in the face. "Which way did the spirit from[r] the LORD go when he went from me to speak to you?" he asked.

25 Micaiah replied, "You will find out on the day you go to hide[h] in an inner room."

26 The king of Israel then ordered, "Take Micaiah and send him back to Amon the ruler of the city and to Joash the king's son 27 and say, 'This is what the king says: Put this fellow in prison[i] and give him nothing but bread and water until I return safely.' "

28 Micaiah declared, "If you ever return safely, the LORD has not spoken[j] through me." Then he added, "Mark my words, all you people!"

Ahab Killed at Ramoth Gilead

22:29-36pp — 2Ch 18:28-34

29 So the king of Israel and Jehoshaphat king of Judah went up to Ramoth Gilead. 30 The king of Israel said to Jehoshaphat, "I will enter the battle in disguise,[k] but you wear your royal robes." So the king of Israel disguised himself and went into battle.

31 Now the king of Aram had ordered his thirty-two chariot commanders, "Do not fight with anyone, small or great, except the king[l] of Israel." 32 When the chariot commanders saw Jehoshaphat, they thought, "Surely this is the king of Israel." So they turned to attack him, but when Jehoshaphat cried out, 33 the chariot commanders saw that he was not the king of Israel and stopped pursuing him.

34 But someone drew his bow[m] at random and hit the king of Israel between the sections of his armor. The king told his chariot driver, "Wheel around and get me out of the fighting. I've been wounded." 35 All day long the battle raged, and the king was propped up in his chariot facing the Arameans. The blood from his wound ran onto the floor of the chariot, and that evening he died. 36 As the sun was setting, a cry spread through the army: "Every man to his town; everyone to his land!"[n]

37 So the king died and was brought to Samaria, and they buried him there. 38 They washed the chariot at a pool in Samaria (where the prostitutes bathed),[s] and the dogs[o] licked up his blood, as the word of the LORD had declared.

39 As for the other events of

22:17 [a] ver 34-36; Nu 27:17; Mt 9:36
22:19 [b] Isa 6:1; Eze 1:26; Da 7:9 [c] Job 1:6; 2:1; Ps 103:20-21; Mt 18:10; Heb 1:7,14
22:22 [d] Jdg 9:23; 1Sa 16:14; 18:10; 19:9; Eze 14:9; 2Th 2:11
22:23 [e] Eze 14:9
22:24 [f] ver 11 [g] Ac 23:2
22:25 [h] 1Ki 20:30
22:27 [i] 2Ch 16:10
22:28 [j] Dt 18:22
22:30 [k] 2Ch 35:32
22:31 [l] 2Sa 17:2
22:34 [m] 2Ch 35:23
22:36 [n] 2Ki 14:12
22:38 [o] 1Ki 21:19

[r] 24 Or *Spirit of* [s] 38 Or *Samaria and cleaned the weapons*

Ahab's reign, including all he did,
the palace he built and inlaid with
ivory,[a] and the cities he fortified,
are they not written in the book of
the annals of the kings of Israel?
40Ahab rested with his fathers. And
Ahaziah his son succeeded him as
king.

Jehoshaphat King of Judah

22:41–50pp — 2Ch 20:31–21:1

41Jehoshaphat son of Asa became king of Judah in the fourth
year of Ahab king of Israel. 42Je-
hoshaphat was thirty-five years old
when he became king, and he
reigned in Jerusalem twenty-five
years. His mother's name was Azubah daughter of Shilhi. 43In everything he walked in the ways of his
father Asa[b] and did not stray from
them; he did what was right in the
eyes of the LORD. The high places,[c]
however, were not removed, and
the people continued to offer sacrifices and burn incense there. 44Je-
hoshaphat was also at peace with
the king of Israel.

45As for the other events of Jehoshaphat's reign, the things he
achieved and his military exploits,
are they not written in the book of
the annals of the kings of Judah?
46He rid the land of the rest of the
male shrine prostitutes[d] who remained there even after the reign
of his father Asa. 47There was then
no king[e] in Edom; a deputy ruled.

48Now Jehoshaphat built a fleet
of trading ships[†][f] to go to Ophir
for gold, but they never set sail—
they were wrecked at Ezion Geber.
49At that time Ahaziah son of Ahab
said to Jehoshaphat, "Let my men
sail with your men," but Jehoshaphat refused.

50Then Jehoshaphat rested with
his fathers and was buried with
them in the city of David his father.
And Jehoram his son succeeded
him.

Ahaziah King of Israel

51Ahaziah son of Ahab became
king of Israel in Samaria in the seventeenth year of Jehoshaphat king
of Judah, and he reigned over Israel
two years. 52He did evil[g] in the
eyes of the LORD, because he
walked in the ways of his father and
mother and in the ways of Jeroboam son of Nebat, who caused Israel
to sin. 53He served and worshiped
Baal[h] and provoked the LORD, the
God of Israel, to anger, just as his
father[i] had done.

22:39 [a] 2Ch 9:17; Am 3:15
22:43 [b] 2Ch 17:3 [c] 1Ki 3:2; 15:14; 2Ki 12:3
22:46 [d] Dt 23:17; 1Ki 14:24; 15:12
22:47 [e] 2Sa 8:14; 2Ki 3:9; 8:20
22:48 [f] 1Ki 9:26; 10:22
22:52 [g] 1Ki 15:26; 21:25
22:53 [h] Jdg 2:11 [i] 1Ki 16:30-32

[†]48 Hebrew *of ships of Tarshish*

2 Kings

Title and Background

See Introduction to 1 Kings.

Author and Date of Writing

See Introduction to 1 Kings.

Theme and Message

2 Kings continues the stories of the great prophets Elijah and Elisha. It also tells the history of the northern and southern kingdoms until they were both finally conquered. In both kingdoms God's prophets continually warned the people that God would punish them if they did not repent of their sins.

Outline

I. Elijah and Elisha (1:1-8:15)
II. Israel and Judah From Joram/Jehoram to Israel's Exile (8:16-17:41)
III. Judah From Hezekiah to the Babylonian Exile (18:1-25:30)

The LORD's Judgment on Ahaziah

1 After Ahab's death, Moab[a] rebelled against Israel. 2Now
Ahaziah had fallen through the lattice of his upper room in Samaria
and injured himself. So he sent
messengers,[b] saying to them, "Go
and consult Baal-Zebub,[c] the god
of Ekron,[d] to see if I will recover[e]
from this injury."
3But the angel[f] of the LORD said
to Elijah[g] the Tishbite, "Go up and
meet the messengers of the king of
Samaria and ask them, 'Is it because there is no God in Israel[h]
that you are going off to consult
Baal-Zebub, the god of Ekron?'
4Therefore this is what the LORD
says: 'You will not leave[i] the bed
you are lying on. You will certainly
die!' " So Elijah went.
5When the messengers returned
to the king, he asked them, "Why
have you come back?"
6"A man came to meet us," they
replied. "And he said to us, 'Go
back to the king who sent you and
tell him, "This is what the LORD
says: Is it because there is no God
in Israel that you are sending men
to consult Baal-Zebub, the god of
Ekron? Therefore you will not leave
the bed you are lying on. You will
certainly die!" ' "
7The king asked them, "What
kind of man was it who came to
meet you and told you this?"
8They replied, "He was a man
with a garment of hair[j] and with a
leather belt around his waist."
The king said, "That was Elijah
the Tishbite."
9Then he sent[k] to Elijah a captain[l] with his company of fifty
men. The captain went up to Elijah, who was sitting on the top of a
hill, and said to him, "Man of God,
the king says, 'Come down!' "
10Elijah answered the captain,
"If I am a man of God, may fire
come down from heaven and consume you and your fifty men!"
Then fire[m] fell from heaven and
consumed the captain and his
men.
11At this the king sent to Elijah
another captain with his fifty men.
The captain said to him, "Man of

1:1 [a]Ge 19:37; 2Sa 8:2; 2Ki 3:5
1:2 [b]ver 16 [c]Mk 3:22 [d]1Sa 6:2; Isa 2:6; 14:29; Mt 10:25 [e]Jdg 18:5; 2Ki 8:7-10
1:3 [f]ver 15; Ge 16:7 [g]1Ki 17:1 [h]1Sa 28:8
1:4 [i]ver 6,16; Ps 41:8
1:8 [j]1Ki 18:7; Zec 13:4; Mt 3:4; Mk 1:6
1:9 [k]2Ki 6:14 [l]Ex 18:25; Isa 3:3
1:10 [m]1Ki 18:38; Lk 9:54; Rev 11:5; 13:13

God, this is what the king says,
'Come down at once!' "
12"If I am a man of God," Elijah
replied, "may fire come down from
heaven and consume you and your
fifty men!" Then the fire of God fell
from heaven and consumed him
and his fifty men.
13So the king sent a third captain
with his fifty men. This third captain went up and fell on his knees
before Elijah. "Man of God," he
begged, "please have respect for
my life[a] and the lives of these fifty
men, your servants! 14See, fire has
fallen from heaven and consumed
the first two captains and all their
men. But now have respect for my
life!"
15The angel[b] of the LORD said to
Elijah, "Go down with him; do not
be afraid[c] of him." So Elijah got up
and went down with him to the
king.
16He told the king, "This is what
the LORD says: Is it because there is
no God in Israel for you to consult
that you have sent messengers[d] to
consult Baal-Zebub, the god of Ekron? Because you have done this,
you will never leave[e] the bed you
are lying on. You will certainly die!"
17So he died,[f] according to the
word of the LORD that Elijah had
spoken.
Because Ahaziah had no son, Joram[a][g] succeeded him as king in
the second year of Jehoram son of
Jehoshaphat king of Judah. 18As
for all the other events of Ahaziah's
reign, and what he did, are they not
written in the book of the annals of
the kings of Israel?

Elijah Taken Up to Heaven

2 When the LORD was about to
take[h] Elijah up to heaven in a
whirlwind,[i] Elijah and Elisha[j]
were on their way from Gilgal.[k]
2Elijah said to Elisha, "Stay here;[l]
the LORD has sent me to Bethel."
But Elisha said, "As surely as the
LORD lives and as you live, I will not
leave you."[m] So they went down to
Bethel.
3The company[n] of the prophets
at Bethel came out to Elisha and
asked, "Do you know that the LORD
is going to take your master from
you today?"
"Yes, I know," Elisha replied,
"but do not speak of it."
4Then Elijah said to him, "Stay
here, Elisha; the LORD has sent me
to Jericho.[o]"
And he replied, "As surely as the
LORD lives and as you live, I will not
leave you." So they went to Jericho.
5The company[p] of the prophets
at Jericho went up to Elisha and
asked him, "Do you know that the
LORD is going to take your master
from you today?"
"Yes, I know," he replied, "but
do not speak of it."
6Then Elijah said to him, "Stay
here;[q] the LORD has sent me to the
Jordan."[r]
And he replied, "As surely as the
LORD lives and as you live, I will not
leave you."[s] So the two of them
walked on.
7Fifty men of the company of the
prophets went and stood at a distance, facing the place where Elijah and Elisha had stopped at the
Jordan. 8Elijah took his cloak,[t]
rolled it up and struck[u] the water
with it. The water divided[v] to the
right and to the left, and the two of
them crossed over on dry[w] ground.
9When they had crossed, Elijah
said to Elisha, "Tell me, what can
I do for you before I am taken from
you?"
"Let me inherit a double[x] portion of your spirit,"[y] Elisha replied.
10"You have asked a difficult
thing," Elijah said, "yet if you see
me when I am taken from you, it
will be yours—otherwise not."
11As they were walking along
and talking together, suddenly a
chariot of fire[z] and horses of fire
appeared and separated the two of
them, and Elijah went up to heav-
en[a] in a whirlwind.[b] 12Elisha saw
this and cried out, "My father! My
father! The chariots[c] and horsemen of Israel!" And Elisha saw him
no more. Then he took hold of his

1:13 [a] 1Sa 26:21; Ps 72:14
1:15 [b] ver 3 [c] Isa 51:12; 57:11; Jer 1:17; Eze 2:6
1:16 [d] ver 2 [e] ver 4
1:17 [f] 2Ki 8:15; Jer 20:6; 28:17 [g] 2Ki 3:1; 8:16
2:1 [h] Ge 5:24; Heb 11:5 [i] ver 11; 1Ki 19:11; Isa 5:28; 66:15; Jer 4:13; Na 1:3 [j] 1Ki 19:16,21 [k] Dt 11:30; 2Ki 4:38
2:2 [l] ver 6 [m] Ru 1:16; 1Sa 1:26; 2Ki 4:30
2:3 [n] 1Sa 10:5; 2Ki 4:1,38
2:4 [o] Jos 3:16; 6:26
2:5 [p] ver 3
2:6 [q] ver 2 [r] Jos 3:15 [s] Ru 1:16
2:8 [t] 1Ki 19:19 [u] ver 14 [v] Ex 14:21 [w] Ex 14:22,29
2:9 [x] Dt 21:17 [y] Nu 11:17
2:11 [z] 2Ki 6:17; Ps 68:17; 104:3,4; Isa 66:15; Hab 3:8; Zec 6:1 [a] Ge 5:24 [b] ver 1
2:12 [c] 2Ki 6:17; 13:14

[a] 17 Hebrew *Jehoram,* a variant of *Joram*

own clothes and tore[a] them apart. 13He picked up the cloak that had fallen from Elijah and went back and stood on the bank of the Jordan. 14Then he took the cloak[b] that had fallen from him and struck[c] the water with it. "Where now is the LORD, the God of Elijah?" he asked. When he struck the water, it divided to the right and to the left, and he crossed over.

15The company[d] of the prophets from Jericho, who were watching, said, "The spirit[e] of Elijah is resting on Elisha." And they went to meet him and bowed to the ground before him. 16"Look," they said, "we your servants have fifty able men. Let them go and look for your master. Perhaps the Spirit[f] of the LORD has picked him up[g] and set him down on some mountain or in some valley."

"No," Elisha replied, "do not send them."

17But they persisted until he was too ashamed[h] to refuse. So he said, "Send them." And they sent fifty men, who searched for three days but did not find him. 18When they returned to Elisha, who was staying in Jericho, he said to them, "Didn't I tell you not to go?"

Healing of the Water

19The men of the city said to Elisha, "Look, our lord, this town is well situated, as you can see, but the water is bad and the land is unproductive."

20"Bring me a new bowl," he said, "and put salt in it." So they brought it to him.

21Then he went out to the spring and threw[i] the salt into it, saying, "This is what the LORD says: 'I have healed this water. Never again will it cause death or make the land unproductive.' " 22And the water has remained wholesome[j] to this day, according to the word Elisha had spoken.

Elisha Is Jeered

23From there Elisha went up to Bethel. As he was walking along the road, some youths came out of the town and jeered[k] at him. "Go on up, you baldhead!" they said. "Go on up, you baldhead!" 24He turned around, looked at them and called down a curse[l] on them in the name[m] of the LORD. Then two bears came out of the woods and mauled forty-two of the youths. 25And he went on to Mount Carmel[n] and from there returned to Samaria.

Moab Revolts

3 Joram[b][o] son of Ahab became king of Israel in Samaria in the eighteenth year of Jehoshaphat king of Judah, and he reigned twelve years. 2He did evil[p] in the eyes of the LORD, but not as his father[q] and mother had done. He got rid of the sacred stone[r] of Baal that his father had made. 3Nevertheless he clung to the sins[s] of Jeroboam son of Nebat, which he had caused Israel to commit; he did not turn away from them.

4Now Mesha king of Moab[t] raised sheep, and he had to supply the king of Israel with a hundred thousand lambs[u] and with the wool of a hundred thousand rams. 5But after Ahab died, the king of Moab rebelled[v] against the king of Israel. 6So at that time King Joram set out from Samaria and mobilized all Israel. 7He also sent this message to Jehoshaphat king of Judah: "The king of Moab has rebelled against me. Will you go with me to fight[w] against Moab?"

"I will go with you," he replied. "I am as you are, my people as your people, my horses as your horses."

8"By what route shall we attack?" he asked.

"Through the Desert of Edom," he answered.

9So the king of Israel set out with the king of Judah and the king of Edom.[x] After a roundabout march of seven days, the army had no more water for themselves or for the animals with them.

10"What!" exclaimed the king of

2:12 [a] Ge 37:29
2:14 [b] 1Ki 19:19 [c] ver 8
2:15 [d] ver 7; 1Sa 10:5 [e] Nu 11:17
2:16 [f] 1Ki 18:12 [g] Ac 8:39
2:17 [h] 2Ki 8:11
2:21 [i] Ex 15:25; 2Ki 4:41; 6:6
2:22 [j] Ex 15:25
2:23 [k] Ex 22:28; 2Ch 36:16; Job 19:18; Ps 31:18
2:24 [l] Ge 4:11; Ne 13:25-27 [m] Dt 18:19
2:25 [n] 1Ki 18:20; 2Ki 4:25
3:1 [o] 2Ki 1:17
3:2 [p] 1Ki 15:26 [q] 1Ki 16:30-32 [r] Ex 23:24; 2Ki 10:18, 26-28
3:3 [s] 1Ki 12:28-32; 14:9,16
3:4 [t] Ge 19:37; 2Ki 1:1 [u] Ezr 7:17; Isa 16:1
3:5 [v] 2Ki 1:1
3:7 [w] 1Ki 22:4
3:9 [x] 1Ki 22:47

[b] *1* Hebrew *Jehoram,* a variant of *Joram;* also in verse 6

Israel. "Has the LORD called us
three kings together only to hand
us over to Moab?"
11But Jehoshaphat asked, "Is
there no prophet of the LORD here,
that we may inquire[a] of the LORD
through him?"
An officer of the king of Israel answered, "Elisha[b] son of Shaphat is
here. He used to pour water on the
hands of Elijah.[c][c]"
12Jehoshaphat said, "The word[d]
of the LORD is with him." So the
king of Israel and Jehoshaphat and
the king of Edom went down to
him.
13Elisha said to the king of Israel, "What do we have to do with
each other? Go to the prophets of
your father and the prophets of
your mother."
"No," the king of Israel answered, "because it was the LORD
who called us three kings together
to hand us over to Moab."
14Elisha said, "As surely as the
LORD Almighty lives, whom I serve,
if I did not have respect for the
presence of Jehoshaphat king of
Judah, I would not look at you or
even notice you. 15But now bring
me a harpist."[e]
While the harpist was playing,
the hand[f] of the LORD came upon
Elisha 16and he said, "This is what
the LORD says: Make this valley full
of ditches. 17For this is what the
LORD says: You will see neither
wind nor rain, yet this valley will be
filled with water,[g] and you, your
cattle and your other animals will
drink. 18This is an easy[h] thing in
the eyes of the LORD; he will also
hand Moab over to you. 19You will
overthrow every fortified city and
every major town. You will cut
down every good tree, stop up all
the springs, and ruin every good
field with stones."
20The next morning, about the
time[i] for offering the sacrifice,
there it was—water flowing from
the direction of Edom! And the
land was filled with water.[j]
21Now all the Moabites had
heard that the kings had come to
fight against them; so every man,
young and old, who could bear
arms was called up and stationed
on the border. 22When they got up
early in the morning, the sun was
shining on the water. To the Moabites across the way, the water
looked red—like blood. 23"That's
blood!" they said. "Those kings
must have fought and slaughtered
each other. Now to the plunder,
Moab!"
24But when the Moabites came
to the camp of Israel, the Israelites
rose up and fought them until they
fled. And the Israelites invaded the
land and slaughtered the Moabites. 25They destroyed the towns,
and each man threw a stone on every good field until it was covered.
They stopped up all the springs and
cut down every good tree. Only Kir
Hareseth[k] was left with its stones
in place, but men armed with
slings surrounded it and attacked it
as well.
26When the king of Moab saw
that the battle had gone against
him, he took with him seven hundred swordsmen to break through
to the king of Edom, but they
failed. 27Then he took his firstborn[l] son, who was to succeed
him as king, and offered him as a
sacrifice on the city wall. The fury
against Israel was great; they withdrew and returned to their own
land.

The Widow's Oil

4 The wife of a man from the
company[m] of the prophets
cried out to Elisha, "Your servant
my husband is dead, and you know
that he revered the LORD. But now
his creditor[n] is coming to take my
two boys as his slaves."
2Elisha replied to her, "How can
I help you? Tell me, what do you
have in your house?"
"Your servant has nothing there
at all," she said, "except a little
oil."[o]
3Elisha said, "Go around and ask
all your neighbors for empty jars.
Don't ask for just a few. 4Then go

3:11 [a] Ge 25:22; 1Ki 22:7 [b] Ge 20:7 [c] 1Ki 19:16
3:12 [d] Nu 11:17
3:15 [e] 1Sa 16:23 [f] Jer 15:17; Eze 1:3
3:17 [g] Ps 107:35; Isa 32:2; 35:6; 41:18
3:18 [h] Ge 18:14; 2Ki 20:10; Isa 49:6; Jer 32:17,27; Mk 10:27
3:20 [i] Ex 29:39-40 [j] Ex 17:6
3:25 [k] ver 19; Isa 15:1; 16:7; Jer 48:31,36
3:27 [l] Dt 12:31; 2Ki 16:3; 21:6; 2Ch 28:3; Ps 106:38; Jer 19:4-5; Am 2:1; Mic 6:7
4:1 [m] 1Sa 10:5; 2Ki 2:3 [n] Ex 22:26; Lev 25:39-43; Ne 5:3-5; Job 22:6; 24:9
4:2 [o] 1Ki 17:12

[c] *11* That is, he was Elijah's personal servant.

inside and shut the door behind you and your sons. Pour oil into all the jars, and as each is filled, put it to one side."

5She left him and afterward shut the door behind her and her sons. They brought the jars to her and she kept pouring. 6When all the jars were full, she said to her son, "Bring me another one."

But he replied, "There is not a jar left." Then the oil stopped flowing.

7She went and told the man of God,[a] and he said, "Go, sell the oil and pay your debts. You and your sons can live on what is left."

The Shunammite's Son Restored to Life

8One day Elisha went to Shunem.[b] And a well-to-do woman was there, who urged him to stay for a meal. So whenever he came by, he stopped there to eat. 9She said to her husband, "I know that this man who often comes our way is a holy man of God. 10Let's make a small room on the roof and put in it a bed and a table, a chair and a lamp for him. Then he can stay[c] there whenever he comes to us."

11One day when Elisha came, he went up to his room and lay down there. 12He said to his servant Gehazi, "Call the Shunammite."[d] So he called her, and she stood before him. 13Elisha said to him, "Tell her, 'You have gone to all this trouble for us. Now what can be done for you? Can we speak on your behalf to the king or the commander of the army?' "

She replied, "I have a home among my own people."

14"What can be done for her?" Elisha asked.

Gehazi said, "Well, she has no son and her husband is old."

15Then Elisha said, "Call her." So he called her, and she stood in the doorway. 16"About this time[e] next year," Elisha said, "you will hold a son in your arms."

"No, my lord," she objected. "Don't mislead your servant, O man of God!"

17But the woman became pregnant, and the next year about that same time she gave birth to a son, just as Elisha had told her.

18The child grew, and one day he went out to his father, who was with the reapers.[f] 19"My head! My head!" he said to his father.

His father told a servant, "Carry him to his mother." 20After the servant had lifted him up and carried him to his mother, the boy sat on her lap until noon, and then he died. 21She went up and laid him on the bed[g] of the man of God, then shut the door and went out.

22She called her husband and said, "Please send me one of the servants and a donkey so I can go to the man of God quickly and return."

23"Why go to him today?" he asked. "It's not the New Moon[h] or the Sabbath."

"It's all right," she said.

24She saddled the donkey and said to her servant, "Lead on; don't slow down for me unless I tell you." 25So she set out and came to the man of God at Mount Carmel.[i]

When he saw her in the distance, the man of God said to his servant Gehazi, "Look! There's the Shunammite! 26Run to meet her and ask her, 'Are you all right? Is your husband all right? Is your child all right?' "

"Everything is all right," she said.

27When she reached the man of God at the mountain, she took hold of his feet. Gehazi came over to push her away, but the man of God said, "Leave her alone! She is in bitter distress,[j] but the LORD has hidden it from me and has not told me why."

28"Did I ask you for a son, my lord?" she said. "Didn't I tell you, 'Don't raise my hopes'?"

29Elisha said to Gehazi, "Tuck your cloak into your belt,[k] take my staff[l] in your hand and run. If you meet anyone, do not greet him, and if anyone greets you, do not answer. Lay my staff on the boy's face."

4:7 [a] 1Ki 12:22
4:8 [b] Jos 19:18
4:10 [c] Mt 10:41; Ro 12:13
4:12 [d] 2Ki 8:1
4:16 [e] Ge 18:10
4:18 [f] Ru 2:3
4:21 [g] ver 32
4:23 [h] Nu 10:10; 1Ch 23:31; Ps 81:3
4:25 [i] 1Ki 18:20; 2Ki 2:25
4:27 [j] 1Sa 1:15
4:29 [k] 1Ki 18:46; 2Ki 2:8,14; 9:1 [l] Ex 4:2; 7:19; 14:16

30But the child's mother said, "As surely as the LORD lives and as you live, I will not leave you." So he got up and followed her.

31Gehazi went on ahead and laid the staff on the boy's face, but there was no sound or response. So Gehazi went back to meet Elisha and told him, "The boy has not awakened."

32When Elisha reached the house, there was the boy lying dead on his couch.[a] 33He went in, shut the door on the two of them and prayed[b] to the LORD. 34Then he got on the bed and lay upon the boy, mouth to mouth, eyes to eyes, hands to hands. As he stretched[c] himself out upon him, the boy's body grew warm. 35Elisha turned away and walked back and forth in the room and then got on the bed and stretched out upon him once more. The boy sneezed seven times[d] and opened his eyes.[e]

36Elisha summoned Gehazi and said, "Call the Shunammite." And he did. When she came, he said, "Take your son."[f] 37She came in, fell at his feet and bowed to the ground. Then she took her son and went out.

Death in the Pot

38Elisha returned to Gilgal[g] and there was a famine[h] in that region. While the company of the prophets was meeting with him, he said to his servant, "Put on the large pot and cook some stew for these men."

39One of them went out into the fields to gather herbs and found a wild vine. He gathered some of its gourds and filled the fold of his cloak. When he returned, he cut them up into the pot of stew, though no one knew what they were. 40The stew was poured out for the men, but as they began to eat it, they cried out, "O man of God, there is death in the pot!" And they could not eat it.

41Elisha said, "Get some flour." He put it into the pot and said, "Serve it to the people to eat." And there was nothing harmful in the pot.[i]

Feeding of a Hundred

42A man came from Baal Shalishah,[j] bringing the man of God twenty loaves[k] of barley bread[l] baked from the first ripe grain, along with some heads of new grain. "Give it to the people to eat," Elisha said.

43"How can I set this before a hundred men?" his servant asked.

But Elisha answered, "Give it to the people to eat.[m] For this is what the LORD says: 'They will eat and have some left over.[n]' " 44Then he set it before them, and they ate and had some left over, according to the word of the LORD.

Naaman Healed of Leprosy

5 Now Naaman was commander of the army of the king of Aram.[o] He was a great man in the sight of his master and highly regarded, because through him the LORD had given victory to Aram. He was a valiant soldier, but he had leprosy.[d][p]

2Now bands[q] from Aram had gone out and had taken captive a young girl from Israel, and she served Naaman's wife. 3She said to her mistress, "If only my master would see the prophet[r] who is in Samaria! He would cure him of his leprosy."

4Naaman went to his master and told him what the girl from Israel had said. 5"By all means, go," the king of Aram replied. "I will send a letter to the king of Israel." So Naaman left, taking with him ten talents[e] of silver, six thousand shekels[f] of gold and ten sets of clothing.[s] 6The letter that he took to the king of Israel read: "With this letter I am sending my servant Naaman to you so that you may cure him of his leprosy."

4:32 [a] ver 21
4:33 [b] 1Ki 17:20; Mt 6:6
4:34 [c] 1Ki 17:21; Ac 20:10
4:35 [d] Jos 6:15 [e] 2Ki 8:5
4:36 [f] Heb 11:35
4:38 [g] 2Ki 2:1 [h] Lev 26:26; 2Ki 8:1
4:41 [i] Ex 15:25; 2Ki 2:21
4:42 [j] 1Sa 9:4 [k] Mt 14:17; 15:36 [l] 1Sa 9:7
4:43 [m] Lk 9:13 [n] Mt 14:20; Jn 6:12
5:1 [o] Ge 10:22; 2Sa 10:19 [p] Ex 4:6; Nu 12:10; Lk 4:27
5:2 [q] 2Ki 6:23; 13:20; 24:2
5:3 [r] Ge 20:7
5:5 [s] ver 22; Ge 24:53; Jdg 14:12; 1Sa 9:7

[d] 1 The Hebrew word was used for various diseases affecting the skin—not necessarily leprosy; also in verses 3, 6, 7, 11 and 27.
[e] 5 That is, about 750 pounds (about 340 kilograms) [f] 5 That is, about 150 pounds (about 70 kilograms)

7As soon as the king of Israel
read the letter,[a] he tore his robes
and said, "Am I God?[b] Can I kill
and bring back to life?[c] Why does
this fellow send someone to me to
be cured of his leprosy? See how he
is trying to pick a quarrel[d] with
me!"
8When Elisha the man of God
heard that the king of Israel had
torn his robes, he sent him this
message: "Why have you torn your
robes? Have the man come to me
and he will know that there is a
prophet[e] in Israel." 9So Naaman
went with his horses and chariots
and stopped at the door of Elisha's
house. 10Elisha sent a messenger
to say to him, "Go, wash[f] yourself
seven times[g] in the Jordan, and
your flesh will be restored and you
will be cleansed."
11But Naaman went away angry
and said, "I thought that he would
surely come out to me and stand
and call on the name of the LORD
his God, wave his hand[h] over the
spot and cure me of my leprosy.
12Are not Abana and Pharpar, the
rivers of Damascus, better than any
of the waters[i] of Israel? Couldn't I
wash in them and be cleansed?" So
he turned and went off in a rage.[j]
13Naaman's servants went to
him and said, "My father,[k] if the
prophet had told you to do some
great thing, would you not have
done it? How much more, then,
when he tells you, 'Wash and be
cleansed'!" 14So he went down and
dipped himself in the Jordan seven
times,[l] as the man of God had told
him, and his flesh was restored[m]
and became clean like that of a
young boy.[n]
15Then Naaman and all his attendants went back to the man of
God[o]. He stood before him and
said, "Now I know[p] that there is no
God in all the world except in Israel. Please accept now a gift[q] from
your servant."
16The prophet answered, "As
surely as the LORD lives, whom I
serve, I will not accept a thing."
And even though Naaman urged
him, he refused.[r]

5:7 [a]2Ki 19:14 [b]Ge 30:2 [c]Dt 32:39; 1Sa 2:6 [d]1Ki 20:7
5:8 [e]1Ki 22:7
5:10 [f]Jn 9:7 [g]Ge 33:3; Lev 14:7
5:11 [h]Ex 7:19
5:12 [i]Isa 8:6 [j]Pr 14:17,29; 19:11; 29:11
5:13 [k]2Ki 6:21; 13:14
5:14 [l]Ge 33:3; Lev 14:7; Jos 6:15 [m]Ex 4:7 [n]Job 33:25; Lk 4:27
5:15 [o]Jos 2:11 [p]Jos 4:24; 1Sa 17:46; Da 2:47 [q]1Sa 9:7; 25:27
5:16 [r]ver 20,26; Ge 14:23; Da 5:17
5:17 [s]Ex 20:24
5:18 [t]2Ki 7:2
5:19 [u]1Sa 1:17; Ac 15:33
5:20 [v]Ex 20:7
5:22 [w]ver 5; Ge 45:22

17"If you will not," said Naaman,
"please let me, your servant, be giv-
en as much earth[s] as a pair of
mules can carry, for your servant
will never again make burnt offerings and sacrifices to any other god
but the LORD. 18But may the LORD
forgive your servant for this one
thing: When my master enters the
temple of Rimmon to bow down
and he is leaning[t] on my arm and
I bow there also—when I bow
down in the temple of Rimmon,
may the LORD forgive your servant
for this."
19"Go in peace,"[u] Elisha said.
After Naaman had traveled some
distance, 20Gehazi, the servant of
Elisha the man of God, said to himself, "My master was too easy on
Naaman, this Aramean, by not accepting from him what he brought.
As surely as the LORD[v] lives, I will
run after him and get something
from him."
21So Gehazi hurried after Naaman. When Naaman saw him running toward him, he got down from
the chariot to meet him. "Is everything all right?" he asked.
22"Everything is all right," Gehazi answered. "My master sent me to
say, 'Two young men from the company of the prophets have just
come to me from the hill country of
Ephraim. Please give them a talent[g] of silver and two sets of clothing.' "[w]
23"By all means, take two talents," said Naaman. He urged Gehazi to accept them, and then tied
up the two talents of silver in two
bags, with two sets of clothing. He
gave them to two of his servants,
and they carried them ahead of Gehazi. 24When Gehazi came to the
hill, he took the things from the
servants and put them away in the
house. He sent the men away and
they left. 25Then he went in and
stood before his master Elisha.
"Where have you been, Gehazi?"
Elisha asked.

[g]22 That is, about 75 pounds (about 34 kilograms)

"Your servant didn't go anywhere," Gehazi answered.

26But Elisha said to him, "Was not my spirit with you when the man got down from his chariot to meet you? Is this the time[a] to take money, or to accept clothes, olive groves, vineyards, flocks, herds, or menservants and maidservants?[b] **27**Naaman's leprosy[c] will cling to you and to your descendants forever." Then Gehazi[d] went from Elisha's presence and he was leprous, as white as snow.[e]

An Axhead Floats

6 The company[f] of the prophets said to Elisha, "Look, the place where we meet with you is too small for us. **2**Let us go to the Jordan, where each of us can get a pole; and let us build a place there for us to live."

And he said, "Go."

3Then one of them said, "Won't you please come with your servants?"

"I will," Elisha replied. **4**And he went with them.

They went to the Jordan and began to cut down trees. **5**As one of them was cutting down a tree, the iron axhead fell into the water. "Oh, my lord," he cried out, "it was borrowed!"

6The man of God asked, "Where did it fall?" When he showed him the place, Elisha cut a stick and threw[g] it there, and made the iron float. **7**"Lift it out," he said. Then the man reached out his hand and took it.

Elisha Traps Blinded Arameans

8Now the king of Aram was at war with Israel. After conferring with his officers, he said, "I will set up my camp in such and such a place."

9The man of God sent word to the king[h] of Israel: "Beware of passing that place, because the Arameans are going down there." **10**So the king of Israel checked on the place indicated by the man of God. Time and again Elisha warned[i] the king, so that he was on his guard in such places.

11This enraged the king of Aram. He summoned his officers and demanded of them, "Will you not tell me which of us is on the side of the king of Israel?"

12"None of us, my lord the king[j]," said one of his officers, "but Elisha, the prophet who is in Israel, tells the king of Israel the very words you speak in your bedroom."

13"Go, find out where he is," the king ordered, "so I can send men and capture him." The report came back: "He is in Dothan."[k] **14**Then he sent[l] horses and chariots and a strong force there. They went by night and surrounded the city.

15When the servant of the man of God got up and went out early the next morning, an army with horses and chariots had surrounded the city. "Oh, my lord, what shall we do?" the servant asked.

16"Don't be afraid,"[m] the prophet answered. "Those who are with us are more[n] than those who are with them."

17And Elisha prayed, "O LORD, open his eyes so he may see." Then the LORD opened the servant's eyes, and he looked and saw the hills full of horses and chariots[o] of fire all around Elisha.

18As the enemy came down toward him, Elisha prayed to the LORD, "Strike these people with blindness."[p] So he struck them with blindness, as Elisha had asked.

19Elisha told them, "This is not the road and this is not the city. Follow me, and I will lead you to the man you are looking for." And he led them to Samaria.

20After they entered the city, Elisha said, "LORD, open the eyes of these men so they can see." Then the LORD opened their eyes and they looked, and there they were, inside Samaria.

21When the king of Israel saw them, he asked Elisha, "Shall I kill them, my father?[q] Shall I kill them?"

5:26 [a]ver 16 [b]Jer 45:5
5:27 [c]Nu 12:10; 2Ki 15:5 [d]Col 3:5 [e]Ex 4:6
6:1 [f]1Sa 10:5; 2Ki 4:38
6:6 [g]Ex 15:25; 2Ki 2:21
6:9 [h]ver 12
6:10 [i]Jer 11:18
6:12 [j]ver 9
6:13 [k]Ge 37:17
6:14 [l]2Ki 1:9
6:16 [m]Ge 15:1 [n]2Ch 32:7; Ps 55:18; Ro 8:31; 1Jn 4:4
6:17 [o]2Ki 2:11,12; Ps 68:17; Zec 6:1-7
6:18 [p]Ge 19:11; Ac 13:11
6:21 [q]2Ki 5:13

22"Do not kill them," he answered. "Would you kill men you
have captured[a] with your own
sword or bow? Set food and water
before them so that they may eat
and drink and then go back to their
master." 23So he prepared a great
feast for them, and after they had
finished eating and drinking, he
sent them away, and they returned
to their master. So the bands[b]
from Aram stopped raiding Israel's
territory.

Famine in Besieged Samaria

24Some time later, Ben-Hadad[c]
king of Aram mobilized his entire
army and marched up and laid
siege[d] to Samaria. 25There was a
great famine[e] in the city; the siege
lasted so long that a donkey's head
sold for eighty shekels[h] of silver,
and a quarter of a cab[i] of seed
pods[i][f] for five shekels.[k]
26As the king of Israel was passing by on the wall, a woman cried
to him, "Help me, my lord the
king!"
27The king replied, "If the LORD
does not help you, where can I get
help for you? From the threshing
floor? From the winepress?"
28Then he asked her, "What's the
matter?"

She answered, "This woman said
to me, 'Give up your son so we may
eat him today, and tomorrow we'll
eat my son.' 29So we cooked my
son and ate[g] him. The next day I
said to her, 'Give up your son so we
may eat him,' but she had hidden
him."
30When the king heard the woman's words, he tore[h] his robes. As
he went along the wall, the people
looked, and there, underneath, he
had sackcloth[i] on his body. 31He
said, "May God deal with me, be it
ever so severely, if the head of Elisha son of Shaphat remains on his
shoulders today!"
32Now Elisha was sitting in his
house, and the elders[j] were sitting
with him. The king sent a messenger ahead, but before he arrived,
Elisha said to the elders, "Don't
you see how this murderer[k] is
sending someone to cut off my
head?[l] Look, when the messenger
comes, shut the door and hold it
shut against him. Is not the sound
of his master's footsteps behind
him?"
33While he was still talking to
them, the messenger came down to
him. And ⌊the king⌋ said, "This disaster is from the LORD. Why should
I wait[m] for the LORD any longer?"

7 Elisha said, "Hear the word of
the LORD. This is what the LORD
says: About this time tomorrow, a
seah[l] of flour will sell for a shekel[m] and two seahs[n] of barley for a
shekel[n] at the gate of Samaria."
2The officer on whose arm the
king was leaning[o] said to the man
of God, "Look, even if the LORD
should open the floodgates[p] of the
heavens, could this happen?"

"You will see it with your own
eyes," answered Elisha, "but you
will not eat[q] any of it!"

The Siege Lifted

3Now there were four men with
leprosy[o][r] at the entrance of the
city gate. They said to each other,
"Why stay here until we die? 4If we
say, 'We'll go into the city'—the
famine is there, and we will die.
And if we stay here, we will die. So
let's go over to the camp of the Arameans and surrender. If they spare
us, we live; if they kill us, then we
die."
5At dusk they got up and went to
the camp of the Arameans. When
they reached the edge of the camp,
not a man was there, 6for the Lord
had caused the Arameans to hear
the sound[s] of chariots and horses
and a great army, so that they said
to one another, "Look, the king of
Israel has hired[t] the Hittite[u] and

6:22 [a]Dt 20:11; 2Ch 28:8-15; Ro 12:20
6:23 [b]2Ki 5:2
6:24 [c]1Ki 15:18; 20:1; 2Ki 8:7 [d]Dt 28:52
6:25 [e]Lev 26:26; Ru 1:1 [f]Isa 36:12
6:29 [g]Lev 26:29; Dt 28:53-55
6:30 [h]2Ki 18:37; Isa 22:15 [i]Ge 37:34; 1Ki 21:27
6:32 [j]Eze 8:1; 14:1; 20:1 [k]1Ki 18:4 [l]ver 31
6:33 [m]Lev 24:11; Job 2:9; 14:14; Isa 40:31
7:1 [n]ver 16
7:2 [o]2Ki 5:18 [p]ver 19; Ge 7:11; Ps 78:23; Mal 3:10 [q]ver 17
7:3 [r]Lev 13:45-46; Nu 5:1-4
7:6 [s]Ex 14:24; 2Sa 5:24; Eze 1:24 [t]2Sa 10:6; Jer 46:21 [u]Nu 13:29

[h]25 That is, about 2 pounds (about 1 kilogram) [i]25 That is, probably about 1/2 pint (about 0.3 liter) [j]25 Or *of dove's dung* [k]25 That is, about 2 ounces (about 55 grams) [l]1 That is, probably about 7 quarts (about 7.3 liters); also in verses 16 and 18 [m]1 That is, about 2/5 ounce (about 11 grams); also in verses 16 and 18 [n]1 That is, probably about 13 quarts (about 15 liters); also in verses 16 and 18 [o]3 The Hebrew word is used for various diseases affecting the skin—not necessarily leprosy; also in verse 8.

Egyptian kings to attack us!" 7So they got up and fled[a] in the dusk and abandoned their tents and their horses and donkeys. They left the camp as it was and ran for their lives.

8The men who had leprosy[b] reached the edge of the camp and entered one of the tents. They ate and drank, and carried away silver, gold and clothes, and went off and hid them. They returned and entered another tent and took some things from it and hid them also.

9Then they said to each other, "We're not doing right. This is a day of good news and we are keeping it to ourselves. If we wait until daylight, punishment will overtake us. Let's go at once and report this to the royal palace."

10So they went and called out to the city gatekeepers and told them, "We went into the Aramean camp and not a man was there—not a sound of anyone—only tethered horses and donkeys, and the tents left just as they were." 11The gatekeepers shouted the news, and it was reported within the palace.

12The king got up in the night and said to his officers, "I will tell you what the Arameans have done to us. They know we are starving; so they have left the camp to hide[c] in the countryside, thinking, 'They will surely come out, and then we will take them alive and get into the city.' "

13One of his officers answered, "Have some men take five of the horses that are left in the city. Their plight will be like that of all the Israelites left here—yes, they will only be like all these Israelites who are doomed. So let us send them to find out what happened."

14So they selected two chariots with their horses, and the king sent them after the Aramean army. He commanded the drivers, "Go and find out what has happened." 15They followed them as far as the Jordan, and they found the whole road strewn with the clothing and equipment the Arameans had thrown away in their headlong flight. So the messengers returned and reported to the king. 16Then the people went out and plundered[d] the camp of the Arameans. So a seah of flour sold for a shekel, and two seahs of barley sold for a shekel,[e] as the LORD had said.

17Now the king had put the officer on whose arm he leaned in charge of the gate, and the people trampled him in the gateway, and he died,[f] just as the man of God had foretold when the king came down to his house. 18It happened as the man of God had said to the king: "About this time tomorrow, a seah of flour will sell for a shekel and two seahs of barley for a shekel at the gate of Samaria."

19The officer had said to the man of God, "Look, even if the LORD should open the floodgates[g] of the heavens, could this happen?" The man of God had replied, "You will see it with your own eyes, but you will not eat any of it!" 20And that is exactly what happened to him, for the people trampled him in the gateway, and he died.

The Shunammite's Land Restored

8 Now Elisha had said to the woman[h] whose son he had restored to life, "Go away with your family and stay for a while wherever you can, because the LORD has decreed a famine[i] in the land that will last seven years."[j] 2The woman proceeded to do as the man of God said. She and her family went away and stayed in the land of the Philistines seven years.

3At the end of the seven years she came back from the land of the Philistines and went to the king to beg for her house and land. 4The king was talking to Gehazi, the servant of the man of God, and had said, "Tell me about all the great things Elisha has done." 5Just as Gehazi was telling the king how Elisha had restored[k] the dead to life, the woman whose son Elisha had brought back to life came to

7:7 [a] Jdg 7:21; Ps 48:4-6; Pr 28:1; Isa 30:17
7:8 [b] Isa 33:23; 35:6
7:12 [c] Jos 8:4; 2Ki 6:25-29
7:16 [d] Isa 33:4,23 [e] ver 1
7:17 [f] ver 2; 2Ki 6:32
7:19 [g] ver 2
8:1 [h] 2Ki 4:8-37 [i] Lev 26:26; Dt 28:22; Ru 1:1 [j] Ge 12:10; Ps 105:16; Hag 1:11
8:5 [k] 2Ki 4:35

beg the king for her house and
land.

Gehazi said, "This is the woman,
my lord the king, and this is her son
whom Elisha restored to life." 6The
king asked the woman about it,
and she told him.

Then he assigned an official to
her case and said to him, "Give
back everything that belonged to
her, including all the income from
her land from the day she left the
country until now."

Hazael Murders Ben-Hadad

7Elisha went to Damascus,[a] and
Ben-Hadad[b] king of Aram was ill.
When the king was told, "The man
of God has come all the way up
here," 8he said to Hazael,[c] "Take a
gift[d] with you and go to meet the
man of God. Consult[e] the LORD
through him; ask him, 'Will I recover from this illness?' "

9Hazael went to meet Elisha,
taking with him as a gift forty cam-
el-loads of all the finest wares of
Damascus. He went in and stood
before him, and said, "Your son
Ben-Hadad king of Aram has sent
me to ask, 'Will I recover from this
illness?' "

10Elisha answered, "Go and say
to him, 'You will certainly recover';[f] but[p] the LORD has revealed to
me that he will in fact die." 11He
stared at him with a fixed gaze until Hazael felt ashamed.[g] Then the
man of God began to weep.[h]

12"Why is my lord weeping?"
asked Hazael.

"Because I know the harm[i] you
will do to the Israelites," he answered. "You will set fire to their
fortified places, kill their young
men with the sword, dash[j] their
little children[k] to the ground, and
rip open[l] their pregnant women."

13Hazael said, "How could your
servant, a mere dog,[m] accomplish
such a feat?"

"The LORD has shown me that
you will become king[n] of Aram,"
answered Elisha.

14Then Hazael left Elisha and returned to his master. When Ben-
Hadad asked, "What did Elisha say

8:7 [a] 2Sa 8:5; 1Ki 11:24 [b] 2Ki 6:24
8:8 [c] 1Ki 19:15 [d] Ge 32:20; 1Sa 9:7; 2Ki 1:2 [e] Jdg 18:5
8:10 [f] Isa 38:1
8:11 [g] Jdg 3:25 [h] Lk 19:41
8:12 [i] 1Ki 19:17; 2Ki 10:32; 12:17; 13:3,7 [j] Ps 137:9; Isa 13:16; Hos 13:16; Na 3:10; Lk 19:44 [k] Ge 34:29 [l] 2Ki 15:16; Am 1:13
8:13 [m] 1Sa 17:43; 2Sa 3:8 [n] 1Ki 19:15
8:15 [o] 2Ki 1:17
8:16 [p] 2Ki 1:17; 3:1 [q] 2Ch 21:1-4
8:18 [r] ver 26; 2Ki 11:1
8:19 [s] Ge 6:13 [t] 2Sa 21:17; 7:13; 1Ki 11:36; Rev 21:23
8:20 [u] 1Ki 22:47
8:22 [v] Ge 27:40 [w] Nu 33:20; Jos 21:13; 2Ki 19:8
8:25 [x] 2Ki 9:29

to you?" Hazael replied, "He told
me that you would certainly recover." 15But the next day he took a
thick cloth, soaked it in water and
spread it over the king's face, so
that he died.[o] Then Hazael succeeded him as king.

Jehoram King of Judah

8:16–24pp — 2Ch 21:5–10,20

16In the fifth year of Joram[p] son
of Ahab king of Israel, when Jehoshaphat was king of Judah, Jehoram[q] son of Jehoshaphat began
his reign as king of Judah. 17He
was thirty-two years old when he
became king, and he reigned in Jerusalem eight years. 18He walked
in the ways of the kings of Israel, as
the house of Ahab had done, for he
married a daughter[r] of Ahab. He
did evil in the eyes of the LORD.
19Nevertheless, for the sake of his
servant David, the LORD was not
willing to destroy[s] Judah. He had
promised to maintain a lamp[t] for
David and his descendants forever.

20In the time of Jehoram, Edom
rebelled against Judah and set up
its own king.[u] 21So Jehoram[q]
went to Zair with all his chariots.
The Edomites surrounded him and
his chariot commanders, but he
rose up and broke through by
night; his army, however, fled back
home. 22To this day Edom has
been in rebellion[v] against Judah.
Libnah[w] revolted at the same time.

23As for the other events of Jehoram's reign, and all he did, are they
not written in the book of the annals of the kings of Judah? 24Jeho-
ram rested with his fathers and was
buried with them in the City of David. And Ahaziah his son succeeded him as king.

Ahaziah King of Judah

8:25–29pp — 2Ch 22:1–6

25In the twelfth[x] year of Joram
son of Ahab king of Israel, Ahaziah
son of Jehoram king of Judah be-

[p] *10* The Hebrew may also be read *Go and say, 'You will certainly not recover,' for.*
[q] *21* Hebrew *Joram,* a variant of *Jehoram;* also in verses 23 and 24

gan to reign. **26**Ahaziah was twenty-two years old when he became
king, and he reigned in Jerusalem
one year. His mother's name was
Athaliah,[a] a granddaughter of
Omri[b] king of Israel. **27**He walked
in the ways of the house of Ahab[c]
and did evil[d] in the eyes of the
LORD, as the house of Ahab had
done, for he was related by marriage to Ahab's family.
28Ahaziah went with Joram son
of Ahab to war against Hazael king
of Aram at Ramoth Gilead.[e] The
Arameans wounded Joram; **29**so
King Joram returned to Jezreel[f] to
recover from the wounds the Arameans had inflicted on him at Ramoth[r] in his battle with Hazael[g]
king of Aram.

Then Ahaziah son of Jehoram
king of Judah went down to Jezreel
to see Joram son of Ahab, because
he had been wounded.

Jehu Anointed King of Israel

9 The prophet Elisha summoned
a man from the company[h] of
the prophets and said to him,
"Tuck your cloak into your belt,[i]
take this flask of oil[j] with you and
go to Ramoth Gilead.[k] **2**When you
get there, look for Jehu son of Jehoshaphat, the son of Nimshi. Go
to him, get him away from his companions and take him into an inner
room. **3**Then take the flask and
pour the oil[l] on his head and declare, 'This is what the LORD says: I
anoint you king over Israel.' Then
open the door and run; don't delay!"
4So the young man, the prophet,
went to Ramoth Gilead. **5**When he
arrived, he found the army officers
sitting together. "I have a message
for you, commander," he said.

"For which of us?" asked Jehu.

"For you, commander," he replied.
6Jehu got up and went into the
house. Then the prophet poured
the oil[m] on Jehu's head and declared, "This is what the LORD, the
God of Israel, says: 'I anoint you
king over the LORD's people Israel.
7You are to destroy the house of

8:26 [a]ver 18 [b]1Ki 16:23
8:27 [c]1Ki 16:30 [d]1Ki 15:26
8:28 [e]Dt 4:43; 1Ki 22:3,29
8:29 [f]2Ki 9:15 [g]1Ki 19:15,17
9:1 [h]1Sa 10:5 [i]2Ki 4:29 [j]1Sa 10:1 [k]2Ki 8:28
9:3 [l]1Ki 19:16
9:6 [m]1Ki 19:16; 2Ch 22:7
9:7 [n]Ge 4:24; Rev 6:10 [o]Dt 32:43 [p]1Ki 18:4; 21:15
9:8 [q]2Ki 10:17 [r]Dt 32:36; 1Sa 25:22; 1Ki 21:21; 2Ki 14:26
9:9 [s]1Ki 14:10; 15:29; 16:3, 11 [t]1Ki 16:3
9:10 [u]ver 35-36; 1Ki 21:23
9:11 [v]Jer 29:26; Jn 10:20; Ac 26:24
9:13 [w]Mt 21:8; Lk 19:36 [x]2Sa 15:10; 1Ki 1:34,39
9:14 [y]Dt 4:43; 2Ki 8:28
9:15 [z]2Ki 8:29
9:16 [a]2Ch 22:7
9:17 [b]Isa 21:6

Ahab your master, and I will
avenge[n] the blood of my servants[o]
the prophets and the blood of all
the LORD's servants shed by Jezebel.[p] **8**The whole house[q] of Ahab
will perish. I will cut off from Ahab
every last male[r] in Israel—slave or
free. **9**I will make the house of
Ahab like the house of Jeroboam[s]
son of Nebat and like the house of
Baasha[t] son of Ahijah. **10**As for
Jezebel, dogs[u] will devour her on
the plot of ground at Jezreel, and
no one will bury her.' " Then he
opened the door and ran.
11When Jehu went out to his fellow officers, one of them asked
him, "Is everything all right? Why
did this madman[v] come to you?"

"You know the man and the sort
of things he says," Jehu replied.
12"That's not true!" they said.
"Tell us."

Jehu said, "Here is what he told
me: 'This is what the LORD says: I
anoint you king over Israel.' "
13They hurried and took their
cloaks and spread[w] them under
him on the bare steps. Then they
blew the trumpet[x] and shouted,
"Jehu is king!"

Jehu Kills Joram and Ahaziah

9:21–29pp — 2Ch 22:7–9

14So Jehu son of Jehoshaphat,
the son of Nimshi, conspired
against Joram. (Now Joram and all
Israel had been defending Ramoth
Gilead[y] against Hazael king of
Aram, **15**but King Joram[s] had returned to Jezreel to recover[z] from
the wounds the Arameans had inflicted on him in the battle with
Hazael king of Aram.) Jehu said, "If
this is the way you feel, don't let
anyone slip out of the city to go and
tell the news in Jezreel." **16**Then he
got into his chariot and rode to Jezreel, because Joram was resting
there and Ahaziah[a] king of Judah
had gone down to see him.
17When the lookout[b] standing
on the tower in Jezreel saw Jehu's

[r]29 Hebrew *Ramah,* a variant of *Ramoth*
[s]15 Hebrew *Jehoram,* a variant of *Joram;* also in verses 17 and 21-24

troops approaching, he called out,
"I see some troops coming."
"Get a horseman," Joram ordered. "Send him to meet them
and ask, 'Do you come in
peace?[a]' "
18The horseman rode off to meet
Jehu and said, "This is what the
king says: 'Do you come in
peace?' "
"What do you have to do with
peace?" Jehu replied. "Fall in behind me."
The lookout reported, "The messenger has reached them, but he
isn't coming back."
19So the king sent out a second
horseman. When he came to them
he said, "This is what the king says:
'Do you come in peace?' "
Jehu replied, "What do you have
to do with peace? Fall in behind
me."
20The lookout reported, "He has
reached them, but he isn't coming
back either. The driving is like[b]
that of Jehu son of Nimshi—he
drives like a madman."
21"Hitch up my chariot," Joram
ordered. And when it was hitched
up, Joram king of Israel and Ahaziah king of Judah rode out, each in
his own chariot, to meet Jehu.
They met him at the plot of ground
that had belonged to Naboth[c] the
Jezreelite. **22**When Joram saw Jehu
he asked, "Have you come in
peace, Jehu?"
"How can there be peace," Jehu
replied, "as long as all the idolatry
and witchcraft of your mother Jezebel[d] abound?"
23Joram turned about and fled,
calling out to Ahaziah, "Treachery,[e] Ahaziah!"
24Then Jehu drew his bow[f] and
shot Joram between the shoulders.
The arrow pierced his heart and he
slumped down in his chariot.
25Jehu said to Bidkar, his chariot
officer, "Pick him up and throw
him on the field that belonged to
Naboth the Jezreelite. Remember
how you and I were riding together
in chariots behind Ahab his father
when the LORD made this prophecy[g] about him: **26**'Yesterday I saw

9:17 [a] 1Sa 16:4
9:20 [b] 2Sa 18:27
9:21 [c] ver 26; 1Ki 21:1-7, 15-19
9:22 [d] 1Ki 16:30-33; 18:19; 2Ch 21:13; Rev 2:20
9:23 [e] 2Ki 11:14
9:24 [f] 1Ki 22:34
9:25 [g] 1Ki 21:19-22, 24-29
9:26 [h] 1Ki 21:19 [i] 1Ki 21:29
9:27 [j] Jdg 1:27 [k] 2Ki 23:29
9:28 [l] 2Ki 14:20; 23:30
9:29 [m] 2Ki 8:25
9:30 [n] Jer 4:30; Eze 23:40
9:31 [o] 1Ki 16:9-10
9:33 [p] Ps 7:5
9:34 [q] 1Ki 16:31; 21:25
9:36 [r] Ps 68:23; Jer 15:3 [s] 1Ki 21:23

the blood of Naboth[h] and the
blood of his sons, declares the
LORD, and I will surely make you
pay for it on this plot of ground, declares the LORD.'[t] Now then, pick
him up and throw him on that plot,
in accordance with the word of the
LORD."[i]
27When Ahaziah king of Judah
saw what had happened, he fled up
the road to Beth Haggan.[u] Jehu
chased him, shouting, "Kill him
too!" They wounded him in his
chariot on the way up to Gur near
Ibleam,[j] but he escaped to Megiddo[k] and died there. **28**His servants
took him by chariot[l] to Jerusalem
and buried him with his fathers in
his tomb in the City of David. **29**(In
the eleventh[m] year of Joram son of
Ahab, Ahaziah had become king of
Judah.)

Jezebel Killed

30Then Jehu went to Jezreel.
When Jezebel heard about it, she
painted[n] her eyes, arranged her
hair and looked out of a window.
31As Jehu entered the gate, she
asked, "Have you come in peace,
Zimri,[o] you murderer of your master?"[v]
32He looked up at the window
and called out, "Who is on my side?
Who?" Two or three eunuchs
looked down at him. **33**"Throw her
down!" Jehu said. So they threw
her down, and some of her blood
spattered the wall and the horses
as they trampled her underfoot.[p]
34Jehu went in and ate and
drank. "Take care of that cursed
woman," he said, "and bury her, for
she was a king's daughter."[q] **35**But
when they went out to bury her,
they found nothing except her
skull, her feet and her hands.
36They went back and told Jehu,
who said, "This is the word of the
LORD that he spoke through his servant Elijah the Tishbite: On the
plot of ground at Jezreel dogs[r] will
devour Jezebel's flesh.[w][s] **37**Jeze-

[t] *26* See 1 Kings 21:19. [u] *27* Or *fled by way of the garden house* [v] *31* Or *"Did Zimri have peace, who murdered his master?"* [w] *36* See 1 Kings 21:23.

bel's body will be like refuse[a] on
the ground in the plot at Jezreel, so
that no one will be able to say,
'This is Jezebel.' "

Ahab's Family Killed

10 Now there were in Samaria[b] seventy sons[c] of the
house of Ahab. So Jehu wrote letters and sent them to Samaria: to
the officials of Jezreel,[x][d] to the elders and to the guardians[e] of
Ahab's children. He said, 2"As
soon as this letter reaches you,
since your master's sons are with
you and you have chariots and
horses, a fortified city and weapons, 3choose the best and most
worthy of your master's sons and
set him on his father's throne.
Then fight for your master's
house."
4But they were terrified and said,
"If two kings could not resist him,
how can we?"
5So the palace administrator,
the city governor, the elders and
the guardians sent this message to
Jehu: "We are your servants[f] and
we will do anything you say. We
will not appoint anyone as king;
you do whatever you think best."
6Then Jehu wrote them a second
letter, saying, "If you are on my
side and will obey me, take the
heads of your master's sons and
come to me in Jezreel by this time
tomorrow."
Now the royal princes, seventy of
them, were with the leading men of
the city, who were rearing them.
7When the letter arrived, these
men took the princes and slaughtered all seventy[g] of them. They
put their heads[h] in baskets and
sent them to Jehu in Jezreel.
8When the messenger arrived, he
told Jehu, "They have brought the
heads of the princes."
Then Jehu ordered, "Put them in
two piles at the entrance of the city
gate until morning."
9The next morning Jehu went
out. He stood before all the people
and said, "You are innocent. It was
I who conspired against my master
and killed him, but who killed all
these? 10Know then, that not a
word the LORD has spoken against
the house of Ahab will fail. The
LORD has done what he promised[i]
through his servant Elijah."[j] 11So
Jehu[k] killed everyone in Jezreel
who remained of the house of
Ahab, as well as all his chief men,
his close friends and his priests,
leaving him no survivor.[l]
12Jehu then set out and went toward Samaria. At Beth Eked of the
Shepherds, 13he met some relatives of Ahaziah king of Judah and
asked, "Who are you?"
They said, "We are relatives of
Ahaziah,[m] and we have come down
to greet the families of the king and
of the queen mother.[n]"
14"Take them alive!" he ordered.
So they took them alive and
slaughtered them by the well of
Beth Eked—forty-two men. He left
no survivor.
15After he left there, he came
upon Jehonadab[o] son of Recab,[p]
who was on his way to meet him.
Jehu greeted him and said, "Are
you in accord with me, as I am with
you?"
"I am," Jehonadab answered.
"If so," said Jehu, "give me your
hand."[q] So he did, and Jehu
helped him up into the chariot.
16Jehu said, "Come with me and
see my zeal[r] for the LORD." Then
he had him ride along in his
chariot.
17When Jehu came to Samaria,
he killed all who were left there of
Ahab's family;[s] he destroyed
them, according to the word of the
LORD spoken to Elijah.

Ministers of Baal Killed

18Then Jehu brought all the people together and said to them,
"Ahab served[t] Baal a little; Jehu
will serve him much. 19Now summon[u] all the prophets of Baal, all
his ministers and all his priests.
See that no one is missing, because
I am going to hold a great sacrifice
for Baal. Anyone who fails to come

9:37 [a] Ps 83:10; Isa 5:25; Jer 8:2; 9:22; 16:4; 25:33; Zep 1:17
10:1 [b] 1Ki 13:32 [c] Jdg 8:30 [d] 1Ki 21:1 [e] ver 5
10:5 [f] Jos 9:8; 1Ki 20:4,32
10:7 [g] 1Ki 21:21 [h] 2Sa 4:8
10:10 [i] 2Ki 9:7-10 [j] 1Ki 21:29
10:11 [k] Hos 1:4 [l] ver 14; Job 18:19
10:13 [m] 2Ki 8:24,29; 2Ch 22:8 [n] 1Ki 2:19
10:15 [o] Jer 35:6, 14-19 [p] 1Ch 2:55; Jer 35:2 [q] Ezr 10:19; Eze 17:18
10:16 [r] Nu 25:13; 1Ki 19:10
10:17 [s] 2Ki 9:8
10:18 [t] Jdg 2:11; 1Ki 16:31-32
10:19 [u] 1Ki 18:19; 22:6

[x] 1 Hebrew; some Septuagint manuscripts and Vulgate *of the city*

will no longer live." But Jehu was acting deceptively in order to destroy the ministers of Baal.

20Jehu said, "Call an assembly[a] in honor of Baal." So they proclaimed it. 21Then he sent word throughout Israel, and all the ministers of Baal came; not one stayed away. They crowded into the temple of Baal until it was full from one end to the other. 22And Jehu said to the keeper of the wardrobe, "Bring robes for all the ministers of Baal." So he brought out robes for them.

23Then Jehu and Jehonadab son of Recab went into the temple of Baal. Jehu said to the ministers of Baal, "Look around and see that no servants of the LORD are here with you—only ministers of Baal." 24So they went in to make sacrifices and burnt offerings. Now Jehu had posted eighty men outside with this warning: "If one of you lets any of the men I am placing in your hands escape, it will be your life for his life."[b]

25As soon as Jehu had finished making the burnt offering, he ordered the guards and officers: "Go in and kill[c] them; let no one escape."[d] So they cut them down with the sword. The guards and officers threw the bodies out and then entered the inner shrine of the temple of Baal. 26They brought the sacred stone[e] out of the temple of Baal and burned it. 27They demolished the sacred stone of Baal and tore down the temple[f] of Baal, and people have used it for a latrine to this day.

28So Jehu[g] destroyed Baal worship in Israel. 29However, he did not turn away from the sins[h] of Jeroboam son of Nebat, which he had caused Israel to commit—the worship of the golden calves[i] at Bethel[j] and Dan.

30The LORD said to Jehu, "Because you have done well in accomplishing what is right in my eyes and have done to the house of Ahab all I had in mind to do, your descendants will sit on the throne of Israel to the fourth generation."[k] 31Yet Jehu was not careful[l] to keep the law of the LORD, the God of Israel, with all his heart. He did not turn away from the sins[m] of Jeroboam, which he had caused Israel to commit.

32In those days the LORD began to reduce[n] the size of Israel. Hazael[o] overpowered the Israelites throughout their territory 33east of the Jordan in all the land of Gilead (the region of Gad, Reuben and Manasseh), from Aroer[p] by the Arnon Gorge through Gilead to Bashan.

34As for the other events of Jehu's reign, all he did, and all his achievements, are they not written in the book of the annals[q] of the kings of Israel?

35Jehu rested with his fathers and was buried in Samaria. And Jehoahaz his son succeeded him as king. 36The time that Jehu reigned over Israel in Samaria was twenty-eight years.

Athaliah and Joash

11:1–21pp — 2Ch 22:10–23:21

11 When Athaliah[r] the mother of Ahaziah saw that her son was dead, she proceeded to destroy the whole royal family. 2But Jehosheba, the daughter of King Jehoram[y] and sister of Ahaziah, took Joash[s] son of Ahaziah and stole him away from among the royal princes, who were about to be murdered. She put him and his nurse in a bedroom to hide him from Athaliah; so he was not killed.[t] 3He remained hidden with his nurse at the temple of the LORD for six years while Athaliah ruled the land.

4In the seventh year Jehoiada sent for the commanders of units of a hundred, the Carites[u] and the guards and had them brought to him at the temple of the LORD. He made a covenant with them and put them under oath at the temple of the LORD. Then he showed them the king's son. 5He commanded them, saying, "This is what you are

10:20 [a] Ex 32:5; Joel 1:14
10:24 [b] 1Ki 20:39
10:25 [c] Ex 22:20; 2Ki 11:18 [d] 1Ki 18:40
10:26 [e] 1Ki 14:23
10:27 [f] 1Ki 16:32
10:28 [g] 1Ki 19:17
10:29 [h] 1Ki 12:30 [i] 1Ki 12:28-29 [j] 1Ki 12:32
10:30 [k] ver 35; 2Ki 15:12
10:31 [l] Pr 4:23 [m] 1Ki 12:30
10:32 [n] 2Ki 13:25 [o] 1Ki 19:17; 2Ki 8:12
10:33 [p] Nu 32:34; Dt 2:36; Jdg 11:26; Isa 17:2
10:34 [q] 1Ki 15:31
11:1 [r] 2Ki 8:18
11:2 [s] ver 21; 2Ki 12:1 [t] Jdg 9:5
11:4 [u] ver 19

[y]2 Hebrew *Joram,* a variant of *Jehoram*

to do: You who are in the three companies that are going on duty on the Sabbath[a]—a third of you guarding the royal palace,[b] 6a third at the Sur Gate, and a third at the gate behind the guard, who take turns guarding the temple— 7and you who are in the other two companies that normally go off Sabbath duty are all to guard the temple for the king. 8Station yourselves around the king, each man with his weapon in his hand. Anyone who approaches your ranks[z] must be put to death. Stay close to the king wherever he goes."

9The commanders of units of a hundred did just as Jehoiada the priest ordered. Each one took his men—those who were going on duty on the Sabbath and those who were going off duty—and came to Jehoiada the priest. 10Then he gave the commanders the spears and shields[c] that had belonged to King David and that were in the temple of the LORD. 11The guards, each with his weapon in his hand, stationed themselves around the king—near the altar and the temple, from the south side to the north side of the temple.

12Jehoiada brought out the king's son and put the crown on him; he presented him with a copy of the covenant[d] and proclaimed him king. They anointed[e] him, and the people clapped their hands[f] and shouted, "Long live the king!"[g]

13When Athaliah heard the noise made by the guards and the people, she went to the people at the temple of the LORD. 14She looked and there was the king, standing by the pillar,[h] as the custom was. The officers and the trumpeters were beside the king, and all the people of the land were rejoicing and blowing trumpets.[i] Then Athaliah tore[j] her robes and called out, "Treason! Treason!"[k]

15Jehoiada the priest ordered the commanders of units of a hundred, who were in charge of the troops: "Bring her out between the ranks[a] and put to the sword anyone who follows her." For the priest had said, "She must not be put to death in the temple[l] of the LORD." 16So they seized her as she reached the place where the horses enter[m] the palace grounds, and there she was put to death.[n]

17Jehoiada then made a covenant[o] between the LORD and the king and people that they would be the LORD's people. He also made a covenant between the king and the people.[p] 18All the people of the land went to the temple[q] of Baal and tore it down. They smashed[r] the altars and idols to pieces and killed Mattan the priest[s] of Baal in front of the altars.

Then Jehoiada the priest posted guards at the temple of the LORD. 19He took with him the commanders of hundreds, the Carites,[t] the guards and all the people of the land, and together they brought the king down from the temple of the LORD and went into the palace, entering by way of the gate of the guards. The king then took his place on the royal throne, 20and all the people of the land rejoiced.[u] And the city was quiet, because Athaliah had been slain with the sword at the palace.

21Joash[b] was seven years old when he began to reign.

Joash Repairs the Temple

12:1–21pp — 2Ch 24:1–14; 24:23–27

12 In the seventh year of Jehu, Joash[c][v] became king, and he reigned in Jerusalem forty years. His mother's name was Zibiah; she was from Beersheba. 2Joash did what was right in the eyes of the LORD all the years Jehoiada the priest instructed him. 3The high places,[w] however, were not removed; the people continued to offer sacrifices and burn incense there.

4Joash said to the priests, "Collect[x] all the money that is brought

11:5 [a] 1Ch 9:25 [b] 1Ki 14:27
11:10 [c] 2Sa 8:7; 1Ch 18:7
11:12 [d] Ex 25:16; 2Ki 23:3 [e] 1Sa 9:16; 1Ki 1:39 [f] Ps 47:1; 98:8; Isa 55:12 [g] 1Sa 10:24
11:14 [h] 1Ki 7:15; 2Ki 23:3; 2Ch 34:31 [i] 1Ki 1:39 [j] Ge 37:29 [k] 2Ki 9:23
11:15 [l] 1Ki 2:30
11:16 [m] Ne 3:28; Jer 31:40 [n] Ge 4:14
11:17 [o] Ex 24:8; 2Sa 5:3; 2Ch 15:12; 23:3; 29:10; 34:31; Ezr 10:3 [p] 2Ki 23:3; Jer 34:8
11:18 [q] 1Ki 16:32 [r] Dt 12:3 [s] 1Ki 18:40; 2Ki 10:25; 23:20
11:19 [t] ver 4
11:20 [u] Pr 11:10; 28:12; 29:2
12:1 [v] 2Ki 11:2
12:3 [w] 1Ki 3:3; 2Ki 14:4; 15:35; 18:4
12:4 [x] 2Ki 22:4

[z]8 Or *approaches the precincts* [a]15 Or *out from the precincts* [b]21 Hebrew *Jehoash,* a variant of *Joash* [c]1 Hebrew *Jehoash,* a variant of *Joash;* also in verses 2, 4, 6, 7 and 18

as sacred offerings[a] to the temple
of the LORD—the money collected
in the census,[b] the money received from personal vows and the
money brought voluntarily[c] to the
temple. **5**Let every priest receive
the money from one of the treasurers, and let it be used to repair
whatever damage is found in the
temple."
6But by the twenty-third year of
King Joash the priests still had not
repaired the temple. **7**Therefore
King Joash summoned Jehoiada
the priest and the other priests and
asked them, "Why aren't you repairing the damage done to the
temple? Take no more money from
your treasurers, but hand it over for
repairing the temple." **8**The priests
agreed that they would not collect
any more money from the people
and that they would not repair the
temple themselves.
9Jehoiada the priest took a chest
and bored a hole in its lid. He
placed it beside the altar, on the
right side as one enters the temple
of the LORD. The priests who guarded the entrance[d] put into the chest
all the money[e] that was brought to
the temple of the LORD. **10**Whenever they saw that there was a large
amount of money in the chest, the
royal secretary[f] and the high
priest came, counted the money
that had been brought into the
temple of the LORD and put it into
bags. **11**When the amount had been
determined, they gave the money
to the men appointed to supervise
the work on the temple. With it
they paid those who worked on the
temple of the LORD—the carpenters and builders, **12**the masons
and stonecutters.[g] They purchased timber and dressed stone
for the repair of the temple of the
LORD, and met all the other expenses of restoring the temple.
13The money brought into the
temple was not spent for making
silver basins, wick trimmers, sprinkling bowls, trumpets or any other
articles of gold[h] or silver for the
temple of the LORD; **14**it was paid to
the workmen, who used it to repair
the temple. **15**They did not require
an accounting from those to whom
they gave the money to pay the
workers, because they acted with
complete honesty.[i] **16**The money
from the guilt offerings[j] and sin
offerings[k] was not brought into the
temple of the LORD; it belonged[l] to
the priests.
17About this time Hazael[m] king
of Aram went up and attacked Gath
and captured it. Then he turned to
attack Jerusalem. **18**But Joash king
of Judah took all the sacred objects
dedicated by his fathers—Jehoshaphat, Jehoram and Ahaziah, the
kings of Judah—and the gifts he
himself had dedicated and all the
gold found in the treasuries of the
temple of the LORD and of the royal
palace, and he sent[n] them to Hazael king of Aram, who then withdrew[o] from Jerusalem.
19As for the other events of the
reign of Joash, and all he did, are
they not written in the book of the
annals of the kings of Judah? **20**His
officials[p] conspired against him
and assassinated[q] him at Beth
Millo,[r] on the road down to Silla.
21The officials who murdered him
were Jozabad son of Shimeath and
Jehozabad son of Shomer. He died
and was buried with his fathers in
the City of David. And Amaziah his
son succeeded him as king.

Jehoahaz King of Israel

13 In the twenty-third year of
Joash son of Ahaziah king
of Judah, Jehoahaz son of Jehu became king of Israel in Samaria, and
he reigned seventeen years. **2**He
did evil[s] in the eyes of the LORD by
following the sins of Jeroboam son
of Nebat, which he had caused Israel to commit, and he did not turn
away from them. **3**So the LORD's anger[t] burned against Israel, and for
a long time he kept them under the
power[u] of Hazael king of Aram and
Ben-Hadad[v] his son.
4Then Jehoahaz sought[w] the
LORD's favor, and the LORD listened
to him, for he saw[x] how severely
the king of Aram was oppressing[y]
Israel. **5**The LORD provided a deliv-

12:4 [a]Ex 35:5 [b]Ex 30:12 [c]Ex 35:29; 1Ch 29:3-9
12:9 [d]Jer 35:4 [e]2Ch 24:8; Mk 12:41; Lk 21:1
12:10 [f]2Sa 8:17
12:12 [g]2Ki 22:5-6
12:13 [h]1Ki 7:48-51; 2Ch 24:14
12:15 [i]2Ki 22:7; 1Co 4:2
12:16 [j]Lev 5:14-19; Nu 18:9 [k]Lev 4:1-35 [l]Lev 7:7
12:17 [m]2Ki 8:12
12:18 [n]1Ki 15:18; 2Ch 21:16-17 [o]1Ki 15:21
12:20 [p]2Ki 14:5 [q]2Ch 24:25 [r]Jdg 9:6
13:2 [s]1Ki 12:26-33
13:3 [t]Dt 31:17; Jdg 2:14 [u]1Ki 8:12; 12:17; 19:17 [v]ver 24
13:4 [w]Dt 4:29; Ps 78:34 [x]Ex 3:7; Dt 26:7 [y]2Ki 14:26

erer[a] for Israel, and they escaped
from the power of Aram. So the Israelites lived in their own homes as
they had before. 6But they did not
turn away from the sins[b] of the
house of Jeroboam, which he had
caused Israel to commit; they continued in them. Also, the Asherah
pole[d][c] remained standing in Samaria.
7Nothing had been left[d] of the
army of Jehoahaz except fifty
horsemen, ten chariots and ten
thousand foot soldiers, for the king
of Aram had destroyed the rest and
made them like the dust[e] at
threshing time.
8As for the other events of the
reign of Jehoahaz, all he did and
his achievements, are they not
written in the book of the annals of
the kings of Israel? 9Jehoahaz rested with his fathers and was buried
in Samaria. And Jehoash[e] his son
succeeded him as king.

Jehoash King of Israel

10In the thirty-seventh year of
Joash king of Judah, Jehoash son
of Jehoahaz became king of Israel
in Samaria, and he reigned sixteen
years. 11He did evil in the eyes of
the LORD and did not turn away
from any of the sins of Jeroboam
son of Nebat, which he had caused
Israel to commit; he continued in
them.
12As for the other events of the
reign of Jehoash, all he did and his
achievements, including his war
against Amaziah[f] king of Judah,
are they not written in the book of
the annals[g] of the kings of Israel?
13Jehoash rested with his fathers,
and Jeroboam[h] succeeded him on
the throne. Jehoash was buried
in Samaria with the kings of Israel.
14Now Elisha was suffering from
the illness from which he died. Jehoash king of Israel went down to
see him and wept over him. "My father! My father!" he cried. "The
chariots[i] and horsemen of Israel!"
15Elisha said, "Get a bow and
some arrows,"[j] and he did so.
16"Take the bow in your hands," he
said to the king of Israel. When he
had taken it, Elisha put his hands
on the king's hands.
17"Open the east window," he
said, and he opened it. "Shoot!"[k]
Elisha said, and he shot. "The
LORD's arrow of victory, the arrow of
victory over Aram!" Elisha declared. "You will completely destroy the Arameans at Aphek."[l]
18Then he said, "Take the arrows," and the king took them. Elisha told him, "Strike the ground."
He struck it three times and
stopped. 19The man of God was angry with him and said, "You should
have struck the ground five or six
times; then you would have defeated Aram and completely destroyed
it. But now you will defeat it only
three times."[m]
20Elisha died and was buried.

Now Moabite raiders[n] used to
enter the country every spring.
21Once while some Israelites were
burying a man, suddenly they saw a
band of raiders; so they threw the
man's body into Elisha's tomb.
When the body touched Elisha's
bones, the man came to life[o] and
stood up on his feet.
22Hazael king of Aram op-
pressed[p] Israel throughout the
reign of Jehoahaz. 23But the LORD
was gracious to them and had compassion and showed concern for
them because of his covenant[q]
with Abraham, Isaac and Jacob. To
this day he has been unwilling to
destroy[r] them or banish them
from his presence.[s]
24Hazael king of Aram died, and
Ben-Hadad[t] his son succeeded
him as king. 25Then Jehoash son of
Jehoahaz recaptured from Ben-Hadad son of Hazael the towns he had
taken in battle from his father Jehoahaz. Three times[u] Jehoash defeated him, and so he recovered[v]
the Israelite towns.

13:5 [a] ver 25; 2Ki 14:25,27
13:6 [b] 1Ki 12:30 [c] 1Ki 16:33
13:7 [d] 2Ki 10:32-33 [e] 2Sa 22:43
13:12 [f] 2Ki 14:15 [g] 1Ki 15:31
13:13 [h] 2Ki 14:23; Hos 1:1
13:14 [i] 2Ki 2:12
13:15 [j] 1Sa 20:20
13:17 [k] Jos 8:18 [l] 1Ki 20:26
13:19 [m] ver 25
13:20 [n] 2Ki 3:7; 24:2
13:21 [o] Mt 27:52
13:22 [p] 1Ki 19:17; 2Ki 8:12
13:23 [q] Ge 13:16-17; Ex 2:24 [r] Dt 29:20 [s] Ex 33:15; 2Ki 14:27; 17:18; 24:3, 20
13:24 [t] ver 3
13:25 [u] ver 18,19 [v] 2Ki 10:32

[d]6 That is, a symbol of the goddess Asherah; here and elsewhere in 2 Kings [e]9 Hebrew *Joash,* a variant of *Jehoash;* also in verses 12-14 and 25

Amaziah King of Judah

14:1–7pp — 2Ch 25:1–4,11–12
14:8–22pp — 2Ch 25:17–26:2

14 In the second year of Jehoash[f] son of Jehoahaz king of Israel, Amaziah son of Joash king of Judah began to reign. [2]He was twenty-five years old when he became king, and he reigned in Jerusalem twenty-nine years. His mother's name was Jehoaddin; she was from Jerusalem. [3]He did what was right in the eyes of the LORD, but not as his father David had done. In everything he followed the example of his father Joash. [4]The high places,[a] however, were not removed; the people continued to offer sacrifices and burn incense there.

[5]After the kingdom was firmly in his grasp, he executed[b] the officials[c] who had murdered his father the king. [6]Yet he did not put the sons of the assassins to death, in accordance with what is written in the Book of the Law[d] of Moses where the LORD commanded: "Fathers shall not be put to death for their children, nor children put to death for their fathers; each is to die for his own sins."[g][e]

[7]He was the one who defeated ten thousand Edomites in the Valley of Salt[f] and captured Sela[g] in battle, calling it Joktheel, the name it has to this day.

[8]Then Amaziah sent messengers to Jehoash son of Jehoahaz, the son of Jehu, king of Israel, with the challenge: "Come, meet me face to face."

[9]But Jehoash king of Israel replied to Amaziah king of Judah: "A thistle[h] in Lebanon sent a message to a cedar in Lebanon, 'Give your daughter to my son in marriage.' Then a wild beast in Lebanon came along and trampled the thistle underfoot. [10]You have indeed defeated Edom and now you are arrogant.[i] Glory in your victory, but stay at home! Why ask for trouble and cause your own downfall and that of Judah also?"

[11]Amaziah, however, would not listen, so Jehoash king of Israel attacked. He and Amaziah king of Judah faced each other at Beth Shemesh[j] in Judah. [12]Judah was routed by Israel, and every man fled to his home.[k] [13]Jehoash king of Israel captured Amaziah king of Judah, the son of Joash, the son of Ahaziah, at Beth Shemesh. Then Jehoash went to Jerusalem and broke down the wall[l] of Jerusalem from the Ephraim Gate[m] to the Corner Gate[n]—a section about six hundred feet long.[h] [14]He took all the gold and silver and all the articles found in the temple of the LORD and in the treasuries of the royal palace. He also took hostages and returned to Samaria.

[15]As for the other events of the reign of Jehoash, what he did and his achievements, including his war[o] against Amaziah king of Judah, are they not written in the book of the annals of the kings of Israel? [16]Jehoash rested with his fathers and was buried in Samaria with the kings of Israel. And Jeroboam his son succeeded him as king.

[17]Amaziah son of Joash king of Judah lived for fifteen years after the death of Jehoash son of Jehoahaz king of Israel. [18]As for the other events of Amaziah's reign, are they not written in the book of the annals of the kings of Judah?

[19]They conspired[p] against him in Jerusalem, and he fled to Lachish,[q] but they sent men after him to Lachish and killed him there. [20]He was brought back by horse[r] and was buried in Jerusalem with his fathers, in the City of David.

[21]Then all the people of Judah took Azariah,[i][s] who was sixteen years old, and made him king in place of his father Amaziah. [22]He was the one who rebuilt Elath[t] and restored it to Judah after Amaziah rested with his fathers.

14:4 [a] 2Ki 12:3; 16:4
14:5 [b] 2Ki 21:24 [c] 2Ki 12:20
14:6 [d] Dt 28:61 [e] Nu 26:11; Job 21:20; Jer 31:30; 44:3; Eze 18:4,20
14:7 [f] 2Sa 8:13; 2Ch 25:11 [g] Jdg 1:36
14:9 [h] Jdg 9:8-15
14:10 [i] Dt 8:14; 2Ch 26:16; 32:25
14:11 [j] Jos 15:10
14:12 [k] 2Sa 18:17
14:13 [l] 1Ki 3:1; 2Ch 33:14; 36:19; Jer 39:2 [m] Ne 8:16; 12:39 [n] 2Ch 25:23; Jer 31:38; Zec 14:10
14:15 [o] 2Ki 13:12
14:19 [p] 2Ki 12:20 [q] Jos 10:3; 2Ki 18:14,17
14:20 [r] 2Ki 9:28
14:21 [s] 2Ki 15:1; 2Ch 26:23
14:22 [t] 1Ki 9:26; 2Ki 16:6

[f]*1* Hebrew *Joash,* a variant of *Jehoash*; also in verses 13, 23 and 27 [g]*6* Deut. 24:16
[h]*13* Hebrew *four hundred cubits* (about 180 meters) [i]*21* Also called *Uzziah*

Jeroboam II King of Israel

23In the fifteenth year of Amaziah son of Joash king of Judah, Jeroboam[a] son of Jehoash king of Israel became king in Samaria, and he
reigned forty-one years. **24**He did
evil in the eyes of the LORD and did
not turn away from any of the sins
of Jeroboam son of Nebat, which
he had caused Israel to commit.[b]
25He was the one who restored the
boundaries of Israel from Lebo[i]
Hamath[c] to the Sea of the Arabah,[k][d] in accordance with the
word of the LORD, the God of Israel,
spoken through his servant Jonah[e]
son of Amittai, the prophet from
Gath Hepher.

26The LORD had seen how bitterly
everyone in Israel, whether slave or
free,[f] was suffering;[g] there was no
one to help them.[h] **27**And since
the LORD had not said he would blot
out[i] the name of Israel from under
heaven, he saved[j] them by the
hand of Jeroboam son of Jehoash.

28As for the other events of Jeroboam's reign, all he did, and his
military achievements, including
how he recovered for Israel both
Damascus[k] and Hamath,[l] which
had belonged to Yaudi,[l] are they
not written in the book of the annals[m] of the kings of Israel? **29**Jeroboam rested with his fathers, the
kings of Israel. And Zechariah his
son succeeded him as king.

Azariah King of Judah

15:1-7pp — 2Ch 26:3-4,21-23

15 In the twenty-seventh year
of Jeroboam king of Israel,
Azariah[n] son of Amaziah king of
Judah began to reign. **2**He was sixteen years old when he became
king, and he reigned in Jerusalem
fifty-two years. His mother's name
was Jecoliah; she was from Jerusalem. **3**He did what was right in the
eyes of the LORD, just as his father
Amaziah had done. **4**The high
places, however, were not removed; the people continued to offer sacrifices and burn incense
there.

5The LORD afflicted[o] the king
with leprosy[m] until the day he died,
and he lived in a separate
house.[n][p] Jotham[q] the king's son
had charge of the palace[r] and governed the people of the land.

6As for the other events of Azariah's reign, and all he did, are they
not written in the book of the annals of the kings of Judah? **7**Azariah rested[s] with his fathers and was
buried near them in the City of David. And Jotham[t] his son succeeded him as king.

Zechariah King of Israel

8In the thirty-eighth year of Azariah king of Judah, Zechariah son
of Jeroboam became king of Israel
in Samaria, and he reigned six
months. **9**He did evil[u] in the eyes
of the LORD, as his fathers had
done. He did not turn away from
the sins of Jeroboam son of Nebat,
which he had caused Israel to commit.

10Shallum son of Jabesh conspired against Zechariah. He attacked him in front of the people,[o]
assassinated[v] him and succeeded
him as king. **11**The other events of
Zechariah's reign are written in the
book of the annals[w] of the kings of
Israel. **12**So the word of the LORD
spoken to Jehu was fulfilled:[x]
"Your descendants will sit on the
throne of Israel to the fourth generation."[p]

Shallum King of Israel

13Shallum son of Jabesh became
king in the thirty-ninth year of Uzziah king of Judah, and he reigned
in Samaria[y] one month. **14**Then
Menahem son of Gadi went from
Tirzah[z] up to Samaria. He attacked Shallum son of Jabesh in
Samaria, assassinated[a] him and
succeeded him as king.

15The other events of Shallum's
reign, and the conspiracy he led,

14:23 [a] 2Ki 13:13
14:24 [b] 1Ki 15:30
14:25 [c] Nu 13:21; 1Ki 8:65 [d] Dt 3:17 [e] Jnh 1:1; Mt 12:39
14:26 [f] Dt 32:36 [g] 2Ki 13:4 [h] Ps 18:41; 22:11; 72:12; 107:12; Isa 63:5; La 1:7
14:27 [i] 2Ki 13:23 [j] Jdg 6:14
14:28 [k] 2Sa 8:5; 1Ki 11:24 [l] 2Ch 8:3 [m] 1Ki 15:31
15:1 [n] ver 32; 2Ki 14:21
15:5 [o] Ge 12:17 [p] Lev 13:46 [q] 2Ch 27:1 [r] Ge 41:40
15:7 [s] Isa 6:1; 14:28 [t] ver 5
15:9 [u] 1Ki 15:26
15:10 [v] 2Ki 12:20
15:11 [w] 1Ki 15:31
15:12 [x] 2Ki 10:30
15:13 [y] ver 1,8
15:14 [z] 1Ki 14:17 [a] 2Ki 12:20

---

[i]25 Or *from the entrance to* [k]25 That is, the Dead Sea [l]28 Or *Judah* [m]5 The Hebrew word was used for various diseases affecting the skin—not necessarily leprosy. [n]5 Or *in a house where he was relieved of responsibility* [o]10 Hebrew; some Septuagint manuscripts *in Ibleam* [p]12 2 Kings 10:30

are written in the book of the annals[a] of the kings of Israel.

16At that time Menahem, starting out from Tirzah, attacked Tiphsah[b] and everyone in the city and its vicinity, because they refused to open[c] their gates. He sacked Tiphsah and ripped open all the pregnant women.

Menahem King of Israel

17In the thirty-ninth year of Azariah king of Judah, Menahem son of Gadi became king of Israel, and he reigned in Samaria ten years. **18**He did evil in the eyes of the LORD. During his entire reign he did not turn away from the sins of Jeroboam son of Nebat, which he had caused Israel to commit.

19Then Pul[q][d] king of Assyria invaded the land, and Menahem gave him a thousand talents[r] of silver to gain his support and strengthen his own hold on the kingdom. **20**Menahem exacted this money from Israel. Every wealthy man had to contribute fifty shekels[s] of silver to be given to the king of Assyria. So the king of Assyria withdrew[e] and stayed in the land no longer.

21As for the other events of Menahem's reign, and all he did, are they not written in the book of the annals of the kings of Israel? **22**Menahem rested with his fathers. And Pekahiah his son succeeded him as king.

Pekahiah King of Israel

23In the fiftieth year of Azariah king of Judah, Pekahiah son of Menahem became king of Israel in Samaria, and he reigned two years. **24**Pekahiah did evil in the eyes of the LORD. He did not turn away from the sins of Jeroboam son of Nebat, which he had caused Israel to commit. **25**One of his chief officers, Pekah[f] son of Remaliah, conspired against him. Taking fifty men of Gilead with him, he assassinated[g] Pekahiah, along with Argob and Arieh, in the citadel of the royal palace at Samaria. So Pekah killed Pekahiah and succeeded him as king.

26The other events of Pekahiah's reign, and all he did, are written in the book of the annals of the kings of Israel.

Pekah King of Israel

27In the fifty-second year of Azariah king of Judah, Pekah[h] son of Remaliah[i] became king of Israel in Samaria, and he reigned twenty years. **28**He did evil in the eyes of the LORD. He did not turn away from the sins of Jeroboam son of Nebat, which he had caused Israel to commit.

29In the time of Pekah king of Israel, Tiglath-Pileser[j] king of Assyria came and took Ijon,[k] Abel Beth Maacah, Janoah, Kedesh and Hazor. He took Gilead and Galilee, including all the land of Naphtali,[l] and deported[m] the people to Assyria. **30**Then Hoshea[n] son of Elah conspired against Pekah son of Remaliah. He attacked and assassinated[o] him, and then succeeded him as king in the twentieth year of Jotham son of Uzziah.

31As for the other events of Pekah's reign, and all he did, are they not written in the book of the annals of the kings of Israel?

Jotham King of Judah

15:33–38pp — 2Ch 27:1-4,7-9

32In the second year of Pekah son of Remaliah king of Israel, Jotham[p] son of Uzziah king of Judah began to reign. **33**He was twenty-five years old when he became king, and he reigned in Jerusalem sixteen years. His mother's name was Jerusha daughter of Zadok. **34**He did what was right[q] in the eyes of the LORD, just as his father Uzziah had done. **35**The high places,[r] however, were not removed; the people continued to offer sacrifices and burn incense there. Jotham rebuilt the Upper Gate[s] of the temple of the LORD.

15:15 [a] 1Ki 15:31
15:16 [b] 1Ki 4:24 [c] 2Ki 8:12; Hos 13:16
15:19 [d] 1Ch 5:6,26
15:20 [e] 2Ki 12:18
15:25 [f] 2Ch 28:6; Isa 7:1 [g] 2Ki 12:20
15:27 [h] 2Ch 28:6; Isa 7:1 [i] Isa 7:4
15:29 [j] 2Ki 16:7; 17:6; 1Ch 5:26; 2Ch 28:20; Jer 50:17 [k] 1Ki 15:20 [l] 2Ki 16:9; 17:24; 2Ch 16:4; Isa 9:1 [m] 2Ki 24:14-16; 1Ch 5:22; Isa 14:6,17; 36:17; 45:13
15:30 [n] 2Ki 17:1 [o] 2Ki 12:20
15:32 [p] 1Ch 5:17
15:34 [q] ver 3; 1Ki 14:8; 2Ch 26:4-5
15:35 [r] 2Ki 12:3 [s] 2Ch 23:20

[q]*19* Also called *Tiglath-Pileser* [r]*19* That is, about 37 tons (about 34 metric tons)
[s]*20* That is, about 1 1/4 pounds (about 0.6 kilogram)

36As for the other events of Jotham's reign, and what he did, are
they not written in the book of the
annals of the kings of Judah? 37(In
those days the LORD began to send
Rezin[a] king of Aram and Pekah
son of Remaliah against Judah.)
38Jotham rested with his fathers
and was buried with them in the
City of David, the city of his father.
And Ahaz his son succeeded him as
king.

Ahaz King of Judah

16:1–20pp — 2Ch 28:1–27

16 In the seventeenth year of
Pekah son of Remaliah,
Ahaz[b] son of Jotham king of Judah
began to reign. 2Ahaz was twenty
years old when he became king,
and he reigned in Jerusalem sixteen years. Unlike David his father,
he did not do what was right[c] in
the eyes of the LORD his God. 3He
walked in the ways of the kings of
Israel and even sacrificed his son[d]
in[t] the fire, following the detestable[e] ways of the nations the LORD
had driven out before the Israelites. 4He offered sacrifices and
burned incense at the high places,
on the hilltops and under every
spreading tree.[f]

5Then Rezin[g] king of Aram and
Pekah son of Remaliah king of Israel marched up to fight against Jerusalem and besieged Ahaz, but they
could not overpower him. 6At that
time, Rezin[h] king of Aram recovered Elath[i] for Aram by driving out
the men of Judah. Edomites then
moved into Elath and have lived
there to this day.

7Ahaz sent messengers to say to
Tiglath-Pileser[j] king of Assyria, "I
am your servant and vassal. Come
up and save[k] me out of the hand of
the king of Aram and of the king of
Israel, who are attacking me."
8And Ahaz took the silver and gold
found in the temple of the LORD and
in the treasuries of the royal palace
and sent it as a gift[l] to the king of
Assyria. 9The king of Assyria com-
plied by attacking Damascus[m] and
capturing it. He deported its inhabitants to Kir[n] and put Rezin to
death.

10Then King Ahaz went to Damascus to meet Tiglath-Pileser
king of Assyria. He saw an altar in
Damascus and sent to Uriah[o] the
priest a sketch of the altar, with detailed plans for its construction.
11So Uriah the priest built an altar
in accordance with all the plans
that King Ahaz had sent from Damascus and finished it before King
Ahaz returned. 12When the king
came back from Damascus and saw
the altar, he approached it and presented offerings[u][p] on it. 13He offered up his burnt offering[q] and
grain offering, poured out his drink
offering, and sprinkled the blood of
his fellowship offerings[v][r] on the
altar. 14The bronze altar[s] that
stood before the LORD he brought
from the front of the temple—from
between the new altar and the temple of the LORD—and put it on the
north side of the new altar.

15King Ahaz then gave these orders to Uriah the priest: "On the
large new altar, offer the morning[t]
burnt offering and the evening
grain offering, the king's burnt offering and his grain offering, and
the burnt offering of all the people
of the land, and their grain offering
and their drink offering. Sprinkle
on the altar all the blood of the
burnt offerings and sacrifices. But I
will use the bronze altar for seeking
guidance."[u] 16And Uriah the
priest did just as King Ahaz had ordered.

17King Ahaz took away the side
panels and removed the basins
from the movable stands. He removed the Sea from the bronze
bulls that supported it and set it on
a stone base.[v] 18He took away the
Sabbath canopy[w] that had been
built at the temple and removed
the royal entryway outside the temple of the LORD, in deference to the
king of Assyria.[w]

19As for the other events of the

[t]3 Or *even made his son pass through*
[u]12 Or *and went up* [v]13 Traditionally *peace offerings* [w]18 Or *the dais of his throne* (see Septuagint)

15:37 [a]2Ki 16:5; Isa 7:1
16:1 [b]Isa 1:1; 14:28
16:2 [c]1Ki 14:8
16:3 [d]Lev 18:21; 2Ki 21:6 [e]Lev 18:3; Dt 9:4; 12:31
16:4 [f]Dt 12:2; Eze 6:13
16:5 [g]2Ki 15:37; Isa 7:1,4
16:6 [h]Isa 9:12 [i]2Ki 14:22; 2Ch 26:2
16:7 [j]2Ki 15:29 [k]Isa 2:6; Jer 2:18; Eze 16:28; Hos 10:6
16:8 [l]2Ki 12:18
16:9 [m]2Ki 15:29 [n]Isa 22:6; Am 1:5; 9:7
16:10 [o]Isa 8:2
16:12 [p]2Ch 26:16
16:13 [q]Lev 6:8-13 [r]Lev 7:11-21
16:14 [s]2Ch 4:1
16:15 [t]Ex 29:38-41 [u]1Sa 9:9
16:17 [v]1Ki 7:27
16:18 [w]Eze 16:28

reign of Ahaz, and what he did, are
they not written in the book of the
annals of the kings of Judah?
20Ahaz rested with his fathers and
was buried with them in the City of
David. And Hezekiah his son succeeded him as king.

Hoshea Last King of Israel

17:3–7pp — 2Ki 18:9–12

17 In the twelfth year of Ahaz
king of Judah, Hoshea[a] son
of Elah became king of Israel in Samaria, and he reigned nine years.
2He did evil in the eyes of the LORD,
but not like the kings of Israel who
preceded him.
3Shalmaneser[b] king of Assyria
came up to attack Hoshea, who
had been Shalmaneser's vassal and
had paid him tribute. 4But the king
of Assyria discovered that Hoshea
was a traitor, for he had sent envoys
to So[x] king of Egypt, and he no
longer paid tribute to the king of
Assyria, as he had done year by
year. Therefore Shalmaneser
seized him and put him in prison.
5The king of Assyria invaded the
entire land, marched against Samaria and laid siege[c] to it for three
years. 6In the ninth year of Hoshea,
the king of Assyria captured Samaria[d] and deported[e] the Israelites to Assyria. He settled them in
Halah, in Gozan[f] on the Habor
River and in the towns of the
Medes.

Israel Exiled Because of Sin

7All this took place because the
Israelites had sinned[g] against the
LORD their God, who had brought
them up out of Egypt[h] from under
the power of Pharaoh king of
Egypt. They worshiped other gods
8and followed the practices of the
nations[i] the LORD had driven out
before them, as well as the practices that the kings of Israel had introduced. 9The Israelites secretly
did things against the LORD their
God that were not right. From
watchtower to fortified city[j] they
built themselves high places in all
their towns. 10They set up sacred
stones and Asherah poles[k] on every high hill and under every
spreading tree.[l] 11At every high
place they burned incense, as the
nations whom the LORD had driven
out before them had done. They
did wicked things that provoked
the LORD to anger. 12They worshiped idols,[m] though the LORD had
said, "You shall not do this."[y]
13The LORD warned Israel and Judah through all his prophets and
seers:[n] "Turn from your evil
ways.[o] Observe my commands and
decrees, in accordance with the entire Law that I commanded your fathers to obey and that I delivered to
you through my servants the
prophets."
14But they would not listen and
were as stiff-necked[p] as their fathers, who did not trust in the LORD
their God. 15They rejected his decrees and the covenant[q] he had
made with their fathers and the
warnings he had given them. They
followed worthless idols[r] and
themselves became worthless.
They imitated the nations[s] around
them although the LORD had
ordered them, "Do not do as
they do," and they did the things
the LORD had forbidden them to
do.
16They forsook all the commands of the LORD their God and
made for themselves two idols cast
in the shape of calves,[t] and an
Asherah[u] pole. They bowed down
to all the starry hosts,[v] and they
worshiped Baal.[w] 17They sacrificed[x] their sons and daughters
in[z] the fire. They practiced divination and sorcery[y] and sold[z]
themselves to do evil in the eyes
of the LORD, provoking him to anger.
18So the LORD was very angry
with Israel and removed them from
his presence. Only the tribe of Judah was left, 19and even Judah did
not keep the commands of the

17:1 [a] 2Ki 15:30
17:3 [b] 2Ki 18:9-12; Hos 10:14
17:5 [c] Hos 13:16
17:6 [d] Hos 13:16 [e] Dt 28:36,64; 2Ki 18:10-11 [f] 1Ch 5:26
17:7 [g] Jos 23:16; Jdg 6:10 [h] Ex 14:15-31
17:8 [i] Lev 18:3; Dt 18:9; 2Ki 16:3
17:9 [j] 2Ki 18:8
17:10 [k] Ex 34:13; Mic 5:14 [l] 1Ki 14:23
17:12 [m] Ex 20:4
17:13 [n] 1Sa 9:9 [o] Jer 18:11; 25:5; 35:15
17:14 [p] Ex 32:9; Dt 31:27; Ac 7:51
17:15 [q] Dt 29:25 [r] Dt 32:21; Ro 1:21-23 [s] Dt 12:30-31
17:16 [t] 1Ki 12:28 [u] 1Ki 14:15,23 [v] 2Ki 21:3 [w] 1Ki 16:31
17:17 [x] Dt 18:10-12; 2Ki 16:3 [y] Lev 19:26 [z] 1Ki 21:20

[x]4 Or *to Sais, to the*; *So* is possibly an abbreviation for *Osorkon.* [y]12 Exodus 20:4, 5 [z]17 Or *They made their sons and daughters pass through*

LORD their God. They followed the
practices Israel had introduced.[a]
20Therefore the LORD rejected all
the people of Israel; he afflicted
them and gave them into the hands
of plunderers,[b] until he thrust
them from his presence.
21When he tore[c] Israel away
from the house of David, they made
Jeroboam son of Nebat their
king.[d] Jeroboam enticed Israel
away from following the LORD and
caused them to commit a great sin.
22The Israelites persisted in all the
sins of Jeroboam and did not turn
away from them 23until the LORD
removed them from his presence,
as he had warned through all his
servants the prophets. So the people of Israel were taken from their
homeland into exile in Assyria, and
they are still there.

Samaria Resettled

24The king of Assyria[e] brought
people from Babylon, Cuthah,
Avva, Hamath and Sepharvaim[f]
and settled them in the towns of
Samaria to replace the Israelites.
They took over Samaria and lived
in its towns. 25When they first lived
there, they did not worship the
LORD; so he sent lions[g] among
them and they killed some of the
people. 26It was reported to the
king of Assyria: "The people you
deported and resettled in the
towns of Samaria do not know what
the god of that country requires.
He has sent lions among them,
which are killing them off, because
the people do not know what he requires."
27Then the king of Assyria gave
this order: "Have one of the priests
you took captive from Samaria go
back to live there and teach the
people what the god of the land requires." 28So one of the priests
who had been exiled from Samaria came to live in Bethel and
taught them how to worship the
LORD.
29Nevertheless, each national
group made its own gods in the several towns[h] where they settled,
and set them up in the shrines[i]
the people of Samaria had made at
the high places.[j] 30The men from
Babylon made Succoth Benoth,
the men from Cuthah made Nergal,
and the men from Hamath made
Ashima; 31the Avvites made Nib-
haz and Tartak, and the Sephar-
vites burned their children in the
fire as sacrifices to Adrammelech[k]
and Anammelech, the gods of
Sepharvaim.[l] 32They worshiped
the LORD, but they also appointed
all sorts[m] of their own people to of-
ficiate for them as priests in the
shrines at the high places. 33They
worshiped the LORD, but they also
served their own gods in accordance with the customs of the nations from which they had been
brought.
34To this day they persist in their
former practices. They neither worship the LORD nor adhere to the decrees and ordinances, the laws and
commands that the LORD gave the
descendants of Jacob, whom he
named Israel.[n] 35When the LORD
made a covenant with the Israelites, he commanded them: "Do not
worship[o] any other gods or bow
down to them, serve them or sacrifice to them. 36But the LORD, who
brought you up out of Egypt with
mighty power and outstretched
arm,[p] is the one you must worship.
To him you shall bow down and to
him offer sacrifices. 37You must always be careful[q] to keep the decrees and ordinances, the laws and
commands he wrote for you. Do
not worship other gods. 38Do not
forget[r] the covenant I have made
with you, and do not worship other
gods. 39Rather, worship the LORD
your God; it is he who will deliver
you from the hand of all your enemies."
40They would not listen, however, but persisted in their former
practices. 41Even while these people were worshiping the LORD,[s]
they were serving their idols. To
this day their children and grandchildren continue to do as their fathers did.

17:19 [a] 1Ki 14:22-23; 2Ki 16:3
17:20 [b] 2Ki 15:29
17:21 [c] 1Ki 11:11 [d] 1Ki 12:20
17:24 [e] Ezr 4:2,10 [f] 2Ki 18:34
17:25 [g] Ge 37:20
17:29 [h] Jer 2:28 [i] 1Ki 12:31 [j] Mic 4:5
17:31 [k] 2Ki 19:37 [l] ver 24
17:32 [m] 1Ki 12:31
17:34 [n] Ge 32:28; 35:10; 1Ki 18:31
17:35 [o] Ex 20:5; Jdg 6:10
17:36 [p] Ex 3:20; 6:6; Ps 136:12
17:37 [q] Dt 5:32
17:38 [r] Dt 4:23; 6:12
17:41 [s] ver 32-33; 1Ki 18:21; Mt 6:24

Hezekiah King of Judah

18:2–4pp — 2Ch 29:1–2; 31:1
18:5–7pp — 2Ch 31:20–21
18:9–12pp — 2Ki 17:3–7

18 In the third year of Hoshea son of Elah king of Israel, Hezekiah[a] son of Ahaz king of Judah began to reign. 2He was twenty-five years old when he became king, and he reigned in Jerusalem twenty-nine years.[b] His mother's name was Abijah[a] daughter of Zechariah. 3He did what was right in the eyes of the LORD, just as his father David[c] had done. 4He removed[d] the high places, smashed the sacred stones[e] and cut down the Asherah poles. He broke into pieces the bronze snake[f] Moses had made, for up to that time the Israelites had been burning incense to it. (It was called[b] Nehushtan.[c])

5Hezekiah trusted[g] in the LORD, the God of Israel. There was no one like him among all the kings of Judah, either before him or after him. 6He held fast[h] to the LORD and did not cease to follow him; he kept the commands the LORD had given Moses. 7And the LORD was with him; he was successful[i] in whatever he undertook. He rebelled[j] against the king of Assyria and did not serve him. 8From watchtower to fortified city,[k] he defeated the Philistines, as far as Gaza and its territory.

9In King Hezekiah's fourth year,[l] which was the seventh year of Hoshea son of Elah king of Israel, Shalmaneser king of Assyria marched against Samaria and laid siege to it. 10At the end of three years the Assyrians took it. So Samaria was captured in Hezekiah's sixth year, which was the ninth year of Hoshea king of Israel. 11The king[m] of Assyria deported Israel to Assyria and settled them in Halah, in Gozan on the Habor River and in towns of the Medes. 12This happened because they had not obeyed the LORD their God, but had violated his covenant[n]—all that Moses the servant of the LORD commanded.[o] They neither listened to the commands[p] nor carried them out.

13In the fourteenth year of King Hezekiah's reign, Sennacherib king of Assyria attacked all the fortified cities of Judah[q] and captured them. 14So Hezekiah king of Judah sent this message to the king of Assyria at Lachish: "I have done wrong.[r] Withdraw from me, and I will pay whatever you demand of me." The king of Assyria exacted from Hezekiah king of Judah three hundred talents[d] of silver and thirty talents[e] of gold. 15So Hezekiah gave[s] him all the silver that was found in the temple of the LORD and in the treasuries of the royal palace.

16At this time Hezekiah king of Judah stripped off the gold with which he had covered the doors and doorposts of the temple of the LORD, and gave it to the king of Assyria.

Sennacherib Threatens Jerusalem

18:13, 17–37pp — Isa 36:1–22
18:17–35pp — 2Ch 32:9–19

17The king of Assyria sent his supreme commander,[t] his chief officer and his field commander with a large army, from Lachish to King Hezekiah at Jerusalem. They came up to Jerusalem and stopped at the aqueduct of the Upper Pool,[u] on the road to the Washerman's Field. 18They called for the king; and Eliakim[v] son of Hilkiah the palace administrator, Shebna[w] the secretary, and Joah son of Asaph the recorder went out to them.

19The field commander said to them, "Tell Hezekiah:

"'This is what the great king, the king of Assyria, says: On what are you basing this confidence of yours? 20You say you have strategy and military strength—but you speak

18:1 [a]Isa 1:1; 2Ch 28:27
18:2 [b]Isa 38:5
18:3 [c]Isa 38:5
18:4 [d]2Ch 31:1 [e]Ex 23:24 [f]Nu 21:9
18:5 [g]2Ki 19:10; 23:25
18:6 [h]Dt 10:20; Jos 23:8; Dt
18:7 [i]Ge 39:3; 1Sa 18:14 [j]2Ki 16:7
18:8 [k]2Ki 17:9; Isa 14:29
18:9 [l]Isa 1:1
18:11 [m]Isa 37:12
18:12 [n]2Ki 17:15 [o]Da 9:6,10 [p]1Ki 9:6
18:13 [q]2Ch 32:1; Isa 1:7; Mic 1:9
18:14 [r]Isa 24:5
18:15 [s]1Ki 15:18; 2Ki 16:8
18:17 [t]Isa 20:1 [u]2Ki 20:20; 2Ch 32:4,30; Isa 7:3
18:18 [v]2Ki 19:2; Isa 22:20 [w]Isa 22:15

[a]2 Hebrew *Abi,* a variant of *Abijah* [b]4 Or *He called it* [c]4 *Nehushtan* sounds like the Hebrew for *bronze* and *snake* and *unclean thing.* [d]14 That is, about 11 tons (about 10 metric tons) [e]14 That is, about 1 ton (about 1 metric ton)

only empty words. On whom
are you depending, that you
rebel against me? **21**Look now,
you are depending on Egypt,[a]
that splintered reed of a
staff,[b] which pierces a man's
hand and wounds him if he
leans on it! Such is Pharaoh
king of Egypt to all who depend on him. **22**And if you say
to me, "We are depending on
the LORD our God"—isn't he
the one whose high places and
altars Hezekiah removed, saying to Judah and Jerusalem,
"You must worship before this
altar in Jerusalem"?
23" 'Come now, make a bargain with my master, the king
of Assyria: I will give you two
thousand horses—if you can
put riders on them! **24**How can
you repulse one officer[c] of the
least of my master's officials,
even though you are depending on Egypt for chariots and
horsemen[f]? **25**Furthermore,
have I come to attack and destroy this place without word
from the LORD?[d] The LORD
himself told me to march
against this country and destroy it.' "

26Then Eliakim son of Hilkiah,
and Shebna and Joah said to the
field commander, "Please speak to
your servants in Aramaic,[e] since
we understand it. Don't speak to us
in Hebrew in the hearing of the
people on the wall."
27But the commander replied,
"Was it only to your master and you
that my master sent me to say
these things, and not to the men
sitting on the wall—who, like you,
will have to eat their own filth and
drink their own urine?"
28Then the commander stood
and called out in Hebrew: "Hear
the word of the great king, the king
of Assyria! **29**This is what the king
says: Do not let Hezekiah deceive[f]
you. He cannot deliver you from my
hand. **30**Do not let Hezekiah persuade you to trust in the LORD when
he says, 'The LORD will surely deliver us; this city will not be given into
the hand of the king of Assyria.'
31"Do not listen to Hezekiah.
This is what the king of Assyria
says: Make peace with me and
come out to me. Then every one of
you will eat from his own vine and
fig tree[g] and drink water from his
own cistern,[h] **32**until I come and
take you to a land like your own, a
land of grain and new wine, a land
of bread and vineyards, a land of
olive trees and honey. Choose life[i]
and not death!
"Do not listen to Hezekiah, for
he is misleading you when he says,
'The LORD will deliver us.' **33**Has
the god[j] of any nation ever delivered his land from the hand of the
king of Assyria? **34**Where are the
gods of Hamath[k] and Arpad?[l]
Where are the gods of Sepharvaim,
Hena and Ivvah? Have they rescued
Samaria from my hand? **35**Who of
all the gods of these countries has
been able to save his land from me?
How then can the LORD deliver Jerusalem from my hand?"[m]
36But the people remained silent
and said nothing in reply, because
the king had commanded, "Do not
answer him."
37Then Eliakim son of Hilkiah
the palace administrator, Shebna
the secretary and Joah son of
Asaph the recorder went to Hezekiah, with their clothes torn,[n] and
told him what the field commander
had said.

Jerusalem's Deliverance Foretold

19:1–13pp — Isa 37:1–13

19 When King Hezekiah heard
this, he tore[o] his clothes
and put on sackcloth and went into
the temple of the LORD. **2**He sent
Eliakim the palace administrator,
Shebna the secretary and the leading priests, all wearing sackcloth,
to the prophet Isaiah[p] son of
Amoz. **3**They told him, "This is
what Hezekiah says: This day is a
day of distress and rebuke and disgrace, as when children come to

18:21 [a] Isa 20:5; Eze 29:6 [b] Isa 30:5,7
18:24 [c] Isa 10:8
18:25 [d] 2Ki 19:6,22
18:26 [e] Ezr 4:7
18:29 [f] 2Ki 19:10
18:31 [g] Nu 13:23; 1Ki 4:25 [h] Jer 14:3; La 4:4
18:32 [i] Dt 8:7-9; 30:19
18:33 [j] 2Ki 19:12; Isa 10:10-11
18:34 [k] 2Ki 17:24; 19:13 [l] Isa 10:9
18:35 [m] Ps 2:1-2
18:37 [n] 2Ki 6:30
19:1 [o] Ge 37:34; 1Ki 21:27; 2Ch 32:20-22
19:2 [p] Isa 1:1

[f] 24 Or *charioteers*

the point of birth and there is no
strength to deliver them. **4**It may be
that the LORD your God will hear all
the words of the field commander,
whom his master, the king of Assyria, has sent to ridicule[a] the living
God, and that he will rebuke[b] him
for the words the LORD your God
has heard. Therefore pray for the
remnant that still survives."

5When King Hezekiah's officials
came to Isaiah, **6**Isaiah said to
them, "Tell your master, 'This is
what the LORD says: Do not be
afraid of what you have heard—
those words with which the under-
lings of the king of Assyria have
blasphemed[c] me. **7**Listen! I am going to put such a spirit in him that
when he hears a certain report, he
will return to his own country, and
there I will have him cut down with
the sword.[d] ' "

8When the field commander
heard that the king of Assyria had
left Lachish,[e] he withdrew and
found the king fighting against Libnah.

9Now Sennacherib received a report that Tirhakah, the Cushite[g]
king ⌞of Egypt⌟, was marching out to
fight against him. So he again sent
messengers to Hezekiah with this
word: **10**"Say to Hezekiah king of
Judah: Do not let the god you depend[f] on deceive[g] you when he
says, 'Jerusalem will not be handed
over to the king of Assyria.' **11**Surely you have heard what the kings of
Assyria have done to all the countries, destroying them completely.
And will you be delivered? **12**Did
the gods of the nations that were
destroyed by my forefathers deliver[h] them: the gods of Gozan,[i] Haran,[j] Rezeph and the people of
Eden who were in Tel Assar?
13Where is the king of Hamath, the
king of Arpad, the king of the city of
Sepharvaim, or of Hena or Ivvah?"[k]

Hezekiah's Prayer

19:14–19pp — Isa 37:14–20

14Hezekiah received the letter
from the messengers and read it.
Then he went up to the temple of
the LORD and spread it out before
the LORD. **15**And Hezekiah prayed
to the LORD: "O LORD, God of Israel,
enthroned between the cherubim,[l] you alone are God over all
the kingdoms of the earth. You
have made heaven and earth.
16Give ear,[m] O LORD, and hear;[n]
open your eyes,[o] O LORD, and see;
listen to the words Sennacherib
has sent to insult the living God.

17"It is true, O LORD, that the Assyrian kings have laid waste these
nations and their lands. **18**They
have thrown their gods into the fire
and destroyed them, for they were
not gods[p] but only wood and
stone, fashioned by men's hands.[q]
19Now, O LORD our God, deliver us
from his hand, so that all kingdoms[r] on earth may know[s] that
you alone, O LORD, are God."

Isaiah Prophesies Sennacherib's Fall

19:20–37pp — Isa 37:21–38
19:35–37pp — 2Ch 32:20–21

20Then Isaiah son of Amoz sent a
message to Hezekiah: "This is what
the LORD, the God of Israel, says: I
have heard[t] your prayer concerning Sennacherib king of Assyria.
21This is the word that the LORD has
spoken against him:

" 'The Virgin Daughter[u] of Zion
despises you and mocks[v]
you.
The Daughter of Jerusalem
tosses her head[w] as you flee.
22Who is it you have insulted and
blasphemed?
Against whom have you
raised your voice
and lifted your eyes in pride?
Against the Holy One[x] of
Israel!
23By your messengers
you have heaped insults on
the Lord.
And you have said,[y]
"With my many chariots[z]
I have ascended the heights of
the mountains,

19:4 [a] 2Ki 18:35 [b] 2Sa 16:12
19:6 [c] 2Ki 18:25
19:7 [d] ver 37
19:8 [e] 2Ki 18:14
19:10 [f] 2Ki 18:5 [g] 2Ki 18:29
19:12 [h] 2Ki 18:33 [i] 2Ki 17:6 [j] Ge 11:31
19:13 [k] 2Ki 18:34
19:15 [l] Ex 25:22
19:16 [m] Ps 31:2 [n] 1Ki 8:29 [o] ver 4; 2Ch 6:40
19:18 [p] Isa 44:9-11; Jer 10:3-10 [q] Ps 115:4; Ac 17:29
19:19 [r] 1Ki 8:43 [s] Ps 83:18
19:20 [t] 2Ki 20:5
19:21 [u] Jer 14:17; La 2:13 [v] Ps 22:7-8 [w] Job 16:4; Ps 109:25
19:22 [x] Ps 71:22; Isa 5:24
19:23 [y] Isa 10:18 [z] Ps 20:7

[g]9 That is, from the upper Nile region

the utmost heights of
Lebanon.
I have cut down its tallest
cedars,
the choicest of its pines.
I have reached its remotest
parts,
the finest of its forests.
24I have dug wells in foreign
lands
and drunk the water there.
With the soles of my feet
I have dried up all the
streams of Egypt."

25" 'Have you not heard?[a]
Long ago I ordained it.
In days of old I planned[b] it;
now I have brought it to
pass,
that you have turned fortified
cities
into piles of stone.[c]
26Their people, drained of power,
are dismayed[d] and put to
shame.
They are like plants in the
field,
like tender green shoots,[e]
like grass sprouting on the roof,
scorched[f] before it grows
up.

27" 'But I know[g] where you stay
and when you come and go
and how you rage against
me.
28Because you rage against me
and your insolence has
reached my ears,
I will put my hook[h] in your
nose
and my bit[i] in your mouth,
and I will make you return[j]
by the way you came.'

29"This will be the sign[k] for you,
O Hezekiah:

"This year you will eat what
grows by itself,[l]
and the second year what
springs from that.
But in the third year sow and
reap,
plant vineyards[m] and eat
their fruit.
30Once more a remnant of the
house of Judah

19:25 [a]Isa 40:21,28 [b]Isa 10:5; 45:7 [c]Mic 1:6
19:26 [d]Ps 6:10 [e]Isa 4:2 [f]Ps 129:6
19:27 [g]Ps 139:1-4
19:28 [h]Eze 19:9; 29:4 [i]Isa 30:28 [j]ver 33
19:29 [k]2Ki 20:8-9; Lk 2:12 [l]Lev 25:5 [m]Ps 107:37
19:30 [n]2Ch 32:22-23
19:31 [o]Isa 9:7
19:33 [p]ver 28
19:34 [q]2Ki 20:6 [r]1Ki 11:12-13
19:35 [s]Ex 12:23 [t]Job 24:24
19:36 [u]Ge 10:11; Jnh 1:2
19:37 [v]ver 7 [w]Ge 8:4 [x]Ezr 4:2

will take root[n] below and
bear fruit above.
31For out of Jerusalem will come
a remnant,
and out of Mount Zion a
band of survivors.

The zeal[o] of the LORD Almighty will
accomplish this.

32"Therefore this is what the
LORD says concerning the king of
Assyria:

"He will not enter this city
or shoot an arrow here.
He will not come before it with
shield
or build a siege ramp against
it.
33By the way that he came he
will return;[p]
he will not enter this city,
declares the LORD.
34I will defend[q] this city and
save it,
for my sake and for the sake
of David[r] my servant."

35That night the angel of the
LORD[s] went out and put to death a
hundred and eighty-five thousand
men in the Assyrian camp. When
the people got up the next morning—there were all the dead bodies![t] 36So Sennacherib king of Assyria broke camp and withdrew. He
returned to Nineveh[u] and stayed
there.
37One day, while he was worshiping in the temple of his god
Nisroch, his sons Adrammelech
and Sharezer cut him down with
the sword,[v] and they escaped to
the land of Ararat.[w] And Esarhaddon[x] his son succeeded him as
king.

Hezekiah's Illness

20:1–11pp — 2Ch 32:24–26; Isa 38:1–8

20 In those days Hezekiah became ill and was at the
point of death. The prophet Isaiah
son of Amoz went to him and said,
"This is what the LORD says: Put
your house in order, because you
are going to die; you will not recover."

2Hezekiah turned his face to the wall and prayed to the LORD, **3**"Remember,[a] O LORD, how I have walked before you faithfully[b] and with wholehearted devotion and have done what is good in your eyes." And Hezekiah wept bitterly.

4Before Isaiah had left the middle court, the word of the LORD came to him: **5**"Go back and tell Hezekiah, the leader of my people, 'This is what the LORD, the God of your father David, says: I have heard[c] your prayer and seen your tears;[d] I will heal you. On the third day from now you will go up to the temple of the LORD. **6**I will add fifteen years to your life. And I will deliver you and this city from the hand of the king of Assyria. I will defend[e] this city for my sake and for the sake of my servant David.' "

7Then Isaiah said, "Prepare a poultice of figs." They did so and applied it to the boil,[f] and he recovered.

8Hezekiah had asked Isaiah, "What will be the sign that the LORD will heal me and that I will go up to the temple of the LORD on the third day from now?"

9Isaiah answered, "This is the LORD's sign[g] to you that the LORD will do what he has promised: Shall the shadow go forward ten steps, or shall it go back ten steps?"

10"It is a simple matter for the shadow to go forward ten steps," said Hezekiah. "Rather, have it go back ten steps."

11Then the prophet Isaiah called upon the LORD, and the LORD made the shadow go back[h] the ten steps it had gone down on the stairway of Ahaz.

Envoys From Babylon

20:12–19pp — Isa 39:1–8
20:20–21pp — 2Ch 32:32–33

12At that time Merodach-Baladan son of Baladan king of Babylon sent Hezekiah letters and a gift, because he had heard of Hezekiah's illness. **13**Hezekiah received the messengers and showed them all that was in his storehouses—the silver, the gold, the spices and the fine oil—his armory and everything found among his treasures. There was nothing in his palace or in all his kingdom that Hezekiah did not show them.

14Then Isaiah the prophet went to King Hezekiah and asked, "What did those men say, and where did they come from?"

"From a distant land," Hezekiah replied. "They came from Babylon."

15The prophet asked, "What did they see in your palace?"

"They saw everything in my palace," Hezekiah said. "There is nothing among my treasures that I did not show them."

16Then Isaiah said to Hezekiah, "Hear the word of the LORD: **17**The time will surely come when everything in your palace, and all that your fathers have stored up until this day, will be carried off to Babylon.[i] Nothing will be left, says the LORD. **18**And some of your descendants,[j] your own flesh and blood, that will be born to you, will be taken away, and they will become eunuchs in the palace of the king of Babylon."

19"The word of the LORD you have spoken is good," Hezekiah replied. For he thought, "Will there not be peace and security in my lifetime?"

20As for the other events of Hezekiah's reign, all his achievements and how he made the pool[k] and the tunnel by which he brought water into the city, are they not written in the book of the annals of the kings of Judah? **21**Hezekiah rested with his fathers. And Manasseh his son succeeded him as king.

Manasseh King of Judah

21:1–10pp — 2Ch 33:1–10
21:17–18pp — 2Ch 33:18–20

21 Manasseh was twelve years old when he became king, and he reigned in Jerusalem fifty-five years. His mother's name was Hephzibah.[l] **2**He did evil[m] in the eyes of the LORD, following the detestable practices[n] of the nations

20:3 [a]Ne 13:22 [b]2Ki 18:3-6
20:5 [c]1Sa 9:16; 1Ki 9:3; 2Ki 19:20 [d]Ps 39:12; 56:8
20:6 [e]2Ki 19:34
20:7 [f]Isa 38:21
20:9 [g]Dt 13:2; Jer 44:29
20:11 [h]Jos 10:13
20:17 [i]2Ki 24:13; 25:13; 2Ch 36:10; Jer 27:22; 52:17-23
20:18 [j]2Ki 24:15; 2Ch 33:11; Da 1:3
20:20 [k]Ne 3:16
21:1 [l]Isa 62:4
21:2 [m]Jer 15:4 [n]2Ki 16:3

the LORD had driven out before the Israelites. 3He rebuilt the high places[a] his father Hezekiah had destroyed; he also erected altars to Baal[b] and made an Asherah pole, as Ahab king of Israel had done. He bowed down to all the starry hosts[c] and worshiped them. 4He built altars[d] in the temple of the LORD, of which the LORD had said, "In Jerusalem I will put my Name."[e] 5In both courts[f] of the temple of the LORD, he built altars to all the starry hosts. 6He sacrificed his own son[g] in[h] the fire, practiced sorcery and divination, and consulted mediums and spiritists.[h] He did much evil in the eyes of the LORD, provoking him to anger.

7He took the carved Asherah pole[i] he had made and put it in the temple, of which the LORD had said to David and to his son Solomon, "In this temple and in Jerusalem, which I have chosen out of all the tribes of Israel, I will put my Name[j] forever. 8I will not again[k] make the feet of the Israelites wander from the land I gave their forefathers, if only they will be careful to do everything I commanded them and will keep the whole Law that my servant Moses[l] gave them." 9But the people did not listen. Manasseh led them astray, so that they did more evil[m] than the nations[n] the LORD had destroyed before the Israelites.

10The LORD said through his servants the prophets: 11"Manasseh king of Judah has committed these detestable sins. He has done more evil[o] than the Amorites[p] who preceded him and has led Judah into sin with his idols. 12Therefore this is what the LORD, the God of Israel, says: I am going to bring such disaster[q] on Jerusalem and Judah that the ears of everyone who hears of it will tingle.[r] 13I will stretch out over Jerusalem the measuring line used against Samaria and the plumb line[s] used against the house of Ahab. I will wipe[t] out Jerusalem as one wipes a dish, wiping it and turning it upside down. 14I will forsake[u] the remnant[v] of my inheritance and hand them over to their enemies. They will be looted and plundered by all their foes, 15because they have done evil[w] in my eyes and have provoked[x] me to anger from the day their forefathers came out of Egypt until this day."

16Moreover, Manasseh also shed so much innocent blood[y] that he filled Jerusalem from end to end—besides the sin that he had caused Judah to commit, so that they did evil in the eyes of the LORD.

17As for the other events of Manasseh's reign, and all he did, including the sin he committed, are they not written in the book of the annals of the kings of Judah? 18Manasseh rested with his fathers and was buried in his palace garden,[z] the garden of Uzza. And Amon his son succeeded him as king.

Amon King of Judah

21:19–24pp — 2Ch 33:21–25

19Amon was twenty-two years old when he became king, and he reigned in Jerusalem two years. His mother's name was Meshullemeth daughter of Haruz; she was from Jotbah. 20He did evil[a] in the eyes of the LORD, as his father Manasseh had done. 21He walked in all the ways of his father; he worshiped the idols his father had worshiped, and bowed down to them. 22He forsook the LORD, the God of his fathers, and did not walk[b] in the way of the LORD.

23Amon's officials conspired against him and assassinated[c] the king in his palace. 24Then the people of the land killed[d] all who had plotted against King Amon, and they made Josiah his son king in his place.

25As for the other events of Amon's reign, and what he did, are they not written in the book of the annals of the kings of Judah? 26He was buried in his grave in the gar-

h6 Or *He made his own son pass through*

21:3 [a]2Ki 18:4 [b]Jdg 6:28; 1Ki 16:32 [c]Dt 17:3; 2Ki 17:16
21:4 [d]Jer 32:34 [e]2Sa 7:13; 1Ki 8:29
21:5 [f]1Ki 7:12; 2Ki 23:12
21:6 [g]Lev 18:21; Dt 18:10; 2Ki 16:3; 17:17 [h]Lev 19:31
21:7 [i]Dt 16:21; 2Ki 23:4 [j]2Sa 7:13; 1Ki 8:29; 9:3; 2Ki 23:27; Jer 32:34
21:8 [k]2Sa 7:10 [l]2Ki 18:12
21:9 [m]Pr 29:12 [n]Dt 9:4
21:11 [o]2Ki 24:3-4 [p]Ge 15:16; 1Ki 21:26
21:12 [q]2Ki 23:26; 24:3; Jer 15:4 [r]1Sa 3:11; Jer 19:3
21:13 [s]Isa 34:11; La 2:8; Am 7:7-9 [t]2Ki 23:27
21:14 [u]Ps 78:58-60 [v]2Ki 19:4; Mic 2:12
21:15 [w]Ex 32:22 [x]Jer 25:7
21:16 [y]2Ki 24:4
21:18 [z]ver 26
21:20 [a]ver 2-6
21:22 [b]1Ki 11:33
21:23 [c]2Ki 12:20; 2Ch 33:24-25
21:24 [d]2Ki 14:5

den of Uzza. And Josiah his son succeeded him as king.

The Book of the Law Found

22:1–20pp — 2Ch 34:1–2,8–28

22 Josiah was eight years old when he became king, and he reigned in Jerusalem thirty-one years. His mother's name was Jedidah daughter of Adaiah; she was from Bozkath.[a] **2**He did what was right[b] in the eyes of the LORD and walked in all the ways of his father David, not turning aside to the right[c] or to the left.

3In the eighteenth year of his reign, King Josiah sent the secretary, Shaphan[d] son of Azaliah, the son of Meshullam, to the temple of the LORD. He said: **4**"Go up to Hilkiah the high priest and have him get ready the money that has been brought into the temple of the LORD, which the doorkeepers have collected[e] from the people. **5**Have them entrust it to the men appointed to supervise the work on the temple. And have these men pay the workers who repair[f] the temple of the LORD— **6**the carpenters, the builders and the masons. Also have them purchase timber and dressed stone to repair the temple.[g] **7**But they need not account for the money entrusted to them, because they are acting faithfully."[h]

8Hilkiah the high priest said to Shaphan the secretary, "I have found the Book of the Law[i] in the temple of the LORD." He gave it to Shaphan, who read it. **9**Then Shaphan the secretary went to the king and reported to him: "Your officials have paid out the money that was in the temple of the LORD and have entrusted it to the workers and supervisors at the temple." **10**Then Shaphan the secretary informed the king, "Hilkiah the priest has given me a book." And Shaphan read from it in the presence of the king.[j]

11When the king heard the words of the Book of the Law, he tore his robes. **12**He gave these orders to Hilkiah the priest, Ahikam[k] son of Shaphan, Acbor son of Micaiah, Shaphan the secretary and Asaiah the king's attendant: **13**"Go and inquire of the LORD for me and for the people and for all Judah about what is written in this book that has been found. Great is the LORD's anger[l] that burns against us because our fathers have not obeyed the words of this book; they have not acted in accordance with all that is written there concerning us."

14Hilkiah the priest, Ahikam, Acbor, Shaphan and Asaiah went to speak to the prophetess Huldah, who was the wife of Shallum son of Tikvah, the son of Harhas, keeper of the wardrobe. She lived in Jerusalem, in the Second District.

15She said to them, "This is what the LORD, the God of Israel, says: Tell the man who sent you to me, **16**'This is what the LORD says: I am going to bring disaster[m] on this place and its people, according to everything written in the book[n] the king of Judah has read. **17**Because they have forsaken[o] me and burned incense to other gods and provoked me to anger by all the idols their hands have made,[1] my anger will burn against this place and will not be quenched.' **18**Tell the king of Judah, who sent you to inquire[p] of the LORD, 'This is what the LORD, the God of Israel, says concerning the words you heard: **19**Because your heart was responsive and you humbled[q] yourself before the LORD when you heard what I have spoken against this place and its people, that they would become accursed[r] and laid waste,[s] and because you tore your robes and wept in my presence, I have heard you, declares the LORD. **20**Therefore I will gather you to your fathers, and you will be buried in peace.[t] Your eyes will not see all the disaster I am going to bring on this place.' "

So they took her answer back to the king.

22:1 [a] Jos 15:39
22:2 [b] Dt 17:19 [c] Dt 5:32
22:3 [d] 2Ch 34:20; Jer 39:14
22:4 [e] 2Ki 12:4-5
22:5 [f] 2Ki 12:5, 11-14
22:6 [g] 2Ki 12:11-12
22:7 [h] 2Ki 12:15
22:8 [i] Dt 31:24
22:10 [j] Jer 36:21
22:12 [k] 2Ki 25:22; Jer 26:24
22:13 [l] Dt 29:24-28; 31:17
22:16 [m] Dt 31:29; Jos 23:15 [n] Dt 29:27; Da 9:11
22:17 [o] Dt 29:25-27
22:18 [p] 2Ch 34:26; Jer 21:2
22:19 [q] Ex 10:3; 1Ki 21:29; Ps 51:17; Isa 57:15; Mic 6:8 [r] Jer 26:6 [s] Lev 26:31
22:20 [t] Isa 57:1

[1] 17 Or *by everything they have done*

Josiah Renews the Covenant

23:1–3pp — 2Ch 34:29–32
23:4–20Ref — 2Ch 34:3–7,33
23:21–23pp — 2Ch 35:1,18–19
23:28–30pp — 2Ch 35:20–36:1

23 Then the king called together all the elders of Judah and Jerusalem. 2He went up to
the temple of the LORD with the
men of Judah, the people of Jerusalem, the priests and the prophets—all the people from the least
to the greatest. He read[a] in their
hearing all the words of the Book of
the Covenant, which had been
found in the temple of the LORD.
3The king stood by the pillar and
renewed the covenant[b] in the
presence of the LORD—to follow[c]
the LORD and keep his commands,
regulations and decrees with all his
heart and all his soul, thus con-
firming the words of the covenant
written in this book. Then all the
people pledged themselves to the
covenant.

4The king ordered Hilkiah the
high priest, the priests next in rank
and the doorkeepers[d] to remove[e]
from the temple of the LORD all the
articles made for Baal and Asherah
and all the starry hosts. He burned
them outside Jerusalem in the
fields of the Kidron Valley and took
the ashes to Bethel. 5He did away
with the pagan priests appointed
by the kings of Judah to burn incense on the high places of the
towns of Judah and on those
around Jerusalem—those who
burned incense to Baal, to the sun
and moon, to the constellations
and to all the starry hosts.[f] 6He
took the Asherah pole from the
temple of the LORD to the Kidron
Valley outside Jerusalem and
burned it there. He ground it to
powder and scattered the dust over
the graves of the common people.[g]
7He also tore down the quarters of
the male shrine prostitutes,[h]
which were in the temple of the
LORD and where women did weav-
ing for Asherah.

8Josiah brought all the priests
from the towns of Judah and desecrated the high places, from Geba[i]
to Beersheba, where the priests
had burned incense. He broke
down the shrines[i] at the gates—at
the entrance to the Gate of Joshua,
the city governor, which is on the
left of the city gate. 9Although the
priests of the high places did not
serve[j] at the altar of the LORD in
Jerusalem, they ate unleavened
bread with their fellow priests.

10He desecrated Topheth,[k]
which was in the Valley of Ben Hinnom,[l] so no one could use it to
sacrifice his son[m] or daughter in[k]
the fire to Molech. 11He removed
from the entrance to the temple of
the LORD the horses that the kings
of Judah had dedicated to the sun.
They were in the court near the
room of an official named Na-
than-Melech. Josiah then burned
the chariots dedicated to the sun.[n]

12He pulled down the altars the
kings of Judah had erected on the
roof[o] near the upper room of Ahaz,
and the altars Manasseh had built
in the two courts[p] of the temple of
the LORD. He removed them from
there, smashed them to pieces and
threw the rubble into the Kidron
Valley. 13The king also desecrated
the high places that were east of
Jerusalem on the south of the Hill
of Corruption—the ones Solomon[q] king of Israel had built for
Ashtoreth the vile goddess of the
Sidonians, for Chemosh the vile
god of Moab, and for Molech[1] the
detestable god of the people of Ammon. 14Josiah smashed[r] the sacred stones and cut down the Asherah poles and covered the sites
with human bones.

15Even the altar[s] at Bethel, the
high place made by Jeroboam[t]
son of Nebat, who had caused Israel to sin—even that altar and high
place he demolished. He burned
the high place and ground it to
powder, and burned the Asherah
pole also. 16Then Josiah[u] looked
around, and when he saw the
tombs that were there on the hillside, he had the bones removed

23:2 [a]Dt 31:11; 2Ki 22:8
23:3 [b]2Ki 11:14,17 [c]Dt 13:4
23:4 [d]2Ki 25:18 [e]2Ki 21:7
23:5 [f]2Ki 21:3; Jer 8:2
23:6 [g]Jer 26:23
23:7 [h]1Ki 14:24; 15:12; Eze 16:16
23:8 [i]1Ki 15:22
23:9 [j]Eze 44:10-14
23:10 [k]Isa 30:33; Jer 7:31,32; 19:6 [l]Jos 15:8 [m]Lev 18:21; Dt 18:10
23:11 [n]Dt 4:19
23:12 [o]Jer 19:13; Zep 1:5 [p]2Ki 21:5
23:13 [q]1Ki 11:7
23:14 [r]Ex 23:24; Dt 7:5,25
23:15 [s]1Ki 13:1-3 [t]1Ki 12:33
23:16 [u]1Ki 13:2

i8 Or *high places* k10 Or *to make his son or daughter pass through* l13 Hebrew *Milcom*

from them and burned on the altar to defile it, in accordance with the word of the LORD proclaimed by the man of God who foretold these things.

17The king asked, "What is that tombstone I see?"

The men of the city said, "It marks the tomb of the man of God who came from Judah and pronounced against the altar of Bethel the very things you have done to it."

18"Leave it alone," he said. "Don't let anyone disturb his bones[a]." So they spared his bones and those of the prophet who had come from Samaria.

19Just as he had done at Bethel, Josiah removed and defiled all the shrines at the high places that the kings of Israel had built in the towns of Samaria that had provoked the LORD to anger. 20Josiah slaughtered[b] all the priests of those high places on the altars and burned human bones[c] on them. Then he went back to Jerusalem.

21The king gave this order to all the people: "Celebrate the Passover[d] to the LORD your God, as it is written in this Book of the Covenant." 22Not since the days of the judges who led Israel, nor throughout the days of the kings of Israel and the kings of Judah, had any such Passover been observed. 23But in the eighteenth year of King Josiah, this Passover was celebrated to the LORD in Jerusalem.

24Furthermore, Josiah got rid of the mediums and spiritists,[e] the household gods,[f] the idols and all the other detestable things seen in Judah and Jerusalem. This he did to fulfill the requirements of the law written in the book that Hilkiah the priest had discovered in the temple of the LORD. 25Neither before nor after Josiah was there a king like him who turned[g] to the LORD as he did—with all his heart and with all his soul and with all his strength, in accordance with all the Law of Moses.

26Nevertheless, the LORD did not turn away from the heat of his fierce anger, which burned against Judah because of all that Manasseh[h] had done to provoke him to anger. 27So the LORD said, "I will remove[i] Judah also from my presence[j] as I removed Israel, and I will reject Jerusalem, the city I chose, and this temple, about which I said, 'There shall my Name be.'[m]"

28As for the other events of Josiah's reign, and all he did, are they not written in the book of the annals of the kings of Judah?

29While Josiah was king, Pharaoh Neco[k] king of Egypt went up to the Euphrates River to help the king of Assyria. King Josiah marched out to meet him in battle, but Neco faced him and killed him at Megiddo.[l] 30Josiah's servants brought his body in a chariot[m] from Megiddo to Jerusalem and buried him in his own tomb. And the people of the land took Jehoahaz son of Josiah and anointed him and made him king in place of his father.

Jehoahaz King of Judah

23:31–34pp — 2Ch 36:2–4

31Jehoahaz[n] was twenty-three years old when he became king, and he reigned in Jerusalem three months. His mother's name was Hamutal[o] daughter of Jeremiah; she was from Libnah. 32He did evil in the eyes of the LORD, just as his fathers had done. 33Pharaoh Neco put him in chains at Riblah[p] in the land of Hamath[n][q] so that he might not reign in Jerusalem, and he imposed on Judah a levy of a hundred talents[o] of silver and a talent[p] of gold. 34Pharaoh Neco made Eliakim[r] son of Josiah king in place of his father Josiah and changed Eliakim's name to Jehoiakim. But he took Jehoahaz and carried him off to Egypt, and there he died.[s] 35Jehoiakim paid Pharaoh

23:18 [a] 1Ki 13:31
23:20 [b] Ex 22:20; 2Ki 10:25; 11:18 [c] 1Ki 13:2
23:21 [d] Ex 12:11; Nu 9:2; Dt 16:1-8
23:24 [e] Lev 19:31; Dt 18:11; 2Ki 21:6 [f] Ge 31:19
23:25 [g] 2Ki 18:5
23:26 [h] 2Ki 21:12; Jer 15:4
23:27 [i] 2Ki 21:13 [j] 2Ki 18:11
23:29 [k] Jer 46:2 [l] Zec 12:11
23:30 [m] 2Ki 9:28
23:31 [n] 1Ch 3:15; Jer 22:11 [o] 2Ki 24:18
23:33 [p] 2Ki 25:6 [q] 1Ki 8:65
23:34 [r] 1Ch 3:15; 2Ch 36:5-8 [s] Jer 22:12; Eze 19:3-4

m27 1 Kings 8:29 n33 Hebrew; Septuagint (see also 2 Chron. 36:3) *Neco at Riblah in Hamath removed him* o33 That is, about 3 3/4 tons (about 3.4 metric tons) p33 That is, about 75 pounds (about 34 kilograms)

Neco the silver and gold he demanded. In order to do so, he taxed
the land and exacted the silver and
gold from the people of the land according to their assessments.[a]

Jehoiakim King of Judah

23:36–24:6pp — 2Ch 36:5–8

36Jehoiakim[b] was twenty-five
years old when he became king,
and he reigned in Jerusalem eleven
years. His mother's name was Zebi-
dah daughter of Pedaiah; she was
from Rumah. 37And he did evil in
the eyes of the LORD, just as his fathers had done.

24 During Jehoiakim's reign,
Nebuchadnezzar[c] king of
Babylon invaded the land, and Jehoiakim became his vassal for
three years. But then he changed
his mind and rebelled against Nebuchadnezzar. 2The LORD sent Babylonian,[q] Aramean,[d] Moabite and
Ammonite raiders against him. He
sent them to destroy[e] Judah, in
accordance with the word of the
LORD proclaimed by his servants
the prophets. 3Surely these things
happened to Judah according to
the LORD's command,[f] in order to
remove them from his presence because of the sins of Manasseh[g]
and all he had done, 4including the
shedding of innocent blood.[h] For
he had filled Jerusalem with innocent blood, and the LORD was not
willing to forgive.

5As for the other events of Jehoiakim's reign, and all he did, are
they not written in the book of the
annals of the kings of Judah? 6Je-
hoiakim rested[i] with his fathers.
And Jehoiachin his son succeeded
him as king.

7The king of Egypt[j] did not
march out from his own country
again, because the king of Babylon[k] had taken all his territory,
from the Wadi of Egypt to the Euphrates River.

Jehoiachin King of Judah

24:8–17pp — 2Ch 36:9–10

8Jehoiachin[l] was eighteen
years old when he became king,
and he reigned in Jerusalem three
months. His mother's name was
Nehushta daughter of Elnathan;
she was from Jerusalem. 9He did
evil in the eyes of the LORD, just as
his father had done.

10At that time the officers of
Nebuchadnezzar[m] king of Babylon
advanced on Jerusalem and laid
siege to it, 11and Nebuchadnezzar
himself came up to the city while
his officers were besieging it. 12Je-
hoiachin king of Judah, his mother, his attendants, his nobles and
his officials all surrendered[n] to
him.

In the eighth year of the reign of
the king of Babylon, he took Jehoiachin prisoner. 13As the LORD had
declared,[o] Nebuchadnezzar removed all the treasures[p] from the
temple of the LORD and from the
royal palace, and took away all the
gold articles[q] that Solomon[r] king
of Israel had made for the temple of
the LORD. 14He carried into exile[s]
all Jerusalem: all the officers and
fighting men, and all the craftsmen
and artisans—a total of ten thousand. Only the poorest[t] people of
the land were left.

15Nebuchadnezzar took Jehoiachin captive to Babylon. He also
took from Jerusalem to Babylon
the king's mother,[u] his wives, his
officials and the leading men[v] of
the land. 16The king of Babylon
also deported to Babylon the entire
force of seven thousand fighting
men, strong and fit for war, and a
thousand craftsmen and artisans.[w]
17He made Mattaniah, Jehoiachin's uncle, king in his place and
changed his name to Zedekiah.[x]

Zedekiah King of Judah

24:18–20pp — 2Ch 36:11–16; Jer 52:1–3

18Zedekiah[y] was twenty-one
years old when he became king,
and he reigned in Jerusalem eleven
years. His mother's name was Hamutal[z] daughter of Jeremiah; she
was from Libnah. 19He did evil in
the eyes of the LORD, just as Jehoiakim had done. 20It was because of

23:35 [a]ver 33
23:36 [b]Jer 26:1
24:1 [c]Jer 25:1,9; Da 1:1
24:2 [d]Jer 35:11 [e]Jer 25:9
24:3 [f]2Ki 18:25 [g]2Ki 21:12; 23:26
24:4 [h]2Ki 21:16
24:6 [i]Jer 22:19
24:7 [j]Ge 15:18 [k]Jer 37:5-7; 46:2
24:8 [l]1Ch 3:16
24:10 [m]Da 1:1
24:12 [n]2Ki 25:27; Jer 22:24-30; 24:1; 25:1; 29:2; 52:28
24:13 [o]2Ki 20:17 [p]2Ki 25:15; Isa 39:6 [q]2Ki 25:14; Jer 20:5 [r]1Ki 7:51
24:14 [s]Jer 24:1; 52:28 [t]2Ki 25:12; Jer 40:7; 52:16
24:15 [u]Jer 22:24-28 [v]Est 2:6; Eze 17:12-14
24:16 [w]Jer 52:28
24:17 [x]1Ch 3:15; 2Ch 36:11; Jer 37:1
24:18 [y]Jer 52:1 [z]2Ki 23:31

[q]2 Or *Chaldean*

the LORD's anger that all this happened to Jerusalem and Judah,
and in the end he thrust[a] them
from his presence.

The Fall of Jerusalem

25:1–12pp — Jer 39:1–10
25:1–21pp — 2Ch 36:17–20; Jer 52:4–27
25:22–26pp — Jer 40:7–9; 41:1–3, 16–18

Now Zedekiah rebelled against
the king of Babylon.

25 So in the ninth year of Zedekiah's reign, on the tenth
day of the tenth month, Nebuchadnezzar[b] king of Babylon marched
against Jerusalem with his whole
army. He encamped outside the
city and built siege works[c] all
around it. **2**The city was kept under
siege until the eleventh year of
King Zedekiah. **3**By the ninth day
of the ⌊fourth⌋[r] month the famine[d]
in the city had become so severe
that there was no food for the people to eat. **4**Then the city wall was
broken through,[e] and the whole
army fled at night through the gate
between the two walls near the
king's garden, though the Babylonians[s] were surrounding[f] the city.
They fled toward the Arabah,[t]
5but the Babylonian[u] army pursued the king and overtook him in
the plains of Jericho. All his soldiers were separated from him and
scattered,[g] **6**and he was captured.[h] He was taken to the king of
Babylon at Riblah,[i] where sentence was pronounced on him.
7They killed the sons of Zedekiah
before his eyes. Then they put out
his eyes, bound him with bronze
shackles and took him to Babylon.[j]

8On the seventh day of the fifth
month, in the nineteenth year of
Nebuchadnezzar king of Babylon,
Nebuzaradan commander of the
imperial guard, an official of the
king of Babylon, came to Jerusalem. **9**He set fire[k] to the temple of
the LORD, the royal palace and all
the houses of Jerusalem. Every important building he burned down.[l]
10The whole Babylonian army, under the commander of the imperial
guard, broke down the walls[m]
around Jerusalem. **11**Nebuzaradan
the commander of the guard carried into exile[n] the people who remained in the city, along with the
rest of the populace and those who
had gone over to the king of Babylon.[o] **12**But the commander left
behind some of the poorest people[p] of the land to work the vineyards and fields.

13The Babylonians broke up the
bronze pillars, the movable stands
and the bronze Sea that were at the
temple of the LORD and they carried
the bronze to Babylon. **14**They also
took away the pots, shovels, wick
trimmers, dishes and all the bronze
articles[q] used in the temple service. **15**The commander of the imperial guard took away the censers
and sprinkling bowls—all that
were made of pure gold or silver.

16The bronze from the two pillars, the Sea and the movable
stands, which Solomon had made
for the temple of the LORD, was
more than could be weighed.
17Each pillar[r] was twenty-seven
feet[v] high. The bronze capital on
top of one pillar was four and a half
feet[w] high and was decorated with
a network and pomegranates of
bronze all around. The other pillar,
with its network, was similar.

18The commander of the guard
took as prisoners Seraiah[s] the
chief priest, Zephaniah[t] the priest
next in rank and the three doorkeepers. **19**Of those still in the city,
he took the officer in charge of the
fighting men and five royal advisers. He also took the secretary who
was chief officer in charge of conscripting the people of the land and
sixty of his men who were found in
the city. **20**Nebuzaradan the commander took them all and brought
them to the king of Babylon at Riblah. **21**There at Riblah, in the land
of Hamath, the king had them executed.

24:20 [a]Dt 4:26; 29:27
25:1 [b]Jer 34:1-7 [c]Eze 24:2
25:3 [d]Jer 14:18; La 4:9
25:4 [e]Eze 33:21 [f]Jer 4:17
25:5 [g]Eze 12:14
25:6 [h]Jer 34:21-22 [i]2Ki 23:33
25:7 [j]Jer 21:7; 32:4-5; Eze 12:11
25:9 [k]Isa 60:7 [l]Ps 74:3-8; Jer 2:15; Am 2:5; Mic 3:12
25:10 [m]Ne 1:3
25:11 [n]2Ki 24:14 [o]2Ki 24:1
25:12 [p]2Ki 24:14
25:14 [q]Ex 27:3; 1Ki 7:47-50
25:17 [r]1Ki 7:15-22
25:18 [s]1Ch 6:14; Ezr 7:1; Ne 11:11 [t]Jer 21:1; 29:25

[r]3 See Jer. 52:6. [s]4 Or *Chaldeans*; also in verses 13, 25 and 26 [t]4 Or *the Jordan Valley* [u]5 Or *Chaldean*; also in verses 10 and 24 [v]17 Hebrew *eighteen cubits* (about 8.1 meters) [w]17 Hebrew *three cubits* (about 1.3 meters)

So Judah went into captivity,
away from her land.[a]
22Nebuchadnezzar king of Babylon appointed Gedaliah[b] son of
Ahikam, the son of Shaphan, to be
over the people he had left behind
in Judah. 23When all the army officers and their men heard that the
king of Babylon had appointed
Gedaliah as governor, they came to
Gedaliah at Mizpah—Ishmael son
of Nethaniah, Johanan son of Kareah, Seraiah son of Tanhumeth
the Netophathite, Jaazaniah the
son of the Maacathite, and their
men. 24Gedaliah took an oath to
reassure them and their men. "Do
not be afraid of the Babylonian officials," he said. "Settle down in
the land and serve the king of
Babylon, and it will go well with
you."
25In the seventh month, however, Ishmael son of Nethaniah, the
son of Elishama, who was of royal
blood, came with ten men and assassinated Gedaliah and also the
men of Judah and the Babylonians
who were with him at Mizpah. 26At
this, all the people from the least to
the greatest, together with the
army officers, fled to Egypt[c] for
fear of the Babylonians.

Jehoiachin Released

25:27–30pp — Jer 52:31–34

27In the thirty-seventh year of
the exile of Jehoiachin king of Judah, in the year Evil-Merodach[x]
became king of Babylon, he released Jehoiachin[d] from prison on
the twenty-seventh day of the
twelfth month. 28He spoke kindly
to him and gave him a seat of hon-
or[e] higher than those of the other
kings who were with him in Babylon. 29So Jehoiachin put aside his
prison clothes and for the rest of
his life ate regularly at the king's
table.[f] 30Day by day the king gave
Jehoiachin a regular allowance as
long as he lived.[g]

25:21 [a] Ge 12:7; Dt 28:64; Jos 23:13; 2Ki 23:27
25:22 [b] Jer 39:14; 40:5,7
25:26 [c] Isa 30:2; Jer 43:7
25:27 [d] 2Ki 24:12; Jer 52:31-34
25:28 [e] Ezr 5:5; Ne 2:1; Da 2:48
25:29 [f] 2Sa 9:7
25:30 [g] Est 2:9; Jer 28:4

[x]27 Also called *Amel-Marduk*

1 Chronicles

Title and Background

The Hebrew title can be translated "the events (or annals) of the days (or years)." The Septuagint (the Greek translation of the Old Testament) translators dubbed the book "the things omitted," indicating that they regarded it as a supplement to Samuel and Kings.

Author and Date of Writing

According to ancient Jewish tradition, Ezra wrote Chronicles, but this cannot be established with certainty. A growing consensus dates Chronicles in the latter half of the fifth century B.C., thus possibly within Ezra's lifetime. It must be acknowledged that the author, if not Ezra, at least shared many basic concerns with that reforming priest.

Theme and Message

Chronicles was written for the exiles who had returned to Israel after the Babylonian captivity, to remind them that they were still God's chosen people. The burning issue was the question of continuity with the past: Is God still interested in us? Are his covenants still in force? Now that we have no Davidic king and are subject to Persia, do God's promises to David still have meaning for us?

Outline

I. Genealogies: From Creation to Restoration (1:1-9:44)
II. The Reign of David (10:1-29:30)

Historical Records From Adam to Abraham

To Noah's Sons

1 Adam,[a] Seth, Enosh, 2Kenan,[b] Mahalalel,[c] Jared,[d]
3Enoch,[e] Methuselah,[f] Lamech,[g] Noah.[h]

4The sons of Noah:[a][i]
Shem, Ham and Japheth.[j]

The Japhethites

1:5–7pp — Ge 10:2-5

5The sons[b] of Japheth:
Gomer, Magog, Madai, Javan, Tubal, Meshech and Tiras.
6The sons of Gomer:
Ashkenaz, Riphath[c] and Togarmah.
7The sons of Javan:
Elishah, Tarshish, the Kittim and the Rodanim.

The Hamites

1:8–16pp — Ge 10:6-20

8The sons of Ham:
Cush, Mizraim,[d] Put and Canaan.
9The sons of Cush:
Seba, Havilah, Sabta, Raamah and Sabteca.
The sons of Raamah:
Sheba and Dedan.
10Cush was the father[e] of

1:1 [a]Ge 5:1-32; Lk 3:36-38
1:2 [b]Ge 5:9 [c]Ge 5:12 [d]Ge 5:15
1:3 [e]Ge 5:18; Jude 1:14 [f]Ge 5:21 [g]Ge 5:25 [h]Ge 5:29
1:4 [i]Ge 6:10; 10:1 [j]Ge 5:32

[a]4 Septuagint; Hebrew does not have *The sons of Noah:* [b]5 *Sons* may mean *descendants* or *successors* or *nations*; also in verses 6-10, 17 and 20. [c]6 Many Hebrew manuscripts and Vulgate (see also Septuagint and Gen. 10:3); most Hebrew manuscripts *Diphath* [d]8 That is, Egypt; also in verse 11 [e]10 *Father* may mean *ancestor* or *predecessor* or *founder*; also in verses 11, 13, 18 and 20.

RULERS OF ISRAEL AND JUDAH

Biblical References	Kings	Years of Reign	Dates of Reign	Notes
1. 1 Ki 12:1-24 14:21-31	***Rehoboam** (J)*	*17 years*	***930-913***	
2. 1 Ki 12:25–14:20	**Jeroboam I** (I)	22 years	**930-909**	
3. 1 Ki 15:1-8	***Abijah** (J)*	*3 years*	***913-910***	
4. 1 Ki 15:9-24	***Asa** (J)*	*41 years*	***910-869***	
5. 1 Ki 15:25-31	**Nadab** (I)	2 years	**909-908**	
6. 1 Ki 15:32–16:7	**Baasha** (I)	24 years	**908-886**	
7. 1 Ki 16:8-14	**Elah** (I)	2 years	**886-885**	
8. 1 Ki 16:15-20	**Zimri** (I)	7 days	**885**	
9. 1 Ki 16:21-22	**Tibni** (I)		**885-880**	Overlap with Omri
10. 1 Ki 16:23-28	**Omri** (I)		885	Made king by the people
			885-880	Overlap with Tibni
		12 years	**885-874**	Official reign = 11 actual years
11. 1 Ki 16:29–22:40	**Ahab** (I)	22 years	**874-853**	Official reign = 21 actual years
12. 1 Ki 22:41-50	***Jehoshaphat** (J)*		*872-869*	*Co-regency with Asa*
		25 years	*872-848*	*Official reign*
			869	*Beginning of sole reign*
			853-848	*Has Jehoram as regent*
13. 1 Ki 22:51– 2 Ki 1:18	**Ahaziah** (I)	2 years	**853-852**	Official reign = 1 yr. actual reign
14. 2 Ki 1:17	**Joram** (I)		852	
2 Ki 3:1–8:15		12 years	**852-841**	Official reign = 11 actual years
15. 2 Ki 8:16-24	***Jehoram** (J)*		***848***	*Beginning of sole reign*
		8 years	***848-841***	*Official reign = 7 actual years*
16. 2 Ki 8:25-29	***Ahaziah** (J)*	*1 year*	*841*	*Nonaccession-year reckoning*
2 Ki 9:29			*841*	*Accession-year reckoning*
17. 2 Ki 9:30–10:36	**Jehu** (I)	28 years	**841-814**	
18. 2 Ki 11	***Athaliah** (J)*	*7 years*	***841-835***	
19. 2 Ki 12	***Joash** (J)*	*40 years*	***835-796***	
20. 2 Ki 13:1-9	**Jehoahaz** (I)	17 years	**814-798**	
21. 2 Ki 13:10-25	**Jehoash** (I)	16 years	**798-782**	

Biblical References	Kings	Years of Reign	Dates of Reign	Notes
22. 2 Ki 14:1-22	***Amaziah** (J)*	*29 years*	***796-767***	
			792-767	*Overlap with Azariah*
23. 2 Ki 14:23-29	**Jeroboam II** (I)		**793-782**	Co-regency with Jehoash
		41 years	**793-753**	Total reign
24. 2 Ki 15:1-7	***Azariah** (J)*		*792-767*	*Overlap with Amaziah*
		52 years	***792-740***	*Total reign*
			767	*Beginning of sole reign*
25. 2 Ki 15:8-12	**Zechariah** (I)	6 months	**753**	
26. 2 Ki 15:13-15	**Shallum** (I)	1 month	**752**	
27. 2 Ki 15:16-22	**Menahem** (I)	10 years	**752-742**	Ruled in Samaria
28. 2 Ki 15:23-26	**Pekahiah** (I)	2 years	**742-740**	
29. 2 Ki 15:27-31	**Pekah** (I)		752-740	In Gilead; overlapping years
		20 years	**752-732**	Total reign
			740	Beginning of sole reign
30. 2 Ki 15:32-38	***Jotham** (J)*		*750-740*	*Co-regency with Azariah*
2 Ki 15:30		*16 years*	***750-735***	*Official reign*
			750-732	*Reign to his 20th year*
			750	*Beginning of co-regency*
31. 2 Ki 16	***Ahaz** (J)*		*735-715*	*Total reign*
		16 years	***732-715***	*From 20th of Jotham*
32. 2 Ki 15:30	**Hoshea** (I)		732	20th of Jotham
2 Ki 17		9 years	**732-722**	
33. 2 Ki 18:1–20:21	***Hezekiah** (J)*	*29 years*	***715-686***	
34. 2 Ki 21:1-18	***Manasseh** (J)*		***697-686***	*Co-regency with Hezekiah*
		55 years	***697-642***	*Total reign*
35. 2 Ki 21:19-26	***Amon** (J)*	*2 years*	***642-640***	
36. 2 Ki 22:1–23:30	***Josiah** (J)*	*31 years*	***640-609***	
37. 2 Ki 23:31-33	***Jehoahaz** (J)*	*3 months*	***609***	
38. 2 Ki 23:34–24:7	***Jehoiakim** (J)*	*11 years*	***609-598***	
39. 2 Ki 24:8-17	***Jehoiachin** (J)*	*3 months*	***598-597***	
40. 2 Ki 24:18–25:26	***Zedekiah** (J)*	*11 years*	***597-586***	

Data and dates in order of sequence
*(J) Italics denote kings of **Judah.*** (I) non-italic type denotes kings of **Israel.**
Adapted from: *A Chronology of the Hebrew Kings* by Edwin R. Thiele.

Nimrod, who grew to be a
mighty warrior on earth.
11 Mizraim was the father of
the Ludites, Anamites,
Lehabites, Naphtuhites,
12 Pathrusites, Casluhites
(from whom the Philistines
came) and Caphtorites.
13 Canaan was the father of
Sidon his firstborn,[f] and
of the Hittites, 14 Jebusites,
Amorites, Girgashites,
15 Hivites, Arkites, Sinites,
16 Arvadites, Zemarites and
Hamathites.

The Semites

1:17–23pp — Ge 10:21–31; 11:10–27

17 The sons of Shem:
Elam, Asshur, Arphaxad,
Lud and Aram.
The sons of Aram[g]:
Uz, Hul, Gether and Meshech.
18 Arphaxad was the father of
Shelah,
and Shelah the father of
Eber.
19 Two sons were born to Eber:
One was named Peleg,[h] because
in his time the earth
was divided; his brother was
named Joktan.
20 Joktan was the father of
Almodad, Sheleph, Hazarmaveth,
Jerah, 21 Hadoram,
Uzal, Diklah, 22 Obal,[i]
Abimael, Sheba, 23 Ophir,
Havilah and Jobab. All
these were sons of Joktan.

24 Shem,[a] Arphaxad,[j] Shelah,
25 Eber, Peleg, Reu,
26 Serug, Nahor, Terah
27 and Abram (that is, Abraham).

The Family of Abraham

28 The sons of Abraham:
Isaac and Ishmael.

Descendants of Hagar

1:29–31pp — Ge 25:12–16

29 These were their descendants:
Nebaioth the firstborn of
Ishmael, Kedar, Adbeel,

1:24 [a] Ge 10:21-25; Lk 3:34-36
1:32 [b] Ge 22:24 [c] Ge 10:7
1:34 [d] Lk 3:34 [e] Ge 21:2-3; Mt 1:2; Ac 7:8 [f] Ge 17:5; 25:25-26
1:35 [g] Ge 36:19 [h] Ge 36:4
1:36 [i] Ex 17:14
1:37 [j] Ge 36:17

Mibsam, 30 Mishma, Dumah,
Massa, Hadad, Tema,
31 Jetur, Naphish and Kedemah.
These were the sons of
Ishmael.

Descendants of Keturah

1:32–33pp — Ge 25:1–4

32 The sons born to Keturah,
Abraham's concubine:[b]
Zimran, Jokshan, Medan,
Midian, Ishbak and Shuah.
The sons of Jokshan:
Sheba and Dedan.[c]
33 The sons of Midian:
Ephah, Epher, Hanoch,
Abida and Eldaah.
All these were descendants of
Keturah.

Descendants of Sarah

1:35–37pp — Ge 36:10–14

34 Abraham[d] was the father of
Isaac.[e]
The sons of Isaac:
Esau and Israel.[f]

Esau's Sons

35 The sons of Esau:[g]
Eliphaz, Reuel,[h] Jeush, Jalam
and Korah.
36 The sons of Eliphaz:
Teman, Omar, Zepho,[k] Gatam
and Kenaz;
by Timna: Amalek.[l][i]
37 The sons of Reuel:[j]
Nahath, Zerah, Shammah
and Mizzah.

The People of Seir in Edom

1:38–42pp — Ge 36:20–28

38 The sons of Seir:
Lotan, Shobal, Zibeon,

[f]13 Or *of the Sidonians, the foremost*
[g]17 One Hebrew manuscript and some Septuagint manuscripts (see also Gen. 10:23); most Hebrew manuscripts do not have this line.
[h]19 *Peleg* means *division.*
[i]22 Some Hebrew manuscripts and Syriac (see also Gen. 10:28); most Hebrew manuscripts *Ebal*
[j]24 Hebrew; some Septuagint manuscripts *Arphaxad, Cainan* (see also note at Gen. 11:10)
[k]36 Many Hebrew manuscripts, some Septuagint manuscripts and Syriac (see also Gen. 36:11); most Hebrew manuscripts *Zephi*
[l]36 Some Septuagint manuscripts (see also Gen. 36:12); Hebrew *Gatam, Kenaz, Timna and Amalek*

Anah, Dishon, Ezer and Dishan.
39The sons of Lotan:
Hori and Homam. Timna was Lotan's sister.
40The sons of Shobal:
Alvan,[m] Manahath, Ebal, Shepho and Onam.
The sons of Zibeon:
Aiah and Anah.[a]
41The son of Anah:
Dishon.
The sons of Dishon:
Hemdan,[n] Eshban, Ithran and Keran.
42The sons of Ezer:
Bilhan, Zaavan and Akan.[o]
The sons of Dishan[p]:
Uz and Aran.

The Rulers of Edom

1:43–54pp — Ge 36:31–43

43These were the kings who reigned in Edom before any Israelite king reigned[q]:
Bela son of Beor, whose city was named Dinhabah.
44When Bela died, Jobab son of Zerah from Bozrah succeeded him as king.
45When Jobab died, Husham from the land of the Temanites[b] succeeded him as king.
46When Husham died, Hadad son of Bedad, who defeated Midian in the country of Moab, succeeded him as king. His city was named Avith.
47When Hadad died, Samlah from Masrekah succeeded him as king.
48When Samlah died, Shaul from Rehoboth on the river[r] succeeded him as king.
49When Shaul died, Baal-Hanan son of Acbor succeeded him as king.
50When Baal-Hanan died, Hadad succeeded him as king. His city was named Pau,[s] and his wife's name was Mehetabel daughter of Matred, the daughter of Me-Zahab. 51Hadad also died.

1:40 [a]Ge 36:2
1:45 [b]Ge 36:11
2:3 [c]Ge 29:35; 38:2-10 [d]Ge 38:5 [e]Ge 38:2 [f]Nu 26:19
2:4 [g]Ge 38:11-30 [h]Ge 11:31 [i]Ge 38:29
2:5 [j]Ge 46:12 [k]Nu 26:21
2:7 [l]Jos 7:1

The chiefs of Edom were:
Timna, Alvah, Jetheth, 52Oholibamah, Elah, Pinon, 53Kenaz, Teman, Mibzar, 54Magdiel and Iram. These were the chiefs of Edom.

Israel's Sons

2:1–2pp — Ge 35:23–26

2 These were the sons of Israel: Reuben, Simeon, Levi, Judah, Issachar, Zebulun, 2Dan, Joseph, Benjamin, Naphtali, Gad and Asher.

Judah

2:5–15pp — Ru 4:18–22; Mt 1:3–6

To Hezron's Sons

3The sons of Judah:[c]
Er, Onan and Shelah.[d] These three were born to him by a Canaanite woman, the daughter of Shua.[e] Er, Judah's firstborn, was wicked in the LORD's sight; so the LORD put him to death.[f] 4Tamar,[g] Judah's daughter-in-law,[h] bore him Perez[i] and Zerah. Judah had five sons in all.
5The sons of Perez:[j]
Hezron[k] and Hamul.
6The sons of Zerah:
Zimri, Ethan, Heman, Calcol and Darda[t]—five in all.
7The son of Carmi:
Achar,[u][l] who brought trouble on Israel by violat-

[m]40 Many Hebrew manuscripts and some Septuagint manuscripts (see also Gen. 36:23); most Hebrew manuscripts *Alian* [n]41 Many Hebrew manuscripts and some Septuagint manuscripts (see also Gen. 36:26); most Hebrew manuscripts *Hamran* [o]42 Many Hebrew and Septuagint manuscripts (see also Gen. 36:27); most Hebrew manuscripts *Zaavan, Jaakan* [p]42 Hebrew *Dishon,* a variant of *Dishan* [q]43 Or *before an Israelite king reigned over them* [r]48 Possibly the Euphrates [s]50 Many Hebrew manuscripts, some Septuagint manuscripts, Vulgate and Syriac (see also Gen. 36:39); most Hebrew manuscripts *Pai* [t]6 Many Hebrew manuscripts, some Septuagint manuscripts and Syriac (see also 1 Kings 4:31); most Hebrew manuscripts *Dara* [u]7 *Achar* means *trouble*; *Achar* is called *Achan* in Joshua.

ing the ban on taking devoted things.[v][a]
8The son of Ethan:
Azariah.
9The sons born to Hezron[b]
were:
Jerahmeel, Ram and Ca-
leb.[w]

From Ram Son of Hezron

10Ram[c] was the father of
Amminadab[d], and Ammin-
adab the father of Nah-
shon,[e] the leader of the
people of Judah. 11Nah-
shon was the father of Salmon,[x] Salmon the father of
Boaz, 12Boaz[f] the father of
Obed and Obed the father
of Jesse.[g]
13Jesse[h] was the father of
Eliab[i] his firstborn; the
second son was Abinadab,
the third Shimea, 14the
fourth Nethanel, the fifth
Raddai, 15the sixth Ozem
and the seventh David.
16Their sisters were Zeruiah[j] and Abigail. Zerui-
ah's[k] three sons were
Abishai, Joab[l] and Asahel.
17Abigail was the mother of
Amasa,[m] whose father was
Jether the Ishmaelite.

Caleb Son of Hezron

18Caleb son of Hezron had children by his wife Azubah
(and by Jerioth). These
were her sons: Jesher, Shobab and Ardon. 19When
Azubah died, Caleb[n] married Ephrath, who bore him
Hur. 20Hur was the father of
Uri, and Uri the father of
Bezalel.[o]
21Later, Hezron lay with the
daughter of Makir the fa-
ther of Gilead[p] (he had
married her when he was
sixty years old), and she
bore him Segub. 22Segub
was the father of Jair, who
controlled twenty-three
towns in Gilead. 23(But Geshur and Aram captured
Havvoth Jair,[y][q] as well as
Kenath[r] with its surrounding settlements—sixty
towns.) All these were
descendants of Makir the
father of Gilead.
24After Hezron died in Caleb
Ephrathah, Abijah the wife
of Hezron bore him Ash-
hur[s] the father[z] of Tekoa.

Jerahmeel Son of Hezron

25The sons of Jerahmeel the
firstborn of Hezron:
Ram his firstborn, Bunah,
Oren, Ozem and[a] Ahijah.
26Jerahmeel had another
wife, whose name was Ata-
rah; she was the mother of
Onam.
27The sons of Ram the firstborn
of Jerahmeel:
Maaz, Jamin and Eker.
28The sons of Onam:
Shammai and Jada.
The sons of Shammai:
Nadab and Abishur.
29Abishur's wife was named Abihail, who bore him Ahban
and Molid.
30The sons of Nadab:
Seled and Appaim. Seled
died without children.
31The son of Appaim:
Ishi, who was the father of
Sheshan.
Sheshan was the father of
Ahlai.
32The sons of Jada, Shammai's
brother:
Jether and Jonathan. Jether
died without children.
33The sons of Jonathan:
Peleth and Zaza.
These were the descendants of
Jerahmeel.
34Sheshan had no sons—only
daughters.
He had an Egyptian servant

2:7 [a]Jos 6:18
2:9 [b]Nu 26:21
2:10 [c]Lk 3:32-33 [d]Ex 6:23 [e]Nu 1:7
2:12 [f]Ru 2:1 [g]Ru 4:17
2:13 [h]Ru 4:17 [i]1Sa 16:6
2:16 [j]1Sa 26:6 [k]2Sa 2:18 [l]2Sa 2:13
2:17 [m]2Sa 17:25
2:19 [n]ver 42,50
2:20 [o]Ex 31:2
2:21 [p]Nu 27:1
2:23 [q]Nu 32:41; Dt 3:14; Jos 13:30 [r]Nu 32:42
2:24 [s]1Ch 4:5

[v]7 The Hebrew term refers to the irrevocable giving over of things or persons to the LORD, often by totally destroying them.
[w]9 Hebrew *Kelubai,* a variant of *Caleb*
[x]*11* Septuagint (see also Ruth 4:21); Hebrew *Salma* [y]*23* *Or captured the settlements of Jair* [z]*24* *Father* may mean *civic leader* or *military leader,* also in verses 42, 45, 49-52 and possibly elsewhere. [a]*25* Or *Oren and Ozem, by*

named Jarha. 35Sheshan gave his daughter in marriage to his servant Jarha, and she bore him Attai.
36Attai was the father of Nathan,
Nathan the father of Zabad,[a]
37Zabad the father of Ephlal,
Ephlal the father of Obed,
38Obed the father of Jehu,
Jehu the father of Azariah,
39Azariah the father of Helez,
Helez the father of Eleasah,
40Eleasah the father of Sismai,
Sismai the father of Shallum,
41Shallum the father of Jekamiah,
and Jekamiah the father of Elishama.

The Clans of Caleb

42The sons of Caleb[b] the brother of Jerahmeel:
Mesha his firstborn, who was the father of Ziph, and his son Mareshah,[b] who was the father of Hebron.
43The sons of Hebron:
Korah, Tappuah, Rekem and Shema. 44Shema was the father of Raham, and Raham the father of Jorkeam. Rekem was the father of Shammai. 45The son of Shammai was Maon[c], and Maon was the father of Beth Zur.[d]
46Caleb's concubine Ephah was the mother of Haran, Moza and Gazez. Haran was the father of Gazez.
47The sons of Jahdai:
Regem, Jotham, Geshan, Pelet, Ephah and Shaaph.
48Caleb's concubine Maacah was the mother of Sheber and Tirhanah. 49She also gave birth to Shaaph the father of Madmannah[e] and to Sheva the father of Macbenah and Gibea. Caleb's daughter was Acsah.[f]
50These were the descendants of Caleb.

The sons of Hur[g] the firstborn of Ephrathah:
Shobal the father of Kiriath Jearim,[h] 51Salma the father of Bethlehem, and Hareph the father of Beth Gader.
52The descendants of Shobal the father of Kiriath Jearim were:
Haroeh, half the Manahathites, 53and the clans of Kiriath Jearim: the Ithrites,[i] Puthites, Shumathites and Mishraites. From these descended the Zorathites and Eshtaolites.
54The descendants of Salma:
Bethlehem, the Netophathites,[j] Atroth Beth Joab, half the Manahathites, the Zorites, 55and the clans of scribes[c] who lived at Jabez: the Tirathites, Shimeathites and Sucathites. These are the Kenites[k] who came from Hammath,[l] the father of the house of Recab.[d][m]

The Sons of David

3:1–4pp — 2Sa 3:2–5
3:5–8pp — 2Sa 5:14–16; 1Ch 14:4–7

3 These were the sons of David[n] born to him in Hebron:
The firstborn was Amnon the son of Ahinoam of Jezreel;[o]
the second, Daniel the son of Abigail[p] of Carmel;
2the third, Absalom the son of Maacah daughter of Talmai king of Geshur;
the fourth, Adonijah[q] the son of Haggith;
3the fifth, Shephatiah the son of Abital;
and the sixth, Ithream, by his wife Eglah.
4These six were born to David in Hebron,[r] where he reigned seven years and six months.[s]
David reigned in Jerusalem thir-

2:36 [a]1Ch 11:41
2:42 [b]ver 19
2:45 [c]Jos 15:55 [d]Jos 15:58
2:49 [e]Jos 15:31 [f]Jos 15:16
2:50 [g]1Ch 4:4 [h]ver 19
2:53 [i]2Sa 23:38
2:54 [j]Ezr 2:22; Ne 7:26; 12:28
2:55 [k]Ge 15:19; Jdg 1:16; Jdg 4:11 [l]Jos 19:35 [m]2Ki 10:15, 23; Jer 35:2-19
3:1 [n]1Ch 14:3; 28:5 [o]Jos 15:56 [p]1Sa 25:42
3:2 [q]1Ki 2:22
3:4 [r]2Sa 5:4; 1Ch 29:27 [s]2Sa 2:11; 5:5

b42 The meaning of the Hebrew for this phrase is uncertain. c55 Or *of the Sopherites* d55 Or *father of Beth Recab*

ty-three years, 5and these were the
children born to him there:
Shammua,[e] Shobab, Na-
than and Solomon. These
four were by Bathsheba[f][a]
daughter of Ammiel. 6There
were also Ibhar, Elishua,[g]
Eliphelet, 7Nogah, Nepheg,
Japhia, 8Elishama, Eliada
and Eliphelet—nine in all.
9All these were the sons of
David, besides his sons by
his concubines. And Ta-
mar[b] was their sister.[c]

The Kings of Judah

10Solomon's son was Rehobo-
am,[d]
Abijah his son,
Asa his son,
Jehoshaphat[e] his son,
11Jehoram[h][f] his son,
Ahaziah[g] his son,
Joash[h] his son,
12Amaziah[i] his son,
Azariah his son,
Jotham[j] his son,
13Ahaz[k] his son,
Hezekiah[l] his son,
Manasseh[m] his son,
14Amon[n] his son,
Josiah[o] his son.
15The sons of Josiah:
Johanan the firstborn,
Jehoiakim[p] the second
son,
Zedekiah[q] the third,
Shallum[r] the fourth.
16The successors of Jehoiakim:
Jehoiachin[i][s] his son,
and Zedekiah.[t]

The Royal Line After the Exile

17The descendants of Jehoia-
chin the captive:
Shealtiel[u] his son, 18Malki-
ram, Pedaiah, Shenazzar,[v]
Jekamiah, Hoshama and
Nedabiah.[w]
19The sons of Pedaiah:
Zerubbabel[x] and Shimei.
The sons of Zerubbabel:
Meshullam and Hananiah.
Shelomith was their sister.
20There were also five others:
Hashubah, Ohel, Berekiah,
Hasadiah and Jushab-He-
sed.
21The descendants of Hananiah:
Pelatiah and Jeshaiah, and
the sons of Rephaiah, of Ar-
nan, of Obadiah and of
Shecaniah.
22The descendants of Shecaniah:
Shemaiah and his sons:
Hattush,[y] Igal, Bariah, Neariah and Shaphat—six in
all.
23The sons of Neariah:
Elioenai, Hizkiah and Azrikam—three in all.
24The sons of Elioenai:
Hodaviah, Eliashib, Pela-
iah, Akkub, Johanan, Delaiah and Anani—seven in
all.

Other Clans of Judah

4 The descendants of Judah:[z]
Perez, Hezron,[a] Carmi, Hur
and Shobal.
2Reaiah son of Shobal was the
father of Jahath, and Jahath
the father of Ahumai and
Lahad. These were the
clans of the Zorathites.
3These were the sons[j] of Etam:
Jezreel, Ishma and Idbash.
Their sister was named
Hazzelelponi. 4Penuel was
the father of Gedor, and
Ezer the father of Hushah.
These were the descendants of
Hur,[b] the firstborn of Ephrathah and father[k] of Bethlehem.[c]
5Ashhur[d] the father of Tekoa
had two wives, Helah and
Naarah.
6Naarah bore him Ahuzzam,
Hepher, Temeni and Haa-

3:5 [a]2Sa 11:3; 12:24
3:9 [b]2Sa 13:1 [c]1Ch 14:4
3:10 [d]1Ki 11:43; 14:21-31; 2Ch 12:16 [e]2Ch 17:1-21:3
3:11 [f]2Ki 8:16-24; 2Ch 21:1 [g]2Ch 22:1-10 [h]2Ki 11:1-12-:21
3:12 [i]2Ki 14:1-22; 2Ch 25:1-28 [j]Isa 1:1; Hos 1:1; Mic 1:1
3:13 [k]2Ki 16:1-20; 2Ch 28:1; Isa 7:1 [l]2Ki 18:1-20:21; 2Ch 29:1; Jer 26:19 [m]2Ch 33:1
3:14 [n]2Ki 21:19-26; 2Ch 33:21; Zep 1:1 [o]2Ch 34:1; Jer 1:2; 3:6; 25:3
3:15 [p]2Ki 23:34 [q]Jer 37:1 [r]2Ki 23:31
3:16 [s]2Ki 24:6,8; Mt 1:11 [t]2Ki 24:18
3:17 [u]Ezr 3:2
3:18 [v]Ezr 1:8; 5:14 [w]Jer 22:30
3:19 [x]Ezr 2:2; 3:2; 5:2; Ne 7:7; 12:1; Hag 1:1; 2:2; Zec 4:6
3:22 [y]Ezr 8:2-3
4:1 [z]Ge 29:35; 46:12; 1Ch 2:3 [a]Nu 26:21
4:4 [b]1Ch 2:50 [c]Ru 1:19
4:5 [d]1Ch 2:24

[e]5 Hebrew *Shimea,* a variant of *Shammua* [f]5 One Hebrew manuscript and Vulgate (see also Septuagint and 2 Samuel 11:3); most Hebrew manuscripts *Bathshua* [g]6 Two Hebrew manuscripts (see also 2 Samuel 5:15 and 1 Chron. 14:5); most Hebrew manuscripts *Elishama* [h]11 Hebrew *Joram,* a variant of *Jehoram* [i]16 Hebrew *Jeconiah,* a variant of *Jehoiachin;* also in verse 17 [j]3 Some Septuagint manuscripts (see also Vulgate); Hebrew *father* [k]4 *Father* may mean *civic leader* or *military leader;* also in verses 12, 14, 17, 18 and possibly elsewhere.

hashtari. These were the
descendants of Naarah.
7The sons of Helah:
Zereth, Zohar, Ethnan, 8and
Koz, who was the father of
Anub and Hazzobebah and
of the clans of Aharhel son
of Harum.

9Jabez was more honorable than
his brothers. His mother had
named him Jabez,[l] saying, "I gave
birth to him in pain." 10Jabez cried
out to the God of Israel, "Oh, that
you would bless me and enlarge my
territory! Let your hand be with me,
and keep me from harm so that I
will be free from pain." And God
granted his request.

11Kelub, Shuhah's brother, was
the father of Mehir, who
was the father of Eshton.
12Eshton was the father of
Beth Rapha, Paseah and Te-
hinnah the father of Ir Nahash.[m] These were the men
of Recah.

13The sons of Kenaz:
Othniel[a] and Seraiah.
The sons of Othniel:
Hathath and Meonothai.[n]
14Meonothai was the father
of Ophrah.
Seraiah was the father of Joab,
the father of Ge Har-
ashim.[o] It was called this
because its people were
craftsmen.
15The sons of Caleb son of Jephunneh:
Iru, Elah and Naam.
The son of Elah:
Kenaz.
16The sons of Jehallelel:
Ziph, Ziphah, Tiria and Asa-
rel.
17The sons of Ezrah:
Jether, Mered, Epher and
Jalon. One of Mered's wives
gave birth to Miriam,[b]
Shammai and Ishbah the father of Eshtemoa. 18(His
Judean wife gave birth to
Jered the father of Gedor,
Heber the father of Soco,
and Jekuthiel the father of
Zanoah.[c]) These were the
children of Pharaoh's
daughter Bithiah, whom
Mered had married.
19The sons of Hodiah's wife, the
sister of Naham:
the father of Keilah[d] the
Garmite, and Eshtemoa the
Maacathite.[e]
20The sons of Shimon:
Amnon, Rinnah, Ben-Ha-
nan and Tilon.
The descendants of Ishi:
Zoheth and Ben-Zoheth.
21The sons of Shelah[f] son of Judah:
Er the father of Lecah, Laa-
dah the father of Mareshah
and the clans of the linen
workers at Beth Ashbea,
22Jokim, the men of Coze-
ba, and Joash and Saraph,
who ruled in Moab and Ja-
shubi Lehem. (These
records are from ancient
times.) 23They were the
potters who lived at Netaim
and Gederah; they stayed
there and worked for the
king.

Simeon

4:28–33pp — Jos 19:2–10

24The descendants of Simeon:[g]
Nemuel, Jamin, Jarib,[h] Zerah and Shaul;
25Shallum was Shaul's son,
Mibsam his son and Mish-
ma his son.
26The descendants of Mishma:
Hammuel his son, Zaccur
his son and Shimei his son.
27Shimei had sixteen sons and
six daughters, but his brothers did
not have many children; so their
entire clan did not become as numerous as the people of Judah.
28They lived in Beersheba,[i] Moladah,[j] Hazar Shual, 29Bilhah,
Ezem,[k] Tolad, 30Bethuel, Hormah,[l] Ziklag, 31Beth Marcaboth,
Hazar Susim, Beth Biri and Shaara-

4:13 [a]Jos 15:17
4:17 [b]Ex 15:20
4:18 [c]Jos 15:34
4:19 [d]Jos 15:44 [e]Dt 3:14
4:21 [f]Ge 38:5
4:24 [g]Ge 29:33 [h]Nu 26:12
4:28 [i]Ge 21:14 [j]Jos 15:26
4:29 [k]Jos 15:29
4:30 [l]Nu 14:45

l9 *Jabez* sounds like the Hebrew for *pain.*
m12 Or *of the city of Nahash* n13 Some Septuagint manuscripts and Vulgate; Hebrew does not have *and Meonothai.*
o14 *Ge Harashim* means *valley of craftsmen.*

im.[a] These were their towns until
the reign of David. 32 Their surrounding villages were Etam, Ain,[b]
Rimmon, Token and Ashan[c]—five
towns— 33 and all the villages
around these towns as far as Baalath.[p] These were their settlements. And they kept a genealogical record.

34 Meshobab, Jamlech, Joshah
son of Amaziah, 35 Joel, Jehu
son of Joshibiah, the son of
Seraiah, the son of Asiel,
36 also Elioenai, Jaakobah,
Jeshohaiah, Asaiah, Adiel, Je-
simiel, Benaiah, 37 and Ziza
son of Shiphi, the son of Allon,
the son of Jedaiah, the son of
Shimri, the son of Shemaiah.

38 The men listed above by name
were leaders of their clans. Their
families increased greatly, 39 and
they went to the outskirts of Gedor[d] to the east of the valley in
search of pasture for their flocks.
40 They found rich, good pasture,
and the land was spacious, peaceful and quiet.[e] Some Hamites had
lived there formerly.

41 The men whose names were
listed came in the days of Hezekiah
king of Judah. They attacked the
Hamites in their dwellings and also
the Meunites[f] who were there and
completely destroyed[q] them, as is
evident to this day. Then they settled in their place, because there
was pasture for their flocks. 42 And
five hundred of these Simeonites,
led by Pelatiah, Neariah, Rephaiah
and Uzziel, the sons of Ishi, invaded the hill country of Seir.[g] 43 They
killed the remaining Amalekites[h]
who had escaped, and they have
lived there to this day.

Reuben

5 The sons of Reuben[i] the firstborn of Israel (he was the firstborn, but when he defiled his father's marriage bed,[j] his rights as
firstborn were given to the sons of
Joseph[k] son of Israel;[l] so he
could not be listed in the genealogical record in accordance with his
birthright,[m] 2 and though Judah[n]
was the strongest of his brothers
and a ruler[o] came from him, the
rights of the firstborn[p] belonged to
Joseph)— 3 the sons of Reuben[q]
the firstborn of Israel:

Hanoch, Pallu,[r] Hezron and
Carmi.

4 The descendants of Joel:
Shemaiah his son, Gog his
son,
Shimei his son, 5 Micah his
son,
Reaiah his son, Baal his
son,
6 and Beerah his son, whom
Tiglath-Pileser[r][s] king of
Assyria took into exile. Beerah was a leader of the Reubenites.

7 Their relatives by clans,[t] listed according to their genealogical records:
Jeiel the chief, Zechariah,
8 and Bela son of Azaz, the
son of Shema, the son of
Joel. They settled in the
area from Aroer[u] to Nebo
and Baal Meon.[v] 9 To the
east they occupied the land
up to the edge of the desert
that extends to the Euphrates River, because their livestock had increased in Gilead.[w]

10 During Saul's reign they
waged war against the Hagrites[x], who were defeated at
their hands; they occupied
the dwellings of the Hagrites
throughout the entire region
east of Gilead.

Gad

11 The Gadites[y] lived next to
them in Bashan, as far as
Salecah:[z]

12 Joel was the chief, Sha-
pham the second, then Ja-
nai and Shaphat, in Bashan.

13 Their relatives, by families,
were:

4:31 [a] Jos 15:36
4:32 [b] Nu 34:11 [c] Jos 15:42
4:39 [d] Jos 15:58
4:40 [e] Jdg 18:7-10
4:41 [f] 2Ch 20:1; 26:7
4:42 [g] Ge 14:6
4:43 [h] 1Sa 15:8; 30:17; 2Sa 8:12; Est 3:1; 9:16
5:1 [i] Ge 29:32 [j] Ge 35:22; 49:4 [k] Ge 48:16,22; 49:26 [l] Ge 48:5 [m] 1Ch 26:10
5:2 [n] Ge 49:10,12 [o] 1Sa 9:16; 12:12; 2Sa 6:21; 1Ch 11:2; 2Ch 7:18; Ps 60:7; Mic 5:2; Mt 2:6 [p] Ge 25:31
5:3 [q] Ge 29:32; 46:9; Ex 6:14; Nu 26:5-11 [r] Nu 26:5
5:6 [s] ver 26; 2Ki 15:19; 16:10; 2Ch 28:20
5:7 [t] ver 17
5:8 [u] Nu 32:34 [v] Jos 13:17
5:9 [w] Nu 32:26; Jos 22:9
5:10 [x] ver 18-21
5:11 [y] Jos 13:24-28 [z] Dt 3:10; Jos 13:11

p33 Some Septuagint manuscripts (see also Joshua 19:8); Hebrew *Baal* q41 The Hebrew term refers to the irrevocable giving over of things or persons to the LORD, often by totally destroying them. r6 Hebrew *Tilgath-Pilneser,* a variant of *Tiglath-Pileser;* also in verse 26

Michael, Meshullam, She-
ba, Jorai, Jacan, Zia and
Eber—seven in all.
14These were the sons of Abihail son of Huri, the son of
Jaroah, the son of Gilead,
the son of Michael, the son
of Jeshishai, the son of Jah-
do, the son of Buz.
15Ahi son of Abdiel, the son of
Guni, was head of their
family.
16The Gadites lived in Gilead, in
Bashan and its outlying villages, and on all the pasturelands of Sharon as far as
they extended.
17All these were entered in the
genealogical records during the
reigns of Jotham[a] king of Judah
and Jeroboam[b] king of Israel.

18The Reubenites, the Gadites
and the half-tribe of Manasseh had
44,760 men ready for military service[c]—able-bodied men who
could handle shield and sword,
who could use a bow, and who were
trained for battle. **19**They waged
war against the Hagrites, Jetur,[d]
Naphish and Nodab. **20**They were
helped[e] in fighting them, and God
handed the Hagrites and all their
allies over to them, because they
cried[f] out to him during the battle. He answered their prayers, because they trusted[g] in him. **21**They
seized the livestock of the Hagrites—fifty thousand camels, two
hundred fifty thousand sheep and
two thousand donkeys. They also
took one hundred thousand people
captive, **22**and many others fell
slain, because the battle[h] was
God's. And they occupied the land
until the exile.[i]

The Half-Tribe of Manasseh

23The people of the half-tribe of
Manasseh were numerous; they
settled in the land from Bashan to
Baal Hermon, that is, to Senir
(Mount Hermon).[j]
24These were the heads of their
families: Epher, Ishi, Eliel, Azriel,
Jeremiah, Hodaviah and Jahdiel.
They were brave warriors, famous
men, and heads of their families.
25But they were unfaithful[k] to the
God of their fathers and prostituted[l] themselves to the gods of the
peoples of the land, whom God had
destroyed before them. **26**So the
God of Israel stirred up the spirit of
Pul[m] king of Assyria (that is, Tiglath-Pileser[n] king of Assyria), who
took the Reubenites, the Gadites
and the half-tribe of Manasseh into
exile. He took them to Halah,[o] Habor, Hara and the river of Gozan,
where they are to this day.

Levi

6 The sons of Levi:[p]
Gershon, Kohath and Mera-
ri.
2The sons of Kohath:
Amram, Izhar, Hebron and
Uzziel.
3The children of Amram:
Aaron, Moses and Miriam.
The sons of Aaron:
Nadab, Abihu,[q] Eleazar
and Ithamar.
4Eleazar was the father of
Phinehas,
Phinehas the father of
Abishua,
5Abishua the father of Bukki,
Bukki the father of Uzzi,
6Uzzi the father of Zerahiah,
Zerahiah the father of Meraioth,
7Meraioth the father of Amariah,
Amariah the father of Ahitub,
8Ahitub the father of Zadok,[r]
Zadok the father of Ahimaaz,
9Ahimaaz the father of Azariah,
Azariah the father of Johanan,
10Johanan the father of Azariah[s] (it was he who served
as priest in the temple Solomon built in Jerusalem),
11Azariah the father of Amariah,
Amariah the father of Ahitub,

5:17 [a]2Ki 15:32 [b]2Ki 14:16,28
5:18 [c]Nu 1:3
5:19 [d]ver 10; Ge 25:15; 1Ch 1:31
5:20 [e]Ps 37:40 [f]1Ki 8:44; 2Ch 13:14; 14:11; Ps 20:7-9; 22:5 [g]Ps 26:1; Da 6:23
5:22 [h]2Ch 32:8 [i]2Ki 15:29; 17:6
5:23 [j]Dt 3:8,9; SS 4:8
5:25 [k]Dt 32:15-18; 2Ki 17:7; 1Ch 9:1; 2Ch 26:16 [l]Ex 34:15
5:26 [m]2Ki 15:19 [n]2Ki 15:29 [o]2Ki 17:6; 18:11
6:1 [p]Ge 46:11; Ex 6:16; Nu 26:57; 1Ch 23:6
6:3 [q]Lev 10:1
6:8 [r]2Sa 8:17; 15:27; Ezr 7:2
6:10 [s]1Ki 4:2; 6:1; 2Ch 3:1; 26:17-18

12Ahitub the father of Zadok,
Zadok the father of Shallum,
13Shallum the father of Hilkiah,[a]
Hilkiah the father of Azariah,
14Azariah the father of Seraiah,[b]
and Seraiah the father of Jehozadak.
15Jehozadak[c] was deported when the LORD sent Judah and Jerusalem into exile by the hand of Nebuchadnezzar.

16The sons of Levi:[d]
Gershon,[s] Kohath and Merari.[e]
17These are the names of the sons of Gershon:
Libni and Shimei.
18The sons of Kohath:
Amram, Izhar, Hebron and Uzziel.
19The sons of Merari:[f]
Mahli and Mushi.
These are the clans of the Levites listed according to their fathers:
20Of Gershon:
Libni his son, Jehath his son,
Zimmah his son, **21**Joah his son,
Iddo his son, Zerah his son and Jeatherai his son.
22The descendants of Kohath:
Amminadab his son, Korah[g] his son,
Assir his son, **23**Elkanah his son,
Ebiasaph his son, Assir his son,
24Tahath his son, Uriel[h] his son,
Uzziah his son and Shaul his son.
25The descendants of Elkanah:
Amasai, Ahimoth,
26Elkanah his son,[t] Zophai his son,
Nahath his son, **27**Eliab his son,
Jeroham his son, Elkanah[i] his son
and Samuel[j] his son.[u]

6:13 [a] 2Ki 22:1-20; 2Ch 34:9; 35:8
6:14 [b] 2Ki 25:18; Ezr 2:2; Ne 11:11
6:15 [c] 2Ki 25:18; Ne 12:1; Hag 1:1,14; 2:2,4; Zec 6:11
6:16 [d] Ge 29:34; Ex 6:16; Nu 3:17-20 [e] Nu 26:57
6:19 [f] Ge 46:11; 1Ch 23:21; 24:26
6:22 [g] Ex 6:24
6:24 [h] 1Ch 15:5
6:27 [i] 1Sa 1:1 [j] 1Sa 1:20
6:28 [k] ver 33; 1Sa 8:2
6:31 [l] 1Ch 25:1; 2Ch 29:25-26; Ne 12:45 [m] 1Ch 9:33; 15:19; Ezr 3:10; Ps 68:25
6:33 [n] 1Ki 4:31; 1Ch 15:17; 25:1 [o] ver 28
6:34 [p] 1Sa 1:1
6:37 [q] Ex 6:24
6:38 [r] Ex 6:21

28The sons of Samuel:
Joel[v][k] the firstborn
and Abijah the second son.
29The descendants of Merari:
Mahli, Libni his son,
Shimei his son, Uzzah his son,
30Shimea his son, Haggiah his son
and Asaiah his son.

The Temple Musicians

6:54-80pp — Jos 21:4-39

31These are the men[l] David put
in charge of the music[m] in the
house of the LORD after the ark
came to rest there. **32**They ministered with music before the tabernacle, the Tent of Meeting, until
Solomon built the temple of the
LORD in Jerusalem. They performed
their duties according to the regulations laid down for them.
33Here are the men who served,
together with their sons:
From the Kohathites:
Heman,[n] the musician,
the son of Joel,[o] the son of Samuel,
34the son of Elkanah,[p] the son of Jeroham,
the son of Eliel, the son of Toah,
35the son of Zuph, the son of Elkanah,
the son of Mahath, the son of Amasai,
36the son of Elkanah, the son of Joel,
the son of Azariah, the son of Zephaniah,
37the son of Tahath, the son of Assir,
the son of Ebiasaph, the son of Korah,[q]
38the son of Izhar,[r] the son of Kohath,

[s]*16* Hebrew *Gershom,* a variant of *Gershon,* also in verses 17, 20, 43, 62 and 71
[t]*26* Some Hebrew manuscripts, Septuagint and Syriac; most Hebrew manuscripts *Ahimoth* [26]*and Elkanah. The sons of Elkanah:*
[u]*27* Some Septuagint manuscripts (see also 1 Samuel 1:19,20 and 1 Chron. 6:33,34); Hebrew does not have *and Samuel his son.*
[v]*28* Some Septuagint manuscripts and Syriac (see also 1 Samuel 8:2 and 1 Chron. 6:33); Hebrew does not have *Joel.*

the son of Levi, the son of Israel;
39 and Heman's associate Asaph,[a] who served at his right hand:
Asaph son of Berekiah, the son of Shimea,[b]
40 the son of Michael, the son of Baaseiah,[w]
the son of Malkijah, 41 the son of Ethni,
the son of Zerah, the son of Adaiah,
42 the son of Ethan, the son of Zimmah,
the son of Shimei, 43 the son of Jahath,
the son of Gershon, the son of Levi;
44 and from their associates, the Merarites, at his left hand:
Ethan son of Kishi, the son of Abdi,
the son of Malluch, 45 the son of Hashabiah,
the son of Amaziah, the son of Hilkiah,
46 the son of Amzi, the son of Bani,
the son of Shemer, 47 the son of Mahli,
the son of Mushi, the son of Merari,
the son of Levi.

48 Their fellow Levites[c] were assigned to all the other duties of the tabernacle, the house of God. 49 But Aaron and his descendants were the ones who presented offerings on the altar[d] of burnt offering and on the altar of incense[e] in connection with all that was done in the Most Holy Place, making atonement for Israel, in accordance with all that Moses the servant of God had commanded.

50 These were the descendants of Aaron:
Eleazar his son, Phinehas his son,
Abishua his son, 51 Bukki his son,
Uzzi his son, Zerahiah his son,
52 Meraioth his son, Amariah his son,
Ahitub his son, 53 Zadok[f] his son
and Ahimaaz his son.

54 These were the locations of their settlements[g] allotted as their territory (they were assigned to the descendants of Aaron who were from the Kohathite clan, because the first lot was for them):

55 They were given Hebron in Judah with its surrounding pasturelands. 56 But the fields and villages around the city were given to Caleb son of Jephunneh.[h]

57 So the descendants of Aaron were given Hebron (a city of refuge), and Libnah,[x][i] Jattir,[j] Eshtemoa, 58 Hilen, Debir,[k] 59 Ashan,[l] Juttah[y] and Beth Shemesh, together with their pasturelands. 60 And from the tribe of Benjamin they were given Gibeon,[z] Geba, Alemeth and Anathoth,[m] together with their pasturelands.

These towns, which were distributed among the Kohathite clans, were thirteen in all.

61 The rest of Kohath's descendants were allotted ten towns from the clans of half the tribe of Manasseh.

62 The descendants of Gershon, clan by clan, were allotted thirteen towns from the tribes of Issachar, Asher and Naphtali, and from the part of the tribe of Manasseh that is in Bashan.

63 The descendants of Merari, clan by clan, were allotted twelve towns from the tribes of Reuben, Gad and Zebulun.

64 So the Israelites gave the Levites these towns[n] and their pasturelands. 65 From the tribes of Judah, Simeon and Benjamin they al-

6:39 [a] 1Ch 25:1,9; 2Ch 29:13; Ne 11:17 [b] 1Ch 15:17
6:48 [c] 1Ch 23:32
6:49 [d] Ex 27:1-8 [e] Ex 30:1-7, 10; 2Ch 26:18
6:53 [f] 2Sa 8:17
6:54 [g] Nu 31:10
6:56 [h] Jos 14:13; 15:13
6:57 [i] Nu 33:20 [j] Jos 15:48
6:58 [k] Jos 10:3
6:59 [l] Jos 15:42
6:60 [m] Jer 1:1
6:64 [n] Nu 35:1-8; Jos 21:3, 41-42

[w] *40* Most Hebrew manuscripts; some Hebrew manuscripts, one Septuagint manuscript and Syriac *Maaseiah* [x] *57* See Joshua 21:13; Hebrew *given the cities of refuge: Hebron, Libnah.* [y] *59* Syriac (see also Septuagint and Joshua 21:16); Hebrew does not have *Juttah.* [z] *60* See Joshua 21:17; Hebrew does not have *Gibeon.*

lotted the previously named towns.
[66]Some of the Kohathite clans
were given as their territory towns
from the tribe of Ephraim.
[67]In the hill country of
Ephraim they were given Shechem (a city of refuge), and
Gezer,[a][a] [68]Jokmeam,[b] Beth
Horon,[c] [69]Aijalon[d] and Gath
Rimmon,[e] together with their
pasturelands.
[70]And from half the tribe of
Manasseh the Israelites gave
Aner and Bileam, together
with their pasturelands, to the
rest of the Kohathite clans.

[71]The Gershonites[f] received
the following:
From the clan of the half-tribe
of Manasseh
they received Golan in Bashan[g] and also Ashtaroth,
together with their pasturelands;
[72]from the tribe of Issachar
they received Kedesh, Daberath,[h] [73]Ramoth and
Anem, together with their
pasturelands;
[74]from the tribe of Asher
they received Mashal, Ab-
don,[i] [75]Hukok[j] and Rehob,[k] together with their
pasturelands;
[76]and from the tribe of Naphtali
they received Kedesh in
Galilee, Hammon[l] and
Kiriathaim,[m] together with
their pasturelands.

[77]The Merarites (the rest of the
Levites) received the following:
From the tribe of Zebulun
they received Jokneam,
Kartah,[b] Rimmono and Tabor, together with their pasturelands;
[78]from the tribe of Reuben
across the Jordan east of
Jericho
they received Bezer[n] in the
desert, Jahzah, [79]Kede-
moth[o] and Mephaath, to-
gether with their pasturelands;
[80]and from the tribe of Gad
they received Ramoth
in Gilead,[p] Mahanaim,[q]
[81]Heshbon and Jazer,[r] together with their pasturelands.[s]

6:67 [a]Jos 10:33
6:68 [b]1Ki 4:12 [c]Jos 10:10
6:69 [d]Jos 10:12 [e]Jos 19:45
6:71 [f]1Ch 23:7 [g]Jos 20:8
6:72 [h]Jos 19:12
6:74 [i]Jos 19:28
6:75 [j]Jos 19:34 [k]Nu 13:21
6:76 [l]Jos 19:28 [m]Nu 32:37
6:78 [n]Jos 20:8
6:79 [o]Dt 2:26
6:80 [p]Jos 20:8 [q]Ge 32:2
6:81 [r]Nu 21:32 [s]2Ch 11:14
7:1 [t]Ge 30:18; Nu 26:23 [u]Ge 46:13
7:6 [v]Ge 46:21; Nu 26:38; 1Ch 8:1-40

Issachar

7 The sons of Issachar:[t]
Tola, Puah,[u] Jashub and
Shimron—four in all.
[2]The sons of Tola:
Uzzi, Rephaiah, Jeriel, Jah-
mai, Ibsam and Samuel—
heads of their families. During the reign of David, the
descendants of Tola listed
as fighting men in their genealogy numbered 22,600.
[3]The son of Uzzi:
Izrahiah.
The sons of Izrahiah:
Michael, Obadiah, Joel and
Isshiah. All five of them
were chiefs. [4]According to
their family genealogy, they
had 36,000 men ready for
battle, for they had many
wives and children.
[5]The relatives who were fighting men belonging to all the
clans of Issachar, as listed
in their genealogy, were
87,000 in all.

Benjamin

[6]Three sons of Benjamin:[v]
Bela, Beker and Jediael.
[7]The sons of Bela:
Ezbon, Uzzi, Uzziel, Jerimoth and Iri, heads of families—five in all. Their genealogical record listed 22,-
034 fighting men.
[8]The sons of Beker:
Zemirah, Joash, Eliezer,
Elioenai, Omri, Jeremoth,
Abijah, Anathoth and Ale-
meth. All these were the
sons of Beker. [9]Their genealogical record listed the
heads of families and 20,-
200 fighting men.

[a]67 See Joshua 21:21; Hebrew *given the cities of refuge: Shechem, Gezer.* [b]77 See Septuagint and Joshua 21:34; Hebrew does not have *Jokneam, Kartah.*

10The son of Jediael:
Bilhan.
The sons of Bilhan:
Jeush, Benjamin, Ehud, Kenaanah, Zethan, Tarshish
and Ahishahar. 11All these
sons of Jediael were heads
of families. There were 17,200 fighting men ready to
go out to war.
12The Shuppites and Huppites were the descendants of Ir, and the Hushites the descendants of Aher.

Naphtali

13The sons of Naphtali:[a]
Jahziel, Guni, Jezer and Shillem[c]—the descendants of Bilhah.

Manasseh

14The descendants of Manasseh:[b]
Asriel was his descendant
through his Aramean concubine. She gave birth to Makir
the father of Gilead.[c] 15Ma-
kir took a wife from among
the Huppites and Shuppites.
His sister's name was Maacah.
Another descendant was named Zelophehad,[d] who had only daughters.
16Makir's wife Maacah gave
birth to a son and named him
Peresh. His brother was named Sheresh, and his sons were Ulam and Rakem.
17The son of Ulam:
Bedan.
These were the sons of Gilead[e] son of Makir, the son of
Manasseh. 18His sister
Hammoleketh gave birth to
Ishhod, Abiezer[f] and Mahlah.
19The sons of Shemida were:
Ahian, Shechem, Likhi and Aniam.

Ephraim

20The descendants of Ephraim:[g]
Shuthelah, Bered his son,
Tahath his son, Eleadah his son,
Tahath his son, 21Zabad his
son
and Shuthelah his son.
Ezer and Elead were killed by the native-born men of Gath, when they went down to seize their livestock.
22Their father Ephraim
mourned for them many days, and his relatives came to
comfort him. 23Then he lay
with his wife again, and she became pregnant and gave birth to a son. He named him Beriah,[d] because there had been misfortune in his family.
24His daughter was Sheerah,
who built Lower and Upper Beth Horon[h] as well as Uzzen Sheerah.
25Rephah was his son, Resheph his son,[e]
Telah his son, Tahan his son,
26Ladan his son, Ammihud his son,
Elishama his son, 27Nun his
son
and Joshua his son.
28Their lands and settlements
included Bethel and its surrounding villages, Naaran to the east, Gezer[i] and its villages to the west, and Shechem and its villages all the way to Ayyah and its villages.
29Along the borders of Manasseh
were Beth Shan,[j] Taanach, Megiddo and Dor,[k] together with their villages. The descendants of Joseph son of Israel lived in these towns.

Asher

30The sons of Asher:[l]
Imnah, Ishvah, Ishvi and Beriah. Their sister was Serah.
31The sons of Beriah:
Heber and Malkiel, who was the father of Birzaith.
32Heber was the father of Japh-

7:13 [a]Ge 30:8; 46:24
7:14 [b]Ge 41:51; Jos 17:1; 1Ch 5:23 [c]Nu 26:30
7:15 [d]Nu 26:33; 36:1-12
7:17 [e]Nu 26:30; 1Sa 12:11
7:18 [f]Jos 17:2
7:20 [g]Ge 41:52; Nu 1:33; 26:35
7:24 [h]Jos 10:10; 16:3,5
7:28 [i]Jos 10:33; 16:7
7:29 [j]Jos 17:11 [k]Jos 11:2
7:30 [l]Ge 46:17; Nu 1:40; 26:44

[c]*13* Some Hebrew and Septuagint manuscripts (see also Gen. 46:24 and Num. 26:49); most Hebrew manuscripts *Shallum* [d]*23 Beriah* sounds like the Hebrew for *misfortune.*
[e]*25* Some Septuagint manuscripts; Hebrew does not have *his son.*

let, Shomer and Hotham
and of their sister Shua.
33 The sons of Japhlet:
Pasach, Bimhal and Ash-
vath.
These were Japhlet's sons.
34 The sons of Shomer:
Ahi, Rohgah,[f] Hubbah and
Aram.
35 The sons of his brother Helem:
Zophah, Imna, Shelesh and
Amal.
36 The sons of Zophah:
Suah, Harnepher, Shual,
Beri, Imrah, 37 Bezer, Hod,
Shamma, Shilshah, Ithran[g]
and Beera.
38 The sons of Jether:
Jephunneh, Pispah and
Ara.
39 The sons of Ulla:
Arah, Hanniel and Rizia.
40 All these were descendants of
Asher—heads of families, choice
men, brave warriors and outstand-
ing leaders. The number of men
ready for battle, as listed in their
genealogy, was 26,000.

The Genealogy of Saul the Benjamite

8:28–38pp — 1Ch 9:34–44

8 Benjamin[a] was the father of
Bela his firstborn,
Ashbel the second son,
Aharah the third,
2 Nohah the fourth and Rapha the fifth.
3 The sons of Bela were:
Addar,[b] Gera, Abihud,[h]
4 Abishua, Naaman, Aho-
ah,[c] 5 Gera, Shephuphan
and Huram.
6 These were the descendants of
Ehud,[d] who were heads of
families of those living in
Geba and were deported to
Manahath:
7 Naaman, Ahijah, and Gera,
who deported them and
who was the father of Uzza
and Ahihud.
8 Sons were born to Shaharaim
in Moab after he had di-
vorced his wives Hushim
and Baara. 9 By his wife Ho-
desh he had Jobab, Zibia,
Mesha, Malcam, 10 Jeuz, Sa-
kia and Mirmah. These
were his sons, heads of families. 11 By Hushim he had
Abitub and Elpaal.
12 The sons of Elpaal:
Eber, Misham, Shemed
(who built Ono[e] and Lod
with its surrounding vil-
lages), 13 and Beriah and
Shema, who were heads of
families of those living in
Aijalon[f] and who drove out
the inhabitants of Gath.[g]
14 Ahio, Shashak, Jeremoth,
15 Zebadiah, Arad, Eder,
16 Michael, Ishpah and Joha
were the sons of Beriah.
17 Zebadiah, Meshullam, Hizki,
Heber, 18 Ishmerai, Izliah
and Jobab were the sons of
Elpaal.
19 Jakim, Zicri, Zabdi, 20 Elienai,
Zillethai, Eliel, 21 Adaiah,
Beraiah and Shimrath were
the sons of Shimei.
22 Ishpan, Eber, Eliel, 23 Abdon,
Zicri, Hanan, 24 Hananiah,
Elam, Anthothijah, 25 Iph-
deiah and Penuel were the
sons of Shashak.
26 Shamsherai, Shehariah, Athaliah, 27 Jaareshiah, Elijah
and Zicri were the sons of
Jeroham.
28 All these were heads of families, chiefs as listed in their genealogy, and they lived in Jerusalem.

29 Jeiel[i] the father[j] of Gibeon
lived in Gibeon.[h]
His wife's name was Maa-
cah, 30 and his firstborn son
was Abdon, followed by Zur,
Kish, Baal, Ner,[k] Nadab,
31 Gedor, Ahio, Zeker 32 and
Mikloth, who was the father
of Shimeah. They too lived

8:1 [a] Ge 46:21; 1Ch 7:6
8:3 [b] Ge 46:21
8:4 [c] 2Sa 23:9
8:6 [d] Jdg 3:12-30; 1Ch 2:52
8:12 [e] Ezr 2:33; Ne 6:2; 7:37; 11:35
8:13 [f] Jos 10:12 [g] Jos 11:22
8:29 [h] Jos 9:3

[f] 34 Or *of his brother Shomer: Rohgah*
[g] 37 Possibly a variant of *Jether*
[h] 3 Or *Gera the father of Ehud*
[i] 29 Some Septuagint manuscripts (see also 1 Chron. 9:35); Hebrew does not have *Jeiel.*
[j] 29 *Father* may mean *civic leader* or *military leader.*
[k] 30 Some Septuagint manuscripts (see also 1 Chron. 9:36); Hebrew does not have *Ner.*

near their relatives in Jerusalem.
[33]Ner[a] was the father of Kish,[b] Kish the father of Saul[c], and Saul the father of Jonathan, Malki-Shua, Abinadab and Esh-Baal.[1d]
[34]The son of Jonathan:[e] Merib-Baal,[mf] who was the father of Micah.
[35]The sons of Micah: Pithon, Melech, Tarea and Ahaz.
[36]Ahaz was the father of Jehoaddah, Jehoaddah was the father of Alemeth, Azmaveth and Zimri, and Zimri was the father of Moza.
[37]Moza was the father of Binea; Raphah was his son, Eleasah his son and Azel his son.
[38]Azel had six sons, and these were their names: Azrikam, Bokeru, Ishmael, Sheariah, Obadiah and Hanan. All these were the sons of Azel.
[39]The sons of his brother Eshek: Ulam his firstborn, Jeush the second son and Eliphelet the third.
[40]The sons of Ulam were brave warriors who could handle the bow. They had many sons and grandsons—150 in all.
All these were the descendants of Benjamin.[g]

9 All Israel was listed in the genealogies recorded in the book of the kings of Israel.

The People in Jerusalem

9:1–17pp — Ne 11:3–19

The people of Judah were taken captive to Babylon because of their unfaithfulness.[h]
[2]Now the first to resettle on their own property in their own towns[i] were some Israelites, priests, Levites and temple servants.[j]
[3]Those from Judah, from Benjamin, and from Ephraim and Manasseh who lived in Jerusalem were:
[4]Uthai son of Ammihud, the son of Omri, the son of Imri, the son of Bani, a descendant of Perez son of Judah.[k]
[5]Of the Shilonites: Asaiah the firstborn and his sons.
[6]Of the Zerahites: Jeuel.
The people from Judah numbered 690.
[7]Of the Benjamites: Sallu son of Meshullam, the son of Hodaviah, the son of Hassenuah;
[8]Ibneiah son of Jeroham; Elah son of Uzzi, the son of Micri; and Meshullam son of Shephatiah, the son of Reuel, the son of Ibnijah.
[9]The people from Benjamin, as listed in their genealogy, numbered 956. All these men were heads of their families.
[10]Of the priests: Jedaiah; Jehoiarib; Jakin;
[11]Azariah son of Hilkiah, the son of Meshullam, the son of Zadok, the son of Meraioth, the son of Ahitub, the official in charge of the house of God;
[12]Adaiah son of Jeroham, the son of Pashhur,[l] the son of Malkijah; and Maasai son of Adiel, the son of Jahzerah, the son of Meshullam, the son of Meshillemith, the son of Immer.
[13]The priests, who were heads of families, numbered 1,760. They were able men, responsible for ministering in the house of God.
[14]Of the Levites: Shemaiah son of Hasshub, the son of Azrikam, the son of Hashabiah, a Merarite;
[15]Bakbakkar, Heresh, Galal and Mattaniah[m] son of Mica, the son of Zicri, the son of Asaph;
[16]Obadiah son of Shemaiah, the son of

8:33 [a] 1Sa 28:19 [b] 1Sa 9:1 [c] 1Sa 14:49 [d] 2Sa 2:8
8:34 [e] 2Sa 9:12 [f] 2Sa 4:4
8:40 [g] Nu 26:38
9:1 [h] 1Ch 5:25
9:2 [i] Jos 9:27; Ezr 2:70 [j] Ezr 2:43,58; 8:20; Ne 7:60
9:4 [k] Ge 38:29; 46:12
9:12 [l] Ezr 2:38; 10:22; Ne 10:3; Jer 21:1; 38:1
9:15 [m] 2Ch 20:14; Ne 11:22

[1]33 Also known as *Ish-Bosheth* [m]34 Also known as *Mephibosheth*

Galal, the son of Jeduthun;
and Berekiah son of Asa,
the son of Elkanah, who
lived in the villages of the
Netophathites.[a]
17The gatekeepers:[b]
Shallum, Akkub, Talmon,
Ahiman and their brothers,
Shallum their chief 18being
stationed at the King's
Gate[c] on the east, up to the
present time. These were
the gatekeepers belonging
to the camp of the Levites.
19Shallum[d] son of Kore,
the son of Ebiasaph, the son
of Korah, and his fellow
gatekeepers from his family
(the Korahites) were re-
sponsible for guarding the
thresholds of the Tent[n] just
as their fathers had been responsible for guarding the
entrance to the dwelling of
the LORD. 20In earlier times
Phinehas[e] son of Eleazar
was in charge of the gatekeepers, and the LORD was
with him. 21Zechariah[f] son
of Meshelemiah was the
gatekeeper at the entrance
to the Tent of Meeting.
22Altogether, those chosen to be
gatekeepers[g] at the thresholds
numbered 212. They were registered by genealogy in their villages.
The gatekeepers had been assigned
to their positions of trust by David
and Samuel the seer.[h] 23They and
their descendants were in charge of
guarding the gates of the house of
the LORD—the house called the
Tent. 24The gatekeepers were on
the four sides: east, west, north and
south. 25Their brothers in their villages had to come from time to
time and share their duties for seven-day[i] periods. 26But the four
principal gatekeepers, who were
Levites, were entrusted with the responsibility for the rooms and treasuries[j] in the house of God.
27They would spend the night stationed around the house of God,[k]
because they had to guard it; and
they had charge of the key[l] for
opening it each morning.

28Some of them were in charge
of the articles used in the temple
service; they counted them when
they were brought in and when
they were taken out. 29Others were
assigned to take care of the furnishings and all the other articles
of the sanctuary,[m] as well as the
flour and wine, and the oil, incense
and spices. 30But some[n] of the
priests took care of mixing the
spices. 31A Levite named Mattithiah, the firstborn son of Shallum the
Korahite, was entrusted with the
responsibility for baking the offering bread. 32Some of their Kohathite brothers were in charge of preparing for every Sabbath the bread
set out on the table.[o]
33Those who were musicians,[p]
heads of Levite families, stayed in
the rooms of the temple and were
exempt from other duties because
they were responsible for the work
day and night.[q]
34All these were heads of Levite
families, chiefs as listed in their genealogy, and they lived in Jerusalem.

The Genealogy of Saul

9:34–44pp — 1Ch 8:28–38

35Jeiel[r] the father[o] of Gibeon
lived in Gibeon.
His wife's name was Maa-
cah, 36and his firstborn son
was Abdon, followed by Zur,
Kish, Baal, Ner, Nadab,
37Gedor, Ahio, Zechariah
and Mikloth. 38Mikloth was
the father of Shimeam.
They too lived near their
relatives in Jerusalem.
39Ner[s] was the father of Kish,[t]
Kish the father of Saul, and
Saul the father of Jona-
than,[u] Malki-Shua, Abinadab and Esh-Baal.[p][v]
40The son of Jonathan:
Merib-Baal,[q][w] who was the
father of Micah.
41The sons of Micah:

9:16 [a]Ne 12:28
9:17 [b]ver 22; 1Ch 26:1; 2Ch 8:14; 31:14; Ezr 2:42; Ne 7:45
9:18 [c]1Ch 26:14; Eze 43:1; 46:1
9:19 [d]Jer 35:4
9:20 [e]Nu 25:7-13
9:21 [f]1Ch 26:2,14
9:22 [g]ver 17; 1Ch 26:1-2; 2Ch 31:15,18 [h]1Sa 9:9
9:25 [i]2Ki 11:5; 2Ch 23:8
9:26 [j]1Ch 26:22
9:27 [k]Nu 3:38; 1Ch 23:30-32 [l]Isa 22:22
9:29 [m]Nu 3:28; 1Ch 23:29
9:30 [n]Ex 30:23-25
9:32 [o]Lev 24:5-8; 1Ch 23:29; 2Ch 13:11
9:33 [p]1Ch 6:31; 25:1-31 [q]Ps 134:1
9:35 [r]1Ch 8:29
9:39 [s]1Ch 8:33 [t]1Sa 9:1 [u]1Sa 13:22 [v]2Sa 2:8
9:40 [w]2Sa 4:4

[n]*19* That is, the temple; also in verses 21 and 23 [o]*35* *Father* may mean *civic leader* or *military leader.* [p]*39* Also known as *Ish-Bosheth* [q]*40* Also known as *Mephibosheth*

Pithon, Melech, Tahrea and Ahaz.[r]

42Ahaz was the father of Jadah, Jadah[s] was the father of Alemeth, Azmaveth and Zimri, and Zimri was the father of Moza. 43Moza was the father of Binea; Rephaiah was his son, Eleasah his son and Azel his son.

44Azel had six sons, and these were their names:

Azrikam, Bokeru, Ishmael, Sheariah, Obadiah and Hanan. These were the sons of Azel.

Saul Takes His Life

10:1–12pp — 1Sa 31:1–13; 2Sa 1:4–12

10 Now the Philistines fought against Israel; the Israelites fled before them, and many fell slain on Mount Gilboa. 2The Philistines pressed hard after Saul and his sons, and they killed his sons Jonathan, Abinadab and Malki-Shua. 3The fighting grew fierce around Saul, and when the archers overtook him, they wounded him.

4Saul said to his armor-bearer, "Draw your sword and run me through, or these uncircumcised fellows will come and abuse me."

But his armor-bearer was terrified and would not do it; so Saul took his own sword and fell on it. 5When the armor-bearer saw that Saul was dead, he too fell on his sword and died. 6So Saul and his three sons died, and all his house died together.

7When all the Israelites in the valley saw that the army had fled and that Saul and his sons had died, they abandoned their towns and fled. And the Philistines came and occupied them.

8The next day, when the Philistines came to strip the dead, they found Saul and his sons fallen on Mount Gilboa. 9They stripped him and took his head and his armor, and sent messengers throughout the land of the Philistines to proclaim the news among their idols and their people. 10They put his armor in the temple of their gods and hung up his head in the temple of Dagon.[a]

11When all the inhabitants of Jabesh Gilead[b] heard of everything the Philistines had done to Saul, 12all their valiant men went and took the bodies of Saul and his sons and brought them to Jabesh. Then they buried their bones under the great tree in Jabesh, and they fasted seven days.

13Saul died[c] because he was unfaithful[d] to the LORD; he did not keep[e] the word of the LORD and even consulted a medium[f] for guidance, 14and did not inquire of the LORD. So the LORD put him to death and turned[g] the kingdom[h] over to David son of Jesse.

David Becomes King Over Israel

11:1–3pp — 2Sa 5:1–3

11 All Israel[i] came together to David at Hebron[j] and said, "We are your own flesh and blood. 2In the past, even while Saul was king, you were the one who led Israel on their military campaigns.[k] And the LORD your God said to you, 'You will shepherd[l] my people Israel, and you will become their ruler.[m]' "

3When all the elders of Israel had come to King David at Hebron, he made a compact with them at Hebron before the LORD, and they anointed[n] David king over Israel, as the LORD had promised through Samuel.

David Conquers Jerusalem

11:4–9pp — 2Sa 5:6–10

4David and all the Israelites marched to Jerusalem (that is, Jebus). The Jebusites[o] who lived there 5said to David, "You will not get in here." Nevertheless, David captured the fortress of Zion, the City of David.

10:10 [a] Jdg 16:23
10:11 [b] Jdg 21:8
10:13 [c] 2Sa 1:1 [d] 1Sa 15:23; 1Ch 5:25 [e] 1Sa 13:13 [f] Lev 19:31; 20:6; Dt 18:9-14; 1Sa 28:7
10:14 [g] 1Ch 12:23 [h] 1Sa 13:14; 15:28
11:1 [i] 1Ch 9:1 [j] Ge 13:18; 23:19
11:2 [k] 1Sa 18:5,16 [l] Ps 78:71; Mt 2:6 [m] 1Ch 5:2
11:3 [n] 1Sa 16:1-13
11:4 [o] Ge 10:16; 15:18-21; Jos 3:10; 15:8; Jdg 1:21; 19:10

[r] *41* Vulgate and Syriac (see also Septuagint and 1 Chron. 8:35); Hebrew does not have *and Ahaz.* [s] *42* Some Hebrew manuscripts and Septuagint (see also 1 Chron. 8:36); most Hebrew manuscripts *Jarah, Jarah*

6David had said, "Whoever leads
the attack on the Jebusites will
become commander-in-chief."
Joab[a] son of Zeruiah went up first,
and so he received the command.
7David then took up residence in
the fortress, and so it was called
the City of David. **8**He built up the
city around it, from the supporting
terraces[t][b] to the surrounding
wall, while Joab restored the rest of
the city. **9**And David became more
and more powerful,[c] because the
LORD Almighty was with him.

David's Mighty Men

11:10–41pp — 2Sa 23:8–39

10These were the chiefs of David's mighty men—they, together
with all Israel,[d] gave his kingship
strong support to extend it over the
whole land, as the LORD had promised[e]— **11**this is the list of David's
mighty men:[f]
Jashobeam,[u] a Hacmonite, was
chief of the officers[v]; he raised his
spear against three hundred men,
whom he killed in one encounter.
12Next to him was Eleazar son of
Dodai the Ahohite, one of the three
mighty men. **13**He was with David
at Pas Dammim when the Philistines gathered there for battle. At a
place where there was a field full of
barley, the troops fled from the
Philistines. **14**But they took their
stand in the middle of the field.
They defended it and struck the
Philistines down, and the LORD
brought about a great victory.[g]
15Three of the thirty chiefs came
down to David to the rock at the
cave of Adullam, while a band of
Philistines was encamped in the
Valley[h] of Rephaim. **16**At that time
David was in the stronghold,[i] and
the Philistine garrison was at Bethlehem. **17**David longed for water
and said, "Oh, that someone would
get me a drink of water from the
well near the gate of Bethlehem!"
18So the Three broke through the
Philistine lines, drew water from
the well near the gate of Bethlehem and carried it back to David.
But he refused to drink it; instead,
he poured[j] it out before the LORD.
19"God forbid that I should do
this!" he said. "Should I drink the
blood of these men who went at the
risk of their lives?" Because they
risked their lives to bring it back,
David would not drink it.
Such were the exploits of the
three mighty men.
20Abishai[k] the brother of Joab
was chief of the Three. He raised
his spear against three hundred
men, whom he killed, and so he became as famous as the Three. **21**He
was doubly honored above the
Three and became their commander, even though he was not included among them.
22Benaiah son of Jehoiada was a
valiant fighter from Kabzeel,[l] who
performed great exploits. He
struck down two of Moab's best
men. He also went down into a pit
on a snowy day and killed a lion.[m]
23And he struck down an Egyptian
who was seven and a half feet[w] tall.
Although the Egyptian had a spear
like a weaver's rod[n] in his hand,
Benaiah went against him with a
club. He snatched the spear from
the Egyptian's hand and killed him
with his own spear. **24**Such were
the exploits of Benaiah son of Jehoiada; he too was as famous as the
three mighty men. **25**He was held
in greater honor than any of the
Thirty, but he was not included
among the Three. And David put
him in charge of his bodyguard.

26The mighty men were:
Asahel[o] the brother of
Joab,
Elhanan son of Dodo from
Bethlehem,
27Shammoth[p] the Harorite,
Helez the Pelonite,
28Ira son of Ikkesh from Te-
koa,
Abiezer[q] from Anathoth,
29Sibbecai[r] the Hushathite,
Ilai the Ahohite,
30Maharai the Netophathite,

11:6 [a] 2Sa 2:13; 8:16
11:8 [b] 2Sa 5:9; 2Ch 32:5
11:9 [c] 2Sa 3:1; Est 9:4
11:10 [d] ver 1 [e] ver 3 1Ch 12:23
11:11 [f] 2Sa 17:10
11:14 [g] Ex 14:30; 1Sa 11:13
11:15 [h] 1Ch 14:9; Isa 17:5
11:16 [i] 2Sa 5:17
11:18 [j] Dt 12:16
11:20 [k] 1Sa 26:6
11:22 [l] Jos 15:21 [m] 1Sa 17:36
11:23 [n] 1Sa 17:7
11:26 [o] 2Sa 2:18
11:27 [p] 1Ch 27:8
11:28 [q] 1Ch 27:12
11:29 [r] 2Sa 21:18

[t] *8* Or *the Millo* [u] *11* Possibly a variant of *Jashob-Baal* [v] *11* Or *Thirty*; some Septuagint manuscripts *Three* (see also 2 Samuel 23:8) [w] *23* Hebrew *five cubits* (about 2.3 meters)

Heled son of Baanah the
Netophathite,
31Ithai son of Ribai from Gibeah in Benjamin,
Benaiah[a] the Pirathonite,[b]
32Hurai from the ravines of
Gaash,
Abiel the Arbathite,
33Azmaveth the Baharumite,
Eliahba the Shaalbonite,
34the sons of Hashem the Gi-
zonite,
Jonathan son of Shagee the
Hararite,
35Ahiam son of Sacar the Hararite,
Eliphal son of Ur,
36Hepher the Mekerathite,
Ahijah the Pelonite,
37Hezro the Carmelite,
Naarai son of Ezbai,
38Joel the brother of Nathan,
Mibhar son of Hagri,
39Zelek the Ammonite,
Naharai the Berothite, the
armor-bearer of Joab son of
Zeruiah,
40Ira the Ithrite,
Gareb the Ithrite,
41Uriah[c] the Hittite,
Zabad[d] son of Ahlai,
42Adina son of Shiza the Reubenite, who was chief of the
Reubenites, and the thirty
with him,
43Hanan son of Maacah,
Joshaphat the Mithnite,
44Uzzia the Ashterathite,[e]
Shama and Jeiel the sons of
Hotham the Aroerite,
45Jediael son of Shimri,
his brother Joha the Tizite,
46Eliel the Mahavite,
Jeribai and Joshaviah the
sons of Elnaam,
Ithmah the Moabite,
47Eliel, Obed and Jaasiel the
Mezobaite.

Warriors Join David

12 These were the men who
came to David at Ziklag,[f]
while he was banished from the
presence of Saul son of Kish (they
were among the warriors who
helped him in battle; 2they were
armed with bows and were able to
shoot arrows or to sling stones
right-handed or left-handed;[g] they
were kinsmen of Saul[h] from the
tribe of Benjamin):

3Ahiezer their chief and Joash
the sons of Shemaah the Gibe-
athite; Jeziel and Pelet the
sons of Azmaveth; Beracah,
Jehu the Anathothite, 4and
Ishmaiah the Gibeonite, a
mighty man among the Thirty,
who was a leader of the Thirty;
Jeremiah, Jahaziel, Johanan,
Jozabad the Gederathite,[i]
5Eluzai, Jerimoth, Bealiah,
Shemariah and Shephatiah
the Haruphite; 6Elkanah, Isshiah, Azarel, Joezer and Jashobeam the Korahites; 7and
Joelah and Zebadiah the sons
of Jeroham from Gedor.[j]

8Some Gadites[k] defected to David at his stronghold in the desert.
They were brave warriors, ready for
battle and able to handle the shield
and spear. Their faces were the
faces of lions,[l] and they were as
swift as gazelles[m] in the mountains.

9Ezer was the chief,
Obadiah the second in command, Eliab the third,
10Mishmannah the fourth, Jeremiah the fifth,
11Attai the sixth, Eliel the seventh,
12Johanan the eighth, Elzabad
the ninth,
13Jeremiah the tenth and Mac-
bannai the eleventh.

14These Gadites were army commanders; the least was a match for
a hundred,[n] and the greatest for a
thousand.[o] 15It was they who
crossed the Jordan in the first
month when it was overflowing all
its banks,[p] and they put to flight
everyone living in the valleys, to
the east and to the west.

16Other Benjamites[q] and some
men from Judah also came to David in his stronghold. 17David went
out to meet them and said to them,
"If you have come to me in peace,
to help me, I am ready to have you
unite with me. But if you have

11:31 [a] 1Ch 27:14 [b] Jdg 12:13
11:41 [c] 2Sa 11:6 [d] 1Ch 2:36
11:44 [e] Dt 1:4
12:1 [f] Jos 15:31; 1Sa 27:2-6
12:2 [g] Jdg 3:15; 20:16 [h] 2Sa 3:19
12:4 [i] Jos 15:36
12:7 [j] Jos 15:58
12:8 [k] Ge 30:11 [l] 2Sa 17:10 [m] 2Sa 2:18
12:14 [n] Lev 26:8 [o] Dt 32:30
12:15 [p] Jos 3:15
12:16 [q] 2Sa 3:19

come to betray me to my enemies
when my hands are free from violence, may the God of our fathers
see it and judge you."
18Then the Spirit[a] came upon
Amasai,[b] chief of the Thirty, and
he said:

"We are yours, O David!
We are with you, O son of
Jesse!
Success,[c] success to you,
and success to those who
help you,
for your God will help
you."

So David received them and
made them leaders of his raiding
bands.
19Some of the men of Manasseh
defected to David when he went
with the Philistines to fight against
Saul. (He and his men did not help
the Philistines because, after con-
sultation, their rulers sent him
away. They said, "It will cost us our
heads if he deserts to his master
Saul.")[d] 20When David went to
Ziklag,[e] these were the men of Manasseh who defected to him: Adnah, Jozabad, Jediael, Michael,
Jozabad, Elihu and Zillethai, leaders of units of a thousand in Manasseh. 21They helped David
against raiding bands, for all of
them were brave warriors, and they
were commanders in his army.
22Day after day men came to help
David, until he had a great army,
like the army of God.[x]

Others Join David at Hebron

23These are the numbers of the
men armed for battle who came to
David at Hebron[f] to turn[g] Saul's
kingdom over to him, as the LORD
had said:[h]
24men of Judah, carrying shield
and spear—6,800 armed for
battle;
25men of Simeon, warriors ready
for battle—7,100;
26men of Levi—4,600, 27includ-
ing Jehoiada, leader of the
family of Aaron, with 3,700
men, 28and Zadok,[i] a brave
young warrior, with 22 officers from his family;
29men of Benjamin,[j] Saul's
kinsmen—3,000, most[k] of
whom had remained loyal
to Saul's house until then;
30men of Ephraim, brave warriors, famous in their own
clans—20,800;
31men of half the tribe of Manasseh, designated by name to
come and make David
king—18,000;
32men of Issachar, who understood the times and knew
what Israel should do[l]—
200 chiefs, with all their relatives under their com-
mand;
33men of Zebulun, experienced
soldiers prepared for battle
with every type of weapon,
to help David with undivided loyalty—50,000;
34men of Naphtali—1,000 officers, together with 37,000
men carrying shields and
spears;
35men of Dan, ready for battle—28,600;
36men of Asher, experienced
soldiers prepared for battle—40,000;
37and from east of the Jordan,
men of Reuben, Gad and
the half-tribe of Manasseh,
armed with every type of
weapon—120,000.
38All these were fighting men
who volunteered to serve in the
ranks. They came to Hebron fully
determined to make David king
over all Israel.[m] All the rest of the
Israelites were also of one mind to
make David king. 39The men spent
three days there with David, eating
and drinking,[n] for their families
had supplied provisions for them.
40Also, their neighbors from as far
away as Issachar, Zebulun and
Naphtali came bringing food on
donkeys, camels, mules and oxen.
There were plentiful supplies[o] of
flour, fig cakes, raisin[p] cakes,

12:18 [a] Jdg 3:10; 6:34; 1Ch 28:12; 2Ch 15:1; 20:14; 24:20 [b] 2Sa 17:25 [c] 1Sa 25:5-6
12:19 [d] 1Sa 29:2-11
12:20 [e] 1Sa 27:6
12:23 [f] 2Sa 2:3-4 [g] 1Ch 10:14 [h] 1Sa 16:1; 1Ch 11:10
12:28 [i] 2Sa 8:17; 1Ch 6:8; 15:11; 16:39; 27:17
12:29 [j] 2Sa 3:19 [k] 2Sa 2:8-9
12:32 [l] Est 1:13
12:38 [m] 2Sa 5:1-3; 1Ch 9:1
12:39 [n] 2Sa 3:20; Isa 25:6-8
12:40 [o] 2Sa 16:1; 17:29 [p] 1Sa 25:18

[x]22 *Or a great and mighty army*

wine, oil, cattle and sheep, for there was joy[a] in Israel.

Bringing Back the Ark

13:1–14pp — 2Sa 6:1–11

13 David conferred with each of his officers, the commanders of thousands and commanders of hundreds. **2**He then said to the whole assembly of Israel, "If it seems good to you and if it is the will of the LORD our God, let us send word far and wide to the rest of our brothers throughout the territories of Israel, and also to the priests and Levites who are with them in their towns and pasturelands, to come and join us. **3**Let us bring the ark of our God back to us,[b] for we did not inquire[c] of[y] it[z] during the reign of Saul." **4**The whole assembly agreed to do this, because it seemed right to all the people.

5So David assembled all the Israelites,[d] from the Shihor River[e] in Egypt to Lebo[a] Hamath,[f] to bring the ark of God from Kiriath Jearim.[g] **6**David and all the Israelites with him went to Baalah[h] of Judah (Kiriath Jearim) to bring up from there the ark of God the LORD, who is enthroned between the cherubim[i]—the ark that is called by the Name.

7They moved the ark of God from Abinadab's[j] house on a new cart, with Uzzah and Ahio guiding it. **8**David and all the Israelites were celebrating with all their might before God, with songs and with harps, lyres, tambourines, cymbals and trumpets.[k]

9When they came to the threshing floor of Kidon, Uzzah reached out his hand to steady the ark, because the oxen stumbled. **10**The LORD's anger[l] burned against Uzzah, and he struck him down[m] because he had put his hand on the ark. So he died there before God.

11Then David was angry because the LORD's wrath had broken out against Uzzah, and to this day that place is called Perez Uzzah.[b][n]

12David was afraid of God that day and asked, "How can I ever bring the ark of God to me?" **13**He did not take the ark to be with him in the City of David. Instead, he took it aside to the house of Obed-Edom[o] the Gittite. **14**The ark of God remained with the family of Obed-Edom in his house for three months, and the LORD blessed his household[p] and everything he had.

David's House and Family

14:1–7pp — 2Sa 5:11–16; 1Ch 3:5–8

14 Now Hiram king of Tyre sent messengers to David, along with cedar logs,[q] stonemasons and carpenters to build a palace for him. **2**And David knew that the LORD had established him as king over Israel and that his kingdom had been highly exalted[r] for the sake of his people Israel.

3In Jerusalem David took more wives and became the father of more sons[s] and daughters. **4**These are the names of the children born to him there:[t] Shammua, Shobab, Nathan, Solomon, **5**Ibhar, Elishua, Elpelet, **6**Nogah, Nepheg, Japhia, **7**Elishama, Beeliada[c] and Eliphelet.

David Defeats the Philistines

14:8–17pp — 2Sa 5:17–25

8When the Philistines heard that David had been anointed king over all Israel,[u] they went up in full force to search for him, but David heard about it and went out to meet them. **9**Now the Philistines had come and raided the Valley[v] of Rephaim; **10**so David inquired of God: "Shall I go and attack the Philistines? Will you hand them over to me?"

The LORD answered him, "Go, I will hand them over to you."

11So David and his men went up to Baal Perazim,[w] and there he defeated them. He said, "As waters break out, God has broken out

12:40 [a] 1Ch 29:22
13:3 [b] 1Sa 7:1-2 [c] 2Ch 1:5
13:5 [d] 1Ch 11:1; 15:3 [e] Jos 13:3 [f] Nu 13:21 [g] 1Sa 6:21; 7:2
13:6 [h] Jos 15:9; 2Sa 6:2 [i] Ex 25:22; 2Ki 19:15
13:7 [j] Nu 4:15; 1Sa 7:1
13:8 [k] 2Sa 6:5; 1Ch 15:16,19, 24; 2Ch 5:12; Ps 92:3
13:10 [l] 1Ch 15:13,15 [m] Lev 10:2
13:11 [n] 1Ch 15:13; Ps 7:11
13:13 [o] 1Ch 15:18, 24; 16:38; 26:4-5,15
13:14 [p] 2Sa 6:11; 1Ch 26:4-5
14:1 [q] 2Ch 2:3; Ezr 3:7
14:2 [r] Nu 24:7; Dt 26:19
14:3 [s] 1Ch 3:1
14:4 [t] 1Ch 3:9
14:8 [u] 1Ch 11:1
14:9 [v] ver 13; Jos 15:8; 1Ch 11:15
14:11 [w] Isa 28:21

[y]3 Or *we neglected* [z]3 Or *him* [a]5 Or *to the entrance to* [b]11 *Perez Uzzah* means *outbreak against Uzzah.* [c]7 A variant of *Eliada*

against my enemies by my hand."
So that place was called Baal Perazim.[d] 12The Philistines had abandoned their gods there, and David
gave orders to burn[a] them in the
fire.[b]

13Once more the Philistines
raided the valley;[c] 14so David inquired of God again, and God answered him, "Do not go straight up,
but circle around them and attack
them in front of the balsam trees.
15As soon as you hear the sound of
marching in the tops of the balsam
trees, move out to battle, because
that will mean God has gone out in
front of you to strike the Philistine
army." 16So David did as God commanded him, and they struck down
the Philistine army, all the way
from Gibeon[d] to Gezer.[e]

17So David's fame[f] spread
throughout every land, and the
LORD made all the nations fear[g]
him.

The Ark Brought to Jerusalem

15:25–16:3pp — 2Sa 6:12–19

15 After David had constructed buildings for himself in
the City of David, he prepared[h] a
place for the ark of God and
pitched[i] a tent for it. 2Then David
said, "No one but the Levites[j] may
carry[k] the ark of God, because the
LORD chose them to carry the ark of
the LORD and to minister[l] before
him forever."

3David assembled all Israel[m] in
Jerusalem to bring up the ark of the
LORD to the place he had prepared
for it. 4He called together the
descendants of Aaron and the Levites:

5From the descendants of Kohath,
Uriel the leader and 120 relatives;
6from the descendants of Merari,
Asaiah the leader and 220 relatives;
7from the descendants of Gershon,[e]
Joel the leader and 130 relatives;
8from the descendants of Elizaphan,[n]
Shemaiah the leader and 200 relatives;
9from the descendants of Hebron,[o]
Eliel the leader and 80 relatives;
10from the descendants of Uzziel,
Amminadab the leader and 112 relatives.

11Then David summoned Za-
dok[p] and Abiathar[q] the priests,
and Uriel, Asaiah, Joel, Shemaiah,
Eliel and Amminadab the Levites.
12He said to them, "You are the
heads of the Levitical families; you
and your fellow Levites are to consecrate[r] yourselves and bring up
the ark of the LORD, the God of Israel, to the place I have prepared for
it. 13It was because you, the Levites,[s] did not bring it up the first
time that the LORD our God broke
out in anger against us.[t] We did
not inquire of him about how to do
it in the prescribed way." 14So the
priests and Levites consecrated
themselves in order to bring up the
ark of the LORD, the God of Israel.
15And the Levites carried the ark of
God with the poles on their shoulders, as Moses had commanded[u]
in accordance with the word of the
LORD.

16David told the leaders of the
Levites to appoint their brothers as
singers[v] to sing joyful songs, accompanied by musical instruments: lyres, harps and cymbals.[w]

17So the Levites appointed Heman[x] son of Joel; from his brothers, Asaph[y] son of Berekiah; and
from their brothers the Merarites,[z]
Ethan son of Kushaiah; 18and with
them their brothers next in rank:
Zechariah,[f] Jaaziel, Shemiramoth,
Jehiel, Unni, Eliab, Benaiah, Maaseiah, Mattithiah, Eliphelehu,

14:12 [a] Ex 32:20 [b] Jos 7:15
14:13 [c] ver 9
14:16 [d] Jos 9:3 [e] Jos 10:33
14:17 [f] Jos 6:27; 2Ch 26:8 [g] Ex 15:14-16; Dt 2:25
15:1 [h] Ps 132:1-18 [i] 1Ch 16:1; 17:1
15:2 [j] Nu 4:15; Dt 10:8; 2Ch 5:5 [k] Dt 31:9 [l] 1Ch 23:13
15:3 [m] 1Ki 8:1; 1Ch 13:5
15:8 [n] Ex 6:22
15:9 [o] Ex 6:18
15:11 [p] 1Ch 12:28 [q] 1Sa 22:20
15:12 [r] Ex 19:14-15; Lev 11:44; 2Ch 35:6
15:13 [s] 1Ki 8:4 [t] 2Sa 6:3; 1Ch 13:7-10
15:15 [u] Ex 25:14; Nu 4:5,15
15:16 [v] Ps 68:25 [w] 1Ch 13:8; 25:1; Ne 12:27,36
15:17 [x] 1Ch 6:33 [y] 1Ch 6:39 [z] 1Ch 6:44

[d] *11 Baal Perazim* means *the lord who breaks out.* [e] *7* Hebrew *Gershom,* a variant of *Gershon* [f] *18* Three Hebrew manuscripts and most Septuagint manuscripts (see also verse 20 and 1 Chron. 16:5); most Hebrew manuscripts *Zechariah son and* or *Zechariah, Ben and*

Mikneiah, Obed-Edom[a] and Jeiel,[g] the gatekeepers.

19 The musicians Heman,[b] Asaph and Ethan were to sound the bronze cymbals; 20 Zechariah, Aziel, Shemiramoth, Jehiel, Unni, Eliab, Maaseiah and Benaiah were to play the lyres according to *alamoth,*[h] 21 and Mattithiah, Eliphelehu, Mikneiah, Obed-Edom, Jeiel and Azaziah were to play the harps, directing according to *sheminith.*[h] 22 Kenaniah the head Levite was in charge of the singing; that was his responsibility because he was skillful at it.

23 Berekiah and Elkanah were to be doorkeepers for the ark. 24 Shebaniah, Joshaphat, Nethanel, Amasai, Zechariah, Benaiah and Eliezer the priests were to blow trumpets[c] before the ark of God. Obed-Edom and Jehiah were also to be doorkeepers for the ark.

25 So David and the elders of Israel and the commanders of units of a thousand went to bring up the ark[d] of the covenant of the LORD from the house of Obed-Edom, with rejoicing. 26 Because God had helped the Levites who were carrying the ark of the covenant of the LORD, seven bulls and seven rams[e] were sacrificed. 27 Now David was clothed in a robe of fine linen, as were all the Levites who were carrying the ark, and as were the singers, and Kenaniah, who was in charge of the singing of the choirs. David also wore a linen ephod. 28 So all Israel brought up the ark of the covenant of the LORD with shouts, with the sounding of rams' horns[f] and trumpets, and of cymbals, and the playing of lyres and harps.

29 As the ark of the covenant of the LORD was entering the City of David, Michal daughter of Saul watched from a window. And when she saw King David dancing and celebrating, she despised him in her heart.

16 They brought the ark of God and set it inside the tent that David had pitched[g] for it, and they presented burnt offerings and fellowship offerings[i] before God. 2 After David had finished sacrificing the burnt offerings and fellowship offerings, he blessed[h] the people in the name of the LORD. 3 Then he gave a loaf of bread, a cake of dates and a cake of raisins to each Israelite man and woman.

4 He appointed some of the Levites to minister[i] before the ark of the LORD, to make petition, to give thanks, and to praise the LORD, the God of Israel: 5 Asaph was the chief, Zechariah second, then Jeiel, Shemiramoth, Jehiel, Mattithiah, Eliab, Benaiah, Obed-Edom and Jeiel. They were to play the lyres and harps, Asaph was to sound the cymbals, 6 and Benaiah and Jahaziel the priests were to blow the trumpets regularly before the ark of the covenant of God.

David's Psalm of Thanks

16:8–22pp — Ps 105:1–15
16:23–33pp — Ps 96:1–13
16:34–36pp — Ps 106:1,47–48

7 That day David first committed to Asaph and his associates this psalm[j] of thanks to the LORD:

8 Give thanks[k] to the LORD, call on his name;
make known among the nations[l] what he has done.
9 Sing to him, sing praise[m] to him;
tell of all his wonderful acts.
10 Glory in his holy name;
let the hearts of those who seek the LORD rejoice.
11 Look to the LORD and his strength;
seek[n] his face always.
12 Remember[o] the wonders he has done,
his miracles,[p] and the judgments he pronounced,
13 O descendants of Israel his servant,
O sons of Jacob, his chosen ones.

15:18 [a] 1Ch 26:4-5
15:19 [b] 1Ch 25:6
15:24 [c] ver 28; 1Ch 16:6; 2Ch 7:6
15:25 [d] 1Ch 13:13; 2Ch 1:4
15:26 [e] Nu 23:1-4,29
15:28 [f] 1Ch 13:8
16:1 [g] 1Ch 15:1
16:2 [h] Ex 39:43
16:4 [i] 1Ch 15:2
16:7 [j] 2Sa 23:1
16:8 [k] ver 34; Ps 136:1 [l] 2Ki 19:19
16:9 [m] Ex 15:1
16:11 [n] 1Ch 28:9; 2Ch 7:14; Ps 24:6; 119:2,58
16:12 [o] Ps 77:11 [p] Ps 78:43

[g] *18* Hebrew; Septuagint (see also verse 21) *Jeiel and Azaziah* [h] *20,21* Probably a musical term [i] *1* Traditionally *peace offerings*; also in verse 2

14He is the LORD our God;
his judgments[a] are in all the earth.
15He remembers[j] his covenant forever,
the word he commanded, for a thousand generations,
16the covenant[b] he made with Abraham,
the oath he swore to Isaac.
17He confirmed it to Jacob[c] as a decree,
to Israel as an everlasting covenant:
18"To you I will give the land of Canaan[d]
as the portion you will inherit."
19When they were but few in number,[e]
few indeed, and strangers in it,
20they[k] wandered from nation to nation,
from one kingdom to another.
21He allowed no man to oppress them;
for their sake he rebuked kings:[f]
22"Do not touch my anointed ones;
do my prophets[g] no harm."
23Sing to the LORD, all the earth;
proclaim his salvation day after day.
24Declare his glory among the nations,
his marvelous deeds among all peoples.
25For great is the LORD and most worthy of praise;[h]
he is to be feared[i] above all gods.[j]
26For all the gods of the nations are idols,
but the LORD made the heavens.[k]
27Splendor and majesty are before him;
strength and joy in his dwelling place.
28Ascribe to the LORD, O families of nations,
ascribe to the LORD glory and strength,[l]
29 ascribe to the LORD the glory due his name.
Bring an offering and come before him;
worship the LORD in the splendor of his[l] holiness.[m]
30Tremble[n] before him, all the earth!
The world is firmly established; it cannot be moved.
31Let the heavens rejoice, let the earth be glad;[o]
let them say among the nations, "The LORD reigns![p]"
32Let the sea resound, and all that is in it;[q]
let the fields be jubilant, and everything in them!
33Then the trees[r] of the forest will sing,
they will sing for joy before the LORD,
for he comes to judge[s] the earth.

34Give thanks[t] to the LORD, for he is good;[u]
his love endures forever.[v]
35Cry out, "Save us, O God our Savior;[w]
gather us and deliver us from the nations,
that we may give thanks to your holy name,
that we may glory in your praise."
36Praise be to the LORD, the God of Israel,[x]
from everlasting to everlasting.

Then all the people said "Amen" and "Praise the LORD."

37David left Asaph and his associates before the ark of the covenant of the LORD to minister there
regularly, according to each day's

16:14 [a]Isa 26:9
16:16 [b]Ge 12:7; 15:18; 17:2; 22:16-18; 26:3; 28:13; 35:11
16:17 [c]Ge 35:9-12
16:18 [d]Ge 13:14-17
16:19 [e]Ge 34:30; Dt 7:7
16:21 [f]Ge 12:17; 20:3; Ex 7:15-18
16:22 [g]Ge 20:7
16:25 [h]Ps 48:1 [i]Ps 76:7; 89:7 [j]Dt 32:39
16:26 [k]Lev 19:4; Ps 102:25
16:28 [l]Ps 29:1-2
16:29 [m]Ps 29:1-2
16:30 [n]Ps 114:7
16:31 [o]Isa 44:23; 49:13 [p]Ps 93:1
16:32 [q]Ps 98:7
16:33 [r]Isa 55:12 [s]Ps 96:10; 98:9
16:34 [t]ver 8 [u]Na 1:7 [v]2Ch 5:13; 7:3; Ezr 3:11; Ps 136:1-26; Jer 33:11
16:35 [w]Mic 7:7
16:36 [x]Dt 27:15; 1Ki 8:15; Ps 72:18-19

j*15* Some Septuagint manuscripts (see also Psalm 105:8); Hebrew *Remember*
k*18-20* One Hebrew manuscript, Septuagint and Vulgate (see also Psalm 105:12); most Hebrew manuscripts *inherit, / 19though you are but few in number, / few indeed, and strangers in it." / 20They*
l*29* Or LORD *with the splendor of*

requirements.[a] **38**He also left
Obed-Edom[b] and his sixty-eight
associates to minister with them.
Obed-Edom son of Jeduthun, and
also Hosah,[c] were gatekeepers.
39David left Zadok[d] the priest
and his fellow priests before the
tabernacle of the LORD at the high
place in Gibeon[e] **40**to present
burnt offerings to the LORD on the
altar of burnt offering regularly,
morning and evening, in accordance with everything written in
the Law[f] of the LORD, which he
had given Israel. **41**With them were
Heman[g] and Jeduthun and the
rest of those chosen and designated by name to give thanks to the
LORD, "for his love endures forever." **42**Heman and Jeduthun were
responsible for the sounding of the
trumpets and cymbals and for the
playing of the other instruments
for sacred song.[h] The sons of Jeduthun were stationed at the gate.
43Then all the people left, each
for his own home, and David returned home to bless his family.

God's Promise to David

17:1-15pp — 2Sa 7:1-17

17 After David was settled in
his palace, he said to Nathan the prophet, "Here I am, living in a palace of cedar, while the
ark of the covenant of the LORD is
under a tent.[i]"
2Nathan replied to David,
"Whatever you have in mind,[j] do
it, for God is with you."
3That night the word of God
came to Nathan, saying:

4"Go and tell my servant
David, 'This is what the LORD
says: You[k] are not the one to
build me a house to dwell in.
5I have not dwelt in a house
from the day I brought Israel
up out of Egypt to this day. I
have moved from one tent site
to another, from one dwelling
place to another. **6**Wherever I
have moved with all the Israelites, did I ever say to any of
their leaders[m] whom I commanded to shepherd my people, "Why have you not built
me a house of cedar?" '
7"Now then, tell my servant
David, 'This is what the LORD
Almighty says: I took you from
the pasture and from following
the flock, to be ruler[l] over my
people Israel. **8**I have been
with you wherever you have
gone, and I have cut off all
your enemies from before you.
Now I will make your name
like the names of the greatest
men of the earth. **9**And I will
provide a place for my people
Israel and will plant them so
that they can have a home of
their own and no longer be disturbed. Wicked people will not
oppress them anymore, as
they did at the beginning
10and have done ever since the
time I appointed leaders[m]
over my people Israel. I will
also subdue all your enemies.
" 'I declare to you that the
LORD will build a house for
you: **11**When your days are
over and you go to be with your
fathers, I will raise up your offspring to succeed you, one of
your own sons, and I will establish his kingdom. **12**He is
the one who will build[n] a
house for me, and I will establish his throne forever.[o] **13**I
will be his father,[p] and he will
be my son.[q] I will never take
my love away from him, as I
took it away from your predecessor. **14**I will set him over my
house and my kingdom forev-
er; his throne[r] will be established forever.[s]' "

15Nathan reported to David all
the words of this entire revelation.

David's Prayer

17:16-27pp — 2Sa 7:18-29

16Then King David went in and
sat before the LORD, and he said:

"Who am I, O LORD God, and
what is my family, that you
have brought me this far?

16:37 [a]2Ch 8:14
16:38 [b]1Ch 13:13 [c]1Ch 26:10
16:39 [d]2Sa 8:17; 1Ch 15:11 [e]1Ki 3:4; 2Ch 1:3
16:40 [f]Ex 29:38; Nu 28:1-8
16:41 [g]1Ch 6:33; 25:1-6; 2Ch 5:13
16:42 [h]2Ch 7:6
17:1 [i]1Ch 15:1
17:2 [j]2Ch 6:7
17:4 [k]1Ch 28:3
17:7 [l]2Sa 6:21
17:10 [m]Jdg 2:16
17:12 [n]1Ki 5:5 [o]2Ch 7:18
17:13 [p]2Co 6:18 [q]Lk 1:32; Heb 1:5*
17:14 [r]1Ki 2:12; 1Ch 28:5 [s]Ps 132:11; Jer 33:17

m6 Traditionally *judges*; also in verse 10

17And as if this were not
enough in your sight, O God,
you have spoken about the future of the house of your servant. You have looked on me
as though I were the most exalted of men, O LORD God.
18"What more can David say
to you for honoring your servant? For you know your servant, 19O LORD. For the sake[a]
of your servant and according
to your will, you have done
this great thing and made
known all these great promises.[b]
20"There is no one like you,
O LORD, and there is no God
but you,[c] as we have heard
with our own ears. 21And who
is like your people Israel—the
one nation on earth whose
God went out to redeem[d] a
people for himself, and to
make a name for yourself, and
to perform great and awesome
wonders by driving out nations
from before your people,
whom you redeemed from
Egypt? 22You made your people Israel your very own forever,[e] and you, O LORD, have become their God.
23"And now, LORD, let the
promise[f] you have made concerning your servant and his
house be established forever.
Do as you promised, 24so that
it will be established and that
your name will be great forever. Then men will say, 'The
LORD Almighty, the God over
Israel, is Israel's God!' And the
house of your servant David
will be established before you.
25"You, my God, have re-
vealed to your servant that you
will build a house for him. So
your servant has found courage to pray to you. 26O LORD,
you are God! You have promised these good things to your
servant. 27Now you have been
pleased to bless the house of
your servant, that it may continue forever in your sight;[g]
for you, O LORD, have blessed
it, and it will be blessed forever."

17:19 [a]2Sa 7:16-17; 2Ki 20:6; Isa 9:7; 37:35; 55:3 [b]2Sa 7:25
17:20 [c]Ex 8:10; 9:14; 15:11; Isa 44:6; 46:9
17:21 [d]Ex 6:6
17:22 [e]Ex 19:5-6
17:23 [f]1Ki 8:25
17:27 [g]Ps 16:11; 21:6
18:2 [h]Nu 21:29
18:3 [i]1Ch 19:6 [j]Ge 2:14
18:4 [k]Ge 49:6
18:5 [l]2Ki 16:9; 1Ch 19:6
18:8 [m]1Ki 7:23; 2Ch 4:12, 15-16
18:11 [n]Nu 24:18

David's Victories

18:1-13pp — 2Sa 8:1-14

18 In the course of time, David
defeated the Philistines
and subdued them, and he took
Gath and its surrounding villages
from the control of the Philistines.
2David also defeated the Moabites,[h] and they became subject to
him and brought tribute.
3Moreover, David fought Hadadezer king of Zobah,[i] as far as Hamath, when he went to establish
his control along the Euphrates
River.[j] 4David captured a thousand of his chariots, seven thousand charioteers and twenty thousand foot soldiers. He hamstrung[k]
all but a hundred of the chariot
horses.
5When the Arameans of Damascus[l] came to help Hadadezer king
of Zobah, David struck down twenty-two thousand of them. 6He put
garrisons in the Aramean kingdom
of Damascus, and the Arameans
became subject to him and brought
tribute. The LORD gave David victory everywhere he went.
7David took the gold shields carried by the officers of Hadadezer
and brought them to Jerusalem.
8From Tebah[n] and Cun, towns
that belonged to Hadadezer, David
took a great quantity of bronze,
which Solomon used to make the
bronze Sea,[m] the pillars and various bronze articles.
9When Tou king of Hamath
heard that David had defeated the
entire army of Hadadezer king of
Zobah, 10he sent his son Hadoram
to King David to greet him and congratulate him on his victory in battle over Hadadezer, who had been
at war with Tou. Hadoram brought
all kinds of articles of gold and silver and bronze.
11King David dedicated these articles to the LORD, as he had done
with the silver and gold he had tak-
en from all these nations: Edom[n]

[n]8 Hebrew *Tibhath*, a variant of *Tebah*

and Moab, the Ammonites and the Philistines, and Amalek.[a]

12Abishai son of Zeruiah struck down eighteen thousand Edomites[b] in the Valley of Salt. 13He put garrisons in Edom, and all the Edomites became subject to David. The LORD gave David victory everywhere he went.

David's Officials

18:14–17pp — 2Sa 8:15–18

14David reigned[c] over all Israel,[d] doing what was just and right for all his people. 15Joab[e] son of Zeruiah was over the army; Jehoshaphat son of Ahilud was recorder; 16Zadok[f] son of Ahitub and Ahimelech[o][g] son of Abiathar were priests; Shavsha was secretary; 17Benaiah son of Jehoiada was over the Kerethites and Pelethites;[h] and David's sons were chief officials at the king's side.

The Battle Against the Ammonites

19:1–19pp — 2Sa 10:1–19

19 In the course of time, Nahash king of the Ammonites[i] died, and his son succeeded him as king. 2David thought, "I will show kindness to Hanun son of Nahash, because his father showed kindness to me." So David sent a delegation to express his sympathy to Hanun concerning his father.

When David's men came to Hanun in the land of the Ammonites to express sympathy to him, 3the Ammonite nobles said to Hanun, "Do you think David is honoring your father by sending men to you to express sympathy? Haven't his men come to you to explore and spy out[j] the country and overthrow it?" 4So Hanun seized David's men, shaved them, cut off their garments in the middle at the buttocks, and sent them away.

5When someone came and told David about the men, he sent messengers to meet them, for they were greatly humiliated. The king said, "Stay at Jericho till your beards have grown, and then come back."

6When the Ammonites realized that they had become a stench[k] in David's nostrils, Hanun and the Ammonites sent a thousand talents[p] of silver to hire chariots and charioteers from Aram Naharaim,[q] Aram Maacah and Zobah.[l] 7They hired thirty-two thousand chariots and charioteers, as well as the king of Maacah with his troops, who came and camped near Medeba,[m] while the Ammonites were mustered from their towns and moved out for battle.

8On hearing this, David sent Joab out with the entire army of fighting men. 9The Ammonites came out and drew up in battle formation at the entrance to their city, while the kings who had come were by themselves in the open country.

10Joab saw that there were battle lines in front of him and behind him; so he selected some of the best troops in Israel and deployed them against the Arameans. 11He put the rest of the men under the command of Abishai[n] his brother, and they were deployed against the Ammonites. 12Joab said, "If the Arameans are too strong for me, then you are to rescue me; but if the Ammonites are too strong for you, then I will rescue you. 13Be strong and let us fight bravely for our people and the cities of our God. The LORD will do what is good in his sight."

14Then Joab and the troops with him advanced to fight the Arameans, and they fled before him. 15When the Ammonites saw that the Arameans were fleeing, they too fled before his brother Abishai and went inside the city. So Joab went back to Jerusalem.

16After the Arameans saw that they had been routed by Israel, they sent messengers and had Ara-

18:11 [a] Nu 24:20
18:12 [b] 1Ki 11:15
18:14 [c] 1Ch 29:26 [d] 1Ch 11:1
18:15 [e] 2Sa 5:6-8; 1Ch 11:6
18:16 [f] 2Sa 8:17; 1Ch 6:8 [g] 1Ch 24:6
18:17 [h] 1Sa 30:14; 2Sa 8:18; 15:18
19:1 [i] Ge 19:38; Jdg 10:17-11:33; 2Ch 20:1-2; Zep 2:8-11
19:3 [j] Nu 21:32
19:6 [k] Ge 34:30 [l] 1Ch 18:3,5,9
19:7 [m] Nu 21:30; Jos 13:9,16
19:11 [n] 1Sa 26:6

[o] *16* Some Hebrew manuscripts, Vulgate and Syriac (see also 2 Samuel 8:17); most Hebrew manuscripts *Abimelech* [p] *6* That is, about 37 tons (about 34 metric tons) [q] *6* That is, Northwest Mesopotamia

means brought from beyond the River,[r] with Shophach the commander of Hadadezer's army leading them.

17When David was told of this, he gathered all Israel[a] and crossed the Jordan; he advanced against them and formed his battle lines opposite them. David formed his lines to meet the Arameans in battle, and they fought against him. 18But they fled before Israel, and David killed seven thousand of their charioteers and forty thousand of their foot soldiers. He also killed Shophach the commander of their army.

19When the vassals of Hadadezer saw that they had been defeated by Israel, they made peace with David and became subject to him.

So the Arameans were not willing to help the Ammonites anymore.

The Capture of Rabbah

20:1–3pp — 2Sa 11:1; 12:29–31

20 In the spring, at the time when kings go off to war, Joab led out the armed forces. He laid waste the land of the Ammonites and went to Rabbah[b] and besieged it, but David remained in Jerusalem. Joab attacked Rabbah and left it in ruins.[c] 2David took the crown from the head of their king[s]—its weight was found to be a talent[t] of gold, and it was set with precious stones—and it was placed on David's head. He took a great quantity of plunder from the city 3and brought out the people who were there, consigning them to labor with saws and with iron picks and axes.[d] David did this to all the Ammonite towns. Then David and his entire army returned to Jerusalem.

War With the Philistines

2:4–8pp — 2Sa 21:15–22

4In the course of time, war broke out with the Philistines, at Gezer.[e] At that time Sibbecai the Hushathite killed Sippai, one of the descendants of the Rephaites,[f] and the Philistines were subjugated.

5In another battle with the Philistines, Elhanan son of Jair killed Lahmi the brother of Goliath the Gittite, who had a spear with a shaft like a weaver's rod.[g]

6In still another battle, which took place at Gath, there was a huge man with six fingers on each hand and six toes on each foot—twenty-four in all. He also was descended from Rapha. 7When he taunted Israel, Jonathan son of Shimea, David's brother, killed him.

8These were descendants of Rapha in Gath, and they fell at the hands of David and his men.

David Numbers the Fighting Men

21:1–26pp — 2Sa 24:1–25

21 Satan[h] rose up against Israel and incited David to take a census[i] of Israel. 2So David said to Joab and the commanders of the troops, "Go and count[j] the Israelites from Beersheba to Dan. Then report back to me so that I may know how many there are."

3But Joab replied, "May the LORD multiply his troops a hundred times over.[k] My lord the king, are they not all my lord's subjects? Why does my lord want to do this? Why should he bring guilt on Israel?"

4The king's word, however, overruled Joab; so Joab left and went throughout Israel and then came back to Jerusalem. 5Joab reported the number of the fighting men to David: In all Israel[l] there were one million one hundred thousand men who could handle a sword, including four hundred and seventy thousand in Judah.

6But Joab did not include Levi and Benjamin in the numbering, because the king's command was repulsive to him. 7This command

19:17 [a] 1Ch 9:1
20:1 [b] Dt 3:11; 2Sa 12:26 [c] Am 1:13-15
20:3 [d] Dt 29:11
20:4 [e] Jos 10:33 [f] Ge 14:5
20:5 [g] 1Sa 17:7
21:1 [h] 2Ch 18:21; Ps 109:6 [i] 2Ch 14:8; 25:5
21:2 [j] 1Ch 27:23-24
21:3 [k] Dt 1:11
21:5 [l] 1Ch 9:1

[r] *16* That is, the Euphrates [s] *2* Or *of Milcom,* that is, Molech [t] *2* That is, about 75 pounds (about 34 kilograms)

was also evil in the sight of God; so
he punished Israel.
8Then David said to God, "I have
sinned greatly by doing this. Now,
I beg you, take away the guilt of
your servant. I have done a very
foolish thing."
9The LORD said to Gad,[a] David's
seer,[b] 10"Go and tell David, 'This
is what the LORD says: I am giving
you three options. Choose one of
them for me to carry out against
you.' "
11So Gad went to David and said
to him, "This is what the LORD says:
'Take your choice: 12three years of
famine,[c] three months of being
swept away[u] before your enemies,
with their swords overtaking you,
or three days of the sword[d] of the
LORD[e]—days of plague in the land,
with the angel of the LORD ravaging
every part of Israel.' Now then, decide how I should answer the one
who sent me."
13David said to Gad, "I am in
deep distress. Let me fall into the
hands of the LORD, for his mercy[f] is
very great; but do not let me fall
into the hands of men."
14So the LORD sent a plague on
Israel, and seventy thousand men
of Israel fell dead.[g] 15And God
sent an angel[h] to destroy Jerusalem.[i] But as the angel was doing
so, the LORD saw it and was
grieved[j] because of the calamity
and said to the angel who was destroying[k] the people, "Enough!
Withdraw your hand." The angel of
the LORD was then standing at the
threshing floor of Araunah[v] the
Jebusite.
16David looked up and saw the
angel of the LORD standing between
heaven and earth, with a drawn
sword in his hand extended over
Jerusalem. Then David and the elders, clothed in sackcloth, fell
facedown.[l]
17David said to God, "Was it not
I who ordered the fighting men to
be counted? I am the one who has
sinned and done wrong. These are
but sheep.[m] What have they done?
O LORD my God, let your hand fall
upon me and my family,[n] but do
not let this plague remain on your
people."
18Then the angel of the LORD ordered Gad to tell David to go up
and build an altar to the LORD on
the threshing floor[o] of Araunah
the Jebusite. 19So David went up in
obedience to the word that Gad
had spoken in the name of the
LORD.
20While Araunah was threshing
wheat,[p] he turned and saw the angel; his four sons who were with
him hid themselves. 21Then David
approached, and when Araunah
looked and saw him, he left the
threshing floor and bowed down
before David with his face to the
ground.
22David said to him, "Let me
have the site of your threshing floor
so I can build an altar to the LORD,
that the plague on the people may
be stopped. Sell it to me at the full
price."
23Araunah said to David, "Take
it! Let my lord the king do whatever
pleases him. Look, I will give the
oxen for the burnt offerings, the
threshing sledges for the wood, and
the wheat for the grain offering. I
will give all this."
24But King David replied to
Araunah, "No, I insist on paying
the full price. I will not take for the
LORD what is yours, or sacrifice a
burnt offering that costs me nothing."
25So David paid Araunah six
hundred shekels[w] of gold for the
site. 26David built an altar to the
LORD there and sacrificed burnt offerings and fellowship offerings.[x]
He called on the LORD, and the LORD
answered him with fire[q] from
heaven on the altar of burnt offering.
27Then the LORD spoke to the angel, and he put his sword back into
its sheath. 28At that time, when
David saw that the LORD had an-

21:9 [a] 1Sa 22:5 [b] 1Sa 9:9
21:12 [c] Dt 32:24 [d] Eze 30:25 [e] Ge 19:13
21:13 [f] Ps 6:4; 86:15; 130:4, 7
21:14 [g] 1Ch 27:24
21:15 [h] Ge 32:1 [i] Ps 125:2 [j] Ge 6:6; Ex 32:14 [k] Ge 19:13
21:16 [l] Nu 14:5; Jos 7:6
21:17 [m] 2Sa 7:8; Ps 74:1 [n] Jnh 1:12
21:18 [o] 2Ch 3:1
21:20 [p] Jdg 6:11
21:26 [q] Lev 9:24; Jdg 6:21

[u] *12* Hebrew; Septuagint and Vulgate (see also 2 Samuel 24:13) *of fleeing* [v] *15* Hebrew *Ornan,* a variant of *Araunah;* also in verses 18-28 [w] *25* That is, about 15 pounds (about 7 kilograms) [x] *26* Traditionally *peace offerings*

swered him on the threshing floor
of Araunah the Jebusite, he offered
sacrifices there. 29The tabernacle
of the LORD, which Moses had made
in the desert, and the altar of burnt
offering were at that time on the
high place at Gibeon.[a] 30But David could not go before it to inquire
of God, because he was afraid of
the sword of the angel of the LORD.

22 Then David said, "The
house of the LORD God[b] is
to be here, and also the altar of
burnt offering for Israel."

Preparations for the Temple

2So David gave orders to assemble the aliens[c] living in Israel, and
from among them he appointed
stonecutters[d] to prepare dressed
stone for building the house of
God. 3He provided a large amount
of iron to make nails for the doors
of the gateways and for the fittings,
and more bronze than could be
weighed.[e] 4He also provided more
cedar logs[f] than could be counted,
for the Sidonians and Tyrians had
brought large numbers of them to
David.

5David said, "My son Solomon is
young[g] and inexperienced, and
the house to be built for the LORD
should be of great magnificence
and fame and splendor in the sight
of all the nations. Therefore I will
make preparations for it." So David
made extensive preparations before his death.

6Then he called for his son Solomon and charged him to build[h] a
house for the LORD, the God of Israel. 7David said to Solomon: "My
son, I had it in my heart[i] to build[j]
a house for the Name[k] of the LORD
my God. 8But this word of the LORD
came to me: 'You have shed much
blood and have fought many
wars.[l] You are not to build a house
for my Name,[m] because you have
shed much blood on the earth in
my sight. 9But you will have a son
who will be a man of peace[n] and
rest, and I will give him rest from
all his enemies on every side. His
name will be Solomon,[y][o] and I
will grant Israel peace and quiet[p]
during his reign. 10He is the one
who will build a house for my
Name.[q] He will be my son,[r] and I
will be his father. And I will establish the throne of his kingdom over
Israel forever.'[s]

11"Now, my son, the LORD be
with[t] you, and may you have success and build the house of the
LORD your God, as he said you
would. 12May the LORD give you
discretion and understanding[u]
when he puts you in command over
Israel, so that you may keep the law
of the LORD your God. 13Then you
will have success if you are careful
to observe the decrees and laws[v]
that the LORD gave Moses for Israel.
Be strong and courageous.[w] Do not
be afraid or discouraged.

14"I have taken great pains to
provide for the temple of the LORD
a hundred thousand talents[z] of
gold, a million talents[a] of silver,
quantities of bronze and iron too
great to be weighed, and wood and
stone. And you may add to them.[x]
15You have many workmen: stonecutters, masons and carpenters, as
well as men skilled in every kind of
work 16in gold and silver, bronze
and iron—craftsmen[y] beyond
number. Now begin the work, and
the LORD be with you."

17Then David ordered[z] all the
leaders of Israel to help his son Solomon. 18He said to them, "Is not
the LORD your God with you? And
has he not granted you rest[a] on every side?[b] For he has handed the
inhabitants of the land over to me,
and the land is subject to the LORD
and to his people. 19Now devote
your heart and soul to seeking the
LORD your God.[c] Begin to build the
sanctuary of the LORD God, so that
you may bring the ark of the covenant of the LORD and the sacred
articles belonging to God into the
temple that will be built for the
Name of the LORD."

21:29 [a] 1Ki 3:4; 1Ch 16:39
22:1 [b] Ge 28:17; 1Ch 21:18-29; 2Ch 3:1
22:2 [c] 1Ki 9:21; Isa 56:6 [d] 1Ki 5:17-18
22:3 [e] ver 14; 1Ki 7:47; 1Ch 29:2-5
22:4 [f] 1Ki 5:6
22:5 [g] 1Ki 3:7; 1Ch 29:1
22:6 [h] Ac 7:47
22:7 [i] 1Ch 17:2 [j] 2Sa 7:2; 1Ki 8:17 [k] Dt 12:5,11
22:8 [l] 1Ki 5:3 [m] 1Ch 28:3
22:9 [n] 1Ki 5:4 [o] 2Sa 12:24 [p] 1Ki 4:20
22:10 [q] 1Ch 17:12 [r] 2Sa 7:13 [s] 2Sa 7:14; 2Ch 6:15
22:11 [t] ver 16
22:12 [u] 1Ki 3:9-12; 2Ch 1:10
22:13 [v] 1Ch 28:7 [w] Dt 31:6; Jos 1:6-9; 1Ch 28:20
22:14 [x] ver 3; 1Ch 29:2-5,19
22:16 [y] ver 11; 2Ch 2:7
22:17 [z] 1Ch 28:1-6
22:18 [a] ver 9; 1Ch 23:25 [b] 2Sa 7:1
22:19 [c] ver 7; 1Ki 8:6; 1Ch 28:9; 2Ch 5:7; 7:14

y9 *Solomon* sounds like and may be derived from the Hebrew for *peace*. z14 That is, about 3,750 tons (about 3,450 metric tons) a14 That is, about 37,500 tons (about 34,500 metric tons)

The Levites

23 When David was old and
full of years, he made his
son Solomon[a] king over Israel.[b]
2He also gathered together all
the leaders of Israel, as well as the
priests and Levites. 3The Levites
thirty years old or more[c] were
counted, and the total number of
men was thirty-eight thousand.[d]
4David said, "Of these, twenty-four
thousand are to supervise[e] the
work of the temple of the LORD and
six thousand are to be officials and
judges.[f] 5Four thousand are to be
gatekeepers and four thousand are
to praise the LORD with the musical
instruments[g] I have provided for
that purpose."[h]
6David divided[i] the Levites into
groups corresponding to the sons
of Levi: Gershon, Kohath and Merari.

Gershonites

7Belonging to the Gershonites:
Ladan and Shimei.
8The sons of Ladan:
Jehiel the first, Zetham and
Joel—three in all.
9The sons of Shimei:
Shelomoth, Haziel and Ha-
ran—three in all.
These were the heads of the
families of Ladan.
10And the sons of Shimei:
Jahath, Ziza,[b] Jeush and
Beriah.
These were the sons of
Shimei—four in all.
11Jahath was the first and
Ziza the second, but Jeush
and Beriah did not have
many sons; so they were
counted as one family with
one assignment.

Kohathites

12The sons of Kohath:[j]
Amram, Izhar, Hebron and
Uzziel—four in all.
13The sons of Amram:[k]
Aaron and Moses.
Aaron was set apart,[l] he
and his descendants forever, to consecrate the most
holy things, to offer sacrifices before the LORD, to
minister before him and to
pronounce blessings[m] in
his name forever. 14The
sons of Moses the man[n] of
God were counted as part of
the tribe of Levi.
15The sons of Moses:
Gershom and Eliezer.[o]
16The descendants of Ger-
shom:[p]
Shubael was the first.
17The descendants of Eliezer:
Rehabiah was the first.
Eliezer had no other sons,
but the sons of Rehabiah
were very numerous.
18The sons of Izhar:
Shelomith was the first.
19The sons of Hebron:[q]
Jeriah the first, Amariah the
second, Jahaziel the third
and Jekameam the fourth.
20The sons of Uzziel:
Micah the first and Isshiah
the second.

Merarites

21The sons of Merari:[r]
Mahli and Mushi.
The sons of Mahli:
Eleazar and Kish.
22Eleazar died without having
sons: he had only daugh-
ters. Their cousins, the sons
of Kish, married them.
23The sons of Mushi:
Mahli, Eder and Jerimoth
—three in all.
24These were the descendants of
Levi by their families—the heads
of families as they were registered
under their names and counted in-
dividually, that is, the workers
twenty years old or more[s] who
served in the temple of the LORD.
25For David had said, "Since the
LORD, the God of Israel, has granted
rest[t] to his people and has come
to dwell in Jerusalem forever, 26the
Levites no longer need to carry the
tabernacle or any of the articles

[b]*10* One Hebrew manuscript, Septuagint and Vulgate (see also verse 11); most Hebrew manuscripts *Zina*

23:1 [a] 1Ki 1:33-39; 1Ch 28:5 [b] 1Ki 1:30; 1Ch 29:28
23:3 [c] ver 24; Nu 8:24 [d] Nu 4:3-49
23:4 [e] Ezr 3:8 [f] 1Ch 26:29; 2Ch 19:8
23:5 [g] 1Ch 15:16 [h] Ne 12:45
23:6 [i] 2Ch 8:14; 29:25
23:12 [j] Ex 6:18
23:13 [k] Ex 6:20; 28:1 [l] Ex 30:7-10; Dt 21:5 [m] Nu 6:23
23:14 [n] Dt 33:1
23:15 [o] Ex 18:4
23:16 [p] 1Ch 26:24-28
23:19 [q] 1Ch 24:23
23:21 [r] 1Ch 24:26
23:24 [s] Nu 4:3; 10:17,21
23:25 [t] 1Ch 22:9

used in its service."[a] 27According to the last instructions of David, the Levites were counted from those twenty years old or more.

28The duty of the Levites was to help Aaron's descendants in the service of the temple of the LORD: to be in charge of the courtyards, the side rooms, the purification[b] of all sacred things and the performance of other duties at the house of God. 29They were in charge of the bread set out on the table,[c] the flour for the grain offerings,[d] the unleavened wafers, the baking and the mixing, and all measurements of quantity and size.[e] 30They were also to stand every morning to thank and praise the LORD. They were to do the same in the evening[f] 31and whenever burnt offerings were presented to the LORD on Sabbaths and at New Moon[g] festivals and at appointed feasts.[h] They were to serve before the LORD regularly in the proper number and in the way prescribed for them.

32And so the Levites[i] carried out their responsibilities for the Tent of Meeting,[j] for the Holy Place and, under their brothers the descendants of Aaron, for the service of the temple of the LORD.[k]

The Divisions of Priests

24 These were the divisions[l] of the sons of Aaron:[m]

The sons of Aaron were Nadab, Abihu, Eleazar and Ithamar.[n] 2But Nadab and Abihu died before their father did,[o] and they had no sons; so Eleazar and Ithamar served as the priests. 3With the help of Zadok[p] a descendant of Eleazar and Ahimelech a descendant of Ithamar, David separated them into divisions for their appointed order of ministering. 4A larger number of leaders were found among Eleazar's descendants than among Ithamar's, and they were divided accordingly: sixteen heads of families from Eleazar's descendants and eight heads of families from Ithamar's descendants. 5They divided them impartially by drawing lots,[q] for there were officials of the sanctuary and officials of God among the descendants of both Eleazar and Ithamar.

6The scribe Shemaiah son of Nethanel, a Levite, recorded their names in the presence of the king and of the officials: Zadok the priest, Ahimelech[r] son of Abiathar and the heads of families of the priests and of the Levites—one family being taken from Eleazar and then one from Ithamar.

7The first lot fell to Jehoiarib,
the second to Jedaiah,[s]
8the third to Harim,[t]
the fourth to Seorim,
9the fifth to Malkijah,
the sixth to Mijamin,
10the seventh to Hakkoz,
the eighth to Abijah,[u]
11the ninth to Jeshua,
the tenth to Shecaniah,
12the eleventh to Eliashib,
the twelfth to Jakim,
13the thirteenth to Huppah,
the fourteenth to Jeshebeab,
14the fifteenth to Bilgah,
the sixteenth to Immer,[v]
15the seventeenth to Hezir,[w]
the eighteenth to Happizzez,
16the nineteenth to Pethahiah,
the twentieth to Jehezkel,
17the twenty-first to Jakin,
the twenty-second to Gamul,
18the twenty-third to Delaiah
and the twenty-fourth to Maaziah.

19This was their appointed order of ministering when they entered the temple of the LORD, according to the regulations prescribed for them by their forefather Aaron, as the LORD, the God of Israel, had commanded him.

The Rest of the Levites

20As for the rest of the descendants of Levi:[x]
from the sons of Amram: Shubael;
from the sons of Shubael: Jehdeiah.
21As for Rehabiah,[y] from his sons:
Isshiah was the first.

23:26 [a] Nu 4:5,15; 7:9; Dt 10:8
23:28 [b] 2Ch 29:15; Ne 13:9; Mal 3:3
23:29 [c] Ex 25:30 [d] Lev 2:4-7; 6:20-23 [e] Lev 19:35-36; 1Ch 9:29,32
23:30 [f] 1Ch 9:33; Ps 134:1
23:31 [g] 2Ki 4:23 [h] Lev 23:4; Nu 28:9-29:39; Isa 1:13-14; Col 2:16
23:32 [i] Nu 1:53; 1Ch 6:48 [j] Nu 3:6-8,38 [k] 2Ch 23:18; 31:2; Eze 44:14
24:1 [l] 1Ch 23:6; 28:13; 2Ch 5:11; 8:14; 23:8; 31:2; 35:4,5; Ezr 6:18 [m] Nu 3:2-4 [n] Ex 6:23
24:2 [o] Lev 10:1-2; Nu 3:4
24:3 [p] 2Sa 8:17
24:5 [q] ver 31; 1Ch 25:8
24:6 [r] 1Ch 18:16
24:7 [s] Ezr 2:36; Ne 12:6
24:8 [t] Ezr 2:39; Ne 10:5
24:10 [u] Ne 12:4,17; Lk 1:5
24:14 [v] Jer 20:1
24:15 [w] Ne 10:20
24:20 [x] 1Ch 23:6
24:21 [y] 1Ch 23:17

22From the Izharites: Shelomoth;
from the sons of Shelomoth: Jahath.
23The sons of Hebron:[a] Jeriah the first,[c] Amariah the second, Jahaziel the third and Jekameam the fourth.
24The son of Uzziel: Micah;
from the sons of Micah: Shamir.
25The brother of Micah: Isshiah;
from the sons of Isshiah: Zechariah.
26The sons of Merari:[b] Mahli and Mushi.
The son of Jaaziah: Beno.
27The sons of Merari:
from Jaaziah: Beno, Shoham, Zaccur and Ibri.
28From Mahli: Eleazar, who had no sons.
29From Kish: the son of Kish: Jerahmeel.
30And the sons of Mushi: Mahli, Eder and Jerimoth.

These were the Levites, according to their families. 31They also
cast lots,[c] just as their brothers
the descendants of Aaron did, in
the presence of King David and of
Zadok, Ahimelech, and the heads
of families of the priests and of the
Levites. The families of the oldest
brother were treated the same as
those of the youngest.

The Singers

25 David, together with the commanders of the army, set apart some of the sons of Asaph,[d] Heman[e] and Jeduthun[f] for the ministry of prophesying,[g] accompanied by harps, lyres and cymbals.[h] Here is the list of the men[i] who performed this service:[j]

2From the sons of Asaph:
Zaccur, Joseph, Nethaniah and Asarelah. The sons of Asaph were under the supervision of Asaph, who prophesied under the king's supervision.
3As for Jeduthun, from his sons:[k]
Gedaliah, Zeri, Jeshaiah, Shimei,[d] Hashabiah and Mattithiah, six in all, under the supervision of their father Jeduthun, who prophesied, using the harp[l] in thanking and praising the LORD.
4As for Heman, from his sons:
Bukkiah, Mattaniah, Uzziel,
Shubael and Jerimoth; Hananiah, Hanani, Eliathah, Giddalti and Romamti-Ezer; Joshbekashah, Mallothi, Hothir
and Mahazioth. 5All these
were sons of Heman the king's
seer. They were given him
through the promises of God
to exalt him.[e] God gave Heman fourteen sons and three
daughters.

6All these men were under the
supervision of their fathers[m] for
the music of the temple of the
LORD, with cymbals, lyres and
harps, for the ministry at the house
of God. Asaph, Jeduthun and Heman[n] were under the supervision
of the king.[o] 7Along with their relatives—all of them trained and
skilled in music for the LORD—they
numbered 288. 8Young and old
alike, teacher as well as student,
cast lots[p] for their duties.

9The first lot, which was for Asaph,[q] fell to Joseph, his sons and relatives,[f] 12[g]
the second to Gedaliah, he and his relatives and sons, 12
10the third to Zaccur, his sons and relatives, 12
11the fourth to Izri,[h] his sons and relatives, 12
12the fifth to Nethaniah, his sons and relatives, 12
13the sixth to Bukkiah, his sons and relatives, 12

24:23 [a] 1Ch 23:19
24:26 [b] 1Ch 6:19; 23:21
24:31 [c] ver 5
25:1 [d] 1Ch 6:39 [e] 1Ch 6:33 [f] 1Ch 16:41, 42; Ne 11:17 [g] 1Sa 10:5; 2Ki 3:15 [h] 1Ch 15:16 [i] 1Ch 6:31 [j] 2Ch 5:12; 8:14; 34:12; 35:15; Ezr 3:10
25:3 [k] 1Ch 16:41-42 [l] Ge 4:21; Ps 33:2
25:6 [m] 1Ch 15:16 [n] 1Ch 15:19 [o] 2Ch 23:18; 29:25
25:8 [p] 1Ch 26:13
25:9 [q] 1Ch 6:39

[c] *23* Two Hebrew manuscripts and some Septuagint manuscripts (see also 1 Chron. 23:19); most Hebrew manuscripts *The sons of Jeriah:* [d] *3* One Hebrew manuscript and some Septuagint manuscripts (see also verse 17); most Hebrew manuscripts do not have *Shimei.* [e] *5* Hebrew *exalt the horn* [f] *9* See Septuagint; Hebrew does not have *his sons and relatives.* [g] *9* See the total in verse 7; Hebrew does not have *twelve.* [h] *11* A variant of *Zeri*

14the seventh to Jesarelah,[i]
his sons and relatives, 12
15the eighth to Jeshaiah,
his sons and relatives, 12
16the ninth to Mattaniah,
his sons and relatives, 12
17the tenth to Shimei,
his sons and relatives, 12
18the eleventh to Azarel,[j]
his sons and relatives, 12
19the twelfth to Hashabiah,
his sons and relatives, 12
20the thirteenth to Shubael,
his sons and relatives, 12
21the fourteenth to Mattithiah,
his sons and relatives, 12
22the fifteenth to Jerimoth,
his sons and relatives, 12
23the sixteenth to Hananiah,
his sons and relatives, 12
24the seventeenth to Joshbekashah,
his sons and relatives, 12
25the eighteenth to Hanani,
his sons and relatives, 12
26the nineteenth to Mallothi,
his sons and relatives, 12
27the twentieth to Eliathah,
his sons and relatives, 12
28the twenty-first to Hothir,
his sons and relatives, 12
29the twenty-second to Giddalti,
his sons and relatives, 12
30the twenty-third to Mahazioth,
his sons and relatives, 12
31the twenty-fourth to Romamti-Ezer,
his sons and relatives, 12[a]

The Gatekeepers

26 The divisions of the gatekeepers:[b]

From the Korahites: Meshelemiah son of Kore, one of the sons of Asaph.
2Meshelemiah had sons:
Zechariah[c] the firstborn,
Jediael the second,
Zebadiah the third,
Jathniel the fourth,
3Elam the fifth,
Jehohanan the sixth
and Eliehoenai the seventh.
4Obed-Edom also had sons:
Shemaiah the firstborn,
Jehozabad the second,
Joah the third,
Sacar the fourth,
Nethanel the fifth,
5Ammiel the sixth,
Issachar the seventh
and Peullethai the eighth.
(For God had blessed Obed-Edom.[d])

6His son Shemaiah also had sons, who were leaders in their father's family because they were very capable men.
7The sons of Shemaiah: Othni, Rephael, Obed and Elzabad; his relatives Elihu and Semakiah were also able men.
8All these were descendants of Obed-Edom; they and their sons and their relatives were capable men with the strength to do the work—descendants of Obed-Edom, 62 in all.
9Meshelemiah had sons and relatives, who were able men—18 in all.

10Hosah the Merarite had sons: Shimri the first (although he was not the firstborn, his father had appointed him the first),[e]
11Hilkiah the second, Tabaliah the third and Zechariah the fourth. The sons and relatives of Hosah were 13 in all.

12These divisions of the gatekeepers, through their chief men, had duties for ministering[f] in the temple of the LORD, just as their relatives had.
13Lots[g] were cast for each gate, according to their families, young and old alike.

14The lot for the East Gate[h] fell to Shelemiah.[k] Then lots were cast for his son Zechariah,[i] a wise counselor, and the lot for the North Gate fell to him.
15The lot for the South Gate fell to Obed-Edom,[j]

25:31 [a] 1Ch 9:33
26:1 [b] 1Ch 9:17
26:2 [c] 1Ch 9:21
26:5 [d] 2Sa 6:10; 1Ch 13:13; 16:38
26:10 [e] Dt 21:16; 1Ch 5:1
26:12 [f] 1Ch 9:22
26:13 [g] 1Ch 24:5,31; 25:8
26:14 [h] 1Ch 9:18 [i] 1Ch 9:21
26:15 [j] 1Ch 13:13; 2Ch 25:24

[i] 14 A variant of *Asarelah* [j] 18 A variant of *Uzziel* [k] 14 A variant of *Meshelemiah*

and the lot for the storehouse fell
to his sons. **16**The lots for the West
Gate and the Shalleketh Gate on
the upper road fell to Shuppim and
Hosah.

Guard was alongside of guard:
17There were six Levites a day on
the east, four a day on the north,
four a day on the south and two at
a time at the storehouse. **18**As for
the court to the west, there were
four at the road and two at the
court itself.

19These were the divisions of the
gatekeepers who were descendants
of Korah and Merari.[a]

The Treasurers and Other Officials

20Their fellow Levites[b] were[1] in
charge of the treasuries of the
house of God and the treasuries for
the dedicated things.[c]

21The descendants of Ladan,
who were Gershonites through Ladan and who were heads of families
belonging to Ladan the Gershon-
ite,[d] were Jehieli, **22**the sons of Jehieli, Zetham and his brother Joel.
They were in charge of the treasuries[e] of the temple of the LORD.

23From the Amramites, the Izharites, the Hebronites and the Uzzielites:[f]

24Shubael,[g] a descendant of
Gershom son of Moses, was
the officer in charge of the
treasuries. **25**His relatives
through Eliezer: Rehabiah
his son, Jeshaiah his son,
Joram his son, Zicri his son
and Shelomith[h] his son.
26Shelomith and his relatives were in charge of all
the treasuries for the things
dedicated[i] by King David,
by the heads of families
who were the commanders
of thousands and com-
manders of hundreds, and
by the other army com-
manders. **27**Some of the
plunder taken in battle they
dedicated for the repair of
the temple of the LORD.
28And everything dedicated
by Samuel the seer[j] and by
Saul son of Kish, Abner son
of Ner and Joab son of Zeruiah, and all the other dedicated things were in the
care of Shelomith and his
relatives.

29From the Izharites: Kenaniah
and his sons were assigned
duties away from the tem-
ple, as officials and judges[k]
over Israel.

30From the Hebronites: Hashabiah[l] and his relatives—
seventeen hundred able
men—were responsible in
Israel west of the Jordan for
all the work of the LORD and
for the king's service. **31**As
for the Hebronites,[m] Jeriah
was their chief according to
the genealogical records of
their families. In the fortieth[n] year of David's reign a
search was made in the
records, and capable men
among the Hebronites were
found at Jazer in Gilead.
32Jeriah had twenty-seven
hundred relatives, who
were able men and heads of
families, and King David
put them in charge of the
Reubenites, the Gadites
and the half-tribe of Manasseh for every matter per-
taining to God and for the
affairs of the king.

Army Divisions

27 This is the list of the Israelites—heads of families,
commanders of thousands and
commanders of hundreds, and
their officers, who served the king
in all that concerned the army divisions that were on duty month by
month throughout the year. Each
division consisted of 24,000 men.

2In charge of the first division, for
the first month, was Jashobe-
am[o] son of Zabdiel. There
were 24,000 men in his division. **3**He was a descendant of

26:19 [a] 2Ch 35:15; Ne 7:1; Eze 44:11
26:20 [b] 2Ch 24:5 [c] 1Ch 28:12
26:21 [d] 1Ch 23:7; 29:8
26:22 [e] 1Ch 9:26
26:23 [f] Nu 3:27
26:24 [g] 1Ch 23:16
26:25 [h] 1Ch 23:18
26:26 [i] 2Sa 8:11
26:28 [j] 1Sa 9:9
26:29 [k] Dt 17:8-13; 1Ch 23:4; Ne 11:16
26:30 [l] 1Ch 27:17
26:31 [m] 1Ch 23:19 [n] 2Sa 5:4
27:2 [o] 2Sa 23:8; 1Ch 11:11

[1]20 Septuagint; Hebrew *As for the Levites, Ahijah was*

Perez and chief of all the army
officers for the first month.
4In charge of the division for the
second month was Dodai[a]
the Ahohite; Mikloth was the
leader of his division. There
were 24,000 men in his division.
5The third army commander, for
the third month, was Benaiah[b] son of Jehoiada the
priest. He was chief and there
were 24,000 men in his division. 6This was the Benaiah
who was a mighty man among
the Thirty and was over the
Thirty. His son Ammizabad
was in charge of his division.
7The fourth, for the fourth month,
was Asahel[c] the brother of
Joab; his son Zebadiah was
his successor. There were 24,-
000 men in his division.
8The fifth, for the fifth month, was
the commander Shamhuth[d]
the Izrahite. There were 24,-
000 men in his division.
9The sixth, for the sixth month,
was Ira[e] the son of Ikkesh the
Tekoite. There were 24,000
men in his division.
10The seventh, for the seventh
month, was Helez[f] the Pelonite, an Ephraimite. There
were 24,000 men in his division.
11The eighth, for the eighth
month, was Sibbecai[g] the
Hushathite, a Zerahite. There
were 24,000 men in his division.
12The ninth, for the ninth month,
was Abiezer[h] the Anathothite, a Benjamite. There were
24,000 men in his division.
13The tenth, for the tenth month,
was Maharai[i] the Netophathite, a Zerahite. There were
24,000 men in his division.
14The eleventh, for the eleventh
month, was Benaiah[j] the Pirathonite, an Ephraimite.
There were 24,000 men in his
division.
15The twelfth, for the twelfth
month, was Heldai[k] the Netophathite, from the family of
Othniel.[l] There were 24,000
men in his division.

Officers of the Tribes

16The officers over the tribes of
Israel:

over the Reubenites: Eliezer
son of Zicri;
over the Simeonites: Shephatiah son of Maacah;
17over Levi: Hashabiah[m] son of
Kemuel;
over Aaron: Zadok;[n]
18over Judah: Elihu, a brother of
David;
over Issachar: Omri son of Michael;
19over Zebulun: Ishmaiah son of
Obadiah;
over Naphtali: Jerimoth son of
Azriel;
20over the Ephraimites: Hoshea
son of Azaziah;
over half the tribe of Manasseh: Joel son of Pedaiah;
21over the half-tribe of Manasseh in Gilead: Iddo son of
Zechariah;
over Benjamin: Jaasiel son of
Abner;
22over Dan: Azarel son of Jeroham.

These were the officers over the
tribes of Israel.

23David did not take the number
of the men twenty years old or
less,[o] because the LORD had promised to make Israel as numerous as
the stars[p] in the sky. 24Joab son of
Zeruiah began to count the men
but did not finish. Wrath came on
Israel on account of this numbering,[q] and the number was not entered in the book[m] of the annals of
King David.

The King's Overseers

25Azmaveth son of Adiel was in
charge of the royal storehouses.

Jonathan son of Uzziah was in
charge of the storehouses in the

27:4 [a] 2Sa 23:9
27:5 [b] 2Sa 23:20
27:7 [c] 2Sa 2:18; 1Ch 11:26
27:8 [d] 1Ch 11:27
27:9 [e] 2Sa 23:26; 1Ch 11:28
27:10 [f] 2Sa 23:26; 1Ch 11:27
27:11 [g] 2Sa 21:18
27:12 [h] 2Sa 23:27; 1Ch 11:28
27:13 [i] 2Sa 23:28; 1Ch 11:30
27:14 [j] 1Ch 11:31
27:15 [k] 2Sa 23:29 [l] Jos 15:17
27:17 [m] 1Ch 26:30 [n] 2Sa 8:17; 1Ch 12:28
27:23 [o] 1Ch 21:2-5 [p] Ge 15:5
27:24 [q] 2Sa 24:15; 1Ch 21:7

[m]*24* Septuagint; Hebrew *number*

outlying districts, in the towns, the villages and the watchtowers.

26 Ezri son of Kelub was in charge of the field workers who farmed the land.

27 Shimei the Ramathite was in charge of the vineyards.

Zabdi the Shiphmite was in charge of the produce of the vineyards for the wine vats.

28 Baal-Hanan the Gederite was in charge of the olive and sycamore-fig[a] trees in the western foothills.

Joash was in charge of the supplies of olive oil.

29 Shitrai the Sharonite was in charge of the herds grazing in Sharon.

Shaphat son of Adlai was in charge of the herds in the valleys.

30 Obil the Ishmaelite was in charge of the camels.

Jehdeiah the Meronothite was in charge of the donkeys.

31 Jaziz the Hagrite[b] was in charge of the flocks.

All these were the officials in charge of King David's property.

32 Jonathan, David's uncle, was a counselor, a man of insight and a scribe. Jehiel son of Hacmoni took care of the king's sons.

33 Ahithophel[c] was the king's counselor.

Hushai[d] the Arkite was the king's friend. 34 Ahithophel was succeeded by Jehoiada son of Benaiah and by Abiathar.[e]

Joab[f] was the commander of the royal army.

David's Plans for the Temple

28 David summoned all the officials[g] of Israel to assemble at Jerusalem: the officers over the tribes, the commanders of the divisions in the service of the king, the commanders of thousands and commanders of hundreds, and the officials in charge of all the property and livestock belonging to the king and his sons, together with the palace officials, the mighty men and all the brave warriors.

27:28 [a] 1Ki 10:27; 2Ch 1:15
27:31 [b] 1Ch 5:10
27:33 [c] 2Sa 15:12 [d] 2Sa 15:37
27:34 [e] 1Ki 1:7 [f] 1Ch 11:6
28:1 [g] 1Ch 11:10; 27:1-31
28:2 [h] 1Ch 17:2 [i] Ps 99:5; 132:7
28:3 [j] 2Sa 7:5 [k] 1Ch 22:8 [l] 1Ki 5:3; 1Ch 17:4
28:4 [m] 1Ch 17:23, 27; 2Ch 6:6 [n] 1Sa 16:1-13 [o] Ge 49:10; 1Ch 5:2
28:5 [p] 1Ch 3:1 [q] 1Ch 22:9; 23:1
28:6 [r] 2Sa 7:13; 1Ch 22:9-10
28:7 [s] 1Ch 22:13
28:8 [t] Dt 6:1 [u] Dt 4:1
28:9 [v] 1Ch 29:19 [w] 1Sa 16:7; Ps 7:9 [x] Ps 40:16; Jer 29:13 [y] Jos 24:20; 2Ch 15:2 [z] Ps 44:23
28:11 [a] Ex 25:9

2 King David rose to his feet and said: "Listen to me, my brothers and my people. I had it in my heart[h] to build a house as a place of rest for the ark of the covenant of the LORD, for the footstool[i] of our God, and I made plans to build it. 3 But God said to me,[j] 'You are not to build a house for my Name,[k] because you are a warrior and have shed blood.'[l]

4 "Yet the LORD, the God of Israel, chose me[m] from my whole family[n] to be king over Israel forever. He chose Judah[o] as leader, and from the house of Judah he chose my family, and from my father's sons he was pleased to make me king over all Israel. 5 Of all my sons—and the LORD has given me many[p]—he has chosen my son Solomon[q] to sit on the throne of the kingdom of the LORD over Israel. 6 He said to me: 'Solomon your son is the one who will build my house and my courts, for I have chosen him to be my son,[r] and I will be his father. 7 I will establish his kingdom forever if he is unswerving in carrying out my commands and laws,[s] as is being done at this time.'

8 "So now I charge you in the sight of all Israel and of the assembly of the LORD, and in the hearing of our God: Be careful to follow all the commands[t] of the LORD your God, that you may possess this good land and pass it on as an inheritance to your descendants forever.[u]

9 "And you, my son Solomon, acknowledge the God of your father, and serve him with wholehearted devotion[v] and with a willing mind, for the LORD searches every heart[w] and understands every motive behind the thoughts. If you seek him,[x] he will be found by you; but if you forsake[y] him, he will reject[z] you forever. 10 Consider now, for the LORD has chosen you to build a temple as a sanctuary. Be strong and do the work."

11 Then David gave his son Solomon the plans[a] for the portico of the temple, its buildings, its store-

rooms, its upper parts, its inner
rooms and the place of atonement.
12He gave him the plans of all that
the Spirit[a] had put in his mind for
the courts of the temple of the LORD
and all the surrounding rooms, for
the treasuries of the temple of God
and for the treasuries for the dedicated things.[b] **13**He gave him instructions for the divisions[c] of the
priests and Levites, and for all the
work of serving in the temple of the
LORD, as well as for all the articles
to be used in its service. **14**He designated the weight of gold for all
the gold articles to be used in various kinds of service, and the weight
of silver for all the silver articles to
be used in various kinds of service:
15the weight of gold for the gold
lampstands[d] and their lamps, with
the weight for each lampstand and
its lamps; and the weight of silver
for each silver lampstand and its
lamps, according to the use of each
lampstand; **16**the weight of gold for
each table[e] for consecrated bread;
the weight of silver for the silver tables; **17**the weight of pure gold for
the forks, sprinkling bowls[f] and
pitchers; the weight of gold for
each gold dish; the weight of silver
for each silver dish; **18**and the
weight of the refined gold for the
altar of incense.[g] He also gave him
the plan for the chariot,[h] that is,
the cherubim of gold that spread
their wings and shelter[i] the ark of
the covenant of the LORD.

19"All this," David said, "I have
in writing from the hand of the
LORD upon me, and he gave me understanding in all the details[j] of
the plan.[k]"

20David also said to Solomon his
son, "Be strong and courageous,[l]
and do the work. Do not be afraid
or discouraged, for the LORD God,
my God, is with you. He will not fail
you or forsake[m] you until all the
work for the service of the temple
of the LORD is finished.[n] **21**The divisions of the priests and Levites
are ready for all the work on the
temple of God, and every willing
man skilled[o] in any craft will help
you in all the work. The officials
and all the people will obey your
every command."

Gifts for Building the Temple

29 Then King David said to the
whole assembly: "My son
Solomon, the one whom God has
chosen, is young and inexperienced.[p] The task is great, because
this palatial structure is not for
man but for the LORD God. **2**With all
my resources I have provided for
the temple of my God—gold[q] for
the gold work, silver for the silver,
bronze for the bronze, iron for the
iron and wood for the wood, as well
as onyx for the settings, turquoise,[n][r] stones of various colors,
and all kinds of fine stone and marble—all of these in large quantities.[s] **3**Besides, in my devotion to
the temple of my God I now give my
personal treasures of gold and silver for the temple of my God, over
and above everything I have provided[t] for this holy temple: **4**three
thousand talents[o] of gold (gold of
Ophir)[u] and seven thousand talents[p] of refined silver,[v] for the
overlaying of the walls of the buildings, **5**for the gold work and the silver work, and for all the work to be
done by the craftsmen. Now, who
is willing to consecrate himself today to the LORD?"

6Then the leaders of families,
the officers of the tribes of Israel,
the commanders of thousands and
commanders of hundreds, and the
officials[w] in charge of the king's
work gave willingly.[x] **7**They[y] gave
toward the work on the temple of
God five thousand talents[q] and ten
thousand darics[r] of gold, ten thousand talents[s] of silver, eighteen
thousand talents[t] of bronze and a
hundred thousand talents[u] of iron.
8Any who had precious stones[z]

28:12 [a] 1Ch 12:18 [b] 1Ch 26:20
28:13 [c] 1Ch 24:1
28:15 [d] Ex 25:31
28:16 [e] Ex 25:23
28:17 [f] Ex 27:3
28:18 [g] Ex 30:1-10 [h] Ex 25:18-22 [i] Ex 25:20
28:19 [j] 1Ki 6:38 [k] Ex 25:9
28:20 [l] Dt 31:6; 1Ch 22:13; 2Ch 19:11; Hag 2:4 [m] Dt 4:31; Jos 24:20 [n] 1Ki 6:14; 2Ch 7:11
28:21 [o] Ex 35:25-36:5
29:1 [p] 1Ki 3:7; 1Ch 22:5; 2Ch 13:7
29:2 [q] ver 7,14,16; Ezr 1:4; 6:5; Hag 2:8 [r] Isa 54:11 [s] 1Ch 22:2-5
29:3 [t] 2Ch 24:10; 31:3; 35:8
29:4 [u] Ge 10:29 [v] 1Ch 22:14
29:6 [w] 1Ch 27:1; 28:1 [x] ver 9; Ex 25:1-8; 35:20-29; 36:2; 2Ch 24:10; Ezr 7:15
29:7 [y] Ex 25:2; Ne 7:70-71
29:8 [z] Ex 35:27

[n]2 The meaning of the Hebrew for this word is uncertain. [o]4 That is, about 110 tons (about 100 metric tons) [p]4 That is, about 260 tons (about 240 metric tons) [q]7 That is, about 190 tons (about 170 metric tons) [r]7 That is, about 185 pounds (about 84 kilograms) [s]7 That is, about 375 tons (about 345 metric tons) [t]7 That is, about 675 tons (about 610 metric tons) [u]7 That is, about 3,750 tons (about 3,450 metric tons)

gave them to the treasury of the
temple of the LORD in the custody
of Jehiel the Gershonite.[a] 9The
people rejoiced at the willing response of their leaders, for they
had given freely and wholeheartedly[b] to the LORD. David the king also
rejoiced greatly.

David's Prayer

10David praised the LORD in the
presence of the whole assembly,
saying,

"Praise be to you, O LORD,
God of our father Israel,
from everlasting to
everlasting.
11Yours, O LORD, is the greatness
and the power[c]
and the glory and the
majesty and the
splendor,
for everything in heaven and
earth is yours.[d]
Yours, O LORD, is the kingdom;
you are exalted as head over
all.[e]
12Wealth and honor[f] come from
you;
you are the ruler[g] of all
things.
In your hands are strength and
power
to exalt and give strength to
all.
13Now, our God, we give you
thanks,
and praise your glorious
name.

14"But who am I, and who are my
people, that we should be able to
give as generously as this? Everything comes from you, and we have
given you only what comes from
your hand. 15We are aliens and
strangers[h] in your sight, as were all
our forefathers. Our days on earth
are like a shadow,[i] without hope.
16O LORD our God, as for all this
abundance that we have provided
for building you a temple for your
Holy Name, it comes from your
hand, and all of it belongs to you.
17I know, my God, that you test the
heart[j] and are pleased with integrity. All these things have I given
willingly and with honest intent.
And now I have seen with joy how
willingly your people who are here
have given to you.[k] 18O LORD, God
of our fathers Abraham, Isaac and
Israel, keep this desire in the
hearts of your people forever, and
keep their hearts loyal to you.
19And give my son Solomon the
wholehearted devotion[l] to keep
your commands, requirements and
decrees[m] and to do everything to
build the palatial structure for
which I have provided."[n]

20Then David said to the whole
assembly, "Praise the LORD your
God." So they all praised the LORD,
the God of their fathers; they
bowed low and fell prostrate before
the LORD and the king.

Solomon Acknowledged as King

29:21–25pp — 1Ki 1:28–53

21The next day they made sacrifices to the LORD and presented
burnt offerings to him:[o] a thousand bulls, a thousand rams and a
thousand male lambs, together
with their drink offerings, and other sacrifices in abundance for all Israel. 22They ate and drank with
great joy[p] in the presence of the
LORD that day.

Then they acknowledged Solomon son of David as king a second
time, anointing him before the
LORD to be ruler and Zadok[q] to be
priest. 23So Solomon sat on the
throne[r] of the LORD as king in
place of his father David. He prospered and all Israel obeyed him.
24All the officers and mighty men,
as well as all of King David's sons,
pledged their submission to King
Solomon.

25The LORD highly exalted Solomon in the sight of all Israel and
bestowed on him royal splendor[s]
such as no king over Israel ever had
before.[t]

The Death of David

29:26–28pp — 1Ki 2:10–12

26David son of Jesse was king[u]

29:8 [a] 1Ch 26:21
29:9 [b] 1Ki 8:61; 2Co 9:7
29:11 [c] Ps 24:8; 59:17; 62:11 [d] Ps 89:11 [e] Rev 5:12-13
29:12 [f] 2Ch 1:12 [g] 2Ch 20:6; Ro 11:36
29:15 [h] Ps 39:12; Heb 11:13 [i] Job 14:2
29:17 [j] Ps 139:23; Pr 15:11; 17:3; Jer 11:20; 17:10 [k] 1Ch 28:9; Ps 15:1-5
29:19 [l] 1Ch 28:9 [m] Ps 72:1 [n] 1Ch 22:14
29:21 [o] 1Ki 8:62
29:22 [p] 1Ch 23:1 [q] 1Ki 1:33-39
29:23 [r] 1Ki 2:12
29:25 [s] 2Ch 1:1,12 [t] 1Ki 3:13; Ecc 2:9
29:26 [u] 1Ch 18:14

over all Israel. **27**He ruled over Israel forty years—seven in Hebron
and thirty-three in Jerusalem.[a]
28He died[b] at a good old age, having enjoyed long life, wealth and
honor. His son Solomon succeeded
him as king.[c]
29As for the events of King David's reign, from beginning to end,
they are written in the records of
Samuel the seer,[d] the records of
Nathan[e] the prophet and the
records of Gad[f] the seer, **30**together with the details of his reign and
power, and the circumstances that
surrounded him and Israel and
the kingdoms of all the other
lands.

29:27 [a] 2Sa 5:4-5; 1Ki 2:11; 1Ch 3:4
29:28 [b] Ge 15:15; Ac 13:36 [c] 1Ch 23:1
29:29 [d] 1Sa 9:9 [e] 2Sa 7:2 [f] 1Sa 22:5

2 Chronicles

Title and Background

See Introduction to 1 Chronicles.

Author and Date of Writing

See Introduction to 1 Chronicles.

Theme and Message

2 Chronicles continues the history of David's royal line. This book, like 1 Chronicles, shows that the people's relationship to God was most important. When the author wrote about the kings, he measured them on the basis of their faithfulness to God. The reigns of evil kings are reported by the author briefly, while the reigns of good kings are described in more detail.

Outline

I. The Reign of Solomon (1:1-9:31)
II. The Kings of Judah (10:1-36:14)
III. The Destruction of Jerusalem (36:15-23)

Solomon Asks for Wisdom

1:2-13pp — 1Ki 3:4-15
1:14-17pp — 1Ki 10:26-29; 2Ch 9:25-28

1 Solomon son of David established[a] himself firmly over his kingdom, for the LORD his God was with[b] him and made him exceedingly great.[c]

2Then Solomon spoke to all Israel[d]—to the commanders of thousands and commanders of hundreds, to the judges and to all the leaders in Israel, the heads of families— **3**and Solomon and the whole assembly went to the high place at Gibeon, for God's Tent of Meeting[e] was there, which Moses[f] the LORD's servant had made in the desert. **4**Now David had brought up the ark[g] of God from Kiriath Jearim to the place he had prepared for it, because he had pitched a tent[h] for it in Jerusalem. **5**But the bronze altar[i] that Bezalel[j] son of Uri, the son of Hur, had made was in Gibeon in front of the tabernacle of the LORD; so Solomon and the assembly inquired[k] of him there. **6**Solomon went up to the bronze altar before the LORD in the Tent of Meeting and offered a thousand burnt offerings on it.

7That night God appeared[l] to Solomon and said to him, "Ask for whatever you want me to give you."

8Solomon answered God, "You have shown great kindness to David my father and have made me[m] king in his place. **9**Now, LORD God, let your promise[n] to my father David be confirmed, for you have made me king over a people who are as numerous as the dust of the earth.[o] **10**Give me wisdom and knowledge, that I may lead[p] this people, for who is able to govern this great people of yours?"

11God said to Solomon, "Since this is your heart's desire and you have not asked for wealth,[q] riches or honor, nor for the death of your enemies, and since you have not asked for a long life but for wisdom and knowledge to govern my people over whom I have made you king, **12**therefore wisdom and knowledge will be given you. And I will also give you wealth, riches

1:1 [a] 1Ki 2:12,26; 2Ch 12:1 [b] Ge 21:22; 39:2; Nu 14:43 [c] 1Ch 29:25
1:2 [d] 1Ch 9:1; 28:1
1:3 [e] Ex 36:8 [f] Ex 40:18
1:4 [g] 2Sa 6:2; 1Ch 15:25 [h] 2Sa 6:17; 1Ch 15:1
1:5 [i] Ex 38:2 [j] Ex 31:2 [k] 1Ch 13:3
1:7 [l] 2Ch 7:12
1:8 [m] 1Ch 23:1; 28:5
1:9 [n] 2Sa 7:25; 1Ki 8:25 [o] Ge 12:2
1:10 [p] Nu 27:17; 2Sa 5:2; Pr 8:15-16
1:11 [q] Dt 17:17

and honor,[a] such as no king who
was before you ever had and none
after you will have.[b]"
13 Then Solomon went to Jerusalem from the high place at Gibeon,
from before the Tent of Meeting.
And he reigned over Israel.
14 Solomon accumulated chariots[c] and horses; he had fourteen
hundred chariots and twelve thousand horses,[a] which he kept in the
chariot cities and also with him in
Jerusalem. 15 The king made silver
and gold[d] as common in Jerusalem as stones, and cedar as plentiful as sycamore-fig trees in the
foothills. 16 Solomon's horses were
imported from Egypt[b] and from
Kue[c]—the royal merchants purchased them from Kue. 17 They imported a chariot[e] from Egypt for
six hundred shekels[d] of silver, and
a horse for a hundred and fifty.[e]
They also exported them to all the
kings of the Hittites and of the Arameans.

Preparations for Building the Temple

2:1-18pp — 1Ki 5:1-16

2 Solomon gave orders to build a
temple[f] for the Name of the
LORD and a royal palace for himself.[g] 2 He conscripted seventy
thousand men as carriers and
eighty thousand as stonecutters in
the hills and thirty-six hundred as
foremen over them.[h]
3 Solomon sent this message to
Hiram[f][i] king of Tyre:

"Send me cedar logs[j] as
you did for my father David
when you sent him cedar to
build a palace to live in. 4 Now
I am about to build a temple[k]
for the Name of the LORD my
God and to dedicate it to him
for burning fragrant incense[l]
before him, for setting out the
consecrated bread[m] regularly,
and for making burnt offerings[n] every morning and evening and on Sabbaths[o] and
New Moons and at the ap-
pointed feasts of the LORD our
God. This is a lasting ordinance for Israel.
5 "The temple I am going to
build will be great,[p] because
our God is greater than all other gods.[q] 6 But who is able to
build a temple for him, since
the heavens, even the highest
heavens, cannot contain
him?[r] Who then am I[s] to
build a temple for him, except
as a place to burn sacrifices
before him?
7 "Send me, therefore, a man
skilled to work in gold and silver, bronze and iron, and in
purple, crimson and blue yarn,
and experienced in the art of
engraving, to work in Judah
and Jerusalem with my skilled
craftsmen,[t] whom my father
David provided.
8 "Send me also cedar, pine
and algum[g] logs from Lebanon, for I know that your men
are skilled in cutting timber
there. My men will work with
yours 9 to provide me with
plenty of lumber, because the
temple I build must be large
and magnificent. 10 I will give
your servants, the woodsmen
who cut the timber, twenty
thousand cors[h] of ground
wheat, twenty thousand cors
of barley, twenty thousand
baths[i] of wine and twenty
thousand baths of olive oil.[u]"

11 Hiram king of Tyre replied by
letter to Solomon:

"Because the LORD loves[v]
his people, he has made you
their king."

12 And Hiram added:

"Praise be to the LORD, the
God of Israel, who made heav-

1:12 [a] 1Ch 29:12 [b] 1Ch 29:25; 2Ch 9:22; Ne 13:26
1:14 [c] 1Sa 8:11; 1Ki 4:26; 9:19
1:15 [d] 1Ki 9:28; Isa 60:5
1:17 [e] SS 1:9
2:1 [f] Dt 12:5 [g] Ecc 2:4
2:2 [h] ver 18; 2Ch 10:4
2:3 [i] 2Sa 5:11 [j] 1Ch 14:1
2:4 [k] ver 1; Dt 12:5 [l] Ex 30:7 [m] Ex 25:30 [n] Ex 29:42; 2Ch 13:11 [o] Nu 28:9-10
2:5 [p] 1Ch 22:5; Ps 135:5 [q] 1Ch 16:25
2:6 [r] 1Ki 8:27; 2Ch 6:18; Jer 23:24 [s] Ex 3:11
2:7 [t] ver 13-14; Ex 35:31; 1Ch 22:16
2:10 [u] Ezr 3:7
2:11 [v] 1Ki 10:9; 2Ch 9:8

[a] *14* Or *charioteers* [b] *16* Or possibly *Muzur,* a region in Cilicia; also in verse 17 [c] *16* Probably Cilicia [d] *17* That is, about 15 pounds (about 7 kilograms) [e] *17* That is, about 3 3/4 pounds (about 1.7 kilograms) [f] *3* Hebrew *Huram,* a variant of *Hiram;* also in verses 11 and 12 [g] *8* Probably a variant of *almug;* possibly juniper [h] *10* That is, probably about 125,000 bushels (about 4,400 kiloliters) [i] *10* That is, probably about 115,000 gallons (about 440 kiloliters)

en and earth![a] He has given
King David a wise son, endowed with intelligence and
discernment, who will build a
temple for the LORD and a palace for himself.
13"I am sending you Huram-Abi,[b] a man of great skill,
14whose mother was from
Dan[c] and whose father was
from Tyre. He is trained[d] to
work in gold and silver, bronze
and iron, stone and wood, and
with purple and blue[e] and
crimson yarn and fine linen.
He is experienced in all kinds
of engraving and can execute
any design given to him. He
will work with your craftsmen
and with those of my lord, David your father.
15"Now let my lord send his
servants the wheat and barley
and the olive oil[f] and wine he
promised, **16**and we will cut all
the logs from Lebanon that
you need and will float them
in rafts by sea down to Joppa.[g] You can then take them
up to Jerusalem."

17Solomon took a census of all
the aliens[h] who were in Israel, after the census[i] his father David
had taken; and they were found to
be 153,600. **18**He assigned[j] 70,-
000 of them to be carriers and 80,-
000 to be stonecutters in the hills,
with 3,600 foremen over them to
keep the people working.

Solomon Builds the Temple

3:1-14pp — 1Ki 6:1-29

3 Then Solomon began to
build[k] the temple of the
LORD[l] in Jerusalem on Mount Moriah, where the LORD had appeared
to his father David. It was on the
threshing floor of Araunah[i][m] the
Jebusite, the place provided by David. **2**He began building on the second day of the second month in the
fourth year of his reign.[n]
3The foundation Solomon laid
for building the temple of God was
sixty cubits long and twenty cubits
wide[k][o] (using the cubit of the old
standard). **4**The portico at the front
of the temple was twenty cubits[l]
long across the width of the building and twenty cubits[m] high.
He overlaid the inside with pure
gold. **5**He paneled the main hall
with pine and covered it with fine
gold and decorated it with palm
tree[p] and chain designs. **6**He
adorned the temple with precious
stones. And the gold he used was
gold of Parvaim. **7**He overlaid the
ceiling beams, doorframes, walls
and doors of the temple with gold,
and he carved cherubim[q] on the
walls.
8He built the Most Holy Place,[r]
its length corresponding to the
width of the temple—twenty cubits long and twenty cubits wide.
He overlaid the inside with six hundred talents[n] of fine gold. **9**The
gold nails[s] weighed fifty shekels.[o]
He also overlaid the upper parts
with gold.
10In the Most Holy Place he
made a pair[t] of sculptured cherubim and overlaid them with gold.
11The total wingspan of the cherubim was twenty cubits. One wing of
the first cherub was five cubits[p]
long and touched the temple wall,
while its other wing, also five cubits long, touched the wing of the
other cherub. **12**Similarly one wing
of the second cherub was five cubits long and touched the other
temple wall, and its other wing,
also five cubits long, touched the
wing of the first cherub. **13**The
wings of these cherubim[u] extended twenty cubits. They stood on
their feet, facing the main hall.[q]
14He made the curtain[v] of blue,
purple and crimson yarn and fine
linen, with cherubim[w] worked into
it.

2:12 [a]Ne 9:6; Ps 8:3; 33:6; 102:25
2:13 [b]1Ki 7:13
2:14 [c]Ex 31:6 [d]Ex 35:31 [e]Ex 35:35
2:15 [f]ver 10; Ezr 3:7
2:16 [g]Jos 19:46; Jnh 1:3
2:17 [h]1Ch 22:2 [i]2Sa 24:2
2:18 [j]ver 2; 1Ch 22:2; 2Ch 8:8
3:1 [k]Ac 7:47 [l]Ge 28:17 [m]2Sa 24:18; 1Ch 21:18
3:2 [n]Ezr 5:11
3:3 [o]Eze 41:2
3:5 [p]Eze 40:16
3:7 [q]Ge 3:24; 1Ki 6:29-35; Eze 41:18
3:8 [r]Ex 26:33
3:9 [s]Ex 26:32
3:10 [t]Ex 25:18
3:13 [u]Ex 25:18
3:14 [v]Ex 26:31,33; Heb 9:3 [w]Ge 3:24

[i]*1* Hebrew *Ornan,* a variant of *Araunah*
[k]*3* That is, about 90 feet (about 27 meters) long and 30 feet (about 9 meters) wide
[l]*4* That is, about 30 feet (about 9 meters); also in verses 8, 11 and 13 [m]*4* Some Septuagint and Syriac manuscripts; Hebrew *and a hundred and twenty* [n]*8* That is, about 23 tons (about 21 metric tons)
[o]*9* That is, about 1 1/4 pounds (about 0.6 kilogram) [p]*11* That is, about 7 1/2 feet (about 2.3 meters); also in verse 15 [q]*13* Or *facing inward*

15In the front of the temple he made two pillars,[a] which ⌞together⌟ were thirty-five cubits[r] long, each with a capital[b] on top measuring five cubits. **16**He made interwoven chains[s][c] and put them on top of the pillars. He also made a hundred pomegranates[d] and attached them to the chains. **17**He erected the pillars in the front of the temple, one to the south and one to the north. The one to the south he named Jakin[t] and the one to the north Boaz.[u]

The Temple's Furnishings

4:2-6,10-5:1pp — 1Ki 7:23-26,38-51

4 He made a bronze altar[e] twenty cubits long, twenty cubits wide and ten cubits high.[v] **2**He made the Sea[f] of cast metal, circular in shape, measuring ten cubits from rim to rim and five cubits[w] high. It took a line of thirty cubits[x] to measure around it. **3**Below the rim, figures of bulls encircled it—ten to a cubit.[y] The bulls were cast in two rows in one piece with the Sea.

4The Sea stood on twelve bulls, three facing north, three facing west, three facing south and three facing east.[g] The Sea rested on top of them, and their hindquarters were toward the center. **5**It was a handbreadth[z] in thickness, and its rim was like the rim of a cup, like a lily blossom. It held three thousand baths.[a]

6He then made ten basins[h] for washing and placed five on the south side and five on the north. In them the things to be used for the burnt offerings[i] were rinsed, but the Sea was to be used by the priests for washing.

7He made ten gold lampstands[j] according to the specifications[k] for them and placed them in the temple, five on the south side and five on the north.

8He made ten tables[l] and placed them in the temple, five on the south side and five on the north. He also made a hundred gold sprinkling bowls.[m]

3:15 [a]1Ki 7:15; Rev 3:12 [b]1Ki 7:22
3:16 [c]1Ki 7:17 [d]1Ki 7:20
4:1 [e]Ex 20:24; 27:1-2; 40:6; 1Ki 8:64; 2Ki 16:14
4:2 [f]Rev 4:6; 15:2
4:4 [g]Nu 2:3-25; Eze 48:30-34; Rev 21:13
4:6 [h]Ex 30:18 [i]Ne 13:5,9; Eze 40:38
4:7 [j]Ex 25:31 [k]Ex 25:40
4:8 [l]Ex 25:23 [m]Nu 4:14
4:9 [n]1Ki 6:36; 2Ki 21:5; 2Ch 33:5
4:11 [o]1Ki 7:14
4:14 [p]1Ki 7:27-30
4:16 [q]1Ki 7:13
4:17 [r]Ge 33:17
4:18 [s]1Ki 7:23

9He made the courtyard[n] of the priests, and the large court and the doors for the court, and overlaid the doors with bronze. **10**He placed the Sea on the south side, at the southeast corner.

11He also made the pots and shovels and sprinkling bowls.

So Huram finished[o] the work he had undertaken for King Solomon in the temple of God:

12the two pillars;
the two bowl-shaped capitals on top of the pillars;
the two sets of network decorating the two bowl-shaped capitals on top of the pillars;
13the four hundred pomegranates for the two sets of network (two rows of pomegranates for each network, decorating the bowl-shaped capitals on top of the pillars);
14the stands[p] with their basins;
15the Sea and the twelve bulls under it;
16the pots, shovels, meat forks and all related articles.

All the objects that Huram-Abi[q] made for King Solomon for the temple of the LORD were of polished bronze. **17**The king had them cast in clay molds in the plain of the Jordan between Succoth[r] and Zarethan.[b] **18**All these things that Solomon made amounted to so much that the weight of the bronze[s] was not determined.

19Solomon also made all the furnishings that were in God's temple:

the golden altar;

[r]*15* That is, about 52 feet (about 16 meters) [s]*16* Or possibly *made chains in the inner sanctuary*; the meaning of the Hebrew for this phrase is uncertain. [t]*17 Jakin* probably means *he establishes.* [u]*17 Boaz* probably means *in him is strength.* [v]*1* That is, about 30 feet (about 9 meters) long and wide, and about 15 feet (about 4.5 meters) high [w]*2* That is, about 7 1/2 feet (about 2.3 meters) [x]*2* That is, about 45 feet (about 13.5 meters) [y]*3* That is, about 1 1/2 feet (about 0.5 meter) [z]*5* That is, about 3 inches (about 8 centimeters) [a]*5* That is, about 17,500 gallons (about 66 kiloliters) [b]*17* Hebrew *Zeredatha,* a variant of *Zarethan*

the tables[a] on which was the
bread of the Presence;
20the lampstands[b] of pure gold
with their lamps, to burn in
front of the inner sanctuary
as prescribed;
21the gold floral work and lamps
and tongs (they were solid
gold);
22the pure gold wick trimmers,
sprinkling bowls, dishes[c]
and censers;[d] and the gold
doors of the temple: the inner doors to the Most Holy
Place and the doors of the
main hall.

5 When all the work Solomon
had done for the temple of the
LORD was finished,[e] he brought in
the things his father David had
dedicated[f]—the silver and gold
and all the furnishings—and he
placed them in the treasuries of
God's temple.

The Ark Brought to the Temple

5:2–6:11pp — 1Ki 8:1-21

2Then Solomon summoned to
Jerusalem the elders of Israel, all
the heads of the tribes and the
chiefs of the Israelite families, to
bring up the ark[g] of the LORD's covenant from Zion, the City of David.
3And all the men of Israel[h] came
together to the king at the time of
the festival in the seventh month.
4When all the elders of Israel had
arrived, the Levites took up the ark,
5and they brought up the ark and
the Tent of Meeting and all the sacred furnishings in it. The priests,
who were Levites,[i] carried them
up; 6and King Solomon and the entire assembly of Israel that had
gathered about him were before
the ark, sacrificing so many sheep
and cattle that they could not be
recorded or counted.
7The priests then brought the
ark[j] of the LORD's covenant to its
place in the inner sanctuary of the
temple, the Most Holy Place, and
put it beneath the wings of the
cherubim. 8The cherubim[k] spread
their wings over the place of the ark
and covered the ark and its carrying
poles. 9These poles were so long
that their ends, extending from the
ark, could be seen from in front of
the inner sanctuary, but not from
outside the Holy Place; and they
are still there today. 10There was
nothing in the ark except[l] the two
tablets[m] that Moses had placed in
it at Horeb, where the LORD made a
covenant with the Israelites after
they came out of Egypt.
11The priests then withdrew
from the Holy Place. All the priests
who were there had consecrated
themselves, regardless of their divisions.[n] 12All the Levites who were
musicians[o]—Asaph, Heman, Jeduthun and their sons and relatives—stood on the east side of the
altar, dressed in fine linen and
playing cymbals, harps and lyres.
They were accompanied by 120
priests sounding trumpets.[p] 13The
trumpeters and singers joined in
unison, as with one voice, to give
praise and thanks to the LORD. Accompanied by trumpets, cymbals
and other instruments, they raised
their voices in praise to the LORD
and sang:

"He is good;
his love endures forever."[q]

Then the temple of the LORD was
filled with a cloud, 14and the
priests could not perform[r] their
service because of the cloud,[s] for
the glory[t] of the LORD filled the
temple of God.

6 Then Solomon said, "The LORD
has said that he would dwell in
a dark cloud;[u] 2I have built a magnificent temple for you, a place for
you to dwell forever.[v]"
3While the whole assembly of Israel was standing there, the king
turned around and blessed them.
4Then he said:

"Praise be to the LORD, the
God of Israel, who with his
hands has fulfilled what he
promised with his mouth to
my father David. For he said,
5'Since the day I brought my
people out of Egypt, I have not
chosen a city in any tribe of Is-

4:19 [a]Ex 25:23,30
4:20 [b]Ex 25:31
4:22 [c]Nu 7:14 [d]Lev 10:1
5:1 [e]1Ki 6:14 [f]2Sa 8:11
5:2 [g]Nu 3:31; 2Sa 6:12; 1Ch 15:25
5:3 [h]1Ch 9:1; 2Ch 7:8-10
5:5 [i]Nu 3:31; 1Ch 15:2
5:7 [j]Rev 11:19
5:8 [k]Ge 3:24
5:10 [l]Heb 9:4 [m]Ex 16:34; Dt 10:2
5:11 [n]1Ch 24:1
5:12 [o]1Ki 10:12; 1Ch 25:1; Ps 68:25 [p]1Ch 13:8; 15:24
5:13 [q]1Ch 16:34, 41; 2Ch 7:3; 20:21; Ezr 3:11; Ps 100:5; 136:1; Jer 33:11
5:14 [r]Ex 40:35; Rev 15:8 [s]Ex 19:16 [t]Ex 29:43; 2Ch 7:2
6:1 [u]Ex 19:9; 1Ki 8:12-50
6:2 [v]Ezr 6:12; 7:15; Ps 135:21

rael to have a temple built for
my Name to be there, nor have
I chosen anyone to be the
leader over my people Israel.
6But now I have chosen Jerusalem[a] for my Name[b] to be
there, and I have chosen David[c] to rule my people Israel.'
7"My father David had it in
his heart[d] to build a temple
for the Name of the LORD, the
God of Israel. 8But the LORD
said to my father David, 'Because it was in your heart to
build a temple for my Name,
you did well to have this in
your heart. 9Nevertheless, you
are not the one to build the
temple, but your son, who is
your own flesh and blood—he
is the one who will build the
temple for my Name.'
10"The LORD has kept the
promise he made. I have succeeded David my father and
now I sit on the throne of Israel, just as the LORD promised,
and I have built the temple for
the Name of the LORD, the God
of Israel. 11There I have placed
the ark, in which is the covenant[e] of the LORD that he
made with the people of Israel."

Solomon's Prayer of Dedication

6:12–40pp — 1Ki 8:22–53
6:41–42pp — Ps 132:8–10

12Then Solomon stood before
the altar of the LORD in front of the
whole assembly of Israel and
spread out his hands. 13Now he
had made a bronze platform,[f] five
cubits[c] long, five cubits wide and
three cubits[d] high, and had placed
it in the center of the outer court.
He stood on the platform and then
knelt down[g] before the whole assembly of Israel and spread out his
hands toward heaven. 14He said:

"O LORD, God of Israel, there
is no God like you[h] in heaven
or on earth—you who keep
your covenant of love[i] with
your servants who continue
wholeheartedly in your way.

6:6 [a]Dt 12:5; Isa 14:1 [b]Ex 20:24; 2Ch 12:13 [c]1Ch 28:4
6:7 [d]1Sa 10:7; 1Ch 17:2; 28:2; Ac 7:46
6:11 [e]Dt 10:2; 2Ch 5:10; Ps 25:10; 50:5
6:13 [f]Ne 8:4 [g]Ps 95:6
6:14 [h]Ex 8:10; 15:11 [i]Dt 7:9
6:15 [j]1Ch 22:10
6:16 [k]2Sa 7:13,15; 1Ki 2:4; 2Ch 7:18; 23:3 [l]Ps 132:12
6:18 [m]Rev 21:3 [n]2Ch 2:6; Ps 11:4; Isa 40:22; 66:1; Ac 7:49
6:20 [o]Ex 3:16; Ps 34:15 [p]Dt 12:11 [q]2Ch 7:14; 30:20
6:21 [r]Ps 51:1; Isa 33:24; 40:2; 43:25; 44:22; 55:7; Mic 7:18
6:22 [s]Ex 22:11
6:23 [t]Isa 3:11; 65:6; Mt 16:27

15You have kept your promise
to your servant David my father; with your mouth you
have promised[j] and with your
hand you have fulfilled it—as
it is today.
16"Now LORD, God of Israel,
keep for your servant David my
father the promises you made
to him when you said, 'You
shall never fail[k] to have a man
to sit before me on the throne
of Israel, if only your sons are
careful in all they do to walk
before me according to my
law,[l] as you have done.'
17And now, O LORD, God of Israel, let your word that you
promised your servant David
come true.
18"But will God really
dwell[m] on earth with men?
The heavens,[n] even the highest heavens, cannot contain
you. How much less this temple I have built! 19Yet give attention to your servant's
prayer and his plea for mercy,
O LORD my God. Hear the cry
and the prayer that your servant is praying in your presence. 20May your eyes[o] be
open toward this temple day
and night, this place of which
you said you would put your
Name[p] there. May you hear[q]
the prayer your servant prays
toward this place. 21Hear the
supplications of your servant
and of your people Israel when
they pray toward this place.
Hear from heaven, your dwelling place; and when you hear,
forgive.[r]
22"When a man wrongs his
neighbor and is required to
take an oath[s] and he comes
and swears the oath before
your altar in this temple,
23then hear from heaven and
act. Judge between your servants, repaying[t] the guilty by
bringing down on his own

[c]*13* That is, about 7 1/2 feet (about 2.3 meters) [d]*13* That is, about 4 1/2 feet (about 1.3 meters)

head what he has done. Declare the innocent not guilty
and so establish his innocence.
24"When your people Israel
have been defeated[a] by an enemy because they have sinned
against you and when they
turn back and confess your
name, praying and making
supplication before you in this
temple, **25**then hear from
heaven and forgive the sin of
your people Israel and bring
them back to the land you
gave to them and their fathers.
26"When the heavens are
shut up and there is no rain[b]
because your people have
sinned against you, and when
they pray toward this place
and confess your name and
turn from their sin because
you have afflicted them,
27then hear from heaven and
forgive[c] the sin of your servants, your people Israel.
Teach them the right way to
live, and send rain on the land
you gave your people for an inheritance.
28"When famine[d] or plague
comes to the land, or blight or
mildew, locusts or grasshoppers, or when enemies besiege
them in any of their cities,
whatever disaster or disease
may come, **29**and when a
prayer or plea is made by any
of your people Israel—each
one aware of his afflictions
and pains, and spreading out
his hands toward this temple— **30**then hear from heav-
en, your dwelling place. Forgive,[e] and deal with each man
according to all he does, since
you know his heart (for you
alone know the hearts of
men),[f] **31**so that they will fear
you[g] and walk in your ways all
the time they live in the land
you gave our fathers.
32"As for the foreigner who
does not belong to your people
Israel but has come[h] from a
distant land because of your
great name and your mighty
hand[i] and your outstretched
arm—when he comes and
prays toward this temple,
33then hear from heaven, your
dwelling place, and do whatever the foreigner[j] asks of
you, so that all the peoples of
the earth may know your name
and fear you, as do your own
people Israel, and may know
that this house I have built
bears your Name.
34"When your people go to
war against their enemies,[k]
wherever you send them, and
when they pray[l] to you toward this city you have chosen
and the temple I have built
for your Name, **35**then hear
from heaven their prayer and
their plea, and uphold their
cause.
36"When they sin against
you—for there is no one who
does not sin[m]—and you become angry with them and
give them over to the enemy,
who takes them captive[n] to a
land far away or near; **37**and if
they have a change of heart[o]
in the land where they are held
captive, and repent and plead
with you in the land of their
captivity and say, 'We have
sinned, we have done wrong
and acted wickedly'; **38**and if
they turn back to you with all
their heart and soul in the land
of their captivity where they
were taken, and pray toward
the land you gave their fathers,
toward the city you have chosen and toward the temple I
have built for your Name;
39then from heaven, your
dwelling place, hear their
prayer and their pleas, and uphold their cause. And forgive
your people, who have sinned
against you.
40"Now, my God, may your
eyes be open and your ears attentive[p] to the prayers offered
in this place.
41"Now arise,[q] O LORD God,

6:24 [a] Lev 26:17
6:26 [b] Lev 26:19; Dt 11:17; 28:24; 2Sa 1:21; 1Ki 17:1
6:27 [c] ver 30,39; 2Ch 7:14
6:28 [d] 2Ch 20:9
6:30 [e] ver 27 [f] 1Sa 16:7; 1Ch 28:9; Ps 7:9; 44:21; Pr 16:2; 17:3
6:31 [g] Ps 103:11, 13; Pr 8:13
6:32 [h] 2Ch 9:6; Jn 12:20; Ac 8:27 [i] Ex 3:19,20
6:33 [j] 2Ch 7:14
6:34 [k] Dt 28:7 [l] 1Ch 5:20
6:36 [m] Job 15:14; Ps 143:2; Ecc 7:20; Jer 17:9; Jas 3:1; 1Jn 1:8-10 [n] Lev 26:44
6:37 [o] 2Ch 7:14; 33:12,19,23; Jer 29:13
6:40 [p] 2Ch 7:15; Ne 1:6,11; Ps 17:1,6
6:41 [q] Isa 33:10

and come to your
resting place,[a]
you and the ark of your
might.
May your priests,[b] O LORD
God, be clothed
with salvation,
may your saints rejoice
in your goodness.[c]
42O LORD God, do not reject
your anointed one.
Remember the great
love[d] promised to
David your servant."

The Dedication of the Temple

7:1–10pp — 1Ki 8:62–66

7 When Solomon finished praying, fire[e] came down from
heaven and consumed the burnt
offering and the sacrifices, and the
glory of the LORD filled[f] the temple.[g] 2The priests could not enter[h] the temple of the LORD because the glory[i] of the LORD filled
it. 3When all the Israelites saw the
fire coming down and the glory of
the LORD above the temple, they
knelt on the pavement with their
faces to the ground, and they worshiped and gave thanks to the
LORD, saying,

"He is good;
his love endures forever."[j]

4Then the king and all the people
offered sacrifices before the LORD.
5And King Solomon offered a sacrifice of twenty-two thousand head
of cattle and a hundred and twenty
thousand sheep and goats. So the
king and all the people dedicated
the temple of God. 6The priests
took their positions, as did the Levites[k] with the LORD's musical instruments,[l] which King David had
made for praising the LORD and
which were used when he gave
thanks, saying, "His love endures
forever." Opposite the Levites, the
priests blew their trumpets, and all
the Israelites were standing.
7Solomon consecrated the middle part of the courtyard in front of
the temple of the LORD, and there
he offered burnt offerings and the
fat of the fellowship offerings,[e] because the bronze altar he had made
could not hold the burnt offerings,
the grain offerings and the fat portions.
8So Solomon observed the festival[m] at that time for seven days,
and all Israel with him—a vast assembly, people from Lebo[f] Hamath to the Wadi of Egypt.[n] 9On
the eighth day they held an assembly, for they had celebrated the
dedication of the altar for seven
days and the festival[o] for seven
days more. 10On the twenty-third
day of the seventh month he sent
the people to their homes, joyful
and glad in heart for the good
things the LORD had done for David
and Solomon and for his people Israel.

The LORD Appears to Solomon

7:11–22pp — 1Ki 9:1–9

11When Solomon had finished
the temple of the LORD and the royal palace, and had succeeded in
carrying out all he had in mind to
do in the temple of the LORD and in
his own palace, 12the LORD appeared to him at night and said:

"I have heard your prayer
and have chosen this place for
myself[p] as a temple for sacrifices.
13"When I shut up the heavens so that there is no rain,[q]
or command locusts to devour
the land or send a plague
among my people, 14if my people, who are called by my
name, will humble[r] themselves and pray and seek my
face[s] and turn[t] from their
wicked ways, then will I hear
from heaven and will forgive[u]
their sin and will heal[v] their
land. 15Now my eyes will be
open and my ears attentive to
the prayers offered in this
place.[w] 16I have chosen[x] and
consecrated this temple so
that my Name may be there

6:41 [a] 1Ch 28:2 [b] Ps 132:16 [c] Ps 116:12
6:42 [d] Ps 89:24,28; Isa 55:3
7:1 [e] Lev 9:24; 1Ki 18:38 [f] Ex 16:10 [g] Ps 26:8
7:2 [h] 1Ki 8:11 [i] Ex 29:43; 40:35; 2Ch 5:14
7:3 [j] 1Ch 16:34; 2Ch 5:13; 20:21
7:6 [k] 1Ch 15:16 [l] 2Ch 5:12
7:8 [m] 2Ch 30:26 [n] Ge 15:18
7:9 [o] Lev 23:36
7:12 [p] Dt 12:5
7:13 [q] 2Ch 6:26-28; Am 4:7
7:14 [r] Lev 26:41; 2Ch 6:37; Jas 4:10 [s] 1Ch 16:11 [t] Isa 55:7; Zec 1:4 [u] 2Ch 6:27 [v] 2Ch 30:20; Isa 30:26; 57:18
7:15 [w] 2Ch 6:40
7:16 [x] ver 12; 2Ch 6:6

[e] 7 Traditionally *peace offerings* [f] 8 Or *from the entrance to*

forever. My eyes and my heart will always be there.

17"As for you, if you walk before me[a] as David your father did, and do all I command, and observe my decrees and laws, **18**I will establish your royal throne, as I covenanted with David your father when I said, 'You shall never fail to have a man[b] to rule over Israel.'[c]

19"But if you[g] turn away[d] and forsake[e] the decrees and commands I have given you[g] and go off to serve other gods and worship them, **20**then I will uproot[f] Israel from my land,[g] which I have given them, and will reject this temple I have consecrated for my Name. I will make it a byword and an object of ridicule[h] among all peoples. **21**And though this temple is now so imposing, all who pass by will be appalled and say,[i] 'Why has the LORD done such a thing to this land and to this temple?' **22**People will answer, 'Because they have forsaken the LORD, the God of their fathers, who brought them out of Egypt, and have embraced other gods, worshiping and serving them—that is why he brought all this disaster on them.'"

Solomon's Other Activities

8:1-18pp — 1Ki 9:10-28

8 At the end of twenty years, during which Solomon built the temple of the LORD and his own palace, **2**Solomon rebuilt the villages that Hiram[h] had given him, and settled Israelites in them. **3**Solomon then went to Hamath Zobah and captured it. **4**He also built up Tadmor in the desert and all the store cities he had built in Hamath. **5**He rebuilt Upper Beth Horon[j] and Lower Beth Horon as fortified cities, with walls and with gates and bars, **6**as well as Baalath and all his store cities, and all the cities for his chariots and for his horses[i]—whatever he desired to build in Jerusalem, in Lebanon and throughout all the territory he ruled.

7All the people left from the Hittites, Amorites, Perizzites, Hivites and Jebusites[k] (these peoples were not Israelites), **8**that is, their descendants remaining in the land, whom the Israelites had not destroyed—these Solomon conscripted[l] for his slave labor force, as it is to this day. **9**But Solomon did not make slaves of the Israelites for his work; they were his fighting men, commanders of his captains, and commanders of his chariots and charioteers. **10**They were also King Solomon's chief officials—two hundred and fifty officials supervising the men.

11Solomon brought Pharaoh's daughter[m] up from the City of David to the palace he had built for her, for he said, "My wife must not live in the palace of David king of Israel, because the places the ark of the LORD has entered are holy."

12On the altar[n] of the LORD that he had built in front of the portico, Solomon sacrificed burnt offerings to the LORD, **13**according to the daily requirement[o] for offerings commanded by Moses for Sabbaths,[p] New Moons and the three[q] annual feasts—the Feast of Unleavened Bread, the Feast of Weeks[r] and the Feast of Tabernacles. **14**In keeping with the ordinance of his father David, he appointed the divisions[s] of the priests for their duties, and the Levites[t] to lead the praise and to assist the priests according to each day's requirement. He also appointed the gatekeepers[u] by divisions for the various gates, because this was what David the man of God[v] had ordered.[w] **15**They did not deviate from the king's commands to the priests or to the Levites in any matter, including that of the treasuries.

7:17 [a]1Ki 9:4
7:18 [b]2Ch 6:16 [c]2Sa 7:13; 2Ch 13:5
7:19 [d]Dt 28:15 [e]Lev 26:14,33
7:20 [f]Dt 29:28 [g]1Ki 14:15 [h]Dt 28:37
7:21 [i]Dt 29:24
8:5 [j]1Ch 7:24; 2Ch 14:7
8:7 [k]Ge 10:16
8:8 [l]1Ki 4:6; 9:21
8:11 [m]1Ki 3:1; 7:8
8:12 [n]1Ki 8:64; 2Ch 4:1; 15:8
8:13 [o]Ex 29:38; Nu 28:3 [p]Nu 28:9 [q]Ex 23:14; Dt 16:16 [r]Ex 23:16
8:14 [s]1Ch 24:1 [t]1Ch 25:1 [u]1Ch 9:17; 26:1 [v]Ne 12:24,36 [w]1Ch 23:6; Ne 12:45

[g]*19* The Hebrew is plural. [h]*2* Hebrew *Huram,* a variant of *Hiram;* also in verse 18
[i]*6* Or *charioteers*

16 All Solomon's work was carried out, from the day the foundation of the temple of the LORD was laid until its completion. So the temple of the LORD was finished.

17 Then Solomon went to Ezion Geber and Elath on the coast of Edom. 18 And Hiram sent him ships commanded by his own officers, men who knew the sea. These, with Solomon's men, sailed to Ophir and brought back four hundred and fifty talents[i] of gold,[a] which they delivered to King Solomon.

The Queen of Sheba Visits Solomon

9:1–12pp — 1Ki 10:1–13

9 When the queen of Sheba[b] heard of Solomon's fame, she came to Jerusalem to test him with hard questions. Arriving with a very great caravan—with camels carrying spices, large quantities of gold, and precious stones—she came to Solomon and talked with him about all she had on her mind. 2 Solomon answered all her questions; nothing was too hard for him to explain to her. 3 When the queen of Sheba saw the wisdom of Solomon,[c] as well as the palace he had built, 4 the food on his table, the seating of his officials, the attending servants in their robes, the cupbearers in their robes and the burnt offerings he made at[k] the temple of the LORD, she was overwhelmed.

5 She said to the king, "The report I heard in my own country about your achievements and your wisdom is true. 6 But I did not believe what they said until I came[d] and saw with my own eyes. Indeed, not even half the greatness of your wisdom was told me; you have far exceeded the report I heard. 7 How happy your men must be! How happy your officials, who continually stand before you and hear your wisdom! 8 Praise be to the LORD your God, who has delighted in you and placed you on his throne[e] as king to rule for the LORD your God. Because of the love of your God for Israel and his desire to uphold them forever, he has made you king[f] over them, to maintain justice and righteousness."

9 Then she gave the king 120 talents[l] of gold,[g] large quantities of spices, and precious stones. There had never been such spices as those the queen of Sheba gave to King Solomon.

10 (The men of Hiram and the men of Solomon brought gold from Ophir;[h] they also brought algumwood[m] and precious stones. 11 The king used the algumwood to make steps for the temple of the LORD and for the royal palace, and to make harps and lyres for the musicians. Nothing like them had ever been seen in Judah.)

12 King Solomon gave the queen of Sheba all she desired and asked for; he gave her more than she had brought to him. Then she left and returned with her retinue to her own country.

Solomon's Splendor

9:13–28pp — 1Ki 10:14–29; 2Ch 1:14–17

13 The weight of the gold that Solomon received yearly was 666 talents,[n] 14 not including the revenues brought in by merchants and traders. Also all the kings of Arabia[i] and the governors of the land brought gold and silver to Solomon.

15 King Solomon made two hundred large shields of hammered gold; six hundred bekas[o] of hammered gold went into each shield. 16 He also made three hundred small shields[j] of hammered gold, with three hundred bekas[p] of gold in each shield. The king put them in the Palace of the Forest of Lebanon.[k]

17 Then the king made a great throne inlaid with ivory[l] and overlaid with pure gold. 18 The throne

8:18 [a]2Ch 9:9
9:1 [b]Ge 10:7; Eze 23:42; Mt 12:42; Lk 11:31
9:3 [c]1Ki 5:12
9:6 [d]2Ch 6:32
9:8 [e]1Ki 2:12; 1Ch 17:14; 28:5; 29:23; 2Ch 13:8 [f]2Ch 2:11
9:9 [g]2Ch 8:18
9:10 [h]2Ch 8:18
9:14 [i]2Ch 17:11; Isa 21:13; Jer 25:24; Eze 27:21; 30:5
9:16 [j]2Ch 12:9 [k]1Ki 7:2
9:17 [l]1Ki 22:39

[i]*18* That is, about 17 tons (about 16 metric tons) [k]*4* Or *the ascent by which he went up to* [l]*9* That is, about 4 1/2 tons (about 4 metric tons) [m]*10* Probably a variant of *almugwood* [n]*13* That is, about 25 tons (about 23 metric tons) [o]*15* That is, about 7 1/2 pounds (about 3.5 kilograms) [p]*16* That is, about 3 3/4 pounds (about 1.7 kilograms)

had six steps, and a footstool of gold was attached to it. On both sides of the seat were armrests, with a lion standing beside each of them. **19**Twelve lions stood on the six steps, one at either end of each step. Nothing like it had ever been made for any other kingdom. **20**All King Solomon's goblets were gold, and all the household articles in the Palace of the Forest of Lebanon were pure gold. Nothing was made of silver, because silver was considered of little value in Solomon's day. **21**The king had a fleet of trading ships[q] manned by Hiram's[r] men. Once every three years it returned, carrying gold, silver and ivory, and apes and baboons.

22King Solomon was greater in riches and wisdom than all the other kings of the earth.[a] **23**All the kings[b] of the earth sought audience with Solomon to hear the wisdom God had put in his heart. **24**Year after year, everyone who came brought a gift[c]—articles of silver and gold, and robes, weapons and spices, and horses and mules.

25Solomon had four thousand stalls for horses and chariots,[d] and twelve thousand horses,[s] which he kept in the chariot cities and also with him in Jerusalem. **26**He ruled[e] over all the kings from the River[t][f] to the land of the Philistines, as far as the border of Egypt.[g] **27**The king made silver as common in Jerusalem as stones, and cedar as plentiful as sycamore-fig trees in the foothills. **28**Solomon's horses were imported from Egypt[u] and from all other countries.

Solomon's Death

9:29–31pp — 1Ki 11:41–43

29As for the other events of Solomon's reign, from beginning to end, are they not written in the records of Nathan[h] the prophet, in the prophecy of Ahijah[i] the Shilonite and in the visions of Iddo the seer concerning Jeroboam[j] son of Nebat? **30**Solomon reigned in Jerusalem over all Israel forty years. **31**Then he rested with his fathers and was buried in the city of David[k] his father. And Rehoboam his son succeeded him as king.

Israel Rebels Against Rehoboam

10:1–11:4pp — 1Ki 12:1–24

10 Rehoboam went to Shechem, for all the Israelites had gone there to make him king. **2**When Jeroboam[l] son of Nebat heard this (he was in Egypt, where he had fled[m] from King Solomon), he returned from Egypt. **3**So they sent for Jeroboam, and he and all Israel[n] went to Rehoboam and said to him: **4**"Your father put a heavy yoke on us,[o] but now lighten the harsh labor and the heavy yoke he put on us, and we will serve you."

5Rehoboam answered, "Come back to me in three days." So the people went away.

6Then King Rehoboam consulted the elders[p] who had served his father Solomon during his lifetime. "How would you advise me to answer these people?" he asked.

7They replied, "If you will be kind to these people and please them and give them a favorable answer,[q] they will always be your servants."

8But Rehoboam rejected[r] the advice the elders[s] gave him and consulted the young men who had grown up with him and were serving him. **9**He asked them, "What is your advice? How should we answer these people who say to me, 'Lighten the yoke your father put on us'?"

10The young men who had grown up with him replied, "Tell the people who have said to you, 'Your father put a heavy yoke on us, but make our yoke lighter'—tell them, 'My little finger is thicker than my father's waist. **11**My father laid on you a heavy yoke; I will make it

9:22 [a]1Ki 3:13; 2Ch 1:12
9:23 [b]1Ki 4:34
9:24 [c]2Ch 32:23; Ps 45:12; 68:29; 72:10; Isa 18:7
9:25 [d]1Sa 8:11; 1Ki 4:26
9:26 [e]1Ki 4:21 [f]Ps 72:8-9 [g]Ge 15:18-21
9:29 [h]2Sa 7:2; 1Ch 29:29 [i]1Ki 11:29 [j]2Ch 10:2
9:31 [k]1Ki 2:10
10:2 [l]2Ch 9:29 [m]1Ki 11:40
10:3 [n]1Ch 9:1
10:4 [o]2Ch 2:2
10:6 [p]Job 8:8-9; 12:12; 15:10; 32:7
10:7 [q]Pr 15:1
10:8 [r]2Sa 17:14 [s]Pr 13:20

[q]*21* Hebrew *of ships that could go to Tarshish*
[r]*21* Hebrew *Huram,* a variant of *Hiram*
[s]*25* Or *charioteers*
[t]*26* That is, the Euphrates
[u]*28* Or possibly *Muzur,* a region in Cilicia

even heavier. My father scourged you with whips; I will scourge you with scorpions.' "

12Three days later Jeroboam and all the people returned to Rehoboam, as the king had said, "Come back to me in three days." 13The king answered them harshly. Rejecting the advice of the elders, 14he followed the advice of the young men and said, "My father made your yoke heavy; I will make it even heavier. My father scourged you with whips; I will scourge you with scorpions." 15So the king did not listen to the people, for this turn of events was from God,[a] to fulfill the word the LORD had spoken to Jeroboam son of Nebat through Ahijah the Shilonite.[b]

16When all Israel[c] saw that the king refused to listen to them, they answered the king:

"What share do we have in
David,[d]
what part in Jesse's son?
To your tents, O Israel!
Look after your own house,
O David!"

So all the Israelites went home. 17But as for the Israelites who were living in the towns of Judah, Rehoboam still ruled over them.

18King Rehoboam sent out Adoniram,[v][e] who was in charge of forced labor, but the Israelites stoned him to death. King Rehoboam, however, managed to get into his chariot and escape to Jerusalem. 19So Israel has been in rebellion against the house of David to this day.

11 When Rehoboam arrived in Jerusalem,[f] he mustered the house of Judah and Benjamin—a hundred and eighty thousand fighting men—to make war against Israel and to regain the kingdom for Rehoboam.

2But this word of the LORD came to Shemaiah[g] the man of God: 3"Say to Rehoboam son of Solomon king of Judah and to all the Israelites in Judah and Benjamin, 4'This is what the LORD says: Do not go up to fight against your brothers.[h] Go home, every one of you, for this is my doing.' " So they obeyed the words of the LORD and turned back from marching against Jeroboam.

Rehoboam Fortifies Judah

5Rehoboam lived in Jerusalem and built up towns for defense in Judah: 6Bethlehem, Etam, Tekoa, 7Beth Zur, Soco, Adullam, 8Gath, Mareshah, Ziph, 9Adoraim, Lachish, Azekah, 10Zorah, Aijalon and Hebron. These were fortified cities in Judah and Benjamin. 11He strengthened their defenses and put commanders in them, with supplies of food, olive oil and wine. 12He put shields and spears in all the cities, and made them very strong. So Judah and Benjamin were his.

13The priests and Levites from all their districts throughout Israel sided with him. 14The Levites[i] even abandoned their pasturelands and property,[j] and came to Judah and Jerusalem because Jeroboam and his sons had rejected them as priests of the LORD. 15And he appointed[k] his own priests[l] for the high places and for the goat[m] and calf[n] idols he had made. 16Those from every tribe of Israel[o] who set their hearts on seeking the LORD, the God of Israel, followed the Levites to Jerusalem to offer sacrifices to the LORD, the God of their fathers. 17They strengthened[p] the kingdom of Judah and supported Rehoboam son of Solomon three years, walking in the ways of David and Solomon during this time.

Rehoboam's Family

18Rehoboam married Mahalath, who was the daughter of David's son Jerimoth and of Abihail, the daughter of Jesse's son Eliab. 19She bore him sons: Jeush, Shemariah and Zaham. 20Then he married Maacah[q] daughter of Absalom, who bore him Abijah,[r] Attai, Ziza and Shelomith. 21Rehoboam loved Maacah daughter of Absalom

10:15 [a]2Ch 11:4; 25:16-20 [b]1Ki 11:29
10:16 [c]1Ch 9:1 [d]ver 19; 2Sa 20:1
10:18 [e]1Ki 5:14
11:1 [f]1Ki 12:21
11:2 [g]2Ch 12:5-7, 15
11:4 [h]2Ch 28:8-11
11:14 [i]Nu 35:2-5 [j]2Ch 13:9
11:15 [k]1Ki 13:33 [l]1Ki 12:31 [m]Lev 17:7 [n]1Ki 12:28; 2Ch 13:8
11:16 [o]2Ch 15:9
11:17 [p]2Ch 12:1
11:20 [q]1Ki 15:2 [r]2Ch 13:2

[v]18 Hebrew *Hadoram,* a variant of *Adoniram*

more than any of his other wives and concubines. In all, he had eighteen wives[a] and sixty concubines, twenty-eight sons and sixty daughters.

22 Rehoboam appointed Abijah[b] son of Maacah to be the chief prince among his brothers, in order to make him king. 23 He acted wisely, dispersing some of his sons throughout the districts of Judah and Benjamin, and to all the fortified cities. He gave them abundant provisions and took many wives for them.

Shishak Attacks Jerusalem

12:9–16pp — 1Ki 14:21, 25–31

12 After Rehoboam's position as king was established[c] and he had become strong,[d] he and all Israel[w] with him abandoned the law of the LORD. 2 Because they had been unfaithful[e] to the LORD, Shishak[f] king of Egypt attacked Jerusalem in the fifth year of King Rehoboam. 3 With twelve hundred chariots and sixty thousand horsemen and the innumerable troops of Libyans, Sukkites and Cushites[x][g] that came with him from Egypt, 4 he captured the fortified cities[h] of Judah and came as far as Jerusalem.

5 Then the prophet Shemaiah[i] came to Rehoboam and to the leaders of Judah who had assembled in Jerusalem for fear of Shishak, and he said to them, "This is what the LORD says, 'You have abandoned me; therefore, I now abandon[j] you to Shishak.' "

6 The leaders of Israel and the king humbled themselves and said, "The LORD is just."[k]

7 When the LORD saw that they humbled themselves, this word of the LORD came to Shemaiah: "Since they have humbled themselves, I will not destroy them but will soon give them deliverance.[l] My wrath will not be poured out on Jerusalem through Shishak. 8 They will, however, become subject[m] to him, so that they may learn the difference between serving me and serving the kings of other lands."

9 When Shishak king of Egypt attacked Jerusalem, he carried off the treasures of the temple of the LORD and the treasures of the royal palace. He took everything, including the gold shields[n] Solomon had made. 10 So King Rehoboam made bronze shields to replace them and assigned these to the commanders of the guard on duty at the entrance to the royal palace. 11 Whenever the king went to the LORD's temple, the guards went with him, bearing the shields, and afterward they returned them to the guardroom.

12 Because Rehoboam humbled himself, the LORD's anger turned from him, and he was not totally destroyed. Indeed, there was some good[o] in Judah.

13 King Rehoboam established himself firmly in Jerusalem and continued as king. He was forty-one years old when he became king, and he reigned seventeen years in Jerusalem, the city the LORD had chosen out of all the tribes of Israel in which to put his Name.[p] His mother's name was Naamah; she was an Ammonite. 14 He did evil because he had not set his heart on seeking the LORD.

15 As for the events of Rehoboam's reign, from beginning to end, are they not written in the records of Shemaiah[q] the prophet and of Iddo the seer that deal with genealogies? There was continual warfare between Rehoboam and Jeroboam. 16 Rehoboam rested with his fathers and was buried in the City of David. And Abijah[r] his son succeeded him as king.

Abijah King of Judah

13:1–2,22–14:1pp — 1Ki 15:1–2,6–8

13 In the eighteenth year of the reign of Jeroboam, Abijah became king of Judah, 2 and he

11:21 [a] Dt 17:17
11:22 [b] Dt 21:15-17
12:1 [c] ver 13 [d] 2Ch 11:17
12:2 [e] 1Ki 14:22-24 [f] 1Ki 11:40
12:3 [g] 2Ch 16:8; Na 3:9
12:4 [h] 2Ch 11:10
12:5 [i] 2Ch 11:2 [j] Dt 28:15; 2Ch 15:2
12:6 [k] Ex 9:27; Da 9:14
12:7 [l] 1Ki 21:29; Ps 78:38
12:8 [m] Dt 28:48
12:9 [n] 2Ch 9:16
12:12 [o] 1Ki 14:13; 2Ch 19:3
12:13 [p] Dt 12:5; 2Ch 6:6
12:15 [q] 2Ch 9:29; 11:2
12:16 [r] 2Ch 11:20

[w] *1* That is, Judah, as frequently in 2 Chronicles [x] *3* That is, people from the upper Nile region

reigned in Jerusalem three years.
His mother's name was Maacah,[y]
a daughter[z] of Uriel of Gibeah.
There was war between Abijah[a]
and Jeroboam.[b] **3**Abijah went into
battle with a force of four hundred
thousand able fighting men, and
Jeroboam drew up a battle line
against him with eight hundred
thousand able troops.
4Abijah stood on Mount Zemara-
im,[c] in the hill country of Ephraim, and said, "Jeroboam and all Israel,[d] listen to me! **5**Don't you
know that the LORD, the God of Israel, has given the kingship of Israel to David and his descendants
forever[e] by a covenant of salt?[f]
6Yet Jeroboam son of Nebat, an official of Solomon son of David, rebelled[g] against his master. **7**Some
worthless scoundrels[h] gathered
around him and opposed Rehoboam son of Solomon when he was
young and indecisive and not
strong enough to resist them.
8"And now you plan to resist the
kingdom of the LORD, which is in
the hands of David's descendants.
You are indeed a vast army and
have with you the golden calves[i]
that Jeroboam made to be your
gods. **9**But didn't you drive out the
priests of the LORD,[j] the sons of
Aaron, and the Levites, and make
priests of your own as the peoples
of other lands do? Whoever comes
to consecrate himself with a young
bull[k] and seven rams may become
a priest of what are not gods.[l]
10"As for us, the LORD is our God,
and we have not forsaken him. The
priests who serve the LORD are sons
of Aaron, and the Levites assist
them. **11**Every morning and evening[m] they present burnt offerings
and fragrant incense to the LORD.
They set out the bread on the ceremonially clean table[n] and light the
lamps on the gold lampstand every
evening. We are observing the requirements of the LORD our God.
But you have forsaken him. **12**God
is with us; he is our leader. His
priests with their trumpets will
sound the battle cry against you.[o]
Men of Israel, do not fight against
the LORD,[p] the God of your fathers,
for you will not succeed."
13Now Jeroboam had sent
troops around to the rear, so that
while he was in front of Judah the
ambush[q] was behind them. **14**Judah turned and saw that they were
being attacked at both front and
rear. Then they cried out[r] to the
LORD. The priests blew their trumpets **15**and the men of Judah raised
the battle cry. At the sound of their
battle cry, God routed Jeroboam
and all Israel[s] before Abijah and
Judah. **16**The Israelites fled before
Judah, and God delivered[t] them
into their hands. **17**Abijah and his
men inflicted heavy losses on
them, so that there were five hundred thousand casualties among
Israel's able men. **18**The men of Israel were subdued on that occasion, and the men of Judah were
victorious because they relied[u] on
the LORD, the God of their fathers.
19Abijah pursued Jeroboam and
took from him the towns of Bethel,
Jeshanah and Ephron, with their
surrounding villages. **20**Jeroboam
did not regain power during the
time of Abijah. And the LORD struck
him down and he died.
21But Abijah grew in strength.
He married fourteen wives and had
twenty-two sons and sixteen
daughters.
22The other events of Abijah's
reign, what he did and what he
said, are written in the annotations
of the prophet Iddo.

14 And Abijah rested with his
fathers and was buried in
the City of David. Asa his son succeeded him as king, and in his days
the country was at peace for ten
years.

Asa King of Judah

14:2–3pp — 1Ki 15:11–12

2Asa did what was good and right
in the eyes of the LORD his God. **3**He
removed the foreign altars and the
high places, smashed the sacred

13:2 [a]2Ch 11:20 [b]1Ki 15:6
13:4 [c]Jos 18:22 [d]1Ch 11:1
13:5 [e]2Sa 7:13 [f]Lev 2:13; Nu 18:19
13:6 [g]1Ki 11:26
13:7 [h]Jdg 9:4
13:8 [i]1Ki 12:28; 2Ch 11:15
13:9 [j]2Ch 11:14-15 [k]Ex 29:35-36 [l]Jer 2:11
13:11 [m]Ex 29:39; 2Ch 2:4 [n]Lev 24:5-9
13:12 [o]Nu 10:8-9 [p]Ac 5:39
13:13 [q]Jos 8:9
13:14 [r]2Ch 14:11
13:15 [s]2Ch 14:12
13:16 [t]2Ch 16:8
13:18 [u]1Ch 5:20; 2Ch 14:11; Ps 22:5

y2 Most Septuagint manuscripts and Syriac (see also 2 Chron. 11:20 and 1 Kings 15:2); Hebrew *Micaiah*   z2 Or *granddaughter*

stones and cut down the Asherah
poles.[a][a] 4He commanded Judah
to seek the LORD, the God of their
fathers, and to obey his laws and
commands. 5He removed the high
places and incense altars[b] in every
town in Judah, and the kingdom
was at peace under him. 6He built
up the fortified cities of Judah,
since the land was at peace. No one
was at war with him during those
years, for the LORD gave him rest.[c]
7"Let us build up these towns,"
he said to Judah, "and put walls
around them, with towers, gates
and bars. The land is still ours, because we have sought the LORD our
God; we sought him and he has giv-
en us rest on every side." So they
built and prospered.
8Asa had an army of three hundred thousand men from Judah,
equipped with large shields and
with spears, and two hundred and
eighty thousand from Benjamin,
armed with small shields and with
bows. All these were brave fighting
men.
9Zerah the Cushite[d] marched
out against them with a vast army[b]
and three hundred chariots, and
came as far as Mareshah.[e] 10Asa
went out to meet him, and they
took up battle positions in the Valley of Zephathah near Mareshah.
11Then Asa called[f] to the LORD
his God and said, "LORD, there is no
one like you to help the powerless
against the mighty. Help us, O LORD
our God, for we rely[g] on you, and
in your name[h] we have come
against this vast army. O LORD, you
are our God; do not let man prevail[i] against you."
12The LORD struck down[j] the
Cushites before Asa and Judah.
The Cushites fled, 13and Asa and
his army pursued them as far as Gerar.[k] Such a great number of Cushites fell that they could not recover;
they were crushed before the LORD
and his forces. The men of Judah
carried off a large amount of plunder. 14They destroyed all the villages around Gerar, for the terror[l]
of the LORD had fallen upon them.
They plundered all these villages,

14:3 [a]Ex 34:13; Dt 7:5; 1Ki 15:12-14
14:5 [b]2Ch 34:4,7
14:6 [c]1Ch 22:9; 2Ch 15:15
14:9 [d]2Ch 12:3; 16:8 [e]2Ch 11:8
14:11 [f]2Ch 13:14 [g]2Ch 13:18 [h]1Sa 17:45 [i]1Sa 14:6; Ps 9:19
14:12 [j]2Ch 13:15
14:13 [k]Ge 10:19
14:14 [l]Ge 35:5; 2Ch 17:10
15:1 [m]Nu 11:25, 26; 24:2; 2Ch 20:14; 24:20
15:2 [n]ver 4,15; 2Ch 20:17 [o]Jas 4:8 [p]Jer 29:13 [q]1Ch 28:9; 2Ch 24:20
15:3 [r]Lev 10:11 [s]2Ch 17:9; La 2:9
15:4 [t]Dt 4:29
15:5 [u]Jdg 5:6
15:6 [v]Mt 24:7
15:7 [w]Jos 1:7,9 [x]Ps 58:11
15:8 [y]2Ch 13:19 [z]2Ch 8:12
15:9 [a]2Ch 11:16-17

since there was much booty there.
15They also attacked the camps of
the herdsmen and carried off
droves of sheep and goats and camels. Then they returned to Jerusalem.

Asa's Reform

15:16–19pp — 1Ki 15:13–16

15 The Spirit of God came
upon[m] Azariah son of
Oded. 2He went out to meet Asa
and said to him, "Listen to me, Asa
and all Judah and Benjamin. The
LORD is with you[n] when you are
with him.[o] If you seek[p] him, he
will be found by you, but if you forsake him, he will forsake you.[q]
3For a long time Israel was without
the true God, without a priest to
teach[r] and without the law.[s] 4But
in their distress they turned to the
LORD, the God of Israel, and sought
him,[t] and he was found by them.
5In those days it was not safe to
travel about,[u] for all the inhabitants of the lands were in great turmoil. 6One nation was being
crushed by another and one city by
another,[v] because God was troubling them with every kind of distress. 7But as for you, be strong[w]
and do not give up, for your work
will be rewarded."[x]
8When Asa heard these words
and the prophecy of Azariah son
of[c] Oded the prophet, he took
courage. He removed the detestable idols from the whole land of
Judah and Benjamin and from the
towns he had captured[y] in the
hills of Ephraim. He repaired the
altar[z] of the LORD that was in front
of the portico of the LORD's temple.
9Then he assembled all Judah
and Benjamin and the people from
Ephraim, Manasseh and Simeon
who had settled among them, for
large numbers[a] had come over to

a3 That is, symbols of the goddess Asherah; here and elsewhere in 2 Chronicles
b9 Hebrew *with an army of a thousand thousands* or *with an army of thousands upon thousands*
c8 Vulgate and Syriac (see also Septuagint and verse 1); Hebrew does not have *Azariah son of.*

him from Israel when they saw that the LORD his God was with him.

10 They assembled at Jerusalem in the third month of the fifteenth year of Asa's reign. 11 At that time they sacrificed to the LORD seven hundred head of cattle and seven thousand sheep and goats from the plunder[a] they had brought back. 12 They entered into a covenant[b] to seek the LORD,[c] the God of their fathers, with all their heart and soul. 13 All who would not seek the LORD, the God of Israel, were to be put to death,[d] whether small or great, man or woman. 14 They took an oath to the LORD with loud acclamation, with shouting and with trumpets and horns. 15 All Judah rejoiced about the oath because they had sworn it wholeheartedly. They sought God[e] eagerly, and he was found by them. So the LORD gave them rest[f] on every side.

16 King Asa also deposed his grandmother Maacah from her position as queen mother, because she had made a repulsive Asherah pole.[g] Asa cut the pole down, broke it up and burned it in the Kidron Valley. 17 Although he did not remove the high places from Israel, Asa's heart was fully committed ⌞to the LORD⌟ all his life. 18 He brought into the temple of God the silver and gold and the articles that he and his father had dedicated.

19 There was no more war until the thirty-fifth year of Asa's reign.

Asa's Last Years

16:1–6pp — 1Ki 15:17–22
16:11–17:1pp — 1Ki 15:23–24

16 In the thirty-sixth year of Asa's reign Baasha[h] king of Israel went up against Judah and fortified Ramah to prevent anyone from leaving or entering the territory of Asa king of Judah.

2 Asa then took the silver and gold out of the treasuries of the LORD's temple and of his own palace and sent it to Ben-Hadad king of Aram, who was ruling in Damascus. 3 "Let there be a treaty[i] between me and you," he said, "as there was between my father and your father. See, I am sending you silver and gold. Now break your treaty with Baasha king of Israel so he will withdraw from me."

4 Ben-Hadad agreed with King Asa and sent the commanders of his forces against the towns of Israel. They conquered Ijon, Dan, Abel Maim[d] and all the store cities of Naphtali. 5 When Baasha heard this, he stopped building Ramah and abandoned his work. 6 Then King Asa brought all the men of Judah, and they carried away from Ramah the stones and timber Baasha had been using. With them he built up Geba and Mizpah.

7 At that time Hanani[j] the seer came to Asa king of Judah and said to him: "Because you relied on the king of Aram and not on the LORD your God, the army of the king of Aram has escaped from your hand. 8 Were not the Cushites[e][k] and Libyans a mighty army with great numbers of chariots and horsemen[f]? Yet when you relied on the LORD, he delivered[l] them into your hand. 9 For the eyes[m] of the LORD range throughout the earth to strengthen those whose hearts are fully committed to him. You have done a foolish[n] thing, and from now on you will be at war."

10 Asa was angry with the seer because of this; he was so enraged that he put him in prison. At the same time Asa brutally oppressed some of the people.

11 The events of Asa's reign, from beginning to end, are written in the book of the kings of Judah and Israel. 12 In the thirty-ninth year of his reign Asa was afflicted with a disease in his feet. Though his disease was severe, even in his illness he did not seek help from the LORD,[o] but only from the physicians. 13 Then in the forty-first year of his reign Asa died and rested with his fathers. 14 They buried him in the tomb that he had cut out for himself in the City of David. They laid

15:11 [a] 2Ch 14:13
15:12 [b] 2Ki 11:17; 2Ch 23:16; 34:31 [c] 1Ch 16:11
15:13 [d] Ex 22:20; Dt 13:9-16
15:15 [e] Dt 4:29 [f] 1Ch 22:9; 2Ch 14:7
15:16 [g] Ex 34:13; 2Ch 14:2-5
16:1 [h] Jer 41:9
16:3 [i] 2Ch 20:35
16:7 [j] 1Ki 16:1
16:8 [k] 2Ch 12:3; 14:9 [l] 2Ch 13:16
16:9 [m] Pr 15:3; Jer 16:17; Zec 4:10 [n] 1Sa 13:13
16:12 [o] Jer 17:5-6

d4 Also known as *Abel Beth Maacah*
e8 That is, people from the upper Nile region
f8 Or *charioteers*

him on a bier covered with spices and various blended perfumes,[a] and they made a huge fire[b] in his honor.

Jehoshaphat King of Judah

17 Jehoshaphat his son succeeded him as king and strengthened himself against Israel. 2He stationed troops in all the fortified cities of Judah and put garrisons in Judah and in the towns of Ephraim that his father Asa had captured.[c]

3The LORD was with Jehoshaphat because in his early years he walked in the ways his father David[d] had followed. He did not consult the Baals 4but sought[e] the God of his father and followed his commands rather than the practices of Israel. 5The LORD established the kingdom under his control; and all Judah brought gifts[f] to Jehoshaphat, so that he had great wealth and honor.[g] 6His heart was devoted[h] to the ways of the LORD; furthermore, he removed the high places[i] and the Asherah poles[j] from Judah.[k]

7In the third year of his reign he sent his officials Ben-Hail, Obadiah, Zechariah, Nethanel and Micaiah to teach[l] in the towns of Judah. 8With them were certain Levites[m]—Shemaiah, Nethaniah, Zebadiah, Asahel, Shemiramoth, Jehonathan, Adonijah, Tobijah and Tob-Adonijah—and the priests Elishama and Jehoram. 9They taught throughout Judah, taking with them the Book of the Law[n] of the LORD; they went around to all the towns of Judah and taught the people.

10The fear[o] of the LORD fell on all the kingdoms of the lands surrounding Judah, so that they did not make war with Jehoshaphat. 11Some Philistines brought Jehoshaphat gifts and silver as tribute, and the Arabs[p] brought him flocks:[q] seven thousand seven hundred rams and seven thousand seven hundred goats.

12Jehoshaphat became more and more powerful; he built forts and store cities in Judah 13and had large supplies in the towns of Judah. He also kept experienced fighting men in Jerusalem. 14Their enrollment[r] by families was as follows:

From Judah, commanders of units of 1,000:
Adnah the commander, with 300,000 fighting men;
15next, Jehohanan the commander, with 280,000;
16next, Amasiah son of Zicri, who volunteered[s] himself for the service of the LORD, with 200,000.
17From Benjamin:[t]
Eliada, a valiant soldier, with 200,000 men armed with bows and shields;
18next, Jehozabad, with 180,000 men armed for battle.

19These were the men who served the king, besides those he stationed in the fortified cities[u] throughout Judah.[v]

Micaiah Prophesies Against Ahab

18:1–27pp — 1Ki 22:1–28

18 Now Jehoshaphat had great wealth and honor,[w] and he allied[x] himself with Ahab[y] by marriage. 2Some years later he went down to visit Ahab in Samaria. Ahab slaughtered many sheep and cattle for him and the people with him and urged him to attack Ramoth Gilead. 3Ahab king of Israel asked Jehoshaphat king of Judah, "Will you go with me against Ramoth Gilead?"

Jehoshaphat replied, "I am as you are, and my people as your people; we will join you in the war." 4But Jehoshaphat also said to the king of Israel, "First seek the counsel of the LORD."

5So the king of Israel brought together the prophets—four hundred men—and asked them, "Shall we go to war against Ramoth Gilead, or shall I refrain?"

"Go," they answered, "for God

16:14 [a]Ge 50:2; Jn 19:39-40 [b]2Ch 21:19; Jer 34:5
17:2 [c]2Ch 15:8
17:3 [d]1Ki 22:43
17:4 [e]1Ki 12:28; 2Ch 22:9
17:5 [f]1Sa 10:27 [g]2Ch 18:1
17:6 [h]1Ki 8:61; 2Ch 15:17 [i]1Ki 15:14; 2Ch 19:3; 20:33 [j]Ex 34:13 [k]2Ch 21:12
17:7 [l]Lev 10:11; Dt 6:4-9; 2Ch 15:3; 35:3
17:8 [m]2Ch 19:8; Ne 8:7-8
17:9 [n]Dt 6:4-9; 28:61
17:10 [o]Ge 35:5; Dt 2:25; 2Ch 14:14
17:11 [p]2Ch 9:14; 26:8 [q]2Ch 21:16
17:14 [r]2Sa 24:2
17:16 [s]Jdg 5:9; 1Ch 29:9
17:17 [t]Nu 1:36
17:19 [u]2Ch 11:10 [v]2Ch 25:5
18:1 [w]2Ch 17:5 [x]2Ch 19:1-3; 22:3 [y]2Ch 21:6

will give it into the king's hand."
6But Jehoshaphat asked, "Is
there not a prophet of the LORD
here whom we can inquire of?"
7The king of Israel answered Jehoshaphat, "There is still one man
through whom we can inquire of
the LORD, but I hate him because he
never prophesies anything good
about me, but always bad. He is
Micaiah son of Imlah."
"The king should not say that,"
Jehoshaphat replied.
8So the king of Israel called one
of his officials and said, "Bring Micaiah son of Imlah at once."
9Dressed in their royal robes, the
king of Israel and Jehoshaphat king
of Judah were sitting on their
thrones at the threshing floor by
the entrance to the gate of Samaria, with all the prophets prophesying before them. 10Now Zedekiah
son of Kenaanah had made iron
horns, and he declared, "This is
what the LORD says: 'With these you
will gore the Arameans until they
are destroyed.' "
11All the other prophets were
prophesying the same thing. "Attack Ramoth Gilead[a] and be victorious," they said, "for the LORD will
give it into the king's hand."
12The messenger who had gone
to summon Micaiah said to him,
"Look, as one man the other
prophets are predicting success for
the king. Let your word agree with
theirs, and speak favorably."
13But Micaiah said, "As surely as
the LORD lives, I can tell him only
what my God says."[b]
14When he arrived, the king
asked him, "Micaiah, shall we go to
war against Ramoth Gilead, or
shall I refrain?"
"Attack and be victorious," he
answered, "for they will be given
into your hand."
15The king said to him, "How
many times must I make you swear
to tell me nothing but the truth in
the name of the LORD?"
16Then Micaiah answered, "I
saw all Israel[c] scattered on the
hills like sheep without a shepherd,[d] and the LORD said, 'These
people have no master. Let each
one go home in peace.' "
17The king of Israel said to Jehoshaphat, "Didn't I tell you that
he never prophesies anything good
about me, but only bad?"
18Micaiah continued, "Therefore hear the word of the LORD: I
saw the LORD sitting on his throne[e]
with all the host of heaven standing
on his right and on his left. 19And
the LORD said, 'Who will entice
Ahab king of Israel into attacking
Ramoth Gilead and going to his
death there?'
"One suggested this, and another that. 20Finally, a spirit came forward, stood before the LORD and
said, 'I will entice him.'
" 'By what means?' the LORD
asked.
21" 'I will go and be a lying spirit[f] in the mouths of all his prophets,' he said.
" 'You will succeed in enticing
him,' said the LORD. 'Go and do it.'
22"So now the LORD has put a lying spirit in the mouths of these
prophets of yours.[g] The LORD has
decreed disaster for you."
23Then Zedekiah son of Kenaanah went up and slapped[h] Micaiah
in the face. "Which way did the
spirit from[g] the LORD go when he
went from me to speak to you?" he
asked.
24Micaiah replied, "You will find
out on the day you go to hide in an
inner room."
25The king of Israel then ordered, "Take Micaiah and send
him back to Amon the ruler of the
city and to Joash the king's son,
26and say, 'This is what the king
says: Put this fellow in prison[i] and
give him nothing but bread and water until I return safely.' "
27Micaiah declared, "If you ever
return safely, the LORD has not spoken through me." Then he added,
"Mark my words, all you people!"

Ahab Killed at Ramoth Gilead

18:28-34pp — 1Ki 22:29-36

28So the king of Israel and Je-

g23 Or *Spirit of*

18:11 [a] 2Ch 22:5
18:13 [b] Nu 22:18,20, 35
18:16 [c] 1Ch 9:1 [d] Nu 27:17; Eze 34:5-8
18:18 [e] Da 7:9
18:21 [f] 1Ch 21:1; Job 1:6; Zec 3:1; Jn 8:44
18:22 [g] Job 12:16; Isa 19:14; Eze 14:9
18:23 [h] Jer 20:2; Mk 14:65; Ac 23:2
18:26 [i] 2Ch 16:10; Heb 11:36

hoshaphat king of Judah went up to Ramoth Gilead. **29**The king of Israel said to Jehoshaphat, "I will enter the battle in disguise, but you wear your royal robes." So the king of Israel disguised[a] himself and went into battle.

30Now the king of Aram had ordered his chariot commanders, "Do not fight with anyone, small or great, except the king of Israel." **31**When the chariot commanders saw Jehoshaphat, they thought, "This is the king of Israel." So they turned to attack him, but Jehoshaphat cried out,[b] and the LORD helped him. God drew them away from him, **32**for when the chariot commanders saw that he was not the king of Israel, they stopped pursuing him.

33But someone drew his bow at random and hit the king of Israel between the sections of his armor. The king told the chariot driver, "Wheel around and get me out of the fighting. I've been wounded." **34**All day long the battle raged, and the king of Israel propped himself up in his chariot facing the Arameans until evening. Then at sunset he died.[c]

19 When Jehoshaphat king of Judah returned safely to his palace in Jerusalem, **2**Jehu[d] the seer, the son of Hanani, went out to meet him and said to the king, "Should you help the wicked[e] and love[h] those who hate the LORD?[f] Because of this, the wrath[g] of the LORD is upon you. **3**There is, however, some good[h] in you, for you have rid the land of the Asherah poles[i] and have set your heart on seeking God.[j]"

Jehoshaphat Appoints Judges

4Jehoshaphat lived in Jerusalem, and he went out again among the people from Beersheba to the hill country of Ephraim and turned them back to the LORD, the God of their fathers. **5**He appointed judges[k] in the land, in each of the fortified cities of Judah. **6**He told them, "Consider carefully what you do,[l] because you are not judging for man[m] but for the LORD, who is with you whenever you give a verdict. **7**Now let the fear of the LORD be upon you. Judge carefully, for with the LORD our God there is no injustice[n] or partiality[o] or bribery."

8In Jerusalem also, Jehoshaphat appointed some of the Levites, priests and heads of Israelite families to administer[p] the law of the LORD and to settle disputes. And they lived in Jerusalem. **9**He gave them these orders: "You must serve faithfully and wholeheartedly in the fear of the LORD. **10**In every case that comes before you from your fellow countrymen who live in the cities—whether bloodshed or other concerns of the law, commands, decrees or ordinances—you are to warn them not to sin against the LORD;[q] otherwise his wrath will come on you and your brothers. Do this, and you will not sin.

11"Amariah the chief priest will be over you in any matter concerning the LORD, and Zebadiah son of Ishmael, the leader of the tribe of Judah, will be over you in any matter concerning the king, and the Levites will serve as officials before you. Act with courage,[r] and may the LORD be with those who do well."

Jehoshaphat Defeats Moab and Ammon

20 After this, the Moabites and Ammonites with some of the Meunites[i][s] came to make war on Jehoshaphat.

2Some men came and told Jehoshaphat, "A vast army is coming against you from Edom,[j] from the other side of the Sea.[k] It is already in Hazazon Tamar[t]" (that is, En Gedi). **3**Alarmed, Jehoshaphat resolved to inquire of the LORD, and he proclaimed a fast[u] for all Judah. **4**The people of Judah came together to seek help from the

18:29 [a]1Sa 28:8
18:31 [b]2Ch 13:14
18:34 [c]2Ch 22:5
19:2 [d]1Ki 16:1 [e]2Ch 16:2-9 [f]Ps 139:21-22 [g]2Ch 24:18; 32:25; Ps 7:11
19:3 [h]1Ki 14:13; 2Ch 12:12 [i]2Ch 17:6 [j]2Ch 18:1; 20:35; 25:7; Ezr 7:10
19:5 [k]Ge 47:6; Ex 18:26
19:6 [l]Lev 19:15 [m]Dt 1:17; 16:18-20; 17:8-13
19:7 [n]Ge 18:25; Dt 32:4 [o]Dt 10:17; Job 34:19; Ro 2:11; Col 3:25
19:8 [p]2Ch 17:8-9
19:10 [q]Dt 17:8-13
19:11 [r]1Ch 28:20
20:1 [s]1Ch 4:41
20:2 [t]Ge 14:7
20:3 [u]1Sa 7:6; 2Ch 19:3; Ezr 8:21; Jer 36:9; Jnh 3:5,7

h2 Or *and make alliances with* i1 Some Septuagint manuscripts; Hebrew *Ammonites*
i2 One Hebrew manuscript; most Hebrew manuscripts, Septuagint and Vulgate *Aram*
k2 That is, the Dead Sea

LORD; indeed, they came from every
town in Judah to seek him.
5Then Jehoshaphat stood up in
the assembly of Judah and Jerusalem at the temple of the LORD in the
front of the new courtyard **6**and
said:

"O LORD, God of our fa-
thers,[a] are you not the God
who is in heaven?[b] You rule
over all the kingdoms[c] of the
nations. Power and might are
in your hand, and no one can
withstand you. **7**O our God,
did you not drive out the inhabitants of this land before
your people Israel and give it
forever to the descendants of
Abraham your friend?[d] **8**They
have lived in it and have built
in it a sanctuary[e] for your
Name, saying, **9**'If calamity
comes upon us, whether the
sword of judgment, or plague
or famine,[f] we will stand in
your presence before this temple that bears your Name and
will cry out to you in our distress, and you will hear us and
save us.'
10"But now here are men
from Ammon, Moab and
Mount Seir, whose territory
you would not allow Israel to
invade when they came from
Egypt;[g] so they turned away
from them and did not destroy
them. **11**See how they are repaying us by coming to drive
us out of the possession[h] you
gave us as an inheritance. **12**O
our God, will you not judge
them?[i] For we have no power
to face this vast army that is
attacking us. We do not know
what to do, but our eyes are
upon you.[j]"

13All the men of Judah, with
their wives and children and little
ones, stood there before the LORD.
14Then the Spirit[k] of the LORD
came upon Jahaziel son of Zechariah, the son of Benaiah, the son of
Jeiel, the son of Mattaniah, a Levite and descendant of Asaph, as
he stood in the assembly.

20:6 [a]Mt 6:9 [b]Dt 4:39 [c]1Ch 29:11-12
20:7 [d]Isa 41:8; Jas 2:23
20:8 [e]2Ch 6:20
20:9 [f]2Ch 6:28
20:10 [g]Nu 20:14-21; Dt 2:4-6,9, 18-19
20:11 [h]Ps 83:1-12
20:12 [i]Jdg 11:27 [j]Ps 25:15; 121:1-2
20:14 [k]2Ch 15:1
20:15 [l]2Ch 32:7 [m]Ex 14:13-14; 1Sa 17:47
20:17 [n]Ex 14:13; 2Ch 15:2
20:18 [o]Ex 4:31
20:20 [p]Isa 7:9 [q]Ge 39:3; Pr 16:3
20:21 [r]1Ch 16:29; Ps 29:2 [s]2Ch 5:13; Ps 136:1
20:22 [t]Jdg 7:22; 2Ch 13:13
20:23 [u]Ge 19:38 [v]2Ch 21:8

15He said: "Listen, King Jehoshaphat and all who live in Judah and
Jerusalem! This is what the LORD
says to you: 'Do not be afraid or discouraged[l] because of this vast
army. For the battle[m] is not yours,
but God's. **16**Tomorrow march
down against them. They will be
climbing up by the Pass of Ziz, and
you will find them at the end of the
gorge in the Desert of Jeruel. **17**You
will not have to fight this battle.
Take up your positions; stand firm
and see[n] the deliverance the LORD
will give you, O Judah and Jerusalem. Do not be afraid; do not be
discouraged. Go out to face them
tomorrow, and the LORD will be
with you.' "
18Jehoshaphat bowed[o] with his
face to the ground, and all the people of Judah and Jerusalem fell
down in worship before the LORD.
19Then some Levites from the Kohathites and Korahites stood up
and praised the LORD, the God of
Israel, with very loud voice.
20Early in the morning they left
for the Desert of Tekoa. As they set
out, Jehoshaphat stood and said,
"Listen to me, Judah and people of
Jerusalem! Have faith[p] in the LORD
your God and you will be upheld;
have faith in his prophets and you
will be successful.[q]" **21**After consulting the people, Jehoshaphat
appointed men to sing to the LORD
and to praise him for the splendor
of his[1] holiness[r] as they went out
at the head of the army, saying:

"Give thanks to the LORD,
for his love endures
forever."[s]

22As they began to sing and
praise, the LORD set ambushes[t]
against the men of Ammon and
Moab and Mount Seir who were invading Judah, and they were defeated. **23**The men of Ammon[u] and
Moab rose up against the men from
Mount Seir[v] to destroy and annihilate them. After they finished
slaughtering the men from Seir,

[1]21 *Or him with the splendor of*

they helped to destroy one another.[a]

24When the men of Judah came to the place that overlooks the desert and looked toward the vast army, they saw only dead bodies lying on the ground; no one had escaped. 25So Jehoshaphat and his men went to carry off their plunder, and they found among them a great amount of equipment and clothing[m] and also articles of value—more than they could take away. There was so much plunder that it took three days to collect it. 26On the fourth day they assembled in the Valley of Beracah, where they praised the LORD. This is why it is called the Valley of Beracah[n] to this day.

27Then, led by Jehoshaphat, all the men of Judah and Jerusalem returned joyfully to Jerusalem, for the LORD had given them cause to rejoice over their enemies. 28They entered Jerusalem and went to the temple of the LORD with harps and lutes and trumpets.

29The fear[b] of God came upon all the kingdoms of the countries when they heard how the LORD had fought[c] against the enemies of Israel. 30And the kingdom of Jehoshaphat was at peace, for his God had given him rest[d] on every side.

The End of Jehoshaphat's Reign

20:31–21:1pp — 1Ki 22:41–50

31So Jehoshaphat reigned over Judah. He was thirty-five years old when he became king of Judah, and he reigned in Jerusalem twenty-five years. His mother's name was Azubah daughter of Shilhi. 32He walked in the ways of his father Asa and did not stray from them; he did what was right in the eyes of the LORD. 33The high places,[e] however, were not removed, and the people still had not set their hearts on the God of their fathers.

34The other events of Jehoshaphat's reign, from beginning to end, are written in the annals of Jehu[f] son of Hanani, which are recorded in the book of the kings of Israel.

35Later, Jehoshaphat king of Judah made an alliance[g] with Ahaziah king of Israel, who was guilty of wickedness.[h] 36He agreed with him to construct a fleet of trading ships.[o] After these were built at Ezion Geber, 37Eliezer son of Dodavahu of Mareshah prophesied against Jehoshaphat, saying, "Because you have made an alliance with Ahaziah, the LORD will destroy what you have made." The ships[i] were wrecked and were not able to set sail to trade.[p]

21 Then Jehoshaphat rested with his fathers and was buried with them in the City of David. And Jehoram[j] his son succeeded him as king. 2Jehoram's brothers, the sons of Jehoshaphat, were Azariah, Jehiel, Zechariah, Azariahu, Michael and Shephatiah. All these were sons of Jehoshaphat king of Israel.[q] 3Their father had given them many gifts[k] of silver and gold and articles of value, as well as fortified cities[l] in Judah, but he had given the kingdom to Jehoram because he was his firstborn son.

Jehoram King of Judah

21:5–10,20pp — 2Ki 8:16–24

4When Jehoram established[m] himself firmly over his father's kingdom, he put all his brothers[n] to the sword along with some of the princes of Israel. 5Jehoram was thirty-two years old when he became king, and he reigned in Jerusalem eight years. 6He walked in the ways of the kings of Israel,[o] as the house of Ahab had done, for he married a daughter of Ahab.[p] He did evil in the eyes of the LORD. 7Nevertheless, because of the covenant the LORD had made with David,[q] the LORD was not willing to

20:23 [a]Jdg 7:22; 1Sa 14:20; Eze 38:21
20:29 [b]Ge 35:5; Dt 2:25; 2Ch 14:14; 17:10 [c]Ex 14:14
20:30 [d]1Ch 22:9; 2Ch 14:6-7; 15:15
20:33 [e]2Ch 17:6; 19:3
20:34 [f]1Ki 16:1
20:35 [g]2Ch 16:3 [h]2Ch 19:1-3
20:37 [i]1Ki 9:26; 2Ch 9:21
21:1 [j]1Ch 3:11
21:3 [k]2Ch 11:23 [l]2Ch 11:10
21:4 [m]1Ki 2:12 [n]Jdg 9:5
21:6 [o]1Ki 12:28-30 [p]2Ch 18:1; 22:3
21:7 [q]2Sa 7:13

m25 Some Hebrew manuscripts and Vulgate; most Hebrew manuscripts *corpses*
n26 *Beracah* means *praise.* o36 Hebrew *of ships that could go to Tarshish* p37 Hebrew *sail for Tarshish* q2 That is, Judah, as frequently in 2 Chronicles

destroy the house of David.[a] He
had promised to maintain a lamp[b]
for him and his descendants forever.
8In the time of Jehoram, Edom[c]
rebelled against Judah and set up
its own king. 9So Jehoram went
there with his officers and all his
chariots. The Edomites surrounded him and his chariot commanders, but he rose up and broke
through by night. 10To this day
Edom has been in rebellion against
Judah.
Libnah[d] revolted at the same
time, because Jehoram had forsak-
en the LORD, the God of his fathers.
11He had also built high places on
the hills of Judah and had caused
the people of Jerusalem to prostitute themselves and had led Judah
astray.
12Jehoram received a letter from
Elijah[e] the prophet, which said:

"This is what the LORD, the
God of your father[f] David,
says: 'You have not walked in
the ways of your father Jehoshaphat or of Asa[g] king of
Judah. 13But you have walked
in the ways of the kings of Israel, and you have led Judah and
the people of Jerusalem to
prostitute themselves, just as
the house of Ahab did.[h] You
have also murdered your own
brothers, members of your father's house, men who were
better[i] than you. 14So now
the LORD is about to strike your
people, your sons, your wives
and everything that is yours,
with a heavy blow. 15You yourself will be very ill with a lingering disease[j] of the bowels,
until the disease causes your
bowels to come out.'"

16The LORD aroused against Jehoram the hostility of the Philistines and of the Arabs[k] who lived
near the Cushites. 17They attacked
Judah, invaded it and carried off all
the goods found in the king's palace, together with his sons and
wives. Not a son was left to him except Ahaziah,[r] the youngest.[l]

21:7 [a]2Sa 7:15; 2Ch 23:3 [b]2Sa 21:17; 1Ki 11:36
21:8 [c]2Ch 20:22-23
21:10 [d]Nu 33:20
21:12 [e]2Ki 1:16-17 [f]2Ch 17:3-6 [g]2Ch 14:2
21:13 [h]ver 6,11; 1Ki 16:29-33 [i]ver 4; 1Ki 2:32
21:15 [j]ver 18-19; Nu 12:10
21:16 [k]2Ch 17:10-11; 22:1; 26:7
21:17 [l]2Ki 12:18; 2Ch 22:1; 25:23; Joel 3:5
21:19 [m]2Ch 16:14
21:20 [n]2Ch 24:25; 28:27; 33:20; Jer 22:18,28
22:1 [o]2Ch 33:25; 36:1 [p]2Ch 23:20-21; 26:1 [q]2Ch 21:16-17
22:3 [r]2Ch 18:1 [s]2Ch 21:6
22:5 [t]2Ch 18:11,34
22:6 [u]1Ki 19:15; 2Ki 8:13-15; 9:15

18After all this, the LORD afflicted
Jehoram with an incurable disease
of the bowels. 19In the course of
time, at the end of the second year,
his bowels came out because of the
disease, and he died in great pain.
His people made no fire in his hon-
or,[m] as they had for his fathers.
20Jehoram was thirty-two years
old when he became king, and he
reigned in Jerusalem eight years.
He passed away, to no one's regret,
and was buried[n] in the City of David, but not in the tombs of the
kings.

Ahaziah King of Judah

22:1–6pp — 2Ki 8:25–29
22:7–9pp — 2Ki 9:21–29

22 The people[o] of Jerusalem[p]
made Ahaziah, Jehoram's
youngest son, king in his place,
since the raiders,[q] who came with
the Arabs into the camp, had killed
all the older sons. So Ahaziah son
of Jehoram king of Judah began to
reign.
2Ahaziah was twenty-two[s] years
old when he became king, and he
reigned in Jerusalem one year. His
mother's name was Athaliah, a
granddaughter of Omri.
3He too walked[r] in the ways of
the house of Ahab,[s] for his mother
encouraged him in doing wrong.
4He did evil in the eyes of the LORD,
as the house of Ahab had done, for
after his father's death they became his advisers, to his undoing.
5He also followed their counsel
when he went with Joram[t] son of
Ahab king of Israel to war against
Hazael king of Aram at Ramoth Gilead.[t] The Arameans wounded Joram; 6so he returned to Jezreel to
recover from the wounds they had
inflicted on him at Ramoth[u] in his
battle with Hazael[u] king of Aram.
Then Ahaziah[v] son of Jehoram
king of Judah went down to Jezreel

[r]17 Hebrew *Jehoahaz,* a variant of *Ahaziah*
[s]2 Some Septuagint manuscripts and Syriac (see also 2 Kings 8:26); Hebrew *forty-two*
[t]5 Hebrew *Jehoram,* a variant of *Joram;* also in verses 6 and 7
[u]6 Hebrew *Ramah,* a variant of *Ramoth*
[v]6 Some Hebrew manuscripts, Septuagint, Vulgate and Syriac (see also 2 Kings 8:29); most Hebrew manuscripts *Azariah*

to see Joram son of Ahab because
he had been wounded.
7Through Ahaziah's[a] visit to Joram, God brought about Ahaziah's
downfall. When Ahaziah arrived,
he went out with Joram to meet
Jehu son of Nimshi, whom the
LORD had anointed to destroy the
house of Ahab. **8**While Jehu was
executing judgment on the house
of Ahab,[b] he found the princes of
Judah and the sons of Ahaziah's
relatives, who had been attending
Ahaziah, and he killed them. **9**He
then went in search of Ahaziah,
and his men captured him while he
was hiding[c] in Samaria. He was
brought to Jehu and put to death.
They buried him, for they said, "He
was a son of Jehoshaphat, who
sought[d] the LORD with all his
heart." So there was no one in the
house of Ahaziah powerful enough
to retain the kingdom.

Athaliah and Joash

22:10–23:21pp — 2Ki 11:1–21

10When Athaliah the mother of
Ahaziah saw that her son was dead,
she proceeded to destroy the whole
royal family of the house of Judah.
11But Jehosheba,[w] the daughter of
King Jehoram, took Joash son of
Ahaziah and stole him away from
among the royal princes who were
about to be murdered and put him
and his nurse in a bedroom. Because Jehosheba,[w] the daughter of
King Jehoram and wife of the priest
Jehoiada, was Ahaziah's sister, she
hid the child from Athaliah so she
could not kill him. **12**He remained
hidden with them at the temple of
God for six years while Athaliah
ruled the land.

23 In the seventh year Jehoiada showed his strength. He
made a covenant with the commanders of units of a hundred: Azariah son of Jeroham, Ishmael son
of Jehohanan, Azariah son of
Obed, Maaseiah son of Adaiah, and
Elishaphat son of Zicri. **2**They went
throughout Judah and gathered
the Levites[e] and the heads of Israelite families from all the towns.
When they came to Jerusalem,
3the whole assembly made a covenant[f] with the king at the temple
of God.
Jehoiada said to them, "The
king's son shall reign, as the LORD
promised concerning the descendants of David.[g] **4**Now this is what
you are to do: A third of you priests
and Levites who are going on duty
on the Sabbath are to keep watch
at the doors, **5**a third of you at the
royal palace and a third at the
Foundation Gate, and all the other
men are to be in the courtyards of
the temple of the LORD. **6**No one is
to enter the temple of the LORD except the priests and Levites on
duty; they may enter because they
are consecrated, but all the other
men are to guard[h] what the LORD
has assigned to them.[x] **7**The Levites are to station themselves
around the king, each man with his
weapons in his hand. Anyone who
enters the temple must be put to
death. Stay close to the king wherever he goes."
8The Levites and all the men of
Judah did just as Jehoiada the
priest ordered.[i] Each one took his
men—those who were going on
duty on the Sabbath and those who
were going off duty—for Jehoiada
the priest had not released any of
the divisions.[j] **9**Then he gave the
commanders of units of a hundred
the spears and the large and small
shields that had belonged to King
David and that were in the temple
of God. **10**He stationed all the men,
each with his weapon in his hand,
around the king—near the altar
and the temple, from the south
side to the north side of the temple.
11Jehoiada and his sons brought
out the king's son and put the
crown on him; they presented him
with a copy[k] of the covenant and
proclaimed him king. They anointed him and shouted, "Long live the
king!"

22:7 [a]2Ki 9:16; 2Ch 10:15
22:8 [b]2Ki 10:13
22:9 [c]Jdg 9:5 [d]2Ch 17:4
23:2 [e]Nu 35:2-5
23:3 [f]2Ki 11:17 [g]2Sa 7:12; 1Ki 2:4; 2Ch 6:16; 7:18; 21:7
23:6 [h]1Ch 23:28-29; Zec 3:7
23:8 [i]2Ki 11:9 [j]1Ch 24:1
23:11 [k]Ex 25:16; Dt 17:18; 1Sa 10:24

[w]*11* Hebrew *Jehoshabeath,* a variant of *Jehosheba* [x]*6* Or *to observe the LORD's command ⌞not to enter⌟*

12When Athaliah heard the noise
of the people running and cheering
the king, she went to them at the
temple of the LORD. 13She looked,
and there was the king,[a] standing
by his pillar[b] at the entrance. The
officers and the trumpeters were
beside the king, and all the people
of the land were rejoicing and
blowing trumpets, and singers with
musical instruments were leading
the praises. Then Athaliah tore her
robes and shouted, "Treason! Treason!"
14Jehoiada the priest sent out
the commanders of units of a hundred, who were in charge of the
troops, and said to them: "Bring
her out between the ranks[y] and
put to the sword anyone who follows her." For the priest had said,
"Do not put her to death at the
temple of the LORD." 15So they
seized her as she reached the entrance of the Horse Gate[c] on the
palace grounds, and there they put
her to death.
16Jehoiada then made a covenant[d] that he and the people and
the king[z] would be the LORD's people. 17All the people went to the
temple of Baal and tore it down.
They smashed the altars and idols
and killed[e] Mattan the priest of
Baal in front of the altars.
18Then Jehoiada placed the
oversight of the temple of the LORD
in the hands of the priests, who
were Levites,[f] to whom David had
made assignments in the temple,[g]
to present the burnt offerings of
the LORD as written in the Law of
Moses, with rejoicing and singing,
as David had ordered. 19He also
stationed doorkeepers[h] at the
gates of the LORD's temple so that
no one who was in any way unclean
might enter.
20He took with him the commanders of hundreds, the nobles,
the rulers of the people and all the
people of the land and brought the
king down from the temple of the
LORD. They went into the palace
through the Upper Gate[i] and seated the king on the royal throne,
21and all the people of the land rejoiced. And the city was quiet, because Athaliah had been slain with
the sword.[j]

Joash Repairs the Temple

24:1–14pp — 2Ki 12:1–16
24:23–27pp — 2Ki 12:17–21

24 Joash was seven years old
when he became king, and
he reigned in Jerusalem forty years.
His mother's name was Zibiah; she
was from Beersheba. 2Joash did
what was right in the eyes of the
LORD[k] all the years of Jehoiada the
priest. 3Jehoiada chose two wives
for him, and he had sons and
daughters.
4Some time later Joash decided
to restore the temple of the LORD.
5He called together the priests and
Levites and said to them, "Go to
the towns of Judah and collect the
money[l] due annually from all Israel,[m] to repair the temple of your
God. Do it now." But the Levites[n]
did not act at once.
6Therefore the king summoned
Jehoiada the chief priest and said
to him, "Why haven't you required
the Levites to bring in from Judah
and Jerusalem the tax imposed by
Moses the servant of the LORD and
by the assembly of Israel for the
Tent of the Testimony?"[o]
7Now the sons of that wicked
woman Athaliah had broken into
the temple of God and had used
even its sacred objects for the Baals.
8At the king's command, a chest
was made and placed outside, at
the gate of the temple of the LORD.
9A proclamation was then issued in
Judah and Jerusalem that they
should bring to the LORD the tax
that Moses the servant of God had
required of Israel in the desert.
10All the officials and all the people brought their contributions
gladly,[p] dropping them into the
chest until it was full. 11Whenever
the chest was brought in by the Levites to the king's officials and they
saw that there was a large amount

23:13 [a] 1Ki 1:41 [b] 1Ki 7:15
23:15 [c] Ne 3:28; Jer 31:40
23:16 [d] 2Ch 29:10; 34:31; Ne 9:38
23:17 [e] Dt 13:6-9
23:18 [f] 1Ch 23:28-32; 2Ch 5:5 [g] 1Ch 23:6; 25:6
23:19 [h] 1Ch 9:22
23:20 [i] 2Ki 15:35
23:21 [j] 2Ch 22:1
24:2 [k] 2Ch 25:2; 26:5
24:5 [l] Ex 30:16; Ne 10:32-33; Mt 17:24 [m] 1Ch 11:1 [n] 1Ch 26:20
24:6 [o] Ex 30:12-16; Nu 1:50
24:10 [p] Ex 25:2; 1Ch 29:3,6,9

[y]14 Or *out from the precincts* [z]16 Or *covenant between the LORD and the people and the king that they* (see 2 Kings 11:17)

of money, the royal secretary and
the officer of the chief priest would
come and empty the chest and carry it back to its place. They did this
regularly and collected a great
amount of money. **12**The king and
Jehoiada gave it to the men who
carried out the work required for
the temple of the LORD. They
hired[a] masons and carpenters to
restore the LORD's temple, and also
workers in iron and bronze to repair the temple.
13The men in charge of the work
were diligent, and the repairs pro-
gressed under them. They rebuilt
the temple of God according to its
original design and reinforced it.
14When they had finished, they
brought the rest of the money to
the king and Jehoiada, and with it
were made articles for the LORD's
temple: articles for the service and
for the burnt offerings, and also
dishes and other objects of gold
and silver. As long as Jehoiada
lived, burnt offerings were presented continually in the temple of the
LORD.
15Now Jehoiada was old and full
of years, and he died at the age of
a hundred and thirty. **16**He was
buried with the kings in the City of
David, because of the good he had
done in Israel for God and his temple.

The Wickedness of Joash

17After the death of Jehoiada,
the officials of Judah came and
paid homage to the king, and he
listened to them. **18**They abandoned[b] the temple of the LORD, the
God of their fathers, and worshiped
Asherah poles and idols.[c] Because
of their guilt, God's anger[d] came
upon Judah and Jerusalem. **19**Although the LORD sent prophets to
the people to bring them back to
him, and though they testified
against them, they would not listen.[e]
20Then the Spirit[f] of God came
upon Zechariah[g] son of Jehoiada
the priest. He stood before the people and said, "This is what God
says: 'Why do you disobey the
LORD's commands? You will not
prosper.[h] Because you have forsaken the LORD, he has forsaken[i]
you.' "
21But they plotted against him,
and by order of the king they
stoned[j] him to death[k] in the
courtyard of the LORD's temple.[l]
22King Joash did not remember the
kindness Zechariah's father Jehoiada had shown him but killed his
son, who said as he lay dying, "May
the LORD see this and call you to
account."[m]
23At the turn of the year,[a] the
army of Aram marched against Joash; it invaded Judah and Jerusalem and killed all the leaders of the
people.[n] They sent all the plunder
to their king in Damascus. **24**Although the Aramean army had
come with only a few men,[o] the
LORD delivered into their hands a
much larger army.[p] Because Judah had forsaken the LORD, the God
of their fathers, judgment was executed on Joash. **25**When the Arameans withdrew, they left Joash
severely wounded. His officials
conspired against him for murdering the son of Jehoiada the priest,
and they killed him in his bed. So
he died and was buried[q] in the City
of David, but not in the tombs of
the kings.
26Those who conspired against
him were Zabad,[b] son of Shimeath
an Ammonite woman, and Jehozabad, son of Shimrith[c][r] a Moabite
woman.[s] **27**The account of his
sons, the many prophecies about
him, and the record of the restoration of the temple of God are written in the annotations on the book
of the kings. And Amaziah his son
succeeded him as king.

Amaziah King of Judah

25:1–4pp — 2Ki 14:1-6
25:11–12pp — 2Ki 14:7
25:17–28pp — 2Ki 14:8-20

25 Amaziah was twenty-five
years old when he became
king, and he reigned in Jerusalem
twenty-nine years. His mother's

24:12 [a]2Ch 34:11
24:18 [b]ver 4; Jos 24:20; 2Ch 7:19 [c]Ex 34:13; 1Ki 14:23; 2Ch 33:3; Jer 17:2 [d]Jos 22:20; 2Ch 19:2
24:19 [e]Nu 11:29; Jer 7:25; Zec 1:4
24:20 [f]Jdg 3:10; 1Ch 12:18; 2Ch 20:14 [g]Mt 23:35; Lk 11:51 [h]Nu 14:41 [i]Dt 31:17; 2Ch 15:2
24:21 [j]Jos 7:25; Ac 7:58-59 [k]Ne 9:26; Jer 26:21 [l]Jer 20:2; Mt 23:35
24:22 [m]Ge 9:5
24:23 [n]2Ki 12:17-18
24:24 [o]2Ch 14:9; 16:8; 20:2,12 [p]Lev 26:23-25; Dt 28:25
24:25 [q]2Ch 21:20
24:26 [r]2Ki 12:21 [s]Ru 1:4

[a]23 Probably in the spring [b]26 A variant of *Jozabad* [c]26 A variant of *Shomer*

name was Jehoaddin[d]; she was from Jerusalem. **2**He did what was right in the eyes of the LORD, but not wholeheartedly.[a] **3**After the kingdom was firmly in his control, he executed the officials who had murdered his father the king. **4**Yet he did not put their sons to death, but acted in accordance with what is written in the Law, in the Book of Moses,[b] where the LORD commanded: "Fathers shall not be put to death for their children, nor children put to death for their fathers; each is to die for his own sins."[e][c]

5Amaziah called the people of Judah together and assigned them according to their families to commanders of thousands and commanders of hundreds for all Judah and Benjamin. He then mustered[d] those twenty years old[e] or more and found that there were three hundred thousand men ready for military service,[f] able to handle the spear and shield. **6**He also hired a hundred thousand fighting men from Israel for a hundred talents[f] of silver.

7But a man of God came to him and said, "O king, these troops from Israel[g] must not march with you, for the LORD is not with Israel—not with any of the people of Ephraim. **8**Even if you go and fight courageously in battle, God will overthrow you before the enemy, for God has the power to help or to overthrow."[h]

9Amaziah asked the man of God, "But what about the hundred talents I paid for these Israelite troops?"

The man of God replied, "The LORD can give you much more than that."[i]

10So Amaziah dismissed the troops who had come to him from Ephraim and sent them home. They were furious with Judah and left for home in a great rage.[j]

11Amaziah then marshaled his strength and led his army to the Valley of Salt, where he killed ten thousand men of Seir. **12**The army of Judah also captured ten thousand men alive, took them to the top of a cliff and threw them down so that all were dashed to pieces.[k]

13Meanwhile the troops that Amaziah had sent back and had not allowed to take part in the war raided Judean towns from Samaria to Beth Horon. They killed three thousand people and carried off great quantities of plunder.

14When Amaziah returned from slaughtering the Edomites, he brought back the gods of the people of Seir. He set them up as his own gods,[l] bowed down to them and burned sacrifices to them. **15**The anger of the LORD burned against Amaziah, and he sent a prophet to him, who said, "Why do you consult this people's gods, which could not save[m] their own people from your hand?"

16While he was still speaking, the king said to him, "Have we appointed you an adviser to the king? Stop! Why be struck down?"

So the prophet stopped but said, "I know that God has determined to destroy you, because you have done this and have not listened to my counsel."

17After Amaziah king of Judah consulted his advisers, he sent this challenge to Jehoash[g] son of Jehoahaz, the son of Jehu, king of Israel: "Come, meet me face to face."

18But Jehoash king of Israel replied to Amaziah king of Judah: "A thistle[n] in Lebanon sent a message to a cedar in Lebanon, 'Give your daughter to my son in marriage.' Then a wild beast in Lebanon came along and trampled the thistle underfoot. **19**You say to yourself that you have defeated Edom, and now you are arrogant and proud. But stay at home! Why ask for trouble and cause your own downfall and that of Judah also?"

20Amaziah, however, would not listen, for God so worked that he might hand them over to Jehoash, because they sought the gods of

25:2 [a]ver 14; 1Ki 8:61; 2Ch 24:2
25:4 [b]Dt 28:61 [c]Nu 26:11; Dt 24:16
25:5 [d]2Sa 24:2 [e]Ex 30:14 [f]Nu 1:3; 1Ch 21:1; 2Ch 17:14-19
25:7 [g]2Ch 16:2-9; 19:1-3
25:8 [h]2Ch 14:11; 20:6
25:9 [i]Dt 8:18; Pr 10:22
25:10 [j]ver 13
25:12 [k]Ps 141:6; Ob 1:3
25:14 [l]Ex 20:3; 2Ch 28:23; Isa 44:15
25:15 [m]Ps 96:5; Isa 36:20
25:18 [n]Jdg 9:8-15

[d]*1* Hebrew *Jehoaddan,* a variant of *Jehoaddin*
[e]*4* Deut. 24:16 [f]*6* That is, about 3 3/4 tons (about 3.4 metric tons); also in verse 9
[g]*17* Hebrew *Joash,* a variant of *Jehoash*; also in verses 18, 21, 23 and 25

Edom.[a] **21**So Jehoash king of Israel attacked. He and Amaziah king
of Judah faced each other at Beth
Shemesh in Judah. **22**Judah was
routed by Israel, and every man
fled to his home. **23**Jehoash king of
Israel captured Amaziah king of Judah, the son of Joash, the son of
Ahaziah,[h] at Beth Shemesh. Then
Jehoash brought him to Jerusalem
and broke down the wall of Jerusalem from the Ephraim Gate[b] to the
Corner Gate[c]—a section about six
hundred feet[i] long. **24**He took all
the gold and silver and all the articles found in the temple of God
that had been in the care of
Obed-Edom,[d] together with the
palace treasures and the hostages,
and returned to Samaria.

25Amaziah son of Joash king of
Judah lived for fifteen years after
the death of Jehoash son of Jehoahaz king of Israel. **26**As for the other
events of Amaziah's reign, from beginning to end, are they not written
in the book of the kings of Judah
and Israel? **27**From the time that
Amaziah turned away from following the LORD, they conspired
against him in Jerusalem and he
fled to Lachish[e], but they sent
men after him to Lachish and
killed him there. **28**He was brought
back by horse and was buried with
his fathers in the City of Judah.

Uzziah King of Judah

26:1–4pp — 2Ki 14:21–22; 15:1–3
26:21–23pp — 2Ki 15:5–7

26 Then all the people of Judah[f] took Uzziah,[j] who
was sixteen years old, and made
him king in place of his father Amaziah. **2**He was the one who rebuilt
Elath and restored it to Judah after
Amaziah rested with his fathers.

3Uzziah was sixteen years old
when he became king, and he
reigned in Jerusalem fifty-two
years. His mother's name was Jecoliah; she was from Jerusalem. **4**He
did what was right in the eyes of
the LORD, just as his father Amaziah
had done. **5**He sought God during
the days of Zechariah, who instructed him in the fear[k] of God.[g]
As long as he sought the LORD, God
gave him success.[h]

6He went to war against the Philistines[i] and broke down the walls
of Gath, Jabneh and Ashdod.[j] He
then rebuilt towns near Ashdod
and elsewhere among the Philistines. **7**God helped him against the
Philistines and against the Arabs[k]
who lived in Gur Baal and against
the Meunites.[l] **8**The Ammonites[m]
brought tribute to Uzziah, and his
fame spread as far as the border of
Egypt, because he had become very
powerful.

9Uzziah built towers in Jerusalem at the Corner Gate,[n] at the
Valley Gate[o] and at the angle of
the wall, and he fortified them.
10He also built towers in the desert
and dug many cisterns, because he
had much livestock in the foothills
and in the plain. He had people
working his fields and vineyards in
the hills and in the fertile lands, for
he loved the soil.

11Uzziah had a well-trained
army, ready to go out by divisions
according to their numbers as mustered by Jeiel the secretary and Maaseiah the officer under the direction of Hananiah, one of the royal
officials. **12**The total number of
family leaders over the fighting
men was 2,600. **13**Under their command was an army of 307,500 men
trained for war, a powerful force to
support the king against his enemies. **14**Uzziah provided shields,
spears, helmets, coats of armor,
bows and slingstones for the entire
army.[p] **15**In Jerusalem he made
machines designed by skillful men
for use on the towers and on the
corner defenses to shoot arrows
and hurl large stones. His fame
spread far and wide, for he was
greatly helped until he became
powerful.

16But after Uzziah became powerful, his pride[q] led to his downfall.[r] He was unfaithful[s] to the

25:20 [a] 1Ki 12:15; 2Ch 10:15; 22:7
25:23 [b] 2Ki 14:13; Ne 8:16; 12:39 [c] 2Ch 26:9; Jer 31:38
25:24 [d] 1Ch 26:15
25:27 [e] Jos 10:3
26:1 [f] 2Ch 22:1
26:5 [g] 2Ch 15:2; 24:2; Da 1:17 [h] 2Ch 27:6
26:6 [i] Isa 2:6; 11:14; 14:29; Jer 25:20 [j] Am 1:8; 3:9
26:7 [k] 2Ch 21:16 [l] 2Ch 20:1
26:8 [m] Ge 19:38; 2Ch 17:11
26:9 [n] 2Ki 14:13; 2Ch 25:23 [o] Ne 2:13; 3:13
26:14 [p] Jer 46:4
26:16 [q] 2Ki 14:10 [r] Dt 32:15; 2Ch 25:19 [s] 1Ch 5:25

[h]*23* Hebrew *Jehoahaz,* a variant of *Ahaziah*
[i]*23* Hebrew *four hundred cubits* (about 180 meters)
[j]*1* Also called *Azariah*
[k]*5* Many Hebrew manuscripts, Septuagint and Syriac; other Hebrew manuscripts *vision*

Lord his God, and entered the temple of the Lord to burn incense[a] on
the altar of incense. 17Azariah[b]
the priest with eighty other courageous priests of the Lord followed
him in. 18They confronted him and
said, "It is not right for you, Uzziah,
to burn incense to the Lord. That is
for the priests,[c] the descendants[d]
of Aaron,[e] who have been consecrated to burn incense.[f] Leave the
sanctuary, for you have been unfaithful; and you will not be honored by the Lord God."
19Uzziah, who had a censer in his
hand ready to burn incense, became angry. While he was raging at
the priests in their presence before
the incense altar in the Lord's temple, leprosy[l][g] broke out on his
forehead. 20When Azariah the chief
priest and all the other priests
looked at him, they saw that he had
leprosy on his forehead, so they
hurried him out. Indeed, he himself was eager to leave, because the
Lord had afflicted him.
21King Uzziah had leprosy until
the day he died. He lived in a separate house[m][h] —leprous, and excluded from the temple of the
Lord. Jotham his son had charge of
the palace and governed the people
of the land.
22The other events of Uzziah's
reign, from beginning to end, are
recorded by the prophet Isaiah[i]
son of Amoz. 23Uzziah[j] rested
with his fathers and was buried
near them in a field for burial that
belonged to the kings, for people
said, "He had leprosy." And Jotham his son succeeded him as
king.[k]

Jotham King of Judah

27:1–4,7–9pp — 2Ki 15:33–38

27 Jotham[l] was twenty-five
years old when he became
king, and he reigned in Jerusalem
sixteen years. His mother's name
was Jerusha daughter of Zadok.
2He did what was right in the eyes
of the Lord, just as his father Uzziah had done, but unlike him he did
not enter the temple of the Lord.
3The people, however, continued
their corrupt practices. 3Jotham rebuilt the Upper Gate of the temple
of the Lord and did extensive work
on the wall at the hill of Ophel.[m]
4He built towns in the Judean hills
and forts and towers in the wooded
areas.
5Jotham made war on the king of
the Ammonites[n] and conquered
them. That year the Ammonites
paid him a hundred talents[n] of silver, ten thousand cors[o] of wheat
and ten thousand cors of barley.
The Ammonites brought him the
same amount also in the second
and third years.
6Jotham grew powerful[o] because he walked steadfastly before
the Lord his God.
7The other events in Jotham's
reign, including all his wars and the
other things he did, are written in
the book of the kings of Israel and
Judah. 8He was twenty-five years
old when he became king, and he
reigned in Jerusalem sixteen years.
9Jotham rested with his fathers
and was buried in the City of David.
And Ahaz his son succeeded him as
king.

Ahaz King of Judah

28:1–27pp — 2Ki 16:1–20

28 Ahaz[p] was twenty years old
when he became king, and
he reigned in Jerusalem sixteen
years. Unlike David his father, he
did not do what was right in the
eyes of the Lord. 2He walked in the
ways of the kings of Israel and also
made cast idols[q] for worshiping
the Baals. 3He burned sacrifices in
the Valley of Ben Hinnom[r] and
sacrificed his sons[s] in the fire, following the detestable[t] ways of the
nations the Lord had driven out before the Israelites. 4He offered sacrifices and burned incense at the

26:16 [a]2Ki 16:12
26:17 [b]1Ki 4:2; 1Ch 6:10
26:18 [c]Nu 16:39 [d]Nu 18:1-7 [e]Ex 30:7 [f]1Ch 6:49
26:19 [g]Nu 12:10; 2Ki 5:25-27
26:21 [h]Ex 4:6; Lev 13:46; 14:8; Nu 5:2; 19:12
26:22 [i]2Ki 15:1; Isa 1:1; 6:1
26:23 [j]Isa 1:1; 6:1 [k]2Ki 14:21; 15:7; Am 1:1
27:1 [l]2Ki 15:5,32; 1Ch 3:12
27:3 [m]2Ch 33:14; Ne 3:26
27:5 [n]Ge 19:38
27:6 [o]2Ch 26:5
28:1 [p]1Ch 3:13; Isa 1:1
28:2 [q]Ex 34:17; 2Ch 22:3
28:3 [r]Jos 15:8; 2Ki 23:10 [s]Lev 18:21; 2Ki 3:27; 2Ch 33:6; Eze 20:26 [t]Dt 18:9; 2Ch 33:2

[l]*19* The Hebrew word was used for various diseases affecting the skin—not necessarily leprosy; also in verses 20, 21 and 23.
[m]*21* *Or in a house where he was relieved of responsibilities*
[n]*5* That is, about 3 3/4 tons (about 3.4 metric tons)
[o]*5* That is, probably about 62,000 bushels (about 2,200 kiloliters)

high places, on the hilltops and under every spreading tree.
5Therefore the LORD his God
handed him over to the king of
Aram.[a] The Arameans defeated
him and took many of his people as
prisoners and brought them to Damascus.
He was also given into the hands
of the king of Israel, who inflicted
heavy casualties on him. **6**In one
day Pekah[b] son of Remaliah killed
a hundred and twenty thousand
soldiers in Judah[c]—because Judah had forsaken the LORD, the God
of their fathers. **7**Zicri, an Ephraimite warrior, killed Maaseiah the
king's son, Azrikam the officer in
charge of the palace, and Elkanah,
second to the king. **8**The Israelites
took captive from their kinsmen[d]
two hundred thousand wives, sons
and daughters. They also took a
great deal of plunder, which they
carried back to Samaria.[e]
9But a prophet of the LORD
named Oded was there, and he
went out to meet the army when it
returned to Samaria. He said to
them, "Because the LORD, the God
of your fathers, was angry[f] with
Judah, he gave them into your
hand. But you have slaughtered
them in a rage that reaches to heav-
en.[g] **10**And now you intend to
make the men and women of Judah and Jerusalem your slaves.[h]
But aren't you also guilty of sins
against the LORD your God? **11**Now
listen to me! Send back your fellow
countrymen you have taken as prisoners, for the LORD's fierce anger
rests on you.[i]"
12Then some of the leaders in
Ephraim—Azariah son of Jehohanan, Berekiah son of Meshillemoth, Jehizkiah son of Shallum,
and Amasa son of Hadlai—confronted those who were arriving
from the war. **13**"You must not
bring those prisoners here," they
said, "or we will be guilty before
the LORD. Do you intend to add to
our sin and guilt? For our guilt is
already great, and his fierce anger
rests on Israel."
14So the soldiers gave up the
prisoners and plunder in the presence of the officials and all the assembly. **15**The men designated by
name took the prisoners, and from
the plunder they clothed all who
were naked. They provided them
with clothes and sandals, food and
drink,[j] and healing balm. All
those who were weak they put on
donkeys. So they took them back
to their fellow countrymen at Jericho, the City of Palms,[k] and returned to Samaria.
16At that time King Ahaz sent to
the king[p] of Assyria[l] for help.
17The Edomites[m] had again come
and attacked Judah and carried
away prisoners,[n] **18**while the Philistines[o] had raided towns in the
foothills and in the Negev of Judah.
They captured and occupied Beth
Shemesh, Aijalon[p] and Gederoth,
as well as Soco, Timnah and Gim-
zo, with their surrounding villages.
19The LORD had humbled Judah because of Ahaz king of Israel,[q] for
he had promoted wickedness in Judah and had been most unfaithful[q] to the LORD. **20**Tiglath-Pileser[r][r] king of Assyria came to him,
but he gave him trouble instead of
help.[s] **21**Ahaz took some of the
things from the temple of the LORD
and from the royal palace and from
the princes and presented them to
the king of Assyria, but that did not
help him.
22In his time of trouble King
Ahaz became even more unfaith-
ful[t] to the LORD. **23**He offered sacrifices to the gods[u] of Damascus,
who had defeated him; for he
thought, "Since the gods of the
kings of Aram have helped them, I
will sacrifice to them so they will
help me."[v] But they were his
downfall and the downfall of all Israel.
24Ahaz gathered together the
furnishings from the temple of
God[w] and took them away.[s] He

28:5 [a] Isa 7:1
28:6 [b] 2Ki 15:25,27 [c] ver 8; Isa 9:21; 11:13
28:8 [d] Dt 28:25-41; 2Ch 11:4 [e] 2Ch 29:9
28:9 [f] 2Ch 25:15; Isa 10:6; 47:6; Zec 1:15 [g] Ezr 9:6; Rev 18:5
28:10 [h] Lev 25:39-46
28:11 [i] 2Ch 11:4; Jas 2:13
28:15 [j] 2Ki 6:22; Pr 25:21-22 [k] Dt 34:3; Jdg 1:16
28:16 [l] 2Ki 16:7
28:17 [m] Ps 137:7; Isa 34:5 [n] 2Ch 29:9
28:18 [o] Eze 16:27,57 [p] Jos 10:12
28:19 [q] 2Ch 21:2
28:20 [r] 2Ki 15:29; 1Ch 5:6 [s] 2Ki 16:7
28:22 [t] Jer 5:3
28:23 [u] 2Ch 25:14 [v] Jer 44:17-18
28:24 [w] 2Ki 16:18

[p] *16* One Hebrew manuscript, Septuagint and Vulgate (see also 2 Kings 16:7); most Hebrew manuscripts *kings* [q] *19* That is, Judah, as frequently in 2 Chronicles [r] *20* Hebrew *Tilgath-Pilneser,* a variant of *Tiglath-Pileser* [s] *24* Or *and cut them up*

shut the doors[a] of the LORD's temple and set up altars[b] at every
street corner in Jerusalem. 25In every town in Judah he built high
places to burn sacrifices to other
gods and provoked the LORD, the
God of his fathers, to anger.
26The other events of his reign
and all his ways, from beginning to
end, are written in the book of the
kings of Judah and Israel. 27Ahaz
rested[c] with his fathers and was
buried[d] in the city of Jerusalem,
but he was not placed in the tombs
of the kings of Israel. And Hezekiah
his son succeeded him as king.

Hezekiah Purifies the Temple

29:1-2pp — 2Ki 18:2-3

29 Hezekiah[e] was twenty-five
years old when he became
king, and he reigned in Jerusalem
twenty-nine years. His mother's
name was Abijah daughter of Zechariah. 2He did what was right in the
eyes of the LORD, just as his father
David[f] had done.
3In the first month of the first
year of his reign, he opened the
doors of the temple of the LORD and
repaired[g] them. 4He brought in
the priests and the Levites, assembled them in the square on the east
side 5and said: "Listen to me, Levites! Consecrate[h] yourselves now
and consecrate the temple of the
LORD, the God of your fathers. Remove all defilement from the sanctuary. 6Our fathers[i] were unfaithful;[j] they did evil in the eyes of the
LORD our God and forsook him.
They turned their faces away from
the LORD's dwelling place and
turned their backs on him. 7They
also shut the doors of the portico
and put out the lamps. They did
not burn incense or present any
burnt offerings at the sanctuary to
the God of Israel. 8Therefore, the
anger of the LORD has fallen on Judah and Jerusalem; he has made
them an object of dread and horror[k] and scorn,[l] as you can see
with your own eyes. 9This is why
our fathers have fallen by the sword
and why our sons and daughters
and our wives are in captivity.[m]
10Now I intend to make a covenant[n] with the LORD, the God of
Israel, so that his fierce anger will
turn away from us. 11My sons, do
not be negligent now, for the LORD
has chosen you to stand before him
and serve him,[o] to minister[p] before him and to burn incense."
12Then these Levites[q] set to
work:
from the Kohathites,
Mahath son of Amasai and
Joel son of Azariah;
from the Merarites,
Kish son of Abdi and Azariah son of Jehallelel;
from the Gershonites,
Joah son of Zimmah and
Eden[r] son of Joah;
13from the descendants of Elizaphan,
Shimri and Jeiel;
from the descendants of
Asaph,[s]
Zechariah and Mattaniah;
14from the descendants of Heman,
Jehiel and Shimei;
from the descendants of Jeduthun,
Shemaiah and Uzziel.
15When they had assembled
their brothers and consecrated
themselves, they went in to purify[t]
the temple of the LORD, as the king
had ordered, following the word of
the LORD. 16The priests went into
the sanctuary of the LORD to purify
it. They brought out to the courtyard of the LORD's temple everything unclean that they found in
the temple of the LORD. The Levites
took it and carried it out to the Kidron Valley.[u] 17They began the consecration on the first day of the first
month, and by the eighth day of the
month they reached the portico of
the LORD. For eight more days they
consecrated the temple of the LORD
itself, finishing on the sixteenth
day of the first month.
18Then they went in to King Hezekiah and reported: "We have purified the entire temple of the LORD,
the altar of burnt offering with all
its utensils, and the table for set-

28:24 [a] 2Ch 29:7 [b] 2Ch 30:14
28:27 [c] Isa 14:28-32 [d] 2Ch 21:20; 24:25
29:1 [e] 1Ch 3:13
29:2 [f] 2Ch 28:1; 34:2
29:3 [g] 2Ch 28:24
29:5 [h] 2Ch 35:6
29:6 [i] Ps 106:6-47; Jer 2:27 [j] 1Ch 5:25; Eze 8:16
29:8 [k] Dt 28:25; 2Ch 24:18 [l] Jer 18:16; 19:8; 25:9,18
29:9 [m] 2Ch 28:5-8, 17
29:10 [n] 2Ch 15:12; 23:16
29:11 [o] Nu 3:6; 8:6, 14 [p] 1Ch 15:2
29:12 [q] Nu 3:17-20 [r] 2Ch 31:15
29:13 [s] 1Ch 6:39
29:15 [t] ver 5; 1Ch 23:28; 2Ch 30:12
29:16 [u] 2Sa 15:23

ting out the consecrated bread, with all its articles. 19We have prepared and consecrated all the articles[a] that King Ahaz removed in his unfaithfulness while he was king. They are now in front of the LORD's altar."

20Early the next morning King Hezekiah gathered the city officials together and went up to the temple of the LORD. 21They brought seven bulls, seven rams, seven male lambs and seven male goats as a sin offering[b] for the kingdom, for the sanctuary and for Judah. The king commanded the priests, the descendants of Aaron, to offer these on the altar of the LORD. 22So they slaughtered the bulls, and the priests took the blood and sprinkled it on the altar; next they slaughtered the rams and sprinkled their blood on the altar; then they slaughtered the lambs and sprinkled their blood[c] on the altar. 23The goats for the sin offering were brought before the king and the assembly, and they laid their hands[d] on them. 24The priests then slaughtered the goats and presented their blood on the altar for a sin offering to atone[e] for all Israel, because the king had ordered the burnt offering and the sin offering for all Israel.

25He stationed the Levites in the temple of the LORD with cymbals, harps and lyres in the way prescribed by David[f] and Gad[g] the king's seer and Nathan the prophet; this was commanded by the LORD through his prophets. 26So the Levites stood ready with David's instruments,[h] and the priests with their trumpets.[i]

27Hezekiah gave the order to sacrifice the burnt offering on the altar. As the offering began, singing to the LORD began also, accompanied by trumpets and the instruments[j] of David king of Israel. 28The whole assembly bowed in worship, while the singers sang and the trumpeters played. All this continued until the sacrifice of the burnt offering was completed.

29When the offerings were finished, the king and everyone present with him knelt down and worshiped.[k] 30King Hezekiah and his officials ordered the Levites to praise the LORD with the words of David and of Asaph the seer. So they sang praises with gladness and bowed their heads and worshiped.

31Then Hezekiah said, "You have now dedicated yourselves to the LORD. Come and bring sacrifices[l] and thank offerings to the temple of the LORD." So the assembly brought sacrifices and thank offerings, and all whose hearts were willing[m] brought burnt offerings.

32The number of burnt offerings the assembly brought was seventy bulls, a hundred rams and two hundred male lambs—all of them for burnt offerings to the LORD. 33The animals consecrated as sacrifices amounted to six hundred bulls and three thousand sheep and goats. 34The priests, however, were too few to skin all the burnt offerings;[n] so their kinsmen the Levites helped them until the task was finished and until other priests had been consecrated,[o] for the Levites had been more conscientious in consecrating themselves than the priests had been. 35There were burnt offerings in abundance, together with the fat[p] of the fellowship offerings[t][q] and the drink offerings[r] that accompanied the burnt offerings.

So the service of the temple of the LORD was reestablished. 36Hezekiah and all the people rejoiced at what God had brought about for his people, because it was done so quickly.

Hezekiah Celebrates the Passover

30 Hezekiah sent word to all Israel and Judah and also wrote letters to Ephraim and Manasseh,[s] inviting them to come to the temple of the LORD in Jerusalem and celebrate the Passover[t] to the LORD, the God of Israel. 2The

29:19 [a] 2Ch 28:24
29:21 [b] Lev 4:13-14
29:22 [c] Lev 4:18
29:23 [d] Lev 4:15
29:24 [e] Ex 29:36; Lev 4:26
29:25 [f] 1Ch 25:6; 2Ch 8:14 [g] 1Sa 22:5; 2Sa 24:11
29:26 [h] 1Ch 15:16 [i] 1Ch 15:24; 23:5; 2Ch 5:12
29:27 [j] 2Ch 23:18
29:29 [k] 2Ch 20:18
29:31 [l] Heb 13:15-16 [m] Ex 25:2; 35:22
29:34 [n] 2Ch 35:11 [o] 2Ch 30:3,15
29:35 [p] Ex 29:13; Lev 3:16 [q] Lev 7:11-21 [r] Nu 15:5-10
30:1 [s] Ge 41:52 [t] Ex 12:11; Nu 28:16

[t]35 Traditionally *peace offerings*

king and his officials and the whole
assembly in Jerusalem decided to
celebrate[a] the Passover in the second month. **3**They had not been
able to celebrate it at the regular
time because not enough priests
had consecrated[b] themselves and
the people had not assembled in
Jerusalem. **4**The plan seemed right
both to the king and to the whole
assembly. **5**They decided to send a
proclamation throughout Israel,
from Beersheba to Dan,[c] calling
the people to come to Jerusalem
and celebrate the Passover to the
LORD, the God of Israel. It had not
been celebrated in large numbers
according to what was written.

6At the king's command, couriers went throughout Israel and Judah with letters from the king and
from his officials, which read:

"People of Israel, return to
the LORD, the God of Abraham,
Isaac and Israel, that he may
return to you who are left, who
have escaped from the hand of
the kings of Assyria. **7**Do not
be like your fathers[d] and
brothers, who were unfaithful
to the LORD, the God of their
fathers, so that he made them
an object of horror,[e] as you
see. **8**Do not be stiff-necked,[f]
as your fathers were; submit to
the LORD. Come to the sanctuary, which he has consecrated
forever. Serve the LORD your
God, so that his fierce anger[g]
will turn away from you. **9**If
you return[h] to the LORD, then
your brothers and your children will be shown compassion[i] by their captors and will
come back to this land, for the
LORD your God is gracious and
compassionate.[j] He will not
turn his face from you if you
return to him."

10The couriers went from town
to town in Ephraim and Manasseh,
as far as Zebulun, but the people
scorned and ridiculed[k] them.
11Nevertheless, some men of Asher, Manasseh and Zebulun humbled themselves and went to Jerusalem.[l] **12**Also in Judah the hand
of God was on the people to give
them unity[m] of mind to carry out
what the king and his officials had
ordered, following the word of the
LORD.

13A very large crowd of people
assembled in Jerusalem to celebrate the Feast of Unleavened
Bread[n] in the second month.
14They removed the altars[o] in Jerusalem and cleared away the incense altars and threw them into
the Kidron Valley.[p]

15They slaughtered the Passover
lamb on the fourteenth day of the
second month. The priests and the
Levites were ashamed and consecrated[q] themselves and brought
burnt offerings to the temple of the
LORD. **16**Then they took up their
regular positions[r] as prescribed in
the Law of Moses the man of God.
The priests sprinkled the blood
handed to them by the Levites.
17Since many in the crowd had not
consecrated themselves, the Levites had to kill[s] the Passover
lambs for all those who were not
ceremonially clean and could not
consecrate ⌞their lambs⌟ to the
LORD. **18**Although most of the many
people who came from Ephraim,
Manasseh, Issachar and Zebulun
had not purified themselves,[t] yet
they ate the Passover, contrary to
what was written. But Hezekiah
prayed for them, saying, "May the
LORD, who is good, pardon everyone
19who sets his heart on seeking
God—the LORD, the God of his fathers—even if he is not clean according to the rules of the sanctuary." **20**And the LORD heard[u] Hezekiah and healed[v] the people.[w]

21The Israelites who were
present in Jerusalem celebrated
the Feast of Unleavened Bread[x]
for seven days with great rejoicing,
while the Levites and priests sang
to the LORD every day, accompanied by the LORD's instruments of
praise.[u]

22Hezekiah spoke encouragingly

30:2 [a] Nu 9:10
30:3 [b] 2Ch 29:34
30:5 [c] Jdg 20:1
30:7 [d] Ps 78:8,57; 106:6; Eze 20:18 [e] 2Ch 29:8
30:8 [f] Ex 32:9 [g] Nu 25:4; 2Ch 29:10
30:9 [h] Dt 30:2-5; Isa 1:16; 55:7 [i] 1Ki 8:50; Ps 106:46 [j] Ex 34:6-7; Dt 4:31; Mic 7:18
30:10 [k] 2Ch 36:16
30:11 [l] ver 25
30:12 [m] Jer 32:39; Eze 11:19; Php 2:13
30:13 [n] Nu 28:16
30:14 [o] 2Ch 28:24 [p] 2Sa 15:23
30:15 [q] 2Ch 29:34
30:16 [r] 2Ch 35:10
30:17 [s] 2Ch 29:34
30:18 [t] Ex 12:43-49; Nu 9:6-10
30:20 [u] 2Ch 6:20 [v] 2Ch 7:14; Mal 4:2 [w] Jas 5:16
30:21 [x] Ex 12:15,17; 13:6

[u] *21* Or *priests praised the LORD every day with resounding instruments belonging to the LORD*

to all the Levites, who showed good
understanding of the service of the
LORD. For the seven days they ate
their assigned portion and offered
fellowship offerings[v] and praised
the LORD, the God of their fathers.
23The whole assembly then
agreed to celebrate[a] the festival
seven more days; so for another
seven days they celebrated joyfully.
24Hezekiah king of Judah provided[b] a thousand bulls and seven
thousand sheep and goats for the
assembly, and the officials provided them with a thousand bulls and
ten thousand sheep and goats. A
great number of priests consecrated themselves. **25**The entire assembly of Judah rejoiced, along with
the priests and Levites and all who
had assembled from Israel[c], including the aliens who had come
from Israel and those who lived in
Judah. **26**There was great joy in Jerusalem, for since the days of Solomon[d] son of David king of Israel
there had been nothing like this in
Jerusalem. **27**The priests and the
Levites stood to bless[e] the people,
and God heard them, for their
prayer reached heaven, his holy
dwelling place.

31 When all this had ended,
the Israelites who were
there went out to the towns of Judah, smashed the sacred stones
and cut down[f] the Asherah poles.
They destroyed the high places and
the altars throughout Judah and
Benjamin and in Ephraim and Manasseh. After they had destroyed
all of them, the Israelites returned
to their own towns and to their own
property.

Contributions for Worship

31:20–21pp — 2Ki 18:5–7

2Hezekiah[g] assigned the priests
and Levites to divisions[h]—each of
them according to their duties as
priests or Levites—to offer burnt
offerings and fellowship offerings,[v] to minister,[i] to give thanks
and to sing praises[j] at the gates of
the LORD's dwelling.[k] **3**The king
contributed[l] from his own possessions for the morning and evening
burnt offerings and for the burnt
offerings on the Sabbaths, New
Moons and appointed feasts as
written in the Law of the LORD.[m]
4He ordered the people living in Jerusalem to give the portion[n] due
the priests and Levites so they
could devote themselves to the
Law of the LORD. **5**As soon as the
order went out, the Israelites generously gave the firstfruits[o] of their
grain, new wine,[p] oil and honey
and all that the fields produced.
They brought a great amount, a
tithe of everything. **6**The men of Israel and Judah who lived in the
towns of Judah also brought a
tithe[q] of their herds and flocks and
a tithe of the holy things dedicated
to the LORD their God, and they
piled them in heaps.[r] **7**They began
doing this in the third month and
finished in the seventh month.[s]
8When Hezekiah and his officials
came and saw the heaps, they
praised the LORD and blessed[t] his
people Israel.
9Hezekiah asked the priests and
Levites about the heaps; **10**and Azariah the chief priest, from the
family of Zadok,[u] answered,
"Since the people began to bring
their contributions to the temple of
the LORD, we have had enough to
eat and plenty to spare, because
the LORD has blessed his people,
and this great amount is left
over."[v]
11Hezekiah gave orders to prepare storerooms in the temple of
the LORD, and this was done.
12Then they faithfully brought in
the contributions, tithes and dedicated gifts. Conaniah,[w] a Levite,
was in charge of these things, and
his brother Shimei was next in
rank. **13**Jehiel, Azaziah, Nahath,
Asahel, Jerimoth, Jozabad,[x] Eliel,
Ismakiah, Mahath and Benaiah
were supervisors under Conaniah
and Shimei his brother, by appointment of King Hezekiah and Azariah
the official in charge of the temple
of God.

30:23 [a] 1Ki 8:65; 2Ch 7:9
30:24 [b] 1Ki 8:5; 2Ch 29:34; 35:7; Ezr 6:17; 8:35
30:25 [c] ver 11
30:26 [d] 2Ch 7:8
30:27 [e] Ex 39:43; Nu 6:23; Dt 26:15; 2Ch 23:18; Ps 68:5
31:1 [f] 2Ki 18:4; 2Ch 32:12; Isa 36:7
31:2 [g] 2Ch 29:9 [h] 1Ch 24:1 [i] 1Ch 15:2 [j] Ps 7:17; 9:2; 47:6; 71:22 [k] 1Ch 23:28-32
31:3 [l] 1Ch 29:3; 2Ch 35:7; Eze 45:17 [m] Nu 28:1-29:40
31:4 [n] Nu 18:8; Dt 18:8; Ne 13:10; Mal 2:7
31:5 [o] Nu 18:12,24; Ne 13:12; Eze 44:30 [p] Dt 12:17
31:6 [q] Lev 27:30; Ne 13:10-12 [r] Dt 14:28; Ru 3:7
31:7 [s] Ex 23:16
31:8 [t] Ps 144:13-15
31:10 [u] 2Sa 8:17 [v] Ex 36:5; Eze 44:30; Mal 3:10-12
31:12 [w] 2Ch 35:9
31:13 [x] 2Ch 35:9

[v] 22,2 Traditionally *peace offerings*

14Kore son of Imnah the Levite, keeper of the East Gate, was in charge of the freewill offerings given to God, distributing the contributions made to the LORD and also the consecrated gifts. 15Eden,[a] Miniamin, Jeshua, Shemaiah, Amariah and Shecaniah assisted him faithfully in the towns[b] of the priests, distributing to their fellow priests according to their divisions, old and young alike.

16In addition, they distributed to the males three years old or more whose names were in the genealogical records[c]—all who would enter the temple of the LORD to perform the daily duties of their various tasks, according to their responsibilities and their divisions. 17And they distributed to the priests enrolled by their families in the genealogical records and likewise to the Levites twenty years old or more, according to their responsibilities and their divisions. 18They included all the little ones, the wives, and the sons and daughters of the whole community listed in these genealogical records. For they were faithful in consecrating themselves.

19As for the priests, the descendants of Aaron, who lived on the farm lands around their towns or in any other towns,[d] men were designated by name to distribute portions to every male among them and to all who were recorded in the genealogies of the Levites.

20This is what Hezekiah did throughout Judah, doing what was good and right and faithful[e] before the LORD his God. 21In everything that he undertook in the service of God's temple and in obedience to the law and the commands, he sought his God and worked wholeheartedly. And so he prospered.[f]

Sennacherib Threatens Jerusalem

32:9–19pp — 2Ki 18:17–35; Isa 36:2–20
32:20–21pp — 2Ki 19:35–37; Isa 37:36–38

32 After all that Hezekiah had so faithfully done, Sennacherib[g] king of Assyria came and invaded Judah. He laid siege to the fortified cities, thinking to conquer them for himself. 2When Hezekiah saw that Sennacherib had come and that he intended to make war on Jerusalem,[h] 3he consulted with his officials and military staff about blocking off the water from the springs outside the city, and they helped him. 4A large force of men assembled, and they blocked all the springs[i] and the stream that flowed through the land. "Why should the kings[w] of Assyria come and find plenty of water?" they said. 5Then he worked hard repairing all the broken sections of the wall[j] and building towers on it. He built another wall outside that one and reinforced the supporting terraces[x][k] of the City of David. He also made large numbers of weapons[l] and shields.

6He appointed military officers over the people and assembled them before him in the square at the city gate and encouraged them with these words: 7"Be strong and courageous.[m] Do not be afraid or discouraged[n] because of the king of Assyria and the vast army with him, for there is a greater power with us than with him.[o] 8With him is only the arm of flesh,[p] but with us[q] is the LORD our God to help us and to fight our battles."[r] And the people gained confidence from what Hezekiah the king of Judah said.

9Later, when Sennacherib king of Assyria and all his forces were laying siege to Lachish,[s] he sent his officers to Jerusalem with this message for Hezekiah king of Judah and for all the people of Judah who were there:

> 10"This is what Sennacherib king of Assyria says: On what are you basing your confidence,[t] that you remain in Jerusalem under siege? 11When Hezekiah says, 'The LORD our God will save us from the hand of the king of Assyria,' he is

31:15 [a] 2Ch 29:12 [b] Jos 21:9-19
31:16 [c] 1Ch 23:3; Ezr 3:4
31:19 [d] ver 12-15; Lev 25:34; Nu 35:2-5
31:20 [e] 2Ki 20:3; 22:2
31:21 [f] Dt 29:9
32:1 [g] 2Ki 18:13-19; Isa 36:1; 37:9, 17,37
32:2 [h] Isa 22:7; Jer 1:15
32:4 [i] 2Ki 18:17; 20:20; Isa 22:9,11; Na 3:14
32:5 [j] 2Ch 25:23; Isa 22:10 [k] 1Ki 9:24; 1Ch 11:8 [l] Isa 22:8
32:7 [m] Dt 31:6; 1Ch 22:13 [n] 2Ch 20:15 [o] Nu 14:9; 2Ki 6:16
32:8 [p] Job 40:9; Isa 52:10; Jer 17:5; 32:21 [q] Dt 3:22; 1Sa 17:45; 2Ch 13:12 [r] 1Ch 5:22; 2Ch 20:17; Ps 20:7; Isa 28:6
32:9 [s] Jos 10:3,31
32:10 [t] Eze 29:16

[w] 4 Hebrew; Septuagint and Syriac *king*
[x] 5 Or *the Millo*

misleading[a] you, to let you die of hunger and thirst. **12**Did not Hezekiah himself remove this god's high places and altars, saying to Judah and Jerusalem, 'You must worship before one altar[b] and burn sacrifices on it'?

13"Do you not know what I and my fathers have done to all the peoples of the other lands? Were the gods of those nations ever able to deliver their land from my hand?[c] **14**Who of all the gods of these nations that my fathers destroyed has been able to save his people from me? How then can your god deliver you from my hand? **15**Now do not let Hezekiah deceive[d] you and mislead you like this. Do not believe him, for no god of any nation or kingdom has been able to deliver[e] his people from my hand or the hand of my fathers.[f] How much less will your god deliver you from my hand!"

16Sennacherib's officers spoke further against the LORD God and against his servant Hezekiah. **17**The king also wrote letters[g] insulting[h] the LORD, the God of Israel, and saying this against him: "Just as the gods[i] of the peoples of the other lands did not rescue their people from my hand, so the god of Hezekiah will not rescue his people from my hand." **18**Then they called out in Hebrew to the people of Jerusalem who were on the wall, to terrify them and make them afraid in order to capture the city. **19**They spoke about the God of Jerusalem as they did about the gods of the other peoples of the world—the work of men's hands.[j]

20King Hezekiah and the prophet Isaiah son of Amoz cried out in prayer to heaven about this. **21**And the LORD sent an angel,[k] who annihilated all the fighting men and the leaders and officers in the camp of the Assyrian king. So he withdrew to his own land in disgrace. And

32:11 [a]Isa 37:10
32:12 [b]2Ch 31:1
32:13 [c]ver 15
32:15 [d]Isa 37:10 [e]Da 3:15 [f]Ex 5:2
32:17 [g]Isa 37:14 [h]Ps 74:22; Isa 37:4,17 [i]2Ki 19:12
32:19 [j]2Ki 19:18; Ps 115:4,4-8; Isa 2:8; 17:8
32:21 [k]Ge 19:13 [l]2Ki 19:7
32:23 [m]2Ch 9:24; 17:5; Isa 45:14; Zec 14:16-17
32:25 [n]2Ki 14:10; 2Ch 26:16 [o]2Ch 19:2; 24:18
32:26 [p]Jer 26:18-19 [q]2Ch 34:27, 28; Isa 39:8
32:27 [r]1Ch 29:12
32:29 [s]1Ch 29:12
32:30 [t]2Ki 18:17 [u]1Ki 1:33
32:31 [v]Isa 39:1 [w]ver 24; Isa 38:7

when he went into the temple of his god, some of his sons cut him down with the sword.[l]

22So the LORD saved Hezekiah and the people of Jerusalem from the hand of Sennacherib king of Assyria and from the hand of all others. He took care of them[y] on every side. **23**Many brought offerings to Jerusalem for the LORD and valuable gifts[m] for Hezekiah king of Judah. From then on he was highly regarded by all the nations.

Hezekiah's Pride, Success and Death

32:24–33pp — 2Ki 20:1–21; Isa 37:21–38; 38:1–8

24In those days Hezekiah became ill and was at the point of death. He prayed to the LORD, who answered him and gave him a miraculous sign. **25**But Hezekiah's heart was proud[n] and he did not respond to the kindness shown him; therefore the LORD's wrath[o] was on him and on Judah and Jerusalem. **26**Then Hezekiah repented[p] of the pride of his heart, as did the people of Jerusalem; therefore the LORD's wrath did not come upon them during the days of Hezekiah.[q]

27Hezekiah had very great riches and honor,[r] and he made treasuries for his silver and gold and for his precious stones, spices, shields and all kinds of valuables. **28**He also made buildings to store the harvest of grain, new wine and oil; and he made stalls for various kinds of cattle, and pens for the flocks. **29**He built villages and acquired great numbers of flocks and herds, for God had given him very great riches.[s]

30It was Hezekiah who blocked[t] the upper outlet of the Gihon[u] spring and channeled the water down to the west side of the City of David. He succeeded in everything he undertook. **31**But when envoys were sent by the rulers of Babylon[v] to ask him about the miraculous sign[w] that had occurred in the

[y]22 Hebrew; Septuagint and Vulgate *He gave them rest*

land, God left him to test[a] him and to know everything that was in his heart.

32The other events of Hezekiah's reign and his acts of devotion are written in the vision of the prophet Isaiah son of Amoz in the book of the kings of Judah and Israel. **33**Hezekiah rested with his fathers and was buried on the hill where the tombs of David's descendants are. All Judah and the people of Jerusalem honored him when he died. And Manasseh his son succeeded him as king.

Manasseh King of Judah

33:1–10pp — 2Ki 21:1–10
33:18–20pp — 2Ki 21:17–18

33 Manasseh[b] was twelve years old when he became king, and he reigned in Jerusalem fifty-five years. **2**He did evil in the eyes of the LORD,[c] following the detestable[d] practices of the nations the LORD had driven out before the Israelites. **3**He rebuilt the high places his father Hezekiah had demolished; he also erected altars to the Baals and made Asherah poles.[e] He bowed down[f] to all the starry hosts and worshiped them. **4**He built altars in the temple of the LORD, of which the LORD had said, "My Name[g] will remain in Jerusalem forever." **5**In both courts of the temple of the LORD,[h] he built altars to all the starry hosts. **6**He sacrificed his sons[i] in[z] the fire in the Valley of Ben Hinnom, practiced sorcery, divination and witchcraft, and consulted mediums[j] and spiritists.[k] He did much evil in the eyes of the LORD, provoking him to anger.

7He took the carved image he had made and put it in God's temple,[l] of which God had said to David and to his son Solomon, "In this temple and in Jerusalem, which I have chosen out of all the tribes of Israel, I will put my Name forever. **8**I will not again make the feet of the Israelites leave the land[m] I assigned to your forefathers, if only they will be careful to do everything I commanded them concerning all the laws, decrees and ordinances given through Moses." **9**But Manasseh led Judah and the people of Jerusalem astray, so that they did more evil than the nations the LORD had destroyed before the Israelites.[n]

10The LORD spoke to Manasseh and his people, but they paid no attention. **11**So the LORD brought against them the army commanders of the king of Assyria, who took Manasseh prisoner,[o] put a hook in his nose, bound him with bronze shackles[p] and took him to Babylon. **12**In his distress he sought the favor of the LORD his God and humbled[q] himself greatly before the God of his fathers. **13**And when he prayed to him, the LORD was moved by his entreaty and listened to his plea; so he brought him back to Jerusalem and to his kingdom. Then Manasseh knew that the LORD is God.

14Afterward he rebuilt the outer wall of the City of David, west of the Gihon[r] spring in the valley, as far as the entrance of the Fish Gate[s] and encircling the hill of Ophel;[t] he also made it much higher. He stationed military commanders in all the fortified cities in Judah.

15He got rid of the foreign gods and removed[u] the image from the temple of the LORD, as well as all the altars he had built on the temple hill and in Jerusalem; and he threw them out of the city. **16**Then he restored the altar of the LORD and sacrificed fellowship offerings[a] and thank offerings[v] on it, and told Judah to serve the LORD, the God of Israel. **17**The people, however, continued to sacrifice at the high places, but only to the LORD their God.

18The other events of Manasseh's reign, including his prayer to his God and the words the seers spoke to him in the name of the LORD, the God of Israel, are written in the annals of the kings of Isra-

32:31 [a] Ge 22:1; Dt 8:16
33:1 [b] 1Ch 3:13
33:2 [c] Jer 15:4 [d] Dt 18:9; 2Ch 28:3
33:3 [e] Dt 16:21-22 [f] Dt 17:3; 2Ch 31:1
33:4 [g] 2Ch 7:16
33:5 [h] 2Ch 4:9
33:6 [i] Lev 18:21; Dt 18:10; 2Ch 28:3 [j] Lev 19:31 [k] 1Sa 28:13
33:7 [l] 2Ch 7:16
33:8 [m] 2Sa 7:10
33:9 [n] Jer 15:4
33:11 [o] Dt 28:36 [p] Ps 149:8
33:12 [q] 2Ch 6:37; 32:26; 1Pe 5:6
33:14 [r] 1Ki 1:33 [s] Ne 3:3; 12:39; Zep 1:10 [t] 2Ch 27:3; Ne 3:26
33:15 [u] ver 3-7; 2Ki 23:12
33:16 [v] Lev 7:11-18

[z] 6 Or *He made his sons pass through*
[a] 16 Traditionally *peace offerings*

el.[b] **19**His prayer and how God was
moved by his entreaty, as well as all
his sins and unfaithfulness, and
the sites where he built high places
and set up Asherah poles and idols
before he humbled[a] himself—all
are written in the records of the
seers.[cb] **20**Manasseh rested with
his fathers and was buried[c] in his
palace. And Amon his son succeeded him as king.

Amon King of Judah

33:21–25pp — 2Ki 21:19–24

21Amon[d] was twenty-two years
old when he became king, and he
reigned in Jerusalem two years.
22He did evil in the eyes of the
LORD, as his father Manasseh had
done. Amon worshiped and offered
sacrifices to all the idols Manasseh
had made. **23**But unlike his father
Manasseh, he did not humble[e]
himself before the LORD; Amon increased his guilt.

24Amon's officials conspired
against him and assassinated him
in his palace. **25**Then the people[f]
of the land killed all who had plotted against King Amon, and they
made Josiah his son king in his
place.

Josiah's Reforms

34:1–2pp — 2Ki 22:1–2
34:3–7Ref — 2Ki 23:4–20
34:8–13pp — 2Ki 22:3–7

34 Josiah[g] was eight years old
when he became king,[h]
and he reigned in Jerusalem thirty-one years. **2**He did what was
right in the eyes of the LORD and
walked in the ways of his father David,[i] not turning aside to the right
or to the left.

3In the eighth year of his reign,
while he was still young, he began
to seek the God[j] of his father David. In his twelfth year he began to
purge Judah and Jerusalem of high
places, Asherah poles, carved idols
and cast images. **4**Under his direction the altars of the Baals were
torn down; he cut to pieces the incense altars that were above them,
and smashed the Asherah poles,[k]
the idols and the images. These he
broke to pieces and scattered over
the graves of those who had sacrificed to them.[l] **5**He burned[m] the
bones of the priests on their altars,
and so he purged Judah and Jerusalem. **6**In the towns of Manasseh,
Ephraim and Simeon, as far as
Naphtali, and in the ruins around
them, **7**he tore down the altars and
the Asherah poles and crushed the
idols to powder[n] and cut to pieces
all the incense altars throughout
Israel. Then he went back to Jerusalem.

8In the eighteenth year of Josiah's reign, to purify the land and
the temple, he sent Shaphan son of
Azaliah and Maaseiah the ruler of
the city, with Joah son of Joahaz,
the recorder, to repair the temple
of the LORD his God.

9They went to Hilkiah[o] the high
priest and gave him the money that
had been brought into the temple
of God, which the Levites who were
the doorkeepers had collected
from the people of Manasseh,
Ephraim and the entire remnant of
Israel and from all the people of Judah and Benjamin and the inhabitants of Jerusalem. **10**Then they
entrusted it to the men appointed
to supervise the work on the LORD's
temple. These men paid the workers who repaired and restored the
temple. **11**They also gave money[p]
to the carpenters and builders to
purchase dressed stone, and timber for joists and beams for the
buildings that the kings of Judah
had allowed to fall into ruin.[q]

12The men did the work faithfully.[r] Over them to direct them were
Jahath and Obadiah, Levites descended from Merari, and Zechariah and Meshullam, descended
from Kohath. The Levites—all who
were skilled in playing musical instruments—[s] **13**had charge of the
laborers[t] and supervised all the
workers from job to job. Some of
the Levites were secretaries,
scribes and doorkeepers.

33:19 [a]2Ch 6:37 [b]2Ki 21:17
33:20 [c]2Ki 21:18; 2Ch 21:20
33:21 [d]1Ch 3:14
33:23 [e]ver 12; Ex 10:3; 2Ch 7:14; Ps 18:27; 147:6; Pr 3:34
33:25 [f]2Ch 22:1
34:1 [g]1Ch 3:14 [h]Zep 1:1
34:2 [i]2Ch 29:2
34:3 [j]1Ki 13:2; 1Ch 16:11; 2Ch 15:2; 33:17,22
34:4 [k]Ex 34:13 [l]Ex 32:20; Lev 26:30; 2Ki 23:11; Mic 1:5
34:5 [m]1Ki 13:2
34:7 [n]Ex 32:20; 2Ch 31:1
34:9 [o]1Ch 6:13; 2Ch 35:8
34:11 [p]2Ch 24:12 [q]2Ch 33:4-7
34:12 [r]2Ki 12:15 [s]1Ch 25:1
34:13 [t]1Ch 23:4

[b]*18* That is, Judah, as frequently in 2 Chronicles [c]*19* One Hebrew manuscript and Septuagint; most Hebrew manuscripts *of Hozai*

The Book of the Law Found

34:14–28pp — 2Ki 22:8–20
34:29–32pp — 2Ki 23:1–3

14While they were bringing out the money that had been taken into the temple of the LORD, Hilkiah the priest found the Book of the Law of the LORD that had been given through Moses. **15**Hilkiah said to Shaphan the secretary, "I have found the Book of the Law[a] in the temple of the LORD." He gave it to Shaphan.

16Then Shaphan took the book to the king and reported to him: "Your officials are doing everything that has been committed to them. **17**They have paid out the money that was in the temple of the LORD and have entrusted it to the supervisors and workers." **18**Then Shaphan the secretary informed the king, "Hilkiah the priest has given me a book." And Shaphan read from it in the presence of the king.

19When the king heard the words of the Law,[b] he tore[c] his robes. **20**He gave these orders to Hilkiah, Ahikam son of Shaphan[d], Abdon son of Micah,[d] Shaphan the secretary and Asaiah the king's attendant: **21**"Go and inquire of the LORD for me and for the remnant in Israel and Judah about what is written in this book that has been found. Great is the LORD's anger that is poured out[e] on us because our fathers have not kept the word of the LORD; they have not acted in accordance with all that is written in this book."

22Hilkiah and those the king had sent with him[e] went to speak to the prophetess[f] Huldah, who was the wife of Shallum son of Tokhath,[f] the son of Hasrah,[g] keeper of the wardrobe. She lived in Jerusalem, in the Second District.

23She said to them, "This is what the LORD, the God of Israel, says: Tell the man who sent you to me, **24**'This is what the LORD says: I am going to bring disaster[g] on this place and its people[h]—all the curses[i] written in the book that has been read in the presence of the king of Judah. **25**Because they have forsaken me[j] and burned incense to other gods and provoked me to anger by all that their hands have made,[h] my anger will be poured out on this place and will not be quenched.' **26**Tell the king of Judah, who sent you to inquire of the LORD, 'This is what the LORD, the God of Israel, says concerning the words you heard: **27**Because your heart was responsive[k] and you humbled[l] yourself before God when you heard what he spoke against this place and its people, and because you humbled yourself before me and tore your robes and wept in my presence, I have heard you, declares the LORD. **28**Now I will gather you to your fathers,[m] and you will be buried in peace. Your eyes will not see all the disaster I am going to bring on this place and on those who live here.' "[n]

So they took her answer back to the king.

29Then the king called together all the elders of Judah and Jerusalem. **30**He went up to the temple of the LORD[o] with the men of Judah, the people of Jerusalem, the priests and the Levites—all the people from the least to the greatest. He read in their hearing all the words of the Book of the Covenant, which had been found in the temple of the LORD. **31**The king stood by his pillar[p] and renewed the covenant[q] in the presence of the LORD—to follow[r] the LORD and keep his commands, regulations and decrees with all his heart and all his soul, and to obey the words of the covenant written in this book.

32Then he had everyone in Jerusalem and Benjamin pledge themselves to it; the people of Jerusalem did this in accordance with the covenant of God, the God of their fathers.

34:15 [a] 2Ki 22:8; Ezr 7:6; Ne 8:1
34:19 [b] Dt 28:3-68 [c] Jos 7:6; Isa 36:22; 37:1
34:20 [d] 2Ki 22:3
34:21 [e] 2Ch 29:8; La 2:4; 4:11; Eze 36:18
34:22 [f] Ex 15:20; Ne 6:14
34:24 [g] Pr 16:4; Isa 3:9; Jer 40:2; 42:10; 44:2, 11 [h] 2Ch 36:14-20 [i] Dt 28:15-68
34:25 [j] 2Ch 33:3-6; Jer 22:9
34:27 [k] 2Ch 12:7; 32:26 [l] Ex 10:3; 2Ch 6:37
34:28 [m] 2Ch 35:20-25 [n] 2Ch 32:26
34:30 [o] 2Ki 23:2; Ne 8:1-3
34:31 [p] 1Ki 7:15; 2Ki 11:14 [q] 2Ki 11:17; 2Ch 23:16; 29:10 [r] Dt 13:4

[d] 20 Also called *Acbor son of Micaiah*
[e] 22 One Hebrew manuscript, Vulgate and Syriac; most Hebrew manuscripts do not have *had sent with him.*
[f] 22 Also called *Tikvah*
[g] 22 Also called *Harhas*
[h] 25 Or *by everything they have done*

33Josiah removed all the detestable[a] idols from all the territory
belonging to the Israelites, and he
had all who were present in Israel
serve the LORD their God. As long
as he lived, they did not fail to
follow the LORD, the God of their
fathers.

Josiah Celebrates the Passover

35:1,18–19pp — 2Ki 23:21–23

35 Josiah celebrated the Passover[b] to the LORD in Jerusalem, and the Passover lamb was
slaughtered on the fourteenth day
of the first month. **2**He appointed
the priests to their duties and encouraged them in the service of the
LORD's temple. **3**He said to the Levites, who instructed[c] all Israel
and who had been consecrated to
the LORD: "Put the sacred ark in the
temple that Solomon son of David
king of Israel built. It is not to be
carried about on your shoulders.
Now serve the LORD your God and
his people Israel. **4**Prepare yourselves by families in your divisions,[d] according to the directions
written by David king of Israel and
by his son Solomon.

5"Stand in the holy place with a
group of Levites for each subdivi-
sion of the families of your fellow
countrymen, the lay people.
6Slaughter the Passover lambs,
consecrate yourselves[e] and prepare ⌞the lambs⌟ for your fellow
countrymen, doing what the LORD
commanded through Moses."

7Josiah provided for all the lay
people who were there a total of
thirty thousand sheep and goats for
the Passover offerings,[f] and also
three thousand cattle—all from
the king's own possessions.[g]

8His officials also contributed[h]
voluntarily to the people and the
priests and Levites. Hilkiah,[i]
Zechariah and Jehiel, the administrators of God's temple, gave the
priests twenty-six hundred Passover offerings and three hundred
cattle. **9**Also Conaniah[j] along with
Shemaiah and Nethanel, his brothers, and Hashabiah, Jeiel and Joza-

34:33 [a]ver 3-7; Dt 18:9
35:1 [b]Ex 12:1-30; Nu 9:3; 28:16
35:3 [c]Dt 33:10; 1Ch 23:26; 2Ch 5:7; 17:7
35:4 [d]ver 10; 1Ch 9:10-13; 24:1; 2Ch 8:14; Ezr 6:18
35:6 [e]Lev 11:44; 2Ch 29:5,15
35:7 [f]2Ch 30:24 [g]2Ch 31:3
35:8 [h]1Ch 29:3; 2Ch 29:31-36 [i]1Ch 6:13
35:9 [j]2Ch 31:12 [k]2Ch 31:13
35:10 [l]ver 4; Ezr 6:18 [m]2Ch 30:16
35:11 [n]2Ch 29:22, 34; 30:17
35:13 [o]Ex 12:2-11; Lev 6:25; 1Sa 2:13-15
35:14 [p]Ex 29:13
35:15 [q]1Ch 25:1; 26:12-19; 2Ch 29:30; Ne 12:46; Ps 68:25

bad,[k] the leaders of the Levites,
provided five thousand Passover offerings and five hundred head of
cattle for the Levites.

10The service was arranged and
the priests stood in their places
with the Levites in their divisions[l]
as the king had ordered.[m] **11**The
Passover lambs were slaughtered,[n]
and the priests sprinkled the blood
handed to them, while the Levites
skinned the animals. **12**They set
aside the burnt offerings to give
them to the subdivisions of the
families of the people to offer to
the LORD, as is written in the Book
of Moses. They did the same with
the cattle. **13**They roasted the Passover animals over the fire as prescribed,[o] and boiled the holy offerings in pots, caldrons and pans and
served them quickly to all the people. **14**After this, they made preparations for themselves and for the
priests, because the priests, the
descendants of Aaron, were sacrificing the burnt offerings and the
fat portions[p] until nightfall. So the
Levites made preparations for
themselves and for the Aaronic
priests.

15The musicians,[q] the descendants of Asaph, were in the places
prescribed by David, Asaph, Heman and Jeduthun the king's seer.
The gatekeepers at each gate did
not need to leave their posts, because their fellow Levites made the
preparations for them.

16So at that time the entire service of the LORD was carried out for
the celebration of the Passover and
the offering of burnt offerings on
the altar of the LORD, as King Josiah
had ordered. **17**The Israelites who
were present celebrated the Passover at that time and observed the
Feast of Unleavened Bread for sev-
en days. **18**The Passover had not
been observed like this in Israel
since the days of the prophet Samuel; and none of the kings of Israel
had ever celebrated such a Passover as did Josiah, with the priests,
the Levites and all Judah and Israel
who were there with the people of
Jerusalem. **19**This Passover was

celebrated in the eighteenth year
of Josiah's reign.

The Death of Josiah

35:20–36:1pp — 2Ki 23:28–30

20After all this, when Josiah had
set the temple in order, Neco king
of Egypt went up to fight at Carchemish[a] on the Euphrates,[b] and Josiah marched out to meet him in
battle. **21**But Neco sent messengers to him, saying, "What quarrel
is there between you and me, O
king of Judah? It is not you I am
attacking at this time, but the
house with which I am at war. God
has told[c] me to hurry; so stop opposing God, who is with me, or he
will destroy you."

22Josiah, however, would not
turn away from him, but disguised[d] himself to engage him in
battle. He would not listen to what
Neco had said at God's command
but went to fight him on the plain
of Megiddo.

23Archers[e] shot King Josiah,
and he told his officers, "Take me
away; I am badly wounded." **24**So
they took him out of his chariot,
put him in the other chariot he had
and brought him to Jerusalem,
where he died. He was buried in
the tombs of his fathers, and all Judah and Jerusalem mourned for
him.

25Jeremiah composed laments
for Josiah, and to this day all the
men and women singers commemorate Josiah in the laments.[f]
These became a tradition in Israel
and are written in the Laments.

26The other events of Josiah's
reign and his acts of devotion, according to what is written in the
Law of the LORD— **27**all the events,
from beginning to end, are written
in the book of the kings of Israel

36 and Judah. **1**And the people
of the land took Jehoahaz
son of Josiah and made him king in
Jerusalem in place of his father.

Jehoahaz King of Judah

36:2–4pp — 2Ki 23:31–34

2Jehoahaz[i] was twenty-three
years old when he became king,
and he reigned in Jerusalem three
months. **3**The king of Egypt de-
throned him in Jerusalem and imposed on Judah a levy of a hundred
talents[j] of silver and a talent[k] of
gold. **4**The king of Egypt made Eliakim, a brother of Jehoahaz, king
over Judah and Jerusalem and
changed Eliakim's name to Jehoiakim. But Neco[g] took Eliakim's
brother Jehoahaz and carried him
off to Egypt.

Jehoiakim King of Judah

36:5–8pp — 2Ki 23:36–24:6

5Jehoiakim[h] was twenty-five
years old when he became king,
and he reigned in Jerusalem eleven
years. He did evil in the eyes of the
LORD his God. **6**Nebuchadnezzar[i]
king of Babylon attacked him and
bound him with bronze shackles to
take him to Babylon.[j] **7**Nebuchadnezzar also took to Babylon articles
from the temple of the LORD and
put them in his temple[l] there.[k]

8The other events of Jehoiakim's
reign, the detestable things he did
and all that was found against him,
are written in the book of the kings
of Israel and Judah. And Jehoiachin his son succeeded him as
king.

Jehoiachin King of Judah

36:9–10pp — 2Ki 24:8–17

9Jehoiachin[l] was eighteen[m]
years old when he became king,
and he reigned in Jerusalem three
months and ten days. He did evil in
the eyes of the LORD. **10**In the
spring, King Nebuchadnezzar sent
for him and brought him to Babylon,[m] together with articles of value from the temple of the LORD, and
he made Jehoiachin's uncle,[n] Zedekiah, king over Judah and Jerusalem.

35:20 [a] Isa 10:9; Jer 46:2 [b] Ge 2:14
35:21 [c] 1Ki 13:18; 2Ki 18:25
35:22 [d] Jdg 5:19; 1Sa 28:8; 2Ch 18:29
35:23 [e] 1Ki 22:34
35:25 [f] Jer 22:10, 15-16
36:4 [g] Jer 22:10-12
36:5 [h] Jer 22:18; 26:1; 35:1
36:6 [i] Jer 25:9; 27:6; Eze 29:18 [j] 2Ch 33:11; Eze 19:9; Da 1:1
36:7 [k] 2Ki 24:13; Ezr 1:7; Da 1:2
36:9 [l] Jer 22:24-28; 52:31
36:10 [m] ver 18; 2Ki 20:17; Ezr 1:7; Jer 22:25; 24:1; 29:1; 37:1; Eze 17:12

[i]2 Hebrew *Joahaz,* a variant of *Jehoahaz;* also in verse 4 [j]3 That is, about 3 3/4 tons (about 3.4 metric tons) [k]3 That is, about 75 pounds (about 34 kilograms) [l]7 Or *palace* [m]9 One Hebrew manuscript, some Septuagint manuscripts and Syriac (see also 2 Kings 24:8); most Hebrew manuscripts *eight* [n]10 Hebrew *brother,* that is, relative (see 2 Kings 24:17)

Zedekiah King of Judah

36:11–16pp — 2Ki 24:18–20; Jer 52:1–3

11Zedekiah[a] was twenty-one years old when he became king, and he reigned in Jerusalem eleven years. **12**He did evil in the eyes of the LORD[b] his God and did not humble[c] himself before Jeremiah the prophet, who spoke the word of the LORD. **13**He also rebelled against King Nebuchadnezzar, who had made him take an oath[d] in God's name. He became stiff-necked[e] and hardened his heart and would not turn to the LORD, the God of Israel. **14**Furthermore, all the leaders of the priests and the people became more and more unfaithful,[f] following all the detestable practices of the nations and defiling the temple of the LORD, which he had consecrated in Jerusalem.

The Fall of Jerusalem

36:17–20pp — 2Ki 25:1–21; Jer 52:4–27
36:22–23pp — Ezr 1:1–3

15The LORD, the God of their fathers, sent word to them through his messengers[g] again and again,[h] because he had pity on his people and on his dwelling place. **16**But they mocked God's messengers, despised his words and scoffed[i] at his prophets until the wrath[j] of the LORD was aroused against his people and there was no remedy.[k] **17**He brought up against them the king of the Babylonians,[o] who killed their young men with the sword in the sanctuary, and spared neither young man[l] nor young woman, old man or aged. God handed all of them over to Nebuchadnezzar.[m] **18**He carried to Babylon all the articles[n] from the temple of God, both large and small, and the treasures of the LORD's temple and the treasures of the king and his officials. **19**They set fire[o] to God's temple[p] and broke down the wall[q] of Jerusalem; they burned all the palaces and destroyed[r] everything of value there.[s]

20He carried into exile[t] to Babylon the remnant, who escaped from the sword, and they became servants[u] to him and his sons until the kingdom of Persia came to power. **21**The land enjoyed its sabbath rests;[v] all the time of its desolation it rested,[w] until the seventy years[x] were completed in fulfillment of the word of the LORD spoken by Jeremiah.

22In the first year of Cyrus[y] king of Persia, in order to fulfill the word of the LORD spoken by Jeremiah, the LORD moved the heart of Cyrus king of Persia to make a proclamation throughout his realm and to put it in writing:

23"This is what Cyrus king of Persia says:

> " 'The LORD, the God of heaven, has given me all the kingdoms of the earth and he has appointed[z] me to build a temple for him at Jerusalem in Judah. Anyone of his people among you—may the LORD his God be with him, and let him go up.' "

36:11 [a] 2Ki 24:17; Jer 27:1; 28:1
36:12 [b] Jer 37:1-39:18 [c] Dt 8:3; 2Ch 7:14; 2Ch 33:23; Jer 21:3-7
36:13 [d] Eze 17:13 [e] 2Ki 17:14; 2Ch 30:8
36:14 [f] 1Ch 5:25
36:15 [g] Isa 5:4; 44:26; Jer 7:25; Hag 1:13; Zec 1:4; Mal 2:7; 3:1 [h] Jer 7:13,25; 25:3-4; 35:14, 15; 44:4-6
36:16 [i] 2Ki 2:23; Pr 1:25; Jer 5:13 [j] Ezr 5:12; Pr 1:30-31 [k] 2Ch 30:10; Pr 29:1; Zec 1:2
36:17 [l] Jer 6:11 [m] Ezr 5:12; Jer 32:28
36:18 [n] ver 7,10
36:19 [o] Jer 11:16; 17:27; 21:10, 14; 22:7; 32:29; 39:8; La 4:11; Eze 20:47; Am 2:5; Zec 11:1 [p] 1Ki 9:8-9 [q] 2Ki 14:13 [r] La 2:6 [s] Ps 79:1-3
36:20 [t] Lev 26:44; 2Ki 24:14; Ezr 2:1; Ne 7:6 [u] Jer 27:7
36:21 [v] Lev 25:4; 26:34 [w] 1Ch 22:9 [x] Jer 1:1; 25:11; 27:22; 29:10; 40:1; Da 9:2; Zec 1:12; 7:5 **36:22** [y] Isa 44:28; 45:1, 13; Jer 25:12; 29:10; Da 1:21; 6:28; 10:1 **36:23** [z] Jdg 4:10

[o] 17 Or *Chaldeans*

Ezra

Title and Background

The books of Ezra and Nehemiah were one book in the earliest Hebrew manuscripts. Origen (A.D. 185-253) is the first writer known to distinguish between two books, which he called I Ezra and II Ezra. Although they were regarded as one book, the caption to Nehemiah 1:1 indicates they were two separate compositions.

Author and Date of Writing

Many scholars have assumed that the author/compiler of Ezra-Nehemiah was also the author of 1,2 Chronicles. This viewpoint is based on certain characteristics common to both. The verses at the end of Chronicles and at the beginning of Ezra are virtually identical, and both of these books exhibit a fondness for lists. But there are also striking differences, so the name of the author cannot be known for certain. Ezra can be dated about 440 B.C.

Theme and Message

Ezra tells of the return of the Jews from exile in Babylon and also of the rebuilding of the temple. The people completed and dedicated the temple in 516 B.C., after being delayed for eighteen years by their enemies from the north. A decree from Darius in 520 B.C. allowed them to finish. Ezra taught the people the law and reformed their religious life so the other nations around them could see they were God's chosen nation.

Outline

I. The First Exiles Return to the Land of Judah (1:1-2:70)
II. The Temple Is Rebuilt (3:1-6:22)
III. Ezra's Return and Ministry (7:1-10:44)

Cyrus Helps the Exiles to Return

1:1-3pp — 2Ch 36:22-23

1 In the first year of Cyrus king of
Persia, in order to fulfill the
word of the LORD spoken by Jeremiah,[a] the LORD moved the heart[b] of
Cyrus king of Persia to make a
proclamation throughout his realm
and to put it in writing:

2"This is what Cyrus king of
Persia says:
" 'The LORD, the God of
heaven, has given me all the
kingdoms of the earth and he
has appointed[c] me to build[d]
a temple for him at Jerusalem
in Judah. 3Anyone of his people among you—may his God
be with him, and let him go up
to Jerusalem in Judah and
build the temple of the LORD,
the God of Israel, the God who
is in Jerusalem. 4And the people of any place where survivors[e] may now be living are to
provide him with silver and
gold, with goods and livestock,
and with freewill offerings[f]
for the temple of God in Jerusalem.' "[g]

5Then the family heads of Judah
and Benjamin,[h] and the priests
and Levites—everyone whose
heart God had moved[i]—prepared
to go up and build the house[j] of
the LORD in Jerusalem. 6All their
neighbors assisted them with articles of silver and gold, with goods

1:1 [a]Jer 25:11-12; 29:10-14 [b]2Ch 36:22, 23
1:2 [c]Isa 44:28; 45:13 [d]Ezr 5:13
1:4 [e]Isa 10:20-22 [f]Nu 15:3; Ps 50:14; 54:6; 116:17 [g]Ezr 4:3; 5:13; 6:3,14
1:5 [h]Ezr 4:1; Ne 11:4 [i]ver 1; Ex 35:20-22; 2Ch 36:22; Hag 1:14; Php 2:13 [j]Ps 127:1

and livestock, and with valuable
gifts, in addition to all the freewill
offerings. 7Moreover, King Cyrus
brought out the articles belonging
to the temple of the LORD, which
Nebuchadnezzar had carried away
from Jerusalem and had placed in
the temple of his god.[a][a] 8Cyrus
king of Persia had them brought by
Mithredath the treasurer, who
counted them out to Sheshbazzar[b]
the prince of Judah.
9This was the inventory:

gold dishes	30
silver dishes	1,000
silver pans[b]	29
10gold bowls	30
matching silver bowls	410
other articles	1,000

11In all, there were 5,400 articles
of gold and of silver. Sheshbazzar
brought all these along when the
exiles came up from Babylon to Jerusalem.

The List of the Exiles Who Returned

2:1-70pp — Ne 7:6-73

2 Now these are the people of
the province who came up
from the captivity of the exiles,[c]
whom Nebuchadnezzar king of
Babylon[d] had taken captive to
Babylon (they returned to Jerusalem and Judah, each to his own
town,[e] 2in company with Zerubbabel,[f] Jeshua,[g] Nehemiah, Seraiah,[h] Reelaiah, Mordecai, Bilshan,
Mispar, Bigvai, Rehum and Baanah):

The list of the men of the people of Israel:

3the descendants of Parosh[i]	2,172
4of Shephatiah	372
5of Arah	775
6of Pahath-Moab (through the line of Jeshua and Joab)	2,812
7of Elam	1,254
8of Zattu	945
9of Zaccai	760
10of Bani	642
11of Bebai	623
12of Azgad	1,222
13of Adonikam[j]	666
14of Bigvai	2,056
15of Adin	454
16of Ater (through Hezekiah)	98
17of Bezai	323
18of Jorah	112
19of Hashum	223
20of Gibbar	95
21the men of Bethlehem[k]	123
22of Netophah	56
23of Anathoth	128
24of Azmaveth	42
25of Kiriath Jearim,[c] Kephirah and Beeroth	743
26of Ramah[l] and Geba	621
27of Micmash	122
28of Bethel and Ai[m]	223
29of Nebo	52
30of Magbish	156
31of the other Elam	1,254
32of Harim	320
33of Lod, Hadid and Ono	725
34of Jericho[n]	345
35of Senaah	3,630

36The priests:

the descendants of Jedaiah[o] (through the family of Jeshua)	973
37of Immer[p]	1,052
38of Pashhur[q]	1,247
39of Harim[r]	1,017

40The Levites:[s]

the descendants of Jeshua[t] and Kadmiel (through the line of Hodaviah)	74

41The singers:[u]

the descendants of Asaph	128

42The gatekeepers[v] of the temple:

the descendants of Shallum, Ater, Talmon, Akkub, Hatita and Shobai	139

1:7 [a] 2Ki 24:13; 2Ch 36:7,10; Ezr 5:14; 6:5
1:8 [b] Ezr 5:14
2:1 [c] 2Ch 36:20; Ne 7:6 [d] 2Ki 24:16; 25:12 [e] Ne 7:73
2:2 [f] 1Ch 3:19 [g] Ezr 3:2 [h] Ne 10:2
2:3 [i] Ezr 8:3
2:13 [j] Ezr 8:13
2:21 [k] Mic 5:2
2:26 [l] Jos 18:25
2:28 [m] Ge 12:8
2:34 [n] 1Ki 16:34; 2Ch 28:15
2:36 [o] 1Ch 24:7
2:37 [p] 1Ch 24:14
2:38 [q] 1Ch 9:12
2:39 [r] 1Ch 24:8
2:40 [s] Ge 29:34; Nu 3:9; Dt 18:6-7; 1Ch 16:4; Ezr 7:7; 8:15; Ne 12:24 [t] Ezr 3:9
2:41 [u] 1Ch 15:16
2:42 [v] 1Sa 3:15; 1Ch 9:17

[a]7 Or *gods* [b]9 The meaning of the Hebrew for this word is uncertain. [c]25 See Septuagint (see also Neh. 7:29); Hebrew *Kiriath Arim.*

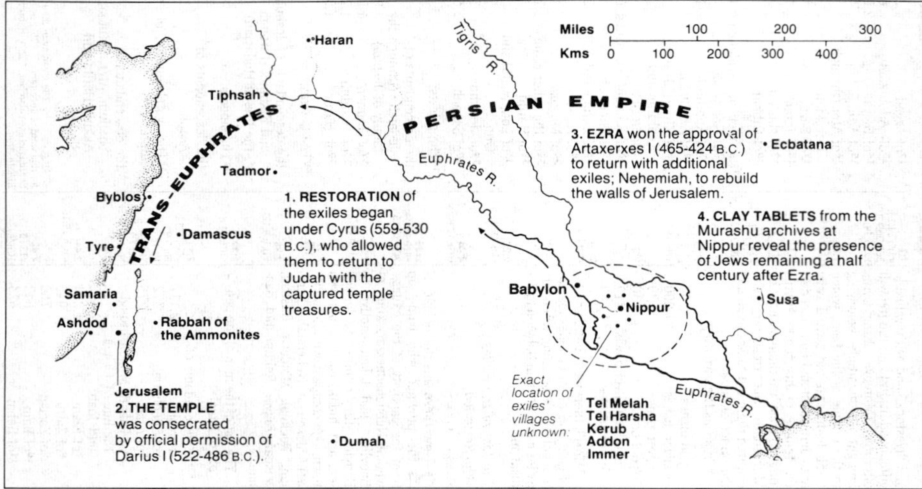
RETURN FROM EXILE
Miles 0 100 200 300
Kms 0 100 200 300 400
Haran
Tigris R.
Tiphsah
PERSIAN EMPIRE
TRANS-EUPHRATES
Tadmor
Euphrates R.
Byblos
Damascus
Tyre
Samaria
Ashdod
Rabbah of the Ammonites
Jerusalem
Dumah
Ecbatana
Babylon
Nippur
Susa
Euphrates R.
1. RESTORATION of the exiles began under Cyrus (559-530 B.C.), who allowed them to return to Judah with the captured temple treasures.
2.THE TEMPLE was consecrated by official permission of Darius I (522-486 B.C.).
3. EZRA won the approval of Artaxerxes I (465-424 B.C.) to return with additional exiles; Nehemiah, to rebuild the walls of Jerusalem.
4. CLAY TABLETS from the Murashu archives at Nippur reveal the presence of Jews remaining a half century after Ezra.
Exact location of exiles' villages unknown:
Tel Melah
Tel Harsha
Kerub
Addon
Immer

43The temple servants:[a]

the descendants of
Ziha, Hasupha, Tabbaoth,
44Keros, Siaha, Padon,
45Lebanah, Hagabah,
Akkub,
46Hagab, Shalmai, Hanan,
47Giddel, Gahar, Reaiah,
48Rezin, Nekoda, Gazzam,
49Uzza, Paseah, Besai,
50Asnah, Meunim,
Nephussim,
51Bakbuk, Hakupha,
Harhur,
52Bazluth, Mehida, Harsha,
53Barkos, Sisera, Temah,
54Neziah and Hatipha

55The descendants of the servants of Solomon:

the descendants of
Sotai, Hassophereth,
Peruda,
56Jaala, Darkon, Giddel,
57Shephatiah, Hattil,
Pokereth-Hazzebaim and
Ami

58The temple servants[b] and
the descendants of the
servants of Solomon 392

59The following came up
from the towns of Tel Melah,
Tel Harsha, Kerub, Addon and
Immer, but they could not
show that their families were
descended[c] from Israel:

60The descendants of
Delaiah, Tobiah and
Nekoda 652

61And from among the priests:

The descendants of
Hobaiah, Hakkoz and
Barzillai (a man who had
married a daughter of
Barzillai the Gileadite[d]
and was called by that
name).
62These searched for their
family records, but they could
not find them and so were excluded from the priesthood[e]
as unclean. 63The governor ordered them not to eat any of
the most sacred food[f] until
there was a priest ministering
with the Urim and Thum-
mim.[g]

64The whole company num-
bered 42,360, 65besides their
7,337 menservants and maidservants; and they also had
200 men and women sing-
ers.[h] 66They had 736
horses,[i] 245 mules, 67435
camels and 6,720 donkeys.

68When they arrived at the house
of the LORD in Jerusalem, some of
the heads of the families[j] gave
freewill offerings toward the rebuilding of the house of God on its
site. 69According to their ability
they gave to the treasury for this
work 61,000 drachmas[d] of gold,
5,000 minas[e] of silver and 100
priestly garments.

70The priests, the Levites, the
singers, the gatekeepers and the
temple servants settled in their
own towns, along with some of the
other people, and the rest of the Israelites settled in their towns.[k]

Rebuilding the Altar

3 When the seventh month came
and the Israelites had settled
in their towns,[l] the people assembled[m] as one man in Jerusalem.
2Then Jeshua[n] son of Jozadak[o]
and his fellow priests and Zerubbabel son of Shealtiel[p] and his associates began to build the altar of
the God of Israel to sacrifice burnt
offerings on it, in accordance with
what is written in the Law of Moses[q] the man of God. 3Despite
their fear[r] of the peoples around
them, they built the altar on its
foundation and sacrificed burnt offerings on it to the LORD, both the
morning and evening sacrifices.[s]
4Then in accordance with what is
written, they celebrated the Feast
of Tabernacles[t] with the required
number of burnt offerings prescribed for each day. 5After that,
they presented the regular burnt
offerings, the New Moon[u] sacri-

2:43 [a] 1Ch 9:2; Ne 11:21
2:58 [b] 1Ki 9:21; 1Ch 9:2
2:59 [c] Nu 1:18
2:61 [d] 2Sa 17:27
2:62 [e] Nu 3:10; 16:39-40
2:63 [f] Lev 2:3,10 [g] Ex 28:30; Nu 27:21
2:65 [h] 2Sa 19:35
2:66 [i] Isa 66:20
2:68 [j] Ex 25:2
2:70 [k] ver 1; 1Ch 9:2; Ne 11:3-4
3:1 [l] Ne 7:73; 8:1 [m] Lev 23:24
3:2 [n] Ezr 2:2; Ne 12:1,8; Hag 2:2 [o] Hag 1:1; Zec 6:11 [p] 1Ch 3:17 [q] Ex 20:24; Dt 12:5-6
3:3 [r] Ezr 4:4; Da 9:25 [s] Ex 29:39; Nu 28:1-8
3:4 [t] Ex 23:16; Nu 29:12-38; Ne 8:14-18; Zec 14:16-19
3:5 [u] Nu 28:3,11, 14; Col 2:16

[d]69 That is, about 1,100 pounds (about 500 kilograms) [e]69 That is, about 3 tons (about 2.9 metric tons)

fices and the sacrifices for all the
appointed sacred feasts of the
LORD,[a] as well as those brought as
freewill offerings to the LORD. **6**On
the first day of the seventh month
they began to offer burnt offerings
to the LORD, though the foundation
of the LORD's temple had not yet
been laid.

Rebuilding the Temple

7Then they gave money to the
masons and carpenters, and gave
food and drink and oil to the people of Sidon and Tyre, so that they
would bring cedar logs[b] by sea
from Lebanon[c] to Joppa, as authorized by Cyrus[d] king of Persia.
8In the second month of the second year after their arrival at the
house of God in Jerusalem, Zerubbabel[e] son of Shealtiel, Jeshua
son of Jozadak and the rest of their
brothers (the priests and the Levites and all who had returned from
the captivity to Jerusalem) began
the work, appointing Levites twenty[f] years of age and older to supervise the building of the house of
the LORD. **9**Jeshua[g] and his sons
and brothers and Kadmiel and his
sons (descendants of Hodaviah[f])
and the sons of Henadad and their
sons and brothers—all Levites—
joined together in supervising
those working on the house of God.
10When the builders laid[h] the
foundation of the temple of the
LORD, the priests in their vestments
and with trumpets,[i] and the Levites (the sons of Asaph) with cymbals, took their places to praise[j]
the LORD, as prescribed by David[k]
king of Israel.[l] **11**With praise and
thanksgiving they sang to the LORD:

"He is good;
his love to Israel endures
forever."[m]

And all the people gave a great
shout[n] of praise to the LORD, because the foundation of the house
of the LORD was laid. **12**But many of
the older priests and Levites and
family heads, who had seen the former temple,[o] wept aloud when
they saw the foundation of this
temple being laid, while many others shouted for joy. **13**No one could
distinguish the sound of the shouts
of joy[p] from the sound of weeping,
because the people made so much
noise. And the sound was heard far
away.

Opposition to the Rebuilding

4 When the enemies of Judah
and Benjamin heard that the
exiles were building a temple for
the LORD, the God of Israel, **2**they
came to Zerubbabel and to the
heads of the families and said, "Let
us help you build because, like
you, we seek your God and have
been sacrificing to him since the
time of Esarhaddon[q] king of Assyria, who brought us here."[r]
3But Zerubbabel, Jeshua and the
rest of the heads of the families of
Israel answered, "You have no part
with us in building a temple to our
God. We alone will build it for the
LORD, the God of Israel, as King Cyrus, the king of Persia, commanded
us."[s]
4Then the peoples around them
set out to discourage the people of
Judah and make them afraid to go
on building.[g][t] **5**They hired counselors to work against them and
frustrate their plans during the entire reign of Cyrus king of Persia
and down to the reign of Darius
king of Persia.

Later Opposition Under Xerxes and Artaxerxes

6At the beginning of the reign of
Xerxes,[h][u] they lodged an accusation against the people of Judah
and Jerusalem.[v]
7And in the days of Artaxerxes[w]
king of Persia, Bishlam, Mithredath, Tabeel and the rest of his associates wrote a letter to Artaxerxes. The letter was written in Aramaic script and in the Aramaic[x]
language.[i,j]

3:5 [a] Lev 23:1-44; Nu 29:39
3:7 [b] 1Ch 14:1 [c] Isa 35:2 [d] Ezr 1:2-4; 6:3
3:8 [e] Zec 4:9 [f] 1Ch 23:24
3:9 [g] Ezr 2:40
3:10 [h] Ezr 5:16 [i] Nu 10:2; 1Ch 16:6 [j] 1Ch 25:1 [k] 1Ch 6:31 [l] Zec 6:12
3:11 [m] 1Ch 16:34, 41; 2Ch 7:3; Ps 107:1; 118:1 [n] Ne 12:24
3:12 [o] Hag 2:3,9
3:13 [p] Job 8:21; Ps 27:6; Isa 16:9
4:2 [q] 2Ki 17:24; 19:37 [r] 2Ki 17:41
4:3 [s] Ezr 1:1-4; Ne 2:20
4:4 [t] Ezr 3:3
4:6 [u] Est 1:1; Da 9:1 [v] Est 3:13; 9:5
4:7 [w] Ezr 7:1; Ne 2:1 [x] 2Ki 18:26; Isa 36:11; Da 2:4

[f]9 Hebrew *Yehudah,* probably a variant of *Hodaviah* [g]4 Or *and troubled them as they built* [h]6 Hebrew *Ahasuerus,* a variant of Xerxes' Persian name [i]7 Or *written in Aramaic and translated* [j]7 The text of Ezra 4:8–6:18 is in Aramaic.

[8]Rehum the commanding officer
and Shimshai the secretary wrote a
letter against Jerusalem to Artaxerxes the king as follows:

[9]Rehum the commanding officer and Shimshai the secretary, together with the rest of
their associates[a]—the judges
and officials over the men
from Tripolis, Persia,[k] Erech
and Babylon, the Elamites of
Susa, [10]and the other people
whom the great and honorable
Ashurbanipal[l] deported and
settled in the city of Samaria
and elsewhere in Trans-Euphrates.[b]

[11](This is a copy of the letter
they sent him.)

To King Artaxerxes,

From your servants, the men
of Trans-Euphrates:

[12]The king should know
that the Jews who came up to
us from you have gone to Jerusalem and are rebuilding that
rebellious and wicked city.
They are restoring the walls
and repairing the founda-
tions.[c]
[13]Furthermore, the king
should know that if this city is
built and its walls are restored,
no more taxes, tribute or
duty[d] will be paid, and the
royal revenues will suffer.
[14]Now since we are under obligation to the palace and it is
not proper for us to see the
king dishonored, we are sending this message to inform the
king, [15]so that a search may be
made in the archives[e] of your
predecessors. In these records
you will find that this city is a
rebellious city, troublesome to
kings and provinces, a place of
rebellion from ancient times.
That is why this city was destroyed.[f] [16]We inform the
king that if this city is built
and its walls are restored, you
will be left with nothing in
Trans-Euphrates.

[17]The king sent this reply:

To Rehum the commanding
officer, Shimshai the secretary
and the rest of their associates
living in Samaria and elsewhere in Trans-Euphrates:[g]

Greetings.

[18]The letter you sent us has
been read and translated in
my presence. [19]I issued an order and a search was made,
and it was found that this city
has a long history of revolt[h]
against kings and has been a
place of rebellion and sedi-
tion. [20]Jerusalem has had
powerful kings ruling over the
whole of Trans-Euphrates,[i]
and taxes, tribute and duty
were paid to them. [21]Now issue an order to these men to
stop work, so that this city will
not be rebuilt until I so order.
[22]Be careful not to neglect
this matter. Why let this threat
grow, to the detriment of the
royal interests?[j]

[23]As soon as the copy of the letter of King Artaxerxes was read to
Rehum and Shimshai the secretary
and their associates,[k] they went
immediately to the Jews in Jerusalem and compelled them by force
to stop.

[24]Thus the work on the house of
God in Jerusalem came to a stand-
still until the second year of the
reign of Darius[l] king of Persia.

Tattenai's Letter to Darius

5 Now Haggai[m] the prophet and
Zechariah[n] the prophet, a
descendant of Iddo, prophesied[o]
to the Jews in Judah and Jerusalem
in the name of the God of Israel,
who was over them. [2]Then Zerubbabel[p] son of Shealtiel and Jeshua[q] son of Jozadak set to work[r] to
rebuild the house of God in Jerusalem. And the prophets of God were
with them, helping them.

4:9 [a]Ezr 5:6; 6:6, 13
4:10 [b]ver 17; Ne 4:2
4:12 [c]Ezr 5:3,9
4:13 [d]Ezr 7:24; Ne 5:4
4:15 [e]Ezr 5:17; 6:1 [f]Est 3:8
4:17 [g]ver 10
4:19 [h]2Ki 18:7
4:20 [i]Ge 15:18-21; Ex 23:31; Jos 1:4; 1Ki 4:21; 1Ch 18:3; Ps 72:8-11
4:22 [j]Da 6:2
4:23 [k]ver 9
4:24 [l]Ne 2:1-8; Da 9:25; Hag 1:1,15; Zec 1:1
5:1 [m]Ezr 6:14; Hag 1:1,3,12; 2:1,10,20 [n]Zec 1:1; 7:1 [o]Hag 1:14-2:9; Zec 4:9-10; 8:9
5:2 [p]1Ch 3:19; Hag 1:14; 2:21; Zec 4:6-10 [q]Ezr 2:2; 3:2 [r]ver 8; Hag 2:2-5

k9 Or *officials, magistrates and governors over the men from* l10 Aramaic *Osnappar,* a variant of *Ashurbanipal*

3At that time Tattenai,[a] governor of Trans-Euphrates, and Shethar-Bozenai[b] and their associates went to them and asked, "Who authorized you to rebuild this temple and restore this structure?"[c] **4**They also asked, "What are the names of the men constructing this building?"[m] **5**But the eye of their God[d] was watching over the elders of the Jews, and they were not stopped until a report could go to Darius and his written reply be received.

6This is a copy of the letter that Tattenai, governor of Trans-Euphrates, and Shethar-Bozenai and their associates, the officials of Trans-Euphrates, sent to King Darius. **7**The report they sent him read as follows:

> To King Darius:
>
> Cordial greetings.
>
> **8**The king should know that we went to the district of Judah, to the temple of the great God. The people are building it with large stones and placing the timbers in the walls. The work[e] is being carried on with diligence and is making rapid progress under their direction.
>
> **9**We questioned the elders and asked them, "Who authorized you to rebuild this temple and restore this structure?"[f] **10**We also asked them their names, so that we could write down the names of their leaders for your information.
>
> **11**This is the answer they gave us:
>
> "We are the servants of the God of heaven and earth, and we are rebuilding the temple[g] that was built many years ago, one that a great king of Israel built and finished. **12**But because our fathers angered[h] the God of heaven, he handed them over to Nebuchadnezzar the Chaldean, king of Babylon, who destroyed this temple and deported the people to Babylon.[i]
>
> **13**"However, in the first year of Cyrus king of Babylon, King Cyrus issued a decree[j] to rebuild this house of God. **14**He even removed from the temple[n] of Babylon the gold and silver articles of the house of God, which Nebuchadnezzar had taken from the temple in Jerusalem and brought to the temple[n] in Babylon.[k]
>
> "Then King Cyrus gave them to a man named Sheshbazzar,[l] whom he had appointed governor, **15**and he told him, 'Take these articles and go and deposit them in the temple in Jerusalem. And rebuild the house of God on its site.' **16**So this Sheshbazzar came and laid the foundations of the house of God[m] in Jerusalem. From that day to the present it has been under construction but is not yet finished."
>
> **17**Now if it pleases the king, let a search be made in the royal archives[n] of Babylon to see if King Cyrus did in fact issue a decree to rebuild this house of God in Jerusalem. Then let the king send us his decision in this matter.

The Decree of Darius

6 King Darius then issued an order, and they searched in the archives[o] stored in the treasury at Babylon. **2**A scroll was found in the citadel of Ecbatana in the province of Media, and this was written on it:

> Memorandum:
>
> **3**In the first year of King Cyrus, the king issued a decree concerning the temple of God in Jerusalem:
>
> Let the temple be rebuilt as

5:3 [a] Ezr 6:6 [b] Ezr 6:6 [c] ver 9; Ezr 1:3; 4:12
5:5 [d] 2Ki 25:28; Ezr 7:6,9,28; 8:18,22,31; Ne 2:8,18; Ps 33:18; Isa 66:14
5:8 [e] ver 2
5:9 [f] Ezr 4:12
5:11 [g] 1Ki 6:1; 2Ch 3:1-2
5:12 [h] 2Ch 36:16 [i] Dt 21:10; 28:36; 2Ki 24:1; 25:8,9,11; Jer 1:3
5:13 [j] Ezr 1:1
5:14 [k] Ezr 1:7; 6:5; Da 5:2 [l] 1Ch 3:18
5:16 [m] Ezr 3:10; 6:15
5:17 [n] Ezr 4:15; 6:1,2
6:1 [o] Ezr 4:15; 5:17

[m]4 See Septuagint; Aramaic *4We told them the names of the men constructing this building.*
[n]14 Or *palace*

a place to present sacrifices, and let its foundations be laid.[a] It is to be ninety feet[o] high and ninety feet wide, 4with three courses[b] of large stones and one of timbers. The costs are to be paid by the royal treasury.[c] 5Also, the gold[d] and silver articles of the house of God, which Nebuchadnezzar took from the temple in Jerusalem and brought to Babylon, are to be returned to their places in the temple in Jerusalem; they are to be deposited in the house of God.[e]

6Now then, Tattenai,[f] governor of Trans-Euphrates, and Shethar-Bozenai[g] and you, their fellow officials of that province, stay away from there. 7Do not interfere with the work on this temple of God. Let the governor of the Jews and the Jewish elders rebuild this house of God on its site.

8Moreover, I hereby decree what you are to do for these elders of the Jews in the construction of this house of God:

The expenses of these men are to be fully paid out of the royal treasury,[h] from the revenues[i] of Trans-Euphrates, so that the work will not stop. 9Whatever is needed—young bulls, rams, male lambs for burnt offerings[j] to the God of heaven, and wheat, salt, wine and oil, as requested by the priests in Jerusalem—must be given them daily without fail, 10so that they may offer sacrifices pleasing to the God of heaven and pray for the well-being of the king and his sons.[k]

11Furthermore, I decree that if anyone changes this edict, a beam is to be pulled from his house and he is to be lifted up and impaled[l] on it. And for this crime his house is to be made a pile of rubble.[m] 12May God, who has caused his Name to dwell there,[n] overthrow any king or people who lifts a hand to change this decree or to destroy this temple in Jerusalem.

I Darius[o] have decreed it. Let it be carried out with diligence.

Completion and Dedication of the Temple

13Then, because of the decree King Darius had sent, Tattenai, governor of Trans-Euphrates, and Shethar-Bozenai and their associates[p] carried it out with diligence. 14So the elders of the Jews continued to build and prosper under the preaching[q] of Haggai the prophet and Zechariah, a descendant of Iddo. They finished building the temple according to the command of the God of Israel and the decrees of Cyrus,[r] Darius[s] and Artaxerxes,[t] kings of Persia. 15The temple was completed on the third day of the month Adar, in the sixth year of the reign of King Darius.[u]

16Then the people of Israel—the priests, the Levites and the rest of the exiles—celebrated the dedication[v] of the house of God with joy. 17For the dedication of this house of God they offered[w] a hundred bulls, two hundred rams, four hundred male lambs and, as a sin offering for all Israel, twelve male goats, one for each of the tribes of Israel. 18And they installed the priests in their divisions[x] and the Levites in their groups[y] for the service of God at Jerusalem, according to what is written in the Book of Moses.[z]

The Passover

19On the fourteenth day of the first month, the exiles celebrated the Passover.[a] 20The priests and Levites had purified themselves and were all ceremonially clean. The Levites slaughtered[b] the Passover lamb for all the exiles, for their brothers the priests and for themselves. 21So the Israelites who had returned from the exile ate it, to-

6:3 [a] Ezr 3:10; Hag 2:3
6:4 [b] 1Ki 6:36 [c] ver 8; Ezr 7:20
6:5 [d] 1Ch 29:2 [e] Ezr 1:7; 5:14
6:6 [f] Ezr 5:3 [g] Ezr 5:3
6:8 [h] ver 4 [i] 1Sa 9:20
6:9 [j] Lev 1:3,10
6:10 [k] Ezr 7:23; 1Ti 2:1-2
6:11 [l] Dt 21:22-23; Est 2:23; 5:14; 9:14 [m] Ezr 7:26; Da 2:5; 3:29
6:12 [n] Ex 20:24; Dt 12:5; 1Ki 9:3; 2Ch 6:2 [o] ver 14
6:13 [p] Ezr 4:9
6:14 [q] Ezr 5:1 [r] Ezr 1:1-4 [s] ver 12 [t] Ezr 7:1; Ne 2:1
6:15 [u] Zec 1:1; 4:9
6:16 [v] 1Ki 8:63; 2Ch 7:5
6:17 [w] 2Sa 6:13; 2Ch 29:21; 30:24; Ezr 8:35
6:18 [x] 1Ch 23:6; 2Ch 35:4; Lk 1:5 [y] 1Ch 24:1 [z] Nu 3:6-9; 8:9-11; 18:1-32
6:19 [a] Ex 12:11; Nu 28:16
6:20 [b] 2Ch 30:15, 17; 35:11

[o]3 Aramaic *sixty cubits* (about 27 meters)

gether with all who had separated themselves[a] from the unclean practices[b] of their Gentile neighbors in order to seek the LORD,[c] the God of Israel. **22**For seven days they celebrated with joy the Feast of Unleavened Bread,[d] because the LORD had filled them with joy by changing the attitude[e] of the king of Assyria, so that he assisted them in the work on the house of God, the God of Israel.

Ezra Comes to Jerusalem

7 After these things, during the reign of Artaxerxes[f] king of Persia, Ezra son of Seraiah, the son of Azariah, the son of Hilkiah,[g] **2**the son of Shallum, the son of Zadok,[h] the son of Ahitub,[i] **3**the son of Amariah, the son of Azariah, the son of Meraioth, **4**the son of Zerahiah, the son of Uzzi, the son of Bukki, **5**the son of Abishua, the son of Phinehas, the son of Eleazar, the son of Aaron the chief priest— **6**this Ezra[j] came up from Babylon. He was a teacher well versed in the Law of Moses, which the LORD, the God of Israel, had given. The king had granted him everything he asked, for the hand of the LORD his God was on him.[k] **7**Some of the Israelites, including priests, Levites, singers, gatekeepers and temple servants, also came up to Jerusalem in the seventh year of King Artaxerxes.[l]

8Ezra arrived in Jerusalem in the fifth month of the seventh year of the king. **9**He had begun his journey from Babylon on the first day of the first month, and he arrived in Jerusalem on the first day of the fifth month, for the gracious hand of his God was on him.[m] **10**For Ezra had devoted himself to the study and observance of the Law of the LORD, and to teaching[n] its decrees and laws in Israel.

King Artaxerxes' Letter to Ezra

11This is a copy of the letter King Artaxerxes had given to Ezra the priest and teacher, a man learned in matters concerning the commands and decrees of the LORD for Israel:

12[p]Artaxerxes, king of kings,[o]

To Ezra the priest, a teacher of the Law of the God of heaven:

Greetings.

13Now I decree that any of the Israelites in my kingdom, including priests and Levites, who wish to go to Jerusalem with you, may go. **14**You are sent by the king and his seven advisers[p] to inquire about Judah and Jerusalem with regard to the Law of your God, which is in your hand. **15**Moreover, you are to take with you the silver and gold that the king and his advisers have freely given[q] to the God of Israel, whose dwelling[r] is in Jerusalem, **16**together with all the silver and gold[s] you may obtain from the province of Babylon, as well as the freewill offerings of the people and priests for the temple of their God in Jerusalem.[t] **17**With this money be sure to buy bulls, rams and male lambs,[u] together with their grain offerings and drink offerings,[v] and sacrifice[w] them on the altar of the temple of your God in Jerusalem.

18You and your brother Jews may then do whatever seems best with the rest of the silver and gold, in accordance with the will of your God. **19**Deliver[x] to the God of Jerusalem all the articles entrusted to you for worship in the temple of your God. **20**And anything else needed for the temple of your God that you may have occasion to supply, you may provide from the royal treasury.[y]

21Now I, King Artaxerxes, order all the treasurers of Trans-Euphrates to provide with diligence whatever Ezra

6:21 [a]Ezr 9:1; Ne 9:2 [b]Dt 18:9; Ezr 9:11; Eze 36:25 [c]1Ch 22:19; Ps 14:2
6:22 [d]Ex 12:17 [e]Ezr 1:1
7:1 [f]Ezr 4:7; 6:14; Ne 2:1 [g]2Ki 22:4
7:2 [h]1Ki 1:8; 1Ch 6:8 [i]Ne 11:11
7:6 [j]Ne 12:36 [k]Ezr 5:5; Isa 41:20
7:7 [l]Ezr 8:1
7:9 [m]ver 6
7:10 [n]ver 25; Dt 33:10; Ne 8:1-8
7:12 [o]Eze 26:7; Da 2:37
7:14 [p]Est 1:14
7:15 [q]1Ch 29:6 [r]1Ch 29:6,9; 2Ch 6:2
7:16 [s]Ezr 8:25 [t]Zec 6:10
7:17 [u]2Ki 3:4 [v]Nu 15:5-12 [w]Dt 12:5-11
7:19 [x]Ezr 5:14; Jer 27:22
7:20 [y]Ezr 6:4

[p]*12* The text of Ezra 7:12-26 is in Aramaic.

the priest, a teacher of the Law
of the God of heaven, may ask
of you— **22**up to a hundred talents[q] of silver, a hundred
cors[r] of wheat, a hundred
baths[s] of wine, a hundred
baths[s] of olive oil, and salt
without limit. **23**Whatever the
God of heaven has prescribed,
let it be done with diligence
for the temple of the God of
heaven. Why should there be
wrath against the realm of the
king and of his sons?[a] **24**You
are also to know that you have
no authority to impose taxes,
tribute or duty[b] on any of the
priests, Levites, singers, gatekeepers, temple servants or
other workers at this house of
God.[c]

25And you, Ezra, in accordance with the wisdom of your
God, which you possess, appoint[d] magistrates and judges
to administer justice to all the
people of Trans-Euphrates—
all who know the laws of your
God. And you are to teach[e]
any who do not know them.
26Whoever does not obey the
law of your God and the law of
the king must surely be punished by death, banishment,
confiscation of property, or
imprisonment.[f]

27Praise be to the LORD, the God
of our fathers, who has put it into
the king's heart[g] to bring honor[h]
to the house of the LORD in Jerusalem in this way **28**and who has extended his good favor[i] to me before the king and his advisers and
all the king's powerful officials. Because the hand of the LORD my God
was on me,[j] I took courage and
gathered leading men from Israel
to go up with me.

List of the Family Heads Returning With Ezra

8 These are the family heads and
those registered with them
who came up with me from Babylon during the reign of King Artaxerxes:[k]

2of the descendants of Phinehas, Gershom;
of the descendants of Ithamar,
Daniel;
of the descendants of David,
Hattush **3**of the descendants of Shecaniah;[l]

of the descendants of Pa-
rosh,[m] Zechariah, and with
him were registered 150
men;
4of the descendants of Pahath-Moab,[n] Eliehoenai
son of Zerahiah, and with
him 200 men;
5of the descendants of Zattu,[t]
Shecaniah son of Jahaziel,
and with him 300 men;
6of the descendants of Adin,[o]
Ebed son of Jonathan, and
with him 50 men;
7of the descendants of Elam,
Jeshaiah son of Athaliah,
and with him 70 men;
8of the descendants of Shephatiah, Zebadiah son of Mi-
chael, and with him 80
men;
9of the descendants of Joab,
Obadiah son of Jehiel, and
with him 218 men;
10of the descendants of Bani,[u]
Shelomith son of Josiphiah,
and with him 160 men;
11of the descendants of Bebai,
Zechariah son of Bebai, and
with him 28 men;
12of the descendants of Azgad,
Johanan son of Hakkatan,
and with him 110 men;
13of the descendants of Adonikam,[p] the last ones, whose
names were Eliphelet, Jeuel and Shemaiah, and with
them 60 men;
14of the descendants of Bigvai,
Uthai and Zaccur, and with
them 70 men.

7:23 [a]Ezr 6:10
7:24 [b]Ezr 4:13 [c]Ezr 8:36
7:25 [d]Ex 18:21,26; Dt 16:18 [e]ver 10; Lev 10:11
7:26 [f]Ezr 6:11
7:27 [g]Ezr 1:1; 6:22 [h]1Ch 29:12
7:28 [i]2Ki 25:28 [j]Ezr 5:5; 9:9
8:1 [k]Ezr 7:7
8:3 [l]1Ch 3:22 [m]Ezr 2:3
8:4 [n]Ezr 2:6
8:6 [o]Ezr 2:15; Ne 7:20; 10:16
8:13 [p]Ezr 2:13

[q]*22* That is, about 3 3/4 tons (about 3.4 metric tons) [r]*22* That is, probably about 600 bushels (about 22 kiloliters) [s]*22* That is, probably about 600 gallons (about 2.2 kiloliters) [t]*5* Some Septuagint manuscripts (also 1 Esdras 8:32); Hebrew does not have *Zattu.* [u]*10* Some Septuagint manuscripts (also 1 Esdras 8:36); Hebrew does not have *Bani.*

The Return to Jerusalem

15I assembled them at the canal that flows toward Ahava,[a] and we camped there three days. When I checked among the people and the priests, I found no Levites[b] there. **16**So I summoned Eliezer, Ariel, Shemaiah, Elnathan, Jarib, Elnathan, Nathan, Zechariah and Meshullam, who were leaders, and Joiarib and Elnathan, who were men of learning, **17**and I sent them to Iddo, the leader in Casiphia. I told them what to say to Iddo and his kinsmen, the temple servants[c] in Casiphia, so that they might bring attendants to us for the house of our God. **18**Because the gracious hand of our God was on us,[d] they brought us Sherebiah, a capable man, from the descendants of Mahli son of Levi, the son of Israel, and Sherebiah's sons and brothers, 18 men; **19**and Hashabiah, together with Jeshaiah from the descendants of Merari, and his brothers and nephews, 20 men. **20**They also brought 220 of the temple servants[e]—a body that David and the officials had established to assist the Levites. All were registered by name.

21There, by the Ahava Canal,[f] I proclaimed a fast, so that we might humble ourselves before our God and ask him for a safe journey[g] for us and our children, with all our possessions. **22**I was ashamed to ask the king for soldiers[h] and horsemen to protect us from enemies on the road, because we had told the king, "The gracious hand of our God is on everyone[i] who looks to him, but his great anger is against all who forsake him.[j]" **23**So we fasted[k] and petitioned our God about this, and he answered our prayer.

24Then I set apart twelve of the leading priests, together with Sherebiah,[l] Hashabiah and ten of their brothers, **25**and I weighed out[m] to them the offering of silver and gold and the articles that the king, his advisers, his officials and all Israel present there had donated for the house of our God. **26**I weighed out to them 650 talents[v] of silver, silver articles weighing 100 talents,[w] 100 talents[w] of gold, **27**20 bowls of gold valued at 1,000 darics,[x] and two fine articles of polished bronze, as precious as gold.

28I said to them, "You as well as these articles are consecrated to the LORD.[n] The silver and gold are a freewill offering to the LORD, the God of your fathers. **29**Guard them carefully until you weigh them out in the chambers of the house of the LORD in Jerusalem before the leading priests and the Levites and the family heads of Israel." **30**Then the priests and Levites received the silver and gold and sacred articles that had been weighed out to be taken to the house of our God in Jerusalem.

31On the twelfth day of the first month we set out from the Ahava Canal[o] to go to Jerusalem. The hand of our God was on us, and he protected us from enemies and bandits along the way. **32**So we arrived in Jerusalem, where we rested three days.[p]

33On the fourth day, in the house of our God, we weighed out the silver and gold and the sacred articles into the hands of Meremoth[q] son of Uriah, the priest. Eleazar son of Phinehas was with him, and so were the Levites Jozabad son of Jeshua and Noadiah son of Binnui.[r] **34**Everything was accounted for by number and weight, and the entire weight was recorded at that time.

35Then the exiles who had returned from captivity sacrificed burnt offerings to the God of Israel: twelve bulls for all Israel, ninety-six rams, seventy-seven male lambs and, as a sin offering, twelve male goats.[s] All this was a burnt offering to the LORD. **36**They also delivered the king's orders[t] to the royal satraps and to the governors of Trans-Euphrates, who then gave

8:15 [a]ver 21,31 [b]Ezr 2:40; 7:7
8:17 [c]Ezr 2:43
8:18 [d]Ezr 5:5
8:20 [e]1Ch 9:2; Ezr 2:43
8:21 [f]ver 15; 2Ch 20:3 [g]Ps 5:8; 107:7
8:22 [h]Ne 2:9; Ezr 7:6,9,28 [i]Ezr 5:5 [j]Dt 31:17; 2Ch 15:2
8:23 [k]2Ch 20:3; 33:13
8:24 [l]ver 18
8:25 [m]ver 33; Ezr 7:15,16
8:28 [n]Lev 21:6; 22:2-3
8:31 [o]ver 15
8:32 [p]Ge 40:13; Ne 2:11
8:33 [q]Ne 3:4,21 [r]Ne 3:24
8:35 [s]2Ch 29:21; Ezr 6:17
8:36 [t]Ezr 7:21-24

[v]*26* That is, about 25 tons (about 22 metric tons) [w]*26* That is, about 3 3/4 tons (about 3.4 metric tons) [x]*27* That is, about 19 pounds (about 8.5 kilograms)

assistance to the people and to the
house of God.[a]

Ezra's Prayer About Intermarriage

9 After these things had been
done, the leaders came to me
and said, "The people of Israel, including the priests and the Levites,
have not kept themselves separate[b] from the neighboring peoples with their detestable practices, like those of the Canaanites,
Hittites, Perizzites, Jebusites, Ammonites,[c] Moabites, Egyptians
and Amorites.[d] 2They have taken
some of their daughters[e] as wives
for themselves and their sons, and
have mingled the holy race[f] with
the peoples around them. And the
leaders and officials have led the
way in this unfaithfulness."[g]

3When I heard this, I tore my tunic and cloak, pulled hair from my
head and beard and sat down appalled. 4Then everyone who trembled[h] at the words of the God of
Israel gathered around me because
of this unfaithfulness of the exiles.
And I sat there appalled until the
evening sacrifice.

5Then, at the evening sacrifice,[i]
I rose from my self-abasement,
with my tunic and cloak torn, and
fell on my knees with my hands
spread out to the LORD my God
6and prayed:

"O my God, I am too
ashamed and disgraced to lift
up my face to you, my God, because our sins are higher than
our heads and our guilt has
reached to the heavens.[j]
7From the days of our forefathers[k] until now, our guilt has
been great. Because of our
sins, we and our kings and our
priests have been subjected to
the sword[l] and captivity,[m] to
pillage and humiliation[n] at
the hand of foreign kings, as it
is today.

8"But now, for a brief moment, the LORD our God has
been gracious[o] in leaving us a
remnant[p] and giving us a firm
place[q] in his sanctuary, and
so our God gives light to our
eyes[r] and a little relief in our
bondage. 9Though we are
slaves,[s] our God has not deserted us in our bondage. He
has shown us kindness[t] in the
sight of the kings of Persia: He
has granted us new life to rebuild the house of our God
and repair its ruins,[u] and he
has given us a wall of protection in Judah and Jerusalem.

10"But now, O our God,
what can we say after this? For
we have disregarded the commands[v] 11you gave through
your servants the prophets
when you said: 'The land you
are entering to possess is a
land polluted[w] by the corruption of its peoples. By their detestable practices[x] they have
filled it with their impurity
from one end to the other.
12Therefore, do not give your
daughters in marriage to their
sons or take their daughters
for your sons. Do not seek a
treaty of friendship with
them[y] at any time, that you
may be strong and eat the
good things of the land and
leave it to your children as an
everlasting inheritance.'

13"What has happened to us
is a result of our evil deeds and
our great guilt, and yet, our
God, you have punished us
less than our sins have deserved[z] and have given us a
remnant like this. 14Shall we
again break your commands
and intermarry[a] with the peoples who commit such detestable practices? Would you not
be angry enough with us to destroy us,[b] leaving us no remnant[c] or survivor? 15O LORD,
God of Israel, you are righteous![d] We are left this day as
a remnant. Here we are before
you in our guilt, though because of it not one of us can
stand[e] in your presence.[f]"

8:36 [a] Est 9:3
9:1 [b] Ezr 6:21; Ne 9:2 [c] Ge 19:38 [d] Ex 13:5
9:2 [e] Ex 34:16 [f] Ex 22:31 [g] Ezr 10:2
9:4 [h] Ezr 10:3
9:5 [i] Ex 29:41
9:6 [j] 2Ch 28:9; Job 42:6; Ps 38:4; Rev 18:5
9:7 [k] 2Ch 29:6 [l] Eze 21:1-32 [m] Dt 28:64 [n] Dt 28:37
9:8 [o] Ps 25:16; Isa 33:2 [p] Ge 45:7 [q] Ecc 12:11; Isa 22:23 [r] Ps 13:3
9:9 [s] Ex 1:14; Ne 9:36 [t] Ezr 7:28 [u] Ps 69:35; Isa 43:1; Jer 32:44
9:10 [v] Dt 11:8; Isa 1:19-20
9:11 [w] Lev 18:25-28 [x] Dt 9:4
9:12 [y] Ex 34:15; Dt 7:3; 23:6
9:13 [z] Job 11:6; Ps 103:10
9:14 [a] Ne 13:27 [b] Dt 9:8 [c] Dt 9:14
9:15 [d] Ge 18:25; Ps 51:4; Jer 12:1; Da 9:7 [e] Ne 9:33; Ps 130:3; Mal 3:2 [f] 1Ki 8:47

The People's Confession of Sin

10 While Ezra was praying and
confessing,[a] weeping and
throwing himself down before the
house of God, a large crowd of Israelites—men, women and children
—gathered around him. They too
wept bitterly. **2**Then Shecaniah son
of Jehiel, one of the descendants of
Elam, said to Ezra, "We have been
unfaithful[b] to our God by marrying
foreign women from the peoples
around us. But in spite of this,
there is still hope for Israel.[c] **3**Now
let us make a covenant[d] before our
God to send away[e] all these wom-
en and their children, in accordance with the counsel of my lord
and of those who fear the commands of our God. Let it be done
according to the Law. **4**Rise up; this
matter is in your hands. We will
support you, so take courage and
do it."

5So Ezra rose up and put the
leading priests and Levites and all
Israel under oath[f] to do what had
been suggested. And they took the
oath. **6**Then Ezra withdrew from
before the house of God and went
to the room of Jehohanan son of
Eliashib. While he was there, he
ate no food and drank no water,[g]
because he continued to mourn
over the unfaithfulness of the exiles.

7A proclamation was then issued
throughout Judah and Jerusalem
for all the exiles to assemble in Jerusalem. **8**Anyone who failed to appear within three days would forfeit all his property, in accordance
with the decision of the officials
and elders, and would himself be
expelled from the assembly of the
exiles.

9Within the three days, all the
men of Judah and Benjamin[h] had
gathered in Jerusalem. And on the
twentieth day of the ninth month,
all the people were sitting in the
square before the house of God,
greatly distressed by the occasion
and because of the rain. **10**Then
Ezra the priest stood up and said to
them, "You have been unfaithful;
you have married foreign women,
adding to Israel's guilt. **11**Now
make confession to the LORD, the
God of your fathers, and do his will.
Separate yourselves from the peoples around you and from your foreign wives."[i]

12The whole assembly responded with a loud voice:[j] "You are
right! We must do as you say. **13**But
there are many people here and it
is the rainy season; so we cannot
stand outside. Besides, this matter
cannot be taken care of in a day or
two, because we have sinned greatly in this thing. **14**Let our officials
act for the whole assembly. Then
let everyone in our towns who has
married a foreign woman come at a
set time, along with the elders and
judges[k] of each town, until the
fierce anger[l] of our God in this
matter is turned away from us."
15Only Jonathan son of Asahel and
Jahzeiah son of Tikvah, supported
by Meshullam and Shabbethai[m]
the Levite, opposed this.

16So the exiles did as was proposed. Ezra the priest selected men
who were family heads, one from
each family division, and all of
them designated by name. On the
first day of the tenth month they
sat down to investigate the cases,
17and by the first day of the first
month they finished dealing with
all the men who had married foreign women.

Those Guilty of Intermarriage

18Among the descendants of the
priests, the following had
married foreign women:[n]

From the descendants of Jeshua[o] son of Jozadak, and his
brothers: Maaseiah, Elie-
zer, Jarib and Gedaliah.
19(They all gave their
hands[p] in pledge to put
away their wives, and for
their guilt they each presented a ram from the flock
as a guilt offering.)[q]

20From the descendants of Immer:[r]
Hanani and Zebadiah.

10:1 [a]2Ch 20:9; Da 9:20
10:2 [b]Ezr 9:2; Ne 13:27 [c]Dt 30:8-10
10:3 [d]2Ch 34:31 [e]Ex 34:16; Dt 7:2-3; Ezr 9:4
10:5 [f]Ne 5:12; 13:25
10:6 [g]Ex 34:28; Dt 9:18
10:9 [h]Ezr 1:5
10:11 [i]ver 3; Dt 24:1; Ne 9:2; Mal 2:10-16
10:12 [j]Jos 6:5
10:14 [k]Dt 16:18 [l]Nu 25:4; 2Ch 29:10; 30:8
10:15 [m]Ne 11:16
10:18 [n]Jdg 3:6 [o]Ezr 2:2
10:19 [p]2Ki 10:15 [q]Lev 5:15; 6:6
10:20 [r]1Ch 24:14

[21]From the descendants of Harim:[a]
Maaseiah, Elijah, Shemaiah, Jehiel and Uzziah.
[22]From the descendants of Pashhur:[b]
Elioenai, Maaseiah, Ishmael, Nethanel, Jozabad and Elasah.

[23]Among the Levites:[c]

Jozabad, Shimei, Kelaiah (that is, Kelita), Pethahiah, Judah and Eliezer.
[24]From the singers:
Eliashib.[d]
From the gatekeepers:
Shallum, Telem and Uri.

[25]And among the other Israelites:

From the descendants of Parosh:[e]
Ramiah, Izziah, Malkijah, Mijamin, Eleazar, Malkijah and Benaiah.
[26]From the descendants of Elam:[f]
Mattaniah, Zechariah, Jehiel, Abdi, Jeremoth and Elijah.
[27]From the descendants of Zattu:
Elioenai, Eliashib, Mattaniah, Jeremoth, Zabad and Aziza.
[28]From the descendants of Bebai:
Jehohanan, Hananiah, Zabbai and Athlai.
[29]From the descendants of Bani:
Meshullam, Malluch, Adaiah, Jashub, Sheal and Jeremoth.

10:21 [a]1Ch 24:8
10:22 [b]1Ch 9:12
10:23 [c]Ne 8:7; 9:4
10:24 [d]Ne 3:1; 12:10; 13:7, 28
10:25 [e]Ezr 2:3
10:26 [f]ver 2

[30]From the descendants of Pahath-Moab:
Adna, Kelal, Benaiah, Maaseiah, Mattaniah, Bezalel, Binnui and Manasseh.
[31]From the descendants of Harim:
Eliezer, Ishijah, Malkijah, Shemaiah, Shimeon,
[32]Benjamin, Malluch and Shemariah.
[33]From the descendants of Hashum:
Mattenai, Mattattah, Zabad, Eliphelet, Jeremai, Manasseh and Shimei.
[34]From the descendants of Bani:
Maadai, Amram, Uel, [35]Benaiah, Bedeiah, Keluhi,
[36]Vaniah, Meremoth, Eliashib, [37]Mattaniah, Mattenai and Jaasu.
[38]From the descendants of Binnui:[y]
Shimei, [39]Shelemiah, Nathan, Adaiah, [40]Macnadebai, Shashai, Sharai, [41]Azarel, Shelemiah, Shemariah,
[42]Shallum, Amariah and Joseph.
[43]From the descendants of Nebo:
Jeiel, Mattithiah, Zabad, Zebina, Jaddai, Joel and Benaiah.

[44]All these had married foreign women, and some of them had children by these wives.[z]

[y]*37,38* See Septuagint (also 1 Esdras 9:34); Hebrew *Jaasu* [38]*and Bani and Binnui,*
[z]*44* Or *and they sent them away with their children*

Nehemiah

Title and Background

See Introduction to Ezra.

Author and Date of Writing

See Introduction to Ezra. Nehemiah can be dated about 430 B.C.

Theme and Message

Nehemiah continues the history of the Jews upon their return from exile in Babylon. Nehemiah went to Jerusalem in 445 B.C. and led the people in repairing the walls. With Ezra, he provided leadership for the people. A recurring theme of this book is the description of the importance of prayer to Nehemiah.

Outline

I. Nehemiah Rebuilds the Walls (1:1-7:3)
II. Change Under Ezra (7:4-10:39)
III. Nehemiah's Plans (11:1-13:31)

Nehemiah's Prayer

1 The words of Nehemiah son of
Hacaliah:

In the month of Kislev[a] in the
twentieth year, while I was in the
citadel of Susa, 2Hanani,[b] one of
my brothers, came from Judah with
some other men, and I questioned
them about the Jewish remnant[c]
that survived the exile, and also
about Jerusalem.
3They said to me, "Those who
survived the exile and are back in
the province are in great trouble
and disgrace. The wall of Jerusalem is broken down, and its gates
have been burned with fire.[d]"
4When I heard these things, I sat
down and wept.[e] For some days I
mourned and fasted[f] and prayed
before the God of heaven. 5Then I
said:

"O LORD, God of heaven, the
great and awesome God,[g]
who keeps his covenant of
love[h] with those who love him
and obey his commands, 6let
your ear be attentive and your
eyes open to hear[i] the
prayer[j] your servant is praying before you day and night
for your servants, the people of
Israel. I confess the sins we Israelites, including myself and
my father's house, have committed against you. 7We have
acted very wickedly[k] toward
you. We have not obeyed the
commands, decrees and laws
you gave your servant Moses.
8"Remember[l] the instruction you gave your servant Moses, saying, 'If you are unfaithful, I will scatter[m] you among
the nations, 9but if you return
to me and obey my com-
mands, then even if your exiled people are at the farthest
horizon, I will gather[n] them
from there and bring them to
the place I have chosen as a
dwelling for my Name.'[o]

10"They are your servants
and your people, whom you redeemed by your great strength
and your mighty hand.[p] 11O
Lord, let your ear be attentive[q] to the prayer of this your

1:1 [a]Ne 10:1; Zec 7:1
1:2 [b]Ne 7:2 [c]Jer 52:28
1:3 [d]2Ki 25:10; Ne 2:3,13,17
1:4 [e]Ps 137:1 [f]Ezr 9:4
1:5 [g]Dt 7:21; Ne 4:14 [h]Ex 20:6; Da 9:4
1:6 [i]1Ki 8:29 [j]Da 9:17
1:7 [k]Dt 28:14-15; Ps 106:6
1:8 [l]2Ki 20:3 [m]Lev 26:33
1:9 [n]Dt 30:4 [o]1Ki 8:48; Jer 29:14
1:10 [p]Ex 32:11; Dt 9:29
1:11 [q]ver 6

servant and to the prayer of your servants who delight in revering your name. Give your servant success today by granting him favor in the presence of this man."

I was cupbearer[a] to the king.

Artaxerxes Sends Nehemiah to Jerusalem

2 In the month of Nisan in the twentieth year of King Artaxerxes,[b] when wine was brought for him, I took the wine and gave it to the king. I had not been sad in his presence before; **2**so the king asked me, "Why does your face look so sad when you are not ill? This can be nothing but sadness of heart."

I was very much afraid, **3**but I said to the king, "May the king live forever![c] Why should my face not look sad when the city[d] where my fathers are buried lies in ruins, and its gates have been destroyed by fire?[e]"

4The king said to me, "What is it you want?"

Then I prayed to the God of heaven, **5**and I answered the king, "If it pleases the king and if your servant has found favor in his sight, let him send me to the city in Judah where my fathers are buried so that I can rebuild it."

6Then the king[f], with the queen sitting beside him, asked me, "How long will your journey take, and when will you get back?" It pleased the king to send me; so I set a time.

7I also said to him, "If it pleases the king, may I have letters to the governors of Trans-Euphrates,[g] so that they will provide me safe-conduct until I arrive in Judah? **8**And may I have a letter to Asaph, keeper of the king's forest, so he will give me timber to make beams for the gates of the citadel[h] by the temple and for the city wall and for the residence I will occupy?" And because the gracious hand of my God was upon me,[i] the king granted my requests. **9**So I went to the governors of Trans-Euphrates and gave them the king's letters. The king had also sent army officers and cavalry[j] with me.

10When Sanballat[k] the Horonite and Tobiah[l] the Ammonite official heard about this, they were very much disturbed that someone had come to promote the welfare of the Israelites.[m]

Nehemiah Inspects Jerusalem's Walls

11I went to Jerusalem, and after staying there three days[n] **12**I set out during the night with a few men. I had not told anyone what my God had put in my heart to do for Jerusalem. There were no mounts with me except the one I was riding on.

13By night I went out through the Valley Gate[o] toward the Jackal[a] Well and the Dung Gate,[p] examining the walls[q] of Jerusalem, which had been broken down, and its gates, which had been destroyed by fire. **14**Then I moved on toward the Fountain Gate[r] and the King's Pool,[s] but there was not enough room for my mount to get through; **15**so I went up the valley by night, examining the wall. Finally, I turned back and reentered through the Valley Gate. **16**The officials did not know where I had gone or what I was doing, because as yet I had said nothing to the Jews or the priests or nobles or officials or any others who would be doing the work.

17Then I said to them, "You see the trouble we are in: Jerusalem lies in ruins, and its gates have been burned with fire.[t] Come, let us rebuild the wall[u] of Jerusalem, and we will no longer be in disgrace.[v]" **18**I also told them about the gracious hand of my God upon me[w] and what the king had said to me.

They replied, "Let us start rebuilding." So they began this good work.

19But when Sanballat the Horonite, Tobiah the Ammonite official and Geshem[x] the Arab heard

1:11 [a]Ge 40:1
2:1 [b]Ezr 7:1
2:3 [c]1Ki 1:31; Da 2:4; 5:10; 6:6,21 [d]Ps 137:6 [e]Ne 1:3
2:6 [f]Ne 5:14; 13:6
2:7 [g]Ezr 8:36
2:8 [h]Ne 7:2 [i]ver 18; Ezr 5:5; 7:6
2:9 [j]Ezr 8:22
2:10 [k]ver 19; Ne 4:1,7 [l]Ne 4:3; 13:4-7 [m]Est 10:3
2:11 [n]Ge 40:13
2:13 [o]2Ch 26:9 [p]Ne 3:13 [q]Ne 1:3
2:14 [r]Ne 3:15 [s]2Ki 18:17
2:17 [t]Ne 1:3 [u]Ps 102:16; Isa 30:13; 58:12 [v]Eze 5:14
2:18 [w]2Sa 2:7
2:19 [x]Ne 6:1,2,6

[a]13 Or *Serpent* or *Fig*

about it, they mocked and ridiculed us.[a] "What is this you are
doing?" they asked. "Are you rebelling against the king?"
20I answered them by saying,
"The God of heaven will give us
success. We his servants will start
rebuilding, but as for you, you have
no share[b] in Jerusalem or any
claim or historic right to it."

Builders of the Wall

3 Eliashib[c] the high priest and
his fellow priests went to work
and rebuilt[d] the Sheep Gate.[e]
They dedicated it and set its doors
in place, building as far as the Tower of the Hundred, which they dedicated, and as far as the Tower of
Hananel.[f] **2**The men of Jericho[g]
built the adjoining section, and
Zaccur son of Imri built next to
them.

3The Fish Gate[h] was rebuilt by
the sons of Hassenaah. They laid
its beams and put its doors and
bolts and bars in place. **4**Meremoth
son of Uriah, the son of Hakkoz, repaired the next section. Next to
him Meshullam son of Berekiah,
the son of Meshezabel, made repairs, and next to him Zadok son of
Baana also made repairs. **5**The next
section was repaired by the men of
Tekoa,[i] but their nobles would
not put their shoulders to the work
under their supervisors.[b]

6The Jeshanah[c] Gate[j] was repaired by Joiada son of Paseah and
Meshullam son of Besodeiah. They
laid its beams and put its doors and
bolts and bars in place. **7**Next to
them, repairs were made by men
from Gibeon[k] and Mizpah—Mela-
tiah of Gibeon and Jadon of Me-
ronoth—places under the authority of the governor of Trans-Euphrates. **8**Uzziel son of Harhaiah, one of
the goldsmiths, repaired the next
section; and Hananiah, one of the
perfume-makers, made repairs
next to that. They restored[d] Jerusalem as far as the Broad Wall.[l]
9Rephaiah son of Hur, ruler of a
half-district of Jerusalem, repaired
the next section. **10**Adjoining this,

2:19 [a]Ps 44:13-16
2:20 [b]Ezr 4:3
3:1 [c]Ezr 10:24 [d]Isa 58:12 [e]ver 32; Ne 12:39 [f]Ne 12:39; Jer 31:38; Zec 14:10
3:2 [g]Ne 7:36
3:3 [h]2Ch 33:14; Ne 12:39
3:5 [i]2Sa 14:2
3:6 [j]Ne 12:39
3:7 [k]Jos 9:3; Ne 2:7
3:8 [l]Ne 12:38
3:11 [m]Ne 12:38
3:13 [n]2Ch 26:9 [o]Jos 15:34 [p]Ne 2:13
3:14 [q]Jer 6:1
3:15 [r]Isa 8:6; Jn 9:7
3:16 [s]Jos 15:58 [t]Ac 2:29
3:17 [u]Jos 15:44

Jedaiah son of Harumaph made repairs opposite his house, and Hattush son of Hashabneiah made repairs next to him. **11**Malkijah son
of Harim and Hasshub son of Pahath-Moab repaired another section and the Tower of the Ovens.[m]
12Shallum son of Hallohesh, ruler
of a half-district of Jerusalem, repaired the next section with the
help of his daughters.

13The Valley Gate[n] was repaired
by Hanun and the residents of Zanoah.[o] They rebuilt it and put its
doors and bolts and bars in place.
They also repaired five hundred
yards[e] of the wall as far as the
Dung Gate.[p]

14The Dung Gate was repaired
by Malkijah son of Recab, ruler of
the district of Beth Hakkerem.[q]
He rebuilt it and put its doors and
bolts and bars in place.

15The Fountain Gate was repaired by Shallun son of Col-Hozeh, ruler of the district of Mizpah.
He rebuilt it, roofing it over and
putting its doors and bolts and bars
in place. He also repaired the wall
of the Pool of Siloam,[f][r] by the
King's Garden, as far as the steps
going down from the City of David.
16Beyond him, Nehemiah son of
Azbuk, ruler of a half-district of
Beth Zur,[s] made repairs up to a
point opposite the tombs[g][t] of David, as far as the artificial pool and
the House of the Heroes.
17Next to him, the repairs were
made by the Levites under Rehum
son of Bani. Beside him, Hashabiah, ruler of half the district of Keilah,[u] carried out repairs for his district. **18**Next to him, the repairs
were made by their countrymen
under Binnui[h] son of Henadad,
ruler of the other half-district of
Keilah. **19**Next to him, Ezer son of

[b]*5* Or *their Lord* or *the governor* [c]*6* Or *Old*
[d]*8* Or *They left out part of* [e]*13* Hebrew *a thousand cubits* (about 450 meters)
[f]*15* Hebrew *Shelah,* a variant of *Shiloah,* that is, Siloam [g]*16* Hebrew; Septuagint, some Vulgate manuscripts and Syriac *tomb*
[h]*18* Two Hebrew manuscripts and Syriac (see also Septuagint and verse 24); most Hebrew manuscripts *Bavvai*

Jeshua, ruler of Mizpah, repaired
another section, from a point facing the ascent to the armory as far
as the angle. **20**Next to him, Baruch
son of Zabbai zealously repaired
another section, from the angle to
the entrance of the house of Eliashib the high priest. **21**Next to him,
Meremoth[a] son of Uriah, the son
of Hakkoz, repaired another section, from the entrance of Eliashib's house to the end of it.

22The repairs next to him were
made by the priests from the surrounding region. **23**Beyond them,
Benjamin and Hasshub made repairs in front of their house; and
next to them, Azariah son of Maaseiah, the son of Ananiah, made repairs beside his house. **24**Next to
him, Binnui[b] son of Henadad repaired another section, from Azariah's house to the angle and the corner, **25**and Palal son of Uzai worked
opposite the angle and the tower
projecting from the upper palace
near the court of the guard.[c] Next
to him, Pedaiah son of Parosh[d]
26and the temple servants[e] living
on the hill of Ophel[f] made repairs
up to a point opposite the Water
Gate[g] toward the east and the projecting tower. **27**Next to them, the
men of Tekoa[h] repaired another
section, from the great projecting
tower[i] to the wall of Ophel.

28Above the Horse Gate,[j] the
priests made repairs, each in front
of his own house. **29**Next to them,
Zadok son of Immer made repairs
opposite his house. Next to him,
Shemaiah son of Shecaniah, the
guard at the East Gate, made repairs. **30**Next to him, Hananiah son
of Shelemiah, and Hanun, the
sixth son of Zalaph, repaired another section. Next to them, Meshullam son of Berekiah made repairs opposite his living quarters.
31Next to him, Malkijah, one of the
goldsmiths, made repairs as far as
the house of the temple servants
and the merchants, opposite the
Inspection Gate, and as far as the
room above the corner; **32**and between the room above the corner
and the Sheep Gate[k] the goldsmiths and merchants made repairs.

Opposition to the Rebuilding

4 When Sanballat[l] heard that
we were rebuilding the wall, he
became angry and was greatly incensed. He ridiculed the Jews,
2and in the presence of his associates[m] and the army of Samaria, he
said, "What are those feeble Jews
doing? Will they restore their wall?
Will they offer sacrifices? Will they
finish in a day? Can they bring the
stones back to life from those
heaps of rubble[n]—burned as they
are?"

3Tobiah[o] the Ammonite, who
was at his side, said, "What they
are building—if even a fox climbed
up on it, he would break down their
wall of stones!"[p]

4Hear us, O our God, for we are
despised.[q] Turn their insults back
on their own heads. Give them over
as plunder in a land of captivity.
5Do not cover up their guilt[r] or
blot out their sins from your
sight,[s] for they have thrown insults in the face of[i] the builders.

6So we rebuilt the wall till all of
it reached half its height, for the
people worked with all their heart.

7But when Sanballat, Tobiah,[t]
the Arabs, the Ammonites and the
men of Ashdod heard that the repairs to Jerusalem's walls had gone
ahead and that the gaps were being
closed, they were very angry. **8**They
all plotted together[u] to come and
fight against Jerusalem and stir up
trouble against it. **9**But we prayed
to our God and posted a guard day
and night to meet this threat.

10Meanwhile, the people in Judah said, "The strength of the laborers[v] is giving out, and there is
so much rubble that we cannot rebuild the wall."

11Also our enemies said, "Before
they know it or see us, we will be
right there among them and will

3:21 [a]Ezr 8:33
3:24 [b]Ezr 8:33
3:25 [c]Jer 32:2; 37:21; 39:14 [d]Ezr 2:3
3:26 [e]Ne 7:46; 11:21 [f]2Ch 33:14 [g]Ne 8:1,3,16; 12:37
3:27 [h]ver 5 [i]Ps 48:12
3:28 [j]2Ki 11:16; 2Ch 23:15; Jer 31:40
3:32 [k]ver 1; Jn 5:2
4:1 [l]Ne 2:10
4:2 [m]Ezr 4:9-10 [n]Ps 79:1; Jer 26:18
4:3 [o]Ne 2:10 [p]Job 13:12; 15:3
4:4 [q]Ps 44:13; 79:12; 123:3-4; Jer 33:24
4:5 [r]Isa 2:9; La 1:22 [s]2Ki 14:27; Ps 51:1; 69:27-28; 109:14; Jer 18:23
4:7 [t]Ne 2:10
4:8 [u]Ps 2:2; 83:1-18
4:10 [v]1Ch 23:4

[i]5 Or *have provoked you to anger before*

kill them and put an end to the work."

12Then the Jews who lived near them came and told us ten times over, "Wherever you turn, they will attack us."

13Therefore I stationed some of the people behind the lowest points of the wall at the exposed places, posting them by families, with their swords, spears and bows. 14After I looked things over, I stood up and said to the nobles, the officials and the rest of the people, "Don't be afraid[a] of them. Remember[b] the Lord, who is great and awesome,[c] and fight[d] for your brothers, your sons and your daughters, your wives and your homes."

15When our enemies heard that we were aware of their plot and that God had frustrated it,[e] we all returned to the wall, each to his own work.

16From that day on, half of my men did the work, while the other half were equipped with spears, shields, bows and armor. The officers posted themselves behind all the people of Judah 17who were building the wall. Those who carried materials did their work with one hand and held a weapon[f] in the other, 18and each of the builders wore his sword at his side as he worked. But the man who sounded the trumpet[g] stayed with me.

19Then I said to the nobles, the officials and the rest of the people, "The work is extensive and spread out, and we are widely separated from each other along the wall. 20Wherever you hear the sound of the trumpet,[h] join us there. Our God will fight[i] for us!"

21So we continued the work with half the men holding spears, from the first light of dawn till the stars came out. 22At that time I also said to the people, "Have every man and his helper stay inside Jerusalem at night, so they can serve us as guards by night and workmen by day." 23Neither I nor my brothers nor my men nor the guards with me took off our clothes; each had his weapon, even when he went for water.[j]

4:14 [a]Ge 28:15; Nu 14:9; Dt 1:29 [b]Ne 1:8 [c]Ne 1:5 [d]2Sa 10:12
4:15 [e]2Sa 17:14; Job 5:12
4:17 [f]Ps 149:6
4:18 [g]Nu 10:2
4:20 [h]Eze 33:3 [i]Ex 14:14; Dt 1:30; 20:4; Jos 10:14
5:3 [j]Ps 109:11 [k]Ge 47:23
5:4 [l]Ezr 4:13
5:5 [m]Ge 29:14 [n]Lev 25:39-43, 47; 2Ki 4:1; Isa 50:1 [o]Dt 15:7-11; 2Ki 4:1
5:7 [p]Ex 22:25-27; Lev 25:35-37; Dt 23:19-20; 24:10-13
5:8 [q]Lev 25:47 [r]Jer 34:8
5:9 [s]Isa 52:5
5:10 [t]Ex 22:25
5:11 [u]Isa 58:6

Nehemiah Helps the Poor

5 Now the men and their wives raised a great outcry against their Jewish brothers. 2Some were saying, "We and our sons and daughters are numerous; in order for us to eat and stay alive, we must get grain."

3Others were saying, "We are mortgaging our fields,[j] our vineyards and our homes to get grain during the famine."[k]

4Still others were saying, "We have had to borrow money to pay the king's tax[l] on our fields and vineyards. 5Although we are of the same flesh and blood[m] as our countrymen and though our sons are as good as theirs, yet we have to subject our sons and daughters to slavery.[n] Some of our daughters have already been enslaved, but we are powerless, because our fields and our vineyards belong to others."[o]

6When I heard their outcry and these charges, I was very angry. 7I pondered them in my mind and then accused the nobles and officials. I told them, "You are exacting usury[p] from your own countrymen!" So I called together a large meeting to deal with them 8and said: "As far as possible, we have bought[q] back our Jewish brothers who were sold to the Gentiles. Now you are selling your brothers, only for them to be sold back to us!" They kept quiet, because they could find nothing to say.[r]

9So I continued, "What you are doing is not right. Shouldn't you walk in the fear of our God to avoid the reproach[s] of our Gentile enemies? 10I and my brothers and my men are also lending the people money and grain. But let the exacting of usury stop![t] 11Give back to them immediately their fields, vineyards, olive groves and houses, and also the usury[u] you are charg-

[j]23 The meaning of the Hebrew for this clause is uncertain.

ing them—the hundredth part of the money, grain, new wine and oil."

12"We will give it back," they said. "And we will not demand anything more from them. We will do as you say."

Then I summoned the priests and made the nobles and officials take an oath[a] to do what they had promised. 13I also shook[b] out the folds of my robe and said, "In this way may God shake out of his house and possessions every man who does not keep this promise. So may such a man be shaken out and emptied!"

At this the whole assembly said, "Amen,"[c] and praised the LORD. And the people did as they had promised.

14Moreover, from the twentieth year of King Artaxerxes,[d] when I was appointed to be their governor[e] in the land of Judah, until his thirty-second year—twelve years—neither I nor my brothers ate the food allotted to the governor. 15But the earlier governors—those preceding me—placed a heavy burden on the people and took forty shekels[k] of silver from them in addition to food and wine. Their assistants also lorded it over the people. But out of reverence for God[f] I did not act like that. 16Instead,[g] I devoted myself to the work on this wall. All my men were assembled there for the work; we[l] did not acquire any land.

17Furthermore, a hundred and fifty Jews and officials ate at my table, as well as those who came to us from the surrounding nations. 18Each day one ox, six choice sheep and some poultry[h] were prepared for me, and every ten days an abundant supply of wine of all kinds. In spite of all this, I never demanded the food allotted to the governor, because the demands were heavy on these people.

19Remember[i] me with favor, O my God, for all I have done for these people.

5:12 [a]Ezr 10:5
5:13 [b]Mt 10:14; Ac 18:6 [c]Dt 27:15-26
5:14 [d]Ne 2:6; 13:6 [e]Ge 42:6; Ezr 6:7; Jer 40:7; Hag 1:1
5:15 [f]Ge 20:11
5:16 [g]2Th 3:7-10
5:18 [h]1Ki 4:23
5:19 [i]Ge 8:1; 2Ki 20:3; Ne 1:8; 13:14, 22,31
6:1 [j]Ne 2:10 [k]Ne 2:19
6:2 [l]1Ch 8:12
6:5 [m]Ne 2:10
6:6 [n]Ne 2:19

Further Opposition to the Rebuilding

6 When word came to Sanballat, Tobiah,[j] Geshem[k] the Arab and the rest of our enemies that I had rebuilt the wall and not a gap was left in it—though up to that time I had not set the doors in the gates— 2Sanballat and Geshem sent me this message: "Come, let us meet together in one of the villages[m] on the plain of Ono.[l]"

But they were scheming to harm me; 3so I sent messengers to them with this reply: "I am carrying on a great project and cannot go down. Why should the work stop while I leave it and go down to you?" 4Four times they sent me the same message, and each time I gave them the same answer.

5Then, the fifth time, Sanballat[m] sent his aide to me with the same message, and in his hand was an unsealed letter 6in which was written:

> "It is reported among the nations—and Geshem[n][n] says it is true—that you and the Jews are plotting to revolt, and therefore you are building the wall. Moreover, according to these reports you are about to become their king 7and have even appointed prophets to make this proclamation about you in Jerusalem: 'There is a king in Judah!' Now this report will get back to the king; so come, let us confer together."

8I sent him this reply: "Nothing like what you are saying is happening; you are just making it up out of your head."

9They were all trying to frighten us, thinking, "Their hands will get too weak for the work, and it will not be completed."

⌞But I prayed,⌟ "Now strengthen my hands."

[k]*15* That is, about 1 pound (about 0.5 kilogram) [l]*16* Most Hebrew manuscripts; some Hebrew manuscripts, Septuagint, Vulgate and Syriac *I* [m]*2* Or *in Kephirim* [n]*6* Hebrew *Gashmu,* a variant of *Geshem*

10 One day I went to the house of Shemaiah son of Delaiah, the son of Mehetabel, who was shut in at his home. He said, "Let us meet in the house of God, inside the temple[a], and let us close the temple doors, because men are coming to kill you—by night they are coming to kill you."

11 But I said, "Should a man like me run away? Or should one like me go into the temple to save his life? I will not go!" 12 I realized that God had not sent him, but that he had prophesied against me[b] because Tobiah and Sanballat[c] had hired him. 13 He had been hired to intimidate me so that I would commit a sin by doing this, and then they would give me a bad name to discredit me.[d]

14 Remember[e] Tobiah and Sanballat,[f] O my God, because of what they have done; remember also the prophetess[g] Noadiah and the rest of the prophets[h] who have been trying to intimidate me.

The Completion of the Wall

15 So the wall was completed on the twenty-fifth of Elul, in fifty-two days. 16 When all our enemies heard about this, all the surrounding nations were afraid and lost their self-confidence, because they realized that this work had been done with the help of our God.

17 Also, in those days the nobles of Judah were sending many letters to Tobiah, and replies from Tobiah kept coming to them. 18 For many in Judah were under oath to him, since he was son-in-law to Shecaniah son of Arah, and his son Jehohanan had married the daughter of Meshullam son of Berekiah. 19 Moreover, they kept reporting to me his good deeds and then telling him what I said. And Tobiah sent letters to intimidate me.

7 After the wall had been rebuilt and I had set the doors in place, the gatekeepers[i] and the singers[j] and the Levites[k] were appointed. 2 I put in charge of Jerusalem my brother Hanani,[l] along with[o] Hananiah[m] the commander of the citadel,[n] because he was a man of integrity and feared[o] God more than most men do. 3 I said to them, "The gates of Jerusalem are not to be opened until the sun is hot. While the gatekeepers are still on duty, have them shut the doors and bar them. Also appoint residents of Jerusalem as guards, some at their posts and some near their own houses."

The List of the Exiles Who Returned

7:6–73pp — Ezr 2:1–70

4 Now the city was large and spacious, but there were few people in it,[p] and the houses had not yet been rebuilt. 5 So my God put it into my heart to assemble the nobles, the officials and the common people for registration by families. I found the genealogical record of those who had been the first to return. This is what I found written there:

6 These are the people of the province who came up from the captivity of the exiles[q] whom Nebuchadnezzar king of Babylon had taken captive (they returned to Jerusalem and Judah, each to his own town, 7 in company with Zerubbabel,[r] Jeshua, Nehemiah, Azariah, Raamiah, Nahamani, Mordecai, Bilshan, Mispereth, Bigvai, Nehum and Baanah):

The list of the men of Israel:

8 the descendants of Parosh	2,172
9 of Shephatiah	372
10 of Arah	652
11 of Pahath-Moab (through the line of Jeshua and Joab)	2,818
12 of Elam	1,254
13 of Zattu	845
14 of Zaccai	760
15 of Binnui	648
16 of Bebai	628

6:10 [a] Nu 18:7
6:12 [b] Eze 13:22-23 [c] Ne 2:10
6:13 [d] Jer 20:10
6:14 [e] Ne 1:8 [f] Ne 2:10 [g] Ex 15:20; Eze 13:17-23; Ac 21:9; Rev 2:20 [h] Ne 13:29; Jer 23:9-40; Zec 13:2-3
7:1 [i] 1Ch 9:27; 26:12-19; Ne 6:1,15 [j] Ps 68:25 [k] Ne 8:9
7:2 [l] Ne 1:2 [m] Ne 10:23 [n] Ne 2:8 [o] 1Ki 18:3
7:4 [p] Ne 11:1
7:6 [q] 2Ch 36:20; Ezr 2:1-70; Ne 1:2
7:7 [r] 1Ch 3:19; Ezr 2:2

o2 Or *Hanani, that is,*

17 of Azgad 2,322
18 of Adonikam 667
19 of Bigvai 2,067
20 of Adin[a] 655
21 of Ater (through
Hezekiah) 98
22 of Hashum 328
23 of Bezai 324
24 of Hariph 112
25 of Gibeon 95

26 the men of Bethlehem
and Netophah[b] 188
27 of Anathoth[c] 128
28 of Beth Azmaveth 42
29 of Kiriath Jearim,
Kephirah[d] and
Beeroth[e] 743
30 of Ramah and Geba 621
31 of Micmash 122
32 of Bethel and Ai[f] 123
33 of the other Nebo 52
34 of the other Elam 1,254
35 of Harim 320
36 of Jericho[g] 345
37 of Lod, Hadid and
Ono[h] 721
38 of Senaah 3,930

39 The priests:

the descendants of Jedaiah
(through the family
of Jeshua) 973
40 of Immer 1,052
41 of Pashhur 1,247
42 of Harim 1,017

43 The Levites:

the descendants of Jeshua
(through Kadmiel through
the line of Hodaviah) 74

44 The singers:[i]

the descendants of
Asaph 148

45 The gatekeepers:[j]

the descendants of
Shallum, Ater, Talmon,
Akkub, Hatita and
Shobai 138

46 The temple servants:[k]

the descendants of
Ziha, Hasupha, Tabbaoth,
47 Keros, Sia, Padon,
48 Lebana, Hagaba, Shalmai,

7:20 [a] Ezr 8:6
7:26 [b] 2Sa 23:28; 1Ch 2:54
7:27 [c] Jos 21:18
7:29 [d] Jos 18:26 [e] Jos 18:25
7:32 [f] Ge 12:8
7:36 [g] Ne 3:2
7:37 [h] 1Ch 8:12
7:44 [i] Ne 11:23
7:45 [j] 1Ch 9:17
7:46 [k] Ne 3:26
7:60 [l] 1Ch 9:2
7:65 [m] Ex 28:30; Ne 8:9

49 Hanan, Giddel, Gahar,
50 Reaiah, Rezin, Nekoda,
51 Gazzam, Uzza, Paseah,
52 Besai, Meunim,
Nephussim,
53 Bakbuk, Hakupha,
Harhur,
54 Bazluth, Mehida, Harsha,
55 Barkos, Sisera, Temah,
56 Neziah and Hatipha

57 The descendants of the servants of Solomon:

the descendants of
Sotai, Sophereth, Perida,
58 Jaala, Darkon, Giddel,
59 Shephatiah, Hattil,
Pokereth-Hazzebaim and
Amon

60 The temple servants and the
descendants of the
servants of Solomon[l] 392

61 The following came up
from the towns of Tel Melah,
Tel Harsha, Kerub, Addon and
Immer, but they could not
show that their families were
descended from Israel:

62 the descendants of
Delaiah, Tobiah and
Nekoda 642

63 And from among the priests:

the descendants of
Hobaiah, Hakkoz and
Barzillai (a man who had
married a daughter of
Barzillai the Gileadite and
was called by that name).

64 These searched for their
family records, but they could
not find them and so were excluded from the priesthood as
unclean. 65 The governor,
therefore, ordered them not to
eat any of the most sacred
food until there should be a
priest ministering with the
Urim and Thummim.[m]

66 The whole company num-
bered 42,360, 67 besides their
7,337 menservants and maidservants; and they also had
245 men and women singers.
68 There were 736 horses, 245

mules,[p] **69**435 camels and 6,720 donkeys.

70Some of the heads of the families contributed to the work. The governor gave to the treasury 1,000 drachmas[q] of gold, 50 bowls and 530 garments for priests. **71**Some of the heads of the families[a] gave to the treasury for the work 20,000 drachmas[r] of gold and 2,200 minas[s] of silver. **72**The total given by the rest of the people was 20,000 drachmas of gold, 2,000 minas[t] of silver and 67 garments for priests.[b]

73The priests, the Levites, the gatekeepers, the singers and the temple servants,[c] along with certain of the people and the rest of the Israelites, settled in their own towns.[d]

Ezra Reads the Law

When the seventh month came and the Israelites had settled in

8 their towns,[e] **1**all the people assembled as one man in the square before the Water Gate.[f] They told Ezra the scribe to bring out the Book of the Law of Moses,[g] which the LORD had commanded for Israel.

2So on the first day of the seventh month[h] Ezra the priest brought the Law[i] before the assembly, which was made up of men and women and all who were able to understand. **3**He read it aloud from daybreak till noon as he faced the square before the Water Gate[j] in the presence of the men, women and others who could understand. And all the people listened attentively to the Book of the Law.

4Ezra the scribe stood on a high wooden platform[k] built for the occasion. Beside him on his right stood Mattithiah, Shema, Anaiah, Uriah, Hilkiah and Maaseiah; and on his left were Pedaiah, Mishael, Malkijah, Hashum, Hashbaddanah, Zechariah and Meshullam.

5Ezra opened the book. All the people could see him because he was standing[l] above them; and as he opened it, the people all stood up. **6**Ezra praised the LORD, the great God; and all the people lifted their hands[m] and responded, "Amen! Amen!" Then they bowed down and worshiped the LORD with their faces to the ground.

7The Levites[n]—Jeshua, Bani, Sherebiah, Jamin, Akkub, Shabbethai, Hodiah, Maaseiah, Kelita, Azariah, Jozabad, Hanan and Pelaiah—instructed[o] the people in the Law while the people were standing there. **8**They read from the Book of the Law of God, making it clear[u] and giving the meaning so that the people could understand what was being read.

9Then Nehemiah the governor, Ezra the priest and scribe, and the Levites[p] who were instructing the people said to them all, "This day is sacred to the LORD your God. Do not mourn or weep."[q] For all the people had been weeping as they listened to the words of the Law.

10Nehemiah said, "Go and enjoy choice food and sweet drinks, and send some to those who have nothing[r] prepared. This day is sacred to our Lord. Do not grieve, for the joy[s] of the LORD is your strength."

11The Levites calmed all the people, saying, "Be still, for this is a sacred day. Do not grieve."

12Then all the people went away to eat and drink, to send portions of food and to celebrate with great joy,[t] because they now understood the words that had been made known to them.

13On the second day of the month, the heads of all the families, along with the priests and the Levites, gathered around Ezra the scribe to give attention to the words of the Law. **14**They found

7:71 [a] 1Ch 29:7
7:72 [b] Ex 25:2
7:73 [c] Ne 1:10; Ps 34:22; 103:21; 113:1; 135:1 [d] Ezr 3:1; Ne 11:1 [e] Ezr 3:1
8:1 [f] Ne 3:26 [g] Dt 28:61; 2Ch 34:15; Ezr 7:6
8:2 [h] Lev 23:23-25; Nu 29:1-6 [i] Dt 31:11
8:3 [j] Ne 3:26
8:4 [k] 2Ch 6:13
8:5 [l] Jdg 3:20
8:6 [m] Ex 4:31; Ezr 9:5; 1Ti 2:8
8:7 [n] Ezr 10:23 [o] Lev 10:11; 2Ch 17:7
8:9 [p] Ne 7:1,65,70 [q] Dt 12:7,12; 16:14-15
8:10 [r] 1Sa 25:8; Lk 14:12-14 [s] Lev 23:40; Dt 12:18; 16:11,14-15
8:12 [t] Est 9:22

[p] *68* Some Hebrew manuscripts (see also Ezra 2:66); most Hebrew manuscripts do not have this verse. [q] *70* That is, about 19 pounds (about 8.5 kilograms) [r] *71* That is, about 375 pounds (about 170 kilograms); also in verse 72 [s] *71* That is, about 1 1/3 tons (about 1.2 metric tons) [t] *72* That is, about 1 1/4 tons (about 1.1 metric tons) [u] *8* Or *God, translating it*

written in the Law, which the LORD
had commanded through Moses,
that the Israelites were to live in
booths during the feast of the seventh month 15and that they should
proclaim this word and spread it
throughout their towns and in Jerusalem: "Go out into the hill
country and bring back branches
from olive and wild olive trees, and
from myrtles, palms and shade
trees, to make booths"—as it is
written.[v]

16So the people went out and
brought back branches and built
themselves booths on their own
roofs, in their courtyards, in the
courts of the house of God and in
the square by the Water Gate and
the one by the Gate of Ephraim.[a]
17The whole company that had returned from exile built booths and
lived in them. From the days of
Joshua son of Nun until that day,
the Israelites had not celebrated[b]
it like this. And their joy was very
great.

18Day after day, from the first
day to the last, Ezra read[c] from the
Book of the Law of God. They celebrated the feast for seven days, and
on the eighth day, in accordance
with the regulation,[d] there was an
assembly.

The Israelites Confess Their Sins

9 On the twenty-fourth day of
the same month, the Israelites
gathered together, fasting and
wearing sackcloth and having dust
on their heads.[e] 2Those of Israelite descent had separated themselves from all foreigners.[f] They
stood in their places and confessed
their sins and the wickedness of
their fathers.[g] 3They stood where
they were and read from the Book
of the Law of the LORD their God for
a quarter of the day, and spent another quarter in confession and in
worshiping the LORD their God.
4Standing on the stairs were the
Levites[h]—Jeshua, Bani, Kadmiel,
Shebaniah, Bunni, Sherebiah, Bani
and Kenani—who called with loud
voices to the LORD their God. 5And
the Levites—Jeshua, Kadmiel,
Bani, Hashabneiah, Sherebiah,
Hodiah, Shebaniah and Pethahiah—said: "Stand up and praise the
LORD your God,[i] who is from everlasting to everlasting.[w]"

"Blessed be your glorious
name, and may it be exalted
above all blessing and praise.
6You alone are the LORD.[j] You
made the heavens,[k] even the
highest heavens, and all their
starry host, the earth[l] and all
that is on it, the seas[m] and all
that is in them.[n] You give life
to everything, and the multitudes of heaven worship you.

7"You are the LORD God,
who chose Abram and brought
him out of Ur of the Chaldeans[o] and named him Abraham.[p] 8You found his heart
faithful to you, and you made
a covenant with him to give to
his descendants the land of
the Canaanites, Hittites, Amorites, Perizzites, Jebusites and
Girgashites.[q] You have kept
your promise[r] because you
are righteous.[s]

9"You saw the suffering of
our forefathers in Egypt;[t] you
heard their cry at the Red
Sea.[x][u] 10You sent miraculous
signs[v] and wonders against
Pharaoh, against all his officials and all the people of his
land, for you knew how arrogantly the Egyptians treated
them. You made a name[w] for
yourself, which remains to this
day. 11You divided the sea before them,[x] so that they
passed through it on dry
ground, but you hurled their
pursuers into the depths, like
a stone into mighty waters.[y]
12By day you led[z] them with a
pillar of cloud,[a] and by night
with a pillar of fire to give
them light on the way they
were to take.

8:16 [a]2Ki 14:13; Ne 12:39
8:17 [b]2Ch 7:8; 8:13; 30:21
8:18 [c]Dt 31:11 [d]Lev 23:36, 40; Nu 29:35
9:1 [e]Jos 7:6; 1Sa 4:12
9:2 [f]Ne 13:3,30 [g]Ezr 10:11; Ps 106:6
9:4 [h]Ezr 10:23
9:5 [i]Ps 78:4
9:6 [j]Dt 6:4 [k]2Ki 19:15 [l]Ge 1:1; Isa 37:16 [m]Ps 95:5 [n]Dt 10:14
9:7 [o]Ge 11:31 [p]Ge 17:5
9:8 [q]Ge 15:18-21 [r]Jos 21:45 [s]Ge 15:6; Ezr 9:15
9:9 [t]Ex 3:7 [u]Ex 14:10-30
9:10 [v]Ex 10:1 [w]Jer 32:20; Da 9:15
9:11 [x]Ex 14:21; Ps 78:13 [y]Ex 15:4-5, 10; Heb 11:29
9:12 [z]Ex 15:13 [a]Ex 13:21

[v]*15* See Lev. 23:37-40. [w]*5* Or *God for ever and ever* [x]*9* Hebrew *Yam Suph*; that is, Sea of Reeds

13"You came down on
Mount Sinai;[a] you spoke[b] to
them from heaven. You gave
them regulations and laws
that are just[c] and right, and
decrees and commands that
are good.[d] **14**You made known
to them your holy Sabbath[e]
and gave them commands, decrees and laws through your
servant Moses. **15**In their hunger you gave them bread from
heaven[f] and in their thirst
you brought them water from
the rock;[g] you told them to go
in and take possession of the
land you had sworn with uplifted hand to give them.[h]
16"But they, our forefathers,
became arrogant and stiff-
necked, and did not obey your
commands.[i] **17**They refused
to listen and failed to remember[j] the miracles you performed among them. They became stiff-necked and in their
rebellion appointed a leader in
order to return to their slavery.[k] But you are a forgiving
God, gracious and compas-
sionate, slow to anger[l] and
abounding in love.[m] Therefore
you did not desert them,[n]
18even when they cast for
themselves an image of a
calf[o] and said, 'This is your
god, who brought you up out
of Egypt,' or when they committed awful blasphemies.
19"Because of your great
compassion you did not abandon them in the desert. By day
the pillar of cloud did not
cease to guide them on their
path, nor the pillar of fire by
night to shine on the way they
were to take. **20**You gave your
good Spirit[p] to instruct them.
You did not withhold your
manna[q] from their mouths,
and you gave them water[r] for
their thirst. **21**For forty years
you sustained them in the
desert; they lacked nothing,[s]
their clothes did not wear out
nor did their feet become
swollen.[t]

22"You gave them kingdoms
and nations, allotting to them
even the remotest frontiers.
They took over the country of
Sihon[y][u] king of Heshbon and
the country of Og king of Bashan.[v] **23**You made their sons
as numerous as the stars in the
sky, and you brought them
into the land that you told
their fathers to enter and possess. **24**Their sons went in and
took possession of the land.[w]
You subdued before them the
Canaanites, who lived in the
land; you handed the Canaanites over to them, along with
their kings and the peoples of
the land, to deal with them as
they pleased. **25**They captured
fortified cities and fertile land;
they took possession of
houses filled with all kinds of
good things, wells already dug,
vineyards, olive groves and
fruit trees in abundance. They
ate to the full and were well-
nourished;[x] they reveled in
your great goodness.[y]
26"But they were disobedient and rebelled against you;
they put your law behind their
backs.[z] They killed your
prophets,[a] who had admonished them in order to turn
them back to you; they committed awful blasphemies.[b]
27So you handed them over to
their enemies,[c] who op-
pressed them. But when they
were oppressed they cried out
to you. From heaven you
heard them, and in your great
compassion[d] you gave them
deliverers, who rescued them
from the hand of their enemies.
28"But as soon as they were
at rest, they again did what
was evil in your sight. Then
you abandoned them to the
hand of their enemies so that
they ruled over them. And

9:13 [a]Ex 19:11 [b]Ex 19:19 [c]Ps 119:137 [d]Ex 20:1

9:14 [e]Ge 2:3; Ex 20:8-11

9:15 [f]Ex 16:4; Jn 6:31 [g]Ex 17:6; Nu 20:7-13 [h]Dt 1:8,21

9:16 [i]Dt 1:26-33; 31:29

9:17 [j]Ps 78:42 [k]Nu 14:1-4 [l]Ex 34:6 [m]Nu 14:17-19 [n]Ps 78:11

9:18 [o]Ex 32:4

9:20 [p]Nu 11:17; Isa 63:11,14 [q]Ex 16:15 [r]Ex 17:6

9:21 [s]Dt 2:7 [t]Dt 8:4

9:22 [u]Nu 21:21 [v]Nu 21:33

9:24 [w]Jos 11:23

9:25 [x]Dt 6:10-12 [y]Nu 13:27; Dt 32:12-15

9:26 [z]1Ki 14:9 [a]Mt 21:35-36 [b]Jdg 2:12-13

9:27 [c]Jdg 2:14 [d]Ps 106:45

[y]*22* One Hebrew manuscript and Septuagint; most Hebrew manuscripts *Sihon, that is, the country of the*

when they cried out to you
again, you heard from heaven,
and in your compassion you
delivered them[a] time after
time.
29"You warned them to re-
turn to your law, but they became arrogant[b] and dis-
obeyed your commands. They
sinned against your ordi-
nances, by which a man will
live if he obeys them.[c] Stubbornly they turned their backs
on you, became stiff-necked
and refused to listen.[d] 30For
many years you were patient
with them. By your Spirit you
admonished them through
your prophets.[e] Yet they paid
no attention, so you handed
them over to the neighboring
peoples. 31But in your great
mercy you did not put an end[f]
to them or abandon them, for
you are a gracious and merciful God.
32"Now therefore, O our
God, the great, mighty[g] and
awesome God, who keeps his
covenant of love,[h] do not let
all this hardship seem trifling
in your eyes—the hardship
that has come upon us, upon
our kings and leaders, upon
our priests and prophets, upon
our fathers and all your people, from the days of the kings
of Assyria until today. 33In all
that has happened to us, you
have been just;[i] you have acted faithfully, while we did
wrong.[j] 34Our kings,[k] our
leaders, our priests and our fathers[l] did not follow your law;
they did not pay attention to
your commands or the warnings you gave them. 35Even
while they were in their kingdom, enjoying your great
goodness[m] to them in the spacious and fertile land you gave
them, they did not serve you[n]
or turn from their evil ways.
36"But see, we are slaves[o]
today, slaves in the land you
gave our forefathers so they
could eat its fruit and the other good things it produces.
37Because of our sins, its
abundant harvest goes to the
kings you have placed over us.
They rule over our bodies and
our cattle as they please. We
are in great distress.[p]

The Agreement of the People

38"In view of all this, we are making a binding agreement,[q] putting
it in writing,[r] and our leaders, our
Levites and our priests are affixing
their seals to it."

10 Those who sealed it were:

Nehemiah the governor,
the son of Hacaliah.

Zedekiah, 2Seraiah,[s] Azariah,
Jeremiah,
3Pashhur,[t] Amariah, Malkijah,
4Hattush, Shebaniah, Malluch,
5Harim,[u] Meremoth, Obadiah,
6Daniel, Ginnethon, Baruch,
7Meshullam, Abijah, Mijamin,
8Maaziah, Bilgai and Shemaiah.
These were the priests.

9The Levites:[v]

Jeshua son of Azaniah, Binnui
of the sons of Henadad,
Kadmiel,
10and their associates: Shebaniah,
Hodiah, Kelita, Pelaiah, Hanan,
11Mica, Rehob, Hashabiah,
12Zaccur, Sherebiah, Shebaniah,
13Hodiah, Bani and Beninu.

14The leaders of the people:

Parosh, Pahath-Moab, Elam,
Zattu, Bani,
15Bunni, Azgad, Bebai,
16Adonijah, Bigvai, Adin,[w]
17Ater, Hezekiah, Azzur,
18Hodiah, Hashum, Bezai,
19Hariph, Anathoth, Nebai,
20Magpiash, Meshullam, Hezir,[x]
21Meshezabel, Zadok, Jaddua,
22Pelatiah, Hanan, Anaiah,
23Hoshea, Hananiah,[y] Hasshub,

9:28 [a]Ps 106:43
9:29 [b]Ps 5:5; Isa 2:11; Jer 43:2 [c]Dt 30:16 [d]Zec 7:11-12
9:30 [e]2Ki 17:13-18; 2Ch 36:16
9:31 [f]Isa 48:9; Jer 4:27
9:32 [g]Ps 24:8 [h]Dt 7:9
9:33 [i]Ge 18:25 [j]Jer 44:3; Da 9:7-8,14
9:34 [k]2Ki 23:11 [l]Jer 44:17
9:35 [m]Isa 63:7 [n]Dt 28:45-48
9:36 [o]Dt 28:48; Ezr 9:9
9:37 [p]Dt 28:33; La 5:5
9:38 [q]2Ch 23:16 [r]Isa 44:5
10:2 [s]Ezr 2:2
10:3 [t]1Ch 9:12
10:5 [u]1Ch 24:8
10:9 [v]Ne 12:1
10:16 [w]Ezr 8:6
10:20 [x]1Ch 24:15
10:23 [y]Ne 7:2

24Hallohesh, Pilha, Shobek,
25Rehum, Hashabnah, Maaseiah,
26Ahiah, Hanan, Anan,
27Malluch, Harim and Baanah.

28"The rest of the people
—priests, Levites, gatekeepers, singers, temple servants[a]
and all who separated themselves from the neighboring
peoples[b] for the sake of the
Law of God, together with
their wives and all their sons
and daughters who are able to
understand— 29all these now
join their brothers the nobles,
and bind themselves with a
curse and an oath[c] to follow
the Law of God given through
Moses the servant of God and
to obey carefully all the commands, regulations and decrees of the LORD our Lord.
30"We promise not to give
our daughters in marriage to
the peoples around us or take
their daughters for our sons.[d]
31"When the neighboring
peoples bring merchandise or
grain to sell on the Sabbath,[e]
we will not buy from them on
the Sabbath or on any holy
day. Every seventh year we will
forgo working the land[f] and
will cancel all debts.[g]
32"We assume the respon-
sibility for carrying out the
commands to give a third of a
shekel[z] each year for the service of the house of our God:
33for the bread set out on the
table;[h] for the regular grain
offerings and burnt offerings;
for the offerings on the Sabbaths, New Moon[i] festivals
and appointed feasts; for the
holy offerings; for sin offerings
to make atonement for Israel;
and for all the duties of the
house of our God.[j]
34"We—the priests, the Levites and the people—have
cast lots[k] to determine when
each of our families is to bring
to the house of our God at set
times each year a contribution
of wood[l] to burn on the altar
of the LORD our God, as it is
written in the Law.
35"We also assume respon-
sibility for bringing to the
house of the LORD each year
the firstfruits[m] of our crops
and of every fruit tree.[n]
36"As it is also written in the
Law, we will bring the firstborn[o] of our sons and of our
cattle, of our herds and of our
flocks to the house of our God,
to the priests ministering
there.[p]
37"Moreover, we will bring
to the storerooms of the house
of our God, to the priests, the
first of our ground meal, of our
⌞grain⌟ offerings, of the fruit of
all our trees and of our new
wine and oil.[q] And we will
bring a tithe[r] of our crops to
the Levites,[s] for it is the Levites who collect the tithes in
all the towns where we work.[t]
38A priest descended from
Aaron is to accompany the Levites when they receive the
tithes, and the Levites are to
bring a tenth of the tithes[u] up
to the house of our God, to the
storerooms of the treasury.
39The people of Israel, including the Levites, are to bring
their contributions of grain,
new wine and oil to the storerooms where the articles for
the sanctuary are kept and
where the ministering priests,
the gatekeepers and the singers stay.
"We will not neglect the
house of our God."[v]

The New Residents of Jerusalem

11:3–19pp — 1Ch 9:1–17

11 Now the leaders of the people settled in Jerusalem,
and the rest of the people cast lots
to bring one out of every ten to live
in Jerusalem,[w] the holy city,[x]
while the remaining nine were to
stay in their own towns.[y] 2The

10:28 [a] Ps 135:1 [b] 2Ch 6:26; Ne 9:2
10:29 [c] Nu 5:21; Ps 119:106
10:30 [d] Ex 34:16; Dt 7:3; Ne 13:23
10:31 [e] Ne 13:16,18; Jer 17:27; Eze 23:38; Am 8:5 [f] Ex 23:11; Lev 25:1-7 [g] Dt 15:1
10:33 [h] Lev 24:6 [i] Nu 10:10; Ps 81:3; Isa 1:14 [j] 2Ch 24:5
10:34 [k] Lev 16:8 [l] Ne 13:31
10:35 [m] Ex 22:29; 23:19; Nu 18:12 [n] Dt 26:1-11
10:36 [o] Ex 13:2; Nu 18:14-16 [p] Ne 13:31
10:37 [q] Lev 23:17; Nu 18:12 [r] Lev 27:30; Nu 18:21 [s] Dt 14:22-29 [t] Eze 44:30
10:38 [u] Nu 18:26
10:39 [v] Dt 12:6; Ne 13:11,12
11:1 [w] Ne 7:4 [x] ver 18; Isa 48:2; 52:1; 64:10; Zec 14:20-21 [y] Ne 7:73

[z] 32 That is, about 1/8 ounce (about 4 grams)

people commended all the men
who volunteered to live in Jerusalem.
3These are the provincial leaders
who settled in Jerusalem (now
some Israelites, priests, Levites,
temple servants and descendants
of Solomon's servants lived in the
towns of Judah, each on his own
property in the various towns,[a]
4while other people from both Judah and Benjamin[b] lived in Jerusalem):[c]

From the descendants of Judah:

Athaiah son of Uzziah, the son
of Zechariah, the son of Amariah, the son of Shephatiah,
the son of Mahalalel, a
descendant of Perez; **5**and Maaseiah son of Baruch, the son
of Col-Hozeh, the son of Haza-
iah, the son of Adaiah, the son
of Joiarib, the son of Zechariah, a descendant of Shelah.
6The descendants of Perez
who lived in Jerusalem totaled
468 able men.

7From the descendants of Benjamin:

Sallu son of Meshullam, the
son of Joed, the son of Pedaiah, the son of Kolaiah, the
son of Maaseiah, the son of
Ithiel, the son of Jeshaiah,
8and his followers, Gabbai and
Sallai—928 men. **9**Joel son of
Zicri was their chief officer,
and Judah son of Hassenuah
was over the Second District of
the city.

10From the priests:

Jedaiah; the son of Joiarib; Jakin; **11**Seraiah[d] son of Hilkiah, the son of Meshullam, the
son of Zadok, the son of Meraioth, the son of Ahitub,[e] su-
pervisor in the house of God,
12and their associates, who
carried on work for the temple—822 men; Adaiah son of
Jeroham, the son of Pelaliah,
the son of Amzi, the son of
Zechariah, the son of Pashhur,
the son of Malkijah, **13**and his
associates, who were heads of
families—242 men; Amashsai
son of Azarel, the son of Ahzai,
the son of Meshillemoth, the
son of Immer, **14**and his[a] associates, who were able
men—128. Their chief officer
was Zabdiel son of Haggedo-
lim.

15From the Levites:

Shemaiah son of Hasshub, the
son of Azrikam, the son of
Hashabiah, the son of Bunni;
16Shabbethai[f] and Jozabad,[g]
two of the heads of the Levites, who had charge of the
outside work of the house of
God; **17**Mattaniah[h] son of
Mica, the son of Zabdi, the son
of Asaph,[i] the director who
led in thanksgiving and prayer;
Bakbukiah, second among his
associates; and Abda son of
Shammua, the son of Galal,
the son of Jeduthun.[j] **18**The
Levites in the holy city[k] totaled 284.

19The gatekeepers:

Akkub, Talmon and their associates, who kept watch at
the gates—172 men.

20The rest of the Israelites, with
the priests and Levites, were in all
the towns of Judah, each on his ancestral property.
21The temple servants[l] lived on
the hill of Ophel, and Ziha and
Gishpa were in charge of them.
22The chief officer of the Levites
in Jerusalem was Uzzi son of Bani,
the son of Hashabiah, the son of
Mattaniah,[m] the son of Mica. Uzzi
was one of Asaph's descendants,
who were the singers responsible
for the service of the house of God.
23The singers[n] were under the
king's orders, which regulated their
daily activity.
24Pethahiah son of Meshezabel,
one of the descendants of Zerah[o]
son of Judah, was the king's agent
in all affairs relating to the people.

11:3 [a] 1Ch 9:2-3; Ezr 2:1
11:4 [b] Ezr 1:5 [c] Ezr 2:70
11:11 [d] 2Ki 25:18; Ezr 2:2 [e] Ezr 7:2
11:16 [f] Ezr 10:15 [g] Ezr 8:33
11:17 [h] 1Ch 9:15; Ne 12:8 [i] 2Ch 5:12 [j] 1Ch 25:1
11:18 [k] Rev 21:2
11:21 [l] Ezr 2:43; Ne 3:26
11:22 [m] 1Ch 9:15
11:23 [n] Ne 7:44
11:24 [o] Ge 38:30

[a] *14* Most Septuagint manuscripts; Hebrew *their*

25As for the villages with their
fields, some of the people of Judah
lived in Kiriath Arba[a] and its surrounding settlements, in Dibon[b]
and its settlements, in Jekabzeel
and its villages, **26**in Jeshua, in
Moladah, in Beth Pelet,[c] **27**in Hazar Shual, in Beersheba[d] and its
settlements, **28**in Ziklag,[e] in Me-
conah and its settlements, **29**in En
Rimmon, in Zorah,[f] in Jarmuth,[g]
30Zanoah, Adullam[h] and their villages, in Lachish[i] and its fields,
and in Azekah[j] and its settlements. So they were living all the
way from Beersheba[k] to the Valley
of Hinnom.
31The descendants of the Benjamites from Geba[l] lived in Micmash,[m] Aija, Bethel and its settlements, **32**in Anathoth,[n] Nob[o] and
Ananiah, **33**in Hazor,[p] Ramah and
Gittaim,[q] **34**in Hadid, Zeboim[r]
and Neballat, **35**in Lod and Ono,[s]
and in the Valley of the Craftsmen.
36Some of the divisions of the
Levites of Judah settled in Benjamin.

Priests and Levites

12 These were the priests[t]
and Levites who returned
with Zerubbabel[u] son of Shealtiel
and with Jeshua:[v]
Seraiah,[w] Jeremiah, Ezra,
2Amariah, Malluch, Hattush,
3Shecaniah, Rehum, Meremoth,
4Iddo,[x] Ginnethon,[b] Abijah,[y]
5Mijamin,[c] Moadiah, Bilgah,
6Shemaiah, Joiarib, Jedaiah,[z]
7Sallu, Amok, Hilkiah and Jedaiah.
These were the leaders of the
priests and their associates in the
days of Jeshua.
8The Levites were Jeshua, Binnui, Kadmiel, Sherebiah, Judah,
and also Mattaniah,[a] who, together with his associates, was in
charge of the songs of thanksgiving. **9**Bakbukiah and Unni, their associates, stood opposite them in
the services.
10Jeshua was the father of Joiakim, Joiakim the father of Eliashib,[b] Eliashib the father of Joiada, **11**Joiada the father of Jonathan, and Jonathan the father of
Jaddua.
12In the days of Joiakim, these
were the heads of the priestly families:
of Seraiah's family, Meraiah;
of Jeremiah's, Hananiah;
13of Ezra's, Meshullam;
of Amariah's, Jehohanan;
14of Malluch's, Jonathan;
of Shecaniah's,[d] Joseph;
15of Harim's, Adna;
of Meremoth's,[e] Helkai;
16of Iddo's,[c] Zechariah;
of Ginnethon's, Meshullam;
17of Abijah's, Zicri;
of Miniamin's and of Moadiah's, Piltai;
18of Bilgah's, Shammua;
of Shemaiah's, Jehonathan;
19of Joiarib's, Mattenai;
of Jedaiah's, Uzzi;
20of Sallu's, Kallai;
of Amok's, Eber;
21of Hilkiah's, Hashabiah;
of Jedaiah's, Nethanel.
22The family heads of the Levites in the days of Eliashib, Joiada, Johanan and Jaddua, as well as
those of the priests, were recorded
in the reign of Darius the Persian.
23The family heads among the
descendants of Levi up to the time
of Johanan son of Eliashib were recorded in the book of the annals.
24And the leaders of the Levites[d]
were Hashabiah, Sherebiah, Jeshua son of Kadmiel, and their associates, who stood opposite them to
give praise and thanksgiving, one
section responding to the other, as
prescribed by David the man of
God.
25Mattaniah, Bakbukiah, Obadiah, Meshullam, Talmon and Akkub
were gatekeepers who guarded the
storerooms at the gates. **26**They
served in the days of Joiakim son of

11:25 [a]Ge 35:27; Jos 14:15 [b]Nu 21:30
11:26 [c]Jos 15:27
11:27 [d]Ge 21:14
11:28 [e]1Sa 27:6
11:29 [f]Jos 15:33 [g]Jos 10:3
11:30 [h]Jos 15:35 [i]Jos 10:3 [j]Jos 10:10 [k]Jos 15:28
11:31 [l]Jos 21:17; Isa 10:29 [m]1Sa 13:2
11:32 [n]Jos 21:18; Isa 10:30 [o]1Sa 21:1
11:33 [p]Jos 11:1 [q]2Sa 4:3
11:34 [r]1Sa 13:18
11:35 [s]1Ch 8:12
12:1 [t]Ne 10:1-8 [u]1Ch 3:19 [v]Ezr 2:2 [w]Ezr 2:2
12:4 [x]Zec 1:1 [y]Lk 1:5
12:6 [z]1Ch 24:7
12:8 [a]Ne 11:17
12:10 [b]Ezr 10:24
12:16 [c]ver 4
12:24 [d]Ezr 2:40

[b]*4* Many Hebrew manuscripts and Vulgate (see also Neh. 12:16); most Hebrew manuscripts *Ginnethoi* [c]*5* A variant of *Miniamin* [d]*14* Very many Hebrew manuscripts, some Septuagint manuscripts and Syriac (see also Neh. 12:3); most Hebrew manuscripts *Shebaniah's* [e]*15* Some Septuagint manuscripts (see also Neh. 12:3); Hebrew *Meraioth's*

Jeshua, the son of Jozadak, and in the days of Nehemiah the governor and of Ezra the priest and scribe.

Dedication of the Wall of Jerusalem

27At the dedication[a] of the wall of Jerusalem, the Levites were sought out from where they lived and were brought to Jerusalem to celebrate joyfully the dedication with songs of thanksgiving and with the music of cymbals,[b] harps and lyres.[c] **28**The singers also were brought together from the region around Jerusalem—from the villages of the Netophathites,[d] **29**from Beth Gilgal, and from the area of Geba and Azmaveth, for the singers had built villages for themselves around Jerusalem. **30**When the priests and Levites had purified themselves ceremonially, they purified the people,[e] the gates and the wall.

31I had the leaders of Judah go up on top[f] of the wall. I also assigned two large choirs to give thanks. One was to proceed on top[g] of the wall to the right, toward the Dung Gate.[f] **32**Hoshaiah and half the leaders of Judah followed them, **33**along with Azariah, Ezra, Meshullam, **34**Judah, Benjamin,[g] Shemaiah, Jeremiah, **35**as well as some priests with trumpets,[h] and also Zechariah son of Jonathan, the son of Shemaiah, the son of Mattaniah, the son of Micaiah, the son of Zaccur, the son of Asaph, **36**and his associates—Shemaiah, Azarel, Milalai, Gilalai, Maai, Nethanel, Judah and Hanani—with musical instruments[i] ⌊prescribed by⌋ David the man of God.[j] Ezra[k] the scribe led the procession. **37**At the Fountain Gate[l] they continued directly up the steps of the City of David on the ascent to the wall and passed above the house of David to the Water Gate[m] on the east.

38The second choir proceeded in the opposite direction. I followed them on top[h] of the wall, together with half the people—past the Tower of the Ovens[n] to the Broad Wall,[o] **39**over the Gate of Ephraim,[p] the Jeshanah[i] Gate,[q] the Fish Gate,[r] the Tower of Hananel[s] and the Tower of the Hundred,[t] as far as the Sheep Gate.[u] At the Gate of the Guard they stopped.

40The two choirs that gave thanks then took their places in the house of God; so did I, together with half the officials, **41**as well as the priests—Eliakim, Maaseiah, Miniamin, Micaiah, Elioenai, Zechariah and Hananiah with their trumpets— **42**and also Maaseiah, Shemaiah, Eleazar, Uzzi, Jehohanan, Malkijah, Elam and Ezer. The choirs sang under the direction of Jezrahiah. **43**And on that day they offered great sacrifices, rejoicing because God had given them great joy. The women and children also rejoiced. The sound of rejoicing in Jerusalem could be heard far away.

44At that time men were appointed to be in charge of the storerooms[v] for the contributions, firstfruits and tithes.[w] From the fields around the towns they were to bring into the storerooms the portions required by the Law for the priests and the Levites, for Judah was pleased with the ministering priests and Levites.[x] **45**They performed the service of their God and the service of purification, as did also the singers and gatekeepers, according to the commands of David[y] and his son Solomon.[z] **46**For long ago, in the days of David and Asaph,[a] there had been directors for the singers and for the songs of praise[b] and thanksgiving to God. **47**So in the days of Zerubbabel and of Nehemiah, all Israel contributed the daily portions for the singers and gatekeepers. They also set aside the portion for the other Levites, and the Levites set aside the portion for the descendants of Aaron.[c]

12:27 [a] Dt 20:5 [b] 2Sa 6:5 [c] 1Ch 15:16, 28; 25:6; Ps 92:3
12:28 [d] 1Ch 2:54; 9:16
12:30 [e] Ex 19:10; Job 1:5
12:31 [f] Ne 2:13
12:34 [g] Ezr 1:5
12:35 [h] Ezr 3:10
12:36 [i] 1Ch 15:16 [j] 2Ch 8:14 [k] Ezr 7:6
12:37 [l] Ne 2:14; 3:15 [m] Ne 3:26
12:38 [n] Ne 3:11 [o] Ne 3:8
12:39 [p] 2Ki 14:13; Ne 8:16 [q] Ne 3:6 [r] 2Ch 33:14; Ne 3:3 [s] Ne 3:1 [t] Ne 3:1 [u] Ne 3:1
12:44 [v] Ne 13:4,13 [w] Lev 27:30 [x] Dt 18:8
12:45 [y] 1Ch 25:1; 2Ch 8:14 [z] 1Ch 6:31; 23:5
12:46 [a] 2Ch 35:15 [b] 2Ch 29:27; Ps 137:4
12:47 [c] Nu 18:21; Dt 18:8

[f]31 Or *go alongside* [g]31 Or *proceed alongside* [h]38 Or *them alongside* [i]39 Or *Old*

Nehemiah's Final Reforms

13 On that day the Book of
Moses was read aloud in
the hearing of the people and there
it was found written that no Ammonite or Moabite should ever be
admitted into the assembly of
God,[a] **2**because they had not met
the Israelites with food and water
but had hired Balaam[b] to call a
curse down on them.[c] (Our God,
however, turned the curse into a
blessing.)[d] **3**When the people
heard this law, they excluded from
Israel all who were of foreign descent.[e]

4Before this, Eliashib the priest
had been put in charge of the storerooms[f] of the house of our God.
He was closely associated with Tobiah,[g] **5**and he had provided him
with a large room formerly used
to store the grain offerings and
incense and temple articles, and
also the tithes[h] of grain, new
wine and oil prescribed for the Levites, singers and gatekeepers, as
well as the contributions for the
priests.

6But while all this was going on,
I was not in Jerusalem, for in the
thirty-second year of Artaxerxes[i]
king of Babylon I had returned to
the king. Some time later I asked
his permission **7**and came back to
Jerusalem. Here I learned about
the evil thing Eliashib[j] had done
in providing Tobiah a room in the
courts of the house of God. **8**I was
greatly displeased and threw all
Tobiah's household goods out of
the room.[k] **9**I gave orders to purify
the rooms,[l] and then I put back
into them the equipment of the
house of God, with the grain offerings and the incense.

10I also learned that the portions
assigned to the Levites had not
been given to them,[m] and that all
the Levites and singers responsible
for the service had gone back to
their own fields. **11**So I rebuked the
officials and asked them, "Why is
the house of God neglected?"[n]
Then I called them together and
stationed them at their posts.

12All Judah brought the tithes[o]
of grain, new wine and oil into the
storerooms.[p] **13**I put Shelemiah
the priest, Zadok the scribe, and a
Levite named Pedaiah in charge of
the storerooms and made Hanan
son of Zaccur, the son of Mattaniah, their assistant, because these
men were considered trustworthy.
They were made responsible for
distributing the supplies to their
brothers.[q]

14Remember[r] me for this, O my
God, and do not blot out what I
have so faithfully done for the
house of my God and its services.

15In those days I saw men in Judah treading winepresses on the
Sabbath and bringing in grain and
loading it on donkeys, together
with wine, grapes, figs and all other
kinds of loads. And they were
bringing all this into Jerusalem on
the Sabbath.[s] Therefore I warned
them against selling food on that
day. **16**Men from Tyre who lived in
Jerusalem were bringing in fish
and all kinds of merchandise and
selling them in Jerusalem on the
Sabbath[t] to the people of Judah.
17I rebuked the nobles of Judah
and said to them, "What is this
wicked thing you are doing—desecrating the Sabbath day? **18**Didn't
your forefathers do the same
things, so that our God brought all
this calamity upon us and upon
this city? Now you are stirring up
more wrath against Israel by desecrating the Sabbath."[u]
19When evening shadows fell on
the gates of Jerusalem before the
Sabbath,[v] I ordered the doors to
be shut and not opened until the
Sabbath was over. I stationed some
of my own men at the gates so that
no load could be brought in on the
Sabbath day. **20**Once or twice the
merchants and sellers of all kinds
of goods spent the night outside Jerusalem. **21**But I warned them and
said, "Why do you spend the night
by the wall? If you do this again, I
will lay hands on you." From that
time on they no longer came on the
Sabbath. **22**Then I commanded the

13:1 [a]ver 23; Dt 23:3
13:2 [b]Nu 22:3-11 [c]Nu 23:7; Dt 23:3 [d]Nu 23:11; Dt 23:4-5
13:3 [e]ver 23; Ne 9:2
13:4 [f]Ne 12:44 [g]Ne 2:10
13:5 [h]Lev 27:30; Nu 18:21
13:6 [i]Ne 2:6; 5:14
13:7 [j]Ezr 10:24
13:8 [k]Mt 21:12-13; Jn 2:13-16
13:9 [l]1Ch 23:28; 2Ch 29:5
13:10 [m]Dt 12:19
13:11 [n]Ne 10:37-39; Hag 1:1-9
13:12 [o]2Ch 31:6 [p]1Ki 7:51; Ne 10:37-39; Mal 3:10
13:13 [q]Ne 12:44; Ac 6:1-5
13:14 [r]Ge 8:1
13:15 [s]Ex 20:8-11; 34:21; Dt 5:12-15; Ne 10:31
13:16 [t]Ne 10:31
13:18 [u]Ne 10:31; Jer 17:21-23
13:19 [v]Lev 23:32

Levites to purify themselves and go
and guard the gates in order to
keep the Sabbath day holy.

Remember[a] me for this also, O
my God, and show mercy to me according to your great love.

23Moreover, in those days I saw
men of Judah who had married[b]
women from Ashdod, Ammon and
Moab.[c] **24**Half of their children
spoke the language of Ashdod or
the language of one of the other
peoples, and did not know how to
speak the language of Judah. **25**I
rebuked them and called curses
down on them. I beat some of the
men and pulled out their hair. I
made them take an oath[d] in God's
name and said: "You are not to give
your daughters in marriage to their
sons, nor are you to take their
daughters in marriage for your sons
or for yourselves. **26**Was it not because of marriages like these that
Solomon king of Israel sinned?
Among the many nations there was
no king like him.[e] He was loved by

13:22 [a]Ge 8:1; Ne 12:30
13:23 [b]Ezr 9:1-2; Mal 2:11 [c]ver 1; Ne 10:30
13:25 [d]Ezr 10:5
13:26 [e]1Ki 3:13; 2Ch 1:12 [f]2Sa 12:25 [g]1Ki 11:3
13:27 [h]Ezr 9:14; 10:2
13:28 [i]Ezr 10:24 [j]Ne 2:10
13:29 [k]Ne 6:14
13:30 [l]Ne 10:30
13:31 [m]Ne 10:34 [n]ver 14,22; Ge 8:1

his God,[f] and God made him king
over all Israel, but even he was led
into sin by foreign women.[g]
27Must we hear now that you too
are doing all this terrible wickedness and are being unfaithful to
our God by marrying[h] foreign
women?"

28One of the sons of Joiada son
of Eliashib[i] the high priest was
son-in-law to Sanballat[j] the Horonite. And I drove him away from
me.

29Remember[k] them, O my God,
because they defiled the priestly
office and the covenant of the
priesthood and of the Levites.

30So I purified the priests and
the Levites of everything foreign,[l]
and assigned them duties, each to
his own task. **31**I also made provision for contributions of wood[m] at
designated times, and for the firstfruits.

Remember[n] me with favor, O
my God.

Esther

Title and Background

This book has the name of its leading character, a beautiful Jewish girl whom King Xerxes of Persia chose to be his queen. The setting is in Susa, the Persian capital during Xerxes' rule (486-465 B.C.).

Author and Date of Writing

We do not know who wrote the book, but it is clear that the author was a Jew, both from the purpose of the book in accounting for the origin of a Jewish festival and from the Jewish nationalism that permeates the story. Many things point to the fact that he was a resident of a Persian city. The earliest date for the book would be shortly after the events narrated, that is, around 460 B.C.; the latest date would be before the Persian empire fell to Greece in 331.

Theme and Message

The central purpose of the author was to record the institution of the annual festival of Purim and to keep alive for later generations the memory of the great deliverance of the Jewish people during the reign of Xerxes. Although the name of God does not appear in the book, his care for his chosen people is clearly shown. Feasting is a prominent theme in Esther (see Outline).

Outline

I. The Feast of Xerxes (1:1-2:18)
II. The Feasts of Esther (2:19-7:10)
III. The Feasts of Purim (8:1-10:3)

Queen Vashti Deposed

1 This is what happened during
the time of Xerxes,[a][a] the Xerxes who ruled over 127 provinces[b]
stretching from India to Cush[b]:[c]
2At that time King Xerxes reigned
from his royal throne in the citadel
of Susa,[d] 3and in the third year of
his reign he gave a banquet[e] for all
his nobles and officials. The military leaders of Persia and Media,
the princes, and the nobles of the
provinces were present.
4For a full 180 days he displayed
the vast wealth of his kingdom and
the splendor and glory of his majesty. 5When these days were over, the
king gave a banquet, lasting seven
days,[f] in the enclosed garden[g] of
the king's palace, for all the people
from the least to the greatest, who
were in the citadel of Susa. 6The
garden had hangings of white and
blue linen, fastened with cords of
white linen and purple material to
silver rings on marble pillars. There
were couches[h] of gold and silver
on a mosaic pavement of porphyry,
marble, mother-of-pearl and other
costly stones. 7Wine was served in
goblets of gold, each one different
from the other, and the royal wine
was abundant, in keeping with the
king's liberality.[i] 8By the king's
command each guest was allowed
to drink in his own way, for the king
instructed all the wine stewards to
serve each man what he wished.
9Queen Vashti also gave a ban
quet[j] for the women in the royal
palace of King Xerxes.

1:1 [a] Ezr 4:6; Da 9:1 [b] Est 9:30; Da 3:2; 6:1 [c] Est 8:9
1:2 [d] Ezr 4:9; Ne 1:1; Est 2:8
1:3 [e] 1Ki 3:15; Est 2:18
1:5 [f] Jdg 14:17 [g] 2Ki 21:18; Est 7:7-8
1:6 [h] Est 7:8; Eze 23:41; Am 3:12; 6:4
1:7 [i] Est 2:18; Da 5:2
1:9 [j] 1Ki 3:15

[a]*1* Hebrew *Ahasuerus,* a variant of Xerxes' Persian name; here and throughout Esther
[b]*1* That is, the upper Nile region

10On the seventh day, when King Xerxes was in high spirits[a] from wine,[b] he commanded the seven eunuchs who served him—Mehuman, Biztha, Harbona,[c] Bigtha, Abagtha, Zethar and Carcas— **11**to bring[d] before him Queen Vashti, wearing her royal crown, in order to display her beauty[e] to the people and nobles, for she was lovely to look at. **12**But when the attendants delivered the king's command, Queen Vashti refused to come. Then the king became furious and burned with anger.[f]

13Since it was customary for the king to consult experts in matters of law and justice, he spoke with the wise men who understood the times[g] **14**and were closest to the king—Carshena, Shethar, Admatha, Tarshish, Meres, Marsena and Memucan, the seven nobles[h] of Persia and Media who had special access to the king and were highest in the kingdom.

15"According to law, what must be done to Queen Vashti?" he asked. "She has not obeyed the command of King Xerxes that the eunuchs have taken to her."

16Then Memucan replied in the presence of the king and the nobles, "Queen Vashti has done wrong, not only against the king but also against all the nobles and the peoples of all the provinces of King Xerxes. **17**For the queen's conduct will become known to all the women, and so they will despise their husbands and say, 'King Xerxes commanded Queen Vashti to be brought before him, but she would not come.' **18**This very day the Persian and Median women of the nobility who have heard about the queen's conduct will respond to all the king's nobles in the same way. There will be no end of disrespect and discord.[i]

19"Therefore, if it pleases the king,[j] let him issue a royal decree and let it be written in the laws of Persia and Media, which cannot be repealed,[k] that Vashti is never again to enter the presence of King Xerxes. Also let the king give her royal position to someone else who is better than she. **20**Then when the king's edict is proclaimed throughout all his vast realm, all the women will respect their husbands, from the least to the greatest."

21The king and his nobles were pleased with this advice, so the king did as Memucan proposed. **22**He sent dispatches to all parts of the kingdom, to each province in its own script and to each people in its own language,[l] proclaiming in each people's tongue that every man should be ruler over his own household.

Esther Made Queen

2 Later when the anger of King Xerxes had subsided,[m] he remembered Vashti and what she had done and what he had decreed about her. **2**Then the king's personal attendants proposed, "Let a search be made for beautiful young virgins for the king. **3**Let the king appoint commissioners in every province of his realm to bring all these beautiful girls into the harem at the citadel of Susa. Let them be placed under the care of Hegai, the king's eunuch, who is in charge of the women; and let beauty treatments be given to them. **4**Then let the girl who pleases the king be queen instead of Vashti." This advice appealed to the king, and he followed it.

5Now there was in the citadel of Susa a Jew of the tribe of Benjamin, named Mordecai son of Jair, the son of Shimei, the son of Kish,[n] **6**who had been carried into exile from Jerusalem by Nebuchadnezzar king of Babylon, among those taken captive with Jehoiachin[c][o] king of Judah.[p] **7**Mordecai had a cousin named Hadassah, whom he had brought up because she had neither father nor mother. This girl, who was also known as Esther,[q] was lovely[r] in form and features, and Mordecai had taken her as his own daughter when her father and mother died.

1:10 [a] Jdg 16:25; Ru 3:7 [b] Ge 14:18; Est 3:15; 5:6; 7:2; Pr 31:4-7; Da 5:1-4 [c] Est 7:9
1:11 [d] SS 2:4 [e] Ps 45:11; Eze 16:14
1:12 [f] Ge 39:19; Est 2:21; 7:7; Pr 19:12
1:13 [g] 1Ch 12:32; Jer 10:7; Da 2:12
1:14 [h] 2Ki 25:19; Ezr 7:14
1:18 [i] Pr 19:13; 27:15
1:19 [j] Ecc 8:4 [k] Est 8:8; Da 6:8,12
1:22 [l] Ne 13:24; Est 8:9; Eph 5:22-24; 1Ti 2:12
2:1 [m] Est 1:19-20; 7:10
2:5 [n] 1Sa 9:1; Est 3:2
2:6 [o] 2Ki 24:6,15; 2Ch 36:10,20 [p] Da 1:1-5; 5:13
2:7 [q] Ge 41:45 [r] Ge 39:6

c6 Hebrew *Jeconiah,* a variant of *Jehoiachin*

8When the king's order and edict had been proclaimed, many girls were brought to the citadel of Susa[a] and put under the care of Hegai. Esther also was taken to the king's palace and entrusted to Hegai, who had charge of the harem. **9**The girl pleased him and won his favor.[b] Immediately he provided her with her beauty treatments and special food.[c] He assigned to her seven maids selected from the king's palace and moved her and her maids into the best place in the harem.

10Esther had not revealed her nationality and family background, because Mordecai had forbidden her to do so.[d] **11**Every day he walked back and forth near the courtyard of the harem to find out how Esther was and what was happening to her.

12Before a girl's turn came to go in to King Xerxes, she had to complete twelve months of beauty treatments prescribed for the women, six months with oil of myrrh and six with perfumes[e] and cosmetics. **13**And this is how she would go to the king: Anything she wanted was given her to take with her from the harem to the king's palace. **14**In the evening she would go there and in the morning return to another part of the harem to the care of Shaashgaz, the king's eunuch who was in charge of the concubines.[f] She would not return to the king unless he was pleased with her and summoned her by name.[g]

15When the turn came for Esther (the girl Mordecai had adopted, the daughter of his uncle Abihail[h]) to go to the king,[i] she asked for nothing other than what Hegai, the king's eunuch who was in charge of the harem, suggested. And Esther won the favor[j] of everyone who saw her. **16**She was taken to King Xerxes in the royal residence in the tenth month, the month of Tebeth, in the seventh year of his reign.

17Now the king was attracted to Esther more than to any of the other women, and she won his favor and approval more than any of the other virgins. So he set a royal crown on her head and made her queen[k] instead of Vashti. **18**And the king gave a great banquet,[l] Esther's banquet, for all his nobles and officials.[m] He proclaimed a holiday throughout the provinces and distributed gifts with royal liberality.[n]

Mordecai Uncovers a Conspiracy

19When the virgins were assembled a second time, Mordecai was sitting at the king's gate.[o] **20**But Esther had kept secret her family background and nationality just as Mordecai had told her to do, for she continued to follow Mordecai's instructions as she had done when he was bringing her up.[p]

21During the time Mordecai was sitting at the king's gate, Bigthana[d] and Teresh, two of the king's officers[q] who guarded the doorway, became angry[r] and conspired to assassinate King Xerxes. **22**But Mordecai found out about the plot and told Queen Esther, who in turn reported it to the king, giving credit to Mordecai. **23**And when the report was investigated and found to be true, the two officials were hanged[s] on a gallows.[e] All this was recorded in the book of the annals[t] in the presence of the king.

Haman's Plot to Destroy the Jews

3 After these events, King Xerxes honored Haman son of Hammedatha, the Agagite,[u] elevating him and giving him a seat of honor higher than that of all the other nobles. **2**All the royal officials at the king's gate knelt down and paid honor to Haman, for the king had commanded this concerning him. But Mordecai would not kneel down or pay him honor.

3Then the royal officials at the king's gate asked Mordecai, "Why

2:8 [a]ver 3,15; Ne 1:1; Est 1:2; Da 8:2
2:9 [b]Ge 39:21 [c]ver 3,12; Ge 37:3; 1Sa 9:22-24; 2Ki 25:30; Eze 16:9-13; Da 1:5
2:10 [d]ver 20
2:12 [e]Pr 27:9; SS 1:3; Isa 3:24
2:14 [f]1Ki 11:3; SS 6:8; Da 5:2 [g]Est 4:11
2:15 [h]Est 9:29 [i]Ps 45:14 [j]Ge 18:3; 30:27; Est 5:8
2:17 [k]Est 1:11; Eze 16:9-13
2:18 [l]1Ki 3:15; Est 1:3 [m]Ge 40:20 [n]Est 1:7
2:19 [o]ver 21; Est 3:2; 4:2; 5:13
2:20 [p]ver 10
2:21 [q]Ge 40:2; Est 6:2 [r]Est 1:12; 3:5; 5:9; 7:7
2:23 [s]Ge 40:19; Ps 7:14-16; Pr 26:27 [t]Est 6:1; 10:2
3:1 [u]ver 10; Ex 17:8-16; Nu 24:7; Dt 25:17-19; 1Sa 14:48; Est 5:11

[d]*21* Hebrew *Bigthan,* a variant of *Bigthana*
[e]*23* Or *were hung* (or *impaled*) *on poles;* similarly elsewhere in Esther

do you disobey the king's command?"[a] **4**Day after day they spoke to him but he refused to comply.[b] Therefore they told Haman about it to see whether Mordecai's behavior would be tolerated, for he had told them he was a Jew.

5When Haman saw that Mordecai would not kneel down or pay him honor, he was enraged.[c] **6**Yet having learned who Mordecai's people were, he scorned the idea of killing only Mordecai. Instead Haman looked for a way[d] to destroy[e] all Mordecai's people, the Jews,[f] throughout the whole kingdom of Xerxes.

7In the twelfth year of King Xerxes, in the first month, the month of Nisan, they cast the *pur*[g] (that is, the lot[h]) in the presence of Haman to select a day and month. And the lot fell on[f] the twelfth month, the month of Adar.[i]

8Then Haman said to King Xerxes, "There is a certain people dispersed and scattered among the peoples in all the provinces of your kingdom whose customs[j] are different from those of all other people and who do not obey[k] the king's laws; it is not in the king's best interest to tolerate them.[l] **9**If it pleases the king, let a decree be issued to destroy them, and I will put ten thousand talents[g] of silver into the royal treasury for the men who carry out this business."[m]

10So the king took his signet ring[n] from his finger and gave it to Haman son of Hammedatha, the Agagite, the enemy of the Jews. **11**"Keep the money," the king said to Haman, "and do with the people as you please."

12Then on the thirteenth day of the first month the royal secretaries were summoned. They wrote out in the script of each province and in the language[o] of each people all Haman's orders to the king's satraps, the governors of the various provinces and the nobles of the various peoples. These were written in the name of King Xerxes himself and sealed[p] with his own ring. **13**Dispatches were sent by couriers to all the king's provinces with the order to destroy, kill and annihilate all the Jews[q]—young and old, women and little children—on a single day, the thirteenth day of the twelfth month, the month of Adar,[r] and to plunder[s] their goods. **14**A copy of the text of the edict was to be issued as law in every province and made known to the people of every nationality so they would be ready for that day.[t]

15Spurred on by the king's command, the couriers went out, and the edict was issued in the citadel of Susa.[u] The king and Haman sat down to drink,[v] but the city of Susa was bewildered.[w]

Mordecai Persuades Esther to Help

4 When Mordecai learned of all that had been done, he tore his clothes,[x] put on sackcloth and ashes,[y] and went out into the city, wailing[z] loudly and bitterly. **2**But he went only as far as the king's gate,[a] because no one clothed in sackcloth was allowed to enter it. **3**In every province to which the edict and order of the king came, there was great mourning among the Jews, with fasting, weeping and wailing. Many lay in sackcloth and ashes.

4When Esther's maids and eunuchs came and told her about Mordecai, she was in great distress. She sent clothes for him to put on instead of his sackcloth, but he would not accept them. **5**Then Esther summoned Hathach, one of the king's eunuchs assigned to attend her, and ordered him to find out what was troubling Mordecai and why.

6So Hathach went out to Mordecai in the open square of the city in front of the king's gate. **7**Mordecai told him everything that had happened to him, including the exact amount of money Haman had

3:3 [a]Est 5:9; Da 3:12
3:4 [b]Ge 39:10
3:5 [c]Est 2:21; 5:9
3:6 [d]Pr 16:25 [e]Ps 74:8; 83:4 [f]Est 9:24
3:7 [g]Est 9:24,26 [h]Lev 16:8; 1Sa 10:21 [i]ver 13; Ezr 6:15; Est 9:19
3:8 [j]Ac 16:20-21 [k]Jer 29:7; Da 6:13 [l]Ezr 4:15
3:9 [m]Est 7:4
3:10 [n]Ge 41:42; Est 7:6; 8:2
3:12 [o]Ne 13:24 [p]Ge 38:18; 1Ki 21:8; Est 8:8-10
3:13 [q]1Sa 15:3; Ezr 4:6; Est 8:10-14 [r]ver 7 [s]Est 8:11; 9:10
3:14 [t]Est 8:8; 9:1
3:15 [u]Est 8:14 [v]Est 1:10 [w]Est 8:15
4:1 [x]Nu 14:6 [y]2Sa 13:19; Eze 27:30-31; Jnh 3:5-6 [z]Ex 11:6; Ps 30:11
4:2 [a]Est 2:19

[f]7 Septuagint; Hebrew does not have *And the lot fell on.* [g]9 That is, about 375 tons (about 345 metric tons)

promised to pay into the royal treasury for the destruction of the
Jews.[a] 8He also gave him a copy of
the text of the edict for their annihilation, which had been published in Susa, to show to Esther
and explain it to her, and he told
him to urge her to go into the king's
presence to beg for mercy and
plead with him for her people.
9Hathach went back and reported to Esther what Mordecai had
said. 10Then she instructed him to
say to Mordecai, 11"All the king's
officials and the people of the royal
provinces know that for any man or
woman who approaches the king in
the inner court without being summoned[b] the king has but one
law:[c] that he be put to death. The
only exception to this is for the
king to extend the gold scepter[d] to
him and spare his life. But thirty
days have passed since I was called
to go to the king."
12When Esther's words were reported to Mordecai, 13he sent back
this answer: "Do not think that because you are in the king's house
you alone of all the Jews will escape. 14For if you remain silent[e] at
this time, relief[f] and deliverance[g]
for the Jews will arise from another
place, but you and your father's
family will perish. And who knows
but that you have come to royal position for such a time as this?"[h]
15Then Esther sent this reply to
Mordecai: 16"Go, gather together
all the Jews who are in Susa, and
fast[i] for me. Do not eat or drink for
three days, night or day. I and my
maids will fast as you do. When this
is done, I will go to the king, even
though it is against the law. And if
I perish, I perish."[j]
17So Mordecai went away and
carried out all of Esther's instructions.

Esther's Request to the King

5 On the third day Esther put on
her royal robes[k] and stood in
the inner court of the palace, in
front of the king's[l] hall. The king
was sitting on his royal throne in
the hall, facing the entrance.

4:7 [a]Est 3:9; 7:4
4:11 [b]Est 2:14 [c]Da 2:9 [d]Est 5:1,2; 8:4
4:14 [e]Ecc 3:7; Isa 62:1; Am 5:13 [f]Est 9:16,22 [g]Ge 45:7; Dt 28:29 [h]Ge 50:20
4:16 [i]2Ch 20:3; Est 9:31 [j]Ge 43:14
5:1 [k]Est 4:16; Eze 16:13 [l]Est 6:4; Pr 21:1
5:2 [m]Est 4:11; 8:4; Pr 21:1
5:3 [n]Est 7:2; Da 5:16; Mk 6:23
5:6 [o]Est 1:10 [p]Mk 6:23 [q]Est 7:2; 9:12
5:8 [r]Est 2:15; 7:3; 8:5 [s]1Ki 3:15; Est 6:14
5:9 [t]Est 2:21; Pr 14:17 [u]Est 3:3,5
5:10 [v]Est 6:13
5:11 [w]Pr 13:16 [x]Est 9:7-10, 13
5:12 [y]Job 22:29; Pr 16:18; 29:23

2When he saw Queen Esther standing in the court, he was pleased
with her and held out to her the
gold scepter that was in his hand.
So Esther approached and touched
the tip of the scepter.[m]
3Then the king asked, "What is
it, Queen Esther? What is your request? Even up to half the kingdom,[n] it will be given you."
4"If it pleases the king," replied
Esther, "let the king, together with
Haman, come today to a banquet I
have prepared for him."
5"Bring Haman at once," the
king said, "so that we may do what
Esther asks."
So the king and Haman went to
the banquet Esther had prepared.
6As they were drinking wine,[o] the
king again asked Esther, "Now
what is your petition? It will be giv-
en you. And what is your request?
Even up to half the kingdom,[p] it
will be granted."[q]
7Esther replied, "My petition
and my request is this: 8If the king
regards me with favor[r] and if it
pleases the king to grant my petition and fulfill my request, let the
king and Haman come tomorrow to
the banquet[s] I will prepare for
them. Then I will answer the king's
question."

Haman's Rage Against Mordecai

9Haman went out that day happy
and in high spirits. But when he
saw Mordecai at the king's gate
and observed that he neither rose
nor showed fear in his presence, he
was filled with rage[t] against Mordecai.[u] 10Nevertheless, Haman restrained himself and went home.
Calling together his friends and
Zeresh,[v] his wife, 11Haman boasted[w] to them about his vast wealth,
his many sons,[x] and all the ways
the king had honored him and how
he had elevated him above the other nobles and officials. 12"And
that's not all," Haman added. "I'm
the only person[y] Queen Esther invited to accompany the king to the
banquet she gave. And she has in-

vited me along with the king tomorrow. 13But all this gives me no satisfaction as long as I see that Jew Mordecai sitting at the king's gate.[a]"

14His wife Zeresh and all his friends said to him, "Have a gallows built, seventy-five feet[h] high,[b] and ask the king in the morning to have Mordecai hanged[c] on it. Then go with the king to the dinner and be happy." This suggestion delighted Haman, and he had the gallows built.

Mordecai Honored

6 That night the king could not sleep;[d] so he ordered the book of the chronicles,[e] the record of his reign, to be brought in and read to him. 2It was found recorded there that Mordecai had exposed Bigthana and Teresh, two of the king's officers who guarded the doorway, who had conspired to assassinate King Xerxes.

3"What honor and recognition has Mordecai received for this?" the king asked.

"Nothing has been done for him,"[f] his attendants answered.

4The king said, "Who is in the court?" Now Haman had just entered the outer court of the palace to speak to the king about hanging Mordecai on the gallows he had erected for him.

5His attendants answered, "Haman is standing in the court."

"Bring him in," the king ordered.

6When Haman entered, the king asked him, "What should be done for the man the king delights to honor?"

Now Haman thought to himself, "Who is there that the king would rather honor than me?" 7So he answered the king, "For the man the king delights to honor, 8have them bring a royal robe[g] the king has worn and a horse[h] the king has ridden, one with a royal crest placed on its head. 9Then let the robe and horse be entrusted to one of the king's most noble princes. Let them robe the man the king delights to honor, and lead him on the horse through the city streets, proclaiming before him, 'This is what is done for the man the king delights to honor![i]' "

10"Go at once," the king commanded Haman. "Get the robe and the horse and do just as you have suggested for Mordecai the Jew, who sits at the king's gate. Do not neglect anything you have recommended."

11So Haman got[j] the robe and the horse. He robed Mordecai, and led him on horseback through the city streets, proclaiming before him, "This is what is done for the man the king delights to honor!"

12Afterward Mordecai returned to the king's gate. But Haman rushed home, with his head covered[k] in grief, 13and told Zeresh[l] his wife and all his friends everything that had happened to him.

His advisers and his wife Zeresh said to him, "Since Mordecai, before whom your downfall[m] has started, is of Jewish origin, you cannot stand against him—you will surely come to ruin!" 14While they were still talking with him, the king's eunuchs arrived and hurried Haman away to the banquet[n] Esther had prepared.

Haman Hanged

7 So the king and Haman went to dine[o] with Queen Esther, 2and as they were drinking wine[p] on that second day, the king again asked, "Queen Esther, what is your petition? It will be given you. What is your request? Even up to half the kingdom,[q] it will be granted.[r]"

3Then Queen Esther answered, "If I have found favor[s] with you, O king, and if it pleases your majesty, grant me my life—this is my petition. And spare my people—this is my request. 4For I and my people have been sold for destruction and slaughter and annihilation.[t] If we had merely been sold as male and female slaves, I would have kept quiet, because no such distress

5:13 [a]Est 2:19
5:14 [b]Est 7:9 [c]Ezr 6:11; Est 6:4
6:1 [d]Da 2:1; 6:18 [e]Est 2:23; 10:2
6:3 [f]Ecc 9:13-16
6:8 [g]Ge 41:42; Isa 52:1 [h]1Ki 1:33
6:9 [i]Ge 41:43
6:11 [j]Ge 41:42
6:12 [k]2Sa 15:30; Jer 14:3,4; Mic 3:7
6:13 [l]Est 5:10 [m]Ps 57:6; Pr 26:27; 28:18
6:14 [n]1Ki 3:15; Est 5:8
7:1 [o]Ge 40:20-22; Mt 22:1-14
7:2 [p]Est 1:10 [q]Est 5:3 [r]Est 9:12
7:3 [s]Est 2:15
7:4 [t]Est 3:9

[h]14 Hebrew *fifty cubits* (about 23 meters)

would justify disturbing the
king.[i]"
5King Xerxes asked Queen Esther, "Who is he? Where is the man
who has dared to do such a thing?"
6Esther said, "The adversary and
enemy is this vile Haman."
Then Haman was terrified before
the king and queen. **7**The king got
up in a rage,[a] left his wine and
went out into the palace garden.[b]
But Haman, realizing that the king
had already decided his fate,[c]
stayed behind to beg Queen Esther
for his life.
8Just as the king returned from
the palace garden to the banquet
hall, Haman was falling on the
couch[d] where Esther was reclining.[e]
The king exclaimed, "Will he
even molest the queen while she is
with me in the house?"[f]
As soon as the word left the
king's mouth, they covered Haman's face.[g] **9**Then Harbona,[h]
one of the eunuchs attending the
king, said, "A gallows seventy-five
feet[j] high[i] stands by Haman's
house. He had it made for Mordecai, who spoke up to help the
king."
The king said, "Hang him on
it!"[j] **10**So they hanged Haman[k] on
the gallows[l] he had prepared for
Mordecai.[m] Then the king's fury
subsided.[n]

The King's Edict in Behalf of the Jews

8 That same day King Xerxes
gave Queen Esther the estate
of Haman,[o] the enemy of the Jews.
And Mordecai came into the presence of the king, for Esther had
told how he was related to her.
2The king took off his signet ring,[p]
which he had reclaimed from Ha-
man, and presented it to Mordecai.
And Esther appointed him over Haman's estate.[q]
3Esther again pleaded with the
king, falling at his feet and weeping. She begged him to put an end
to the evil plan of Haman the Agagite, which he had devised against
the Jews. **4**Then the king extended
the gold scepter[r] to Esther and
she arose and stood before him.
5"If it pleases the king," she said,
"and if he regards me with favor
and thinks it the right thing to do,
and if he is pleased with me, let an
order be written overruling the dispatches that Haman son of Hammedatha, the Agagite, devised and
wrote to destroy the Jews in all the
king's provinces. **6**For how can I
bear to see disaster fall on my people? How can I bear to see the destruction of my family?"[s]
7King Xerxes replied to Queen
Esther and to Mordecai the Jew,
"Because Haman attacked the
Jews, I have given his estate to Esther, and they have hanged him on
the gallows. **8**Now write another
decree[t] in the king's name in behalf of the Jews as seems best
to you, and seal it with the king's
signet ring[u]—for no document
written in the king's name and
sealed with his ring can be revoked."[v]
9At once the royal secretaries
were summoned—on the twenty-
third day of the third month, the
month of Sivan. They wrote out all
Mordecai's orders to the Jews, and
to the satraps, governors and nobles of the 127 provinces stretching from India to Cush.[k][w] These
orders were written in the script of
each province and the language of
each people and also to the Jews in
their own script and language.[x]
10Mordecai wrote in the name of
King Xerxes, sealed the dispatches
with the king's signet ring, and sent
them by mounted couriers, who
rode fast horses especially bred for
the king.
11The king's edict granted the
Jews in every city the right to assemble and protect themselves; to
destroy, kill and annihilate any
armed force of any nationality or

7:7 [a]Ge 34:7; Est 1:12; Pr 19:12; 20:1-2 [b]2Ki 21:18 [c]Est 6:13
7:8 [d]Est 1:6 [e]Ge 39:14 [f]Ge 34:7 [g]Est 6:12
7:9 [h]Est 1:10 [i]Est 5:14 [j]Ps 7:14-16; 9:16; Pr 11:5-6; 26:27; Mt 7:2
7:10 [k]Pr 10:28 [l]Est 9:25 [m]Da 6:24 [n]Est 2:1
8:1 [o]Est 2:7; 7:6; Pr 22:22-23
8:2 [p]Ge 41:42; Est 3:10 [q]Pr 13:22; Da 2:48
8:4 [r]Est 4:11; 5:2
8:6 [s]Est 7:4; 9:1
8:8 [t]Est 3:12-14 [u]Ge 41:42 [v]Est 1:19; Da 6:15
8:9 [w]Est 1:1 [x]Est 1:22

[i]4 Or *quiet, but the compensation our adversary offers cannot be compared with the loss the king would suffer* [j]9 Hebrew *fifty cubits* (about 23 meters) [k]9 That is, the upper Nile region

province that might attack them and their women and children; and to plunder[a] the property of their enemies. **12**The day appointed for the Jews to do this in all the provinces of King Xerxes was the thirteenth day of the twelfth month, the month of Adar.[b] **13**A copy of the text of the edict was to be issued as law in every province and made known to the people of every nationality so that the Jews would be ready on that day[c] to avenge themselves on their enemies.

14The couriers, riding the royal horses, raced out, spurred on by the king's command. And the edict was also issued in the citadel of Susa.

15Mordecai[d] left the king's presence wearing royal garments of blue and white, a large crown of gold and a purple robe of fine linen.[e] And the city of Susa held a joyous celebration.[f] **16**For the Jews it was a time of happiness and joy,[g] gladness and honor.[h] **17**In every province and in every city, wherever the edict of the king went, there was joy[i] and gladness among the Jews, with feasting and celebrating. And many people of other nationalities became Jews because fear[j] of the Jews had seized them.[k]

Triumph of the Jews

9 On the thirteenth day of the twelfth month, the month of Adar,[l] the edict commanded by the king was to be carried out. On this day the enemies of the Jews had hoped to overpower them, but now the tables were turned and the Jews got the upper hand[m] over those who hated them.[n] **2**The Jews assembled in their cities[o] in all the provinces of King Xerxes to attack those seeking their destruction. No one could stand against them,[p] because the people of all the other nationalities were afraid of them. **3**And all the nobles of the provinces, the satraps, the governors and the king's administrators helped the Jews,[q] because fear of Mordecai had seized them. **4**Mordecai was prominent[r] in the palace; his reputation spread throughout the provinces, and he became more and more powerful.[s]

5The Jews struck down all their enemies with the sword, killing and destroying them,[t] and they did what they pleased to those who hated them. **6**In the citadel of Susa, the Jews killed and destroyed five hundred men. **7**They also killed Parshandatha, Dalphon, Aspatha, **8**Poratha, Adalia, Aridatha, **9**Parmashta, Arisai, Aridai and Vaizatha, **10**the ten sons[u] of Haman son of Hammedatha, the enemy of the Jews. But they did not lay their hands on the plunder.[v]

11The number of those slain in the citadel of Susa was reported to the king that same day. **12**The king said to Queen Esther, "The Jews have killed and destroyed five hundred men and the ten sons of Haman in the citadel of Susa. What have they done in the rest of the king's provinces? Now what is your petition? It will be given you. What is your request? It will also be granted."[w]

13"If it pleases the king," Esther answered, "give the Jews in Susa permission to carry out this day's edict tomorrow also, and let Haman's ten sons[x] be hanged[y] on gallows."

14So the king commanded that this be done. An edict was issued in Susa, and they hanged[z] the ten sons of Haman. **15**The Jews in Susa came together on the fourteenth day of the month of Adar, and they put to death in Susa three hundred men, but they did not lay their hands on the plunder.[a]

16Meanwhile, the remainder of the Jews who were in the king's provinces also assembled to protect themselves and get relief[b] from their enemies.[c] They killed seventy-five thousand of them[d] but did not lay their hands on the plunder. **17**This happened on the thirteenth day of the month of Adar, and on the fourteenth they rested and made it a day of feasting[e] and joy.

8:11 [a]Est 9:10,15,16
8:12 [b]Est 3:13; 9:1
8:13 [c]Est 3:14
8:15 [d]Est 9:4 [e]Ge 41:42 [f]Est 3:15
8:16 [g]Ps 97:10-12 [h]Ps 112:4
8:17 [i]Est 9:19,27; Ps 35:27; Pr 11:10 [j]Ex 15:14,16; Dt 11:25 [k]Est 9:3
9:1 [l]Est 8:12 [m]Jer 29:4-7 [n]Est 3:12-14; Pr 22:22-23
9:2 [o]ver 15-18 [p]Est 8:11,17; Ps 71:13,24
9:3 [q]Ezr 8:36
9:4 [r]Ex 11:3 [s]2Sa 3:1; 1Ch 11:9
9:5 [t]Ezr 4:6
9:10 [u]Est 5:11 [v]Ge 14:23; 1Sa 14:32; Est 3:13; 8:11
9:12 [w]Est 5:6; 7:2
9:13 [x]Est 5:11 [y]Dt 21:22-23
9:14 [z]Ezr 6:11
9:15 [a]Ge 14:23; Est 8:11
9:16 [b]Est 4:14 [c]Dt 25:19 [d]1Ch 4:43
9:17 [e]1Ki 3:15

Purim Celebrated

[18]The Jews in Susa, however, had assembled on the thirteenth and fourteenth, and then on the fifteenth they rested and made it a day of feasting and joy.

[19]That is why rural Jews—those living in villages—observe the fourteenth of the month of Adar[a] as a day of joy and feasting, a day for giving presents to each other.[b]

[20]Mordecai recorded these events, and he sent letters to all the Jews throughout the provinces of King Xerxes, near and far, [21]to have them celebrate annually the fourteenth and fifteenth days of the month of Adar [22]as the time when the Jews got relief[c] from their enemies, and as the month when their sorrow was turned into joy and their mourning into a day of celebration.[d] He wrote them to observe the days as days of feasting and joy and giving presents of food[e] to one another and gifts to the poor.

[23]So the Jews agreed to continue the celebration they had begun, doing what Mordecai had written to them. [24]For Haman son of Hammedatha, the Agagite,[f] the enemy of all the Jews, had plotted against the Jews to destroy them and had cast the *pur*[g] (that is, the lot[h]) for their ruin and destruction. [25]But when the plot came to the king's attention,[1] he issued written orders that the evil scheme Haman had devised against the Jews should come back onto his own head,[i] and that he and his sons should be hanged[j] on the gallows.[k] [26](Therefore these days were called Purim, from the word *pur*.[l]) Because of everything written in this letter and because of what they had seen and what had happened to them, [27]the Jews took it upon themselves to establish the custom that they and their descendants and all who join them should without fail observe these two days every year, in the way prescribed and at the time appointed. [28]These days should be remembered and observed in every generation by every family, and in every province and in every city. And these days of Purim should never cease to be celebrated by the Jews, nor should the memory of them die out among their descendants.

[29]So Queen Esther, daughter of Abihail,[m] along with Mordecai the Jew, wrote with full authority to confirm this second letter concerning Purim. [30]And Mordecai sent letters to all the Jews in the 127 provinces[n] of the kingdom of Xerxes—words of goodwill and assurance— [31]to establish these days of Purim at their designated times, as Mordecai the Jew and Queen Esther had decreed for them, and as they had established for themselves and their descendants in regard to their times of fasting[o] and lamentation.[p] [32]Esther's decree confirmed these regulations about Purim, and it was written down in the records.

The Greatness of Mordecai

10 King Xerxes imposed tribute throughout the empire, to its distant shores.[q] [2]And all his acts of power and might, together with a full account of the greatness of Mordecai[r] to which the king had raised him,[s] are they not written in the book of the annals[t] of the kings of Media and Persia? [3]Mordecai the Jew was second[u] in rank[v] to King Xerxes,[w] preeminent among the Jews, and held in high esteem by his many fellow Jews, because he worked for the good of his people and spoke up for the welfare of all the Jews.[x]

9:19 [a]Est 3:7 [b]ver 22; Dt 16:11,14; Ne 8:10,12; Est 2:9; Rev 11:10
9:22 [c]Est 4:14 [d]Ne 8:12; Ps 30:11-12 [e]2Ki 25:30
9:24 [f]Ex 17:8-16 [g]Est 3:7 [h]Lev 16:8
9:25 [i]Ps 7:16 [j]Dt 21:22-23 [k]Est 7:10
9:26 [l]ver 20; Est 3:7
9:29 [m]Est 2:15
9:30 [n]Est 1:1
9:31 [o]Est 4:16 [p]Est 4:1-3
10:1 [q]Ps 72:10; 97:1; Isa 24:15
10:2 [r]Est 8:15; 9:4 [s]Ge 41:44 [t]Est 2:23
10:3 [u]Da 5:7 [v]Ge 41:43 [w]Ge 41:40 [x]Ne 2:10; Jer 29:4-7; Da 6:3

[1]25 Or *when Esther came before the king*

Job

Title and Background

The book of Job is named for its main character, a righteous man who was very rich. Even after losing everything he owned and suffering from a terrible sickness, Job still confessed his trust in God.

Author and Date of Writing

Although most of the book consists of the words of Job and his counselors, Job himself was not the author. We can be sure the author was an Israelite who probably had access to oral and/or written sources from which he composed the book.

Two dates are involved: (1) the date of the man Job and his historical setting, and (2) the date of the inspired writer of the book. The latter could be dated anytime from the reign of Solomon to the exile. The date of the actual events described in this book was most likely between 2000 and 1000 B.C., and probably late in that millennium.

Theme and Message

The book provides a profound statement on the justice of God in light of human suffering. How can the justice of an almighty God be defended in the face of evil, especially human suffering, and even more particularly, the suffering of the innocent? The suffering of the righteous must be seen in the light of the cosmic struggle between God and Satan.

Outline

I. Prologue (1:1-2:13)
II. Dialogue—Dispute: Job and His Friends (3:1-27:23)
III. Interlude on Wisdom (28:1-28)
IV. Monologues: Job, Elihu and God (29:1-42:6)
V. Epilogue (42:7-17)

Prologue

1 In the land of Uz[a] there lived a
man whose name was Job.[b]
This man was blameless[c] and upright; he feared God[d] and shunned
evil. 2 He had seven sons and three
daughters,[e] 3 and he owned seven
thousand sheep, three thousand
camels, five hundred yoke of oxen
and five hundred donkeys, and had
a large number of servants. He was
the greatest man[f] among all the
people of the East.
4 His sons used to take turns
holding feasts in their homes, and
they would invite their three sisters
to eat and drink with them. 5 When
a period of feasting had run its
course, Job would send and have
them purified. Early in the morning
he would sacrifice a burnt offering[g] for each of them, thinking,
"Perhaps my children have
sinned[h] and cursed God[i] in their
hearts." This was Job's regular custom.

Job's First Test

6 One day the angels[a][j] came to
present themselves before the
LORD, and Satan[b] also came with
them.[k] 7 The LORD said to Satan,
"Where have you come from?"
Satan answered the LORD, "From

1:1 [a] Jer 25:20 [b] Eze 14:14, 20; Jas 5:11 [c] Ge 6:9; 17:1 [d] Ge 22:12; Ex 18:21
1:2 [e] Job 42:13
1:3 [f] Job 29:25
1:5 [g] Ge 8:20; Job 42:8 [h] Job 8:4 [i] 1Ki 21:10,13
1:6 [j] Job 38:7 [k] Job 2:1

[a] 6 Hebrew *the sons of God* [b] 6 *Satan* means *accuser.*

roaming through the earth and going back and forth in it."[a]
8Then the LORD said to Satan,
"Have you considered my servant
Job?[b] There is no one on earth like
him; he is blameless and upright, a
man who fears God and shuns
evil."[c]
9"Does Job fear God for nothing?"[d] Satan replied. 10"Have you
not put a hedge around him and his
household and everything he
has?[e] You have blessed the work of
his hands, so that his flocks and
herds are spread throughout the
land.[f] 11But stretch out your hand
and strike everything he has,[g] and
he will surely curse you to your
face."[h]
12The LORD said to Satan, "Very
well, then, everything he has is in
your hands, but on the man himself
do not lay a finger."
Then Satan went out from the
presence of the LORD.
13One day when Job's sons and
daughters were feasting and drinking wine at the oldest brother's
house, 14a messenger came to
Job and said, "The oxen were
plowing and the donkeys were
grazing nearby, 15and the Sabeans[i] attacked and carried them
off. They put the servants to the
sword, and I am the only one who
has escaped to tell you!"
16While he was still speaking,
another messenger came and said,
"The fire of God fell from the sky[j]
and burned up the sheep and the
servants,[k] and I am the only one
who has escaped to tell you!"
17While he was still speaking,
another messenger came and said,
"The Chaldeans[l] formed three
raiding parties and swept down on
your camels and carried them off.
They put the servants to the sword,
and I am the only one who has escaped to tell you!"
18While he was still speaking,
yet another messenger came and
said, "Your sons and daughters
were feasting and drinking wine at
the oldest brother's house, 19when
suddenly a mighty wind[m] swept in
from the desert and struck the four
corners of the house. It collapsed
on them and they are dead, and I
am the only one who has escaped
to tell you!"
20At this, Job got up and tore his
robe[n] and shaved his head. Then
he fell to the ground in worship[o]
21and said:

"Naked I came from my
mother's womb,
and naked I will depart.[c][p]
The LORD gave and the LORD has
taken away;[q]
may the name of the LORD be
praised."[r]

22In all this, Job did not sin by
charging God with wrongdoing.[s]

Job's Second Test

2 On another day the angels[d]
came to present themselves
before the LORD, and Satan also
came with them[t] to present himself before him. 2And the LORD said
to Satan, "Where have you come
from?"
Satan answered the LORD, "From
roaming through the earth and going back and forth in it."
3Then the LORD said to Satan,
"Have you considered my servant
Job? There is no one on earth like
him; he is blameless and upright, a
man who fears God and shuns
evil.[u] And he still maintains his integrity,[v] though you incited me
against him to ruin him without
any reason."[w]
4"Skin for skin!" Satan replied.
"A man will give all he has for his
own life. 5But stretch out your
hand and strike his flesh and
bones,[x] and he will surely curse
you to your face."[y]
6The LORD said to Satan, "Very
well, then, he is in your hands; but
you must spare his life."[z]
7So Satan went out from the
presence of the LORD and afflicted
Job with painful sores from the
soles of his feet to the top of his
head.[a] 8Then Job took a piece of
broken pottery and scraped him-

1:7 [a] 1Pe 5:8
1:8 [b] Jos 1:7; Job 42:7-8 [c] ver 1
1:9 [d] 1Ti 6:5
1:10 [e] Ps 34:7 [f] ver 3; Job 29:6; 31:25; Ps 128:1-2
1:11 [g] Job 19:21 [h] Job 2:5
1:15 [i] Ge 10:7; Job 6:19
1:16 [j] Ge 19:24 [k] Lev 10:2; Nu 11:1-3
1:17 [l] Ge 11:28,31
1:19 [m] Jer 4:11; 13:24
1:20 [n] Ge 37:29 [o] 1Pe 5:6
1:21 [p] Ecc 5:15; 1Ti 6:7 [q] 1Sa 2:7 [r] Job 2:10; Eph 5:20; 1Th 5:18
1:22 [s] Job 2:10
2:1 [t] Job 1:6
2:3 [u] Job 1:1,8 [v] Job 27:6 [w] Job 9:17
2:5 [x] Job 19:20 [y] Job 1:11
2:6 [z] Job 1:12
2:7 [a] Dt 28:35; Job 7:5

[c]21 Or *will return there* [d]1 Hebrew *the sons of God*

self with it as he sat among the
ashes.[a]

9 His wife said to him, "Are you
still holding on to your integrity?
Curse God and die!"

10 He replied, "You are talking
like a foolish[e] woman. Shall we accept
good from God, and not trouble?"[b]

In all this, Job did not sin in
what he said.[c]

Job's Three Friends

11 When Job's three friends, Eliphaz
the Temanite,[d] Bildad the
Shuhite[e] and Zophar the Naamathite,
heard about all the troubles
that had come upon him, they set
out from their homes and met together
by agreement to go and sympathize
with him and comfort
him.[f] 12 When they saw him from a
distance, they could hardly recognize
him; they began to weep
aloud, and they tore their robes
and sprinkled dust on their
heads.[g] 13 Then they sat on the
ground with him for seven days and
seven nights.[h] No one said a word
to him, because they saw how great
his suffering was.

Job Speaks

3 After this, Job opened his
mouth and cursed the day of
his birth. 2 He said:

3 "May the day of my birth
perish,
and the night it was said, 'A
boy is born!'[i]
4 That day—may it turn to
darkness;
may God above not care
about it;
may no light shine upon it.
5 May darkness and deep
shadow[f][j] claim it once
more;
may a cloud settle over it;
may blackness overwhelm its
light.
6 That night—may thick
darkness[k] seize it;
may it not be included
among the days of the
year
nor be entered in any of the
months.
7 May that night be barren;
may no shout of joy be heard
in it.
8 May those who curse days[g]
curse that day,
those who are ready to rouse
Leviathan.[l]
9 May its morning stars become
dark;
may it wait for daylight in
vain
and not see the first rays of
dawn,[m]
10 for it did not shut the doors of
the womb on me
to hide trouble from my
eyes.

11 "Why did I not perish at birth,
and die as I came from the
womb?[n]
12 Why were there knees to
receive me[o]
and breasts that I might be
nursed?
13 For now I would be lying
down[p] in peace;
I would be asleep and at
rest[q]
14 with kings and counselors of
the earth,[r]
who built for themselves
places now lying in
ruins,[s]
15 with rulers[t] who had gold,
who filled their houses with
silver.[u]
16 Or why was I not hidden in the
ground like a stillborn
child,[v]
like an infant who never saw
the light of day?
17 There the wicked cease from
turmoil,
and there the weary are at
rest.[w]
18 Captives also enjoy their ease;
they no longer hear the slave
driver's shout.[x]
19 The small and the great are
there,

2:8 [a] Job 42:6; Jer 6:26; Eze 27:30; Mt 11:21
2:10 [b] Job 1:21 [c] Job 1:22; Ps 39:1; Jas 1:12; 5:11
2:11 [d] Ge 36:11; Jer 49:7 [e] Ge 25:2 [f] Job 42:11; Ro 12:15
2:12 [g] Jos 7:6; Ne 9:1; La 2:10; Eze 27:30
2:13 [h] Ge 50:10; Eze 3:15
3:3 [i] Job 10:18-19; Jer 20:14-18
3:5 [j] Job 10:21,22; Ps 23:4; Jer 2:6; 13:16
3:6 [k] Job 23:17
3:8 [l] Job 41:1,8, 10,25
3:9 [m] Job 41:18
3:11 [n] Job 10:18
3:12 [o] Ge 30:3; Isa 66:12
3:13 [p] Job 17:13 [q] Job 7:8-10, 21; 10:22; 14:10-12; 19:27; 21:13, 23
3:14 [r] Job 12:17 [s] Job 15:28
3:15 [t] Job 12:21 [u] Job 27:17
3:16 [v] Ps 58:8; Ecc 6:3
3:17 [w] Job 17:16
3:18 [x] Job 39:7

[e] *10* The Hebrew word rendered *foolish* denotes moral deficiency. [f] *5* Or *and the shadow of death* [g] *8* Or *the sea*

and the slave is freed from
his master.
20"Why is light given to those in
misery,
and life to the bitter of
soul,[a]
21to those who long for death
that does not come,[b]
who search for it more than
for hidden treasure,[c]
22who are filled with gladness
and rejoice when they reach
the grave?
23Why is life given to a man
whose way is hidden,
whom God has hedged in?[d]
24For sighing comes to me
instead of food;[e]
my groans pour out like
water.[f]
25What I feared has come upon
me;
what I dreaded[g] has
happened to me.
26I have no peace, no quietness;
I have no rest,[h] but only
turmoil."

Eliphaz

4 Then Eliphaz the Temanite replied:

2"If someone ventures a word
with you, will you be
impatient?
But who can keep from
speaking?[i]
3Think how you have instructed
many,
how you have strengthened
feeble hands.[j]
4Your words have supported
those who stumbled;
you have strengthened
faltering knees.[k]
5But now trouble comes to you,
and you are discouraged;
it strikes[l] you, and you are
dismayed.[m]
6Should not your piety be your
confidence[n]
and your blameless[o] ways
your hope?

7"Consider now: Who, being
innocent, has ever
perished?[p]
Where were the upright ever
destroyed?[q]
8As I have observed, those who
plow evil[r]
and those who sow trouble
reap it.[s]
9At the breath of God[t] they are
destroyed;
at the blast of his anger they
perish.[u]
10The lions may roar and growl,
yet the teeth of the great
lions are broken.[v]
11The lion perishes for lack of
prey,[w]
and the cubs of the lioness
are scattered.

12"A word was secretly brought to
me,
my ears caught a whisper[x] of
it.[y]
13Amid disquieting dreams in the
night,
when deep sleep falls on
men,[z]
14fear and trembling seized me
and made all my bones
shake.[a]
15A spirit glided past my face,
and the hair on my body
stood on end.
16It stopped,
but I could not tell what it
was.
A form stood before my eyes,
and I heard a hushed voice:
17'Can a mortal be more
righteous than God?[b]
Can a man be more pure
than his Maker?[c]
18If God places no trust in his
servants,
if he charges his angels with
error,[d]
19how much more those who live
in houses of clay,[e]
whose foundations[f] are in
the dust,[g]
who are crushed more readily
than a moth!
20Between dawn and dusk they
are broken to pieces;
unnoticed, they perish
forever.[h]
21Are not the cords of their tent
pulled up,[i]

3:20 [a] 1Sa 1:10; Jer 20:18; Eze 27:30-31
3:21 [b] Rev 9:6 [c] Pr 2:4
3:23 [d] Job 19:6,8, 12; Ps 88:8; La 3:7
3:24 [e] Job 6:7; 33:20 [f] Ps 42:3,4
3:25 [g] Job 30:15
3:26 [h] Job 7:4,14
4:2 [i] Job 32:20
4:3 [j] Isa 35:3; Heb 12:12
4:4 [k] Isa 35:3; Heb 12:12
4:5 [l] Job 19:21 [m] Job 6:14
4:6 [n] Pr 3:26 [o] Job 1:1
4:7 [p] Job 36:7 [q] Job 8:20; Ps 37:25
4:8 [r] Job 15:35 [s] Pr 22:8; Hos 10:13; Gal 6:7-8
4:9 [t] Job 15:30; Isa 30:33; 2Th 2:8 [u] Job 40:13
4:10 [v] Job 5:15; Ps 58:6
4:11 [w] Job 27:14; Ps 34:10
4:12 [x] Job 26:14 [y] Job 33:14
4:13 [z] Job 33:15
4:14 [a] Jer 23:9; Hab 3:16
4:17 [b] Job 9:2 [c] Job 35:10
4:18 [d] Job 15:15
4:19 [e] Job 10:9 [f] Job 22:16 [g] Ge 2:7
4:20 [h] Job 14:2,20; 20:7; Ps 90:5-6
4:21 [i] Job 8:22

so that they die without
wisdom?'[h][a]

5 "Call if you will, but who will
answer you?
To which of the holy ones[b]
will you turn?
2Resentment kills a fool,
and envy slays the
simple.[c]
3I myself have seen a fool taking
root,[d]
but suddenly his house was
cursed.[e]
4His children are far from
safety,[f]
crushed in court[g] without a
defender.
5The hungry consume his
harvest,[h]
taking it even from among
thorns,
and the thirsty pant after his
wealth.
6For hardship does not spring
from the soil,
nor does trouble sprout from
the ground.
7Yet man is born to trouble[i]
as surely as sparks fly
upward.
8"But if it were I, I would appeal
to God;
I would lay my cause before
him.[j]
9He performs wonders that
cannot be fathomed,[k]
miracles that cannot be
counted.
10He bestows rain on the earth;
he sends water upon the
countryside.[l]
11The lowly he sets on high,[m]
and those who mourn are
lifted to safety.
12He thwarts the plans[n] of the
crafty,
so that their hands achieve
no success.
13He catches the wise in their
craftiness,[o]
and the schemes of the wily
are swept away.
14Darkness[p] comes upon them
in the daytime;
at noon they grope as in the
night.[q]
15He saves the needy[r] from the
sword in their mouth;
he saves them from the
clutches of the
powerful.[s]
16So the poor have hope,
and injustice shuts its
mouth.[t]
17"Blessed is the man whom God
corrects;[u]
so do not despise the
discipline[v] of the
Almighty.[i][w]
18For he wounds, but he also
binds up;[x]
he injures, but his hands also
heal.[y]
19From six calamities he will
rescue you;
in seven no harm will befall
you.[z]
20In famine[a] he will ransom you
from death,
and in battle from the stroke
of the sword.[b]
21You will be protected from the
lash of the tongue,[c]
and need not fear[d] when
destruction comes.
22You will laugh at destruction
and famine,
and need not fear the beasts
of the earth.[e]
23For you will have a covenant
with the stones[f] of the
field,
and the wild animals will be
at peace with you.[g]
24You will know that your tent is
secure;
you will take stock of your
property and find
nothing missing.[h]
25You will know that your
children will be many,[i]
and your descendants like
the grass of the earth.[j]
26You will come to the grave in
full vigor,[k]
like sheaves gathered in
season.
27"We have examined this, and it
is true.

4:21 [a]Job 18:21; 36:12
5:1 [b]Job 15:15
5:2 [c]Pr 12:16
5:3 [d]Ps 37:35; Jer 12:2 [e]Job 24:18
5:4 [f]Job 4:11 [g]Am 5:12
5:5 [h]Job 18:8-10
5:7 [i]Job 14:1
5:8 [j]Ps 35:23; 50:15
5:9 [k]Job 42:3; Ps 40:5
5:10 [l]Job 36:28
5:11 [m]Ps 113:7-8
5:12 [n]Ne 4:15; Ps 33:10
5:13 [o]1Co 3:19*
5:14 [p]Job 12:25 [q]Dt 28:29
5:15 [r]Ps 35:10 [s]Job 4:10
5:16 [t]Ps 107:42
5:17 [u]Jas 1:12 [v]Ps 94:12; Pr 3:11 [w]Heb 12:5-11
5:18 [x]Isa 30:26 [y]1Sa 2:6
5:19 [z]Ps 34:19; 91:10
5:20 [a]Ps 33:19 [b]Ps 144:10
5:21 [c]Ps 31:20 [d]Ps 91:5
5:22 [e]Ps 91:13; Eze 34:25
5:23 [f]Ps 91:12 [g]Isa 11:6-9
5:24 [h]Job 8:6
5:25 [i]Ps 112:2 [j]Ps 72:16; Isa 44:3-4
5:26 [k]Ge 15:15

[h]*21* Some interpreters end the quotation after verse 17. [i]*17* Hebrew *Shaddai*; here and throughout Job

So hear it and apply it to
yourself."

Job

6 Then Job replied:
2"If only my anguish could be weighed
and all my misery be placed on the scales![a]
3It would surely outweigh the sand[b] of the seas—
no wonder my words have been impetuous.[c]
4The arrows[d] of the Almighty are in me,[e]
my spirit drinks[f] in their poison;
God's terrors[g] are marshaled against me.[h]
5Does a wild donkey bray when it has grass,
or an ox bellow when it has fodder?
6Is tasteless food eaten without salt,
or is there flavor in the white of an egg[i]?
7I refuse to touch it;
such food makes me ill.[i]
8"Oh, that I might have my request,
that God would grant what I hope for,[j]
9that God would be willing to crush me,
to let loose his hand and cut me off![k]
10Then I would still have this consolation—
my joy in unrelenting pain—
that I had not denied the words[l] of the Holy One.[m]
11"What strength do I have, that I should still hope?
What prospects, that I should be patient?[n]
12Do I have the strength of stone?
Is my flesh bronze?
13Do I have any power to help myself,[o]
now that success has been driven from me?
14"A despairing man[p] should have the devotion[q] of his friends,
even though he forsakes the fear of the Almighty.
15But my brothers are as undependable as intermittent streams,[r]
as the streams that overflow
16when darkened by thawing ice
and swollen with melting snow,
17but that cease to flow in the dry season,
and in the heat[s] vanish from their channels.
18Caravans turn aside from their routes;
they go up into the wasteland and perish.
19The caravans of Tema[t] look for water,
the traveling merchants of Sheba look in hope.
20They are distressed, because they had been confident;
they arrive there, only to be disappointed.[u]
21Now you too have proved to be of no help;
you see something dreadful and are afraid.[v]
22Have I ever said, 'Give something on my behalf,
pay a ransom for me from your wealth,
23deliver me from the hand of the enemy,
ransom me from the clutches of the ruthless'?
24"Teach me, and I will be quiet;[w]
show me where I have been wrong.
25How painful are honest words![x]
But what do your arguments prove?
26Do you mean to correct what I say,
and treat the words of a despairing man as wind?[y]
27You would even cast lots[z] for the fatherless

6:2 [a]Job 31:6
6:3 [b]Pr 27:3 [c]Job 23:2
6:4 [d]Ps 38:2 [e]Job 16:12,13 [f]Job 21:20 [g]Job 30:15 [h]Ps 88:15-18
6:7 [i]Job 3:24
6:8 [j]Job 14:13
6:9 [k]Nu 11:15; 1Ki 19:4
6:10 [l]Job 22:22; 23:12 [m]Lev 19:2; Isa 57:15
6:11 [n]Job 21:4
6:13 [o]Job 26:2
6:14 [p]Job 4:5 [q]Job 15:4
6:15 [r]Ps 38:11; Jer 15:18
6:17 [s]Job 24:19
6:19 [t]Ge 25:15; Isa 21:14
6:20 [u]Jer 14:3
6:21 [v]Ps 38:11
6:24 [w]Ps 39:1
6:25 [x]Ecc 12:11
6:26 [y]Job 8:2; 15:3
6:27 [z]Joel 3:3; Na 3:10; 2Pe 2:3

i6 The meaning of the Hebrew for this phrase is uncertain.

and barter away your friend.

28"But now be so kind as to look
at me.
Would I lie to your face?[a]
29Relent, do not be unjust;
reconsider, for my integrity is
at stake.[k][b]
30Is there any wickedness on my
lips?[c]
Can my mouth not discern[d]
malice?

7 "Does not man have hard
service[e] on earth?[f]
Are not his days like those of
a hired man?[g]
2Like a slave longing for the
evening shadows,
or a hired man waiting
eagerly for his wages,[h]
3so I have been allotted months
of futility,
and nights of misery have
been assigned to me.[i]
4When I lie down I think, 'How
long before I get up?'[j]
The night drags on, and I
toss till dawn.
5My body is clothed with
worms[k] and scabs,
my skin is broken and
festering.

6"My days are swifter than a
weaver's shuttle,[l]
and they come to an end
without hope.[m]
7Remember, O God, that my life
is but a breath;[n]
my eyes will never see
happiness again.[o]
8The eye that now sees me will
see me no longer;
you will look for me, but I
will be no more.[p]
9As a cloud vanishes and is
gone,
so he who goes down to the
grave[l][q] does not
return.[r]
10He will never come to his
house again;
his place[s] will know him no
more.[t]

11"Therefore I will not keep
silent;[u]
I will speak out in the
anguish of my spirit,
I will complain in the
bitterness of my
soul.[v]
12Am I the sea, or the monster
of the deep,[w]
that you put me under
guard?
13When I think my bed will
comfort me
and my couch will ease my
complaint,[x]
14even then you frighten me with
dreams
and terrify[y] me with visions,
15so that I prefer strangling and
death,[z]
rather than this body of
mine.
16I despise my life;[a] I would not
live forever.
Let me alone; my days have
no meaning.

17"What is man that you make so
much of him,
that you give him so much
attention,[b]
18that you examine him every
morning
and test him every
moment?[c]
19Will you never look away from
me,
or let me alone even for an
instant?[d]
20If I have sinned, what have I
done to you,[e]
O watcher of men?
Why have you made me your
target?[f]
Have I become a burden to
you?[m]
21Why do you not pardon my
offenses
and forgive my sins?[g]
For I will soon lie down in the
dust;[h]
you will search for me, but I
will be no more."

6:28 [a]Job 27:4; 33:1,3; 36:3,4
6:29 [b]Job 23:7,10; 34:5,36; 42:6
6:30 [c]Job 27:4 [d]Job 12:11
7:1 [e]Job 14:14; Isa 40:2 [f]Job 5:7 [g]Job 14:6
7:2 [h]Lev 19:13
7:3 [i]Job 16:7; Ps 6:6
7:4 [j]Dt 28:67
7:5 [k]Job 17:14; Isa 14:11
7:6 [l]Job 9:25 [m]Job 13:15; 17:11,15
7:7 [n]Ps 78:39; Jas 4:14 [o]Job 9:25
7:8 [p]Job 20:7,9, 21
7:9 [q]Job 11:8 [r]2Sa 12:23; Job 30:15
7:10 [s]Job 27:21,23 [t]Job 8:18
7:11 [u]Ps 40:9 [v]1Sa 1:10
7:12 [w]Eze 32:2-3
7:13 [x]Job 9:27
7:14 [y]Job 9:34
7:15 [z]1Ki 19:4
7:16 [a]Job 9:21; 10:1
7:17 [b]Ps 8:4; 144:3; Heb 2:6
7:18 [c]Job 14:3
7:19 [d]Job 9:18
7:20 [e]Job 35:6 [f]Job 16:12
7:21 [g]Job 10:14 [h]Job 10:9; Ps 104:29

k29 Or *my righteousness still stands*
l9 Hebrew *Sheol*
m20 A few manuscripts of the Masoretic Text, an ancient Hebrew scribal tradition and Septuagint; most manuscripts of the Masoretic Text *I have become a burden to myself.*

Bildad

8 Then Bildad the Shuhite replied:

2"How long will you say such things?
Your words are a blustering wind.[a]
3Does God pervert justice?[b]
Does the Almighty pervert what is right?[c]
4When your children sinned against him,
he gave them over to the penalty of their sin.[d]
5But if you will look to God
and plead[e] with the Almighty,
6if you are pure and upright,
even now he will rouse himself on your behalf[f]
and restore you to your rightful place.[g]
7Your beginnings will seem humble,
so prosperous[h] will your future be.

8"Ask the former generations[i]
and find out what their fathers learned,
9for we were born only yesterday and know nothing,[j]
and our days on earth are but a shadow.[k]
10Will they not instruct you and tell you?
Will they not bring forth words from their understanding?
11Can papyrus grow tall where there is no marsh?
Can reeds thrive without water?
12While still growing and uncut,
they wither more quickly than grass.[l]
13Such is the destiny of all who forget God;[m]
so perishes the hope of the godless.[n]
14What he trusts in is fragile[n];
what he relies on is a spider's web.[o]
15He leans on his web,[p] but it gives way;
he clings to it, but it does not hold.[q]
16He is like a well-watered plant in the sunshine,
spreading its shoots[r] over the garden;[s]
17it entwines its roots around a pile of rocks
and looks for a place among the stones.
18But when it is torn from its spot,
that place disowns it and says, 'I never saw you.'[t]
19Surely its life withers[u] away,
and[o] from the soil other plants grow.[v]

20"Surely God does not reject a blameless[w] man
or strengthen the hands of evildoers.[x]
21He will yet fill your mouth with laughter[y]
and your lips with shouts of joy.[z]
22Your enemies will be clothed in shame,[a]
and the tents of the wicked will be no more."[b]

Job

9 Then Job replied:

2"Indeed, I know that this is true.
But how can a mortal be righteous before God?[c]
3Though one wished to dispute with him,
he could not answer him one time out of a thousand.[d]
4His wisdom[e] is profound, his power is vast.[f]
Who has resisted him and come out unscathed?[g]
5He moves mountains without their knowing it
and overturns them in his anger.[h]
6He shakes the earth[i] from its place

8:2 [a]Job 6:26
8:3 [b]Dt 32:4; 2Ch 19:7; Ro 3:5 [c]Ge 18:25
8:4 [d]Job 1:19
8:5 [e]Job 11:13
8:6 [f]Ps 7:6 [g]Job 5:24
8:7 [h]Job 42:12
8:8 [i]Dt 4:32; 32:7; Job 15:18
8:9 [j]Ge 47:9 [k]1Ch 29:15; Job 7:6
8:12 [l]Ps 129:6; Jer 17:6
8:13 [m]Ps 9:17 [n]Job 11:20; 13:16; 15:34; Pr 10:28
8:14 [o]Isa 59:5
8:15 [p]Job 27:18 [q]Ps 49:11
8:16 [r]Ps 80:11 [s]Ps 37:35; Jer 11:16
8:18 [t]Job 7:8; Ps 37:36
8:19 [u]Job 20:5 [v]Ecc 1:4
8:20 [w]Job 1:1 [x]Job 21:30
8:21 [y]Job 5:22 [z]Ps 126:2; 132:16
8:22 [a]Ps 35:26; 109:29; 132:18 [b]Job 18:6,14, 21
9:2 [c]Job 4:17; Ps 143:2; Ro 3:20
9:3 [d]Job 10:2; 40:2
9:4 [e]Job 11:6 [f]Job 36:5 [g]2Ch 13:12
9:5 [h]Mic 1:4
9:6 [i]Isa 2:21; Hag 2:6; Heb 12:26

[n]*14* The meaning of the Hebrew for this word is uncertain. [o]*19* Or *Surely all the joy it has / is that*

and makes its pillars tremble.[a]
7He speaks to the sun and it does not shine;
he seals off the light of the stars.[b]
8He alone stretches out the heavens[c]
and treads on the waves of the sea.[d]
9He is the Maker of the Bear and Orion,
the Pleiades and the constellations of the south.[e]
10He performs wonders[f] that cannot be fathomed,
miracles that cannot be counted.[g]
11When he passes me, I cannot see him;
when he goes by, I cannot perceive him.[h]
12If he snatches away, who can stop him?[i]
Who can say to him, 'What are you doing?'[j]
13God does not restrain his anger;
even the cohorts of Rahab[k] cowered at his feet.

14"How then can I dispute with him?
How can I find words to argue with him?
15Though I were innocent, I could not answer him;[l]
I could only plead[m] with my Judge for mercy.
16Even if I summoned him and he responded,
I do not believe he would give me a hearing.
17He would crush me[n] with a storm[o]
and multiply[p] my wounds for no reason.[q]
18He would not let me regain my breath
but would overwhelm me with misery.[r]
19If it is a matter of strength, he is mighty!
And if it is a matter of justice, who will summon him[p]?

9:6 [a]Job 26:11
9:7 [b]Isa 13:10; Eze 32:8
9:8 [c]Ge 1:6; Ps 104:2-3 [d]Job 38:16; Ps 77:19
9:9 [e]Ge 1:16; Job 38:31; Am 5:8
9:10 [f]Ps 71:15 [g]Job 5:9
9:11 [h]Job 23:8-9; 35:14
9:12 [i]Job 11:10 [j]Isa 45:9; Ro 9:20
9:13 [k]Job 26:12; Ps 89:10; Isa 30:7; 51:9
9:15 [l]Job 10:15 [m]Job 8:5
9:17 [n]Job 16:12 [o]Job 30:22 [p]Job 16:14 [q]Job 2:3
9:18 [r]Job 7:19; 27:2
9:21 [s]Job 1:1 [t]Job 7:16
9:22 [u]Job 10:8; Ecc 9:2,3; Eze 21:3
9:23 [v]Heb 11:36 [w]Job 24:1,12
9:24 [x]Job 10:3; 16:11 [y]Job 12:6
9:25 [z]Job 7:6
9:26 [a]Isa 18:2 [b]Hab 1:8
9:27 [c]Job 7:11
9:28 [d]Job 3:25; Ps 119:120 [e]Job 7:21
9:29 [f]Ps 37:33
9:30 [g]Job 31:7 [h]Jer 2:22
9:32 [i]Ro 9:20 [j]Ps 143:2; Ecc 6:10
9:33 [k]1Sa 2:25

20Even if I were innocent, my mouth would condemn me;
if I were blameless, it would pronounce me guilty.
21"Although I am blameless,[s]
I have no concern for myself;
I despise my own life.[t]
22It is all the same; that is why I say,
'He destroys both the blameless and the wicked.'[u]
23When a scourge[v] brings sudden death,
he mocks the despair of the innocent.[w]
24When a land falls into the hands of the wicked,[x]
he blindfolds its judges.[y]
If it is not he, then who is it?

25"My days are swifter than a runner;[z]
they fly away without a glimpse of joy.
26They skim past like boats of papyrus,[a]
like eagles swooping down on their prey.[b]
27If I say, 'I will forget my complaint,[c]
I will change my expression, and smile,'
28I still dread[d] all my sufferings,
for I know you will not hold me innocent.[e]
29Since I am already found guilty,
why should I struggle in vain?[f]
30Even if I washed myself with soap[q]
and my hands[g] with washing soda,[h]
31you would plunge me into a slime pit
so that even my clothes would detest me.

32"He is not a man like me that I might answer him,[i]
that we might confront each other in court.[j]
33If only there were someone to arbitrate between us,[k]

[p]*19* See Septuagint; Hebrew *me.* [q]*30* Or *snow*

to lay his hand upon us both,
[34]someone to remove God's rod
from me,[a]
so that his terror would
frighten me no more.
[35]Then I would speak up without
fear of him,
but as it now stands with me,
I cannot.[b]

10 "I loathe my very life;[c]
therefore I will give free
rein to my complaint
and speak out in the
bitterness of my
soul.[d]
[2]I will say to God: Do not
condemn me,
but tell me what charges[e]
you have against me.
[3]Does it please you to oppress
me,[f]
to spurn the work of your
hands,[g]
while you smile on the
schemes of the
wicked?[h]
[4]Do you have eyes of flesh?
Do you see as a mortal
sees?[i]
[5]Are your days like those of a
mortal
or your years like those of a
man,[j]
[6]that you must search out my
faults
and probe after my sin[k]—
[7]though you know that I am not
guilty
and that no one can rescue
me from your hand?
[8]"Your hands shaped[l] me and
made me.
Will you now turn and
destroy me?
[9]Remember that you molded me
like clay.[m]
Will you now turn me to dust
again?[n]
[10]Did you not pour me out like
milk
and curdle me like cheese,
[11]clothe me with skin and flesh
and knit me together[o] with
bones and sinews?
[12]You gave me life[p] and showed
me kindness,
and in your providence
watched over my spirit.
[13]"But this is what you concealed
in your heart,
and I know that this was in
your mind:[q]
[14]If I sinned, you would be
watching me
and would not let my offense
go unpunished.[r]
[15]If I am guilty—woe to me![s]
Even if I am innocent, I
cannot lift my head,[t]
for I am full of shame
and drowned in[r] my
affliction.
[16]If I hold my head high, you
stalk me like a lion[u]
and again display your
awesome power against
me.[v]
[17]You bring new witnesses
against me[w]
and increase your anger
toward me;[x]
your forces come against me
wave upon wave.

[18]"Why then did you bring me
out of the womb?[y]
I wish I had died before any
eye saw me.
[19]If only I had never come into
being,
or had been carried straight
from the womb to the
grave!
[20]Are not my few days[z] almost
over?[a]
Turn away from me[b] so I can
have a moment's joy
[21]before I go to the place of no
return,[c]
to the land of gloom and
deep shadow,[s][d]
[22]to the land of deepest night,
of deep shadow and disorder,
where even the light is like
darkness."

Zophar

11 Then Zophar the Naamathite replied:

9:34 [a]Job 13:21; Ps 39:10
9:35 [b]Job 13:21
10:1 [c]1Ki 19:4 [d]Job 7:11
10:2 [e]Job 9:29
10:3 [f]Job 9:22 [g]Job 14:15; Ps 138:8; Isa 64:8 [h]Job 21:16; 22:18
10:4 [i]1Sa 16:7
10:5 [j]Ps 90:2,4; 2Pe 3:8
10:6 [k]Job 14:16
10:8 [l]Ps 119:73
10:9 [m]Isa 64:8 [n]Ge 2:7
10:11 [o]Ps 139:13,15
10:12 [p]Job 33:4
10:13 [q]Job 23:13
10:14 [r]Job 7:21
10:15 [s]Job 9:13; Isa 3:11 [t]Job 9:15
10:16 [u]Isa 38:13; La 3:10 [v]Job 5:9
10:17 [w]Job 16:8 [x]Ru 1:21
10:18 [y]Job 3:11
10:20 [z]Job 14:1 [a]Job 7:19 [b]Job 7:16
10:21 [c]2Sa 12:23; Job 3:13; 16:22 [d]Ps 23:4; 88:12

[r]15 Or *and aware of* [s]21 Or *and the shadow of death*; also in verse 22

2"Are all these words to go
unanswered?[a]
Is this talker to be
vindicated?
3Will your idle talk reduce men
to silence?
Will no one rebuke you when
you mock?[b]
4You say to God, 'My beliefs are
flawless[c]
and I am pure[d] in your
sight.'
5Oh, how I wish that God would
speak,
that he would open his lips
against you
6and disclose to you the secrets
of wisdom,[e]
for true wisdom has two
sides.
Know this: God has even
forgotten some of your
sin.[f]

7"Can you fathom[g] the
mysteries of God?
Can you probe the limits of
the Almighty?
8They are higher than the
heavens[h]—what can you
do?
They are deeper than the
depths of the
grave[t]—what can you
know?
9Their measure is longer than
the earth
and wider than the sea.

10"If he comes along and
confines you in prison
and convenes a court, who
can oppose him?[i]
11Surely he recognizes deceitful
men;
and when he sees evil, does
he not take note?[j]
12But a witless man can no more
become wise
than a wild donkey's colt can
be born a man.[u]

13"Yet if you devote your heart[k]
to him
and stretch out your hands to
him,[l]
14if you put away the sin that is
in your hand
and allow no evil[m] to dwell
in your tent,[n]
15then you will lift up your face[o]
without shame;
you will stand firm and
without fear.
16You will surely forget your
trouble,[p]
recalling it only as waters
gone by.[q]
17Life will be brighter than
noonday,[r]
and darkness will become
like morning.
18You will be secure, because
there is hope;
you will look about you and
take your rest[s] in
safety.[t]
19You will lie down, with no one
to make you afraid,[u]
and many will court your
favor.[v]
20But the eyes of the wicked will
fail,[w]
and escape will elude them;[x]
their hope will become a
dying gasp."[y]

Job

12 Then Job replied:
2"Doubtless you are the
people,
and wisdom will die with
you![z]
3But I have a mind as well as
you;
I am not inferior to you.
Who does not know all these
things?[a]

4"I have become a
laughingstock[b] to my
friends,
though I called upon God
and he answered[c]—
a mere laughingstock, though
righteous and
blameless![d]
5Men at ease have contempt for
misfortune
as the fate of those whose
feet are slipping.

11:2 [a]Job 8:2
11:3 [b]Job 17:2; 21:3
11:4 [c]Job 6:10 [d]Job 10:7
11:6 [e]Job 9:4 [f]Ezr 9:13; Job 15:5
11:7 [g]Ecc 3:11; Ro 11:33
11:8 [h]Job 22:12
11:10 [i]Job 9:12; Rev 3:7
11:11 [j]Job 34:21-25; Ps 10:14
11:13 [k]1Sa 7:3; Ps 78:8 [l]Ps 88:9
11:14 [m]Ps 101:4 [n]Job 22:23
11:15 [o]Job 22:26; 1Jn 3:21
11:16 [p]Isa 65:16 [q]Job 22:11
11:17 [r]Job 22:28; Ps 37:6; Isa 58:8,10
11:18 [s]Ps 3:5 [t]Lev 26:6; Pr 3:24
11:19 [u]Lev 26:6 [v]Isa 45:14
11:20 [w]Dt 28:65; Job 17:5 [x]Job 27:22; 34:22 [y]Job 8:13
12:2 [z]Job 17:10
12:3 [a]Job 13:2
12:4 [b]Job 21:3 [c]Ps 91:15 [d]Job 6:29

[t]*8* Hebrew *than Sheol* [u]*12* Or *wild donkey can be born tame*

6The tents of marauders are
undisturbed,[a]
and those who provoke God
are secure[b]—
those who carry their god in
their hands.[v]
7"But ask the animals, and they
will teach you,
or the birds of the air, and
they will tell you;
8or speak to the earth, and it
will teach you,
or let the fish of the sea
inform you.
9Which of all these does not
know
that the hand of the LORD has
done this?[c]
10In his hand is the life of every
creature
and the breath of all
mankind.[d]
11Does not the ear test words
as the tongue tastes food?[e]
12Is not wisdom found among the
aged?[f]
Does not long life bring
understanding?[g]

13"To God belong wisdom[h] and
power;[i]
counsel and understanding
are his.[j]
14What he tears down[k] cannot
be rebuilt;[l]
the man he imprisons cannot
be released.
15If he holds back the waters,[m]
there is drought;[n]
if he lets them loose, they
devastate the land.[o]
16To him belong strength and
victory;
both deceived and deceiver
are his.[p]
17He leads counselors away
stripped[q]
and makes fools of judges.[r]
18He takes off the shackles[s] put
on by kings
and ties a loincloth[w] around
their waist.
19He leads priests away stripped
and overthrows men long
established.[t]
20He silences the lips of trusted
advisers

12:6 [a]Job 22:18 [b]Job 9:24; 21:9
12:9 [c]Isa 41:20
12:10 [d]Job 27:3; 33:4; Ac 17:28
12:11 [e]Job 34:3
12:12 [f]Job 15:10 [g]Job 32:7,9
12:13 [h]Job 11:6 [i]Job 9:4 [j]Job 32:8; 38:36
12:14 [k]Job 19:10 [l]Job 37:7; Isa 25:2
12:15 [m]1Ki 8:35 [n]1Ki 17:1 [o]Ge 7:11
12:16 [p]Job 13:7,9
12:17 [q]Job 19:9 [r]Job 3:14
12:18 [s]Ps 116:16
12:19 [t]Job 24:12, 22; 34:20,28; 35:9
12:20 [u]Job 32:9
12:22 [v]1Co 4:5 [w]Job 3:5 [x]Da 2:22
12:23 [y]Jer 25:9 [z]Ps 107:38; Isa 9:3; 26:15
12:24 [a]Ps 107:40
12:25 [b]Job 5:14 [c]Ps 107:27; Isa 24:20
13:2 [d]Job 12:3
13:3 [e]Job 23:3-4
13:4 [f]Ps 119:69; Jer 23:32
13:5 [g]Pr 17:28
13:7 [h]Job 36:4
13:8 [i]Lev 19:15
13:9 [j]Job 12:16; Gal 6:7

and takes away the
discernment of elders.[u]
21He pours contempt on nobles
and disarms the mighty.
22He reveals the deep things of
darkness[v]
and brings deep shadows[w]
into the light.[x]
23He makes nations great, and
destroys them;[y]
he enlarges nations,[z] and
disperses them.
24He deprives the leaders of the
earth of their reason;
he sends them wandering
through a trackless
waste.[a]
25They grope in darkness with no
light;[b]
he makes them stagger like
drunkards.[c]

13 "My eyes have seen all
this,
my ears have heard and
understood it.
2What you know, I also know;
I am not inferior to you.[d]
3But I desire to speak to the
Almighty
and to argue my case with
God.[e]
4You, however, smear me with
lies;[f]
you are worthless physicians,
all of you!
5If only you would be altogether
silent!
For you, that would be
wisdom.[g]
6Hear now my argument;
listen to the plea of my lips.
7Will you speak wickedly on
God's behalf?
Will you speak deceitfully for
him?[h]
8Will you show him partiality?[i]
Will you argue the case for
God?
9Would it turn out well if he
examined you?
Could you deceive him as
you might deceive
men?[j]
10He would surely rebuke you

[v]6 Or *secure / in what God's hand brings them*
[w]18 Or *shackles of kings / and ties a belt*

if you secretly showed
partiality.
11Would not his splendor[a] terrify
you?
Would not the dread of him
fall on you?
12Your maxims are proverbs of
ashes;
your defenses are defenses of
clay.

13"Keep silent and let me speak;
then let come to me what
may.
14Why do I put myself in
jeopardy
and take my life in my
hands?
15Though he slay me, yet will I
hope[b] in him;[c]
I will surely[x] defend my
ways to his face.[d]
16Indeed, this will turn out for
my deliverance,[e]
for no godless man would
dare come before him!
17Listen carefully to my words;[f]
let your ears take in what I
say.
18Now that I have prepared my
case,[g]
I know I will be vindicated.
19Can anyone bring charges
against me?[h]
If so, I will be silent and
die.[i]

20"Only grant me these two
things, O God,
and then I will not hide from
you:
21Withdraw your hand[j] far from
me,
and stop frightening me with
your terrors.
22Then summon me and I will
answer,[k]
or let me speak, and you
reply.[l]
23How many wrongs and sins
have I committed?[m]
Show me my offense and my
sin.
24Why do you hide your face[n]
and consider me your
enemy?[o]
25Will you torment a windblown
leaf?[p]
Will you chase after dry
chaff?[q]
26For you write down bitter
things against me
and make me inherit the sins
of my youth.[r]
27You fasten my feet in
shackles;[s]
you keep close watch on all
my paths
by putting marks on the soles
of my feet.

28"So man wastes away like
something rotten,
like a garment eaten by
moths.[t]

14 "Man born of woman
is of few days and full of
trouble.[u]
2He springs up like a flower[v]
and withers away;[w]
like a fleeting shadow,[x] he
does not endure.
3Do you fix your eye on such a
one?[y]
Will you bring him[y] before
you for judgment?[z]
4Who can bring what is pure[a]
from the impure?[b]
No one![c]
5Man's days are determined;
you have decreed the number
of his months[d]
and have set limits he cannot
exceed.
6So look away from him and let
him alone,[e]
till he has put in his time
like a hired man.[f]

7"At least there is hope for a
tree:
If it is cut down, it will
sprout again,
and its new shoots will not
fail.
8Its roots may grow old in the
ground
and its stump die in the soil,
9yet at the scent of water it will
bud
and put forth shoots like a
plant.

13:11 [a]Job 31:23
13:15 [b]Job 7:6 [c]Ps 23:4; Pr 14:32 [d]Job 27:5
13:16 [e]Isa 12:1
13:17 [f]Job 21:2
13:18 [g]Job 23:4
13:19 [h]Job 40:4; Isa 50:8 [i]Job 10:8
13:21 [j]Ps 39:10
13:22 [k]Job 14:15 [l]Job 9:16
13:23 [m]1Sa 26:18
13:24 [n]Dt 32:20; Ps 13:1; Isa 8:17 [o]Job 19:11; La 2:5
13:25 [p]Lev 26:36 [q]Job 21:18; Isa 42:3
13:26 [r]Ps 25:7
13:27 [s]Job 33:11
13:28 [t]Isa 50:9; Jas 5:2
14:1 [u]Job 5:7; Ecc 2:23
14:2 [v]Jas 1:10 [w]Ps 90:5-6 [x]Job 8:9
14:3 [y]Ps 8:4; 144:3 [z]Ps 143:2
14:4 [a]Ps 51:10 [b]Eph 2:1-3 [c]Jn 3:6; Ro 5:12
14:5 [d]Job 21:21
14:6 [e]Job 7:19 [f]Job 7:1,2; Ps 39:13

[x]*15* Or *He will surely slay me; I have no hope — / yet I will* [y]*3* Septuagint, Vulgate and Syriac; Hebrew *me*

10But man dies and is laid low;
he breathes his last and is no more.[a]
11As water disappears from the sea
or a riverbed becomes parched and dry,[b]
12so man lies down and does not rise;
till the heavens are no more,[c] men will not awake
or be roused from their sleep.[d]
13"If only you would hide me in the grave[z]
and conceal me till your anger has passed![e]
If only you would set me a time
and then remember me!
14If a man dies, will he live again?
All the days of my hard service
I will wait for my renewal[a] to come.
15You will call and I will answer you;[f]
you will long for the creature your hands have made.
16Surely then you will count my steps[g]
but not keep track of my sin.[h]
17My offenses will be sealed up in a bag;[i]
you will cover over my sin.[j]
18"But as a mountain erodes and crumbles
and as a rock is moved from its place,
19as water wears away stones
and torrents wash away the soil,
so you destroy man's hope.[k]
20You overpower him once for all, and he is gone;
you change his countenance and send him away.
21If his sons are honored, he does not know it;
if they are brought low, he does not see it.[l]
22He feels but the pain of his own body
and mourns only for himself."

14:10 [a]Job 13:19
14:11 [b]Isa 19:5
14:12 [c]Rev 20:11; 21:1 [d]Ac 3:21
14:13 [e]Isa 26:20
14:15 [f]Job 13:22
14:16 [g]Ps 139:1-3; Pr 5:21; Jer 32:19 [h]Job 10:6
14:17 [i]Dt 32:34 [j]Hos 13:12
14:19 [k]Job 7:6
14:21 [l]Ecc 9:5; Isa 63:16
15:2 [m]Job 6:26
15:5 [n]Job 5:13
15:6 [o]Lk 19:22
15:7 [p]Job 38:21 [q]Ps 90:2; Pr 8:25
15:8 [r]Ro 11:34; 1Co 2:11
15:9 [s]Job 13:2
15:10 [t]Job 32:6-7
15:11 [u]2Co 1:3-4 [v]Zec 1:13 [w]Job 36:16
15:12 [x]Job 11:13
15:14 [y]Job 14:4; 25:4 [z]Pr 20:9; Ecc 7:20

Eliphaz

15 Then Eliphaz the Temanite replied:

2"Would a wise man answer with empty notions
or fill his belly with the hot east wind?[m]
3Would he argue with useless words,
with speeches that have no value?
4But you even undermine piety
and hinder devotion to God.
5Your sin prompts your mouth;
you adopt the tongue of the crafty.[n]
6Your own mouth condemns you, not mine;
your own lips testify against you.[o]

7"Are you the first man ever born?[p]
Were you brought forth before the hills?[q]
8Do you listen in on God's council?[r]
Do you limit wisdom to yourself?
9What do you know that we do not know?
What insights do you have that we do not have?[s]
10The gray-haired and the aged[t] are on our side,
men even older than your father.
11Are God's consolations[u] not enough for you,
words[v] spoken gently to you?[w]
12Why has your heart[x] carried you away,
and why do your eyes flash,
13so that you vent your rage against God
and pour out such words from your mouth?
14"What is man, that he could be pure,
or one born of woman,[y] that he could be righteous?[z]

[z]13 Hebrew *Sheol* [a]14 Or *release*

15 If God places no trust in his
holy ones,
if even the heavens are not
pure in his eyes,[a]
16 how much less man, who is vile
and corrupt,[b]
who drinks up evil like
water![c]

17 "Listen to me and I will explain
to you;
let me tell you what I have
seen,
18 what wise men have declared,
hiding nothing received from
their fathers[d]
19 (to whom alone the land was
given
when no alien passed among
them):
20 All his days the wicked man
suffers torment,
the ruthless through all the
years stored up for
him.[e]
21 Terrifying sounds fill his ears;[f]
when all seems well,
marauders attack him.[g]
22 He despairs of escaping the
darkness;
he is marked for the sword.[h]
23 He wanders about[i]—food for
vultures[b];
he knows the day of darkness
is at hand.[j]
24 Distress and anguish fill him
with terror;
they overwhelm him, like a
king poised to attack,
25 because he shakes his fist at
God
and vaunts himself against
the Almighty,[k]
26 defiantly charging against
him
with a thick, strong shield.

27 "Though his face is covered
with fat
and his waist bulges with
flesh,[l]
28 he will inhabit ruined towns
and houses where no one
lives,[m]
houses crumbling to rubble.[n]
29 He will no longer be rich and
his wealth will not
endure,[o]

15:15 [a] Job 4:18; 25:5
15:16 [b] Ps 14:1 [c] Job 34:7; Pr 19:28
15:18 [d] Job 8:8
15:20 [e] Job 24:1; 27:13-23
15:21 [f] Job 18:11; 20:25 [g] Job 27:20; 1Th 5:3
15:22 [h] Job 19:29; 27:14
15:23 [i] Ps 59:15; 109:10 [j] Job 18:12
15:25 [k] Job 36:9
15:27 [l] Ps 17:10
15:28 [m] Isa 5:9 [n] Job 3:14
15:29 [o] Job 27:16-17
15:30 [p] Job 5:14 [q] Job 22:20 [r] Job 4:9
15:31 [s] Isa 59:4
15:32 [t] Ecc 7:17 [u] Job 22:16; Ps 55:23 [v] Job 18:16
15:33 [w] Hab 3:17
15:34 [x] Job 8:22
15:35 [y] Ps 7:14; Isa 59:4; Hos 10:13
16:2 [z] Job 13:4
16:3 [a] Job 6:26
16:4 [b] Ps 22:7; 109:25; La 2:15; Zep 2:15; Mt 27:39

nor will his possessions
spread over the land.
30 He will not escape the
darkness;[p]
a flame[q] will wither his
shoots,
and the breath of God's
mouth[r] will carry him
away.
31 Let him not deceive himself by
trusting what is
worthless,[s]
for he will get nothing in
return.
32 Before his time[t] he will be
paid in full,[u]
and his branches will not
flourish.[v]
33 He will be like a vine stripped
of its unripe grapes,[w]
like an olive tree shedding its
blossoms.
34 For the company of the godless
will be barren,
and fire will consume the
tents of those who love
bribes.[x]
35 They conceive trouble and give
birth to evil;[y]
their womb fashions deceit."

Job

16 Then Job replied:
2 "I have heard many
things like these;
miserable comforters are you
all![z]
3 Will your long-winded speeches
never end?
What ails you that you keep
on arguing?[a]
4 I also could speak like you,
if you were in my place;
I could make fine speeches
against you
and shake my head[b] at you.
5 But my mouth would
encourage you;
comfort from my lips would
bring you relief.

6 "Yet if I speak, my pain is not
relieved;
and if I refrain, it does not go
away.

[b]23 Or *about, looking for food*

7Surely, O God, you have worn me out;[a]
you have devastated my entire household.
8You have bound me—and it has become a witness;
my gauntness[b] rises up and testifies against me.[c]
9God assails me and tears[d] me in his anger
and gnashes his teeth at me;[e]
my opponent fastens on me his piercing eyes.[f]
10Men open their mouths[g] to jeer at me;
they strike my cheek[h] in scorn
and unite together against me.[i]
11God has turned me over to evil men
and thrown me into the clutches of the wicked.[j]
12All was well with me, but he shattered me;
he seized me by the neck and crushed me.[k]
He has made me his target;[l]
13 his archers surround me.
Without pity, he pierces[m] my kidneys
and spills my gall on the ground.
14Again and again[n] he bursts upon me;
he rushes at me like a warrior.[o]

15"I have sewed sackcloth[p] over my skin
and buried my brow in the dust.
16My face is red with weeping,
deep shadows ring my eyes;
17yet my hands have been free of violence[q]
and my prayer is pure.

18"O earth, do not cover my blood;[r]
may my cry never be laid to rest![s]
19Even now my witness[t] is in heaven;
my advocate is on high.
20My intercessor is my friend[c]
as my eyes pour out[u] tears to God;
21on behalf of a man he pleads[v] with God
as a man pleads for his friend.

22"Only a few years will pass
before I go on the journey of no return.[w]

17 1My spirit is broken,
my days are cut short,
the grave awaits me.[x]
2Surely mockers[y] surround me;
my eyes must dwell on their hostility.

3"Give me, O God, the pledge you demand.[z]
Who else will put up security[a] for me?[b]
4You have closed their minds to understanding;
therefore you will not let them triumph.
5If a man denounces his friends for reward,
the eyes of his children will fail.[c]

6"God has made me a byword[d] to everyone,
a man in whose face people spit.
7My eyes have grown dim with grief;[e]
my whole frame is but a shadow.
8Upright men are appalled at this;
the innocent are aroused[f] against the ungodly.
9Nevertheless, the righteous[g] will hold to their ways,
and those with clean hands[h] will grow stronger.

10"But come on, all of you, try again!
I will not find a wise man among you.[i]
11My days have passed, my plans are shattered,
and so are the desires of my heart.[j]
12These men turn night into day;

16:7 [a]Job 7:3
16:8 [b]Job 19:20 [c]Job 10:17
16:9 [d]Hos 6:1 [e]Ps 35:16; La 2:16; Ac 7:54 [f]Job 13:24
16:10 [g]Ps 22:13 [h]Isa 50:6; La 3:30; Mic 5:1; Ac 23:2 [i]Ps 35:15
16:11 [j]Job 1:15,17
16:12 [k]Job 9:17 [l]La 3:12
16:13 [m]Job 20:24
16:14 [n]Job 9:17 [o]Joel 2:7
16:15 [p]Ge 37:34
16:17 [q]Isa 59:6; Jnh 3:8
16:18 [r]Isa 26:21 [s]Ps 66:18-19
16:19 [t]Ge 31:50; Ro 1:9; 1Th 2:5
16:20 [u]La 2:19
16:21 [v]Ps 9:4
16:22 [w]Ecc 12:5
17:1 [x]Ps 88:3-4
17:2 [y]1Sa 1:6-7
17:3 [z]Ps 119:122 [a]Pr 6:1 [b]Isa 38:14
17:5 [c]Job 11:20
17:6 [d]Job 30:9
17:7 [e]Job 16:8
17:8 [f]Job 22:19
17:9 [g]Pr 4:18 [h]Job 22:30
17:10 [i]Job 12:2
17:11 [j]Job 7:6

[c]20 Or *My friends treat me with scorn*

in the face of darkness they
say, 'Light is near.'
13 If the only home I hope for is
the grave,[d][a]
if I spread out my bed in
darkness,
14 if I say to corruption,[b] 'You are
my father,'
and to the worm,[c] 'My
mother' or 'My sister,'
15 where then is my hope?[d]
Who can see any hope for
me?
16 Will it go down to the gates of
death[d]?[e]
Will we descend together
into the dust?"

Bildad

18 Then Bildad the Shuhite replied:

2 "When will you end these
speeches?
Be sensible, and then we can
talk.
3 Why are we regarded as cattle
and considered stupid in
your sight?[f]
4 You who tear yourself[g] to
pieces in your anger,
is the earth to be abandoned
for your sake?
Or must the rocks be moved
from their place?

5 "The lamp of the wicked is
snuffed out;[h]
the flame of his fire stops
burning.
6 The light in his tent becomes
dark;
the lamp beside him goes
out.
7 The vigor of his step is
weakened;[i]
his own schemes[j] throw him
down.[k]
8 His feet thrust him into a net[l]
and he wanders into its
mesh.
9 A trap seizes him by the heel;
a snare holds him fast.
10 A noose is hidden for him on
the ground;
a trap lies in his path.
11 Terrors startle him on every
side[m]
and dog[n] his every step.
12 Calamity is hungry[o] for him;
disaster is ready for him
when he falls.
13 It eats away parts of his skin;
death's firstborn devours his
limbs.[p]
14 He is torn from the security of
his tent[q]
and marched off to the king
of terrors.
15 Fire resides[e] in his tent;
burning sulfur[r] is scattered
over his dwelling.
16 His roots dry up below[s]
and his branches wither
above.[t]
17 The memory of him perishes
from the earth;
he has no name in the
land.[u]
18 He is driven from light into
darkness[v]
and is banished from the
world.
19 He has no offspring[w] or
descendants[x] among his
people,
no survivor where once he
lived.[y]
20 Men of the west are appalled at
his fate;[z]
men of the east are seized
with horror.
21 Surely such is the dwelling[a] of
an evil man;
such is the place of one who
knows not God."[b]

Job

19 Then Job replied:

2 "How long will you
torment me
and crush me with words?
3 Ten times now you have
reproached me;
shamelessly you attack me.
4 If it is true that I have gone
astray,
my error[c] remains my
concern alone.
5 If indeed you would exalt
yourselves above me[d]

17:13 [a] Job 3:13
17:14 [b] Job 13:28; 30:28,30; Ps 16:10 [c] Job 21:26
17:15 [d] Job 7:6
17:16 [e] Job 3:17-19; Jnh 2:6
18:3 [f] Ps 73:22
18:4 [g] Job 13:14
18:5 [h] Job 21:17; Pr 13:9; 20:20; 24:20
18:7 [i] Pr 4:12 [j] Job 5:13 [k] Job 15:6
18:8 [l] Job 22:10; Ps 9:15; 35:7
18:11 [m] Job 15:21; Jer 6:25; 20:3 [n] Job 20:8
18:12 [o] Isa 8:21
18:13 [p] Zec 14:12
18:14 [q] Job 8:22
18:15 [r] Ps 11:6
18:16 [s] Isa 5:24; Hos 9:1-16; Am 2:9 [t] Job 15:30; Mal 4:1
18:17 [u] Ps 34:16; Pr 2:22; 10:7
18:18 [v] Job 5:14
18:19 [w] Jer 22:30 [x] Isa 14:22 [y] Job 27:14-15
18:20 [z] Ps 37:13; Jer 50:27,31
18:21 [a] Job 21:28 [b] Jer 9:3; 1Th 4:5
19:4 [c] Job 6:24
19:5 [d] Ps 35:26; 38:16; 55:12

[d] *13,16* Hebrew *Sheol* [e] *15* Or *Nothing he had remains*

and use my humiliation
against me,
6then know that God has
wronged me[a]
and drawn his net[b] around
me.

7"Though I cry, 'I've been
wronged!' I get no
response;[c]
though I call for help, there
is no justice.[d]
8He has blocked my way so I
cannot pass;[e]
he has shrouded my paths in
darkness.[f]
9He has stripped[g] me of my
honor
and removed the crown from
my head.[h]
10He tears me down[i] on every
side till I am gone;
he uproots my hope[j] like a
tree.[k]
11His anger[l] burns against me;
he counts me among his
enemies.[m]
12His troops advance in force;[n]
they build a siege ramp[o]
against me
and encamp around my
tent.

13"He has alienated my
brothers[p] from me;
my acquaintances are
completely estranged
from me.[q]
14My kinsmen have gone away;
my friends have forgotten
me.
15My guests and my maidservants
count me a stranger;
they look upon me as an
alien.
16I summon my servant, but he
does not answer,
though I beg him with my
own mouth.
17My breath is offensive to my
wife;
I am loathsome to my own
brothers.
18Even the little boys[r] scorn me;
when I appear, they ridicule
me.
19All my intimate friends[s] detest
me;[t]
those I love have turned
against me.
20I am nothing but skin and
bones;[u]
I have escaped with only
the skin of my
teeth.[f]

21"Have pity on me, my friends,
have pity,
for the hand of God has
struck me.
22Why do you pursue[v] me as
God does?
Will you never get enough
of my flesh?[w]

23"Oh, that my words were
recorded,
that they were written on
a scroll,[x]
24that they were inscribed with
an iron tool on[g]
lead,
or engraved in rock forever!
25I know that my Redeemer[h][y]
lives,[z]
and that in the end he will
stand upon the earth.[i]
26And after my skin has been
destroyed,
yet[j] in[k] my flesh I will see
God;[a]
27I myself will see him
with my own eyes—I, and
not another.
How my heart yearns[b] within
me!

28"If you say, 'How we will hound
him,
since the root of the trouble
lies in him,[l]'
29you should fear the sword
yourselves;
for wrath will bring
punishment by the
sword,[c]
and then you will know that
there is judgment.[m]"[d]

19:6 [a]Job 27:2 [b]Job 18:8
19:7 [c]Job 30:20 [d]Job 9:24; Hab 1:2-4
19:8 [e]Job 3:23; La 3:7 [f]Job 30:26
19:9 [g]Job 12:17 [h]Ps 89:39,44; La 5:16
19:10 [i]Job 12:14 [j]Job 7:6 [k]Job 24:20
19:11 [l]Job 16:9 [m]Job 13:24
19:12 [n]Job 16:13 [o]Job 30:12
19:13 [p]Ps 69:8 [q]Job 16:7; Ps 88:8
19:18 [r]2Ki 2:23
19:19 [s]Ps 55:12-13 [t]Ps 38:11
19:20 [u]Job 33:21; Ps 102:5
19:22 [v]Job 13:25; 16:11 [w]Ps 69:26
19:23 [x]Isa 30:8
19:25 [y]Ps 78:35; Pr 23:11; Isa 43:14; Jer 50:34 [z]Job 16:19
19:26 [a]Ps 17:15; Mt 5:8; 1Co 13:12; 1Jn 3:2
19:27 [b]Ps 73:26
19:29 [c]Job 15:22 [d]Job 22:4; Ps 1:5; 9:7

[f]20 Or *only my gums* [g]24 Or *and* [h]25 Or *defender* [i]25 Or *upon my grave* [j]26 Or *And after I awake, / though this [body] has been destroyed, / then* [k]26 Or */ apart from* [l]28 Many Hebrew manuscripts, Septuagint and Vulgate; most Hebrew manuscripts *me* [m]29 Or */ that you may come to know the Almighty*

Zophar

20 Then Zophar the Naamathite replied:

2"My troubled thoughts prompt me to answer
because I am greatly disturbed.
3I hear a rebuke[a] that dishonors me,
and my understanding inspires me to reply.

4"Surely you know how it has been from of old,
ever since man[n] was placed on the earth,
5that the mirth of the wicked is brief,
the joy of the godless lasts but a moment.[b]
6Though his pride reaches to the heavens
and his head touches the clouds,[c]
7he will perish forever,[d] like his own dung;
those who have seen him will say, 'Where is he?'[e]
8Like a dream[f] he flies away,[g] no more to be found,
banished[h] like a vision of the night.[i]
9The eye that saw him will not see him again;
his place will look on him no more.[j]
10His children[k] must make amends to the poor;
his own hands must give back his wealth.[l]
11The youthful vigor[m] that fills his bones
will lie with him in the dust.[n]

12"Though evil is sweet in his mouth
and he hides it under his tongue,
13though he cannot bear to let it go
and keeps it in his mouth,[o]
14yet his food will turn sour in his stomach;
it will become the venom of serpents within him.
15He will spit out the riches he swallowed;
God will make his stomach vomit them up.
16He will suck the poison[p] of serpents;
the fangs of an adder will kill him.[q]
17He will not enjoy the streams,
the rivers flowing with honey[r] and cream.[s]
18What he toiled for he must give back uneaten;
he will not enjoy the profit from his trading.
19For he has oppressed the poor and left them destitute;[t]
he has seized houses he did not build.

20"Surely he will have no respite from his craving;[u]
he cannot save himself by his treasure.
21Nothing is left for him to devour;
his prosperity will not endure.[v]
22In the midst of his plenty, distress will overtake him;
the full force of misery will come upon him.
23When he has filled his belly,
God will vent his burning anger against him
and rain down his blows upon him.[w]
24Though he flees[x] from an iron weapon,
a bronze-tipped arrow pierces him.
25He pulls it out of his back,
the gleaming point out of his liver.
Terrors[y] will come over him;[z]
26 total darkness[a] lies in wait for his treasures.
A fire unfanned will consume him[b]
and devour what is left in his tent.
27The heavens will expose his guilt;

20:3 [a]Job 19:3
20:5 [b]Job 8:12; Ps 37:35-36; 73:19
20:6 [c]Isa 14:13-14; Ob 1:3-4
20:7 [d]Job 4:20 [e]Job 7:10; 8:18
20:8 [f]Ps 73:20 [g]Job 27:21-23 [h]Job 18:18 [i]Ps 90:5
20:9 [j]Job 7:8
20:10 [k]Job 5:4 [l]Job 27:16-17
20:11 [m]Job 13:26 [n]Job 21:26
20:13 [o]Nu 11:18-20
20:16 [p]Dt 32:32 [q]Dt 32:24
20:17 [r]Dt 32:13 [s]Job 29:6
20:19 [t]Job 24:4,14; 35:9
20:20 [u]Ecc 5:12-14
20:21 [v]Job 15:29
20:23 [w]Ps 78:30-31
20:24 [x]Isa 24:18; Am 5:19
20:25 [y]Job 18:11 [z]Job 16:13
20:26 [a]Job 18:18 [b]Ps 21:9

n4 Or *Adam*

the earth will rise up against him.[a]

28A flood will carry off his house,[b]
rushing waters[o] on the day of God's wrath.[c]

29Such is the fate God allots the wicked,
the heritage appointed for them by God."[d]

Job

21 Then Job replied:

2"Listen carefully to my words;
let this be the consolation you give me.

3Bear with me while I speak,
and after I have spoken, mock on.[e]

4"Is my complaint directed to man?
Why should I not be impatient?[f]

5Look at me and be astonished;
clap your hand over your mouth.[g]

6When I think about this, I am terrified;
trembling seizes my body.

7Why do the wicked live on,
growing old and increasing in power?[h]

8They see their children established around them,
their offspring before their eyes.[i]

9Their homes are safe and free from fear;[j]
the rod of God is not upon them.

10Their bulls never fail to breed;
their cows calve and do not miscarry.[k]

11They send forth their children as a flock;
their little ones dance about.

12They sing to the music of tambourine and harp;
they make merry to the sound of the flute.[l]

13They spend their years in prosperity[m]
and go down to the grave[p] in peace.[q]

20:27 [a]Dt 31:28
20:28 [b]Dt 28:31 [c]Job 21:17, 20,30
20:29 [d]Job 27:13
21:3 [e]Job 16:10
21:4 [f]Job 6:11
21:5 [g]Jdg 18:19; Job 29:9; 40:4
21:7 [h]Job 12:6; Ps 73:3; Jer 12:1; Hab 1:13
21:8 [i]Ps 17:14
21:9 [j]Ps 73:5
21:10 [k]Ex 23:26
21:12 [l]Ps 81:2
21:13 [m]Job 36:11
21:14 [n]Job 22:17 [o]Pr 1:29
21:15 [p]Ex 5:2; Job 34:9; Mal 3:14
21:17 [q]Job 18:5
21:18 [r]Job 13:25; Ps 1:4
21:19 [s]Ex 20:5; Jer 31:29; Eze 18:2
21:20 [t]Ps 75:8; Isa 51:17 [u]Jer 25:15; Rev 14:10
21:21 [v]Job 14:5
21:22 [w]Job 35:11; 36:22; Isa 40:13-14; Ro 11:34 [x]Ps 82:1
21:24 [y]Pr 3:8

14Yet they say to God, 'Leave us alone![n]
We have no desire to know your ways.[o]

15Who is the Almighty, that we should serve him?
What would we gain by praying to him?'[p]

16But their prosperity is not in their own hands,
so I stand aloof from the counsel of the wicked.

17"Yet how often is the lamp of the wicked snuffed out?[q]
How often does calamity come upon them,
the fate God allots in his anger?

18How often are they like straw before the wind,
like chaff[r] swept away by a gale?

19⌊It is said,⌋ 'God stores up a man's punishment for his sons.'[s]
Let him repay the man himself, so that he will know it!

20Let his own eyes see his destruction;
let him drink[t] of the wrath of the Almighty.[r][u]

21For what does he care about the family he leaves behind
when his allotted months[v] come to an end?

22"Can anyone teach knowledge to God,[w]
since he judges even the highest?[x]

23One man dies in full vigor,
completely secure and at ease,

24his body[s] well nourished,
his bones rich with marrow.[y]

25Another man dies in bitterness of soul,

[o]28 Or *The possessions in his house will be carried off, / washed away* [p]13 Hebrew *Sheol* [q]13 Or *in an instant*
[r]17-20 Verses 17 and 18 may be taken as exclamations and 19 and 20 as declarations.
[s]24 The meaning of the Hebrew for this word is uncertain.

never having enjoyed
anything good.
26Side by side they lie in the
dust,
and worms cover them
both.[a]

27"I know full well what you are
thinking,
the schemes by which you
would wrong me.
28You say, 'Where now is the
great man's[b] house,
the tents where wicked men
lived?'[c]
29Have you never questioned
those who travel?
Have you paid no regard to
their accounts—
30that the evil man is spared
from the day of
calamity,[d]
that he is delivered from[t]
the day of wrath?[e]
31Who denounces his conduct to
his face?
Who repays him for what he
has done?
32He is carried to the grave,
and watch is kept over his
tomb.
33The soil in the valley is sweet
to him;[f]
all men follow after him,
and a countless throng goes[u]
before him.[g]

34"So how can you console me[h]
with your nonsense?
Nothing is left of your
answers but falsehood!"

Eliphaz

22 Then Eliphaz the Temanite
replied:

2"Can a man be of benefit to
God?[i]
Can even a wise man benefit
him?
3What pleasure would it give the
Almighty if you were
righteous?
What would he gain if your
ways were blameless?

4"Is it for your piety that he
rebukes you
and brings charges against
you?[j]
5Is not your wickedness great?
Are not your sins[k] endless?
6You demanded security[l] from
your brothers for no
reason;
you stripped men of their
clothing, leaving them
naked.
7You gave no water to the weary
and you withheld food from
the hungry,[m]
8though you were a powerful
man, owning land—
an honored man,[n] living on
it.
9And you sent widows away
empty-handed[o]
and broke the strength of the
fatherless.
10That is why snares are all
around you,
why sudden peril terrifies
you,
11why it is so dark[p] you cannot
see,
and why a flood of water
covers you.[q]

12"Is not God in the heights of
heaven?[r]
And see how lofty are the
highest stars!
13Yet you say, 'What does God
know?[s]
Does he judge through such
darkness?[t]
14Thick clouds[u] veil him, so he
does not see us
as he goes about in the
vaulted heavens.'
15Will you keep to the old
path
that evil men have trod?
16They were carried off before
their time,[v]
their foundations washed
away by a flood.[w]
17They said to God, 'Leave us
alone!
What can the Almighty do to
us?'[x]

21:26 [a]Job 24:20; Ecc 9:2-3; Isa 14:11
21:28 [b]Job 1:3; 12:21; 31:37 [c]Job 8:22
21:30 [d]Pr 16:4 [e]Job 20:22, 28; 2Pe 2:9
21:33 [f]Job 3:22; 17:16; 24:24 [g]Job 3:19
21:34 [h]Job 16:2
22:2 [i]Lk 17:10
22:4 [j]Job 14:3; 19:29; Ps 143:2
22:5 [k]Job 11:6; 15:5
22:6 [l]Ex 22:26; Dt 24:6,17; Eze 18:12,16
22:7 [m]Job 31:17, 21,31
22:8 [n]Isa 3:3; 9:15
22:9 [o]Job 24:3,21
22:11 [p]Job 5:14 [q]Ps 69:1-2; 124:4-5; La 3:54
22:12 [r]Job 11:8
22:13 [s]Ps 10:11; Isa 29:15 [t]Eze 8:12
22:14 [u]Job 26:9
22:16 [v]Job 15:32 [w]Job 14:19; Mt 7:26-27
22:17 [x]Job 21:15

[t]30 Or *man is reserved for the day of calamity, / that he is brought forth to* [u]33 Or */ as a countless throng went*

18Yet it was he who filled their
houses with good
things,[a]
so I stand aloof from the
counsel of the wicked.[b]
19"The righteous see their ruin
and rejoice;[c]
the innocent mock[d] them,
saying,
20'Surely our foes are destroyed,
and fire[e] devours their
wealth.'
21"Submit to God and be at
peace with him;
in this way prosperity will
come to you.[f]
22Accept instruction from his
mouth
and lay up his words in your
heart.
23If you return[g] to the Almighty,
you will be restored:[h]
If you remove wickedness far
from your tent[i]
24and assign your nuggets to the
dust,
your gold of Ophir to the
rocks in the ravines,[j]
25then the Almighty will be your
gold,
the choicest silver for you.[k]
26Surely then you will find
delight in the Almighty[l]
and will lift up your face to
God.
27You will pray to him,[m] and he
will hear you,
and you will fulfill your vows.
28What you decide on will be
done,
and light will shine on your
ways.
29When men are brought low and
you say, 'Lift them up!'
then he will save the
downcast.[n]
30He will deliver even one who is
not innocent,
who will be delivered through
the cleanness of your
hands."[o]

Job

23 Then Job replied:
2"Even today my
complaint[p] is bitter;[q]
his hand[v] is heavy in spite
of[w] my groaning.
3If only I knew where to find
him;
if only I could go to his
dwelling!
4I would state my case[r] before
him
and fill my mouth with
arguments.
5I would find out what he would
answer me,
and consider what he would
say.
6Would he oppose me with great
power?[s]
No, he would not press
charges against me.
7There an upright man could
present his case before
him,[t]
and I would be delivered
forever from my judge.

8"But if I go to the east, he is
not there;
if I go to the west, I do not
find him.
9When he is at work in the
north, I do not see him;
when he turns to the south, I
catch no glimpse of
him.[u]
10But he knows the way that I
take;
when he has tested me,[v] I
will come forth as gold.[w]
11My feet have closely followed
his steps;[x]
I have kept to his way
without turning aside.[y]
12I have not departed from the
commands of his lips;[z]
I have treasured the words of
his mouth more than my
daily bread.[a]

13"But he stands alone, and who
can oppose him?
He does whatever he
pleases.[b]
14He carries out his decree
against me,
and many such plans he still
has in store.[c]

22:18 [a]Job 12:6 [b]Job 21:16
22:19 [c]Ps 58:10; 107:42 [d]Ps 52:6
22:20 [e]Job 15:30
22:21 [f]Ps 34:8-10
22:23 [g]Job 8:5; Isa 31:6; Zec 1:3 [h]Isa 19:22; Ac 20:32 [i]Job 11:14
22:24 [j]Job 31:25
22:25 [k]Isa 33:6
22:26 [l]Job 27:10; Isa 58:14
22:27 [m]Job 33:26; 34:28; Isa 58:9
22:29 [n]Mt 23:12; 1Pe 5:5
22:30 [o]Job 42:7-8
23:2 [p]Job 7:11 [q]Job 6:3
23:4 [r]Job 13:18
23:6 [s]Job 9:4
23:7 [t]Job 13:3
23:9 [u]Job 9:11
23:10 [v]Ps 66:10; 139:1-3 [w]1Pe 1:7
23:11 [x]Ps 17:5 [y]Ps 44:18
23:12 [z]Job 6:10 [a]Jn 4:32,34
23:13 [b]Ps 115:3
23:14 [c]1Th 3:3

[v]2 Septuagint and Syriac; Hebrew / *the hand on me* [w]2 Or *heavy on me in*

15 That is why I am terrified before him;
when I think of all this, I fear him.
16 God has made my heart faint;[a]
the Almighty[b] has terrified me.
17 Yet I am not silenced by the darkness,[c]
by the thick darkness that covers my face.

24

"Why does the Almighty not set times for judgment?[d]
Why must those who know him look in vain for such days?[e]
2 Men move boundary stones;[f]
they pasture flocks they have stolen.
3 They drive away the orphan's donkey
and take the widow's ox in pledge.[g]
4 They thrust the needy from the path
and force all the poor[h] of the land into hiding.[i]
5 Like wild donkeys in the desert,
the poor go about their labor[j] of foraging food;
the wasteland provides food for their children.
6 They gather fodder in the fields
and glean in the vineyards of the wicked.
7 Lacking clothes, they spend the night naked;
they have nothing to cover themselves in the cold.[k]
8 They are drenched by mountain rains
and hug[l] the rocks for lack of shelter.
9 The fatherless[m] child is snatched from the breast;
the infant of the poor is seized for a debt.
10 Lacking clothes, they go about naked;
they carry the sheaves, but still go hungry.
11 They crush olives among the terraces[x];
they tread the winepresses, yet suffer thirst.
12 The groans of the dying rise from the city,
and the souls of the wounded cry out for help.[n]
But God charges no one with wrongdoing.[o]

13 "There are those who rebel against the light,[p]
who do not know its ways
or stay in its paths.[q]
14 When daylight is gone, the murderer rises up
and kills the poor and needy;
in the night he steals forth like a thief.[r]
15 The eye of the adulterer watches for dusk;[s]
he thinks, 'No eye will see me,'[t]
and he keeps his face concealed.
16 In the dark, men break into houses,[u]
but by day they shut themselves in;
they want nothing to do with the light.[v]
17 For all of them, deep darkness is their morning[y];
they make friends with the terrors of darkness.[z]

18 "Yet they are foam[w] on the surface of the water;[x]
their portion of the land is cursed,
so that no one goes to the vineyards.
19 As heat and drought snatch away the melted snow,[y]
so the grave[a][z] snatches away those who have sinned.
20 The womb forgets them,
the worm feasts on them;
evil men are no longer remembered[a]
but are broken like a tree.[b]
21 They prey on the barren and childless woman,

23:16 [a] Dt 20:3; Ps 22:14; Jer 51:46 [b] Job 27:2
23:17 [c] Job 19:8
24:1 [d] Jer 46:10 [e] Ac 1:7
24:2 [f] Dt 19:14; 27:17; Pr 23:10
24:3 [g] Dt 24:6,10, 12,17; Job 22:6
24:4 [h] Job 29:12; 30:25; Ps 41:1 [i] Pr 28:28
24:5 [j] Ps 104:23
24:7 [k] Ex 22:27; Job 22:6
24:8 [l] La 4:5
24:9 [m] Dt 24:17
24:12 [n] Eze 26:15 [o] Job 9:23
24:13 [p] Jn 3:19-20 [q] Isa 5:20
24:14 [r] Ps 10:9
24:15 [s] Pr 7:8-9 [t] Ps 10:11
24:16 [u] Ex 22:2; Mt 6:19 [v] Jn 3:20
24:18 [w] Job 9:26 [x] Job 22:16
24:19 [y] Job 6:17 [z] Job 21:13
24:20 [a] Job 18:17; Pr 10:7 [b] Ps 31:12; Da 4:14

[x] 11 Or *olives between the millstones*; the meaning of the Hebrew for this word is uncertain. [y] 17 Or *them, their morning is like the shadow of death* [z] 17 Or *of the shadow of death* [a] 19 Hebrew *Sheol*

and to the widow show no kindness.[a]
22But God drags away the mighty by his power;
though they become established, they have no assurance of life.[b]
23He may let them rest in a feeling of security,[c]
but his eyes are on their ways.[d]
24For a little while they are exalted, and then they are gone;[e]
they are brought low and gathered up like all others;
they are cut off like heads of grain.[f]
25"If this is not so, who can prove me false
and reduce my words to nothing?"[g]

Bildad

25 Then Bildad the Shuhite replied:

2"Dominion and awe belong to God;[h]
he establishes order in the heights of heaven.
3Can his forces be numbered?
Upon whom does his light not rise?[i]
4How then can a man be righteous before God?
How can one born of woman be pure?[j]
5If even the moon[k] is not bright
and the stars are not pure in his eyes,[l]
6how much less man, who is but a maggot—
a son of man,[m] who is only a worm!"[n]

Job

26 Then Job replied:

2"How you have helped the powerless![o]
How you have saved the arm that is feeble![p]
3What advice you have offered to one without wisdom!
And what great insight you have displayed!
4Who has helped you utter these words?
And whose spirit spoke from your mouth?

5"The dead are in deep anguish,[q]
those beneath the waters and all that live in them.
6Death[b][r] is naked before God;
Destruction[c] lies uncovered.[s]
7He spreads out the northern ⌞skies⌟[t] over empty space;
he suspends the earth over nothing.
8He wraps up the waters[u] in his clouds,[v]
yet the clouds do not burst under their weight.
9He covers the face of the full moon,
spreading his clouds[w] over it.
10He marks out the horizon on the face of the waters[x]
for a boundary between light and darkness.[y]
11The pillars of the heavens quake,
aghast at his rebuke.
12By his power he churned up the sea;[z]
by his wisdom[a] he cut Rahab to pieces.
13By his breath the skies became fair;
his hand pierced the gliding serpent.[b]
14And these are but the outer fringe of his works;
how faint the whisper we hear of him!
Who then can understand the thunder of his power?"[c]

27 And Job continued his discourse:[d]

2"As surely as God lives, who has denied me justice,[e]
the Almighty, who has made me taste bitterness of soul,[f]
3as long as I have life within me,

24:21 [a]Job 22:9
24:22 [b]Dt 28:66
24:23 [c]Job 12:6 [d]Job 11:11
24:24 [e]Job 14:21; Ps 37:10 [f]Isa 17:5
24:25 [g]Job 6:28; 27:4
25:2 [h]Job 9:4; Rev 1:6
25:3 [i]Jas 1:17
25:4 [j]Job 4:17; 14:4
25:5 [k]Job 31:26 [l]Job 15:15
25:6 [m]Job 7:17 [n]Ps 22:6
26:2 [o]Job 6:12 [p]Ps 71:9
26:5 [q]Ps 88:10
26:6 [r]Ps 139:8 [s]Job 41:11; Pr 15:11; Heb 4:13
26:7 [t]Job 9:8
26:8 [u]Pr 30:4 [v]Job 37:11
26:9 [w]Job 22:14; Ps 97:2
26:10 [x]Pr 8:27,29 [y]Job 38:8-11
26:12 [z]Ex 14:21; Isa 51:15; Jer 31:35 [a]Job 12:13
26:13 [b]Isa 27:1
26:14 [c]Job 36:29
27:1 [d]Job 29:1
27:2 [e]Job 34:5 [f]Job 9:18

b6 Hebrew *Sheol* c6 Hebrew *Abaddon*

the breath of God[a] in my
nostrils,
4my lips will not speak
wickedness,
and my tongue will utter no
deceit.[b]
5I will never admit you are in
the right;
till I die, I will not deny my
integrity.[c]
6I will maintain my
righteousness and never
let go of it;
my conscience will not
reproach me as long as I
live.[d]

7"May my enemies be like the
wicked,
my adversaries like the
unjust!
8For what hope has the
godless[e] when he is cut
off,
when God takes away his
life?[f]
9Does God listen to his cry
when distress comes upon
him?[g]
10Will he find delight in the
Almighty?[h]
Will he call upon God at all
times?

11"I will teach you about the
power of God;
the ways of the Almighty I
will not conceal.
12You have all seen this
yourselves.
Why then this meaningless
talk?

13"Here is the fate God allots to
the wicked,
the heritage a ruthless man
receives from the
Almighty:[i]
14However many his children,
their fate is the sword;[j]
his offspring will never have
enough to eat.[k]
15The plague will bury those who
survive him,
and their widows will not
weep for them.[l]
16Though he heaps up silver like
dust
and clothes like piles of
clay,[m]
17what he lays up the righteous
will wear,[n]
and the innocent will divide
his silver.
18The house he builds is like a
moth's cocoon,[o]
like a hut[p] made by a
watchman.
19He lies down wealthy, but
will do so no
more;[q]
when he opens his eyes, all
is gone.
20Terrors overtake him like a
flood;[r]
a tempest snatches him away
in the night.[s]
21The east wind carries him off,
and he is gone;
it sweeps him out of his
place.[t]
22It hurls itself against him
without mercy[u]
as he flees headlong from its
power.[v]
23It claps its hands in derision
and hisses him out of his
place.[w]

28 "There is a mine for silver
and a place where gold is
refined.
2Iron is taken from the earth,
and copper is smelted from
ore.[x]
3Man puts an end to the
darkness;[y]
he searches the farthest
recesses
for ore in the blackest
darkness.
4Far from where people dwell
he cuts a shaft,
in places forgotten by the
foot of man;
far from men he dangles
and sways.
5The earth, from which food
comes,[z]
is transformed below as
by fire;
6sapphires[d] come from its
rocks,

27:3 [a]Job 32:8; 33:4
27:4 [b]Job 6:28
27:5 [c]Job 2:9; 13:15
27:6 [d]Job 2:3
27:8 [e]Job 8:13 [f]Job 11:20; Lk 12:20
27:9 [g]Job 35:12; Pr 1:28; Isa 1:15; Jer 14:12; Mic 3:4
27:10 [h]Job 22:26
27:13 [i]Job 15:20; 20:29
27:14 [j]Dt 28:41; Job 15:22; Hos 9:13 [k]Job 20:10
27:15 [l]Ps 78:64
27:16 [m]Zec 9:3
27:17 [n]Pr 28:8; Ecc 2:26
27:18 [o]Job 8:14 [p]Isa 1:8
27:19 [q]Job 7:8
27:20 [r]Job 15:21 [s]Job 20:8
27:21 [t]Job 7:10; 21:18
27:22 [u]Jer 13:14; Eze 5:11; 24:14 [v]Job 11:20
27:23 [w]Job 18:18
28:2 [x]Dt 8:9
28:3 [y]Ecc 1:13
28:5 [z]Ps 104:14

[d]6 Or *lapis lazuli*; also in verse 16

and its dust contains nuggets
of gold.
7No bird of prey knows that
hidden path,
no falcon's eye has seen it.
8Proud beasts do not set foot
on it,
and no lion prowls there.
9Man's hand assaults the flinty
rock
and lays bare the roots of
the mountains.
10He tunnels through the rock;
his eyes see all its treasures.
11He searches[e] the sources of
the rivers
and brings hidden things
to light.

12"But where can wisdom be
found?[a]
Where does understanding
dwell?
13Man does not comprehend its
worth;[b]
it cannot be found in the
land of the living.
14The deep says, 'It is not in
me';
the sea says, 'It is not
with me.'
15It cannot be bought with the
finest gold,
nor can its price be weighed
in silver.[c]
16It cannot be bought with the
gold of Ophir,
with precious onyx or
sapphires.
17Neither gold nor crystal can
compare with it,
nor can it be had for jewels
of gold.[d]
18Coral and jasper are not worthy
of mention;
the price of wisdom is
beyond rubies.[e]
19The topaz of Cush cannot
compare with it;
it cannot be bought with
pure gold.[f]

20"Where then does wisdom
come from?
Where does understanding
dwell?[g]
21It is hidden from the eyes of
every living thing,

28:12 [a]Ecc 7:24
28:13 [b]Pr 3:15; Mt 13:44-46
28:15 [c]Pr 3:13-14; 8:10-11; 16:16
28:17 [d]Pr 16:16
28:18 [e]Pr 3:15
28:19 [f]Pr 8:19
28:20 [g]ver 23,28
28:22 [h]Job 26:6
28:23 [i]Pr 8:22-31
28:24 [j]Ps 33:13-14 [k]Pr 15:3
28:25 [l]Job 12:15; Ps 135:7
28:26 [m]Job 37:3,8, 11; 38:25,27
28:28 [n]Dt 4:6; Ps 111:10; Pr 1:7; 9:10
29:1 [o]Job 13:12; 27:1
29:2 [p]Jer 31:28
29:3 [q]Job 11:17
29:4 [r]Ps 25:14; Pr 3:32
29:6 [s]Job 20:17 [t]Ps 81:16 [u]Dt 32:13
29:7 [v]Job 31:21

concealed even from the
birds of the air.
22Destruction[f][h] and Death say,
'Only a rumor of it has
reached our ears.'
23God understands the way to it
and he alone knows where it
dwells,[i]
24for he views the ends of the
earth[j]
and sees everything under
the heavens.[k]
25When he established the force
of the wind
and measured out the
waters,[l]
26when he made a decree for the
rain
and a path for the
thunderstorm,[m]
27then he looked at wisdom and
appraised it;
he confirmed it and tested it.
28And he said to man,
'The fear of the Lord—that is
wisdom,
and to shun evil is
understanding.[n]' "

29 Job continued his discourse:[o]

2"How I long for the months
gone by,
for the days when God
watched over me,[p]
3when his lamp shone upon my
head
and by his light I walked
through darkness![q]
4Oh, for the days when I was in
my prime,
when God's intimate
friendship blessed my
house,[r]
5when the Almighty was still
with me
and my children were around
me,
6when my path was drenched
with cream[s]
and the rock[t] poured out for
me streams of olive oil.[u]

7"When I went to the gate[v] of
the city

[e]*11* Septuagint, Aquila and Vulgate; Hebrew *He dams up* [f]*22* Hebrew *Abaddon*

and took my seat in the public square,
[8]the young men saw me and stepped aside
and the old men rose to their feet;
[9]the chief men refrained from speaking
and covered their mouths with their hands;[a]
[10]the voices of the nobles were hushed,
and their tongues stuck to the roof of their mouths.[b]
[11]Whoever heard me spoke well of me,
and those who saw me commended me,
[12]because I rescued the poor[c] who cried for help,
and the fatherless[d] who had none to assist him.[e]
[13]The man who was dying blessed me;[f]
I made the widow's[g] heart sing.
[14]I put on righteousness[h] as my clothing;
justice was my robe and my turban.
[15]I was eyes[i] to the blind
and feet to the lame.
[16]I was a father to the needy;[j]
I took up the case of the stranger.
[17]I broke the fangs of the wicked
and snatched the victims from their teeth.[k]

[18]"I thought, 'I will die in my own house,
my days as numerous as the grains of sand.[l]
[19]My roots will reach to the water,[m]
and the dew will lie all night on my branches.
[20]My glory will remain fresh in me,
the bow[n] ever new in my hand.'[o]

[21]"Men listened to me expectantly,
waiting in silence for my counsel.
[22]After I had spoken, they spoke no more;
my words fell gently on their ears.[p]
[23]They waited for me as for showers
and drank in my words as the spring rain.
[24]When I smiled at them, they scarcely believed it;
the light of my face was precious to them.[g]
[25]I chose the way for them and sat as their chief;
I dwelt as a king[q] among his troops;
I was like one who comforts mourners.[r]

30 "But now they mock me,[s] men younger than I,
whose fathers I would have disdained
to put with my sheep dogs.
[2]Of what use was the strength of their hands to me,
since their vigor had gone from them?
[3]Haggard from want and hunger,
they roamed[h] the parched land
in desolate wastelands at night.
[4]In the brush they gathered salt herbs,
and their food[i] was the root of the broom tree.
[5]They were banished from their fellow men,
shouted at as if they were thieves.
[6]They were forced to live in the dry stream beds,
among the rocks and in holes in the ground.
[7]They brayed among the bushes
and huddled in the undergrowth.
[8]A base and nameless brood,
they were driven out of the land.

[9]"And now their sons mock me[t] in song;[u]

29:9 [a]Job 21:5
29:10 [b]Ps 137:6
29:12 [c]Job 24:4 [d]Job 31:17,21 [e]Ps 72:12; Pr 21:13
29:13 [f]Job 31:20 [g]Job 22:9
29:14 [h]Job 27:6; Ps 132:9; Isa 59:17; 61:10; Eph 6:14
29:15 [i]Nu 10:31
29:16 [j]Job 24:4; Pr 29:7
29:17 [k]Ps 3:7
29:18 [l]Ps 30:6
29:19 [m]Job 18:16; Jer 17:8
29:20 [n]Ps 18:34 [o]Ge 49:24
29:22 [p]Dt 32:2
29:25 [q]Job 1:3; 31:37 [r]Job 4:4
30:1 [s]Job 12:4
30:9 [t]Ps 69:11 [u]Job 12:4; La 3:14,63

g24 The meaning of the Hebrew for this clause is uncertain. h3 Or *gnawed* i4 Or *fuel*

I have become a byword[a]
among them.
10They detest me and keep their
distance;
they do not hesitate to spit
in my face.[b]
11Now that God has unstrung
my bow and afflicted
me,[c]
they throw off restraint[d] in
my presence.
12On my right the tribe[i] attacks;
they lay snares for my feet,[e]
they build their siege ramps
against me.[f]
13They break up my road;[g]
they succeed in destroying
me—
without anyone's helping
them.[k]
14They advance as through a
gaping breach;
amid the ruins they come
rolling in.
15Terrors overwhelm me;[h]
my dignity is driven away as
by the wind,
my safety vanishes like a
cloud.[i]
16"And now my life ebbs away;[j]
days of suffering grip me.
17Night pierces my bones;
my gnawing pains never rest.
18In his great power ⌊God⌋
becomes like clothing
to me[l];
he binds me like the neck
of my garment.
19He throws me into the mud,[k]
and I am reduced to dust
and ashes.
20"I cry out to you, O God, but
you do not answer;[l]
I stand up, but you merely
look at me.
21You turn on me ruthlessly;[m]
with the might of your
hand[n] you attack me.[o]
22You snatch me up and drive
me before the wind;[p]
you toss me about in the
storm.[q]
23I know you will bring me down
to death,[r]
to the place appointed for
all the living.[s]

24"Surely no one lays a hand on a
broken man
when he cries for help in his
distress.[t]
25Have I not wept for those in
trouble?
Has not my soul grieved for
the poor?[u]
26Yet when I hoped for good, evil
came;
when I looked for light, then
came darkness.[v]
27The churning inside me never
stops;[w]
days of suffering confront
me.
28I go about blackened,[x] but not
by the sun;
I stand up in the assembly
and cry for help.[y]
29I have become a brother of
jackals,[z]
a companion of owls.[a]
30My skin grows black and
peels;[b]
my body burns with fever.[c]
31My harp is tuned to
mourning,[d]
and my flute to the sound of
wailing.

31 "I made a covenant with
my eyes
not to look lustfully at a
girl.[e]
2For what is man's lot from God
above,
his heritage from the
Almighty on high?[f]
3Is it not ruin[g] for the wicked,
disaster for those who do
wrong?[h]
4Does he not see my ways[i]
and count my every step?[j]
5"If I have walked in falsehood
or my foot has hurried after
deceit[k]—
6let God weigh me in honest
scales[l]
and he will know that I am
blameless—

30:9 [a]Job 17:6
30:10 [b]Nu 12:14; Dt 25:9; Isa 50:6; Mt 26:67
30:11 [c]Ru 1:21 [d]Ps 32:9
30:12 [e]Ps 140:4-5 [f]Job 19:12
30:13 [g]Isa 3:12
30:15 [h]Job 31:23; Ps 55:4-5 [i]Job 3:25; Hos 13:3
30:16 [j]Job 3:24; Ps 22:14; 42:4
30:19 [k]Ps 69:2,14
30:20 [l]Job 19:7
30:21 [m]Job 19:6,22 [n]Job 16:9,14 [o]Job 10:3
30:22 [p]Job 27:21 [q]Job 9:17
30:23 [r]Job 9:22; 10:8 [s]Job 3:19
30:24 [t]Job 19:7
30:25 [u]Job 24:4; Ps 35:13-14; Ro 12:15
30:26 [v]Job 3:25-26; 19:8; Jer 8:15
30:27 [w]La 2:11
30:28 [x]Ps 38:6; 42:9; 43:2 [y]Job 19:7
30:29 [z]Ps 44:19 [a]Ps 102:6; Mic 1:8
30:30 [b]La 4:8 [c]Ps 102:3
30:31 [d]Isa 24:8
31:1 [e]Mt 5:28
31:2 [f]Job 20:29
31:3 [g]Job 21:30 [h]Job 34:22
31:4 [i]2Ch 16:9 [j]Pr 5:21
31:5 [k]Mic 2:11
31:6 [l]Job 6:2; 27:5-6

[i]*12* The meaning of the Hebrew for this word is uncertain. [k]*13* Or *me. / 'No one can help him,' they say,* [l]*18* Hebrew; Septuagint *⌊God⌋ grasps my clothing*

7 if my steps have turned from the path,[a]
if my heart has been led by my eyes,
or if my hands[b] have been defiled,
8 then may others eat what I have sown,[c]
and may my crops be uprooted.[d]

9 "If my heart has been enticed[e] by a woman,
or if I have lurked at my neighbor's door,
10 then may my wife grind another man's grain,
and may other men sleep with her.[f]
11 For that would have been shameful,
a sin to be judged.[g]
12 It is a fire[h] that burns to Destruction[m];[i]
it would have uprooted my harvest.[j]

13 "If I have denied justice to my menservants and maidservants
when they had a grievance against me,[k]
14 what will I do when God confronts me?
What will I answer when called to account?
15 Did not he who made me in the womb make them?
Did not the same one form us both within our mothers?[l]

16 "If I have denied the desires of the poor[m]
or let the eyes of the widow[n] grow weary,
17 if I have kept my bread to myself,
not sharing it with the fatherless[o]—
18 but from my youth I reared him as would a father,
and from my birth I guided the widow—
19 if I have seen anyone perishing for lack of clothing,[p]
or a needy[q] man without a garment,
20 and his heart did not bless me
for warming him with the fleece from my sheep,
21 if I have raised my hand against the fatherless,[r]
knowing that I had influence in court,
22 then let my arm fall from the shoulder,
let it be broken off at the joint.[s]
23 For I dreaded destruction from God,
and for fear of his splendor[t] I could not do such things.

24 "If I have put my trust in gold[u]
or said to pure gold, 'You are my security,'[v]
25 if I have rejoiced over my great wealth,[w]
the fortune my hands had gained,
26 if I have regarded the sun[x] in its radiance
or the moon moving in splendor,
27 so that my heart was secretly enticed
and my hand offered them a kiss of homage,
28 then these also would be sins to be judged,[y]
for I would have been unfaithful to God on high.

29 "If I have rejoiced at my enemy's misfortune[z]
or gloated over the trouble that came to him[a]—
30 I have not allowed my mouth to sin
by invoking a curse against his life—
31 if the men of my household have never said,
'Who has not had his fill of Job's meat?'[b]—
32 but no stranger had to spend the night in the street,
for my door was always open to the traveler[c]—
33 if I have concealed[d] my sin as men do,[n]

31:7 [a] Job 23:11 [b] Job 9:30
31:8 [c] Lev 26:16; Job 20:18 [d] Mic 6:15
31:9 [e] Job 24:15
31:10 [f] Dt 28:30; Jer 8:10
31:11 [g] Ge 38:24; Lev 20:10; Dt 22:22-24
31:12 [h] Job 15:30 [i] Job 26:6 [j] Job 20:28
31:13 [k] Dt 24:14-15
31:15 [l] Job 10:3
31:16 [m] Job 5:16; 20:19 [n] Job 22:9
31:17 [o] Job 22:7; 29:12
31:19 [p] Job 22:6 [q] Job 24:4
31:21 [r] Job 22:9
31:22 [s] Job 38:15
31:23 [t] Job 13:11
31:24 [u] Job 22:25 [v] Mt 6:24; Mk 10:24
31:25 [w] Ps 62:10
31:26 [x] Eze 8:16
31:28 [y] Dt 17:2-7
31:29 [z] Ob 1:12 [a] Pr 17:5; 24:17-18
31:31 [b] Job 22:7
31:32 [c] Ge 19:2-3; Ro 12:13
31:33 [d] Pr 28:13

[m]12 Hebrew *Abaddon* [n]33 Or *as Adam did*

by hiding[a] my guilt in my
heart
34because I so feared the crowd[b]
and so dreaded the contempt
of the clans
that I kept silent and would
not go outside
35("Oh, that I had someone to
hear me![c]
I sign now my defense—let
the Almighty answer me;
let my accuser[d] put his
indictment in writing.
36Surely I would wear it on my
shoulder,
I would put it on like a
crown.
37I would give him an account of
my every step;
like a prince[e] I would
approach him.)—
38"if my land cries out against
me[f]
and all its furrows are wet
with tears,
39if I have devoured its yield
without payment[g]
or broken the spirit of its
tenants,[h]
40then let briers[i] come up
instead of wheat
and weeds instead of barley."

The words of Job are ended.

Elihu

32 So these three men stopped
answering Job, because he
was righteous in his own eyes.[j]
2But Elihu son of Barakel the Bu-
zite,[k] of the family of Ram, became very angry with Job for justi-
fying himself rather than God.[l]
3He was also angry with the three
friends, because they had found no
way to refute Job, and yet had condemned him.[o] 4Now Elihu had
waited before speaking to
Job because they were older than
he. 5But when he saw that the
three men had nothing more to say,
his anger was aroused.
6So Elihu son of Barakel the Bu-
zite said:

"I am young in years,
and you are old;[m]
that is why I was fearful,
not daring to tell you what I
know.
7I thought, 'Age should speak;
advanced years should teach
wisdom.'
8But it is the spirit[p] in a man,
the breath of the Almighty,[n]
that gives him
understanding.[o]
9It is not only the old[q] who are
wise,[p]
not only the aged who
understand what is right.

10"Therefore I say: Listen to me;
I too will tell you what I
know.
11I waited while you spoke,
I listened to your reasoning;
while you were searching for
words,
12 I gave you my full attention.
But not one of you has proved
Job wrong;
none of you has answered his
arguments.
13Do not say, 'We have found
wisdom;[q]
let God refute him, not man.'
14But Job has not marshaled his
words against me,
and I will not answer him
with your arguments.

15"They are dismayed and have
no more to say;
words have failed them.
16Must I wait, now that they are
silent,
now that they stand there
with no reply?
17I too will have my say;
I too will tell what I know.
18For I am full of words,
and the spirit within me
compels me;
19inside I am like bottled-up
wine,
like new wineskins ready to
burst.
20I must speak and find relief;
I must open my lips and
reply.

31:33 [a]Ge 3:8
31:34 [b]Ex 23:2
31:35 [c]Job 19:7; 30:28 [d]Job 27:7; 35:14
31:37 [e]Job 1:3; 29:25
31:38 [f]Ge 4:10
31:39 [g]1Ki 21:19 [h]Lev 19:13; Jas 5:4
31:40 [i]Ge 3:18
32:1 [j]Job 10:7; 33:9
32:2 [k]Ge 22:21 [l]Job 27:5; 30:21
32:6 [m]Job 15:10
32:8 [n]Job 27:3; 33:4 [o]Pr 2:6
32:9 [p]1Co 1:26
32:13 [q]Jer 9:23

[o]3 Masoretic Text; an ancient Hebrew scribal tradition *Job, and so had condemned God*
[p]8 Or *Spirit*; also in verse 18 [q]9 Or *many*; or *great*

21I will show partiality[a] to no
one,[b]
nor will I flatter any man;
22for if I were skilled in flattery,
my Maker would soon take
me away.

33 "But now, Job, listen to
my words;
pay attention to everything I
say.[c]
2I am about to open my mouth;
my words are on the tip of
my tongue.
3My words come from an
upright heart;
my lips sincerely speak what
I know.[d]
4The Spirit of God has made
me;[e]
the breath of the Almighty[f]
gives me life.
5Answer me[g] then, if you can;
prepare[h] yourself and
confront me.
6I am just like you before God;
I too have been taken from
clay.[i]
7No fear of me should alarm
you,
nor should my hand be heavy
upon you.[j]

8"But you have said in my
hearing—
I heard the very words—
9'I am pure[k] and without sin;[l]
I am clean and free from
guilt.
10Yet God has found fault with
me;
he considers me his enemy.[m]
11He fastens my feet in
shackles;[n]
he keeps close watch on all
my paths.'[o]

12"But I tell you, in this you are
not right,
for God is greater than
man.[p]
13Why do you complain to him[q]
that he answers none of
man's words[r]?
14For God does speak[r]—now
one way, now another—
though man may not perceive
it.
15In a dream,[s] in a vision of the
night,
when deep sleep falls on
men
as they slumber in their
beds,
16he may speak[t] in their ears
and terrify them with
warnings,
17to turn man from wrongdoing
and keep him from pride,
18to preserve his soul from the
pit,[s][u]
his life from perishing by the
sword.[t][v]
19Or a man may be chastened on
a bed of pain
with constant distress in his
bones,[w]
20so that his very being finds
food[x] repulsive
and his soul loathes the
choicest meal.[y]
21His flesh wastes away to
nothing,
and his bones, once hidden,
now stick out.[z]
22His soul draws near to the pit,[u]
and his life to the
messengers of death.[v][a]

23"Yet if there is an angel on his
side
as a mediator, one out of a
thousand,
to tell a man what is right for
him,[b]
24to be gracious to him and say,
'Spare him from going down
to the pit[w];[c]
I have found a ransom for
him'—
25then his flesh is renewed like a
child's;
it is restored as in the days
of his youth.[d]
26He prays to God and finds favor
with him,[e]
he sees God's face and
shouts for joy;[f]
he is restored by God to his
righteous state.[g]

32:21 [a]Lev 19:15; Job 13:10 [b]Mt 22:16
33:1 [c]Job 13:6
33:3 [d]Job 6:28; 27:4; 36:4
33:4 [e]Ge 2:7; Job 10:3 [f]Job 27:3
33:5 [g]ver 32 [h]Job 13:18
33:6 [i]Job 4:19
33:7 [j]Job 9:34; 13:21; 2Co 2:4
33:9 [k]Job 10:7 [l]Job 13:23; 16:17
33:10 [m]Job 13:24
33:11 [n]Job 13:27 [o]Job 14:16
33:12 [p]Ecc 7:20
33:13 [q]Job 40:2; Isa 45:9
33:14 [r]Ps 62:11
33:15 [s]Job 4:13
33:16 [t]Job 36:10,15
33:18 [u]ver 22,24,28, 30 [v]Job 15:22
33:19 [w]Job 30:17
33:20 [x]Ps 107:18 [y]Job 3:24; 6:6
33:21 [z]Job 16:8; 19:20
33:22 [a]Ps 88:3
33:23 [b]Mic 6:8
33:24 [c]Isa 38:17
33:25 [d]2Ki 5:14
33:26 [e]Job 34:28 [f]Job 22:26 [g]Ps 50:15; 51:12

[r]*13* *Or that he does not answer for any of his actions* [s]*18* *Or preserve him from the grave* [t]*18* *Or from crossing the River* [u]*22* *Or He draws near to the grave* [v]*22* *Or to the dead* [w]*24* *Or grave*

27Then he comes to men and says,
'I sinned,[a] and perverted what was right,[b]
but I did not get what I deserved.[c]
28He redeemed my soul from going down to the pit,[x]
and I will live to enjoy the light.'[d]
29"God does all these things to a man[e]—
twice, even three times—
30to turn back his soul from the pit,[y]
that the light of life[f] may shine on him.
31"Pay attention, Job, and listen to me;
be silent, and I will speak.
32If you have anything to say, answer me;
speak up, for I want you to be cleared.
33But if not, then listen to me;
be silent, and I will teach you wisdom.[g]"

34

Then Elihu said:

2"Hear my words, you wise men;
listen to me, you men of learning.
3For the ear tests words
as the tongue tastes food.[h]
4Let us discern for ourselves what is right;
let us learn together what is good.[i]
5"Job says, 'I am innocent,[j]
but God denies me justice.[k]
6Although I am right,
I am considered a liar;
although I am guiltless,
his arrow inflicts an incurable wound.'[l]
7What man is like Job,
who drinks scorn like water?[m]
8He keeps company with evildoers;
he associates with wicked men.[n]
9For he says, 'It profits a man nothing
when he tries to please God.'[o]
10"So listen to me, you men of understanding.
Far be it from God to do evil,[p]
from the Almighty to do wrong.[q]
11He repays a man for what he has done;[r]
he brings upon him what his conduct deserves.[s]
12It is unthinkable that God would do wrong,
that the Almighty would pervert justice.[t]
13Who appointed him over the earth?
Who put him in charge of the whole world?[u]
14If it were his intention
and he withdrew his spirit[z] and breath,[v]
15all mankind would perish together
and man would return to the dust.[w]
16"If you have understanding, hear this;
listen to what I say.
17Can he who hates justice govern?[x]
Will you condemn the just and mighty One?[y]
18Is he not the One who says to kings, 'You are worthless,'
and to nobles, 'You are wicked,'[z]
19who shows no partiality[a] to princes
and does not favor the rich over the poor,[b]
for they are all the work of his hands?[c]
20They die in an instant, in the middle of the night;[d]
the people are shaken and they pass away;
the mighty are removed without human hand.[e]

33:27 [a] 2Sa 12:13 [b] Lk 15:21 [c] Ro 6:21
33:28 [d] Job 22:28
33:29 [e] 1Co 12:6; Eph 1:11; Php 2:13
33:30 [f] Ps 56:13
33:33 [g] Ps 34:11
34:3 [h] Job 12:11
34:4 [i] 1Th 5:21
34:5 [j] Job 33:9 [k] Job 27:2
34:6 [l] Job 6:4
34:7 [m] Job 15:16
34:8 [n] Job 22:15; Ps 50:18
34:9 [o] Job 21:15; 35:3
34:10 [p] Ge 18:25 [q] Dt 32:4; Job 8:3; Ro 9:14
34:11 [r] Ps 62:12; Mt 16:27; Ro 2:6; 2Co 5:10 [s] Jer 32:19; Eze 33:20
34:12 [t] Job 8:3
34:13 [u] Job 38:4,6
34:14 [v] Ps 104:29
34:15 [w] Ge 3:19; Job 9:22
34:17 [x] 2Sa 23:3-4 [y] Job 40:8
34:18 [z] Ex 22:28
34:19 [a] Dt 10:17; Ac 10:34 [b] Lev 19:15 [c] Job 10:3
34:20 [d] Ex 12:29 [e] Job 12:19

[x] 28 Or *redeemed me from going down to the grave* [y] 30 Or *turn him back from the grave* [z] 14 Or *Spirit*

[21]"His eyes are on the ways of
men;
he sees their every step.[a]
[22]There is no dark place,[b] no
deep shadow,[c]
where evildoers can hide.
[23]God has no need to examine
men further,
that they should come before
him for judgment.[d]
[24]Without inquiry he shatters the
mighty[e]
and sets up others in their
place.[f]
[25]Because he takes note of their
deeds,
he overthrows them in the
night and they are
crushed.
[26]He punishes them for their
wickedness
where everyone can see
them,
[27]because they turned from
following him[g]
and had no regard for any of
his ways.[h]
[28]They caused the cry of the poor
to come before him,
so that he heard the cry of
the needy.[i]
[29]But if he remains silent, who
can condemn him?
If he hides his face, who can
see him?
Yet he is over man and nation
alike,
[30] to keep a godless man from
ruling,
from laying snares for the
people.[j]

[31]"Suppose a man says to God,
'I am guilty but will offend
no more.
[32]Teach me what I cannot see;[k]
if I have done wrong, I will
not do so again.'[l]
[33]Should God then reward you on
your terms,
when you refuse to repent?[m]
You must decide, not I;
so tell me what you know.

[34]"Men of understanding declare,
wise men who hear me say to
me,
[35]'Job speaks without
knowledge;[n]
his words lack insight.'
[36]Oh, that Job might be tested
to the utmost
for answering like a wicked
man![o]
[37]To his sin he adds rebellion;
scornfully he claps his
hands[p] among us
and multiplies his words
against God."[q]

35

Then Elihu said:

[2]"Do you think this is
just?
You say, 'I will be cleared by
God.[a]'
[3]Yet you ask him, 'What profit is
it to me,[b]
and what do I gain by not
sinning?'[r]

[4]"I would like to reply to you
and to your friends with
you.
[5]Look up at the heavens[s] and
see;
gaze at the clouds so high
above you.[t]
[6]If you sin, how does that affect
him?
If your sins are many, what
does that do to him?[u]
[7]If you are righteous, what do
you give to him,[v]
or what does he receive[w]
from your hand?[x]
[8]Your wickedness affects only a
man like yourself,
and your righteousness only
the sons of men.

[9]"Men cry out[y] under a load of
oppression;
they plead for relief from the
arm of the powerful.[z]
[10]But no one says, 'Where is God
my Maker,[a]
who gives songs in the
night,[b]
[11]who teaches[c] more to us than
to[c] the beasts of the
earth

34:21 [a]Job 31:4; Pr 15:3
34:22 [b]Ps 139:12 [c]Am 9:2-3
34:23 [d]Job 11:11
34:24 [e]Job 12:19 [f]Da 2:21
34:27 [g]Ps 28:5; Isa 5:12 [h]1Sa 15:11
34:28 [i]Ex 22:23; Job 35:9; Jas 5:4
34:30 [j]Pr 29:2-12
34:32 [k]Job 35:11; Ps 25:4 [l]Job 33:27
34:33 [m]Job 41:11
34:35 [n]Job 35:16; 38:2
34:36 [o]Job 22:15
34:37 [p]Job 27:23 [q]Job 23:2
35:3 [r]Job 9:29-31; 34:9
35:5 [s]Ge 15:5 [t]Job 22:12
35:6 [u]Pr 8:36
35:7 [v]Ro 11:35 [w]Pr 9:12 [x]Job 22:2-3; Lk 17:10
35:9 [y]Ex 2:23 [z]Job 12:19
35:10 [a]Job 27:10; Isa 51:13 [b]Ps 42:8; 149:5; Ac 16:25
35:11 [c]Ps 94:12

[a]2 Or *My righteousness is more than God's*
[b]3 Or *you*
[c]11 Or *teaches us by*

and makes us wiser than[d]
the birds of the air?'
12He does not answer[a] when
men cry out
because of the arrogance of
the wicked.
13Indeed, God does not listen to
their empty plea;
the Almighty pays no
attention to it.[b]
14How much less, then, will he
listen
when you say that you do not
see him,[c]
that your case[d] is before him
and you must wait for him,
15and further, that his anger
never punishes
and he does not take the
least notice of
wickedness.[e]
16So Job opens his mouth with
empty talk;
without knowledge he
multiplies words."[e]

36

Elihu continued:

2"Bear with me a little
longer and I will show
you
that there is more to be said
in God's behalf.
3I get my knowledge from afar;
I will ascribe justice to my
Maker.[f]
4Be assured that my words are
not false;[g]
one perfect in knowledge[h] is
with you.
5"God is mighty, but does not
despise men;[i]
he is mighty, and firm in his
purpose.[j]
6He does not keep the wicked
alive[k]
but gives the afflicted their
rights.[l]
7He does not take his eyes off
the righteous;[m]
he enthrones them with
kings[n]
and exalts them forever.
8But if men are bound in
chains,[o]
held fast by cords of
affliction,
9he tells them what they have
done—
that they have sinned
arrogantly.[p]
10He makes them listen[q] to
correction
and commands them to
repent of their evil.[r]
11If they obey and serve him,[s]
they will spend the rest of
their days in prosperity
and their years in
contentment.
12But if they do not listen,
they will perish by the
sword[f][t]
and die without knowledge.[u]
13"The godless in heart[v] harbor
resentment;
even when he fetters them,
they do not cry for
help.
14They die in their youth,
among male prostitutes of
the shrines.[w]
15But those who suffer he
delivers in their
suffering;
he speaks to them in their
affliction.
16"He is wooing[x] you from the
jaws of distress
to a spacious place free from
restriction,
to the comfort of your table[y]
laden with choice food.
17But now you are laden with the
judgment due the
wicked;
judgment and justice have
taken hold of you.[z]
18Be careful that no one entices
you by riches;
do not let a large bribe turn
you aside.[a]
19Would your wealth
or even all your mighty
efforts
sustain you so you would not
be in distress?
20Do not long for the night,[b]

35:12 [a]Pr 1:28
35:13 [b]Job 27:9; Pr 15:29; Isa 1:15; Jer 11:11
35:14 [c]Job 9:11 [d]Ps 37:6
35:16 [e]Job 34:35,37
36:3 [f]Job 8:3; 37:23
36:4 [g]Job 33:3 [h]Job 37:5,16, 23
36:5 [i]Ps 22:24 [j]Job 12:13
36:6 [k]Job 8:22 [l]Job 5:15
36:7 [m]Ps 33:18 [n]Ps 113:8
36:8 [o]Ps 107:10,14
36:9 [p]Job 15:25
36:10 [q]Job 33:16 [r]2Ki 17:13
36:11 [s]Isa 1:19
36:12 [t]Job 15:22 [u]Job 4:21
36:13 [v]Ro 2:5
36:14 [w]Dt 23:17
36:16 [x]Hos 2:14 [y]Ps 23:5
36:17 [z]Job 22:11
36:18 [a]Job 34:33
36:20 [b]Job 34:20,25

[d]*11* Or *us wise by* [e]*15* Symmachus, Theodotion and Vulgate; the meaning of the Hebrew for this word is uncertain. [f]*12* Or *will cross the River*

to drag people away from their homes.[g]
21 Beware of turning to evil,[a]
which you seem to prefer to affliction.[b]

22 "God is exalted in his power.
Who is a teacher like him?[c]
23 Who has prescribed his ways for him,[d]
or said to him, 'You have done wrong'?[e]
24 Remember to extol his work,[f]
which men have praised in song.[g]
25 All mankind has seen it;
men gaze on it from afar.
26 How great is God—beyond our understanding![h]
The number of his years is past finding out.[i]

27 "He draws up the drops of water,
which distill as rain to the streams[h];[j]
28 the clouds pour down their moisture
and abundant showers fall on mankind.[k]
29 Who can understand how he spreads out the clouds,
how he thunders from his pavilion?[l]
30 See how he scatters his lightning about him,
bathing the depths of the sea.
31 This is the way he governs[i] the nations[m]
and provides food in abundance.[n]
32 He fills his hands with lightning
and commands it to strike its mark.[o]
33 His thunder announces the coming storm;
even the cattle make known its approach.[j]

37 "At this my heart pounds
and leaps from its place.
2 Listen! Listen to the roar of his voice,
to the rumbling that comes from his mouth.[p]
3 He unleashes his lightning beneath the whole heaven
and sends it to the ends of the earth.
4 After that comes the sound of his roar;
he thunders with his majestic voice.
When his voice resounds,
he holds nothing back.
5 God's voice thunders in marvelous ways;
he does great things beyond our understanding.[q]
6 He says to the snow,[r] 'Fall on the earth,'
and to the rain shower, 'Be a mighty downpour.'[s]
7 So that all men he has made may know his work,
he stops every man from his labor.[k][t]
8 The animals take cover;
they remain in their dens.[u]
9 The tempest comes out from its chamber,
the cold from the driving winds.
10 The breath of God produces ice,
and the broad waters become frozen.[v]
11 He loads the clouds with moisture;
he scatters his lightning through them.[w]
12 At his direction they swirl around
over the face of the whole earth
to do whatever he commands them.[x]
13 He brings the clouds to punish men,[y]
or to water his earth[l] and show his love.[z]

14 "Listen to this, Job;
stop and consider God's wonders.
15 Do you know how God controls the clouds

36:21 [a] Ps 66:18 [b] Heb 11:25
36:22 [c] Isa 40:13; 1Co 2:16
36:23 [d] Job 34:13 [e] Job 8:3
36:24 [f] Ps 92:5; 138:5 [g] Ps 59:16; Rev 15:3
36:26 [h] 1Co 13: 12 [i] Job 10:5; Ps 90:2; 102:24; Heb 1:12
36:27 [j] Job 38:28; Ps 147:8
36:28 [k] Job 5:10
36:29 [l] Job 26:14; 37:16
36:31 [m] Job 37:13 [n] Ps 136:25; Ac 14:17
36:32 [o] Job 37:12,15
37:2 [p] Ps 29:3-9
37:5 [q] Job 5:9
37:6 [r] Job 38:22 [s] Job 36:27
37:7 [t] Job 12:14
37:8 [u] Job 38:40; Ps 104:22
37:10 [v] Job 38:29-30; Ps 147:17
37:11 [w] Job 36:27, 29
37:12 [x] Ps 148:8
37:13 [y] 1Sa 12:17 [z] Ex 9:18; 1Ki 18:45; Job 38:27

[g] *20* The meaning of the Hebrew for verses 18-20 is uncertain. [h] *27* Or *distill from the mist as rain* [i] *31* Or *nourishes* [j] *33* Or *announces his coming— / the One zealous against evil* [k] *7* Or */ he fills all men with fear by his power* [l] *13* Or *to favor them*

and makes his lightning
flash?
16Do you know how the clouds
hang poised,
those wonders of him who is
perfect in knowledge?[a]
17You who swelter in your clothes
when the land lies hushed
under the south wind,
18can you join him in spreading
out the skies,[b]
hard as a mirror of cast
bronze?

19"Tell us what we should say to
him;
we cannot draw up our case
because of our darkness.
20Should he be told that I want
to speak?
Would any man ask to be
swallowed up?
21Now no one can look at the
sun,
bright as it is in the skies
after the wind has swept
them clean.
22Out of the north he comes in
golden splendor;
God comes in awesome
majesty.
23The Almighty is beyond our
reach and exalted in
power;[c]
in his justice[d] and great
righteousness, he does
not oppress.[e]
24Therefore, men revere him,[f]
for does he not have regard
for all the wise[g] in
heart?[m]"

The LORD *Speaks*

38 Then the LORD answered
Job out of the storm.[h] He
said:

2"Who is this that darkens my
counsel
with words without
knowledge?[i]
3Brace yourself like a man;
I will question you,
and you shall answer me.[j]

4"Where were you when I laid
the earth's foundation?[k]
Tell me, if you understand.
5Who marked off its
dimensions?[l] Surely you
know!
Who stretched a measuring
line across it?
6On what were its footings set,
or who laid its
cornerstone[m]—
7while the morning stars sang
together
and all the angels[n] shouted
for joy?

8"Who shut up the sea behind
doors[n]
when it burst forth from the
womb,[o]
9when I made the clouds its
garment
and wrapped it in thick
darkness,
10when I fixed limits for it[p]
and set its doors and bars in
place,[q]
11when I said, 'This far you may
come and no farther;
here is where your proud
waves halt'?[r]

12"Have you ever given orders to
the morning,
or shown the dawn its place,
13that it might take the earth by
the edges
and shake the wicked[s] out
of it?
14The earth takes shape like clay
under a seal;
its features stand out like
those of a garment.
15The wicked are denied their
light,[t]
and their upraised arm is
broken.[u]

16"Have you journeyed to the
springs of the sea
or walked in the recesses of
the deep?[v]
17Have the gates of death[w] been
shown to you?
Have you seen the gates of
the shadow of death[o]?
18Have you comprehended the

37:16 [a]Job 36:4
37:18 [b]Job 9:8; Ps 104:2; Isa 44:24
37:23 [c]Job 9:4; 36:4; 1Ti 6:16 [d]Job 8:3 [e]Isa 63:9; Eze 18:23,32
37:24 [f]Mt 10:28 [g]Mt 11:25
38:1 [h]Job 40:6
38:2 [i]Job 35:16; 42:3; 1Ti 1:7
38:3 [j]Job 40:7
38:4 [k]Ps 104:5; Pr 8:29
38:5 [l]Pr 8:29; Isa 40:12
38:6 [m]Job 26:7
38:8 [n]Jer 5:22 [o]Ge 1:9-10
38:10 [p]Ps 33:7; 104:9 [q]Job 26:10
38:11 [r]Ps 89:9
38:13 [s]Ps 104:35
38:15 [t]Job 18:5 [u]Ps 10:15
38:16 [v]Ps 77:19
38:17 [w]Ps 9:13

[m]24 *Or for he does not have regard for any who think they are wise.* [n]7 Hebrew *the sons of God* [o]17 *Or gates of deep shadows*

vast expanses of the
earth?[a]
Tell me, if you know all this.

19"What is the way to the abode
of light?
And where does darkness
reside?
20Can you take them to their
places?
Do you know the paths[b] to
their dwellings?
21Surely you know, for you were
already born![c]
You have lived so many
years!
22"Have you entered the
storehouses of the
snow[d]
or seen the storehouses of
the hail,
23which I reserve for times of
trouble,[e]
for days of war and battle?[f]
24What is the way to the place
where the lightning is
dispersed,
or the place where the east
winds are scattered over
the earth?
25Who cuts a channel for the
torrents of rain,
and a path for the
thunderstorm,[g]
26to water[h] a land where no man
lives,
a desert with no one in it,
27to satisfy a desolate wasteland
and make it sprout with
grass?[i]
28Does the rain have a father?[j]
Who fathers the drops of
dew?
29From whose womb comes the
ice?
Who gives birth to the frost
from the heavens[k]
30when the waters become hard
as stone,
when the surface of the deep
is frozen?[l]

31"Can you bind the beautiful[p]
Pleiades?
Can you loose the cords of
Orion?[m]
32Can you bring forth the
constellations in their
seasons[q]
or lead out the Bear[r] with
its cubs?
33Do you know the laws[n] of the
heavens?
Can you set up ⌞God's[s]⌟
dominion over the earth?

34"Can you raise your voice to
the clouds
and cover yourself with a
flood of water?[o]
35Do you send the lightning bolts
on their way?[p]
Do they report to you, 'Here
we are'?
36Who endowed the heart[t] with
wisdom[q]
or gave understanding[r] to
the mind[t]?
37Who has the wisdom to count
the clouds?
Who can tip over the water
jars of the heavens
38when the dust becomes hard
and the clods of earth stick
together?

39"Do you hunt the prey for the
lioness
and satisfy the hunger of the
lions[s]
40when they crouch in their
dens[t]
or lie in wait in a thicket?
41Who provides food for the
raven[u]
when its young cry out to
God
and wander about for lack of
food?[v]

39 "Do you know when the
mountain goats[w] give
birth?
Do you watch when the doe
bears her fawn?
2Do you count the months till
they bear?
Do you know the time they
give birth?
3They crouch down and bring
forth their young;

38:18 [a]Job 28:24
38:20 [b]Job 26:10
38:21 [c]Job 15:7
38:22 [d]Job 37:6
38:23 [e]Isa 30:30; Eze 13:11 [f]Ex 9:18; Jos 10:11; Rev 16:21
38:25 [g]Job 28:26
38:26 [h]Job 36:27
38:27 [i]Ps 104:14; 107:35
38:28 [j]Ps 147:8; Jer 14:22
38:29 [k]Ps 147:16-17
38:30 [l]Job 37:10
38:31 [m]Job 9:9; Am 5:8
38:33 [n]Ps 148:6; Jer 31:36
38:34 [o]Job 22:11; 36:27-28
38:35 [p]Job 36:32; 37:3
38:36 [q]Job 9:4 [r]Job 32:8; Ps 51:6; Ecc 2:26
38:39 [s]Ps 104:21
38:40 [t]Job 37:8
38:41 [u]Lk 12:24 [v]Ps 147:9; Mt 6:26
39:1 [w]Dt 14:5

[p]31 Or *the twinkling*; or *the chains of the*
[q]32 Or *the morning star in its season*
[r]32 Or *out Leo* [s]33 Or *his*; or *their*
[t]36 The meaning of the Hebrew for this word is uncertain.

their labor pains are ended.
[4]Their young thrive and grow
strong in the wilds;
they leave and do not
return.

[5]"Who let the wild donkey[a] go
free?
Who untied his ropes?
[6]I gave him the wasteland[b] as
his home,
the salt flats as his habitat.[c]
[7]He laughs at the commotion in
the town;
he does not hear a driver's
shout.[d]
[8]He ranges the hills for his
pasture
and searches for any green
thing.

[9]"Will the wild ox[e] consent to
serve you?
Will he stay by your manger
at night?
[10]Can you hold him to the furrow
with a harness?
Will he till the valleys behind
you?
[11]Will you rely on him for his
great strength?
Will you leave your heavy
work to him?
[12]Can you trust him to bring in
your grain
and gather it to your
threshing floor?

[13]"The wings of the ostrich flap
joyfully,
but they cannot compare
with the pinions and
feathers of the stork.
[14]She lays her eggs on the ground
and lets them warm in the
sand,
[15]unmindful that a foot may
crush them,
that some wild animal may
trample them.
[16]She treats her young harshly,[f]
as if they were not hers;
she cares not that her labor
was in vain,
[17]for God did not endow her with
wisdom
or give her a share of good
sense.[g]

39:5 [a]Job 6:5; 11:12; 24:5
39:6 [b]Job 24:5; Ps 107:34; Jer 2:24 [c]Hos 8:9
39:7 [d]Job 3:18
39:9 [e]Nu 23:22; Dt 33:17
39:16 [f]La 4:3
39:17 [g]Job 35:11
39:20 [h]Joel 2:4-5 [i]Jer 8:16
39:21 [j]Jer 8:6
39:24 [k]Jer 4:5,19; Eze 7:14; Am 3:6
39:25 [l]Jos 6:5 [m]Am 1:14; 2:2
39:27 [n]Jer 49:16; Ob 1:4
39:29 [o]Job 9:26
39:30 [p]Mt 24:28; Lk 17:37
40:1 [q]Job 10:2; 13:3; 23:4; 31:35; 33:13

[18]Yet when she spreads her
feathers to run,
she laughs at horse and
rider.

[19]"Do you give the horse his
strength
or clothe his neck with a
flowing mane?
[20]Do you make him leap like a
locust,[h]
striking terror with his proud
snorting?[i]
[21]He paws fiercely, rejoicing in
his strength,
and charges into the fray.[j]
[22]He laughs at fear, afraid of
nothing;
he does not shy away from
the sword.
[23]The quiver rattles against his
side,
along with the flashing spear
and lance.
[24]In frenzied excitement he eats
up the ground;
he cannot stand still when
the trumpet sounds.[k]
[25]At the blast of the trumpet[l] he
snorts, 'Aha!'
He catches the scent of
battle from afar,
the shout of commanders
and the battle cry.[m]

[26]"Does the hawk take flight by
your wisdom
and spread his wings toward
the south?
[27]Does the eagle soar at your
command
and build his nest on high?[n]
[28]He dwells on a cliff and stays
there at night;
a rocky crag is his
stronghold.
[29]From there he seeks out his
food;[o]
his eyes detect it from afar.
[30]His young ones feast on blood,
and where the slain are,
there is he."[p]

40 The LORD said to Job:[q]
[2]"Will the one who
contends with the
Almighty correct him?

Let him who accuses God
answer him!"

3 Then Job answered the LORD:

4 "I am unworthy[a]—how can I
reply to you?
I put my hand over my
mouth.[b]
5 I spoke once, but I have no
answer[c]—
twice, but I will say no
more."[d]

6 Then the LORD spoke to Job out
of the storm:[e]

7 "Brace yourself like a man;
I will question you,
and you shall answer me.[f]
8 "Would you discredit my
justice?[g]
Would you condemn me to
justify yourself?
9 Do you have an arm like
God's,[h]
and can your voice thunder
like his?[i]
10 Then adorn yourself with glory
and splendor,
and clothe yourself in honor
and majesty.[j]
11 Unleash the fury of your
wrath,[k]
look at every proud man and
bring him low,[l]
12 look at every proud man and
humble him,[m]
crush[n] the wicked where
they stand.
13 Bury them all in the dust
together;
shroud their faces in the
grave.
14 Then I myself will admit to you
that your own right hand can
save you.[o]

15 "Look at the behemoth,[u]
which I made along with you
and which feeds on grass like
an ox.
16 What strength he has in his
loins,
what power in the muscles of
his belly!
17 His tail[v] sways like a cedar;
the sinews of his thighs are
close-knit.

40:4 [a] Job 42:6 [b] Job 29:9
40:5 [c] Job 9:3 [d] Job 9:15
40:6 [e] Job 38:1
40:7 [f] Job 38:3; 42:4
40:8 [g] Job 27:2; Ro 3:3
40:9 [h] 2Ch 32:8 [i] Job 37:5; Ps 29:3-4
40:10 [j] Ps 93:1; 104:1
40:11 [k] Isa 42:25; Na 1:6 [l] Isa 2:11,12, 17; Da 4:37
40:12 [m] 1Sa 2:7 [n] Isa 13:11; 63:2-3,6
40:14 [o] Ps 20:6; 60:5; 108:6
40:19 [p] Job 41:33
40:20 [q] Ps 104:14 [r] Ps 104:26
40:22 [s] Isa 44:4
40:24 [t] Job 41:2,7, 26
41:1 [u] Job 3:8; Ps 104:26; Isa 27:1
41:2 [v] Isa 37:29
41:4 [w] Ex 21:6

18 His bones are tubes of bronze,
his limbs like rods of iron.
19 He ranks first among the works
of God,[p]
yet his Maker can approach
him with his sword.
20 The hills bring him their
produce,[q]
and all the wild animals
play[r] nearby.
21 Under the lotus plants he lies,
hidden among the reeds in
the marsh.
22 The lotuses conceal him in
their shadow;
the poplars by the stream[s]
surround him.
23 When the river rages, he is not
alarmed;
he is secure, though the
Jordan should surge
against his mouth.
24 Can anyone capture him by the
eyes,[w]
or trap him and pierce his
nose?[t]

41 "Can you pull in the
leviathan[x][u] with a
fishhook
or tie down his tongue with a
rope?
2 Can you put a cord through his
nose
or pierce his jaw with a
hook?[v]
3 Will he keep begging you for
mercy?
Will he speak to you with
gentle words?
4 Will he make an agreement
with you
for you to take him as your
slave for life?[w]
5 Can you make a pet of him like
a bird
or put him on a leash for
your girls?
6 Will traders barter for him?
Will they divide him up
among the merchants?
7 Can you fill his hide with
harpoons

[u] *15* Possibly the hippopotamus or the elephant [v] *17* Possibly trunk [w] *24* Or *by a water hole* [x] *1* Possibly the crocodile

or his head with fishing
spears?
8If you lay a hand on him,
you will remember the
struggle and never do
it again!
9Any hope of subduing him is
false;
the mere sight of him is
overpowering.
10No one is fierce enough to
rouse him.[a]
Who then is able to stand
against me?[b]
11Who has a claim against me
that I must pay?[c]
Everything under heaven
belongs to me.[d]

12"I will not fail to speak of his
limbs,
his strength and his graceful
form.
13Who can strip off his outer
coat?
Who would approach him
with a bridle?
14Who dares open the doors of
his mouth,
ringed about with his
fearsome teeth?
15His back has[y] rows of shields
tightly sealed together;
16each is so close to the next
that no air can pass between.
17They are joined fast to one
another;
they cling together and
cannot be parted.
18His snorting throws out flashes
of light;
his eyes are like the rays of
dawn.[e]
19Firebrands stream from his
mouth;
sparks of fire shoot out.
20Smoke pours from his nostrils
as from a boiling pot over a
fire of reeds.
21His breath[f] sets coals ablaze,
and flames dart from his
mouth.[g]
22Strength resides in his neck;
dismay goes before him.
23The folds of his flesh are
tightly joined;
they are firm and immovable.

41:10
[a]Job 3:8
[b]Jer 50:44

41:11
[c]Ro 11:35
[d]Ex 19:5; Dt 10:14; Ps 24:1; 50:12; 1Co 10:26

41:18
[e]Job 3:9

41:21
[f]Isa 40:7
[g]Ps 18:8

41:30
[h]Isa 41:15

41:33
[i]Job 40:19

41:34
[j]Job 28:8

42:2
[k]Ge 18:14; Mt 19:26
[l]2Ch 20:6

42:3
[m]Job 38:2
[n]Ps 40:5; 131:1; 139:6

24His chest is hard as rock,
hard as a lower millstone.
25When he rises up, the mighty
are terrified;
they retreat before his
thrashing.
26The sword that reaches him has
no effect,
nor does the spear or the
dart or the javelin.
27Iron he treats like straw
and bronze like rotten
wood.
28Arrows do not make him flee;
slingstones are like chaff to
him.
29A club seems to him but a
piece of straw;
he laughs at the rattling of
the lance.
30His undersides are jagged
potsherds,
leaving a trail in the mud
like a threshing sledge.[h]
31He makes the depths churn
like a boiling caldron
and stirs up the sea like a
pot of ointment.
32Behind him he leaves a
glistening wake;
one would think the deep
had white hair.
33Nothing on earth is his
equal[i]—
a creature without fear.
34He looks down on all that are
haughty;
he is king over all that are
proud.[j]"

Job

42 Then Job replied to the LORD:

2"I know that you can do all
things;[k]
no plan of yours can be
thwarted.[l]
3⌊You asked,⌋ 'Who is this that
obscures my counsel
without knowledge?'[m]
Surely I spoke of things I did
not understand,
things too wonderful for me
to know.[n]

[y]15 Or *His pride is his*

4"You said, 'Listen now, and
I will speak;
I will question you,
and you shall answer
me.'[a]
5My ears had heard of you[b]
but now my eyes have seen
you.[c]
6Therefore I despise myself[d]
and repent in dust and
ashes."[e]

Epilogue

7After the LORD had said these
things to Job, he said to Eliphaz
the Temanite, "I am angry with you
and your two friends,[f] because
you have not spoken of me what is
right, as my servant Job has. 8So
now take seven bulls and seven
rams[g] and go to my servant Job
and sacrifice a burnt offering[h] for
yourselves. My servant Job will
pray for you, and I will accept his
prayer[i] and not deal with you according to your folly.[j] You have
not spoken of me what is right, as
my servant Job has." 9So Eliphaz
the Temanite, Bildad the Shuhite
and Zophar the Naamathite did
what the LORD told them; and the
LORD accepted Job's prayer.
10After Job had prayed for his
friends, the LORD made him prosperous again[k] and gave him twice
as much as he had before.[l] 11All
his brothers and sisters and everyone who had known him before[m]
came and ate with him in his
house. They comforted and consoled him over all the trouble the
LORD had brought upon him, and
each one gave him a piece of silver[z] and a gold ring.
12The LORD blessed the latter
part of Job's life more than the
first. He had fourteen thousand
sheep, six thousand camels, a
thousand yoke of oxen and a thousand donkeys. 13And he also had
seven sons and three daughters.
14The first daughter he named Jemimah, the second Keziah and the
third Keren-Happuch. 15Nowhere
in all the land were there found
women as beautiful as Job's
daughters, and their father granted
them an inheritance along with
their brothers.
16After this, Job lived a hundred
and forty years; he saw his children
and their children to the fourth
generation. 17And so he died, old
and full of years.[n]

42:4 [a]Job 38:3; 40:7
42:5 [b]Job 26:14; Ro 10:17 [c]Jdg 13:22; Isa 6:5; Eph 1:17-18
42:6 [d]Job 40:4 [e]Ezr 9:6
42:7 [f]Job 32:3
42:8 [g]Nu 23:1,29 [h]Job 1:5 [i]Ge 20:17; Jas 5:15-16; 1Jn 5:16 [j]Job 22:30
42:10 [k]Dt 30:3; Ps 14:7 [l]Job 1:3; Ps 85:1-3; 126:5-6
42:11 [m]Job 19:13
42:17 [n]Ge 15:15; 25:8

[z]*11* Hebrew *him a kesitah*; a kesitah was a unit of money of unknown weight and value.

Psalms

Title and Background

The names "Psalms" and "Psalter" come from the Septuagint (the Greek translation of the Old Testament). Both originally referred to stringed instruments (e.g., harp, lyre, lute), then to songs sung with their accompaniment. The traditional Hebrew title means "praises," even though many of the psalms are prayers.

Author and Date of Writing

Of the 150 Psalms, 100 of them are thought to be written by the following authors: David—73; Asaph—12; Sons of Korah—10; Moses—1; Heman the Ezrahite—1; Ethan the Ezrahite—1; and two by Solomon. The rest of the Psalms have no recorded author. The final collection and arrangement of the Psalter was the work of postexilic temple personnel, completed probably in the third century B.C. By the first century A.D. it could be referred to as the "Book of Psalms" (Lk 20:42; Ac 1:20).

Theme and Message

The Psalter is not a book of catechism or doctrine. It is rather for the most part a book of prayer and praise. It speaks to God in prayer and of God in praise and in professions of faith and trust. At the core of the theology of the Psalter is the conviction that the gravitational center of life, but also of history and the whole creation, is God. He is the great King over all, and the One to whom all things are subject.

Outline

Book I. Psalms 1-41
Book II. Psalms 42-72
Book III. Psalms 73-89
Book IV. Psalms 90-106
Book V. Psalms 107-150

BOOK I

Psalms 1–41

Psalm 1

1 Blessed is the man
who does not walk[a] in the counsel of the wicked
or stand in the way of sinners
or sit[b] in the seat of mockers.
2 But his delight[c] is in the law of the LORD,[d]
and on his law he meditates[e] day and night.

3 He is like a tree[f] planted by streams of water,[g]
which yields its fruit[h] in season
and whose leaf does not wither.
Whatever he does prospers.[i]

4 Not so the wicked!
They are like chaff[j]
that the wind blows away.
5 Therefore the wicked will not stand[k] in the judgment,[l]
nor sinners in the assembly of the righteous.

6 For the LORD watches over[m] the way of the righteous,

1:1 [a]Pr 4:14 [b]Ps 26:4; Jer 15:17
1:2 [c]Ps 119:16,35 [d]Ps 119:1 [e]Jos 1:8
1:3 [f]Ps 128:3 [g]Jer 17:8 [h]Eze 47:12 [i]Ge 39:3
1:4 [j]Job 21:18; Isa 17:13
1:5 [k]Ps 5:5 [l]Ps 9:7-8,16
1:6 [m]Ps 37:18; 2Ti 2:19

but the way of the wicked
will perish.[a]

Psalm 2

1Why do the nations conspire[a]
and the peoples plot[b] in
vain?
2The kings[c] of the earth take
their stand
and the rulers gather
together
against the LORD
and against his Anointed[d]
One.[b e]
3"Let us break their chains,"
they say,
"and throw off their
fetters."[f]

4The One enthroned in heaven
laughs;[g]
the Lord scoffs at them.
5Then he rebukes them in his
anger
and terrifies them in his
wrath,[h] saying,
6"I have installed my King[c]
on Zion, my holy hill."

7I will proclaim the decree of the
LORD:

He said to me, "You are my
Son[d];
today I have become your
Father.[e i]
8Ask of me,
and I will make the nations
your inheritance,
the ends of the earth[j] your
possession.
9You will rule them with an iron
scepter[f];[k]
you will dash them to
pieces[l] like pottery.[m]"

10Therefore, you kings, be wise;
be warned, you rulers of the
earth.
11Serve the LORD with fear
and rejoice[n] with
trembling.[o]
12Kiss the Son,[p] lest he be angry
and you be destroyed in your
way,
for his wrath[q] can flare up in a
moment.

1:6 [a]Ps 9:6
2:1 [b]Ps 21:11
2:2 [c]Ps 48:4 [d]Jn 1:41 [e]Ps 74:18,23; Ac 4:25-26*
2:3 [f]Jer 5:5
2:4 [g]Ps 37:13; 59:8; Pr 1:26
2:5 [h]Ps 21:9; 78:49-50
2:7 [i]Ac 13:33*; Heb 1:5*
2:8 [j]Ps 22:27
2:9 [k]Rev 12:5 [l]Ps 89:23 [m]Rev 2:27*
2:11 [n]Heb 12:28 [o]Ps 119:119-120
2:12 [p]Jn 5:23 [q]Rev 6:16 [r]Ps 34:8; Ro 9:33
3:1 [s]2Sa 15:14
3:2 [t]Ps 71:11
3:3 [u]Ge 15:1; Ps 28:7 [v]Ps 27:6
3:4 [w]Ps 2:6
3:5 [x]Lev 26:6; Pr 3:24
3:6 [y]Ps 27:3
3:7 [z]Ps 7:6 [a]Ps 6:4 [b]Job 16:10 [c]Ps 58:6
3:8 [d]Isa 43:3,11
4:1 [e]Ps 25:16 [f]Ps 17:6

Blessed are all who take
refuge[r] in him.

Psalm 3

A psalm of David. When he fled
from his son Absalom.[s]

1O LORD, how many are my foes!
How many rise up against
me!
2Many are saying of me,
"God will not deliver him.[t]"
Selah[g]
3But you are a shield[u] around
me, O LORD;
you bestow glory on me and
lift[h] up my head.[v]
4To the LORD I cry aloud,
and he answers me from his
holy hill.[w] *Selah*
5I lie down and sleep;[x]
I wake again, because the
LORD sustains me.
6I will not fear[y] the tens of
thousands
drawn up against me on
every side.
7Arise,[z] O LORD!
Deliver me,[a] O my God!
Strike[b] all my enemies on the
jaw;
break the teeth[c] of the
wicked.
8From the LORD comes
deliverance.[d]
May your blessing be on your
people. *Selah*

Psalm 4

For the director of music. With
stringed instruments. A psalm
of David.

1Answer me when I call to you,
O my righteous God.
Give me relief from my distress;
be merciful[e] to me and hear
my prayer.[f]

[a]1 Hebrew; Septuagint *rage* [b]2 Or *anointed one* [c]6 Or *king* [d]7 Or *son*; also in verse 12 [e]7 Or *have begotten you* [f]9 Or *will break them with a rod of iron* [g]2 A word of uncertain meaning, occurring frequently in the Psalms; possibly a musical term [h]3 Or *LORD, / my Glorious One, who lifts*

2How long, O men, will you turn
my glory into shame[i]?
How long will you love
delusions and seek false
gods[j]?[a] *Selah*
3Know that the LORD has set
apart the godly[b] for
himself;
the LORD will hear[c] when I
call to him.

4In your anger do not sin;[d]
when you are on your beds,[e]
search your hearts and be
silent. *Selah*
5Offer right sacrifices
and trust in the LORD.[f]
6Many are asking, "Who can
show us any good?"
Let the light of your face
shine upon us,[g] O LORD.
7You have filled my heart[h] with
greater joy[i]
than when their grain and
new wine abound.
8I will lie down and sleep[j] in
peace,
for you alone, O LORD,
make me dwell in safety.[k]

Psalm 5

For the director of music. For flutes. A psalm of David.

1Give ear to my words, O LORD,
consider my sighing.
2Listen to my cry for help,[l]
my King and my God,[m]
for to you I pray.
3In the morning,[n] O LORD, you
hear my voice;
in the morning I lay my
requests before you
and wait in expectation.

4You are not a God who takes
pleasure in evil;
with you the wicked[o] cannot
dwell.
5The arrogant[p] cannot stand[q]
in your presence;
you hate[r] all who do wrong.
6You destroy those who tell
lies;[s]
bloodthirsty and deceitful
men
the LORD abhors.

4:2 [a]Ps 31:6
4:3 [b]Ps 31:23 [c]Ps 6:8
4:4 [d]Eph 4:26* [e]Ps 77:6
4:5 [f]Dt 33:19; Ps 37:3
4:6 [g]Nu 6:25
4:7 [h]Ac 14:17 [i]Isa 9:3
4:8 [j]Ps 3:5 [k]Lev 25:18
5:2 [l]Ps 3:4 [m]Ps 84:3
5:3 [n]Ps 88:13
5:4 [o]Ps 11:5; 92:15
5:5 [p]Ps 73:3 [q]Ps 1:5 [r]Ps 11:5
5:6 [s]Ps 55:23; Rev 21:8
5:7 [t]Ps 138:2
5:8 [u]Ps 31:1 [v]Ps 27:11
5:9 [w]Lk 11:44 [x]Ro 3:13*
5:10 [y]Ps 9:16 [z]Ps 107:11
5:11 [a]Ps 2:12 [b]Ps 69:36 [c]Isa 65:13
5:12 [d]Ps 32:7
6:1 [e]Ps 38:1
6:2 [f]Hos 6:1 [g]Ps 22:14; 31:10
6:3 [h]Jn 12:27 [i]Ps 90:13

7But I, by your great mercy,
will come into your house;
in reverence will I bow down[t]
toward your holy temple.
8Lead me, O LORD, in your
righteousness[u]
because of my enemies—
make straight your way[v]
before me.

9Not a word from their mouth
can be trusted;
their heart is filled with
destruction.
Their throat is an open grave;[w]
with their tongue they speak
deceit.[x]
10Declare them guilty, O God!
Let their intrigues be their
downfall.
Banish them for their many
sins,[y]
for they have rebelled[z]
against you.
11But let all who take refuge in
you be glad;
let them ever sing for joy.[a]
Spread your protection over
them,
that those who love your
name[b] may rejoice in
you.[c]
12For surely, O LORD, you bless
the righteous;
you surround them[d] with
your favor as with a
shield.

Psalm 6

For the director of music. With stringed instruments. According to *sheminith.*[k] A psalm of David.

1O LORD, do not rebuke me in
your anger[e]
or discipline me in your
wrath.
2Be merciful to me, LORD, for I
am faint;
O LORD, heal me,[f] for my
bones are in agony.[g]
3My soul is in anguish.[h]
How long,[i] O LORD, how
long?

[i]2 Or *you dishonor my Glorious One* [j]2 Or *seek lies* [k]Title: Probably a musical term

4Turn, O LORD, and deliver me;
save me because of your unfailing love.[a]
5No one remembers you when he is dead.
Who praises you from the grave[l]?[b]

6I am worn out[c] from groaning;
all night long I flood my bed with weeping
and drench my couch with tears.[d]
7My eyes grow weak[e] with sorrow;
they fail because of all my foes.

8Away from me,[f] all you who do evil,[g]
for the LORD has heard my weeping.
9The LORD has heard my cry for mercy;[h]
the LORD accepts my prayer.
10All my enemies will be ashamed and dismayed;
they will turn back in sudden disgrace.[i]

Psalm 7

A *shiggaion*[m] of David, which he sang to the LORD concerning Cush, a Benjamite.

1O LORD my God, I take refuge in you;
save and deliver me from all who pursue me,[j]
2or they will tear me like a lion[k]
and rip me to pieces with no one to rescue[l] me.

3O LORD my God, if I have done this
and there is guilt on my hands[m]—
4if I have done evil to him who is at peace with me
or without cause have robbed my foe—
5then let my enemy pursue and overtake me;
let him trample my life to the ground
and make me sleep in the dust. *Selah*

6:4 [a]Ps 17:13
6:5 [b]Ps 30:9; 88:10-12; Ecc 9:10; Isa 38:18
6:6 [c]Ps 69:3 [d]Ps 42:3
6:7 [e]Ps 31:9
6:8 [f]Ps 119:115 [g]Mt 7:23; Lk 13:27
6:9 [h]Ps 116:1
6:10 [i]Ps 71:24; 73:19
7:1 [j]Ps 31:15
7:2 [k]Isa 38:13 [l]Ps 50:22
7:3 [m]1Sa 24:11; Isa 59:3
7:6 [n]Ps 94:2 [o]Ps 138:7 [p]Ps 44:23
7:8 [q]Ps 18:20; 96:13
7:9 [r]Jer 11:20 [s]1Ch 28:9; Ps 26:2; Rev 2:23 [t]Ps 37:23
7:10 [u]Ps 125:4
7:11 [v]Ps 50:6
7:12 [w]Dt 32:41
7:14 [x]Job 15:35; Isa 59:4; Jas 1:15
7:15 [y]Job 4:8
7:17 [z]Ps 71:15-16 [a]Ps 9:2

6Arise,[n] O LORD, in your anger;
rise up against the rage of my enemies.[o]
Awake,[p] my God; decree justice.
7Let the assembled peoples gather around you.
Rule over them from on high;
8 let the LORD judge the peoples.
Judge me, O LORD, according to my righteousness,[q]
according to my integrity, O Most High.
9O righteous God,[r]
who searches minds and hearts,[s]
bring to an end the violence of the wicked
and make the righteous secure.[t]

10My shield[n] is God Most High,
who saves the upright in heart.[u]
11God is a righteous judge,[v]
a God who expresses his wrath every day.
12If he does not relent,
he[o] will sharpen his sword;[w]
he will bend and string his bow.
13He has prepared his deadly weapons;
he makes ready his flaming arrows.

14He who is pregnant with evil
and conceives trouble gives birth[x] to disillusionment.
15He who digs a hole and scoops it out
falls into the pit he has made.[y]
16The trouble he causes recoils on himself;
his violence comes down on his own head.

17I will give thanks to the LORD because of his righteousness[z]
and will sing praise[a] to the

[l]5 Hebrew *Sheol* [m]Title: Probably a literary or musical term [n]10 Or *sovereign* [o]12 Or *If a man does not repent, / God*

name of the LORD Most
High.

Psalm 8

For the director of music.
According to *gittith*.[p] A psalm of
David.

1O LORD, our Lord,
how majestic is your name in
all the earth!

You have set your glory
above the heavens.[a]
2From the lips of children and
infants
you have ordained praise[q][b]
because of your enemies,
to silence the foe[c] and the
avenger.

3When I consider your
heavens,[d]
the work of your fingers,
the moon and the stars,[e]
which you have set in place,
4what is man that you are
mindful of him,
the son of man that you care
for him?[f]
5You made him a little lower
than the heavenly
beings[r]
and crowned him with glory
and honor.[g]

6You made him ruler[h] over the
works of your hands;
you put everything under his
feet:[i][j]
7all flocks and herds,
and the beasts of the field,
8the birds of the air,
and the fish of the sea,
all that swim the paths of the
seas.

9O LORD, our Lord,
how majestic is your name in
all the earth![k]

Psalm 9[s]

For the director of music. To
the tune of "The Death of the
Son." A psalm of David.

1I will praise you, O LORD, with
all my heart;[l]

8:1 [a]Ps 57:5; 113:4; 148:13
8:2 [b]Mt 21:16* [c]Ps 44:16; 1Co 1:27
8:3 [d]Ps 89:11 [e]Ps 136:9
8:4 [f]Job 7:17; Ps 144:3; Heb 2:6
8:5 [g]Ps 21:5; 103:4
8:6 [h]Ge 1:28 [i]Heb 2:6-8* [j]1Co 15:25, 27; Eph 1:22
8:9 [k]ver 1
9:1 [l]Ps 86:12 [m]Ps 26:7
9:2 [n]Ps 5:11 [o]Ps 92:1; 83:18
9:4 [p]Ps 140:12 [q]1Pe 2:23
9:5 [r]Pr 10:7
9:6 [s]Ps 34:16
9:7 [t]Ps 89:14
9:8 [u]Ps 96:13
9:9 [v]Ps 32:7
9:10 [w]Ps 91:14 [x]Ps 37:20
9:11 [y]Ps 76:2 [z]Ps 107:22 [a]Ps 105:1
9:12 [b]Ge 9:5

I will tell of all your
wonders.[m]
2I will be glad and rejoice[n]
in you;
I will sing praise to your
name,[o] O Most
High.

3My enemies turn back;
they stumble and perish
before you.
4For you have upheld my right
and my cause;[p]
you have sat on your throne,
judging righteously.[q]
5You have rebuked the nations
and destroyed the
wicked;
you have blotted out their
name[r] for ever and
ever.
6Endless ruin has overtaken the
enemy,
you have uprooted their
cities;
even the memory of them[s]
has perished.

7The LORD reigns forever;
he has established his
throne[t] for judgment.
8He will judge the world in
righteousness;[u]
he will govern the peoples
with justice.
9The LORD is a refuge for the
oppressed,
a stronghold in times of
trouble.[v]
10Those who know your name[w]
will trust in you,
for you, LORD, have never
forsaken[x] those who
seek you.

11Sing praises to the LORD,
enthroned in Zion;[y]
proclaim among the nations[z]
what he has done.[a]
12For he who avenges blood[b]
remembers;
he does not ignore the cry of
the afflicted.

[p]Title: Probably a musical term [q]2 Or *strength* [r]5 Or *than God* [s]Psalms 9 and 10 may have been originally a single acrostic poem, the stanzas of which begin with the successive letters of the Hebrew alphabet. In the Septuagint they constitute one psalm.

13 O LORD, see how my enemies[a]
persecute me!
Have mercy and lift me up
from the gates of death,
14 that I may declare your
praises[b]
in the gates of the Daughter
of Zion
and there rejoice in your
salvation.[c]
15 The nations have fallen into
the pit they have dug;[d]
their feet are caught in the
net they have hidden.[e]
16 The LORD is known by his
justice;
the wicked are ensnared by
the work of their hands.
Higgaion.[t] *Selah*
17 The wicked return to the
grave,[u][f]
all the nations that forget
God.[g]
18 But the needy will not always
be forgotten,
nor the hope[h] of the
afflicted[i] ever perish.

19 Arise, O LORD, let not man
triumph;
let the nations be judged in
your presence.
20 Strike them with terror, O LORD;
let the nations know they are
but men.[j] *Selah*

Psalm 10[v]

1 Why, O LORD, do you stand far
off?[k]
Why do you hide yourself[l] in
times of trouble?

2 In his arrogance the wicked
man hunts down the
weak,
who are caught in the
schemes he devises.
3 He boasts[m] of the cravings of
his heart;
he blesses the greedy and
reviles the LORD.
4 In his pride the wicked does
not seek him;
in all his thoughts there is no
room for God.[n]
5 His ways are always prosperous;
he is haughty and your laws
are far from him;
he sneers at all his enemies.
6 He says to himself, "Nothing
will shake me;
I'll always be happy[o] and
never have trouble."
7 His mouth is full of curses[p]
and lies and threats;[q]
trouble and evil are under his
tongue.[r]
8 He lies in wait near the
villages;
from ambush he murders the
innocent,[s]
watching in secret for his
victims.
9 He lies in wait like a lion in
cover;
he lies in wait to catch the
helpless;[t]
he catches the helpless and
drags them off in his
net.
10 His victims are crushed, they
collapse;
they fall under his strength.
11 He says to himself, "God has
forgotten;[u]
he covers his face and never
sees."

12 Arise, LORD! Lift up your
hand,[v] O God.
Do not forget the helpless.[w]
13 Why does the wicked man
revile God?
Why does he say to himself,
"He won't call me to
account"?
14 But you, O God, do see
trouble[x] and grief;
you consider it to take it in
hand.
The victim commits himself to
you;[y]
you are the helper[z] of the
fatherless.
15 Break the arm of the wicked
and evil man;[a]
call him to account for his
wickedness

9:13 [a]Ps 38:19
9:14 [b]Ps 106:2 [c]Ps 13:5; 51:12
9:15 [d]Ps 7:15-16 [e]Ps 35:8; 57:6
9:17 [f]Ps 49:14 [g]Job 8:13; Ps 50:22
9:18 [h]Ps 71:5; Pr 23:18 [i]Ps 12:5
9:20 [j]Ps 62:9; Isa 31:3
10:1 [k]Ps 22:1,11 [l]Ps 13:1
10:3 [m]Ps 94:4
10:4 [n]Ps 14:1; 36:1
10:6 [o]Rev 18:7
10:7 [p]Ro 3:14* [q]Ps 73:8 [r]Ps 140:3
10:8 [s]Ps 94:6
10:9 [t]Ps 17:12; 59:3; 140:5
10:11 [u]Job 22:13
10:12 [v]Ps 17:7; Mic 5:9 [w]Ps 9:12
10:14 [x]Ps 22:11 [y]Ps 37:5 [z]Ps 68:5
10:15 [a]Ps 37:17

[t]*16* Or *Meditation*; possibly a musical notation
[u]*17* Hebrew *Sheol*
[v]Psalms 9 and 10 may have been originally a single acrostic poem, the stanzas of which begin with the successive letters of the Hebrew alphabet. In the Septuagint they constitute one psalm.

that would not be found out.

16The LORD is King for ever and
ever;[a]
the nations[b] will perish from
his land.
17You hear, O LORD, the desire of
the afflicted;[c]
you encourage them, and you
listen to their cry,
18defending the fatherless[d] and
the oppressed,[e]
in order that man, who is of
the earth, may terrify no
more.

Psalm 11

For the director of music.
Of David.

1In the LORD I take refuge.[f]
How then can you say to
me:
"Flee like a bird to your
mountain.
2For look, the wicked bend their
bows;
they set their arrows[g]
against the strings
to shoot from the shadows
at the upright in heart.[h]
3When the foundations[i] are
being destroyed,
what can the righteous
do[w]?"

4The LORD is in his holy
temple;[j]
the LORD is on his heavenly
throne.[k]
He observes the sons of men;[l]
his eyes examine[m] them.
5The LORD examines the
righteous,[n]
but the wicked[x] and those
who love violence
his soul hates.[o]
6On the wicked he will rain
fiery coals and burning
sulfur;[p]
a scorching wind[q] will be
their lot.

7For the LORD is righteous,[r]
he loves justice;[s]
upright men will see his
face.[t]

10:16 [a]Ps 29:10 [b]Dt 8:20
10:17 [c]1Ch 29:18; Ps 34:15
10:18 [d]Ps 82:3 [e]Ps 9:9
11:1 [f]Ps 56:11
11:2 [g]Ps 7:13 [h]Ps 64:3-4
11:3 [i]Ps 82:5
11:4 [j]Ps 18:6 [k]Ps 103:19 [l]Ps 33:13 [m]Ps 34:15-16
11:5 [n]Ge 22:1; Jas 1:12 [o]Ps 5:5
11:6 [p]Eze 38:22 [q]Jer 4:11-12
11:7 [r]Ps 7:9,11; 45:7 [s]Ps 33:5 [t]Ps 17:15
12:1 [u]Isa 57:1
12:2 [v]Ps 10:7; 41:6; 55:21; Ro 16:18
12:3 [w]Da 7:8; Rev 13:5
12:5 [x]Ps 10:18; 34:6
12:6 [y]2Sa 22:31; Ps 18:30; Pr 30:5
12:7 [z]Ps 37:28
12:8 [a]Ps 55:10-11
13:1 [b]Job 13:24; Ps 44:24
13:2 [c]Ps 42:4

Psalm 12

For the director of music.
According to *sheminith*.[y]
A psalm of David.

1Help, LORD, for the godly are no
more;[u]
the faithful have vanished
from among men.
2Everyone lies to his neighbor;
their flattering lips speak
with deception.[v]
3May the LORD cut off all
flattering lips
and every boastful tongue[w]
4that says, "We will triumph
with our tongues;
we own our lips[z]—who is
our master?"

5"Because of the oppression of
the weak
and the groaning of the
needy,
I will now arise," says the LORD.
"I will protect them[x] from
those who malign them."
6And the words of the LORD are
flawless,[y]
like silver refined in a
furnace of clay,
purified seven times.
7O LORD, you will keep us safe
and protect us from such
people forever.[z]
8The wicked freely strut[a] about
when what is vile is honored
among men.

Psalm 13

For the director of music.
A psalm of David.

1How long, O LORD? Will you
forget me forever?
How long will you hide your
face[b] from me?
2How long must I wrestle with
my thoughts[c]
and every day have sorrow in
my heart?

[w]3 Or *what is the Righteous One doing* [x]5 Or *The LORD, the Righteous One, examines the wicked, /* [y]Title: Probably a musical term [z]4 Or */ our lips are our plowshares*

How long will my enemy
triumph over me?[a]

[3]Look on me and answer,[b]
O LORD my God.
Give light to my eyes,[c] or I
will sleep in death;[d]
[4]my enemy will say, "I have
overcome him,[e]"
and my foes will rejoice
when I fall.

[5]But I trust in your unfailing
love;[f]
my heart rejoices in your
salvation.[g]
[6]I will sing[h] to the LORD,
for he has been good to me.

Psalm 14

14:1–7pp — Ps 53:1–6

For the director of music.
Of David.

[1]The fool[a] says in his heart,
"There is no God."[i]
They are corrupt, their deeds
are vile;
there is no one who does
good.

[2]The LORD looks down from
heaven[j]
on the sons of men
to see if there are any who
understand,[k]
any who seek God.
[3]All have turned aside,
they have together become
corrupt;[l]
there is no one who does
good,[m]
not even one.[n]

[4]Will evildoers never learn—[o]
those who devour my
people[p] as men eat
bread
and who do not call on the
LORD?[q]
[5]There they are, overwhelmed
with dread,
for God is present in the
company of the
righteous.
[6]You evildoers frustrate the
plans of the poor,
but the LORD is their refuge.[r]

[7]Oh, that salvation for Israel
would come out of Zion!
When the LORD restores the
fortunes[s] of his people,
let Jacob rejoice and Israel
be glad!

Psalm 15

A psalm of David.

[1]LORD, who may dwell in your
sanctuary?[t]
Who may live on your holy
hill?[u]

[2]He whose walk is blameless
and who does what is
righteous,
who speaks the truth[v] from his
heart
[3] and has no slander[w] on his
tongue,
who does his neighbor no
wrong
and casts no slur on his
fellowman,
[4]who despises a vile man
but honors[x] those who fear
the LORD,
who keeps his oath[y]
even when it hurts,
[5]who lends his money without
usury[z]
and does not accept a bribe[a]
against the innocent.

He who does these things
will never be shaken.[b]

Psalm 16

A *miktam*[b] of David.

[1]Keep me safe,[c] O God,
for in you I take refuge.[d]

[2]I said to the LORD, "You are my
Lord;
apart from you I have no
good thing."[e]
[3]As for the saints who are in the
land,[f]

13:2 [a]Ps 42:9
13:3 [b]Ps 5:1 [c]Ezr 9:8 [d]Jer 51:39
13:4 [e]Ps 25:2
13:5 [f]Ps 52:8 [g]Ps 9:14
13:6 [h]Ps 116:7
14:1 [i]Ps 10:4
14:2 [j]Ps 33:13 [k]Ps 92:6
14:3 [l]Ps 58:3 [m]Ps 143:2 [n]Ro 3:10-12*
14:4 [o]Ps 82:5 [p]Ps 27:2 [q]Ps 79:6; Isa 64:7
14:6 [r]Ps 9:9; 40:17
14:7 [s]Ps 53:6
15:1 [t]Ps 27:5-6 [u]Ps 24:3-5
15:2 [v]Ps 24:4; Zec 8:3,16; Eph 4:25
15:3 [w]Ex 23:1
15:4 [x]Ac 28:10 [y]Jdg 11:35
15:5 [z]Ex 22:25 [a]Ex 23:8; Dt 16:19 [b]2Pe 1:10
16:1 [c]Ps 17:8 [d]Ps 7:1
16:2 [e]Ps 73:25
16:3 [f]Ps 101:6

[a]*1* The Hebrew words rendered *fool* in Psalms denote one who is morally deficient. [b]Title: Probably a literary or musical term

they are the glorious ones in
whom is all my delight.[c]
4The sorrows[a] of those will
increase
who run after other gods.[b]
I will not pour out their
libations of blood
or take up their names[c] on
my lips.

5LORD, you have assigned me my
portion[d] and my cup;[e]
you have made my lot
secure.
6The boundary lines have fallen
for me in pleasant
places;
surely I have a delightful
inheritance.[f]

7I will praise the LORD, who
counsels me;[g]
even at night[h] my heart
instructs me.
8I have set the LORD always
before me.
Because he is at my right
hand,[i]
I will not be shaken.

9Therefore my heart is glad[j]
and my tongue rejoices;
my body also will rest
secure,[k]
10because you will not abandon
me to the grave,[d]
nor will you let your Holy
One[e] see decay.[l]
11You have made[f] known to me
the path of life;[m]
you will fill me with joy in
your presence,[n]
with eternal pleasures[o] at
your right hand.

Psalm 17

A prayer of David.

1Hear, O LORD, my righteous
plea;
listen to my cry.[p]
Give ear to my prayer—
it does not rise from
deceitful lips.[q]
2May my vindication come from
you;

16:4 [a]Ps 32:10 [b]Ps 106:37-38 [c]Ex 23:13
16:5 [d]Ps 73:26 [e]Ps 23:5
16:6 [f]Ps 78:55; Jer 3:19
16:7 [g]Ps 73:24 [h]Ps 77:6
16:8 [i]Ps 73:23
16:9 [j]Ps 4:7; 30:11 [k]Ps 4:8
16:10 [l]Ac 13:35*
16:11 [m]Mt 7:14 [n]Ac 2:25-28* [o]Ps 36:7-8
17:1 [p]Ps 61:1 [q]Isa 29:13
17:3 [r]Ps 26:2; 66:10 [s]Job 23:10; Jer 50:20 [t]Ps 39:1
17:5 [u]Ps 44:18; 119:133 [v]Ps 18:36
17:6 [w]Ps 86:7 [x]Ps 116:2 [y]Ps 88:2
17:7 [z]Ps 31:21 [a]Ps 20:6
17:8 [b]Dt 32:10
17:9 [c]Ps 31:20; 109:3
17:10 [d]Ps 73:7 [e]1Sa 2:3
17:11 [f]Ps 37:14; 88:17
17:12 [g]Ps 7:2; 10:9
17:13 [h]Ps 7:12; 22:20; 73:18

may your eyes see what is
right.

3Though you probe my heart
and examine me at
night,
though you test me,[r] you
will find nothing;[s]
I have resolved that my
mouth will not sin.[t]
4As for the deeds of men—
by the word of your lips
I have kept myself
from the ways of the violent.
5My steps have held to your
paths;[u]
my feet have not slipped.[v]

6I call on you, O God, for you
will answer me;[w]
give ear to me[x] and hear my
prayer.[y]
7Show the wonder of your great
love,[z]
you who save by your right
hand[a]
those who take refuge in you
from their foes.
8Keep me as the apple of your
eye;[b]
hide me in the shadow of
your wings
9from the wicked who assail me,
from my mortal enemies who
surround me.[c]

10They close up their callous
hearts,[d]
and their mouths speak with
arrogance.[e]
11They have tracked me down,
they now surround me,[f]
with eyes alert, to throw me
to the ground.
12They are like a lion[g] hungry
for prey,
like a great lion crouching in
cover.

13Rise up, O LORD, confront
them, bring them
down;[h]
rescue me from the wicked
by your sword.

c3 Or *As for the pagan priests who are in the land / and the nobles in whom all delight, I said:* d10 Hebrew *Sheol* e10 Or *your faithful one* f11 Or *You will make*

14 O LORD, by your hand save me
from such men,
from men of this world[a]
whose reward is in this
life.
You still the hunger of those
you cherish;
their sons have plenty,
and they store up wealth[b]
for their children.
15 And I—in righteousness I will
see your face;
when I awake, I will be
satisfied with seeing
your likeness.[c]

Psalm 18

18:Title–50pp — 2Sa 22:1-51

For the director of music. Of David the servant of the LORD. He sang to the LORD the words of this song when the LORD delivered him from the hand of all his enemies and from the hand of Saul. He said:

1 I love you, O LORD, my strength.
2 The LORD is my rock,[d] my
fortress and my
deliverer;
my God is my rock, in whom
I take refuge.
He is my shield[e] and the
horn[g] of my salvation,[f]
my stronghold.
3 I call to the LORD, who is
worthy of praise,[g]
and I am saved from my
enemies.
4 The cords of death[h] entangled
me;
the torrents[i] of destruction
overwhelmed me.
5 The cords of the grave[h] coiled
around me;
the snares of death[j]
confronted me.
6 In my distress I called to the
LORD;
I cried to my God for help.
From his temple he heard my
voice;[k]
my cry came before him, into
his ears.

17:14 a Lk 16:8 b Ps 73:3-7
17:15 c Nu 12:8; Ps 4:6-7; 16:11; 1Jn 3:2
18:2 d Ps 19:14 e Ps 59:11 f Ps 75:10
18:3 g Ps 48:1
18:4 h Ps 116:3 i Ps 124:4
18:5 j Ps 116:3
18:6 k Ps 34:15
18:7 l Jdg 5:4 m Ps 68:7-8
18:8 n Ps 50:3
18:9 o Ps 144:5
18:10 p Ps 80:1 q Ps 104:3
18:11 r Dt 4:11; Ps 97:2
18:12 s Ps 104:2 t Ps 97:3
18:13 u Ps 29:3; 104:7
18:14 v Ps 144:6
18:15 w Ps 76:6; 106:9
18:16 x Ps 144:7

7 The earth trembled and
quaked,[l]
and the foundations of the
mountains shook;
they trembled because he
was angry.[m]
8 Smoke rose from his nostrils;
consuming fire[n] came from
his mouth,
burning coals blazed out of
it.
9 He parted the heavens and
came down;[o]
dark clouds were under his
feet.
10 He mounted the cherubim[p]
and flew;
he soared on the wings of the
wind.[q]
11 He made darkness his
covering,[r] his canopy
around him—
the dark rain clouds of the
sky.
12 Out of the brightness of his
presence[s] clouds
advanced,
with hailstones and bolts of
lightning.[t]
13 The LORD thundered[u] from
heaven;
the voice of the Most High
resounded.[i]
14 He shot his arrows and
scattered the enemies,
great bolts of lightning and
routed them.[v]
15 The valleys of the sea were
exposed
and the foundations of the
earth laid bare
at your rebuke,[w] O LORD,
at the blast of breath from
your nostrils.
16 He reached down from on high
and took hold of me;
he drew me out of deep
waters.[x]
17 He rescued me from my
powerful enemy,

g2 *Horn* here symbolizes strength.
h5 Hebrew *Sheol*
i13 Some Hebrew manuscripts and Septuagint (see also 2 Samuel 22:14); most Hebrew manuscripts *resounded, / amid hailstones and bolts of lightning*

from my foes, who were too
strong for me.[a]
18They confronted me in the day
of my disaster,
but the LORD was my
support.[b]
19He brought me out into a
spacious place;[c]
he rescued me because he
delighted in me.[d]

20The LORD has dealt with me
according to my
righteousness;
according to the cleanness of
my hands[e] he has
rewarded me.
21For I have kept the ways of the
LORD;[f]
I have not done evil by
turning[g] from my God.
22All his laws are before me;[h]
I have not turned away from
his decrees.
23I have been blameless before
him
and have kept myself from
sin.
24The LORD has rewarded me
according to my
righteousness,[i]
according to the cleanness of
my hands in his sight.

25To the faithful[j] you show
yourself faithful,
to the blameless you show
yourself blameless,
26to the pure you show yourself
pure,
but to the crooked you show
yourself shrewd.[k]
27You save the humble
but bring low those whose
eyes are haughty.[l]
28You, O LORD, keep my lamp
burning;
my God turns my darkness
into light.[m]
29With your help[n] I can advance
against a troop[i];
with my God I can scale a
wall.

30As for God, his way is perfect;[o]
the word of the LORD is
flawless.[p]
He is a shield
for all who take refuge[q] in
him.
31For who is God besides the
LORD?[r]
And who is the Rock[s] except
our God?
32It is God who arms me with
strength[t]
and makes my way perfect.
33He makes my feet like the feet
of a deer;[u]
he enables me to stand on
the heights.[v]
34He trains my hands for battle;[w]
my arms can bend a bow of
bronze.
35You give me your shield of
victory,
and your right hand
sustains[x] me;
you stoop down to make me
great.
36You broaden the path beneath
me,
so that my ankles do not
turn.

37I pursued my enemies[y] and
overtook them;
I did not turn back till they
were destroyed.
38I crushed them so that they
could not rise;[z]
they fell beneath my feet.[a]
39You armed me with strength for
battle;
you made my adversaries
bow at my feet.
40You made my enemies turn
their backs[b] in flight,
and I destroyed[c] my foes.
41They cried for help, but there
was no one to save
them[d]—
to the LORD, but he did not
answer.[e]
42I beat them as fine as dust
borne on the wind;
I poured them out like mud
in the streets.

43You have delivered me from the
attacks of the people;
you have made me the head
of nations;[f]

18:17 [a]Ps 35:10
18:18 [b]Ps 59:16
18:19 [c]Ps 31:8 [d]Ps 118:5
18:20 [e]Ps 24:4
18:21 [f]2Ch 34:33 [g]Ps 119:102
18:22 [h]Ps 119:30
18:24 [i]1Sa 26:23
18:25 [j]1Ki 8:32; Ps 62:12; Mt 5:7
18:26 [k]Pr 3:34
18:27 [l]Pr 6:17
18:28 [m]Job 18:6; 29:3
18:29 [n]Heb 11:34
18:30 [o]Dt 32:4; Rev 15:3 [p]Ps 12:6 [q]Ps 17:7
18:31 [r]Dt 32:39; 86:8; Isa 45:5, 6,14,18,21 [s]Dt 32:31; 1Sa 2:2
18:32 [t]Isa 45:5
18:33 [u]Hab 3:19 [v]Dt 32:13
18:34 [w]Ps 144:1
18:35 [x]Ps 119:116
18:37 [y]Ps 37:20; 44:5
18:38 [z]Ps 36:12 [a]Ps 47:3
18:40 [b]Ps 21:12 [c]Ps 94:23
18:41 [d]Ps 50:22 [e]Job 27:9; Pr 1:28
18:43 [f]2Sa 8:1-14

i29 *Or can run through a barricade*

people I did not know[a] are
subject to me.
44As soon as they hear me, they
obey me;
foreigners[b] cringe before me.
45They all lose heart;
they come trembling from
their strongholds.[c]

46The LORD lives! Praise be to my
Rock!
Exalted be God my Savior![d]
47He is the God who avenges me,
who subdues nations[e] under
me,
48 who saves[f] me from my
enemies.
You exalted me above my foes;
from violent men you
rescued me.
49Therefore I will praise you
among the nations,
O LORD;
I will sing[g] praises to your
name.[h]
50He gives his king great
victories;
he shows unfailing kindness
to his anointed,
to David[i] and his
descendants forever.[j]

Psalm 19

For the director of music. A
psalm of David.

1The heavens[k] declare[l] the
glory of God;
the skies proclaim the work
of his hands.
2Day after day they pour forth
speech;
night after night they display
knowledge.[m]
3There is no speech or language
where their voice is not
heard.[k]
4Their voice[l] goes out into all
the earth,
their words to the ends of
the world.[n]
In the heavens he has pitched a
tent[o] for the sun,
5 which is like a bridegroom
coming forth from his
pavilion,
like a champion rejoicing to
run his course.
6It rises at one end of the
heavens
and makes its circuit to the
other;[p]
nothing is hidden from its
heat.

7The law of the LORD is
perfect,
reviving the soul.[q]
The statutes of the LORD are
trustworthy,[r]
making wise the simple.[s]
8The precepts of the LORD are
right,[t]
giving joy to the heart.
The commands of the LORD
are radiant,
giving light to the eyes.
9The fear of the LORD is pure,
enduring forever.
The ordinances of the LORD
are sure
and altogether righteous.[u]
10They are more precious than
gold,[v]
than much pure gold;
they are sweeter than
honey,
than honey from the
comb.
11By them is your servant
warned;
in keeping them there is
great reward.

12Who can discern his errors?
Forgive my hidden faults.[w]
13Keep your servant also from
willful sins;
may they not rule over
me.
Then will I be blameless,
innocent of great
transgression.

14May the words of my mouth
and the meditation of
my heart
be pleasing[x] in your sight,
O LORD, my Rock[y] and my
Redeemer.[z]

18:43 [a] Isa 52:15; 55:5
18:44 [b] Ps 66:3
18:45 [c] Mic 7:17
18:46 [d] Ps 51:14
18:47 [e] Ps 47:3
18:48 [f] Ps 59:1
18:49 [g] Ps 108:1 [h] Ro 15:9*
18:50 [i] Ps 144:10 [j] Ps 89:4
19:1 [k] Isa 40:22 [l] Ps 50:6; Ro 1:19
19:2 [m] Ps 74:16
19:4 [n] Ro 10:18* [o] Ps 104:2
19:6 [p] Ps 113:3; Ecc 1:5
19:7 [q] Ps 23:3 [r] Ps 93:5; 111:7 [s] Ps 119:98-100
19:8 [t] Ps 12:6; 119:128
19:9 [u] Ps 119:138, 142
19:10 [v] Pr 8:10
19:12 [w] Ps 51:2; 90:8; 139:6
19:14 [x] Ps 104:34 [y] Ps 18:2 [z] Isa 47:4

k3 Or *They have no speech, there are no words; / no sound is heard from them*
l4 Septuagint, Jerome and Syriac; Hebrew *line*

Psalm 20

For the director of music.
A psalm of David.

1May the LORD answer you when
you are in distress;
may the name of the God of
Jacob[a] protect you.[b]
2May he send you help from the
sanctuary[c]
and grant you support from
Zion.
3May he remember[d] all your
sacrifices
and accept your burnt
offerings.[e] *Selah*
4May he give you the desire of
your heart[f]
and make all your plans
succeed.
5We will shout for joy when you
are victorious
and will lift up our banners[g]
in the name of our God.
May the LORD grant all your
requests.[h]

6Now I know that the LORD saves
his anointed;[i]
he answers him from his holy
heaven
with the saving power of his
right hand.
7Some trust in chariots and
some in horses,[j]
but we trust in the name of
the LORD our God.[k]
8They are brought to their knees
and fall,
but we rise up[l] and stand
firm.[m]
9O LORD, save the king!
Answer[m] us[n] when we call!

Psalm 21

For the director of music.
A psalm of David.

1O LORD, the king rejoices in
your strength.
How great is his joy in the
victories you give![o]
2You have granted him the
desire of his heart[p]
and have not withheld the
request of his lips. *Selah*
3You welcomed him with rich
blessings
and placed a crown of pure
gold[q] on his head.
4He asked you for life, and you
gave it to him—
length of days, for ever and
ever.[r]
5Through the victories[s] you
gave, his glory is
great;
you have bestowed on him
splendor and majesty.
6Surely you have granted him
eternal blessings
and made him glad with the
joy[t] of your presence.[u]
7For the king trusts in the
LORD;
through the unfailing love of
the Most High
he will not be shaken.

8Your hand will lay hold[v] on all
your enemies;
your right hand will seize
your foes.
9At the time of your appearing
you will make them like a
fiery furnace.
In his wrath the LORD will
swallow them up,
and his fire will consume
them.[w]
10You will destroy their
descendants from the
earth,
their posterity from
mankind.[x]
11Though they plot evil[y] against
you
and devise wicked schemes,[z]
they cannot succeed;
12for you will make them turn
their backs[a]
when you aim at them with
drawn bow.

13Be exalted, O LORD, in your
strength;
we will sing and praise your
might.

20:1 [a]Ps 46:7,11 [b]Ps 91:14
20:2 [c]Ps 3:4
20:3 [d]Ac 10:4 [e]Ps 51:19
20:4 [f]Ps 21:2; 145:16,19
20:5 [g]Ps 9:14; 60:4 [h]1Sa 1:17
20:6 [i]Ps 28:8; 41:11; Isa 58:9
20:7 [j]Ps 33:17; Isa 31:1 [k]2Ch 32:8
20:8 [l]Mic 7:8 [m]Ps 37:23
20:9 [n]Ps 3:7; 17:6
21:1 [o]Ps 59:16-17
21:2 [p]Ps 37:4
21:3 [q]2Sa 12:30
21:4 [r]Ps 61:5-6; 91:16; 133:3
21:5 [s]Ps 18:50
21:6 [t]Ps 43:4 [u]1Ch 17:27
21:8 [v]Isa 10:10
21:9 [w]Ps 50:3; La 2:2; Mal 4:1
21:10 [x]Dt 28:18; Ps 37:28
21:11 [y]Ps 2:1 [z]Ps 10:2
21:12 [a]Ps 7:12-13; 18:40

m9 Or *save! / O King, answer*

Psalm 22

For the director of music. To ⌊the tune of⌋ "The Doe of the Morning." A psalm of David.

1My God, my God, why have you
forsaken me?[a]
Why are you so far[b] from
saving me,
so far from the words of my
groaning?
2O my God, I cry out by day, but
you do not answer,
by night,[c] and am not silent.

3Yet you are enthroned as the
Holy One;[d]
you are the praise[e] of
Israel.[n]
4In you our fathers put their
trust;
they trusted and you
delivered them.
5They cried to you and were
saved;
in you they trusted and were
not disappointed.[f]

6But I am a worm[g] and not a
man,
scorned by men[h] and
despised[i] by the people.
7All who see me mock me;
they hurl insults,[j] shaking
their heads:[k]
8"He trusts in the LORD;
let the LORD rescue him.[l]
Let him deliver him,
since he delights[m] in him."

9Yet you brought me out of the
womb;[n]
you made me trust in you
even at my mother's breast.
10From birth[o] I was cast upon
you;
from my mother's womb you
have been my God.
11Do not be far from me,
for trouble is near
and there is no one to help.[p]

12Many bulls[q] surround me;
strong bulls of Bashan[r]
encircle me.
13Roaring lions[s] tearing their
prey
open their mouths wide[t]
against me.
14I am poured out like water,
and all my bones are out of
joint.[u]
My heart has turned to wax;
it has melted away[v] within
me.
15My strength is dried up like a
potsherd,
and my tongue sticks to the
roof of my mouth;[w]
you lay me[o] in the dust[x] of
death.
16Dogs[y] have surrounded me;
a band of evil men has
encircled me,
they have pierced[p][z] my
hands and my feet.
17I can count all my bones;
people stare[a] and gloat over
me.[b]
18They divide my garments
among them
and cast lots[c] for my
clothing.

19But you, O LORD, be not far off;
O my Strength, come
quickly[d] to help me.
20Deliver my life from the sword,
my precious life[e] from the
power of the dogs.
21Rescue me from the mouth of
the lions;
save[q] me from the horns of
the wild oxen.

22I will declare your name to my
brothers;
in the congregation I will
praise you.[f]
23You who fear the LORD, praise
him![g]
All you descendants of Jacob,
honor him!
Revere him,[h] all you
descendants of Israel!
24For he has not despised or
disdained
the suffering of the afflicted
one;

22:1 [a]Mt 27:46*; Mk 15:34* [b]Ps 10:1
22:2 [c]Ps 42:3
22:3 [d]Ps 99:9 [e]Dt 10:21
22:5 [f]Isa 49:23
22:6 [g]Job 25:6; Isa 41:14 [h]Ps 31:11 [i]Isa 49:7; 53:3
22:7 [j]Mt 27:39,44 [k]Mk 15:29
22:8 [l]Ps 91:14 [m]Mt 27:43
22:9 [n]Ps 71:6
22:10 [o]Isa 46:3
22:11 [p]Ps 72:12
22:12 [q]Ps 68:30 [r]Dt 32:14
22:13 [s]Ps 17:12 [t]Ps 35:21
22:14 [u]Ps 31:10 [v]Job 30:16; Da 5:6
22:15 [w]Ps 38:10; Jn 19:28 [x]Ps 104:29
22:16 [y]Ps 59:6 [z]Isa 53:5; Zec 12:10; Jn 19:34
22:17 [a]Lk 23:35 [b]Lk 23:27
22:18 [c]Mt 27:35*; Lk 23:34; Jn 19:24*
22:19 [d]Ps 70:5
22:20 [e]Ps 35:17
22:22 [f]Heb 2:12*
22:23 [g]Ps 86:12; 135:19 [h]Ps 33:8

[n]3 Or *Yet you are holy, / enthroned on the praises of Israel* [o]15 Or */ I am laid* [p]16 Some Hebrew manuscripts, Septuagint and Syriac; most Hebrew manuscripts */ like the lion,* [q]21 Or */ you have heard*

he has not hidden his face[a]
from him
but has listened to his cry for
help.[b]
25From you comes the theme of
my praise in the great
assembly;[c]
before those who fear you[r]
will I fulfill my vows.[d]
26The poor will eat[e] and be
satisfied;
they who seek the LORD will
praise him—[f]
may your hearts live forever!
27All the ends of the earth[g]
will remember and turn to
the LORD,
and all the families of the
nations
will bow down before him,[h]
28for dominion belongs to the
LORD[i]
and he rules over the
nations.
29All the rich[j] of the earth will
feast and worship;
all who go down to the dust[k]
will kneel before him—
those who cannot keep
themselves alive.
30Posterity[l] will serve him;
future generations will be
told about the Lord.
31They will proclaim his
righteousness
to a people yet unborn[m]—
for he has done it.

Psalm 23

A psalm of David.

1The LORD is my shepherd,[n] I
shall not be in want.[o]
2 He makes me lie down in
green pastures,
he leads me beside quiet
waters,[p]
3 he restores my soul.[q]
He guides me in paths of
righteousness[r]
for his name's sake.
4Even though I walk
through the valley of the
shadow of death,[s][s]
I will fear no evil,[t]
for you are with me;[u]
your rod and your staff,
they comfort me.
5You prepare a table before me
in the presence of my
enemies.
You anoint my head with oil;[v]
my cup[w] overflows.
6Surely goodness and love will
follow me
all the days of my life,
and I will dwell in the house of
the LORD
forever.

Psalm 24

Of David. A psalm.

1The earth is the LORD's,[x] and
everything in it,
the world, and all who live in
it;[y]
2for he founded it upon the seas
and established it upon the
waters.
3Who may ascend the hill[z] of
the LORD?
Who may stand in his holy
place?[a]
4He who has clean hands[b] and
a pure heart,[c]
who does not lift up his soul
to an idol
or swear by what is false.[t]
5He will receive blessing from
the LORD
and vindication from God his
Savior.
6Such is the generation of those
who seek him,
who seek your face,[d] O God
of Jacob.[u] *Selah*
7Lift up your heads, O you
gates;[e]
be lifted up, you ancient
doors,
that the King of glory[f] may
come in.
8Who is this King of glory?
The LORD strong and mighty,

22:24 [a]Ps 69:17 [b]Heb 5:7
22:25 [c]Ps 35:18 [d]Ecc 5:4
22:26 [e]Ps 107:9 [f]Ps 40:16
22:27 [g]Ps 2:8 [h]Ps 86:9
22:28 [i]Ps 47:7-8
22:29 [j]Ps 45:12 [k]Isa 26:19
22:30 [l]Ps 102:28
22:31 [m]Ps 78:6
23:1 [n]Isa 40:11; Jn 10:11; 1Pe 2:25 [o]Php 4:19
23:2 [p]Eze 34:14; Rev 7:17
23:3 [q]Ps 19:7 [r]Ps 5:8; 85:13
23:4 [s]Job 10:21-22 [t]Ps 3:6; 27:1 [u]Isa 43:2
23:5 [v]Ps 92:10 [w]Ps 16:5
24:1 [x]Ex 9:29; Job 41:11; Ps 89:11 [y]1Co 10:26*
24:3 [z]Ps 2:6 [a]Ps 15:1; 65:4
24:4 [b]Job 17:9 [c]Mt 5:8
24:6 [d]Ps 27:8
24:7 [e]Isa 26:2 [f]Ps 97:6; 1Co 2:8

[r]25 Hebrew *him* [s]4 Or *through the darkest valley* [t]4 Or *swear falsely* [u]6 Two Hebrew manuscripts and Syriac (see also Septuagint); most Hebrew manuscripts *face, Jacob*

the LORD mighty in battle.[a]
9Lift up your heads, O you gates;
lift them up, you ancient doors,
that the King of glory may come in.
10Who is he, this King of glory?
The LORD Almighty—
he is the King of glory. *Selah*

Psalm 25[v]

Of David.

1To you, O LORD, I lift up my soul;[b]
2 in you I trust,[c] O my God.
Do not let me be put to shame,
nor let my enemies triumph over me.
3No one whose hope is in you
will ever be put to shame,[d]
but they will be put to shame
who are treacherous without excuse.

4Show me your ways, O LORD,
teach me your paths;[e]
5guide me in your truth and teach me,
for you are God my Savior,
and my hope is in you all day long.
6Remember, O LORD, your great mercy and love,[f]
for they are from of old.
7Remember not the sins of my youth[g]
and my rebellious ways;
according to your love[h]
remember me,
for you are good, O LORD.

8Good and upright[i] is the LORD;
therefore he instructs[j]
sinners in his ways.
9He guides[k] the humble in what is right
and teaches them[l] his way.
10All the ways of the LORD are
loving and faithful[m]
for those who keep the
demands of his covenant.[n]
11For the sake of your name,[o]
O LORD,
forgive my iniquity, though it is great.
12Who, then, is the man that fears the LORD?
He will instruct him in the way[p] chosen for him.
13He will spend his days in prosperity,[q]
and his descendants will inherit the land.[r]
14The LORD confides[s] in those who fear him;
he makes his covenant known[t] to them.
15My eyes are ever on the LORD,[u]
for only he will release my feet from the snare.

16Turn to me[v] and be gracious to me,
for I am lonely and afflicted.
17The troubles of my heart have multiplied;
free me from my anguish.[w]
18Look upon my affliction and my distress[x]
and take away all my sins.
19See how my enemies[y] have increased
and how fiercely they hate me!
20Guard my life[z] and rescue me;
let me not be put to shame,
for I take refuge in you.
21May integrity[a] and uprightness protect me,
because my hope is in you.

22Redeem Israel,[b] O God,
from all their troubles!

Psalm 26

Of David.

1Vindicate me, O LORD,
for I have led a blameless life;[c]
I have trusted[d] in the LORD
without wavering.[e]
2Test me,[f] O LORD, and try me,
examine my heart and my mind;[g]
3for your love is ever before me,

24:8 [a]Ps 76:3-6
25:1 [b]Ps 86:4
25:2 [c]Ps 41:11
25:3 [d]Isa 49:23
25:4 [e]Ex 33:13
25:6 [f]Ps 103:17; Isa 63:7,15
25:7 [g]Job 13:26; Jer 3:25 [h]Ps 51:1
25:8 [i]Ps 92:15 [j]Ps 32:8
25:9 [k]Ps 23:3 [l]Ps 27:11
25:10 [m]Ps 40:11 [n]Ps 103:18
25:11 [o]Ps 31:3; 79:9
25:12 [p]Ps 37:23
25:13 [q]Pr 19:23 [r]Ps 37:11
25:14 [s]Pr 3:32 [t]Jn 7:17
25:15 [u]Ps 141:8
25:16 [v]Ps 69:16
25:17 [w]Ps 107:6
25:18 [x]2Sa 16:12
25:19 [y]Ps 3:1
25:20 [z]Ps 86:2
25:21 [a]Ps 41:12
25:22 [b]Ps 130:8
26:1 [c]Ps 7:8; Pr 20:7 [d]Ps 28:7 [e]2Ki 20:3; Heb 10:23
26:2 [f]Ps 17:3 [g]Ps 7:9

[v]This psalm is an acrostic poem, the verses of which begin with the successive letters of the Hebrew alphabet.

and I walk continually[a] in
your truth.
4I do not sit[b] with deceitful
men,
nor do I consort with
hypocrites;
5I abhor[c] the assembly of
evildoers
and refuse to sit with the
wicked.
6I wash my hands in
innocence,[d]
and go about your altar,
O LORD,
7proclaiming aloud your praise
and telling of all your
wonderful deeds.[e]
8I love[f] the house where you
live, O LORD,
the place where your glory
dwells.

9Do not take away my soul
along with sinners,
my life with bloodthirsty
men,[g]
10in whose hands are wicked
schemes,
whose right hands are full of
bribes.[h]
11But I lead a blameless life;
redeem me[i] and be merciful
to me.

12My feet stand on level
ground;[j]
in the great assembly[k] I will
praise the LORD.

Psalm 27

Of David.

1The LORD is my light[l] and my
salvation[m]—
whom shall I fear?
The LORD is the stronghold of
my life—
of whom shall I be afraid?[n]
2When evil men advance against
me
to devour my flesh,[w]
when my enemies and my foes
attack me,
they will stumble and fall.[o]
3Though an army besiege me,
my heart will not fear;[p]
though war break out against
me,
even then will I be
confident.[q]

4One thing[r] I ask of the LORD,
this is what I seek:
that I may dwell in the house
of the LORD
all the days of my life,[s]
to gaze upon the beauty of the
LORD
and to seek him in his
temple.
5For in the day of trouble
he will keep me safe in his
dwelling;
he will hide me[t] in the shelter
of his tabernacle
and set me high upon a
rock.[u]
6Then my head will be exalted[v]
above the enemies who
surround me;
at his tabernacle will I
sacrifice[w] with shouts of
joy;
I will sing and make music to
the LORD.

7Hear my voice when I call,
O LORD;
be merciful to me and
answer me.[x]
8My heart says of you, "Seek
his[x] face!"
Your face, LORD, I will seek.
9Do not hide your face[y] from
me,
do not turn your servant
away in anger;
you have been my helper.
Do not reject me or forsake me,
O God my Savior.
10Though my father and mother
forsake me,
the LORD will receive me.
11Teach me your way, O LORD;
lead me in a straight path[z]
because of my oppressors.
12Do not turn me over to the
desire of my foes,
for false witnesses[a] rise up
against me,
breathing out violence.

26:3 [a]2Ki 20:3
26:4 [b]Ps 1:1
26:5 [c]Ps 31:6; 139:21
26:6 [d]Ps 73:13
26:7 [e]Ps 9:1
26:8 [f]Ps 27:4
26:9 [g]Ps 28:3
26:10 [h]1Sa 8:3
26:11 [i]Ps 69:18
26:12 [j]Ps 27:11; 40:2 [k]Ps 22:22
27:1 [l]Isa 60:19 [m]Ex 15:2 [n]Ps 118:6
27:2 [o]Ps 9:3; 14:4
27:3 [p]Ps 3:6 [q]Job 4:6
27:4 [r]Ps 90:17 [s]Ps 23:6; 26:8
27:5 [t]Ps 17:8; 31:20 [u]Ps 40:2
27:6 [v]Ps 3:3 [w]Ps 107:22
27:7 [x]Ps 13:3
27:9 [y]Ps 69:17
27:11 [z]Ps 5:8; 25:4; 86:11
27:12 [a]Mt 26:60; Ac 9:1

[w]2 Or *to slander me* [x]8 Or *To you, O my heart, he has said, "Seek my*

13I am still confident of this:
I will see the goodness of the
LORD[a]
in the land of the living.[b]
14Wait[c] for the LORD;
be strong and take heart
and wait for the LORD.

Psalm 28

Of David.

1To you I call, O LORD my Rock;
do not turn a deaf ear to me.
For if you remain silent,[d]
I will be like those who have
gone down to the pit.[e]
2Hear my cry for mercy[f]
as I call to you for help,
as I lift up my hands
toward your Most Holy
Place.[g]

3Do not drag me away with the
wicked,
with those who do evil,
who speak cordially with their
neighbors
but harbor malice in their
hearts.[h]
4Repay them for their deeds
and for their evil work;
repay them for what their
hands have done[i]
and bring back upon them
what they deserve.[j]
5Since they show no regard for
the works of the LORD
and what his hands have
done,[k]
he will tear them down
and never build them up
again.

6Praise be to the LORD,
for he has heard my cry for
mercy.
7The LORD is my strength[l] and
my shield;
my heart trusts[m] in him, and
I am helped.
My heart leaps for joy
and I will give thanks to him
in song.[n]

8The LORD is the strength of his
people,

27:13 [a]Ps 31:19 [b]Jer 11:19; Eze 26:20
27:14 [c]Ps 40:1
28:1 [d]Ps 83:1 [e]Ps 88:4
28:2 [f]Ps 138:2; 140:6 [g]Ps 5:7
28:3 [h]Ps 12:2; Ps 26:9; Jer 9:8
28:4 [i]2Ti 4:14; Rev 22:12 [j]Rev 18:6
28:5 [k]Isa 5:12
28:7 [l]Ps 18:1 [m]Ps 13:5 [n]Ps 40:3; 69:30
28:8 [o]Ps 20:6
28:9 [p]Dt 9:29; Ezr 1:4 [q]Isa 40:11 [r]Dt 1:31; 32:11
29:1 [s]1Ch 16:28 [t]Ps 96:7-9
29:2 [u]2Ch 20:21
29:3 [v]Job 37:5 [w]Ps 18:13
29:4 [x]Ps 68:33
29:5 [y]Jdg 9:15
29:6 [z]Ps 114:4 [a]Dt 3:9
29:8 [b]Nu 13:26
29:9 [c]Ps 26:8
29:10 [d]Ge 6:17 [e]Ps 10:16

a fortress of salvation for his
anointed one.[o]
9Save your people and bless
your inheritance;[p]
be their shepherd[q] and carry
them[r] forever.

Psalm 29

A psalm of David.

1Ascribe to the LORD,[s] O mighty
ones,
ascribe to the LORD glory[t]
and strength.
2Ascribe to the LORD the glory
due his name;
worship the LORD in the
splendor of his[y]
holiness.[u]

3The voice[v] of the LORD is over
the waters;
the God of glory thunders,[w]
the LORD thunders over the
mighty waters.
4The voice of the LORD is
powerful;[x]
the voice of the LORD is
majestic.
5The voice of the LORD breaks
the cedars;
the LORD breaks in pieces the
cedars of Lebanon.[y]
6He makes Lebanon skip[z] like a
calf,
Sirion[z][a] like a young wild
ox.
7The voice of the LORD strikes
with flashes of lightning.
8The voice of the LORD shakes
the desert;
the LORD shakes the Desert of
Kadesh.[b]
9The voice of the LORD twists the
oaks[a]
and strips the forests bare.
And in his temple all cry,
"Glory!"[c]

10The LORD sits[b] enthroned over
the flood;[d]
the LORD is enthroned as
King forever.[e]

[y]2 Or *LORD with the splendor of* [z]6 That is, Mount Hermon [a]9 Or *LORD makes the deer give birth* [b]10 Or *sat*

11The LORD gives strength to his people;[a]
the LORD blesses his people with peace.[b]

Psalm 30

A psalm. A song. For the dedication of the temple.[c] Of David.

1I will exalt you, O LORD,
for you lifted me out of the depths
and did not let my enemies gloat over me.[c]
2O LORD my God, I called to you for help[d]
and you healed me.[e]
3O LORD, you brought me up from the grave[d];
you spared me from going down into the pit.[f]

4Sing to the LORD, you saints[g] of his;
praise his holy name.[h]
5For his anger[i] lasts only a moment,
but his favor lasts a lifetime;
weeping may remain for a night,
but rejoicing comes in the morning.[j]

6When I felt secure, I said,
"I will never be shaken."
7O LORD, when you favored me,
you made my mountain[e] stand firm;
but when you hid your face,[k]
I was dismayed.

8To you, O LORD, I called;
to the Lord I cried for mercy:
9"What gain is there in my destruction,[f]
in my going down into the pit?
Will the dust praise you?
Will it proclaim your faithfulness?[l]
10Hear, O LORD, and be merciful to me;
O LORD, be my help."

11You turned my wailing into dancing;
you removed my sackcloth
and clothed me with joy,[m]
12that my heart may sing to you
and not be silent.
O LORD my God, I will give you thanks[n] forever.[o]

Psalm 31

31:1-4pp — Ps 71:1-3

For the director of music. A psalm of David.

1In you, O LORD, I have taken refuge;
let me never be put to shame;
deliver me in your righteousness.
2Turn your ear to me,
come quickly to my rescue;
be my rock of refuge,[p]
a strong fortress to save me.
3Since you are my rock and my fortress,[q]
for the sake of your name[r]
lead and guide me.
4Free me from the trap that is set for me,
for you are my refuge.[s]
5Into your hands I commit my spirit;[t]
redeem me, O LORD, the God of truth.

6I hate those who cling to worthless idols;
I trust in the LORD.[u]
7I will be glad and rejoice in your love,
for you saw my affliction[v]
and knew the anguish[w] of my soul.
8You have not handed me over[x] to the enemy
but have set my feet in a spacious place.

9Be merciful to me, O LORD, for I am in distress;
my eyes grow weak with sorrow,[y]
my soul and my body with grief.
10My life is consumed by anguish

29:11 [a]Ps 28:8 [b]Ps 37:11
30:1 [c]Ps 25:2; 28:9
30:2 [d]Ps 88:13 [e]Ps 6:2
30:3 [f]Ps 28:1; 86:13
30:4 [g]Ps 149:1 [h]Ps 97:12
30:5 [i]Ps 103:9 [j]2Co 4:17
30:7 [k]Dt 31:17; Ps 104:29
30:9 [l]Ps 6:5
30:11 [m]Ps 4:7; Jer 31:4,13
30:12 [n]Ps 16:9 [o]Ps 44:8
31:2 [p]Ps 18:2
31:3 [q]Ps 18:2 [r]Ps 23:3
31:4 [s]Ps 25:15
31:5 [t]Lk 23:46; Ac 7:59
31:6 [u]Jnh 2:8
31:7 [v]Ps 90:14 [w]Ps 10:14; Jn 10:27
31:8 [x]Dt 32:30
31:9 [y]Ps 6:7

[c]Title: Or *palace* [d]3 Hebrew *Sheol* [e]7 Or *hill country* [f]9 Or *there if I am silenced*

and my years by groaning;[a]
my strength fails because of my
affliction,[g]
and my bones grow weak.[b]
11Because of all my enemies,
I am the utter contempt of
my neighbors;[c]
I am a dread to my friends—
those who see me on the
street flee from me.
12I am forgotten by them as
though I were dead;[d]
I have become like broken
pottery.
13For I hear the slander of many;
there is terror on every side;[e]
they conspire against me
and plot to take my life.[f]

14But I trust[g] in you, O LORD;
I say, "You are my God."
15My times[h] are in your hands;
deliver me from my enemies
and from those who pursue
me.
16Let your face shine[i] on your
servant;
save me in your unfailing
love.
17Let me not be put to shame,[j]
O LORD,
for I have cried out to you;
but let the wicked be put to
shame
and lie silent[k] in the grave.[h]
18Let their lying lips[l] be
silenced,
for with pride and contempt
they speak arrogantly[m]
against the righteous.

19How great is your goodness,[n]
which you have stored up for
those who fear you,
which you bestow in the sight
of men[o]
on those who take refuge in
you.
20In the shelter of your presence
you hide[p] them
from the intrigues of men;[q]
in your dwelling you keep them
safe
from accusing tongues.

21Praise be to the LORD,
for he showed his wonderful
love[r] to me
when I was in a besieged
city.[s]
22In my alarm[t] I said,
"I am cut off from your
sight!"
Yet you heard my cry[u] for
mercy
when I called to you for help.

23Love the LORD, all his saints![v]
The LORD preserves the
faithful,[w]
but the proud he pays back[x]
in full.
24Be strong and take heart,[y]
all you who hope in the LORD.

Psalm 32

Of David. A *maskil.*[i]

1Blessed is he
whose transgressions are
forgiven,
whose sins are covered.[z]
2Blessed is the man
whose sin the LORD does not
count against him[a]
and in whose spirit is no
deceit.[b]

3When I kept silent,
my bones wasted away[c]
through my groaning all day
long.
4For day and night
your hand was heavy[d] upon
me;
my strength was sapped
as in the heat of summer.
Selah
5Then I acknowledged my sin to
you
and did not cover up my
iniquity.
I said, "I will confess[e]
my transgressions[f] to the
LORD"—
and you forgave
the guilt of my sin.[g] *Selah*
6Therefore let everyone who is
godly pray to you
while you may be found;[h]
surely when the mighty waters
rise,

31:10 [a]Ps 13:2 [b]Ps 38:3; 39:11
31:11 [c]Job 19:13; Ps 38:11; 64:8; Isa 53:4
31:12 [d]Ps 88:4
31:13 [e]Jer 20:3,10; La 2:22 [f]Mt 27:1
31:14 [g]Ps 140:6
31:15 [h]Job 24:1; Ps 143:9
31:16 [i]Nu 6:25; Ps 4:6
31:17 [j]Ps 25:2-3 [k]Ps 115:17
31:18 [l]Ps 120:2 [m]Ps 94:4
31:19 [n]Ro 11:22 [o]Isa 64:4
31:20 [p]Ps 27:5 [q]Job 5:21
31:21 [r]Ps 17:7 [s]1Sa 23:7
31:22 [t]Ps 116:11 [u]La 3:54
31:23 [v]Ps 34:9 [w]Ps 145:20 [x]Ps 94:2
31:24 [y]Ps 27:14
32:1 [z]Ps 85:2
32:2 [a]Ro 4:7-8*; 2Co 5:19 [b]Jn 1:47
32:3 [c]Ps 31:10
32:4 [d]Job 33:7
32:5 [e]Pr 28:13 [f]Ps 103:12 [g]Lev 26:40
32:6 [h]Ps 69:13; Isa 55:6

[g]*10* Or *guilt* [h]*17* Hebrew *Sheol* [i]Title: Probably a literary or musical term

they will not reach him.[a]
7You are my hiding place;
you will protect me from trouble[b]
and surround me with songs of deliverance.[c] *Selah*

8I will instruct[d] you and teach you in the way you should go;
I will counsel you and watch over[e] you.
9Do not be like the horse or the mule,
which have no understanding
but must be controlled by bit and bridle[f]
or they will not come to you.
10Many are the woes of the wicked,[g]
but the LORD's unfailing love
surrounds the man who trusts[h] in him.

11Rejoice in the LORD[i] and be glad, you righteous;
sing, all you who are upright in heart!

Psalm 33

1Sing joyfully to the LORD, you righteous;
it is fitting[j] for the upright[k] to praise him.
2Praise the LORD with the harp;
make music to him on the ten-stringed lyre.[l]
3Sing to him a new song;[m]
play skillfully, and shout for joy.
4For the word of the LORD is right[n] and true;
he is faithful in all he does.
5The LORD loves righteousness and justice;[o]
the earth is full of his unfailing love.[p]
6By the word[q] of the LORD were the heavens made,
their starry host by the breath of his mouth.
7He gathers the waters of the sea into jars[i];
he puts the deep into storehouses.
8Let all the earth fear the LORD;
let all the people of the world revere him.[r]
9For he spoke, and it came to be;
he commanded,[s] and it stood firm.
10The LORD foils the plans of the nations;[t]
he thwarts the purposes of the peoples.
11But the plans of the LORD stand firm forever,
the purposes[u] of his heart through all generations.
12Blessed is the nation whose God is the LORD,[v]
the people he chose[w] for his inheritance.
13From heaven the LORD looks down
and sees all mankind;[x]
14from his dwelling place[y] he watches
all who live on earth—
15he who forms[z] the hearts of all,
who considers everything they do.[a]
16No king is saved by the size of his army;[b]
no warrior escapes by his great strength.
17A horse[c] is a vain hope for deliverance;
despite all its great strength it cannot save.
18But the eyes[d] of the LORD are on those who fear him,
on those whose hope is in his unfailing love,[e]
19to deliver them from death
and keep them alive in famine.[f]

20We wait[g] in hope for the LORD;
he is our help and our shield.
21In him our hearts rejoice,[h]
for we trust in his holy name.
22May your unfailing love rest upon us, O LORD,
even as we put our hope in you.

32:6 [a]Isa 43:2
32:7 [b]Ps 9:9 [c]Ex 15:1
32:8 [d]Ps 25:8 [e]Ps 33:18
32:9 [f]Pr 26:3
32:10 [g]Ro 2:9 [h]Pr 16:20
32:11 [i]Ps 64:10
33:1 [j]Ps 147:1 [k]Ps 32:11
33:2 [l]Ps 92:3
33:3 [m]Ps 96:1
33:4 [n]Ps 19:8
33:5 [o]Ps 11:7 [p]Ps 119:64
33:6 [q]Heb 11:3
33:8 [r]Ps 67:7; 96:9
33:9 [s]Ge 1:3; Ps 148:5
33:10 [t]Isa 8:10
33:11 [u]Job 23:13
33:12 [v]Ps 144:15 [w]Ex 19:5; Dt 7:6
33:13 [x]Job 28:24; Ps 11:4
33:14 [y]1Ki 8:39
33:15 [z]Job 10:8 [a]Jer 32:19
33:16 [b]Ps 44:6
33:17 [c]Ps 20:7; Pr 21:31
33:18 [d]Job 36:7; Ps 34:15 [e]Ps 147:11
33:19 [f]Job 5:20
33:20 [g]Ps 130:6
33:21 [h]Zec 10:7; Jn 16:22

i7 Or *sea as into a heap*

Psalm 34[k]

Of David. When he pretended to be insane before Abimelech, who drove him away, and he left.

[1]I will extol the LORD at all times;[a]
his praise will always be on my lips.
[2]My soul will boast[b] in the LORD;
let the afflicted hear and rejoice.[c]
[3]Glorify the LORD with me;
let us exalt[d] his name together.

[4]I sought the LORD,[e] and he answered me;
he delivered me from all my fears.
[5]Those who look to him are radiant;[f]
their faces are never covered with shame.[g]
[6]This poor man called, and the LORD heard him;
he saved him out of all his troubles.
[7]The angel of the LORD[h] encamps around those who fear him,
and he delivers them.

[8]Taste and see that the LORD is good;[i]
blessed is the man who takes refuge[j] in him.
[9]Fear the LORD, you his saints,
for those who fear him lack nothing.[k]
[10]The lions may grow weak and hungry,
but those who seek the LORD lack no good thing.[l]

[11]Come, my children, listen to me;
I will teach you[m] the fear of the LORD.
[12]Whoever of you loves life[n]
and desires to see many good days,
[13]keep your tongue from evil
and your lips from speaking lies.[o]
[14]Turn from evil and do good;[p]
seek peace[q] and pursue it.

[15]The eyes of the LORD[r] are on the righteous[s]
and his ears are attentive to their cry;
[16]the face of the LORD is against[t] those who do evil,[u]
to cut off the memory[v] of them from the earth.

[17]The righteous cry out, and the LORD hears[w] them;
he delivers them from all their troubles.
[18]The LORD is close[x] to the brokenhearted[y]
and saves those who are crushed in spirit.

[19]A righteous man may have many troubles,[z]
but the LORD delivers him from them all;[a]
[20]he protects all his bones,
not one of them will be broken.[b]

[21]Evil will slay the wicked;[c]
the foes of the righteous will be condemned.
[22]The LORD redeems[d] his servants;
no one will be condemned who takes refuge in him.

Psalm 35

Of David.

[1]Contend, O LORD, with those who contend with me;
fight[e] against those who fight against me.
[2]Take up shield and buckler;
arise[f] and come to my aid.
[3]Brandish spear and javelin[1]
against those who pursue me.
Say to my soul,
"I am your salvation."

[4]May those who seek my life
be disgraced[g] and put to shame;
may those who plot my ruin
be turned back in dismay.

34:1 [a]Ps 71:6; Eph 5:20
34:2 [b]Jer 9:24; 1Co 1:31 [c]Ps 119:74
34:3 [d]Lk 1:46
34:4 [e]Mt 7:7
34:5 [f]Ps 36:9 [g]Ps 25:3
34:7 [h]2Ki 6:17; Da 6:22
34:8 [i]1Pe 2:3 [j]Ps 2:12
34:9 [k]Ps 23:1
34:10 [l]Ps 84:11
34:11 [m]Ps 32:8
34:12 [n]1Pe 3:10
34:13 [o]1Pe 2:22
34:14 [p]Ps 37:27 [q]Heb 12:14
34:15 [r]Ps 33:18 [s]Job 36:7
34:16 [t]Lev 17:10; Jer 44:11 [u]1Pe 3:10-12* [v]Pr 10:7
34:17 [w]Ps 145:19
34:18 [x]Ps 145:18 [y]Isa 57:15
34:19 [z]ver 17 [a]ver 4,6; Pr 24:16
34:20 [b]Jn 19:36*
34:21 [c]Ps 94:23
34:22 [d]1Ki 1:29; Ps 71:23
35:1 [e]Ps 43:1
35:2 [f]Ps 62:2
35:4 [g]Ps 70:2

[k]This psalm is an acrostic poem, the verses of which begin with the successive letters of the Hebrew alphabet. [1]3 Or *and block the way*

5May they be like chaff[a] before the wind,
with the angel of the LORD driving them away;
6may their path be dark and slippery,
with the angel of the LORD pursuing them.
7Since they hid their net for me without cause
and without cause dug a pit for me,
8may ruin overtake them by surprise—[b]
may the net they hid entangle them,
may they fall into the pit,[c] to their ruin.
9Then my soul will rejoice[d] in the LORD
and delight in his salvation.[e]
10My whole being will exclaim,
"Who is like you,[f] O LORD?
You rescue the poor from those too strong[g] for them,
the poor and needy[h] from those who rob them."
11Ruthless witnesses[i] come forward;
they question me on things I know nothing about.
12They repay me evil for good[j]
and leave my soul forlorn.
13Yet when they were ill, I put on sackcloth
and humbled myself with fasting.[k]
When my prayers returned to me unanswered,
14 I went about mourning
as though for my friend or brother.
I bowed my head in grief
as though weeping for my mother.
15But when I stumbled, they gathered in glee;
attackers gathered against me when I was unaware.
They slandered[l] me without ceasing.
16Like the ungodly they maliciously mocked[m];
they gnashed their teeth[m] at me.

17O Lord, how long[n] will you look on?
Rescue my life from their ravages,
my precious life[o] from these lions.
18I will give you thanks in the great assembly;[p]
among throngs of people I will praise you.[q]
19Let not those gloat over me
who are my enemies without cause;
let not those who hate me without reason[r]
maliciously wink the eye.[s]
20They do not speak peaceably,
but devise false accusations
against those who live quietly in the land.
21They gape[t] at me and say, "Aha! Aha![u]
With our own eyes we have seen it."
22O LORD, you have seen[v] this; be not silent.
Do not be far[w] from me, O Lord.
23Awake,[x] and rise to my defense!
Contend for me, my God and Lord.
24Vindicate me in your righteousness, O LORD my God;
do not let them gloat over me.
25Do not let them think, "Aha, just what we wanted!"
or say, "We have swallowed him up."[y]
26May all who gloat over my distress
be put to shame[z] and confusion;
may all who exalt themselves over me[a]
be clothed with shame and disgrace.
27May those who delight in my vindication[b]
shout for joy[c] and gladness;

35:5 [a]Job 21:18; Ps 1:4; Isa 29:5
35:8 [b]1Th 5:3 [c]Ps 9:15
35:9 [d]Lk 1:47 [e]Isa 61:10
35:10 [f]Ex 15:11 [g]Ps 18:17 [h]Ps 37:14
35:11 [i]Ps 27:12
35:12 [j]Jn 10:32
35:13 [k]Job 30:25; Ps 69:10
35:15 [l]Job 30:1,8
35:16 [m]Job 16:9; La 2:16
35:17 [n]Hab 1:13 [o]Ps 22:20
35:18 [p]Ps 22:25 [q]Ps 22:22
35:19 [r]Ps 38:19; 69:4; Jn 15:25* [s]Ps 13:4; Pr 6:13
35:21 [t]Ps 22:13 [u]Ps 40:15
35:22 [v]Ex 3:7 [w]Ps 10:1; 28:1
35:23 [x]Ps 44:23
35:25 [y]La 2:16
35:26 [z]Ps 40:14; 109:29 [a]Ps 38:16
35:27 [b]Ps 9:4 [c]Ps 32:11

[m]*16* Septuagint; Hebrew may mean *ungodly circle of mockers.*

may they always say, "The LORD
be exalted,
who delights[a] in the
well-being of his
servant."
28My tongue will speak of your
righteousness[b]
and of your praises all day
long.

Psalm 36

For the director of music. Of
David the servant of the LORD.

1An oracle is within my heart
concerning the sinfulness of
the wicked:[n]
There is no fear of God
before his eyes.[c]
2For in his own eyes he flatters
himself
too much to detect or hate
his sin.
3The words of his mouth[d] are
wicked and deceitful;
he has ceased to be wise[e]
and to do good.[f]
4Even on his bed he plots evil;[g]
he commits himself to a
sinful course[h]
and does not reject what is
wrong.[i]

5Your love, O LORD, reaches to
the heavens,
your faithfulness to the skies.
6Your righteousness is like the
mighty mountains,
your justice like the great
deep.[j]
O LORD, you preserve both man
and beast.
7 How priceless is your
unfailing love!
Both high and low among men
find[o] refuge in the shadow of
your wings.[k]
8They feast on the abundance of
your house;[l]
you give them drink from
your river[m] of delights.
9For with you is the fountain of
life;[n]
in your light[o] we see light.

10Continue your love to those
who know you,

35:27 [a]Ps 40:16; 147:11
35:28 [b]Ps 51:14
36:1 [c]Ro 3:18*
36:3 [d]Ps 10:7 [e]Ps 94:8 [f]Jer 4:22
36:4 [g]Pr 4:16; Mic 2:1 [h]Isa 65:2 [i]Ps 52:3; Ro 12:9
36:6 [j]Job 11:8; Ps 77:19; Ro 11:33
36:7 [k]Ru 2:12; Ps 17:8
36:8 [l]Ps 65:4 [m]Job 20:17; Rev 22:1
36:9 [n]Jer 2:13 [o]1Pe 2:9
36:12 [p]Ps 140:10
37:1 [q]Pr 23:17-18 [r]Ps 73:3
37:2 [s]Ps 90:6
37:3 [t]Dt 30:20 [u]Isa 40:11; Jn 10:9
37:4 [v]Isa 58:14
37:5 [w]Ps 4:5; Ps 55:22; Pr 16:3; 1Pe 5:7
37:6 [x]Mic 7:9 [y]Job 11:17
37:7 [z]Ps 62:5; La 3:26 [a]Ps 40:1
37:8 [b]Eph 4:31; Col 3:8

your righteousness to the
upright in heart.
11May the foot of the proud not
come against me,
nor the hand of the wicked
drive me away.
12See how the evildoers lie
fallen—
thrown down, not able to
rise![p]

Psalm 37[p]

Of David.

1Do not fret because of evil
men
or be envious[q] of those who
do wrong;[r]
2for like the grass they will soon
wither,
like green plants they will
soon die away.[s]

3Trust in the LORD and do good;
dwell in the land[t] and enjoy
safe pasture.[u]
4Delight[v] yourself in the LORD
and he will give you the
desires of your heart.

5Commit your way to the LORD;
trust in him[w] and he will do
this:
6He will make your
righteousness[x] shine
like the dawn,[y]
the justice of your cause like
the noonday sun.

7Be still[z] before the LORD and
wait patiently[a] for him;
do not fret when men
succeed in their ways,
when they carry out their
wicked schemes.

8Refrain from anger[b] and turn
from wrath;
do not fret—it leads only to
evil.
9For evil men will be cut off,
but those who hope in the

[n]1 Or *heart: / Sin proceeds from the wicked.* [o]7 Or *love, O God! / Men find*; or *love! / Both heavenly beings and men / find* [p]This psalm is an acrostic poem, the stanzas of which begin with the successive letters of the Hebrew alphabet.

LORD will inherit the
land.[a]

10A little while, and the wicked
will be no more;[b]
though you look for them,
they will not be found.
11But the meek will inherit the
land[c]
and enjoy great peace.

12The wicked plot against the
righteous
and gnash their teeth[d] at
them;
13but the Lord laughs at the
wicked,
for he knows their day is
coming.[e]

14The wicked draw the sword
and bend the bow[f]
to bring down the poor and
needy,[g]
to slay those whose ways are
upright.
15But their swords will pierce
their own hearts,[h]
and their bows will be
broken.

16Better the little that the
righteous have
than the wealth[i] of many
wicked;
17for the power of the wicked will
be broken,[j]
but the LORD upholds the
righteous.

18The days of the blameless are
known to the LORD,[k]
and their inheritance will
endure forever.
19In times of disaster they will
not wither;
in days of famine they will
enjoy plenty.

20But the wicked will perish:
The LORD's enemies will be
like the beauty of the
fields,
they will vanish—vanish like
smoke.[l]

21The wicked borrow and do not
repay,
but the righteous give
generously;[m]
22those the LORD blesses will
inherit the land,
but those he curses[n] will be
cut off.

23If the LORD delights[o] in a
man's way,
he makes his steps firm;[p]
24though he stumble, he will not
fall,[q]
for the LORD upholds[r] him
with his hand.

25I was young and now I am old,
yet I have never seen the
righteous forsaken[s]
or their children begging
bread.
26They are always generous and
lend freely;
their children will be
blessed.[t]

27Turn from evil and do good;[u]
then you will dwell in the
land forever.
28For the LORD loves the just
and will not forsake his
faithful ones.

They will be protected forever,
but the offspring of the
wicked will be cut off;[v]
29the righteous will inherit the
land[w]
and dwell in it forever.

30The mouth of the righteous
man utters wisdom,
and his tongue speaks what
is just.
31The law of his God is in his
heart;[x]
his feet do not slip.[y]

32The wicked lie in wait[z] for the
righteous,
seeking their very lives;
33but the LORD will not leave
them in their power
or let them be condemned
when brought to trial.[a]

34Wait for the LORD[b]
and keep his way.
He will exalt you to inherit the
land;
when the wicked are cut off,
you will see[c] it.

37:9 [a]Isa 57:13; 60:21
37:10 [b]Job 7:10; 24:24
37:11 [c]Mt 5:5
37:12 [d]Ps 35:16
37:13 [e]1Sa 26:10; Ps 2:4
37:14 [f]Ps 11:2 [g]Ps 35:10
37:15 [h]Ps 9:16
37:16 [i]Pr 15:16
37:17 [j]Job 38:15; Ps 10:15
37:18 [k]Ps 1:6
37:20 [l]Ps 102:3
37:21 [m]Ps 112:5
37:22 [n]Job 5:3; Pr 3:33
37:23 [o]Ps 147:11 [p]1Sa 2:9
37:24 [q]Pr 24:16 [r]Ps 145:14; 147:6
37:25 [s]Heb 13:5
37:26 [t]Ps 147:13
37:27 [u]Ps 34:14
37:28 [v]Ps 21:10; Isa 14:20
37:29 [w]ver 9; Pr 2:21
37:31 [x]Dt 6:6; Ps 40:8; Isa 51:7 [y]ver 23
37:32 [z]Ps 10:8
37:33 [a]Ps 109:31; 2Pe 2:9
37:34 [b]Ps 27:14 [c]Ps 52:6

[35]I have seen a wicked and
ruthless man
flourishing[a] like a green tree
in its native soil,
[36]but he soon passed away and
was no more;
though I looked for him, he
could not be found.[b]

[37]Consider the blameless, observe
the upright;
there is a future[q] for the
man of peace.[c]
[38]But all sinners will be
destroyed;
the future[r] of the wicked
will be cut off.[d]

[39]The salvation[e] of the righteous
comes from the LORD;
he is their stronghold in time
of trouble.[f]
[40]The LORD helps[g] them and
delivers[h] them;
he delivers them from the
wicked and saves them,
because they take refuge in
him.

Psalm 38

A psalm of David. A petition.

[1]O LORD, do not rebuke me in
your anger
or discipline me in your
wrath.[i]
[2]For your arrows[j] have pierced
me,
and your hand has come
down upon me.
[3]Because of your wrath there is
no health in my body;
my bones[k] have no
soundness because of
my sin.
[4]My guilt has overwhelmed me
like a burden too heavy to
bear.[l]

[5]My wounds fester and are
loathsome
because of my sinful folly.[m]
[6]I am bowed down and brought
very low;
all day long I go about
mourning.[n]
[7]My back is filled with searing
pain;[o]
there is no health in my
body.
[8]I am feeble and utterly
crushed;
I groan[p] in anguish of heart.

[9]All my longings lie open before
you, O Lord;
my sighing[q] is not hidden
from you.
[10]My heart pounds, my strength
fails[r] me;
even the light has gone from
my eyes.[s]
[11]My friends and companions
avoid me because of my
wounds;[t]
my neighbors stay far away.
[12]Those who seek my life set
their traps,[u]
those who would harm me
talk of my ruin;[v]
all day long they plot
deception.[w]

[13]I am like a deaf man, who
cannot hear,
like a mute, who cannot
open his mouth;
[14]I have become like a man who
does not hear,
whose mouth can offer no
reply.
[15]I wait[x] for you, O LORD;
you will answer,[y] O Lord my
God.
[16]For I said, "Do not let them
gloat[z]
or exalt themselves over me
when my foot slips."[a]

[17]For I am about to fall,
and my pain is ever with me.
[18]I confess my iniquity;[b]
I am troubled by my sin.
[19]Many are those who are my
vigorous enemies;[c]
those who hate me without
reason[d] are numerous.
[20]Those who repay my good with
evil[e]
slander me when I pursue
what is good.

37:35 [a]Job 5:3
37:36 [b]Job 20:5
37:37 [c]Isa 57:1-2
37:38 [d]Ps 1:4
37:39 [e]Ps 3:8 [f]Ps 9:9
37:40 [g]1Ch 5:20 [h]Isa 31:5
38:1 [i]Ps 6:1
38:2 [j]Job 6:4; Ps 32:4
38:3 [k]Ps 6:2; Isa 1:6
38:4 [l]Ezr 9:6
38:5 [m]Ps 69:5
38:6 [n]Job 30:28; Ps 35:14; 42:9
38:7 [o]Ps 102:3
38:8 [p]Ps 22:1
38:9 [q]Job 3:24; Ps 6:6; 10:17
38:10 [r]Ps 31:10 [s]Ps 6:7
38:11 [t]Ps 31:11
38:12 [u]Ps 140:5 [v]Ps 35:4; 54:3 [w]Ps 35:20
38:15 [x]Ps 39:7 [y]Ps 17:6
38:16 [z]Ps 35:26 [a]Ps 13:4
38:18 [b]Ps 32:5
38:19 [c]Ps 18:17 [d]Ps 35:19
38:20 [e]Ps 35:12; 1Jn 3:12

[q]37 Or *there will be posterity* [r]38 Or *posterity*

[21]O LORD, do not forsake me;
be not far[a] from me, O my God.
[22]Come quickly to help me,[b]
O Lord my Savior.[c]

Psalm 39

For the director of music. For Jeduthun. A psalm of David.

[1]I said, "I will watch my ways[d]
and keep my tongue from sin;[e]
I will put a muzzle on my mouth
as long as the wicked are in my presence."
[2]But when I was silent[f] and still,
not even saying anything good,
my anguish increased.
[3]My heart grew hot within me,
and as I meditated, the fire burned;
then I spoke with my tongue:

[4]"Show me, O LORD, my life's end
and the number of my days;[g]
let me know how fleeting is my life.[h]
[5]You have made my days[i] a mere handbreadth;
the span of my years is as nothing before you.
Each man's life is but a breath.[j] *Selah*
[6]Man is a mere phantom[k] as he goes to and fro:
He bustles about, but only in vain;[l]
he heaps up wealth, not knowing who will get it.[m]

[7]"But now, Lord, what do I look for?
My hope is in you.[n]
[8]Save me[o] from all my transgressions;[p]
do not make me the scorn of fools.
[9]I was silent; I would not open my mouth,[q]
for you are the one who has done this.
[10]Remove your scourge from me;
I am overcome by the blow of your hand.[r]
[11]You rebuke[s] and discipline men for their sin;
you consume their wealth like a moth[t]—
each man is but a breath. *Selah*

[12]"Hear my prayer, O LORD,
listen to my cry for help;
be not deaf to my weeping.
For I dwell with you as an alien,[u]
a stranger,[v] as all my fathers were.
[13]Look away from me, that I may rejoice again
before I depart and am no more."[w]

Psalm 40

40:13–17pp — Ps 70:1–5

For the director of music. Of David. A psalm.

[1]I waited patiently[x] for the LORD;
he turned to me and heard my cry.[y]
[2]He lifted me out of the slimy pit,
out of the mud and mire;[z]
he set my feet on a rock[a]
and gave me a firm place to stand.
[3]He put a new song[b] in my mouth,
a hymn of praise to our God.
Many will see and fear
and put their trust in the LORD.

[4]Blessed is the man[c]
who makes the LORD his trust,[d]
who does not look to the proud,
to those who turn aside to false gods.[s]
[5]Many, O LORD my God,
are the wonders[e] you have done.
The things you planned for us

38:21 [a]Ps 35:22
38:22 [b]Ps 40:13 [c]Ps 27:1
39:1 [d]1Ki 2:4 [e]Job 2:10; Jas 3:2
39:2 [f]Ps 38:13
39:4 [g]Ps 90:12 [h]Ps 103:14
39:5 [i]Ps 89:45 [j]Ps 62:9
39:6 [k]1Pe 1:24 [l]Ps 127:2 [m]Lk 12:20
39:7 [n]Ps 38:15
39:8 [o]Ps 51:9 [p]Ps 44:13
39:9 [q]Job 2:10
39:10 [r]Job 9:34; Ps 32:4
39:11 [s]2Pe 2:16 [t]Job 13:28
39:12 [u]1Pe 2:11 [v]Heb 11:13
39:13 [w]Job 10:21; 14:10
40:1 [x]Ps 27:14 [y]Ps 34:15
40:2 [z]Ps 69:14 [a]Ps 27:5
40:3 [b]Ps 33:3
40:4 [c]Ps 34:8 [d]Ps 84:12
40:5 [e]Ps 136:4

[s]4 Or *to falsehood*

no one can recount[a] to you;
were I to speak and tell of them,
they would be too many to declare.

6 Sacrifice and offering you did not desire,[b]
but my ears you have pierced[t,u];
burnt offerings[c] and sin offerings
you did not require.
7 Then I said, "Here I am, I have come—
it is written about me in the scroll.[v]
8 I desire to do your will,[d] O my God;
your law is within my heart."[e]

9 I proclaim righteousness in the great assembly;[f]
I do not seal my lips,
as you know,[g] O LORD.
10 I do not hide your righteousness in my heart;
I speak of your faithfulness[h] and salvation.
I do not conceal your love and your truth
from the great assembly.[i]

11 Do not withhold your mercy from me, O LORD;
may your love[j] and your truth[k] always protect me.
12 For troubles[l] without number surround me;
my sins have overtaken me, and I cannot see.[m]
They are more than the hairs of my head,[n]
and my heart fails[o] within me.

13 Be pleased, O LORD, to save me;
O LORD, come quickly to help me.[p]
14 May all who seek to take my life
be put to shame and confusion;
may all who desire my ruin[q]
be turned back in disgrace.
15 May those who say to me, "Aha! Aha!"
be appalled at their own shame.
16 But may all who seek you
rejoice and be glad in you;
may those who love your salvation always say,
"The LORD be exalted!"[r]
17 Yet I am poor and needy;
may the Lord think of me.
You are my help and my deliverer;
O my God, do not delay.[s]

Psalm 41

For the director of music.
A psalm of David.

1 Blessed is he who has regard for the weak;[t]
the LORD delivers him in times of trouble.
2 The LORD will protect him and preserve his life;
he will bless him in the land[u]
and not surrender him to the desire of his foes.[v]
3 The LORD will sustain him on his sickbed
and restore him from his bed of illness.

4 I said, "O LORD, have mercy[w] on me;
heal me, for I have sinned[x] against you."
5 My enemies say of me in malice,
"When will he die and his name perish?[y]"
6 Whenever one comes to see me,
he speaks falsely,[z] while his heart gathers slander;[a]
then he goes out and spreads it abroad.

7 All my enemies whisper together[b] against me;
they imagine the worst for me, saying,

40:5 [a] Ps 139:18; Isa 55:8
40:6 [b] 1Sa 15:22; Am 5:22 [c] Isa 1:11
40:8 [d] Jn 4:34 [e] Ps 37:31
40:9 [f] Ps 22:25 [g] Jos 22:22; Ps 119:13
40:10 [h] Ps 89:1 [i] Ac 20:20
40:11 [j] Pr 20:28 [k] Ps 43:3
40:12 [l] Ps 116:3 [m] Ps 38:4 [n] Ps 69:4 [o] Ps 73:26
40:13 [p] Ps 70:1
40:14 [q] Ps 35:4
40:16 [r] Ps 35:27
40:17 [s] Ps 70:5
41:1 [t] Ps 82:3-4; Pr 14:21
41:2 [u] Ps 37:22 [v] Ps 27:12
41:4 [w] Ps 6:2 [x] Ps 51:4
41:5 [y] Ps 38:12
41:6 [z] Ps 12:2 [a] Pr 26:24
41:7 [b] Ps 56:5; 71:10-11

[t] 6 Hebrew; Septuagint *but a body you have prepared for me* (see also Symmachus and Theodotion) [u] 6 Or *opened* [v] 7 Or *come / with the scroll written for me*

8"A vile disease has beset him;
he will never get up from the
place where he lies."
9Even my close friend,[a] whom I
trusted,
he who shared my bread,
has lifted up his heel against
me.[b]

10But you, O LORD, have mercy
on me;
raise me up,[c] that I may
repay them.
11I know that you are pleased
with me,[d]
for my enemy does not
triumph over me.[e]
12In my integrity you uphold
me[f]
and set me in your presence
forever.[g]

13Praise be to the LORD, the God
of Israel,[h]
from everlasting to
everlasting.
Amen and Amen.[i]

BOOK II

Psalms 42–72

Psalm 42[w]

For the director of music. A *maskil*[x] of the Sons of Korah.

1As the deer pants for streams
of water,
so my soul pants[j] for you,
O God.
2My soul thirsts[k] for God, for
the living God.[l]
When can I go[m] and meet
with God?
3My tears[n] have been my food
day and night,
while men say to me all day
long,
"Where is your God?"[o]
4These things I remember
as I pour out my soul:
how I used to go with the
multitude,
leading the procession to the
house of God,[p]
with shouts of joy and
thanksgiving[q]
among the festive throng.

5Why are you downcast,[r] O my
soul?
Why so disturbed within me?
Put your hope in God,[s]
for I will yet praise him,
my Savior[t] and 6my God.

My[y] soul is downcast within
me;
therefore I will remember
you
from the land of the Jordan,
the heights of Hermon—from
Mount Mizar.
7Deep calls to deep
in the roar of your waterfalls;
all your waves and breakers
have swept over me.[u]

8By day the LORD directs his
love,[v]
at night[w] his song[x] is with
me—
a prayer to the God of my
life.

9I say to God my Rock,
"Why have you forgotten me?
Why must I go about
mourning,[y]
oppressed by the enemy?"
10My bones suffer mortal agony
as my foes taunt me,
saying to me all day long,
"Where is your God?"

11Why are you downcast, O my
soul?
Why so disturbed within me?
Put your hope in God,
for I will yet praise him,
my Savior and my God.[z]

Psalm 43[w]

1Vindicate me, O God,
and plead my cause[a] against
an ungodly nation;
rescue me from deceitful and
wicked men.[b]

[w]In many Hebrew manuscripts Psalms 42 and 43 constitute one psalm. [x]Title: Probably a literary or musical term [y]5,6 A few Hebrew manuscripts, Septuagint and Syriac; most Hebrew manuscripts *praise him for his saving help. / 6O my God, my*

41:9 [a]2Sa 15:12; Ps 55:12 [b]Job 19:19; Ps 55:20; Mt 26:23; Jn 13:18*
41:10 [c]Ps 3:3
41:11 [d]Ps 147:11 [e]Ps 25:2
41:12 [f]Ps 37:17 [g]Job 36:7
41:13 [h]Ps 72:18 [i]Ps 89:52; 106:48
42:1 [j]Ps 119:131
42:2 [k]Ps 63:1 [l]Jer 10:10 [m]Ps 43:4
42:3 [n]Ps 80:5 [o]Ps 79:10
42:4 [p]Isa 30:29 [q]Ps 100:4
42:5 [r]Ps 38:6; 77:3 [s]La 3:24 [t]Ps 44:3
42:7 [u]Ps 88:7; Jnh 2:3
42:8 [v]Ps 57:3 [w]Job 35:10 [x]Ps 63:6; 149:5
42:9 [y]Ps 38:6
42:11 [z]Ps 43:5
43:1 [a]1Sa 24:15; Ps 26:1; 35:1 [b]Ps 5:6

2You are God my stronghold.
Why have you rejected[a] me?
Why must I go about mourning,
oppressed by the enemy?[b]
3Send forth your light[c] and your truth,
let them guide me;
let them bring me to your holy mountain,[d]
to the place where you dwell.[e]
4Then will I go to the altar[f] of God,
to God, my joy and my delight.
I will praise you with the harp,[g]
O God, my God.

5Why are you downcast, O my soul?
Why so disturbed within me?
Put your hope in God,
for I will yet praise him,
my Savior and my God.[h]

Psalm 44

For the director of music. Of the Sons of Korah. A *maskil*.[z]

1We have heard with our ears, O God;
our fathers have told us[i]
what you did in their days,
in days long ago.
2With your hand you drove out[j] the nations
and planted[k] our fathers;
you crushed the peoples
and made our fathers flourish.[l]
3It was not by their sword[m] that they won the land,
nor did their arm bring them victory;
it was your right hand, your arm,[n]
and the light of your face, for you loved[o] them.

4You are my King[p] and my God,
who decrees[a] victories for Jacob.
5Through you we push back our enemies;
through your name we trample[q] our foes.
6I do not trust in my bow,[r]
my sword does not bring me victory;
7but you give us victory[s] over our enemies,
you put our adversaries to shame.[t]
8In God we make our boast[u] all day long,
and we will praise your name forever.[v] *Selah*

9But now you have rejected[w] and humbled us;
you no longer go out with our armies.[x]
10You made us retreat[y] before the enemy,
and our adversaries have plundered us.
11You gave us up to be devoured like sheep[z]
and have scattered us among the nations.[a]
12You sold your people for a pittance,[b]
gaining nothing from their sale.

13You have made us a reproach to our neighbors,[c]
the scorn[d] and derision of those around us.
14You have made us a byword among the nations;
the peoples shake their heads[e] at us.
15My disgrace is before me all day long,
and my face is covered with shame
16at the taunts of those who reproach and revile[f] me,
because of the enemy, who is bent on revenge.

17All this happened to us,
though we had not forgotten[g] you
or been false to your covenant.
18Our hearts had not turned[h] back;
our feet had not strayed from your path.

43:2 [a]Ps 44:9 [b]Ps 42:9
43:3 [c]Ps 36:9 [d]Ps 42:4 [e]Ps 84:1
43:4 [f]Ps 26:6 [g]Ps 33:2
43:5 [h]Ps 42:6
44:1 [i]Ex 12:26; Ps 78:3
44:2 [j]Ps 78:55 [k]Ex 15:17 [l]Ps 80:9
44:3 [m]Dt 8:17; Jos 24:12 [n]Ps 77:15 [o]Dt 4:37; 7:7-8
44:4 [p]Ps 74:12
44:5 [q]Ps 108:13
44:6 [r]Ps 33:16
44:7 [s]Ps 136:24 [t]Ps 53:5
44:8 [u]Ps 34:2 [v]Ps 30:12
44:9 [w]Ps 74:1 [x]Ps 60:1,10
44:10 [y]Lev 26:17; Jos 7:8; Ps 89:41
44:11 [z]Ro 8:36 [a]Dt 4:27; 28:64; Ps 106:27
44:12 [b]Isa 52:3; Jer 15:13; 52:3; Jer 15:13
44:13 [c]Ps 79:4; 80:6 [d]Dt 28:37
44:14 [e]Ps 109:25; Jer 24:9
44:16 [f]Ps 74:10
44:17 [g]Ps 78:7,57; Da 9:13
44:18 [h]Job 23:11

[z]Title: Probably a literary or musical term
[a]4 Septuagint, Aquila and Syriac; Hebrew *King, O God; / command*

19But you crushed[a] us and made us a haunt for jackals
and covered us over with deep darkness.[b]

20If we had forgotten[c] the name of our God
or spread out our hands to a foreign god,[d]
21would not God have discovered it,
since he knows the secrets of the heart?[e]
22Yet for your sake we face death all day long;
we are considered as sheep to be slaughtered.[f]

23Awake,[g] O Lord! Why do you sleep?[h]
Rouse yourself! Do not reject us forever.[i]
24Why do you hide your face[j]
and forget our misery and oppression?[k]

25We are brought down to the dust;[l]
our bodies cling to the ground.
26Rise up[m] and help us;
redeem[n] us because of your unfailing love.

Psalm 45

For the director of music. To ⌞the tune of⌟ "Lilies." Of the Sons of Korah. A *maskil.* [b] A wedding song.

1My heart is stirred by a noble theme
as I recite my verses for the king;
my tongue is the pen of a skillful writer.

2You are the most excellent of men
and your lips have been anointed with grace,[o]
since God has blessed you forever.
3Gird your sword[p] upon your side, O mighty one;[q]
clothe yourself with splendor and majesty.

44:19 [a]Ps 51:8 [b]Job 3:5
44:20 [c]Ps 78:11 [d]Dt 6:14; Ps 81:9
44:21 [e]Ps 139:1-2; Jer 17:10
44:22 [f]Isa 53:7; Ro 8:36*
44:23 [g]Ps 7:6 [h]Ps 78:65 [i]Ps 77:7
44:24 [j]Job 13:24 [k]Ps 42:9
44:25 [l]Ps 119:25
44:26 [m]Ps 35:2 [n]Ps 25:22
45:2 [o]Lk 4:22
45:3 [p]Heb 4:12; Rev 1:16 [q]Isa 9:6
45:4 [r]Rev 6:2
45:6 [s]Ps 93:2; 98:9
45:7 [t]Ps 33:5 [u]Isa 61:1 [v]Ps 21:6; Heb 1:8-9*
45:8 [w]SS 1:3
45:9 [x]SS 6:8 [y]1Ki 2:19
45:10 [z]Dt 21:13
45:11 [a]Ps 95:6 [b]Isa 54:5
45:12 [c]Ps 22:29; Isa 49:23
45:13 [d]Isa 61:10
45:14 [e]SS 1:4

4In your majesty ride forth victoriously[r]
in behalf of truth, humility and righteousness;
let your right hand display awesome deeds.
5Let your sharp arrows pierce the hearts of the king's enemies;
let the nations fall beneath your feet.
6Your throne, O God, will last for ever and ever;[s]
a scepter of justice will be the scepter of your kingdom.
7You love righteousness[t] and hate wickedness;
therefore God, your God, has set you above your companions
by anointing[u] you with the oil of joy.[v]
8All your robes are fragrant[w] with myrrh and aloes and cassia;
from palaces adorned with ivory
the music of the strings makes you glad.
9Daughters of kings[x] are among your honored women;
at your right hand[y] is the royal bride in gold of Ophir.

10Listen, O daughter, consider and give ear:
Forget your people[z] and your father's house.
11The king is enthralled by your beauty;
honor[a] him, for he is your lord.[b]
12The Daughter of Tyre will come with a gift,[c c]
men of wealth will seek your favor.
13All glorious[d] is the princess within ⌞her chamber⌟;
her gown is interwoven with gold.
14In embroidered garments she is led to the king;[e]

[b]Title: Probably a literary or musical term
[c]*12* Or *A Tyrian robe is among the gifts*

her virgin companions follow her
and are brought to you.
15They are led in with joy and gladness;
they enter the palace of the king.
16Your sons will take the place of your fathers;
you will make them princes throughout the land.
17I will perpetuate your memory through all generations;[a]
therefore the nations will praise you[b] for ever and ever.

Psalm 46

For the director of music. Of the Sons of Korah. According to *alamoth*.[d] A song.

1God is our refuge[c] and strength,
an ever-present[d] help in trouble.
2Therefore we will not fear,[e]
though the earth give way[f]
and the mountains fall[g] into the heart of the sea,
3though its waters roar[h] and foam
and the mountains quake with their surging. *Selah*

4There is a river whose streams make glad the city of God,[i]
the holy place where the Most High dwells.
5God is within her,[j] she will not fall;
God will help[k] her at break of day.
6Nations[l] are in uproar, kingdoms[m] fall;
he lifts his voice, the earth melts.[n]

7The LORD Almighty is with us;[o]
the God of Jacob is our fortress.[p] *Selah*

8Come and see the works of the LORD,[q]

45:17 [a]Mal 1:11 [b]Ps 138:4
46:1 [c]Ps 9:9; 14:6 [d]Dt 4:7
46:2 [e]Ps 23:4 [f]Ps 82:5 [g]Ps 18:7
46:3 [h]Ps 93:3
46:4 [i]Ps 48:1,8; Isa 60:14
46:5 [j]Isa 12:6; Eze 43:7 [k]Ps 37:40
46:6 [l]Ps 2:1 [m]Ps 68:32 [n]Mic 1:4
46:7 [o]2Ch 13:12 [p]Ps 9:9
46:8 [q]Ps 66:5 [r]Isa 61:4
46:9 [s]Isa 2:4 [t]Ps 76:3 [u]Eze 39:9
46:10 [v]Ps 100:3 [w]Isa 2:11
47:1 [x]Ps 98:8; Isa 55:12 [y]Ps 106:47
47:2 [z]Dt 7:21 [a]Mal 1:14
47:3 [b]Ps 18:39,47
47:4 [c]1Pe 1:4
47:5 [d]Ps 68:33; 98:6
47:6 [e]Ps 68:4; 89:18
47:7 [f]Zec 14:9 [g]Col 3:16
47:8 [h]1Ch 16:31

the desolations[r] he has brought on the earth.
9He makes wars[s] cease to the ends of the earth;
he breaks the bow[t] and shatters the spear,
he burns the shields[e] with fire.[u]
10"Be still, and know that I am God;[v]
I will be exalted[w] among the nations,
I will be exalted in the earth."

11The LORD Almighty is with us;
the God of Jacob is our fortress. *Selah*

Psalm 47

For the director of music. Of the Sons of Korah. A psalm.

1Clap your hands,[x] all you nations;
shout to God with cries of joy.[y]
2How awesome[z] is the LORD Most High,
the great King[a] over all the earth!
3He subdued[b] nations under us,
peoples under our feet.
4He chose our inheritance[c] for us,
the pride of Jacob, whom he loved. *Selah*

5God has ascended amid shouts of joy,
the LORD amid the sounding of trumpets.[d]
6Sing praises[e] to God, sing praises;
sing praises to our King, sing praises.
7For God is the King of all the earth;[f]
sing to him a psalm[f][g] of praise.
8God reigns[h] over the nations;
God is seated on his holy throne.

[d]Title: Probably a musical term [e]9 Or *chariots* [f]7 Or *a maskil* (probably a literary or musical term)

9 The nobles of the nations
assemble
as the people of the God of
Abraham,
for the kings[g] of the earth
belong to God;[a]
he is greatly exalted.[b]

Psalm 48

A song. A psalm of the Sons of Korah.

1 Great is the LORD,[c] and most
worthy of praise,
in the city of our God,[d] his
holy mountain.[e]
2 It is beautiful[f] in its loftiness,
the joy of the whole earth.
Like the utmost heights of
Zaphon[h] is Mount Zion,
the[i] city of the Great King.[g]
3 God is in her citadels;
he has shown himself to be
her fortress.[h]

4 When the kings joined forces,
when they advanced
together,[i]
5 they saw ⌞her⌟ and were
astounded;
they fled in terror.[j]
6 Trembling seized them there,
pain like that of a woman in
labor.
7 You destroyed them like ships
of Tarshish
shattered by an east wind.[k]

8 As we have heard,
so have we seen
in the city of the LORD
Almighty,
in the city of our God:
God makes her secure
forever.[l] *Selah*

9 Within your temple, O God,
we meditate on your
unfailing love.[m]
10 Like your name,[n] O God,
your praise reaches to the
ends of the earth;[o]
your right hand is filled with
righteousness.
11 Mount Zion rejoices,
the villages of Judah are glad
because of your judgments.[p]

12 Walk about Zion, go around
her,
count her towers,
13 consider well her ramparts,
view her citadels,[q]
that you may tell of them to
the next generation.[r]
14 For this God is our God for
ever and ever;
he will be our guide[s] even to
the end.

Psalm 49

For the director of music. Of the Sons of Korah. A psalm.

1 Hear this, all you peoples;[t]
listen, all who live in this
world,[u]
2 both low and high,
rich and poor alike:
3 My mouth will speak words of
wisdom;[v]
the utterance from my heart
will give
understanding.[w]
4 I will turn my ear to a
proverb;[x]
with the harp I will expound
my riddle:[y]

5 Why should I fear[z] when evil
days come,
when wicked deceivers
surround me—
6 those who trust in their
wealth[a]
and boast of their great
riches?
7 No man can redeem the life of
another
or give to God a ransom for
him—
8 the ransom for a life is
costly,
no payment is ever
enough—[b]
9 that he should live on[c] forever
and not see decay.

10 For all can see that wise men
die;[d]

47:9 [a] Ps 72:11; 89:18 [b] Ps 97:9
48:1 [c] Ps 96:4 [d] Ps 46:4 [e] Isa 2:2-3; Mic 4:1; Zec 8:3
48:2 [f] Ps 50:2; La 2:15 [g] Mt 5:35
48:3 [h] Ps 46:7
48:4 [i] 2Sa 10:1-19
48:5 [j] Ex 15:16
48:7 [k] Jer 18:17; Eze 27:26
48:8 [l] Ps 87:5
48:9 [m] Ps 26:3
48:10 [n] Dt 28:58; Jos 7:9 [o] Isa 41:10
48:11 [p] Ps 97:8
48:13 [q] ver 3; Ps 122:7 [r] Ps 78:6
48:14 [s] Ps 23:4
49:1 [t] Ps 78:1 [u] Ps 33:8
49:3 [v] Ps 37:30 [w] Ps 119:130
49:4 [x] Ps 78:2 [y] Nu 12:8
49:5 [z] Ps 23:4
49:6 [a] Job 31:24
49:8 [b] Mt 16:26
49:9 [c] Ps 22:29; 89:48
49:10 [d] Ecc 2:16

g9 Or *shields* h2 *Zaphon* can refer to a sacred mountain or the direction north. i2 Or *earth, / Mount Zion, on the northern side / of the*

the foolish and the senseless
alike perish
and leave their wealth to
others.[a]
11Their tombs will remain their
houses[j] forever,
their dwellings for endless
generations,
though they had[k] named[b]
lands after themselves.

12But man, despite his riches,
does not endure;
he is[l] like the beasts that
perish.

13This is the fate of those who
trust in themselves,[c]
and of their followers, who
approve their sayings.
Selah
14Like sheep they are destined
for the grave,[m][d]
and death will feed on
them.
The upright will rule[e] over
them in the morning;
their forms will decay in the
grave,[m]
far from their princely
mansions.
15But God will redeem my life[n]
from the grave;[f]
he will surely take me to
himself.[g] *Selah*

16Do not be overawed when a
man grows rich,
when the splendor of his
house increases;
17for he will take nothing with
him when he dies,
his splendor will not descend
with him.[h]
18Though while he lived he
counted himself
blessed—[i]
and men praise you when
you prosper—
19he will join the generation of
his fathers,[j]
who will never see the light[k]
⌞of life⌟.

20A man who has riches without
understanding
is like the beasts that
perish.[l]

Psalm 50

A psalm of Asaph.

1The Mighty One, God, the
Lord,[m]
speaks and summons the
earth
from the rising of the sun to
the place where it
sets.[n]
2From Zion, perfect in beauty,[o]
God shines forth.[p]
3Our God comes[q] and will not
be silent;
a fire devours before him,[r]
and around him a tempest
rages.
4He summons the heavens
above,
and the earth,[s] that he may
judge his people:
5"Gather to me my consecrated
ones,[t]
who made a covenant[u] with
me by sacrifice."
6And the heavens proclaim[v] his
righteousness,
for God himself is judge.[w]
Selah

7"Hear, O my people, and I will
speak,
O Israel, and I will testify[x]
against you:
I am God, your God.[y]
8I do not rebuke you for your
sacrifices
or your burnt offerings,[z]
which are ever before
me.
9I have no need of a bull[a] from
your stall
or of goats from your
pens,
10for every animal of the forest is
mine,
and the cattle on a thousand
hills.[b]
11I know every bird in the
mountains,

49:10 [a]Ecc 2:18,21
49:11 [b]Ge 4:17; Dt 3:14
49:13 [c]Lk 12:20
49:14 [d]Job 24:19; Ps 9:17 [e]Da 7:18; Mal 4:3; 1Co 6:2; Rev 2:26
49:15 [f]Ps 56:13; Hos 13:14 [g]Ps 73:24
49:17 [h]Ps 17:14; 1Ti 6:7
49:18 [i]Dt 29:19; Lk 12:19
49:19 [j]Ge 15:15 [k]Job 33:30
49:20 [l]Ecc 3:19
50:1 [m]Jos 22:22 [n]Ps 113:3
50:2 [o]Ps 48:2 [p]Dt 33:2; Ps 80:1
50:3 [q]Ps 96:13 [r]Ps 97:3; Da 7:10
50:4 [s]Dt 4:26; Isa 1:2
50:5 [t]Ps 30:4 [u]Ex 24:7
50:6 [v]Ps 89:5 [w]Ps 75:7
50:7 [x]Ps 81:8 [y]Ex 20:2
50:8 [z]Ps 40:6; Hos 6:6
50:9 [a]Ps 69:31
50:10 [b]Ps 104:24

[j]*11* Septuagint and Syriac; Hebrew *In their thoughts their houses will remain* [k]*11* Or / *for they have* [l]*12* Hebrew; Septuagint and Syriac read verse 12 the same as verse 20. [m]*14* Hebrew *Sheol*; also in verse 15 [n]*15* Or *soul*

and the creatures of the field
are mine.
[12]If I were hungry I would not
tell you,
for the world[a] is mine, and
all that is in it.
[13]Do I eat the flesh of bulls
or drink the blood of
goats?
[14]Sacrifice thank offerings[b] to
God,
fulfill your vows[c] to the
Most High,
[15]and call[d] upon me in the day
of trouble;
I will deliver you, and you
will honor[e] me."

[16]But to the wicked, God says:

"What right have you to recite
my laws
or take my covenant on your
lips?[f]
[17]You hate my instruction
and cast my words behind[g]
you.
[18]When you see a thief, you
join[h] with him;
you throw in your lot with
adulterers.
[19]You use your mouth for
evil
and harness your tongue to
deceit.[i]
[20]You speak continually against
your brother[j]
and slander your own
mother's son.
[21]These things you have done
and I kept silent;[k]
you thought I was
altogether[o] like you.
But I will rebuke you
and accuse[l] you to your
face.

[22]"Consider this, you who forget
God,[m]
or I will tear you to pieces,
with none to rescue:[n]
[23]He who sacrifices thank
offerings honors me,
and he prepares the way[o]
so that I may show him[p] the
salvation of God.[p]"

50:12 [a]Ex 19:5
50:14 [b]Heb 13:15 [c]Dt 23:21
50:15 [d]Ps 81:7 [e]Ps 22:23
50:16 [f]Isa 29:13
50:17 [g]Ne 9:26; Ro 2:21-22
50:18 [h]Ro 1:32; 1Ti 5:22
50:19 [i]Ps 10:7; 52:2
50:20 [j]Mt 10:21
50:21 [k]Ecc 8:11; Isa 42:14 [l]Ps 90:8
50:22 [m]Job 8:13; Ps 9:17 [n]Ps 7:2
50:23 [o]Ps 85:13 [p]Ps 91:16
51:1 [q]Ac 3:19 [r]Isa 43:25; Col 2:14
51:2 [s]1Jn 1:9 [t]Heb 9:14
51:3 [u]Isa 59:12
51:4 [v]Ge 20:6; Lk 15:21 [w]Ro 3:4*
51:5 [x]Job 14:4
51:6 [y]Pr 2:6 [z]Ps 15:2
51:7 [a]Lev 14:4; Heb 9:19 [b]Isa 1:18
51:8 [c]Isa 35:10
51:9 [d]Jer 16:17
51:10 [e]Ps 78:37; Ac 15:9 [f]Eze 18:31

Psalm 51

For the director of music. A psalm of David. When the prophet Nathan came to him after David had committed adultery with Bathsheba.

[1]Have mercy on me, O God,
according to your unfailing
love;
according to your great
compassion
blot out[q] my
transgressions.[r]
[2]Wash away[s] all my iniquity
and cleanse[t] me from my
sin.

[3]For I know my transgressions,
and my sin is always before
me.[u]
[4]Against you, you only, have I
sinned
and done what is evil in your
sight,[v]
so that you are proved right
when you speak
and justified when you
judge.[w]
[5]Surely I was sinful[x] at birth,
sinful from the time my
mother conceived me.
[6]Surely you desire truth in the
inner parts[q];
you teach[r] me wisdom[y] in
the inmost place.[z]

[7]Cleanse me with hyssop,[a] and
I will be clean;
wash me, and I will be whiter
than snow.[b]
[8]Let me hear joy and gladness;[c]
let the bones you have
crushed rejoice.
[9]Hide your face from my sins[d]
and blot out all my iniquity.

[10]Create in me a pure heart,[e]
O God,
and renew a steadfast spirit
within me.[f]
[11]Do not cast me from your
presence

[o]21 *Or thought the 'I AM' was* [p]23 *Or and to him who considers his way / I will show*
[q]6 The meaning of the Hebrew for this phrase is uncertain. [r]6 *Or you desired . . . ; / you taught*

or take your Holy Spirit[a]
from me.
12Restore to me the joy of your
salvation[b]
and grant me a willing spirit,
to sustain me.

13Then I will teach transgressors
your ways,[c]
and sinners will turn back to
you.[d]
14Save me from bloodguilt,[e]
O God,
the God who saves me,[f]
and my tongue will sing of
your righteousness.[g]
15O Lord, open my lips,[h]
and my mouth will declare
your praise.
16You do not delight in
sacrifice,[i] or I would
bring it;
you do not take pleasure in
burnt offerings.
17The sacrifices of God are[s] a
broken spirit;
a broken and contrite heart,[j]
O God, you will not despise.

18In your good pleasure make
Zion[k] prosper;
build up the walls of
Jerusalem.
19Then there will be righteous
sacrifices,[l]
whole burnt offerings[m] to
delight you;
then bulls[n] will be offered
on your altar.

Psalm 52

For the director of music. A *maskil*[t] of David. When Doeg the Edomite[o] had gone to Saul and told him: "David has gone to the house of Ahimelech."

1Why do you boast of evil, you
mighty man?
Why do you boast[p] all day
long,
you who are a disgrace in the
eyes of God?
2Your tongue plots destruction;
it is like a sharpened razor,[q]
you who practice deceit.[r]
3You love evil rather than good,
falsehood[s] rather than
speaking the truth. *Selah*
4You love every harmful word,
O you deceitful tongue![t]

5Surely God will bring you down
to everlasting ruin:
He will snatch you up and
tear[u] you from your
tent;
he will uproot[v] you from the
land of the living.[w]
Selah
6The righteous will see and fear;
they will laugh[x] at him,
saying,
7"Here now is the man
who did not make God his
stronghold
but trusted in his great wealth[y]
and grew strong by
destroying others!"
8But I am like an olive tree[z]
flourishing in the house of
God;
I trust[a] in God's unfailing love
for ever and ever.
9I will praise you forever[b] for
what you have done;
in your name I will hope, for
your name is good.[c]
I will praise you in the
presence of your saints.

Psalm 53

53:1-6pp — Ps 14:1-7

For the director of music.
According to *mahalath.*[u]
A *maskil*[t] of David.

1The fool[d] says in his heart,
"There is no God."[e]
They are corrupt, and their
ways are vile;
there is no one who does
good.
2God looks down from heaven[f]
on the sons of men
to see if there are any who
understand,
any who seek God.[g]
3Everyone has turned away,

51:11 [a]Eph 4:30
51:12 [b]Ps 13:5
51:13 [c]Ac 9:21-22 [d]Ps 22:27
51:14 [e]2Sa 12:9 [f]Ps 25:5 [g]Ps 35:28
51:15 [h]Ps 9:14
51:16 [i]1Sa 15:22; Ps 40:6
51:17 [j]Ps 34:18
51:18 [k]Ps 102:16; Isa 51:3
51:19 [l]Ps 4:5 [m]Ps 66:13 [n]Ps 66:15
52:1 [o]1Sa 22:9 [p]Ps 94:4
52:2 [q]Ps 57:4 [r]Ps 50:19
52:3 [s]Jer 9:5
52:4 [t]Ps 120:2,3
52:5 [u]Isa 22:19 [v]Pr 2:22 [w]Ps 27:13
52:6 [x]Job 22:19; Ps 37:34; 40:3
52:7 [y]Ps 49:6
52:8 [z]Jer 11:16 [a]Ps 13:5
52:9 [b]Ps 30:12 [c]Ps 54:6
53:1 [d]Ps 14:1-7; Ro 3:10 [e]Ps 10:4
53:2 [f]Ps 33:13 [g]2Ch 15:2

[s]17 Or *My sacrifice, O God, is* [t]Title: Probably a literary or musical term [u]Title: Probably a musical term

they have together become
corrupt;
there is no one who does good,
not even one.[a]

4Will the evildoers never learn—
those who devour my people
as men eat bread
and who do not call on God?
5There they were, overwhelmed
with dread,
where there was nothing to
dread.[b]
God scattered the bones[c] of
those who attacked you;
you put them to shame, for
God despised them.

6Oh, that salvation for Israel
would come out of Zion!
When God restores the
fortunes of his people,
let Jacob rejoice and Israel
be glad!

Psalm 54

For the director of music. With stringed instruments. A *maskil*[v] of David. When the Ziphites had gone to Saul and said, "Is not David hiding among us?"

1Save me, O God, by your
name;[d]
vindicate me by your might.[e]
2Hear my prayer, O God;[f]
listen to the words of my
mouth.

3Strangers are attacking me;[g]
ruthless men seek my life[h]—
men without regard for
God.[i] *Selah*
4Surely God is my help;[j]
the Lord is the one who
sustains me.[k]

5Let evil recoil[l] on those who
slander me;
in your faithfulness[m] destroy
them.

6I will sacrifice a freewill
offering[n] to you;
I will praise your name,
O LORD,
for it is good.[o]
7For he has delivered me[p] from
all my troubles,
and my eyes have looked in
triumph on my foes.[q]

Psalm 55

For the director of music. With stringed instruments. A *maskil*[v] of David.

1Listen to my prayer, O God,
do not ignore my plea;[r]
2 hear me and answer me.[s]
My thoughts trouble me and I
am distraught[t]
3 at the voice of the enemy,
at the stares of the wicked;
for they bring down suffering
upon me[u]
and revile me in their
anger.[v]

4My heart is in anguish within
me;
the terrors[w] of death assail
me.
5Fear and trembling[x] have beset
me;
horror has overwhelmed me.
6I said, "Oh, that I had the
wings of a dove!
I would fly away and be at
rest—
7I would flee far away
and stay in the desert; *Selah*
8I would hurry to my place of
shelter,
far from the tempest and
storm.[y]"

9Confuse the wicked, O Lord,
confound their speech,
for I see violence and strife[z]
in the city.
10Day and night they prowl about
on its walls;
malice and abuse are within
it.
11Destructive forces[a] are at work
in the city;
threats and lies[b] never leave
its streets.

12If an enemy were insulting me,
I could endure it;

53:3 [a]Ro 3:10-12*
53:5 [b]Lev 26:17 [c]Eze 6:5
54:1 [d]Ps 20:1 [e]2Ch 20:6
54:2 [f]Ps 5:1; 55:1
54:3 [g]Ps 86:14 [h]Ps 40:14 [i]Ps 36:1
54:4 [j]Ps 118:7 [k]Ps 41:12
54:5 [l]Ps 94:23 [m]Ps 89:49; 143:12
54:6 [n]Ps 50:14 [o]Ps 52:9
54:7 [p]Ps 34:6 [q]Ps 59:10
55:1 [r]Ps 27:9; 61:1
55:2 [s]Ps 66:19 [t]Ps 77:3; Isa 38:14
55:3 [u]2Sa 16:6-8; Ps 17:9 [v]Ps 71:11
55:4 [w]Ps 116:3
55:5 [x]Job 21:6; Ps 119:120
55:8 [y]Isa 4:6
55:9 [z]Jer 6:7
55:11 [a]Ps 5:9 [b]Ps 10:7

[v]Title. Probably a literary or musical term

if a foe were raising himself
against me,
I could hide from him.
13But it is you, a man like
myself,
my companion, my close
friend,[a]
14with whom I once enjoyed
sweet fellowship
as we walked with the throng
at the house of God.[b]

15Let death take my enemies by
surprise;[c]
let them go down alive to the
grave,[w][d]
for evil finds lodging among
them.

16But I call to God,
and the LORD saves me.
17Evening,[e] morning[f] and noon
I cry out in distress,
and he hears my voice.
18He ransoms me unharmed
from the battle waged against
me,
even though many oppose
me.
19God, who is enthroned
forever,[g]
will hear[h] them and afflict
them— *Selah*
men who never change their
ways
and have no fear of God.

20My companion attacks his
friends;[i]
he violates his covenant.[j]
21His speech is smooth as butter,
yet war is in his heart;
his words are more soothing
than oil,[k]
yet they are drawn swords.[l]

22Cast your cares on the LORD
and he will sustain you;[m]
he will never let the
righteous fall.[n]
23But you, O God, will bring
down the wicked
into the pit[o] of corruption;
bloodthirsty and deceitful
men[p]
will not live out half their
days.[q]

But as for me, I trust in you.[r]

55:13 [a]2Sa 15:12; Ps 41:9
55:14 [b]Ps 42:4
55:15 [c]Ps 64:7 [d]Nu 16:30,33
55:17 [e]Ps 141:2; Ac 3:1 [f]Ps 5:3
55:19 [g]Dt 33:27 [h]Ps 78:59
55:20 [i]Ps 7:4 [j]Ps 89:34
55:21 [k]Pr 5:3 [l]Ps 28:3; Ps 57:4; 59:7
55:22 [m]Ps 37:5; Mt 6:25-34; 1Pe 5:7 [n]Ps 37:24
55:23 [o]Ps 73:18 [p]Ps 5:6 [q]Job 15:32; Pr 10:27 [r]Ps 25:2
56:1 [s]Ps 57:1-3
56:2 [t]Ps 57:3 [u]Ps 35:1
56:3 [v]Ps 55:4-5
56:4 [w]Ps 118:6; Heb 13:6
56:5 [x]Ps 41:7
56:6 [y]Ps 59:3 [z]Ps 71:10
56:7 [a]Ps 36:12; 55:23
56:8 [b]Mal 3:16
56:9 [c]Ps 9:3 [d]Ps 102:2 [e]Ro 8:31
56:12 [f]Ps 50:14

Psalm 56

For the director of music. To ⌞the tune of,⌟ "A Dove on Distant Oaks." Of David. A *miktam.*[x] When the Philistines had seized him in Gath.

1Be merciful to me, O God, for
men hotly pursue me;[s]
all day long they press their
attack.
2My slanderers pursue me all
day long;[t]
many are attacking me in
their pride.[u]

3When I am afraid,[v]
I will trust in you.
4In God, whose word I praise,
in God I trust; I will not be
afraid.
What can mortal man do to
me?[w]

5All day long they twist my
words;[x]
they are always plotting to
harm me.
6They conspire,[y] they lurk,
they watch my steps,
eager to take my life.[z]
7On no account let them
escape;
in your anger, O God, bring
down the nations.[a]
8Record my lament;
list my tears on your
scroll[y]—
are they not in your record?[b]

9Then my enemies will turn
back[c]
when I call for help.[d]
By this I will know that God
is for me.[e]
10In God, whose word I praise,
in the LORD, whose word I
praise—
11in God I trust; I will not be
afraid.
What can man do to me?

12I am under vows[f] to you,
O God;

[w] *15* Hebrew *Sheol* [x] Title: Probably a literary or musical term [y] *8* Or *I put my tears in your wineskin*

I will present my thank
offerings to you.
13 For you have delivered me[z]
from death[a]
and my feet from stumbling,
that I may walk before God
in the light of life.[a][b]

Psalm 57

57:7–11pp — Ps 108:1–5

For the director of music. ⌞To the tune of⌟ "Do Not Destroy." Of David. A *miktam.*[b] When he had fled from Saul into the cave.

1 Have mercy on me, O God,
have mercy on me,
for in you my soul takes
refuge.[c]
I will take refuge in the shadow
of your wings[d]
until the disaster has
passed.[e]
2 I cry out to God Most High,
to God, who fulfills ⌞his
purpose⌟ for me.[f]
3 He sends from heaven and
saves me,[g]
rebuking those who hotly
pursue me;[h] *Selah*
God sends his love and his
faithfulness.[i]
4 I am in the midst of lions;[j]
I lie among ravenous
beasts—
men whose teeth are spears
and arrows,
whose tongues are sharp
swords.[k]
5 Be exalted, O God, above the
heavens;
let your glory be over all the
earth.[l]
6 They spread a net for my feet—
I was bowed down[m] in
distress.
They dug a pit[n] in my path—
but they have fallen into it
themselves.[o] *Selah*
7 My heart is steadfast, O God,
my heart is steadfast;[p]
I will sing and make music.
8 Awake, my soul!
Awake, harp and lyre![q]

56:13 [a]Ps 116:8 [b]Job 33:30
57:1 [c]Ps 2:12 [d]Ps 17:8 [e]Isa 26:20
57:2 [f]Ps 138:8
57:3 [g]Ps 18:9,16 [h]Ps 56:1 [i]Ps 40:11
57:4 [j]Ps 35:17 [k]Ps 55:21; Pr 30:14
57:5 [l]Ps 108:5
57:6 [m]Ps 145:14 [n]Ps 35:7 [o]Ps 7:15; Pr 28:10
57:7 [p]Ps 108:1
57:8 [q]Ps 16:9; 30:12; 150:3
57:10 [r]Ps 36:5; 103:11
57:11 [s]ver 5
58:1 [t]Ps 82:2
58:2 [u]Ps 94:20; Mal 3:15
58:4 [v]Ps 140:3; Ecc 10:11
58:6 [w]Ps 3:7 [x]Job 4:10
58:7 [y]Jos 7:5; Ps 112:10 [z]Ps 64:3
58:8 [a]Job 3:16

I will awaken the dawn.
9 I will praise you, O Lord,
among the nations;
I will sing of you among the
peoples.
10 For great is your love, reaching
to the heavens;
your faithfulness reaches to
the skies.[r]
11 Be exalted, O God, above the
heavens;
let your glory be over all the
earth.[s]

Psalm 58

For the director of music. ⌞To the tune of⌟ "Do Not Destroy." Of David. A *miktam.*[b]

1 Do you rulers indeed speak
justly?[t]
Do you judge uprightly
among men?
2 No, in your heart you devise
injustice,
and your hands mete out
violence on the earth.[u]
3 Even from birth the wicked go
astray;
from the womb they are
wayward and speak lies.
4 Their venom is like the venom
of a snake,[v]
like that of a cobra that has
stopped its ears,
5 that will not heed the tune of
the charmer,
however skillful the
enchanter may be.
6 Break the teeth in their
mouths, O God;[w]
tear out, O LORD, the fangs of
the lions![x]
7 Let them vanish like water that
flows away;[y]
when they draw the bow, let
their arrows be
blunted.[z]
8 Like a slug melting away as it
moves along,
like a stillborn child,[a] may
they not see the sun.

[z]*13* Or *my soul* [a]*13* Or *the land of the living*
[b]Title: Probably a literary or musical term

9 Before your pots can feel ⌊the
heat of⌋ the thorns[a]—
whether they be green or
dry—the wicked will be
swept away.[c][b]
10 The righteous will be glad
when they are avenged,[c]
when they bathe their feet in
the blood of the
wicked.[d]
11 Then men will say,
"Surely the righteous still are
rewarded;
surely there is a God who
judges the earth."[e]

Psalm 59

For the director of music. ⌊To the
tune of⌋ "Do Not Destroy." Of
David. A *miktam*.[d] When Saul
had sent men to watch David's
house in order to kill him.

1 Deliver me from my enemies,
O God;[f]
protect me from those who
rise up against me.
2 Deliver me from evildoers
and save me from
bloodthirsty men.[g]
3 See how they lie in wait for me!
Fierce men conspire[h] against
me
for no offense or sin of mine,
O LORD.
4 I have done no wrong, yet they
are ready to attack me.[i]
Arise to help me; look on my
plight!
5 O LORD God Almighty, the God
of Israel,
rouse yourself to punish all
the nations;
show no mercy to wicked
traitors.[j] *Selah*
6 They return at evening,
snarling like dogs,[k]
and prowl about the city.
7 See what they spew from their
mouths—
they spew out swords[l] from
their lips,
and they say, "Who can hear
us?"[m]
8 But you, O LORD, laugh at
them;[n]
you scoff at all those
nations.[o]
9 O my Strength, I watch for
you;
you, O God, are my
fortress,[p] 10 my loving
God.

God will go before me
and will let me gloat over
those who slander
me.
11 But do not kill them, O Lord
our shield,[e][q]
or my people will forget.[r]
In your might make them
wander about,
and bring them down.[s]
12 For the sins of their mouths,[t]
for the words of their lips,[u]
let them be caught in their
pride.[v]
For the curses and lies they
utter,
13 consume them in wrath,
consume them till they are
no more.[w]
Then it will be known to the
ends of the earth
that God rules over Jacob.[x]
Selah
14 They return at evening,
snarling like dogs,
and prowl about the
city.
15 They wander about for
food[y]
and howl if not satisfied.
16 But I will sing of your
strength,[z]
in the morning[a] I will sing
of your love;[b]
for you are my fortress,
my refuge in times of
trouble.[c]
17 O my Strength, I sing praise
to you;
you, O God, are my fortress,
my loving God.

58:9 [a]Ps 118:12 [b]Pr 10:25
58:10 [c]Ps 64:10; 91:8 [d]Ps 68:23
58:11 [e]Ps 9:8; 18:20
59:1 [f]Ps 143:9
59:2 [g]Ps 139:19
59:3 [h]Ps 56:6
59:4 [i]Ps 35:19,23
59:5 [j]Jer 18:23
59:6 [k]ver 14
59:7 [l]Ps 57:4 [m]Ps 10:11
59:8 [n]Ps 37:13; Pr 1:26 [o]Ps 2:4
59:9 [p]Ps 9:9; 62:2
59:11 [q]Ps 84:9 [r]Dt 4:9 [s]Ps 106:27
59:12 [t]Ps 10:7 [u]Pr 12:13 [v]Zep 3:11
59:13 [w]Ps 104:35 [x]Ps 83:18
59:15 [y]Job 15:23
59:16 [z]Ps 21:13 [a]Ps 88:13 [b]Ps 101:1 [c]Ps 46:1

[c]*9* The meaning of the Hebrew for this verse is uncertain [d]Title: Probably a literary or musical term [e]*11* Or *sovereign*

Psalm 60

60:5–12pp — Ps 108:6–13

For the director of music. To ⌞the tune of⌟ "The Lily of the Covenant." A *miktam*[f] of David. For teaching. When he fought Aram Naharaim[g] and Aram Zobah,[h] and when Joab returned and struck down twelve thousand Edomites in the Valley of Salt.

1You have rejected us,[a] O God,
and burst forth upon us;
you have been angry[b]—now
restore us![c]
2You have shaken the land[d] and
torn it open;
mend its fractures,[e] for it is
quaking.
3You have shown your people
desperate times;[f]
you have given us wine that
makes us stagger.[g]

4But for those who fear you, you
have raised a banner
to be unfurled against the
bow. *Selah*

5Save us and help us with your
right hand,[h]
that those you love[i] may be
delivered.
6God has spoken from his
sanctuary:
"In triumph I will parcel out
Shechem[j]
and measure off the Valley of
Succoth.
7Gilead[k] is mine, and Manasseh
is mine;
Ephraim is my helmet,
Judah[l] my scepter.[m]
8Moab is my washbasin,
upon Edom I toss my sandal;
over Philistia I shout in
triumph.[n]"

9Who will bring me to the
fortified city?
Who will lead me to Edom?
10Is it not you, O God, you who
have rejected us
and no longer go out with
our armies?[o]
11Give us aid against the enemy,
for the help of man is
worthless.[p]
12With God we will gain the
victory,
and he will trample down our
enemies.[q]

60:1 [a]2Sa 5:20; Ps 44:9 [b]Ps 79:5 [c]Ps 80:3
60:2 [d]Ps 18:7 [e]2Ch 7:14
60:3 [f]Ps 71:20 [g]Isa 51:17; Jer 25:16
60:5 [h]Ps 17:7; 108:6 [i]Ps 127:2
60:6 [j]Ge 12:6
60:7 [k]Jos 13:31 [l]Dt 33:17 [m]Ge 49:10
60:8 [n]2Sa 8:1
60:10 [o]Jos 7:12; Ps 44:9; 108:11
60:11 [p]Ps 146:3
60:12 [q]Nu 24:18; Ps 44:5
61:1 [r]Ps 64:1 [s]Ps 86:6
61:2 [t]Ps 77:3 [u]Ps 18:2
61:3 [v]Ps 62:7 [w]Pr 18:10
61:4 [x]Ps 23:6 [y]Ps 91:4
61:5 [z]Ps 56:12 [a]Ps 86:11
61:6 [b]Ps 21:4
61:7 [c]Ps 41:12 [d]Ps 40:11
61:8 [e]Ps 65:1; 71:22
62:1 [f]Ps 33:20

Psalm 61

For the director of music. With stringed instruments. Of David.

1Hear my cry, O God;[r]
listen to my prayer.[s]

2From the ends of the earth I
call to you,
I call as my heart grows
faint;[t]
lead me to the rock[u] that is
higher than I.
3For you have been my refuge,[v]
a strong tower against the
foe.[w]

4I long to dwell[x] in your tent
forever
and take refuge in the shelter
of your wings.[y] *Selah*
5For you have heard my vows,[z]
O God;
you have given me the
heritage of those who
fear your name.[a]

6Increase the days of the king's
life,
his years for many
generations.[b]
7May he be enthroned in God's
presence forever;[c]
appoint your love and
faithfulness to protect
him.[d]

8Then will I ever sing praise to
your name[e]
and fulfill my vows day after
day.

Psalm 62

For the director of music. For Jeduthun. A psalm of David.

1My soul finds rest[f] in God
alone;

[f]Title: Probably a literary or musical term
[g]Title: That is, Arameans of Northwest Mesopotamia
[h]Title: That is, Arameans of central Syria

my salvation comes from
him.
2He alone is my rock[a] and my
salvation;
he is my fortress, I will never
be shaken.

3How long will you assault a
man?
Would all of you throw him
down—
this leaning wall,[b] this
tottering fence?
4They fully intend to topple him
from his lofty place;
they take delight in lies.
With their mouths they bless,
but in their hearts they
curse.[c] *Selah*

5Find rest, O my soul, in God
alone;
my hope comes from him.
6He alone is my rock and my
salvation;
he is my fortress, I will not
be shaken.
7My salvation and my honor
depend on God[i];
he is my mighty rock, my
refuge.[d]
8Trust in him at all times,
O people;
pour out your hearts to
him,[e]
for God is our refuge. *Selah*

9Lowborn men are but a
breath,[f]
the highborn are but a lie;
if weighed on a balance,[g] they
are nothing;
together they are only a
breath.
10Do not trust in extortion
or take pride in stolen
goods;[h]
though your riches increase,
do not set your heart on
them.[i]

11One thing God has spoken,
two things have I heard:
that you, O God, are strong,
12 and that you, O Lord, are
loving.
Surely you will reward each
person
according to what he has
done.[j]

Psalm 63

A psalm of David. When he was
in the Desert of Judah.

1O God, you are my God,
earnestly I seek you;
my soul thirsts for you,[k]
my body longs for you,
in a dry and weary land
where there is no water.

2I have seen you in the
sanctuary[l]
and beheld your power and
your glory.
3Because your love is better
than life,[m]
my lips will glorify you.
4I will praise you as long as I
live,[n]
and in your name I will lift
up my hands.[o]
5My soul will be satisfied as
with the richest of
foods;[p]
with singing lips my mouth
will praise you.

6On my bed I remember you;
I think of you through the
watches of the night.[q]
7Because you are my help,[r]
I sing in the shadow of your
wings.
8My soul clings to you;
your right hand upholds
me.[s]

9They who seek my life will be
destroyed;[t]
they will go down to the
depths of the earth.[u]
10They will be given over to the
sword
and become food for jackals.

11But the king will rejoice in
God;
all who swear by God's name
will praise him,[v]
while the mouths of liars will
be silenced.

i7 Or *I God Most High is my salvation and my honor*

62:2 [a]Ps 89:26
62:3 [b]Isa 30:13
62:4 [c]Ps 28:3
62:7 [d]Ps 46:1; 85:9; Jer 3:23
62:8 [e]1Sa 1:15; Ps 42:4; La 2:19
62:9 [f]Ps 39:5,11 [g]Isa 40:15
62:10 [h]Isa 61:8 [i]Job 31:25; 1Ti 6:6-10
62:12 [j]Job 34:11; Mt 16:27
63:1 [k]Ps 42:2; 84:2
63:2 [l]Ps 27:4
63:3 [m]Ps 69:16
63:4 [n]Ps 104:33 [o]Ps 28:2
63:5 [p]Ps 36:8
63:6 [q]Ps 42:8
63:7 [r]Ps 27:9
63:8 [s]Ps 18:35
63:9 [t]Ps 40:14 [u]Ps 55:15
63:11 [v]Dt 6:13; Ps 21:1; Isa 45:23

Psalm 64

For the director of music.
A psalm of David.

1Hear me, O God, as I voice my complaint;[a]
protect my life from the threat of the enemy.[b]
2Hide me from the conspiracy of the wicked,[c]
from that noisy crowd of evildoers.

3They sharpen their tongues like swords
and aim their words like deadly arrows.[d]
4They shoot from ambush at the innocent man;[e]
they shoot at him suddenly, without fear.[f]

5They encourage each other in evil plans,
they talk about hiding their snares;
they say, "Who will see them[i]?"[g]
6They plot injustice and say,
"We have devised a perfect plan!"
Surely the mind and heart of man are cunning.

7But God will shoot them with arrows;
suddenly they will be struck down.
8He will turn their own tongues against them[h]
and bring them to ruin;
all who see them will shake their heads[i] in scorn.
9All mankind will fear;
they will proclaim the works of God
and ponder what he has done.[j]
10Let the righteous rejoice in the LORD
and take refuge in him;[k]
let all the upright in heart praise him![l]

64:1 [a]Ps 55:2 [b]Ps 140:1
64:2 [c]Ps 56:6; 59:2
64:3 [d]Ps 58:7
64:4 [e]Ps 11:2 [f]Ps 55:19
64:5 [g]Ps 10:11
64:8 [h]Ps 9:3; Pr 18:7 [i]Ps 22:7
64:9 [j]Jer 51:10
64:10 [k]Ps 25:20 [l]Ps 32:11
65:1 [m]Ps 116:18
65:2 [n]Isa 66:23
65:3 [o]Ps 38:4 [p]Heb 9:14
65:4 [q]Ps 4:3; 33:12 [r]Ps 36:8
65:5 [s]Ps 85:4 [t]Ps 107:23
65:6 [u]Ps 93:1
65:7 [v]Mt 8:26 [w]Isa 17:12-13
65:9 [x]Ps 68:9-10 [y]Ps 46:4; 104:14

Psalm 65

For the director of music. A psalm of David. A song.

1Praise awaits[k] you, O God, in Zion;
to you our vows will be fulfilled.[m]
2O you who hear prayer,
to you all men will come.[n]
3When we were overwhelmed by sins,[o]
you forgave[l] our transgressions.[p]
4Blessed are those you choose[q]
and bring near to live in your courts!
We are filled with the good things of your house,[r]
of your holy temple.

5You answer us with awesome deeds of righteousness,
O God our Savior,[s]
the hope of all the ends of the earth
and of the farthest seas,[t]
6who formed the mountains by your power,
having armed yourself with strength,[u]
7who stilled the roaring of the seas,[v]
the roaring of their waves,
and the turmoil of the nations.[w]
8Those living far away fear your wonders;
where morning dawns and evening fades
you call forth songs of joy.

9You care for the land and water it;[x]
you enrich it abundantly.
The streams of God are filled with water
to provide the people with grain,[y]
for so you have ordained it.[m]
10You drench its furrows
and level its ridges;
you soften it with showers

i5 Or *us* k1 Or *befits*; the meaning of the Hebrew for this word is uncertain. l3 Or *made atonement for* m9 Or *for that is how you prepare the land*

and bless its crops.
11You crown the year with your
bounty,
and your carts overflow with
abundance.
12The grasslands of the desert
overflow;[a]
the hills are clothed with
gladness.
13The meadows are covered with
flocks[b]
and the valleys are mantled
with grain;[c]
they shout for joy and sing.[d]

Psalm 66

For the director of music.
A song. A psalm.

1Shout with joy to God, all the
earth![e]
2 Sing the glory of his name;[f]
make his praise glorious!
3Say to God, "How awesome are
your deeds![g]
So great is your power
that your enemies cringe[h]
before you.
4All the earth bows down[i] to
you;
they sing praise[j] to you,
they sing praise to your
name." *Selah*
5Come and see what God has
done,
how awesome his works[k] in
man's behalf!
6He turned the sea into dry
land,[l]
they passed through the
waters on foot—
come, let us rejoice in him.
7He rules forever[m] by his power,
his eyes watch[n] the
nations—
let not the rebellious[o] rise
up against him. *Selah*
8Praise[p] our God, O peoples,
let the sound of his praise be
heard;
9he has preserved our lives
and kept our feet from
slipping.[q]
10For you, O God, tested us;
you refined us like silver.[r]

65:12 [a]Job 28:26
65:13 [b]Ps 144:13 [c]Ps 72:16 [d]Ps 98:8; Isa 55:12
66:1 [e]Ps 100:1
66:2 [f]Ps 79:9
66:3 [g]Ps 65:5 [h]Ps 18:44
66:4 [i]Ps 22:27 [j]Ps 67:3
66:5 [k]Ps 106:22
66:6 [l]Ex 14:22
66:7 [m]Ps 145:13 [n]Ps 11:4 [o]Ps 140:8
66:8 [p]Ps 98:4
66:9 [q]Ps 121:3
66:10 [r]Ps 17:3; Isa 48:10; Zec 13:9; 1Pe 1:6-7
66:11 [s]La 1:13
66:12 [t]Isa 51:23 [u]Isa 43:2
66:13 [v]Ecc 5:4
66:15 [w]Nu 6:14; Ps 51:19
66:16 [x]Ps 34:11 [y]Ps 71:15,24
66:18 [z]Job 36:21; Isa 1:15; Jas 4:3
66:19 [a]Ps 116:1-2
66:20 [b]Ps 22:24; 68:35
67:1 [c]Nu 6:24-26; Ps 4:6
67:2 [d]Isa 52:10 [e]Tit 2:11

11You brought us into prison
and laid burdens[s] on our
backs.
12You let men ride over our
heads;[t]
we went through fire and
water,
but you brought us to a place
of abundance.[u]

13I will come to your temple with
burnt offerings
and fulfill my vows[v] to
you—
14vows my lips promised and my
mouth spoke
when I was in trouble.
15I will sacrifice fat animals to
you
and an offering of rams;
I will offer bulls and goats.[w]
Selah

16Come and listen,[x] all you who
fear God;
let me tell[y] you what he has
done for me.
17I cried out to him with my
mouth;
his praise was on my tongue.
18If I had cherished sin in my
heart,
the Lord would not have
listened;[z]
19but God has surely listened
and heard my voice[a] in
prayer.
20Praise be to God,
who has not rejected[b] my
prayer
or withheld his love from me!

Psalm 67

For the director of music. With
stringed instruments. A psalm.
A song.

1May God be gracious to us and
bless us
and make his face shine
upon us,[c] *Selah*
2that your ways may be known
on earth,
your salvation[d] among all
nations.[e]

3May the peoples praise you,
O God;

may all the peoples praise
you.
4May the nations be glad and
sing for joy,
for you rule the peoples
justly[a]
and guide the nations of the
earth. *Selah*
5May the peoples praise you,
O God;
may all the peoples praise
you.
6Then the land will yield its
harvest,[b]
and God, our God, will bless
us.
7God will bless us,
and all the ends of the earth
will fear him.[c]

Psalm 68

For the director of music. Of David. A psalm. A song.

1May God arise, may his
enemies be scattered;
may his foes flee[d] before
him.
2As smoke[e] is blown away by
the wind,
may you blow them away;
as wax melts[f] before the fire,
may the wicked perish before
God.
3But may the righteous be glad
and rejoice[g] before God;
may they be happy and
joyful.

4Sing to God, sing praise to his
name,[h]
extol him who rides on the
clouds[n][i]—
his name is the LORD[j]—
and rejoice before him.
5A father to the fatherless,[k] a
defender of widows,[l]
is God in his holy dwelling.[m]
6God sets the lonely in
families,[o][n]
he leads forth the prisoners[o]
with singing;
but the rebellious live in a
sun-scorched land.[p]

7When you went out[q] before
your people, O God,
when you marched through
the wasteland, *Selah*
8the earth shook,
the heavens poured down
rain,[r]
before God, the One of Sinai,[s]
before God, the God of
Israel.
9You gave abundant showers,[t]
O God;
you refreshed your weary
inheritance.
10Your people settled in it,
and from your bounty,
O God, you provided[u] for
the poor.

11The Lord announced the word,
and great was the company
of those who proclaimed
it:
12"Kings and armies flee[v] in
haste;
in the camps men divide the
plunder.
13Even while you sleep among
the campfires,[p][w]
the wings of ⌊my⌋ dove are
sheathed with silver,
its feathers with shining
gold."
14When the Almighty[q]
scattered[x] the kings in
the land,
it was like snow fallen on
Zalmon.

15The mountains of Bashan are
majestic mountains;
rugged are the mountains of
Bashan.
16Why gaze in envy, O rugged
mountains,
at the mountain where God
chooses[y] to reign,
where the LORD himself will
dwell forever?
17The chariots of God are tens of
thousands
and thousands of
thousands;[z]
the Lord ⌊has come⌋ from
Sinai into his sanctuary.
18When you ascended on high,

67:4 [a]Ps 96:10-13
67:6 [b]Lev 26:4; Ps 85:12; Eze 34:27
67:7 [c]Ps 33:8
68:1 [d]Nu 10:35; Isa 33:3
68:2 [e]Hos 13:3 [f]Isa 9:18; Mic 1:4
68:3 [g]Ps 32:11
68:4 [h]Ps 66:2 [i]Dt 33:26 [j]Ex 6:3; Ps 83:18
68:5 [k]Ps 10:14 [l]Dt 10:18 [m]Dt 26:15
68:6 [n]Ps 113:9 [o]Ac 12:6 [p]Ps 107:34
68:7 [q]Ex 13:21; Jdg 4:14
68:8 [r]Jdg 5:4 [s]Ex 19:16,18
68:9 [t]Dt 11:11
68:10 [u]Ps 74:19
68:12 [v]Jos 10:16
68:13 [w]Ge 49:14
68:14 [x]Jos 10:10
68:16 [y]Dt 12:5
68:17 [z]Dt 33:2; Da 7:10

[n]4 Or *I prepare the way for him who rides through the deserts* [o]6 Or *the desolate in a homeland* [p]13 Or *saddlebags* [q]14 Hebrew *Shaddai*

you led captives[a] in your
train;
you received gifts from
men,[b]
even from[r] the rebellious—
that you,[s] O LORD God,
might dwell there.

19Praise be to the Lord, to God
our Savior,[c]
who daily bears our
burdens.[d] *Selah*
20Our God is a God who saves;
from the Sovereign LORD
comes escape from
death.[e]

21Surely God will crush the
heads[f] of his enemies,
the hairy crowns of those
who go on in their sins.
22The Lord says, "I will bring
them from Bashan;
I will bring them from the
depths of the sea,[g]
23that you may plunge your feet
in the blood of your
foes,[h]
while the tongues of your
dogs[i] have their share."

24Your procession has come into
view, O God,
the procession of my God
and King into the
sanctuary.[j]
25In front are the singers, after
them the musicians;
with them are the maidens
playing tambourines.[k]
26Praise God in the great
congregation;
praise the LORD in the
assembly of Israel.[l]
27There is the little tribe[m] of
Benjamin, leading them,
there the great throng of
Judah's princes,
and there the princes of
Zebulun and of Naphtali.

28Summon your power, O God[t];
show us your strength,
O God, as you have
done before.
29Because of your temple at
Jerusalem
kings will bring you gifts.[n]

68:18 [a]Jdg 5:12 [b]Eph 4:8*
68:19 [c]Ps 65:5 [d]Ps 55:22
68:20 [e]Ps 56:13
68:21 [f]Ps 110:5; Hab 3:13
68:22 [g]Nu 21:33
68:23 [h]Ps 58:10 [i]1Ki 21:19
68:24 [j]Ps 63:2
68:25 [k]Jdg 11:34; 1Ch 13:8
68:26 [l]Ps 26:12; Isa 48:1
68:27 [m]1Sa 9:21
68:29 [n]Ps 72:10
68:30 [o]Ps 22:12 [p]Ps 89:10
68:31 [q]Isa 19:19; 45:14
68:33 [r]Ps 18:10 [s]Ps 29:4
68:34 [t]Ps 29:1
68:35 [u]Ps 29:11 [v]Ps 66:20
69:1 [w]Jnh 2:5
69:2 [x]Ps 40:2
69:3 [y]Ps 6:6 [z]Ps 119:82; Isa 38:14
69:4 [a]Jn 15:25*

30Rebuke the beast among the
reeds,
the herd of bulls[o] among the
calves of the nations.
Humbled, may it bring bars of
silver.
Scatter the nations[p] who
delight in war.
31Envoys will come from Egypt;[q]
Cush[u] will submit herself to
God.

32Sing to God, O kingdoms of the
earth,
sing praise to the Lord, *Selah*
33to him who rides[r] the ancient
skies above,
who thunders with mighty
voice.[s]
34Proclaim the power[t] of God,
whose majesty is over Israel,
whose power is in the skies.
35You are awesome, O God, in
your sanctuary;
the God of Israel gives power
and strength to his
people.[u]

Praise be to God![v]

Psalm 69

For the director of music. To ⌊the tune of⌋ "Lilies." Of David.

1Save me, O God,
for the waters have come up
to my neck.[w]
2I sink in the miry depths,[x]
where there is no foothold.
I have come into the deep
waters;
the floods engulf me.
3I am worn out calling for
help;[y]
my throat is parched.
My eyes fail,[z]
looking for my God.
4Those who hate me without
reason[a]
outnumber the hairs of my
head;

[r]*18* Or *gifts for men, / even* [s]*18* Or *they*
[t]*28* Many Hebrew manuscripts, Septuagint and Syriac; most Hebrew manuscripts *Your God has summoned power for you* [u]*31* That is, the upper Nile region

many are my enemies without
cause,[a]
those who seek to destroy
me.
I am forced to restore
what I did not steal.

5You know my folly,[b] O God;
my guilt is not hidden from
you.[c]

6May those who hope in you
not be disgraced because of
me,
O Lord, the LORD Almighty;
may those who seek you
not be put to shame because
of me,
O God of Israel.
7For I endure scorn for your
sake,[d]
and shame covers my face.[e]
8I am a stranger to my brothers,
an alien to my own mother's
sons;[f]
9for zeal for your house
consumes me,[g]
and the insults of those who
insult you fall on me.[h]
10When I weep and fast,[i]
I must endure scorn;
11when I put on sackcloth,[j]
people make sport of me.
12Those who sit at the gate mock
me,
and I am the song of the
drunkards.[k]

13But I pray to you, O LORD,
in the time of your favor;[l]
in your great love,[m] O God,
answer me with your sure
salvation.
14Rescue me from the mire,
do not let me sink;
deliver me from those who hate
me,
from the deep waters.[n]
15Do not let the floodwaters[o]
engulf me
or the depths swallow me
up[p]
or the pit close its mouth
over me.
16Answer me, O LORD, out of the
goodness of your love;[q]
in your great mercy turn to
me.

17Do not hide your face[r] from
your servant;
answer me quickly, for I am
in trouble.[s]
18Come near and rescue me;
redeem[t] me because of my
foes.

19You know how I am scorned,[u]
disgraced and shamed;
all my enemies are before
you.
20Scorn has broken my heart
and has left me helpless;
I looked for sympathy, but
there was none,
for comforters,[v] but I found
none.[w]
21They put gall in my food
and gave me vinegar for my
thirst.[x]

22May the table set before them
become a snare;
may it become retribution
and[v] a trap.
23May their eyes be darkened so
they cannot see,
and their backs be bent
forever.[y]
24Pour out your wrath[z] on them;
let your fierce anger overtake
them.
25May their place be deserted;[a]
let there be no one to dwell
in their tents.[b]
26For they persecute those you
wound
and talk about the pain of
those you hurt.[c]
27Charge them with crime upon
crime;[d]
do not let them share in your
salvation.[e]
28May they be blotted out of the
book of life[f]
and not be listed with the
righteous.[g]

29I am in pain and distress;
may your salvation, O God,
protect me.[h]

30I will praise God's name in
song[i]
and glorify him[j] with
thanksgiving.

69:4 [a]Ps 35:19; 38:19
69:5 [b]Ps 38:5 [c]Ps 44:21
69:7 [d]Jer 15:15 [e]Ps 44:15
69:8 [f]Ps 31:11; Isa 53:3
69:9 [g]Jn 2:17* [h]Ps 89:50-51; Ro 15:3*
69:10 [i]Ps 35:13
69:11 [j]Ps 35:13
69:12 [k]Job 30:9
69:13 [l]Isa 49:8; 2Co 6:2 [m]Ps 51:1
69:14 [n]ver 2; Ps 144:7
69:15 [o]Ps 124:4-5 [p]Nu 16:33
69:16 [q]Ps 63:3
69:17 [r]Ps 27:9 [s]Ps 66:14
69:18 [t]Ps 49:15
69:19 [u]Ps 22:6
69:20 [v]Job 16:2 [w]Isa 63:5
69:21 [x]Mt 27:34; Mk 15:23; Jn 19:28-30
69:23 [y]Isa 6:9-10; Ro 11:9-10*
69:24 [z]Ps 79:6
69:25 [a]Mt 23:38 [b]Ac 1:20*
69:26 [c]Isa 53:4; Zec 1:15
69:27 [d]Ne 4:5 [e]Ps 109:14; Isa 26:10
69:28 [f]Ex 32:32-33; Lk 10:20; Php 4:3 [g]Eze 13:9
69:29 [h]Ps 59:1; 70:5
69:30 [i]Ps 28:7 [j]Ps 34:3

[v]22 Or *snare / and their fellowship become*

31This will please the LORD more
than an ox,
more than a bull with its
horns and hoofs.[a]
32The poor will see and be
glad[b]—
you who seek God, may your
hearts live![c]
33The LORD hears the needy[d]
and does not despise his
captive people.

34Let heaven and earth praise
him,
the seas and all that move in
them,[e]
35for God will save Zion[f]
and rebuild the cities of
Judah.[g]
Then people will settle there
and possess it;
36 the children of his servants
will inherit it,
and those who love his name
will dwell there.[h]

Psalm 70

70:1–5pp — Ps 40:13–17

For the director of music. Of David. A petition.

1Hasten, O God, to save me;
O LORD, come quickly to help
me.[i]
2May those who seek my life[j]
be put to shame and
confusion;
may all who desire my ruin
be turned back in disgrace.[k]
3May those who say to me,
"Aha! Aha!"
turn back because of their
shame.
4But may all who seek you
rejoice and be glad in you;
may those who love your
salvation always say,
"Let God be exalted!"

5Yet I am poor and needy;[l]
come quickly to me,[m]
O God.
You are my help and my
deliverer;
O LORD, do not delay.

Psalm 71

71:1–3pp — Ps 31:1–4

1In you, O LORD, I have taken
refuge;
let me never be put to
shame.[n]
2Rescue me and deliver me in
your righteousness;
turn your ear[o] to me and
save me.
3Be my rock of refuge,
to which I can always go;
give the command to save me,
for you are my rock and my
fortress.[p]
4Deliver me, O my God, from
the hand of the
wicked,[q]
from the grasp of evil and
cruel men.

5For you have been my hope,
O Sovereign LORD,
my confidence[r] since my
youth.
6From birth[s] I have relied on
you;
you brought me forth from
my mother's womb.[t]
I will ever praise[u] you.
7I have become like a portent[v]
to many,
but you are my strong
refuge.[w]
8My mouth[x] is filled with your
praise,
declaring your splendor[y] all
day long.

9Do not cast[z] me away when I
am old;[a]
do not forsake me when my
strength is gone.
10For my enemies speak against
me;
those who wait to kill[b] me
conspire[c] together.
11They say, "God has forsaken
him;
pursue him and seize him,
for no one will rescue[d] him."
12Be not far[e] from me, O God;
come quickly, O my God, to
help[f] me.
13May my accusers perish in
shame;

69:31 [a]Ps 50:9-13
69:32 [b]Ps 34:2 [c]Ps 22:26
69:33 [d]Ps 12:5; 68:6
69:34 [e]Ps 96:11; 148:1; Isa 44:23; 49:13; 55:12
69:35 [f]Ob 1:17 [g]Ps 51:18; Isa 44:26
69:36 [h]Ps 37:29; 102:28
70:1 [i]Ps 40:13
70:2 [j]Ps 35:4 [k]Ps 35:26
70:5 [l]Ps 40:17 [m]Ps 141:1
71:1 [n]Ps 25:2-3; 31:1
71:2 [o]Ps 17:6
71:3 [p]Ps 18:2; 31:2-3; 44:4
71:4 [q]Ps 140:4
71:5 [r]Job 4:6; Jer 17:7
71:6 [s]Ps 22:10 [t]Ps 22:9; Isa 46:3 [u]Ps 9:1; 34:1; 52:9; 119:164; 145:2
71:7 [v]Isa 8:18; 1Co 4:9 [w]2Sa 22:3; Ps 61:3
71:8 [x]Ps 51:15; 63:5 [y]Ps 35:28; 96:6; 104:1
71:9 [z]Ps 51:11 [a]ver 18; Ps 92:14; Isa 46:4
71:10 [b]Ps 10:8; 59:3; Pr 1:18 [c]Ps 31:13; 56:6; Mt 12:14
71:11 [d]Ps 7:2
71:12 [e]Ps 35:22; 38:21 [f]Ps 38:22; 70:1

may those who want to harm
me
be covered with scorn and
disgrace.[a]
14But as for me, I will always
have hope;[b]
I will praise you more and
more.
15My mouth will tell[c] of your
righteousness,
of your salvation all day long,
though I know not its
measure.
16I will come and proclaim your
mighty acts,[d] O
Sovereign LORD;
I will proclaim your
righteousness, yours
alone.
17Since my youth, O God, you
have taught[e] me,
and to this day I declare your
marvelous deeds.[f]
18Even when I am old and gray,[g]
do not forsake me, O God,
till I declare your power to the
next generation,
your might to all who are to
come.[h]

19Your righteousness reaches to
the skies,[i] O God,
you who have done great
things.[j]
Who, O God, is like you?[k]
20Though you have made me see
troubles,[l] many and
bitter,
you will restore[m] my life
again;
from the depths of the earth
you will again bring me up.
21You will increase my honor[n]
and comfort[o] me once again.

22I will praise you with the harp[p]
for your faithfulness, O my
God;
I will sing praise to you with
the lyre,[q]
O Holy One of Israel.[r]
23My lips will shout for joy
when I sing praise to you—
I, whom you have
redeemed.[s]
24My tongue will tell of your
righteous acts

71:13 [a]ver 24
71:14 [b]Ps 130:7
71:15 [c]Ps 35:28; 40:5
71:16 [d]Ps 106:2
71:17 [e]Dt 4:5 [f]Ps 26:7
71:18 [g]ver 9 [h]Ps 22:30,31; 78:4
71:19 [i]Ps 36:5; 57:10 [j]Ps 126:2; Lk 1:49 [k]Ps 35:10
71:20 [l]Ps 60:3 [m]Hos 6:2
71:21 [n]Ps 18:35 [o]Ps 23:4; 86:17; Isa 12:1; 49:13
71:22 [p]Ps 33:2 [q]Ps 92:3; 144:9 [r]2Ki 19:22
71:23 [s]Ps 103:4
71:24 [t]Ps 35:28 [u]ver 13
72:2 [v]Isa 9:7; 11:4-5; 32:1
72:4 [w]Isa 11:4
72:6 [x]Dt 32:2; Hos 6:3
72:7 [y]Ps 92:12; Isa 2:4
72:8 [z]Ex 23:31 [a]Zec 9:10
72:10 [b]Ge 10:7 [c]2Ch 9:24

all day long,[t]
for those who wanted to harm
me[u]
have been put to shame and
confusion.

Psalm 72

Of Solomon.

1Endow the king with your
justice, O God,
the royal son with your
righteousness.
2He will[w] judge your people in
righteousness,[v]
your afflicted ones with
justice.
3The mountains will bring
prosperity to the people,
the hills the fruit of
righteousness.
4He will defend the afflicted
among the people
and save the children of the
needy;[w]
he will crush the oppressor.

5He will endure[x] as long as the
sun,
as long as the moon, through
all generations.
6He will be like rain[x] falling on
a mown field,
like showers watering the
earth.
7In his days the righteous will
flourish;[y]
prosperity will abound till
the moon is no more.

8He will rule from sea to sea
and from the River[y][z] to the
ends of the earth.[z][a]
9The desert tribes will bow
before him
and his enemies will lick the
dust.
10The kings of Tarshish and of
distant shores
will bring tribute to him;
the kings of Sheba[b] and Seba
will present him gifts.[c]

[w]2 Or *May he*; similarly in verses 3-11 and 17
[x]5 Septuagint; Hebrew *You will be feared*
[y]8 That is, the Euphrates
[z]8 Or *the end of the land*

11All kings will bow down to him
and all nations will serve
him.
12For he will deliver the needy
who cry out,
the afflicted who have no
one to help.
13He will take pity on the weak
and the needy
and save the needy from
death.
14He will rescue[a] them from
oppression and
violence,
for precious[b] is their
blood in his
sight.

15Long may he live!
May gold from Sheba[c] be
given him.
May people ever pray for
him
and bless him all day
long.
16Let grain abound throughout
the land;
on the tops of the hills may
it sway.
Let its fruit flourish like
Lebanon;[d]
let it thrive like the grass of
the field.
17May his name endure
forever;[e]
may it continue as long as
the sun.[f]
All nations will be blessed
through him,
and they will call him
blessed.[g]

18Praise be to the LORD God,
the God of
Israel,[h]
who alone does marvelous
deeds.[i]
19Praise be to his glorious name
forever;
may the whole earth be filled
with his glory.[j]
Amen and Amen.[k]

20This concludes the prayers
of David son of
Jesse.

72:14 [a]Ps 69:18 [b]1Sa 26:21; Ps 116:15
72:15 [c]Isa 60:6
72:16 [d]Ps 104:16
72:17 [e]Ex 3:15 [f]Ps 89:36 [g]Ge 12:3; Lk 1:48
72:18 [h]1Ch 29:10; Ps 41:13; 106:48 [i]Job 5:9
72:19 [j]Nu 14:21; Ne 9:5 [k]Ps 41:13
73:1 [l]Mt 5:8
73:3 [m]Ps 37:1; Pr 23:17 [n]Job 21:7; Jer 12:1
73:5 [o]Job 21:9
73:6 [p]Ge 41:42 [q]Ps 109:18
73:7 [r]Ps 17:10
73:8 [s]Ps 17:10; Jude 16

BOOK III

Psalms 73–89

Psalm 73

A psalm of Asaph.

1Surely God is good to Israel,
to those who are pure in
heart.[l]

2But as for me, my feet had
almost slipped;
I had nearly lost my foothold.
3For I envied[m] the arrogant
when I saw the prosperity of
the wicked.[n]

4They have no struggles;
their bodies are healthy and
strong.[a]
5They are free[o] from the
burdens common to
man;
they are not plagued by
human ills.
6Therefore pride is their
necklace;[p]
they clothe themselves with
violence.[q]
7From their callous hearts[r]
comes iniquity[b];
the evil conceits of their
minds know no limits.
8They scoff, and speak with
malice;
in their arrogance[s] they
threaten oppression.
9Their mouths lay claim to
heaven,
and their tongues take
possession of the earth.
10Therefore their people turn to
them
and drink up waters in
abundance.[c]
11They say, "How can God know?
Does the Most High have
knowledge?"

12This is what the wicked are
like—

[a]*4* With a different word division of the Hebrew; Masoretic Text *struggles at their death; / their bodies are healthy* [b]*7* Syriac (see also Septuagint); Hebrew *Their eyes bulge with fat* [c]*10* The meaning of the Hebrew for this verse is uncertain.

always carefree, they increase
in wealth.[a]

13Surely in vain[b] have I kept my
heart pure;
in vain have I washed my
hands in innocence.[c]
14All day long I have been
plagued;
I have been punished every
morning.

15If I had said, "I will speak
thus,"
I would have betrayed your
children.
16When I tried to understand[d] all
this,
it was oppressive to me
17till I entered the sanctuary[e] of
God;
then I understood their final
destiny.[f]

18Surely you place them on
slippery ground;[g]
you cast them down to ruin.
19How suddenly[h] are they
destroyed,
completely swept away by
terrors!
20As a dream[i] when one
awakes,[j]
so when you arise, O Lord,
you will despise them as
fantasies.

21When my heart was grieved
and my spirit embittered,
22I was senseless[k] and ignorant;
I was a brute beast[l] before
you.

23Yet I am always with you;
you hold me by my right
hand.
24You guide[m] me with your
counsel,[n]
and afterward you will take
me into glory.
25Whom have I in heaven but
you?
And earth has nothing I
desire besides you.[o]
26My flesh and my heart[p] may
fail,[q]
but God is the strength of my
heart
and my portion forever.

73:12 [a]Ps 49:6
73:13 [b]Job 21:15; 34:9 [c]Ps 26:6
73:16 [d]Ecc 8:17
73:17 [e]Ps 77:13 [f]Ps 37:38
73:18 [g]Ps 35:6
73:19 [h]Isa 47:11
73:20 [i]Job 20:8 [j]Ps 78:65
73:22 [k]Ps 49:10; 92:6 [l]Ecc 3:18
73:24 [m]Ps 48:14 [n]Ps 32:8
73:25 [o]Php 3:8
73:26 [p]Ps 84:2 [q]Ps 40:12
73:27 [r]Ps 119:155
73:28 [s]Heb 10:22; Jas 4:8 [t]Ps 40:5
74:1 [u]Dt 29:20; Ps 44:23 [v]Ps 79:13; 95:7; 100:3
74:2 [w]Ex 15:16 [x]Dt 32:7 [y]Ex 15:13 [z]Ps 68:16
74:4 [a]La 2:7 [b]Nu 2:2
74:5 [c]Jer 46:22
74:6 [d]1Ki 6:18
74:8 [e]Ps 83:4
74:9 [f]1Sa 3:1

27Those who are far from you will
perish;[r]
you destroy all who are
unfaithful to you.
28But as for me, it is good to be
near God.[s]
I have made the Sovereign
LORD my refuge;
I will tell of all your deeds.[t]

Psalm 74

A *maskil*[d] of Asaph.

1Why have you rejected us
forever,[u] O God?
Why does your anger smolder
against the sheep of your
pasture?[v]
2Remember the people you
purchased[w] of old,[x]
the tribe of your inheritance,
whom you redeemed[y]—
Mount Zion, where you
dwelt.[z]
3Turn your steps toward these
everlasting ruins,
all this destruction the
enemy has brought on
the sanctuary.

4Your foes roared[a] in the place
where you met with us;
they set up their standards[b]
as signs.
5They behaved like men
wielding axes
to cut through a thicket of
trees.[c]
6They smashed all the carved[d]
paneling
with their axes and hatchets.
7They burned your sanctuary to
the ground;
they defiled the dwelling
place of your Name.
8They said in their hearts, "We
will crush[e] them
completely!"
They burned every place
where God was
worshiped in the land.
9We are given no miraculous
signs;
no prophets[f] are left,

[d]Title: Probably a literary or musical term

and none of us knows how
long this will be.

10 How long will the enemy mock
you, O God?
Will the foe revile[a] your
name forever?
11 Why do you hold back your
hand, your right hand?[b]
Take it from the folds of your
garment and destroy
them!

12 But you, O God, are my king[c]
from of old;
you bring salvation upon the
earth.
13 It was you who split open the
sea[d] by your power;
you broke the heads of the
monster[e] in the waters.
14 It was you who crushed the
heads of Leviathan
and gave him as food to the
creatures of the desert.
15 It was you who opened up
springs[f] and streams;
you dried up[g] the ever
flowing rivers.
16 The day is yours, and yours
also the night;
you established the sun and
moon.[h]
17 It was you who set all the
boundaries[i] of the
earth;
you made both summer and
winter.[j]

18 Remember how the enemy has
mocked you, O LORD,
how foolish people[k] have
reviled your name.
19 Do not hand over the life of
your dove to wild beasts;
do not forget the lives of your
afflicted[l] people forever.
20 Have regard for your
covenant,[m]
because haunts of violence
fill the dark places of
the land.
21 Do not let the oppressed[n]
retreat in disgrace;
may the poor and needy[o]
praise your name.

22 Rise up, O God, and defend
your cause;
remember how fools[p] mock
you all day long.
23 Do not ignore the clamor of
your adversaries,[q]
the uproar of your enemies,
which rises continually.

Psalm 75

For the director of music. To the
tune of "Do Not Destroy." A
psalm of Asaph. A song.

1 We give thanks to you, O God,
we give thanks, for your
Name is near;[r]
men tell of your wonderful
deeds.[s]

2 You say, "I choose the
appointed time;
it is I who judge uprightly.
3 When the earth and all its
people quake,[t]
it is I who hold its pillars[u]
firm. *Selah*
4 To the arrogant I say, 'Boast no
more,'
and to the wicked, 'Do not
lift up your horns.[v]
5 Do not lift your horns against
heaven;
do not speak with
outstretched neck.' "

6 No one from the east or the
west
or from the desert can exalt
a man.
7 But it is God who judges:[w]
He brings one down, he
exalts another.[x]
8 In the hand of the LORD is a
cup
full of foaming wine mixed[y]
with spices;
he pours it out, and all the
wicked of the earth
drink it down to its very
dregs.[z]

9 As for me, I will declare[a] this
forever;
I will sing praise to the God
of Jacob.
10 I will cut off the horns of all
the wicked,

74:10 [a] Ps 44:16
74:11 [b] La 2:3
74:12 [c] Ps 44:4
74:13 [d] Ex 14:21 [e] Isa 51:9; Eze 29:3
74:15 [f] Ex 17:6; Nu 20:11 [g] Jos 2:10; 3:13
74:16 [h] Ge 1:16; Ps 136:7-9
74:17 [i] Dt 32:8; Ac 17:26 [j] Ge 8:22
74:18 [k] Dt 32:6; Ps 39:8
74:19 [l] Ps 9:18
74:20 [m] Ge 17:7; Ps 106:45
74:21 [n] Ps 103:6 [o] Ps 35:10
74:22 [p] Ps 53:1
74:23 [q] Ps 65:7
75:1 [r] Ps 145:18 [s] Ps 44:1; 71:16
75:3 [t] Isa 24:19 [u] 1Sa 2:8
75:4 [v] Zec 1:21
75:7 [w] Ps 50:6 [x] 1Sa 2:7; Ps 147:6; Da 2:21
75:8 [y] Pr 23:30 [z] Job 21:20; Jer 25:15
75:9 [a] Ps 40:10

but the horns of the
righteous will be lifted
up.[a]

Psalm 76

For the director of music. With stringed instruments. A psalm of Asaph. A song.

1In Judah God is known;
his name is great in
Israel.
2His tent is in Salem,[b]
his dwelling place in Zion.
3There he broke the flashing
arrows,
the shields and the swords,
the weapons of war.[c]
Selah

4You are resplendent with
light,
more majestic than
mountains rich with
game.
5Valiant men lie plundered,
they sleep their last
sleep;[d]
not one of the warriors
can lift his hands.
6At your rebuke, O God of
Jacob,
both horse and chariot[e] lie
still.
7You alone are to be feared.[f]
Who can stand[g] before you
when you are angry?[h]
8From heaven you pronounced
judgment,
and the land feared[i] and
was quiet—
9when you, O God, rose up to
judge,[j]
to save all the afflicted of
the land. *Selah*
10Surely your wrath against men
brings you praise,[k]
and the survivors of your
wrath are restrained.[e]
11Make vows to the LORD your
God and fulfill them;[l]
let all the neighboring lands
bring gifts[m] to the One to be
feared.
12He breaks the spirit of rulers;
he is feared by the kings of
the earth.

75:10 [a]Ps 89:17; 92:10; 148:14
76:2 [b]Ge 14:18
76:3 [c]Ps 46:9
76:5 [d]Ps 13:3
76:6 [e]Ex 15:1
76:7 [f]1Ch 16:25 [g]Ezr 9:15; Rev 6:17 [h]Ps 2:5; Na 1:6
76:8 [i]1Ch 16:30; 2Ch 20:29-30
76:9 [j]Ps 9:8
76:10 [k]Ex 9:16; Ro 9:17
76:11 [l]Ps 50:14; Ecc 5:4-5 [m]2Ch 32:23; Ps 68:29
77:1 [n]Ps 3:4
77:2 [o]Ps 50:15; Isa 26:9,16 [p]Job 11:13 [q]Ge 37:35
77:3 [r]Ps 143:4
77:5 [s]Dt 32:7; Ps 44:1; 143:5; Isa 51:9
77:7 [t]Ps 85:1
77:8 [u]2Pe 3:9
77:9 [v]Ps 25:6; 40:11; 51:1 [w]Isa 49:15
77:10 [x]Ps 31:22
77:11 [y]Ps 143:5

Psalm 77

For the director of music. For Jeduthun. Of Asaph. A psalm.

1I cried out to God[n] for help;
I cried out to God to hear
me.
2When I was in distress,[o] I
sought the Lord;
at night I stretched out
untiring hands[p]
and my soul refused to be
comforted.[q]

3I remembered you, O God, and
I groaned;
I mused, and my spirit grew
faint.[r] *Selah*
4You kept my eyes from closing;
I was too troubled to speak.
5I thought about the former
days,[s]
the years of long ago;
6I remembered my songs in the
night.
My heart mused and my
spirit inquired:

7"Will the Lord reject forever?
Will he never show his
favor[t] again?
8Has his unfailing love vanished
forever?
Has his promise[u] failed for
all time?
9Has God forgotten to be
merciful?[v]
Has he in anger withheld his
compassion?[w]" *Selah*

10Then I thought, "To this I will
appeal:
the years of the right hand[x]
of the Most High."
11I will remember the deeds of
the LORD;
yes, I will remember your
miracles[y] of long ago.
12I will meditate on all your
works
and consider all your mighty
deeds.

13Your ways, O God, are holy.

[e]10 Or *Surely the wrath of men brings you praise, / and with the remainder of wrath you arm yourself*

What god is so great as our
God?[a]
14You are the God who performs
miracles;
you display your power
among the peoples.
15With your mighty arm you
redeemed your people,[b]
the descendants of Jacob and
Joseph. *Selah*

16The waters[c] saw you, O God,
the waters saw you and
writhed;[d]
the very depths were
convulsed.
17The clouds poured down
water,[e]
the skies resounded with
thunder;
your arrows flashed back and
forth.
18Your thunder was heard in the
whirlwind,
your lightning lit up the
world;
the earth trembled and
quaked.[f]
19Your path led through the
sea,[g]
your way through the mighty
waters,
though your footprints were
not seen.

20You led your people[h] like a
flock[i]
by the hand of Moses and
Aaron.

Psalm 78

A *maskil*[f] of Asaph.

1O my people, hear my
teaching;[j]
listen to the words of my
mouth.
2I will open my mouth in
parables,[k]
I will utter hidden things,
things from of old—
3what we have heard and
known,
what our fathers have told
us.[l]
4We will not hide them from
their children;[m]
we will tell the next
generation
the praiseworthy deeds[n] of the
LORD,
his power, and the wonders
he has done.
5He decreed statutes[o] for
Jacob[p]
and established the law in
Israel,
which he commanded our
forefathers
to teach their children,
6so the next generation would
know them,
even the children yet to be
born,[q]
and they in turn would tell
their children.
7Then they would put their trust
in God
and would not forget[r] his
deeds
but would keep his
commands.[s]
8They would not be like their
forefathers[t]—
a stubborn[u] and rebellious[v]
generation,
whose hearts were not loyal to
God,
whose spirits were not
faithful to him.

9The men of Ephraim, though
armed with bows,[w]
turned back on the day of
battle;[x]
10they did not keep God's
covenant[y]
and refused to live by his
law.
11They forgot what he had
done,[z]
the wonders he had shown
them.
12He did miracles[a] in the sight
of their fathers
in the land of Egypt,[b] in the
region of Zoan.[c]
13He divided the sea[d] and led
them through;
he made the water stand firm
like a wall.[e]

77:13 [a]Ex 15:11; Ps 71:19; 86:8
77:15 [b]Ex 6:6; Dt 9:29
77:16 [c]Ex 14:21,28; Hab 3:8 [d]Ps 114:4; Hab 3:10
77:17 [e]Jdg 5:4
77:18 [f]Jdg 5:4
77:19 [g]Hab 3:15
77:20 [h]Ex 13:21 [i]Ps 78:52; Isa 63:11
78:1 [j]Isa 51:4; 55:3
78:2 [k]Ps 49:4; Mt 13:35*
78:3 [l]Ps 44:1
78:4 [m]Dt 11:19 [n]Ps 26:7; 71:17
78:5 [o]Ps 19:7; 81:5 [p]Ps 147:19
78:6 [q]Ps 22:31; 102:18
78:7 [r]Dt 6:12 [s]Dt 5:29
78:8 [t]2Ch 30:7 [u]Ex 32:9 [v]ver 37; Isa 30:9
78:9 [w]ver 57; 1Ch 12:2 [x]Jdg 20:39
78:10 [y]2Ki 17:15
78:11 [z]Ps 106:13
78:12 [a]Ps 106:22 [b]Ex 7-12 [c]Nu 13:22
78:13 [d]Ex 14:21; Ps 136:13 [e]Ex 15:8

[f]Title: Probably a literary or musical term

[14]He guided them with the cloud
by day
and with light from the fire
all night.[a]
[15]He split the rocks[b] in the
desert
and gave them water as
abundant as the seas;
[16]he brought streams out of a
rocky crag
and made water flow down
like rivers.

[17]But they continued to sin[c]
against him,
rebelling in the desert
against the Most High.
[18]They willfully put God to the
test[d]
by demanding the food they
craved.[e]
[19]They spoke against God,[f]
saying,
"Can God spread a table in
the desert?
[20]When he struck the rock, water
gushed out,[g]
and streams flowed
abundantly.
But can he also give us food?
Can he supply meat[h] for his
people?"
[21]When the LORD heard them, he
was very angry;
his fire broke out[i] against
Jacob,
and his wrath rose against
Israel,
[22]for they did not believe in God
or trust[j] in his deliverance.
[23]Yet he gave a command to the
skies above
and opened the doors of the
heavens;[k]
[24]he rained down manna[l] for the
people to eat,
he gave them the grain of
heaven.
[25]Men ate the bread of angels;
he sent them all the food
they could eat.
[26]He let loose the east wind[m]
from the heavens
and led forth the south wind
by his power.
[27]He rained meat down on them
like dust,

78:14 [a]Ex 13:21; Ps 105:39
78:15 [b]Nu 20:11; 1Co 10:4
78:17 [c]Dt 9:22; Isa 63:10; Heb 3:16
78:18 [d]1Co 10:9 [e]Ex 16:2; Nu 11:4
78:19 [f]Nu 21:5
78:20 [g]Nu 20:11 [h]Nu 11:18
78:21 [i]Nu 11:1
78:22 [j]Dt 1:32; Heb 3:19
78:23 [k]Ge 7:11; Mal 3:10
78:24 [l]Ex 16:4; Jn 6:31*
78:26 [m]Nu 11:31
78:29 [n]Nu 11:20
78:30 [o]Nu 11:33
78:31 [p]Isa 10:16
78:32 [q]ver 11 [r]ver 22
78:33 [s]Nu 14:29,35
78:34 [t]Hos 5:15
78:35 [u]Dt 32:4 [v]Dt 9:26
78:36 [w]Eze 33:31
78:37 [x]ver 8; Ac 8:21
78:38 [y]Ex 34:6 [z]Isa 48:10 [a]Nu 14:18,20
78:39 [b]Ge 6:3; Ps 103:14 [c]Job 7:7; Jas 4:14
78:40 [d]Heb 3:16 [e]Ps 95:8; 106:14

flying birds like sand on the
seashore.
[28]He made them come down
inside their camp,
all around their tents.
[29]They ate till they had more
than enough,[n]
for he had given them what
they craved.
[30]But before they turned from
the food they craved,
even while it was still in
their mouths,[o]
[31]God's anger rose against them;
he put to death the
sturdiest[p] among them,
cutting down the young men
of Israel.
[32]In spite of all this, they kept on
sinning;
in spite of his wonders,[q]
they did not believe.[r]
[33]So he ended their days in
futility[s]
and their years in terror.
[34]Whenever God slew them, they
would seek[t] him;
they eagerly turned to him
again.
[35]They remembered that God was
their Rock,[u]
that God Most High was
their Redeemer.[v]
[36]But then they would flatter him
with their mouths,[w]
lying to him with their
tongues;
[37]their hearts were not loyal[x] to
him,
they were not faithful to his
covenant.
[38]Yet he was merciful;[y]
he forgave[z] their
iniquities[a]
and did not destroy them.
Time after time he restrained
his anger
and did not stir up his full
wrath.
[39]He remembered that they were
but flesh,[b]
a passing breeze[c] that does
not return.
[40]How often they rebelled[d]
against him in the
desert[e]

and grieved him[a] in the
wasteland!
41Again and again they put God
to the test;[b]
they vexed the Holy One of
Israel.[c]
42They did not remember his
power—
the day he redeemed them
from the oppressor,
43the day he displayed his
miraculous signs in
Egypt,
his wonders in the region of
Zoan.
44He turned their rivers to
blood;[d]
they could not drink from
their streams.
45He sent swarms of flies[e] that
devoured them,
and frogs[f] that devastated
them.
46He gave their crops to the
grasshopper,
their produce to the locust.[g]
47He destroyed their vines with
hail[h]
and their sycamore-figs with
sleet.
48He gave over their cattle to the
hail,
their livestock[i] to bolts of
lightning.
49He unleashed against them his
hot anger,[j]
his wrath, indignation and
hostility—
a band of destroying angels.
50He prepared a path for his
anger;
he did not spare them from
death
but gave them over to the
plague.
51He struck down all the
firstborn of Egypt,[k]
the firstfruits of manhood in
the tents of Ham.[l]
52But he brought his people out
like a flock;[m]
he led them like sheep
through the desert.
53He guided them safely, so they
were unafraid;
but the sea engulfed[n] their
enemies.[o]

78:40 [a]Eph 4:30
78:41 [b]Nu 14:22 [c]2Ki 19:22; Ps 89:18
78:44 [d]Ex 7:20-21; Ps 105:29
78:45 [e]Ex 8:24; Ps 105:31 [f]Ex 8:2,6
78:46 [g]Ex 10:13
78:47 [h]Ex 9:23; Ps 105:32
78:48 [i]Ex 9:25
78:49 [j]Ex 15:7
78:51 [k]Ex 12:29; Ps 135:8 [l]Ps 105:23; 106:22
78:52 [m]Ps 77:20
78:53 [n]Ex 14:28 [o]Ps 106:10
78:54 [p]Ex 15:17; Ps 44:3
78:55 [q]Ps 44:2 [r]Jos 13:7
78:57 [s]Eze 20:27 [t]Hos 7:16
78:58 [u]Jdg 2:12 [v]Lev 26:30 [w]Ex 20:4; Dt 32:21
78:59 [x]Dt 32:19
78:60 [y]Jos 18:1
78:61 [z]Ps 132:8 [a]1Sa 4:17
78:63 [b]Nu 11:1 [c]Jer 7:34; 16:9
78:64 [d]1Sa 4:17; 22:18
78:65 [e]Ps 44:23
78:66 [f]1Sa 5:6

54Thus he brought them to the
border of his holy land,
to the hill country his right
hand[p] had taken.
55He drove out nations[q] before
them
and allotted their lands to
them as an
inheritance;[r]
he settled the tribes of Israel
in their homes.

56But they put God to the test
and rebelled against the
Most High;
they did not keep his
statutes.
57Like their fathers[s] they were
disloyal and faithless,
as unreliable as a faulty
bow.[t]
58They angered him[u] with their
high places;[v]
they aroused his jealousy
with their idols.[w]
59When God heard them, he was
very angry;
he rejected Israel[x]
completely.
60He abandoned the tabernacle
of Shiloh,[y]
the tent he had set up among
men.
61He sent ⌊the ark of⌋ his might[z]
into captivity,[a]
his splendor into the hands
of the enemy.
62He gave his people over to the
sword;
he was very angry with his
inheritance.
63Fire consumed[b] their young
men,
and their maidens had no
wedding songs;[c]
64their priests were put to the
sword,[d]
and their widows could not
weep.
65Then the Lord awoke as from
sleep,[e]
as a man wakes from the
stupor of wine.
66He beat back his enemies;
he put them to everlasting
shame.[f]

[67]Then he rejected the tents of Joseph,
he did not choose the tribe of Ephraim;
[68]but he chose the tribe of Judah,
Mount Zion,[a] which he loved.
[69]He built his sanctuary like the heights,
like the earth that he established forever.
[70]He chose David[b] his servant
and took him from the sheep pens;
[71]from tending the sheep he brought him
to be the shepherd[c] of his people Jacob,
of Israel his inheritance.
[72]And David shepherded them with integrity of heart;[d]
with skillful hands he led them.

Psalm 79

A psalm of Asaph.

[1]O God, the nations have invaded your inheritance;[e]
they have defiled your holy temple,
they have reduced Jerusalem to rubble.[f]
[2]They have given the dead bodies of your servants
as food to the birds of the air,
the flesh of your saints to the beasts of the earth.[g]
[3]They have poured out blood like water
all around Jerusalem,
and there is no one to bury the dead.[h]
[4]We are objects of reproach to our neighbors,
of scorn and derision to those around us.[i]

[5]How long,[j] O LORD? Will you be angry[k] forever?
How long will your jealousy burn like fire?[l]
[6]Pour out your wrath[m] on the nations
that do not acknowledge[n] you,
on the kingdoms
that do not call on your name;[o]
[7]for they have devoured Jacob
and destroyed his homeland.
[8]Do not hold against us the sins of the fathers;[p]
may your mercy come quickly to meet us,
for we are in desperate need.[q]

[9]Help us,[r] O God our Savior,
for the glory of your name;
deliver us and forgive our sins
for your name's sake.[s]
[10]Why should the nations say,
"Where is their God?"[t]
Before our eyes, make known among the nations
that you avenge[u] the outpoured blood of your servants.
[11]May the groans of the prisoners come before you;
by the strength of your arm
preserve those condemned to die.

[12]Pay back into the laps[v] of our neighbors seven times[w]
the reproach they have hurled at you, O Lord.
[13]Then we your people, the sheep of your pasture,[x]
will praise you forever;[y]
from generation to generation
we will recount your praise.

Psalm 80

For the director of music. To ⌊the tune of⌋ "The Lilies of the Covenant." Of Asaph. A psalm.

[1]Hear us, O Shepherd of Israel,
you who lead Joseph like a flock;[z]
you who sit enthroned between the cherubim,[a] shine forth
[2] before Ephraim, Benjamin and Manasseh.[b]
Awaken[c] your might;

78:68 [a]Ps 87:2
78:70 [b]1Sa 16:1
78:71 [c]2Sa 5:2; Ps 28:9
78:72 [d]1Ki 9:4
79:1 [e]Ps 74:2 [f]2Ki 25:9
79:2 [g]Dt 28:26; Jer 7:33
79:3 [h]Jer 16:4
79:4 [i]Ps 44:13; 80:6
79:5 [j]Ps 74:10 [k]Ps 74:1; 85:5 [l]Dt 29:20; Ps 89:46; Zep 3:8
79:6 [m]Ps 69:24; Rev 16:1 [n]Jer 10:25; 2Th 1:8 [o]Ps 14:4
79:8 [p]Isa 64:9 [q]Ps 116:6; 142:6
79:9 [r]2Ch 14:11 [s]Ps 25:11; 31:3; Jer 14:7
79:10 [t]Ps 42:10 [u]Ps 94:1
79:12 [v]Isa 65:6; Jer 32:18 [w]Ge 4:15
79:13 [x]Ps 74:1; 95:7 [y]Ps 44:8
80:1 [z]Ps 77:20 [a]Ex 25:22
80:2 [b]Nu 2:18-24 [c]Ps 35:23

come and save us.

3 Restore[a] us,[b] O God;
make your face shine upon us,
that we may be saved.

4 O LORD God Almighty,
how long will your anger smolder
against the prayers of your people?
5 You have fed them with the bread of tears;
you have made them drink tears by the bowlful.[c]
6 You have made us a source of contention to our neighbors,
and our enemies mock us.[d]

7 Restore us, O God Almighty;
make your face shine upon us,
that we may be saved.

8 You brought a vine[e] out of Egypt;
you drove out[f] the nations and planted it.
9 You cleared the ground for it,
and it took root and filled the land.
10 The mountains were covered with its shade,
the mighty cedars with its branches.
11 It sent out its boughs to the Sea,[g]
its shoots as far as the River.[h][g]
12 Why have you broken down its walls[h]
so that all who pass by pick its grapes?
13 Boars from the forest ravage[i] it
and the creatures of the field feed on it.
14 Return to us, O God Almighty!
Look down from heaven and see![j]
Watch over this vine,
15 the root your right hand has planted,
the son[i] you have raised up for yourself.

16 Your vine is cut down, it is burned with fire;

80:3 [a]Ps 85:4; La 5:21 [b]Nu 6:25
80:5 [c]Ps 42:3; Isa 30:20
80:6 [d]Ps 79:4
80:8 [e]Isa 5:1-2; Jer 2:21 [f]Jos 13:6; Ac 7:45
80:11 [g]Ps 72:8
80:12 [h]Ps 89:40; Isa 5:5
80:13 [i]Jer 5:6
80:14 [j]Isa 63:15
80:16 [k]Ps 39:11; 76:6
81:1 [l]Ps 66:1
81:2 [m]Ex 15:20 [n]Ps 92:3
81:5 [o]Ex 11:4 [p]Ps 114:1
81:6 [q]Isa 9:4
81:7 [r]Ex 2:23; Ps 50:15 [s]Ex 19:19

at your rebuke[k] your people perish.
17 Let your hand rest on the man at your right hand,
the son of man you have raised up for yourself.
18 Then we will not turn away from you;
revive us, and we will call on your name.

19 Restore us, O LORD God Almighty;
make your face shine upon us,
that we may be saved.

Psalm 81

For the director of music. According to *gittith*.[j] Of Asaph.

1 Sing for joy to God our strength;
shout aloud to the God of Jacob![l]
2 Begin the music, strike the tambourine,[m]
play the melodious harp[n] and lyre.

3 Sound the ram's horn at the New Moon,
and when the moon is full, on the day of our Feast;
4 this is a decree for Israel,
an ordinance of the God of Jacob.
5 He established it as a statute for Joseph
when he went out against Egypt,[o]
where we heard a language we did not understand.[k][p]

6 He says, "I removed the burden from their shoulders;[q]
their hands were set free from the basket.
7 In your distress you called[r] and I rescued you,
I answered[s] you out of a thundercloud;

[g]*11* Probably the Mediterranean [h]*11* That is, the Euphrates [i]*15* Or *branch* [j]Title: Probably a musical term [k]*5* Or *I and we heard a voice we had not known*

I tested you at the waters of
Meribah.[a] *Selah*
8"Hear, O my people,[b] and I
will warn you—
if you would but listen to
me, O Israel!
9You shall have no foreign god[c]
among you;
you shall not bow down to an
alien god.
10I am the LORD your God,
who brought you up out of
Egypt.[d]
Open wide your mouth and I
will fill[e] it.

11"But my people would not
listen to me;
Israel would not submit to
me.[f]
12So I gave them over[g] to their
stubborn hearts
to follow their own devices.

13"If my people would but listen
to me,[h]
if Israel would follow my
ways,
14how quickly would I subdue[i]
their enemies
and turn my hand against[j]
their foes!
15Those who hate the LORD would
cringe before him,
and their punishment would
last forever.
16But you would be fed with the
finest of wheat;[k]
with honey from the rock I
would satisfy you."

Psalm 82

A psalm of Asaph.

1God presides in the great
assembly;
he gives judgment[l] among
the "gods":

2"How long will you[l] defend
the unjust
and show partiality[m] to the
wicked?[n] *Selah*
3Defend the cause of the weak
and fatherless;[o]
maintain the rights of the
poor[p] and oppressed.
4Rescue the weak and needy;
deliver them from the hand
of the wicked.

5"They know nothing, they
understand nothing.[q]
They walk about in
darkness;[r]
all the foundations[s] of the
earth are shaken.

6"I said, 'You are "gods";[t]
you are all sons of the Most
High.'
7But you will die[u] like mere
men;
you will fall like every other
ruler."

8Rise up,[v] O God, judge the
earth,
for all the nations are your
inheritance.[w]

Psalm 83

A song. A psalm of Asaph.

1O God, do not keep silent;[x]
be not quiet, O God, be not
still.
2See how your enemies are
astir,[y]
how your foes rear their
heads.[z]
3With cunning they conspire[a]
against your people;
they plot against those you
cherish.
4"Come," they say, "let us
destroy[b] them as a
nation,
that the name of Israel be
remembered[c] no more."

5With one mind they plot
together;[d]
they form an alliance against
you—
6the tents of Edom[e] and the
Ishmaelites,
of Moab[f] and the Hagrites,[g]
7Gebal,[m][h] Ammon and Amalek,
Philistia, with the people of
Tyre.[i]
8Even Assyria has joined them

81:7 [a]Ex 17:7 **81:8** [b]Ps 50:7 **81:9** [c]Ex 20:3; Dt 32:12; Isa 43:12 **81:10** [d]Ex 20:2 [e]Ps 107:9 **81:11** [f]Ex 32:1-6 **81:12** [g]Ac 7:42; Ro 1:24 **81:13** [h]Dt 5:29; Isa 48:18 **81:14** [i]Ps 47:3 [j]Am 1:8 **81:16** [k]Dt 32:14 **82:1** [l]Ps 58:11; Isa 3:13 **82:2** [m]Dt 1:17 [n]Ps 58:1-2; Pr 18:5 **82:3** [o]Dt 24:17 [p]Jer 22:16 **82:5** [q]Ps 14:4; Mic 3:1 [r]Isa 59:9 [s]Ps 11:3 **82:6** [t]Jn 10:34* **82:7** [u]Ps 49:12; Eze 31:14 **82:8** [v]Ps 12:5 [w]Ps 2:8; Rev 11:15 **83:1** [x]Ps 28:1; 35:22 **83:2** [y]Ps 2:1; Isa 17:12 [z]Jdg 8:28; Ps 81:15 **83:3** [a]Ps 31:13 **83:4** [b]Est 3:6 [c]Jer 11:19 **83:5** [d]Ps 2:2 **83:6** [e]Ps 137:7 [f]2Ch 20:1 [g]Ge 25:16 **83:7** [h]Jos 13:5 [i]Eze 27:3

[l]2 The Hebrew is plural. [m]7 That is, Byblos

to lend strength to the
descendants of Lot.[a]
Selah

9Do to them as you did to
Midian,[b]
as you did to Sisera and
Jabin at the river
Kishon,[c]
10who perished at Endor
and became like refuse[d] on
the ground.
11Make their nobles like Oreb
and Zeeb,[e]
all their princes like Zebah
and Zalmunna,[f]
12who said, "Let us take
possession[g]
of the pasturelands of God."

13Make them like tumbleweed,
O my God,
like chaff[h] before the wind.
14As fire consumes the forest
or a flame sets the
mountains ablaze,[i]
15so pursue them with your
tempest
and terrify them with your
storm.[j]
16Cover their faces with shame[k]
so that men will seek your
name, O LORD.

17May they ever be ashamed and
dismayed;
may they perish in disgrace.[l]
18Let them know that you, whose
name is the LORD—
that you alone are the Most
High over all the earth.[m]

Psalm 84

For the director of music.
According to *gittith*.[n] Of the
Sons of Korah. A psalm.

1How lovely is your dwelling
place,[n]
O LORD Almighty!
2My soul yearns,[o] even faints,
for the courts of the LORD;
my heart and my flesh cry out
for the living God.

3Even the sparrow has found a
home,

83:8 [a]Dt 2:9
83:9 [b]Jdg 7:1-23 [c]Jdg 4:23-24
83:10 [d]Zep 1:17
83:11 [e]Jdg 7:25 [f]Jdg 8:12,21
83:12 [g]2Ch 20:11
83:13 [h]Ps 35:5; Isa 17:13
83:14 [i]Dt 32:22; Isa 9:18
83:15 [j]Job 9:17
83:16 [k]Ps 109:29; 132:18
83:17 [l]Ps 35:4
83:18 [m]Ps 59:13
84:1 [n]Ps 27:4; 43:3; 132:5
84:2 [o]Ps 42:1-2
84:3 [p]Ps 43:4 [q]Ps 5:2
84:5 [r]Ps 81:1 [s]Jer 31:6
84:6 [t]Joel 2:23
84:7 [u]Pr 4:18 [v]Dt 16:16
84:9 [w]Ps 59:11 [x]1Sa 16:6; Ps 2:2; 132:17
84:10 [y]1Ch 23:5
84:11 [z]Isa 60:19; Rev 21:23 [a]Ge 15:1 [b]Ps 34:10
84:12 [c]Ps 2:12

and the swallow a nest for
herself,
where she may have her
young—
a place near your altar,[p]
O LORD Almighty, my King
and my God.[q]
4Blessed are those who dwell in
your house;
they are ever praising you.
Selah

5Blessed are those whose
strength[r] is in you,
who have set their hearts on
pilgrimage.[s]
6As they pass through the Valley
of Baca,
they make it a place of
springs;
the autumn[t] rains also cover
it with pools.[o]
7They go from strength to
strength,[u]
till each appears[v] before
God in Zion.

8Hear my prayer, O LORD God
Almighty;
listen to me, O God of Jacob.
Selah
9Look upon our shield,[p][w]
O God;
look with favor on your
anointed one.[x]

10Better is one day in your courts
than a thousand elsewhere;
I would rather be a
doorkeeper[y] in the
house of my God
than dwell in the tents of the
wicked.
11For the LORD God is a sun[z] and
shield;[a]
the LORD bestows favor and
honor;
no good thing does he
withhold[b]
from those whose walk is
blameless.

12O LORD Almighty,
blessed[c] is the man who
trusts in you.

[n]Title: Probably a musical term [o]6 Or *blessings* [p]9 Or *sovereign*

Psalm 85

For the director of music. Of the Sons of Korah. A psalm.

1You showed favor to your land,
O LORD;
you restored the fortunes[a] of Jacob.
2You forgave[b] the iniquity[c] of your people
and covered all their sins.
Selah
3You set aside all your wrath[d]
and turned from your fierce anger.[e]

4Restore[f] us again, O God our Savior,
and put away your displeasure toward us.
5Will you be angry with us forever?[g]
Will you prolong your anger through all generations?
6Will you not revive[h] us again,
that your people may rejoice in you?
7Show us your unfailing love, O LORD,
and grant us your salvation.

8I will listen to what God the LORD will say;
he promises peace[i] to his people, his saints—
but let them not return to folly.
9Surely his salvation[j] is near those who fear him,
that his glory[k] may dwell in our land.

10Love and faithfulness[l] meet together;
righteousness[m] and peace kiss each other.
11Faithfulness springs forth from the earth,
and righteousness[n] looks down from heaven.
12The LORD will indeed give what is good,[o]
and our land will yield[p] its harvest.
13Righteousness goes before him
and prepares the way for his steps.

85:1 [a]Ps 14:7; Jer 30:18; Eze 39:25
85:2 [b]Nu 14:19 [c]Ps 78:38
85:3 [d]Ps 106:23 [e]Ex 32:12; Dt 13:17; Ps 78:38; Jnh 3:9
85:4 [f]Ps 80:3,7
85:5 [g]Ps 79:5
85:6 [h]Ps 80:18; Hab 3:2
85:8 [i]Zec 9:10
85:9 [j]Isa 46:13 [k]Zec 2:5
85:10 [l]Ps 89:14; Pr 3:3 [m]Ps 72:2-3; Isa 32:17
85:11 [n]Isa 45:8
85:12 [o]Ps 84:11; Jas 1:17 [p]Lev 26:4; Ps 67:6; Zec 8:12
86:1 [q]Ps 17:6
86:2 [r]Ps 25:2; 31:14
86:3 [s]Ps 4:1; 57:1 [t]Ps 88:9
86:4 [u]Ps 25:1; 143:8
86:5 [v]Ex 34:6; Ne 9:17; Ps 103:8; 145:8; Joel 2:13; Jnh 4:2
86:7 [w]Ps 50:15
86:8 [x]Ex 15:11; Dt 3:24; Ps 89:6
86:9 [y]Ps 66:4; Rev 15:4 [z]Isa 43:7
86:10 [a]Ps 72:18 [b]Dt 6:4; Mk 12:29; 1Co 8:4
86:11 [c]Ps 25:5 [d]Jer 32:39

Psalm 86

A prayer of David.

1Hear, O LORD, and answer[q] me,
for I am poor and needy.
2Guard my life, for I am devoted to you.
You are my God; save your servant
who trusts in you.[r]
3Have mercy[s] on me, O Lord,
for I call[t] to you all day long.
4Bring joy to your servant,
for to you, O Lord,
I lift[u] up my soul.

5You are forgiving and good, O Lord,
abounding in love[v] to all who call to you.
6Hear my prayer, O LORD;
listen to my cry for mercy.
7In the day of my trouble[w] I will call to you,
for you will answer me.

8Among the gods there is none like you,[x] O Lord;
no deeds can compare with yours.
9All the nations you have made
will come and worship[y] before you, O Lord;
they will bring glory[z] to your name.
10For you are great and do marvelous deeds;[a]
you alone[b] are God.

11Teach me your way,[c] O LORD,
and I will walk in your truth;
give me an undivided[d] heart,
that I may fear your name.
12I will praise you, O Lord my God, with all my heart;
I will glorify your name forever.
13For great is your love toward me;
you have delivered me from the depths of the grave.[q]
14The arrogant are attacking me, O God;

[q]13 Hebrew *Sheol*

a band of ruthless men seeks
my life—
men without regard for you.[a]
15But you, O Lord, are a
compassionate and
gracious[b] God,
slow to anger, abounding in
love and faithfulness.[c]
16Turn to me and have mercy on
me;
grant your strength to your
servant
and save the son of your
maidservant.[r][d]
17Give me a sign of your
goodness,
that my enemies may see it
and be put to shame,
for you, O LORD, have helped
me and comforted me.

Psalm 87

Of the Sons of Korah. A psalm.
A song.

1He has set his foundation on
the holy mountain;
2 the LORD loves the gates of
Zion[e]
more than all the dwellings
of Jacob.
3Glorious things are said of you,
O city of God:[f] *Selah*
4"I will record Rahab[s][g] and
Babylon
among those who
acknowledge me—
Philistia too, and Tyre[h], along
with Cush[t]—
and will say, 'This[u] one was
born in Zion.[i]' "
5Indeed, of Zion it will be said,
"This one and that one were
born in her,
and the Most High himself
will establish her."
6The LORD will write in the
register[j] of the peoples:
"This one was born in Zion."
Selah
7As they make music[k] they will
sing,
"All my fountains[l] are in
you."

86:14 [a]Ps 54:3
86:15 [b]Ps 103:8 [c]Ex 34:6; Ne 9:17; Joel 2:13
86:16 [d]Ps 116:16
87:2 [e]Ps 78:68
87:3 [f]Ps 46:4; Isa 60:1
87:4 [g]Job 9:13 [h]Ps 45:12 [i]Isa 19:25
87:6 [j]Ps 69:28; Isa 4:3; Eze 13:9
87:7 [k]Ps 149:3 [l]Ps 36:9
88:1 [m]Ps 51:14 [n]Ps 22:2; 27:9; Lk 18:7
88:3 [o]Ps 107:18,26
88:4 [p]Ps 28:1
88:5 [q]Ps 31:22; Isa 53:8
88:6 [r]Ps 69:15; La 3:55
88:7 [s]Ps 42:7
88:8 [t]Job 19:13; Ps 31:11 [u]Jer 32:2
88:9 [v]Ps 38:10 [w]Ps 86:3 [x]Job 11:13; Ps 143:6

Psalm 88

A song. A psalm of the Sons of
Korah. For the director of music.
According to *mahalath
leannoth.*[v] A *maskil*[w] of Heman
the Ezrahite.

1O LORD, the God who saves
me,[m]
day and night I cry out[n]
before you.
2May my prayer come before
you;
turn your ear to my cry.
3For my soul is full of trouble
and my life draws near the
grave.[x][o]
4I am counted among those who
go down to the pit;[p]
I am like a man without
strength.
5I am set apart with the dead,
like the slain who lie in the
grave,
whom you remember no more,
who are cut off[q] from your
care.
6You have put me in the lowest
pit,
in the darkest depths.[r]
7Your wrath lies heavily upon
me;
you have overwhelmed me
with all your waves.[s]
Selah
8You have taken from me my
closest friends[t]
and have made me repulsive
to them.
I am confined[u] and cannot
escape;
9 my eyes[v] are dim with grief.
I call[w] to you, O LORD, every
day;
I spread out my hands[x] to
you.
10Do you show your wonders to
the dead?

[r]16 Or *save your faithful son* [s]4 A poetic name for Egypt [t]4 That is, the upper Nile region [u]4 Or *"O Rahab and Babylon, / Philistia, Tyre and Cush, / I will record concerning those who acknowledge me: / 'This* [v]Title: Possibly a tune, "The Suffering of Affliction" [w]Title: Probably a literary or musical term [x]3 Hebrew *Sheol*

Do those who are dead rise
up and praise you?[a]
Selah
11Is your love declared in the
grave,
your faithfulness[b] in
Destruction[y]?
12Are your wonders known in the
place of darkness,
or your righteous deeds in
the land of oblivion?

13But I cry to you for help,[c]
O LORD;
in the morning[d] my prayer
comes before you.[e]
14Why, O LORD, do you reject[f]
me
and hide your face[g] from
me?
15From my youth I have been
afflicted and close to
death;
I have suffered your terrors[h]
and am in despair.
16Your wrath has swept over me;
your terrors have destroyed
me.
17All day long they surround me
like a flood;[i]
they have completely
engulfed me.
18You have taken my
companions[j] and loved
ones from me;
the darkness is my closest
friend.

Psalm 89

A *maskil*[z] of Ethan the Ezrahite.

1I will sing[k] of the LORD's great
love forever;
with my mouth I will make
your faithfulness
known[l] through all
generations.
2I will declare that your love
stands firm forever,
that you established your
faithfulness in heaven
itself.[m]

3You said, "I have made a
covenant with my
chosen one,

88:10 [a]Ps 6:5
88:11 [b]Ps 30:9
88:13 [c]Ps 30:2 [d]Ps 5:3 [e]Ps 119:147
88:14 [f]Ps 43:2 [g]Job 13:24; Ps 13:1
88:15 [h]Job 6:4
88:17 [i]Ps 22:16; 124:4
88:18 [j]ver 8; Job 19:13; Ps 38:11
89:1 [k]Ps 59:16; Ps 101:1 [l]Ps 36:5; 40:10
89:2 [m]Ps 36:5
89:4 [n]2Sa 7:12-16; 1Ki 8:16; Ps 132:11-12; Isa 9:7; Lk 1:33
89:5 [o]Ps 19:1
89:6 [p]Ps 113:5
89:7 [q]Ps 47:2
89:8 [r]Ps 71:19
89:9 [s]Ps 65:7
89:10 [t]Ps 87:4 [u]Ps 68:1
89:11 [v]1Ch 29:11; Ps 24:1 [w]Ge 1:1
89:12 [x]Jos 19:22 [y]Dt 3:8; Jos 12:1 [z]Ps 98:8
89:14 [a]Ps 97:2
89:15 [b]Ps 44:3

I have sworn to David my
servant,
4'I will establish your line
forever
and make your throne firm
through all
generations.' "[n] *Selah*

5The heavens[o] praise your
wonders, O LORD,
your faithfulness too, in the
assembly of the holy
ones.
6For who in the skies above can
compare with the LORD?
Who is like the LORD among
the heavenly beings?[p]
7In the council of the holy ones
God is greatly feared;
he is more awesome than all
who surround him.[q]
8O LORD God Almighty, who is
like you?[r]
You are mighty, O LORD, and
your faithfulness
surrounds you.

9You rule over the surging sea;
when its waves mount up,
you still them.[s]
10You crushed Rahab[t] like one
of the slain;
with your strong arm you
scattered[u] your enemies.
11The heavens are yours, and
yours also the earth;[v]
you founded the world and
all that is in it.[w]
12You created the north and the
south;
Tabor[x] and Hermon[y] sing
for joy[z] at your name.
13Your arm is endued with power;
your hand is strong, your
right hand exalted.

14Righteousness and justice are
the foundation of your
throne;[a]
love and faithfulness go
before you.
15Blessed are those who have
learned to acclaim you,
who walk in the light[b] of
your presence, O LORD.

[y]*11* Hebrew *Abaddon* [z]Title: Probably a literary or musical term

16They rejoice in your name[a] all
day long;
they exult in your
righteousness.
17For you are their glory and
strength,
and by your favor you exalt
our horn.[a][b]
18Indeed, our shield[b] belongs to
the LORD,
our king[c] to the Holy One of
Israel.

19Once you spoke in a vision,
to your faithful people you
said:
"I have bestowed strength on a
warrior;
I have exalted a young man
from among the people.
20I have found David[d] my
servant;[e]
with my sacred oil I have
anointed[f] him.
21My hand will sustain him;
surely my arm will strengthen
him.[g]
22No enemy will subject him to
tribute;
no wicked man will oppress[h]
him.
23I will crush his foes before
him[i]
and strike down his
adversaries.[j]
24My faithful love will be with
him,[k]
and through my name his
horn[c] will be exalted.
25I will set his hand over the sea,
his right hand over the
rivers.[l]
26He will call out to me, 'You are
my Father,[m]
my God, the Rock my
Savior.'[n]
27I will also appoint him my
firstborn,[o]
the most exalted[p] of the
kings[q] of the earth.
28I will maintain my love to him
forever,
and my covenant with him
will never fail.[r]
29I will establish his line forever,
his throne as long as the
heavens endure.[s]

30"If his sons forsake my law
and do not follow my
statutes,
31if they violate my decrees
and fail to keep my
commands,
32I will punish their sin with the
rod,
their iniquity with flogging;[t]
33but I will not take my love from
him,[u]
nor will I ever betray my
faithfulness.
34I will not violate my covenant
or alter what my lips have
uttered.[v]
35Once for all, I have sworn by
my holiness—
and I will not lie to David—
36that his line will continue
forever
and his throne endure before
me like the sun;
37it will be established forever
like the moon,
the faithful witness in the
sky." *Selah*

38But you have rejected,[w] you
have spurned,
you have been very angry
with your anointed one.
39You have renounced the
covenant with your
servant
and have defiled his crown in
the dust.[x]
40You have broken through all his
walls[y]
and reduced his
strongholds[z] to ruins.
41All who pass by have plundered
him;
he has become the scorn of
his neighbors.[a]
42You have exalted the right
hand of his foes;
you have made all his
enemies rejoice.[b]
43You have turned back the edge
of his sword
and have not supported him
in battle.[c]

89:16 [a]Ps 105:3
89:17 [b]Ps 75:10; 92:10; 148:14
89:18 [c]Ps 47:9
89:20 [d]Ac 13:22 [e]Ps 78:70 [f]1Sa 16:1,12
89:21 [g]Ps 18:35
89:22 [h]2Sa 7:10
89:23 [i]Ps 18:40 [j]2Sa 7:9
89:24 [k]2Sa 7:15
89:25 [l]Ps 72:8
89:26 [m]2Sa 7:14 [n]2Sa 22:47
89:27 [o]Col 1:18 [p]Nu 24:7 [q]Rev 1:5; 19:16
89:28 [r]ver 33-34; Isa 55:3
89:29 [s]ver 4,36; Dt 11:21; Jer 33:17
89:32 [t]2Sa 7:14
89:33 [u]2Sa 7:15
89:34 [v]Nu 23:19
89:38 [w]Dt 32:19; 1Ch 28:9; Ps 44:9
89:39 [x]La 5:16
89:40 [y]Ps 80:12 [z]La 2:2
89:41 [a]Ps 44:13
89:42 [b]Ps 13:2; 80:6
89:43 [c]Ps 44:10

[a]17 *Horn* here symbolizes strong one.
[b]18 Or *sovereign* [c]24 *Horn* here symbolizes strength.

44You have put an end to his
splendor
and cast his throne to the
ground.
45You have cut short the days of
his youth;
you have covered him with a
mantle of shame.[a] *Selah*
46How long, O LORD? Will you
hide yourself forever?
How long will your wrath
burn like fire?[b]
47Remember how fleeting is my
life.[c]
For what futility you have
created all men!
48What man can live and not see
death,
or save himself from the
power of the grave[d]?[d]
Selah
49O Lord, where is your former
great love,
which in your faithfulness
you swore to David?
50Remember, Lord, how your
servant has[e] been
mocked,[e]
how I bear in my heart the
taunts of all the nations,
51the taunts with which your
enemies have mocked,
O LORD,
with which they have mocked
every step of your
anointed one.[f]

52Praise be to the LORD forever!
Amen and Amen.[g]

BOOK IV

Psalms 90–106

Psalm 90

A prayer of Moses the man of
God.

1Lord, you have been our
dwelling place[h]
throughout all generations.
2Before the mountains were
born[i]
or you brought forth the
earth and the world,
from everlasting to
everlasting you are
God.[j]

3You turn men back to dust,
saying, "Return to dust,
O sons of men."[k]
4For a thousand years in your
sight
are like a day that has just
gone by,
or like a watch in the night.[l]
5You sweep men away[m] in the
sleep of death;
they are like the new grass of
the morning—
6though in the morning it
springs up new,
by evening it is dry and
withered.[n]

7We are consumed by your anger
and terrified by your
indignation.
8You have set our iniquities
before you,
our secret sins[o] in the light
of your presence.
9All our days pass away under
your wrath;
we finish our years with a
moan.[p]
10The length of our days is
seventy years—
or eighty, if we have the
strength;
yet their span[f] is but trouble
and sorrow,
for they quickly pass, and we
fly away.[q]
11Who knows the power of your
anger?
For your wrath is as great as
the fear that is due
you.[r]
12Teach us to number our days[s]
aright,
that we may gain a heart of
wisdom.[t]
13Relent, O LORD! How long[u] will
it be?
Have compassion on your
servants.[v]

89:45 [a]Ps 44:15; 109:29
89:46 [b]Ps 79:5
89:47 [c]Job 7:7; Ps 39:5
89:48 [d]Ps 22:29; 49:9
89:50 [e]Ps 69:19
89:51 [f]Ps 74:10
89:52 [g]Ps 41:13; 72:19
90:1 [h]Dt 33:27; Eze 11:16
90:2 [i]Job 15:7; Pr 8:25 [j]Ps 102:24-27
90:3 [k]Ge 3:19; Job 34:15
90:4 [l]2Pe 3:8
90:5 [m]Ps 73:20; Isa 40:6
90:6 [n]Mt 6:30; Jas 1:10
90:8 [o]Ps 19:12
90:9 [p]Ps 78:33
90:10 [q]Job 20:8
90:11 [r]Ps 76:7
90:12 [s]Ps 39:4 [t]Dt 32:29
90:13 [u]Ps 6:3 [v]Dt 32:36; Ps 135:14

[d]48 Hebrew *Sheol* [e]50 Or *your servants have* [f]10 Or *yet the best of them*

[14]Satisfy[a] us in the morning with
your unfailing love,
that we may sing for joy[b]
and be glad all our
days.[c]
[15]Make us glad for as many days
as you have afflicted us,
for as many years as we have
seen trouble.
[16]May your deeds be shown to
your servants,
your splendor to their
children.[d]
[17]May the favor[g] of the Lord our
God rest upon us;
establish the work of our
hands for us—
yes, establish the work of our
hands.[e]

Psalm 91

[1]He who dwells in the shelter[f]
of the Most High
will rest in the shadow[g] of
the Almighty.[h]
[2]I will say[i] of the LORD, "He is
my refuge[h] and my
fortress,
my God, in whom I trust."
[3]Surely he will save you from
the fowler's snare[i]
and from the deadly
pestilence.[j]
[4]He will cover you with his
feathers,
and under his wings you will
find refuge;[k]
his faithfulness will be your
shield[l] and rampart.
[5]You will not fear[m] the terror of
night,
nor the arrow that flies by
day,
[6]nor the pestilence that stalks in
the darkness,
nor the plague that destroys
at midday.
[7]A thousand may fall at your
side,
ten thousand at your right
hand,
but it will not come near
you.
[8]You will only observe with your
eyes
and see the punishment of
the wicked.[n]
[9]If you make the Most High
your dwelling—
even the LORD, who is my
refuge—
[10]then no harm[o] will befall you,
no disaster will come near
your tent.
[11]For he will command his
angels[p] concerning you
to guard you in all your
ways;[q]
[12]they will lift you up in their
hands,
so that you will not strike
your foot against a
stone.[r]
[13]You will tread upon the lion
and the cobra;
you will trample the great
lion and the serpent.[s]

[14]"Because he loves me," says
the LORD, "I will rescue
him;
I will protect him, for he
acknowledges my name.
[15]He will call upon me, and I will
answer him;
I will be with him in trouble,
I will deliver him and honor
him.[t]
[16]With long life[u] will I satisfy
him
and show him my
salvation.[v]"

Psalm 92

A psalm. A song. For the
Sabbath day.

[1]It is good to praise the LORD
and make music to your
name,[w] O Most High,[x]
[2]to proclaim your love in the
morning[y]
and your faithfulness at
night,
[3]to the music of the ten-stringed
lyre
and the melody of the harp.[z]

90:14 [a]Ps 103:5 [b]Ps 85:6 [c]Ps 31:7
90:16 [d]Ps 44:1; Hab 3:2
90:17 [e]Isa 26:12
91:1 [f]Ps 31:20 [g]Ps 17:8
91:2 [h]Ps 142:5
91:3 [i]Ps 124:7; Pr 6:5 [j]1Ki 8:37
91:4 [k]Ps 17:8 [l]Ps 35:2
91:5 [m]Job 5:21
91:8 [n]Ps 37:34; 58:10; Mal 1:5
91:10 [o]Pr 12:21
91:11 [p]Heb 1:14 [q]Ps 34:7
91:12 [r]Mt 4:6*; Lk 4:10-11*
91:13 [s]Da 6:22; Lk 10:19
91:15 [t]1Sa 2:30; Ps 50:15; Jn 12:26
91:16 [u]Dt 6:2; Ps 21:4 [v]Ps 50:23
92:1 [w]Ps 147:1 [x]Ps 135:3
92:2 [y]Ps 89:1
92:3 [z]1Sa 10:5; Ne 12:27; Ps 33:2

[g]17 Or *beauty* [h]1 Hebrew *Shaddai*
[i]2 Or *He says*

4 For you make me glad by your
deeds, O LORD;
I sing for joy at the works of
your hands.[a]
5 How great are your works,[b]
O LORD,
how profound your
thoughts![c]
6 The senseless man[d] does not
know,
fools do not understand,
7 that though the wicked spring
up like grass
and all evildoers flourish,
they will be forever destroyed.

8 But you, O LORD, are exalted
forever.

9 For surely your enemies,
O LORD,
surely your enemies will
perish;
all evildoers will be
scattered.[e]
10 You have exalted my horn[i][f]
like that of a wild ox;
fine oils[g] have been poured
upon me.
11 My eyes have seen the defeat of
my adversaries;
my ears have heard the rout
of my wicked foes.[h]

12 The righteous will flourish like
a palm tree,
they will grow like a cedar of
Lebanon;[i]
13 planted in the house of the
LORD,
they will flourish in the
courts of our God.[j]
14 They will still bear fruit[k] in old
age,
they will stay fresh and
green,
15 proclaiming, "The LORD is
upright;
he is my Rock, and there is
no wickedness in him.[l]"

Psalm 93

1 The LORD reigns,[m] he is robed
in majesty;[n]
the LORD is robed in majesty
and is armed with strength.[o]
The world is firmly established;
it cannot be moved.[p]
2 Your throne was established
long ago;
you are from all eternity.[q]

3 The seas[r] have lifted up,
O LORD,
the seas have lifted up their
voice;
the seas have lifted up their
pounding waves.
4 Mightier than the thunder[s] of
the great waters,
mightier than the breakers of
the sea—
the LORD on high is mighty.

5 Your statutes stand firm;
holiness[t] adorns your house
for endless days, O LORD.

Psalm 94

1 O LORD, the God who avenges,[u]
O God who avenges, shine
forth.[v]
2 Rise up, O Judge[w] of the earth;
pay back[x] to the proud what
they deserve.
3 How long will the wicked,
O LORD,
how long will the wicked be
jubilant?

4 They pour out arrogant[y] words;
all the evildoers are full of
boasting.[z]
5 They crush your people,[a]
O LORD;
they oppress your
inheritance.
6 They slay the widow and the
alien;
they murder the fatherless.
7 They say, "The LORD does not
see;[b]
the God of Jacob pays no
heed."

8 Take heed, you senseless
ones[c] among the
people;
you fools, when will you
become wise?
9 Does he who implanted the ear
not hear?

92:4 [a] Ps 8:6; 143:5
92:5 [b] Rev 15:3 [c] Ps 40:5; 139:17; Isa 28:29; Ro 11:33
92:6 [d] Ps 73:22
92:9 [e] Ps 68:1; 89:10
92:10 [f] Ps 89:17 [g] Ps 23:5
92:11 [h] Ps 54:7; 91:8
92:12 [i] Ps 1:3; 52:8; Jer 17:8; Hos 14:6
92:13 [j] Ps 100:4
92:14 [k] Jn 15:2
92:15 [l] Job 34:10
93:1 [m] Ps 97:1 [n] Ps 104:1 [o] Ps 65:6 [p] Ps 96:10
93:2 [q] Ps 45:6
93:3 [r] Ps 96:11
93:4 [s] Ps 65:7
93:5 [t] Ps 29:2
94:1 [u] Na 1:2; Ro 12:19 [v] Ps 80:1
94:2 [w] Ge 18:25 [x] Ps 31:23
94:4 [y] Ps 31:18 [z] Ps 52:1
94:5 [a] Isa 3:15
94:7 [b] Job 22:14; Ps 10:11
94:8 [c] Ps 92:6

[i] *10 Horn* here symbolizes strength.

Does he who formed the eye
not see?[a]
10Does he who disciplines
nations not punish?
Does he who teaches[b] man
lack knowledge?
11The LORD knows the thoughts
of man;
he knows that they are
futile.[c]

12Blessed is the man you
discipline,[d] O LORD,
the man you teach[e] from
your law;
13you grant him relief from days
of trouble,
till a pit[f] is dug for the
wicked.
14For the LORD will not reject his
people;[g]
he will never forsake his
inheritance.
15Judgment will again be
founded on
righteousness,[h]
and all the upright in heart
will follow it.

16Who will rise up[i] for me
against the wicked?
Who will take a stand for me
against evildoers?[j]
17Unless the LORD had given me
help,[k]
I would soon have dwelt in
the silence of death.
18When I said, "My foot is
slipping,[l]"
your love, O LORD, supported
me.
19When anxiety was great within
me,
your consolation brought joy
to my soul.

20Can a corrupt throne be allied
with you—
one that brings on misery by
its decrees?[m]
21They band together[n] against
the righteous
and condemn the innocent[o]
to death.
22But the LORD has become my
fortress,
and my God the rock in
whom I take refuge.[p]
23He will repay[q] them for their
sins
and destroy them for their
wickedness;
the LORD our God will destroy
them.

Psalm 95

1Come, let us sing for joy to the
LORD;
let us shout aloud[r] to the
Rock[s] of our salvation.
2Let us come before him[t] with
thanksgiving
and extol him with music[u]
and song.

3For the LORD is the great God,[v]
the great King above all
gods.[w]
4In his hand are the depths of
the earth,
and the mountain peaks
belong to him.
5The sea is his, for he made it,
and his hands formed the dry
land.[x]

6Come, let us bow down[y] in
worship,
let us kneel[z] before the LORD
our Maker;[a]
7for he is our God
and we are the people of his
pasture,[b]
the flock under his care.

Today, if you hear his voice,
8 do not harden your hearts as
you did at Meribah,[k][c]
as you did that day at
Massah[l] in the desert,
9where your fathers tested[d] and
tried me,
though they had seen what I
did.
10For forty years[e] I was angry
with that generation;
I said, "They are a people
whose hearts go astray,
and they have not known my
ways."
11So I declared on oath[f] in my
anger,

94:9 [a]Ex 4:11; Pr 20:12
94:10 [b]Job 35:11; Isa 28:26
94:11 [c]1Co 3:20*
94:12 [d]Job 5:17; Heb 12:5 [e]Dt 8:3
94:13 [f]Ps 55:23
94:14 [g]1Sa 12:22; Ps 37:28; Ro 11:2
94:15 [h]Ps 97:2
94:16 [i]Nu 10:35; Ps 17:13 [j]Ps 59:2
94:17 [k]Ps 124:2
94:18 [l]Ps 38:16
94:20 [m]Ps 58:2
94:21 [n]Ps 56:6 [o]Ps 106:38; Pr 17:15,26
94:22 [p]Ps 18:2; 59:9
94:23 [q]Ps 7:16
95:1 [r]Ps 81:1 [s]2Sa 22:47
95:2 [t]Mic 6:6 [u]Ps 81:2; Eph 5:19
95:3 [v]Ps 48:1; 145:3 [w]Ps 96:4; 97:9
95:5 [x]Ge 1:9; Ps 146:6
95:6 [y]Php 2:10 [z]2Ch 6:13 [a]Ps 100:3; 149:2; Isa 17:7; Da 6:10-11; Hos 8:14
95:7 [b]Ps 74:1; 79:13
95:8 [c]Ex 17:7
95:9 [d]Nu 14:22; Ps 78:18; 1Co 10:9
95:10 [e]Ac 7:36; Heb 3:17
95:11 [f]Nu 14:23

[k]8 *Meribah* means *quarreling.* [l]8 *Massah* means *testing.*

"They shall never enter my
rest."[a]

Psalm 96

96:1–13pp — 1Ch 16:23–33

1 Sing to the LORD[b] a new song;
sing to the LORD, all the
earth.
2 Sing to the LORD, praise his
name;
proclaim his salvation[c] day
after day.
3 Declare his glory among the
nations,
his marvelous deeds among
all peoples.

4 For great is the LORD and most
worthy of praise;[d]
he is to be feared[e] above all
gods.[f]
5 For all the gods of the nations
are idols,
but the LORD made the
heavens.[g]
6 Splendor and majesty are
before him;
strength and glory[h] are in
his sanctuary.

7 Ascribe to the LORD,[i]
O families of nations,[j]
ascribe to the LORD glory and
strength.
8 Ascribe to the LORD the glory
due his name;
bring an offering[k] and come
into his courts.
9 Worship the LORD in the
splendor of his[m]
holiness;[l]
tremble[m] before him, all the
earth.[n]

10 Say among the nations, "The
LORD reigns.[o]"
The world is firmly
established, it cannot be
moved;[p]
he will judge the peoples
with equity.[q]
11 Let the heavens rejoice, let the
earth be glad;[r]
let the sea resound, and all
that is in it;
12 let the fields be jubilant, and
everything in them.

95:11 [a] Dt 1:35; Heb 4:3,5*
96:1 [b] 1Ch 16:23
96:2 [c] Ps 71:15
96:4 [d] Ps 18:3; 145:3 [e] Ps 89:7 [f] Ps 95:3
96:5 [g] Ps 115:15
96:6 [h] Ps 29:1
96:7 [i] Ps 29:1 [j] Ps 22:27
96:8 [k] Ps 45:12; 72:10
96:9 [l] Ps 29:2 [m] Ps 114:7 [n] Ps 33:8
96:10 [o] Ps 97:1 [p] Ps 93:1 [q] Ps 67:4
96:11 [r] Ps 97:1; 98:7; Isa 49:13
96:12 [s] Isa 44:23 [t] Ps 65:13
96:13 [u] Rev 19:11
97:1 [v] Ps 96:10 [w] Ps 96:11
97:2 [x] Ex 19:9; Ps 18:11 [y] Ps 89:14
97:3 [z] Da 7:10 [a] Hab 3:5 [b] Ps 18:8
97:4 [c] Ps 104:32
97:5 [d] Ps 46:2,6; Mic 1:4 [e] Jos 3:11
97:6 [f] Ps 50:6 [g] Ps 19:1
97:7 [h] Lev 26:1 [i] Jer 10:14 [j] Heb 1:6
97:8 [k] Ps 48:11
97:9 [l] Ps 83:18; 95:3 [m] Ex 18:11
97:10 [n] Ps 34:14; Am 5:15; Ro 12:9 [o] Pr 2:8

Then all the trees of the
forest[s] will sing for
joy;[t]
13 they will sing before the
LORD, for he comes,
he comes to judge[u] the
earth.
He will judge the world in
righteousness
and the peoples in his truth.

Psalm 97

1 The LORD reigns,[v] let the earth
be glad;[w]
let the distant shores rejoice.

2 Clouds and thick darkness[x]
surround him;
righteousness and justice are
the foundation of his
throne.[y]
3 Fire[z] goes before[a] him
and consumes[b] his foes on
every side.
4 His lightning lights up the
world;
the earth sees and
trembles.[c]
5 The mountains melt[d] like wax
before the LORD,
before the Lord of all the
earth.[e]
6 The heavens proclaim his
righteousness,[f]
and all the peoples see his
glory.[g]

7 All who worship images[h] are
put to shame,[i]
those who boast in idols—
worship him,[j] all you gods!

8 Zion hears and rejoices
and the villages of Judah are
glad
because of your judgments,[k]
O LORD.
9 For you, O LORD, are the Most
High over all the earth;[l]
you are exalted[m] far above
all gods.

10 Let those who love the LORD
hate evil,[n]
for he guards the lives of his
faithful ones[o]

m9 Or *LORD with the splendor of*

and delivers[a] them from the hand of the wicked.[b]
11Light is shed[c] upon the righteous
and joy on the upright in heart.
12Rejoice in the LORD, you who are righteous,
and praise his holy name.[d]

Psalm 98

A psalm.

1Sing to the LORD a new song,[e]
for he has done marvelous things;[f]
his right hand[g] and his holy arm[h]
have worked salvation for him.
2The LORD has made his salvation known[i]
and revealed his righteousness to the nations.
3He has remembered[j] his love
and his faithfulness to the house of Israel;
all the ends of the earth have seen
the salvation of our God.

4Shout for joy[k] to the LORD, all the earth,
burst into jubilant song with music;
5make music to the LORD with the harp,[l]
with the harp and the sound of singing,[m]
6with trumpets[n] and the blast of the ram's horn—
shout for joy before the LORD, the King.[o]

7Let the sea resound, and everything in it,
the world, and all who live in it.[p]
8Let the rivers clap their hands,
let the mountains[q] sing together for joy;
9let them sing before the LORD,
for he comes to judge the earth.
He will judge the world in righteousness
and the peoples with equity.[r]

Psalm 99

1The LORD reigns,[s]
let the nations tremble;
he sits enthroned between the cherubim,[t]
let the earth shake.
2Great is the LORD[u] in Zion;
he is exalted[v] over all the nations.
3Let them praise your great and awesome name[w]—
he is holy.

4The King is mighty, he loves justice[x]—
you have established equity;[y]
in Jacob you have done
what is just and right.
5Exalt[z] the LORD our God
and worship at his footstool;
he is holy.

6Moses[a] and Aaron were among his priests,
Samuel[b] was among those who called on his name;
they called on the LORD
and he answered[c] them.
7He spoke to them from the pillar of cloud;[d]
they kept his statutes and the decrees he gave them.

8O LORD our God,
you answered them;
you were to Israel[n] a forgiving God,[e]
though you punished their misdeeds.[o]
9Exalt the LORD our God
and worship at his holy mountain,
for the LORD our God is holy.

Psalm 100

A psalm. For giving thanks.

1Shout for joy[f] to the LORD, all the earth.

97:10 [a]Da 3:28 [b]Ps 37:40; Jer 15:21
97:11 [c]Job 22:28
97:12 [d]Ps 30:4
98:1 [e]Ps 96:1 [f]Ps 96:3 [g]Ex 15:6 [h]Isa 52:10
98:2 [i]Isa 52:10
98:3 [j]Lk 1:54
98:4 [k]Isa 44:23
98:5 [l]Ps 92:3 [m]Isa 51:3
98:6 [n]Nu 10:10 [o]Ps 47:7
98:7 [p]Ps 24:1
98:8 [q]Isa 55:12
98:9 [r]Ps 96:10
99:1 [s]Ps 97:1 [t]Ex 25:22
99:2 [u]Ps 48:1 [v]Ps 97:9; 113:4
99:3 [w]Ps 76:1
99:4 [x]Ps 11:7 [y]Ps 98:9
99:5 [z]Ps 132:7
99:6 [a]Ex 24:6 [b]Jer 15:1 [c]1Sa 7:9
99:7 [d]Ex 33:9
99:8 [e]Nu 14:20
100:1 [f]Ps 98:4

[n]8 Hebrew *them* [o]8 Or / *an avenger of the wrongs done to them*

2 Worship the LORD with gladness;
come before him[a] with joyful songs.
3 Know that the LORD is God.[b]
It is he who made us,[c] and we are his[p];
we are his people, the sheep of his pasture.[d]

4 Enter his gates with thanksgiving
and his courts with praise;
give thanks to him and praise his name.[e]
5 For the LORD is good[f] and his love endures forever;[g]
his faithfulness[h] continues through all generations.

Psalm 101

Of David. A psalm.

1 I will sing of your love[i] and justice;
to you, O LORD, I will sing praise.
2 I will be careful to lead a blameless life—
when will you come to me?

I will walk in my house
with blameless heart.
3 I will set before my eyes
no vile thing.[j]

The deeds of faithless men I hate;[k]
they will not cling to me.
4 Men of perverse heart[l] shall be far from me;
I will have nothing to do with evil.

5 Whoever slanders his neighbor[m] in secret,
him will I put to silence;
whoever has haughty eyes[n] and a proud heart,
him will I not endure.

6 My eyes will be on the faithful in the land,
that they may dwell with me;
he whose walk is blameless[o]
will minister to me.

7 No one who practices deceit
will dwell in my house;
no one who speaks falsely
will stand in my presence.

8 Every morning[p] I will put to silence
all the wicked[q] in the land;
I will cut off every evildoer[r]
from the city of the LORD.[s]

Psalm 102

A prayer of an afflicted man. When he is faint and pours out his lament before the LORD.

1 Hear my prayer, O LORD;
let my cry for help[t] come to you.
2 Do not hide your face[u] from me
when I am in distress.
Turn your ear to me;
when I call, answer me quickly.

3 For my days vanish like smoke;[v]
my bones burn like glowing embers.
4 My heart is blighted and withered like grass;[w]
I forget to eat my food.
5 Because of my loud groaning
I am reduced to skin and bones.
6 I am like a desert owl,[x]
like an owl among the ruins.
7 I lie awake;[y] I have become
like a bird alone[z] on a roof.
8 All day long my enemies taunt me;
those who rail against me
use my name as a curse.
9 For I eat ashes as my food
and mingle my drink with tears[a]
10 because of your great wrath,[b]
for you have taken me up
and thrown me aside.
11 My days are like the evening shadow;[c]
I wither away like grass.

12 But you, O LORD, sit enthroned forever;[d]
your renown endures[e]
through all generations.

100:2 [a] Ps 95:2
100:3 [b] Ps 46:10 [c] Job 10:3 [d] Ps 74:1; Eze 34:31
100:4 [e] Ps 116:17
100:5 [f] 1Ch 16:34; Ps 25:8 [g] Ezr 3:11; Ps 106:1 [h] Ps 119:90
101:1 [i] Ps 51:14; 89:1; 145:7
101:3 [j] Dt 15:9 [k] Ps 40:4
101:4 [l] Pr 11:20
101:5 [m] Ps 50:20 [n] Ps 10:5; Pr 6:17
101:6 [o] Ps 119:1
101:8 [p] Jer 21:12 [q] Ps 75:10 [r] Ps 118:10-12 [s] Ps 46:4
102:1 [t] Ex 2:23
102:2 [u] Ps 69:17
102:3 [v] Jas 4:14
102:4 [w] Ps 37:2
102:6 [x] Job 30:29; Isa 34:11
102:7 [y] Ps 77:4 [z] Ps 38:11
102:9 [a] Ps 42:3
102:10 [b] Ps 38:3
102:11 [c] Job 14:2
102:12 [d] Ps 9:7 [e] Ps 135:13

p3 Or *and not we ourselves*

13You will arise and have
compassion[a] on Zion,
for it is time to show favor to
her;
the appointed time has
come.
14For her stones are dear to your
servants;
her very dust moves them to
pity.
15The nations will fear[b] the
name of the LORD,
all the kings[c] of the earth
will revere your glory.
16For the LORD will rebuild Zion
and appear in his glory.[d]
17He will respond to the prayer[e]
of the destitute;
he will not despise their plea.

18Let this be written[f] for a
future generation,
that a people not yet
created[g] may praise the
LORD:
19"The LORD looked down[h] from
his sanctuary on high,
from heaven he viewed the
earth,
20to hear the groans of the
prisoners[i]
and release those condemned
to death."
21So the name of the LORD will be
declared[j] in Zion
and his praise in Jerusalem
22when the peoples and the
kingdoms
assemble to worship the
LORD.

23In the course of my life[q] he
broke my strength;
he cut short my days.
24So I said:
"Do not take me away, O my
God, in the midst of my
days;
your years go on[k] through all
generations.
25In the beginning[l] you laid the
foundations of the earth,
and the heavens are the work
of your hands.
26They will perish,[m] but you
remain;
they will all wear out like a
garment.
Like clothing you will change
them
and they will be discarded.
27But you remain the same,[n]
and your years will never
end.
28The children of your servants[o]
will live in your
presence;
their descendants[p] will be
established before you."

102:13 [a]Isa 60:10
102:15 [b]1Ki 8:43 [c]Ps 138:4
102:16 [d]Isa 60:1-2
102:17 [e]Ne 1:6
102:18 [f]Ro 15:4 [g]Ps 22:31
102:19 [h]Dt 26:15
102:20 [i]Ps 79:11
102:21 [j]Ps 22:22
102:24 [k]Ps 90:2; Isa 38:10
102:25 [l]Ge 1:1; Heb 1:10-12*
102:26 [m]Isa 34:4; Mt 24:35; 2Pe 3:7-10; Rev 20:11
102:27 [n]Mal 3:6; Heb 13:8; Jas 1:17
102:28 [o]Ps 69:36 [p]Ps 89:4

Psalm 103

Of David.

1Praise the LORD, O my soul;[q]
all my inmost being, praise
his holy name.
2Praise the LORD, O my soul,
and forget not all his
benefits—
3who forgives all your sins[r]
and heals[s] all your diseases,
4who redeems your life from the
pit
and crowns you with love
and compassion,
5who satisfies your desires with
good things
so that your youth is renewed
like the eagle's.[t]

6The LORD works righteousness
and justice for all the
oppressed.

7He made known[u] his ways[v] to
Moses,
his deeds[w] to the people of
Israel:
8The LORD is compassionate and
gracious,[x]
slow to anger, abounding in
love.
9He will not always accuse,
nor will he harbor his anger
forever;[y]
10he does not treat us as our sins
deserve[z]
or repay us according to our
iniquities.
11For as high as the heavens are
above the earth,
so great is his love[a] for those
who fear him;

103:1 [q]Ps 104:1
103:3 [r]Ps 130:8 [s]Ex 15:26
103:5 [t]Isa 40:31
103:7 [u]Ps 99:7; 147:19 [v]Ex 33:13 [w]Ps 106:22
103:8 [x]Ex 34:6; Ps 86:15; Jas 5:11
103:9 [y]Ps 30:5; Isa 57:16; Jer 3:5,12; Mic 7:18
103:10 [z]Ezr 9:13
103:11 [a]Ps 57:10

q23 Or *By his power*

12as far as the east is from the
west,
so far has he removed our
transgressions[a] from us.
13As a father has compassion[b]
on his children,
so the LORD has compassion
on those who fear him;
14for he knows how we are
formed,[c]
he remembers that we are
dust.
15As for man, his days are like
grass,[d]
he flourishes like a flower[e]
of the field;
16the wind blows[f] over it and it
is gone,
and its place[g] remembers it
no more.
17But from everlasting to
everlasting
the LORD's love is with those
who fear him,
and his righteousness with
their children's
children—
18with those who keep his
covenant
and remember to obey his
precepts.[h]
19The LORD has established his
throne in heaven,
and his kingdom rules[i] over
all.
20Praise the LORD, you his
angels,[j]
you mighty ones[k] who do his
bidding,
who obey his word.
21Praise the LORD, all his
heavenly hosts,[l]
you his servants who do his
will.
22Praise the LORD, all his works[m]
everywhere in his dominion.

Praise the LORD, O my soul.

Psalm 104

1Praise the LORD, O my soul.[n]

O LORD my God, you are very
great;
you are clothed with
splendor and majesty.
2He wraps[o] himself in light as
with a garment;
he stretches out the
heavens[p] like a tent
3 and lays the beams[q] of his
upper chambers on their
waters.
He makes the clouds[r] his
chariot
and rides on the wings of the
wind.[s]
4He makes winds his
messengers,[r][t]
flames of fire[u] his servants.

5He set the earth[v] on its
foundations;
it can never be moved.
6You covered it[w] with the
deep[x] as with a
garment;
the waters stood above the
mountains.
7But at your rebuke[y] the waters
fled,
at the sound of your thunder
they took to flight;
8they flowed over the
mountains,
they went down into the
valleys,
to the place you assigned[z]
for them.
9You set a boundary they cannot
cross;
never again will they cover
the earth.

10He makes springs[a] pour water
into the ravines;
it flows between the
mountains.
11They give water to all the
beasts of the field;
the wild donkeys quench
their thirst.
12The birds of the air[b] nest by
the waters;
they sing among the
branches.
13He waters the mountains[c]
from his upper
chambers;
the earth is satisfied by the
fruit of his work.

103:12 [a]2Sa 12:13
103:13 [b]Mal 3:17
103:14 [c]Isa 29:16
103:15 [d]Ps 90:5 [e]Job 14:2; Jas 1:10; 1Pe 1:24
103:16 [f]Isa 40:7 [g]Job 7:10
103:18 [h]Dt 7:9
103:19 [i]Ps 47:2
103:20 [j]Ps 148:2; Heb 1:14 [k]Ps 29:1
103:21 [l]1Ki 22:19
103:22 [m]Ps 145:10
104:1 [n]Ps 103:22
104:2 [o]Da 7:9 [p]Isa 40:22
104:3 [q]Am 9:6 [r]Isa 19:1 [s]Ps 18:10
104:4 [t]Ps 148:8; Heb 1:7* [u]2Ki 2:11
104:5 [v]Job 26:7; Ps 24:1-2
104:6 [w]Ge 7:19 [x]Ge 1:2
104:7 [y]Ps 18:15
104:8 [z]Ps 33:7
104:10 [a]Ps 107:33; Isa 41:18
104:12 [b]Mt 8:20
104:13 [c]Ps 147:8; Jer 10:13

[r]4 Or *angels*

14He makes grass grow[a] for the
cattle,
and plants for man to
cultivate—
bringing forth food[b] from the
earth:
15wine[c] that gladdens the heart
of man,
oil[d] to make his face
shine,
and bread that sustains his
heart.
16The trees of the LORD are well
watered,
the cedars of Lebanon that
he planted.
17There the birds[e] make their
nests;
the stork has its home in the
pine trees.
18The high mountains belong to
the wild goats;
the crags are a refuge for the
coneys.[s][f]
19The moon marks off the
seasons,[g]
and the sun[h] knows when to
go down.
20You bring darkness,[i] it
becomes night,[j]
and all the beasts of the
forest[k] prowl.
21The lions roar for their prey
and seek their food from
God.[l]
22The sun rises, and they steal
away;
they return and lie down in
their dens.[m]
23Then man goes out to his
work,[n]
to his labor until evening.

24How many are your works,[o]
O LORD!
In wisdom you made[p] them
all;
the earth is full of your
creatures.
25There is the sea,[q] vast and
spacious,
teeming with creatures
beyond number—
living things both large and
small.
26There the ships[r] go to and fro,

104:14 [a]Job 38:27; Ps 147:8 [b]Ge 1:30; Job 28:5
104:15 [c]Jdg 9:13 [d]Ps 23:5; 92:10; Lk 7:46
104:17 [e]ver 12
104:18 [f]Pr 30:26
104:19 [g]Ge 1:14 [h]Ps 19:6
104:20 [i]Isa 45:7 [j]Ps 74:16 [k]Ps 50:10
104:21 [l]Job 38:39; Ps 145:15; Joel 1:20
104:22 [m]Job 37:8
104:23 [n]Ge 3:19
104:24 [o]Ps 40:5 [p]Pr 3:19
104:25 [q]Ps 69:34
104:26 [r]Ps 107:23; Eze 27:9 [s]Job 41:1
104:27 [t]Job 36:31; Ps 136:25; 145:15; 147:9
104:28 [u]Ps 145:16
104:29 [v]Dt 31:17 [w]Job 34:14; Ecc 12:7
104:31 [x]Ge 1:31
104:32 [y]Ps 97:4 [z]Ex 19:18 [a]Ps 144:5
104:33 [b]Ps 63:4
104:34 [c]Ps 9:2
104:35 [d]Ps 37:38 [e]Ps 105:45; 106:48
105:1 [f]1Ch 16:34 [g]Ps 99:6

and the leviathan,[s] which
you formed to frolic
there.

27These all look to you
to give them their food[t] at
the proper time.
28When you give it to them,
they gather it up;
when you open your hand,
they are satisfied[u] with good
things.
29When you hide your face,[v]
they are terrified;
when you take away their
breath,
they die and return to the
dust.[w]
30When you send your Spirit,
they are created,
and you renew the face of
the earth.

31May the glory of the LORD
endure forever;
may the LORD rejoice in his
works[x]—
32he who looks at the earth, and
it trembles,[y]
who touches the
mountains,[z] and they
smoke.[a]

33I will sing[b] to the LORD all my
life;
I will sing praise to my God
as long as I live.
34May my meditation be pleasing
to him,
as I rejoice[c] in the LORD.
35But may sinners vanish[d] from
the earth
and the wicked be no more.

Praise the LORD, O my soul.

Praise the LORD.[t][e]

Psalm 105

105:1–15pp — 1Ch 16:8–22

1Give thanks to the LORD,[f] call
on his name;[g]
make known among the
nations what he has
done.

[s]*18* That is, the hyrax or rock badger
[t]*35* Hebrew *Hallelu Yah*; in the Septuagint this line stands at the beginning of Psalm 105.

[2]Sing to him,[a] sing praise to him;
tell of all his wonderful acts.
[3]Glory in his holy name;
let the hearts of those who seek the LORD rejoice.
[4]Look to the LORD and his strength;
seek his face[b] always.
[5]Remember the wonders[c] he has done,
his miracles, and the judgments he pronounced,[d]
[6]O descendants of Abraham his servant,[e]
O sons of Jacob, his chosen[f] ones.
[7]He is the LORD our God;
his judgments are in all the earth.

[8]He remembers his covenant[g] forever,
the word he commanded, for a thousand generations,
[9]the covenant he made with Abraham,[h]
the oath he swore to Isaac.
[10]He confirmed it[i] to Jacob as a decree,
to Israel as an everlasting covenant:
[11]"To you I will give the land of Canaan[j]
as the portion you will inherit."

[12]When they were but few in number,[k]
few indeed, and strangers in it,[l]
[13]they wandered from nation to nation,
from one kingdom to another.
[14]He allowed no one to oppress[m] them;
for their sake he rebuked kings:[n]
[15]"Do not touch[o] my anointed ones;
do my prophets no harm."

[16]He called down famine[p] on the land
and destroyed all their supplies of food;
[17]and he sent a man before them—
Joseph, sold as a slave.[q]
[18]They bruised his feet with shackles,[r]
his neck was put in irons,
[19]till what he foretold[s] came to pass,
till the word of the LORD proved him true.
[20]The king sent and released him,
the ruler of peoples set him free.[t]
[21]He made him master of his household,
ruler over all he possessed,
[22]to instruct his princes[u] as he pleased
and teach his elders wisdom.

[23]Then Israel entered Egypt;[v]
Jacob lived as an alien in the land of Ham.
[24]The LORD made his people very fruitful;
he made them too numerous[w] for their foes,
[25]whose hearts he turned[x] to hate his people,
to conspire[y] against his servants.
[26]He sent Moses[z] his servant,
and Aaron, whom he had chosen.[a]
[27]They performed[b] his miraculous signs among them,
his wonders in the land of Ham.
[28]He sent darkness[c] and made the land dark—
for had they not rebelled against his words?
[29]He turned their waters into blood,[d]
causing their fish to die.[e]
[30]Their land teemed with frogs,[f]
which went up into the bedrooms of their rulers.
[31]He spoke, and there came swarms of flies,[g]
and gnats[h] throughout their country.
[32]He turned their rain into hail,[i]

105:2 [a]Ps 96:1
105:4 [b]Ps 27:8
105:5 [c]Ps 40:5 [d]Ps 77:11
105:6 [e]ver 42 [f]Ps 106:5
105:8 [g]Ps 106:45; Lk 1:72
105:9 [h]Ge 12:7; 17:2; 22:16-18; Gal 3:15-18
105:10 [i]Ge 28:13-15
105:11 [j]Ge 13:15; 15:18
105:12 [k]Ge 34:30; Dt 7:7 [l]Ge 23:4; Heb 11:9
105:14 [m]Ge 35:5 [n]Ge 12:17-20
105:15 [o]Ge 26:11
105:16 [p]Ge 41:54; Lev 26:26; Isa 3:1; Eze 4:16
105:17 [q]Ge 37:28; 45:5; Ac 7:9
105:18 [r]Ge 40:15
105:19 [s]Ge 40:20-22
105:20 [t]Ge 41:14
105:22 [u]Ge 41:43-44
105:23 [v]Ge 46:6; Ac 13:17
105:24 [w]Ex 1:7,9
105:25 [x]Ex 4:21 [y]Ex 1:6-10; Ac 7:19
105:26 [z]Ex 3:10 [a]Nu 16:5; 17:5-8
105:27 [b]Ex 7:8-12:51
105:28 [c]Ex 10:22
105:29 [d]Ps 78:44 [e]Ex 7:21
105:30 [f]Ex 8:2,6
105:31 [g]Ex 8:21-24 [h]Ex 8:16-18
105:32 [i]Ex 9:22-25

with lightning throughout
their land;
33he struck down their vines[a]
and fig trees
and shattered the trees of
their country.
34He spoke, and the locusts
came,[b]
grasshoppers without
number;
35they ate up every green thing
in their land,
ate up the produce of their
soil.
36Then he struck down all the
firstborn[c] in their land,
the firstfruits of all their
manhood.

37He brought out Israel, laden
with silver and gold,[d]
and from among their tribes
no one faltered.
38Egypt was glad when they
left,
because dread of Israel[e] had
fallen on them.
39He spread out a cloud[f] as a
covering,
and a fire to give light at
night.[g]
40They asked,[h] and he brought
them quail[i]
and satisfied them with the
bread of heaven.[j]
41He opened the rock,[k] and
water gushed out;
like a river it flowed in the
desert.

42For he remembered his holy
promise[l]
given to his servant
Abraham.
43He brought out his people
with rejoicing,[m]
his chosen ones with shouts
of joy;
44he gave them the lands of the
nations,[n]
and they fell heir to what
others had toiled
for—
45that they might keep his
precepts
and observe his laws.[o]

Praise the LORD.[u]

Psalm 106

106:1,47-48pp — 1Ch 16:34-36

1Praise the LORD.[v]

Give thanks to the LORD, for he
is good;[p]
his love endures forever.
2Who can proclaim the mighty
acts[q] of the LORD
or fully declare his praise?
3Blessed are they who maintain
justice,
who constantly do what is
right.[r]
4Remember me,[s] O LORD, when
you show favor to your
people,
come to my aid when you
save them,
5that I may enjoy the
prosperity[t] of your
chosen ones,
that I may share in the joy[u]
of your nation
and join your inheritance in
giving praise.

6We have sinned,[v] even as our
fathers did;
we have done wrong and
acted wickedly.
7When our fathers were in
Egypt,
they gave no thought to your
miracles;
they did not remember[w] your
many kindnesses,
and they rebelled by the
sea,[x] the Red Sea.[w]
8Yet he saved them for his
name's sake,[y]
to make his mighty power
known.
9He rebuked[z] the Red Sea, and
it dried up;[a]
he led them through[b] the
depths as through a
desert.
10He saved them[c] from the hand
of the foe;
from the hand of the enemy
he redeemed them.[d]

105:33 [a]Ps 78:47
105:34 [b]Ex 10:4, 12-15
105:36 [c]Ex 12:29
105:37 [d]Ex 12:35
105:38 [e]Ex 12:33; 15:16
105:39 [f]Ex 13:21 [g]Ne 9:12; Ps 78:14
105:40 [h]Ps 78:18,24 [i]Ex 16:13 [j]Jn 6:31
105:41 [k]Ex 17:6; Nu 20:11; Ps 78:15-16; 1Co 10:4
105:42 [l]Ge 15:13-16
105:43 [m]Ex 15:1-18; Ps 106:12
105:44 [n]Jos 13:6-7
105:45 [o]Dt 4:40; 6:21-24
106:1 [p]Ps 100:5; 105:1
106:2 [q]Ps 145:4,12
106:3 [r]Ps 15:2
106:4 [s]Ps 119:132
106:5 [t]Ps 1:3 [u]Ps 118:15
106:6 [v]Da 9:5
106:7 [w]Ps 78:11,42 [x]Ex 14:11-12
106:8 [y]Ex 9:16
106:9 [z]Ps 18:15 [a]Ex 14:21; Na 1:4 [b]Isa 63:11-14
106:10 [c]Ex 14:30 [d]Ps 107:2

[u]45 Hebrew *Hallelu Yah* [v]1 Hebrew *Hallelu Yah*; also in verse 48 [w]7 Hebrew *Yam Suph*; that is, Sea of Reeds; also in verses 9 and 22

11The waters covered[a] their
adversaries;
not one of them survived.
12Then they believed his
promises
and sang his praise.[b]

13But they soon forgot[c] what he
had done
and did not wait for his
counsel.
14In the desert they gave in to
their craving;
in the wasteland they put
God to the test.[d]
15So he gave them[e] what they
asked for,
but sent a wasting disease[f]
upon them.

16In the camp they grew
envious[g] of Moses
and of Aaron, who was
consecrated to the LORD.
17The earth opened[h] up and
swallowed Dathan;
it buried the company of
Abiram.
18Fire blazed[i] among their
followers;
a flame consumed the
wicked.

19At Horeb they made a calf[j]
and worshiped an idol cast
from metal.
20They exchanged their Glory[k]
for an image of a bull, which
eats grass.
21They forgot the God[l] who
saved them,
who had done great things[m]
in Egypt,
22miracles in the land of Ham[n]
and awesome deeds by the
Red Sea.
23So he said he would destroy[o]
them—
had not Moses, his chosen
one,
stood in the breach[p] before
him
to keep his wrath from
destroying them.

24Then they despised the
pleasant land;[q]
they did not believe[r] his
promise.

25They grumbled[s] in their tents
and did not obey the LORD.
26So he swore[t] to them with
uplifted hand
that he would make them fall
in the desert,[u]
27make their descendants fall
among the nations
and scatter[v] them
throughout the lands.

28They yoked themselves to the
Baal of Peor[w]
and ate sacrifices offered to
lifeless gods;
29they provoked the LORD to
anger by their wicked
deeds,
and a plague broke out
among them.
30But Phinehas stood up and
intervened,
and the plague was
checked.[x]
31This was credited to him[y] as
righteousness
for endless generations to
come.

32By the waters of Meribah[z] they
angered the LORD,
and trouble came to Moses
because of them;
33for they rebelled against the
Spirit of God,
and rash words came from
Moses' lips.[x][a]

34They did not destroy[b] the
peoples
as the LORD had
commanded[c] them,
35but they mingled[d] with the
nations
and adopted their customs.
36They worshiped their idols,[e]
which became a snare to
them.
37They sacrificed their sons[f]
and their daughters to
demons.
38They shed innocent blood,
the blood of their sons[g] and
daughters,
whom they sacrificed to the
idols of Canaan,

[x]33 Or *against his spirit, / and rash words came from his lips*

106:11 [a]Ex 14:28; 15:5
106:12 [b]Ex 15:1-21
106:13 [c]Ex 15:24
106:14 [d]1Co 10:9
106:15 [e]Nu 11:31 [f]Isa 10:16
106:16 [g]Nu 16:1-3
106:17 [h]Dt 11:6
106:18 [i]Nu 16:35
106:19 [j]Ex 32:4
106:20 [k]Jer 2:11; Ro 1:23
106:21 [l]Ps 78:11 [m]Dt 10:21
106:22 [n]Ps 105:27
106:23 [o]Ex 32:10 [p]Ex 32:11-14
106:24 [q]Dt 8:7; Eze 20:6 [r]Heb 3:18-19
106:25 [s]Nu 14:2
106:26 [t]Eze 20:15; Heb 3:11 [u]Nu 14:28-35
106:27 [v]Lev 26:33; Ps 44:11
106:28 [w]Nu 25:2-3; Hos 9:10
106:30 [x]Nu 25:8
106:31 [y]Nu 25:11-13
106:32 [z]Nu 20:2-13; Ps 81:7
106:33 [a]Nu 20:8-12
106:34 [b]Jdg 1:21 [c]Dt 7:16
106:35 [d]Jdg 3:5-6
106:36 [e]Jdg 2:12
106:37 [f]2Ki 16:3; 17:17
106:38 [g]Nu 35:33

and the land was desecrated
by their blood.
39They defiled themselves[a] by
what they did;
by their deeds they
prostituted[b] themselves.

40Therefore the LORD was angry[c]
with his people
and abhorred his
inheritance.[d]
41He handed them over[e] to the
nations,
and their foes ruled over
them.
42Their enemies oppressed them
and subjected them to their
power.
43Many times he delivered them,
but they were bent on
rebellion[f]
and they wasted away in
their sin.

44But he took note of their
distress
when he heard their cry;[g]
45for their sake he remembered
his covenant[h]
and out of his great love[i] he
relented.
46He caused them to be pitied[j]
by all who held them captive.

47Save us, O LORD our God,
and gather us[k] from the
nations,
that we may give thanks to
your holy name
and glory in your praise.

48Praise be to the LORD, the God
of Israel,
from everlasting to
everlasting.
Let all the people say,
"Amen!"[l]

Praise the LORD.

BOOK V

Psalms 107–150

Psalm 107

1Give thanks to the LORD,[m] for
he is good;
his love endures forever.
2Let the redeemed[n] of the LORD
say this—
those he redeemed from the
hand of the foe,
3those he gathered[o] from the
lands,
from east and west, from
north and south.[y]

4Some wandered in desert[p]
wastelands,
finding no way to a city
where they could settle.
5They were hungry and thirsty,
and their lives ebbed away.
6Then they cried out[q] to the
LORD in their trouble,
and he delivered them from
their distress.
7He led them by a straight way[r]
to a city where they could
settle.
8Let them give thanks to the
LORD for his unfailing
love
and his wonderful deeds for
men,
9for he satisfies[s] the thirsty
and fills the hungry with
good things.[t]

10Some sat in darkness[u] and the
deepest gloom,
prisoners suffering in iron
chains,[v]
11for they had rebelled[w] against
the words of God
and despised the counsel[x] of
the Most High.
12So he subjected them to bitter
labor;
they stumbled, and there was
no one to help.[y]
13Then they cried to the LORD in
their trouble,
and he saved them from their
distress.
14He brought them out of
darkness and the
deepest gloom
and broke away their
chains.[z]
15Let them give thanks to the
LORD for his unfailing
love

106:39 [a] Eze 20:18 [b] Lev 17:7; Nu 15:39
106:40 [c] Jdg 2:14; Ps 78:59 [d] Dt 9:29
106:41 [e] Jdg 2:14; Ne 9:27
106:43 [f] Jdg 2:16-19
106:44 [g] Jdg 3:9; 10:10
106:45 [h] Lev 26:42; Ps 105:8 [i] Jdg 2:18
106:46 [j] Ezr 9:9; Jer 42:12
106:47 [k] Ps 147:2
106:48 [l] Ps 41:13
107:1 [m] Ps 106:1
107:2 [n] Ps 106:10
107:3 [o] Ps 106:47; Isa 43:5-6
107:4 [p] Nu 14:33; 32:13
107:6 [q] Ps 50:15
107:7 [r] Ezr 8:21
107:9 [s] Ps 22:26; Lk 1:53 [t] Ps 34:10
107:10 [u] Lk 1:79 [v] Job 36:8
107:11 [w] Ps 106:7; La 3:42 [x] 2Ch 36:16
107:12 [y] Ps 22:11
107:14 [z] Ps 116:16; Lk 13:16; Ac 12:7

y3 Hebrew *north and the sea*

and his wonderful deeds for men,
16for he breaks down gates of bronze
and cuts through bars of iron.

17Some became fools through their rebellious ways
and suffered affliction[a] because of their iniquities.
18They loathed all food[b]
and drew near the gates of death.[c]
19Then they cried to the LORD in their trouble,
and he saved them from their distress.
20He sent forth his word[d] and healed them;[e]
he rescued[f] them from the grave.[g]
21Let them give thanks to the LORD for his unfailing love
and his wonderful deeds for men.
22Let them sacrifice thank offerings[h]
and tell of his works[i] with songs of joy.

23Others went out on the sea in ships;
they were merchants on the mighty waters.
24They saw the works of the LORD,
his wonderful deeds in the deep.
25For he spoke[j] and stirred up a tempest[k]
that lifted high the waves.[l]
26They mounted up to the heavens and went down to the depths;
in their peril their courage melted[m] away.
27They reeled and staggered like drunken men;
they were at their wits' end.
28Then they cried out to the LORD in their trouble,
and he brought them out of their distress.
29He stilled the storm[n] to a whisper;
the waves[o] of the sea were hushed.
30They were glad when it grew calm,
and he guided them to their desired haven.
31Let them give thanks to the LORD for his unfailing love
and his wonderful deeds for men.
32Let them exalt him in the assembly[p] of the people
and praise him in the council of the elders.

33He turned rivers into a desert,[q]
flowing springs into thirsty ground,
34and fruitful land into a salt waste,[r]
because of the wickedness of those who lived there.
35He turned the desert into pools of water[s]
and the parched ground into flowing springs;
36there he brought the hungry to live,
and they founded a city where they could settle.
37They sowed fields and planted vineyards[t]
that yielded a fruitful harvest;
38he blessed them, and their numbers greatly increased,[u]
and he did not let their herds diminish.

39Then their numbers decreased,[v] and they were humbled
by oppression, calamity and sorrow;
40he who pours contempt on nobles[w]
made them wander in a trackless waste.[x]
41But he lifted the needy[y] out of their affliction
and increased their families like flocks.
42The upright see and rejoice,[z]
but all the wicked shut their mouths.[a]

107:17 [a] Isa 65:6-7; La 3:39
107:18 [b] Job 33:20 [c] Job 33:22; Ps 9:13; 88:3
107:20 [d] Mt 8:8 [e] Ps 103:3 [f] Job 33:28 [g] Ps 30:3; 49:15
107:22 [h] Lev 7:12; Ps 50:14; 116:17 [i] Ps 9:11; 73:28; 118:17
107:25 [j] Ps 105:31 [k] Jnh 1:4 [l] Ps 93:3
107:26 [m] Ps 22:14
107:29 [n] Mt 8:26 [o] Ps 89:9
107:32 [p] Ps 22:22,25; 35:18
107:33 [q] 1Ki 17:1; Ps 74:15
107:34 [r] Ge 13:10; 14:3; 19:25
107:35 [s] Ps 114:8; Isa 41:18
107:37 [t] Isa 65:21
107:38 [u] Ge 12:2; 17:16,20; Ex 1:7
107:39 [v] 2Ki 10:32; Eze 5:12
107:40 [w] Job 12:21 [x] Job 12:24
107:41 [y] 1Sa 2:8; Ps 113:7-9
107:42 [z] Job 22:19 [a] Job 5:16; Ps 63:11; Ro 3:19

43Whoever is wise,[a] let him heed
these things
and consider the great love[b]
of the LORD.

Psalm 108

108:1–5pp — Ps 57:7–11
108:6–13pp — Ps 60:5–12

A song. A psalm of David.

1My heart is steadfast, O God;
I will sing and make music
with all my soul.
2Awake, harp and lyre!
I will awaken the dawn.
3I will praise you, O LORD,
among the nations;
I will sing of you among the
peoples.
4For great is your love, higher
than the heavens;
your faithfulness reaches to
the skies.
5Be exalted, O God, above the
heavens,
and let your glory be over all
the earth.[c]

6Save us and help us with your
right hand,
that those you love may be
delivered.
7God has spoken from his
sanctuary:
"In triumph I will parcel out
Shechem
and measure off the Valley of
Succoth.
8Gilead is mine, Manasseh is
mine;
Ephraim is my helmet,
Judah[d] my scepter.
9Moab is my washbasin,
upon Edom I toss my sandal;
over Philistia I shout in
triumph."

10Who will bring me to the
fortified city?
Who will lead me to Edom?
11Is it not you, O God, you who
have rejected us
and no longer go out with
our armies?[e]
12Give us aid against the enemy,
for the help of man is
worthless.
13With God we will gain the
victory,
and he will trample down our
enemies.

Psalm 109

For the director of music.
Of David. A psalm.

1O God, whom I praise,
do not remain silent,[f]
2for wicked and deceitful men
have opened their mouths
against me;
they have spoken against me
with lying tongues.[g]
3With words of hatred[h] they
surround me;
they attack me without
cause.[i]
4In return for my friendship they
accuse me,
but I am a man of prayer.[j]
5They repay me evil for good,[k]
and hatred for my friendship.

6Appoint[z] an evil man[a] to
oppose him;
let an accuser[b][l] stand at his
right hand.
7When he is tried, let him be
found guilty,
and may his prayers
condemn[m] him.
8May his days be few;
may another take his place[n]
of leadership.
9May his children be fatherless
and his wife a widow.[o]
10May his children be wandering
beggars;
may they be driven[c] from
their ruined homes.
11May a creditor seize all he has;
may strangers plunder the
fruits of his labor.[p]
12May no one extend kindness to
him
or take pity[q] on his
fatherless children.
13May his descendants be cut
off,[r]
their names blotted out[s]

107:43 [a]Jer 9:12; Hos 14:9 [b]Ps 64:9
108:5 [c]Ps 57:5
108:8 [d]Ge 49:10
108:11 [e]Ps 44:9
109:1 [f]Ps 83:1
109:2 [g]Ps 52:4; 120:2
109:3 [h]Ps 69:4 [i]Ps 35:7; Jn 15:25
109:4 [j]Ps 69:13
109:5 [k]Ps 35:12; 38:20
109:6 [l]Zec 3:1
109:7 [m]Pr 28:9
109:8 [n]Ac 1:20*
109:9 [o]Ex 22:24
109:11 [p]Job 5:5
109:12 [q]Isa 9:17
109:13 [r]Job 18:19; Ps 37:28 [s]Pr 10:7

[z]6 Or *⌊They say:⌋ "Appoint* (with quotation marks at the end of verse 19) [a]6 Or *the Evil One* [b]6 Or *let Satan*
[c]10 Septuagint; Hebrew *sought*

from the next
generation.
14May the iniquity of his fathers[a]
be remembered before
the LORD;
may the sin of his mother
never be blotted out.
15May their sins always remain
before the LORD,
that he may cut off the
memory[b] of them from
the earth.

16For he never thought of doing a
kindness,
but hounded to death the
poor
and the needy[c] and the
brokenhearted.[d]
17He loved to pronounce a
curse—
may it[d] come on him;[e]
he found no pleasure in
blessing—
may it be[e] far from him.
18He wore cursing[f] as his
garment;
it entered into his body like
water,[g]
into his bones like oil.
19May it be like a cloak wrapped
about him,
like a belt tied forever
around him.
20May this be the LORD's
payment[h] to my
accusers,
to those who speak evil[i] of
me.
21But you, O Sovereign LORD,
deal well with me for your
name's sake;[j]
out of the goodness of your
love,[k] deliver me.
22For I am poor and needy,
and my heart is wounded
within me.
23I fade away like an evening
shadow;[l]
I am shaken off like a locust.
24My knees give[m] way from
fasting;
my body is thin and gaunt.
25I am an object of scorn[n] to my
accusers;
when they see me, they
shake their heads.[o]

26Help me,[p] O LORD my God;
save me in accordance with
your love.
27Let them know[q] that it is your
hand,
that you, O LORD, have done
it.
28They may curse,[r] but you will
bless;
when they attack they will be
put to shame,
but your servant will
rejoice.[s]
29My accusers will be clothed
with disgrace
and wrapped in shame[t] as in
a cloak.
30With my mouth I will greatly
extol the LORD;
in the great throng[u] I will
praise him.
31For he stands at the right
hand[v] of the needy one,
to save his life from those
who condemn him.

Psalm 110

Of David. A psalm.

1The LORD says[w] to my Lord:
"Sit at my right hand
until I make your enemies
a footstool for your feet."[x]

2The LORD will extend your
mighty scepter[y] from
Zion;
you will rule in the midst of
your enemies.
3Your troops will be willing
on your day of battle.
Arrayed in holy majesty,[z]
from the womb of the dawn
you will receive the dew of
your youth.[f]

4The LORD has sworn
and will not change his
mind:[a]
"You are a priest forever,[b]
in the order of
Melchizedek.[c]"

109:14 [a]Ex 20:5; Ne 4:5; Jer 18:23
109:15 [b]Job 18:17; Ps 34:16
109:16 [c]Ps 37:14,32 [d]Ps 34:18
109:17 [e]Pr 14:14; Eze 35:6
109:18 [f]Ps 73:6 [g]Nu 5:22
109:20 [h]Ps 94:23; 2Ti 4:14 [i]Ps 71:10
109:21 [j]Ps 79:9 [k]Ps 69:16
109:23 [l]Ps 102:11
109:24 [m]Heb 12:12
109:25 [n]Ps 22:6 [o]Mt 27:39; Mk 15:29
109:26 [p]Ps 119:86
109:27 [q]Job 37:7
109:28 [r]2Sa 16:12 [s]Isa 65:14
109:29 [t]Ps 35:26; 132:18
109:30 [u]Ps 35:18; 111:1
109:31 [v]Ps 16:8; 73:23; 121:5
110:1 [w]Mt 22:44*; Mk 12:36*; Lk 20:42*; Ac 2:34* [x]1Co 15:25
110:2 [y]Ps 45:6
110:3 [z]Jdg 5:2; Ps 96:9
110:4 [a]Nu 23:19 [b]Heb 5:6*; 7:21* [c]Heb 7:15-17*

[d]17 *Or curse, / and it has* [e]17 *Or blessing, / and it is* [f]3 *Or / your young men will come to you like the dew*

5 The Lord is at your right
hand;[a]
he will crush kings[b] on the
day of his wrath.[c]
6 He will judge the nations,[d]
heaping up the dead[e]
and crushing the rulers[f] of
the whole earth.
7 He will drink from a brook
beside the way[g];
therefore he will lift up his
head.[g]

Psalm 111[h]

1 Praise the LORD.[i]

I will extol the LORD with all my
heart
in the council of the upright
and in the assembly.

2 Great are the works[h] of the
LORD;
they are pondered by all who
delight in them.
3 Glorious and majestic are his
deeds,
and his righteousness
endures forever.
4 He has caused his wonders to
be remembered;
the LORD is gracious and
compassionate.[i]
5 He provides food[j] for those
who fear him;
he remembers his covenant
forever.
6 He has shown his people the
power of his works,
giving them the lands of
other nations.
7 The works of his hands are
faithful and just;
all his precepts are
trustworthy.[k]
8 They are steadfast for ever[l]
and ever,
done in faithfulness and
uprightness.
9 He provided redemption[m] for
his people;
he ordained his covenant
forever—
holy and awesome[n] is his
name.
10 The fear of the LORD is the
beginning of wisdom;[o]
all who follow his precepts
have good
understanding.[p]
To him belongs eternal
praise.[q]

Psalm 112[h]

1 Praise the LORD.[i]

Blessed is the man who fears
the LORD,[r]
who finds great delight[s] in
his commands.

2 His children will be mighty in
the land;
the generation of the upright
will be blessed.
3 Wealth and riches are in his
house,
and his righteousness
endures forever.
4 Even in darkness light dawns[t]
for the upright,
for the gracious and
compassionate and
righteous[u] man.[j]
5 Good will come to him who is
generous and lends
freely,[v]
who conducts his affairs with
justice.
6 Surely he will never be
shaken;
a righteous man will be
remembered[w] forever.
7 He will have no fear of bad
news;
his heart is steadfast,[x]
trusting in the LORD.
8 His heart is secure, he will
have no fear;
in the end he will look
in triumph on his
foes.[y]
9 He has scattered abroad his
gifts to the poor,[z]
his righteousness endures
forever;
his horn[k] will be lifted[a]
high in honor.

110:5 [a] Ps 16:8 [b] Ps 2:12 [c] Ps 2:5; Ro 2:5
110:6 [d] Isa 2:4 [e] Isa 66:24 [f] Ps 68:21
110:7 [g] Ps 27:6
111:2 [h] Ps 92:5; 143:5
111:4 [i] Ps 103:8
111:5 [j] Mt 6:26, 31-33
111:7 [k] Ps 19:7; Rev 15:3
111:8 [l] Isa 40:8; Mt 5:18
111:9 [m] Lk 1:68 [n] Ps 99:3; Lk 1:49
111:10 [o] Pr 9:10 [p] Ecc 12:13 [q] Ps 145:2
112:1 [r] Ps 128:1 [s] Ps 119:14, 16,47,92
112:4 [t] Job 11:17 [u] Ps 97:11
112:5 [v] Ps 37:21,26
112:6 [w] Pr 10:7
112:7 [x] Ps 57:7; Pr 1:33
112:8 [y] Ps 59:10
112:9 [z] 2Co 9:9* [a] Ps 75:10

g7 Or / *The One who grants succession will set him in authority* h This psalm is an acrostic poem, the lines of which begin with the successive letters of the Hebrew alphabet. i1 Hebrew *Hallelu Yah* j4 Or / *for the LORD is gracious and compassionate and righteous* k9 *Horn* here symbolizes dignity.

10The wicked man will see[a] and
be vexed,
he will gnash his teeth[b] and
waste away;[c]
the longings of the wicked
will come to nothing.[d]

Psalm 113

1Praise the LORD.[1]

Praise, O servants of the LORD,[e]
praise the name of the LORD.
2Let the name of the LORD be
praised,
both now and forevermore.[f]
3From the rising of the sun[g] to
the place where it sets,
the name of the LORD is to be
praised.

4The LORD is exalted[h] over all
the nations,
his glory above the heavens.[i]
5Who is like the LORD our God,[j]
the One who sits enthroned[k]
on high,
6who stoops down to look[l]
on the heavens and the
earth?

7He raises the poor[m] from the
dust
and lifts the needy[n] from the
ash heap;
8he seats them[o] with princes,
with the princes of their
people.
9He settles the barren[p] woman
in her home
as a happy mother of
children.

Praise the LORD.

Psalm 114

1When Israel came out of
Egypt,[q]
the house of Jacob from a
people of foreign tongue,
2Judah became God's sanctuary,
Israel his dominion.

3The sea looked and fled,[r]
the Jordan turned back;[s]
4the mountains skipped like
rams,
the hills like lambs.

5Why was it, O sea, that you
fled,
O Jordan, that you turned
back,
6you mountains, that you
skipped like rams,
you hills, like lambs?

7Tremble, O earth,[t] at the
presence of the Lord,
at the presence of the God of
Jacob,
8who turned the rock into a
pool,
the hard rock into springs of
water.[u]

Psalm 115

115:4–11pp — Ps 135:15–20

1Not to us, O LORD, not to us
but to your name be the
glory,[v]
because of your love and
faithfulness.

2Why do the nations say,
"Where is their God?"[w]
3Our God is in heaven;[x]
he does whatever pleases
him.[y]
4But their idols are silver and
gold,
made by the hands of men.[z]
5They have mouths, but cannot
speak,[a]
eyes, but they cannot see;
6they have ears, but cannot
hear,
noses, but they cannot smell;
7they have hands, but cannot
feel,
feet, but they cannot walk;
nor can they utter a sound
with their throats.
8Those who make them will be
like them,
and so will all who trust in
them.

9O house of Israel, trust in the
LORD—
he is their help and shield.
10O house of Aaron,[b] trust in the
LORD—
he is their help and shield.

112:10 [a]Ps 86:17 [b]Ps 37:12 [c]Ps 58:7-8 [d]Pr 11:7
113:1 [e]Ps 135:1
113:2 [f]Da 2:20
113:3 [g]Isa 59:19; Mal 1:11
113:4 [h]Ps 99:2 [i]Ps 8:1; 97:9
113:5 [j]Ps 89:6 [k]Ps 103:19
113:6 [l]Ps 11:4; 138:6; Isa 57:15
113:7 [m]1Sa 2:8 [n]Ps 107:41
113:8 [o]Job 36:7
113:9 [p]1Sa 2:5; Ps 68:6; Isa 54:1
114:1 [q]Ex 13:3
114:3 [r]Ex 14:21; Ps 77:16 [s]Jos 3:16
114:7 [t]Ps 96:9
114:8 [u]Ex 17:6; Nu 20:11; Ps 107:35
115:1 [v]Ps 96:8; Isa 48:11; Eze 36:32
115:2 [w]Ps 42:3; 79:10
115:3 [x]Ps 103:19 [y]Ps 135:6; Da 4:35
115:4 [z]Dt 4:28; Jer 10:3-5
115:5 [a]Jer 10:5
115:10 [b]Ps 118:3

[1]1 Hebrew *Hallelu Yah*; also in verse 9

11You who fear him, trust in the LORD—
he is their help and shield.

12The LORD remembers us and will bless us:
He will bless the house of Israel,
he will bless the house of Aaron,
13he will bless those who fear[a] the LORD—
small and great alike.

14May the LORD make you increase,[b]
both you and your children.
15May you be blessed by the LORD,
the Maker of heaven[c] and earth.

16The highest heavens belong to the LORD,[d]
but the earth he has given[e] to man.
17It is not the dead[f] who praise the LORD,
those who go down to silence;
18it is we who extol the LORD,
both now and forevermore.[g]

Praise the LORD.[m]

Psalm 116

1I love the LORD,[h] for he heard my voice;
he heard my cry[i] for mercy.
2Because he turned his ear[j] to me,
I will call on him as long as I live.

3The cords of death[k] entangled me,
the anguish of the grave[n] came upon me;
I was overcome by trouble and sorrow.
4Then I called on the name[l] of the LORD:
"O LORD, save me![m]"

5The LORD is gracious and righteous;[n]
our God is full of compassion.

115:13 [a]Ps 128:1,4
115:14 [b]Dt 1:11
115:15 [c]Ge 1:1; 14:19; Ps 96:5
115:16 [d]Ps 89:11 [e]Ps 8:6-8
115:17 [f]Ps 6:5; 88:10-12; Isa 38:18
115:18 [g]Ps 113:2; Da 2:20
116:1 [h]Ps 18:1 [i]Ps 66:19
116:2 [j]Ps 40:1
116:3 [k]Ps 18:4-5
116:4 [l]Ps 118:5 [m]Ps 22:20
116:5 [n]Ezr 9:15; Ne 9:8; Ps 103:8; 145:17
116:6 [o]Ps 19:7; 79:8
116:7 [p]Jer 6:16; Mt 11:29 [q]Ps 13:6
116:8 [r]Ps 56:13
116:9 [s]Ps 27:13
116:10 [t]2Co 4:13*
116:11 [u]Ro 3:4
116:13 [v]Ps 16:5; 80:18
116:14 [w]Ps 22:25; Jnh 2:9
116:15 [x]Ps 72:14
116:16 [y]Ps 119:125; 143:12 [z]Ps 86:16
116:17 [a]Lev 7:12; Ps 50:14
116:19 [b]Ps 96:8; 135:2

6The LORD protects the simplehearted;
when I was in great need,[o]
he saved me.

7Be at rest[p] once more, O my soul,
for the LORD has been good[q] to you.

8For you, O LORD, have delivered my soul[r] from death,
my eyes from tears,
my feet from stumbling,
9that I may walk before the LORD
in the land of the living.[s]
10I believed;[t] therefore[o] I said,
"I am greatly afflicted."
11And in my dismay I said,
"All men are liars."[u]

12How can I repay the LORD
for all his goodness to me?
13I will lift up the cup of salvation
and call on the name[v] of the LORD.
14I will fulfill my vows[w] to the LORD
in the presence of all his people.

15Precious in the sight[x] of the LORD
is the death of his saints.
16O LORD, truly I am your servant;[y]
I am your servant, the son of your maidservant[p];[z]
you have freed me from my chains.

17I will sacrifice a thank offering[a] to you
and call on the name of the LORD.
18I will fulfill my vows to the LORD
in the presence of all his people,
19in the courts[b] of the house of the LORD—
in your midst, O Jerusalem.

Praise the LORD.[m]

[m]18,19 Hebrew *Hallelu Yah* [n]3 Hebrew *Sheol* [o]10 *Or believed even when* [p]16 *Or servant, your faithful son*

Psalm 117

1Praise the LORD, all you nations;[a]
extol him, all you peoples.
2For great is his love toward us,
and the faithfulness of the LORD[b] endures forever.

Praise the LORD.[q]

Psalm 118

1Give thanks to the LORD,[c] for he is good;
his love endures forever.[d]

2Let Israel say:[e]
"His love endures forever."
3Let the house of Aaron say:
"His love endures forever."
4Let those who fear the LORD say:
"His love endures forever."

5In my anguish[f] I cried to the LORD,
and he answered[g] by setting me free.
6The LORD is with me;[h] I will not be afraid.
What can man do to me?[i]
7The LORD is with me; he is my helper.[j]
I will look in triumph on my enemies.[k]

8It is better to take refuge in the LORD[l]
than to trust in man.[m]
9It is better to take refuge in the LORD
than to trust in princes.[n]

10All the nations surrounded me,
but in the name of the LORD I cut them off.[o]
11They surrounded me[p] on every side,[q]
but in the name of the LORD I cut them off.
12They swarmed around me like bees,[r]
but they died out as quickly as burning thorns;[s]
in the name of the LORD I cut them off.

13I was pushed back and about to fall,
but the LORD helped me.[t]
14The LORD is my strength[u] and my song;
he has become my salvation.[v]

15Shouts of joy[w] and victory
resound in the tents of the righteous:
"The LORD's right hand[x] has done mighty things!
16 The LORD's right hand is lifted high;
the LORD's right hand has done mighty things!"

17I will not die[y] but live,
and will proclaim[z] what the LORD has done.
18The LORD has chastened me severely,
but he has not given me over to death.[a]

19Open for me the gates[b] of righteousness;
I will enter and give thanks to the LORD.
20This is the gate of the LORD
through which the righteous may enter.[c]
21I will give you thanks, for you answered me;[d]
you have become my salvation.

22The stone the builders rejected
has become the capstone;[e]
23the LORD has done this,
and it is marvelous in our eyes.
24This is the day the LORD has made;
let us rejoice and be glad in it.

25O LORD, save us;
O LORD, grant us success.
26Blessed is he who comes[f] in the name of the LORD.
From the house of the LORD we bless you.[r]
27The LORD is God,
and he has made his light shine[g] upon us.
With boughs in hand, join in the festal procession

117:1 [a]Ro 15:11*
117:2 [b]Ps 100:5
118:1 [c]1Ch 16:8 [d]Ps 106:1; 136:1
118:2 [e]Ps 115:9
118:5 [f]Ps 120:1 [g]Ps 18:19
118:6 [h]Heb 13:6* [i]Ps 27:1; 56:4
118:7 [j]Ps 54:4 [k]Ps 59:10
118:8 [l]Ps 40:4 [m]Jer 17:5
118:9 [n]Ps 146:3
118:10 [o]Ps 18:40
118:11 [p]Ps 88:17 [q]Ps 3:6
118:12 [r]Dt 1:44 [s]Ps 58:9
118:13 [t]Ps 86:17; 140:4
118:14 [u]Ex 15:2 [v]Isa 12:2
118:15 [w]Ps 68:3 [x]Ps 89:13
118:17 [y]Ps 6:5; Hab 1:12 [z]Ex 15:6; Ps 73:28
118:18 [a]2Co 6:9
118:19 [b]Isa 26:2
118:20 [c]Ps 24:7; Isa 35:8; Rev 22:14
118:21 [d]Ps 116:1
118:22 [e]Mt 21:42; Mk 12:10; Lk 20:17*; Ac 4:11*; 1Pe 2:7*
118:26 [f]Mt 21:9*; Mk 11:9*; Lk 13:35*; 19:38*; Jn 12:13*
118:27 [g]1Pe 2:9

[q]2 Hebrew *Hallelu Yah* [r]26 The Hebrew is plural.

up[s] to the horns of the altar.

28You are my God, and I will give
you thanks;
you are my God,[a] and I will
exalt[b] you.

29Give thanks to the LORD, for he
is good;
his love endures forever.

Psalm 119[t]

א Aleph

1Blessed are they whose ways
are blameless,
who walk[c] according to the
law of the LORD.
2Blessed are they who keep his
statutes
and seek him with all their
heart.[d]
3They do nothing wrong;[e]
they walk in his ways.
4You have laid down precepts
that are to be fully obeyed.
5Oh, that my ways were
steadfast
in obeying your decrees!
6Then I would not be put to
shame
when I consider all your
commands.
7I will praise you with an
upright heart
as I learn your righteous
laws.
8I will obey your decrees;
do not utterly forsake me.

ב Beth

9How can a young man keep his
way pure?
By living according to your
word.[f]
10I seek you with all my heart;[g]
do not let me stray from your
commands.[h]
11I have hidden your word in my
heart[i]
that I might not sin against
you.
12Praise be to you, O LORD;
teach me your decrees.[j]
13With my lips I recount
all the laws that come from
your mouth.[k]
14I rejoice in following your
statutes
as one rejoices in great
riches.
15I meditate on your precepts[l]
and consider your ways.
16I delight[m] in your decrees;
I will not neglect your word.

ג Gimel

17Do good to your servant,[n] and
I will live;
I will obey your word.
18Open my eyes that I may see
wonderful things in your law.
19I am a stranger on earth;[o]
do not hide your commands
from me.
20My soul is consumed[p] with
longing
for your laws[q] at all times.
21You rebuke the arrogant, who
are cursed
and who stray[r] from your
commands.
22Remove from me scorn[s] and
contempt,
for I keep your statutes.
23Though rulers sit together and
slander me,
your servant will meditate on
your decrees.
24Your statutes are my delight;
they are my counselors.

ד Daleth

25I am laid low in the dust;[t]
preserve my life[u] according
to your word.
26I recounted my ways and you
answered me;
teach me your decrees.[v]
27Let me understand the
teaching of your
precepts;
then I will meditate on your
wonders.[w]
28My soul is weary with sorrow;[x]
strengthen me[y] according to
your word.

118:28 [a] Isa 25:1 [b] Ex 15:2
119:1 [c] Ps 128:1
119:2 [d] Dt 6:5
119:3 [e] 1Jn 3:9; 5:18
119:9 [f] 2Ch 6:16
119:10 [g] 2Ch 15:15 [h] ver 21,118
119:11 [i] Ps 37:31; Lk 2:19,51
119:12 [j] ver 26
119:13 [k] Ps 40:9
119:15 [l] Ps 1:2
119:16 [m] Ps 1:2
119:17 [n] Ps 13:6; 116:7
119:19 [o] 1Ch 29:15; Ps 39:12; 2Co 5:6; Heb 11:13
119:20 [p] Ps 42:2; 84:2 [q] Ps 63:1
119:21 [r] ver 10
119:22 [s] Ps 39:8
119:25 [t] Ps 44:25 [u] Ps 143:11
119:26 [v] Ps 25:4; 27:11; 86:11
119:27 [w] Ps 145:5
119:28 [x] Ps 107:26 [y] Ps 20:2; 1Pe 5:10

[s]27 Or *Bind the festal sacrifice with ropes / and take it* [t]This psalm is an acrostic poem; the verses of each stanza begin with the same letter of the Hebrew alphabet.

29Keep me from deceitful ways;
be gracious to me through your law.
30I have chosen the way of truth;
I have set my heart on your laws.
31I hold fast[a] to your statutes, O LORD;
do not let me be put to shame.
32I run in the path of your commands,
for you have set my heart free.

ה He

33Teach me,[b] O LORD, to follow your decrees;
then I will keep them to the end.
34Give me understanding, and I will keep your law
and obey it with all my heart.
35Direct me in the path of your commands,
for there I find delight.
36Turn my heart[c] toward your statutes
and not toward selfish gain.[d]
37Turn my eyes away from worthless things;
preserve my life[e] according to your word.[u]
38Fulfill your promise[f] to your servant,
so that you may be feared.
39Take away the disgrace I dread,
for your laws are good.
40How I long[g] for your precepts!
Preserve my life in your righteousness.

ו Waw

41May your unfailing love come to me, O LORD,
your salvation according to your promise;
42then I will answer[h] the one who taunts me,
for I trust in your word.
43Do not snatch the word of truth from my mouth,
for I have put my hope in your laws.
44I will always obey your law,
for ever and ever.
45I will walk about in freedom,
for I have sought out your precepts.
46I will speak of your statutes before kings[i]
and will not be put to shame,
47for I delight in your commands
because I love them.
48I lift up my hands to[v] your commands, which I love,
and I meditate on your decrees.

ז Zayin

49Remember your word to your servant,
for you have given me hope.
50My comfort in my suffering is this:
Your promise preserves my life.[j]
51The arrogant mock me[k] without restraint,
but I do not turn[l] from your law.
52I remember[m] your ancient laws, O LORD,
and I find comfort in them.
53Indignation grips me[n] because of the wicked,
who have forsaken your law.[o]
54Your decrees are the theme of my song
wherever I lodge.
55In the night I remember[p] your name, O LORD,
and I will keep your law.
56This has been my practice:
I obey your precepts.

ח Heth

57You are my portion,[q] O LORD;
I have promised to obey your words.
58I have sought your face with all my heart;
be gracious to me[r] according to your promise.[s]
59I have considered my ways[t]
and have turned my steps to your statutes.
60I will hasten and not delay

119:31 [a]Dt 11:22
119:33 [b]ver 12
119:36 [c]1Ki 8:58 [d]Eze 33:31; Mk 7:21-22; Lk 12:15; Heb 13:5
119:37 [e]Ps 71:20; Isa 33:15
119:38 [f]2Sa 7:25
119:40 [g]ver 20
119:42 [h]Pr 27:11
119:46 [i]Mt 10:18; Ac 26:1-2
119:50 [j]Ro 15:4
119:51 [k]Jer 20:7 [l]ver 157; Job 23:11; Ps 44:18
119:52 [m]Ps 103:18
119:53 [n]Ezr 9:3 [o]Ps 89:30
119:55 [p]Ps 63:6
119:57 [q]Ps 16:5; La 3:24
119:58 [r]1Ki 13:6 [s]ver 41
119:59 [t]Lk 15:17-18

[u]37 Two manuscripts of the Masoretic Text and Dead Sea Scrolls; most manuscripts of the Masoretic Text *life in your way* [v]48 Or *for*

to obey your commands.
61Though the wicked bind me with ropes,
I will not forget[a] your law.
62At midnight[b] I rise to give you thanks
for your righteous laws.
63I am a friend to all who fear you,[c]
to all who follow your precepts.
64The earth is filled with your love,[d] O LORD;
teach me your decrees.

ט Teth

65Do good to your servant
according to your word, O LORD.
66Teach me knowledge and good judgment,
for I believe in your commands.
67Before I was afflicted I went astray,[e]
but now I obey your word.
68You are good,[f] and what you do is good;
teach me your decrees.[g]
69Though the arrogant have smeared me with lies,[h]
I keep your precepts with all my heart.
70Their hearts are callous[i] and unfeeling,
but I delight in your law.
71It was good for me to be afflicted
so that I might learn your decrees.
72The law from your mouth is more precious to me
than thousands of pieces of silver and gold.[j]

י Yodh

73Your hands made me[k] and formed me;
give me understanding to learn your commands.
74May those who fear you rejoice[l] when they see me,
for I have put my hope in your word.

119:61 [a]Ps 140:5
119:62 [b]Ac 16:25
119:63 [c]Ps 101:6-7
119:64 [d]Ps 33:5
119:67 [e]Jer 31:18-19; Heb 12:11
119:68 [f]Ps 106:1; 107:1; Mt 19:17 [g]ver 12
119:69 [h]Job 13:4; Ps 109:2
119:70 [i]Ps 17:10; Isa 6:10; Ac 28:27
119:72 [j]Ps 19:10; Pr 8:10-11,19
119:73 [k]Job 10:8; Ps 100:3; 138:8; 139:13-16
119:74 [l]Ps 34:2
119:75 [m]Heb 12:5-11
119:77 [n]ver 41
119:78 [o]Jer 50:32 [p]ver 86,161
119:81 [q]Ps 84:2
119:82 [r]Ps 69:3; La 2:11
119:84 [s]Ps 39:4; Rev 6:10
119:85 [t]Ps 35:7; Jer 18:20,22
119:86 [u]Ps 35:19 [v]Ps 109:26 [w]ver 78
119:87 [x]Isa 58:2

75I know, O LORD, that your laws are righteous,
and in faithfulness[m] you have afflicted me.
76May your unfailing love be my comfort,
according to your promise to your servant.
77Let your compassion[n] come to me that I may live,
for your law is my delight.
78May the arrogant[o] be put to shame for wronging me without cause;[p]
but I will meditate on your precepts.
79May those who fear you turn to me,
those who understand your statutes.
80May my heart be blameless toward your decrees,
that I may not be put to shame.

כ Kaph

81My soul faints[q] with longing for your salvation,
but I have put my hope in your word.
82My eyes fail,[r] looking for your promise;
I say, "When will you comfort me?"
83Though I am like a wineskin in the smoke,
I do not forget your decrees.
84How long[s] must your servant wait?
When will you punish my persecutors?
85The arrogant dig pitfalls[t] for me,
contrary to your law.
86All your commands are trustworthy;[u]
help me,[v] for men persecute me without cause.[w]
87They almost wiped me from the earth,
but I have not forsaken[x] your precepts.
88Preserve my life according to your love,
and I will obey the statutes of your mouth.

ל Lamedh

89Your word, O LORD, is eternal;[a]
it stands firm in the heavens.
90Your faithfulness[b] continues
through all generations;
you established the earth,
and it endures.[c]
91Your laws endure[d] to this day,
for all things serve you.
92If your law had not been my
delight,
I would have perished in my
affliction.
93I will never forget your
precepts,
for by them you have
preserved my life.
94Save me, for I am yours;
I have sought out your
precepts.
95The wicked are waiting to
destroy me,
but I will ponder your
statutes.
96To all perfection I see a limit;
but your commands are
boundless.

מ Mem

97Oh, how I love your law!
I meditate[e] on it all day
long.
98Your commands make me
wiser[f] than my enemies,
for they are ever with me.
99I have more insight than all
my teachers,
for I meditate on your
statutes.
100I have more understanding
than the elders,
for I obey your precepts.[g]
101I have kept my feet[h] from
every evil path
so that I might obey your
word.
102I have not departed from your
laws,
for you yourself have taught
me.
103How sweet are your words to
my taste,
sweeter than honey[i] to my
mouth![j]
104I gain understanding from your
precepts;
therefore I hate every wrong
path.[k]

נ Nun

105Your word is a lamp to my
feet
and a light[l] for my path.
106I have taken an oath[m] and
confirmed it,
that I will follow your
righteous laws.
107I have suffered much;
preserve my life, O LORD,
according to your word.
108Accept, O LORD, the willing
praise of my mouth,[n]
and teach me your laws.
109Though I constantly take my
life in my hands,[o]
I will not forget your law.
110The wicked have set a snare[p]
for me,
but I have not strayed[q] from
your precepts.
111Your statutes are my heritage
forever;
they are the joy of my heart.
112My heart is set on keeping
your decrees
to the very end.[r]

ס Samekh

113I hate double-minded men,[s]
but I love your law.
114You are my refuge and my
shield;[t]
I have put my hope[u] in your
word.
115Away from me,[v] you evildoers,
that I may keep the
commands of my God!
116Sustain me[w] according to your
promise, and I will live;
do not let my hopes be
dashed.[x]
117Uphold me, and I will be
delivered;
I will always have regard for
your decrees.
118You reject all who stray from
your decrees,
for their deceitfulness is in
vain.
119All the wicked of the earth
you discard like dross;[y]
therefore I love your statutes.

119:89 [a]Mt 24:34-35; 1Pe 1:25
119:90 [b]Ps 36:5 [c]Ps 148:6; Ecc 1:4
119:91 [d]Jer 33:25
119:97 [e]Ps 1:2
119:98 [f]Dt 4:6
119:100 [g]Job 32:7-9
119:101 [h]Pr 1:15
119:103 [i]Ps 19:10; Pr 8:11 [j]Pr 24:13-14
119:104 [k]ver 128
119:105 [l]Pr 6:23
119:106 [m]Ne 10:29
119:108 [n]Hos 14:2; Heb 13:15
119:109 [o]Jdg 12:3; Job 13:14
119:110 [p]Ps 140:5; 141:9 [q]ver 10
119:112 [r]ver 33
119:113 [s]Jas 1:8
119:114 [t]Ps 32:7; 91:1 [u]ver 74
119:115 [v]Ps 6:8; 139:19; Mt 7:23
119:116 [w]Ps 54:4 [x]Ps 25:2; Ro 5:5; 9:33
119:119 [y]Eze 22:18,19

120My flesh trembles[a] in fear of
you;
I stand in awe of your laws.

ע Ayin

121I have done what is righteous
and just;
do not leave me to my
oppressors.
122Ensure your servant's
well-being;[b]
let not the arrogant oppress
me.
123My eyes fail, looking for your
salvation,
looking for your righteous
promise.[c]
124Deal with your servant
according to your love
and teach me your decrees.[d]
125I am your servant;[e] give me
discernment
that I may understand your
statutes.
126It is time for you to act,
O LORD;
your law is being broken.
127Because I love your commands
more than gold,[f] more than
pure gold,
128and because I consider all
your precepts right,
I hate every wrong path.[g]

פ Pe

129Your statutes are wonderful;
therefore I obey them.
130The unfolding of your words
gives light;[h]
it gives understanding to the
simple.[i]
131I open my mouth and pant,[j]
longing for your commands.[k]
132Turn to me and have mercy[l]
on me,
as you always do to those
who love your name.
133Direct my footsteps according
to your word;[m]
let no sin rule[n] over me.
134Redeem me from the
oppression of men,[o]
that I may obey your
precepts.
135Make your face shine[p] upon
your servant
and teach me your decrees.
136Streams of tears[q] flow from
my eyes,
for your law is not obeyed.[r]

צ Tsadhe

137Righteous are you,[s] O LORD,
and your laws are right.[t]
138The statutes you have laid
down are righteous;[u]
they are fully trustworthy.
139My zeal wears me out,[v]
for my enemies ignore your
words.
140Your promises have been
thoroughly tested,[w]
and your servant loves them.
141Though I am lowly and
despised,[x]
I do not forget your precepts.
142Your righteousness is
everlasting
and your law is true.[y]
143Trouble and distress have
come upon me,
but your commands are my
delight.
144Your statutes are forever right;
give me understanding[z] that
I may live.

ק Qoph

145I call with all my heart;
answer me, O LORD,
and I will obey your decrees.
146I call out to you; save me
and I will keep your statutes.
147I rise before dawn[a] and cry
for help;
I have put my hope in your
word.
148My eyes stay open through the
watches of the night,[b]
that I may meditate on your
promises.
149Hear my voice in accordance
with your love;
preserve my life, O LORD,
according to your laws.
150Those who devise wicked
schemes are near,
but they are far from your
law.
151Yet you are near,[c] O LORD,
and all your commands are
true.[d]

119:120 [a] Hab 3:16
119:122 [b] Job 17:3
119:123 [c] ver 82
119:124 [d] ver 12
119:125 [e] Ps 116:16
119:127 [f] Ps 19:10
119:128 [g] ver 104,163
119:130 [h] Pr 6:23 [i] Ps 19:7
119:131 [j] Ps 42:1 [k] ver 20
119:132 [l] Ps 25:16; 106:4
119:133 [m] Ps 17:5 [n] Ps 19:13; Ro 6:12
119:134 [o] Ps 142:6; Lk 1:74
119:135 [p] Nu 6:25; Ps 4:6
119:136 [q] Jer 9:1,18 [r] Eze 9:4
119:137 [s] Ezr 9:15; Jer 12:1 [t] Ne 9:13
119:138 [u] Ps 19:7
119:139 [v] Ps 69:9; Jn 2:17
119:140 [w] Ps 12:6
119:141 [x] Ps 22:6
119:142 [y] Ps 19:7
119:144 [z] Ps 19:9
119:147 [a] Ps 5:3; 57:8; 108:2
119:148 [b] Ps 63:6
119:151 [c] Ps 34:18; 145:18 [d] ver 142

152Long ago I learned from your statutes
that you established them to last forever.[a]

ר Resh

153Look upon my suffering[b] and deliver me,
for I have not forgotten[c] your law.
154Defend my cause[d] and redeem me;[e]
preserve my life according to your promise.
155Salvation is far from the wicked,
for they do not seek out[f] your decrees.
156Your compassion is great, O LORD;
preserve my life[g] according to your laws.
157Many are the foes who persecute me,[h]
but I have not turned from your statutes.
158I look on the faithless with loathing,[i]
for they do not obey your word.
159See how I love your precepts;
preserve my life, O LORD, according to your love.
160All your words are true;
all your righteous laws are eternal.

ש Sin and Shin

161Rulers persecute me[j] without cause,
but my heart trembles at your word.
162I rejoice in your promise
like one who finds great spoil.[k]
163I hate and abhor falsehood
but I love your law.
164Seven times a day I praise you
for your righteous laws.
165Great peace[l] have they who love your law,
and nothing can make them stumble.
166I wait for your salvation,[m] O LORD,
and I follow your commands.

119:152 [a]Lk 21:33
119:153 [b]La 5:1 [c]Pr 3:1
119:154 [d]Mic 7:9 [e]1Sa 24:15
119:155 [f]Job 5:4
119:156 [g]2Sa 24:14
119:157 [h]Ps 7:1
119:158 [i]Ps 139:21
119:161 [j]1Sa 24:11
119:162 [k]1Sa 30:16
119:165 [l]Pr 3:2; Isa 26:3,12; 32:17
119:166 [m]Ge 49:18
119:168 [n]Pr 5:21
119:169 [o]Ps 18:6
119:170 [p]Ps 28:2 [q]Ps 31:2
119:171 [r]Ps 51:15 [s]Ps 94:12
119:173 [t]Ps 37:24 [u]Jos 24:22
119:174 [v]ver 166
119:175 [w]Isa 55:3
119:176 [x]Isa 53:6
120:1 [y]Ps 102:2; Jnh 2:2
120:2 [z]Pr 12:22 [a]Ps 52:4
120:4 [b]Ps 45:5

167I obey your statutes,
for I love them greatly.
168I obey your precepts and your statutes,
for all my ways are known[n] to you.

ת Taw

169May my cry come[o] before you, O LORD;
give me understanding according to your word.
170May my supplication come[p] before you;
deliver me[q] according to your promise.
171May my lips overflow with praise,[r]
for you teach me[s] your decrees.
172May my tongue sing of your word,
for all your commands are righteous.
173May your hand be ready to help[t] me,
for I have chosen[u] your precepts.
174I long for your salvation,[v] O LORD,
and your law is my delight.
175Let me live[w] that I may praise you,
and may your laws sustain me.
176I have strayed like a lost sheep.[x]
Seek your servant,
for I have not forgotten your commands.

Psalm 120

A song of ascents.

1I call on the LORD in my distress,[y]
and he answers me.
2Save me, O LORD, from lying lips[z]
and from deceitful tongues.[a]
3What will he do to you,
and what more besides,
O deceitful tongue?
4He will punish you with a warrior's sharp arrows,[b]

with burning coals of the
broom tree.

5Woe to me that I dwell in
Meshech,
that I live among the tents of
Kedar![a]
6Too long have I lived
among those who hate peace.
7I am a man of peace;
but when I speak, they are
for war.

Psalm 121

A song of ascents.

1I lift up my eyes to the hills—
where does my help come
from?
2My help comes from the LORD,
the Maker of heaven and
earth.[b]

3He will not let your foot slip—
he who watches over you will
not slumber;
4indeed, he who watches over
Israel
will neither slumber nor
sleep.

5The LORD watches over[c] you—
the LORD is your shade at
your right hand;
6the sun[d] will not harm you by
day,
nor the moon by night.

7The LORD will keep you from all
harm[e]—
he will watch over your life;
8the LORD will watch over your
coming and going
both now and forevermore.[f]

Psalm 122

A song of ascents. Of David.

1I rejoiced with those who said
to me,
"Let us go to the house of
the LORD."
2Our feet are standing
in your gates, O Jerusalem.

3Jerusalem is built like a city
that is closely compacted
together.
4That is where the tribes go up,
the tribes of the LORD,
to praise the name of the LORD
according to the statute given
to Israel.
5There the thrones for judgment
stand,
the thrones of the house of
David.

6Pray for the peace of
Jerusalem:
"May those who love[g] you
be secure.
7May there be peace within your
walls
and security within your
citadels."
8For the sake of my brothers
and friends,
I will say, "Peace be within
you."
9For the sake of the house of
the LORD our God,
I will seek your prosperity.[h]

Psalm 123

A song of ascents.

1I lift up my eyes to you,
to you whose throne[i] is in
heaven.
2As the eyes of slaves look to
the hand of their master,
as the eyes of a maid look to
the hand of her mistress,
so our eyes look to the LORD[j]
our God,
till he shows us his mercy.

3Have mercy on us, O LORD,
have mercy on us,
for we have endured much
contempt.
4We have endured much ridicule
from the proud,
much contempt from the
arrogant.

Psalm 124

A song of ascents. Of David.

1If the LORD had not been on our
side—
let Israel say[k]—

120:5 [a] Ge 25:13; Jer 49:28
121:2 [b] Ps 115:15; 124:8
121:5 [c] Isa 25:4
121:6 [d] Ps 91:5; Isa 49:10; Rev 7:16
121:7 [e] Ps 41:2; 91:10-12
121:8 [f] Dt 28:6
122:6 [g] Ps 51:18
122:9 [h] Ne 2:10
123:1 [i] Ps 11:4; 121:1; 141:8
123:2 [j] Ps 25:15
124:1 [k] Ps 129:1

2 if the LORD had not been on our side
when men attacked us,
3 when their anger flared against us,
they would have swallowed us alive;
4 the flood would have engulfed us,
the torrent would have swept over us,
5 the raging waters
would have swept us away.

6 Praise be to the LORD,
who has not let us be torn by their teeth.
7 We have escaped like a bird
out of the fowler's snare;[a]
the snare has been broken,
and we have escaped.
8 Our help is in the name of the LORD,
the Maker of heaven[b] and earth.

Psalm 125

A song of ascents.

1 Those who trust in the LORD are like Mount Zion,
which cannot be shaken[c]
but endures forever.
2 As the mountains surround Jerusalem,
so the LORD surrounds[d] his people
both now and forevermore.
3 The scepter of the wicked will not remain[e]
over the land allotted to the righteous,
for then the righteous might use
their hands to do evil.[f]

4 Do good, O LORD,[g] to those who are good,
to those who are upright in heart.[h]
5 But those who turn[i] to crooked ways[j]
the LORD will banish with the evildoers.

Peace be upon Israel.[k]

Psalm 126

A song of ascents.

1 When the LORD brought back[l] the captives to[w] Zion,
we were like men who dreamed.[x]
2 Our mouths were filled with laughter,
our tongues with songs of joy.[m]
Then it was said among the nations,
"The LORD has done great things[n] for them."
3 The LORD has done great things for us,
and we are filled with joy.[o]

4 Restore our fortunes,[y] O LORD,
like streams in the Negev.[p]
5 Those who sow in tears
will reap with songs of joy.[q]
6 He who goes out weeping,
carrying seed to sow,
will return with songs of joy,
carrying sheaves with him.

Psalm 127

A song of ascents. Of Solomon.

1 Unless the LORD builds[r] the house,
its builders labor in vain.
Unless the LORD watches[s] over the city,
the watchmen stand guard in vain.
2 In vain you rise early
and stay up late,
toiling for food[t] to eat—
for he grants sleep[u] to[z] those he loves.

3 Sons are a heritage from the LORD,
children a reward[v] from him.
4 Like arrows in the hands of a warrior
are sons born in one's youth.
5 Blessed is the man
whose quiver is full of them.

[w]*1 Or* LORD *restored the fortunes of* [x]*1 Or men restored to health* [y]*4 Or Bring back our captives* [z]*2 Or eat— / for while they sleep he provides for*

124:7 [a]Ps 91:3; Pr 6:5
124:8 [b]Ge 1:1; Ps 121:2; 134:3
125:1 [c]Ps 46:5
125:2 [d]Ps 121:8; Zec 2:4-5
125:3 [e]Ps 89:22; Pr 22:8; Isa 14:5 [f]1Sa 24:10; Ps 55:20
125:4 [g]Ps 119:68 [h]Ps 7:10; 36:10; 94:15
125:5 [i]Job 23:11 [j]Pr 2:15; Isa 59:8 [k]Ps 128:6
126:1 [l]Ps 85:1; Hos 6:11
126:2 [m]Job 8:21; Ps 51:14 [n]Ps 71:19
126:3 [o]Isa 25:9
126:4 [p]Isa 35:6; 43:19
126:5 [q]Isa 35:10
127:1 [r]Ps 78:69 [s]Ps 121:4
127:2 [t]Ge 3:17 [u]Job 11:18
127:3 [v]Ge 33:5

They will not be put to shame
when they contend with their
enemies[a] in the gate.

Psalm 128

A song of ascents.

[1]Blessed are all who fear the
LORD,[b]
who walk in his ways.[c]
[2]You will eat the fruit of your
labor;[d]
blessings and prosperity[e]
will be yours.
[3]Your wife will be like a fruitful
vine[f]
within your house;
your sons will be like olive
shoots[g]
around your table.
[4]Thus is the man blessed
who fears the LORD.

[5]May the LORD bless you from
Zion[h]
all the days of your life;
may you see the prosperity of
Jerusalem,
[6] and may you live to see your
children's children.[i]

Peace be upon Israel.[j]

Psalm 129

A song of ascents.

[1]They have greatly oppressed me
from my youth[k]—
let Israel say[l]—
[2]they have greatly oppressed me
from my youth,
but they have not gained the
victory[m] over me.
[3]Plowmen have plowed my back
and made their furrows long.
[4]But the LORD is righteous;[n]
he has cut me free from the
cords of the wicked.

[5]May all who hate Zion[o]
be turned back in shame.[p]
[6]May they be like grass on the
roof,
which withers[q] before it can
grow;
[7]with it the reaper cannot fill
his hands,
nor the one who gathers fill
his arms.
[8]May those who pass by not say,
"The blessing of the LORD be
upon you;
we bless you[r] in the name
of the LORD."

Psalm 130

A song of ascents.

[1]Out of the depths[s] I cry to
you, O LORD;
[2] O Lord, hear my voice.[t]
Let your ears be attentive[u]
to my cry for mercy.

[3]If you, O LORD, kept a record of
sins,
O Lord, who could stand?[v]
[4]But with you there is
forgiveness;[w]
therefore you are feared.[x]

[5]I wait for the LORD,[y] my soul
waits,
and in his word[z] I put my
hope.
[6]My soul waits for the Lord
more than watchmen[a] wait
for the morning,
more than watchmen wait for
the morning.[b]

[7]O Israel, put your hope[c] in the
LORD,
for with the LORD is unfailing
love
and with him is full
redemption.
[8]He himself will redeem[d] Israel
from all their sins.

Psalm 131

A song of ascents. Of David.

[1]My heart is not proud,[e]
O LORD,
my eyes are not haughty;
I do not concern myself with
great matters
or things too wonderful for
me.
[2]But I have stilled and quieted
my soul;
like a weaned child with its
mother,

127:5 [a]Pr 27:11
128:1 [b]Ps 112:1 [c]Ps 119:1-3
128:2 [d]Isa 3:10 [e]Ecc 8:12
128:3 [f]Eze 19:10 [g]Ps 52:8; 144:12
128:5 [h]Ps 20:2; 134:3
128:6 [i]Ge 50:23; Job 42:16 [j]Ps 125:5
129:1 [k]Ps 88:15; Hos 2:15 [l]Ps 124:1
129:2 [m]Mt 16:18
129:4 [n]Ps 119:137
129:5 [o]Mic 4:11 [p]Ps 71:13
129:6 [q]Ps 37:2
129:8 [r]Ru 2:4; Ps 118:26
130:1 [s]Ps 42:7; 69:2; La 3:55
130:2 [t]Ps 28:2 [u]2Ch 6:40; Ps 64:1
130:3 [v]Ps 76:7; 143:2
130:4 [w]Ex 34:7; Isa 55:7; Jer 33:8 [x]1Ki 8:40
130:5 [y]Ps 27:14; 33:20; Isa 8:17 [z]Ps 119:81
130:6 [a]Ps 63:6 [b]Ps 119:147
130:7 [c]Ps 131:3
130:8 [d]Lk 1:68
131:1 [e]Ps 101:5; Ro 12:16

like a weaned child is my
soul[a] within me.

3O Israel, put your hope[b] in the LORD
both now and forevermore.

Psalm 132

132:8–10pp — 2Ch 6:41–42

A song of ascents.

1O LORD, remember David
and all the hardships he endured.

2He swore an oath to the LORD
and made a vow to the
Mighty One of Jacob:[c]
3"I will not enter my house
or go to my bed—
4I will allow no sleep to my eyes,
no slumber to my eyelids,
5till I find a place[d] for the LORD,
a dwelling for the Mighty
One of Jacob."
6We heard it in Ephrathah,[e]
we came upon it in the fields
of Jaar[a]:[b][f]
7"Let us go to his dwelling
place;[g]
let us worship at his
footstool[h]—
8arise, O LORD,[i] and come to
your resting place,
you and the ark of your
might.
9May your priests be clothed
with righteousness;[j]
may your saints sing for joy."
10For the sake of David your
servant,
do not reject your anointed
one.

11The LORD swore an oath to
David,[k]
a sure oath that he will not
revoke:
"One of your own
descendants[l]
I will place on your throne—
12if your sons keep my covenant
and the statutes I teach
them,
then their sons will sit
on your throne[m] for ever and
ever."

13For the LORD has chosen Zion,[n]
he has desired it for his
dwelling:
14"This is my resting place for
ever and ever;[o]
here I will sit enthroned, for I
have desired it—
15I will bless her with abundant
provisions;
her poor will I satisfy with
food.[p]
16I will clothe her priests[q] with
salvation,
and her saints will ever sing
for joy.
17"Here I will make a horn[c]
grow[r] for David
and set up a lamp[s] for my
anointed one.
18I will clothe his enemies with
shame,[t]
but the crown on his head
will be resplendent."

Psalm 133

A song of ascents. Of David.

1How good and pleasant it is
when brothers live together[u]
in unity!
2It is like precious oil poured on
the head,[v]
running down on the beard,
running down on Aaron's
beard,
down upon the collar of his
robes.
3It is as if the dew of Hermon[w]
were falling on Mount Zion.
For there the LORD bestows his
blessing,[x]
even life forevermore.[y]

Psalm 134

A song of ascents.

1Praise the LORD, all you
servants[z] of the LORD

131:2 [a]Mt 18:3; 1Co 14:20
131:3 [b]Ps 130:7
132:2 [c]Ge 49:24
132:5 [d]Ac 7:46
132:6 [e]1Sa 17:12 [f]1Sa 7:2
132:7 [g]Ps 5:7 [h]Ps 99:5
132:8 [i]Nu 10:35; Ps 78:61
132:9 [j]Job 29:14; Isa 61:3,10
132:11 [k]Ps 89:3-4,35 [l]2Sa 7:12
132:12 [m]Lk 1:32; Ac 2:30
132:13 [n]Ps 48:1-2
132:14 [o]Ps 68:16
132:15 [p]Ps 107:9; 147:14
132:16 [q]2Ch 6:41
132:17 [r]Eze 29:21; Lk 1:69 [s]1Ki 11:36; 2Ch 21:7
132:18 [t]Ps 35:26; 109:29
133:1 [u]Ge 13:8; Heb 13:1
133:2 [v]Ex 30:25
133:3 [w]Dt 4:48 [x]Lev 25:21; Dt 28:8 [y]Ps 42:8
134:1 [z]Ps 135:1-2

[a]6 That is, Kiriath Jearim [b]6 Or *heard of it in Ephrathah, / we found it in the fields of Jaar.* (And no quotes around verses 7-9)
[c]17 *Horn* here symbolizes strong one, that is, king.

who minister by night[a] in the house of the LORD.
[2]Lift up your hands[b] in the sanctuary
and praise the LORD.

[3]May the LORD, the Maker of heaven[c] and earth,
bless you from Zion.[d]

Psalm 135

135:15–20pp – Ps 115:4–11

[1]Praise the LORD.[d]

Praise the name of the LORD;
praise him, you servants[e] of the LORD,
[2]you who minister in the house[f] of the LORD,
in the courts[g] of the house of our God.

[3]Praise the LORD, for the LORD is good;[h]
sing praise to his name, for that is pleasant.[i]
[4]For the LORD has chosen Jacob[j] to be his own,
Israel to be his treasured possession.[k]

[5]I know that the LORD is great,[l]
that our Lord is greater than all gods.[m]
[6]The LORD does whatever pleases him,[n]
in the heavens and on the earth,
in the seas and all their depths.
[7]He makes clouds rise from the ends of the earth;
he sends lightning with the rain[o]
and brings out the wind[p] from his storehouses.[q]

[8]He struck down the firstborn[r] of Egypt,
the firstborn of men and animals.
[9]He sent his signs[s] and wonders into your midst, O Egypt,
against Pharaoh and all his servants.[t]
[10]He struck down many[u] nations
and killed mighty kings—

134:1 [a]1Ch 9:33
134:2 [b]Ps 28:2; 1Ti 2:8
134:3 [c]Ps 124:8 [d]Ps 128:5
135:1 [e]Ps 113:1; 134:1
135:2 [f]Lk 2:37 [g]Ps 116:19
135:3 [h]Ps 119:68 [i]Ps 147:1
135:4 [j]Dt 10:15; 1Pe 2:9 [k]Ex 19:5; Dt 7:6
135:5 [l]Ps 48:1 [m]Ps 97:9
135:6 [n]Ps 115:3
135:7 [o]Jer 10:13; Zec 10:1 [p]Job 28:25 [q]Job 38:22
135:8 [r]Ex 12:12; Ps 78:51
135:9 [s]Dt 6:22 [t]Ps 136:10-15
135:10 [u]Nu 21:21-25; Ps 136:17-21
135:11 [v]Nu 21:21 [w]Jos 12:7-24
135:12 [x]Ps 78:55
135:13 [y]Ex 3:15 [z]Ps 102:12
135:14 [a]Dt 32:36
135:21 [b]Ps 134:3
136:1 [c]Ps 106:1 [d]1Ch 16:34; 2Ch 20:21

[11]Sihon[v] king of the Amorites,
Og king of Bashan
and all the kings of Canaan[w]—
[12]and he gave their land as an inheritance,[x]
an inheritance to his people Israel.

[13]Your name, O LORD, endures forever,[y]
your renown,[z] O LORD, through all generations.
[14]For the LORD will vindicate his people
and have compassion on his servants.[a]

[15]The idols of the nations are silver and gold,
made by the hands of men.
[16]They have mouths, but cannot speak,
eyes, but they cannot see;
[17]they have ears, but cannot hear,
nor is there breath in their mouths.
[18]Those who make them will be like them,
and so will all who trust in them.

[19]O house of Israel, praise the LORD;
O house of Aaron, praise the LORD;
[20]O house of Levi, praise the LORD;
you who fear him, praise the LORD.
[21]Praise be to the LORD from Zion,[b]
to him who dwells in Jerusalem.

Praise the LORD.

Psalm 136

[1]Give thanks to the LORD, for he is good.[c]
His love endures forever.[d]

[d]*1* Hebrew *Hallelu Yah*; also in verses 3 and 21

[2]Give thanks to the God of
gods.[a]
His love endures forever.
[3]Give thanks to the Lord of
lords:
His love endures forever.

[4]to him who alone does great
wonders,[b]
His love endures forever.
[5]who by his understanding[c]
made the heavens,[d]
His love endures forever.
[6]who spread out the earth[e]
upon the waters,[f]
His love endures forever.
[7]who made the great lights[g]—
His love endures forever.
[8]the sun to govern[h] the day,
His love endures forever.
[9]the moon and stars to govern
the night;
His love endures forever.

[10]to him who struck down the
firstborn[i] of Egypt
His love endures forever.
[11]and brought Israel out[j] from
among them
His love endures forever.
[12]with a mighty hand and
outstretched arm;[k]
His love endures forever.

[13]to him who divided the Red
Sea[e][l] asunder
His love endures forever.
[14]and brought Israel through[m]
the midst of it,
His love endures forever.
[15]but swept Pharaoh and his
army into the Red Sea;[n]
His love endures forever.

[16]to him who led his people
through the desert,[o]
His love endures forever.
[17]who struck down great kings,[p]
His love endures forever.
[18]and killed mighty kings[q]—
His love endures forever.
[19]Sihon king of the Amorites[r]
His love endures forever.
[20]and Og king of Bashan—
His love endures forever.
[21]and gave their land[s] as an
inheritance,
His love endures forever.
[22]an inheritance to his servant
Israel;
His love endures forever.

[23]to the One who remembered
us[t] in our low estate
His love endures forever.
[24]and freed us from our
enemies,[u]
His love endures forever.
[25]and who gives food[v] to every
creature.
His love endures forever.

[26]Give thanks to the God of
heaven.
His love endures forever.

Psalm 137

[1]By the rivers of Babylon[w] we
sat and wept[x]
when we remembered
Zion.
[2]There on the poplars
we hung our harps,
[3]for there our captors asked us
for songs,
our tormentors demanded[y]
songs of joy;
they said, "Sing us one of the
songs of Zion!"

[4]How can we sing the songs of
the LORD
while in a foreign land?
[5]If I forget you, O Jerusalem,
may my right hand forget ⌊its
skill⌋.
[6]May my tongue cling to the
roof[z] of my mouth
if I do not remember
you,
if I do not consider Jerusalem
my highest joy.

[7]Remember, O LORD, what the
Edomites[a] did
on the day Jerusalem
fell.[b]
"Tear it down," they cried,
"tear it down to its
foundations!"

[8]O Daughter of Babylon,
doomed to destruction,[c]

136:2 [a]Dt 10:17
136:4 [b]Ps 72:18
136:5 [c]Pr 3:19; Jer 51:15 [d]Ge 1:1
136:6 [e]Ge 1:9; Jer 10:12 [f]Ps 24:2
136:7 [g]Ge 1:14,16
136:8 [h]Ge 1:16
136:10 [i]Ex 12:29; Ps 135:8
136:11 [j]Ex 6:6; 12:51
136:12 [k]Dt 4:34; Ps 44:3
136:13 [l]Ex 14:21; Ps 78:13
136:14 [m]Ex 14:22
136:15 [n]Ex 14:27; Ps 135:9
136:16 [o]Ex 13:18
136:17 [p]Ps 135:9-12
136:18 [q]Dt 29:7
136:19 [r]Nu 21:21-25
136:21 [s]Jos 12:1
136:23 [t]Ps 113:7
136:24 [u]Ps 107:2
136:25 [v]Ps 104:27; 145:15
137:1 [w]Eze 1:1,3 [x]Ne 1:4
137:3 [y]Ps 80:6
137:6 [z]Eze 3:26
137:7 [a]Jer 49:7; La 4:21-22; Eze 25:12 [b]Ob 1:11
137:8 [c]Isa 13:1,19; Jer 25:12,26; Jer 50:15; Rev 18:6

[e]*13* Hebrew *Yam Suph*; that is, Sea of Reeds; also in verse 15

happy is he who repays you
for what you have done to us—
9he who seizes your infants
and dashes them[a] against the rocks.

Psalm 138

Of David.

1I will praise you, O LORD, with all my heart;
before the "gods"[b] I will sing your praise.
2I will bow down toward your holy temple[c]
and will praise your name
for your love and your faithfulness,
for you have exalted above all things
your name and your word.[d]
3When I called, you answered me;
you made me bold and stouthearted.[e]

4May all the kings of the earth[f] praise you, O LORD,
when they hear the words of your mouth.
5May they sing of the ways of the LORD,
for the glory of the LORD is great.

6Though the LORD is on high, he looks upon the lowly,[g]
but the proud[h] he knows from afar.
7Though I walk[i] in the midst of trouble,
you preserve my life;
you stretch out your hand against the anger of my foes,[j]
with your right hand[k] you save me.[l]
8The LORD will fulfill ⌞his purpose⌟[m] for me;
your love, O LORD, endures forever—
do not abandon the works of your hands.[n]

Psalm 139

For the director of music.
Of David. A psalm.

1O LORD, you have searched me[o]
and you know[p] me.
2You know when I sit and when I rise;[q]
you perceive my thoughts[r] from afar.
3You discern my going out and my lying down;
you are familiar with all my ways.[s]
4Before a word is on my tongue
you know it completely,[t] O LORD.

5You hem me in[u]—behind and before;
you have laid your hand upon me.
6Such knowledge is too wonderful for me,
too lofty[v] for me to attain.

7Where can I go from your Spirit?
Where can I flee[w] from your presence?
8If I go up to the heavens,[x] you are there;
if I make my bed[y] in the depths,[f] you are there.
9If I rise on the wings of the dawn,
if I settle on the far side of the sea,
10even there your hand will guide me,[z]
your right hand will hold me fast.

11If I say, "Surely the darkness will hide me
and the light become night around me,"
12even the darkness will not be dark[a] to you;
the night will shine like the day,
for darkness is as light to you.

137:9 [a] 2Ki 8:12; Isa 13:16
138:1 [b] Ps 95:3; 96:4
138:2 [c] 1Ki 8:29; Ps 5:7; 28:2 [d] Isa 42:21
138:3 [e] Ps 28:7
138:4 [f] Ps 102:15
138:6 [g] Ps 113:6; Isa 57:15 [h] Pr 3:34; Jas 4:6
138:7 [i] Ps 23:4 [j] Jer 51:25 [k] Ps 20:6 [l] Ps 71:20
138:8 [m] Ps 57:2; Php 1:6 [n] Job 10:3,8; 14:15
139:1 [o] Ps 17:3 [p] Jer 12:3
139:2 [q] 2Ki 19:27 [r] Mt 9:4; Jn 2:24
139:3 [s] Job 31:4
139:4 [t] Heb 4:13
139:5 [u] Ps 34:7
139:6 [v] Job 42:3; Ro 11:33
139:7 [w] Jer 23:24; Jnh 1:3
139:8 [x] Am 9:2-3 [y] Pr 15:11
139:10 [z] Ps 23:3
139:12 [a] Job 34:22; Da 2:22

f8 Hebrew *Sheol*

13For you created my inmost being;[a]
you knit me together[b] in my mother's womb.
14I praise you because I am fearfully and wonderfully made;
your works are wonderful,[c]
I know that full well.
15My frame was not hidden from you
when I was made in the secret place.
When I was woven together[d] in the depths of the earth,[e]
16 your eyes saw my unformed body.
All the days ordained for me
were written in your book
before one of them came to be.

17How precious to[g] me are your thoughts, O God![f]
How vast is the sum of them!
18Were I to count them,
they would outnumber the grains of sand.
When I awake,
I am still with you.
19If only you would slay the wicked,[g] O God!
Away from me,[h] you bloodthirsty men!
20They speak of you with evil intent;
your adversaries misuse your name.[i]
21Do I not hate those[j] who hate you, O LORD,
and abhor those who rise up against you?
22I have nothing but hatred for them;
I count them my enemies.

23Search me,[k] O God, and know my heart;[l]
test me and know my anxious thoughts.
24See if there is any offensive way in me,
and lead me[m] in the way everlasting.

139:13 [a]Ps 119:73 [b]Job 10:11
139:14 [c]Ps 40:5
139:15 [d]Job 10:11 [e]Ps 63:9
139:17 [f]Ps 40:5
139:19 [g]Isa 11:4 [h]Ps 119:115
139:20 [i]Jude 15
139:21 [j]2Ch 19:2; Ps 31:6; 119:113; Ps 119:158
139:23 [k]Job 31:6; Ps 26:2 [l]Jer 11:20
139:24 [m]Ps 5:8; 143:10; Pr 15:9
140:1 [n]Ps 17:13 [o]Ps 18:48
140:2 [p]Ps 36:4; 56:6
140:3 [q]Ps 57:4 [r]Ps 58:4; Jas 3:8
140:4 [s]Ps 141:9 [t]Ps 71:4
140:5 [u]Ps 31:4; 35:7
140:6 [v]Ps 16:2 [w]Ps 116:1; 143:1
140:7 [x]Ps 28:8
140:8 [y]Ps 10:2-3
140:9 [z]Ps 7:16
140:10 [a]Ps 11:6; 21:9
140:11 [b]Ps 34:21

Psalm 140

For the director of music.
A psalm of David.

1Rescue me,[n] O LORD, from evil men;
protect me from men of violence,[o]
2who devise evil plans[p] in their hearts
and stir up war every day.
3They make their tongues as sharp as[q] a serpent's;
the poison of vipers[r] is on their lips. *Selah*
4Keep me,[s] O LORD, from the hands of the wicked;[t]
protect me from men of violence
who plan to trip my feet.
5Proud men have hidden a snare for me;
they have spread out the cords of their net
and have set traps[u] for me along my path. *Selah*
6O LORD, I say to you, "You are my God."[v]
Hear, O LORD, my cry for mercy.[w]
7O Sovereign LORD,[x] my strong deliverer,
who shields my head in the day of battle—
8do not grant the wicked[y] their desires, O LORD;
do not let their plans succeed,
or they will become proud. *Selah*

9Let the heads of those who surround me
be covered with the trouble their lips have caused.[z]
10Let burning coals fall upon them;
may they be thrown into the fire,[a]
into miry pits, never to rise.
11Let slanderers not be established in the land;
may disaster hunt down men of violence.[b]

g17 *Or concerning*

12 I know that the LORD secures
justice for the poor
and upholds the cause[a] of
the needy.[b]
13 Surely the righteous will praise
your name[c]
and the upright will live[d]
before you.

Psalm 141

A psalm of David.

1 O LORD, I call to you; come
quickly[e] to me.
Hear my voice[f] when I call
to you.
2 May my prayer be set before
you like incense;[g]
may the lifting up of my
hands[h] be like the
evening sacrifice.[i]

3 Set a guard over my mouth,
O LORD;
keep watch over the door of
my lips.
4 Let not my heart be drawn to
what is evil,
to take part in wicked deeds
with men who are evildoers;
let me not eat of their
delicacies.[j]

5 Let a righteous man[h] strike
me—it is a kindness;
let him rebuke me[k]—it is oil
on my head.[l]
My head will not refuse it.

Yet my prayer is ever against
the deeds of evildoers;
6 their rulers will be thrown
down from the cliffs,
and the wicked will learn
that my words were well
spoken.
7 ⌊They will say,⌋ "As one plows
and breaks up the earth,
so our bones have been
scattered at the mouth[m]
of the grave.[i]"

8 But my eyes are fixed[n] on you,
O Sovereign LORD;
in you I take refuge[o]—do
not give me over to
death.

9 Keep me[p] from the snares they
have laid for me,
from the traps set[q] by
evildoers.
10 Let the wicked fall[r] into their
own nets,
while I pass by in safety.

Psalm 142

A *maskil*[j] of David. When he
was in the cave. A prayer.

1 I cry aloud to the LORD;
I lift up my voice to the LORD
for mercy.[s]
2 I pour out my complaint[t]
before him;
before him I tell my trouble.

3 When my spirit grows faint[u]
within me,
it is you who know my way.
In the path where I walk
men have hidden a snare for
me.
4 Look to my right and see;
no one is concerned for me.
I have no refuge;
no one cares[v] for my life.

5 I cry to you, O LORD;
I say, "You are my refuge,[w]
my portion[x] in the land of
the living."[y]
6 Listen to my cry,[z]
for I am in desperate need;[a]
rescue me from those who
pursue me,
for they are too strong for
me.
7 Set me free from my prison,[b]
that I may praise your name.

Then the righteous will gather
about me
because of your goodness to
me.[c]

Psalm 143

A psalm of David.

1 O LORD, hear my prayer,
listen to my cry for mercy;[d]

140:12 [a] Ps 9:4 [b] Ps 35:10
140:13 [c] Ps 97:12 [d] Ps 11:7
141:1 [e] Ps 22:19; 70:5 [f] Ps 143:1
141:2 [g] Rev 5:8; 8:3 [h] 1Ti 2:8 [i] Ex 29:39,41
141:4 [j] Pr 23:6
141:5 [k] Pr 9:8 [l] Ps 23:5
141:7 [m] Ps 53:5
141:8 [n] Ps 25:15 [o] Ps 2:12
141:9 [p] Ps 140:4 [q] Ps 38:12
141:10 [r] Ps 35:8
142:1 [s] Ps 30:8
142:2 [t] Isa 26:16
142:3 [u] Ps 140:5; 143:4,7
142:4 [v] Ps 31:11; Jer 30:17
142:5 [w] Ps 46:1 [x] Ps 16:5 [y] Ps 27:13
142:6 [z] Ps 17:1 [a] Ps 79:8; 116:6
142:7 [b] Ps 146:7 [c] Ps 13:6
143:1 [d] Ps 140:6

[h] 5 Or *Let the Righteous One* [i] 7 Hebrew *Sheol* [j] Title: Probably a literary or musical term

in your faithfulness[a] and
righteousness[b]
come to my relief.
2Do not bring your servant into
judgment,
for no one living is
righteous[c] before you.

3The enemy pursues me,
he crushes me to the
ground;
he makes me dwell in
darkness
like those long dead.
4So my spirit grows faint within
me;
my heart within me is
dismayed.[d]

5I remember[e] the days of long
ago;
I meditate on all your works
and consider what your
hands have done.
6I spread out my hands[f] to
you;
my soul thirsts for you like a
parched land. *Selah*
7Answer me quickly,[g] O LORD;
my spirit fails.
Do not hide your face[h] from
me
or I will be like those who go
down to the pit.
8Let the morning bring me word
of your unfailing love,[i]
for I have put my trust in
you.
Show me the way[j] I should
go,
for to you I lift up my
soul.[k]
9Rescue me from my enemies,[l]
O LORD,
for I hide myself in you.
10Teach me to do your will,
for you are my God;
may your good Spirit
lead[m] me on level ground.

11For your name's sake, O LORD,
preserve my life;[n]
in your righteousness,[o] bring
me out of trouble.
12In your unfailing love, silence
my enemies;
destroy all my foes,[p]
for I am your servant.[q]

143:1 [a]Ps 89:1-2 [b]Ps 71:2
143:2 [c]Ps 14:3; Ecc 7:20; Ro 3:20
143:4 [d]Ps 142:3
143:5 [e]Ps 77:6
143:6 [f]Ps 63:1; 88:9
143:7 [g]Ps 69:17 [h]Ps 27:9; 28:1
143:8 [i]Ps 46:5; 90:14 [j]Ps 27:11 [k]Ps 25:1-2
143:9 [l]Ps 31:15
143:10 [m]Ne 9:20; Ps 23:3; 25:4-5
143:11 [n]Ps 119:25 [o]Ps 31:1
143:12 [p]Ps 52:5; 54:5 [q]Ps 116:16
144:1 [r]Ps 18:2,34
144:2 [s]Ps 59:9; 91:2 [t]Ps 84:9
144:3 [u]Ps 8:4; Heb 2:6
144:4 [v]Ps 39:11; 102:11
144:5 [w]Ps 18:9; Isa 64:1 [x]Ps 104:32
144:6 [y]Ps 7:12-13; 18:14
144:7 [z]Ps 69:2 [a]Ps 18:44
144:8 [b]Ps 12:2
144:9 [c]Ps 33:2-3
144:10 [d]Ps 18:50

Psalm 144

Of David.

1Praise be to the LORD my
Rock,[r]
who trains my hands for war,
my fingers for battle.
2He is my loving God and my
fortress,[s]
my stronghold and my
deliverer,
my shield,[t] in whom I take
refuge,
who subdues peoples[k] under
me.

3O LORD, what is man[u] that you
care for him,
the son of man that you
think of him?
4Man is like a breath;
his days are like a fleeting
shadow.[v]

5Part your heavens,[w] O LORD,
and come down;
touch the mountains, so that
they smoke.[x]
6Send forth lightning and scatter
⌞the enemies⌟;
shoot your arrows[y] and rout
them.
7Reach down your hand from on
high;
deliver me and rescue me
from the mighty waters,[z]
from the hands of
foreigners[a]
8whose mouths are full of lies,[b]
whose right hands are
deceitful.

9I will sing a new song to you,
O God;
on the ten-stringed lyre[c] I
will make music to you,
10to the One who gives victory to
kings,
who delivers his servant
David[d] from the deadly
sword.

11Deliver me and rescue me
from the hands of foreigners

k2 Many manuscripts of the Masoretic Text, Dead Sea Scrolls, Aquila, Jerome and Syriac; most manuscripts of the Masoretic Text *subdues my people*

whose mouths are full of lies,
whose right hands are deceitful.[a]

12Then our sons in their youth
will be like well-nurtured plants,[b]
and our daughters will be like pillars
carved to adorn a palace.
13Our barns will be filled
with every kind of provision.
Our sheep will increase by thousands,
by tens of thousands in our fields;
14 our oxen will draw heavy loads.[1]
There will be no breaching of walls,
no going into captivity,
no cry of distress in our streets.

15Blessed are the people[c] of whom this is true;
blessed are the people whose God is the LORD.

Psalm 145[m]

A psalm of praise. Of David.

1I will exalt you,[d] my God the King;[e]
I will praise your name for ever and ever.
2Every day I will praise[f] you
and extol your name for ever and ever.

3Great is the LORD and most worthy of praise;
his greatness no one can fathom.[g]
4One generation[h] will commend your works to another;
they will tell of your mighty acts.
5They will speak of the glorious splendor of your majesty,
and I will meditate on your wonderful works.[n][i]
6They will tell of the power of your awesome works,[j]
and I will proclaim[k] your great deeds.
7They will celebrate your abundant goodness[l]
and joyfully sing of your righteousness.[m]

8The LORD is gracious and compassionate,[n]
slow to anger and rich in love.[o]
9The LORD is good[p] to all;
he has compassion on all he has made.
10All you have made will praise you,[q] O LORD;
your saints will extol you.[r]
11They will tell of the glory of your kingdom
and speak of your might,
12so that all men may know of your mighty acts[s]
and the glorious splendor of your kingdom.
13Your kingdom is an everlasting kingdom,[t]
and your dominion endures through all generations.

The LORD is faithful to all his promises
and loving toward all he has made.[o]
14The LORD upholds[u] all those who fall
and lifts up all[v] who are bowed down.
15The eyes of all look to you,
and you give them their food[w] at the proper time.
16You open your hand
and satisfy the desires[x] of every living thing.

17The LORD is righteous in all his ways
and loving toward all he has made.

144:11 [a]Ps 12:2; Isa 44:20
144:12 [b]Ps 128:3
144:15 [c]Ps 33:12
145:1 [d]Ps 30:1; 34:1 [e]Ps 5:2
145:2 [f]Ps 71:6
145:3 [g]Job 5:9; Ps 147:5; Ro 11:33
145:4 [h]Isa 38:19
145:5 [i]Ps 119:27
145:6 [j]Ps 66:3 [k]Dt 32:3
145:7 [l]Isa 63:7 [m]Ps 51:14
145:8 [n]Ps 86:15 [o]Ex 34:6; Nu 14:18
145:9 [p]Ps 100:5
145:10 [q]Ps 19:1 [r]Ps 68:26
145:12 [s]Ps 105:1
145:13 [t]1Ti 1:17; 2Pe 1:11
145:14 [u]Ps 37:24 [v]Ps 146:8
145:15 [w]Ps 104:27; 136:25
145:16 [x]Ps 104:28

[1]14 Or *our chieftains will be firmly established*
[m]This psalm is an acrostic poem, the verses of which (including verse 13b) begin with the successive letters of the Hebrew alphabet.
[n]5 Dead Sea Scrolls and Syriac (see also Septuagint); Masoretic Text *On the glorious splendor of your majesty / and on your wonderful works I will meditate*
[o]13 One manuscript of the Masoretic Text, Dead Sea Scrolls and Syriac (see also Septuagint); most manuscripts of the Masoretic Text do not have the last two lines of verse 13.

18The LORD is near[a] to all who
call on him,[b]
to all who call on him in
truth.
19He fulfills the desires[c] of those
who fear him;
he hears their cry[d] and saves
them.
20The LORD watches over all who
love him,[e]
but all the wicked he will
destroy.[f]

21My mouth will speak[g] in praise
of the LORD.
Let every creature[h] praise
his holy name
for ever and ever.

Psalm 146

1Praise the LORD.[p]

Praise the LORD,[i] O my soul.
2 I will praise the LORD all my
life;[j]
I will sing praise to my God
as long as I live.

3Do not put your trust in
princes,[k]
in mortal men,[l] who cannot
save.
4When their spirit departs, they
return to the ground;[m]
on that very day their plans
come to nothing.[n]

5Blessed is he[o] whose help[p] is
the God of Jacob,
whose hope is in the LORD his
God,
6the Maker of heaven[q] and
earth,
the sea, and everything in
them—
the LORD, who remains
faithful[r] forever.
7He upholds the cause of the
oppressed[s]
and gives food to the
hungry.[t]
The LORD sets prisoners free,[u]
8 the LORD gives sight to the
blind,[v]
the LORD lifts up those who are
bowed down,
the LORD loves the righteous.

145:18 [a]Dt 4:7 [b]Jn 4:24
145:19 [c]Ps 37:4 [d]Pr 15:29
145:20 [e]Ps 31:23; 97:10 [f]Ps 9:5
145:21 [g]Ps 71:8 [h]Ps 65:2
146:1 [i]Ps 103:1
146:2 [j]Ps 104:33
146:3 [k]Ps 118:9 [l]Isa 2:22
146:4 [m]Ps 104:29; Ecc 12:7 [n]Ps 33:10; 1Co 2:6
146:5 [o]Ps 144:15; Jer 17:7 [p]Ps 71:5
146:6 [q]Ps 115:15; Ac 14:15; Rev 14:7 [r]Ps 117:2
146:7 [s]Ps 103:6 [t]Ps 107:9 [u]Ps 68:6
146:8 [v]Mt 9:30
146:9 [w]Ex 22:22; Dt 10:18; Ps 68:5
146:10 [x]Ex 15:18; Ps 10:16
147:1 [y]Ps 135:3 [z]Ps 33:1
147:2 [a]Ps 102:16 [b]Dt 30:3
147:4 [c]Isa 40:26
147:5 [d]Ps 48:1 [e]Isa 40:28
147:6 [f]Ps 146:8-9
147:7 [g]Ps 33:3
147:8 [h]Job 38:26 [i]Ps 104:14
147:9 [j]Ps 104:27-28; Mt 6:26 [k]Job 38:41
147:10 [l]1Sa 16:7 [m]Ps 33:16-17

9The LORD watches over the
alien
and sustains the fatherless
and the widow,[w]
but he frustrates the ways of
the wicked.

10The LORD reigns[x] forever,
your God, O Zion, for all
generations.

Praise the LORD.

Psalm 147

1Praise the LORD.[q]

How good it is to sing praises
to our God,
how pleasant[y] and fitting to
praise him![z]

2The LORD builds up
Jerusalem;[a]
he gathers the exiles[b] of
Israel.
3He heals the brokenhearted
and binds up their wounds.

4He determines the number of
the stars[c]
and calls them each by
name.
5Great is our Lord[d] and mighty
in power;
his understanding has no
limit.[e]
6The LORD sustains the humble[f]
but casts the wicked to the
ground.

7Sing to the LORD[g] with
thanksgiving;
make music to our God on
the harp.
8He covers the sky with clouds;
he supplies the earth with
rain[h]
and makes grass grow[i] on
the hills.
9He provides food[j] for the
cattle
and for the young ravens[k]
when they call.

10His pleasure is not in the
strength[l] of the horse,[m]

p1 Hebrew *Hallelu Yah*; also in verse 10
q1 Hebrew *Hallelu Yah*; also in verse 20

nor his delight in the legs of a man;
11the LORD delights in those who fear him,
who put their hope in his unfailing love.

12Extol the LORD, O Jerusalem;
praise your God, O Zion,
13for he strengthens the bars of your gates
and blesses your people within you.
14He grants peace[a] to your borders
and satisfies you[b] with the finest of wheat.

15He sends his command[c] to the earth;
his word runs swiftly.
16He spreads the snow[d] like wool
and scatters the frost[e] like ashes.
17He hurls down his hail like pebbles.
Who can withstand his icy blast?
18He sends his word[f] and melts them;
he stirs up his breezes, and the waters flow.

19He has revealed his word to Jacob,
his laws and decrees[g] to Israel.
20He has done this for no other nation;[h]
they do not know his laws.

Praise the LORD.

Psalm 148

1Praise the LORD.[r]

Praise the LORD from the heavens,
praise him in the heights above.
2Praise him, all his angels,[i]
praise him, all his heavenly hosts.
3Praise him, sun and moon,
praise him, all you shining stars.
4Praise him, you highest heavens
and you waters above the skies.[j]
5Let them praise the name of the LORD,
for he commanded[k] and they were created.
6He set them in place for ever and ever;
he gave a decree[l] that will never pass away.

7Praise the LORD from the earth,
you great sea creatures[m] and all ocean depths,
8lightning and hail, snow and clouds,
stormy winds that do his bidding,[n]
9you mountains and all hills,[o]
fruit trees and all cedars,
10wild animals and all cattle,
small creatures and flying birds,
11kings of the earth and all nations,
you princes and all rulers on earth,
12young men and maidens,
old men and children.

13Let them praise the name of the LORD,[p]
for his name alone is exalted;
his splendor is above the earth and the heavens.[q]
14He has raised up for his people a horn,[s][r]
the praise of all his saints,
of Israel, the people close to his heart.

Praise the LORD.

Psalm 149

1Praise the LORD.[t][s]

Sing to the LORD a new song,
his praise in the assembly[t] of the saints.

147:14 [a]Isa 60:17-18 [b]Ps 132:15
147:15 [c]Job 37:12
147:16 [d]Job 37:6 [e]Job 38:29
147:18 [f]Ps 33:9
147:19 [g]Dt 33:4; Mal 4:4
147:20 [h]Dt 4:7-8, 32-34
148:2 [i]Ps 103:20
148:4 [j]Ge 1:7; 1Ki 8:27
148:5 [k]Ge 1:1,6; Ps 33:6,9
148:6 [l]Job 38:33; Ps 89:37; Jer 33:25
148:7 [m]Ps 74:13-14
148:8 [n]Ps 147:15-18
148:9 [o]Isa 44:23; 49:13; 55:12
148:13 [p]Isa 12:4 [q]Ps 8:1; 113:4
148:14 [r]Ps 75:10
149:1 [s]Ps 33:2 [t]Ps 35:18

[r]*1* Hebrew *Hallelu Yah*; also in verse 14
[s]*14* *Horn* here symbolizes strong one, that is, king.
[t]*1* Hebrew *Hallelu Yah*; also in verse 9

[2]Let Israel rejoice in their Maker;
let the people of Zion be glad in their King.[a]
[3]Let them praise his name with dancing
and make music to him with tambourine and harp.[b]
[4]For the LORD takes delight[c] in his people;
he crowns the humble with salvation.[d]
[5]Let the saints rejoice[e] in this honor
and sing for joy on their beds.[f]

[6]May the praise of God be in their mouths[g]
and a double-edged[h] sword in their hands,
[7]to inflict vengeance on the nations
and punishment on the peoples,
[8]to bind their kings with fetters,
their nobles with shackles of iron,
[9]to carry out the sentence written against them.[i]
This is the glory of all his saints.[j]
Praise the LORD.

Psalm 150

[1]Praise the LORD.[u]
Praise God in his sanctuary;[k]
praise him in his mighty heavens.[l]
[2]Praise him for his acts of power;[m]
praise him for his surpassing greatness.[n]
[3]Praise him with the sounding of the trumpet,
praise him with the harp and lyre,[o]
[4]praise him with tambourine and dancing,[p]
praise him with the strings[q] and flute,
[5]praise him with the clash of cymbals,[r]
praise him with resounding cymbals.

[6]Let everything[s] that has breath praise the LORD.

Praise the LORD.

149:2 [a]Ps 47:6; Zec 9:9
149:3 [b]Ps 81:2; 150:4
149:4 [c]Ps 35:27 [d]Ps 132:16
149:5 [e]Ps 132:16 [f]Job 35:10
149:6 [g]Ps 66:17 [h]Heb 4:12; Rev 1:16
149:9 [i]Dt 7:1; Eze 28:26 [j]Ps 148:14
150:1 [k]Ps 102:19 [l]Ps 19:1
150:2 [m]Dt 3:24 [n]Ps 145:5-6
150:3 [o]Ps 149:3
150:4 [p]Ex 15:20 [q]Isa 38:20
150:5 [r]1Ch 13:8; 15:16
150:6 [s]Ps 145:21

[u]*1* Hebrew *Hallelu Yah*; also in verse 6

Proverbs

Title and Background

The Hebrew word translated "proverb" is also translated "taunt" (Isa 14:4), "oracle" (Nu 23:7,18) and "parable" (Eze 17:2), so its meaning is considerably broader than the English term. Most proverbs are short, compact statements that express a truth about human behavior. A common feature of the proverbs is the use of figurative language.

Author and Date of Writing

Although the book begins with a title ascribing the proverbs to Solomon, it is clear from later chapters that he was not the only author of the book (see Outline). Since Solomon has a prominent role in the book, most of Proverbs would stem from the tenth century B.C. and Israel's united kingdom.

Theme and Message

According to the prologue (1:1-7), Proverbs was written to give "prudence to the simple, knowledge and discretion to the young" (1:4), and to make wise men wiser (1:5). Acquiring wisdom and knowing how to avoid the pitfalls of folly will lead to health and success. Although Proverbs is a practical book dealing with the art of living, it bases wisdom solidly on the fear of the Lord (1:7).

Outline

I. Prologue: Purpose and Theme (1:1-7)
II. The Superiority of the Way of Wisdom (1:8-9:18)
III. The Proverbs of Solomon (10:1-22:16)
IV. Sayings of the Wise (22:17-24:34)
V. More Proverbs of Solomon (25:1-29:27)
VI. The Words of Agur and Lemuel (30:1-31:9)
VII. Epilogue: The Excellent Wife (31:10-31)

Prologue: Purpose and Theme

1 The proverbs of Solomon[a] son of David, king of Israel:[b]

2 for attaining wisdom and discipline;
for understanding words of insight;
3 for acquiring a disciplined and prudent life,
doing what is right and just and fair;
4 for giving prudence to the simple,[c]
knowledge and discretion[d] to the young—
5 let the wise listen and add to their learning,[e]
and let the discerning get guidance—
6 for understanding proverbs and parables,[f]
the sayings and riddles[g] of the wise.

7 The fear of the LORD[h] is the beginning of knowledge,
but fools[a] despise wisdom and discipline.

1:1 [a] 1Ki 4:29-34 [b] Pr 10:1; 25:1; Ecc 1:1
1:4 [c] Pr 8:5 [d] Pr 2:10-11; 8:12
1:5 [e] Pr 9:9
1:6 [f] Ps 49:4; 78:2 [g] Nu 12:8
1:7 [h] Job 28:28; Ps 111:10; Pr 9:10; 15:33; Ecc 12:13

[a]7 The Hebrew words rendered *fool* in Proverbs, and often elsewhere in the Old Testament, denote one who is morally deficient.

Exhortations to Embrace Wisdom

Warning Against Enticement

8Listen, my son,[a] to your father's instruction
and do not forsake your mother's teaching.[b]
9They will be a garland to grace your head
and a chain to adorn your neck.[c]

10My son, if sinners entice[d] you,
do not give in[e] to them.[f]
11If they say, "Come along with us;
let's lie in wait[g] for someone's blood,
let's waylay some harmless soul;
12let's swallow them alive, like the grave,[b]
and whole, like those who go down to the pit;[h]
13we will get all sorts of valuable things
and fill our houses with plunder;
14throw in your lot with us,
and we will share a common purse"—
15my son, do not go along with them,
do not set foot[i] on their paths;[j]
16for their feet rush into sin,
they are swift to shed blood.[k]
17How useless to spread a net
in full view of all the birds!
18These men lie in wait for their own blood;
they waylay only themselves!
19Such is the end of all who go after ill-gotten gain;
it takes away the lives of those who get it.[l]

Warning Against Rejecting Wisdom

20Wisdom calls aloud[m] in the street,
she raises her voice in the public squares;
21at the head of the noisy streets[c] she cries out,
in the gateways of the city she makes her speech:

22"How long will you simple ones[d][n] love your simple ways?
How long will mockers delight in mockery
and fools hate knowledge?
23If you had responded to my rebuke,
I would have poured out my heart to you
and made my thoughts known to you.
24But since you rejected me when I called[o]
and no one gave heed when I stretched out my hand,
25since you ignored all my advice
and would not accept my rebuke,
26I in turn will laugh[p] at your disaster;
I will mock when calamity overtakes you[q]—
27when calamity overtakes you like a storm,
when disaster sweeps over you like a whirlwind,
when distress and trouble overwhelm you.

28"Then they will call to me but I will not answer;[r]
they will look for me but will not find me.[s]
29Since they hated knowledge
and did not choose to fear the LORD,[t]
30since they would not accept my advice
and spurned my rebuke,[u]
31they will eat the fruit of their ways
and be filled with the fruit of their schemes.[v]
32For the waywardness of the simple will kill them,
and the complacency of fools will destroy them;[w]

1:8 [a]Pr 4:1 [b]Pr 6:20
1:9 [c]Pr 4:1-9
1:10 [d]Ge 39:7 [e]Dt 13:8 [f]Pr 16:29; Eph 5:11
1:11 [g]Ps 10:8
1:12 [h]Ps 28:1
1:15 [i]Ps 119:101 [j]Ps 1:1; Pr 4:14
1:16 [k]Pr 6:18; Isa 59:7
1:19 [l]Pr 15:27
1:20 [m]Pr 8:1; 9:1-3,13-15
1:22 [n]Pr 8:5; 9:4, 16
1:24 [o]Isa 65:12; 66:4; Jer 7:13; Zec 7:11
1:26 [p]Ps 2:4 [q]Pr 6:15; 10:24
1:28 [r]1Sa 8:18; Isa 1:15; Jer 11:11; Mic 3:4 [s]Job 27:9; Pr 8:17; Eze 8:18; Zec 7:13
1:29 [t]Job 21:14
1:30 [u]ver 25; Ps 81:11
1:31 [v]Job 4:8; Pr 14:14; Isa 3:11; Jer 6:19
1:32 [w]Jer 2:19

[b]12 Hebrew *Sheol* [c]21 Hebrew; Septuagint / *on the tops of the walls* [d]22 The Hebrew word rendered *simple* in Proverbs generally denotes one without moral direction and inclined to evil.

33 but whoever listens to me will
live in safety[a]
and be at ease, without fear
of harm."[b]

Moral Benefits of Wisdom

2 My son, if you accept my
words
and store up my commands
within you,
2 turning your ear to wisdom
and applying your heart to
understanding,[c]
3 and if you call out for insight
and cry aloud for
understanding,
4 and if you look for it as for
silver
and search for it as for
hidden treasure,[d]
5 then you will understand the
fear of the LORD
and find the knowledge of
God.[e]
6 For the LORD gives wisdom,[f]
and from his mouth come
knowledge and
understanding.
7 He holds victory in store for the
upright,
he is a shield[g] to those
whose walk is
blameless,[h]
8 for he guards the course of the
just
and protects the way of his
faithful ones.[i]

9 Then you will understand what
is right and just
and fair—every good path.
10 For wisdom will enter your
heart,[j]
and knowledge will be
pleasant to your soul.
11 Discretion will protect you,
and understanding will guard
you.[k]

12 Wisdom will save you from the
ways of wicked men,
from men whose words are
perverse,
13 who leave the straight paths
to walk in dark ways,[l]
14 who delight in doing wrong

1:33 [a] Ps 25:12; Pr 3:23 [b] Ps 112:8
2:2 [c] Pr 22:17
2:4 [d] Job 3:21; Pr 3:14; Mt 13:44
2:5 [e] Pr 1:7
2:6 [f] 1Ki 3:9,12; Jas 1:5
2:7 [g] Pr 30:5-6 [h] Ps 84:11
2:8 [i] 1Sa 2:9; Ps 66:9
2:10 [j] Pr 14:33
2:11 [k] Pr 4:6; 6:22
2:13 [l] Pr 4:19; Jn 3:19
2:14 [m] Pr 10:23; Jer 11:15
2:15 [n] Ps 125:5 [o] Pr 21:8
2:16 [p] Pr 5:1-6; 6:20-29; 7:5-27
2:17 [q] Mal 2:14
2:18 [r] Pr 7:27
2:19 [s] Ecc 7:26
2:21 [t] Ps 37:29
2:22 [u] Job 18:17; Ps 37:38 [v] Dt 28:63; Pr 10:30
3:1 [w] Pr 4:5
3:2 [x] Pr 4:10
3:3 [y] Ex 13:9; Pr 6:21; 7:3; 2Co 3:3
3:4 [z] 1Sa 2:26; Lk 2:52
3:5 [a] Ps 37:3,5

and rejoice in the
perverseness of evil,[m]
15 whose paths are crooked[n]
and who are devious in their
ways.[o]

16 It will save you also from the
adulteress,[p]
from the wayward wife with
her seductive words,
17 who has left the partner of her
youth
and ignored the covenant she
made before God.[e][q]
18 For her house leads down to
death
and her paths to the spirits
of the dead.[r]
19 None who go to her return
or attain the paths of life.[s]

20 Thus you will walk in the ways
of good men
and keep to the paths of the
righteous.
21 For the upright will live in the
land,[t]
and the blameless will
remain in it;
22 but the wicked will be cut off
from the land,[u]
and the unfaithful will be
torn from it.[v]

Further Benefits of Wisdom

3 My son, do not forget my
teaching,[w]
but keep my commands in
your heart,
2 for they will prolong your life
many years[x]
and bring you prosperity.
3 Let love and faithfulness never
leave you;
bind them around your neck,
write them on the tablet of
your heart.[y]
4 Then you will win favor and a
good name
in the sight of God and
man.[z]
5 Trust in the LORD[a] with all
your heart
and lean not on your own
understanding;

[e] 17 *Or covenant of her God*

6in all your ways acknowledge
him,
and he will make your
paths[a] straight.[f][b]

7Do not be wise in your own
eyes;[c]
fear the LORD and shun evil.[d]
8This will bring health to your
body[e]
and nourishment to your
bones.[f]

9Honor the LORD with your
wealth,
with the firstfruits[g] of all
your crops;
10then your barns will be filled[h]
to overflowing,
and your vats will brim over
with new wine.[i]

11My son, do not despise the
LORD's discipline[j]
and do not resent his rebuke,
12because the LORD disciplines
those he loves,[k]
as a father[g] the son he
delights in.[l]

13Blessed is the man who finds
wisdom,
the man who gains
understanding,
14for she is more profitable than
silver
and yields better returns than
gold.[m]
15She is more precious than
rubies;[n]
nothing you desire can
compare with her.[o]
16Long life is in her right hand;
in her left hand are riches
and honor.[p]
17Her ways are pleasant ways,
and all her paths are peace.[q]
18She is a tree of life[r] to those
who embrace her;
those who lay hold of her
will be blessed.

19By wisdom the LORD laid the
earth's foundations,[s]
by understanding he set the
heavens[t] in place;
20by his knowledge the deeps
were divided,
and the clouds let drop the
dew.

21My son, preserve sound
judgment and
discernment,
do not let them out of your
sight;[u]
22they will be life for you,
an ornament to grace your
neck.[v]
23Then you will go on your way
in safety,
and your foot will not
stumble;[w]
24when you lie down,[x] you will
not be afraid;
when you lie down, your
sleep[y] will be sweet.
25Have no fear of sudden disaster
or of the ruin that overtakes
the wicked,
26for the LORD will be your
confidence
and will keep your foot[z]
from being snared.

27Do not withhold good from
those who deserve it,
when it is in your power to
act.
28Do not say to your neighbor,
"Come back later; I'll give it
tomorrow"—
when you now have it with
you.[a]
29Do not plot harm against your
neighbor,
who lives trustfully near you.
30Do not accuse a man for no
reason—
when he has done you no
harm.

31Do not envy[b] a violent man
or choose any of his ways,
32for the LORD detests a perverse
man[c]
but takes the upright into his
confidence.[d]

33The LORD's curse[e] is on the
house of the wicked,[f]
but he blesses the home of
the righteous.[g]
34He mocks proud mockers

3:6 [a] 1Ch 28:9 [b] Pr 16:3; Isa 45:13
3:7 [c] Ro 12:16 [d] Job 1:1; Pr 16:6
3:8 [e] Pr 4:22 [f] Job 21:24
3:9 [g] Ex 22:29; 23:19; Dt 26:1-15
3:10 [h] Dt 28:8 [i] Joel 2:24
3:11 [j] Job 5:17
3:12 [k] Pr 13:24; Rev 3:19 [l] Dt 8:5; Heb 12:5-6*
3:14 [m] Job 28:15; Pr 8:19; 16:16
3:15 [n] Job 28:18 [o] Pr 8:11
3:16 [p] Pr 8:18
3:17 [q] Pr 16:7; Mt 11:28-30
3:18 [r] Ge 2:9; Pr 11:30; Rev 2:7
3:19 [s] Ps 104:24 [t] Pr 8:27-29
3:21 [u] Pr 4:20-22
3:22 [v] Pr 1:8-9
3:23 [w] Ps 37:24; Pr 4:12
3:24 [x] Lev 26:6; Ps 3:5 [y] Job 11:18
3:26 [z] 1Sa 2:9
3:28 [a] Lev 19:13; Dt 24:15
3:31 [b] Ps 37:1; Pr 24:1-2
3:32 [c] Pr 11:20 [d] Job 29:4; Ps 25:14
3:33 [e] Dt 11:28; Mal 2:2 [f] Zec 5:4 [g] Ps 1:3

[f]6 Or *will direct your paths* [g]12 Hebrew; Septuagint / *and he punishes*

but gives grace to the
humble.[a]
35The wise inherit honor,
but fools he holds up to
shame.

Wisdom Is Supreme

4 Listen, my sons,[b] to a
father's instruction;
pay attention and gain
understanding.
2I give you sound learning,
so do not forsake my
teaching.
3When I was a boy in my
father's house,
still tender, and an only child
of my mother,
4he taught me and said,
"Lay hold of my words with
all your heart;
keep my commands and you
will live.[c]
5Get wisdom,[d] get
understanding;
do not forget my words or
swerve from them.
6Do not forsake wisdom, and
she will protect you;[e]
love her, and she will watch
over you.
7Wisdom is supreme; therefore
get wisdom.
Though it cost all[f] you
have,[h] get
understanding.[g]
8Esteem her, and she will exalt
you;
embrace her, and she will
honor you.[h]
9She will set a garland of grace
on your head
and present you with a crown
of splendor.[i]"

10Listen, my son, accept what I
say,
and the years of your life will
be many.[j]
11I guide[k] you in the way of
wisdom
and lead you along straight
paths.
12When you walk, your steps will
not be hampered;
when you run, you will not
stumble.[l]

3:34 [a]Jas 4:6*; 1Pe 5:5*
4:1 [b]Pr 1:8
4:4 [c]Pr 7:2
4:5 [d]Pr 16:16
4:6 [e]2Th 2:10
4:7 [f]Mt 13:44-46 [g]Pr 23:23
4:8 [h]1Sa 2:30; Pr 3:18
4:9 [i]Pr 1:8-9
4:10 [j]Pr 3:2
4:11 [k]1Sa 12:23
4:12 [l]Job 18:7; Pr 3:23
4:13 [m]Pr 3:22
4:14 [n]Ps 1:1; Pr 1:15
4:16 [o]Ps 36:4; Mic 2:1
4:18 [p]Isa 26:7 [q]2Sa 23:4; Da 12:3; Mt 5:14; Php 2:15
4:19 [r]Job 18:5; Pr 2:13; Isa 59:9-10; Jn 12:35
4:20 [s]Pr 5:1
4:21 [t]Pr 3:21; 7:1-2
4:22 [u]Pr 3:8; 12:18
4:23 [v]Mt 12:34; Lk 6:45
4:26 [w]Heb 12:13*

13Hold on to instruction, do not
let it go;
guard it well, for it is your
life.[m]
14Do not set foot on the path of
the wicked
or walk in the way of evil
men.[n]
15Avoid it, do not travel on it;
turn from it and go on your
way.
16For they cannot sleep till they
do evil;[o]
they are robbed of slumber
till they make someone
fall.
17They eat the bread of
wickedness
and drink the wine of
violence.

18The path of the righteous[p] is
like the first gleam of
dawn,
shining ever brighter till the
full light of day.[q]
19But the way of the wicked is
like deep darkness;[r]
they do not know what
makes them stumble.

20My son, pay attention to what I
say;
listen closely to my words.[s]
21Do not let them out of your
sight,[t]
keep them within your heart;
22for they are life to those who
find them
and health to a man's whole
body.[u]
23Above all else, guard your
heart,
for it is the wellspring of
life.[v]
24Put away perversity from your
mouth;
keep corrupt talk far from
your lips.
25Let your eyes look straight
ahead,
fix your gaze directly before
you.
26Make level[i] paths for your
feet[w]

[h]7 Or *Whatever else you get* [i]26 Or *Consider the*

and take only ways that are firm.
27Do not swerve to the right or the left;[a]
keep your foot from evil.

Warning Against Adultery

5 My son, pay attention to my wisdom,
listen well to my words[b] of insight,
2that you may maintain discretion
and your lips may preserve knowledge.
3For the lips of an adulteress drip honey,
and her speech is smoother than oil;[c]
4but in the end she is bitter as gall,[d]
sharp as a double-edged sword.
5Her feet go down to death;
her steps lead straight to the grave.[i][e]
6She gives no thought to the way of life;
her paths are crooked, but she knows it not.[f]
7Now then, my sons, listen[g] to me;
do not turn aside from what I say.
8Keep to a path far from her,[h]
do not go near the door of her house,
9lest you give your best strength to others
and your years to one who is cruel,
10lest strangers feast on your wealth
and your toil enrich another man's house.
11At the end of your life you will groan,
when your flesh and body are spent.
12You will say, "How I hated discipline!
How my heart spurned correction![i]
13I would not obey my teachers
or listen to my instructors.

4:27 [a]Dt 5:32; 28:14
5:1 [b]Pr 4:20; 22:17
5:3 [c]Ps 55:21; Pr 2:16; 7:5
5:4 [d]Ecc 7:26
5:5 [e]Pr 7:26-27
5:6 [f]Pr 30:20
5:7 [g]Pr 7:24
5:8 [h]Pr 7:1-27
5:12 [i]Pr 1:29; 12:1
5:18 [j]SS 4:12-15 [k]Ecc 9:9; Mal 2:14
5:19 [l]SS 2:9; 4:5
5:21 [m]Ps 119:168; Hos 7:2 [n]Job 14:16; Job 31:4; 34:21; Pr 15:3; Jer 16:17; 32:19; Heb 4:13
5:22 [o]Ps 9:16 [p]Nu 32:23; Ps 7:15-16; Pr 1:31-32
5:23 [q]Job 4:21; 36:12
6:1 [r]Pr 17:18 [s]Pr 11:15; 22:26-27

14I have come to the brink of utter ruin
in the midst of the whole assembly."
15Drink water from your own cistern,
running water from your own well.
16Should your springs overflow in the streets,
your streams of water in the public squares?
17Let them be yours alone,
never to be shared with strangers.
18May your fountain[j] be blessed,
and may you rejoice in the wife of your youth.[k]
19A loving doe, a graceful deer[l]—
may her breasts satisfy you always,
may you ever be captivated by her love.
20Why be captivated, my son, by an adulteress?
Why embrace the bosom of another man's wife?
21For a man's ways are in full view[m] of the LORD,
and he examines all his paths.[n]
22The evil deeds of a wicked man ensnare him;[o]
the cords of his sin hold him fast.[p]
23He will die for lack of discipline,[q]
led astray by his own great folly.

Warnings Against Folly

6 My son, if you have put up security for your neighbor,[r]
if you have struck hands in pledge[s] for another,
2if you have been trapped by what you said,
ensnared by the words of your mouth,
3then do this, my son, to free yourself,

i5 Hebrew *Sheol*

since you have fallen into
your neighbor's hands:
Go and humble yourself;
press your plea with your
neighbor!
4Allow no sleep to your eyes,
no slumber to your eyelids.[a]
5Free yourself, like a gazelle
from the hand of the
hunter,
like a bird from the snare of
the fowler.[b]

6Go to the ant, you sluggard;[c]
consider its ways and be
wise!
7It has no commander,
no overseer or ruler,
8yet it stores its provisions in
summer
and gathers its food at
harvest.[d]

9How long will you lie there,
you sluggard?[e]
When will you get up from
your sleep?
10A little sleep, a little slumber,
a little folding of the hands
to rest[f]—
11and poverty[g] will come on you
like a bandit
and scarcity like an armed
man.[k]

12A scoundrel and villain,
who goes about with a
corrupt mouth,
13 who winks with his eye,[h]
signals with his feet
and motions with his fingers,
14 who plots evil[i] with deceit
in his heart—
he always stirs up
dissension.[j]
15Therefore disaster will overtake
him in an instant;
he will suddenly be
destroyed—without
remedy.[k]

16There are six things the LORD
hates,
seven that are detestable to
him:
17 haughty eyes,
a lying tongue,[l]
hands that shed innocent
blood,[m]
18 a heart that devises wicked
schemes,
feet that are quick to rush
into evil,[n]
19 a false witness[o] who pours
out lies
and a man who stirs up
dissension among
brothers.[p]

Warning Against Adultery

20My son, keep your father's
commands
and do not forsake your
mother's teaching.[q]
21Bind them upon your heart
forever;
fasten them around your
neck.[r]
22When you walk, they will guide
you;
when you sleep, they will
watch over you;
when you awake, they will
speak to you.
23For these commands are a
lamp,
this teaching is a light,[s]
and the corrections of
discipline
are the way to life,
24keeping you from the immoral
woman,
from the smooth tongue of
the wayward wife.[t]
25Do not lust in your heart after
her beauty
or let her captivate you with
her eyes,
26for the prostitute reduces you
to a loaf of bread,
and the adulteress preys
upon your very life.[u]
27Can a man scoop fire into his
lap
without his clothes being
burned?
28Can a man walk on hot coals
without his feet being
scorched?
29So is he who sleeps[v] with
another man's wife;[w]
no one who touches her will
go unpunished.

6:4 [a]Ps 132:4
6:5 [b]Ps 91:3
6:6 [c]Pr 20:4
6:8 [d]Pr 10:4
6:9 [e]Pr 24:30-34
6:10 [f]Pr 24:33
6:11 [g]Pr 24:30-34
6:13 [h]Ps 35:19
6:14 [i]Mic 2:1 [j]ver 16-19
6:15 [k]2Ch 36:16
6:17 [l]Ps 120:2; Pr 12:22 [m]Dt 19:10; Isa 1:15; 59:7
6:18 [n]Ge 6:5
6:19 [o]Ps 27:12 [p]ver 12-15
6:20 [q]Pr 1:8
6:21 [r]Pr 3:3; 7:1-3
6:23 [s]Ps 19:8; 119:105
6:24 [t]Pr 2:16; 7:5
6:26 [u]Pr 7:22-23; 29:3
6:29 [v]Ex 20:14 [w]Pr 2:16-19; 5:8

[k]11 Or *like a vagrant / and scarcity like a beggar*

30Men do not despise a thief if he steals
to satisfy his hunger when he is starving.
31Yet if he is caught, he must pay sevenfold,[a]
though it costs him all the wealth of his house.
32But a man who commits adultery[b] lacks judgment;[c]
whoever does so destroys himself.
33Blows and disgrace are his lot,
and his shame will never[d] be wiped away;
34for jealousy[e] arouses a husband's fury,[f]
and he will show no mercy when he takes revenge.
35He will not accept any compensation;
he will refuse the bribe, however great it is.[g]

Warning Against the Adulteress

7 My son,[h] keep my words
and store up my commands within you.
2Keep my commands and you will live;[i]
guard my teachings as the apple of your eye.
3Bind them on your fingers;
write them on the tablet of your heart.[j]
4Say to wisdom, "You are my sister,"
and call understanding your kinsman;
5they will keep you from the adulteress,
from the wayward wife with her seductive words.[k]

6At the window of my house
I looked out through the lattice.
7I saw among the simple,
I noticed among the young men,
a youth who lacked judgment.[l]
8He was going down the street near her corner,
walking along in the direction of her house
9at twilight,[m] as the day was fading,
as the dark of night set in.

10Then out came a woman to meet him,
dressed like a prostitute and with crafty intent.
11(She is loud[n] and defiant,
her feet never stay at home;
12now in the street, now in the squares,
at every corner she lurks.)[o]
13She took hold of him[p] and kissed him
and with a brazen face she said:[q]

14"I have fellowship offerings[l][r] at home;
today I fulfilled my vows.
15So I came out to meet you;
I looked for you and have found you!
16I have covered my bed
with colored linens from Egypt.
17I have perfumed my bed[s]
with myrrh,[t] aloes and cinnamon.
18Come, let's drink deep of love till morning;
let's enjoy ourselves with love![u]
19My husband is not at home;
he has gone on a long journey.
20He took his purse filled with money
and will not be home till full moon."

21With persuasive words she led him astray;
she seduced him with her smooth talk.[v]
22All at once he followed her
like an ox going to the slaughter,
like a deer[m] stepping into a noose[n][w]
23 till an arrow pierces[x] his liver,
like a bird darting into a snare,

6:31 [a]Ex 22:1-14
6:32 [b]Ex 20:14 [c]Pr 7:7; 9:4, 16
6:33 [d]Pr 5:9-14
6:34 [e]Nu 5:14 [f]Ge 34:7
6:35 [g]Job 31:9-11; SS 8:7
7:1 [h]Pr 1:8; 2:1
7:2 [i]Pr 4:4
7:3 [j]Dt 6:8; Pr 3:3
7:5 [k]ver 21; Job 31:9; Pr 2:16; 6:24
7:7 [l]Pr 1:22; 6:32
7:9 [m]Job 24:15
7:11 [n]Pr 9:13; 1Ti 5:13
7:12 [o]Pr 8:1-36; 23:26-28
7:13 [p]Ge 39:12 [q]Pr 1:20
7:14 [r]Lev 7:11-18
7:17 [s]Est 1:6; Isa 57:7; Eze 23:41; Am 6:4 [t]Ge 37:25
7:18 [u]Ge 39:7
7:21 [v]Pr 5:3
7:22 [w]Job 18:10
7:23 [x]Job 15:22; 16:13

[l]14 Traditionally *peace offerings*
[m]22 Syriac (see also Septuagint); Hebrew *fool*
[n]22 The meaning of the Hebrew for this line is uncertain.

little knowing it will cost him
his life.[a]

24Now then, my sons, listen[b] to
me;
pay attention to what I say.
25Do not let your heart turn to
her ways
or stray into her paths.[c]
26Many are the victims she has
brought down;
her slain are a mighty throng.
27Her house is a highway to the
grave,[o]
leading down to the
chambers of death.[d]

Wisdom's Call

8 Does not wisdom call out?[e]
Does not understanding raise
her voice?
2On the heights along the way,
where the paths meet, she
takes her stand;
3beside the gates leading into
the city,
at the entrances, she cries
aloud:[f]
4"To you, O men, I call out;
I raise my voice to all
mankind.
5You who are simple,[g] gain
prudence;[h]
you who are foolish, gain
understanding.
6Listen, for I have worthy things
to say;
I open my lips to speak what
is right.
7My mouth speaks what is
true,[i]
for my lips detest
wickedness.
8All the words of my mouth are
just;
none of them is crooked or
perverse.
9To the discerning all of them
are right;
they are faultless to those
who have knowledge.
10Choose my instruction instead
of silver,
knowledge rather than choice
gold,[j]
11for wisdom is more precious[k]
than rubies,
and nothing you desire can
compare with her.[l]

12"I, wisdom, dwell together with
prudence;
I possess knowledge and
discretion.[m]
13To fear the LORD is to hate
evil;[n]
I hate[o] pride and arrogance,
evil behavior and perverse
speech.
14Counsel and sound judgment
are mine;
I have understanding and
power.[p]
15By me kings reign
and rulers[q] make laws that
are just;
16by me princes govern,
and all nobles who rule on
earth.[p]
17I love those who love me,[r]
and those who seek me find
me.[s]
18With me are riches and
honor,[t]
enduring wealth and
prosperity.[u]
19My fruit is better than fine
gold;
what I yield surpasses choice
silver.[v]
20I walk in the way of
righteousness,
along the paths of justice,
21bestowing wealth on those who
love me
and making their treasuries
full.[w]

22"The LORD brought me forth as
the first of his works,[q,r]
before his deeds of old;
23I was appointed[s] from eternity,
from the beginning, before
the world began.
24When there were no oceans, I
was given birth,
when there were no springs
abounding with water;[x]

7:23 [a]Pr 6:26; Ecc 7:26; 9:12
7:24 [b]Pr 1:8-9; 5:7; 8:32
7:25 [c]Pr 5:7-8
7:27 [d]Pr 2:18; 5:5; 9:18; Rev 22:15
8:1 [e]Pr 1:20; 9:3
8:3 [f]Job 29:7
8:5 [g]Pr 1:22 [h]Pr 1:4
8:7 [i]Ps 37:30; Jn 8:14
8:10 [j]Pr 3:14-15
8:11 [k]Job 28:17-19 [l]Pr 3:13-15
8:12 [m]Pr 1:4
8:13 [n]Pr 16:6 [o]Jer 44:4
8:14 [p]Pr 21:22; Ecc 7:19
8:15 [q]Da 2:21; Ro 13:1
8:17 [r]1Sa 2:30; Ps 91:14; Jn 14:21-24 [s]Pr 1:28; Jas 1:5
8:18 [t]Pr 3:16 [u]Dt 8:18; Mt 6:33
8:19 [v]Pr 3:13-14; 10:20
8:21 [w]Pr 24:4
8:24 [x]Ge 7:11

[o]27 Hebrew *Sheol* [p]16 Many Hebrew manuscripts and Septuagint; most Hebrew manuscripts *and nobles—all righteous rulers* [q]22 Or *way*; or *dominion* [r]22 Or *The LORD possessed me at the beginning of his work*; or *The LORD brought me forth at the beginning of his work* [s]23 Or *fashioned*

25before the mountains were settled in place,
before the hills, I was given birth,[a]
26before he made the earth or its fields
or any of the dust of the world.[b]
27I was there when he set the heavens in place,[c]
when he marked out the horizon on the face of the deep,
28when he established the clouds above
and fixed securely the fountains of the deep,
29when he gave the sea its boundary[d]
so the waters would not overstep his command,[e]
and when he marked out the foundations of the earth.[f]
30 Then I was the craftsman at his side.[g]
I was filled with delight day after day,
rejoicing always in his presence,
31rejoicing in his whole world
and delighting in mankind.[h]

32"Now then, my sons, listen to me;
blessed are[i] those who keep my ways.[j]
33Listen to my instruction and be wise;
do not ignore it.
34Blessed is the man who listens[k] to me,
watching daily at my doors,
waiting at my doorway.
35For whoever finds me[l] finds life
and receives favor from the LORD.[m]
36But whoever fails to find me harms himself;[n]
all who hate me love death."

Invitations of Wisdom and of Folly

9 Wisdom has built[o] her house;
she has hewn out its seven pillars.
2She has prepared her meat and mixed her wine;
she has also set her table.[p]
3She has sent out her maids, and she calls[q]
from the highest point of the city.[r]
4"Let all who are simple come in here!"
she says to those who lack judgment.[s]
5"Come, eat my food
and drink the wine I have mixed.[t]
6Leave your simple ways and you will live;[u]
walk in the way of understanding.

7"Whoever corrects a mocker invites insult;
whoever rebukes a wicked man incurs abuse.[v]
8Do not rebuke a mocker[w] or he will hate you;
rebuke a wise man and he will love you.[x]
9Instruct a wise man and he will be wiser still;
teach a righteous man and he will add to his learning.[y]

10"The fear of the LORD[z] is the beginning of wisdom,
and knowledge of the Holy One is understanding.
11For through me your days will be many,
and years will be added to your life.[a]
12If you are wise, your wisdom will reward you;
if you are a mocker, you alone will suffer."

13The woman Folly is loud;[b]
she is undisciplined and without knowledge.[c]
14She sits at the door of her house,
on a seat at the highest point of the city,[d]
15calling out to those who pass by,
who go straight on their way.

8:25 [a]Job 15:7
8:26 [b]Ps 90:2
8:27 [c]Pr 3:19
8:29 [d]Ge 1:9; Job 38:10; Ps 16:6 [e]Ps 104:9 [f]Job 38:5
8:30 [g]Jn 1:1-3
8:31 [h]Ps 16:3; 104:1-30
8:32 [i]Lk 11:28 [j]Ps 119:1-2
8:34 [k]Pr 3:13,18
8:35 [l]Pr 3:13-18 [m]Pr 12:2
8:36 [n]Pr 15:32
9:1 [o]Eph 2:20-22; 1Pe 2:5
9:2 [p]Lk 14:16-23
9:3 [q]Pr 8:1-3 [r]ver 14
9:4 [s]Pr 6:32
9:5 [t]Isa 55:1
9:6 [u]Pr 8:35
9:7 [v]Pr 23:9
9:8 [w]Pr 15:12 [x]Ps 141:5
9:9 [y]Pr 1:5,7
9:10 [z]Job 28:28; Pr 1:7
9:11 [a]Pr 3:16; 10:27
9:13 [b]Pr 7:11 [c]Pr 5:6
9:14 [d]ver 3

16"Let all who are simple come
in here!"
she says to those who lack
judgment.
17"Stolen water is sweet;
food eaten in secret is
delicious![a]"
18But little do they know that the
dead are there,
that her guests are in the
depths of the grave.[t][b]

Proverbs of Solomon

10 The proverbs of Solomon:[c]
A wise son brings joy to
his father,[d]
but a foolish son grief to his
mother.

2Ill-gotten treasures are of no
value,[e]
but righteousness delivers
from death.[f]

3The LORD does not let the
righteous go hungry[g]
but he thwarts the craving of
the wicked.

4Lazy hands make a man poor,[h]
but diligent hands bring
wealth.[i]

5He who gathers crops in
summer is a wise son,
but he who sleeps during
harvest is a disgraceful
son.

6Blessings crown the head of the
righteous,
but violence overwhelms the
mouth of the wicked.[u][j]

7The memory of the righteous[k]
will be a blessing,
but the name of the wicked[l]
will rot.[m]

8The wise in heart accept
commands,
but a chattering fool comes
to ruin.[n]

9The man of integrity[o] walks
securely,[p]
but he who takes crooked
paths will be found
out.[q]

9:17 [a]Pr 20:17
9:18 [b]Pr 2:18; 7:26-27
10:1 [c]Pr 1:1 [d]Pr 15:20; 29:3
10:2 [e]Pr 21:6 [f]Pr 11:4,19
10:3 [g]Mt 6:25-34
10:4 [h]Pr 19:15 [i]Pr 12:24; 13:4; 21:5
10:6 [j]ver 8,11,14
10:7 [k]Ps 112:6 [l]Ps 109:13 [m]Ps 9:6
10:8 [n]Mt 7:24-27
10:9 [o]Isa 33:15 [p]Ps 23:4 [q]Pr 28:18
10:10 [r]Ps 35:19
10:11 [s]Ps 37:30; Pr 13:12,14, 19 [t]ver 6
10:12 [u]Pr 17:9; 1Co 13:4-7; 1Pe 4:8
10:13 [v]ver 31 [w]Pr 26:3
10:14 [x]Pr 18:6,7
10:15 [y]Pr 18:11 [z]Pr 19:7
10:16 [a]Pr 11:18-19
10:17 [b]Pr 6:23
10:19 [c]Pr 17:28; Ecc 5:3; Jas 1:19; 3:2-12
10:21 [d]Pr 5:22-23; Hos 4:1,6,14

10He who winks maliciously[r]
causes grief,
and a chattering fool comes
to ruin.

11The mouth of the righteous is a
fountain of life,[s]
but violence overwhelms the
mouth of the wicked.[t]

12Hatred stirs up dissension,
but love covers over all
wrongs.[u]

13Wisdom is found on the lips of
the discerning,[v]
but a rod is for the back of
him who lacks
judgment.[w]

14Wise men store up knowledge,
but the mouth of a fool
invites ruin.[x]

15The wealth of the rich is their
fortified city,[y]
but poverty is the ruin of the
poor.[z]

16The wages of the righteous
bring them life,
but the income of the wicked
brings them
punishment.[a]

17He who heeds discipline shows
the way to life,[b]
but whoever ignores
correction leads others
astray.

18He who conceals his hatred has
lying lips,
and whoever spreads slander
is a fool.

19When words are many, sin is
not absent,
but he who holds his tongue
is wise.[c]

20The tongue of the righteous is
choice silver,
but the heart of the wicked is
of little value.

21The lips of the righteous
nourish many,
but fools die for lack of
judgment.[d]

[t]*18* Hebrew *Sheol* [u]*6* Or *but the mouth of the wicked conceals violence*; also in verse 11

[22]The blessing of the LORD brings wealth,[a]
and he adds no trouble to it.

[23]A fool finds pleasure in evil conduct,[b]
but a man of understanding delights in wisdom.

[24]What the wicked dreads[c] will overtake him;
what the righteous desire will be granted.[d]

[25]When the storm has swept by, the wicked are gone,
but the righteous stand firm[e] forever.[f]

[26]As vinegar to the teeth and smoke to the eyes,
so is a sluggard to those who send him.[g]

[27]The fear of the LORD adds length to life,[h]
but the years of the wicked are cut short.[i]

[28]The prospect of the righteous is joy,
but the hopes of the wicked come to nothing.[j]

[29]The way of the LORD is a refuge for the righteous,
but it is the ruin of those who do evil.[k]

[30]The righteous will never be uprooted,
but the wicked will not remain in the land.[l]

[31]The mouth of the righteous brings forth wisdom,[m]
but a perverse tongue will be cut out.

[32]The lips of the righteous know what is fitting,[n]
but the mouth of the wicked only what is perverse.

11 The LORD abhors dishonest scales,[o]
but accurate weights are his delight.[p]

[2]When pride comes, then comes disgrace,[q]
but with humility comes wisdom.[r]

[3]The integrity of the upright guides them,
but the unfaithful are destroyed by their duplicity.[s]

[4]Wealth is worthless in the day of wrath,[t]
but righteousness delivers from death.[u]

[5]The righteousness of the blameless makes a straight way for them,
but the wicked are brought down by their own wickedness.[v]

[6]The righteousness of the upright delivers them,
but the unfaithful are trapped by evil desires.

[7]When a wicked man dies, his hope perishes;
all he expected from his power comes to nothing.[w]

[8]The righteous man is rescued from trouble,
and it comes on the wicked instead.[x]

[9]With his mouth the godless destroys his neighbor,
but through knowledge the righteous escape.

[10]When the righteous prosper, the city rejoices;[y]
when the wicked perish, there are shouts of joy.

[11]Through the blessing of the upright a city is exalted,
but by the mouth of the wicked it is destroyed.[z]

[12]A man who lacks judgment derides his neighbor,[a]
but a man of understanding holds his tongue.

[13]A gossip betrays a confidence,[b]
but a trustworthy man keeps a secret.

[14]For lack of guidance a nation falls,[c]
but many advisers make victory sure.[d]

10:22 [a]Ge 24:35; Ps 37:22
10:23 [b]Pr 2:14; 15:21
10:24 [c]Isa 66:4 [d]Ps 145:17-19; Mt 5:6; 1Jn 5:14-15
10:25 [e]Ps 15:5 [f]Pr 12:3,7; Mt 7:24-27
10:26 [g]Pr 26:6
10:27 [h]Pr 9:10-11 [i]Job 15:32
10:28 [j]Job 8:13; Pr 11:7
10:29 [k]Pr 21:15
10:30 [l]Ps 37:9, 28-29; Pr 2:20-22
10:31 [m]Ps 37:30
10:32 [n]Ecc 10:12
11:1 [o]Lev 19:36; Dt 25:13-16; Pr 20:10,23 [p]Pr 16:11
11:2 [q]Pr 16:18 [r]Pr 18:12; 29:23
11:3 [s]Pr 13:6
11:4 [t]Eze 7:19; Zep 1:18 [u]Ge 7:1; Pr 10:2
11:5 [v]Pr 5:21-23
11:7 [w]Pr 10:28
11:8 [x]Pr 21:18
11:10 [y]Pr 28:12
11:11 [z]Pr 29:8
11:12 [a]Pr 14:21
11:13 [b]Lev 19:16; Pr 20:19; 1Ti 5:13
11:14 [c]Pr 20:18 [d]Pr 15:22; 24:6

15He who puts up security[a] for
another will surely
suffer,
but whoever refuses to strike
hands in pledge is safe.

16A kindhearted woman gains
respect,[b]
but ruthless men gain only
wealth.

17A kind man benefits himself,
but a cruel man brings
trouble on himself.

18The wicked man earns
deceptive wages,
but he who sows
righteousness reaps a
sure reward.[c]

19The truly righteous man attains
life,
but he who pursues evil goes
to his death.

20The LORD detests men of
perverse heart
but he delights in those
whose ways are
blameless.[d]

21Be sure of this: The wicked will
not go unpunished,
but those who are righteous
will go free.[e]

22Like a gold ring in a pig's snout
is a beautiful woman who
shows no discretion.

23The desire of the righteous
ends only in good,
but the hope of the wicked
only in wrath.

24One man gives freely, yet gains
even more;
another withholds unduly,
but comes to poverty.

25A generous man will prosper;
he who refreshes others will
himself be refreshed.[f]

26People curse the man who
hoards grain,
but blessing crowns him who
is willing to sell.

27He who seeks good finds
goodwill,
but evil comes to him who
searches for it.[g]

28Whoever trusts in his riches
will fall,[h]
but the righteous will thrive
like a green leaf.[i]

29He who brings trouble on his
family will inherit only
wind,
and the fool will be servant
to the wise.[j]

30The fruit of the righteous is a
tree of life,[k]
and he who wins souls is
wise.

31If the righteous receive their
due[l] on earth,
how much more the ungodly
and the sinner!

12 Whoever loves discipline
loves knowledge,
but he who hates correction
is stupid.[m]

2A good man obtains favor from
the LORD,
but the LORD condemns a
crafty man.

3A man cannot be established
through wickedness,
but the righteous cannot be
uprooted.[n]

4A wife of noble character is her
husband's crown,
but a disgraceful wife is like
decay in his bones.[o]

5The plans of the righteous are
just,
but the advice of the wicked
is deceitful.

6The words of the wicked lie in
wait for blood,
but the speech of the upright
rescues them.[p]

7Wicked men are overthrown
and are no more,[q]
but the house of the
righteous stands firm.[r]

8A man is praised according to
his wisdom,
but men with warped minds
are despised.

11:15 [a]Pr 6:1
11:16 [b]Pr 31:31
11:18 [c]Hos 10:12-13
11:20 [d]1Ch 29:17; Ps 119:1; Pr 12:2,22
11:21 [e]Pr 16:5
11:25 [f]Mt 5:7; 2Co 9:6-9
11:27 [g]Est 7:10; Ps 7:15-16
11:28 [h]Job 31:24-28; Ps 49:6; 52:7; Mk 10:25; 1Ti 6:17 [i]Ps 1:3; 92:12-14; Jer 17:8
11:29 [j]Pr 14:19
11:30 [k]Jas 5:20
11:31 [l]Pr 13:21; Jer 25:29; 1Pe 4:18
12:1 [m]Pr 9:7-9; 15:5,10,12,32
12:3 [n]Pr 10:25
12:4 [o]Pr 14:30
12:6 [p]Pr 14:3
12:7 [q]Ps 37:36 [r]Pr 10:25

9Better to be a nobody and yet
have a servant
than pretend to be somebody
and have no food.

10A righteous man cares for the
needs of his animal,
but the kindest acts of the
wicked are cruel.

11He who works his land will
have abundant food,
but he who chases fantasies
lacks judgment.[a]

12The wicked desire the plunder
of evil men,
but the root of the righteous
flourishes.

13An evil man is trapped by his
sinful talk,[b]
but a righteous man escapes
trouble.[c]

14From the fruit of his lips a man
is filled with good
things[d]
as surely as the work of his
hands rewards him.[e]

15The way of a fool seems right
to him,[f]
but a wise man listens to
advice.

16A fool shows his annoyance at
once,
but a prudent man overlooks
an insult.[g]

17A truthful witness gives honest
testimony,
but a false witness tells
lies.[h]

18Reckless words pierce like a
sword,[i]
but the tongue of the wise
brings healing.[j]

19Truthful lips endure forever,
but a lying tongue lasts only
a moment.

20There is deceit in the hearts of
those who plot evil,
but joy for those who
promote peace.

21No harm befalls the
righteous,[k]
but the wicked have their fill
of trouble.

22The LORD detests lying lips,[l]
but he delights in men who
are truthful.[m]

23A prudent man keeps his
knowledge to himself,[n]
but the heart of fools blurts
out folly.

24Diligent hands will rule,
but laziness ends in slave
labor.[o]

25An anxious heart weighs a man
down,[p]
but a kind word cheers him
up.

26A righteous man is cautious in
friendship,[v]
but the way of the wicked
leads them astray.

27The lazy man does not roast[w]
his game,
but the diligent man prizes
his possessions.

28In the way of righteousness
there is life;[q]
along that path is
immortality.

13 A wise son heeds his
father's instruction,
but a mocker does not listen
to rebuke.[r]

2From the fruit of his lips a man
enjoys good things,[s]
but the unfaithful have a
craving for violence.

3He who guards his lips[t] guards
his life,[u]
but he who speaks rashly will
come to ruin.[v]

4The sluggard craves and gets
nothing,
but the desires of the diligent
are fully satisfied.

5The righteous hate what is
false,
but the wicked bring shame
and disgrace.

12:11 [a]Pr 28:19
12:13 [b]Pr 18:7 [c]Pr 21:23; 2Pe 2:9
12:14 [d]Pr 13:2; 15:23; 18:20 [e]Isa 3:10-11
12:15 [f]Pr 14:12; 16:2,25; Lk 18:11
12:16 [g]Pr 29:11
12:17 [h]Pr 14:5,25
12:18 [i]Ps 57:4 [j]Pr 15:4
12:21 [k]Ps 91:10
12:22 [l]Pr 6:17; Rev 22:15 [m]Pr 11:20
12:23 [n]Pr 10:14; 13:16
12:24 [o]Pr 10:4
12:25 [p]Pr 15:13; Isa 50:4
12:28 [q]Dt 30:15
13:1 [r]Pr 10:1
13:2 [s]Pr 12:14
13:3 [t]Jas 3:2 [u]Pr 21:23 [v]Pr 18:7, 20-21

[v]26 Or *man is a guide to his neighbor*
[w]27 The meaning of the Hebrew for this word is uncertain.

6Righteousness guards the man of integrity,
but wickedness overthrows the sinner.[a]

7One man pretends to be rich, yet has nothing;
another pretends to be poor, yet has great wealth.[b]

8A man's riches may ransom his life,
but a poor man hears no threat.

9The light of the righteous shines brightly,
but the lamp of the wicked is snuffed out.[c]

10Pride only breeds quarrels,
but wisdom is found in those who take advice.

11Dishonest money dwindles away,[d]
but he who gathers money little by little makes it grow.

12Hope deferred makes the heart sick,
but a longing fulfilled is a tree of life.

13He who scorns instruction will pay for it,[e]
but he who respects a command is rewarded.

14The teaching of the wise is a fountain of life,[f]
turning a man from the snares of death.[g]

15Good understanding wins favor,
but the way of the unfaithful is hard.[x]

16Every prudent man acts out of knowledge,
but a fool exposes his folly.[h]

17A wicked messenger falls into trouble,
but a trustworthy envoy brings healing.[i]

18He who ignores discipline comes to poverty and shame,
but whoever heeds correction is honored.[j]

19A longing fulfilled is sweet to the soul,
but fools detest turning from evil.

20He who walks with the wise grows wise,
but a companion of fools suffers harm.[k]

21Misfortune pursues the sinner,
but prosperity is the reward of the righteous.[l]

22A good man leaves an inheritance for his children's children,
but a sinner's wealth is stored up for the righteous.[m]

23A poor man's field may produce abundant food,
but injustice sweeps it away.

24He who spares the rod hates his son,
but he who loves him is careful to discipline him.[n]

25The righteous eat to their hearts' content,
but the stomach of the wicked goes hungry.[o]

14 The wise woman builds her house,[p]
but with her own hands the foolish one tears hers down.

2He whose walk is upright fears the LORD,
but he whose ways are devious despises him.

3A fool's talk brings a rod to his back,
but the lips of the wise protect them.[q]

4Where there are no oxen, the manger is empty,
but from the strength of an ox comes an abundant harvest.

5A truthful witness does not deceive,

13:6 [a]Pr 11:3,5
13:7 [b]2Co 6:10
13:9 [c]Job 18:5; Pr 4:18-19; 24:20
13:11 [d]Pr 10:2
13:13 [e]Nu 15:31; 2Ch 36:16
13:14 [f]Pr 10:11 [g]Pr 14:27
13:16 [h]Pr 12:23
13:17 [i]Pr 25:13
13:18 [j]Pr 15:5,31-32
13:20 [k]Pr 15:31
13:21 [l]Ps 32:10
13:22 [m]Job 27:17; Ecc 2:26
13:24 [n]Pr 19:18; 22:15; 23:13-14; 29:15,17; Heb 12:7
13:25 [o]Ps 34:10; Pr 10:3
14:1 [p]Pr 24:3
14:3 [q]Pr 12:6

[x]15 Or *unfaithful does not endure*

but a false witness pours out
lies.[a]

6The mocker seeks wisdom and
finds none,
but knowledge comes easily
to the discerning.

7Stay away from a foolish man,
for you will not find
knowledge on his lips.

8The wisdom of the prudent is
to give thought to their
ways,
but the folly of fools is
deception.[b]

9Fools mock at making amends
for sin,
but goodwill is found among
the upright.

10Each heart knows its own
bitterness,
and no one else can share its
joy.

11The house of the wicked will
be destroyed,
but the tent of the upright
will flourish.[c]

12There is a way that seems right
to a man,[d]
but in the end it leads to
death.[e]

13Even in laughter[f] the heart
may ache,
and joy may end in grief.

14The faithless will be fully
repaid for their ways,[g]
and the good man rewarded
for his.[h]

15A simple man believes
anything,
but a prudent man gives
thought to his steps.

16A wise man fears the LORD and
shuns evil,[i]
but a fool is hotheaded and
reckless.

17A quick-tempered man does
foolish things,[j]
and a crafty man is hated.

18The simple inherit folly,
but the prudent are crowned
with knowledge.

19Evil men will bow down in the
presence of the good,
and the wicked at the gates
of the righteous.[k]

20The poor are shunned even by
their neighbors,
but the rich have many
friends.[l]

21He who despises his neighbor
sins,[m]
but blessed is he who is kind
to the needy.[n]

22Do not those who plot evil go
astray?
But those who plan what is
good find[y] love and
faithfulness.

23All hard work brings a profit,
but mere talk leads only to
poverty.

24The wealth of the wise is their
crown,
but the folly of fools yields
folly.

25A truthful witness saves lives,
but a false witness is
deceitful.[o]

26He who fears the LORD has a
secure fortress,[p]
and for his children it will be
a refuge.

27The fear of the LORD is a
fountain of life,
turning a man from the
snares of death.[q]

28A large population is a king's
glory,
but without subjects a prince
is ruined.

29A patient man has great
understanding,
but a quick-tempered man
displays folly.[r]

30A heart at peace gives life to
the body,
but envy rots the bones.[s]

31He who oppresses the poor

14:5 [a]Pr 6:19; 12:17
14:8 [b]ver 24
14:11 [c]Pr 3:33; 12:7
14:12 [d]Pr 12:15 [e]Pr 16:25
14:13 [f]Ecc 2:2
14:14 [g]Pr 1:31 [h]Pr 12:14
14:16 [i]Pr 22:3
14:17 [j]ver 29
14:19 [k]Pr 11:29
14:20 [l]Pr 19:4,7
14:21 [m]Pr 11:12 [n]Ps 41:1; Pr 19:17
14:25 [o]ver 5
14:26 [p]Pr 18:10; 19:23; Isa 33:6
14:27 [q]Pr 13:14
14:29 [r]Ecc 7:8-9; Jas 1:19
14:30 [s]Pr 12:4

[y]22 Or *show*

shows contempt for their Maker,[a]
but whoever is kind to the needy honors God.

32When calamity comes, the wicked are brought down,[b]
but even in death the righteous have a refuge.[c]

33Wisdom reposes in the heart of the discerning[d]
and even among fools she lets herself be known.[z]

34Righteousness exalts a nation,[e]
but sin is a disgrace to any people.

35A king delights in a wise servant,
but a shameful servant incurs his wrath.[f]

15 A gentle answer turns away wrath,[g]
but a harsh word stirs up anger.

2The tongue of the wise commends knowledge,
but the mouth of the fool gushes folly.[h]

3The eyes[i] of the LORD are everywhere,[j]
keeping watch on the wicked and the good.[k]

4The tongue that brings healing is a tree of life,
but a deceitful tongue crushes the spirit.

5A fool spurns his father's discipline,
but whoever heeds correction shows prudence.[l]

6The house of the righteous contains great treasure,[m]
but the income of the wicked brings them trouble.

7The lips of the wise spread knowledge;
not so the hearts of fools.

8The LORD detests the sacrifice of the wicked,[n]

14:31 [a]Pr 17:5
14:32 [b]Pr 6:15 [c]Job 13:15; 2Ti 4:18
14:33 [d]Pr 2:6-10
14:34 [e]Pr 11:11
14:35 [f]Mt 24:45-51; 25:14-30
15:1 [g]Pr 25:15
15:2 [h]Pr 12:23
15:3 [i]2Ch 16:9 [j]Job 31:4; Heb 4:13 [k]Job 34:21; Jer 16:17
15:5 [l]Pr 13:1
15:6 [m]Pr 8:21
15:8 [n]Pr 21:27; Isa 1:11; Jer 6:20 [o]ver 29
15:9 [p]Pr 21:21; 1Ti 6:11
15:10 [q]Pr 1:31-32; 5:12
15:11 [r]Job 26:6; Ps 139:8 [s]2Ch 6:30; Ps 44:21
15:12 [t]Am 5:10
15:13 [u]Pr 12:25; 17:22; 18:14
15:14 [v]Pr 18:15
15:15 [w]ver 13
15:16 [x]Ps 37:16-17; Pr 16:8; 1Ti 6:6
15:17 [y]Pr 17:1
15:18 [z]Pr 26:21 [a]Ge 13:8
15:19 [b]Pr 22:5
15:20 [c]Pr 10:1

but the prayer of the upright pleases him.[o]

9The LORD detests the way of the wicked
but he loves those who pursue righteousness.[p]

10Stern discipline awaits him who leaves the path;
he who hates correction will die.[q]

11Death and Destruction[a] lie open before the LORD[r]—
how much more the hearts of men![s]

12A mocker resents correction;[t]
he will not consult the wise.

13A happy heart makes the face cheerful,
but heartache crushes the spirit.[u]

14The discerning heart seeks knowledge,[v]
but the mouth of a fool feeds on folly.

15All the days of the oppressed are wretched,
but the cheerful heart has a continual feast.[w]

16Better a little with the fear of the LORD
than great wealth with turmoil.[x]

17Better a meal of vegetables where there is love
than a fattened calf with hatred.[y]

18A hot-tempered man stirs up dissension,[z]
but a patient man calms a quarrel.[a]

19The way of the sluggard is blocked with thorns,[b]
but the path of the upright is a highway.

20A wise son brings joy to his father,[c]
but a foolish man despises his mother.

[z]33 Hebrew; Septuagint and Syriac / *but in the heart of fools she is not known* [a]11 Hebrew *Sheol and Abaddon*

[21]Folly delights a man who lacks
judgment,[a]
but a man of understanding
keeps a straight course.

[22]Plans fail for lack of counsel,
but with many advisers they
succeed.[b]

[23]A man finds joy in giving an
apt reply[c]—
and how good is a timely
word![d]

[24]The path of life leads upward
for the wise
to keep him from going down
to the grave.[b]

[25]The LORD tears down the proud
man's house[e]
but he keeps the widow's
boundaries intact.[f]

[26]The LORD detests the thoughts
of the wicked,[g]
but those of the pure are
pleasing to him.

[27]A greedy man brings trouble to
his family,
but he who hates bribes will
live.[h]

[28]The heart of the righteous
weighs its answers,[i]
but the mouth of the wicked
gushes evil.

[29]The LORD is far from the wicked
but he hears the prayer of
the righteous.[j]

[30]A cheerful look brings joy to
the heart,
and good news gives health
to the bones.

[31]He who listens to a life-giving
rebuke
will be at home among the
wise.[k]

[32]He who ignores discipline
despises himself,[l]
but whoever heeds correction
gains understanding.

[33]The fear of the LORD[m] teaches a
man wisdom,[c]
and humility comes before
honor.[n]

15:21 [a]Pr 10:23
15:22 [b]Pr 11:14
15:23 [c]Pr 12:14 [d]Pr 25:11
15:25 [e]Pr 12:7 [f]Dt 19:14; Ps 68:5-6; Pr 23:10-11
15:26 [g]Pr 6:16
15:27 [h]Ex 23:8; Isa 33:15
15:28 [i]1Pe 3:15
15:29 [j]Ps 145:18-19
15:31 [k]ver 5
15:32 [l]Pr 1:7
15:33 [m]Pr 1:7 [n]Pr 18:12
16:1 [o]Pr 19:21
16:2 [p]Pr 21:2
16:3 [q]Ps 37:5-6; Pr 3:5-6
16:4 [r]Isa 43:7 [s]Ro 9:22
16:5 [t]Pr 6:16 [u]Pr 11:20-21
16:6 [v]Pr 14:16
16:8 [w]Ps 37:16
16:9 [x]Jer 10:23
16:11 [y]Pr 11:1
16:12 [z]Pr 25:5

16 To man belong the plans
of the heart,
but from the LORD comes the
reply of the tongue.[o]

[2]All a man's ways seem
innocent to him,
but motives are weighed by
the LORD.[p]

[3]Commit to the LORD whatever
you do,
and your plans will
succeed.[q]

[4]The LORD works out everything
for his own ends[r]—
even the wicked for a day of
disaster.[s]

[5]The LORD detests all the proud
of heart.[t]
Be sure of this: They will not
go unpunished.[u]

[6]Through love and faithfulness
sin is atoned for;
through the fear of the LORD
a man avoids evil.[v]

[7]When a man's ways are
pleasing to the LORD,
he makes even his enemies
live at peace with him.

[8]Better a little with
righteousness
than much gain[w] with
injustice.

[9]In his heart a man plans his
course,
but the LORD determines his
steps.[x]

[10]The lips of a king speak as an
oracle,
and his mouth should not
betray justice.

[11]Honest scales and balances are
from the LORD;
all the weights in the bag are
of his making.[y]

[12]Kings detest wrongdoing,
for a throne is established
through righteousness.[z]

[13]Kings take pleasure in honest
lips;

[b]24 Hebrew *Sheol* [c]33 Or *Wisdom teaches the fear of the LORD*

they value a man who speaks
the truth.[a]

14A king's wrath is a messenger
of death,[b]
but a wise man will appease
it.

15When a king's face brightens, it
means life;[c]
his favor is like a rain cloud
in spring.

16How much better to get
wisdom than gold,
to choose understanding
rather than silver![d]

17The highway of the upright
avoids evil;
he who guards his way
guards his life.

18Pride goes before destruction,
a haughty spirit before a
fall.[e]

19Better to be lowly in spirit and
among the oppressed
than to share plunder with
the proud.

20Whoever gives heed to
instruction prospers,
and blessed is he who trusts
in the LORD.[f]

21The wise in heart are called
discerning,
and pleasant words promote
instruction.[d][g]

22Understanding is a fountain of
life to those who have
it,[h]
but folly brings punishment
to fools.

23A wise man's heart guides his
mouth,
and his lips promote
instruction.[e]

24Pleasant words are a
honeycomb,
sweet to the soul and healing
to the bones.[i]

25There is a way that seems right
to a man,[j]
but in the end it leads to
death.[k]

16:13 [a]Pr 14:35
16:14 [b]Pr 19:12
16:15 [c]Job 29:24
16:16 [d]Pr 8:10,19
16:18 [e]Pr 11:2; 18:12
16:20 [f]Ps 2:12; 34:8; Pr 19:8; Jer 17:7
16:21 [g]ver 23
16:22 [h]Pr 13:14
16:24 [i]Pr 24:13-14
16:25 [j]Pr 12:15 [k]Pr 14:12
16:27 [l]Jas 3:6
16:28 [m]Pr 15:18 [n]Pr 17:9
16:29 [o]Pr 1:10; 12:26
16:31 [p]Pr 20:29
16:33 [q]Pr 18:18; 29:26
17:1 [r]Pr 15:16,17
17:3 [s]Pr 27:21 [t]1Ch 29:17; Ps 26:2; Jer 17:10

26The laborer's appetite works for
him;
his hunger drives him on.

27A scoundrel plots evil,
and his speech is like a
scorching fire.[l]

28A perverse man stirs up
dissension,[m]
and a gossip separates close
friends.[n]

29A violent man entices his
neighbor
and leads him down a path
that is not good.[o]

30He who winks with his eye is
plotting perversity;
he who purses his lips is
bent on evil.

31Gray hair is a crown of
splendor;[p]
it is attained by a righteous
life.

32Better a patient man than a
warrior,
a man who controls his
temper than one who
takes a city.

33The lot is cast into the lap,
but its every decision is from
the LORD.[q]

17 Better a dry crust with
peace and quiet
than a house full of
feasting,[f] with strife.[r]

2A wise servant will rule over a
disgraceful son,
and will share the
inheritance as one of the
brothers.

3The crucible for silver and the
furnace for gold,[s]
but the LORD tests the
heart.[t]

4A wicked man listens to evil
lips;
a liar pays attention to a
malicious tongue.

5He who mocks the poor shows

[d]21 Or *words make a man persuasive*
[e]23 Or *mouth / and makes his lips persuasive*
[f]1 Hebrew *sacrifices*

contempt for their Maker;[a]
whoever gloats over disaster[b] will not go unpunished.[c]

[6]Children's children[d] are a crown to the aged,
and parents are the pride of their children.

[7]Arrogant[g] lips are unsuited to a fool—
how much worse lying lips to a ruler!

[8]A bribe is a charm to the one who gives it;
wherever he turns, he succeeds.

[9]He who covers over an offense promotes love,[e]
but whoever repeats the matter separates close friends.[f]

[10]A rebuke impresses a man of discernment
more than a hundred lashes a fool.

[11]An evil man is bent only on rebellion;
a merciless official will be sent against him.

[12]Better to meet a bear robbed of her cubs
than a fool in his folly.

[13]If a man pays back evil[g] for good,
evil will never leave his house.

[14]Starting a quarrel is like breaching a dam;
so drop the matter before a dispute breaks out.[h]

[15]Acquitting the guilty and condemning the innocent[i]—
the LORD detests them both.[j]

[16]Of what use is money in the hand of a fool,
since he has no desire to get wisdom?[k]

[17]A friend loves at all times,
and a brother is born for adversity.

[18]A man lacking in judgment strikes hands in pledge
and puts up security for his neighbor.[l]

[19]He who loves a quarrel loves sin;
he who builds a high gate invites destruction.

[20]A man of perverse heart does not prosper;
he whose tongue is deceitful falls into trouble.

[21]To have a fool for a son brings grief;
there is no joy for the father of a fool.[m]

[22]A cheerful heart is good medicine,
but a crushed spirit dries up the bones.[n]

[23]A wicked man accepts a bribe[o] in secret
to pervert the course of justice.

[24]A discerning man keeps wisdom in view,
but a fool's eyes[p] wander to the ends of the earth.

[25]A foolish son brings grief to his father
and bitterness to the one who bore him.[q]

[26]It is not good to punish an innocent man,[r]
or to flog officials for their integrity.

[27]A man of knowledge uses words with restraint,
and a man of understanding is even-tempered.[s]

[28]Even a fool is thought wise if he keeps silent,
and discerning if he holds his tongue.[t]

18 An unfriendly man pursues selfish ends;
he defies all sound judgment.

17:5 [a]Pr 14:31 [b]Job 31:29 [c]Ob 1:12
17:6 [d]Pr 13:22
17:9 [e]Pr 10:12 [f]Pr 16:28
17:13 [g]Ps 109:4-5; Jer 18:20
17:14 [h]Pr 20:3
17:15 [i]Pr 18:5 [j]Ex 23:6-7; Isa 5:23
17:16 [k]Pr 23:23
17:18 [l]Pr 6:1-5; 11:15; 22:26-27
17:21 [m]Pr 10:1
17:22 [n]Ps 22:15; Pr 15:13
17:23 [o]Ex 23:8
17:24 [p]Ecc 2:14
17:25 [q]Pr 10:1
17:26 [r]Pr 18:5
17:27 [s]Pr 14:29; Jas 1:19
17:28 [t]Job 13:5

[g]7 Or *Eloquent*

2A fool finds no pleasure in understanding
but delights in airing his own opinions.[a]

3When wickedness comes, so does contempt,
and with shame comes disgrace.

4The words of a man's mouth are deep waters,
but the fountain of wisdom is a bubbling brook.

5It is not good to be partial to the wicked[b]
or to deprive the innocent of justice.[c]

6A fool's lips bring him strife,
and his mouth invites a beating.

7A fool's mouth is his undoing,
and his lips are a snare[d] to his soul.[e]

8The words of a gossip are like choice morsels;
they go down to a man's inmost parts.[f]

9One who is slack in his work
is brother to one who destroys.[g]

10The name of the LORD is a strong tower;[h]
the righteous run to it and are safe.

11The wealth of the rich is their fortified city;[i]
they imagine it an unscalable wall.

12Before his downfall a man's heart is proud,
but humility comes before honor.[j]

13He who answers before listening—
that is his folly and his shame.[k]

14A man's spirit sustains him in sickness,
but a crushed spirit who can bear?[l]

15The heart of the discerning acquires knowledge;[m]
the ears of the wise seek it out.

16A gift[n] opens the way for the giver
and ushers him into the presence of the great.

17The first to present his case seems right,
till another comes forward and questions him.

18Casting the lot settles disputes[o]
and keeps strong opponents apart.

19An offended brother is more unyielding than a fortified city,
and disputes are like the barred gates of a citadel.

20From the fruit of his mouth a man's stomach is filled;
with the harvest from his lips he is satisfied.[p]

21The tongue has the power of life and death,
and those who love it will eat its fruit.[q]

22He who finds a wife finds what is good[r]
and receives favor from the LORD.[s]

23A poor man pleads for mercy,
but a rich man answers harshly.

24A man of many companions may come to ruin,
but there is a friend who sticks closer than a brother.[t]

19 Better a poor man whose walk is blameless
than a fool whose lips are perverse.[u]

2It is not good to have zeal without knowledge,
nor to be hasty and miss the way.[v]

3A man's own folly ruins his life,

18:2 [a]Pr 12:23
18:5 [b]Lev 19:15; Pr 24:23-25; 28:21 [c]Ps 82:2; Pr 17:15
18:7 [d]Ps 140:9 [e]Ps 64:8; Pr 10:14; 12:13; 13:3; Ecc 10:12
18:8 [f]Pr 26:22
18:9 [g]Pr 28:24
18:10 [h]2Sa 22:3; Ps 61:3
18:11 [i]Pr 10:15
18:12 [j]Pr 11:2; 15:33; 16:18
18:13 [k]Pr 20:25; Jn 7:51
18:14 [l]Pr 15:13; 17:22
18:15 [m]Pr 15:14
18:16 [n]Ge 32:20
18:18 [o]Pr 16:33
18:20 [p]Pr 12:14
18:21 [q]Pr 13:2-3; Mt 12:37
18:22 [r]Pr 12:4 [s]Pr 19:14; 31:10
18:24 [t]Pr 17:17; Jn 15:13-15
19:1 [u]Pr 28:6
19:2 [v]Pr 29:20

yet his heart rages against
the LORD.

4Wealth brings many friends,
but a poor man's friend
deserts him.[a]

5A false witness[b] will not go
unpunished,
and he who pours out lies
will not go free.[c]

6Many curry favor with a ruler,[d]
and everyone is the friend of
a man who gives gifts.[e]

7A poor man is shunned by all
his relatives—
how much more do his
friends avoid him!
Though he pursues them with
pleading,
they are nowhere to be
found.[h][f]

8He who gets wisdom loves his
own soul;
he who cherishes
understanding
prospers.[g]

9A false witness will not go
unpunished,
and he who pours out lies
will perish.[h]

10It is not fitting for a fool[i] to
live in luxury—
how much worse for a slave
to rule over princes![j]

11A man's wisdom gives him
patience;[k]
it is to his glory to overlook
an offense.

12A king's rage is like the roar of
a lion,
but his favor is like dew[l] on
the grass.[m]

13A foolish son is his father's
ruin,[n]
and a quarrelsome wife is
like a constant
dripping.[o]

14Houses and wealth are
inherited from parents,[p]
but a prudent wife is from
the LORD.[q]

15Laziness brings on deep sleep,
and the shiftless man goes
hungry.[r]

16He who obeys instructions
guards his life,
but he who is contemptuous
of his ways will die.[s]

17He who is kind to the poor
lends to the LORD,
and he will reward him for
what he has done.[t]

18Discipline your son, for in that
there is hope;
do not be a willing party to
his death.[u]

19A hot-tempered man must pay
the penalty;
if you rescue him, you will
have to do it again.

20Listen to advice and accept
instruction,[v]
and in the end you will be
wise.[w]

21Many are the plans in a man's
heart,
but it is the LORD's purpose
that prevails.[x]

22What a man desires is unfailing
love[i];
better to be poor than a liar.

23The fear of the LORD leads to
life:
Then one rests content,
untouched by trouble.[y]

24The sluggard buries his hand in
the dish;
he will not even bring it back
to his mouth![z]

25Flog a mocker, and the simple
will learn prudence;
rebuke a discerning man, and
he will gain knowledge.[a]

26He who robs his father and
drives out his mother[b]
is a son who brings shame
and disgrace.

27Stop listening to instruction,
my son,

19:4 [a]Pr 14:20
19:5 [b]Ex 23:1 [c]Dt 19:19; Pr 21:28
19:6 [d]Pr 29:26 [e]Pr 17:8; 18:16
19:7 [f]ver 4; Ps 38:11
19:8 [g]Pr 16:20
19:9 [h]ver 5
19:10 [i]Pr 26:1 [j]Pr 30:21-23; Ecc 10:5-7
19:11 [k]Pr 16:32
19:12 [l]Ps 133:3 [m]Pr 16:14-15
19:13 [n]Pr 10:1 [o]Pr 21:9
19:14 [p]2Co 12:14 [q]Pr 18:22
19:15 [r]Pr 6:9; 10:4
19:16 [s]Pr 16:17; Lk 10:28
19:17 [t]Mt 10:42; 2Co 9:6-8
19:18 [u]Pr 13:24; 23:13-14
19:20 [v]Pr 4:1 [w]Pr 12:15
19:21 [x]Ps 33:11; Pr 16:9; Isa 14:24,27
19:23 [y]Ps 25:13; Pr 12:21; 1Ti 4:8
19:24 [z]Pr 26:15
19:25 [a]Pr 9:9; 21:11
19:26 [b]Pr 28:24

h7 The meaning of the Hebrew for this sentence is uncertain. i22 Or *A man's greed is his shame*

and you will stray from the
words of knowledge.

28A corrupt witness mocks at
justice,
and the mouth of the wicked
gulps down evil.[a]

29Penalties are prepared for
mockers,
and beatings for the backs of
fools.[b]

20 Wine is a mocker and beer
a brawler;
whoever is led astray by them
is not wise.[c]

2A king's wrath is like the roar
of a lion;[d]
he who angers him forfeits
his life.[e]

3It is to a man's honor to avoid
strife,
but every fool is quick to
quarrel.[f]

4A sluggard does not plow in
season;
so at harvest time he looks
but finds nothing.

5The purposes of a man's heart
are deep waters,
but a man of understanding
draws them out.

6Many a man claims to have
unfailing love,
but a faithful man who can
find?[g]

7The righteous man leads a
blameless life;
blessed are his children after
him.[h]

8When a king sits on his throne
to judge,
he winnows out all evil with
his eyes.[i]

9Who can say, "I have kept my
heart pure;
I am clean and without
sin"?[j]

10Differing weights and differing
measures—
the LORD detests them both.[k]

19:28 [a]Job 15:16
19:29 [b]Pr 26:3
20:1 [c]Pr 31:4
20:2 [d]Pr 19:12 [e]Pr 8:36
20:3 [f]Pr 17:14
20:6 [g]Ps 12:1
20:7 [h]Ps 37:25-26; 112:2
20:8 [i]ver 26; Pr 25:4-5
20:9 [j]1Ki 8:46; Ecc 7:20; 1Jn 1:8
20:10 [k]ver 23; Pr 11:1
20:11 [l]Mt 7:16
20:12 [m]Ps 94:9
20:13 [n]Pr 6:11; 19:15
20:16 [o]Ex 22:26 [p]Pr 27:13
20:17 [q]Pr 9:17
20:18 [r]Pr 11:14; 24:6
20:19 [s]Pr 11:13
20:20 [t]Pr 30:11 [u]Ex 21:17; Job 18:5
20:22 [v]Pr 24:29 [w]Ro 12:19

11Even a child is known by his
actions,
by whether his conduct is
pure[l] and right.

12Ears that hear and eyes that
see—
the LORD has made them
both.[m]

13Do not love sleep or you will
grow poor;[n]
stay awake and you will have
food to spare.

14"It's no good, it's no good!"
says the buyer;
then off he goes and boasts
about his purchase.

15Gold there is, and rubies in
abundance,
but lips that speak
knowledge are a rare
jewel.

16Take the garment of one who
puts up security for a
stranger;
hold it in pledge[o] if he does
it for a wayward
woman.[p]

17Food gained by fraud tastes
sweet to a man,[q]
but he ends up with a mouth
full of gravel.

18Make plans by seeking advice;
if you wage war, obtain
guidance.[r]

19A gossip betrays a confidence;[s]
so avoid a man who talks too
much.

20If a man curses his father or
mother,[t]
his lamp will be snuffed out
in pitch darkness.[u]

21An inheritance quickly gained
at the beginning
will not be blessed at the
end.

22Do not say, "I'll pay you back
for this wrong!"[v]
Wait for the LORD, and he will
deliver you.[w]

23The LORD detests differing
weights,

and dishonest scales do not please him.[a]

24A man's steps are directed by the LORD.
How then can anyone understand his own way?[b]

25It is a trap for a man to dedicate something rashly
and only later to consider his vows.[c]

26A wise king winnows out the wicked;
he drives the threshing wheel over them.[d]

27The lamp of the LORD searches the spirit of a man[i];
it searches out his inmost being.

28Love and faithfulness keep a king safe;
through love his throne is made secure.[e]

29The glory of young men is their strength,
gray hair the splendor of the old.[f]

30Blows and wounds cleanse[g] away evil,
and beatings purge the inmost being.

21 The king's heart is in the hand of the LORD;
he directs it like a watercourse wherever he pleases.

2All a man's ways seem right to him,
but the LORD weighs the heart.[h]

3To do what is right and just
is more acceptable to the LORD than sacrifice.[i]

4Haughty eyes[j] and a proud heart,
the lamp of the wicked, are sin!

5The plans of the diligent lead to profit[k]
as surely as haste leads to poverty.

6A fortune made by a lying tongue
is a fleeting vapor and a deadly snare.[k][l]

7The violence of the wicked will drag them away,
for they refuse to do what is right.

8The way of the guilty is devious,[m]
but the conduct of the innocent is upright.

9Better to live on a corner of the roof
than share a house with a quarrelsome wife.[n]

10The wicked man craves evil;
his neighbor gets no mercy from him.

11When a mocker is punished,
the simple gain wisdom;
when a wise man is instructed, he gets knowledge.[o]

12The Righteous One[l] takes note of the house of the wicked
and brings the wicked to ruin.[p]

13If a man shuts his ears to the cry of the poor,
he too will cry out and not be answered.[q]

14A gift given in secret soothes anger,
and a bribe concealed in the cloak pacifies great wrath.[r]

15When justice is done, it brings joy to the righteous
but terror to evildoers.[s]

16A man who strays from the path of understanding
comes to rest in the company of the dead.[t]

20:23 [a]ver 10
20:24 [b]Jer 10:23
20:25 [c]Ecc 5:2,4-5
20:26 [d]ver 8
20:28 [e]Pr 29:14
20:29 [f]Pr 16:31
20:30 [g]Pr 22:15
21:2 [h]Pr 16:2; 24:12; Lk 16:15
21:3 [i]1Sa 15:22; Pr 15:8; Isa 1:11; Hos 6:6; Mic 6:6-8
21:4 [j]Pr 6:17
21:5 [k]Pr 10:4; 28:22
21:6 [l]2Pe 2:3
21:8 [m]Pr 2:15
21:9 [n]Pr 25:24
21:11 [o]Pr 19:25
21:12 [p]Pr 14:11
21:13 [q]Mt 18:30-34; Jas 2:13
21:14 [r]Pr 18:16; 19:6
21:15 [s]Pr 10:29
21:16 [t]Ps 49:14

i27 Or *The spirit of man is the LORD's lamp*
k6 Some Hebrew manuscripts, Septuagint and Vulgate; most Hebrew manuscripts *vapor for those who seek death*
l12 Or *The righteous man*

[17]He who loves pleasure will
become poor;
whoever loves wine and oil
will never be rich.[a]

[18]The wicked become a ransom[b]
for the righteous,
and the unfaithful for the
upright.

[19]Better to live in a desert
than with a quarrelsome and
ill-tempered wife.[c]

[20]In the house of the wise are
stores of choice food and
oil,
but a foolish man devours all
he has.

[21]He who pursues righteousness
and love
finds life, prosperity[m] and
honor.[d]

[22]A wise man attacks the city of
the mighty[e]
and pulls down the
stronghold in which they
trust.

[23]He who guards his mouth[f] and
his tongue
keeps himself from
calamity.[g]

[24]The proud and arrogant[h]
man—"Mocker" is his
name;
he behaves with overweening
pride.

[25]The sluggard's craving will be
the death of him,[i]
because his hands refuse to
work.

[26]All day long he craves for more,
but the righteous give
without sparing.[j]

[27]The sacrifice of the wicked is
detestable[k]—
how much more so when
brought with evil
intent![l]

[28]A false witness will perish,[m]
and whoever listens to him
will be destroyed
forever.[n]

21:17 [a]Pr 23:20-21, 29-35
21:18 [b]Pr 11:8; Isa 43:3
21:19 [c]ver 9
21:21 [d]Mt 5:6
21:22 [e]Ecc 9:15-16
21:23 [f]Jas 3:2 [g]Pr 12:13; 13:3
21:24 [h]Ps 1:1; Pr 1:22; Isa 16:6; Jer 48:29
21:25 [i]Pr 13:4
21:26 [j]Ps 37:26; Mt 5:42; Eph 4:28
21:27 [k]Isa 66:3; Jer 6:20; Am 5:22 [l]Pr 15:8
21:28 [m]Pr 19:5
21:30 [n]Jer 9:23 [o]Isa 8:10; Ac 5:39
21:31 [p]Ps 3:8; 33:12-19; Isa 31:1
22:1 [q]Ecc 7:1
22:2 [r]Job 31:15
22:3 [s]Pr 14:16 [t]Pr 27:12
22:5 [u]Pr 15:19
22:6 [v]Eph 6:4
22:8 [w]Job 4:8 [x]Ps 125:3
22:9 [y]2Co 9:6 [z]Pr 19:17

[29]A wicked man puts up a bold
front,
but an upright man gives
thought to his ways.

[30]There is no wisdom,[n] no
insight, no plan
that can succeed against the
LORD.[o]

[31]The horse is made ready for the
day of battle,
but victory rests with the
LORD.[p]

22 A good name is more
desirable than great
riches;
to be esteemed is better than
silver or gold.[q]

[2]Rich and poor have this in
common:
The LORD is the Maker of
them all.[r]

[3]A prudent man sees danger and
takes refuge,[s]
but the simple keep going
and suffer for it.[t]

[4]Humility and the fear of the
LORD
bring wealth and honor and
life.

[5]In the paths of the wicked lie
thorns and snares,[u]
but he who guards his soul
stays far from them.

[6]Train[o] a child in the way he
should go,[v]
and when he is old he will
not turn from it.

[7]The rich rule over the poor,
and the borrower is servant
to the lender.

[8]He who sows wickedness reaps
trouble,[w]
and the rod of his fury will
be destroyed.[x]

[9]A generous man will himself be
blessed,[y]
for he shares his food with
the poor.[z]

[m]21 Or *righteousness* [n]28 Or / *but the words of an obedient man will live on* [o]6 Or *Start*

10Drive out the mocker, and out goes strife;
quarrels and insults are ended.[a]

11He who loves a pure heart and whose speech is gracious
will have the king for his friend.[b]

12The eyes of the LORD keep watch over knowledge,
but he frustrates the words of the unfaithful.

13The sluggard says, "There is a lion outside!"[c]
or, "I will be murdered in the streets!"

14The mouth of an adulteress is a deep pit;[d]
he who is under the LORD's wrath will fall into it.[e]

15Folly is bound up in the heart of a child,
but the rod of discipline will drive it far from him.[f]

16He who oppresses the poor to increase his wealth
and he who gives gifts to the rich—both come to poverty.

Sayings of the Wise

17Pay attention and listen to the sayings of the wise;[g]
apply your heart to what I teach,
18for it is pleasing when you keep them in your heart
and have all of them ready on your lips.
19So that your trust may be in the LORD,
I teach you today, even you.
20Have I not written thirty[p] sayings for you,
sayings of counsel and knowledge,
21teaching you true and reliable words,[h]
so that you can give sound answers
to him who sent you?

22Do not exploit the poor[i] because they are poor
and do not crush the needy in court,[j]
23for the LORD will take up their case[k]
and will plunder those who plunder them.[l]

24Do not make friends with a hot-tempered man,
do not associate with one easily angered,
25or you may learn his ways
and get yourself ensnared.[m]

26Do not be a man who strikes hands in pledge[n]
or puts up security for debts;
27if you lack the means to pay,
your very bed will be snatched from under you.[o]

28Do not move an ancient boundary stone[p]
set up by your forefathers.

29Do you see a man skilled in his work?
He will serve[q] before kings;
he will not serve before obscure men.

23 When you sit to dine with a ruler,
note well what[q] is before you,
2and put a knife to your throat
if you are given to gluttony.
3Do not crave his delicacies,[r]
for that food is deceptive.

4Do not wear yourself out to get rich;
have the wisdom to show restraint.
5Cast but a glance at riches, and they are gone,
for they will surely sprout wings
and fly off to the sky like an eagle.[s]

6Do not eat the food of a stingy man,
do not crave his delicacies;[t]
7for he is the kind of man

22:10 [a]Pr 18:6; 26:20
22:11 [b]Pr 16:13; Mt 5:8
22:13 [c]Pr 26:13
22:14 [d]Pr 2:16; 5:3-5; 7:5; 23:27 [e]Ecc 7:26
22:15 [f]Pr 13:24; 23:14
22:17 [g]Pr 5:1
22:21 [h]Lk 1:3-4; 1Pe 3:15
22:22 [i]Zec 7:10 [j]Ex 23:6; Mal 3:5
22:23 [k]Ps 12:5 [l]1Sa 25:39; Pr 23:10-11
22:25 [m]1Co 15:33
22:26 [n]Pr 11:15
22:27 [o]Pr 17:18
22:28 [p]Dt 19:14; Pr 23:10
22:29 [q]Ge 41:46
23:3 [r]ver 6-8
23:5 [s]Pr 27:24
23:6 [t]Ps 141:4

p20 *Or not formerly written;* or *not written excellent* q1 *Or who*

who is always thinking about
the cost.[r]
"Eat and drink," he says to
you,
but his heart is not with you.
8You will vomit up the little you
have eaten
and will have wasted your
compliments.

9Do not speak to a fool,
for he will scorn the wisdom
of your words.[a]

10Do not move an ancient
boundary stone[b]
or encroach on the fields of
the fatherless,
11for their Defender[c] is strong;
he will take up their case
against you.[d]

12Apply your heart to instruction
and your ears to words of
knowledge.

13Do not withhold discipline
from a child;
if you punish him with the
rod, he will not die.
14Punish him with the rod
and save his soul from
death.[s]

15My son, if your heart is wise,
then my heart will be glad;
16my inmost being will rejoice
when your lips speak what is
right.[e]

17Do not let your heart envy[f]
sinners,
but always be zealous for the
fear of the LORD.
18There is surely a future hope
for you,
and your hope will not be cut
off.[g]

19Listen, my son, and be wise,
and keep your heart on the
right path.
20Do not join those who drink
too much wine[h]
or gorge themselves on meat,
21for drunkards and gluttons
become poor,[i]
and drowsiness clothes them
in rags.

22Listen to your father, who gave
you life,
and do not despise your
mother when she is
old.[j]
23Buy the truth and do not sell
it;
get wisdom, discipline and
understanding.[k]
24The father of a righteous man
has great joy;
he who has a wise son
delights in him.[l]
25May your father and mother be
glad;
may she who gave you birth
rejoice!

26My son,[m] give me your heart
and let your eyes keep to my
ways,[n]
27for a prostitute is a deep pit[o]
and a wayward wife is a
narrow well.
28Like a bandit she lies in wait,[p]
and multiplies the unfaithful
among men.

29Who has woe? Who has sorrow?
Who has strife? Who has
complaints?
Who has needless bruises?
Who has bloodshot eyes?
30Those who linger over wine,[q]
who go to sample bowls of
mixed wine.
31Do not gaze at wine when it is
red,
when it sparkles in the cup,
when it goes down smoothly!
32In the end it bites like a snake
and poisons like a viper.
33Your eyes will see strange
sights
and your mind imagine
confusing things.
34You will be like one sleeping
on the high seas,
lying on top of the rigging.
35"They hit me," you will say,
"but I'm not hurt!
They beat me, but I don't
feel it!
When will I wake up
so I can find another drink?"

23:9 [a]Pr 1:7; 9:7; Mt 7:6
23:10 [b]Dt 19:14; Pr 22:28
23:11 [c]Job 19:25 [d]Pr 22:22-23
23:16 [e]ver 24; Pr 27:11
23:17 [f]Ps 37:1; Pr 28:14
23:18 [g]Ps 9:18; Pr 24:14, 19-20
23:20 [h]Isa 5:11,22; Ro 13:13; Eph 5:18
23:21 [i]Pr 21:17
23:22 [j]Lev 19:32; Pr 1:8; 30:17; Eph 6:1-2
23:23 [k]Pr 4:7
23:24 [l]ver 15-16; Pr 10:1; 15:20
23:26 [m]Pr 3:1; 5:1-6 [n]Ps 18:21; Pr 4:4
23:27 [o]Pr 22:14
23:28 [p]Pr 7:11-12; Ecc 7:26
23:30 [q]Ps 75:8; Isa 5:11; Eph 5:18

[r]7 Or *for as he thinks within himself, / so he is*; or *for as he puts on a feast, / so he is*
[s]14 Hebrew *Sheol*

24 Do not envy[a] wicked
men,
do not desire their company;
2for their hearts plot violence,
and their lips talk about
making trouble.[b]

3By wisdom a house is built,[c]
and through understanding it
is established;
4through knowledge its rooms
are filled
with rare and beautiful
treasures.[d]

5A wise man has great power,
and a man of knowledge
increases strength;
6for waging war you need
guidance,
and for victory many
advisers.[e]

7Wisdom is too high for a fool;
in the assembly at the gate
he has nothing to say.

8He who plots evil
will be known as a schemer.
9The schemes of folly are sin,
and men detest a mocker.

10If you falter in times of trouble,
how small is your strength![f]
11Rescue those being led away to
death;
hold back those staggering
toward slaughter.[g]
12If you say, "But we knew
nothing about this,"
does not he who weighs[h] the
heart perceive it?
Does not he who guards your
life know it?
Will he not repay each
person according to what
he has done?[i]

13Eat honey, my son, for it is
good;
honey from the comb is
sweet to your taste.
14Know also that wisdom is
sweet to your soul;
if you find it, there is a
future hope for you,
and your hope will not be cut
off.[j][k]

15Do not lie in wait like an

24:1 [a]Ps 37:1; 73:3; Pr 3:31-32; 23:17-18
24:2 [b]Ps 10:7
24:3 [c]Pr 14:1
24:4 [d]Pr 8:21
24:6 [e]Pr 11:14; 20:18; Lk 14:31
24:10 [f]Job 4:5; Jer 51:46; Heb 12:3
24:11 [g]Ps 82:4; Isa 58:6-7
24:12 [h]Pr 21:2 [i]Job 34:11; Ps 62:12; Ro 2:6*
24:14 [j]Ps 119:103; Pr 16:24 [k]Pr 23:18
24:16 [l]Job 5:19; Ps 34:19; Mic 7:8
24:17 [m]Ob 1:12 [n]Job 31:29
24:19 [o]Ps 37:1
24:20 [p]Job 18:5; Pr 13:9; 23:17-18
24:21 [q]Ro 13:1-5; 1Pe 2:17
24:23 [r]Pr 1:6 [s]Lev 19:15 [t]Pr 28:21
24:24 [u]Pr 17:15

outlaw against a
righteous man's house,
do not raid his dwelling
place;
16for though a righteous man
falls seven times, he
rises again,
but the wicked are brought
down by calamity.[l]

17Do not gloat[m] when your
enemy falls;
when he stumbles, do not let
your heart rejoice,[n]
18or the LORD will see and
disapprove
and turn his wrath away from
him.

19Do not fret[o] because of evil
men
or be envious of the wicked,
20for the evil man has no future
hope,
and the lamp of the wicked
will be snuffed out.[p]

21Fear the LORD and the king,[q]
my son,
and do not join with the
rebellious,
22for those two will send sudden
destruction upon them,
and who knows what
calamities they can
bring?

Further Sayings of the Wise

23These also are sayings of the
wise:[r]

To show partiality[s] in judging
is not good:[t]
24Whoever says to the guilty,
"You are innocent"[u]—
peoples will curse him and
nations denounce him.
25But it will go well with those
who convict the guilty,
and rich blessing will come
upon them.

26An honest answer
is like a kiss on the lips.

27Finish your outdoor work
and get your fields ready;
after that, build your house.

28Do not testify against your

neighbor without
cause,[a]
or use your lips to deceive.
29Do not say, "I'll do to him as
he has done to me;
I'll pay that man back for
what he did."[b]

30I went past the field of the
sluggard,[c]
past the vineyard of the man
who lacks judgment;
31thorns had come up
everywhere,
the ground was covered with
weeds,
and the stone wall was in
ruins.
32I applied my heart to what I
observed
and learned a lesson from
what I saw:
33A little sleep, a little slumber,
a little folding of the hands
to rest[d]—
34and poverty will come on you
like a bandit
and scarcity like an armed
man.[t][e]

More Proverbs of Solomon

25 These are more proverbs[f] of Solomon, copied by the men of Hezekiah king of Judah:[g]

2It is the glory of God to conceal
a matter;
to search out a matter is the
glory of kings.[h]

3As the heavens are high and
the earth is deep,
so the hearts of kings are
unsearchable.

4Remove the dross from the
silver,
and out comes material for[u]
the silversmith;
5remove the wicked from the
king's presence,[i]
and his throne will be
established[j] through
righteousness.[k]

6Do not exalt yourself in the
king's presence,
and do not claim a place
among great men;

24:28 [a]Ps 7:4; Pr 25:18; Eph 4:25
24:29 [b]Pr 20:22; Mt 5:38-41; Ro 12:17
24:30 [c]Pr 6:6-11; 26:13-16
24:33 [d]Pr 6:10
24:34 [e]Pr 10:4; Ecc 10:18
25:1 [f]1Ki 4:32 [g]Pr 1:1
25:2 [h]Pr 16:10-15
25:5 [i]Pr 20:8 [j]2Sa 7:13 [k]Pr 16:12; 29:14
25:7 [l]Lk 14:7-10
25:8 [m]Mt 5:25-26
25:11 [n]ver 12; Pr 15:23
25:12 [o]ver 11; Ps 141:5; Pr 13:18; 15:31
25:13 [p]Pr 10:26; 13:17
25:15 [q]Ecc 10:4 [r]Pr 15:1
25:16 [s]ver 27

7it is better for him to say to
you, "Come up here,"[l]
than for him to humiliate
you before a nobleman.

What you have seen with your
eyes
8 do not bring[v] hastily to
court,
for what will you do in the end
if your neighbor puts you to
shame?[m]

9If you argue your case with a
neighbor,
do not betray another man's
confidence,
10or he who hears it may shame
you
and you will never lose your
bad reputation.

11A word aptly spoken
is like apples of gold in
settings of silver.[n]

12Like an earring of gold or an
ornament of fine gold
is a wise man's rebuke to a
listening ear.[o]

13Like the coolness of snow at
harvest time
is a trustworthy messenger to
those who send him;
he refreshes the spirit of his
masters.[p]

14Like clouds and wind without
rain
is a man who boasts of gifts
he does not give.

15Through patience a ruler can
be persuaded,[q]
and a gentle tongue can
break a bone.[r]

16If you find honey, eat just
enough—
too much of it, and you will
vomit.[s]
17Seldom set foot in your
neighbor's house—
too much of you, and he will
hate you.

[t]34 *Or like a vagrant / and scarcity like a beggar* [u]4 *Or comes a vessel from*
[v]7,8 *Or nobleman / on whom you had set your eyes. /* [8]*Do not go*

18Like a club or a sword or a sharp arrow
is the man who gives false testimony against his neighbor.[a]

19Like a bad tooth or a lame foot
is reliance on the unfaithful in times of trouble.

20Like one who takes away a garment on a cold day,
or like vinegar poured on soda,
is one who sings songs to a heavy heart.

21If your enemy is hungry, give him food to eat;
if he is thirsty, give him water to drink.

22In doing this, you will heap burning coals[b] on his head,
and the LORD will reward you.[c]

23As a north wind brings rain,
so a sly tongue brings angry looks.

24Better to live on a corner of the roof
than share a house with a quarrelsome wife.[d]

25Like cold water to a weary soul
is good news from a distant land.[e]

26Like a muddied spring or a polluted well
is a righteous man who gives way to the wicked.

27It is not good to eat too much honey,[f]
nor is it honorable to seek one's own honor.[g]

28Like a city whose walls are broken down
is a man who lacks self-control.

26

Like snow in summer or rain[h] in harvest,
honor is not fitting for a fool.[i]

2Like a fluttering sparrow or a darting swallow,
an undeserved curse does not come to rest.[j]

3A whip for the horse, a halter for the donkey,[k]
and a rod for the backs of fools![l]

4Do not answer a fool according to his folly,
or you will be like him yourself.[m]

5Answer a fool according to his folly,
or he will be wise in his own eyes.[n]

6Like cutting off one's feet or drinking violence
is the sending of a message by the hand of a fool.[o]

7Like a lame man's legs that hang limp
is a proverb in the mouth of a fool.[p]

8Like tying a stone in a sling
is the giving of honor to a fool.[q]

9Like a thornbush in a drunkard's hand
is a proverb in the mouth of a fool.[r]

10Like an archer who wounds at random
is he who hires a fool or any passer-by.

11As a dog returns to its vomit,[s]
so a fool repeats his folly.[t]

12Do you see a man wise in his own eyes?[u]
There is more hope for a fool than for him.[v]

13The sluggard says,[w] "There is a lion in the road,
a fierce lion roaming the streets!"[x]

14As a door turns on its hinges,
so a sluggard turns on his bed.[y]

15The sluggard buries his hand in the dish;
he is too lazy to bring it back to his mouth.[z]

25:18 [a] Ps 57:4; Pr 12:18
25:22 [b] Ps 18:8 [c] 2Sa 16:12; 2Ch 28:15; Mt 5:44; Ro 12:20*
25:24 [d] Pr 21:9
25:25 [e] Pr 15:30
25:27 [f] ver 16 [g] Pr 27:2; Mt 23:12
26:1 [h] 1Sa 12:17 [i] ver 8; Pr 19:10
26:2 [j] Nu 23:8; Dt 23:5
26:3 [k] Ps 32:9 [l] Pr 10:13
26:4 [m] ver 5; Isa 36:21
26:5 [n] ver 4; Pr 3:7
26:6 [o] Pr 10:26
26:7 [p] ver 9
26:8 [q] ver 1
26:9 [r] ver 7
26:11 [s] 2Pe 2:22* [t] Ex 8:15; Ps 85:8
26:12 [u] Pr 3:7 [v] Pr 29:20
26:13 [w] Pr 6:6-11; 24:30-34 [x] Pr 22:13
26:14 [y] Pr 6:9
26:15 [z] Pr 19:24

16 The sluggard is wiser in his own eyes
than seven men who answer discreetly.

17 Like one who seizes a dog by the ears
is a passer-by who meddles in a quarrel not his own.

18 Like a madman shooting
firebrands or deadly arrows
19 is a man who deceives his neighbor
and says, "I was only joking!"

20 Without wood a fire goes out;
without gossip a quarrel dies down.[a]

21 As charcoal to embers and as wood to fire,
so is a quarrelsome man for kindling strife.[b]

22 The words of a gossip are like choice morsels;
they go down to a man's inmost parts.[c]

23 Like a coating of glaze[w] over earthenware
are fervent lips with an evil heart.

24 A malicious man disguises himself with his lips,[d]
but in his heart he harbors deceit.[e]
25 Though his speech is charming,[f] do not believe him,
for seven abominations fill his heart.[g]
26 His malice may be concealed by deception,
but his wickedness will be exposed in the assembly.

27 If a man digs a pit,[h] he will fall into it;[i]
if a man rolls a stone, it will roll back on him.[j]

28 A lying tongue hates those it hurts,
and a flattering mouth[k] works ruin.

27

Do not boast[l] about tomorrow,
for you do not know what a day may bring forth.[m]

2 Let another praise you, and not your own mouth;
someone else, and not your own lips.[n]

3 Stone is heavy and sand[o] a burden,
but provocation by a fool is heavier than both.

4 Anger is cruel and fury overwhelming,
but who can stand before jealousy?[p]

5 Better is open rebuke
than hidden love.

6 Wounds from a friend can be trusted,
but an enemy multiplies kisses.[q]

7 He who is full loathes honey,
but to the hungry even what is bitter tastes sweet.

8 Like a bird that strays from its nest[r]
is a man who strays from his home.

9 Perfume[s] and incense bring joy to the heart,
and the pleasantness of one's friend springs from his earnest counsel.

10 Do not forsake your friend and the friend of your father,
and do not go to your brother's house when disaster[t] strikes you—
better a neighbor nearby than a brother far away.
11 Be wise, my son, and bring joy to my heart;[u]
then I can answer anyone who treats me with contempt.[v]

12 The prudent see danger and take refuge,
but the simple keep going and suffer for it.[w]

13 Take the garment of one who

26:20 [a] Pr 22:10
26:21 [b] Pr 14:17; 15:18
26:22 [c] Pr 18:8
26:24 [d] Ps 31:18 [e] Ps 41:6; Pr 10:18; 12:20
26:25 [f] Ps 28:3 [g] Jer 9:4-8
26:27 [h] Ps 7:15 [i] Est 6:13 [j] Est 2:23; 7:9; Ps 35:8; 141:10; Pr 28:10; 29:6; Isa 50:11
26:28 [k] Ps 12:3; Pr 29:5
27:1 [l] 1Ki 20:11 [m] Mt 6:34; Lk 12:19-20; Jas 4:13-16
27:2 [n] Pr 25:27
27:3 [o] Job 6:3
27:4 [p] Nu 5:14
27:6 [q] Ps 141:5; Pr 28:23
27:8 [r] Isa 16:2
27:9 [s] Est 2:12; Ps 45:8
27:10 [t] Pr 17:17; 18:24
27:11 [u] Pr 10:1; 23:15-16 [v] Ge 24:60
27:12 [w] Pr 22:3

[w] *23* With a different word division of the Hebrew; Masoretic Text *of silver dross*

puts up security for a
stranger;
hold it in pledge if he does it
for a wayward woman.[a]

14If a man loudly blesses his
neighbor early in the
morning,
it will be taken as a curse.

15A quarrelsome wife is like
a constant dripping[b] on a
rainy day;
16restraining her is like
restraining the wind
or grasping oil with the hand.

17As iron sharpens iron,
so one man sharpens
another.

18He who tends a fig tree will eat
its fruit,[c]
and he who looks after his
master will be honored.[d]

19As water reflects a face,
so a man's heart reflects the
man.

20Death and Destruction[x] are
never satisfied,[e]
and neither are the eyes of
man.[f]

21The crucible for silver and the
furnace for gold,[g]
but man is tested by the
praise he receives.

22Though you grind a fool in a
mortar,
grinding him like grain with a
pestle,
you will not remove his folly
from him.

23Be sure you know the condition
of your flocks,[h]
give careful attention to your
herds;
24for riches do not endure
forever,[i]
and a crown is not secure for
all generations.
25When the hay is removed and
new growth appears
and the grass from the hills
is gathered in,
26the lambs will provide you with
clothing,

27:13 [a]Pr 20:16
27:15 [b]Est 1:18; Pr 19:13
27:18 [c]1Co 9:7 [d]Lk 19:12-27
27:20 [e]Pr 30:15-16; Hab 2:5 [f]Ecc 1:8; 6:7
27:21 [g]Pr 17:3
27:23 [h]Pr 12:10
27:24 [i]Pr 23:5
28:1 [j]2Ki 7:7 [k]Lev 26:17; Ps 53:5 [l]Ps 138:3
28:6 [m]Pr 19:1
28:7 [n]Pr 23:19-21
28:8 [o]Ex 18:21 [p]Job 27:17; Pr 13:22 [q]Ps 112:9; Pr 14:31; Lk 14:12-14
28:9 [r]Ps 66:18; 109:7; Pr 15:8; Isa 1:13
28:10 [s]Pr 26:27

and the goats with the price
of a field.
27You will have plenty of goats'
milk
to feed you and your family
and to nourish your servant
girls.

28 The wicked man flees[j]
though no one pursues,[k]
but the righteous are as bold
as a lion.[l]

2When a country is rebellious, it
has many rulers,
but a man of understanding
and knowledge
maintains order.

3A ruler[y] who oppresses the
poor
is like a driving rain that
leaves no crops.

4Those who forsake the law
praise the wicked,
but those who keep the law
resist them.

5Evil men do not understand
justice,
but those who seek the LORD
understand it fully.

6Better a poor man whose walk
is blameless
than a rich man whose ways
are perverse.[m]

7He who keeps the law is a
discerning son,
but a companion of gluttons
disgraces his father.[n]

8He who increases his wealth by
exorbitant interest[o]
amasses it for another,[p] who
will be kind to the
poor.[q]

9If anyone turns a deaf ear to
the law,
even his prayers are
detestable.[r]

10He who leads the upright along
an evil path
will fall into his own trap,[s]

[x]20 Hebrew *Sheol and Abaddon* [y]3 Or *A poor man*

but the blameless will receive
a good inheritance.

11A rich man may be wise in his
own eyes,
but a poor man who has
discernment sees
through him.

12When the righteous triumph,
there is great elation;[a]
but when the wicked rise to
power, men go into
hiding.[b]

13He who conceals his sins[c]
does not prosper,
but whoever confesses and
renounces them finds
mercy.[d]

14Blessed is the man who always
fears the LORD,
but he who hardens his heart
falls into trouble.

15Like a roaring lion or a
charging bear
is a wicked man ruling over a
helpless people.

16A tyrannical ruler lacks
judgment,
but he who hates ill-gotten
gain will enjoy a long
life.

17A man tormented by the guilt
of murder
will be a fugitive[e] till death;
let no one support him.

18He whose walk is blameless is
kept safe,
but he whose ways are
perverse will suddenly
fall.[f]

19He who works his land will
have abundant food,
but the one who chases
fantasies will have his
fill of poverty.[g]

20A faithful man will be richly
blessed,
but one eager to get rich will
not go unpunished.[h]

21To show partiality is not
good[i]—
yet a man will do wrong for a
piece of bread.[j]

22A stingy man is eager to get
rich
and is unaware that poverty
awaits him.[k]

23He who rebukes a man will in
the end gain more favor
than he who has a flattering
tongue.[l]

24He who robs his father or
mother[m]
and says, "It's not wrong"—
he is partner to him who
destroys.[n]

25A greedy man stirs up
dissension,
but he who trusts in the
LORD[o] will prosper.

26He who trusts in himself is a
fool,[p]
but he who walks in wisdom
is kept safe.

27He who gives to the poor will
lack nothing,[q]
but he who closes his eyes to
them receives many
curses.

28When the wicked rise to power,
people go into hiding;[r]
but when the wicked perish,
the righteous thrive.

29

A man who remains
stiff-necked after many
rebukes
will suddenly be
destroyed—without
remedy.[s]

2When the righteous thrive, the
people rejoice;[t]
when the wicked rule, the
people groan.[u]

3A man who loves wisdom
brings joy to his father,[v]
but a companion of
prostitutes squanders his
wealth.[w]

4By justice a king gives a
country stability,[x]
but one who is greedy for
bribes tears it down.

28:12 [a] 2Ki 11:20 [b] Pr 11:10; 29:2
28:13 [c] Job 31:33 [d] Ps 32:1-5; 1Jn 1:9
28:17 [e] Ge 9:6
28:18 [f] Pr 10:9
28:19 [g] Pr 12:11
28:20 [h] ver 22; Pr 10:6; 1Ti 6:9
28:21 [i] Pr 18:5 [j] Eze 13:19
28:22 [k] ver 20; Pr 23:6
28:23 [l] Pr 27:5-6
28:24 [m] Pr 19:26 [n] Pr 18:9
28:25 [o] Pr 29:25
28:26 [p] Ps 4:5; Pr 3:5
28:27 [q] Dt 15:7; 24:19; Pr 19:17; 22:9
28:28 [r] ver 12
29:1 [s] 2Ch 36:16; Pr 6:15
29:2 [t] Est 8:15 [u] Pr 28:12
29:3 [v] Pr 10:1 [w] Pr 5:8-10; Lk 15:11-32
29:4 [x] Pr 8:15-16

5Whoever flatters his neighbor
is spreading a net for his
feet.
6An evil man is snared by his
own sin,[a]
but a righteous one can sing
and be glad.
7The righteous care about
justice for the poor,[b]
but the wicked have no such
concern.
8Mockers stir up a city,
but wise men turn away
anger.[c]
9If a wise man goes to court
with a fool,
the fool rages and scoffs, and
there is no peace.
10Bloodthirsty men hate a man of
integrity
and seek to kill the upright.[d]
11A fool gives full vent to his
anger,
but a wise man keeps
himself under control.[e]
12If a ruler listens to lies,
all his officials become
wicked.
13The poor man and the
oppressor have this in
common:
The LORD gives sight to the
eyes of both.[f]
14If a king judges the poor with
fairness,
his throne will always be
secure.[g]
15The rod of correction imparts
wisdom,
but a child left to himself
disgraces his mother.[h]
16When the wicked thrive, so
does sin,
but the righteous will see
their downfall.[i]
17Discipline your son, and he will
give you peace;
he will bring delight to your
soul.[j]
18Where there is no revelation,

29:6 [a]Ecc 9:12
29:7 [b]Job 29:16; Ps 41:1; Pr 31:8-9
29:8 [c]Pr 11:11; 16:14
29:10 [d]1Jn 3:12
29:11 [e]Pr 12:16; 19:11
29:13 [f]Pr 22:2; Mt 5:45
29:14 [g]Ps 72:1-5; Pr 16:12
29:15 [h]Pr 10:1; 13:24; 17:21, 25
29:16 [i]Ps 37:35-36; 58:10; 91:8; 92:11
29:17 [j]ver 15; Pr 10:1
29:18 [k]Ps 1:1-2; 119:1-2; Jn 13:17
29:20 [l]Pr 26:12; Jas 1:19
29:22 [m]Pr 14:17; 15:18; 26:21
29:23 [n]Pr 11:2; 15:33; 16:18; Isa 66:2; Mt 23:12
29:24 [o]Lev 5:1
29:25 [p]Pr 28:25
29:26 [q]Pr 19:6
29:27 [r]ver 10

the people cast off
restraint;
but blessed is he who keeps
the law.[k]
19A servant cannot be corrected
by mere words;
though he understands, he
will not respond.
20Do you see a man who speaks
in haste?
There is more hope for a fool
than for him.[l]
21If a man pampers his servant
from youth,
he will bring grief[z] in the
end.
22An angry man stirs up
dissension,
and a hot-tempered one
commits many sins.[m]
23A man's pride brings him low,
but a man of lowly spirit
gains honor.[n]
24The accomplice of a thief is his
own enemy;
he is put under oath and
dare not testify.[o]
25Fear of man will prove to be a
snare,
but whoever trusts in the
LORD[p] is kept safe.
26Many seek an audience with a
ruler,[q]
but it is from the LORD that
man gets justice.
27The righteous detest the
dishonest;
the wicked detest the
upright.[r]

Sayings of Agur

30 The sayings of Agur son of
Jakeh—an oracle[a]:

This man declared to Ithiel,
to Ithiel and to Ucal:[b]

[z]*21* The meaning of the Hebrew for this word is uncertain. [a]*1* Or *Jakeh of Massa*
[b]*1* Masoretic Text; with a different word division of the Hebrew *declared, "I am weary, O God; / I am weary, O God, and faint.*

2"I am the most ignorant of
men;
I do not have a man's
understanding.
3I have not learned wisdom,
nor have I knowledge of the
Holy One.[a]
4Who has gone up[b] to heaven
and come down?
Who has gathered up the
wind in the hollow[c] of
his hands?
Who has wrapped up the
waters[d] in his cloak?[e]
Who has established all the
ends of the earth?
What is his name,[f] and the
name of his son?
Tell me if you know!

5"Every word of God is
flawless;[g]
he is a shield[h] to those who
take refuge in him.
6Do not add[i] to his words,
or he will rebuke you and
prove you a liar.

7"Two things I ask of you,
O LORD;
do not refuse me before I
die:
8Keep falsehood and lies far
from me;
give me neither poverty nor
riches,
but give me only my daily
bread.[j]
9Otherwise, I may have too
much and disown[k] you
and say, 'Who is the LORD?'[l]
Or I may become poor and
steal,
and so dishonor the name of
my God.[m]

10"Do not slander a servant to his
master,
or he will curse you, and you
will pay for it.

11"There are those who curse
their fathers
and do not bless their
mothers;[n]
12those who are pure in their
own eyes[o]

30:3 [a]Pr 9:10
30:4 [b]Ps 24:1-2; Jn 3:13; Eph 4:7-10 [c]Ps 104:3; Isa 40:12 [d]Job 26:8; 38:8-9 [e]Ge 1:2 [f]Rev 19:12
30:5 [g]Ps 12:6; 18:30 [h]Ge 15:1; Ps 84:11
30:6 [i]Dt 4:2; 12:32; Rev 22:18
30:8 [j]Mt 6:11
30:9 [k]Jos 24:27; Isa 1:4; 59:13 [l]Dt 6:12; 8:10-14; Hos 13:6 [m]Dt 8:12
30:11 [n]Pr 20:20
30:12 [o]Pr 16:2; Lk 18:11 [p]Jer 2:23,35
30:13 [q]2Sa 22:28; Job 41:34; Ps 131:1; Pr 6:17
30:14 [r]Job 4:11; 29:17; Ps 3:7 [s]Ps 57:4 [t]Job 24:9; Ps 14:4 [u]Am 8:4; Mic 2:2 [v]Job 19:22
30:15 [w]Pr 27:20
30:16 [x]Pr 27:20; Isa 5:14; 14:9, 11; Hab 2:5
30:17 [y]Dt 21:18-21; Pr 23:22 [z]Job 15:23
30:20 [a]Pr 5:6
30:22 [b]Pr 19:10; 29:2

and yet are not cleansed of
their filth;[p]
13those whose eyes are ever so
haughty,[q]
whose glances are so
disdainful;
14those whose teeth[r] are swords
and whose jaws are set with
knives[s]
to devour[t] the poor[u] from the
earth,
the needy from among
mankind.[v]

15"The leech has two daughters.
'Give! Give!' they cry.

"There are three things that are
never satisfied,[w]
four that never say,
'Enough!':
16the grave,[c][x] the barren womb,
land, which is never satisfied
with water,
and fire, which never says,
'Enough!'

17"The eye that mocks[y] a father,
that scorns obedience to a
mother,
will be pecked out by the
ravens of the valley,
will be eaten by the
vultures.[z]

18"There are three things that are
too amazing for me,
four that I do not
understand:
19the way of an eagle in the sky,
the way of a snake on a rock,
the way of a ship on the high
seas,
and the way of a man with a
maiden.

20"This is the way of an
adulteress:
She eats and wipes her
mouth
and says, 'I've done nothing
wrong.'[a]

21"Under three things the earth
trembles,
under four it cannot bear up:
22a servant who becomes king,[b]
a fool who is full of food,

[c]16 Hebrew *Sheol*

23an unloved woman who is married,
and a maidservant who displaces her mistress.

24"Four things on earth are small,
yet they are extremely wise:
25Ants are creatures of little strength,
yet they store up their food in the summer;[a]
26coneys[d][b] are creatures of little power,
yet they make their home in the crags;
27locusts[c] have no king,
yet they advance together in ranks;
28a lizard can be caught with the hand,
yet it is found in kings' palaces.

29"There are three things that are stately in their stride,
four that move with stately bearing:
30a lion, mighty among beasts,
who retreats before nothing;
31a strutting rooster, a he-goat,
and a king with his army around him.[e]

32"If you have played the fool and exalted yourself,
or if you have planned evil,
clap your hand over your mouth![d]
33For as churning the milk produces butter,
and as twisting the nose produces blood,
so stirring up anger produces strife."

Sayings of King Lemuel

31 The sayings[e] of King Lemuel—an oracle[f] his mother taught him:

2"O my son, O son of my womb,
O son of my vows,[g][f]
3do not spend your strength on women,
your vigor on those who ruin kings.[g]

4"It is not for kings, O Lemuel—
not for kings to drink wine,[h]
not for rulers to crave beer,
5lest they drink[i] and forget what the law decrees,[j]
and deprive all the oppressed of their rights.
6Give beer to those who are perishing,
wine[k] to those who are in anguish;
7let them drink[l] and forget their poverty
and remember their misery no more.

8"Speak[m] up for those who cannot speak for themselves,
for the rights of all who are destitute.
9Speak up and judge fairly;
defend the rights of the poor and needy."[n]

Epilogue: The Wife of Noble Character

10[h]A wife of noble character[o] who can find?[p]
She is worth far more than rubies.
11Her husband[q] has full confidence in her
and lacks nothing of value.[r]
12She brings him good, not harm,
all the days of her life.
13She selects wool and flax
and works with eager hands.[s]
14She is like the merchant ships,
bringing her food from afar.
15She gets up while it is still dark;
she provides food for her family
and portions for her servant girls.
16She considers a field and buys it;
out of her earnings she plants a vineyard.

30:25 [a]Pr 6:6-8
30:26 [b]Ps 104:18
30:27 [c]Ex 10:4
30:32 [d]Job 21:5; 29:9
31:1 [e]Pr 22:17
31:2 [f]Jdg 11:30; Isa 49:15
31:3 [g]Dt 17:17; 1Ki 11:3; Ne 13:26; Pr 5:1-14
31:4 [h]Pr 20:1; Ecc 10:16-17; Isa 5:22
31:5 [i]1Ki 16:9 [j]Pr 16:12; Hos 4:11
31:6 [k]Ge 14:18
31:7 [l]Est 1:10
31:8 [m]1Sa 19:4; Job 29:12-17
31:9 [n]Lev 19:15; Dt 1:16; Pr 24:23; 29:7; Isa 1:17; Jer 22:16
31:10 [o]Ru 3:11; Pr 12:4; 18:22 [p]Pr 8:35; 19:14
31:11 [q]Ge 2:18 [r]Pr 12:4
31:13 [s]1Ti 2:9-10

[d]*26* That is, the hyrax or rock badger
[e]*31* Or *king secure against revolt*
[f]*1* Or *of Lemuel king of Massa, which*
[g]*2* Or */ the answer to my prayers*
[h]*10* Verses 10-31 are an acrostic, each verse beginning with a successive letter of the Hebrew alphabet.

[17]She sets about her work
vigorously;
her arms are strong for her
tasks.
[18]She sees that her trading is
profitable,
and her lamp does not go out
at night.
[19]In her hand she holds the
distaff
and grasps the spindle with
her fingers.
[20]She opens her arms to the
poor
and extends her hands to
the needy.[a]
[21]When it snows, she has no fear
for her household;
for all of them are clothed in
scarlet.
[22]She makes coverings for her
bed;
she is clothed in fine linen
and purple.
[23]Her husband is respected at
the city gate,
where he takes his seat
among the elders[b] of
the land.

31:20
[a]Dt 15:11; Eph 4:28; Heb 13:16

31:23
[b]Ex 3:16; Ru 4:1,11; Pr 12:4

31:26
[c]Pr 10:31

31:31
[d]Pr 11:16

[24]She makes linen garments and
sells them,
and supplies the merchants
with sashes.
[25]She is clothed with strength
and dignity;
she can laugh at the days to
come.
[26]She speaks with wisdom,
and faithful instruction is on
her tongue.[c]
[27]She watches over the affairs of
her household
and does not eat the bread of
idleness.
[28]Her children arise and call her
blessed;
her husband also, and he
praises her:
[29]"Many women do noble things,
but you surpass them all."
[30]Charm is deceptive, and beauty
is fleeting;
but a woman who fears the
LORD is to be praised.
[31]Give her the reward she has
earned,
and let her works bring her
praise[d] at the city gate.

Ecclesiastes

Title and Background

The writer's title ("Teacher") comes from a Hebrew root word related to "assembly" or "congregation." Perhaps the Teacher also held an office in the assembly. The Septuagint word for "Teacher" is *ecclesiastes,* from which most English titles of the book are taken.

Author and Date of Writing

No time period or writer's name is mentioned in the book, but several passages strongly suggest that Solomon is the author. Though some date the book as late as the third century B.C., Solomonic authorship would demand a date of the tenth century B.C.

Theme and Message

Life not centered on God is purposeless and meaningless. Without him, nothing else can satisfy (2:25). With him, all of life and his other good gifts are to be gratefully received and used and enjoyed to the full (2:26; 11:8). The book contains the philosophical and theological reflections of an old man, most of whose life was meaningless because he had not himself relied on God.

Outline

I. Introduction: Working to Accumulate Things to Achieve Happiness Is Profitless (1:1-11)
II. Life Is to Be Enjoyed as a Gift From God (1:12-11:6)
III. Man Should Begin Enjoying Life in His Youth, Remembering That God Will Judge (11:7-12:7)
IV. Conclusion: Reverently Trust in and Obey God (12:8-14)

Everything Is Meaningless

1 The words of the Teacher,[a][a] son of David, king in Jerusalem:[b]

2"Meaningless! Meaningless!"
says the Teacher.
"Utterly meaningless!
Everything is meaningless."[c]

3What does man gain from all
his labor
at which he toils under the
sun?[d]
4Generations come and
generations go,
but the earth remains
forever.[e]
5The sun rises and the sun sets,
and hurries back to where it
rises.[f]
6The wind blows to the south
and turns to the north;
round and round it goes,
ever returning on its course.
7All streams flow into the sea,
yet the sea is never full.
To the place the streams come
from,
there they return again.[g]
8All things are wearisome,
more than one can say.
The eye never has enough of
seeing,[h]
nor the ear its fill of hearing.
9What has been will be again,
what has been done will be
done again;[i]

1:1 [a]ver 12; Ecc 7:27; 12:10 [b]Pr 1:1
1:2 [c]Ps 39:5-6; 62:9; 144:4; Ecc 12:8; Ro 8:20-21
1:3 [d]Ecc 2:11,22; 3:9; 5:15-16
1:4 [e]Ps 104:5; 119:90
1:5 [f]Ps 19:5-6
1:7 [g]Job 36:28
1:8 [h]Pr 27:20
1:9 [i]Ecc 2:12; 3:15

[a]*1* Or *leader of the assembly;* also in verses 2 and 12

there is nothing new under
the sun.
10Is there anything of which one
can say,
"Look! This is something
new"?
It was here already, long ago;
it was here before our time.
11There is no remembrance of
men of old,
and even those who are yet
to come
will not be remembered
by those who follow.[a]

Wisdom Is Meaningless

12I, the Teacher,[b] was king over
Israel in Jerusalem. 13I devoted
myself to study and to explore by
wisdom all that is done under heav-
en. What a heavy burden God has
laid on men![c] 14I have seen all the
things that are done under the sun;
all of them are meaningless, a
chasing after the wind.[d]

15What is twisted cannot be
straightened;[e]
what is lacking cannot be
counted.

16I thought to myself, "Look, I
have grown and increased in wisdom more than anyone who has
ruled over Jerusalem before me;[f] I
have experienced much of wisdom
and knowledge." 17Then I applied
myself to the understanding of wisdom,[g] and also of madness and
folly,[h] but I learned that this, too,
is a chasing after the wind.

18For with much wisdom comes
much sorrow;
the more knowledge, the
more grief.[i]

Pleasures Are Meaningless

2 I thought in my heart, "Come
now, I will test you with pleasure[j] to find out what is good."
But that also proved to be meaningless. 2"Laughter,"[k] I said, "is
foolish. And what does pleasure accomplish?" 3I tried cheering myself
with wine,[l] and embracing folly[m]—my mind still guiding me
with wisdom. I wanted to see what
was worthwhile for men to do under heaven during the few days of
their lives.

4I undertook great projects: I
built houses for myself[n] and planted vineyards.[o] 5I made gardens
and parks and planted all kinds of
fruit trees in them. 6I made reservoirs to water groves of flourishing
trees. 7I bought male and female
slaves and had other slaves who
were born in my house. I also
owned more herds and flocks than
anyone in Jerusalem before me. 8I
amassed silver and gold[p] for myself, and the treasure of kings and
provinces. I acquired men and
women singers,[q] and a harem[b] as
well—the delights of the heart of
man. 9I became greater by far than
anyone in Jerusalem before me.[r]
In all this my wisdom stayed with
me.

10I denied myself nothing my
eyes desired;
I refused my heart no
pleasure.
My heart took delight in all my
work,
and this was the reward for
all my labor.
11Yet when I surveyed all that my
hands had done
and what I had toiled to
achieve,
everything was meaningless, a
chasing after the wind;[s]
nothing was gained under the
sun.[t]

Wisdom and Folly Are Meaningless

12Then I turned my thoughts to
consider wisdom,
and also madness and folly.[u]
What more can the king's
successor do
than what has already been
done?[v]
13I saw that wisdom[w] is better
than folly,[x]
just as light is better than
darkness.

b8 The meaning of the Hebrew for this phrase is uncertain.

1:11 [a]Ecc 2:16
1:12 [b]ver 1
1:13 [c]Ge 3:17; Ecc 3:10
1:14 [d]Ecc 2:11,17
1:15 [e]Ecc 7:13
1:16 [f]1Ki 3:12; 4:30; Ecc 2:9
1:17 [g]Ecc 7:23 [h]Ecc 2:3,12; 7:25
1:18 [i]Ecc 2:23; 12:12
2:1 [j]Ecc 7:4; 8:15; Lk 12:19
2:2 [k]Pr 14:13; Ecc 7:6
2:3 [l]ver 24-25; Ecc 3:12-13 [m]Ecc 1:17
2:4 [n]1Ki 7:1-12 [o]SS 8:11
2:8 [p]1Ki 9:28; 10:10,14,21 [q]2Sa 19:35
2:9 [r]1Ch 29:25; Ecc 1:16
2:11 [s]Ecc 1:14 [t]Ecc 1:3
2:12 [u]Ecc 1:17 [v]Ecc 1:9; 7:25
2:13 [w]Ecc 7:19; 9:18 [x]Ecc 7:11-12

14The wise man has eyes in his head,
while the fool walks in the darkness;
but I came to realize
that the same fate overtakes them both.[a]

15Then I thought in my heart,
"The fate of the fool will overtake me also.
What then do I gain by being wise?"[b]
I said in my heart,
"This too is meaningless."
16For the wise man, like the fool, will not be long remembered;
in days to come both will be forgotten.[c]
Like the fool, the wise man too must die!

Toil Is Meaningless

17So I hated life, because the
work that is done under the sun
was grievous to me. All of it is
meaningless, a chasing after the
wind.[d] 18I hated all the things I
had toiled for under the sun, because I must leave them to the one
who comes after me.[e] 19And who
knows whether he will be a wise
man or a fool? Yet he will have control over all the work into which I
have poured my effort and skill under the sun. This too is meaningless. 20So my heart began to despair over all my toilsome labor under the sun. 21For a man may do
his work with wisdom, knowledge
and skill, and then he must leave
all he owns to someone who has
not worked for it. This too is meaningless and a great misfortune.
22What does a man get for all the
toil and anxious striving with
which he labors under the sun?[f]
23All his days his work is pain and
grief;[g] even at night his mind does
not rest. This too is meaningless.
24A man can do nothing better
than to eat and drink[h] and find
satisfaction in his work.[i] This too,
I see, is from the hand of God,[j]
25for without him, who can eat or
find enjoyment? 26To the man who
pleases him, God gives wisdom,
knowledge and happiness, but to
the sinner he gives the task of gathering and storing up wealth[k] to
hand it over to the one who pleases
God.[l] This too is meaningless, a
chasing after the wind.

A Time for Everything

3 There is a time[m] for everything,
and a season for every activity under heaven:

2 a time to be born and a time to die,
a time to plant and a time to uproot,
3 a time to kill and a time to heal,
a time to tear down and a time to build,
4 a time to weep and a time to laugh,
a time to mourn and a time to dance,
5 a time to scatter stones and a time to gather them,
a time to embrace and a time to refrain,
6 a time to search and a time to give up,
a time to keep and a time to throw away,
7 a time to tear and a time to mend,
a time to be silent[n] and a time to speak,
8 a time to love and a time to hate,
a time for war and a time for peace.

9What does the worker gain from
his toil?[o] 10I have seen the burden
God has laid on men.[p] 11He has
made everything beautiful in its
time.[q] He has also set eternity in
the hearts of men; yet they cannot
fathom[r] what God has done from
beginning to end.[s] 12I know that
there is nothing better for men
than to be happy and do good while
they live. 13That everyone may eat
and drink,[t] and find satisfaction[u]
in all his toil—this is the gift of
God.[v] 14I know that everything

2:14 [a]Ps 49:10; Pr 17:24; Ecc 3:19; 6:6; 7:2; 9:3,11-12
2:15 [b]Ecc 6:8
2:16 [c]Ecc 1:11; 9:5
2:17 [d]Ecc 4:2
2:18 [e]Ps 39:6; 49:10
2:22 [f]Ecc 1:3; 3:9
2:23 [g]Job 5:7; 14:1; Ecc 1:18
2:24 [h]Ecc 8:15; 1Co 15:32 [i]Ecc 3:22 [j]Ecc 3:12-13; 5:17-19; 9:7-10
2:26 [k]Job 27:17 [l]Pr 13:22
3:1 [m]ver 11,17; Ecc 8:6
3:7 [n]Am 5:13
3:9 [o]Ecc 1:3
3:10 [p]Ecc 1:13
3:11 [q]ver 1 [r]Job 11:7; Ecc 8:17 [s]Job 28:23; Ro 11:33
3:13 [t]Ecc 2:3 [u]Ps 34:12 [v]Dt 12:7,18; Ecc 2:24; 5:19

God does will endure forever; nothing can be added to it and nothing taken from it. God does it so that men will revere him.[a]

[15]Whatever is has already been,[b]
and what will be has been before;[c]
and God will call the past to account.[c]

[16]And I saw something else under the sun:

In the place of judgment—wickedness was there,
in the place of justice—wickedness was there.

[17]I thought in my heart,

"God will bring to judgment[d]
both the righteous and the wicked,
for there will be a time for every activity,
a time for every deed."[e]

[18]I also thought, "As for men,
God tests them so that they may
see that they are like the animals.[f]
[19]Man's fate[g] is like that of the animals;
the same fate awaits them
both: As one dies, so dies the other.
All have the same breath[d]; man
has no advantage over the animal.
Everything is meaningless. [20]All go
to the same place; all come from
dust, and to dust all return.[h]
[21]Who knows if the spirit of man
rises upward[i] and if the spirit of
the animal[e] goes down into the
earth?"
[22]So I saw that there is nothing
better for a man than to enjoy his
work,[j] because that is his lot.[k]
For who can bring him to see what
will happen after him?

Oppression, Toil, Friendlessness

4 Again I looked and saw all the oppression[l] that was taking place under the sun:

I saw the tears of the oppressed—
and they have no comforter;
power was on the side of their oppressors—
and they have no comforter.[m]
[2]And I declared that the dead,[n]
who had already died,
are happier than the living,
who are still alive.[o]
[3]But better than both
is he who has not yet been,[p]
who has not seen the evil
that is done under the sun.[q]

[4]And I saw that all labor and all achievement spring from man's envy of his neighbor. This too is meaningless, a chasing after the wind.[r]

[5]The fool folds his hands[s]
and ruins himself.
[6]Better one handful with tranquillity
than two handfuls with toil[t]
and chasing after the wind.

[7]Again I saw something meaningless under the sun:

[8]There was a man all alone;
he had neither son nor brother.
There was no end to his toil,
yet his eyes were not content[u] with his wealth.
"For whom am I toiling," he asked,
"and why am I depriving myself of enjoyment?"
This too is meaningless—
a miserable business!

[9]Two are better than one,
because they have a good return for their work:
[10]If one falls down,
his friend can help him up.
But pity the man who falls
and has no one to help him up!
[11]Also, if two lie down together,
they will keep warm.
But how can one keep warm alone?

3:14 [a]Job 23:15; Ecc 5:7; 7:18; 8:12-13; Jas 1:17
3:15 [b]Ecc 6:10 [c]Ecc 1:9
3:17 [d]Job 19:29; Ecc 11:9; Mt 16:27; Ro 2:6-8; 2Th 1:6-7 [e]ver 1
3:18 [f]Ps 73:22
3:19 [g]Ecc 2:14
3:20 [h]Ge 2:7; 3:19; Job 34:15
3:21 [i]Ecc 12:7
3:22 [j]Ecc 2:24; 5:18 [k]Job 31:2
4:1 [l]Ps 12:5; Ecc 3:16 [m]La 1:16
4:2 [n]Jer 20:17-18; 22:10 [o]Job 3:17; 10:18
4:3 [p]Job 3:16; Ecc 6:3 [q]Job 3:22
4:4 [r]Ecc 1:14
4:5 [s]Pr 6:10
4:6 [t]Pr 15:16-17; 16:8
4:8 [u]Pr 27:20

[c]15 Or *God calls back the past* [d]19 Or *spirit* [e]21 Or *Who knows the spirit of man, which rises upward, or the spirit of the animal, which*

12Though one may be
overpowered,
two can defend themselves.
A cord of three strands is not
quickly broken.

Advancement Is Meaningless

13Better a poor but wise youth
than an old but foolish king who no
longer knows how to take warning.
14The youth may have come from
prison to the kingship, or he may
have been born in poverty within
his kingdom. 15I saw that all who
lived and walked under the sun followed the youth, the king's successor. 16There was no end to all the
people who were before them. But
those who came later were not
pleased with the successor. This
too is meaningless, a chasing after
the wind.

Stand in Awe of God

5 Guard your steps when you go
to the house of God. Go near to
listen rather than to offer the sacrifice of fools, who do not know that
they do wrong.

2Do not be quick with your
mouth,
do not be hasty in your heart
to utter anything before
God.[a]
God is in heaven
and you are on earth,
so let your words be few.[b]
3As a dream[c] comes when there
are many cares,
so the speech of a fool when
there are many words.[d]

4When you make a vow to God,
do not delay in fulfilling it.[e] He
has no pleasure in fools; fulfill your
vow.[f] 5It is better not to vow than
to make a vow and not fulfill it.[g]
6Do not let your mouth lead you
into sin. And do not protest to the
⌞temple⌟ messenger, "My vow was a
mistake." Why should God be angry at what you say and destroy the
work of your hands? 7Much dream-
ing and many words are meaningless. Therefore stand in awe of
God.[h]

5:2 [a]Jdg 11:35 [b]Job 6:24; Pr 10:19; 20:25
5:3 [c]Job 20:8 [d]Ecc 10:14
5:4 [e]Dt 23:21; Jdg 11:35; Ps 119:60 [f]Nu 30:2; Ps 66:13-14; 76:11
5:5 [g]Nu 30:2-4; Pr 20:25; Jnh 2:9; Ac 5:4
5:7 [h]Ecc 3:14; 12:13
5:8 [i]Ps 12:5; Ecc 4:1
5:12 [j]Job 20:20
5:13 [k]Ecc 6:1-2
5:15 [l]Job 1:21 [m]Ps 49:17; 1Ti 6:7 [n]Ecc 1:3
5:16 [o]Pr 11:29; Ecc 1:3

Riches Are Meaningless

8If you see the poor oppressed[i]
in a district, and justice and rights
denied, do not be surprised at such
things; for one official is eyed by a
higher one, and over them both are
others higher still. 9The increase
from the land is taken by all; the
king himself profits from the fields.

10Whoever loves money never has
money enough;
whoever loves wealth is never
satisfied with his
income.
This too is meaningless.

11As goods increase,
so do those who consume
them.
And what benefit are they to
the owner
except to feast his eyes on
them?

12The sleep of a laborer is sweet,
whether he eats little or
much,
but the abundance of a rich
man
permits him no sleep.[j]

13I have seen a grievous evil under the sun:[k]

wealth hoarded to the harm of
its owner,
14 or wealth lost through some
misfortune,
so that when he has a son
there is nothing left for him.
15Naked a man comes from his
mother's womb,
and as he comes, so he
departs.[l]
He takes nothing from his
labor[m]
that he can carry in his
hand.[n]

16This too is a grievous evil:

As a man comes, so he departs,
and what does he gain,
since he toils for the wind?[o]
17All his days he eats in
darkness,
with great frustration,
affliction and anger.

18Then I realized that it is good
and proper for a man to eat and
drink,[a] and to find satisfaction in
his toilsome labor[b] under the sun
during the few days of life God has
given him—for this is his lot.
19Moreover, when God gives any
man wealth and possessions,[c] and
enables him to enjoy them,[d] to accept his lot[e] and be happy in his
work—this is a gift of God.[f] 20He
seldom reflects on the days of his
life, because God keeps him occupied with gladness of heart.[g]

6 I have seen another evil under
the sun, and it weighs heavily
on men: 2God gives a man wealth,
possessions and honor, so that he
lacks nothing his heart desires, but
God does not enable him to enjoy
them,[h] and a stranger enjoys them
instead. This is meaningless, a
grievous evil.[i]

3A man may have a hundred children and live many years; yet no
matter how long he lives, if he cannot enjoy his prosperity and does
not receive proper burial, I say that
a stillborn[j] child is better off than
he.[k] 4It comes without meaning, it
departs in darkness, and in darkness its name is shrouded.
5Though it never saw the sun or
knew anything, it has more rest
than does that man— 6even if he
lives a thousand years twice over
but fails to enjoy his prosperity. Do
not all go to the same place?

7All man's efforts are for his
mouth,
yet his appetite is never
satisfied.[l]
8What advantage has a wise man
over a fool?[m]
What does a poor man gain
by knowing how to conduct
himself before others?
9Better what the eye sees
than the roving of the
appetite.
This too is meaningless,
a chasing after the wind.[n]

10Whatever exists has already
been named,
and what man is has been
known;
no man can contend
with one who is stronger
than he.
11The more the words,
the less the meaning,
and how does that profit
anyone?

12For who knows what is good
for a man in life, during the few and
meaningless days[o] he passes
through like a shadow?[p] Who can
tell him what will happen under
the sun after he is gone?

Wisdom

7 A good name is better than
fine perfume,[q]
and the day of death better
than the day of birth.
2It is better to go to a house of
mourning
than to go to a house of
feasting,
for death[r] is the destiny[s] of
every man;
the living should take this to
heart.
3Sorrow is better than
laughter,[t]
because a sad face is good
for the heart.
4The heart of the wise is in the
house of mourning,
but the heart of fools is in
the house of pleasure.[u]
5It is better to heed a wise
man's rebuke[v]
than to listen to the song of
fools.
6Like the crackling of thorns[w]
under the pot,
so is the laughter[x] of fools.
This too is meaningless.

7Extortion turns a wise man into
a fool,
and a bribe[y] corrupts the
heart.

8The end of a matter is better
than its beginning,
and patience[z] is better than
pride.
9Do not be quickly provoked[a] in
your spirit,
for anger resides in the lap of
fools.

5:18 [a] Ecc 2:3 [b] Ecc 2:10,24
5:19 [c] 1Ch 29:12; 2Ch 1:12 [d] Ecc 6:2 [e] Job 31:2 [f] Ecc 2:24; 3:13
5:20 [g] Dt 12:7,18
6:2 [h] Ps 17:14; Ecc 5:19 [i] Ecc 5:13
6:3 [j] Job 3:16; Ecc 4:3 [k] Job 3:3
6:7 [l] Pr 16:26; 27:20
6:8 [m] Ecc 2:15
6:9 [n] Ecc 1:14
6:12 [o] Job 10:20 [p] Job 14:2; Ps 39:6; Jas 4:14
7:1 [q] Pr 22:1; SS 1:3
7:2 [r] Pr 11:19 [s] Ps 90:12
7:3 [t] Pr 14:13
7:4 [u] Ecc 2:1; Jer 16:8
7:5 [v] Ps 141:5; Pr 13:18; 15:31-32
7:6 [w] Ps 58:9; 118:12 [x] Ecc 2:2
7:7 [y] Ex 18:21; 23:8; Dt 16:19
7:8 [z] Pr 14:29; Gal 5:22; Eph 4:2
7:9 [a] Mt 5:22; Pr 14:17; Jas 1:19

10Do not say, "Why were the old
days better than these?"
For it is not wise to ask such
questions.

11Wisdom, like an inheritance, is
a good thing[a]
and benefits those who see
the sun.[b]
12Wisdom is a shelter
as money is a shelter,
but the advantage of knowledge
is this:
that wisdom preserves the
life of its possessor.

13Consider what God has done:[c]

Who can straighten
what he has made crooked?[d]
14When times are good, be
happy;
but when times are bad,
consider:
God has made the one
as well as the other.
Therefore, a man cannot
discover
anything about his future.

15In this meaningless life[e] of
mine I have seen both of these:

a righteous man perishing in
his righteousness,
and a wicked man living long
in his wickedness.[f]
16Do not be overrighteous,
neither be overwise—
why destroy yourself?
17Do not be overwicked,
and do not be a fool—
why die before your time?[g]
18It is good to grasp the one
and not let go of the other.
The man who fears God[h]
will avoid all
⌞extremes⌟.[f]

19Wisdom[i] makes one wise man
more powerful[j]
than ten rulers in a city.

20There is not a righteous man[k]
on earth
who does what is right and
never sins.[l]

21Do not pay attention to every
word people say,
or you[m] may hear your
servant cursing you—
22for you know in your heart
that many times you yourself
have cursed others.

23All this I tested by wisdom and
I said,

"I am determined to be
wise"[n]—
but this was beyond me.
24Whatever wisdom may be,
it is far off and most
profound—
who can discover it?[o]
25So I turned my mind to
understand,
to investigate and to search
out wisdom and the
scheme of things[p]
and to understand the stupidity
of wickedness
and the madness of folly.[q]

26I find more bitter than death
the woman who is a snare,[r]
whose heart is a trap
and whose hands are chains.
The man who pleases God will
escape her,
but the sinner she will
ensnare.[s]

27"Look," says the Teacher,[g][t]
"this is what I have discovered:

"Adding one thing to another
to discover the scheme
of things—
28 while I was still searching
but not finding—
I found one ⌞upright⌟ man
among a thousand,
but not one ⌞upright⌟ woman[u]
among them all.
29This only have I found:
God made mankind upright,
but men have gone in search
of many schemes."

8 Who is like the wise man?
Who knows the explanation
of things?
Wisdom brightens a man's face
and changes its hard
appearance.

7:11 [a]Pr 8:10-11; Ecc 2:13 [b]Ecc 11:7
7:13 [c]Ecc 2:24 [d]Ecc 1:15
7:15 [e]Job 7:7 [f]Ecc 8:12-14; Jer 12:1
7:17 [g]Job 15:32; Ps 55:23
7:18 [h]Ecc 3:14
7:19 [i]Ecc 2:13 [j]Ecc 9:13-18
7:20 [k]Ps 14:3 [l]1Ki 8:46; 2Ch 6:36; Pr 20:9; Ro 3:23
7:21 [m]Pr 30:10
7:23 [n]Ecc 1:17; Ro 1:22
7:24 [o]Job 28:12
7:25 [p]Job 28:3 [q]Ecc 1:17
7:26 [r]Ex 10:7; Jdg 14:15 [s]Pr 2:16-19; 5:3-5; 7:23; 22:14
7:27 [t]Ecc 1:1
7:28 [u]1Ki 11:3

f18 Or will follow them both *g27 Or leader of the assembly*

Obey the King

2Obey the king's command, I
say, because you took an oath before God. **3**Do not be in a hurry to
leave the king's presence.[a] Do not
stand up for a bad cause, for he will
do whatever he pleases. **4**Since a
king's word is supreme, who can
say to him, "What are you doing?[b]"

5Whoever obeys his command
    will come to no harm,
  and the wise heart will know
    the proper time and
    procedure.
6For there is a proper time and
    procedure for every
    matter,[c]
  though a man's misery
    weighs heavily upon
    him.
7Since no man knows the future,
  who can tell him what is to
    come?
8No man has power over the
    wind to contain it[h];
  so no one has power over the
    day of his death.
As no one is discharged in time
    of war,
  so wickedness will not
    release those who
    practice it.

9All this I saw, as I applied my
mind to everything done under the
sun. There is a time when a man
lords it over others to his own[i]
hurt. **10**Then too, I saw the wicked
buried[d]—those who used to come
and go from the holy place and receive praise[j] in the city where they
did this. This too is meaningless.
11When the sentence for a crime
is not quickly carried out, the
hearts of the people are filled with
schemes to do wrong. **12**Although a
wicked man commits a hundred
crimes and still lives a long time, I
know that it will go better[e] with
God-fearing men,[f] who are reverent before God.[g] **13**Yet because
the wicked do not fear God,[h] it will
not go well with them, and their
days[i] will not lengthen like a
shadow.
14There is something else meaningless that occurs on earth: righteous men who get what the wicked deserve, and wicked men who
get what the righteous deserve.[j]
This too, I say, is meaningless.[k]
15So I commend the enjoyment of
life[l], because nothing is better for
a man under the sun than to eat
and drink[m] and be glad.[n] Then joy
will accompany him in his work all
the days of the life God has given
him under the sun.
16When I applied my mind to
know wisdom[o] and to observe
man's labor on earth[p]—his eyes
not seeing sleep day or night—
17then I saw all that God has
done.[q] No one can comprehend
what goes on under the sun. Despite all his efforts to search it out,
man cannot discover its meaning.
Even if a wise man claims he
knows, he cannot really comprehend it.[r]

A Common Destiny for All

9 So I reflected on all this and
concluded that the righteous
and the wise and what they do are
in God's hands, but no man knows
whether love or hate awaits him.[s]
2All share a common destiny—the
righteous and the wicked, the good
and the bad,[k] the clean and the
unclean, those who offer sacrifices
and those who do not.

As it is with the good man,
  so with the sinner;
as it is with those who take
    oaths,
  so with those who are afraid
    to take them.[t]

3This is the evil in everything
that happens under the sun: The
same destiny overtakes all.[u] The
hearts of men, moreover, are full of
evil and there is madness in their
hearts while they live,[v] and afterward they join the dead.[w] **4**Anyone
who is among the living has

8:3 [a]Ecc 10:4
8:4 [b]Job 9:12; Est 1:19; Da 4:35
8:6 [c]Ecc 3:1
8:10 [d]Ecc 1:11
8:12 [e]Dt 12:28; Ps 37:11, 18-19; Pr 1:32-33; Isa 3:10-11 [f]Ex 1:20 [g]Ecc 3:14
8:13 [h]Ecc 3:14; Isa 3:11 [i]Dt 4:40; Job 5:26; Ps 34:12; Isa 65:20
8:14 [j]Job 21:7; Ps 73:14; Mal 3:15 [k]Ecc 7:15
8:15 [l]Ps 42:8 [m]Ex 32:6; Ecc 2:3 [n]Ecc 2:24; 3:12-13; 5:18; 9:7
8:16 [o]Ecc 1:17 [p]Ecc 1:13
8:17 [q]Job 28:3 [r]Job 5:9; 28:23; Ecc 3:11; Ro 11:33
9:1 [s]Dt 33:3; Job 12:10; Ecc 10:14
9:2 [t]Job 9:22; Ecc 2:14; 6:6; 7:2
9:3 [u]Job 9:22; Ecc 2:14 [v]Jer 11:8; 13:10; 16:12; 17:9 [w]Job 21:26

[h]*8* Or *over his spirit to retain it* [i]*9* Or *to their* [j]*10* Some Hebrew manuscripts and Septuagint (Aquila); most Hebrew manuscripts *and are forgotten* [k]*2* Septuagint (Aquila), Vulgate and Syriac; Hebrew does not have *and the bad.*

hope[l]—even a live dog is better off
than a dead lion!

5For the living know that they
will die,
but the dead know nothing;[a]
they have no further reward,
and even the memory of
them[b] is forgotten.[c]
6Their love, their hate
and their jealousy have long
since vanished;
never again will they have a
part
in anything that happens
under the sun.[d]

7Go, eat your food with gladness,
and drink your wine[e] with a joyful
heart,[f] for it is now that God favors
what you do. 8Always be clothed in
white,[g] and always anoint your
head with oil. 9Enjoy life with your
wife,[h] whom you love, all the days
of this meaningless life that God
has given you under the sun— all
your meaningless days. For this is
your lot[i] in life and in your toilsome labor under the sun. 10What-
ever[j] your hand finds to do, do it
with all your might,[k] for in the
grave,[m l] where you are going,
there is neither working nor planning nor knowledge nor wisdom.[m]

11I have seen something else under the sun:

The race is not to the swift
or the battle to the strong,[n]
nor does food come to the
wise[o]
or wealth to the brilliant
or favor to the learned;
but time and chance[p] happen
to them all.[q]

12Moreover, no man knows
when his hour will come:

As fish are caught in a cruel
net,
or birds are taken in a snare,
so men are trapped by evil
times[r]
that fall unexpectedly upon
them.[s]

Wisdom Better Than Folly

13I also saw under the sun this
example of wisdom[t] that greatly
impressed me: 14There was once a
small city with only a few people in
it. And a powerful king came
against it, surrounded it and built
huge siegeworks against it. 15Now
there lived in that city a man poor
but wise, and he saved the city by
his wisdom. But nobody remembered that poor man.[u] 16So I said,
"Wisdom is better than strength."
But the poor man's wisdom is despised, and his words are no longer
heeded.[v]

17The quiet words of the wise are
more to be heeded
than the shouts of a ruler of
fools.
18Wisdom[w] is better than
weapons of war,
but one sinner destroys much
good.

10 As dead flies give perfume
a bad smell,
so a little folly[x] outweighs
wisdom and honor.
2The heart of the wise inclines
to the right,
but the heart of the fool to
the left.
3Even as he walks along the
road,
the fool lacks sense
and shows everyone[y] how
stupid he is.
4If a ruler's anger rises against
you,
do not leave your post;[z]
calmness can lay great errors
to rest.[a]

5There is an evil I have seen
under the sun,
the sort of error that arises
from a ruler:
6Fools are put in many high
positions,[b]
while the rich occupy the low
ones.
7I have seen slaves on
horseback,
while princes go on foot like
slaves.[c]

9:5 [a]Job 14:21 [b]Ps 9:6 [c]Ecc 1:11; 2:16; Isa 26:14
9:6 [d]Job 21:21
9:7 [e]Nu 6:20 [f]Ecc 2:24; 8:15
9:8 [g]Ps 23:5; Rev 3:4
9:9 [h]Pr 5:18 [i]Job 31:2
9:10 [j]1Sa 10:7 [k]Ecc 11:6; Ro 12:11; Col 3:23 [l]Nu 16:33 [m]Ecc 2:24
9:11 [n]Am 2:14-15 [o]Job 32:13; Isa 47:10; Jer 9:23 [p]Ecc 2:14 [q]Dt 8:18
9:12 [r]Pr 29:6 [s]Ps 73:22; Ecc 2:14; 8:7
9:13 [t]2Sa 20:22
9:15 [u]Ge 40:14; Ecc 1:11; 2:16; 4:13
9:16 [v]Pr 21:22; Ecc 7:19
9:18 [w]ver 16
10:1 [x]Pr 13:16; 18:2
10:3 [y]Pr 13:16; 18:2
10:4 [z]Ecc 8:3 [a]Pr 16:14; 25:15
10:6 [b]Pr 29:2
10:7 [c]Pr 19:10

l4 Or *What then is to be chosen? With all who live, there is hope* m10 Hebrew *Sheol*

8Whoever digs a pit may fall into it;[a]
whoever breaks through a wall may be bitten by a snake.[b]
9Whoever quarries stones may be injured by them;
whoever splits logs may be endangered by them.[c]

10If the ax is dull
and its edge unsharpened,
more strength is needed
but skill will bring success.

11If a snake bites before it is charmed,
there is no profit for the charmer.[d]

12Words from a wise man's mouth are gracious,[e]
but a fool is consumed by his own lips.[f]
13At the beginning his words are folly;
at the end they are wicked madness—
14 and the fool multiplies words.[g]

No one knows what is coming—
who can tell him what will happen after him?[h]

15A fool's work wearies him;
he does not know the way to town.

16Woe to you, O land whose king was a servant[n][i]
and whose princes feast in the morning.
17Blessed are you, O land whose king is of noble birth
and whose princes eat at a proper time—
for strength and not for drunkenness.[j]

18If a man is lazy, the rafters sag;
if his hands are idle, the house leaks.[k]

19A feast is made for laughter,
and wine[l] makes life merry,
but money is the answer for everything.

20Do not revile the king[m] even in your thoughts,
or curse the rich in your bedroom,
because a bird of the air may carry your words,
and a bird on the wing may report what you say.

Bread Upon the Waters

11 Cast[n] your bread upon the waters,
for after many days you will find it again.[o]
2Give portions to seven, yes to eight,
for you do not know what disaster may come upon the land.

3If clouds are full of water,
they pour rain upon the earth.
Whether a tree falls to the south or to the north,
in the place where it falls, there will it lie.
4Whoever watches the wind will not plant;
whoever looks at the clouds will not reap.

5As you do not know the path of the wind,[p]
or how the body is formed[o] in a mother's womb,[q]
so you cannot understand the work of God,
the Maker of all things.

6Sow your seed in the morning,
and at evening let not your hands be idle,[r]
for you do not know which will succeed,
whether this or that,
or whether both will do equally well.

Remember Your Creator While Young

7Light is sweet,
and it pleases the eyes to see the sun.[s]

10:8 [a] Ps 7:15; 57:6; Pr 26:27 [b] Est 2:23; Ps 9:16; Am 5:19
10:9 [c] Pr 26:27
10:11 [d] Ps 58:5; Isa 3:3
10:12 [e] Pr 10:32 [f] Pr 10:14; 14:3; 15:2; 18:7
10:14 [g] Pr 15:2; Ecc 5:3; 6:12; 8:7 [h] Ecc 9:1
10:16 [i] Isa 3:4-5,12
10:17 [j] Dt 14:26; 1Sa 25:36; Pr 31:4
10:18 [k] Pr 20:4; 24:30-34
10:19 [l] Ge 14:18; Jdg 9:13
10:20 [m] Ex 22:28
11:1 [n] ver 6; Isa 32:20; Hos 10:12 [o] Dt 24:19; Pr 19:17; Mt 10:42
11:5 [p] Jn 3:8-10 [q] Ps 139:14-16
11:6 [r] Ecc 9:10
11:7 [s] Ecc 7:11

[n]16 Or *king is a child* [o]5 Or *know how life (or the spirit) / enters the body being formed*

8However many years a man
may live,
let him enjoy them all.
But let him remember[a] the
days of darkness,
for they will be many.
Everything to come is
meaningless.

9Be happy, young man, while
you are young,
and let your heart give you
joy in the days of your
youth.
Follow the ways of your heart
and whatever your eyes see,
but know that for all these
things
God will bring you to
judgment.[b]
10So then, banish anxiety[c] from
your heart
and cast off the troubles of
your body,
for youth and vigor are
meaningless.[d]

12 Remember[e] your Creator
in the days of your youth,
before the days of trouble[f]
come
and the years approach when
you will say,
"I find no pleasure in
them"—
2before the sun and the light
and the moon and the stars
grow dark,
and the clouds return after
the rain;
3when the keepers of the house
tremble,
and the strong men stoop,
when the grinders cease
because they are few,
and those looking through
the windows grow dim;
4when the doors to the street
are closed
and the sound of grinding
fades;
when men rise up at the sound
of birds,
but all their songs grow
faint;[g]
5when men are afraid of heights
and of dangers in the streets;
when the almond tree blossoms
and the grasshopper drags
himself along
and desire no longer is
stirred.
Then man goes to his eternal
home[h]
and mourners[i] go about the
streets.

6Remember him—before the
silver cord is severed,
or the golden bowl is broken;
before the pitcher is shattered
at the spring,
or the wheel broken at the
well,
7and the dust returns[j] to the
ground it came from,
and the spirit returns to
God[k] who gave it.[l]

8"Meaningless! Meaningless!"
says the Teacher.[p]
"Everything is meaningless![m]"

The Conclusion of the Matter

9Not only was the Teacher wise,
but also he imparted knowledge to
the people. He pondered and
searched out and set in order
many proverbs.[n] 10The Teacher
searched to find just the right
words, and what he wrote was upright and true.[o]
11The words of the wise are like
goads, their collected sayings like
firmly embedded nails[p]—given by
one Shepherd. 12Be warned, my
son, of anything in addition to
them.
Of making many books there is
no end, and much study wearies
the body.[q]

13Now all has been heard;
here is the conclusion of the
matter:
Fear God and keep his
commandments,[r]
for this is the whole ⌞duty⌟ of
man.[s]
14For God will bring every deed
into judgment,[t]
including every hidden
thing,[u]
whether it is good or evil.

11:8 [a] Ecc 12:1
11:9 [b] Job 19:29; Ecc 2:24; 3:17; 12:14; Ro 14:10
11:10 [c] Ps 94:19 [d] Ecc 2:24
12:1 [e] Ecc 11:8 [f] 2Sa 19:35
12:4 [g] Jer 25:10
12:5 [h] Job 17:13; 10:21 [i] Jer 9:17; Am 5:16
12:7 [j] Ge 3:19; Job 34:15; Ps 146:4 [k] Ecc 3:21 [l] Job 20:8; Zec 12:1
12:8 [m] Ecc 1:2
12:9 [n] 1Ki 4:32
12:10 [o] Pr 22:20-21
12:11 [p] Ezr 9:8
12:12 [q] Ecc 1:18
12:13 [r] Dt 4:2; 10:12 [s] Mic 6:8
12:14 [t] Ecc 3:17 [u] Mt 10:26; 1Co 4:5

p8 Or *the leader of the assembly;* also in verses 9 and 10

Song of Songs

Title and Background

The title in the Hebrew text is "Solomon's Song of Songs," meaning a song either by, for or about Solomon. The phrase "Song of Songs" means the greatest of songs.

Author and Date of Writing

Verse 1 seems to ascribe authorship to Solomon. He is referred to seven times in the book, but whether he was the author remains an open question. Consistency of language, style, tone, perspective and recurring refrains seems to argue for a single author. If Solomon is the author, the Song can be dated in the tenth century B.C.

Theme and Message

In ancient Israel everything human came to expression in words. In the Song, love finds words—inspired words that disclose its exquisite charm and beauty as one of God's choicest gifts. The woman's voice of love in the Song suggests that love and wisdom draw men powerfully with the subtlety and mystery of a woman's allurements. God intends that such love be a normal part of marital life in his good creation.

Outline

I. Courtship (1:1-3:5)
II. Wedding Procession (3:6-11)
III. Expressions of Love (4:1-5:1)
IV. Conflict and Solution (5:2-6:13)
V. More Expressions of Love (7:1-8:4)
VI. Conclusion (8:5-14)

---

1 Solomon's Song of Songs.[a]

Beloved[a]

[2]Let him kiss me with the kisses
of his mouth—
for your love[b] is more
delightful than wine.
[3]Pleasing is the fragrance of
your perfumes;[c]
your name[d] is like perfume
poured out.
No wonder the maidens[e]
love you!
[4]Take me away with you—let us
hurry!
Let the king bring me into
his chambers.[f]

Friends

We rejoice and delight in you[b];
we will praise your love more
than wine.

Beloved

How right they are to adore
you!

[5]Dark am I, yet lovely,[g]
O daughters of Jerusalem,[h]

1:1 [a] 1Ki 4:32
1:2 [b] SS 4:10
1:3 [c] SS 4:10 [d] Ecc 7:1 [e] Ps 45:14
1:4 [f] Ps 45:15
1:5 [g] SS 2:14; 4:3 [h] SS 2:7; 5:8; 5:16

[a]Primarily on the basis of the gender of the Hebrew pronouns used, male and female speakers are indicated in the margins by the captions *Lover* and *Beloved* respectively. The words of others are marked *Friends*. In some instances the divisions and their captions are debatable. [b]*4* The Hebrew is masculine singular.

dark like the tents of Kedar,
like the tent curtains of Solomon.[c]
6Do not stare at me because I am dark,
because I am darkened by the sun.
My mother's sons were angry with me
and made me take care of the vineyards;[a]
my own vineyard I have neglected.
7Tell me, you whom I love,
where you graze your flock
and where you rest your sheep[b] at midday.
Why should I be like a veiled woman
beside the flocks of your friends?

Friends

8If you do not know, most beautiful of women,[c]
follow the tracks of the sheep
and graze your young goats
by the tents of the shepherds.

Lover

9I liken you, my darling, to a mare
harnessed to one of the chariots[d] of Pharaoh.
10Your cheeks[e] are beautiful with earrings,
your neck with strings of jewels.[f]
11We will make you earrings of gold,
studded with silver.

Beloved

12While the king was at his table,
my perfume spread its fragrance.[g]
13My lover is to me a sachet of myrrh
resting between my breasts.
14My lover is to me a cluster of henna[h] blossoms
from the vineyards of En Gedi.[i]

Lover

15How beautiful[j] you are, my darling!
Oh, how beautiful!
Your eyes are doves.[k]

Beloved

16How handsome you are, my lover!
Oh, how charming!
And our bed is verdant.

Lover

17The beams of our house are cedars;[l]
our rafters are firs.

Beloved[d]

2 I am a rose[e][m] of Sharon,[n]
a lily[o] of the valleys.

Lover

2Like a lily among thorns
is my darling among the maidens.

Beloved

3Like an apple tree among the trees of the forest
is my lover[p] among the young men.
I delight[q] to sit in his shade,
and his fruit is sweet to my taste.[r]
4He has taken me to the banquet hall,[s]
and his banner[t] over me is love.
5Strengthen me with raisins,
refresh me with apples,[u]
for I am faint with love.[v]
6His left arm is under my head,
and his right arm embraces me.[w]
7Daughters of Jerusalem, I charge you[x]
by the gazelles and by the does of the field:
Do not arouse or awaken love
until it so desires.[y]

8Listen! My lover!
Look! Here he comes,

1:6 [a]Ps 69:8; SS 8:12
1:7 [b]SS 3:1-4; Isa 13:20
1:8 [c]SS 5:9; 6:1
1:9 [d]2Ch 1:17
1:10 [e]SS 5:13 [f]Isa 61:10
1:12 [g]SS 4:11-14
1:14 [h]SS 4:13 [i]1Sa 23:29
1:15 [j]SS 4:7 [k]SS 2:14; 4:1; 5:2,12; 6:9
1:17 [l]1Ki 6:9
2:1 [m]Isa 35:1 [n]S 1Ch 27:29 [o]SS 5:13; Hos 14:5
2:3 [p]SS 1:14 [q]SS 1:4 [r]SS 4:16
2:4 [s]Est 1:11 [t]Nu 1:52
2:5 [u]SS 7:8 [v]SS 5:8
2:6 [w]SS 8:3
2:7 [x]SS 5:8 [y]SS 3:5; 8:4

[c]5 Or *Salma* [d]1 Or *Lover* [e]1 Possibly a member of the crocus family

leaping across the mountains,
bounding over the hills.[a]
9My lover is like a gazelle[b] or a young stag.[c]
Look! There he stands behind our wall,
gazing through the windows,
peering through the lattice.
10My lover spoke and said to me,
"Arise, my darling,
my beautiful one, and come with me.
11See! The winter is past;
the rains are over and gone.
12Flowers appear on the earth;
the season of singing has come,
the cooing of doves
is heard in our land.
13The fig tree forms its early fruit;[d]
the blossoming[e] vines spread their fragrance.
Arise, come, my darling;
my beautiful one, come with me."

Lover

14My dove[f] in the clefts of the rock,
in the hiding places on the mountainside,
show me your face,
let me hear your voice;
for your voice is sweet,
and your face is lovely.[g]
15Catch for us the foxes,[h]
the little foxes
that ruin the vineyards,[i]
our vineyards that are in bloom.[j]

Beloved

16My lover is mine and I am his;[k]
he browses among the lilies.[l]
17Until the day breaks
and the shadows flee,[m]
turn, my lover,[n]
and be like a gazelle
or like a young stag[o]
on the rugged hills.[f][p]

3 All night long on my bed
I looked[q] for the one my heart loves;
I looked for him but did not find him.
2I will get up now and go about the city,
through its streets and squares;
I will search for the one my heart loves.
So I looked for him but did not find him.
3The watchmen found me
as they made their rounds in the city.[r]
"Have you seen the one my heart loves?"
4Scarcely had I passed them
when I found the one my heart loves.
I held him and would not let him go
till I had brought him to my mother's house,[s]
to the room of the one who conceived me.[t]
5Daughters of Jerusalem, I charge you[u]
by the gazelles and by the does of the field:
Do not arouse or awaken love
until it so desires.[v]

6Who is this coming up from the desert[w]
like a column of smoke,
perfumed with myrrh[x] and incense
made from all the spices[y] of the merchant?
7Look! It is Solomon's carriage,
escorted by sixty warriors,[z]
the noblest of Israel,
8all of them wearing the sword,
all experienced in battle,
each with his sword at his side,
prepared for the terrors of the night.[a]
9King Solomon made for himself the carriage;
he made it of wood from Lebanon.
10Its posts he made of silver,
its base of gold.
Its seat was upholstered with purple,
its interior lovingly inlaid

2:8 [a]ver 17; SS 8:14
2:9 [b]2Sa 2:18 [c]ver 17; SS 8:14
2:13 [d]Isa 28:4; Jer 24:2; Hos 9:10; Mic 7:1; Na 3:12 [e]SS 7:12
2:14 [f]Ge 8:8; SS 1:15 [g]SS 1:5; 8:13
2:15 [h]Jdg 15:4 [i]SS 1:6 [j]SS 7:12
2:16 [k]SS 7:10 [l]SS 4:5; 6:3
2:17 [m]SS 4:6 [n]SS 1:14 [o]ver 9 [p]ver 8
3:1 [q]SS 5:6; Isa 26:9
3:3 [r]SS 5:7
3:4 [s]SS 8:2 [t]SS 6:9
3:5 [u]SS 2:7 [v]SS 8:4
3:6 [w]SS 8:5 [x]SS 1:13; 4:6, 14 [y]Ex 30:34
3:7 [z]1Sa 8:11
3:8 [a]Job 15:22; Ps 91:5

[f]17 *Or the hills of Bether*

by[g] the daughters of
Jerusalem.
11Come out, you daughters of
Zion,[a]
and look at King Solomon
wearing the crown,
the crown with which his
mother crowned him
on the day of his wedding,
the day his heart rejoiced.[b]

Lover

4 How beautiful you are, my
darling!
Oh, how beautiful!
Your eyes behind your veil
are doves.[c]
Your hair is like a flock of goats
descending from Mount
Gilead.[d]
2Your teeth are like a flock of
sheep just shorn,
coming up from the washing.
Each has its twin;
not one of them is alone.[e]
3Your lips are like a scarlet
ribbon;
your mouth[f] is lovely.
Your temples behind your veil
are like the halves of a
pomegranate.[g]
4Your neck is like the tower[h] of
David,
built with elegance[h];
on it hang a thousand shields,[i]
all of them shields of
warriors.
5Your two breasts[j] are like two
fawns,
like twin fawns of a gazelle[k]
that browse among the
lilies.[l]
6Until the day breaks
and the shadows flee,[m]
I will go to the mountain of
myrrh[n]
and to the hill of incense.
7All beautiful[o] you are, my
darling;
there is no flaw in you.

8Come with me from Lebanon,
my bride,[p]
come with me from Lebanon.
Descend from the crest of
Amana,
from the top of Senir,[q] the
summit of Hermon,[r]
from the lions' dens
and the mountain haunts of
the leopards.
9You have stolen my heart, my
sister, my bride;
you have stolen my heart
with one glance of your eyes,
with one jewel of your
necklace.[s]
10How delightful[t] is your love[u],
my sister, my bride!
How much more pleasing is
your love than wine,
and the fragrance of your
perfume than any spice!
11Your lips drop sweetness as the
honeycomb, my bride;
milk and honey are under
your tongue.[v]
The fragrance of your
garments is like that of
Lebanon.[w]
12You are a garden locked up, my
sister, my bride;
you are a spring enclosed, a
sealed fountain.[x]
13Your plants are an orchard of
pomegranates[y]
with choice fruits,
with henna[z] and nard,
14 nard and saffron,
calamus and cinnamon,[a]
with every kind of incense
tree,
with myrrh[b] and aloes
and all the finest spices.[c]
15You are[i] a garden fountain,
a well of flowing water
streaming down from
Lebanon.

Beloved

16Awake, north wind,
and come, south wind!
Blow on my garden,
that its fragrance may spread
abroad.
Let my lover come into his
garden
and taste its choice fruits.[d]

3:11 [a] Isa 4:4 [b] Isa 62:5
4:1 [c] SS 1:15; 5:12 [d] SS 6:5; Mic 7:14
4:2 [e] SS 6:6
4:3 [f] SS 5:16 [g] SS 6:7
4:4 [h] SS 7:4 [i] Eze 27:10
4:5 [j] SS 7:3 [k] Pr 5:19 [l] SS 2:16; 6:2-3
4:6 [m] SS 2:17 [n] ver 14
4:7 [o] SS 1:15
4:8 [p] SS 5:1 [q] Dt 3:9 [r] 1Ch 5:23
4:9 [s] Ge 41:42
4:10 [t] SS 7:6 [u] SS 1:2
4:11 [v] Ps 19:10; SS 5:1 [w] Hos 14:6
4:12 [x] Pr 5:15-18
4:13 [y] SS 6:11; 7:12 [z] SS 1:14
4:14 [a] Ex 30:23 [b] SS 3:6 [c] SS 1:12
4:16 [d] SS 2:3; 5:1

[g]10 Or *its inlaid interior a gift of love / from*
[h]4 The meaning of the Hebrew for this word is uncertain.
[i]15 Or *I am* (spoken by the *Beloved*)

Lover

5 I have come into my garden,
my sister, my bride;[a]
I have gathered my myrrh
with my spice.
I have eaten my honeycomb
and my honey;
I have drunk my wine and
my milk.[b]

Friends

Eat, O friends, and drink;
drink your fill, O lovers.

Beloved

2I slept but my heart was awake.
Listen! My lover is knocking:
"Open to me, my sister, my
darling,
my dove, my flawless[c] one.[d]
My head is drenched with dew,
my hair with the dampness
of the night."
3I have taken off my robe—
must I put it on again?
I have washed my feet—
must I soil them again?
4My lover thrust his hand
through the
latch-opening;
my heart began to pound for
him.
5I arose to open for my lover,
and my hands dripped with
myrrh,[e]
my fingers with flowing myrrh,
on the handles of the lock.
6I opened for my lover,[f]
but my lover had left; he was
gone.[g]
My heart sank at his
departure.[i]
I looked[h] for him but did not
find him.
I called him but he did not
answer.
7The watchmen found me
as they made their rounds in
the city.[i]
They beat me, they bruised me;
they took away my cloak,
those watchmen of the walls!
8O daughters of Jerusalem, I
charge you[j]—
if you find my lover,
what will you tell him?
Tell him I am faint with
love.[k]

Friends

9How is your beloved better
than others,
most beautiful of women?[l]
How is your beloved better
than others,
that you charge us so?

Beloved

10My lover is radiant and ruddy,
outstanding among ten
thousand.[m]
11His head is purest gold;
his hair is wavy
and black as a raven.
12His eyes are like doves[n]
by the water streams,
washed in milk,[o]
mounted like jewels.
13His cheeks[p] are like beds of
spice[q]
yielding perfume.
His lips are like lilies[r]
dripping with myrrh.
14His arms are rods of gold
set with chrysolite.
His body is like polished ivory
decorated with sapphires.[k][s]
15His legs are pillars of marble
set on bases of pure gold.
His appearance is like
Lebanon,[t]
choice as its cedars.
16His mouth[u] is sweetness itself;
he is altogether lovely.
This is my lover,[v] this my
friend,
O daughters of Jerusalem.[w]

Friends

6 Where has your lover[x] gone,
most beautiful of women?[y]
Which way did your lover turn,
that we may look for him
with you?

Beloved

2My lover has gone[z] down to
his garden,[a]
to the beds of spices,[b]
to browse in the gardens

5:1 [a]SS 4:8 [b]SS 4:11; Isa 55:1
5:2 [c]SS 4:7 [d]SS 6:9
5:5 [e]ver 13
5:6 [f]SS 6:1 [g]SS 6:2 [h]SS 3:1
5:7 [i]SS 3:3
5:8 [j]SS 2:7; 3:5 [k]SS 2:5
5:9 [l]SS 1:8; 6:1
5:10 [m]Ps 45:2
5:12 [n]SS 1:15; 4:1 [o]Ge 49:12
5:13 [p]SS 1:10 [q]SS 6:2 [r]SS 2:1
5:14 [s]Job 28:6
5:15 [t]1Ki 4:33; SS 7:4
5:16 [u]SS 4:3 [v]SS 7:9 [w]SS 1:5
6:1 [x]SS 5:6 [y]SS 1:8
6:2 [z]SS 5:6 [a]SS 4:12 [b]SS 5:13

[i]6 Or *heart had gone out to him when he spoke*
[k]14 Or *lapis lazuli*

and to gather lilies.
3I am my lover's and my lover is mine;[a]
he browses among the lilies.[b]

Lover

4You are beautiful, my darling, as Tirzah,[c]
lovely as Jerusalem,[d]
majestic as troops with banners.[e]
5Turn your eyes from me;
they overwhelm me.
Your hair is like a flock of goats
descending from Gilead.[f]
6Your teeth are like a flock of sheep
coming up from the washing.
Each has its twin,
not one of them is alone.[g]
7Your temples behind your veil[h]
are like the halves of a pomegranate.[i]
8Sixty queens[j] there may be,
and eighty concubines,[k]
and virgins beyond number;
9but my dove,[l] my perfect one,[m] is unique,
the only daughter of her mother,
the favorite of the one who bore her.[n]
The maidens saw her and called her blessed;
the queens and concubines praised her.

Friends

10Who is this that appears like the dawn,
fair as the moon, bright as the sun,
majestic as the stars in procession?

Lover

11I went down to the grove of nut trees
to look at the new growth in the valley,
to see if the vines had budded
or the pomegranates were in bloom.[o]
12Before I realized it,
my desire set me among the royal chariots of my people.[1]

Friends

13Come back, come back, O Shulammite;
come back, come back, that we may gaze on you!

Lover

Why would you gaze on the Shulammite
as on the dance[p] of Mahanaim?

7 How beautiful your sandaled feet,
O prince's[q] daughter!
Your graceful legs are like jewels,
the work of a craftsman's hands.
2Your navel is a rounded goblet
that never lacks blended wine.
Your waist is a mound of wheat
encircled by lilies.
3Your breasts[r] are like two fawns,
twins of a gazelle.
4Your neck is like an ivory tower.[s]
Your eyes are the pools of Heshbon[t]
by the gate of Bath Rabbim.
Your nose is like the tower of Lebanon[u]
looking toward Damascus.
5Your head crowns you like Mount Carmel.[v]
Your hair is like royal tapestry;
the king is held captive by its tresses.
6How beautiful[w] you are and how pleasing,
O love, with your delights![x]
7Your stature is like that of the palm,
and your breasts[y] like clusters of fruit.
8I said, "I will climb the palm tree;

6:3 [a]SS 7:10 [b]SS 2:16
6:4 [c]Jos 12:24 [d]Ps 48:2; 50:2 [e]ver 10
6:5 [f]SS 4:1
6:6 [g]SS 4:2
6:7 [h]Ge 24:65 [i]SS 4:3
6:8 [j]Ps 45:9 [k]Ge 22:24
6:9 [l]SS 1:15 [m]SS 5:2 [n]SS 3:4
6:11 [o]SS 7:12
6:13 [p]Ex 15:20
7:1 [q]Ps 45:13
7:3 [r]SS 4:5
7:4 [s]Ps 144:12; SS 4:4 [t]Nu 21:26 [u]SS 5:15
7:5 [v]Isa 35:2
7:6 [w]SS 1:15 [x]SS 4:10
7:7 [y]SS 4:5

[1]12 Or *among the chariots of Amminadab;* or *among the chariots of the people of the prince*

I will take hold of its fruit."
May your breasts be like the clusters of the vine,
the fragrance of your breath like apples,[a]
9 and your mouth like the best wine.

Beloved

May the wine go straight to my lover,[b]
flowing gently over lips and teeth.[m]
10 I belong to my lover,
and his desire[c] is for me.[d]
11 Come, my lover, let us go to the countryside,
let us spend the night in the villages.[n]
12 Let us go early to the vineyards[e]
to see if the vines have budded,[f]
if their blossoms[g] have opened,
and if the pomegranates[h] are in bloom[i]—
there I will give you my love.
13 The mandrakes[j] send out their fragrance,
and at our door is every delicacy,
both new and old,
that I have stored up for you, my lover.[k]

8 If only you were to me like a brother,
who was nursed at my mother's breasts!
Then, if I found you outside,
I would kiss you,
and no one would despise me.
2 I would lead you
and bring you to my mother's house[l]—
she who has taught me.
I would give you spiced wine to drink,
the nectar of my pomegranates.
3 His left arm is under my head
and his right arm embraces me.[m]
4 Daughters of Jerusalem, I charge you:
Do not arouse or awaken love
until it so desires.[n]

7:8 [a]SS 2:5
7:9 [b]S S 5:16
7:10 [c]Ps 45:11 [d]SS 2:16; 6:3
7:12 [e]SS 1:6 [f]SS 2:15 [g]SS 2:13 [h]SS 4:13 [i]SS 6:11
7:13 [j]Ge 30:14 [k]SS 4:16
8:2 [l]SS 3:4
8:3 [m]SS 2:6
8:4 [n]SS 2:7; 3:5
8:5 [o]SS 3:6 [p]SS 3:4
8:6 [q]SS 1:2 [r]Nu 5:14
8:7 [s]Pr 6:35

Friends

5 Who is this coming up from the desert[o]
leaning on her lover?

Beloved

Under the apple tree I roused you;
there your mother conceived[p] you,
there she who was in labor gave you birth.
6 Place me like a seal over your heart,
like a seal on your arm;
for love[q] is as strong as death,
its jealousy[o][r] unyielding as the grave.[p]
It burns like blazing fire,
like a mighty flame.[q]
7 Many waters cannot quench love;
rivers cannot wash it away.
If one were to give
all the wealth of his house for love,
it[r] would be utterly scorned.[s]

Friends

8 We have a young sister,
and her breasts are not yet grown.
What shall we do for our sister
for the day she is spoken for?
9 If she is a wall,
we will build towers of silver on her.
If she is a door,
we will enclose her with panels of cedar.

Beloved

10 I am a wall,
and my breasts are like towers.
Thus I have become in his eyes

[m]9 Septuagint, Aquila, Vulgate and Syriac; Hebrew *lips of sleepers* [n]11 Or *henna bushes* [o]6 Or *ardor* [p]6 Hebrew *Sheol* [q]6 Or / *like the very flame of the Lord* [r]7 Or *he*

like one bringing
contentment.
11Solomon had a vineyard[a] in
Baal Hamon;
he let out his vineyard to
tenants.
Each was to bring for its fruit
a thousand shekels[s][b] of
silver.
12But my own vineyard[c] is mine
to give;
the thousand shekels are for
you, O Solomon,
and two hundred[t] are for
those who tend its fruit.

Lover

13You who dwell in the gardens
with friends in attendance,
let me hear your voice!

Beloved

14Come away, my lover,
and be like a gazelle[d]
or like a young stag[e]
on the spice-laden
mountains.[f]

8:11 [a]Ecc 2:4 [b]Isa 7:23
8:12 [c]SS 1:6
8:14 [d]Pr 5:19 [e]SS 2:9 [f]SS 2:8,17

[s]*11* That is, about 25 pounds (about 11.5 kilograms); also in verse 12 [t]*12* That is, about 5 pounds (about 2.3 kilograms)

Isaiah

Title and Background

The book is named after the prophet whose message it records. Isaiah wrote during the stormy period marking the expansion of the Assyrian empire and the decline of Israel. He warned Judah that her sin would bring captivity at the hands of Babylon. Although the fall of Jerusalem would not take place until 586 B.C., Isaiah assumes its demise and proceeds to predict the restoration of the people from captivity. The decree of Cyrus would allow the Jews to return home, a deliverance that prefigured the greater salvation from sin through Jesus Christ. Significantly, Isaiah's name means "The LORD saves."

Author and Date of Writing

Isaiah son of Amoz was the greatest of the writing prophets and a contemporary of Amos, Hosea and Micah. Most of the events discussed in chapters 1-39 occurred during Isaiah's ministry, so it is likely they were completed around 700 B.C. He lived until at least 681 and may have written chapters 40-66 during his later years.

Theme and Message

Isaiah unveils the full dimensions of God's judgment and salvation. The awful judgment to be unleashed on Israel and all who defy God is called "the day of the LORD." The Lord's kingdom on earth, with its righteous Ruler and his righteous subjects, is the goal toward which the book of Isaiah steadily moves. The restored earth and the restored people will then conform to the divine ideal, and all will result in the praise and glory of the Holy One of Israel.

Outline

I. Rebuke and Promise (1:1-6:13)
II. Immanuel and His Kingdom (7:1-12:6)
III. Judgment Against the Nations (13:1-23:18)
IV. Judgment and Promise (24:1-27:13)
V. Six Woes on Israel and Assyria (28:1-33:24)
VI. Judgment and Promise (34:1-35:10)
VII. From the Assyrian Threat to the Babylonian Exile (36:1-39:8)
VIII. Deliverance and Restoration of Israel (40:1-48:22)
IX. The Servant's Ministry and Israel's Restoration (49:1-57:21)
X. Everlasting Deliverance and Judgment (58:1-66:24)

---

1 The vision[a] concerning Judah and Jerusalem[b] that Isaiah son of Amoz saw[c] during the reigns of Uzziah,[d] Jotham, Ahaz[e] and Hezekiah, kings of Judah.

A Rebellious Nation

2Hear, O heavens! Listen, O earth!
For the LORD has spoken:[f]
"I reared children and brought them up,
but they have rebelled[g] against me.
3The ox knows his master,
the donkey his owner's manger,
but Israel does not know,[h]
my people do not understand."
4Ah, sinful nation,

1:1 [a]Nu 12:6 [b]Isa 40:9 [c]Isa 2:1 [d]2Ch 26:22 [e]2Ki 16:1
1:2 [f]Mic 1:2 [g]Isa 30:1,9; 65:2
1:3 [h]Jer 8:7; 9:3, 6

a people loaded with guilt,
a brood of evildoers,[a]
children given to corruption!
They have forsaken the LORD;
they have spurned the Holy
One[b] of Israel
and turned their backs on
him.

5Why should you be beaten
anymore?
Why do you persist in
rebellion?[c]
Your whole head is injured,
your whole heart afflicted.[d]
6From the sole of your foot to
the top of your head
there is no soundness[e]—
only wounds and welts
and open sores,
not cleansed or bandaged[f]
or soothed with oil.[g]

7Your country is desolate,[h]
your cities burned with fire;
your fields are being stripped
by foreigners
right before you,
laid waste as when
overthrown by strangers.
8The Daughter of Zion is left
like a shelter in a vineyard,
like a hut[i] in a field of
melons,
like a city under siege.
9Unless the LORD Almighty
had left us some survivors,[j]
we would have become like
Sodom,
we would have been like
Gomorrah.[k]

10Hear the word of the LORD,[l]
you rulers of Sodom;[m]
listen to the law[n] of our God,
you people of Gomorrah!
11"The multitude of your
sacrifices—
what are they to me?" says
the LORD.
"I have more than enough of
burnt offerings,
of rams and the fat of
fattened animals;[o]
I have no pleasure
in the blood of bulls[p] and
lambs and goats.[q]

12When you come to appear
before me,
who has asked this of you,[r]
this trampling of my courts?
13Stop bringing meaningless
offerings![s]
Your incense[t] is detestable
to me.
New Moons, Sabbaths and
convocations[u]—
I cannot bear your evil
assemblies.
14Your New Moon festivals and
your appointed feasts[v]
my soul hates.
They have become a burden to
me;
I am weary[w] of bearing them.
15When you spread out your
hands in prayer,
I will hide[x] my eyes from
you;
even if you offer many prayers,
I will not listen.
Your hands are full of blood;[y]
16 wash and make yourselves
clean.
Take your evil deeds
out of my sight![z]
Stop doing wrong,[a]
17 learn to do right!
Seek justice,[b]
encourage the oppressed.[a]
Defend the cause of the
fatherless,[c]
plead the case of the widow.

18"Come now, let us reason
together,"[d]
says the LORD.
"Though your sins are like
scarlet,
they shall be as white as
snow;[e]
though they are red as crimson,
they shall be like wool.
19If you are willing and obedient,
you will eat the best from the
land;[f]
20but if you resist and rebel,
you will be devoured by the
sword."[g]
For the mouth of the
LORD has spoken.[h]

21See how the faithful city

1:4 [a]Isa 14:20 [b]Isa 5:19,24
1:5 [c]Isa 31:6 [d]Isa 33:6,24
1:6 [e]Ps 38:3 [f]Isa 30:26; Jer 8:22 [g]Lk 10:34
1:7 [h]Lev 26:34
1:8 [i]Job 27:18
1:9 [j]Isa 10:20-22; 37:4,31-32 [k]Ge 19:24; Ro 9:29*
1:10 [l]Isa 28:14 [m]Isa 3:9; Eze 16:49; Ro 9:29; Rev 11:8 [n]Isa 8:20
1:11 [o]Ps 50:8 [p]Jer 6:20 [q]1Sa 15:22; Mal 1:10
1:12 [r]Ex 23:17
1:13 [s]Isa 66:3 [t]Jer 7:9 [u]1Ch 23:31
1:14 [v]Lev 23:1-44; Nu 28:11-29:39; Isa 29:1 [w]Isa 7:13; 43:22,24
1:15 [x]Isa 8:17; 59:2; Mic 3:4 [y]Isa 59:3
1:16 [z]Isa 52:11 [a]Isa 55:7; Jer 25:5
1:17 [b]Zep 2:3 [c]Ps 82:3
1:18 [d]Isa 41:1; 43:9,26 [e]Ps 51:7; Rev 7:14
1:19 [f]Dt 30:15 16; Isa 55:2
1:20 [g]Isa 3:25; 65:12 [h]Isa 34:16; 40:5; 58:14; Mic 4:4

[a]17 Or / *rebuke the oppressor*

has become a harlot![a]
She once was full of justice;
righteousness used to dwell in her—
but now murderers!
22 Your silver has become dross,
your choice wine is diluted with water.
23 Your rulers are rebels,
companions of thieves;
they all love bribes[b]
and chase after gifts.
They do not defend the cause of the fatherless;
the widow's case does not come before them.[c]
24 Therefore the Lord, the LORD Almighty,
the Mighty One of Israel, declares:
"Ah, I will get relief from my foes
and avenge[d] myself on my enemies.
25 I will turn my hand against you;
I will thoroughly purge away your dross
and remove all your impurities.[e]
26 I will restore your judges as in days of old,[f]
your counselors as at the beginning.
Afterward you will be called
the City of Righteousness,[g]
the Faithful City.[h]"
27 Zion will be redeemed with justice,
her penitent ones with righteousness.[i]
28 But rebels and sinners will both be broken,
and those who forsake the LORD will perish.[j]
29 "You will be ashamed because of the sacred oaks[k]
in which you have delighted;
you will be disgraced because of the gardens[l]
that you have chosen.
30 You will be like an oak with fading leaves,
like a garden without water.
31 The mighty man will become tinder
and his work a spark;
both will burn together,
with no one to quench the fire.[m]"

The Mountain of the LORD

2:1-4pp — Mic 4:1-3

2 This is what Isaiah son of Amoz saw concerning Judah and Jerusalem:[n]

2 In the last days

the mountain[o] of the LORD's temple will be established
as chief among the mountains;
it will be raised above the hills,
and all nations will stream to it.

3 Many peoples will come and say,

"Come, let us go up to the mountain of the LORD,
to the house of the God of Jacob.
He will teach us his ways,
so that we may walk in his paths."
The law[p] will go out from Zion,
the word of the LORD from Jerusalem.[q]
4 He will judge between the nations
and will settle disputes for many peoples.
They will beat their swords into plowshares
and their spears into pruning hooks.[r]
Nation will not take up sword against nation,[s]
nor will they train for war anymore.

5 Come, O house of Jacob,[t]
let us walk in the light[u] of the LORD.

The Day of the LORD

6 You have abandoned[v] your people,
the house of Jacob.
They are full of superstitions from the East;

1:21 [a] Isa 57:3-9; Jer 2:20
1:23 [b] Ex 23:8 [c] Isa 10:2; Jer 5:28; Eze 22:6-7; Zec 7:10
1:24 [d] Isa 35:4; 59:17; 61:2; 63:4
1:25 [e] Eze 22:22; Mal 3:3
1:26 [f] Jer 33:7,11 [g] Isa 33:5; 62:1; Zec 8:3 [h] Isa 60:14; 62:2
1:27 [i] Isa 35:10; 62:12; 63:4
1:28 [j] Ps 9:5; Isa 24:20; 66:24; 2Th 1:8-9
1:29 [k] Isa 57:5 [l] Isa 65:3; 66:17
1:31 [m] Isa 5:24; 9:18-19; 26:11; 33:14; 66:15-16,24
2:1 [n] Isa 1:1
2:2 [o] Isa 27:13; 56:7; 66:20; Mic 4:7
2:3 [p] Isa 51:4,7 [q] Lk 24:47
2:4 [r] Joel 3:10 [s] Ps 46:9; Isa 9:5; 11:6-9; 32:18; Hos 2:18; Zec 9:10
2:5 [t] Isa 58:1 [u] Isa 60:1, 19-20; 1Jn 1:5,7
2:6 [v] Dt 31:17

they practice divination like
the Philistines[a]
and clasp hands[b] with
pagans.[c]
7Their land is full of silver and
gold;
there is no end to their
treasures.
Their land is full of horses;[d]
there is no end to their
chariots.[e]
8Their land is full of idols;[f]
they bow down to the work
of their hands,
to what their fingers[g] have
made.
9So man will be brought low[h]
and mankind humbled[i]—
do not forgive them.[b][j]

10Go into the rocks,
hide in the ground
from dread of the LORD
and the splendor of his
majesty![k]
11The eyes of the arrogant man
will be humbled
and the pride[l] of men
brought low;
the LORD alone will be exalted
in that day.

12The LORD Almighty has a day in
store
for all the proud and lofty,
for all that is exalted[m]
(and they will be humbled),[n]
13for all the cedars of Lebanon,
tall and lofty,
and all the oaks of Bashan,[o]
14for all the towering mountains
and all the high hills,[p]
15for every lofty tower
and every fortified wall,[q]
16for every trading ship[c][r]
and every stately vessel.
17The arrogance of man will be
brought low
and the pride of men
humbled;
the LORD alone will be exalted
in that day,[s]
18 and the idols will totally
disappear.[t]

19Men will flee to caves in the
rocks
and to holes in the ground

2:6 [a]2Ki 1:2 [b]Pr 6:1 [c]2Ki 16:7
2:7 [d]Dt 17:16 [e]Isa 31:1; Mic 5:10
2:8 [f]Isa 10:9-11 [g]Isa 17:8
2:9 [h]Ps 62:9 [i]Isa 5:15 [j]Ne 4:5
2:10 [k]2Th 1:9; Rev 6:15-16
2:11 [l]Isa 5:15; 37:23
2:12 [m]Isa 24:4,21; Mal 4:1 [n]Job 40:11
2:13 [o]Zec 11:2
2:14 [p]Isa 30:25; 40:4
2:15 [q]Isa 25:2,12
2:16 [r]1Ki 10:22
2:17 [s]ver 11
2:18 [t]Isa 21:9
2:19 [u]Heb 12:26
2:20 [v]Lev 11:19
2:21 [w]ver 19
2:22 [x]Ps 146:3; Jer 17:5 [y]Ps 8:4; 144:3; Isa 40:15; Jas 4:14
3:1 [z]Lev 26:26 [a]Isa 5:13; Eze 4:16
3:2 [b]Eze 17:13 [c]2Ki 24:14; Isa 9:14-15
3:4 [d]Ecc 10:16 fn
3:5 [e]Isa 9:19; Jer 9:8; Mic 7:2,6

from dread of the LORD
and the splendor of his
majesty,
when he rises to shake the
earth.[u]
20In that day men will throw
away
to the rodents and bats[v]
their idols of silver and idols of
gold,
which they made to worship.
21They will flee to caverns in the
rocks
and to the overhanging crags
from dread of the LORD
and the splendor of his
majesty,
when he rises to shake the
earth.[w]

22Stop trusting in man,[x]
who has but a breath in his
nostrils.
Of what account is he?[y]

Judgment on Jerusalem and Judah

3 See now, the Lord,
the LORD Almighty,
is about to take from Jerusalem
and Judah
both supply and support:
all supplies of food[z] and all
supplies of water,[a]
2 the hero and warrior,[b]
the judge and prophet,
the soothsayer and elder,[c]
3the captain of fifty and man of
rank,
the counselor, skilled
craftsman and clever
enchanter.

4I will make boys their officials;
mere children will govern
them.[d]
5People will oppress each
other—
man against man, neighbor
against neighbor.[e]
The young will rise up against
the old,
the base against the
honorable.

b9 Or *not raise them up* c16 Hebrew *every ship of Tarshish*

6A man will seize one of his brothers
at his father's home, and say,
"You have a cloak, you be our leader;
take charge of this heap of ruins!"
7But in that day he will cry out,
"I have no remedy.[a]
I have no food or clothing in my house;
do not make me the leader of the people."

8Jerusalem staggers,
Judah is falling;[b]
their words[c] and deeds are against the LORD,
defying[d] his glorious presence.
9The look on their faces testifies against them;
they parade their sin like Sodom;[e]
they do not hide it.
Woe to them!
They have brought disaster[f] upon themselves.

10Tell the righteous it will be well[g] with them,
for they will enjoy the fruit of their deeds.[h]
11Woe to the wicked! Disaster[i] is upon them!
They will be paid back for what their hands have done.

12Youths[j] oppress my people,
women rule over them.
O my people, your guides lead you astray;[k]
they turn you from the path.

13The LORD takes his place in court;
he rises to judge[l] the people.
14The LORD enters into judgment[m]
against the elders and leaders of his people:
"It is you who have ruined my vineyard;
the plunder[n] from the poor is in your houses.
15What do you mean by crushing my people[o]
and grinding the faces of the poor?"
declares the Lord, the LORD Almighty.

16The LORD says,
"The women of Zion[p] are haughty,
walking along with outstretched necks,
flirting with their eyes,
tripping along with mincing steps,
with ornaments jingling on their ankles.
17Therefore the Lord will bring sores on the heads of the women of Zion;
the LORD will make their scalps bald."

18In that day the Lord will
snatch away their finery: the ban-
gles and headbands and crescent
necklaces,[q] 19the earrings and
bracelets and veils, 20the head-
dresses[r] and ankle chains and
sashes, the perfume bottles and
charms, 21the signet rings and nose
rings, 22the fine robes and the
capes and cloaks, the purses 23and
mirrors, and the linen garments
and tiaras and shawls.

24Instead of fragrance[s] there will be a stench;
instead of a sash,[t] a rope;
instead of well-dressed hair, baldness;[u]
instead of fine clothing, sackcloth;[v]
instead of beauty,[w] branding.
25Your men will fall by the sword,[x]
your warriors in battle.
26The gates of Zion will lament and mourn;[y]
destitute, she will sit on the ground.[z]

4 In that day seven women will take hold of one man[a]
and say, "We will eat our own food[b]
and provide our own clothes;
only let us be called by your name.
Take away our disgrace!"[c]

3:7 [a]Eze 34:4; Hos 5:13
3:8 [b]Isa 1:7 [c]Isa 9:15,17 [d]Ps 73:9,11
3:9 [e]Ge 13:13 [f]Pr 8:36; Ro 6:23
3:10 [g]Dt 28:1-14 [h]Ps 128:2
3:11 [i]Dt 28:15-68
3:12 [j]ver 4 [k]Isa 9:16
3:13 [l]Mic 6:2
3:14 [m]Job 22:4 [n]Job 24:9; Jas 2:6
3:15 [o]Ps 94:5
3:16 [p]SS 3:11
3:18 [q]Jdg 8:21
3:20 [r]Ex 39:28
3:24 [s]Est 2:12 [t]Pr 31:24 [u]Isa 22:12 [v]La 2:10; Eze 27:30-31 [w]1Pe 3:3
3:25 [x]Isa 1:20
3:26 [y]Jer 14:2 [z]La 2:10
4:1 [a]Isa 13:12 [b]2Th 3:12 [c]Ge 30:23

The Branch of the Lord

2In that day the Branch of the
Lord[a] will be beautiful and glorious, and the fruit[b] of the land will
be the pride and glory of the survivors in Israel. **3**Those who are left
in Zion, who remain[c] in Jerusalem, will be called holy,[d] all who
are recorded[e] among the living in
Jerusalem. **4**The Lord will wash
away the filth[f] of the women of
Zion; he will cleanse the blood-
stains[g] from Jerusalem by a spirit[d] of judgment[h] and a spirit[d] of
fire.[i] **5**Then the Lord will create
over all of Mount Zion and over
those who assemble there a cloud
of smoke by day and a glow of flaming fire by night;[j] over all the glory[k] will be a canopy. **6**It will be a
shelter[l] and shade from the heat
of the day, and a refuge[m] and hiding place from the storm and rain.

The Song of the Vineyard

5 I will sing for the one I love
a song about his vineyard:[n]
My loved one had a vineyard
on a fertile hillside.
2He dug it up and cleared it of
stones
and planted it with the
choicest vines.[o]
He built a watchtower in it
and cut out a winepress as
well.
Then he looked for a crop of
good grapes,
but it yielded only bad
fruit.[p]

3"Now you dwellers in
Jerusalem and men of
Judah,
judge between me and my
vineyard.[q]
4What more could have been
done for my vineyard
than I have done for it?[r]
When I looked for good grapes,
why did it yield only bad?
5Now I will tell you
what I am going to do to my
vineyard:
I will take away its hedge,
and it will be destroyed;

4:2 [a]Isa 11:1-5; 53:2; Jer 23:5-6; Zec 3:8; 6:12 [b]Ps 72:16
4:3 [c]Ro 11:5 [d]Isa 52:1; 60:21 [e]Lk 10:20
4:4 [f]Isa 3:24 [g]Isa 1:15 [h]Isa 28:6 [i]Isa 1:31; Mt 3:11
4:5 [j]Ex 13:21 [k]Isa 60:1
4:6 [l]Ps 27:5 [m]Isa 25:4
5:1 [n]Ps 80:8-9
5:2 [o]Jer 2:21 [p]Mt 21:19; Mk 11:13; Lk 13:6
5:3 [q]Mt 21:40
5:4 [r]2Ch 36:15; Jer 2:5-7; Mic 6:3-4; Mt 23:37
5:5 [s]Ps 80:12 [t]Isa 28:3,18; La 1:15; Lk 21:24
5:6 [u]Isa 7:23,24; Heb 6:8
5:7 [v]Ps 80:8 [w]Isa 59:15
5:8 [x]Jer 22:13 [y]Mic 2:2; Hab 2:9-12
5:9 [z]Isa 22:14 [a]Isa 6:11-12; Mt 23:38
5:10 [b]Lev 26:26
5:11 [c]Pr 23:29-30

I will break down its wall,[s]
and it will be trampled.[t]
6I will make it a wasteland,
neither pruned nor
cultivated,
and briers and thorns[u] will
grow there.
I will command the clouds
not to rain on it."

7The vineyard[v] of the Lord
Almighty
is the house of Israel,
and the men of Judah
are the garden of his delight.
And he looked for justice,[w] but
saw bloodshed;
for righteousness, but heard
cries of distress.

Woes and Judgments

8Woe[x] to you who add house to
house
and join field to field[y]
till no space is left
and you live alone in the
land.

9The Lord Almighty has declared
in my hearing:[z]

"Surely the great houses will
become desolate,[a]
the fine mansions left
without occupants.
10A ten-acre[e] vineyard will
produce only a bath[f] of
wine,
a homer[g] of seed only an
ephah[h] of grain."[b]

11Woe to those who rise early in
the morning
to run after their drinks,
who stay up late at night
till they are inflamed with
wine.[c]
12They have harps and lyres at
their banquets,
tambourines and flutes and
wine,

[d]4 Or *the Spirit* [e]*10* Hebrew *ten-yoke,* that is, the land plowed by 10 yoke of oxen in one day [f]*10* That is, probably about 6 gallons (about 22 liters) [g]*10* That is, probably about 6 bushels (about 220 liters)
[h]*10* That is, probably about 3/5 bushel (about 22 liters)

but they have no regard[a] for
the deeds of the LORD,
no respect for the work of his
hands.[b]
13Therefore my people will go
into exile[c]
for lack of understanding;[d]
their men of rank will die of
hunger
and their masses will be
parched with thirst.
14Therefore the grave[i][e] enlarges
its appetite
and opens its mouth[f]
without limit;
into it will descend their nobles
and masses
with all their brawlers and
revelers.
15So man will be brought low[g]
and mankind humbled,[h]
the eyes of the arrogant[i]
humbled.
16But the LORD Almighty will be
exalted by his justice,[j]
and the holy God will show
himself holy[k] by his
righteousness.
17Then sheep will graze as in
their own pasture;[l]
lambs will feed[j] among the
ruins of the rich.

18Woe to those who draw sin
along with cords of
deceit,
and wickedness[m] as with cart
ropes,
19to those who say, "Let God
hurry,
let him hasten his work
so we may see it.
Let it approach,
let the plan of the Holy One
of Israel come,
so we may know it."[n]

20Woe to those who call evil good
and good evil,
who put darkness for light
and light for darkness,[o]
who put bitter for sweet
and sweet for bitter.[p]

21Woe to those who are wise in
their own eyes[q]
and clever in their own sight.

22Woe to those who are heroes at
drinking wine[r]
and champions at mixing
drinks,
23who acquit the guilty for a
bribe,[s]
but deny justice[t] to the
innocent.[u]
24Therefore, as tongues of fire
lick up straw
and as dry grass sinks down
in the flames,
so their roots will decay[v]
and their flowers blow away
like dust;
for they have rejected the law
of the LORD Almighty
and spurned the word[w] of
the Holy One of Israel.
25Therefore the LORD's anger[x]
burns against his people;
his hand is raised and he
strikes them down.
The mountains shake,
and the dead bodies are like
refuse[y] in the streets.

Yet for all this, his anger is not
turned away,[z]
his hand is still upraised.[a]

26He lifts up a banner for the
distant nations,
he whistles[b] for those at the
ends of the earth.[c]
Here they come,
swiftly and speedily!
27Not one of them grows tired or
stumbles,
not one slumbers or sleeps;
not a belt is loosened at the
waist,[d]
not a sandal thong is
broken.[e]
28Their arrows are sharp,[f]
all their bows[g] are strung;
their horses' hoofs seem like
flint,
their chariot wheels like a
whirlwind.
29Their roar is like that of the
lion,[h]
they roar like young lions;
they growl as they seize[i] their
prey

5:12 [a]Job 34:27 [b]Ps 28:5; Am 6:5-6
5:13 [c]Hos 4:6 [d]Isa 1:3; Hos 4:6
5:14 [e]Pr 30:16 [f]Nu 16:30
5:15 [g]Isa 10:33 [h]Isa 2:9 [i]Isa 2:11
5:16 [j]Isa 28:17; 30:18; 33:5; 61:8 [k]Isa 29:23
5:17 [l]Isa 7:25; Zep 2:6,14
5:18 [m]Isa 59:4-8; Jer 23:14
5:19 [n]Jer 17:15; Eze 12:22; 2Pe 3:4
5:20 [o]Mt 6:22-23; Lk 11:34-35 [p]Am 5:7
5:21 [q]Pr 3:7; Ro 12:16; 1Co 3:18-20
5:22 [r]Pr 23:20
5:23 [s]Ex 23:8 [t]Isa 10:2 [u]Ps 94:21; Jas 5:6
5:24 [v]Job 18:16 [w]Isa 8:6; 30:9,12
5:25 [x]2Ki 22:13 [y]2Ki 9:37 [z]Jer 4:8; Da 9:16 [a]Isa 9:12,17, 21; 10:4
5:26 [b]Isa 7:18; Zec 10:8 [c]Dt 28:49; Isa 13:5; 18:3
5:27 [d]Job 12:18 [e]Joel 2:7-8
5:28 [f]Ps 45:5 [g]Ps 7:12
5:29 [h]Jer 51:38; Zep 3:3; Zec 11:3 [i]Isa 10:6; 49:24-25

[i]14 Hebrew *Sheol* [j]17 Septuagint; Hebrew / *strangers will eat*

and carry it off with no one
to rescue.[a]
30 In that day they will roar over it
like the roaring of the sea.[b]
And if one looks at the land,
he will see darkness and
distress;[c]
even the light will be
darkened[d] by the
clouds.

Isaiah's Commission

6 In the year that King Uzziah[e]
died,[f] I saw the Lord[g] seated
on a throne,[h] high and exalted,
and the train of his robe filled the
temple. 2 Above him were seraphs,[i] each with six wings: With
two wings they covered their faces,
with two they covered their feet,[j]
and with two they were flying. 3 And
they were calling to one another:

"Holy, holy, holy is the LORD
Almighty;
the whole earth is full of his
glory."[k]

4 At the sound of their voices the
doorposts and thresholds shook
and the temple was filled with
smoke.
5 "Woe to me!" I cried. "I am ruined! For I am a man of unclean
lips, and I live among a people of
unclean lips,[l] and my eyes have
seen the King,[m] the LORD Almighty."
6 Then one of the seraphs flew to
me with a live coal in his hand,
which he had taken with tongs
from the altar. 7 With it he touched
my mouth and said, "See, this has
touched your lips;[n] your guilt is
taken away and your sin atoned
for.[o]"
8 Then I heard the voice[p] of the
Lord saying, "Whom shall I send?
And who will go for us?"
And I said, "Here am I. Send
me!"
9 He said, "Go[q] and tell this people:

" 'Be ever hearing, but never
understanding;
be ever seeing, but never
perceiving.'[r]
10 Make the heart of this people
calloused;[s]
make their ears dull
and close their eyes.[k]
Otherwise they might see with
their eyes,
hear with their ears,[t]
understand with their hearts,
and turn and be healed."[u]

11 Then I said, "For how long,
O Lord?"[v]
And he answered:

"Until the cities lie ruined[w]
and without inhabitant,
until the houses are left
deserted
and the fields ruined and
ravaged,
12 until the LORD has sent
everyone far away[x]
and the land is utterly
forsaken.[y]
13 And though a tenth remains[z]
in the land,
it will again be laid waste.
But as the terebinth and oak
leave stumps when they are
cut down,
so the holy seed will be the
stump in the land."[a]

The Sign of Immanuel

7 When Ahaz son of Jotham, the
son of Uzziah, was king of Judah, King Rezin[b] of Aram[c] and
Pekah[d] son of Remaliah king of Israel marched up to fight against Jerusalem, but they could not overpower it.
2 Now the house of David[e] was
told, "Aram has allied itself with[l]
Ephraim[f]"; so the hearts of Ahaz
and his people were shaken, as the
trees of the forest are shaken by the
wind.
3 Then the LORD said to Isaiah,
"Go out, you and your son Shear-
Jashub,[m] to meet Ahaz at the end
of the aqueduct of the Upper Pool,
on the road to thc Washerman's

5:29 [a] Isa 42:22; Mic 5:8
5:30 [b] Lk 21:25 [c] Isa 8:22; Jer 4:23-28 [d] Joel 2:10
6:1 [e] 2Ch 26:22,23 [f] 2Ki 15:7 [g] Jn 12:41 [h] Rev 4:2
6:2 [i] Rev 4:8 [j] Eze 1:11
6:3 [k] Ps 72:19; Rev 4:8
6:5 [l] Jer 9:3-8 [m] Jer 51:57
6:7 [n] Jer 1:9 [o] 1Jn 1:7
6:8 [p] Ac 9:4
6:9 [q] Eze 3:11 [r] Mt 13:15*; Lk 8:10*
6:10 [s] Dt 32:15; Ps 119:70 [t] Jer 5:21 [u] Mt 13:13-15; Mk 4:12*; Ac 28:26-27*
6:11 [v] Ps 79:5 [w] Lev 26:31
6:12 [x] Dt 28:64 [y] Jer 4:29
6:13 [z] Isa 1:9 [a] Job 14:7
7:1 [b] 2Ki 15:37 [c] 2Ch 28:5 [d] 2Ki 15:25
7:2 [e] ver 13; Isa 22:22 [f] Isa 9:9

[k] 9,10 Hebrew; Septuagint *'You will be ever hearing, but never understanding; / you will be ever seeing, but never perceiving.' / 10This people's heart has become calloused; / they hardly hear with their ears, / and they have closed their eyes*
[l] 2 Or *has set up camp in*
[m] 3 *Shear-Jashub* means *a remnant will return.*

Field.[a] **4**Say to him, 'Be careful,
keep calm[b] and don't be afraid.[c]
Do not lose heart[d] because of
these two smoldering stubs[e] of
firewood—because of the fierce
anger[f] of Rezin and Aram and of
the son of Remaliah. **5**Aram,
Ephraim and Remaliah's son have
plotted your ruin, saying, **6**"Let us
invade Judah; let us tear it apart
and divide it among ourselves, and
make the son of Tabeel king over
it." **7**Yet this is what the Sovereign
LORD says:

" 'It will not take place,
it will not happen,[g]
8for the head of Aram is
Damascus,[h]
and the head of Damascus is
only Rezin.
Within sixty-five years
Ephraim will be too
shattered[i] to be a
people.
9The head of Ephraim is
Samaria,
and the head of Samaria is
only Remaliah's son.
If you do not stand firm in your
faith,[j]
you will not stand at all.' "[k]

10Again the LORD spoke to Ahaz,
11"Ask the LORD your God for a
sign, whether in the deepest
depths or in the highest heights."
12But Ahaz said, "I will not ask;
I will not put the LORD to the test."
13Then Isaiah said, "Hear now,
you house of David! Is it not
enough to try the patience of men?
Will you try the patience of my
God[l] also? **14**Therefore the Lord
himself will give you[n] a sign: The
virgin will be with child and will
give birth to a son,[m] and[o] will call
him Immanuel.[p][n] **15**He will eat
curds and honey[o] when he knows
enough to reject the wrong and
choose the right. **16**But before the
boy knows[p] enough to reject the
wrong and choose the right, the
land of the two kings you dread will
be laid waste.[q] **17**The LORD will
bring on you and on your people
and on the house of your father a
time unlike any since Ephraim

7:3 [a]2Ki 18:17; Isa 36:2
7:4 [b]Isa 30:15 [c]Isa 35:4 [d]Dt 20:3 [e]Zec 3:2 [f]Isa 10:24
7:7 [g]Isa 8:10; Ac 4:25
7:8 [h]Ge 14:15 [i]Isa 17:1-3
7:9 [j]2Ch 20:20 [k]Isa 8:6-8; 30:12-14
7:13 [l]Isa 25:1
7:14 [m]Lk 1:31 [n]Isa 8:8,10; Mt 1:23*
7:15 [o]ver 22
7:16 [p]Isa 8:4 [q]Isa 17:3; Hos 5:9,13; Am 1:3-5
7:17 [r]1Ki 12:16 [s]2Ch 28:20
7:18 [t]Isa 5:26 [u]Isa 13:5
7:19 [v]Isa 2:19
7:20 [w]Isa 10:15 [x]Isa 8:7; 10:5
7:23 [y]Isa 5:6
7:25 [z]Isa 5:17
8:1 [a]Isa 30:8; Hab 2:2 [b]ver 3; Hab 2:2
8:2 [c]2Ki 16:10
8:4 [d]Isa 7:16 [e]Isa 7:8

broke away[r] from Judah—he will
bring the king of Assyria.[s]"
18In that day the LORD will whis-
tle[t] for flies from the distant
streams of Egypt and for bees from
the land of Assyria.[u] **19**They will all
come and settle in the steep ravines and in the crevices[v] in the
rocks, on all the thornbushes and
at all the water holes. **20**In that day
the Lord will use[w] a razor hired
from beyond the River[q]—the king
of Assyria[x]—to shave your head
and the hair of your legs, and to
take off your beards also. **21**In that
day, a man will keep alive a young
cow and two goats. **22**And because
of the abundance of the milk they
give, he will have curds to eat. All
who remain in the land will eat
curds and honey. **23**In that day, in
every place where there were a
thousand vines worth a thousand
silver shekels,[r] there will be only
briers and thorns.[y] **24**Men will go
there with bow and arrow, for the
land will be covered with briers and
thorns. **25**As for all the hills once
cultivated by the hoe, you will no
longer go there for fear of the briers
and thorns; they will become
places where cattle are turned
loose and where sheep run.[z]

Assyria, the LORD's Instrument

8 The LORD said to me, "Take a
large scroll[a] and write on it
with an ordinary pen: Maher-Shalal-Hash-Baz.[s][b] **2**And I will call in
Uriah[c] the priest and Zechariah
son of Jeberekiah as reliable witnesses for me."
3Then I went to the prophetess,
and she conceived and gave birth
to a son. And the LORD said to me,
"Name him Maher-Shalal-Hash-
Baz. **4**Before the boy knows[d] how
to say 'My father' or 'My mother,'
the wealth of Damascus and the
plunder of Samaria will be carried
off by the king of Assyria.[e]"

[n]*14* The Hebrew is plural. [o]*14* Masoretic Text; Dead Sea Scrolls *and he* or *and they*
[p]*14 Immanuel* means *God with us.*
[q]*20* That is, the Euphrates [r]*23* That is, about 25 pounds (about 11.5 kilograms)
[s]*1 Maher-Shalal-Hash-Baz* means *quick to the plunder, swift to the spoil*; also in verse 3.

5 The LORD spoke to me again:

6 "Because this people has
rejected[a]
the gently flowing waters of
Shiloah[b]
and rejoices over Rezin
and the son of Remaliah,[c]
7 therefore the Lord is about to
bring against them
the mighty floodwaters[d] of
the River[t]—
the king of Assyria[e] with all
his pomp.
It will overflow all its channels,
run over all its banks
8 and sweep on into Judah,
swirling over it,
passing through it and
reaching up to the neck.
Its outspread wings will cover
the breadth of your land,
O Immanuel[u]!"[f]

9 Raise the war cry,[v][g] you
nations, and be
shattered!
Listen, all you distant lands.
Prepare[h] for battle, and be
shattered!
Prepare for battle, and be
shattered!
10 Devise your strategy, but it will
be thwarted;[i]
propose your plan, but it will
not stand,[j]
for God is with us.[w][k]

Fear God

11 The LORD spoke to me with his
strong hand upon me,[l] warning
me not to follow[m] the way of this
people. He said:

12 "Do not call conspiracy[n]
everything that these people
call conspiracy[x];
do not fear what they fear,
and do not dread it.[o]
13 The LORD Almighty is the one
you are to regard as
holy,[p]
he is the one you are to fear,
he is the one you are to
dread,[q]
14 and he will be a sanctuary;[r]
but for both houses of Israel
he will be
a stone that causes men to
stumble
and a rock that makes them
fall.[s]
And for the people of
Jerusalem he will be
a trap and a snare.[t]
15 Many of them will stumble;[u]
they will fall and be broken,
they will be snared and
captured."

16 Bind up the testimony
and seal[v] up the law among
my disciples.
17 I will wait[w] for the LORD,
who is hiding[x] his face from
the house of Jacob.
I will put my trust in him.

18 Here am I, and the children
the LORD has given me.[y] We are
signs[z] and symbols in Israel from
the LORD Almighty, who dwells on
Mount Zion.[a]

19 When men tell you to consult[b]
mediums and spiritists, who whisper and mutter,[c] should not a people inquire of their God? Why consult the dead on behalf of the living? 20 To the law[d] and to the
testimony! If they do not speak according to this word, they have no
light[e] of dawn. 21 Distressed and
hungry, they will roam through the
land; when they are famished, they
will become enraged and, looking
upward, will curse[f] their king and
their God. 22 Then they will look toward the earth and see only distress and darkness and fearful
gloom, and they will be thrust into
utter darkness.[g]

To Us a Child Is Born

9 Nevertheless, there will be no
more gloom for those who were
in distress. In the past he humbled
the land of Zebulun and the land of
Naphtali,[h] but in the future he will
honor Galilee of the Gentiles, by
the way of the sea, along the Jordan—

8:6 [a] Isa 5:24 [b] Jn 9:7 [c] Isa 7:1
8:7 [d] Isa 17:12-13 [e] Isa 7:20
8:8 [f] Isa 7:14
8:9 [g] Isa 17:12-13 [h] Joel 3:9
8:10 [i] Job 5:12 [j] Isa 7:7 [k] Isa 7:14; Ro 8:31
8:11 [l] Eze 3:14 [m] Eze 2:8
8:12 [n] Isa 7:2; 30:1 [o] 1Pe 3:14*
8:13 [p] Nu 20:12 [q] Isa 29:23
8:14 [r] Isa 4:6; Eze 11:16 [s] Lk 2:34; Ro 9:33*; 1Pe 2:8* [t] Isa 24:17-18
8:15 [u] Isa 28:13; 59:10; Lk 20:18; Ro 9:32
8:16 [v] Isa 29:11-12
8:17 [w] Hab 2:3 [x] Dt 31:17; Isa 54:8
8:18 [y] Heb 2:13* [z] Lk 2:34 [a] Ps 9:11
8:19 [b] 1Sa 28:8 [c] Isa 29:4
8:20 [d] Isa 1:10; Lk 16:29 [e] Mic 3:6
8:21 [f] Rev 16:11
8:22 [g] ver 20; Isa 5:30
9:1 [h] 2Ki 15:29

[t] 7 That is, the Euphrates [u] 8 *Immanuel* means *God with us.* [v] 9 Or *Do your worst* [w] 10 Hebrew *Immanuel* [x] 12 Or *Do not call for a treaty / every time these people call for a treaty*

2The people walking in darkness
have seen a great light;[a]
on those living in the land of
the shadow of death[y][b]
a light has dawned.[c]
3You have enlarged the nation
and increased their joy;
they rejoice before you
as people rejoice at the
harvest,
as men rejoice
when dividing the plunder.
4For as in the day of Midian's
defeat,[d]
you have shattered
the yoke[e] that burdens them,
the bar across their
shoulders,[f]
the rod of their oppressor.[g]
5Every warrior's boot used in
battle
and every garment rolled in
blood
will be destined for burning,[h]
will be fuel for the fire.
6For to us a child is born,[i]
to us a son is given,[j]
and the government[k] will be
on his shoulders.
And he will be called
Wonderful Counselor,[z][l]
Mighty God,[m]
Everlasting Father, Prince of
Peace.[n]
7Of the increase of his
government and peace
there will be no end.[o]
He will reign on David's throne
and over his kingdom,
establishing and upholding it
with justice[p] and
righteousness
from that time on and
forever.
The zeal[q] of the LORD Almighty
will accomplish this.

The LORD's Anger Against Israel

8The Lord has sent a message
against Jacob;
it will fall on Israel.
9All the people will know it—
Ephraim and the inhabitants
of Samaria[r]—
who say with pride
and arrogance[s] of heart,
10"The bricks have fallen down,
but we will rebuild with
dressed stone;
the fig trees have been felled,
but we will replace them
with cedars."
11But the LORD has strengthened
Rezin's[t] foes against
them
and has spurred their
enemies on.
12Arameans[u] from the east and
Philistines[v] from the
west
have devoured[w] Israel with
open mouth.

Yet for all this, his anger is not
turned away,
his hand is still upraised.[x]

13But the people have not
returned to him who
struck[y] them,
nor have they sought[z] the
LORD Almighty.
14So the LORD will cut off from
Israel both head and tail,
both palm branch and reed[a]
in a single day;[b]
15the elders[c] and prominent men
are the head,
the prophets who teach lies
are the tail.
16Those who guide[d] this people
mislead them,
and those who are guided are
led astray.[e]
17Therefore the Lord will take no
pleasure in the young
men,[f]
nor will he pity[g] the
fatherless and widows,
for everyone is ungodly[h] and
wicked,[i]
every mouth speaks
vileness.[j]

Yet for all this, his anger is not
turned away,
his hand is still upraised.[k]

18Surely wickedness burns like a
fire;[l]

9:2 [a]Eph 5:8 [b]Lk 1:79 [c]Mt 4:15-16*
9:4 [d]Jdg 7:25 [e]Isa 14:25 [f]Isa 10:27 [g]Isa 14:4; 49:26; 51:13; 54:14
9:5 [h]Isa 2:4
9:6 [i]Isa 53:2; Lk 2:11 [j]Jn 3:16 [k]Mt 28:18 [l]Isa 28:29 [m]Isa 10:21; 11:2 [n]Isa 26:3,12; 66:12
9:7 [o]Da 2:44; Lk 1:33 [p]Isa 11:4; 16:5; 32:1,16 [q]Isa 37:32; 59:17
9:9 [r]Isa 7:9 [s]Isa 46:12
9:11 [t]Isa 7:8
9:12 [u]2Ki 16:6 [v]2Ch 28:18 [w]Ps 79:7 [x]Isa 5:25
9:13 [y]Jer 5:3 [z]Isa 31:1; Hos 7:7,10
9:14 [a]Isa 19:15 [b]Rev 18:8
9:15 [c]Isa 3:2-3
9:16 [d]Mt 15:14; 23:16,24 [e]Isa 3:12
9:17 [f]Jer 18:21 [g]Isa 27:11 [h]Isa 10:6 [i]Isa 1:4 [j]Mt 12:34 [k]Isa 5:25
9:18 [l]Mal 4:1

[y]2 Or *land of darkness* [z]6 Or *Wonderful, Counselor*

it consumes briers and thorns,
it sets the forest thickets ablaze,[a]
so that it rolls upward in a column of smoke.
19By the wrath[b] of the LORD Almighty
the land will be scorched
and the people will be fuel for the fire;[c]
no one will spare his brother.[d]
20On the right they will devour,
but still be hungry;[e]
on the left they will eat,[f]
but not be satisfied.
Each will feed on the flesh of his own offspring[a]:
21 Manasseh will feed on Ephraim, and Ephraim on Manasseh;
together they will turn against Judah.[g]

Yet for all this, his anger is not turned away,
his hand is still upraised.[h]

10 Woe to those who make unjust laws,
to those who issue oppressive decrees,[i]
2to deprive[j] the poor of their rights
and withhold justice from the oppressed of my people,[k]
making widows their prey
and robbing the fatherless.
3What will you do on the day of reckoning,[l]
when disaster[m] comes from afar?
To whom will you run for help?[n]
Where will you leave your riches?
4Nothing will remain but to cringe among the captives[o]
or fall among the slain.[p]

Yet for all this, his anger is not turned away,[q]
his hand is still upraised.

9:18 [a]Ps 83:14
9:19 [b]Isa 13:9,13 [c]Isa 1:31 [d]Mic 7:2,6
9:20 [e]Lev 26:26 [f]Isa 49:26
9:21 [g]2Ch 28:6 [h]Isa 5:25
10:1 [i]Ps 58:2
10:2 [j]Isa 3:14 [k]Isa 5:23
10:3 [l]Job 31:14; Hos 9:7 [m]Lk 19:44 [n]Isa 20:6
10:4 [o]Isa 24:22 [p]Isa 22:2; 34:3; 66:16 [q]Isa 5:25
10:5 [r]Isa 14:25; Zep 2:13 [s]Jer 51:20 [t]Isa 13:3,5, 13; 30:30; 66:14
10:6 [u]Isa 9:17 [v]Isa 9:19 [w]Isa 5:29
10:7 [x]Ge 50:20; Ac 4:23-28
10:8 [y]2Ki 18:24
10:9 [z]Ge 10:10 [a]2Ch 35:20 [b]2Ki 17:6 [c]2Ki 16:9
10:10 [d]2Ki 19:18
10:12 [e]Isa 28:21-22; 65:7 [f]2Ki 19:31 [g]Jer 50:18
10:13 [h]Isa 37:24; Da 4:30 [i]Eze 28:4

God's Judgment on Assyria

5"Woe to the Assyrian,[r] the rod of my anger,
in whose hand is the club[s] of my wrath![t]
6I send him against a godless[u] nation,
I dispatch him against a people who anger me,[v]
to seize loot and snatch plunder,[w]
and to trample them down like mud in the streets.
7But this is not what he intends,[x]
this is not what he has in mind;
his purpose is to destroy,
to put an end to many nations.
8'Are not my commanders[y] all kings?' he says.
9 'Has not Calno[z] fared like Carchemish?[a]
Is not Hamath like Arpad,
and Samaria[b] like Damascus?[c]
10As my hand seized the kingdoms of the idols,[d]
kingdoms whose images excelled those of Jerusalem and Samaria—
11shall I not deal with Jerusalem and her images
as I dealt with Samaria and her idols?' "

12When the Lord has finished all
his work[e] against Mount Zion[f]
and Jerusalem, he will say, "I will
punish the king of Assyria[g] for the
willful pride of his heart and the
haughty look in his eyes. 13For he
says:

" 'By the strength of my hand I have done this,[h]
and by my wisdom, because I have understanding.
I removed the boundaries of nations,
I plundered their treasures;[i]
like a mighty one I subdued[b] their kings.

[a]20 Or *arm* [b]13 Or / *I subdued the mighty,*

14As one reaches into a nest,[a]
so my hand reached for the
wealth[b] of the nations;
as men gather abandoned eggs,
so I gathered all the
countries;
not one flapped a wing,
or opened its mouth to
chirp.' "
15Does the ax raise itself above
him who swings it,
or the saw boast against him
who uses it?[c]
As if a rod were to wield him
who lifts it up,
or a club[d] brandish him who
is not wood!
16Therefore, the Lord, the LORD
Almighty,
will send a wasting disease[e]
upon his sturdy warriors;
under his pomp[f] a fire will be
kindled
like a blazing flame.
17The Light of Israel will become
a fire,[g]
their Holy One[h] a flame;
in a single day it will burn and
consume
his thorns[i] and his briers.[j]
18The splendor of his forests[k]
and fertile fields
it will completely destroy,
as when a sick man wastes
away.
19And the remaining trees of his
forests will be so few[l]
that a child could write them
down.

The Remnant of Israel

20In that day[m] the remnant of
Israel,
the survivors of the house of
Jacob,
will no longer rely[n] on him
who struck them down[o]
but will truly rely[p] on the
LORD,
the Holy One of Israel.
21A remnant[q] will return,[c] a
remnant of Jacob
will return to the Mighty God.[r]
22Though your people, O Israel,
be like the sand by the
sea,
only a remnant will return.[s]
Destruction has been decreed,[t]
overwhelming and righteous.
23The Lord, the LORD Almighty,
will carry out
the destruction decreed upon
the whole land.[u]

24Therefore, this is what the
Lord, the LORD Almighty, says:

"O my people who live in
Zion,[v]
do not be afraid of the
Assyrians,
who beat[w] you with a rod
and lift up a club against
you, as Egypt did.
25Very soon[x] my anger against
you will end
and my wrath[y] will be
directed to their
destruction."

26The LORD Almighty will lash[z]
them with a whip,
as when he struck down
Midian[a] at the rock of
Oreb;
and he will raise his staff over
the waters,[b]
as he did in Egypt.
27In that day their burden will be
lifted from your
shoulders,
their yoke[c] from your neck;[d]
the yoke will be broken
because you have grown so
fat.[d]

28They enter Aiath;
they pass through Migron;[e]
they store supplies at
Micmash.[f]
29They go over the pass, and
say,
"We will camp overnight at
Geba."
Ramah[g] trembles;
Gibeah of Saul flees.
30Cry out, O Daughter of
Gallim![h]
Listen, O Laishah!
Poor Anathoth![i]
31Madmenah is in flight;

10:14 [a]Jer 49:16; Ob 1:4 [b]Job 31:25
10:15 [c]Isa 45:9; Ro 9:20-21 [d]ver 5
10:16 [e]ver 18; Isa 17:4 [f]Isa 8:7
10:17 [g]Isa 31:9 [h]Isa 37:23 [i]Nu 11:1-3 [j]Isa 9:18
10:18 [k]2Ki 19:23
10:19 [l]Isa 21:17
10:20 [m]Isa 11:10,11 [n]2Ki 16:7 [o]2Ch 28:20 [p]Isa 17:7
10:21 [q]Isa 6:13 [r]Isa 9:6
10:22 [s]Ro 9:27-28 [t]Isa 28:22; Da 9:27
10:23 [u]Isa 28:22; Ro 9:27-28*
10:24 [v]Ps 87:5-6 [w]Ex 5:14
10:25 [x]Isa 17:14 [y]ver 5; Da 11:36
10:26 [z]Isa 37:36-38 [a]Isa 9:4 [b]Ex 14:16
10:27 [c]Isa 9:4 [d]Isa 14:25
10:28 [e]1Sa 14:2 [f]1Sa 13:2
10:29 [g]Jos 18:25
10:30 [h]1Sa 25:44 [i]Ne 11:32

[c]*21* Hebrew *shear-jashub*; also in verse 22
[d]*27* Hebrew; Septuagint *broken / from your shoulders*

the people of Gebim take
cover.
32This day they will halt at
Nob;[a]
they will shake their fist
at the mount of the Daughter
of Zion,[b]
at the hill of Jerusalem.

33See, the Lord, the LORD
Almighty,
will lop off the boughs with
great power.
The lofty trees will be felled,
the tall[c] ones will be
brought low.
34He will cut down the forest
thickets with an ax;
Lebanon will fall before the
Mighty One.

The Branch From Jesse

11 A shoot will come up from
the stump of Jesse;[d]
from his roots a Branch[e] will
bear fruit.
2The Spirit[f] of the LORD will
rest on him—
the Spirit of wisdom[g] and of
understanding,
the Spirit of counsel and of
power,[h]
the Spirit of knowledge and
of the fear of the LORD—
3and he will delight in the fear
of the LORD.

He will not judge by what he
sees with his eyes,[i]
or decide by what he hears
with his ears;[j]
4but with righteousness[k] he will
judge the needy,
with justice[l] he will give
decisions for the poor[m]
of the earth.
He will strike[n] the earth with
the rod of his mouth;
with the breath[o] of his lips
he will slay the wicked.
5Righteousness will be his belt
and faithfulness[p] the sash
around his waist.[q]

6The wolf will live with the
lamb,[r]
the leopard will lie down
with the goat,

10:32 [a] 1Sa 21:1 [b] Jer 6:23
10:33 [c] Am 2:9
11:1 [d] ver 10; Isa 9:7; Rev 5:5 [e] Isa 4:2
11:2 [f] Isa 42:1; 48:16; 61:1; Mt 3:16; Jn 1:32-33 [g] Eph 1:17 [h] 2Ti 1:7
11:3 [i] Jn 7:24 [j] Jn 2:25
11:4 [k] Ps 72:2 [l] Isa 9:7 [m] Isa 3:14 [n] Mal 4:6 [o] Job 4:9; 2Th 2:8
11:5 [p] Isa 25:1 [q] Eph 6:14
11:6 [r] Isa 65:25
11:9 [s] Job 5:23 [t] Ps 98:2-3; Isa 52:10 [u] Isa 45:6,14; Hab 2:14
11:10 [v] Jn 12:32 [w] Isa 49:23; Lk 2:32 [x] Ro 15:12* [y] Isa 14:3; 28:12; 32:17-18
11:11 [z] Isa 10:20 [a] Isa 19:24; Hos 11:11; Mic 7:12; Zec 10:10 [b] Ge 10:22 [c] Isa 42:4,10, 12; 66:19
11:12 [d] Zep 3:10
11:13 [e] Jer 3:18; Eze 37:16-17, 22; Hos 1:11

the calf and the lion and the
yearling[e] together;
and a little child will lead
them.
7The cow will feed with the
bear,
their young will lie down
together,
and the lion will eat straw
like the ox.
8The infant will play near the
hole of the cobra,
and the young child put his
hand into the viper's
nest.
9They will neither harm nor
destroy[s]
on all my holy mountain,
for the earth[t] will be full of
the knowledge[u] of the
LORD
as the waters cover the sea.

10In that day the Root of Jesse
will stand as a banner[v] for the peoples; the nations[w] will rally to
him,[x] and his place of rest[y] will be
glorious. 11In that day[z] the Lord
will reach out his hand a second
time to reclaim the remnant that is
left of his people from Assyria,[a]
from Lower Egypt, from Upper
Egypt,[f] from Cush,[g] from Elam,[b]
from Babylonia,[h] from Hamath
and from the islands[c] of the sea.

12He will raise a banner for the
nations
and gather the exiles of
Israel;
he will assemble the scattered
people[d] of Judah
from the four quarters of the
earth.
13Ephraim's jealousy will vanish,
and Judah's enemies[i] will
be cut off;
Ephraim will not be jealous of
Judah,
nor Judah hostile toward
Ephraim.[e]
14They will swoop down on the
slopes of Philistia to the
west;

[e]6 Hebrew; Septuagint *lion will feed*
[f]11 Hebrew *from Pathros*
[g]11 That is, the upper Nile region
[h]11 Hebrew *Shinar*
[i]13 Or *hostility*

together they will plunder
the people to the east.
They will lay hands on Edom[a]
and Moab,[b]
and the Ammonites will be
subject to them.
15The LORD will dry up
the gulf of the Egyptian sea;
with a scorching wind he will
sweep his hand[c]
over the Euphrates River.[j][d]
He will break it up into seven
streams
so that men can cross over in
sandals.
16There will be a highway[e] for
the remnant of his
people
that is left from Assyria,
as there was for Israel
when they came up from
Egypt.[f]

Songs of Praise

12 In that day you will say:
"I will praise[g] you,
O LORD.
Although you were angry
with me,
your anger has turned away
and you have comforted me.
2Surely God is my salvation;
I will trust[h] and not be
afraid.
The LORD, the LORD, is my
strength and my song;
he has become my
salvation.[i]"
3With joy you will draw water[j]
from the wells of salvation.

4In that day you will say:

"Give thanks to the LORD, call
on his name;[k]
make known among the
nations what he has
done,
and proclaim that his name
is exalted.
5Sing[l] to the LORD, for he has
done glorious things;[m]
let this be known to all the
world.
6Shout aloud and sing for joy,
people of Zion,
for great is the Holy One of
Israel[n] among you.[o]"

A Prophecy Against Babylon

13 An oracle concerning Babylon that Isaiah son of Amoz saw:

2Raise a banner[p] on a bare
hilltop,
shout to them;
beckon to them
to enter the gates of the
nobles.
3I have commanded my holy
ones;
I have summoned my
warriors[q] to carry out
my wrath—
those who rejoice[r] in my
triumph.

4Listen, a noise on the
mountains,
like that of a great
multitude![s]
Listen, an uproar among the
kingdoms,
like nations massing
together!
The LORD Almighty is mustering
an army for war.
5They come from faraway lands,
from the ends of the
heavens[t]—
the LORD and the weapons of
his wrath—
to destroy[u] the whole
country.

6Wail,[v] for the day[w] of the LORD
is near;
it will come like destruction
from the Almighty.[k]
7Because of this, all hands will
go limp,
every man's heart will melt.[x]
8Terror[y] will seize them,
pain and anguish will grip
them;
they will writhe like a woman
in labor.
They will look aghast at each
other,
their faces aflame.[z]

11:14 [a]Da 11:41; Joel 3:19 [b]Isa 16:14; 25:10
11:15 [c]Isa 19:16 [d]Isa 7:20
11:16 [e]Isa 19:23; 62:10 [f]Ex 14:26-31
12:1 [g]Isa 25:1
12:2 [h]Isa 26:3 [i]Ex 15:2; Ps 118:14
12:3 [j]Jn 4:10,14
12:4 [k]Ps 105:1; Isa 24:15
12:5 [l]Ex 15:1 [m]Ps 98:1
12:6 [n]Isa 49:26 [o]Zep 3:14-17
13:2 [p]Jer 50:2; 51:27
13:3 [q]Joel 3:11 [r]Ps 149:2
13:4 [s]Joel 3:14
13:5 [t]Isa 5:26 [u]Isa 24:1
13:6 [v]Eze 30:2 [w]Isa 2:12; Joel 1:15
13:7 [x]Eze 21:7
13:8 [y]Isa 21:4 [z]Na 2:10

[j]15 Hebrew *the River* [k]6 Hebrew *Shaddai*

[9]See, the day of the LORD is coming
—a cruel day, with wrath and fierce anger—
to make the land desolate
and destroy the sinners within it.
[10]The stars of heaven and their constellations
will not show their light.
The rising sun[a] will be darkened[b]
and the moon will not give its light.[c]
[11]I will punish[d] the world for its evil,
the wicked for their sins.
I will put an end to the arrogance of the haughty
and will humble the pride of the ruthless.
[12]I will make man[e] scarcer than pure gold,
more rare than the gold of Ophir.
[13]Therefore I will make the heavens tremble;[f]
and the earth will shake from its place
at the wrath of the LORD Almighty,
in the day of his burning anger.
[14]Like a hunted gazelle,
like sheep without a shepherd,[g]
each will return to his own people,
each will flee to his native land.[h]
[15]Whoever is captured will be thrust through;
all who are caught will fall[i] by the sword.[j]
[16]Their infants[k] will be dashed to pieces before their eyes;
their houses will be looted and their wives ravished.

[17]See, I will stir up[l] against them the Medes,
who do not care for silver
and have no delight in gold.[m]
[18]Their bows will strike down the young men;
they will have no mercy on infants
nor will they look with compassion on children.
[19]Babylon, the jewel of kingdoms,
the glory[n] of the Babylonians'[1] pride,
will be overthrown[o] by God
like Sodom and Gomorrah.[p]
[20]She will never be inhabited[q]
or lived in through all generations;
no Arab[r] will pitch his tent there,
no shepherd will rest his flocks there.
[21]But desert creatures[s] will lie there,
jackals will fill her houses;
there the owls will dwell,
and there the wild goats will leap about.
[22]Hyenas will howl in her strongholds,[t]
jackals[u] in her luxurious palaces.
Her time is at hand,[v]
and her days will not be prolonged.

14

[1]The LORD will have compassion[w] on Jacob;
once again he will choose[x] Israel
and will settle them in their own land.
Aliens[y] will join them
and unite with the house of Jacob.
[2]Nations will take them
and bring[z] them to their own place.
And the house of Israel will possess the nations[a]
as menservants and maidservants in the LORD's land.
They will make captives of their captors
and rule over their oppressors.[b]

[3]On the day the LORD gives you
relief[c] from suffering and turmoil

13:10 [a]Isa 24:23 [b]Isa 5:30; Rev 8:12 [c]Eze 32:7; Mt 24:29*; Mk 13:24*
13:11 [d]Isa 3:11; 11:4; 26:21
13:12 [e]Isa 4:1
13:13 [f]Isa 34:4; 51:6; Hag 2:6
13:14 [g]1Ki 22:17 [h]Jer 50:16
13:15 [i]Jer 51:4 [j]Isa 14:19; Jer 50:25
13:16 [k]Ps 137:9
13:17 [l]Jer 51:1 [m]Pr 6:34-35
13:19 [n]Da 4:30 [o]Rev 14:8 [p]Ge 19:24
13:20 [q]Isa 14:23; 34:10-15 [r]2Ch 17:11
13:21 [s]Rev 18:2
13:22 [t]Isa 25:2 [u]Isa 34:13 [v]Jer 51:33
14:1 [w]Ps 102:13; Isa 49:10,13; 54:7-8,10 [x]Isa 41:8; 44:1; 49:7; Zec 1:17; 2:12 [y]Eph 2:12-19
14:2 [z]Isa 60:9 [a]Isa 49:7,23 [b]Isa 60:14; 61:5
14:3 [c]Isa 11:10

[1]19 Or *Chaldeans'*

and cruel bondage, 4you will take
up this taunt[a] against the king of
Babylon:

How the oppressor[b] has come
to an end!
How his fury[m] has ended!
5The LORD has broken the rod of
the wicked,[c]
the scepter of the rulers,
6which in anger struck down
peoples[d]
with unceasing blows,
and in fury subdued nations
with relentless aggression.[e]
7All the lands are at rest and at
peace;
they break into singing.[f]
8Even the pine trees[g] and the
cedars of Lebanon
exult over you and say,
"Now that you have been laid
low,
no woodsman comes to cut
us down."

9The grave[n][h] below is all astir
to meet you at your coming;
it rouses the spirits of the
departed to greet you—
all those who were leaders in
the world;
it makes them rise from their
thrones—
all those who were kings over
the nations.
10They will all respond,
they will say to you,
"You also have become weak,
as we are;
you have become like us."[i]
11All your pomp has been
brought down to the
grave,
along with the noise of your
harps;
maggots are spread out beneath
you
and worms[j] cover you.

12How you have fallen[k] from
heaven,
O morning star,[l] son of the
dawn!
You have been cast down to
the earth,
you who once laid low the
nations!
13You said in your heart,
"I will ascend[m] to heaven;
I will raise my throne[n]
above the stars of God;
I will sit enthroned on the
mount of assembly,
on the utmost heights of the
sacred mountain.[o]
14I will ascend above the tops of
the clouds;
I will make myself like the
Most High."[o]
15But you are brought down to
the grave,
to the depths[p] of the pit.

16Those who see you stare at
you,
they ponder your fate:[q]
"Is this the man who shook the
earth
and made kingdoms tremble,
17the man who made the world a
desert,[r]
who overthrew its cities
and would not let his
captives go home?"

18All the kings of the nations lie
in state,
each in his own tomb.
19But you are cast out[s] of your
tomb
like a rejected branch;
you are covered with the slain,
with those pierced by the
sword,
those who descend to the
stones of the pit.[t]
Like a corpse trampled
underfoot,
20 you will not join them in
burial,
for you have destroyed your
land
and killed your people.

The offspring[u] of the wicked[v]
will never be mentioned[w]
again.
21Prepare a place to slaughter his
sons

14:4 [a]Hab 2:6 [b]Isa 9:4
14:5 [c]Ps 125:3
14:6 [d]Isa 10:14 [e]Isa 47:6
14:7 [f]Ps 98:1; 126:1-3
14:8 [g]Eze 31:16
14:9 [h]Eze 32:21
14:10 [i]Eze 32:21
14:11 [j]Isa 51:8
14:12 [k]Isa 34:4; Lk 10:18 [l]2Pe 1:19; Rev 2:28; 8:10; 9:1
14:13 [m]Da 5:23; 8:10; Mt 11:23 [n]Eze 28:2; 2Th 2:4
14:14 [o]Isa 47:8; 2Th 2:4
14:15 [p]Mt 11:23; Lk 10:15
14:16 [q]Jer 50:23
14:17 [r]Joel 2:3
14:19 [s]Isa 22:16-18 [t]Jer 41:7-9
14:20 [u]Job 18:19 [v]Isa 1:4 [w]Ps 21:10

[m]*4* Dead Sea Scrolls, Septuagint and Syriac; the meaning of the word in the Masoretic Text is uncertain. [n]*9* Hebrew *Sheol*; also in verses 11 and 15 [o]*13* Or *the north*; Hebrew *Zaphon*

for the sins of their
forefathers;[a]
they are not to rise to inherit
the land
and cover the earth with
their cities.

22"I will rise up against them,"
declares the LORD Almighty.
"I will cut off from Babylon her
name and survivors,
her offspring and
descendants,[b]"
declares the LORD.
23"I will turn her into a place for
owls[c]
and into swampland;
I will sweep her with the broom
of destruction,"
declares the LORD Almighty.

A Prophecy Against Assyria

24The LORD Almighty has sworn,[d]

"Surely, as I have planned, so it
will be,
and as I have purposed, so it
will stand.[e]
25I will crush the Assyrian[f] in
my land;
on my mountains I will
trample him down.
His yoke[g] will be taken from
my people,
and his burden removed from
their shoulders.[h]"

26This is the plan[i] determined
for the whole world;
this is the hand[j] stretched
out over all nations.
27For the LORD Almighty has
purposed, and who can
thwart him?
His hand is stretched out,
and who can turn it
back?[k]

A Prophecy Against the Philistines

28This oracle[l] came in the year
King Ahaz[m] died:

29Do not rejoice, all you
Philistines,[n]
that the rod that struck you
is broken;
from the root of that snake will
spring up a viper,[o]
its fruit will be a darting,
venomous serpent.
30The poorest of the poor will
find pasture,
and the needy[p] will lie down
in safety.[q]
But your root I will destroy by
famine;[r]
it will slay[s] your survivors.

31Wail, O gate![t] Howl, O city!
Melt away, all you
Philistines!
A cloud of smoke comes from
the north,[u]
and there is not a straggler in
its ranks.
32What answer shall be given
to the envoys[v] of that
nation?
"The LORD has established
Zion,[w]
and in her his afflicted
people will find
refuge.[x]"

A Prophecy Against Moab

16:6–12pp — Jer 48:29–36

15 An oracle concerning
Moab:[y]

Ar in Moab is ruined,[z]
destroyed in a night!
Kir in Moab is ruined,
destroyed in a night!
2Dibon goes up to its temple,
to its high places[a] to weep;
Moab wails over Nebo and
Medeba.
Every head is shaved[b]
and every beard cut off.
3In the streets they wear
sackcloth;
on the roofs and in the
public squares[c]
they all wail,
prostrate with weeping.[d]
4Heshbon and Elealeh[e] cry out,
their voices are heard all the
way to Jahaz.
Therefore the armed men of
Moab cry out,
and their hearts are faint.
5My heart cries out over Moab;[f]

14:21 [a]Ex 20:5; Lev 26:39
14:22 [b]1Ki 14:10; Job 18:19
14:23 [c]Isa 34:11-15; Zep 2:14
14:24 [d]Isa 45:23 [e]Ac 4:28
14:25 [f]Isa 10:5,12 [g]Isa 9:4 [h]Isa 10:27
14:26 [i]Isa 23:9 [j]Ex 15:12
14:27 [k]2Ch 20:6; Isa 43:13; Da 4:35
14:28 [l]Isa 13:1 [m]2Ki 16:20
14:29 [n]2Ch 26:6 [o]Isa 11:8
14:30 [p]Isa 3:15 [q]Isa 7:21-22 [r]Isa 8:21; 9:20; 51:19 [s]Jer 25:16
14:31 [t]Isa 3:26 [u]Jer 1:14
14:32 [v]Isa 37:9 [w]Ps 87:2,5; Isa 44:28; 54:11 [x]Isa 4:6; Jas 2:5
15:1 [y]Isa 11:14 [z]Jer 48:24,41
15:2 [a]Jer 48:35 [b]Lev 21:5
15:3 [c]Jer 48:38 [d]Isa 22:4
15:4 [e]Nu 32:3
15:5 [f]Jer 48:31

her fugitives flee as far as
Zoar,
as far as Eglath Shelishiyah.
They go up the way to Luhith,
weeping as they go;
on the road to Horonaim[a]
they lament their
destruction.[b]
6The waters of Nimrim are dried
up[c]
and the grass is withered;[d]
the vegetation is gone
and nothing green is left.
7So the wealth they have
acquired[e] and stored up
they carry away over the
Ravine of the Poplars.
8Their outcry echoes along the
border of Moab;
their wailing reaches as far as
Eglaim,
their lamentation as far as
Beer Elim.
9Dimon's[p] waters are full of
blood,
but I will bring still more
upon Dimon[p]—
a lion[f] upon the fugitives of
Moab
and upon those who remain
in the land.

16 Send lambs[g] as tribute
to the ruler of the land,
from Sela,[h] across the desert,
to the mount of the Daughter
of Zion.[i]
2Like fluttering birds
pushed from the nest,[j]
so are the women of Moab
at the fords of the Arnon.[k]

3"Give us counsel,
render a decision.
Make your shadow like night—
at high noon.
Hide the fugitives,[l]
do not betray the refugees.
4Let the Moabite fugitives stay
with you;
be their shelter from the
destroyer."
The oppressor[m] will come to an
end,
and destruction will cease;
the aggressor will vanish
from the land.

5In love a throne[n] will be
established;
in faithfulness a man will sit
on it—
one from the house[q] of
David[o]—
one who in judging seeks
justice[p]
and speeds the cause of
righteousness.

6We have heard of Moab's[q]
pride[r]—
her overweening pride and
conceit,
her pride and her insolence—
but her boasts are empty.
7Therefore the Moabites wail,[s]
they wail together for Moab.
Lament and grieve
for the men[r][t] of Kir
Hareseth.[u]
8The fields of Heshbon wither,
the vines of Sibmah also.
The rulers of the nations
have trampled down the
choicest vines,
which once reached Jazer
and spread toward the
desert.
Their shoots spread out
and went as far as the sea.
9So I weep,[v] as Jazer weeps,
for the vines of Sibmah.
O Heshbon, O Elealeh,
I drench you with tears!
The shouts of joy over your
ripened fruit
and over your harvests[w] have
been stilled.
10Joy and gladness are taken
away from the
orchards;[x]
no one sings or shouts in the
vineyards;
no one treads[y] out wine at the
presses,[z]
for I have put an end to the
shouting.
11My heart laments for Moab[a]
like a harp,
my inmost being[b] for Kir
Hareseth.

15:5 [a]Jer 48:3,34 [b]Jer 4:20; 48:5
15:6 [c]Isa 19:5-7; Jer 48:34 [d]Joel 1:12
15:7 [e]Isa 30:6; Jer 48:36
15:9 [f]2Ki 17:25
16:1 [g]2Ki 3:4 [h]2Ki 14:7 [i]Isa 10:32
16:2 [j]Pr 27:8 [k]Nu 21:13-14; Jer 48:20
16:3 [l]1Ki 18:4
16:4 [m]Isa 9:4
16:5 [n]Da 7:14; Mic 4:7 [o]Lk 1:32 [p]Isa 9:7
16:6 [q]Am 2:1; Zep 2:8 [r]Ob 1:3; Zep 2:10
16:7 [s]Jer 48:20 [t]1Ch 16:3 [u]2Ki 3:25
16:9 [v]Isa 15:3 [w]Jer 40:12
16:10 [x]Isa 24:7-8 [y]Jdg 9:27 [z]Job 24:11
16:11 [a]Isa 15:5 [b]Isa 63:15; Hos 11:8; Php 2:1

p9 Masoretic Text; Dead Sea Scrolls, some Septuagint manuscripts and Vulgate *Dibon*
q5 Hebrew *tent* r7 Or "*raisin cakes*," a wordplay

12When Moab appears at her high
place,
she only wears herself out;
when she goes to her shrine[a]
to pray,
it is to no avail.[b]

13This is the word the LORD has
already spoken concerning Moab.
14But now the LORD says: "Within
three years, as a servant bound by
contract would count them,
Moab's splendor and all her many
people will be despised,[c] and her
survivors will be very few and feeble."[d]

An Oracle Against Damascus

17 An oracle concerning Damascus:[e]

"See, Damascus will no longer
be a city
but will become a heap of
ruins.[f]
2The cities of Aroer will be
deserted
and left to flocks,[g] which
will lie down,
with no one to make them
afraid.[h]
3The fortified city will disappear
from Ephraim,
and royal power from
Damascus;
the remnant of Aram will be
like the glory[i] of the
Israelites,"[j]
declares the LORD
Almighty.

4"In that day the glory of Jacob
will fade;
the fat of his body will
waste[k] away.
5It will be as when a reaper
gathers the standing
grain
and harvests[l] the grain with
his arm—
as when a man gleans heads of
grain
in the Valley of Rephaim.
6Yet some gleanings will
remain,[m]
as when an olive tree is
beaten,[n]
leaving two or three olives on
the topmost branches,
four or five on the fruitful
boughs,"
declares the LORD, the
God of Israel.

7In that day men will look[o] to
their Maker
and turn their eyes to the
Holy One[p] of Israel.
8They will not look to the altars,
the work of their hands,[q]
and they will have no regard for
the Asherah poles[s]
and the incense altars their
fingers have made.

9In that day their strong cities,
which they left because of the Israelites, will be like places abandoned to thickets and undergrowth. And all will be desolation.

10You have forgotten[r] God your
Savior;[s]
you have not remembered
the Rock, your fortress.
Therefore, though you set out
the finest plants
and plant imported vines,
11though on the day you set
them out, you make
them grow,
and on the morning[t] when
you plant them, you
bring them to bud,
yet the harvest will be as
nothing[u]
in the day of disease and
incurable pain.[v]

12Oh, the raging of many
nations—
they rage like the raging
sea![w]
Oh, the uproar of the peoples—
they roar like the roaring of
great waters!
13Although the peoples roar like
the roar of surging
waters,
when he rebukes[x] them they
flee[y] far away,
driven before the wind like
chaff[z] on the hills,

16:12 [a]Isa 15:2 [b]1Ki 18:29
16:14 [c]Isa 25:10; Jer 48:42 [d]Isa 21:17
17:1 [e]Ge 14:15; Jer 49:23; Ac 9:2 [f]Isa 25:2; Am 1:3; Zec 9:1
17:2 [g]Isa 7:21; Eze 25:5 [h]Jer 7:33; Mic 4:4
17:3 [i]ver 4; Hos 9:11 [j]Isa 7:8,16; 8:4
17:4 [k]Isa 10:16
17:5 [l]ver 11; Jer 51:33; Joel 3:13; Mt 13:30
17:6 [m]Dt 4:27; Isa 24:13 [n]Isa 27:12
17:7 [o]Isa 10:20 [p]Mic 7:7
17:8 [q]Isa 2:18,20; 30:22
17:10 [r]Isa 51:13 [s]Ps 68:19; Isa 12:2
17:11 [t]Ps 90:6 [u]Hos 8:7 [v]Job 4:8
17:12 [w]Ps 18:4; Jer 6:23; Lk 21:25
17:13 [x]Ps 9:5 [y]Isa 13:14 [z]Isa 41:2, 15-16

[s]*8* That is, symbols of the goddess Asherah

like tumbleweed before a
gale.[a]
14In the evening, sudden terror!
Before the morning, they are
gone![b]
This is the portion of those
who loot us,
the lot of those who plunder
us.

A Prophecy Against Cush

18 Woe to the land of
whirring wings[t]
along the rivers of Cush,[u][c]
2which sends envoys by sea
in papyrus[d] boats over the
water.

Go, swift messengers,
to a people tall and
smooth-skinned,
to a people feared far and
wide,
an aggressive[e] nation of
strange speech,
whose land is divided by
rivers.[f]

3All you people of the world,
you who live on the earth,
when a banner[g] is raised on
the mountains,
you will see it,
and when a trumpet sounds,
you will hear it.
4This is what the LORD says to
me:
"I will remain quiet and will
look on from my
dwelling place,[h]
like shimmering heat in the
sunshine,
like a cloud of dew[i] in the
heat of harvest."
5For, before the harvest, when
the blossom is gone
and the flower becomes a
ripening grape,
he will cut off the shoots with
pruning knives,
and cut down and take away
the spreading
branches.[j]
6They will all be left to the
mountain birds of prey
and to the wild animals;[k]
the birds will feed on them all
summer,
the wild animals all winter.

7At that time gifts will be
brought to the LORD Almighty

from a people tall and
smooth-skinned,
from a people feared far and
wide,
an aggressive nation of strange
speech,
whose land is divided by
rivers—

the gifts will be brought to Mount
Zion, the place of the Name of the
LORD Almighty.[l]

A Prophecy About Egypt

19 An oracle[m] concerning
Egypt:[n][o]

See, the LORD rides on a swift
cloud[p]
and is coming to Egypt.
The idols of Egypt tremble
before him,
and the hearts of the
Egyptians melt[q] within
them.

2"I will stir up Egyptian against
Egyptian—
brother will fight against
brother,[r]
neighbor against neighbor,
city against city,
kingdom against kingdom.[s]
3The Egyptians will lose heart,
and I will bring their plans to
nothing;
they will consult the idols and
the spirits of the dead,
the mediums and the
spiritists.[t]
4I will hand the Egyptians over
to the power of a cruel
master,
and a fierce king[u] will rule
over them,"
declares the Lord, the LORD
Almighty.

5The waters of the river will dry
up,[v]

17:13 [a]Job 21:18
17:14 [b]2Ki 19:35
18:1 [c]Isa 20:3-5; Eze 30:4-5,9; Zep 2:12; 3:10
18:2 [d]Ex 2:3 [e]Ge 10:8-9; 2Ch 12:3 [f]ver 7
18:3 [g]Isa 5:26
18:4 [h]Isa 26:21; Hos 5:15 [i]Isa 26:19; Hos 14:5
18:5 [j]Isa 17:10-11; Eze 17:6
18:6 [k]Isa 56:9; Jer 7:33; Eze 32:4; 39:17
18:7 [l]Ps 68:31
19:1 [m]Isa 13:1; Jer 43:12 [n]Joel 3:19 [o]Ex 12:12 [p]Ps 18:10; 104:3; Rev 1:7 [q]Jos 2:11
19:2 [r]Jdg 7:22; Mt 10:21,36 [s]2Ch 20:23
19:3 [t]Isa 8:19; 47:13; Da 2:2,10
19:4 [u]Isa 20:4; Jer 46:26; Eze 29:19
19:5 [v]Jer 51:36

[t]*1* Or *of locusts* [u]*1* That is, the upper Nile region

and the riverbed will be
parched and dry.
6 The canals will stink;[a]
the streams of Egypt will
dwindle and dry up.[b]
The reeds and rushes will
wither,[c]
7 also the plants along the
Nile,
at the mouth of the river.
Every sown field[d] along the
Nile
will become parched, will
blow away and be no
more.
8 The fishermen[e] will groan and
lament,
all who cast hooks[f] into the
Nile;
those who throw nets on the
water
will pine away.
9 Those who work with combed
flax will despair,
the weavers of fine linen[g]
will lose hope.
10 The workers in cloth will be
dejected,
and all the wage earners will
be sick at heart.

11 The officials of Zoan[h] are
nothing but fools;
the wise counselors of
Pharaoh give senseless
advice.
How can you say to Pharaoh,
"I am one of the wise
men,[i]
a disciple of the ancient
kings"?

12 Where are your wise men[j]
now?
Let them show you and make
known
what the LORD Almighty
has planned[k] against Egypt.
13 The officials of Zoan have
become fools,
the leaders of Memphis[v][l]
are deceived;
the cornerstones of her peoples
have led Egypt astray.
14 The LORD has poured into them
a spirit of dizziness;[m]
they make Egypt stagger in all
that she does,
as a drunkard staggers
around in his vomit.
15 There is nothing Egypt can
do—
head or tail, palm branch or
reed.[n]

16 In that day the Egyptians will
be like women.[o] They will shudder
with fear[p] at the uplifted hand[q]
that the LORD Almighty raises
against them. 17 And the land of Judah will bring terror to the Egyptians; everyone to whom Judah is
mentioned will be terrified, because of what the LORD Almighty is
planning[r] against them.
18 In that day five cities in Egypt
will speak the language of Canaan
and swear allegiance[s] to the LORD
Almighty. One of them will be
called the City of Destruction.[w]
19 In that day there will be an altar[t] to the LORD in the heart of
Egypt, and a monument[u] to the
LORD at its border. 20 It will be a sign
and witness to the LORD Almighty
in the land of Egypt. When they cry
out to the LORD because of their oppressors, he will send them a savior
and defender, and he will rescue[v]
them. 21 So the LORD will make himself known to the Egyptians, and in
that day they will acknowledge[w]
the LORD. They will worship[x] with
sacrifices and grain offerings; they
will make vows to the LORD and
keep them. 22 The LORD will strike[y]
Egypt with a plague; he will strike
them and heal them. They will
turn[z] to the LORD, and he will respond to their pleas and heal[a]
them.
23 In that day there will be a highway[b] from Egypt to Assyria. The
Assyrians will go to Egypt and the
Egyptians to Assyria. The Egyptians and Assyrians will worship[c]
together. 24 In that day Israel will
be the third, along with Egypt and
Assyria, a blessing on the earth.
25 The LORD Almighty will bless
them, saying, "Blessed be Egypt

19:6 [a]Ex 7:18 [b]Isa 37:25; Eze 30:12 [c]Isa 15:6
19:7 [d]Isa 23:3
19:8 [e]Eze 47:10 [f]Hab 1:15
19:9 [g]Pr 7:16; Eze 27:7
19:11 [h]Nu 13:22 [i]1Ki 4:30; Ac 7:22
19:12 [j]1Co 1:20 [k]Isa 14:24; Ro 9:17
19:13 [l]Jer 2:16; Eze 30:13,16
19:14 [m]Mt 17:17
19:15 [n]Isa 9:14
19:16 [o]51:30; Na 3:13 [p]Heb 10:31 [q]Isa 11:15
19:17 [r]Isa 14:24
19:18 [s]Zep 3:9
19:19 [t]Jos 22:10 [u]Ge 28:18
19:20 [v]Isa 49:24-26
19:21 [w]Isa 11:9 [x]Isa 56:7; Mal 1:11
19:22 [y]Heb 12:11 [z]Isa 45:14; Hos 14:1 [a]Dt 32:39
19:23 [b]Isa 11:16 [c]Isa 27:13

[v]*13* Hebrew *Noph* [w]*18* Most manuscripts of the Masoretic Text; some manuscripts of the Masoretic Text, Dead Sea Scrolls and Vulgate *City of the Sun* (that is, Heliopolis)

my people,[a] Assyria my handi-
work,[b] and Israel my inheritance.[c]"

A Prophecy Against Egypt and Cush

20 In the year that the supreme commander,[d] sent
by Sargon king of Assyria, came to
Ashdod and attacked and captured
it— 2 at that time the LORD spoke
through Isaiah son of Amoz.[e] He
said to him, "Take off the sackcloth[f] from your body and the sandals[g] from your feet." And he did
so, going around stripped[h] and
barefoot.[i]
3 Then the LORD said, "Just as my
servant Isaiah has gone stripped
and barefoot for three years, as a
sign[j] and portent against Egypt
and Cush,[x][k] 4 so the king[l] of Assyria will lead away stripped and
barefoot the Egyptian captives and
Cushite exiles, young and old,
with buttocks bared—to Egypt's
shame.[m] 5 Those who trusted in
Cush and boasted in Egypt[n] will be
afraid and put to shame. 6 In that
day the people who live on this
coast will say, 'See what has happened to those we relied on, those
we fled to for help[o] and deliverance from the king of Assyria! How
then can we escape?[p]' "

A Prophecy Against Babylon

21 An oracle concerning the Desert[q] by the Sea:

Like whirlwinds sweeping
through the southland,[r]
an invader comes from the
desert,
from a land of terror.

2 A dire[s] vision has been shown
to me:
The traitor betrays,[t] the
looter takes loot.
Elam,[u] attack! Media, lay
siege!
I will bring to an end all the
groaning she caused.

3 At this my body is racked with
pain,
pangs seize me, like those of
a woman in labor;[v]
I am staggered by what I hear,
I am bewildered by what I
see.
4 My heart falters,
fear makes me tremble;
the twilight I longed for
has become a horror to me.

5 They set the tables,
they spread the rugs,
they eat, they drink![w]
Get up, you officers,
oil the shields!

6 This is what the Lord says to me:

"Go, post a lookout
and have him report what he
sees.
7 When he sees chariots[x]
with teams of horses,
riders on donkeys
or riders on camels,
let him be alert,
fully alert."

8 And the lookout[y][y] shouted,

"Day after day, my lord, I stand
on the watchtower;
every night I stay at my post.
9 Look, here comes a man in a
chariot
with a team of horses.
And he gives back the answer:
'Babylon[z] has fallen,[a] has
fallen!
All the images of its gods[b]
lie shattered on the
ground!' "

10 O my people, crushed on the
threshing floor,[c]
I tell you what I have heard
from the LORD Almighty,
from the God of Israel.

A Prophecy Against Edom

11 An oracle concerning Dumah[z]:[d]

Someone calls to me from
Seir,[e]

19:25 [a] Ps 100:3 [b] Isa 29:23; 45:11; 60:21; 64:8; Eph 2:10 [c] Hos 2:23
20:1 [d] 2Ki 18:17
20:2 [e] Isa 13:1 [f] Zec 13:4; Mt 3:4 [g] Eze 24:17,23 [h] 1Sa 19:24 [i] Mic 1:8
20:3 [j] Isa 8:18 [k] Isa 37:9; 43:3
20:4 [l] Isa 19:4 [m] Isa 47:3; Jer 13:22,26
20:5 [n] 2Ki 18:21; Isa 30:5
20:6 [o] Isa 10:3 [p] Jer 30:15-17; Mt 23:33; 1Th 5:3; Heb 2:3
21:1 [q] Isa 13:21; Jer 51:43 [r] Zec 9:14
21:2 [s] Ps 60:3 [t] Isa 33:1 [u] Isa 22:6; Jer 49:34
21:3 [v] Ps 48:6; Isa 26:17
21:5 [w] Jer 51:39, 57; Da 5:2
21:7 [x] ver 9
21:8 [y] Hab 2:1
21:9 [z] Rev 14:8 [a] Jer 51:8; Rev 18:2 [b] Isa 46:1; Jer 50:2; 51:44
21:10 [c] Jer 51:33
21:11 [d] Ge 25:14 [e] Ge 32:3

[x] 3 That is, the upper Nile region; also in verse 5 [y] 8 Dead Sea Scrolls and Syriac; Masoretic Text *A lion* [z] 11 *Dumah* means *silence* or *stillness,* a wordplay on *Edom.*

"Watchman, what is left of
the night?
Watchman, what is left of the
night?"
12 The watchman replies,
"Morning is coming, but also
the night.
If you would ask, then ask;
and come back yet again."

A Prophecy Against Arabia

13 An oracle[a] concerning Arabia:

You caravans of Dedanites,
who camp in the thickets of
Arabia,
14 bring water for the thirsty;
you who live in Tema,[b]
bring food for the fugitives.
15 They flee[c] from the sword,
from the drawn sword,
from the bent bow
and from the heat of battle.

16 This is what the Lord says to
me: "Within one year, as a servant
bound by contract[d] would count
it, all the pomp[e] of Kedar[f] will
come to an end. 17 The survivors of
the bowmen, the warriors of Kedar,
will be few.[g]" The LORD, the God of
Israel, has spoken.

A Prophecy About Jerusalem

22 An oracle[h] concerning the Valley[i] of Vision:

What troubles you now,
that you have all gone up on
the roofs,
2 O town full of commotion,
O city of tumult and
revelry?[j]
Your slain were not killed by
the sword,
nor did they die in battle.
3 All your leaders have fled
together;
they have been captured
without using the bow.
All you who were caught were
taken prisoner together,
having fled while the enemy
was still far away.
4 Therefore I said, "Turn away
from me;
let me weep[k] bitterly.
Do not try to console me
over the destruction of my
people."[l]

5 The Lord, the LORD Almighty,
has a day
of tumult and trampling and
terror[m]
in the Valley of Vision,
a day of battering down walls
and of crying out to the
mountains.
6 Elam[n] takes up the quiver,[o]
with her charioteers and
horses;
Kir[p] uncovers the shield.
7 Your choicest valleys are full of
chariots,
and horsemen are posted at
the city gates;[q]
8 the defenses of Judah are
stripped away.

And you looked in that day
to the weapons[r] in the
Palace of the Forest;[s]
9 you saw that the City of David
had many breaches in its
defenses;
you stored up water
in the Lower Pool.[t]
10 You counted the buildings in
Jerusalem
and tore down houses to
strengthen the wall.
11 You built a reservoir between
the two walls[u]
for the water of the Old
Pool,[v]
but you did not look to the
One who made it,
or have regard for the One
who planned it long ago.

12 The Lord, the LORD Almighty,
called you on that day
to weep[w] and to wail,
to tear out your hair[x] and
put on sackcloth.[y]
13 But see, there is joy and
revelry,
slaughtering of cattle and
killing of sheep,
eating of meat and drinking
of wine![z]
"Let us eat and drink," you say,
"for tomorrow we die!"[a]

14 The LORD Almighty has revealed this in my hearing:[b] "Till

21:13 [a] Isa 13:1
21:14 [b] Ge 25:15
21:15 [c] Isa 13:14
21:16 [d] Isa 16:14 [e] Isa 17:3 [f] Ps 120:5; Isa 60:7
21:17 [g] Isa 10:19
22:1 [h] Isa 13:1 [i] Ps 125:2; Jer 21:13; Joel 3:2,12,14
22:2 [j] Isa 32:13
22:4 [k] Isa 15:3; Lk 19:41 [l] Jer 9:1
22:5 [m] La 1:5
22:6 [n] Isa 21:2 [o] Jer 49:35 [p] 2Ki 16:9
22:7 [q] 2Ch 32:1-2
22:8 [r] 2Ch 32:5 [s] 1Ki 7:2
22:9 [t] 2Ch 32:4
22:11 [u] 2Ki 25:4; Jer 39:4 [v] 2Ch 32:4
22:12 [w] Joel 2:17 [x] Mic 1:16 [y] Joel 1:13
22:13 [z] Isa 5:22; 28:7-8; 56:12; Lk 17:26-29 [a] 1Co 15:32*
22:14 [b] Isa 5:9

your dying day this sin will not be
atoned[a] for," says the Lord, the
LORD Almighty.

15 This is what the Lord, the LORD
Almighty, says:

"Go, say to this steward,
to Shebna,[b] who is in charge
of the palace:
16 What are you doing here and
who gave you permission
to cut out a grave[c] for
yourself here,
hewing your grave on the
height
and chiseling your resting
place in the rock?

17 "Beware, the LORD is about to
take firm hold of you
and hurl you away, O you
mighty man.
18 He will roll you up tightly like
a ball
and throw[d] you into a large
country.
There you will die
and there your splendid
chariots will remain—
you disgrace to your master's
house!
19 I will depose you from your
office,
and you will be ousted from
your position.

20 "In that day I will summon my
servant, Eliakim[e] son of Hilkiah.
21 I will clothe him with your robe
and fasten your sash around him
and hand your authority over to
him. He will be a father to those
who live in Jerusalem and to the
house of Judah. 22 I will place on
his shoulder the key[f] to the house
of David;[g] what he opens no one
can shut, and what he shuts no one
can open.[h] 23 I will drive him like a
peg[i] into a firm place;[j] he will be
a seat[a] of honor[k] for the house of
his father. 24 All the glory of his
family will hang on him: its offspring and offshoots—all its lesser
vessels, from the bowls to all the
jars.

25 "In that day," declares the
LORD Almighty, "the peg[l] driven
into the firm place will give way; it
will be sheared off and will fall, and
the load hanging on it will be cut
down." The LORD has spoken.[m]

A Prophecy About Tyre

23 An oracle concerning
Tyre:[n]

Wail, O ships[o] of Tarshish![p]
For Tyre is destroyed
and left without house or
harbor.
From the land of Cyprus[b]
word has come to them.

2 Be silent, you people of the
island
and you merchants of Sidon,
whom the seafarers have
enriched.
3 On the great waters
came the grain of the Shihor;
the harvest of the Nile[c][q] was
the revenue of Tyre,[r]
and she became the
marketplace of the
nations.

4 Be ashamed, O Sidon,[s] and
you, O fortress of the
sea,
for the sea has spoken:
"I have neither been in labor
nor given birth;
I have neither reared sons
nor brought up
daughters."
5 When word comes to Egypt,
they will be in anguish at the
report from Tyre.

6 Cross over to Tarshish;
wail, you people of the
island.
7 Is this your city of revelry,[t]
the old, old city,
whose feet have taken her
to settle in far-off lands?
8 Who planned this against Tyre,
the bestower of crowns,
whose merchants are princes,
whose traders are renowned
in the earth?

22:14 [a] Isa 13:11; 26:21; 30:13-14; Eze 24:13
22:15 [b] 2Ki 18:18; Isa 36:3
22:16 [c] Mt 27:60
22:18 [d] Isa 17:13
22:20 [e] 2Ki 18:18; Isa 36:3
22:22 [f] Rev 3:7 [g] Isa 7:2 [h] Job 12:14
22:23 [i] Zec 10:4 [j] Ezr 9:8 [k] 1Sa 2:7-8; Job 36:7
22:25 [l] ver 23 [m] Isa 46:11; Mic 4:4
23:1 [n] Jos 19:29; 1Ki 5:1; Jer 47:4; Eze 26,27,28; Joel 3:4-8; Am 1:9-10; Zec 9:2-4 [o] 1Ki 10:22 [p] Ge 10:4; Isa 2:16 *fn*
23:3 [q] Isa 19:7 [r] Eze 27:3
23:4 [s] Ge 10:15,19
23:7 [t] Isa 22:2; 32:13

[a] *23* Or *throne* [b] *1,12* Hebrew *Kittim*
[c] *2,3* Masoretic Text; one Dead Sea Scroll *Sidon, / who cross over the sea; / your envoys*
3are on the great waters. / The grain of the Shihor, / the harvest of the Nile,

[9]The LORD Almighty planned it,
to bring low[a] the pride of all glory
and to humble[b] all who are renowned[c] on the earth.

[10]Till[d] your land as along the Nile,
O Daughter of Tarshish,
for you no longer have a harbor.
[11]The LORD has stretched out his hand[d] over the sea
and made its kingdoms tremble.
He has given an order
concerning Phoenicia[e]
that her fortresses be destroyed.[e]
[12]He said, "No more of your reveling,[f]
O Virgin Daughter[g] of Sidon, now crushed!

"Up, cross over to Cyprus[f];
even there you will find no rest."
[13]Look at the land of the Babylonians,[g]
this people that is now of no account!
The Assyrians[h] have made it
a place for desert creatures;
they raised up their siege towers,
they stripped its fortresses bare
and turned it into a ruin.[i]
[14]Wail, you ships of Tarshish;[j]
your fortress is destroyed!

[15]At that time Tyre[k] will be forgotten for seventy years, the span
of a king's life. But at the end of
these seventy years, it will happen
to Tyre as in the song of the prostitute:

[16]"Take up a harp, walk through the city,
O prostitute forgotten;
play the harp well, sing many a song,
so that you will be remembered."

[17]At the end of seventy years, the
LORD will deal with Tyre. She will
return to her hire as a prostitute[l]
and will ply her trade with all the
kingdoms on the face of the earth.
[18]Yet her profit and her earnings
will be set apart for the LORD;[m] they
will not be stored up or hoarded.
Her profits will go to those who live
before the LORD,[n] for abundant
food and fine clothes.

The LORD's Devastation of the Earth

24 See, the LORD is going to lay waste the earth[o]
and devastate it;
he will ruin its face
and scatter its inhabitants—
[2]it will be the same
for priest as for people,[p]
for master as for servant,
for mistress as for maid,
for seller as for buyer,[q]
for borrower as for lender,
for debtor as for creditor.[r]
[3]The earth will be completely laid waste
and totally plundered.[s]
The LORD has spoken this word.

[4]The earth dries up and withers,
the world languishes and withers,
the exalted[t] of the earth languish.
[5]The earth is defiled[u] by its people;
they have disobeyed[v] the laws,
violated the statutes
and broken the everlasting covenant.
[6]Therefore a curse consumes the earth;
its people must bear their guilt.
Therefore earth's inhabitants are burned up,[w]
and very few are left.
[7]The new wine dries up and the vine withers;[x]
all the merrymakers groan.[y]
[8]The gaiety of the tambourines[z] is stilled,

23:9 [a]Job 40:11 [b]Isa 13:11 [c]Isa 5:13; 9:15
23:11 [d]Ex 14:21 [e]Isa 25:2; Zec 9:3-4
23:12 [f]Rev 18:22 [g]Isa 47:1
23:13 [h]Isa 10:5 [i]Isa 10:7
23:14 [j]Isa 2:16 *fn*
23:15 [k]Jer 25:22
23:17 [l]Eze 16:26; Na 3:4; Rev 17:1
23:18 [m]Ex 28:36; Ps 72:10 [n]Isa 60:5-9; Mic 4:13
24:1 [o]ver 20; Isa 2:19-21; 33:9
24:2 [p]Hos 4:9 [q]Eze 7:12 [r]Lev 25:35-37; Dt 23:19-20
24:3 [s]Isa 6:11-12
24:4 [t]Isa 2:12
24:5 [u]Ge 3:17; Nu 35:33 [v]Isa 10:6; 59:12
24:6 [w]Isa 1:31
24:7 [x]Joel 1:10-12 [y]Isa 16:8-10
24:8 [z]Isa 5:12

[d]*10* Dead Sea Scrolls and some Septuagint manuscripts; Masoretic Text *Go through*
[e]*11* Hebrew *Canaan* [f]*1,12* Hebrew *Kittim*
[g]*13* Or *Chaldeans*

the noise[a] of the revelers
has stopped,
the joyful harp[b] is silent.[c]
9No longer do they drink wine[d]
with a song;
the beer is bitter[e] to its
drinkers.
10The ruined city lies desolate;
the entrance to every house
is barred.
11In the streets they cry out for
wine;
all joy turns to gloom,[f]
all gaiety is banished from
the earth.
12The city is left in ruins,
its gate is battered to pieces.
13So will it be on the earth
and among the nations,
as when an olive tree is
beaten,[g]
or as when gleanings are left
after the grape harvest.

14They raise their voices, they
shout for joy;[h]
from the west they acclaim
the LORD's majesty.
15Therefore in the east give
glory[i] to the LORD;
exalt[j] the name of the LORD,
the God of Israel,
in the islands of the sea.
16From the ends of the earth we
hear singing:
"Glory[k] to the Righteous
One."

But I said, "I waste away, I
waste away!
Woe to me!
The treacherous betray!
With treachery the
treacherous betray![l]"
17Terror and pit and snare[m] await
you,
O people of the earth.
18Whoever flees at the sound of
terror
will fall into a pit;
whoever climbs out of the pit
will be caught in a snare.

The floodgates of the heavens[n]
are opened,
the foundations of the earth
shake.[o]
19The earth is broken up,
the earth is split asunder,[p]
the earth is thoroughly
shaken.
20The earth reels like a
drunkard,[q]
it sways like a hut in the
wind;
so heavy upon it is the guilt of
its rebellion[r]
that it falls—never to rise
again.

21In that day the LORD will
punish[s]
the powers in the heavens
above
and the kings on the earth
below.
22They will be herded together
like prisoners[t] bound in a
dungeon;[u]
they will be shut up in prison
and be punished[h] after many
days.[v]
23The moon will be abashed, the
sun[w] ashamed;
for the LORD Almighty will
reign[x]
on Mount Zion[y] and in
Jerusalem,
and before its elders,
gloriously.[z]

Praise to the LORD

25 O LORD, you are my God;
I will exalt you and praise
your name,
for in perfect faithfulness
you have done marvelous
things,[a]
things planned[b] long ago.
2You have made the city a heap
of rubble,[c]
the fortified[d] town a ruin,
the foreigners' stronghold[e] a
city no more;
it will never be rebuilt.
3Therefore strong peoples will
honor you;
cities of ruthless[f] nations
will revere you.
4You have been a refuge[g] for
the poor,
a refuge for the needy in his
distress,

24:8 [a]Jer 7:34; 16:9; 25:10; Hos 2:11 [b]Rev 18:22 [c]Eze 26:13
24:9 [d]Isa 5:11,22 [e]Isa 5:20
24:11 [f]Isa 16:10; 32:13; Jer 14:3
24:13 [g]Isa 17:6
24:14 [h]Isa 12:6
24:15 [i]Isa 66:19 [j]Isa 25:3; Mal 1:11
24:16 [k]Isa 28:5 [l]Isa 21:2; Jer 5:11
24:17 [m]Jer 48:43
24:18 [n]Ge 7:11 [o]Ps 18:7
24:19 [p]Dt 11:6
24:20 [q]Isa 19:14 [r]Isa 1:2,28; 43:27
24:21 [s]Isa 10:12
24:22 [t]Isa 10:4 [u]Isa 42:7,22 [v]Eze 38:8
24:23 [w]Isa 13:10 [x]Rev 22:5 [y]Heb 12:22 [z]Isa 60:19
25:1 [a]Ps 98:1 [b]Nu 23:19
25:2 [c]Isa 17:1 [d]Isa 17:3 [e]Isa 13:22
25:3 [f]Isa 13:11
25:4 [g]Isa 4:6; 17:10; 27:5; 33:16

h22 Or *released*

a shelter from the storm
and a shade from the heat.
For the breath of the ruthless[a]
is like a storm driving against a wall
5 and like the heat of the desert.
You silence[b] the uproar of foreigners;
as heat is reduced by the shadow of a cloud,
so the song of the ruthless is stilled.

6 On this mountain[c] the LORD Almighty will prepare
a feast[d] of rich food for all peoples,
a banquet of aged wine—
the best of meats and the finest of wines.[e]
7 On this mountain he will destroy
the shroud[f] that enfolds all peoples,
the sheet that covers all nations;
8 he will swallow up death[g] forever.
The Sovereign LORD will wipe away the tears[h]
from all faces;
he will remove the disgrace[i] of his people
from all the earth.
The LORD has spoken.

9 In that day they will say,

"Surely this is our God;[j]
we trusted in him, and he saved[k] us.
This is the LORD, we trusted in him;
let us rejoice[l] and be glad in his salvation."

10 The hand of the LORD will rest on this mountain;
but Moab[m] will be trampled under him
as straw is trampled down in the manure.
11 They will spread out their hands in it,
as a swimmer spreads out his hands to swim.
God will bring down[n] their pride[o]
despite the cleverness[i] of their hands.
12 He will bring down your high fortified walls
and lay them low;[p]
he will bring them down to the ground,
to the very dust.

A Song of Praise

26

In that day this song will be sung in the land of Judah:

We have a strong city;[q]
God makes salvation
its walls[r] and ramparts.
2 Open the gates
that the righteous[s] nation may enter,
the nation that keeps faith.
3 You will keep in perfect peace
him whose mind is steadfast,
because he trusts in you.
4 Trust[t] in the LORD forever,
for the LORD, the LORD, is the Rock eternal.
5 He humbles those who dwell on high,
he lays the lofty city low;
he levels it to the ground[u]
and casts it down to the dust.
6 Feet trample it down—
the feet of the oppressed,
the footsteps of the poor.[v]

7 The path of the righteous is level;
O upright One, you make the way of the righteous smooth.[w]
8 Yes, LORD, walking in the way of your laws,[j][x]
we wait for you;
your name[y] and renown
are the desire of our hearts.
9 My soul yearns for you in the night;
in the morning my spirit longs[z] for you.
When your judgments come upon the earth,
the people of the world learn righteousness.[a]

[i] *11* The meaning of the Hebrew for this word is uncertain. [j] *8* Or *judgments*

25:4 [a] Isa 29:5; 49:25
25:5 [b] Jer 51:55
25:6 [c] Isa 2:2 [d] Isa 1:19; Mt 8:11; 22:4 [e] Pr 9:2
25:7 [f] 2Co 3:15-16; Eph 4:18
25:8 [g] Hos 13:14; 1Co 15:54-55* [h] Isa 30:19; 35:10; 51:11; 65:19; Rev 7:17; 21:4 [i] Mt 5:11; 1Pe 4:14
25:9 [j] Isa 40:9 [k] Ps 20:5; Isa 33:22; 35:4; 49:25-26,26; 60:16 [l] Isa 35:2,10
25:10 [m] Am 2:1-3
25:11 [n] Isa 5:25; 14:26; 16:14 [o] Job 40:12
25:12 [p] Isa 15:1
26:1 [q] Isa 14:32 [r] Isa 60:18
26:2 [s] Isa 54:14; 58:8; 62:2
26:4 [t] Isa 12:2; 50:10
26:5 [u] Isa 25:12
26:6 [v] Isa 3:15
26:7 [w] Isa 42:16
26:8 [x] Isa 56:1 [y] Isa 12:4
26:9 [z] Ps 63:1; 78:34; Isa 55:6 [a] Mt 6:33

10 Though grace is shown to the
wicked,
they do not learn
righteousness;
even in a land of uprightness
they go on doing evil[a]
and regard[b] not the majesty
of the LORD.
11 O LORD, your hand is lifted
high,
but they do not see[c] it.
Let them see your zeal for your
people and be put to
shame;
let the fire[d] reserved for your
enemies consume them.

12 LORD, you establish peace for
us;
all that we have
accomplished you have
done for us.
13 O LORD, our God, other lords[e]
besides you have ruled
over us,
but your name alone do we
honor.[f]
14 They are now dead,[g] they live
no more;
those departed spirits do not
rise.
You punished them and
brought them to ruin;[h]
you wiped out all memory of
them.
15 You have enlarged the nation,
O LORD;
you have enlarged the
nation.
You have gained glory for
yourself;
you have extended all the
borders[i] of the land.

16 LORD, they came to you in their
distress;[j]
when you disciplined them,
they could barely whisper a
prayer.[k]
17 As a woman with child and
about to give birth[k]
writhes and cries out in her
pain,
so were we in your presence,
O LORD.
18 We were with child, we writhed
in pain,
but we gave birth[l] to wind.

26:10 [a]Isa 32:6 [b]Isa 22:12-13; Hos 11:7; Jn 5:37-38; Ro 2:4
26:11 [c]Isa 44:9,18 [d]Heb 10:27
26:13 [e]Isa 2:8; 10:5, 11 [f]Isa 63:7
26:14 [g]Dt 4:28 [h]Isa 10:3
26:15 [i]Isa 33:17
26:16 [j]Hos 5:15
26:17 [k]Jn 16:21
26:18 [l]Isa 33:11; 59:4 [m]Ps 17:14
26:19 [n]Isa 25:8; Eph 5:14 [o]Eze 37:1-14; Da 12:2
26:20 [p]Ex 12:23 [q]Ps 91:1,4 [r]Ps 30:5; Isa 54:7-8
26:21 [s]Jude 1:14 [t]Mic 1:3 [u]Isa 13:9,11; 30:12-14 [v]Job 16:18; Lk 11:50-51
27:1 [w]Isa 34:6; 66:16 [x]Job 3:8 [y]Ps 74:13
27:2 [z]Jer 2:21
27:3 [a]Isa 58:11
27:4 [b]Isa 10:17; Mt 3:12; Heb 6:8

We have not brought salvation[m]
to the earth;
we have not given birth to
people of the world.

19 But your dead[n] will live;
their bodies will rise.
You who dwell in the dust,
wake up and shout for joy.
Your dew is like the dew of the
morning;
the earth will give birth to
her dead.[o]

20 Go, my people, enter your
rooms
and shut the doors[p] behind
you;
hide[q] yourselves for a little
while
until his wrath has passed
by.[r]
21 See, the LORD is coming[s] out
of his dwelling[t]
to punish[u] the people of the
earth for their sins.
The earth will disclose the
blood[v] shed upon her;
she will conceal her slain no
longer.

Deliverance of Israel

27 In that day,
the LORD will punish with
his sword,[w]
his fierce, great and powerful
sword,
Leviathan[x] the gliding serpent,
Leviathan the coiling serpent;
he will slay the monster[y] of
the sea.

2 In that day—

"Sing about a fruitful
vineyard:[z]
3 I, the LORD, watch over it;
I water[a] it continually.
I guard it day and night
so that no one may harm it.
4 I am not angry.
If only there were briers and
thorns confronting me!
I would march against them
in battle;
I would set them all on fire.[b]

[k]*16* The meaning of the Hebrew for this clause is uncertain.

5Or else let them come to me for refuge;[a]
let them make peace[b] with me,
yes, let them make peace with me."

6In days to come Jacob will take root,
Israel will bud and blossom[c]
and fill all the world with fruit.[d]

7Has the LORD struck her
as he struck[e] down those who struck her?
Has she been killed
as those were killed who killed her?
8By warfare[l] and exile[f] you contend with her—
with his fierce blast he drives her out,
as on a day the east wind blows.
9By this, then, will Jacob's guilt be atoned for,
and this will be the full fruitage of the removal of his sin:[g]
When he makes all the altar stones
to be like chalk stones crushed to pieces,
no Asherah poles[m][h] or incense altars
will be left standing.
10The fortified city stands desolate,[i]
an abandoned settlement, forsaken like the desert;
there the calves graze,
there they lie down;[j]
they strip its branches bare.
11When its twigs are dry, they are broken off
and women come and make fires with them.
For this is a people without understanding;[k]
so their Maker has no compassion on them,
and their Creator[l] shows them no favor.[m]

12In that day the LORD will thresh
from the flowing Euphrates[n] to the
Wadi of Egypt,[n] and you, O Israelites, will be gathered[o] up one by
one. 13And in that day a great
trumpet[p] will sound. Those who
were perishing in Assyria and those
who were exiled in Egypt[q] will
come and worship the LORD on the
holy mountain in Jerusalem.

Woe to Ephraim

28 Woe to that wreath, the pride of Ephraim's[r] drunkards,
to the fading flower, his glorious beauty,
set on the head of a fertile valley[s]—
to that city, the pride of those laid low by wine![t]
2See, the Lord has one who is powerful[u] and strong.
Like a hailstorm[v] and a destructive wind,[w]
like a driving rain and a flooding[x] downpour,
he will throw it forcefully to the ground.
3That wreath, the pride of Ephraim's[y] drunkards,
will be trampled underfoot.
4That fading flower, his glorious beauty,
set on the head of a fertile valley,[z]
will be like a fig[a] ripe before harvest—
as soon as someone sees it and takes it in his hand,
he swallows it.

5In that day the LORD Almighty
will be a glorious crown,[b]
a beautiful wreath
for the remnant of his people.
6He will be a spirit of justice[c]
to him who sits in judgment,[d]
a source of strength
to those who turn back the battle[e] at the gate.

7And these also stagger from wine[f]
and reel[g] from beer:

27:5 [a]Isa 25:4 [b]Job 22:21; Ro 5:1; 2Co 5:20
27:6 [c]Hos 14:5-6 [d]Isa 37:31
27:7 [e]Isa 37:36-38
27:8 [f]Isa 50:1; 54:7
27:9 [g]Ro 11:27* [h]Ex 34:13
27:10 [i]Isa 32:14; Jer 26:6 [j]Isa 17:2
27:11 [k]Dt 32:28; Isa 1:3; Jer 8:7 [l]Dt 32:18; Isa 43:1,7,15; 44:1-2,21,24 [m]Isa 9:17
27:12 [n]Ge 15:18 [o]Dt 30:4; Isa 11:12; 17:6
27:13 [p]Lev 25:9; Mt 24:31 [q]Isa 19:21,25
28:1 [r]ver 3; Isa 9:9 [s]ver 4 [t]Hos 7:5
28:2 [u]Isa 40:10 [v]Isa 30:30; Eze 13:11 [w]Isa 29:6 [x]Isa 8:7
28:3 [y]ver 1
28:4 [z]ver 1 [a]Hos 9:10; Na 3:12
28:5 [b]Isa 62:3
28:6 [c]Isa 11:2-4; 32:1,16 [d]Jn 5:30 [e]2Ch 32:8
28:7 [f]Isa 22:13 [g]Isa 56:10-12

[l]*8* See Septuagint; the meaning of the Hebrew for this word is uncertain. [m]*9* That is, symbols of the goddess Asherah
[n]*12* Hebrew *River*

Priests[a] and prophets[b] stagger
from beer
and are befuddled with wine;
they reel from beer,
they stagger when seeing
visions,[c]
they stumble when rendering
decisions.
8All the tables are covered with
vomit[d]
and there is not a spot
without filth.

9"Who is it he is trying to
teach?[e]
To whom is he explaining his
message?
To children weaned[f] from
their milk,[g]
to those just taken from the
breast?
10For it is:
Do and do, do and do,
rule on rule, rule on rule[o];
a little here, a little there."

11Very well then, with foreign lips
and strange tongues[h]
God will speak to this
people,[i]
12to whom he said,
"This is the resting place, let
the weary rest";[j]
and, "This is the place of
repose"—
but they would not listen.
13So then, the word of the LORD
to them will become:
Do and do, do and do,
rule on rule, rule on rule;
a little here, a little there—
so that they will go and fall
backward,
be injured[k] and snared and
captured.[l]

14Therefore hear the word of the
LORD,[m] you scoffers
who rule this people in
Jerusalem.
15You boast, "We have entered
into a covenant with
death,
with the grave[p] we have
made an agreement.
When an overwhelming scourge
sweeps by,[n]
it cannot touch us,
for we have made a lie[o] our
refuge
and falsehood[q] our hiding
place.[p]"

16So this is what the Sovereign
LORD says:

"See, I lay a stone in Zion,
a tested stone,[q]
a precious cornerstone for a
sure foundation;
the one who trusts will never
be dismayed.[r]
17I will make justice[s] the
measuring line
and righteousness the plumb
line;[t]
hail will sweep away your
refuge, the lie,
and water will overflow your
hiding place.
18Your covenant with death will
be annulled;
your agreement with the
grave will not stand.[u]
When the overwhelming
scourge sweeps by,[v]
you will be beaten down[w] by
it.
19As often as it comes it will
carry you away;[x]
morning after morning, by
day and by night,
it will sweep through."

The understanding of this
message
will bring sheer terror.[y]
20The bed is too short to stretch
out on,
the blanket too narrow to
wrap around you.[z]
21The LORD will rise up as he did
at Mount Perazim,[a]
he will rouse himself as in
the Valley of Gibeon[b]—
to do his work,[c] his strange
work,
and perform his task, his
alien task.
22Now stop your mocking,
or your chains will become
heavier;

28:7 [a]Isa 24:2 [b]Isa 9:15 [c]Isa 29:11; Hos 4:11
28:8 [d]Jer 48:26
28:9 [e]ver 26; Isa 30:20; 48:17; 50:4; 54:13 [f]Ps 131:2 [g]Heb 5:12-13
28:11 [h]Isa 33:19 [i]1Co 14:21*
28:12 [j]Isa 11:10; Mt 11:28-29
28:13 [k]Mt 21:44 [l]Isa 8:15
28:14 [m]Isa 1:10
28:15 [n]ver 2,18; Isa 8:7-8; 30:28; Da 11:22 [o]Isa 9:15 [p]Isa 29:15
28:16 [q]Ps 118:22; Isa 8:14-15; Mt 21:42; Ac 4:11; Eph 2:20 [r]Ro 9:33*; 10:11*; 1Pe 2:6*
28:17 [s]Isa 5:16 [t]2Ki 21:13
28:18 [u]Isa 7:7 [v]ver 15 [w]Da 8:13
28:19 [x]2Ki 24:2 [y]Job 18:11
28:20 [z]Isa 59:6
28:21 [a]1Ch 14:11 [b]Jos 10:10, 12; 1Ch 14:16 [c]Isa 10:12; Lk 19:41-44

[o]*10* Hebrew / *sav lasav sav lasav / kav lakav kav lakav* (possibly meaningless sounds; perhaps a mimicking of the prophet's words); also in verse 13 [p]*15* Hebrew *Sheol*; also in verse 18 [q]*15* Or *false gods*

the Lord, the LORD Almighty,
has told me
of the destruction decreed[a]
against the whole land.[b]

23Listen and hear my voice;
pay attention and hear what I say.
24When a farmer plows for planting, does he plow continually?
Does he keep on breaking up and harrowing the soil?
25When he has leveled the surface,
does he not sow caraway and scatter cummin?[c]
Does he not plant wheat in its place,[r]
barley in its plot,[r]
and spelt[d] in its field?
26His God instructs him
and teaches him the right way.

27Caraway is not threshed with a sledge,
nor is a cartwheel rolled over cummin;
caraway is beaten out with a rod,
and cummin with a stick.
28Grain must be ground to make bread;
so one does not go on threshing it forever.
Though he drives the wheels of his threshing cart over it,
his horses do not grind it.
29All this also comes from the LORD Almighty,
wonderful in counsel[e] and magnificent in wisdom.[f]

Woe to David's City

29 Woe[g] to you, Ariel, Ariel,[h]
the city where David settled!
Add year to year
and let your cycle of festivals[i] go on.
2Yet I will besiege Ariel;
she will mourn and lament,[j]
she will be to me like an altar hearth.[s]
3I will encamp against you all around;
I will encircle[k] you with towers
and set up my siege works against you.
4Brought low, you will speak from the ground;
your speech will mumble[l] out of the dust.
Your voice will come ghostlike from the earth;
out of the dust your speech will whisper.

5But your many enemies will become like fine dust,
the ruthless hordes like blown chaff.[m]
Suddenly,[n] in an instant,
6 the LORD Almighty will come
with thunder and earthquake[o] and great noise,
with windstorm and tempest and flames of a devouring fire.
7Then the hordes of all the nations[p] that fight against Ariel,
that attack her and her fortress and besiege her,
will be as it is with a dream,[q]
with a vision in the night—
8as when a hungry man dreams that he is eating,
but he awakens,[r] and his hunger remains;
as when a thirsty man dreams that he is drinking,
but he awakens faint, with his thirst unquenched.
So will it be with the hordes of all the nations
that fight against Mount Zion.

9Be stunned and amazed,
blind yourselves and be sightless;
be drunk,[s] but not from wine,[t]
stagger, but not from beer.
10The LORD has brought over you a deep sleep:
He has sealed your eyes[u] (the prophets);[v]

28:22 [a]Isa 10:22 [b]Isa 10:23
28:25 [c]Mt 23:23 [d]Ex 9:32
28:29 [e]Isa 9:6 [f]Ro 11:33
29:1 [g]Isa 22:12-13 [h]2Sa 5:9 [i]Isa 1:14
29:2 [j]Isa 3:26; La 2:5
29:3 [k]Lk 19:43-44
29:4 [l]Isa 8:19
29:5 [m]Isa 17:13 [n]Isa 17:14; 1Th 5:3
29:6 [o]Mt 24:7; Mk 13:8; Lk 21:11; Rev 11:19
29:7 [p]Mic 4:11-12; Zec 12:9 [q]Job 20:8
29:8 [r]Ps 73:20
29:9 [s]Isa 51:17 [t]Isa 51:21-22
29:10 [u]Ps 69:23; Isa 6:9-10; Ro 11:8* [v]Mic 3:6

[r]25 The meaning of the Hebrew for this word is uncertain. [s]2 The Hebrew for *altar hearth* sounds like the Hebrew for *Ariel.*

he has covered your heads
(the seers).[a]

11For you this whole vision is
nothing but words sealed[b] in a
scroll. And if you give the scroll to
someone who can read, and say to
him, "Read this, please," he will
answer, "I can't; it is sealed." 12Or
if you give the scroll to someone
who cannot read, and say, "Read
this, please," he will answer, "I
don't know how to read."

13The Lord says:

"These people come near to me
with their mouth
and honor me with their lips,
but their hearts are far from
me.[c]
Their worship of me
is made up only of rules
taught by men.[t][d]
14Therefore once more I will
astound these people
with wonder upon wonder;[e]
the wisdom of the wise[f] will
perish,
the intelligence of the
intelligent will vanish.[g]"
15Woe to those who go to great
depths
to hide their plans from the
LORD,
who do their work in darkness
and think,
"Who sees us?[h] Who will
know?"[i]
16You turn things upside down,
as if the potter were thought
to be like the clay!
Shall what is formed say to him
who formed it,
"He did not make me"?
Can the pot say of the potter,[j]
"He knows nothing"?
17In a very short time, will not
Lebanon be turned into
a fertile field[k]
and the fertile field seem like
a forest?[l]
18In that day the deaf[m] will hear
the words of the scroll,
and out of gloom and
darkness
the eyes of the blind will
see.[n]

29:10 [a] 1Sa 9:9
29:11 [b] Isa 8:16; Mt 13:11; Rev 5:1-2
29:13 [c] Eze 33:31 [d] Mt 15:8-9*; Mk 7:6-7*; Col 2:22
29:14 [e] Hab 1:5 [f] Jer 8:9; 49:7 [g] Isa 6:9-10; 1Co 1:19*
29:15 [h] Ps 10:11-13; 94:7; Isa 57:12 [i] Job 22:13
29:16 [j] Isa 45:9; 64:8; Ro 9:20-21*
29:17 [k] Ps 84:6 [l] Isa 32:15
29:18 [m] Mk 7:37 [n] Isa 32:3; 35:5; Mt 11:5
29:19 [o] Isa 61:1; Mt 5:5; 11:29 [p] Isa 14:30; Mt 11:5; Jas 1:9; 2:5
29:20 [q] Isa 28:22 [r] Isa 59:4; Mic 2:1
29:21 [s] Am 5:10,15 [t] Isa
29:22 [u] Isa 41:8; 63:16 [v] Isa 49:23
29:23 [w] Isa 49:20-26 [x] Isa 19:25
29:24 [y] Isa 28:7; Heb 5:2 [z] Isa 41:20; 60:16 [a] Isa 30:21
30:1 [b] Isa 29:15 [c] Isa 1:2 [d] Isa 8:12
30:2 [e] Isa 31:1 [f] Nu 27:21 [g] Isa 36:9

19Once more the humble[o] will
rejoice in the LORD;
the needy[p] will rejoice in the
Holy One of Israel.
20The ruthless will vanish,
the mockers[q] will disappear,
and all who have an eye for
evil[r] will be cut down—
21those who with a word make a
man out to be guilty,
who ensnare the defender in
court[s]
and with false testimony
deprive the innocent of
justice.[t]

22Therefore this is what the
LORD, who redeemed Abraham,[u]
says to the house of Jacob:

"No longer will Jacob be
ashamed;[v]
no longer will their faces
grow pale.
23When they see among them
their children,[w]
the work of my hands,[x]
they will keep my name holy;
they will acknowledge the
holiness of the Holy One
of Jacob,
and will stand in awe of the
God of Israel.
24Those who are wayward[y] in
spirit will gain
understanding;[z]
those who complain will
accept instruction."[a]

Woe to the Obstinate Nation

30 "Woe[b] to the obstinate
children,"[c]
declares the LORD,
"to those who carry out plans
that are not mine,
forming an alliance,[d] but not
by my Spirit,
heaping sin upon sin;
2who go down to Egypt[e]
without consulting[f] me;
who look for help to Pharaoh's
protection,[g]
to Egypt's shade for refuge.

[t]13 Hebrew; Septuagint *They worship me in vain; / their teachings are but rules taught by men*

3But Pharaoh's protection will
be to your shame,
Egypt's shade will bring you
disgrace.[a]
4Though they have officials in
Zoan[b]
and their envoys have arrived
in Hanes,
5everyone will be put to shame
because of a people[c] useless
to them,
who bring neither help nor
advantage,
but only shame and
disgrace."

6An oracle concerning the animals of the Negev:

Through a land of hardship and
distress,[d]
of lions and lionesses,
of adders and darting
snakes,[e]
the envoys carry their riches on
donkeys' backs,
their treasures[f] on the
humps of camels,
to that unprofitable nation,
7 to Egypt, whose help is
utterly useless.
Therefore I call her
Rahab the Do-Nothing.
8Go now, write it on a tablet for
them,
inscribe it on a scroll,[g]
that for the days to come
it may be an everlasting
witness.
9These are rebellious people,
deceitful[h] children,
children unwilling to listen
to the LORD's
instruction.[i]
10They say to the seers,
"See no more visions[j]!"
and to the prophets,
"Give us no more visions of
what is right!
Tell us pleasant things,[k]
prophesy illusions.[l]
11Leave this way,
get off this path,
and stop confronting[m] us
with the Holy One of Israel!"

12Therefore, this is what the
Holy One of Israel says:

"Because you have rejected this
message,[n]
relied on oppression[o]
and depended on deceit,
13this sin will become for you
like a high wall,[p] cracked
and bulging,
that collapses[q] suddenly,[r]
in an instant.
14It will break in pieces like
pottery,[s]
shattered so mercilessly
that among its pieces not a
fragment will be found
for taking coals from a hearth
or scooping water out of a
cistern."

15This is what the Sovereign
LORD, the Holy One of Israel, says:

"In repentance and rest is your
salvation,
in quietness and trust[t] is
your strength,
but you would have none of
it.
16You said, 'No, we will flee on
horses.'[u]
Therefore you will flee!
You said, 'We will ride off on
swift horses.'
Therefore your pursuers will
be swift!
17A thousand will flee
at the threat of one;
at the threat of five[v]
you will all flee[w] away,
till you are left
like a flagstaff on a
mountaintop,
like a banner on a hill."
18Yet the LORD longs[x] to be
gracious to you;
he rises to show you
compassion.
For the LORD is a God of
justice.[y]
Blessed are all who wait for
him![z]

19O people of Zion, who live in
Jerusalem, you will weep no
more.[a] How gracious he will be
when you cry for help! As soon as
he hears, he will answer[b] you.
20Although the Lord gives you the
bread[c] of adversity and the water

30:3 [a] Isa 20:4-5; 36:6
30:4 [b] Isa 19:11
30:5 [c] ver 7
30:6 [d] Ex 5:10,21; Isa 8:22; Jer 11:4 [e] Dt 8:15 [f] Isa 15:7
30:8 [g] Isa 8:1; Hab 2:2
30:9 [h] Isa 28:15; 59:3-4 [i] Isa 1:10
30:10 [j] Jer 11:21; Am 7:13 [k] 1Ki 22:8 [l] Eze 13:7; Ro 16:18
30:11 [m] Job 21:14
30:12 [n] Isa 5:24 [o] Isa 5:7
30:13 [p] Ps 62:3 [q] 1Ki 20:30 [r] Isa 29:5
30:14 [s] Ps 2:9; Jer 19:10-11
30:15 [t] Isa 32:17
30:16 [u] Isa 31:1,3
30:17 [v] Lev 26:8; Jos 23:10 [w] Lev 26:36; Dt 28:25
30:18 [x] Isa 42:14; 2Pe 3:9,15 [y] Isa 5:16 [z] Isa 25:9
30:19 [a] Isa 60:20; 61:3 [b] Ps 50:15; Isa 58:9; 65:24; Mt 7:7-11
30:20 [c] 1Ki 22:27

of affliction, your teachers will be
hidden[a] no more; with your own
eyes you will see them. 21Whether
you turn to the right or to the left,
your ears will hear a voice[b] behind
you, saying, "This is the way; walk
in it." 22Then you will defile your
idols[c] overlaid with silver and your
images covered with gold; you will
throw them away like a menstrual
cloth and say to them, "Away with
you!"

23He will also send you rain[d] for
the seed you sow in the ground,
and the food that comes from the
land will be rich and plentiful. In
that day your cattle will graze in
broad meadows.[e] 24The oxen and
donkeys that work the soil will eat
fodder and mash, spread out with
fork[f] and shovel. 25In the day of
great slaughter, when the towers[g]
fall, streams of water will flow[h] on
every high mountain and every
lofty hill. 26The moon will shine
like the sun,[i] and the sunlight will
be seven times brighter, like the
light of seven full days, when the
LORD binds up the bruises of his
people and heals[j] the wounds he
inflicted.

27See, the Name[k] of the LORD
comes from afar,
with burning anger[l] and
dense clouds of smoke;
his lips are full of wrath,[m]
and his tongue is a
consuming fire.
28His breath[n] is like a rushing
torrent,
rising up to the neck.[o]
He shakes the nations in the
sieve[p] of destruction;
he places in the jaws of the
peoples
a bit[q] that leads them
astray.
29And you will sing
as on the night you celebrate
a holy festival;
your hearts will rejoice
as when people go up with
flutes
to the mountain[r] of the LORD,
to the Rock of Israel.

30:20 [a]Ps 74:9; Am 8:11
30:21 [b]Isa 29:24
30:22 [c]Ex 32:4
30:23 [d]Isa 65:21-22 [e]Ps 65:13
30:24 [f]Mt 3:12; Lk 3:17
30:25 [g]Isa 2:15 [h]Isa 41:18
30:26 [i]Isa 24:23; 60:19-20; Rev 21:23; 22:5 [j]Dt 32:39; Isa 1:5
30:27 [k]Isa 59:19 [l]Isa 66:14 [m]Isa 10:5
30:28 [n]Isa 11:4 [o]Isa 8:8 [p]Am 9:9 [q]2Ki 19:28; Isa 37:29
30:29 [r]Ps 42:4
30:31 [s]Isa 10:5,12 [t]Isa 11:4
30:32 [u]Isa 11:15; Eze 32:10
30:33 [v]2Ki 23:10 [w]Ge 19:24
31:1 [x]Dt 17:16; Isa 30:2,5 [y]Isa 2:7 [z]Ps 20:7; Da 9:13
31:2 [a]Ro 16:27 [b]Isa 45:7 [c]Nu 23:19 [d]Isa 32:6
31:3 [e]Isa 36:9 [f]Eze 28:9; 2Th 2:4

30The LORD will cause men to
hear his majestic voice
and will make them see his
arm coming down
with raging anger and
consuming fire,
with cloudburst,
thunderstorm and hail.
31The voice of the LORD will
shatter Assyria;[s]
with his scepter he will
strike[t] them down.
32Every stroke the LORD lays on
them
with his punishing rod
will be to the music of
tambourines and harps,
as he fights them in battle
with the blows of his
arm.[u]
33Topheth[v] has long been
prepared;
it has been made ready for
the king.
Its fire pit has been made deep
and wide,
with an abundance of fire
and wood;
the breath of the LORD,
like a stream of burning
sulfur,[w]
sets it ablaze.

Woe to Those Who Rely on Egypt

31 Woe to those who go
down to Egypt[x] for help,
who rely on horses,
who trust in the multitude of
their chariots[y]
and in the great strength of
their horsemen,
but do not look to the Holy
One of Israel,
or seek help from the
LORD.[z]
2Yet he too is wise[a] and can
bring disaster;[b]
he does not take back his
words.[c]
He will rise up against the
house of the wicked,[d]
against those who help
evildoers.
3But the Egyptians[e] are men
and not God;[f]

their horses are flesh and not
spirit.
When the LORD stretches out
his hand,[a]
he who helps will stumble,
he who is helped[b] will fall;
both will perish together.

4This is what the LORD says to me:

"As a lion[c] growls,
a great lion over his prey—
and though a whole band of
shepherds
is called together against
him,
he is not frightened by their
shouts
or disturbed by their
clamor—
so the LORD Almighty will come
down[d]
to do battle on Mount Zion
and on its heights.
5Like birds hovering overhead,
the LORD Almighty will
shield[e] Jerusalem;
he will shield it and deliver[f]
it,
he will 'pass over' it and will
rescue it."

6Return to him you have so greatly revolted against, O Israelites.
7For in that day every one of you will reject the idols of silver and gold[g] your sinful hands have made.

8"Assyria[h] will fall by a sword
that is not of man;
a sword, not of mortals, will
devour[i] them.
They will flee before the
sword
and their young men will be
put to forced labor.[j]
9Their stronghold[k] will fall
because of terror;
at sight of the battle
standard their
commanders will panic,"
declares the LORD,
whose fire[l] is in Zion,
whose furnace is in
Jerusalem.

31:3 [a]Isa 9:17,21 [b]Isa 30:5-7
31:4 [c]Nu 24:9; Hos 11:10; Am 3:8 [d]Isa 42:13
31:5 [e]Ps 91:4 [f]Isa 37:35; 38:6
31:7 [g]Isa 2:20; 30:22
31:8 [h]Isa 10:12 [i]Isa 14:25; 37:7 [j]Ge 49:15
31:9 [k]Dt 32:31,37 [l]Isa 10:17
32:1 [m]Eze 37:24 [n]Ps 72:1-4; Isa 9:7
32:2 [o]Isa 4:6
32:3 [p]Isa 29:18
32:4 [q]Isa 29:24
32:5 [r]1Sa 25:25
32:6 [s]Pr 19:3 [t]Isa 9:17 [u]Isa 9:16 [v]Isa 3:15
32:7 [w]Jer 5:26-28 [x]Mic 7:3 [y]Isa 61:1
32:8 [z]Pr 11:25
32:9 [a]Isa 28:23 [b]Isa 47:8; Am 6:1; Zep 2:15
32:10 [c]Isa 5:5-6; 24:7

The Kingdom of Righteousness

32 See, a king[m] will reign in
righteousness
and rulers will rule with
justice.[n]
2Each man will be like a
shelter[o] from the wind
and a refuge from the storm,
like streams of water in the
desert
and the shadow of a great
rock in a thirsty land.

3Then the eyes of those who see
will no longer be
closed,[p]
and the ears of those who
hear will listen.
4The mind of the rash will know
and understand,[q]
and the stammering tongue
will be fluent and clear.
5No longer will the fool[r] be
called noble
nor the scoundrel be highly
respected.
6For the fool speaks folly,[s]
his mind is busy with evil:
He practices ungodliness[t]
and spreads error[u]
concerning the LORD;
the hungry he leaves empty[v]
and from the thirsty he
withholds water.
7The scoundrel's methods are
wicked,[w]
he makes up evil schemes[x]
to destroy the poor with lies,
even when the plea of the
needy[y] is just.
8But the noble man makes
noble plans,
and by noble deeds[z] he
stands.

The Women of Jerusalem

9You women who are so
complacent,
rise up and listen[a] to me;
you daughters who feel
secure,[b]
hear what I have to say!
10In little more than a year
you who feel secure will
tremble;
the grape harvest will fail,[c]

and the harvest of fruit will
not come.
11Tremble, you complacent
women;
shudder, you daughters who
feel secure!
Strip off your clothes,[a]
put sackcloth around your
waists.
12Beat your breasts[b] for the
pleasant fields,
for the fruitful vines
13and for the land of my
people,
a land overgrown with thorns
and briers[c]—
yes, mourn for all houses of
merriment
and for this city of revelry.[d]
14The fortress[e] will be
abandoned,
the noisy city deserted;[f]
citadel and watchtower[g] will
become a wasteland
forever,
the delight of donkeys,[h] a
pasture for flocks,
15till the Spirit[i] is poured upon
us from on high,
and the desert becomes a
fertile field,[j]
and the fertile field seems
like a forest.[k]
16Justice will dwell in the
desert
and righteousness live in the
fertile field.
17The fruit of righteousness will
be peace;[l]
the effect of righteousness
will be quietness and
confidence[m] forever.
18My people will live in peaceful
dwelling places,
in secure homes,
in undisturbed places of
rest.[n]
19Though hail[o] flattens the
forest[p]
and the city is leveled[q]
completely,
20how blessed you will be,
sowing[r] your seed by every
stream,
and letting your cattle and
donkeys range free.[s]

32:11 [a]Isa 47:2
32:12 [b]Na 2:7
32:13 [c]Isa 5:6 [d]Isa 22:2
32:14 [e]Isa 13:22 [f]Isa 6:11; 27:10 [g]Isa 34:13 [h]Ps 104:11
32:15 [i]Isa 11:2; Joel 2:28 [j]Ps 107:35; Isa 35:1-2 [k]Isa 29:17
32:17 [l]Ps 119:165; Ro 14:17; Jas 3:18 [m]Isa 30:15
32:18 [n]Hos 2:18-23
32:19 [o]Isa 28:17; 30:30 [p]Isa 10:19; Zec 11:2 [q]Isa 24:10; 27:10
32:20 [r]Ecc 11:1 [s]Isa 30:24
33:1 [t]Hab 2:8; Mt 7:2 [u]Isa 21:2
33:2 [v]Isa 40:10; 51:9; 59:16 [w]Isa 25:9
33:3 [x]Isa 59:16-18
33:5 [y]Ps 97:9 [z]Isa 28:6 [a]Isa 1:26
33:6 [b]Isa 51:6 [c]Isa 11:2-3; Mt 6:33
33:7 [d]2Ki 18:37
33:8 [e]Jdg 5:6; Isa 35:8
33:9 [f]Isa 3:26 [g]Isa 2:13; 35:2 [h]Isa 24:4

Distress and Help

33 Woe to you, O destroyer,
you who have not been
destroyed!
Woe to you, O traitor,
you who have not been
betrayed!
When you stop destroying,
you will be destroyed;[t]
when you stop betraying,
you will be betrayed.[u]

2O LORD, be gracious to us;
we long for you.
Be our strength[v] every
morning,
our salvation[w] in time of
distress.
3At the thunder of your voice,
the peoples flee;
when you rise up,[x] the
nations scatter.
4Your plunder, O nations, is
harvested as by young
locusts;
like a swarm of locusts men
pounce on it.

5The LORD is exalted,[y] for he
dwells on high;
he will fill Zion with justice[z]
and righteousness.[a]
6He will be the sure foundation
for your times,
a rich store of salvation[b] and
wisdom and knowledge;
the fear[c] of the LORD is the
key to this treasure.[u]

7Look, their brave men cry aloud
in the streets;
the envoys[d] of peace weep
bitterly.
8The highways are deserted,
no travelers are on the
roads.[e]
The treaty is broken,
its witnesses[v] are despised,
no one is respected.
9The land mourns[w][f] and wastes
away,
Lebanon[g] is ashamed and
withers;[h]
Sharon is like the Arabah,

[u]6 Or *is a treasure from him* [v]8 Dead Sea Scrolls; Masoretic Text / *the cities* [w]9 Or *dries up*

and Bashan and Carmel drop
their leaves.
10"Now will I arise,[a]" says the
LORD.
"Now will I be exalted;
now will I be lifted up.
11You conceive[b] chaff,
you give birth[c] to straw;
your breath is a fire[d] that
consumes you.
12The peoples will be burned as
if to lime;
like cut thornbushes they
will be set ablaze.[e]"

13You who are far away,[f] hear[g]
what I have done;
you who are near,
acknowledge my power!
14The sinners in Zion are
terrified;
trembling[h] grips the godless:
"Who of us can dwell with the
consuming fire?[i]
Who of us can dwell with
everlasting burning?"
15He who walks righteously[j]
and speaks what is right,[k]
who rejects gain from extortion
and keeps his hand from
accepting bribes,
who stops his ears against plots
of murder
and shuts his eyes[l] against
contemplating evil—
16this is the man who will dwell
on the heights,
whose refuge[m] will be the
mountain fortress.[n]
His bread will be supplied,
and water will not fail[o]
him.

17Your eyes will see the king[p] in
his beauty
and view a land that
stretches afar.[q]
18In your thoughts you will
ponder the former
terror:[r]
"Where is that chief officer?
Where is the one who took
the revenue?
Where is the officer in charge
of the towers?"
19You will see those arrogant
people no more,
those people of an obscure
speech,
with their strange,
incomprehensible
tongue.[s]
20Look upon Zion, the city of our
festivals;
your eyes will see Jerusalem,
a peaceful abode,[t] a tent
that will not be moved;[u]
its stakes will never be pulled
up,
nor any of its ropes broken.
21There the LORD will be our
Mighty One.
It will be like a place of
broad rivers and
streams.[v]
No galley with oars will ride
them,
no mighty ship will sail
them.
22For the LORD is our judge,[w]
the LORD is our lawgiver,[x]
the LORD is our king;[y]
it is he who will save[z] us.

23Your rigging hangs loose:
The mast is not held secure,
the sail is not spread.
Then an abundance of spoils
will be divided
and even the lame[a] will
carry off plunder.[b]
24No one living in Zion will say,
"I am ill";[c]
and the sins of those who
dwell there will be
forgiven.[d]

Judgment Against the Nations

34 Come near, you nations,
and listen;
pay attention, you peoples![e]
Let the earth[f] hear, and all
that is in it,
the world, and all that comes
out of it![g]
2The LORD is angry with all
nations;
his wrath is upon all their
armies.
He will totally destroy[x][h] them,

x2 The Hebrew term refers to the irrevocable giving over of things or persons to the LORD, often by totally destroying them; also in verse 5.

33:10 [a]Ps 12:5; Isa 2:21
33:11 [b]Ps 7:14; Isa 59:4; Jas 1:15 [c]Isa 26:18 [d]Isa 1:31
33:12 [e]Isa 10:17
33:13 [f]Ps 48:10; 49:1 [g]Isa 49:1
33:14 [h]Isa 32:11 [i]Isa 30:30; Heb 12:29
33:15 [j]Isa 58:8 [k]Ps 15:2; 24:4 [l]Ps 119:37
33:16 [m]Isa 25:4 [n]Isa 26:1 [o]Isa 49:10
33:17 [p]Isa 6:5 [q]Isa 26:15
33:18 [r]Isa 17:14
33:19 [s]Isa 28:11; Jer 5:15
33:20 [t]Isa 32:18 [u]Ps 46:5; 125:1-2
33:21 [v]Isa 41:18; 48:18; 66:12
33:22 [w]Isa 11:4 [x]Isa 2:3; Jas 4:12 [y]Ps 89:18 [z]Isa 25:9
33:23 [a]2Ki 7:8 [b]2Ki 7:16
33:24 [c]Isa 30:26 [d]Jer 50:20; 1Jn 1:7 9
34:1 [e]Isa 41:1; 43:9 [f]Ps 49:1 [g]Dt 32:1
34:2 [h]Isa 13:5

he will give them over to
slaughter.[a]
3Their slain will be thrown out,
their dead bodies will send
up a stench;[b]
the mountains will be soaked
with their blood.[c]
4All the stars of the heavens will
be dissolved[d]
and the sky rolled up[e] like a
scroll;
all the starry host will fall[f]
like withered leaves from the
vine,
like shriveled figs from the
fig tree.

5My sword[g] has drunk its fill in
the heavens;
see, it descends in judgment
on Edom,[h]
the people I have totally
destroyed.[i]
6The sword of the LORD is
bathed in blood,
it is covered with fat—
the blood of lambs and goats,
fat from the kidneys of rams.
For the LORD has a sacrifice in
Bozrah
and a great slaughter in
Edom.
7And the wild oxen will fall with
them,
the bull calves and the great
bulls.[j]
Their land will be drenched
with blood,
and the dust will be soaked
with fat.

8For the LORD has a day of
vengeance,[k]
a year of retribution, to
uphold Zion's cause.
9Edom's streams will be turned
into pitch,
her dust into burning sulfur;
her land will become blazing
pitch!
10It will not be quenched night
and day;
its smoke will rise forever.[l]
From generation to generation
it will lie desolate;[m]
no one will ever pass through
it again.

34:2 [a]Isa 30:25
34:3 [b]Joel 2:20; Am 4:10 [c]ver 7; Eze 14:19; 35:6; 38:22
34:4 [d]Isa 13:13; 2Pe 3:10 [e]Eze 32:7-8 [f]Joel 2:31; Mt 24:29*; Rev 6:13
34:5 [g]Dt 32:41-42; Jer 46:10; Eze 21:5 [h]Am 1:11-12 [i]Isa 24:6; Mal 1:4
34:7 [j]Ps 68:30
34:8 [k]Isa 63:4
34:10 [l]Rev 14:10-11; 19:3 [m]Isa 13:20; 24:1; Eze 29:12; Mal 1:3
34:11 [n]Zep 2:14; Rev 18:2 [o]2Ki 21:13; La 2:8
34:12 [p]Jer 27:20; 39:6 [q]Isa 41:11-12
34:13 [r]Isa 13:22; 32:13 [s]Ps 44:19; Jer 9:11; 10:22
34:14 [t]Isa 13:22
34:15 [u]Dt 14:13
34:16 [v]Isa 30:8 [w]Isa 1:20; 58:14
34:17 [x]Isa 17:14; Jer 13:25 [y]ver 10

11The desert owl[y][n] and screech
owl[y] will possess it;
the great owl[y] and the raven
will nest there.
God will stretch out over Edom
the measuring line of chaos
and the plumb line[o] of
desolation.
12Her nobles will have nothing
there to be called a
kingdom,
all her princes[p] will vanish[q]
away.
13Thorns will overrun her
citadels,
nettles and brambles her
strongholds.[r]
She will become a haunt for
jackals,[s]
a home for owls.
14Desert creatures will meet with
hyenas,[t]
and wild goats will bleat to
each other;
there the night creatures will
also repose
and find for themselves
places of rest.
15The owl will nest there and lay
eggs,
she will hatch them, and care
for her young under the
shadow of her wings;
there also the falcons[u] will
gather,
each with its mate.

16Look in the scroll[v] of the LORD
and read:
None of these will be missing,
not one will lack her mate.
For it is his mouth[w] that has
given the order,
and his Spirit will gather
them together.
17He allots their portions;[x]
his hand distributes them by
measure.
They will possess it forever
and dwell there from
generation to
generation.[y]

[y]11 The precise identification of these birds is uncertain.

Joy of the Redeemed

35 The desert[a] and the
parched land will be
glad;
the wilderness will rejoice
and blossom.[b]
Like the crocus, 2it will burst
into bloom;
it will rejoice greatly and
shout for joy.[c]
The glory of Lebanon[d] will be
given to it,
the splendor of Carmel[e] and
Sharon;
they will see the glory of the
LORD,
the splendor of our God.[f]

3Strengthen the feeble hands,
steady the knees[g] that give
way;
4say to those with fearful hearts,
"Be strong, do not fear;
your God will come,
he will come with
vengeance;[h]
with divine retribution
he will come to save you."

5Then will the eyes of the blind
be opened[i]
and the ears of the deaf[j]
unstopped.
6Then will the lame[k] leap like a
deer,
and the mute tongue[l] shout
for joy.
Water will gush forth in the
wilderness
and streams[m] in the desert.
7The burning sand will become
a pool,
the thirsty ground bubbling
springs.[n]
In the haunts where jackals[o]
once lay,
grass and reeds and papyrus
will grow.

8And a highway[p] will be there;
it will be called the Way of
Holiness.[q]
The unclean[r] will not journey
on it;
it will be for those who walk
in that Way;
wicked fools will not go
about on it.[z]

35:1 [a]Isa 27:10; 41:18-19 [b]Isa 51:3
35:2 [c]Isa 25:9; 55:12 [d]Isa 32:15 [e]SS 7:5 [f]Isa 25:9
35:3 [g]Job 4:4; Heb 12:12
35:4 [h]Isa 1:24; 34:8
35:5 [i]Mt 11:5; Jn 9:6-7 [j]Isa 29:18; 50:4
35:6 [k]Mt 15:30; Jn 5:8-9; Ac 3:8 [l]Isa 32:4; Mt 9:32-33; 12:22; Lk 11:14 [m]Isa 41:18; Jn 7:38
35:7 [n]Isa 49:10 [o]Isa 13:22
35:8 [p]Isa 11:16; 33:8; Mt 7:13-14 [q]Isa 4:3; 1Pe 1:15 [r]Isa 52:1
35:9 [s]Isa 30:6 [t]Isa 34:14 [u]Isa 51:11; 62:12; 63:4
35:10 [v]Isa 25:9 [w]Isa 30:19; 51:11; Rev 7:17; 21:4
36:1 [x]2Ch 32:1
36:2 [y]Isa 7:3
36:3 [z]Isa 22:20-21 [a]2Ki 18:18
36:5 [b]2Ki 18:7
36:6 [c]Isa 30:2,5 [d]Eze 29:6-7

9No lion[s] will be there,
nor will any ferocious beast[t]
get up on it;
they will not be found there.
But only the redeemed[u] will
walk there,
10 and the ransomed of the
LORD will return.
They will enter Zion with
singing;
everlasting joy[v] will crown
their heads.
Gladness and joy will overtake
them,
and sorrow and sighing will
flee away.[w]

Sennacherib Threatens Jerusalem

36:1–22pp — 2Ki 18:13,17–37; 2Ch 32:9–19

36 In the fourteenth year of
King Hezekiah's reign, Sennacherib[x] king of Assyria attacked
all the fortified cities of Judah and
captured them. 2Then the king of
Assyria sent his field commander
with a large army from Lachish to
King Hezekiah at Jerusalem. When
the commander stopped at the aqueduct of the Upper Pool, on the
road to the Washerman's Field,[y]
3Eliakim[z] son of Hilkiah the palace administrator, Shebna[a] the
secretary, and Joah son of Asaph
the recorder went out to him.
4The field commander said to
them, "Tell Hezekiah,

" 'This is what the great
king, the king of Assyria, says:
On what are you basing this
confidence of yours? 5You say
you have strategy and military
strength—but you speak only
empty words. On whom are
you depending, that you rebel[b] against me? 6Look now,
you are depending on Egypt,[c]
that splintered reed[d] of a
staff, which pierces a man's
hand and wounds him if he
leans on it! Such is Pharaoh
king of Egypt to all who depend on him. 7And if you say
to me, "We are depending on

[z]8 Or / *the simple will not stray from it*

the LORD our God"—isn't he the one whose high places and altars Hezekiah removed,[a] saying to Judah and Jerusalem, "You must worship before this altar"?[b]

8" 'Come now, make a bargain with my master, the king of Assyria: I will give you two thousand horses—if you can put riders on them! 9How then can you repulse one officer of the least of my master's officials, even though you are depending on Egypt[c] for chariots and horsemen?[d] 10Furthermore, have I come to attack and destroy this land without the LORD? The LORD himself told[e] me to march against this country and destroy it.' "

11Then Eliakim, Shebna and Joah said to the field commander, "Please speak to your servants in Aramaic,[f] since we understand it. Don't speak to us in Hebrew in the hearing of the people on the wall."

12But the commander replied, "Was it only to your master and you that my master sent me to say these things, and not to the men sitting on the wall—who, like you, will have to eat their own filth and drink their own urine?"

13Then the commander stood and called out in Hebrew,[g] "Hear the words of the great king, the king of Assyria! 14This is what the king says: Do not let Hezekiah deceive you. He cannot deliver you! 15Do not let Hezekiah persuade you to trust in the LORD when he says, 'The LORD will surely deliver us; this city will not be given into the hand of the king of Assyria.'[h]

16"Do not listen to Hezekiah. This is what the king of Assyria says: Make peace with me and come out to me. Then every one of you will eat from his own vine and fig tree[i] and drink water from his own cistern,[j] 17until I come and take you to a land like your own—a land of grain and new wine, a land of bread and vineyards.

18"Do not let Hezekiah mislead you when he says, 'The LORD will deliver us.' Has the god of any nation ever delivered his land from the hand of the king of Assyria? 19Where are the gods of Hamath and Arpad? Where are the gods of Sepharvaim? Have they rescued Samaria from my hand? 20Who of all the gods[k] of these countries has been able to save his land from me? How then can the LORD deliver Jerusalem from my hand?"

21But the people remained silent and said nothing in reply, because the king had commanded, "Do not answer him."[l]

22Then Eliakim son of Hilkiah the palace administrator, Shebna the secretary, and Joah son of Asaph the recorder went to Hezekiah, with their clothes torn, and told him what the field commander had said.

Jerusalem's Deliverance Foretold

37:1-13pp — 2Ki 19:1-13

37 When King Hezekiah heard this, he tore his clothes and put on sackcloth and went into the temple of the LORD. 2He sent Eliakim the palace administrator, Shebna the secretary, and the leading priests, all wearing sackcloth, to the prophet Isaiah son of Amoz.[m] 3They told him, "This is what Hezekiah says: This day is a day of distress and rebuke and disgrace, as when children come to the point of birth[n] and there is no strength to deliver them. 4It may be that the LORD your God will hear the words of the field commander, whom his master, the king of Assyria, has sent to ridicule the living God, and that he will rebuke him for the words the LORD your God has heard.[o] Therefore pray for the remnant[p] that still survives."

5When King Hezekiah's officials came to Isaiah, 6Isaiah said to them, "Tell your master, 'This is what the LORD says: Do not be afraid[q] of what you have heard—those words with which the under-

36:7 [a] 2Ki 18:4 [b] Dt 12:2-5
36:9 [c] Isa 31:3 [d] Isa 30:2-5
36:10 [e] 1Ki 13:18
36:11 [f] Ezr 4:7
36:13 [g] 2Ch 32:18
36:15 [h] Isa 37:10
36:16 [i] 1Ki 4:25; Zec 3:10 [j] Pr 5:15
36:20 [k] 1Ki 20:23
36:21 [l] Pr 9:7-8; 26:4
37:2 [m] Isa 1:1
37:3 [n] Isa 26:18; 66:9; Hos 13:13
37:4 [o] Isa 36:13, 18-20 [p] Isa 1:9
37:6 [q] Isa 7:4

lings of the king of Assyria have
blasphemed me. 7 Listen! I am going to put a spirit in him so that
when he hears a certain report,[a]
he will return to his own country,
and there I will have him cut down
with the sword.' "

8 When the field commander
heard that the king of Assyria had
left Lachish, he withdrew and
found the king fighting against Libnah.[b]

9 Now Sennacherib received a report[c] that Tirhakah, the Cushite[a]
king ⌞of Egypt⌟, was marching out to
fight against him. When he heard
it, he sent messengers to Hezekiah
with this word: 10 "Say to Hezekiah
king of Judah: Do not let the god
you depend on deceive you when
he says, 'Jerusalem will not be
handed over to the king of Assyria.'[d] 11 Surely you have heard what
the kings of Assyria have done to
all the countries, destroying them
completely. And will you be delivered?[e] 12 Did the gods of the nations that were destroyed by my
forefathers[f] deliver them—the
gods of Gozan, Haran,[g] Rezeph
and the people of Eden who were
in Tel Assar? 13 Where is the king of
Hamath, the king of Arpad, the
king of the city of Sepharvaim, or of
Hena or Ivvah?"

Hezekiah's Prayer

37:14–20pp — 2Ki 19:14–19

14 Hezekiah received the letter
from the messengers and read it.
Then he went up to the temple of
the LORD and spread it out before
the LORD. 15 And Hezekiah prayed
to the LORD: 16 "O LORD Almighty,
God of Israel, enthroned between
the cherubim, you alone are God[h]
over all the kingdoms of the earth.
You have made heaven and earth.
17 Give ear, O LORD, and hear;[i]
open your eyes, O LORD, and see;[j]
listen to all the words Sennacherib
has sent to insult the living God.

18 "It is true, O LORD, that the Assyrian kings have laid waste all
these peoples and their lands.[k]
19 They have thrown their gods into
the fire and destroyed them,[l] for
they were not gods[m] but only wood
and stone, fashioned by human
hands. 20 Now, O LORD our God, deliver us from his hand, so that all
kingdoms on earth may know that
you alone, O LORD, are God.[b][n]"

Sennacherib's Fall

37:21–38pp — 2Ki 19:20–37; 2Ch 32:20–21

21 Then Isaiah son of Amoz[o] sent
a message to Hezekiah: "This is
what the LORD, the God of Israel,
says: Because you have prayed to
me concerning Sennacherib king of
Assyria, 22 this is the word the LORD
has spoken against him:

"The Virgin Daughter of Zion
despises and mocks you.
The Daughter of Jerusalem
tosses her head[p] as you flee.
23 Who is it you have insulted and
blasphemed?[q]
Against whom have you
raised your voice
and lifted your eyes in pride?[r]
Against the Holy One of
Israel!
24 By your messengers
you have heaped insults on
the Lord.
And you have said,
'With my many chariots
I have ascended the heights of
the mountains,
the utmost heights of
Lebanon.[s]
I have cut down its tallest
cedars,
the choicest of its pines.
I have reached its remotest
heights,
the finest of its forests.
25 I have dug wells in foreign
lands[c]
and drunk the water there.
With the soles of my feet
I have dried up all the
streams of Egypt.[t]'
26 "Have you not heard?
Long ago I ordained[u] it.

37:7 [a]ver 9
37:8 [b]Nu 33:20
37:9 [c]ver 7
37:10 [d]Isa 36:15
37:11 [e]Isa 36:18-20
37:12 [f]2Ki 18:11 [g]Ge 11:31; 12:1-4; Ac 7:2
37:16 [h]Dt 10:17; Ps 86:10; 136:2-3
37:17 [i]2Ch 6:40 [j]Da 9:18
37:18 [k]2Ki 15:29; Na 2:11-12
37:19 [l]Isa 26:14 [m]Isa 41:24,29
37:20 [n]Ps 46:10
37:21 [o]ver 2
37:22 [p]Job 16:4
37:23 [q]ver 4 [r]Isa 2:11
37:24 [s]Isa 14:8
37:25 [t]Dt 11:10
37:26 [u]Ac 2:23; 4:27-28; 1Pe 2:8

[a]*9* That is, from the upper Nile region
[b]*20* Dead Sea Scrolls (see also 2 Kings 19:19); Masoretic Text *alone are the LORD*
[c]*25* Dead Sea Scrolls (see also 2 Kings 19:24); Masoretic Text does not have *in foreign lands.*

In days of old I planned[a] it;
now I have brought it to pass,
that you have turned fortified cities
into piles of stone.[b]
27Their people, drained of power,
are dismayed and put to shame.
They are like plants in the field,
like tender green shoots,
like grass sprouting on the roof,[c]
scorched[d] before it grows up.

28"But I know where you stay
and when you come and go[d]
and how you rage[e] against me.
29Because you rage against me
and because your insolence[f]
has reached my ears,
I will put my hook in your nose[g]
and my bit in your mouth,
and I will make you return
by the way you came.[h]

30"This will be the sign for you, O Hezekiah:

"This year you will eat what grows by itself,
and the second year what springs from that.
But in the third year sow and reap,
plant vineyards and eat their fruit.
31Once more a remnant of the house of Judah
will take root below and bear fruit[i] above.
32For out of Jerusalem will come a remnant,
and out of Mount Zion a band of survivors.
The zeal[j] of the LORD Almighty
will accomplish this.

33"Therefore this is what the LORD says concerning the king of Assyria:

"He will not enter this city
or shoot an arrow here.
He will not come before it with shield
or build a siege ramp against it.
34By the way that he came he will return;[k]
he will not enter this city,"
declares the LORD.
35"I will defend[l] this city and save it,
for my sake[m] and for the sake of David[n] my servant!"

36Then the angel of the LORD
went out and put to death a hundred and eighty-five thousand men
in the Assyrian[o] camp. When the
people got up the next morning
—there were all the dead bodies!
37So Sennacherib king of Assyria
broke camp and withdrew. He returned to Nineveh[p] and stayed
there.
38One day, while he was worshiping in the temple of his god
Nisroch, his sons Adrammelech
and Sharezer cut him down with
the sword, and they escaped to the
land of Ararat.[q] And Esarhaddon
his son succeeded him as king.

Hezekiah's Illness

38:1–8pp — 2Ki 20:1–11; 2Ch 32:24–26

38 In those days Hezekiah became ill and was at the
point of death. The prophet Isaiah
son of Amoz[r] went to him and
said, "This is what the LORD says:
Put your house in order,[s] because
you are going to die; you will not
recover."
2Hezekiah turned his face to the
wall and prayed to the LORD, 3"Remember, O LORD, how I have
walked[t] before you faithfully and
with wholehearted devotion[u] and
have done what is good in your
eyes.[v]" And Hezekiah wept[w] bitterly.
4Then the word of the LORD came
to Isaiah: 5"Go and tell Hezekiah,
'This is what the LORD, the God of
your father David, says: I have

37:26 [a]Isa 10:6; 25:1 [b]Isa 25:2
37:27 [c]Ps 129:6
37:28 [d]Ps 139:1-3 [e]Ps 2:1
37:29 [f]Isa 10:12 [g]Isa 30:28; Eze 38:4 [h]ver 34
37:31 [i]Isa 27:6
37:32 [j]Isa 9:7
37:34 [k]ver 29
37:35 [l]Isa 31:5; 38:6 [m]Isa 43:25; 48:9,11 [n]2Ki 20:6
37:36 [o]Isa 10:12
37:37 [p]Ge 10:11
37:38 [q]Ge 8:4; Jer 51:27
38:1 [r]Isa 37:2 [s]2Sa 17:23
38:3 [t]Ne 13:14; Ps 26:3 [u]1Ch 29:19 [v]Dt 6:18 [w]Ps 6:8

[d]27 Some manuscripts of the Masoretic Text, Dead Sea Scrolls and some Septuagint manuscripts (see also 2 Kings 19:26); most manuscripts of the Masoretic Text *roof / and terraced fields*

heard your prayer and seen your
tears; I will add fifteen years[a] to
your life. 6And I will deliver you
and this city from the hand of the
king of Assyria. I will defend[b] this
city.
7" 'This is the LORD's sign[c] to
you that the LORD will do what he
has promised: 8I will make the
shadow cast by the sun go back the
ten steps it has gone down on the
stairway of Ahaz.' " So the sunlight
went back the ten steps it had gone
down.[d]

9A writing of Hezekiah king of
Judah after his illness and recovery:

10I said, "In the prime of my
life[e]
must I go through the gates
of death[ef]
and be robbed of the rest of
my years?[g]"
11I said, "I will not again see the
LORD,
the LORD, in the land of the
living;[h]
no longer will I look on
mankind,
or be with those who now
dwell in this world.[f]
12Like a shepherd's tent[i] my
house
has been pulled down[j] and
taken from me.
Like a weaver I have rolled[k] up
my life,
and he has cut me off from
the loom;[l]
day and night[m] you made an
end of me.
13I waited patiently till
dawn,
but like a lion he broke[n] all
my bones;[o]
day and night you made an
end of me.
14I cried like a swift or thrush,
I moaned like a mourning
dove.[p]
My eyes grew weak as I looked
to the heavens.
I am troubled; O Lord, come
to my aid!"[q]
15But what can I say?
He has spoken to me, and he
himself has done this.[r]
I will walk humbly[s] all my
years
because of this anguish of
my soul.[t]
16Lord, by such things men live;
and my spirit finds life in
them too.
You restored me to health
and let me live.[u]
17Surely it was for my benefit
that I suffered such anguish.
In your love you kept me
from the pit[v] of destruction;
you have put all my sins[w]
behind your back.[x]
18For the grave[ey] cannot praise
you,
death cannot sing your
praise;[z]
those who go down to the pit[a]
cannot hope for your
faithfulness.
19The living, the living—they
praise[b] you,
as I am doing today;
fathers tell their children[c]
about your faithfulness.
20The LORD will save me,
and we will sing[d] with
stringed instruments[e]
all the days of our lives[f]
in the temple[g] of the LORD.

21Isaiah had said, "Prepare a
poultice of figs and apply it to the
boil, and he will recover."
22Hezekiah had asked, "What
will be the sign that I will go up to
the temple of the LORD?"

Envoys From Babylon

39:1-8pp — 2Ki 20:12-19

39 At that time Merodach-Baladan son of Baladan king of
Babylon[h] sent Hezekiah letters
and a gift, because he had heard of
his illness and recovery. 2Hezekiah
received the envoys[i] gladly and
showed them what was in his storehouses—the silver, the gold,[j] the
spices, the fine oil, his entire ar-

38:5 [a]2Ki 18:2
38:6 [b]Isa 31:5; 37:35
38:7 [c]Isa 7:11,14
38:8 [d]Jos 10:13
38:10 [e]Ps 102:24 [f]Ps 107:18; 2Co 1:9 [g]Job 17:11
38:11 [h]Ps 27:13; 116:9
38:12 [i]2Co 5:1,4; 2Pe 1:13-14 [j]Job 4:21 [k]Heb 1:12 [l]Job 7:6 [m]Ps 73:14
38:13 [n]Ps 51:8 [o]Job 10:16; Da 6:24
38:14 [p]Isa 59:11 [q]Job 17:3
38:15 [r]Ps 39:9 [s]1Ki 21:27 [t]Job 7:11
38:16 [u]Ps 119:25
38:17 [v]Ps 30:3 [w]Jer 31:34 [x]Isa 43:25; Mic 7:19
38:18 [y]Ecc 9:10 [z]Ps 6:5; 88:10-11; 115:17 [a]Ps 30:9
38:19 [b]Dt 6:7; Ps 118:17; 119:175 [c]Dt 11:19
38:20 [d]Ps 68:25 [e]Ps 33:2 [f]Ps 116:2 [g]Ps 116:17-19
39:1 [h]2Ch 32:31
39:2 [i]2Ch 32:31 [j]2Ki 18:15

[e]*10,18* Hebrew *Sheol* [f]*11* A few Hebrew manuscripts; most Hebrew manuscripts *in the place of cessation*

mory and everything found among
his treasures. There was nothing in
his palace or in all his kingdom
that Hezekiah did not show them.
3Then Isaiah the prophet went to
King Hezekiah and asked, "What
did those men say, and where did
they come from?"
"From a distant land,[a]" Hezekiah replied. "They came to me from
Babylon."
4The prophet asked, "What did
they see in your palace?"
"They saw everything in my palace," Hezekiah said. "There is
nothing among my treasures that I
did not show them."
5Then Isaiah said to Hezekiah,
"Hear the word of the LORD Almighty: 6The time will surely come
when everything in your palace,
and all that your fathers have
stored up until this day, will be carried off to Babylon.[b] Nothing will
be left, says the LORD. 7And some of
your descendants, your own flesh
and blood who will be born to you,
will be taken away, and they will
become eunuchs in the palace of
the king of Babylon.[c]"
8"The word of the LORD you have
spoken is good," Hezekiah replied.
For he thought, "There will be
peace and security in my lifetime.[d]"

Comfort for God's People

40 Comfort, comfort[e] my
people,
says your God.
2Speak tenderly[f] to Jerusalem,
and proclaim to her
that her hard service has been
completed,[g]
that her sin has been paid
for,
that she has received from the
LORD's hand
double[h] for all her sins.

3A voice of one calling:
"In the desert prepare
the way[i] for the LORD[g];
make straight in the wilderness
a highway for our God.[h][j]
4Every valley shall be raised up,
every mountain and hill
made low;
the rough ground shall become
level,[k]
the rugged places a plain.
5And the glory of the LORD will
be revealed,
and all mankind together will
see it.[l]
For the mouth of the
LORD has spoken."[m]

6A voice says, "Cry out."
And I said, "What shall I
cry?"

"All men are like grass,[n]
and all their glory is like the
flowers of the field.
7The grass withers and the
flowers fall,
because the breath[o] of the
LORD blows on them.
Surely the people are grass.
8The grass withers and the
flowers fall,
but the word[p] of our God
stands forever.[q]"

9You who bring good tidings[r] to
Zion,
go up on a high mountain.
You who bring good tidings to
Jerusalem,[i]
lift up your voice with a
shout,
lift it up, do not be afraid;
say to the towns of Judah,
"Here is your God!"[s]
10See, the Sovereign LORD
comes[t] with power,
and his arm[u] rules[v] for him.
See, his reward[w] is with him,
and his recompense
accompanies him.
11He tends his flock like a
shepherd:[x]
He gathers the lambs in his
arms
and carries them close to his
heart;
he gently leads those that
have young.

39:3 [a]Dt 28:49
39:6 [b]2Ki 24:13; Jer 20:5
39:7 [c]2Ki 24:15; Da 1:1-7
39:8 [d]2Ch 32:26
40:1 [e]Isa 12:1; 49:13; 51:3, 12; 52:9; 61:2; 66:13; Jer 31:13; Zep 3:14-17; 2Co 1:3
40:2 [f]Isa 35:4 [g]Isa 41:11-13; 49:25 [h]Isa 61:7; Jer 16:18; Zec 9:12; Rev 18:6
40:3 [i]Mal 3:1 [j]Mt 3:3*; Mk 1:3*; Jn 1:23*
40:4 [k]Isa 45:2,13
40:5 [l]Isa 52:10; Lk 3:4-6* [m]Isa 1:20; 58:14
40:6 [n]Job 14:2
40:7 [o]Job 41:21
40:8 [p]Isa 55:11; 59:21 [q]Mt 5:18; 1Pe 1:24-25*
40:9 [r]Isa 52:7-10; 61:1; Ro 10:15 [s]Isa 25:9
40:10 [t]Rev 22:7 [u]Isa 59:16 [v]Isa 9:6-7 [w]Isa 62:11; Rev 22:12
40:11 [x]Eze 34:23; Mic 5:4; Jn 10:11

g3 Or *A voice of one calling in the desert: / "Prepare the way for the LORD* h3 Hebrew; Septuagint *make straight the paths of our God* i9 Or *O Zion, bringer of good tidings, / go up on a high mountain. / O Jerusalem, bringer of good tidings*

12Who has measured the waters[a]
in the hollow of his
hand,[b]
or with the breadth of his
hand marked off the
heavens?[c]
Who has held the dust of the
earth in a basket,
or weighed the mountains on
the scales
and the hills in a balance?
13Who has understood the mind[i]
of the LORD,
or instructed him as his
counselor?[d]
14Whom did the LORD consult to
enlighten him,
and who taught him the right
way?
Who was it that taught him
knowledge[e]
or showed him the path of
understanding?

15Surely the nations are like a
drop in a bucket;
they are regarded as dust on
the scales;
he weighs the islands as
though they were fine
dust.
16Lebanon is not sufficient for
altar fires,
nor its animals[f] enough for
burnt offerings.
17Before him all the nations[g] are
as nothing;[h]
they are regarded by him as
worthless
and less than nothing.[i]

18To whom, then, will you
compare God?[j]
What image[k] will you
compare him to?
19As for an idol,[l] a craftsman
casts it,
and a goldsmith[m] overlays it
with gold[n]
and fashions silver chains for
it.
20A man too poor to present such
an offering
selects wood that will not
rot.
He looks for a skilled craftsman
to set up an idol that will not
topple.[o]

40:12 [a]Job 38:10 [b]Pr 30:4 [c]Heb 1:10-12
40:13 [d]Ro 11:34*; 1Co 2:16*
40:14 [e]Job 21:22; Col 2:3
40:16 [f]Ps 50:9-11; Mic 6:7; Heb 10:5-9
40:17 [g]Isa 30:28 [h]Isa 29:7 [i]Da 4:35
40:18 [j]Ex 8:10; 1Sa 2:2; Isa 46:5 [k]Ac 17:29
40:19 [l]Ps 115:4 [m]Isa 41:7; Jer 10:3 [n]Isa 2:20
40:20 [o]1Sa 5:3
40:21 [p]Ps 19:1; 50:6; Ac 14:17 [q]Ro 1:19 [r]Isa 48:13; 51:13
40:22 [s]Nu 13:33; Ps 104:2; Isa 42:5 [t]Job 22:14 [u]Job 36:29
40:23 [v]Isa 34:12 [w]Job 12:21; Ps 107:40
40:24 [x]Isa 41:16
40:25 [y]ver 18
40:26 [z]Isa 51:6 [a]Ps 89:11-13; Isa 42:5 [b]Ps 147:4 [c]Isa 34:16
40:27 [d]Job 27:2; Lk 18:7-8
40:28 [e]ver 21 [f]Ps 90:2

21Do you not know?
Have you not heard?
Has it not been told[p] you from
the beginning?
Have you not understood[q]
since the earth was
founded?[r]
22He sits enthroned above the
circle of the earth,
and its people are like
grasshoppers.[s]
He stretches out the heavens
like a canopy,[t]
and spreads them out like a
tent[u] to live in.
23He brings princes[v] to naught
and reduces the rulers of this
world to nothing.[w]
24No sooner are they planted,
no sooner are they sown,
no sooner do they take root
in the ground,
than he blows[x] on them and
they wither,
and a whirlwind sweeps them
away like chaff.

25"To whom will you compare
me?[y]
Or who is my equal?" says
the Holy One.
26Lift your eyes and look to the
heavens:[z]
Who created[a] all these?
He who brings out the starry
host[b] one by one,
and calls them each by
name.
Because of his great power and
mighty strength,
not one of them is missing.[c]

27Why do you say, O Jacob,
and complain, O Israel,
"My way is hidden from the
LORD;
my cause is disregarded by
my God"?[d]
28Do you not know?
Have you not heard?[e]
The LORD is the everlasting[f]
God,
the Creator of the ends of
the earth.
He will not grow tired or weary,

[i]13 Or *Spirit*; or *spirit*

and his understanding no
one can fathom.[a]
29He gives strength to the weary[b]
and increases the power of
the weak.
30Even youths grow tired and
weary,
and young men[c] stumble
and fall;
31but those who hope[d] in the
LORD
will renew their strength.[e]
They will soar on wings like
eagles;[f]
they will run and not grow
weary,
they will walk and not be
faint.[g]

The Helper of Israel

41 "Be silent[h] before me,
you islands![i]
Let the nations renew their
strength!
Let them come forward[j] and
speak;
let us meet together[k] at the
place of judgment.

2"Who has stirred[l] up one from
the east,[m]
calling him in righteousness
to his service[k]?
He hands nations over to him
and subdues kings before
him.
He turns them to dust[n] with
his sword,
to windblown chaff[o] with his
bow.
3He pursues them and moves on
unscathed,
by a path his feet have not
traveled before.
4Who has done this and carried
it through,
calling forth the generations
from the beginning?[p]
I, the LORD—with the first of
them
and with the last[q]—I am
he."

5The islands[r] have seen it and
fear;
the ends of the earth
tremble.

40:28 [a]Ps 147:5; Ro 11:33
40:29 [b]Isa 50:4; Jer 31:25
40:30 [c]Isa 9:17; Jer 6:11; 9:21
40:31 [d]Lk 18:1 [e]2Co 4:16 [f]Ex 19:4; Ps 103:5 [g]2Co 4:1; Heb 12:1-3
41:1 [h]Hab 2:20; Zec 2:13 [i]Isa 11:11 [j]Isa 48:16 [k]Isa 1:18; 34:1; 50:8
41:2 [l]Ezr 1:2 [m]ver 25; Isa 45:1,13 [n]2Sa 22:43 [o]Isa 40:24
41:4 [p]ver 26; Isa 46:10 [q]Isa 44:6; 48:12; Rev 1:8,17; 22:13
41:5 [r]Eze 26:17-18
41:7 [s]Isa 40:19
41:8 [t]Isa 29:22; 51:2; 63:16 [u]2Ch 20:7; Jas 2:23
41:9 [v]Isa 11:12 [w]Dt 7:6
41:10 [x]Jos 1:9; Isa 43:2,5; Ro 8:31 [y]ver 13-14; Isa 44:2; 49:8
41:11 [z]Isa 17:12 [a]Isa 45:24 [b]Ex 23:22 [c]Isa 29:8
41:12 [d]Ps 37:35-36 [e]Isa 17:14
41:13 [f]Isa 42:6; 45:1 [g]ver 10

They approach and come
forward;
6 each helps the other
and says to his brother, "Be
strong!"
7The craftsman encourages the
goldsmith,[s]
and he who smooths with the
hammer
spurs on him who strikes the
anvil.
He says of the welding, "It is
good."
He nails down the idol so it
will not topple.

8"But you, O Israel, my servant,
Jacob, whom I have chosen,
you descendants of
Abraham[t] my friend,[u]
9I took you from the ends of the
earth,[v]
from its farthest corners I
called you.
I said, 'You are my servant';
I have chosen[w] you and have
not rejected you.
10So do not fear, for I am with
you;[x]
do not be dismayed, for I am
your God.
I will strengthen you and help[y]
you;
I will uphold you with my
righteous right hand.

11"All who rage[z] against you
will surely be ashamed and
disgraced;[a]
those who oppose[b] you
will be as nothing and
perish.[c]
12Though you search for your
enemies,
you will not find them.[d]
Those who wage war against
you
will be as nothing[e] at all.
13For I am the LORD, your God,
who takes hold of your right
hand[f]
and says to you, Do not fear;
I will help[g] you.
14Do not be afraid, O worm
Jacob,
O little Israel,

[k]2 Or *I whom victory meets at every step*

for I myself will help you,"
declares the LORD,
your Redeemer, the Holy One
of Israel.
15"See, I will make you into a
threshing sledge,[a]
new and sharp, with many
teeth.
You will thresh the mountains
and crush them,
and reduce the hills to chaff.
16You will winnow[b] them, the
wind will pick them up,
and a gale will blow them
away.
But you will rejoice in the LORD
and glory[c] in the Holy One
of Israel.

17"The poor and needy search for
water,[d]
but there is none;
their tongues are parched
with thirst.
But I the LORD will answer[e]
them;
I, the God of Israel, will not
forsake them.
18I will make rivers flow[f] on
barren heights,
and springs within the
valleys.
I will turn the desert[g] into
pools of water,
and the parched ground into
springs.[h]
19I will put in the desert
the cedar and the acacia, the
myrtle and the olive.
I will set pines in the
wasteland,
the fir and the cypress
together,[i]
20so that people may see and
know,
may consider and
understand,
that the hand of the LORD has
done this,
that the Holy One of Israel
has created[j] it.

21"Present your case," says the
LORD.
"Set forth your arguments,"
says Jacob's King.[k]
22"Bring in ⌞your idols⌟ to tell us
what is going to happen.[l]
Tell us what the former things
were,
so that we may consider
them
and know their final
outcome.
Or declare to us the things to
come,[m]
23 tell us what the future holds,
so we may know[n] that you
are gods.
Do something, whether good or
bad,[o]
so that we will be dismayed
and filled with fear.
24But you are less than nothing[p]
and your works are utterly
worthless;
he who chooses you is
detestable.[q]

25"I have stirred up one from the
north,[r] and he comes—
one from the rising sun who
calls on my name.
He treads[s] on rulers as if they
were mortar,
as if he were a potter
treading the clay.
26Who told of this from the
beginning, so we could
know,
or beforehand, so we could
say, 'He was right'?
No one told of this,
no one foretold it,
no one heard any words[t]
from you.
27I was the first to tell[u] Zion,
'Look, here they are!'
I gave to Jerusalem a
messenger of good
tidings.[v]
28I look but there is no one[w]—
no one among them to give
counsel,[x]
no one to give answer when I
ask them.
29See, they are all false!
Their deeds amount to
nothing;[y]
their images are but wind[z]
and confusion.

The Servant of the LORD

42 "Here is my servant,
whom I uphold,

41:15 [a]Mic 4:13
41:16 [b]Jer 51:2 [c]Isa 45:25
41:17 [d]Isa 43:20 [e]Isa 30:19
41:18 [f]Isa 30:25 [g]Isa 43:19 [h]Isa 35:7
41:19 [i]Isa 60:13
41:20 [j]Job 12:9
41:21 [k]Isa 43:15
41:22 [l]Isa 43:9; 45:21 [m]Isa 46:10
41:23 [n]Isa 42:9; 44:7-8; 45:3 [o]Jer 10:5
41:24 [p]Isa 37:19; 44:9; 1Co 8:4 [q]Ps 115:8
41:25 [r]ver 2 [s]2Sa 22:43
41:26 [t]Hab 2:18-19
41:27 [u]Isa 48:3,16 [v]Isa 40:9
41:28 [w]Isa 50:2; 59:16; 63:5 [x]Isa 40:13-14
41:29 [y]ver 24 [z]Jer 5:13

my chosen one[a] in whom I delight;
I will put my Spirit[b] on him
and he will bring justice to the nations.
2He will not shout or cry out,
or raise his voice in the streets.
3A bruised reed he will not break,
and a smoldering wick he will not snuff out.
In faithfulness he will bring forth justice;[c]
4 he will not falter or be discouraged
till he establishes justice on earth.
In his law the islands will put their hope."[d]

5This is what God the LORD says—
he who created the heavens and stretched them out,
who spread out the earth and all that comes out of it,[e]
who gives breath[f] to its people,
and life to those who walk on it:
6"I, the LORD, have called[g] you in righteousness;[h]
I will take hold of your hand.
I will keep[i] you and will make you
to be a covenant[j] for the people
and a light for the Gentiles,[k]
7to open eyes that are blind,[l]
to free[m] captives from prison[n]
and to release from the dungeon those who sit in darkness.

8"I am the LORD; that is my name![o]
I will not give my glory to another[p]
or my praise to idols.
9See, the former things have taken place,
and new things I declare;
before they spring into being
I announce them to you."

42:1 [a]Isa 43:10; Lk 9:35; 1Pe 2:4,6 [b]Isa 11:2; Mt 3:16-17; Jn 3:34
42:3 [c]Ps 72:2
42:4 [d]Ge 49:10; Mt 12:18-21*
42:5 [e]Ps 24:2 [f]Ac 17:25
42:6 [g]Isa 43:1 [h]Jer 23:6 [i]Isa 26:3 [j]Isa 49:8 [k]Lk 2:32; Ac 13:47
42:7 [l]Isa 35:5 [m]Isa 49:9; 61:1 [n]Lk 4:19; 2Ti 2:26; Heb 2:14-15
42:8 [o]Ex 3:15 [p]Isa 48:11
42:10 [q]Ps 33:3; 40:3; 98:1 [r]Isa 49:6 [s]1Ch 16:32; Ps 96:11
42:11 [t]Isa 32:16 [u]Isa 60:7 [v]Isa 52:7; Na 1:15
42:12 [w]Isa 24:15
42:13 [x]Isa 9:6 [y]Isa 26:11 [z]Hos 11:10 [a]Isa 66:14
42:15 [b]Eze 38:20 [c]Isa 50:2; Na 1:4-6
42:16 [d]Lk 1:78-79 [e]Isa 32:3 [f]Lk 3:5 [g]Heb 13:5

Song of Praise to the LORD

10Sing to the LORD a new song,[q]
his praise from the ends of the earth,[r]
you who go down to the sea, and all that is in it,[s]
you islands, and all who live in them.
11Let the desert[t] and its towns raise their voices;
let the settlements where Kedar[u] lives rejoice.
Let the people of Sela sing for joy;
let them shout from the mountaintops.[v]
12Let them give glory[w] to the LORD
and proclaim his praise in the islands.
13The LORD will march out like a mighty[x] man,
like a warrior he will stir up his zeal;[y]
with a shout[z] he will raise the battle cry
and will triumph over his enemies.[a]

14"For a long time I have kept silent,
I have been quiet and held myself back.
But now, like a woman in childbirth,
I cry out, I gasp and pant.
15I will lay waste[b] the mountains and hills
and dry up all their vegetation;
I will turn rivers into islands
and dry up[c] the pools.
16I will lead[d] the blind[e] by ways they have not known,
along unfamiliar paths I will guide them;
I will turn the darkness into light before them
and make the rough places smooth.[f]
These are the things I will do;
I will not forsake[g] them.
17But those who trust in idols,
who say to images, 'You are our gods,'

will be turned back in utter
shame.[a]

Israel Blind and Deaf

18“Hear, you deaf;[b]
look, you blind, and see!
19Who is blind[c] but my
servant,[d]
and deaf like the messenger[e]
I send?
Who is blind like the one
committed[f] to me,
blind like the servant of the
LORD?
20You have seen many things, but
have paid no attention;
your ears are open, but you
hear nothing.”[g]
21It pleased the LORD
for the sake of his
righteousness
to make his law[h] great and
glorious.
22But this is a people plundered
and looted,
all of them trapped in pits[i]
or hidden away in prisons.[j]
They have become plunder,
with no one to rescue them;
they have been made loot,
with no one to say, “Send
them back.”

23Which of you will listen to this
or pay close attention[k] in
time to come?
24Who handed Jacob over to
become loot,
and Israel to the plunderers?
Was it not the LORD,
against whom we have
sinned?
For they would not follow[l] his
ways;
they did not obey his law.
25So he poured out on them his
burning anger,
the violence of war.
It enveloped them in flames,[m]
yet they did not
understand;
it consumed them, but they
did not take it to heart.[n]

Israel's Only Savior

43 But now, this is what the
LORD says—
he who created you, O Jacob,
he who formed[o] you,
O Israel:[p]
“Fear not, for I have
redeemed[q] you;
I have summoned you by
name;[r] you are mine.
2When you pass through the
waters,[s]
I will be with you;[t]
and when you pass through the
rivers,
they will not sweep over you.
When you walk through the
fire,[u]
you will not be burned;
the flames will not set you
ablaze.[v]
3For I am the LORD, your God,[w]
the Holy One of Israel, your
Savior;
I give Egypt for your ransom,
Cush[1][x] and Seba in your
stead.[y]
4Since you are precious and
honored in my sight,
and because I love[z] you,
I will give men in exchange for
you,
and people in exchange for
your life.
5Do not be afraid,[a] for I am
with you;[b]
I will bring your children[c]
from the east
and gather you from the
west.
6I will say to the north, ‘Give
them up!’
and to the south,[d] ‘Do not
hold them back.’
Bring my sons from afar
and my daughters[e] from the
ends of the earth—
7everyone who is called by my
name,[f]
whom I created for my glory,
whom I formed and made.[g]”
8Lead out those who have eyes
but are blind,[h]
who have ears but are deaf.[i]
9All the nations gather
together[j]
and the peoples assemble.

42:17 [a]Ps 97:7; Isa 1:29; 44:11; 45:16
42:18 [b]Isa 35:5
42:19 [c]Isa 43:8; Eze 12:2 [d]Isa 41:8-9 [e]Isa 44:26 [f]Isa 26:3
42:20 [g]Jer 6:10
42:21 [h]ver 4
42:22 [i]Isa 24:18 [j]Isa 24:22
42:23 [k]Isa 48:18
42:24 [l]Isa 30:15
42:25 [m]2Ki 25:9 [n]Isa 29:13; 47:7; 57:1,11; Hos 7:9
43:1 [o]ver 7 [p]Ge 32:28; Isa 44:21 [q]Isa 44:2,6 [r]Isa 42:6; 45:3-4
43:2 [s]Isa 8:7 [t]Dt 31:6,8 [u]Isa 29:6; 30:27 [v]Ps 66:12; Da 3:25-27
43:3 [w]Ex 20:2 [x]Isa 20:3 [y]Pr 21:18
43:4 [z]Isa 63:9
43:5 [a]Isa 44:2 [b]Jer 30:10-11 [c]Isa 41:8
43:6 [d]Ps 107:3 [e]2Co 6:18
43:7 [f]Isa 56:5; 63:19; Jas 2:7 [g]ver 1,21; Ps 100:3; Eph 2:10; Eph 2:10
43:8 [h]Isa 6:9-10 [i]Isa 42:20; Eze 12:2
43:9 [j]Isa 41:1

[1]3 That is, the upper Nile region

Which of them foretold[a] this
and proclaimed to us the
former things?
Let them bring in their
witnesses to prove they
were right,
so that others may hear and
say, "It is true."
10"You are my witnesses,"
declares the LORD,
"and my servant[b] whom I
have chosen,
so that you may know and
believe me
and understand that I am he.
Before me no god[c] was
formed,
nor will there be one after
me.
11I, even I, am the LORD,
and apart from me there is
no savior.[d]
12I have revealed and saved and
proclaimed—
I, and not some foreign god[e]
among you.
You are my witnesses,[f]"
declares the LORD, "that I
am God.
13 Yes, and from ancient days[g]
I am he.
No one can deliver out of my
hand.
When I act, who can reverse
it?"[h]

God's Mercy and Israel's Unfaithfulness

14This is what the LORD says—
your Redeemer, the Holy One
of Israel:
"For your sake I will send to
Babylon
and bring down as fugitives[i]
all the Babylonians,[m][j]
in the ships in which they
took pride.
15I am the LORD, your Holy One,
Israel's Creator, your King."
16This is what the LORD says—
he who made a way through
the sea,
a path through the mighty
waters,[k]
17who drew out[l] the chariots
and horses,

43:9 [a]Isa 41:26
43:10 [b]Isa 41:8-9 [c]Isa 44:6,8
43:11 [d]Isa 45:21
43:12 [e]Dt 32:12; Ps 81:9 [f]Isa 44:8
43:13 [g]Ps 90:2 [h]Job 9:12; Isa 14:27
43:14 [i]Isa 13:14-15 [j]Isa 23:13
43:16 [k]Ps 77:19; Isa 11:15; 51:10
43:17 [l]Ps 118:12; Isa 1:31 [m]Ex 14:9
43:19 [n]2Co 5:17; Rev 21:5 [o]Ex 17:6; Nu 20:11
43:20 [p]Isa 13:22 [q]Isa 48:21
43:21 [r]Ps 102:18; 1Pe 2:9
43:22 [s]Isa 30:11
43:23 [t]Zec 7:5-6; Mal 1:6-8 [u]Am 5:25 [v]Jer 7:22 [w]Ex 30:35; Lev 2:1
43:24 [x]Ex 30:23 [y]Isa 1:14; 7:13 [z]Mal 2:17
43:25 [a]Ac 3:19 [b]Isa 37:35; Eze 36:22 [c]Isa 38:17; Jer 31:34

the army and reinforcements
together,[m]
and they lay there, never to rise
again,
extinguished, snuffed out
like a wick:
18"Forget the former things;
do not dwell on the past.
19See, I am doing a new thing![n]
Now it springs up; do you
not perceive it?
I am making a way in the
desert[o]
and streams in the
wasteland.
20The wild animals honor me,
the jackals[p] and the owls,
because I provide water[q] in the
desert
and streams in the
wasteland,
to give drink to my people, my
chosen,
21 the people I formed for
myself
that they may proclaim my
praise.[r]

22"Yet you have not called upon
me, O Jacob,
you have not wearied
yourselves for me,
O Israel.[s]
23You have not brought me sheep
for burnt offerings,
nor honored[t] me with your
sacrifices.[u]
I have not burdened you with
grain offerings
nor wearied you with
demands[v] for incense.[w]
24You have not bought any
fragrant calamus[x] for
me,
or lavished on me the fat of
your sacrifices.
But you have burdened me
with your sins
and wearied[y] me with your
offenses.[z]

25"I, even I, am he who blots out
your transgressions,[a] for my
own sake,[b]
and remembers your sins no
more.[c]

[m]14 Or *Chaldeans*

26Review the past for me,
let us argue the matter together;[a]
state the case[b] for your innocence.
27Your first father sinned;
your spokesmen[c] rebelled against me.
28So I will disgrace the dignitaries of your temple,
and I will consign Jacob to destruction[n]
and Israel to scorn.[d]

Israel the Chosen

44 "But now listen, O Jacob, my servant,[e]
Israel, whom I have chosen.
2This is what the LORD says—
he who made you, who formed you in the womb,
and who will help[f] you:
Do not be afraid, O Jacob, my servant,
Jeshurun,[g] whom I have chosen.
3For I will pour water[h] on the thirsty land,
and streams on the dry ground;
I will pour out my Spirit[i] on your offspring,
and my blessing on your descendants.[j]
4They will spring up like grass in a meadow,
like poplar trees[k] by flowing streams.[l]
5One will say, 'I belong to the LORD';
another will call himself by the name of Jacob;
still another will write on his hand,[m] 'The LORD's,'[n]
and will take the name Israel.

The LORD, Not Idols

6"This is what the LORD says—
Israel's King[o] and Redeemer,[p] the LORD Almighty:
I am the first and I am the last;[q]
apart from me there is no God.
7Who then is like me? Let him proclaim it.
Let him declare and lay out before me
what has happened since I established my ancient people,
and what is yet to come—
yes, let him foretell[r] what will come.
8Do not tremble, do not be afraid.
Did I not proclaim this and foretell it long ago?
You are my witnesses. Is there any God[s] besides me?
No, there is no other Rock;[t]
I know not one."
9All who make idols are nothing,
and the things they treasure are worthless.[u]
Those who would speak up for them are blind;
they are ignorant, to their own shame.
10Who shapes a god and casts an idol,
which can profit him nothing?[v]
11He and his kind will be put to shame;[w]
craftsmen are nothing but men.
Let them all come together and take their stand;
they will be brought down to terror and infamy.[x]
12The blacksmith[y] takes a tool
and works with it in the coals;
he shapes an idol with hammers,
he forges it with the might of his arm.[z]
He gets hungry and loses his strength;
he drinks no water and grows faint.
13The carpenter[a] measures with a line

43:26 [a]Isa 1:18 [b]Isa 41:1; 50:8
43:27 [c]Isa 9:15; 28:7; Jer 5:31
43:28 [d]Jer 24:9; Eze 5:15
44:1 [e]ver 21; Jer 30:10; 46:27-28
44:2 [f]Isa 41:10 [g]Dt 32:15
44:3 [h]Joel 3:18 [i]Joel 2:28; Ac 2:17 [j]Isa 61:9; 65:23
44:4 [k]Lev 23:40 [l]Job 40:22
44:5 [m]Ex 13:9 [n]Zec 8:20-22
44:6 [o]Isa 41:21 [p]Isa 43:1 [q]Isa 41:4; Rev 1:8,17; 22:13
44:7 [r]Isa 41:22,26
44:8 [s]Isa 43:10 [t]Dt 4:35; 1Sa 2:2
44:9 [u]Isa 41:24
44:10 [v]Isa 41:29; Jer 10:5; Ac 19:26
44:11 [w]Isa 1:29 [x]Isa 42:17
44:12 [y]Isa 40:19; 41:6-7 [z]Jer 10:3-5; Ac 17:29
44:13 [a]Isa 41:7

[n]28 The Hebrew term refers to the irrevocable giving over of things or persons to the LORD, often by totally destroying them.

and makes an outline with a
marker;
he roughs it out with chisels
and marks it with compasses.
He shapes it in the form of
man,[a]
of man in all his glory,
that it may dwell in a
shrine.[b]
14He cut down cedars,
or perhaps took a cypress or
oak.
He let it grow among the trees
of the forest,
or planted a pine, and the
rain made it grow.
15It is man's fuel[c] for burning;
some of it he takes and
warms himself,
he kindles a fire and bakes
bread.
But he also fashions a god and
worships it;
he makes an idol and bows[d]
down to it.
16Half of the wood he burns in
the fire;
over it he prepares his meal,
he roasts his meat and eats
his fill.
He also warms himself and
says,
"Ah! I am warm; I see the
fire."
17From the rest he makes a god,
his idol;
he bows down to it and
worships.
He prays[e] to it and says,
"Save[f] me; you are my god."
18They know nothing, they
understand[g] nothing;
their eyes[h] are plastered over
so they cannot see,
and their minds closed so
they cannot understand.
19No one stops to think,
no one has the knowledge or
understanding[i] to say,
"Half of it I used for fuel;
I even baked bread over its
coals,
I roasted meat and I ate.
Shall I make a detestable[j]
thing from what is left?
Shall I bow down to a block
of wood?"
20He feeds on ashes,[k] a
deluded[l] heart misleads
him;
he cannot save himself, or
say,
"Is not this thing in my right
hand a lie?[m]"

21"Remember[n] these things,
O Jacob,
for you are my servant,
O Israel.
I have made you, you are my
servant;[o]
O Israel, I will not forget
you.[p]
22I have swept away[q] your
offenses like a cloud,
your sins like the morning
mist.
Return[r] to me,
for I have redeemed[s] you."

23Sing for joy,[t] O heavens, for
the LORD has done this;
shout aloud, O earth[u]
beneath.
Burst into song, you
mountains,[v]
you forests and all your trees,
for the LORD has redeemed
Jacob,
he displays his glory[w] in
Israel.

Jerusalem to Be Inhabited

24"This is what the LORD says—
your Redeemer,[x] who formed
you in the womb:

I am the LORD,
who has made all things,
who alone stretched out the
heavens,[y]
who spread out the earth by
myself,

25who foils[z] the signs of false
prophets
and makes fools of diviners,[a]
who overthrows the learning of
the wise[b]
and turns it into nonsense,[c]
26who carries out the words[d] of
his servants
and fulfills[e] the predictions
of his messengers,

44:13 [a]Ps 115:4-7 [b]Jdg 17:4-5
44:15 [c]ver 19 [d]2Ch 25:14
44:17 [e]1Ki 18:26 [f]Isa 45:20
44:18 [g]Isa 1:3 [h]Isa 6:9-10
44:19 [i]Isa 5:13; 27:11; 45:20 [j]Dt 27:15
44:20 [k]Ps 102:9 [l]Job 15:31; Ro 1:21-23, 28; 2Th 2:11; 2Ti 3:13 [m]Isa 59:3,4, 13; Ro 1:25
44:21 [n]Isa 46:8; Zec 10:9 [o]ver 1-2 [p]Isa 49:15
44:22 [q]Isa 43:25; Ac 3:19 [r]Isa 55:7 [s]1Co 6:20
44:23 [t]Isa 42:10 [u]Ps 148:7 [v]Ps 98:8 [w]Isa 61:3
44:24 [x]Isa 43:14 [y]Isa 42:5
44:25 [z]Ps 33:10 [a]Isa 47:13 [b]1Co 1:27 [c]2Sa 15:31; 1Co 1:19-20
44:26 [d]Zec 1:6 [e]Isa 55:11; Mt 5:18

who says of Jerusalem, 'It shall
be inhabited,'
of the towns of Judah, 'They
shall be built,'
and of their ruins, 'I will
restore them,'[a]
27who says to the watery deep,
'Be dry,
and I will dry up your
streams,'
28who says of Cyrus,[b] 'He is my
shepherd
and will accomplish all that I
please;
he will say of Jerusalem,[c]
"Let it be rebuilt,"
and of the temple,[d] "Let its
foundations be laid." '

45 "This is what the LORD
says to his anointed,
to Cyrus, whose right hand I
take hold[e] of
to subdue nations[f] before him
and to strip kings of their
armor,
to open doors before him
so that gates will not be
shut:
2I will go before you
and will level[g] the
mountains[o];
I will break down gates of
bronze
and cut through bars of
iron.[h]
3I will give you the treasures[i] of
darkness,
riches stored in secret
places,[j]
so that you may know[k] that I
am the LORD,
the God of Israel, who
summons you by name.[l]
4For the sake of Jacob my
servant,[m]
of Israel my chosen,
I summon you by name
and bestow on you a title of
honor,
though you do not
acknowledge[n] me.
5I am the LORD, and there is no
other;[o]
apart from me there is no
God.[p]
I will strengthen you,[q]
though you have not
acknowledged me,
6so that from the rising of the
sun
to the place of its setting[r]
men may know there is none
besides me.[s]
I am the LORD, and there is
no other.
7I form the light and create
darkness,
I bring prosperity and create
disaster;[t]
I, the LORD, do all these
things.

8"You heavens above, rain[u]
down righteousness;[v]
let the clouds shower it
down.
Let the earth open wide,
let salvation[w] spring up,
let righteousness grow with it;
I, the LORD, have created it.

9"Woe to him who quarrels[x]
with his Maker,
to him who is but a potsherd
among the potsherds on
the ground.
Does the clay say to the
potter,[y]
'What are you making?'
Does your work say,
'He has no hands'?
10Woe to him who says to his
father,
'What have you begotten?'
or to his mother,
'What have you brought to
birth?'

11"This is what the LORD says—
the Holy One of Israel, and
its Maker:
Concerning things to come,
do you question me about
my children,
or give me orders about the
work of my hands?[z]
12It is I who made the earth
and created mankind upon it.
My own hands stretched out
the heavens;[a]

44:26 [a]Isa 49:8-21
44:28 [b]2Ch 36:22 [c]Isa 14:32 [d]Ezr 1:2-4
45:1 [e]Ps 73:23; Isa 41:13; 42:6 [f]Jer 50:35
45:2 [g]Isa 40:4 [h]Ps 107:16; Jer 51:30
45:3 [i]Jer 50:37 [j]Jer 41:8 [k]Isa 41:23 [l]Ex 33:12; Isa 43:1
45:4 [m]Isa 41:8-9 [n]Ac 17:23
45:5 [o]Isa 44:8 [p]Ps 18:31 [q]Ps 18:39
45:6 [r]Isa 43:5; Mal 1:11 [s]ver 5,18
45:7 [t]Isa 31:2; Am 3:6
45:8 [u]Ps 72:6; Joel 3:18 [v]Ps 85:11; Isa 60:21; 61:10,11; Hos 10:12 [w]Isa 12:3
45:9 [x]Job 15:25 [y]Isa 29:16; Ro 9:20-21*
45:11 [z]Isa 19:25
45:12 [a]Ge 2:1; Isa 42:5

o2 Dead Sea Scrolls and Septuagint; the meaning of the word in the Masoretic Text is uncertain.

I marshaled their starry
hosts.[a]
13I will raise up Cyrus[p][b] in my
righteousness:
I will make all his ways
straight.
He will rebuild my city
and set my exiles free,
but not for a price or reward,[c]
says the LORD Almighty."

14This is what the LORD says:

"The products of Egypt and the
merchandise of Cush,[q]
and those tall Sabeans—
they will come over to you
and will be yours;
they will trudge behind you,
coming over to you in
chains.[d]
They will bow down before you
and plead[e] with you, saying,
'Surely God is with you,[f] and
there is no other;
there is no other god.' "
15Truly you are a God who
hides[g] himself,
O God and Savior of Israel.
16All the makers of idols will be
put to shame and
disgraced;[h]
they will go off into disgrace
together.
17But Israel will be saved[i] by the
LORD
with an everlasting
salvation;[j]
you will never be put to shame
or disgraced,
to ages everlasting.

18For this is what the LORD
says—
he who created the heavens,
he is God;
he who fashioned and made
the earth,
he founded it;
he did not create it to be
empty,[k]
but formed it to be
inhabited[l]—
he says:
"I am the LORD,
and there is no other.[m]
19I have not spoken in secret,[n]

45:12
[a]Ne 9:6

45:13
[b]2Ch 36:22; Isa 41:2
[c]Isa 52:3

45:14
[d]Isa 14:1-2
[e]Jer 16:19; Zec 8:20-23
[f]1Co 14:25

45:15
[g]Ps 44:24

45:16
[h]Isa 44:9,11

45:17
[i]Ro 11:26
[j]Isa 26:4

45:18
[k]Ge 1:2
[l]Ge 1:26; Isa 42:5
[m]ver 5

45:19
[n]Isa 48:16
[o]Isa 41:8
[p]Dt 30:11

45:20
[q]Isa 43:9
[r]Isa 44:19
[s]Isa 46:1; Jer 10:5
[t]Isa 44:17; 46:6-7

45:21
[u]Isa 41:22
[v]ver 5

45:22
[w]Zec 12:10
[x]Nu 21:8-9; 2Ch 20:12
[y]Isa 49:6,12

45:23
[z]Ge 22:16
[a]Heb 6:13
[b]Isa 55:11
[c]Ps 63:11; Isa 19:18; Ro 14:11*; Php 2:10-11

45:24
[d]Jer 33:16
[e]Isa 41:11

45:25
[f]Isa 41:16

46:1
[g]Isa 21:9; Jer 50:2; 51:44

from somewhere in a land of
darkness;
I have not said to Jacob's
descendants,[o]
'Seek me in vain.'
I, the LORD, speak the truth;
I declare what is right.[p]

20"Gather together[q] and come;
assemble, you fugitives from
the nations.
Ignorant[r] are those who carry[s]
about idols of wood,
who pray to gods that cannot
save.[t]
21Declare what is to be, present
it—
let them take counsel
together.
Who foretold[u] this long ago,
who declared it from the
distant past?
Was it not I, the LORD?
And there is no God apart
from me,[v]
a righteous God and a Savior;
there is none but me.

22"Turn[w] to me and be saved,[x]
all you ends of the earth;[y]
for I am God, and there is no
other.
23By myself I have sworn,[z]
my mouth has uttered in all
integrity[a]
a word that will not be
revoked:[b]
Before me every knee will bow;
by me every tongue will
swear.[c]
24They will say of me, 'In the
LORD alone
are righteousness[d] and
strength.' "
All who have raged against him
will come to him and be put
to shame.[e]
25But in the LORD all the
descendants of Israel
will be found righteous and
will exult.[f]

Gods of Babylon

46 Bel[g] bows down, Nebo
stoops low;

[p]13 Hebrew *him* [q]14 That is, the upper Nile region

their idols are borne by
beasts of burden.[r]
The images that are carried[a]
about are burdensome,
a burden for the weary.
2They stoop and bow down
together;
unable to rescue the
burden,
they themselves go off into
captivity.[b]

3"Listen[c] to me, O house of
Jacob,
all you who remain of the
house of Israel,
you whom I have upheld since
you were conceived,
and have carried since your
birth.
4Even to your old age and gray
hairs[d]
I am he,[e] I am he who will
sustain you.
I have made you and I will
carry you;
I will sustain you and I will
rescue you.

5"To whom will you compare me
or count me equal?
To whom will you liken me
that we may be
compared?[f]
6Some pour out gold from their
bags
and weigh out silver on the
scales;
they hire a goldsmith[g] to make
it into a god,
and they bow down and
worship it.[h]
7They lift it to their shoulders
and carry[i] it;
they set it up in its place,
and there it stands.
From that spot it cannot
move.
Though one cries out to it, it
does not answer;
it cannot save[j] him from his
troubles.

8"Remember[k] this, fix it in
mind,
take it to heart, you rebels.
9Remember the former things,
those of long ago;[l]
I am God, and there is no
other;
I am God, and there is none
like me.[m]
10I make known the end from the
beginning,
from ancient times,[n] what is
still to come.
I say: My purpose will stand,[o]
and I will do all that I please.
11From the east I summon a bird
of prey;
from a far-off land, a man to
fulfill my purpose.
What I have said, that will I
bring about;
what I have planned, that
will I do.
12Listen[p] to me, you
stubborn-hearted,
you who are far from
righteousness.[q]
13I am bringing my righteousness
near,
it is not far away;
and my salvation will not be
delayed.
I will grant salvation to Zion,
my splendor[r] to Israel.

The Fall of Babylon

47 "Go down, sit in the dust,
Virgin Daughter[s] of
Babylon;
sit on the ground without a
throne,
Daughter of the
Babylonians.[s][t]
No more will you be called
tender or delicate.[u]
2Take millstones[v] and grind[w]
flour;
take off your veil.[x]
Lift up your skirts,[y] bare your
legs,
and wade through the
streams.
3Your nakedness[z] will be
exposed
and your shame[a] uncovered.
I will take vengeance;[b]
I will spare no one."
4Our Redeemer—the LORD
Almighty is his name[c]—

46:1 [a]Isa 45:20
46:2 [b]Jdg 18:17-18; 2Sa 5:21
46:3 [c]ver 12
46:4 [d]Ps 71:18 [e]Isa 43:13
46:5 [f]Isa 40:18,25
46:6 [g]Isa 40:19 [h]Isa 44:17
46:7 [i]ver 1 [j]Isa 44:17; Isa 45:20
46:8 [k]Isa 44:21
46:9 [l]Dt 32:7 [m]Isa 45:5,21
46:10 [n]Isa 45:21 [o]Pr 19:21; Ac 5:39
46:12 [p]ver 3 [q]Ps 119:150; Isa 48:1; Jer 2:5
46:13 [r]Isa 44:23
47:1 [s]Isa 23:12 [t]Ps 137:8; Jer 50:42; 51:33; Zec 2:7 [u]Dt 28:56
47:2 [v]Ex 11:5; Mt 24:41 [w]Jdg 16:21 [x]Ge 24:65 [y]Isa 32:11
47:3 [z]Eze 16:37; Na 3:5 [a]Isa 20:4 [b]Isa 34:8
47:4 [c]Jer 50:34

[r]1 Or *are but beasts and cattle* [s]1 Or *Chaldeans;* also in verse 5

is the Holy One of Israel.

5"Sit in silence, go into
darkness,[a]
Daughter of the Babylonians;
no more will you be called
queen of kingdoms.[b]
6I was angry[c] with my people
and desecrated my
inheritance;
I gave them into your hand,[d]
and you showed them no
mercy.
Even on the aged
you laid a very heavy yoke.
7You said, 'I will continue
forever—
the eternal queen!'[e]
But you did not consider these
things
or reflect[f] on what might
happen.[g]

8"Now then, listen, you wanton
creature,
lounging in your security[h]
and saying to yourself,
'I am, and there is none
besides me.[i]
I will never be a widow[j]
or suffer the loss of children.'
9Both of these will overtake you
in a moment,[k] on a single
day:
loss of children[l] and
widowhood.
They will come upon you in
full measure,
in spite of your many
sorceries[m]
and all your potent spells.[n]
10You have trusted[o] in your
wickedness
and have said, 'No one sees
me.'[p]
Your wisdom[q] and knowledge
mislead[r] you
when you say to yourself,
'I am, and there is none
besides me.'
11Disaster will come upon you,
and you will not know how
to conjure it away.
A calamity will fall upon you
that you cannot ward off with
a ransom;
a catastrophe you cannot
foresee
will suddenly[s] come upon
you.

12"Keep on, then, with your
magic spells
and with your many
sorceries,[t]
which you have labored at
since childhood.
Perhaps you will succeed,
perhaps you will cause terror.
13All the counsel you have
received has only worn
you out![u]
Let your astrologers[v] come
forward,
those stargazers who make
predictions month by
month,
let them save[w] you from
what is coming upon
you.
14Surely they are like stubble;[x]
the fire will burn them up.
They cannot even save
themselves
from the power of the
flame.[y]
Here are no coals to warm
anyone;
here is no fire to sit by.
15That is all they can do for
you—
these you have labored with
and trafficked[z] with since
childhood.
Each of them goes on in his
error;
there is not one that can
save you.

Stubborn Israel

48 "Listen to this, O house of
Jacob,
you who are called by the
name of Israel
and come from the line of
Judah,
you who take oaths in the
name of the LORD
and invoke[a] the God of
Israel—
but not in truth[b] or
righteousness—
2you who call yourselves citizens
of the holy city[c]

47:5 [a] Isa 13:10 [b] Isa 13:19
47:6 [c] 2Ch 28:9 [d] Isa 10:13
47:7 [e] ver 5; Rev 18:7 [f] Isa 42:23,25 [g] Dt 32:29
47:8 [h] Isa 32:9 [i] Isa 45:6; Zep 2:15 [j] Rev 18:7
47:9 [k] Ps 73:19; 1Th 5:3; Rev 18:8-10 [l] Isa 13:18 [m] Na 3:4 [n] Rev 18:23
47:10 [o] Ps 52:7; 62:10 [p] Isa 29:15 [q] Isa 5:21 [r] Isa 44:20
47:11 [s] 1Th 5:3
47:12 [t] ver 9
47:13 [u] Isa 57:10; Jer 51:58 [v] Isa 44:25 [w] ver 15
47:14 [x] Isa 5:24; Na 1:10 [y] Isa 10:17; Jer 51:30,32, 58
47:15 [z] Rev 18:11
48:1 [a] Isa 58:2 [b] Jer 4:2
48:2 [c] Isa 52:1

and rely[a] on the God of
Israel—
the LORD Almighty is his
name:
3I foretold the former things[b]
long ago,
my mouth announced[c] them
and I made them known;
then suddenly I acted, and
they came to pass.
4For I knew how stubborn[d] you
were;
the sinews of your neck[e]
were iron,
your forehead[f] was
bronze.
5Therefore I told you these
things long ago;
before they happened I
announced them to you
so that you could not say,
'My idols did them;[g]
my wooden image and metal
god ordained them.'
6You have heard these things;
look at them all.
Will you not admit them?

"From now on I will tell you of
new things,
of hidden things unknown to
you.
7They are created now, and not
long ago;
you have not heard of them
before today.
So you cannot say,
'Yes, I knew of them.'
8You have neither heard nor
understood;
from of old your ear has not
been open.
Well do I know how
treacherous you are;
you were called a rebel[h]
from birth.
9For my own name's sake I
delay my wrath;[i]
for the sake of my praise I
hold it back from you,
so as not to cut you off.[j]
10See, I have refined you, though
not as silver;
I have tested you in the
furnace[k] of affliction.
11For my own sake,[l] for my own
sake, I do this.
How can I let myself be
defamed?[m]
I will not yield my glory to
another.[n]

Israel Freed

12"Listen[o] to me, O Jacob,
Israel, whom I have called:
I am he;
I am the first and I am the
last.[p]
13My own hand laid the
foundations of the
earth,[q]
and my right hand spread out
the heavens;[r]
when I summon them,
they all stand up together.[s]

14"Come together,[t] all of you,
and listen:
Which of ⌊the idols⌋ has
foretold these things?
The LORD's chosen ally
will carry out his purpose[u]
against Babylon;
his arm will be against the
Babylonians.[t]
15I, even I, have spoken;
yes, I have called[v] him.
I will bring him,
and he will succeed in his
mission.

16"Come near[w] me and listen to
this:

"From the first announcement I
have not spoken in
secret;[x]
at the time it happens, I am
there."

And now the Sovereign LORD
has sent[y] me,
with his Spirit.

17This is what the LORD says—
your Redeemer,[z] the Holy
One[a] of Israel:
"I am the LORD your God,
who teaches you what is best
for you,
who directs[b] you in the
way[c] you should go.
18If only you had paid attention[d]
to my commands,

48:2 [a]Isa 10:20; Mic 3:11; Ro 2:17
48:3 [b]Isa 41:22 [c]Isa 45:21
48:4 [d]Dt 31:27 [e]Ex 32:9; Ac 7:51 [f]Eze 3:9
48:5 [g]Jer 44:15-18
48:8 [h]Dt 9:7,24; Ps 58:3
48:9 [i]Ps 78:38; Isa 30:18 [j]Ne 9:31
48:10 [k]1Ki 8:51
48:11 [l]1Sa 12:22; Isa 37:35 [m]Dt 32:27; Jer 14:7,21; Eze 20:9,14, 22,44 [n]Isa 42:8
48:12 [o]Isa 46:3 [p]Isa 41:4; Rev 1:17; 22:13
48:13 [q]Heb 1:10-12 [r]Ex 20:11 [s]Isa 40:26
48:14 [t]Isa 43:9 [u]Isa 46:10-11
48:15 [v]Isa 45:1
48:16 [w]Isa 41:1 [x]Isa 45:19 [y]Zec 2:9,11
48:17 [z]Isa 49:7 [a]Isa 43:14 [b]Isa 49:10 [c]Ps 32:8
48:18 [d]Dt 32:29

[t]14 Or *Chaldeans*; also in verse 20

your peace[a] would have
been like a river,
your righteousness[b] like the
waves of the sea.
19Your descendants would have
been like the sand,
your children like its
numberless grains;[c]
their name would never be cut
off[d]
nor destroyed from before
me."

20Leave Babylon,
flee[e] from the Babylonians!
Announce this with shouts of
joy[f]
and proclaim it.
Send it out to the ends of the
earth;
say, "The LORD has
redeemed[g] his servant
Jacob."
21They did not thirst[h] when he
led them through the
deserts;
he made water flow[i] for
them from the rock;
he split the rock
and water gushed out.[j]

22"There is no peace," says the
LORD, "for the wicked."[k]

The Servant of the LORD

49 Listen to me, you islands;
hear this, you distant
nations:
Before I was born[l] the LORD
called[m] me;
from my birth he has made
mention of my name.
2He made my mouth like a
sharpened sword,[n]
in the shadow of his hand he
hid me;
he made me into a polished
arrow
and concealed me in his
quiver.
3He said to me, "You are my
servant,[o]
Israel, in whom I will display
my splendor.[p]"
4But I said, "I have labored to
no purpose;

48:18 [a]Ps 119:165; Isa 66:12 [b]Isa 45:8
48:19 [c]Ge 22:17 [d]Isa 56:5; 66:22
48:20 [e]Jer 50:8; 51:6,45; Zec 2:6-7; Rev 18:4 [f]Isa 49:13 [g]Isa 52:9; 63:9
48:21 [h]Isa 41:17 [i]Isa 30:25 [j]Ex 17:6; Nu 20:11; Ps 105:41; Isa 35:6
48:22 [k]Isa 57:21
49:1 [l]Isa 44:24; 46:3; Mt 1:20 [m]Isa 7:14; 9:6; 44:2; Jer 1:5; Gal 1:15
49:2 [n]Isa 11:4; Rev 1:16
49:3 [o]Zec 3:8 [p]Isa 44:23
49:4 [q]Isa 65:23 [r]Isa 35:4
49:5 [s]Isa 11:12 [t]Isa 43:4
49:6 [u]Lk 2:32 [v]Ac 13:47*
49:7 [w]Isa 48:17 [x]Ps 22:6; 69:7-9 [y]Isa 52:15
49:8 [z]Ps 69:13 [a]2Co 6:2* [b]Isa 26:3 [c]Isa 42:6 [d]Isa 44:26

I have spent my strength in
vain[q] and for nothing.
Yet what is due me is in the
LORD's hand,
and my reward[r] is with my
God."

5And now the LORD says—
he who formed me in the
womb to be his servant
to bring Jacob back to him
and gather Israel[s] to
himself,
for I am honored[t] in the eyes
of the LORD
and my God has been my
strength—
6he says:
"It is too small a thing for you
to be my servant
to restore the tribes of Jacob
and bring back those of
Israel I have kept.
I will also make you a light for
the Gentiles,[u]
that you may bring my
salvation to the ends of
the earth."[v]

7This is what the LORD says—
the Redeemer and Holy One
of Israel[w]—
to him who was despised[x] and
abhorred by the nation,
to the servant of rulers:
"Kings[y] will see you and rise
up,
princes will see and bow
down,
because of the LORD, who is
faithful,
the Holy One of Israel, who
has chosen you."

Restoration of Israel

8This is what the LORD says:

"In the time of my favor[z] I will
answer you,
and in the day of salvation I
will help you;[a]
I will keep[b] you and will make
you
to be a covenant for the
people,[c]
to restore the land[d]
and to reassign its desolate
inheritances,

9to say to the captives,[a] 'Come out,'
and to those in darkness, 'Be free!'

"They will feed beside the roads
and find pasture on every barren hill.[b]
10They will neither hunger nor thirst,[c]
nor will the desert heat or the sun beat upon them.[d]
He who has compassion[e] on them will guide them
and lead them beside springs[f] of water.
11I will turn all my mountains into roads,
and my highways[g] will be raised up.[h]
12See, they will come from afar[i]—
some from the north, some from the west,
some from the region of Aswan.[u]"

13Shout for joy, O heavens;
rejoice, O earth;
burst into song, O mountains![j]
For the LORD comforts[k] his people
and will have compassion on his afflicted ones.

14But Zion said, "The LORD has forsaken me,
the Lord has forgotten me."
15"Can a mother forget the baby at her breast
and have no compassion on the child she has borne?
Though she may forget,
I will not forget you![l]
16See, I have engraved[m] you on the palms of my hands;
your walls[n] are ever before me.
17Your sons hasten back,
and those who laid you waste[o] depart from you.
18Lift up your eyes and look around;
all your sons gather[p] and come to you.
As surely as I live,[q]" declares the LORD,
"you will wear[r] them all as ornaments;
you will put them on, like a bride.

19"Though you were ruined and made desolate[s]
and your land laid waste,[t]
now you will be too small for your people,[u]
and those who devoured you will be far away.
20The children born during your bereavement
will yet say in your hearing,
'This place is too small for us;
give us more space to live in.'[v]
21Then you will say in your heart,
'Who bore me these?
I was bereaved and barren;
I was exiled and rejected.[w]
Who brought these up?
I was left[x] all alone,
but these—where have they come from?' "

22This is what the Sovereign
LORD says:

"See, I will beckon to the Gentiles,
I will lift up my banner[y] to the peoples;
they will bring your sons in their arms
and carry your daughters on their shoulders.[z]
23Kings[a] will be your foster fathers,
and their queens your nursing mothers.[b]
They will bow down before you with their faces to the ground;
they will lick the dust[c] at your feet.
Then you will know that I am the LORD;[d]
those who hope in me will not be disappointed."

24Can plunder be taken from warriors,[e]

[u]12 Dead Sea Scrolls; Masoretic Text *Sinim*

49:9 [a]Isa 42:7; 61:1; Lk 4:19 [b]Isa 41:18
49:10 [c]Isa 33:16 [d]Ps 121:6; Rev 7:16 [e]Isa 14:1 [f]Isa 35:7
49:11 [g]Isa 11:16 [h]Isa 40:4
49:12 [i]Isa 43:5-6
49:13 [j]Isa 44:23 [k]Isa 40:1
49:15 [l]Isa 44:21
49:16 [m]SS 8:6 [n]Ps 48:12-13; Isa 62:6
49:17 [o]Isa 10:6
49:18 [p]Isa 43:5; 54:7; Isa 60:4 [q]Isa 45:23 [r]Isa 52:1
49:19 [s]Isa 54:1,3 [t]Isa 5:6 [u]Zec 10:10
49:20 [v]Isa 54:1-3
49:21 [w]Isa 5:13 [x]Isa 1:8
49:22 [y]Isa 11:10 [z]Isa 60:4
49:23 [a]Isa 60:3, 10-11 [b]Isa 60:16 [c]Ps 72:9 [d]Mic 7:17
49:24 [e]Mt 12:29; Lk 11:21

or captives rescued from the
fierce[v]?

25But this is what the LORD says:

"Yes, captives[a] will be taken
from warriors,[b]
and plunder retrieved from
the fierce;
I will contend with those who
contend with you,
and your children I will
save.[c]
26I will make your oppressors[d]
eat[e] their own flesh;
they will be drunk on their
own blood,[f] as with
wine.
Then all mankind will know[g]
that I, the LORD, am your
Savior,
your Redeemer, the Mighty
One of Jacob."

Israel's Sin and the Servant's Obedience

50 This is what the LORD says:
"Where is your mother's
certificate of divorce[h]
with which I sent her away?
Or to which of my creditors
did I sell[i] you?
Because of your sins you were
sold;[j]
because of your
transgressions your
mother was sent away.
2When I came, why was there no
one?
When I called, why was there
no one to answer?[k]
Was my arm too short[l] to
ransom you?
Do I lack the strength[m] to
rescue you?
By a mere rebuke I dry up the
sea,[n]
I turn rivers into a desert;
their fish rot for lack of water
and die of thirst.
3I clothe the sky with darkness
and make sackcloth[o] its
covering."

4The Sovereign LORD has given
me an instructed
tongue,[p]
to know the word that
sustains the weary.[q]
He wakens me morning by
morning,[r]
wakens my ear to listen like
one being taught.
5The Sovereign LORD has opened
my ears,[s]
and I have not been
rebellious;[t]
I have not drawn back.
6I offered my back to those who
beat[u] me,
my cheeks to those who
pulled out my beard;
I did not hide my face
from mocking and spitting.[v]
7Because the Sovereign LORD
helps[w] me,
I will not be disgraced.
Therefore have I set my face
like flint,[x]
and I know I will not be put
to shame.
8He who vindicates me is near.
Who then will bring charges
against me?[y]
Let us face each other![z]
Who is my accuser?
Let him confront me!
9It is the Sovereign LORD who
helps[a] me.
Who is he that will condemn
me?
They will all wear out like a
garment;
the moths[b] will eat them up.

10Who among you fears the LORD
and obeys the word of his
servant?[c]
Let him who walks in the dark,
who has no light,
trust[d] in the name of the LORD
and rely on his God.
11But now, all you who light fires
and provide yourselves with
flaming torches,[e]
go, walk in the light of your
fires[f]
and of the torches you have
set ablaze.
This is what you shall receive
from my hand:

49:25 [a]Isa 14:2 [b]Jer 50:33-34 [c]Isa 25:9; 35:4
49:26 [d]Isa 9:4 [e]Isa 9:20 [f]Rev 16:6 [g]Eze 39:7
50:1 [h]Dt 24:1; Jer 3:8; Hos 2:2 [i]Ne 5:5; Mt 18:25 [j]Dt 32:30; Isa 52:3
50:2 [k]Isa 41:28 [l]Nu 11:23; Isa 59:1 [m]Ge 18:14 [n]Ex 14:22; Jos 3:16
50:3 [o]Rev 6:12
50:4 [p]Ex 4:12 [q]Mt 11:28 [r]Ps 5:3; 119:147; 143:8
50:5 [s]Isa 35:5 [t]Mt 26:39; Jn 8:29; 14:31; 15:10; Ac 26:19; Heb 5:8
50:6 [u]Isa 53:5; Mt 27:30; Mk 14:65; 15:19; Lk 22:63 [v]La 3:30; Mt 26:67
50:7 [w]Isa 42:1 [x]Eze 3:8-9
50:8 [y]Isa 43:26; Ro 8:32-34 [z]Isa 41:1
50:9 [a]Isa 41:10 [b]Job 13:28; Isa 51:8
50:10 [c]Isa 49:3 [d]Isa 26:4
50:11 [e]Pr 26:18 [f]Jas 3:6

[v]*24* Dead Sea Scrolls, Vulgate and Syriac (see also Septuagint and verse 25); Masoretic Text *righteous*

You will lie down in
torment.[a]

Everlasting Salvation for Zion

51 "Listen[b] to me, you who
pursue righteousness[c]
and who seek the LORD:
Look to the rock from which
you were cut
and to the quarry from which
you were hewn;
2look to Abraham,[d] your father,
and to Sarah, who gave you
birth.
When I called him he was but
one,
and I blessed him and made
him many.[e]
3The LORD will surely comfort[f]
Zion
and will look with
compassion on all her
ruins;[g]
he will make her deserts like
Eden,[h]
her wastelands like the
garden of the LORD.
Joy and gladness[i] will be
found in her,
thanksgiving and the sound
of singing.

4"Listen to me, my people;[j]
hear me, my nation:
The law will go out from me;
my justice[k] will become a
light to the nations.[l]
5My righteousness draws near
speedily,
my salvation is on the way,[m]
and my arm[n] will bring
justice to the nations.
The islands will look to me
and wait in hope for my arm.
6Lift up your eyes to the
heavens,
look at the earth beneath;
the heavens will vanish like
smoke,[o]
the earth will wear out like a
garment[p]
and its inhabitants die like
flies.
But my salvation will last
forever,
my righteousness will never
fail.

7"Hear me, you who know what
is right,[q]
you people who have my law
in your hearts:[r]
Do not fear the reproach of
men
or be terrified by their
insults.[s]
8For the moth will eat them up
like a garment;[t]
the worm will devour them
like wool.
But my righteousness will last
forever,[u]
my salvation through all
generations."

9Awake, awake! Clothe yourself
with strength,[v]
O arm of the LORD;
awake, as in days gone by,
as in generations of old.[w]
Was it not you who cut Rahab
to pieces,
who pierced that monster[x]
through?
10Was it not you who dried up
the sea,[y]
the waters of the great deep,
who made a road in the depths
of the sea
so that the redeemed might
cross over?
11The ransomed[z] of the LORD
will return.
They will enter Zion with
singing;
everlasting joy will crown
their heads.
Gladness and joy[a] will
overtake them,
and sorrow and sighing will
flee away.[b]

12"I, even I, am he who
comforts[c] you.
Who are you that you fear
mortal men,[d]
the sons of men, who are but
grass,[e]
13that you forget[f] the LORD your
Maker,[g]
who stretched out the
heavens[h]
and laid the foundations of
the earth,
that you live in constant
terror[i] every day

50:11 [a]Isa 65:13-15
51:1 [b]Isa 46:3 [c]ver 7; Ps 94:15; Ro 9:30-31
51:2 [d]Isa 29:22; Ro 4:16; Heb 11:11 [e]Ge 12:2
51:3 [f]Isa 40:1 [g]Isa 52:9 [h]Ge 2:8 [i]Isa 25:9; 66:10
51:4 [j]Ps 50:7 [k]Isa 2:4 [l]Isa 42:4,6
51:5 [m]Isa 46:13 [n]Isa 40:10; 63:1,5
51:6 [o]Mt 24:35; 2Pe 3:10 [p]Ps 102:25-26
51:7 [q]ver 1 [r]Ps 37:31 [s]Mt 5:11; Ac 5:41
51:8 [t]Isa 50:9 [u]ver 6
51:9 [v]Isa 52:1 [w]Dt 4:34 [x]Ps 74:13
51:10 [y]Ex 14:22
51:11 [z]Isa 35:9 [a]Jer 33:11 [b]Rev 7:17
51:12 [c]2Co 1:4 [d]Ps 118:6; Isa 2:22 [e]Isa 40:6-7; 1Pe 1:24
51:13 [f]Isa 17:10 [g]Isa 45:11 [h]Ps 104:2; Isa 48:13 [i]Isa 7:4

because of the wrath of the oppressor,
who is bent on destruction?
For where is the wrath of the oppressor?
14 The cowering prisoners will soon be set free;
they will not die in their dungeon,
nor will they lack bread.[a]
15For I am the LORD your God,
who churns up the sea[b] so that its waves roar—
the LORD Almighty is his name.
16I have put my words in your mouth[c]
and covered you with the shadow of my hand[d]—
I who set the heavens in place,
who laid the foundations of the earth,
and who say to Zion, 'You are my people.' "

The Cup of the LORD's Wrath

17Awake, awake![e]
Rise up, O Jerusalem,
you who have drunk from the hand of the LORD
the cup of his wrath,[f]
you who have drained to its dregs
the goblet that makes men stagger.[g]
18Of all the sons[h] she bore
there was none to guide her;[i]
of all the sons she reared
there was none to take her by the hand.
19These double calamities[j] have come upon you—
who can comfort you?—
ruin and destruction, famine[k] and sword—
who can[w] console you?
20Your sons have fainted;
they lie at the head of every street,[l]
like antelope caught in a net.
They are filled with the wrath of the LORD
and the rebuke of your God.

21Therefore hear this, you afflicted one,
made drunk,[m] but not with wine.
22This is what your Sovereign LORD says,
your God, who defends[n] his people:
"See, I have taken out of your hand
the cup[o] that made you stagger;
from that cup, the goblet of my wrath,
you will never drink again.
23I will put it into the hands of your tormentors,[p]
who said to you,
'Fall prostrate[q] that we may walk[r] over you.'
And you made your back like the ground,
like a street to be walked over."

52 Awake, awake,[s] O Zion,
clothe yourself with strength.[t]
Put on your garments of splendor,[u]
O Jerusalem, the holy city.[v]
The uncircumcised and defiled
will not enter you again.[w]
2Shake off your dust;[x]
rise up, sit enthroned,
O Jerusalem.
Free yourself from the chains on your neck,
O captive Daughter of Zion.

3For this is what the LORD says:

"You were sold for nothing,[y]
and without money[z] you will be redeemed."

4For this is what the Sovereign LORD says:

"At first my people went down to Egypt[a] to live;
lately, Assyria has oppressed them.

5"And now what do I have here?" declares the LORD.

"For my people have been taken away for nothing,

51:14 [a]Isa 49:10
51:15 [b]Jer 31:35
51:16 [c]Dt 18:18; Isa 59:21 [d]Ex 33:22
51:17 [e]Isa 52:1 [f]Job 21:20; Rev 14:10; 16:19 [g]Ps 60:3
51:18 [h]Ps 88:18 [i]Isa 49:21
51:19 [j]Isa 47:9 [k]Isa 14:30
51:20 [l]Isa 5:25; Jer 14:16
51:21 [m]ver 17; Isa 29:9
51:22 [n]Isa 49:25 [o]ver 17
51:23 [p]Isa 49:26; Jer 25:15-17, 26,28; 49:12 [q]Zec 12:2 [r]Jos 10:24
52:1 [s]Isa 51:17 [t]Isa 51:9 [u]Ex 28:2,40; Ps 110:3; Zec 3:4 [v]Ne 11:1; Mt 4:5; Rev 21:2 [w]Na 1:15; Rev 21:27
52:2 [x]Isa 29:4
52:3 [y]Ps 44:12 [z]Isa 45:13
52:4 [a]Ge 46:6

[w]*19* Dead Sea Scrolls, Septuagint, Vulgate and Syriac; Masoretic Text / *how can I*

and those who rule them
mock,[x]"
declares the LORD.
"And all day long
my name is constantly
blasphemed.[a]
6Therefore my people will
know[b] my name;
therefore in that day they
will know
that it is I who foretold it.
Yes, it is I."

7How beautiful on the
mountains
are the feet of those who
bring good news,[c]
who proclaim peace,[d]
who bring good tidings,
who proclaim salvation,
who say to Zion,
"Your God reigns!"[e]
8Listen! Your watchmen[f] lift up
their voices;
together they shout for joy.
When the LORD returns to
Zion,
they will see it with their
own eyes.
9Burst into songs of joy[g]
together,
you ruins[h] of Jerusalem,
for the LORD has comforted his
people,
he has redeemed
Jerusalem.[i]
10The LORD will lay bare his holy
arm
in the sight of all the
nations,[j]
and all the ends of the earth
will see
the salvation[k] of our God.

11Depart,[l] depart, go out from
there!
Touch no unclean thing![m]
Come out from it and be
pure,[n]
you who carry the vessels of
the LORD.
12But you will not leave in
haste[o]
or go in flight;
for the LORD will go before
you,[p]
the God of Israel will be your
rear guard.[q]

52:5 [a]Eze 36:20; Ro 2:24*
52:6 [b]Isa 49:23
52:7 [c]Isa 40:9; Ro 10:15* [d]Na 1:15; Eph 6:15 [e]Ps 93:1
52:8 [f]Isa 62:6
52:9 [g]Ps 98:4 [h]Isa 51:3 [i]Isa 48:20
52:10 [j]Isa 66:18 [k]Ps 98:2-3; Lk 3:6
52:11 [l]Isa 48:20 [m]Isa 1:16; 2Co 6:17* [n]2Ti 2:19
52:12 [o]Ex 12:11 [p]Mic 2:13 [q]Ex 14:19
52:13 [r]Isa 42:1 [s]Isa 57:15; Php 2:9
52:15 [t]Ro 15:21*; Eph 3:4-5
53:1 [u]Ro 10:16* [v]Jn 12:38*
53:2 [w]Isa 52:14
53:3 [x]ver 4,10; Lk 18:31 33 [y]Ps 22:6; Jn 1:10-11
53:4 [z]Mt 8:17* [a]Jn 19:7

The Suffering and Glory of the Servant

13See, my servant[r] will act
wisely[y];
he will be raised and lifted
up and highly exalted.[s]
14Just as there were many who
were appalled at him[z]—
his appearance was so
disfigured beyond that of
any man
and his form marred beyond
human likeness—
15so will he sprinkle many
nations,[a]
and kings will shut their
mouths because of him.
For what they were not told,
they will see,
and what they have not
heard, they will
understand.[t]

53 Who has believed our
message[u]
and to whom has the arm of
the LORD been
revealed?[v]
2He grew up before him like a
tender shoot,
and like a root out of dry
ground.
He had no beauty or majesty to
attract us to him,
nothing in his appearance[w]
that we should desire
him.
3He was despised and rejected
by men,
a man of sorrows, and
familiar with suffering.[x]
Like one from whom men hide
their faces
he was despised,[y] and we
esteemed him not.

4Surely he took up our
infirmities
and carried our sorrows,[z]
yet we considered him stricken
by God,[a]
smitten by him, and afflicted.

[x]5 Dead Sea Scrolls and Vulgate; Masoretic Text *wail* [y]13 Or *will prosper* [z]14 Hebrew *you* [a]15 Hebrew; Septuagint *so will many nations marvel at him*

5But he was pierced for our
transgressions,[a]
he was crushed for our
iniquities;
the punishment that brought us
peace was upon him,
and by his wounds we are
healed.[b]
6We all, like sheep, have gone
astray,
each of us has turned to his
own way;
and the LORD has laid on him
the iniquity of us all.

7He was oppressed and afflicted,
yet he did not open his
mouth;[c]
he was led like a lamb to the
slaughter,
and as a sheep before her
shearers is silent,
so he did not open his
mouth.
8By oppression[b] and judgment
he was taken away.
And who can speak of his
descendants?
For he was cut off from the
land of the living;[d]
for the transgression[e] of my
people he was stricken.[c]
9He was assigned a grave with
the wicked,
and with the rich[f] in his
death,
though he had done no
violence,[g]
nor was any deceit in his
mouth.[h]

10Yet it was the LORD's will[i] to
crush[j] him and cause
him to suffer,[k]
and though the LORD makes[d]
his life a guilt offering,
he will see his offspring[l] and
prolong his days,
and the will of the LORD will
prosper in his hand.
11After the suffering[m] of his soul,
he will see the light ⌞of life⌟[e]
and be satisfied[f];
by his knowledge[g] my
righteous servant will
justify[n] many,
and he will bear their
iniquities.
12Therefore I will give him a
portion among the
great,[h][o]
and he will divide the spoils
with the strong,[i]
because he poured out his life
unto death,[p]
and was numbered with the
transgressors.[q]
For he bore the sin of many,
and made intercession for
the transgressors.

The Future Glory of Zion

54 "Sing, O barren woman,
you who never bore a
child;
burst into song, shout for joy,
you who were never in labor;
because more are the children[r]
of the desolate woman
than of her who has a
husband,[s]"
says the LORD.
2"Enlarge the place of your
tent,[t]
stretch your tent curtains
wide,
do not hold back;
lengthen your cords,
strengthen your stakes.[u]
3For you will spread out to the
right and to the left;
your descendants will
dispossess nations
and settle in their desolate[v]
cities.

4"Do not be afraid; you will not
suffer shame.
Do not fear disgrace; you will
not be humiliated.
You will forget the shame of
your youth
and remember no more the
reproach[w] of your
widowhood.

53:5 [a] Ro 4:25; 1Co 15:3; Heb 9:28 [b] 1Pe 2:24-25
53:7 [c] Mk 14:61
53:8 [d] Da 9:26; Ac 8:32-33* [e] ver 12
53:9 [f] Mt 27:57-60 [g] Isa 42:1-3 [h] 1Pe 2:22*
53:10 [i] Isa 46:10 [j] ver 5 [k] ver 3 [l] Ps 22:30
53:11 [m] Jn 10:14-18 [n] Ro 5:18-19
53:12 [o] Php 2:9 [p] Mt 26:28,38, 39,42 [q] Mk 15:27*; Lk 22:37*; 23:32
54:1 [r] Isa 49:20 [s] 1Sa 2:5; Gal 4:27*
54:2 [t] Isa 49:19-20 [u] Ex 35:18; 39:40
54:3 [v] Isa 49:19
54:4 [w] Isa 51:7

b8 Or *From arrest* c8 Or *away. / Yet who of his generation considered / that he was cut off from the land of the living / for the transgression of my people, / to whom the blow was due?* d10 Hebrew *though you make* e11 Dead Sea Scrolls (see also Septuagint); Masoretic Text does not have *the light of life.* f11 Or (with Masoretic Text) 11*He will see the result of the suffering of his soul / and be satisfied* g11 Or *by knowledge of him* h12 Or *many* i12 Or *numerous*

5For your Maker is your husband[a]—
the LORD Almighty is his name—
the Holy One of Israel is your Redeemer;[b]
he is called the God of all the earth.[c]
6The LORD will call you back[d]
as if you were a wife deserted[e] and distressed in spirit—
a wife who married young,
only to be rejected," says your God.
7"For a brief moment[f] I abandoned you,
but with deep compassion I will bring you back.[g]
8In a surge of anger[h]
I hid my face from you for a moment,
but with everlasting kindness[i]
I will have compassion on you,"
says the LORD your Redeemer.

9"To me this is like the days of Noah,
when I swore that the waters of Noah would never again cover the earth.[j]
So now I have sworn not to be angry[k] with you,
never to rebuke you again.
10Though the mountains be shaken[l]
and the hills be removed,
yet my unfailing love for you will not be shaken[m]
nor my covenant[n] of peace be removed,"
says the LORD, who has compassion[o] on you.

11"O afflicted[p] city, lashed by storms[q] and not comforted,[r]
I will build you with stones of turquoise,[i][s]
your foundations[t] with sapphires.[k]
12I will make your battlements of rubies,
your gates of sparkling jewels,
and all your walls of precious stones.
13All your sons will be taught by the LORD,[u]
and great will be your children's peace.[v]
14In righteousness you will be established:
Tyranny[w] will be far from you;
you will have nothing to fear.
Terror will be far removed;
it will not come near you.
15If anyone does attack you, it will not be my doing;
whoever attacks you will surrender[x] to you.

16"See, it is I who created the blacksmith
who fans the coals into flame
and forges a weapon fit for its work.
And it is I who have created the destroyer to work havoc;
17 no weapon forged against you will prevail,[y]
and you will refute[z] every tongue that accuses you.
This is the heritage of the servants of the LORD,
and this is their vindication from me,"
declares the LORD.

Invitation to the Thirsty

55 "Come, all you who are thirsty,[a]
come to the waters;
and you who have no money,
come, buy[b] and eat!
Come, buy wine and milk[c]
without money and without cost.[d]
2Why spend money on what is not bread,
and your labor on what does not satisfy?[e]
Listen, listen to me, and eat what is good,[f]
and your soul will delight in the richest of fare.
3Give ear and come to me;
hear me, that your soul may live.[g]
I will make an everlasting covenant[h] with you,

54:5 [a]Jer 3:14 [b]Isa 48:17 [c]Isa 6:3
54:6 [d]Isa 49:14-21 [e]Isa 50:1-2; 62:4,12
54:7 [f]Isa 26:20 [g]Isa 49:18
54:8 [h]Isa 60:10 [i]ver 10
54:9 [j]Ge 8:21 [k]Isa 12:1
54:10 [l]Ps 46:2 [m]Isa 51:6 [n]Ps 89:34 [o]ver 8
54:11 [p]Isa 14:32 [q]Isa 28:2; 29:6 [r]Isa 51:19 [s]1Ch 29:2; Rev 21:18 [t]Isa 28:16; Rev 21:19-20
54:13 [u]Jn 6:45* [v]Isa 48:18
54:14 [w]Isa 9:4
54:15 [x]Isa 41:11-16
54:17 [y]Isa 29:8 [z]Isa 45:24-25
55:1 [a]Jn 4:14; 7:37 [b]La 5:4; Mt 13:44; Rev 3:18 [c]SS 5:1 [d]Hos 14:4; Mt 10:8; Rev 21:6
55:2 [e]Ps 22:26; Ecc 6:2; Hos 8:7 [f]Isa 1:19
55:3 [g]Lev 18:5; Ro 10:5 [h]Isa 61:8

[i]*11* The meaning of the Hebrew for this word is uncertain [k]*11* Or *lapis lazuli*

my faithful love[a] promised
to David.[b]
4See, I have made him a witness
to the peoples,
a leader and commander[c] of
the peoples.
5Surely you will summon
nations[d] you know not,
and nations that do not know
you will hasten to you,
because of the LORD your God,
the Holy One of Israel,
for he has endowed you with
splendor."[e]

6Seek the LORD while he may be
found;[f]
call[g] on him while he is
near.
7Let the wicked forsake his way
and the evil man his
thoughts.[h]
Let him turn[i] to the LORD, and
he will have mercy[j] on
him,
and to our God, for he will
freely pardon.[k]

8"For my thoughts are not your
thoughts,
neither are your ways my
ways,"[l]
declares the LORD.
9"As the heavens are higher
than the earth,[m]
so are my ways higher than
your ways
and my thoughts than your
thoughts.
10As the rain[n] and the snow
come down from heaven,
and do not return to it
without watering the earth
and making it bud and flourish,
so that it yields seed for the
sower and bread for the
eater,[o]
11so is my word that goes out
from my mouth:
It will not return to me
empty,[p]
but will accomplish what I
desire
and achieve the purpose[q] for
which I sent it.
12You will go out in joy
and be led forth in peace;[r]
the mountains and hills
will burst into song before
you,
and all the trees[s] of the field
will clap their hands.[t]
13Instead of the thornbush will
grow the pine tree,
and instead of briers[u] the
myrtle[v] will grow.
This will be for the LORD's
renown,[w]
for an everlasting sign,
which will not be destroyed."

Salvation for Others

56 This is what the LORD says:
"Maintain justice[x]
and do what is right,
for my salvation[y] is close at
hand
and my righteousness will
soon be revealed.
2Blessed[z] is the man who does
this,
the man who holds it fast,
who keeps the Sabbath[a]
without desecrating it,
and keeps his hand from
doing any evil."

3Let no foreigner who has bound
himself to the LORD say,
"The LORD will surely exclude
me from his people."
And let not any eunuch[b]
complain,
"I am only a dry tree."

4For this is what the LORD says:

"To the eunuchs who keep my
Sabbaths,
who choose what pleases me
and hold fast to my
covenant—
5to them I will give within my
temple and its walls[c]
a memorial and a name
better than sons and
daughters;
I will give them an everlasting
name
that will not be cut off.[d]
6And foreigners who bind
themselves to the LORD
to serve[e] him,
to love the name of the LORD,
and to worship him,

55:3 [a]Isa 54:8 [b]Ac 13:34*
55:4 [c]Jer 30:9; Eze 34:23-24
55:5 [d]Isa 49:6 [e]Isa 60:9
55:6 [f]Ps 32:6; Isa 49:8; 2Co 6:1-2 [g]Isa 65:24
55:7 [h]Isa 32:7; 59:7 [i]Isa 44:22 [j]Isa 54:10 [k]Isa 1:18; 40:2
55:8 [l]Isa 53:6
55:9 [m]Ps 103:11
55:10 [n]Isa 30:23 [o]2Co 9:10
55:11 [p]Isa 45:23 [q]Isa 44:26
55:12 [r]Isa 54:10,13 [s]1Ch 16:33 [t]Ps 98:8
55:13 [u]Isa 5:6 [v]Isa 41:19 [w]Isa 63:12
56:1 [x]Isa 1:17 [y]Ps 85:9
56:2 [z]Ps 119:2 [a]Ex 20:8,10; Isa 58:13
56:3 [b]Jer 38:7 *fn*; Ac 8:27
56:5 [c]Isa 26:1; 60:18 [d]Isa 48:19; 55:13
56:6 [e]Isa 60:7,10; 61:5

all who keep the Sabbath[a]
without desecrating it
and who hold fast to my
covenant—
7these I will bring to my holy
mountain[b]
and give them joy in my
house of prayer.
Their burnt offerings and
sacrifices[c]
will be accepted on my altar;
for my house will be called
a house of prayer for all
nations."[d][e]
8The Sovereign LORD declares—
he who gathers the exiles of
Israel:
"I will gather[f] still others to
them
besides those already
gathered."

God's Accusation Against the Wicked

9Come, all you beasts of the
field,[g]
come and devour, all you
beasts of the forest!
10Israel's watchmen[h] are blind,
they all lack knowledge;
they are all mute dogs,
they cannot bark;
they lie around and dream,
they love to sleep.[i]
11They are dogs with mighty
appetites;
they never have enough.
They are shepherds[j] who lack
understanding;[k]
they all turn to their own
way,
each seeks his own gain.[l]
12"Come," each one cries, "let
me get wine!
Let us drink our fill of beer!
And tomorrow will be like
today,
or even far better."[m]

57 The righteous perish,[n]
and no one ponders it in
his heart;[o]
devout men are taken away,
and no one understands
that the righteous are taken
away
to be spared from evil.[p]
2Those who walk uprightly[q]
enter into peace;
they find rest as they lie in
death.

3"But you—come here, you sons
of a sorceress,
you offspring of adulterers[r]
and prostitutes![s]
4Whom are you mocking?
At whom do you sneer
and stick out your tongue?
Are you not a brood of rebels,
the offspring of liars?
5You burn with lust among the
oaks
and under every spreading
tree;[t]
you sacrifice your children[u] in
the ravines
and under the overhanging
crags.
6The idols[v] among the smooth
stones of the ravines are
your portion;
they, they are your lot.
Yes, to them you have poured
out drink offerings[w]
and offered grain offerings.
In the light of these things,
should I relent?[x]
7You have made your bed on a
high and lofty hill;[y]
there you went up to offer
your sacrifices.
8Behind your doors and your
doorposts
you have put your pagan
symbols.
Forsaking me, you uncovered
your bed,
you climbed into it and
opened it wide;
you made a pact with those
whose beds you love,[z]
and you looked on their
nakedness.[a]
9You went to Molech[l] with
olive oil
and increased your perfumes.
You sent your ambassadors[m][b]
far away;
you descended to the grave[n]
itself!

56:6 [a]ver 2,4
56:7 [b]Isa 2:2 [c]Ro 12:1; Heb 13:15 [d]Mt 21:13*; Lk 19:46* [e]Mk 11:17*
56:8 [f]Isa 11:12; 60:3-11; Jn 10:16
56:9 [g]Isa 18:6; Jer 12:9
56:10 [h]Eze 3:17 [i]Na 3:18
56:11 [j]Eze 34:2 [k]Isa 1:3 [l]Isa 57:17; Eze 13:19; Mic 3:11
56:12 [m]Ps 10:6; Lk 12:18-19
57:1 [n]Ps 12:1 [o]Isa 42:25 [p]2Ki 22:20
57:2 [q]Isa 26:7
57:3 [r]Mt 16:4 [s]Isa 1:21
57:5 [t]2Ki 16:4 [u]Lev 18:21; Ps 106:37-38; Eze 16:20
57:6 [v]Jer 3:9 [w]Jer 7:18 [x]Jer 5:9,29; 9:9
57:7 [y]Jer 3:6; Eze 16:16
57:8 [z]Eze 16:26; 23:7 [a]Eze 23:18
57:9 [b]Eze 23:16,40

l9 Or *to the king* m9 Or *idols*
n9 Hebrew *Sheol*

10You were wearied by all your
ways,
but you would not say, 'It is
hopeless.'[a]
You found renewal of your
strength,
and so you did not faint.

11"Whom have you so dreaded
and feared[b]
that you have been false to
me,
and have neither remembered[c]
me
nor pondered this in your
hearts?
Is it not because I have long
been silent[d]
that you do not fear me?
12I will expose your righteousness
and your works,[e]
and they will not benefit you.
13When you cry out[f] for help,
let your collection ⌞of idols⌟
save you!
The wind will carry all of them
off,
a mere breath will blow them
away.
But the man who makes me his
refuge
will inherit the land[g]
and possess my holy
mountain."[h]

Comfort for the Contrite

14And it will be said:

"Build up, build up, prepare
the road!
Remove the obstacles out of
the way of my people."[i]
15For this is what the high and
lofty[j] One says—
he who lives forever,[k] whose
name is holy:
"I live in a high and holy place,
but also with him who is
contrite[l] and lowly in
spirit,[m]
to revive the spirit of the lowly
and to revive the heart of the
contrite.[n]
16I will not accuse forever,
nor will I always be angry,[o]
for then the spirit of man
would grow faint before
me—

57:10 [a]Jer 2:25; 18:12
57:11 [b]Pr 29:25 [c]Jer 2:32; 3:21 [d]Ps 50:21
57:12 [e]Isa 29:15; Mic 3:2-4,8
57:13 [f]Jer 22:20; 30:15 [g]Ps 37:9 [h]Isa 65:9-11
57:14 [i]Isa 62:10; Jer 18:15
57:15 [j]Isa 52:13 [k]Dt 33:27 [l]Ps 147:3 [m]Ps 34:18; 51:17; Isa 66:2 [n]Isa 61:1
57:16 [o]Ps 85:5; 103:9; Mic 7:18
57:17 [p]Isa 56:11 [q]Isa 1:4
57:18 [r]Isa 30:26 [s]Isa 61:1-3
57:19 [t]Isa 6:7; Heb 13:15 [u]Eph 2:17 [v]Ac 2:39
57:20 [w]Job 18:5-21
57:21 [x]Isa 59:8 [y]Isa 48:22
58:1 [z]Isa 40:6 [a]Isa 48:8
58:2 [b]Isa 48:1; Tit 1:16; Jas 4:8 [c]Isa 29:13
58:3 [d]Lev 16:29 [e]Mal 3:14 [f]Isa 22:13; Zec 7:5-6

the breath of man that I have
created.
17I was enraged by his sinful
greed;[p]
I punished him, and hid my
face in anger,
yet he kept on in his willful
ways.[q]
18I have seen his ways, but I will
heal[r] him;
I will guide him and restore
comfort[s] to him,
19 creating praise on the lips[t]
of the mourners in
Israel.
Peace, peace,[u] to those far and
near,"[v]
says the LORD. "And I will
heal them."
20But the wicked[w] are like the
tossing sea,
which cannot rest,
whose waves cast up mire
and mud.
21"There is no peace," [x] says my
God, "for the wicked."[y]

True Fasting

58 "Shout it aloud,[z] do not
hold back.
Raise your voice like a
trumpet.
Declare to my people their
rebellion[a]
and to the house of Jacob
their sins.
2For day after day they seek[b]
me out;
they seem eager to know my
ways,
as if they were a nation that
does what is right
and has not forsaken the
commands of its God.
They ask me for just decisions
and seem eager for God to
come near[c] them.
3'Why have we fasted,'[d] they
say,
'and you have not seen it?
Why have we humbled
ourselves,
and you have not noticed?'[e]

"Yet on the day of your fasting,
you do as you please[f]
and exploit all your workers.

4Your fasting ends in quarreling
and strife,[a]
and in striking each other
with wicked fists.
You cannot fast as you do
today
and expect your voice to be
heard[b] on high.
5Is this the kind of fast[c] I have
chosen,
only a day for a man to
humble[d] himself?
Is it only for bowing one's head
like a reed
and for lying on sackcloth
and ashes?[e]
Is that what you call a fast,
a day acceptable to the LORD?
6"Is not this the kind of fasting I
have chosen:
to loose the chains of
injustice[f]
and untie the cords of the
yoke,
to set the oppressed[g] free
and break every yoke?
7Is it not to share your food with
the hungry[h]
and to provide the poor
wanderer with
shelter[i]—
when you see the naked, to
clothe[j] him,
and not to turn away from
your own flesh and
blood?[k]
8Then your light will break forth
like the dawn,[l]
and your healing[m] will
quickly appear;
then your righteousness[o] will
go before you,
and the glory of the LORD will
be your rear guard.[n]
9Then you will call,[o] and the
LORD will answer;
you will cry for help, and he
will say: Here am I.

"If you do away with the yoke
of oppression,
with the pointing finger[p] and
malicious talk,[q]
10and if you spend yourselves in
behalf of the hungry
and satisfy the needs of the
oppressed,[r]
then your light[s] will rise in the
darkness,
and your night will become
like the noonday.[t]
11The LORD will guide you always;
he will satisfy your needs[u] in
a sun-scorched land
and will strengthen your
frame.
You will be like a well-watered
garden,[v]
like a spring[w] whose waters
never fail.
12Your people will rebuild the
ancient ruins[x]
and will raise up the age-old
foundations;[y]
you will be called Repairer of
Broken Walls,
Restorer of Streets with
Dwellings.

13"If you keep your feet from
breaking the Sabbath[z]
and from doing as you please
on my holy day,
if you call the Sabbath a
delight[a]
and the LORD's holy day
honorable,
and if you honor it by not going
your own way
and not doing as you please
or speaking idle words,
14then you will find your joy[b] in
the LORD,
and I will cause you to ride
on the heights[c] of the
land
and to feast on the
inheritance of your
father Jacob."
The mouth of the LORD
has spoken.[d]

Sin, Confession and Redemption

59 Surely the arm of the LORD
is not too short[e] to
save,
nor his ear too dull to hear.[f]
2But your iniquities have
separated
you from your God;

58:4 [a] 1Ki 21:9-13; Isa 59:6 [b] Isa 59:2
58:5 [c] Zec 7:5 [d] 1Ki 21:27 [e] Job 2:8
58:6 [f] Ne 5:10-11 [g] Jer 34:9
58:7 [h] Eze 18:16; Lk 3:11 [i] Isa 16:4; Heb 13:2 [j] Job 31:19-20; Mt 25:36 [k] Ge 29:14; Lk 10:31-32
58:8 [l] Job 11:17 [m] Isa 30:26 [n] Ex 14:19
58:9 [o] Ps 50:15 [p] Pr 6:13 [q] Ps 12:2; Isa 59:13
58:10 [r] Dt 15:7-8 [s] Isa 42:16 [t] Job 11:17
58:11 [u] Ps 107:9 [v] SS 4:15 [w] Jn 4:14
58:12 [x] Isa 49:8 [y] Isa 44:28
58:13 [z] Isa 56:2 [a] Ps 84:2,10
58:14 [b] Job 22:26 [c] Dt 32:13 [d] Isa 1:20
59:1 [e] Nu 11:23; Isa 50:2 [f] Isa 58:9; 65:24

o8 *Or your righteous One*

your sins have hidden his face from you,
so that he will not hear.[a]
3 For your hands are stained with blood,[b]
your fingers with guilt.
Your lips have spoken lies,
and your tongue mutters wicked things.
4 No one calls for justice;
no one pleads his case with integrity.
They rely on empty arguments and speak lies;
they conceive trouble and give birth to evil.[c]
5 They hatch the eggs of vipers
and spin a spider's web.[d]
Whoever eats their eggs will die,
and when one is broken, an adder is hatched.
6 Their cobwebs are useless for clothing;
they cannot cover themselves with what they make.[e]
Their deeds are evil deeds,
and acts of violence[f] are in their hands.
7 Their feet rush into sin;
they are swift to shed innocent blood.[g]
Their thoughts are evil thoughts;[h]
ruin and destruction mark their ways.[i]
8 The way of peace they do not know;
there is no justice in their paths.
They have turned them into crooked roads;
no one who walks in them will know peace.[j]

9 So justice is far from us,
and righteousness does not reach us.
We look for light, but all is darkness;[k]
for brightness, but we walk in deep shadows.
10 Like the blind[l] we grope along the wall,
feeling our way like men without eyes.
At midday we stumble[m] as if it were twilight;
among the strong, we are like the dead.[n]
11 We all growl like bears;
we moan mournfully like doves.[o]
We look for justice, but find none;
for deliverance, but it is far away.

12 For our offenses[p] are many in your sight,
and our sins testify[q] against us.
Our offenses are ever with us,
and we acknowledge our iniquities:
13 rebellion and treachery against the LORD,
turning our backs[r] on our God,
fomenting oppression[s] and revolt,
uttering lies[t] our hearts have conceived.
14 So justice is driven back,
and righteousness[u] stands at a distance;
truth[v] has stumbled in the streets,
honesty cannot enter.
15 Truth is nowhere to be found,
and whoever shuns evil becomes a prey.

The LORD looked and was displeased
that there was no justice.
16 He saw that there was no one,[w]
he was appalled that there was no one to intervene;
so his own arm worked salvation[x] for him,
and his own righteousness sustained him.
17 He put on righteousness as his breastplate,[y]
and the helmet[z] of salvation on his head;
he put on the garments[a] of vengeance
and wrapped himself in zeal[b] as in a cloak.
18 According to what they have done,

59:2 [a] Isa 1:15; 58:4
59:3 [b] Isa 1:15
59:4 [c] Job 15:35; Ps 7:14
59:5 [d] Job 8:14
59:6 [e] Isa 28:20 [f] Isa 58:4
59:7 [g] Pr 6:17 [h] Mk 7:21-22 [i] Ro 3:15-17*
59:8 [j] Isa 57:21; Lk 1:79
59:9 [k] Isa 5:30; 8:20
59:10 [l] Dt 28:29 [m] Isa 8:15 [n] La 3:6
59:11 [o] Isa 38:14; Eze 7:16
59:12 [p] Ezr 9:6 [q] Isa 3:9
59:13 [r] Pr 30:9; Mt 10:33; Tit 1:16 [s] Isa 5:7 [t] Mk 7:21-22
59:14 [u] Isa 1:21 [v] Isa 48:1
59:16 [w] Isa 41:28 [x] Ps 98:1; Isa 63:5
59:17 [y] Eph 6:14 [z] Eph 6:17; 1Th 5:8 [a] Isa 63:3 [b] Isa 9:7

so will he repay
wrath to his enemies
and retribution to his foes;
he will repay the islands
their due.
19From the west,[a] men will fear
the name of the LORD,
and from the rising of the
sun,[b] they will revere
his glory.
For he will come like a pent-up
flood
that the breath of the LORD
drives along.[p]
20"The Redeemer will come to
Zion,
to those in Jacob who repent
of their sins,"[c]
declares the LORD.

21"As for me, this is my covenant
with them," says the LORD. "My
Spirit,[d] who is on you, and my
words that I have put in your
mouth will not depart from your
mouth, or from the mouths of your
children, or from the mouths of
their descendants from this time
on and forever," says the LORD.

The Glory of Zion

60 "Arise,[e] shine, for your
light[f] has come,
and the glory of the LORD
rises upon you.
2See, darkness covers the earth
and thick darkness[g] is over
the peoples,
but the LORD rises upon you
and his glory appears over
you.
3Nations[h] will come to your
light,
and kings[i] to the brightness
of your dawn.

4"Lift up your eyes and look
about you:
All assemble[j] and come to
you;
your sons come from afar,
and your daughters[k] are
carried on the arm.[l]
5Then you will look and be
radiant,
your heart will throb and
swell with joy;

59:19 [a]Isa 49:12 [b]Ps 113:3
59:20 [c]Ac 2:38-39; Ro 11:26-27*
59:21 [d]Isa 11:2; 44:3
60:1 [e]Isa 52:2 [f]Eph 5:14
60:2 [g]Jer 13:16; Col 1:13
60:3 [h]Isa 45:14; Rev 21:24 [i]Isa 49:23
60:4 [j]Isa 11:12 [k]Isa 43:6 [l]Isa 49:20-22
60:6 [m]Ge 25:2 [n]Ge 25:4 [o]Ps 72:10 [p]Isa 43:23; Mt 2:11 [q]Isa 42:10
60:7 [r]Ge 25:13 [s]ver 13; Hag 2:3,7,9
60:8 [t]Isa 49:21
60:9 [u]Isa 11:11 [v]Isa 2:16 *fn* [w]Isa 14:2; 43:6 [x]Isa 55:5
60:10 [y]Isa 14:1-2 [z]Isa 49:23; Rev 21:24 [a]Isa 54:8
60:11 [b]ver 18; Isa 62:10, Rev 21:25 [c]ver 5; Rev 21:26 [d]Ps 149:8
60:12 [e]Isa 14:2

the wealth on the seas will be
brought to you,
to you the riches of the
nations will come.
6Herds of camels will cover your
land,
young camels of Midian[m]
and Ephah.[n]
And all from Sheba[o] will come,
bearing gold and incense[p]
and proclaiming the praise[q]
of the LORD.
7All Kedar's[r] flocks will be
gathered to you,
the rams of Nebaioth will
serve you;
they will be accepted as
offerings on my altar,
and I will adorn my glorious
temple.[s]

8"Who are these[t] that fly along
like clouds,
like doves to their nests?
9Surely the islands[u] look to me;
in the lead are the ships of
Tarshish,[q][v]
bringing[w] your sons from afar,
with their silver and gold,
to the honor of the LORD your
God,
the Holy One of Israel,
for he has endowed you with
splendor.[x]

10"Foreigners[y] will rebuild your
walls,
and their kings[z] will serve
you.
Though in anger I struck you,
in favor I will show you
compassion.[a]
11Your gates[b] will always stand
open,
they will never be shut, day
or night,
so that men may bring you the
wealth of the nations[c]—
their kings[d] led in triumphal
procession.
12For the nation or kingdom that
will not serve[e] you will
perish;
it will be utterly ruined.

[p]19 Or *When the enemy comes in like a flood, / the Spirit of the LORD will put him to flight*
[q]9 Or *the trading ships*

13"The glory of Lebanon[a] will
come to you,
the pine, the fir and the
cypress together,[b]
to adorn the place of my
sanctuary;
and I will glorify the place of
my feet.[c]
14The sons of your oppressors[d]
will come bowing before
you;
all who despise you will bow
down[e] at your feet
and will call you the City of the
LORD,
Zion[f] of the Holy One of
Israel.

15"Although you have been
forsaken[g] and hated,
with no one traveling[h]
through,
I will make you the everlasting
pride[i]
and the joy[j] of all
generations.
16You will drink the milk of
nations
and be nursed[k] at royal
breasts.
Then you will know that I, the
LORD, am your Savior,
your Redeemer,[l] the Mighty
One of Jacob.
17Instead of bronze I will bring
you gold,
and silver in place of iron.
Instead of wood I will bring you
bronze,
and iron in place of stones.
I will make peace your governor
and righteousness your ruler.
18No longer will violence be
heard in your land,
nor ruin or destruction
within your borders,
but you will call your walls
Salvation[m]
and your gates Praise.
19The sun will no more be your
light by day,
nor will the brightness of the
moon shine on you,
for the LORD will be your
everlasting light,[n]
and your God will be your
glory.[o]
20Your sun[p] will never set again,
and your moon will wane no
more;
the LORD will be your
everlasting light,
and your days of sorrow[q] will
end.
21Then will all your people be
righteous[r]
and they will possess[s] the
land forever.
They are the shoot I have
planted,[t]
the work of my hands,[u]
for the display of my
splendor.[v]
22The least of you will become a
thousand,
the smallest a mighty nation.
I am the LORD;
in its time I will do this
swiftly."

The Year of the LORD's Favor

61 The Spirit[w] of the
Sovereign LORD is on me,
because the LORD has
anointed[x] me
to preach good news to the
poor.[y]
He has sent me to bind up[z]
the brokenhearted,
to proclaim freedom for the
captives[a]
and release from darkness for
the prisoners,[r]
2to proclaim the year of the
LORD's favor[b]
and the day of vengeance[c] of
our God,
to comfort[d] all who mourn,
3 and provide for those who
grieve in Zion—
to bestow on them a crown of
beauty
instead of ashes,
the oil of gladness
instead of mourning,
and a garment of praise
instead of a spirit of despair.
They will be called oaks of
righteousness,
a planting of the LORD
for the display of his
splendor.[e]

60:13 [a]Isa 35:2 [b]Isa 41:19 [c]1Ch 28:2; Ps 132:7
60:14 [d]Isa 14:2 [e]Isa 49:23; Rev 3:9 [f]Heb 12:22
60:15 [g]Isa 1:7-9; 6:12 [h]Isa 33:8 [i]Isa 4:2 [j]Isa 65:18
60:16 [k]Isa 49:23; 66:11,12 [l]Isa 59:20
60:18 [m]Isa 26:1
60:19 [n]Rev 22:5 [o]Zec 2:5; Rev 21:23
60:20 [p]Isa 30:26 [q]Isa 35:10
60:21 [r]Rev 21:27 [s]Ps 37:11,22; Isa 57:13; 61:7 [t]Mt 15:13 [u]Isa 19:25; 29:23; Eph 2:10 [v]Isa 52:1
61:1 [w]Isa 11:2 [x]Ps 45:7 [y]Mt 11:5; Lk 7:22 [z]Isa 57:15 [a]Isa 42:7; 49:9
61:2 [b]Isa 49:8; Lk 4:18-19* [c]Isa 34:8 [d]Isa 57:18; Mt 5:4
61:3 [e]Isa 60:20-21

[r]1 Hebrew; Septuagint *the blind*

4They will rebuild the ancient ruins[a]
and restore the places long devastated;
they will renew the ruined cities
that have been devastated for generations.
5Aliens[b] will shepherd your flocks;
foreigners will work your fields and vineyards.
6And you will be called priests[c] of the LORD,
you will be named ministers of our God.
You will feed on the wealth[d] of nations,
and in their riches you will boast.

7Instead of their shame
my people will receive a double[e] portion,
and instead of disgrace
they will rejoice in their inheritance;
and so they will inherit a double portion in their land,
and everlasting joy will be theirs.

8"For I, the LORD, love justice;[f]
I hate robbery and iniquity.
In my faithfulness I will reward them
and make an everlasting covenant[g] with them.
9Their descendants will be known among the nations
and their offspring among the peoples.
All who see them will acknowledge
that they are a people the LORD has blessed."

10I delight greatly in the LORD;
my soul rejoices[h] in my God.
For he has clothed me with garments of salvation
and arrayed me in a robe of righteousness,[i]
as a bridegroom adorns his head like a priest,
and as a bride[j] adorns herself with her jewels.
11For as the soil makes the sprout come up
and a garden causes seeds to grow,
so the Sovereign LORD will make righteousness[k] and praise
spring up before all nations.

Zion's New Name

62 For Zion's sake I will not keep silent,
for Jerusalem's sake I will not remain quiet,
till her righteousness[l] shines out like the dawn,
her salvation like a blazing torch.
2The nations[m] will see your righteousness,
and all kings your glory;
you will be called by a new name[n]
that the mouth of the LORD will bestow.
3You will be a crown[o] of splendor in the LORD's hand,
a royal diadem in the hand of your God.
4No longer will they call you Deserted,[p]
or name your land Desolate.
But you will be called Hephzibah,[s]
and your land Beulah[t];
for the LORD will take delight[q] in you,
and your land will be married.[r]
5As a young man marries a maiden,
so will your sons[u] marry you;
as a bridegroom rejoices over his bride,
so will your God rejoice[s] over you.
6I have posted watchmen[t] on your walls, O Jerusalem;
they will never be silent day or night.
You who call on the LORD,

61:4 [a]Isa 49:8; Eze 36:33; Am 9:14
61:5 [b]Isa 14:1-2
61:6 [c]Ex 19:6; 1Pe 2:5 [d]Isa 60:11
61:7 [e]Isa 40:2; Zec 9:12
61:8 [f]Ps 11:7; Isa 5:16 [g]Isa 55:3
61:10 [h]Isa 25:9; Hab 3:18 [i]Ps 132:9; Isa 52:1 [j]Isa 49:18; Rev 21:2
61:11 [k]Ps 85:11
62:1 [l]Isa 1:26
62:2 [m]Isa 52:10; 60:3 [n]ver 4,12
62:3 [o]Isa 28:5; Zec 9:16; 1Th 2:19
62:4 [p]Isa 54:6 [q]Jer 32:41; Zep 3:17 [r]Jer 3:14; Hos 2:19
62:5 [s]Isa 65:19
62:6 [t]Isa 52:8; Eze 3:17

s4 *Hephzibah* means *my delight is in her.*
t4 *Beulah* means *married.*
u5 Or *Builder*

give yourselves no rest,
7and give him no rest[a] till he
establishes Jerusalem
and makes her the praise of
the earth.

8The LORD has sworn by his right
hand
and by his mighty arm:
"Never again will I give your
grain[b]
as food for your enemies,
and never again will foreigners
drink the new wine
for which you have toiled;
9but those who harvest it will
eat it
and praise the LORD,
and those who gather the
grapes will drink it
in the courts of my
sanctuary."

10Pass through, pass through the
gates![c]
Prepare the way for the
people.
Build up, build up the
highway![d][e]
Remove the stones.
Raise a banner[f] for the
nations.

11The LORD has made
proclamation
to the ends of the earth:
"Say to the Daughter of Zion,[g]
'See, your Savior comes![h]
See, his reward is with him,
and his recompense
accompanies him.' "[i]
12They will be called[j] the Holy
People,[k]
the Redeemed[l] of the LORD;
and you will be called Sought
After,
the City No Longer
Deserted.[m]

God's Day of Vengeance and Redemption

63 Who is this coming from
Edom,
from Bozrah,[n] with his
garments stained
crimson?
Who is this, robed in splendor,
striding forward in the
greatness of his
strength?

"It is I, speaking in righteousness,
mighty to save."[o]

2Why are your garments red,
like those of one treading the
winepress?

3"I have trodden the winepress[p]
alone;
from the nations no one was
with me.
I trampled them in my anger
and trod them down in my
wrath;[q]
their blood spattered my
garments,[r]
and I stained all my clothing.
4For the day of vengeance was
in my heart,
and the year of my
redemption has come.
5I looked, but there was no
one[s] to help,
I was appalled that no one
gave support;
so my own arm[t] worked
salvation for me,
and my own wrath sustained
me.[u]
6I trampled the nations in my
anger;
in my wrath I made them
drunk[v]
and poured their blood[w] on
the ground."

Praise and Prayer

7I will tell of the kindnesses[x] of
the LORD,
the deeds for which he is to
be praised,
according to all the LORD has
done for us—
yes, the many good things he
has done
for the house of Israel,
according to his
compassion[y] and many
kindnesses.
8He said, "Surely they are my
people,[z]
sons who will not be false to
me";

62:7 [a]Mt 15:21-28; Lk 18:1-8
62:8 [b]Dt 28:30-33; Isa 1:7; Jer 5:17
62:10 [c]Isa 60:11 [d]Isa 57:14 [e]Isa 11:16 [f]Isa 11:10
62:11 [g]Zec 9:9; Mt 21:5 [h]Rev 22:12 [i]Isa 40:10
62:12 [j]ver 4 [k]1Pe 2:9 [l]Isa 35:9 [m]Isa 42:16
63:1 [n]Am 1:12 [o]Zep 3:17
63:3 [p]Rev 14:20; 19:15 [q]Isa 22:5 [r]Rev 19:13
63:5 [s]Isa 41:28 [t]Ps 44:3; 98:1 [u]Isa 59:16
63:6 [v]Isa 29:9 [w]Isa 34:3
63:7 [x]Isa 54:8 [y]Ps 51:1; Eph 2:4
63:8 [z]Isa 51:4

and so he became their
Savior.
9In all their distress he too was
distressed,
and the angel of his
presence[a] saved them.
In his love and mercy he
redeemed[b] them;
he lifted them up and
carried[c] them
all the days of old.
10Yet they rebelled[d]
and grieved his Holy Spirit.[e]
So he turned and became their
enemy[f]
and he himself fought against
them.

11Then his people recalled[v] the
days of old,
the days of Moses and his
people—
where is he who brought them
through the sea,[g]
with the shepherd of his
flock?
Where is he who set
his Holy Spirit[h] among
them,
12who sent his glorious arm of
power
to be at Moses' right hand,
who divided the waters[i] before
them,
to gain for himself everlasting
renown,
13who led[j] them through the
depths?
Like a horse in open country,
they did not stumble;[k]
14like cattle that go down to the
plain,
they were given rest by the
Spirit of the LORD.
This is how you guided your
people
to make for yourself a
glorious name.
15Look down from heaven[l] and
see
from your lofty throne,[m] holy
and glorious.
Where are your zeal[n] and your
might?
Your tenderness and
compassion[o] are
withheld from us.

16But you are our Father,
though Abraham does not
know us
or Israel acknowledge[p] us;
you, O LORD, are our Father,
our Redeemer[q] from of old
is your name.
17Why, O LORD, do you make us
wander from your ways
and harden our hearts so we
do not revere[r] you?
Return[s] for the sake of your
servants,
the tribes that are your
inheritance.
18For a little while your people
possessed your holy
place,
but now our enemies have
trampled down your
sanctuary.[t]
19We are yours from of old;
but you have not ruled over
them,
they have not been called by
your name.[w]

64 Oh, that you would rend
the heavens[u] and come
down,[v]
that the mountains[w] would
tremble before you!
2As when fire sets twigs ablaze
and causes water to boil,
come down to make your name
known to your enemies
and cause the nations to
quake[x] before you!
3For when you did awesome[y]
things that we did not
expect,
you came down, and the
mountains trembled
before you.
4Since ancient times no one has
heard,
no ear has perceived,
no eye has seen any God
besides you,
who acts on behalf of those
who wait for him.[z]
5You come to the help of those
who gladly do right,[a]

63:9 [a]Ex 33:14 [b]Dt 7:7-8 [c]Dt 1:31
63:10 [d]Ps 78:40 [e]Ps 51:11; Ac 7:51; Eph 4:30 [f]Ps 106:40
63:11 [g]Ex 14:22,30 [h]Nu 11:17
63:12 [i]Ex 14:21-22; Isa 11:15
63:13 [j]Dt 32:12 [k]Jer 31:9
63:15 [l]Dt 26:15; Ps 80:14 [m]Ps 123:1 [n]Isa 9:7; 26:11 [o]Jer 31:20; Hos 11:8
63:16 [p]Job 14:21 [q]Isa 41:14; 44:6
63:17 [r]Isa 29:13 [s]Nu 10:36
63:18 [t]Ps 74:3-8
64:1 [u]Ps 18:9; 144:5 [v]Mic 1:3 [w]Ex 19:18
64:2 [x]Ps 99:1; Jer 5:22; 33:9
64:3 [y]Ps 65:5
64:4 [z]Isa 30:18; 1Co 2:9*
64:5 [a]Isa 26:8

[v]11 Or *But may he recall* [w]19 Or *We are like those you have never ruled, / like those never called by your name*

who remember your ways.
But when we continued to sin
against them,
you were angry.
How then can we be saved?
6All of us have become like one
who is unclean,
and all our righteous[a] acts
are like filthy rags;
we all shrivel up like a leaf,[b]
and like the wind our sins
sweep us away.
7No one[c] calls on your name
or strives to lay hold of you;
for you have hidden[d] your face
from us
and made us waste away[e]
because of our sins.

8Yet, O LORD, you are our
Father.[f]
We are the clay, you are the
potter;[g]
we are all the work of your
hand.
9Do not be angry[h] beyond
measure, O LORD;
do not remember our sins[i]
forever.
Oh, look upon us, we pray,
for we are all your people.
10Your sacred cities have become
a desert;
even Zion is a desert,
Jerusalem a desolation.
11Our holy and glorious temple,[j]
where our fathers
praised you,
has been burned with fire,
and all that we treasured[k]
lies in ruins.
12After all this, O LORD, will you
hold yourself back?[l]
Will you keep silent[m] and
punish us beyond
measure?

Judgment and Salvation

65 "I revealed myself to those
who did not ask for me;
I was found by those who did
not seek me.[n]
To a nation[o] that did not call
on my name,
I said, 'Here am I, here am I.'
2All day long I have held out my
hands
to an obstinate people,[p]
who walk in ways not good,
pursuing their own
imaginations[q]—
3a people who continually
provoke me
to my very face,[r]
offering sacrifices in gardens[s]
and burning incense on altars
of brick;
4who sit among the graves
and spend their nights
keeping secret vigil;
who eat the flesh of pigs,[t]
and whose pots hold broth of
unclean meat;
5who say, 'Keep away; don't
come near me,
for I am too sacred[u] for you!'
Such people are smoke in my
nostrils,
a fire that keeps burning all
day.

6"See, it stands written before
me:
I will not keep silent[v] but
will pay back[w] in full;
I will pay it back into their
laps[x]—
7both your sins[y] and the sins of
your fathers,"[z]
says the LORD.
"Because they burned sacrifices
on the mountains
and defied me on the
hills,[a]
I will measure into their laps
the full payment for their
former deeds."

8This is what the LORD says:

"As when juice is still found in
a cluster of grapes
and men say, 'Don't destroy
it,
there is yet some good in it,'
so will I do in behalf of my
servants;
I will not destroy them all.
9I will bring forth descendants[b]
from Jacob,
and from Judah those who
will possess[c] my
mountains;
my chosen people will inherit
them,

64:6 [a]Isa 46:12; 48:1 [b]Ps 90:5-6
64:7 [c]Isa 59:4 [d]Dt 31:18; Isa 1:15; 54:8 [e]Isa 9:18
64:8 [f]Isa 63:16 [g]Isa 29:16
64:9 [h]Isa 57:17; 60:10 [i]Isa 43:25
64:11 [j]Ps 74:3-7 [k]La 1:7,10
64:12 [l]Ps 74:10-11; Isa 42:14 [m]Ps 83:1
65:1 [n]Hos 1:10; Ro 9:24-26; 10:20* [o]Eph 2:12
65:2 [p]Isa 1:2,23; Ro 10:21* [q]Ps 81:11-12; Isa 66:18
65:3 [r]Job 1:11 [s]Isa 1:29
65:4 [t]Lev 11:7
65:5 [u]Mt 9:11; Lk 7:39; 18:9-12
65:6 [v]Ps 50:3 [w]Jer 16:18 [x]Ps 79:12
65:7 [y]Isa 22:14 [z]Ex 20:5 [a]Isa 57:7
65:9 [b]Isa 45:19 [c]Am 9:11-15

and there will my servants
live.[a]
10Sharon[b] will become a pasture
for flocks,
and the Valley of Achor[c] a
resting place for herds,
for my people who seek[d]
me.
11"But as for you who forsake[e]
the LORD
and forget my holy mountain,
who spread a table for Fortune
and fill bowls of mixed wine
for Destiny,
12I will destine you for the
sword,[f]
and you will all bend down
for the slaughter;
for I called but you did not
answer,[g]
I spoke but you did not
listen.[h]
You did evil in my sight
and chose what displeases
me."

13Therefore this is what the Sovereign LORD says:

"My servants will eat,[i]
but you will go hungry;
my servants will drink,
but you will go thirsty;[j]
my servants will rejoice,
but you will be put to
shame.[k]
14My servants will sing
out of the joy of their hearts,
but you will cry out[l]
from anguish of heart
and wail in brokenness of
spirit.
15You will leave your name
to my chosen ones as a
curse;[m]
the Sovereign LORD will put you
to death,
but to his servants he will
give another name.
16Whoever invokes a blessing in
the land
will do so by the God of
truth;[n]
he who takes an oath in the
land
will swear[o] by the God of
truth.
For the past troubles will be
forgotten
and hidden from my eyes.

New Heavens and a New Earth

17"Behold, I will create
new heavens and a new
earth.[p]
The former things will not be
remembered,[q]
nor will they come to mind.
18But be glad and rejoice[r]
forever
in what I will create,
for I will create Jerusalem to be
a delight
and its people a joy.
19I will rejoice[s] over Jerusalem
and take delight in my
people;
the sound of weeping and of
crying[t]
will be heard in it no more.
20"Never again will there be in it
an infant who lives but a few
days,
or an old man who does not
live out his years;[u]
he who dies at a hundred
will be thought a mere youth;
he who fails to reach[x] a
hundred
will be considered accursed.
21They will build houses[v] and
dwell in them;
they will plant vineyards and
eat their fruit.[w]
22No longer will they build
houses and others live in
them,
or plant and others eat.
For as the days of a tree,[x]
so will be the days[y] of my
people;
my chosen ones will long enjoy
the works of their hands.
23They will not toil in vain
or bear children doomed to
misfortune;
for they will be a people
blessed[z] by the LORD,
they and their descendants[a]
with them.

65:9 [a]Isa 32:18
65:10 [b]Isa 35:2 [c]Jos 7:26 [d]Isa 51:1
65:11 [e]Dt 29:24-25; Isa 1:28
65:12 [f]Isa 27:1 [g]Pr 1:24-25; Isa 41:28; 66:4 [h]2Ch 36:15-16; Jer 7:13
65:13 [i]Isa 1:19 [j]Isa 41:17 [k]Isa 44:9
65:14 [l]Mt 8:12; Lk 13:28
65:15 [m]Zec 8:13
65:16 [n]Ps 31:5 [o]Isa 19:18
65:17 [p]Isa 66:22; 2Pe 3:13 [q]Isa 43:18; Jer 3:16
65:18 [r]Ps 98:1-9; Isa 25:9
65:19 [s]Isa 35:10; 62:5 [t]Isa 25:8; Rev 7:17
65:20 [u]Ecc 8:13
65:21 [v]Isa 32:18 [w]Isa 37:30; Am 9:14
65:22 [x]Ps 92:12-14 [y]Ps 21:4; 91:16
65:23 [z]Dt 28:3-12; Isa 61:9 [a]Ac 2:39

[x]20 Or *I the sinner who reaches*

24Before they call[a] I will answer;
while they are still speaking[b]
I will hear.
25The wolf and the lamb[c] will
feed together,
and the lion will eat straw
like the ox,
but dust will be the
serpent's[d] food.
They will neither harm nor
destroy
on all my holy mountain,"
says the LORD.

Judgment and Hope

66 This is what the LORD says:
"Heaven is my throne,[e]
and the earth is my
footstool.[f]
Where is the house[g] you will
build for me?
Where will my resting place
be?
2Has not my hand made all
these things,[h]
and so they came into
being?"
declares the LORD.
"This is the one I esteem:
he who is humble and
contrite in spirit,[i]
and trembles at my word.[j]
3But whoever sacrifices a bull[k]
is like one who kills a man,
and whoever offers a lamb,
like one who breaks a dog's
neck;
whoever makes a grain offering
is like one who presents pig's
blood,
and whoever burns memorial
incense,[l]
like one who worships an
idol.
They have chosen their own
ways,[m]
and their souls delight in
their abominations;
4so I also will choose harsh
treatment for them
and will bring upon them
what they dread.[n]
For when I called, no one
answered,[o]
when I spoke, no one
listened.
They did evil[p] in my sight
and chose what displeases
me."[q]

5Hear the word of the LORD,
you who tremble at his word:
"Your brothers who hate[r] you,
and exclude you because of
my name, have said,
'Let the LORD be glorified,
that we may see your joy!'
Yet they will be put to
shame.[s]
6Hear that uproar from the city,
hear that noise from the
temple!
It is the sound of the LORD
repaying[t] his enemies all
they deserve.

7"Before she goes into labor,[u]
she gives birth;
before the pains come upon
her,
she delivers a son.[v]
8Who has ever heard of such a
thing?
Who has ever seen[w] such
things?
Can a country be born in a day
or a nation be brought forth
in a moment?
Yet no sooner is Zion in labor
than she gives birth to her
children.
9Do I bring to the moment of
birth[x]
and not give delivery?" says
the LORD.
"Do I close up the womb
when I bring to delivery?"
says your God.
10"Rejoice[y] with Jerusalem and
be glad for her,
all you who love[z] her;
rejoice greatly with her,
all you who mourn over her.
11For you will nurse[a] and be
satisfied
at her comforting breasts;
you will drink deeply
and delight in her
overflowing abundance."

12For this is what the LORD says:

"I will extend peace to her like
a river,[b]

65:24 [a]Isa 55:6 [b]Da 9:20-23; 10:12
65:25 [c]Isa 11:6 [d]Ge 3:14; Mic 7:17
66:1 [e]Mt 23:22 [f]1Ki 8:27; Mt 5:34-35 [g]2Sa 7:7; Jn 4:20-21; Ac 7:48; 17:24
66:2 [h]Isa 40:26; Ac 7:50* [i]Isa 57:15; Mt 5:3-4; Lk 18:13-14 [j]Ezr 9:4
66:3 [k]Isa 1:11 [l]Lev 2:2 [m]Isa 57:17
66:4 [n]Pr 10:24 [o]Pr 1:24; Jer 7:13 [p]2Ki 21:2,4,6 [q]Isa 65:12
66:5 [r]Ps 38:20; Isa 60:15 [s]Lk 13:17
66:6 [t]Isa 65:6; Joel 3:7
66:7 [u]Isa 54:1 [v]Rev 12:5
66:8 [w]Isa 64:4
66:9 [x]Isa 37:3
66:10 [y]Dt 32:43; Ro 15:10 [z]Ps 26:8
66:11 [a]Isa 60:16
66:12 [b]Isa 48:18

and the wealth[a] of nations
like a flooding stream;
you will nurse and be carried[b]
on her arm
and dandled on her knees.
13As a mother comforts her child,
so will I comfort[c] you;
and you will be comforted
over Jerusalem."

14When you see this, your heart
will rejoice
and you will flourish like
grass;
the hand of the LORD will be
made known to his
servants,
but his fury[d] will be shown
to his foes.
15See, the LORD is coming with
fire,
and his chariots[e] are like a
whirlwind;
he will bring down his anger
with fury,
and his rebuke[f] with flames
of fire.
16For with fire[g] and with his
sword[h]
the LORD will execute
judgment upon all men,
and many will be those slain
by the LORD.

17"Those who consecrate and
purify themselves to go into the
gardens,[i] following the one in the
midst of[y] those who eat the flesh
of pigs[j] and rats and other abominable things—they will meet their
end[k] together," declares the LORD.
18"And I, because of their actions and their imaginations, am
about to come[z] and gather all nations and tongues, and they will
come and see my glory.
19"I will set a sign[l] among
them, and I will send some of those
who survive to the nations—to Tarshish,[m] to the Libyans[a] and Lydi-
ans[n] (famous as archers), to Tubal[o] and Greece, and to the distant
islands[p] that have not heard of my
fame or seen my glory.[q] They will
proclaim my glory among the nations. 20And they will bring all your
brothers, from all the nations, to
my holy mountain in Jerusalem as
an offering to the LORD—on horses,
in chariots and wagons, and on
mules and camels," says the LORD.
"They will bring them, as the Israelites bring their grain offerings, to
the temple of the LORD in ceremonially clean vessels.[r] 21And I
will select some of them also to be
priests[s] and Levites," says the
LORD.

22"As the new heavens and the
new earth[t] that I make will endure
before me," declares the LORD, "so
will your name and descendants
endure.[u] 23From one New Moon
to another and from one Sabbath[v]
to another, all mankind will come
and bow down[w] before me," says
the LORD. 24"And they will go out
and look upon the dead bodies of
those who rebelled against me;
their worm[x] will not die, nor will
their fire be quenched,[y] and they
will be loathsome to all mankind."

66:12 [a]Ps 72:3; Isa 60:5; 61:6 [b]Isa 60:4
66:13 [c]Isa 40:1; 2Co 1:4
66:14 [d]Isa 10:5
66:15 [e]Ps 68:17 [f]Ps 9:5
66:16 [g]Isa 30:30 [h]Isa 27:1
66:17 [i]Isa 1:29 [j]Lev 11:7 [k]Ps 37:20; Isa 1:28
66:19 [l]Isa 11:10; 49:22 [m]Isa 2:16 [n]Eze 27:10 [o]Ge 10:2 [p]Isa 11:11 [q]1Ch 16:24; Isa 24:15
66:20 [r]Isa 52:11
66:21 [s]Ex 19:6; Isa 61:6; 1Pe 2:5,9
66:22 [t]Isa 65:17; Heb 12:26-27; 2Pe 3:13; Rev 21:1 [u]Jn 10:27-29; 1Pe 1:4-5
66:23 [v]Eze 46:1-3 [w]Isa 19:21
66:24 [x]Isa 14:11 [y]Isa 1:31; Mk 9:48*

[y]*17* Or *gardens behind one of your temples, and* [z]*18* The meaning of the Hebrew for this clause is uncertain. [a]*19* Some Septuagint manuscripts *Put* (Libyans); Hebrew *Pul*

Jeremiah

Title and Background

The book is named after the prophet whose ministry it records. Jeremiah prophesied in Judah during the reigns of Josiah and succeeding kings up to the Babylonian exile. It was a period of storm and stress when the doom of entire nations—including Judah itself—was being sealed. After Josiah's reign, Jeremiah was often in danger from political and religious leaders who were angry because of his messages. Through all this, God protected Jeremiah so he could continue to warn the wicked and comfort those who trusted in God.

Author and Date of Writing

The book preserves an account of the prophetic ministry of Jeremiah, whose personal life and struggles are known to us in greater depth and detail than those of any other Old Testament prophet. His prophetic ministry began in 626 B.C. and ended sometime after 586.

Theme and Message

Jeremiah was always conscious of his call from the Lord to be a prophet, and as such proclaimed words that were spoken first by God himself and were therefore certain of fulfillment. Judgment is one of the all-pervasive themes in his writings, though he was careful to point out that repentance, if sincere, would postpone the inevitable. For Jeremiah, God was ultimate. His theology conceived of the Lord as the Creator of all that exists, as all-powerful and as everywhere present. At the same time, God is very much concerned about individual people and their accountability to him.

Outline

I. The Call of Jeremiah (1:1-19)
II. Warnings and Exhortations to Judah (2:1-29:32)
III. Promises of Restoration (30:1-33:26)
IV. Historical Insertion (34:1-35:19)
V. The Sufferings of Jeremiah (36:1-38:28)
VI. The Fall of Jerusalem and Its Aftermath (39:1-45:5)
VII. Judgment Against the Nations (46:1-51:64)
VIII. Historical Appendix (52:1-34)

---

1 The words of Jeremiah son of
Hilkiah, one of the priests at
Anathoth[a] in the territory of Benjamin. 2The word of the LORD came
to him in the thirteenth year of the
reign of Josiah son of Amon king of
Judah, 3and through the reign of
Jehoiakim[b] son of Josiah king of
Judah, down to the fifth month of
the eleventh year of Zedekiah[c] son
of Josiah king of Judah, when the
people of Jerusalem went into exile.[d]

The Call of Jeremiah

4The word of the LORD came to
me, saying,

5"Before I formed you in the
womb I knew[a][e] you,
before you were born[f] I set
you apart;

1:1 [a]Jos 21:18; 1Ch 6:60; Jer 32:7-9
1:3 [b]2Ki 23:34 [c]2Ki 24:17; Jer 39:2 [d]Jer 52:15
1:5 [e]Ps 139:16 [f]Isa 49:1

[a]5 Or *chose*

I appointed you as a prophet
to the nations.[a]"

6"Ah, Sovereign LORD," I said, "I
do not know how to speak;[b] I am
only a child."[c]

7But the LORD said to me, "Do
not say, 'I am only a child.' You
must go to everyone I send you to
and say whatever I command you.
8Do not be afraid[d] of them, for I
am with you[e] and will rescue you,"
declares the LORD.

9Then the LORD reached out his
hand and touched[f] my mouth and
said to me, "Now, I have put my
words in your mouth.[g] 10See, today I appoint you over nations and
kingdoms to uproot and tear down,
to destroy and overthrow, to build
and to plant."[h]

11The word of the LORD came to
me: "What do you see, Jeremiah?"[i]

"I see the branch of an almond
tree," I replied.

12The LORD said to me, "You
have seen correctly, for I am watching[b] to see that my word is fulfilled."

13The word of the LORD came to
me again: "What do you see?"[j]

"I see a boiling pot, tilting away
from the north," I answered.

14The LORD said to me, "From
the north disaster will be poured
out on all who live in the land. 15I
am about to summon all the peoples of the northern kingdoms,"
declares the LORD.

"Their kings will come and set
up their thrones
in the entrance of the gates
of Jerusalem;
they will come against all her
surrounding walls
and against all the towns of
Judah.[k]
16I will pronounce my judgments
on my people
because of their wickedness[l]
in forsaking me,[m]
in burning incense to other
gods[n]
and in worshiping what their
hands have made.

17"Get yourself ready! Stand up
and say to them whatever I command you. Do not be terrified[o] by
them, or I will terrify you before
them. 18Today I have made you[p] a
fortified city, an iron pillar and a
bronze wall to stand against the
whole land—against the kings of
Judah, its officials, its priests and
the people of the land. 19They will
fight against you but will not overcome you, for I am with you[q] and
will rescue[r] you," declares the
LORD.

Israel Forsakes God

2 The word of the LORD came to
me: 2"Go and proclaim in the
hearing of Jerusalem:

" 'I remember the devotion of
your youth,[s]
how as a bride you loved me
and followed me through the
desert,[t]
through a land not sown.
3Israel was holy[u] to the LORD,[v]
the firstfruits[w] of his harvest;
all who devoured[x] her were
held guilty,[y]
and disaster overtook
them,' "
declares the LORD.

4Hear the word of the LORD,
O house of Jacob,
all you clans of the house of
Israel.

5This is what the LORD says:

"What fault did your fathers
find in me,
that they strayed so far from
me?
They followed worthless idols
and became worthless[z]
themselves.
6They did not ask, 'Where is the
LORD,
who brought us up out of
Egypt[a]
and led us through the barren
wilderness,
through a land of deserts[b]
and rifts,[c]

1:5 [a]ver 10; Jer 25:15-26
1:6 [b]Ex 4:10; 6:12 [c]1Ki 3:7
1:8 [d]Eze 2:6 [e]Jos 1:5; Jer 15:20
1:9 [f]Isa 6:7 [g]Ex 4:12
1:10 [h]Jer 18:7-10; 24:6; 31:4,28
1:11 [i]Jer 24:3; Am 7:8
1:13 [j]Zec 4:2
1:15 [k]Jer 4:16; 9:11
1:16 [l]Dt 28:20 [m]Jer 17:13 [n]Jer 7:9; 19:4
1:17 [o]Eze 2:6
1:18 [p]Isa 50:7
1:19 [q]Jer 20:11 [r]ver 8
2:2 [s]Eze 16:8-14, 60; Hos 2:15 [t]Dt 2:7
2:3 [u]Dt 7:6 [v]Ex 19:6 [w]Jas 1:18; Rev 14:4 [x]Isa 41:11; Jer 30:16 [y]Jer 50:7
2:5 [z]2Ki 17:15
2:6 [a]Hos 13:4 [b]Dt 8:15 [c]Dt 32:10

[b]*12* The Hebrew for *watching* sounds like the Hebrew for *almond tree.*

a land of drought and darkness,[c]
a land where no one travels and no one lives?'
7I brought you into a fertile land
to eat its fruit and rich produce.[a]
But you came and defiled my land
and made my inheritance detestable.[b]
8The priests did not ask, 'Where is the LORD?'
Those who deal with the law did not know me;[c]
the leaders rebelled against me.
The prophets prophesied by Baal,[d]
following worthless idols.[e]

9"Therefore I bring charges[f] against you again,"
declares the LORD.
"And I will bring charges against your children's children.
10Cross over to the coasts of Kittim[d] and look,
send to Kedar[e] and observe closely;
see if there has ever been anything like this:
11Has a nation ever changed its gods?
(Yet they are not gods[g] at all.)
But my people have exchanged their[f] Glory[h]
for worthless idols.
12Be appalled at this, O heavens,
and shudder with great horror,"
declares the LORD.
13"My people have committed two sins:
They have forsaken me,
the spring of living water,[i]
and have dug their own cisterns,
broken cisterns that cannot hold water.
14Is Israel a servant, a slave[j] by birth?
Why then has he become plunder?

2:7 [a]Nu 13:27; Dt 8:7-9; 11:10-12 [b]Ps 106:34-39; Jer 16:18
2:8 [c]Jer 4:22 [d]Jer 23:13 [e]Jer 16:19
2:9 [f]Eze 20:35-36; Mic 6:2
2:11 [g]Isa 37:19; Jer 16:20 [h]Ps 106:20; Ro 1:23
2:13 [i]Ps 36:9; Jn 4:14
2:14 [j]Ex 4:22
2:15 [k]Jer 4:7; 50:17 [l]Isa 1:7
2:16 [m]Isa 19:13 [n]Jer 43:7-9
2:17 [o]Jer 4:18
2:18 [p]Isa 30:2 [q]Jos 13:3
2:19 [r]Jer 3:11,22 [s]Isa 3:9; Hos 5:5 [t]Job 20:14; Am 8:10 [u]Ps 36:1
2:20 [v]Lev 26:13 [w]Isa 57:7; Jer 17:2 [x]Dt 12:2
2:21 [y]Ex 15:17 [z]Ps 80:8 [a]Isa 5:4

15Lions[k] have roared;
they have growled at him.
They have laid waste[l] his land;
his towns are burned and deserted.
16Also, the men of Memphis[g][m] and Tahpanhes[n]
have shaved the crown of your head.[h]
17Have you not brought this on yourselves[o]
by forsaking the LORD your God
when he led you in the way?
18Now why go to Egypt[p]
to drink water from the Shihor[i]?[q]
And why go to Assyria
to drink water from the River[j]?
19Your wickedness will punish you;
your backsliding[r] will rebuke[s] you.
Consider then and realize
how evil and bitter[t] it is for you
when you forsake the LORD your God
and have no awe[u] of me,"
declares the Lord, the LORD Almighty.

20"Long ago you broke off your yoke[v]
and tore off your bonds;
you said, 'I will not serve you!'
Indeed, on every high hill[w]
and under every spreading tree[x]
you lay down as a prostitute.
21I had planted[y] you like a choice vine[z]
of sound and reliable stock.
How then did you turn against me
into a corrupt,[a] wild vine?
22Although you wash yourself with soda

[c]6 Or *and the shadow of death* [d]10 That is, Cyprus and western coastlands [e]10 The home of Bedouin tribes in the Syro-Arabian desert [f]11 Masoretic Text; an ancient Hebrew scribal tradition *my* [g]16 Hebrew *Noph* [h]16 Or *have cracked your skull* [i]18 That is, a branch of the Nile [j]18 That is, the Euphrates

and use an abundance of soap,
the stain of your guilt is still before me,"
declares the Sovereign LORD.

23"How can you say, 'I am not defiled;[a]
I have not run after the Baals'?[b]
See how you behaved in the valley;[c]
consider what you have done.
You are a swift she-camel running[d] here and there,
24a wild donkey[e] accustomed to the desert,
sniffing the wind in her craving—
in her heat who can restrain her?
Any males that pursue her need not tire themselves;
at mating time they will find her.
25Do not run until your feet are bare
and your throat is dry.
But you said, 'It's no use!
I love foreign gods,[f]
and I must go after them.'

26"As a thief is disgraced[g] when he is caught,
so the house of Israel is disgraced—
they, their kings and their officials,
their priests and their prophets.
27They say to wood, 'You are my father,'
and to stone,[h] 'You gave me birth.'
They have turned their backs to me
and not their faces;[i]
yet when they are in trouble,[j] they say,
'Come and save us!'
28Where then are the gods[k] you made for yourselves?
Let them come if they can save you
when you are in trouble![l]
For you have as many gods
as you have towns,[m]
O Judah.

29"Why do you bring charges against me?
You have all[n] rebelled against me,"
declares the LORD.
30"In vain I punished your people;
they did not respond to correction.
Your sword has devoured your prophets[o]
like a ravening lion.

31"You of this generation, consider the word of the LORD:

"Have I been a desert to Israel
or a land of great darkness?[p]
Why do my people say, 'We are free to roam;
we will come to you no more'?
32Does a maiden forget her jewelry,
a bride her wedding ornaments?
Yet my people have forgotten me,
days without number.
33How skilled you are at pursuing love!
Even the worst of women can learn from your ways.
34On your clothes men find
the lifeblood[q] of the innocent poor,
though you did not catch them breaking in.[r]
Yet in spite of all this
35 you say, 'I am innocent;
he is not angry with me.'
But I will pass judgment[s] on you
because you say, 'I have not sinned.'[t]
36Why do you go about so much,
changing[u] your ways?
You will be disappointed by Egypt[v]
as you were by Assyria.
37You will also leave that place
with your hands on your head,[w]
for the LORD has rejected those you trust;

2:23 [a] Pr 30:12 [b] Jer 9:14 [c] Jer 7:31 [d] ver 33; Jer 31:22
2:24 [e] Jer 14:6
2:25 [f] Dt 32:16; Jer 3:13; 14:10
2:26 [g] Jer 48:27
2:27 [h] Jer 3:9 [i] Jer 18:17; 32:33 [j] Jdg 10:10; Isa 26:16
2:28 [k] Isa 45:20 [l] Dt 32:37 [m] 2Ki 17:29; Jer 11:13
2:29 [n] Jer 5:1; 6:13; Da 9:11
2:30 [o] Ne 9:26; Ac 7:52; 1Th 2:15
2:31 [p] Isa 45:19
2:34 [q] 2Ki 21:16 [r] Ex 22:2
2:35 [s] Jer 25:31 [t] 1Jn 1:8,10
2:36 [u] Jer 31:22 [v] Isa 30:2,3,7
2:37 [w] 2Sa 13:19

you will not be helped[a] by
them.

3 "If a man divorces[b] his wife
and she leaves him and
marries another man,
should he return to her again?
Would not the land be
completely defiled?
But you have lived as a
prostitute with many
lovers[c]—
would you now return to
me?"
declares the LORD.
2 "Look up to the barren heights
and see.
Is there any place where you
have not been ravished?
By the roadside[d] you sat
waiting for lovers,
sat like a nomad[k] in the
desert.
You have defiled the land[e]
with your prostitution and
wickedness.
3 Therefore the showers have
been withheld,[f]
and no spring rains[g] have
fallen.
Yet you have the brazen look of
a prostitute;
you refuse to blush with
shame.[h]
4 Have you not just called to me:
'My Father,[i] my friend from
my youth,[j]
5 will you always be angry?[k]
Will your wrath continue
forever?'
This is how you talk,
but you do all the evil you
can."

Unfaithful Israel

6 During the reign of King Josiah,
the LORD said to me, "Have you
seen what faithless Israel has
done? She has gone up on every
high hill and under every spreading
tree[l] and has committed adultery[m] there. 7 I thought that after
she had done all this she would return to me but she did not, and her
unfaithful sister[n] Judah saw it. 8 I
gave faithless Israel her certificate
of divorce and sent her away because of all her adulteries. Yet I
saw that her unfaithful sister Judah
had no fear;[o] she also went out
and committed adultery. 9 Because
Israel's immorality mattered so little to her, she defiled the land[p]
and committed adultery with
stone[q] and wood.[r] 10 In spite of all
this, her unfaithful sister Judah did
not return to me with all her heart,
but only in pretense,[s]" declares
the LORD.

11 The LORD said to me, "Faithless Israel is more righteous[t] than
unfaithful[u] Judah. 12 Go, proclaim
this message toward the north:[v]

" 'Return,[w] faithless Israel,'
declares the LORD,
'I will frown on you no
longer,
for I am merciful,' declares the
LORD,
'I will not be angry[x] forever.
13 Only acknowledge[y] your
guilt—
you have rebelled against the
LORD your God,
you have scattered your favors
to foreign gods[z]
under every spreading tree,[a]
and have not obeyed[b] me,' "
declares the LORD.

14 "Return,[c] faithless people,"
declares the LORD, "for I am your
husband. I will choose you—one
from a town and two from a clan
—and bring you to Zion. 15 Then I
will give you shepherds[d] after my
own heart, who will lead you with
knowledge and understanding.
16 In those days, when your numbers have increased greatly in the
land," declares the LORD, "men will
no longer say, 'The ark of the covenant of the LORD.' It will never enter their minds or be remembered;[e] it will not be missed, nor
will another one be made. 17 At that
time they will call Jerusalem The
Throne[f] of the LORD, and all nations will gather in Jerusalem to
honor[g] the name of the LORD. No
longer will they follow the stubbornness of their evil hearts.[h] 18 In

2:37 [a] Jer 37:7
3:1 [b] Dt 24:1-4 [c] Jer 2:20,25; Eze 16:26,29
3:2 [d] Ge 38:14; Eze 16:25 [e] Jer 2:7
3:3 [f] Lev 26:19 [g] Jer 14:4 [h] Jer 6:15; 8:12; Zep 3:5
3:4 [i] ver 19 [j] Jer 2:2
3:5 [k] Ps 103:9; Isa 57:16
3:6 [l] Jer 17:2 [m] Jer 2:20
3:7 [n] Eze 16:46
3:8 [o] Eze 16:47; 23:11
3:9 [p] ver 2 [q] Isa 57:6 [r] Jer 2:27
3:10 [s] Jer 12:2
3:11 [t] Eze 16:52; 23:11 [u] ver 7
3:12 [v] 2Ki 17:3-6 [w] ver 14; Jer 31:21,22; Eze 33:11 [x] Ps 86:15
3:13 [y] Dt 30:1-3; Jer 14:20; 1Jn 1:9 [z] Jer 2:25 [a] Dt 12:2 [b] ver 25
3:14 [c] Hos 2:19
3:15 [d] Ac 20:28
3:16 [e] Isa 65:17
3:17 [f] Jer 17:12; Eze 43:7 [g] Isa 60:9 [h] Jer 11:8

[k] 2 Or *an Arab*

those days the house of Judah will
join the house of Israel,[a] and together[b] they will come from a
northern[c] land to the land[d] I gave
your forefathers as an inheritance.

19"I myself said,

" 'How gladly would I treat you
like sons
and give you a desirable
land,
the most beautiful
inheritance of any
nation.'
I thought you would call me
'Father'[e]
and not turn away from
following me.
20But like a woman unfaithful to
her husband,
so you have been unfaithful
to me, O house of
Israel,"
declares the LORD.

21A cry is heard on the barren
heights,[f]
the weeping and pleading of
the people of Israel,
because they have perverted
their ways
and have forgotten the LORD
their God.

22"Return,[g] faithless people;
I will cure[h] you of
backsliding."

"Yes, we will come to you,
for you are the LORD our God.
23Surely the ⌊idolatrous⌋
commotion on the hills
and mountains is a
deception;
surely in the LORD our God
is the salvation[i] of Israel.
24From our youth shameful[j]
gods have consumed
the fruits of our fathers'
labor—
their flocks and herds,
their sons and daughters.
25Let us lie down in our shame,[k]
and let our disgrace cover us.
We have sinned against the
LORD our God,
both we and our fathers;
from our youth[l] till this day
we have not obeyed the LORD
our God."

4 "If you will return[m], O Israel,
return to me,"
declares the LORD.
"If you put your detestable
idols[n] out of my sight
and no longer go astray,
2and if in a truthful, just and
righteous way
you swear,[o] 'As surely as the
LORD lives,'[p]
then the nations will be
blessed[q] by him
and in him they will glory."

3This is what the LORD says to the
men of Judah and to Jerusalem:

"Break up your unplowed
ground[r]
and do not sow among
thorns.[s]
4Circumcise yourselves to the
LORD,
circumcise your hearts,[t]
you men of Judah and people
of Jerusalem,
or my wrath[u] will break out
and burn like fire
because of the evil you have
done—
burn with no one to quench[v]
it.

Disaster From the North

5"Announce in Judah and
proclaim in Jerusalem
and say:
'Sound the trumpet
throughout the land!'
Cry aloud and say:
'Gather together!
Let us flee to the fortified
cities!'[w]
6Raise the signal to go to Zion!
Flee for safety without delay!
For I am bringing disaster from
the north,[x]
even terrible destruction."
7A lion[y] has come out of his
lair;
a destroyer of nations has set
out.
He has left his place
to lay waste[z] your land.

3:18 [a]Hos 1:11 [b]Isa 11:13; Jer 50:4 [c]Jer 16:15; 31:8 [d]Am 9:15
3:19 [e]ver 4; Isa 63:16
3:21 [f]ver 2
3:22 [g]Hos 14:4 [h]Jer 33:6; Hos 6:1
3:23 [i]Ps 3:8; Jer 17:14
3:24 [j]Hos 9:10
3:25 [k]Ezr 9:6 [l]Jer 22:21
4:1 [m]Jer 3:1,22; Joel 2:12 [n]Jer 35:15
4:2 [o]Dt 10:20; Isa 65:16 [p]Jer 12:16 [q]Ge 22:18; Gal 3:8
4:3 [r]Hos 10:12 [s]Mk 4:18
4:4 [t]Dt 10:16; Jer 9:26; Ro 2:28-29 [u]Zep 2:2 [v]Am 5:6
4:5 [w]Jos 10:20; Jer 8:14
4:6 [x]Jer 1:13-15; 50:3
4:7 [y]2Ki 24:1; Jer 2:15 [z]Isa 1:7

Your towns will lie in ruins[a]
without inhabitant.
8So put on sackcloth,[b]
lament and wail,
for the fierce anger[c] of the
LORD
has not turned away from
us.

9"In that day," declares the
LORD,
"the king and the officials
will lose heart,
the priests will be horrified,
and the prophets will be
appalled."[d]

10Then I said, "Ah, Sovereign
LORD, how completely you have deceived[e] this people and Jerusalem
by saying, 'You will have peace,'[f]
when the sword is at our throats."
11At that time this people and
Jerusalem will be told, "A scorching wind[g] from the barren heights
in the desert blows toward my people, but not to winnow or cleanse;
12a wind too strong for that comes
from me.[1] Now I pronounce my
judgments[h] against them."

13Look! He advances like the
clouds,[i]
his chariots[j] come like a
whirlwind,[k]
his horses are swifter than
eagles.[l]
Woe to us! We are ruined!
14O Jerusalem, wash[m] the evil
from your heart and be
saved.
How long will you harbor
wicked thoughts?
15A voice is announcing from
Dan,[n]
proclaiming disaster from the
hills of Ephraim.
16"Tell this to the nations,
proclaim it to Jerusalem:
'A besieging army is coming
from a distant land,
raising a war cry[o] against the
cities of Judah.
17They surround[p] her like men
guarding a field,
because she has rebelled[q]
against me,' "
declares the LORD.

18"Your own conduct and
actions[r]
have brought this upon you.[s]
This is your punishment.
How bitter[t] it is!
How it pierces to the heart!"

19Oh, my anguish, my anguish![u]
I writhe in pain.
Oh, the agony of my heart!
My heart pounds within me,
I cannot keep silent.[v]
For I have heard the sound of
the trumpet;
I have heard the battle cry.[w]
20Disaster follows disaster;[x]
the whole land lies in ruins.
In an instant my tents[y] are
destroyed,
my shelter in a moment.
21How long must I see the battle
standard
and hear the sound of the
trumpet?

22"My people are fools;[z]
they do not know me.[a]
They are senseless children;
they have no understanding.
They are skilled in doing evil;[b]
they know not how to do
good."[c]

23I looked at the earth,
and it was formless and
empty;[d]
and at the heavens,
and their light was gone.
24I looked at the mountains,
and they were quaking;[e]
all the hills were swaying.
25I looked, and there were no
people;
every bird in the sky had
flown away.[f]
26I looked, and the fruitful land
was a desert;
all its towns lay in ruins
before the LORD, before his
fierce anger.

27This is what the LORD says:

"The whole land will be ruined,
though I will not destroy[g] it
completely.
28Therefore the earth will
mourn[h]

[1]*12* Or *comes at my command*

4:7 [a]Jer 25:9
4:8 [b]Isa 22:12; Jer 6:26 [c]Jer 30:24
4:9 [d]Isa 29:9
4:10 [e]2Th 2:11 [f]Jer 14:13
4:11 [g]Eze 17:10; Hos 13:15
4:12 [h]Jer 1:16
4:13 [i]Isa 19:1 [j]Isa 66:15 [k]Isa 5:28 [l]Dt 28:49; Hab 1:8
4:14 [m]Jas 4:8
4:15 [n]Jer 8:16
4:16 [o]Eze 21:22
4:17 [p]2Ki 25:1,4 [q]Jer 5:23
4:18 [r]Ps 107:17; Isa 50:1 [s]Jer 2:17 [t]Jer 2:19
4:19 [u]Isa 16:11; 22:4; Jer 9:10 [v]Jer 20:9 [w]Nu 10:9
4:20 [x]Ps 42:7; Eze 7:26 [y]Jer 10:20
4:22 [z]Jer 10:8 [a]Jer 2:8 [b]Jer 13:23; 1Co 14:20 [c]Ro 16:19
4:23 [d]Ge 1:2
4:24 [e]Isa 5:25; Eze 38:20
4:25 [f]Jer 9:10; 12:4; Zep 1:3
4:27 [g]Jer 5:10,18; 12:12; 30:11; 46:28
4:28 [h]Jer 12:4,11; 14:2; Hos 4:3

and the heavens above grow
dark,[a]
because I have spoken and will
not relent,[b]
I have decided and will not
turn back.[c]"

29At the sound of horsemen and
archers[d]
every town takes to flight.[e]
Some go into the thickets;
some climb up among the
rocks.
All the towns are deserted;[f]
no one lives in them.

30What are you doing,[g]
O devastated one?
Why dress yourself in scarlet
and put on jewels[h] of gold?
Why shade your eyes with
paint?[i]
You adorn yourself in vain.
Your lovers[j] despise you;
they seek your life.

31I hear a cry as of a woman in
labor,[k]
a groan as of one bearing her
first child—
the cry of the Daughter of Zion
gasping for breath,[l]
stretching out her hands[m]
and saying,
"Alas! I am fainting;
my life is given over to
murderers."

Not One Is Upright

5 "Go up and down[n] the
streets of Jerusalem,
look around and consider,
search through her squares.
If you can find but one
person[o]
who deals honestly and seeks
the truth,
I will forgive[p] this city.
2Although they say, 'As surely as
the LORD lives,'[q]
still they are swearing
falsely."

3O LORD, do not your eyes[r] look
for truth?
You struck[s] them, but they
felt no pain;
you crushed them, but they
refused correction.[t]
They made their faces harder
than stone[u]
and refused to repent.
4I thought, "These are only the
poor;
they are foolish,
for they do not know[v] the way
of the LORD,
the requirements of their
God.
5So I will go to the leaders[w]
and speak to them;
surely they know the way of the
LORD,
the requirements of their
God."
But with one accord they too
had broken off the yoke
and torn off the bonds.[x]
6Therefore a lion from the forest
will attack them,
a wolf from the desert will
ravage them,
a leopard[y] will lie in wait near
their towns
to tear to pieces any who
venture out,
for their rebellion is great
and their backslidings
many.[z]

7"Why should I forgive you?
Your children have forsaken
me
and sworn[a] by gods that are
not gods.[b]
I supplied all their needs,
yet they committed
adultery[c]
and thronged to the houses
of prostitutes.
8They are well-fed, lusty
stallions,
each neighing for another
man's wife.[d]
9Should I not punish them for
this?"[e]
declares the LORD.
"Should I not avenge myself
on such a nation as this?

10"Go through her vineyards and
ravage them,
but do not destroy them
completely.[f]
Strip off her branches,

4:28 [a]Isa 5:30; 50:3 [b]Nu 23:19 [c]Jer 23:20; 30:24
4:29 [d]Jer 6:23 [e]2Ki 25:4 [f]ver 7
4:30 [g]Isa 10:3-4 [h]Eze 23:40 [i]2Ki 9:30 [j]La 1:2; Eze 23:9,22
4:31 [k]Jer 13:21 [l]Isa 42:14 [m]Isa 1:15; La 1:17
5:1 [n]2Ch 16:9; Eze 22:30 [o]Ge 18:32 [p]Ge 18:24
5:2 [q]Jer 4:2
5:3 [r]2Ch 16:9 [s]Isa 9:13 [t]Jer 2:30; Zep 3:2 [u]Jer 7:26; 19:15; Eze 3:8-9
5:4 [v]Jer 8:7
5:5 [w]Mic 3:1,9 [x]Ps 2:3; Jer 2:20
5:6 [y]Hos 13:7 [z]Jer 30:14
5:7 [a]Jos 23:7; Zep 1:5 [b]Dt 32:21; Jer 2:11; Gal 4:8 [c]Nu 25:1
5:8 [d]Jer 29:23; Eze 22:11
5:9 [e]ver 29; Jer 9:9
5:10 [f]Jer 4:27

for these people do not
belong to the LORD.
11The house of Israel and the
house of Judah
have been utterly unfaithful[a]
to me,"
declares the LORD.
12They have lied about the LORD;
they said, "He will do
nothing!
No harm will come to us;[b]
we will never see sword or
famine.[c]
13The prophets[d] are but wind
and the word is not in them;
so let what they say be done
to them."
14Therefore this is what the LORD
God Almighty says:
"Because the people have
spoken these words,
I will make my words in your
mouth[e] a fire[f]
and these people the wood it
consumes.
15O house of Israel," declares the
LORD,
"I am bringing a distant
nation[g] against you—
an ancient and enduring
nation,
a people whose language[h]
you do not know,
whose speech you do not
understand.
16Their quivers are like an open
grave;
all of them are mighty
warriors.
17They will devour[i j] your
harvests and food,
devour[k l] your sons and
daughters;
they will devour[m] your flocks
and herds,
devour your vines and fig
trees.
With the sword they will
destroy
the fortified cities in which
you trust.[n]

18"Yet even in those days," declares the LORD, "I will not destroy[o] you completely. 19And
when the people ask,[p] 'Why has
the LORD our God done all this to
us?' you will tell them, 'As you have
forsaken me and served foreign
gods[q] in your own land, so now
you will serve foreigners[r] in a land
not your own.'

20"Announce this to the house of
Jacob
and proclaim it in Judah:
21Hear this, you foolish and
senseless people,
who have eyes[s] but do not
see,
who have ears but do not
hear:[t]
22Should you not fear[u] me?"
declares the LORD.
"Should you not tremble in
my presence?
I made the sand a boundary for
the sea,
an everlasting barrier it
cannot cross.
The waves may roll, but they
cannot prevail;
they may roar, but they
cannot cross it.
23But these people have stubborn
and rebellious[v] hearts;
they have turned aside and
gone away.
24They do not say to themselves,
'Let us fear the LORD our
God,
who gives autumn and spring
rains[w] in season,
who assures us of the regular
weeks of harvest.'[x]
25Your wrongdoings have kept
these away;
your sins have deprived you
of good.
26"Among my people are wicked
men
who lie in wait[y] like men
who snare birds
and like those who set traps
to catch men.
27Like cages full of birds,
their houses are full of
deceit;[z]
they have become rich[a] and
powerful
28 and have grown fat[b] and
sleek.
Their evil deeds have no limit;

5:11 [a] Jer 3:20
5:12 [b] Jer 23:17 [c] 2Ch 36:16; Jer 14:13
5:13 [d] Jer 14:15
5:14 [e] Jer 1:9; Hos 6:5 [f] Jer 23:29
5:15 [g] Dt 28:49; Isa 5:26; Jer 4:16 [h] Isa 28:11
5:17 [i] Jer 8:16 [j] Lev 26:16 [k] Jer 50:7,17 [l] Dt 28:32 [m] Dt 28:31 [n] Dt 28:33
5:18 [o] Jer 4:27
5:19 [p] Dt 29:24-26; 1Ki 9:9 [q] Jer 16:13 [r] Dt 28:48
5:21 [s] Isa 6:10; Eze 12:2 [t] Mt 13:15; Mk 8:18
5:22 [u] Dt 28:58
5:23 [v] Dt 21:18
5:24 [w] Ps 147:8; Joel 2:23 [x] Ge 8:22; Ac 14:17
5:26 [y] Ps 10:8; Pr 1:11
5:27 [z] Jer 9:6 [a] Jer 12:1
5:28 [b] Dt 32:15

they do not plead the case of
the fatherless[a] to win it,
they do not defend the rights
of the poor.[b]
29Should I not punish them for
this?"
declares the LORD.
"Should I not avenge myself
on such a nation as this?

30"A horrible[c] and shocking
thing
has happened in the land:
31The prophets prophesy lies,[d]
the priests rule by their own
authority,
and my people love it this way.
But what will you do in the
end?

Jerusalem Under Siege

6 "Flee for safety, people of
Benjamin!
Flee from Jerusalem!
Sound the trumpet in Tekoa![e]
Raise the signal over Beth
Hakkerem![f]
For disaster looms out of the
north,[g]
even terrible destruction.
2I will destroy the Daughter of
Zion,
so beautiful and delicate.
3Shepherds[h] with their flocks
will come against her;
they will pitch their tents
around[i] her,
each tending his own
portion."

4"Prepare for battle against her!
Arise, let us attack at noon![j]
But, alas, the daylight is fading,
and the shadows of evening
grow long.
5So arise, let us attack at night
and destroy her fortresses!"

6This is what the LORD Almighty
says:

"Cut down the trees[k]
and build siege ramps[l]
against Jerusalem.
This city must be punished;
it is filled with oppression.
7As a well pours out its water,
so she pours out her
wickedness.
Violence[m] and destruction[n]
resound in her;
her sickness and wounds are
ever before me.
8Take warning, O Jerusalem,
or I will turn away[o] from you
and make your land desolate
so no one can live in it."

9This is what the LORD Almighty
says:

"Let them glean the remnant of
Israel
as thoroughly as a vine;
pass your hand over the
branches again,
like one gathering grapes."

10To whom can I speak and give
warning?
Who will listen to me?
Their ears are closed[m][p]
so they cannot hear.
The word[q] of the LORD is
offensive to them;
they find no pleasure in it.
11But I am full of the wrath[r] of
the LORD,
and I cannot hold it in.[s]

"Pour it out on the children in
the street
and on the young men[t]
gathered together;
both husband and wife will be
caught in it,
and the old, those weighed
down with years.
12Their houses will be turned
over to others,[u]
together with their fields and
their wives,[v]
when I stretch out my hand[w]
against those who live in the
land,"
declares the LORD.
13"From the least to the greatest,
all are greedy for gain;[x]
prophets and priests alike,
all practice deceit.[y]
14They dress the wound of my
people
as though it were not serious.
'Peace, peace,' they say,

5:28 [a]Zec 7:10 [b]Isa 1:23; Jer 7:6
5:30 [c]Jer 23:14; Hos 6:10
5:31 [d]Eze 13:6; Mic 2:11
6:1 [e]2Ch 11:6 [f]Ne 3:14 [g]Jer 4:6
6:3 [h]Jer 12:10 [i]2Ki 25:4; Lk 19:43
6:4 [j]Jer 15:8
6:6 [k]Dt 20:19-20 [l]Jer 32:24
6:7 [m]Ps 55:9; Eze 7:11,23 [n]Jer 20:8
6:8 [o]Eze 23:18; Hos 9:12
6:10 [p]Ac 7:51 [q]Jer 20:8
6:11 [r]Jer 7:20 [s]Job 32:20; Jer 20:9 [t]Jer 9:21
6:12 [u]Dt 28:30 [v]Jer 8:10; 38:22 [w]Isa 5:25
6:13 [x]Isa 56:11 [y]Jer 8:10

[m]10 Hebrew *uncircumcised*

when there is no peace.[a]
15Are they ashamed of their
loathsome conduct?
No, they have no shame at
all;
they do not even know how
to blush.[b]
So they will fall among the
fallen;
they will be brought down
when I punish them,"
says the LORD.

16This is what the LORD says:

"Stand at the crossroads and
look;
ask for the ancient paths,[c]
ask where the good way[d] is,
and walk in it,
and you will find rest[e] for
your souls.
But you said, 'We will not
walk in it.'
17I appointed watchmen[f] over
you and said,
'Listen to the sound of the
trumpet!'
But you said, 'We will not
listen.'[g]
18Therefore hear, O nations;
observe, O witnesses,
what will happen to them.
19Hear, O earth:[h]
I am bringing disaster on this
people,
the fruit of their schemes,[i]
because they have not listened
to my words
and have rejected my law.[j]
20What do I care about incense
from Sheba
or sweet calamus[k] from a
distant land?
Your burnt offerings are not
acceptable;[l]
your sacrifices[m] do not
please me."[n]

21Therefore this is what the LORD
says:

"I will put obstacles before this
people.
Fathers and sons alike will
stumble[o] over them;
neighbors and friends will
perish."

22This is what the LORD says:

"Look, an army is coming
from the land of the
north;[p]
a great nation is being stirred
up
from the ends of the earth.
23They are armed with bow and
spear;
they are cruel and show no
mercy.[q]
They sound like the roaring sea
as they ride on their horses;[r]
they come like men in battle
formation
to attack you, O Daughter of
Zion."

24We have heard reports about
them,
and our hands hang limp.
Anguish[s] has gripped us,
pain like that of a woman in
labor.[t]
25Do not go out to the fields
or walk on the roads,
for the enemy has a sword,
and there is terror on every
side.[u]
26O my people, put on
sackcloth[v]
and roll in ashes;[w]
mourn with bitter wailing
as for an only son,[x]
for suddenly the destroyer
will come upon us.

27"I have made you a tester[y] of
metals
and my people the ore,
that you may observe
and test their ways.
28They are all hardened
rebels,[z]
going about to slander.[a]
They are bronze and iron;[b]
they all act corruptly.
29The bellows blow fiercely
to burn away the lead with
fire,
but the refining goes on in
vain;
the wicked are not purged
out.
30They are called rejected silver,
because the LORD has
rejected them."[c]

6:14 [a] Jer 4:10; 8:11; Eze 13:10
6:15 [b] Jer 3:3; 8:10-12
6:16 [c] Jer 18:15 [d] Ps 119:3 [e] Mt 11:29
6:17 [f] Eze 3:17 [g] Jer 11:7-8; 25:4
6:19 [h] Isa 1:2; Jer 22:29 [i] Pr 1:31 [j] Jer 8:9
6:20 [k] Ex 30:23 [l] Am 5:22 [m] Ps 50:8-10; Jer 7:21; Mic 6:7-8 [n] Isa 1:11
6:21 [o] Isa 8:14
6:22 [p] Jer 1:15; 10:22
6:23 [q] Isa 13:18 [r] Jer 4:29
6:24 [s] Jer 4:19 [t] Jer 4:31; 50:41-43
6:25 [u] Jer 49:29
6:26 [v] Jer 4:8 [w] Jer 25:34; Mic 1:10 [x] Zec 12:10
6:27 [y] Jer 9:7
6:28 [z] Jer 5:23 [a] Jer 9:4 [b] Eze 22:18
6:30 [c] Ps 119:119; Jer 7:29; Hos 9:17

False Religion Worthless

7 This is the word that came to
Jeremiah from the LORD:
2"Stand[a] at the gate of the LORD's
house and there proclaim this message:

" 'Hear the word of the LORD, all
you people of Judah who come
through these gates to worship the
LORD. 3This is what the LORD Almighty, the God of Israel, says: Reform your ways[b] and your actions,
and I will let you live in this place.
4Do not trust in deceptive[c] words
and say, "This is the temple of the
LORD, the temple of the LORD, the
temple of the LORD!" 5If you really
change your ways and your actions
and deal with each other justly,[d]
6if you do not oppress the alien, the
fatherless or the widow and do not
shed innocent blood[e] in this
place, and if you do not follow other gods[f] to your own harm, 7then
I will let you live in this place, in
the land[g] I gave your forefathers
for ever and ever. 8But look, you are
trusting in deceptive words that are
worthless.

9" 'Will you steal and murder,
commit adultery and perjury,[n]
burn incense to Baal[h] and follow
other gods[i] you have not known,
10and then come and stand before
me in this house,[j] which bears my
Name, and say, "We are safe"—
safe to do all these detestable
things? 11Has this house,[k] which
bears my Name, become a den of
robbers[l] to you? But I have been
watching![m] declares the LORD.

12" 'Go now to the place in Shiloh[n] where I first made a dwelling
for my Name, and see what I did[o]
to it because of the wickedness of
my people Israel. 13While you were
doing all these things, declares the
LORD, I spoke to you again and
again,[p] but you did not listen;[q] I
called you, but you did not answer.[r] 14Therefore, what I did to
Shiloh I will now do to the house
that bears my Name,[s] the temple
you trust in, the place I gave to you
and your fathers. 15I will thrust you
from my presence, just as I did all
your brothers, the people of Ephraim.'[t]

16"So do not pray for this people
nor offer any plea[u] or petition for
them; do not plead with me, for I
will not listen to you. 17Do you not
see what they are doing in the
towns of Judah and in the streets of
Jerusalem? 18The children gather
wood, the fathers light the fire, and
the women knead the dough and
make cakes of bread for the Queen
of Heaven.[v] They pour out drink
offerings[w] to other gods to provoke[x] me to anger. 19But am I the
one they are provoking? declares
the LORD. Are they not rather harming themselves, to their own
shame?[y]

20" 'Therefore this is what the
Sovereign LORD says: My anger[z]
and my wrath will be poured out on
this place, on man and beast, on
the trees of the field and on the
fruit of the ground, and it will burn
and not be quenched.

21" 'This is what the LORD Almighty, the God of Israel, says: Go
ahead, add your burnt offerings to
your other sacrifices[a] and eat[b] the
meat yourselves! 22For when I
brought your forefathers out of
Egypt and spoke to them, I did not
just give them commands about
burnt offerings and sacrifices,[c]
23but I gave them this command:
Obey[d] me, and I will be your God
and you will be my people.[e] Walk
in all the ways I command you, that
it may go well[f] with you. 24But
they did not listen or pay attention;[g] instead, they followed the
stubborn inclinations of their evil
hearts. They went backward and
not forward. 25From the time your
forefathers left Egypt until now,
day after day, again and again I sent
you my servants the prophets.[h]
26But they did not listen to me or
pay attention. They were stiff-
necked and did more evil than their
forefathers.'[i]

27"When you tell[j] them all this,
they will not listen[k] to you; when
you call to them, they will not an-

7:2 [a] Jer 17:19
7:3 [b] Jer 18:11; 26:13
7:4 [c] Mic 3:11
7:5 [d] Jer 22:3
7:6 [e] Jer 2:34; 19:4 [f] Dt 8:19
7:7 [g] Dt 4:40
7:9 [h] Jer 11:13,17 [i] Ex 20:3
7:10 [j] Jer 32:34; Eze 23:38-39
7:11 [k] Isa 56:7 [l] Mt 21:13*; Mk 11:17*; Lk 19:46* [m] Jer 29:23
7:12 [n] Jos 18:1 [o] 1Sa 4:10-11, 22; Ps 78:60-64
7:13 [p] 2Ch 36:15 [q] Isa 65:12 [r] Jer 35:17
7:14 [s] 1Ki 9:7
7:15 [t] Ps 78:67
7:16 [u] Ex 32:10; Dt 9:14; Jer 15:1
7:18 [v] Jer 44:17-19 [w] Jer 19:13 [x] 1Ki 14:9
7:19 [y] Jer 9:19
7:20 [z] Jer 42:18; La 2:3-5
7:21 [a] Isa 1:11; Am 5:21-22 [b] Hos 8:13
7:22 [c] 1Sa 15:22; Ps 51:16; Hos 6:6
7:23 [d] Ex 19:5 [e] Lev 26:12 [f] Ex 15:26
7:24 [g] Ps 81:11-12; Jer 11:8
7:25 [h] Jer 25:4
7:26 [i] Jer 16:12
7:27 [j] Eze 2:7 [k] Eze 3:7

n9 Or *and swear by false gods*

swer. 28Therefore say to them,
'This is the nation that has not
obeyed the LORD its God or responded to correction. Truth has
perished; it has vanished from their
lips. 29Cut off[a] your hair and throw
it away; take up a lament on the
barren heights, for the LORD has rejected and abandoned[b] this generation that is under his wrath.

The Valley of Slaughter

30" 'The people of Judah have
done evil in my eyes, declares the
LORD. They have set up their detestable idols[c] in the house that bears
my Name and have defiled[d] it.
31They have built the high places
of Topheth[e] in the Valley of Ben
Hinnom to burn their sons and
daughters[f] in the fire—something
I did not command, nor did it enter
my mind.[g] 32So beware, the days
are coming, declares the LORD,
when people will no longer call it
Topheth or the Valley of Ben Hinnom, but the Valley of Slaughter,[h]
for they will bury[i] the dead in Topheth until there is no more room.
33Then the carcasses of this people
will become food[j] for the birds of
the air and the beasts of the earth,
and there will be no one to frighten
them away. 34I will bring an end to
the sounds[k] of joy and gladness
and to the voices of bride and
bridegroom[l] in the towns of Judah
and the streets of Jerusalem, for
the land will become desolate.[m]

8 " 'At that time, declares the
LORD, the bones of the kings
and officials of Judah, the bones of
the priests and prophets, and the
bones of the people of Jerusalem
will be removed from their graves.
2They will be exposed to the sun
and the moon and all the stars of
the heavens, which they have loved
and served[n] and which they have
followed and consulted and worshiped. They will not be gathered
up or buried, but will be like refuse
lying on the ground. 3Wherever I
banish them, all the survivors of
this evil nation will prefer death to
life,[o] declares the LORD Almighty.'

7:29 [a] Job 1:20; Isa 15:2; Mic 1:16 [b] Jer 6:30
7:30 [c] Eze 7:20-22 [d] Jer 32:34
7:31 [e] 2Ki 23:10 [f] Ps 106:38 [g] Jer 19:5
7:32 [h] Jer 19:6 [i] Jer 19:11
7:33 [j] Dt 28:26
7:34 [k] Isa 24:8; Eze 26:13 [l] Rev 18:23 [m] Lev 26:34
8:2 [n] 2Ki 23:5; Ac 7:42
8:3 [o] Job 3:22; Rev 9:6
8:4 [p] Pr 24:16
8:5 [q] Jer 5:27 [r] Jer 7:24; 9:6
8:6 [s] Rev 9:20 [t] Ps 14:1-3
8:7 [u] Isa 1:3; Jer 5:4-5
8:8 [v] Ro 2:17
8:9 [w] Jer 6:15 [x] Jer 6:19
8:10 [y] Jer 6:12 [z] Isa 56:11

Sin and Punishment

4"Say to them, 'This is what the
LORD says:

" 'When men fall down, do they
not get up?[p]
When a man turns away,
does he not return?
5Why then have these people
turned away?
Why does Jerusalem always
turn away?
They cling to deceit;[q]
they refuse to return.[r]
6I have listened attentively,
but they do not say what is
right.
No one repents[s] of his
wickedness,
saying, "What have I done?"
Each pursues his own course[t]
like a horse charging into
battle.
7Even the stork in the sky
knows her appointed
seasons,
and the dove, the swift and the
thrush
observe the time of their
migration.
But my people do not know[u]
the requirements of the
LORD.

8" 'How can you say, "We are
wise,
for we have the law[v] of the
LORD,"
when actually the lying pen of
the scribes
has handled it falsely?
9The wise[w] will be put to
shame;
they will be dismayed and
trapped.
Since they have rejected the
word[x] of the LORD,
what kind of wisdom do they
have?
10Therefore I will give their wives
to other men
and their fields to new
owners.[y]
From the least to the greatest,
all are greedy for gain;[z]
prophets and priests alike,
all practice deceit.

11They dress the wound of my
people
as though it were not
serious.
"Peace, peace," they say,
when there is no peace.[a]
12Are they ashamed of their
loathsome conduct?
No, they have no shame[b] at
all;
they do not even know how
to blush.
So they will fall among the
fallen;
they will be brought down
when they are
punished,[c]
says the LORD.[d]

13" 'I will take away their harvest,
declares the LORD.
There will be no grapes on
the vine.[e]
There will be no figs[f] on the
tree,
and their leaves will wither.[g]
What I have given them
will be taken[h] from
them.[o]' "

14"Why are we sitting here?
Gather together!
Let us flee to the fortified
cities[i]
and perish there!
For the LORD our God has
doomed us to perish
and given us poisoned
water[j] to drink,
because we have sinned[k]
against him.
15We hoped for peace[l]
but no good has come,
for a time of healing
but there was only terror.[m]
16The snorting of the enemy's
horses
is heard from Dan;[n]
at the neighing of their
stallions
the whole land trembles.
They have come to devour
the land and everything in it,
the city and all who live
there."

17"See, I will send venomous
snakes[o] among you,
vipers that cannot be
charmed,[p]
and they will bite you,"
declares the LORD.

18O my Comforter[p] in sorrow,
my heart is faint[q] within me.
19Listen to the cry of my people
from a land far away:[r]
"Is the LORD not in Zion?
Is her King no longer there?"

"Why have they provoked me to
anger with their images,
with their worthless foreign
idols?"[s]

20"The harvest is past,
the summer has ended,
and we are not saved."

21Since my people are crushed, I
am crushed;
I mourn,[t] and horror grips
me.
22Is there no balm in Gilead?[u]
Is there no physician there?
Why then is there no healing[v]
for the wound of my people?

9 1Oh, that my head were a
spring of water
and my eyes a fountain of
tears!
I would weep[w] day and night
for the slain of my people.[x]
2Oh, that I had in the desert
a lodging place for travelers,
so that I might leave my people
and go away from them;
for they are all adulterers,[y]
a crowd of unfaithful people.

3"They make ready their tongue
like a bow, to shoot lies;[z]
it is not by truth
that they triumph[q] in the
land.
They go from one sin to
another;
they do not acknowledge
me,"
declares the LORD.
4"Beware of your friends;
do not trust your brothers.[a]

8:11 [a]Jer 6:14
8:12 [b]Jer 3:3 [c]Ps 52:5-7; Isa 3:9 [d]Jer 6:15
8:13 [e]Joel 1:7 [f]Lk 13:6 [g]Mt 21:19 [h]Jer 5:17
8:14 [i]Jer 4:5; Jer 35:11 [j]Dt 29:18; Jer 9:15; 23:15 [k]Jer 14:7,20
8:15 [l]ver 11 [m]Jer 14:19
8:16 [n]Jer 4:15
8:17 [o]Nu 21:6; Dt 32:24 [p]Ps 58:5
8:18 [q]La 5:17
8:19 [r]Jer 9:16 [s]Dt 32:21
8:21 [t]Jer 14:17
8:22 [u]Ge 37:25 [v]Jer 30:12
9:1 [w]Jer 13:17; La 2:11,18 [x]Isa 22:4
9:2 [y]Jer 5:7-8; 23:10; Hos 4:2
9:3 [z]Ps 64:3
9:4 [a]Mic 7:5-6

[o]13 The meaning of the Hebrew for this sentence is uncertain. [p]18 The meaning of the Hebrew for this word is uncertain.
[q]3 Or *lies; / they are not valiant for truth*

For every brother is a
deceiver,[r][a]
and every friend a slanderer.
5 Friend deceives friend,
and no one speaks the truth.
They have taught their tongues
to lie;
they weary themselves with
sinning.
6 You[s] live in the midst of
deception;[b]
in their deceit they refuse to
acknowledge me,"
declares the LORD.

7 Therefore this is what the LORD
Almighty says:

"See, I will refine[c] and test[d]
them,
for what else can I do
because of the sin of my
people?
8 Their tongue[e] is a deadly
arrow;
it speaks with deceit.
With his mouth each speaks
cordially to his neighbor,
but in his heart he sets a
trap[f] for him.
9 Should I not punish them for
this?"
declares the LORD.
"Should I not avenge[g] myself
on such a nation as this?"

10 I will weep and wail for the
mountains
and take up a lament
concerning the desert
pastures.
They are desolate and
untraveled,
and the lowing of cattle is
not heard.
The birds of the air[h] have fled
and the animals are gone.

11 "I will make Jerusalem a heap
of ruins,
a haunt of jackals;[i]
and I will lay waste the towns
of Judah
so no one can live there."[j]

12 What man is wise[k] enough to
understand this? Who has been instructed by the LORD and can explain it? Why has the land been ru-

9:4 [a] Ge 27:35
9:6 [b] Jer 5:27
9:7 [c] Isa 1:25 [d] Jer 6:27
9:8 [e] ver 3 [f] Jer 5:26
9:9 [g] Jer 5:9,29
9:10 [h] Jer 4:25; 12:4; Hos 4:3
9:11 [i] Isa 34:13 [j] Isa 25:2; Jer 26:9
9:12 [k] Ps 107:43; Hos 14:9
9:13 [l] 2Ch 7:19; Ps 89:30-32
9:14 [m] Jer 2:8,23 [n] Jer 7:24
9:15 [o] La 3:15 [p] Jer 8:14
9:16 [q] Lev 26:33 [r] Dt 28:64 [s] Eze 5:2 [t] Jer 44:27; Eze 5:12
9:17 [u] 2Ch 35:25; Ecc 12:5; Am 5:16
9:18 [v] Jer 14:17
9:19 [w] Jer 4:13
9:20 [x] Isa 32:9-13

ined and laid waste like a desert
that no one can cross?
13 The LORD said, "It is because
they have forsaken my law, which I
set before them; they have not
obeyed me or followed my law.[l]
14 Instead, they have followed[m] the
stubbornness of their hearts;[n] they
have followed the Baals, as their fathers taught them." 15 Therefore,
this is what the LORD Almighty, the
God of Israel, says: "See, I will
make this people eat bitter food[o]
and drink poisoned water.[p] 16 I will
scatter them among nations[q] that
neither they nor their fathers have
known,[r] and I will pursue them
with the sword[s] until I have destroyed them."[t]

17 This is what the LORD Almighty
says:

"Consider now! Call for the
wailing women[u] to
come;
send for the most skillful of
them.
18 Let them come quickly
and wail over us
till our eyes overflow with tears
and water streams from our
eyelids.[v]
19 The sound of wailing is heard
from Zion:
'How ruined[w] we are!
How great is our shame!
We must leave our land
because our houses are in
ruins.'"
20 Now, O women, hear the word
of the LORD;
open your ears to the words
of his mouth.
Teach your daughters how to
wail;
teach one another a
lament.[x]
21 Death has climbed in through
our windows
and has entered our
fortresses;
it has cut off the children from
the streets

[r] 4 Or *a deceiving Jacob* [s] 6 That is, Jeremiah (the Hebrew is singular)

and the young men[a] from
the public squares.

22Say, "This is what the LORD declares:

" 'The dead bodies of men will
lie
like refuse[b] on the open
field,
like cut grain behind the
reaper,
with no one to gather
them.' "

23This is what the LORD says:

"Let not the wise man boast of
his wisdom[c]
or the strong man boast of
his strength[d]
or the rich man boast of his
riches,[e]
24but let him who boasts boast[f]
about this:
that he understands and
knows me,
that I am the LORD,[g] who
exercises kindness,[h]
justice and righteousness[i]
on earth,
for in these I delight,"
declares the LORD.

25"The days are coming," declares the LORD, "when I will punish
all who are circumcised only in the
flesh[j]— 26Egypt, Judah, Edom,
Ammon, Moab and all who live in
the desert in distant places.[t][k] For
all these nations are really uncircumcised, and even the whole
house of Israel is uncircumcised in
heart.[l]"

God and Idols

10:12–16pp — Jer 51:15–19

10 Hear what the LORD says to you, O house of Israel.
2This is what the LORD says:

"Do not learn the ways of the
nations[m]
or be terrified by signs in the
sky,
though the nations are
terrified by them.
3For the customs of the peoples
are worthless;
they cut a tree out of the
forest,
and a craftsman[n] shapes it
with his chisel.
4They adorn it with silver and
gold;
they fasten it with hammer
and nails
so it will not totter.[o]
5Like a scarecrow in a melon
patch,
their idols cannot speak;[p]
they must be carried
because they cannot walk.[q]
Do not fear them;
they can do no harm
nor can they do any good."[r]

6No one is like you, O LORD;
you are great,[s]
and your name is mighty in
power.
7Who should not revere you,
O King of the nations?[t]
This is your due.
Among all the wise men of the
nations
and in all their kingdoms,
there is no one like you.
8They are all senseless and
foolish;[u]
they are taught by worthless
wooden idols.
9Hammered silver is brought
from Tarshish
and gold from Uphaz.
What the craftsman and
goldsmith have made[v]
is then dressed in blue and
purple—
all made by skilled workers.
10But the LORD is the true God;
he is the living God, the
eternal King.
When he is angry, the earth
trembles;
the nations cannot endure
his wrath.[w]

11"Tell them this: 'These gods,
who did not make the heavens and
the earth, will perish[x] from the
earth and from under the heavens.' "[u]

9:21 [a] 2Ch 36:17
9:22 [b] Jer 8:2
9:23 [c] Ecc 9:11 [d] 1Ki 20:11 [e] Eze 28:4-5
9:24 [f] 1Co 1:31*; Gal 6:14 [g] 2Co 10:17* [h] Ps 51:1; Mic 7:18 [i] Ps 36:6
9:25 [j] Ro 2:8-9
9:26 [k] Jer 25:23 [l] Lev 26:41; Ac 7:51; Ro 2:28
10:2 [m] Lev 20:23
10:3 [n] Isa 40:19
10:4 [o] Isa 41:7
10:5 [p] 1Co 12:2 [q] Ps 115:5,7 [r] Isa 41:24; 46:7
10:6 [s] Ps 48:1
10:7 [t] Ps 22:28; Rev 15:4
10:8 [u] Isa 40:19; Jer 4:22
10:9 [v] Ps 115:4; Isa 40:19
10:10 [w] Ps 76:7
10:11 [x] Ps 96:5; Isa 2:18

[t] 26 Or *desert and who clip the hair by their foreheads* [u] 11 The text of this verse is in Aramaic.

12But God made the earth by his power;
he founded the world by his wisdom
and stretched out the heavens[a] by his understanding.
13When he thunders,[b] the waters in the heavens roar;
he makes clouds rise from the ends of the earth.
He sends lightning with the rain[c]
and brings out the wind from his storehouses.

14Everyone is senseless and without knowledge;
every goldsmith is shamed by his idols.
His images are a fraud;
they have no breath in them.
15They are worthless,[d] the objects of mockery;
when their judgment comes, they will perish.
16He who is the Portion[e] of Jacob is not like these,
for he is the Maker of all things,[f]
including Israel, the tribe of his inheritance[g]—
the LORD Almighty is his name.[h]

Coming Destruction

17Gather up your belongings[i] to leave the land,
you who live under siege.
18For this is what the LORD says:
"At this time I will hurl[j] out those who live in this land;
I will bring distress on them
so that they may be captured."

19Woe to me because of my injury!
My wound[k] is incurable!
Yet I said to myself,
"This is my sickness, and I must endure[l] it."
20My tent[m] is destroyed;
all its ropes are snapped.
My sons are gone from me and are no more;[n]
no one is left now to pitch my tent
or to set up my shelter.
21The shepherds are senseless
and do not inquire of the LORD;
so they do not prosper
and all their flock is scattered.[o]
22Listen! The report is coming—
a great commotion from the land of the north!
It will make the towns of Judah desolate,
a haunt of jackals.[p]

Jeremiah's Prayer

23I know, O LORD, that a man's life is not his own;
it is not for man to direct his steps.[q]
24Correct me, LORD, but only with justice—
not in your anger,[r]
lest you reduce me to nothing.[s]
25Pour out your wrath on the nations[t]
that do not acknowledge you,
on the peoples who do not call on your name.[u]
For they have devoured[v] Jacob;
they have devoured him completely
and destroyed his homeland.[w]

The Covenant Is Broken

11 This is the word that came to Jeremiah from the LORD:
2"Listen to the terms of this covenant and tell them to the people of Judah and to those who live in Jerusalem.
3Tell them that this is what the LORD, the God of Israel, says: 'Cursed[x] is the man who does not obey the terms of this covenant—
4the terms I commanded your forefathers when I brought them out of Egypt, out of the iron-smelting furnace.[y]' I said, 'Obey[z] me and do everything I command you, and you will be my people,[a] and I will be your God.
5Then I will fulfill the oath I

10:12 [a]Ge 1:1,8; Job 9:8; Isa 40:22
10:13 [b]Job 36:29 [c]Ps 135:7
10:15 [d]Isa 41:24; Jer 14:22
10:16 [e]Dt 32:9; Ps 119:57 [f]ver 12 [g]Ps 74:2 [h]Jer 31:35; 32:18
10:17 [i]Eze 12:3-12
10:18 [j]1Sa 25:29
10:19 [k]Jer 14:17 [l]Mic 7:9
10:20 [m]Jer 4:20 [n]Jer 31:15; La 1:5
10:21 [o]Jer 23:2
10:22 [p]Jer 9:11
10:23 [q]Pr 20:24
10:24 [r]Ps 6:1; 38:1 [s]Jer 30:11
10:25 [t]Zep 3:8 [u]Job 18:21; Ps 14:4 [v]Ps 79:7; Jer 8:16 [w]Ps 79:6-7
11:3 [x]Dt 27:26; Gal 3:10
11:4 [y]Dt 4:20; 1Ki 8:51 [z]Ex 24:8 [a]Jer 7:23; 31:33

swore[a] to your forefathers, to give them a land flowing with milk and honey'—the land you possess today."

I answered, "Amen, LORD."

6The LORD said to me, "Proclaim all these words in the towns of Judah and in the streets of Jerusalem: 'Listen to the terms of this covenant and follow[b] them. 7From the time I brought your forefathers up from Egypt until today, I warned them again and again,[c] saying, "Obey me." 8But they did not listen or pay attention;[d] instead, they followed the stubbornness of their evil hearts. So I brought on them all the curses[e] of the covenant I had commanded them to follow but that they did not keep.' "

9Then the LORD said to me, "There is a conspiracy[f] among the people of Judah and those who live in Jerusalem. 10They have returned to the sins of their forefathers,[g] who refused to listen to my words. They have followed other gods[h] to serve them. Both the house of Israel and the house of Judah have broken the covenant I made with their forefathers. 11Therefore this is what the LORD says: 'I will bring on them a disaster[i] they cannot escape. Although they cry[j] out to me, I will not listen[k] to them. 12The towns of Judah and the people of Jerusalem will go and cry out to the gods to whom they burn incense,[l] but they will not help them at all when disaster[m] strikes. 13You have as many gods as you have towns, O Judah; and the altars you have set up to burn incense[n] to that shameful[o] god Baal are as many as the streets of Jerusalem.'

14"Do not pray[p] for this people nor offer any plea or petition for them, because I will not listen[q] when they call to me in the time of their distress.

15"What is my beloved doing in
my temple
as she works out her evil
schemes with many?
Can consecrated meat avert
⌊your punishment⌋?
When you engage in your
wickedness,
then you rejoice.[v]"

16The LORD called you a thriving
olive tree
with fruit beautiful in form.
But with the roar of a mighty
storm
he will set it on fire,[r]
and its branches will be
broken.[s]

17The LORD Almighty, who planted[t] you, has decreed disaster for you, because the house of Israel and the house of Judah have done evil and provoked me to anger by burning incense to Baal.[u]

Plot Against Jeremiah

18Because the LORD revealed their plot to me, I knew it, for at that time he showed me what they were doing. 19I had been like a gentle lamb led to the slaughter; I did not realize that they had plotted[v] against me, saying,

"Let us destroy the tree and its
fruit;
let us cut him off from the
land of the living,[w]
that his name be
remembered[x] no more."
20But, O LORD Almighty, you who
judge righteously
and test the heart and
mind,[y]
let me see your vengeance
upon them,
for to you I have committed
my cause.

21"Therefore this is what the LORD says about the men of Anathoth who are seeking your life[z] and saying, 'Do not prophesy in the name of the LORD or you will die[a] by our hands'— 22therefore this is what the LORD Almighty says: 'I will punish them. Their young men[b] will die by the sword, their sons and daughters by famine. 23Not

11:5 [a]Ex 13:5; Dt 7:12; Ps 105:8-11
11:6 [b]Dt 15:5; Ro 2:13; Jas 1:22
11:7 [c]2Ch 36:15
11:8 [d]Jer 7:26 [e]Lev 26:14-43
11:9 [f]Eze 22:25
11:10 [g]Dt 9:7 [h]Jdg 2:12-13
11:11 [i]2Ki 22:16 [j]Jer 14:12; Eze 8:18 [k]ver 14; Pr 1:28; Isa 1:15; Zec 7:13
11:12 [l]Jer 44:17 [m]Dt 32:37
11:13 [n]Jer 7:9 [o]Jer 3:24
11:14 [p]Ex 32:10 [q]ver 11
11:16 [r]Jer 21:14 [s]Isa 27:11; Ro 11:17-24
11:17 [t]Isa 5:2; Jer 12:2 [u]Jer 7:9
11:19 [v]Jer 18:18; 20:10 [w]Job 28:13; Isa 53:8 [x]Ps 83:4
11:20 [y]Ps 7:9
11:21 [z]Jer 12:6 [a]Jer 26:8,11; 38:4
11:22 [b]Jer 18:21

[v]15 Or *Could consecrated meat avert your punishment? / Then you would rejoice*

even a remnant[a] will be left to them, because I will bring disaster on the men of Anathoth in the year of their punishment.[b]' "

Jeremiah's Complaint

12 You are always righteous,[c] O LORD,
when I bring a case before you.
Yet I would speak with you about your justice:
Why does the way of the wicked prosper?[d]
Why do all the faithless live at ease?
2You have planted[e] them, and they have taken root;
they grow and bear fruit.
You are always on their lips
but far from their hearts.[f]
3Yet you know me, O LORD;
you see me and test[g] my thoughts about you.
Drag them off like sheep to be butchered!
Set them apart for the day of slaughter![h]
4How long will the land lie parched[w][i]
and the grass in every field be withered?[j]
Because those who live in it are wicked,
the animals and birds have perished.[k]
Moreover, the people are saying,
"He will not see what happens to us."

God's Answer

5"If you have raced with men on foot
and they have worn you out,
how can you compete with horses?
If you stumble in safe country,[x]
how will you manage in the thickets[l] by[y] the Jordan?
6Your brothers, your own family—
even they have betrayed you;
they have raised a loud cry against you.[m]
Do not trust them,
though they speak well of you.[n]

7"I will forsake my house,
abandon[o] my inheritance;
I will give the one I love
into the hands of her enemies.
8My inheritance has become to me
like a lion in the forest.
She roars at me;
therefore I hate her.[p]
9Has not my inheritance become to me
like a speckled bird of prey
that other birds of prey surround and attack?
Go and gather all the wild beasts;
bring them to devour.[q]
10Many shepherds[r] will ruin my vineyard
and trample down my field;
they will turn my pleasant field
into a desolate wasteland.[s]
11It will be made a wasteland,
parched and desolate before me;[t]
the whole land will be laid waste
because there is no one who cares.
12Over all the barren heights in the desert
destroyers will swarm,
for the sword of the LORD[u] will devour
from one end of the land to the other;[v]
no one will be safe.
13They will sow wheat but reap thorns;
they will wear themselves out but gain nothing.[w]
So bear the shame of your harvest
because of the LORD's fierce anger."[x]

14This is what the LORD says: "As for all my wicked neighbors who

11:23 [a]Jer 6:9 [b]Jer 23:12
12:1 [c]Ezr 9:15 [d]Jer 5:27-28
12:2 [e]Jer 11:17 [f]Isa 29:13; Jer 3:10; Mt 15:8; Tit 1:16
12:3 [g]Ps 7:9; 11:5; 139:1-4; Jer 11:20 [h]Jer 17:18
12:4 [i]Jer 4:28 [j]Joel 1:10-12 [k]Jer 4:25; 9:10
12:5 [l]Jer 49:19; 50:44
12:6 [m]Pr 26:24-25; Jer 9:4 [n]Ps 12:2
12:7 [o]Jer 7:29
12:8 [p]Hos 9:15; Am 6:8
12:9 [q]Isa 56:9; Jer 15:3; Eze 23:25
12:10 [r]Jer 23:1 [s]Isa 5:1-7
12:11 [t]ver 4; Isa 42:25; Jer 23:10
12:12 [u]Jer 47:6 [v]Jer 3:2
12:13 [w]Lev 26:20; Dt 28:38; Mic 6:15; Hag 1:6 [x]Jer 4:26

[w]4 Or *land mourn* [x]5 Or *If you put your trust in a land of safety* [y]5 Or *the flooding of*

seize the inheritance I gave my people Israel, I will uproot[a] them from their lands and I will uproot the house of Judah from among them. **15**But after I uproot them, I will again have compassion and will bring[b] each of them back to his own inheritance and his own country. **16**And if they learn well the ways of my people and swear by my name, saying, 'As surely as the LORD lives'[c]—even as they once taught my people to swear by Baal[d]—then they will be established among my people.[e] **17**But if any nation does not listen, I will completely uproot and destroy[f] it," declares the LORD.

A Linen Belt

13 This is what the LORD said to me: "Go and buy a linen belt and put it around your waist, but do not let it touch water." **2**So I bought a belt, as the LORD directed, and put it around my waist.

3Then the word of the LORD came to me a second time: **4**"Take the belt you bought and are wearing around your waist, and go now to Perath[z] and hide it there in a crevice in the rocks." **5**So I went and hid it at Perath, as the LORD told me.[g]

6Many days later the LORD said to me, "Go now to Perath and get the belt I told you to hide there." **7**So I went to Perath and dug up the belt and took it from the place where I had hidden it, but now it was ruined and completely useless.

8Then the word of the LORD came to me: **9**"This is what the LORD says: 'In the same way I will ruin the pride of Judah and the great pride[h] of Jerusalem. **10**These wicked people, who refuse to listen to my words, who follow the stubbornness of their hearts[i] and go after other gods[j] to serve and worship them, will be like this belt—completely useless! **11**For as a belt is bound around a man's waist, so I bound the whole house of Israel and the whole house of Judah to me,' declares the LORD, 'to be my people for my renown[k] and praise and honor.[l] But they have not listened.'[m]

Wineskins

12"Say to them: 'This is what the LORD, the God of Israel, says: Every wineskin should be filled with wine.' And if they say to you, 'Don't we know that every wineskin should be filled with wine?' **13**then tell them, 'This is what the LORD says: I am going to fill with drunkenness[n] all who live in this land, including the kings who sit on David's throne, the priests, the prophets and all those living in Jerusalem. **14**I will smash them one against the other, fathers and sons alike, declares the LORD. I will allow no pity or mercy or compassion[o] to keep me from destroying[p] them.' "

Threat of Captivity

15Hear and pay attention,
do not be arrogant,
for the LORD has spoken.
16Give glory[q] to the LORD your God
before he brings the darkness,
before your feet stumble[r]
on the darkening hills.
You hope for light,
but he will turn it to thick darkness
and change it to deep gloom.[s]
17But if you do not listen,[t]
I will weep in secret
because of your pride;
my eyes will weep bitterly,
overflowing with tears,[u]
because the LORD's flock[v]
will be taken captive.[w]
18Say to the king and to the queen mother,
"Come down from your thrones,
for your glorious crowns
will fall from your heads."
19The cities in the Negev will be shut up,
and there will be no one to open them.

[z]4 Or possibly *the Euphrates*; also in verses 5-7

12:14 [a]Zec 2:7-9
12:15 [b]Am 9:14-15
12:16 [c]Jer 4:2 [d]Jos 23:7 [e]Isa 49:6; Jer 3:17
12:17 [f]Isa 60:12
13:5 [g]Ex 40:16
13:9 [h]Lev 26:19
13:10 [i]Jer 11:8; 16:12 [j]Jer 9:14
13:11 [k]Jer 32:20; 33:9 [l]Ex 19:5-6 [m]Jer 7:26
13:13 [n]Ps 60:3; 75:8; Isa 51:17; 63:6; Jer 51:57
13:14 [o]Jer 16:5 [p]Dt 29:20; Eze 5:10
13:16 [q]Jos 7:19 [r]Jer 23:12 [s]Isa 59:9
13:17 [t]Mal 2:2 [u]Jer 9:1 [v]Ps 80:1; Jer 23:1 [w]Jer 14:18

All Judah[a] will be carried into
exile,
carried completely away.

20Lift up your eyes and see
those who are coming from
the north.[b]
Where is the flock[c] that was
entrusted to you,
the sheep of which you
boasted?
21What will you say when ⌊the
LORD⌋ sets over you
those you cultivated as your
special allies?[d]
Will not pain grip you
like that of a woman in
labor?[e]
22And if you ask yourself,
"Why has this happened to
me?"—
it is because of your many
sins[f]
that your skirts have been
torn off
and your body mistreated.[g]
23Can the Ethiopian[a] change his
skin
or the leopard its spots?
Neither can you do good
who are accustomed to doing
evil.

24"I will scatter you like chaff[h]
driven by the desert wind.[i]
25This is your lot,
the portion[j] I have decreed
for you,"
declares the LORD,
"because you have forgotten
me
and trusted in false gods.
26I will pull up your skirts over
your face
that your shame may be
seen[k]—
27your adulteries and lustful
neighings,
your shameless
prostitution![l]
I have seen your detestable
acts
on the hills and in the
fields.[m]
Woe to you, O Jerusalem!
How long will you be
unclean?"[n]

13:19 [a]Jer 20:4; 52:30
13:20 [b]Jer 6:22; Hab 1:6 [c]Jer 23:2
13:21 [d]Jer 38:22 [e]Jer 4:31
13:22 [f]Jer 9:2-6; 16:10-12 [g]Eze 16:37; Na 3:5-6
13:24 [h]Ps 1:4 [i]Lev 26:33
13:25 [j]Job 20:29; Mt 24:51
13:26 [k]La 1:8; Eze 16:37; Hos 2:10
13:27 [l]Jer 2:20 [m]Eze 6:13 [n]Hos 8:5
14:2 [o]Isa 3:26; Jer 8:21
14:3 [p]2Ki 18:31; Job 6:19-20 [q]2Sa 15:30
14:4 [r]Jer 3:3
14:5 [s]Isa 15:6
14:6 [t]Job 39:5-6; Jer 2:24
14:7 [u]Hos 5:5 [v]Jer 5:6 [w]Jer 8:14
14:8 [x]Jer 17:13
14:9 [y]Isa 50:2 [z]Jer 8:19 [a]Isa 63:19; Jer 15:16

Drought, Famine, Sword

14 This is the word of the LORD to Jeremiah concerning the drought:

2"Judah mourns,[o]
her cities languish;
they wail for the land,
and a cry goes up from
Jerusalem.
3The nobles send their servants
for water;
they go to the cisterns
but find no water.[p]
They return with their jars
unfilled;
dismayed and despairing,
they cover their heads.[q]
4The ground is cracked
because there is no rain in
the land;[r]
the farmers are dismayed
and cover their heads.
5Even the doe in the field
deserts her newborn fawn
because there is no grass.[s]
6Wild donkeys stand on the
barren heights[t]
and pant like jackals;
their eyesight fails
for lack of pasture."
7Although our sins testify[u]
against us,
O LORD, do something for the
sake of your name.
For our backsliding[v] is great;
we have sinned[w] against you.
8O Hope[x] of Israel,
its Savior in times of distress,
why are you like a stranger in
the land,
like a traveler who stays only
a night?
9Why are you like a man taken
by surprise,
like a warrior powerless to
save?[y]
You are among[z] us, O LORD,
and we bear your name;[a]
do not forsake us!

10This is what the LORD says
about this people:

"They greatly love to wander;

[a]23 Hebrew *Cushite* (probably a person from the upper Nile region)

they do not restrain their
feet.[a]
So the LORD does not accept[b]
them;
he will now remember[c] their
wickedness
and punish them for their
sins."[d]

[11]Then the LORD said to me, "Do
not pray[e] for the well-being of this
people. [12]Although they fast, I will
not listen to their cry;[f] though
they offer burnt offerings[g] and
grain offerings, I will not accept[h]
them. Instead, I will destroy them
with the sword, famine and
plague."
[13]But I said, "Ah, Sovereign
LORD, the prophets keep telling
them, 'You will not see the sword
or suffer famine.[i] Indeed, I will
give you lasting peace in this
place.' "
[14]Then the LORD said to me,
"The prophets are prophesying
lies[j] in my name. I have not sent[k]
them or appointed them or spoken
to them. They are prophesying to
you false visions,[l] divinations,[m]
idolatries[b] and the delusions of
their own minds. [15]Therefore, this
is what the LORD says about the
prophets who are prophesying in
my name: I did not send them, yet
they are saying, 'No sword or famine will touch this land.' Those
same prophets will perish[n] by
sword and famine.[o] [16]And the
people they are prophesying to will
be thrown out into the streets of Jerusalem because of the famine and
sword. There will be no one to
bury[p] them or their wives, their
sons or their daughters.[q] I will
pour out on them the calamity they
deserve.[r]

[17]"Speak this word to them:

" 'Let my eyes overflow with
tears[s]
night and day without
ceasing;
for my virgin daughter—my
people—
has suffered a grievous
wound,
a crushing blow.[t]
[18]If I go into the country,
I see those slain by the
sword;
if I go into the city,
I see the ravages of famine.[u]
Both prophet and priest
have gone to a land they
know not.' "

[19]Have you rejected Judah
completely?[v]
Do you despise Zion?
Why have you afflicted us
so that we cannot be
healed?[w]
We hoped for peace
but no good has come,
for a time of healing
but there is only terror.[x]
[20]O LORD, we acknowledge our
wickedness
and the guilt of our fathers;
we have indeed sinned[y]
against you.
[21]For the sake of your name[z] do
not despise us;
do not dishonor your glorious
throne.[a]
Remember your covenant with
us
and do not break it.
[22]Do any of the worthless idols of
the nations bring rain?[b]
Do the skies themselves send
down showers?
No, it is you, O LORD our God.
Therefore our hope is in you,
for you are the one who does
all this.

15 Then the LORD said to me:
"Even if Moses[c] and Samuel[d] were to stand before me, my
heart would not go out to this people.[e] Send them away from my
presence![f] Let them go! [2]And if
they ask you, 'Where shall we go?'
tell them, 'This is what the LORD
says:

" 'Those destined for death, to
death;
those for the sword, to the
sword;[g]
those for starvation, to
starvation;[h]

14:10 [a]Ps 119:101; Jer 2:25 [b]Jer 6:20; Am 5:22 [c]Hos 9:9 [d]Jer 44:21-23; Hos 8:13
14:11 [e]Ex 32:10
14:12 [f]Isa 1:15; Jer 11:11 [g]Jer 7:21 [h]Jer 6:20
14:13 [i]Jer 5:12
14:14 [j]Jer 27:14 [k]Jer 23:21,32 [l]Jer 23:16 [m]Eze 12:24
14:15 [n]Eze 14:9 [o]Jer 5:12-13
14:16 [p]Ps 79:3 [q]Jer 7:33 [r]Pr 1:31
14:17 [s]Jer 9:1 [t]Jer 8:21
14:18 [u]Eze 7:15
14:19 [v]Jer 7:29 [w]Jer 30:12-13 [x]Jer 8:15
14:20 [y]Da 9:7-8
14:21 [z]ver 7 [a]Jer 3:17
14:22 [b]Ps 135:7
15:1 [c]Ex 32:11; Nu 14:13-20 [d]1Sa 7:9 [e]Jer 7:16; Eze 14:14,20 [f]2Ki 17:20
15:2 [g]Jer 43:11 [h]Jer 14:12

[b]14 Or *visions, worthless divinations*

those for captivity, to
captivity.'[a]

3"I will send four kinds of destroyers[b] against them," declares the LORD, "the sword to kill and the dogs to drag away and the birds[c] of the air and the beasts of the earth to devour and destroy.[d] 4I will make them abhorrent[e] to all the kingdoms of the earth[f] because of what Manasseh[g] son of Hezekiah king of Judah did in Jerusalem.

5"Who will have pity[h] on you,
O Jerusalem?
Who will mourn for you?
Who will stop to ask how you
are?
6You have rejected[i] me,"
declares the LORD.
"You keep on backsliding.
So I will lay hands[j] on you
and destroy you;
I can no longer show
compassion.
7I will winnow them with a
winnowing fork
at the city gates of the land.
I will bring bereavement and
destruction on my
people,[k]
for they have not changed
their ways.
8I will make their widows more
numerous
than the sand of the sea.
At midday I will bring a
destroyer[l]
against the mothers of their
young men;
suddenly I will bring down on
them
anguish and terror.
9The mother of seven will grow
faint[m]
and breathe her last.
Her sun will set while it is still
day;
she will be disgraced and
humiliated.
I will put the survivors to the
sword[n]
before their enemies,"
declares the LORD.

10Alas, my mother, that you gave
me birth,[o]
a man with whom the whole
land strives and
contends![p]
I have neither lent[q] nor
borrowed,
yet everyone curses me.

11The LORD said,

"Surely I will deliver you[r] for a
good purpose;
surely I will make your
enemies plead[s] with
you
in times of disaster and
times of distress.
12"Can a man break iron—
iron from the north[t]—or
bronze?
13Your wealth and your treasures
I will give as plunder,
without charge,[u]
because of all your sins
throughout your country.[v]
14I will enslave you to your
enemies
in[c] a land you do not
know,[w]
for my anger will kindle a fire[x]
that will burn against you."
15You understand, O LORD;
remember me and care for
me.
Avenge me on my
persecutors.[y]
You are long-suffering—do not
take me away;
think of how I suffer
reproach for your sake.[z]
16When your words came, I ate[a]
them;
they were my joy and my
heart's delight,[b]
for I bear your name,[c]
O LORD God Almighty.
17I never sat[d] in the company of
revelers,
never made merry with them;
I sat alone because your hand
was on me
and you had filled me with
indignation.
18Why is my pain unending

15:2 [a]Rev 13:10
15:3 [b]Lev 26:16 [c]Dt 28:26 [d]Lev 26:22; Eze 14:21
15:4 [e]Jer 24:9; 29:18 [f]Dt 28:25 [g]2Ki 21:2; 23:26-27
15:5 [h]Isa 51:19; Jer 13:14; 21:7; Na 3:7
15:6 [i]Jer 6:19; 7:24 [j]Zep 1:4
15:7 [k]Jer 18:21
15:8 [l]Jer 6:4
15:9 [m]1Sa 2:5 [n]Jer 21:7
15:10 [o]Job 3:1 [p]Jer 1:19 [q]Lev 25:36
15:11 [r]Jer 40:4 [s]Jer 21:1-2; 37:3; 42:1-3
15:12 [t]Jer 28:14
15:13 [u]Ps 44:12 [v]Jer 17:3
15:14 [w]Dt 28:36; Jer 16:13 [x]Dt 32:22; Ps 21:9
15:15 [y]Jer 12:3 [z]Ps 69:7-9
15:16 [a]Eze 3:3; Rev 10:10 [b]Ps 119:72, 103 [c]Jer 14:9
15:17 [d]Ps 1:1; 26:4-5; Jer 16:8

[c]14 Some Hebrew manuscripts, Septuagint and Syriac (see also Jer. 17:4); most Hebrew manuscripts *I will cause your enemies to bring you / into*

and my wound grievous and
incurable?[a]
Will you be to me like a
deceptive brook,
like a spring that fails?[b]

19Therefore this is what the LORD
says:

"If you repent, I will restore
you
that you may serve[c] me;
if you utter worthy, not
worthless, words,
you will be my spokesman.
Let this people turn to you,
but you must not turn to
them.
20I will make you a wall to this
people,
a fortified wall of bronze;
they will fight against you
but will not overcome you,
for I am with you
to rescue and save you,"[d]
declares the LORD.
21"I will save you from the hands
of the wicked
and redeem[e] you from the
grasp of the cruel."[f]

Day of Disaster

16 Then the word of the LORD
came to me: **2**"You must
not marry[g] and have sons or
daughters in this place." **3**For this
is what the LORD says about the
sons and daughters born in this
land and about the women who are
their mothers and the men who are
their fathers:[h] **4**"They will die of
deadly diseases. They will not be
mourned or buried[i] but will be
like refuse lying on the ground.[j]
They will perish by sword and famine, and their dead bodies will become food for the birds of the air
and the beasts of the earth."[k]

5For this is what the LORD says:
"Do not enter a house where there
is a funeral meal; do not go to
mourn or show sympathy, because
I have withdrawn my blessing, my
love and my pity from this people,"
declares the LORD. **6**"Both high and
low will die in this land.[l] They will
not be buried or mourned, and no
one will cut[m] himself or shave[n] his
head for them. **7**No one will offer
food to comfort those who mourn[o]
for the dead—not even for a father
or a mother—nor will anyone give
them a drink to console them.

8"And do not enter a house
where there is feasting and sit
down to eat and drink.[p] **9**For this
is what the LORD Almighty, the God
of Israel, says: Before your eyes and
in your days I will bring an end to
the sounds[q] of joy and gladness
and to the voices of bride and
bridegroom in this place.[r]

10"When you tell these people
all this and they ask you, 'Why has
the LORD decreed such a great disaster against us? What wrong have
we done? What sin have we committed against the LORD our God?'[s]
11then say to them, 'It is because
your fathers forsook me,' declares
the LORD, 'and followed other gods
and served and worshiped them.
They forsook me and did not keep
my law.[t] **12**But you have behaved
more wickedly than your fathers.[u]
See how each of you is following
the stubbornness of his evil heart[v]
instead of obeying me. **13**So I will
throw you out of this land into a
land neither you nor your fathers
have known,[w] and there you will
serve other gods[x] day and night,
for I will show you no favor.'[y]

14"However, the days are coming," declares the LORD, "when men
will no longer say, 'As surely as the
LORD lives, who brought the Israelites up out of Egypt,'[z] **15**but they
will say, 'As surely as the LORD lives,
who brought the Israelites up out
of the land of the north and out of
all the countries where he had banished them.'[a] For I will restore[b]
them to the land I gave their forefathers.

16"But now I will send for many
fishermen," declares the LORD,
"and they will catch them.[c] After
that I will send for many hunters,
and they will hunt[d] them down on
every mountain and hill and from
the crevices of the rocks.[e] **17**My
eyes are on all their ways; they are
not hidden[f] from me, nor is their
sin concealed from my eyes.[g] **18**I

15:18 [a]Jer 30:15; Mic 1:9 [b]Job 6:15
15:19 [c]Zec 3:7
15:20 [d]Jer 20:11; Eze 3:8
15:21 [e]Jer 50:34 [f]Ge 48:16
16:2 [g]1Co 7:26-27
16:3 [h]Jer 6:21
16:4 [i]Jer 25:33 [j]Ps 83:10; Jer 9:22 [k]Ps 79:1-3; Jer 15:3; 34:20
16:6 [l]Eze 9:5-6 [m]Lev 19:28 [n]Jer 41:5; 47:5
16:7 [o]Eze 24:17; Hos 9:4
16:8 [p]Ecc 7:2-4; Jer 15:17
16:9 [q]Isa 24:8; Eze 26:13; Hos 2:11 [r]Rev 18:23
16:10 [s]Dt 29:24; Jer 5:19
16:11 [t]Dt 29:25-26; 1Ki 9:9; Ps 106:35-43; Jer 22:9
16:12 [u]Jer 7:26 [v]Ecc 9:3; Jer 13:10
16:13 [w]Dt 28:36; Jer 5:19 [x]Dt 4:28 [y]Jer 15:5
16:14 [z]Dt 15:15; Jer 23:7-8
16:15 [a]Isa 11:11; Jer 23:8 [b]Jer 24:6
16:16 [c]Am 4:2; Hab 1:14-15 [d]Am 9:3; Mic 7:2 [e]1Sa 26:20
16:17 [f]1Co 4:5; Heb 4:13 [g]Pr 15:3

will repay them double[a] for their wickedness and their sin, because they have defiled my land[b] with the lifeless forms of their vile images and have filled my inheritance with their detestable idols."

19O LORD, my strength and my fortress,
my refuge in time of distress,
to you the nations will come[c]
from the ends of the earth
and say,
"Our fathers possessed nothing
but false gods,[d]
worthless idols that did them
no good.
20Do men make their own gods?
Yes, but they are not gods!"[e]

21"Therefore I will teach them—
this time I will teach them
my power and might.
Then they will know
that my name is the LORD.

17 "Judah's sin is engraved
with an iron tool,[f]
inscribed with a flint point,
on the tablets of their hearts[g]
and on the horns of their
altars.
2Even their children remember
their altars and Asherah
poles[d][h]
beside the spreading trees
and on the high hills.[i]
3My mountain in the land
and your[e] wealth and all
your treasures
I will give away as plunder,[j]
together with your high
places,[k]
because of sin throughout
your country.[l]
4Through your own fault you
will lose
the inheritance[m] I gave you.
I will enslave you to your
enemies[n]
in a land[o] you do not know,
for you have kindled my anger,
and it will burn[p] forever."

5This is what the LORD says:

"Cursed is the one who trusts
in man,[q]
who depends on flesh for his
strength
and whose heart turns away
from the LORD.
6He will be like a bush in the
wastelands;
he will not see prosperity
when it comes.
He will dwell in the parched
places of the desert,
in a salt[r] land where no one
lives.

7"But blessed is the man who
trusts[s] in the LORD,
whose confidence is in him.
8He will be like a tree planted
by the water
that sends out its roots by
the stream.
It does not fear when heat
comes;
its leaves are always green.
It has no worries in a year of
drought[t]
and never fails to bear
fruit."[u]

9The heart[v] is deceitful above
all things
and beyond cure.
Who can understand it?

10"I the LORD search the heart[w]
and examine the mind,[x]
to reward[y] a man according to
his conduct,
according to what his deeds
deserve."[z]

11Like a partridge that hatches
eggs it did not lay
is the man who gains riches
by unjust means.
When his life is half gone, they
will desert him,
and in the end he will prove
to be a fool.[a]

12A glorious throne,[b] exalted
from the beginning,
is the place of our sanctuary.
13O LORD, the hope[c] of Israel,
all who forsake[d] you will be
put to shame.
Those who turn away from you

16:18 [a]Isa 40:2; Rev 18:6 [b]Nu 35:34; Jer 2:7
16:19 [c]Isa 2:2; Jer 3:17 [d]Ps 4:2
16:20 [e]Ps 115:4-7; Isa 37:19; Jer 2:11
17:1 [f]Job 19:24 [g]Pr 3:3; 2Co 3:3
17:2 [h]2Ch 24:18 [i]Jer 2:20
17:3 [j]2Ki 24:13 [k]Jer 26:18; Mic 3:12 [l]Jer 15:13
17:4 [m]La 5:2 [n]Dt 28:48; Jer 12:7 [o]Jer 16:13 [p]Jer 7:20; 15:14
17:5 [q]Isa 2:22; 30:1-3
17:6 [r]Dt 29:23; Job 39:6
17:7 [s]Ps 34:8; 40:4; Pr 16:20
17:8 [t]Jer 14:1-6 [u]Ps 1:3; 92:12-14
17:9 [v]Ecc 9:3; Mt 13:15; Mk 7:21-22
17:10 [w]1Sa 16:7; Rev 2:23 [x]Ps 17:3; 139:23; Jer 11:20; 20:12; Ro 8:27 [y]Ps 62:12; Jer 32:19 [z]Ro 2:6
17:11 [a]Lk 12:20
17:12 [b]Jer 3:17
17:13 [c]Jer 14:8 [d]Isa 1:28; Jer 2:17

[d]2 That is, symbols of the goddess Asherah
[e]2,3 Or *hills / 3and the mountains of the land. / Your*

will be written in the
dust
because they have forsaken
the LORD,
the spring of living water.

14Heal me, O LORD, and I will be
healed;
save me and I will be saved,
for you are the one I praise.[a]
15They keep saying to me,
"Where is the word of the
LORD?
Let it now be fulfilled!"[b]
16I have not run away from being
your shepherd;
you know I have not desired
the day of despair.
What passes my lips is open
before you.
17Do not be a terror[c] to me;
you are my refuge[d] in the
day of disaster.
18Let my persecutors be put to
shame,
but keep me from shame;
let them be terrified,
but keep me from terror.
Bring on them the day of
disaster;
destroy them with double
destruction.[e]

Keeping the Sabbath Holy

19This is what the LORD said to
me: "Go and stand at the gate of
the people, through which the
kings of Judah go in and out; stand
also at all the other gates of Jerusalem.[f] 20Say to them, 'Hear the
word of the LORD, O kings of Judah
and all people of Judah and everyone living in Jerusalem[g] who
come through these gates.[h] 21This
is what the LORD says: Be careful
not to carry a load on the Sabbath[i]
day or bring it through the gates of
Jerusalem. 22Do not bring a load
out of your houses or do any work
on the Sabbath, but keep the Sabbath day holy, as I commanded
your forefathers.[j] 23Yet they did
not listen or pay attention;[k] they
were stiff-necked[l] and would not
listen or respond to discipline.[m]
24But if you are careful to obey me,
declares the LORD, and bring no
load through the gates of this city
on the Sabbath, but keep the Sabbath day holy by not doing any
work on it, 25then kings who sit on
David's throne[n] will come through
the gates of this city with their officials. They and their officials will
come riding in chariots and on
horses, accompanied by the men of
Judah and those living in Jerusalem, and this city will be inhabited
forever. 26People will come from
the towns of Judah and the villages
around Jerusalem, from the territory of Benjamin and the western
foothills, from the hill country and
the Negev,[o] bringing burnt offerings and sacrifices, grain offerings,
incense and thank offerings to the
house of the LORD. 27But if you do
not obey[p] me to keep the Sabbath
day holy by not carrying any load as
you come through the gates of Jerusalem on the Sabbath day, then I
will kindle an unquenchable fire[q]
in the gates of Jerusalem that will
consume her fortresses.' "[r]

At the Potter's House

18 This is the word that came
to Jeremiah from the LORD:
2"Go down to the potter's house,
and there I will give you my message." 3So I went down to the potter's house, and I saw him working
at the wheel. 4But the pot he was
shaping from the clay was marred
in his hands; so the potter formed
it into another pot, shaping it as
seemed best to him.

5Then the word of the LORD came
to me: 6"O house of Israel, can I
not do with you as this potter
does?" declares the LORD. "Like
clay[s] in the hand of the potter, so
are you in my hand, O house of Israel. 7If at any time I announce that
a nation or kingdom is to be uprooted,[t] torn down and destroyed,
8and if that nation I warned repents of its evil, then I will relent[u]
and not inflict on it the disaster[v] I
had planned. 9And if at another
time I announce that a nation or
kingdom is to be built[w] up and
planted, 10and if it does evil[x] in my
sight and does not obey me, then I

17:14 [a] Ps 109:1
17:15 [b] Isa 5:19; 2Pe 3:4
17:17 [c] Ps 88:15-16 [d] Jer 16:19; Na 1:7
17:18 [e] Ps 35:1-8
17:19 [f] Jer 7:2; 26:2
17:20 [g] Jer 19:3 [h] Jer 22:2
17:21 [i] Nu 15:32-36; Ne 13:15-21; Jn 5:10
17:22 [j] Ex 20:8; 31:13; Isa 56:2-6; Eze 20:12
17:23 [k] Jer 7:26 [l] Jer 19:15 [m] Jer 7:28
17:25 [n] 2Sa 7:13; Isa 9:7; Jer 22:2,4; Lk 1:32
17:26 [o] Jer 32:44; 33:13; Zec 7:7
17:27 [p] Jer 22:5 [q] Jer 7:20 [r] 2Ki 25:9; Am 2:5
18:6 [s] Isa 45:9; Ro 9:20-21
18:7 [t] Jer 1:10
18:8 [u] Jer 26:13; Jnh 3:8-10 [v] Eze 18:21; Hos 11:8-9
18:9 [w] Jer 1:10; 31:28
18:10 [x] Eze 33:18

will reconsider[a] the good I had intended to do for it.

11"Now therefore say to the people of Judah and those living in Jerusalem, 'This is what the LORD
says: Look! I am preparing a disaster[b] for you and devising a plan
against you. So turn[c] from your
evil ways,[d] each one of you, and
reform your ways and your actions.'
12But they will reply, 'It's no use.[e]
We will continue with our own
plans; each of us will follow the
stubbornness of his evil heart.' "

13Therefore this is what the LORD
says:

"Inquire among the nations:
    Who has ever heard anything
        like this?[f]
A most horrible[g] thing has
        been done
    by Virgin Israel.
14Does the snow of Lebanon
    ever vanish from its rocky
        slopes?
Do its cool waters from distant
        sources
    ever cease to flow?[f]
15Yet my people have forgotten
        me;
    they burn incense to
        worthless idols,[h]
which made them stumble in
        their ways
    and in the ancient paths.[i]
They made them walk in
        bypaths
    and on roads not built up.[j]
16Their land will be laid waste,[k]
    an object of lasting scorn;[l]
all who pass by will be appalled
    and will shake their heads.[m]
17Like a wind[n] from the east,
    I will scatter them before
        their enemies;
I will show them my back and
        not my face[o]
    in the day of their disaster."

18They said, "Come, let's make
plans[p] against Jeremiah; for the
teaching of the law by the priest[q]
will not be lost, nor will counsel
from the wise, nor the word from
the prophets.[r] So come, let's attack him with our tongues[s] and
pay no attention to anything he
says."

19Listen to me, O LORD;
    hear what my accusers are
        saying!
20Should good be repaid with
        evil?
    Yet they have dug a pit[t] for
        me.
Remember that I stood before
        you
    and spoke in their behalf[u]
    to turn your wrath away from
        them.
21So give their children over to
        famine;[v]
    hand them over to the power
        of the sword.
Let their wives be made
        childless and widows;[w]
    let their men be put to
        death,
    their young men slain by the
        sword in battle.
22Let a cry[x] be heard from their
        houses
    when you suddenly bring
        invaders against them,
for they have dug a pit to
        capture me
    and have hidden snares[y] for
        my feet.
23But you know, O LORD,
    all their plots to kill[z] me.
Do not forgive[a] their crimes
    or blot out their sins from
        your sight.
Let them be overthrown before
        you;
    deal with them in the time of
        your anger.

19 This is what the LORD says:
"Go and buy a clay jar from
a potter.[b] Take along some of the
elders[c] of the people and of the
priests 2and go out to the Valley of
Ben Hinnom,[d] near the entrance
of the Potsherd Gate. There proclaim the words I tell you, 3and say,
'Hear the word of the LORD, O
kings[e] of Judah and people of Jerusalem. This is what the LORD Almighty, the God of Israel, says: Lis-

18:10 [a] 1Sa 2:29-30
18:11 [b] Jer 4:6 [c] 2Ki 17:13; Isa 1:16-19 [d] Jer 7:3
18:12 [e] Isa 57:10; Jer 2:25
18:13 [f] Isa 66:8; Jer 2:10 [g] Jer 5:30
18:15 [h] Jer 10:15 [i] Jer 6:16 [j] Isa 57:14; 62:10
18:16 [k] Jer 25:9 [l] Jer 19:8 [m] Ps 22:7
18:17 [n] Jer 13:24 [o] Jer 2:27
18:18 [p] Jer 11:19 [q] Mal 2:7 [r] Jer 5:13 [s] Ps 52:2
18:20 [t] Ps 35:7; 57:6 [u] Ps 106:23
18:21 [v] Jer 11:22 [w] Ps 109:9
18:22 [x] Jer 6:26 [y] Ps 140:5
18:23 [z] Jer 11:21 [a] Ps 109:14
19:1 [b] Jer 18:2 [c] Nu 11:17
19:2 [d] Jos 15:8
19:3 [e] Jer 17:20

[f] 14 The meaning of the Hebrew for this sentence is uncertain.

ten! I am going to bring a disaster[a] on this place that will make the ears of everyone who hears of it tingle.[b] **4**For they have forsaken[c] me and made this a place of foreign gods; they have burned sacrifices[d] in it to gods that neither they nor their fathers nor the kings of Judah ever knew, and they have filled this place with the blood of the innocent.[e] **5**They have built the high places of Baal to burn their sons[f] in the fire as offerings to Baal—something I did not command or mention, nor did it enter my mind.[g] **6**So beware, the days are coming, declares the LORD, when people will no longer call this place Topheth or the Valley of Ben Hinnom,[h] but the Valley of Slaughter.[i]

7" 'In this place I will ruin[g] the plans of Judah and Jerusalem. I will make them fall by the sword before their enemies,[j] at the hands of those who seek their lives, and I will give their carcasses[k] as food[l] to the birds of the air and the beasts of the earth. **8**I will devastate this city and make it an object of scorn;[m] all who pass by will be appalled and will scoff because of all its wounds. **9**I will make them eat[n] the flesh of their sons and daughters, and they will eat one another's flesh during the stress of the siege imposed on them by the enemies[o] who seek their lives.'

10"Then break the jar[p] while those who go with you are watching, **11**and say to them, 'This is what the LORD Almighty says: I will smash[q] this nation and this city just as this potter's jar is smashed and cannot be repaired. They will bury[r] the dead in Topheth until there is no more room. **12**This is what I will do to this place and to those who live here, declares the LORD. I will make this city like Topheth. **13**The houses[s] in Jerusalem and those of the kings of Judah will be defiled like this place, Topheth—all the houses where they burned incense on the roofs to all the starry hosts[t] and poured out drink offerings[u] to other gods.' "

14Jeremiah then returned from Topheth, where the LORD had sent him to prophesy, and stood in the court[v] of the LORD's temple and said to all the people, **15**"This is what the LORD Almighty, the God of Israel, says: 'Listen! I am going to bring on this city and the villages around it every disaster I pronounced against them, because they were stiff-necked[w] and would not listen to my words.' "

Jeremiah and Pashhur

20 When the priest Pashhur son of Immer,[x] the chief officer[y] in the temple of the LORD, heard Jeremiah prophesying these things, **2**he had Jeremiah the prophet beaten[z] and put in the stocks[a] at the Upper Gate of Benjamin[b] at the LORD's temple. **3**The next day, when Pashhur released him from the stocks, Jeremiah said to him, "The LORD's name for you is not Pashhur, but Magor-Missabib.[h][c] **4**For this is what the LORD says: 'I will make you a terror to yourself and to all your friends; with your own eyes[d] you will see them fall by the sword of their enemies. I will hand[e] all Judah over to the king of Babylon, who will carry[f] them away to Babylon or put them to the sword. **5**I will hand over to their enemies all the wealth[g] of this city—all its products, all its valuables and all the treasures of the kings of Judah. They will take it away[h] as plunder and carry it off to Babylon. **6**And you, Pashhur, and all who live in your house will go into exile to Babylon. There you will die and be buried, you and all your friends to whom you have prophesied[i] lies.' "

Jeremiah's Complaint

7O LORD, you deceived[i] me, and
I was deceived[i];
you overpowered me and
prevailed.
I am ridiculed all day long;

19:3 [a]Jer 6:19 [b]1Sa 3:11
19:4 [c]Dt 28:20; Isa 65:11 [d]Lev 18:21 [e]2Ki 21:16; Jer 2:34
19:5 [f]Lev 18:21; Ps 106:37-38 [g]Jer 7:31; 32:35
19:6 [h]Jos 15:8 [i]Jer 7:32
19:7 [j]Lev 26:17; Dt 28:25 [k]Jer 16:4; 34:20 [l]Ps 79:2
19:8 [m]Jer 18:16
19:9 [n]Lev 26:29; Dt 28:49-57; La 4:10 [o]Isa 9:20
19:10 [p]ver 1
19:11 [q]Ps 2:9; Isa 30:14 [r]Jer 7:32
19:13 [s]Jer 32:29; 52:13 [t]Dt 4:19; Ac 7:42 [u]Jer 7:18; Eze 20:28
19:14 [v]2Ch 20:5; Jer 26:2
19:15 [w]Ne 9:16; Jer 7:26; 17:23
20:1 [x]1Ch 24:14 [y]2Ki 25:18
20:2 [z]Jer 1:19 [a]Job 13:27 [b]Jer 37:13; 38:7; Zec 14:10
20:3 [c]ver 10
20:4 [d]Jer 29:21 [e]Jer 21:10 [f]Jer 52:27
20:5 [g]Jer 17:3 [h]2Ki 20:17
20:6 [i]Jer 14:15; La 2:14

g7 The Hebrew for *ruin* sounds like the Hebrew for *jar* (see verses 1 and 10).
h3 *Magor-Missabib* means *terror on every side.*
i7 Or *persuaded*

everyone mocks me.
8Whenever I speak, I cry out
proclaiming violence and
destruction.[a]
So the word of the LORD has
brought me
insult and reproach[b] all day
long.
9But if I say, "I will not mention
him
or speak any more in his
name,"
his word is in my heart like a
fire,[c]
a fire shut up in my bones.
I am weary of holding it in;[d]
indeed, I cannot.
10I hear many whispering,
"Terror[e] on every side!
Report[f] him! Let's report
him!"
All my friends[g]
are waiting for me to slip,[h]
saying,
"Perhaps he will be deceived;
then we will prevail[i] over
him
and take our revenge on
him."

11But the LORD[j] is with me like a
mighty warrior;
so my persecutors[k] will
stumble and not
prevail.[l]
They will fail and be thoroughly
disgraced;[m]
their dishonor will never be
forgotten.
12O LORD Almighty, you who
examine the righteous
and probe the heart and
mind,[n]
let me see your vengeance[o]
upon them,
for to you I have committed[p]
my cause.
13Sing to the LORD!
Give praise to the LORD!
He rescues[q] the life of the
needy
from the hands of the
wicked.

14Cursed be the day I was born![r]
May the day my mother bore
me not be blessed!

15Cursed be the man who
brought my father the
news,
who made him very glad,
saying,
"A child is born to you—a
son!"
16May that man be like the
towns[s]
the LORD overthrew without
pity.
May he hear wailing in the
morning,
a battle cry at noon.
17For he did not kill me in the
womb,[t]
with my mother as my grave,
her womb enlarged forever.
18Why did I ever come out of the
womb
to see trouble and sorrow
and to end my days in
shame?[u]

God Rejects Zedekiah's Request

21 The word came to Jeremiah
from the LORD when King
Zedekiah[v] sent to him Pashhur[w]
son of Malkijah and the priest
Zephaniah[x] son of Maaseiah. They
said: 2"Inquire[y] now of the LORD
for us because Nebuchadnezzar[i][z]
king of Babylon is attacking us.
Perhaps the LORD will perform wonders[a] for us as in times past so that
he will withdraw from us."
3But Jeremiah answered them,
"Tell Zedekiah, 4'This is what the
LORD, the God of Israel, says: I am
about to turn[b] against you the
weapons of war that are in your
hands, which you are using to fight
the king of Babylon and the Babylonians[k] who are outside the wall
besieging[c] you. And I will gather
them inside this city. 5I myself will
fight against you with an outstretched hand[d] and a mighty arm
in anger and fury and great wrath.
6I will strike down those who live in
this city—both men and animals
—and they will die of a terrible

i2 Hebrew *Nebuchadrezzar,* of which *Nebuchadnezzar* is a variant; here and often in Jeremiah and Ezekiel k4 Or *Chaldeans;* also in verse 9

20:8 [a] Jer 6:7 [b] 2Ch 36:16; Jer 6:10
20:9 [c] Ps 39:3 [d] Job 32:18-20; Ac 4:20
20:10 [e] Ps 31:13; Jer 6:25 [f] Isa 29:21 [g] Ps 41:9 [h] Lk 11:53-54 [i] 1Ki 19:2
20:11 [j] Jer 1:8; Ro 8:31 [k] Jer 17:18 [l] Jer 15:20 [m] Jer 23:40
20:12 [n] Jer 17:10 [o] Ps 54:7; 59:10 [p] Ps 62:8; Jer 11:20
20:13 [q] Ps 35:10
20:14 [r] Job 3:3; Jer 15:10
20:16 [s] Ge 19:25
20:17 [t] Job 10:18-19
20:18 [u] Ps 90:9
21:1 [v] 2Ki 24:18; Jer 52:1 [w] Jer 38:1 [x] 2Ki 25:18; Jer 29:25; 37:3
21:2 [y] Jer 37:3,7 [z] 2Ki 25:1 [a] Ps 44:1-4; Jer 32:17
21:4 [b] Jer 32:5 [c] Jer 37:8-10
21:5 [d] Jer 6:12

plague.[a] 7After that, declares the
LORD, I will hand over Zedekiah[b]
king of Judah, his officials and the
people in this city who survive the
plague, sword and famine, to Nebuchadnezzar king of Babylon[c] and
to their enemies who seek their
lives. He will put them to the
sword; he will show them no mercy
or pity or compassion.'[d]
8"Furthermore, tell the people,
'This is what the LORD says: See, I
am setting before you the way of
life and the way of death. 9Whoever
stays in this city will die by the
sword, famine or plague.[e] But
whoever goes out and surrenders to
the Babylonians who are besieging
you will live, he will escape with his
life.[f] 10I have determined to do
this city harm[g] and not good, declares the LORD. It will be given into
the hands[h] of the king of Babylon,
and he will destroy it with fire.'[i]
11"Moreover, say to the royal
house[j] of Judah, 'Hear the word of
the LORD; 12O house of David, this
is what the LORD says:

" 'Administer justice[k] every
morning;
rescue from the hand of his
oppressor
the one who has been
robbed,
or my wrath will break out and
burn like fire
because of the evil you have
done—
burn with no one to quench[l]
it.
13I am against[m] you, ⌊Jerusalem,⌋
you who live above this
valley[n]
on the rocky plateau,
declares the LORD—
you who say, "Who can come
against us?
Who can enter our
refuge?"[o]
14I will punish you as your
deeds[p] deserve,
declares the LORD.
I will kindle a fire[q] in your
forests[r]
that will consume everything
around you.' "

Judgment Against Evil Kings

22 This is what the LORD says:
"Go down to the palace of
the king of Judah and proclaim this
message there: 2'Hear the word of
the LORD, O king of Judah, you who
sit on David's throne[s]—you, your
officials and your people who come
through these gates.[t] 3This is
what the LORD says: Do what is
just[u] and right. Rescue from the
hand of his oppressor[v] the one
who has been robbed. Do no wrong
or violence to the alien, the fatherless or the widow,[w] and do not
shed innocent blood in this place.
4For if you are careful to carry out
these commands, then kings[x] who
sit on David's throne will come
through the gates of this palace,
riding in chariots and on horses,
accompanied by their officials and
their people. 5But if you do not
obey[y] these commands, declares
the LORD, I swear[z] by myself that
this palace will become a ruin.' "
6For this is what the LORD says
about the palace of the king of Judah:

"Though you are like Gilead to
me,
like the summit of Lebanon,
I will surely make you like a
desert,[a]
like towns not inhabited.
7I will send destroyers[b] against
you,
each man with his weapons,
and they will cut[c] up your fine
cedar beams
and throw them into the fire.

8"People from many nations will
pass by this city and will ask one
another, 'Why has the LORD done
such a thing to this great city?'[d]
9And the answer will be: 'Because
they have forsaken the covenant of
the LORD their God and have worshiped and served other gods.[e]' "

10Do not weep for the dead[f]
⌊king⌋ or mourn[g] his
loss;
rather, weep bitterly for him
who is exiled,
because he will never return

21:6 [a]Jer 14:12
21:7 [b]2Ki 25:7; Jer 52:9 [c]Jer 37:17; 39:5 [d]2Ch 36:17; Eze 7:9; Hab 1:6
21:9 [e]Jer 14:12 [f]Jer 38:2,17; 39:18; 45:5
21:10 [g]Jer 44:11,27; Am 9:4 [h]Jer 32:28; 38:2-3 [i]Jer 52:13
21:11 [j]Jer 13:18
21:12 [k]Jer 22:3 [l]Isa 1:31
21:13 [m]Eze 13:8 [n]Ps 125:2 [o]Jer 49:4; Ob 1:3-4
21:14 [p]Isa 3:10-11 [q]2Ch 36:19; Jer 52:13 [r]Eze 20:47
22:2 [s]Jer 17:25; Lk 1:32 [t]Jer 17:20
22:3 [u]Mic 6:8; Zec 7:9 [v]Ps 72:4; Jer 21:12 [w]Ex 22:22
22:4 [x]Jer 17:25
22:5 [y]Jer 17:27 [z]Heb 6:13
22:6 [a]Mic 3:12
22:7 [b]Jer 4:7 [c]Isa 10:34
22:8 [d]Dt 29:25-26; 1Ki 9:8-9; Jer 16:10-11
22:9 [e]2Ki 22:17; 2Ch 34:25
22:10 [f]Ecc 4:2 [g]ver 18

nor see his native land again.

[11]For this is what the LORD says
about Shallum[1][a] son of Josiah,
who succeeded his father as king of
Judah but has gone from this
place: "He will never return. [12]He
will die[b] in the place where they
have led him captive; he will not
see this land again."

[13]"Woe to him who builds[c] his
palace by
unrighteousness,
his upper rooms by injustice,
making his countrymen work
for nothing,
not paying[d] them for their
labor.
[14]He says, 'I will build myself a
great palace[e]
with spacious upper rooms.'
So he makes large windows in
it,
panels it with cedar[f]
and decorates it in red.

[15]"Does it make you a king
to have more and more
cedar?
Did not your father have food
and drink?
He did what was right and
just,[g]
so all went well[h] with him.
[16]He defended the cause of the
poor and needy,[i]
and so all went well.
Is that not what it means to
know me?"
declares the LORD.
[17]"But your eyes and your heart
are set only on dishonest
gain,
on shedding innocent blood[j]
and on oppression and
extortion."

[18]Therefore this is what the LORD
says about Jehoiakim son of Josiah
king of Judah:

"They will not mourn for him:
'Alas, my brother! Alas, my
sister!'
They will not mourn for him:
'Alas, my master! Alas, his
splendor!'

22:11 [a]2Ki 23:31
22:12 [b]2Ki 23:34
22:13 [c]Mic 3:10; Hab 2:9 [d]Lev 19:13; Jas 5:4
22:14 [e]Isa 5:8-9 [f]2Sa 7:2
22:15 [g]2Ki 23:25 [h]Ps 128:2; Isa 3:10
22:16 [i]Ps 72:1-4, 12-13
22:17 [j]2Ki 24:4
22:19 [k]Jer 36:30
22:20 [l]Nu 27:12
22:21 [m]Jer 3:25; 32:30 [n]Jer 7:23-28
22:23 [o]Jer 4:31
22:24 [p]2Ki 24:6,8; Jer 37:1
22:25 [q]2Ki 24:16; Jer 34:20
22:26 [r]2Ki 24:8; 2Ch 36:10
22:28 [s]Ps 31:12; Jer 48:38; Hos 8:8

[19]He will have the burial of a
donkey—
dragged away and thrown[k]
outside the gates of
Jerusalem."

[20]"Go up to Lebanon and cry out,
let your voice be heard in
Bashan,
cry out from Abarim,[l]
for all your allies are
crushed.
[21]I warned you when you felt
secure,
but you said, 'I will not
listen!'
This has been your way from
your youth;[m]
you have not obeyed[n] me.
[22]The wind will drive all your
shepherds away,
and your allies will go into
exile.
Then you will be ashamed and
disgraced
because of all your
wickedness.
[23]You who live in 'Lebanon,[m]'
who are nestled in cedar
buildings,
how you will groan when pangs
come upon you,
pain[o] like that of a woman
in labor!

[24]"As surely as I live," declares
the LORD, "even if you, Jehoiachin[n][p] son of Jehoiakim king of
Judah, were a signet ring on my
right hand, I would still pull you
off. [25]I will hand you over[q] to
those who seek your life, those you
fear—to Nebuchadnezzar king of
Babylon and to the Babylonians.[o]
[26]I will hurl[r] you and the mother
who gave you birth into another
country, where neither of you was
born, and there you both will die.
[27]You will never come back to the
land you long to return to."

[28]Is this man Jehoiachin a
despised, broken pot,[s]
an object no one wants?

[l]*11* Also called *Jehoahaz* [m]*23* That is, the palace in Jerusalem (see 1 Kings 7:2) [n]*24* Hebrew *Coniah,* a variant of *Jehoiachin;* also in verse 28 [o]*25* Or *Chaldeans*

Why will he and his children be
hurled[a] out,
cast into a land[b] they do not
know?
29O land,[c] land, land,
hear the word of the LORD!
30This is what the LORD says:
"Record this man as if
childless,[d]
a man who will not prosper[e]
in his lifetime,
for none of his offspring will
prosper,
none will sit on the throne[f]
of David
or rule anymore in Judah."

The Righteous Branch

23 "Woe to the shepherds[g]
who are destroying and
scattering[h] the sheep of my pasture!"[i] declares the LORD. 2There-
fore this is what the LORD, the God
of Israel, says to the shepherds who
tend my people: "Because you have
scattered my flock and driven them
away and have not bestowed care
on them, I will bestow punishment
on you for the evil[j] you have
done," declares the LORD. 3"I myself will gather the remnant[k] of my
flock out of all the countries where
I have driven them and will bring
them back to their pasture, where
they will be fruitful and increase in
number. 4I will place shepherds[l]
over them who will tend them, and
they will no longer be afraid[m] or
terrified, nor will any be missing,[n]" declares the LORD.

5"The days are coming,"
declares the LORD,
"when I will raise up to
David[p] a righteous
Branch,[o]
a King who will reign[p] wisely
and do what is just and
right[q] in the land.
6In his days Judah will be saved
and Israel will live in safety.
This is the name[r] by which he
will be called:
The LORD Our
Righteousness.[s]

7"So then, the days are coming,"
declares the LORD, "when people

22:28 [a]Jer 15:1 [b]Jer 17:4
22:29 [c]Jer 6:19; Mic 1:2
22:30 [d]1Ch 3:18; Mt 1:12 [e]Jer 10:21 [f]Ps 94:20
23:1 [g]Jer 10:21; Eze 34:1-10; Zec 11:15-17 [h]Isa 56:11 [i]Eze 34:31
23:2 [j]Jer 21:12
23:3 [k]Isa 11:10-12; Jer 32:37; Eze 34:11-16
23:4 [l]Jer 3:15; 31:10; Eze 34:23 [m]Jer 30:10; 46:27-28 [n]Jn 6:39
23:5 [o]Isa 4:2 [p]Isa 9:7 [q]Isa 11:1; Zec 6:12
23:6 [r]Jer 33:16; Mt 1:21-23 [s]Ro 3:21-22; 1Co 1:30
23:7 [t]Jer 16:14
23:8 [u]Isa 43:5-6; Am 9:14-15
23:9 [v]Jer 20:8-9
23:10 [w]Jer 9:2 [x]Ps 107:34; Jer 9:10 [y]Hos 4:2-3
23:11 [z]Jer 6:13; 8:10; Zep 3:4 [a]Jer 7:10
23:12 [b]Ps 35:6; Jer 13:16 [c]Jer 11:23
23:13 [d]Jer 2:8
23:14 [e]Jer 5:30 [f]Jer 29:23

will no longer say, 'As surely as the
LORD lives, who brought the Israelites up out of Egypt,'[t] 8but they
will say, 'As surely as the LORD lives,
who brought the descendants of Israel up out of the land of the north
and out of all the countries where
he had banished them.' Then they
will live in their own land."[u]

Lying Prophets

9Concerning the prophets:

My heart is broken within me;
all my bones tremble.
I am like a drunken man,
like a man overcome by
wine,
because of the LORD
and his holy words.[v]
10The land is full of adulterers;[w]
because of the curse[q] the
land lies parched[r]
and the pastures[x] in the
desert are withered.[y]
The ⌊prophets⌋ follow an evil
course
and use their power unjustly.

11"Both prophet and priest are
godless;[z]
even in my temple[a] I find
their wickedness,"
declares the LORD.
12"Therefore their path will
become slippery;[b]
they will be banished to
darkness
and there they will fall.
I will bring disaster on them
in the year they are
punished,[c]"
declares the LORD.

13"Among the prophets of
Samaria
I saw this repulsive thing:
They prophesied by Baal[d]
and led my people Israel
astray.
14And among the prophets of
Jerusalem
I have seen something
horrible:[e]
They commit adultery and
live a lie.[f]

p5 Or *up from David's line* q10 Or *because of these things* r10 Or *land mourns*

They strengthen the hands of
evildoers,[a]
so that no one turns from his
wickedness.
They are all like Sodom[b] to
me;
the people of Jerusalem are
like Gomorrah."[c]

15Therefore, this is what the
LORD Almighty says concerning the
prophets:

"I will make them eat bitter
food
and drink poisoned water,[d]
because from the prophets of
Jerusalem
ungodliness has spread
throughout the land."

16This is what the LORD Almighty
says:

"Do not listen[e] to what the
prophets are prophesying
to you;
they fill you with false hopes.
They speak visions[f] from their
own minds,
not from the mouth[g] of the
LORD.
17They keep saying to those who
despise me,
'The LORD says: You will have
peace.'[h]
And to all who follow the
stubbornness[i] of their
hearts
they say, 'No harm[j] will
come to you.'
18But which of them has stood in
the council of the LORD
to see or to hear his word?
Who has listened and heard
his word?
19See, the storm[k] of the LORD
will burst out in wrath,
a whirlwind swirling down
on the heads of the wicked.
20The anger[l] of the LORD will not
turn back[m]
until he fully accomplishes
the purposes of his heart.
In days to come
you will understand it
clearly.
21I did not send[n] these prophets,

23:14 [a]Eze 13:22 [b]Ge 18:20 [c]Isa 1:9-10; Jer 20:16
23:15 [d]Jer 8:14; 9:15
23:16 [e]Jer 27:9-10, 14; Mt 7:15 [f]Jer 14:14 [g]Jer 9:20
23:17 [h]Jer 8:11 [i]Jer 13:10 [j]Jer 5:12; Am 9:10; Mic 3:11
23:19 [k]Jer 25:32; 30:23
23:20 [l]2Ki 23:26 [m]Jer 30:24
23:21 [n]Jer 14:14; 27:15
23:22 [o]Jer 25:5; Zec 1:4
23:23 [p]Ps 139:1-10
23:24 [q]Job 22:12-14 [r]1Ki 8:27
23:25 [s]Jer 14:14 [t]ver 28,32; Jer 29:8
23:26 [u]1Ti 4:1-2
23:27 [v]Dt 13:1-3; Jer 29:8 [w]Jdg 3:7; 8:33-34
23:29 [x]Jer 5:14
23:30 [y]Ps 34:16 [z]Dt 18:20; Jer 14:15
23:31 [a]ver 17
23:32 [b]ver 25 [c]Jer 7:8; La 2:14

yet they have run with their
message;
I did not speak to them,
yet they have prophesied.
22But if they had stood in my
council,
they would have proclaimed
my words to my people
and would have turned[o] them
from their evil ways
and from their evil deeds.

23"Am I only a God nearby,[p]"
declares the LORD,
"and not a God far away?
24Can anyone hide[q] in secret
places
so that I cannot see him?"
declares the LORD.
"Do not I fill heaven and
earth?"[r]
declares the LORD.

25"I have heard what the prophets say who prophesy lies[s] in my
name. They say, 'I had a dream![t] I
had a dream!'
26How long will this
continue in the hearts of these lying prophets, who prophesy the delusions[u] of their own minds?
27They think the dreams they tell
one another will make my people
forget[v] my name, just as their fathers forgot[w] my name through
Baal worship.
28Let the prophet
who has a dream tell his dream, but
let the one who has my word speak
it faithfully. For what has straw to
do with grain?" declares the LORD.
29"Is not my word like fire,"[x] declares the LORD, "and like a hammer that breaks a rock in pieces?
30"Therefore," declares the
LORD, "I am against[y] the prophets[z] who steal from one another
words supposedly from me.
31Yes,"
declares the LORD, "I am against
the prophets who wag their own
tongues and yet declare, 'The LORD
declares.'[a]
32Indeed, I am against
those who prophesy false
dreams,[b]" declares the LORD.
"They tell them and lead my people astray with their reckless lies,
yet I did not send or appoint them.
They do not benefit[c] these people in the least," declares the
LORD.

False Oracles and False Prophets

33"When these people, or a prophet or a priest, ask you, 'What is the oracle[s][a] of the LORD?' say to them, 'What oracle?[t] I will forsake[b] you, declares the LORD.' 34If a prophet or a priest or anyone else claims, 'This is the oracle[c] of the LORD,' I will punish[d] that man and his household. 35This is what each of you keeps on saying to his friend or relative: 'What is the LORD's answer?'[e] or 'What has the LORD spoken?' 36But you must not mention 'the oracle of the LORD' again, because every man's own word becomes his oracle and so you distort[f] the words of the living God, the LORD Almighty, our God. 37This is what you keep saying to a prophet: 'What is the LORD's answer to you?' or 'What has the LORD spoken?' 38Although you claim, 'This is the oracle of the LORD,' this is what the LORD says: You used the words, 'This is the oracle of the LORD,' even though I told you that you must not claim, 'This is the oracle of the LORD.' 39Therefore, I will surely forget you and cast[g] you out of my presence along with the city I gave to you and your fathers. 40I will bring upon you everlasting disgrace[h]—everlasting shame that will not be forgotten."

Two Baskets of Figs

24 After Jehoiachin[u][i] son of Jehoiakim king of Judah and the officials, the craftsmen and the artisans of Judah were carried into exile from Jerusalem to Babylon by Nebuchadnezzar king of Babylon, the LORD showed me two baskets of figs[j] placed in front of the temple of the LORD. 2One basket had very good figs, like those that ripen early; the other basket had very poor[k] figs, so bad they could not be eaten.

3Then the LORD asked me, "What do you see,[l] Jeremiah?"

"Figs," I answered. "The good ones are very good, but the poor ones are so bad they cannot be eaten."

4Then the word of the LORD came to me: 5"This is what the LORD, the God of Israel, says: 'Like these good figs, I regard as good the exiles from Judah, whom I sent away from this place to the land of the Babylonians.[v] 6My eyes will watch over them for their good, and I will bring them back[m] to this land. I will build[n] them up and not tear them down; I will plant them and not uproot them. 7I will give them a heart to know me, that I am the LORD. They will be my people,[o] and I will be their God, for they will return[p] to me with all their heart.[q]

8" 'But like the poor[r] figs, which are so bad they cannot be eaten,' says the LORD, 'so will I deal with Zedekiah king of Judah, his officials[s] and the survivors[t] from Jerusalem, whether they remain in this land or live in Egypt.[u] 9I will make them abhorrent[v] and an offense to all the kingdoms of the earth, a reproach and a byword,[w] an object of ridicule and cursing,[x] wherever I banish[y] them. 10I will send the sword,[z] famine and plague[a] against them until they are destroyed from the land I gave to them and their fathers.' "

Seventy Years of Captivity

25 The word came to Jeremiah concerning all the people of Judah in the fourth year of Jehoiakim[b] son of Josiah king of Judah, which was the first year of Nebuchadnezzar[c] king of Babylon. 2So Jeremiah the prophet said to all the people of Judah[d] and to all those living in Jerusalem: 3For twenty-three years—from the thirteenth year of Josiah[e] son of Amon king of Judah until this very day—the word of the LORD has come to me and I have spoken to you again and again,[f] but you have not listened.[g]

23:33 [a]Mal 1:1 [b]ver 39
23:34 [c]La 2:14 [d]Zec 13:3
23:35 [e]Jer 33:3; 42:4
23:36 [f]Gal 1:7-8; 2Pe 3:16
23:39 [g]Jer 7:15
23:40 [h]Jer 20:11; Eze 5:14-15
24:1 [i]2Ki 24:16; 2Ch 36:9; Jer 29:2 [j]Am 8:1-2
24:2 [k]Isa 5:4
24:3 [l]Jer 1:11; Am 8:2
24:6 [m]Jer 29:10; Eze 11:17 [n]Jer 33:7; 42:10
24:7 [o]Isa 51:16; Jer 31:33; Heb 8:10 [p]Jer 32:40 [q]Eze 11:19
24:8 [r]Jer 29:17 [s]Jer 39:6 [t]Jer 39:9 [u]Jer 44:1,26
24:9 [v]Jer 15:4; 34:17 [w]Dt 28:25; 1Ki 9:7 [x]Jer 29:18 [y]Dt 28:37
24:10 [z]Isa 51:19 [a]Jer 27:8
25:1 [b]2Ki 24:2; Jer 36:1 [c]2Ki 24:1
25:2 [d]Jer 18:11
25:3 [e]Jer 1:2 [f]Jer 11:7; 26:5 [g]Jer 7:26

[s]33 Or *burden* (see Septuagint and Vulgate) [t]33 Hebrew; Septuagint and Vulgate *'You are the burden.* (The Hebrew for *oracle* and *burden* is the same.) [u]1 Hebrew *Jeconiah,* a variant of *Jehoiachin* [v]5 Or *Chaldeans*

4And though the LORD has sent all his servants the prophets[a] to you again and again, you have not listened or paid any attention. 5They said, "Turn now, each of you, from your evil ways and your evil practices, and you can stay in the land the LORD gave to you and your fathers for ever and ever. 6Do not follow other gods[b] to serve and worship them; do not provoke me to anger with what your hands have made. Then I will not harm you."

7"But you did not listen to me," declares the LORD, "and you have provoked me with what your hands have made,[c] and you have brought harm[d] to yourselves."

8Therefore the LORD Almighty says this: "Because you have not listened to my words, 9I will summon[e] all the peoples of the north[f] and my servant[g] Nebuchadnezzar king of Babylon," declares the LORD, "and I will bring them against this land and its inhabitants and against all the surrounding nations. I will completely destroy[w] them and make them an object of horror and scorn,[h] and an everlasting ruin. 10I will banish from them the sounds[i] of joy and gladness, the voices of bride and bridegroom,[j] the sound of millstones[k] and the light of the lamp.[l] 11This whole country will become a desolate wasteland,[m] and these nations will serve the king of Babylon seventy years.[n]

12"But when the seventy years[o] are fulfilled, I will punish the king of Babylon and his nation, the land of the Babylonians,[x] for their guilt," declares the LORD, "and will make it desolate[p] forever. 13I will bring upon that land all the things I have spoken against it, all that are written in this book and prophesied by Jeremiah against all the nations. 14They themselves will be enslaved[q] by many nations[r] and great kings; I will repay[s] them according to their deeds and the work of their hands."

The Cup of God's Wrath

15This is what the LORD, the God of Israel, said to me: "Take from my hand this cup[t] filled with the wine of my wrath and make all the nations to whom I send you drink it. 16When they drink it, they will stagger[u] and go mad[v] because of the sword I will send among them."

17So I took the cup from the LORD's hand and made all the nations to whom he sent[w] me drink it: 18Jerusalem and the towns of Judah, its kings and officials, to make them a ruin and an object of horror and scorn and cursing,[x] as they are today;[y] 19Pharaoh king of Egypt, his attendants, his officials and all his people, 20and all the foreign people there; all the kings of Uz;[z] all the kings of the Philistines (those of Ashkelon,[a] Gaza, Ekron, and the people left at Ashdod); 21Edom, Moab and Ammon;[b] 22all the kings of Tyre and Sidon;[c] the kings of the coastlands[d] across the sea; 23Dedan, Tema, Buz and all who are in distant places[y];[e] 24all the kings of Arabia[f] and all the kings of the foreign people who live in the desert; 25all the kings of Zimri, Elam[g] and Media; 26and all the kings of the north,[h] near and far, one after the other—all the kingdoms on the face of the earth. And after all of them, the king of Sheshach[z][i] will drink it too.

27"Then tell them, 'This is what the LORD Almighty, the God of Israel, says: Drink, get drunk[j] and vomit, and fall to rise no more because of the sword[k] I will send among you.' 28But if they refuse to take the cup from your hand and drink, tell them, 'This is what the LORD Almighty says: You must drink it! 29See, I am beginning to bring disaster[l] on the city that bears my Name,[m] and will you indeed go unpunished?[n] You will not go unpunished, for I am calling down a sword upon all[o] who live

25:4 [a]Jer 7:25
25:6 [b]Dt 8:19
25:7 [c]Dt 32:21 [d]2Ki 21:15
25:9 [e]Isa 13:3-5 [f]Jer 1:15 [g]Jer 27:6 [h]Jer 18:16
25:10 [i]Isa 24:8; Eze 26:13 [j]Jer 7:34 [k]Ecc 12:3-4 [l]Rev 18:22-23
25:11 [m]Jer 4:26-27; 12:11-12 [n]2Ch 36:21
25:12 [o]Jer 29:10 [p]Isa 13:19-22; 14:22-23
25:14 [q]Jer 27:7 [r]Jer 50:9; 51:27-28 [s]Jer 51:6
25:15 [t]Isa 51:17; Ps 75:8; Rev 14:10
25:16 [u]Na 3:11 [v]Jer 51:7
25:17 [w]Jer 1:10
25:18 [x]Jer 24:9 [y]Jer 44:22
25:20 [z]Job 1:1 [a]Jer 47:5
25:21 [b]Jer 49:1
25:22 [c]Jer 47:4 [d]Jer 31:10
25:23 [e]Jer 9:26; 49:32
25:24 [f]2Ch 9:14
25:25 [g]Ge 10:22
25:26 [h]Jer 50:3,9 [i]Jer 51:41
25:27 [j]ver 16,28; Hab 2:16 [k]Eze 21:4
25:29 [l]Jer 13:12-14 [m]1Pe 4:17 [n]Pr 11:31 [o]ver 30-31

[w]9 The Hebrew term refers to the irrevocable giving over of things or persons to the LORD, often by totally destroying them. [x]12 Or *Chaldeans* [y]23 Or *who clip the hair by their foreheads* [z]26 *Sheshach* is a cryptogram for Babylon.

on the earth, declares the LORD Almighty.'
30"Now prophesy all these words
against them and say to them:

" 'The LORD will roar[a] from on
high;
he will thunder[b] from his
holy dwelling
and roar mightily against his
land.
He will shout like those who
tread the grapes,
shout against all who live on
the earth.
31The tumult will resound to the
ends of the earth,
for the LORD will bring
charges[c] against the
nations;
he will bring judgment on all
mankind
and put the wicked to the
sword,' "
declares the LORD.

32This is what the LORD Almighty
says:

"Look! Disaster is spreading
from nation to nation;[d]
a mighty storm[e] is rising
from the ends of the earth."

33At that time those slain[f] by the
LORD will be everywhere—from one
end of the earth to the other. They
will not be mourned or gathered[g]
up or buried,[h] but will be like refuse lying on the ground.

34Weep and wail, you shepherds;
roll[i] in the dust, you leaders
of the flock.
For your time to be
slaughtered[j] has come;
you will fall and be shattered
like fine pottery.
35The shepherds will have
nowhere to flee,
the leaders of the flock no
place to escape.[k]
36Hear the cry of the shepherds,
the wailing of the leaders of
the flock,
for the LORD is destroying
their pasture.
37The peaceful meadows will be
laid waste
because of the fierce anger of
the LORD.
38Like a lion[l] he will leave his
lair,
and their land will become
desolate
because of the sword[a] of the
oppressor
and because of the LORD's
fierce anger.

Jeremiah Threatened With Death

26 Early in the reign of Jehoiakim[m] son of Josiah king of
Judah, this word came from the
LORD: 2"This is what the LORD says:
Stand in the courtyard[n] of the
LORD's house and speak to all the
people of the towns of Judah who
come to worship in the house of
the LORD. Tell[o] them everything I
command you; do not omit[p] a
word. 3Perhaps they will listen and
each will turn[q] from his evil way.
Then I will relent[r] and not bring
on them the disaster I was planning
because of the evil they have done.
4Say to them, 'This is what the
LORD says: If you do not listen[s] to
me and follow my law,[t] which I
have set before you, 5and if you do
not listen to the words of my servants the prophets, whom I have
sent to you again and again
(though you have not listened[u]),
6then I will make this house like
Shiloh[v] and this city an object of
cursing[w] among all the nations of
the earth.' "
7The priests, the prophets and
all the people heard Jeremiah
speak these words in the house of
the LORD. 8But as soon as Jeremiah
finished telling all the people everything the LORD had commanded
him to say, the priests, the prophets and all the people seized him
and said, "You must die! 9Why do
you prophesy in the LORD's name
that this house will be like Shiloh
and this city will be desolate and
deserted?"[x] And all the people

25:30 [a] Isa 16:10; 42:13 [b] Joel 3:16; Am 1:2
25:31 [c] Hos 4:1; Joel 3:2; Mic 6:2
25:32 [d] Isa 34:2 [e] Jer 23:19
25:33 [f] Isa 66:16; Eze 39:17-20 [g] Jer 16:4 [h] Ps 79:3
25:34 [i] Jer 6:26 [j] Isa 34:6; Jer 50:27
25:35 [k] Job 11:20
25:38 [l] Jer 4:7
26:1 [m] 2Ki 23:36
26:2 [n] Jer 19:14 [o] Jer 1:17; Mt 28:20; Ac 20:27 [p] Dt 4:2
26:3 [q] Jer 36:7 [r] Jer 18:8
26:4 [s] Lev 26:14 [t] 1Ki 9:6
26:5 [u] Jer 25:4
26:6 [v] Jos 18:1 [w] 2Ki 22:19
26:9 [x] Jer 9:11

[a] *38* Some Hebrew manuscripts and Septuagint (see also Jer. 46:16 and 50:16); most Hebrew manuscripts *anger*

crowded around Jeremiah in the house of the LORD.

10When the officials of Judah heard about these things, they went up from the royal palace to the house of the LORD and took their places at the entrance of the New Gate of the LORD's house. 11Then the priests and the prophets said to the officials and all the people, "This man should be sentenced to death[a] because he has prophesied against this city. You have heard it with your own ears!"

12Then Jeremiah said to all the officials[b] and all the people: "The LORD sent me to prophesy[c] against this house and this city all the things you have heard.[d] 13Now reform[e] your ways and your actions and obey the LORD your God. Then the LORD will relent and not bring the disaster he has pronounced against you. 14As for me, I am in your hands;[f] do with me whatever you think is good and right. 15Be assured, however, that if you put me to death, you will bring the guilt of innocent blood on yourselves and on this city and on those who live in it, for in truth the LORD has sent me to you to speak all these words in your hearing."

16Then the officials[g] and all the people said to the priests and the prophets, "This man should not be sentenced to death![h] He has spoken to us in the name of the LORD our God."

17Some of the elders of the land stepped forward and said to the entire assembly of people, 18"Micah[i] of Moresheth prophesied in the days of Hezekiah king of Judah. He told all the people of Judah, 'This is what the LORD Almighty says:

" 'Zion[j] will be plowed like a
field,
Jerusalem will become a
heap of rubble,[k]
the temple hill[l] a mound
overgrown with
thickets.'[b][m]

19"Did Hezekiah king of Judah or anyone else in Judah put him to death? Did not Hezekiah[n] fear the LORD and seek his favor? And did not the LORD relent,[o] so that he did not bring the disaster[p] he pronounced against them? We are about to bring a terrible disaster[q] on ourselves!"

20(Now Uriah son of Shemaiah from Kiriath Jearim[r] was another man who prophesied in the name of the LORD; he prophesied the same things against this city and this land as Jeremiah did. 21When King Jehoiakim[s] and all his officers and officials heard his words, the king sought to put him to death. But Uriah heard of it and fled[t] in fear to Egypt. 22King Jehoiakim, however, sent Elnathan[u] son of Acbor to Egypt, along with some other men. 23They brought Uriah out of Egypt and took him to King Jehoiakim, who had him struck down with a sword and his body thrown into the burial place of the common people.)

24Furthermore, Ahikam[v] son of Shaphan supported Jeremiah, and so he was not handed over to the people to be put to death.

Judah to Serve Nebuchadnezzar

27 Early in the reign of Zedekiah[c][w] son of Josiah king of Judah, this word came to Jeremiah from the LORD: 2This is what the LORD said to me: "Make a yoke[x] out of straps and crossbars and put it on your neck. 3Then send word to the kings of Edom, Moab, Ammon,[y] Tyre and Sidon through the envoys who have come to Jerusalem to Zedekiah king of Judah. 4Give them a message for their masters and say, 'This is what the LORD Almighty, the God of Israel, says: "Tell this to your masters: 5With my great power and outstretched arm[z] I made the earth and its people and the animals that are on it, and I give[a] it to anyone I please. 6Now I will hand all your

26:11 [a]Dt 18:20; Jer 18:23; 38:4; Mt 26:66; Ac 6:11
26:12 [b]Jer 1:18 [c]Am 7:15; Ac 4:18-20; 5:29 [d]ver 2,15
26:13 [e]Jer 7:5; Joel 2:12-14
26:14 [f]Jer 38:5
26:16 [g]Ac 23:9 [h]Ac 5:34-39; 23:29
26:18 [i]Mic 1:1 [j]Isa 2:3 [k]Ne 4:2; Jer 9:11 [l]Mic 4:1; Zec 8:3 [m]Jer 17:3
26:19 [n]2Ch 32:24-26; Isa 37:14-20 [o]Ex 32:14; 2Sa 24:16 [p]Jer 44:7 [q]Hab 2:10
26:20 [r]Jos 9:17
26:21 [s]1Ki 19:2 [t]Mt 10:23
26:22 [u]Jer 36:12,25
26:24 [v]2Ki 22:12
27:1 [w]2Ch 36:11
27:2 [x]Jer 28:10,13
27:3 [y]Jer 25:21
27:5 [z]Dt 9:29 [a]Ps 115:16

[b]*18* Micah 3:12 [c]*1* A few Hebrew manuscripts and Syriac (see also Jer. 27:3, 12 and 28:1); most Hebrew manuscripts *Jehoiakim* (Most Septuagint manuscripts do not have this verse.)

countries over to my servant[a] Nebuchadnezzar[b] king of Babylon; I
will make even the wild animals
subject to him.[c] **7**All nations will
serve[d] him and his son and his
grandson until the time[e] for his
land comes; then many nations
and great kings will subjugate[f]
him.
8" ' "If, however, any nation or
kingdom will not serve Nebuchadnezzar king of Babylon or bow its
neck under his yoke, I will punish
that nation with the sword, famine
and plague, declares the LORD, until I destroy it by his hand. **9**So do
not listen to your prophets, your diviners, your interpreters of dreams,
your mediums[g] or your sorcerers
who tell you, 'You will not serve the
king of Babylon.' **10**They prophesy
lies[h] to you that will only serve to
remove you far from your lands; I
will banish you and you will perish.
11But if any nation will bow its
neck under the yoke[i] of the king of
Babylon and serve him, I will let
that nation remain in its own land
to till it and to live there, declares
the LORD." ' "
12I gave the same message to
Zedekiah king of Judah. I said,
"Bow your neck under the yoke of
the king of Babylon; serve him and
his people, and you will live. **13**Why
will you and your people die[j] by
the sword, famine and plague with
which the LORD has threatened any
nation that will not serve the king
of Babylon? **14**Do not listen to the
words of the prophets who say to
you, 'You will not serve the king of
Babylon,' for they are prophesying
lies[k] to you. **15**'I have not sent[l]
them,' declares the LORD. 'They are
prophesying lies in my name.[m]
Therefore, I will banish you and
you will perish,[n] both you and the
prophets who prophesy to you.' "
16Then I said to the priests and
all these people, "This is what the
LORD says: Do not listen to the
prophets who say, 'Very soon now
the articles[o] from the LORD's house
will be brought back from Babylon.' They are prophesying lies to
you. **17**Do not listen to them. Serve
the king of Babylon, and you will
live. Why should this city become a
ruin? **18**If they are prophets and
have the word of the LORD, let them
plead[p] with the LORD Almighty
that the furnishings remaining in
the house of the LORD and in the
palace of the king of Judah and in
Jerusalem not be taken to Babylon.
19For this is what the LORD Almighty says about the pillars, the
Sea,[q] the movable stands and the
other furnishings[r] that are left in
this city, **20**which Nebuchadnezzar
king of Babylon did not take away
when he carried[s] Jehoiachin[d][t]
son of Jehoiakim king of Judah
into exile from Jerusalem to Babylon, along with all the nobles of
Judah and Jerusalem— **21**yes, this
is what the LORD Almighty, the God
of Israel, says about the things that
are left in the house of the LORD and
in the palace of the king of Judah
and in Jerusalem: **22**'They will be
taken[u] to Babylon and there they
will remain until the day[v] I come
for them,' declares the LORD. 'Then
I will bring[w] them back and restore
them to this place.' "

The False Prophet Hananiah

28 In the fifth month of that
same year, the fourth year,
early in the reign of Zedekiah[x]
king of Judah, the prophet Hananiah son of Azzur, who was from Gibeon,[y] said to me in the house of
the LORD in the presence of the
priests and all the people: **2**"This is
what the LORD Almighty, the God of
Israel, says: 'I will break the yoke[z]
of the king of Babylon. **3**Within two
years I will bring back to this place
all the articles[a] of the LORD's
house that Nebuchadnezzar king of
Babylon removed from here and
took to Babylon. **4**I will also bring
back to this place Jehoiachin[d][b]
son of Jehoiakim king of Judah and
all the other exiles from Judah who
went to Babylon,' declares the
LORD, 'for I will break the yoke of
the king of Babylon.' "

27:6 [a] Jer 25:9 [b] Jer 21:7; Eze 29:18-20 [c] Jer 28:14; Da 2:37-38
27:7 [d] 2Ch 36:20 [e] Jer 25:12 [f] Jer 25:14; Da 5:28
27:9 [g] Dt 18:11
27:10 [h] Jer 23:25
27:11 [i] Jer 21:9
27:13 [j] Eze 18:31
27:14 [k] Jer 14:14
27:15 [l] Jer 23:21 [m] Jer 29:9 [n] Jer 6:15
27:16 [o] 2Ki 24:13; 2Ch 36:7,10; Jer 28:3; Da 1:2
27:18 [p] 1Sa 7:8
27:19 [q] 2Ki 25:13 [r] Jer 52:17-23
27:20 [s] 2Ch 36:10; Jer 24:1 [t] Jer 22:24
27:22 [u] 2Ki 25:13 [v] 2Ch 36:21 [w] Ezr 1:7; 7:19
28:1 [x] Jer 27:1,3 [y] Jos 9:3
28:2 [z] Jer 27:12
28:3 [a] 2Ki 24:13
28:4 [b] Jer 22:24-27

[d] *20,4* Hebrew *Jeconiah,* a variant of *Jehoiachin*

5 Then the prophet Jeremiah replied to the prophet Hananiah before the priests and all the people who were standing in the house of the LORD. 6 He said, "Amen! May the LORD do so! May the LORD fulfill the words you have prophesied by bringing the articles of the LORD's house and all the exiles back to this place from Babylon. 7 Nevertheless, listen to what I have to say in your hearing and in the hearing of all the people: 8 From early times the prophets who preceded you and me have prophesied war, disaster and plague[a] against many countries and great kingdoms. 9 But the prophet who prophesies peace will be recognized as one truly sent by the LORD only if his prediction comes true.[b]"

10 Then the prophet Hananiah took the yoke[c] off the neck of the prophet Jeremiah and broke it, 11 and he said[d] before all the people, "This is what the LORD says: 'In the same way will I break the yoke of Nebuchadnezzar king of Babylon off the neck of all the nations within two years.' " At this, the prophet Jeremiah went on his way.

12 Shortly after the prophet Hananiah had broken the yoke off the neck of the prophet Jeremiah, the word of the LORD came to Jeremiah: 13 "Go and tell Hananiah, 'This is what the LORD says: You have broken a wooden yoke, but in its place you will get a yoke of iron. 14 This is what the LORD Almighty, the God of Israel, says: I will put an iron yoke[e] on the necks of all these nations to make them serve[f] Nebuchadnezzar king of Babylon, and they will serve him. I will even give him control over the wild animals.[g]' "

15 Then the prophet Jeremiah said to Hananiah the prophet, "Listen, Hananiah! The LORD has not sent[h] you, yet you have persuaded this nation to trust in lies.[i] 16 Therefore, this is what the LORD says: 'I am about to remove you from the face of the earth.[j] This very year you are going to die, because you have preached rebellion[k] against the LORD.' "

17 In the seventh month of that same year, Hananiah the prophet died.

A Letter to the Exiles

29 This is the text of the letter that the prophet Jeremiah sent from Jerusalem to the surviving elders among the exiles and to the priests, the prophets and all the other people Nebuchadnezzar had carried into exile from Jerusalem to Babylon.[l] 2 (This was after King Jehoiachin[e][m] and the queen mother, the court officials and the leaders of Judah and Jerusalem, the craftsmen and the artisans had gone into exile from Jerusalem.) 3 He entrusted the letter to Elasah son of Shaphan and to Gemariah son of Hilkiah, whom Zedekiah king of Judah sent to King Nebuchadnezzar in Babylon. It said:

4 This is what the LORD Almighty, the God of Israel, says to all those I carried[n] into exile from Jerusalem to Babylon: 5 "Build[o] houses and settle down; plant gardens and eat what they produce. 6 Marry and have sons and daughters; find wives for your sons and give your daughters in marriage, so that they too may have sons and daughters. Increase in number there; do not decrease. 7 Also, seek the peace and prosperity of the city to which I have carried you into exile. Pray[p] to the LORD for it, because if it prospers, you too will prosper." 8 Yes, this is what the LORD Almighty, the God of Israel, says: "Do not let the prophets and diviners among you deceive[q] you. Do not listen to the dreams you encourage them to have.[r] 9 They are prophesying lies[s] to you in my name. I have not sent them," declares the LORD.

10 This is what the LORD says: "When seventy years[t] are

28:8 [a] Lev 26:14-17; Isa 5:5-7
28:9 [b] Dt 18:22
28:10 [c] Jer 27:2
28:11 [d] Jer 14:14; 27:10
28:14 [e] Dt 28:48 [f] Jer 25:11 [g] Jer 27:6
28:15 [h] Jer 29:31 [i] Jer 20:6; 29:21; La 2:14; Eze 13:6
28:16 [j] Ge 7:4 [k] Dt 13:5; Jer 29:32
29:1 [l] 2Ch 36:10
29:2 [m] 2Ki 24:12; Jer 22:24-28
29:4 [n] Jer 24:5
29:5 [o] ver 28
29:7 [p] Ezr 6:10; 1Ti 2:1-2
29:8 [q] Jer 37:9 [r] Jer 23:27
29:9 [s] Jer 14:14; 27:15
29:10 [t] 2Ch 36:21; Jer 25:12; Da 9:2

e2 Hebrew *Jeconiah*, a variant of *Jehoiachin*

completed for Babylon, I will
come to you and fulfill my gracious promise to bring you
back[a] to this place. **11**For I
know the plans[b] I have for
you," declares the LORD,
"plans to prosper you and not
to harm you, plans to give you
hope and a future. **12**Then you
will call upon me and come
and pray to me, and I will listen[c] to you. **13**You will seek[d]
me and find me when you seek
me with all your heart.[e] **14**I
will be found by you," declares
the LORD, "and will bring you
back[f] from captivity.[f] I will
gather you from all the nations
and places where I have banished you," declares the LORD,
"and will bring you back to the
place from which I carried you
into exile."[g]

15You may say, "The LORD
has raised up prophets for us
in Babylon," **16**but this is what
the LORD says about the king
who sits on David's throne and
all the people who remain in
this city, your countrymen
who did not go with you into
exile— **17**yes, this is what the
LORD Almighty says: "I will
send the sword, famine and
plague[h] against them and I
will make them like poor figs[i]
that are so bad they cannot be
eaten. **18**I will pursue them
with the sword, famine and
plague and will make them abhorrent[j] to all the kingdoms
of the earth and an object of
cursing and horror,[k] of scorn
and reproach, among all the
nations where I drive them.
19For they have not listened to
my words,"[l] declares the
LORD, "words that I sent to
them again and again by my
servants the prophets.[m] And
you exiles have not listened either," declares the LORD.

20Therefore, hear the word
of the LORD, all you exiles
whom I have sent[n] away from
Jerusalem to Babylon. **21**This
is what the LORD Almighty, the
God of Israel, says about Ahab
son of Kolaiah and Zedekiah
son of Maaseiah, who are
prophesying lies[o] to you in my
name: "I will hand them over
to Nebuchadnezzar king of
Babylon, and he will put them
to death before your very eyes.
22Because of them, all the exiles from Judah who are in
Babylon will use this curse:
'The LORD treat you like Zedekiah and Ahab, whom the king
of Babylon burned[p] in the
fire.' **23**For they have done
outrageous things in Israel;
they have committed adul-
tery[q] with their neighbors'
wives and in my name have
spoken lies, which I did not
tell them to do. I know[r] it and
am a witness to it," declares
the LORD.

Message to Shemaiah

24Tell Shemaiah the Nehelamite, **25**"This is what the LORD Almighty, the God of Israel, says: You
sent letters in your own name to all
the people in Jerusalem, to Zephaniah[s] son of Maaseiah the priest,
and to all the other priests. You
said to Zephaniah, **26**'The LORD has
appointed you priest in place of Jehoiada to be in charge of the house
of the LORD; you should put any
madman[t] who acts like a prophet
into the stocks[u] and neck-irons.
27So why have you not repri-
manded Jeremiah from Anathoth,
who poses as a prophet among
you? **28**He has sent this message[v]
to us in Babylon: It will be a long
time.[w] Therefore build[x] houses
and settle down; plant gardens and
eat what they produce.' "

29Zephaniah the priest, however,
read the letter to Jeremiah the
prophet. **30**Then the word of the
LORD came to Jeremiah: **31**"Send
this message to all the exiles: 'This
is what the LORD says about Shemaiah[y] the Nehelamite: Because
Shemaiah has prophesied to you,
even though I did not send[z] him,

29:10 [a]Jer 21:22
29:11 [b]Ps 40:5
29:12 [c]Ps 145:19
29:13 [d]Mt 7:7 [e]Dt 4:29; Jer 24:7
29:14 [f]Dt 30:3; Jer 30:3 [g]Jer 23:3-4
29:17 [h]Jer 27:8 [i]Jer 24:8-10
29:18 [j]Jer 15:4 [k]Dt 28:25; Jer 42:18
29:19 [l]Jer 6:19 [m]Jer 25:4
29:20 [n]Jer 24:5
29:21 [o]ver 9; Jer 14:14
29:22 [p]Da 3:6
29:23 [q]Jer 23:14 [r]Heb 4:13
29:25 [s]2Ki 25:18; Jer 21:1
29:26 [t]2Ki 9:11; Hos 9:7; Jn 10:20 [u]Jer 20:2
29:28 [v]ver 1 [w]ver 10 [x]ver 5
29:31 [y]ver 24 [z]Jer 14:14; 28:15

[f]14 Or *will restore your fortunes*

and has led you to believe a lie,
32 this is what the LORD says: I will
surely punish Shemaiah the Nehelamite and his descendants.[a] He
will have no one left among this
people, nor will he see the good[b]
things I will do for my people, declares the LORD, because he has
preached rebellion[c] against me.' "

Restoration of Israel

30 This is the word that came
to Jeremiah from the LORD:
2 "This is what the LORD, the God of
Israel, says: 'Write[d] in a book all
the words I have spoken to you.
3 The days are coming,' declares
the LORD, 'when I will bring[e] my
people Israel and Judah back from
captivity[g] and restore[f] them to
the land I gave their forefathers to
possess,' says the LORD."

4 These are the words the LORD
spoke concerning Israel and Judah:
5 "This is what the LORD says:

" 'Cries of fear[g] are heard—
terror, not peace.
6 Ask and see:
Can a man bear children?
Then why do I see every strong
man
with his hands on his
stomach like a woman in
labor,[h]
every face turned deathly
pale?
7 How awful that day[i] will be!
None will be like it.
It will be a time of trouble[j] for
Jacob,
but he will be saved[k] out of
it.

8 " 'In that day,' declares the
LORD Almighty,
'I will break the yoke[l] off
their necks
and will tear off their bonds;
no longer will foreigners
enslave them.[m]
9 Instead, they will serve the
LORD their God
and David[n] their king,[o]
whom I will raise up for
them.

10 " 'So do not fear,[p] O Jacob my
servant;[q]
do not be dismayed,
O Israel,'
declares the LORD.
'I will surely save[r] you out of a
distant place,
your descendants from the
land of their exile.
Jacob will again have peace
and security,[s]
and no one will make him
afraid.
11 I am with you and will save
you,'
declares the LORD.
'Though I completely destroy
all the nations
among which I scatter you,
I will not completely
destroy[t] you.
I will discipline[u] you but only
with justice;
I will not let you go entirely
unpunished.'[v]

12 "This is what the LORD says:

" 'Your wound is incurable,
your injury beyond healing.[w]
13 There is no one to plead your
cause,
no remedy for your sore,
no healing[x] for you.
14 All your allies[y] have forgotten
you;
they care nothing for you.
I have struck you as an enemy[z]
would
and punished you as would
the cruel,[a]
because your guilt is so great
and your sins[b] so many.
15 Why do you cry out over your
wound,
your pain that has no cure?
Because of your great guilt and
many sins
I have done these things to
you.

16 " 'But all who devour[c] you will
be devoured;
all your enemies will go into
exile.[d]

29:32 [a] 1Sa 2:30-33 [b] ver 10 [c] Jer 28:16
30:2 [d] Isa 30:8
30:3 [e] Jer 29:14 [f] Jer 16:15
30:5 [g] Jer 6:25
30:6 [h] Jer 4:31
30:7 [i] Isa 2:12; Joel 2:11 [j] Zep 1:15 [k] ver 10
30:8 [l] Isa 9:4 [m] Eze 34:27
30:9 [n] Isa 55:3-4; Lk 1:69; Ac 2:30; 13:23 [o] Eze 34:23-24; 37:24; Hos 3:5
30:10 [p] Isa 43:5; Jer 46:27-28 [q] Isa 44:2 [r] Jer 29:14 [s] Isa 35:9
30:11 [t] Jer 4:27; 46:28 [u] Jer 10:24 [v] Am 9:8
30:12 [w] Jer 15:18
30:13 [x] Jer 8:22; 14:19; 46:11
30:14 [y] Jer 22:20; La 1:2 [z] Job 13:24 [a] Job 30:21 [b] Jer 5:6
30:16 [c] Isa 33:1; Jer 2:3; 10:25 [d] Isa 14:2; Joel 3:4-8

g3 Or *will restore the fortunes of my people Israel and Judah*

Those who plunder[a] you will
be plundered;
all who make spoil of you I
will despoil.
17But I will restore you to health
and heal your wounds,'
declares the LORD,
'because you are called an
outcast,[b]
Zion for whom no one cares.'

18"This is what the LORD says:

" 'I will restore the fortunes[c] of
Jacob's tents
and have compassion[d] on
his dwellings;
the city will be rebuilt[e] on her
ruins,
and the palace will stand in
its proper place.
19From them will come songs[f]
of thanksgiving[g]
and the sound of rejoicing.[h]
I will add to their numbers,[i]
and they will not be
decreased;
I will bring them honor,[j]
and they will not be
disdained.
20Their children[k] will be as in
days of old,
and their community will be
established[l] before me;
I will punish all who oppress
them.
21Their leader[m] will be one of
their own;
their ruler will arise from
among them.
I will bring him near[n] and he
will come close to me,
for who is he who will devote
himself
to be close to me?'
declares the LORD.
22" 'So you will be my people,
and I will be your God.' "

23See, the storm[o] of the LORD
will burst out in wrath,
a driving wind swirling down
on the heads of the wicked.
24The fierce anger[p] of the LORD
will not turn back[q]
until he fully accomplishes
the purposes of his heart.
In days to come
you will understand[r] this.

31 "At that time," declares the
LORD, "I will be the God[s] of
all the clans of Israel, and they will
be my people."
2This is what the LORD says:

"The people who survive the
sword
will find favor[t] in the desert;
I will come to give rest[u] to
Israel."

3The LORD appeared to us in the
past,[h] saying:

"I have loved[v] you with an
everlasting love;
I have drawn[w] you with
loving-kindness.
4I will build you up again
and you will be rebuilt,
O Virgin Israel.
Again you will take up your
tambourines
and go out to dance with the
joyful.[x]
5Again you will plant vineyards
on the hills of Samaria;[y]
the farmers will plant them
and enjoy their fruit.[z]
6There will be a day when
watchmen cry out
on the hills of Ephraim,
'Come, let us go up to Zion,
to the LORD our God.' "[a]

7This is what the LORD says:

"Sing with joy for Jacob;
shout for the foremost[b] of
the nations.
Make your praises heard, and
say,
'O LORD, save[c] your people,
the remnant[d] of Israel.'
8See, I will bring them from the
land of the north[e]
and gather[f] them from the
ends of the earth.
Among them will be the blind[g]
and the lame,[h]
expectant mothers and
women in labor;
a great throng will return.
9They will come with weeping;[i]

[h]3 Or *LORD has appeared to us from afar*

30:16 [a]Jer 50:10
30:17 [b]Jer 33:24
30:18 [c]ver 3; Jer 31:23 [d]Ps 102:13 [e]Jer 31:4,24, 38
30:19 [f]Isa 35:10; 51:11 [g]Isa 51:3 [h]Ps 126:1-2; Jer 31:4 [i]Jer 33:22 [j]Isa 60:9
30:20 [k]Isa 54:13; Jer 31:17 [l]Isa 54:14
30:21 [m]ver 9 [n]Nu 16:5
30:23 [o]Jer 23:19
30:24 [p]Jer 4:8 [q]Jer 4:28 [r]Jer 23:19-20
31:1 [s]Jer 30:22
31:2 [t]Nu 14:20 [u]Ex 33:14
31:3 [v]Dt 4:37 [w]Hos 11:4
31:4 [x]Jer 30:19
31:5 [y]Jer 50:19 [z]Isa 65:21; Am 9:14
31:6 [a]Isa 2:3; Jer 50:4-5; Mic 4:2
31:7 [b]Dt 28:13; Isa 61:9 [c]Ps 14:7; 28:9 [d]Isa 37:31
31:8 [e]Jer 3:18; 23:8 [f]Dt 30:4; Eze 34:12-14 [g]Isa 42:16 [h]Eze 34:16; Mic 4:6
31:9 [i]Ps 126:5

they will pray as I bring them back.
I will lead[a] them beside streams of water
on a level[b] path where they will not stumble,
because I am Israel's father,[c]
and Ephraim is my firstborn son.

10"Hear the word of the LORD, O nations;
proclaim it in distant coastlands:[d]
'He who scattered Israel will gather[e] them
and will watch over his flock like a shepherd.'[f]
11For the LORD will ransom Jacob
and redeem[g] them from the hand of those stronger[h] than they.
12They will come and shout for joy on the heights[i] of Zion;
they will rejoice in the bounty[j] of the LORD—
the grain, the new wine and the oil,[k]
the young of the flocks and herds.
They will be like a well-watered garden,[l]
and they will sorrow[m] no more.
13Then maidens will dance and be glad,
young men and old as well.
I will turn their mourning[n] into gladness;
I will give them comfort and joy[o] instead of sorrow.
14I will satisfy[p] the priests with abundance,
and my people will be filled with my bounty,"
declares the LORD.

15This is what the LORD says:

"A voice is heard in Ramah,[q]
mourning and great weeping,
Rachel weeping for her children
and refusing to be comforted,[r]
because her children are no more."[s]

16This is what the LORD says:

"Restrain your voice from weeping
and your eyes from tears,[t]
for your work will be rewarded,[u]"
declares the LORD.
"They will return[v] from the land of the enemy.
17So there is hope for your future,"
declares the LORD.
"Your children will return to their own land.

18"I have surely heard Ephraim's moaning:
'You disciplined[w] me like an unruly calf,[x]
and I have been disciplined.
Restore[y] me, and I will return,
because you are the LORD my God.
19After I strayed,[z]
I repented;
after I came to understand,
I beat[a] my breast.
I was ashamed and humiliated
because I bore the disgrace of my youth.'
20Is not Ephraim my dear son,
the child in whom I delight?
Though I often speak against him,
I still remember[b] him.
Therefore my heart yearns for him;
I have great compassion[c] for him,"
declares the LORD.

21"Set up road signs;
put up guideposts.
Take note of the highway,[d]
the road that you take.
Return,[e] O Virgin[f] Israel,
return to your towns.
22How long will you wander,[g]
O unfaithful[h] daughter?
The LORD will create a new thing on earth—
a woman will surround[i] a man."

23This is what the LORD Almighty, the God of Israel, says: "When I bring them back from cap-

[i]22 Or *will go about seeking;* or *will protect*

31:9 [a]Isa 63:13 [b]Isa 49:11 [c]Ex 4:22; Jer 3:4
31:10 [d]Isa 66:19; Jer 25:22 [e]Jer 50:19 [f]Isa 40:11; Eze 34:12
31:11 [g]Isa 44:23; 48:20 [h]Ps 142:6
31:12 [i]Eze 17:23; Mic 4:1 [j]Joel 3:18 [k]Hos 2:21-22 [l]Isa 58:11 [m]Isa 65:19; Jn 16:22; Rev 7:17
31:13 [n]Isa 61:3 [o]Ps 30:11; Isa 51:11
31:14 [p]ver 25
31:15 [q]Jos 18:25 [r]Ge 37:35 [s]Jer 10:20; Mt 2:17-18*
31:16 [t]Isa 25:8; 30:19 [u]Ru 2:12 [v]Jer 30:3; Eze 11:17
31:18 [w]Job 5:17 [x]Hos 4:16 [y]Ps 80:3
31:19 [z]Eze 36:31 [a]Eze 21:12; Lk 18:13
31:20 [b]Hos 4:4; 11:8 [c]Isa 55:7; 63:15; Mic 7:18
31:21 [d]Jer 50:5 [e]Isa 52:11 [f]ver 4
31:22 [g]Jer 2:23 [h]Jer 3:6

tivity,[i][a] the people in the land of
Judah and in its towns will once
again use these words: 'The LORD
bless you, O righteous dwelling,[b]
O sacred mountain.'[c] 24People
will live[d] together in Judah and all
its towns—farmers and those who
move about with their flocks. 25I
will refresh the weary and satisfy
the faint."[e]

26At this I awoke[f] and looked
around. My sleep had been pleasant to me.

27"The days are coming," declares the LORD, "when I will plant[g]
the house of Israel and the house of
Judah with the offspring of men
and of animals. 28Just as I watched
over them to uproot and tear down,
and to overthrow, destroy and bring
disaster,[h] so I will watch over them
to build and to plant,"[i] declares
the LORD. 29"In those days people
will no longer say,

'The fathers[j] have eaten sour
grapes,
and the children's teeth are
set on edge.'[k]

30Instead, everyone will die for his
own sin;[l] whoever eats sour
grapes—his own teeth will be set
on edge.

31"The time is coming," declares
the LORD,
"when I will make a new
covenant[m]
with the house of Israel
and with the house of Judah.
32It will not be like the
covenant[n]
I made with their
forefathers[o]
when I took them by the hand
to lead them out of Egypt,
because they broke my
covenant,
though I was a husband to[k]
them,[l]"
declares the LORD.
33"This is the covenant I will
make with the house of
Israel
after that time," declares the
LORD.
"I will put my law in their
minds
and write it on their hearts.[p]
I will be their God,
and they will be my people.[q]
34No longer will a man teach[r]
his neighbor,
or a man his brother, saying,
'Know the LORD,'
because they will all know[s]
me,
from the least of them to the
greatest,"
declares the LORD.
"For I will forgive[t] their
wickedness
and will remember their
sins[u] no more."

35This is what the LORD says,

he who appoints[v] the sun
to shine by day,
who decrees the moon and
stars
to shine by night,[w]
who stirs up the sea
so that its waves roar—
the LORD Almighty is his
name:[x]
36"Only if these decrees[y] vanish
from my sight,"
declares the LORD,
"will the descendants[z] of Israel
ever cease
to be a nation before me."

37This is what the LORD says:

"Only if the heavens above can
be measured[a]
and the foundations of the
earth below be searched
out
will I reject[b] all the
descendants of Israel
because of all they have
done,"
declares the LORD.

38"The days are coming," declares the LORD, "when this city will
be rebuilt[c] for me from the Tower
of Hananel[d] to the Corner Gate.[e]
39The measuring line will stretch
from there straight to the hill of Ga-

31:23 [a]Jer 30:18 [b]Isa 1:26 [c]Ps 48:1; Zec 8:3
31:24 [d]Zec 8:4-8
31:25 [e]Jn 4:14
31:26 [f]Zec 4:1
31:27 [g]Eze 36:9-11; Hos 2:23
31:28 [h]Jer 18:8; 44:27 [i]Jer 1:10
31:29 [j]La 5:7 [k]Eze 18:2
31:30 [l]Isa 3:11; Gal 6:7
31:31 [m]Jer 32:40; Eze 37:26; Lk 22:20; Heb 8:8-12*; 10:16-17
31:32 [n]Ex 24:8 [o]Dt 5:3
31:33 [p]2Co 3:3 [q]Jer 24:7; Heb 10:16
31:34 [r]1Jn 2:27 [s]Jn 6:45 [t]Isa 54:13; Jer 33:8; 50:20 [u]Ro 11:27; Mic 7:19; Heb 10:17*
31:35 [v]Ps 136:7-9 [w]Ge 1:16 [x]Jer 10:16
31:36 [y]Isa 54:9-10; Jer 33:20-26 [z]Ps 89:36-37
31:37 [a]Jer 33:22 [b]Jer 33:24-26; Ro 11:1-5
31:38 [c]Jer 30:18 [d]Ne 3:1 [e]2Ki 14:13; Zec 14:10

i23 Or *I restore their fortunes* k32 Hebrew; Septuagint and Syriac / *and I turned away from* l32 Or *was their master*

reb and then turn to Goah. **40**The
whole valley[a] where dead bodies[b]
and ashes are thrown, and all the
terraces out to the Kidron Valley[c]
on the east as far as the corner of
the Horse Gate,[d] will be holy[e] to
the LORD. The city will never again
be uprooted or demolished."

Jeremiah Buys a Field

32 This is the word that came
to Jeremiah from the LORD
in the tenth[f] year of Zedekiah king
of Judah, which was the eighteenth[g] year of Nebuchadnezzar.
2The army of the king of Babylon
was then besieging Jerusalem, and
Jeremiah the prophet was confined
in the courtyard of the guard[h] in
the royal palace of Judah.
3Now Zedekiah king of Judah
had imprisoned him there, saying,
"Why do you prophesy[i] as you do?
You say, 'This is what the LORD
says: I am about to hand this city
over to the king of Babylon, and he
will capture[j] it. **4**Zedekiah king of
Judah will not escape[k] out of the
hands of the Babylonians[m] but will
certainly be handed over to the
king of Babylon, and will speak
with him face to face and see him
with his own eyes. **5**He will take[l]
Zedekiah to Babylon, where he will
remain until I deal with him, declares the LORD. If you fight against
the Babylonians, you will not succeed.' "[m]
6Jeremiah said, "The word of the
LORD came to me: **7**Hanamel son of
Shallum your uncle is going to
come to you and say, 'Buy my field
at Anathoth, because as nearest
relative it is your right and duty[n] to
buy it.'
8"Then, just as the LORD had
said, my cousin Hanamel came to
me in the courtyard of the guard
and said, 'Buy my field at Anathoth
in the territory of Benjamin. Since
it is your right to redeem it and possess it, buy it for yourself.'
"I knew that this was the word of
the LORD; **9**so I bought the field at
Anathoth from my cousin Hanamel
and weighed out for him seventeen
shekels[n] of silver.[o] **10**I signed and
sealed the deed, had it witnessed,[p]
and weighed out the silver on the
scales. **11**I took the deed of purchase—the sealed copy containing
the terms and conditions, as well
as the unsealed copy— **12**and I
gave this deed to Baruch[q] son of
Neriah,[r] the son of Mahseiah, in
the presence of my cousin Hanamel and of the witnesses who had
signed the deed and of all the Jews
sitting in the courtyard of the
guard.
13"In their presence I gave Baruch these instructions: **14**'This is
what the LORD Almighty, the God of
Israel, says: Take these documents,
both the sealed and unsealed copies of the deed of purchase, and put
them in a clay jar so they will last
a long time. **15**For this is what the
LORD Almighty, the God of Israel,
says: Houses, fields and vineyards
will again be bought in this land.'[s]
16"After I had given the deed of
purchase to Baruch son of Neriah,
I prayed to the LORD:

17"Ah, Sovereign LORD,[t] you
have made the heavens and
the earth by your great power
and outstretched arm.[u] Nothing is too hard[v] for you. **18**You
show love[w] to thousands but
bring the punishment for the
fathers' sins into the laps of
their children[x] after them. O
great and powerful God,
whose name is the LORD Almighty,[y] **19**great are your purposes and mighty are your
deeds.[z] Your eyes are open to
all the ways of men;[a] you reward everyone according to
his conduct and as his deeds
deserve.[b] **20**You performed
miraculous signs and wonders
in Egypt[c] and have continued
them to this day, both in Israel
and among all mankind, and
have gained the renown that is
still yours. **21**You brought your
people Israel out of Egypt with
signs and wonders, by a

31:40 [a] Jer 7:31-32 [b] Jer 8:2 [c] 2Sa 15:23; Jn 18:1 [d] 2Ki 11:16 [e] Joel 3:17; Zec 14:21
32:1 [f] 2Ki 25:1 [g] Jer 25:1; 39:1
32:2 [h] Ne 3:25; Jer 37:21
32:3 [i] Jer 26:8-9 [j] ver 28; Jer 34:2-3
32:4 [k] Jer 38:18,23; 39:5-7; 52:9
32:5 [l] Jer 39:7; Eze 12:13 [m] Jer 21:4
32:7 [n] Lev 25:24-25; Ru 4:3-4; Mt 27:10*
32:9 [o] Ge 23:16
32:10 [p] Ru 4:9
32:12 [q] ver 16; Jer 36:4; 43:3,6; 45:1 [r] Jer 51:59
32:15 [s] ver 43-44; Jer 30:18; Am 9:14-15
32:17 [t] Jer 1:6 [u] 2Ki 19:15; Ps 102:25 [v] Mt 19:26
32:18 [w] Dt 5:10 [x] Ex 20:5 [y] Jer 10:16
32:19 [z] Isa 28:29 [a] Pr 5:21; Jer 16:17 [b] Jer 17:10; Mt 16:27
32:20 [c] Ex 9:16

m4 Or *Chaldeans*; also in verses 5, 24, 25, 28, 29 and 43 n9 That is, about 7 ounces (about 200 grams)

mighty hand[a] and an outstretched arm and with great
terror.[b] **22**You gave them this
land you had sworn to give
their forefathers, a land flowing with milk and honey.[c]
23They came in and took possession[d] of it, but they did not
obey you or follow your law;[e]
they did not do what you commanded them to do. So you
brought all this disaster[f]
upon them.

24"See how the siege ramps
are built up to take the city.
Because of the sword, famine
and plague,[g] the city will be
handed over to the Babylonians who are attacking it. What
you said[h] has happened, as
you now see. **25**And though
the city will be handed over to
the Babylonians, you, O Sovereign LORD, say to me, 'Buy the
field with silver and have the
transaction witnessed.' "

26Then the word of the LORD
came to Jeremiah: **27**"I am the
LORD, the God of all mankind.[i] Is
anything too hard for me? **28**Therefore, this is what the LORD says: I
am about to hand this city over to
the Babylonians and to Nebuchadnezzar[j] king of Babylon, who will
capture it.[k] **29**The Babylonians
who are attacking this city will
come in and set it on fire; they will
burn it down,[l] along with the
houses[m] where the people provoked me to anger by burning incense on the roofs to Baal and by
pouring out drink offerings[n] to
other gods.
30"The people of Israel and Judah have done nothing but evil in
my sight from their youth;[o] indeed, the people of Israel have
done nothing but provoke[p] me
with what their hands have made,[q]
declares the LORD. **31**From the day
it was built until now, this city has
so aroused my anger and wrath that
I must remove[r] it from my sight.
32The people of Israel and Judah
have provoked me by all the evil[s]
they have done—they, their kings
and officials, their priests and
prophets, the men of Judah and
the people of Jerusalem. **33**They
turned their backs[t] to me and not
their faces; though I taught[u] them
again and again, they would not listen or respond to discipline.
34They set up their abominable
idols in the house that bears my
Name and defiled[v] it. **35**They built
high places for Baal in the Valley of
Ben Hinnom to sacrifice their sons
and daughters° to Molech,[w]
though I never commanded, nor
did it enter my mind,[x] that they
should do such a detestable thing
and so make Judah sin.

36"You are saying about this city,
'By the sword, famine and plague[y]
it will be handed over to the king of
Babylon'; but this is what the LORD,
the God of Israel, says: **37**I will
surely gather[z] them from all the
lands where I banish them in my
furious anger and great wrath; I will
bring them back to this place and
let them live in safety.[a] **38**They will
be my people,[b] and I will be their
God. **39**I will give them singleness[c]
of heart and action, so that they
will always fear me for their own
good and the good of their children
after them. **40**I will make an everlasting covenant[d] with them: I will
never stop doing good to them, and
I will inspire them to fear me, so
that they will never turn away from
me.[e] **41**I will rejoice in doing them
good[f] and will assuredly plant[g]
them in this land with all my heart
and soul.

42"This is what the LORD says: As
I have brought all this great calamity on this people, so I will give
them all the prosperity I have
promised[h] them. **43**Once more
fields will be bought[i] in this land
of which you say, 'It is a desolate
waste, without men or animals, for
it has been handed over to the Babylonians.' **44**Fields will be bought
for silver, and deeds[j] will be
signed, sealed and witnessed in the
territory of Benjamin, in the vil-

°35 *Or to make their sons and daughters pass through ⌊the fire⌋*

32:21 [a]Ex 6:6; 1Ch 17:21; Da 9:15 [b]Dt 26:8
32:22 [c]Ex 3:8; Jer 11:5
32:23 [d]Ps 44:2; 78:54-55 [e]Ne 9:26; Jer 11:8 [f]Da 9:14
32:24 [g]Jer 14:12 [h]Dt 4:25-26; Jos 23:15-16
32:27 [i]Nu 16:22
32:28 [j]2Ch 36:17 [k]ver 3
32:29 [l]2Ch 36:19; Jer 21:10; 37:8,10; 52:13 [m]Jer 19:13 [n]Jer 44:18
32:30 [o]Jer 22:21 [p]Jer 8:19 [q]Jer 25:7
32:31 [r]2Ki 23:27; 24:3
32:32 [s]Isa 1:4-6; Da 9:8
32:33 [t]Jer 2:27; Eze 8:16 [u]Jer 7:13
32:34 [v]Jer 7:30
32:35 [w]Lev 18:21 [x]Jer 7:31; 19:5
32:36 [y]ver 24
32:37 [z]Jer 23:3,6 [a]Dt 30:3; Eze 34:28
32:38 [b]Jer 24:7; 2Co 6:16*
32:39 [c]Eze 11:19
32:40 [d]Isa 55:3 [e]Jer 24:7
32:41 [f]Dt 30:9 [g]Jer 24:6; 31:28; Am 9:15
32:42 [h]Jer 31:28
32:43 [i]ver 15
32:44 [j]ver 10

lages around Jerusalem, in the towns of Judah and in the towns of the hill country, of the western foothills and of the Negev,[a] because I will restore[b] their fortunes,[p] declares the LORD."

Promise of Restoration

33 While Jeremiah was still confined in the courtyard[c] of the guard, the word of the LORD came to him a second time: 2"This is what the LORD says, he who made the earth,[d] the LORD who formed it and established it—the LORD is his name:[e] 3'Call[f] to me and I will answer you and tell you great and unsearchable things you do not know.' 4For this is what the LORD, the God of Israel, says about the houses in this city and the royal palaces of Judah that have been torn down to be used against the siege[g] ramps[h] and the sword 5in the fight with the Babylonians[q]: 'They will be filled with the dead bodies of the men I will slay in my anger and wrath.[i] I will hide my face[j] from this city because of all its wickedness.

6" 'Nevertheless, I will bring health and healing to it; I will heal my people and will let them enjoy abundant peace and security. 7I will bring Judah[k] and Israel back from captivity[r][l] and will rebuild them as they were before.[m] 8I will cleanse[n] them from all the sin they have committed against me and will forgive[o] all their sins of rebellion against me. 9Then this city will bring me renown, joy, praise[p] and honor[q] before all nations on earth that hear of all the good things I do for it; and they will be in awe and will tremble at the abundant prosperity and peace I provide for it.'

10"This is what the LORD says: 'You say about this place, "It is a desolate waste, without men or animals."[r] Yet in the towns of Judah and the streets of Jerusalem that are deserted, inhabited by neither men nor animals, there will be heard once more 11the sounds of joy and gladness,[s] the voices of bride and bridegroom, and the voices of those who bring thank offerings[t] to the house of the LORD, saying,

"Give thanks to the LORD
Almighty,
for the LORD is good;[u]
his love endures forever."[v]

For I will restore the fortunes of the land as they were before,' says the LORD.

12"This is what the LORD Almighty says: 'In this place, desolate[w] and without men or animals—in all its towns there will again be pastures for shepherds to rest their flocks.[x] 13In the towns of the hill country, of the western foothills and of the Negev,[y] in the territory of Benjamin, in the villages around Jerusalem and in the towns of Judah, flocks will again pass under the hand[z] of the one who counts them,' says the LORD.

14" 'The days are coming,' declares the LORD, 'when I will fulfill the gracious promise[a] I made to the house of Israel and to the house of Judah.

15" 'In those days and at that
time
I will make a righteous[b]
Branch[c] sprout from
David's line;
he will do what is just and
right in the land.
16In those days Judah will be
saved[d]
and Jerusalem will live in
safety.
This is the name by which it[s]
will be called:
The LORD Our
Righteousness.'[e]

17For this is what the LORD says: 'David will never fail[f] to have a man to sit on the throne of the house of Israel, 18nor will the priests, who are Levites,[g] ever fail to have a man to stand before me continually to offer burnt offerings, to burn grain offerings and to present sacrifices.[h]' "

32:44 [a]Jer 17:26 [b]Jer 33:7,11, 26
33:1 [c]Jer 32:2-3; 37:21; 38:28
33:2 [d]Jer 10:16 [e]Ex 3:15; 15:3
33:3 [f]Isa 55:6; Jer 29:12
33:4 [g]Eze 4:2 [h]Jer 32:24; Hab 1:10
33:5 [i]Jer 21:4-7 [j]Isa 8:17
33:7 [k]Jer 32:44 [l]Jer 30:3; Am 9:14 [m]Isa 1:26
33:8 [n]Heb 9:13-14 [o]Jer 31:34; Mic 7:18; Zec 13:1
33:9 [p]Jer 13:11 [q]Isa 62:7; Jer 3:17
33:10 [r]Jer 32:43
33:11 [s]Isa 51:3 [t]Lev 7:12 [u]1Ch 16:8; Ps 136:1 [v]1Ch 16:34; 2Ch 5:13; Ps 100:4-5
33:12 [w]Jer 32:43 [x]Isa 65:10; Eze 34:11-15
33:13 [y]Jer 17:26 [z]Lev 27:32
33:14 [a]Jer 29:10
33:15 [b]Ps 72:2 [c]Isa 4:2; 11:1; Jer 23:5
33:16 [d]Isa 45:17 [e]1Co 1:30
33:17 [f]2Sa 7:13; 1Ki 2:4; Ps 89:29-37; Lk 1:33
33:18 [g]Dt 18:1 [h]Heb 13:15

[p]44 Or *will bring them back from captivity* [q]5 Or *Chaldeans* [r]7 Or *will restore the fortunes of Judah and Israel* [s]16 Or *he*

19The word of the LORD came to
Jeremiah: 20"This is what the LORD
says: 'If you can break my covenant
with the day[a] and my covenant
with the night, so that day and
night no longer come at their appointed time, 21then my covenant[b] with David my servant—
and my covenant with the Levites
who are priests ministering before
me—can be broken and David will
no longer have a descendant to
reign on his throne.[c] 22I will make
the descendants of David my servant and the Levites who minister
before me as countless[d] as the
stars of the sky and as measureless
as the sand on the seashore.' "

23The word of the LORD came to
Jeremiah: 24"Have you not noticed
that these people are saying, 'The
LORD has rejected the two kingdoms[t][e] he chose'? So they despise[f] my people and no longer regard them as a nation.[g] 25This is
what the LORD says: 'If I have not
established my covenant with day
and night[h] and the fixed laws of
heaven and earth,[i] 26then I will reject[j] the descendants of Jacob[k]
and David my servant and will not
choose one of his sons to rule over
the descendants of Abraham, Isaac
and Jacob. For I will restore their
fortunes[u][l] and have compassion
on them.' "

Warning to Zedekiah

34 While Nebuchadnezzar
king of Babylon and all his
army and all the kingdoms and
peoples[m] in the empire he ruled
were fighting against Jerusalem[n]
and all its surrounding towns, this
word came to Jeremiah from the
LORD: 2"This is what the LORD, the
God of Israel, says: Go to Zedekiah[o] king of Judah and tell him,
'This is what the LORD says: I am
about to hand this city over to the
king of Babylon, and he will burn it
down.[p] 3You will not escape from
his grasp but will surely be captured and handed over[q] to him.
You will see the king of Babylon
with your own eyes, and he will
speak with you face to face. And
you will go to Babylon.
4" 'Yet hear the promise of the
LORD, O Zedekiah king of Judah.
This is what the LORD says concerning you: You will not die by the
sword; 5you will die peacefully. As
people made a funeral fire[r] in hon-
or of your fathers, the former kings
who preceded you, so they will
make a fire in your honor and lament, "Alas,[s] O master!" I myself
make this promise, declares the
LORD.' "

6Then Jeremiah the prophet told
all this to Zedekiah king of Judah,
in Jerusalem, 7while the army of
the king of Babylon was fighting
against Jerusalem and the other
cities of Judah that were still holding out—Lachish[t] and Azekah.[u]
These were the only fortified cities
left in Judah.

Freedom for Slaves

8The word came to Jeremiah
from the LORD after King Zedekiah
had made a covenant with all the
people[v] in Jerusalem to proclaim
freedom[w] for the slaves. 9Everyone
was to free his Hebrew slaves, both
male and female; no one was to
hold a fellow Jew in bondage.[x]
10So all the officials and people
who entered into this covenant
agreed that they would free their
male and female slaves and no
longer hold them in bondage. They
agreed, and set them free. 11But afterward they changed their minds
and took back the slaves they had
freed and enslaved them again.
12Then the word of the LORD
came to Jeremiah: 13"This is what
the LORD, the God of Israel, says: I
made a covenant with your forefathers[y] when I brought them out of
Egypt, out of the land of slavery. I
said, 14'Every seventh year each of
you must free any fellow Hebrew
who has sold himself to you. After
he has served you six years, you
must let him go free.'[v][z] Your fathers, however, did not listen to me

33:20 [a]Ps 89:36
33:21 [b]Ps 89:34 [c]2Ch 7:18
33:22 [d]Ge 15:5
33:24 [e]Eze 37:22 [f]Ne 4:4 [g]Jer 30:17
33:25 [h]Jer 31:35-36 [i]Ps 74:16-17
33:26 [j]Jer 31:37 [k]Isa 14:1 [l]ver 7
34:1 [m]Jer 27:7 [n]2Ki 25:1; Jer 39:1
34:2 [o]2Ch 36:11 [p]ver 22; Jer 32:29; 37:8
34:3 [q]2Ki 25:7; Jer 21:7; 32:4
34:5 [r]2Ch 16:14; 21:19 [s]Jer 22:18
34:7 [t]Jos 10:3 [u]Jos 10:10; 2Ch 11:9
34:8 [v]2Ki 11:17 [w]Ex 21:2; Lev 25:10, 39-41; Ne 5:5-8
34:9 [x]Lev 25:39-46
34:13 [y]Ex 24:8
34:14 [z]Ex 21:2

[t]24 Or *families* [u]26 Or *will bring them back from captivity* [v]14 Deut. 15:12

or pay attention[a] to me. **15**Recently you repented and did what is
right in my sight: Each of you proclaimed freedom to his countrymen.[b] You even made a covenant
before me in the house that bears
my Name.[c] **16**But now you have
turned around[d] and profaned[e] my
name; each of you has taken back
the male and female slaves you had
set free to go where they wished.
You have forced them to become
your slaves again.

17"Therefore, this is what the
LORD says: You have not obeyed me;
you have not proclaimed freedom
for your fellow countrymen. So I
now proclaim 'freedom' for you,[f]
declares the LORD—'freedom' to
fall by the sword, plague and famine. I will make you abhorrent to all
the kingdoms of the earth.[g] **18**The
men who have violated my covenant and have not fulfilled the
terms of the covenant they made
before me, I will treat like the calf
they cut in two and then walked
between its pieces.[h] **19**The leaders
of Judah and Jerusalem, the court
officials,[i] the priests and all the
people of the land who walked between the pieces of the calf, **20**I will
hand over[j] to their enemies who
seek their lives.[k] Their dead bodies will become food for the birds of
the air and the beasts of the
earth.[l]

21"I will hand Zedekiah[m] king of
Judah and his officials[n] over to
their enemies who seek their lives,
to the army of the king of Babylon,
which has withdrawn[o] from you.
22I am going to give the order, declares the LORD, and I will bring
them back to this city. They will
fight against it, take[p] it and burn[q]
it down. And I will lay waste the
towns of Judah so no one can live
there."

The Recabites

35 This is the word that came
to Jeremiah from the LORD
during the reign of Jehoiakim[r] son
of Josiah king of Judah: **2**"Go to the
Recabite[s] family and invite them
to come to one of the side rooms[t]
of the house of the LORD and give
them wine to drink."

3So I went to get Jaazaniah son
of Jeremiah, the son of Habazzini-
ah, and his brothers and all his
sons—the whole family of the Recabites. **4**I brought them into the
house of the LORD, into the room of
the sons of Hanan son of Igdaliah
the man of God.[u] It was next to the
room of the officials, which was
over that of Maaseiah son of Shallum[v] the doorkeeper.[w] **5**Then I set
bowls full of wine and some cups
before the men of the Recabite
family and said to them, "Drink
some wine."

6But they replied, "We do not
drink wine, because our forefather
Jonadab[x] son of Recab gave us
this command: 'Neither you nor
your descendants must ever drink
wine.[y] **7**Also you must never build
houses, sow seed or plant vineyards; you must never have any of
these things, but must always live
in tents.[z] Then you will live a long
time in the land[a] where you are
nomads.' **8**We have obeyed everything our forefather[b] Jonadab son
of Recab commanded us. Neither
we nor our wives nor our sons and
daughters have ever drunk wine **9**or
built houses to live in or had vineyards, fields or crops.[c] **10**We have
lived in tents and have fully obeyed
everything our forefather Jonadab
commanded us. **11**But when Nebuchadnezzar king of Babylon invaded[d] this land, we said, 'Come, we
must go to Jerusalem[e] to escape
the Babylonian[w] and Aramean armies.' So we have remained in Jerusalem."

12Then the word of the LORD
came to Jeremiah, saying: **13**"This
is what the LORD Almighty, the God
of Israel, says: Go and tell the men
of Judah and the people of Jerusalem, 'Will you not learn a lesson[f]
and obey my words?' declares the
LORD. **14**'Jonadab son of Recab ordered his sons not to drink wine
and this command has been kept.
To this day they do not drink wine,

34:14 [a]Dt 15:12; 2Ki 17:14
34:15 [b]ver 8 [c]Jer 7:10-11; 32:34
34:16 [d]Eze 3:20; 18:24 [e]Ex 20:7; Lev 19:12
34:17 [f]Mt 7:2; Gal 6:7 [g]Dt 28:25,64; Jer 29:18
34:18 [h]Ge 15:10
34:19 [i]Zep 3:3-4
34:20 [j]Jer 21:7 [k]Jer 11:21 [l]Dt 28:26; Jer 7:33; 19:7
34:21 [m]Jer 32:4 [n]Jer 39:6; 52:24-27 [o]Jer 37:5
34:22 [p]Jer 39:1-2 [q]Jer 39:8
35:1 [r]2Ch 36:5
35:2 [s]2Ki 10:15; 1Ch 2:55 [t]1Ki 6:5
35:4 [u]Dt 33:1 [v]1Ch 9:19 [w]2Ki 12:9
35:6 [x]2Ki 10:15 [y]Lev 10:9; Nu 6:2-4; Lk 1:15
35:7 [z]Heb 11:9 [a]Ex 20:12; Eph 6:2-3
35:8 [b]Pr 1:8; Col 3:20
35:9 [c]1Ti 6:6
35:11 [d]2Ki 24:1 [e]Jer 8:14
35:13 [f]Jer 6:10; 32:33

[w]*11* Or *Chaldean*

because they obey their forefather's command. But I have spoken to you again and again,[a] yet you have not obeyed[b] me. **15**Again and again I sent all my servants the prophets[c] to you. They said, "Each of you must turn[d] from your wicked ways and reform[e] your actions; do not follow other gods to serve them. Then you will live in the land[f] I have given to you and your fathers." But you have not paid attention or listened[g] to me. **16**The descendants of Jonadab son of Recab have carried out the command their forefather[h] gave them, but these people have not obeyed me.'

17"Therefore, this is what the LORD God Almighty, the God of Israel, says: 'Listen! I am going to bring on Judah and on everyone living in Jerusalem every disaster[i] I pronounced against them. I spoke to them, but they did not listen;[j] I called to them, but they did not answer.' "[k]

18Then Jeremiah said to the family of the Recabites, "This is what the LORD Almighty, the God of Israel, says: 'You have obeyed the command of your forefather Jonadab and have followed all his instructions and have done everything he ordered.' **19**Therefore, this is what the LORD Almighty, the God of Israel, says: 'Jonadab son of Recab will never fail[l] to have a man to serve[m] me.' "

Jehoiakim Burns Jeremiah's Scroll

36 In the fourth year of Jehoiakim[n] son of Josiah king of Judah, this word came to Jeremiah from the LORD: **2**"Take a scroll[o] and write on it all the words I have spoken to you concerning Israel, Judah and all the other nations from the time I began speaking to you in the reign of Josiah[p] till now. **3**Perhaps[q] when the people of Judah hear[r] about every disaster I plan to inflict on them, each of them will turn[s] from his wicked way; then I will forgive[t] their wickedness and their sin."

35:14 [a]Jer 7:13; 25:3 [b]Isa 30:9
35:15 [c]Jer 7:25 [d]Jer 26:3 [e]Isa 1:16-17; Jer 4:1; 18:11; Eze 18:30 [f]Jer 25:5 [g]Jer 7:26
35:16 [h]Mal 1:6
35:17 [i]Jos 23:15; Jer 21:4-7 [j]Pr 1:24; Ro 10:21 [k]Isa 65:12; 66:4; Jer 7:13
35:19 [l]Jer 33:17 [m]Jer 15:19
36:1 [n]2Ch 36:5
36:2 [o]Ex 17:14; Jer 30:2; Hab 2:2 [p]Jer 1:2; 25:3
36:3 [q]ver 7; Eze 12:3 [r]Mk 4:12 [s]Jer 26:3; Jnh 3:8; Ac 3:19 [t]Jer 18:8
36:4 [u]Jer 32:12 [v]ver 18 [w]Eze 2:9
36:6 [x]ver 9
36:7 [y]Jer 26:3 [z]Dt 31:17
36:9 [a]ver 22 [b]2Ch 20:3
36:10 [c]Jer 52:25 [d]Jer 26:10
36:12 [e]Jer 26:22
36:14 [f]ver 21

4So Jeremiah called Baruch[u] son of Neriah, and while Jeremiah dictated[v] all the words the LORD had spoken to him, Baruch wrote them on the scroll.[w] **5**Then Jeremiah told Baruch, "I am restricted; I cannot go to the LORD's temple. **6**So you go to the house of the LORD on a day of fasting[x] and read to the people from the scroll the words of the LORD that you wrote as I dictated. Read them to all the people of Judah who come in from their towns. **7**Perhaps they will bring their petition before the LORD, and each will turn[y] from his wicked ways, for the anger[z] and wrath pronounced against this people by the LORD are great."

8Baruch son of Neriah did everything Jeremiah the prophet told him to do; at the LORD's temple he read the words of the LORD from the scroll. **9**In the ninth month[a] of the fifth year of Jehoiakim son of Josiah king of Judah, a time of fasting[b] before the LORD was proclaimed for all the people in Jerusalem and those who had come from the towns of Judah. **10**From the room of Gemariah son of Shaphan the secretary,[c] which was in the upper courtyard at the entrance of the New Gate[d] of the temple, Baruch read to all the people at the LORD's temple the words of Jeremiah from the scroll.

11When Micaiah son of Gemariah, the son of Shaphan, heard all the words of the LORD from the scroll, **12**he went down to the secretary's room in the royal palace, where all the officials were sitting: Elishama the secretary, Delaiah son of Shemaiah, Elnathan[e] son of Acbor, Gemariah son of Shaphan, Zedekiah son of Hananiah, and all the other officials. **13**After Micaiah told them everything he had heard Baruch read to the people from the scroll, **14**all the officials sent Jehudi[f] son of Nethaniah, the son of Shelemiah, the son of Cushi, to say to Baruch, "Bring the scroll from which you have read to the people and come." So Baruch son of Neriah went to them with the scroll in his hand. 15They said to him, "Sit down, please, and read it to us."

So Baruch read it to them. 16When they heard all these words, they looked at each other in fear and said to Baruch, "We must report all these words to the king." 17Then they asked Baruch, "Tell us, how did you come to write all this? Did Jeremiah dictate it?"

18"Yes," Baruch replied, "he dictated[a] all these words to me, and I wrote them in ink on the scroll."

19Then the officials said to Baruch, "You and Jeremiah, go and hide.[b] Don't let anyone know where you are."

20After they put the scroll in the room of Elishama the secretary, they went to the king in the courtyard and reported everything to him. 21The king sent Jehudi[c] to get the scroll, and Jehudi brought it from the room of Elishama the secretary and read it to the king[d] and all the officials standing beside him. 22It was the ninth month and the king was sitting in the winter apartment,[e] with a fire burning in the firepot in front of him. 23Whenever Jehudi had read three or four columns of the scroll, the king cut them off with a scribe's knife and threw them into the firepot, until the entire scroll was burned in the fire.[f] 24The king and all his attendants who heard all these words showed no fear,[g] nor did they tear their clothes.[h] 25Even though Elnathan, Delaiah and Gemariah urged the king not to burn the scroll, he would not listen to them. 26Instead, the king commanded Jerahmeel, a son of the king, Seraiah son of Azriel and Shelemiah son of Abdeel to arrest[i] Baruch the scribe and Jeremiah the prophet. But the LORD had hidden[j] them.

27After the king burned the scroll containing the words that Baruch had written at Jeremiah's dictation,[k] the word of the LORD came to Jeremiah: 28"Take another scroll and write on it all the words that were on the first scroll, which Jehoiakim king of Judah burned up. 29Also tell Jehoiakim king of Judah, 'This is what the LORD says: You burned that scroll and said, "Why did you write on it that the king of Babylon would certainly come and destroy this land and cut off both men and animals from it?"[l] 30Therefore, this is what the LORD says about Jehoiakim king of Judah: He will have no one to sit on the throne of David; his body will be thrown out[m] and exposed to the heat by day and the frost by night. 31I will punish him and his children and his attendants for their wickedness; I will bring on them and those living in Jerusalem and the people of Judah every disaster[n] I pronounced against them, because they have not listened.' "

32So Jeremiah took another scroll and gave it to the scribe Baruch son of Neriah, and as Jeremiah dictated,[o] Baruch wrote[p] on it all the words of the scroll that Jehoiakim king of Judah had burned[q] in the fire. And many similar words were added to them.

Jeremiah in Prison

37 Zedekiah[r] son of Josiah was made king[s] of Judah by Nebuchadnezzar king of Babylon; he reigned in place of Jehoiachin[x][t] son of Jehoiakim. 2Neither he nor his attendants nor the people of the land paid any attention[u] to the words the LORD had spoken through Jeremiah the prophet.

3King Zedekiah, however, sent Jehucal son of Shelemiah with the priest Zephaniah[v] son of Maaseiah to Jeremiah the prophet with this message: "Please pray[w] to the LORD our God for us."

4Now Jeremiah was free to come and go among the people, for he had not yet been put in prison.[x] 5Pharaoh's army had marched out of Egypt,[y] and when the Babylonians[y] who were besieging Jerusalem heard the report about them,

36:18 [a]ver 4
36:19 [b]1Ki 17:3
36:21 [c]ver 14 [d]2Ki 22:10
36:22 [e]Am 3:15
36:23 [f]1Ki 22:8
36:24 [g]Ps 36:1 [h]Ge 37:29; 2Ki 22:11; Isa 37:1
36:26 [i]Mt 23:34 [j]Jer 15:21
36:27 [k]ver 4
36:29 [l]Isa 30:10
36:30 [m]Jer 22:19
36:31 [n]Pr 29:1
36:32 [o]ver 4 [p]Ex 34:1 [q]ver 23
37:1 [r]2Ki 24:17 [s]Eze 17:13 [t]2Ki 24:8,12; 2Ch 36:10; Jer 22:24
37:2 [u]2Ki 24:19; 2Ch 36:12,14
37:3 [v]Jer 29:25; 52:24 [w]1Ki 13:6; Jer 21:1-2; 42:2
37:4 [x]ver 15; Jer 32:2
37:5 [y]Eze 17:15

x1 Hebrew *Coniah,* a variant of *Jehoiachin*
y5 Or *Chaldeans;* also in verses 8, 9, 13 and 14

they withdrew[a] from Jerusalem.[b]
6Then the word of the LORD came
to Jeremiah the prophet: 7"This is
what the LORD, the God of Israel,
says: Tell the king of Judah, who
sent you to inquire[c] of me, 'Pharaoh's army, which has marched out
to support you, will go back to its
own land, to Egypt.[d] 8Then the
Babylonians will return and attack
this city; they will capture it and
burn[e] it down.'
9"This is what the LORD says: Do
not deceive[f] yourselves, thinking,
'The Babylonians will surely leave
us.' They will not! 10Even if you
were to defeat the entire Babylonian[z] army that is attacking you and
only wounded men were left in
their tents, they would come out
and burn this city down."
11After the Babylonian army had
withdrawn[g] from Jerusalem because of Pharaoh's army, 12Jeremi-
ah started to leave the city to go to
the territory of Benjamin to get his
share of the property[h] among the
people there. 13But when he
reached the Benjamin Gate, the
captain of the guard, whose name
was Irijah son of Shelemiah, the
son of Hananiah, arrested him and
said, "You are deserting to the Babylonians!"
14"That's not true!" Jeremiah
said. "I am not deserting to the
Babylonians." But Irijah would not
listen to him; instead, he arrested[i]
Jeremiah and brought him to the
officials. 15They were angry with
Jeremiah and had him beaten[j]
and imprisoned in the house[k] of
Jonathan the secretary, which they
had made into a prison.
16Jeremiah was put into a vaulted cell in a dungeon, where he remained a long time. 17Then King
Zedekiah sent for him and had him
brought to the palace, where he
asked[l] him privately,[m] "Is there
any word from the LORD?"
"Yes," Jeremiah replied, "you
will be handed over[n] to the king of
Babylon."
18Then Jeremiah said to King
Zedekiah, "What crime[o] have I
committed against you or your officials or this people, that you have
put me in prison? 19Where are your
prophets who prophesied to you,
'The king of Babylon will not attack you or this land'? 20But now,
my lord the king, please listen. Let
me bring my petition before you:
Do not send me back to the house
of Jonathan the secretary, or I will
die there."
21King Zedekiah then gave orders for Jeremiah to be placed in
the courtyard of the guard and giv-
en bread from the street of the bakers each day until all the bread[p] in
the city was gone.[q] So Jeremiah
remained in the courtyard of the
guard.[r]

Jeremiah Thrown Into a Cistern

38 Shephatiah son of Mattan,
Gedaliah son of Pashhur,
Jehucal[a][s] son of Shelemiah, and
Pashhur son of Malkijah heard
what Jeremiah was telling all the
people when he said, 2"This is
what the LORD says: 'Whoever stays
in this city will die by the sword,
famine or plague,[t] but whoever
goes over to the Babylonians[b] will
live. He will escape with his life; he
will live.'[u] 3And this is what the
LORD says: 'This city will certainly
be handed over to the army of the
king of Babylon, who will capture
it.' "[v]
4Then the officials[w] said to the
king, "This man should be put to
death.[x] He is discouraging the soldiers who are left in this city, as
well as all the people, by the things
he is saying to them. This man is
not seeking the good of these people but their ruin."
5"He is in your hands," King
Zedekiah answered. "The king can
do nothing to oppose you."
6So they took Jeremiah and put
him into the cistern of Malkijah,
the king's son, which was in the
courtyard of the guard.[y] They lowered Jeremiah by ropes into the

37:5 [a] Jer 34:21 [b] 2Ki 24:7
37:7 [c] 2Ki 22:18 [d] Jer 2:36; La 4:17
37:8 [e] Jer 34:22; 39:8
37:9 [f] Jer 29:8
37:11 [g] ver 5
37:12 [h] Jer 32:9
37:14 [i] Jer 40:4
37:15 [j] Jer 20:2 [k] Jer 38:26
37:17 [l] Jer 15:11 [m] Jer 38:16 [n] Jer 21:7
37:18 [o] 1Sa 26:18; Jn 10:32; Ac 25:8
37:21 [p] Isa 33:16; Jer 38:9 [q] 2Ki 25:3; Jer 52:6 [r] Jer 32:2; 38:6,13,28
38:1 [s] Jer 37:3
38:2 [t] Jer 34:17 [u] Jer 21:9; 39:18; 45:5
38:3 [v] Jer 21:4,10; 32:3
38:4 [w] Jer 36:12 [x] Jer 26:11
38:6 [y] Jer 37:21

[z] *10* Or *Chaldean;* also in verse 11
[a] *1* Hebrew *Jucal,* a variant of *Jehucal*
[b] *2* Or *Chaldeans;* also in verses 18, 19 and 23

cistern; it had no water in it, only
mud, and Jeremiah sank down into
the mud.
7But Ebed-Melech,[a] a Cush-
ite,[c] an official[d][b] in the royal palace, heard that they had put Jeremiah into the cistern. While the
king was sitting in the Benjamin
Gate,[c] 8Ebed-Melech went out of
the palace and said to him, 9"My
lord the king, these men have acted
wickedly in all they have done to
Jeremiah the prophet. They have
thrown him into a cistern, where he
will starve to death when there is
no longer any bread[d] in the city."
10Then the king commanded
Ebed-Melech the Cushite, "Take
thirty men from here with you and
lift Jeremiah the prophet out of the
cistern before he dies."
11So Ebed-Melech took the men
with him and went to a room under
the treasury in the palace. He took
some old rags and worn-out clothes
from there and let them down with
ropes to Jeremiah in the cistern.
12Ebed-Melech the Cushite said to
Jeremiah, "Put these old rags and
worn-out clothes under your arms
to pad the ropes." Jeremiah did so,
13and they pulled him up with the
ropes and lifted him out of the cistern. And Jeremiah remained in
the courtyard of the guard.[e]

Zedekiah Questions Jeremiah Again

14Then King Zedekiah sent for
Jeremiah the prophet and had him
brought to the third entrance to the
temple of the LORD. "I am going to
ask you something," the king said
to Jeremiah. "Do not hide[f] anything from me."
15Jeremiah said to Zedekiah, "If
I give you an answer, will you not
kill me? Even if I did give you counsel, you would not listen to me."
16But King Zedekiah swore this
oath secretly[g] to Jeremiah: "As
surely as the LORD lives, who has
given us breath,[h] I will neither kill
you nor hand you over to those who
are seeking your life."[i]
17Then Jeremiah said to Zedekiah, "This is what the LORD God Almighty, the God of Israel, says: 'If
you surrender to the officers of the
king of Babylon, your life will be
spared and this city will not be
burned down; you and your family
will live.[j] 18But if you will not surrender to the officers of the king of
Babylon, this city will be handed
over[k] to the Babylonians and they
will burn[l] it down; you yourself
will not escape[m] from their
hands.' "
19King Zedekiah said to Jeremiah, "I am afraid[n] of the Jews who
have gone over[o] to the Babylonians, for the Babylonians may hand
me over to them and they will mistreat me."
20"They will not hand you over,"
Jeremiah replied. "Obey[p] the LORD
by doing what I tell you. Then it
will go well with you, and your
life[q] will be spared. 21But if you
refuse to surrender, this is what the
LORD has revealed to me: 22All the
women[r] left in the palace of the
king of Judah will be brought out to
the officials of the king of Babylon.
Those women will say to you:

" 'They misled you and
overcame you—
those trusted friends of
yours.
Your feet are sunk in the mud;
your friends have deserted
you.'

23"All your wives and children[s]
will be brought out to the Babylonians. You yourself will not escape
from their hands but will be captured[t] by the king of Babylon; and
this city will[e] be burned down."
24Then Zedekiah said to Jeremiah, "Do not let anyone know about
this conversation, or you may die.
25If the officials hear that I talked
with you, and they come to you and
say, 'Tell us what you said to the
king and what the king said to you;
do not hide it from us or we will kill
you,' 26then tell them, 'I was pleading with the king not to send me

38:7 [a] Jer 39:16 [b] Ac 8:27 [c] Job 29:7
38:9 [d] Jer 37:21
38:13 [e] Jer 37:21
38:14 [f] 1Sa 3:17
38:16 [g] Jer 37:17 [h] Isa 42:5; 57:16 [i] ver 4
38:17 [j] 2Ki 24:12; Jer 21:9
38:18 [k] ver 3; Jer 34:3 [l] Jer 37:8 [m] Jer 24:8; 32:4
38:19 [n] Isa 51:12; Jn 12:42 [o] Jer 39:9
38:20 [p] Jer 11:4 [q] Isa 55:3
38:22 [r] Jer 6:12
38:23 [s] 2Ki 25:6 [t] Jer 41:10

c7 Probably from the upper Nile region
d7 Or *a eunuch*
e23 Or *and you will cause this city to*

back to Jonathan's house[a] to die there.' "

[27]All the officials did come to Jeremiah and question him, and he told them everything the king had ordered him to say. So they said no more to him, for no one had heard his conversation with the king.

[28]And Jeremiah remained in the courtyard of the guard[b] until the day Jerusalem was captured.

The Fall of Jerusalem

39:1–10pp — 2Ki 25:1–12; Jer 52:4–16

39 This is how Jerusalem was taken: [1]In the ninth year of Zedekiah king of Judah, in the tenth month, Nebuchadnezzar king of Babylon marched against Jerusalem with his whole army and laid siege[c] to it. [2]And on the ninth day of the fourth month of Zedekiah's eleventh year, the city wall was broken through. [3]Then all the officials[d] of the king of Babylon came and took seats in the Middle Gate: Nergal-Sharezer of Samgar, Nebo-Sarsekim[f] a chief officer, Nergal-Sharezer a high official and all the other officials of the king of Babylon. [4]When Zedekiah king of Judah and all the soldiers saw them, they fled; they left the city at night by way of the king's garden, through the gate between the two walls, and headed toward the Arabah.[g]

[5]But the Babylonian[h] army pursued them and overtook Zedekiah[e] in the plains of Jericho. They captured him and took him to Nebuchadnezzar king of Babylon at Riblah[f] in the land of Hamath, where he pronounced sentence on him. [6]There at Riblah the king of Babylon slaughtered the sons of Zedekiah before his eyes and also killed all the nobles of Judah. [7]Then he put out Zedekiah's eyes[g] and bound him with bronze shackles to take him to Babylon.[h]

[8]The Babylonians[i] set fire[i] to the royal palace and the houses of the people and broke down the walls[j] of Jerusalem. [9]Nebuzaradan commander of the imperial guard carried into exile to Babylon the people who remained in the city, along with those who had gone over to him, and the rest of the people.[k] [10]But Nebuzaradan the commander of the guard left behind in the land of Judah some of the poor people, who owned nothing; and at that time he gave them vineyards and fields.

[11]Now Nebuchadnezzar king of Babylon had given these orders about Jeremiah through Nebuzaradan commander of the imperial guard: [12]"Take him and look after him; don't harm[l] him but do for him whatever he asks." [13]So Nebuzaradan the commander of the guard, Nebushazban a chief officer, Nergal-Sharezer a high official and all the other officers of the king of Babylon [14]sent and had Jeremiah taken out of the courtyard of the guard.[m] They turned him over to Gedaliah son of Ahikam,[n] the son of Shaphan, to take him back to his home. So he remained among his own people.[o]

[15]While Jeremiah had been confined in the courtyard of the guard, the word of the LORD came to him: [16]"Go and tell Ebed-Melech[p] the Cushite, 'This is what the LORD Almighty, the God of Israel, says: I am about to fulfill my words against this city through disaster,[q] not prosperity. At that time they will be fulfilled before your eyes. [17]But I will rescue[r] you on that day, declares the LORD; you will not be handed over to those you fear. [18]I will save you; you will not fall by the sword[s] but will escape with your life,[t] because you trust[u] in me, declares the LORD.' "

Jeremiah Freed

40 The word came to Jeremiah from the LORD after Nebuzaradan commander of the imperial guard had released him at Ramah. He had found Jeremiah bound in chains among all the cap-

38:26 [a]Jer 37:15
38:28 [b]Jer 37:21; 39:14
39:1 [c]2Ki 25:1; Jer 52:4; Eze 24:2
39:3 [d]Jer 21:4
39:5 [e]Jer 32:4 [f]2Ki 23:33
39:7 [g]Eze 12:13 [h]Jer 32:5
39:8 [i]Jer 38:18 [j]Ne 1:3
39:9 [k]Jer 40:1
39:12 [l]Pr 16:7; 1Pe 3:13
39:14 [m]Jer 38:28 [n]2Ki 22:12 [o]Jer 40:5
39:16 [p]Jer 38:7 [q]Jer 21:10; Da 9:12
39:17 [r]Ps 41:1-2
39:18 [s]Jer 45:5 [t]Jer 21:9; 38:2 [u]Jer 17:7

f3 Or *Nergal-Sharezer, Samgar-Nebo, Sarsekim*
g4 Or *the Jordan Valley* h5 Or *Chaldean*
i8 Or *Chaldeans*

tives from Jerusalem and Judah
who were being carried into exile
to Babylon. 2When the commander
of the guard found Jeremiah, he
said to him, "The LORD your God
decreed this disaster for this
place.[a] 3And now the LORD has
brought it about; he has done just
as he said he would. All this happened because you people sinned[b]
against the LORD and did not obey[c]
him. 4But today I am freeing you
from the chains on your wrists.
Come with me to Babylon, if you
like, and I will look after you; but if
you do not want to, then don't
come. Look, the whole country lies
before you; go wherever you
please."[d] 5However, before Jeremiah turned to go,[i] Nebuzaradan
added, "Go back to Gedaliah[e] son
of Ahikam, the son of Shaphan,
whom the king of Babylon has appointed over the towns of Judah,
and live with him among the people, or go anywhere else you
please."[f]

Then the commander gave him
provisions and a present and let
him go. 6So Jeremiah went to Gedaliah son of Ahikam at Mizpah[g]
and stayed with him among the
people who were left behind in the
land.

Gedaliah Assassinated

40:7-9; 41:1-3pp — 2Ki 25:22-26

7When all the army officers and
their men who were still in the
open country heard that the king of
Babylon had appointed Gedaliah
son of Ahikam as governor over the
land and had put him in charge of
the men, women and children who
were the poorest[h] in the land and
who had not been carried into exile
to Babylon, 8they came to Gedaliah at Mizpah[i]—Ishmael[j] son of
Nethaniah, Johanan and Jonathan
the sons of Kareah, Seraiah son of
Tanhumeth, the sons of Ephai the
Netophathite,[k] and Jaazaniah[k]
the son of the Maacathite,[l] and
their men. 9Gedaliah son of Ahikam, the son of Shaphan, took an
oath to reassure them and their
men. "Do not be afraid to serve[m]
the Babylonians,[l]" he said. "Settle
down in the land and serve the king
of Babylon, and it will go well with
you.[n] 10I myself will stay at Mizpah[o] to represent you before the
Babylonians who come to us, but
you are to harvest the wine, summer fruit and oil, and put them in
your storage jars, and live in the
towns you have taken over."[p]

11When all the Jews in Moab,[q]
Ammon, Edom and all the other
countries heard that the king of
Babylon had left a remnant in Judah and had appointed Gedaliah
son of Ahikam, the son of Shaphan,
as governor over them, 12they all
came back to the land of Judah, to
Gedaliah at Mizpah, from all the
countries where they had been
scattered.[r] And they harvested an
abundance of wine and summer
fruit.

13Johanan son of Kareah and all
the army officers still in the open
country came to Gedaliah at Mizpah[s] 14and said to him, "Don't you
know that Baalis king of the Ammonites[t] has sent Ishmael son of
Nethaniah to take your life?" But
Gedaliah son of Ahikam did not believe them.

15Then Johanan son of Kareah
said privately to Gedaliah in Mizpah, "Let me go and kill Ishmael
son of Nethaniah, and no one will
know it. Why should he take your
life and cause all the Jews who are
gathered around you to be scattered and the remnant of Judah to
perish?"

16But Gedaliah son of Ahikam
said to Johanan son of Kareah,
"Don't do such a thing! What you
are saying about Ishmael is not
true."

41 In the seventh month Ishmael[u] son of Nethaniah,
the son of Elishama, who was of
royal blood and had been one of
the king's officers, came with ten
men to Gedaliah son of Ahikam at

40:2 [a] Jer 50:7
40:3 [b] Da 9:11 [c] Dt 29:24-28; Ro 2:5-9
40:4 [d] Ge 13:9; Jer 39:11-12
40:5 [e] 2Ki 25:22 [f] Jer 39:14
40:6 [g] Jdg 20:1; 1Sa 7:5-17
40:7 [h] Jer 39:10
40:8 [i] ver 13 [j] ver 14; Jer 41:1,2 [k] 2Sa 23:28 [l] Dt 3:14
40:9 [m] Jer 27:11 [n] Jer 38:20
40:10 [o] ver 6 [p] Dt 1:39
40:11 [q] Nu 25:1
40:12 [r] Jer 43:5
40:13 [s] ver 8
40:14 [t] 2Sa 10:1-19; Jer 25:21; 41:10
41:1 [u] Jer 40:8

i5 Or *Jeremiah answered* k8 Hebrew *Jezaniah,* a variant of *Jaazaniah* l9 Or *Chaldeans;* also in verse 10

Mizpah. While they were eating together there, **2**Ishmael[a] son of
Nethaniah and the ten men who
were with him got up and struck
down Gedaliah son of Ahikam, the
son of Shaphan, with the sword,
killing the one whom the king of
Babylon had appointed[b] as governor over the land.[c] **3**Ishmael also
killed all the Jews who were with
Gedaliah at Mizpah, as well as the
Babylonian[m] soldiers who were
there.

4The day after Gedaliah's assas-
sination, before anyone knew
about it, **5**eighty men who had
shaved off their beards,[d] torn their
clothes and cut themselves came
from Shechem,[e] Shiloh[f] and Samaria,[g] bringing grain offerings
and incense with them to the
house of the LORD.[h] **6**Ishmael son
of Nethaniah went out from Mizpah to meet them, weeping[i] as he
went. When he met them, he said,
"Come to Gedaliah son of Ahikam." **7**When they went into the
city, Ishmael son of Nethaniah and
the men who were with him
slaughtered them and threw them
into a cistern. **8**But ten of them
said to Ishmael, "Don't kill us! We
have wheat and barley, oil and honey, hidden in a field."[j] So he let
them alone and did not kill them
with the others. **9**Now the cistern
where he threw all the bodies of the
men he had killed along with Gedaliah was the one King Asa[k] had
made as part of his defense[l]
against Baasha[m] king of Israel. Ishmael son of Nethaniah filled it with
the dead.

10Ishmael made captives of all
the rest of the people[n] who were in
Mizpah—the king's daughters
along with all the others who were
left there, over whom Nebuzaradan
commander of the imperial guard
had appointed Gedaliah son of
Ahikam. Ishmael son of Nethaniah
took them captive and set out to
cross over to the Ammonites.[o]

11When Johanan[p] son of Kareah
and all the army officers who were
with him heard about all the
crimes Ishmael son of Nethaniah
had committed, **12**they took all
their men and went to fight Ishmael son of Nethaniah. They caught
up with him near the great pool[q] in
Gibeon. **13**When all the people[r]
Ishmael had with him saw Johanan
son of Kareah and the army officers
who were with him, they were glad.
14All the people Ishmael had taken
captive at Mizpah turned and went
over to Johanan son of Kareah.
15But Ishmael son of Nethaniah
and eight of his men escaped[s]
from Johanan and fled to the Ammonites.

Flight to Egypt

16Then Johanan son of Kareah
and all the army officers who were
with him led away all the survivors[t] from Mizpah whom he had
recovered from Ishmael son of
Nethaniah after he had assassinated Gedaliah son of Ahikam: the
soldiers, women, children and
court officials he had brought from
Gibeon. **17**And they went on, stopping at Geruth Kimham[u] near
Bethlehem on their way to Egypt[v]
18to escape the Babylonians.[n]
They were afraid[w] of them because
Ishmael son of Nethaniah had
killed Gedaliah[x] son of Ahikam,
whom the king of Babylon had appointed as governor over the land.

42 Then all the army officers,
including Johanan[y] son of
Kareah and Jezaniah[o] son of Hoshaiah, and all the people from the
least to the greatest[z] approached
2Jeremiah the prophet and said to
him, "Please hear our petition and
pray[a] to the LORD your God for this
entire remnant.[b] For as you now
see, though we were once many,
now only a few[c] are left. **3**Pray that
the LORD your God will tell us
where we should go and what we
should do."[d]

4"I have heard you," replied Jeremiah the prophet. "I will certainly
pray[e] to the LORD your God as you
have requested; I will tell you ev-

41:2 [a]Ps 41:9; 109:5 [b]Jer 40:5 [c]2Sa 3:27; 20:9-10
41:5 [d]Lev 19:27 [e]Ge 33:18; Jdg 9:1-57; 1Ki 12:1 [f]Jos 18:1 [g]1Ki 16:24 [h]2Ki 25:9
41:6 [i]2Sa 3:16
41:8 [j]Isa 45:3
41:9 [k]1Ki 15:22; 2Ch 16:6 [l]Jdg 6:2 [m]2Ch 16:1
41:10 [n]Jer 40:7,12 [o]Jer 40:14
41:11 [p]Jer 40:8
41:12 [q]2Sa 2:13
41:13 [r]ver 10
41:15 [s]Job 21:30; Pr 28:17
41:16 [t]Jer 43:4
41:17 [u]2Sa 19:37 [v]Jer 42:14
41:18 [w]Isa 51:12; Jer 42:16; Lk 12:4-5 [x]Jer 40:5
42:1 [y]Jer 40:13; 41:11 [z]Jer 6:13; 44:12
42:2 [a]Jer 36:7; Ac 8:24; Jas 5:16 [b]Isa 1:9 [c]Lev 26:22; La 1:1
42:3 [d]Ps 86:11; Pr 3:6
42:4 [e]Ex 8:29; 1Sa 12:23

[m]3 Or *Chaldean* [n]*18* Or *Chaldeans*
[o]*1* Hebrew; Septuagint (see also 43:2) *Azariah*

erything the LORD says and will
keep nothing back from you."[a]
5Then they said to Jeremiah,
"May the LORD be a true and faithful witness[b] against us if we do not
act in accordance with everything
the LORD your God sends you to tell
us. 6Whether it is favorable or unfa-
vorable, we will obey the LORD our
God, to whom we are sending you,
so that it will go well[c] with us, for
we will obey[d] the LORD our God."
7Ten days later the word of the
LORD came to Jeremiah. 8So he
called together Johanan son of Kareah and all the army officers[e] who
were with him and all the people
from the least to the greatest. 9He
said to them, "This is what the
LORD, the God of Israel, to whom
you sent me to present your petition, says:[f] 10'If you stay in this
land, I will build[g] you up and not
tear you down; I will plant[h] you
and not uproot you,[i] for I am
grieved over the disaster I have inflicted on you.[j] 11Do not be afraid
of the king of Babylon,[k] whom you
now fear.[l] Do not be afraid of him,
declares the LORD, for I am with you
and will save[m] you and deliver you
from his hands.[n] 12I will show you
compassion so that he will have
compassion on you and restore you
to your land.'[o]
13"However, if you say, 'We will
not stay in this land,' and so disobey[p] the LORD your God, 14and if
you say, 'No, we will go and live in
Egypt,[q] where we will not see war
or hear the trumpet or be hungry
for bread,' 15then hear the word of
the LORD, O remnant of Judah. This
is what the LORD Almighty, the God
of Israel, says: 'If you are determined to go to Egypt and you do go
to settle there, 16then the sword[r]
you fear will overtake you there,
and the famine you dread will follow you into Egypt, and there you
will die. 17Indeed, all who are determined to go to Egypt to settle
there will die by the sword, famine
and plague;[s] not one of them will
survive or escape the disaster I will
bring on them.' 18This is what the
LORD Almighty, the God of Israel,
says: 'As my anger and wrath[t] have
been poured out on those who
lived in Jerusalem,[u] so will my
wrath be poured out on you when
you go to Egypt. You will be an object of cursing and horror,[v] of condemnation and reproach; you will
never see this place again.'[w]
19"O remnant of Judah, the LORD
has told you, 'Do not go to Egypt.'[x]
Be sure of this: I warn you today
20that you made a fatal mistake[p]
when you sent me to the LORD your
God and said, 'Pray to the LORD our
God for us; tell us everything he
says and we will do it.'[y] 21I have
told you today, but you still have
not obeyed the LORD your God in all
he sent me to tell you.[z] 22So now,
be sure of this: You will die by the
sword, famine and plague[a] in the
place where you want to go to settle."[b]

43 When Jeremiah finished
telling the people all the
words of the LORD their God—everything the LORD had sent him to
tell them[c]— 2Azariah son of Hoshaiah and Johanan[d] son of Kareah and all the arrogant men said to
Jeremiah, "You are lying! The LORD
our God has not sent you to say,
'You must not go to Egypt to settle
there.' 3But Baruch son of Neriah
is inciting you against us to hand
us over to the Babylonians,[q] so
they may kill us or carry us into exile to Babylon."[e]
4So Johanan son of Kareah and
all the army officers and all the
people disobeyed the LORD's command[f] to stay in the land of Judah.[g] 5Instead, Johanan son of
Kareah and all the army officers led
away all the remnant of Judah who
had come back to live in the land of
Judah from all the nations where
they had been scattered.[h] 6They
also led away all the men, women
and children and the king's daughters whom Nebuzaradan commander of the imperial guard had
left with Gedaliah son of Ahikam,
the son of Shaphan, and Jeremiah

42:4 [a] 1Ki 22:14; 1Sa 3:17
42:5 [b] Ge 31:50
42:6 [c] Dt 5:29; 6:3; Jer 7:23 [d] Ex 24:7; Jos 24:24
42:8 [e] ver 1
42:9 [f] 2Ki 22:15
42:10 [g] Jer 24:6 [h] Jer 31:28 [i] Eze 36:36 [j] Jer 18:8
42:11 [k] Jer 27:11 [l] Nu 14:9 [m] Isa 43:5 [n] Jer 1:8; Ro 8:31
42:12 [o] Ps 106:44-46
42:13 [p] Jer 44:16
42:14 [q] Nu 11:4-5
42:16 [r] Eze 11:8
42:17 [s] ver 22; Jer 44:13
42:18 [t] Dt 29:18-20; Jer 7:20 [u] 2Ch 36:19; Jer 39:1-9 [v] Jer 29:18 [w] Jer 22:10
42:19 [x] Dt 17:16; Isa 30:7
42:20 [y] ver 2
42:21 [z] Eze 2:7; Zec 7:11-12
42:22 [a] ver 17; Eze 6:11 [b] Hos 9:6
43:1 [c] Jer 26:8; 42:9-22
43:2 [d] Jer 42:1
43:3 [e] Jer 38:4
43:4 [f] Jer 42:5-6 [g] Jer 42:10
43:5 [h] Jer 40:12

p20 *Or you erred in your hearts* q3 *Or Chaldeans*

the prophet and Baruch son of Neriah. **7**So they entered Egypt in disobedience to the LORD and went as
far as Tahpanhes.[a]

8In Tahpanhes[b] the word of the
LORD came to Jeremiah: **9**"While
the Jews are watching, take some
large stones with you and bury
them in clay in the brick pavement
at the entrance to Pharaoh's palace
in Tahpanhes. **10**Then say to them,
'This is what the LORD Almighty,
the God of Israel, says: I will send
for my servant[c] Nebuchadnezzar
king of Babylon, and I will set his
throne over these stones I have
buried here; he will spread his royal
canopy above them. **11**He will
come and attack Egypt,[d] bringing
death to those destined for death,
captivity to those destined for captivity, and the sword to those destined for the sword.[e] **12**He[r] will
set fire to the temples of the gods[f]
of Egypt; he will burn their temples
and take their gods captive. As a
shepherd wraps[g] his garment
around him, so will he wrap Egypt
around himself and depart from
there unscathed. **13**There in the
temple of the sun[s] in Egypt he will
demolish the sacred pillars and will
burn down the temples of the gods
of Egypt.' "

Disaster Because of Idolatry

44 This word came to Jeremiah concerning all the Jews
living in Lower Egypt—in Migdol,[h]
Tahpanhes[i] and Memphis[t][j]—
and in Upper Egypt[u][k] **2**"This is
what the LORD Almighty, the God of
Israel, says: You saw the great disaster I brought on Jerusalem and
on all the towns of Judah. Today
they lie deserted and in ruins[l] **3**because of the evil they have done.
They provoked me to anger by
burning incense and by worshiping
other gods[m] that neither they nor
you nor your fathers[n] ever knew.
4Again and again[o] I sent my servants the prophets,[p] who said, 'Do
not do this detestable thing that I
hate!' **5**But they did not listen or
pay attention; they did not turn
from their wickedness or stop
burning incense to other gods.[q]
6Therefore, my fierce anger was
poured out; it raged against the
towns of Judah and the streets of
Jerusalem and made them the desolate ruins they are today.

7"Now this is what the LORD God
Almighty, the God of Israel, says:
Why bring such great disaster[r] on
yourselves by cutting off from Judah the men and women,[s] the
children and infants, and so leave
yourselves without a remnant?
8Why provoke me to anger with
what your hands have made,[t]
burning incense to other gods in
Egypt, where you have come to
live?[u] You will destroy yourselves
and make yourselves an object of
cursing and reproach[v] among all
the nations on earth. **9**Have you
forgotten the wickedness committed by your fathers and by the kings
and queens of Judah and the wickedness committed by you and your
wives in the land of Judah and the
streets of Jerusalem?[w] **10**To this
day they have not humbled themselves or shown reverence, nor
have they followed my law[x] and
the decrees I set before you and
your fathers.[y]

11"Therefore, this is what the
LORD Almighty, the God of Israel,
says: I am determined to bring disaster[z] on you and to destroy all
Judah. **12**I will take away the remnant[a] of Judah who were determined to go to Egypt to settle
there. They will all perish in Egypt;
they will fall by the sword or die
from famine. From the least to the
greatest, they will die by sword or
famine.[b] They will become an object of cursing and horror, of condemnation and reproach.[c] **13**I will
punish those who live in Egypt with
the sword, famine and plague,[d] as
I punished Jerusalem. **14**None of
the remnant of Judah who have
gone to live in Egypt will escape or
survive to return to the land of Judah, to which they long to return

43:7 [a]Jer 2:16; 44:1
43:8 [b]Jer 2:16
43:10 [c]Isa 44:28; Jer 25:9; 27:6
43:11 [d]Jer 46:13-26; Eze 29:19-20 [e]Jer 15:2; 44:13; Zec 11:9
43:12 [f]Jer 46:25; Eze 30:13 [g]Ps 104:2; 109:18-19
44:1 [h]Ex 14:2 [i]Jer 43:7,8 [j]Isa 19:13 [k]Isa 11:11; Jer 46:14
44:2 [l]Isa 6:11; Jer 9:11; 34:22
44:3 [m]ver 8; Dt 13:6-11; 29:26 [n]Dt 32:17; Jer 19:4
44:4 [o]Jer 7:13 [p]Jer 7:25; 25:4; 26:5
44:5 [q]Jer 11:8-10
44:7 [r]Jer 26:19 [s]Jer 51:22
44:8 [t]Jer 25:6-7 [u]1Co 10:22 [v]Jer 42:18
44:9 [w]ver 17,21
44:10 [x]Jos 1:7 [y]1Ki 9:6-9
44:11 [z]Jer 21:10; Am 9:4
44:12 [a]ver 7 [b]Isa 1:28 [c]Jer 29:18; 42:15-18
44:13 [d]Jer 42:17

[r]*12* Or *I* [s]*13* Or *in Heliopolis* [t]*1* Hebrew *Noph* [u]*1* Hebrew *in Pathros*

and live; none will return except a
few fugitives."[a]
15Then all the men who knew
that their wives were burning incense to other gods, along with all
the women who were present—a
large assembly—and all the people
living in Lower and Upper Egypt,[v]
said to Jeremiah, **16**"We will not
listen[b] to the message you have
spoken to us in the name of the
LORD! **17**We will certainly do everything we said we would:[c] We will
burn incense to the Queen of Heav-
en[d] and will pour out drink offerings to her just as we and our fathers, our kings and our officials
did in the towns of Judah and in
the streets of Jerusalem. At that
time we had plenty of food and
were well off and suffered no
harm.[e] **18**But ever since we
stopped burning incense to the
Queen of Heaven and pouring out
drink offerings to her, we have had
nothing and have been perishing
by sword and famine.[f]"
19The women added, "When we
burned incense to the Queen of
Heaven[g] and poured out drink offerings to her, did not our husbands know that we were making
cakes like her image and pouring
out drink offerings to her?"
20Then Jeremiah said to all the
people, both men and women, who
were answering him, **21**"Did not
the LORD remember[h] and think
about the incense[i] burned in the
towns of Judah and the streets of
Jerusalem[j] by you and your fathers,[k] your kings and your officials and the people of the land?
22When the LORD could no longer
endure your wicked actions and
the detestable things you did, your
land became an object of cursing[l]
and a desolate waste without inhabitants, as it is today.[m] **23**Because you have burned incense and
have sinned against the LORD and
have not obeyed him or followed
his law or his decrees or his stipulations, this disaster[n] has come
upon you, as you now see."[o]
24Then Jeremiah said to all the
people, including the women,[p]
"Hear the word of the LORD, all you
people of Judah in Egypt.[q] **25**This
is what the LORD Almighty, the God
of Israel, says: You and your wives
have shown by your actions what
you promised when you said, 'We
will certainly carry out the vows we
made to burn incense and pour out
drink offerings to the Queen of
Heaven.'[r]
"Go ahead then, do what you
promised! Keep your vows![s] **26**But
hear the word of the LORD, all Jews
living in Egypt: 'I swear[t] by my
great name,' says the LORD, 'that no
one from Judah living anywhere in
Egypt will ever again invoke my
name or swear, "As surely as the
Sovereign LORD lives."[u] **27**For I am
watching over them for harm,[v] not
for good; the Jews in Egypt will perish by sword and famine until they
are all destroyed. **28**Those who escape the sword and return to the
land of Judah from Egypt will be
very few.[w] Then the whole remnant of Judah who came to live in
Egypt will know whose word will
stand—mine or theirs.[x]
29" 'This will be the sign to you
that I will punish you in this place,'
declares the LORD, 'so that you will
know that my threats of harm
against you will surely stand.'[y]
30This is what the LORD says: 'I am
going to hand Pharaoh[z] Hophra
king of Egypt over to his enemies
who seek his life, just as I handed
Zedekiah[a] king of Judah over to
Nebuchadnezzar king of Babylon,
the enemy who was seeking his
life.' "[b]

A Message to Baruch

45 This is what Jeremiah the
prophet told Baruch[c] son
of Neriah in the fourth year of Jehoiakim[d] son of Josiah king of Judah, after Baruch had written on a
scroll the words Jeremiah was then
dictating: **2**"This is what the LORD,
the God of Israel, says to you, Baruch: **3**You said, 'Woe to me! The
LORD has added sorrow to my pain;

44:14 [a]ver 28; Jer 22:24-27; Ro 9:27
44:16 [b]Jer 11:8-10
44:17 [c]Dt 23:23 [d]ver 25; Jer 7:18 [e]Hos 2:5-13
44:18 [f]Mal 3:13-15
44:19 [g]Jer 7:18
44:21 [h]Isa 64:9; Jer 14:10 [i]Jer 11:13 [j]ver 9 [k]Ps 79:8
44:22 [l]Jer 25:18 [m]Ge 19:13; Ps 107:33-34
44:23 [n]Jer 40:2 [o]1Ki 9:9; Jer 7:13-15; Da 9:11-12
44:24 [p]ver 15 [q]Jer 43:7
44:25 [r]ver 17 [s]Eze 20:39
44:26 [t]Ge 22:16; Isa 48:1; Heb 6:13-17 [u]Dt 32:40; Ps 50:16
44:27 [v]Jer 31:28
44:28 [w]ver 13-14; Isa 10:19 [x]ver 17,25-26
44:29 [y]Pr 19:21
44:30 [z]Jer 46:26; Eze 30:21 [a]2Ki 25:1-7 [b]Jer 39:5
45:1 [c]Jer 32:12; 36:4,18,32 [d]2Ch 36:5

[v]15 Hebrew *in Egypt and Pathros*

I am worn out with groaning[a] and
find no rest.' "
4 The LORD said, "Say this to him:
'This is what the LORD says: I will
overthrow what I have built and
uproot what I have planted,[b]
throughout the land.[c] 5 Should you
then seek great things for yourself?
Seek them not.[d] For I will bring disaster on all people, declares the
LORD, but wherever you go I will let
you escape with your life.' "[e]

A Message About Egypt

46 This is the word of the LORD
that came to Jeremiah the
prophet concerning the nations:[f]

2 Concerning Egypt:

This is the message against the
army of Pharaoh Neco[g] king of
Egypt, which was defeated at Carchemish[h] on the Euphrates River
by Nebuchadnezzar king of Babylon in the fourth year of Jehoiakim[i] son of Josiah king of Judah:

3 "Prepare your shields,[j] both
large and small,
and march out for battle!
4 Harness the horses,
mount the steeds!
Take your positions
with helmets on!
Polish[k] your spears,
put on your armor![l]
5 What do I see?
They are terrified,
they are retreating,
their warriors are defeated.
They flee[m] in haste
without looking back,
and there is terror[n] on every
side,"
declares the LORD.
6 "The swift cannot flee[o]
nor the strong escape.
In the north by the River
Euphrates
they stumble and fall.[p]
7 "Who is this that rises like the
Nile,
like rivers of surging
waters?[q]
8 Egypt rises like the Nile,
like rivers of surging waters.
She says, 'I will rise and cover
the earth;
I will destroy cities and their
people.'
9 Charge, O horses!
Drive furiously,
O charioteers![r]
March on, O warriors—
men of Cush[w] and Put who
carry shields,
men of Lydia[s] who draw the
bow.
10 But that day[t] belongs to the
Lord, the LORD
Almighty—
a day of vengeance, for
vengeance on his foes.
The sword will devour[u] till it is
satisfied,
till it has quenched its thirst
with blood.
For the Lord, the LORD
Almighty, will offer
sacrifice[v]
in the land of the north by
the River Euphrates.
11 "Go up to Gilead and get
balm,[w]
O Virgin[x] Daughter of Egypt.
But you multiply remedies in
vain;
there is no healing[y] for you.
12 The nations will hear of your
shame;
your cries will fill the earth.
One warrior will stumble over
another;
both will fall[z] down
together."

13 This is the message the LORD
spoke to Jeremiah the prophet
about the coming of Nebuchadnezzar king of Babylon to attack
Egypt:[a]

14 "Announce this in Egypt, and
proclaim it in Migdol;
proclaim it also in Memphis[x]
and Tahpanhes:[b]
'Take your positions and get
ready,
for the sword devours those
around you.'

45:3 [a] Ps 69:3
45:4 [b] Jer 11:17 [c] Isa 5:5-7; Jer 18:7-10
45:5 [d] Mt 6:25-27, 33 [e] Jer 21:9; 38:2; 39:18
46:1 [f] Jer 1:10; 25:15-38
46:2 [g] 2Ki 23:29 [h] 2Ch 35:20 [i] Jer 45:1
46:3 [j] Isa 21:5; Jer 51:11-12
46:4 [k] Eze 21:9-11 [l] 1Sa 17:5,38; 2Ch 26:14; Ne 4:16
46:5 [m] ver 21 [n] Jer 49:29
46:6 [o] Isa 30:16 [p] ver 12,16; Da 11:19
46:7 [q] Jer 47:2
46:9 [r] Jer 47:3 [s] Isa 66:19
46:10 [t] Joel 1:15 [u] Dt 32:42 [v] Zep 1:7
46:11 [w] Jer 8:22 [x] Isa 47:1 [y] Jer 30:13; Mic 1:9
46:12 [z] Isa 19:4; Na 3:8-10
46:13 [a] Isa 19:1
46:14 [b] Jer 43:8

w9 That is, the upper Nile region
x14 Hebrew *Noph*; also in verse 19

15Why will your warriors be laid low?
They cannot stand, for the LORD will push them down.[a]
16They will stumble[b] repeatedly;
they will fall[c] over each other.
They will say, 'Get up, let us go back
to our own people and our native lands,
away from the sword of the oppressor.'
17There they will exclaim,
'Pharaoh king of Egypt is only a loud noise;
he has missed his opportunity.[d]'
18"As surely as I live," declares the King,[e]
whose name is the LORD Almighty,
"one will come who is like Tabor[f] among the mountains,
like Carmel[g] by the sea.
19Pack your belongings for exile,[h]
you who live in Egypt,
for Memphis will be laid waste
and lie in ruins without inhabitant.

20"Egypt is a beautiful heifer,
but a gadfly is coming
against her from the north.[i]
21The mercenaries[j] in her ranks
are like fattened calves.
They too will turn and flee[k] together,
they will not stand their ground,
for the day[l] of disaster is coming upon them,
the time for them to be punished.
22Egypt will hiss like a fleeing serpent
as the enemy advances in force;
they will come against her with axes,
like men who cut down trees.
23They will chop down her forest,"
declares the LORD,

46:15 [a]Isa 66:15-16
46:16 [b]Lev 26:37 [c]ver 6
46:17 [d]Isa 19:11-16
46:18 [e]Jer 48:15 [f]Jos 19:22 [g]1Ki 18:42
46:19 [h]Isa 20:4
46:20 [i]ver 24; Jer 47:2
46:21 [j]2Ki 7:6 [k]ver 5 [l]Ps 37:13
46:23 [m]Jdg 7:12
46:24 [n]Jer 1:15
46:25 [o]Eze 30:14; Na 3:8 [p]Jer 43:12 [q]Isa 20:6
46:26 [r]Jer 44:30 [s]Eze 32:11 [t]Eze 29:11-16
46:27 [u]Isa 41:13; 43:5 [v]Isa 11:11; Jer 50:19
46:28 [w]Isa 8:9-10 [x]Jer 4:27
47:1 [y]Ge 10:19; Am 1:6; Zec 9:5-7

"dense though it be.
They are more numerous than locusts,[m]
they cannot be counted.
24The Daughter of Egypt will be put to shame,
handed over to the people of the north.[n]"

25The LORD Almighty, the God of
Israel, says: "I am about to bring
punishment on Amon god of
Thebes,[y][o] on Pharaoh, on Egypt
and her gods[p] and her kings, and
on those who rely[q] on Pharaoh. 26I
will hand them over[r] to those who
seek their lives, to Nebuchadnezzar king[s] of Babylon and his officers. Later, however, Egypt will be
inhabited[t] as in times past," declares the LORD.

27"Do not fear,[u] O Jacob my servant;
do not be dismayed, O Israel.
I will surely save you out of a distant place,
your descendants from the land of their exile.[v]
Jacob will again have peace and security,
and no one will make him afraid.
28Do not fear, O Jacob my servant,
for I am with you,"[w] declares the LORD.
"Though I completely destroy[x] all the nations
among which I scatter you,
I will not completely destroy you.
I will discipline you but only with justice;
I will not let you go entirely unpunished."

A Message About the Philistines

47 This is the word of the LORD that came to Jeremiah the prophet concerning the Philistines before Pharaoh attacked Gaza:[y]

2This is what the LORD says:

[y]25 Hebrew *No*

"See how the waters are rising
in the north;[a]
they will become an
overflowing torrent.
They will overflow the land and
everything in it,
the towns and those who live
in them.
The people will cry out;
all who dwell in the land will
wail
3at the sound of the hoofs of
galloping steeds,
at the noise of enemy
chariots
and the rumble of their
wheels.
Fathers will not turn to help
their children;
their hands will hang limp.
4For the day has come
to destroy all the Philistines
and to cut off all survivors
who could help Tyre[b] and
Sidon.[c]
The LORD is about to destroy
the Philistines,[d]
the remnant from the coasts
of Caphtor.[z][e]
5Gaza will shave[f] her head in
mourning;
Ashkelon[g] will be silenced.
O remnant on the plain,
how long will you cut
yourselves?

6" 'Ah, sword[h] of the LORD,'
⌞you cry,⌟
'how long till you rest?
Return to your scabbard;
cease and be still.'
7But how can it rest
when the LORD has
commanded it,
when he has ordered it
to attack Ashkelon and the
coast?"

A Message About Moab

48:29–36pp — Isa 16:6–12

48 Concerning Moab:

This is what the LORD Almighty, the God of Israel, says:

"Woe to Nebo,[i] for it will be
ruined.
Kiriathaim[j] will be disgraced
and captured;
the stronghold[a] will be
disgraced and shattered.
2Moab will be praised[k] no
more;
in Heshbon[b][l] men will plot
her downfall:
'Come, let us put an end to
that nation.'
You too, O Madmen,[c] will be
silenced;
the sword will pursue you.
3Listen to the cries from
Horonaim,[m]
cries of great havoc and
destruction.
4Moab will be broken;
her little ones will cry out.[d]
5They go up the way to Luhith,[n]
weeping bitterly as they go;
on the road down to Horonaim
anguished cries over the
destruction are heard.
6Flee! Run for your lives;
become like a bush[e] in the
desert.[o]
7Since you trust in your deeds
and riches,
you too will be taken captive,
and Chemosh[p] will go into
exile,[q]
together with his priests and
officials.
8The destroyer will come against
every town,
and not a town will escape.
The valley will be ruined
and the plateau destroyed,
because the LORD has
spoken.
9Put salt on Moab,
for she will be laid waste[f];
her towns will become
desolate,
with no one to live in them.

10"A curse on him who is lax in
doing the LORD's work!
A curse on him who keeps

47:2 [a] Isa 8:7; 14:31
47:4 [b] Am 1:9-10; Zec 9:2-4 [c] Jer 25:22 [d] Ge 10:14; Joel 3:4 [e] Dt 2:23
47:5 [f] Jer 41:5; Mic 1:16 [g] Jer 25:20
47:6 [h] Jer 12:12
48:1 [i] Nu 32:38 [j] Nu 32:37
48:2 [k] Isa 16:14 [l] Nu 21:25
48:3 [m] Isa 15:5
48:5 [n] Isa 15:5
48:6 [o] Jer 17:6
48:7 [p] Nu 21:29 [q] Isa 46:1-2; Jer 49:3

[z]4 That is, Crete [a]1 Or / *Misgab* [b]2 The Hebrew for *Heshbon* sounds like the Hebrew for *plot.* [c]2 The name of the Moabite town Madmen sounds like the Hebrew for *be silenced.* [d]4 Hebrew; Septuagint / *proclaim it to Zoar* [e]6 Or *like Aroer* [f]9 Or *Give wings to Moab, / for she will fly away*

his sword[a] from bloodshed![b]

11"Moab has been at rest[c] from
youth,
like wine left on its dregs,[d]
not poured from one jar to
another—
she has not gone into exile.
So she tastes as she did,
and her aroma is unchanged.
12But days are coming,"
declares the LORD,
"when I will send men who
pour from jars,
and they will pour her out;
they will empty her jars
and smash her jugs.
13Then Moab will be ashamed[e]
of Chemosh,
as the house of Israel was
ashamed
when they trusted in Bethel.

14"How can you say, 'We are
warriors,[f]
men valiant in battle'?
15Moab will be destroyed and her
towns invaded;
her finest young men will go
down in the slaughter,[g]"
declares the King,[h] whose
name is the LORD
Almighty.[i]
16"The fall of Moab is at hand;[j]
her calamity will come
quickly.
17Mourn for her, all who live
around her,
all who know her fame;
say, 'How broken is the mighty
scepter,
how broken the glorious
staff!'

18"Come down from your glory
and sit on the parched
ground,[k]
O inhabitants of the
Daughter of Dibon,[l]
for he who destroys Moab
will come up against you
and ruin your fortified
cities.[m]
19Stand by the road and watch,
you who live in Aroer.[n]
Ask the man fleeing and the
woman escaping,

48:10 [a]Jer 47:6 [b]1Ki 20:42; 2Ki 13:15-19
48:11 [c]Zec 1:15 [d]Zep 1:12
48:13 [e]Hos 10:6
48:14 [f]Ps 33:16
48:15 [g]Jer 50:27 [h]Jer 46:18 [i]Jer 51:57
48:16 [j]Isa 13:22
48:18 [k]Isa 47:1 [l]Nu 21:30; Jos 13:9 [m]ver 8
48:19 [n]Dt 2:36
48:20 [o]Isa 16:7 [p]Nu 21:13
48:21 [q]Nu 21:23; Isa 15:4 [r]Jos 13:18
48:22 [s]Jos 13:9,17
48:23 [t]Jos 13:17
48:24 [u]Am 2:2
48:25 [v]Ps 75:10 [w]Ps 10:15; Eze 30:21
48:26 [x]Jer 25:16,27
48:27 [y]Jer 2:26 [z]Job 16:4; Jer 18:16 [a]Mic 7:8-10
48:28 [b]Ps 55:6-7 [c]Jdg 6:2
48:29 [d]Job 40:12; Isa 16:6
48:31 [e]Isa 15:5-8

ask them, 'What has
happened?'
20Moab is disgraced, for she is
shattered.
Wail[o] and cry out!
Announce by the Arnon[p]
that Moab is destroyed.
21Judgment has come to the
plateau—
to Holon, Jahzah[q] and
Mephaath,[r]
22 to Dibon,[s] Nebo and Beth
Diblathaim,
23 to Kiriathaim, Beth Gamul
and Beth Meon,[t]
24 to Kerioth[u] and
Bozrah—
to all the towns of Moab, far
and near.
25Moab's horn[g][v] is cut off;
her arm[w] is broken,"
declares the LORD.

26"Make her drunk,[x]
for she has defied the LORD.
Let Moab wallow in her vomit;
let her be an object of
ridicule.
27Was not Israel the object of
your ridicule?[y]
Was she caught among
thieves,
that you shake your head[z] in
scorn[a]
whenever you speak of her?
28Abandon your towns and dwell
among the rocks,
you who live in Moab.
Be like a dove[b] that makes its
nest
at the mouth of a cave.[c]
29"We have heard of Moab's
pride[d]—
her overweening pride and
conceit,
her pride and arrogance
and the haughtiness of her
heart.
30I know her insolence but it is
futile,"
declares the LORD,
"and her boasts accomplish
nothing.
31Therefore I wail[e] over Moab,
for all Moab I cry out,

[g]25 *Horn* here symbolizes strength.

I moan for the men of Kir
Hareseth.[a]
32I weep for you, as Jazer weeps,
O vines of Sibmah.[b]
Your branches spread as far as
the sea;
they reached as far as the sea
of Jazer.
The destroyer has fallen
on your ripened fruit and
grapes.
33Joy and gladness are gone
from the orchards and fields
of Moab.
I have stopped the flow of
wine[c] from the presses;
no one treads them with
shouts of joy.[d]
Although there are shouts,
they are not shouts of joy.
34"The sound of their cry rises
from Heshbon to Elealeh[e]
and Jahaz,[f]
from Zoar[g] as far as
Horonaim[h] and Eglath
Shelishiyah,
for even the waters of
Nimrim are dried up.[i]
35In Moab I will put an end
to those who make offerings
on the high places[j]
and burn incense[k] to their
gods,"
declares the LORD.
36"So my heart laments[l] for
Moab like a flute;
it laments like a flute for the
men of Kir Hareseth.
The wealth they acquired[m] is
gone.
37Every head is shaved[n]
and every beard cut off;
every hand is slashed
and every waist is covered
with sackcloth.[o]
38On all the roofs in Moab
and in the public squares
there is nothing but mourning,
for I have broken Moab
like a jar[p] that no one
wants,"
declares the LORD.
39"How shattered she is! How
they wail!
How Moab turns her back in
shame!
Moab has become an object of
ridicule,
an object of horror to all
those around her."

40This is what the LORD says:

"Look! An eagle is swooping[q]
down,
spreading its wings[r] over
Moab.
41Kerioth[h] will be captured
and the strongholds taken.
In that day the hearts of
Moab's warriors
will be like the heart of a
woman in labor.[s]
42Moab will be destroyed[t] as a
nation[u]
because she defied[v] the
LORD.
43Terror and pit and snare[w] await
you,
O people of Moab,"
declares the LORD.
44"Whoever flees[x] from the terror
will fall into a pit,
whoever climbs out of the pit
will be caught in a snare;
for I will bring upon Moab
the year[y] of her
punishment,"
declares the LORD.

45"In the shadow of Heshbon
the fugitives stand helpless,
for a fire has gone out from
Heshbon,
a blaze from the midst of
Sihon;[z]
it burns the foreheads of Moab,
the skulls[a] of the noisy
boasters.
46Woe to you, O Moab![b]
The people of Chemosh are
destroyed;
your sons are taken into exile
and your daughters into
captivity.

47"Yet I will restore[c] the
fortunes of Moab
in days to come,"
declares the LORD.

Here ends the judgment on Moab.

48:31 [a]2Ki 3:25
48:32 [b]Isa 16:8-9
48:33 [c]Isa 16:10 [d]Joel 1:12
48:34 [e]Nu 32:3 [f]Isa 15:4 [g]Ge 13:10 [h]Isa 15:5 [i]Isa 15:6
48:35 [j]Isa 15:2; 16:12 [k]Jer 11:13
48:36 [l]Isa 16:11 [m]Isa 15:7
48:37 [n]Isa 15:2; Jer 41:5 [o]Ge 37:34
48:38 [p]Jer 22:28
48:40 [q]Dt 28:49; Hab 1:8 [r]Isa 8:8
48:41 [s]Isa 21:3
48:42 [t]Ps 83:4; Isa 16:14 [u]ver 2 [v]ver 26
48:43 [w]Isa 24:17
48:44 [x]1Ki 19:17; Isa 24:18 [y]Jer 11:23
48:45 [z]Nu 21:21, 26-28 [a]Nu 24:17
48:46 [b]Nu 21:29
48:47 [c]Jer 12:15; 49:6,39

[h]41 Or *The cities*

A Message About Ammon

49 Concerning the Ammonites:[a]

This is what the LORD says:

"Has Israel no sons?
Has she no heirs?
Why then has Molech[i] taken possession of Gad?
Why do his people live in its towns?
2But the days are coming,"
declares the LORD,
"when I will sound the battle cry[b]
against Rabbah[c] of the Ammonites;
it will become a mound of ruins,
and its surrounding villages will be set on fire.
Then Israel will drive out those who drove her out,[d]"
says the LORD.
3"Wail, O Heshbon, for Ai[e] is destroyed!
Cry out, O inhabitants of Rabbah!
Put on sackcloth and mourn;
rush here and there inside the walls,
for Molech will go into exile,[f]
together with his priests and officials.
4Why do you boast of your valleys,
boast of your valleys so fruitful?
O unfaithful daughter,
you trust in your riches[g]
and say,
'Who will attack me?'[h]
5I will bring terror on you
from all those around you,"
declares the Lord, the LORD Almighty.
"Every one of you will be driven away,
and no one will gather the fugitives.

6"Yet afterward, I will restore[i] the fortunes of the Ammonites,"
declares the LORD.

49:1 [a]Am 1:13; Zep 2:8-9
49:2 [b]Jer 4:19 [c]Dt 3:11 [d]Isa 14:2; Eze 21:28-32; 25:2-11
49:3 [e]Jos 8:28 [f]Jer 48:7
49:4 [g]Jer 9:23; 1Ti 6:17 [h]Jer 21:13
49:6 [i]ver 39; Jer 48:47
49:7 [j]Ge 25:30; Eze 25:12 [k]Ge 36:11,15, 34
49:8 [l]Jer 25:23
49:10 [m]Mal 1:2-5
49:11 [n]Hos 14:3
49:12 [o]Jer 25:15 [p]Jer 25:28-29
49:13 [q]Ge 22:16 [r]Ge 36:33; Isa 34:6

A Message About Edom

49:9–10pp — Ob 5–6
49:14–16pp — Ob 1–4

7Concerning Edom:[j]

This is what the LORD Almighty says:

"Is there no longer wisdom in Teman?[k]
Has counsel perished from the prudent?
Has their wisdom decayed?
8Turn and flee, hide in deep caves,
you who live in Dedan,[l]
for I will bring disaster on Esau
at the time I punish him.
9If grape pickers came to you,
would they not leave a few grapes?
If thieves came during the night,
would they not steal only as much as they wanted?
10But I will strip Esau bare;
I will uncover his hiding places,
so that he cannot conceal himself.
His children, relatives and neighbors will perish,
and he will be no more.[m]
11Leave your orphans;[n] I will protect their lives.
Your widows too can trust in me."

12This is what the LORD says: "If
those who do not deserve to drink
the cup[o] must drink it, why should
you go unpunished?[p] You will not
go unpunished, but must drink it.
13I swear[q] by myself," declares the
LORD, "that Bozrah[r] will become a
ruin and an object of horror, of reproach and of cursing; and all its
towns will be in ruins forever."

14I have heard a message from the LORD:
An envoy was sent to the nations to say,
"Assemble yourselves to attack it!
Rise up for battle!"

[i]*1* Or *their king*; Hebrew *malcam*; also in verse 3

15"Now I will make you small
among the nations,
despised among men.
16The terror you inspire
and the pride of your
heart have deceived
you,
you who live in the clefts of the
rocks,
who occupy the heights of
the hill.
Though you build your nest[a]
as high as the eagle's,
from there I will bring you
down,"
declares the LORD.
17"Edom will become an object
of horror;[b]
all who pass by will be
appalled and will scoff
because of all its wounds.[c]
18As Sodom and Gomorrah[d]
were overthrown,
along with their neighboring
towns,"
says the LORD,
"so no one will live there;
no man will dwell[e] in it.

19"Like a lion coming up from
Jordan's thickets[f]
to a rich pastureland,
I will chase Edom from its land
in an instant.
Who is the chosen one I will
appoint for this?
Who is like me and who can
challenge me?[g]
And what shepherd can stand
against me?"
20Therefore, hear what the LORD
has planned against
Edom,
what he has purposed[h]
against those who live in
Teman:
The young of the flock[i] will be
dragged away;
he will completely destroy[j]
their pasture because of
them.
21At the sound of their fall the
earth will tremble;[k]
their cry[l] will resound to the
Red Sea.[i]
22Look! An eagle will soar and
swoop[m] down,
spreading its wings over
Bozrah.
In that day the hearts of
Edom's warriors
will be like the heart of a
woman in labor.[n]

A Message About Damascus

23Concerning Damascus:[o]

"Hamath[p] and Arpad[q] are
dismayed,
for they have heard bad
news.
They are disheartened,
troubled like[k] the restless
sea.[r]
24Damascus has become feeble,
she has turned to flee
and panic has gripped her;
anguish and pain have seized
her,
pain like that of a woman in
labor.
25Why has the city of renown not
been abandoned,
the town in which I delight?
26Surely, her young men will fall
in the streets;
all her soldiers will be
silenced[s] in that day,"
declares the LORD
Almighty.
27"I will set fire[t] to the walls of
Damascus;
it will consume the fortresses
of Ben-Hadad.[u]"

A Message About Kedar and Hazor

28Concerning Kedar[v] and the
kingdoms of Hazor, which Nebuchadnezzar king of Babylon attacked:

This is what the LORD says:

"Arise, and attack Kedar
and destroy the people of the
East.[w]
29Their tents and their flocks will
be taken;
their shelters will be carried
off
with all their goods and
camels.

49:16 [a]Job 39:27; Am 9:2
49:17 [b]ver 13 [c]Jer 50:13; Eze 35:7
49:18 [d]Ge 19:24; Dt 29:23 [e]ver 33
49:19 [f]Jer 12:5 [g]Jer 50:44
49:20 [h]Isa 14:27 [i]Jer 50:45 [j]Mal 1:3-4
49:21 [k]Eze 26:15 [l]Jer 50:46; Eze 26:18
49:22 [m]Hos 8:1 [n]Isa 13:8; Jer 48:40-41
49:23 [o]Ge 14:15; 2Ch 16:2; Ac 9:2 [p]Isa 10:9; Am 6:2; Zec 9:2 [q]2Ki 18:34 [r]Ge 49:4; Isa 57:20
49:26 [s]Jer 50:30
49:27 [t]Jer 43:12; Am 1:4 [u]1Ki 15:18
49:28 [v]Ge 25:13 [w]Jdg 6:3

[i]21 Hebrew *Yam Suph*; that is, Sea of Reeds
[k]23 Hebrew *on* or *by*

Men will shout to them,
'Terror[a] on every side!'

30"Flee quickly away!
Stay in deep caves, you who
live in Hazor,"
declares the LORD.
"Nebuchadnezzar king of
Babylon has plotted
against you;
he has devised a plan against
you.

31"Arise and attack a nation at
ease,
which lives in confidence,"
declares the LORD,
"a nation that has neither gates
nor bars;[b]
its people live alone.
32Their camels will become
plunder,
and their large herds will be
booty.
I will scatter to the winds those
who are in distant
places[1c]
and will bring disaster on
them from every side,"
declares the LORD.
33"Hazor will become a haunt of
jackals,
a desolate[d] place forever.
No one will live there;
no man will dwell[e] in it."

A Message About Elam

34This is the word of the LORD
that came to Jeremiah the prophet
concerning Elam,[f] early in the
reign of Zedekiah[g] king of Judah:

35This is what the LORD Almighty
says:

"See, I will break the bow[h] of
Elam,
the mainstay of their might.
36I will bring against Elam the
four winds[i]
from the four quarters of the
heavens;
I will scatter them to the four
winds,
and there will not be a
nation
where Elam's exiles do not
go.

49:29 [a]Jer 6:25; 46:5
49:31 [b]Eze 38:11
49:32 [c]Jer 9:26
49:33 [d]Jer 10:22 [e]ver 18; Jer 51:37
49:34 [f]Ge 10:22 [g]2Ki 24:18
49:35 [h]Isa 22:6
49:36 [i]ver 32
49:37 [j]Jer 30:24 [k]Jer 9:16
49:39 [l]Jer 48:47
50:1 [m]Ge 10:10; Isa 13:1
50:2 [n]Jer 4:16 [o]Jer 51:31 [p]Isa 46:1 [q]Jer 51:47
50:3 [r]ver 13; Isa 14:22-23 [s]Zep 1:3
50:4 [t]Jer 3:18; Hos 1:11 [u]Ezr 3:12; Jer 31:9 [v]Hos 3:5

37I will shatter Elam before their
foes,
before those who seek their
lives;
I will bring disaster upon them,
even my fierce anger,"[j]
declares the LORD.
"I will pursue them with the
sword[k]
until I have made an end of
them.
38I will set my throne in Elam
and destroy her king and
officials,"
declares the LORD.

39"Yet I will restore[l] the
fortunes of Elam
in days to come,"
declares the LORD.

A Message About Babylon

51:15–19pp — Jer 10:12–16

50 This is the word the LORD
spoke through Jeremiah
the prophet concerning Babylon[m]
and the land of the Babylonians[m]:

2"Announce and proclaim[n]
among the nations,
lift up a banner and proclaim
it;
keep nothing back, but say,
'Babylon will be captured;[o]
Bel[p] will be put to shame,
Marduk[q] filled with terror.
Her images will be put to
shame
and her idols filled with
terror.'
3A nation from the north will
attack her
and lay waste her land.
No one will live[r] in it;
both men and animals[s] will
flee away.

4"In those days, at that time,"
declares the LORD,
"the people of Israel and the
people of Judah
together[t]
will go in tears[u] to seek[v]
the LORD their God.
5They will ask the way to Zion

[1]32 Or *who clip the hair by their foreheads*
[m]1 Or *Chaldeans*; also in verses 8, 25, 35 and 45

and turn their faces toward
it.
They will come[a] and bind
themselves to the LORD
in an everlasting covenant[b]
that will not be forgotten.

6"My people have been lost
sheep;[c]
their shepherds have led
them astray
and caused them to roam on
the mountains.
They wandered over mountain
and hill[d]
and forgot their own resting
place.[e]
7Whoever found them devoured
them;
their enemies said, 'We are
not guilty,[f]
for they sinned against the
LORD, their true pasture,
the LORD, the hope[g] of their
fathers.'

8"Flee[h] out of Babylon;
leave the land of the
Babylonians,
and be like the goats that
lead the flock.
9For I will stir up and bring
against Babylon
an alliance of great nations
from the land of the
north.
They will take up their
positions against her,
and from the north she will
be captured.
Their arrows will be like skilled
warriors
who do not return
empty-handed.
10So Babylonia[n] will be
plundered;
all who plunder her will have
their fill,"
declares the LORD.

11"Because you rejoice and are
glad,
you who pillage my
inheritance,[i]
because you frolic like a heifer
threshing grain
and neigh like stallions,

50:5 [a]Jer 33:7 [b]Isa 55:3; Jer 32:40; Heb 8:6-10
50:6 [c]Isa 53:6; Mt 9:36; 10:6 [d]Jer 3:6; Eze 34:6 [e]ver 19
50:7 [f]Jer 2:3 [g]Jer 14:8
50:8 [h]Isa 48:20; Jer 51:6; Rev 18:4
50:11 [i]Isa 47:6
50:13 [j]Jer 18:16 [k]Jer 49:17
50:14 [l]ver 29,42
50:15 [m]Jer 51:14 [n]Jer 51:44,58 [o]Jer 51:6 [p]Ps 137:8; Rev 18:6
50:16 [q]Jer 25:38 [r]Isa 13:14 [s]Jer 51:9
50:17 [t]Jer 2:15 [u]2Ki 17:6 [v]2Ki 24:10,14 [w]2Ki 25:7

12your mother will be greatly
ashamed;
she who gave you birth will
be disgraced.
She will be the least of the
nations—
a wilderness, a dry land, a
desert.
13Because of the LORD's anger she
will not be inhabited
but will be completely
desolate.
All who pass Babylon will be
horrified and scoff[j]
because of all her wounds.[k]

14"Take up your positions around
Babylon,
all you who draw the bow.[l]
Shoot at her! Spare no arrows,
for she has sinned against
the LORD.
15Shout[m] against her on every
side!
She surrenders, her towers
fall,
her walls[n] are torn down.
Since this is the vengeance[o] of
the LORD,
take vengeance on her;
do to her[p] as she has done
to others.
16Cut off from Babylon the sower,
and the reaper with his sickle
at harvest.
Because of the sword[q] of the
oppressor
let everyone return to his
own people,[r]
let everyone flee to his own
land.[s]

17"Israel is a scattered flock
that lions[t] have chased
away.
The first to devour him
was the king[u] of Assyria;
the last to crush his bones
was Nebuchadnezzar[v] king[w]
of Babylon."

18Therefore this is what the LORD
Almighty, the God of Israel, says:

"I will punish the king of
Babylon and his land

[n]10 *Or Chaldea*

as I punished the king[a] of
Assyria.[b]
19But I will bring[c] Israel back to
his own pasture
and he will graze on Carmel
and Bashan;
his appetite will be satisfied
on the hills[d] of Ephraim and
Gilead.
20In those days, at that time,"
declares the LORD,
"search will be made for
Israel's guilt,
but there will be none,
and for the sins[e] of Judah,
but none will be found,
for I will forgive[f] the
remnant[g] I spare.

21"Attack the land of Merathaim
and those who live in
Pekod.[h]
Pursue, kill and completely
destroy° them,"
declares the LORD
"Do everything I have
commanded you.
22The noise[i] of battle is in the
land,
the noise of great
destruction!
23How broken and shattered
is the hammer of the whole
earth!
How desolate[j] is Babylon
among the nations!
24I set a trap[k] for you,
O Babylon,
and you were caught before
you knew it;
you were found and captured[l]
because you opposed[m] the
LORD.
25The LORD has opened his
arsenal
and brought out the
weapons[n] of his wrath,
for the Sovereign LORD Almighty
has work to do
in the land of the
Babylonians.[o]
26Come against her from afar.
Break open her granaries;
pile her up like heaps of
grain.
Completely destroy[p] her
and leave her no remnant.

50:18 [a]Isa 10:12 [b]Eze 31:3
50:19 [c]Jer 31:10; Eze 34:13 [d]Jer 31:5; 33:12
50:20 [e]Mic 7:18,19 [f]Jer 31:34 [g]Isa 1:9
50:21 [h]Eze 23:23
50:22 [i]Jer 4:19-21; 51:54
50:23 [j]Isa 14:16
50:24 [k]Da 5:30-31 [l]Jer 51:31 [m]Job 9:4
50:25 [n]Isa 13:5 [o]Jer 51:25,55
50:26 [p]Isa 14:22-23
50:28 [q]Isa 48:20; Jer 51:10 [r]ver 15
50:29 [s]ver 14 [t]Rev 18:6 [u]Jer 51:56 [v]Isa 47:10
50:30 [w]Isa 13:18; Jer 49:26
50:31 [x]Jer 21:13
50:32 [y]Jer 21:14; 49:27
50:33 [z]Isa 58:6 [a]Isa 14:17

27Kill all her young bulls;
let them go down to the
slaughter!
Woe to them! For their day has
come,
the time for them to be
punished.
28Listen to the fugitives and
refugees from Babylon
declaring in Zion[q]
how the LORD our God has
taken vengeance,[r]
vengeance for his temple.

29"Summon archers against
Babylon,
all those who draw the
bow.[s]
Encamp all around her;
let no one escape.
Repay[t] her for her deeds;[u]
do to her as she has done.
For she has defied[v] the LORD,
the Holy One of Israel.
30Therefore, her young men[w] will
fall in the streets;
all her soldiers will be
silenced in that day,"
declares the LORD.
31"See, I am against[x] you,
O arrogant one,"
declares the Lord, the LORD
Almighty,
"for your day has come,
the time for you to be
punished.
32The arrogant one will stumble
and fall
and no one will help her up;
I will kindle a fire[y] in her
towns
that will consume all who are
around her."

33This is what the LORD Almighty
says:

"The people of Israel are
oppressed,[z]
and the people of Judah as
well.
All their captors hold them
fast,
refusing to let them go.[a]

°21 The Hebrew term refers to the irrevocable giving over of things or persons to the LORD, often by totally destroying them; also in verse 26.

34Yet their Redeemer is strong;
the LORD Almighty[a] is his name.
He will vigorously defend their cause[b]
so that he may bring rest[c] to their land,
but unrest to those who live in Babylon.

35"A sword[d] against the Babylonians!"
declares the LORD—
"against those who live in Babylon
and against her officials and wise[e] men!
36A sword against her false prophets!
They will become fools.
A sword against her warriors![f]
They will be filled with terror.
37A sword against her horses and chariots[g]
and all the foreigners in her ranks!
They will become women.[h]
A sword against her treasures!
They will be plundered.
38A drought on[p] her waters!
They will dry[i] up.
For it is a land of idols,[j]
idols that will go mad with terror.

39"So desert creatures and hyenas will live there,
and there the owl will dwell.
It will never again be inhabited
or lived in from generation to generation.[k]
40As God overthrew Sodom and Gomorrah[l]
along with their neighboring towns,"
declares the LORD,
"so no one will live there;
no man will dwell in it.

41"Look! An army is coming from the north;[m]
a great nation and many kings
are being stirred up from the ends of the earth.[n]
42They are armed with bows[o] and spears;
they are cruel and without mercy.[p]
They sound like the roaring sea[q]
as they ride on their horses;
they come like men in battle formation
to attack you, O Daughter of Babylon.[r]
43The king of Babylon has heard reports about them,
and his hands hang limp.
Anguish has gripped him,
pain like that of a woman in labor.
44Like a lion coming up from Jordan's thickets
to a rich pastureland,
I will chase Babylon from its land in an instant.
Who is the chosen[s] one I will appoint for this?
Who is like me and who can challenge me?[t]
And what shepherd can stand against me?"
45Therefore, hear what the LORD has planned against Babylon,
what he has purposed[u] against the land of the Babylonians:
The young of the flock will be dragged away;
he will completely destroy their pasture because of them.
46At the sound of Babylon's capture the earth will tremble;
its cry[v] will resound among the nations.

51 This is what the LORD says:
"See, I will stir up the spirit of a destroyer
against Babylon and the people of Leb Kamai.[q]
2I will send foreigners to Babylon
to winnow[w] her and to devastate her land;
they will oppose her on every side

50:34 [a]Jer 51:19 [b]Jer 15:21; 51:36 [c]Isa 14:7
50:35 [d]Jer 47:6 [e]Da 5:7
50:36 [f]Jer 49:22
50:37 [g]Jer 51:21 [h]Jer 51:30; Na 3:13
50:38 [i]Jer 51:36 [j]ver 2
50:39 [k]Isa 13:19-22; 34:13-15; Jer 51:37; Rev 18:2
50:40 [l]Ge 19:24
50:41 [m]Jer 6:22 [n]Isa 13:4; Jer 51:22-28
50:42 [o]ver 14 [p]Isa 13:18 [q]Isa 5:30 [r]Jer 6:23
50:44 [s]Nu 16:5 [t]Job 41:10; Isa 46:9; Jer 49:19
50:45 [u]Ps 33:11; Isa 14:24; Jer 51:11
50:46 [v]Rev 18:9-10
51:2 [w]Isa 41:16; Jer 15:7; Mt 3:12

[p]38 Or *A sword against* [q]1 *Leb Kamai* is a cryptogram for Chaldea, that is, Babylonia.

in the day of her disaster.
3Let not the archer string his bow,[a]
nor let him put on his armor.[b]
Do not spare her young men;
completely destroy[r] her army.
4They will fall[c] down slain in Babylon,[s]
fatally wounded in her streets.[d]
5For Israel and Judah have not been forsaken[e]
by their God, the LORD Almighty,
though their land[t] is full of guilt[f]
before the Holy One of Israel.

6"Flee[g] from Babylon!
Run for your lives!
Do not be destroyed because of her sins.[h]
It is time for the LORD's vengeance;[i]
he will pay[j] her what she deserves.
7Babylon was a gold cup[k] in the LORD's hand;
she made the whole earth drunk.
The nations drank her wine;
therefore they have now gone mad.
8Babylon will suddenly fall[l] and be broken.
Wail over her!
Get balm[m] for her pain;
perhaps she can be healed.
9" 'We would have healed Babylon,
but she cannot be healed;
let us leave[n] her and each go to his own land,
for her judgment[o] reaches to the skies,
it rises as high as the clouds.'
10" 'The LORD has vindicated[p] us;
come, let us tell in Zion
what the LORD our God has done.'[q]

11"Sharpen the arrows,[r]
take up the shields![s]
The LORD has stirred up the kings of the Medes,[t]
because his purpose[u] is to destroy Babylon.
The LORD will take vengeance,
vengeance for his temple.[v]
12Lift up a banner against the walls of Babylon!
Reinforce the guard,
station the watchmen,
prepare an ambush!
The LORD will carry out his purpose,
his decree against the people of Babylon.
13You who live by many waters[w]
and are rich in treasures,[x]
your end has come,
the time for you to be cut off.
14The LORD Almighty has sworn by himself:[y]
I will surely fill you with men, as with a swarm of locusts,[z]
and they will shout[a] in triumph over you.

15"He made the earth by his power;
he founded the world by his wisdom
and stretched[b] out the heavens by his understanding.
16When he thunders,[c] the waters in the heavens roar;
he makes clouds rise from the ends of the earth.
He sends lightning with the rain
and brings out the wind from his storehouses.[d]

17"Every man is senseless and without knowledge;
every goldsmith is shamed by his idols.
His images are a fraud;[e]
they have no breath in them.
18They are worthless,[f] the objects of mockery;

51:3 [a]Jer 50:29 [b]Jer 46:4
51:4 [c]Isa 13:15 [d]Jer 49:26; 50:30
51:5 [e]Isa 54:6-8 [f]Hos 4:1
51:6 [g]Jer 50:8 [h]Nu 16:26; Rev 18:4 [i]Jer 50:15 [j]Jer 25:14
51:7 [k]Jer 25:15-16; Rev 14:8-10; 17:4
51:8 [l]Isa 21:9; Rev 14:8 [m]Jer 46:11
51:9 [n]Isa 13:14; Jer 50:16 [o]Rev 18:4-5
51:10 [p]Mic 7:9 [q]Jer 50:28
51:11 [r]Jer 50:9 [s]Jer 46:4 [t]ver 28 [u]Jer 50:45 [v]Jer 50:28
51:13 [w]Rev 17:1,15 [x]Isa 45:3; Hab 2:9
51:14 [y]Am 6:8 [z]ver 27; Na 3:15 [a]Jer 50:15
51:15 [b]Ge 1:1; Job 9:8; Ps 104:2
51:16 [c]Ps 18:11-13 [d]Ps 135:7; Jnh 1:4
51:17 [e]Isa 44:20; Hab 2:18-19
51:18 [f]Jer 18:15

r3 The Hebrew term refers to the irrevocable giving over of things or persons to the LORD, often by totally destroying them. s4 Or *Chaldea* t5 Or / *and the land of the Babylonians*,

when their judgment comes,
they will perish.
19He who is the Portion of Jacob
is not like these,
for he is the Maker of all
things,
including the tribe of his
inheritance—
the LORD Almighty is his
name.

20"You are my war club,[a]
my weapon for battle—
with you I shatter[b] nations,
with you I destroy kingdoms,
21with you I shatter horse and
rider,[c]
with you I shatter chariot
and driver,
22with you I shatter man and
woman,
with you I shatter old man
and youth,
with you I shatter young man
and maiden,[d]
23with you I shatter shepherd and
flock,
with you I shatter farmer and
oxen,
with you I shatter governors
and officials.[e]

24"Before your eyes I will repay[f]
Babylon and all who live in Babylonia[u] for all the wrong they have
done in Zion," declares the LORD.

25"I am against you, O destroying
mountain,
you who destroy the whole
earth,"
declares the LORD.
"I will stretch out my hand
against you,
roll you off the cliffs,
and make you a burned-out
mountain.[g]
26No rock will be taken from you
for a cornerstone,
nor any stone for a
foundation,
for you will be desolate[h]
forever,"
declares the LORD.

27"Lift up a banner[i] in the land!
Blow the trumpet among the
nations!

51:20 [a]Isa 10:5 [b]Mic 4:13
51:21 [c]Ex 15:1
51:22 [d]2Ch 36:17; Isa 13:17-18
51:23 [e]ver 57
51:24 [f]Jer 50:15
51:25 [g]Zec 4:7
51:26 [h]ver 29; Isa 13:19-22; Jer 50:12
51:27 [i]Isa 13:2; Jer 50:2 [j]Jer 25:14 [k]Ge 8:4 [l]Ge 10:3
51:28 [m]ver 11
51:29 [n]ver 43; Isa 13:20
51:30 [o]Jer 50:36 [p]Isa 19:16 [q]Isa 45:2; La 2:9; Na 3:13
51:31 [r]2Sa 18:19-31
51:32 [s]Jer 50:36
51:33 [t]Isa 21:10 [u]Isa 17:5; Hos 6:11
51:34 [v]Jer 50:17

Prepare the nations for battle
against her;
summon against her these
kingdoms:[j]
Ararat,[k] Minni and
Ashkenaz.[l]
Appoint a commander against
her;
send up horses like a swarm
of locusts.
28Prepare the nations for battle
against her—
the kings of the Medes,[m]
their governors and all their
officials,
and all the countries they
rule.
29The land trembles and writhes,
for the LORD's purposes
against Babylon stand—
to lay waste the land of
Babylon
so that no one will live
there.[n]
30Babylon's warriors[o] have
stopped fighting;
they remain in their
strongholds.
Their strength is exhausted;
they have become like
women.[p]
Her dwellings are set on fire;
the bars[q] of her gates are
broken.
31One courier[r] follows another
and messenger follows
messenger
to announce to the king of
Babylon
that his entire city is
captured,
32the river crossings seized,
the marshes set on fire,
and the soldiers terrified.[s]"

33This is what the LORD Almighty, the God of Israel, says:
"The Daughter of Babylon is
like a threshing floor[t]
at the time it is trampled;
the time to harvest[u] her will
soon come."
34"Nebuchadnezzar[v] king of
Babylon has devoured
us,

[u]24 Or *Chaldea*; also in verse 35

he has thrown us into confusion,
he has made us an empty jar.
Like a serpent he has swallowed us
and filled his stomach with our delicacies,
and then has spewed us out.
35May the violence done to our flesh[v] be upon Babylon,"
say the inhabitants of Zion.
"May our blood be on those who live in Babylonia,"
says Jerusalem.[a]

36Therefore, this is what the LORD says:

"See, I will defend your cause[b]
and avenge[c] you;
I will dry up[d] her sea
and make her springs dry.
37Babylon will be a heap of ruins,
a haunt[e] of jackals,
an object of horror and scorn,
a place where no one lives.[f]
38Her people all roar like young lions,
they growl like lion cubs.
39But while they are aroused,
I will set out a feast for them
and make them drunk,
so that they shout with laughter—
then sleep forever and not awake,"
declares the LORD.[g]
40"I will bring them down
like lambs to the slaughter,
like rams and goats.

41"How Sheshach[w][h] will be captured,[i]
the boast of the whole earth seized!
What a horror Babylon will be
among the nations!
42The sea will rise over Babylon;
its roaring waves[j] will cover her.
43Her towns will be desolate,
a dry and desert land,
a land where no one lives,
through which no man travels.[k]
44I will punish Bel[l] in Babylon
and make him spew out[m]
what he has swallowed.
The nations will no longer
stream to him.
And the wall[n] of Babylon
will fall.

45"Come out[o] of her, my people!
Run[p] for your lives!
Run from the fierce anger of the LORD.
46Do not lose heart or be afraid[q]
when rumors[r] are heard in the land;
one rumor comes this year,
another the next,
rumors of violence in the land
and of ruler against ruler.
47For the time will surely come
when I will punish the idols[s] of Babylon;
her whole land will be disgraced[t]
and her slain will all lie fallen within her.
48Then heaven and earth and all that is in them
will shout[u] for joy over Babylon,
for out of the north[v]
destroyers will attack her,"
declares the LORD.

49"Babylon must fall because of Israel's slain,
just as the slain in all the earth
have fallen because of Babylon.[w]
50You who have escaped the sword,
leave[x] and do not linger!
Remember[y] the LORD in a distant land,
and think on Jerusalem."

51"We are disgraced,[z]
for we have been insulted
and shame covers our faces,
because foreigners have entered
the holy places of the LORD's house."[a]

52"But days are coming," declares the LORD,

51:35 [a]ver 24; Ps 137:8
51:36 [b]Ps 140:12; Jer 50:34; La 3:58 [c]ver 6; Ro 12:19 [d]Jer 50:38
51:37 [e]Isa 13:22; Rev 18:2 [f]Jer 50:13,39
51:39 [g]ver 57
51:41 [h]Jer 25:26 [i]Isa 13:19
51:42 [j]Isa 8:7
51:43 [k]ver 29,62; Isa 13:20; Jer 2:6
51:44 [l]Isa 46:1 [m]ver 34 [n]ver 58; Jer 50:15
51:45 [o]Rev 18:4 [p]ver 6; Isa 48:20; Jer 50:8
51:46 [q]Jer 46:27 [r]2Ki 19:7
51:47 [s]ver 52; Isa 46:1-2; Jer 50:2 [t]Jer 50:12
51:48 [u]Isa 44:23; Rev 18:20 [v]ver 11
51:49 [w]Ps 137:8; Jer 50:29
51:50 [x]ver 45 [y]Ps 137:6
51:51 [z]Ps 44:13-16; 79:4 [a]La 1:10

[v]35 Or *done to us and to our children*
[w]41 *Sheshach* is a cryptogram for Babylon.

"when I will punish her
idols,[a]
and throughout her land
the wounded will groan.
53 Even if Babylon reaches the
sky[b]
and fortifies her lofty
stronghold,
I will send destroyers[c]
against her,"
declares the LORD.

54 "The sound of a cry comes
from Babylon,
the sound of great
destruction[d]
from the land of the
Babylonians.[x]
55 The LORD will destroy Babylon;
he will silence her noisy din.
Waves[e] of enemies will rage
like great waters;
the roar of their voices will
resound.
56 A destroyer[f] will come against
Babylon;
her warriors will be captured,
and their bows will be
broken.[g]
For the LORD is a God of
retribution;
he will repay[h] in full.
57 I will make her officials and
wise men drunk,
her governors, officers and
warriors as well;
they will sleep[i] forever and not
awake,"
declares the King,[j] whose
name is the LORD
Almighty.

58 This is what the LORD Almighty
says:

"Babylon's thick wall[k] will be
leveled
and her high gates set on
fire;
the peoples[l] exhaust
themselves for nothing,
the nations' labor is only fuel
for the flames."[m]

59 This is the message Jeremiah
gave to the staff officer Seraiah son
of Neriah,[n] the son of Mahseiah,
when he went to Babylon with Zedekiah[o] king of Judah in the

51:52 [a]ver 47
51:53 [b]Ge 11:4; Isa 14:13-14 [c]Jer 49:16
51:54 [d]Jer 50:22
51:55 [e]Ps 18:4
51:56 [f]ver 48 [g]Ps 46:9 [h]ver 6; Ps 94:1-2; Hab 2:8
51:57 [i]Ps 76:5; Jer 25:27 [j]Jer 46:18; 48:15
51:58 [k]ver 44 [l]ver 64 [m]Hab 2:13
51:59 [n]Jer 36:4 [o]Jer 52:1 [p]Jer 28:1
51:60 [q]Jer 30:2; 36:2
51:62 [r]Isa 13:20; Jer 50:13,39
51:64 [s]ver 58 [t]Job 31:40
52:1 [u]2Ki 24:17 [v]Jos 10:29; 2Ki 8:22
52:2 [w]Jer 36:30
52:3 [x]Isa 3:1 [y]Eze 17:12-16
52:4 [z]Zec 8:19 [a]2Ki 25:1-7; Jer 39:1 [b]Eze 24:1-2
52:6 [c]Isa 3:1

fourth[p] year of his reign. 60 Jeremiah had written on a scroll[q] about
all the disasters that would come
upon Babylon—all that had been
recorded concerning Babylon.
61 He said to Seraiah, "When you
get to Babylon, see that you read all
these words aloud. 62 Then say, 'O
LORD, you have said you will destroy
this place, so that neither man nor
animal will live in it; it will be desolate[r] forever.' 63 When you finish
reading this scroll, tie a stone to it
and throw it into the Euphrates.
64 Then say, 'So will Babylon sink
to rise no more because of the disaster I will bring upon her. And
her people[s] will fall.' "

The words of Jeremiah end[t]
here.

The Fall of Jerusalem

52:1–3pp — 2Ki 24:18–20; 2Ch 36:11–16
52:4–16pp — Jer 39:1–10
52:4–21pp — 2Ki 25:1–21; 2Ch 36:17–20

52 Zedekiah[u] was twenty-one
years old when he became
king, and he reigned in Jerusalem
eleven years. His mother's name
was Hamutal daughter of Jeremiah; she was from Libnah.[v] 2 He did
evil in the eyes of the LORD, just as
Jehoiakim[w] had done. 3 It was because of the LORD's anger that all
this happened to Jerusalem and
Judah,[x] and in the end he thrust
them from his presence.

Now Zedekiah rebelled[y] against
the king of Babylon.

4 So in the ninth year of Zedekiah's reign, on the tenth[z] day of the
tenth month, Nebuchadnezzar
king of Babylon marched against
Jerusalem[a] with his whole army.
They camped outside the city and
built siege works all around it.[b]
5 The city was kept under siege until the eleventh year of King Zedekiah.

6 By the ninth day of the fourth
month the famine in the city had
become so severe that there was no
food for the people to eat.[c] 7 Then
the city wall was broken through,
and the whole army fled. They left

[x]54 Or *Chaldeans*

the city at night through the gate
between the two walls near the
king's garden, though the Babylonians[y] were surrounding the city.
They fled toward the Arabah,[z]
8but the Babylonian[a] army pursued King Zedekiah and overtook
him in the plains of Jericho. All his
soldiers were separated from him
and scattered, **9**and he was captured.[a]

He was taken to the king of Babylon at Riblah[b] in the land of Hamath,[c] where he pronounced sentence on him. **10**There at Riblah
the king of Babylon slaughtered
the sons[d] of Zedekiah before his
eyes; he also killed all the officials
of Judah. **11**Then he put out Zedekiah's eyes, bound him with bronze
shackles and took him to Babylon,
where he put him in prison till the
day of his death.[e]

12On the tenth day of the fifth[f]
month, in the nineteenth year of
Nebuchadnezzar king of Babylon,
Nebuzaradan[g] commander of the
imperial guard, who served the
king of Babylon, came to Jerusalem. **13**He set fire[h] to the temple[i]
of the LORD, the royal palace and all
the houses of Jerusalem. Every important building he burned down.
14The whole Babylonian army under the commander of the imperial
guard broke down all the walls[j]
around Jerusalem. **15**Nebuzaradan
the commander of the guard carried into exile some of the poorest
people and those who remained in
the city, along with the rest of the
craftsmen[b] and those who had
gone over to the king of Babylon.
16But Nebuzaradan left behind[k]
the rest of the poorest people of the
land to work the vineyards and
fields.

17The Babylonians broke up the
bronze pillars,[l] the movable
stands[m] and the bronze Sea[n] that
were at the temple of the LORD and
they carried all the bronze to Babylon.[o] **18**They also took away the
pots, shovels, wick trimmers,
sprinkling bowls, dishes and all the
bronze articles used in the temple
service.[p] **19**The commander of the
imperial guard took away the basins, censers,[q] sprinkling bowls,
pots, lampstands, dishes and bowls
used for drink offerings—all that
were made of pure gold or silver.

20The bronze from the two pillars, the Sea and the twelve bronze
bulls under it, and the movable
stands, which King Solomon had
made for the temple of the LORD,
was more than could be weighed.[r]
21Each of the pillars was eighteen
cubits high and twelve cubits in
circumference[c]; each was four fingers thick, and hollow.[s] **22**The
bronze capital[t] on top of the one
pillar was five cubits[d] high and was
decorated with a network and
pomegranates of bronze all around.
The other pillar, with its pomegranates, was similar. **23**There were
ninety-six pomegranates on the
sides; the total number of pomegranates[u] above the surrounding
network was a hundred.

24The commander of the guard
took as prisoners Seraiah[v] the
chief priest, Zephaniah[w] the priest
next in rank and the three doorkeepers. **25**Of those still in the city,
he took the officer in charge of the
fighting men, and seven royal advisers. He also took the secretary
who was chief officer in charge of
conscripting the people of the land
and sixty of his men who were
found in the city. **26**Nebuzaradan[x]
the commander took them all and
brought them to the king of Babylon at Riblah. **27**There at Riblah,
in the land of Hamath, the king had
them executed.

So Judah went into captivity,
away[y] from her land. **28**This is the
number of the people Nebuchadnezzar carried into exile:[z]

in the seventh year, 3,023
Jews;
29in Nebuchadnezzar's eighteenth year,

52:9 [a]Jer 32:4 [b]Nu 34:11 [c]Nu 13:21
52:10 [d]Jer 22:30
52:11 [e]Eze 12:13
52:12 [f]Zec 7:5; 8:19 [g]Jer 39:9
52:13 [h]2Ch 36:19; Ps 74:8; La 2:6 [i]Ps 79:1; Mic 3:12
52:14 [j]Ne 1:3
52:16 [k]Jer 40:6
52:17 [l]1Ki 7:15 [m]1Ki 7:27-37 [n]1Ki 7:23 [o]Jer 27:19-22
52:18 [p]Ex 27:3; 1Ki 7:45
52:19 [q]1Ki 7:50
52:20 [r]1Ki 7:47
52:21 [s]1Ki 7:15
52:22 [t]1Ki 7:16
52:23 [u]1Ki 7:20
52:24 [v]2Ki 25:18 [w]Jer 21:1; 37:3
52:26 [x]ver 12
52:27 [y]Jer 20:4
52:28 [z]2Ki 24:14-16; 2Ch 36:20

[y]7 Or *Chaldeans;* also in verse 17 [z]7 Or *the Jordan Valley* [a]8 Or *Chaldean;* also in verse 14 [b]*15* Or *populace* [c]*21* That is, about 27 feet (about 8.1 meters) high and 18 feet (about 5.4 meters) in circumference [d]*22* That is, about 7 1/2 feet (about 2.3 meters)

832 people from Jerusalem;
30in his twenty-third year,
745 Jews taken into exile by Nebuzaradan the commander of the imperial guard.
There were 4,600 people in all.

Jehoiachin Released

52:31-34pp — 2Ki 25:27-30

31In the thirty-seventh year of
the exile of Jehoiachin king of Judah, in the year Evil-Merodach[e] became king of Babylon, he released Jehoiachin king of Judah and freed him from prison on the twenty-fifth day of the twelfth month.
32He spoke kindly to him and gave him a seat of honor higher than those of the other kings who were with him in Babylon.
33So Jehoiachin put aside his prison clothes and for the rest of his life ate regularly at the king's table.[a]
34Day by day the king of Babylon gave Jehoiachin a regular allowance[b] as long as he lived, till the day of his death.

52:33 [a] 2Sa 9:7
52:34 [b] 2Sa 9:10

[e]*31* Also called *Amel-Marduk*

Lamentations

Title and Background

Because of its subject matter, the book is referred to in Jewish tradition as "Lamentations." It was written as a reminder of the fall of Jerusalem and of the burning of the temple.

Author and Date of Writing

Although the writer of Lamentations is anonymous, ancient Jewish and Christian tradition ascribes it to Jeremiah. Since he was an eyewitness to the divine judgment on Jerusalem in 586 B.C., it is reasonable to assume he was the author. The book was probably written shortly after 586.

Theme and Message

Lamentations is the only Old Testament book that consists solely of laments. Jeremiah recognizes that the judgment on Jerusalem and the temple is the judgment of a righteous God. The book that begins with a lament (1:1-2) rightly ends in repentance (5:21-22). Knowing that God is merciful, the author appeals for mercy in prayer to God. In the middle of the book, the theology of Lamentations reaches its apex as it focuses on the goodness of God. In spite of all evidence to the contrary, "his compassions never fail."

Outline

I. Jerusalem's Misery and Desolation (1:1-22)
II. The Lord's Anger Against His People (2:1-22)
III. Judah's Complaint and the Basis for Consolation (3:1-66)
IV. The Contrast Between Zion's Past and Present (4:1-22)
V. Judah's Appeal for God's Forgiveness (5:1-22)

1[a] How deserted lies the city,
once so full of people!
How like a widow[a] is she,
who once was great[b] among
the nations!
She who was queen among the
provinces
has now become a slave.[c]

2Bitterly she weeps[d] at night,
tears are upon her cheeks.
Among all her lovers[e]
there is none to comfort her.
All her friends have betrayed[f]
her;
they have become her
enemies.[g]

3After affliction and harsh labor,
Judah has gone into exile.[h]
She dwells among the nations;
she finds no resting place.[i]
All who pursue her have
overtaken her
in the midst of her distress.

4The roads to Zion mourn,
for no one comes to her
appointed feasts.
All her gateways are desolate,[j]
her priests groan,
her maidens grieve,
and she is in bitter anguish.[k]

5Her foes have become her
masters;
her enemies are at ease.
The LORD has brought her
grief[l]

1:1 [a] Isa 47:8 [b] 1Ki 4:21 [c] Isa 3:26; Jer 40:9
1:2 [d] Ps 6:6 [e] Jer 3:1 [f] Jer 4:30; Mic 7:5 [g] ver 16
1:3 [h] Jer 13:19 [i] Dt 28:65
1:4 [j] Jer 9:11 [k] Joel 1:8-13
1:5 [l] Jer 30:15

[a]This chapter is an acrostic poem, the verses of which begin with the successive letters of the Hebrew alphabet.

because of her many sins.
Her children have gone into exile,[a]
captive before the foe.

6All the splendor has departed
from the Daughter of Zion.[b]
Her princes are like deer
that find no pasture;
in weakness they have fled
before the pursuer.

7In the days of her affliction and wandering
Jerusalem remembers all the treasures
that were hers in days of old.
When her people fell into enemy hands,
there was no one to help her.[c]
Her enemies looked at her
and laughed at her destruction.

8Jerusalem has sinned[d] greatly
and so has become unclean.
All who honored her despise her,
for they have seen her nakedness;[e]
she herself groans[f]
and turns away.

9Her filthiness clung to her skirts;
she did not consider her future.[g]
Her fall[h] was astounding;
there was none to comfort[i] her.
"Look, O LORD, on my affliction,[j]
for the enemy has triumphed."

10The enemy laid hands
on all her treasures;[k]
she saw pagan nations
enter her sanctuary[l]—
those you had forbidden[m]
to enter your assembly.

11All her people groan[n]
as they search for bread;[o]
they barter their treasures for food
to keep themselves alive.
"Look, O LORD, and consider,
for I am despised."

1:5 [a]Jer 39:9; 52:28-30
1:6 [b]Jer 13:18
1:7 [c]Jer 37:7; La 4:17
1:8 [d]ver 20; Isa 59:2-13 [e]Jer 13:22,26 [f]ver 21,22
1:9 [g]Dt 32:28-29; Isa 47:7; Eze 24:13 [h]Jer 13:18 [i]Ecc 4:1; Jer 16:7 [j]Ps 25:18
1:10 [k]Isa 64:11 [l]Ps 74:7-8; Jer 51:51 [m]Dt 23:3
1:11 [n]Ps 38:8 [o]Jer 52:6
1:12 [p]Jer 18:16 [q]ver 18 [r]Isa 13:13; Jer 30:24
1:13 [s]Job 30:30 [t]Jer 44:6 [u]Hab 3:16
1:14 [v]Dt 28:48; Isa 47:6 [w]Jer 32:5
1:15 [x]Jer 37:10 [y]Isa 41:2 [z]Isa 28:18; Jer 18:21
1:16 [a]La 2:11,18; 3:48-49 [b]Ps 69:20; Ecc 4:1 [c]ver 2; Jer 13:17; 14:17
1:17 [d]Jer 4:31

12"Is it nothing to you, all you who pass by?[p]
Look around and see.
Is any suffering like my suffering[q]
that was inflicted on me,
that the LORD brought on me
in the day of his fierce anger?[r]

13"From on high he sent fire,
sent it down into my bones.[s]
He spread a net for my feet
and turned me back.
He made me desolate,[t]
faint[u] all the day long.

14"My sins have been bound into a yoke[b];[v]
by his hands they were woven together.
They have come upon my neck
and the Lord has sapped my strength.
He has handed me over[w]
to those I cannot withstand.

15"The Lord has rejected
all the warriors in my midst;[x]
he has summoned an army[y]
against me
to[c] crush my young men.[z]
In his winepress the Lord has trampled
the Virgin Daughter of Judah.

16"This is why I weep
and my eyes overflow with tears.[a]
No one is near to comfort[b] me,
no one to restore my spirit.
My children are destitute
because the enemy has prevailed."[c]

17Zion stretches out her hands,[d]
but there is no one to comfort her.
The LORD has decreed for Jacob
that his neighbors become his foes;
Jerusalem has become
an unclean thing among them.

18"The LORD is righteous,

b*14* Most Hebrew manuscripts; Septuagint *He kept watch over my sins* c*15* Or *has set a time for me / when he will*

yet I rebelled[a] against his
command.
Listen, all you peoples;
look upon my suffering.[b]
My young men and maidens
have gone into exile.[c]

19"I called to my allies
but they betrayed me.
My priests and my elders
perished[d] in the city
while they searched for food
to keep themselves alive.

20"See, O LORD, how distressed[e]
I am!
I am in torment[f] within,
and in my heart I am disturbed,
for I have been most
rebellious.
Outside, the sword bereaves;
inside, there is only death.[g]

21"People have heard my
groaning,[h]
but there is no one to
comfort me.[i]
All my enemies have heard of
my distress;
they rejoice[j] at what you
have done.
May you bring the day[k] you
have announced
so they may become like me.

22"Let all their wickedness come
before you;
deal with them
as you have dealt with me
because of all my sins.[l]
My groans are many
and my heart is faint."

2[d] How the Lord has covered
the Daughter of Zion
with the cloud of his
anger[e]![m]
He has hurled down the
splendor of Israel
from heaven to earth;
he has not remembered his
footstool[n]
in the day of his anger.

2Without pity[o] the Lord has
swallowed[p] up
all the dwellings of Jacob;
in his wrath he has torn down
the strongholds[q] of the
Daughter of Judah.
He has brought her kingdom
and its princes
down to the ground[r] in
dishonor.

3In fierce anger he has cut off
every horn[f][s] of Israel.
He has withdrawn his right
hand[t]
at the approach of the
enemy.
He has burned in Jacob like a
flaming fire
that consumes everything
around it.[u]

4Like an enemy he has strung
his bow;[v]
his right hand is ready.
Like a foe he has slain
all who were pleasing to the
eye;[w]
he has poured out his wrath
like fire[x]
on the tent of the Daughter
of Zion.

5The Lord is like an enemy;[y]
he has swallowed up Israel.
He has swallowed up all her
palaces
and destroyed her
strongholds.[z]
He has multiplied mourning
and lamentation
for the Daughter of Judah.[a]

6He has laid waste his dwelling
like a garden;
he has destroyed his place of
meeting.[b]
The LORD has made Zion forget
her appointed feasts and her
Sabbaths;[c]
in his fierce anger he has
spurned
both king and priest.[d]

7The Lord has rejected his altar
and abandoned his
sanctuary.

1:18 [a] 1Sa 12:14 [b] ver 12 [c] Dt 28:32,41
1:19 [d] Jer 14:15; La 2:20
1:20 [e] Jer 4:19 [f] La 2:11 [g] Dt 32:25; Eze 7:15
1:21 [h] ver 8 [i] ver 4 [j] La 2:15 [k] Isa 47:11; Jer 30:16
1:22 [l] Ne 4:5
2:1 [m] La 3:44 [n] Ps 99:5; 132:7
2:2 [o] La 3:43 [p] Ps 21:9 [q] Ps 89:39-40; Mic 5:11 [r] Isa 25:12
2:3 [s] Ps 75:5,10 [t] Ps 74:11 [u] Isa 42:25; Jer 21:4-5,14
2:4 [v] Job 16:13; La 3:12-13 [w] Eze 24:16, 25 [x] Isa 42:25; Jer 7:20
2:5 [y] Jer 30:14 [z] ver 2 [a] Jer 9:17-20
2:6 [b] Jer 52:13 [c] La 1:4; Zep 3:18 [d] La 4:16

[d]This chapter is an acrostic poem, the verses of which begin with the successive letters of the Hebrew alphabet. [e]*1* Or *How the Lord in his anger / has treated the Daughter of Zion with contempt* [f]*3* Or / *all the strength*; or *every king*; *horn* here symbolizes strength.

He has handed over to the enemy
the walls of her palaces;[a]
they have raised a shout in the house of the LORD
as on the day of an appointed feast.

8The LORD determined to tear down
the wall around the Daughter of Zion.
He stretched out a measuring line[b]
and did not withhold his hand from destroying.
He made ramparts and walls lament;
together they wasted away.[c]

9Her gates[d] have sunk into the ground;
their bars he has broken and destroyed.
Her king and her princes are exiled[e] among the nations,
the law[f] is no more,
and her prophets no longer find visions[g] from the LORD.

10The elders of the Daughter of Zion
sit on the ground in silence;
they have sprinkled dust on their heads[h]
and put on sackcloth.[i]
The young women of Jerusalem
have bowed their heads to the ground.[j]

11My eyes fail from weeping,[k]
I am in torment within,[l]
my heart is poured out[m] on the ground
because my people are destroyed,
because children and infants faint[n]
in the streets of the city.

12They say to their mothers,
"Where is bread and wine?"
as they faint like wounded men
in the streets of the city,
as their lives ebb away
in their mothers' arms.[o]

13What can I say for you?
With what can I compare you,
O Daughter of Jerusalem?
To what can I liken you,
that I may comfort you,
O Virgin Daughter of Zion?[p]
Your wound is as deep as the sea.[q]
Who can heal you?

14The visions of your prophets
were false and worthless;
they did not expose your sin
to ward off your captivity.[r]
The oracles they gave you
were false and misleading.[s]

15All who pass your way
clap their hands at you;[t]
they scoff[u] and shake their heads
at the Daughter of Jerusalem:
"Is this the city that was called
the perfection of beauty,[v]
the joy of the whole earth?"[w]

16All your enemies open their mouths
wide against you;[x]
they scoff and gnash their teeth[y]
and say, "We have swallowed her up.[z]
This is the day we have waited for;
we have lived to see it."

17The LORD has done what he planned;
he has fulfilled his word,
which he decreed long ago.[a]
He has overthrown you without pity,[b]
he has let the enemy gloat over you,
he has exalted the horn[g] of your foes.[c]

18The hearts of the people
cry out to the Lord.[d]
O wall of the Daughter of Zion,
let your tears[e] flow like a river
day and night;[f]
give yourself no relief,
your eyes no rest.[g]

19Arise, cry out in the night,

[g]17 *Horn* here symbolizes strength.

2:7 [a]Ps 74:7-8; Isa 64:11; Jer 33:4-5
2:8 [b]2Ki 21:13; Isa 34:11 [c]Isa 3:26
2:9 [d]Ne 1:3 [e]Dt 28:36; 2Ki 24:15 [f]2Ch 15:3 [g]Jer 14:14
2:10 [h]Job 2:12 [i]Isa 15:3 [j]Job 2:13; Isa 3:26
2:11 [k]La 1:16; 3:48-51 [l]La 1:20 [m]ver 19; Ps 22:14 [n]La 4:4
2:12 [o]La 4:4
2:13 [p]Isa 37:22 [q]Jer 14:17; La 1:12
2:14 [r]Isa 58:1 [s]Jer 2:8; 23:25-32, 33-40; 29:9; Eze 13:3; 22:28
2:15 [t]Eze 25:6 [u]Jer 19:8 [v]Ps 50:2 [w]Ps 48:2
2:16 [x]Ps 56:2; La 3:46 [y]Job 16:9 [z]Ps 35:25
2:17 [a]Dt 28:15-45 [b]ver 2; Eze 5:11 [c]Ps 89:42
2:18 [d]Ps 119:145 [e]La 1:16 [f]Jer 9:1 [g]La 3:49

as the watches of the night
begin;
pour out your heart[a] like water
in the presence of the Lord.[b]
Lift up your hands to him
for the lives of your children,
who faint[c] from hunger
at the head of every street.

20"Look, O LORD, and consider:
Whom have you ever treated
like this?
Should women eat their
offspring,[d]
the children they have cared
for?[e]
Should priest and prophet be
killed[f]
in the sanctuary of the Lord?

21"Young and old lie together
in the dust of the streets;
my young men and maidens
have fallen by the sword.[g]
You have slain them in the day
of your anger;
you have slaughtered them
without pity.[h]

22"As you summon to a feast day,
so you summoned against me
terrors[i] on every side.
In the day of the LORD's anger
no one escaped or survived;
those I cared for and reared,[j]
my enemy has destroyed."

3[h] I am the man who has seen
affliction
by the rod of his wrath.[k]
2He has driven me away and
made me walk
in darkness[l] rather than
light;
3indeed, he has turned his hand
against me[m]
again and again, all day long.

4He has made my skin and my
flesh grow old
and has broken my bones.[n]
5He has besieged me and
surrounded me
with bitterness[o] and
hardship.[p]
6He has made me dwell in
darkness
like those long dead.[q]

7He has walled me in so I
cannot escape;[r]
he has weighed me down
with chains.[s]
8Even when I call out or cry for
help,
he shuts out my prayer.[t]
9He has barred my way with
blocks of stone;
he has made my paths
crooked.[u]

10Like a bear lying in wait,
like a lion in hiding,
11he dragged me from the path
and mangled[v] me
and left me without help.
12He drew his bow[w]
and made me the target[x] for
his arrows.[y]

13He pierced my heart
with arrows from his quiver.[z]
14I became the laughingstock[a] of
all my people;
they mock me in song[b] all
day long.
15He has filled me with bitter
herbs
and sated me with gall.[c]

16He has broken my teeth with
gravel;[d]
he has trampled me in the
dust.
17I have been deprived of peace;
I have forgotten what
prosperity is.
18So I say, "My splendor is gone
and all that I had hoped from
the LORD."[e]

19I remember my affliction and
my wandering,
the bitterness and the gall.
20I well remember them,
and my soul is downcast[f]
within me.[g]
21Yet this I call to mind
and therefore I have hope:

22Because of the LORD's great
love we are not
consumed,

2:19 [a]1Sa 1:15; Ps 62:8 [b]Isa 26:9 [c]Isa 51:20
2:20 [d]Dt 28:53; Jer 19:9 [e]La 4:10 [f]Ps 78:64; Jer 14:15
2:21 [g]2Ch 36:17; Ps 78:62-63; Jer 6:11 [h]Jer 13:14; La 3:43; Zec 11:6
2:22 [i]Ps 31:13; Jer 6:25 [j]Hos 9:13
3:1 [k]Job 19:21; Ps 88:7
3:2 [l]Jer 4:23
3:3 [m]Isa 5:25
3:4 [n]Ps 51:8; Isa 38:13; Jer 50:17
3:5 [o]ver 19 [p]Jer 23:15
3:6 [q]Ps 88:5-6
3:7 [r]Job 3:23 [s]Jer 40:4
3:8 [t]Job 30:20; Ps 22:2
3:9 [u]Isa 63:17; Hos 2:6
3:11 [v]Hos 6:1
3:12 [w]La 2:4 [x]Job 7:20 [y]Ps 7:12-13; 38:2
3:13 [z]Job 6:4
3:14 [a]Jer 20:7 [b]Job 30:9
3:15 [c]Jer 9:15
3:16 [d]Pr 20:17
3:18 [e]Job 17:15
3:20 [f]Ps 42:5 [g]Ps 42:11

[h]This chapter is an acrostic poem; the verses of each stanza begin with the successive letters of the Hebrew alphabet, and the verses within each stanza begin with the same letter.

for his compassions never
fail.[a]
23They are new every morning;
great is your faithfulness.[b]
24I say to myself, "The LORD is
my portion;[c]
therefore I will wait for him."
25The LORD is good to those
whose hope is in him,
to the one who seeks him;[d]
26it is good to wait quietly
for the salvation of the
LORD.[e]
27It is good for a man to bear the
yoke
while he is young.
28Let him sit alone in silence,[f]
for the LORD has laid it on
him.
29Let him bury his face in the
dust—
there may yet be hope.[g]
30Let him offer his cheek to one
who would strike him,[h]
and let him be filled with
disgrace.
31For men are not cast off
by the Lord forever.[i]
32Though he brings grief, he will
show compassion,
so great is his unfailing
love.[j]
33For he does not willingly bring
affliction
or grief to the children of
men.[k]
34To crush underfoot
all prisoners in the land,
35to deny a man his rights
before the Most High,
36to deprive a man of justice—
would not the Lord see such
things?[l]
37Who can speak and have it
happen
if the Lord has not decreed
it?[m]
38Is it not from the mouth of the
Most High
that both calamities and
good things come?[n]
39Why should any living man
complain
when punished for his sins?[o]

3:22 [a]Ps 78:38; Mal 3:6
3:23 [b]Zep 3:5
3:24 [c]Ps 16:5
3:25 [d]Isa 25:9; 30:18
3:26 [e]Ps 37:7; 40:1
3:28 [f]Jer 15:17
3:29 [g]Jer 31:17
3:30 [h]Job 16:10; Isa 50:6
3:31 [i]Ps 94:14; Isa 54:7
3:32 [j]Ps 78:38; Hos 11:8
3:33 [k]Eze 33:11
3:36 [l]Jer 22:3; Hab 1:13
3:37 [m]Ps 33:9-11
3:38 [n]Job 2:10; Isa 45:7; Jer 32:42
3:39 [o]Jer 30:15; Mic 7:9
3:40 [p]2Co 13:5 [q]Ps 119:59; 139:23-24
3:41 [r]Ps 25:1; 28:2
3:42 [s]Da 9:5 [t]Jer 5:7-9
3:43 [u]La 2:2,17,21
3:44 [v]Ps 97:2 [w]ver 8
3:45 [x]1Co 4:13
3:46 [y]La 2:16
3:47 [z]Jer 48:43 [a]Isa 24:17-18; 51:19
3:48 [b]La 1:16 [c]La 2:11
3:49 [d]Jer 14:17
3:50 [e]Isa 63:15
3:52 [f]Ps 35:7
3:53 [g]Jer 37:16
3:54 [h]Ps 69:2; Jnh 2:3-5
3:55 [i]Ps 130:1; Jnh 2:2
3:56 [j]Ps 55:1

40Let us examine our ways and
test them,[p]
and let us return to the
LORD.[q]
41Let us lift up our hearts and
our hands
to God in heaven,[r] and say:
42"We have sinned and rebelled[s]
and you have not forgiven.[t]
43"You have covered yourself with
anger and pursued us;
you have slain without pity.[u]
44You have covered yourself with
a cloud[v]
so that no prayer[w] can get
through.
45You have made us scum[x] and
refuse
among the nations.
46"All our enemies have opened
their mouths
wide against us.[y]
47We have suffered terror and
pitfalls,[z]
ruin and destruction."[a]
48Streams of tears flow from my
eyes[b]
because my people are
destroyed.[c]
49My eyes will flow unceasingly,
without relief,[d]
50until the LORD looks down
from heaven and sees.[e]
51What I see brings grief to my
soul
because of all the women of
my city.
52Those who were my enemies
without cause
hunted me like a bird.[f]
53They tried to end my life in a
pit[g]
and threw stones at me;
54the waters closed over my
head,[h]
and I thought I was about to
be cut off.
55I called on your name, O LORD,
from the depths of the pit.[i]
56You heard my plea:[j] "Do not
close your ears
to my cry for relief."

57You came near when I called
you,
and you said, "Do not fear."[a]
58O Lord, you took up my case;[b]
you redeemed my life.[c]
59You have seen, O LORD, the
wrong done to me.[d]
Uphold my cause!
60You have seen the depth of
their vengeance,
all their plots against me.[e]
61O LORD, you have heard their
insults,
all their plots against me—
62what my enemies whisper and
mutter
against me all day long.[f]
63Look at them! Sitting or
standing,
they mock me in their songs.
64Pay them back what they
deserve, O LORD,
for what their hands have
done.[g]
65Put a veil over their hearts,[h]
and may your curse be on
them!
66Pursue them in anger and
destroy them
from under the heavens of
the LORD.

4[i] How the gold has lost its
luster,
the fine gold become dull!
The sacred gems are scattered
at the head of every street.[i]
2How the precious sons of Zion,
once worth their weight in
gold,
are now considered as pots of
clay,
the work of a potter's hands!
3Even jackals offer their breasts
to nurse their young,
but my people have become
heartless
like ostriches in the desert.[j]
4Because of thirst the infant's
tongue
sticks to the roof of its
mouth;[k]
the children beg for bread,
but no one gives it to them.[l]

3:57 [a]Isa 41:10
3:58 [b]Jer 51:36 [c]Ps 34:22; Jer 50:34
3:59 [d]Jer 18:19-20
3:60 [e]Jer 11:20; 18:18
3:62 [f]Eze 36:3
3:64 [g]Ps 28:4
3:65 [h]Isa 6:10
4:1 [i]Eze 7:19
4:3 [j]Job 39:16
4:4 [k]Ps 22:15 [l]La 2:11,12
4:5 [m]Jer 6:2 [n]Am 6:3-7
4:6 [o]Ge 19:25
4:8 [p]Job 30:28 [q]Ps 102:3-5
4:9 [r]Jer 15:2; 16:4
4:10 [s]Lev 26:29; Dt 28:53-57; Jer 19:9; La 2:20; Eze 5:10
4:11 [t]Jer 17:27 [u]Dt 32:22; Jer 7:20; Eze 22:31

5Those who once ate delicacies
are destitute in the streets.
Those nurtured in purple[m]
now lie on ash heaps.[n]
6The punishment of my people
is greater than that of
Sodom,[o]
which was overthrown in a
moment
without a hand turned to
help her.
7Their princes were brighter
than snow
and whiter than milk,
their bodies more ruddy than
rubies,
their appearance like
sapphires.[j]
8But now they are blacker[p] than
soot;
they are not recognized in
the streets.
Their skin has shriveled on
their bones;[q]
it has become as dry as a
stick.
9Those killed by the sword are
better off
than those who die of
famine;
racked with hunger, they waste
away
for lack of food from the
field.[r]
10With their own hands
compassionate women
have cooked their own
children,[s]
who became their food
when my people were
destroyed.
11The LORD has given full vent to
his wrath;
he has poured out his fierce
anger.
He kindled a fire[t] in Zion
that consumed her
foundations.[u]
12The kings of the earth did not
believe,

[i]This chapter is an acrostic poem, the verses of which begin with the successive letters of the Hebrew alphabet. [j]7 Or *lapis lazuli*

nor did any of the world's
people,
that enemies and foes could
enter
the gates of Jerusalem.[a]

13But it happened because of the
sins of her prophets
and the iniquities of her
priests,[b]
who shed within her
the blood of the righteous.

14Now they grope through the
streets
like men who are blind.[c]
They are so defiled with
blood[d]
that no one dares to touch
their garments.

15"Go away! You are unclean!"
men cry to them.
"Away! Away! Don't touch
us!"
When they flee and wander
about,
people among the nations
say,
"They can stay here no
longer."[e]

16The LORD himself has scattered
them;
he no longer watches over
them.[f]
The priests are shown no
honor,
the elders[g] no favor.

17Moreover, our eyes failed,
looking in vain[h] for help;[i]
from our towers we watched
for a nation[j] that could not
save us.

18Men stalked us at every step,
so we could not walk in our
streets.
Our end was near, our days
were numbered,
for our end had come.[k]

19Our pursuers were swifter
than eagles[l] in the sky;
they chased us[m] over the
mountains
and lay in wait for us in the
desert.

20The LORD's anointed,[n] our very
life breath,
was caught in their traps.[o]
We thought that under his
shadow
we would live among the
nations.

21Rejoice and be glad,
O Daughter of Edom,
you who live in the land of
Uz.
But to you also the cup[p] will
be passed;
you will be drunk and
stripped naked.[q]

22O Daughter of Zion, your
punishment will end;[r]
he will not prolong your
exile.
But, O Daughter of Edom, he
will punish your sin
and expose your
wickedness.[s]

5 Remember, O LORD, what has
happened to us;
look, and see our disgrace.[t]
2Our inheritance[u] has been
turned over to aliens,
our homes[v] to foreigners.
3We have become orphans and
fatherless,
our mothers like widows.[w]
4We must buy the water we
drink;
our wood can be had only at
a price.[x]
5Those who pursue us are at our
heels;
we are weary[y] and find no
rest.
6We submitted to Egypt and
Assyria[z]
to get enough bread.
7Our fathers sinned and are no
more,
and we bear their
punishment.[a]
8Slaves[b] rule over us,
and there is none to free us
from their hands.[c]
9We get our bread at the risk of
our lives
because of the sword in the
desert.

4:12 [a] 1Ki 9:9; Jer 21:13
4:13 [b] Jer 5:31; 6:13; Eze 22:28; Mic 3:11
4:14 [c] Isa 59:10 [d] Jer 2:34; 19:4
4:15 [e] Lev 13:46
4:16 [f] Isa 9:14-16 [g] La 5:12
4:17 [h] Isa 20:5; Eze 29:16 [i] La 1:7 [j] Jer 37:7
4:18 [k] Eze 7:2-12; Am 8:2
4:19 [l] Dt 28:49 [m] Isa 5:26-28
4:20 [n] 2Sa 19:21 [o] Jer 39:5; Eze 12:12-13; 19:4,8
4:21 [p] Jer 25:15 [q] Isa 34:6-10; Am 1:11-12; Ob 1:16
4:22 [r] Isa 40:2; Jer 33:8 [s] Ps 137:7; Mal 1:4
5:1 [t] Ps 44:13-16; 89:50
5:2 [u] Ps 79:1 [v] Zep 1:13
5:3 [w] Jer 15:8; 18:21
5:4 [x] Isa 3:1
5:5 [y] Ne 9:37
5:6 [z] Hos 9:3
5:7 [a] Jer 14:20; 16:12
5:8 [b] Ne 5:15 [c] Zec 11:6

10Our skin is hot as an oven,
feverish from hunger.[a]
11Women have been ravished[b] in Zion,
and virgins in the towns of Judah.
12Princes have been hung up by their hands;
elders are shown no respect.[c]
13Young men toil at the millstones;
boys stagger under loads of wood.
14The elders are gone from the city gate;
the young men have stopped their music.[d]
15Joy is gone from our hearts;
our dancing has turned to mourning.[e]
16The crown[f] has fallen from our head.
Woe to us, for we have sinned![g]
17Because of this our hearts[h] are faint,
because of these things our eyes[i] grow dim
18for Mount Zion, which lies desolate,[j]
with jackals prowling over it.

19You, O LORD, reign forever;
your throne endures[k] from generation to generation.
20Why do you always forget us?[l]
Why do you forsake us so long?
21Restore[m] us to yourself,
O LORD, that we may return;
renew our days as of old
22unless you have utterly rejected us
and are angry with us beyond measure.[n]

5:10 [a] La 4:8-9
5:11 [b] Zec 14:2
5:12 [c] La 4:16
5:14 [d] Isa 24:8; Jer 7:34
5:15 [e] Jer 25:10
5:16 [f] Ps 89:39 [g] Isa 3:11
5:17 [h] Isa 1:5 [i] Ps 6:7
5:18 [j] Mic 3:12
5:19 [k] Ps 45:6; 102:12,24-27
5:20 [l] Ps 13:1; 44:24
5:21 [m] Ps 80:3
5:22 [n] Isa 64:9

Ezekiel

Title and Background

This book is named after the prophet Ezekiel, whose name means "God is strong." The Babylonians laid siege to Jerusalem in 588 B.C., and in 586 the city and temple were burned. Israel's monarchy was ended; the City of David and the Lord's temple were no more.

Author and Date of Writing

Ezekiel was among the more than 3,000 Jews exiled to Babylon by Nebuchadnezzar in 597 B.C., and there among the exiles he received his call to become a prophet. As a priest-prophet called to minister to the exiles, his message had much to do with the temple and its ritual. Since the book of Ezekiel contains more dates than any other Biblical book, its prophecies can be dated with considerable precision. Ezekiel's period of activity coincides with Jerusalem's darkest hour. His messages are dated between 593 and 571 B.C.

Theme and Message

Nowhere in the Bible are God's initiative and control over all creation expressed more clearly and pervasively than in Ezekiel. This sovereign God resolved that he would be known and acknowledged, for at least 65 times we read the clause (or variations): "Then they will know that I am the LORD." God's total sovereignty is also evident in his mobility. He was not limited to the temple; he can respond to his people under any circumstance.

Outline

I. Ezekiel's Call and Commission (1:1-3:27)
II. Judgment Against Judah and Jerusalem (4:1-24:27)
III. Judgment Against the Nations (25:1-32:32)
IV. Preparation for Restoration (33:1-39:29)
V. Renewed Worship (40:1-48:35)

The Living Creatures and the Glory of the LORD

1 In the[a] thirtieth year, in the
fourth month on the fifth day,
while I was among the exiles[a] by
the Kebar River, the heavens were
opened[b] and I saw visions[c] of
God.
2On the fifth of the month—it
was the fifth year of the exile of
King Jehoiachin[d]— 3the word of
the LORD came to Ezekiel the
priest, the son of Buzi,[b] by the Kebar River in the land of the Babylonians.[c] There the hand of the LORD
was upon him.[e]
4I looked, and I saw a windstorm
coming out of the north[f]—an im-
mense cloud with flashing lightning and surrounded by brilliant
light. The center of the fire looked
like glowing metal,[g] 5and in the
fire was what looked like four living
creatures.[h] In appearance their
form was that of a man,[i] 6but each
of them had four faces[j] and four
wings. 7Their legs were straight;
their feet were like those of a calf
and gleamed like burnished
bronze.[k] 8Under their wings on
their four sides they had the hands
of a man.[l] All four of them had

1:1 [a]Eze 11:24-25 [b]Mt 3:16; Ac 7:56 [c]Ex 24:10
1:2 [d]2Ki 24:15
1:3 [e]2Ki 3:15; Eze 3:14,22
1:4 [f]Jer 1:14 [g]Eze 8:2
1:5 [h]Rev 4:6 [i]ver 26
1:6 [j]Eze 10:14
1:7 [k]Da 10:6; Rev 1:15
1:8 [l]Eze 10:8

[a]1 Or *my* [b]3 Or *Ezekiel son of Buzi the priest* [c]3 Or *Chaldeans*

faces and wings, **9**and their wings touched one another. Each one went straight ahead; they did not turn as they moved.[a]

10Their faces looked like this: Each of the four had the face of a man, and on the right side each had the face of a lion, and on the left the face of an ox; each also had the face of an eagle.[b] **11**Such were their faces. Their wings[c] were spread out upward; each had two wings, one touching the wing of another creature on either side, and two wings covering its body. **12**Each one went straight ahead. Wherever the spirit would go, they would go, without turning as they went. **13**The appearance of the living creatures was like burning coals of fire or like torches. Fire moved back and forth among the creatures; it was bright, and lightning[d] flashed out of it. **14**The creatures sped back and forth like flashes of lightning.[e]

15As I looked at the living creatures, I saw a wheel on the ground beside each creature with its four faces. **16**This was the appearance and structure of the wheels: They sparkled like chrysolite,[f] and all four looked alike. Each appeared to be made like a wheel intersecting a wheel. **17**As they moved, they would go in any one of the four directions the creatures faced; the wheels did not turn[g] about[d] as the creatures went. **18**Their rims were high and awesome, and all four rims were full of eyes[h] all around.

19When the living creatures moved, the wheels beside them moved; and when the living creatures rose from the ground, the wheels also rose. **20**Wherever the spirit would go, they would go,[i] and the wheels would rise along with them, because the spirit of the living creatures was in the wheels. **21**When the creatures moved, they also moved; when the creatures stood still, they also stood still; and when the creatures rose from the ground, the wheels rose along with them, because the spirit of the living creatures was in the wheels.[j]

22Spread out above the heads of the living creatures was what looked like an expanse,[k] sparkling like ice, and awesome. **23**Under the expanse their wings were stretched out one toward the other, and each had two wings covering its body. **24**When the creatures moved, I heard the sound of their wings, like the roar of rushing waters, like the voice[l] of the Almighty,[e] like the tumult of an army.[m] When they stood still, they lowered their wings.

25Then there came a voice from above the expanse over their heads as they stood with lowered wings. **26**Above the expanse over their heads was what looked like a throne of sapphire,[f][n] and high above on the throne was a figure like that of a man.[o] **27**I saw that from what appeared to be his waist up he looked like glowing metal, as if full of fire, and that from there down he looked like fire; and brilliant light surrounded him.[p] **28**Like the appearance of a rainbow[q] in the clouds on a rainy day, so was the radiance around him.[r]

This was the appearance of the likeness of the glory[s] of the LORD. When I saw it, I fell facedown,[t] and I heard the voice of one speaking.

Ezekiel's Call

2 He said to me, "Son of man, stand[u] up on your feet and I will speak to you." **2**As he spoke, the Spirit came into me and raised me[v] to my feet, and I heard him speaking to me.

3He said: "Son of man, I am sending you to the Israelites, to a rebellious nation that has rebelled against me; they and their fathers have been in revolt against me to this very day.[w] **4**The people to whom I am sending you are obstinate and stubborn.[x] Say to them, 'This is what the Sovereign LORD says.' **5**And whether they listen or fail to listen[y]—for they are a rebel-

1:9 [a]Eze 10:22
1:10 [b]Eze 10:14; Rev 4:7
1:11 [c]Isa 6:2
1:13 [d]Rev 4:5
1:14 [e]Ps 29:7
1:16 [f]Eze 10:9-11; Da 10:6
1:17 [g]ver 9
1:18 [h]Eze 10:12; Rev 4:6
1:20 [i]ver 12
1:21 [j]Eze 10:17
1:22 [k]Eze 10:1
1:24 [l]Eze 10:5; 43:2; Da 10:6; Rev 1:15; 19:6 [m]2Ki 7:6
1:26 [n]Ex 24:10; Eze 10:1 [o]Rev 1:13
1:27 [p]Eze 8:2
1:28 [q]Ge 9:13; Rev 10:1 [r]Rev 4:2 [s]Eze 8:4 [t]Eze 3:23; Da 8:17; Rev 1:17
2:1 [u]Da 10:11
2:2 [v]Eze 3:24; Da 8:18
2:3 [w]Jer 3:25; Eze 20:8-24
2:4 [x]Eze 3:7
2:5 [y]Eze 3:11

[d]17 Or *aside* [e]24 Hebrew *Shaddai* [f]26 Or *lapis lazuli*

lious house[a]—they will know that
a prophet has been among them.[b]
6And you, son of man, do not be
afraid[c] of them or their words. Do
not be afraid, though briers and
thorns[d] are all around you and you
live among scorpions. Do not be
afraid of what they say or terrified
by them, though they are a rebellious house.[e] **7**You must speak my
words to them, whether they listen
or fail to listen, for they are rebellious.[f] **8**But you, son of man, listen
to what I say to you. Do not rebel
like that rebellious house;[g] open
your mouth and eat[h] what I give
you."

9Then I looked, and I saw a
hand[i] stretched out to me. In it
was a scroll, **10**which he unrolled
before me. On both sides of it were
written words of lament and
mourning and woe.[j]

3 And he said to me, "Son of
man, eat what is before you,
eat this scroll; then go and speak to
the house of Israel." **2**So I opened
my mouth, and he gave me the
scroll to eat.

3Then he said to me, "Son of
man, eat this scroll I am giving you
and fill your stomach with it." So I
ate[k] it, and it tasted as sweet as
honey[l] in my mouth.

4He then said to me: "Son of
man, go now to the house of Israel
and speak my words to them. **5**You
are not being sent to a people of
obscure speech and difficult language,[m] but to the house of Israel— **6**not to many peoples of obscure speech and difficult language, whose words you cannot
understand. Surely if I had sent you
to them, they would have listened
to you.[n] **7**But the house of Israel is
not willing to listen to you because
they are not willing to listen to me,
for the whole house of Israel is
hardened and obstinate.[o] **8**But I
will make you as unyielding and
hardened as they are.[p] **9**I will make
your forehead like the hardest
stone, harder than flint. Do not be
afraid of them or terrified by them,
though they are a rebellious
house.[q]"

10And he said to me, "Son of
man, listen carefully and take to
heart all the words I speak to you.
11Go now to your countrymen in
exile and speak to them. Say to
them, 'This is what the Sovereign
LORD says,' whether they listen or
fail to listen.[r]"

12Then the Spirit lifted me up,[s]
and I heard behind me a loud rumbling sound—May the glory of the
LORD be praised in his dwelling
place!— **13**the sound of the wings
of the living creatures brushing
against each other and the sound
of the wheels beside them, a loud
rumbling sound.[t] **14**The Spirit
then lifted me up and took me
away, and I went in bitterness and
in the anger of my spirit, with the
strong hand of the LORD upon me.
15I came to the exiles who lived at
Tel Abib near the Kebar River.[u]
And there, where they were living,
I sat among them for seven days[v]
—overwhelmed.

Warning to Israel

16At the end of seven days the
word of the LORD came to me:[w]
17"Son of man, I have made you a
watchman[x] for the house of Israel;
so hear the word I speak and give
them warning from me. **18**When I
say to a wicked man, 'You will surely die,' and you do not warn him or
speak out to dissuade him from his
evil ways in order to save his life,
that wicked man will die for[g] his
sin, and I will hold you accountable
for his blood.[y] **19**But if you do warn
the wicked man and he does not
turn from his wickedness or from
his evil ways, he will die for his sin;
but you will have saved yourself.[z]

20"Again, when a righteous man
turns from his righteousness and
does evil, and I put a stumbling
block before him, he will die. Since
you did not warn him, he will die
for his sin. The righteous things he
did will not be remembered, and I
will hold you accountable for his
blood.[a] **21**But if you do warn the
righteous man not to sin and he

2:5 [a]Eze 3:27 [b]Eze 33:33
2:6 [c]Jer 1:8,17 [d]Isa 9:18; Mic 7:4 [e]Eze 3:9
2:7 [f]Jer 1:7; Eze 3:10-11
2:8 [g]Isa 50:5 [h]Jer 15:16; Rev 10:9
2:9 [i]Eze 8:3
2:10 [j]Rev 8:13
3:3 [k]Jer 15:16 [l]Ps 19:10; Ps 119:103; Rev 10:9-10
3:5 [m]Isa 28:11; Jnh 1:2
3:6 [n]Mt 11:21-23
3:7 [o]Eze 2:4; Jn 15:20-23
3:8 [p]Jer 1:18
3:9 [q]Isa 50:7; Eze 2:6; Mic 3:8
3:11 [r]Eze 2:4-5,7
3:12 [s]Eze 8:3; Ac 8:39
3:13 [t]Eze 1:24; 10:5,16-17
3:15 [u]Ps 137:1 [v]Job 2:13
3:16 [w]Jer 42:7
3:17 [x]Isa 52:8; Jer 6:17; Eze 33:7-9
3:18 [y]ver 20; Eze 33:6
3:19 [z]2Ki 17:13; Eze 14:14,20; Ac 18:6; 20:26; 1Ti 4:14-16
3:20 [a]Ps 125:5; Eze 18:24; 33:12,18

[g]*18* Or *in;* also in verses 19 and 20

does not sin, he will surely live because he took warning, and you will have saved yourself.[a]"

22The hand of the LORD[b] was upon me there, and he said to me, "Get up and go[c] out to the plain,[d] and there I will speak to you." 23So I got up and went out to the plain. And the glory of the LORD was standing there, like the glory I had seen by the Kebar River,[e] and I fell facedown.[f]

24Then the Spirit came into me and raised me[g] to my feet. He spoke to me and said: "Go, shut yourself inside your house. 25And you, son of man, they will tie with ropes; you will be bound so that you cannot go out among the people.[h] 26I will make your tongue stick to the roof of your mouth so that you will be silent and unable to rebuke them, though they are a rebellious house.[i] 27But when I speak to you, I will open your mouth and you shall say to them, 'This is what the Sovereign LORD says.'[j] Whoever will listen let him listen, and whoever will refuse let him refuse; for they are a rebellious house.[k]

Siege of Jerusalem Symbolized

4 "Now, son of man, take a clay tablet, put it in front of you and draw the city of Jerusalem on it. 2Then lay siege to it: Erect siege works against it, build a ramp[l] up to it, set up camps against it and put battering rams around it.[m] 3Then take an iron pan, place it as an iron wall between you and the city and turn your face toward it. It will be under siege, and you shall besiege it. This will be a sign[n] to the house of Israel.[o]

4"Then lie on your left side and put the sin of the house of Israel upon yourself.[h] You are to bear their sin for the number of days you lie on your side. 5I have assigned you the same number of days as the years of their sin. So for 390 days you will bear the sin of the house of Israel.

6"After you have finished this, lie down again, this time on your right side, and bear the sin of the house of Judah. I have assigned you 40 days, a day for each year.[p] 7Turn your face toward the siege of Jerusalem and with bared arm prophesy against her. 8I will tie you up with ropes so that you cannot turn from one side to the other until you have finished the days of your siege.[q]

9"Take wheat and barley, beans and lentils, millet and spelt;[r] put them in a storage jar and use them to make bread for yourself. You are to eat it during the 390 days you lie on your side. 10Weigh out twenty shekels[i] of food to eat each day and eat it at set times. 11Also measure out a sixth of a hin[j] of water and drink it at set times. 12Eat the food as you would a barley cake; bake it in the sight of the people, using human excrement[s] for fuel." 13The LORD said, "In this way the people of Israel will eat defiled food among the nations where I will drive them."[t]

14Then I said, "Not so, Sovereign LORD![u] I have never defiled myself. From my youth until now I have never eaten anything found dead[v] or torn by wild animals. No unclean meat has ever entered my mouth.[w]"

15"Very well," he said, "I will let you bake your bread over cow manure instead of human excrement."

16He then said to me: "Son of man, I will cut off[x] the supply of food in Jerusalem. The people will eat rationed food in anxiety and drink rationed water in despair,[y] 17for food and water will be scarce. They will be appalled at the sight of each other and will waste away because of[k] their sin.[z]

5 "Now, son of man, take a sharp sword and use it as a barber's razor[a] to shave[b] your head and your beard.[c] Then take a set of scales and divide up the hair. 2When the days of your siege come

3:21 [a]Ac 20:31
3:22 [b]Eze 1:3 [c]Ac 9:6 [d]Eze 8:4
3:23 [e]Eze 1:1 [f]Eze 1:28
3:24 [g]Eze 2:2
3:25 [h]Eze 4:8
3:26 [i]Eze 2:5; 24:27; 33:22
3:27 [j]ver 11 [k]Eze 12:3; 24:27; 33:22
4:2 [l]Jer 6:6 [m]Eze 21:22
4:3 [n]Isa 8:18; 20:3; Eze 12:3-6; 24:24,27 [o]Jer 39:1
4:6 [p]Nu 14:34; Da 9:24-26; 12:11-12
4:8 [q]Eze 3:25
4:9 [r]Isa 28:25
4:12 [s]Isa 36:12
4:13 [t]Hos 9:3
4:14 [u]Jer 1:6; Eze 9:8; 20:49 [v]Lev 11:39 [w]Ex 22:31; Dt 14:3; Ac 10:14
4:16 [x]Ps 105:16; Eze 5:16 [y]ver 10-11; Lev 26:26; Isa 3:1; Eze 12:19
4:17 [z]Lev 26:39; Eze 24:23; 33:10
5:1 [a]Isa 7:20 [b]Eze 44:20 [c]Lev 21:5

[h]*4* Or *your side* [i]*10* That is, about 8 ounces (about 0.2 kilogram) [j]*11* That is, about 2/3 quart (about 0.6 liter) [k]*17* Or *away in*

to an end, burn a third of the hair
with fire inside the city. Take a
third and strike it with the sword
all around the city. And scatter a
third to the wind. For I will pursue
them with drawn sword.[a] **3**But
take a few strands of hair and tuck
them away in the folds of your garment.[b] **4**Again, take a few of these
and throw them into the fire and
burn them up. A fire will spread
from there to the whole house of
Israel.
5"This is what the Sovereign
LORD says: This is Jerusalem, which
I have set in the center of the nations, with countries all around
her. **6**Yet in her wickedness she has
rebelled against my laws and decrees more than the nations and
countries around her. She has rejected my laws and has not followed my decrees.[c]
7"Therefore this is what the Sovereign LORD says: You have been
more unruly than the nations
around you and have not followed
my decrees or kept my laws. You
have not even[1] conformed to the
standards of the nations around
you.[d]
8"Therefore this is what the Sovereign LORD says: I myself am
against you, Jerusalem, and I will
inflict punishment on you in the
sight of the nations.[e] **9**Because of
all your detestable idols, I will do to
you what I have never done before
and will never do again.[f] **10**Therefore in your midst fathers will eat
their children, and children will eat
their fathers.[g] I will inflict punishment on you and will scatter all
your survivors to the winds.[h]
11Therefore as surely as I live, declares the Sovereign LORD, because
you have defiled my sanctuary with
all your vile images[i] and detestable practices,[j] I myself will withdraw my favor; I will not look on
you with pity or spare you.[k] **12**A
third of your people will die of the
plague or perish by famine inside
you; a third will fall by the sword
outside your walls; and a third I will
scatter to the winds and pursue
with drawn sword.[l]

13"Then my anger will cease and
my wrath[m] against them will subside, and I will be avenged.[n] And
when I have spent my wrath upon
them, they will know that I the
LORD have spoken in my zeal.
14"I will make you a ruin and a
reproach among the nations
around you, in the sight of all who
pass by.[o] **15**You will be a reproach
and a taunt, a warning and an object of horror to the nations around
you when I inflict punishment on
you in anger and in wrath and with
stinging rebuke.[p] I the LORD have
spoken.[q] **16**When I shoot at you
with my deadly and destructive arrows of famine, I will shoot to destroy you. I will bring more and
more famine upon you and cut off
your supply of food.[r] **17**I will send
famine and wild beasts against
you, and they will leave you childless. Plague and bloodshed[s] will
sweep through you, and I will bring
the sword against you. I the LORD
have spoken.[t]"

A Prophecy Against the Mountains of Israel

6 The word of the LORD came to
me: **2**"Son of man, set your
face against the mountains[u] of Israel; prophesy against them **3**and
say: 'O mountains of Israel, hear
the word of the Sovereign LORD.
This is what the Sovereign LORD
says to the mountains and hills, to
the ravines and valleys:[v] I am
about to bring a sword against you,
and I will destroy your high
places.[w] **4**Your altars will be demolished and your incense altars[x]
will be smashed; and I will slay
your people in front of your idols. **5**I
will lay the dead bodies of the Israelites in front of their idols, and I
will scatter your bones[y] around
your altars. **6**Wherever you live, the
towns will be laid waste and the
high places demolished, so that
your altars will be laid waste and
devastated, your idols[z] smashed
and ruined, your incense altars[a]

5:2 [a]ver 12; Lev 26:33
5:3 [b]Jer 39:10
5:6 [c]Jer 11:10; Eze 16:47-51; Zec 7:11
5:7 [d]2Ch 33:9; Jer 2:10-11; Eze 16:47
5:8 [e]Eze 15:7
5:9 [f]Da 9:12; Mt 24:21
5:10 [g]Lev 26:29; La 2:20 [h]Lev 26:33; Ps 44:11; Eze 12:14; Zec 2:6
5:11 [i]Eze 7:20 [j]2Ch 36:14; Eze 8:6 [k]Eze 7:4,9
5:12 [l]ver 2,17; Jer 15:2; 21:9; Eze 6:11-12; 12:14
5:13 [m]Eze 21:17; 36:6 [n]Isa 1:24
5:14 [o]Lev 26:32; Ne 2:17; Ps 74:3-10; 79:1-4
5:15 [p]1Ki 9:7; Jer 22:8-9; 24:9 [q]Eze 25:17
5:16 [r]Dt 32:24
5:17 [s]Eze 38:22 [t]Eze 14:21
6:2 [u]Eze 36:1
6:3 [v]Eze 36:4 [w]Lev 26:30
6:4 [x]2Ch 14:5
6:5 [y]Jer 8:1-2
6:6 [z]Mic 1:7; Zec 13:2 [a]Lev 26:30

[1]7 Most Hebrew manuscripts; some Hebrew manuscripts and Syriac *You have*

broken down, and what you have
made wiped out.[a] 7Your people
will fall slain among you, and you
will know that I am the LORD.

8" 'But I will spare some, for
some of you will escape[b] the sword
when you are scattered among the
lands and nations.[c] 9Then in the
nations where they have been carried captive, those who escape will
remember me—how I have been
grieved[d] by their adulterous
hearts, which have turned away
from me, and by their eyes, which
have lusted after their idols.[e] They
will loathe themselves for the evil
they have done and for all their detestable practices.[f] 10And they
will know that I am the LORD; I did
not threaten in vain to bring this
calamity on them.

11" 'This is what the Sovereign
LORD says: Strike your hands together and stamp your feet and cry
out "Alas!" because of all the wicked and detestable practices of the
house of Israel, for they will fall by
the sword, famine and plague.[g]
12He that is far away will die of the
plague, and he that is near will fall
by the sword, and he that survives
and is spared will die of famine. So
will I spend my wrath upon them.[h]
13And they will know that I am the
LORD, when their people lie slain
among their idols around their altars, on every high hill and on all
the mountaintops, under every
spreading tree and every leafy
oak[i]—places where they offered
fragrant incense to all their idols.[j]
14And I will stretch out my hand[k]
against them and make the land a
desolate waste from the desert to
Diblah[m]—wherever they live. Then
they will know that I am the
LORD.[l] ' "

The End Has Come

7 The word of the LORD came to
me: 2"Son of man, this is what
the Sovereign LORD says to the land
of Israel: The end![m] The end has
come upon the four corners[n] of the
land. 3The end is now upon you
and I will unleash my anger against
you. I will judge you according to
your conduct and repay you for all
your detestable practices. 4I will
not look on you with pity[o] or spare
you; I will surely repay you for your
conduct and the detestable practices among you. Then you will
know that I am the LORD.

5"This is what the Sovereign
LORD says: Disaster![p] An unheard-of[n] disaster is coming. 6The
end has come! The end has come!
It has roused itself against you. It
has come! 7Doom has come upon
you—you who dwell in the land.
The time has come, the day is
near;[q] there is panic, not joy, upon
the mountains. 8I am about to pour
out my wrath[r] on you and spend
my anger against you; I will judge
you according to your conduct and
repay you for all your detestable
practices.[s] 9I will not look on you
with pity or spare you; I will repay
you in accordance with your conduct and the detestable practices
among you. Then you will know
that it is I the LORD who strikes the
blow.

10"The day is here! It has come!
Doom has burst forth, the rod[t] has
budded, arrogance has blossomed!
11Violence has grown into[o] a rod
to punish wickedness; none of the
people will be left, none of that
crowd—no wealth, nothing of value.[u] 12The time has come, the day
has arrived. Let not the buyer rejoice nor the seller grieve, for wrath
is upon the whole crowd.[v] 13The
seller will not recover the land he
has sold as long as both of them
live, for the vision concerning the
whole crowd will not be reversed.
Because of their sins, not one of
them will preserve his life.[w]
14Though they blow the trumpet
and get everything ready, no one
will go into battle, for my wrath is
upon the whole crowd.

15"Outside is the sword, inside
are plague and famine; those in the

6:6 [a]Isa 6:11; Eze 5:14
6:8 [b]Jer 44:28 [c]Isa 6:13; Jer 44:14; Eze 12:16; 14:22
6:9 [d]Ps 78:40; Isa 7:13 [e]Eze 20:7,24 [f]Eze 20:43; 36:31
6:11 [g]Eze 5:12; 21:14,17; 25:6
6:12 [h]Eze 5:12
6:13 [i]Isa 57:5 [j]1Ki 14:23; Jer 2:20; Eze 20:28; Hos 4:13
6:14 [k]Isa 5:25 [l]Eze 14:13
7:2 [m]Am 8:2,10 [n]Rev 7:1; 20:8
7:4 [o]Eze 5:11
7:5 [p]2Ki 21:12
7:7 [q]Eze 12:23; Zep 1:14
7:8 [r]Isa 42:25; Eze 9:8; 14:19; Na 1:6 [s]Eze 20:8,21; 36:19
7:10 [t]Ps 89:32; Isa 10:5
7:11 [u]Jer 16:6; Zep 1:18
7:12 [v]ver 7; Isa 5:13-14; Eze 30:3
7:13 [w]Lev 25:24-28

[m]*14* Most Hebrew manuscripts; a few Hebrew manuscripts *Riblah* [n]*5* Most Hebrew manuscripts; some Hebrew manuscripts and Syriac *Disaster after* [o]*11* Or *The violent one has become*

country will die by the sword, and
those in the city will be devoured
by famine and plague.[a] **16**All who
survive and escape will be in the
mountains, moaning like doves[b]
of the valleys, each because of his
sins.[c] **17**Every hand will go limp,[d]
and every knee will become as
weak as water. **18**They will put on
sackcloth and be clothed with terror.[e] Their faces will be covered
with shame and their heads will be
shaved.[f] **19**They will throw their
silver into the streets, and their
gold will be an unclean thing. Their
silver and gold will not be able to
save them in the day of the LORD's
wrath.[g] They will not satisfy their
hunger or fill their stomachs with
it, for it has made them stumble[h]
into sin.[i] **20**They were proud of
their beautiful jewelry and used it
to make their detestable idols and
vile images.[j] Therefore I will turn
these into an unclean thing for
them. **21**I will hand it all over as
plunder to foreigners and as loot to
the wicked of the earth, and they
will defile it.[k] **22**I will turn my
face[l] away from them, and they
will desecrate my treasured place;
robbers will enter it and desecrate
it.

23"Prepare chains, because the
land is full of bloodshed[m] and the
city is full of violence. **24**I will bring
the most wicked of the nations to
take possession of their houses; I
will put an end to the pride of the
mighty, and their sanctuaries[n] will
be desecrated.[o] **25**When terror
comes, they will seek peace, but
there will be none.[p] **26**Calamity
upon calamity[q] will come, and rumor upon rumor. They will try to
get a vision from the prophet; the
teaching of the law by the priest
will be lost, as will the counsel of
the elders.[r] **27**The king will
mourn, the prince will be clothed
with despair,[s] and the hands of
the people of the land will tremble.
I will deal with them according to
their conduct,[t] and by their own
standards I will judge them. Then
they will know that I am the
LORD.[u]"

Idolatry in the Temple

8 In the sixth year, in the sixth
month on the fifth day, while I
was sitting in my house and the elders[v] of Judah were sitting before[w] me, the hand of the Sovereign LORD came upon me there.[x] **2**I
looked, and I saw a figure like that
of a man.[p] From what appeared to
be his waist down he was like fire,
and from there up his appearance
was as bright as glowing metal.[y]
3He stretched out what looked like
a hand and took me by the hair of
my head. The Spirit lifted me up[z]
between earth and heaven and in
visions of God he took me to Jerusalem, to the entrance to the north
gate of the inner court, where the
idol that provokes to jealousy[a]
stood. **4**And there before me was
the glory[b] of the God of Israel, as
in the vision I had seen in the
plain.[c]

5Then he said to me, "Son of
man, look toward the north." So I
looked, and in the entrance north
of the gate of the altar I saw this
idol[d] of jealousy.

6And he said to me, "Son of man,
do you see what they are doing—
the utterly detestable[e] things the
house of Israel is doing here, things
that will drive me far from my sanctuary? But you will see things that
are even more detestable."

7Then he brought me to the entrance to the court. I looked, and I
saw a hole in the wall. **8**He said to
me, "Son of man, now dig into the
wall." So I dug into the wall and
saw a doorway there.

9And he said to me, "Go in and
see the wicked and detestable
things they are doing here." **10**So I
went in and looked, and I saw portrayed all over the walls all kinds of
crawling things and detestable animals and all the idols of the house
of Israel.[f] **11**In front of them stood
seventy elders of the house of Israel, and Jaazaniah son of Shaphan
was standing among them. Each
had a censer[g] in his hand, and a

7:15 [a]Dt 32:25; Jer 14:18; La 1:20; Eze 5:12
7:16 [b]Isa 59:11 [c]Ezr 9:15; Eze 6:8
7:17 [d]Isa 13:7; Eze 21:7; 22:14
7:18 [e]Ps 55:5 [f]Isa 15:2-3; Eze 27:31; Am 8:10
7:19 [g]Eze 13:5; Zep 1:7,18 [h]Eze 14:3 [i]Pr 11:4
7:20 [j]Jer 7:30
7:21 [k]2Ki 24:13
7:22 [l]Eze 39:23-24
7:23 [m]2Ki 21:16
7:24 [n]Eze 24:21 [o]2Ch 7:20; Eze 28:7
7:25 [p]Eze 13:10,16
7:26 [q]Jer 4:20 [r]Isa 47:11; Eze 20:1-3; Mic 3:6
7:27 [s]Ps 109:19; Eze 26:16 [t]Eze 18:20 [u]ver 4
8:1 [v]Eze 14:1 [w]Eze 33:31 [x]Eze 1:1-3
8:2 [y]Eze 1:4, 26-27
8:3 [z]Eze 3:12; 11:1 [a]Ex 20:5; Dt 32:16
8:4 [b]Eze 1:28 [c]Eze 3:22
8:5 [d]Ps 78:58; Jer 32:34
8:6 [e]Eze 5:11
8:10 [f]Ex 20:4
8:11 [g]Nu 16:17

[p]2 Or *saw a fiery figure*

fragrant cloud of incense[a] was rising.
12He said to me, "Son of man,
have you seen what the elders of
the house of Israel are doing in the
darkness, each at the shrine of his
own idol? They say, 'The LORD does
not see[b] us; the LORD has forsaken
the land.' " **13**Again, he said, "You
will see them doing things that are
even more detestable."
14Then he brought me to the entrance to the north gate of the
house of the LORD, and I saw wom-
en sitting there, mourning for Tam-
muz. **15**He said to me, "Do you see
this, son of man? You will see
things that are even more detestable than this."
16He then brought me into the
inner court of the house of the
LORD, and there at the entrance to
the temple, between the portico
and the altar,[c] were about twenty-five men. With their backs toward the temple of the LORD and
their faces toward the east, they
were bowing down to the sun in the
east.[d]
17He said to me, "Have you seen
this, son of man? Is it a trivial matter for the house of Judah to do the
detestable things they are doing
here? Must they also fill the land
with violence[e] and continually
provoke me to anger?[f] Look at
them putting the branch to their
nose! **18**Therefore I will deal with
them in anger; I will not look on
them with pity[g] or spare them. Although they shout in my ears, I will
not listen[h] to them."

Idolaters Killed

9 Then I heard him call out in a
loud voice, "Bring the guards
of the city here, each with a weapon in his hand." **2**And I saw six men
coming from the direction of the
upper gate, which faces north, each
with a deadly weapon in his hand.
With them was a man clothed in
linen[i] who had a writing kit at his
side. They came in and stood beside the bronze altar.
3Now the glory[j] of the God of
Israel went up from above the cherubim,[k] where it had been, and
moved to the threshold of the temple. Then the LORD called to the
man clothed in linen who had the
writing kit at his side **4**and said to
him, "Go throughout the city of Jerusalem and put a mark[l] on the
foreheads of those who grieve and
lament[m] over all the detestable
things that are done in it.[n]"
5As I listened, he said to the others, "Follow him through the city
and kill, without showing pity[o] or
compassion. **6**Slaughter old men,
young men and maidens, women
and children, but do not touch anyone who has the mark. Begin at my
sanctuary." So they began with the
elders[p] who were in front of the
temple.[q]
7Then he said to them, "Defile
the temple and fill the courts with
the slain. Go!" So they went out
and began killing throughout the
city. **8**While they were killing and I
was left alone, I fell facedown,[r]
crying out, "Ah, Sovereign LORD!
Are you going to destroy the entire
remnant of Israel in this outpour-
ing of your wrath on Jerusalem?[s]"
9He answered me, "The sin of
the house of Israel and Judah is exceedingly great; the land is full of
bloodshed and the city is full of injustice.[t] They say, 'The LORD has
forsaken the land; the LORD does
not see.'[u] **10**So I will not look on
them with pity[v] or spare them, but
I will bring down on their own
heads what they have done.[w]"
11Then the man in linen with the
writing kit at his side brought back
word, saying, "I have done as you
commanded."

The Glory Departs From the Temple

10 I looked, and I saw the likeness of a throne[x] of sapphire[q][y] above the expanse[z] that
was over the heads of the cherubim. **2**The LORD said to the man
clothed in linen,[a] "Go in among
the wheels[b] beneath the cherubim. Fill[c] your hands with burning

8:11 [a] Nu 16:35
8:12 [b] Ps 10:11; Isa 29:15; Eze 9:9
8:16 [c] Joel 2:17 [d] Dt 4:19; 17:3; Job 31:28; Jer 2:27; Eze 11:1,12
8:17 [e] Eze 9:9 [f] Eze 16:26
8:18 [g] Eze 9:10; 24:14 [h] Isa 1:15; Jer 11:11; Mic 3:4; Zec 7:13
9:2 [i] Lev 16:4; Eze 10:2; Rev 15:6
9:3 [j] Eze 10:4 [k] Eze 11:22
9:4 [l] Ex 12:7; 2Co 1:22; Rev 7:3; 9:4 [m] Ps 119:136; Jer 13:17; Eze 21:6 [n] Ps 119:53
9:5 [o] Eze 5:11
9:6 [p] Eze 8:11-13, 16 [q] 2Ch 36:17; Jer 25:29; 1Pe 4:17
9:8 [r] Jos 7:6 [s] Eze 11:13; Am 7:1-6
9:9 [t] Eze 22:29 [u] Job 22:13; Eze 8:12
9:10 [v] Eze 7:4; 8:18 [w] Isa 65:6; Eze 11:21
10:1 [x] Rev 4:2 [y] Ex 24:10 [z] Eze 1:22
10:2 [a] Eze 9:2 [b] Eze 1:15 [c] Rev 8:5

[q] 1 Or *lapis lazuli*

coals from among the cherubim and scatter them over the city." And as I watched, he went in.

3Now the cherubim were standing on the south side of the temple when the man went in, and a cloud filled the inner court. 4Then the glory of the LORD[a] rose from above the cherubim and moved to the threshold of the temple. The cloud filled the temple, and the court was full of the radiance of the glory of the LORD. 5The sound of the wings of the cherubim could be heard as far away as the outer court, like the voice[b] of God Almighty[r] when he speaks.

6When the LORD commanded the man in linen, "Take fire from among the wheels, from among the cherubim," the man went in and stood beside a wheel. 7Then one of the cherubim reached out his hand to the fire that was among them. He took up some of it and put it into the hands of the man in linen, who took it and went out. 8(Under the wings of the cherubim could be seen what looked like the hands of a man.)[c]

9I looked, and I saw beside the cherubim four wheels, one beside each of the cherubim; the wheels sparkled like chrysolite.[d] 10As for their appearance, the four of them looked alike; each was like a wheel intersecting a wheel. 11As they moved, they would go in any one of the four directions the cherubim faced; the wheels did not turn about[s] as the cherubim went. The cherubim went in whatever direction the head faced, without turning as they went. 12Their entire bodies, including their backs, their hands and their wings, were completely full of eyes,[e] as were their four wheels.[f] 13I heard the wheels being called "the whirling wheels." 14Each of the cherubim[g] had four faces:[h] One face was that of a cherub, the second the face of a man, the third the face of a lion, and the fourth the face of an eagle.[i]

15Then the cherubim rose upward. These were the living creatures[j] I had seen by the Kebar River. 16When the cherubim moved, the wheels beside them moved; and when the cherubim spread their wings to rise from the ground, the wheels did not leave their side. 17When the cherubim stood still, they also stood still; and when the cherubim rose, they rose with them, because the spirit of the living creatures was in them.[k]

18Then the glory of the LORD departed from over the threshold of the temple and stopped above the cherubim.[l] 19While I watched, the cherubim spread their wings and rose from the ground, and as they went, the wheels went with them.[m] They stopped at the entrance to the east gate of the LORD's house, and the glory of the God of Israel was above them.

20These were the living creatures I had seen beneath the God of Israel by the Kebar River,[n] and I realized that they were cherubim. 21Each had four faces[o] and four wings,[p] and under their wings was what looked like the hands of a man. 22Their faces had the same appearance as those I had seen by the Kebar River. Each one went straight ahead.

Judgment on Israel's Leaders

11 Then the Spirit lifted me up and brought me to the gate of the house of the LORD that faces east. There at the entrance to the gate were twenty-five men, and I saw among them Jaazaniah son of Azzur and Pelatiah son of Benaiah, leaders of the people.[q] 2The LORD said to me, "Son of man, these are the men who are plotting evil and giving wicked advice in this city. 3They say, 'Will it not soon be time to build houses?[t] This city is a cooking pot,[r] and we are the meat.'[s] 4Therefore prophesy[t] against them; prophesy, son of man."

5Then the Spirit of the LORD came upon me, and he told me to say: "This is what the LORD says:

10:4 [a]Eze 1:28; 9:3
10:5 [b]Job 40:9; Eze 1:24
10:8 [c]Eze 1:8
10:9 [d]Eze 1:15-16; Rev 21:20
10:12 [e]Rev 4:6-8 [f]Eze 1:15-21
10:14 [g]1Ki 7:36 [h]Eze 1:6 [i]Eze 1:10; Rev 4:7
10:15 [j]Eze 1:3,5
10:17 [k]Eze 1:20-21
10:18 [l]Ps 18:10
10:19 [m]Eze 11:1,22
10:20 [n]Eze 1:1
10:21 [o]Eze 41:18 [p]Eze 1:6
11:1 [q]Eze 8:16; 10:19; 43:4-5
11:3 [r]Jer 1:13; Eze 24:3 [s]ver 7,11
11:4 [t]Eze 3:4,17

[r]5 Hebrew *El-Shaddai* [s]11 Or *aside*
[t]3 Or *This is not the time to build houses.*

That is what you are saying, O
house of Israel, but I know what is
going through your mind.[a] **6**You
have killed many people in this city
and filled its streets with the
dead.[b]
7"Therefore this is what the Sovereign LORD says: The bodies you
have thrown there are the meat and
this city is the pot, but I will drive
you out of it.[c] **8**You fear the sword,
and the sword is what I will bring
against you, declares the Sovereign
LORD.[d] **9**I will drive you out of the
city and hand you over[e] to foreigners and inflict punishment on
you.[f] **10**You will fall by the sword,
and I will execute judgment on you
at the borders of Israel.[g] Then you
will know that I am the LORD.
11This city will not be a pot[h] for
you, nor will you be the meat in it;
I will execute judgment on you at
the borders of Israel. **12**And you
will know that I am the LORD, for
you have not followed my decrees[i]
or kept my laws but have conformed to the standards of the nations around you.[j]"
13Now as I was prophesying, Pelatiah[k] son of Benaiah died. Then I
fell facedown and cried out in a
loud voice, "Ah, Sovereign LORD!
Will you completely destroy the
remnant of Israel?[l]"
14The word of the LORD came to
me: **15**"Son of man, your brothers
—your brothers who are your blood
relatives[u] and the whole house of
Israel—are those of whom the people of Jerusalem have said, 'They
are[v] far away from the LORD; this
land was given to us as our possession.'[m]

Promised Return of Israel

16"Therefore say: 'This is what
the Sovereign LORD says: Although
I sent them far away among the nations and scattered them among
the countries, yet for a little while
I have been a sanctuary[n] for them
in the countries where they have
gone.'
17"Therefore say: 'This is what
the Sovereign LORD says: I will gather you from the nations and bring
you back from the countries where
you have been scattered, and I will
give you back the land of Israel
again.'[o]
18"They will return to it and remove all its vile images[p] and detestable idols.[q] **19**I will give them
an undivided heart[r] and put a new
spirit in them; I will remove from
them their heart of stone[s] and give
them a heart of flesh.[t] **20**Then
they will follow my decrees and be
careful to keep my laws.[u] They will
be my people, and I will be their
God.[v] **21**But as for those whose
hearts are devoted to their vile images and detestable idols, I will
bring down on their own heads
what they have done, declares the
Sovereign LORD.[w]"
22Then the cherubim, with the
wheels beside them, spread their
wings, and the glory of the God of
Israel was above them.[x] **23**The glory[y] of the LORD went up from within the city and stopped above the
mountain[z] east of it. **24**The Spirit[a] lifted me up and brought me to
the exiles in Babylonia[w] in the vision[b] given by the Spirit of God.
Then the vision I had seen went
up from me, **25**and I told the exiles
everything the LORD had shown
me.[c]

The Exile Symbolized

12 The word of the LORD came
to me: **2**"Son of man, you
are living among a rebellious people. They have eyes to see but do
not see and ears to hear but do not
hear, for they are a rebellious people.[d]
3"Therefore, son of man, pack
your belongings for exile and in the
daytime, as they watch, set out and
go from where you are to another
place. Perhaps[e] they will understand,[f] though they are a rebellious house.[g] **4**During the daytime,
while they watch, bring out your
belongings packed for exile. Then
in the evening, while they are

11:5 [a]Jer 17:10
11:6 [b]Eze 7:23; 22:6
11:7 [c]Eze 24:3-13; Mic 3:2-3
11:8 [d]Pr 10:24
11:9 [e]Ps 106:41 [f]Dt 28:36; Eze 5:8
11:10 [g]2Ki 14:25
11:11 [h]ver 3
11:12 [i]Lev 18:4; Eze 18:9 [j]Eze 8:10
11:13 [k]ver 1 [l]Eze 9:8
11:15 [m]Eze 33:24
11:16 [n]Ps 90:1; 91:9; Isa 8:14
11:17 [o]Jer 3:18; 24:5-6; Eze 28:25; 34:13
11:18 [p]Eze 5:11 [q]Eze 37:23
11:19 [r]Jer 32:39 [s]Zec 7:12 [t]Eze 18:31; 36:26; 2Co 3:3
11:20 [u]Ps 105:45 [v]Eze 14:11; 36:26-28
11:21 [w]Eze 9:10; 16:43
11:22 [x]Eze 10:19
11:23 [y]Eze 8:4; 10:4 [z]Zec 14:4
11:24 [a]Eze 8:3 [b]2Co 12:2-4
11:25 [c]Eze 3:4,11
12:2 [d]Isa 6:10; Eze 2:6-8; Mt 13:15
12:3 [e]Jer 36:3 [f]Jer 26:3 [g]2Ti 2:25-26

[u]15 Or *are in exile with you* (see Septuagint and Syriac) [v]15 Or *those to whom the people of Jerusalem have said, 'Stay* [w]24 Or *Chaldea*

watching, go out like those who go into exile.[a] 5While they watch, dig through the wall and take your belongings out through it. 6Put them on your shoulder as they are watching and carry them out at dusk. Cover your face so that you cannot see the land, for I have made you a sign[b] to the house of Israel."

7So I did as I was commanded.[c] During the day I brought out my things packed for exile. Then in the evening I dug through the wall with my hands. I took my belongings out at dusk, carrying them on my shoulders while they watched.

8In the morning the word of the LORD came to me: 9"Son of man, did not that rebellious house of Israel ask you, 'What are you doing?'[d]

10"Say to them, 'This is what the Sovereign LORD says: This oracle concerns the prince in Jerusalem and the whole house of Israel who are there.' 11Say to them, 'I am a sign to you.'

"As I have done, so it will be done to them. They will go into exile as captives.[e]

12"The prince among them will put his things on his shoulder at dusk[f] and leave, and a hole will be dug in the wall for him to go through. He will cover his face so that he cannot see the land.[g] 13I will spread my net[h] for him, and he will be caught in my snare;[i] I will bring him to Babylonia, the land of the Chaldeans, but he will not see[j] it, and there he will die.[k] 14I will scatter to the winds all those around him—his staff and all his troops—and I will pursue them with drawn sword.[l]

15"They will know that I am the LORD, when I disperse them among the nations and scatter them through the countries. 16But I will spare a few of them from the sword, famine and plague, so that in the nations where they go they may acknowledge all their detestable practices. Then they will know that I am the LORD.[m]"

17The word of the LORD came to me: 18"Son of man, tremble as you eat your food,[n] and shudder in fear as you drink your water. 19Say to the people of the land: 'This is what the Sovereign LORD says about those living in Jerusalem and in the land of Israel: They will eat their food in anxiety and drink their water in despair, for their land will be stripped of everything[o] in it because of the violence of all who live there.[p] 20The inhabited towns will be laid waste and the land will be desolate. Then you will know that I am the LORD.[q]' "

21The word of the LORD came to me: 22"Son of man, what is this proverb you have in the land of Israel: 'The days go by and every vision comes to nothing'?[r] 23Say to them, 'This is what the Sovereign LORD says: I am going to put an end to this proverb, and they will no longer quote it in Israel.' Say to them, 'The days are near when every vision will be fulfilled.[s] 24For there will be no more false visions or flattering divinations[t] among the people of Israel. 25But I the LORD will speak what I will, and it shall be fulfilled without delay. For in your days, you rebellious house, I will fulfill whatever I say, declares the Sovereign LORD.[u]' "

26The word of the LORD came to me: 27"Son of man, the house of Israel is saying, 'The vision he sees is for many years from now, and he prophesies about the distant future.'[v]

28"Therefore say to them, 'This is what the Sovereign LORD says: None of my words will be delayed any longer; whatever I say will be fulfilled, declares the Sovereign LORD.' "

False Prophets Condemned

13 The word of the LORD came to me: 2"Son of man, prophesy against the prophets of Israel who are now prophesying. Say to those who prophesy out of their own imagination: 'Hear the word of the LORD![w] 3This is what the Sovereign LORD says: Woe to the foolish[x]

12:4 [a]ver 12; Jer 39:4
12:6 [b]ver 12; Isa 8:18; 20:3; Eze 4:3; 24:24
12:7 [c]Eze 24:18; 37:10
12:9 [d]Eze 17:12; 20:49; 24:19
12:11 [e]2Ki 25:7; Jer 15:2; 52:15
12:12 [f]Jer 39:4 [g]Jer 52:7
12:13 [h]Eze 17:20; 19:8; Hos 7:12 [i]Isa 24:17-18 [j]Jer 39:7 [k]Jer 52:11; Eze 17:16
12:14 [l]2Ki 25:5; Eze 5:10,12
12:16 [m]Jer 22:8-9; Eze 6:8-10; 14:22
12:18 [n]La 5:9; Eze 4:16
12:19 [o]Eze 6:6-14; Mic 7:13; Zec 7:14 [p]Eze 4:16; 23:33
12:20 [q]Isa 7:23-24; Jer 4:7
12:22 [r]Eze 11:3; Am 6:3; 2Pe 3:4
12:23 [s]Ps 37:13; Joel 2:1; Zep 1:14
12:24 [t]Jer 14:14; Eze 13:23; Zec 13:2-4
12:25 [u]Isa 14:24; Hab 1:5
12:27 [v]Da 10:14
13:2 [w]ver 17; Jer 23:16; 37:19

[x]3 Or *wicked*

prophets[a] who follow their own
spirit and have seen nothing![b]
4Your prophets, O Israel, are like
jackals among ruins. **5**You have not
gone up to the breaks in the wall to
repair[c] it for the house of Israel so
that it will stand firm in the battle
on the day of the LORD.[d] **6**Their visions are false and their divinations
a lie. They say, "The LORD declares," when the LORD has not sent
them; yet they expect their words
to be fulfilled.[e] **7**Have you not
seen false visions and uttered lying
divinations when you say, "The
LORD declares," though I have not
spoken?
8" 'Therefore this is what the
Sovereign LORD says: Because of
your false words and lying visions,
I am against you, declares the Sovereign LORD. **9**My hand will be
against the prophets who see false
visions and utter lying divinations.
They will not belong to the council
of my people or be listed in the
records[f] of the house of Israel, nor
will they enter the land of Israel.
Then you will know that I am the
Sovereign LORD.[g]
10" 'Because they lead my people astray,[h] saying, "Peace," when
there is no peace, and because,
when a flimsy wall is built, they
cover it with whitewash,[i] **11**therefore tell those who cover it with
whitewash that it is going to fall.
Rain will come in torrents, and I
will send hailstones hurtling down,
and violent winds will burst forth.[j]
12When the wall collapses, will
people not ask you, "Where is the
whitewash you covered it with?"
13" 'Therefore this is what the
Sovereign LORD says: In my wrath I
will unleash a violent wind, and in
my anger hailstones[k] and torrents
of rain will fall with destructive
fury.[l] **14**I will tear down the wall
you have covered with whitewash
and will level it to the ground so
that its foundation[m] will be laid
bare. When it[y] falls,[n] you will be
destroyed in it; and you will know
that I am the LORD. **15**So I will
spend my wrath against the wall
and against those who covered it

13:3 [a]La 2:14 [b]Jer 23:25-32
13:5 [c]Isa 58:12; Eze 22:30 [d]Eze 7:19
13:6 [e]Jer 28:15; Eze 22:28
13:9 [f]Jer 17:13 [g]Eze 20:38
13:10 [h]Jer 50:6 [i]Eze 7:25; 22:28
13:11 [j]Eze 38:22
13:13 [k]Rev 11:19; 16:21 [l]Ex 9:25; Isa 30:30
13:14 [m]Mic 1:6 [n]Jer 6:15
13:16 [o]Isa 57:21; Jer 6:14
13:17 [p]Rev 2:20 [q]ver 2
13:19 [r]Eze 20:39; 22:26 [s]Pr 28:21
13:21 [t]Ps 91:3
13:22 [u]Jer 23:14; Eze 33:14-16
13:23 [v]ver 6; Eze 12:24 [w]Mic 3:6
14:1 [x]Eze 8:1; 20:1

with whitewash. I will say to you,
"The wall is gone and so are those
who whitewashed it, **16**those
prophets of Israel who prophesied
to Jerusalem and saw visions of
peace for her when there was no
peace, declares the Sovereign
LORD.[o]" '
17"Now, son of man, set your
face against the daughters[p] of your
people who prophesy out of their
own imagination. Prophesy against
them[q] **18**and say, 'This is what the
Sovereign LORD says: Woe to the
women who sew magic charms on
all their wrists and make veils of
various lengths for their heads in
order to ensnare people. Will you
ensnare the lives of my people but
preserve your own? **19**You have profaned[r] me among my people for a
few handfuls of barley and scraps
of bread. By lying to my people,
who listen to lies, you have killed
those who should not have died
and have spared those who should
not live.[s]
20" 'Therefore this is what the
Sovereign LORD says: I am against
your magic charms with which you
ensnare people like birds and I will
tear them from your arms; I will set
free the people that you ensnare
like birds. **21**I will tear off your veils
and save my people from your
hands, and they will no longer fall
prey to your power. Then you will
know that I am the LORD.[t] **22**Because you disheartened the righteous with your lies, when I had
brought them no grief, and because
you encouraged the wicked not to
turn from their evil ways and so
save their lives,[u] **23**therefore you
will no longer see false visions or
practice divination.[v] I will save my
people from your hands. And then
you will know that I am the
LORD.[w]' "

Idolaters Condemned

14 Some of the elders of Israel
came to me and sat down in
front of me.[x] **2**Then the word of
the LORD came to me: **3**"Son of

[y]14 *Or the city*

man, these men have set up idols
in their hearts and put wicked
stumbling blocks[a] before their
faces. Should I let them inquire of
me at all?[b] **4**Therefore speak to
them and tell them, 'This is what
the Sovereign LORD says: When any
Israelite sets up idols in his heart
and puts a wicked stumbling block
before his face and then goes to a
prophet, I the LORD will answer him
myself in keeping with his great
idolatry. **5**I will do this to recapture
the hearts of the people of Israel,
who have all deserted[c] me for their
idols.'[d]

6"Therefore say to the house of
Israel, 'This is what the Sovereign
LORD says: Repent! Turn from your
idols and renounce all your detestable practices![e]

7" 'When any Israelite or any
alien[f] living in Israel separates
himself from me and sets up idols
in his heart and puts a wicked
stumbling block before his face
and then goes to a prophet to inquire of me, I the LORD will answer
him myself. **8**I will set my face
against[g] that man and make him
an example and a byword.[h] I will
cut him off from my people. Then
you will know that I am the LORD.

9" 'And if the prophet[i] is enticed[j] to utter a prophecy, I the
LORD have enticed that prophet,
and I will stretch out my hand
against him and destroy him from
among my people Israel.[k] **10**They
will bear their guilt—the prophet
will be as guilty as the one who
consults him. **11**Then the people of
Israel will no longer stray[l] from
me, nor will they defile themselves
anymore with all their sins. They
will be my people, and I will be
their God, declares the Sovereign
LORD.[m]' "

Judgment Inescapable

12The word of the LORD came to
me: **13**"Son of man, if a country
sins against me by being unfaithful
and I stretch out my hand against it
to cut off its food supply[n] and send
famine upon it and kill its men and
their animals,[o] **14**even if these
three men—Noah,[p] Daniel[z][q] and
Job[r]—were in it, they could save
only themselves by their righteousness,[s] declares the Sovereign
LORD.

15"Or if I send wild beasts[t]
through that country and they
leave it childless and it becomes
desolate so that no one can pass
through it because of the beasts,[u]
16as surely as I live, declares the
Sovereign LORD, even if these three
men were in it, they could not save
their own sons or daughters. They
alone would be saved, but the land
would be desolate.[v]

17"Or if I bring a sword[w] against
that country and say, 'Let the
sword pass throughout the land,'
and I kill its men and their animals,[x] **18**as surely as I live, declares the Sovereign LORD, even if
these three men were in it, they
could not save their own sons or
daughters. They alone would be
saved.

19"Or if I send a plague into that
land and pour out my wrath[y] upon
it through bloodshed, killing its
men and their animals,[z] **20**as surely as I live, declares the Sovereign
LORD, even if Noah, Daniel and
Job were in it, they could save neither son nor daughter. They would
save only themselves by their righteousness.[a]

21"For this is what the Sovereign
LORD says: How much worse will it
be when I send against Jerusalem
my four dreadful judgments—
sword and famine and wild beasts
and plague—to kill its men and
their animals![b] **22**Yet there will be
some survivors—sons and daughters who will be brought out of it.[c]
They will come to you, and when
you see their conduct[d] and their
actions, you will be consoled regarding the disaster I have brought
upon Jerusalem—every disaster I
have brought upon it. **23**You will be
consoled when you see their conduct and their actions, for you will

14:3 [a]ver 7; Eze 7:19 [b]Isa 1:15; Eze 20:31
14:5 [c]Zec 11:8 [d]Jer 2:11
14:6 [e]Isa 2:20; 30:22
14:7 [f]Ex 12:48; 20:10
14:8 [g]Eze 15:7 [h]Eze 5:15
14:9 [i]Jer 14:15 [j]Jer 4:10 [k]1Ki 22:23
14:11 [l]Eze 48:11 [m]Eze 11:19-20; 37:23
14:13 [n]Lev 26:26 [o]Eze 5:16; 6:14; 15:8
14:14 [p]Ge 6:8 [q]ver 20; Eze 28:3; Da 1:6; 6:13 [r]Job 1:1 [s]Job 42:9; Jer 15:1; Eze 18:20
14:15 [t]Eze 5:17 [u]Lev 26:22
14:16 [v]Eze 18:20
14:17 [w]Lev 26:25; Eze 5:12; 21:3-4 [x]Eze 25:13; Zep 1:3
14:19 [y]Eze 7:8 [z]Eze 38:22
14:20 [a]ver 14
14:21 [b]Jer 15:3; Eze 5:17; 33:27; Am 4:6-10; Rev 6:8
14:22 [c]Eze 12:16 [d]Eze 20:43

[z]*14* Or *Danel*; the Hebrew spelling may suggest a person other than the prophet Daniel; also in verse 20.

know that I have done nothing in it without cause, declares the Sovereign LORD.[a]"

Jerusalem, A Useless Vine

15 The word of the LORD came to me: 2"Son of man, how is the wood of a vine[b] better than that of a branch on any of the trees in the forest? 3Is wood ever taken from it to make anything useful? Do they make pegs from it to hang things on? 4And after it is thrown on the fire as fuel and the fire burns both ends and chars the middle, is it then useful for anything?[c] 5If it was not useful for anything when it was whole, how much less can it be made into something useful when the fire has burned it and it is charred?

6"Therefore this is what the Sovereign LORD says: As I have given the wood of the vine among the trees of the forest as fuel for the fire, so will I treat the people living in Jerusalem. 7I will set my face against[d] them. Although they have come out of the fire, the fire will yet consume them. And when I set my face against them, you will know that I am the LORD.[e] 8I will make the land desolate[f] because they have been unfaithful,[g] declares the Sovereign LORD."

An Allegory of Unfaithful Jerusalem

16 The word of the LORD came to me: 2"Son of man, confront Jerusalem with her detestable practices[h] 3and say, 'This is what the Sovereign LORD says to Jerusalem: Your ancestry[i] and birth were in the land of the Canaanites; your father was an Amorite and your mother a Hittite.[j] 4On the day you were born[k] your cord was not cut, nor were you washed with water to make you clean, nor were you rubbed with salt or wrapped in cloths. 5No one looked on you with pity or had compassion enough to do any of these things for you. Rather, you were thrown out into the open field, for on the day you were born you were despised.

6" 'Then I passed by and saw you kicking about in your blood, and as you lay there in your blood I said to you, "Live!"[a][l] 7I made you grow[m] like a plant of the field. You grew up and developed and became the most beautiful of jewels.[b] Your breasts were formed and your hair grew, you who were naked and bare.[n]

8" 'Later I passed by, and when I looked at you and saw that you were old enough for love, I spread the corner of my garment[o] over you and covered your nakedness. I gave you my solemn oath and entered into a covenant with you, declares the Sovereign LORD, and you became mine.[p]

9" 'I bathed[c] you with water and washed[q] the blood from you and put ointments on you. 10I clothed you with an embroidered[r] dress and put leather sandals on you. I dressed you in fine linen[s] and covered you with costly garments.[t] 11I adorned you with jewelry:[u] I put bracelets[v] on your arms and a necklace[w] around your neck, 12and I put a ring on your nose,[x] earrings on your ears and a beautiful crown[y] on your head. 13So you were adorned with gold and silver; your clothes were of fine linen and costly fabric and embroidered cloth. Your food was fine flour, honey and olive oil.[z] You became very beautiful and rose to be a queen.[a] 14And your fame[b] spread among the nations on account of your beauty,[c] because the splendor I had given you made your beauty perfect, declares the Sovereign LORD.

15" 'But you trusted in your beauty and used your fame to become a prostitute. You lavished your favors on anyone who passed by[d] and your beauty became

14:23 [a]Jer 22:8-9
15:2 [b]Isa 5:1-7; Jer 2:21; Hos 10:1
15:4 [c]Eze 19:14; Jn 15:6
15:7 [d]Ps 34:16; Eze 14:8 [e]Isa 24:18; Am 9:1-4
15:8 [f]Eze 14:13 [g]Eze 17:20
16:2 [h]Eze 20:4; 22:2
16:3 [i]Eze 21:30 [j]ver 45
16:4 [k]Hos 2:3
16:6 [l]Ex 19:4
16:7 [m]Dt 1:10 [n]Ex 1:7
16:8 [o]Ru 3:9 [p]Jer 2:2; Hos 2:7,19-20
16:9 [q]Ru 3:3
16:10 [r]Ex 26:36 [s]Eze 27:16 [t]ver 18
16:11 [u]Eze 23:40 [v]Isa 3:19; Eze 23:42 [w]Ge 41:42
16:12 [x]Isa 3:21 [y]Isa 28:5; Jer 13:18
16:13 [z]1Sa 10:1 [a]Dt 32:13-14; 1Ki 4:21
16:14 [b]1Ki 10:24 [c]La 2:15
16:15 [d]ver 25

a6 A few Hebrew manuscripts, Septuagint and Syriac; most Hebrew manuscripts *"Live!" And as you lay there in your blood I said to you, "Live!"* b7 Or *became mature* c9 Or *I had bathed*

his.[d][a] **16**You took some of your
garments to make gaudy high
places, where you carried on your
prostitution.[b] Such things should
not happen, nor should they ever
occur. **17**You also took the fine jewelry I gave you, the jewelry made of
my gold and silver, and you made
for yourself male idols and engaged
in prostitution with them.[c] **18**And
you took your embroidered clothes
to put on them, and you offered my
oil and incense before them. **19**Also
the food I provided for you—the
fine flour, olive oil and honey I gave
you to eat—you offered as fragrant
incense before them. That is what
happened, declares the Sovereign
LORD.[d]

20" 'And you took your sons and
daughters[e] whom you bore to me[f]
and sacrificed them as food to the
idols. Was your prostitution not
enough?[g] **21**You slaughtered my
children and sacrificed them[e] to
the idols.[h] **22**In all your detestable
practices and your prostitution you
did not remember the days of your
youth,[i] when you were naked
and bare, kicking about in your
blood.[j]

23" 'Woe! Woe to you, declares
the Sovereign LORD. In addition to
all your other wickedness, **24**you
built a mound for yourself and
made a lofty shrine[k] in every public square.[l] **25**At the head of every
street you built your lofty shrines
and degraded your beauty, offering
your body with increasing promiscuity to anyone who passed by.[m]
26You engaged in prostitution with
the Egyptians, your lustful neighbors, and provoked[n] me to anger
with your increasing promiscuity.[o]
27So I stretched out my hand[p]
against you and reduced your territory; I gave you over to the greed of
your enemies, the daughters of the
Philistines,[q] who were shocked by
your lewd conduct. **28**You engaged
in prostitution with the Assyrians[r]
too, because you were insatiable;
and even after that, you still were
not satisfied. **29**Then you increased
your promiscuity to include Babylonia,[f][s] a land of merchants, but
even with this you were not satisfied.

30" 'How weak-willed you are,
declares the Sovereign LORD, when
you do all these things, acting like
a brazen prostitute![t] **31**When you
built your mounds at the head of
every street and made your lofty
shrines[u] in every public square,
you were unlike a prostitute, because you scorned payment.

32" 'You adulterous wife! You
prefer strangers to your own husband! **33**Every prostitute receives a
fee, but you give gifts[v] to all your
lovers, bribing them to come to you
from everywhere for your illicit favors.[w] **34**So in your prostitution
you are the opposite of others; no
one runs after you for your favors.
You are the very opposite, for you
give payment and none is given to
you.

35" 'Therefore, you prostitute,
hear the word of the LORD! **36**This is
what the Sovereign LORD says: Because you poured out your wealth[g]
and exposed your nakedness in
your promiscuity with your lovers,
and because of all your detestable
idols, and because you gave them
your children's blood,[x] **37**therefore I am going to gather all your
lovers, with whom you found pleasure, those you loved as well as
those you hated. I will gather them
against you from all around and
will strip you in front of them, and
they will see all your nakedness.[y]
38I will sentence you to the punishment of women who commit adultery and who shed blood;[z] I will
bring upon you the blood vengeance of my wrath and jealous anger.[a] **39**Then I will hand you over
to your lovers, and they will tear
down your mounds and destroy
your lofty shrines. They will strip
you of your clothes and take your
fine jewelry and leave you naked
and bare.[b] **40**They will bring a mob
against you, who will stone[c] you

16:15 [a]Isa 57:8; Jer 2:20; Eze 23:3; 27:3
16:16 [b]2Ki 23:7
16:17 [c]Eze 7:20
16:19 [d]Hos 2:8
16:20 [e]Jer 7:31 [f]Ex 13:2 [g]Ps 106:37-38; Isa 57:5; Eze 23:37
16:21 [h]2Ki 17:17; Jer 19:5
16:22 [i]Jer 2:2; Hos 11:1 [j]ver 6
16:24 [k]ver 31; Isa 57:7 [l]Ps 78:58; Jer 2:20; 3:2; Eze 20:28
16:25 [m]ver 15; Pr 9:14
16:26 [n]Eze 8:17 [o]Eze 20:8; 23:19-21
16:27 [p]Eze 20:33 [q]2Ch 28:18
16:28 [r]2Ki 16:7
16:29 [s]Eze 23:14-17
16:30 [t]Jer 3:3
16:31 [u]ver 24
16:33 [v]Isa 30:6; 57:9 [w]Hos 8:9-10
16:36 [x]Jer 19:5; Eze 23:10
16:37 [y]Jer 13:22
16:38 [z]Eze 23:45 [a]Lev 20:10; Eze 23:25
16:39 [b]Eze 23:26; Hos 2:3
16:40 [c]Jn 8:5,7

[d]*15* Most Hebrew manuscripts; one Hebrew manuscript (see some Septuagint manuscripts) *by. Such a thing should not happen* [e]*21* Or *and made them pass through the fire,* [f]*29* Or *Chaldea* [g]*36* Or *lust*

and hack you to pieces with their swords. **41**They will burn down[a] your houses and inflict punishment on you in the sight of many women.[b] I will put a stop[c] to your prostitution, and you will no longer pay your lovers. **42**Then my wrath against you will subside and my jealous anger will turn away from you; I will be calm and no longer angry.[d]

43" 'Because you did not remember[e] the days of your youth but enraged me with all these things, I will surely bring down[f] on your head what you have done, declares the Sovereign LORD. Did you not add lewdness to all your other detestable practices?[g]

44" 'Everyone who quotes proverbs will quote this proverb about you: "Like mother, like daughter." **45**You are a true daughter of your mother, who despised her husband and her children; and you are a true sister of your sisters, who despised their husbands and their children. Your mother was a Hittite and your father an Amorite.[h] **46**Your older sister was Samaria, who lived to the north of you with her daughters; and your younger sister, who lived to the south of you with her daughters, was Sodom.[i] **47**You not only walked in their ways and copied their detestable practices, but in all your ways you soon became more depraved than they.[j] **48**As surely as I live, declares the Sovereign LORD, your sister Sodom and her daughters never did what you and your daughters have done.[k]

49" 'Now this was the sin of your sister Sodom:[l] She and her daughters were arrogant,[m] overfed and unconcerned; they did not help the poor and needy.[n] **50**They were haughty and did detestable things before me. Therefore I did away with them as you have seen.[o] **51**Samaria did not commit half the sins you did. You have done more detestable things than they, and have made your sisters seem righteous by all these things you have done.[p] **52**Bear your disgrace, for you have furnished some justification for your sisters. Because your sins were more vile than theirs, they appear more righteous than you. So then, be ashamed and bear your disgrace, for you have made your sisters appear righteous.

53" 'However, I will restore[q] the fortunes of Sodom and her daughters and of Samaria and her daughters, and your fortunes along with them, **54**so that you may bear your disgrace[r] and be ashamed of all you have done in giving them comfort. **55**And your sisters, Sodom with her daughters and Samaria with her daughters, will return to what they were before; and you and your daughters will return to what you were before.[s] **56**You would not even mention your sister Sodom in the day of your pride, **57**before your wickedness was uncovered. Even so, you are now scorned by the daughters of Edom[h][t] and all her neighbors and the daughters of the Philistines—all those around you who despise you. **58**You will bear the consequences of your lewdness and your detestable practices, declares the LORD.[u]

59" 'This is what the Sovereign LORD says: I will deal with you as you deserve, because you have despised my oath by breaking the covenant.[v] **60**Yet I will remember the covenant I made with you in the days of your youth, and I will establish an everlasting covenant[w] with you. **61**Then you will remember your ways and be ashamed[x] when you receive your sisters, both those who are older than you and those who are younger. I will give them to you as daughters, but not on the basis of my covenant with you. **62**So I will establish my covenant with you, and you will know that I am the LORD.[y] **63**Then, when I make atonement[z] for you for all you have done, you will remember and be ashamed and never again open your mouth[a] because of your

16:41 [a]Dt 13:16 [b]Eze 23:10 [c]Eze 23:27,48
16:42 [d]Isa 54:9; Eze 5:13; 39:29
16:43 [e]Ps 78:42 [f]Eze 22:31 [g]ver 22; Eze 11:21
16:45 [h]Eze 23:2
16:46 [i]Ge 13:10-13; Eze 23:4
16:47 [j]2Ki 21:9; Eze 5:7
16:48 [k]Mt 10:15; 11:23-24
16:49 [l]Ge 13:13 [m]Ps 138:6 [n]Eze 18:7,12, 16; Lk 12:16-20
16:50 [o]Ge 18:20-21; 19:5
16:51 [p]Jer 3:8-11
16:53 [q]Isa 19:24-25
16:54 [r]Jer 2:26; Eze 14:22
16:55 [s]Mal 3:4
16:57 [t]2Ki 16:6
16:58 [u]Eze 23:49
16:59 [v]Eze 17:19
16:60 [w]Jer 32:40; Eze 37:26
16:61 [x]Eze 20:43
16:62 [y]Jer 24:7; Eze 20:37, 43-44; Hos 2:19-20
16:63 [z]Ps 65:3; 79:9 [a]Ro 3:19

[h]57 Many Hebrew manuscripts and Syriac; most Hebrew manuscripts, Septuagint and Vulgate *Aram*

humiliation, declares the Sovereign LORD.[a]' "

Two Eagles and a Vine

17 The word of the LORD came
to me: 2"Son of man, set
forth an allegory and tell the house
of Israel a parable.[b] 3Say to them,
'This is what the Sovereign LORD
says: A great eagle[c] with powerful
wings, long feathers and full plumage of varied colors came to Lebanon.[d] Taking hold of the top of a
cedar, 4he broke off its topmost
shoot and carried it away to a land
of merchants, where he planted it
in a city of traders.
5" 'He took some of the seed of
your land and put it in fertile soil.
He planted it like a willow by abundant water,[e] 6and it sprouted and
became a low, spreading vine. Its
branches turned toward him, but
its roots remained under it. So it
became a vine and produced
branches and put out leafy boughs.
7" 'But there was another great
eagle with powerful wings and full
plumage. The vine now sent out its
roots toward him from the plot
where it was planted and stretched
out its branches to him for water.[f]
8It had been planted in good soil by
abundant water so that it would
produce branches, bear fruit and
become a splendid vine.'
9"Say to them, 'This is what the
Sovereign LORD says: Will it thrive?
Will it not be uprooted and
stripped of its fruit so that it withers? All its new growth will wither.
It will not take a strong arm or
many people to pull it up by the
roots. 10Even if it[g] is transplanted,
will it thrive? Will it not wither
completely when the east wind
strikes it—wither away in the plot
where it grew?' "
11Then the word of the LORD
came to me: 12"Say to this rebellious house, 'Do you not know
what these things mean?[h]' Say to
them: 'The king of Babylon went to
Jerusalem and carried off her king
and her nobles,[i] bringing them
back with him to Babylon.[j]
13Then he took a member of the
royal family and made a treaty with
him, putting him under oath.[k] He
also carried away the leading men
of the land, 14so that the kingdom
would be brought low,[l] unable to
rise again, surviving only by keeping his treaty. 15But the king rebelled[m] against him by sending his
envoys to Egypt to get horses and a
large army.[n] Will he succeed? Will
he who does such things escape?
Will he break the treaty and yet escape?[o]
16" 'As surely as I live, declares
the Sovereign LORD, he shall die[p]
in Babylon, in the land of the king
who put him on the throne, whose
oath he despised and whose treaty
he broke.[q] 17Pharaoh[r] with his
mighty army and great horde will
be of no help to him in war, when
ramps[s] are built and siege works
erected to destroy many lives.[t]
18He despised the oath by breaking
the covenant. Because he had giv-
en his hand in pledge[u] and yet did
all these things, he shall not escape.
19" 'Therefore this is what the
Sovereign LORD says: As surely as I
live, I will bring down on his head
my oath that he despised and my
covenant that he broke.[v] 20I will
spread my net[w] for him, and he will
be caught in my snare. I will bring
him to Babylon and execute judgment[x] upon him there because he
was unfaithful to me. 21All his fleeing troops will fall by the sword,[y]
and the survivors[z] will be scattered to the winds.[a] Then you will
know that I the LORD have spoken.
22" 'This is what the Sovereign
LORD says: I myself will take a shoot
from the very top of a cedar and
plant it; I will break off a tender
sprig from its topmost shoots and
plant it on a high and lofty mountain.[b] 23On the mountain heights
of Israel I will plant it; it will produce branches and bear fruit and
become a splendid cedar. Birds of
every kind will nest in it; they will
find shelter in the shade of its
branches.[c] 24All the trees of the
field[d] will know that I the LORD
bring down the tall tree and make

16:63 [a]Ps 39:9; Da 9:7-8
17:2 [b]Eze 20:49
17:3 [c]Hos 8:1 [d]Jer 22:23
17:5 [e]Dt 8:7-9; Isa 44:4
17:7 [f]Eze 31:4
17:10 [g]Hos 13:15
17:12 [h]Eze 12:9 [i]2Ki 24:15 [j]Eze 24:19
17:13 [k]2Ch 36:13
17:14 [l]Eze 29:14
17:15 [m]Jer 52:3 [n]Dt 17:16 [o]Jer 34:3; 38:18
17:16 [p]Jer 52:11; Eze 12:13 [q]2Ki 24:17
17:17 [r]Jer 37:7 [s]Eze 4:2 [t]Isa 36:6; Jer 37:5; Eze 29:6-7
17:18 [u]1Ch 29:24
17:19 [v]Eze 16:59
17:20 [w]Eze 12:13; 32:3 [x]Jer 2:35; Eze 20:36
17:21 [y]Eze 12:14 [z]2Ki 25:11 [a]2Ki 25:5
17:22 [b]Jer 23:5; Eze 20:40; 36:1,36; 37:22
17:23 [c]Ps 92:12; Isa 2:2; Eze 31:6; Da 4:12; Hos 14:5-7; Mt 13:32
17:24 [d]Ps 96:12

the low tree grow tall. I dry up the
green tree and make the dry tree
flourish.

" 'I the LORD have spoken, and I
will do it.[a]' "

The Soul Who Sins Will Die

18 The word of the LORD came
to me: **2**"What do you people mean by quoting this proverb
about the land of Israel:

" 'The fathers eat sour grapes,
and the children's teeth are
set on edge'?[b]

3"As surely as I live, declares the
Sovereign LORD, you will no longer
quote this proverb in Israel. **4**For
every living soul belongs to me, the
father as well as the son—both
alike belong to me. The soul who
sins is the one who will die.[c]

5"Suppose there is a righteous
man
who does what is just and
right.
6He does not eat at the
mountain[d] shrines
or look to the idols[e] of the
house of Israel.
He does not defile his
neighbor's wife
or lie with a woman during
her period.
7He does not oppress[f] anyone,
but returns what he took in
pledge[g] for a loan.
He does not commit robbery
but gives his food to the
hungry
and provides clothing for the
naked.[h]
8He does not lend at usury
or take excessive interest.[i][i]
He withholds his hand from
doing wrong
and judges fairly[j] between
man and man.
9He follows my decrees
and faithfully keeps my laws.
That man is righteous;[k]
he will surely live,[l]
declares the Sovereign
LORD.

10"Suppose he has a violent son,
who sheds blood[m] or does any of
these other things[j] **11**(though the
father has done none of them):

"He eats at the mountain
shrines.
He defiles his neighbor's wife.
12He oppresses the poor[n] and
needy.
He commits robbery.
He does not return what he
took in pledge.
He looks to the idols.
He does detestable things.[o]
13He lends at usury and takes
excessive interest.[p]

Will such a man live? He will not!
Because he has done all these detestable things, he will surely be
put to death and his blood will be
on his own head.[q]

14"But suppose this son has a
son who sees all the sins his father
commits, and though he sees
them, he does not do such things:[r]

15"He does not eat at the
mountain shrines
or look to the idols of the
house of Israel.
He does not defile his
neighbor's wife.
16He does not oppress anyone
or require a pledge for a
loan.
He does not commit robbery
but gives his food to the
hungry
and provides clothing for the
naked.[s]
17He withholds his hand from
sin[k]
and takes no usury or
excessive interest.
He keeps my laws and follows
my decrees.

He will not die for his father's sin;
he will surely live. **18**But his father
will die for his own sin, because he
practiced extortion, robbed his
brother and did what was wrong
among his people.

19"Yet you ask, 'Why does the
son not share the guilt of his fa-

17:24 [a]Eze 19:12; 21:26; 22:14; Am 9:11
18:2 [b]Isa 3:15; Jer 31:29; La 5:7
18:4 [c]ver 20; Isa 42:5; Ro 6:23
18:6 [d]Eze 22:9 [e]Dt 4:19; Eze 6:13; 20:24
18:7 [f]Ex 22:21 [g]Ex 22:26; Dt 24:12 [h]Dt 15:11; Mt 25:36
18:8 [i]Ex 22:25; Lev 25:35-37; Dt 23:19-20 [j]Zec 8:16
18:9 [k]Hab 2:4 [l]Lev 18:5; Eze 20:11; Am 5:4
18:10 [m]Ex 21:12
18:12 [n]Am 4:1 [o]2Ki 21:11; Isa 59:6-7; Jer 22:17; Eze 8:6,17
18:13 [p]Ex 22:25 [q]Eze 33:4-5
18:14 [r]2Ch 34:21; Pr 23:24
18:16 [s]Ps 41:1; Isa 58:10

[i]*8* Or *take interest*; similarly in verses 13 and 17 [j]*10* Or *things to a brother*
[k]*17* Septuagint (see also verse 8); Hebrew *from the poor*

ther?' Since the son has done what
is just and right and has been careful to keep all my decrees, he will
surely live.[a] 20The soul who sins is
the one who will die. The son will
not share the guilt of the father, nor
will the father share the guilt of the
son. The righteousness of the righteous man will be credited to him,
and the wickedness of the wicked
will be charged against him.[b]
21"But if a wicked man turns
away from all the sins he has committed and keeps all my decrees
and does what is just and right, he
will surely live; he will not die.[c]
22None of the offenses he has committed will be remembered against
him. Because of the righteous
things he has done, he will live.[d]
23Do I take any pleasure in the
death of the wicked? declares the
Sovereign LORD. Rather, am I not
pleased[e] when they turn from
their ways and live?[f]
24"But if a righteous man turns
from his righteousness and commits sin and does the same detestable things the wicked man does,
will he live? None of the righteous
things he has done will be remembered. Because of the unfaithfulness he is guilty of and because of
the sins he has committed, he will
die.[g]
25"Yet you say, 'The way of the
Lord is not just.' Hear, O house of
Israel: Is my way unjust?[h] Is it not
your ways that are unjust? 26If a
righteous man turns from his righteousness and commits sin, he will
die for it; because of the sin he has
committed he will die. 27But if a
wicked man turns away from the
wickedness he has committed and
does what is just and right, he will
save his life.[i] 28Because he considers all the offenses he has committed and turns away from them,
he will surely live; he will not die.
29Yet the house of Israel says, 'The
way of the Lord is not just.' Are my
ways unjust, O house of Israel? Is it
not your ways that are unjust?
30"Therefore, O house of Israel, I
will judge you, each one according
to his ways, declares the Sovereign
LORD. Repent![j] Turn away from all
your offenses; then sin will not be
your downfall.[k] 31Rid yourselves
of all the offenses you have committed, and get a new heart[l] and a
new spirit. Why will you die, O
house of Israel?[m] 32For I take no
pleasure in the death of anyone,
declares the Sovereign LORD. Repent and live![n]

A Lament for Israel's Princes

19 "Take up a lament[o] concerning the princes[p] of Israel 2and say:

" 'What a lioness was your
mother
among the lions!
She lay down among the young
lions
and reared her cubs.
3She brought up one of her
cubs,
and he became a strong lion.
He learned to tear the prey
and he devoured men.
4The nations heard about him
and he was trapped in their
pit.
They led him with hooks
to the land of Egypt.[q]

5" 'When she saw her hope
unfulfilled,
her expectation gone,
she took another of her cubs
and made him a strong
lion.[r]
6He prowled among the lions,
for he was now a strong lion.
He learned to tear the prey
and he devoured men.[s]
7He broke down[1] their
strongholds
and devastated[t] their towns.
The land and all who were in it
were terrified by his roaring.
8Then the nations[u] came
against him,
those from regions round
about.
They spread their net for him,
and he was trapped in their
pit.[v]

18:19 [a]Ex 20:5; Dt 5:9; Jer 15:4; Zec 1:3-6
18:20 [b]Dt 24:16; 1Ki 8:32; 2Ki 14:6; Isa 3:11; Mt 16:27; Ro 2:9
18:21 [c]Eze 33:12,19
18:22 [d]Ps 18:20-24; Isa 43:25; Mic 7:19
18:23 [e]Ps 147:11 [f]Eze 33:11; 1Ti 2:4
18:24 [g]1Sa 15:11; 2Ch 24:17-20; Eze 3:20; 20:27; 2Pe 2:20-22
18:25 [h]Ge 18:25; Jer 12:1; Eze 33:17; Zep 3:5; Mal 2:17; 3:13-15
18:27 [i]Isa 1:18
18:30 [j]Mt 3:2 [k]Eze 7:3; 33:20; Hos 12:6
18:31 [l]Ps 51:10 [m]Isa 1:16-17; Eze 11:19; 36:26
18:32 [n]Eze 33:11
19:1 [o]Eze 26:17; 27:2,32 [p]2Ki 24:6
19:4 [q]2Ki 23:33-34; 2Ch 36:4
19:5 [r]2Ki 23:34
19:6 [s]2Ki 24:9; 2Ch 36:9
19:7 [t]Eze 30:12
19:8 [u]2Ki 24:2 [v]2Ki 24:11

[1]7 Targum (see Septuagint); Hebrew *He knew*

9With hooks they pulled him
into a cage
and brought him to the king
of Babylon.[a]
They put him in prison,
so his roar was heard no
longer
on the mountains of Israel.[b]

10" 'Your mother was like a vine
in your vineyard[m]
planted by the water;
it was fruitful and full of
branches
because of abundant water.[c]
11Its branches were strong,
fit for a ruler's scepter.
It towered high
above the thick foliage,
conspicuous for its height
and for its many branches.[d]
12But it was uprooted[e] in fury
and thrown to the ground.
The east wind made it shrivel,
it was stripped of its fruit;
its strong branches withered
and fire consumed them.[f]
13Now it is planted in the
desert,[g]
in a dry and thirsty land.[h]
14Fire spread from one of its
main[n] branches
and consumed[i] its fruit.
No strong branch is left on it
fit for a ruler's scepter.'[j]

This is a lament and is to be used
as a lament."

Rebellious Israel

20 In the seventh year, in the
fifth month on the tenth
day, some of the elders of Israel
came to inquire of the LORD, and
they sat down in front of me.[k]
2Then the word of the LORD came
to me: 3"Son of man, speak to the
elders of Israel and say to them,
'This is what the Sovereign LORD
says: Have you come to inquire[l] of
me? As surely as I live, I will not let
you inquire of me, declares the
Sovereign LORD.[m]'
4"Will you judge them? Will you
judge them, son of man? Then confront them with the detestable
practices of their fathers[n] 5and say
to them: 'This is what the Sovereign LORD says: On the day I chose[o]
Israel, I swore with uplifted hand to
the descendants of the house of Jacob and revealed myself to them in
Egypt. With uplifted hand I said to
them, "I am the LORD your God.[p]"
6On that day I swore to them that
I would bring them out of Egypt
into a land I had searched out for
them, a land flowing with milk and
honey,[q] the most beautiful of all
lands.[r] 7And I said to them, "Each
of you, get rid of the vile images[s]
you have set your eyes on, and do
not defile yourselves with the idols
of Egypt. I am the LORD your
God.[t]"
8" 'But they rebelled against me
and would not listen to me; they
did not get rid of the vile images
they had set their eyes on, nor did
they forsake the idols of Egypt.[u] So
I said I would pour out my wrath on
them and spend my anger against
them in Egypt.[v] 9But for the sake
of my name I did what would keep
it from being profaned in the eyes
of the nations they lived among
and in whose sight I had revealed
myself to the Israelites by bringing
them out of Egypt.[w] 10Therefore I
led them out of Egypt and brought
them into the desert.[x] 11I gave
them my decrees and made known
to them my laws, for the man who
obeys them will live by them.[y]
12Also I gave them my Sabbaths as
a sign[z] between us, so they would
know that I the LORD made them
holy.
13" 'Yet the people of Israel rebelled[a] against me in the desert.
They did not follow my decrees but
rejected my laws—although the
man who obeys them will live by
them—and they utterly desecrated
my Sabbaths. So I said I would pour
out my wrath[b] on them and destroy them in the desert.[c] 14But
for the sake of my name I did what
would keep it from being profaned
in the eyes of the nations in whose
sight I had brought them out.[d]

19:9 [a]2Ch 36:6 [b]2Ki 24:15
19:10 [c]Ps 80:8-11
19:11 [d]Eze 31:3; Da 4:11
19:12 [e]Eze 17:10 [f]Isa 27:11; Eze 28:17; Hos 13:15
19:13 [g]Eze 20:35 [h]Hos 2:3
19:14 [i]Eze 20:47 [j]Eze 15:4
20:1 [k]Eze 8:1
20:3 [l]Eze 14:3 [m]Mic 3:7
20:4 [n]Eze 16:2; 22:2; Mt 23:32
20:5 [o]Dt 7:6 [p]Ex 6:7
20:6 [q]Ex 3:8; Jer 32:22 [r]Dt 8:7; Ps 48:2; Da 8:9
20:7 [s]Ex 20:4 [t]Ex 20:2; Lev 18:3; Dt 29:18
20:8 [u]Eze 7:8 [v]Isa 63:10
20:9 [w]Eze 36:22; 39:7
20:10 [x]Ex 13:18
20:11 [y]Lev 18:5; Dt 4:7-8; Ro 10:5
20:12 [z]Ex 31:13
20:13 [a]Ps 78:40 [b]Dt 9:8 [c]Nu 14:29; Ps 95:8-10; Isa 56:6
20:14 [d]Eze 36:23

[m]*10* Two Hebrew manuscripts; most Hebrew manuscripts *your blood* [n]*14* Or *from under its*

15Also with uplifted hand I swore
to them in the desert that I would
not bring them into the land I had
given them—a land flowing with
milk and honey, most beautiful of
all lands[a]— **16**because they rejected my laws and did not follow my
decrees and desecrated my Sabbaths. For their hearts[b] were devoted to their idols.[c] **17**Yet I
looked on them with pity and did
not destroy them or put an end to
them in the desert. **18**I said to their
children in the desert, "Do not follow the statutes of your fathers[d] or
keep their laws or defile yourselves
with their idols. **19**I am the LORD
your God;[e] follow my decrees and
be careful to keep my laws.[f]
20Keep my Sabbaths holy, that
they may be a sign between us.
Then you will know that I am the
LORD your God.[g]"

21" 'But the children rebelled
against me: They did not follow my
decrees, they were not careful to
keep my laws—although the man
who obeys them will live by them
—and they desecrated my Sabbaths. So I said I would pour out
my wrath on them and spend my
anger against them in the desert.
22But I withheld[h] my hand, and for
the sake of my name I did what
would keep it from being profaned
in the eyes of the nations in whose
sight I had brought them out.
23Also with uplifted hand I swore
to them in the desert that I would
disperse them among the nations
and scatter[i] them through the
countries, **24**because they had not
obeyed my laws but had rejected
my decrees and desecrated my
Sabbaths,[j] and their eyes ⌊lusted⌋
after[k] their fathers' idols.[l] **25**I also
gave them over[m] to statutes that
were not good and laws they could
not live by;[n] **26**I let them become
defiled through their gifts—the
sacrifice of every firstborn[o]—that I
might fill them with horror so they
would know that I am the LORD.[o']

27"Therefore, son of man, speak
to the people of Israel and say to
them, 'This is what the Sovereign
LORD says: In this also your fathers

20:15 [a]Ps 95:11; 106:26
20:16 [b]Nu 15:39 [c]Am 5:26
20:18 [d]Zec 1:4
20:19 [e]Ex 20:2 [f]Dt 5:32-33; 6:1-2; 8:1; 11:1; 12:1
20:20 [g]Jer 17:22
20:22 [h]Ps 78:38
20:23 [i]Lev 26:33; Dt 28:64
20:24 [j]ver 13 [k]Eze 6:9 [l]ver 16
20:25 [m]Ps 81:12 [n]2Th 2:11
20:26 [o]2Ki 17:17
20:27 [p]Ro 2:24 [q]Eze 18:24
20:28 [r]Ps 78:55,58 [s]Eze 6:13
20:30 [t]ver 43 [u]Jer 16:12
20:31 [v]Eze 16:20 [w]Ps 106:37-39; Jer 7:31
20:33 [x]Jer 21:5
20:34 [y]2Co 6:17* [z]Isa 27:12-13; S Jer 44:6; La 2:4
20:35 [a]Jer 2:35
20:36 [b]Nu 11:1-35; 1Co 10:5-10
20:37 [c]Lev 27:32; Jer 33:13 [d]Eze 16:62
20:38 [e]Eze 34:17-22; Am 9:9-10

blasphemed[p] me by forsaking
me:[q] **28**When I brought them into
the land[r] I had sworn to give them
and they saw any high hill or any
leafy tree, there they offered their
sacrifices, made offerings that provoked me to anger, presented their
fragrant incense and poured out
their drink offerings.[s] **29**Then I
said to them: What is this high
place you go to?' " (It is called Bamah[p] to this day.)

Judgment and Restoration

30"Therefore say to the house of
Israel: 'This is what the Sovereign
LORD says: Will you defile yourselves[t] the way your fathers did
and lust after their vile images?[u]
31When you offer your gifts—the
sacrifice of your sons[v] in[q] the
fire—you continue to defile yourselves with all your idols to this
day. Am I to let you inquire of me,
O house of Israel? As surely as I
live, declares the Sovereign LORD, I
will not let you inquire of me.[w]

32" 'You say, "We want to be like
the nations, like the peoples of the
world, who serve wood and stone."
But what you have in mind will
never happen. **33**As surely as I live,
declares the Sovereign LORD, I will
rule over you with a mighty hand
and an outstretched arm and with
outpoured wrath.[x] **34**I will bring
you from the nations[y] and gather
you from the countries where you
have been scattered—with a
mighty hand and an outstretched
arm and with outpoured wrath.[z]
35I will bring you into the desert of
the nations and there, face to face,
I will execute judgment[a] upon
you. **36**As I judged your fathers in
the desert of the land of Egypt, so
I will judge you, declares the Sovereign LORD.[b] **37**I will take note of
you as you pass under my rod,[c]
and I will bring you into the bond of
the covenant.[d] **38**I will purge[e] you
of those who revolt and rebel
against me. Although I will bring

[o]26 Or *—making every firstborn pass through ⌊the fire⌋*   [p]29 *Bamah* means *high place*
[q]31 Or *—making your sons pass through*

them out of the land where they are
living, yet they will not enter the
land of Israel. Then you will know
that I am the LORD.[a]
39" 'As for you, O house of Israel,
this is what the Sovereign LORD
says: Go and serve your idols,[b] every one of you! But afterward you
will surely listen to me and no longer profane my holy name with your
gifts and idols.[c] **40**For on my holy
mountain, the high mountain of Israel, declares the Sovereign LORD,
there in the land the entire house
of Israel will serve me, and there I
will accept them. There I will require your offerings[d] and your
choice gifts,[r] along with all your
holy sacrifices.[e] **41**I will accept you
as fragrant incense when I bring
you out from the nations and gather you from the countries where
you have been scattered, and I will
show myself holy[f] among you in
the sight of the nations.[g] **42**Then
you will know that I am the LORD,[h]
when I bring you into the land of
Israel,[i] the land I had sworn with
uplifted hand to give to your fathers. **43**There you will remember
your conduct and all the actions by
which you have defiled yourselves,
and you will loathe yourselves for
all the evil you have done.[j] **44**You
will know that I am the LORD, when
I deal with you for my name's
sake[k] and not according to your
evil ways and your corrupt practices, O house of Israel, declares
the Sovereign LORD.[l]' "

Prophecy Against the South

45The word of the LORD came to
me: **46**"Son of man, set your face
toward the south; preach against
the south and prophesy against[m]
the forest of the southland.[n] **47**Say
to the southern forest: 'Hear the
word of the LORD. This is what the
Sovereign LORD says: I am about to
set fire to you, and it will consume
all your trees, both green and dry.
The blazing flame will not be
quenched, and every face from
south to north will be scorched by
it.[o] **48**Everyone will see that I the
LORD have kindled it; it will not be
quenched.[p]' "
49Then I said, "Ah, Sovereign
LORD! They are saying of me, 'Isn't
he just telling parables?[q]' "

Babylon, God's Sword of Judgment

21 The word of the LORD came
to me: **2**"Son of man, set
your face against Jerusalem and
preach against the sanctuary.
Prophesy against[r] the land of Israel **3**and say to her: 'This is what the
LORD says: I am against you.[s] I will
draw my sword from its scabbard
and cut off from you both the righteous and the wicked.[t] **4**Because I
am going to cut off the righteous
and the wicked, my sword will be
unsheathed against everyone from
south to north.[u] **5**Then all people
will know that I the LORD have
drawn my sword from its scabbard;
it will not return[v] again.'[w]
6"Therefore groan, son of man!
Groan before them with broken
heart and bitter grief.[x] **7**And when
they ask you, 'Why are you groaning?' you shall say, 'Because of the
news that is coming. Every heart
will melt and every hand go limp;[y]
every spirit will become faint and
every knee become as weak as water.' It is coming! It will surely take
place, declares the Sovereign
LORD."
8The word of the LORD came to
me: **9**"Son of man, prophesy and
say, 'This is what the Lord says:

" 'A sword, a sword,
sharpened and polished—
10sharpened for the slaughter,[z]
polished to flash like
lightning!

" 'Shall we rejoice in the scepter
of my son ⌞Judah⌟? The sword despises every such stick.

11" 'The sword is appointed to be
polished,[a]
to be grasped with the hand;
it is sharpened and polished,

20:38 [a]Ps 95:11; Jer 44:14; Eze 13:9; Mal 3:3; Heb 4:3
20:39 [b]Jer 44:25 [c]Isa 1:13; Eze 43:7; Am 4:4
20:40 [d]Isa 60:7 [e]Isa 56:7; Mal 3:4
20:41 [f]Eze 28:25; 36:23 [g]Eze 11:17
20:42 [h]Eze 38:23 [i]Eze 34:13; 36:24
20:43 [j]Eze 6:9; 16:61; Hos 5:15
20:44 [k]Eze 36:22 [l]Eze 24:24
20:46 [m]Eze 21:2; Am 7:16 [n]Isa 30:6; Jer 13:19
20:47 [o]Isa 9:18-19; 13:8; Jer 21:14
20:48 [p]Jer 7:20
20:49 [q]Mt 13:13; Jn 16:25
21:2 [r]Eze 20:46
21:3 [s]Jer 21:13 [t]ver 9-11; Job 9:22
21:4 [u]Eze 20:47
21:5 [v]ver 30 [w]Na 1:9
21:6 [x]Isa 22:4
21:7 [y]Eze 22:14; 7:17
21:10 [z]Ps 110:5-6; Isa 34:5-6
21:11 [a]Jer 46:4

[r]40 Or *and the gifts of your firstfruits*

made ready for the hand of
the slayer.
12Cry out and wail, son of man,
for it is against my people;
it is against all the princes of
Israel.
They are thrown to the sword
along with my people.
Therefore beat your breast.[a]

13" 'Testing will surely come.
And what if the scepter ⌞of Judah⌟,
which the sword despises, does not
continue? declares the Sovereign
LORD.'

14"So then, son of man, prophesy
and strike your hands[b]
together.
Let the sword strike twice,
even three times.
It is a sword for slaughter—
a sword for great slaughter,
closing in on them from
every side.[c]
15So that hearts may melt[d]
and the fallen be many,
I have stationed the sword for
slaughter[s]
at all their gates.
Oh! It is made to flash like
lightning,
it is grasped for slaughter.[e]
16O sword, slash to the right,
then to the left,
wherever your blade is
turned.
17I too will strike my hands[f]
together,
and my wrath[g] will subside.
I the LORD have spoken."

18The word of the LORD came to
me: 19"Son of man, mark out two
roads for the sword of the king of
Babylon to take, both starting from
the same country. Make a signpost
where the road branches off to the
city. 20Mark out one road for the
sword to come against Rabbah of
the Ammonites[h] and another
against Judah and fortified Jerusalem. 21For the king of Babylon will
stop at the fork in the road, at the
junction of the two roads, to seek
an omen: He will cast lots[i] with
arrows, he will consult his idols, he
will examine the liver.[j] 22Into his
right hand will come the lot for Jerusalem, where he is to set up battering rams, to give the command
to slaughter, to sound the battle
cry, to set battering rams against
the gates, to build a ramp and to
erect siege works.[k] 23It will seem
like a false omen to those who have
sworn allegiance to him, but he
will remind[l] them of their guilt
and take them captive.

24"Therefore this is what the
Sovereign LORD says: 'Because you
people have brought to mind your
guilt by your open rebellion, revealing your sins in all that you do—because you have done this, you will
be taken captive.

25" 'O profane and wicked
prince of Israel, whose day has
come, whose time of punishment
has reached its climax,[m] 26this is
what the Sovereign LORD says: Take
off the turban, remove the crown.[n]
It will not be as it was: The lowly
will be exalted and the exalted will
be brought low.[o] 27A ruin! A ruin!
I will make it a ruin! It will not be
restored until he comes to whom it
rightfully belongs; to him I will give
it.'[p]

28"And you, son of man, prophesy and say, 'This is what the Sovereign LORD says about the Ammonites[q] and their insults:

" 'A sword,[r] a sword,
drawn for the slaughter,
polished to consume
and to flash like lightning!
29Despite false visions concerning
you
and lying divinations about
you,
it will be laid on the necks
of the wicked who are to be
slain,
whose day has come,
whose time of punishment
has reached its climax.[s]
30Return the sword to its
scabbard.[t]
In the place where you were
created,
in the land of your ancestry,[u]

21:12 [a]Jer 31:19
21:14 [b]Nu 24:10 [c]Eze 6:11; 30:24
21:15 [d]2Sa 17:10 [e]Ps 22:14
21:17 [f]ver 14; Eze 22:13 [g]Eze 5:13
21:20 [h]Dt 3:11; Jer 49:2; Am 1:14
21:21 [i]Pr 16:33 [j]Nu 22:7; 23:23
21:22 [k]Eze 4:2; 26:9
21:23 [l]Nu 5:15
21:25 [m]Eze 35:5
21:26 [n]Jer 13:18 [o]Ps 75:7; Eze 17:24
21:27 [p]Ps 2:6; Jer 23:5-6; Eze 37:24; Hag 2:21-22
21:28 [q]Zep 2:8 [r]Jer 12:12
21:29 [s]ver 25; Eze 22:28; 35:5
21:30 [t]Jer 47:6 [u]Eze 16:3

[s]*15* Septuagint; the meaning of the Hebrew for this word is uncertain.

I will judge you.
31 I will pour out my wrath upon
you
and breathe out my fiery
anger[a] against you;
I will hand you over to brutal
men,
men skilled in destruction.[b]
32 You will be fuel for the fire,[c]
your blood will be shed in
your land,
you will be remembered[d] no
more;
for I the LORD have spoken.' "

Jerusalem's Sins

22 The word of the LORD came
to me: 2 "Son of man, will
you judge her? Will you judge this
city of bloodshed?[e] Then confront
her with all her detestable practices[f] 3 and say: 'This is what the
Sovereign LORD says: O city that
brings on herself doom by shedding
blood[g] in her midst and defiles
herself by making idols, 4 you have
become guilty because of the blood
you have shed[h] and have become
defiled by the idols you have made.
You have brought your days to a
close, and the end of your years has
come.[i] Therefore I will make you
an object of scorn to the nations
and a laughingstock to all the
countries.[j] 5 Those who are near
and those who are far away will
mock you, O infamous city, full of
turmoil.
6 " 'See how each of the princes
of Israel who are in you uses his
power to shed blood.[k] 7 In you they
have treated father and mother
with contempt;[l] in you they have
oppressed the alien and mistreated
the fatherless and the widow.[m]
8 You have despised my holy things
and desecrated my Sabbaths.[n] 9 In
you are slanderous men[o] bent on
shedding blood; in you are those
who eat at the mountain shrines[p]
and commit lewd acts.[q] 10 In you
are those who dishonor their fathers' bed; in you are those who violate women during their period,
when they are ceremonially unclean.[r] 11 In you one man commits
a detestable offense with his neighbor's wife, another shamefully defiles his daughter-in-law,[s] and another violates his sister,[t] his own
father's daughter. 12 In you men accept bribes[u] to shed blood; you
take usury and excessive interest[t]
and make unjust gain from your
neighbors[v] by extortion. And you
have forgotten me, declares the
Sovereign LORD.
13 " 'I will surely strike my
hands[w] together at the unjust
gain[x] you have made and at the
blood[y] you have shed in your
midst. 14 Will your courage endure
or your hands be strong in the day
I deal with you? I the LORD have
spoken,[z] and I will do it.[a] 15 I will
disperse you among the nations
and scatter[b] you through the
countries; and I will put an end to
your uncleanness.[c] 16 When you
have been defiled[u] in the eyes of
the nations, you will know that I
am the LORD.' "
17 Then the word of the LORD
came to me: 18 "Son of man, the
house of Israel has become dross[d]
to me; all of them are the copper,
tin, iron and lead left inside a furnace. They are but the dross of silver.[e] 19 Therefore this is what the
Sovereign LORD says: 'Because you
have all become dross, I will gather
you into Jerusalem. 20 As men gather silver, copper, iron, lead and tin
into a furnace to melt it with a fiery
blast, so will I gather you in my anger and my wrath and put you inside the city and melt you.[f] 21 I will
gather you and I will blow on you
with my fiery wrath, and you will be
melted inside her. 22 As silver is
melted[g] in a furnace, so you will
be melted inside her, and you will
know that I the LORD have poured
out my wrath upon you.' "[h]
23 Again the word of the LORD
came to me: 24 "Son of man, say to
the land, 'You are a land that has
had no rain or showers[v] in the day
of wrath.'[i] 25 There is a conspira-

21:31 [a] Eze 22:20-21 [b] Jer 51:20-23
21:32 [c] Mal 4:1 [d] Eze 25:10
22:2 [e] Eze 24:6,9; Na 3:1 [f] Eze 16:2
22:3 [g] ver 6,13,27; Eze 23:37,45
22:4 [h] 2Ki 21:16 [i] Eze 21:25 [j] Eze 5:14
22:6 [k] Isa 1:23
22:7 [l] Dt 5:16; 27:16 [m] Ex 22:21-22
22:8 [n] Eze 23:38-39
22:9 [o] Lev 19:16 [p] Eze 18:11 [q] Hos 4:10,14
22:10 [r] Lev 18:8,19
22:11 [s] Lev 18:15 [t] Lev 18:9; 2Sa 13:14
22:12 [u] Dt 27:25; Mic 7:3 [v] Lev 19:13
22:13 [w] Eze 21:17 [x] Isa 33:15 [y] ver 3
22:14 [z] Eze 24:14 [a] Eze 17:24; 21:7
22:15 [b] Dt 4:27; Zec 7:14 [c] Eze 23:27
22:18 [d] Ps 119:119; Isa 1:22 [e] Jer 6:28-30
22:20 [f] Mal 3:2
22:22 [g] Isa 1:25 [h] Eze 20:8,33
22:24 [i] Eze 24:13

t12 Or *usury and interest* u16 Or *When I have allotted you your inheritance*
v24 Septuagint; Hebrew *has not been cleansed or rained on*

cy[a] of her princes[w] within her like
a roaring lion tearing its prey; they
devour people,[b] take treasures and
precious things and make many
widows[c] within her. **26**Her priests
do violence to my law[d] and profane my holy things; they do not
distinguish between the holy and
the common;[e] they teach that
there is no difference between the
unclean and the clean;[f] and they
shut their eyes to the keeping of my
Sabbaths, so that I am profaned
among them.[g] **27**Her officials
within her are like wolves tearing
their prey; they shed blood and kill
people to make unjust gain.[h]
28Her prophets whitewash[i] these
deeds for them by false visions and
lying divinations. They say, 'This is
what the Sovereign LORD says'—
when the LORD has not spoken.[j]
29The people of the land practice
extortion and commit robbery;
they oppress the poor and needy
and mistreat the alien,[k] denying
them justice.[l]
30"I looked for a man among
them who would build up the
wall[m] and stand before me in the
gap on behalf of the land so I would
not have to destroy it, but I found
none.[n] **31**So I will pour out my
wrath on them and consume them
with my fiery anger, bringing
down[o] on their own heads all they
have done, declares the Sovereign
LORD.[p]"

Two Adulterous Sisters

23 The word of the LORD came
to me: **2**"Son of man, there
were two women, daughters of the
same mother.[q] **3**They became
prostitutes in Egypt,[r] engaging in
prostitution[s] from their youth. In
that land their breasts were fon-
dled and their virgin bosoms caressed. **4**The older was named Oholah, and her sister was Oholibah.
They were mine and gave birth to
sons and daughters. Oholah is Samaria, and Oholibah is Jerusalem.
5"Oholah engaged in prostitution while she was still mine; and
she lusted after her lovers, the Assyrians[t]—warriors[u] **6**clothed in
blue, governors and commanders,
all of them handsome young men,
and mounted horsemen. **7**She gave
herself as a prostitute to all the
elite of the Assyrians and defiled
herself with all the idols of everyone she lusted after.[v] **8**She did not
give up the prostitution she began
in Egypt,[w] when during her youth
men slept with her, caressed her
virgin bosom and poured out their
lust upon her.[x]
9"Therefore I handed her over[y]
to her lovers, the Assyrians, for
whom she lusted.[z] **10**They
stripped[a] her naked, took away
her sons and daughters and killed
her with the sword. She became a
byword among women,[b] and punishment was inflicted on her.[c]
11"Her sister Oholibah saw this,
yet in her lust and prostitution she
was more depraved than her sis-
ter.[d] **12**She too lusted after the Assyrians—governors and command-
ers, warriors in full dress, mounted
horsemen, all handsome young
men.[e] **13**I saw that she too defiled
herself; both of them went the
same way.
14"But she carried her prostitution still further. She saw men portrayed on a wall,[f] figures of Chaldeans[x] portrayed in red,[g] **15**with
belts around their waists and flowing turbans on their heads; all of
them looked like Babylonian chariot officers, natives of Chaldea.[y]
16As soon as she saw them, she
lusted after them and sent messengers to them in Chaldea. **17**Then
the Babylonians came to her, to the
bed of love, and in their lust they
defiled her. After she had been defiled by them, she turned away
from them in disgust. **18**When she
carried on her prostitution openly
and exposed her nakedness, I
turned away[h] from her in disgust,
just as I had turned away from her
sister.[i] **19**Yet she became more
and more promiscuous as she recalled the days of her youth, when

22:25 [a]Jer 11:9 [b]Hos 6:9 [c]Jer 15:8
22:26 [d]Mal 2:7-8 [e]Eze 44:23 [f]Lev 10:10 [g]1Sa 2:12-17; Jer 2:8,26; Hag 2:11-14
22:27 [h]Isa 1:23
22:28 [i]Eze 13:10 [j]Eze 13:2,6-7
22:29 [k]Ex 22:21; 23:9 [l]Isa 5:7
22:30 [m]Eze 13:5 [n]Ps 106:23; Jer 5:1
22:31 [o]Eze 16:43 [p]Eze 7:8-9; 9:10; Ro 2:8
23:2 [q]Jer 3:7; Eze 16:45
23:3 [r]Jos 24:14 [s]Lev 17:7
23:5 [t]2Ki 16:7; Hos 5:13 [u]Hos 8:9
23:7 [v]Hos 5:3; 6:10
23:8 [w]Ex 32:4 [x]Eze 16:15
23:9 [y]2Ki 18:11 [z]Hos 11:5
23:10 [a]Hos 2:10 [b]Eze 16:41 [c]Eze 16:36
23:11 [d]Jer 3:8-11; Eze 16:51
23:12 [e]2Ki 16:7-15; 2Ch 28:16
23:14 [f]Eze 8:10 [g]Jer 22:14
23:18 [h]Ps 78:59; 106:40; Jer 6:8 [i]Jer 12:8; Am 5:21

[w]*25* Septuagint; Hebrew *prophets* [x]*14* Or *Babylonians* [y]*15* Or *Babylonia*; also in verse 16

she was a prostitute in Egypt.
20There she lusted after her lovers,
whose genitals were like those of
donkeys and whose emission was
like that of horses. **21**So you longed
for the lewdness of your youth,
when in Egypt your bosom was caressed and your young breasts fon-
dled.[z][a]
22"Therefore, Oholibah, this is
what the Sovereign LORD says: I will
stir up your lovers against you,
those you turned away from in disgust, and I will bring them against
you from every side[b]— **23**the Babylonians[c] and all the Chaldeans,
the men of Pekod[d] and Shoa and
Koa, and all the Assyrians with
them, handsome young men, all of
them governors and commanders,
chariot officers and men of high
rank, all mounted on horses.[e]
24They will come against you with
weapons,[a] chariots and wagons[f]
and with a throng of people; they
will take up positions against you
on every side with large and small
shields and with helmets. I will
turn you over to them for punishment,[g] and they will punish you
according to their standards. **25**I
will direct my jealous anger against
you, and they will deal with you in
fury. They will cut off your noses
and your ears, and those of you
who are left will fall by the sword.
They will take away your sons and
daughters,[h] and those of you who
are left will be consumed by fire.[i]
26They will also strip[j] you of your
clothes and take your fine jewel-
ry.[k] **27**So I will put a stop[l] to the
lewdness and prostitution you began in Egypt. You will not look on
these things with longing or remember Egypt anymore.
28"For this is what the Sovereign
LORD says: I am about to hand you
over[m] to those you hate, to those
you turned away from in disgust.
29They will deal with you in hatred
and take away everything you have
worked for. They will leave you naked and bare, and the shame of
your prostitution will be exposed.
Your lewdness and promiscuity[n]
30have brought this upon you, because you lusted after the nations
and defiled yourself with their
idols.[o] **31**You have gone the way of
your sister; so I will put her cup[p]
into your hand.[q]
32"This is what the Sovereign
LORD says:

"You will drink your sister's
cup,
a cup large and deep;
it will bring scorn and derision,
for it holds so much.[r]
33You will be filled with
drunkenness and sorrow,
the cup of ruin and
desolation,
the cup of your sister
Samaria.[s]
34You will drink it[t] and drain it
dry;
you will dash it to pieces
and tear your breasts.

I have spoken, declares the Sovereign LORD.

35"Therefore this is what the
Sovereign LORD says: Since you
have forgotten[u] me and thrust me
behind your back,[v] you must bear
the consequences of your lewdness
and prostitution."
36The LORD said to me: "Son of
man, will you judge Oholah and
Oholibah? Then confront[w] them
with their detestable practices,[x]
37for they have committed adultery
and blood is on their hands. They
committed adultery with their
idols; they even sacrificed their
children, whom they bore to me,[b]
as food for them.[y] **38**They have
also done this to me: At that same
time they defiled my sanctuary and
desecrated my Sabbaths. **39**On the
very day they sacrificed their children to their idols, they entered my
sanctuary and desecrated[z] it. That
is what they did in my house.[a]
40"They even sent messengers
for men who came from far away,[b]
and when they arrived you bathed
yourself for them, painted your

23:21 [a]Eze 16:26
23:22 [b]Eze 16:37
23:23 [c]2Ki 20:14-18 [d]Jer 50:21 [e]2Ki 24:2
23:24 [f]Jer 47:3; Eze 26:7,10; Na 2:4 [g]Jer 39:5-6
23:25 [h]ver 47 [i]Eze 20:47-48
23:26 [j]Jer 13:22 [k]Isa 3:18-23; Eze 16:39
23:27 [l]Eze 16:41
23:28 [m]Jer 34:20
23:29 [n]Dt 28:48
23:30 [o]Eze 6:9
23:31 [p]Jer 25:15 [q]2Ki 21:13
23:32 [r]Ps 60:3; Isa 51:17; Jer 25:15
23:33 [s]Jer 25:15-16
23:34 [t]Ps 75:8; Isa 51:17
23:35 [u]Isa 17:10; Jer 3:21 [v]1Ki 14:9
23:36 [w]Eze 16:2 [x]Isa 58:1; Eze 22:2; Mic 3:8
23:37 [y]Eze 16:36
23:39 [z]2Ki 21:4 [a]Jer 7:10
23:40 [b]Isa 57:9

[z]*21* Syriac (see also verse 3); Hebrew *caressed because of your young breasts* [a]*24* The meaning of the Hebrew for this word is uncertain. [b]*37* Or *even made the children they bore to me pass through ⌞the fire⌟*

eyes[a] and put on your jewelry.[b]
41You sat on an elegant couch,[c]
with a table[d] spread before it on
which you had placed the incense
and oil that belonged to me.
42"The noise of a carefree crowd
was around her; Sabeans[c] were
brought from the desert along with
men from the rabble, and they put
bracelets[e] on the arms of the
woman and her sister and beautiful
crowns on their heads.[f] 43Then I
said about the one worn out by
adultery, 'Now let them use her as
a prostitute,[g] for that is all she is.'
44And they slept with her. As men
sleep with a prostitute, so they
slept with those lewd women, Oholah and Oholibah. 45But righteous
men will sentence them to the
punishment of women who commit adultery and shed blood, because they are adulterous and
blood is on their hands.[h]
46"This is what the Sovereign
LORD says: Bring a mob[i] against
them and give them over to terror
and plunder. 47The mob will stone
them and cut them down with their
swords; they will kill their sons and
daughters and burn[j] down their
houses.[k]
48"So I will put an end to lewdness in the land, that all women
may take warning and not imitate
you.[l] 49You will suffer the penalty
for your lewdness and bear the consequences of your sins of idolatry.
Then you will know that I am the
Sovereign LORD.[m]"

The Cooking Pot

24 In the ninth year, in the
tenth month on the tenth
day, the word of the LORD came to
me:[n] 2"Son of man, record this
date, this very date, because the
king of Babylon has laid siege to Jerusalem this very day.[o] 3Tell this
rebellious house[p] a parable[q] and
say to them: 'This is what the Sovereign LORD says:

" 'Put on the cooking pot;[r] put
it on
and pour water into it.
4Put into it the pieces of meat,
all the choice pieces—the leg
and the shoulder.
Fill it with the best of these
bones;
5 take the pick of the flock.[s]
Pile wood beneath it for the
bones;
bring it to a boil
and cook the bones in it.[t]

6" 'For this is what the Sovereign
LORD says:

" 'Woe to the city of
bloodshed,[u]
to the pot now encrusted,
whose deposit will not go
away!
Empty it piece by piece
without casting lots[v] for
them.

7" 'For the blood she shed is in
her midst:
She poured it on the bare
rock;
she did not pour it on the
ground,
where the dust would cover
it.[w]
8To stir up wrath and take
revenge
I put her blood on the bare
rock,
so that it would not be
covered.

9" 'Therefore this is what the Sovereign LORD says:

" 'Woe to the city of bloodshed!
I, too, will pile the wood high.
10So heap on the wood
and kindle the fire.
Cook the meat well,
mixing in the spices;
and let the bones be charred.
11Then set the empty pot on the
coals
till it becomes hot and its
copper glows
so its impurities may be melted
and its deposit burned
away.[x]
12It has frustrated all efforts;
its heavy deposit has not
been removed,
not even by fire.

23:40 [a]2Ki 9:30 [b]Jer 4:30; Eze 16:13-19
23:41 [c]Est 1:6; Pr 7:17; Am 6:4 [d]Isa 65:11; Eze 44:16
23:42 [e]Ge 24:30 [f]Eze 16:11-12
23:43 [g]ver 3
23:45 [h]Lev 20:10; Eze 16:38; Hos 6:5
23:46 [i]Eze 16:40
23:47 [j]2Ch 36:19 [k]2Ch 36:17; Eze 16:40-41
23:48 [l]2Pe 2:6
23:49 [m]Eze 7:4; 9:10; 20:38
24:1 [n]Eze 8:1
24:2 [o]2Ki 25:1; Jer 39:1; 52:4
24:3 [p]Isa 1:2; Eze 2:3,6 [q]Eze 17:2; 20:49 [r]Jer 1:13; Eze 11:3
24:5 [s]Jer 52:10 [t]Jer 52:24-27
24:6 [u]Eze 22:2 [v]Ob 1:11; Na 3:10
24:7 [w]Lev 17:13
24:11 [x]Jer 21:10; Eze 22:15

c42 Or *drunkards*

13"'Now your impurity is lewdness. Because I tried to cleanse you
but you would not be cleansed
from your impurity, you will not be
clean again until my wrath against
you has subsided.[a]

14"'I the LORD have spoken. The
time has come for me to act. I will
not hold back; I will not have pity,
nor will I relent. You will be judged
according to your conduct and your
actions,[b] declares the Sovereign
LORD.[c]'"

Ezekiel's Wife Dies

15The word of the LORD came to
me: 16"Son of man, with one blow
I am about to take away from you
the delight of your eyes. Yet do not
lament or weep or shed any tears.[d]
17Groan quietly; do not mourn for
the dead. Keep your turban fastened and your sandals on your
feet; do not cover the lower part of
your face or eat the customary food
⌞of mourners⌟.[e]"

18So I spoke to the people in the
morning, and in the evening my
wife died. The next morning I did
as I had been commanded.

19Then the people asked me,
"Won't you tell us what these
things have to do with us?[f]"

20So I said to them, "The word of
the LORD came to me: 21Say to the
house of Israel, 'This is what the
Sovereign LORD says: I am about to
desecrate my sanctuary—the
stronghold in which you take pride,
the delight of your eyes,[g] the object of your affection. The sons and
daughters[h] you left behind will fall
by the sword.[i] 22And you will do
as I have done. You will not cover
the lower part of your face or eat
the customary food ⌞of mourners⌟.[j]
23You will keep your turbans on
your heads and your sandals on
your feet. You will not mourn[k] or
weep but will waste away because
of[d] your sins and groan among
yourselves.[l] 24Ezekiel will be a
sign[m] to you; you will do just as he
has done. When this happens, you
will know that I am the Sovereign
LORD.'

25"And you, son of man, on the
day I take away their stronghold,
their joy and glory, the delight of
their eyes, their heart's desire, and
their sons and daughters[n] as
well— 26on that day a fugitive will
come to tell you[o] the news. 27At
that time your mouth will be
opened; you will speak with him
and will no longer be silent. So you
will be a sign to them, and they will
know that I am the LORD.[p]"

A Prophecy Against Ammon

25 The word of the LORD came
to me: 2"Son of man, set
your face against the Ammonites[q]
and prophesy against them.[r] 3Say
to them, 'Hear the word of the Sovereign LORD. This is what the Sovereign LORD says: Because you said
"Aha![s]" over my sanctuary when it
was desecrated and over the land of
Israel when it was laid waste and
over the people of Judah when they
went into exile,[t] 4therefore I am
going to give you to the people of
the East[u] as a possession. They
will set up their camps and pitch
their tents among you; they will eat
your fruit and drink your milk.[v] 5I
will turn Rabbah[w] into a pasture
for camels and Ammon into a resting place for sheep.[x] Then you will
know that I am the LORD. 6For this
is what the Sovereign LORD says:
Because you have clapped your
hands and stamped your feet, rejoicing with all the malice of your
heart against the land of Israel,[y]
7therefore I will stretch out my
hand[z] against you and give you as
plunder to the nations. I will cut
you off from the nations and exterminate you from the countries. I
will destroy[a] you, and you will
know that I am the LORD.[b]'"

A Prophecy Against Moab

8"This is what the Sovereign
LORD says: 'Because Moab[c] and
Seir said, "Look, the house of Ju-
dah has become like all the other

24:13 [a]Jer 6:28-30; Eze 16:42; 22:24
24:14 [b]Eze 36:19 [c]Eze 18:30
24:16 [d]Jer 13:17; 16:5; 22:10
24:17 [e]Jer 16:7
24:19 [f]Eze 12:9; 37:18
24:21 [g]Ps 27:4 [h]Eze 23:25 [i]Jer 7:14,15; Eze 23:47
24:22 [j]Jer 16:7
24:23 [k]Job 27:15 [l]Ps 78:64
24:24 [m]Isa 20:3; Eze 4:3; 12:11
24:25 [n]Jer 11:22
24:26 [o]1Sa 4:12; Job 1:15-19
24:27 [p]Eze 3:26; 33:22
25:2 [q]Eze 21:28; Zep 2:8-9 [r]Jer 49:1-6
25:3 [s]Eze 26:2; 36:2 [t]Pr 17:5
25:4 [u]Jdg 6:3 [v]Dt 28:33,51; Jdg 6:33
25:5 [w]Dt 3:11; Eze 21:20 [x]Isa 17:2
25:6 [y]Ob 1:12; Zep 2:8
25:7 [z]Zep 1:4 [a]Eze 21:31 [b]Am 1:14-15
25:8 [c]Jer 48:1; Am 2:1

[d]23 Or *away in*

nations," **9**therefore I will expose the flank of Moab, beginning at its frontier towns—Beth Jeshimoth[a], Baal Meon[b] and Kiriathaim[c]—the glory of that land. **10**I will give Moab along with the Ammonites to the people of the East as a possession, so that the Ammonites will not be remembered[d] among the nations; **11**and I will inflict punishment on Moab. Then they will know that I am the LORD.' "

A Prophecy Against Edom

12"This is what the Sovereign LORD says: 'Because Edom[e] took revenge on the house of Judah and became very guilty by doing so, **13**therefore this is what the Sovereign LORD says: I will stretch out my hand against Edom and kill its men and their animals.[f] I will lay it waste, and from Teman to Dedan[g] they will fall by the sword. **14**I will take vengeance on Edom by the hand of my people Israel, and they will deal with Edom in accordance with my anger[h] and my wrath; they will know my vengeance, declares the Sovereign LORD.' "

A Prophecy Against Philistia

15"This is what the Sovereign LORD says: 'Because the Philistines[i] acted in vengeance and took revenge with malice in their hearts, and with ancient hostility sought to destroy Judah, **16**therefore this is what the Sovereign LORD says: I am about to stretch out my hand against the Philistines,[j] and I will cut off the Kerethites[k] and destroy those remaining along the coast. **17**I will carry out great vengeance on them and punish them in my wrath. Then they will know that I am the LORD, when I take vengeance on them.' "

A Prophecy Against Tyre

26 In the eleventh year, on the first day of the month, the word of the LORD came to me: **2**"Son of man, because Tyre[l] has said of Jerusalem, 'Aha![m] The gate to the nations is broken, and its doors have swung open to me; now that she lies in ruins I will prosper,' **3**therefore this is what the Sovereign LORD says: I am against you, O Tyre, and I will bring many nations against you, like the sea[n] casting up its waves. **4**They will destroy[o] the walls of Tyre[p] and pull down her towers; I will scrape away her rubble and make her a bare rock. **5**Out in the sea[q] she will become a place to spread fishnets, for I have spoken, declares the Sovereign LORD. She will become plunder[r] for the nations, **6**and her settlements on the mainland will be ravaged by the sword. Then they will know that I am the LORD.

7"For this is what the Sovereign LORD says: From the north I am going to bring against Tyre Nebuchadnezzar[e][s] king of Babylon, king of kings,[t] with horses and chariots,[u] with horsemen and a great army. **8**He will ravage your settlements on the mainland with the sword; he will set up siege works[v] against you, build a ramp[w] up to your walls and raise his shields against you. **9**He will direct the blows of his battering rams against your walls and demolish your towers with his weapons. **10**His horses will be so many that they will cover you with dust. Your walls will tremble at the noise of the war horses, wagons and chariots[x] when he enters your gates as men enter a city whose walls have been broken through. **11**The hoofs[y] of his horses will trample all your streets; he will kill your people with the sword, and your strong pillars[z] will fall to the ground.[a] **12**They will plunder your wealth and loot your merchandise; they will break down your walls and demolish your fine houses and throw your stones, timber and rubble into the sea.[b] **13**I will put an end[c] to your noisy songs, and the music of your harps[d] will be heard no more.[e] **14**I will make you a bare rock, and you will become a place

25:9 [a] Nu 33:49 [b] Nu 32:3; Jos 13:17 [c] Nu 32:37; Jos 13:19
25:10 [d] Eze 21:32
25:12 [e] 2Ch 28:17
25:13 [f] Eze 29:8 [g] Jer 25:23
25:14 [h] Eze 35:11
25:15 [i] 2Ch 28:18
25:16 [j] Jer 47:1-7 [k] 1Sa 30:14; Zep 2:4-5
26:2 [l] 2Sa 5:11; Isa 23 [m] Eze 25:3
26:3 [n] Isa 5:30; Jer 50:42; 51:42
26:4 [o] Isa 23:1,11 [p] Am 1:10
26:5 [q] Eze 27:32 [r] Eze 29:19
26:7 [s] Jer 27:6 [t] Ezr 7:12; Da 2:37 [u] Eze 23:24; Na 2:3-4
26:8 [v] Jer 6:6 [w] Eze 21:22
26:10 [x] Jer 4:13
26:11 [y] Isa 5:28 [z] Jer 43:13 [a] Isa 26:5
26:12 [b] Isa 23:8; Eze 27:3-27; 28:8
26:13 [c] Jer 7:34 [d] Isa 14:11 [e] Jer 25:10; Rev 18:22

[e]7 Hebrew *Nebuchadrezzar,* of which *Nebuchadnezzar* is a variant; here and often in Ezekiel and Jeremiah

to spread fishnets. You will never
be rebuilt,[a] for I the LORD have spoken, declares the Sovereign LORD.
15"This is what the Sovereign
LORD says to Tyre: Will not the
coastlands[b] tremble[c] at the
sound of your fall, when the
wounded groan and the slaughter
takes place in you? 16Then all the
princes of the coast will step down
from their thrones and lay aside
their robes and take off their embroidered garments. Clothed[d]
with terror, they will sit on the
ground, trembling[e] every moment,
appalled[f] at you. 17Then they will
take up a lament[g] concerning you
and say to you:

" 'How you are destroyed,
O city of renown,
peopled by men of the sea!
You were a power on the seas,
you and your citizens;
you put your terror
on all who lived there.[h]
18Now the coastlands tremble
on the day of your fall;
the islands in the sea
are terrified at your
collapse.'[i]

19"This is what the Sovereign
LORD says: When I make you a desolate city, like cities no longer inhabited, and when I bring the
ocean depths over you and its vast
waters cover you,[j] 20then I will
bring you down with those who go
down to the pit,[k] to the people of
long ago. I will make you dwell in
the earth below, as in ancient ruins, with those who go down to the
pit, and you will not return or take
your place[f] in the land of the living.[l] 21I will bring you to a horrible
end and you will be no more. You
will be sought, but you will never
again be found, declares the Sovereign LORD."[m]

A Lament for Tyre

27 The word of the LORD came
to me: 2"Son of man, take
up a lament concerning Tyre. 3Say
to Tyre, situated at the gateway to
the sea,[n] merchant of peoples on
many coasts, 'This is what the Sovereign LORD says:

" 'You say, O Tyre,
"I am perfect in beauty.[o]"
4Your domain was on the high
seas;
your builders brought your
beauty to perfection.
5They made all your timbers
of pine trees from Senir[g];[p]
they took a cedar from
Lebanon
to make a mast for you.
6Of oaks[q] from Bashan
they made your oars;
of cypress wood[h] from the
coasts of Cyprus[i][r]
they made your deck, inlaid
with ivory.
7Fine embroidered linen from
Egypt was your sail
and served as your banner;
your awnings were of blue and
purple[s]
from the coasts of Elishah.
8Men of Sidon and Arvad[t] were
your oarsmen;
your skilled men, O Tyre,
were aboard as your
seamen.[u]
9Veteran craftsmen of Gebal[j][v]
were on board
as shipwrights to caulk your
seams.
All the ships of the sea and
their sailors
came alongside to trade for
your wares.

10" 'Men of Persia,[w] Lydia and
Put[x]
served as soldiers in your
army.
They hung their shields and
helmets on your walls,
bringing you splendor.
11Men of Arvad and Helech
manned your walls on every
side;
men of Gammad
were in your towers.

26:14 [a] Job 12:14; Mal 1:4
26:15 [b] Eze 27:35 [c] Jer 49:21
26:16 [d] Job 8:22 [e] Hos 11:10 [f] Eze 32:10
26:17 [g] Eze 19:1; 27:32 [h] Isa 14:12
26:18 [i] Isa 23:5; 41:5; Eze 27:35
26:19 [j] Isa 8:7-8
26:20 [k] Eze 32:18; Am 9:2; Jnh 2:2,6 [l] Eze 32:24,30
26:21 [m] Eze 27:36; 28:19; Rev 18:21
27:3 [n] ver 33 [o] Eze 28:2
27:5 [p] Dt 3:9
27:6 [q] Nu 21:33; Jer 22:20; Zec 11:2 [r] Ge 10:4; Isa 23:12
27:7 [s] Ex 25:4; Jer 10:9
27:8 [t] Ge 10:18 [u] 1Ki 9:27
27:9 [v] Jos 13:5; 1Ki 5:18
27:10 [w] Eze 38:5 [x] Eze 30:5

f20 Septuagint; Hebrew *return, and I will give glory* g5 That is, Hermon h6 Targum; the Masoretic Text has a different division of the consonants. i6 Hebrew *Kittim* j9 That is, Byblos

They hung their shields around
your walls;
they brought your beauty to
perfection.

12 " 'Tarshish[a] did business with
you because of your great wealth of
goods;[b] they exchanged silver,
iron, tin and lead for your merchandise.

13 " 'Greece, Tubal and Meshech[c] traded with you; they exchanged slaves[d] and articles of
bronze for your wares.

14 " 'Men of Beth Togarmah[e] exchanged work horses, war horses
and mules for your merchandise.

15 " 'The men of Rhodes[k][f] traded with you, and many coastlands[g]
were your customers; they paid you
with ivory[h] tusks and ebony.

16 " 'Aram[l][i] did business with
you because of your many products; they exchanged turquoise,[j]
purple fabric, embroidered work,
fine linen, coral and rubies for your
merchandise.

17 " 'Judah and Israel traded with
you; they exchanged wheat from
Minnith[k] and confections,[m] honey, oil and balm for your wares.

18 " 'Damascus,[l] because of
your many products and great
wealth of goods, did business with
you in wine from Helbon and wool
from Zahar.

19 " 'Danites and Greeks from
Uzal bought your merchandise;
they exchanged wrought iron, cassia and calamus for your wares.

20 " 'Dedan traded in saddle
blankets with you.

21 " 'Arabia and all the princes of
Kedar[m] were your customers; they
did business with you in lambs,
rams and goats.

22 " 'The merchants of Sheba[n]
and Raamah traded with you; for
your merchandise they exchanged
the finest of all kinds of spices[o]
and precious stones, and gold.

23 " 'Haran,[p] Canneh and Eden[q]
and merchants of Sheba, Asshur
and Kilmad traded with you. 24 In
your marketplace they traded with
you beautiful garments, blue fabric, embroidered work and multi-
colored rugs with cords twisted and
tightly knotted.

25 " 'The ships of Tarshish[r] serve
as carriers for your wares.
You are filled with heavy cargo
in the heart of the sea.
26 Your oarsmen take you
out to the high seas.
But the east wind[s] will break
you to pieces
in the heart of the sea.
27 Your wealth,[t] merchandise and
wares,
your mariners, seamen and
shipwrights,
your merchants and all your
soldiers,
and everyone else on board
will sink into the heart of the
sea
on the day of your shipwreck.
28 The shorelands will quake[u]
when your seamen cry out.
29 All who handle the oars
will abandon their ships;
the mariners and all the
seamen
will stand on the shore.
30 They will raise their voice
and cry bitterly over you;
they will sprinkle dust[v] on
their heads
and roll[w] in ashes.[x]
31 They will shave their heads
because of you
and will put on sackcloth.
They will weep[y] over you with
anguish of soul
and with bitter mourning.[z]
32 As they wail and mourn over
you,
they will take up a lament[a]
concerning you:
"Who was ever silenced like
Tyre,
surrounded by the sea?"
33 When your merchandise went
out on the seas,
you satisfied many nations;
with your great wealth[b] and
your wares

27:12 [a] Ge 10:4 [b] ver 18,33
27:13 [c] Ge 10:2; Isa 66:19; Eze 38:2 [d] Rev 18:13
27:14 [e] Ge 10:3; Eze 38:6
27:15 [f] Ge 10:7 [g] Jer 25:22 [h] 1Ki 10:22; Rev 18:12
27:16 [i] Jdg 10:6; Isa 7:1-8 [j] Eze 28:13
27:17 [k] Jdg 11:33
27:18 [l] Ge 14:15; Eze 47:16-18
27:21 [m] Ge 25:13; Isa 60:7
27:22 [n] Ge 10:7,28; 1Ki 10:1-2; Isa 60:6 [o] Ge 43:11
27:23 [p] 2Ki 19:12 [q] Isa 37:12
27:25 [r] Isa 2:16 *fn*
27:26 [s] Ps 48:7; Jer 18:17
27:27 [t] Pr 11:4
27:28 [u] Eze 26:15
27:30 [v] 2Sa 1:2 [w] Jer 6:26 [x] Rev 18:18-19
27:31 [y] Isa 16:9 [z] Isa 22:12; Eze 7:18
27:32 [a] Eze 26:17
27:33 [b] ver 12; Eze 28:4-5

[k] *15* Septuagint; Hebrew *Dedan* [l] *16* Most Hebrew manuscripts; some Hebrew manuscripts and Syriac *Edom* [m] *17* The meaning of the Hebrew for this word is uncertain.

you enriched the kings of the
earth.
34Now you are shattered by the
sea
in the depths of the waters;
your wares and all your
company
have gone down with you.[a]
35All who live in the coastlands[b]
are appalled at you;
their kings shudder with horror
and their faces are distorted
with fear.
36The merchants among the
nations hiss at you;[c]
you have come to a horrible
end
and will be no more.[d]' "

A Prophecy Against the King of Tyre

28 The word of the LORD came
to me: 2"Son of man, say to
the ruler of Tyre, 'This is what the
Sovereign LORD says:

" 'In the pride of your heart
you say, "I am a god;
I sit on the throne[e] of a god
in the heart of the seas."
But you are a man and not a
god,
though you think you are as
wise as a god.[f]
3Are you wiser than Daniel[n]?[g]
Is no secret hidden from
you?
4By your wisdom and
understanding
you have gained wealth for
yourself
and amassed gold and silver
in your treasuries.[h]
5By your great skill in trading
you have increased your
wealth,
and because of your wealth
your heart has grown proud.[i]

6" 'Therefore this is what the
Sovereign LORD says:

" 'Because you think you are
wise,
as wise as a god,
7I am going to bring foreigners
against you,
the most ruthless of
nations;[j]
they will draw their swords
against your beauty and
wisdom
and pierce your shining
splendor.
8They will bring you down to the
pit,[k]
and you will die a violent
death
in the heart of the seas.[l]
9Will you then say, "I am a
god,"
in the presence of those who
kill you?
You will be but a man, not a
god,
in the hands of those who
slay you.
10You will die the death of the
uncircumcised[m]
at the hands of foreigners.

I have spoken, declares the Sovereign LORD.' "

11The word of the LORD came to
me: 12"Son of man, take up a lament[n] concerning the king of Tyre
and say to him: 'This is what the
Sovereign LORD says:

" 'You were the model of
perfection,
full of wisdom and perfect in
beauty.[o]
13You were in Eden,[p]
the garden of God;[q]
every precious stone adorned
you:
ruby, topaz and emerald,
chrysolite, onyx and jasper,
sapphire,[o] turquoise[r] and
beryl.[p]
Your settings and mountings[q]
were made of gold;
on the day you were created
they were prepared.
14You were anointed[s] as a
guardian cherub,[t]
for so I ordained you.

27:34 [a]Zec 9:4
27:35 [b]Eze 26:15
27:36 [c]Jer 18:16; 19:8; 49:17; 50:13; Zep 2:15 [d]Ps 37:10,36; Eze 26:21
28:2 [e]Isa 14:13 [f]Ps 9:20; 82:6-7; Isa 31:3; 2Th 2:4
28:3 [g]Da 1:20; 5:11-12
28:4 [h]Zec 9:3
28:5 [i]Job 31:25; Ps 52:7; 62:10; Hos 12:8; 13:6
28:7 [j]Eze 30:11; 31:12; 32:12; Hab 1:6
28:8 [k]Eze 32:30 [l]Eze 27:27
28:10 [m]Eze 31:18; 32:19,24
28:12 [n]Eze 19:1 [o]Eze 27:2-4
28:13 [p]Ge 2:8 [q]Eze 31:8-9 [r]Eze 27:16
28:14 [s]Ex 30:26; 40:9 [t]Ex 25:17-20

n3 Or *Danel*; the Hebrew spelling may suggest a person other than the prophet Daniel.
o13 Or *lapis lazuli* p13 The precise identification of some of these precious stones is uncertain. q13 The meaning of the Hebrew for this phrase is uncertain.

You were on the holy mount of God;
you walked among the fiery stones.
15You were blameless in your ways
from the day you were created
till wickedness was found in you.
16Through your widespread trade
you were filled with violence,[a]
and you sinned.
So I drove you in disgrace from the mount of God,
and I expelled you,
O guardian cherub,[b]
from among the fiery stones.
17Your heart became proud[c]
on account of your beauty,
and you corrupted your wisdom
because of your splendor.
So I threw you to the earth;
I made a spectacle of you
before kings.
18By your many sins and dishonest trade
you have desecrated your sanctuaries.
So I made a fire come out from you,
and it consumed you,
and I reduced you to ashes[d] on the ground
in the sight of all who were watching.
19All the nations who knew you
are appalled at you;
you have come to a horrible end
and will be no more.[e]' "

A Prophecy Against Sidon

20The word of the LORD came to
me: 21"Son of man, set your face
against[f] Sidon;[g] prophesy against
her 22and say: 'This is what the
Sovereign LORD says:

" 'I am against you, O Sidon,
and I will gain glory[h] within you.
They will know that I am the LORD,
when I inflict punishment[i] on her

28:16 [a]Hab 2:17 [b]Ge 3:24
28:17 [c]Eze 31:10
28:18 [d]Mal 4:3
28:19 [e]Jer 51:64; Eze 26:21; 27:36
28:21 [f]Eze 6:2 [g]Ge 10:15; Jer 25:22
28:22 [h]Eze 39:13 [i]Eze 30:19
28:23 [j]Eze 38:22
28:24 [k]Nu 33:55; Jos 23:13; Eze 2:6
28:25 [l]Ps 106:47; Jer 32:37 [m]Isa 11:12 [n]Eze 20:41 [o]Jer 23:8; Eze 11:17; 34:27; 37:25
28:26 [p]Jer 23:6 [q]Isa 65:21; Jer 32:15; Eze 38:8; Am 9:14-15
29:1 [r]ver 17; Eze 26:1
29:2 [s]Jer 25:19 [t]Isa 19:1-17; Jer 46:2; Eze 30:1-26; 31:1-18; 32:1-32
29:3 [u]Jer 44:30 [v]Ps 74:13; Isa 27:1; Eze 32:2
29:4 [w]2Ki 19:28 [x]Eze 38:4

and show myself holy within her.
23I will send a plague upon her
and make blood flow in her streets.
The slain will fall within her,
with the sword against her on every side.
Then they will know that I am the LORD.[j]

24" 'No longer will the people of
Israel have malicious neighbors
who are painful briers and sharp
thorns.[k] Then they will know that
I am the Sovereign LORD.
25" 'This is what the Sovereign
LORD says: When I gather[l] the people of Israel from the nations where
they have been scattered,[m] I will
show myself holy[n] among them in
the sight of the nations. Then they
will live in their own land, which I
gave to my servant Jacob.[o] 26They
will live there in safety[p] and will
build houses and plant vineyards;
they will live in safety when I inflict
punishment on all their neighbors
who maligned them. Then they will
know that I am the LORD their
God.[q]' "

A Prophecy Against Egypt

29 In the tenth year, in the
tenth month on the twelfth
day, the word of the LORD came to
me:[r] 2"Son of man, set your face
against Pharaoh king of Egypt[s]
and prophesy against him and
against all Egypt.[t] 3Speak to him
and say: 'This is what the Sovereign
LORD says:

" 'I am against you, Pharaoh[u]
king of Egypt,
you great monster[v] lying
among your streams.
You say, "The Nile is mine;
I made it for myself."
4But I will put hooks[w] in your jaws
and make the fish of your streams stick to your scales.
I will pull you out from among your streams,
with all the fish sticking to your scales.[x]

5I will leave you in the desert,
you and all the fish of your
streams.
You will fall on the open field
and not be gathered or
picked up.
I will give you as food
to the beasts of the earth and
the birds of the air.[a]

6Then all who live in Egypt will
know that I am the LORD.

" 'You have been a staff of reed[b]
for the house of Israel. 7When they
grasped you with their hands, you
splintered[c] and you tore open
their shoulders; when they leaned
on you, you broke and their backs
were wrenched.[r][d]
8" 'Therefore this is what the
Sovereign LORD says: I will bring a
sword against you and kill your
men and their animals.[e] 9Egypt
will become a desolate wasteland.
Then they will know that I am the
LORD.
" 'Because you said, "The Nile is
mine; I made it,[f]" 10therefore I am
against you and against your
streams, and I will make the land of
Egypt a ruin and a desolate waste
from Migdol to Aswan,[g] as far as
the border of Cush.[s] 11No foot of
man or animal will pass through it;
no one will live there for forty
years.[h] 12I will make the land of
Egypt desolate among devastated
lands, and her cities will lie desolate forty years among ruined cities. And I will disperse the Egyptians among the nations and scatter them through the countries.[i]
13" 'Yet this is what the Sovereign LORD says: At the end of forty
years I will gather the Egyptians
from the nations where they were
scattered. 14I will bring them back
from captivity and return them to
Upper Egypt,[t][j] the land of their
ancestry. There they will be a lowly[k] kingdom. 15It will be the lowliest of kingdoms and will never
again exalt itself above the other
nations.[l] I will make it so weak
that it will never again rule over the
nations. 16Egypt will no longer be a
source of confidence[m] for the people of Israel but will be a reminder
of their sin in turning to her for
help. Then they will know that I am
the Sovereign LORD.[n]' "

17In the twenty-seventh year, in
the first month on the first day, the
word of the LORD came to me:[o]
18"Son of man, Nebuchadnezzar[p]
king of Babylon drove his army in a
hard campaign against Tyre; every
head was rubbed bare[q] and every
shoulder made raw. Yet he and his
army got no reward from the campaign he led against Tyre. 19There-
fore this is what the Sovereign LORD
says: I am going to give Egypt to
Nebuchadnezzar king of Babylon,
and he will carry off its wealth. He
will loot and plunder the land as
pay for his army.[r] 20I have given
him Egypt as a reward for his efforts because he and his army did it
for me, declares the Sovereign
LORD.[s]

21"On that day I will make a
horn[u][t] grow for the house of Israel, and I will open your mouth[u]
among them. Then they will know
that I am the LORD.[v]"

A Lament for Egypt

30 The word of the LORD came
to me: 2"Son of man, prophesy and say: 'This is what the Sovereign LORD says:

" 'Wail[w] and say,
"Alas for that day!"
3For the day is near,[x]
the day of the LORD[y] is
near—
a day of clouds,
a time of doom for the
nations.
4A sword will come against
Egypt,
and anguish will come upon
Cush.[v]
When the slain fall in Egypt,
her wealth will be carried
away

29:5 [a]Jer 7:33; 34:20; Eze 32:4-6; 39:4
29:6 [b]2Ki 18:21; Isa 36:6
29:7 [c]Isa 36:6 [d]Eze 17:15-17
29:8 [e]Eze 14:17; 32:11-13
29:9 [f]Eze 30:7-8, 13-19
29:10 [g]Eze 30:6
29:11 [h]Eze 32:13
29:12 [i]Jer 46:19; Eze 30:7,23, 26
29:14 [j]Eze 30:14 [k]Eze 17:14
29:15 [l]Zec 10:11
29:16 [m]Isa 36:4,6 [n]Isa 30:2; Hos 8:13
29:17 [o]Eze 24:1
29:18 [p]Jer 27:6; Eze 26:7-8 [q]Jer 48:37
29:19 [r]Jer 43:10-13; Eze 30:4,10, 24-25
29:20 [s]Isa 10:6-7; 45:1; Jer 25:9
29:21 [t]Ps 132:17 [u]Eze 33:22 [v]Eze 24:27
30:2 [w]Isa 13:6
30:3 [x]Eze 7:7; Joel 2:1,11; Ob 1:15 [y]ver 18; Eze 7:12,19

[r]7 Syriac (see also Septuagint and Vulgate); Hebrew *and you caused their backs to stand*
[s]*10* That is, the upper Nile region
[t]*14* Hebrew *to Pathros* [u]*21* *Horn* here symbolizes strength. [v]*4* That is, the upper Nile region; also in verses 5 and 9

and her foundations torn
down.[a]

5Cush and Put,[b] Lydia and all Arabia, Libya[w] and the people[c] of the
covenant land will fall by the sword
along with Egypt.

6" 'This is what the LORD says:

" 'The allies of Egypt will fall
and her proud strength will
fail.
From Migdol to Aswan[d]
they will fall by the sword
within her,
declares the Sovereign
LORD.
7" 'They will be desolate
among desolate lands,
and their cities will lie
among ruined cities.[e]
8Then they will know that I am
the LORD,
when I set fire to Egypt
and all her helpers are
crushed.

9" 'On that day messengers will
go out from me in ships to frighten
Cush[f] out of her complacency.
Anguish[g] will take hold of them on
the day of Egypt's doom, for it is
sure to come.[h]

10" 'This is what the Sovereign
LORD says:

" 'I will put an end to the
hordes of Egypt
by the hand of
Nebuchadnezzar king of
Babylon.[i]
11He and his army—the most
ruthless of nations[j]—
will be brought in to destroy
the land.
They will draw their swords
against Egypt
and fill the land with the
slain.
12I will dry up[k] the streams of
the Nile[l]
and sell the land to evil men;
by the hand of foreigners
I will lay waste the land and
everything in it.

I the LORD have spoken.

13" 'This is what the Sovereign
LORD says:

" 'I will destroy the idols[m]
and put an end to the images
in Memphis.[x][n]
No longer will there be a prince
in Egypt,[o]
and I will spread fear
throughout the land.
14I will lay[p] waste Upper Egypt,[y]
set fire to Zoan[q]
and inflict punishment on
Thebes.[z][r]
15I will pour out my wrath on
Pelusium,[a]
the stronghold of Egypt,
and cut off the hordes of
Thebes.
16I will set fire to Egypt;
Pelusium will writhe in
agony.
Thebes will be taken by storm;
Memphis will be in constant
distress.
17The young men of
Heliopolis[b][s] and
Bubastis[c]
will fall by the sword,
and the cities themselves will
go into captivity.
18Dark will be the day at
Tahpanhes
when I break the yoke of
Egypt;[t]
there her proud strength will
come to an end.
She will be covered with
clouds,
and her villages will go into
captivity.[u]
19So I will inflict punishment on
Egypt,
and they will know that I am
the LORD.' "

20In the eleventh year, in the
first month on the seventh day, the
word of the LORD came to me:[v]
21"Son of man, I have broken the
arm[w] of Pharaoh king of Egypt. It
has not been bound up for heal-

30:4 [a]Eze 29:19
30:5 [b]Eze 27:10 [c]Jer 25:20
30:6 [d]Eze 29:10
30:7 [e]Eze 29:12
30:9 [f]Isa 18:1-2 [g]Isa 23:5 [h]Eze 32:9-10
30:10 [i]Eze 29:19
30:11 [j]Eze 28:7
30:12 [k]Isa 19:6 [l]Eze 29:9
30:13 [m]Jer 43:12 [n]Isa 19:13 [o]Zec 10:11
30:14 [p]Eze 29:14 [q]Ps 78:12,43 [r]Jer 46:25
30:17 [s]Ge 41:45
30:18 [t]Lev 26:13 [u]ver 3
30:20 [v]Eze 26:1; 29:17; 31:1
30:21 [w]Jer 48:25

[w]5 Hebrew *Cub* [x]13 Hebrew *Noph;* also in verse 16 [y]14 Hebrew *waste Pathros* [z]14 Hebrew *No;* also in verses 15 and 16 [a]15 Hebrew *Sin;* also in verse 16 [b]17 Hebrew *Awen* (or *On*) [c]17 Hebrew *Pi Beseth*

ing[a] or put in a splint so as to become strong enough to hold a
sword. **22**Therefore this is what the
Sovereign LORD says: I am against
Pharaoh king of Egypt.[b] I will
break both his arms, the good arm
as well as the broken one, and
make the sword fall from his
hand.[c] **23**I will disperse the Egyptians among the nations and scatter them through the countries.[d]
24I will strengthen[e] the arms of
the king of Babylon and put my
sword[f] in his hand, but I will break
the arms of Pharaoh, and he will
groan before him like a mortally
wounded man. **25**I will strengthen
the arms of the king of Babylon,
but the arms of Pharaoh will fall
limp. Then they will know that I am
the LORD, when I put my sword into
the hand of the king of Babylon and
he brandishes it against Egypt. **26**I
will disperse the Egyptians among
the nations and scatter them
through the countries. Then they
will know that I am the LORD.[g]"

A Cedar in Lebanon

31 In the eleventh year,[h] in
the third month on the first
day, the word of the LORD came to
me:[i] **2**"Son of man, say to Pharaoh
king of Egypt and to his hordes:

" 'Who can be compared with
you in majesty?
3Consider Assyria, once a cedar
in Lebanon,
with beautiful branches
overshadowing the
forest;
it towered on high,
its top above the thick
foliage.[j]
4The waters nourished it,
deep springs made it grow
tall;
their streams flowed
all around its base
and sent their channels
to all the trees of the field.
5So it towered higher
than all the trees of the field;
its boughs increased
and its branches grew long,
spreading because of
abundant waters.[k]
6All the birds of the air
nested in its boughs,
all the beasts of the field
gave birth under its branches;
all the great nations
lived in its shade.[l]
7It was majestic in beauty,
with its spreading boughs,
for its roots went down
to abundant waters.
8The cedars[m] in the garden of
God
could not rival it,
nor could the pine trees
equal its boughs,
nor could the plane trees
compare with its branches—
no tree in the garden of God
could match its beauty.[n]
9I made it beautiful
with abundant branches,
the envy of all the trees of
Eden[o]
in the garden of God.[p]

10" 'Therefore this is what the
Sovereign LORD says: Because it
towered on high, lifting its top
above the thick foliage, and because it was proud[q] of its height,
11I handed it over to the ruler of the
nations, for him to deal with according to its wickedness. I cast it
aside,[r] **12**and the most ruthless of
foreign nations[s] cut it down and
left it. Its boughs fell on the mountains and in all the valleys;[t] its
branches lay broken in all the ravines of the land. All the nations of
the earth came out from under its
shade and left it.[u] **13**All the birds
of the air settled on the fallen tree,
and all the beasts of the field were
among its branches.[v] **14**Therefore
no other trees by the waters are
ever to tower proudly on high, lifting their tops above the thick foliage. No other trees so well-watered are ever to reach such a
height; they are all destined for
death,[w] for the earth below, among
mortal men, with those who go
down to the pit.[x]

15" 'This is what the Sovereign
LORD says: On the day it was

30:21 [a]Jer 30:13; 46:11
30:22 [b]Jer 46:25 [c]Ps 37:17
30:23 [d]Eze 29:12
30:24 [e]Zec 10:6,12 [f]Eze 21:14; Zep 2:12
30:26 [g]Eze 29:12
31:1 [h]Jer 52:5 [i]Eze 30:20
31:3 [j]Isa 10:34
31:5 [k]Eze 17:5
31:6 [l]Eze 17:23; Mt 13:32
31:8 [m]Ps 80:10 [n]Ge 2:8-9
31:9 [o]Ge 2:8 [p]Ge 13:10; Eze 28:13
31:10 [q]Isa 14:13-14; Eze 28:17
31:11 [r]Da 5:20
31:12 [s]Eze 28:7 [t]Eze 32:5; 35:8 [u]Eze 32:11-12; Da 4:14
31:13 [v]Isa 18:6; Eze 29:5; 32:4
31:14 [w]Ps 82:7 [x]Ps 63:9; Eze 26:20; 32:24

brought down to the grave[d] I covered the deep springs with mourning for it; I held back its streams,
and its abundant waters were restrained. Because of it I clothed
Lebanon with gloom, and all the
trees of the field withered away. 16I
made the nations tremble[a] at the
sound of its fall when I brought it
down to the grave with those who
go down to the pit. Then all the
trees[b] of Eden, the choicest and
best of Lebanon, all the trees that
were well-watered, were consoled[c] in the earth below.[d]
17Those who lived in its shade, its
allies among the nations, had also
gone down to the grave with it,
joining those killed by the sword.[e]
18" 'Which of the trees of Eden
can be compared with you in splendor and majesty? Yet you, too, will
be brought down with the trees of
Eden to the earth below; you will
lie among the uncircumcised,[f]
with those killed by the sword.

" 'This is Pharaoh and all his hordes, declares the Sovereign LORD.' "

A Lament for Pharaoh

32 In the twelfth year, in the
twelfth month on the first
day, the word of the LORD came to
me:[g] 2"Son of man, take up a lament[h] concerning Pharaoh king of
Egypt and say to him:

" 'You are like a lion[i] among
the nations;
you are like a monster in the
seas
thrashing about in your
streams,
churning the water with your
feet
and muddying the streams.[j]

3" 'This is what the Sovereign LORD says:

" 'With a great throng of people
I will cast my net over you,
and they will haul you up in
my net.[k]
4I will throw you on the land
and hurl you on the open
field.
I will let all the birds of the air
settle on you
and all the beasts of the
earth gorge themselves
on you.[l]
5I will spread your flesh on the
mountains
and fill the valleys[m] with
your remains.
6I will drench the land with your
flowing blood[n]
all the way to the mountains,
and the ravines will be filled
with your flesh.
7When I snuff you out, I will
cover the heavens
and darken their stars;
I will cover the sun with a
cloud,
and the moon will not give
its light.[o]
8All the shining lights in the
heavens
I will darken over you;
I will bring darkness over
your land,
declares the Sovereign
LORD.
9I will trouble the hearts of
many peoples
when I bring about your
destruction among the
nations,
among[e] lands you have not
known.
10I will cause many peoples to be
appalled at you,
and their kings will shudder
with horror because of
you
when I brandish my sword
before them.
On the day[p] of your downfall
each of them will tremble
every moment for his life.[q]

11" 'For this is what the Sovereign LORD says:

" 'The sword of the king of
Babylon[r]
will come against you.
12I will cause your hordes to fall
by the swords of mighty
men—

31:16 [a]Eze 26:15 [b]Isa 14:8 [c]Eze 14:22; 32:31 [d]Isa 14:15; Eze 32:18
31:17 [e]Ps 9:17
31:18 [f]Jer 9:26; Eze 32:19,21
32:1 [g]Eze 31:1; 33:21
32:2 [h]Eze 19:1; 27:2 [i]Eze 19:3,6; Na 2:11-13 [j]Eze 29:3; 34:18
32:3 [k]Eze 12:13
32:4 [l]Isa 18:6; Eze 31:12-13
32:5 [m]Eze 31:12
32:6 [n]Isa 34:3
32:7 [o]Isa 13:10; 34:4; Eze 30:3; Joel 2:2,31; 3:15; Mt 24:29; Rev 8:12
32:10 [p]Jer 46:10 [q]Eze 26:16; 27:35
32:11 [r]Jer 46:26

[d]*15* Hebrew *Sheol;* also in verses 16 and 17
[e]*9* Hebrew; Septuagint *bring you into captivity among the nations, / to*

the most ruthless of all
nations.[a]
They will shatter the pride of
Egypt,
and all her hordes will be
overthrown.[b]
13I will destroy all her cattle
from beside abundant waters
no longer to be stirred by the
foot of man
or muddied by the hoofs of
cattle.[c]
14Then I will let her waters settle
and make her streams flow
like oil,
declares the Sovereign
LORD.
15When I make Egypt desolate
and strip the land of
everything in it,
when I strike down all who live
there,
then they will know that I
am the LORD.[d]

16"This is the lament[e] they will
chant for her. The daughters of the
nations will chant it; for Egypt and
all her hordes they will chant it, declares the Sovereign LORD."

17In the twelfth year, on the fifteenth day of the month, the word
of the LORD came to me:[f] 18"Son of
man, wail for the hordes of Egypt
and consign[g] to the earth below
both her and the daughters of
mighty nations, with those who go
down to the pit.[h] 19Say to them,
'Are you more favored than others?
Go down and be laid among the uncircumcised.'[i] 20They will fall
among those killed by the sword.
The sword is drawn; let her be
dragged[j] off with all her hordes.
21From within the grave[f][k] the
mighty leaders will say of Egypt
and her allies, 'They have come
down and they lie with the uncircumcised, with those killed by the
sword.'
22"Assyria is there with her
whole army; she is surrounded by
the graves of all her slain, all who
have fallen by the sword. 23Their
graves are in the depths of the pit[l]
and her army lies around her grave.
All who had spread terror in the

32:12 [a]Eze 28:7 [b]Eze 31:11-12
32:13 [c]Eze 29:8,11
32:15 [d]Ex 7:5; 14:4, 18; Ps 107:33-34; Eze 6:7
32:16 [e]2Sa 1:17; 2Ch 35:25; Eze 26:17
32:17 [f]ver 1
32:18 [g]Jer 1:10 [h]Eze 31:14, 16; Mic 1:8
32:19 [i]ver 29-30; Eze 28:10; 31:18
32:20 [j]Ps 28:3
32:21 [k]Isa 14:9
32:23 [l]Isa 14:15
32:24 [m]Ge 10:22 [n]Jer 49:37 [o]Job 28:13 [p]Eze 26:20
32:26 [q]Ge 10:2; Eze 27:13
32:29 [r]Isa 34:5-15; Jer 49:7; Eze 35:15; Ob 1:1 [s]Eze 25:12-14
32:30 [t]Jer 25:26; Eze 38:6; 39:2 [u]Jer 25:22; Eze 28:21
32:31 [v]Eze 14:22; 31:16

land of the living are slain, fallen by
the sword.
24"Elam[m] is there, with all her
hordes around her grave. All of
them are slain, fallen by the
sword.[n] All who had spread terror
in the land of the living[o] went
down uncircumcised to the earth
below. They bear their shame with
those who go down to the pit.[p] 25A
bed is made for her among the
slain, with all her hordes around
her grave. All of them are uncircumcised, killed by the sword. Because their terror had spread in the
land of the living, they bear their
shame with those who go down to
the pit; they are laid among the
slain.
26"Meshech and Tubal[q] are
there, with all their hordes around
their graves. All of them are uncircumcised, killed by the sword because they spread their terror in
the land of the living. 27Do they not
lie with the other uncircumcised
warriors who have fallen, who went
down to the grave with their weapons of war, whose swords were
placed under their heads? The
punishment for their sins rested on
their bones, though the terror of
these warriors had stalked through
the land of the living.
28"You too, O Pharaoh, will be
broken and will lie among the uncircumcised, with those killed by
the sword.
29"Edom[r] is there, her kings
and all her princes; despite their
power, they are laid with those
killed by the sword. They lie with
the uncircumcised, with those who
go down to the pit.[s]
30"All the princes of the north[t]
and all the Sidonians[u] are there;
they went down with the slain in
disgrace despite the terror caused
by their power. They lie uncircumcised with those killed by the
sword and bear their shame with
those who go down to the pit.
31"Pharaoh—he and all his
army—will see them and he will be
consoled[v] for all his hordes that

[f]21 Hebrew *Sheol*; also in verse 27

were killed by the sword, declares
the Sovereign LORD. **32**Although I
had him spread terror in the land of
the living, Pharaoh and all his
hordes will be laid among the uncircumcised, with those killed by
the sword, declares the Sovereign
LORD."

Ezekiel a Watchman

33 The word of the LORD came
to me: **2**"Son of man, speak
to your countrymen and say to
them: 'When I bring the sword[a]
against a land, and the people of
the land choose one of their men
and make him their watchman,[b]
3and he sees the sword coming
against the land and blows the
trumpet[c] to warn the people,
4then if anyone hears the trumpet
but does not take warning[d] and
the sword comes and takes his life,
his blood will be on his own head.[e]
5Since he heard the sound of the
trumpet but did not take warning,
his blood will be on his own head.
If he had taken warning, he would
have saved himself. **6**But if the
watchman sees the sword coming
and does not blow the trumpet to
warn the people and the sword
comes and takes the life of one of
them, that man will be taken away
because of his sin, but I will hold
the watchman accountable for his
blood.'[f]

7"Son of man, I have made you a
watchman for the house of Israel;
so hear the word I speak and give
them warning from me.[g] **8**When I
say to the wicked, 'O wicked man,
you will surely die,[h]' and you do
not speak out to dissuade him from
his ways, that wicked man will die
for[g] his sin, and I will hold you accountable for his blood.[i] **9**But if
you do warn the wicked man to
turn from his ways and he does not
do so, he will die for his sin, but you
will have saved yourself.[j]

10"Son of man, say to the house
of Israel, 'This is what you are saying: "Our offenses and sins weigh
us down, and we are wasting
away[k] because of[h] them. How
then can we live?[l]" ' **11**Say to
them, 'As surely as I live, declares
the Sovereign LORD, I take no pleasure in the death of the wicked, but
rather that they turn from their
ways and live.[m] Turn! Turn from
your evil ways! Why will you die, O
house of Israel?'[n]

12"Therefore, son of man, say to
your countrymen, 'The righteousness of the righteous man will not
save him when he disobeys, and
the wickedness of the wicked man
will not cause him to fall when he
turns from it. The righteous man, if
he sins, will not be allowed to live
because of his former righteousness.'[o] **13**If I tell the righteous man
that he will surely live, but then he
trusts in his righteousness and
does evil, none of the righteous
things he has done will be remembered; he will die for the evil he has
done.[p] **14**And if I say to the wicked
man, 'You will surely die,' but he
then turns away from his sin and
does what is just[q] and right— **15**if
he gives back what he took in
pledge for a loan, returns what he
has stolen,[r] follows the decrees
that give life, and does no evil, he
will surely live; he will not die.[s]
16None of the sins he has committed will be remembered against
him. He has done what is just and
right; he will surely live.[t]

17"Yet your countrymen say,
'The way of the Lord is not just.'
But it is their way that is not just.
18If a righteous man turns from his
righteousness and does evil, he will
die for it.[u] **19**And if a wicked man
turns away from his wickedness
and does what is just and right, he
will live by doing so. **20**Yet, O house
of Israel, you say, 'The way of the
Lord is not just.' But I will judge
each of you according to his own
ways."

Jerusalem's Fall Explained

21In the twelfth year of our exile,
in the tenth month on the fifth day,
a man who had escaped[v] from Jerusalem came to me and said, "The
city has fallen![w]" **22**Now the eve-

33:2 [a]Jer 12:12 [b]Eze 3:11
33:3 [c]Hos 8:1
33:4 [d]2Ch 25:16 [e]Jer 6:17; Eze 18:13; Zec 1:4; Ac 18:6
33:6 [f]Eze 3:18
33:7 [g]Jer 26:2; Eze 3:17
33:8 [h]ver 14 [i]Eze 18:4
33:9 [j]Eze 3:17-19
33:10 [k]Eze 24:23 [l]Lev 26:39; Eze 4:17
33:11 [m]Eze 18:32; 2Pe 3:9 [n]Eze 18:23
33:12 [o]2Ch 7:14; Eze 3:20
33:13 [p]Eze 18:24; Heb 10:38; 2Pe 2:20-21
33:14 [q]Eze 18:27
33:15 [r]Ex 22:1-4; Lev 6:2-5 [s]Eze 20:11; Lk 19:8
33:16 [t]Isa 43:25; Eze 18:22
33:18 [u]Eze 3:20; Eze 18:26
33:21 [v]Eze 24:26 [w]2Ki 25:4,10; Jer 39:1-2; Eze 32:1

[g]8 Or *in;* also in verse 9 [h]10 Or *away in*

ning before the man arrived, the
hand of the LORD was upon me,[a]
and he opened my mouth[b] before
the man came to me in the morning. So my mouth was opened and
I was no longer silent.[c]
23 Then the word of the LORD
came to me: 24 "Son of man, the
people living in those ruins[d] in the
land of Israel are saying, 'Abraham
was only one man, yet he possessed the land. But we are many;
surely the land has been given to us
as our possession.'[e] 25 Therefore
say to them, 'This is what the Sovereign LORD says: Since you eat
meat with the blood[f] still in it and
look to your idols and shed blood,
should you then possess the
land?[g] 26 You rely on your sword,
you do detestable things, and
each of you defiles his neighbor's
wife.[h] Should you then possess
the land?'
27 "Say this to them: 'This is what
the Sovereign LORD says: As surely
as I live, those who are left in the
ruins will fall by the sword, those
out in the country I will give to the
wild animals to be devoured, and
those in strongholds and caves will
die of a plague.[i] 28 I will make the
land a desolate waste, and her
proud strength will come to an end,
and the mountains of Israel will become desolate so that no one will
cross them. 29 Then they will know
that I am the LORD, when I have
made the land a desolate waste because of all the detestable things
they have done.'
30 "As for you, son of man, your
countrymen are talking together
about you by the walls and at the
doors of the houses, saying to each
other, 'Come and hear the message
that has come from the LORD.' 31 My
people come to you, as they usually
do, and sit before[j] you to listen to
your words, but they do not put
them into practice. With their
mouths they express devotion, but
their hearts are greedy for unjust
gain.[k] 32 Indeed, to them you are
nothing more than one who sings
love songs with a beautiful voice
and plays an instrument well, for
they hear your words but do not put
them into practice.[l]
33 "When all this comes true—
and it surely will—then they will
know that a prophet has been
among them.[m]"

Shepherds and Sheep

34 The word of the LORD came
to me: 2 "Son of man, prophesy against the shepherds of Israel;
prophesy and say to them: 'This is
what the Sovereign LORD says: Woe
to the shepherds of Israel who only
take care of themselves! Should
not shepherds take care of the
flock?[n] 3 You eat the curds, clothe
yourselves with the wool and
slaughter the choice animals, but
you do not take care of the flock.[o]
4 You have not strengthened the
weak or healed the sick or bound
up the injured. You have not
brought back the strays or searched
for the lost. You have ruled them
harshly and brutally.[p] 5 So they
were scattered because there was
no shepherd,[q] and when they were
scattered they became food for all
the wild animals.[r] 6 My sheep wandered over all the mountains and
on every high hill. They were scattered over the whole earth, and no
one searched or looked for them.[s]
7 " 'Therefore, you shepherds,
hear the word of the LORD: 8 As surely as I live, declares the Sovereign
LORD, because my flock lacks a
shepherd and so has been plundered and has become food for all
the wild animals, and because my
shepherds did not search for my
flock but cared for themselves rather than for my flock, 9 therefore, O
shepherds, hear the word of the
LORD: 10 This is what the Sovereign
LORD says: I am against[t] the shepherds and will hold them accountable for my flock. I will remove
them from tending the flock so that
the shepherds can no longer feed
themselves. I will rescue[u] my flock
from their mouths, and it will no
longer be food for them.[v]
11 " 'For this is what the Sovereign LORD says: I myself will search
for my sheep and look after them.

33:22 [a] Eze 1:3 [b] Lk 1:64 [c] Eze 3:26-27; 24:27
33:24 [d] Eze 36:4 [e] Isa 51:2; Jer 40:7; Eze 11:15; Ac 7:5
33:25 [f] Ge 9:4; Dt 12:16 [g] Jer 7:9-10; Eze 22:6,27
33:26 [h] Eze 22:11
33:27 [i] 1Sa 13:6; Isa 2:19; Jer 42:22; Eze 39:4
33:31 [j] Eze 8:1 [k] Ps 78:36-37; Isa 29:13; Eze 22:27; Mt 13:22; 1Jn 3:18
33:32 [l] Mk 6:20
33:33 [m] 1Sa 3:20; Jer 28:9; Eze 2:5
34:2 [n] Ps 78:70-72; Isa 40:11; Jer 3:15; 23:1; Mic 3:11; Jn 10:11; 21:15-17
34:3 [o] Isa 56:11; Eze 22:27; Zec 11:16
34:4 [p] Zec 11:15-17
34:5 [q] Nu 27:17 [r] ver 28; Isa 56:9
34:6 [s] Ps 142:4; 1Pe 2:25
34:10 [t] Jer 21:13 [u] Ps 72:14 [v] 1Sa 2:29-30; Zec 10:3

12As a shepherd[a] looks after his scattered flock when he is with them, so will I look after my sheep. I will rescue them from all the places where they were scattered on a day of clouds and darkness.[b] **13**I will bring them out from the nations and gather them from the countries, and I will bring them into their own land. I will pasture them on the mountains of Israel, in the ravines and in all the settlements in the land.[c] **14**I will tend them in a good pasture, and the mountain heights of Israel[d] will be their grazing land. There they will lie down in good grazing land, and there they will feed in a rich pasture[e] on the mountains of Israel.[f] **15**I myself will tend my sheep and have them lie down, declares the Sovereign LORD.[g] **16**I will search for the lost and bring back the strays. I will bind up the injured and strengthen the weak,[h] but the sleek and the strong I will destroy. I will shepherd the flock with justice.[i]

17" 'As for you, my flock, this is what the Sovereign LORD says: I will judge between one sheep and another, and between rams and goats.[j] **18**Is it not enough for you to feed on the good pasture? Must you also trample the rest of your pasture with your feet? Is it not enough for you to drink clear water? Must you also muddy the rest with your feet? **19**Must my flock feed on what you have trampled and drink what you have muddied with your feet?

20" 'Therefore this is what the Sovereign LORD says to them: See, I myself will judge between the fat sheep and the lean sheep. **21**Because you shove with flank and shoulder, butting all the weak sheep with your horns[k] until you have driven them away, **22**I will save my flock, and they will no longer be plundered. I will judge between one sheep and another.[l] **23**I will place over them one shepherd, my servant David, and he will tend[m] them; he will tend them and be their shepherd. **24**I the LORD will be their God,[n] and my servant David will be prince among them. I the LORD have spoken.[o]

25" 'I will make a covenant of peace with them and rid the land of wild beasts[p] so that they may live in the desert and sleep in the forests in safety.[q] **26**I will bless[r] them and the places surrounding my hill.[i] I will send down showers in season;[s] there will be showers of blessing.[t] **27**The trees of the field will yield their fruit and the ground will yield its crops; the people will be secure in their land. They will know that I am the LORD, when I break the bars of their yoke[u] and rescue them from the hands of those who enslaved them.[v] **28**They will no longer be plundered by the nations, nor will wild animals devour them. They will live in safety, and no one will make them afraid.[w] **29**I will provide for them a land renowned[x] for its crops, and they will no longer be victims of famine[y] in the land or bear the scorn[z] of the nations.[a] **30**Then they will know that I, the LORD their God, am with them and that they, the house of Israel, are my people, declares the Sovereign LORD.[b] **31**You my sheep, the sheep of my pasture,[c] are people, and I am your God, declares the Sovereign LORD.' "

A Prophecy Against Edom

35 The word of the LORD came to me: **2**"Son of man, set your face against Mount Seir; prophesy against it **3**and say: 'This is what the Sovereign LORD says: I am against you, Mount Seir, and I will stretch out my hand[d] against you and make you a desolate waste.[e] **4**I will turn your towns into ruins and you will be desolate. Then you will know that I am the LORD.[f]

5" 'Because you harbored an ancient hostility and delivered the Israelites over to the sword at the time of their calamity, the time

34:12 [a] Isa 40:11; Jer 31:10; Lk 19:10 [b] Eze 30:3
34:13 [c] Jer 23:3
34:14 [d] Eze 20:40 [e] Ps 23:2 [f] Eze 36:29-30
34:15 [g] Ps 23:1-2
34:16 [h] Mic 4:6 [i] Isa 10:16; Lk 5:32
34:17 [j] Mt 25:32-33
34:21 [k] Dt 33:17
34:22 [l] Ps 72:12-14; Jer 23:2-3
34:23 [m] Isa 40:11
34:24 [n] Eze 36:28 [o] Jer 30:9
34:25 [p] Lev 26:6 [q] Isa 11:6-9; Hos 2:18
34:26 [r] Ge 12:2 [s] Ps 68:9 [t] Dt 11:13-15; Isa 44:3
34:27 [u] Lev 26:13 [v] Jer 30:8
34:28 [w] Jer 30:10; Eze 39:26
34:29 [x] Isa 4:2 [y] Eze 36:29 [z] Eze 36:6 [a] Eze 36:15
34:30 [b] Eze 14:11; 37:27
34:31 [c] Ps 100:3; Jer 23:1
35:3 [d] Jer 6:12 [e] Eze 25:12-14
35:4 [f] ver 9

[i]26 Or *I will make them and the places surrounding my hill a blessing*

their punishment reached its climax,[a] **6**therefore as surely as I live, declares the Sovereign LORD, I will give you over to bloodshed and it will pursue you.[b] Since you did not hate bloodshed, bloodshed will pursue you. **7**I will make Mount Seir a desolate waste and cut off from it all who come and go. **8**I will fill your mountains with the slain; those killed by the sword will fall on your hills and in your valleys and in all your ravines.[c] **9**I will make you desolate forever; your towns will not be inhabited. Then you will know that I am the LORD.[d]

10" 'Because you have said, "These two nations and countries will be ours and we will take possession[e] of them," even though I the LORD was there, **11**therefore as surely as I live, declares the Sovereign LORD, I will treat you in accordance with the anger[f] and jealousy you showed in your hatred of them and I will make myself known among them when I judge you.[g] **12**Then you will know that I the LORD have heard all the contemptible things you have said against the mountains of Israel. You said, "They have been laid waste and have been given over to us to devour."[h] **13**You boasted against me and spoke against me without restraint, and I heard it.[i] **14**This is what the Sovereign LORD says: While the whole earth rejoices, I will make you desolate.[j] **15**Because you rejoiced[k] when the inheritance of the house of Israel became desolate, that is how I will treat you. You will be desolate, O Mount Seir,[l] you and all of Edom.[m] Then they will know that I am the LORD.' "

A Prophecy to the Mountains of Israel

36 "Son of man, prophesy to the mountains of Israel and say, 'O mountains of Israel, hear the word of the LORD. **2**This is what the Sovereign LORD says: The enemy said of you, "Aha![n] The ancient heights[o] have become our possession.[p]" ' **3**Therefore prophesy and say, 'This is what the Sovereign LORD says: Because they ravaged and hounded you from every side so that you became the possession of the rest of the nations and the object of people's malicious talk and slander,[q] **4**therefore, O mountains of Israel, hear the word of the Sovereign LORD: This is what the Sovereign LORD says to the mountains and hills, to the ravines and valleys,[r] to the desolate ruins and the deserted towns that have been plundered and ridiculed by the rest of the nations around you[s]— **5**this is what the Sovereign LORD says: In my burning zeal I have spoken against the rest of the nations, and against all Edom, for with glee and with malice in their hearts they made my land their own possession so that they might plunder its pastureland.'[t] **6**Therefore prophesy concerning the land of Israel and say to the mountains and hills, to the ravines and valleys: 'This is what the Sovereign LORD says: I speak in my jealous wrath because you have suffered the scorn of the nations.[u] **7**Therefore this is what the Sovereign LORD says: I swear with uplifted hand that the nations around you will also suffer scorn.

8" 'But you, O mountains of Israel, will produce branches and fruit[v] for my people Israel, for they will soon come home. **9**I am concerned for you and will look on you with favor; you will be plowed and sown, **10**and I will multiply the number of people upon you, even the whole house of Israel. The towns will be inhabited and the ruins rebuilt.[w] **11**I will increase the number of men and animals upon you, and they will be fruitful and become numerous. I will settle people on you as in the past[x] and will make you prosper more than before.[y] Then you will know that I am the LORD. **12**I will cause people, my people Israel, to walk upon you. They will possess you, and you will be their inheritance;[z] you will never again deprive them of their children.

35:5 [a] Ps 137:7; Eze 21:29
35:6 [b] Isa 63:2-6
35:8 [c] Eze 31:12
35:9 [d] Jer 49:13
35:10 [e] Ps 83:12; Eze 36:2,5
35:11 [f] Eze 25:14 [g] Ps 9:16; Mt 7:2
35:12 [h] Jer 50:7
35:13 [i] Da 11:36
35:14 [j] Jer 51:48
35:15 [k] Ob 1:12 [l] ver 3 [m] Isa 34:5-6, 11; Jer 50:11-13; La 4:21
36:2 [n] Eze 25:3 [o] Dt 32:13 [p] Eze 35:10
36:3 [q] Ps 44:13-14
36:4 [r] Eze 6:3 [s] Dt 11:11; Ps 79:4; Eze 34:28
36:5 [t] Jer 50:11; Eze 25:12-14; 35:10,15
36:6 [u] Ps 123:3-4; Eze 34:29
36:8 [v] Isa 27:6
36:10 [w] ver 33; Isa 49:17-23
36:11 [x] Mic 7:14 [y] Jer 31:28; Eze 16:55
36:12 [z] Eze 47:14,22

[13]" 'This is what the Sovereign LORD says: Because people say to you, "You devour men[a] and deprive your nation of its children," [14]therefore you will no longer devour men or make your nation childless, declares the Sovereign LORD. [15]No longer will I make you hear the taunts of the nations, and no longer will you suffer the scorn of the peoples or cause your nation to fall, declares the Sovereign LORD.[b]' "

[16]Again the word of the LORD came to me: [17]"Son of man, when the people of Israel were living in their own land, they defiled it by their conduct and their actions. Their conduct was like a woman's monthly uncleanness in my sight.[c] [18]So I poured out[d] my wrath on them because they had shed blood in the land and because they had defiled it with their idols. [19]I dispersed them among the nations, and they were scattered[e] through the countries; I judged them according to their conduct and their actions.[f] [20]And wherever they went among the nations they profaned[g] my holy name, for it was said of them, 'These are the LORD's people, and yet they had to leave his land.'[h] [21]I had concern for my holy name, which the house of Israel profaned among the nations where they had gone.[i]

[22]"Therefore say to the house of Israel, 'This is what the Sovereign LORD says: It is not for your sake, O house of Israel, that I am going to do these things, but for the sake of my holy name, which you have profaned[j] among the nations where you have gone.[k] [23]I will show the holiness of my great name, which has been profaned among the nations, the name you have profaned among them. Then the nations will know that I am the LORD, declares the Sovereign LORD, when I show myself holy[l] through you before their eyes.[m]

[24]" 'For I will take you out of the nations; I will gather you from all the countries and bring you back into your own land.[n] [25]I will sprinkle[o] clean water on you, and you will be clean; I will cleanse[p] you from all your impurities and from all your idols.[q] [26]I will give you a new heart[r] and put a new spirit in you; I will remove from you your heart of stone and give you a heart of flesh.[s] [27]And I will put my Spirit[t] in you and move you to follow my decrees and be careful to keep my laws. [28]You will live in the land I gave your forefathers; you will be my people,[u] and I will be your God.[v] [29]I will save you from all your uncleanness. I will call for the grain and make it plentiful and will not bring famine[w] upon you. [30]I will increase the fruit of the trees and the crops of the field, so that you will no longer suffer disgrace among the nations because of famine.[x] [31]Then you will remember your evil ways and wicked deeds, and you will loathe yourselves for your sins and detestable practices.[y] [32]I want you to know that I am not doing this for your sake, declares the Sovereign LORD. Be ashamed and disgraced for your conduct, O house of Israel![z]

[33]" 'This is what the Sovereign LORD says: On the day I cleanse you from all your sins, I will resettle your towns, and the ruins will be rebuilt. [34]The desolate land will be cultivated instead of lying desolate in the sight of all who pass through it. [35]They will say, "This land that was laid waste has become like the garden of Eden;[a] the cities that were lying in ruins, desolate and destroyed, are now fortified and inhabited.[b]" [36]Then the nations around you that remain will know that I the LORD have rebuilt what was destroyed and have replanted what was desolate. I the LORD have spoken, and I will do it.'[c]

[37]"This is what the Sovereign LORD says: Once again I will yield to the plea of the house of Israel and do this for them: I will make their people as numerous as sheep, [38]as numerous as the flocks for offerings[d] at Jerusalem during her appointed feasts. So will the ruined cities be filled with flocks of peo-

36:13 [a] Nu 13:32
36:15 [b] Ps 89:50-51; Eze 34:29
36:17 [c] Jer 2:7
36:18 [d] 2Ch 34:21
36:19 [e] Dt 28:64 [f] Eze 39:24
36:20 [g] Ro 2:24 [h] Isa 52:5; Jer 33:24; Eze 12:16
36:21 [i] Ps 74:18; Isa 48:9
36:22 [j] Ro 2:24* [k] Ps 106:8
36:23 [l] Eze 20:41 [m] Ps 126:2; Isa 5:16
36:24 [n] Eze 34:13; 37:21
36:25 [o] Heb 9:13; 10:22 [p] Ps 51:2,7 [q] Zec 13:2
36:26 [r] Jer 24:7 [s] Ps 51:10; Eze 11:19
36:27 [t] Eze 37:14
36:28 [u] Jer 30:22 [v] Eze 14:11; 37:14,27
36:29 [w] Eze 34:29
36:30 [x] Lev 26:4-5; Eze 34:27; Hos 2:21-22
36:31 [y] Eze 6:9; 20:43
36:32 [z] Dt 9:5
36:35 [a] Joel 2:3 [b] Isa 51:3
36:36 [c] Eze 17:22; 22:14; 37:14; 39:27-28
36:38 [d] 1Ki 8:63; 2Ch 35:7-9

ple. Then they will know that I am the LORD."

The Valley of Dry Bones

37 The hand of the LORD was upon me,[a] and he brought me out by the Spirit[b] of the LORD and set me in the middle of a valley;[c] it was full of bones.[d] **2**He led me back and forth among them, and I saw a great many bones on the floor of the valley, bones that were very dry. **3**He asked me, "Son of man, can these bones live?"

I said, "O Sovereign LORD, you alone know.[e]"

4Then he said to me, "Prophesy to these bones and say to them, 'Dry bones, hear the word of the LORD![f] **5**This is what the Sovereign LORD says to these bones: I will make breath[i] enter you, and you will come to life.[g] **6**I will attach tendons to you and make flesh come upon you and cover you with skin; I will put breath in you, and you will come to life. Then you will know that I am the LORD.[h]' "

7So I prophesied as I was commanded. And as I was prophesying, there was a noise, a rattling sound, and the bones came together, bone to bone. **8**I looked, and tendons and flesh appeared on them and skin covered them, but there was no breath in them.

9Then he said to me, "Prophesy to the breath;[i] prophesy, son of man, and say to it, 'This is what the Sovereign LORD says: Come from the four winds, O breath, and breathe into these slain, that they may live.' " **10**So I prophesied as he commanded me, and breath entered them; they came to life and stood up on their feet—a vast army.[j]

11Then he said to me: "Son of man, these bones are the whole house of Israel. They say, 'Our bones are dried up and our hope is gone; we are cut off.'[k] **12**Therefore prophesy and say to them: 'This is what the Sovereign LORD says: O my people, I am going to open your graves and bring you up from them; I will bring you back to the land of Israel.[l] **13**Then you, my people, will know that I am the LORD, when I open your graves and bring you up from them. **14**I will put my Spirit[m] in you and you will live, and I will settle you in your own land. Then you will know that I the LORD have spoken, and I have done it, declares the LORD.[n]' "

One Nation Under One King

15The word of the LORD came to me: **16**"Son of man, take a stick of wood and write on it, 'Belonging to Judah and the Israelites[o] associated with him.[p]' Then take another stick of wood, and write on it, 'Ephraim's stick, belonging to Joseph and all the house of Israel associated with him.' **17**Join them together into one stick so that they will become one in your hand.[q]

18"When your countrymen ask you, 'Won't you tell us what you mean by this?'[r] **19**say to them, 'This is what the Sovereign LORD says: I am going to take the stick of Joseph—which is in Ephraim's hand—and of the Israelite tribes associated with him, and join it to Judah's stick, making them a single stick of wood, and they will become one in my hand.'[s] **20**Hold before their eyes the sticks you have written on **21**and say to them, 'This is what the Sovereign LORD says: I will take the Israelites out of the nations where they have gone. I will gather them from all around and bring them back into their own land.[t] **22**I will make them one nation in the land, on the mountains of Israel. There will be one king over all of them and they will never again be two nations or be divided into two kingdoms.[u] **23**They will no longer defile[v] themselves with their idols and vile images or with any of their offenses, for I will save them from all their sinful backsliding,[k] and I will cleanse them. They

37:1 [a]Eze 1:3; 8:3 [b]Eze 11:24; Lk 4:1; Ac 8:39 [c]Jer 7:32 [d]Jer 8:2; Eze 40:1
37:3 [e]Dt 32:39; 1Sa 2:6; Isa 26:19
37:4 [f]Jer 22:29
37:5 [g]Ge 2:7; Ps 104:29-30
37:6 [h]Eze 38:23; Joel 2:27; 3:17
37:9 [i]Ps 104:30
37:10 [j]Rev 11:11
37:11 [k]La 3:54
37:12 [l]Dt 32:39; 1Sa 2:6; Isa 26:19; Hos 13:14; Am 9:14-15
37:14 [m]Joel 2:28-29 [n]Eze 36:27-28, 36
37:16 [o]1Ki 12:20; 2Ch 10:17-19 [p]Nu 17:2-3; 2Ch 15:9
37:17 [q]ver 24; Isa 11:13; Jer 50:4; Hos 1:11
37:18 [r]Eze 24:19
37:19 [s]Zec 10:6
37:21 [t]Isa 43:5-6; Eze 36:24; 39:27
37:22 [u]Isa 11:13; Jer 3:18; Hos 1:11
37:23 [v]Eze 36:25; 43:7

i5 The Hebrew for this word can also mean *wind* or *spirit* (see verses 6-14). k23 Many Hebrew manuscripts (see also Septuagint); most Hebrew manuscripts *all their dwelling places where they sinned* will be my people, and I will be their God.[a]

24 "'My servant David[b] will be king over them, and they will all have one shepherd.[c] They will follow my laws and be careful to keep my decrees.[d] 25 They will live in the land I gave to my servant Jacob, the land where your fathers lived.[e] They and their children and their children's children will live there forever,[f] and David my servant will be their prince forever.[g] 26 I will make a covenant of peace[h] with them; it will be an everlasting covenant. I will establish them and increase their numbers,[i] and I will put my sanctuary among them forever.[j] 27 My dwelling place[k] will be with them; I will be their God, and they will be my people.[l] 28 Then the nations will know that I the LORD make Israel holy,[m] when my sanctuary is among them forever.'"

A Prophecy Against Gog

38 The word of the LORD came to me: 2 "Son of man, set your face against Gog, of the land of Magog,[n] the chief prince of[l] Meshech and Tubal;[o] prophesy against him 3 and say: 'This is what the Sovereign LORD says: I am against you, O Gog, chief prince of[m] Meshech and Tubal.[p] 4 I will turn you around, put hooks[q] in your jaws and bring you out with your whole army—your horses, your horsemen fully armed, and a great horde with large and small shields, all of them brandishing their swords.[r] 5 Persia, Cush[n][s] and Put[t] will be with them, all with shields and helmets, 6 also Gomer[u] with all its troops, and Beth Togarmah[v] from the far north with all its troops—the many nations with you.

7 "'Get ready; be prepared,[w] you and all the hordes gathered about you, and take command of them. 8 After many days[x] you will be called to arms. In future years you will invade a land that has recovered from war, whose people were gathered from many nations[y] to the mountains of Israel, which had long been desolate. They had been brought out from the nations, and now all of them live in safety.[z] 9 You and all your troops and the many nations with you will go up, advancing like a storm;[a] you will be like a cloud[b] covering the land.

10 "'This is what the Sovereign LORD says: On that day thoughts will come into your mind and you will devise an evil scheme.[c] 11 You will say, "I will invade a land of unwalled villages; I will attack a peaceful and unsuspecting people—all of them living without walls and without gates and bars.[d] 12 I will plunder and loot and turn my hand against the resettled ruins and the people gathered from the nations, rich in livestock and goods, living at the center of the land." 13 Sheba[e] and Dedan and the merchants of Tarshish and all her villages[o] will say to you, "Have you come to plunder? Have you gathered your hordes to loot, to carry off silver and gold, to take away livestock and goods and to seize much plunder?"[f]'

14 "Therefore, son of man, prophesy and say to Gog: 'This is what the Sovereign LORD says: In that day, when my people Israel are living in safety,[g] will you not take notice of it? 15 You will come from your place in the far north, you and many nations with you, all of them riding on horses, a great horde, a mighty army.[h] 16 You will advance against my people Israel like a cloud[i] that covers the land. In days to come, O Gog, I will bring you against my land, so that the nations may know me when I show myself holy through you before their eyes.[j]

17 "'This is what the Sovereign LORD says: Are you not the one I spoke of in former days by my servants the prophets of Israel? At that time they prophesied for years that I would bring you against

37:23 [a] Eze 11:18; 36:28
37:24 [b] Hos 3:5 [c] Isa 40:11; Eze 34:23 [d] Ps 78:70-71
37:25 [e] Eze 28:25 [f] Am 9:15 [g] Isa 11:1
37:26 [h] Isa 55:3 [i] Jer 30:19 [j] Eze 16:62
37:27 [k] Lev 26:11; Jn 1:14 [l] 2Co 6:16*
37:28 [m] Ex 31:13; Eze 20:12
38:2 [n] Ge 10:2 [o] Rev 20:8
38:3 [p] Eze 39:1
38:4 [q] 2Ki 19:28 [r] Eze 29:4; Da 11:40
38:5 [s] Ge 10:6 [t] Eze 27:10
38:6 [u] Ge 10:2 [v] Eze 27:14
38:7 [w] Isa 8:9
38:8 [x] Isa 24:22 [y] Isa 11:11 [z] Jer 23:6
38:9 [a] Isa 28:2 [b] Jer 4:13; Joel 2:2
38:10 [c] Ps 36:4; Mic 2:1
38:11 [d] Jer 49:31; Zec 2:4
38:13 [e] Eze 27:22 [f] Isa 10:6; Jer 15:13
38:14 [g] ver 8; Zec 2:5
38:15 [h] Eze 39:2
38:16 [i] ver 9 [j] Isa 29:23; Eze 39:21

[l]2 Or *the prince of Rosh,* [m]3 Or *Gog, prince of Rosh,* [n]5 That is, the upper Nile region [o]13 Or *her strong lions*

them. **18**This is what will happen in that day: When Gog attacks the land of Israel, my hot anger will be aroused, declares the Sovereign LORD. **19**In my zeal and fiery wrath I declare that at that time there shall be a great earthquake in the land of Israel.[a] **20**The fish of the sea, the birds of the air, the beasts of the field, every creature that moves along the ground, and all the people on the face of the earth will tremble at my presence. The mountains will be overturned, the cliffs will crumble and every wall will fall to the ground.[b] **21**I will summon a sword[c] against Gog on all my mountains, declares the Sovereign LORD. Every man's sword will be against his brother.[d] **22**I will execute judgment[e] upon him with plague and bloodshed; I will pour down torrents of rain, hailstones[f] and burning sulfur on him and on his troops and on the many nations with him. **23**And so I will show my greatness and my holiness, and I will make myself known in the sight of many nations. Then they will know that I am the LORD.[g]'

39 "Son of man, prophesy against Gog and say: 'This is what the Sovereign LORD says: I am against you, O Gog, chief prince of[p] Meshech and Tubal.[h] **2**I will turn you around and drag you along. I will bring you from the far north and send you against the mountains of Israel. **3**Then I will strike your bow[i] from your left hand and make your arrows[j] drop from your right hand. **4**On the mountains of Israel you will fall, you and all your troops and the nations with you. I will give you as food to all kinds of carrion birds and to the wild animals.[k] **5**You will fall in the open field, for I have spoken, declares the Sovereign LORD. **6**I will send fire[l] on Magog and on those who live in safety in the coastlands,[m] and they will know that I am the LORD.

7" 'I will make known my holy name among my people Israel. I will no longer let my holy name be profaned,[n] and the nations will know that I the LORD am the Holy One in Israel.[o] **8**It is coming! It will surely take place, declares the Sovereign LORD. This is the day I have spoken of.

9" 'Then those who live in the towns of Israel will go out and use the weapons for fuel and burn them up—the small and large shields, the bows and arrows, the war clubs and spears. For seven years they will use them for fuel.[p] **10**They will not need to gather wood from the fields or cut it from the forests, because they will use the weapons for fuel. And they will plunder those who plundered them and loot those who looted them, declares the Sovereign LORD.[q]

11" 'On that day I will give Gog a burial place in Israel, in the valley of those who travel east toward[q] the Sea.[r] It will block the way of travelers, because Gog and all his hordes will be buried there. So it will be called the Valley of Hamon Gog.[s][r]

12" 'For seven months the house of Israel will be burying them in order to cleanse the land.[s] **13**All the people of the land will bury them, and the day I am glorified[t] will be a memorable day for them, declares the Sovereign LORD.

14" 'Men will be regularly employed to cleanse the land. Some will go throughout the land and, in addition to them, others will bury those that remain on the ground. At the end of the seven months they will begin their search. **15**As they go through the land and one of them sees a human bone, he will set up a marker beside it until the gravediggers have buried it in the Valley of Hamon Gog. **16**(Also a town called Hamonah[t] will be there.) And so they will cleanse the land.'

17"Son of man, this is what the Sovereign LORD says: Call out to every kind of bird[u] and all the wild

[p]1 Or *Gog, prince of Rosh,* [q]11 Or *of* [r]11 That is, the Dead Sea [s]11 *Hamon Gog* means *hordes of Gog.* [t]16 *Hamonah* means *horde.*

38:19 [a]Ps 18:7; Eze 5:13; Hag 2:6,21
38:20 [b]Hos 4:3; Na 1:5
38:21 [c]Eze 14:17 [d]1Sa 14:20; 2Ch 20:23; Hag 2:22
38:22 [e]Isa 66:16; Jer 25:31 [f]Ps 18:12; Rev 16:21
38:23 [g]Eze 36:23
39:1 [h]Eze 38:2,3
39:3 [i]Hos 1:5 [j]Ps 76:3
39:4 [k]ver 17-20; Eze 29:5; 33:27
39:6 [l]Eze 30:8; Am 1:4 [m]Jer 25:22
39:7 [n]Ex 20:7 [o]Isa 12:6; Eze 36:16,23
39:9 [p]Ps 46:9
39:10 [q]Isa 14:2; 33:1; Hab 2:8
39:11 [r]Eze 38:2
39:12 [s]Dt 21:23
39:13 [t]Eze 28:22
39:17 [u]Rev 19:17

animals: 'Assemble and come together from all around to the sacrifice I am preparing for you, the great sacrifice on the mountains of Israel. There you will eat flesh and drink blood. **18**You will eat the flesh of mighty men and drink the blood of the princes of the earth as if they were rams and lambs, goats and bulls—all of them fattened animals from Bashan.[a] **19**At the sacrifice I am preparing for you, you will eat fat till you are glutted and drink blood till you are drunk. **20**At my table you will eat your fill of horses and riders, mighty men and soldiers of every kind,' declares the Sovereign LORD.[b]

21"I will display my glory among the nations, and all the nations will see the punishment I inflict and the hand I lay upon them.[c] **22**From that day forward the house of Israel will know that I am the LORD their God. **23**And the nations will know that the people of Israel went into exile for their sin, because they were unfaithful to me. So I hid my face from them and handed them over to their enemies, and they all fell by the sword.[d] **24**I dealt with them according to their uncleanness and their offenses, and I hid my face from them.[e]

25"Therefore this is what the Sovereign LORD says: I will now bring Jacob back from captivity[u][f] and will have compassion[g] on all the people of Israel, and I will be zealous for my holy name.[h] **26**They will forget their shame and all the unfaithfulness they showed toward me when they lived in safety[i] in their land with no one to make them afraid.[j] **27**When I have brought them back from the nations and have gathered them from the countries of their enemies, I will show myself holy through them in the sight of many nations.[k] **28**Then they will know that I am the LORD their God, for though I sent them into exile among the nations, I will gather them to their own land, not leaving any behind. **29**I will no longer hide my face from them, for I will pour out my Spirit[l] on the house of Israel, declares the Sovereign LORD."

The New Temple Area

40 In the twenty-fifth year of our exile, at the beginning of the year, on the tenth of the month, in the fourteenth year after the fall of the city[m]—on that very day the hand of the LORD was upon me[n] and he took me there. **2**In visions[o] of God he took me to the land of Israel and set me on a very high mountain,[p] on whose south side were some buildings that looked like a city. **3**He took me there, and I saw a man whose appearance was like bronze;[q] he was standing in the gateway with a linen cord and a measuring rod[r] in his hand. **4**The man said to me, "Son of man, look with your eyes and hear with your ears and pay attention to everything I am going to show you, for that is why you have been brought here. Tell[s] the house of Israel everything you see.[t]"

The East Gate to the Outer Court

5I saw a wall completely surrounding the temple area. The length of the measuring rod in the man's hand was six long cubits, each of which was a cubit[v] and a handbreadth.[w] He measured[u] the wall; it was one measuring rod thick and one rod high.

6Then he went to the gate facing east.[v] He climbed its steps and measured the threshold of the gate; it was one rod deep.[x] **7**The alcoves[w] for the guards were one rod long and one rod wide, and the projecting walls between the alcoves were five cubits thick. And the threshold of the gate next to the portico facing the temple was one rod deep.

8Then he measured the portico

39:18 [a]Ps 22:12; Jer 51:40
39:20 [b]Rev 19:17-18
39:21 [c]Ex 9:16; Isa 37:20; Eze 38:16
39:23 [d]Isa 1:15; 59:2; Jer 22:8-9; 44:23
39:24 [e]Jer 2:17,19; 4:18; Eze 36:19
39:25 [f]Jer 33:7; Eze 34:13 [g]Jer 30:18 [h]Isa 27:12-13
39:26 [i]1Ki 4:25 [j]Isa 17:2; Eze 34:28; Mic 4:4
39:27 [k]Eze 36:23-24; 37:21; 38:16
39:29 [l]Joel 2:28; Ac 2:17
40:1 [m]2Ki 25:7; Jer 39:1-10; 52:4-11; Eze 33:21 [n]Eze 1:3
40:2 [o]Da 7:1,7 [p]Eze 17:22; Rev 21:10
40:3 [q]Eze 1:7; Da 10:6; Rev 1:15 [r]Eze 47:3; Zec 2:1-2; Rev 11:1; 21:15
40:4 [s]Jer 26:2 [t]Eze 44:5
40:5 [u]Eze 42:20
40:6 [v]Eze 8:16
40:7 [w]ver 36

[u]25 Or *now restore the fortunes of Jacob*
[v]5 The common cubit was about 1 1/2 feet (about 0.5 meter). [w]5 That is, about 3 inches (about 8 centimeters)
[x]6 Septuagint; Hebrew *deep, the first threshold, one rod deep*

of the gateway; 9it[y] was eight cubits deep and its jambs were two
cubits thick. The portico of the
gateway faced the temple.
10Inside the east gate were three
alcoves on each side; the three had
the same measurements, and the
faces of the projecting walls on
each side had the same measurements. 11Then he measured the
width of the entrance to the gateway; it was ten cubits and its length
was thirteen cubits. 12In front of
each alcove was a wall one cubit
high, and the alcoves were six cubits square. 13Then he measured
the gateway from the top of the rear
wall of one alcove to the top of the
opposite one; the distance was
twenty-five cubits from one parapet opening to the opposite one.
14He measured along the faces of
the projecting walls all around the
inside of the gateway—sixty cubits. The measurement was up to
the portico[z] facing the courtyard.[a][a] 15The distance from the
entrance of the gateway to the far
end of its portico was fifty cubits.
16The alcoves and the projecting
walls inside the gateway were sur-
mounted by narrow parapet openings all around, as was the portico;
the openings all around faced inward. The faces of the projecting
walls were decorated with palm
trees.[b]

The Outer Court

17Then he brought me into the
outer court.[c] There I saw some
rooms and a pavement that had
been constructed all around the
court; there were thirty rooms[d]
along the pavement.[e] 18It abutted
the sides of the gateways and was
as wide as they were long; this was
the lower pavement. 19Then he
measured the distance from the inside of the lower gateway to the
outside of the inner court;[f] it was
a hundred cubits[g] on the east side
as well as on the north.

The North Gate

20Then he measured the length
and width of the gate facing north,
leading into the outer court. 21Its
alcoves[h]—three on each side—its
projecting walls and its portico had
the same measurements as those
of the first gateway. It was fifty cubits long and twenty-five cubits
wide. 22Its openings, its portico[i]
and its palm tree decorations had
the same measurements as those
of the gate facing east. Seven steps
led up to it, with its portico opposite them. 23There was a gate to the
inner court facing the north gate,
just as there was on the east. He
measured from one gate to the opposite one; it was a hundred cubits.[j]

The South Gate

24Then he led me to the south
side and I saw a gate facing south.
He measured its jambs and its portico, and they had the same measurements as the others. 25The
gateway and its portico had narrow
openings all around, like the openings of the others. It was fifty cubits
long and twenty-five cubits wide.[k]
26Seven steps led up to it, with its
portico opposite them; it had palm
tree decorations on the faces of the
projecting walls on each side.[l]
27The inner court[m] also had a gate
facing south, and he measured
from this gate to the outer gate on
the south side; it was a hundred cubits.

Gates to the Inner Court

28Then he brought me into the
inner court through the south gate,
and he measured the south gate; it
had the same measurements[n] as
the others. 29Its alcoves, its projecting walls and its portico had
the same measurements as the
others. The gateway and its portico
had openings all around. It was fifty cubits long and twenty-five cubits wide. 30(The porticoes[o] of the
gateways around the inner court

40:14 [a]Ex 27:9
40:16 [b]ver 21-22; 2Ch 3:5; Eze 41:26
40:17 [c]Rev 11:2 [d]Eze 41:6 [e]Eze 42:1
40:19 [f]Eze 46:1 [g]ver 23,27
40:21 [h]ver 7
40:22 [i]ver 49
40:23 [j]ver 19
40:25 [k]ver 33
40:26 [l]ver 22
40:27 [m]ver 32
40:28 [n]ver 35
40:30 [o]ver 21

[y]8,9 Many Hebrew manuscripts, Septuagint, Vulgate and Syriac; most Hebrew manuscripts *gateway facing the temple; it was one rod deep.* [9]*Then he measured the portico of the gateway; it* [z]*14* Septuagint; Hebrew *projecting wall* [a]*14* The meaning of the Hebrew for this verse is uncertain.

were twenty-five cubits wide and
five cubits deep.) **31**Its portico[a]
faced the outer court; palm trees
decorated its jambs, and eight
steps led up to it.

32Then he brought me to the inner court on the east side, and he
measured the gateway; it had the
same measurements as the others.
33Its alcoves, its projecting walls
and its portico had the same measurements as the others. The gateway and its portico had openings
all around. It was fifty cubits long
and twenty-five cubits wide. **34**Its
portico[b] faced the outer court;
palm trees decorated the jambs on
either side, and eight steps led up
to it.

35Then he brought me to the
north gate[c] and measured it. It
had the same measurements as the
others, **36**as did its alcoves,[d] its
projecting walls and its portico,
and it had openings all around. It
was fifty cubits long and twenty-
five cubits wide. **37**Its portico[b]
faced the outer court; palm trees
decorated the jambs on either side,
and eight steps led up to it.

The Rooms for Preparing Sacrifices

38A room with a doorway was by
the portico in each of the inner
gateways, where the burnt offerings[e] were washed. **39**In the portico of the gateway were two tables
on each side, on which the burnt
offerings,[f] sin offerings[g] and guilt
offerings[h] were slaughtered. **40**By
the outside wall of the portico of
the gateway, near the steps at the
entrance to the north gateway were
two tables, and on the other side of
the steps were two tables. **41**So
there were four tables on one side
of the gateway and four on the other—eight tables in all—on which
the sacrifices were slaughtered.
42There were also four tables of
dressed stone[i] for the burnt offerings, each a cubit and a half long,
a cubit and a half wide and a cubit
high. On them were placed the
utensils for slaughtering the burnt
offerings and the other sacrifices.[j]
43And double-pronged hooks, each
a handbreadth long, were attached
to the wall all around. The tables
were for the flesh of the offerings.

Rooms for the Priests

44Outside the inner gate, within
the inner court, were two rooms,
one[c] at the side of the north gate
and facing south, and another at
the side of the south[d] gate and facing north. **45**He said to me, "The
room facing south is for the priests
who have charge of the temple,[k]
46and the room facing north[l] is for
the priests who have charge of the
altar.[m] These are the sons of Zadok,[n] who are the only Levites who
may draw near to the LORD to minister before him.[o]"

47Then he measured the court: It
was square—a hundred cubits long
and a hundred cubits wide. And the
altar was in front of the temple.

The Temple

48He brought me to the portico
of the temple[p] and measured the
jambs of the portico; they were five
cubits wide on either side. The
width of the entrance was fourteen
cubits and its projecting walls
were[e] three cubits wide on either
side. **49**The portico[q] was twenty
cubits wide, and twelve[f] cubits
from front to back. It was reached
by a flight of stairs,[g] and there
were pillars[r] on each side of the
jambs.

41 Then the man brought me
to the outer sanctuary[s] and
measured the jambs; the width of
the jambs was six cubits[h] on each
side.[i] **2**The entrance was ten cubits wide, and the projecting walls
on each side of it were five cubits
wide. He also measured the outer

40:31 [a]ver 22
40:34 [b]ver 22
40:35 [c]Eze 44:4; 47:2
40:36 [d]ver 7
40:38 [e]2Ch 4:6; Eze 42:13
40:39 [f]Eze 46:2 [g]Lev 4:3,28 [h]Lev 7:1
40:42 [i]Ex 20:25 [j]ver 39
40:45 [k]1Ch 9:23
40:46 [l]Eze 42:13 [m]Nu 18:5 [n]1Ki 2:35 [o]Nu 16:5; Eze 43:19; 44:15; 45:4; 48:11
40:48 [p]1Ki 6:2
40:49 [q]ver 22; 1Ki 6:3 [r]1Ki 7:15
41:1 [s]ver 23

[b]*37* Septuagint (see also verses 31 and 34); Hebrew *jambs* [c]*44* Septuagint; Hebrew *were rooms for singers, which were*
[d]*44* Septuagint; Hebrew *east*
[e]*48* Septuagint; Hebrew *entrance was*
[f]*49* Septuagint; Hebrew *eleven*
[g]*49* Hebrew; Septuagint *Ten steps led up to it*
[h]*1* The common cubit was about 1 1/2 feet (about 0.5 meter). [i]*1* One Hebrew manuscript and Septuagint; most Hebrew manuscripts *side, the width of the tent*

sanctuary; it was forty cubits long and twenty cubits wide.[a]

3Then he went into the inner sanctuary and measured the jambs of the entrance; each was two cubits wide. The entrance was six cubits wide, and the projecting walls on each side of it were seven cubits wide. 4And he measured the length of the inner sanctuary; it was twenty cubits, and its width was twenty cubits across the end of the outer sanctuary.[b] He said to me, "This is the Most Holy Place.[c]"

5Then he measured the wall of the temple; it was six cubits thick, and each side room around the temple was four cubits wide. 6The side rooms were on three levels, one above another, thirty[d] on each level. There were ledges all around the wall of the temple to serve as supports for the side rooms, so that the supports were not inserted into the wall of the temple.[e] 7The side rooms all around the temple were wider at each successive level. The structure surrounding the temple was built in ascending stages, so that the rooms widened as one went upward. A stairway[f] went up from the lowest floor to the top floor through the middle floor.

8I saw that the temple had a raised base all around it, forming the foundation of the side rooms. It was the length of the rod, six long cubits. 9The outer wall of the side rooms was five cubits thick. The open area between the side rooms of the temple 10and the ⌞priests'⌟ rooms was twenty cubits wide all around the temple. 11There were entrances to the side rooms from the open area, one on the north and another on the south; and the base adjoining the open area was five cubits wide all around.

12The building facing the temple courtyard on the west side was seventy cubits wide. The wall of the building was five cubits thick all around, and its length was ninety cubits.

13Then he measured the temple; it was a hundred cubits long, and the temple courtyard and the building with its walls were also a hundred cubits long. 14The width of the temple courtyard on the east, including the front of the temple, was a hundred cubits.[g]

15Then he measured the length of the building facing the courtyard at the rear of the temple, including its galleries[h] on each side; it was a hundred cubits.

The outer sanctuary, the inner sanctuary and the portico facing the court, 16as well as the thresholds and the narrow windows[i] and galleries around the three of them—everything beyond and including the threshold was covered with wood. The floor, the wall up to the windows, and the windows were covered.[j] 17In the space above the outside of the entrance to the inner sanctuary and on the walls at regular intervals all around the inner and outer sanctuary 18were carved[k] cherubim[l] and palm trees.[m] Palm trees alternated with cherubim. Each cherub had two faces:[n] 19the face of a man toward the palm tree on one side and the face of a lion toward the palm tree on the other. They were carved all around the whole temple.[o] 20From the floor to the area above the entrance, cherubim and palm trees were carved on the wall of the outer sanctuary.

21The outer sanctuary[p] had a rectangular doorframe, and the one at the front of the Most Holy Place was similar. 22There was a wooden altar[q] three cubits high and two cubits square[i]; its corners, its base[k] and its sides were of wood. The man said to me, "This is the table[r] that is before the LORD." 23Both the outer sanctuary[s] and the Most Holy Place had double doors.[t] 24Each door had two leaves—two hinged leaves[u] for each door. 25And on the doors of the outer sanctuary were carved cherubim and palm trees like those carved on the walls, and there was a wooden overhang on the front of

41:2 [a]2Ch 3:3
41:4 [b]1Ki 6:20 [c]Ex 26:33; Heb 9:3-8
41:6 [d]Eze 40:17 [e]1Ki 6:5
41:7 [f]1Ki 6:8
41:14 [g]Eze 40:47
41:15 [h]Eze 42:3
41:16 [i]1Ki 6:4 [j]ver 25-26; 1Ki 6:15; Eze 42:3
41:18 [k]1Ki 6:18 [l]Ex 37:7; 2Ch 3:7 [m]1Ki 6:29; 7:36 [n]Eze 10:21
41:19 [o]Eze 10:14
41:21 [p]ver 1
41:22 [q]Ex 30:1 [r]Ex 25:23; Eze 23:41; 44:16; Mal 1:7,12
41:23 [s]ver 1 [t]1Ki 6:32
41:24 [u]1Ki 6:34

i22 Septuagint; Hebrew *long*
k22 Septuagint; Hebrew *length*

the portico. **26**On the sidewalls of the portico were narrow windows with palm trees carved on each side. The side rooms of the temple also had overhangs.[a]

Rooms for the Priests

42 Then the man led me northward into the outer court and brought me to the rooms[b] opposite the temple courtyard[c] and opposite the outer wall on the north side.[d] **2**The building whose door faced north was a hundred cubits[l] long and fifty cubits wide. **3**Both in the section twenty cubits from the inner court and in the section opposite the pavement of the outer court, gallery[e] faced gallery at the three levels.[f] **4**In front of the rooms was an inner passageway ten cubits wide and a hundred cubits[m] long. Their doors were on the north.[g] **5**Now the upper rooms were narrower, for the galleries took more space from them than from the rooms on the lower and middle floors of the building. **6**The rooms on the third floor had no pillars, as the courts had; so they were smaller in floor space than those on the lower and middle floors. **7**There was an outer wall parallel to the rooms and the outer court; it extended in front of the rooms for fifty cubits. **8**While the row of rooms on the side next to the outer court was fifty cubits long, the row on the side nearest the sanctuary was a hundred cubits long. **9**The lower rooms had an entrance[h] on the east side as one enters them from the outer court.

10On the south side[n] along the length of the wall of the outer court, adjoining the temple courtyard and opposite the outer wall, were rooms[i] **11**with a passageway in front of them. These were like the rooms on the north; they had the same length and width, with similar exits and dimensions. Similar to the doorways on the north **12**were the doorways of the rooms on the south. There was a doorway at the beginning of the passageway that was parallel to the corresponding wall extending eastward, by which one enters the rooms.

13Then he said to me, "The north[j] and south rooms facing the temple courtyard are the priests' rooms, where the priests who approach the LORD will eat the most holy offerings. There they will put the most holy offerings—the grain offerings, the sin offerings[k] and the guilt offerings[l]—for the place is holy.[m] **14**Once the priests enter the holy precincts, they are not to go into the outer court until they leave behind the garments[n] in which they minister, for these are holy. They are to put on other clothes before they go near the places that are for the people.[o]"

15When he had finished measuring what was inside the temple area, he led me out by the east gate[p] and measured the area all around: **16**He measured the east side with the measuring rod; it was five hundred cubits.[o] **17**He measured the north side; it was five hundred cubits[p] by the measuring rod. **18**He measured the south side; it was five hundred cubits by the measuring rod. **19**Then he turned to the west side and measured; it was five hundred cubits by the measuring rod. **20**So he measured[q] the area on all four sides. It had a wall around it,[r] five hundred cubits long and five hundred cubits wide,[s] to separate the holy from the common.[t]

The Glory Returns to the Temple

43 Then the man brought me to the gate facing east,[u] **2**and I saw the glory of the God of Israel coming from the east. His voice was like the roar of rushing waters,[v] and the land was radiant with his glory.[w] **3**The vision I saw was like the vision I had seen when

41:26 [a]ver 15-16; Eze 40:16
42:1 [b]ver 13 [c]Eze 41:12-14 [d]Eze 40:17
42:3 [e]Eze 41:15 [f]Eze 41:16
42:4 [g]Eze 46:19
42:9 [h]Eze 44:5; 46:19
42:10 [i]ver 1
42:13 [j]Eze 40:46 [k]Lev 10:17; 6:25 [l]Lev 14:13 [m]Ex 29:31; Lev 6:29; 7:6; 10:12-13; Nu 18:9-10
42:14 [n]Eze 44:19 [o]Ex 29:9; Lev 8:7-9
42:15 [p]Eze 43:1
42:20 [q]Eze 40:5 [r]Zec 2:5 [s]Eze 45:2; Rev 21:16 [t]Eze 22:26
43:1 [u]Eze 10:19; 42:15; 44:1; 46:1
43:2 [v]Rev 1:15 [w]Isa 6:3; Eze 11:23; Rev 18:1

l*2* The common cubit was about 1 1/2 feet (about 0.5 meter). m*4* Septuagint and Syriac; Hebrew *and one cubit* n*10* Septuagint; Hebrew *Eastward* o*16* See Septuagint of verse 17; Hebrew *rods*; also in verses 18 and 19. p*17* Septuagint; Hebrew *rods*

he[q] came to destroy the city and
like the visions I had seen by the
Kebar River, and I fell facedown.
4The glory[a] of the LORD entered
the temple through the gate facing
east.[b] **5**Then the Spirit[c] lifted me
up[d] and brought me into the inner
court, and the glory of the LORD
filled the temple.

6While the man was standing beside me, I heard someone speaking
to me from inside the temple. **7**He
said: "Son of man, this is the place
of my throne and the place for the
soles of my feet. This is where I will
live among the Israelites forever.
The house of Israel will never again
defile my holy name—neither they
nor their kings—by their prostitution[r] and the lifeless idols[s] of
their kings at their high places.[e]
8When they placed their threshold
next to my threshold and their
doorposts beside my doorposts,
with only a wall between me and
them, they defiled my holy name
by their detestable practices. So I
destroyed them in my anger. **9**Now
let them put away from me their
prostitution and the lifeless idols
of their kings, and I will live among
them forever.[f]

10"Son of man, describe the temple to the people of Israel, that they
may be ashamed[g] of their sins. Let
them consider the plan, **11**and if
they are ashamed of all they have
done, make known to them the design of the temple—its arrangement, its exits and entrances—its
whole design and all its regulations[t] and laws. Write these down
before them so that they may be
faithful to its design and follow all
its regulations.[h]

12"This is the law of the temple:
All the surrounding area[i] on top of
the mountain will be most holy.
Such is the law of the temple.

The Altar

13"These are the measurements
of the altar[j] in long cubits, that
cubit being a cubit[u] and a handbreadth[v]: Its gutter is a cubit deep
and a cubit wide, with a rim of one

43:4 [a]Eze 1:28 [b]Eze 10:19
43:5 [c]Eze 11:24 [d]Eze 3:12; 8:3
43:7 [e]Lev 26:30
43:9 [f]Eze 37:26-28
43:10 [g]Eze 16:61
43:11 [h]Eze 44:5
43:12 [i]Eze 40:2
43:13 [j]2Ch 4:1
43:15 [k]Ex 27:2
43:17 [l]Ex 20:26
43:18 [m]Ex 40:29 [n]Lev 1:5,11; Heb 9:21-22
43:19 [o]Lev 4:3; Eze 45:18-19 [p]Eze 44:15 [q]Nu 16:40; Eze 40:46
43:20 [r]ver 17 [s]Lev 16:19
43:21 [t]Ex 29:14; Heb 13:11
43:23 [u]Ex 29:1
43:24 [v]Lev 2:13; Mk 9:49-50

span[w] around the edge. And this is
the height of the altar: **14**From the
gutter on the ground up to the lower ledge it is two cubits high and a
cubit wide, and from the smaller
ledge up to the larger ledge it is
four cubits high and a cubit wide.
15The altar hearth is four cubits
high, and four horns[k] project upward from the hearth. **16**The altar
hearth is square, twelve cubits long
and twelve cubits wide. **17**The upper ledge also is square, fourteen
cubits long and fourteen cubits
wide, with a rim of half a cubit and
a gutter of a cubit all around. The
steps[l] of the altar face east."

18Then he said to me, "Son of
man, this is what the Sovereign
LORD says: These will be the regulations for sacrificing burnt offerings[m] and sprinkling blood[n] upon
the altar when it is built: **19**You are
to give a young bull[o] as a sin offering to the priests, who are Levites,
of the family of Zadok,[p] who come
near[q] to minister before me, declares the Sovereign LORD. **20**You
are to take some of its blood and
put it on the four horns of the altar
and on the four corners of the upper ledge[r] and all around the rim,
and so purify the altar[s] and make
atonement for it. **21**You are to take
the bull for the sin offering and
burn it in the designated part of the
temple area outside the sanctuary.[t]

22"On the second day you are to
offer a male goat without defect for
a sin offering, and the altar is to be
purified as it was purified with the
bull. **23**When you have finished pu-
rifying it, you are to offer a young
bull and a ram from the flock, both
without defect.[u] **24**You are to offer
them before the LORD, and the
priests are to sprinkle salt[v] on

q3 Some Hebrew manuscripts and Vulgate; most Hebrew manuscripts *I*   r7 Or *their spiritual adultery*; also in verse 9   s7 Or *the corpses*; also in verse 9   t11 Some Hebrew manuscripts and Septuagint; most Hebrew manuscripts *regulations and its whole design*   u13 The common cubit was about 1 1/2 feet (about 0.5 meter).   v13 That is, about 3 inches (about 8 centimeters)   w13 That is, about 9 inches (about 22 centimeters)

them and sacrifice them as a burnt
offering to the LORD.
25"For seven days[a] you are to
provide a male goat daily for a sin
offering; you are also to provide a
young bull and a ram from the
flock, both without defect.[b] 26For
seven days they are to make atonement for the altar and cleanse it;
thus they will dedicate it. 27At the
end of these days, from the eighth
day[c] on, the priests are to present
your burnt offerings and fellowship
offerings[x][d] on the altar. Then I
will accept you, declares the Sovereign LORD."

The Prince, the Levites, the Priests

44 Then the man brought me
back to the outer gate of the
sanctuary, the one facing east,[e]
and it was shut. 2The LORD said to
me, "This gate is to remain shut. It
must not be opened; no one may
enter through it.[f] It is to remain
shut because the LORD, the God of
Israel, has entered through it. 3The
prince himself is the only one who
may sit inside the gateway to eat in
the presence[g] of the LORD. He is to
enter by way of the portico of the
gateway and go out the same
way.[h]"
4Then the man brought me by
way of the north gate to the front of
the temple. I looked and saw the
glory of the LORD filling the temple[i] of the LORD, and I fell facedown.[j]
5The LORD said to me, "Son of
man, look carefully, listen closely
and give attention to everything I
tell you concerning all the regulations regarding the temple of the
LORD. Give attention to the entrance of the temple and all the exits of the sanctuary.[k] 6Say to the
rebellious house[l] of Israel, 'This is
what the Sovereign LORD says:
Enough of your detestable practices, O house of Israel! 7In addition to all your other detestable
practices, you brought foreigners
uncircumcised in heart[m] and flesh
into my sanctuary, desecrating my
temple while you offered me food,
fat and blood, and you broke my
covenant.[n] 8Instead of carrying
out your duty in regard to my holy
things, you put others in charge of
my sanctuary.[o] 9This is what the
Sovereign LORD says: No foreigner
uncircumcised in heart and flesh is
to enter my sanctuary, not even the
foreigners who live among the Israelites.[p]
10" 'The Levites who went far
from me when Israel went astray[q]
and who wandered from me after
their idols must bear the consequences of their sin.[r] 11They may
serve in my sanctuary, having
charge of the gates of the temple
and serving in it; they may slaughter the burnt offerings[s] and sacrifices for the people and stand before the people and serve them.[t]
12But because they served them in
the presence of their idols and
made the house of Israel fall into
sin, therefore I have sworn with uplifted hand[u] that they must bear
the consequences of their sin, declares the Sovereign LORD.[v] 13They
are not to come near to serve me as
priests or come near any of my holy
things or my most holy offerings;
they must bear the shame[w] of their
detestable practices.[x] 14Yet I will
put them in charge of the duties of
the temple and all the work that is
to be done in it.[y]
15" 'But the priests, who are Levites and descendants of Zadok
and who faithfully carried out the
duties of my sanctuary when the Israelites went astray from me, are to
come near to minister before me;
they are to stand before me to offer
sacrifices of fat and blood, declares
the Sovereign LORD.[z] 16They alone
are to enter my sanctuary; they
alone are to come near my table[a]
to minister before me and perform
my service.[b]
17" 'When they enter the gates of
the inner court, they are to wear
linen clothes;[c] they must not wear
any woolen garment while ministering at the gates of the inner

43:25 [a] Lev 8:33 [b] Ex 29:37
43:27 [c] Lev 9:1 [d] Lev 17:5
44:1 [e] Eze 43:1
44:2 [f] Eze 43:4-5
44:3 [g] Ex 24:9-11 [h] Eze 46:2,8
44:4 [i] Isa 6:4; Rev 15:8 [j] Eze 1:28; 3:23
44:5 [k] Eze 40:4; 43:10-11
44:6 [l] Eze 3:9
44:7 [m] Lev 26:41 [n] Ge 17:14; Ex 12:48; Lev 22:25
44:8 [o] Lev 22:2; Nu 18:7
44:9 [p] Joel 3:17; Zec 14:21
44:10 [q] 2Ki 23:8 [r] Nu 18:23
44:11 [s] 2Ch 29:34 [t] Nu 3:5-37; 16:9; 1Ch 26:12-19
44:12 [u] Ps 106:26 [v] 2Ki 16:10-16
44:13 [w] Eze 16:61 [x] Nu 18:3
44:14 [y] Nu 18:4; 1Ch 23:28-32
44:15 [z] Jer 33:18; Eze 40:46; Zec 3:7
44:16 [a] Eze 41:22 [b] Nu 18:5
44:17 [c] Ex 39:27-28; Rev 19:8

[x]27 Traditionally *peace offerings*

court or inside the temple. **18**They are to wear linen turbans[a] on their heads and linen undergarments[b] around their waists. They must not wear anything that makes them perspire.[c] **19**When they go out into the outer court where the people are, they are to take off the clothes they have been ministering in and are to leave them in the sacred rooms, and put on other clothes, so that they do not consecrate[d] the people by means of their garments.[e]

20" 'They must not shave their heads or let their hair grow long, but they are to keep the hair of their heads trimmed.[f] **21**No priest is to drink wine when he enters the inner court.[g] **22**They must not marry widows or divorced women; they may marry only virgins of Israelite descent or widows of priests.[h] **23**They are to teach my people the difference between the holy and the common[i] and show them how to distinguish between the unclean and the clean.[j]

24" 'In any dispute, the priests are to serve as judges[k] and decide it according to my ordinances. They are to keep my laws and my decrees for all my appointed feasts, and they are to keep my Sabbaths holy.[l]

25" 'A priest must not defile himself by going near a dead person; however, if the dead person was his father or mother, son or daughter, brother or unmarried sister, then he may defile himself.[m] **26**After he is cleansed, he must wait seven days.[n] **27**On the day he goes into the inner court of the sanctuary to minister in the sanctuary, he is to offer a sin offering for himself, declares the Sovereign LORD.

28" 'I am to be the only inheritance[o] the priests have. You are to give them no possession in Israel; I will be their possession. **29**They will eat the grain offerings, the sin offerings and the guilt offerings; and everything in Israel devoted[y] to the LORD[p] will belong to them.[q] **30**The best of all the firstfruits[r] and of all your special gifts will belong to the priests. You are to give them the first portion of your ground meal[s] so that a blessing[t] may rest on your household.[u] **31**The priests must not eat anything, bird or animal, found dead or torn by wild animals.[v]

Division of the Land

45 " 'When you allot the land as an inheritance,[w] you are to present to the LORD a portion of the land as a sacred district, 25,000 cubits long and 20,000[z] cubits wide; the entire area will be holy.[x] **2**Of this, a section 500 cubits square[y] is to be for the sanctuary, with 50 cubits around it for open land. **3**In the sacred district, measure off a section 25,000 cubits[a] long and 10,000 cubits[b] wide. In it will be the sanctuary, the Most Holy Place. **4**It will be the sacred portion of the land for the priests,[z] who minister in the sanctuary and who draw near to minister before the LORD. It will be a place for their houses as well as a holy place for the sanctuary.[a] **5**An area 25,000 cubits long and 10,000 cubits wide will belong to the Levites, who serve in the temple, as their possession for towns to live in.[c][b]

6" 'You are to give the city as its property an area 5,000 cubits wide and 25,000 cubits long, adjoining the sacred portion; it will belong to the whole house of Israel.[c]

7" 'The prince will have the land bordering each side of the area formed by the sacred district and the property of the city. It will extend westward from the west side and eastward from the east side, running lengthwise from the western to the eastern border parallel to one of the tribal portions.[d] **8**This land will be his possession in Israel. And my princes will no longer oppress my people but will allow

44:18 [a]Ex 28:39; Isa 3:20 [b]Ex 28:42 [c]Lev 16:4
44:19 [d]Lev 6:27; Eze 46:20 [e]Lev 6:10-11; Eze 42:14
44:20 [f]Lev 21:5; Nu 6:5
44:21 [g]Lev 10:9
44:22 [h]Lev 21:7
44:23 [i]Eze 22:26 [j]Mal 2:7
44:24 [k]Dt 17:8-9; 1Ch 23:4 [l]2Ch 19:8
44:25 [m]Lev 21:1-4
44:26 [n]Nu 19:14
44:28 [o]Nu 18:20; Dt 10:9; 18:1-2; Jos 13:33
44:29 [p]Lev 27:21 [q]Nu 18:9,14
44:30 [r]Nu 18:12-13 [s]Nu 15:18-21 [t]Mal 3:10 [u]Ne 10:35-37
44:31 [v]Ex 22:31; Lev 22:8
45:1 [w]Eze 47:21-22 [x]Eze 48:8-9, 29
45:2 [y]Eze 42:20
45:4 [z]Eze 40:46 [a]Eze 48:10-11
45:5 [b]Eze 48:13
45:6 [c]Eze 48:15-18
45:7 [d]Eze 48:21

[y]*29* The Hebrew term refers to the irrevocable giving over of things or persons to the LORD.
[z]*1* Septuagint (see also verses 3 and 5 and 48:9); Hebrew *10,000* [a]*3* That is, about 7 miles (about 12 kilometers) [b]*3* That is, about 3 miles (about 5 kilometers)
[c]*5* Septuagint; Hebrew *temple; they will have as their possession 20 rooms*

the house of Israel to possess the land according to their tribes.[a]

9 “ ‘This is what the Sovereign LORD says: You have gone far enough, O princes of Israel! Give up your violence and oppression and do what is just and right.[b] Stop dispossessing my people, declares the Sovereign LORD. 10 You are to use accurate scales,[c] an accurate ephah[d][d] and an accurate bath.[e] 11 The ephah[e] and the bath are to be the same size, the bath containing a tenth of a homer[f] and the ephah a tenth of a homer; the homer is to be the standard measure for both. 12 The shekel[g] is to consist of twenty gerahs.[f] Twenty shekels plus twenty-five shekels plus fifteen shekels equal one mina.[h]

Offerings and Holy Days

13 “ ‘This is the special gift you are to offer: a sixth of an ephah from each homer of wheat and a sixth of an ephah from each homer of barley. 14 The prescribed portion of oil, measured by the bath, is a tenth of a bath from each cor (which consists of ten baths or one homer, for ten baths are equivalent to a homer). 15 Also one sheep is to be taken from every flock of two hundred from the well-watered pastures of Israel. These will be used for the grain offerings, burnt offerings[g] and fellowship offerings[i] to make atonement[h] for the people, declares the Sovereign LORD. 16 All the people of the land will participate in this special gift for the use of the prince in Israel. 17 It will be the duty of the prince to provide the burnt offerings, grain offerings and drink offerings at the festivals, the New Moons and the Sabbaths[i]—at all the appointed feasts of the house of Israel. He will provide the sin offerings, grain offerings, burnt offerings and fellowship offerings to make atonement for the house of Israel.[j]

18 “ ‘This is what the Sovereign LORD says: In the first month[k] on the first day you are to take a young bull without defect[l] and purify the sanctuary.[m] 19 The priest is to take some of the blood of the sin offering and put it on the doorposts of the temple, on the four corners of the upper ledge[n] of the altar[o] and on the gateposts of the inner court. 20 You are to do the same on the seventh day of the month for anyone who sins unintentionally[p] or through ignorance; so you are to make atonement for the temple.

21 “ ‘In the first month on the fourteenth day you are to observe the Passover,[q] a feast lasting seven days, during which you shall eat bread made without yeast. 22 On that day the prince is to provide a bull as a sin offering for himself and for all the people of the land.[r] 23 Every day during the seven days of the Feast he is to provide seven bulls and seven rams[s] without defect as a burnt offering to the LORD, and a male goat for a sin offering.[t] 24 He is to provide as a grain offering[u] an ephah for each bull and an ephah for each ram, along with a hin[j] of oil for each ephah.[v]

25 “ ‘During the seven days of the Feast,[w] which begins in the seventh month on the fifteenth day, he is to make the same provision for sin offerings, burnt offerings, grain offerings and oil.[x]

46

“ ‘This is what the Sovereign LORD says: The gate of the inner court[y] facing east[z] is to be shut on the six working days, but on the Sabbath day and on the day of the New Moon[a] it is to be opened. 2 The prince is to enter from the outside through the portico[b] of the gateway and stand by the gatepost. The priests are to sacrifice his burnt offering and his fellowship offerings.[k] He is to worship at the threshold of the gateway and then go out, but the gate

45:8 [a] Nu 26:53; Eze 46:18
45:9 [b] Jer 22:3; Zec 7:9-10; 8:16
45:10 [c] Dt 25:15; Pr 11:1; Am 8:4-6; Mic 6:10-11 [d] Lev 19:36
45:11 [e] Isa 5:10
45:12 [f] Ex 30:13; Lev 27:25; Nu 3:47
45:15 [g] Lev 1:4 [h] Lev 6:30
45:17 [i] Lev 23:38; Isa 66:23 [j] 1Ki 8:62; 2Ch 31:3; Eze 46:4-12
45:18 [k] Ex 12:2 [l] Lev 22:20; Heb 9:14 [m] Lev 16:16, 33
45:19 [n] Eze 43:17 [o] Lev 16:18-19; Eze 43:20
45:20 [p] Lev 4:27
45:21 [q] Ex 12:11; Lev 23:5-6
45:22 [r] Lev 4:14
45:23 [s] Job 42:8 [t] Nu 28:16-25
45:24 [u] Nu 28:12-13 [v] Eze 46:5-7
45:25 [w] Dt 16:13 [x] Lev 23:34-43; Nu 29:12-38
46:1 [y] Eze 40:19 [z] 1Ch 9:18 [a] ver 6; Isa 66:23
46:2 [b] ver 8

[d] *10* An ephah was a dry measure. [e] *10* A bath was a liquid measure. [f] *11* A homer was a dry measure. [g] *12* A shekel weighed about 2/5 ounce (about 11.5 grams). [h] *12* That is, 60 shekels; the common mina was 50 shekels. [i] *15* Traditionally *peace offerings*; also in verse 17 [j] *24* That is, probably about 4 quarts (about 4 liters) [k] *2* Traditionally *peace offerings*; also in verse 12

will not be shut until evening.[a] 3On the Sabbaths and New Moons the people of the land are to worship in the presence of the LORD at the entrance to that gateway.[b] 4The burnt offering the prince brings to the LORD on the Sabbath day is to be six male lambs and a ram, all without defect. 5The grain offering given with the ram is to be an ephah,[l] and the grain offering with the lambs is to be as much as he pleases, along with a hin[m] of oil for each ephah.[c] 6On the day of the New Moon[d] he is to offer a young bull, six lambs and a ram, all without defect. 7He is to provide as a grain offering one ephah with the bull, one ephah with the ram, and with the lambs as much as he wants to give, along with a hin of oil with each ephah.[e] 8When the prince enters, he is to go in through the portico[f] of the gateway, and he is to come out the same way.[g]

9" 'When the people of the land come before the LORD at the appointed feasts,[h] whoever enters by the north gate to worship is to go out the south gate; and whoever enters by the south gate is to go out the north gate. No one is to return through the gate by which he entered, but each is to go out the opposite gate. 10The prince is to be among them, going in when they go in and going out when they go out.[i]

11" 'At the festivals and the appointed feasts, the grain offering is to be an ephah with a bull, an ephah with a ram, and with the lambs as much as one pleases, along with a hin of oil for each ephah.[j] 12When the prince provides[k] a freewill offering[l] to the LORD—whether a burnt offering or fellowship offerings—the gate facing east is to be opened for him. He shall offer his burnt offering or his fellowship offerings as he does on the Sabbath day. Then he shall go out, and after he has gone out, the gate will be shut.[m]

13" 'Every day you are to provide a year-old lamb without defect for a burnt offering to the LORD; morning by morning you shall provide it.[n] 14You are also to provide with it morning by morning a grain offering, consisting of a sixth of an ephah with a third of a hin of oil to moisten the flour. The presenting of this grain offering to the LORD is a lasting ordinance.[o] 15So the lamb and the grain offering and the oil shall be provided morning by morning for a regular[p] burnt offering.[q]

16" 'This is what the Sovereign LORD says: If the prince makes a gift from his inheritance to one of his sons, it will also belong to his descendants; it is to be their property by inheritance.[r] 17If, however, he makes a gift from his inheritance to one of his servants, the servant may keep it until the year of freedom;[s] then it will revert to the prince. His inheritance belongs to his sons only; it is theirs. 18The prince must not take any of the inheritance[t] of the people, driving them off their property. He is to give his sons their inheritance out of his own property, so that none of my people will be separated from his property.' "

19Then the man brought me through the entrance[u] at the side of the gate to the sacred rooms facing north, which belonged to the priests, and showed me a place at the western end. 20He said to me, "This is the place where the priests will cook the guilt offering and the sin offering and bake the grain offering, to avoid bringing them into the outer court and consecrating[v] the people."[w]

21He then brought me to the outer court and led me around to its four corners, and I saw in each corner another court. 22In the four corners of the outer court were enclosed[n] courts, forty cubits long and thirty cubits wide; each of the courts in the four corners was the same size. 23Around the inside of each of the four courts was a ledge

46:2 [a]ver 12; Eze 44:3
46:3 [b]Lk 1:10
46:5 [c]ver 11; Eze 45:24
46:6 [d]ver 1; Nu 10:10
46:7 [e]Eze 45:24
46:8 [f]ver 2 [g]Eze 44:3
46:9 [h]Ex 23:14; 34:20
46:10 [i]2Sa 6:14-15; Ps 42:4
46:11 [j]ver 5
46:12 [k]Eze 45:17 [l]Lev 7:16 [m]ver 2
46:13 [n]Ex 29:38; Nu 28:3
46:14 [o]Da 8:11
46:15 [p]Ex 29:42 [q]Ex 29:38; Nu 28:5-6
46:16 [r]2Ch 21:3
46:17 [s]Lev 25:10
46:18 [t]Lev 25:23; Eze 45:8; Mic 2:1-2
46:19 [u]Eze 42:9
46:20 [v]Lev 6:27 [w]Zec 14:20

l5 That is, probably about 3/5 bushel (about 22 liters) m5 That is, probably about 4 quarts (about 4 liters) n22 The meaning of the Hebrew for this word is uncertain.

of stone, with places for fire built
all around under the ledge. **24**He
said to me, "These are the kitchens
where those who minister at the
temple will cook the sacrifices of
the people."

The River From the Temple

47 The man brought me back
to the entrance of the temple, and I saw water[a] coming out
from under the threshold of the
temple toward the east (for the
temple faced east). The water was
coming down from under the south
side of the temple, south of the altar.[b] **2**He then brought me out
through the north gate and led me
around the outside to the outer
gate facing east, and the water was
flowing from the south side.

3As the man went eastward with
a measuring line[c] in his hand, he
measured off a thousand cubits[o]
and then led me through water that
was ankle-deep. **4**He measured off
another thousand cubits and led
me through water that was knee-
deep. He measured off another
thousand and led me through water that was up to the waist. **5**He
measured off another thousand,
but now it was a river that I could
not cross, because the water had
risen and was deep enough to swim
in—a river that no one could
cross.[d] **6**He asked me, "Son of
man, do you see this?"

Then he led me back to the bank
of the river. **7**When I arrived there,
I saw a great number of trees on
each side of the river.[e] **8**He said to
me, "This water flows toward the
eastern region and goes down into
the Arabah,[p][f] where it enters the
Sea.[q] When it empties into the
Sea,[q] the water there becomes
fresh.[g] **9**Swarms of living creatures
will live wherever the river flows.
There will be large numbers of fish,
because this water flows there and
makes the salt water fresh; so
where the river flows everything
will live.[h] **10**Fishermen[i] will
stand along the shore; from En
Gedi[j] to En Eglaim there will be
places for spreading nets.[k] The
fish will be of many kinds[l]—like
the fish of the Great Sea.[r][m] **11**But
the swamps and marshes will not
become fresh; they will be left for
salt.[n] **12**Fruit trees of all kinds will
grow on both banks of the river.[o]
Their leaves will not wither, nor
will their fruit[p] fail. Every month
they will bear, because the water
from the sanctuary flows to them.
Their fruit will serve for food and
their leaves for healing.[q]"

The Boundaries of the Land

13This is what the Sovereign
LORD says: "These are the boundaries[r] by which you are to divide
the land for an inheritance among
the twelve tribes of Israel, with two
portions for Joseph.[s] **14**You are to
divide it equally among them. Because I swore with uplifted hand to
give it to your forefathers, this land
will become your inheritance.[t]

15"This is to be the boundary of
the land:

"On the north side it will run
from the Great Sea by the
Hethlon road[u] past Lebo[s]
Hamath to Zedad, **16**Berothah[t][v] and Sibraim (which
lies on the border between
Damascus and Hamath),[w] as
far as Hazer Hatticon, which
is on the border of Hauran.
17The boundary will extend
from the sea to Hazar Enan,[u]
along the northern border of
Damascus, with the border of
Hamath to the north. This
will be the north boundary.[x]
18"On the east side the boundary
will run between Hauran and
Damascus, along the Jordan
between Gilead and the land
of Israel, to the eastern sea

47:1 [a]Isa 55:1 [b]Ps 46:4; Joel 3:18; Rev 22:1
47:3 [c]Eze 40:3
47:5 [d]Isa 11:9; Hab 2:14
47:7 [e]ver 12; Rev 22:2
47:8 [f]Dt 3:17; Jos 3:16 [g]Isa 41:18
47:9 [h]Isa 12:3; 55:1; Jn 4:14; 7:37-38
47:10 [i]Mt 4:19 [j]Jos 15:62 [k]Eze 26:5 [l]Ps 104:25; Mt 13:47 [m]Nu 34:6
47:11 [n]Dt 29:23
47:12 [o]ver 7; Rev 22:2 [p]Ps 1:3 [q]Ge 2:9; Jer 17:8
47:13 [r]Nu 34:2-12 [s]Ge 48:5
47:14 [t]Ge 12:7; Dt 1:8; Eze 20:5-6
47:15 [u]Eze 48:1
47:16 [v]2Sa 8:8 [w]Nu 13:21; Eze 48:1
47:17 [x]Eze 48:1

[o]3 That is, about 1,500 feet (about 450 meters) [p]8 Or *the Jordan Valley* [q]8 That is, the Dead Sea [r]10 That is, the Mediterranean; also in verses 15, 19 and 20 [s]15 Or *past the entrance to* [t]15,16 See Septuagint and Ezekiel 48:1; Hebrew *road to go into Zedad, 16Hamath, Berothah* [u]17 Hebrew *Enon,* a variant of *Enan*

and as far as Tamar.[v] This
will be the east boundary.
19"On the south side it will run
from Tamar as far as the waters of Meribah Kadesh,[a]
then along the Wadi ⌞of
Egypt⌟,[b] to the Great Sea.[c]
This will be the south boundary.
20"On the west side, the Great
Sea will be the boundary to a
point opposite Lebo[w] Hamath.[d] This will be the west
boundary.[e]

21"You are to distribute this land
among yourselves according to the
tribes of Israel. 22You are to allot it
as an inheritance for yourselves
and for the aliens[f] who have settled among you and who have children. You are to consider them as
native-born Israelites; along with
you they are to be allotted an inheritance among the tribes of Israel.[g]
23In whatever tribe the alien settles, there you are to give him his
inheritance," declares the Sovereign LORD.

The Division of the Land

48 "These are the tribes, listed
by name: At the northern
frontier, Dan[h] will have one portion; it will follow the Hethlon
road[i] to Lebo[x] Hamath;[j] Hazar
Enan and the northern border of
Damascus next to Hamath will be
part of its border from the east side
to the west side.
2"Asher[k] will have one portion;
it will border the territory of Dan
from east to west.
3"Naphtali[l] will have one portion; it will border the territory of
Asher from east to west.
4"Manasseh[m] will have one portion; it will border the territory of
Naphtali from east to west.
5"Ephraim[n] will have one portion; it will border the territory of
Manasseh[o] from east to west.[p]
6"Reuben[q] will have one portion; it will border the territory of
Ephraim from east to west.
7"Judah[r] will have one portion;
it will border the territory of Reuben from east to west.
8"Bordering the territory of Judah from east to west will be the
portion you are to present as a special gift. It will be 25,000 cubits[y]
wide, and its length from east to
west will equal one of the tribal
portions; the sanctuary will be in
the center of it.[s]
9"The special portion you are to
offer to the LORD will be 25,000 cubits long and 10,000 cubits[z]
wide.[t] 10This will be the sacred
portion for the priests. It will be
25,000 cubits long on the north
side, 10,000 cubits wide on the
west side, 10,000 cubits wide on
the east side and 25,000 cubits
long on the south side. In the center of it will be the sanctuary of the
LORD.[u] 11This will be for the consecrated priests, the Zadokites,[v]
who were faithful in serving me[w]
and did not go astray as the Levites
did when the Israelites went
astray.[x] 12It will be a special gift to
them from the sacred portion of
the land, a most holy portion, bordering the territory of the Levites.
13"Alongside the territory of the
priests, the Levites will have an allotment 25,000 cubits long and
10,000 cubits wide. Its total length
will be 25,000 cubits and its width
10,000 cubits.[y] 14They must not
sell or exchange any of it. This is
the best of the land and must not
pass into other hands, because it is
holy to the LORD.[z]
15"The remaining area, 5,000
cubits wide and 25,000 cubits
long, will be for the common use of
the city, for houses and for pastureland. The city will be in the center
of it 16and will have these measurements: the north side 4,500 cubits,
the south side 4,500 cubits, the
east side 4,500 cubits, and the
west side 4,500 cubits.[a] 17The
pastureland for the city will be 250

47:19 [a]Dt 32:51 [b]Isa 27:12 [c]Eze 48:28
47:20 [d]Eze 48:1 [e]Nu 34:6
47:22 [f]Isa 14:1 [g]Nu 26:55-56; Isa 56:6-7; Ro 10:12; Eph 2:12-16; 3:6; Col 3:11
48:1 [h]Ge 30:6 [i]Eze 47:15-17 [j]Eze 47:20
48:2 [k]Jos 19:24-31
48:3 [l]Jos 19:32-39
48:4 [m]Jos 17:1-11
48:5 [n]Jos 16:5-9 [o]Jos 17:7-10 [p]Jos 17:17
48:6 [q]Jos 13:15-21
48:7 [r]Jos 15:1-63
48:8 [s]ver 21
48:9 [t]Eze 45:1
48:10 [u]ver 21; Eze 45:3-4
48:11 [v]2Sa 8:17 [w]Lev 8:35 [x]Eze 14:11; 44:15
48:13 [y]Eze 45:5
48:14 [z]Lev 25:34; 27:10,28
48:16 [a]Rev 21:16

[v]*18* Septuagint and Syriac; Hebrew *Israel. You will measure to the eastern sea* [w]*20* Or *opposite the entrance to* [x]*1* Or *to the entrance to* [y]*8* That is, about 7 miles (about 12 kilometers) [z]*9* That is, about 3 miles (about 5 kilometers)

cubits on the north, 250 cubits on
the south, 250 cubits on the east,
and 250 cubits on the west. **18**What
remains of the area, bordering on
the sacred portion and running the
length of it, will be 10,000 cubits
on the east side and 10,000 cubits
on the west side. Its produce will
supply food for the workers of the
city.[a] **19**The workers from the city
who farm it will come from all the
tribes of Israel. **20**The entire portion will be a square, 25,000 cubits
on each side. As a special gift you
will set aside the sacred portion,
along with the property of the city.
21"What remains on both sides
of the area formed by the sacred
portion and the city property will
belong to the prince. It will extend
eastward from the 25,000 cubits of
the sacred portion to the eastern
border, and westward from the 25,-
000 cubits to the western border.
Both these areas running the
length of the tribal portions will belong to the prince, and the sacred
portion with the temple sanctuary
will be in the center of them.[b] **22**So
the property of the Levites and the
property of the city will lie in the
center of the area that belongs to
the prince. The area belonging to
the prince will lie between the border of Judah and the border of Benjamin.
23"As for the rest of the tribes:
Benjamin[c] will have one portion;
it will extend from the east side to
the west side.
24"Simeon[d] will have one portion; it will border the territory of
Benjamin from east to west.
25"Issachar[e] will have one portion; it will border the territory of
Simeon from east to west.
26"Zebulun[f] will have one portion; it will border the territory of
Issachar from east to west.
27"Gad[g] will have one portion; it
will border the territory of Zebulun
from east to west.
28"The southern boundary of
Gad will run south from Tamar[h] to
the waters of Meribah Kadesh,
then along the Wadi ⌞of Egypt⌟ to
the Great Sea.[a][i]
29"This is the land you are to allot as an inheritance to the tribes of
Israel, and these will be their portions," declares the Sovereign
LORD.

The Gates of the City

30"These will be the exits of the
city: Beginning on the north side,
which is 4,500 cubits long, **31**the
gates of the city will be named after
the tribes of Israel. The three gates
on the north side will be the gate of
Reuben, the gate of Judah and the
gate of Levi.
32"On the east side, which is
4,500 cubits long, will be three
gates: the gate of Joseph, the gate
of Benjamin and the gate of Dan.
33"On the south side, which
measures 4,500 cubits, will be
three gates: the gate of Simeon, the
gate of Issachar and the gate of
Zebulun.
34"On the west side, which is
4,500 cubits long, will be three
gates: the gate of Gad, the gate of
Asher and the gate of Naphtali.
35"The distance all around will
be 18,000 cubits.
"And the name of the city from
that time on will be:

THE LORD IS THERE.[j]"

48:18 [a]Eze 45:6
48:21 [b]ver 8,10; Eze 45:7
48:23 [c]Jos 18:11-28
48:24 [d]Ge 29:33; Jos 19:1-9
48:25 [e]Jos 19:17-23
48:26 [f]Jos 19:10-16
48:27 [g]Jos 13:24-28
48:28 [h]Ge 14:7 [i]Eze 47:19
48:35 [j]Isa 12:6; 24:23; Jer 3:17; 14:9; Jer 33:16; Joel 3:21; Zec 2:10; Rev 21:3

[a]*28* That is, the Mediterranean

Daniel

Title and Background

Daniel records events that took place during Israel's captivity and encourages the people to trust in the God who controls all history.

Author and Date of Writing

In several passages, such as 9:2 and 10:2, the book itself mentions Daniel as the author. Jesus himself referred to Daniel as the author (Mt 24:15). Objective evidence indicates that the book was written about 530 B.C., shortly after the capture of Babylon by Cyrus in 539.

Theme and Message

The theological theme of the book is God's sovereignty: "The Most High God is sovereign over the kingdoms of men" (5:21). Daniel's visions always show God as triumphant. The climax of his sovereignty is described in Revelation 11:15 (compare Da 2:44; 7:27).

Outline

I. Introduction: The Setting (1:1-21)
II. The Destinies of the Nations (2:1-7:28)
  A. Nebuchadnezzar's Dreams (2:1-4:37)
  B. Belshazzar's and Babylon's Downfall (5:1-31)
  C. Daniel's Deliverance and Dream (6:1-7:28)
III. The Destiny of Israel (8:1-12:13)
  A. Daniel's Vision of a Ram and a Goat (8:1-27)
  B. Daniel's Prayer and the Seventy "Sevens" (9:1-27)
  C. Daniel's Vision of Israel's Future (10:1-12:13)

Daniel's Training in Babylon

1 In the third year of the reign of
Jehoiakim king of Judah, Nebuchadnezzar[a] king of Babylon
came to Jerusalem and besieged
it.[b] 2 And the Lord delivered Jehoiakim king of Judah into his hand,
along with some of the articles
from the temple of God. These he
carried off to the temple of his god
in Babylonia[a] and put in the treasure house of his god.[c]
3 Then the king ordered Ashpe-
naz, chief of his court officials, to
bring in some of the Israelites from
the royal family and the nobility[d]— 4 young men without any
physical defect, handsome, showing aptitude for every kind of learning, well informed, quick to understand, and qualified to serve in the
king's palace. He was to teach
them the language and literature of
the Babylonians.[b] 5 The king assigned them a daily amount of food
and wine[e] from the king's table.
They were to be trained for three
years, and after that they were to
enter the king's service.[f]
6 Among these were some from
Judah: Daniel,[g] Hananiah, Mishael and Azariah. 7 The chief official
gave them new names: to Daniel,
the name Belteshazzar;[h] to Hananiah, Shadrach; to Mishael, Meshach; and to Azariah, Abednego.[i]
8 But Daniel resolved not to defile[j] himself with the royal food

1:1 [a] 2Ki 24:1 [b] 2Ch 36:6
1:2 [c] 2Ch 36:7; Jer 27:19-20; Zec 5:5-11
1:3 [d] 2Ki 20:18; 24:15; Isa 39:7
1:5 [e] ver 8,10 [f] ver 19
1:6 [g] Eze 14:14
1:7 [h] Da 4:8; 5:12 [i] Da 2:49; 3:12
1:8 [j] Eze 4:13-14

a2 Hebrew *Shinar* b4 Or *Chaldeans*

and wine, and he asked the chief official for permission not to defile himself this way. **9**Now God had caused the official to show favor[a] and sympathy[b] to Daniel, **10**but the official told Daniel, "I am afraid of my lord the king, who has assigned your[c] food and drink. Why should he see you looking worse than the other young men your age? The king would then have my head because of you."

11Daniel then said to the guard whom the chief official had appointed over Daniel, Hananiah, Mishael and Azariah, **12**"Please test your servants for ten days: Give us nothing but vegetables to eat and water to drink. **13**Then compare our appearance with that of the young men who eat the royal food, and treat your servants in accordance with what you see." **14**So he agreed to this and tested them for ten days.

15At the end of the ten days they looked healthier and better nourished than any of the young men who ate the royal food.[c] **16**So the guard took away their choice food and the wine they were to drink and gave them vegetables instead.[d]

17To these four young men God gave knowledge and understanding[e] of all kinds of literature and learning.[f] And Daniel could understand visions and dreams of all kinds.[g]

18At the end of the time[h] set by the king to bring them in, the chief official presented them to Nebuchadnezzar. **19**The king talked with them, and he found none equal to Daniel, Hananiah, Mishael and Azariah; so they entered the king's service.[i] **20**In every matter of wisdom and understanding about which the king questioned them, he found them ten times better than all the magicians and enchanters in his whole kingdom.[j]

21And Daniel remained there until the first year of King Cyrus.[k]

1:9 [a]Ge 39:21; Pr 16:7 [b]1Ki 8:50; Ps 106:46
1:15 [c]Ex 23:25
1:16 [d]ver 12-13
1:17 [e]1Ki 3:12 [f]Da 2:23; Jas 1:5 [g]Da 2:19,30; 7:1; 8:1
1:18 [h]ver 5
1:19 [i]Ge 41:46
1:20 [j]1Ki 4:30; Da 2:13,28
1:21 [k]Da 6:28; 10:1
2:1 [l]Job 33:15,18; Da 4:5 [m]Ge 41:8 [n]Est 6:1; Da 6:18
2:2 [o]Ge 41:8 [p]Ex 7:11 [q]ver 10; Da 5:7 [r]Da 4:6
2:3 [s]Da 4:5
2:4 [t]Ezr 4:7 [u]Da 3:9; 5:10
2:5 [v]ver 12 [w]Ezr 6:11; Da 3:29
2:6 [x]ver 48; Da 5:7,16
2:9 [y]Est 4:11 [z]Isa 41:22-24
2:10 [a]ver 27
2:11 [b]Da 5:11

Nebuchadnezzar's Dream

2 In the second year of his reign, Nebuchadnezzar had dreams;[l] his mind was troubled[m] and he could not sleep.[n] **2**So the king summoned the magicians,[o] enchanters, sorcerers[p] and astrologers[d][q] to tell him what he had dreamed.[r] When they came in and stood before the king, **3**he said to them, "I have had a dream that troubles[s] me and I want to know what it means.[e]"

4Then the astrologers answered the king in Aramaic,[f][t] "O king, live forever![u] Tell your servants the dream, and we will interpret it."

5The king replied to the astrologers, "This is what I have firmly decided: If you do not tell me what my dream was and interpret it, I will have you cut into pieces[v] and your houses turned into piles of rubble.[w] **6**But if you tell me the dream and explain it, you will receive from me gifts and rewards and great honor.[x] So tell me the dream and interpret it for me."

7Once more they replied, "Let the king tell his servants the dream, and we will interpret it."

8Then the king answered, "I am certain that you are trying to gain time, because you realize that this is what I have firmly decided: **9**If you do not tell me the dream, there is just one penalty[y] for you. You have conspired to tell me misleading and wicked things, hoping the situation will change. So then, tell me the dream, and I will know that you can interpret it for me."[z]

10The astrologers answered the king, "There is not a man on earth who can do what the king asks! No king, however great and mighty, has ever asked such a thing of any magician or enchanter or astrologer.[a] **11**What the king asks is too difficult. No one can reveal it to the king except the gods,[b] and they do not live among men."

c*10* The Hebrew for *your* and *you* in this verse is plural. d*2* Or *Chaldeans*; also in verses 4, 5 and 10 e*3* Or *was* f*4* The text from here through chapter 7 is in Aramaic.

12This made the king so angry and furious[a] that he ordered the execution[b] of all the wise men of Babylon. 13So the decree was issued to put the wise men to death, and men were sent to look for Daniel and his friends to put them to death.[c]

14When Arioch, the commander of the king's guard, had gone out to put to death the wise men of Babylon, Daniel spoke to him with wisdom and tact. 15He asked the king's officer, "Why did the king issue such a harsh decree?" Arioch then explained the matter to Daniel. 16At this, Daniel went in to the king and asked for time, so that he might interpret the dream for him.

17Then Daniel returned to his house and explained the matter to his friends Hananiah, Mishael and Azariah.[d] 18He urged them to plead for mercy[e] from the God of heaven concerning this mystery,[f] so that he and his friends might not be executed with the rest of the wise men of Babylon. 19During the night the mystery[g] was revealed to Daniel in a vision.[h] Then Daniel praised the God of heaven 20and said:

"Praise be to the name of God
  for ever and ever;[i]
 wisdom and power[j] are his.
21He changes times and
  seasons;[k]
 he sets up kings and
  deposes[l] them.
He gives wisdom[m] to the wise
 and knowledge to the
  discerning.
22He reveals deep and hidden
  things;[n]
 he knows what lies in
  darkness,[o]
 and light[p] dwells with him.
23I thank and praise you, O God
  of my fathers:[q]
 You have given me wisdom[r]
  and power,
you have made known to me
  what we asked of you,
 you have made known to us
  the dream of the king."

Daniel Interprets the Dream

24Then Daniel went to Arioch,[s] whom the king had appointed to execute the wise men of Babylon, and said to him, "Do not execute the wise men of Babylon. Take me to the king, and I will interpret his dream for him."

25Arioch took Daniel to the king at once and said, "I have found a man among the exiles from Judah[t] who can tell the king what his dream means."

26The king asked Daniel (also called Belteshazzar),[u] "Are you able to tell me what I saw in my dream and interpret it?"

27Daniel replied, "No wise man, enchanter, magician or diviner can explain to the king the mystery he has asked about,[v] 28but there is a God in heaven who reveals mysteries.[w] He has shown King Nebuchadnezzar what will happen in days to come.[x] Your dream and the visions that passed through your mind[y] as you lay on your bed are these:

29"As you were lying there, O king, your mind turned to things to come, and the revealer of mysteries showed you what is going to happen. 30As for me, this mystery has been revealed[z] to me, not because I have greater wisdom than other living men, but so that you, O king, may know the interpretation and that you may understand what went through your mind.

31"You looked, O king, and there before you stood a large statue—an enormous, dazzling statue,[a] awesome in appearance. 32The head of the statue was made of pure gold, its chest and arms of silver, its belly and thighs of bronze, 33its legs of iron, its feet partly of iron and partly of baked clay. 34While you were watching, a rock was cut out, but not by human hands.[b] It struck the statue on its feet of iron and clay and smashed them.[c] 35Then the iron, the clay, the bronze, the silver and the gold were broken to pieces at the same time and became like chaff on a threshing floor in the

2:12 [a]Da 3:13,19 [b]ver 5
2:13 [c]Da 1:20
2:17 [d]Da 1:6
2:18 [e]Isa 37:4 [f]Jer 33:3
2:19 [g]ver 28 [h]Job 33:15; Da 1:17
2:20 [i]Ps 113:2; 145:1-2 [j]Jer 32:19
2:21 [k]Da 7:25 [l]Job 12:19; Ps 75:6-7 [m]Jas 1:5
2:22 [n]Job 12:22; Ps 25:14; Da 5:11 [o]Ps 139:11-12; Jer 23:24; Heb 4:13 [p]Isa 45:7; Jas 1:17
2:23 [q]Ex 3:15 [r]Da 1:17
2:24 [s]ver 14
2:25 [t]Da 1:6; 5:13; 6:13
2:26 [u]Da 1:7
2:27 [v]ver 10
2:28 [w]Ge 40:8; Am 4:13 [x]Ge 49:1; Da 10:14 [y]Da 4:5
2:30 [z]Isa 45:3; Da 1:17; Am 4:13
2:31 [a]Hab 1:7
2:34 [b]Zec 4:6 [c]ver 44-45; Ps 2:9; Isa 60:12; Da 8:25

summer. The wind swept them away[a] without leaving a trace. But the rock that struck the statue became a huge mountain[b] and filled the whole earth.

36“This was the dream, and now we will interpret it to the king. 37You, O king, are the king of kings.[c] The God of heaven has given you dominion[d] and power and might and glory; 38in your hands he has placed mankind and the beasts of the field and the birds of the air. Wherever they live, he has made you ruler over them all.[e] You are that head of gold.

39“After you, another kingdom will rise, inferior to yours. Next, a third kingdom, one of bronze, will rule over the whole earth. 40Finally, there will be a fourth kingdom, strong as iron—for iron breaks and smashes everything—and as iron breaks things to pieces, so it will crush and break all the others.[f] 41Just as you saw that the feet and toes were partly of baked clay and partly of iron, so this will be a divided kingdom; yet it will have some of the strength of iron in it, even as you saw iron mixed with clay. 42As the toes were partly iron and partly clay, so this kingdom will be partly strong and partly brittle. 43And just as you saw the iron mixed with baked clay, so the people will be a mixture and will not remain united, any more than iron mixes with clay.

44“In the time of those kings, the God of heaven will set up a kingdom that will never be destroyed, nor will it be left to another people. It will crush[g] all those kingdoms[h] and bring them to an end, but it will itself endure forever.[i] 45This is the meaning of the vision of the rock[j] cut out of a mountain, but not by human hands[k]—a rock that broke the iron, the bronze, the clay, the silver and the gold to pieces.

“The great God has shown the king what will take place in the future. The dream is true and the interpretation is trustworthy.”

46Then King Nebuchadnezzar fell prostrate[l] before Daniel and paid him honor and ordered that an offering[m] and incense be presented to him. 47The king said to Daniel, “Surely your God is the God of gods[n] and the Lord of kings[o] and a revealer of mysteries,[p] for you were able to reveal this mystery.”

48Then the king placed Daniel in a high position and lavished many gifts on him. He made him ruler over the entire province of Babylon and placed him in charge of all its wise men.[q] 49Moreover, at Daniel's request the king appointed Shadrach, Meshach and Abednego administrators over the province of Babylon,[r] while Daniel himself remained at the royal court.

The Image of Gold and the Fiery Furnace

3 King Nebuchadnezzar made an image[s] of gold, ninety feet high and nine feet[g] wide, and set it up on the plain of Dura in the province of Babylon. 2He then summoned the satraps, prefects, governors, advisers, treasurers, judges, magistrates and all the other provincial officials[t] to come to the dedication of the image he had set up. 3So the satraps, prefects, governors, advisers, treasurers, judges, magistrates and all the other provincial officials assembled for the dedication of the image that King Nebuchadnezzar had set up, and they stood before it.

4Then the herald loudly proclaimed, “This is what you are commanded to do, O peoples, nations and men of every language:[u] 5As soon as you hear the sound of the horn, flute, zither, lyre, harp, pipes and all kinds of music, you must fall down and worship the image of gold that King Nebuchadnezzar has set up.[v] 6Whoever does not fall down and worship will immediately be thrown into a blazing furnace.”[w]

7Therefore, as soon as they heard the sound of the horn, flute,

2:35 [a] Ps 1:4; 37:10; Isa 17:13 [b] Isa 2:3, Mic 4:1
2:37 [c] Eze 26:7 [d] Jer 27:7
2:38 [e] Jer 27:6; Da 4:21-22
2:40 [f] Da 7:7,23
2:44 [g] Ps 2:9; 1Co 15:24 [h] Isa 60:12 [i] Ps 145:13; Isa 9:7; Da 4:34; 6:26; 7:14,27; Mic 4:7,13; Lk 1:33
2:45 [j] Isa 28:16 [k] Da 8:25
2:46 [l] Da 8:17; Ac 10:25 [m] Ac 14:13
2:47 [n] Da 11:36 [o] Da 4:25 [p] ver 22,28
2:48 [q] ver 6; Da 4:9; 5:11
2:49 [r] Da 1:7
3:1 [s] Isa 46:6; Jer 16:20; Hab 2:19
3:2 [t] ver 27; Da 6:7
3:4 [u] Da 4:1; 6:25
3:5 [v] ver 10,15
3:6 [w] ver 11,15, 21; Jer 29:22; Da 6:7; Mt 13:42,50; Rev 13:15

[g]1 Aramaic *sixty cubits high and six cubits wide* (about 27 meters high and 2.7 meters wide)

zither, lyre, harp and all kinds of music, all the peoples, nations and men of every language fell down and worshiped the image of gold that King Nebuchadnezzar had set up.[a]

8At this time some astrologers[h][b] came forward and denounced the Jews. **9**They said to King Nebuchadnezzar, "O king, live forever![c] **10**You have issued a decree,[d] O king, that everyone who hears the sound of the horn, flute, zither, lyre, harp, pipes and all kinds of music must fall down and worship the image of gold,[e] **11**and that whoever does not fall down and worship will be thrown into a blazing furnace. **12**But there are some Jews whom you have set over the affairs of the province of Babylon—Shadrach, Meshach and Abednego[f]—who pay no attention[g] to you, O king. They neither serve your gods nor worship the image of gold you have set up."[h]

13Furious[i] with rage, Nebuchadnezzar summoned Shadrach, Meshach and Abednego. So these men were brought before the king, **14**and Nebuchadnezzar said to them, "Is it true, Shadrach, Meshach and Abednego, that you do not serve my gods[j] or worship the image[k] of gold I have set up? **15**Now when you hear the sound of the horn, flute, zither, lyre, harp, pipes and all kinds of music, if you are ready to fall down and worship the image I made, very good. But if you do not worship it, you will be thrown immediately into a blazing furnace. Then what god[l] will be able to rescue[m] you from my hand?"

16Shadrach, Meshach and Abednego[n] replied to the king, "O Nebuchadnezzar, we do not need to defend ourselves before you in this matter. **17**If we are thrown into the blazing furnace, the God we serve is able to save[o] us from it, and he will rescue[p] us from your hand, O king. **18**But even if he does not, we want you to know, O king, that we will not serve your gods or worship the image of gold you have set up.[q]"

19Then Nebuchadnezzar was furious with Shadrach, Meshach and Abednego, and his attitude toward them changed. He ordered the furnace heated seven[r] times hotter than usual **20**and commanded some of the strongest soldiers in his army to tie up Shadrach, Meshach and Abednego and throw them into the blazing furnace. **21**So these men, wearing their robes, trousers, turbans and other clothes, were bound and thrown into the blazing furnace. **22**The king's command was so urgent and the furnace so hot that the flames of the fire killed the soldiers who took up Shadrach, Meshach and Abednego,[s] **23**and these three men, firmly tied, fell into the blazing furnace.

24Then King Nebuchadnezzar leaped to his feet in amazement and asked his advisers, "Weren't there three men that we tied up and threw into the fire?"

They replied, "Certainly, O king."

25He said, "Look! I see four men walking around in the fire, unbound and unharmed, and the fourth looks like a son of the gods."

26Nebuchadnezzar then approached the opening of the blazing furnace and shouted, "Shadrach, Meshach and Abednego, servants of the Most High God,[t] come out! Come here!"

So Shadrach, Meshach and Abednego came out of the fire, **27**and the satraps, prefects, governors and royal advisers[u] crowded around them.[v] They saw that the fire[w] had not harmed their bodies, nor was a hair of their heads singed; their robes were not scorched, and there was no smell of fire on them.

28Then Nebuchadnezzar said, "Praise be to the God of Shadrach, Meshach and Abednego, who has sent his angel[x] and rescued his servants! They trusted[y] in him and

3:7 [a]ver 5
3:8 [b]Da 2:10
3:9 [c]Ne 2:3; Da 5:10; 6:6
3:10 [d]Da 6:12 [e]ver 4-6
3:12 [f]Da 2:49 [g]Da 6:13 [h]Est 3:3
3:13 [i]Da 2:12
3:14 [j]Isa 46:1; Jer 50:2 [k]ver 1
3:15 [l]Isa 36:18-20 [m]Ex 5:2; 2Ch 32:15
3:16 [n]Da 1:7
3:17 [o]Ps 27:1-2 [p]Job 5:19; Jer 1:8
3:18 [q]ver 28; Jos 24:15
3:19 [r]Lev 26:18-28
3:22 [s]Da 1:7
3:26 [t]Da 4:2,34
3:27 [u]ver 2 [v]Isa 43:2; Heb 11:32-34 [w]Da 6:23
3:28 [x]Ps 34:7; Da 6:22; Ac 5:19 [y]Job 13:15; Ps 26:1; 84:12; Jer 17:7

[h]8 Or *Chaldeans*

defied the king's command and
were willing to give up their lives
rather than serve or worship any
god except their own God.[a]
29Therefore I decree[b] that the people of any nation or language who
say anything against the God of
Shadrach, Meshach and Abednego
be cut into pieces and their houses
be turned into piles of rubble,[c] for
no other god can save[d] in this
way."
30Then the king promoted Shadrach, Meshach and Abednego in
the province of Babylon.[e]

Nebuchadnezzar's Dream of a Tree

4 King Nebuchadnezzar,
To the peoples, nations
and men of every language,[f]
who live in all the world:

May you prosper greatly![g]

2It is my pleasure to tell you
about the miraculous signs[h]
and wonders that the Most
High God[i] has performed for
me.

3How great are his signs,
how mighty his wonders![j]
His kingdom is an eternal kingdom;
his dominion endures[k]
from generation to generation.

4I, Nebuchadnezzar, was at
home in my palace, contented[l] and prosperous. 5I had a
dream[m] that made me afraid.
As I was lying in my bed, the
images and visions that
passed through my mind[n] terrified me. 6So I commanded
that all the wise men of Babylon be brought before me to
interpret[o] the dream for me.
7When the magicians,[p] enchanters, astrologers[i] and diviners[q] came, I told them the
dream, but they could not interpret it for me.[r] 8Finally,
Daniel came into my presence
and I told him the dream. (He
is called Belteshazzar,[s] after
the name of my god, and the
spirit of the holy gods[t] is in
him.)
9I said, "Belteshazzar,
chief[u] of the magicians, I
know that the spirit of the holy
gods[v] is in you, and no mystery is too difficult for you.
Here is my dream; interpret it
for me. 10These are the visions
I saw while lying in my bed:[w]
I looked, and there before me
stood a tree in the middle of
the land. Its height was enormous.[x] 11The tree grew large
and strong and its top touched
the sky; it was visible to the
ends of the earth. 12Its leaves
were beautiful, its fruit abundant, and on it was food for all.
Under it the beasts of the field
found shelter, and the birds of
the air lived in its branches;[y]
from it every creature was fed.
13"In the visions I saw while
lying in my bed,[z] I looked,
and there before me was a
messenger,[j] a holy one,[a]
coming down from heaven.
14He called in a loud voice:
'Cut down the tree and trim off
its branches; strip off its leaves
and scatter its fruit. Let the
animals flee from under it and
the birds from its branches.[b]
15But let the stump and its
roots, bound with iron and
bronze, remain in the ground,
in the grass of the field.
" 'Let him be drenched with
the dew of heaven, and let him
live with the animals among
the plants of the earth. 16Let
his mind be changed from that
of a man and let him be given
the mind of an animal, till sev-
en times[k] pass by for him.[c]
17" 'The decision is an-
nounced by messengers, the
holy ones declare the verdict,
so that the living may know
that the Most High[d] is sover-

3:28 [a]ver 18
3:29 [b]Da 6:26 [c]Ezr 6:11 [d]Da 6:27
3:30 [e]Da 2:49
4:1 [f]Da 3:4 [g]Da 6:25
4:2 [h]Ps 74:9 [i]Da 3:26
4:3 [j]Ps 105:27; Da 6:27 [k]Da 2:44
4:4 [l]Ps 30:6
4:5 [m]Da 2:1 [n]Da 2:28
4:6 [o]Da 2:2
4:7 [p]Ge 41:8 [q]Isa 44:25; Da 2:2 [r]Da 2:10
4:8 [s]Da 1:7 [t]Da 5:11,14
4:9 [u]Da 2:48 [v]Da 5:11-12
4:10 [w]ver 5 [x]Eze 31:3-4
4:12 [y]Eze 17:23; Mt 13:32
4:13 [z]Da 7:1 [a]ver 23; Dt 33:2; Da 8:13
4:14 [b]Eze 31:12; Mt 3:10
4:16 [c]ver 23,32
4:17 [d]ver 2,25; Ps 83:18

[i]7 Or *Chaldeans* [j]13 Or *watchman*; also in verses 17 and 23 [k]16 Or *years*; also in verses 23, 25 and 32

eign[a] over the kingdoms of men and gives them to anyone he wishes and sets over them the lowliest[b] of men.'

18"This is the dream that I, King Nebuchadnezzar, had. Now, Belteshazzar, tell me what it means, for none of the wise men in my kingdom can interpret it for me.[c] But you can,[d] because the spirit of the holy gods is in you."[e]

Daniel Interprets the Dream

19Then Daniel (also called Belteshazzar) was greatly perplexed for a time, and his thoughts terrified[f] him. So the king said, "Belteshazzar, do not let the dream or its meaning alarm you."

Belteshazzar answered, "My lord, if only the dream applied to your enemies and its meaning to your adversaries! **20**The tree you saw, which grew large and strong, with its top touching the sky, visible to the whole earth, **21**with beautiful leaves and abundant fruit, providing food for all, giving shelter to the beasts of the field, and having nesting places in its branches for the birds of the air— **22**you, O king, are that tree![g] You have become great and strong; your greatness has grown until it reaches the sky, and your dominion extends to distant parts of the earth.[h]

23"You, O king, saw a messenger, a holy one,[i] coming down from heaven and saying, 'Cut down the tree and destroy it, but leave the stump, bound with iron and bronze, in the grass of the field, while its roots remain in the ground. Let him be drenched with the dew of heaven; let him live like the wild animals, until seven times pass by for him.'[j]

24"This is the interpretation, O king, and this is the decree[k] the Most High has issued against my lord the king: **25**You will be driven away from people and will live with the wild animals; you will eat grass like cattle and be drenched with the dew of heaven. Seven times will pass by for you until you acknowledge that the Most High[l] is sovereign over the kingdoms of men and gives them to anyone he wishes.[m] **26**The command to leave the stump of the tree with its roots[n] means that your kingdom will be restored to you when you acknowledge that Heaven rules.[o] **27**Therefore, O king, be pleased to accept my advice: Renounce your sins by doing what is right, and your wickedness by being kind to the oppressed.[p] It may be that then your prosperity will continue.[q]"

The Dream Is Fulfilled

28All this happened[r] to King Nebuchadnezzar. **29**Twelve months later, as the king was walking on the roof of the royal palace of Babylon, **30**he said, "Is not this the great Babylon I have built as the royal residence, by my mighty power and for the glory of my majesty?"[s]

31The words were still on his lips when a voice came from heaven, "This is what is decreed for you, King Nebuchadnezzar: Your royal authority has been taken from you. **32**You will be driven away from people and will live with the wild animals; you will eat grass like cattle. Seven times will pass by for you until you acknowledge that the Most High is sovereign over the kingdoms of men and gives them to anyone he wishes."

33Immediately what had been said about Nebuchadnezzar was fulfilled. He was driven away from people and

4:17 [a] Jer 27:5-7; Da 2:21; 5:18-21 [b] Da 11:21
4:18 [c] Ge 41:8; Da 5:8,15 [d] Ge 41:15 [e] ver 7-9
4:19 [f] Da 7:15,28; 8:27; 10:16-17
4:22 [g] 2Sa 12:7 [h] Jer 27:7; Da 2:37-38; 5:18-19
4:23 [i] ver 13 [j] Da 5:21
4:24 [k] Job 40:12; Ps 107:40
4:25 [l] ver 17; Ps 83:18 [m] Jer 27:5; Da 5:21
4:26 [n] ver 15 [o] Da 2:37
4:27 [p] Isa 55:6-7 [q] 1Ki 21:29; Ps 41:3; Eze 18:22
4:28 [r] Nu 23:19
4:30 [s] Isa 37:24-25; Da 5:20; Hab 2:4

THE NEO-BABYLONIAN EMPIRE 626-539 B.C.

MEDIAN EMPIRE

Caspian Sea

Khorsabad

Tigris R.

ASSYRIA

Carchemish

Haran

Nineveh

Euphrates R.

Babylon boasted one of the world's seven wonders, the famed Hanging Gardens, as well as a staged temple-tower 295 feet high and, according to Herodotus, several colossal gold statues weighing many tons.

Hamath

Route of Judahite Exiles

ARAM

Great Sea

Sidon

Tyre

Damascus

Arabian Desert

Tigris R.

ELAM

Susa

Babylon

Nippur

Jerusalem

BABYLONIA

Ur

Euphrates R.

Lower Sea

Miles 0 100 200 300

Kms 0 100 200 300 400 500

ate grass like cattle. His body was drenched with the dew of heaven until his hair grew like the feathers of an eagle and his nails like the claws of a bird.[a]

34At the end of that time, I, Nebuchadnezzar, raised my eyes toward heaven, and my sanity was restored. Then I praised the Most High; I honored and glorified him who lives forever.[b]

His dominion is an eternal
  dominion;
 his kingdom endures from
  generation to
  generation.[c]
35All the peoples of the earth
 are regarded as nothing.[d]
He does as he pleases[e]
 with the powers of heaven
 and the peoples of the earth.
No one can hold back his hand
 or say to him: "What have
  you done?"[f]

36At the same time that my sanity was restored, my honor and splendor were returned to me for the glory of my kingdom.[g] My advisers and nobles sought me out, and I was restored to my throne and became even greater than before. **37**Now I, Nebuchadnezzar, praise and exalt and glorify the King of heaven, because everything he does is right and all his ways are just.[h] And those who walk in pride he is able to humble.[i]

The Writing on the Wall

5 King Belshazzar gave a great banquet[j] for a thousand of his nobles and drank wine with them. **2**While Belshazzar was drinking his wine, he gave orders to bring in the gold and silver goblets[k] that Nebuchadnezzar his father[l] had taken from the temple in Jerusalem, so that the king and his nobles, his wives and his concubines might drink from them.[l] **3**So they brought in the gold goblets that had been taken from the temple of God in Jerusalem, and the king and his nobles, his wives and his concubines drank from them. **4**As they drank the wine, they praised the gods of gold and silver, of bronze, iron, wood and stone.[m]

5Suddenly the fingers of a human hand appeared and wrote on the plaster of the wall, near the lampstand in the royal palace. The king watched the hand as it wrote. **6**His face turned pale and he was so frightened[n] that his knees knocked together and his legs gave way.[o]

7The king called out for the enchanters, astrologers[m] and diviners[p] to be brought and said to these wise[q] men of Babylon, "Whoever reads this writing and tells me what it means will be clothed in purple and have a gold chain placed around his neck,[r] and he will be made the third highest ruler in the kingdom."[s]

8Then all the king's wise men came in, but they could not read the writing or tell the king what it meant.[t] **9**So King Belshazzar became even more terrified[u] and his face grew more pale. His nobles were baffled.

10The queen,[n] hearing the voices of the king and his nobles, came into the banquet hall. "O king, live forever!"[v] she said. "Don't be alarmed! Don't look so pale! **11**There is a man in your kingdom who has the spirit of the holy gods[w] in him. In the time of your father he was found to have insight and intelligence and wisdom[x] like that of the gods. King Nebuchadnezzar your father—your father the king, I say—appointed him chief of the magicians, enchanters, astrologers and diviners.[y] **12**This man Daniel, whom the king called Belteshazzar,[z] was found to have a keen mind and knowledge and understanding, and also the ability to interpret dreams, explain riddles

4:33 [a]Da 5:20-21
4:34 [b]Da 12:7; Rev 4:10 [c]Ps 145:13; Da 2:44; 5:21; 6:26; Lk 1:33
4:35 [d]Isa 40:17 [e]Ps 115:3; 135:6 [f]Isa 45:9; Ro 9:20
4:36 [g]Pr 22:4
4:37 [h]Dt 32:4; Ps 33:4-5 [i]Ex 18:11; Job 40:11-12; Da 5:20,23
5:1 [j]Est 1:3
5:2 [k]2Ki 24:13; Jer 52:19 [l]Est 1:7; Da 1:2
5:4 [m]Ps 135:15-18; Hab 2:19; Rev 9:20
5:6 [n]Da 4:5 [o]Eze 7:17
5:7 [p]Isa 44:25 [q]Da 4:6-7 [r]Ge 41:42 [s]Da 2:5-6,48; 6:2-3
5:8 [t]Da 2:10,27
5:9 [u]Isa 21:4
5:10 [v]Da 3:9
5:11 [w]Da 4:8-9,19 [x]ver 14; Da 1:17 [y]Da 2:47-48
5:12 [z]Da 1:7

[l]*2* Or *ancestor*; or *predecessor*; also in verses 11, 13 and 18 [m]*7* Or *Chaldeans*; also in verse 11 [n]*10* Or *queen mother*

and solve difficult problems.[a] Call
for Daniel, and he will tell you what
the writing means."
13So Daniel was brought before
the king, and the king said to him,
"Are you Daniel, one of the exiles
my father the king brought from
Judah?[b] 14I have heard that the
spirit of the gods is in you and that
you have insight, intelligence and
outstanding wisdom. 15The wise
men and enchanters were brought
before me to read this writing and
tell me what it means, but they
could not explain it. 16Now I have
heard that you are able to give interpretations and to solve difficult
problems. If you can read this writing and tell me what it means, you
will be clothed in purple and have
a gold chain placed around your
neck, and you will be made the
third highest ruler in the kingdom."
17Then Daniel answered the
king, "You may keep your gifts for
yourself and give your rewards to
someone else.[c] Nevertheless, I
will read the writing for the king
and tell him what it means.
18"O king, the Most High God
gave your father Nebuchadnezzar
sovereignty and greatness and glory and splendor.[d] 19Because of the
high position he gave him, all the
peoples and nations and men of every language dreaded and feared
him. Those the king wanted to put
to death, he put to death;[e] those
he wanted to spare, he spared;
those he wanted to promote, he
promoted; and those he wanted to
humble, he humbled. 20But when
his heart became arrogant and
hardened with pride,[f] he was deposed from his royal throne and
stripped[g] of his glory.[h] 21He was
driven away from people and given
the mind of an animal; he lived
with the wild donkeys and ate grass
like cattle; and his body was
drenched with the dew of heaven,
until he acknowledged that the
Most High God is sovereign[i] over
the kingdoms of men and sets over
them anyone he wishes.[j]
22"But you his son,[o] O Belshaz

5:12 [a]ver 14-16; Da 6:3
5:13 [b]Da 6:13
5:17 [c]2Ki 5:16
5:18 [d]Jer 27:7; Da 2:37-38
5:19 [e]Da 2:12-13; 3:6
5:20 [f]Da 4:30 [g]Jer 13:18 [h]Job 40:12; Isa 14:13-15
5:21 [i]Eze 17:24 [j]Da 4:16-17, 35
5:22 [k]Ex 10:3; 2Ch 33:23
5:23 [l]Jer 50:29 [m]Ps 115:4-8; Hab 2:19 [n]Job 12:10 [o]Job 31:4; Jer 10:23
5:26 [p]Jer 27:7 [q]Isa 13:6
5:27 [r]Ps 62:9
5:28 [s]Isa 13:17 [t]Da 6:28
5:30 [u]ver 1 [v]Isa 21:9; Jer 51:31
5:31 [w]Da 6:1; 9:1
6:1 [x]Da 5:31 [y]Est 1:1

zar, have not humbled[k] yourself,
though you knew all this. 23In-
stead, you have set yourself up
against[l] the Lord of heaven. You
had the goblets from his temple
brought to you, and you and your
nobles, your wives and your concubines drank wine from them. You
praised the gods of silver and gold,
of bronze, iron, wood and stone,
which cannot see or hear or understand.[m] But you did not honor the
God who holds in his hand your
life[n] and all your ways.[o] 24There-
fore he sent the hand that wrote
the inscription.
25"This is the inscription that
was written:

MENE, MENE, TEKEL, PARSIN[p]

26"This is what these words
mean:

Mene[q]: God has numbered the days[p] of your reign and brought it to an end.[q]
27*Tekel*[r]: You have been weighed on the scales and found wanting.[r]
28*Peres*[s]: Your kingdom is divided and given to the Medes[s] and Persians."[t]

29Then at Belshazzar's command, Daniel was clothed in purple, a gold chain was placed around
his neck, and he was proclaimed
the third highest ruler in the kingdom.
30That very night Belshazzar,[u]
king of the Babylonians,[t] was
slain,[v] 31and Darius[w] the Mede
took over the kingdom, at the age
of sixty-two.

Daniel in the Den of Lions

6 It pleased Darius[x] to appoint
120 satraps[y] to rule through-

[o]22 Or *descendant*; or *successor*
[p]25 Aramaic *UPARSIN* (that is, *AND PARSIN*)
[q]26 *Mene* can mean *numbered* or *mina* (a unit of money).
[r]27 *Tekel* can mean *weighed* or *shekel*.
[s]28 *Peres* (the singular of *Parsin*) can mean *divided* or *Persia* or *a half mina* or *a half shekel*.
[t]30 Or *Chaldeans*

out the kingdom, **2**with three administrators over them, one of whom was Daniel.[a] The satraps were made accountable[b] to them so that the king might not suffer loss. **3**Now Daniel so distinguished himself among the administrators and the satraps by his exceptional qualities that the king planned to set him over the whole kingdom.[c] **4**At this, the administrators and the satraps tried to find grounds for charges against Daniel in his conduct of government affairs, but they were unable to do so. They could find no corruption in him, because he was trustworthy and neither corrupt nor negligent. **5**Finally these men said, "We will never find any basis for charges against this man Daniel unless it has something to do with the law of his God."[d]

6So the administrators and the satraps went as a group to the king and said: "O King Darius, live forever![e] **7**The royal administrators, prefects, satraps, advisers and governors[f] have all agreed that the king should issue an edict and enforce the decree that anyone who prays to any god or man during the next thirty days, except to you, O king, shall be thrown into the lions' den.[g] **8**Now, O king, issue the decree and put it in writing so that it cannot be altered—in accordance with the laws of the Medes and Persians, which cannot be repealed."[h] **9**So King Darius put the decree in writing.

10Now when Daniel learned that the decree had been published, he went home to his upstairs room where the windows opened toward[i] Jerusalem. Three times a day he got down on his knees[j] and prayed, giving thanks to his God, just as he had done before.[k] **11**Then these men went as a group and found Daniel praying and asking God for help. **12**So they went to the king and spoke to him about his royal decree: "Did you not publish a decree that during the next thirty days anyone who prays to any god or man except to you, O king, would be thrown into the lions' den?"

The king answered, "The decree stands—in accordance with the laws of the Medes and Persians, which cannot be repealed."[l]

13Then they said to the king, "Daniel, who is one of the exiles from Judah,[m] pays no attention[n] to you, O king, or to the decree you put in writing. He still prays three times a day." **14**When the king heard this, he was greatly distressed;[o] he was determined to rescue Daniel and made every effort until sundown to save him.

15Then the men went as a group to the king and said to him, "Remember, O king, that according to the law of the Medes and Persians no decree or edict that the king issues can be changed."[p]

16So the king gave the order, and they brought Daniel and threw him into the lions' den.[q] The king said to Daniel, "May your God, whom you serve continually, rescue[r] you!"

17A stone was brought and placed over the mouth of the den, and the king sealed[s] it with his own signet ring and with the rings of his nobles, so that Daniel's situation might not be changed. **18**Then the king returned to his palace and spent the night without eating[t] and without any entertainment being brought to him. And he could not sleep.[u]

19At the first light of dawn, the king got up and hurried to the lions' den. **20**When he came near the den, he called to Daniel in an anguished voice, "Daniel, servant of the living God, has your God, whom you serve continually, been able to rescue you from the lions?"[v]

21Daniel answered, "O king, live forever![w] **22**My God sent his angel,[x] and he shut the mouths of the lions.[y] They have not hurt me, because I was found innocent in his sight.[z] Nor have I ever done any wrong before you, O king."

23The king was overjoyed and gave orders to lift Daniel out of the

6:2 [a]Da 2:48-49 [b]Ezr 4:22
6:3 [c]Ge 41:41; Est 10:3; Da 5:12-14
6:5 [d]Ac 24:13-16
6:6 [e]Ne 2:3; Da 2:4
6:7 [f]Da 3:2 [g]Ps 59:3; 64:2-6; Da 3:6
6:8 [h]Est 1:19
6:10 [i]1Ki 8:48-49 [j]Ps 95:6 [k]Ac 5:29
6:12 [l]Est 1:19; Da 3:8-12
6:13 [m]Da 2:25; 5:13 [n]Est 3:8; Da 3:12
6:14 [o]Mk 6:26
6:15 [p]Est 8:8
6:16 [q]ver 7 [r]Job 5:19; Ps 37:39-40
6:17 [s]Mt 27:66
6:18 [t]2Sa 12:17 [u]Est 6:1; Da 2:1
6:20 [v]Da 3:17
6:21 [w]Da 2:4
6:22 [x]Da 3:28 [y]Ps 91:11-13; Heb 11:33 [z]Ac 12:11; 2Ti 4:17

den. And when Daniel was lifted
from the den, no wound[a] was
found on him, because he had
trusted[b] in his God.
24At the king's command, the
men who had falsely accused Daniel were brought in and thrown into
the lions' den,[c] along with their
wives and children.[d] And before
they reached the floor of the den,
the lions overpowered them and
crushed all their bones.[e]
25Then King Darius wrote to all
the peoples, nations and men of every language throughout the land:

"May you prosper greatly![f]

26"I issue a decree that in
every part of my kingdom people must fear and reverence
the God of Daniel.[g]

"For he is the living God
and he endures forever;
his kingdom will not be
destroyed,
his dominion will never
end.[h]
27He rescues and he saves;
he performs signs and
wonders[i]
in the heavens and on the
earth.
He has rescued Daniel
from the power of the
lions."[j]

28So Daniel prospered during
the reign of Darius and the reign of
Cyrus[u][k] the Persian.

Daniel's Dream of Four Beasts

7 In the first year of Belshazzar[l]
king of Babylon, Daniel had a
dream, and visions passed through
his mind[m] as he was lying on his
bed. He wrote[n] down the sub-
stance of his dream.
2Daniel said: "In my vision at
night I looked, and there before me
were the four winds of heaven[o]
churning up the great sea. 3Four
great beasts,[p] each different from
the others, came up out of the sea.
4"The first was like a lion,[q] and
it had the wings of an eagle.[r] I
watched until its wings were torn
off and it was lifted from the

6:23 [a]Da 3:27 [b]1Ch 5:20
6:24 [c]Dt 19:18-19; Est 7:9-10; Ps 54:5 [d]Dt 24:16; 2Ki 14:6 [e]Isa 38:13
6:25 [f]Da 4:1
6:26 [g]Ps 99:1-3; Da 3:29 [h]Da 2:44; 4:34
6:27 [i]Da 4:3 [j]ver 22
6:28 [k]2Ch 36:22; Da 1:21
7:1 [l]Da 5:1 [m]Da 1:17 [n]Jer 36:4
7:2 [o]Rev 7:1
7:3 [p]Rev 13:1
7:4 [q]Jer 4:7 [r]Eze 17:3
7:5 [s]Da 2:39
7:6 [t]Rev 13:2
7:7 [u]Da 2:40 [v]Rev 12:3
7:8 [w]Da 8:9 [x]Rev 9:7 [y]Ps 12:3; Rev 13:5-6
7:9 [z]Rev 1:14 [a]Eze 1:15; 10:6
7:10 [b]Ps 50:3; 97:3; Isa 30:27 [c]Dt 33:2; Ps 68:17; Rev 5:11

ground so that it stood on two feet
like a man, and the heart of a man
was given to it.
5"And there before me was a second beast, which looked like a
bear. It was raised up on one of its
sides, and it had three ribs in its
mouth between its teeth. It was
told, 'Get up and eat your fill of
flesh!'[s]
6"After that, I looked, and there
before me was another beast, one
that looked like a leopard.[t] And
on its back it had four wings like
those of a bird. This beast had four
heads, and it was given authority to
rule.
7"After that, in my vision at night
I looked, and there before me was
a fourth beast—terrifying and
frightening and very powerful. It
had large iron[u] teeth; it crushed
and devoured its victims and trampled underfoot whatever was left. It
was different from all the former
beasts, and it had ten horns.[v]
8"While I was thinking about the
horns, there before me was another
horn, a little[w] one, which came up
among them; and three of the first
horns were uprooted before it. This
horn had eyes like the eyes of a
man[x] and a mouth that spoke
boastfully.[y]
9"As I looked,

"thrones were set in place,
and the Ancient of Days took
his seat.
His clothing was as white as
snow;
the hair of his head was
white like wool.[z]
His throne was flaming with
fire,
and its wheels[a] were all
ablaze.
10A river of fire[b] was flowing,
coming out from before
him.[c]
Thousands upon thousands
attended him;
ten thousand times ten
thousand stood before
him.

[u]28 *Or Darius, that is, the reign of Cyrus*

The court was seated,
and the books[a] were opened.

11"Then I continued to watch because of the boastful words the horn was speaking. I kept looking until the beast was slain and its body destroyed and thrown into the blazing fire.[b] 12(The other beasts had been stripped of their authority, but were allowed to live for a period of time.)

13"In my vision at night I looked, and there before me was one like a son of man,[c] coming with the clouds of heaven.[d] He approached the Ancient of Days and was led into his presence. 14He was given authority,[e] glory and sovereign power; all peoples, nations and men of every language worshiped him.[f] His dominion is an everlasting dominion that will not pass away, and his kingdom is one that will never be destroyed.[g]

The Interpretation of the Dream

15"I, Daniel, was troubled in spirit, and the visions that passed through my mind disturbed me.[h] 16I approached one of those standing there and asked him the true meaning of all this.

"So he told me and gave me the interpretation[i] of these things: 17'The four great beasts are four kingdoms that will rise from the earth. 18But the saints of the Most High will receive the kingdom and will possess it forever—yes, for ever and ever.'[j]

19"Then I wanted to know the true meaning of the fourth beast, which was different from all the others and most terrifying, with its iron teeth and bronze claws—the beast that crushed and devoured its victims and trampled underfoot whatever was left. 20I also wanted to know about the ten horns on its head and about the other horn that came up, before which three of them fell—the horn that looked more imposing than the others and that had eyes and a mouth that spoke boastfully. 21As I watched, this horn was waging war against the saints and defeating them,[k] 22until the Ancient of Days came and pronounced judgment in favor of the saints of the Most High, and the time came when they possessed the kingdom.

23"He gave me this explanation: 'The fourth beast is a fourth kingdom that will appear on earth. It will be different from all the other kingdoms and will devour the whole earth, trampling it down and crushing it.[l] 24The ten horns[m] are ten kings who will come from this kingdom. After them another king will arise, different from the earlier ones; he will subdue three kings. 25He will speak against the Most High[n] and oppress his saints and try to change the set times[o] and the laws. The saints will be handed over to him for a time, times and half a time.[v][p]

26" 'But the court will sit, and his power will be taken away and completely destroyed forever. 27Then the sovereignty, power and greatness of the kingdoms under the whole heaven will be handed over to the saints, the people of the Most High. His kingdom will be an everlasting[q] kingdom, and all rulers will worship[r] and obey him.'

28"This is the end of the matter. I, Daniel, was deeply troubled[s] by my thoughts, and my face turned pale, but I kept the matter to myself."

Daniel's Vision of a Ram and a Goat

8 In the third year of King Belshazzar's reign, I, Daniel, had a vision, after the one that had already appeared to me. 2In my vision I saw myself in the citadel of Susa[t] in the province of Elam;[u] in the vision I was beside the Ulai Canal. 3I looked up,[v] and there before me was a ram with two horns, standing beside the canal, and the horns were long. One of the horns was longer than the other but grew

7:10 [a] Rev 20:11-15
7:11 [b] Rev 19:20
7:13 [c] Mt 8:20*; Rev 1:13* [d] Mt 24:30; Rev 1:7
7:14 [e] Mt 28:18 [f] Ps 72:11; 102:22; 1Co 15:27; Eph 1:22 [g] Da 2:44; Heb 12:28; Rev 11:15
7:15 [h] Da 4:19
7:16 [i] Da 8:16; 9:22; Zec 1:9
7:18 [j] Isa 60:12-14; Rev 2:26; 20:4
7:21 [k] Rev 13:7
7:23 [l] Da 2:40
7:24 [m] Rev 17:12
7:25 [n] Isa 37:23; Da 11:36 [o] Da 2:21 [p] Da 8:24; 12:7; Rev 12:14
7:27 [q] Da 2:44; 4:34; Lk 1:33; Rev 11:15; 22:5 [r] Ps 22:27; 72:11; 86:9
7:28 [s] Da 4:19
8:2 [t] Est 1:2 [u] Ge 10:22
8:3 [v] Da 10:5

[v]25 *Or for a year, two years and half a year*

up later. 4I watched the ram as he
charged toward the west and the
north and the south. No animal
could stand against him, and none
could rescue from his power. He
did as he pleased[a] and became
great.
5As I was thinking about this,
suddenly a goat with a prominent
horn between his eyes came from
the west, crossing the whole earth
without touching the ground. 6He
came toward the two-horned ram I
had seen standing beside the canal
and charged at him in great rage. 7I
saw him attack the ram furiously,
striking the ram and shattering his
two horns. The ram was powerless
to stand against him; the goat
knocked him to the ground and
trampled on him,[b] and none could
rescue the ram from his power.
8The goat became very great, but at
the height of his power his large
horn was broken off,[c] and in its
place four prominent horns grew
up toward the four winds of heav-
en.[d]
9Out of one of them came another horn, which started small but
grew in power to the south and to
the east and toward the Beautiful
Land.[e] 10It grew until it reached[f]
the host of the heavens, and it
threw some of the starry host down
to the earth[g] and trampled[h] on
them. 11It set itself up to be as
great as the Prince of the host;[i] it
took away the daily sacrifice[j] from
him, and the place of his sanctuary
was brought low.[k] 12Because of rebellion, the host ⌞of the saints⌟[w]
and the daily sacrifice were given
over to it. It prospered in everything it did, and truth was thrown
to the ground.
13Then I heard a holy one[l]
speaking, and another holy one
said to him, "How long will it take
for the vision to be fulfilled[m]—the
vision concerning the daily sacrifice, the rebellion that causes desolation, and the surrender of the
sanctuary and of the host that will
be trampled[n] underfoot?"
14He said to me, "It will take
2,300 evenings and mornings; then
the sanctuary will be reconsecra-
ted"[o]

The Interpretation of the Vision

15While I, Daniel, was watching
the vision[p] and trying to understand it, there before me stood one
who looked like a man.[q] 16And I
heard a man's voice from the Ulai
calling, "Gabriel,[r] tell this man
the meaning of the vision."
17As he came near the place
where I was standing, I was terrified and fell prostrate.[s] "Son of
man," he said to me, "understand
that the vision concerns the time of
the end."[t]
18While he was speaking to me,
I was in a deep sleep, with my face
to the ground.[u] Then he touched
me and raised me to my feet.[v]
19He said: "I am going to tell you
what will happen later in the time
of wrath, because the vision concerns the appointed time of the
end.[x][w] 20The two-horned ram that
you saw represents the kings of
Media and Persia. 21The shaggy
goat is the king of Greece,[x] and
the large horn between his eyes is
the first king.[y] 22The four horns
that replaced the one that was broken off represent four kingdoms
that will emerge from his nation
but will not have the same power.
23"In the latter part of their
reign, when rebels have become
completely wicked, a stern-faced
king, a master of intrigue, will
arise. 24He will become very
strong, but not by his own power.
He will cause astounding devastation and will succeed in whatever
he does. He will destroy the mighty
men and the holy people.[z] 25He
will cause deceit to prosper, and he
will consider himself superior.
When they feel secure, he will destroy many and take his stand
against the Prince of princes.[a] Yet
he will be destroyed, but not by human power.[b]
26"The vision of the evenings
and mornings that has been given

8:4 [a]Da 11:3,16
8:7 [b]Da 7:7
8:8 [c]2Ch 26:16-21; Da 5:20 [d]Da 7:2; Rev 7:1
8:9 [e]Da 11:16
8:10 [f]Isa 14:13 [g]Rev 12:4 [h]Da 7:7
8:11 [i]Da 11:36-37 [j]Eze 46:13-14 [k]Da 11:31; 12:11
8:13 [l]Da 4:23 [m]Da 12:6 [n]Lk 21:24; Rev 11:2
8:14 [o]Da 12:11-12
8:15 [p]ver 1 [q]Da 10:16-18
8:16 [r]Da 9:21; Lk 1:19
8:17 [s]Eze 1:28; Da 2:46; Rev 1:17 [t]Hab 2:3
8:18 [u]Da 10:9 [v]Eze 2:2; Da 10:16-18
8:19 [w]Hab 2:3
8:21 [x]Da 10:20 [y]Da 11:3
8:24 [z]Da 7:25; 11:36
8:25 [a]Da 11:36 [b]Da 2:34; 11:21

[w]*12* Or *rebellion, the armies* [x]*19* Or *because the end will be at the appointed time*

you is true,[a] but seal[b] up the vision, for it concerns the distant future."[c]
27 I, Daniel, was exhausted and
lay ill for several days. Then I got
up and went about the king's business.[d] I was appalled[e] by the vision; it was beyond understanding.

Daniel's Prayer

9 In the first year of Darius[f] son
of Xerxes[y] (a Mede by descent), who was made ruler over
the Babylonian[z] kingdom— 2 in
the first year of his reign, I, Daniel,
understood from the Scriptures,
according to the word of the LORD
given to Jeremiah the prophet, that
the desolation of Jerusalem would
last seventy[g] years. 3 So I turned to
the Lord God and pleaded with him
in prayer and petition, in fasting,
and in sackcloth and ashes.[h]
4 I prayed to the LORD my God and
confessed:

"O Lord, the great and awesome God,[i] who keeps his
covenant of love[j] with all who
love him and obey his commands, 5 we have sinned and
done wrong.[k] We have been
wicked and have rebelled; we
have turned away[l] from your
commands and laws.[m] 6 We
have not listened to your servants the prophets,[n] who
spoke in your name to our
kings, our princes and our fathers, and to all the people of
the land.
7 "Lord, you are righteous,
but this day we are covered
with shame[o]—the men of Judah and people of Jerusalem
and all Israel, both near and
far, in all the countries where
you have scattered[p] us because of our unfaithfulness to
you.[q] 8 O LORD, we and our
kings, our princes and our fathers are covered with shame
because we have sinned
against you. 9 The Lord our
God is merciful and forgiving,[r] even though we have rebelled against him;[s] 10 we
have not obeyed the LORD our
God or kept the laws he gave
us through his servants the
prophets.[t] 11 All Israel has
transgressed your law and
turned away, refusing to obey
you.

"Therefore the curses and
sworn judgments written in
the Law of Moses, the servant
of God, have been poured out
on us, because we have
sinned[u] against you. 12 You
have fulfilled[v] the words spoken against us and against our
rulers by bringing upon us
great disaster. Under the
whole heaven nothing has ever
been done like what has been
done to Jerusalem.[w] 13 Just as
it is written in the Law of Moses, all this disaster has come
upon us, yet we have not
sought the favor of the LORD
our God by turning from our
sins and giving attention to
your truth.[x] 14 The LORD did
not hesitate to bring the disaster[y] upon us, for the LORD our
God is righteous in everything
he does; yet we have not
obeyed him.[z]
15 "Now, O Lord our God,
who brought your people out
of Egypt with a mighty hand[a]
and who made for yourself a
name[b] that endures to this
day, we have sinned, we have
done wrong. 16 O Lord, in
keeping with all your righteous acts,[c] turn away your
anger and your wrath from Jerusalem,[d] your city, your holy
hill.[e] Our sins and the iniquities of our fathers have made
Jerusalem and your people an
object of scorn[f] to all those
around us.
17 "Now, our God, hear the
prayers and petitions of your
servant. For your sake, O Lord,
look with favor[g] on your desolate sanctuary. 18 Give ear, O
God, and hear; open your eyes
and see[h] the desolation of the

8:26 [a] Da 10:1 [b] Rev 22:10 [c] Da 10:14
8:27 [d] Da 2:48 [e] Da 7:28
9:1 [f] Da 5:31
9:2 [g] 2Ch 36:21; Jer 29:10; Zec 7:5
9:3 [h] Ne 1:4; Jer 29:12
9:4 [i] Dt 7:21 [j] Dt 7:9
9:5 [k] Ps 106:6 [l] Isa 53:6 [m] ver 11; La 1:20
9:6 [n] 2Ch 36:16; Jer 44:5
9:7 [o] Ps 44:15 [p] Dt 4:27; Am 9:9 [q] Jer 3:25
9:9 [r] Ps 130:4 [s] Ne 9:17; Jer 14:7
9:10 [t] 2Ki 17:13-15; 18:12
9:11 [u] Isa 1:4-6; Jer 8:5-10
9:12 [v] Isa 44:26; Zec 1:6 [w] Jer 44:2-6; Eze 5:9
9:13 [x] Isa 9:13; Jer 2:30
9:14 [y] Jer 44:27 [z] Ne 9:33
9:15 [a] Jer 32:21 [b] Ne 9:10
9:16 [c] Ps 31:1 [d] Jer 32:32 [e] Zec 8:3 [f] Eze 5:14
9:17 [g] Nu 6:24-26; Ps 80:19
9:18 [h] Ps 80:14

[y]1 Hebrew *Ahasuerus* [z]1 Or *Chaldean*

city that bears your Name.[a]
We do not make requests of
you because we are righteous,
but because of your great mercy. 19O Lord, listen! O Lord,
forgive![b] O Lord, hear and act!
For your sake, O my God, do
not delay, because your city
and your people bear your
Name."

The Seventy "Sevens"

20While I was speaking and praying, confessing my sin and the sin
of my people Israel and making my
request to the LORD my God for his
holy hill[c]— 21while I was still in
prayer, Gabriel,[d] the man I had
seen in the earlier vision, came to
me in swift flight about the time of
the evening sacrifice.[e] 22He instructed me and said to me, "Daniel, I have now come to give you insight and understanding. 23As soon
as you began to pray, an answer
was given, which I have come to
tell you, for you are highly esteemed.[f] Therefore, consider the
message and understand the vision:[g]

24"Seventy 'sevens'[a] are decreed for your people and your holy
city to finish[b] transgression, to put
an end to sin, to atone[h] for wickedness, to bring in everlasting righteousness,[i] to seal up vision and
prophecy and to anoint the most
holy.[c]

25"Know and understand this:
From the issuing of the decree[d] to
restore and rebuild[j] Jerusalem
until the Anointed One,[e][k] the ruler, comes, there will be seven 'sevens,' and sixty-two 'sevens.' It will
be rebuilt with streets and a
trench, but in times of trouble.
26After the sixty-two 'sevens,' the
Anointed One will be cut off[l] and
will have nothing.[f] The people of
the ruler who will come will destroy the city and the sanctuary.
The end will come like a flood:[m]
War will continue until the end,
and desolations have been decreed. 27He will confirm a covenant with many for one 'seven.'[g]
In the middle of the 'seven'[g] he
will put an end to sacrifice and offering. And on a wing ⌊of the tem-
ple⌋ he will set up an abomination
that causes desolation, until the
end that is decreed[n] is poured out
on him.[h]"[i]

Daniel's Vision of a Man

10 In the third year of Cyrus[o]
king of Persia, a revelation
was given to Daniel (who was
called Belteshazzar).[p] Its message
was true[q] and it concerned a great
war.[j] The understanding of the
message came to him in a vision.

2At that time I, Daniel,
mourned[r] for three weeks. 3I ate
no choice food; no meat or wine
touched my lips; and I used no lotions at all until the three weeks
were over.

4On the twenty-fourth day of the
first month, as I was standing on
the bank of the great river, the Tigris,[s] 5I looked up and there before me was a man dressed in lin-
en,[t] with a belt of the finest gold[u]
around his waist. 6His body was
like chrysolite, his face like lightning,[v] his eyes like flaming
torches,[w] his arms and legs like the
gleam of burnished bronze,[x] and
his voice like the sound of a multitude.

7I, Daniel, was the only one who
saw the vision; the men with me
did not see it,[y] but such terror
overwhelmed them that they fled
and hid themselves. 8So I was left
alone,[z] gazing at this great vision;
I had no strength left,[a] my face
turned deathly pale and I was helpless.[b] 9Then I heard him speaking,
and as I listened to him, I fell into
a deep sleep, my face to the
ground.[c]

10A hand touched me[d] and set
me trembling on my hands and

9:18 [a]Isa 37:17; Jer 7:10-12; 25:29
9:19 [b]Ps 44:23
9:20 [c]ver 3; Ps 145:18; Isa 58:9
9:21 [d]Da 8:16; Lk 1:19 [e]Ex 29:39
9:23 [f]Da 10:19; Lk 1:28 [g]Da 10:11-12; Mt 24:15
9:24 [h]Isa 53:10 [i]Isa 56:1
9:25 [j]Ezr 4:24 [k]Jn 4:25
9:26 [l]Isa 53:8 [m]Na 1:8
9:27 [n]Isa 10:22
10:1 [o]Da 1:21 [p]Da 1:7 [q]Da 8:26
10:2 [r]Ezr 9:4
10:4 [s]Ge 2:14
10:5 [t]Eze 9:2; Rev 15:6 [u]Jer 10:9
10:6 [v]Mt 17:2 [w]Rev 19:12 [x]Rev 1:15
10:7 [y]2Ki 6:17-20; Ac 9:7
10:8 [z]Ge 32:24 [a]Da 8:27 [b]Hab 3:16
10:9 [c]Da 8:18
10:10 [d]Jer 1:9

[a]24 Or *'weeks'*; also in verses 25 and 26 [b]24 Or *restrain* [c]24 Or *Most Holy Place*; or *most holy One* [d]25 Or *word* [e]25 Or *an anointed one*; also in verse 26 [f]26 Or *off and will have no one*; or *off, but not for himself* [g]27 Or *'week'* [h]27 Or *it* [i]27 Or *And one who causes desolation will come upon the pinnacle of the abominable ⌊temple⌋, until the end that is decreed is poured out on the desolated ⌊city⌋* [j]1 Or *true and burdensome*

knees.[a] 11He said, "Daniel, you who are highly esteemed,[b] consider carefully the words I am about to speak to you, and stand up,[c] for I have now been sent to you." And when he said this to me, I stood up trembling.

12Then he continued, "Do not be afraid, Daniel. Since the first day that you set your mind to gain understanding and to humble[d] yourself before your God, your words were heard, and I have come in response to them.[e] 13But the prince of the Persian kingdom resisted me twenty-one days. Then Michael,[f] one of the chief princes, came to help me, because I was detained there with the king of Persia. 14Now I have come to explain[g] to you what will happen to your people in the future, for the vision concerns a time yet to come.[h]"

15While he was saying this to me, I bowed with my face toward the ground and was speechless.[i] 16Then one who looked like a man[k] touched my lips, and I opened my mouth and began to speak.[j] I said to the one standing before me, "I am overcome with anguish[k] because of the vision, my lord, and I am helpless. 17How can I, your servant, talk with you, my lord? My strength is gone and I can hardly breathe."[l]

18Again the one who looked like a man touched[m] me and gave me strength. 19"Do not be afraid, O man highly esteemed," he said. "Peace![n] Be strong now; be strong."[o]

When he spoke to me, I was strengthened and said, "Speak, my lord, since you have given me strength."[p]

20So he said, "Do you know why I have come to you? Soon I will return to fight against the prince of Persia, and when I go, the prince of Greece[q] will come; 21but first I will tell you what is written in the Book of Truth.[r] (No one supports me against them except Michael,[s] your prince. 11 1And in the first year of Darius[t] the

10:10 [a]Rev 1:17
10:11 [b]Da 9:23 [c]Eze 2:1
10:12 [d]Da 9:3 [e]Da 9:20
10:13 [f]ver 21; Da 12:1; Jude 1:9
10:14 [g]Da 9:22 [h]Da 2:28; 8:26; Hab 2:3
10:15 [i]Eze 24:27; Lk 1:20
10:16 [j]Isa 6:7; Jer 1:9; Da 8:15-18 [k]Isa 21:3
10:17 [l]Da 4:19
10:18 [m]ver 16
10:19 [n]Jdg 6:23; Isa 35:4 [o]Jos 1:9 [p]Isa 6:1-8
10:20 [q]Da 8:21; 11:2
10:21 [r]Da 11:2 [s]ver 13; Jude 1:9
11:1 [t]Da 5:31
11:2 [u]Da 10:21 [v]Da 10:20
11:3 [w]Da 8:4,21
11:4 [x]Da 7:2; 8:22
11:7 [y]ver 6
11:8 [z]Isa 37:19; 46:1-2 [a]Jer 43:12

Mede, I took my stand to support and protect him.)

The Kings of the South and the North

2"Now then, I tell you the truth:[u] Three more kings will appear in Persia, and then a fourth, who will be far richer than all the others. When he has gained power by his wealth, he will stir up everyone against the kingdom of Greece.[v] 3Then a mighty king will appear, who will rule with great power and do as he pleases.[w] 4After he has appeared, his empire will be broken up and parceled out toward the four winds of heaven.[x] It will not go to his descendants, nor will it have the power he exercised, because his empire will be uprooted and given to others.

5"The king of the South will become strong, but one of his commanders will become even stronger than he and will rule his own kingdom with great power. 6After some years, they will become allies. The daughter of the king of the South will go to the king of the North to make an alliance, but she will not retain her power, and he and his power[l] will not last. In those days she will be handed over, together with her royal escort and her father[m] and the one who supported her.

7"One from her family line will arise to take her place. He will attack the forces of the king of the North[y] and enter his fortress; he will fight against them and be victorious. 8He will also seize their gods,[z] their metal images and their valuable articles of silver and gold and carry them off to Egypt.[a] For some years he will leave the king of the North alone. 9Then the king of the North will invade the realm of the king of the South but will retreat to his own country.

[k]*16* Most manuscripts of the Masoretic Text; one manuscript of the Masoretic Text, Dead Sea Scrolls and Septuagint *Then something that looked like a man's hand* [l]*6* Or *offspring* [m]*6* Or *child* (see Vulgate and Syriac)

10His sons will prepare for war and
assemble a great army, which will
sweep on like an irresistible flood[a]
and carry the battle as far as his fortress.
11"Then the king of the South
will march out in a rage and fight
against the king of the North, who
will raise a large army, but it will be
defeated.[b] 12When the army is carried off, the king of the South will
be filled with pride and will slaughter many thousands, yet he will not
remain triumphant. 13For the king
of the North will muster another
army, larger than the first; and after
several years, he will advance with
a huge army fully equipped.
14"In those times many will rise
against the king of the South. The
violent men among your own people will rebel in fulfillment of the
vision, but without success.
15Then the king of the North will
come and build up siege ramps[c]
and will capture a fortified city.
The forces of the South will be
powerless to resist; even their best
troops will not have the strength to
stand. 16The invader will do as he
pleases;[d] no one will be able to
stand against him.[e] He will establish himself in the Beautiful Land
and will have the power to destroy
it.[f] 17He will determine to come
with the might of his entire kingdom and will make an alliance with
the king of the South. And he will
give him a daughter in marriage in
order to overthrow the kingdom,
but his plans[n] will not succeed[g] or
help him. 18Then he will turn his
attention to the coastlands[h] and
will take many of them, but a commander will put an end to his insolence and will turn his insolence
back upon him.[i] 19After this, he
will turn back toward the fortresses
of his own country but will stumble
and fall,[j] to be seen no more.[k]
20"His successor will send out a
tax collector to maintain the royal
splendor.[l] In a few years, however,
he will be destroyed, yet not in anger or in battle.
21"He will be succeeded by a
contemptible[m] person who has not
been given the honor of royalty.[n]
He will invade the kingdom when
its people feel secure, and he will
seize it through intrigue. 22Then an
overwhelming army will be swept
away before him; both it and a
prince of the covenant will be destroyed.[o] 23After coming to an
agreement with him, he will act deceitfully,[p] and with only a few people he will rise to power. 24When
the richest provinces feel secure,
he will invade them and will
achieve what neither his fathers
nor his forefathers did. He will distribute plunder, loot and wealth
among his followers.[q] He will plot
the overthrow of fortresses—but
only for a time.
25"With a large army he will stir
up his strength and courage against
the king of the South. The king of
the South will wage war with a
large and very powerful army, but
he will not be able to stand because of the plots devised against
him. 26Those who eat from the
king's provisions will try to destroy
him; his army will be swept away,
and many will fall in battle. 27The
two kings, with their hearts bent on
evil,[r] will sit at the same table and
lie[s] to each other, but to no avail,
because an end will still come at
the appointed time.[t] 28The king of
the North will return to his own
country with great wealth, but his
heart will be set against the holy
covenant. He will take action
against it and then return to his
own country.
29"At the appointed time he will
invade the South again, but this
time the outcome will be different
from what it was before. 30Ships of
the western coastlands[o][u] will oppose him, and he will lose heart.
Then he will turn back and vent his
fury against the holy covenant. He
will return and show favor to those
who forsake the holy covenant.
31"His armed forces will rise up
to desecrate the temple fortress
and will abolish the daily sacrifice.
Then they will set up the abomina-

11:10 [a]Isa 8:8; Jer 46:8; Da 9:26
11:11 [b]Da 8:7-8
11:15 [c]Eze 4:2
11:16 [d]Da 8:4 [e]Jos 1:5; Da 8:7 [f]Da 8:9
11:17 [g]Ps 20:4
11:18 [h]Isa 66:19; Jer 25:22 [i]Hos 12:14
11:19 [j]Ps 27:2 [k]Ps 37:36; Eze 26:21
11:20 [l]Isa 60:17
11:21 [m]Da 4:17 [n]Da 8:25
11:22 [o]Da 8:10-11
11:23 [p]Da 8:25
11:24 [q]Ne 9:25
11:27 [r]Ps 64:6 [s]Ps 12:2; Jer 9:5 [t]Hab 2:3
11:30 [u]Ge 10:4

[n]17 Or *but she* [o]30 Hebrew *of Kittim*

tion that causes desolation.[a]
32With flattery he will corrupt
those who have violated the covenant, but the people who know
their God will firmly resist[b] him.
33"Those who are wise will instruct[c] many, though for a time
they will fall by the sword or be
burned or captured or plundered.[d]
34When they fall, they will receive
a little help, and many who are not
sincere[e] will join them. 35Some of
the wise will stumble, so that they
may be refined,[f] purified and
made spotless until the time of the
end, for it will still come at the appointed time.

The King Who Exalts Himself

36"The king will do as he
pleases. He will exalt and magnify
himself above every god and will
say unheard-of things[g] against the
God of gods.[h] He will be successful until the time of wrath[i] is completed, for what has been determined must take place. 37He will
show no regard for the gods of his
fathers or for the one desired by
women, nor will he regard any god,
but will exalt himself above them
all. 38Instead of them, he will hon-
or a god of fortresses; a god unknown to his fathers he will honor
with gold and silver, with precious
stones and costly gifts. 39He will
attack the mightiest fortresses with
the help of a foreign god and will
greatly honor those who acknowledge him. He will make them rulers over many people and will distribute the land at a price.[p]
40"At the time of the end the
king of the South[j] will engage him
in battle, and the king of the North
will storm[k] out against him with
chariots and cavalry and a great
fleet of ships. He will invade many
countries and sweep through them
like a flood.[l] 41He will also invade
the Beautiful Land. Many countries will fall, but Edom,[m] Moab[n]
and the leaders of Ammon will be
delivered from his hand. 42He will
extend his power over many countries; Egypt will not escape. 43He
will gain control of the treasures of
gold and silver and all the riches of
Egypt,[o] with the Libyans[p] and
Nubians in submission. 44But reports from the east and the north
will alarm him, and he will set out
in a great rage to destroy and annihilate many. 45He will pitch his
royal tents between the seas at[q]
the beautiful holy mountain. Yet
he will come to his end, and no one
will help him.

The End Times

12 "At that time Michael,[q] the
great prince who protects
your people, will arise. There will
be a time of distress[r] such as has
not happened from the beginning
of nations until then. But at that
time your people—everyone whose
name is found written in the
book[s]—will be delivered.[t] 2Mul-
titudes who sleep in the dust of the
earth will awake: some to everlasting life, others to shame and everlasting contempt.[u] 3Those who are
wise[r][v] will shine[w] like the brightness of the heavens, and those who
lead many to righteousness, like
the stars for ever and ever.[x] 4But
you, Daniel, close up and seal[y]
the words of the scroll until the
time of the end.[z] Many will go
here and there to increase knowledge."

5Then I, Daniel, looked, and
there before me stood two others,
one on this bank of the river and
one on the opposite bank.[a] 6One
of them said to the man clothed in
linen,[b] who was above the waters
of the river, "How long will it be before these astonishing things are
fulfilled?"[c]
7The man clothed in linen, who
was above the waters of the river,
lifted his right hand and his left
hand toward heaven, and I heard
him swear by him who lives forever,[d] saying, "It will be for a time,
times and half a time.[s][e] When the
power of the holy people[f] has

11:31 [a]Da 8:11-13; 9:27; Mt 24:15*; Mk 13:14*
11:32 [b]Mic 5:7-9
11:33 [c]Mal 2:7 [d]Mt 24:9; Jn 16:2; Heb 11:32-38
11:34 [e]Mt 7:15; Ro 16:18
11:35 [f]Ps 78:38; Da 12:10; Zec 13:9; Jn 15:2
11:36 [g]Rev 13:5-6 [h]Dt 10:17; Isa 14:13-14; Da 7:25; 8:11-12,25; 2Th 2:4 [i]Isa 10:25; 26:20
11:40 [j]Isa 21:1 [k]Isa 5:28 [l]Eze 38:4
11:41 [m]Isa 11:14 [n]Jer 48:47
11:43 [o]Eze 30:4 [p]2Ch 12:3; Na 3:9
12:1 [q]Da 10:13 [r]Da 9:12; Mt 24:21; Mk 13:19; Rev 16:18 [s]Ex 32:32; Ps 56:8 [t]Jer 30:7
12:2 [u]Isa 26:19; Mt 25:46; Jn 5:28-29
12:3 [v]Da 11:33 [w]Mt 13:43; Jn 5:35 [x]1Co 15:42
12:4 [y]Isa 8:16 [z]ver 9,13; Rev 22:10
12:5 [a]Da 10:4
12:6 [b]Eze 9:2 [c]Da 8:13
12:7 [d]Rev 10:5-6 [e]Da 7:25 [f]Da 8:24

[p]39 Or *land for a reward* [q]45 Or *the sea and* [r]3 Or *who impart wisdom* [s]7 Or *a year, two years and half a year*

been finally broken, all these things will be completed.[a]"

[8]I heard, but I did not understand. So I asked, "My lord, what will the outcome of all this be?"

[9]He replied, "Go your way, Daniel, because the words are closed up and sealed until the time of the end.[b] [10]Many will be purified, made spotless and refined,[c] but the wicked will continue to be wicked.[d] None of the wicked will understand, but those who are wise will understand.[e]

[11]"From the time that the daily sacrifice is abolished and the abomination that causes desolation[f] is set up, there will be 1,290 days. [12]Blessed is the one who waits[g] for and reaches the end of the 1,335 days.[h]

[13]"As for you, go your way till the end. You will rest,[i] and then at the end of the days you will rise to receive your allotted inheritance.[j]"

12:7 [a]Lk 21:24; Rev 10:7
12:9 [b]ver 4
12:10 [c]Da 11:35 [d]Isa 32:7; Rev 22:11 [e]Hos 14:9
12:11 [f]Da 8:11; 9:27; Mt 24:15*; Mk 13:14*
12:12 [g]Isa 30:18 [h]Da 8:14
12:13 [i]Isa 57:2 [j]Ps 16:5; Rev 14:13

Hosea

Title and Background

The book is named after the prophet whose message it preserves. Hosea's time encompasses the tragic last days of the northern kingdom (Israel), during which six kings reigned within twenty-five years. Assyria was expanding westward, and in about 733 B.C. they dismembered Israel. Then in 722-721 B.C. Samaria was captured and its people exiled. The northern kingdom was at an end.

Author and Date of Writing

Hosea prophesied about the middle of the eighth century B.C., shortly after the ministry of Amos. Amos threatened God's judgment on Israel at the hands of an unnamed enemy; Hosea identifies that enemy as Assyria. Hosea stands first in the division of the Bible called the Minor Prophets (Hosea-Malachi).

Theme and Message

In the first half of the book, Hosea's family life is made a symbolic action to convey the message Hosea had from the Lord for his people. The Lord loved his covenant people and would take them back, however often they would wander. The second half of the book gives the details of Israel's involvement in Canaanite religion. Like other prophetic books, Hosea carried a call to repentance. The alternative to destruction is to forsake idols and return to the Lord.

Outline

I. The Unfaithful Wife and the Faithful Husband (1:1-3:5)
II. The Unfaithful Nation and the Faithful God (4:1-14:9)
   A. Israel's Unfaithfulness (4:1-6:3)
   B. Israel's Punishment (6:4-10:15)
   C. The Lord's Faithful Love (11:1-14:9)

---

1 The word of the LORD that
came to Hosea son of Beeri
during the reigns of Uzziah, Jotham, Ahaz and Hezekiah, kings of
Judah,[a] and during the reign of
Jeroboam[b] son of Jehoash[a] king
of Israel:[c]

Hosea's Wife and Children

2 When the LORD began to speak
through Hosea, the LORD said to
him, "Go, take to yourself an adulterous[d] wife and children of unfaithfulness, because the land is
guilty of the vilest adultery[e] in de-
parting from the LORD." 3 So he married Gomer daughter of Diblaim,
and she conceived and bore him a
son.

4 Then the LORD said to Hosea,
"Call him Jezreel,[f] because I will
soon punish the house of Jehu for
the massacre at Jezreel, and I will
put an end to the kingdom of Israel. 5 In that day I will break Israel's
bow in the Valley of Jezreel.[g]"
6 Gomer[h] conceived again and
gave birth to a daughter. Then the
LORD said to Hosea, "Call her Lo-
Ruhamah,[b] for I will no longer
show love to the house of Israel,[i]
that I should at all forgive them.
7 Yet I will show love to the house of
Judah; and I will save them—not
by bow,[j] sword or battle, or by

1:1 [a] Isa 1:1; Mic 1:1 [b] 2Ki 13:13 [c] Am 1:1
1:2 [d] Jer 3:1; Hos 2:2,5; 3:1 [e] Dt 31:16; Jer 3:14; Eze 23:3-21; Hos 5:3
1:4 [f] 2Ki 10:1-14; Hos 2:22
1:5 [g] 2Ki 15:29
1:6 [h] ver 3 [i] Hos 2:4
1:7 [j] Ps 44:6

a1 Hebrew *Joash*, a variant of *Jehoash*
b6 *Lo-Ruhamah* means *not loved.*

horses and horsemen, but by the
LORD their God.[a]"
8After she had weaned Lo-Ruhamah, Gomer had another son.
9Then the LORD said, "Call him
Lo-Ammi,[c] for you are not my people, and I am not your God.
10"Yet the Israelites will be like
the sand on the seashore, which
cannot be measured or counted.[b]
In the place where it was said to
them, 'You are not my people,' they
will be called 'sons of the living
God.'[c] 11The people of Judah and
the people of Israel will be reunited,[d] and they will appoint one
leader[e] and will come up out of
the land,[f] for great will be the day
of Jezreel.

2 "Say of your brothers, 'My people,' and of your sisters, 'My
loved one.'[g]

Israel Punished and Restored

2"Rebuke your mother,[h] rebuke
her,
for she is not my wife,
and I am not her husband.
Let her remove the adulterous[i]
look from her face
and the unfaithfulness from
between her breasts.
3Otherwise I will strip her naked
and make her as bare as on
the day she was born;[j]
I will make her like a desert,[k]
turn her into a parched land,
and slay her with thirst.
4I will not show my love to her
children,[l]
because they are the children
of adultery.
5Their mother has been
unfaithful
and has conceived them in
disgrace.
She said, 'I will go after my
lovers,[m]
who give me my food and my
water,
my wool and my linen, my
oil and my drink.'[n]
6Therefore I will block her path
with thornbushes;
I will wall her in so that she
cannot find her way.[o]
7She will chase after her lovers
but not catch them;
she will look for them but
not find them.[p]
Then she will say,
'I will go back to my husband
as at first,[q]
for then I was better off[r]
than now.'
8She has not acknowledged[s]
that I was the one
who gave her the grain, the
new wine and oil,
who lavished on her the silver
and gold—
which they used for Baal.[t]

9"Therefore I will take away my
grain[u] when it ripens,
and my new wine[v] when it is
ready.
I will take back my wool and
my linen,
intended to cover her
nakedness.
10So now I will expose her
lewdness
before the eyes of her lovers;
no one will take her out of
my hands.[w]
11I will stop[x] all her
celebrations:
her yearly festivals, her New
Moons,
her Sabbath days—all her
appointed feasts.[y]
12I will ruin her vines[z] and her
fig trees,
which she said were her pay
from her lovers;
I will make them a thicket,[a]
and wild animals will devour
them.[b]
13I will punish her for the days
she burned incense to the
Baals;[c]
she decked herself with rings
and jewelry,[d]
and went after her lovers,[e]
but me she forgot,[f]"
declares the LORD.

14"Therefore I am now going to
allure her;
I will lead her into the desert
and speak tenderly to her.

1:7 [a]Zec 4:6
1:10 [b]Ge 22:17; Jer 33:22 [c]ver 9; Ro 9:26*
1:11 [d]Isa 11:12,13 [e]Jer 23:5-8 [f]Eze 37:15-28
2:1 [g]ver 23
2:2 [h]ver 5; Isa 50:1; Hos 1:2 [i]Eze 23:45
2:3 [j]Eze 16:4,22 [k]Isa 32:13-14
2:4 [l]Eze 8:18
2:5 [m]Jer 3:6 [n]Jer 44:17-18
2:6 [o]Job 3:23; 19:8; La 3:9
2:7 [p]Hos 5:13 [q]Jer 2:2; 3:1 [r]Eze 16:8
2:8 [s]Isa 1:3 [t]Eze 16:15-19; Hos 8:4
2:9 [u]Hos 8:7 [v]Hos 9:2
2:10 [w]Eze 16:37
2:11 [x]Jer 7:34 [y]Isa 1:14; Jer 16:9; Hos 3:4; Am 8:10
2:12 [z]Isa 7:23; Jer 8:13 [a]Isa 5:6 [b]Hos 13:8
2:13 [c]Hos 11:2 [d]Eze 16:17 [e]Hos 4:13 [f]Hos 4:6; 8:14; 13:6

c9 *Lo-Ammi* means *not my people.*

15 There I will give her back her
vineyards,
and will make the Valley of
Achor[d][a] a door of hope.
There she will sing[e][b] as in the
days of her youth,[c]
as in the day she came up
out of Egypt.[d]

16 "In that day," declares the
LORD,
"you will call me 'my
husband';
you will no longer call me
'my master.[f]'
17 I will remove the names of the
Baals from her lips;[e]
no longer will their names be
invoked.[f]
18 In that day I will make a
covenant for them
with the beasts of the field
and the birds of the air
and the creatures that move
along the ground.[g]
Bow and sword and battle
I will abolish[h] from the land,
so that all may lie down in
safety.[i]
19 I will betroth[j] you to me
forever;
I will betroth you in[g]
righteousness and
justice,[k]
in[h] love and compassion.
20 I will betroth you in
faithfulness,
and you will acknowledge[l]
the LORD.

21 "In that day I will respond,"
declares the LORD—
"I will respond[m] to the skies,
and they will respond to the
earth;
22 and the earth will respond to
the grain,
the new wine and oil,[n]
and they will respond to
Jezreel.[i]
23 I will plant[o] her for myself in
the land;
I will show my love to the
one I called 'Not my
loved one.[j][p]'
I will say to those called 'Not
my people,[k]' 'You are
my people';[q]
and they will say, 'You are
my God.[r]' "

2:15 [a]Jos 7:24,26 [b]Ex 15:1-18 [c]Jer 2:2 [d]Hos 12:9
2:17 [e]Ex 23:13; Ps 16:4 [f]Jos 23:7
2:18 [g]Job 5:22 [h]Isa 2:4 [i]Jer 23:6; Eze 34:25
2:19 [j]Isa 62:4 [k]Isa 1:27
2:20 [l]Jer 31:34; Hos 6:6; 13:4
2:21 [m]Isa 55:10; Zec 8:12
2:22 [n]Jer 31:12; Joel 2:19
2:23 [o]Jer 31:27 [p]Hos 1:6 [q]Hos 1:10 [r]Ro 9:25*; 1Pe 2:10
3:1 [s]Hos 1:2 [t]2Sa 6:19
3:4 [u]Hos 13:11 [v]Da 11:31; Hos 2:11 [w]Jdg 17:5-6; Zec 10:2
3:5 [x]Eze 34:23-24 [y]Jer 50:4-5
4:1 [z]Jer 7:28
4:2 [a]Hos 7:3; 10:4 [b]Hos 6:9 [c]Hos 7:1
4:3 [d]Jer 4:28

Hosea's Reconciliation With His Wife

3 The LORD said to me, "Go,
show your love to your wife
again, though she is loved by another and is an adulteress.[s] Love
her as the LORD loves the Israelites,
though they turn to other gods and
love the sacred raisin cakes.[t]"
2 So I bought her for fifteen shekels[l] of silver and about a homer
and a lethek[m] of barley. 3 Then I
told her, "You are to live with[n] me
many days; you must not be a prostitute or be intimate with any man,
and I will live with[n] you."
4 For the Israelites will live many
days without king or prince,[u] without sacrifice[v] or sacred stones,
without ephod or idol.[w] 5 Afterward
the Israelites will return and seek
the LORD their God and David their
king.[x] They will come trembling to
the LORD and to his blessings in the
last days.[y]

The Charge Against Israel

4 Hear the word of the LORD,
you Israelites,
because the LORD has a
charge to bring
against you who live in the
land:
"There is no faithfulness, no
love,
no acknowledgment[z] of God
in the land.
2 There is only cursing,[o] lying[a]
and murder,[b]
stealing[c] and adultery;
they break all bounds,
and bloodshed follows
bloodshed.
3 Because of this the land
mourns,[p][d]

[d]15 *Achor* means *trouble.* [e]15 Or *respond* [f]16 Hebrew *baal* [g]19 Or *with;* also in verse 20 [h]19 Or *with* [i]22 *Jezreel* means *God plants.* [j]23 Hebrew *Lo-Ruhamah* [k]23 Hebrew *Lo-Ammi* [l]2 That is, about 6 ounces (about 170 grams) [m]2 That is, probably about 10 bushels (about 330 liters) [n]3 Or *wait for* [o]2 That is, to pronounce a curse upon [p]3 Or *dries up*

and all who live in it waste
away;[a]
the beasts of the field and the
birds of the air
and the fish of the sea are
dying.[b]

4"But let no man bring a charge,
let no man accuse another,
for your people are like those
who bring charges against a
priest.[c]
5You stumble[d] day and night,
and the prophets stumble
with you.
So I will destroy your
mother[e]—
6 my people are destroyed from
lack of knowledge.[f]

"Because you have rejected
knowledge,
I also reject you as my
priests;
because you have ignored the
law[g] of your God,
I also will ignore your
children.
7The more the priests increased,
the more they sinned against
me;
they exchanged[q] their[r]
Glory[h] for something
disgraceful.[i]
8They feed on the sins of my
people
and relish their wickedness.[j]
9And it will be: Like people, like
priests.[k]
I will punish both of them
for their ways
and repay them for their
deeds.[l]

10"They will eat but not have
enough;[m]
they will engage in
prostitution but not
increase,
because they have deserted[n]
the LORD
to give themselves 11to
prostitution,[o]
to old wine and new,
which take away the
understanding[p] 12of my
people.
They consult a wooden idol[q]
and are answered by a stick
of wood.[r]
A spirit of prostitution leads
them astray;[s]
they are unfaithful to their
God.
13They sacrifice on the
mountaintops
and burn offerings on the
hills,
under oak,[t] poplar and
terebinth,
where the shade is
pleasant.[u]
Therefore your daughters turn
to prostitution[v]
and your daughters-in-law to
adultery.[w]

14"I will not punish your
daughters
when they turn to
prostitution,
nor your daughters-in-law
when they commit adultery,
because the men themselves
consort with harlots[x]
and sacrifice with shrine
prostitutes—
a people without
understanding will come
to ruin!

15"Though you commit adultery,
O Israel,
let not Judah become guilty.

"Do not go to Gilgal;[y]
do not go up to Beth Aven.[s]
And do not swear, 'As surely
as the LORD lives!'
16The Israelites are stubborn,
like a stubborn heifer.
How then can the LORD pasture
them
like lambs[z] in a meadow?
17Ephraim is joined to idols;
leave him alone!
18Even when their drinks are
gone,
they continue their
prostitution;

4:3 [a]Isa 33:9 [b]Jer 4:25; Zep 1:3
4:4 [c]Dt 17:12; Eze 3:26
4:5 [d]Eze 14:7 [e]Hos 2:2
4:6 [f]Hos 2:13; Mal 2:7-8 [g]Hos 8:1,12
4:7 [h]Hab 2:16 [i]Hos 10:1,6; 13:6
4:8 [j]Isa 56:11; Mic 3:11
4:9 [k]Isa 24:2 [l]Jer 5:31; Hos 8:13; 9:9, 15
4:10 [m]Lev 26:26; Mic 6:14 [n]Hos 7:14; 9:17
4:11 [o]Hos 5:4 [p]Pr 20:1
4:12 [q]Jer 2:27 [r]Hab 2:19 [s]Isa 44:20
4:13 [t]Isa 1:29 [u]Jer 3:6; Hos 11:2 [v]Jer 2:20; Am 7:17 [w]Hos 2:13
4:14 [x]ver 11
4:15 [y]Hos 9:15; 12:11; Am 4:4
4:16 [z]Isa 5:17; 7:25

[q]7 Syriac and an ancient Hebrew scribal tradition; Masoretic Text *I will exchange*
[r]7 Masoretic Text; an ancient Hebrew scribal tradition *my*
[s]15 *Beth Aven* means *house of wickedness* (a name for Bethel, which means *house of God*).

their rulers dearly love
shameful ways.
19A whirlwind[a] will sweep them
away,
and their sacrifices will bring
them shame.[b]

Judgment Against Israel

5 "Hear this, you priests!
Pay attention, you Israelites!
Listen, O royal house!
This judgment is against you:
You have been a snare[c] at
Mizpah,
a net spread out on Tabor.
2The rebels are deep in
slaughter.[d]
I will discipline all of them.[e]
3I know all about Ephraim;
Israel is not hidden from me.
Ephraim, you have now turned
to prostitution;
Israel is corrupt.[f]

4"Their deeds do not permit
them
to return to their God.
A spirit of prostitution[g] is in
their heart;
they do not acknowledge[h]
the LORD.
5Israel's arrogance testifies[i]
against them;
the Israelites, even Ephraim,
stumble in their sin;
Judah also stumbles with
them.
6When they go with their flocks
and herds
to seek the LORD,[j]
they will not find him;
he has withdrawn[k] himself
from them.
7They are unfaithful[l] to the
LORD;
they give birth to
illegitimate[m] children.
Now their New Moon festivals
will devour[n] them and their
fields.

8"Sound the trumpet in
Gibeah,[o]
the horn in Ramah.[p]
Raise the battle cry in Beth
Aven[t];[q]
lead on, O Benjamin.

4:19 [a]Hos 12:1; 13:15 [b]Isa 1:29
5:1 [c]Hos 6:9; 9:8
5:2 [d]Hos 4:2 [e]Hos 9:15
5:3 [f]Hos 6:10
5:4 [g]Hos 4:11 [h]Hos 4:6
5:5 [i]Hos 7:10
5:6 [j]Mic 6:6-7 [k]Pr 1:28; Isa 1:15; Eze 8:6
5:7 [l]Hos 6:7 [m]Hos 2:4 [n]Hos 2:11-12
5:8 [o]Hos 9:9; 10:9 [p]Isa 10:29 [q]Hos 4:15
5:9 [r]Isa 37:3; Hos 9:11-17 [s]Isa 46:10; Zec 1:6
5:10 [t]Dt 19:14 [u]Eze 7:8
5:11 [v]Hos 9:16; Mic 6:16
5:12 [w]Isa 51:8
5:13 [x]Hos 7:11; 8:9 [y]Hos 10:6 [z]Hos 14:3 [a]Jer 30:12
5:14 [b]Am 3:4 [c]Mic 5:8
5:15 [d]Hos 3:5 [e]Jer 2:27 [f]Isa 64:9
6:1 [g]Hos 5:14 [h]Dt 32:39; Jer 30:17; Hos 14:4
6:2 [i]Ps 30:5

9Ephraim will be laid waste
on the day of reckoning.[r]
Among the tribes of Israel
I proclaim what is certain.[s]
10Judah's leaders are like those
who move boundary stones.[t]
I will pour out my wrath[u] on
them
like a flood of water.
11Ephraim is oppressed,
trampled in judgment,
intent on pursuing idols.[u][v]
12I am like a moth[w] to Ephraim,
like rot to the people of
Judah.

13"When Ephraim saw his
sickness,
and Judah his sores,
then Ephraim turned to
Assyria,[x]
and sent to the great king for
help.[y]
But he is not able to cure[z]
you,
not able to heal your sores.[a]
14For I will be like a lion[b] to
Ephraim,
like a great lion to Judah.
I will tear them to pieces and
go away;
I will carry them off, with no
one to rescue them.[c]
15Then I will go back to my place
until they admit their guilt.
And they will seek my face;[d]
in their misery[e] they will
earnestly seek me.[f]"

Israel Unrepentant

6 "Come, let us return to the
LORD.
He has torn us to pieces[g]
but he will heal us;
he has injured us
but he will bind up our
wounds.[h]
2After two days he will revive
us;[i]
on the third day he will
restore us,
that we may live in his
presence.

[t]8 *Beth Aven* means *house of wickedness* (a name for Bethel, which means *house of God*).
[u]11 The meaning of the Hebrew for this word is uncertain.

3 Let us acknowledge the LORD;
let us press on to
acknowledge him.
As surely as the sun rises,
he will appear;
he will come to us like the
winter rains,[a]
like the spring rains that
water the earth.[b]"

4 "What can I do with you,
Ephraim?[c]
What can I do with you,
Judah?
Your love is like the morning
mist,
like the early dew that
disappears.[d]
5 Therefore I cut you in pieces
with my prophets,
I killed you with the words of
my mouth;[e]
my judgments flashed like
lightning upon you.[f]
6 For I desire mercy, not
sacrifice,[g]
and acknowledgment[h] of
God rather than burnt
offerings.
7 Like Adam,[v] they have broken
the covenant[i]—
they were unfaithful[j] to me
there.
8 Gilead is a city of wicked men,
stained with footprints of
blood.
9 As marauders lie in ambush for
a man,
so do bands of priests;
they murder on the road to
Shechem,
committing shameful
crimes.[k]
10 I have seen a horrible[l] thing
in the house of Israel.
There Ephraim is given to
prostitution
and Israel is defiled.[m]

11 "Also for you, Judah,
a harvest[n] is appointed.

"Whenever I would restore
the fortunes of my
people,

7 1 whenever I would heal Israel,
the sins of Ephraim are
exposed
and the crimes of Samaria
revealed.[o]
They practice deceit,[p]
thieves break into houses,[q]
bandits rob in the streets;
2 but they do not realize
that I remember[r] all their
evil deeds.
Their sins engulf them;[s]
they are always before me.

3 "They delight the king with
their wickedness,
the princes with their lies.[t]
4 They are all adulterers,[u]
burning like an oven
whose fire the baker need not
stir
from the kneading of the
dough till it rises.
5 On the day of the festival of
our king
the princes become inflamed
with wine,[v]
and he joins hands with the
mockers.
6 Their hearts are like an oven;[w]
they approach him with
intrigue.
Their passion smolders all
night;
in the morning it blazes like
a flaming fire.
7 All of them are hot as an oven;
they devour their rulers.
All their kings fall,
and none of them calls[x] on
me.

8 "Ephraim mixes[y] with the
nations;
Ephraim is a flat cake not
turned over.
9 Foreigners sap his strength,[z]
but he does not realize it.
His hair is sprinkled with gray,
but he does not notice.
10 Israel's arrogance testifies
against him,[a]
but despite all this
he does not return to the LORD
his God
or search[b] for him.

11 "Ephraim is like a dove,[c]
easily deceived and
senseless—

6:3 [a] Joel 2:23 [b] Ps 72:6
6:4 [c] Hos 11:8 [d] Hos 7:1; 13:3
6:5 [e] Jer 1:9-10; 23:29 [f] Heb 4:12
6:6 [g] Isa 1:11; Mt 9:13*; 12:7* [h] Hos 2:20
6:7 [i] Hos 8:1 [j] Hos 5:7
6:9 [k] Jer 7:9-10; Eze 22:9; Hos 7:1
6:10 [l] Jer 5:30 [m] Hos 5:3
6:11 [n] Jer 51:33; Joel 3:13
7:1 [o] Hos 6:4 [p] ver 13 [q] Hos 4:2
7:2 [r] Jer 14:10; Hos 8:13 [s] Jer 2:19
7:3 [t] Hos 4:2; Mic 7:3
7:4 [u] Jer 9:2
7:5 [v] Isa 28:1,7
7:6 [w] Ps 21:9
7:7 [x] ver 16
7:8 [y] ver 11; Ps 106:35; Hos 5:13
7:9 [z] Isa 1:7; Hos 8:7
7:10 [a] Hos 5:5 [b] Isa 9:13
7:11 [c] Hos 11:11

v7 Or *As at Adam*; or *Like men*

now calling to Egypt,
now turning to Assyria.[a]
12When they go, I will throw my
net[b] over them;
I will pull them down like
birds of the air.
When I hear them flocking
together,
I will catch them.
13Woe[c] to them,
because they have strayed[d]
from me!
Destruction to them,
because they have rebelled
against me!
I long to redeem them
but they speak lies against
me.[e]
14They do not cry out to me from
their hearts[f]
but wail upon their beds.
They gather together[w] for grain
and new wine[g]
but turn away from me.[h]
15I trained them and
strengthened them,
but they plot evil[i] against
me.
16They do not turn to the Most
High;
they are like a faulty bow.[j]
Their leaders will fall by the
sword
because of their insolent
words.
For this they will be ridiculed[k]
in the land of Egypt.[l]

Israel to Reap the Whirlwind

8 "Put the trumpet to your lips!
An eagle[m] is over the house
of the LORD
because the people have
broken my covenant
and rebelled against my
law.[n]
2Israel cries out to me,
'O our God, we acknowledge
you!'
3But Israel has rejected what is
good;
an enemy will pursue him.
4They set up kings without my
consent;
they choose princes without
my approval.[o]
With their silver and gold
they make idols[p] for
themselves
to their own destruction.
5Throw out your calf-idol,
O Samaria![q]
My anger burns against them.
How long will they be
incapable of purity?[r]
6 They are from Israel!
This calf—a craftsman has
made it;
it is not God.
It will be broken in pieces,
that calf of Samaria.
7"They sow the wind
and reap the whirlwind.[s]
The stalk has no head;
it will produce no flour.
Were it to yield grain,
foreigners would swallow it
up.[t]
8Israel is swallowed up;[u]
now she is among the
nations
like a worthless[v] thing.
9For they have gone up to
Assyria
like a wild donkey wandering
alone.
Ephraim has sold herself to
lovers.
10Although they have sold
themselves among the
nations,
I will now gather them
together.[w]
They will begin to waste away[x]
under the oppression of the
mighty king.
11"Though Ephraim built many
altars for sin offerings,
these have become altars for
sinning.[y]
12I wrote for them the many
things of my law,
but they regarded them as
something alien.
13They offer sacrifices given to
me
and they eat[z] the meat,
but the LORD is not pleased
with them.

7:11 [a]Hos 5:13; 12:1
7:12 [b]Eze 12:13
7:13 [c]Hos 9:12 [d]Jer 14:10; Eze 34:4-6; Hos 9:17 [e]ver 1; Mt 23:37
7:14 [f]Jer 3:10 [g]Am 2:8 [h]Hos 13:16
7:15 [i]Na 1:9,11
7:16 [j]Ps 78:9,57 [k]Eze 23:32 [l]Hos 9:3
8:1 [m]Dt 28:49; Jer 4:13 [n]Hos 4:6; 6:7
8:4 [o]Hos 13:10 [p]Hos 2:8
8:5 [q]Hos 10:5 [r]Jer 13:27
8:7 [s]Pr 22:8; Isa 66:15; Hos 10:12-13; Na 1:3 [t]Hos 2:9
8:8 [u]Jer 51:34 [v]Jer 22:28
8:10 [w]Eze 16:37; 22:20 [x]Jer 42:2
8:11 [y]Hos 10:1; 12:11
8:13 [z]Jer 7:21

[w]*14* Most Hebrew manuscripts; some Hebrew manuscripts and Septuagint *They slash themselves*

Now he will remember[a] their
wickedness
and punish their sins:[b]
They will return to Egypt.[c]
14Israel has forgotten[d] his Maker
and built palaces;
Judah has fortified many
towns.
But I will send fire upon their
cities
that will consume their
fortresses."[e]

Punishment for Israel

9 Do not rejoice, O Israel;
do not be jubilant[f] like the
other nations.
For you have been unfaithful[g]
to your God;
you love the wages of a
prostitute
at every threshing floor.
2Threshing floors and
winepresses will not feed
the people;
the new wine[h] will fail them.
3They will not remain[i] in the
LORD's land;
Ephraim will return to
Egypt[j]
and eat unclean[x] food in
Assyria.[k]
4They will not pour out wine
offerings to the LORD,
nor will their sacrifices
please[l] him.
Such sacrifices will be to them
like the bread of
mourners;
all who eat them will be
unclean.[m]
This food will be for
themselves;
it will not come into the
temple of the LORD.

5What will you do[n] on the day
of your appointed
feasts,[o]
on the festival days of the
LORD?
6Even if they escape from
destruction,
Egypt will gather them,
and Memphis[p] will bury
them.

8:13 [a]Hos 7:2 [b]Hos 4:9 [c]Hos 9:3,6
8:14 [d]Dt 32:18; Hos 2:13 [e]Jer 17:27
9:1 [f]Isa 22:12-13 [g]Hos 10:5
9:2 [h]Hos 2:9
9:3 [i]Lev 25:23 [j]Hos 8:13 [k]Eze 4:13; Hos 7:11
9:4 [l]Jer 6:20; Hos 8:13 [m]Hag 2:13-14
9:5 [n]Isa 10:3; Jer 5:31 [o]Hos 2:11
9:6 [p]Isa 19:13 [q]Isa 5:6; Hos 10:8
9:7 [r]Isa 34:8; Jer 10:15; Mic 7:4 [s]Jer 16:18 [t]Isa 44:25; La 2:14; Eze 14:9-10
9:8 [u]Hos 5:1
9:9 [v]Jdg 19:16-30; Hos 5:8; 10:9 [w]Hos 8:13
9:10 [x]Nu 25:1-5; Ps 106:28-29 [y]Jer 11:13; Hos 4:14
9:11 [z]Hos 4:7; 10:5 [a]ver 14
9:12 [b]Hos 7:13 [c]Dt 31:17

Their treasures of silver will be
taken over by briers,
and thorns[q] will overrun
their tents.
7The days of punishment[r] are
coming,
the days of reckoning are at
hand.
Let Israel know this.
Because your sins[s] are so
many
and your hostility so great,
the prophet is considered a
fool,[t]
the inspired man a maniac.
8The prophet, along with my
God,
is the watchman over
Ephraim,[y]
yet snares[u] await him on all
his paths,
and hostility in the house of
his God.
9They have sunk deep into
corruption,
as in the days of Gibeah.[v]
God will remember[w] their
wickedness
and punish them for their
sins.

10"When I found Israel,
it was like finding grapes in
the desert;
when I saw your fathers,
it was like seeing the early
fruit on the fig tree.
But when they came to Baal
Peor,[x]
they consecrated themselves
to that shameful idol[y]
and became as vile as the
thing they loved.
11Ephraim's glory will fly away
like a bird[z]—
no birth, no pregnancy, no
conception.[a]
12Even if they rear children,
I will bereave them of every
one.
Woe[b] to them
when I turn away from
them![c]
13I have seen Ephraim, like Tyre,

[x]3 That is, ceremonially unclean [y]8 Or *The prophet is the watchman over Ephraim, / the people of my God*

planted in a pleasant place.[a]
But Ephraim will bring out
their children to the slayer."

14Give them, O LORD—
what will you give them?
Give them wombs that miscarry
and breasts that are dry.[b]

15"Because of all their
wickedness in Gilgal,[c]
I hated them there.
Because of their sinful deeds,[d]
I will drive them out of my
house.
I will no longer love them;
all their leaders are
rebellious.[e]
16Ephraim[f] is blighted,
their root is withered,
they yield no fruit.[g]
Even if they bear children,
I will slay[h] their cherished
offspring."

17My God will reject them
because they have not
obeyed[i] him;
they will be wanderers
among the nations.[j]

10 Israel was a spreading
vine;[k]
he brought forth fruit for
himself.
As his fruit increased,
he built more altars;[l]
as his land prospered,
he adorned his sacred
stones.[m]
2Their heart is deceitful,[n]
and now they must bear their
guilt.[o]
The LORD will demolish their
altars[p]
and destroy their sacred
stones.[q]

3Then they will say, "We have
no king
because we did not revere
the LORD.
But even if we had a king,
what could he do for us?"
4They make many promises,
take false oaths[r]
and make agreements;[s]
therefore lawsuits spring up

9:13 [a]Eze 27:3
9:14 [b]ver 11; Lk 23:29
9:15 [c]Hos 4:15 [d]Hos 7:2 [e]Isa 1:23; Hos 4:9; 5:2
9:16 [f]Hos 5:11 [g]Hos 8:7 [h]ver 12
9:17 [i]Hos 4:10 [j]Dt 28:65; Hos 7:13
10:1 [k]Eze 15:2 [l]1Ki 14:23 [m]Hos 8:11; 12:11
10:2 [n]1Ki 18:21 [o]Hos 13:16 [p]ver 8 [q]Mic 5:13
10:4 [r]Hos 4:2 [s]Eze 17:19; Am 5:7
10:5 [t]Hos 5:8 [u]2Ki 23:5 [v]Hos 8:5; 9:1, 3,11
10:6 [w]Hos 11:5 [x]Hos 5:13 [y]Isa 30:3; Hos 4:7
10:7 [z]Hos 13:11
10:8 [a]1Ki 12:28-30; Hos 4:13 [b]Hos 9:6 [c]ver 2; Isa 32:13 [d]Lk 23:30*; Rev 6:16
10:9 [e]Hos 5:8
10:10 [f]Eze 5:13; Hos 4:9

like poisonous weeds in a
plowed field.
5The people who live in Samaria
fear
for the calf-idol of Beth
Aven.[z][t]
Its people will mourn over it,
and so will its idolatrous
priests,[u]
those who had rejoiced over its
splendor,
because it is taken from
them into exile.[v]
6It will be carried to Assyria[w]
as tribute for the great
king.[x]
Ephraim will be disgraced;[y]
Israel will be ashamed of its
wooden idols.[a]
7Samaria and its king will float
away[z]
like a twig on the surface of
the waters.
8The high places of
wickedness[b][a] will be
destroyed—
it is the sin of Israel.
Thorns[b] and thistles will grow
up
and cover their altars.[c]
Then they will say to the
mountains, "Cover us!"
and to the hills, "Fall on
us!"[d]

9"Since the days of Gibeah,[e]
you have sinned,
O Israel,
and there you have
remained.[c]
Did not war overtake
the evildoers in Gibeah?
10When I please, I will punish[f]
them;
nations will be gathered
against them
to put them in bonds for
their double sin.
11Ephraim is a trained heifer
that loves to thresh;
so I will put a yoke
on her fair neck.

[z]5 *Beth Aven* means *house of wickedness* (a name for Bethel, which means *house of God*). [a]6 Or *its counsel* [b]8 Hebrew *aven,* a reference to Beth Aven (a derogatory name for Bethel) [c]9 Or *there a stand was taken*

I will drive Ephraim,
Judah must plow,
and Jacob must break up the ground.
12Sow for yourselves righteousness,[a]
reap the fruit of unfailing love,
and break up your unplowed ground;[b]
for it is time to seek[c] the LORD,
until he comes
and showers righteousness[d] on you.
13But you have planted wickedness,
you have reaped evil,[e]
you have eaten the fruit of deception.
Because you have depended on your own strength
and on your many warriors,[f]
14the roar of battle will rise against your people,
so that all your fortresses will be devastated[g]—
as Shalman devastated Beth Arbel on the day of battle,
when mothers were dashed to the ground with their children.[h]
15Thus will it happen to you, O Bethel,
because your wickedness is great.
When that day dawns,
the king of Israel will be completely destroyed.[i]

God's Love for Israel

11 "When Israel was a child, I loved him,
and out of Egypt I called my son.[j]
2But the more I[d] called Israel,
the further they went from me.[e]
They sacrificed to the Baals[k]
and they burned incense to images.[l]
3It was I who taught Ephraim to walk,
taking them by the arms;[m]
but they did not realize
it was I who healed[n] them.
4I led them with cords of human kindness,
with ties of love;[o]
I lifted the yoke[p] from their neck
and bent down to feed[q] them.

5"Will they not return to Egypt[r]
and will not Assyria[s] rule over them
because they refuse to repent?
6Swords[t] will flash in their cities,
will destroy the bars of their gates
and put an end to their plans.
7My people are determined to turn from me.[u]
Even if they call to the Most High,
he will by no means exalt them.

8"How can I give you up, Ephraim?[v]
How can I hand you over, Israel?
How can I treat you like Admah?
How can I make you like Zeboiim?[w]
My heart is changed within me;
all my compassion is aroused.
9I will not carry out my fierce anger,[x]
nor will I turn and devastate[y] Ephraim.
For I am God, and not man[z]—
the Holy One among you.
I will not come in wrath.[f]
10They will follow the LORD;
he will roar like a lion.
When he roars,
his children will come trembling from the west.[a]
11They will come trembling like birds from Egypt,
like doves from Assyria.[b]

10:12 [a]Pr 11:18 [b]Jer 4:3 [c]Hos 12:6 [d]Isa 45:8
10:13 [e]Job 4:8; Hos 7:3; 11:12; Gal 6:7-8 [f]Ps 33:16
10:14 [g]Isa 17:3 [h]Hos 13:16
10:15 [i]ver 7
11:1 [j]Ex 4:22; Hos 12:9,13; 13:4; Mt 2:15*
11:2 [k]Hos 2:13 [l]2Ki 17:15; Isa 65:7; Jer 18:15
11:3 [m]Dt 1:31; Hos 7:15 [n]Jer 30:17
11:4 [o]Jer 31:2-3 [p]Lev 26:13 [q]Ex 16:32; Ps 78:25
11:5 [r]Hos 7:16 [s]Hos 10:6
11:6 [t]Hos 13:16
11:7 [u]Jer 3:6-7; 8:5
11:8 [v]Hos 6:4 [w]Ge 14:8
11:9 [x]Dt 13:17; Jer 30:11 [y]Mal 3:6 [z]Nu 23:19
11:10 [a]Hos 6:1-3
11:11 [b]Isa 11:11

d2 Some Septuagint manuscripts; Hebrew *they* e2 Septuagint; Hebrew *them* f9 Or *come against any city*

I will settle them in their
homes,"
declares the LORD.

Israel's Sin

12 Ephraim has surrounded me
with lies,[a]
the house of Israel with
deceit.
And Judah is unruly against
God,
even against the faithful Holy
One.

12

1 Ephraim feeds on the
wind;[b]
he pursues the east wind all
day
and multiplies lies and
violence.
He makes a treaty with Assyria
and sends olive oil to
Egypt.[c]
2 The LORD has a charge[d] to
bring against Judah;
he will punish Jacob[g]
according to his ways
and repay him according to
his deeds.[e]
3 In the womb he grasped his
brother's heel;[f]
as a man he struggled[g] with
God.
4 He struggled with the angel
and overcame him;
he wept and begged for his
favor.
He found him at Bethel[h]
and talked with him there—
5 the LORD God Almighty,
the LORD is his name[i] of
renown!
6 But you must return to your
God;
maintain love and justice,[j]
and wait for your God
always.[k]

7 The merchant uses dishonest
scales;[l]
he loves to defraud.
8 Ephraim boasts,
"I am very rich; I have
become wealthy.[m]
With all my wealth they will
not find in me
any iniquity or sin."

9 "I am the LORD your God,
⌊who brought you⌋ out of[h]
Egypt;[n]
I will make you live in tents[o]
again,
as in the days of your
appointed feasts.
10 I spoke to the prophets,
gave them many visions
and told parables[p] through
them."[q]

11 Is Gilead wicked?[r]
Its people are worthless!
Do they sacrifice bulls in
Gilgal?[s]
Their altars will be like piles
of stones
on a plowed field.[t]
12 Jacob fled to the country of
Aram[i];[u]
Israel served to get a wife,
and to pay for her he tended
sheep.[v]
13 The LORD used a prophet to
bring Israel up from
Egypt,
by a prophet he cared for
him.[w]
14 But Ephraim has bitterly
provoked him to anger;
his Lord will leave upon him
the guilt of his
bloodshed[x]
and will repay him for his
contempt.[y]

The LORD's Anger Against Israel

13

When Ephraim spoke,
men trembled;[z]
he was exalted[a] in Israel.
But he became guilty of Baal
worship[b] and died.
2 Now they sin more and more;
they make idols for
themselves from their
silver,[c]
cleverly fashioned images,
all of them the work of
craftsmen.
It is said of these people,
"They offer human sacrifice

11:12 [a] Hos 4:2
12:1 [b] Eze 17:10 [c] 2Ki 17:4
12:2 [d] Mic 6:2 [e] Hos 4:9
12:3 [f] Ge 25:26 [g] Ge 32:24-29
12:4 [h] Ge 28:12-15; 35:15
12:5 [i] Ex 3:15
12:6 [j] Mic 6:8 [k] Hos 6:1-3; 10:12; Mic 7:7
12:7 [l] Am 8:5
12:8 [m] Ps 62:10; Rev 3:17
12:9 [n] Lev 23:43; Hos 11:1 [o] Ne 8:17
12:10 [p] Eze 20:49 [q] 2Ki 17:13; Jer 7:25
12:11 [r] Hos 6:8 [s] Hos 4:15 [t] Hos 8:11
12:12 [u] Ge 28:5 [v] Ge 29:18
12:13 [w] Ex 13:3; Isa 63:11-14
12:14 [x] Eze 18:13 [y] Da 11:18
13:1 [z] Jdg 12:1 [a] Jdg 8:1 [b] Hos 11:2
13:2 [c] Isa 46:6; Jer 10:4

g2 *Jacob* means *he grasps the heel* (figuratively, *he deceives*). h9 Or *God / ever since you were in* i12 That is, Northwest Mesopotamia

and kiss[i] the calf-idols.[a]"
3Therefore they will be like the
morning mist,
like the early dew that
disappears,[b]
like chaff[c] swirling from a
threshing floor,[d]
like smoke[e] escaping
through a window.

4"But I am the LORD your God,
⌊who brought you⌋ out of[k]
Egypt.[f]
You shall acknowledge no God
but me,[g]
no Savior[h] except me.
5I cared for you in the desert,
in the land of burning heat.
6When I fed them, they were
satisfied;
when they were satisfied,
they became proud;
then they forgot me.[i]
7So I will come upon them like
a lion,
like a leopard I will lurk by
the path.
8Like a bear robbed of her
cubs,[j]
I will attack them and rip
them open.
Like a lion I will devour them;
a wild animal will tear them
apart.[k]

9"You are destroyed, O Israel,
because you are against
me,[l] against your
helper.[m]
10Where is your king,[n] that he
may save you?
Where are your rulers in all
your towns,
of whom you said,
'Give me a king and
princes'?[o]
11So in my anger I gave you a
king,
and in my wrath I took him
away.[p]
12The guilt of Ephraim is stored
up,
his sins are kept on record.[q]
13Pains as of a woman in
childbirth[r] come to
him,
but he is a child without
wisdom;
when the time arrives,
he does not come to the
opening of the womb.[s]

14"I will ransom them from the
power of the grave[l];[t]
I will redeem them from
death.
Where, O death, are your
plagues?
Where, O grave,[l] is your
destruction?[u]

"I will have no compassion,
15 even though he thrives[v]
among his brothers.
An east wind[w] from the LORD
will come,
blowing in from the desert;
his spring will fail
and his well dry up.[x]
His storehouse will be
plundered[y]
of all its treasures.
16The people of Samaria must
bear their guilt,[z]
because they have rebelled[a]
against their God.
They will fall by the sword;[b]
their little ones will be
dashed[c] to the ground,
their pregnant women[d]
ripped open."

Repentance to Bring Blessing

14 Return, O Israel, to the
LORD your God.
Your sins have been your
downfall![e]
2Take words with you
and return to the LORD.
Say to him:
"Forgive all our sins
and receive us graciously,[f]
that we may offer the fruit of
our lips.[m][g]
3Assyria cannot save us;
we will not mount
war-horses.[h]
We will never again say 'Our
gods'[i]
to what our own hands have
made,

13:2 [a]Isa 44:17-20
13:3 [b]Hos 6:4 [c]Isa 17:13 [d]Da 2:35 [e]Ps 68:2
13:4 [f]Hos 12:9 [g]Ex 20:3 [h]Isa 43:11; 45:21-22
13:6 [i]Dt 32:12-15; Hos 2:13
13:8 [j]2Sa 17:8 [k]Ps 50:22
13:9 [l]Jer 2:17-19 [m]Dt 33:29
13:10 [n]2Ki 17:4 [o]1Sa 8:6; Hos 8:4
13:11 [p]1Ki 14:10; Hos 10:7
13:12 [q]Dt 32:34
13:13 [r]Isa 13:8; Mic 4:9-10 [s]Isa 66:9
13:14 [t]Ps 49:15; Eze 37:12-13 [u]1Co 15:55*
13:15 [v]Hos 10:1 [w]Eze 19:12 [x]Jer 51:36 [y]Jer 20:5
13:16 [z]Hos 10:2 [a]Hos 7:14 [b]Hos 11:6 [c]2Ki 8:12; Hos 10:14 [d]2Ki 15:16; Isa 13:16
14:1 [e]Hos 5:5
14:2 [f]Mic 7:18-19 [g]Heb 13:15
14:3 [h]Ps 33:17; Isa 31:1 [i]Hos 8:6

[i]2 Or *"Men who sacrifice / kiss* [k]4 Or *God / ever since you were in* [l]14 Hebrew *Sheol* [m]2 Or *offer our lips as sacrifices of bulls*

for in you the fatherless[a]
find compassion."

4"I will heal[b] their waywardness
and love them freely,[c]
for my anger has turned away
from them.
5I will be like the dew to Israel;
he will blossom like a lily.[d]
Like a cedar of Lebanon[e]
he will send down his roots;[f]
6 his young shoots will grow.
His splendor will be like an
olive tree,[g]
his fragrance like a cedar of
Lebanon.[h]
7Men will dwell again in his
shade.[i]
He will flourish like the
grain.
He will blossom like a vine,
and his fame will be like the
wine[j] from Lebanon.[k]
8O Ephraim, what more have I[n]
to do with idols?[l]
I will answer him and care
for him.
I am like a green pine tree;
your fruitfulness comes from
me."

9Who is wise?[m] He will realize
these things.
Who is discerning? He will
understand them.[n]
The ways of the LORD are
right;[o]
the righteous walk[p] in them,
but the rebellious stumble in
them.

14:3 [a] Ps 10:14; 68:5
14:4 [b] Hos 6:1 [c] Zep 3:17
14:5 [d] SS 2:1 [e] Isa 35:2 [f] Job 29:19
14:6 [g] Ps 52:8 [h] SS 4:11
14:7 [i] Ps 91:1-4 [j] Hos 2:22 [k] Eze 17:23
14:8 [l] ver 3
14:9 [m] Ps 107:43 [n] Pr 10:29; Isa 1:28 [o] Ps 111:7-8; Ac 13:10 [p] Isa 26:7

[n]8 Or *What more has Ephraim*

Joel

Title and Background

Joel was a common Old Testament name meaning "The LORD is God." Locust plagues were frequent occurrences in the Near East for millennia, and Joel envisions one coming on Israel as a judgment from God.

Author and Date of Writing

The book contains no references to datable historical events, but a good case can be made for its being written about 830 B.C., during the reign of King Joash and at a time when Jehoiada the high priest was regent in Judah.

Theme and Message

Joel sees in the massive locust plague and severe drought devastating Judah a harbinger of the "great and dreadful day of the LORD" (2:31). Confronted with this crisis, he calls on everyone to repent. He sees this day as a day of punishment for unfaithful Israel as well as for her neighbors. Restoration and blessing will come only after judgment and repentance.

Outline

I. A Foretaste of the Day of the Lord (1:1-2:17)
  A. A Call to Mourning and Prayer (1:2-14)
  B. The Announcement of the Day of the Lord (1:15-2:11)
  C. A Call to Repentance (2:12-17)
II. Salvation in the Day of the Lord (2:18-3:21)
  A. The Lord's Restoration of Judah (2:18-27)
  B. The Lord's Renewal of His People (2:28-32)
  C. The Coming of the Day of the Lord (3:1-21)

---

1 The word of the LORD that came[a] to Joel[b] son of Pethuel.

An Invasion of Locusts

2Hear this,[c] you elders;
listen, all who live in the land.[d]
Has anything like this ever happened in your days
or in the days of your forefathers?[e]
3Tell it to your children,[f]
and let your children tell it to their children,
and their children to the next generation.
4What the locust swarm has left
the great locusts have eaten;
what the great locusts have left
the young locusts have eaten;
what the young locusts have left
other locusts[a] have eaten.[g]
5Wake up, you drunkards, and weep!
Wail, all you drinkers of wine;[h]
wail because of the new wine,
for it has been snatched from your lips.
6A nation has invaded my land,
powerful and without number;[i]
it has the teeth[j] of a lion,
the fangs of a lioness.

1:1 [a]Jer 1:2 [b]Ac 2:16
1:2 [c]Hos 5:1 [d]Hos 4:1 [e]Joel 2:2
1:3 [f]Ex 10:2; Ps 78:4
1:4 [g]Dt 28:39; Na 3:15
1:5 [h]Joel 3:3
1:6 [i]Joel 2:2,11, 25 [j]Rev 9:8

a4 The precise meaning of the four Hebrew words used here for locusts is uncertain.

7It has laid waste[a] my vines
and ruined my fig trees.[b]
It has stripped off their bark
and thrown it away,
leaving their branches white.

8Mourn like a virgin[b] in
sackcloth[c]
grieving for the husband[c] of
her youth.
9Grain offerings and drink
offerings[d]
are cut off from the house of
the LORD.
The priests are in mourning,
those who minister before
the LORD.
10The fields are ruined,
the ground is dried up[d];[e]
the grain is destroyed,
the new wine[f] is dried up,
the oil fails.
11Despair, you farmers,[g]
wail, you vine growers;
grieve for the wheat and the
barley,
because the harvest of the
field is destroyed.[h]
12The vine is dried up
and the fig tree is withered;
the pomegranate, the palm and
the apple tree—
all the trees of the field—are
dried up.[i]
Surely the joy of mankind
is withered away.

A Call to Repentance

13Put on sackcloth,[j] O priests,
and mourn;
wail, you who minister[k]
before the altar.
Come, spend the night in
sackcloth,
you who minister before my
God;
for the grain offerings and drink
offerings[l]
are withheld from the house
of your God.
14Declare a holy fast;[m]
call a sacred assembly.
Summon the elders
and all who live in the land
to the house of the LORD your
God,
and cry out[n] to the LORD.

1:7 [a]Isa 5:6 [b]Am 4:9
1:8 [c]ver 13; Isa 22:12; Am 8:10
1:9 [d]Hos 9:4; Joel 2:14,17
1:10 [e]Isa 24:4 [f]Hos 9:2
1:11 [g]Jer 14:3-4; Am 5:16 [h]Isa 17:11
1:12 [i]Hag 2:19
1:13 [j]Jer 4:8 [k]Joel 2:17 [l]ver 9
1:14 [m]2Ch 20:3 [n]Jnh 3:8
1:15 [o]Jer 30:7 [p]Isa 13:6,9; Joel 2:1,11,31
1:16 [q]Isa 3:7 [r]Dt 12:7
1:17 [s]Isa 17:10-11
1:19 [t]Ps 50:15 [u]Am 7:4 [v]Jer 9:10
1:20 [w]Ps 104:21 [x]1Ki 17:7
2:1 [y]Jer 4:5 [z]ver 15 [a]Joel 1:15; Zep 1:14-16 [b]Ob 1:15
2:2 [c]Am 5:18 [d]Da 9:12 [e]Joel 1:6 [f]Joel 1:2

15Alas for that[o] day!
For the day of the LORD[p] is
near;
it will come like destruction
from the Almighty.[e]

16Has not the food been cut off[q]
before our very eyes—
joy and gladness
from the house of our God?[r]
17The seeds are shriveled
beneath the clods.[f][s]
The storehouses are in ruins,
the granaries have been
broken down,
for the grain has dried up.
18How the cattle moan!
The herds mill about
because they have no pasture;
even the flocks of sheep are
suffering.

19To you, O LORD, I call,[t]
for fire[u] has devoured the
open pastures[v]
and flames have burned up
all the trees of the field.
20Even the wild animals pant for
you;[w]
the streams of water have
dried up[x]
and fire has devoured the
open pastures.

An Army of Locusts

2 Blow the trumpet[y] in Zion;[z]
sound the alarm on my holy
hill.
Let all who live in the land
tremble,
for the day of the LORD[a] is
coming.
It is close at hand[b]—
2 a day of darkness[c] and
gloom,[d]
a day of clouds and
blackness.
Like dawn spreading across the
mountains
a large and mighty army[e]
comes,
such as never was of old[f]
nor ever will be in ages to
come.

[b]8 Or *young woman* [c]8 Or *betrothed* [d]10 Or *ground mourns* [e]15 Hebrew *Shaddai* [f]17 The meaning of the Hebrew for this word is uncertain.

3Before them fire devours,
behind them a flame blazes.
Before them the land is like the
garden of Eden,[a]
behind them, a desert
waste[b]—
nothing escapes them.
4They have the appearance of
horses;[c]
they gallop along like cavalry.
5With a noise like that of
chariots[d]
they leap over the
mountaintops,
like a crackling fire[e]
consuming stubble,
like a mighty army drawn up
for battle.

6At the sight of them, nations
are in anguish;[f]
every face turns pale.[g]
7They charge like warriors;
they scale walls like soldiers.
They all march in line,
not swerving[h] from their
course.
8They do not jostle each other;
each marches straight ahead.
They plunge through defenses
without breaking ranks.
9They rush upon the city;
they run along the wall.
They climb into the houses;
like thieves they enter
through the windows.[i]

10Before them the earth shakes,[j]
the sky trembles,
the sun and moon are
darkened,[k]
and the stars no longer
shine.[l]
11The LORD[m] thunders
at the head of his army;
his forces are beyond number,
and mighty are those who
obey his command.
The day of the LORD is great;[n]
it is dreadful.
Who can endure it?[o]

Rend Your Heart

12"Even now," declares the LORD,
"return[p] to me with all your
heart,
with fasting and weeping and
mourning."
13Rend your heart[q]
and not your garments.[r]
Return to the LORD your God,
for he is gracious and
compassionate,
slow to anger and abounding in
love,[s]
and he relents from sending
calamity.[t]
14Who knows? He may turn[u] and
have pity
and leave behind a
blessing[v]—
grain offerings and drink
offerings[w]
for the LORD your God.

15Blow the trumpet[x] in Zion,
declare a holy fast,[y]
call a sacred assembly.[z]
16Gather the people,
consecrate[a] the assembly;
bring together the elders,
gather the children,
those nursing at the breast.
Let the bridegroom[b] leave his
room
and the bride her chamber.
17Let the priests, who minister
before the LORD,
weep between the temple
porch and the altar.[c]
Let them say, "Spare your
people, O LORD.
Do not make your
inheritance an object of
scorn,[d]
a byword among the nations.
Why should they say among the
peoples,
'Where is their God?[e]' "

The LORD's Answer

18Then the LORD will be jealous[f]
for his land
and take pity on his people.

19The LORD will reply[g] to them:

"I am sending you grain, new
wine and oil,[g]
enough to satisfy you fully;
never again will I make you

2:3 [a]Ge 2:8 [b]Ps 105:34-35
2:4 [c]Rev 9:7
2:5 [d]Rev 9:9 [e]Isa 5:24; 30:30
2:6 [f]Isa 13:8 [g]Na 2:10
2:7 [h]Isa 5:27
2:9 [i]Jer 9:21
2:10 [j]Ps 18:7 [k]Mt 24:29 [l]Isa 13:10; Eze 32:8
2:11 [m]Joel 1:15 [n]Zep 1:14; Rev 18:8 [o]Eze 22:14
2:12 [p]Jer 4:1; Hos 12:6
2:13 [q]Ps 34:18; Isa 57:15 [r]Job 1:20 [s]Ex 34:6 [t]Jer 18:8
2:14 [u]Jer 26:3 [v]Hag 2:19 [w]Joel 1:13
2:15 [x]Nu 10:2 [y]Jer 36:9 [z]Joel 1:14
2:16 [a]Ex 19:10,22 [b]Ps 19:5
2:17 [c]Eze 8:16; Mt 23:35 [d]Dt 9:26-29; Ps 44:13 [e]Ps 42:3
2:18 [f]Zec 1:14
2:19 [g]Jer 31:12

[g]*18,19* Or LORD *was jealous . . . / and took pity . . . / 19The* LORD *replied*

an object of scorn[a] to the
nations.

20"I will drive the northern
army[b] far from you,
pushing it into a parched and
barren land,
with its front columns going
into the eastern[c] sea[h]
and those in the rear into the
western sea.[i]
And its stench[d] will go up;
its smell will rise."

Surely he has done great
things.[j]
21 Be not afraid,[e] O land;
be glad and rejoice.
Surely the LORD has done great
things.[f]
22 Be not afraid, O wild
animals,
for the open pastures are
becoming green.[g]
The trees are bearing their
fruit;
the fig tree and the vine yield
their riches.[h]
23Be glad, O people of Zion,
rejoice[i] in the LORD your
God,
for he has given you
the autumn rains in
righteousness.[k]
He sends you abundant
showers,
both autumn and spring
rains,[j] as before.
24The threshing floors will be
filled with grain;
the vats will overflow[k] with
new wine[l] and oil.

25"I will repay you for the years
the locusts have eaten—
the great locust and the
young locust,
the other locusts and the
locust swarm[l]—
my great army that I sent
among you.
26You will have plenty to eat,
until you are full,[m]
and you will praise[n] the
name of the LORD your
God,
who has worked wonders[o]
for you;

2:19 [a]Eze 34:29
2:20 [b]Jer 1:14-15 [c]Zec 14:8 [d]Isa 34:3
2:21 [e]Isa 54:4; Zep 3:16-17 [f]Ps 126:3
2:22 [g]Ps 65:12 [h]Joel 1:18-20
2:23 [i]Ps 149:2; Isa 12:6; 41:16; Hab 3:18; Zec 10:7 [j]Lev 26:4
2:24 [k]Lev 26:10; Mal 3:10 [l]Am 9:13
2:26 [m]Lev 26:5 [n]Isa 62:9 [o]Ps 126:3; Isa 25:1
2:27 [p]Joel 3:17
2:28 [q]Eze 39:29
2:29 [r]1Co 12:13; Gal 3:28
2:30 [s]Lk 21:11 [t]Mk 13:24-25
2:31 [u]Mt 24:29 [v]Isa 13:9-10; Mal 4:1,5
2:32 [w]Ac 2:17-21*; Ro 10:13* [x]Isa 46:13 [y]Ob 1:17 [z]Isa 11:11; Mic 4:7; Ro 9:27
3:1 [a]Jer 16:15

never again will my people be
shamed.
27Then you will know that I am
in Israel,
that I am the LORD[p] your
God,
and that there is no other;
never again will my people be
shamed.

The Day of the LORD

28"And afterward,
I will pour out my Spirit[q] on
all people.
Your sons and daughters will
prophesy,
your old men will dream
dreams,
your young men will see
visions.
29Even on my servants,[r] both
men and women,
I will pour out my Spirit in
those days.
30I will show wonders in the
heavens[s]
and on the earth,[t]
blood and fire and billows of
smoke.
31The sun will be turned to
darkness[u]
and the moon to blood
before the coming of the
great and dreadful day of
the LORD.[v]
32And everyone who calls
on the name of the LORD will
be saved;[w]
for on Mount Zion[x] and in
Jerusalem
there will be deliverance,[y]
as the LORD has said,
among the survivors[z]
whom the LORD calls.

The Nations Judged

3 "In those days and at that
time,
when I restore the fortunes[a]
of Judah and Jerusalem,

[h]*20* That is, the Dead Sea [i]*20* That is, the Mediterranean [j]*20* Or *rise. / Surely it has done great things."* [k]*23* Or */ the teacher for righteousness:* [l]*25* The precise meaning of the four Hebrew words used here for locusts is uncertain.

[2]I will gather all nations
and bring them down to the
Valley of Jehoshaphat.[m]
There I will enter into
judgment[a] against them
concerning my inheritance,
my people Israel,
for they scattered my people
among the nations
and divided up my land.
[3]They cast lots for my people
and traded boys for
prostitutes;
they sold girls for wine[b]
that they might drink.

[4]"Now what have you against
me, O Tyre and Sidon[c] and all you
regions of Philistia? Are you repaying me for something I have done?
If you are paying me back, I will
swiftly and speedily return on your
own heads what you have done.[d]
[5]For you took my silver and my
gold and carried off my finest treasures to your temples.[e] [6]You sold
the people of Judah and Jerusalem
to the Greeks, that you might send
them far from their homeland.

[7]"See, I am going to rouse them
out of the places to which you sold
them,[f] and I will return on your
own heads what you have done. [8]I
will sell your sons[g] and daughters
to the people of Judah,[h] and they
will sell them to the Sabeans, a nation far away." The LORD has spoken.

[9]Proclaim this among the
nations:
Prepare for war![i]
Rouse the warriors![j]
Let all the fighting men draw
near and attack.
[10]Beat your plowshares into
swords
and your pruning hooks[k]
into spears.
Let the weakling[l] say,
"I am strong!"
[11]Come quickly, all you nations
from every side,
and assemble[m] there.

Bring down your warriors,[n]
O LORD!

3:2 [a]Eze 36:5
3:3 [b]Am 2:6
3:4 [c]Mt 11:21 [d]Isa 34:8
3:5 [e]2Ch 21:16-17
3:7 [f]Isa 43:5-6; Jer 23:8
3:8 [g]Isa 60:14 [h]Isa 14:2
3:9 [i]Isa 8:9 [j]Jer 46:4
3:10 [k]Isa 2:4; Mic 4:3 [l]Zec 12:8
3:11 [m]Eze 38:15-16; Zep 3:8 [n]Isa 13:3
3:12 [o]Isa 2:4
3:13 [p]Hos 6:11; Mt 13:39; Rev 14:15-19 [q]Rev 14:20
3:14 [r]Isa 34:2-8; Joel 1:15
3:16 [s]Am 1:2 [t]Eze 38:19 [u]Jer 16:19
3:17 [v]Joel 2:27 [w]Isa 4:3
3:18 [x]Ex 3:8 [y]Isa 30:25; 35:6 [z]Rev 22:1-2 [a]Eze 47:1; Am 9:13

[12]"Let the nations be roused;
let them advance into the
Valley of Jehoshaphat,
for there I will sit
to judge[o] all the nations on
every side.
[13]Swing the sickle,
for the harvest[p] is ripe.
Come, trample the grapes,
for the winepress[q] is full
and the vats overflow—
so great is their wickedness!"

[14]Multitudes, multitudes
in the valley of decision!
For the day of the LORD[r] is
near
in the valley of decision.
[15]The sun and moon will be
darkened,
and the stars no longer
shine.
[16]The LORD will roar from Zion
and thunder from
Jerusalem;[s]
the earth and the sky will
tremble.[t]
But the LORD will be a refuge
for his people,
a stronghold[u] for the people
of Israel.

Blessings for God's People

[17]"Then you will know that I, the
LORD your God,[v]
dwell in Zion,[w] my holy
hill.
Jerusalem will be holy;
never again will foreigners
invade her.

[18]"In that day the mountains will
drip new wine,
and the hills will flow with
milk;[x]
all the ravines of Judah will
run with water.[y]
A fountain will flow out of the
LORD's house[z]
and will water the valley of
acacias.[n][a]
[19]But Egypt will be desolate,
Edom a desert waste,

[m]2 *Jehoshaphat* means *the LORD judges*; also in verse 12. [n]18 Or *Valley of Shittim*

because of violence[a] done
to the people of
Judah,
in whose land they shed
innocent blood.
20 Judah will be inhabited
forever[b]
and Jerusalem through all
generations.
21 Their bloodguilt, which I have
not pardoned,
I will pardon.[c]"

The LORD dwells in Zion!

3:19 [a] Ob 1:10
3:20 [b] Am 9:15
3:21 [c] Eze 36:25

Amos

Title and Background

The concurrent reigns of Uzziah of Judah and Jeroboam II of Israel were marked by a period of peace and prosperity. Prosperity was accompanied by an almost unprecedented degree of social corruption, and it is to this that the book of Amos is addressed.

Author and Date of Writing

Amos was a herdsman from the small town of Tekoa; he was not a man of the court like Isaiah, or a priest like Jeremiah. Though he lived in Judah, he was sent to announce God's judgment on the northern kingdom (Israel). Amos prophesied during the reigns of Uzziah and Jeroboam II. The main part of his ministry was probably carried out about 760-750 B.C., and this book can be dated during that time.

Theme and Message

The dominant theme is clearly stated in 5:24, which calls for social justice as the indispensable expression of true piety. Amos was a vigorous spokesman for God's justice and righteousness. He condemns all who make themselves powerful or rich at the expense of others.

Outline

I. Judgments on Israel's Neighbors (1:1-2:5)
II. Judgment on Israel (2:6-16)
III. Oracles Against Israel (3:1-5:17)
IV. Announcements of Exile (5:18-6:14)
V. Visions of Divine Retribution (7:1-9:10)
VI. Restoration of Israel (9:11-15)

---

1 The words of Amos, one of the
shepherds of Tekoa[a]—what
he saw concerning Israel two years
before the earthquake,[b] when Uzziah[c] was king of Judah and Jeroboam[d] son of Jehoash[a] was king
of Israel.[e]
2He said:

"The LORD roars[f] from Zion
and thunders from
Jerusalem;[g]
the pastures of the shepherds
dry up,[b]
and the top of Carmel[h]
withers."[i]

Judgment on Israel's Neighbors

3This is what the LORD says:

"For three sins of Damascus,[j]
even for four, I will not turn
back ⌊my wrath⌋.[k]
Because she threshed Gilead
with sledges having iron
teeth,
4I will send fire[l] upon the
house of Hazael
that will consume the
fortresses[m] of
Ben-Hadad.[n]
5I will break down the gate[o] of
Damascus;
I will destroy the king who is
in[c] the Valley of Aven[d]

1:1 [a] 2Sa 14:2 [b] Zec 14:5 [c] 2Ch 26:23 [d] 2Ki 14:23 [e] Hos 1:1
1:2 [f] Isa 42:13 [g] Joel 3:16 [h] Am 9:3 [i] Jer 12:4
1:3 [j] Isa 8:4; 17:1-3 [k] Am 2:6
1:4 [l] Jer 49:27 [m] Jer 17:27 [n] 1Ki 20:1; 2Ki 6:24
1:5 [o] Jer 51:30

[a]*1* Hebrew *Joash,* a variant of *Jehoash*
[b]*2* Or *shepherds mourn*
[c]*5* Or *the inhabitants of*
[d]*5* *Aven* means *wickedness.*

and the one who holds the scepter in Beth Eden.
The people of Aram will go into exile to Kir,[a]"
says the LORD.

6This is what the LORD says:

"For three sins of Gaza,[b]
even for four, I will not turn back ⌞my wrath⌟.
Because she took captive whole communities
and sold them to Edom,[c]
7I will send fire upon the walls of Gaza
that will consume her fortresses.
8I will destroy the king[e] of Ashdod[d]
and the one who holds the scepter in Ashkelon.
I will turn my hand[e] against Ekron,
till the last of the Philistines[f] is dead,"
says the Sovereign LORD.[g]

9This is what the LORD says:

"For three sins of Tyre,[h]
even for four, I will not turn back ⌞my wrath⌟.
Because she sold whole communities of captives to Edom,
disregarding a treaty of brotherhood,
10I will send fire upon the walls of Tyre
that will consume her fortresses.[i]"

11This is what the LORD says:

"For three sins of Edom,[j]
even for four, I will not turn back ⌞my wrath⌟.
Because he pursued his brother with a sword,
stifling all compassion,[f]
because his anger raged continually
and his fury flamed unchecked,[k]
12I will send fire upon Teman[l]
that will consume the fortresses of Bozrah."

13This is what the LORD says:

"For three sins of Ammon,[m]
even for four, I will not turn back ⌞my wrath⌟.
Because he ripped open the pregnant women[n] of Gilead
in order to extend his borders,
14I will set fire to the walls of Rabbah[o]
that will consume her fortresses
amid war cries[p] on the day of battle,
amid violent winds on a stormy day.
15Her king[g] will go into exile,
he and his officials together,"
says the LORD.

2 This is what the LORD says:
"For three sins of Moab,
even for four, I will not turn back ⌞my wrath⌟.
Because he burned, as if to lime,
the bones of Edom's king,
2I will send fire upon Moab
that will consume the fortresses of Kerioth.[h]
Moab will go down in great tumult
amid war cries and the blast of the trumpet.
3I will destroy her ruler[q]
and kill all her officials with him,"[r]
says the LORD.

4This is what the LORD says:

"For three sins of Judah,[s]
even for four, I will not turn back ⌞my wrath⌟.
Because they have rejected the law[t] of the LORD
and have not kept his decrees,[u]
because they have been led astray[v] by false gods,[i][w]
the gods[j] their ancestors followed,[x]

1:5 [a] 2Ki 16:9
1:6 [b] 1Sa 6:17; Zep 2:4 [c] Ob 1:11
1:8 [d] 2Ch 26:6 [e] Ps 81:14 [f] Eze 25:16 [g] Isa 14:28-32; Zep 2:4-7
1:9 [h] 1Ki 5:1; 9:11-14; Isa 23:1-18; Jer 25:22; Joel 3:4; Mt 11:21
1:10 [i] Zec 9:1-4
1:11 [j] Nu 20:14-21; 2Ch 28:17; Jer 49:7-22 [k] Eze 25:12-14
1:12 [l] Ob 1:9-10
1:13 [m] Jer 49:1-6; Eze 21:28; 25:2-7 [n] Hos 13:16
1:14 [o] Dt 3:11 [p] Am 2:2
2:3 [q] Ps 2:10 [r] Isa 40:23
2:4 [s] 2Ki 17:19; Hos 12:2 [t] Jer 6:19 [u] Eze 20:24 [v] Isa 9:16 [w] Isa 28:15 [x] 2Ki 22:13; Jer 16:12

[e]8 Or *inhabitants* [f]11 Or *sword / and destroyed his allies* [g]15 Or / *Molech;* Hebrew *malcam* [h]2 Or *of her cities* [i]4 Or *by lies* [j]4 Or *lies*

5I will send fire upon Judah
that will consume the
fortresses of
Jerusalem.[a]"

Judgment on Israel

6This is what the LORD says:

"For three sins of Israel,
even for four, I will not turn
back ⌊my wrath⌋.
They sell the righteous for
silver,
and the needy for a pair of
sandals.[b]
7They trample on the heads of
the poor
as upon the dust of the
ground
and deny justice to the
oppressed.
Father and son use the same
girl
and so profane my holy
name.[c]
8They lie down beside every
altar
on garments taken in
pledge.[d]
In the house of their god
they drink wine[e] taken as
fines.

9"I destroyed the Amorite[f]
before them,
though he was tall as the
cedars
and strong as the oaks.
I destroyed his fruit above
and his roots[g] below.

10"I brought you up out of
Egypt,[h]
and I led you forty years in
the desert[i]
to give you the land of the
Amorites.[j]
11I also raised up prophets[k] from
among your sons
and Nazirites[l] from among
your young men.
Is this not true, people of
Israel?"
declares the LORD.
12"But you made the Nazirites
drink wine
and commanded the
prophets not to
prophesy.[m]

13"Now then, I will crush you
as a cart crushes when
loaded with grain.
14The swift will not escape,
the strong[n] will not muster
their strength,
and the warrior will not save
his life.[o]
15The archer[p] will not stand his
ground,
the fleet-footed soldier will
not get away,
and the horseman will not
save his life.
16Even the bravest warriors[q]
will flee naked on that day,"
declares the LORD.

Witnesses Summoned Against Israel

3 Hear this word the LORD has
spoken against you, O people
of Israel—against the whole family
I brought up out of Egypt:[r]

2"You only have I chosen[s]
of all the families of the earth;
therefore I will punish you
for all your sins.[t]"

3Do two walk together
unless they have agreed to do
so?
4Does a lion roar in the thicket
when he has no prey?[u]
Does he growl in his den
when he has caught nothing?
5Does a bird fall into a trap on
the ground
where no snare has been set?
Does a trap spring up from the
earth
when there is nothing to
catch?
6When a trumpet sounds in a
city,
do not the people tremble?
When disaster comes to a city,
has not the LORD caused it?[v]

7Surely the Sovereign LORD does
nothing
without revealing his plan[w]
to his servants the
prophets.[x]

2:5 [a]Jer 17:27; Hos 8:14
2:6 [b]Joel 3:3; Am 8:6
2:7 [c]Am 5:11-12; 8:4
2:8 [d]Ex 22:26 [e]Am 4:1; 6:6
2:9 [f]Nu 21:23-26; Jos 10:12 [g]Eze 17:9; Mal 4:1
2:10 [h]Ex 20:2; Am 3:1 [i]Dt 2:7 [j]Ex 3:8; Am 9:7
2:11 [k]Dt 18:18; Jer 7:25 [l]Nu 6:2-3; Jdg 13:5
2:12 [m]Isa 30:10; Jer 11:21; Am 7:12-13; Mic 2:6
2:14 [n]Jer 9:23 [o]Ps 33:16; Isa 30:16-17
2:15 [p]Eze 39:3
2:16 [q]Jer 48:41
3:1 [r]Am 2:10
3:2 [s]Dt 7:6; Lk 12:47 [t]Jer 14:10
3:4 [u]Ps 104:21; Hos 5:14
3:6 [v]Isa 14:24-27; 45:7
3:7 [w]Ge 18:17; Da 9:22; Jn 15:15; Rev 10:7 [x]Jer 23:22

[8]The lion has roared—
who will not fear?
The Sovereign LORD has
spoken—
who can but prophesy?[a]
[9]Proclaim to the fortresses of
Ashdod
and to the fortresses of
Egypt:
"Assemble yourselves on the
mountains of Samaria;[b]
see the great unrest within
her
and the oppression among
her people."

[10]"They do not know how to do
right,[c]" declares the
LORD,
"who hoard plunder[d] and
loot in their
fortresses."[e]

[11]Therefore this is what the Sovereign LORD says:

"An enemy will overrun the
land;
he will pull down your
strongholds
and plunder your
fortresses.[f]"

[12]This is what the LORD says:

"As a shepherd saves from the
lion's[g] mouth
only two leg bones or a piece
of an ear,
so will the Israelites be
saved,
those who sit in Samaria
on the edge of their beds
and in Damascus on their
couches.[kh]"

[13]"Hear this and testify[i] against
the house of Jacob," declares the
Lord, the LORD God Almighty.

[14]"On the day I punish Israel for
her sins,
I will destroy the altars of
Bethel;[j]
the horns of the altar will be
cut off
and fall to the ground.
[15]I will tear down the winter
house[k]

3:8 [a]Jer 20:9; Jnh 1:1-3; 3:1-3; Ac 4:20
3:9 [b]Am 4:1; 6:1
3:10 [c]Jer 4:22; Am 5:7; 6:12 [d]Hab 2:8 [e]Zep 1:9
3:11 [f]Am 2:5; 6:14
3:12 [g]1Sa 17:34 [h]Am 6:4
3:13 [i]Eze 2:7
3:14 [j]Am 5:5-6
3:15 [k]Jer 36:22 [l]Jdg 3:20 [m]1Ki 22:39
4:1 [n]Ps 22:12; Eze 39:18 [o]Am 3:9 [p]Am 2:8; 5:11; 8:6
4:2 [q]Am 6:8
4:3 [r]Eze 12:5
4:4 [s]Hos 4:15 [t]Nu 28:3 [u]Dt 14:28 [v]Eze 20:39; Am 5:21-22
4:5 [w]Lev 7:13 [x]Lev 22:18-21

along with the summer
house;[l]
the houses adorned with ivory[m]
will be destroyed
and the mansions will be
demolished,"
declares the LORD.

Israel Has Not Returned to God

4 Hear this word, you cows of
Bashan[n] on Mount
Samaria,[o]
you women who oppress the
poor and crush the
needy
and say to your husbands,
"Bring us some
drinks![p]"
[2]The Sovereign LORD has sworn
by his holiness:
"The time will surely come
when you will be taken away[q]
with hooks,
the last of you with
fishhooks.
[3]You will each go straight out
through breaks in the wall,[r]
and you will be cast out
toward Harmon,[l]"
declares the LORD.
[4]"Go to Bethel and sin;
go to Gilgal[s] and sin yet
more.
Bring your sacrifices every
morning,[t]
your tithes[u] every three
years.[mv]
[5]Burn leavened bread[w] as a
thank offering
and brag about your freewill
offerings[x]—
boast about them, you
Israelites,
for this is what you love to
do,"
declares the Sovereign
LORD.

[6]"I gave you empty stomachs[n]
in every city

[k]12 The meaning of the Hebrew for this line is uncertain. [l]3 Masoretic Text; with a different word division of the Hebrew (see Septuagint) *out, O mountain of oppression* [m]4 Or *tithes on the third day* [n]6 Hebrew *you cleanness of teeth*

and lack of bread in every
town,
yet you have not returned to
me,"
declares the LORD.[a]

7"I also withheld rain from you
when the harvest was still
three months away.
I sent rain on one town,
but withheld it from
another.[b]
One field had rain;
another had none and dried
up.
8People staggered from town to
town for water[c]
but did not get enough to
drink,
yet you have not returned[d]
to me,"
declares the LORD.[e]

9"Many times I struck your
gardens and vineyards,
I struck them with blight and
mildew.[f]
Locusts devoured your fig and
olive trees,[g]
yet you have not returned[h]
to me,"
declares the LORD.

10"I sent plagues[i] among you
as I did to Egypt.
I killed your young men with
the sword,
along with your captured
horses.
I filled your nostrils with the
stench of your camps,
yet you have not returned to
me,"
declares the LORD.[j]

11"I overthrew some of you
as I[o] overthrew Sodom and
Gomorrah.[k]
You were like a burning stick
snatched from the fire,
yet you have not returned to
me,"
declares the LORD.

12"Therefore this is what I will do
to you, Israel,
and because I will do this to
you,
prepare to meet your God,
O Israel."

13He who forms the mountains,[l]
creates the wind,
and reveals his thoughts[m] to
man,
he who turns dawn to darkness,
and treads the high places of
the earth[n]—
the LORD God Almighty is his
name.[o]

A Lament and Call to Repentance

5 Hear this word, O house of Israel, this lament[p] I take up
concerning you:

2"Fallen is Virgin[q] Israel,
never to rise again,
deserted in her own land,
with no one to lift her up.[r]"

3This is what the Sovereign LORD
says:

"The city that marches out a
thousand strong for
Israel
will have only a hundred left;
the town that marches out a
hundred strong
will have only ten left.[s]"

4This is what the LORD says to the
house of Israel:

"Seek me and live;[t]
5 do not seek Bethel,
do not go to Gilgal,[u]
do not journey to
Beersheba.[v]
For Gilgal will surely go into
exile,
and Bethel will be reduced to
nothing.[p][w]"
6Seek[x] the LORD and live,[y]
or he will sweep through the
house of Joseph like a
fire;[z]
it will devour,
and Bethel[a] will have no one
to quench it.
7You who turn justice into
bitterness[b]

4:6 [a]Isa 3:1; Jer 5:3; Hag 2:17
4:7 [b]Ex 9:4,26; Dt 11:17; 2Ch 7:13
4:8 [c]Eze 4:16-17 [d]Jer 3:7 [e]Jer 14:4
4:9 [f]Dt 28:22 [g]Joel 1:7 [h]Jer 3:10; Hag 2:17
4:10 [i]Ex 9:3; Dt 28:27 [j]Isa 9:13
4:11 [k]Ge 19:24; Jer 23:14
4:13 [l]Ps 65:6 [m]Da 2:28 [n]Mic 1:3 [o]Isa 47:4; Am 5:8,27; 9:6
5:1 [p]Eze 19:1
5:2 [q]Jer 14:17 [r]Jer 50:32; Am 8:14
5:3 [s]Isa 6:13; Am 6:9
5:4 [t]Isa 55:3; Jer 29:13
5:5 [u]1Sa 11:14; Am 4:4 [v]Am 8:14 [w]1Sa 7:16
5:6 [x]Isa 55:6 [y]ver 14 [z]Dt 4:24 [a]Am 3:14
5:7 [b]Am 6:12

[o]*11* Hebrew *God* [p]*5* Or *grief*; or *wickedness*; Hebrew *aven*, a reference to Beth Aven (a derogatory name for Bethel)

and cast righteousness to the
ground
8(he who made the Pleiades and
Orion,[a]
who turns blackness into
dawn[b]
and darkens day into night,[c]
who calls for the waters of the
sea
and pours them out over the
face of the land—
the LORD is his name[d]—
9he flashes destruction on the
stronghold
and brings the fortified city
to ruin),[e]
10you hate the one who reproves
in court[f]
and despise him who tells
the truth.[g]

11You trample on the poor[h]
and force him to give you
grain.
Therefore, though you have
built stone mansions,[i]
you will not live in them;
though you have planted lush
vineyards,
you will not drink their
wine.[j]
12For I know how many are your
offenses
and how great your sins.

You oppress the righteous and
take bribes
and you deprive the poor of
justice in the courts.[k]
13Therefore the prudent man
keeps quiet in such
times,
for the times are evil.

14Seek good, not evil,
that you may live.
Then the LORD God Almighty
will be with you,
just as you say he is.
15Hate evil,[l] love good;
maintain justice in the
courts.
Perhaps the LORD God Almighty
will have mercy[m]
on the remnant[n] of Joseph.

16Therefore this is what the
Lord, the LORD God Almighty, says:

5:8 [a]Job 9:9 [b]Isa 42:16 [c]Ps 104:20; Am 8:9 [d]Ps 104:6-9; Am 4:13
5:9 [e]Mic 5:11
5:10 [f]Isa 29:21 [g]1Ki 22:8
5:11 [h]Am 8:6 [i]Am 3:15 [j]Mic 6:15
5:12 [k]Isa 5:23; Am 2:6-7
5:15 [l]Ps 97:10; Ro 12:9 [m]Joel 2:14 [n]Mic 5:7,8
5:16 [o]Jer 9:17 [p]Joel 1:11
5:17 [q]Ex 12:12 [r]Isa 16:10; Jer 48:33
5:18 [s]Joel 1:15 [t]Joel 2:2 [u]Isa 5:19,30; Jer 30:7
5:19 [v]Job 20:24; Isa 24:17-18; Jer 15:2-3; 48:44
5:20 [w]Isa 13:10; Zep 1:15
5:21 [x]Lev 26:31 [y]Isa 1:11-16
5:22 [z]Am 4:4; Mic 6:6-7 [a]Isa 66:3
5:23 [b]Am 6:5
5:24 [c]Jer 22:3 [d]Mic 6:8
5:25 [e]Isa 43:23

"There will be wailing[o] in all
the streets
and cries of anguish in every
public square.
The farmers[p] will be
summoned to weep
and the mourners to wail.
17There will be wailing in all the
vineyards,
for I will pass through[q] your
midst,"
says the LORD.[r]

The Day of the LORD

18Woe to you who long
for the day of the LORD![s]
Why do you long for the day of
the LORD?
That day will be darkness,[t]
not light.[u]
19It will be as though a man fled
from a lion
only to meet a bear,
as though he entered his house
and rested his hand on the
wall
only to have a snake bite
him.[v]
20Will not the day of the LORD be
darkness, not light—
pitch-dark, without a ray of
brightness?[w]

21"I hate, I despise your religious
feasts;[x]
I cannot stand your
assemblies.[y]
22Even though you bring me
burnt offerings and grain
offerings,
I will not accept them.
Though you bring choice
fellowship offerings,[q]
I will have no regard for
them.[z][a]
23Away with the noise of your
songs!
I will not listen to the music
of your harps.[b]
24But let justice[c] roll on like a
river,
righteousness like a
never-failing stream![d]

25"Did you bring me sacrifices[e]
and offerings

[q]22 Traditionally *peace offerings*

forty years[a] in the desert,
O house of Israel?
26You have lifted up the shrine of
your king,
the pedestal of your idols,
the star of your god[r]—
which you made for
yourselves.
27Therefore I will send you into
exile beyond Damascus,"
says the LORD, whose name is
God Almighty.[b]

Woe to the Complacent

6 Woe to you[c] who are
complacent in Zion,
and to you who feel secure
on Mount Samaria,
you notable men of the
foremost nation,
to whom the people of Israel
come![d]
2Go to Calneh[e] and look at it;
go from there to great
Hamath,[f]
and then go down to Gath[g]
in Philistia.
Are they better off than[h] your
two kingdoms?
Is their land larger than
yours?
3You put off the evil day
and bring near a reign of
terror.[i]
4You lie on beds inlaid with
ivory
and lounge on your couches.
You dine on choice lambs
and fattened calves.[j]
5You strum away on your harps[k]
like David
and improvise on musical
instruments.[l]
6You drink wine[m] by the bowlful
and use the finest lotions,
but you do not grieve[n] over
the ruin of Joseph.
7Therefore you will be among
the first to go into exile;
your feasting and lounging
will end.

The LORD Abhors the Pride of Israel

8The Sovereign LORD has sworn
by himself[o]—the LORD God Almighty declares:

"I abhor[p] the pride of Jacob[q]
and detest his fortresses;
I will deliver up[r] the city
and everything in it.[s]"

9If ten[t] men are left in one
house, they too will die. 10And if a
relative who is to burn the bodies[u]
comes to carry them out of the
house and asks anyone still hiding
there, "Is anyone with you?" and he
says, "No," then he will say,
"Hush![v] We must not mention the
name of the LORD."

11For the LORD has given the
command,
and he will smash the great
house[w] into pieces
and the small house into
bits.[x]

12Do horses run on the rocky
crags?
Does one plow there with
oxen?
But you have turned justice
into poison[y]
and the fruit of righteousness
into bitterness[z]—
13you who rejoice in the
conquest of Lo Debar[s]
and say, "Did we not take
Karnaim[t] by our own
strength?[a]"

14For the LORD God Almighty
declares,
"I will stir up a nation[b]
against you, O house of
Israel,
that will oppress you all the
way
from Lebo[u] Hamath[c] to the
valley of the Arabah.[d]"

Locusts, Fire and a Plumb Line

7 This is what the Sovereign
LORD showed me:[e] He was preparing swarms of locusts[f] after the

5:25 [a]Dt 32:17
5:27 [b]Am 4:13; Ac 7:42-43*
6:1 [c]Lk 6:24 [d]Isa 32:9-11
6:2 [e]Ge 10:10 [f]2Ki 18:34 [g]2Ch 26:6 [h]Na 3:8
6:3 [i]Isa 56:12; Am 9:10
6:4 [j]Eze 34:2-3; Am 3:12
6:5 [k]Isa 5:12; Am 5:23 [l]1Ch 15:16
6:6 [m]Am 2:8 [n]Eze 9:4
6:8 [o]Ge 22:16; Heb 6:13 [p]Lev 26:30 [q]Ps 47:4 [r]Am 4:2 [s]Dt 32:19
6:9 [t]Am 5:3
6:10 [u]1Sa 31:12 [v]Am 8:3
6:11 [w]Am 3:15 [x]Isa 55:11
6:12 [y]Hos 10:4 [z]Am 5:7
6:13 [a]Job 8:15; Isa 28:14-15
6:14 [b]Jer 5:15 [c]1Ki 8:65 [d]Am 3:11
7:1 [e]Am 8:1 [f]Joel 1:4

[r]26 *Or lifted up Sakkuth your king / and Kaiwan your idols, / your star-gods*; Septuagint *lifted up the shrine of Molech / and the star of your god Rephan, / their idols* [s]13 *Lo Debar* means *nothing.* [t]13 *Karnaim* means *horns*; *horn* here symbolizes strength. [u]14 Or *from the entrance to*

king's share had been harvested
and just as the second crop was
coming up. 2When they had
stripped the land clean,[a] I cried
out, "Sovereign LORD, forgive! How
can Jacob survive?[b] He is so
small![c]"
3So the LORD relented.[d]
"This will not happen," the LORD
said.[e]
4This is what the Sovereign LORD
showed me: The Sovereign LORD
was calling for judgment by fire;[f]
it dried up the great deep and devoured[g] the land. 5Then I cried
out, "Sovereign LORD, I beg you,
stop! How can Jacob survive? He is
so small![h]"
6So the LORD relented.[i]
"This will not happen either,"
the Sovereign LORD said.

7This is what he showed me: The
Lord was standing by a wall that
had been built true to plumb, with
a plumb line in his hand. 8And the
LORD asked me, "What do you see,[j]
Amos?[k]"
"A plumb line,[l]" I replied.
Then the Lord said, "Look, I am
setting a plumb line among my
people Israel; I will spare them no
longer.[m]

9"The high places of Isaac will
be destroyed
and the sanctuaries[n] of
Israel will be ruined;
with my sword I will rise
against the house of
Jeroboam.[o]"

Amos and Amaziah

10Then Amaziah the priest of
Bethel[p] sent a message to Jeroboam[q] king of Israel: "Amos is raising a conspiracy[r] against you in
the very heart of Israel. The land
cannot bear all his words.[s] 11For
this is what Amos is saying:

" 'Jeroboam will die by the
sword,
and Israel will surely go into
exile,
away from their native
land.' "

12Then Amaziah said to Amos,
"Get out, you seer! Go back to the
land of Judah. Earn your bread
there and do your prophesying
there.[t] 13Don't prophesy anymore
at Bethel, because this is the king's
sanctuary and the temple of the
kingdom.[u]"
14Amos answered Amaziah, "I
was neither a prophet[v] nor a
prophet's son, but I was a shepherd, and I also took care of sycamore-fig trees. 15But the LORD took
me from tending the flock[w] and
said to me, 'Go, prophesy to my
people Israel.'[x] 16Now then, hear
the word of the LORD. You say,

" 'Do not prophesy against[y]
Israel,
and stop preaching against
the house of Isaac.'

17"Therefore this is what the
LORD says:

" 'Your wife will become a
prostitute[z] in the city,
and your sons and daughters
will fall by the sword.
Your land will be measured and
divided up,
and you yourself will die in a
pagan[v] country.
And Israel will certainly go into
exile,
away from their native
land.[a]' "

A Basket of Ripe Fruit

8 This is what the Sovereign
LORD showed me: a basket of
ripe fruit. 2"What do you see,[b]
Amos?[c]" he asked.
"A basket of ripe fruit," I answered.
Then the LORD said to me, "The
time is ripe for my people Israel; I
will spare them no longer.[d]
3"In that day," declares the Sovereign LORD, "the songs in the temple will turn to wailing.[w][e] Many,
many bodies—flung everywhere!
Silence![f]"

4Hear this, you who trample the
needy

7:2 [a]Ex 10:15 [b]Isa 37:4 [c]Eze 11:13
7:3 [d]Dt 32:36; Jer 26:19; Jnh 3:10 [e]Hos 11:8
7:4 [f]Isa 66:16 [g]Dt 32:22
7:5 [h]ver 1-2; Joel 2:17
7:6 [i]Jnh 3:10
7:8 [j]Jer 1:11,13 [k]Isa 28:17; La 2:8; Am 8:2 [l]2Ki 21:13 [m]Jer 15:6; Eze 7:2-9
7:9 [n]Lev 26:31 [o]2Ki 15:9; Isa 63:18; Hos 10:8
7:10 [p]1Ki 12:32 [q]2Ki 14:23 [r]Jer 38:4 [s]Jer 26:8-11
7:12 [t]Mt 8:34
7:13 [u]Am 2:12; Ac 4:18
7:14 [v]2Ki 2:5; 4:38
7:15 [w]2Sa 7:8 [x]Jer 7:1-2; Eze 2:3-4
7:16 [y]Eze 20:46; Mic 2:6
7:17 [z]Hos 4:13 [a]2Ki 17:6; Eze 4:13; Hos 9:3
8:2 [b]Jer 24:3 [c]Am 7:8 [d]Eze 7:2-9
8:3 [e]Am 5:16 [f]Am 5:23; 6:10

[v]17 Hebrew *an unclean* [w]3 Or *"the temple singers will wail*

and do away with the poor[a]
of the land,[b]

5saying,

"When will the New Moon be
over
that we may sell grain,
and the Sabbath be ended
that we may market
wheat?"—
skimping the measure,
boosting the price
and cheating with dishonest
scales,[c]
6buying the poor with silver
and the needy for a pair of
sandals,
selling even the sweepings
with the wheat.[d]

7The LORD has sworn by the Pride
of Jacob:[e] "I will never forget[f]
anything they have done.

8"Will not the land tremble[g] for
this,
and all who live in it mourn?
The whole land will rise like
the Nile;
it will be stirred up and then
sink
like the river of Egypt.[h]

9"In that day," declares the Sovereign LORD,

"I will make the sun go down
at noon
and darken the earth in
broad daylight.[i]
10I will turn your religious feasts
into mourning
and all your singing into
weeping.
I will make all of you wear
sackcloth[j]
and shave your heads.
I will make that time like
mourning for an only
son[k]
and the end of it like a bitter
day.[l]

11"The days are coming,"
declares the Sovereign
LORD,
"when I will send a famine
through the land—
not a famine of food or a thirst
for water,
but a famine of hearing the
words of the LORD.[m]
12Men will stagger from sea to
sea
and wander from north to
east,
searching for the word of the
LORD,
but they will not find it.[n]

13"In that day

"the lovely young women and
strong young men
will faint because of thirst.[o]
14They who swear by the shame[x]
of Samaria,
or say, 'As surely as your god
lives, O Dan,'[p]
or, 'As surely as the god[y] of
Beersheba[q] lives'—
they will fall,
never to rise again.[r]"

Israel to Be Destroyed

9 I saw the Lord standing by the
altar, and he said:

"Strike the tops of the pillars
so that the thresholds shake.
Bring them down on the
heads[s] of all the people;
those who are left I will kill
with the sword.
Not one will get away,
none will escape.
2Though they dig down to the
depths of the grave,[z][t]
from there my hand will take
them.
Though they climb up to the
heavens,[u]
from there I will bring them
down.[v]
3Though they hide themselves
on the top of Carmel,[w]
there I will hunt them down
and seize them.[x]
Though they hide from me at
the bottom of the sea,
there I will command the
serpent to bite them.[y]
4Though they are driven into
exile by their enemies,

8:4 [a] Pr 30:14 [b] Ps 14:4; Am 2:7
8:5 [c] 2Ki 4:23; Ne 13:15-16; Hos 12:7; Mic 6:10-11
8:6 [d] Am 2:6
8:7 [e] Am 6:8 [f] Hos 8:13
8:8 [g] Hos 4:3 [h] Ps 18:7; Jer 46:8; Am 9:5
8:9 [i] Job 5:14; Isa 59:9-10; Jer 15:9; Am 5:8; Mic 3:6
8:10 [j] Jer 48:37 [k] Jer 6:26; Zec 12:10 [l] Eze 7:18
8:11 [m] 1Sa 3:1; 2Ch 15:3; Eze 7:26
8:12 [n] Eze 20:3,31
8:13 [o] Isa 41:17; Hos 2:3
8:14 [p] 1Ki 12:29 [q] Am 5:5 [r] Am 5:2
9:1 [s] Ps 68:21
9:2 [t] Ps 139:8 [u] Jer 51:53 [v] Ob 1:4
9:3 [w] Am 1:2 [x] Ps 139:8-10 [y] Jer 16:16 17

[x]14 Or *by Ashima;* or *by the idol* [y]14 Or *power* [z]2 Hebrew *to Sheol*

there I will command the
sword[a] to slay them.
I will fix my eyes upon them
for evil[b] and not for
good.[c]"[d]

5The Lord, the LORD Almighty,
he who touches the earth
and it melts,[e]
and all who live in it
mourn—
the whole land rises like the
Nile,
then sinks like the river of
Egypt[f]—
6he who builds his lofty palace[a]
in the heavens
and sets its foundation[b] on
the earth,
who calls for the waters of the
sea
and pours them out over the
face of the land—
the LORD is his name.[g]

7"Are not you Israelites
the same to me as the
Cushites[c]?"[h]
declares the LORD.
"Did I not bring Israel up from
Egypt,
the Philistines from
Caphtor[d][i]
and the Arameans from
Kir?[j]

8"Surely the eyes of the
Sovereign LORD
are on the sinful kingdom.
I will destroy it
from the face of the earth—
yet I will not totally destroy
the house of Jacob,"
declares the LORD.[k]
9"For I will give the command,
and I will shake the house of
Israel
among all the nations
as grain[l] is shaken in a sieve,[m]
and not a pebble will reach
the ground.
10All the sinners among my
people
will die by the sword,
all those who say,
'Disaster will not overtake or
meet us.'[n]

Israel's Restoration

11"In that day I will restore
David's fallen tent.
I will repair its broken places,
restore its ruins,
and build it as it used to
be,[o]
12so that they may possess the
remnant of Edom[p]
and all the nations that bear
my name,[e][q]"
declares the LORD, who
will do these things.[r]

13"The days are coming," declares the LORD,

"when the reaper will be
overtaken by the
plowman[s]
and the planter by the one
treading grapes.
New wine will drip from the
mountains
and flow from all the hills.[t]
14I will bring back my exiled[f]
people Israel;
they will rebuild the ruined
cities[u] and live in them.
They will plant vineyards and
drink their wine;
they will make gardens and
eat their fruit.[v]
15I will plant[w] Israel in their own
land,
never again to be uprooted
from the land I have given
them,"
says the LORD your
God.[x]

9:4 [a]Lev 26:33; Eze 5:12 [b]Jer 21:10 [c]Jer 39:16 [d]Jer 44:11
9:5 [e]Ps 46:2; Mic 1:4 [f]Am 8:8
9:6 [g]Ps 104:1-3, 5-6,13; Am 5:8
9:7 [h]Isa 20:4; 43:3 [i]Dt 2:23; Jer 47:4 [j]2Ki 16:9; Isa 22:6; Am 1:5; 2:10
9:8 [k]Jer 44:27
9:9 [l]Lk 22:31 [m]Isa 30:28
9:10 [n]Am 6:3
9:11 [o]Ps 80:12
9:12 [p]Nu 24:18 [q]Isa 43:7 [r]Ac 15:16-17*
9:13 [s]Lev 26:5 [t]Joel 3:18
9:14 [u]Isa 61:4 [v]Jer 30:18; 31:28; Eze 28:25-26
9:15 [w]Isa 60:21 [x]Jer 24:6; Eze 34:25-28; 37:12,25

[a]6 The meaning of the Hebrew for this phrase is uncertain. [b]6 The meaning of the Hebrew for this word is uncertain. [c]7 That is, people from the upper Nile region [d]7 That is, Crete [e]12 Hebrew; Septuagint *so that the remnant of men / and all the nations that bear my name may seek ⌞the Lord⌟* [f]14 Or *will restore the fortunes of my*

Obadiah

Title and Background

Obadiah's name means "servant of the LORD." The prophecy centers around an ancient feud between Edom and Israel. The Edomites were descendants of Esau, who carried a grudge against Israel because Jacob had cheated their ancestor out of his birthright.

Author and Date of Writing

The author is Obadiah. The date and place of composition are uncertain. A date between 853 and 841 B.C. is suggested by relating verses 11-14 to the invasion of Jerusalem by Philistines and Arabians during Jehoram's reign (2 Kings 8:20-22). An exilic date is arrived at by relating those verses to the Babylonian attacks on Jerusalem (605-586 B.C.).

Theme and Message

Its theme is that Edom is proud of her own security and has gloated over God's people when Israel was devastated by foreign powers, but her participation in that disaster will bring on God's wrath. Edom herself will be destroyed, but Mount Zion and Israel will be delivered, and God's kingdom will triumph.

Outline

I. The Doom of Edom (1-14)
II. Edom in the Day of the Lord (15-21)

---

1 The vision of Obadiah.

1–4pp — Jer 49:14–16
5–6pp — Jer 49:9–10

This is what the Sovereign LORD says about Edom[a]—

We have heard a message from the LORD:
An envoy[b] was sent to the nations to say,
"Rise, and let us go against her for battle"[c]—

2 "See, I will make you small among the nations;
you will be utterly despised.
3 The pride[d] of your heart has deceived you,
you who live in the clefts of the rocks[a]
and make your home on the heights,
you who say to yourself,
'Who can bring me down to the ground?'[e]
4 Though you soar like the eagle
and make your nest[f] among the stars,
from there I will bring you down,"[g]
declares the LORD.[h]
5 "If thieves came to you,
if robbers in the night—
Oh, what a disaster awaits you—
would they not steal only as much as they wanted?
If grape pickers came to you,
would they not leave a few grapes?[i]
6 But how Esau will be ransacked,
his hidden treasures pillaged!
7 All your allies[j] will force you to the border;

1:1 [a] Isa 63:1-6; Jer 49:7-22; Eze 25:12-14; Am 1:11-12 [b] Isa 18:2 [c] Jer 6:4-5
1:3 [d] Isa 16:6 [e] Isa 14:13-15; Rev 18:7
1:4 [f] Hab 2:9 [g] Isa 14:13 [h] Job 20:6
1:5 [i] Dt 24:21
1:7 [j] Jer 30:14

[a] 3 Or *of Sela*

your friends will deceive and
overpower you;
those who eat your bread[a] will
set a trap for you,[b]
but you will not detect it.

8"In that day," declares the
LORD,
"will I not destroy[b] the wise
men of Edom,
men of understanding in the
mountains of Esau?
9Your warriors, O Teman,[c] will
be terrified,
and everyone in Esau's
mountains
will be cut down in the
slaughter.
10Because of the violence[d]
against your brother
Jacob,[e]
you will be covered with
shame;
you will be destroyed
forever.[f]
11On the day you stood aloof
while strangers carried off his
wealth
and foreigners entered his gates
and cast lots[g] for Jerusalem,
you were like one of them.
12You should not look down on
your brother
in the day of his misfortune,
nor rejoice[h] over the people of
Judah
in the day of their
destruction,[i]
nor boast so much
in the day of their trouble.[j]
13You should not march through
the gates of my people
in the day of their disaster,
nor look down on them in their
calamity[k]
in the day of their disaster,
nor seize their wealth
in the day of their disaster.
14You should not wait at the
crossroads
to cut down their fugitives,
nor hand over their survivors
in the day of their trouble.

15"The day of the LORD is near[l]
for all nations.
As you have done, it will be
done to you;
your deeds[m] will return upon
your own head.
16Just as you drank on my holy
hill,
so all the nations will drink[n]
continually;
they will drink and drink
and be as if they had never
been.
17But on Mount Zion will be
deliverance;[o]
it will be holy,[p]
and the house of Jacob
will possess its inheritance.
18The house of Jacob will be a
fire
and the house of Joseph a
flame;
the house of Esau will be
stubble,
and they will set it on fire
and consume[q] it.
There will be no survivors
from the house of Esau."
The LORD has spoken.

19People from the Negev will
occupy
the mountains of Esau,
and people from the foothills
will possess
the land of the Philistines.[r]
They will occupy the fields of
Ephraim and Samaria,[s]
and Benjamin will possess
Gilead.
20This company of Israelite exiles
who are in Canaan
will possess the land, as far
as Zarephath;[t]
the exiles from Jerusalem who
are in Sepharad
will possess the towns of the
Negev.[u]
21Deliverers will go up on[c]
Mount Zion
to govern the mountains of
Esau.
And the kingdom will be the
LORD's.[v]

1:7 [a]Ps 41:9
1:8 [b]Job 5:12; Isa 29:14
1:9 [c]Ge 36:11,34
1:10 [d]Joel 3:19 [e]Ps 137:7; Am 1:11-12 [f]Eze 35:9
1:11 [g]Na 3:10
1:12 [h]Eze 35:15 [i]Pr 17:5 [j]Mic 4:11
1:13 [k]Eze 35:5
1:15 [l]Eze 30:3 [m]Jer 50:29; Hab 2:8
1:16 [n]Jer 25:15; 49:12
1:17 [o]Am 9:11-15 [p]Isa 4:3
1:18 [q]Zec 12:6
1:19 [r]Isa 11:14 [s]Jer 31:5
1:20 [t]1Ki 17:9-10 [u]Jer 33:13
1:21 [v]Ps 22:28; Zec 14:9,16; Rev 11:15

[b]7 The meaning of the Hebrew for this clause is uncertain. [c]21 Or *from*

Jonah

Title and Background

The book is named after its principal character, whose name means "dove." The events in the book took place probably during the eighth century, when the Assyrians were a feared and despised enemy.

Author and Date of Writing

Traditionally, the book has been ascribed to Jonah son of Amittai, though nowhere in the book is it plainly stated. To accept that the book is authored by Jonah would necessitate a date no later than the third quarter of the eighth century B.C.

Theme and Message

The theme that runs throughout the four chapters of the book is God's great mercy to Gentile nations through repentance. The book also depicts the larger scope of God's purpose for Israel: that she might rediscover the truth of his concern for the whole creation and that she might better understand her own role in carrying out that concern.

Outline

- I. Jonah Flees His Mission (1:1-2:10)
  - A. Jonah's Commission and Flight (1:1-3)
  - B. The Endangered Sailors' Cry to Their Gods (1:4-6)
  - C. Jonah's Disobedience Exposed (1:7-10)
  - D. Jonah's Punishment, Deliverance and Prayer of Thanksgiving (1:11-2:10)
- II. Jonah Reluctantly Fulfills His Mission (3:1-4:11)
  - A. Jonah's Renewed Commission and Obedience (3:1-4)
  - B. The Endangered Ninevites' Repentant Appeal to the Lord (3:5-9)
  - C. The Ninevites' Repentance Acknowledged (3:10-4:4)
  - D. Jonah's Deliverance and Rebuke (4:5-11)

Jonah Flees From the Lord

1 The word of the Lord came
to Jonah[a] son of Amittai:[b]
2"Go to the great city of Nineveh[c]
and preach against it, because its
wickedness has come up before
me."
3But Jonah ran[d] away from the
Lord and headed for Tarshish. He
went down to Joppa,[e] where he
found a ship bound for that port.
After paying the fare, he went
aboard and sailed for Tarshish to
flee from the Lord.
4Then the Lord sent a great wind
on the sea, and such a violent
storm arose that the ship threatened to break up.[f] 5All the sailors
were afraid and each cried out to
his own god. And they threw the
cargo into the sea to lighten the
ship.[g]
But Jonah had gone below deck,
where he lay down and fell into a
deep sleep. 6The captain went to
him and said, "How can you sleep?
Get up and call[h] on your god! Maybe he will take notice of us, and we
will not perish."[i]
7Then the sailors said to each
other, "Come, let us cast lots to
find out who is responsible for this
calamity."[j] They cast lots and the
lot fell on Jonah.
8So they asked him, "Tell us,
who is responsible for making all

1:1 [a]Mt 12:39-41 [b]2Ki 14:25
1:2 [c]Ge 10:11
1:3 [d]Ps 139:7 [e]Jos 19:46; Ac 9:36,43
1:4 [f]Ps 107:23-26
1:5 [g]Ac 27:18-19
1:6 [h]Jnh 3:8 [i]Ps 107:28
1:7 [j]Jos 7:10-18; 1Sa 14:42

this trouble for us? What do you
do? Where do you come from?
What is your country? From what
people are you?"
9He answered, "I am a Hebrew
and I worship the LORD, the God of
heaven,[a] who made the sea and
the land.[b]"
10This terrified them and they
asked, "What have you done?"
(They knew he was running away
from the LORD, because he had already told them so.)
11The sea was getting rougher
and rougher. So they asked him,
"What should we do to you to make
the sea calm down for us?"
12"Pick me up and throw me into
the sea," he replied, "and it will become calm. I know that it is my
fault that this great storm has come
upon you."[c]
13Instead, the men did their best
to row back to land. But they could
not, for the sea grew even wilder
than before.[d] 14Then they cried to
the LORD, "O LORD, please do not let
us die for taking this man's life. Do
not hold us accountable for killing
an innocent man,[e] for you, O LORD,
have done as you pleased."[f]
15Then they took Jonah and threw
him overboard, and the raging sea
grew calm.[g] 16At this the men
greatly feared[h] the LORD, and they
offered a sacrifice to the LORD and
made vows to him.
17But the LORD provided a great
fish to swallow Jonah,[i] and Jonah
was inside the fish three days and
three nights.

Jonah's Prayer

2 From inside the fish Jonah
prayed to the LORD his God.
2He said:

"In my distress I called to the
LORD,[j]
and he answered me.
From the depths of the grave[a]
I called for help,
and you listened to my cry.
3You hurled me into the deep,[k]
into the very heart of the
seas,
and the currents swirled
about me;
all your waves and breakers
swept over me.[l]
4I said, 'I have been banished
from your sight;[m]
yet I will look again
toward your holy temple.'
5The engulfing waters
threatened me,[b]
the deep surrounded me;
seaweed was wrapped around
my head.[n]
6To the roots of the mountains I
sank down;
the earth beneath barred me
in forever.
But you brought my life up
from the pit,
O LORD my God.

7"When my life was ebbing
away,
I remembered[o] you, LORD,
and my prayer[p] rose to you,
to your holy temple.[q]

8"Those who cling to worthless
idols[r]
forfeit the grace that could
be theirs.
9But I, with a song of
thanksgiving,
will sacrifice[s] to you.
What I have vowed[t] I will
make good.
Salvation[u] comes from the
LORD."

10And the LORD commanded the
fish, and it vomited Jonah onto dry
land.

Jonah Goes to Nineveh

3 Then the word of the LORD
came to Jonah[v] a second
time: 2"Go to the great city of Nineveh and proclaim to it the message
I give you."
3Jonah obeyed the word of the
LORD and went to Nineveh. Now
Nineveh was a very important
city—a visit required three days.
4On the first day, Jonah started
into the city. He proclaimed: "Forty more days and Nineveh will be

1:9 [a]Ac 17:24 [b]Ps 146:6
1:12 [c]2Sa 24:17; 1Ch 21:17
1:13 [d]Pr 21:30
1:14 [e]Dt 21:8 [f]Ps 115:3
1:15 [g]Ps 107:29; Lk 8:24
1:16 [h]Mk 4:41
1:17 [i]Mt 12:40; 16:4; Lk 11:30
2:2 [j]Ps 18:6; 120:1
2:3 [k]Ps 88:6 [l]Ps 42:7
2:4 [m]Ps 31:22
2:5 [n]Ps 69:1-2
2:7 [o]Ps 77:11-12 [p]2Ch 30:27 [q]Ps 11:4; 18:6
2:8 [r]2Ki 17:15; Jer 10:8
2:9 [s]Ps 50:14,23; Hos 14:2 [t]Ecc 5:4-5 [u]Ps 3:8
3:1 [v]Jnh 1:1

[a]2 Hebrew *Sheol* [b]5 Or *waters were at my throat*

overturned." 5The Ninevites believed God. They declared a fast,
and all of them, from the greatest
to the least, put on sackcloth.[a]
6When the news reached the
king of Nineveh, he rose from his
throne, took off his royal robes,
covered himself with sackcloth and
sat down in the dust.[b] 7Then he
issued a proclamation in Nineveh:

"By the decree of the king and
his nobles:

> Do not let any man or beast,
> herd or flock, taste anything;
> do not let them eat or drink.[c]
> 8But let man and beast be cov-
> ered with sackcloth. Let every-
> one call[d] urgently on God. Let
> them give up their evil ways
> and their violence. 9Who
> knows?[e] God may yet relent
> and with compassion turn[f]
> from his fierce anger so that
> we will not perish."

10When God saw what they did
and how they turned from their evil
ways, he had compassion[g] and did
not bring upon them the destruction[h] he had threatened.[i]

Jonah's Anger at the LORD's Compassion

4 But Jonah was greatly displeased and became angry.[j]
2He prayed to the LORD, "O LORD, is
this not what I said when I was still
at home? That is why I was so quick
to flee to Tarshish. I knew[k] that
you are a gracious and compassionate God, slow to anger and abounding in love,[l] a God who relents
from sending calamity.[m] 3Now, O
LORD, take away my life,[n] for it is
better for me to die[o] than to live."
4But the LORD replied, "Have you
any right to be angry?"[p]
5Jonah went out and sat down at
a place east of the city. There he
made himself a shelter, sat in its
shade and waited to see what
would happen to the city. 6Then
the LORD God provided a vine and
made it grow up over Jonah to give
shade for his head to ease his dis-
comfort, and Jonah was very happy
about the vine. 7But at dawn the
next day God provided a worm,
which chewed the vine so that it
withered.[q] 8When the sun rose,
God provided a scorching east
wind, and the sun blazed on Jonah's head so that he grew faint.
He wanted to die, and said, "It
would be better for me to die than
to live."
9But God said to Jonah, "Do you
have a right to be angry about the
vine?"

"I do," he said. "I am angry
enough to die."
10But the LORD said, "You have
been concerned about this vine,
though you did not tend it or make
it grow. It sprang up overnight and
died overnight. 11But Nineveh[r]
has more than a hundred and twenty thousand people who cannot tell
their right hand from their left, and
many cattle as well. Should I not
be concerned[s] about that great
city?"

3:5 [a] Da 9:3; Lk 11:32
3:6 [b] Job 2:8,13; Eze 27:30-31
3:7 [c] 2Ch 20:3
3:8 [d] Ps 130:1; Jnh 1:6
3:9 [e] 2Sa 12:22 [f] Joel 2:14
3:10 [g] Am 7:6 [h] Jer 18:8 [i] Ex 32:14
4:1 [j] ver 4; Lk 15:28
4:2 [k] Jer 20:7-8 [l] Ex 34:6; Ps 86:5,15 [m] Joel 2:13
4:3 [n] 1Ki 19:4 [o] Job 7:15
4:4 [p] Mt 20:11-15
4:7 [q] Joel 1:12
4:11 [r] Jnh 1:2; 3:2 [s] Jnh 3:10

Micah

Title and Background

The book is named after Micah, a shortened form of Micaiah, meaning "Who is like the LORD?" Judah had enjoyed comparative economic prosperity when Micah came on the scene. This prosperity placed wealth and power in the hands of a few and brought with it social injustice.

Author and Date of Writing

Little is known about Micah beyond what can be learned from the book itself. He was deeply sensitive to the social ills of his day, especially as they affected the small towns and villages of his homeland. Micah prophesied sometime between 750 and 686 B.C., and his book was written prior to 686.

Theme and Message

Micah's message alternated between oracles of doom and oracles of hope. The theme is judgment and deliverance by God. Micah also stresses that God hates idolatry, injustice, rebellion and empty ritualism, but he delights in pardoning the penitent.

Outline

I. Judgment Against Israel and Judah (1:1-3:12)
II. Hope for Israel and Judah (4:1-5:15)
III. The Lord's Case Against Israel (6:1-16)
IV. Gloom Turns to Triumph (7:1-20)

---

1 The word of the LORD that came to Micah of Moresheth[a] during the reigns of Jotham,[b] Ahaz[c] and Hezekiah, kings of Judah[d]—the vision[e] he saw concerning Samaria and Jerusalem.

2Hear, O peoples, all of you,[f]
listen, O earth[g] and all who are in it,
that the Sovereign LORD may witness[h] against you,
the Lord from his holy temple.[i]

Judgment Against Samaria and Jerusalem

3Look! The LORD is coming from his dwelling[j] place;
he comes down and treads the high places of the earth.[k]
4The mountains melt[l] beneath him
and the valleys split apart,[m]
like wax before the fire,
like water rushing down a slope.
5All this is because of Jacob's transgression,
because of the sins of the house of Israel.
What is Jacob's transgression?
Is it not Samaria?[n]
What is Judah's high place?
Is it not Jerusalem?
6"Therefore I will make Samaria a heap of rubble,
a place for planting vineyards.
I will pour her stones[o] into the valley
and lay bare her foundations.[p]

1:1 [a] Jer 26:18 [b] 1Ch 3:12 [c] 1Ch 3:13 [d] Hos 1:1 [e] Isa 1:1
1:2 [f] Ps 50:7 [g] Jer 6:19 [h] Ge 31:50; Dt 4:26; Isa 1:2 [i] Ps 11:4
1:3 [j] Isa 18:4 [k] Am 4:13
1:4 [l] Ps 46:2,6 [m] Nu 16:31; Na 1:5
1:5 [n] Am 8:14
1:6 [o] Am 5:11 [p] Eze 13:14

[7]All her idols[a] will be broken to
pieces;
all her temple gifts will be
burned with fire;
I will destroy all her
images.[b]
Since she gathered her gifts
from the wages of
prostitutes,[c]
as the wages of prostitutes
they will again be used."

Weeping and Mourning

[8]Because of this I will weep[d]
and wail;
I will go about barefoot and
naked.
I will howl like a jackal
and moan like an owl.
[9]For her wound[e] is incurable;
it has come to Judah.[f]
It[a] has reached the very gate[g]
of my people,
even to Jerusalem itself.
[10]Tell it not in Gath[b];
weep not at all.[c]
In Beth Ophrah[d]
roll in the dust.
[11]Pass on in nakedness[h] and
shame,
you who live in Shaphir.[e]
Those who live in Zaanan[f]
will not come out.
Beth Ezel is in mourning;
its protection is taken from
you.
[12]Those who live in Maroth[g]
writhe in pain,
waiting for relief,[i]
because disaster has come from
the LORD,
even to the gate of
Jerusalem.
[13]You who live in Lachish,[h][j]
harness the team to the
chariot.
You were the beginning of sin
to the Daughter of Zion,
for the transgressions of Israel
were found in you.
[14]Therefore you will give parting
gifts[k]
to Moresheth Gath.
The town of Aczib[i][l] will prove
deceptive[m]
to the kings of Israel.

[15]I will bring a conqueror against
you
who live in Mareshah.[j][n]
He who is the glory of Israel
will come to Adullam.[o]
[16]Shave[p] your heads in mourning
for the children in whom you
delight;
make yourselves as bald as the
vulture,
for they will go from you into
exile.

Man's Plans and God's

2 Woe to those who plan
iniquity,
to those who plot evil on
their beds![q]
At morning's light they carry it
out
because it is in their power
to do it.
[2]They covet fields[r] and seize
them,
and houses, and take them.
They defraud[s] a man of his
home,
a fellowman of his
inheritance.

[3]Therefore, the LORD says:

"I am planning disaster[t]
against this people,
from which you cannot save
yourselves.
You will no longer walk
proudly,[u]
for it will be a time of
calamity.
[4]In that day men will ridicule
you;
they will taunt you with this
mournful song:
'We are utterly ruined;[v]
my people's possession is
divided up.
He takes it from me!

1:7 [a]Eze 6:6 [b]Dt 9:21 [c]Dt 23:17-18
1:8 [d]Isa 15:3
1:9 [e]Jer 46:11 [f]2Ki 18:13 [g]Isa 3:26
1:11 [h]Eze 23:29
1:12 [i]Jer 14:19
1:13 [j]Jos 10:3
1:14 [k]2Ki 16:8 [l]Jos 15:44 [m]Jer 15:18
1:15 [n]Jos 15:44 [o]Jos 12:15
1:16 [p]Job 1:20
2:1 [q]Ps 36:4
2:2 [r]Isa 5:8 [s]Jer 22:17
2:3 [t]Jer 18:11; Am 3:1-2 [u]Isa 2:12
2:4 [v]Jer 4:13

[a]9 Or *He* [b]*10 Gath* sounds like the Hebrew for *tell.* [c]*10* Hebrew; Septuagint may suggest *not in Acco.* The Hebrew for *in Acco* sounds like the Hebrew for *weep.* [d]*10 Beth Ophrah* means *house of dust.* [e]*11 Shaphir* means *pleasant.* [f]*11 Zaanan* sounds like the Hebrew for *come out.* [g]*12 Maroth* sounds like the Hebrew for *bitter.* [h]*13 Lachish* sounds like the Hebrew for *team.* [i]*14 Aczib* means *deception.* [j]*15 Mareshah* sounds like the Hebrew for *conqueror.*

He assigns our fields to
traitors.' "

5Therefore you will have no one
in the assembly of the
LORD
to divide the land[a] by lot.

False Prophets

6"Do not prophesy," their
prophets say.
"Do not prophesy about
these things;
disgrace[b] will not overtake
us.[c]"
7Should it be said, O house of
Jacob:
"Is the Spirit of the LORD
angry?
Does he do such things?"

"Do not my words do good[d]
to him whose ways are
upright?[e]
8Lately my people have risen up
like an enemy.
You strip off the rich robe
from those who pass by
without a care,
like men returning from
battle.
9You drive the women of my
people
from their pleasant homes.[f]
You take away my blessing
from their children forever.
10Get up, go away!
For this is not your resting
place,[g]
because it is defiled,[h]
it is ruined, beyond all
remedy.
11If a liar and deceiver[i] comes
and says,
'I will prophesy for you
plenty of wine and beer,'
he would be just the prophet
for this people![j]

Deliverance Promised

12"I will surely gather all of you,
O Jacob;
I will surely bring together
the remnant[k] of Israel.
I will bring them together like
sheep in a pen,
like a flock in its pasture;
the place will throng with
people.
13One who breaks open the way
will go up before[l] them;
they will break through the
gate and go out.
Their king will pass through
before them,
the LORD at their head."

Leaders and Prophets Rebuked

3 Then I said,
"Listen, you leaders[m] of
Jacob,
you rulers of the house of
Israel.
Should you not know justice,
2 you who hate good and love
evil;
who tear the skin from my
people
and the flesh from their
bones;[n]
3who eat my people's flesh,[o]
strip off their skin
and break their bones in
pieces;[p]
who chop them up like meat
for the pan,
like flesh for the pot?[q]"

4Then they will cry out to the
LORD,
but he will not answer
them.[r]
At that time he will hide his
face[s] from them
because of the evil they have
done.

5This is what the LORD says:

"As for the prophets
who lead my people astray,[t]
if one feeds them,
they proclaim 'peace';
if he does not,
they prepare to wage war
against him.
6Therefore night will come over
you, without visions,
and darkness, without
divination.[u]
The sun will set for the
prophets,[v]
and the day will go dark for
them.
7The seers will be ashamed[w]

2:5 [a] Jos 18:4
2:6 [b] Mic 6:16 [c] Am 2:12
2:7 [d] Ps 119:65 [e] Ps 15:2; 84:11
2:9 [f] Jer 10:20
2:10 [g] Dt 12:9 [h] Lev 18:25-29; Ps 106:38-39
2:11 [i] Jer 5:31 [j] Isa 30:10
2:12 [k] Mic 4:7; 5:7; 7:18
2:13 [l] Isa 52:12
3:1 [m] Jer 5:5
3:2 [n] Ps 53:4; Eze 22:27
3:3 [o] Ps 14:4 [p] Zep 3:3 [q] Eze 11:7
3:4 [r] Ps 18:41; Isa 1:15 [s] Dt 31:17
3:5 [t] Isa 3:12; 9:16
3:6 [u] Isa 8:19-22 [v] Isa 29:10
3:7 [w] Mic 7:16

and the diviners disgraced.[a]
They will all cover their faces
because there is no answer
from God."

8But as for me, I am filled with
power,
with the Spirit of the LORD,
and with justice and might,
to declare to Jacob his
transgression,
to Israel his sin.[b]
9Hear this, you leaders of the
house of Jacob,
you rulers of the house of
Israel,
who despise justice
and distort all that is right;[c]
10who build[d] Zion with
bloodshed,[e]
and Jerusalem with
wickedness.[f]
11Her leaders judge for a bribe,
her priests teach for a price,
and her prophets tell
fortunes for money.[g]
Yet they lean upon the LORD
and say,
"Is not the LORD among
us?
No disaster will come upon
us."[h]
12Therefore because of you,
Zion will be plowed like a
field,
Jerusalem will become a heap
of rubble,[i]
the temple hill a mound
overgrown with thickets.

The Mountain of the LORD

4:1–3pp — Isa 2:1–4

4 In the last days
the mountain[j] of the LORD's
temple will be
established
as chief among the
mountains;
it will be raised above the
hills,[k]
and peoples will stream to
it.[l]

2Many nations will come and
say,

"Come, let us go up to the
mountain of the LORD,[m]
to the house of the God of
Jacob.[n]
He will teach us his ways,[o]
so that we may walk in his
paths."
The law will go out from Zion,
the word of the LORD from
Jerusalem.
3He will judge between many
peoples
and will settle disputes for
strong nations far and
wide.[p]
They will beat their swords into
plowshares
and their spears into pruning
hooks.[q]
Nation will not take up sword
against nation,
nor will they train for war
anymore.[r]
4Every man will sit under his
own vine
and under his own fig tree,[s]
and no one will make them
afraid,[t]
for the LORD Almighty has
spoken.[u]
5All the nations may walk
in the name of their gods;[v]
we will walk in the name of the
LORD
our God for ever and ever.[w]

The LORD's Plan

6"In that day," declares the LORD,

"I will gather the lame;
I will assemble the exiles[x]
and those I have brought to
grief.[y]
7I will make the lame a
remnant,[z]
those driven away a strong
nation.
The LORD will rule over them in
Mount Zion
from that day and forever.[a]
8As for you, O watchtower of the
flock,
O stronghold[k] of the
Daughter of Zion,
the former dominion will be
restored[b] to you;

3:7 [a] Isa 44:25
3:8 [b] Isa 58:1
3:9 [c] Ps 58:1-2; Isa 1:23
3:10 [d] Jer 22:13 [e] Hab 2:12 [f] Eze 22:27
3:11 [g] Isa 1:23; Jer 6:13; Hos 4:8,18 [h] Jer 7:4
3:12 [i] Jer 26:18
4:1 [j] Zec 8:3 [k] Eze 17:22 [l] Ps 22:27; 86:9; Jer 3:17
4:2 [m] Jer 31:6 [n] Zec 2:11; 14:16 [o] Ps 25:8-9; Isa 54:13
4:3 [p] Isa 11:4 [q] Joel 3:10 [r] Isa 2:4
4:4 [s] 1Ki 4:25 [t] Lev 26:6 [u] Isa 1:20; Zec 3:10
4:5 [v] 2Ki 17:29 [w] Jos 24:14-15; Isa 26:8; Zec 10:12
4:6 [x] Ps 147:2 [y] Eze 34:13, 16; 37:21; Zep 3:19
4.7 [z] Mic 2:12 [a] Da 7:14; Lk 1:33; Rev 11:15
4:8 [b] Isa 1:26

[k]8 Or *hill*

kingship will come to the
Daughter of Jerusalem."

9Why do you now cry aloud—
have you no king?[a]
Has your counselor perished,
that pain seizes you like that
of a woman in labor?[b]
10Writhe in agony, O Daughter of
Zion,
like a woman in labor,
for now you must leave the city
to camp in the open field.
You will go to Babylon;[c]
there you will be rescued.
There the LORD will redeem[d]
you
out of the hand of your
enemies.

11But now many nations
are gathered against you.
They say, "Let her be defiled,
let our eyes gloat[e] over
Zion!"
12But they do not know
the thoughts of the LORD;
they do not understand his
plan,[f]
he who gathers them like
sheaves to the threshing
floor.
13"Rise and thresh, O Daughter
of Zion,
for I will give you horns of
iron;
I will give you hoofs of bronze
and you will break to pieces
many nations."[g]
You will devote their ill-gotten
gains to the LORD,
their wealth to the Lord of
all the earth.

A Promised Ruler From Bethlehem

5 Marshal your troops, O city
of troops,[1]
for a siege is laid against us.
They will strike Israel's ruler
on the cheek[h] with a rod.

2"But you, Bethlehem[i]
Ephrathah,[j]
though you are small among
the clans[m] of Judah,
out of you will come for me
one who will be ruler over
Israel,
whose origins[n] are from of
old,[k]
from ancient times.[o]"[l]

3Therefore Israel will be
abandoned
until the time when she who
is in labor gives birth
and the rest of his brothers
return
to join the Israelites.

4He will stand and shepherd his
flock[m]
in the strength of the LORD,
in the majesty of the name of
the LORD his God.
And they will live securely, for
then his greatness[n]
will reach to the ends of the
earth.
5 And he will be their peace.[o]

Deliverance and Destruction

When the Assyrian invades[p]
our land
and marches through our
fortresses,
we will raise against him seven
shepherds,
even eight leaders of men.[q]
6They will rule[p] the land of
Assyria with the sword,
the land of Nimrod[r] with
drawn sword.[q][s]
He will deliver us from the
Assyrian
when he invades our land
and marches into our
borders.[t]

7The remnant[u] of Jacob will be
in the midst of many peoples
like dew from the LORD,
like showers on the grass,[v]
which do not wait for man
or linger for mankind.
8The remnant of Jacob will be
among the nations,
in the midst of many
peoples,

4:9 [a]Jer 8:19 [b]Jer 30:6
4:10 [c]2Ki 20:18; Isa 43:14 [d]Isa 48:20
4:11 [e]La 2:16; Ob 1:12
4:12 [f]Isa 55:8; Ro 11:33-34
4:13 [g]Da 2:44
5:1 [h]La 3:30
5:2 [i]Jn 7:42 [j]Ge 48:7 [k]Ps 102:25 [l]Mt 2:6*
5:4 [m]Isa 40:11; 49:9; Eze 34:11-15, 23; Mic 7:14 [n]Isa 52:13; Lk 1:32
5:5 [o]Isa 9:6; Lk 2:14; Col 1:19-20 [p]Isa 8:7 [q]Isa 10:24-27
5:6 [r]Ge 10:8 [s]Zep 2:13 [t]Na 2:11-13
5:7 [u]Mic 2:12 [v]Isa 44:4

[1]1 Or *Strengthen your walls, O walled city*
[m]2 Or *rulers* [n]2 Hebrew *goings out*
[o]2 Or *from days of eternity* [p]6 Or *crush*
[q]6 Or *Nimrod in its gates*

like a lion among the beasts of the forest,[a]
like a young lion among flocks of sheep,
which mauls and mangles[b] as it goes,
and no one can rescue.[c]
9Your hand will be lifted up[d] in triumph over your enemies,
and all your foes will be destroyed.

10"In that day," declares the LORD,

"I will destroy your horses from among you
and demolish your chariots.[e]
11I will destroy the cities[f] of your land
and tear down all your strongholds.[g]
12I will destroy your witchcraft
and you will no longer cast spells.[h]
13I will destroy your carved images
and your sacred stones from among you;
you will no longer bow down
to the work of your hands.[i]
14I will uproot from among you
your Asherah poles[r][j]
and demolish your cities.
15I will take vengeance[k] in anger and wrath
upon the nations that have not obeyed me."

The LORD's Case Against Israel

6 Listen to what the LORD says:
"Stand up, plead your case before the mountains;[l]
let the hills hear what you have to say.
2Hear,[m] O mountains, the LORD's accusation;[n]
listen, you everlasting foundations of the earth.
For the LORD has a case against his people;
he is lodging a charge[o] against Israel.

3"My people, what have I done to you?

5:8 [a]Ge 49:9 [b]Mic 4:13; Zec 10:5 [c]Ps 50:22; Hos 5:14
5:9 [d]Ps 10:12
5:10 [e]Hos 14:3; Zec 9:10
5:11 [f]Isa 6:11 [g]Hos 10:14; Am 5:9
5:12 [h]Dt 18:10-12; Isa 2:6; 8:19
5:13 [i]Eze 6:9; Zec 13:2
5:14 [j]Ex 34:13
5:15 [k]Isa 65:12
6:1 [l]Ps 50:1; Eze 6:2
6:2 [m]Dt 32:1 [n]Hos 12:2 [o]Ps 50:7
6:3 [p]Jer 2:5
6:4 [q]Dt 7:8 [r]Ex 4:16 [s]Ps 77:20 [t]Ex 15:20
6:5 [u]Nu 22:5-6 [v]Nu 25:1 [w]Jos 5:9-10 [x]Jdg 5:11; 1Sa 12:7
6:6 [y]Ps 40:6-8; 51:16-17
6:7 [z]Isa 40:16 [a]Ps 50:8-10 [b]Lev 18:21 [c]2Ki 16:3
6:8 [d]Isa 1:17; Jer 22:3 [e]Isa 57:15 [f]Dt 10:12-13; 1Sa 15:22; Hos 6:6

How have I burdened[p] you? Answer me.
4I brought you up out of Egypt
and redeemed you from the land of slavery.[q]
I sent Moses[r] to lead you,
also Aaron[s] and Miriam.[t]
5My people, remember
what Balak[u] king of Moab counseled
and what Balaam son of Beor answered.
Remember ⌊your journey⌋ from Shittim[v] to Gilgal,[w]
that you may know the righteous acts[x] of the LORD."

6With what shall I come before the LORD
and bow down before the exalted God?
Shall I come before him with burnt offerings,
with calves a year old?[y]
7Will the LORD be pleased with thousands of rams,[z]
with ten thousand rivers of oil?[a]
Shall I offer my firstborn[b] for my transgression,
the fruit of my body for the sin of my soul?[c]
8He has showed you, O man, what is good.
And what does the LORD require of you?
To act justly[d] and to love mercy
and to walk humbly[e] with your God.[f]

Israel's Guilt and Punishment

9Listen! The LORD is calling to the city—
and to fear your name is wisdom—
"Heed the rod and the One who appointed it.[s]
10Am I still to forget, O wicked house,
your ill-gotten treasures

[r]*14* That is, symbols of the goddess Asherah
[s]*9* The meaning of the Hebrew for this line is uncertain.

and the short ephah,[t] which
is accursed?[a]
11Shall I acquit a man with
dishonest scales,[b]
with a bag of false weights?
12Her rich men are violent;[c]
her people are liars[d]
and their tongues speak
deceitfully.[e]
13Therefore, I have begun to
destroy[f] you,
to ruin you because of your
sins.
14You will eat but not be
satisfied;[g]
your stomach will still be
empty.[u]
You will store up but save
nothing,[h]
because what you save I will
give to the sword.
15You will plant but not
harvest;[i]
you will press olives but not
use the oil on
yourselves,
you will crush grapes but not
drink the wine.[j]
16You have observed the statutes
of Omri[k]
and all the practices of
Ahab's[l] house,
and you have followed their
traditions.[m]
Therefore I will give you over to
ruin[n]
and your people to derision;
you will bear the scorn[o] of
the nations.[v]"

Israel's Misery

7 What misery is mine!
I am like one who gathers
summer fruit
at the gleaning of the
vineyard;
there is no cluster of grapes to
eat,
none of the early figs that I
crave.
2The godly have been swept
from the land;[p]
not one upright man
remains.
All men lie in wait to shed
blood;[q]
each hunts his brother with a
net.[r]
3Both hands are skilled in doing
evil;[s]
the ruler demands gifts,
the judge accepts bribes,
the powerful dictate what
they desire—
they all conspire together.
4The best of them is like a
brier,[t]
the most upright worse than
a thorn hedge.
The day of your watchmen has
come,
the day God visits you.
Now is the time of their
confusion.[u]
5Do not trust a neighbor;
put no confidence in a
friend.[v]
Even with her who lies in your
embrace
be careful of your words.
6For a son dishonors his father,
a daughter rises up against
her mother,[w]
a daughter-in-law against her
mother-in-law—
a man's enemies are the
members of his own
household.[x]

7But as for me, I watch in
hope[y] for the LORD,
I wait for God my Savior;
my God will hear[z] me.

Israel Will Rise

8Do not gloat over me,[a] my
enemy!
Though I have fallen, I will
rise.[b]
Though I sit in darkness,
the LORD will be my light.[c]
9Because I have sinned against
him,
I will bear the LORD's wrath,[d]
until he pleads my case
and establishes my right.
He will bring me out into the
light;
I will see his righteousness.[e]

6:10 [a]Eze 45:9-10; Am 3:10; 8:4-6
6:11 [b]Lev 19:36; Hos 12:7
6:12 [c]Isa 1:23 [d]Isa 3:8 [e]Jer 9:3
6:13 [f]Isa 1:7; 6:11
6:14 [g]Isa 9:20 [h]Isa 30:6
6:15 [i]Dt 28:38; Jer 12:13 [j]Am 5:11; Zep 1:13
6:16 [k]1Ki 16:25 [l]1Ki 16:29-33 [m]Jer 7:24 [n]Jer 25:9 [o]Jer 51:51
7:2 [p]Ps 12:1 [q]Mic 3:10 [r]Jer 5:26
7:3 [s]Pr 4:16
7:4 [t]Eze 2:6 [u]Isa 22:5; Hos 9:7
7:5 [v]Jer 9:4
7:6 [w]Eze 22:7 [x]Mt 10:35-36*
7:7 [y]Ps 130:5; Isa 25:9 [z]Ps 4:3
7:8 [a]Pr 24:17 [b]Ps 37:24; Am 9:11 [c]Isa 9:2
7:9 [d]La 3:39-40 [e]Isa 46:13

[t]*10* An ephah was a dry measure. [u]*14* The meaning of the Hebrew for this word is uncertain. [v]*16* Septuagint; Hebrew *scorn due my people*

10Then my enemy will see it
and will be covered with shame,[a]
she who said to me,
"Where is the LORD your God?"
My eyes will see her downfall;[b]
even now she will be trampled[c] underfoot
like mire in the streets.

11The day for building your walls[d] will come,
the day for extending your boundaries.
12In that day people will come to you
from Assyria and the cities of Egypt,
even from Egypt to the Euphrates
and from sea to sea
and from mountain to mountain.[e]
13The earth will become desolate
because of its inhabitants,
as the result of their deeds.[f]

Prayer and Praise

14Shepherd[g] your people with your staff,[h]
the flock of your inheritance,
which lives by itself in a forest,
in fertile pasturelands.[w]
Let them feed in Bashan and Gilead[i]
as in days long ago.

15"As in the days when you came out of Egypt,
I will show them my wonders.[j]"

16Nations will see and be ashamed,[k]
deprived of all their power.
They will lay their hands on their mouths
and their ears will become deaf.
17They will lick dust like a snake,
like creatures that crawl on the ground.
They will come trembling out of their dens;
they will turn in fear[l] to the LORD our God
and will be afraid of you.
18Who is a God like you,
who pardons sin[m] and forgives[n] the transgression
of the remnant[o] of his inheritance?[p]
You do not stay angry[q] forever
but delight to show mercy.[r]
19You will again have compassion on us;
you will tread our sins underfoot
and hurl all our iniquities[s] into the depths of the sea.[t]
20You will be true to Jacob,
and show mercy to Abraham,
as you pledged on oath to our fathers[u]
in days long ago.

7:10 [a] Ps 35:26 [b] Isa 51:23 [c] Zec 10:5
7:11 [d] Isa 54:11
7:12 [e] Isa 19:23-25
7:13 [f] Isa 3:10-11
7:14 [g] Mic 5:4 [h] Ps 23:4 [i] Jer 50:19
7:15 [j] Ex 3:20; Ps 78:12
7:16 [k] Isa 26:11
7:17 [l] Isa 25:3; 49:23; 59:19
7:18 [m] Isa 43:25; Jer 50:20 [n] Ps 103:8-13 [o] Mic 2:12 [p] Ex 34:9 [q] Ps 103:9 [r] Jer 32:41
7:19 [s] Isa 43:25 [t] Jer 31:34
7:20 [u] Dt 7:8; Lk 1:72

[w] *14 Or in the middle of Carmel*

Nahum

Title and Background

The name Nahum means "comfort" or "consolation." During Jonah's time, Nineveh repented and their destruction was temporarily averted. Not long after that, however, Nineveh reverted to its extreme wickedness, brutality and pride.

Author and Date of Writing

Nothing is known about Nahum except his hometown (Elkosh), but even its precise location is uncertain. In all three chapters Nahum prophesied Nineveh's fall, which was fulfilled in 612 B.C. Nahum therefore probably uttered this oracle between 663 and 612, perhaps near the end of this period.

Theme and Message

The focal point of the whole book is the Lord's judgment on Nineveh for her oppression, cruelty, idolatry and wickedness. God's righteous and just kingdom will ultimately triumph, for kingdoms built on wickedness and tyranny must eventually fall, as Assyria did.

Finally, Nahum declares the universal sovereignty of God. God is Lord of history and of all nations; as such he controls their destinies.

Outline

I. The Lord's Anger Against Nineveh (1:1-15)
II. Nineveh's Fall (2:1-13)
III. Woe to Nineveh (3:1-19)

---

1 An oracle[a] concerning Nineveh.[b] The book of the vision of Nahum the Elkoshite.

The LORD's Anger Against Nineveh

2The LORD is a jealous[c] and
avenging God;
the LORD takes vengeance[d]
and is filled with wrath.
The LORD takes vengeance on
his foes
and maintains his wrath
against his enemies.
3The LORD is slow to anger[e] and
great in power;
the LORD will not leave the
guilty unpunished.[f]
His way is in the whirlwind and
the storm,
and clouds[g] are the dust of
his feet.

1:1 [a] Isa 13:1; 19:1; Jer 23:33-34 [b] Jnh 1:2; Na 2:8; Zep 2:13
1:2 [c] Ex 20:5 [d] Dt 32:41; Ps 94:1
1:3 [e] Ne 9:17 [f] Ex 34:7 [g] Ps 104:3
1:4 [h] Isa 33:9
1:5 [i] Ex 19:18 [j] Mic 1:4
1:6 [k] Mal 3:2 [l] Jer 10:10 [m] 1Ki 19:11

4He rebukes the sea and dries it
up;
he makes all the rivers run
dry.
Bashan and Carmel[h] wither
and the blossoms of Lebanon
fade.
5The mountains quake[i] before
him
and the hills melt away.[j]
The earth trembles at his
presence,
the world and all who live in
it.
6Who can withstand his
indignation?
Who can endure[k] his fierce
anger?
His wrath is poured out like
fire;[l]
the rocks are shattered[m]
before him.

7The LORD is good,[a]
a refuge in times of trouble.
He cares for[b] those who trust
in him,
8 but with an overwhelming
flood
he will make an end of
⌞Nineveh⌟;
he will pursue his foes into
darkness.
9Whatever they plot against the
LORD
he[a] will bring to an end;
trouble will not come a
second time.
10They will be entangled among
thorns[c]
and drunk from their wine;
they will be consumed like
dry stubble.[b][d]
11From you, ⌞O Nineveh,⌟ has one
come forth
who plots evil against the
LORD
and counsels wickedness.

12This is what the LORD says:

"Although they have allies and
are numerous,
they will be cut off[e] and
pass away.
Although I have afflicted you,
⌞O Judah,⌟
I will afflict you no more.[f]
13Now I will break their yoke[g]
from your neck
and tear your shackles away."

14The LORD has given a command
concerning you,
⌞Nineveh⌟:
"You will have no
descendants to bear your
name.[h]
I will destroy the carved
images[i] and cast idols
that are in the temple of your
gods.
I will prepare your grave,[j]
for you are vile."

15Look, there on the mountains,
the feet of one who brings
good news,[k]
who proclaims peace![l]
Celebrate your festivals,[m]
O Judah,
and fulfill your vows.
No more will the wicked invade
you;[n]
they will be completely
destroyed.

Nineveh to Fall

2 An attacker[o] advances
against you, ⌞Nineveh⌟.
Guard the fortress,
watch the road,
brace yourselves,
marshal all your strength!

2The LORD will restore[p] the
splendor[q] of Jacob
like the splendor of Israel,
though destroyers have laid
them waste
and have ruined their vines.

3The shields of his soldiers are
red;
the warriors are clad in
scarlet.[r]
The metal on the chariots
flashes
on the day they are made
ready;
the spears of pine are
brandished.[c]
4The chariots[s] storm through
the streets,
rushing back and forth
through the squares.
They look like flaming torches;
they dart about like
lightning.

5He summons his picked troops,
yet they stumble[t] on their
way.
They dash to the city wall;
the protective shield is put in
place.
6The river gates[u] are thrown
open
and the palace collapses.
7It is decreed[d] that ⌞the city⌟
be exiled and carried away.
Its slave girls moan[v] like doves
and beat upon their
breasts.[w]

1:7 [a]Jer 33:11 [b]Ps 1:6
1:10 [c]2Sa 23:6 [d]Isa 5:24; Mal 4:1
1:12 [e]Isa 10:34 [f]Isa 54:6-8; La 3:31-32
1:13 [g]Isa 9:4
1:14 [h]Isa 14:22 [i]Mic 5:13 [j]Eze 32:22-23
1:15 [k]Isa 40:9; Ro 10:15 [l]Isa 52:7 [m]Lev 23:2-4 [n]Isa 52:1
2:1 [o]Jer 51:20
2:2 [p]Eze 37:23 [q]Isa 60:15
2:3 [r]Eze 23:14-15
2:4 [s]Jer 4:13
2:5 [t]Jer 46:12
2:6 [u]Na 3:13
2:7 [v]Isa 59:11 [w]Isa 32:12

[a]9 Or *What do you foes plot against the LORD? / He* [b]10 The meaning of the Hebrew for this verse is uncertain. [c]3 Hebrew; Septuagint and Syriac / *the horsemen rush to and fro* [d]7 The meaning of the Hebrew for this word is uncertain.

8Nineveh is like a pool,
and its water is draining away.
"Stop! Stop!" they cry,
but no one turns back.
9Plunder the silver!
Plunder the gold!
The supply is endless,
the wealth from all its treasures!
10She is pillaged, plundered, stripped!
Hearts melt, knees give way,
bodies tremble, every face grows pale.[a]

11Where now is the lions' den,[b]
the place where they fed their young,
where the lion and lioness went,
and the cubs, with nothing to fear?
12The lion killed[c] enough for his cubs
and strangled the prey for his mate,
filling his lairs with the kill
and his dens with the prey.

13"I am against[d] you,"
declares the LORD Almighty.
"I will burn up your chariots in smoke,[e]
and the sword will devour your young lions.
I will leave you no prey on the earth.
The voices of your messengers
will no longer be heard."

Woe to Nineveh

3 Woe to the city of blood,[f]
full of lies,
full of plunder,
never without victims!
2The crack of whips,
the clatter of wheels,
galloping horses
and jolting chariots!
3Charging cavalry,
flashing swords
and glittering spears!
Many casualties,
piles of dead,
bodies without number,
people stumbling over the corpses[g]—
4all because of the wanton lust of a harlot,
alluring, the mistress of sorceries,[h]
who enslaved nations by her prostitution[i]
and peoples by her witchcraft.

5"I am against[j] you," declares the LORD Almighty.
"I will lift your skirts[k] over your face.
I will show the nations your nakedness[l]
and the kingdoms your shame.
6I will pelt you with filth,[m]
I will treat you with contempt[n]
and make you a spectacle.[o]
7All who see you will flee from you and say,
'Nineveh[p] is in ruins—who will mourn for her?'[q]
Where can I find anyone to comfort[r] you?"

8Are you better than[s] Thebes,[e][t]
situated on the Nile,[u]
with water around her?
The river was her defense,
the waters her wall.
9Cush[f][v] and Egypt were her boundless strength;
Put[w] and Libya[x] were among her allies.
10Yet she was taken captive[y]
and went into exile.
Her infants were dashed[z] to pieces
at the head of every street.
Lots were cast for her nobles,
and all her great men were put in chains.
11You too will become drunk;[a]
you will go into hiding[b]
and seek refuge from the enemy.

12All your fortresses are like fig trees
with their first ripe fruit;

2:10 [a] Isa 29:22
2:11 [b] Isa 5:29
2:12 [c] Jer 51:34
2:13 [d] Jer 21:13; Na 3:5 [e] Ps 46:9
3:1 [f] Eze 22:2; Mic 3:10
3:3 [g] 2Ki 19:35; Isa 34:3
3:4 [h] Isa 47:9 [i] Isa 23:17; Eze 16:25-29
3:5 [j] Na 2:13 [k] Jer 13:22 [l] Isa 47:3
3:6 [m] Job 9:31 [n] 1Sa 2:30; Jer 51:37 [o] Isa 14:16
3:7 [p] Na 1:1 [q] Jer 15:5 [r] Isa 51:19
3:8 [s] Am 6:2 [t] Jer 46:25 [u] Isa 19:6-9
3:9 [v] 2Ch 12:3 [w] Eze 27:10 [x] Eze 30:5
3:10 [y] Isa 20:4 [z] Isa 13:16; Hos 13:16
3:11 [a] Isa 49:26 [b] Isa 2:10

[e] 8 Hebrew *No Amon* [f] 9 That is, the upper Nile region

when they are shaken,
the figs[a] fall into the mouth of the eater.
13Look at your troops—
they are all women![b]
The gates[c] of your land
are wide open to your enemies;
fire has consumed their bars.[d]

14Draw water for the siege,[e]
strengthen your defenses![f]
Work the clay,
tread the mortar,
repair the brickwork!
15There the fire will devour you;
the sword will cut you down
and, like grasshoppers, consume you.
Multiply like grasshoppers,
multiply like locusts![g]
16You have increased the number of your merchants
till they are more than the stars of the sky,
but like locusts they strip the land
and then fly away.
17Your guards are like locusts,[h]
your officials like swarms of locusts
that settle in the walls on a cold day—
but when the sun appears they fly away,
and no one knows where.

18O king of Assyria, your shepherds[g] slumber;[i]
your nobles lie down to rest.[j]
Your people are scattered[k] on the mountains
with no one to gather them.
19Nothing can heal your wound;[l]
your injury is fatal.
Everyone who hears the news about you
claps his hands[m] at your fall,
for who has not felt
your endless cruelty?

3:12 [a] Isa 28:4
3:13 [b] Isa 19:16; Jer 50:37 [c] Na 2:6 [d] Isa 45:2
3:14 [e] 2Ch 32:4 [f] Na 2:1
3:15 [g] Joel 1:4
3:17 [h] Jer 51:27
3:18 [i] Ps 76:5-6 [j] Isa 56:10 [k] 1Ki 22:17
3:19 [l] Jer 30:13; Mic 1:9 [m] Job 27:23; La 2:15; Zep 2:15

[g] 18 Or *rulers*

Habakkuk

Title and Background

The title of the book is the author's name and apparently comes from a Hebrew root meaning "to clasp" or "to embrace." Habakkuk prayed and prophesied in times of crisis. The international scene was shocked by events of far-reaching import. Internally the people of God were caught up in a crisis of religious and moral bewilderment.

Author and Date of Writing

Little is known about the author except his name and that he was a contemporary of Jeremiah. He was a man of vigorous faith, a faith rooted deeply in the religious traditions of Israel. The prophecy is generally dated a little before or after the battle of Carchemish (605 B.C.).

Theme and Message

Habakkuk was written as a dialogue or conversation between God and the prophet. He saw that the leaders were oppressing the poor, so he asked why God allowed the wicked to prosper. Having received replies, he responds with a beautiful confession of faith. His confession became a public expression and appears to have been used as a psalm.

Outline

I. Habakkuk's First Question and God's Answer (1:1-11)
II. Habakkuk's Second Question and God's Answer (1:12-2:20)
III. Habakkuk's Prayer (3:1-19)

---

1 The oracle[a] that Habakkuk the prophet received.

Habakkuk's Complaint

[2]How long, O LORD, must I call
for help,
but you do not listen?[b]
Or cry out to you, "Violence!"
but you do not save?[c]
[3]Why do you make me look at
injustice?
Why do you tolerate[d] wrong?
Destruction and violence[e] are
before me;
there is strife,[f] and conflict
abounds.
[4]Therefore the law[g] is
paralyzed,
and justice never prevails.
The wicked hem in the
righteous,
so that justice is perverted.[h]

The LORD's Answer

[5]"Look at the nations and
watch—
and be utterly amazed.[i]
For I am going to do something
in your days
that you would not believe,
even if you were told.[j]
[6]I am raising up the
Babylonians,[a][k]
that ruthless and impetuous
people,
who sweep across the whole
earth
to seize dwelling places not
their own.[l]
[7]They are a feared and dreaded
people;[m]
they are a law to themselves

1:1 [a]Na 1:1
1:2 [b]Ps 13:1-2; 22:1-2 [c]Jer 14:9
1:3 [d]ver 13 [e]Jer 20:8 [f]Ps 55:9
1:4 [g]Ps 119:126 [h]Job 19:7; Isa 1:23; 5:20; Eze 9:9
1:5 [i]Isa 29:9 [j]Ac 13:41*
1:6 [k]2Ki 24:2 [l]Jer 13:20
1:7 [m]Isa 18:7; Jer 39:5-9

[a]6 Or *Chaldeans*

and promote their own honor.
8 Their horses are swifter[a] than leopards,
fiercer than wolves at dusk.
Their cavalry gallops headlong;
their horsemen come from afar.
They fly like a vulture swooping to devour;
9 they all come bent on violence.
Their hordes[b] advance like a desert wind
and gather prisoners[b] like sand.
10 They deride kings
and scoff at rulers.[c]
They laugh at all fortified cities;
they build earthen ramps and capture them.
11 Then they sweep past like the wind[d] and go on—
guilty men, whose own strength is their god."[e]

Habakkuk's Second Complaint

12 O LORD, are you not from everlasting?
My God, my Holy One,[f] we will not die.
O LORD, you have appointed[g] them to execute judgment;
O Rock, you have ordained them to punish.
13 Your eyes are too pure to look on evil;
you cannot tolerate wrong.[h]
Why then do you tolerate the treacherous?
Why are you silent while the wicked
swallow up those more righteous than themselves?
14 You have made men like fish in the sea,
like sea creatures that have no ruler.
15 The wicked foe pulls all of them up with hooks,[i]
he catches them in his net,[j]
he gathers them up in his dragnet;

1:8 [a]Jer 4:13
1:9 [b]Hab 2:5
1:10 [c]2Ch 36:6
1:11 [d]Jer 4:11-12 [e]Da 4:30
1:12 [f]Isa 31:1 [g]Isa 10:6
1:13 [h]La 3:34-36
1:15 [i]Isa 19:8 [j]Jer 16:16
1:16 [k]Jer 44:8
1:17 [l]Isa 14:6; 19:8
2:1 [m]Isa 21:8 [n]Ps 48:13 [o]Ps 85:8 [p]Ps 5:3
2:2 [q]Rev 1:19
2:3 [r]Da 8:17; 10:14 [s]Ps 27:14 [t]Eze 12:25; Heb 10:37-38
2:4 [u]Ro 1:17*; Gal 3:11*; Heb 10:37-38*
2:5 [v]Pr 20:1 [w]Pr 27:20; 30:15-16
2:6 [x]Isa 14:4

and so he rejoices and is glad.
16 Therefore he sacrifices to his net
and burns incense[k] to his dragnet,
for by his net he lives in luxury
and enjoys the choicest food.
17 Is he to keep on emptying his net,
destroying nations without mercy?[l]

2 I will stand at my watch[m]
and station myself on the ramparts;[n]
I will look to see what he will say[o] to me,
and what answer I am to give to this complaint.[c][p]

The LORD's Answer

2 Then the LORD replied:

"Write[q] down the revelation
and make it plain on tablets
so that a herald[d] may run with it.
3 For the revelation awaits an appointed time;
it speaks of the end[r]
and will not prove false.
Though it linger, wait[s] for it;
it[e] will certainly come and will not delay.[t]

4 "See, he is puffed up;
his desires are not upright—
but the righteous will live by his faith[f][u]—
5 indeed, wine[v] betrays him;
he is arrogant and never at rest.
Because he is as greedy as the grave[g]
and like death is never satisfied,[w]
he gathers to himself all the nations
and takes captive all the peoples.

6 "Will not all of them taunt[x]

[b]9 The meaning of the Hebrew for this word is uncertain. [c]1 Or *and what to answer when I am rebuked* [d]2 Or *so that whoever reads it* [e]3 Or *Though he linger, wait for him; / he* [f]4 Or *faithfulness* [g]5 Hebrew *Sheol*

him with ridicule and scorn, saying,

" 'Woe to him who piles up
stolen goods
and makes himself wealthy
by extortion![a]
How long must this go on?'
7Will not your debtors[h]
suddenly arise?
Will they not wake up and
make you tremble?
Then you will become their
victim.[b]
8Because you have plundered
many nations,
the peoples who are left will
plunder you.[c]
For you have shed man's
blood;[d]
you have destroyed lands and
cities and everyone in
them.

9"Woe to him who builds[e] his
realm by unjust gain
to set his nest on high,
to escape the clutches of
ruin!
10You have plotted the ruin[f] of
many peoples,
shaming[g] your own house
and forfeiting your life.
11The stones[h] of the wall will cry
out,
and the beams of the
woodwork will echo it.

12"Woe to him who builds a city
with bloodshed[i]
and establishes a town by
crime!
13Has not the LORD Almighty
determined
that the people's labor is
only fuel for the fire,[j]
that the nations exhaust
themselves for
nothing?[k]
14For the earth will be filled with
the knowledge of the
glory[l] of the LORD,
as the waters cover the sea.[m]

15"Woe to him who gives drink to
his neighbors,
pouring it from the wineskin
till they are drunk,
so that he can gaze on their
naked bodies.
16You will be filled with shame[n]
instead of glory.
Now it is your turn! Drink
and be exposed![i][o]
The cup[p] from the LORD's right
hand is coming around
to you,
and disgrace will cover your
glory.
17The violence[q] you have done
to Lebanon will
overwhelm you,
and your destruction of
animals will terrify you.[r]
For you have shed man's
blood;[s]
you have destroyed lands and
cities and everyone in
them.

18"Of what value is an idol,[t]
since a man has carved
it?
Or an image that teaches
lies?
For he who makes it trusts in
his own creation;
he makes idols that cannot
speak.[u]
19Woe to him who says to wood,
'Come to life!'
Or to lifeless stone, 'Wake
up!'[v]
Can it give guidance?
It is covered with gold and
silver;[w]
there is no breath in it.
20But the LORD is in his holy
temple;[x]
let all the earth be silent[y]
before him."

Habakkuk's Prayer

3 A prayer of Habakkuk the prophet. On *shigionoth*.[j]

2LORD, I have heard[z] of your
fame;
I stand in awe[a] of your
deeds, O LORD.
Renew[b] them in our day,

2:6 [a]Am 2:8
2:7 [b]Pr 29:1
2:8 [c]Isa 33:1; Zec 2:8-9 [d]ver 17
2:9 [e]Jer 22:13
2:10 [f]Jer 26:19 [g]ver 16
2:11 [h]Jos 24:27; Lk 19:40
2:12 [i]Mic 3:10
2:13 [j]Isa 50:11 [k]Isa 47:13
2:14 [l]Nu 14:21 [m]Isa 11:9
2:16 [n]ver 10 [o]La 4:21 [p]Isa 51:22
2:17 [q]Jer 51:35 [r]Jer 50:15 [s]ver 8
2:18 [t]Jer 5:21 [u]Ps 115:4-5; Jer 10:14
2:19 [v]1Ki 18:27 [w]Jer 10:4
2:20 [x]Ps 11:4 [y]Isa 41:1
3:2 [z]Ps 44:1 [a]Ps 119:120 [b]Ps 85:6

[h]7 Or *creditors* [i]16 Masoretic Text; Dead Sea Scrolls, Aquila, Vulgate and Syriac (see also Septuagint) *and stagger* [j]1 Probably a literary or musical term

in our time make them
known;
in wrath remember mercy.[a]

[3]God came from Teman,
the Holy One from Mount
Paran. *Selah*[k]
His glory covered the heavens
and his praise filled the
earth.[b]
[4]His splendor was like the
sunrise;
rays flashed from his hand,
where his power was hidden.
[5]Plague went before him;
pestilence followed his steps.
[6]He stood, and shook the earth;
he looked, and made the
nations tremble.
The ancient mountains
crumbled
and the age-old hills
collapsed.[c]
His ways are eternal.
[7]I saw the tents of Cushan in
distress,
the dwellings of Midian[d] in
anguish.[e]

[8]Were you angry with the
rivers,[f] O LORD?
Was your wrath against the
streams?
Did you rage against the sea
when you rode with your
horses
and your victorious
chariots?[g]
[9]You uncovered your bow,
you called for many arrows.[h]
Selah
You split the earth with rivers;
10 the mountains saw you and
writhed.
Torrents of water swept by;
the deep roared[i]
and lifted its waves[j] on
high.
[11]Sun and moon stood still[k] in
the heavens
at the glint of your flying
arrows,[l]
at the lightning of your
flashing spear.
[12]In wrath you strode through the
earth
and in anger you threshed[m]
the nations.
[13]You came out to deliver[n] your
people,
to save your anointed one.
You crushed[o] the leader of the
land of wickedness,
you stripped him from head
to foot. *Selah*
[14]With his own spear you pierced
his head
when his warriors stormed
out to scatter us,[p]
gloating as though about to
devour
the wretched[q] who were in
hiding.
[15]You trampled the sea with your
horses,
churning the great waters.[r]
[16]I heard and my heart pounded,
my lips quivered at the
sound;
decay crept into my bones,
and my legs trembled.
Yet I will wait patiently for the
day of calamity
to come on the nation
invading us.
[17]Though the fig tree does not
bud
and there are no grapes on
the vines,
though the olive crop fails
and the fields produce no
food,[s]
though there are no sheep in
the pen
and no cattle in the stalls,[t]
[18]yet I will rejoice in the LORD,[u]
I will be joyful in God my
Savior.

[19]The Sovereign LORD is my
strength;[v]
he makes my feet like the
feet of a deer,
he enables me to go on the
heights.[w]

For the director of music. On
my stringed instruments.

3:2 [a]Isa 54:8
3:3 [b]Ps 48:10
3:6 [c]Ps 114:1-6
3:7 [d]Jdg 7:24-25 [e]Ex 15:14
3:8 [f]Ex 7:20 [g]Ps 68:17
3:9 [h]Ps 7:12-13
3:10 [i]Ps 98:7 [j]Ps 93:3
3:11 [k]Jos 10:13 [l]Ps 18:14
3:12 [m]Isa 41:15
3:13 [n]Ps 20:6; 28:8 [o]Ps 68:21; 110:6
3:14 [p]Jdg 7:22 [q]Ps 64:2-5
3:15 [r]Ex 15:8; Ps 77:19
3:17 [s]Joel 1:10-12, 18 [t]Jer 5:17
3:18 [u]Isa 61:10; Php 4:4
3:19 [v]Dt 33:29; Ps 46:1-5 [w]Dt 32:13; 2Sa 22:34; Ps 18:33

k3 A word of uncertain meaning; possibly a musical term; also in verses 9 and 13

Zephaniah

Title and Background

The name Zephaniah means "The LORD hides (or protects)."

The religious state of Judah declined markedly following the death of Hezekiah, but Josiah launched a sweeping reform. He was backed by Jeremiah and Nahum, but their calls for repentance fell on deaf ears. Judah became ripe for judgment.

Author and Date of Writing

The prophet was evidently a person of considerable social standing in Judah. He was a fourth-generation descendant of King Hezekiah. Zephaniah shows great familiarity with court circles and current political issues. According to 1:1, Zephaniah prophesied during the reign of King Josiah (640-609 B.C.), so this prophecy could have been written about 630 B.C.

Theme and Message

The intent of the author was to announce to Judah God's approaching judgment. His main theme was the coming of the day of the Lord, when God would severely punish the nations. He portrays the stark horror of that ordeal, but also makes it clear that God will yet be merciful toward his people.

Outline

I. Introduction (1:1-3)
II. The Day of the Lord Coming on Judah and the Nations (1:4-18)
III. God's Judgment on the Nations (2:1-3:8)
IV. Redemption of the Remnant (3:9-20)

---

1 The word of the LORD that came to Zephaniah son of Cushi, the son of Gedaliah, the son of Amariah, the son of Hezekiah, during the reign of Josiah[a] son of Amon king of Judah:

Warning of Coming Destruction

2"I will sweep away everything
from the face of the earth,"[b]
declares the LORD.
3"I will sweep away both men
and animals;
I will sweep away the birds of
the air[c]
and the fish of the sea.
The wicked will have only
heaps of rubble[a]
when I cut off man from the
face of the earth,"[d]
declares the LORD.

1:1 [a] 2Ki 22:1; 2Ch 34:1-35:25
1:2 [b] Ge 6:7
1:3 [c] Jer 4:25 [d] Hos 4:3
1:4 [e] Jer 6:12 [f] Mic 5:13 [g] Hos 10:5
1:5 [h] Jer 5:7
1:6 [i] Isa 1:4; Jer 2:13

Against Judah

4"I will stretch out my hand[e]
against Judah
and against all who live in
Jerusalem.
I will cut off from this place
every remnant of Baal,[f]
the names of the pagan and
the idolatrous priests[g]—
5those who bow down on the
roofs
to worship the starry host,
those who bow down and swear
by the LORD
and who also swear by
Molech,[b][h]
6those who turn back from
following[i] the LORD

[a]3 The meaning of the Hebrew for this line is uncertain. [b]5 Hebrew *Malcam,* that is, Milcom

and neither seek[a] the LORD
nor inquire[b] of him.
7Be silent[c] before the Sovereign LORD,
for the day of the LORD[d] is near.
The LORD has prepared a sacrifice;[e]
he has consecrated those he has invited.
8On the day of the LORD's sacrifice
I will punish[f] the princes
and the king's sons[g]
and all those clad
in foreign clothes.
9On that day I will punish
all who avoid stepping on the threshold,[c]
who fill the temple of their gods
with violence and deceit.[h]

10"On that day," declares the LORD,
"a cry will go up from the Fish Gate,[i]
wailing from the New Quarter,
and a loud crash from the hills.
11Wail,[j] you who live in the market district[d];
all your merchants will be wiped out,
all who trade with[e] silver
will be ruined.[k]
12At that time I will search Jerusalem with lamps
and punish those who are complacent,[l]
who are like wine left on its dregs,[m]
who think, 'The LORD will do nothing,[n]
either good or bad.'
13Their wealth will be plundered,[o]
their houses demolished.
They will build houses
but not live in them;
they will plant vineyards
but not drink the wine.[p]

The Great Day of the LORD

14"The great day of the LORD[q] is near[r]—

1:6 [a]Isa 9:13 [b]Hos 7:7
1:7 [c]Hab 2:20; Zec 2:13 [d]ver 14; Isa 13:6 [e]Isa 34:6; Jer 46:10
1:8 [f]Isa 24:21 [g]Jer 39:6
1:9 [h]Am 3:10
1:10 [i]2Ch 33:14
1:11 [j]Jas 5:1 [k]Hos 9:6
1:12 [l]Am 6:1 [m]Jer 48:11 [n]Eze 8:12
1:13 [o]Jer 15:13 [p]Dt 28:30,39; Am 5:11; Mic 6:15
1:14 [q]ver 7; Joel 1:15 [r]Eze 7:7
1:15 [s]Isa 22:5; Joel 2:2
1:16 [t]Jer 4:19 [u]Isa 2:15
1:17 [v]Isa 59:10 [w]Ps 79:3 [x]Jer 9:22
1:18 [y]Eze 7:19 [z]ver 2-3; Zep 3:8 [a]Ge 6:7
2:1 [b]2Ch 20:4; Joel 1:14 [c]Jer 3:3; 6:15
2:2 [d]Isa 17:13; Hos 13:3 [e]La 4:11
2:3 [f]Am 5:6 [g]Ps 45:4; Am 5:14-15

near and coming quickly.
Listen! The cry on the day of the LORD will be bitter,
the shouting of the warrior there.
15That day will be a day of wrath,
a day of distress and anguish,
a day of trouble and ruin,
a day of darkness and gloom,
a day of clouds and blackness,[s]
16a day of trumpet and battle cry[t]
against the fortified cities
and against the corner towers.[u]
17I will bring distress on the people
and they will walk like blind[v] men,
because they have sinned against the LORD.
Their blood will be poured out[w] like dust
and their entrails like filth.[x]
18Neither their silver nor their gold
will be able to save them
on the day of the LORD's wrath.[y]
In the fire of his jealousy
the whole world will be consumed,[z]
for he will make a sudden end
of all who live in the earth.[a]"

2 Gather together,[b] gather together,
O shameful[c] nation,
2before the appointed time arrives
and that day sweeps on like chaff,[d]
before the fierce anger[e] of the LORD comes upon you,
before the day of the LORD's wrath comes upon you.
3Seek[f] the LORD, all you humble of the land,
you who do what he commands.
Seek righteousness, seek humility;[g]

[c]9 See 1 Samuel 5:5. [d]11 Or *the Mortar* [e]11 Or *in*

perhaps you will be
sheltered[a]
on the day of the LORD's
anger.

Against Philistia

4Gaza[b] will be abandoned
and Ashkelon left in ruins.
At midday Ashdod will be
emptied
and Ekron uprooted.
5Woe to you who live by the sea,
O Kerethite[c] people;
the word of the LORD is against
you,[d]
O Canaan, land of the
Philistines.
"I will destroy you,
and none will be left."[e]

6The land by the sea, where the
Kerethites[f] dwell,
will be a place for shepherds
and sheep pens.[f]
7It will belong to the remnant of
the house of Judah;
there they will find pasture.
In the evening they will lie
down
in the houses of Ashkelon.
The LORD their God will care for
them;
he will restore their
fortunes.[g][g]

Against Moab and Ammon

8"I have heard the insults[h] of
Moab
and the taunts of the
Ammonites,
who insulted[i] my people
and made threats against
their land.
9Therefore, as surely as I live,"
declares the LORD Almighty,
the God of Israel,
"surely Moab[j] will become like
Sodom,[k]
the Ammonites[l] like
Gomorrah—
a place of weeds and salt pits,
a wasteland forever.
The remnant of my people will
plunder[m] them;
the survivors of my nation
will inherit their land."[n]

2:3 [a]Ps 57:1
2:4 [b]Am 1:6,7-8; Zec 9:5-7
2:5 [c]Eze 25:16 [d]Am 3:1 [e]Isa 14:30
2:6 [f]Isa 5:17
2:7 [g]Ps 126:4; Jer 32:44
2:8 [h]Jer 48:27 [i]Eze 25:3
2:9 [j]Isa 15:1-16:14; Jer 48:1-47 [k]Dt 29:23 [l]Jer 49:1-6; Eze 25:1-7 [m]Isa 11:14 [n]Am 2:1-3
2:10 [o]Isa 16:6 [p]Jer 48:27
2:11 [q]Joel 2:11 [r]Zep 1:4 [s]Zep 3:9
2:12 [t]Isa 18:1; 20:4 [u]Jer 46:10
2:13 [v]Na 1:1 [w]Mic 5:6
2:14 [x]Isa 14:23
2:15 [y]Isa 32:9 [z]Isa 47:8 [a]Eze 28:2 [b]Na 3:19
3:1 [c]Jer 6:6 [d]Eze 23:30
3:2 [e]Jer 22:21 [f]Jer 7:28

10This is what they will get in
return for their pride,[o]
for insulting[p] and mocking
the people of the LORD
Almighty.
11The LORD will be awesome[q] to
them
when he destroys all the
gods[r] of the land.
The nations on every shore will
worship him,[s]
every one in its own land.

Against Cush

12"You too, O Cushites,[h][t]
will be slain by my sword."[u]

Against Assyria

13He will stretch out his hand
against the north
and destroy Assyria,
leaving Nineveh[v] utterly
desolate
and dry as the desert.[w]
14Flocks and herds will lie down
there,
creatures of every kind.
The desert owl[x] and the
screech owl
will roost on her columns.
Their calls will echo through
the windows,
rubble will be in the
doorways,
the beams of cedar will be
exposed.
15This is the carefree[y] city
that lived in safety.[z]
She said to herself,
"I am, and there is none
besides me."[a]
What a ruin she has become,
a lair for wild beasts!
All who pass by her scoff[b]
and shake their fists.

The Future of Jerusalem

3 Woe to the city of
oppressors,[c]
rebellious and defiled![d]
2She obeys[e] no one,
she accepts no correction.[f]

[f]6 The meaning of the Hebrew for this word is uncertain. [g]7 Or *will bring back their captives* [h]12 That is, people from the upper Nile region

She does not trust in the LORD,
she does not draw near[a] to her God.
3 Her officials are roaring lions,
her rulers are evening wolves,[b]
who leave nothing for the morning.
4 Her prophets are arrogant;
they are treacherous[c] men.
Her priests profane the sanctuary
and do violence to the law.[d]
5 The LORD within her is righteous;
he does no wrong.[e]
Morning by morning he dispenses his justice,
and every new day he does not fail,
yet the unrighteous know no shame.

6 "I have cut off nations;
their strongholds are demolished.
I have left their streets deserted,
with no one passing through.
Their cities are destroyed;[f]
no one will be left—no one at all.
7 I said to the city,
'Surely you will fear me
and accept correction!'
Then her dwelling would not be cut off,
nor all my punishments come upon her.
But they were still eager
to act corruptly[g] in all they did.
8 Therefore wait[h] for me,"
declares the LORD,
"for the day I will stand up to testify.[i]
I have decided to assemble the nations,[i]
to gather the kingdoms
and to pour out my wrath on them
all my fierce anger.
The whole world will be consumed[j]
by the fire of my jealous anger.

3:2 [a] Ps 73:28; Jer 5:3
3:3 [b] Eze 22:27
3:4 [c] Jer 9:4 [d] Eze 22:26
3:5 [e] Dt 32:4
3:6 [f] Lev 26:31
3:7 [g] Hos 9:9
3:8 [h] Ps 27:14 [i] Joel 3:2 [j] Zep 1:18
3:9 [k] Zep 2:11 [l] Isa 19:18
3:10 [m] Ps 68:31 [n] Isa 60:7
3:11 [o] Joel 2:26-27
3:12 [p] Isa 14:32 [q] Na 1:7
3:13 [r] Isa 10:21; Mic 4:7 [s] Ps 119:3 [t] Rev 14:5 [u] Eze 34:15; Zep 2:7 [v] Eze 34:25-28
3:14 [w] Zec 2:10 [x] Isa 12:6
3:15 [y] Eze 37:26-28 [z] Isa 54:14
3:16 [a] Job 4:3; Isa 35:3-4; Heb 12:12

9 "Then will I purify the lips of the peoples,
that all of them may call[k] on the name of the LORD
and serve[l] him shoulder to shoulder.
10 From beyond the rivers of Cush[i][m]
my worshipers, my scattered people,
will bring me offerings.[n]
11 On that day you will not be put to shame[o]
for all the wrongs you have done to me,
because I will remove from this city
those who rejoice in their pride.
Never again will you be haughty
on my holy hill.
12 But I will leave within you
the meek[p] and humble,
who trust[q] in the name of the LORD.
13 The remnant[r] of Israel will do no wrong;[s]
they will speak no lies,[t]
nor will deceit be found in their mouths.
They will eat and lie down[u]
and no one will make them afraid.[v]"

14 Sing, O Daughter of Zion;[w]
shout aloud,[x] O Israel!
Be glad and rejoice with all your heart,
O Daughter of Jerusalem!
15 The LORD has taken away your punishment,
he has turned back your enemy.
The LORD, the King of Israel, is with you;[y]
never again will you fear[z] any harm.
16 On that day they will say to Jerusalem,
"Do not fear, O Zion;
do not let your hands hang limp.[a]
17 The LORD your God is with you,

[i] 8 Septuagint and Syriac; Hebrew *will rise up to plunder* [i] 10 That is, the upper Nile region

he is mighty to save.[a]
He will take great delight[b] in
you,
he will quiet you with his
love,
he will rejoice over you with
singing."

18"The sorrows for the appointed
feasts
I will remove from you;
they are a burden and a
reproach to you.[k]
19At that time I will deal
with all who oppressed you;
I will rescue the lame
and gather those who have
been scattered.[c]
I will give them praise[d] and
honor
in every land where they
were put to shame.
20At that time I will gather you;
at that time I will bring[e] you
home.
I will give you honor[f] and
praise
among all the peoples of the
earth
when I restore your fortunes[l][g]
before your very eyes,"
says the LORD.

3:17 [a] Isa 63:1 [b] Isa 62:4
3:19 [c] Eze 34:16; Mic 4:6 [d] Isa 60:18
3:20 [e] Jer 29:14; Eze 37:12 [f] Isa 56:5; 66:22 [g] Joel 3:1

[k] *18* Or *"I will gather you who mourn for the appointed feasts; / your reproach is a burden to you* [l] *20* Or *I bring back your captives*

Haggai

Title and Background

The book is named for its author, and the name means "festal" or "festival."

In 538 B.C. Cyrus issued a decree allowing the Jews to return to Jerusalem and rebuild the temple. The Samaritans and other neighbors opposed the project vigorously and managed to halt work until Darius the Great became king. Haggai began to preach in Darius's second year.

Author and Date of Writing

Haggai was a prophet who, along with Zechariah, encouraged the returned exiles to rebuild the temple. Based on 2:3, Haggai may have witnessed the destruction of Solomon's temple. If so, he was about 80 years old during his ministry recorded in this book. The messages of Haggai were given during a four-month period in 520 B.C.

Theme and Message

Haggai clearly shows the consequences of disobedience and the blessings of obedience. When the people give priority to God and his house, they are blessed. Obedience brings the encouragement and strength of the Spirit of God.

Outline

I. First Message: The Call to Rebuild the Temple (1:1-11)
II. The Response of Zerubbabel and the People (1:12-15)
III. Second Message: The Temple to Be Filled With Glory (2:1-9)
IV. Third Message: A Defiled People Purified and Blessed (2:10-19)
V. Fourth Message: The Promise to Zerubbabel (2:20-23)

A Call to Build the House of the Lord

1 In the second year of King Darius,[a] on the first day of the
sixth month, the word of the LORD
came through the prophet Haggai[b]
to Zerubbabel[c] son of Shealtiel,
governor[d] of Judah, and to Joshua[a][e] son of Jehozadak,[f] the high
priest:
2This is what the LORD Almighty
says: "These people say, 'The time
has not yet come for the LORD's
house to be built.' "
3Then the word of the LORD came
through the prophet Haggai:[g] 4"Is
it a time for you yourselves to be
living in your paneled houses,[h]
while this house remains a ruin?[i]"
5Now this is what the LORD
Almighty says: "Give careful
thought[j] to your ways. 6You have
planted much, but have harvested
little.[k] You eat, but never have
enough. You drink, but never have
your fill. You put on clothes, but
are not warm. You earn wages,[l]
only to put them in a purse with
holes in it."
7This is what the LORD Almighty
says: "Give careful thought to your
ways. 8Go up into the mountains
and bring down timber and build
the house, so that I may take pleasure[m] in it and be honored," says
the LORD. 9"You expected much,
but see, it turned out to be little.
What you brought home, I blew
away. Why?" declares the LORD Al-

1:1 [a]Ezr 4:24 [b]Ezr 5:1 [c]Mt 1:12-13 [d]Ezr 5:3 [e]Ezr 2:2 [f]1Ch 6:15; Ezr 3:2
1:3 [g]Ezr 5:1
1:4 [h]2Sa 7:2 [i]ver 9; Jer 33:12
1:5 [j]La 3:40
1:6 [k]Dt 28:38 [l]Hag 2:16; Zec 8:10
1:8 [m]Ps 132:13-14

[a]*1* A variant of *Jeshua;* here and elsewhere in Haggai

mighty. "Because of my house,
which remains a ruin,[a] while each
of you is busy with his own house.
10Therefore, because of you the
heavens have withheld their dew
and the earth its crops.[b] **11**I called
for a drought[c] on the fields and the
mountains, on the grain, the new
wine, the oil and whatever the
ground produces, on men and cattle, and on the labor of your
hands.[d]"

12Then Zerubbabel[e] son of Shealtiel, Joshua son of Jehozadak,
the high priest, and the whole remnant[f] of the people obeyed[g] the
voice of the LORD their God and the
message of the prophet Haggai, because the LORD their God had sent
him. And the people feared[h] the
LORD.

13Then Haggai, the LORD's messenger, gave this message of the
LORD to the people: "I am with[i]
you," declares the LORD. **14**So the
LORD stirred up the spirit of Zerubbabel[j] son of Shealtiel, governor
of Judah, and the spirit of Joshua
son of Jehozadak, the high priest,
and the spirit of the whole remnant[k] of the people. They came
and began to work on the house of
the LORD Almighty, their God, **15**on
the twenty-fourth day of the sixth
month[l] in the second year of King
Darius.

The Promised Glory of the New House

2 On the twenty-first day of the
seventh month, the word of the
LORD came through the prophet
Haggai: **2**"Speak to Zerubbabel son
of Shealtiel, governor of Judah, to
Joshua son of Jehozadak, the high
priest, and to the remnant of the
people. Ask them, **3**'Who of you is
left who saw this house[m] in its former glory? How does it look to you
now? Does it not seem to you like
nothing?[n] **4**But now be strong, O
Zerubbabel,' declares the LORD. 'Be
strong,[o] O Joshua son of Jehozadak, the high priest. Be strong, all
you people of the land,' declares
the LORD, 'and work. For I am
with[p] you,' declares the LORD Almighty. **5**'This is what I covenanted
with you when you came out of
Egypt.[q] And my Spirit[r] remains
among you. Do not fear.'

6"This is what the LORD Almighty
says: 'In a little while[s] I will once
more shake the heavens and the
earth,[t] the sea and the dry land. **7**I
will shake all nations, and the desired of all nations will come, and
I will fill this house[u] with glory,'
says the LORD Almighty. **8**'The silver is mine and the gold is mine,'
declares the LORD Almighty. **9**'The
glory[v] of this present house will be
greater than the glory of the former
house,' says the LORD Almighty.
'And in this place I will grant
peace,' declares the LORD Almighty."

Blessings for a Defiled People

10On the twenty-fourth day of
the ninth month,[w] in the second
year of Darius, the word of the LORD
came to the prophet Haggai:
11"This is what the LORD Almighty
says: 'Ask the priests[x] what the
law says: **12**If a person carries consecrated meat in the fold of his garment, and that fold touches some
bread or stew, some wine, oil or
other food, does it become consecrated?[y]' "

The priests answered, "No."

13Then Haggai said, "If a person
defiled by contact with a dead body
touches one of these things, does it
become defiled?"

"Yes," the priests replied, "it becomes defiled.[z]"

14Then Haggai said, " 'So it is
with this people and this nation in
my sight,' declares the LORD.
'Whatever they do and whatever
they offer[a] there is defiled.

15" 'Now give careful thought[b]
to this from this day on[b]—consider how things were before one
stone was laid[c] on another in the

1:9 [a] ver 4
1:10 [b] Lev 26:19; Dt 28:23
1:11 [c] Dt 28:22; 1Ki 17:1 [d] Hag 2:17
1:12 [e] ver 1 [f] ver 14; Isa 1:9; Hag 2:2 [g] Isa 50:10 [h] Dt 31:12
1:13 [i] Mt 28:20; Ro 8:31
1:14 [j] Ezr 5:2 [k] ver 12
1:15 [l] ver 1
2:3 [m] Ezr 3:12 [n] Zec 4:10
2:4 [o] 1Ch 28:20; Zec 8:9; Eph 6:10 [p] 2Sa 5:10; Ac 7:9
2:5 [q] Ex 29:46 [r] Ne 9:20; Isa 63:11
2:6 [s] Isa 10:25 [t] Heb 12:26*
2:7 [u] Isa 60:7
2:9 [v] Ps 85:9
2:10 [w] ver 1
2:11 [x] Lev 10:10-11; Dt 17:8-11; Mal 2:7
2:12 [y] Lev 6:27; Mt 23:19
2:13 [z] Lev 22:4-6
2:14 [a] Isa 1:13
2:15 [b] Hag 1:5 [c] Ezr 3:10

[b]15 *Or to the days past*

LORD's temple. 16When anyone
came to a heap of twenty measures, there were only ten. When
anyone went to a wine vat to draw
fifty measures, there were only
twenty.[a] 17I struck all the work of
your hands[b] with blight,[c] mildew
and hail, yet you did not turn to
me,' declares the LORD.[d] 18'From
this day on, from this twenty-
fourth day of the ninth month, give
careful thought to the day when
the foundation[e] of the LORD's temple was laid. Give careful thought:
19Is there yet any seed left in the
barn? Until now, the vine and the
fig tree, the pomegranate and the
olive tree have not borne fruit.

" 'From this day on I will bless
you.' "

2:16 [a] Hag 1:6
2:17 [b] Hag 1:11 [c] Dt 28:22; 1Ki 8:37; Am 4:9 [d] Am 4:6
2:18 [e] Zec 8:9
2:21 [f] Ezr 5:2
2:22 [g] Da 2:44 [h] Mic 5:10 [i] Jdg 7:22
2:23 [j] Isa 43:10

Zerubbabel the LORD's Signet Ring

20The word of the LORD came to
Haggai a second time on the twenty-fourth day of the month: 21"Tell
Zerubbabel[f] governor of Judah
that I will shake the heavens and
the earth. 22I will overturn royal
thrones and shatter the power of
the foreign kingdoms.[g] I will overthrow chariots[h] and their drivers;
horses and their riders will fall,
each by the sword of his brother.[i]

23" 'On that day,' declares the
LORD Almighty, 'I will take you, my
servant[j] Zerubbabel son of Shealtiel,' declares the LORD, 'and I will
make you like my signet ring, for I
have chosen you,' declares the
LORD Almighty."

Zechariah

Title and Background

The book is named after its author, and the title means "The LORD remembers." Zechariah's prophetic ministry took place in the postexilic period, the time of the Jewish restoration from Babylonian captivity. His prophecies began two months after Haggai's first message.

Author and Date of Writing

Zechariah was not only a prophet but also a priest. He was among those who returned to Judah in 538 B.C. He was a contemporary of Haggai but continued his ministry long after him. The book of Zechariah was probably written sometime before 480 B.C.

Theme and Message

Zechariah was concerned about the rebuilding of the temple, and in his first message he warned the people they were to listen to God's message through the prophets. He was also interested in their spiritual renewal. Zechariah also contains many Messianic passages: he predicted Christ's coming in lowliness (6:12), his humanity (6:12; 13:7), his rejection and betrayal for thirty pieces of silver (11:12-13), his being struck by the sword of the Lord (13:7), his priesthood (6:13), his kingship (6:13; 9:9; 14:9,16), his coming in glory (14:4), his building of the Lord's temple (6:12-13), his reign (9:10,14) and his establishment of enduring peace and prosperity (3:10; 9:9-10).

Outline

I. A Call to Repentance (1:1-6)
II. Eight Visions (1:7-6:8)
III. The Crowning of Joshua the High Priest (6:9-15)
IV. Fasting and the Future (7:1-8:23)
V. The Advent and Rejection of the Messiah (9:1-11:17)
VI. The Advent and Redemption of the Messiah (12:1-14:21)

A Call to Return to the LORD

1 In the eighth month of the second year of Darius,[a] the word
of the LORD came to the prophet
Zechariah[b] son of Berekiah,[c] the
son of Iddo:[d]
2"The LORD was very angry[e] with
your forefathers. **3**Therefore tell
the people: This is what the LORD
Almighty says: 'Return to me,' declares the LORD Almighty, 'and I
will return to you,'[f] says the LORD
Almighty. **4**Do not be like your
forefathers,[g] to whom the earlier
prophets proclaimed: This is what
the LORD Almighty says: 'Turn from
your evil ways[h] and your evil practices.' But they would not listen or
pay attention to me,[i] declares the
LORD. **5**Where are your forefathers
now? And the prophets, do they
live forever? **6**But did not my words
and my decrees, which I commanded my servants the prophets, overtake your forefathers?
"Then they repented and said,
'The LORD Almighty has done to us
what our ways and practices deserve,[j] just as he determined to
do.'"

1:1 [a]Ezr 4:24; 6:15 [b]Ezr 5:1 [c]Mt 23:35; Lk 11:51 [d]ver 7; Ne 12:4
1:2 [e]2Ch 36:16
1:3 [f]Mal 3:7
1:4 [g]2Ch 36:15 [h]Ps 106:6 [i]2Ch 24:19; Ps 78:8
1:6 [j]Jer 12:14-17; La 2:17

The Man Among the Myrtle Trees

7On the twenty-fourth day of the eleventh month, the month of Shebat, in the second year of Darius, the word of the LORD came to the prophet Zechariah son of Berekiah, the son of Iddo.

8During the night I had a vision—and there before me was a man riding a red[a] horse! He was standing among the myrtle trees in a ravine. Behind him were red, brown and white horses.[b]

9I asked, "What are these, my lord?"

The angel[c] who was talking with me answered, "I will show you what they are."

10Then the man standing among the myrtle trees explained, "They are the ones the LORD has sent to go throughout the earth."[d]

11And they reported to the angel of the LORD, who was standing among the myrtle trees, "We have gone throughout the earth and found the whole world at rest and in peace."[e]

12Then the angel of the LORD said, "LORD Almighty, how long will you withhold mercy from Jerusalem and from the towns of Judah, which you have been angry with these seventy[f] years?" 13So the LORD spoke kind and comforting words to the angel who talked with me.[g]

14Then the angel who was speaking to me said, "Proclaim this word: This is what the LORD Almighty says: 'I am very jealous[h] for Jerusalem and Zion, 15but I am very angry with the nations that feel secure.[i] I was only a little angry, but they added to the calamity.'[j]

16"Therefore, this is what the LORD says: 'I will return[k] to Jerusalem with mercy, and there my house will be rebuilt. And the measuring line[l] will be stretched out over Jerusalem,' declares the LORD Almighty.

17"Proclaim further: This is what the LORD Almighty says: 'My towns will again overflow with prosperity, and the LORD will again comfort[m] Zion and choose[n] Jerusalem.' "[o]

Four Horns and Four Craftsmen

18Then I looked up—and there before me were four horns! 19I asked the angel who was speaking to me, "What are these?"

He answered me, "These are the horns[p] that scattered Judah, Israel and Jerusalem."

20Then the LORD showed me four craftsmen. 21I asked, "What are these coming to do?"

He answered, "These are the horns that scattered Judah so that no one could raise his head, but the craftsmen have come to terrify them and throw down these horns of the nations who lifted up their horns[q] against the land of Judah to scatter its people."[r]

A Man With a Measuring Line

2 Then I looked up—and there before me was a man with a measuring line in his hand! 2I asked, "Where are you going?"

He answered me, "To measure Jerusalem, to find out how wide and how long it is."[s]

3Then the angel who was speaking to me left, and another angel came to meet him 4and said to him: "Run, tell that young man, 'Jerusalem will be a city without walls[t] because of the great number[u] of men and livestock in it. 5And I myself will be a wall[v] of fire around it,' declares the LORD, 'and I will be its glory[w] within.'

6"Come! Come! Flee from the land of the north," declares the LORD, "for I have scattered you to the four winds of heaven,"[x] declares the LORD.

7"Come, O Zion! Escape, you who live in the Daughter of Babylon!"[y] 8For this is what the LORD Almighty says: "After he has honored me and has sent me against the nations that have plundered you—for whoever touches you touches the apple of his eye[z]— 9I

1:8 [a] Rev 6:4 [b] Zec 6:2-7
1:9 [c] Zec 4:1,4-5
1:10 [d] Zec 6:5-8
1:11 [e] Isa 14:7
1:12 [f] Da 9:2
1:13 [g] Zec 4:1
1:14 [h] Joel 2:18; Zec 8:2
1:15 [i] Jer 48:11 [j] Ps 123:3-4; Am 1:11
1:16 [k] Zec 8:3 [l] Zec 2:1-2
1:17 [m] Isa 51:3 [n] Isa 14:1 [o] Zec 2:12
1:19 [p] Am 6:13
1:21 [q] Ps 75:4 [r] Ps 75:10
2:2 [s] Eze 40:3; Rev 21:15
2:4 [t] Eze 38:11 [u] Isa 49:20; Jer 30:19; 33:22
2:5 [v] Isa 26:1 [w] Rev 21:23
2:6 [x] Eze 17:21
2:7 [y] Isa 48:20
2:8 [z] Dt 32:10

will surely raise my hand against
them so that their slaves will plunder them.[a][a] Then you will know
that the LORD Almighty has sent
me.[b]

10"Shout and be glad, O Daughter of Zion.[c] For I am coming,[d]
and I will live among you,"[e] declares the LORD. 11"Many nations
will be joined with the LORD in that
day and will become my people. I
will live among you and you will
know that the LORD Almighty has
sent me to you. 12The LORD will inherit[f] Judah as his portion in the
holy land and will again choose[g]
Jerusalem. 13Be still[h] before the
LORD, all mankind, because he has
roused himself from his holy dwelling."

Clean Garments for the High Priest

3 Then he showed me Joshua[b][i]
the high priest standing before
the angel of the LORD, and Satan[c][j]
standing at his right side to accuse
him. 2The LORD said to Satan, "The
LORD rebuke you,[k] Satan! The
LORD, who has chosen[l] Jerusalem,
rebuke you! Is not this man a burning stick snatched from the fire?"[m]

3Now Joshua was dressed in
filthy clothes as he stood before
the angel. 4The angel said to those
who were standing before him,
"Take off his filthy clothes."

Then he said to Joshua, "See, I
have taken away your sin,[n] and I
will put rich garments[o] on you."

5Then I said, "Put a clean turban[p] on his head." So they put a
clean turban on his head and
clothed him, while the angel of the
LORD stood by.

6The angel of the LORD gave this
charge to Joshua: 7"This is what
the LORD Almighty says: 'If you will
walk in my ways and keep my requirements, then you will govern
my house[q] and have charge of my
courts, and I will give you a place
among these standing here.

8" 'Listen, O high priest Joshua
and your associates seated before
you, who are men symbolic[r] of
things to come: I am going to bring
my servant, the Branch.[s] 9See, the
stone I have set in front of Joshua!
There are seven eyes[d] on that one
stone,[t] and I will engrave an inscription on it,' says the LORD Almighty, 'and I will remove the sin[u]
of this land in a single day.

10" 'In that day each of you will
invite his neighbor to sit under his
vine and fig tree,[v]' declares the
LORD Almighty."

The Gold Lampstand and the Two Olive Trees

4 Then the angel who talked
with me returned and wak-
ened[w] me, as a man is wakened
from his sleep.[x] 2He asked me,
"What do you see?"[y]

I answered, "I see a solid gold
lampstand[z] with a bowl at the top
and seven lights[a] on it, with seven
channels to the lights. 3Also there
are two olive trees[b] by it, one on
the right of the bowl and the other
on its left."

4I asked the angel who talked
with me, "What are these, my
lord?"

5He answered, "Do you not know
what these are?"

"No, my lord," I replied.[c]

6So he said to me, "This is the
word of the LORD to Zerubbabel:[d]
'Not by might nor by power, but by
my Spirit,'[e] says the LORD Almighty.

7"What[e] are you, O mighty
mountain? Before Zerubbabel you
will become level ground.[f] Then
he will bring out the capstone[g] to
shouts of 'God bless it! God bless
it!' "

8Then the word of the LORD came
to me: 9"The hands of Zerubbabel
have laid the foundation[h] of this
temple; his hands will also complete it.[i] Then you will know that
the LORD Almighty has sent me[j] to
you.

10"Who despises the day of small
things?[k] Men will rejoice when

2:9 [a]Isa 14:2 [b]Zec 4:9
2:10 [c]Zep 3:14 [d]Zec 9:9 [e]Lev 26:12; Zec 8:3
2:12 [f]Dt 32:9; Ps 33:12; Jer 10:16 [g]Zec 1:17
2:13 [h]Hab 2:20
3:1 [i]Hag 1:1; Zec 6:11 [j]Ps 109:6
3:2 [k]Jude 1:9 [l]Isa 14:1 [m]Am 4:11; Jude 1:23
3:4 [n]Eze 36:25; Mic 7:18 [o]Isa 52:1; Rev 19:8
3:5 [p]Ex 29:6
3:7 [q]Dt 17:8-11; Eze 44:15-16
3:8 [r]Eze 12:11 [s]Isa 4:2
3:9 [t]Isa 28:16 [u]Jer 50:20
3:10 [v]1Ki 4:25; Mic 4:4
4:1 [w]Da 8:18 [x]Jer 31:26
4:2 [y]Jer 1:13 [z]Ex 25:31; Rev 1:12 [a]Rev 4:5
4:3 [b]ver 11; Rev 11:4
4:5 [c]Zec 1:9
4:6 [d]Ezr 5:2 [e]Isa 11:2-4; Hos 1:7
4:7 [f]Jer 51:25 [g]Ps 118:22
4:9 [h]Ezr 3:11 [i]Ezr 3:8; 6:15; Zec 6:12 [j]Zec 2:9
4:10 [k]Hag 2:3

[a]*8,9* Or *says after . . . eye: 9"I . . . plunder them."* [b]*1* A variant of *Joshua;* here and elsewhere in Zechariah [c]*1 Satan* means *accuser.* [d]*9* Or *facets* [e]*7* Or *Who*

they see the plumb line in the hand
of Zerubbabel.
"(These seven are the eyes[a] of
the LORD, which range throughout
the earth.)"
11Then I asked the angel, "What
are these two olive trees[b] on the
right and the left of the lampstand?"
12Again I asked him, "What are
these two olive branches beside
the two gold pipes that pour out
golden oil?"
13He replied, "Do you not know
what these are?"
"No, my lord," I said.
14So he said, "These are the two
who are anointed[c] to[f] serve the
Lord of all the earth."

The Flying Scroll

5 I looked again—and there before me was a flying scroll![d]
2He asked me, "What do you
see?"
I answered, "I see a flying scroll,
thirty feet long and fifteen feet
wide.[g]"
3And he said to me, "This is the
curse[e] that is going out over the
whole land; for according to what it
says on one side, every thief[f] will
be banished, and according to what
it says on the other, everyone who
swears falsely[g] will be banished.
4The LORD Almighty declares, 'I will
send it out, and it will enter the
house of the thief and the house of
him who swears falsely by my
name. It will remain in his house
and destroy it, both its timbers and
its stones.[h]' "

The Woman in a Basket

5Then the angel who was speaking to me came forward and said to
me, "Look up and see what this is
that is appearing."
6I asked, "What is it?"
He replied, "It is a measuring
basket.[h]" And he added, "This is
the iniquity[i] of the people
throughout the land."
7Then the cover of lead was
raised, and there in the basket sat
a woman! 8He said, "This is wickedness," and he pushed her back
into the basket and pushed the
lead cover down over its mouth.[i]
9Then I looked up—and there
before me were two women, with
the wind in their wings! They had
wings like those of a stork,[j] and
they lifted up the basket between
heaven and earth.
10"Where are they taking the
basket?" I asked the angel who was
speaking to me.
11He replied, "To the country of
Babylonia[i][k] to build a house[l] for
it. When it is ready, the basket will
be set there in its place."[m]

Four Chariots

6 I looked up again—and there
before me were four chariots[n]
coming out from between two
mountains—mountains of bronze!
2The first chariot had red horses,
the second black,[o] 3the third
white,[p] and the fourth dappled—
all of them powerful. 4I asked the
angel who was speaking to me,
"What are these, my lord?"
5The angel answered me, "These
are the four spirits[k][q] of heaven,
going out from standing in the
presence of the Lord of the whole
world. 6The one with the black
horses is going toward the north
country, the one with the white
horses toward the west,[l] and the
one with the dappled horses toward the south."
7When the powerful horses went
out, they were straining to go
throughout the earth.[r] And he
said, "Go throughout the earth!" So
they went throughout the earth.
8Then he called to me, "Look,
those going toward the north country have given my Spirit[m] rest[s] in
the land of the north."

A Crown for Joshua

9The word of the LORD came to
me: 10"Take silver and gold from
the exiles Heldai, Tobijah and Je-

4:10 [a]Zec 3:9; Rev 5:6
4:11 [b]ver 3; Rev 11:4
4:14 [c]Ex 29:7; 40:15; Da 9:24-26; Zec 3:1-7
5:1 [d]Eze 2:9; Rev 5:1
5:3 [e]Isa 24:6; 43:28; Mal 3:9; 4:6 [f]Ex 20:15; Mal 3:8 [g]Isa 48:1
5:4 [h]Lev 14:34-45; Hab 2:9-11; Mal 3:5
5:8 [i]Mic 6:11
5:9 [j]Lev 11:19
5:11 [k]Ge 10:10 [l]Jer 29:5,28 [m]Da 1:2
6:1 [n]ver 5
6:2 [o]Rev 6:5
6:3 [p]Rev 6:2
6:5 [q]Eze 37:9; Mt 24:31; Rev 7:1
6:7 [r]Zec 1:10
6:8 [s]Eze 5:13; 24:13

[f]14 Or *two who bring oil and* [g]2 Hebrew *twenty cubits long and ten cubits wide* (about 9 meters long and 4.5 meters wide)
[h]6 Hebrew *an ephah*; also in verses 7-11
[i]6 Or *appearance* [i]11 Hebrew *Shinar*
[k]5 Or *winds* [l]6 Or *horses after them*
[m]8 Or *spirit*

daiah, who have arrived from Babylon.[a] Go the same day to the house of Josiah son of Zephaniah. **11**Take the silver and gold and make a crown,[b] and set it on the head of the high priest, Joshua[c] son of Jehozadak.[d] **12**Tell him this is what the LORD Almighty says: 'Here is the man whose name is the Branch,[e] and he will branch out from his place and build the temple of the LORD.[f] **13**It is he who will build the temple of the LORD, and he will be clothed with majesty and will sit and rule on his throne. And he will be a priest[g] on his throne. And there will be harmony between the two.' **14**The crown will be given to Heldai,[n] Tobijah, Jedaiah and Hen[o] son of Zephaniah as a memorial in the temple of the LORD. **15**Those who are far away will come and help to build the temple of the LORD,[h] and you will know that the LORD Almighty has sent me to you.[i] This will happen if you diligently obey[j] the LORD your God."

Justice and Mercy, Not Fasting

7 In the fourth year of King Darius, the word of the LORD came to Zechariah on the fourth day of the ninth month, the month of Kislev.[k] **2**The people of Bethel had sent Sharezer and Regem-Melech, together with their men, to entreat[l] the LORD **3**by asking the priests of the house of the LORD Almighty and the prophets, "Should I mourn[m] and fast in the fifth[n] month, as I have done for so many years?"

4Then the word of the LORD Almighty came to me: **5**"Ask all the people of the land and the priests, 'When you fasted[o] and mourned in the fifth and seventh months for the past seventy years, was it really for me that you fasted? **6**And when you were eating and drinking, were you not just feasting for yourselves? **7**Are these not the words the LORD proclaimed through the earlier prophets[p] when Jerusalem and its surrounding towns were at rest[q] and prosperous, and the Negev and the western foothills[r] were settled?' "

8And the word of the LORD came again to Zechariah: **9**"This is what the LORD Almighty says: 'Administer true justice;[s] show mercy and compassion to one another. **10**Do not oppress the widow or the fatherless, the alien[t] or the poor. In your hearts do not think evil of each other.'[u]

11"But they refused to pay attention; stubbornly they turned their backs and stopped up their ears.[v] **12**They made their hearts as hard as flint[w] and would not listen to the law or to the words that the LORD Almighty had sent by his Spirit through the earlier prophets.[x] So the LORD Almighty was very angry.[y]

13" 'When I called, they did not listen;[z] so when they called, I would not listen,'[a] says the LORD Almighty.[b] **14**'I scattered[c] them with a whirlwind[d] among all the nations, where they were strangers. The land was left so desolate behind them that no one could come or go. This is how they made the pleasant land desolate.[e]' "

The LORD Promises to Bless Jerusalem

8 Again the word of the LORD Almighty came to me. **2**This is what the LORD Almighty says: "I am very jealous for Zion; I am burning with jealousy for her."

3This is what the LORD says: "I will return[f] to Zion and dwell in Jerusalem.[g] Then Jerusalem will be called the City of Truth, and the mountain of the LORD Almighty will be called the Holy Mountain."

4This is what the LORD Almighty says: "Once again men and women of ripe old age will sit in the streets of Jerusalem,[h] each with cane in hand because of his age. **5**The city streets will be filled with boys and girls playing there.[i]"

6This is what the LORD Almighty says: "It may seem marvelous to

6:10 [a]Ezr 7:14-16; Jer 28:6
6:11 [b]Ps 21:3 [c]Zec 3:1 [d]Ezr 3:2
6:12 [e]Isa 4:2; Zec 3:8 [f]Ezr 3:8-10; Zec 4:6-9
6:13 [g]Ps 110:4
6:15 [h]Isa 60:10 [i]Zec 2:9-11 [j]Isa 58:12; Jer 7:23; Zec 3:7
7:1 [k]Ne 1:1
7:2 [l]Jer 26:19; Zec 8:21
7:3 [m]Zec 12:12-14 [n]Jer 52:12-14; Zec 8:19
7:5 [o]Isa 58:5
7:7 [p]Zec 1:4 [q]Jer 22:21 [r]Jer 17:26
7:9 [s]Zec 8:16
7:10 [t]Ex 22:21 [u]Ex 22:22; Isa 1:17
7:11 [v]Jer 8:5; 11:10; 17:23
7:12 [w]Jer 17:1; Eze 11:19 [x]Ne 9:29 [y]Da 9:12
7:13 [z]Pr 1:24 [a]Isa 1:15; Jer 11:11; 14:12; Mic 3:4 [b]Pr 1:28
7:14 [c]Dt 4:27; 28:64-67 [d]Jer 23:19 [e]Jer 44:6
8:3 [f]Zec 1:16 [g]Zec 2:10
8:4 [h]Isa 65:20
8:5 [i]Jer 30:20; 31:13

[n]14 Syriac; Hebrew *Helem* [o]14 Or *and the gracious one, the*

the remnant of this people at that
time,[a] but will it seem marvelous
to me?[b]" declares the LORD Almighty.
7This is what the LORD Almighty
says: "I will save my people from
the countries of the east and the
west.[c] **8**I will bring them back[d] to
live in Jerusalem; they will be my
people,[e] and I will be faithful and
righteous to them as their God."
9This is what the LORD Almighty
says: "You who now hear these
words spoken by the prophets[f]
who were there when the foundation was laid for the house of the
LORD Almighty, let your hands be
strong[g] so that the temple may be
built. **10**Before that time there were
no wages[h] for man or beast. No
one could go about his business
safely because of his enemy, for I
had turned every man against his
neighbor. **11**But now I will not deal
with the remnant of this people as
I did in the past,"[i] declares the
LORD Almighty.
12"The seed will grow well, the
vine will yield its fruit,[j] the ground
will produce its crops,[k] and the
heavens will drop their dew.[l] I will
give all these things as an inheritance[m] to the remnant of this people. **13**As you have been an object
of cursing[n] among the nations, O
Judah and Israel, so will I save you,
and you will be a blessing.[o] Do not
be afraid, but let your hands be
strong."
14This is what the LORD Almighty
says: "Just as I had determined to
bring disaster[p] upon you and
showed no pity when your fathers
angered me," says the LORD Almighty, **15**"so now I have determined to do good[q] again to Jerusalem and Judah. Do not be afraid.
16These are the things you are to
do: Speak the truth[r] to each other,
and render true and sound judgment in your courts;[s] **17**do not plot
evil[t] against your neighbor, and do
not love to swear falsely.[u] I hate all
this," declares the LORD.
18Again the word of the LORD Almighty came to me. **19**This is what
the LORD Almighty says: "The fasts
of the fourth,[v] fifth,[w] seventh[x]
and tenth[y] months will become
joyful[z] and glad occasions and
happy festivals for Judah. Therefore love truth[a] and peace."
20This is what the LORD Almighty
says: "Many peoples and the inhabitants of many cities will yet
come, **21**and the inhabitants of one
city will go to another and say, 'Let
us go at once to entreat[b] the LORD
and seek the LORD Almighty. I myself am going.' **22**And many peoples and powerful nations will
come to Jerusalem to seek the LORD
Almighty and to entreat him."[c]
23This is what the LORD Almighty
says: "In those days ten men from
all languages and nations will take
firm hold of one Jew by the hem of
his robe and say, 'Let us go with
you, because we have heard that
God is with you.' "[d]

Judgment on Israel's Enemies

An Oracle

9 The word of the LORD is
against the land of
Hadrach
and will rest upon
Damascus[e]—
for the eyes of men and all the
tribes of Israel
are on the LORD—[p]
2and upon Hamath[f] too, which
borders on it,
and upon Tyre[g] and Sidon,
though they are very
skillful.
3Tyre has built herself a
stronghold;
she has heaped up silver like
dust,
and gold like the dirt of the
streets.[h]
4But the Lord will take away her
possessions
and destroy her power on the
sea,
and she will be consumed by
fire.[i]
5Ashkelon will see it and fear;
Gaza will writhe in agony,

8:6 [a]Ps 118:23; 126:1-3 [b]Jer 32:17,27
8:7 [c]Ps 107:3; Isa 11:11; 43:5
8:8 [d]Zec 10:10 [e]Eze 11:19-20; 36:28; Zec 2:11
8:9 [f]Ezr 5:1 [g]Hag 2:4
8:10 [h]Hag 1:6
8:11 [i]Isa 12:1
8:12 [j]Joel 2:22 [k]Ps 67:6 [l]Ge 27:28 [m]Ob 1:17
8:13 [n]Jer 42:18 [o]Ge 12:2
8:14 [p]Jer 31:28; Eze 24:14
8:15 [q]ver 13; Jer 29:11; Mic 7:18-20
8:16 [r]Ps 15:2; Eph 4:25 [s]Zec 7:9
8:17 [t]Pr 3:29 [u]Pr 6:16-19
8:19 [v]Jer 39:2 [w]Jer 52:12 [x]2Ki 25:25 [y]Jer 52:4 [z]Ps 30:11 [a]ver 16
8:21 [b]Zec 7:2
8:22 [c]Ps 117:1; Isa 60:3; Zec 2:11
8:23 [d]Isa 45:14; 1Co 14:25
9:1 [e]Isa 17:1
9:2 [f]Jer 49:23 [g]Eze 28:1-19
9:3 [h]Job 27:16; Eze 28:4
9:4 [i]Isa 23:1; Eze 26:3-5; 28:18

[p]1 Or *Damascus. / For the eye of the LORD is on all mankind, / as well as on the tribes of Israel,*

and Ekron too, for her hope will wither.
Gaza will lose her king
and Ashkelon will be deserted.
6Foreigners will occupy Ashdod,
and I will cut off the pride of the Philistines.
7I will take the blood from their mouths,
the forbidden food from between their teeth.
Those who are left will belong to our God
and become leaders in Judah,
and Ekron will be like the Jebusites.
8But I will defend my house
against marauding forces.
Never again will an oppressor overrun my people,
for now I am keeping watch.[a]

The Coming of Zion's King

9Rejoice greatly, O Daughter of Zion!
Shout, Daughter of Jerusalem!
See, your king[q] comes to you,
righteous and having salvation,[b]
gentle and riding on a donkey,
on a colt, the foal of a donkey.[c]
10I will take away the chariots from Ephraim
and the war-horses from Jerusalem,
and the battle bow will be broken.[d]
He will proclaim peace to the nations.
His rule will extend from sea to sea
and from the River[r] to the ends of the earth.[s][e]
11As for you, because of the blood of my covenant[f] with you,
I will free your prisoners[g] from the waterless pit.
12Return to your fortress,[h] O prisoners of hope;
even now I announce that I will restore twice as much to you.
13I will bend Judah as I bend my bow
and fill it with Ephraim.[i]
I will rouse your sons, O Zion,
against your sons, O Greece,[j]
and make you like a warrior's sword.[k]

The LORD Will Appear

14Then the LORD will appear over them;[l]
his arrow will flash like lightning.[m]
The Sovereign LORD will sound the trumpet;
he will march in the storms[n] of the south,
15 and the LORD Almighty will shield[o] them.
They will destroy
and overcome with slingstones.
They will drink and roar as with wine;
they will be full like a bowl
used for sprinkling[t] the corners[p] of the altar.
16The LORD their God will save them on that day
as the flock of his people.
They will sparkle in his land
like jewels in a crown.[q]
17How attractive and beautiful they will be!
Grain will make the young men thrive,
and new wine the young women.

The LORD Will Care for Judah

10 Ask the LORD for rain in the springtime;
it is the LORD who makes the storm clouds.
He gives showers of rain to men,
and plants of the field to everyone.
2The idols[r] speak deceit,

9:8 [a]Isa 52:1; 54:14
9:9 [b]Isa 9:6-7; 43:3-11; Jer 23:5-6; Zep 3:14-15; Zec 2:10 [c]Mt 21:5*; Jn 12:15*
9:10 [d]Hos 1:7; 2:18; Mic 4:3; 5:10; Zec 10:4 [e]Ps 72:8
9:11 [f]Ex 24:8 [g]Isa 42:7
9:12 [h]Joel 3:16
9:13 [i]Isa 49:2 [j]Joel 3:6 [k]Jer 51:20
9:14 [l]Isa 31:5 [m]Ps 18:14; Hab 3:11 [n]Isa 21:1; 66:15
9:15 [o]Isa 37:35; Zec 12:8 [p]Ex 27:2
9:16 [q]Isa 62:3; Jer 31:11
10:2 [r]Eze 21:21

[q]9 Or *King* [r]10 That is, the Euphrates
[s]10 Or *the end of the land* [t]15 Or *bowl, / like*

diviners see visions that lie;
they tell dreams that are false,
they give comfort in vain.
Therefore the people wander like sheep
oppressed for lack of a shepherd.[a]

3"My anger burns against the shepherds,
and I will punish the leaders;[b]
for the LORD Almighty will care for his flock, the house of Judah,
and make them like a proud horse in battle.
4From Judah will come the cornerstone,
from him the tent peg,[c]
from him the battle bow,[d]
from him every ruler.
5Together they[u] will be like mighty men
trampling the muddy streets in battle.[e]
Because the LORD is with them,
they will fight and overthrow the horsemen.[f]

6"I will strengthen the house of Judah
and save the house of Joseph.
I will restore them
because I have compassion on them.[g]
They will be as though
I had not rejected them,
for I am the LORD their God
and I will answer[h] them.
7The Ephraimites will become like mighty men,
and their hearts will be glad as with wine.[i]
Their children will see it and be joyful;
their hearts will rejoice in the LORD.
8I will signal[j] for them
and gather them in.
Surely I will redeem them;
they will be as numerous[k] as before.
9Though I scatter them among the peoples,
yet in distant lands they will remember me.[l]
They and their children will survive,
and they will return.
10I will bring them back from Egypt
and gather them from Assyria.[m]
I will bring them to Gilead[n] and Lebanon,
and there will not be room[o] enough for them.
11They will pass through the sea of trouble;
the surging sea will be subdued
and all the depths of the Nile will dry up.[p]
Assyria's pride[q] will be brought down
and Egypt's scepter[r] will pass away.
12I will strengthen them in the LORD
and in his name they will walk,[s]"
declares the LORD.

11 Open your doors, O Lebanon,[t]
so that fire may devour your cedars!
2Wail, O pine tree, for the cedar has fallen;
the stately trees are ruined!
Wail, oaks of Bashan;
the dense forest[u] has been cut down!
3Listen to the wail of the shepherds;
their rich pastures are destroyed!
Listen to the roar of the lions;
the lush thicket of the Jordan is ruined![v]

Two Shepherds

4This is what the LORD my God says: "Pasture the flock marked for slaughter. 5Their buyers slaughter them and go unpunished. Those who sell them say, 'Praise the LORD, I am rich!' Their own shepherds do not spare them.[w] 6For I will no

10:2 [a]Eze 34:5; Hos 3:4; Mt 9:36
10:3 [b]Jer 25:34
10:4 [c]Isa 22:23 [d]Zec 9:10
10:5 [e]2Sa 22:43 [f]Am 2:15; Hag 2:22
10:6 [g]Zec 8:7-8 [h]Zec 13:9
10:7 [i]Zec 9:15
10:8 [j]Isa 5:26 [k]Jer 33:22; Eze 36:11
10:9 [l]Eze 6:9
10:10 [m]Isa 11:11 [n]Jer 50:19 [o]Isa 49:19
10:11 [p]Isa 19:5-7; 51:10 [q]Zep 2:13 [r]Eze 30:13
10:12 [s]Mic 4:5
11:1 [t]Eze 31:3
11:2 [u]Isa 32:19
11:3 [v]Jer 2:15; 50:44
11:5 [w]Jer 50:7; Eze 34:2-3

[u]4,5 *Or ruler, all of them together.* / [5]*They*

longer have pity on the people of the land," declares the LORD. "I will hand everyone over to his neighbor[a] and his king. They will oppress the land, and I will not rescue them from their hands."[b]

7So I pastured the flock marked for slaughter, particularly the oppressed of the flock. Then I took two staffs and called one Favor and the other Union, and I pastured the flock. 8In one month I got rid of the three shepherds.

The flock detested me, and I grew weary of them 9and said, "I will not be your shepherd. Let the dying die, and the perishing perish.[c] Let those who are left eat one another's flesh."

10Then I took my staff called Favor[d] and broke it, revoking[e] the covenant I had made with all the nations. 11It was revoked on that day, and so the afflicted of the flock who were watching me knew it was the word of the LORD.

12I told them, "If you think it best, give me my pay; but if not, keep it." So they paid me thirty pieces of silver.[f]

13And the LORD said to me, "Throw it to the potter"—the handsome price at which they priced me! So I took the thirty pieces of silver and threw them into the house of the LORD to the potter.[g]

14Then I broke my second staff called Union, breaking the brotherhood between Judah and Israel.

15Then the LORD said to me, "Take again the equipment of a foolish shepherd. 16For I am going to raise up a shepherd over the land who will not care for the lost, or seek the young, or heal the injured, or feed the healthy, but will eat the meat of the choice sheep, tearing off their hoofs.

17"Woe to the worthless shepherd,[h]
who deserts the flock!
May the sword strike his arm[i]
and his right eye!
May his arm be completely withered,
his right eye totally blinded!"[j]

Jerusalem's Enemies to Be Destroyed

An Oracle

12 This is the word of the LORD concerning Israel. The LORD, who stretches out the heavens,[k] who lays the foundation of the earth,[l] and who forms the spirit of man[m] within him, declares: 2"I am going to make Jerusalem a cup[n] that sends all the surrounding peoples reeling.[o] Judah[p] will be besieged as well as Jerusalem. 3On that day, when all the nations[q] of the earth are gathered against her, I will make Jerusalem an immovable rock[r] for all the nations. All who try to move it will injure[s] themselves. 4On that day I will strike every horse with panic and its rider with madness," declares the LORD. "I will keep a watchful eye over the house of Judah, but I will blind all the horses of the nations.[t] 5Then the leaders of Judah will say in their hearts, 'The people of Jerusalem are strong, because the LORD Almighty is their God.'

6"On that day I will make the leaders of Judah like a firepot[u] in a woodpile, like a flaming torch among sheaves. They will consume[v] right and left all the surrounding peoples, but Jerusalem will remain intact in her place.

7"The LORD will save the dwellings of Judah first, so that the honor of the house of David and of Jerusalem's inhabitants may not be greater than that of Judah.[w] 8On that day the LORD will shield[x] those who live in Jerusalem, so that the feeblest among them will be like David, and the house of David will be like God,[y] like the Angel of the LORD going before[z] them. 9On that day I will set out to destroy all the nations that attack Jerusalem.[a]

11:6 [a]Zec 14:13 [b]Isa 9:19-21; Jer 13:14; Mic 5:8; 7:2-6
11:9 [c]Jer 15:2; 43:11
11:10 [d]ver 7 [e]Ps 89:39; Jer 14:21
11:12 [f]Ex 21:32; Mt 26:15
11:13 [g]Mt 27:9-10*; Ac 1:18-19
11:17 [h]Jer 23:1 [i]Eze 30:21-22 [j]Jer 23:1
12:1 [k]Isa 42:5; Jer 51:15 [l]Ps 102:25; Heb 1:10 [m]Isa 57:16
12:2 [n]Ps 75:8 [o]Isa 51:23 [p]Zec 14:14
12:3 [q]Zec 14:2 [r]Da 2:34-35 [s]Mt 21:44
12:4 [t]Ps 76:6
12:6 [u]Isa 10:17-18; Zec 11:1 [v]Ob 1:18
12:7 [w]Jer 30:18; Am 9:11
12:8 [x]Joel 3:16; Zec 9:15 [y]Ps 82:6 [z]Mic 7:8
12:9 [a]Zec 14:2-3

Mourning for the One They Pierced

10"And I will pour out on the
house of David and the inhabitants
of Jerusalem a spirit[v] of grace and
supplication.[a] They will look on[w]
me, the one they have pierced,[b]
and they will mourn for him as one
mourns for an only child, and
grieve bitterly for him as one
grieves for a firstborn son. 11On
that day the weeping in Jerusalem
will be great, like the weeping of
Hadad Rimmon in the plain of Megiddo.[c] 12The land will mourn,[d]
each clan by itself, with their wives
by themselves: the clan of the
house of David and their wives, the
clan of the house of Nathan and
their wives, 13the clan of the house
of Levi and their wives, the clan of
Shimei and their wives, 14and all
the rest of the clans and their
wives.

Cleansing From Sin

13 "On that day a fountain[e]
will be opened to the house
of David and the inhabitants of Jerusalem, to cleanse[f] them from
sin and impurity.
2"On that day, I will banish the
names of the idols[g] from the land,
and they will be remembered no
more," declares the LORD Almighty.
"I will remove both the prophets[h]
and the spirit of impurity from the
land. 3And if anyone still prophesies, his father and mother, to
whom he was born, will say to him,
'You must die, because you have
told lies in the LORD's name.' When
he prophesies, his own parents will
stab him.[i]
4"On that day every prophet will
be ashamed[j] of his prophetic vision. He will not put on a prophet's
garment[k] of hair[l] in order to deceive. 5He will say, 'I am not a
prophet. I am a farmer; the land
has been my livelihood since my
youth.[x][m] 6If someone asks him,
'What are these wounds on your
body[y]?' he will answer, 'The
wounds I was given at the house of
my friends.'

12:10 [a] Isa 44:3; Eze 39:29; Joel 2:28-29 [b] Jn 19:34, 37*; Rev 1:7
12:11 [c] 2Ki 23:29
12:12 [d] Mt 24:30; Rev 1:7
13:1 [e] Jer 17:13 [f] Ps 51:2; Heb 9:14
13:2 [g] Ex 23:13; Eze 36:25; Hos 2:17 [h] 1Ki 22:22; Jer 23:14-15
13:3 [i] Dt 13:6-11; 18:20; Jer 23:34; Eze 14:9
13:4 [j] Jer 6:15; Mic 3:6-7 [k] Mt 3:4 [l] 2Ki 1:8; Isa 20:2
13:5 [m] Am 7:14
13:7 [n] Jer 47:6 [o] Isa 40:11; 53:4; Eze 37:24 [p] Mt 26:31*; Mk 14:27*
13:8 [q] Eze 5:2-4,12
13:9 [r] Mal 3:2 [s] Isa 48:10; 1Pe 1:6-7 [t] Ps 50:15 [u] Zec 10:6 [v] Jer 30:22 [w] Jer 29:12
14:1 [x] Isa 13:9; Mal 4:1
14:2 [y] Isa 13:6; Zec 13:8
14:3 [z] Zec 9:14-15
14:4 [a] Eze 11:23

The Shepherd Struck, the Sheep Scattered

7"Awake, O sword,[n] against my
shepherd,[o]
against the man who is close
to me!"
declares the LORD Almighty.
"Strike the shepherd,
and the sheep will be
scattered,[p]
and I will turn my hand
against the little ones.
8In the whole land," declares
the LORD,
"two-thirds will be struck
down and perish;
yet one-third will be left in
it.[q]
9This third I will bring into the
fire;[r]
I will refine them like silver[s]
and test them like gold.
They will call[t] on my name
and I will answer[u] them;
I will say, 'They are my
people,'[v]
and they will say, 'The LORD
is our God.[w]' "

The LORD Comes and Reigns

14 A day of the LORD[x] is coming when your plunder will
be divided among you.
2I will gather all the nations to
Jerusalem to fight against it; the
city will be captured, the houses
ransacked, and the women raped.
Half of the city will go into exile,
but the rest of the people will not
be taken from the city.[y]
3Then the LORD will go out and
fight[z] against those nations, as he
fights in the day of battle. 4On that
day his feet will stand on the
Mount of Olives,[a] east of Jerusalem, and the Mount of Olives will
be split in two from east to west,
forming a great valley, with half of
the mountain moving north and
half moving south. 5You will flee by
my mountain valley, for it will extend to Azel. You will flee as you

[v]10 Or *the Spirit* [w]10 Or *to* [x]5 Or *farmer; a man sold me in my youth* [y]6 Or *wounds between your hands*

fled from the earthquake[z][a] in the
days of Uzziah king of Judah. Then
the LORD my God will come,[b] and
all the holy ones with him.[c]
6On that day there will be no
light,[d] no cold or frost. 7It will be
a unique[e] day, without daytime or
nighttime[f]—a day known to the
LORD. When evening comes, there
will be light.[g]
8On that day living water[h] will
flow out from Jerusalem, half to
the eastern[i] sea[a] and half to the
western sea,[b] in summer and in
winter.
9The LORD will be king over the
whole earth.[j] On that day there
will be one LORD, and his name the
only name.[k]
10The whole land, from Geba[l]
to Rimmon, south of Jerusalem,
will become like the Arabah. But
Jerusalem will be raised up[m] and
remain in its place,[n] from the Benjamin Gate to the site of the First
Gate, to the Corner Gate, and from
the Tower of Hananel to the royal
winepresses. 11It will be inhabited;
never again will it be destroyed. Jerusalem will be secure.[o]
12This is the plague with which
the LORD will strike all the nations
that fought against Jerusalem:
Their flesh will rot while they are
still standing on their feet, their
eyes will rot in their sockets, and
their tongues will rot in their
mouths.[p] 13On that day men will
be stricken by the LORD with great
panic. Each man will seize the
hand of another, and they will attack each other.[q] 14Judah[r] too
will fight at Jerusalem. The wealth
of all the surrounding nations will
be collected[s]—great quantities of
gold and silver and clothing. 15A
similar plague[t] will strike the
horses and mules, the camels and
donkeys, and all the animals in
those camps.
16Then the survivors from all the
nations that have attacked Jerusalem will go up year after year to
worship the King, the LORD Almighty, and to celebrate the Feast
of Tabernacles.[u] 17If any of the
peoples of the earth do not go up to
Jerusalem to worship the King, the
LORD Almighty, they will have no
rain.[v] 18If the Egyptian people do
not go up and take part, they will
have no rain. The LORD[c] will bring
on them the plague he inflicts on
the nations that do not go up to celebrate the Feast of Tabernacles.[w]
19This will be the punishment of
Egypt and the punishment of all
the nations that do not go up to celebrate the Feast of Tabernacles.
20On that day HOLY TO THE LORD
will be inscribed on the bells of the
horses, and the cooking pots[x] in
the LORD's house will be like the sacred bowls[y] in front of the altar.
21Every pot in Jerusalem and Judah will be holy[z] to the LORD Almighty, and all who come to sacrifice will take some of the pots and
cook in them. And on that day[a]
there will no longer be a Canaanite[d][b] in the house of the LORD Almighty.[c]

14:5 [a] Am 1:1 [b] Isa 29:6; 66:15-16 [c] Mt 16:27; 25:31
14:6 [d] Isa 13:10; Jer 4:23
14:7 [e] Jer 30:7 [f] Rev 21:23-25; 22:5 [g] Isa 30:26
14:8 [h] Eze 47:1-12; Jn 7:38; Rev 22:1-2 [i] Joel 2:20
14:9 [j] Dt 6:4; Isa 45:24; Rev 11:15 [k] Eph 4:5-6
14:10 [l] 1Ki 15:22 [m] Jer 30:18; Am 9:11 [n] Zec 12:6
14:11 [o] Eze 34:25-28
14:12 [p] Lev 26:16; Dt 28:22
14:13 [q] Zec 11:6
14:14 [r] Zec 12:2 [s] Isa 23:18
14:15 [t] ver 12
14:16 [u] Isa 60:6-9
14:17 [v] Jer 14:4; Am 4:7
14:18 [w] ver 12
14:20 [x] Eze 46:20 [y] Zec 9:15
14:21 [z] Ro 14:6-7; 1Co 10:31 [a] Ne 8:10 [b] Zec 9:8 [c] Eze 44:9

[z]5 Or *5My mountain valley will be blocked and will extend to Azel. It will be blocked as it was blocked because of the earthquake* [a]8 That is, the Dead Sea [b]8 That is, the Mediterranean [c]18 Or *part, then the LORD* [d]21 Or *merchant*

Malachi

Title and Background

The temple had been rebuilt, but times of prosperity had not come. The people were suffering drought, famine and blighted crops, and they met these conditions with indifference and spiritual lethargy. They had forgotten God and treated him with dishonor. They had also married foreign women. Against such a background Malachi, meaning "my messenger," was written.

Author and Date of Writing

Since the term "my messenger" occurs in 3:1, and since both prophets and priests were called messengers of the Lord, some have thought "Malachi" only a title that tradition has given the author. There is no certainty about this, however, and it seems likely that Malachi was in fact the author's name. The book was written probably 433-430 B.C.

Theme and Message

Malachi's message is filled with indictments and warnings. He rebukes the Jews for doubting God's love (1:2-5) and for the faithlessness of both priests (1:6-2:9) and people (2:10-16). How quickly the nation had forgotten! Only through repentance and reformation will the people again experience God's blessing (3:6-12). That "great and dreadful day of the LORD" (4:5) was coming, and Malachi both reassures and warns his people.

Outline

I. God's Covenant Love for Israel (1:1-5)
II. Israel's Unfaithfulness (1:6-2:16)
  A. The Unfaithfulness of the Priests (1:6-2:9)
  B. The Unfaithfulness of the People (2:10-16)
III. The Lord's Coming (2:17-4:6)

---

1 An oracle:[a] The word[b] of the
LORD to Israel through Malachi.[a]

Jacob Loved, Esau Hated

2"I have loved[c] you," says the
LORD.
"But you ask, 'How have you
loved us?'
"Was not Esau Jacob's brother?"
the LORD says. "Yet I have loved Jacob,[d] 3but Esau I have hated, and
I have turned his mountains into a
wasteland[e] and left his inheritance to the desert jackals.[f]"
4Edom may say, "Though we
have been crushed, we will rebuild[g] the ruins."
But this is what the LORD Almighty says: "They may build, but
I will demolish. They will be called
the Wicked Land, a people always
under the wrath of the LORD.[h] 5You
will see it with your own eyes and
say, 'Great[i] is the LORD—even beyond the borders of Israel!'[j]

Blemished Sacrifices

6"A son honors his father, and a
servant his master. If I am a father,
where is the honor due me? If I am
a master, where is the respect[k]
due me?" says the LORD Almighty.[l]
"It is you, O priests, who show contempt for my name.

1:1 [a] Na 1:1 [b] 1Pe 4:11
1:2 [c] Dt 4:37 [d] Ro 9:13*
1:3 [e] Isa 34:10 [f] Eze 35:3-9
1:4 [g] Isa 9:10 [h] Eze 25:12-14
1:5 [i] Ps 35:27; Mic 5:4 [j] Am 1:11-12
1:6 [k] Isa 1:2 [l] Job 5:17

[a] *1 Malachi* means *my messenger.*

"But you ask, 'How have we shown contempt for your name?'

7"You place defiled food[a] on my altar.

"But you ask, 'How have we defiled you?'

"By saying that the LORD's table is contemptible. **8**When you bring blind animals for sacrifice, is that not wrong? When you sacrifice crippled or diseased animals,[b] is that not wrong? Try offering them to your governor! Would he be pleased with you? Would he accept you?" says the LORD Almighty.[c]

9"Now implore God to be gracious to us. With such offerings[d] from your hands, will he accept you?"—says the LORD Almighty.

10"Oh, that one of you would shut the temple doors, so that you would not light useless fires on my altar! I am not pleased[e] with you," says the LORD Almighty, "and I will accept no offering[f] from your hands. **11**My name will be great among the nations, from the rising to the setting of the sun. In every place incense[g] and pure offerings will be brought to my name, because my name will be great among the nations," says the LORD Almighty.

12"But you profane it by saying of the Lord's table, 'It is defiled,' and of its food,[h] 'It is contemptible.' **13**And you say, 'What a burden!'[i] and you sniff at it contemptuously," says the LORD Almighty.

"When you bring injured, crippled or diseased animals and offer them as sacrifices, should I accept them from your hands?" says the LORD. **14**"Cursed is the cheat who has an acceptable male in his flock and vows to give it, but then sacrifices a blemished animal[j] to the Lord. For I am a great king,[k]" says the LORD Almighty, "and my name is to be feared among the nations.

Admonition for the Priests

2 "And now this admonition is for you, O priests.[l] **2**If you do not listen, and if you do not set your heart to honor my name," says the LORD Almighty, "I will send a curse[m] upon you, and I will curse your blessings. Yes, I have already cursed them, because you have not set your heart to honor me.

3"Because of you I will rebuke[b] your descendants[c]; I will spread on your faces the offal[n] from your festival sacrifices, and you will be carried off with it.[o] **4**And you will know that I have sent you this admonition so that my covenant with Levi[p] may continue," says the LORD Almighty. **5**"My covenant was with him, a covenant[q] of life and peace,[r] and I gave them to him; this called for reverence and he revered me and stood in awe of my name. **6**True instruction[s] was in his mouth and nothing false was found on his lips. He walked with me in peace and uprightness, and turned many from sin.[t]

7"For the lips of a priest[u] ought to preserve knowledge, and from his mouth men should seek instruction[v]—because he is the messenger[w] of the LORD Almighty. **8**But you have turned from the way and by your teaching have caused many to stumble;[x] you have violated the covenant with Levi," says the LORD Almighty. **9**"So I have caused you to be despised[y] and humiliated before all the people, because you have not followed my ways but have shown partiality in matters of the law."

Judah Unfaithful

10Have we not all one Father[d]?[z] Did not one God create us? Why do we profane the covenant[a] of our fathers by breaking faith with one another?

11Judah has broken faith. A detestable thing has been committed in Israel and in Jerusalem: Judah has desecrated the sanctuary the LORD loves, by marrying[b] the daughter of a foreign god.[c] **12**As for the man who does this, whoever he may be, may the LORD cut him off[d]

1:7 [a]ver 12; Lev 21:6
1:8 [b]Lev 22:22; Dt 15:21 [c]Isa 43:23
1:9 [d]Lev 23:33-44
1:10 [e]Hos 5:6 [f]Isa 1:11-14; Jer 14:12
1:11 [g]Isa 60:6-7; Rev 8:3
1:12 [h]ver 7
1:13 [i]Isa 43:22-24
1:14 [j]Lev 22:18-21 [k]1Ti 6:15
2:1 [l]ver 7
2:2 [m]Dt 28:20
2:3 [n]Ex 29:14 [o]1Ki 14:10
2:4 [p]Nu 3:12
2:5 [q]Dt 33:9 [r]Nu 25:12
2:6 [s]Dt 33:10 [t]Jer 23:22; Jas 5:19-20
2:7 [u]Jer 18:18 [v]Lev 10:11 [w]Nu 27:21
2:8 [x]Jer 18:15
2:9 [y]1Sa 2:30
2:10 [z]1Co 8:6 [a]Ex 19:5
2:11 [b]Ne 13:23 [c]Ezr 9:1; Jer 3:7-9
2:12 [d]Eze 24:21

b3 Or *cut off* (see Septuagint) c3 Or *will blight your grain* d10 Or *father*

from the tents of Jacob[e]—even though he brings offerings[a] to the LORD Almighty.

[13]Another thing you do: You flood the LORD's altar with tears. You weep and wail because he no longer pays attention[b] to your offerings or accepts them with pleasure from your hands. [14]You ask, "Why?" It is because the LORD is acting as the witness between you and the wife of your youth,[c] because you have broken faith with her, though she is your partner, the wife of your marriage covenant.

[15]Has not ⌊the LORD⌋ made them one?[d] In flesh and spirit they are his. And why one? Because he was seeking godly offspring.[f][e] So guard yourself in your spirit, and do not break faith with the wife of your youth.

[16]"I hate divorce,[f]" says the LORD God of Israel, "and I hate a man's covering himself[g] with violence as well as with his garment," says the LORD Almighty.

So guard yourself in your spirit, and do not break faith.

The Day of Judgment

[17]You have wearied[g] the LORD with your words.

"How have we wearied him?" you ask.

By saying, "All who do evil are good in the eyes of the LORD, and he is pleased with them" or "Where is the God of justice?"

3 "See, I will send my messenger, who will prepare the way before me.[h] Then suddenly the Lord you are seeking will come to his temple; the messenger of the covenant, whom you desire, will come," says the LORD Almighty.

[2]But who can endure[i] the day of his coming? Who can stand when he appears? For he will be like a refiner's fire[j] or a launderer's soap. [3]He will sit as a refiner and purifier of silver;[k] he will purify[l] the Levites and refine them like gold and silver. Then the LORD will have men who will bring offerings in righteousness, [4]and the offerings[m] of Judah and Jerusalem will be acceptable to the LORD, as in days gone by, as in former years.[n]

[5]"So I will come near to you for judgment. I will be quick to testify against sorcerers, adulterers and perjurers,[o] against those who defraud laborers of their wages,[p] who oppress the widows[q] and the fatherless, and deprive aliens of justice, but do not fear me," says the LORD Almighty.

Robbing God

[6]"I the LORD do not change.[r] So you, O descendants of Jacob, are not destroyed. [7]Ever since the time of your forefathers you have turned away[s] from my decrees and have not kept them. Return to me, and I will return to you,"[t] says the LORD Almighty.

"But you ask, 'How are we to return?'

[8]"Will a man rob God? Yet you rob me.

"But you ask, 'How do we rob you?'

"In tithes[u] and offerings. [9]You are under a curse—the whole nation of you—because you are robbing me. [10]Bring the whole tithe into the storehouse,[v] that there may be food in my house. Test me in this," says the LORD Almighty, "and see if I will not throw open the floodgates[w] of heaven and pour out so much blessing that you will not have room enough for it. [11]I will prevent pests from devouring your crops, and the vines in your fields will not cast their fruit," says the LORD Almighty. [12]"Then all the nations will call you blessed,[x] for yours will be a delightful land,"[y] says the LORD Almighty.

[13]"You have said harsh things[z] against me," says the LORD.

"Yet you ask, 'What have we said against you?'

[14]"You have said, 'It is futile[a] to serve God. What did we gain by car-

2:12 [a]Mal 1:10
2:13 [b]Jer 14:12
2:14 [c]Pr 5:18
2:15 [d]Ge 2:24; Mt 19:4-6 [e]1Co 7:14
2:16 [f]Dt 24:1; Mt 5:31-32; 19:4-9
2:17 [g]Isa 43:24
3:1 [h]Isa 40:3; Mt 11:10*; Mk 1:2*; Lk 7:27*
3:2 [i]Eze 22:14; Rev 6:17 [j]Zec 13:9; Mt 3:10-12
3:3 [k]Da 12:10 [l]Isa 1:25
3:4 [m]2Ch 7:12; Ps 51:19; Mal 1:11 [n]2Ch 7:3
3:5 [o]Jer 7:9 [p]Lev 19:13; Jas 5:4 [q]Ex 22:22
3:6 [r]Nu 23:19; Jas 1:17
3:7 [s]Jer 7:26; Ac 7:51 [t]Zec 1:3
3:8 [u]Ne 13:10-12
3:10 [v]Ne 13:12 [w]2Ki 7:2
3:12 [x]Isa 61:9 [y]Isa 62:4
3:13 [z]Mal 2:17
3:14 [a]Ps 73:13

[e]12 Or *[12]May the LORD cut off from the tents of Jacob anyone who gives testimony in behalf of the man who does this* [f]15 Or *[15]But the one ⌊who is our father⌋ did not do this, not as long as life remained in him. And what was he seeking? An offspring from God* [g]16 Or *his wife*

rying out his requirements and going about like mourners[a] before
the LORD Almighty? **15**But now we
call the arrogant blessed. Certainly
the evildoers[b] prosper, and even
those who challenge God escape.' "

16Then those who feared the
LORD talked with each other, and
the LORD listened and heard.[c] A
scroll[d] of remembrance was written in his presence concerning
those who feared the LORD and honored his name.

17"They will be mine," says the
LORD Almighty, "in the day when I
make up my treasured posses-
sion.[h][e] I will spare[f] them, just as
in compassion a man spares his
son who serves him. **18**And you will
again see the distinction between
the righteous[g] and the wicked, between those who serve God and
those who do not.

The Day of the LORD

4 "Surely the day is coming;[h] it
will burn like a furnace. All the
arrogant and every evildoer will be
stubble,[i] and that day that is coming will set them on fire," says the
LORD Almighty. "Not a root or a
branch will be left to them. **2**But for
you who revere my name, the sun
of righteousness[j] will rise with
healing[k] in its wings. And you will
go out and leap[l] like calves released from the stall. **3**Then you
will trample[m] down the wicked;
they will be ashes[n] under the soles
of your feet on the day when I do
these things," says the LORD Almighty.

4"Remember the law[o] of my servant Moses, the decrees and laws I
gave him at Horeb for all Israel.

5"See, I will send you the prophet Elijah[p] before that great and
dreadful day of the LORD comes.[q]
6He will turn the hearts of the fathers to their children,[r] and the
hearts of the children to their fathers; or else I will come and
strike[s] the land with a curse."[t]

3:14 [a] Isa 58:3
3:15 [b] Jer 7:10
3:16 [c] Ps 34:15 [d] Ps 56:8
3:17 [e] Dt 7:6 [f] Ps 103:13; Isa 26:20
3:18 [g] Ge 18:25
4:1 [h] Joel 2:31 [i] Isa 5:24; Ob 1:18
4:2 [j] Lk 1:78; Eph 5:14 [k] Isa 30:26 [l] Isa 35:6
4:3 [m] Job 40:12 [n] Eze 28:18
4:4 [o] Ps 147:19
4:5 [p] Mt 11:14; Lk 1:17 [q] Joel 2:31
4:6 [r] Lk 1:17 [s] Isa 11:4; Rev 19:15 [t] Zec 5:3

[h] *17* Or *Almighty, "my treasured possession, in the day when I act*

FROM MALACHI TO CHRIST

THE PERSIAN PERIOD 450-330 B.C.

For about 200 years after Nehemiah's time the Persians controlled Judah, but the Jews were allowed to carry on their religious observances and were not interfered with. During this time Judah was ruled by high priests who were responsible to the Jewish government.

THE HELLENISTIC PERIOD 330-166 B.C.

In 333 B.C. the Persian armies stationed in Macedonia were defeated by Alexander the Great. He was convinced that Greek culture was the one force that could unify the world. Alexander permitted the Jews to observe *their laws and even* granted them exemption from tribute or tax during their sabbath years. The Greek conquest prepared the way for the translation of the OT into Greek (Septuagint version) c. 250 B.C.

		Malachi c. 430 B.C.
	410	
	400 B.C.	
	390	
	380	
	370	
	360	
	350	
	340	
Rule of Alexander the Great	330	334-323 Alexander the Great conquers the East; 330-328 Alexander's years of power
	320	320 Ptolemy (I) Soter conquers Jerusalem
Rule of the Ptolemies of Egypt	310	311 Seleucus conquers Babylon; Seleucid dynasty begins
	300	
	290	
	280	
	270	
	260	
	250	
	240	
	230	226 Antiochus III (the Great) of Syria overpowers Palestine
	220	223-187 Antiochus becomes Seleucid ruler of Syria
	210	
	200	198 Antiochus defeats Egypt and gains control of Palestine
	190	

THE HASMONEAN PERIOD
166-63 B.C.

When this historical period began, the Jews were being greatly oppressed. The Ptolemies had been tolerant of the Jews and their religious practices but the Seleucid rulers were determined to force Hellenism on them. Copies of the Scriptures were ordered destroyed and laws were enforced with extreme cruelty. The oppressed Jews revolted, led by Judas the Maccabee.

THE ROMAN PERIOD
63 B.C. . . .

In the year 63 B.C. Pompey, the Roman general, captured Jerusalem, and the provinces of Palestine became subject to Rome. The local government was entrusted part of the time to princes and the rest of the time to procurators who were appointed by the emperors. Herod the Great was ruler of all Palestine at the time of Christ's birth.

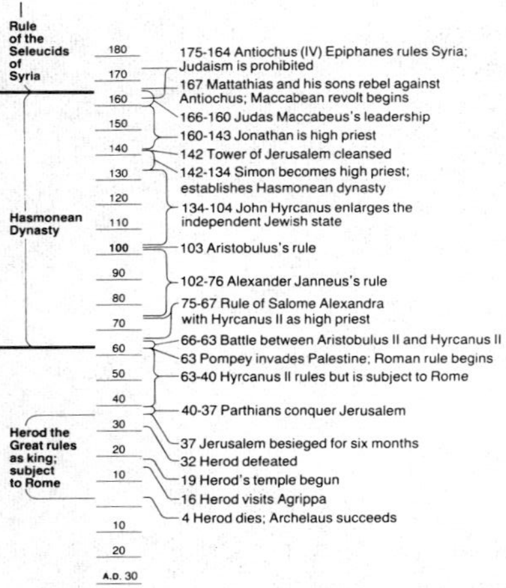

Rule of the Seleucids of Syria

Hasmonean Dynasty

Herod the Great rules as king; subject to Rome

180
170
160
150
140
130
120
110
100
90
80
70
60
50
40
30
20
10

10
20
A.D. 30

175-164 Antiochus (IV) Epiphanes rules Syria; Judaism is prohibited
167 Mattathias and his sons rebel against Antiochus; Maccabean revolt begins
166-160 Judas Maccabeus's leadership
160-143 Jonathan is high priest
142 Tower of Jerusalem cleansed
142-134 Simon becomes high priest; establishes Hasmonean dynasty
134-104 John Hyrcanus enlarges the independent Jewish state
103 Aristobulus's rule
102-76 Alexander Janneus's rule
75-67 Rule of Salome Alexandra with Hyrcanus II as high priest
66-63 Battle between Aristobulus II and Hyrcanus II
63 Pompey invades Palestine; Roman rule begins
63-40 Hyrcanus II rules but is subject to Rome
40-37 Parthians conquer Jerusalem
37 Jerusalem besieged for six months
32 Herod defeated
19 Herod's temple begun
16 Herod visits Agrippa
4 Herod dies; Archelaus succeeds

The New Testament

Matthew

Title and Background

The Gospel of Matthew was so named to distinguish it from the other Gospel accounts. There is only one gospel, but four accounts of it. So we have here Matthew's version of the "good news" from God. Matthew's name means "gift of the LORD."

Author and Date of Writing

All four of the canonical Gospels are anonymous, but the early church fathers were unanimous in holding that Matthew was the author of this Gospel. He was a tax collector and was also known as Levi. The Gospel was most likely written before the destruction of Jerusalem in A.D. 70.

Theme and Message

Matthew's main purpose is to prove to his Jewish readers that Jesus is their Messiah. He quotes the Old Testament often and uses the phrase "kingdom of heaven" frequently. The whole Gospel is woven around five great discourses: (1) chapters 5-7; (2) chapter 10; (3) chapter 13; (4) chapter 18; (5) chapters 24-25.

Outline

I. The Birth and Early Years of Jesus (1:1-2:23)
II. The Beginnings of Jesus' Ministry (3:1-4:11)
III. Jesus' Ministry in Galilee (4:12-14:12)
IV. Jesus' Withdrawals From Galilee (14:13-17:20)
V. Jesus' Last Ministry in Galilee (17:22-18:35)
VI. Jesus' Ministry in Judea and Perea (19:1-20:34)
VII. Passion Week (21:1-27:66)
VIII. The Resurrection (28:1-20)

The Genealogy of Jesus

1:1–17pp — Lk 3:23–38
1:3–6pp — Ru 4:18–22
1:7–11pp — 1Ch 3:10–17

1 A record of the genealogy of Jesus Christ the son of David,[a] the son of Abraham:[b]

2 Abraham was the father of Isaac,[c]
Isaac the father of Jacob,[d]
Jacob the father of Judah and his brothers,[e]
3 Judah the father of Perez and Zerah, whose mother was Tamar,[f]
Perez the father of Hezron,
Hezron the father of Ram,
4 Ram the father of Amminadab,
Amminadab the father of Nahshon,
Nahshon the father of Salmon,
5 Salmon the father of Boaz, whose mother was Rahab,
Boaz the father of Obed, whose mother was Ruth,
Obed the father of Jesse,
6 and Jesse the father of King David.[g]

David was the father of Solomon, whose mother had been Uriah's wife,[h]
7 Solomon the father of Rehoboam,
Rehoboam the father of Abijah,

1:1 [a] 2Sa 7:12-16; Isa 9:6,7; 11:1; Jer 23:5,6; Mt 9:27; Lk 1:32,69; Ro 1:3; Rev 22:16 [b] Ge 22:18; Gal 3:16
1:2 [c] Ge 21:3,12 [d] Ge 25:26 [e] Ge 29:35
1:3 [f] Ge 38:27-30
1:6 [g] 1Sa 16:1; 17:12 [h] 2Sa 12:24

Abijah the father of Asa,
8 Asa the father of Jehoshaphat,
Jehoshaphat the father of Jehoram,
Jehoram the father of Uzziah,
9 Uzziah the father of Jotham,
Jotham the father of Ahaz,
Ahaz the father of Hezekiah,
10 Hezekiah the father of Manasseh,[a]
Manasseh the father of Amon,
Amon the father of Josiah,
11 and Josiah the father of Jeconiah[a] and his brothers at the time of the exile to Babylon.[b]

12 After the exile to Babylon:
Jeconiah was the father of Shealtiel,[c]
Shealtiel the father of Zerubbabel,[d]
13 Zerubbabel the father of Abiud,
Abiud the father of Eliakim,
Eliakim the father of Azor,
14 Azor the father of Zadok,
Zadok the father of Akim,
Akim the father of Eliud,
15 Eliud the father of Eleazar,
Eleazar the father of Matthan,
Matthan the father of Jacob,
16 and Jacob the father of Joseph, the husband of Mary,[e] of whom was born Jesus, who is called Christ.[f]

17 Thus there were fourteen generations in all from Abraham to David, fourteen from David to the exile to Babylon, and fourteen from the exile to the Christ.[b]

The Birth of Jesus Christ

18 This is how the birth of Jesus
Christ came about: His mother
Mary was pledged to be married to
Joseph, but before they came together, she was found to be with
child through the Holy Spirit.[g]
19 Because Joseph her husband was
a righteous man and did not want
to expose her to public disgrace,
he had in mind to divorce[h] her
quietly.

20 But after he had considered
this, an angel of the Lord appeared
to him in a dream and said, "Joseph son of David, do not be afraid
to take Mary home as your wife, because what is conceived in her is
from the Holy Spirit. 21 She will
give birth to a son, and you are to
give him the name Jesus,[c i] because he will save his people from
their sins."[j]

22 All this took place to fulfill
what the Lord had said through the
prophet: 23 "The virgin will be with
child and will give birth to a son,
and they will call him Immanuel"[d k]—which means, "God with
us."

24 When Joseph woke up, he did
what the angel of the Lord had
commanded him and took Mary
home as his wife. 25 But he had no
union with her until she gave birth
to a son. And he gave him the name
Jesus.[l]

The Visit of the Magi

2 After Jesus was born in Bethlehem in Judea,[m] during the
time of King Herod,[n] Magi[e] from
the east came to Jerusalem 2 and
asked, "Where is the one who has
been born king of the Jews?[o] We
saw his star[p] in the east[f] and have
come to worship him."

3 When King Herod heard this he
was disturbed, and all Jerusalem
with him. 4 When he had called together all the people's chief priests
and teachers of the law, he asked
them where the Christ[g] was to be
born. 5 "In Bethlehem[q] in Judea,"
they replied, "for this is what the
prophet has written:

1:10 [a] 2Ki 20:21
1:11 [b] 2Ki 24:14-16; Jer 27:20; Da 1:1,2
1:12 [c] 1Ch 3:17 [d] 1Ch 3:19; Ezr 3:2
1:16 [e] Lk 1:27 [f] Mt 27:17
1:18 [g] Lk 1:35
1:19 [h] Dt 24:1
1:21 [i] Lk 1:31 [j] Lk 2:11; Ac 5:31; 13:23,28
1:23 [k] Isa 7:14; 8:8, 10
1:25 [l] ver 21
2:1 [m] Lk 2:4-7 [n] Lk 1:5
2:2 [o] Jer 23:5; Mt 27:11; Mk 15:2; Jn 1:49; 18:33-37 [p] Nu 24:17
2:5 [q] Jn 7:42

[a] *11* That is, Jehoiachin; also in verse 12
[b] *17* Or *Messiah.* "The Christ" (Greek) and "the Messiah" (Hebrew) both mean "the Anointed One."
[c] *21* *Jesus* is the Greek form of *Joshua,* which means *the LORD saves.*
[d] *23* Isaiah 7:14
[e] *1* Traditionally *Wise Men*
[f] *2* Or *star when it rose*
[g] *4* Or *Messiah*

6" 'But you, Bethlehem, in the
land of Judah,
are by no means least among
the rulers of Judah;
for out of you will come a ruler
who will be the shepherd of
my people Israel.'[h]"[a]

7Then Herod called the Magi secretly and found out from them the
exact time the star had appeared.
8He sent them to Bethlehem and
said, "Go and make a careful
search for the child. As soon as you
find him, report to me, so that I too
may go and worship him."
9After they had heard the king,
they went on their way, and the star
they had seen in the east[i] went
ahead of them until it stopped over
the place where the child was.
10When they saw the star, they
were overjoyed. 11On coming to
the house, they saw the child with
his mother Mary, and they bowed
down and worshiped him.[b] Then
they opened their treasures and
presented him with gifts[c] of gold
and of incense and of myrrh. 12And
having been warned[d] in a dream[e]
not to go back to Herod, they returned to their country by another
route.

The Escape to Egypt

13When they had gone, an angel[f] of the Lord appeared to Joseph in a dream.[g] "Get up," he
said, "take the child and his mother and escape to Egypt. Stay there
until I tell you, for Herod is going to
search for the child to kill him."
14So he got up, took the child
and his mother during the night
and left for Egypt, 15where he
stayed until the death of Herod.
And so was fulfilled what the Lord
had said through the prophet: "Out
of Egypt I called my son."[j][h]
16When Herod realized that he
had been outwitted by the Magi, he
was furious, and he gave orders to
kill all the boys in Bethlehem and
its vicinity who were two years old
and under, in accordance with the
time he had learned from the Magi.

2:6 [a]Mic 5:2; 2Sa 5:2
2:11 [b]Isa 60:3 [c]Ps 72:10
2:12 [d]Heb 11:7 [e]ver 13,19,22; Mt 27:19
2:13 [f]Ac 5:19 [g]ver 12,19,22
2:15 [h]Hos 11:1; Ex 4:22,23
2:18 [i]Jer 31:15
2:19 [j]ver 12,13,22
2:22 [k]ver 12,13,19; Mt 27:19 [l]Lk 2:39
2:23 [m]Lk 1:26; Jn 1:45,46 [n]Mt 1:22 [o]Mk 1:24
3:1 [p]Lk 1:13, 57-66; 3:2-19
3:2 [q]Da 2:44; Mt 4:17; 6:10; Lk 11:20; 21:31; Jn 3:3, 5; Ac 1:3,6
3:3 [r]Isa 40:3; Mal 3:1; Lk 1:76; Jn 1:23
3:4 [s]2Ki 1:8 [t]Lev 11:22

17Then what was said through the
prophet Jeremiah was fulfilled:

18"A voice is heard in Ramah,
weeping and great mourning,
Rachel weeping for her children
and refusing to be comforted,
because they are no more."[k][i]

The Return to Nazareth

19After Herod died, an angel of
the Lord appeared in a dream[j] to
Joseph in Egypt 20and said, "Get
up, take the child and his mother
and go to the land of Israel, for
those who were trying to take the
child's life are dead."
21So he got up, took the child
and his mother and went to the
land of Israel. 22But when he heard
that Archelaus was reigning in Judea in place of his father Herod, he
was afraid to go there. Having been
warned in a dream,[k] he withdrew
to the district of Galilee,[l] 23and he
went and lived in a town called
Nazareth.[m] So was fulfilled[n] what
was said through the prophets: "He
will be called a Nazarene."[o]

John the Baptist Prepares the Way

3:1–12pp — Mk 1:3–8; Lk 3:2–17

3 In those days John the Baptist[p] came, preaching in the
Desert of Judea 2and saying, "Repent, for the kingdom of heaven[q]
is near." 3This is he who was spoken of through the prophet Isaiah:

"A voice of one calling in the
desert,
'Prepare the way for the Lord,
make straight paths for
him.' "[l][r]

4John's clothes were made of
camel's hair, and he had a leather
belt around his waist.[s] His food
was locusts[t] and wild honey.
5People went out to him from Jerusalem and all Judea and the whole
region of the Jordan. 6Confessing
their sins, they were baptized by
him in the Jordan River.

[h]6 Micah 5:2 [i]9 Or *seen when it rose* [j]15 Hosea 11:1 [k]18 Jer. 31:15 [l]3 Isaiah 40:3

7But when he saw many of the
Pharisees and Sadducees coming
to where he was baptizing, he said
to them: "You brood of vipers![a]
Who warned you to flee from the
coming wrath?[b] 8Produce fruit in
keeping with repentance.[c] 9And
do not think you can say to yourselves, 'We have Abraham as our
father.' I tell you that out of these
stones God can raise up children
for Abraham. 10The ax is already at
the root of the trees, and every tree
that does not produce good fruit
will be cut down and thrown into
the fire.[d]

11"I baptize you with[m] water for
repentance. But after me will come
one who is more powerful than I,
whose sandals I am not fit to carry.
He will baptize you with the Holy
Spirit[e] and with fire.[f] 12His winnowing fork is in his hand, and he
will clear his threshing floor, gathering his wheat into the barn and
burning up the chaff with unquenchable fire."[g]

The Baptism of Jesus

3:13–17pp — Mk 1:9–11; Lk 3:21,22; Jn 1:31–34

13Then Jesus came from Galilee
to the Jordan to be baptized by
John.[h] 14But John tried to deter
him, saying, "I need to be baptized
by you, and do you come to me?"

15Jesus replied, "Let it be so
now; it is proper for us to do this to
fulfill all righteousness." Then
John consented.

16As soon as Jesus was baptized,
he went up out of the water. At that
moment heaven was opened, and
he saw the Spirit of God[i] descending like a dove and lighting on him.
17And a voice from heaven[j] said,
"This is my Son,[k] whom I love;
with him I am well pleased."[l]

The Temptation of Jesus

4:1–11pp — Mk 1:12,13; Lk 4:1–13

4 Then Jesus was led by the Spirit into the desert to be tempted
by the devil. 2After fasting forty
days and forty nights,[m] he was
hungry. 3The tempter[n] came to
him and said, "If you are the Son of
God,[o] tell these stones to become
bread."

4Jesus answered, "It is written:
'Man does not live on bread alone,
but on every word that comes from
the mouth of God.'[n]"[p]

5Then the devil took him to the
holy city[q] and had him stand on
the highest point of the temple.
6"If you are the Son of God," he
said, "throw yourself down. For it is
written:

" 'He will command his angels
concerning you,
and they will lift you up in
their hands,
so that you will not strike your
foot against a
stone.'[o]"[r]

7Jesus answered him, "It is also
written: 'Do not put the Lord your
God to the test.'[p]"[s]

8Again, the devil took him to a
very high mountain and showed
him all the kingdoms of the world
and their splendor. 9"All this I will
give you," he said, "if you will bow
down and worship me."

10Jesus said to him, "Away from
me, Satan![t] For it is written: 'Worship the Lord your God, and serve
him only.'[q]"[u]

11Then the devil left him, and
angels came and attended him.[v]

Jesus Begins to Preach

12When Jesus heard that John
had been put in prison,[w] he returned to Galilee.[x] 13Leaving Nazareth, he went and lived in Capernaum,[y] which was by the lake in
the area of Zebulun and Naphtali— 14to fulfill what was said
through the prophet Isaiah:

15"Land of Zebulun and land of
Naphtali,
the way to the sea, along the
Jordan,
Galilee of the Gentiles—
16the people living in darkness
have seen a great light;
on those living in the land of
the shadow of death

3:7 [a]Mt 12:34; 23:33 [b]Ro 1:18; 1Th 1:10
3:8 [c]Ac 26:20
3:10 [d]Mt 7:19; Lk 13:6-9; Jn 15:2,6
3:11 [e]Mk 1:8 [f]Isa 4:4; Ac 2:3,4
3:12 [g]Mt 13:30
3:13 [h]Mk 1:4
3:16 [i]Isa 11:2; 42:1
3:17 [j]Mt 17:5; Jn 12:28 [k]Ps 2:7; 2Pe 1:17,18 [l]Isa 42:1; Mt 12:18; 17:5; Mk 1:11; 9:7; Lk 9:35
4:2 [m]Ex 34:28; 1Ki 19:8
4:3 [n]1Th 3:5 [o]Mt 3:17; Jn 5:25; Ac 9:20
4:4 [p]Dt 8:3
4:5 [q]Ne 11:1; Da 9:24; Mt 27:53
4:6 [r]Ps 91:11,12
4:7 [s]Dt 6:16
4:10 [t]1Ch 21:1 [u]Dt 6:13
4:11 [v]Mt 26:53; Lk 22:43; Heb 1:14
4:12 [w]Mt 14:3 [x]Mk 1:14
4:13 [y]Mk 1:21; Lk 4:23,31; Jn 2:12; 4:46, 47

[m]*11* Or *in* [n]*4* Deut. 8:3 [o]*6* Psalm 91:11,12 [p]*7* Deut. 6:16 [q]*10* Deut. 6:13

a light has dawned."[r][a]

17 From that time on Jesus began
to preach, "Repent, for the kingdom of heaven[b] is near."

The Calling of the First Disciples

4:18–22pp — Mk 1:16–20; Lk 5:2–11; Jn 1:35–42

18 As Jesus was walking beside
the Sea of Galilee,[c] he saw two
brothers, Simon called Peter[d] and
his brother Andrew. They were
casting a net into the lake, for they
were fishermen. 19 "Come, follow
me,"[e] Jesus said, "and I will make
you fishers of men." 20 At once they
left their nets and followed him.

21 Going on from there, he saw
two other brothers, James son of
Zebedee and his brother John.[f]
They were in a boat with their father Zebedee, preparing their nets.
Jesus called them, 22 and immediately they left the boat and their father and followed him.

Jesus Heals the Sick

23 Jesus went throughout Galilee,[g] teaching in their synagogues,[h] preaching the good
news[i] of the kingdom,[j] and healing every disease and sickness
among the people.[k] 24 News about
him spread all over Syria,[l] and
people brought to him all who were
ill with various diseases, those suffering severe pain, the demon-possessed,[m] those having seizures,[n]
and the paralyzed,[o] and he healed
them. 25 Large crowds from Galilee,
the Decapolis,[s] Jerusalem, Judea
and the region across the Jordan
followed him.[p]

The Beatitudes

5:3–12pp — Lk 6:20–23

5 Now when he saw the crowds,
he went up on a mountainside
and sat down. His disciples came
to him, 2 and he began to teach
them, saying:

3 "Blessed are the poor in spirit,
for theirs is the kingdom of
heaven.[q]
4 Blessed are those who mourn,
for they will be comforted.[r]
5 Blessed are the meek,
for they will inherit the
earth.[s]
6 Blessed are those who hunger
and thirst for
righteousness,
for they will be filled.[t]
7 Blessed are the merciful,
for they will be shown mercy.
8 Blessed are the pure in heart,[u]
for they will see God.[v]
9 Blessed are the peacemakers,
for they will be called sons of
God.[w]
10 Blessed are those who are
persecuted because of
righteousness,[x]
for theirs is the kingdom of
heaven.

11 "Blessed are you when people
insult you,[y] persecute you and
falsely say all kinds of evil against
you because of me. 12 Rejoice and
be glad,[z] because great is your reward in heaven, for in the same way
they persecuted the prophets who
were before you.[a]

Salt and Light

13 "You are the salt of the earth.
But if the salt loses its saltiness,
how can it be made salty again? It
is no longer good for anything, except to be thrown out and trampled
by men.[b]

14 "You are the light of the
world.[c] A city on a hill cannot be
hidden. 15 Neither do people light a
lamp and put it under a bowl. Instead they put it on its stand, and
it gives light to everyone in the
house.[d] 16 In the same way, let
your light shine before men, that
they may see your good deeds and
praise[e] your Father in heaven.

The Fulfillment of the Law

17 "Do not think that I have come
to abolish the Law or the Prophets;
I have not come to abolish them
but to fulfill them.[f] 18 I tell you the
truth, until heaven and earth dis-

4:16 [a] Isa 9:1,2; Lk 2:32 **4:17** [b] Mt 3:2 **4:18** [c] Mt 15:29; Mk 7:31; Jn 6:1 [d] Mt 16:17,18 **4:19** [e] Mk 10:21,28,52 **4:21** [f] Mt 20:20 **4:23** [g] Mk 1:39; Lk 4:15,44 [h] Mt 9:35; 13:54; Mk 1:21; Lk 4:15; Jn 6:59 [i] Mk 1:14 [j] Mt 3:2; Ac 20:25 [k] Mt 8:16; 15:30; Ac 10:38 **4:24** [l] Lk 2:2 [m] Mt 8:16,28; 9:32; 15:22; Mk 1:32; 5:15,16,18 [n] Mt 17:15 [o] Mt 8:6; 9:2; Mk 2:3 **4:25** [p] Mk 3:7,8; Lk 6:17 **5:3** [q] ver 10,19; Mt 25:34 **5:4** [r] Isa 61:2,3; Rev 7:17 **5:5** [s] Ps 37:11; Ro 4:13 **5:6** [t] Isa 55:1,2 **5:8** [u] Ps 24:3,4 [v] Heb 12:14; Rev 22:4 **5:9** [w] ver 44,45; Ro 8:14 **5:10** [x] 1Pe 3:14 **5:11** [y] 1Pe 4:14 **5:12** [z] Ac 5:41; 1Pe 4:13,16 [a] Mt 23:31,37; Ac 7:52; 1Th 2:15 **5:13** [b] Mk 9:50; Lk 14:34,35 **5:14** [c] Jn 8:12 **5:15** [d] Mk 4:21; Lk 8:16

5:16 [e] Mt 9:8 **5:17** [f] Ro 3:31

[r] *16* Isaiah 9:1,2 [s] *25* That is, the Ten Cities

appear, not the smallest letter, not
the least stroke of a pen, will by any
means disappear from the Law until everything is accomplished.[a]
19Anyone who breaks one of the
least of these commandments[b]
and teaches others to do the same
will be called least in the kingdom
of heaven, but whoever practices
and teaches these commands will
be called great in the kingdom of
heaven. **20**For I tell you that unless
your righteousness surpasses that
of the Pharisees and the teachers of
the law, you will certainly not enter
the kingdom of heaven.

Murder

5:25,26pp — Lk 12:58,59

21"You have heard that it was
said to the people long ago, 'Do not
murder,[t][c] and anyone who murders will be subject to judgment.'
22But I tell you that anyone who is
angry with his brother[u] will be subject to judgment.[d] Again, anyone
who says to his brother, 'Raca,[v]' is
answerable to the Sanhedrin.[e] But
anyone who says, 'You fool!' will be
in danger of the fire of hell.[f]
23"Therefore, if you are offering
your gift at the altar and there remember that your brother has
something against you, **24**leave
your gift there in front of the altar.
First go and be reconciled to your
brother; then come and offer your
gift.
25"Settle matters quickly with
your adversary who is taking you to
court. Do it while you are still with
him on the way, or he may hand
you over to the judge, and the judge
may hand you over to the officer,
and you may be thrown into prison.
26I tell you the truth, you will not
get out until you have paid the last
penny.[w]

Adultery

27"You have heard that it was
said, 'Do not commit adultery.'[x][g]
28But I tell you that anyone who
looks at a woman lustfully has already committed adultery with her
in his heart.[h] **29**If your right eye
causes you to sin,[i] gouge it out
and throw it away. It is better for
you to lose one part of your body
than for your whole body to be
thrown into hell. **30**And if your
right hand causes you to sin, cut it
off and throw it away. It is better for
you to lose one part of your body
than for your whole body to go into
hell.

Divorce

31"It has been said, 'Anyone who
divorces his wife must give her a
certificate of divorce.'[y][j] **32**But I
tell you that anyone who divorces
his wife, except for marital unfaithfulness, causes her to become an
adulteress, and anyone who marries the divorced woman commits
adultery.[k]

Oaths

33"Again, you have heard that it
was said to the people long ago,
'Do not break your oath,[l] but keep
the oaths you have made to the
Lord.'[m] **34**But I tell you, Do not
swear at all:[n] either by heaven, for
it is God's throne;[o] **35**or by the
earth, for it is his footstool; or by
Jerusalem, for it is the city of the
Great King.[p] **36**And do not swear
by your head, for you cannot make
even one hair white or black.
37Simply let your 'Yes' be 'Yes,'
and your 'No,' 'No';[q] anything beyond this comes from the evil
one.[r]

An Eye for an Eye

38"You have heard that it was
said, 'Eye for eye, and tooth for
tooth.'[z][s] **39**But I tell you, Do not
resist an evil person. If someone
strikes you on the right cheek, turn
to him the other also.[t] **40**And if
someone wants to sue you and take
your tunic, let him have your cloak
as well. **41**If someone forces you to
go one mile, go with him two miles.
42Give to the one who asks you,

5:18 [a]Lk 16:17
5:19 [b]Jas 2:10
5:21 [c]Ex 20:13; Dt 5:17
5:22 [d]1Jn 3:15 [e]Mt 26:59 [f]Jas 3:6
5:27 [g]Ex 20:14; Dt 5:18
5:28 [h]Pr 6:25
5:29 [i]Mt 18:6,8,9; Mk 9:42-47
5:31 [j]Dt 24:1-4
5:32 [k]Lk 16:18
5:33 [l]Lev 19:12 [m]Nu 30:2; Dt 23:21; Mt 23:16-22
5:34 [n]Jas 5:12 [o]Isa 66:1; Mt 23:22
5:35 [p]Ps 48:2
5:37 [q]Jas 5:12 [r]Mt 6:13; 13:19,38; Jn 17:15; 2Th 3:3; 1Jn 2:13,14; 3:12; 5:18,19
5:38 [s]Ex 21:24; Lev 24:20; Dt 19:21
5:39 [t]Lk 6:29; Ro 12:17,19; 1Co 6:7; 1Pe 3:9

[t]*21* Exodus 20:13 [u]*22* Some manuscripts *brother without cause* [v]*22* An Aramaic term of contempt [w]*26* Greek *kodrantes* [x]*27* Exodus 20:14 [y]*31* Deut. 24:1 [z]*38* Exodus 21:24; Lev. 24:20; Deut. 19:21

and do not turn away from the one
who wants to borrow from you.[a]

Love for Enemies

43"You have heard that it was
said, 'Love your neighbor[a][b] and
hate your enemy.'[c] 44But I tell
you: Love your enemies[b] and pray
for those who persecute you,[d]
45that you may be sons[e] of your
Father in heaven. He causes his
sun to rise on the evil and the good,
and sends rain on the righteous
and the unrighteous.[f] 46If you love
those who love you, what reward
will you get?[g] Are not even the tax
collectors doing that? 47And if you
greet only your brothers, what are
you doing more than others? Do
not even pagans do that? 48Be perfect, therefore, as your heavenly
Father is perfect.[h]

Giving to the Needy

6 "Be careful not to do your 'acts
of righteousness' before men,
to be seen by them.[i] If you do, you
will have no reward from your Father in heaven.

2"So when you give to the needy,
do not announce it with trumpets,
as the hypocrites do in the synagogues and on the streets, to be
honored by men. I tell you the
truth, they have received their reward in full. 3But when you give to
the needy, do not let your left hand
know what your right hand is doing, 4so that your giving may be in
secret. Then your Father, who sees
what is done in secret, will reward
you.[j]

Prayer

6:9–13pp — Lk 11:2–4

5"And when you pray, do not be
like the hypocrites, for they love to
pray standing[k] in the synagogues
and on the street corners to be seen
by men. I tell you the truth, they
have received their reward in full.
6But when you pray, go into your
room, close the door and pray to
your Father,[l] who is unseen. Then
your Father, who sees what is done
in secret, will reward you. 7And
when you pray, do not keep on bab-
bling[m] like pagans, for they think
they will be heard because of their
many words.[n] 8Do not be like
them, for your Father knows what
you need[o] before you ask him.

9"This, then, is how you should
pray:

"'Our Father in heaven,
hallowed be your name,
10your kingdom[p] come,
your will be done[q]
on earth as it is in heaven.
11Give us today our daily bread.[r]
12Forgive us our debts,
as we also have forgiven our
debtors.[s]
13And lead us not into
temptation,[t]
but deliver us from the evil
one.[c][u]

14For if you forgive men when they
sin against you, your heavenly Father will also forgive you.[v] 15But if
you do not forgive men their sins,
your Father will not forgive your
sins.[w]

Fasting

16"When you fast, do not look
somber[x] as the hypocrites do, for
they disfigure their faces to show
men they are fasting. I tell you the
truth, they have received their reward in full. 17But when you fast,
put oil on your head and wash your
face, 18so that it will not be obvious
to men that you are fasting, but
only to your Father, who is unseen;
and your Father, who sees what is
done in secret, will reward you.[y]

Treasures in Heaven

6:22,23pp — Lk 11:34–36

19"Do not store up for yourselves
treasures on earth,[z] where moth
and rust destroy,[a] and where
thieves break in and steal. 20But
store up for yourselves treasures in
heaven,[b] where moth and rust do
not destroy, and where thieves do

5:42 [a]Dt 15:8; Lk 6:30
5:43 [b]Lev 19:18 [c]Dt 23:6
5:44 [d]Lk 6:27,28; 23:34; Ac 7:60; Ro 12:14; 1Co 4:12; 1Pe 2:23
5:45 [e]ver 9 [f]Job 25:3
5:46 [g]Lk 6:32
5:48 [h]Lev 19:2; 1Pe 1:16
6:1 [i]Mt 23:5
6:4 [j]ver 6,18; Col 3:23,24
6:5 [k]Mk 11:25; Lk 18:10-14
6:6 [l]2Ki 4:33
6:7 [m]Ecc 5:2 [n]1Ki 18:26-29
6:8 [o]ver 32
6:10 [p]Mt 3:2 [q]Mt 26:39
6:11 [r]Pr 30:8
6:12 [s]Mt 18:21-35
6:13 [t]Jas 1:13 [u]Mt 5:37
6:14 [v]Mt 18:21-35; Mk 11:25,26; Eph 4:32; Col 3:13
6:15 [w]Mt 18:35
6:16 [x]Isa 58:5
6:18 [y]ver 4,6
6:19 [z]Pr 23:4; Heb 13:5 [a]Jas 5:2,3
6:20 [b]Mt 19:21; Lk 12:33; 18:22; 1Ti 6:19

[a]43 Lev. 19:18 [b]44 Some late manuscripts *enemies, bless those who curse you, do good to those who hate you* [c]13 Or *from evil*; some late manuscripts *one, / for yours is the kingdom and the power and the glory forever. Amen.*

not break in and steal.[a] **21**For where your treasure is, there your heart will be also.[b]

22"The eye is the lamp of the body. If your eyes are good, your whole body will be full of light. **23**But if your eyes are bad, your whole body will be full of darkness. If then the light within you is darkness, how great is that darkness!

24"No one can serve two masters. Either he will hate the one and love the other, or he will be devoted to the one and despise the other. You cannot serve both God and Money.[c]

Do Not Worry

6:25–33pp — Lk 12:22–31

25"Therefore I tell you, do not worry[d] about your life, what you will eat or drink; or about your body, what you will wear. Is not life more important than food, and the body more important than clothes? **26**Look at the birds of the air; they do not sow or reap or store away in barns, and yet your heavenly Father feeds them.[e] Are you not much more valuable than they?[f] **27**Who of you by worrying can add a single hour to his life[d]?[g]

28"And why do you worry about clothes? See how the lilies of the field grow. They do not labor or spin. **29**Yet I tell you that not even Solomon in all his splendor[h] was dressed like one of these. **30**If that is how God clothes the grass of the field, which is here today and tomorrow is thrown into the fire, will he not much more clothe you, O you of little faith?[i] **31**So do not worry, saying, 'What shall we eat?' or 'What shall we drink?' or 'What shall we wear?' **32**For the pagans run after all these things, and your heavenly Father knows that you need them.[j] **33**But seek first his kingdom and his righteousness, and all these things will be given to you as well.[k] **34**Therefore do not worry about tomorrow, for tomorrow will worry about itself. Each day has enough trouble of its own.

6:20 [a]Lk 12:33
6:21 [b]Lk 12:34
6:24 [c]Lk 16:13
6:25 [d]ver 27,28,31, 34; Lk 10:41; 12:11,22; Php 4:6; 1Pe 5:7
6:26 [e]Job 38:41; Ps 147:9 [f]Mt 10:29-31
6:27 [g]Ps 39:5
6:29 [h]1Ki 10:4-7
6:30 [i]Mt 8:26; 14:31; 16:8
6:32 [j]ver 8
6:33 [k]Mt 19:29; Mk 10:29-30
7:1 [l]Lk 6:37; Ro 14:4,10, 13; 1Co 4:5; Jas 4:11,12
7:2 [m]Mk 4:24; Lk 6:38
7:7 [n]Mt 21:22; Mk 11:24; Jn 14:13,14; 15:7,16; 16:23,24; Jas 1:5-8; 4:2, 3; 1Jn 3:22; 5:14,15
7:8 [o]Pr 8:17; Jer 29:12,13
7:12 [p]Lk 6:31 [q]Ro 13:8-10; Gal 5:14
7:13 [r]Lk 13:24

Judging Others

7:3–5pp — Lk 6:41,42

7 "Do not judge, or you too will be judged.[l] **2**For in the same way you judge others, you will be judged, and with the measure you use, it will be measured to you.[m]

3"Why do you look at the speck of sawdust in your brother's eye and pay no attention to the plank in your own eye? **4**How can you say to your brother, 'Let me take the speck out of your eye,' when all the time there is a plank in your own eye? **5**You hypocrite, first take the plank out of your own eye, and then you will see clearly to remove the speck from your brother's eye.

6"Do not give dogs what is sacred; do not throw your pearls to pigs. If you do, they may trample them under their feet, and then turn and tear you to pieces.

Ask, Seek, Knock

7:7–11pp — Lk 11:9–13

7"Ask and it will be given to you;[n] seek and you will find; knock and the door will be opened to you. **8**For everyone who asks receives; he who seeks finds;[o] and to him who knocks, the door will be opened.

9"Which of you, if his son asks for bread, will give him a stone? **10**Or if he asks for a fish, will give him a snake? **11**If you, then, though you are evil, know how to give good gifts to your children, how much more will your Father in heaven give good gifts to those who ask him! **12**So in everything, do to others what you would have them do to you,[p] for this sums up the Law and the Prophets.[q]

The Narrow and Wide Gates

13"Enter through the narrow gate.[r] For wide is the gate and broad is the road that leads to destruction, and many enter through it. **14**But small is the gate and narrow the road that leads to life, and only a few find it.

[d]27 Or *single cubit to his height*

A Tree and Its Fruit

15 "Watch out for false prophets.[a] They come to you in sheep's clothing, but inwardly they are ferocious wolves.[b] 16 By their fruit you will recognize them.[c] Do people pick grapes from thornbushes, or figs from thistles?[d] 17 Likewise every good tree bears good fruit, but a bad tree bears bad fruit. 18 A good tree cannot bear bad fruit, and a bad tree cannot bear good fruit. 19 Every tree that does not bear good fruit is cut down and thrown into the fire.[e] 20 Thus, by their fruit you will recognize them.

21 "Not everyone who says to me, 'Lord, Lord,'[f] will enter the kingdom of heaven, but only he who does the will of my Father who is in heaven.[g] 22 Many will say to me on that day,[h] 'Lord, Lord, did we not prophesy in your name, and in your name drive out demons and perform many miracles?'[i] 23 Then I will tell them plainly, 'I never knew you. Away from me, you evildoers!'[j]

The Wise and Foolish Builders

7:24–27pp — Lk 6:47–49

24 "Therefore everyone who hears these words of mine and puts them into practice[k] is like a wise man who built his house on the rock. 25 The rain came down, the streams rose, and the winds blew and beat against that house; yet it did not fall, because it had its foundation on the rock. 26 But everyone who hears these words of mine and does not put them into practice is like a foolish man who built his house on sand. 27 The rain came down, the streams rose, and the winds blew and beat against that house, and it fell with a great crash."

28 When Jesus had finished saying these things,[l] the crowds were amazed at his teaching,[m] 29 because he taught as one who had authority, and not as their teachers of the law.

7:15 [a] Jer 23:16; Mt 24:24; Mk 13:22; Lk 6:26; 2Pe 2:1; 1Jn 4:1; Rev 16:13 [b] Ac 20:29
7:16 [c] Mt 12:33; Lk 6:44 [d] Jas 3:12
7:19 [e] Mt 3:10
7:21 [f] Hos 8:2; Mt 25:11 [g] Ro 2:13; Jas 1:22
7:22 [h] Mt 10:15 [i] 1Co 13:1-3
7:23 [j] Ps 6:8; Mt 25:12,41; Lk 13:25-27
7:24 [k] Jas 1:22-25
7:28 [l] Mt 11:1; 13:53; 19:1; 26:1 [m] Mt 13:54; Mk 1:22; 6:2; Lk 4:32; Jn 7:46
8:2 [n] Lk 5:12 [o] Mt 9:18; 15:25; 18:26; 20:20
8:4 [p] Mt 9:30; Mk 5:43; 7:36; 8:30 [q] Lev 14:2-32
8:8 [r] Ps 107:20
8:10 [s] Mt 15:28
8:11 [t] Ps 107:3; Isa 49:12; 59:19; Mal 1:11 [u] Lk 13:29
8:12 [v] Mt 13:38 [w] Mt 13:42, 50; 22:13; 24:51; 25:30; Lk 13:28

The Man With Leprosy

8:2–4pp — Mk 1:40–44; Lk 5:12–14

8 When he came down from the mountainside, large crowds followed him. 2 A man with leprosy[e][n] came and knelt before him[o] and said, "Lord, if you are willing, you can make me clean."

3 Jesus reached out his hand and touched the man. "I am willing," he said. "Be clean!" Immediately he was cured[f] of his leprosy. 4 Then Jesus said to him, "See that you don't tell anyone.[p] But go, show yourself to the priest and offer the gift Moses commanded,[q] as a testimony to them."

The Faith of the Centurion

8:5–13pp — Lk 7:1–10

5 When Jesus had entered Capernaum, a centurion came to him, asking for help. 6 "Lord," he said, "my servant lies at home paralyzed and in terrible suffering."

7 Jesus said to him, "I will go and heal him."

8 The centurion replied, "Lord, I do not deserve to have you come under my roof. But just say the word, and my servant will be healed.[r] 9 For I myself am a man under authority, with soldiers under me. I tell this one, 'Go,' and he goes; and that one, 'Come,' and he comes. I say to my servant, 'Do this,' and he does it."

10 When Jesus heard this, he was astonished and said to those following him, "I tell you the truth, I have not found anyone in Israel with such great faith.[s] 11 I say to you that many will come from the east and the west,[t] and will take their places at the feast with Abraham, Isaac and Jacob in the kingdom of heaven.[u] 12 But the subjects of the kingdom[v] will be thrown outside, into the darkness, where there will be weeping and gnashing of teeth."[w]

13 Then Jesus said to the centurion, "Go! It will be done just as you

[e]2 The Greek word was used for various diseases affecting the skin—not necessarily leprosy. [f]3 Greek *made clean*

believed it would."[a] And his servant was healed at that very hour.

Jesus Heals Many

8:14–16pp — Mk 1:29–34; Lk 4:38–41

14When Jesus came into Peter's house, he saw Peter's mother-in-law lying in bed with a fever. 15He touched her hand and the fever left her, and she got up and began to wait on him.

16When evening came, many who were demon-possessed were brought to him, and he drove out the spirits with a word and healed all the sick.[b] 17This was to fulfill[c] what was spoken through the prophet Isaiah:

> "He took up our infirmities
> and carried our diseases."[g][d]

The Cost of Following Jesus

8:19–22pp — Lk 9:57–60

18When Jesus saw the crowd around him, he gave orders to cross to the other side of the lake.[e] 19Then a teacher of the law came to him and said, "Teacher, I will follow you wherever you go."

20Jesus replied, "Foxes have holes and birds of the air have nests, but the Son of Man[f] has no place to lay his head."

21Another disciple said to him, "Lord, first let me go and bury my father."

22But Jesus told him, "Follow me,[g] and let the dead bury their own dead."

Jesus Calms the Storm

8:23–27pp — Mk 4:36–41; Lk 8:22–25
8:23–27Ref — Mt 14:22–33

23Then he got into the boat and his disciples followed him. 24Without warning, a furious storm came up on the lake, so that the waves swept over the boat. But Jesus was sleeping. 25The disciples went and woke him, saying, "Lord, save us! We're going to drown!"

26He replied, "You of little faith,[h] why are you so afraid?" Then he got up and rebuked the winds and the waves, and it was completely calm.[i]

8:13 [a]Mt 9:22
8:16 [b]Mt 4:23,24
8:17 [c]Mt 1:22 [d]Isa 53:4
8:18 [e]Mk 4:35
8:20 [f]Da 7:13; Mt 12:8,32, 40; 16:13,27, 28; 17:9; 19:28; Mk 2:10; 8:31
8:22 [g]Mt 4:19
8:26 [h]Mt 6:30 [i]Ps 65:7; 89:9; 107:29
8:28 [j]Mt 4:24
8:29 [k]Jdg 11:12; 2Sa 16:10; 1Ki 17:18; Mk 1:24; Lk 4:34; Jn 2:4 [l]2Pe 2:4
8:34 [m]Lk 5:8; Ac 16:39
9:1 [n]Mt 4:13
9:2 [o]Mt 4:24 [p]ver 22 [q]Jn 16:33 [r]Lk 7:48
9:3 [s]Mt 26:65; Jn 10:33
9:4 [t]Ps 94:11; Mt 12:25; Lk 6:8; 9:47; 11:17

27The men were amazed and asked, "What kind of man is this? Even the winds and the waves obey him!"

The Healing of Two Demon-possessed Men

8:28–34pp — Mk 5:1–17; Lk 8:26–37

28When he arrived at the other side in the region of the Gadarenes,[h] two demon-possessed[j] men coming from the tombs met him. They were so violent that no one could pass that way. 29"What do you want with us,[k] Son of God?" they shouted. "Have you come here to torture us before the appointed time?"[l]

30Some distance from them a large herd of pigs was feeding. 31The demons begged Jesus, "If you drive us out, send us into the herd of pigs."

32He said to them, "Go!" So they came out and went into the pigs, and the whole herd rushed down the steep bank into the lake and died in the water. 33Those tending the pigs ran off, went into the town and reported all this, including what had happened to the demon-possessed men. 34Then the whole town went out to meet Jesus. And when they saw him, they pleaded with him to leave their region.[m]

Jesus Heals a Paralytic

9:2–8pp — Mk 2:3–12; Lk 5:18–26

9 Jesus stepped into a boat, crossed over and came to his own town.[n] 2Some men brought to him a paralytic,[o] lying on a mat. When Jesus saw their faith,[p] he said to the paralytic, "Take heart,[q] son; your sins are forgiven."[r]

3At this, some of the teachers of the law said to themselves, "This fellow is blaspheming!"[s]

4Knowing their thoughts,[t] Jesus said, "Why do you entertain evil thoughts in your hearts? 5Which is easier: to say, 'Your sins are forgiven,' or to say, 'Get up and

[g]17 Isaiah 53:4 [h]28 Some manuscripts *Gergesenes*; others *Gerasenes*

walk'? **6**But so that you may know that the Son of Man[a] has authority on earth to forgive sins. . . ." Then he said to the paralytic, "Get up, take your mat and go home." **7**And the man got up and went home. **8**When the crowd saw this, they were filled with awe; and they praised God,[b] who had given such authority to men.

The Calling of Matthew

9:9-13pp — Mk 2:14-17; Lk 5:27-32

9As Jesus went on from there, he saw a man named Matthew sitting at the tax collector's booth. "Follow me," he told him, and Matthew got up and followed him.

10While Jesus was having dinner at Matthew's house, many tax collectors and "sinners" came and ate with him and his disciples. **11**When the Pharisees saw this, they asked his disciples, "Why does your teacher eat with tax collectors and 'sinners'?"[c]

12On hearing this, Jesus said, "It is not the healthy who need a doctor, but the sick. **13**But go and learn what this means: 'I desire mercy, not sacrifice.'[i][d] For I have not come to call the righteous, but sinners."[e]

Jesus Questioned About Fasting

9:14-17pp — Mk 2:18-22; Lk 5:33-39

14Then John's disciples came and asked him, "How is it that we and the Pharisees fast,[f] but your disciples do not fast?"

15Jesus answered, "How can the guests of the bridegroom mourn while he is with them?[g] The time will come when the bridegroom will be taken from them; then they will fast.[h]

16"No one sews a patch of unshrunk cloth on an old garment, for the patch will pull away from the garment, making the tear worse. **17**Neither do men pour new wine into old wineskins. If they do, the skins will burst, the wine will run out and the wineskins will be ruined. No, they pour new wine into new wineskins, and both are preserved."

A Dead Girl and a Sick Woman

9:18-26pp — Mk 5:22-43; Lk 8:41-56

18While he was saying this, a ruler came and knelt before him[i] and said, "My daughter has just died. But come and put your hand on her,[j] and she will live." **19**Jesus got up and went with him, and so did his disciples.

20Just then a woman who had been subject to bleeding for twelve years came up behind him and touched the edge of his cloak.[k] **21**She said to herself, "If I only touch his cloak, I will be healed."

22Jesus turned and saw her. "Take heart, daughter," he said, "your faith has healed you."[l] And the woman was healed from that moment.[m]

23When Jesus entered the ruler's house and saw the flute players and the noisy crowd,[n] **24**he said, "Go away. The girl is not dead[o] but asleep."[p] But they laughed at him. **25**After the crowd had been put outside, he went in and took the girl by the hand, and she got up. **26**News of this spread through all that region.[q]

Jesus Heals the Blind and Mute

27As Jesus went on from there, two blind men followed him, calling out, "Have mercy on us, Son of David!"[r]

28When he had gone indoors, the blind men came to him, and he asked them, "Do you believe that I am able to do this?"

"Yes, Lord," they replied.

29Then he touched their eyes and said, "According to your faith will it be done to you";[s] **30**and their sight was restored. Jesus warned them sternly, "See that no one knows about this."[t] **31**But they went out and spread the news about him all over that region.[u]

32While they were going out, a

9:6 [a] Mt 8:20
9:8 [b] Mt 5:16; 15:31; Lk 7:16; 13:13; 17:15; 23:47; Jn 15:8; Ac 4:21; 11:18; 21:20
9:11 [c] Mt 11:19; Lk 5:30; 15:2; Gal 2:15
9:13 [d] Hos 6:6; Mic 6:6-8; Mt 12:7 [e] 1Ti 1:15
9:14 [f] Lk 18:12
9:15 [g] Jn 3:29 [h] Ac 13:2,3; 14:23
9:18 [i] Mt 8:2 [j] Mk 5:23
9:20 [k] Mt 14:36; Mk 3:10
9:22 [l] Mk 10:52; Lk 7:50; 17:19; 18:42 [m] Mt 15:28
9:23 [n] 2Ch 35:25; Jer 9:17,18
9:24 [o] Ac 20:10 [p] Jn 11:11-14
9:26 [q] Mt 4:24
9:27 [r] Mt 15:22; Mk 10:47; Lk 18:38-39
9:29 [s] ver 22
9:30 [t] Mt 8:4
9:31 [u] ver 26; Mk 7:36

[i] 13 Hosea 6:6

man who was demon-possessed[a]
and could not talk[b] was brought to
Jesus. 33And when the demon was
driven out, the man who had been
mute spoke. The crowd was
amazed and said, "Nothing like
this has ever been seen in Israel."[c]
34But the Pharisees said, "It is by
the prince of demons that he drives
out demons."[d]

The Workers Are Few

35Jesus went through all the
towns and villages, teaching in
their synagogues, preaching the
good news of the kingdom and
healing every disease and sickness.[e] 36When he saw the crowds,
he had compassion on them,[f] because they were harassed and helpless, like sheep without a shepherd.[g] 37Then he said to his disciples, "The harvest[h] is plentiful but
the workers are few.[i] 38Ask the
Lord of the harvest, therefore, to
send out workers into his harvest
field."

Jesus Sends Out the Twelve

10:2–4pp — Mk 3:16–19; Lk 6:14–16; Ac 1:13
10:9–15pp — Mk 6:8–11; Lk 9:3–5; 10:4–12
10:19–22pp — Mk 13:11–13; Lk 21:12–17
10:26–33pp — Lk 12:2–9
10:34,35pp — Lk 12:51–53

10 He called his twelve disciples to him and gave them
authority to drive out evil[i] spirits[j]
and to heal every disease and sickness.
2These are the names of the
twelve apostles: first, Simon (who
is called Peter) and his brother Andrew; James son of Zebedee, and
his brother John; 3Philip and Bartholomew; Thomas and Matthew
the tax collector; James son of Alphaeus, and Thaddaeus; 4Simon
the Zealot and Judas Iscariot, who
betrayed him.[k]
5These twelve Jesus sent out
with the following instructions:
"Do not go among the Gentiles or
enter any town of the Samaritans.[l]
6Go rather to the lost sheep of Israel.[m] 7As you go, preach this message: 'The kingdom of heaven[n] is
near.' 8Heal the sick, raise the
dead, cleanse those who have leprosy,[k] drive out demons. Freely
you have received, freely give. 9Do
not take along any gold or silver or
copper in your belts;[o] 10take no
bag for the journey, or extra tunic,
or sandals or a staff; for the worker
is worth his keep.[p]
11"Whatever town or village you
enter, search for some worthy person there and stay at his house until you leave. 12As you enter the
home, give it your greeting.[q] 13If
the home is deserving, let your
peace rest on it; if it is not, let your
peace return to you. 14If anyone
will not welcome you or listen to
your words, shake the dust off your
feet[r] when you leave that home or
town. 15I tell you the truth, it will
be more bearable for Sodom and
Gomorrah[s] on the day of judgment[t] than for that town.[u] 16I am
sending you out like sheep among
wolves.[v] Therefore be as shrewd as
snakes and as innocent as doves.[w]
17"Be on your guard against
men; they will hand you over to the
local councils[x] and flog you in
their synagogues.[y] 18On my account you will be brought before
governors and kings[z] as witnesses
to them and to the Gentiles. 19But
when they arrest you, do not worry
about what to say or how to say it.[a]
At that time you will be given what
to say, 20for it will not be you
speaking, but the Spirit of your Father[b] speaking through you.
21"Brother will betray brother to
death, and a father his child; children will rebel against their parents[c] and have them put to death.
22All men will hate you because of
me, but he who stands firm to the
end will be saved.[d] 23When you are
persecuted in one place, flee to another. I tell you the truth, you will
not finish going through the cities
of Israel before the Son of Man
comes.
24"A student is not above his
teacher, nor a servant above his
master.[e] 25It is enough for the stu-

9:32 [a]Mt 4:24 [b]Mt 12:22-24 **9:33** [c]Mk 2:12 **9:34** [d]Mt 12:24; Lk 11:15 **9:35** [e]Mt 4:23 **9:36** [f]Mt 14:14 [g]Nu 27:17; Eze 34:5,6; Zec 10:2; Mk 6:34 **9:37** [h]Jn 4:35 [i]Lk 10:2 **10:1** [j]Mk 3:13-15; Lk 9:1 **10:4** [k]Mt 26:14-16, 25,47; Jn 13:2,26,27 **10:5** [l]2Ki 17:24; Lk 9:52; Jn 4:4-26,39, 40; Ac 8:5,25 **10:6** [m]Jer 50:6; Mt 15:24 **10:7** [n]Mt 3:2 **10:9** [o]Lk 22:35 **10:10** [p]1Ti 5:18 **10:12** [q]1Sa 25:6 **10:14** [r]Ne 5:13; Lk 10:11; Ac 13:51 **10:15** [s]2Pe 2:6 [t]Mt 12:36; 2Pe 2:9; 1Jn 4:17 [u]Mt 11:22,24 **10:16** [v]Lk 10:3 [w]Ro 16:19 **10:17** [x]Mt 5:22 [y]Mt 23:34; Mk 13:9; Ac 5:40; 26:11 **10:18** [z]Ac 25:24-26 **10:19** [a]Ex 4:12 **10:20** [b]Ac 4:8 **10:21** [c]ver 35,36; Mic 7:6 **10:22** [d]Mt 24:13; Mk 13:13 **10:24** [e]Lk 6:40; Jn 13:16; 15:20

i1 Greek *unclean* k8 The Greek word was used for various diseases affecting the skin—not necessarily leprosy.

dent to be like his teacher, and the servant like his master. If the head of the house has been called Beelzebub,[l][a] how much more the members of his household!

26"So do not be afraid of them. There is nothing concealed that will not be disclosed, or hidden that will not be made known.[b] 27What I tell you in the dark, speak in the daylight; what is whispered in your ear, proclaim from the roofs. 28Do not be afraid of those who kill the body but cannot kill the soul. Rather, be afraid of the One[c] who can destroy both soul and body in hell. 29Are not two sparrows sold for a penny[m]? Yet not one of them will fall to the ground apart from the will of your Father. 30And even the very hairs of your head are all numbered.[d] 31So don't be afraid; you are worth more than many sparrows.[e]

32"Whoever acknowledges me before men,[f] I will also acknowledge him before my Father in heaven. 33But whoever disowns me before men, I will disown him before my Father in heaven.[g]

34"Do not suppose that I have come to bring peace to the earth. I did not come to bring peace, but a sword. 35For I have come to turn

" 'a man against his father,
a daughter against her mother,
a daughter-in-law against her mother-in-law[h] —
36 a man's enemies will be the members of his own household.'[n][i]

37"Anyone who loves his father or mother more than me is not worthy of me; anyone who loves his son or daughter more than me is not worthy of me;[j] 38and anyone who does not take his cross and follow me is not worthy of me.[k] 39Whoever finds his life will lose it, and whoever loses his life for my sake will find it.[l]

40"He who receives you receives me,[m] and he who receives me receives the one who sent me.[n] 41Anyone who receives a prophet because he is a prophet will receive a prophet's reward, and anyone who receives a righteous man because he is a righteous man will receive a righteous man's reward. 42And if anyone gives even a cup of cold water to one of these little ones because he is my disciple, I tell you the truth, he will certainly not lose his reward."[o]

Jesus and John the Baptist

11:2-19pp — Lk 7:18-35

11 After Jesus had finished instructing his twelve disciples,[p] he went on from there to teach and preach in the towns of Galilee.[o]

2When John heard in prison[q] what Christ was doing, he sent his disciples 3to ask him, "Are you the one who was to come,[r] or should we expect someone else?"

4Jesus replied, "Go back and report to John what you hear and see: 5The blind receive sight, the lame walk, those who have leprosy[p] are cured, the deaf hear, the dead are raised, and the good news is preached to the poor.[s] 6Blessed is the man who does not fall away on account of me."[t]

7As John's[u] disciples were leaving, Jesus began to speak to the crowd about John: "What did you go out into the desert to see? A reed swayed by the wind? 8If not, what did you go out to see? A man dressed in fine clothes? No, those who wear fine clothes are in kings' palaces. 9Then what did you go out to see? A prophet?[v] Yes, I tell you, and more than a prophet. 10This is the one about whom it is written:

" 'I will send my messenger ahead of you,
who will prepare your way before you.'[q][w]

10:25 [a]Mk 3:22
10:26 [b]Mk 4:22; Lk 8:17
10:28 [c]Isa 8:12,13; Heb 10:31
10:30 [d]1Sa 14:45; 2Sa 14:11; Lk 21:18; Ac 27:34
10:31 [e]Mt 12:12
10:32 [f]Ro 10:9
10:33 [g]Mk 8:38; 2Ti 2:12
10:35 [h]ver 21
10:36 [i]Mic 7:6
10:37 [j]Lk 14:26
10:38 [k]Mt 16:24; Lk 14:27
10:39 [l]Lk 17:33; Jn 12:25
10:40 [m]Mt 18:5; Gal 4:14 [n]Lk 9:48; Jn 12:44; 13:20
10:42 [o]Mt 25:40; Mk 9:41; Heb 6:10
11:1 [p]Mt 7:28
11:2 [q]Mt 14:3
11:3 [r]Ps 118:26; Jn 11:27; Heb 10:37
11:5 [s]Isa 35:4-6; 61:1; Lk 4:18, 19
11:6 [t]Mt 13:21
11:7 [u]Mt 3:1
11:9 [v]Mt 21:26; Lk 1:76
11:10 [w]Mal 3:1; Mk 1:2

[l]*25* Greek *Beezeboul* or *Beelzeboul*
[m]*29* Greek *an assarion* [n]*36* Micah 7:6
[o]*1* Greek *in their towns* [p]*5* The Greek word was used for various diseases affecting the skin—not necessarily leprosy. [q]*10* Mal. 3:1

11I tell you the truth: Among those
born of women there has not risen
anyone greater than John the Baptist; yet he who is least in the kingdom of heaven is greater than he.
12From the days of John the Baptist until now, the kingdom of
heaven has been forcefully advancing, and forceful men lay hold of it.
13For all the Prophets and the Law
prophesied until John. 14And if you
are willing to accept it, he is the
Elijah who was to come.[a] 15He
who has ears, let him hear.[b]

16"To what can I compare this
generation? They are like children
sitting in the marketplaces and
calling out to others:

17" 'We played the flute for you,
and you did not dance;
we sang a dirge,
and you did not mourn.'

18For John came neither eating[c]
nor drinking,[d] and they say, 'He
has a demon.' 19The Son of Man
came eating and drinking, and they
say, 'Here is a glutton and a drunkard, a friend of tax collectors and
"sinners." '[e] But wisdom is proved
right by her actions."

Woe on Unrepentant Cities

11:21–23pp – Lk 10:13–15

20Then Jesus began to denounce
the cities in which most of his miracles had been performed, because
they did not repent. 21"Woe to you,
Korazin! Woe to you, Bethsaida![f]
If the miracles that were performed
in you had been performed in Tyre
and Sidon,[g] they would have repented long ago in sackcloth and
ashes.[h] 22But I tell you, it will be
more bearable for Tyre and Sidon
on the day of judgment than for
you.[i] 23And you, Capernaum,[j]
will you be lifted up to the skies?
No, you will go down to the
depths.[r][k] If the miracles that
were performed in you had been
performed in Sodom, it would have
remained to this day. 24But I tell
you that it will be more bearable for
Sodom on the day of judgment
than for you."[l]

11:14 [a]Mal 4:5; Mt 17:10-13; Mk 9:11-13; Lk 1:17; Jn 1:21
11:15 [b]Mt 13:9,43; Mk 4:23; Lk 14:35; Rev 2:7
11:18 [c]Mt 3:4 [d]Lk 1:15
11:19 [e]Mt 9:11
11:21 [f]Mk 6:45; Lk 9:10; Jn 12:21 [g]Mt 15:21; Lk 6:17; Ac 12:20 [h]Jnh 3:5-9
11:22 [i]ver 24; Mt 10:15
11:23 [j]Mt 4:13 [k]Isa 14:13-15
11:24 [l]Mt 10:15
11:25 [m]Lk 22:42; Jn 11:41 [n]1Co 1:26-29
11:27 [o]Mt 28:18 [p]Jn 3:35; 13:3; 17:2 [q]Jn 10:15
11:28 [r]Jn 7:37
11:29 [s]Jn 13:15; Php 2:5; 1Pe 2:21; 1Jn 2:6 [t]Jer 6:16
11:30 [u]1Jn 5:3
12:1 [v]Dt 23:25
12:2 [w]ver 10; Lk 13:14; 14:3; Jn 5:10; 7:23; 9:16
12:3 [x]1Sa 21:6
12:4 [y]Lev 24:5,9
12:5 [z]Nu 28:9,10; Jn 7:22,23
12:6 [a]ver 41,42
12:7 [b]Hos 6:6; Mic 6:6-8; Mt 9:13
12:8 [c]Mt 8:20

Rest for the Weary

11:25–27pp – Lk 10:21,22

25At that time Jesus said, "I
praise you, Father,[m] Lord of heav-
en and earth, because you have
hidden these things from the wise
and learned, and revealed them to
little children.[n] 26Yes, Father, for
this was your good pleasure.

27"All things have been committed to me[o] by my Father.[p] No one
knows the Son except the Father,
and no one knows the Father except the Son and those to whom
the Son chooses to reveal him.[q]

28"Come to me,[r] all you who are
weary and burdened, and I will give
you rest. 29Take my yoke upon you
and learn from me,[s] for I am gentle
and humble in heart, and you will
find rest for your souls.[t] 30For my
yoke is easy and my burden is
light."[u]

Lord of the Sabbath

12:1–8pp – Mk 2:23–28; Lk 6:1–5
12:9–14pp – Mk 3:1–6; Lk 6:6–11

12 At that time Jesus went
through the grainfields on
the Sabbath. His disciples were
hungry and began to pick some
heads of grain[v] and eat them.
2When the Pharisees saw this, they
said to him, "Look! Your disciples
are doing what is unlawful on the
Sabbath."[w]

3He answered, "Haven't you
read what David did when he and
his companions were hungry?[x]
4He entered the house of God, and
he and his companions ate the consecrated bread—which was not
lawful for them to do, but only for
the priests.[y] 5Or haven't you read
in the Law that on the Sabbath the
priests in the temple desecrate the
day[z] and yet are innocent? 6I tell
you that one[s] greater than the
temple is here.[a] 7If you had known
what these words mean, 'I desire
mercy, not sacrifice,'[t][b] you would
not have condemned the innocent.
8For the Son of Man[c] is Lord of the
Sabbath."

[r]23 Greek *Hades* [s]6 Or *something*; also in verses 41 and 42 [t]7 Hosea 6:6

9Going on from that place, he
went into their synagogue, 10and a
man with a shriveled hand was
there. Looking for a reason to accuse Jesus, they asked him, "Is it
lawful to heal on the Sabbath?"[a]
11He said to them, "If any of you
has a sheep and it falls into a pit on
the Sabbath, will you not take hold
of it and lift it out?[b] 12How much
more valuable is a man than a
sheep![c] Therefore it is lawful to do
good on the Sabbath."
13Then he said to the man,
"Stretch out your hand." So he
stretched it out and it was completely restored, just as sound as
the other. 14But the Pharisees went
out and plotted how they might kill
Jesus.[d]

God's Chosen Servant

15Aware of this, Jesus withdrew
from that place. Many followed
him, and he healed all their sick,[e]
16warning them not to tell who he
was.[f] 17This was to fulfill what
was spoken through the prophet
Isaiah:

18"Here is my servant whom I
have chosen,
the one I love, in whom I
delight;[g]
I will put my Spirit on him,
and he will proclaim justice
to the nations.
19He will not quarrel or cry out;
no one will hear his voice in
the streets.
20A bruised reed he will not
break,
and a smoldering wick he
will not snuff out,
till he leads justice to victory.
21 In his name the nations will
put their hope."[u][h]

Jesus and Beelzebub

12:25–29pp — Mk 3:23–27; Lk 11:17–22

22Then they brought him a demon-possessed man who was blind
and mute, and Jesus healed him,
so that he could both talk and
see.[i] 23All the people were astonished and said, "Could this be the
Son of David?"[j]
24But when the Pharisees heard
this, they said, "It is only by Beelzebub,[v][k] the prince of demons, that
this fellow drives out demons."[l]
25Jesus knew their thoughts[m]
and said to them, "Every kingdom
divided against itself will be ruined, and every city or household
divided against itself will not
stand. 26If Satan[n] drives out Satan,
he is divided against himself. How
then can his kingdom stand? 27And
if I drive out demons by Beelzebub,
by whom do your people[o] drive
them out? So then, they will be
your judges. 28But if I drive out demons by the Spirit of God, then the
kingdom of God has come upon
you.
29"Or again, how can anyone enter a strong man's house and carry
off his possessions unless he first
ties up the strong man? Then he
can rob his house.
30"He who is not with me is
against me, and he who does not
gather with me scatters.[p] 31And so
I tell you, every sin and blasphemy
will be forgiven men, but the blasphemy against the Spirit will not be
forgiven.[q] 32Anyone who speaks a
word against the Son of Man will be
forgiven, but anyone who speaks
against the Holy Spirit will not be
forgiven, either in this age[r] or in
the age to come.[s]
33"Make a tree good and its fruit
will be good, or make a tree bad
and its fruit will be bad, for a tree
is recognized by its fruit.[t] 34You
brood of vipers,[u] how can you who
are evil say anything good? For out
of the overflow of the heart the
mouth speaks.[v] 35The good man
brings good things out of the good
stored up in him, and the evil man
brings evil things out of the evil
stored up in him. 36But I tell you
that men will have to give account
on the day of judgment for every
careless word they have spoken.
37For by your words you will be ac-
quitted, and by your words you will
be condemned."

12:10 [a]ver 2; Lk 13:14; 14:3; Jn 9:16
12:11 [b]Lk 14:5
12:12 [c]Mt 10:31
12:14 [d]Mt 26:4; 27:1; Mk 3:6; Lk 6:11; Jn 5:18; 11:53
12:15 [e]Mt 4:23
12:16 [f]Mt 8:4
12:18 [g]Mt 3:17
12:21 [h]Isa 42:1-4
12:22 [i]Mt 4:24; 9:32-33
12:23 [j]Mt 9:27
12:24 [k]Mk 3:22 [l]Mt 9:34
12:25 [m]Mt 9:4
12:26 [n]Mt 4:10
12:27 [o]Ac 19:13
12:30 [p]Mk 9:40; Lk 11:23
12:31 [q]Mk 3:28,29; Lk 12:10
12:32 [r]Tit 2:12 [s]Mk 10:30; Lk 20:34,35; Eph 1:21; Heb 6:5
12:33 [t]Mt 7:16,17; Lk 6:43,44
12:34 [u]Mt 3:7; 23:33 [v]Mt 15:18; Lk 6:45

[u]*21* Isaiah 42:1-4 [v]*24* Greek *Beezeboul* or *Beelzeboul*; also in verse 27

The Sign of Jonah

12:39–42pp — Lk 11:29–32
12:43–45pp — Lk 11:24–26

38Then some of the Pharisees and teachers of the law said to him, "Teacher, we want to see a miraculous sign from you."[a]

39He answered, "A wicked and adulterous generation asks for a miraculous sign! But none will be given it except the sign of the prophet Jonah.[b] **40**For as Jonah was three days and three nights in the belly of a huge fish,[c] so the Son of Man[d] will be three days and three nights in the heart of the earth.[e] **41**The men of Nineveh[f] will stand up at the judgment with this generation and condemn it; for they repented at the preaching of Jonah,[g] and now one[w] greater than Jonah is here. **42**The Queen of the South will rise at the judgment with this generation and condemn it; for she came[h] from the ends of the earth to listen to Solomon's wisdom, and now one greater than Solomon is here.

43"When an evil[x] spirit comes out of a man, it goes through arid places seeking rest and does not find it. **44**Then it says, 'I will return to the house I left.' When it arrives, it finds the house unoccupied, swept clean and put in order. **45**Then it goes and takes with it seven other spirits more wicked than itself, and they go in and live there. And the final condition of that man is worse than the first.[i] That is how it will be with this wicked generation."

Jesus' Mother and Brothers

12:46–50pp — Mk 3:31–35; Lk 8:19–21

46While Jesus was still talking to the crowd, his mother[j] and brothers[k] stood outside, wanting to speak to him. **47**Someone told him, "Your mother and brothers are standing outside, wanting to speak to you."[y]

48He replied to him, "Who is my mother, and who are my brothers?" **49**Pointing to his disciples, he said, "Here are my mother and my brothers. **50**For whoever does the will of my Father in heaven[l] is my brother and sister and mother."

The Parable of the Sower

13:1–15pp — Mk 4:1–12; Lk 8:4–10
13:16,17pp — Lk 10:23,24
13:18–23pp — Mk 4:13–20; Lk 8:11–15

13 That same day Jesus went out of the house[m] and sat by the lake. **2**Such large crowds gathered around him that he got into a boat[n] and sat in it, while all the people stood on the shore. **3**Then he told them many things in parables, saying: "A farmer went out to sow his seed. **4**As he was scattering the seed, some fell along the path, and the birds came and ate it up. **5**Some fell on rocky places, where it did not have much soil. It sprang up quickly, because the soil was shallow. **6**But when the sun came up, the plants were scorched, and they withered because they had no root. **7**Other seed fell among thorns, which grew up and choked the plants. **8**Still other seed fell on good soil, where it produced a crop—a hundred,[o] sixty or thirty times what was sown. **9**He who has ears, let him hear."[p]

10The disciples came to him and asked, "Why do you speak to the people in parables?"

11He replied, "The knowledge of the secrets of the kingdom of heaven has been given to you,[q] but not to them. **12**Whoever has will be given more, and he will have an abundance. Whoever does not have, even what he has will be taken from him.[r] **13**This is why I speak to them in parables:

> "Though seeing, they do not
> see;
> though hearing, they do not
> hear or understand.[s]

14In them is fulfilled the prophecy of Isaiah:

> " 'You will be ever hearing but
> never understanding;

12:38 [a]Mt 16:1; Mk 8:11,12; Lk 11:16; Jn 2:18; 6:30; 1Co 1:22
12:39 [b]Mt 16:4; Lk 11:29
12:40 [c]Jnh 1:17 [d]Mt 8:20 [e]Mt 16:21
12:41 [f]Jnh 1:2 [g]Jnh 3:5
12:42 [h]1Ki 10:1; 2Ch 9:1
12:45 [i]2Pe 2:20
12:46 [j]Mt 1:18; 2:11,13,14, 20; Lk 1:43; 2:33,34,48, 51; Jn 2:1,5; 19:25,26 [k]Mt 13:55; Jn 2:12; 7:3, 5; Ac 1:14; 1Co 9:5; Gal 1:19
12:50 [l]Jn 15:14
13:1 [m]ver 36; Mt 9:28
13:2 [n]Lk 5:3
13:8 [o]Ge 26:12
13:9 [p]Mt 11:15
13:11 [q]Mt 11:25; 16:17; 19:11; Jn 6:65; 1Co 2:10,14; Col 1:27; 1Jn 2:20,27
13:12 [r]Mt 25:29; Lk 19:26
13:13 [s]Dt 29:4; Jer 5:21; Eze 12:2

[w]41 Or *something*; also in verse 42
[x]43 Greek *unclean*
[y]47 Some manuscripts do not have verse 47.

you will be ever seeing but
never perceiving.
15For this people's heart has
become calloused;
they hardly hear with their
ears,
and they have closed their
eyes.
Otherwise they might see with
their eyes,
hear with their ears,
understand with their hearts
and turn, and I would heal
them.'[z][a]

16But blessed are your eyes because they see, and your ears because they hear.[b] 17For I tell you
the truth, many prophets and righteous men longed to see what you
see[c] but did not see it, and to hear
what you hear but did not hear it.
18"Listen then to what the parable of the sower means: 19When
anyone hears the message about
the kingdom[d] and does not understand it, the evil one[e] comes and
snatches away what was sown in
his heart. This is the seed sown
along the path. 20The one who received the seed that fell on rocky
places is the man who hears the
word and at once receives it with
joy. 21But since he has no root, he
lasts only a short time. When trouble or persecution comes because
of the word, he quickly falls away.[f]
22The one who received the seed
that fell among the thorns is the
man who hears the word, but the
worries of this life and the deceitfulness of wealth[g] choke it, making it unfruitful. 23But the one who
received the seed that fell on good
soil is the man who hears the word
and understands it. He produces a
crop, yielding a hundred, sixty or
thirty times what was sown."[h]

The Parable of the Weeds

24Jesus told them another parable: "The kingdom of heaven is
like[i] a man who sowed good seed
in his field. 25But while everyone
was sleeping, his enemy came and
sowed weeds among the wheat,
and went away. 26When the wheat
sprouted and formed heads, then
the weeds also appeared.
27"The owner's servants came
to him and said, 'Sir, didn't you
sow good seed in your field?
Where then did the weeds come
from?'
28" 'An enemy did this,' he replied.
"The servants asked him, 'Do
you want us to go and pull them
up?'
29" 'No,' he answered, 'because
while you are pulling the weeds,
you may root up the wheat with
them. 30Let both grow together until the harvest. At that time I will
tell the harvesters: First collect the
weeds and tie them in bundles to
be burned; then gather the wheat
and bring it into my barn.' "[j]

The Parables of the Mustard Seed and the Yeast

13:31,32pp — Mk 4:30–32
13:31–33pp — Lk 13:18–21

31He told them another parable:
"The kingdom of heaven is like[k] a
mustard seed,[l] which a man took
and planted in his field. 32Though
it is the smallest of all your seeds,
yet when it grows, it is the largest of
garden plants and becomes a tree,
so that the birds of the air come
and perch in its branches."[m]
33He told them still another parable: "The kingdom of heaven is
like[n] yeast that a woman took and
mixed into a large amount[a] of
flour[o] until it worked all through
the dough."[p]
34Jesus spoke all these things to
the crowd in parables; he did not
say anything to them without using
a parable.[q] 35So was fulfilled what
was spoken through the prophet:

"I will open my mouth in
parables,
I will utter things hidden
since the creation of the
world."[b][r]

13:15 [a]Isa 6:9,10; Jn 12:40; Ac 28:26,27; Ro 11:8
13:16 [b]Mt 16:17
13:17 [c]Jn 8:56; Heb 11:13; 1Pe 1:10-12
13:19 [d]Mt 4:23 [e]Mt 5:37
13:21 [f]Mt 11:6
13:22 [g]Mt 19:23; 1Ti 6:9,10,17
13:23 [h]ver 8
13:24 [i]ver 31,33,45, 47; Mt 18:23; 20:1; 22:2; 25:1; Mk 4:26,30
13:30 [j]Mt 3:12
13:31 [k]ver 24 [l]Mt 17:20; Lk 17:6
13:32 [m]Ps 104:12; Eze 17:23; 31:6; Da 4:12
13:33 [n]ver 24 [o]Ge 18:6 [p]Gal 5:9
13:34 [q]Mk 4:33; Jn 16:25
13:35 [r]Ps 78:2; Ro 16:25,26; 1Co 2:7; Eph 3:9; Col 1:26

[z]*15* Isaiah 6:9,10 [a]*33* Greek *three satas* (probably about 1/2 bushel or 22 liters)
[b]*35* Psalm 78:2

The Parable of the Weeds Explained

36Then he left the crowd and went into the house. His disciples came to him and said, "Explain to us the parable[a] of the weeds in the field."

37He answered, "The one who sowed the good seed is the Son of Man.[b] **38**The field is the world, and the good seed stands for the sons of the kingdom. The weeds are the sons of the evil one,[c] **39**and the enemy who sows them is the devil. The harvest[d] is the end of the age,[e] and the harvesters are angels.[f]

40"As the weeds are pulled up and burned in the fire, so it will be at the end of the age. **41**The Son of Man[g] will send out his angels,[h] and they will weed out of his kingdom everything that causes sin and all who do evil. **42**They will throw them into the fiery furnace, where there will be weeping and gnashing of teeth.[i] **43**Then the righteous will shine like the sun[j] in the kingdom of their Father. He who has ears, let him hear.[k]

The Parables of the Hidden Treasure and the Pearl

44"The kingdom of heaven is like[l] treasure hidden in a field. When a man found it, he hid it again, and then in his joy went and sold all he had and bought that field.[m]

45"Again, the kingdom of heaven is like[n] a merchant looking for fine pearls. **46**When he found one of great value, he went away and sold everything he had and bought it.

The Parable of the Net

47"Once again, the kingdom of heaven is like[o] a net that was let down into the lake and caught all kinds[p] of fish. **48**When it was full, the fishermen pulled it up on the shore. Then they sat down and collected the good fish in baskets, but threw the bad away. **49**This is how it will be at the end of the age. The angels will come and separate the wicked from the righteous[q] **50**and throw them into the fiery furnace, where there will be weeping and gnashing of teeth.[r]

51"Have you understood all these things?" Jesus asked.

"Yes," they replied.

52He said to them, "Therefore every teacher of the law who has been instructed about the kingdom of heaven is like the owner of a house who brings out of his storeroom new treasures as well as old."

A Prophet Without Honor

13:54–58pp — Mk 6:1–6

53When Jesus had finished these parables,[s] he moved on from there. **54**Coming to his hometown, he began teaching the people in their synagogue,[t] and they were amazed.[u] "Where did this man get this wisdom and these miraculous powers?" they asked. **55**"Isn't this the carpenter's son?[v] Isn't his mother's[w] name Mary, and aren't his brothers James, Joseph, Simon and Judas? **56**Aren't all his sisters with us? Where then did this man get all these things?" **57**And they took offense[x] at him.

But Jesus said to them, "Only in his hometown and in his own house is a prophet without honor."[y]

58And he did not do many miracles there because of their lack of faith.

John the Baptist Beheaded

14:1–12pp — Mk 6:14–29

14 At that time Herod[z] the tetrarch heard the reports about Jesus,[a] **2**and he said to his attendants, "This is John the Baptist;[b] he has risen from the dead! That is why miraculous powers are at work in him."

3Now Herod had arrested John and bound him and put him in prison[c] because of Herodias, his brother Philip's wife,[d] **4**for John had been saying to him: "It is not lawful for you to have her."[e] **5**Herod wanted to kill John, but he was

13:36 [a]Mt 15:15
13:37 [b]Mt 8:20
13:38 [c]Jn 8:44,45; 1Jn 3:10
13:39 [d]Joel 3:13 [e]Mt 24:3; 28:20 [f]Rev 14:15
13:41 [g]Mt 8:20 [h]Mt 24:31
13:42 [i]ver 50; Mt 8:12
13:43 [j]Da 12:3 [k]Mt 11:15
13:44 [l]ver 24 [m]Isa 55:1; Php 3:7,8
13:45 [n]ver 24
13:47 [o]ver 24 [p]Mt 22:10
13:49 [q]Mt 25:32
13:50 [r]Mt 8:12
13:53 [s]Mt 7:28
13:54 [t]Mt 4:23 [u]Mt 7:28
13:55 [v]Lk 3:23; Jn 6:42 [w]Mt 12:46
13:57 [x]Jn 6:61 [y]Lk 4:24; Jn 4:44
14:1 [z]Mk 8:15; Lk 3:1,19; 13:31; 23:7,8; Ac 4:27; 12:1 [a]Lk 9:7-9
14:2 [b]Mt 3:1
14:3 [c]Mt 4:12; 11:2 [d]Lk 3:19,20
14:4 [e]Lev 18:16; 20:21

afraid of the people, because they considered him a prophet.[a]

[6]On Herod's birthday the daughter of Herodias danced for them and pleased Herod so much [7]that he promised with an oath to give her whatever she asked. [8]Prompted by her mother, she said, "Give me here on a platter the head of John the Baptist." [9]The king was distressed, but because of his oaths and his dinner guests, he ordered that her request be granted [10]and had John beheaded[b] in the prison. [11]His head was brought in on a platter and given to the girl, who carried it to her mother. [12]John's disciples came and took his body and buried it.[c] Then they went and told Jesus.

Jesus Feeds the Five Thousand

14:13–21pp — Mk 6:32–44; Lk 9:10–17; Jn 6:1–13
14:13–21Ref — Mt 15:32–38

[13]When Jesus heard what had happened, he withdrew by boat privately to a solitary place. Hearing of this, the crowds followed him on foot from the towns. [14]When Jesus landed and saw a large crowd, he had compassion on them[d] and healed their sick.[e]

[15]As evening approached, the disciples came to him and said, "This is a remote place, and it's already getting late. Send the crowds away, so they can go to the villages and buy themselves some food."

[16]Jesus replied, "They do not need to go away. You give them something to eat."

[17]"We have here only five loaves[f] of bread and two fish," they answered.

[18]"Bring them here to me," he said. [19]And he directed the people to sit down on the grass. Taking the five loaves and the two fish and looking up to heaven, he gave thanks and broke the loaves.[g] Then he gave them to the disciples, and the disciples gave them to the people. [20]They all ate and were satisfied, and the disciples picked up twelve basketfuls of broken pieces that were left over. [21]The number of those who ate was about five thousand men, besides women and children.

Jesus Walks on the Water

14:22–33pp — Mk 6:45–51; Jn 6:15–21
14:34–36pp — Mk 6:53–56

[22]Immediately Jesus made the disciples get into the boat and go on ahead of him to the other side, while he dismissed the crowd. [23]After he had dismissed them, he went up on a mountainside by himself to pray.[h] When evening came, he was there alone, [24]but the boat was already a considerable distance[c] from land, buffeted by the waves because the wind was against it.

[25]During the fourth watch of the night Jesus went out to them, walking on the lake. [26]When the disciples saw him walking on the lake, they were terrified. "It's a ghost,"[i] they said, and cried out in fear.

[27]But Jesus immediately said to them: "Take courage![j] It is I. Don't be afraid."[k]

[28]"Lord, if it's you," Peter replied, "tell me to come to you on the water."

[29]"Come," he said.

Then Peter got down out of the boat, walked on the water and came toward Jesus. [30]But when he saw the wind, he was afraid and, beginning to sink, cried out, "Lord, save me!"

[31]Immediately Jesus reached out his hand and caught him. "You of little faith,"[l] he said, "why did you doubt?"

[32]And when they climbed into the boat, the wind died down. [33]Then those who were in the boat worshiped him, saying, "Truly you are the Son of God."[m]

[34]When they had crossed over, they landed at Gennesaret. [35]And when the men of that place recognized Jesus, they sent word to all the surrounding country. People brought all their sick to him [36]and begged him to let the sick just

14:5 [a]Mt 11:9
14:10 [b]Mt 17:12
14:12 [c]Ac 8:2
14:14 [d]Mt 9:36 [e]Mt 4:23
14:17 [f]Mt 16:9
14:19 [g]1Sa 9:13; Mt 26:26; Mk 8:6; Lk 24:30; Ac 2:42; 27:35; 1Ti 4:4
14:23 [h]Lk 3:21
14:26 [i]Lk 24:37
14:27 [j]Mt 9:2; Ac 23:11 [k]Da 10:12; Mt 17:7; 28:10; Lk 1:13,30; 2:10; Ac 18:9; 23:11; Rev 1:17
14:31 [l]Mt 6:30
14:33 [m]Ps 2:7; Mt 4:3

[c]24 Greek *many stadia*

touch the edge of his cloak,[a] and
all who touched him were healed.

Clean and Unclean

15:1–20pp — Mk 7:1–23

15 Then some Pharisees and
teachers of the law came to
Jesus from Jerusalem and asked,
2"Why do your disciples break the
tradition of the elders? They don't
wash their hands before they
eat!"[b]
3Jesus replied, "And why do you
break the command of God for the
sake of your tradition? 4For God
said, 'Honor your father and mother'[d][c] and 'Anyone who curses his
father or mother must be put to
death.'[e][d] 5But you say that if a
man says to his father or mother,
'Whatever help you might otherwise have received from me is a gift
devoted to God,' 6he is not to 'hon-
or his father[f]' with it. Thus you
nullify the word of God for the sake
of your tradition. 7You hypocrites!
Isaiah was right when he prophesied about you:

8" 'These people honor me with
their lips,
but their hearts are far from
me.
9They worship me in vain;
their teachings are but rules
taught by men.'[e][g][f]"

10Jesus called the crowd to him
and said, "Listen and understand.
11What goes into a man's mouth
does not make him 'unclean,'[g] but
what comes out of his mouth, that
is what makes him 'unclean.' "[h]
12Then the disciples came to
him and asked, "Do you know that
the Pharisees were offended when
they heard this?"
13He replied, "Every plant that
my heavenly Father has not planted[i] will be pulled up by the roots.
14Leave them; they are blind
guides.[h][j] If a blind man leads a
blind man, both will fall into a
pit."[k]
15Peter said, "Explain the parable to us."[l]
16"Are you still so dull?"[m] Jesus
asked them. 17"Don't you see that
whatever enters the mouth goes
into the stomach and then out of
the body? 18But the things that
come out of the mouth come from
the heart,[n] and these make a man
'unclean.' 19For out of the heart
come evil thoughts, murder, adultery, sexual immorality, theft, false
testimony, slander.[o] 20These are
what make a man 'unclean';[p] but
eating with unwashed hands does
not make him 'unclean.' "

The Faith of the Canaanite Woman

15:21–28pp — Mk 7:24–30

21Leaving that place, Jesus withdrew to the region of Tyre and Sidon.[q] 22A Canaanite woman from
that vicinity came to him, crying
out, "Lord, Son of David,[r] have
mercy on me! My daughter is suffering terribly from demon-posses-
sion."[s]
23Jesus did not answer a word.
So his disciples came to him and
urged him, "Send her away, for she
keeps crying out after us."
24He answered, "I was sent only
to the lost sheep of Israel."[t]
25The woman came and knelt
before him.[u] "Lord, help me!" she
said.
26He replied, "It is not right to
take the children's bread and toss
it to their dogs."
27"Yes, Lord," she said, "but
even the dogs eat the crumbs that
fall from their masters' table."
28Then Jesus answered, "Wom-
an, you have great faith![v] Your request is granted." And her daughter was healed from that very hour.

Jesus Feeds the Four Thousand

15:29–31pp — Mk 7:31–37
15:32–39pp — Mk 8:1–10
15:32–39Ref — Mt 14:13–21

29Jesus left there and went along
the Sea of Galilee. Then he went up
on a mountainside and sat down.

14:36 [a]Mt 9:20
15:2 [b]Lk 11:38
15:4 [c]Ex 20:12; Dt 5:16; Eph 6:2 [d]Ex 21:17; Lev 20:9
15:9 [e]Col 2:20-22 [f]Isa 29:13; Mal 2:2
15:11 [g]Ac 10:14,15 [h]ver 18
15:13 [i]Isa 60:21; 61:3; Jn 15:2
15:14 [j]Mt 23:16,24; Ro 2:19 [k]Lk 6:39
15:15 [l]Mt 13:36
15:16 [m]Mt 16:9
15:18 [n]Mt 12:34; Lk 6:45; Jas 3:6
15:19 [o]Gal 5:19-21
15:20 [p]Ro 14:14
15:21 [q]Mt 11:21
15:22 [r]Mt 9:27 [s]Mt 4:24
15:24 [t]Mt 10:6,23; Ro 15:8
15:25 [u]Mt 8:2
15:28 [v]Mt 9:22

[d]4 Exodus 20:12; Deut. 5:16 [e]4 Exodus 21:17; Lev. 20:9 [f]6 Some manuscripts *father or his mother* [g]9 Isaiah 29:13 [h]14 Some manuscripts *guides of the blind*

30Great crowds came to him, bringing the lame, the blind, the crippled, the mute and many others, and laid them at his feet; and he healed them.[a] 31The people were amazed when they saw the mute speaking, the crippled made well, the lame walking and the blind seeing. And they praised the God of Israel.[b]

32Jesus called his disciples to him and said, "I have compassion for these people;[c] they have already been with me three days and have nothing to eat. I do not want to send them away hungry, or they may collapse on the way."

33His disciples answered, "Where could we get enough bread in this remote place to feed such a crowd?"

34"How many loaves do you have?" Jesus asked.

"Seven," they replied, "and a few small fish."

35He told the crowd to sit down on the ground. 36Then he took the seven loaves and the fish, and when he had given thanks, he broke them[d] and gave them to the disciples, and they in turn to the people. 37They all ate and were satisfied. Afterward the disciples picked up seven basketfuls of broken pieces that were left over.[e] 38The number of those who ate was four thousand, besides women and children. 39After Jesus had sent the crowd away, he got into the boat and went to the vicinity of Magadan.

The Demand for a Sign

16:1–12pp — Mk 8:11–21

16 The Pharisees and Sadducees[f] came to Jesus and tested him by asking him to show them a sign from heaven.[g]

2He replied,[i] "When evening comes, you say, 'It will be fair weather, for the sky is red,' 3and in the morning, 'Today it will be stormy, for the sky is red and overcast.' You know how to interpret the appearance of the sky, but you cannot interpret the signs of the times.[h] 4A wicked and adulterous generation looks for a miraculous sign, but none will be given it except the sign of Jonah."[i] Jesus then left them and went away.

The Yeast of the Pharisees and Sadducees

5When they went across the lake, the disciples forgot to take bread. 6"Be careful," Jesus said to them. "Be on your guard against the yeast of the Pharisees and Sadducees."[j]

7They discussed this among themselves and said, "It is because we didn't bring any bread."

8Aware of their discussion, Jesus asked, "You of little faith,[k] why are you talking among yourselves about having no bread? 9Do you still not understand? Don't you remember the five loaves for the five thousand, and how many basketfuls you gathered?[l] 10Or the seven loaves for the four thousand, and how many basketfuls you gathered?[m] 11How is it you don't understand that I was not talking to you about bread? But be on your guard against the yeast of the Pharisees and Sadducees." 12Then they understood that he was not telling them to guard against the yeast used in bread, but against the teaching of the Pharisees and Sadducees.[n]

Peter's Confession of Christ

16:13–16pp — Mk 8:27–29; Lk 9:18–20

13When Jesus came to the region of Caesarea Philippi, he asked his disciples, "Who do people say the Son of Man is?"

14They replied, "Some say John the Baptist;[o] others say Elijah; and still others, Jeremiah or one of the prophets."[p]

15"But what about you?" he asked. "Who do you say I am?"

16Simon Peter answered, "You are the Christ,[j] the Son of the living God."[q]

15:30 [a] Mt 4:23
15:31 [b] Mt 9:8
15:32 [c] Mt 9:36
15:36 [d] Mt 14:19
15:37 [e] Mt 16:10
16:1 [f] Ac 4:1 [g] Mt 12:38
16:3 [h] Lk 12:54-56
16:4 [i] Mt 12:39
16:6 [j] Lk 12:1
16:8 [k] Mt 6:30
16:9 [l] Mt 14:17-21
16:10 [m] Mt 15:34-38
16:12 [n] Ac 4:1
16:14 [o] Mt 3:1; 14:2 [p] Mk 6:15; Jn 1:21
16:16 [q] Mt 4:3; Ps 42:2; Jn 11:27; Ac 14:15; 2Co 6:16; 1Th 1:9; 1Ti 3:15; Heb 10:31; 12:22

i2 Some early manuscripts do not have the rest of verse 2 and all of verse 3. j16 Or *Messiah*; also in verse 20

17Jesus replied, "Blessed are
you, Simon son of Jonah, for this
was not revealed to you by man,[a]
but by my Father in heaven. 18And
I tell you that you are Peter,[k][b] and
on this rock I will build my
church,[c] and the gates of Hades[l]
will not overcome it.[m] 19I will give
you the keys[d] of the kingdom of
heaven; whatever you bind on
earth will be[n] bound in heaven,
and whatever you loose on earth
will be[n] loosed in heaven."[e]
20Then he warned his disciples not
to tell anyone[f] that he was the
Christ.

Jesus Predicts His Death

16:21–28pp — Mk 8:31–9:1; Lk 9:22–27

21From that time on Jesus began
to explain to his disciples that he
must go to Jerusalem and suffer
many things[g] at the hands of the
elders, chief priests and teachers of
the law, and that he must be killed
and on the third day[h] be raised to
life.[i]

22Peter took him aside and began to rebuke him. "Never, Lord!"
he said. "This shall never happen
to you!"

23Jesus turned and said to Peter,
"Get behind me, Satan![j] You are a
stumbling block to me; you do not
have in mind the things of God, but
the things of men."

24Then Jesus said to his disciples, "If anyone would come after
me, he must deny himself and take
up his cross and follow me.[k] 25For
whoever wants to save his life[o] will
lose it, but whoever loses his life
for me will find it.[l] 26What good
will it be for a man if he gains the
whole world, yet forfeits his soul?
Or what can a man give in exchange for his soul? 27For the Son
of Man[m] is going to come[n] in his
Father's glory with his angels, and
then he will reward each person according to what he has done.[o] 28I
tell you the truth, some who are
standing here will not taste death
before they see the Son of Man
coming in his kingdom."

The Transfiguration

17:1–8pp — Lk 9:28–36
17:1–13pp — Mk 9:2–13

17 After six days Jesus took
with him Peter, James and
John the brother of James, and led
them up a high mountain by themselves. 2There he was transfigured
before them. His face shone like
the sun, and his clothes became as
white as the light. 3Just then there
appeared before them Moses and
Elijah, talking with Jesus.

4Peter said to Jesus, "Lord, it is
good for us to be here. If you wish,
I will put up three shelters—one
for you, one for Moses and one for
Elijah."

5While he was still speaking, a
bright cloud enveloped them, and
a voice from the cloud said, "This
is my Son, whom I love; with him
I am well pleased.[p] Listen to
him!"[q]

6When the disciples heard this,
they fell facedown to the ground,
terrified. 7But Jesus came and
touched them. "Get up," he said.
"Don't be afraid."[r] 8When they
looked up, they saw no one except
Jesus.

9As they were coming down the
mountain, Jesus instructed them,
"Don't tell anyone[s] what you have
seen, until the Son of Man[t] has
been raised from the dead."[u]

10The disciples asked him, "Why
then do the teachers of the law say
that Elijah must come first?"

11Jesus replied, "To be sure, Elijah comes and will restore all
things.[v] 12But I tell you, Elijah has
already come,[w] and they did not
recognize him, but have done to
him everything they wished.[x] In
the same way the Son of Man is going to suffer[y] at their hands."
13Then the disciples understood
that he was talking to them about
John the Baptist.

16:17 [a] 1Co 15:50; Gal 1:16; Eph 6:12; Heb 2:14
16:18 [b] Jn 1:42 [c] Eph 2:20
16:19 [d] Isa 22:22; Rev 3:7 [e] Mt 18:18; Jn 20:23
16:20 [f] Mk 8:30
16:21 [g] Mk 10:34; Lk 17:25 [h] Jn 2:19 [i] Mt 17:22,23; Mk 9:31; Lk 9:22; 18:31-33; 24:6,7
16:23 [j] Mt 4:10
16:24 [k] Mt 10:38; Lk 14:27
16:25 [l] Jn 12:25
16:27 [m] Mt 8:20 [n] Ac 1:11 [o] Job 34:11; Ps 62:12; Jer 17:10; Ro 2:6; 2Co 5:10; Rev 22:12
17:5 [p] Mt 3:17; 2Pe 1:17 [q] Ac 3:22,23
17:7 [r] Mt 14:27
17:9 [s] Mk 8:30 [t] Mt 8:20 [u] Mt 16:21
17:11 [v] Mal 4:6; Lk 1:16,17
17:12 [w] Mt 11:14 [x] Mt 14:3,10 [y] Mt 16:21

[k] *18 Peter* means *rock.* [l] *18* Or *hell* [m] *18* Or *not prove stronger than it* [n] *19* Or *have been* [o] *25* The Greek word means either *life* or *soul;* also in verse 26.

The Healing of a Boy With a Demon

17:14–19pp — Mk 9:14–28; Lk 9:37–42

14When they came to the crowd,
a man approached Jesus and knelt
before him. 15"Lord, have mercy on
my son," he said. "He has seizures[a] and is suffering greatly. He
often falls into the fire or into the
water. 16I brought him to your disciples, but they could not heal
him."
17"O unbelieving and perverse
generation," Jesus replied, "how
long shall I stay with you? How
long shall I put up with you? Bring
the boy here to me." 18Jesus rebuked the demon, and it came out
of the boy, and he was healed from
that moment.
19Then the disciples came to
Jesus in private and asked, "Why
couldn't we drive it out?"
20He replied, "Because you have
so little faith. I tell you the truth, if
you have faith[b] as small as a mustard seed,[c] you can say to this
mountain, 'Move from here to
there' and it will move.[d] Nothing
will be impossible for you.[p]"
22When they came together in
Galilee, he said to them, "The Son
of Man[e] is going to be betrayed
into the hands of men. 23They will
kill him,[f] and on the third day[g] he
will be raised to life."[h] And the disciples were filled with grief.

The Temple Tax

24After Jesus and his disciples
arrived in Capernaum, the collectors of the two-drachma tax[i] came
to Peter and asked, "Doesn't your
teacher pay the temple tax[q]?"
25"Yes, he does," he replied.
When Peter came into the house,
Jesus was the first to speak. "What
do you think, Simon?" he asked.
"From whom do the kings of the
earth collect duty and taxes[j]—
from their own sons or from others?"
26"From others," Peter answered.
"Then the sons are exempt,"
Jesus said to him. 27"But so that
we may not offend[k] them, go to
the lake and throw out your line.
Take the first fish you catch; open
its mouth and you will find a
four-drachma coin. Take it and
give it to them for my tax and
yours."

The Greatest in the Kingdom of Heaven

18:1–5pp — Mk 9:33–37; Lk 9:46–48

18 At that time the disciples
came to Jesus and asked,
"Who is the greatest in the kingdom of heaven?"
2He called a little child and had
him stand among them. 3And he
said: "I tell you the truth, unless
you change and become like little
children,[l] you will never enter the
kingdom of heaven.[m] 4Therefore,
whoever humbles himself like this
child is the greatest in the kingdom
of heaven.[n]
5"And whoever welcomes a little
child like this in my name welcomes me.[o] 6But if anyone causes
one of these little ones who believe
in me to sin,[p] it would be better for
him to have a large millstone hung
around his neck and to be drowned
in the depths of the sea.[q]
7"Woe to the world because of
the things that cause people to sin!
Such things must come, but woe to
the man through whom they
come![r] 8If your hand or your foot
causes you to sin,[s] cut it off and
throw it away. It is better for you to
enter life maimed or crippled than
to have two hands or two feet and
be thrown into eternal fire. 9And if
your eye causes you to sin,[t] gouge
it out and throw it away. It is better
for you to enter life with one eye
than to have two eyes and be
thrown into the fire of hell.[u]

The Parable of the Lost Sheep

18:12–14pp — Lk 15:4–7

10"See that you do not look
down on one of these little ones.
For I tell you that their angels[v] in

17:15 [a]Mt 4:24
17:20 [b]Mt 21:21 [c]Mt 13:31; Mk 11:23; Lk 17:6 [d]1Co 13:2
17:22 [e]Mt 8:20
17:23 [f]Ac 2:23; 3:13 [g]Mt 16:21 [h]Mt 16:21
17:24 [i]Ex 30:13
17:25 [j]Mt 22:17-21; Ro 13:7
17:27 [k]Jn 6:61
18:3 [l]Mt 19:14; 1Pe 2:2 [m]Mt 3:2
18:4 [n]Mk 9:35
18:5 [o]Mt 10:40
18:6 [p]Mt 5:29 [q]Mk 9:42; Lk 17:2
18:7 [r]Lk 17:1
18:8 [s]Mt 5:29; Mk 9:43,45
18:9 [t]Mt 5:29 [u]Mt 5:22
18:10 [v]Ge 48:16; Ps 34:7; Ac 12:11,15; Heb 1:14

p20 Some manuscripts *you.* 21*But this kind does not go out except by prayer and fasting.*
q24 Greek *the two drachmas*

heaven always see the face of my
Father in heaven.[r]
12"What do you think? If a man
owns a hundred sheep, and one of
them wanders away, will he not
leave the ninety-nine on the hills
and go to look for the one that wandered off? **13**And if he finds it, I tell
you the truth, he is happier about
that one sheep than about the
ninety-nine that did not wander
off. **14**In the same way your Father
in heaven is not willing that any of
these little ones should be lost.

A Brother Who Sins Against You

15"If your brother sins against
you,[s] go and show him his fault,[a]
just between the two of you. If he
listens to you, you have won your
brother over. **16**But if he will not
listen, take one or two others
along, so that 'every matter may be
established by the testimony of two
or three witnesses.'[t][b] **17**If he refuses to listen to them, tell it to the
church;[c] and if he refuses to listen
even to the church, treat him as
you would a pagan or a tax collector.[d]
18"I tell you the truth, whatever
you bind on earth will be[u] bound
in heaven, and whatever you loose
on earth will be[u] loosed in heav-
en.[e]
19"Again, I tell you that if two of
you on earth agree about anything
you ask for, it will be done for you[f]
by my Father in heaven. **20**For
where two or three come together
in my name, there am I with them."

The Parable of the Unmerciful Servant

21Then Peter came to Jesus and
asked, "Lord, how many times
shall I forgive my brother when he
sins against me?[g] Up to seven
times?"[h]
22Jesus answered, "I tell you, not
seven times, but seventy-seven
times.[v][i]
23"Therefore, the kingdom of
heaven is like[j] a king who wanted
to settle accounts[k] with his servants. **24**As he began the settlement, a man who owed him ten
thousand talents[w] was brought to
him. **25**Since he was not able to
pay,[l] the master ordered that he
and his wife and his children and
all that he had be sold[m] to repay
the debt.
26"The servant fell on his knees
before him.[n] 'Be patient with me,'
he begged, 'and I will pay back everything.' **27**The servant's master
took pity on him, canceled the debt
and let him go.
28"But when that servant went
out, he found one of his fellow servants who owed him a hundred denarii.[x] He grabbed him and began
to choke him. 'Pay back what you
owe me!' he demanded.
29"His fellow servant fell to his
knees and begged him, 'Be patient
with me, and I will pay you back.'
30"But he refused. Instead, he
went off and had the man thrown
into prison until he could pay the
debt. **31**When the other servants
saw what had happened, they were
greatly distressed and went and
told their master everything that
had happened.
32"Then the master called the
servant in. 'You wicked servant,' he
said, 'I canceled all that debt of
yours because you begged me to.
33Shouldn't you have had mercy on
your fellow servant just as I had on
you?' **34**In anger his master turned
him over to the jailers to be tortured, until he should pay back all
he owed.
35"This is how my heavenly Father will treat each of you unless
you forgive your brother from your
heart."[o]

Divorce

19:1–9pp — Mk 10:1–12

19 When Jesus had finished
saying these things,[p] he

18:15 [a] Lev 19:17; Lk 17:3; Gal 6:1; Jas 5:19,20
18:16 [b] Nu 35:30; Dt 17:6; 19:15; Jn 8:17; 2Co 13:1; 1Ti 5:19; Heb 10:28
18:17 [c] 1Co 6:1-6 [d] Ro 16:17; 2Th 3:6,14
18:18 [e] Mt 16:19; Jn 20:23
18:19 [f] Mt 7:7
18:21 [g] Mt 6:14 [h] Lk 17:4
18:22 [i] Ge 4:24
18:23 [j] Mt 13:24 [k] Mt 25:19
18:25 [l] Lk 7:42 [m] Lev 25:39; 2Ki 4:1; Ne 5:5,8
18:26 [n] Mt 8:2
18:35 [o] Mt 6:14; Jas 2:13
19:1 [p] Mt 7:28

[r] 10 Some manuscripts *heaven.* [11] *The Son of Man came to save what was lost.* [s] 15 Some manuscripts do not have *against you.* [t] 16 Deut. 19:15 [u] 18 Or *have been* [v] 22 Or *seventy times seven* [w] 24 That is, millions of dollars [x] 28 That is, a few dollars

left Galilee and went into the region of Judea to the other side of
the Jordan. **2**Large crowds followed
him, and he healed them[a] there.
3Some Pharisees came to him to
test him. They asked, "Is it lawful
for a man to divorce his wife[b] for
any and every reason?"
4"Haven't you read," he replied,
"that at the beginning the Creator
'made them male and female,'[y][c]
5and said, 'For this reason a man
will leave his father and mother
and be united to his wife, and the
two will become one flesh'[z]?[d] **6**So
they are no longer two, but one.
Therefore what God has joined together, let man not separate."
7"Why then," they asked, "did
Moses command that a man give
his wife a certificate of divorce and
send her away?"[e]
8Jesus replied, "Moses permitted you to divorce your wives because your hearts were hard. But it
was not this way from the beginning. **9**I tell you that anyone who
divorces his wife, except for marital unfaithfulness, and marries another woman commits adultery."[f]
10The disciples said to him, "If
this is the situation between a husband and wife, it is better not to
marry."
11Jesus replied, "Not everyone
can accept this word, but only
those to whom it has been given.[g]
12For some are eunuchs because
they were born that way; others
were made that way by men; and
others have renounced marriage[a]
because of the kingdom of heaven.
The one who can accept this
should accept it."

The Little Children and Jesus

19:13–15pp — Mk 10:13–16; Lk 18:15–17

13Then little children were
brought to Jesus for him to place
his hands on them[h] and pray for
them. But the disciples rebuked
those who brought them.
14Jesus said, "Let the little children come to me, and do not hinder them, for the kingdom of heav-
en belongs[i] to such as these."[j]
15When he had placed his hands on
them, he went on from there.

The Rich Young Man

19:16–29pp Mk 10:17–30; Lk 18:18–30

16Now a man came up to Jesus
and asked, "Teacher, what good
thing must I do to get eternal
life[k]?"[l]
17"Why do you ask me about
what is good?" Jesus replied.
"There is only One who is good. If
you want to enter life, obey the
commandments."[m]
18"Which ones?" the man inquired.
Jesus replied, " 'Do not murder,
do not commit adultery,[n] do not
steal, do not give false testimony,
19honor your father and mother,'[b][o] and 'love your neighbor as
yourself.'[c]"[p]
20"All these I have kept," the
young man said. "What do I still
lack?"
21Jesus answered, "If you want
to be perfect,[q] go, sell your possessions and give to the poor,[r] and
you will have treasure in heaven.[s]
Then come, follow me."
22When the young man heard
this, he went away sad, because he
had great wealth.
23Then Jesus said to his disciples, "I tell you the truth, it is hard
for a rich man[t] to enter the kingdom of heaven. **24**Again I tell you,
it is easier for a camel to go through
the eye of a needle than for a rich
man to enter the kingdom of God."
25When the disciples heard this,
they were greatly astonished and
asked, "Who then can be saved?"
26Jesus looked at them and said,
"With man this is impossible, but
with God all things are possible."[u]
27Peter answered him, "We have
left everything to follow you![v]
What then will there be for us?"
28Jesus said to them, "I tell you
the truth, at the renewal of all
things, when the Son of Man sits on
his glorious throne,[w] you who have

19:2 [a]Mt 4:23
19:3 [b]Mt 5:31
19:4 [c]Ge 1:27; 5:2
19:5 [d]Ge 2:24; 1Co 6:16; Eph 5:31
19:7 [e]Dt 24:1-4; Mt 5:31
19:9 [f]Mt 5:32; Lk 16:18
19:11 [g]Mt 13:11; 1Co 7:7-9,17
19:13 [h]Mk 5:23
19:14 [i]Mt 25:34 [j]Mt 18:3; 1Pe 2:2
19:16 [k]Mt 25:46 [l]Lk 10:25
19:17 [m]Lev 18:5
19:18 [n]Jas 2:11
19:19 [o]Ex 20:12-16; Dt 5:16-20 [p]Lev 19:18; Mt 5:43
19:21 [q]Mt 5:48 [r]Lk 12:33; Ac 2:45; 4:34-35 [s]Mt 6:20
19:23 [t]Mt 13:22; 1Ti 6:9,10
19:26 [u]Ge 18:14; Job 42:2; Jer 32:17; Zec 8:6; Lk 1:37; 18:27; Ro 4:21
19:27 [v]Mt 4:19
19:28 [w]Mt 20:21; 25:31

[y]*4* Gen. 1:27 [z]*5* Gen. 2:24 [a]*12* Or *have made themselves eunuchs*
[b]*19* Exodus 20:12-16; Deut. 5:16-20
[c]*19* Lev. 19:18

followed me will also sit on twelve
thrones, judging the twelve tribes
of Israel.[a] **29**And everyone who has
left houses or brothers or sisters or
father or mother[d] or children or
fields for my sake will receive a
hundred times as much and will inherit eternal life.[b] **30**But many who
are first will be last, and many who
are last will be first.[c]

The Parable of the Workers in the Vineyard

20 "For the kingdom of heaven
is like[d] a landowner who
went out early in the morning to
hire men to work in his vineyard.[e]
2He agreed to pay them a denarius
for the day and sent them into his
vineyard.

3"About the third hour he went
out and saw others standing in the
marketplace doing nothing. **4**He
told them, 'You also go and work in
my vineyard, and I will pay you
whatever is right.' **5**So they went.

"He went out again about the
sixth hour and the ninth hour and
did the same thing. **6**About the
eleventh hour he went out and
found still others standing around.
He asked them, 'Why have you
been standing here all day long doing nothing?'

7" 'Because no one has hired us,'
they answered.

"He said to them, 'You also go
and work in my vineyard.'

8"When evening came,[f] the
owner of the vineyard said to his
foreman, 'Call the workers and pay
them their wages, beginning with
the last ones hired and going on to
the first.'

9"The workers who were hired
about the eleventh hour came and
each received a denarius. **10**So
when those came who were hired
first, they expected to receive
more. But each one of them also
received a denarius. **11**When they
received it, they began to grumble[g] against the landowner.
12'These men who were hired last
worked only one hour,' they said,
'and you have made them equal to
us who have borne the burden of
the work and the heat[h] of the day.'

13"But he answered one of them,
'Friend,[i] I am not being unfair to
you. Didn't you agree to work for a
denarius? **14**Take your pay and go.
I want to give the man who was
hired last the same as I gave you.
15Don't I have the right to do what
I want with my own money? Or are
you envious because I am generous?'[j]

16"So the last will be first, and
the first will be last."[k]

Jesus Again Predicts His Death

20:17–19pp — Mk 10:32–34; Lk 18:31–33

17Now as Jesus was going up to
Jerusalem, he took the twelve disciples aside and said to them,
18"We are going up to Jerusalem,[l]
and the Son of Man[m] will be betrayed to the chief priests and the
teachers of the law.[n] They will
condemn him to death **19**and will
turn him over to the Gentiles to be
mocked and flogged[o] and crucified.[p] On the third day[q] he will be
raised to life!"[r]

A Mother's Request

20:20–28pp — Mk 10:35–45

20Then the mother of Zebedee's
sons[s] came to Jesus with her sons
and, kneeling down,[t] asked a favor
of him.

21"What is it you want?" he
asked.

She said, "Grant that one of
these two sons of mine may sit at
your right and the other at your left
in your kingdom."[u]

22"You don't know what you are
asking," Jesus said to them. "Can
you drink the cup[v] I am going to
drink?"

"We can," they answered.

23Jesus said to them, "You will
indeed drink from my cup,[w] but to
sit at my right or left is not for me
to grant. These places belong to
those for whom they have been prepared by my Father."

24When the ten heard about this,
they were indignant[x] with the two

19:28 [a] Lk 22:28-30; Rev 3:21; 4:4; 20:4
19:29 [b] Mt 6:33; 25:46
19:30 [c] Mt 20:16; Mk 10:31; Lk 13:30
20:1 [d] Mt 13:24 [e] Mt 21:28,33
20:8 [f] Lev 19:13; Dt 24:15
20:11 [g] Jnh 4:1
20:12 [h] Jnh 4:8; Lk 12:55; Jas 1:11
20:13 [i] Mt 22:12; 26:50
20:15 [j] Dt 15:9; Mk 7:22
20:16 [k] Mt 19:30
20:18 [l] Lk 9:51 [m] Mt 8:20 [n] Mt 16:21; 27:1,2
20:19 [o] Mt 16:21 [p] Ac 2:23 [q] Mt 16:21 [r] Mt 16:21
20:20 [s] Mt 4:21 [t] Mt 8:2
20:21 [u] Mt 19:28
20:22 [v] Isa 51:17,22; Jer 49:12; Mt 26:39,42; Mk 14:36; Lk 22:42; Jn 18:11
20:23 [w] Ac 12:2; Rev 1:9
20:24 [x] Lk 22:24,25

d29 Some manuscripts *mother or wife*

brothers. **25**Jesus called them together and said, "You know that
the rulers of the Gentiles lord it
over them, and their high officials
exercise authority over them.
26Not so with you. Instead, whoever wants to become great among
you must be your servant,[a] **27**and
whoever wants to be first must be
your slave— **28**just as the Son of
Man[b] did not come to be served,
but to serve,[c] and to give his life as
a ransom[d] for many."

Two Blind Men Receive Sight

20:29-34pp — Mk 10:46-52; Lk 18:35-43

29As Jesus and his disciples were
leaving Jericho, a large crowd followed him. **30**Two blind men were
sitting by the roadside, and when
they heard that Jesus was going by,
they shouted, "Lord, Son of David,[e] have mercy on us!"
31The crowd rebuked them and
told them to be quiet, but they
shouted all the louder, "Lord, Son
of David, have mercy on us!"
32Jesus stopped and called
them. "What do you want me to do
for you?" he asked.
33"Lord," they answered, "we
want our sight."
34Jesus had compassion on
them and touched their eyes. Immediately they received their sight
and followed him.

The Triumphal Entry

21:1-9pp — Mk 11:1-10; Lk 19:29-38
21:4-9pp — Jn 12:12-15

21 As they approached Jerusalem and came to Bethphage
on the Mount of Olives,[f] Jesus
sent two disciples, **2**saying to them,
"Go to the village ahead of you, and
at once you will find a donkey tied
there, with her colt by her. Untie
them and bring them to me. **3**If
anyone says anything to you, tell
him that the Lord needs them, and
he will send them right away."
4This took place to fulfill what
was spoken through the prophet:

5"Say to the Daughter of Zion,
'See, your king comes to you,
gentle and riding on a donkey,
on a colt, the foal of a
donkey.' "[e][g]

6The disciples went and did as
Jesus had instructed them. **7**They
brought the donkey and the colt,
placed their cloaks on them, and
Jesus sat on them. **8**A very large
crowd spread their cloaks[h] on the
road, while others cut branches
from the trees and spread them on
the road. **9**The crowds that went
ahead of him and those that followed shouted,

"Hosanna[f] to the Son of
David!"[i]

"Blessed is he who comes in
the name of the
Lord!"[g][j]

"Hosanna[f] in the highest!"[k]

10When Jesus entered Jerusalem, the whole city was stirred and
asked, "Who is this?"
11The crowds answered, "This is
Jesus, the prophet[l] from Nazareth
in Galilee."

Jesus at the Temple

21:12-16pp — Mk 11:15-18; Lk 19:45-47

12Jesus entered the temple area
and drove out all who were buying[m] and selling there. He overturned the tables of the money
changers[n] and the benches of
those selling doves.[o] **13**"It is written," he said to them, " 'My house
will be called a house of prayer,'[h][p]
but you are making it a 'den of robbers.' "[i][q]
14The blind and the lame came
to him at the temple, and he healed
them.[r] **15**But when the chief
priests and the teachers of the law
saw the wonderful things he did
and the children shouting in the
temple area, "Hosanna to the Son
of David,"[s] they were indignant.[t]
16"Do you hear what these children are saying?" they asked him.

20:26 [a]Mt 23:11; Mk 9:35
20:28 [b]Mt 8:20 [c]Lk 22:27; Jn 13:13-16; 2Co 8:9; Php 2:7 [d]Isa 53:10; Mt 26:28; 1Ti 2:6; Tit 2:14; Heb 9:28; 1Pe 1:18,19
20:30 [e]Mt 9:27
21:1 [f]Mt 24:3; 26:30; Mk 14:26; Lk 19:37; 21:37; 22:39; Jn 8:1; Ac 1:12
21:5 [g]Zec 9:9; Isa 62:11
21:8 [h]2Ki 9:13
21:9 [i]ver 15; Mt 9:27 [j]Ps 118:26; Mt 23:39 [k]Lk 2:14
21:11 [l]Lk 7:16,39; 24:19; Jn 1:21,25; 6:14; 7:40
21:12 [m]Dt 14:26 [n]Ex 30:13 [o]Lev 1:14
21:13 [p]Isa 56:7 [q]Jer 7:11
21:14 [r]Mt 4:23
21:15 [s]ver 9; Mt 9:27 [t]Lk 19:39

[e]5 Zech. 9:9 [f]9 A Hebrew expression meaning "Save!" which became an exclamation of praise; also in verse 15
[g]9 Psalm 118:26 [h]*13* Isaiah 56:7
[i]*13* Jer. 7:11

"Yes," replied Jesus, "have you never read,

" 'From the lips of children and infants
you have ordained praise'[i]?"[a]

17 And he left them and went out of the city to Bethany,[b] where he spent the night.

The Fig Tree Withers

21:18–22pp — Mk 11:12–14,20–24

18 Early in the morning, as he was on his way back to the city, he was hungry. 19 Seeing a fig tree by the road, he went up to it but found nothing on it except leaves. Then he said to it, "May you never bear fruit again!" Immediately the tree withered.[c]

20 When the disciples saw this, they were amazed. "How did the fig tree wither so quickly?" they asked.

21 Jesus replied, "I tell you the truth, if you have faith and do not doubt,[d] not only can you do what was done to the fig tree, but also you can say to this mountain, 'Go, throw yourself into the sea,' and it will be done. 22 If you believe, you will receive whatever you ask for[e] in prayer."

The Authority of Jesus Questioned

21:23–27pp — Mk 11:27–33; Lk 20:1–8

23 Jesus entered the temple courts, and, while he was teaching, the chief priests and the elders of the people came to him. "By what authority[f] are you doing these things?" they asked. "And who gave you this authority?"

24 Jesus replied, "I will also ask you one question. If you answer me, I will tell you by what authority I am doing these things. 25 John's baptism—where did it come from? Was it from heaven, or from men?"

They discussed it among themselves and said, "If we say, 'From heaven,' he will ask, 'Then why didn't you believe him?' 26 But if we say, 'From men'—we are afraid of the people, for they all hold that John was a prophet."[g]

27 So they answered Jesus, "We don't know."

Then he said, "Neither will I tell you by what authority I am doing these things.

The Parable of the Two Sons

28 "What do you think? There was a man who had two sons. He went to the first and said, 'Son, go and work today in the vineyard.'[h]

29 " 'I will not,' he answered, but later he changed his mind and went.

30 "Then the father went to the other son and said the same thing. He answered, 'I will, sir,' but he did not go.

31 "Which of the two did what his father wanted?"

"The first," they answered.

Jesus said to them, "I tell you the truth, the tax collectors[i] and the prostitutes[j] are entering the kingdom of God ahead of you. 32 For John came to you to show you the way of righteousness,[k] and you did not believe him, but the tax collectors[l] and the prostitutes[m] did. And even after you saw this, you did not repent[n] and believe him.

The Parable of the Tenants

21:33–46pp — Mk 12:1–12; Lk 20:9–19

33 "Listen to another parable: There was a landowner who planted[o] a vineyard. He put a wall around it, dug a winepress in it and built a watchtower.[p] Then he rented the vineyard to some farmers and went away on a journey.[q] 34 When the harvest time approached, he sent his servants[r] to the tenants to collect his fruit.

35 "The tenants seized his servants; they beat one, killed another, and stoned a third.[s] 36 Then he sent other servants[t] to them, more than the first time, and the tenants treated them the same way. 37 Last of all, he sent his son to them. 'They will respect my son,' he said.

38 "But when the tenants saw the

21:16 [a] Ps 8:2
21:17 [b] Mt 26:6; Mk 11:1; Lk 24:50; Jn 11:1,18; 12:1
21:19 [c] Isa 34:4; Jer 8:13
21:21 [d] Mt 17:20; Lk 17:6; 1Co 13:2; Jas 1:6
21:22 [e] Mt 7:7
21:23 [f] Ac 4:7; 7:27
21:26 [g] Mt 11:9; Mk 6:20
21:28 [h] ver 33; Mt 20:1
21:31 [i] Lk 7:29 [j] Lk 7:50
21:32 [k] Mt 3:1-12 [l] Lk 3:12,13; 7:29 [m] Lk 7:36-50 [n] Lk 7:30
21:33 [o] Ps 80:8 [p] Isa 5:1-7 [q] Mt 25:14,15
21:34 [r] Mt 22:3
21:35 [s] 2Ch 24:21; Mt 23:34,37; Heb 11:36,37
21:36 [t] Mt 22:4

[i] 16 Psalm 8:2

son, they said to each other, 'This
is the heir.[a] Come, let's kill him[b]
and take his inheritance.'[c] 39So
they took him and threw him out of
the vineyard and killed him.
40"Therefore, when the owner of
the vineyard comes, what will he
do to those tenants?"
41"He will bring those wretches
to a wretched end,"[d] they replied,
"and he will rent the vineyard to
other tenants,[e] who will give him
his share of the crop at harvest
time."
42Jesus said to them, "Have you
never read in the Scriptures:

" 'The stone the builders
rejected
has become the capstone[k];
the Lord has done this,
and it is marvelous in our
eyes'[l]?[f]

43"Therefore I tell you that the
kingdom of God will be taken away
from you[g] and given to a people
who will produce its fruit. 44He
who falls on this stone will be broken to pieces, but he on whom it
falls will be crushed."[m][h]
45When the chief priests and the
Pharisees heard Jesus' parables,
they knew he was talking about
them. 46They looked for a way to
arrest him, but they were afraid of
the crowd because the people held
that he was a prophet.[i]

The Parable of the Wedding Banquet

22:2–14Ref – Lk 14:16–24

22 Jesus spoke to them again
in parables, saying: 2"The
kingdom of heaven is like[j] a king
who prepared a wedding banquet
for his son. 3He sent his servants[k]
to those who had been invited to
the banquet to tell them to come,
but they refused to come.
4"Then he sent some more servants[l] and said, 'Tell those who
have been invited that I have prepared my dinner: My oxen and fattened cattle have been butchered,
and everything is ready. Come to
the wedding banquet.'
5"But they paid no attention and
went off—one to his field, another
to his business. 6The rest seized his
servants, mistreated them and
killed them. 7The king was enraged. He sent his army and destroyed those murderers[m] and
burned their city.
8"Then he said to his servants,
'The wedding banquet is ready, but
those I invited did not deserve to
come. 9Go to the street corners[n]
and invite to the banquet anyone
you find.' 10So the servants went
out into the streets and gathered
all the people they could find, both
good and bad,[o] and the wedding
hall was filled with guests.
11"But when the king came in to
see the guests, he noticed a man
there who was not wearing wedding clothes. 12'Friend,'[p] he
asked, 'how did you get in here
without wedding clothes?' The
man was speechless.
13"Then the king told the attendants, 'Tie him hand and foot, and
throw him outside, into the darkness, where there will be weeping
and gnashing of teeth.'[q]
14"For many are invited, but few
are chosen."[r]

Paying Taxes to Caesar

22:15–22pp – Mk 12:13–17; Lk 20:20–26

15Then the Pharisees went out
and laid plans to trap him in his
words. 16They sent their disciples
to him along with the Herodians.[s]
"Teacher," they said, "we know
you are a man of integrity and that
you teach the way of God in accordance with the truth. You aren't
swayed by men, because you pay
no attention to who they are. 17Tell
us then, what is your opinion? Is it
right to pay taxes[t] to Caesar or
not?"
18But Jesus, knowing their evil
intent, said, "You hypocrites, why
are you trying to trap me? 19Show
me the coin used for paying the
tax." They brought him a denarius,
20and he asked them, "Whose por-

21:38 [a] Heb 1:2 [b] Mt 12:14 [c] Ps 2:8
21:41 [d] Mt 8:11,12 [e] Ac 13:46; 18:6; 28:28
21:42 [f] Ps 118:22,23; Ac 4:11; 1Pe 2:7
21:43 [g] Mt 8:12
21:44 [h] Lk 2:34
21:46 [i] ver 11,26
22:2 [j] Mt 13:24
22:3 [k] Mt 21:34
22:4 [l] Mt 21:36
22:7 [m] Lk 19:27
22:9 [n] Eze 21:21
22:10 [o] Mt 13:47,48
22:12 [p] Mt 20:13; 26:50
22:13 [q] Mt 8:12
22:14 [r] Rev 17:14
22:16 [s] Mk 3:6
22:17 [t] Mt 17:25

[k]42 Or *cornerstone* [l]42 Psalm 118:22,23
[m]44 Some manuscripts do not have verse 44.

trait is this? And whose inscription?"
21"Caesar's," they replied.
Then he said to them, "Give to
Caesar what is Caesar's,[a] and to
God what is God's."
22When they heard this, they
were amazed. So they left him and
went away.[b]

Marriage at the Resurrection

22:23–33pp — Mk 12:18–27; Lk 20:27–40

23That same day the Sadducees,[c] who say there is no resurrection,[d] came to him with a question. 24"Teacher," they said, "Moses told us that if a man dies
without having children, his brother must marry the widow and have
children for him.[e] 25Now there
were seven brothers among us. The
first one married and died, and
since he had no children, he left his
wife to his brother. 26The same
thing happened to the second and
third brother, right on down to the
seventh. 27Finally, the woman
died. 28Now then, at the resurrection, whose wife will she be of the
seven, since all of them were married to her?"
29Jesus replied, "You are in error
because you do not know the Scriptures[f] or the power of God. 30At
the resurrection people will neither
marry nor be given in marriage;[g]
they will be like the angels in heav-
en. 31But about the resurrection of
the dead—have you not read what
God said to you, 32'I am the God of
Abraham, the God of Isaac, and the
God of Jacob'[n]?[h] He is not the
God of the dead but of the living."
33When the crowds heard this,
they were astonished at his teaching.[i]

The Greatest Commandment

22:34–40pp — Mk 12:28–31

34Hearing that Jesus had silenced the Sadducees,[j] the Pharisees got together. 35One of them,
an expert in the law,[k] tested him
with this question: 36"Teacher,
which is the greatest commandment in the Law?"
37Jesus replied: " 'Love the Lord
your God with all your heart and
with all your soul and with all your
mind.'[o][l] 38This is the first and
greatest commandment. 39And the
second is like it: 'Love your neighbor as yourself.'[p][m] 40All the Law
and the Prophets hang on these
two commandments."[n]

Whose Son Is the Christ?

22:41–46pp — Mk 12:35–37; Lk 20:41–44

41While the Pharisees were gathered together, Jesus asked them,
42"What do you think about the
Christ[q]? Whose son is he?"
"The son of David,"[o] they replied.
43He said to them, "How is it
then that David, speaking by the
Spirit, calls him 'Lord'? For he
says,

44" 'The Lord said to my Lord:
"Sit at my right hand
until I put your enemies
under your feet." '[r][p]

45If then David calls him 'Lord,'
how can he be his son?" 46No one
could say a word in reply, and from
that day on no one dared to ask him
any more questions.[q]

Seven Woes

23:1–7pp — Mk 12:38,39; Lk 20:45,46
23:37–39pp — Lk 13:34,35

23 Then Jesus said to the
crowds and to his disciples:
2"The teachers of the law[r] and the
Pharisees sit in Moses' seat. 3So
you must obey them and do everything they tell you. But do not do
what they do, for they do not practice what they preach. 4They tie up
heavy loads and put them on men's
shoulders, but they themselves are
not willing to lift a finger to move
them.[s]
5"Everything they do is done for
men to see:[t] They make their phy-
lacteries[s][u] wide and the tassels
on their garments[v] long; 6they love
the place of honor at banquets and

22:21 [a]Ro 13:7
22:22 [b]Mk 12:12
22:23 [c]Ac 4:1 [d]Ac 23:8; 1Co 15:12
22:24 [e]Dt 25:5,6
22:29 [f]Jn 20:9
22:30 [g]Mt 24:38
22:32 [h]Ex 3:6; Ac 7:32
22:33 [i]Mt 7:28
22:34 [j]Ac 4:1
22:35 [k]Lk 7:30; 10:25; 11:45; 14:3
22:37 [l]Dt 6:5
22:39 [m]Lev 19:18; Mt 5:43; 19:19; Gal 5:14
22:40 [n]Mt 7:12
22:42 [o]Mt 9:27
22:44 [p]Ps 110:1; Ac 2:34,35; 1Co 15:25; Heb 1:13; 10:13
22:46 [q]Mk 12:34; Lk 20:40
23:2 [r]Ezr 7:6,25; Ne 8:4
23:4 [s]Lk 11:46; Ac 15:10; Gal 6:13
23:5 [t]Mt 6:1,2,5,16 [u]Ex 13:9; Dt 6:8 [v]Nu 15:38; Dt 22:12

[n]32 Exodus 3:6 [o]37 Deut. 6:5 [p]39 Lev. 19:18 [q]42 Or *Messiah* [r]44 Psalm 110:1
[s]5 That is, boxes containing Scripture verses, worn on forehead and arm

JEWISH SECTS

PHARISEES

Their roots can be traced to the second century B.C. — to the Hasidim.

1. Along with the Torah, they accepted as equally inspired and authoritative, all material contained within the oral tradition.
2. On free will and determination, they held to a mediating view that made it impossible for either free will or the sovereignty of God to cancel out the other.
3. They accepted a rather developed hierarchy of angels and demons.
4. They taught that there was a future for the dead.
5. They believed in the immortality of the soul and in reward and retribution after death.
6. They were champions of human equality.
7. The emphasis of their teaching was ethical rather than theological.

SADDUCEES

They probably had their beginning during the Hasmonean period (166-63 B.C.). Their demise occurred c. A.D. 70 with the fall of Jerusalem.

1. They denied that the oral law was authoritative and binding.
2. They interpreted Mosaic law more literally than did the Pharisees.
3. They were very exacting in Levitical purity.
4. They attributed all to free will.
5. They argued there is neither resurrection of the dead nor a future life.
6. They rejected a belief in angels and demons.
7. They rejected the idea of a spiritual world.
8. Only the books of Moses were canonical Scripture.

ESSENES

They probably originated among the Hasidim, along with the Pharisees, from whom they later separated (I Maccabees 2:42; 7:13). They were a group of very strict and zealous Jews who took part with the Maccabeans in a revolt against the Syrians, c. 165-155 B.C.

1. They followed a strict observance of the purity laws of the Torah.
2. They were notable for their communal ownership of property.
3. They had a strong sense of mutual responsibility.
4. Daily worship was an important feature along with a daily study of their sacred scriptures.
5. Solemn oaths of piety and obedience had to be taken.
6. Sacrifices were offered on holy days and during sacred seasons.
7. Marriage was not condemned in principle but was avoided.
8. They attributed all that happened to fate.

ZEALOTS

They originated during the reign of Herod the Great c. 6 B.C. and ceased to exist in A.D. 73 at Masada.

1. They opposed payment of tribute for taxes to a pagan emperor, saying that allegiance was due only to God.
2. They held a fierce loyalty to the Jewish traditions.
3. They were opposed to the use of the Greek language in Palestine.
4. They prophesied the coming of the time of salvation.

the most important seats in the
synagogues;[a] **7**they love to be
greeted in the marketplaces and to
have men call them 'Rabbi.'[b]
8"But you are not to be called
'Rabbi,' for you have only one Master and you are all brothers. **9**And
do not call anyone on earth 'father,' for you have one Father,[c]
and he is in heaven. **10**Nor are you
to be called 'teacher,' for you have
one Teacher, the Christ.[t] **11**The
greatest among you will be your
servant.[d] **12**For whoever exalts
himself will be humbled, and whoever humbles himself will be exalted.[e]
13"Woe to you, teachers of the
law and Pharisees, you hypocrites![f] You shut the kingdom of
heaven in men's faces. You yourselves do not enter, nor will you let
those enter who are trying to.[u][g]
15"Woe to you, teachers of the
law and Pharisees, you hypocrites!
You travel over land and sea to win
a single convert,[h] and when he becomes one, you make him twice as
much a son of hell[i] as you are.
16"Woe to you, blind guides![j]
You say, 'If anyone swears by the
temple, it means nothing; but if
anyone swears by the gold of the
temple, he is bound by his oath.'[k]
17You blind fools! Which is greater:
the gold, or the temple that makes
the gold sacred?[l] **18**You also say,
'If anyone swears by the altar, it
means nothing; but if anyone
swears by the gift on it, he is bound
by his oath.' **19**You blind men!
Which is greater: the gift, or the altar that makes the gift sacred?[m]
20Therefore, he who swears by the
altar swears by it and by everything
on it. **21**And he who swears by the
temple swears by it and by the one
who dwells[n] in it. **22**And he who
swears by heaven swears by God's
throne and by the one who sits on
it.[o]
23"Woe to you, teachers of the
law and Pharisees, you hypocrites!
You give a tenth[p] of your spices
—mint, dill and cummin. But you
have neglected the more important
matters of the law—justice, mercy

23:6 [a]Lk 11:43; 14:7; 20:46
23:7 [b]ver 8; Mk 9:5; 10:51; Jn 1:38,49
23:9 [c]Mal 1:6; Mt 7:11
23:11 [d]Mt 20:26; Mk 9:35
23:12 [e]Lk 14:11
23:13 [f]ver 15,23,25, 27,29 [g]Lk 11:52
23:15 [h]Ac 2:11; 6:5; 13:43 [i]Mt 5:22
23:16 [j]ver 24; Mt 15:14 [k]Mt 5:33-35
23:17 [l]Ex 30:29
23:19 [m]Ex 29:37
23:21 [n]1Ki 8:13; Ps 26:8
23:22 [o]Ps 11:4; Mt 5:34
23:23 [p]Lev 27:30 [q]Mic 6:8; Lk 11:42
23:24 [r]ver 16
23:25 [s]Mk 7:4 [t]Lk 11:39
23:27 [u]Lk 11:44; Ac 23:3
23:29 [v]Lk 11:47,48
23:31 [w]Ac 7:51-52
23:32 [x]1Th 2:16
23:33 [y]Mt 3:7; 12:34 [z]Mt 5:22
23:34 [a]2Ch 36:15, 16; Lk 11:49 [b]Mt 10:17 [c]Mt 10:23
23:35 [d]Ge 4:8; Heb 11:4 [e]Zec 1:1 [f]2Ch 24:21

and faithfulness.[q] You should
have practiced the latter, without
neglecting the former. **24**You blind
guides![r] You strain out a gnat but
swallow a camel.
25"Woe to you, teachers of the
law and Pharisees, you hypocrites!
You clean the outside of the cup
and dish,[s] but inside they are full
of greed and self-indulgence.[t]
26Blind Pharisee! First clean the
inside of the cup and dish, and
then the outside also will be clean.
27"Woe to you, teachers of the
law and Pharisees, you hypocrites!
You are like whitewashed tombs,[u]
which look beautiful on the outside but on the inside are full of
dead men's bones and everything
unclean. **28**In the same way, on the
outside you appear to people as
righteous but on the inside you are
full of hypocrisy and wickedness.
29"Woe to you, teachers of the
law and Pharisees, you hypocrites!
You build tombs for the prophets[v]
and decorate the graves of the righteous. **30**And you say, 'If we had
lived in the days of our forefathers,
we would not have taken part with
them in shedding the blood of the
prophets.' **31**So you testify against
yourselves that you are the descendants of those who murdered the
prophets.[w] **32**Fill up, then, the
measure[x] of the sin of your forefathers!
33"You snakes! You brood of vipers![y] How will you escape being
condemned to hell?[z] **34**Therefore I
am sending you prophets and wise
men and teachers. Some of them
you will kill and crucify;[a] others
you will flog in your synagogues[b]
and pursue from town to town.[c]
35And so upon you will come all
the righteous blood that has been
shed on earth, from the blood of
righteous Abel[d] to the blood of
Zechariah son of Berekiah,[e] whom
you murdered between the temple
and the altar.[f] **36**I tell you the

[t]10 Or *Messiah* [u]13 Some manuscripts *to.* [14]*Woe to you, teachers of the law and Pharisees, you hypocrites! You devour widows' houses and for a show make lengthy prayers. Therefore you will be punished more severely.*

truth, all this will come upon this generation.[a]

37"O Jerusalem, Jerusalem, you who kill the prophets and stone those sent to you,[b] how often I have longed to gather your children together, as a hen gathers her chicks under her wings, but you were not willing. **38**Look, your house is left to you desolate.[c] **39**For I tell you, you will not see me again until you say, 'Blessed is he who comes in the name of the Lord.'[v]"[d]

Signs of the End of the Age

24:1–51pp — Mk 13:1–37; Lk 21:5–36

24 Jesus left the temple and was walking away when his disciples came up to him to call his attention to its buildings. **2**"Do you see all these things?" he asked. "I tell you the truth, not one stone here will be left on another;[e] every one will be thrown down."

3As Jesus was sitting on the Mount of Olives,[f] the disciples came to him privately. "Tell us," they said, "when will this happen, and what will be the sign of your coming and of the end of the age?"

4Jesus answered: "Watch out that no one deceives you. **5**For many will come in my name, claiming, 'I am the Christ,[w]' and will deceive many.[g] **6**You will hear of wars and rumors of wars, but see to it that you are not alarmed. Such things must happen, but the end is still to come. **7**Nation will rise against nation, and kingdom against kingdom.[h] There will be famines[i] and earthquakes in various places. **8**All these are the beginning of birth pains.

9"Then you will be handed over to be persecuted[j] and put to death,[k] and you will be hated by all nations because of me. **10**At that time many will turn away from the faith and will betray and hate each other, **11**and many false prophets[l] will appear and deceive many people. **12**Because of the increase of wickedness, the love of most will grow cold, **13**but he who stands firm to the end will be saved.[m] **14**And this gospel of the kingdom[n] will be preached in the whole world[o] as a testimony to all nations, and then the end will come.

15"So when you see standing in the holy place[p] 'the abomination that causes desolation,'[x][q] spoken of through the prophet Daniel—let the reader understand— **16**then let those who are in Judea flee to the mountains. **17**Let no one on the roof of his house[r] go down to take anything out of the house. **18**Let no one in the field go back to get his cloak. **19**How dreadful it will be in those days for pregnant women and nursing mothers![s] **20**Pray that your flight will not take place in winter or on the Sabbath. **21**For then there will be great distress, unequaled from the beginning of the world until now—and never to be equaled again.[t] **22**If those days had not been cut short, no one would survive, but for the sake of the elect[u] those days will be shortened. **23**At that time if anyone says to you, 'Look, here is the Christ!' or, 'There he is!' do not believe it.[v] **24**For false Christs and false prophets will appear and perform great signs and miracles[w] to deceive even the elect—if that were possible. **25**See, I have told you ahead of time.

26"So if anyone tells you, 'There he is, out in the desert,' do not go out; or, 'Here he is, in the inner rooms,' do not believe it. **27**For as lightning[x] that comes from the east is visible even in the west, so will be the coming of the Son of Man.[y] **28**Wherever there is a carcass, there the vultures will gather.[z]

29"Immediately after the distress of those days

" 'the sun will be darkened,
and the moon will not give
its light;
the stars will fall from the sky,
and the heavenly bodies will
be shaken.'[y][a]

23:36 [a]Mt 10:23; 24:34
23:37 [b]2Ch 24:21; Mt 5:12
23:38 [c]1Ki 9:7,8; Jer 22:5
23:39 [d]Ps 118:26; Mt 21:9
24:2 [e]Lk 19:44
24:3 [f]Mt 21:1
24:5 [g]ver 11,23,24; 1Jn 2:18
24:7 [h]Isa 19:2 [i]Ac 11:28
24:9 [j]Mt 10:17 [k]Jn 16:2
24:11 [l]Mt 7:15
24:13 [m]Mt 10:22
24:14 [n]Mt 4:23 [o]Ro 10:18; Col 1:6,23; Lk 2:1; 4:5; Ac 11:28; 17:6; Rev 3:10; 16:14
24:15 [p]Ac 6:13 [q]Da 9:27; 11:31; 12:11
24:17 [r]1Sa 9:25; Mt 10:27; Lk 12:3; Ac 10:9
24:19 [s]Lk 23:29
24:21 [t]Da 12:1; Joel 2:2
24:22 [u]ver 24,31
24:23 [v]Lk 17:23; 21:8
24:24 [w]2Th 2:9-11; Rev 13:13
24:27 [x]Lk 17:24 [y]Mt 8:20
24:28 [z]Lk 17:37
24:29 [a]Isa 13:10; 34:4; Eze 32:7; Joel 2:10,31; Zep 1:15; Rev 6:12,13; 8:12

[v]*39* Psalm 118:26 [w]*5* Or *Messiah*; also in verse 23 [x]*15* Daniel 9:27; 11:31; 12:11 [y]*29* Isaiah 13:10; 34:4

30 "At that time the sign of the
Son of Man will appear in the sky,
and all the nations of the earth will
mourn. They will see the Son of
Man coming on the clouds of the
sky,[a] with power and great glory.
31 And he will send his angels[b]
with a loud trumpet call,[c] and they
will gather his elect from the four
winds, from one end of the heavens
to the other.

32 "Now learn this lesson from
the fig tree: As soon as its twigs get
tender and its leaves come out, you
know that summer is near. 33 Even
so, when you see all these things,
you know that it[z] is near, right at
the door.[d] 34 I tell you the truth,
this generation[a] will certainly not
pass away until all these things
have happened.[e] 35 Heaven and
earth will pass away, but my words
will never pass away.[f]

The Day and Hour Unknown

24:37–39pp — Lk 17:26,27
24:45–51pp — Lk 12:42–46

36 "No one knows about that day
or hour, not even the angels in
heaven, nor the Son,[b] but only the
Father.[g] 37 As it was in the days of
Noah,[h] so it will be at the coming
of the Son of Man. 38 For in the days
before the flood, people were eating and drinking, marrying and giving in marriage,[i] up to the day
Noah entered the ark; 39 and they
knew nothing about what would
happen until the flood came and
took them all away. That is how it
will be at the coming of the Son of
Man. 40 Two men will be in the
field; one will be taken and the other left.[j] 41 Two women will be
grinding with a hand mill; one will
be taken and the other left.[k]

42 "Therefore keep watch, because you do not know on what day
your Lord will come.[l] 43 But understand this: If the owner of the
house had known at what time of
night the thief was coming,[m] he
would have kept watch and would
not have let his house be broken
into. 44 So you also must be ready,[n]
because the Son of Man will come
at an hour when you do not expect
him.

45 "Who then is the faithful and
wise servant,[o] whom the master
has put in charge of the servants in
his household to give them their
food at the proper time? 46 It will be
good for that servant whose master
finds him doing so when he returns.[p] 47 I tell you the truth, he
will put him in charge of all his possessions.[q] 48 But suppose that servant is wicked and says to himself,
'My master is staying away a long
time,' 49 and he then begins to beat
his fellow servants and to eat and
drink with drunkards.[r] 50 The master of that servant will come on a
day when he does not expect him
and at an hour he is not aware of.
51 He will cut him to pieces and assign him a place with the hypocrites, where there will be weeping
and gnashing of teeth.[s]

The Parable of the Ten Virgins

25 "At that time the kingdom
of heaven will be like[t] ten
virgins who took their lamps[u] and
went out to meet the bridegroom.[v]
2 Five of them were foolish and five
were wise.[w] 3 The foolish ones took
their lamps but did not take any oil
with them. 4 The wise, however,
took oil in jars along with their
lamps. 5 The bridegroom was a long
time in coming, and they all became drowsy and fell asleep.[x]

6 "At midnight the cry rang out:
'Here's the bridegroom! Come out
to meet him!'

7 "Then all the virgins woke up
and trimmed their lamps. 8 The
foolish ones said to the wise, 'Give
us some of your oil; our lamps are
going out.'[y]

9 " 'No,' they replied, 'there may
not be enough for both us and you.
Instead, go to those who sell oil
and buy some for yourselves.'

10 "But while they were on their
way to buy the oil, the bridegroom
arrived. The virgins who were ready
went in with him to the wedding

24:30 [a] Da 7:13; Rev 1:7
24:31 [b] Mt 13:41 [c] Isa 27:13; Zec 9:14; 1Co 15:52; 1Th 4:16; Rev 8:2; 10:7; 11:15
24:33 [d] Jas 5:9
24:34 [e] Mt 16:28; 23:36
24:35 [f] Mt 5:18
24:36 [g] Ac 1:7
24:37 [h] Ge 6:5; 7:6-23
24:38 [i] Mt 22:30
24:40 [j] Lk 17:34
24:41 [k] Lk 17:35
24:42 [l] Mt 25:13; Lk 12:40
24:43 [m] Lk 12:39
24:44 [n] 1Th 5:6
24:45 [o] Mt 25:21,23
24:46 [p] Rev 16:15
24:47 [q] Mt 25:21,23
24:49 [r] Lk 21:34
24:51 [s] Mt 8:12
25:1 [t] Mt 13:24 [u] Lk 12:35-38; Ac 20:8; Rev 4:5 [v] Rev 19:7; 21:2
25:2 [w] Mt 24:45
25:5 [x] 1Th 5:6
25:8 [y] Lk 12:35

[z] 33 Or *he* [a] 34 Or *race* [b] 36 Some manuscripts do not have *nor the Son.*

banquet.[a] And the door was shut.

11"Later the others also came. 'Sir! Sir!' they said. 'Open the door for us!'

12"But he replied, 'I tell you the truth, I don't know you.'

13"Therefore keep watch, because you do not know the day or the hour.[b]

The Parable of the Talents

25:14–30Ref — Lk 19:12–27

14"Again, it will be like a man going on a journey,[c] who called his servants and entrusted his property to them. **15**To one he gave five talents[c] of money, to another two talents, and to another one talent, each according to his ability.[d] Then he went on his journey. **16**The man who had received the five talents went at once and put his money to work and gained five more. **17**So also, the one with the two talents gained two more. **18**But the man who had received the one talent went off, dug a hole in the ground and hid his master's money.

19"After a long time the master of those servants returned and settled accounts with them.[e] **20**The man who had received the five talents brought the other five. 'Master,' he said, 'you entrusted me with five talents. See, I have gained five more.'

21"His master replied, 'Well done, good and faithful servant! You have been faithful with a few things; I will put you in charge of many things.[f] Come and share your master's happiness!'

22"The man with the two talents also came. 'Master,' he said, 'you entrusted me with two talents; see, I have gained two more.'

23"His master replied, 'Well done, good and faithful servant! You have been faithful with a few things; I will put you in charge of many things.[g] Come and share your master's happiness!'

24"Then the man who had received the one talent came. 'Master,' he said, 'I knew that you are a hard man, harvesting where you have not sown and gathering where you have not scattered seed. **25**So I was afraid and went out and hid your talent in the ground. See, here is what belongs to you.'

26"His master replied, 'You wicked, lazy servant! So you knew that I harvest where I have not sown and gather where I have not scattered seed? **27**Well then, you should have put my money on deposit with the bankers, so that when I returned I would have received it back with interest.

28" 'Take the talent from him and give it to the one who has the ten talents. **29**For everyone who has will be given more, and he will have an abundance. Whoever does not have, even what he has will be taken from him.[h] **30**And throw that worthless servant outside, into the darkness, where there will be weeping and gnashing of teeth.'[i]

The Sheep and the Goats

31"When the Son of Man comes[j] in his glory, and all the angels with him, he will sit on his throne[k] in heavenly glory. **32**All the nations will be gathered before him, and he will separate[l] the people one from another as a shepherd separates the sheep from the goats.[m] **33**He will put the sheep on his right and the goats on his left.

34"Then the King will say to those on his right, 'Come, you who are blessed by my Father; take your inheritance, the kingdom[n] prepared for you since the creation of the world.[o] **35**For I was hungry and you gave me something to eat, I was thirsty and you gave me something to drink, I was a stranger and you invited me in,[p] **36**I needed clothes and you clothed me,[q] I was sick and you looked after me,[r] I was in prison and you came to visit me.'[s]

37"Then the righteous will answer him, 'Lord, when did we see you hungry and feed you, or thirsty

25:10 [a]Rev 19:9
25:13 [b]Mt 24:42,44; Mk 13:35; Lk 12:40
25:14 [c]Mt 21:33; Lk 19:12
25:15 [d]Mt 18:24,25
25:19 [e]Mt 18:23
25:21 [f]ver 23; Mt 24:45,47; Lk 16:10
25:23 [g]ver 21
25:29 [h]Mt 13:12; Mk 4:25; Lk 8:18; 19:26
25:30 [i]Mt 8:12
25:31 [j]Mt 16:27; Lk 17:30 [k]Mt 19:28
25:32 [l]Mal 3:18 [m]Eze 34:17, 20
25:34 [n]Mt 3:2; 5:3, 10,19; 19:14; Ac 20:32; 1Co 15:50; Gal 5:21; Jas 2:5 [o]Heb 4:3; 9:26; Rev 13:8; 17:8
25:35 [p]Job 31:32; Isa 58:7; Eze 18:7; Heb 13:2
25:36 [q]Isa 58:7; Eze 18:7; Jas 2:15,16 [r]Jas 1:27 [s]2Ti 1:16

[c]*15* A talent was worth more than a thousand dollars.

and give you something to drink?
38When did we see you a stranger
and invite you in, or needing
clothes and clothe you? 39When
did we see you sick or in prison and
go to visit you?'

40"The King will reply, 'I tell you
the truth, whatever you did for one
of the least of these brothers of
mine, you did for me.'[a]

41"Then he will say to those on
his left, 'Depart from me,[b] you
who are cursed, into the eternal
fire[c] prepared for the devil and his
angels.[d] 42For I was hungry and
you gave me nothing to eat, I was
thirsty and you gave me nothing to
drink, 43I was a stranger and you
did not invite me in, I needed
clothes and you did not clothe me,
I was sick and in prison and you did
not look after me.'

44"They also will answer, 'Lord,
when did we see you hungry or
thirsty or a stranger or needing
clothes or sick or in prison, and did
not help you?'

45"He will reply, 'I tell you the
truth, whatever you did not do for
one of the least of these, you did
not do for me.'[e]

46"Then they will go away to
eternal punishment, but the righteous to eternal life."[f][g]

The Plot Against Jesus

26:2–5pp — Mk 14:1,2; Lk 22:1,2

26 When Jesus had finished
saying all these things,[h] he
said to his disciples, 2"As you
know, the Passover[i] is two days
away—and the Son of Man will be
handed over to be crucified."

3Then the chief priests and the
elders of the people assembled[j] in
the palace of the high priest, whose
name was Caiaphas,[k] 4and they
plotted to arrest Jesus in some sly
way and kill him.[l] 5"But not during the Feast," they said, "or there
may be a riot[m] among the people."

Jesus Anointed at Bethany

26:6–13pp — Mk 14:3–9
26:6–13Ref — Lk 7:37,38; Jn 12:1–8

6While Jesus was in Bethany[n] in
the home of a man known as Simon
the Leper, 7a woman came to him
with an alabaster jar of very expensive perfume, which she poured on
his head as he was reclining at the
table.

8When the disciples saw this,
they were indignant. "Why this
waste?" they asked. 9"This perfume could have been sold at a
high price and the money given to
the poor."

10Aware of this, Jesus said to
them, "Why are you bothering this
woman? She has done a beautiful
thing to me. 11The poor you will always have with you,[o] but you will
not always have me. 12When she
poured this perfume on my body,
she did it to prepare me for burial.[p] 13I tell you the truth, wherever
this gospel is preached throughout
the world, what she has done will
also be told, in memory of her."

Judas Agrees to Betray Jesus

26:14–16pp — Mk 14:10,11; Lk 22:3–6

14Then one of the Twelve—the
one called Judas Iscariot[q]—went
to the chief priests 15and asked,
"What are you willing to give me if
I hand him over to you?" So they
counted out for him thirty silver
coins.[r] 16From then on Judas
watched for an opportunity to hand
him over.

The Lord's Supper

26:17–19pp — Mk 14:12–16; Lk 22:7–13
26:20–24pp — Mk 14:17–21
26:26–29pp — Mk 14:22–25; Lk 22:17–20; 1Co 11:23–25

17On the first day of the Feast of
Unleavened Bread,[s] the disciples
came to Jesus and asked, "Where
do you want us to make preparations for you to eat the Passover?"

18He replied, "Go into the city to
a certain man and tell him, 'The
Teacher says: My appointed time[t]
is near. I am going to celebrate the
Passover with my disciples at your
house.' " 19So the disciples did as
Jesus had directed them and prepared the Passover.

20When evening came, Jesus was
reclining at the table with the

25:40 [a] Pr 19:17; Mt 10:40,42; Heb 6:10; 13:2
25:41 [b] Mt 7:23 [c] Isa 66:24; Mt 3:12; 5:22; Mk 9:43,48; Lk 3:17; Jude 7 [d] 2Pe 2:4
25:45 [e] Pr 14:31; 17:5
25:46 [f] Mt 19:29; Jn 3:15,16,36; 17:2,3; Ro 2:7; Gal 6:8; 5:11, 13,20 [g] Da 12:2; Jn 5:29; Ac 24:15; Ro 2:7,8; Gal 6:8
26:1 [h] Mt 7:28
26:2 [i] Jn 11:55; 13:1
26:3 [j] Ps 2:2 [k] ver 57; Jn 11:47-53; 18:13,14,24, 28
26:4 [l] Mt 12:14
26:5 [m] Mt 27:24
26:6 [n] Mt 21:17
26:11 [o] Dt 15:11
26:12 [p] Jn 19:40
26:14 [q] ver 25,47; Mt 10:4
26:15 [r] Ex 21:32; Zec 11:12
26:17 [s] Ex 12:18-20
26:18 [t] Jn 7:6,8,30; 12:23; 13:1; 17:1

Twelve. 21And while they were eating, he said, "I tell you the truth,
one of you will betray me."[a]

22They were very sad and began
to say to him one after the other,
"Surely not I, Lord?"

23Jesus replied, "The one who
has dipped his hand into the bowl
with me will betray me.[b] 24The
Son of Man will go just as it is written about him.[c] But woe to that
man who betrays the Son of Man! It
would be better for him if he had
not been born."

25Then Judas, the one who
would betray him, said, "Surely not
I, Rabbi?"[d]

Jesus answered, "Yes, it is
you."[d]

26While they were eating, Jesus
took bread, gave thanks and broke
it,[e] and gave it to his disciples,
saying, "Take and eat; this is my
body."

27Then he took the cup, gave
thanks and offered it to them, saying, "Drink from it, all of you.
28This is my blood of the[e] covenant,[f] which is poured out for
many for the forgiveness of sins.[g]
29I tell you, I will not drink of this
fruit of the vine from now on until
that day when I drink it anew with
you[h] in my Father's kingdom."

30When they had sung a hymn,
they went out to the Mount of Olives.[i]

Jesus Predicts Peter's Denial

26:31–35pp — Mk 14:27–31; Lk 22:31–34

31Then Jesus told them, "This
very night you will all fall away on
account of me,[j] for it is written:

" 'I will strike the shepherd,
and the sheep of the flock
will be scattered.'[f][k]

32But after I have risen, I will go
ahead of you into Galilee."[l]

33Peter replied, "Even if all fall
away on account of you, I never
will."

34"I tell you the truth," Jesus answered, "this very night, before the
rooster crows, you will disown me
three times."[m]

35But Peter declared, "Even if I
have to die with you,[n] I will never
disown you." And all the other disciples said the same.

Gethsemane

26:36–46pp — Mk 14:32–42; Lk 22:40–46

36Then Jesus went with his disciples to a place called Gethsemane, and he said to them, "Sit here
while I go over there and pray."
37He took Peter and the two sons
of Zebedee[o] along with him, and
he began to be sorrowful and troubled. 38Then he said to them, "My
soul is overwhelmed with sorrow[p]
to the point of death. Stay here and
keep watch with me."[q]

39Going a little farther, he fell
with his face to the ground and
prayed, "My Father, if it is possible,
may this cup[r] be taken from me.
Yet not as I will, but as you will."[s]

40Then he returned to his disciples and found them sleeping.
"Could you men not keep watch
with me[t] for one hour?" he asked
Peter. 41"Watch and pray so that
you will not fall into temptation.[u]
The spirit is willing, but the body is
weak."

42He went away a second time
and prayed, "My Father, if it is not
possible for this cup to be taken
away unless I drink it, may your
will be done."

43When he came back, he again
found them sleeping, because their
eyes were heavy. 44So he left them
and went away once more and
prayed the third time, saying the
same thing.

45Then he returned to the disciples and said to them, "Are you still
sleeping and resting? Look, the
hour[v] is near, and the Son of Man
is betrayed into the hands of sinners. 46Rise, let us go! Here comes
my betrayer!"

Jesus Arrested

26:47–56pp — Mk 14:43–50; Lk 22:47–53

47While he was still speaking,

26:21 [a]Lk 22:21-23; Jn 13:21
26:23 [b]Ps 41:9; Jn 13:18
26:24 [c]Isa 53; Da 9:26; Mk 9:12; Lk 24:25-27, 46; Ac 17:2,3; 26:22,23
26:25 [d]Mt 23:7
26:26 [e]Mt 14:19; 1Co 10:16
26:28 [f]Ex 24:6-8; Heb 9:20 [g]Mt 20:28; Mk 1:4
26:29 [h]Ac 10:41
26:30 [i]Mt 21:1; Mk 14:26
26:31 [j]Mt 11:6 [k]Zec 13:7; Jn 16:32
26:32 [l]Mt 28:7,10, 16
26:34 [m]ver 75; Jn 13:38
26:35 [n]Jn 13:37
26:37 [o]Mt 4:21
26:38 [p]Jn 12:27 [q]ver 40,41
26:39 [r]Mt 20:22 [s]ver 42; Ps 40:6-8; Isa 50:5; Jn 5:30; 6:38
26:40 [t]ver 38
26:41 [u]Mt 6:13
26:45 [v]ver 18

[d]25 Or *"You yourself have said it"*
[e]28 Some manuscripts *the new*
[f]31 Zech. 13:7

Judas, one of the Twelve, arrived.
With him was a large crowd armed
with swords and clubs, sent from
the chief priests and the elders of
the people. 48Now the betrayer had
arranged a signal with them: "The
one I kiss is the man; arrest him."
49Going at once to Jesus, Judas
said, "Greetings, Rabbi!"[a] and
kissed him.

50Jesus replied, "Friend,[b] do
what you came for."[g]

Then the men stepped forward,
seized Jesus and arrested him.
51With that, one of Jesus' companions reached for his sword,[c] drew
it out and struck the servant of the
high priest, cutting off his ear.[d]

52"Put your sword back in its
place," Jesus said to him, "for all
who draw the sword will die by the
sword.[e] 53Do you think I cannot
call on my Father, and he will at
once put at my disposal more than
twelve legions of angels?[f] 54But
how then would the Scriptures be
fulfilled[g] that say it must happen
in this way?"

55At that time Jesus said to the
crowd, "Am I leading a rebellion,
that you have come out with
swords and clubs to capture me?
Every day I sat in the temple courts
teaching,[h] and you did not arrest
me. 56But this has all taken place
that the writings of the prophets
might be fulfilled."[i] Then all the
disciples deserted him and fled.

Before the Sanhedrin

26:57–68pp — Mk 14:53–65; Jn 18:12,13,19–24

57Those who had arrested Jesus
took him to Caiaphas,[j] the high
priest, where the teachers of the
law and the elders had assembled.
58But Peter followed him at a distance, right up to the courtyard of
the high priest.[k] He entered and
sat down with the guards[l] to see
the outcome.

59The chief priests and the
whole Sanhedrin[m] were looking for
false evidence against Jesus so that
they could put him to death. 60But
they did not find any, though many
false witnesses[n] came forward.

Finally two[o] came forward
61and declared, "This fellow said, 'I
am able to destroy the temple of
God and rebuild it in three
days.' "[p]

62Then the high priest stood up
and said to Jesus, "Are you not going to answer? What is this testimony that these men are bringing
against you?" 63But Jesus remained silent.[q]

The high priest said to him, "I
charge you under oath[r] by the living God:[s] Tell us if you are the
Christ,[h] the Son of God."

64"Yes, it is as you say," Jesus replied. "But I say to all of you: In the
future you will see the Son of Man
sitting at the right hand of the
Mighty One[t] and coming on the
clouds of heaven."[u]

65Then the high priest tore his
clothes[v] and said, "He has spoken
blasphemy! Why do we need any
more witnesses? Look, now you
have heard the blasphemy. 66What
do you think?"

"He is worthy of death,"[w] they
answered.

67Then they spit in his face and
struck him with their fists.[x] Others
slapped him 68and said, "Prophesy
to us, Christ. Who hit you?"[y]

Peter Disowns Jesus

26:69–75pp — Mk 14:66–72; Lk 22:55–62; Jn 18:16–18,25–27

69Now Peter was sitting out in
the courtyard, and a servant girl
came to him. "You also were with
Jesus of Galilee," she said.

70But he denied it before them
all. "I don't know what you're talking about," he said.

71Then he went out to the gateway, where another girl saw him
and said to the people there, "This
fellow was with Jesus of Nazareth."

72He denied it again, with an
oath: "I don't know the man!"

73After a little while, those
standing there went up to Peter
and said, "Surely you are one of

26:49 [a]ver 25
26:50 [b]Mt 20:13; 22:12
26:51 [c]Lk 22:36,38 [d]Jn 18:10
26:52 [e]Ge 9:6; Rev 13:10
26:53 [f]2Ki 6:17; Da 7:10; Mt 4:11
26:54 [g]ver 24
26:55 [h]Mk 12:35; Lk 21:37; Jn 7:14,28; 18:20
26:56 [i]ver 24
26:57 [j]ver 3
26:58 [k]Jn 18:15 [l]Jn 7:32,45, 46
26:59 [m]Mt 5:22
26:60 [n]Ps 27:12; 35:11; Ac 6:13 [o]Dt 19:15
26:61 [p]Jn 2:19
26:63 [q]Mt 27:12,14 [r]Lev 5:1 [s]Mt 16:16
26:64 [t]Ps 110:1 [u]Da 7:13; Rev 1:7
26:65 [v]Mk 14:63
26:66 [w]Lev 24:16; Jn 19:7
26:67 [x]Mt 16:21; 27:30
26:68 [y]Lk 22:63-65

[g]50 Or *"Friend, why have you come?"*
[h]63 Or *Messiah;* also in verse 68

them, for your accent gives you away."

74Then he began to call down curses on himself and he swore to them, "I don't know the man!"

Immediately a rooster crowed. **75**Then Peter remembered the word Jesus had spoken: "Before the rooster crows, you will disown me three times."[a] And he went outside and wept bitterly.

Judas Hangs Himself

27 Early in the morning, all the chief priests and the elders of the people came to the decision to put Jesus to death.[b] **2**They bound him, led him away and handed him over[c] to Pilate, the governor.[d]

3When Judas, who had betrayed him,[e] saw that Jesus was condemned, he was seized with remorse and returned the thirty silver coins[f] to the chief priests and the elders. **4**"I have sinned," he said, "for I have betrayed innocent blood."

"What is that to us?" they replied. "That's your responsibility."[g]

5So Judas threw the money into the temple[h] and left. Then he went away and hanged himself.[i]

6The chief priests picked up the coins and said, "It is against the law to put this into the treasury, since it is blood money." **7**So they decided to use the money to buy the potter's field as a burial place for foreigners. **8**That is why it has been called the Field of Blood[j] to this day. **9**Then what was spoken by Jeremiah the prophet was fulfilled:[k] "They took the thirty silver coins, the price set on him by the people of Israel, **10**and they used them to buy the potter's field, as the Lord commanded me."[i][l]

Jesus Before Pilate

27:11–26pp — Mk 15:2–15; Lk 23:2,3, 18–25; Jn 18:29–19:16

11Meanwhile Jesus stood before the governor, and the governor asked him, "Are you the king of the Jews?"[m]

"Yes, it is as you say," Jesus replied.

12When he was accused by the chief priests and the elders, he gave no answer.[n] **13**Then Pilate asked him, "Don't you hear the testimony they are bringing against you?"[o] **14**But Jesus made no reply,[p] not even to a single charge—to the great amazement of the governor.

15Now it was the governor's custom at the Feast to release a prisoner[q] chosen by the crowd. **16**At that time they had a notorious prisoner, called Barabbas. **17**So when the crowd had gathered, Pilate asked them, "Which one do you want me to release to you: Barabbas, or Jesus who is called Christ?"[r] **18**For he knew it was out of envy that they had handed Jesus over to him.

19While Pilate was sitting on the judge's seat,[s] his wife sent him this message: "Don't have anything to do with that innocent[t] man, for I have suffered a great deal today in a dream[u] because of him."

20But the chief priests and the elders persuaded the crowd to ask for Barabbas and to have Jesus executed.[v]

21"Which of the two do you want me to release to you?" asked the governor.

"Barabbas," they answered.

22"What shall I do, then, with Jesus who is called Christ?"[w] Pilate asked.

They all answered, "Crucify him!"

23"Why? What crime has he committed?" asked Pilate.

But they shouted all the louder, "Crucify him!"

24When Pilate saw that he was getting nowhere, but that instead an uproar[x] was starting, he took water and washed his hands[y] in front of the crowd. "I am innocent of this man's blood,"[z] he said. "It is your responsibility!"[a]

25All the people answered, "Let his blood be on us and on our children!"[b]

[i]*10* See Zech. 11:12,13; Jer. 19:1-13; 32:6-9.

26:75 [a]ver 34; Jn 13:38
27:1 [b]Mt 12:14; Mk 15:1; Lk 22:66
27:2 [c]Mt 20:19 [d]Mk 15:1; Lk 13:1; Ac 3:13; 1Ti 6:13
27:3 [e]Mt 10:4 [f]Mt 26:14,15
27:4 [g]ver 24
27:5 [h]Lk 1:9,21 [i]Ac 1:18
27:8 [j]Ac 1:19
27:9 [k]Mt 1:22
27:10 [l]Zec 11:12,13; Jer 32:6-9
27:11 [m]Mt 2:2
27:12 [n]Mt 26:63; Mk 14:61; Jn 19:9
27:13 [o]Mt 26:62
27:14 [p]Mk 14:61
27:15 [q]Jn 18:39
27:17 [r]ver 22; Mt 1:16
27:19 [s]Jn 19:13 [t]ver 24 [u]Ge 20:6; Nu 12:6; 1Ki 3:5; Job 33:14-16; Mt 1:20; 2:12, 13,19,22
27:20 [v]Ac 3:14
27:22 [w]Mt 1:16
27:24 [x]Mt 26:5 [y]Ps 26:6 [z]Dt 21:6-8 [a]ver 4
27:25 [b]Jos 2:19; Ac 5:28

[26]Then he released Barabbas to them. But he had Jesus flogged,[a] and handed him over to be crucified.

The Soldiers Mock Jesus

27:27–31pp — Mk 15:16–20

[27]Then the governor's soldiers took Jesus into the Praetorium[b] and gathered the whole company of soldiers around him. [28]They stripped him and put a scarlet robe on him,[c] [29]and then twisted together a crown of thorns and set it on his head. They put a staff in his right hand and knelt in front of him and mocked him. "Hail, king of the Jews!" they said.[d] [30]They spit on him, and took the staff and struck him on the head again and again.[e] [31]After they had mocked him, they took off the robe and put his own clothes on him. Then they led him away to crucify him.[f]

The Crucifixion

27:33–44pp — Mk 15:22–32; Lk 23:33–43; Jn 19:17–24

[32]As they were going out,[g] they met a man from Cyrene,[h] named Simon, and they forced him to carry the cross.[i] [33]They came to a place called Golgotha (which means The Place of the Skull).[j] [34]There they offered Jesus wine to drink, mixed with gall;[k] but after tasting it, he refused to drink it. [35]When they had crucified him, they divided up his clothes by casting lots.[i][l] [36]And sitting down, they kept watch[m] over him there. [37]Above his head they placed the written charge against him: THIS IS JESUS, THE KING OF THE JEWS. [38]Two robbers were crucified with him,[n] one on his right and one on his left. [39]Those who passed by hurled insults at him, shaking their heads[o] [40]and saying, "You who are going to destroy the temple and build it in three days,[p] save yourself![q] Come down from the cross, if you are the Son of God!"[r]

[41]In the same way the chief priests, the teachers of the law and the elders mocked him. [42]"He saved others," they said, "but he can't save himself! He's the King of Israel![s] Let him come down now from the cross, and we will believe[t] in him. [43]He trusts in God. Let God rescue him[u] now if he wants him, for he said, 'I am the Son of God.' " [44]In the same way the robbers who were crucified with him also heaped insults on him.

The Death of Jesus

27:45–56pp — Mk 15:33–41; Lk 23:44–49

[45]From the sixth hour until the ninth hour darkness[v] came over all the land. [46]About the ninth hour Jesus cried out in a loud voice, *"Eloi, Eloi,*[k] *lama sabachthani?"*—which means, "My God, my God, why have you forsaken me?"[l][w]

[47]When some of those standing there heard this, they said, "He's calling Elijah."

[48]Immediately one of them ran and got a sponge. He filled it with wine vinegar,[x] put it on a stick, and offered it to Jesus to drink. [49]The rest said, "Now leave him alone. Let's see if Elijah comes to save him."

[50]And when Jesus had cried out again in a loud voice, he gave up his spirit.[y]

[51]At that moment the curtain of the temple[z] was torn in two from top to bottom. The earth shook and the rocks split.[a] [52]The tombs broke open and the bodies of many holy people who had died were raised to life. [53]They came out of the tombs, and after Jesus' resurrection they went into the holy city[b] and appeared to many people.

[54]When the centurion and those with him who were guarding[c] Jesus saw the earthquake and all that had happened, they were terri-

27:26 [a]Isa 53:5; Jn 19:1
27:27 [b]Jn 18:28,33; 19:9
27:28 [c]Jn 19:2
27:29 [d]Isa 53:3; Jn 19:2,3
27:30 [e]Mt 16:21; 26:67
27:31 [f]Isa 53:7
27:32 [g]Heb 13:12 [h]Ac 2:10; 6:9; 11:20; 13:1 [i]Mk 15:21; Lk 23:26
27:33 [j]Jn 19:17
27:34 [k]ver 48; Ps 69:21
27:35 [l]Ps 22:18
27:36 [m]ver 54
27:38 [n]Isa 53:12
27:39 [o]Ps 22:7; 109:25; La 2:15
27:40 [p]Mt 26:61; Jn 2:19 [q]ver 42 [r]Mt 4:3,6
27:42 [s]Jn 1:49; 12:13 [t]Jn 3:15
27:43 [u]Ps 22:8
27:45 [v]Am 8:9
27:46 [w]Ps 22:1
27:48 [x]ver 34; Ps 69:21
27:50 [y]Jn 19:30
27:51 [z]Ex 26:31-33; Heb 9:3,8 [a]ver 54
27:53 [b]Mt 4:5
27:54 [c]ver 36

i35 A few late manuscripts *lots that the word spoken by the prophet might be fulfilled: "They divided my garments among themselves and cast lots for my clothing"* (Psalm 22:18)
k46 Some manuscripts *Eli, Eli* l46 Psalm 22:1

fied, and exclaimed, "Surely he was the Son[m] of God!"[a]

55Many women were there, watching from a distance. They had followed Jesus from Galilee to care for his needs.[b] **56**Among them were Mary Magdalene, Mary the mother of James and Joses, and the mother of Zebedee's sons.[c]

The Burial of Jesus

27:57–61pp — Mk 15:42–47; Lk 23:50–56; Jn 19:38–42

57As evening approached, there came a rich man from Arimathea, named Joseph, who had himself become a disciple of Jesus. **58**Going to Pilate, he asked for Jesus' body, and Pilate ordered that it be given to him. **59**Joseph took the body, wrapped it in a clean linen cloth, **60**and placed it in his own new tomb[d] that he had cut out of the rock. He rolled a big stone in front of the entrance to the tomb and went away. **61**Mary Magdalene and the other Mary were sitting there opposite the tomb.

The Guard at the Tomb

62The next day, the one after Preparation Day, the chief priests and the Pharisees went to Pilate. **63**"Sir," they said, "we remember that while he was still alive that deceiver said, 'After three days I will rise again.'[e] **64**So give the order for the tomb to be made secure until the third day. Otherwise, his disciples may come and steal the body and tell the people that he has been raised from the dead. This last deception will be worse than the first."

65"Take a guard,"[f] Pilate answered. "Go, make the tomb as secure as you know how." **66**So they went and made the tomb secure by putting a seal[g] on the stone[h] and posting the guard.[i]

The Resurrection

28:1–8pp — Mk 16:1–8; Lk 24:1–10

28 After the Sabbath, at dawn on the first day of the week, Mary Magdalene and the other Mary[j] went to look at the tomb.

2There was a violent earthquake,[k] for an angel[l] of the Lord came down from heaven and, going to the tomb, rolled back the stone and sat on it. **3**His appearance was like lightning, and his clothes were white as snow.[m] **4**The guards were so afraid of him that they shook and became like dead men.

5The angel said to the women, "Do not be afraid,[n] for I know that you are looking for Jesus, who was crucified. **6**He is not here; he has risen, just as he said.[o] Come and see the place where he lay. **7**Then go quickly and tell his disciples: 'He has risen from the dead and is going ahead of you into Galilee.[p] There you will see him.' Now I have told you."

8So the women hurried away from the tomb, afraid yet filled with joy, and ran to tell his disciples. **9**Suddenly Jesus met them.[q] "Greetings," he said. They came to him, clasped his feet and worshiped him. **10**Then Jesus said to them, "Do not be afraid. Go and tell my brothers[r] to go to Galilee; there they will see me."

The Guards' Report

11While the women were on their way, some of the guards[s] went into the city and reported to the chief priests everything that had happened. **12**When the chief priests had met with the elders and devised a plan, they gave the soldiers a large sum of money, **13**telling them, "You are to say, 'His disciples came during the night and stole him away while we were asleep.' **14**If this report gets to the governor,[t] we will satisfy him and keep you out of trouble." **15**So the soldiers took the money and did as they were instructed. And this story has been widely circulated among the Jews to this very day.

The Great Commission

16Then the eleven disciples went

27:54 [a] Mt 4:3; 17:5
27:55 [b] Lk 8:2,3
27:56 [c] Mk 15:47; Lk 24:10; Jn 19:25
27:60 [d] Mt 27:66; 28:2; Mk 16:4
27:63 [e] Mt 16:21
27:65 [f] ver 66; Mt 28:11
27:66 [g] Da 6:17 [h] ver 60; Mt 28:2 [i] Mt 28:11
28:1 [j] Mt 27:56
28:2 [k] Mt 27:51 [l] Jn 20:12
28:3 [m] Da 10:6; Mk 9:3; Jn 20:12
28:5 [n] ver 10; Mt 14:27
28:6 [o] Mt 16:21
28:7 [p] ver 10,16; Mt 26:32
28:9 [q] Jn 20:14-18
28:10 [r] Jn 20:17; Ro 8:29; Heb 2:11-13, 17
28:11 [s] Mt 27:65,66
28:14 [t] Mt 27:2

m54 Or *a son*

to Galilee, to the mountain where
Jesus had told them to go.[a]
17When they saw him, they worshiped him; but some doubted.
18Then Jesus came to them and
said, "All authority in heaven and
on earth has been given to me.[b]
19Therefore go and make disciples
of all nations,[c] baptizing them in[n]
the name of the Father and of the
Son and of the Holy Spirit,[d] 20and
teaching[e] them to obey everything
I have commanded you. And surely
I am with you[f] always, to the very
end of the age."[g]

28:16 [a] ver 7,10; Mt 26:32 **28:18** [b] Da 7:13,14; Lk 10:22; Jn 3:35; 17:2; 1Co 15:27; Eph 1:20-22; Php 2:9,10 **28:19** [c] Mk 16:15, 16; Lk 24:47; Ac 1:8; 14:21 [d] Ac 2:38; 8:16; Ro 6:3,4 **28:20** [e] Ac 2:42 [f] Mt 18:20; Ac 18:10 [g] Mt 13:39

[n] *19* Or *into*; see Acts 8:16; 19:5; Romans 6:3; 1 Cor. 1:13; 10:2 and Gal. 3:27.

Mark

Title and Background

The early church fathers agreed that Mark's Gospel reproduces the preaching of Peter. Peter's personality can be found on almost every page, and the main characteristic of this Gospel is action.

Author and Date of Writing

Mark was the son of Mary (Ac 12:12) and the cousin of Barnabas (Col 4:10). He accompanied Paul and Barnabas on their first missionary journey. Paul speaks of him as his companion in Rome and pays high tribute to his service. It is believed that Mark is the first of the Gospels, and therefore it can be dated about A.D. 55.

Theme and Message

The book of Mark stresses facts and actions rather than themes or topics. Although it is the shortest of the four Gospels, it is often the most detailed. Jewish customs are carefully explained for Roman readers, and one of Mark's purposes was to demonstrate the deity of Christ. He tells the stories of Christ's ministry, especially his miracles. Mark spends one-third of the book telling the events of Christ's last week on earth, ending with his death and resurrection.

Outline

I. The Beginnings of Jesus' Ministry (1:1-13)
II. Jesus' Ministry in Galilee (1:14-6:29)
III. Withdrawals From Galilee (6:30-9:32)
IV. Final Ministry in Galilee (9:33-50)
V. Jesus' Ministry in Judea and Perea (10:1-52)
VI. The Passion of Jesus (11:1-15:47)
VII. The Resurrection of Jesus (16:1-20)

John the Baptist Prepares the Way

1:2-8pp – Mt 3:1-11; Lk 3:2-16

1 The beginning of the gospel about Jesus Christ, the Son of God.[a][a]

2 It is written in Isaiah the prophet:

"I will send my messenger
ahead of you,
who will prepare your
way"[b][b]—
3 "a voice of one calling in the
desert,
'Prepare the way for the Lord,
make straight paths for
him.' "[c][c]

4 And so John[d] came, baptizing in
the desert region and preaching a
baptism of repentance[e] for the forgiveness of sins.[f] 5 The whole Judean countryside and all the people of Jerusalem went out to him.
Confessing their sins, they were
baptized by him in the Jordan River. 6 John wore clothing made of
camel's hair, with a leather belt
around his waist, and he ate locusts[g] and wild honey. 7 And this
was his message: "After me will
come one more powerful than I,
the thongs of whose sandals I am
not worthy to stoop down and un-

1:1 [a]Mt 4:3
1:2 [b]Mal 3:1; Mt 11:10; Lk 7:27
1:3 [c]Isa 40:3; Jn 1:23
1:4 [d]Mt 3:1 [e]Ac 13:24 [f]Lk 1:77
1:6 [g]Lev 11:22

[a]*1* Some manuscripts do not have *the Son of God.* [b]*2* Mal. 3:1 [c]*3* Isaiah 40:3

tie.[a] **8**I baptize you with[d] water, but he will baptize you with the Holy Spirit."[b]

The Baptism and Temptation of Jesus

1:9–11pp — Mt 3:13–17; Lk 3:21,22
1:12,13pp — Mt 4:1–11; Lk 4:1–13

9At that time Jesus came from Nazareth[c] in Galilee and was baptized by John in the Jordan. **10**As Jesus was coming up out of the water, he saw heaven being torn open and the Spirit descending on him like a dove.[d] **11**And a voice came from heaven: "You are my Son,[e] whom I love; with you I am well pleased."

12At once the Spirit sent him out into the desert, **13**and he was in the desert forty days, being tempted by Satan.[f] He was with the wild animals, and angels attended him.

The Calling of the First Disciples

1:16–20pp — Mt 4:18–22; Lk 5:2–11; Jn 1:35–42

14After John was put in prison, Jesus went into Galilee,[g] proclaiming the good news of God.[h] **15**"The time has come,"[i] he said. "The kingdom of God is near. Repent and believe the good news!"[j]

16As Jesus walked beside the Sea of Galilee, he saw Simon and his brother Andrew casting a net into the lake, for they were fishermen. **17**"Come, follow me," Jesus said, "and I will make you fishers of men." **18**At once they left their nets and followed him.

19When he had gone a little farther, he saw James son of Zebedee and his brother John in a boat, preparing their nets. **20**Without delay he called them, and they left their father Zebedee in the boat with the hired men and followed him.

Jesus Drives Out an Evil Spirit

1:21–28pp — Lk 4:31–37

21They went to Capernaum, and when the Sabbath came, Jesus went into the synagogue and began to teach.[k] **22**The people were amazed at his teaching, because he taught them as one who had authority, not as the teachers of the law.[l] **23**Just then a man in their synagogue who was possessed by an evil[e] spirit cried out, **24**"What do you want with us,[m] Jesus of Nazareth?[n] Have you come to destroy us? I know who you are—the Holy One of God!"[o]

25"Be quiet!" said Jesus sternly. "Come out of him!"[p] **26**The evil spirit shook the man violently and came out of him with a shriek.[q]

27The people were all so amazed[r] that they asked each other, "What is this? A new teaching—and with authority! He even gives orders to evil spirits and they obey him." **28**News about him spread quickly over the whole region[s] of Galilee.

Jesus Heals Many

1:29–31pp — Mt 8:14,15; Lk 4:38,39
1:32–34pp — Mt 8:16,17; Lk 4:40,41

29As soon as they left the synagogue,[t] they went with James and John to the home of Simon and Andrew. **30**Simon's mother-in-law was in bed with a fever, and they told Jesus about her. **31**So he went to her, took her hand and helped her up.[u] The fever left her and she began to wait on them.

32That evening after sunset the people brought to Jesus all the sick and demon-possessed.[v] **33**The whole town gathered at the door, **34**and Jesus healed many who had various diseases.[w] He also drove out many demons, but he would not let the demons speak because they knew who he was.[x]

Jesus Prays in a Solitary Place

1:35–38pp — Lk 4:42,43

35Very early in the morning, while it was still dark, Jesus got up, left the house and went off to a solitary place, where he prayed.[y] **36**Simon and his companions went to look for him, **37**and when they found him, they exclaimed: "Everyone is looking for you!"

1:7 [a]Ac 13:25
1:8 [b]Isa 44:3; Joel 2:28; Ac 1:5; 2:4; 11:16; 19:4-6
1:9 [c]Mt 2:23
1:10 [d]Jn 1:32
1:11 [e]Mt 3:17
1:13 [f]Mt 4:10
1:14 [g]Mt 4:12 [h]Mt 4:23
1:15 [i]Gal 4:4; Eph 1:10 [j]Ac 20:21
1:21 [k]Mt 4:23; Mk 10:1
1:22 [l]Mt 7:28,29
1:24 [m]Mt 8:29 [n]Mt 2:23; Lk 24:19; Ac 24:5 [o]Lk 1:35; Jn 6:69; Ac 3:14
1:25 [p]ver 34
1:26 [q]Mk 9:20
1:27 [r]Mk 10:24,32
1:28 [s]Mt 9:26
1:29 [t]ver 21,23
1:31 [u]Lk 7:14
1:32 [v]Mt 4:24
1:34 [w]Mt 4:23 [x]Mk 3:12; Ac 16:17,18
1:35 [y]Lk 3:21

[d]8 Or *in* [e]23 Greek *unclean*; also in verses 26 and 27

38Jesus replied, "Let us go somewhere else—to the nearby villages—so I can preach there also.
That is why I have come."[a] 39So he
traveled throughout Galilee,
preaching in their synagogues[b]
and driving out demons.[c]

A Man With Leprosy

1:40–44pp — Mt 8:2–4; Lk 5:12–14

40A man with leprosy[f] came to
him and begged him on his
knees,[d] "If you are willing, you can
make me clean."
41Filled with compassion, Jesus
reached out his hand and touched
the man. "I am willing," he said.
"Be clean!" 42Immediately the leprosy left him and he was cured.
43Jesus sent him away at once
with a strong warning: 44"See that
you don't tell this to anyone.[e] But
go, show yourself to the priest[f]
and offer the sacrifices that Moses
commanded for your cleansing,[g]
as a testimony to them." 45Instead
he went out and began to talk freely, spreading the news. As a result,
Jesus could no longer enter a town
openly but stayed outside in lonely
places.[h] Yet the people still came
to him from everywhere.[i]

Jesus Heals a Paralytic

2:3–12pp — Mt 9:2–8; Lk 5:18–26

2 A few days later, when Jesus
again entered Capernaum, the
people heard that he had come
home. 2So many[j] gathered that
there was no room left, not even
outside the door, and he preached
the word to them. 3Some men
came, bringing to him a paralytic,[k]
carried by four of them. 4Since they
could not get him to Jesus because
of the crowd, they made an opening in the roof above Jesus and, after digging through it, lowered the
mat the paralyzed man was lying
on. 5When Jesus saw their faith, he
said to the paralytic, "Son, your
sins are forgiven."[l]
6Now some teachers of the law
were sitting there, thinking to
themselves, 7"Why does this fellow
talk like that? He's blaspheming!
Who can forgive sins but God
alone?"[m]
8Immediately Jesus knew in his
spirit that this was what they were
thinking in their hearts, and he
said to them, "Why are you thinking these things? 9Which is easier:
to say to the paralytic, 'Your sins
are forgiven,' or to say, 'Get up,
take your mat and walk'? 10But
that you may know that the Son of
Man[n] has authority on earth to forgive sins . . . ." He said to the paralytic, 11"I tell you, get up, take your
mat and go home." 12He got up,
took his mat and walked out in full
view of them all. This amazed everyone and they praised God,[o] saying, "We have never seen anything
like this!"[p]

The Calling of Levi

2:14–17pp — Mt 9:9–13; Lk 5:27–32

13Once again Jesus went out beside the lake. A large crowd came
to him,[q] and he began to teach
them. 14As he walked along, he
saw Levi son of Alphaeus sitting at
the tax collector's booth. "Follow
me,"[r] Jesus told him, and Levi got
up and followed him.
15While Jesus was having dinner
at Levi's house, many tax collectors and "sinners" were eating with
him and his disciples, for there
were many who followed him.
16When the teachers of the law
who were Pharisees[s] saw him eating with the "sinners" and tax collectors, they asked his disciples:
"Why does he eat with tax collectors and 'sinners'?"[t]
17On hearing this, Jesus said to
them, "It is not the healthy who
need a doctor, but the sick. I have
not come to call the righteous, but
sinners."[u]

Jesus Questioned About Fasting

2:18–22pp — Mt 9:14–17; Lk 5:33–38

18Now John's disciples and the
Pharisees were fasting.[v] Some

[f]40 The Greek word was used for various diseases affecting the skin—not necessarily leprosy.

1:38 [a]Isa 61:1
1:39 [b]Mt 4:23 [c]Mt 4:24
1:40 [d]Mk 10:17
1:44 [e]Mt 8:4 [f]Lev 13:49 [g]Lev 14:1-32
1:45 [h]Lk 5:15,16 [i]Mk 2:13; Lk 5:17; Jn 6:2
2:2 [j]ver 13; Mk 1:45
2:3 [k]Mt 4:24
2:5 [l]Lk 7:48
2:7 [m]Isa 43:25
2:10 [n]Mt 8:20
2:12 [o]Mt 9:8 [p]Mt 9:33
2:13 [q]Mk 1:45; Lk 5:15; Jn 6:2
2:14 [r]Mt 4:19
2:16 [s]Ac 23:9 [t]Mt 9:11
2:17 [u]Lk 19:10; 1Ti 1:15
2:18 [v]Mt 6:16-18; Ac 13:2

people came and asked Jesus, "How is it that John's disciples and the disciples of the Pharisees are fasting, but yours are not?"

19Jesus answered, "How can the guests of the bridegroom fast while he is with them? They cannot, so long as they have him with them. **20**But the time will come when the bridegroom will be taken from them,[a] and on that day they will fast.

21"No one sews a patch of unshrunk cloth on an old garment. If he does, the new piece will pull away from the old, making the tear worse. **22**And no one pours new wine into old wineskins. If he does, the wine will burst the skins, and both the wine and the wineskins will be ruined. No, he pours new wine into new wineskins."

Lord of the Sabbath

2:23–28pp — Mt 12:1–8; Lk 6:1–5
3:1–6pp — Mt 12:9–14; Lk 6:6–11

23One Sabbath Jesus was going through the grainfields, and as his disciples walked along, they began to pick some heads of grain.[b] **24**The Pharisees said to him, "Look, why are they doing what is unlawful on the Sabbath?"[c]

25He answered, "Have you never read what David did when he and his companions were hungry and in need? **26**In the days of Abiathar the high priest,[d] he entered the house of God and ate the consecrated bread, which is lawful only for priests to eat.[e] And he also gave some to his companions."[f]

27Then he said to them, "The Sabbath was made for man,[g] not man for the Sabbath.[h] **28**So the Son of Man[i] is Lord even of the Sabbath."

3 Another time he went into the synagogue,[j] and a man with a shriveled hand was there. **2**Some of them were looking for a reason to accuse Jesus, so they watched him closely[k] to see if he would heal him on the Sabbath.[l] **3**Jesus said to the man with the shriveled hand, "Stand up in front of everyone."

4Then Jesus asked them, "Which is lawful on the Sabbath: to do good or to do evil, to save life or to kill?" But they remained silent.

5He looked around at them in anger and, deeply distressed at their stubborn hearts, said to the man, "Stretch out your hand." He stretched it out, and his hand was completely restored. **6**Then the Pharisees went out and began to plot with the Herodians[m] how they might kill Jesus.[n]

Crowds Follow Jesus

3:7–12pp — Mt 12:15,16; Lk 6:17–19

7Jesus withdrew with his disciples to the lake, and a large crowd from Galilee followed.[o] **8**When they heard all he was doing, many people came to him from Judea, Jerusalem, Idumea, and the regions across the Jordan and around Tyre and Sidon.[p] **9**Because of the crowd he told his disciples to have a small boat ready for him, to keep the people from crowding him. **10**For he had healed many,[q] so that those with diseases were pushing forward to touch him.[r] **11**Whenever the evil[g] spirits saw him, they fell down before him and cried out, "You are the Son of God."[s] **12**But he gave them strict orders not to tell who he was.[t]

The Appointing of the Twelve Apostles

3:16–19pp — Mt 10:2–4; Lk 6:14–16; Ac 1:13

13Jesus went up on a mountainside and called to him those he wanted, and they came to him.[u] **14**He appointed twelve—designating them apostles[h][v]—that they might be with him and that he might send them out to preach **15**and to have authority to drive out demons.[w] **16**These are the twelve he appointed: Simon (to whom he gave the name Peter);[x] **17**James son of Zebedee and his brother John (to them he gave the name Boanerges, which means Sons of

2:20 [a] Lk 17:22
2:23 [b] Dt 23:25
2:24 [c] Mt 12:2
2:26 [d] 1Ch 24:6; 2Sa 8:17 [e] Lev 24:5-9 [f] 1Sa 21:1-6
2:27 [g] Ex 23:12; Dt 5:14 [h] Col 2:16
2:28 [i] Mt 8:20
3:1 [j] Mt 4:23; Mk 1:21
3:2 [k] Mt 12:10 [l] Lk 14:1
3:6 [m] Mt 22:16; Mk 12:13 [n] Mt 12:14
3:7 [o] Mt 4:25
3:8 [p] Mt 11:21
3:10 [q] Mt 4:23 [r] Mt 9:20
3:11 [s] Mt 4:3; Mk 1:23,24
3:12 [t] Mt 8:4; Mk 1:24,25, 34; Ac 16:17, 18
3:13 [u] Mt 5:1
3:14 [v] Mk 6:30
3:15 [w] Mt 10:1
3:16 [x] Jn 1:42

[g]*11* Greek *unclean;* also in verse 30
[h]*14* Some manuscripts do not have *designating them apostles.*

Thunder); **18**Andrew, Philip, Bartholomew, Matthew, Thomas,
James son of Alphaeus, Thaddaeus, Simon the Zealot **19**and Judas
Iscariot, who betrayed him.

Jesus and Beelzebub

3:23–27pp — Mt 12:25–29; Lk 11:17–22

20Then Jesus entered a house,
and again a crowd gathered,[a] so
that he and his disciples were not
even able to eat.[b] **21**When his family heard about this, they went to
take charge of him, for they said,
"He is out of his mind."[c]
22And the teachers of the law
who came down from Jerusalem[d]
said, "He is possessed by Beelzebub[i]![e] By the prince of demons he
is driving out demons."[f]
23So Jesus called them and
spoke to them in parables:[g] "How
can Satan[h] drive out Satan? **24**If a
kingdom is divided against itself,
that kingdom cannot stand. **25**If a
house is divided against itself, that
house cannot stand. **26**And if Satan
opposes himself and is divided, he
cannot stand; his end has come.
27In fact, no one can enter a strong
man's house and carry off his possessions unless he first ties up the
strong man. Then he can rob his
house.[i] **28**I tell you the truth, all
the sins and blasphemies of men
will be forgiven them. **29**But whoever blasphemes against the Holy
Spirit will never be forgiven; he is
guilty of an eternal sin."[j]
30He said this because they were
saying, "He has an evil spirit."

Jesus' Mother and Brothers

3:31–35pp — Mt 12:46–50; Lk 8:19–21

31Then Jesus' mother and brothers arrived.[k] Standing outside,
they sent someone in to call him.
32A crowd was sitting around him,
and they told him, "Your mother
and brothers are outside looking
for you."
33"Who are my mother and my
brothers?" he asked.
34Then he looked at those seated in a circle around him and said,

3:20 [a] ver 7 [b] Mk 6:31
3:21 [c] Jn 10:20; Ac 26:24
3:22 [d] Mt 15:1 [e] Mt 10:25; 11:18; 12:24; Jn 7:20; 8:48, 52; 10:20 [f] Mt 9:34
3:23 [g] Mk 4:2 [h] Mt 4:10
3:27 [i] Isa 49:24,25
3:29 [j] Mt 12:31,32; Lk 12:10
3:31 [k] ver 21
4:1 [l] Mk 2:13; 3:7
4:2 [m] ver 11; Mk 3:23
4:3 [n] ver 26
4:8 [o] Jn 15:5; Col 1:6
4:9 [p] ver 23; Mt 11:15
4:11 [q] Mt 3:2 [r] 1Co 5:12,13; Col 4:5; 1Th 4:12; 1Ti 3:7
4:12 [s] Isa 6:9,10; Mt 13:13-15

"Here are my mother and my
brothers! **35**Whoever does God's
will is my brother and sister and
mother."

The Parable of the Sower

4:1–12pp — Mt 13:1–15; Lk 8:4–10
4:13–20pp — Mt 13:18–23; Lk 8:11–15

4 Again Jesus began to teach by
the lake.[l] The crowd that
gathered around him was so large
that he got into a boat and sat in it
out on the lake, while all the people were along the shore at the water's edge. **2**He taught them many
things by parables,[m] and in his
teaching said: **3**"Listen! A farmer
went out to sow his seed.[n] **4**As he
was scattering the seed, some fell
along the path, and the birds came
and ate it up. **5**Some fell on rocky
places, where it did not have much
soil. It sprang up quickly, because
the soil was shallow. **6**But when the
sun came up, the plants were
scorched, and they withered because they had no root. **7**Other
seed fell among thorns, which grew
up and choked the plants, so that
they did not bear grain. **8**Still other
seed fell on good soil. It came up,
grew and produced a crop, multi-
plying thirty, sixty, or even a hundred times."[o]
9Then Jesus said, "He who has
ears to hear, let him hear."[p]
10When he was alone, the
Twelve and the others around him
asked him about the parables.
11He told them, "The secret of the
kingdom of God[q] has been given to
you. But to those on the outside[r]
everything is said in parables **12**so
that,

" 'they may be ever seeing but
never perceiving,
and ever hearing but never
understanding;
otherwise they might turn and
be forgiven!'[j]"[s]

13Then Jesus said to them,
"Don't you understand this para-

[i] *22* Greek *Beezeboul* or *Beelzeboul*
[j] *12* Isaiah 6:9,10

ble? How then will you understand any parable? **14**The farmer sows the word.[a] **15**Some people are like seed along the path, where the word is sown. As soon as they hear it, Satan[b] comes and takes away the word that was sown in them. **16**Others, like seed sown on rocky places, hear the word and at once receive it with joy. **17**But since they have no root, they last only a short time. When trouble or persecution comes because of the word, they quickly fall away. **18**Still others, like seed sown among thorns, hear the word; **19**but the worries of this life, the deceitfulness of wealth[c] and the desires for other things come in and choke the word, making it unfruitful. **20**Others, like seed sown on good soil, hear the word, accept it, and produce a crop—thirty, sixty or even a hundred times what was sown."

A Lamp on a Stand

21He said to them, "Do you bring in a lamp to put it under a bowl or a bed? Instead, don't you put it on its stand?[d] **22**For whatever is hidden is meant to be disclosed, and whatever is concealed is meant to be brought out into the open.[e] **23**If anyone has ears to hear, let him hear."[f]

24"Consider carefully what you hear," he continued. "With the measure you use, it will be measured to you—and even more.[g] **25**Whoever has will be given more; whoever does not have, even what he has will be taken from him."[h]

The Parable of the Growing Seed

26He also said, "This is what the kingdom of God is like.[i] A man scatters seed on the ground. **27**Night and day, whether he sleeps or gets up, the seed sprouts and grows, though he does not know how. **28**All by itself the soil produces grain—first the stalk, then the head, then the full kernel in the head. **29**As soon as the grain is ripe, he puts the sickle to it, because the harvest has come."[j]

The Parable of the Mustard Seed

4:30–32pp — Mt 13:31,32; Lk 13:18,19

30Again he said, "What shall we say the kingdom of God is like,[k] or what parable shall we use to describe it? **31**It is like a mustard seed, which is the smallest seed you plant in the ground. **32**Yet when planted, it grows and becomes the largest of all garden plants, with such big branches that the birds of the air can perch in its shade."

33With many similar parables Jesus spoke the word to them, as much as they could understand.[l] **34**He did not say anything to them without using a parable.[m] But when he was alone with his own disciples, he explained everything.

Jesus Calms the Storm

4:35–41pp — Mt 8:18,23–27; Lk 8:22–25

35That day when evening came, he said to his disciples, "Let us go over to the other side." **36**Leaving the crowd behind, they took him along, just as he was, in the boat.[n] There were also other boats with him. **37**A furious squall came up, and the waves broke over the boat, so that it was nearly swamped. **38**Jesus was in the stern, sleeping on a cushion. The disciples woke him and said to him, "Teacher, don't you care if we drown?"

39He got up, rebuked the wind and said to the waves, "Quiet! Be still!" Then the wind died down and it was completely calm.

40He said to his disciples, "Why are you so afraid? Do you still have no faith?"[o]

41They were terrified and asked each other, "Who is this? Even the wind and the waves obey him!"

4:14 [a] Mk 16:20; Lk 1:2; Ac 4:31; 8:4; 16:6; 17:11; Php 1:14
4:15 [b] Mt 4:10
4:19 [c] Mt 19:23; 1Ti 6:9,10,17; 1Jn 2:15-17
4:21 [d] Mt 5:15
4:22 [e] Jer 16:17; Mt 10:26; Lk 8:17; 12:2
4:23 [f] ver 9; Mt 11:15
4:24 [g] Mt 7:2; Lk 6:38
4:25 [h] Mt 13:12; 25:29
4:26 [i] Mt 13:24
4:29 [j] Rev 14:15
4:30 [k] Mt 13:24
4:33 [l] Jn 16:12
4:34 [m] Jn 16:25
4:36 [n] ver 1; Mk 3:9; 5:2, 21; 6:32,45
4:40 [o] Mt 14:31; Mk 16:14

The Healing of a Demon-possessed Man

5:1–17pp — Mt 8:28–34; Lk 8:26–37
5:18–20pp — Lk 8:38,39

5 They went across the lake to the region of the Gerasenes.[k] **2**When Jesus got out of the boat,[a] a man with an evil[l] spirit[b] came from the tombs to meet him. **3**This man lived in the tombs, and no one could bind him any more, not even with a chain. **4**For he had often been chained hand and foot, but he tore the chains apart and broke the irons on his feet. No one was strong enough to subdue him. **5**Night and day among the tombs and in the hills he would cry out and cut himself with stones.

6When he saw Jesus from a distance, he ran and fell on his knees in front of him. **7**He shouted at the top of his voice, "What do you want with me,[c] Jesus, Son of the Most High God?[d] Swear to God that you won't torture me!" **8**For Jesus had said to him, "Come out of this man, you evil spirit!"

9Then Jesus asked him, "What is your name?"

"My name is Legion,"[e] he replied, "for we are many." **10**And he begged Jesus again and again not to send them out of the area.

11A large herd of pigs was feeding on the nearby hillside. **12**The demons begged Jesus, "Send us among the pigs; allow us to go into them." **13**He gave them permission, and the evil spirits came out and went into the pigs. The herd, about two thousand in number, rushed down the steep bank into the lake and were drowned.

14Those tending the pigs ran off and reported this in the town and countryside, and the people went out to see what had happened. **15**When they came to Jesus, they saw the man who had been possessed by the legion[f] of demons,[g] sitting there, dressed and in his right mind; and they were afraid. **16**Those who had seen it told the people what had happened to the demon-possessed man—and told about the pigs as well. **17**Then the people began to plead with Jesus to leave their region.

18As Jesus was getting into the boat, the man who had been demon-possessed begged to go with him. **19**Jesus did not let him, but said, "Go home to your family and tell them[h] how much the Lord has done for you, and how he has had mercy on you." **20**So the man went away and began to tell in the Decapolis[m][i] how much Jesus had done for him. And all the people were amazed.

A Dead Girl and a Sick Woman

5:22–43pp — Mt 9:18–26; Lk 8:41–56

21When Jesus had again crossed over by boat to the other side of the lake,[j] a large crowd gathered around him while he was by the lake.[k] **22**Then one of the synagogue rulers,[l] named Jairus, came there. Seeing Jesus, he fell at his feet **23**and pleaded earnestly with him, "My little daughter is dying. Please come and put your hands on[m] her so that she will be healed and live." **24**So Jesus went with him.

A large crowd followed and pressed around him. **25**And a woman was there who had been subject to bleeding[n] for twelve years. **26**She had suffered a great deal under the care of many doctors and had spent all she had, yet instead of getting better she grew worse. **27**When she heard about Jesus, she came up behind him in the crowd and touched his cloak, **28**because she thought, "If I just touch his clothes,[o] I will be healed." **29**Immediately her bleeding stopped and she felt in her body that she was freed from her suffering.[p]

30At once Jesus realized that power[q] had gone out from him. He turned around in the crowd and asked, "Who touched my clothes?"

5:2 [a] Mk 4:1 [b] Mk 1:23
5:7 [c] Mt 8:29 [d] Mt 4:3; Lk 1:32; 6:35; Ac 16:17; Heb 7:1
5:9 [e] ver 15
5:15 [f] ver 9 [g] ver 16, 18; Mt 4:24
5:19 [h] Mt 8:4
5:20 [i] Mt 4:25; Mk 7:31
5:21 [j] Mt 9:1 [k] Mk 4:1
5:22 [l] ver 35,36,38; Lk 13:14; Ac 13:15; 18:8,17
5:23 [m] Mt 19:13; Mk 6:5; 7:32; 8:23; 16:18; Lk 4:40; 13:13; Ac 6:6
5:25 [n] Lev 15:25-30
5:28 [o] Mt 9:20
5:29 [p] ver 34
5:30 [q] Lk 5:17; 6:19

[k] *1* Some manuscripts *Gadarenes*; other manuscripts *Gergesenes* [l] *2* Greek *unclean*; also in verses 8 and 13 [m] *20* That is, the Ten Cities

31"You see the people crowding against you," his disciples answered, "and yet you can ask, 'Who touched me?' "

32But Jesus kept looking around to see who had done it. 33Then the woman, knowing what had happened to her, came and fell at his feet and, trembling with fear, told him the whole truth. 34He said to her, "Daughter, your faith has healed you.[a] Go in peace[b] and be freed from your suffering."

35While Jesus was still speaking, some men came from the house of Jairus, the synagogue ruler.[c] "Your daughter is dead," they said. "Why bother the teacher any more?"

36Ignoring what they said, Jesus told the synagogue ruler, "Don't be afraid; just believe."

37He did not let anyone follow him except Peter, James and John the brother of James.[d] 38When they came to the home of the synagogue ruler,[e] Jesus saw a commotion, with people crying and wailing loudly. 39He went in and said to them, "Why all this commotion and wailing? The child is not dead but asleep."[f] 40But they laughed at him.

After he put them all out, he took the child's father and mother and the disciples who were with him, and went in where the child was. 41He took her by the hand[g] and said to her, *"Talitha koum!"* (which means, "Little girl, I say to you, get up!").[h] 42Immediately the girl stood up and walked around (she was twelve years old). At this they were completely astonished. 43He gave strict orders not to let anyone know about this,[i] and told them to give her something to eat.

A Prophet Without Honor

6:1–6pp — Mt 13:54–58

6 Jesus left there and went to his hometown,[j] accompanied by his disciples. 2When the Sabbath came,[k] he began to teach in the synagogue,[l] and many who heard him were amazed.[m]

"Where did this man get these things?" they asked. "What's this wisdom that has been given him, that he even does miracles! 3Isn't this the carpenter? Isn't this Mary's son and the brother of James, Joseph,[n] Judas and Simon?[n] Aren't his sisters here with us?" And they took offense at him.[o]

4Jesus said to them, "Only in his hometown, among his relatives and in his own house is a prophet without honor."[p] 5He could not do any miracles there, except lay his hands on[q] a few sick people and heal them. 6And he was amazed at their lack of faith.

Jesus Sends Out the Twelve

6:7–11pp — Mt 10:1,9–14; Lk 9:1,3–5

Then Jesus went around teaching from village to village.[r] 7Calling the Twelve to him,[s] he sent them out two by two[t] and gave them authority over evil[o] spirits.[u]

8These were his instructions: "Take nothing for the journey except a staff—no bread, no bag, no money in your belts. 9Wear sandals but not an extra tunic. 10Whenever you enter a house, stay there until you leave that town. 11And if any place will not welcome you or listen to you, shake the dust off your feet[v] when you leave, as a testimony against them."

12They went out and preached that people should repent.[w] 13They drove out many demons and anointed many sick people with oil[x] and healed them.

John the Baptist Beheaded

6:14–29pp — Mt 14:1–12
6:14–16pp — Lk 9:7–9

14King Herod heard about this, for Jesus' name had become well known. Some were saying,[p] "John the Baptist[y] has been raised from the dead, and that is why miraculous powers are at work in him."

15Others said, "He is Elijah."[z]

And still others claimed, "He is a

5:34 [a]Mt 9:22 [b]Ac 15:33
5:35 [c]ver 22
5:37 [d]Mt 4:21
5:38 [e]ver 22
5:39 [f]Mt 9:24
5:41 [g]Mk 1:31 [h]Lk 7:14; Ac 9:40
5:43 [i]Mt 8:4
6:1 [j]Mt 2:23
6:2 [k]Mk 1:21 [l]Mt 4:23 [m]Mt 7:28
6:3 [n]Mt 12:46 [o]Mt 11:6; Jn 6:61
6:4 [p]Lk 4:24; Jn 4:44
6:5 [q]Mk 5:23
6:6 [r]Mt 9:35; Mk 1:39; Lk 13:22
6:7 [s]Mk 3:13 [t]Dt 17:6; Lk 10:1 [u]Mt 10:1
6:11 [v]Mt 10:14
6:12 [w]Lk 9:6
6:13 [x]Jas 5:14
6:14 [y]Mt 3:1
6:15 [z]Mal 4:5

n3 Greek *Joses,* a variant of *Joseph*
o7 Greek *unclean*
p14 Some early manuscripts *He was saying*

prophet,[a] like one of the prophets
of long ago."[b]
16But when Herod heard this, he
said, "John, the man I beheaded,
has been raised from the dead!"
17For Herod himself had given
orders to have John arrested, and
he had him bound and put in prison.[c] He did this because of Herodias, his brother Philip's wife,
whom he had married. **18**For John
had been saying to Herod, "It is not
lawful for you to have your brother's wife."[d] **19**So Herodias nursed a
grudge against John and wanted to
kill him. But she was not able to,
20because Herod feared John and
protected him, knowing him to be
a righteous and holy man.[e] When
Herod heard John, he was greatly
puzzled[q]; yet he liked to listen to
him.
21Finally the opportune time
came. On his birthday Herod gave
a banquet[f] for his high officials
and military commanders and the
leading men of Galilee.[g] **22**When
the daughter of Herodias came in
and danced, she pleased Herod
and his dinner guests.
The king said to the girl, "Ask me
for anything you want, and I'll give
it to you." **23**And he promised her
with an oath, "Whatever you ask I
will give you, up to half my kingdom."[h]
24She went out and said to her
mother, "What shall I ask for?"
"The head of John the Baptist,"
she answered.
25At once the girl hurried in to
the king with the request: "I want
you to give me right now the head
of John the Baptist on a platter."
26The king was greatly distressed, but because of his oaths
and his dinner guests, he did not
want to refuse her. **27**So he immediately sent an executioner with orders to bring John's head. The man
went, beheaded John in the prison,
28and brought back his head on a
platter. He presented it to the girl,
and she gave it to her mother. **29**On
hearing of this, John's disciples
came and took his body and laid it
in a tomb.

Jesus Feeds the Five Thousand

6:32–44pp — Mt 14:13–21; Lk 9:10–17; Jn 6:5–13
6:32–44Ref — Mk 8:2–9

30The apostles[i] gathered around
Jesus and reported to him all they
had done and taught.[j] **31**Then, because so many people were coming
and going that they did not even
have a chance to eat,[k] he said to
them, "Come with me by yourselves to a quiet place and get
some rest."
32So they went away by themselves in a boat[l] to a solitary place.
33But many who saw them leaving
recognized them and ran on foot
from all the towns and got there
ahead of them. **34**When Jesus landed and saw a large crowd, he had
compassion on them, because they
were like sheep without a shepherd.[m] So he began teaching them
many things.
35By this time it was late in the
day, so his disciples came to him.
"This is a remote place," they said,
"and it's already very late. **36**Send
the people away so they can go to
the surrounding countryside and
villages and buy themselves something to eat."
37But he answered, "You give
them something to eat."[n]
They said to him, "That would
take eight months of a man's
wages[r]! Are we to go and spend
that much on bread and give it to
them to eat?"
38"How many loaves do you
have?" he asked. "Go and see."
When they found out, they said,
"Five—and two fish."[o]
39Then Jesus directed them to
have all the people sit down in
groups on the green grass. **40**So
they sat down in groups of hundreds and fifties. **41**Taking the five
loaves and the two fish and looking
up to heaven, he gave thanks and
broke the loaves.[p] Then he gave
them to his disciples to set before
the people. He also divided the two
fish among them all. **42**They all ate
and were satisfied, **43**and the disci-

6:15 [a]Mt 21:11 [b]Mt 16:14; Mk 8:28
6:17 [c]Mt 4:12; 11:2; Lk 3:19, 20
6:18 [d]Lev 18:16; 20:21
6:20 [e]Mt 11:9; 21:26
6:21 [f]Est 1:3; 2:18 [g]Lk 3:1
6:23 [h]Est 5:3,6; 7:2
6:30 [i]Mt 10:2; Lk 9:10; 17:5; 22:14; 24:10; Ac 1:2,26 [j]Lk 9:10
6:31 [k]Mk 3:20
6:32 [l]ver 45; Mk 4:36
6:34 [m]Mt 9:36
6:37 [n]2Ki 4:42-44
6:38 [o]Mt 15:34; Mk 8:5
6:41 [p]Mt 14:19

[q]20 Some early manuscripts *he did many things* [r]37 Greek *take two hundred denarii*

ples picked up twelve basketfuls of
broken pieces of bread and fish.
44The number of the men who had
eaten was five thousand.

Jesus Walks on the Water

6:45–51pp — Mt 14:22–32; Jn 6:15–21
6:53–56pp — Mt 14:34–36

45Immediately Jesus made his
disciples get into the boat[a] and go
on ahead of him to Bethsaida,[b]
while he dismissed the crowd.
46After leaving them, he went up
on a mountainside to pray.[c]
47When evening came, the boat
was in the middle of the lake, and
he was alone on land. 48He saw the
disciples straining at the oars, because the wind was against them.
About the fourth watch of the night
he went out to them, walking on
the lake. He was about to pass by
them, 49but when they saw him
walking on the lake, they thought
he was a ghost.[d] They cried out,
50because they all saw him and
were terrified.

Immediately he spoke to them
and said, "Take courage! It is I.
Don't be afraid."[e] 51Then he
climbed into the boat[f] with them,
and the wind died down.[g] They
were completely amazed, 52for
they had not understood about the
loaves; their hearts were hardened.[h]

53When they had crossed over,
they landed at Gennesaret and an-
chored there.[i] 54As soon as they
got out of the boat, people recognized Jesus. 55They ran throughout
that whole region and carried the
sick on mats to wherever they
heard he was. 56And wherever he
went—into villages, towns or
countryside—they placed the sick
in the marketplaces. They begged
him to let them touch even the
edge of his cloak,[j] and all who
touched him were healed.

Clean and Unclean

7:1–23pp — Mt 15:1–20

7 The Pharisees and some of the
teachers of the law who had
come from Jerusalem gathered
around Jesus and 2saw some of his
disciples eating food with hands
that were "unclean,"[k] that is, unwashed. 3(The Pharisees and all
the Jews do not eat unless they give
their hands a ceremonial washing,
holding to the tradition of the elders.[l] 4When they come from the
marketplace they do not eat unless
they wash. And they observe many
other traditions, such as the washing of cups, pitchers and kettles.[s])[m]

5So the Pharisees and teachers
of the law asked Jesus, "Why don't
your disciples live according to the
tradition of the elders[n] instead of
eating their food with 'unclean'
hands?"

6He replied, "Isaiah was right
when he prophesied about you
hypocrites; as it is written:

" 'These people honor me with
their lips,
but their hearts are far from
me.
7They worship me in vain;
their teachings are but rules
taught by men.'[t][o]

8You have let go of the commands
of God and are holding on to the
traditions of men."[p]

9And he said to them: "You have
a fine way of setting aside the commands of God in order to observe[u]
your own traditions![q] 10For Moses
said, 'Honor your father and your
mother,'[v][r] and, 'Anyone who
curses his father or mother must be
put to death.'[w][s] 11But you say[t]
that if a man says to his father or
mother: 'Whatever help you might
otherwise have received from me is
Corban' (that is, a gift devoted to
God), 12then you no longer let him
do anything for his father or mother. 13Thus you nullify the word of
God[u] by your tradition[v] that you
have handed down. And you do
many things like that."

14Again Jesus called the crowd

6:45 [a]ver 32 [b]Mt 11:21
6:46 [c]Lk 3:21
6:49 [d]Lk 24:37
6:50 [e]Mt 14:27
6:51 [f]ver 32 [g]Mk 4:39
6:52 [h]Mk 8:17-21
6:53 [i]Jn 6:24,25
6:56 [j]Mt 9:20
7:2 [k]Ac 10:14,28; 11:8; Ro 14:14
7:3 [l]ver 5,8,9,13; Lk 11:38
7:4 [m]Mt 23:25; Lk 11:39
7:5 [n]ver 3; Gal 1:14; Col 2:8
7:7 [o]Isa 29:13
7:8 [p]ver 3
7:9 [q]ver 3
7:10 [r]Ex 20:12; Dt 5:16 [s]Ex 21:17; Lev 20:9
7:11 [t]Mt 23:16,18
7:13 [u]Heb 4:12 [v]ver 3

[s]4 Some early manuscripts *pitchers, kettles and dining couches* [t]6,7 Isaiah 29:13 [u]9 Some manuscripts *set up* [v]10 Exodus 20:12; Deut. 5:16 [w]10 Exodus 21:17; Lev. 20:9

to him and said, "Listen to me, everyone, and understand this. 15Nothing outside a man can make him 'unclean' by going into him. Rather, it is what comes out of a man that makes him 'unclean.'[x]"

17After he had left the crowd and entered the house, his disciples asked him[a] about this parable. 18"Are you so dull?" he asked. "Don't you see that nothing that enters a man from the outside can make him 'unclean'? 19For it doesn't go into his heart but into his stomach, and then out of his body." (In saying this, Jesus declared all foods[b] "clean.")[c]

20He went on: "What comes out of a man is what makes him 'unclean.' 21For from within, out of men's hearts, come evil thoughts, sexual immorality, theft, murder, adultery, 22greed,[d] malice, deceit, lewdness, envy, slander, arrogance and folly. 23All these evils come from inside and make a man 'unclean.' "

The Faith of a Syrophoenician Woman

7:24–30pp – Mt 15:21–28

24Jesus left that place and went to the vicinity of Tyre.[y][e] He entered a house and did not want anyone to know it; yet he could not keep his presence secret. 25In fact, as soon as she heard about him, a woman whose little daughter was possessed by an evil[z] spirit[f] came and fell at his feet. 26The woman was a Greek, born in Syrian Phoenicia. She begged Jesus to drive the demon out of her daughter.

27"First let the children eat all they want," he told her, "for it is not right to take the children's bread and toss it to their dogs."

28"Yes, Lord," she replied, "but even the dogs under the table eat the children's crumbs."

29Then he told her, "For such a reply, you may go; the demon has left your daughter."

30She went home and found her child lying on the bed, and the demon gone.

7:17 [a] Mk 9:28
7:19 [b] Ro 14:1-12; Col 2:16; 1Ti 4:3-5 [c] Ac 10:15
7:22 [d] Mt 20:15
7:24 [e] Mt 11:21
7:25 [f] Mt 4:24
7:31 [g] ver 24; Mt 11:21 [h] Mt 4:18 [i] Mt 4:25; Mk 5:20
7:32 [j] Mt 9:32; Lk 11:14 [k] Mk 5:23
7:33 [l] Mk 8:23
7:34 [m] Mk 6:41; Jn 11:41 [n] Mk 8:12
7:35 [o] Isa 35:5,6
7:36 [p] Mt 8:4
8:2 [q] Mt 9:36

The Healing of a Deaf and Mute Man

7:31–37pp – Mt 15:29–31

31Then Jesus left the vicinity of Tyre[g] and went through Sidon, down to the Sea of Galilee[h] and into the region of the Decapolis.[a][i] 32There some people brought to him a man who was deaf and could hardly talk,[j] and they begged him to place his hand on[k] the man.

33After he took him aside, away from the crowd, Jesus put his fingers into the man's ears. Then he spit[l] and touched the man's tongue. 34He looked up to heaven[m] and with a deep sigh[n] said to him, *"Ephphatha!"* (which means, "Be opened!"). 35At this, the man's ears were opened, his tongue was loosened and he began to speak plainly.[o]

36Jesus commanded them not to tell anyone.[p] But the more he did so, the more they kept talking about it. 37People were overwhelmed with amazement. "He has done everything well," they said. "He even makes the deaf hear and the mute speak."

Jesus Feeds the Four Thousand

8:1–9pp – Mt 15:32–39
8:1–9Ref – Mk 6:32–44
8:11–21pp – Mt 16:1–12

8 During those days another large crowd gathered. Since they had nothing to eat, Jesus called his disciples to him and said, 2"I have compassion for these people;[q] they have already been with me three days and have nothing to eat. 3If I send them home hungry, they will collapse on the way, because some of them have come a long distance."

4His disciples answered, "But where in this remote place can anyone get enough bread to feed them?"

[x]15 Some early manuscripts *'unclean.' 16If anyone has ears to hear, let him hear.*
[y]24 Many early manuscripts *Tyre and Sidon*
[z]25 Greek *unclean*
[a]31 That is, the Ten Cities

5"How many loaves do you have?" Jesus asked.

"Seven," they replied.

6He told the crowd to sit down on the ground. When he had taken the seven loaves and given thanks, he broke them and gave them to his disciples to set before the people, and they did so. 7They had a few small fish as well; he gave thanks for them also and told the disciples to distribute them.[a] 8The people ate and were satisfied. Afterward the disciples picked up seven basketfuls of broken pieces that were left over.[b] 9About four thousand men were present. And having sent them away, 10he got into the boat with his disciples and went to the region of Dalmanutha.

11The Pharisees came and began to question Jesus. To test him, they asked him for a sign from heaven.[c] 12He sighed deeply[d] and said, "Why does this generation ask for a miraculous sign? I tell you the truth, no sign will be given to it." 13Then he left them, got back into the boat and crossed to the other side.

The Yeast of the Pharisees and Herod

14The disciples had forgotten to bring bread, except for one loaf they had with them in the boat. 15"Be careful," Jesus warned them. "Watch out for the yeast[e] of the Pharisees[f] and that of Herod."[g]

16They discussed this with one another and said, "It is because we have no bread."

17Aware of their discussion, Jesus asked them: "Why are you talking about having no bread? Do you still not see or understand? Are your hearts hardened?[h] 18Do you have eyes but fail to see, and ears but fail to hear? And don't you remember? 19When I broke the five loaves for the five thousand, how many basketfuls of pieces did you pick up?"

"Twelve,"[i] they replied.

20"And when I broke the seven loaves for the four thousand, how many basketfuls of pieces did you pick up?"

They answered, "Seven."[j]

21He said to them, "Do you still not understand?"[k]

The Healing of a Blind Man at Bethsaida

22They came to Bethsaida,[l] and some people brought a blind man[m] and begged Jesus to touch him. 23He took the blind man by the hand and led him outside the village. When he had spit[n] on the man's eyes and put his hands on[o] him, Jesus asked, "Do you see anything?"

24He looked up and said, "I see people; they look like trees walking around."

25Once more Jesus put his hands on the man's eyes. Then his eyes were opened, his sight was restored, and he saw everything clearly. 26Jesus sent him home, saying, "Don't go into the village.[b]"

Peter's Confession of Christ

8:27–29pp — Mt 16:13–16; Lk 9:18–20

27Jesus and his disciples went on to the villages around Caesarea Philippi. On the way he asked them, "Who do people say I am?"

28They replied, "Some say John the Baptist;[p] others say Elijah;[q] and still others, one of the prophets."

29"But what about you?" he asked. "Who do you say I am?"

Peter answered, "You are the Christ.[c]"[r]

30Jesus warned them not to tell anyone about him.[s]

Jesus Predicts His Death

8:31 — 9:1pp — Mt 16:21–28; Lk 9:22–27

31He then began to teach them that the Son of Man[t] must suffer many things[u] and be rejected by the elders, chief priests and teachers of the law,[v] and that he must

8:7 [a] Mt 14:19
8:8 [b] ver 20
8:11 [c] Mt 12:38
8:12 [d] Mk 7:34
8:15 [e] 1Co 5:6-8 [f] Lk 12:1 [g] Mt 14:1; Mk 12:13
8:17 [h] Isa 6:9,10; Mk 6:52
8:19 [i] Mt 14:20; Mk 6:41-44; Lk 9:17; Jn 6:13
8:20 [j] ver 6-9; Mt 15:37
8:21 [k] Mk 6:52
8:22 [l] Mt 11:21 [m] Mk 10:46; Jn 9:1
8:23 [n] Mk 7:33 [o] Mk 5:23
8:28 [p] Mt 3:1 [q] Mal 4:5
8:29 [r] Jn 6:69; 11:27
8:30 [s] Mt 8:4; 16:20; 17:9; Mk 9:9; Lk 9:21
8:31 [t] Mt 8:20 [u] Mt 16:21 [v] Mt 27:1,2

[b]26 Some manuscripts *Don't go and tell anyone in the village* [c]29 Or *Messiah*. "The Christ" (Greek) and "the Messiah" (Hebrew) both mean "the Anointed One."

be killed[a] and after three days[b] rise again.[c] **32**He spoke plainly[d] about this, and Peter took him aside and began to rebuke him.

33But when Jesus turned and looked at his disciples, he rebuked Peter. "Get behind me, Satan!"[e] he said. "You do not have in mind the things of God, but the things of men."

34Then he called the crowd to him along with his disciples and said: "If anyone would come after me, he must deny himself and take up his cross and follow me.[f] **35**For whoever wants to save his life[d] will lose it, but whoever loses his life for me and for the gospel will save it.[g] **36**What good is it for a man to gain the whole world, yet forfeit his soul? **37**Or what can a man give in exchange for his soul? **38**If anyone is ashamed of me and my words in this adulterous and sinful generation, the Son of Man[h] will be ashamed of him[i] when he comes[j] in his Father's glory with the holy angels."

9 And he said to them, "I tell you the truth, some who are standing here will not taste death before they see the kingdom of God come[k] with power."[l]

The Transfiguration

9:2–8pp — Lk 9:28–36
9:2–13pp — Mt 17:1–13

2After six days Jesus took Peter, James and John[m] with him and led them up a high mountain, where they were all alone. There he was transfigured before them. **3**His clothes became dazzling white,[n] whiter than anyone in the world could bleach them. **4**And there appeared before them Elijah and Moses, who were talking with Jesus.

5Peter said to Jesus, "Rabbi,[o] it is good for us to be here. Let us put up three shelters—one for you, one for Moses and one for Elijah." **6**(He did not know what to say, they were so frightened.)

7Then a cloud appeared and enveloped them, and a voice came from the cloud:[p] "This is my Son, whom I love. Listen to him!"[q]

8Suddenly, when they looked around, they no longer saw anyone with them except Jesus.

9As they were coming down the mountain, Jesus gave them orders not to tell anyone[r] what they had seen until the Son of Man[s] had risen from the dead. **10**They kept the matter to themselves, discussing what "rising from the dead" meant.

11And they asked him, "Why do the teachers of the law say that Elijah must come first?"

12Jesus replied, "To be sure, Elijah does come first, and restores all things. Why then is it written that the Son of Man[t] must suffer much[u] and be rejected?[v] **13**But I tell you, Elijah has come,[w] and they have done to him everything they wished, just as it is written about him."

The Healing of a Boy With an Evil Spirit

9:14–28; 30–32pp — Mt 17:14–19; 22,23; Lk 9:37–45

14When they came to the other disciples, they saw a large crowd around them and the teachers of the law arguing with them. **15**As soon as all the people saw Jesus, they were overwhelmed with wonder and ran to greet him.

16"What are you arguing with them about?" he asked.

17A man in the crowd answered, "Teacher, I brought you my son, who is possessed by a spirit that has robbed him of speech. **18**Whenever it seizes him, it throws him to the ground. He foams at the mouth, gnashes his teeth and becomes rigid. I asked your disciples to drive out the spirit, but they could not."

19"O unbelieving generation," Jesus replied, "how long shall I stay with you? How long shall I put up with you? Bring the boy to me."

20So they brought him. When the spirit saw Jesus, it immediately threw the boy into a convulsion. He

8:31 [a]Ac 2:23; 3:13 [b]Mt 16:21 [c]Mt 16:21
8:32 [d]Jn 18:20
8:33 [e]Mt 4:10
8:34 [f]Mt 10:38; Lk 14:27
8:35 [g]Jn 12:25
8:38 [h]Mt 8:20 [i]Mt 10:33; Lk 12:9 [j]1Th 2:19
9:1 [k]Mk 13:30; Lk 22:18 [l]Mt 24:30; 25:31
9:2 [m]Mt 4:21
9:3 [n]Mt 28:3
9:5 [o]Mt 23:7
9:7 [p]Ex 24:16 [q]Mt 3:17
9:9 [r]Mk 8:30 [s]Mt 8:20
9:12 [t]Mt 8:20 [u]Mt 16:21 [v]Lk 23:11
9:13 [w]Mt 11:14

[d]35 The Greek word means either *life* or *soul*; also in verse 36.

fell to the ground and rolled
around, foaming at the mouth.[a]
21Jesus asked the boy's father,
"How long has he been like this?"
"From childhood," he answered.
22"It has often thrown him into fire
or water to kill him. But if you can
do anything, take pity on us and
help us."
23" 'If you can'?" said Jesus. "Everything is possible for him who believes."[b]
24Immediately the boy's father
exclaimed, "I do believe; help me
overcome my unbelief!"
25When Jesus saw that a crowd
was running to the scene,[c] he rebuked the evil[e] spirit. "You deaf
and mute spirit," he said, "I command you, come out of him and
never enter him again."
26The spirit shrieked, convulsed
him violently and came out. The
boy looked so much like a corpse
that many said, "He's dead." **27**But
Jesus took him by the hand and
lifted him to his feet, and he stood
up.
28After Jesus had gone indoors,
his disciples asked him privately,[d]
"Why couldn't we drive it out?"
29He replied, "This kind can
come out only by prayer.[f]"
30They left that place and passed
through Galilee. Jesus did not want
anyone to know where they were,
31because he was teaching his disciples. He said to them, "The Son
of Man[e] is going to be betrayed
into the hands of men. They will
kill him,[f] and after three days[g] he
will rise."[h] **32**But they did not understand what he meant[i] and were
afraid to ask him about it.

Who Is the Greatest?

9:33–37pp — Mt 18:1–5; Lk 9:46–48

33They came to Capernaum.[j]
When he was in the house,[k] he
asked them, "What were you arguing about on the road?" **34**But they
kept quiet because on the way they
had argued about who was the
greatest.[l]
35Sitting down, Jesus called the
Twelve and said, "If anyone wants
to be first, he must be the very last,
and the servant of all."[m]
36He took a little child and had
him stand among them. Taking
him in his arms,[n] he said to them,
37"Whoever welcomes one of these
little children in my name welcomes me; and whoever welcomes
me does not welcome me but the
one who sent me."[o]

Whoever Is Not Against Us Is for Us

9:38–40pp — Lk 9:49,50

38"Teacher," said John, "we saw
a man driving out demons in your
name and we told him to stop, because he was not one of us."[p]
39"Do not stop him," Jesus said.
"No one who does a miracle in my
name can in the next moment say
anything bad about me, **40**for whoever is not against us is for us.[q] **41**I
tell you the truth, anyone who gives
you a cup of water in my name because you belong to Christ will certainly not lose his reward.[r]

Causing to Sin

42"And if anyone causes one of
these little ones who believe in me
to sin,[s] it would be better for him
to be thrown into the sea with a
large millstone tied around his
neck.[t] **43**If your hand causes you
to sin,[u] cut it off. It is better for you
to enter life maimed than with two
hands to go into hell,[v] where the
fire never goes out.[g][w] **45**And if
your foot causes you to sin,[x] cut it
off. It is better for you to enter life
crippled than to have two feet and
be thrown into hell.[h][y] **47**And if
your eye causes you to sin,[z] pluck
it out. It is better for you to enter
the kingdom of God with one eye
than to have two eyes and be
thrown into hell,[a] **48**where

" 'their worm does not die,

9:20 [a]Mk 1:26
9:23 [b]Mt 21:21; Mk 11:23; Jn 11:40
9:25 [c]ver 15
9:28 [d]Mk 7:17
9:31 [e]Mt 8:20 [f]ver 12; Ac 2:23; 3:13 [g]Mt 16:21 [h]Mt 16:21
9:32 [i]Lk 2:50; 9:45; 18:34; Jn 12:16
9:33 [j]Mt 4:13 [k]Mk 1:29
9:34 [l]Lk 22:24
9:35 [m]Mt 18:4; 20:26; Mk 10:43; Lk 22:26
9:36 [n]Mk 10:16
9:37 [o]Mt 10:40
9:38 [p]Nu 11:27-29
9:40 [q]Mt 12:30; Lk 11:23
9:41 [r]Mt 10:42
9:42 [s]Mt 5:29 [t]Mt 18:6; Lk 17:2
9:43 [u]Mt 5:29 [v]Mt 5:30; 18:8 [w]Mt 25:41
9:45 [x]Mt 5:29 [y]Mt 18:8
9:47 [z]Mt 5:29 [a]Mt 5:29; 18:9

[e]*25* Greek *unclean* [f]*29* Some manuscripts *prayer and fasting* [g]*43* Some manuscripts *out,* [44]*where / " 'their worm does not die, / and the fire is not quenched.'* [h]*45* Some manuscripts *hell,* [46]*where / " 'their worm does not die, / and the fire is not quenched.'*

and the fire is not
quenched.'[i][a]

49Everyone will be salted[b] with
fire.
50"Salt is good, but if it loses its
saltiness, how can you make it
salty again?[c] Have salt in yourselves,[d] and be at peace with each
other."[e]

Divorce

10:1–12pp — Mt 19:1–9

10 Jesus then left that place
and went into the region of
Judea and across the Jordan.[f]
Again crowds of people came to
him, and as was his custom, he
taught them.[g]
2Some Pharisees[h] came and
tested him by asking, "Is it lawful
for a man to divorce his wife?"
3"What did Moses command
you?" he replied.
4They said, "Moses permitted a
man to write a certificate of divorce
and send her away."[i]
5"It was because your hearts
were hard[j] that Moses wrote you
this law," Jesus replied. 6"But at
the beginning of creation God
'made them male and female.'[j][k]
7'For this reason a man will leave
his father and mother and be united to his wife,[k] 8and the two will
become one flesh.'[l][l] So they are
no longer two, but one. 9Therefore
what God has joined together, let
man not separate."
10When they were in the house
again, the disciples asked Jesus
about this. 11He answered, "Anyone who divorces his wife and marries another woman commits adultery against her.[m] 12And if she divorces her husband and marries
another man, she commits adultery."[n]

The Little Children and Jesus

10:13–16pp — Mt 19:13–15; Lk 18:15–17

13People were bringing little
children to Jesus to have him
touch them, but the disciples rebuked them. 14When Jesus saw
this, he was indignant. He said to
them, "Let the little children come

9:48 [a]Isa 66:24; Mt 25:41
9:49 [b]Lev 2:13
9:50 [c]Mt 5:13; Lk 14:34,35 [d]Col 4:6 [e]Ro 12:18; 2Co 13:11; 1Th 5:13
10:1 [f]Mk 1:5; Jn 10:40; 11:7 [g]Mt 4:23; Mk 2:13; 4:2; 6:6,34
10:2 [h]Mk 2:16
10:4 [i]Dt 24:1-4; Mt 5:31
10:5 [j]Ps 95:8; Heb 3:15
10:6 [k]Ge 1:27; 5:2
10:8 [l]Ge 2:24; 1Co 6:16
10:11 [m]Mt 5:32; Lk 16:18
10:12 [n]Ro 7:3; 1Co 7:10,11
10:14 [o]Mt 25:34
10:15 [p]Mt 18:3
10:16 [q]Mk 9:36
10:17 [r]Mk 1:40 [s]Lk 10:25; Ac 20:32
10:19 [t]Ex 20:12-16; Dt 5:16-20
10:21 [u]Ac 2:45 [v]Mt 6:20; Lk 12:33 [w]Mt 4:19
10:23 [x]Ps 52:7; 62:10; 1Ti 6:9,10,17
10:24 [y]Mt 7:13,14
10:25 [z]Lk 12:16-20

to me, and do not hinder them, for
the kingdom of God belongs to
such as these.[o] 15I tell you the
truth, anyone who will not receive
the kingdom of God like a little
child will never enter it."[p] 16And
he took the children in his arms,[q]
put his hands on them and blessed
them.

The Rich Young Man

10:17–31pp — Mt 19:16–30; Lk 18:18–30

17As Jesus started on his way, a
man ran up to him and fell on his
knees[r] before him. "Good teacher," he asked, "what must I do to
inherit eternal life?"[s]
18"Why do you call me good?"
Jesus answered. "No one is good
—except God alone. 19You know
the commandments: 'Do not murder, do not commit adultery, do not
steal, do not give false testimony,
do not defraud, honor your father
and mother.'[m]"[t]
20"Teacher," he declared, "all
these I have kept since I was a
boy."
21Jesus looked at him and loved
him. "One thing you lack," he said.
"Go, sell everything you have and
give to the poor,[u] and you will have
treasure in heaven.[v] Then come,
follow me."[w]
22At this the man's face fell. He
went away sad, because he had
great wealth.
23Jesus looked around and said
to his disciples, "How hard it is for
the rich[x] to enter the kingdom of
God!"
24The disciples were amazed at
his words. But Jesus said again,
"Children, how hard it is[n] to enter
the kingdom of God![y] 25It is easier
for a camel to go through the eye of
a needle than for a rich man to enter the kingdom of God."[z]
26The disciples were even more
amazed, and said to each other,
"Who then can be saved?"
27Jesus looked at them and said,

[i]*48* Isaiah 66:24 [j]*6* Gen. 1:27 [k]*7* Some early manuscripts do not have *and be united to his wife.* [l]*8* Gen. 2:24 [m]*19* Exodus 20:12-16; Deut. 5:16-20 [n]*24* Some manuscripts *is for those who trust in riches*

"With man this is impossible, but
not with God; all things are possible with God."[a]
28Peter said to him, "We have
left everything to follow you!"[b]
29"I tell you the truth," Jesus replied, "no one who has left home or
brothers or sisters or mother or father or children or fields for me and
the gospel 30will fail to receive a
hundred times as much[c] in this
present age (homes, brothers, sisters, mothers, children and fields
—and with them, persecutions)
and in the age to come,[d] eternal
life.[e] 31But many who are first will
be last, and the last first."[f]

Jesus Again Predicts His Death

10:32–34pp — Mt 20:17–19; Lk 18:31–33

32They were on their way up to
Jerusalem, with Jesus leading the
way, and the disciples were astonished, while those who followed
were afraid. Again he took the
Twelve[g] aside and told them what
was going to happen to him. 33"We
are going up to Jerusalem,"[h] he
said, "and the Son of Man[i] will be
betrayed to the chief priests and
teachers of the law.[j] They will
condemn him to death and will
hand him over to the Gentiles,
34who will mock him and spit on
him, flog him[k] and kill him.[l]
Three days later[m] he will rise."[n]

The Request of James and John

10:35–45pp — Mt 20:20–28

35Then James and John, the
sons of Zebedee, came to him.
"Teacher," they said, "we want you
to do for us whatever we ask."
36"What do you want me to do
for you?" he asked.
37They replied, "Let one of us sit
at your right and the other at your
left in your glory."[o]
38"You don't know what you are
asking,"[p] Jesus said. "Can you
drink the cup[q] I drink or be baptized with the baptism I am baptized with?"[r]
39"We can," they answered.
Jesus said to them, "You will
drink the cup I drink and be baptized with the baptism I am baptized with,[s] 40but to sit at my right
or left is not for me to grant. These
places belong to those for whom
they have been prepared."
41When the ten heard about this,
they became indignant with James
and John. 42Jesus called them together and said, "You know that
those who are regarded as rulers of
the Gentiles lord it over them, and
their high officials exercise authority over them. 43Not so with you.
Instead, whoever wants to become
great among you must be your servant,[t] 44and whoever wants to be
first must be slave of all. 45For even
the Son of Man did not come to
be served, but to serve,[u] and to
give his life as a ransom for
many."[v]

Blind Bartimaeus Receives His Sight

10:46–52pp — Mt 20:29–34; Lk 18:35–43

46Then they came to Jericho. As
Jesus and his disciples, together
with a large crowd, were leaving the
city, a blind man, Bartimaeus (that
is, the Son of Timaeus), was sitting
by the roadside begging. 47When
he heard that it was Jesus of Nazareth,[w] he began to shout, "Jesus,
Son of David,[x] have mercy on me!"
48Many rebuked him and told
him to be quiet, but he shouted all
the more, "Son of David, have mercy on me!"
49Jesus stopped and said, "Call
him."
So they called to the blind man,
"Cheer up! On your feet! He's calling you." 50Throwing his cloak
aside, he jumped to his feet and
came to Jesus.
51"What do you want me to do
for you?" Jesus asked him.
The blind man said, "Rabbi,[y] I
want to see."
52"Go," said Jesus, "your faith
has healed you."[z] Immediately he
received his sight and followed[a]
Jesus along the road.

10:27 [a] Mt 19:26
10:28 [b] Mt 4:19
10:30 [c] Mt 6:33 [d] Mt 12:32 [e] Mt 25:46
10:31 [f] Mt 19:30
10:32 [g] Mk 3:16-19
10:33 [h] Lk 9:51 [i] Mt 8:20 [j] Mt 27:1,2
10:34 [k] Mt 16:21 [l] Ac 2:23; 3:13 [m] Mt 16:21 [n] Mt 16:21
10:37 [o] Mt 19:28
10:38 [p] Job 38:2 [q] Mt 20:22 [r] Lk 12:50
10:39 [s] Ac 12:2; Rev 1:9
10:43 [t] Mk 9:35
10:45 [u] Mt 20:28 [v] Mt 20:28
10:47 [w] Mk 1:24 [x] Mt 9:27
10:51 [y] Mt 23:7
10:52 [z] Mt 9:22 [a] Mt 4:19

The Triumphal Entry

11:1–10pp — Mt 21:1–9; Lk 19:29–38
11:7–10pp — Jn 12:12–15

11 As they approached Jerusalem and came to Bethphage
and Bethany[a] at the Mount of Olives,[b] Jesus sent two of his disciples, **2**saying to them, "Go to the
village ahead of you, and just as
you enter it, you will find a colt tied
there, which no one has ever ridden.[c] Untie it and bring it here. **3**If
anyone asks you, 'Why are you doing this?' tell him, 'The Lord needs
it and will send it back here shortly.' "
4They went and found a colt outside in the street, tied at a doorway.[d] As they untied it, **5**some
people standing there asked,
"What are you doing, untying that
colt?" **6**They answered as Jesus had
told them to, and the people let
them go. **7**When they brought the
colt to Jesus and threw their cloaks
over it, he sat on it. **8**Many people
spread their cloaks on the road,
while others spread branches they
had cut in the fields. **9**Those who
went ahead and those who followed shouted,

"Hosanna![o]"

"Blessed is he who comes in
the name of the
Lord!"[p][e]

10"Blessed is the coming
kingdom of our father
David!"

"Hosanna in the highest!"[f]

11Jesus entered Jerusalem and
went to the temple. He looked
around at everything, but since it
was already late, he went out to
Bethany with the Twelve.[g]

Jesus Clears the Temple

11:12–14pp — Mt 21:18–22
11:15–18pp — Mt 21:12–16; Lk 19:45–47; Jn 2:13–16

12The next day as they were leaving Bethany, Jesus was hungry.
13Seeing in the distance a fig tree
in leaf, he went to find out if it had
any fruit. When he reached it, he
found nothing but leaves, because
it was not the season for figs.[h]
14Then he said to the tree, "May no
one ever eat fruit from you again."
And his disciples heard him say it.
15On reaching Jerusalem, Jesus
entered the temple area and began
driving out those who were buying
and selling there. He overturned
the tables of the money changers
and the benches of those selling
doves, **16**and would not allow anyone to carry merchandise through
the temple courts. **17**And as he
taught them, he said, "Is it not
written:

" 'My house will be called
a house of prayer for all
nations'[q]?[i]

But you have made it 'a den of robbers.'[r]"[j]

18The chief priests and the
teachers of the law heard this and
began looking for a way to kill him,
for they feared him,[k] because the
whole crowd was amazed at his
teaching.[l]
19When evening came, they[s]
went out of the city.[m]

The Withered Fig Tree

11:20–24pp — Mt 21:19–22

20In the morning, as they went
along, they saw the fig tree withered from the roots. **21**Peter remembered and said to Jesus, "Rabbi,[n] look! The fig tree you cursed
has withered!"
22"Have[t] faith in God," Jesus
answered. **23**"I tell you the truth, if
anyone says to this mountain, 'Go,
throw yourself into the sea,' and
does not doubt in his heart but believes that what he says will happen, it will be done for him.[o]
24Therefore I tell you, whatever
you ask for in prayer, believe that
you have received it, and it will be
yours.[p] **25**And when you stand
praying, if you hold anything

11:1 [a]Mt 21:17 [b]Mt 21:1
11:2 [c]Nu 19:2; Dt 21:3; 1Sa 6:7
11:4 [d]Mk 14:16
11:9 [e]Ps 118:25, 26; Mt 23:39
11:10 [f]Lk 2:14
11:11 [g]Mt 21:12,17
11:13 [h]Lk 13:6-9
11:17 [i]Isa 56:7 [j]Jer 7:11
11:18 [k]Mt 21:46; Mk 12:12; Lk 20:19 [l]Mt 7:28
11:19 [m]Lk 21:37
11:21 [n]Mt 23:7
11:23 [o]Mt 21:21
11:24 [p]Mt 7:7

[o]9 A Hebrew expression meaning "Save!" which became an exclamation of praise; also in verse 10 [p]9 Psalm 118:25,26 [q]17 Isaiah 56:7 [r]17 Jer. 7:11 [s]19 Some early manuscripts *he* [t]22 Some early manuscripts *If you have*

against anyone, forgive him, so that
your Father in heaven may forgive
you your sins.[u]"[a]

The Authority of Jesus Questioned

11:27–33pp — Mt 21:23–27; Lk 20:1–8

27They arrived again in Jerusalem, and while Jesus was walking
in the temple courts, the chief
priests, the teachers of the law and
the elders came to him. 28"By what
authority are you doing these
things?" they asked. "And who
gave you authority to do this?"

29Jesus replied, "I will ask you
one question. Answer me, and I
will tell you by what authority I am
doing these things. 30John's baptism—was it from heaven, or from
men? Tell me!"

31They discussed it among
themselves and said, "If we say,
'From heaven,' he will ask, 'Then
why didn't you believe him?' 32But
if we say, 'From men' . . . ." (They
feared the people, for everyone
held that John really was a prophet.)[b]

33So they answered Jesus, "We
don't know."

Jesus said, "Neither will I tell
you by what authority I am doing
these things."

The Parable of the Tenants

12:1–12pp — Mt 21:33–46; Lk 20:9–19

12 He then began to speak to
them in parables: "A man
planted a vineyard.[c] He put a wall
around it, dug a pit for the winepress and built a watchtower. Then
he rented the vineyard to some
farmers and went away on a journey. 2At harvest time he sent a servant to the tenants to collect from
them some of the fruit of the vineyard. 3But they seized him, beat
him and sent him away empty-
handed. 4Then he sent another servant to them; they struck this man
on the head and treated him
shamefully. 5He sent still another,
and that one they killed. He sent
many others; some of them they
beat, others they killed.

6"He had one left to send, a son,
whom he loved. He sent him last of
all,[d] saying, 'They will respect my
son.'

7"But the tenants said to one another, 'This is the heir. Come, let's
kill him, and the inheritance will
be ours.' 8So they took him and
killed him, and threw him out of
the vineyard.

9"What then will the owner of
the vineyard do? He will come and
kill those tenants and give the vineyard to others. 10Haven't you read
this scripture:

" 'The stone the builders
rejected
has become the capstone[v];[e]
11the Lord has done this,
and it is marvelous in our
eyes'[w]?"[f]

12Then they looked for a way to
arrest him because they knew he
had spoken the parable against
them. But they were afraid of the
crowd;[g] so they left him and went
away.[h]

Paying Taxes to Caesar

12:13–17pp — Mt 22:15–22; Lk 20:20–26

13Later they sent some of the
Pharisees and Herodians[i] to Jesus
to catch him[j] in his words. 14They
came to him and said, "Teacher,
we know you are a man of integrity.
You aren't swayed by men, because
you pay no attention to who they
are; but you teach the way of God
in accordance with the truth. Is it
right to pay taxes to Caesar or not?
15Should we pay or shouldn't we?"

But Jesus knew their hypocrisy.
"Why are you trying to trap me?" he
asked. "Bring me a denarius and let
me look at it." 16They brought the
coin, and he asked them, "Whose
portrait is this? And whose inscription?"

"Caesar's," they replied.

17Then Jesus said to them, "Give
to Caesar what is Caesar's and to
God what is God's."[k]

11:25 [a]Mt 6:14
11:32 [b]Mt 11:9
12:1 [c]Isa 5:1-7
12:6 [d]Heb 1:1-3
12:10 [e]Ac 4:11
12:11 [f]Ps 118:22,23
12:12 [g]Mk 11:18 [h]Mt 22:22
12:13 [i]Mt 22:16; Mk 3:6 [j]Mt 12:10
12:17 [k]Ro 13:7

[u]25 Some manuscripts *sins.* 26*But if you do not forgive, neither will your Father who is in heaven forgive your sins.* [v]10 Or *cornerstone* [w]11 Psalm 118:22,23

And they were amazed at him.

Marriage at the Resurrection

12:18–27pp — Mt 22:23–33; Lk 20:27–38

18 Then the Sadducees,[a] who
say there is no resurrection,[b] came
to him with a question. 19 "Teacher," they said, "Moses wrote for us
that if a man's brother dies and
leaves a wife but no children, the
man must marry the widow and
have children for his brother.[c]
20 Now there were seven brothers.
The first one married and died
without leaving any children.
21 The second one married the widow, but he also died, leaving no
child. It was the same with the
third. 22 In fact, none of the seven
left any children. Last of all, the
woman died too. 23 At the resurrection[x] whose wife will she be, since
the seven were married to her?"

24 Jesus replied, "Are you not in
error because you do not know the
Scriptures[d] or the power of God?
25 When the dead rise, they will neither marry nor be given in marriage; they will be like the angels in
heaven.[e] 26 Now about the dead
rising—have you not read in the
book of Moses, in the account of
the bush, how God said to him, 'I
am the God of Abraham, the God of
Isaac, and the God of Jacob'[y]?[f]
27 He is not the God of the dead,
but of the living. You are badly mistaken!"

The Greatest Commandment

12:28–34pp — Mt 22:34–40

28 One of the teachers of the
law[g] came and heard them debat-
ing. Noticing that Jesus had given
them a good answer, he asked him,
"Of all the commandments, which
is the most important?"

29 "The most important one," answered Jesus, "is this: 'Hear, O Israel, the Lord our God, the Lord is
one.[z] 30 Love the Lord your God
with all your heart and with all your
soul and with all your mind and
with all your strength.'[a][h] 31 The
second is this: 'Love your neighbor
as yourself.'[b][i] There is no commandment greater than these."

32 "Well said, teacher," the man
replied. "You are right in saying
that God is one and there is no other but him.[j] 33 To love him with all
your heart, with all your understanding and with all your strength,
and to love your neighbor as yourself is more important than all
burnt offerings and sacrifices."[k]

34 When Jesus saw that he had
answered wisely, he said to him,
"You are not far from the kingdom
of God."[l] And from then on no one
dared ask him any more questions.[m]

Whose Son Is the Christ?

12:35–37pp — Mt 22:41–46; Lk 20:41–44
12:38–40pp — Mt 23:1–7; Lk 20:45–47

35 While Jesus was teaching in
the temple courts,[n] he asked,
"How is it that the teachers of the
law say that the Christ[c] is the son
of David?[o] 36 David himself, speaking by the Holy Spirit,[p] declared:

" 'The Lord said to my Lord:
"Sit at my right hand
until I put your enemies
under your feet." '[d][q]

37 David himself calls him 'Lord.'
How then can he be his son?"

The large crowd[r] listened to
him with delight.

38 As he taught, Jesus said,
"Watch out for the teachers of the
law. They like to walk around in
flowing robes and be greeted in the
marketplaces, 39 and have the most
important seats in the synagogues
and the places of honor at banquets.[s] 40 They devour widows'
houses and for a show make
lengthy prayers. Such men will be
punished most severely."

The Widow's Offering

12:41–44pp — Lk 21:1–4

41 Jesus sat down opposite the
place where the offerings were

12:18 [a]Ac 4:1 [b]Ac 23:8; 1Co 15:12
12:19 [c]Dt 25:5
12:24 [d]2Ti 3:15-17
12:25 [e]1Co 15:42, 49,52
12:26 [f]Ex 3:6
12:28 [g]Lk 10:25-28; 20:39
12:30 [h]Dt 6:4,5
12:31 [i]Lev 19:18; Mt 5:43
12:32 [j]Dt 4:35,39; Isa 45:6,14; 46:9
12:33 [k]1Sa 15:22; Hos 6:6; Mic 6:6-8; Heb 10:8
12:34 [l]Mt 3:2 [m]Mt 22:46; Lk 20:40
12:35 [n]Mt 26:55 [o]Mt 9:27
12:36 [p]2Sa 23:2 [q]Ps 110:1; Mt 22:44
12:37 [r]Jn 12:9
12:39 [s]Lk 11:43

[x]23 Some manuscripts *resurrection, when men rise from the dead,* [y]26 Exodus 3:6
[z]29 Or *the Lord our God is one Lord*
[a]30 Deut. 6:4,5 [b]31 Lev. 19:18 [c]35 Or *Messiah* [d]36 Psalm 110:1

put[a] and watched the crowd putting their money into the temple
treasury. Many rich people threw in
large amounts. 42But a poor widow
came and put in two very small
copper coins,[e] worth only a frac-
tion of a penny.[f]
43Calling his disciples to him,
Jesus said, "I tell you the truth, this
poor widow has put more into the
treasury than all the others. 44They
all gave out of their wealth; but
she, out of her poverty, put in everything—all she had to live on."[b]

Signs of the End of the Age

13:1-37pp — Mt 24:1-51; Lk 21:5-36

13 As he was leaving the temple, one of his disciples said
to him, "Look, Teacher! What massive stones! What magnificent
buildings!"
2"Do you see all these great
buildings?" replied Jesus. "Not one
stone here will be left on another;
every one will be thrown down."[c]
3As Jesus was sitting on the
Mount of Olives[d] opposite the
temple, Peter, James, John[e] and
Andrew asked him privately, 4"Tell
us, when will these things happen?
And what will be the sign that they
are all about to be fulfilled?"
5Jesus said to them: "Watch out
that no one deceives you.[f] 6Many
will come in my name, claiming, 'I
am he,' and will deceive many.
7When you hear of wars and rumors
of wars, do not be alarmed. Such
things must happen, but the end is
still to come. 8Nation will rise
against nation, and kingdom
against kingdom. There will be
earthquakes in various places, and
famines. These are the beginning
of birth pains.
9"You must be on your guard.
You will be handed over to the local
councils and flogged in the synagogues.[g] On account of me you
will stand before governors and
kings as witnesses to them. 10And
the gospel must first be preached
to all nations. 11Whenever you are
arrested and brought to trial, do
not worry beforehand about what
to say. Just say whatever is given
you at the time, for it is not you
speaking, but the Holy Spirit.[h]
12"Brother will betray brother to
death, and a father his child. Children will rebel against their parents and have them put to death.[i]
13All men will hate you because of
me,[j] but he who stands firm to the
end will be saved.[k]
14"When you see 'the abomination that causes desolation'[g][l]
standing where it[h] does not belong—let the reader understand
—then let those who are in Judea
flee to the mountains. 15Let no one
on the roof of his house go down or
enter the house to take anything
out. 16Let no one in the field go
back to get his cloak. 17How dreadful it will be in those days for pregnant women and nursing moth-
ers![m] 18Pray that this will not take
place in winter, 19because those
will be days of distress unequaled
from the beginning, when God created the world,[n] until now—and
never to be equaled again.[o] 20If
the Lord had not cut short those
days, no one would survive. But for
the sake of the elect, whom he has
chosen, he has shortened them.
21At that time if anyone says to
you, 'Look, here is the Christ[i]!' or,
'Look, there he is!' do not believe
it.[p] 22For false Christs and false
prophets[q] will appear and perform
signs and miracles[r] to deceive the
elect—if that were possible. 23So
be on your guard;[s] I have told you
everything ahead of time.
24"But in those days, following
that distress,

" 'the sun will be darkened,
and the moon will not give
its light;
25the stars will fall from the sky,
and the heavenly bodies will
be shaken.'[j][t]

26"At that time men will see the
Son of Man coming in clouds[u]
with great power and glory. 27And

12:41 [a] 2Ki 12:9; Jn 8:20
12:44 [b] 2Co 8:12
13:2 [c] Lk 19:44
13:3 [d] Mt 21:1 [e] Mt 4:21
13:5 [f] ver 22; Jer 29:8; Eph 5:6; 2Th 2:3, 10-12; 1Ti 4:1; 2Ti 3:13; 1Jn 4:6
13:9 [g] Mt 10:17
13:11 [h] Mt 10:19,20; Lk 12:11,12
13:12 [i] Mic 7:6; Mt 10:21; Lk 12:51-53
13:13 [j] Jn 15:21 [k] Mt 10:22
13:14 [l] Da 9:27; 11:31; 12:11
13:17 [m] Lk 23:29
13:19 [n] Mk 10:6 [o] Da 9:26; 12:1; Joel 2:2
13:21 [p] Lk 17:23; 21:8
13:22 [q] Mt 7:15 [r] Jn 4:48; 2Th 2:9,10
13:23 [s] 2Pe 3:17
13:25 [t] Isa 13:10; 34:4; Mt 24:29
13:26 [u] Da 7:13; Mt 16:27; Rev 1:7

[e] *42* Greek *two lepta* [f] *42* Greek *kodrantes*
[g] *14* Daniel 9:27; 11:31; 12:11 [h] *14* Or *he*; also in verse 29 [i] *21* Or *Messiah*
[j] *25* Isaiah 13:10; 34:4

he will send his angels and gather
his elect from the four winds, from
the ends of the earth to the ends of
the heavens.[a]
28"Now learn this lesson from
the fig tree: As soon as its twigs get
tender and its leaves come out, you
know that summer is near. 29Even
so, when you see these things happening, you know that it is near,
right at the door. 30I tell you the
truth, this generation[k b] will certainly not pass away until all these
things have happened.[c] 31Heaven
and earth will pass away, but my
words will never pass away.[d]

The Day and Hour Unknown

32"No one knows about that day
or hour, not even the angels in
heaven, nor the Son, but only the
Father.[e] 33Be on guard! Be
alert![l f] You do not know when
that time will come. 34It's like a
man going away: He leaves his
house and puts his servants[g] in
charge, each with his assigned
task, and tells the one at the door
to keep watch.
35"Therefore keep watch because you do not know when the
owner of the house will come
back—whether in the evening, or
at midnight, or when the rooster
crows, or at dawn. 36If he comes
suddenly, do not let him find you
sleeping. 37What I say to you, I say
to everyone: 'Watch!' "[h]

Jesus Anointed at Bethany

14:1-11pp — Mt 26:2-16
14:1,2,10,11pp — Lk 22:1-6
14:3-8Ref — Jn 12:1-8

14 Now the Passover[i] and the
Feast of Unleavened Bread
were only two days away, and the
chief priests and the teachers of
the law were looking for some sly
way to arrest Jesus and kill him.[j]
2"But not during the Feast," they
said, "or the people may riot."
3While he was in Bethany,[k] reclining at the table in the home of
a man known as Simon the Leper,
a woman came with an alabaster
jar of very expensive perfume,
made of pure nard. She broke the
jar and poured the perfume on his
head.[l]
4Some of those present were saying indignantly to one another,
"Why this waste of perfume? 5It
could have been sold for more than
a year's wages[m] and the money giv-
en to the poor." And they rebuked
her harshly.
6"Leave her alone," said Jesus.
"Why are you bothering her? She
has done a beautiful thing to me.
7The poor you will always have
with you, and you can help them
any time you want.[m] But you will
not always have me. 8She did what
she could. She poured perfume on
my body beforehand to prepare for
my burial.[n] 9I tell you the truth,
wherever the gospel is preached
throughout the world,[o] what she
has done will also be told, in memory of her."
10Then Judas Iscariot, one of the
Twelve,[p] went to the chief priests
to betray Jesus to them.[q] 11They
were delighted to hear this and
promised to give him money. So he
watched for an opportunity to hand
him over.

The Lord's Supper

14:12-26pp — Mt 26:17-30; Lk 22:7-23
14:22-25pp — 1Co 11:23-25

12On the first day of the Feast of
Unleavened Bread, when it was
customary to sacrifice the Passover
lamb,[r] Jesus' disciples asked him,
"Where do you want us to go and
make preparations for you to eat
the Passover?"
13So he sent two of his disciples,
telling them, "Go into the city, and
a man carrying a jar of water will
meet you. Follow him. 14Say to the
owner of the house he enters, 'The
Teacher asks: Where is my guest
room, where I may eat the Passover
with my disciples?' 15He will show
you a large upper room,[s] furnished
and ready. Make preparations for
us there."
16The disciples left, went into
the city and found things just as

13:27 [a]Zec 2:6
13:30 [b]Lk 17:25 [c]Mk 9:1
13:31 [d]Mt 5:18
13:32 [e]Ac 1:7; 1Th 5:1,2
13:33 [f]1Th 5:6
13:34 [g]Mt 25:14
13:37 [h]Lk 12:35-40
14:1 [i]Jn 11:55; 13:1 [j]Mt 12:14
14:3 [k]Mt 21:17 [l]Lk 7:37-39
14:7 [m]Dt 15:11
14:8 [n]Jn 19:40
14:9 [o]Mt 24:14; Mk 16:15
14:10 [p]Mk 3:16-19 [q]Mt 10:4
14:12 [r]Ex 12:1-11; Dt 16:1-4; 1Co 5:7
14:15 [s]Ac 1:13

k30 Or *race* l33 Some manuscripts *alert and pray* m5 Greek *than three hundred denarii*

Jesus had told them. So they prepared the Passover.
17When evening came, Jesus arrived with the Twelve. 18While they
were reclining at the table eating,
he said, "I tell you the truth, one of
you will betray me—one who is
eating with me."
19They were saddened, and one
by one they said to him, "Surely
not I?"
20"It is one of the Twelve," he replied, "one who dips bread into the
bowl with me.[a] 21The Son of
Man[b] will go just as it is written
about him. But woe to that man
who betrays the Son of Man! It
would be better for him if he had
not been born."
22While they were eating, Jesus
took bread, gave thanks and broke
it,[c] and gave it to his disciples,
saying, "Take it; this is my body."
23Then he took the cup, gave
thanks and offered it to them, and
they all drank from it.[d]
24"This is my blood of the[n] covenant,[e] which is poured out for
many," he said to them. 25"I tell
you the truth, I will not drink again
of the fruit of the vine until that day
when I drink it anew in the kingdom of God."[f]
26When they had sung a hymn,
they went out to the Mount of Olives.[g]

Jesus Predicts Peter's Denial

14:27-31pp — Mt 26:31-35

27"You will all fall away," Jesus
told them, "for it is written:

" 'I will strike the shepherd,
and the sheep will be
scattered.'[o][h]

28But after I have risen, I will go
ahead of you into Galilee."[i]
29Peter declared, "Even if all fall
away, I will not."
30"I tell you the truth," Jesus answered, "today—yes, tonight—before the rooster crows twice[p] you
yourself will disown me three
times."[j]
31But Peter insisted emphatical-
ly, "Even if I have to die with you,[k]
I will never disown you." And all
the others said the same.

Gethsemane

14:32-42pp — Mt 26:36-46; Lk 22:40-46

32They went to a place called
Gethsemane, and Jesus said to his
disciples, "Sit here while I pray."
33He took Peter, James and John[l]
along with him, and he began to be
deeply distressed and troubled.
34"My soul is overwhelmed with
sorrow to the point of death,"[m] he
said to them. "Stay here and keep
watch."
35Going a little farther, he fell to
the ground and prayed that if possible the hour[n] might pass from
him. 36"*Abba*,[q] Father,"[o] he said,
"everything is possible for you.
Take this cup[p] from me. Yet not
what I will, but what you will."[q]
37Then he returned to his disciples and found them sleeping. "Simon," he said to Peter, "are you
asleep? Could you not keep watch
for one hour? 38Watch and pray so
that you will not fall into temptation.[r] The spirit is willing, but the
body is weak."[s]
39Once more he went away and
prayed the same thing. 40When he
came back, he again found them
sleeping, because their eyes were
heavy. They did not know what to
say to him.
41Returning the third time, he
said to them, "Are you still sleeping and resting? Enough! The
hour[t] has come. Look, the Son of
Man is betrayed into the hands of
sinners. 42Rise! Let us go! Here
comes my betrayer!"

Jesus Arrested

14:43-50pp — Mt 26:47-56; Lk 22:47-50; Jn 18:3-11

43Just as he was speaking, Judas,[u] one of the Twelve, appeared.
With him was a crowd armed with
swords and clubs, sent from the
chief priests, the teachers of the
law, and the elders.

14:20 [a]Jn 13:18-27
14:21 [b]Mt 8:20
14:22 [c]Mt 14:19
14:23 [d]1Co 10:16
14:24 [e]Mt 26:28
14:25 [f]Mt 3:2
14:26 [g]Mt 21:1
14:27 [h]Zec 13:7
14:28 [i]Mk 16:7
14:30 [j]ver 66-72; Lk 22:34; Jn 13:38
14:31 [k]Lk 22:33; Jn 13:37
14:33 [l]Mt 4:21
14:34 [m]Jn 12:27
14:35 [n]ver 41; Mt 26:18
14:36 [o]Ro 8:15; Gal 4:6 [p]Mt 20:22 [q]Mt 26:39
14:38 [r]Mt 6:13 [s]Ro 7:22,23
14:41 [t]ver 35; Mt 26:18
14:43 [u]Mt 10:4

[n]*24* Some manuscripts *the new* [o]*27* Zech. 13:7 [p]*30* Some early manuscripts do not have *twice*. [q]*36* Aramaic for *Father*

44Now the betrayer had arranged
a signal with them: "The one I kiss
is the man; arrest him and lead him
away under guard." **45**Going at
once to Jesus, Judas said, "Rabbi!"[a] and kissed him. **46**The men
seized Jesus and arrested him.
47Then one of those standing near
drew his sword and struck the servant of the high priest, cutting off
his ear.

48"Am I leading a rebellion,"
said Jesus, "that you have come
out with swords and clubs to capture me? **49**Every day I was with
you, teaching in the temple
courts,[b] and you did not arrest me.
But the Scriptures must be fulfilled."[c] **50**Then everyone deserted
him and fled.[d]

51A young man, wearing nothing
but a linen garment, was following
Jesus. When they seized him, **52**he
fled naked, leaving his garment behind.

Before the Sanhedrin

14:53–65pp — Mt 26:57–68; Jn 18:12,13,19–24
14:61–63pp — Lk 22:67–71

53They took Jesus to the high
priest, and all the chief priests, elders and teachers of the law came
together. **54**Peter followed him at a
distance, right into the courtyard of
the high priest.[e] There he sat with
the guards and warmed himself at
the fire.[f]

55The chief priests and the
whole Sanhedrin[g] were looking for
evidence against Jesus so that they
could put him to death, but they
did not find any. **56**Many testified
falsely against him, but their statements did not agree.

57Then some stood up and gave
this false testimony against him:
58"We heard him say, 'I will destroy
this man-made temple and in three
days will build another,[h] not made
by man.'" **59**Yet even then their
testimony did not agree.

60Then the high priest stood up
before them and asked Jesus, "Are
you not going to answer? What is
this testimony that these men are
bringing against you?" **61**But Jesus
remained silent and gave no answer.[i]

Again the high priest asked him,
"Are you the Christ,[r] the Son of
the Blessed One?"[j]

62"I am," said Jesus. "And you
will see the Son of Man sitting at
the right hand of the Mighty One
and coming on the clouds of heav-
en."[k]

63The high priest tore his
clothes.[l] "Why do we need any
more witnesses?" he asked. **64**"You
have heard the blasphemy. What
do you think?"

They all condemned him as worthy of death.[m] **65**Then some began
to spit at him; they blindfolded
him, struck him with their fists,
and said, "Prophesy!" And the
guards took him and beat him.[n]

Peter Disowns Jesus

14:66–72pp — Mt 26:69–75; Lk 22:56–62;
Jn 18:16–18,25–27

66While Peter was below in the
courtyard,[o] one of the servant girls
of the high priest came by. **67**When
she saw Peter warming himself,[p]
she looked closely at him.

"You also were with that Nazarene, Jesus,"[q] she said.

68But he denied it. "I don't know
or understand what you're talking
about,"[r] he said, and went out
into the entryway.[s]

69When the servant girl saw him
there, she said again to those
standing around, "This fellow is
one of them." **70**Again he denied
it.[s]

After a little while, those standing near said to Peter, "Surely you
are one of them, for you are a Galilean."[t]

71He began to call down curses
on himself, and he swore to them,
"I don't know this man you're talking about."[u]

72Immediately the rooster
crowed the second time.[t] Then

[r]*61* Or *Messiah* [s]*68* Some early manuscripts *entryway and the rooster crowed*
[t]*72* Some early manuscripts do not have *the second time.*

14:45 [a]Mt 23:7
14:49 [b]Mt 26:55 [c]Isa 53:7-12; Mt 1:22
14:50 [d]ver 27
14:54 [e]Mt 26:3 [f]Jn 18:18
14:55 [g]Mt 5:22
14:58 [h]Mk 15:29; Jn 2:19
14:61 [i]Isa 53:7; Mt 27:12,14; Mk 15:5; Lk 23:9; Jn 19:9 [j]Mt 16:16; Jn 4:25,26
14:62 [k]Rev 1:7
14:63 [l]Lev 10:6; 21:10; Nu 14:6; Ac 14:14
14:64 [m]Lev 24:16
14:65 [n]Mt 16:21
14:66 [o]ver 54
14:67 [p]ver 54 [q]Mk 1:24
14:68 [r]ver 30,72
14:70 [s]ver 30,68,72 [t]Ac 2:7
14:71 [u]ver 30,72

Peter remembered the word Jesus
had spoken to him: “Before the
rooster crows twice[u] you will disown me three times.”[a] And he
broke down and wept.

Jesus Before Pilate

15:2–15pp — Mt 27:11–26; Lk 23:2,3,18–25;
Jn 18:29–19:16

15 Very early in the morning,
the chief priests, with the
elders, the teachers of the law[b]
and the whole Sanhedrin,[c]
reached a decision. They bound
Jesus, led him away and handed
him over to Pilate.[d]
2“Are you the king of the
Jews?”[e] asked Pilate.
“Yes, it is as you say,” Jesus replied.
3The chief priests accused him
of many things. 4So again Pilate
asked him, “Aren’t you going to answer? See how many things they
are accusing you of.”
5But Jesus still made no reply,[f]
and Pilate was amazed.
6Now it was the custom at the
Feast to release a prisoner whom
the people requested. 7A man
called Barabbas was in prison with
the insurrectionists who had committed murder in the uprising.
8The crowd came up and asked Pilate to do for them what he usually
did.
9“Do you want me to release to
you the king of the Jews?”[g] asked
Pilate, 10knowing it was out of envy
that the chief priests had handed Jesus over to him. 11But the
chief priests stirred up the crowd
to have Pilate release Barabbas[h]
instead.
12“What shall I do, then, with
the one you call the king of the
Jews?” Pilate asked them.
13“Crucify him!” they shouted.
14“Why? What crime has he
committed?” asked Pilate.
But they shouted all the louder,
“Crucify him!”
15Wanting to satisfy the crowd,
Pilate released Barabbas to them.
He had Jesus flogged,[i] and handed him over to be crucified.

14:72 [a]ver 30,68
15:1 [b]Mt 27:1; Lk 22:66 [c]Mt 5:22 [d]Mt 27:2
15:2 [e]ver 9,12,18, 26; Mt 2:2
15:5 [f]Mk 14:61
15:9 [g]ver 2
15:11 [h]Ac 3:14
15:15 [i]Isa 53:6
15:16 [j]Jn 18:28,33; 19:9
15:18 [k]ver 2
15:20 [l]Heb 13:12
15:21 [m]Mt 27:32 [n]Ro 16:13 [o]Mt 27:32; Lk 23:26
15:23 [p]ver 36; Ps 69:21; Pr 31:6
15:24 [q]Ps 22:18
15:26 [r]ver 2
15:29 [s]Ps 22:7; 109:25 [t]Mk 14:58; Jn 2:19
15:31 [u]Ps 22:7

The Soldiers Mock Jesus

15:16–20pp — Mt 27:27–31

16The soldiers led Jesus away
into the palace[j] (that is, the Praetorium) and called together the
whole company of soldiers. 17They
put a purple robe on him, then
twisted together a crown of thorns
and set it on him. 18And they began
to call out to him, “Hail, king of the
Jews!”[k] 19Again and again they
struck him on the head with a staff
and spit on him. Falling on their
knees, they paid homage to him.
20And when they had mocked him,
they took off the purple robe and
put his own clothes on him. Then
they led him out[l] to crucify him.

The Crucifixion

15:22–32pp — Mt 27:33–44; Lk 23:33–43;
Jn 19:17–24

21A certain man from Cyrene,[m]
Simon, the father of Alexander and
Rufus,[n] was passing by on his way
in from the country, and they
forced him to carry the cross.[o]
22They brought Jesus to the place
called Golgotha (which means The
Place of the Skull). 23Then they offered him wine mixed with
myrrh,[p] but he did not take it.
24And they crucified him. Dividing
up his clothes, they cast lots[q] to
see what each would get.
25It was the third hour when they
crucified him. 26The written notice
of the charge against him read: THE
KING OF THE JEWS.[r] 27They crucified
two robbers with him, one on his
right and one on his left.[v] 29Those
who passed by hurled insults at
him, shaking their heads[s] and saying, “So! You who are going to destroy the temple and build it in
three days,[t] 30come down from
the cross and save yourself!”
31In the same way the chief
priests and the teachers of the law
mocked him[u] among themselves.
“He saved others,” they said, “but
he can’t save himself! 32Let this

[u]72 Some early manuscripts do not have *twice.* [v]27 Some manuscripts *left,* 28*and the scripture was fulfilled which says, “He was counted with the lawless ones”* (Isaiah 53:12)

Christ,[w][a] this King of Israel,[b]
come down now from the cross,
that we may see and believe."
Those crucified with him also
heaped insults on him.

The Death of Jesus

15:33–41pp – Mt 27:45–56; Lk 23:44–49

33At the sixth hour darkness
came over the whole land until the
ninth hour.[c] 34And at the ninth
hour Jesus cried out in a loud
voice, *"Eloi, Eloi, lama sabachthani?"*—which means, "My God, my
God, why have you forsaken
me?"[x][d]

35When some of those standing
near heard this, they said, "Listen,
he's calling Elijah."

36One man ran, filled a sponge
with wine vinegar,[e] put it on a
stick, and offered it to Jesus to
drink. "Now leave him alone. Let's
see if Elijah comes to take him
down," he said.

37With a loud cry, Jesus
breathed his last.[f]

38The curtain of the temple was
torn in two from top to bottom.[g]
39And when the centurion,[h] who
stood there in front of Jesus, heard
his cry and[y] saw how he died, he
said, "Surely this man was the
Son[z] of God!"[i]

40Some women were watching
from a distance.[j] Among them
were Mary Magdalene, Mary the
mother of James the younger and
of Joses, and Salome.[k] 41In Galilee these women had followed him
and cared for his needs. Many other women who had come up with
him to Jerusalem were also there.[l]

The Burial of Jesus

15:42–47pp – Mt 27:57–61; Lk 23:50–56; Jn 19:38–42

42It was Preparation Day (that is,
the day before the Sabbath).[m] So
as evening approached, 43Joseph
of Arimathea, a prominent member
of the Council,[n] who was himself
waiting for the kingdom of God,[o]
went boldly to Pilate and asked for
Jesus' body. 44Pilate was surprised
to hear that he was already dead.
Summoning the centurion, he
asked him if Jesus had already
died. 45When he learned from the
centurion[p] that it was so, he gave
the body to Joseph. 46So Joseph
bought some linen cloth, took
down the body, wrapped it in the
linen, and placed it in a tomb cut
out of rock. Then he rolled a stone
against the entrance of the tomb.[q]
47Mary Magdalene and Mary the
mother of Joses[r] saw where he
was laid.

The Resurrection

16:1–8pp – Mt 28:1–8; Lk 24:1–10

16 When the Sabbath was
over, Mary Magdalene,
Mary the mother of James, and Salome bought spices[s] so that they
might go to anoint Jesus' body.
2Very early on the first day of the
week, just after sunrise, they were
on their way to the tomb 3and they
asked each other, "Who will roll
the stone away from the entrance
of the tomb?"[t]

4But when they looked up, they
saw that the stone, which was very
large, had been rolled away. 5As
they entered the tomb, they saw a
young man dressed in a white
robe[u] sitting on the right side, and
they were alarmed.

6"Don't be alarmed," he said.
"You are looking for Jesus the Nazarene,[v] who was crucified. He has
risen! He is not here. See the place
where they laid him. 7But go, tell
his disciples and Peter, 'He is going
ahead of you into Galilee. There
you will see him,[w] just as he told
you.' "[x]

8Trembling and bewildered, the
women went out and fled from the
tomb. They said nothing to anyone,
because they were afraid.

[The earliest manuscripts and some other ancient witnesses do not have Mark 16:9–20.]

15:32 [a]Mk 14:61 [b]ver 2
15:33 [c]Am 8:9
15:34 [d]Ps 22:1
15:36 [e]ver 23; Ps 69:21
15:37 [f]Jn 19:30
15:38 [g]Heb 10:19, 20
15:39 [h]ver 45 [i]Mk 1:1,11; 9:7; Mt 4:3
15:40 [j]Ps 38:11 [k]Mk 16:1; Lk 24:10; Jn 19:25
15:41 [l]Mt 27:55,56; Lk 8:2,3
15:42 [m]Mt 27:62; Jn 19:31
15:43 [n]Mt 5:22 [o]Mt 3:2; Lk 2:25,38
15:45 [p]ver 39
15:46 [q]Mk 16:3
15:47 [r]ver 40
16:1 [s]Lk 23:56; Jn 19:39,40
16:3 [t]Mk 15:46
16:5 [u]Jn 20:12
16:6 [v]Mk 1:24
16:7 [w]Jn 21:1-23 [x]Mk 14:28

[w]*32* Or *Messiah* [x]*34* Psalm 22:1
[y]*39* Some manuscripts do not have *heard his cry and* [z]*39* Or *a son*

9 When Jesus rose early on the
first day of the week, he appeared
first to Mary Magdalene,[a] out of
whom he had driven seven demons. 10 She went and told those
who had been with him and who
were mourning and weeping.
11 When they heard that Jesus was
alive and that she had seen him,
they did not believe it.[b]

12 Afterward Jesus appeared in a
different form to two of them while
they were walking in the country.[c]
13 These returned and reported it to
the rest; but they did not believe
them either.

14 Later Jesus appeared to the
Eleven as they were eating; he rebuked them for their lack of faith
and their stubborn refusal to believe those who had seen him after
he had risen.[d]

15 He said to them, "Go into all
the world and preach the good
news to all creation.[e] 16 Whoever
believes and is baptized will be
saved, but whoever does not believe will be condemned.[f] 17 And
these signs will accompany those
who believe: In my name they will
drive out demons;[g] they will speak
in new tongues;[h] 18 they will pick
up snakes[i] with their hands; and
when they drink deadly poison, it
will not hurt them at all; they will
place their hands on[j] sick people,
and they will get well."

19 After the Lord Jesus had spoken to them, he was taken up into
heaven[k] and he sat at the right
hand of God.[l] 20 Then the disciples went out and preached everywhere, and the Lord worked with
them and confirmed his word by
the signs that accompanied it.

16:9 [a] Jn 20:11-18 **16:11** [b] ver 13,14; Lk 24:11 **16:12** [c] Lk 24:13-32 **16:14** [d] Lk 24:36-43 **16:15** [e] Mt 28:18-20; Lk 24:47,48 **16:16** [f] Jn 3:16,18, 36; Ac 16:31 **16:17** [g] Mk 9:38; Lk 10:17; Ac 5:16; 8:7; 16:18; 19:13-16 [h] Ac 2:4; 10:46; 19:6; 1Co 12:10,28, 30 **16:18** [i] Lk 10:19; Ac 28:3-5 [j] Ac 6:6 **16:19** [k] Lk 24:50,51; Jn 6:62; Ac 1:9-11; 1Ti 3:16 [l] Ps 110:1; Ro 8:34; Col 3:1; Heb 1:3; 12:2

Luke

Title and Background

The Gospel of Luke has been called the most beautiful book ever written. Luke's writing shows him to be a highly educated man, one who wrote from a Greek background and viewpoint. He wrote especially with Gentiles in mind, for he explained Jewish customs and traced the genealogy of Jesus back to Adam.

Author and Date of Writing

The author's name does not appear in the book, but much unmistakable evidence points to Luke. This Gospel is a companion volume to the book of Acts, and the language and structure of these books indicate that both were written by the same person. Luke was probably a Gentile by birth, well educated in Greek culture, a physician by profession and a companion of Paul at various times. The book was probably written between A.D. 59 and 63.

Theme and Message

Luke tells us in the first four verses of his book that he wrote this Gospel to give the true and complete story of Jesus' life. He wrote the fullest and most orderly story of his life. One of Luke's interests in writing this book was to show that Jesus loved all kinds of people. In the parables especially, he wrote about the poor and oppressed. The theme of joy is felt throughout the book, as Christ's coming brought joy as well as hope and salvation to a sinful world.

Outline

I. The Preface (1:1-4)
II. The Coming of Jesus (1:5-2:52)
III. Jesus' Preparation for His Ministry (3:1-4:13)
IV. Jesus' Ministry in Galilee (4:14-9:9)
V. Jesus' Withdrawals From Galilee (9:10-50)
VI. Jesus' Ministry in Judea (9:51-13:21)
VII. Jesus' Ministry in and Near Perea (13:22-19:27)
VIII. Jesus' Sacrifice and Triumph (19:28-24:53)

Introduction

1:1–4Ref – Ac 1:1

1 Many have undertaken to draw
up an account of the things
that have been fulfilled[a] among
us, **2**just as they were handed down
to us by those who from the first[a]
were eyewitnesses[b] and servants
of the word.[c] **3**Therefore, since I
myself have carefully investigated
everything from the beginning, it
seemed good also to me to write an
orderly account[d] for you, most excellent[e] Theophilus,[f] **4**so that
you may know the certainty of the
things you have been taught.[g]

The Birth of John the Baptist Foretold

5In the time of Herod king of Judea[h] there was a priest named
Zechariah, who belonged to the
priestly division of Abijah;[i] his
wife Elizabeth was also a descendant of Aaron. **6**Both of them were
upright in the sight of God, observing all the Lord's commandments

1:2 [a] Mk 1:1; Jn 15:27; Ac 1:21,22 [b] Heb 2:3; 1Pe 5:1; 2Pe 1:16; 1Jn 1:1 [c] Mk 4:14
1:3 [d] Ac 11:4 [e] Ac 24:3; 26:25 [f] Ac 1:1
1:4 [g] Jn 20:31
1:5 [h] Mt 2:1 [i] 1Ch 24:10

[a] *1* Or *been surely believed*

and regulations blamelessly.[a]
7But they had no children, because
Elizabeth was barren; and they
were both well along in years.
8Once when Zechariah's division
was on duty and he was serving as
priest before God,[b] 9he was chosen by lot, according to the custom
of the priesthood, to go into the
temple of the Lord and burn incense.[c] 10And when the time for
the burning of incense came, all
the assembled worshipers were
praying outside.[d]
11Then an angel[e] of the Lord appeared to him, standing at the right
side of the altar of incense.[f]
12When Zechariah saw him, he was
startled and was gripped with
fear.[g] 13But the angel said to him:
"Do not be afraid,[h] Zechariah;
your prayer has been heard. Your
wife Elizabeth will bear you a son,
and you are to give him the name
John.[i] 14He will be a joy and delight to you, and many will rejoice
because of his birth,[j] 15for he will
be great in the sight of the Lord. He
is never to take wine or other fermented drink,[k] and he will be
filled with the Holy Spirit even
from birth.[b][l] 16Many of the people of Israel will he bring back to
the Lord their God. 17And he will
go on before the Lord,[m] in the spirit and power of Elijah,[n] to turn the
hearts of the fathers to their children[o] and the disobedient to the
wisdom of the righteous—to make
ready a people prepared for the
Lord."
18Zechariah asked the angel,
"How can I be sure of this? I am an
old man and my wife is well along
in years."[p]
19The angel answered, "I am Gabriel.[q] I stand in the presence of
God, and I have been sent to speak
to you and to tell you this good
news. 20And now you will be silent
and not able to speak[r] until the
day this happens, because you did
not believe my words, which will
come true at their proper time."
21Meanwhile, the people were
waiting for Zechariah and wondering why he stayed so long in the
temple. 22When he came out, he
could not speak to them. They realized he had seen a vision in the
temple, for he kept making signs[s]
to them but remained unable to
speak.
23When his time of service was
completed, he returned home.
24After this his wife Elizabeth became pregnant and for five months
remained in seclusion. 25"The
Lord has done this for me," she
said. "In these days he has shown
his favor and taken away my disgrace[t] among the people."

The Birth of Jesus Foretold

26In the sixth month, God sent
the angel Gabriel[u] to Nazareth,[v] a
town in Galilee, 27to a virgin
pledged to be married to a man
named Joseph,[w] a descendant of
David. The virgin's name was Mary.
28The angel went to her and said,
"Greetings, you who are highly favored! The Lord is with you."
29Mary was greatly troubled at
his words and wondered what kind
of greeting this might be. 30But the
angel said to her, "Do not be
afraid,[x] Mary, you have found favor with God. 31You will be with
child and give birth to a son, and
you are to give him the name
Jesus.[y] 32He will be great and will
be called the Son of the Most
High.[z] The Lord God will give him
the throne of his father David,
33and he will reign over the house
of Jacob forever; his kingdom[a] will
never end."[b]
34"How will this be," Mary asked
the angel, "since I am a virgin?"
35The angel answered, "The
Holy Spirit will come upon you,[c]
and the power of the Most High[d]
will overshadow you. So the holy
one[e] to be born will be called[c] the
Son of God.[f] 36Even Elizabeth
your relative is going to have a
child in her old age, and she who
was said to be barren is in her sixth
month. 37For nothing is impossible
with God."[g]

1:6 [a]Ge 7:1; 1Ki 9:4 **1:8** [b]1Ch 24:19; 2Ch 8:14 **1:9** [c]Ex 30:7,8; 1Ch 23:13; 2Ch 29:11 **1:10** [d]Lev 16:17 **1:11** [e]Ac 5:19 [f]Ex 30:1-10 **1:12** [g]Jdg 6:22,23; 13:22 **1:13** [h]ver 30; Mt 14:27 [i]ver 60,63 **1:14** [j]ver 58 **1:15** [k]Nu 6:3; Jdg 13:4; Lk 7:33 [l]Jer 1:5; Gal 1:15 **1:17** [m]ver 76 [n]Mt 11:14 [o]Mal 4:5,6 **1:18** [p]ver 34; Ge 17:17 **1:19** [q]ver 26; Mt 18:10; Da 8:16; 9:21 **1:20** [r]Eze 3:26 **1:22** [s]ver 62 **1:25** [t]Ge 30:23; Isa 4:1 **1:26** [u]ver 19 [v]Mt 2:23 **1:27** [w]Mt 1:16,18, 20; Lk 2:4 **1:30** [x]ver 13; Mt 14:27 **1:31** [y]Isa 7:14; Mt 1:21,25; Lk 2:21 **1:32** [z]ver 35,76; Mk 5:7 **1:33** [a]Mt 28:18 [b]Da 2:44; 7:14,27; Mic 4:7; Heb 1:8 **1:35** [c]Mt 1:18 [d]ver 32,76 [e]Mk 1:24 [f]Mt 4:3 **1:37** [g]Mt 19:26

[b]*15* Or *from his mother's womb* [c]*35* Or *So the child to be born will be called holy,*

all these things and pondered them
in her heart.[a] 20The shepherds returned, glorifying and praising
God[b] for all the things they had
heard and seen, which were just as
they had been told.

Jesus Presented in the Temple

21On the eighth day, when it was
time to circumcise him,[c] he was
named Jesus, the name the angel
had given him before he had been
conceived.[d]
22When the time of their purification according to the Law of Moses[e] had been completed, Joseph
and Mary took him to Jerusalem to
present him to the Lord 23(as it is
written in the Law of the Lord, "Every firstborn male is to be consecrated to the Lord"[f]),[f] 24and to
offer a sacrifice in keeping with
what is said in the Law of the Lord:
"a pair of doves or two young pigeons."[g][g]
25Now there was a man in Jerusalem called Simeon, who was
righteous and devout.[h] He was
waiting for the consolation of Israel,[i] and the Holy Spirit was upon
him. 26It had been revealed to him
by the Holy Spirit that he would
not die before he had seen the
Lord's Christ. 27Moved by the Spirit, he went into the temple courts.
When the parents brought in the
child Jesus to do for him what the
custom of the Law required,[j]
28Simeon took him in his arms and
praised God, saying:

29"Sovereign Lord, as you have
promised,[k]
you now dismiss[h] your
servant in peace.[l]
30For my eyes have seen your
salvation,[m]
31 which you have prepared in
the sight of all people,
32a light for revelation to the
Gentiles
and for glory to your people
Israel."[n]

33The child's father and mother
marveled at what was said about
him. 34Then Simeon blessed them
and said to Mary, his mother:[o]

2:19 [a]ver 51
2:20 [b]Mt 9:8
2:21 [c]Lk 1:59 [d]Lk 1:31
2:22 [e]Lev 12:2-8
2:23 [f]Ex 13:2,12, 15; Nu 3:13
2:24 [g]Lev 12:8
2:25 [h]Lk 1:6 [i]ver 38; Isa 52:9; Lk 23:51
2:27 [j]ver 22
2:29 [k]ver 26 [l]Ac 2:24
2:30 [m]Isa 52:10; Lk 3:6
2:32 [n]Isa 42:6; 49:6; Ac 13:47; 26:23
2:34 [o]Mt 12:46 [p]Isa 8:14; Mt 21:44; 1Co 1:23; 2Co 2:16; 1Pe 2:7,8
2:36 [q]Ac 21:9
2:37 [r]1Ti 5:9 [s]Ac 13:3; 14:23; 1Ti 5:5
2:38 [t]ver 25; Isa 40:2; Lk 1:68; 24:21
2:39 [u]ver 51; Mt 2:23
2:40 [v]ver 52; Lk 1:80
2:41 [w]Ex 23:15; Dt 16:1-8
2:47 [x]Mt 7:28

"This child is destined to cause the
falling[p] and rising of many in Israel, and to be a sign that will be spoken against, 35so that the thoughts
of many hearts will be revealed.
And a sword will pierce your own
soul too."
36There was also a prophetess,[q]
Anna, the daughter of Phanuel, of
the tribe of Asher. She was very old;
she had lived with her husband sev-
en years after her marriage, 37and
then was a widow until she was
eighty-four.[i][r] She never left the
temple but worshiped night and
day, fasting and praying.[s] 38Com-
ing up to them at that very moment, she gave thanks to God and
spoke about the child to all who
were looking forward to the redemption of Jerusalem.[t]
39When Joseph and Mary had
done everything required by the
Law of the Lord, they returned to
Galilee to their own town of Nazareth.[u] 40And the child grew and
became strong; he was filled with
wisdom, and the grace of God was
upon him.[v]

The Boy Jesus at the Temple

41Every year his parents went to
Jerusalem for the Feast of the Passover.[w] 42When he was twelve years
old, they went up to the Feast, according to the custom. 43After the
Feast was over, while his parents
were returning home, the boy Jesus
stayed behind in Jerusalem, but
they were unaware of it. 44Think-
ing he was in their company, they
traveled on for a day. Then they began looking for him among their
relatives and friends. 45When they
did not find him, they went back to
Jerusalem to look for him. 46After
three days they found him in the
temple courts, sitting among the
teachers, listening to them and
asking them questions. Everyone
who heard him was amazed[x] at his
understanding and his answers.
48When his parents saw him, they

[f]23 Exodus 13:2,12 [g]24 Lev. 12:8
[h]29 Or *promised, / now dismiss* [i]37 Or
widow for eighty-four years

were astonished. His mother[a] said
to him, "Son, why have you treated
us like this? Your father[b] and I
have been anxiously searching for
you."

49"Why were you searching for
me?" he asked. "Didn't you know I
had to be in my Father's house?"[c]
50But they did not understand
what he was saying to them.[d]

51Then he went down to Nazareth with them[e] and was obedient
to them. But his mother treasured
all these things in her heart.[f]
52And Jesus grew in wisdom and
stature, and in favor with God and
men.[g]

John the Baptist Prepares the Way

3:2–10pp — Mt 3:1–10; Mk 1:3–5
3:16,17pp — Mt 3:11,12; Mk 1:7,8

3 In the fifteenth year of the
reign of Tiberius Caesar—
when Pontius Pilate[h] was governor
of Judea, Herod[i] tetrarch of Galilee, his brother Philip tetrarch of
Iturea and Traconitis, and Lysanias
tetrarch of Abilene— **2**during the
high priesthood of Annas and Caiaphas,[j] the word of God came to
John[k] son of Zechariah[l] in the
desert. **3**He went into all the country around the Jordan, preaching a
baptism of repentance for the forgiveness of sins.[m] **4**As is written in
the book of the words of Isaiah the
prophet:

"A voice of one calling in the
desert,
'Prepare the way for the Lord,
make straight paths for him.
5Every valley shall be filled in,
every mountain and hill
made low.
The crooked roads shall
become straight,
the rough ways smooth.
6And all mankind will see God's
salvation.' "[j][n]

7John said to the crowds coming
out to be baptized by him, "You
brood of vipers![o] Who warned you
to flee from the coming wrath?[p]
8Produce fruit in keeping with repentance. And do not begin to say
to yourselves, 'We have Abraham
as our father.'[q] For I tell you that
out of these stones God can raise
up children for Abraham. **9**The ax
is already at the root of the trees,
and every tree that does not produce good fruit will be cut down
and thrown into the fire."[r]

10"What should we do then?"[s]
the crowd asked.

11John answered, "The man
with two tunics should share with
him who has none, and the one
who has food should do the
same."[t]

12Tax collectors also came to be
baptized.[u] "Teacher," they asked,
"what should we do?"

13"Don't collect any more than
you are required to,"[v] he told
them.

14Then some soldiers asked him,
"And what should we do?"

He replied, "Don't extort money
and don't accuse people falsely[w]
—be content with your pay."

15The people were waiting expectantly and were all wondering
in their hearts if John[x] might possibly be the Christ.[k][y] **16**John answered them all, "I baptize you
with[l] water.[z] But one more powerful than I will come, the thongs of
whose sandals I am not worthy to
untie. He will baptize you with the
Holy Spirit and with fire.[a] **17**His
winnowing fork[b] is in his hand to
clear his threshing floor and to
gather the wheat into his barn, but
he will burn up the chaff with unquenchable fire."[c] **18**And with
many other words John exhorted
the people and preached the good
news to them.

19But when John rebuked Herod[d] the tetrarch because of Herodias, his brother's wife, and all the
other evil things he had done,
20Herod added this to them all: He
locked John up in prison.[e]

2:48 [a] Mt 12:46 [b] Lk 3:23; 4:22
2:49 [c] Jn 2:16
2:50 [d] Mk 9:32
2:51 [e] ver 39; Mt 2:23 [f] ver 19
2:52 [g] ver 40; 1Sa 2:26; Lk 1:80
3:1 [h] Mt 27:2 [i] Mt 14:1
3:2 [j] Mt 26:3; Jn 18:13; Ac 4:6 [k] Mt 3:1 [l] Lk 1:13
3:3 [m] ver 16; Mk 1:4
3:6 [n] Isa 40:3-5; Ps 98:2; Isa 42:16; 52:10; Lk 2:30
3:7 [o] Mt 12:34; 23:33 [p] Ro 1:18
3:8 [q] Isa 51:2; Lk 19:9; Jn 8:33,39; Ac 13:26; Ro 4:1,11,12, 16,17; Gal 3:7
3:9 [r] Mt 3:10
3:10 [s] ver 12,14; Ac 2:37; 16:30
3:11 [t] Isa 58:7
3:12 [u] Lk 7:29
3:13 [v] Lk 19:8
3:14 [w] Ex 23:1; Lev 19:11
3:15 [x] Mt 3:1 [y] Jn 1:19,20; Ac 13:25
3:16 [z] ver 3; Mk 1:4 [a] Jn 1:26,33; Ac 1:5; 11:16; 19:4
3:17 [b] Isa 30:24 [c] Mt 13:30; 25:41
3:19 [d] ver 1
3:20 [e] Mt 14:3,4; Mk 6:17-18

j6 Isaiah 40:3-5 k15 Or *Messiah* l16 Or *in*

The Baptism and Genealogy of Jesus

3:21,22pp — Mt 3:13–17; Mk 1:9–11
3:23–38pp — Mt 1:1–17

21When all the people were being baptized, Jesus was baptized
too. And as he was praying,[a] heav-
en was opened **22**and the Holy Spirit descended on him[b] in bodily
form like a dove. And a voice came
from heaven: "You are my Son,[c]
whom I love; with you I am well
pleased."[d]

23Now Jesus himself was about
thirty years old when he began his
ministry.[e] He was the son, so it
was thought, of Joseph,[f]

the son of Heli, **24**the son of
Matthat,
the son of Levi, the son of
Melki,
the son of Jannai, the son of
Joseph,
25the son of Mattathias, the son
of Amos,
the son of Nahum, the son of
Esli,
the son of Naggai, **26**the son of
Maath,
the son of Mattathias, the son
of Semein,
the son of Josech, the son of
Joda,
27the son of Joanan, the son of
Rhesa,
the son of Zerubbabel,[g] the
son of Shealtiel,
the son of Neri, **28**the son of
Melki,
the son of Addi, the son of Co-
sam,
the son of Elmadam, the son
of Er,
29the son of Joshua, the son of
Eliezer,
the son of Jorim, the son of
Matthat,
the son of Levi, **30**the son of
Simeon,
the son of Judah, the son of
Joseph,
the son of Jonam, the son of
Eliakim,
31the son of Melea, the son of
Menna,
the son of Mattatha, the son of
Nathan,[h]
the son of David, **32**the son of
Jesse,
the son of Obed, the son of
Boaz,
the son of Salmon,[m] the son of
Nahshon,
33the son of Amminadab, the
son of Ram,[n]
the son of Hezron, the son of
Perez,[i]
the son of Judah, **34**the son of
Jacob,
the son of Isaac, the son of
Abraham,
the son of Terah, the son of
Nahor,[j]
35the son of Serug, the son of
Reu,
the son of Peleg, the son of
Eber,
the son of Shelah, **36**the son of
Cainan,
the son of Arphaxad,[k] the son
of Shem,
the son of Noah, the son of Lamech,[l]
37the son of Methuselah, the
son of Enoch,
the son of Jared, the son of
Mahalalel,
the son of Kenan, **38**the son of
Enosh,
the son of Seth, the son of
Adam,
the son of God.[m]

The Temptation of Jesus

4:1–13pp — Mt 4:1–11; Mk 1:12,13

4 Jesus, full of the Holy Spirit,[n]
returned from the Jordan[o] and
was led by the Spirit[p] in the desert,
2where for forty days[q] he was
tempted by the devil. He ate nothing during those days, and at the
end of them he was hungry.

3The devil said to him, "If you
are the Son of God, tell this stone
to become bread."

4Jesus answered, "It is written:
'Man does not live on bread
alone.'[o]"[r]

3:21 [a] Mt 14:23; Mk 1:35; 6:46; Lk 5:16; 6:12; 9:18,28; 11:1
3:22 [b] Isa 42:1; Jn 1:32,33; Ac 10:38 [c] Mt 3:17 [d] Mt 3:17
3:23 [e] Mt 4:17; Ac 1:1 [f] Lk 1:27
3:27 [g] Mt 1:12
3:31 [h] 2Sa 5:14; 1Ch 3:5
3:33 [i] Ru 4:18-22; 1Ch 2:10-12
3:34 [j] Ge 11:24,26
3:36 [k] Ge 11:12 [l] Ge 5:28-32
3:38 [m] Ge 5:1,2,6-9
4:1 [n] ver 14,18 [o] Lk 3:3,21 [p] Lk 2:27
4:2 [q] Ex 34:28; 1Ki 19:8
4:4 [r] Dt 8:3

[m]*32* Some early manuscripts *Sala*
[n]*33* Some manuscripts *Amminadab, the son of Admin, the son of Arni*; other manuscripts vary widely.
[o]*4* Deut. 8:3

[5]The devil led him up to a high
place and showed him in an instant
all the kingdoms of the world.[a]
[6]And he said to him, "I will give you
all their authority and splendor, for
it has been given to me,[b] and I can
give it to anyone I want to. [7]So if
you worship me, it will all be
yours."

[8]Jesus answered, "It is written:
'Worship the Lord your God and
serve him only.'[p]"[c]

[9]The devil led him to Jerusalem
and had him stand on the highest
point of the temple. "If you are the
Son of God," he said, "throw yourself down from here. [10]For it is
written:

" 'He will command his angels
concerning you
to guard you carefully;
[11]they will lift you up in their
hands,
so that you will not strike
your foot against a
stone.'[q]"[d]

[12]Jesus answered, "It says: 'Do
not put the Lord your God to the
test.'[r]"[e]

[13]When the devil had finished all
this tempting,[f] he left him[g] until
an opportune time.

Jesus Rejected at Nazareth

[14]Jesus returned to Galilee[h] in
the power of the Spirit, and news
about him spread through the
whole countryside.[i] [15]He taught
in their synagogues,[j] and everyone
praised him.

[16]He went to Nazareth,[k] where
he had been brought up, and on the
Sabbath day he went into the synagogue,[l] as was his custom. And he
stood up to read. [17]The scroll of the
prophet Isaiah was handed to him.
Unrolling it, he found the place
where it is written:

[18]"The Spirit of the Lord is on
me,[m]
because he has anointed me
to preach good news to the
poor.
He has sent me to proclaim
freedom for the prisoners
and recovery of sight for the
blind,
to release the oppressed,
[19] to proclaim the year of the
Lord's favor."[s][n]

[20]Then he rolled up the scroll,
gave it back to the attendant and
sat down.[o] The eyes of everyone in
the synagogue were fastened on
him, [21]and he began by saying to
them, "Today this scripture is fulfilled in your hearing."

[22]All spoke well of him and were
amazed at the gracious words that
came from his lips. "Isn't this Joseph's son?" they asked.[p]

[23]Jesus said to them, "Surely
you will quote this proverb to me:
'Physician, heal yourself! Do here
in your hometown[q] what we have
heard that you did in Capernaum.' "[r]

[24]"I tell you the truth," he continued, "no prophet is accepted in
his hometown.[s] [25]I assure you
that there were many widows in Israel in Elijah's time, when the sky
was shut for three and a half years
and there was a severe famine
throughout the land.[t] [26]Yet Elijah
was not sent to any of them, but to
a widow in Zarephath in the region
of Sidon.[u] [27]And there were many
in Israel with leprosy[t] in the time
of Elisha the prophet, yet not one
of them was cleansed—only Naaman the Syrian."[v]

[28]All the people in the synagogue were furious when they
heard this. [29]They got up, drove
him out of the town,[w] and took
him to the brow of the hill on which
the town was built, in order to
throw him down the cliff. [30]But he
walked right through the crowd
and went on his way.[x]

Jesus Drives Out an Evil Spirit

4:31–37pp — Mk 1:21–28

[31]Then he went down to Capernaum,[y] a town in Galilee, and on

4:5 [a]Mt 24:14
4:6 [b]Jn 12:31; 14:30; 1Jn 5:19
4:8 [c]Dt 6:13
4:11 [d]Ps 91:11,12
4:12 [e]Dt 6:16
4:13 [f]Heb 4:15 [g]Jn 14:30
4:14 [h]Mt 4:12 [i]Mt 9:26
4:15 [j]Mt 4:23
4:16 [k]Mt 2:23 [l]Mt 13:54
4:18 [m]Jn 3:34
4:19 [n]Isa 61:1,2; Lev 25:10
4:20 [o]ver 17; Mt 26:55
4:22 [p]Mt 13:54,55; Jn 6:42; 7:15
4:23 [q]ver 16 [r]Mk 1:21-28; 2:1-12
4:24 [s]Mt 13:57; Jn 4:44
4:25 [t]1Ki 17:1; 18:1; Jas 5:17,18
4:26 [u]1Ki 17:8-16; Mt 11:21
4:27 [v]2Ki 5:1-14
4:29 [w]Nu 15:35; Ac 7:58; Heb 13:12
4:30 [x]Jn 8:59; 10:39
4:31 [y]ver 23; Mt 4:13

[p]*8* Deut. 6:13 [q]*11* Psalm 91:11,12
[r]*12* Deut. 6:16 [s]*19* Isaiah 61:1,2
[t]*27* The Greek word was used for various diseases affecting the skin—not necessarily leprosy.

the Sabbath began to teach the people. 32They were amazed at his teaching,[a] because his message had authority.[b]

33In the synagogue there was a man possessed by a demon, an evil[u] spirit. He cried out at the top of his voice, 34"Ha! What do you want with us,[c] Jesus of Nazareth?[d] Have you come to destroy us? I know who you are[e]—the Holy One of God!"[f]

35"Be quiet!" Jesus said sternly.[g] "Come out of him!" Then the demon threw the man down before them all and came out without injuring him.

36All the people were amazed[h] and said to each other, "What is this teaching? With authority[i] and power he gives orders to evil spirits and they come out!" 37And the news about him spread throughout the surrounding area.[j]

Jesus Heals Many

4:38–41pp — Mt 8:14–17
4:38–43pp — Mk 1:29–38

38Jesus left the synagogue and went to the home of Simon. Now Simon's mother-in-law was suffering from a high fever, and they asked Jesus to help her. 39So he bent over her and rebuked[k] the fever, and it left her. She got up at once and began to wait on them.

40When the sun was setting, the people brought to Jesus all who had various kinds of sickness, and laying his hands on each one,[l] he healed them.[m] 41Moreover, demons came out of many people, shouting, "You are the Son of God!"[n] But he rebuked[o] them and would not allow them to speak,[p] because they knew he was the Christ.[v]

42At daybreak Jesus went out to a solitary place. The people were looking for him and when they came to where he was, they tried to keep him from leaving them. 43But he said, "I must preach the good news of the kingdom of God[q] to the other towns also, because that is why I was sent." 44And he kept on preaching in the synagogues of Judea.[w][r]

The Calling of the First Disciples

5:1–11pp — Mt 4:18–22; Mk 1:16–20; Jn 1:40–42

5 One day as Jesus was standing by the Lake of Gennesaret,[x] with the people crowding around him and listening to the word of God,[s] 2he saw at the water's edge two boats, left there by the fishermen, who were washing their nets. 3He got into one of the boats, the one belonging to Simon, and asked him to put out a little from shore. Then he sat down and taught the people from the boat.[t]

4When he had finished speaking, he said to Simon, "Put out into deep water, and let down[y] the nets for a catch."[u]

5Simon answered, "Master,[v] we've worked hard all night and haven't caught anything.[w] But because you say so, I will let down the nets."

6When they had done so, they caught such a large number of fish that their nets began to break.[x] 7So they signaled their partners in the other boat to come and help them, and they came and filled both boats so full that they began to sink.

8When Simon Peter saw this, he fell at Jesus' knees and said, "Go away from me, Lord; I am a sinful man!"[y] 9For he and all his companions were astonished at the catch of fish they had taken, 10and so were James and John, the sons of Zebedee, Simon's partners.

Then Jesus said to Simon, "Don't be afraid;[z] from now on you will catch men." 11So they pulled their boats up on shore, left everything and followed him.[a]

The Man With Leprosy

5:12–14pp — Mt 8:2–4; Mk 1:40–44

12While Jesus was in one of the

4:32 [a]Mt 7:28 [b]ver 36; Mt 7:29
4:34 [c]Mt 8:29 [d]Mk 1:24 [e]Jas 2:19 [f]ver 41; Mk 1:24
4:35 [g]ver 39,41; Mt 8:26; Lk 8:24
4:36 [h]Mt 7:28 [i]ver 32; Mt 7:29; Mt 10:1
4:37 [j]ver 14; Mt 9:26
4:39 [k]ver 35,41
4:40 [l]Mk 5:23 [m]Mt 4:23
4:41 [n]Mt 4:3 [o]ver 35 [p]Mt 8:4
4:43 [q]Mt 3:2
4:44 [r]Mt 4:23
5:1 [s]Mk 4:14; Heb 4:12
5:3 [t]Mt 13:2
5:4 [u]Jn 21:6
5:5 [v]Lk 8:24,45; 9:33,49; 17:13 [w]Jn 21:3
5:6 [x]Jn 21:11
5:8 [y]Ge 18:27; Job 42:6; Isa 6:5
5:10 [z]Mt 14:27
5:11 [a]ver 28; Mt 4:19

[u]33 Greek *unclean*; also in verse 36 [v]41 Or *Messiah* [w]44 Or *the land of the Jews*; some manuscripts *Galilee* [x]1 That is, Sea of Galilee [y]4 The Greek verb is plural.

towns, a man came along who was
covered with leprosy.[z][a] When he
saw Jesus, he fell with his face to
the ground and begged him, "Lord,
if you are willing, you can make me
clean."
13Jesus reached out his hand
and touched the man. "I am willing," he said. "Be clean!" And immediately the leprosy left him.
14Then Jesus ordered him,
"Don't tell anyone,[b] but go, show
yourself to the priest and offer the
sacrifices that Moses commanded[c] for your cleansing, as a testimony to them."
15Yet the news about him spread
all the more,[d] so that crowds of
people came to hear him and to be
healed of their sicknesses. **16**But
Jesus often withdrew to lonely
places and prayed.[e]

Jesus Heals a Paralytic

5:18–26pp — Mt 9:2–8; Mk 2:3–12

17One day as he was teaching,
Pharisees and teachers of the
law,[f] who had come from every village of Galilee and from Judea and
Jerusalem, were sitting there. And
the power of the Lord was present
for him to heal the sick.[g] **18**Some
men came carrying a paralytic on a
mat and tried to take him into the
house to lay him before Jesus.
19When they could not find a way
to do this because of the crowd,
they went up on the roof and lowered him on his mat through the
tiles into the middle of the crowd,
right in front of Jesus.
20When Jesus saw their faith, he
said, "Friend, your sins are forgiven."[h]
21The Pharisees and the teachers of the law began thinking to
themselves, "Who is this fellow
who speaks blasphemy? Who can
forgive sins but God alone?"[i]
22Jesus knew what they were
thinking and asked, "Why are you
thinking these things in your
hearts? **23**Which is easier: to say,
'Your sins are forgiven,' or to say,
'Get up and walk'? **24**But that you
may know that the Son of Man[j]
has authority on earth to forgive
sins. . . ." He said to the paralyzed
man, "I tell you, get up, take your
mat and go home." **25**Immediately
he stood up in front of them, took
what he had been lying on and
went home praising God. **26**Everyone was amazed and gave praise to
God.[k] They were filled with awe
and said, "We have seen remarkable things today."

The Calling of Levi

5:27–32pp — Mt 9:9–13; Mk 2:14–17

27After this, Jesus went out and
saw a tax collector by the name of
Levi sitting at his tax booth. "Follow me,"[l] Jesus said to him, **28**and
Levi got up, left everything and followed him.[m]
29Then Levi held a great banquet
for Jesus at his house, and a large
crowd of tax collectors[n] and others
were eating with them. **30**But the
Pharisees and the teachers of the
law who belonged to their sect[o]
complained to his disciples, "Why
do you eat and drink with tax collectors and 'sinners'?"[p]
31Jesus answered them, "It is
not the healthy who need a doctor,
but the sick. **32**I have not come to
call the righteous, but sinners to
repentance."[q]

Jesus Questioned About Fasting

5:33–39pp — Mt 9:14–17; Mk 2:18–22

33They said to him, "John's disciples[r] often fast and pray, and so
do the disciples of the Pharisees,
but yours go on eating and drinking."
34Jesus answered, "Can you
make the guests of the bridegroom[s] fast while he is with them?
35But the time will come when the
bridegroom will be taken from
them;[t] in those days they will
fast."
36He told them this parable: "No
one tears a patch from a new garment and sews it on an old one. If

5:12 [a]Mt 8:2
5:14 [b]Mt 8:4 [c]Lev 14:2-32
5:15 [d]Mt 9:26
5:16 [e]Mt 14:23; Lk 3:21
5:17 [f]Mt 15:1; Lk 2:46 [g]Mk 5:30; Lk 6:19
5:20 [h]Lk 7:48,49
5:21 [i]Isa 43:25
5:24 [j]Mt 8:20
5:26 [k]Mt 9:8
5:27 [l]Mt 4:19
5:28 [m]ver 11; Mt 4:19
5:29 [n]Lk 15:1
5:30 [o]Ac 23:9 [p]Mt 9:11
5:32 [q]Jn 3:17
5:33 [r]Lk 7:18; Jn 1:35; 3:25, 26
5:34 [s]Jn 3:29
5:35 [t]Lk 9:22; 17:22; Jn 16:5-7

[z]*12* The Greek word was used for various diseases affecting the skin—not necessarily leprosy.

he does, he will have torn the new
garment, and the patch from the
new will not match the old. 37 And
no one pours new wine into old
wineskins. If he does, the new wine
will burst the skins, the wine will
run out and the wineskins will be
ruined. 38 No, new wine must be
poured into new wineskins. 39 And
no one after drinking old wine
wants the new, for he says, 'The old
is better.' "

Lord of the Sabbath

6:1–11pp — Mt 12:1–14; Mk 2:23–3:6

6 One Sabbath Jesus was going
through the grainfields, and
his disciples began to pick some
heads of grain, rub them in their
hands and eat the kernels.[a] 2 Some
of the Pharisees asked, "Why are
you doing what is unlawful on the
Sabbath?"[b]

3 Jesus answered them, "Have
you never read what David did
when he and his companions were
hungry?[c] 4 He entered the house of
God, and taking the consecrated
bread, he ate what is lawful only for
priests to eat.[d] And he also gave
some to his companions." 5 Then
Jesus said to them, "The Son of
Man[e] is Lord of the Sabbath."

6 On another Sabbath[f] he went
into the synagogue and was teaching, and a man was there whose
right hand was shriveled. 7 The
Pharisees and the teachers of the
law were looking for a reason to accuse Jesus, so they watched him
closely[g] to see if he would heal on
the Sabbath.[h] 8 But Jesus knew
what they were thinking[i] and said
to the man with the shriveled hand,
"Get up and stand in front of everyone." So he got up and stood there.

9 Then Jesus said to them, "I ask
you, which is lawful on the Sabbath: to do good or to do evil, to
save life or to destroy it?"

10 He looked around at them all,
and then said to the man, "Stretch
out your hand." He did so, and his
hand was completely restored.
11 But they were furious[j] and began to discuss with one another
what they might do to Jesus.

The Twelve Apostles

6:13–16pp — Mt 10:2–4; Mk 3:16–19; Ac 1:13

12 One of those days Jesus went
out to a mountainside to pray, and
spent the night praying to God.[k]
13 When morning came, he called
his disciples to him and chose
twelve of them, whom he also designated apostles:[l] 14 Simon (whom
he named Peter), his brother Andrew, James, John, Philip, Bartholomew, 15 Matthew,[m] Thomas,
James son of Alphaeus, Simon who
was called the Zealot, 16 Judas son
of James, and Judas Iscariot, who
became a traitor.

Blessings and Woes

6:20–23pp — Mt 5:3–12

17 He went down with them and
stood on a level place. A large
crowd of his disciples was there
and a great number of people from
all over Judea, from Jerusalem, and
from the coast of Tyre and Sidon,[n]
18 who had come to hear him and to
be healed of their diseases. Those
troubled by evil[a] spirits were
cured, 19 and the people all tried to
touch him,[o] because power was
coming from him and healing them
all.[p]

20 Looking at his disciples, he
said:

"Blessed are you who are poor,
for yours is the kingdom of
God.[q]
21 Blessed are you who hunger
now,
for you will be satisfied.[r]
Blessed are you who weep now,
for you will laugh.[s]
22 Blessed are you when men hate
you,
when they exclude you[t] and
insult you[u]
and reject your name as evil,
because of the Son of
Man.[v]

6:1 [a] Dt 23:25
6:2 [b] Mt 12:2
6:3 [c] 1Sa 21:6
6:4 [d] Lev 24:5,9
6:5 [e] Mt 8:20
6:6 [f] ver 1
6:7 [g] Mt 12:10 [h] Mt 12:2
6:8 [i] Mt 9:4
6:11 [j] Jn 5:18
6:12 [k] Lk 3:21
6:13 [l] Mk 6:30
6:15 [m] Mt 9:9
6:17 [n] Mt 4:25; Mt 11:21; Mk 3:7,8
6:19 [o] Mt 9:20 [p] Mt 14:36; Mk 5:30; Lk 5:17
6:20 [q] Mt 25:34
6:21 [r] Isa 55:1,2; Mt 5:6 [s] Isa 61:2,3; Mt 5:4; Rev 7:17
6:22 [t] Jn 9:22; 16:2 [u] Isa 51:7 [v] Jn 15:21

[a] *18* Greek *unclean*

23"Rejoice in that day and leap
for joy,[a] because great is your reward in heaven. For that is how
their fathers treated the prophets.[b]

24"But woe to you who are rich,[c]
for you have already received
your comfort.[d]
25Woe to you who are well fed
now,
for you will go hungry.[e]
Woe to you who laugh now,
for you will mourn and
weep.[f]
26Woe to you when all men speak
well of you,
for that is how their fathers
treated the false
prophets.[g]

Love for Enemies

6:29,30pp — Mt 5:39–42

27"But I tell you who hear me:
Love your enemies, do good to
those who hate you,[h] 28bless those
who curse you, pray for those who
mistreat you.[i] 29If someone
strikes you on one cheek, turn to
him the other also. If someone
takes your cloak, do not stop him
from taking your tunic. 30Give to
everyone who asks you, and if anyone takes what belongs to you, do
not demand it back.[j] 31Do to others as you would have them do to
you.[k]

32"If you love those who love
you, what credit is that to you?[l]
Even 'sinners' love those who love
them. 33And if you do good to
those who are good to you, what
credit is that to you? Even 'sinners'
do that. 34And if you lend to those
from whom you expect repayment,
what credit is that to you?[m] Even
'sinners' lend to 'sinners,' expecting to be repaid in full. 35But love
your enemies, do good to them,[n]
and lend to them without expecting to get anything back. Then your
reward will be great, and you will
be sons[o] of the Most High,[p] because he is kind to the ungrateful
and wicked. 36Be merciful,[q] just
as your Father[r] is merciful.

Judging Others

6:37–42pp — Mt 7:1–5

37"Do not judge, and you will not
be judged.[s] Do not condemn, and
you will not be condemned. Forgive, and you will be forgiven.[t]
38Give, and it will be given to you.
A good measure, pressed down,
shaken together and running over,
will be poured into your lap.[u] For
with the measure you use, it will be
measured to you."[v]

39He also told them this parable:
"Can a blind man lead a blind
man? Will they not both fall into a
pit?[w] 40A student is not above his
teacher, but everyone who is fully
trained will be like his teacher.[x]

41"Why do you look at the speck
of sawdust in your brother's eye
and pay no attention to the plank
in your own eye? 42How can you
say to your brother, 'Brother, let
me take the speck out of your eye,'
when you yourself fail to see the
plank in your own eye? You hypocrite, first take the plank out of
your eye, and then you will see
clearly to remove the speck from
your brother's eye.

A Tree and Its Fruit

6:43,44pp — Mt 7:16,18,20

43"No good tree bears bad fruit,
nor does a bad tree bear good fruit.
44Each tree is recognized by its
own fruit.[y] People do not pick figs
from thornbushes, or grapes from
briers. 45The good man brings good
things out of the good stored up in
his heart, and the evil man brings
evil things out of the evil stored up
in his heart. For out of the overflow
of his heart his mouth speaks.[z]

The Wise and Foolish Builders

6:47–49pp — Mt 7:24–27

46"Why do you call me, 'Lord,
Lord,'[a] and do not do what I say?[b]
47I will show you what he is like
who comes to me and hears my
words and puts them into practice.[c] 48He is like a man building
a house, who dug down deep and
laid the foundation on rock. When

6:23 [a]Mt 5:12 [b]Mt 5:12
6:24 [c]Jas 5:1 [d]Lk 16:25
6:25 [e]Isa 65:13 [f]Pr 14:13
6:26 [g]Mt 7:15
6:27 [h]ver 35; Mt 5:44; Ro 12:20
6:28 [i]Mt 5:44
6:30 [j]Dt 15:7,8,10; Pr 21:26
6:31 [k]Mt 7:12
6:32 [l]Mt 5:46
6:34 [m]Mt 5:42
6:35 [n]ver 27 [o]Ro 8:14 [p]Mk 5:7
6:36 [q]Jas 2:13 [r]Mt 5:48; 6:1; Lk 11:2; 12:32; Ro 8:15; Eph 4:6; 1Pe 1:17; 1Jn 1:3; 3:1
6:37 [s]Mt 7:1 [t]Mt 6:14
6:38 [u]Ps 79:12; Isa 65:6,7 [v]Mt 7:2; Mk 4:24
6:39 [w]Mt 15:14
6:40 [x]Mt 10:24; Jn 13:16
6:44 [y]Mt 12:33
6:45 [z]Pr 4:23; Mt 12:34,35; Mk 7:20
6:46 [a]Jn 13:13 [b]Mal 1:6; Mt 7:21
6:47 [c]Lk 8:21; 11:28; Jas 1:22-25

a flood came, the torrent struck
that house but could not shake it,
because it was well built. **49**But the
one who hears my words and does
not put them into practice is like a
man who built a house on the
ground without a foundation. The
moment the torrent struck that
house, it collapsed and its destruction was complete."

The Faith of the Centurion

7:1–10pp — Mt 8:5–13

7 When Jesus had finished saying all this[a] in the hearing of
the people, he entered Capernaum.
2There a centurion's servant,
whom his master valued highly,
was sick and about to die. **3**The
centurion heard of Jesus and sent
some elders of the Jews to him,
asking him to come and heal his
servant. **4**When they came to Jesus,
they pleaded earnestly with him,
"This man deserves to have you do
this, **5**because he loves our nation
and has built our synagogue." **6**So
Jesus went with them.

He was not far from the house
when the centurion sent friends to
say to him: "Lord, don't trouble
yourself, for I do not deserve to
have you come under my roof.
7That is why I did not even consider myself worthy to come to you.
But say the word, and my servant
will be healed.[b] **8**For I myself am a
man under authority, with soldiers
under me. I tell this one, 'Go,' and
he goes; and that one, 'Come,' and
he comes. I say to my servant, 'Do
this,' and he does it."

9When Jesus heard this, he was
amazed at him, and turning to the
crowd following him, he said, "I tell
you, I have not found such great
faith even in Israel." **10**Then the
men who had been sent returned to
the house and found the servant
well.

Jesus Raises a Widow's Son

7:11–16Ref — 1Ki 17:17–24; 2Ki 4:32–37; Mk 5:21–24,35–43; Jn 11:1–44

11Soon afterward, Jesus went to
a town called Nain, and his disciples and a large crowd went along
with him. **12**As he approached the
town gate, a dead person was being
carried out—the only son of his
mother, and she was a widow. And
a large crowd from the town was
with her. **13**When the Lord[c] saw
her, his heart went out to her and
he said, "Don't cry."

14Then he went up and touched
the coffin, and those carrying it
stood still. He said, "Young man, I
say to you, get up!"[d] **15**The dead
man sat up and began to talk, and
Jesus gave him back to his mother.

16They were all filled with awe[e]
and praised God.[f] "A great prophet[g] has appeared among us," they
said. "God has come to help his
people."[h] **17**This news about Jesus
spread throughout Judea[b] and the
surrounding country.[i]

Jesus and John the Baptist

7:18–35pp — Mt 11:2–19

18John's[j] disciples[k] told him
about all these things. Calling two
of them, **19**he sent them to the Lord
to ask, "Are you the one who was to
come, or should we expect someone else?"

20When the men came to Jesus,
they said, "John the Baptist sent us
to you to ask, 'Are you the one who
was to come, or should we expect
someone else?' "

21At that very time Jesus cured
many who had diseases, sicknesses[l] and evil spirits, and gave
sight to many who were blind. **22**So
he replied to the messengers, "Go
back and report to John what you
have seen and heard: The blind receive sight, the lame walk, those
who have leprosy[c] are cured, the
deaf hear, the dead are raised, and
the good news is preached to the
poor.[m] **23**Blessed is the man who
does not fall away on account of
me."

24After John's messengers left,
Jesus began to speak to the crowd
about John: "What did you go out

7:1 [a]Mt 7:28
7:7 [b]Ps 107:20
7:13 [c]ver 19; Lk 10:1; 13:15; 17:5; 22:61; 24:34; Jn 11:2
7:14 [d]Mt 9:25; Mk 1:31; Lk 8:54; Jn 11:43; Ac 9:40
7:16 [e]Lk 1:65 [f]Mt 9:8 [g]ver 39; Mt 21:11 [h]Lk 1:68
7:17 [i]Mt 9:26
7:18 [j]Mt 3:1 [k]Lk 5:33
7:21 [l]Mt 4:23
7:22 [m]Isa 29:18, 19; 35:5,6; 61:1,2; Lk 4:18

[b]*17* Or *the land of the Jews* [c]*22* The Greek word was used for various diseases affecting the skin—not necessarily leprosy.

into the desert to see? A reed swayed by the wind? **25**If not, what did you go out to see? A man dressed in fine clothes? No, those who wear expensive clothes and indulge in luxury are in palaces. **26**But what did you go out to see? A prophet?[a] Yes, I tell you, and more than a prophet. **27**This is the one about whom it is written:

> " 'I will send my messenger
> ahead of you,
> who will prepare your way
> before you.'[d][b]

28I tell you, among those born of women there is no one greater than John; yet the one who is least in the kingdom of God[c] is greater than he."

29(All the people, even the tax collectors, when they heard Jesus' words, acknowledged that God's way was right, because they had been baptized by John.[d] **30**But the Pharisees and experts in the law[e] rejected God's purpose for themselves, because they had not been baptized by John.)

31"To what, then, can I compare the people of this generation? What are they like? **32**They are like children sitting in the marketplace and calling out to each other:

> " 'We played the flute for you,
> and you did not dance;
> we sang a dirge,
> and you did not cry.'

33For John the Baptist came neither eating bread nor drinking wine,[f] and you say, 'He has a demon.' **34**The Son of Man came eating and drinking, and you say, 'Here is a glutton and a drunkard, a friend of tax collectors and "sinners." '[g] **35**But wisdom is proved right by all her children."

Jesus Anointed by a Sinful Woman

7:37–39Ref – Mt 26:6–13; Mk 14:3–9; Jn 12:1–8
7:41,42Ref – Mt 18:23–34

36Now one of the Pharisees invited Jesus to have dinner with him, so he went to the Pharisee's house and reclined at the table. **37**When a woman who had lived a sinful life in that town learned that Jesus was eating at the Pharisee's house, she brought an alabaster jar of perfume, **38**and as she stood behind him at his feet weeping, she began to wet his feet with her tears. Then she wiped them with her hair, kissed them and poured perfume on them.

39When the Pharisee who had invited him saw this, he said to himself, "If this man were a prophet,[h] he would know who is touching him and what kind of woman she is—that she is a sinner."

40Jesus answered him, "Simon, I have something to tell you."

"Tell me, teacher," he said.

41"Two men owed money to a certain moneylender. One owed him five hundred denarii,[e] and the other fifty. **42**Neither of them had the money to pay him back, so he canceled the debts of both. Now which of them will love him more?"

43Simon replied, "I suppose the one who had the bigger debt canceled."

"You have judged correctly," Jesus said.

44Then he turned toward the woman and said to Simon, "Do you see this woman? I came into your house. You did not give me any water for my feet,[i] but she wet my feet with her tears and wiped them with her hair. **45**You did not give me a kiss,[j] but this woman, from the time I entered, has not stopped kissing my feet. **46**You did not put oil on my head,[k] but she has poured perfume on my feet. **47**Therefore, I tell you, her many sins have been forgiven—for she loved much. But he who has been forgiven little loves little."

48Then Jesus said to her, "Your sins are forgiven."[l]

49The other guests began to say among themselves, "Who is this who even forgives sins?"

50Jesus said to the woman,

7:26 [a]Mt 11:9
7:27 [b]Mal 3:1; Mt 11:10; Mk 1:2
7:28 [c]Mt 3:2
7:29 [d]Mt 21:32; Mk 1:5; Lk 3:12
7:30 [e]Mt 22:35
7:33 [f]Lk 1:15
7:34 [g]Lk 5:29,30; 15:1,2
7:39 [h]ver 16; Mt 21:11
7:44 [i]Ge 18:4; 19:2; 43:24; Jdg 19:21; Jn 13:4-14; 1Ti 5:10
7:45 [j]Lk 22:47,48; Ro 16:16
7:46 [k]Ps 23:5; Ecc 9:8
7:48 [l]Mt 9:2

[d]*27* Mal. 3:1 [e]*41* A denarius was a coin worth about a day's wages.

"Your faith has saved you;[a] go in peace."[b]

The Parable of the Sower

8:4–15pp — Mt 13:2–23; Mk 4:1–20

8 After this, Jesus traveled about from one town and village to another, proclaiming the good news of the kingdom of God.[c] The Twelve were with him, 2and also some women who had been cured of evil spirits and diseases: Mary (called Magdalene)[d] from whom seven demons had come out; 3Joanna the wife of Cuza, the manager of Herod's[e] household; Susanna; and many others. These women were helping to support them out of their own means.

4While a large crowd was gathering and people were coming to Jesus from town after town, he told this parable: 5"A farmer went out to sow his seed. As he was scattering the seed, some fell along the path; it was trampled on, and the birds of the air ate it up. 6Some fell on rock, and when it came up, the plants withered because they had no moisture. 7Other seed fell among thorns, which grew up with it and choked the plants. 8Still other seed fell on good soil. It came up and yielded a crop, a hundred times more than was sown."

When he said this, he called out, "He who has ears to hear, let him hear."[f]

9His disciples asked him what this parable meant. 10He said, "The knowledge of the secrets of the kingdom of God has been given to you,[g] but to others I speak in parables, so that,

" 'though seeing, they may not see;
though hearing, they may not understand.'[f][h]

11"This is the meaning of the parable: The seed is the word of God.[i] 12Those along the path are the ones who hear, and then the devil comes and takes away the word from their hearts, so that they may not believe and be saved. 13Those on the rock are the ones who receive the word with joy when they hear it, but they have no root. They believe for a while, but in the time of testing they fall away.[j] 14The seed that fell among thorns stands for those who hear, but as they go on their way they are choked by life's worries, riches[k] and pleasures, and they do not mature. 15But the seed on good soil stands for those with a noble and good heart, who hear the word, retain it, and by persevering produce a crop.

A Lamp on a Stand

16"No one lights a lamp and hides it in a jar or puts it under a bed. Instead, he puts it on a stand, so that those who come in can see the light.[l] 17For there is nothing hidden that will not be disclosed, and nothing concealed that will not be known or brought out into the open.[m] 18Therefore consider carefully how you listen. Whoever has will be given more; whoever does not have, even what he thinks he has will be taken from him."[n]

Jesus' Mother and Brothers

8:19–21pp — Mt 12:46–50; Mk 3:31–35

19Now Jesus' mother and brothers came to see him, but they were not able to get near him because of the crowd. 20Someone told him, "Your mother and brothers[o] are standing outside, wanting to see you."

21He replied, "My mother and brothers are those who hear God's word and put it into practice."[p]

Jesus Calms the Storm

8:22–25pp — Mt 8:23–27; Mk 4:36–41
8:22–25Ref — Mk 6:47–52; Jn 6:16–21

22One day Jesus said to his disciples, "Let's go over to the other side of the lake." So they got into a boat and set out. 23As they sailed, he fell asleep. A squall came down on the lake, so that the boat was being swamped, and they were in great danger.

7:50 [a] Mt 9:22; Mk 5:34; Lk 8:48 [b] Ac 15:33
8:1 [c] Mt 4:23
8:2 [d] Mt 27:55,56
8:3 [e] Mt 14:1
8:8 [f] Mt 11:15
8:10 [g] Mt 13:11 [h] Isa 6:9; Mt 13:13,14
8:11 [i] Heb 4:12
8:13 [j] Mt 11:6
8:14 [k] Mt 19:23; 1Ti 6:9,10,17
8:16 [l] Mt 5:15; Mk 4:21; Lk 11:33
8:17 [m] Mt 10:26; Mk 4:22; Lk 12:2
8:18 [n] Mt 13:12; 25:29; Lk 19:26
8:20 [o] Jn 7:5
8:21 [p] Lk 6:47; 11:28; Jn 14:21

[f]10 Isaiah 6:9

24The disciples went and woke him, saying, "Master, Master,[a] we're going to drown!"

He got up and rebuked[b] the wind and the raging waters; the storm subsided, and all was calm.[c] 25"Where is your faith?" he asked his disciples.

In fear and amazement they asked one another, "Who is this? He commands even the winds and the water, and they obey him."

The Healing of a Demon-possessed Man

8:26–37pp — Mt 8:28–34
8:26–39pp — Mk 5:1–20

26They sailed to the region of the Gerasenes,[g] which is across the lake from Galilee. 27When Jesus stepped ashore, he was met by a demon-possessed man from the town. For a long time this man had not worn clothes or lived in a house, but had lived in the tombs. 28When he saw Jesus, he cried out and fell at his feet, shouting at the top of his voice, "What do you want with me,[d] Jesus, Son of the Most High God?[e] I beg you, don't torture me!" 29For Jesus had commanded the evil[h] spirit to come out of the man. Many times it had seized him, and though he was chained hand and foot and kept under guard, he had broken his chains and had been driven by the demon into solitary places.

30Jesus asked him, "What is your name?"

"Legion," he replied, because many demons had gone into him. 31And they begged him repeatedly not to order them to go into the Abyss.[f]

32A large herd of pigs was feeding there on the hillside. The demons begged Jesus to let them go into them, and he gave them permission. 33When the demons came out of the man, they went into the pigs, and the herd rushed down the steep bank into the lake[g] and was drowned.

34When those tending the pigs saw what had happened, they ran off and reported this in the town and countryside, 35and the people went out to see what had happened. When they came to Jesus, they found the man from whom the demons had gone out, sitting at Jesus' feet,[h] dressed and in his right mind; and they were afraid. 36Those who had seen it told the people how the demon-possessed[i] man had been cured. 37Then all the people of the region of the Gerasenes asked Jesus to leave them,[j] because they were overcome with fear. So he got into the boat and left.

38The man from whom the demons had gone out begged to go with him, but Jesus sent him away, saying, 39"Return home and tell how much God has done for you." So the man went away and told all over town how much Jesus had done for him.

A Dead Girl and a Sick Woman

8:40–56pp — Mt 9:18–26; Mk 5:22–43

40Now when Jesus returned, a crowd welcomed him, for they were all expecting him. 41Then a man named Jairus, a ruler of the synagogue,[k] came and fell at Jesus' feet, pleading with him to come to his house 42because his only daughter, a girl of about twelve, was dying.

As Jesus was on his way, the crowds almost crushed him. 43And a woman was there who had been subject to bleeding[l] for twelve years,[i] but no one could heal her. 44She came up behind him and touched the edge of his cloak,[m] and immediately her bleeding stopped.

45"Who touched me?" Jesus asked.

When they all denied it, Peter said, "Master,[n] the people are crowding and pressing against you."

46But Jesus said, "Someone

8:24 [a]Lk 5:5 [b]Lk 4:35,39, 41 [c]Ps 107:29; Jnh 1:15
8:28 [d]Mt 8:29 [e]Mk 5:7
8:31 [f]Rev 9:1,2,11; 11:7; 17:8; 20:1,3
8:33 [g]ver 22,23
8:35 [h]Lk 10:39
8:36 [i]Mt 4:24
8:37 [j]Ac 16:39
8:41 [k]ver 49; Mk 5:22
8:43 [l]Lev 15:25-30
8:44 [m]Mt 9:20
8:45 [n]Lk 5:5

[g]*26* Some manuscripts *Gadarenes;* other manuscripts *Gergesenes;* also in verse 37
[h]*29* Greek *unclean*
[i]*43* Many manuscripts *years, and she had spent all she had on doctors*

touched me;[a] I know that power has gone out from me."[b]

47Then the woman, seeing that she could not go unnoticed, came trembling and fell at his feet. In the presence of all the people, she told why she had touched him and how she had been instantly healed. **48**Then he said to her, "Daughter, your faith has healed you.[c] Go in peace."[d]

49While Jesus was still speaking, someone came from the house of Jairus, the synagogue ruler.[e] "Your daughter is dead," he said. "Don't bother the teacher any more."

50Hearing this, Jesus said to Jairus, "Don't be afraid; just believe, and she will be healed."

51When he arrived at the house of Jairus, he did not let anyone go in with him except Peter, John and James,[f] and the child's father and mother. **52**Meanwhile, all the people were wailing and mourning[g] for her. "Stop wailing," Jesus said. "She is not dead but asleep."[h]

53They laughed at him, knowing that she was dead. **54**But he took her by the hand and said, "My child, get up!"[i] **55**Her spirit returned, and at once she stood up. Then Jesus told them to give her something to eat. **56**Her parents were astonished, but he ordered them not to tell anyone what had happened.[j]

Jesus Sends Out the Twelve

9:3–5pp — Mt 10:9–15; Mk 6:8–11
9:7–9pp — Mt 14:1,2; Mk 6:14–16

9 When Jesus had called the Twelve together, he gave them power and authority to drive out all demons[k] and to cure diseases,[l] **2**and he sent them out to preach the kingdom of God[m] and to heal the sick. **3**He told them: "Take nothing for the journey—no staff, no bag, no bread, no money, no extra tunic.[n] **4**Whatever house you enter, stay there until you leave that town. **5**If people do not welcome you, shake the dust off your feet when you leave their town, as a testimony against them."[o] **6**So

8:46 [a] Mt 14:36; Mk 3:10 [b] Lk 5:17; 6:19
8:48 [c] Mt 9:22 [d] Ac 15:33
8:49 [e] ver 41
8:51 [f] Mt 4:21
8:52 [g] Lk 23:27 [h] Mt 9:24; Jn 11:11,13
8:54 [i] Lk 7:14
8:56 [j] Mt 8:4
9:1 [k] Mt 10:1 [l] Mt 4:23; Lk 5:17
9:2 [m] Mt 3:2
9:3 [n] Lk 10:4; 22:35
9:5 [o] Mt 10:14
9:7 [p] Mt 14:1 [q] Mt 3:1 [r] ver 19
9:8 [s] Mt 11:14 [t] ver 19; Jn 1:21
9:9 [u] Lk 23:8
9:10 [v] Mk 6:30 [w] Mt 11:21
9:11 [x] ver 2; Mt 3:2
9:16 [y] Mt 14:19

they set out and went from village to village, preaching the gospel and healing people everywhere.

7Now Herod[p] the tetrarch heard about all that was going on. And he was perplexed, because some were saying that John[q] had been raised from the dead,[r] **8**others that Elijah had appeared,[s] and still others that one of the prophets of long ago had come back to life.[t] **9**But Herod said, "I beheaded John. Who, then, is this I hear such things about?" And he tried to see him.[u]

Jesus Feeds the Five Thousand

9:10–17pp — Mt 14:13–21; Mk 6:32–44; Jn 6:5–13
9:13–17Ref — 2Ki 4:42–44

10When the apostles[v] returned, they reported to Jesus what they had done. Then he took them with him and they withdrew by themselves to a town called Bethsaida,[w] **11**but the crowds learned about it and followed him. He welcomed them and spoke to them about the kingdom of God,[x] and healed those who needed healing.

12Late in the afternoon the Twelve came to him and said, "Send the crowd away so they can go to the surrounding villages and countryside and find food and lodging, because we are in a remote place here."

13He replied, "You give them something to eat."

They answered, "We have only five loaves of bread and two fish—unless we go and buy food for all this crowd." **14**(About five thousand men were there.)

But he said to his disciples, "Have them sit down in groups of about fifty each." **15**The disciples did so, and everybody sat down. **16**Taking the five loaves and the two fish and looking up to heaven, he gave thanks and broke them.[y] Then he gave them to the disciples to set before the people. **17**They all ate and were satisfied, and the disciples picked up twelve basketfuls of broken pieces that were left over.

Peter's Confession of Christ

9:18–20pp — Mt 16:13–16; Mk 8:27–29
9:22–27pp — Mt 16:21–28; Mk 8:31–9:1

18Once when Jesus was praying[a] in private and his disciples were with him, he asked them, "Who do the crowds say I am?"

19They replied, "Some say John the Baptist;[b] others say Elijah; and still others, that one of the prophets of long ago has come back to life."[c]

20"But what about you?" he asked. "Who do you say I am?"

Peter answered, "The Christ[i] of God."[d]

21Jesus strictly warned them not to tell this to anyone.[e] **22**And he said, "The Son of Man[f] must suffer many things[g] and be rejected by the elders, chief priests and teachers of the law,[h] and he must be killed[i] and on the third day[j] be raised to life."[k]

23Then he said to them all: "If anyone would come after me, he must deny himself and take up his cross daily and follow me.[l] **24**For whoever wants to save his life will lose it, but whoever loses his life for me will save it.[m] **25**What good is it for a man to gain the whole world, and yet lose or forfeit his very self? **26**If anyone is ashamed of me and my words, the Son of Man will be ashamed of him[n] when he comes in his glory and in the glory of the Father and of the holy angels.[o] **27**I tell you the truth, some who are standing here will not taste death before they see the kingdom of God."

The Transfiguration

9:28–36pp — Mt 17:1–8; Mk 9:2–8

28About eight days after Jesus said this, he took Peter, John and James[p] with him and went up onto a mountain to pray.[q] **29**As he was praying, the appearance of his face changed, and his clothes became as bright as a flash of lightning. **30**Two men, Moses and Elijah, **31**appeared in glorious splendor, talking with Jesus. They spoke about his departure,[r] which he was about to bring to fulfillment at Jerusalem. **32**Peter and his companions were very sleepy,[s] but when they became fully awake, they saw his glory and the two men standing with him. **33**As the men were leaving Jesus, Peter said to him, "Master,[t] it is good for us to be here. Let us put up three shelters—one for you, one for Moses and one for Elijah." (He did not know what he was saying.)

34While he was speaking, a cloud appeared and enveloped them, and they were afraid as they entered the cloud. **35**A voice came from the cloud, saying, "This is my Son, whom I have chosen;[u] listen to him."[v] **36**When the voice had spoken, they found that Jesus was alone. The disciples kept this to themselves, and told no one at that time what they had seen.[w]

The Healing of a Boy With an Evil Spirit

9:37–42,43–45pp — Mt 17:14–18, 22,23; Mk 9:14–27, 30–32

37The next day, when they came down from the mountain, a large crowd met him. **38**A man in the crowd called out, "Teacher, I beg you to look at my son, for he is my only child. **39**A spirit seizes him and he suddenly screams; it throws him into convulsions so that he foams at the mouth. It scarcely ever leaves him and is destroying him. **40**I begged your disciples to drive it out, but they could not."

41"O unbelieving and perverse generation,"[x] Jesus replied, "how long shall I stay with you and put up with you? Bring your son here."

42Even while the boy was coming, the demon threw him to the ground in a convulsion. But Jesus rebuked the evil[k] spirit, healed the boy and gave him back to his father. **43**And they were all amazed at the greatness of God.

While everyone was marveling at all that Jesus did, he said to his disciples, **44**"Listen carefully to what I am about to tell you: The Son of

9:18 [a]Lk 3:21
9:19 [b]Mt 3:1 [c]ver 7,8
9:20 [d]Jn 1:49; 6:66-69; 11:27
9:21 [e]Mt 16:20; Mk 8:30
9:22 [f]Mt 8:20 [g]Mt 16:21 [h]Mt 27:1,2 [i]Ac 2:23; 3:13 [j]Mt 16:21 [k]Mt 16:21
9:23 [l]Mt 10:38; Lk 14:27
9:24 [m]Jn 12:25
9:26 [n]Mt 10:33; Lk 12:9; 2Ti 2:12 [o]Mt 16:27
9:28 [p]Mt 4:21 [q]Lk 3:21
9:31 [r]2Pe 1:15
9:32 [s]Mt 26:43
9:33 [t]Lk 5:5
9:35 [u]Isa 42:1 [v]Mt 3:17
9:36 [w]Mt 17:9
9:41 [x]Dt 32:5

i20 Or *Messiah*   k42 Greek *unclean*

Man is going to be betrayed into the hands of men."[a] **45**But they did not understand what this meant. It was hidden from them, so that they did not grasp it,[b] and they were afraid to ask him about it.

Who Will Be the Greatest?

9:46–48pp — Mt 18:1–5
9:46–50pp — Mk 9:33–40

46An argument started among the disciples as to which of them would be the greatest.[c] **47**Jesus, knowing their thoughts,[d] took a little child and had him stand beside him. **48**Then he said to them, "Whoever welcomes this little child in my name welcomes me; and whoever welcomes me welcomes the one who sent me.[e] For he who is least among you all—he is the greatest."[f]

49"Master,"[g] said John, "we saw a man driving out demons in your name and we tried to stop him, because he is not one of us."

50"Do not stop him," Jesus said, "for whoever is not against you is for you."[h]

Samaritan Opposition

51As the time approached for him to be taken up to heaven,[i] Jesus resolutely set out for Jerusalem.[j] **52**And he sent messengers on ahead, who went into a Samaritan[k] village to get things ready for him; **53**but the people there did not welcome him, because he was heading for Jerusalem. **54**When the disciples James and John[l] saw this, they asked, "Lord, do you want us to call fire down from heaven to destroy them[l]?"[m] **55**But Jesus turned and rebuked them, **56**and[m] they went to another village.

The Cost of Following Jesus

9:57–60pp — Mt 8:19–22

57As they were walking along the road,[n] a man said to him, "I will follow you wherever you go."

58Jesus replied, "Foxes have holes and birds of the air have nests, but the Son of Man[o] has no place to lay his head."

59He said to another man, "Follow me."[p]

But the man replied, "Lord, first let me go and bury my father."

60Jesus said to him, "Let the dead bury their own dead, but you go and proclaim the kingdom of God."[q]

61Still another said, "I will follow you, Lord; but first let me go back and say good-by to my family."[r]

62Jesus replied, "No one who puts his hand to the plow and looks back is fit for service in the kingdom of God."

Jesus Sends Out the Seventy-two

10:4–12pp — Lk 9:3–5
10:13–15,21,22pp — Mt 11:21–23,25–27
10:23,24pp — Mt 13:16,17

10 After this the Lord[s] appointed seventy-two[n] others[t] and sent them two by two[u] ahead of him to every town and place where he was about to go.[v] **2**He told them, "The harvest is plentiful, but the workers are few. Ask the Lord of the harvest, therefore, to send out workers into his harvest field.[w] **3**Go! I am sending you out like lambs among wolves.[x] **4**Do not take a purse or bag or sandals; and do not greet anyone on the road.

5"When you enter a house, first say, 'Peace to this house.' **6**If a man of peace is there, your peace will rest on him; if not, it will return to you. **7**Stay in that house, eating and drinking whatever they give you, for the worker deserves his wages.[y] Do not move around from house to house.

8"When you enter a town and are welcomed, eat what is set before you.[z] **9**Heal the sick who are there and tell them, 'The kingdom of God[a] is near you.' **10**But when you enter a town and are not wel-

9:44 [a]ver 22
9:45 [b]Mk 9:32
9:46 [c]Lk 22:24
9:47 [d]Mt 9:4
9:48 [e]Mt 10:40 [f]Mk 9:35
9:49 [g]Lk 5:5
9:50 [h]Mt 12:30; Lk 11:23
9:51 [i]Mk 16:19 [j]Lk 13:22; 17:11; 18:31; 19:28
9:52 [k]Mt 10:5
9:54 [l]Mt 4:21 [m]2Ki 1:10,12
9:57 [n]ver 51
9:58 [o]Mt 8:20
9:59 [p]Mt 4:19
9:60 [q]Mt 3:2
9:61 [r]1Ki 19:20
10:1 [s]Lk 7:13 [t]Lk 9:1,2,51, 52 [u]Mk 6:7 [v]Mt 10:1
10:2 [w]Mt 9:37,38; Jn 4:35
10:3 [x]Mt 10:16
10:7 [y]Mt 10:10; 1Co 9:14; 1Ti 5:18
10:8 [z]1Co 10:27
10:9 [a]Mt 3:2; 10:7

[l]*54* Some manuscripts *them, even as Elijah did*
[m]*55,56* Some manuscripts *them. And he said, "You do not know what kind of spirit you are of, for the Son of Man did not come to destroy men's lives, but to save them."* *56And*
[n]*1* Some manuscripts *seventy;* also in verse 17

comed, go into its streets and say,
[11]'Even the dust of your town that
sticks to our feet we wipe off
against you.[a] Yet be sure of this:
The kingdom of God is near.'[b] [12]I
tell you, it will be more bearable on
that day for Sodom[c] than for that
town.[d]
[13]"Woe to you,[e] Korazin! Woe to
you, Bethsaida! For if the miracles
that were performed in you had
been performed in Tyre and Sidon,
they would have repented long ago,
sitting in sackcloth[f] and ashes.
[14]But it will be more bearable for
Tyre and Sidon at the judgment
than for you. [15]And you, Capernaum,[g] will you be lifted up to the
skies? No, you will go down to the
depths.[o]
[16]"He who listens to you listens
to me; he who rejects you rejects
me; but he who rejects me rejects
him who sent me."[h]
[17]The seventy-two[i] returned
with joy and said, "Lord, even the
demons submit to us in your
name."[j]
[18]He replied, "I saw Satan[k] fall
like lightning from heaven.[l] [19]I
have given you authority to trample
on snakes[m] and scorpions and to
overcome all the power of the enemy; nothing will harm you. [20]However, do not rejoice that the spirits
submit to you, but rejoice that your
names are written in heaven."[n]
[21]At that time Jesus, full of joy
through the Holy Spirit, said, "I
praise you, Father, Lord of heaven
and earth, because you have hidden these things from the wise and
learned, and revealed them to little
children.[o] Yes, Father, for this was
your good pleasure.
[22]"All things have been committed to me by my Father.[p] No one
knows who the Son is except the
Father, and no one knows who the
Father is except the Son and those
to whom the Son chooses to reveal
him."[q]
[23]Then he turned to his disciples
and said privately, "Blessed are the
eyes that see what you see. [24]For I
tell you that many prophets and
kings wanted to see what you see
but did not see it, and to hear what
you hear but did not hear it."[r]

The Parable of the Good Samaritan

10:25–28pp — Mt 22:34–40; Mk 12:28–31

[25]On one occasion an expert in
the law stood up to test Jesus.
"Teacher," he asked, "what must I
do to inherit eternal life?"[s]
[26]"What is written in the Law?"
he replied. "How do you read it?"
[27]He answered: " 'Love the Lord
your God with all your heart and
with all your soul and with all your
strength and with all your
mind'[p];[t] and, 'Love your neighbor
as yourself.'[q]"[u]
[28]"You have answered correctly," Jesus replied. "Do this and you
will live."[v]
[29]But he wanted to justify himself,[w] so he asked Jesus, "And who
is my neighbor?"
[30]In reply Jesus said: "A man
was going down from Jerusalem to
Jericho, when he fell into the
hands of robbers. They stripped
him of his clothes, beat him and
went away, leaving him half dead.
[31]A priest happened to be going
down the same road, and when he
saw the man, he passed by on the
other side.[x] [32]So too, a Levite,
when he came to the place and saw
him, passed by on the other side.
[33]But a Samaritan,[y] as he traveled,
came where the man was; and
when he saw him, he took pity on
him. [34]He went to him and bandaged his wounds, pouring on oil
and wine. Then he put the man on
his own donkey, took him to an inn
and took care of him. [35]The next
day he took out two silver coins[r]
and gave them to the innkeeper.
'Look after him,' he said, 'and
when I return, I will reimburse you
for any extra expense you may
have.'
[36]"Which of these three do you
think was a neighbor to the man
who fell into the hands of robbers?"

10:11 [a]Mt 10:14; Mk 6:11 [b]ver 9
10:12 [c]Mt 10:15 [d]Mt 11:24
10:13 [e]Lk 6:24-26 [f]Rev 11:3
10:15 [g]Mt 4:13
10:16 [h]Mt 10:40; Jn 13:20
10:17 [i]ver 1 [j]Mk 16:17
10:18 [k]Mt 4:10 [l]Isa 14:12; Rev 9:1; 12:8, 9
10:19 [m]Mk 16:18; Ac 28:3-5
10:20 [n]Ex 32:32; Ps 69:28; Da 12:1; Php 4:3; Heb 12:23; Rev 13:8; 20:12; 21:27
10:21 [o]1Co 1:26-29
10:22 [p]Mt 28:18 [q]Jn 1:18
10:24 [r]1Pe 1:10-12
10:25 [s]Mt 19:16; Lk 18:18
10:27 [t]Dt 6:5 [u]Lev 19:18; Mt 5:43
10:28 [v]Lev 18:5; Ro 7:10
10:29 [w]Lk 16:15
10:31 [x]Lev 21:1-3
10:33 [y]Mt 10:5

[o]*15* Greek *Hades* [p]*27* Deut. 6:5 [q]*27* Lev. 19:18 [r]*35* Greek *two denarii*

37The expert in the law replied,
"The one who had mercy on him."
Jesus told him, "Go and do likewise."

At the Home of Martha and Mary

38As Jesus and his disciples were
on their way, he came to a village
where a woman named Martha[a]
opened her home to him. 39She
had a sister called Mary,[b] who sat
at the Lord's feet[c] listening to
what he said. 40But Martha was
distracted by all the preparations
that had to be made. She came to
him and asked, "Lord, don't you
care[d] that my sister has left me to
do the work by myself? Tell her to
help me!"
41"Martha, Martha," the Lord
answered, "you are worried[e] and
upset about many things, 42but
only one thing is needed.[s][f] Mary
has chosen what is better, and it
will not be taken away from her."

Jesus' Teaching on Prayer

11:2–4pp — Mt 6:9–13
11:9–13pp — Mt 7:7–11

11 One day Jesus was praying[g] in a certain place.
When he finished, one of his disciples said to him, "Lord,[h] teach us
to pray, just as John taught his disciples."
2He said to them, "When you
pray, say:

"'Father,[t]
hallowed be your name,
your kingdom[i] come.[u]
3Give us each day our daily
bread.
4Forgive us our sins,
for we also forgive everyone
who sins against us.[v][j]
And lead us not into
temptation.[w]'"[k]

5Then he said to them, "Suppose
one of you has a friend, and he goes
to him at midnight and says,
'Friend, lend me three loaves of
bread, 6because a friend of mine on
a journey has come to me, and I
have nothing to set before him.'
7"Then the one inside answers,

10:38 [a]Jn 11:1; 12:2
10:39 [b]Jn 11:1; 12:3 [c]Lk 8:35
10:40 [d]Mk 4:38
10:41 [e]Mt 6:25-34; Lk 12:11,22
10:42 [f]Ps 27:4
11:1 [g]Lk 3:21 [h]Jn 13:13
11:2 [i]Mt 3:2
11:4 [j]Mt 18:35; Mk 11:25 [k]Mt 26:41; Jas 1:13
11:8 [l]Lk 18:1-6
11:9 [m]Mt 7:7
11:14 [n]Mt 9:32,33
11:15 [o]Mk 3:22 [p]Mt 9:34
11:16 [q]Mt 12:38
11:17 [r]Mt 9:4
11:18 [s]Mt 4:10

'Don't bother me. The door is already locked, and my children are
with me in bed. I can't get up and
give you anything.' 8I tell you,
though he will not get up and give
him the bread because he is his
friend, yet because of the man's
boldness[x] he will get up and give
him as much as he needs.[l]
9"So I say to you: Ask and it will
be given to you;[m] seek and you will
find; knock and the door will be
opened to you. 10For everyone who
asks receives; he who seeks finds;
and to him who knocks, the door
will be opened.
11"Which of you fathers, if your
son asks for[y] a fish, will give him a
snake instead? 12Or if he asks for
an egg, will give him a scorpion?
13If you then, though you are evil,
know how to give good gifts to your
children, how much more will your
Father in heaven give the Holy
Spirit to those who ask him!"

Jesus and Beelzebub

11:14,15, 17–22, 24–26pp — Mt 12:22,24–29, 43–45
11:17–22pp — Mk 3:23–27

14Jesus was driving out a demon
that was mute. When the demon
left, the man who had been mute
spoke, and the crowd was
amazed.[n] 15But some of them
said, "By Beelzebub,[z][o] the prince
of demons, he is driving out demons."[p] 16Others tested him by
asking for a sign from heaven.[q]
17Jesus knew their thoughts[r]
and said to them: "Any kingdom divided against itself will be ruined,
and a house divided against itself
will fall. 18If Satan[s] is divided
against himself, how can his kingdom stand? I say this because you
claim that I drive out demons by
Beelzebub. 19Now if I drive out de-

[s]42 Some manuscripts *but few things are needed—or only one* [t]2 Some manuscripts *Our Father in heaven* [u]2 Some manuscripts *come. May your will be done on earth as it is in heaven.* [v]4 Greek *everyone who is indebted to us* [w]4 Some manuscripts *temptation but deliver us from the evil one* [x]8 Or *persistence* [y]11 Some manuscripts *for bread, will give him a stone; or if he asks for* [z]15 Greek *Beezeboul* or *Beelzeboul*; also in verses 18 and 19

mons by Beelzebub, by whom do
your followers drive them out? So
then, they will be your judges.
20But if I drive out demons by the
finger of God,[a] then the kingdom
of God[b] has come to you.

21"When a strong man, fully
armed, guards his own house, his
possessions are safe. 22But when
someone stronger attacks and
overpowers him, he takes away the
armor in which the man trusted
and divides up the spoils.

23"He who is not with me is
against me, and he who does not
gather with me, scatters.[c]

24"When an evil[a] spirit comes
out of a man, it goes through arid
places seeking rest and does not
find it. Then it says, 'I will return to
the house I left.' 25When it arrives,
it finds the house swept clean and
put in order. 26Then it goes and
takes seven other spirits more
wicked than itself, and they go in
and live there. And the final condition of that man is worse than the
first."[d]

27As Jesus was saying these
things, a woman in the crowd
called out, "Blessed is the mother
who gave you birth and nursed
you."[e]

28He replied, "Blessed rather are
those who hear the word of God[f]
and obey it."[g]

The Sign of Jonah

11:29–32pp — Mt 12:39–42

29As the crowds increased, Jesus
said, "This is a wicked generation.
It asks for a miraculous sign,[h] but
none will be given it except the
sign of Jonah.[i] 30For as Jonah was
a sign to the Ninevites, so also will
the Son of Man be to this generation. 31The Queen of the South will
rise at the judgment with the men
of this generation and condemn
them; for she came from the ends
of the earth to listen to Solomon's
wisdom,[j] and now one[b] greater
than Solomon is here. 32The men
of Nineveh will stand up at the
judgment with this generation and
condemn it; for they repented at
the preaching of Jonah,[k] and now
one greater than Jonah is here.

The Lamp of the Body

11:34,35pp — Mt 6:22,23

33"No one lights a lamp and puts
it in a place where it will be hidden,
or under a bowl. Instead he puts it
on its stand, so that those who
come in may see the light.[l] 34Your
eye is the lamp of your body. When
your eyes are good, your whole
body also is full of light. But when
they are bad, your body also is full
of darkness. 35See to it, then, that
the light within you is not darkness. 36Therefore, if your whole
body is full of light, and no part of
it dark, it will be completely lighted, as when the light of a lamp
shines on you."

Six Woes

37When Jesus had finished
speaking, a Pharisee invited him to
eat with him; so he went in and reclined at the table.[m] 38But the
Pharisee, noticing that Jesus did
not first wash before the meal,[n]
was surprised.

39Then the Lord[o] said to him,
"Now then, you Pharisees clean
the outside of the cup and dish, but
inside you are full of greed and
wickedness.[p] 40You foolish people![q] Did not the one who made
the outside make the inside also?
41But give what is inside the dish[c]
to the poor,[r] and everything will
be clean for you.[s]

42"Woe to you Pharisees, because you give God a tenth[t] of
your mint, rue and all other kinds
of garden herbs, but you neglect
justice and the love of God.[u] You
should have practiced the latter
without leaving the former undone.[v]

43"Woe to you Pharisees, because you love the most important
seats in the synagogues and greetings in the marketplaces.[w]

44"Woe to you, because you are

11:20 [a] Ex 8:19 [b] Mt 3:2
11:23 [c] Mt 12:30; Mk 9:40; Lk 9:50
11:26 [d] 2Pe 2:20
11:27 [e] Lk 23:29
11:28 [f] Heb 4:12 [g] Pr 8:32; Lk 6:47; 8:21; Jn 14:21
11:29 [h] ver 16; Mt 12:38 [i] Jnh 1:17; Mt 16:4
11:31 [j] 1Ki 10:1; 2Ch 9:1
11:32 [k] Jnh 3:5
11:33 [l] Mt 5:15; Mk 4:21; Lk 8:16
11:37 [m] Lk 7:36; 14:1
11:38 [n] Mk 7:3,4
11:39 [o] Lk 7:13 [p] Mt 23:25,26; Mk 7:20-23
11:40 [q] Lk 12:20; 1Co 15:36
11:41 [r] Lk 12:33 [s] Ac 10:15
11:42 [t] Lk 18:12 [u] Dt 6:5; Mic 6:8 [v] Mt 23:23
11:43 [w] Mt 23:6,7; Mk 12:38-39; Lk 14:7; 20:46

a24 Greek *unclean* b31 Or *something*; also in verse 32 c41 Or *what you have*

like unmarked graves,[a] which men
walk over without knowing it."
45One of the experts in the law[b]
answered him, "Teacher, when you
say these things, you insult us
also."
46Jesus replied, "And you experts in the law, woe to you, because you load people down with
burdens they can hardly carry, and
you yourselves will not lift one finger to help them.[c]
47"Woe to you, because you
build tombs for the prophets, and it
was your forefathers who killed
them. 48So you testify that you approve of what your forefathers did;
they killed the prophets, and you
build their tombs.[d] 49Because of
this, God in his wisdom[e] said, 'I
will send them prophets and apostles, some of whom they will kill
and others they will persecute.'[f]
50Therefore this generation will be
held responsible for the blood of all
the prophets that has been shed
since the beginning of the world,
51from the blood of Abel[g] to the
blood of Zechariah,[h] who was
killed between the altar and the
sanctuary. Yes, I tell you, this generation will be held responsible for
it all.[i]
52"Woe to you experts in the law,
because you have taken away the
key to knowledge. You yourselves
have not entered, and you have
hindered those who were entering."[j]
53When Jesus left there, the
Pharisees and the teachers of the
law began to oppose him fiercely
and to besiege him with questions,
54waiting to catch him in something he might say.[k]

Warnings and Encouragements

12:2–9pp — Mt 10:26–33

12 Meanwhile, when a crowd
of many thousands had
gathered, so that they were trampling on one another, Jesus began
to speak first to his disciples, saying: "Be on your guard against the
yeast of the Pharisees, which is hypocrisy.[l] 2There is nothing concealed that will not be disclosed, or
hidden that will not be made
known.[m] 3What you have said in
the dark will be heard in the daylight, and what you have whispered
in the ear in the inner rooms will be
proclaimed from the roofs.
4"I tell you, my friends,[n] do not
be afraid of those who kill the body
and after that can do no more. 5But
I will show you whom you should
fear: Fear him who, after the killing
of the body, has power to throw you
into hell. Yes, I tell you, fear him.[o]
6Are not five sparrows sold for two
pennies[d]? Yet not one of them is
forgotten by God. 7Indeed, the very
hairs of your head are all numbered.[p] Don't be afraid; you are
worth more than many sparrows.[q]
8"I tell you, whoever acknowledges me before men, the Son of
Man will also acknowledge him before the angels of God.[r] 9But he
who disowns me before men will be
disowned[s] before the angels of
God. 10And everyone who speaks a
word against the Son of Man[t] will
be forgiven, but anyone who blasphemes against the Holy Spirit will
not be forgiven.[u]
11"When you are brought before
synagogues, rulers and authorities,
do not worry about how you will defend yourselves or what you will
say,[v] 12for the Holy Spirit will
teach you at that time what you
should say."[w]

The Parable of the Rich Fool

13Someone in the crowd said to
him, "Teacher, tell my brother to
divide the inheritance with me."
14Jesus replied, "Man, who appointed me a judge or an arbiter
between you?" 15Then he said to
them, "Watch out! Be on your
guard against all kinds of greed; a
man's life does not consist in the
abundance of his possessions."[x]
16And he told them this parable:
"The ground of a certain rich man
produced a good crop. 17He
thought to himself, 'What shall I

11:44 [a] Mt 23:27
11:45 [b] Mt 22:35
11:46 [c] Mt 23:4
11:48 [d] Mt 23:29-32; Ac 7:51-53
11:49 [e] 1Co 1:24,30; Col 2:3 [f] Mt 23:34
11:51 [g] Ge 4:8 [h] 2Ch 24:20,21 [i] Mt 23:35,36
11:52 [j] Mt 23:13
11:54 [k] Mt 12:10; Mk 12:13
12:1 [l] Mt 16:6,11,12; Mk 8:15
12:2 [m] Mk 4:22; Lk 8:17
12:4 [n] Jn 15:14,15
12:5 [o] Heb 10:31
12:7 [p] Mt 10:30 [q] Mt 12:12
12:8 [r] Lk 15:10
12:9 [s] Mk 8:38; 2Ti 2:12
12:10 [t] Mt 8:20 [u] Mt 12:31,32; Mk 3:28-29; 1Jn 5:16
12:11 [v] Mt 10:17,19; Mk 13:11; Lk 21:12,14
12:12 [w] Ex 4:12; Mt 10:20; Mk 13:11; Lk 21:15
12:15 [x] Job 20:20; 31:24; Ps 62:10

d6 Greek *two assaria*

do? I have no place to store my
crops.'
18"Then he said, 'This is what I'll
do. I will tear down my barns and
build bigger ones, and there I will
store all my grain and my goods.
19And I'll say to myself, "You have
plenty of good things laid up for
many years. Take life easy; eat,
drink and be merry."'
20"But God said to him, 'You
fool![a] This very night your life will
be demanded from you.[b] Then
who will get what you have prepared for yourself?'[c]
21"This is how it will be with
anyone who stores up things for
himself but is not rich toward
God."[d]

Do Not Worry

12:22–31pp — Mt 6:25–33

22Then Jesus said to his disciples: "Therefore I tell you, do not
worry about your life, what you will
eat; or about your body, what you
will wear. 23Life is more than food,
and the body more than clothes.
24Consider the ravens: They do not
sow or reap, they have no storeroom or barn; yet God feeds
them.[e] And how much more valuable you are than birds! 25Who of
you by worrying can add a single
hour to his life[e]? 26Since you cannot do this very little thing, why do
you worry about the rest?
27"Consider how the lilies grow.
They do not labor or spin. Yet I tell
you, not even Solomon in all his
splendor[f] was dressed like one of
these. 28If that is how God clothes
the grass of the field, which is here
today, and tomorrow is thrown into
the fire, how much more will he
clothe you, O you of little faith![g]
29And do not set your heart on
what you will eat or drink; do not
worry about it. 30For the pagan
world runs after all such things,
and your Father[h] knows that you
need them.[i] 31But seek his kingdom,[j] and these things will be giv-
en to you as well.[k]
32"Do not be afraid,[l] little flock,
for your Father has been pleased to
give you the kingdom.[m] 33Sell your
possessions and give to the poor.[n]
Provide purses for yourselves that
will not wear out, a treasure in
heaven[o] that will not be exhausted, where no thief comes near and
no moth destroys.[p] 34For where
your treasure is, there your heart
will be also.[q]

Watchfulness

12:35,36pp — Mt 25:1–13; Mk 13:33–37
12:39,40; 42–46pp — Mt 24:43–51

35"Be dressed ready for service
and keep your lamps burning,
36like men waiting for their master
to return from a wedding banquet,
so that when he comes and knocks
they can immediately open the
door for him. 37It will be good for
those servants whose master finds
them watching when he comes.[r] I
tell you the truth, he will dress
himself to serve, will have them re-
cline at the table and will come and
wait on them.[s] 38It will be good for
those servants whose master finds
them ready, even if he comes in the
second or third watch of the night.
39But understand this: If the owner
of the house had known at what
hour the thief[t] was coming, he
would not have let his house be
broken into. 40You also must be
ready,[u] because the Son of Man
will come at an hour when you do
not expect him."
41Peter asked, "Lord, are you
telling this parable to us, or to everyone?"
42The Lord[v] answered, "Who
then is the faithful and wise manager, whom the master puts in
charge of his servants to give them
their food allowance at the proper
time? 43It will be good for that servant whom the master finds doing
so when he returns. 44I tell you the
truth, he will put him in charge of
all his possessions. 45But suppose
the servant says to himself, 'My
master is taking a long time in
coming,' and he then begins to
beat the menservants and maidservants and to eat and drink and get

12:20 [a] Jer 17:11; Lk 11:40 [b] Job 27:8 [c] Ps 39:6; 49:10
12:21 [d] ver 33
12:24 [e] Job 38:41; Ps 147:9
12:27 [f] 1Ki 10:4-7
12:28 [g] Mt 6:30
12:30 [h] Lk 6:36 [i] Mt 6:8
12:31 [j] Mt 3:2 [k] Mt 19:29
12:32 [l] Mt 14:27 [m] Mt 25:34
12:33 [n] Mt 19:21; Ac 2:45 [o] Mt 6:20 [p] Jas 5:2
12:34 [q] Mt 6:21
12:37 [r] Mt 24:42,46; 25:13 [s] Mt 20:28
12:39 [t] Mt 6:19; 1Th 5:2; 2Pe 3:10; Rev 3:3; 16:15
12:40 [u] Mk 13:33; Lk 21:36
12:42 [v] Lk 7:13

[e]25 Or *single cubit to his height*

drunk. 46The master of that servant will come on a day when he does not expect him and at an hour he is not aware of.[a] He will cut him to pieces and assign him a place with the unbelievers.

47"That servant who knows his master's will and does not get ready or does not do what his master wants will be beaten with many blows.[b] 48But the one who does not know and does things deserving punishment will be beaten with few blows.[c] From everyone who has been given much, much will be demanded; and from the one who has been entrusted with much, much more will be asked.

Not Peace but Division

12:51–53pp — Mt 10:34–36

49"I have come to bring fire on the earth, and how I wish it were already kindled! 50But I have a baptism[d] to undergo, and how distressed I am until it is completed![e] 51Do you think I came to bring peace on earth? No, I tell you, but division. 52From now on there will be five in one family divided against each other, three against two and two against three. 53They will be divided, father against son and son against father, mother against daughter and daughter against mother, mother-in-law against daughter-in-law and daughter-in-law against mother-in-law."[f]

Interpreting the Times

54He said to the crowd: "When you see a cloud rising in the west, immediately you say, 'It's going to rain,' and it does.[g] 55And when the south wind blows, you say, 'It's going to be hot,' and it is. 56Hypocrites! You know how to interpret the appearance of the earth and the sky. How is it that you don't know how to interpret this present time?[h]

57"Why don't you judge for yourselves what is right? 58As you are going with your adversary to the magistrate, try hard to be reconciled to him on the way, or he may drag you off to the judge, and the judge turn you over to the officer, and the officer throw you into prison.[i] 59I tell you, you will not get out until you have paid the last penny.[f]"[j]

Repent or Perish

13 Now there were some present at that time who told Jesus about the Galileans whose blood Pilate[k] had mixed with their sacrifices. 2Jesus answered, "Do you think that these Galileans were worse sinners than all the other Galileans because they suffered this way?[l] 3I tell you, no! But unless you repent, you too will all perish. 4Or those eighteen who died when the tower in Siloam[m] fell on them—do you think they were more guilty than all the others living in Jerusalem? 5I tell you, no! But unless you repent,[n] you too will all perish."

6Then he told this parable: "A man had a fig tree, planted in his vineyard, and he went to look for fruit on it, but did not find any.[o] 7So he said to the man who took care of the vineyard, 'For three years now I've been coming to look for fruit on this fig tree and haven't found any. Cut it down![p] Why should it use up the soil?'

8" 'Sir,' the man replied, 'leave it alone for one more year, and I'll dig around it and fertilize it. 9If it bears fruit next year, fine! If not, then cut it down.' "

A Crippled Woman Healed on the Sabbath

10On a Sabbath Jesus was teaching in one of the synagogues,[q] 11and a woman was there who had been crippled by a spirit for eighteen years.[r] She was bent over and could not straighten up at all. 12When Jesus saw her, he called her forward and said to her, "Woman, you are set free from your infirmity." 13Then he put his hands on her,[s] and immediately she

12:46 [a] ver 40
12:47 [b] Dt 25:2
12:48 [c] Lev 5:17; Nu 15:27-30
12:50 [d] Mk 10:38 [e] Jn 19:30
12:53 [f] Mic 7:6; Mt 10:21
12:54 [g] Mt 16:2
12:56 [h] Mt 16:3
12:58 [i] Mt 5:25
12:59 [j] Mt 5:26; Mk 12:42
13:1 [k] Mt 27:2
13:2 [l] Jn 9:2,3
13:4 [m] Jn 9:7,11
13:5 [n] Mt 3:2; Ac 2:38
13:6 [o] Isa 5:2; Jer 8:13; Mt 21:19
13:7 [p] Mt 3:10
13:10 [q] Mt 4:23
13:11 [r] ver 16
13:13 [s] Mk 5:23

[f]59 Greek *lepton*

straightened up and praised God.
14 Indignant because Jesus had
healed on the Sabbath,[a] the synagogue ruler[b] said to the people,
"There are six days for work.[c] So
come and be healed on those days,
not on the Sabbath."
15 The Lord answered him, "You
hypocrites! Doesn't each of you on
the Sabbath untie his ox or donkey
from the stall and lead it out to give
it water?[d] 16 Then should not this
woman, a daughter of Abraham,[e]
whom Satan[f] has kept bound for
eighteen long years, be set free on
the Sabbath day from what bound
her?"
17 When he said this, all his opponents were humiliated,[g] but the
people were delighted with all the
wonderful things he was doing.

The Parables of the Mustard Seed and the Yeast

13:18,19pp — Mk 4:30–32
13:18–21pp — Mt 13:31–33

18 Then Jesus asked, "What is
the kingdom of God[h] like?[i] What
shall I compare it to? 19 It is like a
mustard seed, which a man took
and planted in his garden. It grew
and became a tree,[j] and the birds
of the air perched in its
branches."[k]
20 Again he asked, "What shall I
compare the kingdom of God to?
21 It is like yeast that a woman took
and mixed into a large amount[g] of
flour until it worked all through the
dough."[l]

The Narrow Door

22 Then Jesus went through the
towns and villages, teaching as he
made his way to Jerusalem.[m]
23 Someone asked him, "Lord, are
only a few people going to be
saved?"
He said to them, 24 "Make every
effort to enter through the narrow
door,[n] because many, I tell you,
will try to enter and will not be able
to. 25 Once the owner of the house
gets up and closes the door, you
will stand outside knocking and
pleading, 'Sir, open the door for
us.'
"But he will answer, 'I don't
know you or where you come
from.'[o]
26 "Then you will say, 'We ate
and drank with you, and you taught
in our streets.'
27 "But he will reply, 'I don't
know you or where you come from.
Away from me, all you evildoers!'[p]
28 "There will be weeping there,
and gnashing of teeth,[q] when you
see Abraham, Isaac and Jacob and
all the prophets in the kingdom of
God, but you yourselves thrown
out. 29 People will come from east
and west[r] and north and south,
and will take their places at the
feast in the kingdom of God. 30 Indeed there are those who are last
who will be first, and first who will
be last."[s]

Jesus' Sorrow for Jerusalem

13:34,35pp — Mt 23:37–39
13:34,35Ref — Lk 19:41

31 At that time some Pharisees
came to Jesus and said to him,
"Leave this place and go somewhere else. Herod[t] wants to kill
you."
32 He replied, "Go tell that fox, 'I
will drive out demons and heal
people today and tomorrow, and on
the third day I will reach my goal.'[u]
33 In any case, I must keep going today and tomorrow and the next
day—for surely no prophet[v] can
die outside Jerusalem!
34 "O Jerusalem, Jerusalem, you
who kill the prophets and stone
those sent to you, how often I have
longed to gather your children together, as a hen gathers her chicks
under her wings,[w] but you were not
willing! 35 Look, your house is left
to you desolate.[x] I tell you, you
will not see me again until you say,
'Blessed is he who comes in the
name of the Lord.'[h]"[y]

Jesus at a Pharisee's House

14:8–10Ref — Pr 25:6,7

14 One Sabbath, when Jesus
went to eat in the house of

13:14 [a]Mt 12:2; Lk 14:3 [b]Mk 5:22 [c]Ex 20:9
13:15 [d]Lk 14:5
13:16 [e]Lk 3:8; 19:9 [f]Mt 4:10
13:17 [g]Isa 66:5
13:18 [h]Mt 3:2 [i]Mt 13:24
13:19 [j]Lk 17:6 [k]Mt 13:32
13:21 [l]1Co 5:6
13:22 [m]Lk 9:51
13:24 [n]Mt 7:13
13:25 [o]Mt 7:23; 25:10-12
13:27 [p]Mt 7:23; 25:41
13:28 [q]Mt 8:12
13:29 [r]Mt 8:11
13:30 [s]Mt 19:30
13:31 [t]Mt 14:1
13:32 [u]Heb 2:10
13:33 [v]Mt 21:11
13:34 [w]Mt 23:37
13:35 [x]Jer 12:17; 22:5 [y]Ps 118:26; Mt 21:9; Lk 19:38

[g]*21* Greek *three satas* (probably about 1/2 bushel or 22 liters) [h]*35* Psalm 118:26

a prominent Pharisee,[a] he was being carefully watched.[b] **2**There in front of him was a man suffering from dropsy. **3**Jesus asked the Pharisees and experts in the law,[c] "Is it lawful to heal on the Sabbath or not?"[d] **4**But they remained silent. So taking hold of the man, he healed him and sent him away.

5Then he asked them, "If one of you has a son[i] or an ox that falls into a well on the Sabbath day, will you not immediately pull him out?"[e] **6**And they had nothing to say.

7When he noticed how the guests picked the places of honor at the table,[f] he told them this parable: **8**"When someone invites you to a wedding feast, do not take the place of honor, for a person more distinguished than you may have been invited. **9**If so, the host who invited both of you will come and say to you, 'Give this man your seat.' Then, humiliated, you will have to take the least important place. **10**But when you are invited, take the lowest place, so that when your host comes, he will say to you, 'Friend, move up to a better place.' Then you will be honored in the presence of all your fellow guests. **11**For everyone who exalts himself will be humbled, and he who humbles himself will be exalted."[g]

12Then Jesus said to his host, "When you give a luncheon or dinner, do not invite your friends, your brothers or relatives, or your rich neighbors; if you do, they may invite you back and so you will be repaid. **13**But when you give a banquet, invite the poor, the crippled, the lame, the blind,[h] **14**and you will be blessed. Although they cannot repay you, you will be repaid at the resurrection of the righteous."[i]

The Parable of the Great Banquet

14:16–24Ref – Mt 22:2–14

15When one of those at the table with him heard this, he said to Jesus, "Blessed is the man who will eat at the feast[j] in the kingdom of God."[k]

16Jesus replied: "A certain man was preparing a great banquet and invited many guests. **17**At the time of the banquet he sent his servant to tell those who had been invited, 'Come, for everything is now ready.'

18"But they all alike began to make excuses. The first said, 'I have just bought a field, and I must go and see it. Please excuse me.'

19"Another said, 'I have just bought five yoke of oxen, and I'm on my way to try them out. Please excuse me.'

20"Still another said, 'I just got married, so I can't come.'

21"The servant came back and reported this to his master. Then the owner of the house became angry and ordered his servant, 'Go out quickly into the streets and alleys of the town and bring in the poor, the crippled, the blind and the lame.'[l]

22" 'Sir,' the servant said, 'what you ordered has been done, but there is still room.'

23"Then the master told his servant, 'Go out to the roads and country lanes and make them come in, so that my house will be full. **24**I tell you, not one of those men who were invited will get a taste of my banquet.' "[m]

The Cost of Being a Disciple

25Large crowds were traveling with Jesus, and turning to them he said: **26**"If anyone comes to me and does not hate his father and mother, his wife and children, his brothers and sisters—yes, even his own life—he cannot be my disciple.[n] **27**And anyone who does not carry his cross and follow me cannot be my disciple.[o]

28"Suppose one of you wants to build a tower. Will he not first sit down and estimate the cost to see if he has enough money to complete it? **29**For if he lays the foundation and is not able to finish it,

14:1 [a]Lk 7:36; 11:37 [b]Mt 12:10
14:3 [c]Mt 22:35 [d]Mt 12:2
14:5 [e]Lk 13:15
14:7 [f]Lk 11:43
14:11 [g]Mt 23:12; Lk 18:14
14:13 [h]ver 21
14:14 [i]Ac 24:15
14:15 [j]Isa 25:6; Mt 26:29; Lk 13:29; Rev 19:9 [k]Mt 3:2
14:21 [l]ver 13
14:24 [m]Mt 21:43; Ac 13:46
14:26 [n]Mt 10:37; Jn 12:25
14:27 [o]Mt 10:38; Lk 9:23

[i]5 Some manuscripts *donkey*

everyone who sees it will ridicule him, **30**saying, 'This fellow began to build and was not able to finish.'

31"Or suppose a king is about to go to war against another king. Will he not first sit down and consider whether he is able with ten thousand men to oppose the one coming against him with twenty thousand? **32**If he is not able, he will send a delegation while the other is still a long way off and will ask for terms of peace. **33**In the same way, any of you who does not give up everything he has cannot be my disciple.[a]

34"Salt is good, but if it loses its saltiness, how can it be made salty again?[b] **35**It is fit neither for the soil nor for the manure pile; it is thrown out.[c]

"He who has ears to hear, let him hear."[d]

The Parable of the Lost Sheep

15:4-7pp — Mt 18:12-14

15 Now the tax collectors[e] and "sinners" were all gathering around to hear him. **2**But the Pharisees and the teachers of the law muttered, "This man welcomes sinners and eats with them."[f]

3Then Jesus told them this parable:[g] **4**"Suppose one of you has a hundred sheep and loses one of them. Does he not leave the ninety-nine in the open country and go after the lost sheep until he finds it?[h] **5**And when he finds it, he joyfully puts it on his shoulders **6**and goes home. Then he calls his friends and neighbors together and says, 'Rejoice with me; I have found my lost sheep.'[i] **7**I tell you that in the same way there will be more rejoicing in heaven over one sinner who repents than over ninety-nine righteous persons who do not need to repent.[j]

The Parable of the Lost Coin

8"Or suppose a woman has ten silver coins[i] and loses one. Does she not light a lamp, sweep the house and search carefully until she finds it? **9**And when she finds it, she calls her friends and neighbors together and says, 'Rejoice with me; I have found my lost coin.'[k] **10**In the same way, I tell you, there is rejoicing in the presence of the angels of God over one sinner who repents."[l]

The Parable of the Lost Son

11Jesus continued: "There was a man who had two sons.[m] **12**The younger one said to his father, 'Father, give me my share of the estate.'[n] So he divided his property[o] between them.

13"Not long after that, the younger son got together all he had, set off for a distant country and there squandered his wealth[p] in wild living. **14**After he had spent everything, there was a severe famine in that whole country, and he began to be in need. **15**So he went and hired himself out to a citizen of that country, who sent him to his fields to feed pigs.[q] **16**He longed to fill his stomach with the pods that the pigs were eating, but no one gave him anything.

17"When he came to his senses, he said, 'How many of my father's hired men have food to spare, and here I am starving to death! **18**I will set out and go back to my father and say to him: Father, I have sinned[r] against heaven and against you. **19**I am no longer worthy to be called your son; make me like one of your hired men.' **20**So he got up and went to his father.

"But while he was still a long way off, his father saw him and was filled with compassion for him; he ran to his son, threw his arms around him and kissed him.[s]

21"The son said to him, 'Father, I have sinned against heaven and against you.[t] I am no longer worthy to be called your son.[k]'

22"But the father said to his servants, 'Quick! Bring the best robe[u] and put it on him. Put a ring on his finger[v] and sandals on his feet.

14:33 Php 3:7,8
14:34 [b]Mk 9:50
14:35 [c]Mt 5:13 [d]Mt 11:15
15:1 [e]Lk 5:29
15:2 [f]Mt 9:11
15:3 [g]Mt 13:3
15:4 [h]Ps 23; 119:176; Jer 31:10; Eze 34:11-16; Lk 5:32; 19:10
15:6 [i]ver 9
15:7 [j]ver 10
15:9 [k]ver 6
15:10 [l]ver 7
15:11 [m]Mt 21:28
15:12 [n]Dt 21:17 [o]ver 30
15:13 [p]ver 30; Lk 16:1
15:15 [q]Lev 11:7
15:18 [r]Lev 26:40; Mt 3:2
15:20 [s]Ge 45:14,15; 46:29; Ac 20:37
15:21 [t]Ps 51:4
15:22 [u]Zec 3:4; Rev 6:11 [v]Ge 41:42

i8 Greek *ten drachmas,* each worth about a day's wages k21 Some early manuscripts *son. Make me like one of your hired men.*

23Bring the fattened calf and kill it. Let's have a feast and celebrate. 24For this son of mine was dead and is alive again;[a] he was lost and is found.' So they began to celebrate.[b]

25"Meanwhile, the older son was in the field. When he came near the house, he heard music and dancing. 26So he called one of the servants and asked him what was going on. 27'Your brother has come,' he replied, 'and your father has killed the fattened calf because he has him back safe and sound.'

28"The older brother became angry[c] and refused to go in. So his father went out and pleaded with him. 29But he answered his father, 'Look! All these years I've been slaving for you and never disobeyed your orders. Yet you never gave me even a young goat so I could celebrate with my friends. 30But when this son of yours who has squandered your property[d] with prostitutes[e] comes home, you kill the fattened calf for him!'

31" 'My son,' the father said, 'you are always with me, and everything I have is yours. 32But we had to celebrate and be glad, because this brother of yours was dead and is alive again; he was lost and is found.' "[f]

The Parable of the Shrewd Manager

16 Jesus told his disciples: "There was a rich man whose manager was accused of wasting his possessions.[g] 2So he called him in and asked him, 'What is this I hear about you? Give an account of your management, because you cannot be manager any longer.'

3"The manager said to himself, 'What shall I do now? My master is taking away my job. I'm not strong enough to dig, and I'm ashamed to beg— 4I know what I'll do so that, when I lose my job here, people will welcome me into their houses.'

5"So he called in each one of his

15:24 [a]Eph 2:1,5; 5:14; 1Ti 5:6 [b]ver 32
15:28 [c]Jnh 4:1
15:30 [d]ver 12,13 [e]Pr 29:3
15:32 [f]ver 24; Mal 3:17
16:1 [g]Lk 15:13,30
16:8 [h]Ps 17:14 [i]Ps 18:26 [j]Jn 12:36; Eph 5:8; 1Th 5:5
16:9 [k]ver 11,13 [l]Mt 19:21; Lk 12:33
16:10 [m]Mt 25:21, 23; Lk 19:17
16:11 [n]ver 9,13
16:13 [o]ver 9,11; Mt 6:24
16:14 [p]1Ti 3:3 [q]Lk 23:35
16:15 [r]Lk 10:29 [s]1Sa 16:7; Rev 2:23
16:16 [t]Mt 11:12,13

master's debtors. He asked the first, 'How much do you owe my master?'

6" 'Eight hundred gallons[l] of olive oil,' he replied.

"The manager told him, 'Take your bill, sit down quickly, and make it four hundred.'

7"Then he asked the second, 'And how much do you owe?'

" 'A thousand bushels[m] of wheat,' he replied.

"He told him, 'Take your bill and make it eight hundred.'

8"The master commended the dishonest manager because he had acted shrewdly. For the people of this world[h] are more shrewd[i] in dealing with their own kind than are the people of the light.[j] 9I tell you, use worldly wealth[k] to gain friends for yourselves, so that when it is gone, you will be welcomed into eternal dwellings.[l]

10"Whoever can be trusted with very little can also be trusted with much,[m] and whoever is dishonest with very little will also be dishonest with much. 11So if you have not been trustworthy in handling worldly wealth,[n] who will trust you with true riches? 12And if you have not been trustworthy with someone else's property, who will give you property of your own?

13"No servant can serve two masters. Either he will hate the one and love the other, or he will be devoted to the one and despise the other. You cannot serve both God and Money."[o]

14The Pharisees, who loved money,[p] heard all this and were sneering at Jesus.[q] 15He said to them, "You are the ones who justify yourselves[r] in the eyes of men, but God knows your hearts.[s] What is highly valued among men is detestable in God's sight.

Additional Teachings

16"The Law and the Prophets were proclaimed until John.[t]

[l]6 Greek *one hundred batous* (probably about 3 kiloliters) [m]7 Greek *one hundred korous* (probably about 35 kiloliters)

Since that time, the good news of
the kingdom of God is being
preached,[a] and everyone is forcing
his way into it. **17**It is easier for
heaven and earth to disappear than
for the least stroke of a pen to drop
out of the Law.[b]
18"Anyone who divorces his wife
and marries another woman commits adultery, and the man who
marries a divorced woman commits adultery.[c]

The Rich Man and Lazarus

19"There was a rich man who
was dressed in purple and fine lin-
en and lived in luxury every day.[d]
20At his gate was laid a beggar[e]
named Lazarus, covered with sores
21and longing to eat what fell from
the rich man's table.[f] Even the
dogs came and licked his sores.
22"The time came when the beggar died and the angels carried him
to Abraham's side. The rich man
also died and was buried. **23**In
hell,[n] where he was in torment, he
looked up and saw Abraham far
away, with Lazarus by his side.
24So he called to him, 'Father
Abraham,[g] have pity on me and
send Lazarus to dip the tip of his
finger in water and cool my tongue,
because I am in agony in this
fire.'[h]
25"But Abraham replied, 'Son,
remember that in your lifetime you
received your good things, while
Lazarus received bad things,[i] but
now he is comforted here and you
are in agony.[j] **26**And besides all
this, between us and you a great
chasm has been fixed, so that
those who want to go from here to
you cannot, nor can anyone cross
over from there to us.'
27"He answered, 'Then I beg
you, father, send Lazarus to my father's house, **28**for I have five
brothers. Let him warn them,[k] so
that they will not also come to this
place of torment.'
29"Abraham replied, 'They have
Moses[l] and the Prophets;[m] let
them listen to them.'
30" 'No, father Abraham,'[n] he
said, 'but if someone from the dead
goes to them, they will repent.'
31"He said to him, 'If they do not
listen to Moses and the Prophets,
they will not be convinced even if
someone rises from the dead.' "

Sin, Faith, Duty

17 Jesus said to his disciples:
"Things that cause people
to sin[o] are bound to come, but woe
to that person through whom they
come.[p] **2**It would be better for him
to be thrown into the sea with a
millstone tied around his neck
than for him to cause one of these
little ones[q] to sin.[r] **3**So watch
yourselves.
"If your brother sins, rebuke
him,[s] and if he repents, forgive
him.[t] **4**If he sins against you seven
times in a day, and seven times
comes back to you and says, 'I repent,' forgive him."[u]
5The apostles[v] said to the
Lord,[w] "Increase our faith!"
6He replied, "If you have faith as
small as a mustard seed,[x] you can
say to this mulberry tree, 'Be uprooted and planted in the sea,' and
it will obey you.[y]
7"Suppose one of you had a servant plowing or looking after the
sheep. Would he say to the servant
when he comes in from the field,
'Come along now and sit down to
eat'? **8**Would he not rather say,
'Prepare my supper, get yourself
ready and wait on me[z] while I eat
and drink; after that you may eat
and drink'? **9**Would he thank the
servant because he did what he was
told to do? **10**So you also, when you
have done everything you were told
to do, should say, 'We are unworthy
servants; we have only done our
duty.' "[a]

Ten Healed of Leprosy

11Now on his way to Jerusalem,[b] Jesus traveled along the border between Samaria and Galilee.[c]
12As he was going into a village, ten

16:16 [a]Mt 4:23
16:17 [b]Mt 5:18
16:18 [c]Mt 5:31,32; 19:9; Mk 10:11; Ro 7:2,3; 1Co 7:10,11
16:19 [d]Eze 16:49
16:20 [e]Ac 3:2
16:21 [f]Mt 15:27
16:24 [g]ver 30; Lk 3:8 [h]Mt 5:22
16:25 [i]Ps 17:14 [j]Lk 6:21,24, 25
16:28 [k]Ac 2:40; 20:23; 1Th 4:6
16:29 [l]Lk 24:27,44; Jn 5:45-47; Ac 15:21 [m]Lk 4:17; Jn 1:45
16:30 [n]ver 24; Lk 3:8
17:1 [o]Mt 5:29 [p]Mt 18:7
17:2 [q]Mk 10:24; Lk 10:21 [r]Mt 5:29
17:3 [s]Mt 18:15 [t]Eph 4:32; Col 3:13
17:4 [u]Mt 18:21,22
17:5 [v]Mk 6:30 [w]Lk 7:13
17:6 [x]Mt 13:31; 17:20; Lk 13:19 [y]Mt 21:21; Mk 9:23
17:8 [z]Lk 12:37
17:10 [a]1Co 9:16
17:11 [b]Lk 9:51 [c]Lk 9:51,52; Jn 4:3,4

[n]23 Greek *Hades*

men who had leprosy[o][a] met him. They stood at a distance[b] **13**and called out in a loud voice, "Jesus, Master,[c] have pity on us!"

14When he saw them, he said, "Go, show yourselves to the priests."[d] And as they went, they were cleansed.

15One of them, when he saw he was healed, came back, praising God[e] in a loud voice. **16**He threw himself at Jesus' feet and thanked him—and he was a Samaritan.[f]

17Jesus asked, "Were not all ten cleansed? Where are the other nine? **18**Was no one found to return and give praise to God except this foreigner?" **19**Then he said to him, "Rise and go; your faith has made you well."[g]

The Coming of the Kingdom of God

17:26,27pp — Mt 24:37–39

20Once, having been asked by the Pharisees when the kingdom of God would come,[h] Jesus replied, "The kingdom of God does not come with your careful observation, **21**nor will people say, 'Here it is,' or 'There it is,'[i] because the kingdom of God is within[p] you."

22Then he said to his disciples, "The time is coming when you will long to see one of the days of the Son of Man,[j] but you will not see it.[k] **23**Men will tell you, 'There he is!' or 'Here he is!' Do not go running off after them.[l] **24**For the Son of Man in his day[q] will be like the lightning,[m] which flashes and lights up the sky from one end to the other. **25**But first he must suffer many things[n] and be rejected[o] by this generation.[p]

26"Just as it was in the days of Noah,[q] so also will it be in the days of the Son of Man. **27**People were eating, drinking, marrying and being given in marriage up to the day Noah entered the ark. Then the flood came and destroyed them all.

28"It was the same in the days of Lot.[r] People were eating and drinking, buying and selling, planting and building. **29**But the day Lot left Sodom, fire and sulfur rained down from heaven and destroyed them all.

30"It will be just like this on the day the Son of Man is revealed.[s] **31**On that day no one who is on the roof of his house, with his goods inside, should go down to get them. Likewise, no one in the field should go back for anything.[t] **32**Remember Lot's wife![u] **33**Whoever tries to keep his life will lose it, and whoever loses his life will preserve it.[v] **34**I tell you, on that night two people will be in one bed; one will be taken and the other left. **35**Two women will be grinding grain together; one will be taken and the other left.[r]"[w]

37"Where, Lord?" they asked.

He replied, "Where there is a dead body, there the vultures will gather."[x]

The Parable of the Persistent Widow

18 Then Jesus told his disciples a parable to show them that they should always pray and not give up.[y] **2**He said: "In a certain town there was a judge who neither feared God nor cared about men. **3**And there was a widow in that town who kept coming to him with the plea, 'Grant me justice[z] against my adversary.'

4"For some time he refused. But finally he said to himself, 'Even though I don't fear God or care about men, **5**yet because this widow keeps bothering me, I will see that she gets justice, so that she won't eventually wear me out with her coming!'"[a]

6And the Lord[b] said, "Listen to what the unjust judge says. **7**And will not God bring about justice for his chosen ones, who cry out[c] to him day and night? Will he keep putting them off? **8**I tell you, he will see that they get justice, and quick-

17:12 [a]Mt 8:2 [b]Lev 13:45,46
17:13 [c]Lk 5:5
17:14 [d]Lev 14:2; Mt 8:4
17:15 [e]Mt 9:8
17:16 [f]Mt 10:5
17:19 [g]Mt 9:22
17:20 [h]Mt 3:2
17:21 [i]ver 23
17:22 [j]Mt 8:20 [k]Mt 9:15; Lk 5:35
17:23 [l]Mt 24:23; Mk 13:21; Lk 21:8
17:24 [m]Mt 24:27
17:25 [n]Mt 16:21 [o]Lk 9:22; 18:32 [p]Mk 13:30; Lk 21:32
17:26 [q]Ge 7:6-24
17:28 [r]Ge 19:1-28
17:30 [s]Mt 10:23; 16:27; 24:3, 27,37,39; 25:31; 1Co 1:7; 1Th 2:19; 2Th 1:7; 2:8; 2Pe 3:4; Rev 1:7
17:31 [t]Mt 24:17,18; Mk 13:15-16
17:32 [u]Ge 19:26
17:33 [v]Jn 12:25
17:35 [w]Mt 24:41
17:37 [x]Mt 24:28
18:1 [y]Isa 40:31; Lk 11:5-8; Ac 1:14; Ro 12:12; Eph 6:18; Col 4:2; 1Th 5:17
18:3 [z]Isa 1:17
18:5 [a]Lk 11:8
18:6 [b]Lk 7:13
18:7 [c]Ex 22:23; Ps 88:1; Rev 6:10

[o]*12* The Greek word was used for various diseases affecting the skin—not necessarily leprosy. [p]*21* Or *among* [q]*24* Some manuscripts do not have *in his day.*
[r]*35* Some manuscripts *left.* *36Two men will be in the field; one will be taken and the other left.*

ly. However, when the Son of Man[a] comes,[b] will he find faith on the earth?"

The Parable of the Pharisee and the Tax Collector

9To some who were confident of their own righteousness[c] and looked down on everybody else,[d] Jesus told this parable: 10"Two men went up to the temple to pray,[e] one a Pharisee and the other a tax collector. 11The Pharisee stood up[f] and prayed about[s] himself: 'God, I thank you that I am not like other men—robbers, evildoers, adulterers—or even like this tax collector. 12I fast[g] twice a week and give a tenth[h] of all I get.'

13"But the tax collector stood at a distance. He would not even look up to heaven, but beat his breast[i] and said, 'God, have mercy on me, a sinner.'[j]

14"I tell you that this man, rather than the other, went home justified before God. For everyone who exalts himself will be humbled, and he who humbles himself will be exalted."[k]

The Little Children and Jesus

18:15–17pp — Mt 19:13–15; Mk 10:13–16

15People were also bringing babies to Jesus to have him touch them. When the disciples saw this, they rebuked them. 16But Jesus called the children to him and said, "Let the little children come to me, and do not hinder them, for the kingdom of God belongs to such as these. 17I tell you the truth, anyone who will not receive the kingdom of God like a little child[l] will never enter it."

The Rich Ruler

18:18–30pp — Mt 19:16–29; Mk 10:17–30

18A certain ruler asked him, "Good teacher, what must I do to inherit eternal life?"[m]

19"Why do you call me good?" Jesus answered. "No one is good—except God alone. 20You know the commandments: 'Do not commit adultery, do not murder, do not steal, do not give false testimony, honor your father and mother.'[t]"[n]

21"All these I have kept since I was a boy," he said.

22When Jesus heard this, he said to him, "You still lack one thing. Sell everything you have and give to the poor,[o] and you will have treasure in heaven.[p] Then come, follow me."

23When he heard this, he became very sad, because he was a man of great wealth. 24Jesus looked at him and said, "How hard it is for the rich to enter the kingdom of God![q] 25Indeed, it is easier for a camel to go through the eye of a needle than for a rich man to enter the kingdom of God."

26Those who heard this asked, "Who then can be saved?"

27Jesus replied, "What is impossible with men is possible with God."[r]

28Peter said to him, "We have left all we had to follow you!"[s]

29"I tell you the truth," Jesus said to them, "no one who has left home or wife or brothers or parents or children for the sake of the kingdom of God 30will fail to receive many times as much in this age and, in the age to come,[t] eternal life."[u]

Jesus Again Predicts His Death

18:31–33pp — Mt 20:17–19; Mk 10:32–34

31Jesus took the Twelve aside and told them, "We are going up to Jerusalem,[v] and everything that is written by the prophets[w] about the Son of Man[x] will be fulfilled. 32He will be handed over to the Gentiles.[y] They will mock him, insult him, spit on him, flog him[z] and kill him.[a] 33On the third day[b] he will rise again."[c]

34The disciples did not understand any of this. Its meaning was hidden from them, and they did not know what he was talking about.[d]

[s] *11* Or *to* [t] *20* Exodus 20:12-16; Deut. 5:16-20

18:8 [a] Mt 8:20 [b] Mt 16:27
18:9 [c] Lk 16:15 [d] Isa 65:5
18:10 [e] Ac 3:1
18:11 [f] Mt 6:5; Mk 11:25
18:12 [g] Isa 58:3; Mt 9:14 [h] Mal 3:8; Lk 11:42
18:13 [i] Isa 66:2; Jer 31:19; Lk 23:48 [j] Lk 5:32; 1Ti 1:15
18:14 [k] Mt 23:12; Lk 14:11
18:17 [l] Mt 11:25; 18:3
18:18 [m] Lk 10:25
18:20 [n] Ex 20:12-16; Dt 5:16-20; Ro 13:9
18:22 [o] Ac 2:45 [p] Mt 6:20
18:24 [q] Pr 11:28
18:27 [r] Mt 19:26
18:28 [s] Mt 4:19
18:30 [t] Mt 12:32 [u] Mt 25:46
18:31 [v] Lk 9:51 [w] Ps 22; Isa 53 [x] Mt 8:20
18:32 [y] Lk 23:1 [z] Mt 16:21 [a] Ac 2:23
18:33 [b] Mt 16:21 [c] Mt 16:21
18:34 [d] Mk 9:32; Lk 9:45

A Blind Beggar Receives His Sight

18:35–43pp — Mt 20:29–34; Mk 10:46–52

35As Jesus approached Jericho,[a] a blind man was sitting by
the roadside begging. **36**When he
heard the crowd going by, he asked
what was happening. **37**They told
him, "Jesus of Nazareth is passing
by."[b]
38He called out, "Jesus, Son of
David,[c] have mercy[d] on me!"
39Those who led the way rebuked him and told him to be quiet, but he shouted all the more,
"Son of David, have mercy on
me!"[e]
40Jesus stopped and ordered the
man to be brought to him. When he
came near, Jesus asked him,
41"What do you want me to do for
you?"
"Lord, I want to see," he replied.
42Jesus said to him, "Receive
your sight; your faith has healed
you."[f] **43**Immediately he received
his sight and followed Jesus, praising God. When all the people saw
it, they also praised God.[g]

Zacchaeus the Tax Collector

19 Jesus entered Jericho[h] and
was passing through. **2**A
man was there by the name of Zacchaeus; he was a chief tax collector
and was wealthy. **3**He wanted to
see who Jesus was, but being a
short man he could not, because of
the crowd. **4**So he ran ahead and
climbed a sycamore-fig[i] tree to
see him, since Jesus was coming
that way.[j]
5When Jesus reached the spot,
he looked up and said to him, "Zacchaeus, come down immediately. I
must stay at your house today." **6**So
he came down at once and welcomed him gladly.
7All the people saw this and began to mutter, "He has gone to be
the guest of a 'sinner.' "[k]
8But Zacchaeus stood up and
said to the Lord,[l] "Look, Lord!
Here and now I give half of my possessions to the poor, and if I have
cheated anybody out of anything,[m]
I will pay back four times the
amount."[n]
9Jesus said to him, "Today salvation has come to this house, because this man, too, is a son of
Abraham.[o] **10**For the Son of Man
came to seek and to save what was
lost."[p]

The Parable of the Ten Minas

19:12–27Ref — Mt 25:14–30

11While they were listening to
this, he went on to tell them a parable, because he was near Jerusalem and the people thought that
the kingdom of God[q] was going to
appear at once.[r] **12**He said: "A
man of noble birth went to a distant country to have himself appointed king and then to return.
13So he called ten of his servants[s]
and gave them ten minas.[u] 'Put
this money to work,' he said, 'until
I come back.'
14"But his subjects hated him
and sent a delegation after him to
say, 'We don't want this man to be
our king.'
15"He was made king, however,
and returned home. Then he sent
for the servants to whom he had
given the money, in order to find
out what they had gained with it.
16"The first one came and said,
'Sir, your mina has earned ten
more.'
17" 'Well done, my good servant!'[t] his master replied. 'Because you have been trustworthy in
a very small matter, take charge of
ten cities.'[u]
18"The second came and said,
'Sir, your mina has earned five
more.'
19"His master answered, 'You
take charge of five cities.'
20"Then another servant came
and said, 'Sir, here is your mina; I
have kept it laid away in a piece of
cloth. **21**I was afraid of you, because you are a hard man. You take
out what you did not put in and
reap what you did not sow.'[v]
22"His master replied, 'I will
judge you by your own words,[w] you

18:35 [a]Lk 19:1
18:37 [b]Lk 19:4
18:38 [c]ver 39; Mt 9:27 [d]Mt 17:15; Lk 18:13
18:39 [e]ver 38
18:42 [f]Mt 9:22
18:43 [g]Mt 9:8; Lk 13:17
19:1 [h]Lk 18:35
19:4 [i]1Ki 10:27; 1Ch 27:28; Isa 9:10 [j]Lk 18:37
19:7 [k]Mt 9:11
19:8 [l]Lk 7:13 [m]Lk 3:12,13 [n]Ex 22:1; Lev 6:4,5; Nu 5:7; 2Sa 12:6
19:9 [o]Lk 3:8; 13:16; Ro 4:16; Gal 3:7
19:10 [p]Eze 34:12, 16; Jn 3:17
19:11 [q]Mt 3:2 [r]Lk 17:20; Ac 1:6
19:13 [s]Mk 13:34
19:17 [t]Pr 27:18 [u]Lk 16:10
19:21 [v]Mt 25:24
19:22 [w]2Sa 1:16; Job 15:6

[u]*13* A mina was about three months' wages.

wicked servant! You knew, did you, that I am a hard man, taking out what I did not put in, and reaping what I did not sow?[a] **23**Why then didn't you put my money on deposit, so that when I came back, I could have collected it with interest?'

24"Then he said to those standing by, 'Take his mina away from him and give it to the one who has ten minas.'

25" 'Sir,' they said, 'he already has ten!'

26"He replied, 'I tell you that to everyone who has, more will be given, but as for the one who has nothing, even what he has will be taken away.[b] **27**But those enemies of mine who did not want me to be king over them—bring them here and kill them in front of me.' "

The Triumphal Entry

19:29–38pp — Mt 21:1–9; Mk 11:1–10
19:35–38pp — Jn 12:12–15

28After Jesus had said this, he went on ahead, going up to Jerusalem.[c] **29**As he approached Bethphage and Bethany[d] at the hill called the Mount of Olives,[e] he sent two of his disciples, saying to them, **30**"Go to the village ahead of you, and as you enter it, you will find a colt tied there, which no one has ever ridden. Untie it and bring it here. **31**If anyone asks you, 'Why are you untying it?' tell him, 'The Lord needs it.' "

32Those who were sent ahead went and found it just as he had told them.[f] **33**As they were untying the colt, its owners asked them, "Why are you untying the colt?"

34They replied, "The Lord needs it."

35They brought it to Jesus, threw their cloaks on the colt and put Jesus on it. **36**As he went along, people spread their cloaks[g] on the road.

37When he came near the place where the road goes down the Mount of Olives,[h] the whole crowd of disciples began joyfully to praise God in loud voices for all the miracles they had seen:

38"Blessed is the king who comes
in the name of the
Lord!"[v][i]

"Peace in heaven and glory in
the highest!"[j]

39Some of the Pharisees in the crowd said to Jesus, "Teacher, rebuke your disciples!"[k]

40"I tell you," he replied, "if they keep quiet, the stones will cry out."[l]

41As he approached Jerusalem and saw the city, he wept over it[m] **42**and said, "If you, even you, had only known on this day what would bring you peace—but now it is hidden from your eyes. **43**The days will come upon you when your enemies will build an embankment against you and encircle you and hem you in on every side.[n] **44**They will dash you to the ground, you and the children within your walls.[o] They will not leave one stone on another,[p] because you did not recognize the time of God's coming[q] to you."

Jesus at the Temple

19:45,46pp — Mt 21:12–16; Mk 11:15–18; Jn 2:13–16

45Then he entered the temple area and began driving out those who were selling. **46**"It is written," he said to them, " 'My house will be a house of prayer'[w];[r] but you have made it 'a den of robbers.'[x]"[s]

47Every day he was teaching at the temple.[t] But the chief priests, the teachers of the law and the leaders among the people were trying to kill him.[u] **48**Yet they could not find any way to do it, because all the people hung on his words.

The Authority of Jesus Questioned

20:1–8pp — Mt 21:23–27; Mk 11:27–33

20 One day as he was teaching the people in the temple courts[v] and preaching the gospel,[w] the chief priests and the teachers of the law, together with

[v]*38* Psalm 118:26 [w]*46* Isaiah 56:7
[x]*46* Jer. 7:11

19:22 [a]Mt 25:26
19:26 [b]Mt 13:12; 25:29; Lk 8:18
19:28 [c]Mk 10:32; Lk 9:51
19:29 [d]Mt 21:17 [e]Mt 21:1
19:32 [f]Lk 22:13
19:36 [g]2Ki 9:13
19:37 [h]Mt 21:1
19:38 [i]Ps 118:26; Lk 13:35 [j]Lk 2:14
19:39 [k]Mt 21:15,16
19:40 [l]Hab 2:11
19:41 [m]Isa 22:4; Lk 13:34,35
19:43 [n]Isa 29:3; Jer 6:6; Eze 4:2; 26:8; Lk 21:20
19:44 [o]Ps 137:9 [p]Mt 24:2; Mk 13:2; Lk 21:6 [q]1Pe 2:12
19:46 [r]Isa 56:7 [s]Jer 7:11
19:47 [t]Mt 26:55 [u]Mt 12:14; Mk 11:18
20:1 [v]Mt 26:55 [w]Lk 8:1

the elders, came up to him. 2"Tell
us by what authority you are doing
these things," they said. "Who gave
you this authority?"[a]
3He replied, "I will also ask you
a question. Tell me, 4John's baptism[b]—was it from heaven, or
from men?"
5They discussed it among themselves and said, "If we say, 'From
heaven,' he will ask, 'Why didn't
you believe him?' 6But if we say,
'From men,' all the people[c] will
stone us, because they are persuaded that John was a prophet."[d]
7So they answered, "We don't
know where it was from."
8Jesus said, "Neither will I tell
you by what authority I am doing
these things."

The Parable of the Tenants

20:9–19pp — Mt 21:33–46; Mk 12:1–12

9He went on to tell the people
this parable: "A man planted a
vineyard,[e] rented it to some farmers and went away for a long time.[f]
10At harvest time he sent a servant
to the tenants so they would give
him some of the fruit of the vineyard. But the tenants beat him and
sent him away empty-handed.
11He sent another servant, but that
one also they beat and treated
shamefully and sent away empty-
handed. 12He sent still a third, and
they wounded him and threw him
out.
13"Then the owner of the vineyard said, 'What shall I do? I will
send my son, whom I love;[g] perhaps they will respect him.'
14"But when the tenants saw
him, they talked the matter over.
'This is the heir,' they said. 'Let's
kill him, and the inheritance will
be ours.' 15So they threw him out
of the vineyard and killed him.
"What then will the owner of the
vineyard do to them? 16He will
come and kill those tenants[h] and
give the vineyard to others."
When the people heard this, they
said, "May this never be!"
17Jesus looked directly at them
and asked, "Then what is the
meaning of that which is written:

" 'The stone the builders
rejected
has become the
capstone'[y][z]?[i]

18Everyone who falls on that stone
will be broken to pieces, but he on
whom it falls will be crushed."[j]
19The teachers of the law and
the chief priests looked for a way to
arrest him[k] immediately, because
they knew he had spoken this parable against them. But they were
afraid of the people.[l]

Paying Taxes to Caesar

20:20–26pp — Mt 22:15–22; Mk 12:13–17

20Keeping a close watch on him,
they sent spies, who pretended to
be honest. They hoped to catch
Jesus in something he said[m] so
that they might hand him over to
the power and authority of the governor.[n] 21So the spies questioned
him: "Teacher, we know that you
speak and teach what is right, and
that you do not show partiality but
teach the way of God in accordance
with the truth.[o] 22Is it right for us
to pay taxes to Caesar or not?"
23He saw through their duplicity
and said to them, 24"Show me a denarius. Whose portrait and inscription are on it?"
25"Caesar's," they replied.
He said to them, "Then give to
Caesar what is Caesar's,[p] and to
God what is God's."
26They were unable to trap him
in what he had said there in public.
And astonished by his answer, they
became silent.

The Resurrection and Marriage

20:27–40pp — Mt 22:23–33; Mk 12:18–27

27Some of the Sadducees,[q] who
say there is no resurrection,[r] came
to Jesus with a question. 28"Teacher," they said, "Moses wrote for us
that if a man's brother dies and
leaves a wife but no children, the
man must marry the widow and
have children for his brother.[s]

20:2 [a]Jn 2:18; Ac 4:7; 7:27
20:4 [b]Mk 1:4
20:6 [c]Lk 7:29 [d]Mt 11:9
20:9 [e]Isa 5:1-7 [f]Mt 25:14
20:13 [g]Mt 3:17
20:16 [h]Lk 19:27
20:17 [i]Ps 118:22; Ac 4:11
20:18 [j]Isa 8:14,15
20:19 [k]Lk 19:47 [l]Mk 11:18
20:20 [m]Mt 12:10 [n]Mt 27:2
20:21 [o]Jn 3:2
20:25 [p]Lk 23:2; Ro 13:7
20:27 [q]Ac 4:1 [r]Ac 23:8; 1Co 15:12
20:28 [s]Dt 25:5

[y]17 Or *cornerstone* [z]17 Psalm 118:22

29Now there were seven brothers.
The first one married a woman and
died childless. 30The second 31and
then the third married her, and in
the same way the seven died, leaving no children. 32Finally, the
woman died too. 33Now then, at
the resurrection whose wife will
she be, since the seven were married to her?"

34Jesus replied, "The people of
this age marry and are given in marriage. 35But those who are considered worthy of taking part in that
age[a] and in the resurrection from
the dead will neither marry nor be
given in marriage, 36and they can
no longer die; for they are like the
angels. They are God's children,[b]
since they are children of the resurrection. 37But in the account of the
bush, even Moses showed that the
dead rise, for he calls the Lord 'the
God of Abraham, and the God of
Isaac, and the God of Jacob.'[a][c]
38He is not the God of the dead,
but of the living, for to him all are
alive."

39Some of the teachers of the
law responded, "Well said, teacher!" 40And no one dared to ask him
any more questions.[d]

Whose Son Is the Christ?

20:41–47pp — Mt 22:41–23:7; Mk 12:35–40

41Then Jesus said to them, "How
is it that they say the Christ[b] is the
Son of David?[e] 42David himself
declares in the Book of Psalms:

" 'The Lord said to my Lord:
"Sit at my right hand
43until I make your enemies
a footstool for your feet." '[c][f]

44David calls him 'Lord.' How then
can he be his son?"

45While all the people were listening, Jesus said to his disciples,
46"Beware of the teachers of the
law. They like to walk around in
flowing robes and love to be greeted in the marketplaces and have
the most important seats in the
synagogues and the places of honor
at banquets.[g] 47They devour widows' houses and for a show make
lengthy prayers. Such men will be
punished most severely."

The Widow's Offering

21:1–4pp — Mk 12:41–44

21 As he looked up, Jesus saw
the rich putting their gifts
into the temple treasury.[h] 2He also
saw a poor widow put in two very
small copper coins.[d] 3"I tell you
the truth," he said, "this poor widow has put in more than all the others. 4All these people gave their
gifts out of their wealth; but she
out of her poverty put in all she had
to live on."[i]

Signs of the End of the Age

21:5–36pp — Mt 24; Mk 13
21:12–17pp — Mt 10:17–22

5Some of his disciples were re-
marking about how the temple was
adorned with beautiful stones and
with gifts dedicated to God. But
Jesus said, 6"As for what you see
here, the time will come when not
one stone will be left on another;[j]
every one of them will be thrown
down."

7"Teacher," they asked, "when
will these things happen? And
what will be the sign that they are
about to take place?"

8He replied: "Watch out that you
are not deceived. For many will
come in my name, claiming, 'I am
he,' and, 'The time is near.' Do not
follow them.[k] 9When you hear of
wars and revolutions, do not be
frightened. These things must happen first, but the end will not come
right away."

10Then he said to them: "Nation
will rise against nation, and kingdom against kingdom.[l] 11There
will be great earthquakes, famines
and pestilences in various places,
and fearful events and great signs
from heaven.[m]

20:35 [a]Mt 12:32
20:36 [b]Jn 1:12; 1Jn 3:1-2
20:37 [c]Ex 3:6
20:40 [d]Mt 22:46; Mk 12:34
20:41 [e]Mt 1:1
20:43 [f]Ps 110:1; Mt 22:44
20:46 [g]Lk 11:43
21:1 [h]Mt 27:6; Jn 8:20
21:4 [i]2Co 8:12
21:6 [j]Lk 19:44
21:8 [k]Lk 17:23
21:10 [l]2Ch 15:6; Isa 19:2
21:11 [m]Isa 29:6; Joel 2:30

[a]*37* Exodus 3:6
[b]*41* Or *Messiah*
[c]*43* Psalm 110:1
[d]*2* Greek *two lepta*

12“But before all this, they will
lay hands on you and persecute
you. They will deliver you to synagogues and prisons, and you will be
brought before kings and governors, and all on account of my
name. **13**This will result in your being witnesses to them.[a] **14**But
make up your mind not to worry
beforehand how you will defend
yourselves.[b] **15**For I will give you[c]
words and wisdom that none of
your adversaries will be able to resist or contradict. **16**You will be betrayed even by parents, brothers,
relatives and friends,[d] and they
will put some of you to death. **17**All
men will hate you because of me.[e]
18But not a hair of your head will
perish.[f] **19**By standing firm you
will gain life.[g]

20“When you see Jerusalem being surrounded by armies,[h] you
will know that its desolation is
near. **21**Then let those who are in
Judea flee to the mountains, let
those in the city get out, and let
those in the country not enter the
city.[i] **22**For this is the time of punishment[j] in fulfillment[k] of all
that has been written. **23**How
dreadful it will be in those days for
pregnant women and nursing
mothers! There will be great distress in the land and wrath against
this people. **24**They will fall by the
sword and will be taken as prisoners to all the nations. Jerusalem
will be trampled[l] on by the Gentiles until the times of the Gentiles
are fulfilled.

25“There will be signs in the sun,
moon and stars. On the earth, nations will be in anguish and per-
plexity at the roaring and tossing of
the sea.[m] **26**Men will faint from terror, apprehensive of what is coming
on the world, for the heavenly bodies will be shaken.[n] **27**At that time
they will see the Son of Man[o] coming in a cloud[p] with power and
great glory. **28**When these things
begin to take place, stand up and
lift up your heads, because your redemption is drawing near.”[q]

29He told them this parable:
“Look at the fig tree and all the
trees. **30**When they sprout leaves,
you can see for yourselves and
know that summer is near. **31**Even
so, when you see these things happening, you know that the kingdom
of God[r] is near.

32“I tell you the truth, this generation[e][s] will certainly not pass
away until all these things have
happened. **33**Heaven and earth will
pass away, but my words will never
pass away.[t]

34“Be careful, or your hearts will
be weighed down with dissipation,
drunkenness and the anxieties of
life,[u] and that day will close on you
unexpectedly[v] like a trap. **35**For it
will come upon all those who live
on the face of the whole earth. **36**Be
always on the watch, and pray[w]
that you may be able to escape all
that is about to happen, and that
you may be able to stand before the
Son of Man.”

37Each day Jesus was teaching
at the temple,[x] and each evening
he went out[y] to spend the night on
the hill called the Mount of Olives,[z] **38**and all the people came
early in the morning to hear him at
the temple.[a]

Judas Agrees to Betray Jesus

22:1,2pp — Mt 26:2-5; Mk 14:1,2,10,11

22 Now the Feast of Unleavened Bread, called the
Passover, was approaching,[b] **2**and
the chief priests and the teachers
of the law were looking for some
way to get rid of Jesus,[c] for they
were afraid of the people. **3**Then
Satan[d] entered Judas, called Iscariot,[e] one of the Twelve. **4**And Judas went to the chief priests and
the officers of the temple guard[f]
and discussed with them how he
might betray Jesus. **5**They were delighted and agreed to give him
money.[g] **6**He consented, and
watched for an opportunity to hand
Jesus over to them when no crowd
was present.

21:13 [a]Php 1:12
21:14 [b]Lk 12:11
21:15 [c]Lk 12:12
21:16 [d]Lk 12:52,53
21:17 [e]Jn 15:21
21:18 [f]Mt 10:30
21:19 [g]Mt 10:22
21:20 [h]Lk 19:43
21:21 [i]Lk 17:31
21:22 [j]Isa 63:4; Da 9:24-27; Hos 9:7 [k]Mt 1:22
21:24 [l]Isa 5:5; 63:18; Da 8:13; Rev 11:2
21:25 [m]2Pe 3:10,12
21:26 [n]Mt 24:29
21:27 [o]Mt 8:20 [p]Rev 1:7
21:28 [q]Lk 18:7
21:31 [r]Mt 3:2
21:32 [s]Lk 11:50; 17:25
21:33 [t]Mt 5:18
21:34 [u]Mk 4:19 [v]Lk 12:40,46; 1Th 5:2-7
21:36 [w]Mt 26:41
21:37 [x]Mt 26:55 [y]Mk 11:19 [z]Mt 21:1
21:38 [a]Jn 8:2
22:1 [b]Jn 11:55
22:2 [c]Mt 12:14
22:3 [d]Mt 4:10; Jn 13:2 [e]Mt 10:4
22:4 [f]ver 52; Ac 4:1; 5:24
22:5 [g]Zec 11:12

[e]32 Or *race*

The Last Supper

22:7–13pp — Mt 26:17–19; Mk 14:12–16
22:17–20pp — Mt 26:26–29; Mk 14:22–25; 1Co 11:23–25
22:21–23pp — Mt 26:21–24; Mk 14:18–21; Jn 13:21–30
22:25–27pp — Mt 20:25–28; Mk 10:42–45
22:33,34pp — Mt 26:33–35; Mk 14:29–31; Jn 13:37,38

7Then came the day of Unleavened Bread on which the Passover
lamb had to be sacrificed.[a] **8**Jesus
sent Peter and John,[b] saying, "Go
and make preparations for us to eat
the Passover."
9"Where do you want us to prepare for it?" they asked.
10He replied, "As you enter the
city, a man carrying a jar of water
will meet you. Follow him to the
house that he enters, **11**and say to
the owner of the house, 'The
Teacher asks: Where is the guest
room, where I may eat the Passover
with my disciples?' **12**He will show
you a large upper room, all furnished. Make preparations there."
13They left and found things just
as Jesus had told them.[c] So they
prepared the Passover.
14When the hour came, Jesus
and his apostles[d] reclined at the
table.[e] **15**And he said to them, "I
have eagerly desired to eat this
Passover with you before I suffer.[f]
16For I tell you, I will not eat it
again until it finds fulfillment in
the kingdom of God."[g]
17After taking the cup, he gave
thanks and said, "Take this and divide it among you. **18**For I tell you
I will not drink again of the fruit of
the vine until the kingdom of God
comes."
19And he took bread, gave
thanks and broke it,[h] and gave it to
them, saying, "This is my body giv-
en for you; do this in remembrance
of me."
20In the same way, after the supper he took the cup, saying, "This
cup is the new covenant[i] in my
blood, which is poured out for you.
21But the hand of him who is going
to betray me is with mine on the
table.[j] **22**The Son of Man[k] will go
as it has been decreed,[l] but woe to
that man who betrays him." **23**They
began to question among themselves which of them it might be
who would do this.
24Also a dispute arose among
them as to which of them was considered to be greatest.[m] **25**Jesus
said to them, "The kings of the
Gentiles lord it over them; and
those who exercise authority over
them call themselves Benefactors.
26But you are not to be like that.
Instead, the greatest among you
should be like the youngest,[n] and
the one who rules like the one who
serves.[o] **27**For who is greater, the
one who is at the table or the one
who serves? Is it not the one who is
at the table? But I am among you as
one who serves.[p] **28**You are those
who have stood by me in my trials.
29And I confer on you a kingdom,[q]
just as my Father conferred one on
me, **30**so that you may eat and
drink at my table in my kingdom[r]
and sit on thrones, judging the
twelve tribes of Israel.[s]
31"Simon, Simon, Satan has
asked[t] to sift you[f] as wheat.[u]
32But I have prayed for you,[v] Simon, that your faith may not fail.
And when you have turned back,
strengthen your brothers."[w]
33But he replied, "Lord, I am
ready to go with you to prison and
to death."[x]
34Jesus answered, "I tell you, Peter, before the rooster crows today,
you will deny three times that you
know me."
35Then Jesus asked them,
"When I sent you without purse,
bag or sandals,[y] did you lack anything?"
"Nothing," they answered.
36He said to them, "But now if
you have a purse, take it, and also
a bag; and if you don't have a
sword, sell your cloak and buy one.
37It is written: 'And he was numbered with the transgressors'[g];[z]
and I tell you that this must be fulfilled in me. Yes, what is written
about me is reaching its fulfillment."

22:7 [a] Ex 12:18-20; Dt 16:5-8; Mk 14:12
22:8 [b] Ac 3:1,11; 4:13,19; 8:14
22:13 [c] Lk 19:32
22:14 [d] Mk 6:30 [e] Mt 26:20; Mk 14:17,18
22:15 [f] Mt 16:21
22:16 [g] Lk 14:15; Rev 19:9
22:19 [h] Mt 14:19
22:20 [i] Ex 24:8; Isa 42:6; Jer 31:31-34; Zec 9:11; 2Co 3:6; Heb 8:6; 9:15
22:21 [j] Ps 41:9
22:22 [k] Mt 8:20 [l] Ac 2:23; 4:28
22:24 [m] Mk 9:34; Lk 9:46
22:26 [n] 1Pe 5:5 [o] Mk 9:35; Lk 9:48
22:27 [p] Mt 20:28; Lk 12:37
22:29 [q] Mt 25:34; 2Ti 2:12
22:30 [r] Lk 14:15 [s] Mt 19:28
22:31 [t] Job 1:6-12 [u] Am 9:9
22:32 [v] Jn 17:9,15; Ro 8:34 [w] Jn 21:15-17
22:33 [x] Jn 11:16
22:35 [y] Mt 10:9,10; Lk 9:3; 10:4
22:37 [z] Isa 53:12

[f] *31* The Greek is plural. [g] *37* Isaiah 53:12

38The disciples said, "See, Lord, here are two swords."

"That is enough," he replied.

Jesus Prays on the Mount of Olives

22:40–46pp — Mt 26:36–46; Mk 14:32–42

39Jesus went out as usual[a] to the Mount of Olives,[b] and his disciples followed him. 40On reaching the place, he said to them, "Pray that you will not fall into temptation."[c] 41He withdrew about a stone's throw beyond them, knelt down[d] and prayed, 42"Father, if you are willing, take this cup[e] from me; yet not my will, but yours be done."[f] 43An angel from heaven appeared to him and strengthened him.[g] 44And being in anguish, he prayed more earnestly, and his sweat was like drops of blood falling to the ground.[h]

45When he rose from prayer and went back to the disciples, he found them asleep, exhausted from sorrow. 46"Why are you sleeping?" he asked them. "Get up and pray so that you will not fall into temptation."[h]

Jesus Arrested

22:47–53pp — Mt 26:47–56; Mk 14:43–50; Jn 18:3–11

47While he was still speaking a crowd came up, and the man who was called Judas, one of the Twelve, was leading them. He approached Jesus to kiss him, 48but Jesus asked him, "Judas, are you betraying the Son of Man with a kiss?"

49When Jesus' followers saw what was going to happen, they said, "Lord, should we strike with our swords?"[i] 50And one of them struck the servant of the high priest, cutting off his right ear.

51But Jesus answered, "No more of this!" And he touched the man's ear and healed him.

52Then Jesus said to the chief priests, the officers of the temple guard,[j] and the elders, who had come for him, "Am I leading a rebellion, that you have come with swords and clubs? 53Every day I was with you in the temple courts,[k] and you did not lay a hand on me. But this is your hour[l]—when darkness reigns."[m]

Peter Disowns Jesus

22:55–62pp — Mt 26:69–75; Mk 14:66–72; Jn 18:16–18,25–27

54Then seizing him, they led him away and took him into the house of the high priest.[n] Peter followed at a distance.[o] 55But when they had kindled a fire in the middle of the courtyard and had sat down together, Peter sat down with them. 56A servant girl saw him seated there in the firelight. She looked closely at him and said, "This man was with him."

57But he denied it. "Woman, I don't know him," he said.

58A little later someone else saw him and said, "You also are one of them."

"Man, I am not!" Peter replied.

59About an hour later another asserted, "Certainly this fellow was with him, for he is a Galilean."[p]

60Peter replied, "Man, I don't know what you're talking about!" Just as he was speaking, the rooster crowed. 61The Lord[q] turned and looked straight at Peter. Then Peter remembered the word the Lord had spoken to him: "Before the rooster crows today, you will disown me three times."[r] 62And he went outside and wept bitterly.

The Guards Mock Jesus

22:63–65pp — Mt 26:67,68; Mk 14:65; Jn 18:22,23

63The men who were guarding Jesus began mocking and beating him. 64They blindfolded him and demanded, "Prophesy! Who hit you?" 65And they said many other insulting things to him.[s]

22:39 [a]Lk 21:37 [b]Mt 21:1
22:40 [c]Mt 6:13
22:41 [d]Lk 18:11
22:42 [e]Mt 20:22 [f]Mt 26:39
22:43 [g]Mt 4:11; Mk 1:13
22:46 [h]ver 40
22:49 [i]ver 38
22:52 [j]ver 4
22:53 [k]Mt 26:55 [l]Jn 12:27 [m]Mt 8:12; Jn 1:5; 3:20
22:54 [n]Mt 26:57; Mk 14:53 [o]Mt 26:58; Mk 14:54; Jn 18:15
22:59 [p]Lk 23:6
22:61 [q]Lk 7:13 [r]ver 34
22:65 [s]Mt 16:21

[h]*44* Some early manuscripts do not have verses 43 and 44.

Jesus Before Pilate and Herod

22:67–71pp — Mt 26:63–66; Mk 14:61–63; Jn 18:19–21
23:2,3pp — Mt 27:11–14; Mk 15:2–5; Jn 18:29–37
23:18–25pp — Mt 27:15–26; Mk 15:6–15; Jn 18:39–19:16

66At daybreak the council[a] of
the elders of the people, both the
chief priests and teachers of the
law, met together,[b] and Jesus was
led before them. **67**"If you are the
Christ,[i]" they said, "tell us."

Jesus answered, "If I tell you,
you will not believe me, **68**and if I
asked you, you would not answer.[c]
69But from now on, the Son of Man
will be seated at the right hand of
the mighty God."[d]

70They all asked, "Are you then
the Son of God?"[e]

He replied, "You are right in saying I am."[f]

71Then they said, "Why do we
need any more testimony? We have
heard it from his own lips."

23 Then the whole assembly
rose and led him off to Pi-
late.[g] **2**And they began to accuse
him, saying, "We have found this
man subverting our nation.[h] He
opposes payment of taxes to Caesar[i] and claims to be Christ,[j] a
king."[j]

3So Pilate asked Jesus, "Are you
the king of the Jews?"

"Yes, it is as you say," Jesus replied.

4Then Pilate announced to the
chief priests and the crowd, "I find
no basis for a charge against this
man."[k]

5But they insisted, "He stirs
up the people all over Judea[k] by
his teaching. He started in Galilee[l] and has come all the way
here."

6On hearing this, Pilate asked if
the man was a Galilean.[m] **7**When
he learned that Jesus was under
Herod's jurisdiction, he sent him
to Herod,[n] who was also in Jerusalem at that time.

8When Herod saw Jesus, he was
greatly pleased, because for a long
time he had been wanting to see
him.[o] From what he had heard
about him, he hoped to see him
perform some miracle. **9**He plied
him with many questions, but
Jesus gave him no answer.[p] **10**The
chief priests and the teachers of
the law were standing there, vehe-
mently accusing him. **11**Then Herod and his soldiers ridiculed and
mocked him. Dressing him in an elegant robe,[q] they sent him back to
Pilate. **12**That day Herod and Pilate
became friends[r]—before this they
had been enemies.

13Pilate called together the chief
priests, the rulers and the people,
14and said to them, "You brought
me this man as one who was inciting the people to rebellion. I have
examined him in your presence
and have found no basis for your
charges against him.[s] **15**Neither
has Herod, for he sent him back to
us; as you can see, he has done
nothing to deserve death. **16**Therefore, I will punish him[t] and then
release him.[l]"

18With one voice they cried out,
"Away with this man! Release Barabbas to us!"[u] **19**(Barabbas had
been thrown into prison for an insurrection in the city, and for murder.)

20Wanting to release Jesus, Pilate appealed to them again. **21**But
they kept shouting, "Crucify him!
Crucify him!"

22For the third time he spoke to
them: "Why? What crime has this
man committed? I have found in
him no grounds for the death penalty. Therefore I will have him punished and then release him."[v]

23But with loud shouts they in-
sistently demanded that he be crucified, and their shouts prevailed.
24So Pilate decided to grant their
demand. **25**He released the man
who had been thrown into prison
for insurrection and murder, the
one they asked for, and surrendered Jesus to their will.

22:66 [a]Mt 5:22 [b]Mt 27:1; Mk 15:1
22:68 [c]Lk 20:3-8
22:69 [d]Mk 16:19
22:70 [e]Mt 4:3 [f]Mt 27:11; Lk 23:3
23:1 [g]Mt 27:2; Mk 15:1; Jn 18:28
23:2 [h]ver 14 [i]Lk 20:22 [j]Jn 19:12
23:4 [k]ver 14,22,41; Mt 27:23; Jn 18:38; 1Ti 6:13; 2Co 5:21
23:5 [l]Mk 1:14
23:6 [m]Lk 22:59
23:7 [n]Mt 14:1; Lk 3:1
23:8 [o]Lk 9:9
23:9 [p]Mk 14:61
23:11 [q]Mk 15:17-19; Jn 19:2,3
23:12 [r]Ac 4:27
23:14 [s]ver 4
23:16 [t]ver 22; Mt 27:26; Jn 19:1; Ac 16:37; 2Co 11:23,24
23:18 [u]Ac 3:13,14
23:22 [v]ver 16

[i]67 Or *Messiah* [j]2 Or *Messiah*; also in verses 35 and 39 [k]5 Or *over the land of the Jews* [l]16 Some manuscripts *him."* [17]*Now he was obliged to release one man to them at the Feast.*

The Crucifixion

23:33-43pp — Mt 27:33-44; Mk 15:22-32; Jn 19:17-24

26As they led him away, they
seized Simon from Cyrene,[a] who
was on his way in from the country,
and put the cross on him and made
him carry it behind Jesus.[b] **27**A
large number of people followed
him, including women who
mourned and wailed[c] for him.
28Jesus turned and said to them,
"Daughters of Jerusalem, do not
weep for me; weep for yourselves
and for your children.[d] **29**For the
time will come when you will say,
'Blessed are the barren women, the
wombs that never bore and the
breasts that never nursed!'[e]
30Then

" 'they will say to the
mountains, "Fall on us!"
and to the hills, "Cover
us!" '[m][f]

31For if men do these things when
the tree is green, what will happen
when it is dry?"[g]

32Two other men, both criminals, were also led out with him to
be executed.[h] **33**When they came
to the place called the Skull, there
they crucified him, along with the
criminals—one on his right, the
other on his left. **34**Jesus said, "Father,[i] forgive them, for they do not
know what they are doing."[n][j] And
they divided up his clothes by casting lots.[k]

35The people stood watching,
and the rulers even sneered at
him.[l] They said, "He saved others;
let him save himself if he is the
Christ of God, the Chosen One."[m]

36The soldiers also came up and
mocked him.[n] They offered him
wine vinegar[o] **37**and said, "If you
are the king of the Jews,[p] save
yourself."

38There was a written notice
above him, which read: THIS IS THE
KING OF THE JEWS.[q]

39One of the criminals who hung
there hurled insults at him: "Aren't
you the Christ? Save yourself and
us!"[r]

40But the other criminal rebuked him. "Don't you fear God,"
he said, "since you are under the
same sentence? **41**We are punished
justly, for we are getting what our
deeds deserve. But this man has
done nothing wrong."[s]

42Then he said, "Jesus, remember me when you come into your
kingdom.[o]"[t]

43Jesus answered him, "I tell you
the truth, today you will be with me
in paradise."[u]

Jesus' Death

23:44-49pp — Mt 27:45-56; Mk 15:33-41

44It was now about the sixth
hour, and darkness came over the
whole land until the ninth hour,[v]
45for the sun stopped shining. And
the curtain of the temple[w] was
torn in two.[x] **46**Jesus called out
with a loud voice,[y] "Father, into
your hands I commit my spirit."[z]
When he had said this, he breathed
his last.[a]

47The centurion, seeing what
had happened, praised God[b] and
said, "Surely this was a righteous
man." **48**When all the people who
had gathered to witness this sight
saw what took place, they beat
their breasts[c] and went away.
49But all those who knew him, including the women who had followed him from Galilee,[d] stood at
a distance,[e] watching these
things.

Jesus' Burial

23:50-56pp — Mt 27:57-61; Mk 15:42-47; Jn 19:38-42

50Now there was a man named
Joseph, a member of the Council, a
good and upright man, **51**who had
not consented to their decision and
action. He came from the Judean
town of Arimathea and he was
waiting for the kingdom of God.[f]
52Going to Pilate, he asked for
Jesus' body. **53**Then he took it

23:26 [a]Mt 27:32 [b]Mk 15:21; Jn 19:17
23:27 [c]Lk 8:52
23:28 [d]Lk 19:41-44; 21:23,24
23:29 [e]Mt 24:19
23:30 [f]Hos 10:8; Isa 2:19; Rev 6:16
23:31 [g]Eze 20:47
23:32 [h]Isa 53:12; Mt 27:38; Mk 15:27; Jn 19:18
23:34 [i]Mt 11:25 [j]Mt 5:44 [k]Ps 22:18
23:35 [l]Ps 22:17 [m]Isa 42:1
23:36 [n]Ps 22:7 [o]Ps 69:21; Mt 27:48
23:37 [p]Lk 4:3,9
23:38 [q]Mt 2:2
23:39 [r]ver 35,37
23:41 [s]ver 4
23:42 [t]Mt 16:27
23:43 [u]2Co 12:3,4; Rev 2:7
23:44 [v]Am 8:9
23:45 [w]Ex 26:31-33; Heb 9:3,8 [x]Heb 10:19, 20
23:46 [y]Mt 27:50 [z]Ps 31:5; 1Pe 2:23 [a]Jn 19:30
23:47 [b]Mt 9:8
23:48 [c]Lk 18:13
23:49 [d]Lk 8:2 [e]Ps 38:11
23:51 [f]Lk 2:25,38

m*30* Hosea 10:8 n*34* Some early manuscripts do not have this sentence.
o*42* Some manuscripts *come with your kingly power*

down, wrapped it in linen cloth and placed it in a tomb cut in the rock, one in which no one had yet been laid. **54**It was Preparation Day,[a] and the Sabbath was about to begin.

55The women who had come with Jesus from Galilee[b] followed Joseph and saw the tomb and how his body was laid in it. **56**Then they went home and prepared spices and perfumes.[c] But they rested on the Sabbath in obedience to the commandment.[d]

The Resurrection

24:1–10pp — Mt 28:1–8; Mk 16:1–8; Jn 20:1–8

24 On the first day of the week, very early in the morning, the women took the spices they had prepared[e] and went to the tomb. **2**They found the stone rolled away from the tomb, **3**but when they entered, they did not find the body of the Lord Jesus.[f] **4**While they were wondering about this, suddenly two men in clothes that gleamed like lightning[g] stood beside them. **5**In their fright the women bowed down with their faces to the ground, but the men said to them, "Why do you look for the living among the dead? **6**He is not here; he has risen! Remember how he told you, while he was still with you in Galilee:[h] **7**'The Son of Man[i] must be delivered into the hands of sinful men, be crucified and on the third day be raised again.' "[j] **8**Then they remembered his words.[k]

9When they came back from the tomb, they told all these things to the Eleven and to all the others. **10**It was Mary Magdalene, Joanna, Mary the mother of James, and the others with them[l] who told this to the apostles.[m] **11**But they did not believe[n] the women, because their words seemed to them like nonsense. **12**Peter, however, got up and ran to the tomb. Bending over, he saw the strips of linen lying by themselves,[o] and he went away,[p] wondering to himself what had happened.

On the Road to Emmaus

13Now that same day two of them were going to a village called Emmaus, about seven miles[p] from Jerusalem.[q] **14**They were talking with each other about everything that had happened. **15**As they talked and discussed these things with each other, Jesus himself came up and walked along with them;[r] **16**but they were kept from recognizing him.[s]

17He asked them, "What are you discussing together as you walk along?"

They stood still, their faces downcast. **18**One of them, named Cleopas,[t] asked him, "Are you only a visitor to Jerusalem and do not know the things that have happened there in these days?"

19"What things?" he asked.

"About Jesus of Nazareth,"[u] they replied. "He was a prophet,[v] powerful in word and deed before God and all the people. **20**The chief priests and our rulers[w] handed him over to be sentenced to death, and they crucified him; **21**but we had hoped that he was the one who was going to redeem Israel.[x] And what is more, it is the third day[y] since all this took place. **22**In addition, some of our women amazed us.[z] They went to the tomb early this morning **23**but didn't find his body. They came and told us that they had seen a vision of angels, who said he was alive. **24**Then some of our companions went to the tomb and found it just as the women had said, but him they did not see."[a]

25He said to them, "How foolish you are, and how slow of heart to believe all that the prophets have spoken! **26**Did not the Christ[q] have to suffer these things and then enter his glory?"[b] **27**And beginning with Moses[c] and all the Prophets,[d] he explained to them what was said in all the Scriptures concerning himself.[e]

28As they approached the village to which they were going, Jesus

23:54 [a] Mt 27:62
23:55 [b] ver 49
23:56 [c] Mk 16:1; Lk 24:1 [d] Ex 12:16; 20:10
24:1 [e] Lk 23:56
24:3 [f] ver 23,24
24:4 [g] Jn 20:12
24:6 [h] Mt 17:22,23; Mk 9:30-31; Lk 9:22; 24:44
24:7 [i] Mt 8:20 [j] Mt 16:21
24:8 [k] Jn 2:22
24:10 [l] Lk 8:1-3 [m] Mk 6:30
24:11 [n] Mk 16:11
24:12 [o] Jn 20:3-7 [p] Jn 20:10
24:13 [q] Mk 16:12
24:15 [r] ver 36
24:16 [s] Jn 20:14; 21:4
24:18 [t] Jn 19:25
24:19 [u] Mk 1:24 [v] Mt 21:11
24:20 [w] Lk 23:13
24:21 [x] Lk 1:68; 2:38; 21:28 [y] Mt 16:21
24:22 [z] ver 1-10
24:24 [a] ver 12
24:26 [b] Heb 2:10; 1Pe 1:11
24:27 [c] Ge 3:15; Nu 21:9; Dt 18:15 [d] Isa 7:14; 9:6; 40:10,11; 53; Eze 34:23; Da 9:24; Mic 7:20; Mal 3:1 [e] Jn 1:45

[p] *13* Greek *sixty stadia* (about 11 kilometers)
[q] *26* Or *Messiah*; also in verse 46

RESURRECTION APPEARANCES

Event	Date	Matthew	Mark	Luke	John	Acts	I Corinthians
At the empty tomb outside Jerusalem	Early Sunday morning	28:1-10	16:1-8	24:1-12	20:1-9		
To Mary Magdalene at the tomb	Early Sunday morning		16:9-11		20:11-18		
To two travelers on the road to Emmaus	Sunday at midday		16:12-13	24:13-32			
To Peter in Jerusalem	During the day on Sunday			24:34			15:5
To the ten disciples in the upper room	Sunday evening			24:36-43	20:19-25		
To the eleven disciples in the upper room	One week later		16:14		20:26-31		15:5
To seven disciples fishing on the Sea of Galilee	One day at daybreak				21:1-23		
To the eleven disciples on the mountain in Galilee	Some time later	28:16-20	16:15-18				
To more than 500	Some time later						15:6
To James	Some time later						15:7
At the Ascension on the Mt. of Olives	Forty days after the resurrection			24:44-51		1:3-8	

acted as if he were going farther.
29But they urged him strongly,
"Stay with us, for it is nearly evening; the day is almost over." So he
went in to stay with them.
30When he was at the table with
them, he took bread, gave thanks,
broke it[a] and began to give it to
them. **31**Then their eyes were
opened and they recognized him,[b]
and he disappeared from their
sight. **32**They asked each other,
"Were not our hearts burning within us[c] while he talked with us on
the road and opened the Scriptures[d] to us?"
33They got up and returned at
once to Jerusalem. There they
found the Eleven and those with
them, assembled together **34**and
saying, "It is true! The Lord has ris-
en and has appeared to Simon."[e]
35Then the two told what had happened on the way, and how Jesus
was recognized by them when he
broke the bread.[f]

Jesus Appears to the Disciples

36While they were still talking
about this, Jesus himself stood
among them and said to them,
"Peace be with you."[g]
37They were startled and frightened, thinking they saw a ghost.[h]
38He said to them, "Why are you
troubled, and why do doubts rise in
your minds? **39**Look at my hands
and my feet. It is I myself! Touch
me and see;[i] a ghost does not have
flesh and bones, as you see I have."
40When he had said this, he
showed them his hands and feet.
41And while they still did not believe it because of joy and amazement, he asked them, "Do you have
anything here to eat?" **42**They gave
him a piece of broiled fish, **43**and
he took it and ate it in their presence.[j]
44He said to them, "This is what
I told you while I was still with
you:[k] Everything must be fulfilled[l] that is written about me in
the Law of Moses,[m] the Prophets
and the Psalms."[n]
45Then he opened their minds so
they could understand the Scriptures. **46**He told them, "This is
what is written: The Christ will suffer and rise from the dead on the
third day, **47**and repentance and
forgiveness of sins will be preached
in his name[o] to all nations,[p] beginning at Jerusalem. **48**You are
witnesses[q] of these things. **49**I am
going to send you what my Father
has promised;[r] but stay in the city
until you have been clothed with
power from on high."

The Ascension

50When he had led them out to
the vicinity of Bethany,[s] he lifted
up his hands and blessed them.
51While he was blessing them, he
left them and was taken up into
heaven.[t] **52**Then they worshiped
him and returned to Jerusalem
with great joy. **53**And they stayed
continually at the temple,[u] praising God.

24:30 [a] Mt 14:19
24:31 [b] ver 16
24:32 [c] Ps 39:3 [d] ver 27,45
24:34 [e] 1Co 15:5
24:35 [f] ver 30,31
24:36 [g] Jn 20:19,21, 26; 14:27
24:37 [h] Mk 6:49
24:39 [i] Jn 20:27; 1Jn 1:1
24:43 [j] Ac 10:41
24:44 [k] Lk 9:45; 18:34 [l] Mt 16:21; Lk 9:22,44; 18:31-33; 22:37 [m] ver 27 [n] Ps 2; 16; 22; 69; 72; 110; 118
24:47 [o] Ac 5:31; 10:43; 13:38 [p] Mt 28:19
24:48 [q] Ac 1:8; 2:32; 5:32; 13:31; 1Pe 5:1
24:49 [r] Jn 14:16; Ac 1:4
24:50 [s] Mt 21:17
24:51 [t] 2Ki 2:11
24:53 [u] Ac 2:46

John

Title and Background

The Gospel of John was greatly influenced by the Old Testament. The prologue, with its account of the origin of light and life, is evocative of the Genesis account of creation. Reminders of the Passover also occur frequently in John. His name means "The LORD is gracious."

Author and Date of Writing

The author is the apostle John, "the disciple whom Jesus loved." He knew Jewish life well and referred often to Jewish customs. John's account has many touches that were obviously based on the recollections of an eyewitness. The date of writing was probably about A.D. 85 or a little later.

Theme and Message

The writer states his main purpose clearly in 20:31. He may have had Greek readers mainly in mind, and his primary intention was evangelism. John's purpose is not so much to present new evidence as it is to clarify issues on which the evidence will be either accepted or rejected. He writes not so much to inform the reader as to confront him with the necessity to "believe."

Outline

I. Prologue (1:1-18)
II. Beginnings of Jesus' Ministry (1:19-51)
III. Jesus' Ministry: Signs and Discourses (2:1-11:57)
IV. Passion Week (12:1-19:42)
V. The Resurrection (20:1-29)
VI. Statement of Purpose (20:30-31)
VII. Epilogue (21:1-25)

The Word Became Flesh

1 *In the beginning* was the
Word,[a] and the Word was with
God,[b] and the Word was God.[c]
2He was with God in the beginning.[d]
3Through him all things were
made; without him nothing was
made that has been made.[e] 4In
him was life,[f] and that life was the
light[g] of men. 5The light shines in
the darkness, but the darkness has
not understood[a] it.[h]
6There came a man who was sent
from God; his name was John.[i]
7He came as a witness to testify[j]
concerning that light, so that
through him all men might believe.[k] 8He himself was not the
light; he came only as a witness to
the light. 9The true light[l] that
gives light to every man[m] was coming into the world.[b]
10He was in the world, and
though the world was made
through him,[n] the world did not
recognize him. 11He came to that
which was his own, but his own did
not receive him. 12Yet to all who
received him, to those who believed[o] in his name,[p] he gave the
right to become children of
God[q]— 13children born not of nat-

1:1 [a]Rev 19:13 [b]Jn 17:5; 1Jn 1:2 [c]Php 2:6 **1:2** [d]Ge 1:1 **1:3** [e]1Co 8:6; Col 1:16; Heb 1:2 **1:4** [f]Jn 5:26; 11:25; 14:6 [g]Jn 8:12 **1:5** [h]Jn 3:19 **1:6** [i]Mt 3:1 **1:7** [j]ver 15,19,32 [k]ver 12 **1:9** [l]1Jn 2:8 [m]Isa 49:6 **1:10** [n]Heb 1:2 **1:12** [o]ver 7 [p]1Jn 3:23 [q]Gal 3:26

[a]5 *Or darkness, and the darkness has not overcome* [b]9 Or *This was the true light that gives light to every man who comes into the world*

ural descent,[c] nor of human decision or a husband's will, but born
of God.[a]

14The Word became flesh[b] and
made his dwelling among us. We
have seen his glory, the glory of the
One and Only,[d] who came from
the Father, full of grace and
truth.[c]

15John testifies[d] concerning
him. He cries out, saying, "This
was he of whom I said, 'He who
comes after me has surpassed me
because he was before me.' "[e]
16From the fullness[f] of his grace
we have all received one blessing
after another. 17For the law was
given through Moses;[g] grace and
truth came through Jesus Christ.[h]
18No one has ever seen God,[i] but
God the One and Only,[d,e j] who is
at the Father's side, has made him
known.

John the Baptist Denies Being the Christ

19Now this was John's testimony
when the Jews[k] of Jerusalem sent
priests and Levites to ask him who
he was. 20He did not fail to confess,
but confessed freely, "I am not the
Christ.[f]"[l]

21They asked him, "Then who
are you? Are you Elijah?"[m]

He said, "I am not."

"Are you the Prophet?"[n]

He answered, "No."

22Finally they said, "Who are
you? Give us an answer to take
back to those who sent us. What do
you say about yourself?"

23John replied in the words of
Isaiah the prophet, "I am the voice
of one calling in the desert,[o]
'Make straight the way for the
Lord.' "[g p]

24Now some Pharisees who had
been sent 25questioned him, "Why
then do you baptize if you are not
the Christ, nor Elijah, nor the
Prophet?"

26"I baptize with[h] water," John
replied, "but among you stands
one you do not know. 27He is the
one who comes after me,[q] the
thongs of whose sandals I am not
worthy to untie."

28This all happened at Bethany
on the other side of the Jordan,[r]
where John was baptizing.

Jesus the Lamb of God

29The next day John saw Jesus
coming toward him and said,
"Look, the Lamb of God,[s] who
takes away the sin of the world!
30This is the one I meant when I
said, 'A man who comes after me
has surpassed me because he was
before me.'[t] 31I myself did not
know him, but the reason I came
baptizing with water was that he
might be revealed to Israel."

32Then John gave this testimony: "I saw the Spirit come down
from heaven as a dove and remain
on him.[u] 33I would not have
known him, except that the one
who sent me to baptize with water[v] told me, 'The man on whom
you see the Spirit come down and
remain is he who will baptize with
the Holy Spirit.'[w] 34I have seen and
I testify that this is the Son of
God."[x]

Jesus' First Disciples

1:40–42pp — Mt 4:18–22; Mk 1:16–20; Lk 5:2–11

35The next day John[y] was there
again with two of his disciples.
36When he saw Jesus passing by,
he said, "Look, the Lamb of
God!"[z]

37When the two disciples heard
him say this, they followed Jesus.
38Turning around, Jesus saw them
following and asked, "What do you
want?"

They said, "Rabbi"[a] (which
means Teacher), "where are you
staying?"

39"Come," he replied, "and you
will see."

1:13 [a] Jn 3:6; Jas 1:18; 1Pe 1:23; 1Jn 3:9
1:14 [b] Gal 4:4; Php 2:7,8; 1Ti 3:16; Heb 2:14 [c] Jn 14:6
1:15 [d] ver 7 [e] ver 30; Mt 3:11
1:16 [f] Eph 1:23; Col 1:19
1:17 [g] Jn 7:19 [h] ver 14
1:18 [i] Ex 33:20; Jn 6:46; Col 1:15; 1Ti 6:16 [j] Jn 3:16,18; 1Jn 4:9
1:19 [k] Jn 2:18; 5:10,16; 6:41, 52
1:20 [l] Jn 3:28; Lk 3:15,16
1:21 [m] Mt 11:14 [n] Dt 18:15
1:23 [o] Mt 3:1 [p] Isa 40:3
1:27 [q] ver 15,30
1:28 [r] Jn 3:26; 10:40
1:29 [s] ver 36; Isa 53:7; 1Pe 1:19; Rev 5:6
1:30 [t] ver 15,27
1:32 [u] Mt 3:16; Mk 1:10
1:33 [v] Mk 1:4 [w] Mt 3:11; Mk 1:8
1:34 [x] ver 49; Mt 4:3
1:35 [y] Mt 3:1
1:36 [z] ver 29
1:38 [a] ver 49; Mt 23:7

[c]13 Greek *of bloods* [d]14,18 Or *the Only Begotten* [e]18 Some manuscripts *but the only* (or *only begotten*) *Son* [f]20 Or *Messiah*. "The Christ" (Greek) and "the Messiah" (Hebrew) both mean "the Anointed One"; also in verse 25. [g]23 Isaiah 40:3 [h]26 Or *in*; also in verses 31 and 33

So they went and saw where he was staying, and spent that day with him. It was about the tenth hour.

40Andrew, Simon Peter's brother, was one of the two who heard what John had said and who had followed Jesus. **41**The first thing Andrew did was to find his brother Simon and tell him, "We have found the Messiah" (that is, the Christ).[a] **42**And he brought him to Jesus.

Jesus looked at him and said, "You are Simon son of John. You will be called[b] Cephas" (which, when translated, is Peter[i]).[c]

Jesus Calls Philip and Nathanael

43The next day Jesus decided to leave for Galilee. Finding Philip,[d] he said to him, "Follow me."[e]

44Philip, like Andrew and Peter, was from the town of Bethsaida.[f] **45**Philip found Nathanael[g] and told him, "We have found the one Moses wrote about in the Law,[h] and about whom the prophets also wrote[i]—Jesus of Nazareth,[j] the son of Joseph."[k]

46"Nazareth! Can anything good come from there?"[l] Nathanael asked.

"Come and see," said Philip.

47When Jesus saw Nathanael approaching, he said of him, "Here is a true Israelite,[m] in whom there is nothing false."[n]

48"How do you know me?" Nathanael asked.

Jesus answered, "I saw you while you were still under the fig tree before Philip called you."

49Then Nathanael declared, "Rabbi,[o] you are the Son of God;[p] you are the King of Israel."[q]

50Jesus said, "You believe[j] because I told you I saw you under the fig tree. You shall see greater things than that." **51**He then added, "I tell you[k] the truth, you[k] shall see heaven open,[r] and the angels of God ascending and descending[s] on the Son of Man."[t]

1:41 [a]Jn 4:25
1:42 [b]Ge 17:5,15 [c]Mt 16:18
1:43 [d]Mt 10:3; Jn 6:5-7; 12:21,22; 14:8,9 [e]Mt 4:19
1:44 [f]Mt 11:21; Jn 12:21
1:45 [g]Jn 21:2 [h]Lk 24:27 [i]Lk 24:27 [j]Mt 2:23; Mk 1:24 [k]Lk 3:23
1:46 [l]Jn 7:41,42, 52
1:47 [m]Ro 9:4,6 [n]Ps 32:2
1:49 [o]ver 38; Mt 23:7 [p]ver 34; Mt 4:3 [q]Mt 2:2; 27:42; Jn 12:13
1:51 [r]Mt 3:16 [s]Ge 28:12 [t]Mt 8:20
2:1 [u]Jn 4:46; 21:2 [v]Mt 12:46
2:4 [w]Jn 19:26 [x]Mt 8:29 [y]Mt 26:18; Jn 7:6
2:5 [z]Ge 41:55
2:6 [a]Mk 7:3,4; Jn 3:25
2:9 [b]Jn 4:46
2:11 [c]ver 23; Jn 3:2; 4:48; 6:2,14,26,30; 12:37; 20:30 [d]Jn 1:14 [e]Ex 14:31
2:12 [f]Mt 4:13 [g]Mt 12:46
2:13 [h]Jn 11:55 [i]Dt 16:1-6; Lk 2:41

Jesus Changes Water to Wine

2 On the third day a wedding took place at Cana in Galilee.[u] Jesus' mother[v] was there, **2**and Jesus and his disciples had also been invited to the wedding. **3**When the wine was gone, Jesus' mother said to him, "They have no more wine."

4"Dear woman,[w] why do you involve me?"[x] Jesus replied. "My time[y] has not yet come."

5His mother said to the servants, "Do whatever he tells you."[z]

6Nearby stood six stone water jars, the kind used by the Jews for ceremonial washing,[a] each holding from twenty to thirty gallons.[l]

7Jesus said to the servants, "Fill the jars with water"; so they filled them to the brim.

8Then he told them, "Now draw some out and take it to the master of the banquet."

They did so, **9**and the master of the banquet tasted the water that had been turned into wine.[b] He did not realize where it had come from, though the servants who had drawn the water knew. Then he called the bridegroom aside **10**and said, "Everyone brings out the choice wine first and then the cheaper wine after the guests have had too much to drink; but you have saved the best till now."

11This, the first of his miraculous signs,[c] Jesus performed at Cana in Galilee. He thus revealed his glory,[d] and his disciples put their faith in him.[e]

Jesus Clears the Temple

2:14–16pp — Mt 21:12,13; Mk 11:15–17; Lk 19:45,46

12After this he went down to Capernaum[f] with his mother and brothers[g] and his disciples. There they stayed for a few days.

13When it was almost time for the Jewish Passover,[h] Jesus went up to Jerusalem.[i] **14**In the temple

[i]*42* Both *Cephas* (Aramaic) and *Peter* (Greek) mean *rock*. [j]*50* Or *Do you believe . . . ?* [k]*51* The Greek is plural. [l]*6* Greek *two to three metretes* (probably about 75 to 115 liters)

courts he found men selling cattle,
sheep and doves, and others sitting
at tables exchanging money. 15So
he made a whip out of cords, and
drove all from the temple area,
both sheep and cattle; he scattered
the coins of the money changers
and overturned their tables. 16To
those who sold doves he said, "Get
these out of here! How dare you
turn my Father's house[a] into a
market!"

17His disciples remembered that
it is written: "Zeal for your house
will consume me."[m][b]

18Then the Jews demanded of
him, "What miraculous sign can
you show us to prove your authority
to do all this?"[c]

19Jesus answered them, "Destroy
this temple, and I will raise it
again in three days."[d]

20The Jews replied, "It has taken
forty-six years to build this temple,
and you are going to raise it in
three days?" 21But the temple he
had spoken of was his body.[e] 22After
he was raised from the dead, his
disciples recalled what he had
said.[f] Then they believed the
Scripture and the words that Jesus
had spoken.

23Now while he was in Jerusalem
at the Passover Feast,[g] many
people saw the miraculous signs he
was doing and believed in his
name.[n] 24But Jesus would not entrust
himself to them, for he knew
all men. 25He did not need man's
testimony about man, for he knew
what was in a man.[h]

Jesus Teaches Nicodemus

3 Now there was a man of the
Pharisees named Nicodemus,[i]
a member of the Jewish ruling
council.[j] 2He came to Jesus at
night and said, "Rabbi, we know
you are a teacher who has come
from God. For no one could perform
the miraculous signs[k] you are
doing if God were not with him."[l]

3In reply Jesus declared, "I tell
you the truth, no one can see the
kingdom of God unless he is born
again.[o]"[m]

4"How can a man be born when
he is old?" Nicodemus asked.
"Surely he cannot enter a second
time into his mother's womb to be
born!"

5Jesus answered, "I tell you the
truth, no one can enter the kingdom
of God unless he is born of water
and the Spirit.[n] 6Flesh gives
birth to flesh, but the Spirit[p] gives
birth to spirit.[o] 7You should not be
surprised at my saying, 'You[q] must
be born again.' 8The wind blows
wherever it pleases. You hear its
sound, but you cannot tell where it
comes from or where it is going. So
it is with everyone born of the
Spirit."

9"How can this be?"[p] Nicodemus
asked.

10"You are Israel's teacher,"[q]
said Jesus, "and do you not understand
these things? 11I tell you the
truth, we speak of what we know,[r]
and we testify to what we have
seen, but still you people do not accept
our testimony.[s] 12I have spoken
to you of earthly things and
you do not believe; how then will
you believe if I speak of heavenly
things? 13No one has ever gone
into heaven[t] except the one who
came from heaven[u]—the Son of
Man.[r] 14Just as Moses lifted up
the snake in the desert,[v] so the
Son of Man must be lifted up,[w]
15that everyone who believes[x] in
him may have eternal life.[s]

16"For God so loved[y] the world
that he gave his one and only Son,[t]
that whoever believes in him shall
not perish but have eternal life.[z]
17For God did not send his Son into
the world[a] to condemn the world,
but to save the world through
him.[b] 18Whoever believes in him is
not condemned,[c] but whoever
does not believe stands condemned
already because he has
not believed in the name of God's
one and only Son.[u][d] 19This is the
verdict: Light[e] has come into the

2:16 [a]Lk 2:49
2:17 [b]Ps 69:9
2:18 [c]Mt 12:38
2:19 [d]Mt 26:61; 27:40; Mk 14:58; 15:29
2:21 [e]1Co 6:19
2:22 [f]Lk 24:5-8; Jn 12:16; 14:26
2:23 [g]ver 13
2:25 [h]Mt 9:4; Jn 6:61,64; 13:11
3:1 [i]Jn 7:50; 19:39 [j]Lk 23:13
3:2 [k]Jn 9:16,33 [l]Ac 2:22; 10:38
3:3 [m]Jn 1:13; 1Pe 1:23
3:5 [n]Tit 3:5
3:6 [o]Jn 1:13; 1Co 15:50
3:9 [p]Jn 6:52,60
3:10 [q]Lk 2:46
3:11 [r]Jn 1:18; 7:16,17 [s]ver 32
3:13 [t]Pr 30:4; Ac 2:34; Eph 4:8-10 [u]Jn 6:38,42
3:14 [v]Nu 21:8,9 [w]Jn 8:28; 12:32
3:15 [x]ver 16,36
3:16 [y]Ro 5:8; Eph 2:4; 1Jn 4:9,10 [z]ver 36; Jn 6:29,40; 11:25,26
3:17 [a]Jn 6:29,57; 10:36; 11:42; 17:8,21; 20:21 [b]Jn 12:47; 1Jn 4:14
3:18 [c]Jn 5:24 [d]1Jn 4:9
3:19 [e]Jn 1:4; 8:12

[m]17 Psalm 69:9 [n]23 Or *and believed in him* [o]3 Or *born from above*; also in verse 7 [p]6 Or *but spirit* [q]7 The Greek is plural. [r]13 Some manuscripts *Man, who is in heaven* [s]15 Or *believes may have eternal life in him* [t]16 Or *his only begotten Son* [u]18 Or *God's only begotten Son*

world, but men loved darkness instead of light because their deeds
were evil. **20**Everyone who does evil
hates the light, and will not come
into the light for fear that his deeds
will be exposed.[a] **21**But whoever
lives by the truth comes into the
light, so that it may be seen plainly
that what he has done has been
done through God."[v]

John the Baptist's Testimony About Jesus

22After this, Jesus and his disciples went out into the Judean
countryside, where he spent some
time with them, and baptized.[b]
23Now John also was baptizing at
Aenon near Salim, because there
was plenty of water, and people
were constantly coming to be baptized. **24**(This was before John was
put in prison.)[c] **25**An argument developed between some of John's
disciples and a certain Jew[w] over
the matter of ceremonial washing.[d] **26**They came to John and
said to him, "Rabbi,[e] that man
who was with you on the other side
of the Jordan—the one you testified[f] about—well, he is baptizing,
and everyone is going to him."
27To this John replied, "A man
can receive only what is given him
from heaven. **28**You yourselves can
testify that I said, 'I am not the
Christ[x] but am sent ahead of
him.'[g] **29**The bride belongs to the
bridegroom.[h] The friend who at-
tends the bridegroom waits and listens for him, and is full of joy when
he hears the bridegroom's voice.
That joy is mine, and it is now complete.[i] **30**He must become greater;
I must become less.
31"The one who comes from
above[j] is above all; the one who is
from the earth belongs to the earth,
and speaks as one from the earth.[k]
The one who comes from heaven is
above all. **32**He testifies to what he
has seen and heard,[l] but no one
accepts his testimony.[m] **33**The
man who has accepted it has certi-
fied that God is truthful. **34**For the
one whom God has sent[n] speaks
the words of God, for God[y] gives
the Spirit[o] without limit. **35**The
Father loves the Son and has
placed everything in his hands.[p]
36Whoever believes in the Son has
eternal life,[q] but whoever rejects
the Son will not see life, for God's
wrath remains on him."[z]

Jesus Talks With a Samaritan Woman

4 The Pharisees heard that Jesus
was gaining and baptizing
more disciples than John,[r] **2**although in fact it was not Jesus who
baptized, but his disciples. **3**When
the Lord learned of this, he left Judea[s] and went back once more to
Galilee.
4Now he had to go through Samaria. **5**So he came to a town in Samaria called Sychar, near the plot
of ground Jacob had given to his
son Joseph.[t] **6**Jacob's well was
there, and Jesus, tired as he was
from the journey, sat down by the
well. It was about the sixth hour.
7When a Samaritan woman
came to draw water, Jesus said to
her, "Will you give me a drink?"
8(His disciples had gone into the
town[u] to buy food.)
9The Samaritan woman said to
him, "You are a Jew and I am a Samaritan[v] woman. How can you ask
me for a drink?" (For Jews do not
associate with Samaritans.[a])
10Jesus answered her, "If you
knew the gift of God and who it is
that asks you for a drink, you would
have asked him and he would have
given you living water."[w]
11"Sir," the woman said, "you
have nothing to draw with and the
well is deep. Where can you get this
living water? **12**Are you greater
than our father Jacob, who gave us
the well[x] and drank from it himself, as did also his sons and his
flocks and herds?"
13Jesus answered, "Everyone

3:20 [a]Eph 5:11,13
3:22 [b]Jn 4:2
3:24 [c]Mt 4:12; 14:3
3:25 [d]Jn 2:6
3:26 [e]Mt 23:7 [f]Jn 1:7-
3:28 [g]Jn 1:20,23
3:29 [h]Mt 9:15 [i]Jn 16:24; 17:13; Php 2:2; 1Jn 1:4; 2Jn 12
3:31 [j]ver 13 [k]Jn 8:23; 1Jn 4:5
3:32 [l]Jn 8:26; 15:15 [m]ver 11
3:34 [n]ver 17 [o]Mt 12:18; Lk 4:18; Ac 10:38
3:35 [p]Mt 28:18; Jn 5:20,22; 17:2
3:36 [q]ver 15; Jn 5:24; 6:47
4:1 [r]Jn 3:22,26
4:3 [s]Jn 3:22
4:5 [t]Ge 33:19; 48:22; Jos 24:32
4:8 [u]ver 5,39
4:9 [v]Mt 10:5; Lk 9:52,53
4:10 [w]Isa 44:3; Jer 2:13; Zec 14:8; Jn 7:37,38; Rev 21:6; 22:1,17
4:12 [x]ver 6

[v]*21* Some interpreters end the quotation after verse 15. [w]*25* Some manuscripts *and certain Jews* [x]*28* Or *Messiah* [y]*34* Greek *he* [z]*36* Some interpreters end the quotation after verse 30. [a]*9* Or *do not use dishes Samaritans have used*

who drinks this water will be
thirsty again, **14**but whoever drinks
the water I give him will never
thirst.[a] Indeed, the water I give
him will become in him a spring of
water[b] welling up to eternal
life."[c]
15The woman said to him, "Sir,
give me this water so that I won't
get thirsty[d] and have to keep coming here to draw water."
16He told her, "Go, call your husband and come back."
17"I have no husband," she replied.
Jesus said to her, "You are right
when you say you have no husband. **18**The fact is, you have had
five husbands, and the man you
now have is not your husband.
What you have just said is quite
true."
19"Sir," the woman said, "I can
see that you are a prophet.[e] **20**Our
fathers worshiped on this mountain,[f] but you Jews claim that the
place where we must worship is in
Jerusalem."[g]
21Jesus declared, "Believe me,
woman, a time is coming[h] when
you will worship the Father neither
on this mountain nor in Jerusalem.[i] **22**You Samaritans worship
what you do not know;[j] we worship what we do know, for salvation
is from the Jews.[k] **23**Yet a time is
coming and has now come[l] when
the true worshipers will worship
the Father in spirit[m] and truth, for
they are the kind of worshipers the
Father seeks. **24**God is spirit,[n] and
his worshipers must worship in
spirit and in truth."
25The woman said, "I know that
Messiah" (called Christ)[o] "is coming. When he comes, he will explain everything to us."
26Then Jesus declared, "I who
speak to you am he."[p]

The Disciples Rejoin Jesus

27Just then his disciples returned[q] and were surprised to find
him talking with a woman. But no
one asked, "What do you want?" or
"Why are you talking with her?"
28Then, leaving her water jar, the
woman went back to the town and
said to the people, **29**"Come, see a
man who told me everything I ever
did.[r] Could this be the Christ[b]?"[s]
30They came out of the town and
made their way toward him.
31Meanwhile his disciples urged
him, "Rabbi,[t] eat something."
32But he said to them, "I have
food to eat[u] that you know nothing
about."
33Then his disciples said to each
other, "Could someone have
brought him food?"
34"My food," said Jesus, "is to do
the will[v] of him who sent me and
to finish his work.[w] **35**Do you not
say, 'Four months more and then
the harvest'? I tell you, open your
eyes and look at the fields! They
are ripe for harvest.[x] **36**Even now
the reaper draws his wages, even
now he harvests[y] the crop for eternal life,[z] so that the sower and the
reaper may be glad together.
37Thus the saying 'One sows and
another reaps'[a] is true. **38**I sent
you to reap what you have not
worked for. Others have done the
hard work, and you have reaped the
benefits of their labor."

Many Samaritans Believe

39Many of the Samaritans from
that town[b] believed in him because of the woman's testimony,
"He told me everything I ever
did."[c] **40**So when the Samaritans
came to him, they urged him to
stay with them, and he stayed two
days. **41**And because of his words
many more became believers.
42They said to the woman, "We
no longer believe just because of
what you said; now we have heard
for ourselves, and we know that
this man really is the Savior of the
world."[d]

Jesus Heals the Official's Son

43After the two days[e] he left for
Galilee. **44**(Now Jesus himself had
pointed out that a prophet has no
honor in his own country.)[f]
45When he arrived in Galilee, the

4:14 [a]Jn 6:35 [b]Jn 7:38 [c]Mt 25:46
4:15 [d]Jn 6:34
4:19 [e]Mt 21:11
4:20 [f]Dt 11:29; Jos 8:33 [g]Lk 9:53
4:21 [h]Jn 5:28; 16:2 [i]Mal 1:11; 1Ti 2:8
4:22 [j]2Ki 17:28-41 [k]Isa 2:3; Ro 3:1,2; 9:4, 5
4:23 [l]Jn 5:25; 16:32 [m]Php 3:3
4:24 [n]Php 3:3
4:25 [o]Mt 1:16
4:26 [p]Jn 8:24; 9:35-37
4:27 [q]ver 8
4:29 [r]ver 17,18 [s]Mt 12:23; Jn 7:26,31
4:31 [t]Mt 23:7
4:32 [u]Job 23:12; Mt 4:4; Jn 6:27
4:34 [v]Mt 26:39; Jn 6:38; 17:4; 19:30 [w]Jn 19:30
4:35 [x]Mt 9:37; Lk 10:2
4:36 [y]Ro 1:13 [z]Mt 25:46
4:37 [a]Job 31:8; Mic 6:15
4:39 [b]ver 5 [c]ver 29
4:42 [d]Lk 2:11; 1Jn 4:14
4:43 [e]ver 40
4:44 [f]Mt 13:57; Lk 4:24

[b]29 Or *Messiah*

Galileans welcomed him. They had seen all that he had done in Jerusalem at the Passover Feast,[a] for they also had been there.

46Once more he visited Cana in Galilee, where he had turned the water into wine.[b] And there was a certain royal official whose son lay sick at Capernaum. **47**When this man heard that Jesus had arrived in Galilee from Judea,[c] he went to him and begged him to come and heal his son, who was close to death.

48"Unless you people see miraculous signs and wonders,"[d] Jesus told him, "you will never believe."

49The royal official said, "Sir, come down before my child dies."

50Jesus replied, "You may go. Your son will live."

The man took Jesus at his word and departed. **51**While he was still on the way, his servants met him with the news that his boy was living. **52**When he inquired as to the time when his son got better, they said to him, "The fever left him yesterday at the seventh hour."

53Then the father realized that this was the exact time at which Jesus had said to him, "Your son will live." So he and all his household[e] believed.

54This was the second miraculous sign[f] that Jesus performed, having come from Judea to Galilee.

The Healing at the Pool

5 *Some time later,* Jesus went up to Jerusalem for a feast of the Jews. **2**Now there is in Jerusalem near the Sheep Gate[g] a pool, which in Aramaic[h] is called Bethesda[c] and which is surrounded by five covered colonnades. **3**Here a great number of disabled people used to lie—the blind, the lame, the paralyzed.[d] **5**One who was there had been an invalid for thirty-eight years. **6**When Jesus saw him lying there and learned that he had been in this condition for a long time, he asked him, "Do you want to get well?"

7"Sir," the invalid replied, "I have no one to help me into the pool when the water is stirred. While I am trying to get in, someone else goes down ahead of me."

8Then Jesus said to him, "Get up! Pick up your mat and walk."[i] **9**At once the man was cured; he picked up his mat and walked.

The day on which this took place was a Sabbath,[j] **10**and so the Jews[k] said to the man who had been healed, "It is the Sabbath; the law forbids you to carry your mat."[l]

11But he replied, "The man who made me well said to me, 'Pick up your mat and walk.' "

12So they asked him, "Who is this fellow who told you to pick it up and walk?"

13The man who was healed had no idea who it was, for Jesus had slipped away into the crowd that was there.

14Later Jesus found him at the temple and said to him, "See, you are well again. Stop sinning[m] or something worse may happen to you." **15**The man went away and told the Jews[n] that it was Jesus who had made him well.

Life Through the Son

16So, because Jesus was doing these things on the Sabbath, the Jews persecuted him. **17**Jesus said to them, "My Father is always at his work[o] to this very day, and I, too, am working." **18**For this reason the Jews tried all the harder to kill him;[p] not only was he breaking the Sabbath, but he was even calling God his own Father, making himself equal with God.[q]

19Jesus gave them this answer: "I tell you the truth, the Son can do nothing by himself;[r] he can do only what he sees his Father doing, because whatever the Father does the Son also does. **20**For the Father loves the Son[s] and shows him all

4:45 [a]Jn 2:23
4:46 [b]Jn 2:1-11
4:47 [c]ver 3,54
4:48 [d]Da 4:2,3; Jn 2:11; Ac 2:43; 14:3; Ro 15:19; 2Co 12:12; Heb 2:4
4:53 [e]Ac 11:14
4:54 [f]ver 48; Jn 2:11
5:2 [g]Ne 3:1; 12:39 [h]Jn 19:13,17, 20; 20:16; Ac 21:40; 22:2; 26:14
5:8 [i]Mt 9:5,6; Mk 2:11; Lk 5:24
5:9 [j]Jn 9:14
5:10 [k]ver 16 [l]Ne 13:15-22; Jer 17:21; Mt 12:2
5:14 [m]Mk 2:5; Jn 8:11
5:15 [n]Jn 1:19
5:17 [o]Jn 9:4; 14:10
5:18 [p]Jn 7:1 [q]Jn 10:30,33; 19:7
5:19 [r]ver 30; Jn 8:28
5:20 [s]Jn 3:35

[c]2 Some manuscripts *Bethzatha;* other manuscripts *Bethsaida* [d]3 Some less important manuscripts *paralyzed—and they waited for the moving of the waters.* [4]*From time to time an angel of the Lord would come down and stir up the waters. The first one into the pool after each such disturbance would be cured of whatever disease he had.*

he does. Yes, to your amazement he will show him even greater things than these.[a] **21**For just as the Father raises the dead and gives them life,[b] even so the Son gives life[c] to whom he is pleased to give it. **22**Moreover, the Father judges no one, but has entrusted all judgment to the Son,[d] **23**that all may honor the Son just as they honor the Father. He who does not honor the Son does not honor the Father, who sent him.[e]

24"I tell you the truth, whoever hears my word and believes him who sent me has eternal life and will not be condemned;[f] he has crossed over from death to life.[g] **25**I tell you the truth, a time is coming and has now come[h] when the dead will hear[i] the voice of the Son of God and those who hear will live. **26**For as the Father has life in himself, so he has granted the Son to have life in himself. **27**And he has given him authority to judge[j] because he is the Son of Man.

28"Do not be amazed at this, for a time is coming[k] when all who are in their graves will hear his voice **29**and come out—those who have done good will rise to live, and those who have done evil will rise to be condemned.[l] **30**By myself I can do nothing;[m] I judge only as I hear, and my judgment is just,[n] for I seek not to please myself but him who sent me.[o]

Testimonies About Jesus

31"If I testify about myself, my testimony is not valid.[p] **32**There is another who testifies in my favor,[q] and I know that his testimony about me is valid.

33"You have sent to John and he has testified[r] to the truth. **34**Not that I accept human testimony;[s] but I mention it that you may be saved. **35**John was a lamp that burned and gave light,[t] and you chose for a time to enjoy his light.

36"I have testimony weightier than that of John.[u] For the very work that the Father has given me to finish, and which I am doing,[v] testifies that the Father has sent me.[w] **37**And the Father who sent me has himself testified concerning me.[x] You have never heard his voice nor seen his form,[y] **38**nor does his word dwell in you,[z] for you do not believe the one he sent.[a] **39**You diligently study[e] the Scriptures[b] because you think that by them you possess eternal life. These are the Scriptures that testify about me,[c] **40**yet you refuse to come to me to have life.

41"I do not accept praise from men,[d] **42**but I know you. I know that you do not have the love of God in your hearts. **43**I have come in my Father's name, and you do not accept me; but if someone else comes in his own name, you will accept him. **44**How can you believe if you accept praise from one another, yet make no effort to obtain the praise that comes from the only God[f]?[e]

45"But do not think I will accuse you before the Father. Your accuser is Moses,[f] on whom your hopes are set.[g] **46**If you believed Moses, you would believe me, for he wrote about me.[h] **47**But since you do not believe what he wrote, how are you going to believe what I say?"[i]

Jesus Feeds the Five Thousand

6:1-13pp — Mt 14:13-21; Mk 6:32-44; Lk 9:10-17

6 Some time after this, Jesus crossed to the far shore of the Sea of Galilee (that is, the Sea of Tiberias), **2**and a great crowd of people followed him because they saw the miraculous signs[j] he had performed on the sick. **3**Then Jesus went up on a mountainside[k] and sat down with his disciples. **4**The Jewish Passover Feast[l] was near.

5When Jesus looked up and saw a great crowd coming toward him, he said to Philip,[m] "Where shall we buy bread for these people to eat?" **6**He asked this only to test him, for

5:20 [a]Jn 14:12 **5:21** [b]Ro 4:17; 8:11 [c]Jn 11:25 **5:22** [d]ver 27; Jn 9:39; Ac 10:42; 17:31 **5:23** [e]Lk 10:16; 1Jn 2:23 **5:24** [f]Jn 3:18 [g]1Jn 3:14 **5:25** [h]Jn 4:23 [i]Jn 8:43,47 **5:27** [j]ver 22; Ac 10:42; 17:31 **5:28** [k]Jn 4:21 **5:29** [l]Da 12:2; Mt 25:46 **5:30** [m]ver 19 [n]Jn 8:16 [o]Mt 26:39; Jn 4:34; 6:38 **5:31** [p]Jn 8:14 **5:32** [q]ver 37; Jn 8:18 **5:33** [r]Jn 1:7 **5:34** [s]1Jn 5:9 **5:35** [t]2Pe 1:19 **5:36** [u]1Jn 5:9 [v]Jn 14:11; 15:24 [w]Jn 3:17; 10:25 **5:37** [x]Jn 8:18 [y]Dt 4:12; 1Ti 1:17; Jn 1:18 **5:38** [z]1Jn 2:14 [a]Jn 3:17 **5:39** [b]Ro 2:17,18 [c]Lk 24:27,44; Ac 13:27 **5:41** [d]ver 44 **5:44** [e]Ro 2:29 **5:45** [f]Jn 9:28 [g]Ro 2:17 **5:46** [h]Ge 3:15; Lk 24:27,44; Ac 26:22 **5:47** [i]Lk 16:29,31 **6:2** [j]Jn 2:11 **6:3** [k]ver 15 **6:4** [l]Jn 2:13; 11:55 **6:5** [m]Jn 1:43

e39 Or *Study diligently* (the imperative)
f44 Some early manuscripts *the Only One*

he already had in mind what he was
going to do.
7Philip answered him, "Eight
months' wages[g] would not buy
enough bread for each one to have
a bite!"
8Another of his disciples, Andrew, Simon Peter's brother,[a]
spoke up, **9**"Here is a boy with five
small barley loaves and two small
fish, but how far will they go among
so many?"[b]
10Jesus said, "Have the people
sit down." There was plenty of
grass in that place, and the men sat
down, about five thousand of them.
11Jesus then took the loaves, gave
thanks,[c] and distributed to those
who were seated as much as they
wanted. He did the same with the
fish.
12When they had all had enough
to eat, he said to his disciples,
"Gather the pieces that are left
over. Let nothing be wasted." **13**So
they gathered them and filled
twelve baskets with the pieces of
the five barley loaves left over by
those who had eaten.
14After the people saw the miraculous sign[d] that Jesus did, they
began to say, "Surely this is the
Prophet who is to come into the
world."[e] **15**Jesus, knowing that
they intended to come and make
him king[f] by force, withdrew again
to a mountain by himself.[g]

Jesus Walks on the Water

6:16–21pp — Mt 14:22–33; Mk 6:47–51

16When evening came, his disciples went down to the lake,
17where they got into a boat and
set off across the lake for Capernaum. By now it was dark, and Jesus
had not yet joined them. **18**A strong
wind was blowing and the waters
grew rough. **19**When they had
rowed three or three and a half
miles,[h] they saw Jesus approaching the boat, walking on the water;[h] and they were terrified. **20**But
he said to them, "It is I; don't be
afraid."[i] **21**Then they were willing
to take him into the boat, and immediately the boat reached the
shore where they were heading.
22The next day the crowd that
had stayed on the opposite shore of
the lake[j] realized that only one
boat had been there, and that
Jesus had not entered it with his
disciples, but that they had gone
away alone.[k] **23**Then some boats
from Tiberias[l] landed near the
place where the people had eaten
the bread after the Lord had given
thanks.[m] **24**Once the crowd realized that neither Jesus nor his disciples were there, they got into the
boats and went to Capernaum in
search of Jesus.

Jesus the Bread of Life

25When they found him on the
other side of the lake, they asked
him, "Rabbi,[n] when did you get
here?"
26Jesus answered, "I tell you the
truth, you are looking for me,[o] not
because you saw miraculous
signs[p] but because you ate the
loaves and had your fill. **27**Do not
work for food that spoils, but for
food that endures[q] to eternal
life,[r] which the Son of Man[s] will
give you. On him God the Father
has placed his seal[t] of approval."
28Then they asked him, "What
must we do to do the works God
requires?"
29Jesus answered, "The work of
God is this: to believe[u] in the one
he has sent."[v]
30So they asked him, "What miraculous sign[w] then will you give
that we may see it and believe
you?[x] What will you do? **31**Our
forefathers ate the manna[y] in the
desert; as it is written: 'He gave
them bread from heaven to
eat.'[i]"[z]
32Jesus said to them, "I tell you
the truth, it is not Moses who has
given you the bread from heaven,
but it is my Father who gives you
the true bread from heaven. **33**For
the bread of God is he who comes

6:8 [a]Jn 1:40
6:9 [b]2Ki 4:43
6:11 [c]ver 23; Mt 14:19
6:14 [d]Jn 2:11 [e]Dt 18:15,18; Mt 11:3; 21:11
6:15 [f]Jn 18:36 [g]Mt 14:23; Mk 6:46
6:19 [h]Job 9:8
6:20 [i]Mt 14:27
6:22 [j]ver 2 [k]ver 15-21
6:23 [l]ver 1 [m]ver 11
6:25 [n]Mt 23:7
6:26 [o]ver 24 [p]ver 30; Jn 2:11
6:27 [q]Isa 55:2 [r]ver 54; Mt 25:46; Jn 4:14 [s]Mt 8:20 [t]Ro 4:11; 1Co 9:2; 2Co 1:22; Eph 1:13; 4:30; 2Ti 2:19; Rev 7:3
6:29 [u]1Jn 3:23 [v]Jn 3:17
6:30 [w]Jn 2:11 [x]Mt 12:38
6:31 [y]Nu 11:7-9 [z]Ex 16:4,15; Ne 9:15; Ps 78:24; 105:40

[g]7 Greek *two hundred denarii* [h]19 Greek *rowed twenty-five or thirty stadia* (about 5 or 6 kilometers) [i]31 Exodus 16:4; Neh. 9:15; Psalm 78:24,25

down from heaven[a] and gives life
to the world."
34"Sir," they said, "from now on
give us this bread."[b]
35Then Jesus declared, "I am the
bread of life.[c] He who comes to me
will never go hungry, and he who
believes in me will never be
thirsty.[d] **36**But as I told you, you
have seen me and still you do not
believe. **37**All that the Father gives
me[e] will come to me, and whoever
comes to me I will never drive
away. **38**For I have come down from
heaven not to do my will but to do
the will of him who sent me.[f]
39And this is the will of him who
sent me, that I shall lose none of all
that he has given me,[g] but raise
them up at the last day.[h] **40**For my
Father's will is that everyone who
looks to the Son and believes in
him shall have eternal life,[i] and I
will raise him up at the last day."
41At this the Jews began to
grumble about him because he
said, "I am the bread that came
down from heaven." **42**They said,
"Is this not Jesus, the son of Joseph,[j] whose father and mother
we know?[k] How can he now say, 'I
came down from heaven'?"[l]
43"Stop grumbling among yourselves," Jesus answered. **44**"No one
can come to me unless the Father
who sent me draws him,[m] and I will
raise him up at the last day. **45**It is
written in the Prophets: 'They will
all be taught by God.'[i][n] Everyone
who listens to the Father and
learns from him comes to me. **46**No
one has seen the Father except the
one who is from God;[o] only he has
seen the Father. **47**I tell you the
truth, he who believes has everlasting life. **48**I am the bread of life.[p]
49Your forefathers ate the manna
in the desert, yet they died.[q] **50**But
here is the bread that comes down
from heaven,[r] which a man may
eat and not die. **51**I am the living
bread that came down from heav-
en. If anyone eats of this bread, he
will live forever. This bread is my
flesh, which I will give for the life of
the world."[s]
52Then the Jews began to argue
sharply among themselves,[t] "How
can this man give us his flesh to
eat?"
53Jesus said to them, "I tell you
the truth, unless you eat the flesh
of the Son of Man[u] and drink his
blood, you have no life in you.
54Whoever eats my flesh and
drinks my blood has eternal life,
and I will raise him up at the last
day.[v] **55**For my flesh is real food
and my blood is real drink. **56**Whoever eats my flesh and drinks my
blood remains in me, and I in
him.[w] **57**Just as the living Father
sent me[x] and I live because of the
Father, so the one who feeds on me
will live because of me. **58**This is
the bread that came down from
heaven. Your forefathers ate manna and died, but he who feeds on
this bread will live forever."[y] **59**He
said this while teaching in the synagogue in Capernaum.

Many Disciples Desert Jesus

60On hearing it, many of his disciples[z] said, "This is a hard teaching. Who can accept it?"
61Aware that his disciples were
grumbling about this, Jesus said to
them, "Does this offend you?[a]
62What if you see the Son of Man
ascend to where he was before![b]
63The Spirit gives life;[c] the flesh
counts for nothing. The words I
have spoken to you are spirit[k] and
they are life. **64**Yet there are some
of you who do not believe." For
Jesus had known[d] from the beginning which of them did not believe
and who would betray him. **65**He
went on to say, "This is why I told
you that no one can come to me
unless the Father has enabled
him."[e]
66From this time many of his disciples[f] turned back and no longer
followed him.
67"You do not want to leave too,
do you?" Jesus asked the Twelve.[g]
68Simon Peter answered him,[h]
"Lord, to whom shall we go? You
have the words of eternal life. **69**We

6:33 [a]ver 50
6:34 [b]Jn 4:15
6:35 [c]ver 48,51 [d]Jn 4:14
6:37 [e]ver 39; Jn 17:2,6,9,24
6:38 [f]Jn 4:34; 5:30
6:39 [g]Jn 10:28; 17:12; 18:9 [h]ver 40,44,54
6:40 [i]Jn 3:15,16
6:42 [j]Lk 4:22 [k]Jn 7:27,28 [l]ver 38,62
6:44 [m]ver 65; Jer 31:3; Jn 12:32
6:45 [n]Isa 54:13; Jer 31:33,34; Heb 8:10,11; 10:16
6:46 [o]Jn 1:18; 5:37; 7:29
6:48 [p]ver 35,51
6:49 [q]ver 31,58
6:50 [r]ver 33
6:51 [s]Heb 10:10
6:52 [t]Jn 7:43; 9:16; 10:19
6:53 [u]Mt 8:20
6:54 [v]ver 39
6:56 [w]Jn 15:4-7; 1Jn 3:24; 4:15
6:57 [x]Jn 3:17
6:58 [y]ver 49-51; Jn 3:36
6:60 [z]ver 66
6:61 [a]Mt 11:6
6:62 [b]Mk 16:19; Jn 3:13; 17:5
6:63 [c]2Co 3:6
6:64 [d]Jn 2:25
6:65 [e]ver 37,44
6:66 [f]ver 60
6:67 [g]Mt 10:2
6:68 [h]Mt 16:16

[i]*45* Isaiah 54:13 [k]*63* Or *Spirit*

believe and know that you are the
Holy One of God."[a]

70Then Jesus replied, "Have I
not chosen you,[b] the Twelve? Yet
one of you is a devil!"[c] **71**(He
meant Judas, the son of Simon Iscariot, who, though one of the
Twelve, was later to betray him.)

Jesus Goes to the Feast of Tabernacles

7 After this, Jesus went around
in Galilee, purposely staying
away from Judea because the
Jews[d] there were waiting to take
his life.[e] **2**But when the Jewish
Feast of Tabernacles[f] was near,
3Jesus' brothers[g] said to him,
"You ought to leave here and go to
Judea, so that your disciples may
see the miracles you do. **4**No one
who wants to become a public figure acts in secret. Since you are doing these things, show yourself to
the world." **5**For even his own
brothers did not believe in him.[h]

6Therefore Jesus told them,
"The right time[i] for me has not yet
come; for you any time is right.
7The world cannot hate you, but it
hates me[j] because I testify that
what it does is evil.[k] **8**You go to the
Feast. I am not yet[l] going up to
this Feast, because for me the right
time[l] has not yet come." **9**Having
said this, he stayed in Galilee.

10However, after his brothers
had left for the Feast, he went also,
not publicly, but in secret. **11**Now
at the Feast the Jews were watching for him[m] and asking, "Where is
that man?"

12Among the crowds there was
widespread whispering about him.
Some said, "He is a good man."

Others replied, "No, he deceives
the people."[n] **13**But no one would
say anything publicly about him for
fear of the Jews.[o]

Jesus Teaches at the Feast

14Not until halfway through the
Feast did Jesus go up to the temple
courts and begin to teach.[p] **15**The
Jews[q] were amazed and asked,
"How did this man get such learn-
ing[r] without having studied?"[s]

16Jesus answered, "My teaching
is not my own. It comes from him
who sent me.[t] **17**If anyone chooses
to do God's will, he will find out[u]
whether my teaching comes from
God or whether I speak on my own.
18He who speaks on his own does
so to gain honor for himself,[v] but
he who works for the honor of the
one who sent him is a man of truth;
there is nothing false about him.
19Has not Moses given you the
law?[w] Yet not one of you keeps the
law. Why are you trying to kill
me?"[x]

20"You are demon-possessed,"[y]
the crowd answered. "Who is trying
to kill you?"

21Jesus said to them, "I did one
miracle, and you are all astonished.
22Yet, because Moses gave you circumcision[z] (though actually it did
not come from Moses, but from the
patriarchs),[a] you circumcise a
child on the Sabbath. **23**Now if a
child can be circumcised on the
Sabbath so that the law of Moses
may not be broken, why are you angry with me for healing the whole
man on the Sabbath? **24**Stop judging by mere appearances, and
make a right judgment."[b]

Is Jesus the Christ?

25At that point some of the people of Jerusalem began to ask,
"Isn't this the man they are trying
to kill? **26**Here he is, speaking publicly, and they are not saying a word
to him. Have the authorities[c]
really concluded that he is the
Christ[m]? **27**But we know where this
man is from;[d] when the Christ
comes, no one will know where he
is from."

28Then Jesus, still teaching in
the temple courts,[e] cried out,
"Yes, you know me, and you know
where I am from.[f] I am not here on
my own, but he who sent me is
true.[g] You do not know him, **29**but

l8 Some early manuscripts do not have *yet.*
m26 Or *Messiah*; also in verses 27, 31, 41 and 42

6:69 [a]Mk 8:29; Lk 9:20
6:70 [b]Jn 15:16,19 [c]Jn 13:27
7:1 [d]Jn 1:19 [e]Jn 5:18
7:2 [f]Lev 23:34; Dt 16:16
7:3 [g]Mt 12:46
7:5 [h]Mk 3:21
7:6 [i]Mt 26:18
7:7 [j]Jn 15:18,19 [k]Jn 3:19,20
7:8 [l]ver 6
7:11 [m]Jn 11:56
7:12 [n]ver 40,43
7:13 [o]Jn 9:22; 12:42; 19:38
7:14 [p]ver 28; Mt 26:55
7:15 [q]Jn 1:19 [r]Ac 26:24 [s]Mt 13:54
7:16 [t]Jn 3:11; 14:24
7:17 [u]Ps 25:14; Jn 8:43
7:18 [v]Jn 5:41; 8:50,54
7:19 [w]Jn 1:17 [x]ver 1; Mt 12:14
7:20 [y]Jn 8:48; 10:20
7:22 [z]Lev 12:3 [a]Ge 17:10-14
7:24 [b]Isa 11:3,4; Jn 8:15
7:26 [c]ver 48
7:27 [d]Mt 13:55; Lk 4:22
7:28 [e]ver 14 [f]Jn 8:14 [g]Jn 8:26,42

I know him[a] because I am from
him and he sent me."
30At this they tried to seize him,
but no one laid a hand on him,[b]
because his time had not yet come.
31Still, many in the crowd put their
faith in him.[c] They said, "When
the Christ comes, will he do more
miraculous signs[d] than this man?"
32The Pharisees heard the crowd
whispering such things about him.
Then the chief priests and the
Pharisees sent temple guards to arrest him.
33Jesus said, "I am with you for
only a short time,[e] and then I go to
the one who sent me.[f] **34**You will
look for me, but you will not find
me; and where I am, you cannot
come."[g]
35The Jews said to one another,
"Where does this man intend to go
that we cannot find him? Will he go
where our people live scattered[h]
among the Greeks,[i] and teach the
Greeks? **36**What did he mean when
he said, 'You will look for me, but
you will not find me,' and 'Where I
am, you cannot come'?"
37On the last and greatest day of
the Feast,[j] Jesus stood and said in
a loud voice, "If anyone is thirsty,
let him come to me and drink.[k]
38Whoever believes in me, as[n] the
Scripture has said,[l] streams of living water[m] will flow from within
him."[n] **39**By this he meant the
Spirit,[o] whom those who believed
in him were later to receive.[p] Up to
that time the Spirit had not been
given, since Jesus had not yet been
glorified.[q]
40On hearing his words, some of
the people said, "Surely this man is
the Prophet."[r]
41Others said, "He is the Christ."
Still others asked, "How can the
Christ come from Galilee?[s]
42Does not the Scripture say that
the Christ will come from David's
family[o][t] and from Bethlehem,[u]
the town where David lived?"
43Thus the people were divided[v]
because of Jesus. **44**Some wanted
to seize him, but no one laid a hand
on him.[w]

Unbelief of the Jewish Leaders

45Finally the temple guards
went back to the chief priests and
Pharisees, who asked them, "Why
didn't you bring him in?"
46"No one ever spoke the way
this man does,"[x] the guards declared.
47"You mean he has deceived
you also?"[y] the Pharisees retorted.
48"Has any of the rulers or of the
Pharisees believed in him?[z] **49**No!
But this mob that knows nothing of
the law—there is a curse on them."
50Nicodemus,[a] who had gone to
Jesus earlier and who was one of
their own number, asked, **51**"Does
our law condemn anyone without
first hearing him to find out what
he is doing?"
52They replied, "Are you from
Galilee, too? Look into it, and you
will find that a prophet[p] does not
come out of Galilee."[b]

[The earliest manuscripts and many other ancient witnesses do not have John 7:53–8:11.]

53Then each went to his own
home.
8 But Jesus went to the Mount of
Olives.[c] **2**At dawn he appeared
again in the temple courts, where
all the people gathered around
him, and he sat down to teach
them.[d] **3**The teachers of the law
and the Pharisees brought in a
woman caught in adultery. They
made her stand before the group
4and said to Jesus, "Teacher, this
woman was caught in the act of
adultery. **5**In the Law Moses commanded us to stone such women.[e]
Now what do you say?" **6**They were
using this question as a trap,[f] in
order to have a basis for accusing
him.[g]
But Jesus bent down and started
to write on the ground with his fin-

7:29 [a]Mt 11:27
7:30 [b]ver 32,44; Jn 10:39
7:31 [c]Jn 8:30 [d]Jn 2:11
7:33 [e]Jn 13:33; 16:16 [f]Jn 16:5,10, 17,28
7:34 [g]Jn 8:21; 13:33
7:35 [h]Jas 1:1 [i]Jn 12:20; 1Pe 1:1
7:37 [j]Lev 23:36 [k]Isa 55:1; Rev 22:17
7:38 [l]Isa 58:11 [m]Jn 4:10 [n]Jn 4:14
7:39 [o]Joel 2:28; Ac 2:17,33 [p]Jn 20:22 [q]Jn 12:23; 13:31,32
7:40 [r]Mt 21:11; Jn 1:21
7:41 [s]ver 52; Jn 1:46
7:42 [t]Mt 1:1 [u]Mic 5:2; Mt 2:5,6; Lk 2:4
7:43 [v]Jn 9:16; 10:19
7:44 [w]ver 30
7:46 [x]Mt 7:28
7:47 [y]ver 12
7:48 [z]Jn 12:42
7:50 [a]Jn 3:1; 19:39
7:52 [b]ver 41
8:1 [c]Mt 21:1
8:2 [d]ver 20; Mt 26:55
8:5 [e]Lev 20:10; Dt 22:22
8:6 [f]Mt 22:15,18 [g]Mt 12:10

[n]37,38 Or / *If anyone is thirsty, let him come to me. / And let him drink,* [38]*who believes in me. / As* [o]42 Greek *seed* [p]52 Two early manuscripts *the Prophet*

ger. 7When they kept on question-
ing him, he straightened up and
said to them, "If any one of you is
without sin, let him be the first to
throw a stone[a] at her."[b] 8Again he
stooped down and wrote on the
ground.
9At this, those who heard began
to go away one at a time, the older
ones first, until only Jesus was left,
with the woman still standing
there. 10Jesus straightened up and
asked her, "Woman, where are
they? Has no one condemned
you?"
11"No one, sir," she said.
"Then neither do I condemn
you,"[c] Jesus declared. "Go now
and leave your life of sin."[d]

The Validity of Jesus' Testimony

12When Jesus spoke again to the
people, he said, "I am[e] the light of
the world.[f] Whoever follows me
will never walk in darkness, but
will have the light of life."[g]
13The Pharisees challenged him,
"Here you are, appearing as your
own witness; your testimony is not
valid."[h]
14Jesus answered, "Even if I testify on my own behalf, my testimony is valid, for I know where I came
from and where I am going.[i] But
you have no idea where I come
from[j] or where I am going. 15You
judge by human standards;[k] I pass
judgment on no one.[l] 16But if I do
judge, my decisions are right, because I am not alone. I stand with
the Father, who sent me.[m] 17In
your own Law it is written that the
testimony of two men is valid.[n] 18I
am one who testifies for myself; my
other witness is the Father, who
sent me."[o]
19Then they asked him, "Where
is your father?"
"You do not know me or my Father,"[p] Jesus replied. "If you knew
me, you would know my Father
also."[q] 20He spoke these words
while teaching[r] in the temple area
near the place where the offerings
were put.[s] Yet no one seized him,
because his time had not yet
come.[t]
21Once more Jesus said to them,
"I am going away, and you will look
for me, and you will die[u] in your
sin. Where I go, you cannot
come."[v]
22This made the Jews ask, "Will
he kill himself? Is that why he says,
'Where I go, you cannot come'?"
23But he continued, "You are
from below; I am from above. You
are of this world; I am not of this
world.[w] 24I told you that you would
die in your sins; if you do not believe that I am ⌊the one I claim to
be⌋,[q][x] you will indeed die in your
sins."
25"Who are you?" they asked.
"Just what I have been claiming
all along," Jesus replied. 26"I have
much to say in judgment of you.
But he who sent me is reliable,[y]
and what I have heard from him I
tell the world."[z]
27They did not understand that
he was telling them about his Father. 28So Jesus said, "When you
have lifted up the Son of Man,[a]
then you will know that I am ⌊the
one I claim to be⌋ and that I do
nothing on my own but speak just
what the Father has taught me.
29The one who sent me is with me;
he has not left me alone,[b] for I always do what pleases him."[c]
30Even as he spoke, many put their
faith in him.[d]

The Children of Abraham

31To the Jews who had believed
him, Jesus said, "If you hold to my
teaching,[e] you are really my disciples. 32Then you will know the
truth, and the truth will set you
free."[f]
33They answered him, "We are
Abraham's descendants[r][g] and
have never been slaves of anyone.
How can you say that we shall be
set free?"
34Jesus replied, "I tell you the

8:7 [a]Dt 17:7 [b]Ro 2:1,22
8:11 [c]Jn 3:17 [d]Jn 5:14
8:12 [e]Jn 6:35 [f]Jn 1:4; 12:35 [g]Pr 4:18; Mt 5:14
8:13 [h]Jn 5:31
8:14 [i]Jn 13:3; 16:28 [j]Jn 7:28; 9:29
8:15 [k]Jn 7:24 [l]Jn 3:17
8:16 [m]Jn 5:30
8:17 [n]Dt 17:6; Mt 18:16
8:18 [o]Jn 5:37
8:19 [p]Jn 16:3 [q]Jn 14:7; 1Jn 2:23
8:20 [r]Mt 26:55 [s]Mk 12:41 [t]Mt 26:18; Jn 7:30
8:21 [u]Eze 3:18 [v]Jn 7:34; 13:33
8:23 [w]Jn 3:31; 17:14
8:24 [x]Jn 4:26; 13:19
8:26 [y]Jn 7:28 [z]Jn 3:32; 15:15
8:28 [a]Jn 3:14; 5:19; 12:32
8:29 [b]ver 16; Jn 16:32 [c]Jn 4:34; 5:30; 6:38
8:30 [d]Jn 7:31
8:31 [e]Jn 15:7; 2Jn 9
8:32 [f]Ro 8:2; Jas 2:12
8:33 [g]ver 37,39; Mt 3:9

[q]24 Or *I am he*; also in verse 28 [r]33 Greek *seed*; also in verse 37

truth, everyone who sins is a slave
to sin.[a] 35Now a slave has no permanent place in the family, but a
son belongs to it forever.[b] 36So if
the Son sets you free, you will be
free indeed. 37I know you are Abraham's descendants. Yet you are
ready to kill me,[c] because you
have no room for my word. 38I am
telling you what I have seen in the
Father's presence,[d] and you do
what you have heard from your father.[s]"

39"Abraham is our father," they
answered.

"If you were Abraham's children,"[e] said Jesus, "then you
would[t] do the things Abraham
did. 40As it is, you are determined
to kill me, a man who has told you
the truth that I heard from God.[f]
Abraham did not do such things.
41You are doing the things your
own father does."[g]

"We are not illegitimate children," they protested. "The only
Father we have is God himself."[h]

The Children of the Devil

42Jesus said to them, "If God
were your Father, you would love
me,[i] for I came from God[j] and
now am here. I have not come on
my own;[k] but he sent me.[l] 43Why
is my language not clear to you?
Because you are unable to hear
what I say. 44You belong to your father, the devil,[m] and you want to
carry out your father's desire.[n] He
was a murderer from the beginning, not holding to the truth, for
there is no truth in him. When he
lies, he speaks his native language,
for he is a liar and the father of
lies.[o] 45Yet because I tell the
truth,[p] you do not believe me!
46Can any of you prove me guilty of
sin? If I am telling the truth, why
don't you believe me? 47He who
belongs to God hears what God
says.[q] The reason you do not hear
is that you do not belong to God."

The Claims of Jesus About Himself

48The Jews answered him,

8:34 [a]Ro 6:16; 2Pe 2:19
8:35 [b]Gal 4:30
8:37 [c]ver 39,40
8:38 [d]Jn 5:19,30; 14:10,24
8:39 [e]ver 37; Ro 9:7; Gal 3:7
8:40 [f]ver 26
8:41 [g]ver 38,44 [h]Isa 63:16; 64:8
8:42 [i]1Jn 5:1 [j]Jn 16:27; 17:8 [k]Jn 7:28 [l]Jn 3:17
8:44 [m]1Jn 3:8 [n]ver 38,41 [o]Ge 3:4
8:45 [p]Jn 18:37
8:47 [q]Jn 18:37; 1Jn 4:6
8:48 [r]Mt 10:5 [s]ver 52; Jn 7:20
8:50 [t]ver 54; Jn 5:41
8:51 [u]Jn 11:26
8:53 [v]Jn 4:12
8:54 [w]ver 50 [x]Jn 16:14; 17:1,5
8:55 [y]ver 19 [z]Jn 7:28,29 [a]Jn 15:10
8:56 [b]ver 37,39 [c]Mt 13:17; Heb 11:13
8:58 [d]Jn 1:2; 17:5, 24 [e]Ex 3:14
8:59 [f]Lev 24:16; Jn 10:31; 11:8 [g]Jn 12:36
9:2 [h]Mt 23:7 [i]ver 34; Lk 13:2; Ac 28:4 [j]Eze 18:20 [k]Ex 20:5; Job 21:19
9:3 [l]Jn 11:4

"Aren't we right in saying that you
are a Samaritan[r] and demon-possessed?"[s]

49"I am not possessed by a demon," said Jesus, "but I honor my
Father and you dishonor me. 50I
am not seeking glory for myself;[t]
but there is one who seeks it, and
he is the judge. 51I tell you the
truth, if anyone keeps my word, he
will never see death."[u]

52At this the Jews exclaimed,
"Now we know that you are demon-possessed! Abraham died and
so did the prophets, yet you say
that if anyone keeps your word, he
will never taste death. 53Are you
greater than our father Abraham?[v]
He died, and so did the prophets.
Who do you think you are?"

54Jesus replied, "If I glorify myself,[w] my glory means nothing. My
Father, whom you claim as your
God, is the one who glorifies me.[x]
55Though you do not know him,[y] I
know him.[z] If I said I did not, I
would be a liar like you, but I do
know him and keep his word.[a]
56Your father Abraham[b] rejoiced
at the thought of seeing my day; he
saw it[c] and was glad."

57"You are not yet fifty years
old," the Jews said to him, "and
you have seen Abraham!"

58"I tell you the truth," Jesus answered, "before Abraham was
born,[d] I am!"[e] 59At this, they
picked up stones to stone him,[f]
but Jesus hid himself,[g] slipping
away from the temple grounds.

Jesus Heals a Man Born Blind

9 As he went along, he saw a
man blind from birth. 2His disciples asked him, "Rabbi,[h] who
sinned,[i] this man[j] or his parents,[k] that he was born blind?"

3"Neither this man nor his parents sinned," said Jesus, "but this
happened so that the work of God
might be displayed in his life.[l] 4As

[s]38 Or *presence. Therefore do what you have heard from the Father.* [t]39 Some early manuscripts *"If you are Abraham's children," said Jesus, "then*

long as it is day,[a] we must do the
work of him who sent me. Night is
coming, when no one can work.
5While I am in the world, I am the
light of the world."[b]
6Having said this, he spit[c] on
the ground, made some mud with
the saliva, and put it on the man's
eyes. **7**"Go," he told him, "wash in
the Pool of Siloam"[d] (this word
means Sent). So the man went and
washed, and came home seeing.[e]
8His neighbors and those who
had formerly seen him begging
asked, "Isn't this the same man
who used to sit and beg?"[f] **9**Some
claimed that he was.
Others said, "No, he only looks
like him."
But he himself insisted, "I am
the man."
10"How then were your eyes
opened?" they demanded.
11He replied, "The man they call
Jesus made some mud and put it
on my eyes. He told me to go to
Siloam and wash. So I went and
washed, and then I could see."[g]
12"Where is this man?" they
asked him.
"I don't know," he said.

The Pharisees Investigate the Healing

13They brought to the Pharisees
the man who had been blind.
14Now the day on which Jesus had
made the mud and opened the
man's eyes was a Sabbath.[h]
15Therefore the Pharisees also
asked him how he had received his
sight.[i] "He put mud on my eyes,"
the man replied, "and I washed,
and now I see."
16Some of the Pharisees said,
"This man is not from God, for he
does not keep the Sabbath."[j]
But others asked, "How can a
sinner do such miraculous signs?"
So they were divided.[k]
17Finally they turned again to
the blind man, "What have you to
say about him? It was your eyes he
opened."
The man replied, "He is a prophet."[l]

9:4 [a]Jn 11:9; 12:35
9:5 [b]Jn 1:4; 8:12; 12:46
9:6 [c]Mk 7:33; 8:23
9:7 [d]ver 11; 2Ki 5:10; Lk 13:4 [e]Isa 35:5; Jn 11:37
9:8 [f]Ac 3:2,10
9:11 [g]ver 7
9:14 [h]Jn 5:9
9:15 [i]ver 10
9:16 [j]Mt 12:2 [k]Jn 6:52; 7:43; 10:19
9:17 [l]Mt 21:11
9:18 [m]Jn 1:19
9:22 [n]Jn 7:13 [o]ver 34; Lk 6:22 [p]Jn 12:42; 16:2
9:23 [q]ver 21
9:24 [r]Jos 7:19 [s]ver 16
9:27 [t]ver 15
9:28 [u]Jn 5:45
9:29 [v]Jn 8:14
9:31 [w]Ge 18:23-32; Ps 34:15,16; 66:18; 145:19,20; Pr 15:29; Isa 1:15; 59:1,2; Jn 15:7; Jas 5:16-18; 1Jn 5:14,15
9:33 [x]ver 16; Jn 3:2

18The Jews[m] still did not believe
that he had been blind and had received his sight until they sent for
the man's parents. **19**"Is this your
son?" they asked. "Is this the one
you say was born blind? How is it
that now he can see?"
20"We know he is our son," the
parents answered, "and we know
he was born blind. **21**But how he
can see now, or who opened his
eyes, we don't know. Ask him. He
is of age; he will speak for himself."
22His parents said this because
they were afraid of the Jews,[n] for
already the Jews had decided that
anyone who acknowledged that
Jesus was the Christ[u] would be put
out[o] of the synagogue.[p] **23**That
was why his parents said, "He is of
age; ask him."[q]
24A second time they summoned
the man who had been blind. "Give
glory to God,[v]"[r] they said. "We
know this man is a sinner."[s]
25He replied, "Whether he is a
sinner or not, I don't know. One
thing I do know. I was blind but
now I see!"
26Then they asked him, "What
did he do to you? How did he open
your eyes?"
27He answered, "I have told you
already[t] and you did not listen.
Why do you want to hear it again?
Do you want to become his disciples, too?"
28Then they hurled insults at
him and said, "You are this fellow's
disciple! We are disciples of Moses![u] **29**We know that God spoke to
Moses, but as for this fellow, we
don't even know where he comes
from."[v]
30The man answered, "Now that
is remarkable! You don't know
where he comes from, yet he
opened my eyes. **31**We know that
God does not listen to sinners. He
listens to the godly man who does
his will.[w] **32**Nobody has ever heard
of opening the eyes of a man born
blind. **33**If this man were not from
God,[x] he could do nothing."

[u]*22* Or *Messiah* [v]*24* A solemn charge to tell the truth (see Joshua 7:19)

34To this they replied, "You were steeped in sin at birth;[a] how dare you lecture us!" And they threw him out.[b]

Spiritual Blindness

35Jesus heard that they had thrown him out, and when he found him, he said, "Do you believe in the Son of Man?"

36"Who is he, sir?" the man asked. "Tell me so that I may believe in him."[c]

37Jesus said, "You have now seen him; in fact, he is the one speaking with you."[d]

38Then the man said, "Lord, I believe," and he worshiped him.[e]

39Jesus said, "For judgment[f] I have come into this world,[g] so that the blind will see[h] and those who see will become blind."[i]

40Some Pharisees who were with him heard him say this and asked, "What? Are we blind too?"[j]

41Jesus said, "If you were blind, you would not be guilty of sin; but now that you claim you can see, your guilt remains.[k]

The Shepherd and His Flock

10 "I tell you the truth, the man who does not enter the sheep pen by the gate, but climbs in by some other way, is a thief and a robber. **2**The man who enters by the gate is the shepherd of his sheep.[l] **3**The watchman opens the gate for him, and the sheep listen to his voice.[m] He calls his own sheep by name and leads them out. **4**When he has brought out all his own, he goes on ahead of them, and his sheep follow him because they know his voice. **5**But they will never follow a stranger; in fact, they will run away from him because they do not recognize a stranger's voice." **6**Jesus used this figure of speech,[n] but they did not understand what he was telling them.

7Therefore Jesus said again, "I tell you the truth, I am the gate for the sheep. **8**All who ever came before me[o] were thieves and robbers, but the sheep did not listen to them. **9**I am the gate; whoever enters through me will be saved.[w] He will come in and go out, and find pasture. **10**The thief comes only to steal and kill and destroy; I have come that they may have life, and have it to the full.

11"I am the good shepherd.[p] The good shepherd lays down his life for the sheep.[q] **12**The hired hand is not the shepherd who owns the sheep. So when he sees the wolf coming, he abandons the sheep and runs away.[r] Then the wolf attacks the flock and scatters it. **13**The man runs away because he is a hired hand and cares nothing for the sheep.

14"I am the good shepherd;[s] I know my sheep[t] and my sheep know me— **15**just as the Father knows me and I know the Father[u]—and I lay down my life for the sheep. **16**I have other sheep[v] that are not of this sheep pen. I must bring them also. They too will listen to my voice, and there shall be one flock[w] and one shepherd.[x] **17**The reason my Father loves me is that I lay down my life[y]—only to take it up again. **18**No one takes it from me, but I lay it down of my own accord.[z] I have authority to lay it down and authority to take it up again. This command I received from my Father."[a]

19At these words the Jews were again divided.[b] **20**Many of them said, "He is demon-possessed[c] and raving mad.[d] Why listen to him?"

21But others said, "These are not the sayings of a man possessed by a demon.[e] Can a demon open the eyes of the blind?"[f]

The Unbelief of the Jews

22Then came the Feast of Dedication[x] at Jerusalem. It was winter, **23**and Jesus was in the temple area walking in Solomon's Colonnade.[g] **24**The Jews[h] gathered around him, saying, "How long will

9:34 [a]ver 2 [b]ver 22,35; Isa 66:5
9:36 [c]Ro 10:14
9:37 [d]Jn 4:26
9:38 [e]Mt 28:9
9:39 [f]Jn 5:22 [g]Jn 3:19 [h]Lk 4:18 [i]Mt 13:13
9:40 [j]Ro 2:19
9:41 [k]Jn 15:22,24
10:2 [l]ver 11,14
10:3 [m]ver 4,5,14, 16,27
10:6 [n]Jn 16:25
10:8 [o]Jer 23:1,2
10:11 [p]ver 14; Isa 40:11; Eze 34:11-16, 23; Heb 13:20; 1Pe 5:4; Rev 7:17 [q]Jn 15:13; 1Jn 3:16
10:12 [r]Zec 11:16,17
10:14 [s]ver 11 [t]ver 27
10:15 [u]Mt 11:27
10:16 [v]Isa 56:8 [w]Jn 11:52; Eph 2:11-19 [x]Eze 37:24; 1Pe 2:25
10:17 [y]ver 11,15,18
10:18 [z]Mt 26:53 [a]Jn 15:10; Php 2:8; Heb 5:8
10:19 [b]Jn 7:43; 9:16
10:20 [c]Jn 7:20 [d]Mk 3:21
10:21 [e]Mt 4:24 [f]Ex 4:11; Jn 9:32,33
10:23 [g]Ac 3:11; 5:12
10:24 [h]Jn 1:19

[w]9 Or *kept safe* [x]22 That is, Hanukkah

you keep us in suspense? If you are
the Christ,[y] tell us plainly."[a]

25Jesus answered, "I did tell
you,[b] but you do not believe. The
miracles I do in my Father's name
speak for me,[c] 26but you do not
believe because you are not my
sheep.[d] 27My sheep listen to my
voice; I know them,[e] and they follow me.[f] 28I give them eternal life,
and they shall never perish; no one
can snatch them out of my hand.[g]
29My Father, who has given them
to me,[h] is greater than all[z];[i] no
one can snatch them out of my Father's hand. 30I and the Father are
one."[j]

31Again the Jews picked up
stones to stone him,[k] 32but Jesus
said to them, "I have shown you
many great miracles from the Father. For which of these do you
stone me?"

33"We are not stoning you for
any of these," replied the Jews,
"but for blasphemy, because you, a
mere man, claim to be God."[l]

34Jesus answered them, "Is it
not written in your Law,[m] 'I have
said you are gods'[a]?[n] 35If he
called them 'gods,' to whom the
word of God came—and the Scripture cannot be broken— 36what
about the one whom the Father set
apart[o] as his very own[p] and sent
into the world?[q] Why then do you
accuse me of blasphemy because I
said, 'I am God's Son'?[r] 37Do not
believe me unless I do what my Father does.[s] 38But if I do it, even
though you do not believe me, believe the miracles, that you may
know and understand that the Father is in me, and I in the Father."[t]
39Again they tried to seize him,[u]
but he escaped their grasp.[v]

40Then Jesus went back across
the Jordan[w] to the place where
John had been baptizing in the early days. Here he stayed 41and many
people came to him. They said,
"Though John never performed a
miraculous sign,[x] all that John
said about this man was true."[y]
42And in that place many believed
in Jesus.[z]

10:24 [a]Jn 16:25,29
10:25 [b]Jn 8:58 [c]Jn 5:36
10:26 [d]Jn 8:47
10:27 [e]ver 14 [f]ver 4
10:28 [g]Jn 6:39
10:29 [h]Jn 17:2,6,24 [i]Jn 14:28
10:30 [j]Jn 17:21-23
10:31 [k]Jn 8:59
10:33 [l]Lev 24:16; Jn 5:18
10:34 [m]Jn 8:17; Ro 3:19 [n]Ps 82:6
10:36 [o]Jer 1:5 [p]Jn 6:69 [q]Jn 3:17 [r]Jn 5:17,18
10:37 [s]ver 25; Jn 15:24
10:38 [t]Jn 14:10,11, 20; 17:21
10:39 [u]Jn 7:30 [v]Lk 4:30; Jn 8:59
10:40 [w]Jn 1:28
10:41 [x]Jn 2:11; 3:30 [y]Jn 1:26,27, 30,34
10:42 [z]Jn 7:31
11:1 [a]Mt 21:17 [b]Lk 10:38
11:2 [c]Mk 14:3; Lk 7:38; Jn 12:3
11:3 [d]ver 5,36
11:4 [e]ver 40; Jn 9:3
11:7 [f]Jn 10:40
11:8 [g]Mt 23:7 [h]Jn 8:59; 10:31
11:9 [i]Jn 9:4; 12:35
11:11 [j]ver 3 [k]Ac 7:60
11:13 [l]Mt 9:24
11:16 [m]Mt 10:3; Jn 14:5; 20:24-28; 21:2; Ac 1:13

The Death of Lazarus

11 Now a man named Lazarus
was sick. He was from Bethany,[a] the village of Mary and her
sister Martha.[b] 2This Mary, whose
brother Lazarus now lay sick, was
the same one who poured perfume
on the Lord and wiped his feet with
her hair.[c] 3So the sisters sent word
to Jesus, "Lord, the one you love[d]
is sick."

4When he heard this, Jesus said,
"This sickness will not end in
death. No, it is for God's glory[e] so
that God's Son may be glorified
through it." 5Jesus loved Martha
and her sister and Lazarus. 6Yet
when he heard that Lazarus was
sick, he stayed where he was two
more days.

7Then he said to his disciples,
"Let us go back to Judea."[f]

8"But Rabbi,"[g] they said, "a
short while ago the Jews tried to
stone you,[h] and yet you are going
back there?"

9Jesus answered, "Are there not
twelve hours of daylight? A man
who walks by day will not stumble,
for he sees by this world's light.[i]
10It is when he walks by night that
he stumbles, for he has no light."

11After he had said this, he went
on to tell them, "Our friend[j] Lazarus has fallen asleep;[k] but I am going there to wake him up."

12His disciples replied, "Lord, if
he sleeps, he will get better."
13Jesus had been speaking of his
death, but his disciples thought he
meant natural sleep.[l]

14So then he told them plainly,
"Lazarus is dead, 15and for your
sake I am glad I was not there, so
that you may believe. But let us go
to him."

16Then Thomas[m] (called Didymus) said to the rest of the disciples, "Let us also go, that we may
die with him."

[y]24 Or *Messiah* [z]29 Many early manuscripts *What my Father has given me is greater than all* [a]34 Psalm 82:6

Jesus Comforts the Sisters

17On his arrival, Jesus found
that Lazarus had already been in
the tomb for four days.[a] 18Betha-
ny[b] was less than two miles[b] from
Jerusalem, 19and many Jews had
come to Martha and Mary to comfort them in the loss of their brother.[c] 20When Martha heard that
Jesus was coming, she went out to
meet him, but Mary stayed at
home.[d]
21"Lord," Martha said to Jesus,
"if you had been here, my brother
would not have died.[e] 22But I
know that even now God will give
you whatever you ask."[f]
23Jesus said to her, "Your brother will rise again."
24Martha answered, "I know he
will rise again in the resurrection[g]
at the last day."
25Jesus said to her, "I am the resurrection and the life.[h] He who believes in me will live, even though
he dies; 26and whoever lives and
believes in me will never die. Do
you believe this?"
27"Yes, Lord," she told him, "I
believe that you are the Christ,[c][i]
the Son of God,[j] who was to come
into the world."[k]
28And after she had said this, she
went back and called her sister
Mary aside. "The Teacher[l] is
here," she said, "and is asking for
you." 29When Mary heard this, she
got up quickly and went to him.
30Now Jesus had not yet entered
the village, but was still at the
place where Martha had met him.[m]
31When the Jews who had been
with Mary in the house, comforting
her,[n] noticed how quickly she got
up and went out, they followed her,
supposing she was going to the
tomb to mourn there.
32When Mary reached the place
where Jesus was and saw him, she
fell at his feet and said, "Lord, if
you had been here, my brother
would not have died."[o]
33When Jesus saw her weeping,
and the Jews who had come along
with her also weeping, he was
deeply moved[p] in spirit and troubled.[q] 34"Where have you laid
him?"
"Come and see, Lord," they replied.
35Jesus wept.[r]
36Then the Jews said, "See how
he loved him!"[s]
37But some of them said, "Could
not he who opened the eyes of the
blind man[t] have kept this man
from dying?"[u]

Jesus Raises Lazarus From the Dead

38Jesus, once more deeply
moved,[v] came to the tomb. It was
a cave with a stone laid across the
entrance.[w] 39"Take away the
stone," he said.
"But, Lord," said Martha, the sister of the dead man, "by this time
there is a bad odor, for he has been
there four days."[x]
40Then Jesus said, "Did I not tell
you that if you believed,[y] you
would see the glory of God?"[z]
41So they took away the stone.
Then Jesus looked up[a] and said,
"Father,[b] I thank you that you
have heard me. 42I knew that you
always hear me, but I said this for
the benefit of the people standing
here,[c] that they may believe that
you sent me."[d]
43When he had said this, Jesus
called in a loud voice, "Lazarus,
come out!"[e] 44The dead man
came out, his hands and feet
wrapped with strips of linen,[f] and
a cloth around his face.[g]
Jesus said to them, "Take off the
grave clothes and let him go."

The Plot to Kill Jesus

45Therefore many of the Jews
who had come to visit Mary,[h] and
had seen what Jesus did,[i] put
their faith in him.[j] 46But some of
them went to the Pharisees and
told them what Jesus had done.
47Then the chief priests and the
Pharisees[k] called a meeting[l] of
the Sanhedrin.[m]
"What are we accomplishing?"

[b]18 Greek *fifteen stadia* (about 3 kilometers)
[c]27 Or *Messiah*

11:17 [a]ver 6,39
11:18 [b]ver 1
11:19 [c]ver 31; Job 2:11
11:20 [d]Lk 10:38-42
11:21 [e]ver 32,37
11:22 [f]ver 41,42; Jn 9:31
11:24 [g]Da 12:2; Jn 5:28,29; Ac 24:15
11:25 [h]Jn 1:4
11:27 [i]Lk 2:11 [j]Mt 16:16 [k]Jn 6:14
11:28 [l]Mt 26:18; Jn 13:13
11:30 [m]ver 20
11:31 [n]ver 19
11:32 [o]ver 21
11:33 [p]ver 38 [q]Jn 12:27
11:35 [r]Lk 19:41
11:36 [s]ver 3
11:37 [t]Jn 9:6,7 [u]ver 21,32
11:38 [v]ver 33 [w]Mt 27:60; Lk 24:2; Jn 20:1
11:39 [x]ver 17
11:40 [y]ver 23-25 [z]ver 4
11:41 [a]Jn 17:1 [b]Mt 11:25
11:42 [c]Jn 12:30 [d]Jn 3:17
11:43 [e]Lk 7:14
11:44 [f]Jn 19:40 [g]Jn 20:7
11:45 [h]ver 19 [i]Jn 2:23 [j]Ex 14:31; Jn 7:31
11:47 [k]ver 57 [l]Mt 26:3 [m]Mt 5:22

they asked. "Here is this man performing many miraculous signs.[a]
48If we let him go on like this, everyone will believe in him, and
then the Romans will come and
take away both our place[d] and our
nation."

49Then one of them, named Caiaphas,[b] who was high priest that
year,[c] spoke up, "You know nothing at all! **50**You do not realize that
it is better for you that one man die
for the people than that the whole
nation perish."[d]

51He did not say this on his own,
but as high priest that year he
prophesied that Jesus would die
for the Jewish nation, **52**and not
only for that nation but also for the
scattered children of God, to bring
them together and make them
one.[e] **53**So from that day on they
plotted to take his life.[f]

54Therefore Jesus no longer
moved about publicly among the
Jews.[g] Instead he withdrew to a region near the desert, to a village
called Ephraim, where he stayed
with his disciples.

55When it was almost time for
the Jewish Passover,[h] many went
up from the country to Jerusalem
for their ceremonial cleansing[i] before the Passover. **56**They kept
looking for Jesus,[j] and as they
stood in the temple area they asked
one another, "What do you think?
Isn't he coming to the Feast at all?"
57But the chief priests and Pharisees had given orders that if anyone
found out where Jesus was, he
should report it so that they might
arrest him.

Jesus Anointed at Bethany

12:1–8Ref — Mt 26:6–13; Mk 14:3–9; Lk 7:37–39

12 Six days before the Passover,[k] Jesus arrived at
Bethany,[l] where Lazarus lived,
whom Jesus had raised from the
dead. **2**Here a dinner was given in
Jesus' honor. Martha served,[m]
while Lazarus was among those reclining at the table with him.
3Then Mary took about a pint[e] of
pure nard, an expensive perfume;[n]
she poured it on Jesus' feet and
wiped his feet with her hair.[o] And
the house was filled with the fragrance of the perfume.

4But one of his disciples, Judas
Iscariot, who was later to betray
him,[p] objected, **5**"Why wasn't this
perfume sold and the money given
to the poor? It was worth a year's
wages.[f]" **6**He did not say this because he cared about the poor but
because he was a thief; as keeper of
the money bag,[q] he used to help
himself to what was put into it.

7"Leave her alone," Jesus replied. "⌊It was intended⌋ that she
should save this perfume for the
day of my burial.[r] **8**You will always
have the poor among you,[s] but you
will not always have me."

9Meanwhile a large crowd of
Jews found out that Jesus was
there and came, not only because
of him but also to see Lazarus,
whom he had raised from the
dead.[t] **10**So the chief priests made
plans to kill Lazarus as well, **11**for
on account of him[u] many of the
Jews were going over to Jesus and
putting their faith in him.[v]

The Triumphal Entry

12:12–15pp — Mt 21:4–9; Mk 11:7–10; Lk 19:35–38

12The next day the great crowd
that had come for the Feast heard
that Jesus was on his way to Jerusalem. **13**They took palm branches
and went out to meet him, shouting,

"Hosanna![g]"

"Blessed is he who comes in
the name of the
Lord!"[h][w]

"Blessed is the King of
Israel!"[x]

14Jesus found a young donkey and
sat upon it, as it is written,

15"Do not be afraid, O Daughter
of Zion;

11:47 [a]Jn 2:11
11:49 [b]Mt 26:3 [c]ver 51; Jn 18:13,14
11:50 [d]Jn 18:14
11:52 [e]Isa 49:6; Jn 10:16
11:53 [f]Mt 12:14
11:54 [g]Jn 7:1
11:55 [h]Ex 12:13,23,27; Mt 26:1,2; Mk 14:1; Jn 13:1 [i]2Ch 30:17,18
11:56 [j]Jn 7:11
12:1 [k]Jn 11:55 [l]Mt 21:17
12:2 [m]Lk 10:38-42
12:3 [n]Mk 14:3 [o]Jn 11:2
12:4 [p]Mt 10:4
12:6 [q]Jn 13:29
12:7 [r]Jn 19:40
12:8 [s]Dt 15:11
12:9 [t]Jn 11:43,44
12:11 [u]ver 17,18; Jn 11:45 [v]Jn 7:31
12:13 [w]Ps 118:25,26 [x]Jn 1:49

[d]*48* Or *temple* [e]*3* Greek *a litra* (probably about 0.5 liter) [f]*5* Greek *three hundred denarii* [g]*13* A Hebrew expression meaning "Save!" which became an exclamation of praise [h]*13* Psalm 118:25, 26

see, your king is coming,
seated on a donkey's
colt."[i][a]

16 At first his disciples did not
understand all this.[b] Only after
Jesus was glorified[c] did they realize that these things had been written about him and that they had
done these things to him.
17 Now the crowd that was with
him[d] when he called Lazarus from
the tomb and raised him from the
dead continued to spread the word.
18 Many people, because they had
heard that he had given this miraculous sign,[e] went out to meet him.
19 So the Pharisees said to one another, "See, this is getting us nowhere. Look how the whole world
has gone after him!"[f]

Jesus Predicts His Death

20 Now there were some Greeks[g]
among those who went up to worship at the Feast. 21 They came to
Philip, who was from Bethsaida[h]
in Galilee, with a request. "Sir,"
they said, "we would like to see
Jesus." 22 Philip went to tell Andrew; Andrew and Philip in turn
told Jesus.
23 Jesus replied, "The hour has
come for the Son of Man to be glorified.[i] 24 I tell you the truth, unless a kernel of wheat falls to the
ground and dies,[j] it remains only
a single seed. But if it dies, it produces many seeds. 25 The man who
loves his life will lose it, while the
man who hates his life in this world
will keep it[k] for eternal life.
26 Whoever serves me must follow
me; and where I am, my servant
also will be.[l] My Father will honor
the one who serves me.
27 "Now my heart is troubled,[m]
and what shall I say? 'Father,[n]
save me from this hour'?[o] No, it
was for this very reason I came to
this hour. 28 Father, glorify your
name!"

Then a voice came from heav-
en,[p] "I have glorified it, and will
glorify it again." 29 The crowd that
was there and heard it said it had
thundered; others said an angel
had spoken to him.
30 Jesus said, "This voice was for
your benefit,[q] not mine. 31 Now is
the time for judgment on this
world;[r] now the prince of this
world[s] will be driven out. 32 But I,
when I am lifted up from the
earth,[t] will draw all men to myself."[u] 33 He said this to show the
kind of death he was going to die.[v]
34 The crowd spoke up, "We have
heard from the Law that the
Christ[j] will remain forever,[w] so
how can you say, 'The Son of Man[x]
must be lifted up'?[y] Who is this
'Son of Man'?"
35 Then Jesus told them, "You
are going to have the light[z] just a
little while longer. Walk while you
have the light,[a] before darkness
overtakes you.[b] The man who
walks in the dark does not know
where he is going. 36 Put your trust
in the light while you have it, so
that you may become sons of
light."[c] When he had finished
speaking, Jesus left and hid himself from them.[d]

The Jews Continue in Their Unbelief

37 Even after Jesus had done all
these miraculous signs[e] in their
presence, they still would not believe in him. 38 This was to fulfill
the word of Isaiah the prophet:

"Lord, who has believed our
message
and to whom has the arm of
the Lord been
revealed?"[k][f]

39 For this reason they could not
believe, because, as Isaiah says
elsewhere:

40 "He has blinded their eyes
and deadened their hearts,
so they can neither see with
their eyes,
nor understand with their
hearts,
nor turn—and I would heal
them."[l][g]

12:15 [a] Zec 9:9 **12:16** [b] Mk 9:32 [c] Jn 2:22; 7:39; 14:26 **12:17** [d] Jn 11:42 **12:18** [e] ver 11 **12:19** [f] Jn 11:47,48 **12:20** [g] Jn 7:35; Ac 11:20 **12:21** [h] Mt 11:21; Jn 1:44 **12:23** [i] Jn 13:32; 17:1 **12:24** [j] 1Co 15:36 **12:25** [k] Mt 10:39; Mk 8:35; Lk 14:26 **12:26** [l] Jn 14:3; 17:24; 2Co 5:8; 1Th 4:17 **12:27** [m] Mt 26:38, 39; Jn 11:33, 38; 13:21 [n] Mt 11:25 [o] ver 23 **12:28** [p] Mt 3:17 **12:30** [q] Jn 11:42 **12:31** [r] Jn 16:11 [s] Jn 14:30; 16:11; 2Co 4:4; Eph 2:2; 1Jn 4:4 **12:32** [t] ver 34; Jn 3:14; 8:28 [u] Jn 6:44 **12:33** [v] Jn 18:32 **12:34** [w] Ps 110:4; Isa 9:7; Eze 37:25; Da 7:14 [x] Mt 8:20 [y] Jn 3:14 **12:35** [z] ver 46 [a] Eph 5:8 [b] 1Jn 2:11 **12:36** [c] Lk 16:8 [d] Jn 8:59 **12:37** [e] Jn 2:11 **12:38** [f] Isa 53:1; Ro 10:16 **12:40** [g] Isa 6:10; Mt 13:13,15

[i] *15* Zech. 9:9 [j] *34* Or *Messiah*
[k] *38* Isaiah 53:1 [l] *40* Isaiah 6:10

41Isaiah said this because he saw Jesus' glory[a] and spoke about him.[b]

42Yet at the same time many even among the leaders believed in him.[c] But because of the Pharisees[d] they would not confess their faith for fear they would be put out of the synagogue;[e] 43for they loved praise from men more than praise from God.[f]

44Then Jesus cried out, "When a man believes in me, he does not believe in me only, but in the one who sent me.[g] 45When he looks at me, he sees the one who sent me.[h] 46I have come into the world as a light,[i] so that no one who believes in me should stay in darkness.

47"As for the person who hears my words but does not keep them, I do not judge him. For I did not come to judge the world, but to save it.[j] 48There is a judge for the one who rejects me and does not accept my words; that very word which I spoke will condemn him[k] at the last day. 49For I did not speak of my own accord, but the Father who sent me commanded me[l] what to say and how to say it. 50I know that his command leads to eternal life. So whatever I say is just what the Father has told me to say."

Jesus Washes His Disciples' Feet

13 *It was just before the Passover Feast.*[m] Jesus knew that the time had come[n] for him to leave this world and go to the Father.[o] Having loved his own who were in the world, he now showed them the full extent of his love.[m]

2The evening meal was being served, and the devil had already prompted Judas Iscariot, son of Simon, to betray Jesus. 3Jesus knew that the Father had put all things under his power,[p] and that he had come from God[q] and was returning to God; 4so he got up from the meal, took off his outer clothing, and wrapped a towel around his waist. 5After that, he poured water into a basin and began to wash his disciples' feet,[r] drying them with the towel that was wrapped around him.

6He came to Simon Peter, who said to him, "Lord, are you going to wash my feet?"

7Jesus replied, "You do not realize now what I am doing, but later you will understand."[s]

8"No," said Peter, "you shall never wash my feet."

Jesus answered, "Unless I wash you, you have no part with me."

9"Then, Lord," Simon Peter replied, "not just my feet but my hands and my head as well!"

10Jesus answered, "A person who has had a bath needs only to wash his feet; his whole body is clean. And you are clean,[t] though not every one of you." 11For he knew who was going to betray him, and that was why he said not every one was clean.

12When he had finished washing their feet, he put on his clothes and returned to his place. "Do you understand what I have done for you?" he asked them. 13"You call me 'Teacher'[u] and 'Lord,'[v] and rightly so, for that is what I am. 14Now that I, your Lord and Teacher, have washed your feet, you also should wash one another's feet.[w] 15I have set you an example that you should do as I have done for you.[x] 16I tell you the truth, no servant is greater than his master,[y] nor is a messenger greater than the one who sent him. 17Now that you know these things, you will be blessed if you do them.[z]

Jesus Predicts His Betrayal

18"I am not referring to all of you;[a] I know those I have chosen.[b] But this is to fulfill the scripture: 'He who shares my bread[c] has lifted up his heel[d] against me.'[n][e]

19"I am telling you now before it happens, so that when it does happen you will believe[f] that I am

12:41 [a]Isa 6:1-4 [b]Lk 24:27
12:42 [c]ver 11; Jn 7:48 [d]Jn 7:13 [e]Jn 9:22
12:43 [f]Jn 5:44
12:44 [g]Mt 10:40; Jn 5:24
12:45 [h]Jn 14:9
12:46 [i]Jn 1:4; 3:19; 8:12; 9:5
12:47 [j]Jn 3:17
12:48 [k]Jn 5:45
12:49 [l]Jn 14:31
13:1 [m]Jn 11:55 [n]Jn 12:23 [o]Jn 16:28
13:3 [p]Mt 28:18 [q]Jn 8:42; 16:27,28,30
13:5 [r]Lk 7:44
13:7 [s]ver 12
13:10 [t]Jn 15:3
13:13 [u]Jn 11:28 [v]Lk 6:46; 1Co 12:3; Php 2:11
13:14 [w]1Pe 5:5
13:15 [x]Mt 11:29
13:16 [y]Mt 10:24; Lk 6:40; Jn 15:20
13:17 [z]Mt 7:24,25; Lk 11:28; Jas 1:25
13:18 [a]ver 10 [b]Jn 15:16,19 [c]Mt 26:23 [d]Jn 6:70 [e]Ps 41:9
13:19 [f]Jn 14:29; 16:4

[m]*1 Or he loved them to the last* [n]*18* Psalm 41:9

He.[a] **20**I tell you the truth, whoever accepts anyone I send accepts me; and whoever accepts me accepts the one who sent me."[b]

21After he had said this, Jesus was troubled in spirit[c] and testified, "I tell you the truth, one of you is going to betray me."[d]

22His disciples stared at one another, at a loss to know which of them he meant. **23**One of them, the disciple whom Jesus loved,[e] was reclining next to him. **24**Simon Peter motioned to this disciple and said, "Ask him which one he means."

25Leaning back against Jesus, he asked him, "Lord, who is it?"[f]

26Jesus answered, "It is the one to whom I will give this piece of bread when I have dipped it in the dish." Then, dipping the piece of bread, he gave it to Judas Iscariot, son of Simon. **27**As soon as Judas took the bread, Satan entered into him.[g]

"What you are about to do, do quickly," Jesus told him, **28**but no one at the meal understood why Jesus said this to him. **29**Since Judas had charge of the money,[h] some thought Jesus was telling him to buy what was needed for the Feast, or to give something to the poor. **30**As soon as Judas had taken the bread, he went out. And it was night.[i]

Jesus Predicts Peter's Denial

13:37,38pp — Mt 26:33–35; Mk 14:29–31; Lk 22:33,34

31When he was gone, Jesus said, "Now is the Son of Man glorified[j] and God is glorified in him.[k] **32**If God is glorified in him,[o] God will glorify the Son in himself,[l] and will glorify him at once.

33"My children, I will be with you only a little longer. You will look for me, and just as I told the Jews, so I tell you now: Where I am going, you cannot come.[m]

34"A new command[n] I give you: Love one another.[o] As I have loved you, so you must love one another.[p] **35**By this all men will know that you are my disciples, if you love one another."[q]

36Simon Peter asked him, "Lord, where are you going?"

Jesus replied, "Where I am going, you cannot follow now,[r] but you will follow later."[s]

37Peter asked, "Lord, why can't I follow you now? I will lay down my life for you."

38Then Jesus answered, "Will you really lay down your life for me? I tell you the truth, before the rooster crows, you will disown me three times![t]

Jesus Comforts His Disciples

14 "Do not let your hearts be troubled.[u] Trust in God[p]; trust also in me. **2**In my Father's house are many rooms; if it were not so, I would have told you. I am going there[v] to prepare a place for you. **3**And if I go and prepare a place for you, I will come back and take you to be with me that you also may be where I am.[w] **4**You know the way to the place where I am going."

Jesus the Way to the Father

5Thomas[x] said to him, "Lord, we don't know where you are going, so how can we know the way?"

6Jesus answered, "I am the way[y] and the truth and the life.[z] No one comes to the Father except through me. **7**If you really knew me, you would know[q] my Father as well.[a] From now on, you do know him and have seen him."

8Philip said, "Lord, show us the Father and that will be enough for us."

9Jesus answered: "Don't you know me, Philip, even after I have been among you such a long time? Anyone who has seen me has seen the Father.[b] How can you say, 'Show us the Father'? **10**Don't you believe that I am in the Father, and that the Father is in me?[c] The words I say to you are not just my

13:19 [a]Jn 8:24
13:20 [b]Mt 10:40; Lk 10:16
13:21 [c]Jn 12:27 [d]Mt 26:21
13:23 [e]Jn 19:26; 20:2; 21:7,20
13:25 [f]Jn 21:20
13:27 [g]Lk 22:3
13:29 [h]Jn 12:6
13:30 [i]Lk 22:53
13:31 [j]Jn 7:39 [k]Jn 14:13; 17:4; 1Pe 4:11
13:32 [l]Jn 17:1
13:33 [m]Jn 7:33,34
13:34 [n]1Jn 2:7-11; 3:11 [o]Lev 19:18; 1Th 4:9; 1Pe 1:22 [p]Jn 15:12; Eph 5:2; 1Jn 4:10,11
13:35 [q]1Jn 3:14; 4:20
13:36 [r]ver 33; Jn 14:2 [s]Jn 21:18,19; 2Pe 1:14
13:38 [t]Jn 18:27
14:1 [u]ver 27
14:2 [v]Jn 13:33,36
14:3 [w]Jn 12:26
14:5 [x]Jn 11:16
14:6 [y]Jn 10:9 [z]Jn 11:25
14:7 [a]Jn 8:19
14:9 [b]Jn 12:45; Col 1:15; Heb 1:3
14:10 [c]Jn 10:38

o32 Many early manuscripts do not have *If God is glorified in him.* p1 Or *You trust in God* q7 Some early manuscripts *If you really have known me, you will know*

own.[a] Rather, it is the Father, living in me, who is doing his work.
11Believe me when I say that I am
in the Father and the Father is in
me; or at least believe on the evidence of the miracles them-
selves.[b] **12**I tell you the truth, anyone who has faith[c] in me will do
what I have been doing.[d] He will
do even greater things than these,
because I am going to the Father.
13And I will do whatever you ask[e]
in my name, so that the Son may
bring glory to the Father. **14**You
may ask me for anything in my
name, and I will do it.

Jesus Promises the Holy Spirit

15"If you love me, you will obey
what I command.[f] **16**And I will ask
the Father, and he will give you another Counselor[g] to be with you
forever— **17**the Spirit of truth.[h]
The world cannot accept him,[i] because it neither sees him nor
knows him. But you know him, for
he lives with you and will be[r] in
you. **18**I will not leave you as orphans; I will come to you.[j] **19**Before long, the world will not see me
anymore, but you will see me.[k] Because I live, you also will live.[l]
20On that day you will realize that
I am in my Father,[m] and you are in
me, and I am in you. **21**Whoever has
my commands and obeys them, he
is the one who loves me.[n] He who
loves me will be loved by my Father,[o] and I too will love him and
show myself to him."

22Then Judas[p] (not Judas Iscariot) said, "But, Lord, why do you
intend to show yourself to us and
not to the world?"[q]

23Jesus replied, "If anyone loves
me, he will obey my teaching.[r] My
Father will love him, and we will
come to him and make our home
with him.[s] **24**He who does not love
me will not obey my teaching.
These words you hear are not my
own; they belong to the Father who
sent me.[t]

25"All this I have spoken while
still with you. **26**But the Counsel-
or,[u] the Holy Spirit, whom the Father will send in my name,[v] will
teach you all things[w] and will remind you of everything I have said
to you.[x] **27**Peace I leave with you;
my peace I give you.[y] I do not give
to you as the world gives. Do not let
your hearts be troubled and do not
be afraid.

28"You heard me say, 'I am going
away and I am coming back to
you.'[z] If you loved me, you would
be glad that I am going to the Father,[a] for the Father is greater
than I.[b] **29**I have told you now before it happens, so that when it
does happen you will believe.[c] **30**I
will not speak with you much longer, for the prince of this world[d] is
coming. He has no hold on me,
31but the world must learn that I
love the Father and that I do exactly what my Father has commanded
me.[e]

"Come now; let us leave.

The Vine and the Branches

15 "I am the true vine,[f] and
my Father is the gardener.
2He cuts off every branch in me
that bears no fruit, while every
branch that does bear fruit he
prunes[s] so that it will be even
more fruitful. **3**You are already
clean because of the word I have
spoken to you.[g] **4**Remain in me,
and I will remain in you.[h] No
branch can bear fruit by itself; it
must remain in the vine. Neither
can you bear fruit unless you remain in me.

5"I am the vine; you are the
branches. If a man remains in me
and I in him, he will bear much
fruit;[i] apart from me you can do
nothing. **6**If anyone does not remain in me, he is like a branch that
is thrown away and withers; such
branches are picked up, thrown
into the fire and burned.[j] **7**If you
remain in me and my words remain
in you, ask whatever you wish, and
it will be given you.[k] **8**This is to my
Father's glory,[l] that you bear

14:10 [a]Jn 5:19
14:11 [b]Jn 5:36; 10:38
14:12 [c]Mt 21:21 [d]Lk 10:17
14:13 [e]Mt 7:7
14:15 [f]ver 21,23; Jn 15:10; 1Jn 5:3
14:16 [g]Jn 15:26; 16:7
14:17 [h]Jn 15:26; 16:13; 1Jn 4:6 [i]1Co 2:14
14:18 [j]ver 3,28
14:19 [k]Jn 7:33,34; 16:16 [l]Jn 6:57
14:20 [m]Jn 10:38
14:21 [n]1Jn 5:3 [o]1Jn 2:5
14:22 [p]Lk 6:16; Ac 1:13 [q]Ac 10:41
14:23 [r]ver 15 [s]1Jn 2:24; Rev 3:20
14:24 [t]Jn 7:16
14:26 [u]Jn 15:26; 16:7 [v]Ac 2:33 [w]Jn 16:13; 1Jn 2:20,27 [x]Jn 2:22
14:27 [y]Jn 16:33; Php 4:7; Col 3:15
14:28 [z]ver 2-4,18 [a]Jn 5:18 [b]Jn 10:29; Php 2:6
14:29 [c]Jn 13:19; 16:4
14:30 [d]Jn 12:31
14:31 [e]Jn 10:18; 12:49
15:1 [f]Isa 5:1-7
15:3 [g]Jn 13:10; 17:17; Eph 5:26
15:4 [h]Jn 6:56; 1Jn 2:6
15:5 [i]ver 16
15:6 [j]ver 2 **15:7** [k]Mt 7:7 **15:8** [l]Mt 5:16

[r]*17* Some early manuscripts *and is* [s]*2* The Greek for *prunes* also means *cleans.*

much fruit, showing yourselves to
be my disciples.[a]
9"As the Father has loved me,[b]
so have I loved you. Now remain in
my love. 10If you obey my commands,[c] you will remain in my
love, just as I have obeyed my Father's commands and remain in his
love. 11I have told you this so that
my joy may be in you and that your
joy may be complete.[d] 12My command is this: Love each other as I
have loved you.[e] 13Greater love
has no one than this, that he lay
down his life for his friends.[f]
14You are my friends[g] if you do
what I command.[h] 15I no longer
call you servants, because a servant
does not know his master's business. Instead, I have called you
friends, for everything that I
learned from my Father I have
made known to you.[i] 16You did
not choose me, but I chose you and
appointed you[j] to go and bear
fruit—fruit that will last. Then the
Father will give you whatever you
ask in my name. 17This is my command: Love each other.[k]

The World Hates the Disciples

18"If the world hates you,[l] keep
in mind that it hated me first. 19If
you belonged to the world, it would
love you as its own. As it is, you do
not belong to the world, but I have
chosen you[m] out of the world. That
is why the world hates you.[n] 20Re-
member the words I spoke to you:
'No servant is greater than his master.'[t][o] If they persecuted me, they
will persecute you also.[p] If they
obeyed my teaching, they will obey
yours also. 21They will treat you
this way because of my name,[q] for
they do not know the One who sent
me.[r] 22If I had not come and spoken to them, they would not be
guilty of sin. Now, however, they
have no excuse for their sin.[s] 23He
who hates me hates my Father as
well. 24If I had not done among
them what no one else did,[t] they
would not be guilty of sin. But now
they have seen these miracles, and
yet they have hated both me and
my Father. 25But this is to fulfill
what is written in their Law: 'They
hated me without reason.'[u][u]
26"When the Counselor[v] comes,
whom I will send to you from the
Father,[w] the Spirit of truth[x] who
goes out from the Father, he will
testify about me.[y] 27And you also
must testify,[z] for you have been
with me from the beginning.[a]

16 "All this[b] I have told you so
that you will not go astray.[c]
2They will put you out of the synagogue;[d] in fact, a time is coming
when anyone who kills you will
think he is offering a service to
God.[e] 3They will do such things
because they have not known the
Father or me.[f] 4I have told you
this, so that when the time comes
you will remember[g] that I warned
you. I did not tell you this at first
because I was with you.

The Work of the Holy Spirit

5"Now I am going to him who
sent me,[h] yet none of you asks me,
'Where are you going?'[i] 6Because
I have said these things, you are
filled with grief. 7But I tell you the
truth: It is for your good that I am
going away. Unless I go away, the
Counselor[j] will not come to you;
but if I go, I will send him to you.[k]
8When he comes, he will convict
the world of guilt[v] in regard to sin
and righteousness and judgment:
9in regard to sin,[l] because men do
not believe in me; 10in regard to
righteousness,[m] because I am going to the Father, where you can
see me no longer; 11and in regard
to judgment, because the prince of
this world[n] now stands condemned.
12"I have much more to say to
you, more than you can now bear.[o]
13But when he, the Spirit of
truth,[p] comes, he will guide you
into all truth.[q] He will not speak
on his own; he will speak only what
he hears, and he will tell you what
is yet to come. 14He will bring glory

15:8 [a]Jn 8:31 **15:9** [b]Jn 17:23,24,26 **15:10** [c]Jn 14:15 **15:11** [d]Jn 17:13 **15:12** [e]Jn 13:34 **15:13** [f]Jn 10:11; Ro 5:7,8 **15:14** [g]Lk 12:4 [h]Mt 12:50 **15:15** [i]Jn 8:26 **15:16** [j]Jn 6:70; 13:18 **15:17** [k]ver 12 **15:18** [l]1Jn 3:13 **15:19** [m]ver 16 [n]Jn 17:14 **15:20** [o]Jn 13:16 [p]2Ti 3:12 **15:21** [q]Mt 10:22 [r]Jn 16:3 **15:22** [s]Jn 9:41; Ro 1:20 **15:24** [t]Jn 5:36 **15:25** [u]Ps 35:19; 69:4 **15:26** [v]Jn 14:16 [w]Jn 14:26 [x]Jn 14:17 [y]1Jn 5:7 **15:27** [z]Lk 24:48; 1Jn 1:2; 4:14 [a]Lk 1:2 **16:1** [b]Jn 15:18-27 [c]Mt 11:6 **16:2** [d]Jn 9:22 [e]Isa 66:5; Ac 26:9,10; Rev 6:9 **16:3** [f]Jn 15:21; 17:25; 1Jn 3:1 **16:4** [g]Jn 13:19 **16:5** [h]Jn 7:33 [i]Jn 13:36; 14:5 **16:7** [j]Jn 14:16,26; 15:26 [k]Jn 7:39 **16:9** [l]Jn 15:22 **16:10** [m]Ac 3:14; 7:52; 1Pe 3:18 **16:11** [n]Jn 12:31 **16:12** [o]Mk 4:33 **16:13** [p]Jn 14:17 [q]Jn 14:26

[t]*20* John 13:16 [u]*25* Psalms 35:19; 69:4
[v]*8* Or *will expose the guilt of the world*

to me by taking from what is mine
and making it known to you. **15**All
that belongs to the Father is
mine.[a] That is why I said the Spirit
will take from what is mine and
make it known to you.
16"In a little while[b] you will see
me no more, and then after a little
while you will see me."[c]

The Disciples' Grief Will Turn to Joy

17Some of his disciples said to
one another, "What does he mean
by saying, 'In a little while you will
see me no more, and then after a
little while you will see me,'[d] and
'Because I am going to the Father'?"[e]
18They kept asking,
"What does he mean by 'a little
while'? We don't understand what
he is saying."
19Jesus saw that they wanted to
ask him about this, so he said to
them, "Are you asking one another
what I meant when I said, 'In a little
while you will see me no more,
and then after a little while you will
see me'? **20**I tell you the truth, you
will weep and mourn[f] while the
world rejoices. You will grieve, but
your grief will turn to joy.[g] **21**A
woman giving birth to a child has
pain[h] because her time has come;
but when her baby is born she forgets
the anguish because of her joy
that a child is born into the world.
22So with you: Now is your time of
grief,[i] but I will see you again[j]
and you will rejoice, and no one
will take away your joy. **23**In that
day you will no longer ask me anything.
I tell you the truth, my Father
will give you whatever you ask
in my name.[k] **24**Until now you
have not asked for anything in my
name. Ask and you will receive,
and your joy will be complete.[l]
25"Though I have been speaking
figuratively,[m] a time is coming[n]
when I will no longer use this kind
of language but will tell you plainly
about my Father. **26**In that day you
will ask in my name.[o] I am not saying
that I will ask the Father on
your behalf. **27**No, the Father himself
loves you because you have
loved me[p] and have believed that I
came from God. **28**I came from the
Father and entered the world; now
I am leaving the world and going
back to the Father."[q]
29Then Jesus' disciples said,
"Now you are speaking clearly and
without figures of speech.[r] **30**Now
we can see that you know all things
and that you do not even need to
have anyone ask you questions.
This makes us believe that you
came from God."
31"You believe at last!"[w] Jesus
answered. **32**"But a time is coming,[s]
and has come, when you will
be scattered,[t] each to his own
home. You will leave me all alone.
Yet I am not alone, for my Father is
with me.[u]
33"I have told you these things,
so that in me you may have
peace.[v] In this world you will have
trouble.[w] But take heart! I have
overcome[x] the world."

Jesus Prays for Himself

17 After Jesus said this, he
looked toward heaven[y] and
prayed:

"Father, the time has come.
Glorify your Son, that your Son
may glorify you.[z] **2**For you
granted him authority over all
people that he might give eternal
life to all those you have
given him.[a] **3**Now this is eternal
life: that they may know
you, the only true God, and
Jesus Christ, whom you have
sent.[b] **4**I have brought you
glory[c] on earth by completing
the work you gave me to do.[d]
5And now, Father, glorify me
in your presence with the glory
I had with you[e] before the
world began.[f]

Jesus Prays for His Disciples

6"I have revealed you[x][g] to
those whom you gave me[h] out
of the world. They were yours;
you gave them to me and they

16:15 [a]Jn 17:10
16:16 [b]Jn 7:33 [c]Jn 14:18-24
16:17 [d]ver 16 [e]ver 5
16:20 [f]Lk 23:27 [g]Jn 20:20
16:21 [h]Isa 26:17; 1Th 5:3
16:22 [i]ver 6 [j]ver 16
16:23 [k]Mt 7:7; Jn 15:16
16:24 [l]Jn 3:29; 15:11
16:25 [m]Mt 13:34; Jn 10:6 [n]ver 2
16:26 [o]ver 23,24
16:27 [p]Jn 14:21,23
16:28 [q]Jn 13:3
16:29 [r]ver 25
16:32 [s]ver 2,25 [t]Mt 26:31 [u]Jn 8:16,29
16:33 [v]Jn 14:27 [w]Jn 15:18-21 [x]Ro 8:37; 1Jn 4:4
17:1 [y]Jn 11:41 [z]Jn 12:23; 13:31,32
17:2 [a]ver 6,9,24; Da 7:14; Jn 6:37,39
17:3 [b]ver 8,18,21, 23,25; Jn 3:17
17:4 [c]Jn 13:31 [d]Jn 4:34
17:5 [e]Php 2:6 [f]Jn 1:2
17:6 [g]ver 26 [h]ver 2; Jn 6:37,39

[w]31 Or *"Do you now believe?"* [x]6 Greek *your name*; also in verse 26

have obeyed your word. 7Now
they know that everything you
have given me comes from
you. 8For I gave them the
words you gave me[a] and they
accepted them. They knew
with certainty that I came
from you,[b] and they believed
that you sent me.[c] 9I pray for
them.[d] I am not praying for
the world, but for those you
have given me, for they are
yours. 10All I have is yours,
and all you have is mine.[e] And
glory has come to me through
them. 11I will remain in the
world no longer, but they are
still in the world,[f] and I am
coming to you.[g] Holy Father,
protect them by the power of
your name—the name you
gave me—so that they may be
one[h] as we are one.[i] 12While
I was with them, I protected
them and kept them safe by
that name you gave me. None
has been lost[j] except the one
doomed to destruction[k] so
that Scripture would be fulfilled.

13"I am coming to you now,
but I say these things while I
am still in the world, so that
they may have the full measure
of my joy[l] within them.
14I have given them your word
and the world has hated
them,[m] for they are not of the
world any more than I am of
the world.[n] 15My prayer is not
that you take them out of the
world but that you protect
them from the evil one.[o]
16They are not of the world,
even as I am not of it.[p]
17Sanctify[y] them by the truth;
your word is truth.[q] 18As you
sent me into the world,[r] I
have sent them into the
world.[s] 19For them I sanctify
myself, that they too may be
truly sanctified.

Jesus Prays for All Believers

20"My prayer is not for them
alone. I pray also for those
who will believe in me through
their message, 21that all of
them may be one, Father, just
as you are in me and I am in
you.[t] May they also be in us
so that the world may believe
that you have sent me.[u] 22I
have given them the glory that
you gave me, that they may be
one as we are one:[v] 23I in
them and you in me. May they
be brought to complete unity
to let the world know that you
sent me[w] and have loved
them[x] even as you have loved
me.

24"Father, I want those you
have given me to be with me
where I am,[y] and to see my
glory,[z] the glory you have given
me because you loved me
before the creation of the
world.[a]

25"Righteous Father, though
the world does not know you,[b]
I know you, and they know that
you have sent me.[c] 26I have
made you known to them,[d] and
will continue to make you
known in order that the love
you have for me may be in
them[e] and that I myself may
be in them."

Jesus Arrested

18:3–11pp — Mt 26:47–56; Mk 14:43–50; Lk 22:47–53

18 When he had finished praying,
Jesus left with his disciples
and crossed the Kidron Valley.[f]
On the other side there was
an olive grove,[g] and he and his
disciples went into it.[h]

2Now Judas, who betrayed him,
knew the place, because Jesus had
often met there with his disciples.[i]
3So Judas came to the
grove, guiding[j] a detachment of
soldiers and some officials from
the chief priests and Pharisees.[k]
They were carrying torches, lanterns
and weapons.

4Jesus, knowing all that was going
to happen to him,[l] went out

17:8 [a]ver 14,26 [b]Jn 16:27 [c]ver 3,18,21,23,25; Jn 3:17
17:9 [d]Lk 22:32
17:10 [e]Jn 16:15
17:11 [f]Jn 13:1 [g]Jn 7:33 [h]ver 21-23 [i]Jn 10:30
17:12 [j]Jn 6:39 [k]Jn 6:70
17:13 [l]Jn 3:29
17:14 [m]Jn 15:19 [n]Jn 8:23
17:15 [o]Mt 5:37
17:16 [p]ver 14
17:17 [q]Jn 15:3
17:18 [r]ver 3,8,21,23,25 [s]Jn 20:21
17:21 [t]Jn 10:38 [u]ver 3,8,18,23,25; Jn 3:17
17:22 [v]Jn 14:20
17:23 [w]Jn 3:17 [x]Jn 16:27
17:24 [y]Jn 12:26 [z]Jn 1:14 [a]ver 5; Mt 25:34
17:25 [b]Jn 15:21; 16:3 [c]ver 3,8,18,21,23; Jn 3:17; 7:29; 16:27
17:26 [d]ver 6 [e]Jn 15:9
18:1 [f]2Sa 15:23 [g]ver 26 [h]Mt 26:36
18:2 [i]Lk 21:37; 22:39
18:3 [j]Ac 1:16 [k]ver 12
18:4 [l]Jn 6:64; 13:1,11

y17 Greek *hagiazo (set apart for sacred use* or *make holy)*; also in verse 19

and asked them, "Who is it you want?"[a]

5"Jesus of Nazareth," they replied.

"I am he," Jesus said. (And Judas the traitor was standing there with them.) **6**When Jesus said, "I am he," they drew back and fell to the ground.

7Again he asked them, "Who is it you want?"[b]

And they said, "Jesus of Nazareth."

8"I told you that I am he," Jesus answered. "If you are looking for me, then let these men go." **9**This happened so that the words he had spoken would be fulfilled: "I have not lost one of those you gave me."[z][c]

10Then Simon Peter, who had a sword, drew it and struck the high priest's servant, cutting off his right ear. (The servant's name was Malchus.)

11Jesus commanded Peter, "Put your sword away! Shall I not drink the cup[d] the Father has given me?"

Jesus Taken to Annas

18:12,13pp — Mt 26:57

12Then the detachment of soldiers with its commander and the Jewish officials[e] arrested Jesus. They bound him **13**and brought him first to Annas, who was the father-in-law of Caiaphas,[f] the high priest that year. **14**Caiaphas was the one who had advised the Jews that it would be good if one man died for the people.[g]

Peter's First Denial

18:16–18pp — Mt 26:69,70; Mk 14:66–68; Lk 22:55–57

15Simon Peter and another disciple were following Jesus. Because this disciple was known to the high priest,[h] he went with Jesus into the high priest's courtyard,[i] **16**but Peter had to wait outside at the door. The other disciple, who was known to the high priest, came back, spoke to the girl on duty there and brought Peter in.

17"You are not one of his disciples, are you?" the girl at the door asked Peter.

He replied, "I am not."[j]

18It was cold, and the servants and officials stood around a fire[k] they had made to keep warm. Peter also was standing with them, warming himself.[l]

The High Priest Questions Jesus

18:19–24pp — Mt 26:59–68; Mk 14:55–65; Lk 22:63–71

19Meanwhile, the high priest questioned Jesus about his disciples and his teaching.

20"I have spoken openly to the world," Jesus replied. "I always taught in synagogues[m] or at the temple,[n] where all the Jews come together. I said nothing in secret.[o] **21**Why question me? Ask those who heard me. Surely they know what I said."

22When Jesus said this, one of the officials[p] nearby struck him in the face.[q] "Is this the way you answer the high priest?" he demanded.

23"If I said something wrong," Jesus replied, "testify as to what is wrong. But if I spoke the truth, why did you strike me?"[r] **24**Then Annas sent him, still bound, to Caiaphas[s] the high priest.[a]

Peter's Second and Third Denials

18:25–27pp — Mt 26:71–75; Mk 14:69–72; Lk 22:58–62

25As Simon Peter stood warming himself,[t] he was asked, "You are not one of his disciples, are you?"

He denied it, saying, "I am not."[u]

26One of the high priest's servants, a relative of the man whose ear Peter had cut off,[v] challenged him, "Didn't I see you with him in the olive grove?"[w] **27**Again Peter denied it, and at that moment a rooster began to crow.[x]

18:4 [a]ver 7
18:7 [b]ver 4
18:9 [c]Jn 17:12
18:11 [d]Mt 20:22
18:12 [e]ver 3
18:13 [f]ver 24; Mt 26:3
18:14 [g]Jn 11:49-51
18:15 [h]Mt 26:3 [i]Mt 26:58; Mk 14:54; Lk 22:54
18:17 [j]ver 25
18:18 [k]Jn 21:9 [l]Mk 14:54,67
18:20 [m]Mt 4:23 [n]Mt 26:55 [o]Jn 7:26
18:22 [p]ver 3 [q]Mt 16:21; Jn 19:3
18:23 [r]Mt 5:39; Ac 23:2-5
18:24 [s]ver 13; Mt 26:3
18:25 [t]ver 18 [u]ver 17
18:26 [v]ver 10 [w]ver 1
18:27 [x]Jn 13:38

[z]9 John 6:39 [a]24 Or *(Now Annas had sent him, still bound, to Caiaphas the high priest.)*

Jesus Before Pilate

18:29–40pp — Mt 27:11–18,20–23; Mk 15:2–15; Lk 23:2,3,18–25

28 Then the Jews led Jesus from Caiaphas to the palace of the Roman governor.[a] By now it was early morning, and to avoid ceremonial uncleanness the Jews did not enter the palace;[b] they wanted to be able to eat the Passover.[c] **29** So Pilate came out to them and asked, "What charges are you bringing against this man?"

30 "If he were not a criminal," they replied, "we would not have handed him over to you."

31 Pilate said, "Take him yourselves and judge him by your own law."

"But we have no right to execute anyone," the Jews objected. **32** This happened so that the words Jesus had spoken indicating the kind of death he was going to die[d] would be fulfilled.

33 Pilate then went back inside the palace,[e] summoned Jesus and asked him, "Are you the king of the Jews?"[f]

34 "Is that your own idea," Jesus asked, "or did others talk to you about me?"

35 "Am I a Jew?" Pilate replied. "It was your people and your chief priests who handed you over to me. What is it you have done?"

36 Jesus said, "My kingdom[g] is not of this world. If it were, my servants would fight to prevent my arrest by the Jews.[h] But now my kingdom is from another place."[i]

37 "You are a king, then!" said Pilate.

Jesus answered, "You are right in saying I am a king. In fact, for this *reason I was born, and for this I* came into the world, to testify to the truth.[j] Everyone on the side of truth listens to me."[k]

38 "What is truth?" Pilate asked. With this he went out again to the Jews and said, "I find no basis for a charge against him.[l] **39** But it is your custom for me to release to you one prisoner at the time of the Passover. Do you want me to release 'the king of the Jews'?"

40 They shouted back, "No, not him! Give us Barabbas!" Now Barabbas had taken part in a rebellion.[m]

Jesus Sentenced to be Crucified

19:1–16pp — Mt 27:27–31; Mk 15:16–20

19 Then Pilate took Jesus and had him flogged.[n] **2** The soldiers twisted together a crown of thorns and put it on his head. They clothed him in a purple robe **3** and went up to him again and again, saying, "Hail, king of the Jews!"[o] And they struck him in the face.[p]

4 Once more Pilate came out and said to the Jews, "Look, I am bringing him out[q] to you to let you know that I find no basis for a charge against him."[r] **5** When Jesus came out wearing the crown of thorns and the purple robe,[s] Pilate said to them, "Here is the man!"

6 As soon as the chief priests and their officials saw him, they shouted, "Crucify! Crucify!"

But Pilate answered, "You take him and crucify him.[t] As for me, I find no basis for a charge against him."[u]

7 The Jews insisted, "We have a law, and according to that law he must die,[v] because he claimed to be the Son of God."[w]

8 When Pilate heard this, he was even more afraid, **9** and he went back inside the palace.[x] "Where do you come from?" he asked Jesus, but Jesus gave him no answer.[y] **10** "Do you refuse to speak to me?" Pilate said. "Don't you realize I have power either to free you or to crucify you?"

11 Jesus answered, "You would have no power over me if it were not given to you from above.[z] Therefore the one who handed me over to you[a] is guilty of a greater sin."

12 From then on, Pilate tried to set Jesus free, but the Jews kept shouting, "If you let this man go,

18:28 [a] Mt 27:2; Mk 15:1; Lk 23:1 [b] ver 33; Jn 19:9 [c] Jn 11:55
18:32 [d] Mt 20:19; 26:2; Jn 3:14; 8:28; 12:32, 33
18:33 [e] ver 28,29; Jn 19:9 [f] Lk 23:3; Mt 2:2
18:36 [g] Mt 3:2 [h] Mt 26:53 [i] Lk 17:21; Jn 6:15
18:37 [j] Jn 3:32 [k] Jn 8:47; 1Jn 4:6
18:38 [l] Lk 23:4; Jn 19:4,6
18:40 [m] Ac 3:14
19:1 [n] Dt 25:3; Isa 50:6; 53:5; Mt 27:26
19:3 [o] Mt 27:29 [p] Jn 18:22
19:4 [q] Jn 18:38 [r] ver 6; Lk 23:4
19:5 [s] ver 2
19:6 [t] Ac 3:13 [u] ver 4; Lk 23:4
19:7 [v] Lev 24:16 [w] Mt 26:63-66; Jn 5:18; 10:33
19:9 [x] Jn 18:33 [y] Mk 14:61
19:11 [z] Ro 13:1 [a] Jn 18:28-30; Ac 3:13

you are no friend of Caesar. Anyone who claims to be a king[a] opposes Caesar."

13When Pilate heard this, he brought Jesus out and sat down on the judge's seat[b] at a place known as the Stone Pavement (which in Aramaic[c] is Gabbatha). **14**It was the day of Preparation[d] of Passover Week, about the sixth hour.[e]

"Here is your king,"[f] Pilate said to the Jews.

15But they shouted, "Take him away! Take him away! Crucify him!"

"Shall I crucify your king?" Pilate asked.

"We have no king but Caesar," the chief priests answered.

16Finally Pilate handed him over to them to be crucified.[g]

The Crucifixion

19:17–24pp — Mt 27:33–44; Mk 15:22–32; Lk 23:33–43

So the soldiers took charge of Jesus. **17**Carrying his own cross,[h] he went out to the place of the Skull[i] (which in Aramaic[j] is called Golgotha). **18**Here they crucified him, and with him two others[k]—one on each side and Jesus in the middle.

19Pilate had a notice prepared and fastened to the cross. It read: JESUS OF NAZARETH,[l] THE KING OF THE JEWS.[m] **20**Many of the Jews read this sign, for the place where Jesus was crucified was near the city,[n] and the sign was written in Aramaic, Latin and Greek. **21**The chief priests of the Jews protested to Pilate, "Do not write 'The King of the Jews,' but that this man claimed to be king of the Jews."[o]

22Pilate answered, "What I have written, I have written."

23When the soldiers crucified Jesus, they took his clothes, dividing them into four shares, one for each of them, with the undergarment remaining. This garment was seamless, woven in one piece from top to bottom.

24"Let's not tear it," they said to one another. "Let's decide by lot who will get it."

19:12 [a] Lk 23:2
19:13 [b] Mt 27:19 [c] Jn 5:2
19:14 [d] Mt 27:62 [e] Mk 15:25 [f] ver 19,21
19:16 [g] Mt 27:26; Mk 15:15; Lk 23:25
19:17 [h] Ge 22:6; Lk 14:27; 23:26 [i] Lk 23:33 [j] Jn 5:2
19:18 [k] Lk 23:32
19:19 [l] Mk 1:24 [m] ver 14,21
19:20 [n] Heb 13:12
19:21 [o] ver 14
19:24 [p] ver 28,36,37; Mt 1:22 [q] Ps 22:18
19:25 [r] Mt 27:55,56; Mk 15:40,41; Lk 23:49 [s] Mt 12:46 [t] Lk 24:18
19:26 [u] Mt 12:46 [v] Jn 13:23
19:28 [w] ver 30; Jn 13:1 [x] ver 24,36,37
19:29 [y] Ps 69:21
19:30 [z] Lk 12:50; Jn 17:4
19:31 [a] ver 14,42 [b] Dt 21:23; Jos 8:29; 10:26,27
19:32 [c] ver 18
19:34 [d] Zec 12:10 [e] 1Jn 5:6,8
19:35 [f] Lk 24:48 [g] Jn 15:27; 21:24

This happened that the scripture might be fulfilled[p] which said,

"They divided my garments
among them
and cast lots for my
clothing."[b][q]

So this is what the soldiers did.

25Near the cross[r] of Jesus stood his mother,[s] his mother's sister, Mary the wife of Clopas, and Mary Magdalene.[t] **26**When Jesus saw his mother[u] there, and the disciple whom he loved[v] standing nearby, he said to his mother, "Dear woman, here is your son," **27**and to the disciple, "Here is your mother." From that time on, this disciple took her into his home.

The Death of Jesus

19:29,30pp — Mt 27:48,50; Mk 15:36,37; Lk 23:36

28Later, knowing that all was now completed,[w] and so that the Scripture would be fulfilled,[x] Jesus said, "I am thirsty." **29**A jar of wine vinegar[y] was there, so they soaked a sponge in it, put the sponge on a stalk of the hyssop plant, and lifted it to Jesus' lips. **30**When he had received the drink, Jesus said, "It is finished." With that, he bowed his head and gave up his spirit.

31Now it was the day of Preparation,[a] and the next day was to be a special Sabbath. Because the Jews did not want the bodies left on the crosses[b] during the Sabbath, they asked Pilate to have the legs broken and the bodies taken down. **32**The soldiers therefore came and broke the legs of the first man who had been crucified with Jesus, and then those of the other.[c] **33**But when they came to Jesus and found that he was already dead, they did not break his legs. **34**Instead, one of the soldiers pierced[d] Jesus' side with a spear, bringing a sudden flow of blood and water.[e] **35**The man who saw it[f] has given testimony, and his testimony is true.[g] He knows that he tells the truth, and he testifies

[b]*24* Psalm 22:18

so that you also may believe.
36These things happened so that
the scripture would be fulfilled:[a]
"Not one of his bones will be broken,"[c][b] **37**and, as another scripture says, "They will look on the
one they have pierced."[d][c]

The Burial of Jesus

19:38–42pp — Mt 27:57–61; Mk 15:42–47; Lk 23:50–56

38Later, Joseph of Arimathea
asked Pilate for the body of Jesus.
Now Joseph was a disciple of
Jesus, but secretly because he
feared the Jews. With Pilate's permission, he came and took the
body away. **39**He was accompanied
by Nicodemus,[d] the man who earlier had visited Jesus at night. Nicodemus brought a mixture of
myrrh and aloes, about seventy-
five pounds.[e] **40**Taking Jesus'
body, the two of them wrapped it,
with the spices, in strips of linen.[e]
This was in accordance with Jewish burial customs.[f] **41**At the place
where Jesus was crucified, there
was a garden, and in the garden a
new tomb, in which no one had
ever been laid. **42**Because it was
the Jewish day of Preparation[g] and
since the tomb was nearby,[h] they
laid Jesus there.

The Empty Tomb

20:1–8pp — Mt 28:1–8; Mk 16:1–8; Lk 24:1–10

20 Early on the first day of the
week, while it was still dark,
Mary Magdalene[i] went to the
tomb and saw that the stone had
been removed from the entrance.[j]
2So she came running to Simon Peter and the other disciple, the one
Jesus loved,[k] and said, "They have
taken the Lord out of the tomb,
and we don't know where they have
put him!"[l]
3So Peter and the other disciple
started for the tomb.[m] **4**Both were
running, but the other disciple outran Peter and reached the tomb
first. **5**He bent over and looked in[n]
at the strips of linen[o] lying there
but did not go in. **6**Then Simon Peter, who was behind him, arrived
and went into the tomb. He saw the
strips of linen lying there, **7**as well
as the burial cloth that had been
around Jesus' head.[p] The cloth
was folded up by itself, separate
from the linen. **8**Finally the other
disciple, who had reached the
tomb first,[q] also went inside. He
saw and believed. **9**(They still did
not understand from Scripture[r]
that Jesus had to rise from the
dead.)[s]

Jesus Appears to Mary Magdalene

10Then the disciples went back
to their homes, **11**but Mary stood
outside the tomb crying. As she
wept, she bent over to look into the
tomb[t] **12**and saw two angels in
white,[u] seated where Jesus' body
had been, one at the head and the
other at the foot.
13They asked her, "Woman, why
are you crying?"[v]
"They have taken my Lord
away," she said, "and I don't know
where they have put him."[w] **14**At
this, she turned around and saw
Jesus standing there,[x] but she did
not realize that it was Jesus.[y]
15"Woman," he said, "why are
you crying?[z] Who is it you are
looking for?"
Thinking he was the gardener,
she said, "Sir, if you have carried
him away, tell me where you have
put him, and I will get him."
16Jesus said to her, "Mary."
She turned toward him and cried
out in Aramaic,[a] "Rabboni!"[b]
(which means Teacher).
17Jesus said, "Do not hold on to
me, for I have not yet returned to
the Father. Go instead to my brothers[c] and tell them, 'I am returning
to my Father[d] and your Father, to
my God and your God.' "
18Mary Magdalene[e] went to the
disciples[f] with the news: "I have
seen the Lord!" And she told them
that he had said these things to
her.

19:36 [a]ver 24,28,37; Mt 1:22 [b]Ex 12:46; Nu 9:12; Ps 34:20
19:37 [c]Zec 12:10; Rev 1:7
19:39 [d]Jn 3:1; 7:50
19:40 [e]Lk 24:12; Jn 11:44; 20:5,7 [f]Mt 26:12
19:42 [g]ver 14,31 [h]ver 20,41
20:1 [i]ver 18; Jn 19:25 [j]Mt 27:60,66
20:2 [k]Jn 13:23 [l]ver 13
20:3 [m]Lk 24:12
20:5 [n]ver 11 [o]Jn 19:40
20:7 [p]Jn 11:44
20:8 [q]ver 4
20:9 [r]Mt 22:29; Jn 2:22 [s]Lk 24:26,46
20:11 [t]ver 5
20:12 [u]Mt 28:2,3; Mk 16:5; Lk 24:4; Ac 5:19
20:13 [v]ver 15 [w]ver 2
20:14 [x]Mt 28:9; Mk 16:9 [y]Lk 24:16; Jn 21:4
20:15 [z]ver 13
20:16 [a]Jn 5:2 [b]Mt 23:7
20:17 [c]Mt 28:10 [d]Jn 7:33
20:18 [e]ver 1 [f]Lk 24:10,22,23

[c]36 Exodus 12:46; Num. 9:12; Psalm 34:20
[d]37 Zech. 12:10 [e]39 Greek *a hundred litrai* (about 34 kilograms)

Jesus Appears to His Disciples

19On the evening of that first day
of the week, when the disciples
were together, with the doors
locked for fear of the Jews,[a] Jesus
came and stood among them and
said, "Peace[b] be with you!" **20**After he said this, he showed them
his hands and side.[d] The disciples
were overjoyed[e] when they saw
the Lord.

21Again Jesus said, "Peace be
with you![f] As the Father has sent
me,[g] I am sending you."[h] **22**And
with that he breathed on them and
said, "Receive the Holy Spirit.[i]
23If you forgive anyone his sins,
they are forgiven; if you do not forgive them, they are not forgiven."[j]

Jesus Appears to Thomas

24Now Thomas[k] (called Didymus), one of the Twelve, was not
with the disciples when Jesus
came. **25**So the other disciples told
him, "We have seen the Lord!"

But he said to them, "Unless I
see the nail marks in his hands and
put my finger where the nails were,
and put my hand into his side,[l] I
will not believe it."[m]

26A week later his disciples were
in the house again, and Thomas
was with them. Though the doors
were locked, Jesus came and stood
among them and said, "Peace[n] be
with you!"[o] **27**Then he said to
Thomas, "Put your finger here; see
my hands. Reach out your hand
and put it into my side. Stop doubting and believe."[p]

28Thomas said to him, "My Lord
and my God!"

29Then Jesus told him, "Because
you have seen me, you have believed;[q] blessed are those who
have not seen and yet have believed."[r]

30Jesus did many other miraculous signs[s] in the presence of his
disciples, which are not recorded
in this book.[t] **31**But these are written that you may[f] believe[u] that
Jesus is the Christ, the Son of
God,[v] and that by believing you
may have life in his name.[w]

Jesus and the Miraculous Catch of Fish

21 Afterward Jesus appeared
again to his disciples,[x] by
the Sea of Tiberias.[gy] It happened
this way: **2**Simon Peter, Thomas[z]
(called Didymus), Nathanael[a]
from Cana in Galilee,[b] the sons of
Zebedee,[c] and two other disciples
were together. **3**"I'm going out to
fish," Simon Peter told them, and
they said, "We'll go with you." So
they went out and got into the
boat, but that night they caught
nothing.[d]

4Early in the morning, Jesus
stood on the shore, but the disciples did not realize that it was
Jesus.[e]

5He called out to them,
"Friends, haven't you any fish?"

"No," they answered.

6He said, "Throw your net on the
right side of the boat and you will
find some." When they did, they
were unable to haul the net in because of the large number of fish.[f]

7Then the disciple whom Jesus
loved[g] said to Peter, "It is the
Lord!" As soon as Simon Peter
heard him say, "It is the Lord," he
wrapped his outer garment around
him (for he had taken it off) and
jumped into the water. **8**The other
disciples followed in the boat, tow-
ing the net full of fish, for they were
not far from shore, about a hundred yards.[h] **9**When they landed,
they saw a fire[h] of burning coals
there with fish on it,[i] and some
bread.

10Jesus said to them, "Bring
some of the fish you have just
caught."

11Simon Peter climbed aboard
and dragged the net ashore. It was
full of large fish, 153, but even with
so many the net was not torn.
12Jesus said to them, "Come and
have breakfast." None of the disciples dared ask him, "Who are you?"
They knew it was the Lord. **13**Jesus
came, took the bread and gave it to

20:19 [a]Jn 7:13 [b]Jn 14:27 [c]ver 21,26; Lk 24:36-39
20:20 [d]Lk 24:39,40; Jn 19:34 [e]Jn 16:20,22
20:21 [f]ver 19 [g]Jn 3:17 [h]Mt 28:19; Jn 17:18
20:22 [i]Jn 7:39; Ac 2:38; 8:15-17; 19:2; Gal 3:2
20:23 [j]Mt 16:19; 18:18
20:24 [k]Jn 11:16
20:25 [l]ver 20 [m]Mk 16:11
20:26 [n]Jn 14:27 [o]ver 21
20:27 [p]ver 25; Lk 24:40
20:29 [q]Jn 3:15 [r]1Pe 1:8
20:30 [s]Jn 2:11 [t]Jn 21:25
20:31 [u]Jn 3:15; 19:35 [v]Mt 4:3 [w]Mt 25:46
21:1 [x]Jn 20:19,26 [y]Jn 6:1
21:2 [z]Jn 11:16 [a]Jn 1:45 [b]Jn 2:1 [c]Mt 4:21
21:3 [d]Lk 5:5
21:4 [e]Lk 24:16; Jn 20:14
21:6 [f]Lk 5:4-7
21:7 [g]Jn 13:23
21:9 [h]Jn 18:18 [i]ver 10,13

[f]*31* Some manuscripts *may continue to*
[g]*1* That is, Sea of Galilee [h]*8* Greek *about two hundred cubits* (about 90 meters)

them, and did the same with the
fish.[a] **14**This was now the third
time Jesus appeared to his disciples[b] after he was raised from the
dead.

Jesus Reinstates Peter

15When they had finished eating, Jesus said to Simon Peter, "Simon son of John, do you truly love
me more than these?"
"Yes, Lord," he said, "you know
that I love you."[c]
Jesus said, "Feed my lambs."[d]
16Again Jesus said, "Simon son
of John, do you truly love me?"
He answered, "Yes, Lord, you
know that I love you."
Jesus said, "Take care of my
sheep."[e]
17The third time he said to him,
"Simon son of John, do you love
me?"
Peter was hurt because Jesus
asked him the third time, "Do you
love me?"[f] He said, "Lord, you
know all things;[g] you know that I
love you."
Jesus said, "Feed my sheep.[h] **18**I
tell you the truth, when you were
younger you dressed yourself and
went where you wanted; but when
you are old you will stretch out
your hands, and someone else will
dress you and lead you where you
do not want to go." **19**Jesus said
this to indicate the kind of death[i]
by which Peter would glorify God.[j]
Then he said to him, "Follow
me!"
20Peter turned and saw that the
disciple whom Jesus loved[k] was
following them. (This was the one
who had leaned back against Jesus
at the supper and had said, "Lord,
who is going to betray you?")[l]
21When Peter saw him, he asked,
"Lord, what about him?"
22Jesus answered, "If I want him
to remain alive until I return,[m]
what is that to you? You must follow me."[n] **23**Because of this, the
rumor spread among the brothers[o]
that this disciple would not die.
But Jesus did not say that he would
not die; he only said, "If I want him
to remain alive until I return, what
is that to you?"
24This is the disciple who testifies to these things[p] and who
wrote them down. We know that
his testimony is true.[q]
25Jesus did many other things as
well.[r] If every one of them were
written down, I suppose that even
the whole world would not have
room for the books that would be
written.

21:13 [a]ver 9
21:14 [b]Jn 20:19,26
21:15 [c]Mt 26:33,35; Jn 13:37 [d]Lk 12:32
21:16 [e]Mt 2:6; Ac 20:28; 1Pe 5:2,3
21:17 [f]Jn 13:38 [g]Jn 16:30 [h]ver 16
21:19 [i]Jn 12:33; 18:32 [j]2Pe 1:14
21:20 [k]ver 7; Jn 13:23 [l]Jn 13:25
21:22 [m]Mt 16:27; 1Co 4:5; Rev 2:25 [n]ver 19
21:23 [o]Ac 1:16
21:24 [p]Jn 15:27 [q]Jn 19:35
21:25 [r]Jn 20:30

Acts

Title and Background

The book of Acts provides the basic history of the spread of Christianity during the thirty years immediately following the death and resurrection of Jesus Christ. It serves as a link between the Gospels and the Letters. It can be called "The Acts of the Holy Spirit," because it teaches about the coming and work of the Spirit.

Author and Date of Writing

Although the author does not name himself, evidence outside the Scriptures and inferences from the book itself lead to the conclusion that the author was Luke. A likely date for the book of Acts is A.D. 63.

Theme and Message

The theme of the work is best summarized in 1:8. Luke weaves together different interests and emphases as he relates the beginnings and expansion of the church. The design of the book revolves around (1) key persons: Peter and Paul; (2) important topics and events: the role of the Holy Spirit, pioneer missionary outreach to new fields, conversions, the growth of the church, and life in the Christian community; (3) significant problems: conflict between Jew and Gentile, persecution of the church by some Jewish elements, trials before Jews and Romans, confrontations with Gentiles, and other hardships in the ministry; (4) geographical advances: from Jerusalem to Rome.

Outline

I. Peter and the Beginnings of the Church in Palestine (1:1-12:25)
  A. "Throughout Judea, Galilee and Samaria" (1:1-9:31; see 9:31)
  B. "As far as Phoenicia, Cyprus and Antioch" (9:32-12:25; see 11:19)
II. Paul and the Expansion of the Church From Antioch to Rome (13:1-28:31)
  A. "Throughout the Region of Phrygia and Galatia" (13:1-15:35; see 16:6)
  B. "Over to Macedonia" (15:36-21:16; see 16:9)
  C. "To Rome" (21:17-28:31; see 28:14)

Jesus Taken Up Into Heaven

1 In my former book,[a] Theophilus, I wrote about all that Jesus
began to do and to teach[b] **2**until
the day he was taken up to heav-
en,[c] after giving instructions[d]
through the Holy Spirit to the apostles[e] he had chosen.[f] **3**After his
suffering, he showed himself to
these men and gave many convinc-
ing proofs that he was alive. He appeared to them[g] over a period of
forty days and spoke about the
kingdom of God. **4**On one occasion, while he was eating with
them, he gave them this command:
"Do not leave Jerusalem, but wait
for the gift my Father promised, which you have heard me
speak about.[h] **5**For John baptized
with[a] water, but in a few days you
will be baptized with the Holy Spirit."
6So when they met together,
they asked him, "Lord, are you at
this time going to restore[i] the
kingdom to Israel?"
7He said to them: "It is not for
you to know the times or dates the
Father has set by his own authori-

1:1 [a]Lk 1:1-4 [b]Lk 3:23
1:2 [c]ver 9,11; Mk 16:19 [d]Mt 28:19,20 [e]Mk 6:30 [f]Jn 13:18
1:3 [g]Mt 28:17; Lk 24:34,36; Jn 20:19,26; 21:1,14; 1Co 15:5-7
1:4 [h]Lk 24:49; Jn 14:16; Ac 2:33
1:6 [i]Mt 17:11

[a]5 Or *in*

ty.[a] **8**But you will receive power when the Holy Spirit comes on you;[b] and you will be my witnesses[c] in Jerusalem, and in all Judea and Samaria,[d] and to the ends of the earth."[e]

9After he said this, he was taken up[f] before their very eyes, and a cloud hid him from their sight.

10They were looking intently up into the sky as he was going, when suddenly two men dressed in white[g] stood beside them. **11**"Men of Galilee,"[h] they said, "why do you stand here looking into the sky? This same Jesus, who has been taken from you into heaven, will come back[i] in the same way you have seen him go into heaven."

Matthias Chosen to Replace Judas

12Then they returned to Jerusalem[j] from the hill called the Mount of Olives,[k] a Sabbath day's walk[b] from the city. **13**When they arrived, they went upstairs to the room[l] where they were staying. Those present were Peter, John, James and Andrew; Philip and Thomas, Bartholomew and Matthew; James son of Alphaeus and Simon the Zealot, and Judas son of James.[m] **14**They all joined together constantly in prayer,[n] along with the women[o] and Mary the mother of Jesus, and with his brothers.[p]

15In those days Peter stood up among the believers[c] (a group numbering about a hundred and twenty) **16**and said, "Brothers, the Scripture had to be fulfilled[q] which the Holy Spirit spoke long ago through the mouth of David concerning Judas,[r] who served as guide for those who arrested Jesus— **17**he was one of our number[s] and shared in this ministry."[t]

18(With the reward[u] he got for his wickedness, Judas bought a field;[v] there he fell headlong, his body burst open and all his intestines spilled out. **19**Everyone in Jerusalem heard about this, so they called that field in their language Akeldama, that is, Field of Blood.)

20"For," said Peter, "it is written in the book of Psalms,

> " 'May his place be deserted;
> let there be no one to dwell
> in it,'[d][w]

and,

> " 'May another take his place of
> leadership.'[e][x]

21Therefore it is necessary to choose one of the men who have been with us the whole time the Lord Jesus went in and out among us, **22**beginning from John's baptism[y] to the time when Jesus was taken up from us. For one of these must become a witness[z] with us of his resurrection."

23So they proposed two men: Joseph called Barsabbas (also known as Justus) and Matthias. **24**Then they prayed,[a] "Lord, you know everyone's heart.[b] Show us which of these two you have chosen **25**to take over this apostolic ministry, which Judas left to go where he belongs." **26**Then they cast lots, and the lot fell to Matthias; so he was added to the eleven apostles.[c]

The Holy Spirit Comes at Pentecost

2 When the day of Pentecost[d] came, they were all together[e] in one place. **2**Suddenly a sound like the blowing of a violent wind came from heaven and filled the whole house where they were sitting.[f] **3**They saw what seemed to be tongues of fire that separated and came to rest on each of them. **4**All of them were filled with the Holy Spirit and began to speak in other tongues[f][g] as the Spirit enabled them.

5Now there were staying in Jerusalem God-fearing[h] Jews from every nation under heaven. **6**When they heard this sound, a crowd came together in bewilderment, because each one heard them

b*12* That is, about 3/4 mile (about 1,100 meters) c*15* Greek *brothers* d*20* Psalm 69:25 e*20* Psalm 109:8 f*4* Or *languages*; also in verse 11

1:7 [a]Mt 24:36
1:8 [b]Ac 2:1-4 [c]Lk 24:48 [d]Ac 8:1-25 [e]Mt 28:19
1:9 [f]ver 2
1:10 [g]Lk 24:4; Jn 20:12
1:11 [h]Ac 2:7 [i]Mt 16:27
1:12 [j]Lk 24:52 [k]Mt 21:1
1:13 [l]Ac 9:37; 20:8 [m]Mt 10:2-4; Mk 3:16-19; Lk 6:14-16
1:14 [n]Ac 2:42; 6:4 [o]Lk 23:49,55 [p]Mt 12:46
1:16 [q]ver 20 [r]Jn 13:18
1:17 [s]Jn 6:70,71 [t]ver 25
1:18 [u]Mt 26:14,15 [v]Mt 27:3-10
1:20 [w]Ps 69:25 [x]Ps 109:8
1:22 [y]Mk 1:4 [z]ver 8
1:24 [a]Ac 6:6; 14:23 [b]1Sa 16:7; Jer 17:10; Ac 15:8; Rev 2:23
1:26 [c]Ac 2:14
2:1 [d]Lev 23:15,16; Ac 20:16 [e]Ac 1:14
2:2 [f]Ac 4:31
2:4 [g]Mk 16:17; 1Co 12:10
2:5 [h]Ac 8:2

speaking in his own language. 7Ut-
terly amazed,[a] they asked: "Are
not all these men who are speaking
Galileans?[b] 8Then how is it that
each of us hears them in his own
native language? 9Parthians,
Medes and Elamites; residents of
Mesopotamia, Judea and Cappa-
docia,[c] Pontus[d] and Asia,[e]
10Phrygia[f] and Pamphylia,[g]
Egypt and the parts of Libya near
Cyrene;[h] visitors from Rome
11(both Jews and converts to Judaism); Cretans and Arabs—we hear
them declaring the wonders of God
in our own tongues!" 12Amazed
and perplexed, they asked one another, "What does this mean?"
13Some, however, made fun of
them and said, "They have had too
much wine.[g]"[i]

Peter Addresses the Crowd

14Then Peter stood up with the
Eleven, raised his voice and addressed the crowd: "Fellow Jews
and all of you who live in Jerusalem, let me explain this to you; listen carefully to what I say. 15These
men are not drunk, as you suppose.
It's only nine in the morning![j]
16No, this is what was spoken by
the prophet Joel:

17" 'In the last days, God says,
I will pour out my Spirit on
all people.[k]
Your sons and daughters will
prophesy,[l]
your young men will see
visions,
your old men will dream
dreams.
18Even on my servants, both men
and women,
I will pour out my Spirit in
those days,
and they will prophesy.[m]
19I will show wonders in the
heaven above
and signs on the earth below,
blood and fire and billows of
smoke.
20The sun will be turned to
darkness
and the moon to blood[n]

2:7 [a]ver 12 [b]Ac 1:11
2:9 [c]1Pe 1:1 [d]Ac 18:2 [e]Ac 16:6; Ro 16:5; 1Co 16:19; 2Co 1:8
2:10 [f]Ac 16:6; 18:23 [g]Ac 13:13; 15:38 [h]Mt 27:32
2:13 [i]1Co 14:23
2:15 [j]1Th 5:7
2:17 [k]Isa 44:3; Jn 7:37-39; Ac 10:45 [l]Ac 21:9
2:18 [m]Ac 21:9-12
2:20 [n]Mt 24:29
2:21 [o]Ro 10:13
2:22 [p]Jn 4:48; Ac 10:38 [q]Jn 3:2
2:23 [r]Lk 22:22; Ac 3:18; 4:28 [s]Lk 24:20; Ac 3:13
2:24 [t]ver 32; 1Co 6:14; 2Co 4:14; Eph 1:20; Col 2:12; Heb 13:20; 1Pe 1:21 [u]Jn 20:9
2:27 [v]ver 31; Ac 13:35
2:29 [w]Ac 7:8,9 [x]Ac 13:36; 1Ki 2:10 [y]Ne 3:16
2:30 [z]2Sa 7:12; Ps 132:11
2:31 [a]Ps 16:10

before the coming of the
great and glorious day of
the Lord.
21And everyone who calls
on the name of the Lord will
be saved.'[h][o]

22"Men of Israel, listen to this:
Jesus of Nazareth was a man accredited by God to you by miracles,
wonders and signs,[p] which God
did among you through him,[q] as
you yourselves know. 23This man
was handed over to you by God's
set purpose and foreknowledge;[r]
and you, with the help of wicked
men,[i] put him to death by nailing
him to the cross.[s] 24But God
raised him from the dead,[t] freeing
him from the agony of death, because it was impossible for death
to keep its hold on him.[u] 25David
said about him:

" 'I saw the Lord always before
me.
Because he is at my right hand,
I will not be shaken.
26Therefore my heart is glad and
my tongue rejoices;
my body also will live in
hope,
27because you will not abandon
me to the grave,
nor will you let your Holy
One see decay.[v]
28You have made known to me
the paths of life;
you will fill me with joy in
your presence.'[j]

29"Brothers, I can tell you confidently that the patriarch[w] David
died and was buried,[x] and his
tomb is here[y] to this day. 30But he
was a prophet and knew that God
had promised him on oath that he
would place one of his descendants
on his throne.[z] 31Seeing what was
ahead, he spoke of the resurrection
of the Christ,[k] that he was not
abandoned to the grave, nor did his
body see decay.[a] 32God has raised

g*13* Or *sweet wine* h*21* Joel 2:28-32
i*23* Or *of those not having the law* (that is, Gentiles) j*28* Psalm 16:8-11 k*31* Or *Messiah.* "The Christ" (Greek) and "the Messiah" (Hebrew) both mean "the Anointed One"; also in verse 36.

COUNTRIES OF PEOPLE MENTIONED AT PENTECOST

ASIA—Provinces of the Roman empire
Media—Provinces of the Parthian empire
Rome —Cities
CRETE—Island
(1) (2) (3) etc.—Numbers indicate sequence listed in Ac 2:9-11
Rome (13)
Black Sea
Caspian Sea
PONTUS (7)
CAPPA-DOCIA (6)
ASIA (8)
PHRYGIA (9)
PAMPHYLIA (10)
Parthian empire (1)
Meso-potamia (4)
Ecbatana
Media (2)
Susa
Elam (3)
Mediterranean Sea
CRETE (14)
Cyrene
(12) CYRENE
Jerusalem
JUDEA (5)
(11) EGYPT
Red Sea
ARABIA (15)
Miles 0 200 400 600 800 1000
Kms 0 300 600 900 1200 1500

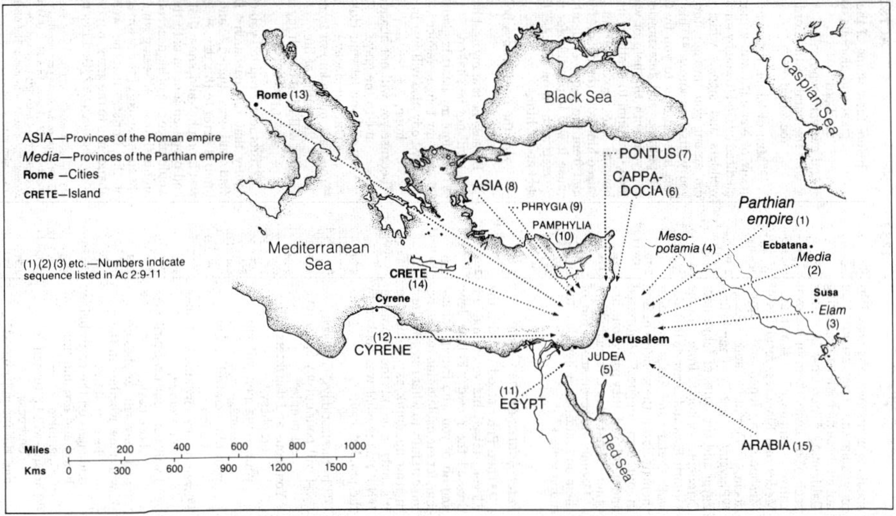

this Jesus to life,[a] and we are all witnesses[b] of the fact. **33**Exalted[c] to the right hand of God,[d] he has received from the Father[e] the promised Holy Spirit[f] and has poured out[g] what you now see and hear. **34**For David did not ascend to heaven, and yet he said,

" 'The Lord said to my Lord:
"Sit at my right hand
35until I make your enemies
a footstool for your feet." '[l][h]

36"Therefore let all Israel be assured of this: God has made this Jesus, whom you crucified, both Lord and Christ."[i]

37When the people heard this, they were cut to the heart and said to Peter and the other apostles, "Brothers, what shall we do?"[j]

38Peter replied, "Repent and be baptized,[k] every one of you, in the name of Jesus Christ for the forgiveness of your sins.[l] And you will receive the gift of the Holy Spirit. **39**The promise is for you and your children[m] and for all who are far off[n]—for all whom the Lord our God will call."

40With many other words he warned them; and he pleaded with them, "Save yourselves from this corrupt generation."[o] **41**Those who accepted his message were baptized, and about three thousand were added to their number that day.

The Fellowship of the Believers

42They devoted themselves to the apostles' teaching and to the fellowship, to the breaking of bread and to prayer.[p] **43**Everyone was filled with awe, and many wonders and miraculous signs were done by the apostles.[q] **44**All the believers were together and had everything in common.[r] **45**Selling their possessions and goods, they gave to anyone as he had need.[s] **46**Every day they continued to meet together in the temple courts.[t] They broke bread[u] in their homes and ate together with glad and sincere hearts, **47**praising God and enjoying the favor of all the people.[v] And the Lord added to their number[w] daily those who were being saved.

2:32 [a]ver 24 [b]Ac 1:8
2:33 [c]Php 2:9 [d]Mk 16:19 [e]Ac 1:4 [f]Jn 7:39; 14:26 [g]Ac 10:45
2:35 [h]Ps 110:1; Mt 22:44
2:36 [i]Lk 2:11
2:37 [j]Lk 3:10,12, 14
2:38 [k]Ac 8:12,16, 36,38; 22:16 [l]Lk 24:47; Ac 3:19
2:39 [m]Isa 44:3 [n]Ac 10:45; Eph 2:13
2:40 [o]Dt 32:5
2:42 [p]Ac 1:14
2:43 [q]Ac 5:12
2:44 [r]Ac 4:32
2:45 [s]Mt 19:21
2:46 [t]Lk 24:53; Ac 5:21,42 [u]Ac 20:7
2:47 [v]Ro 14:18 [w]ver 41; Ac 5:14
3:1 [x]Lk 22:8 [y]Ac 2:46 [z]Ps 55:17
3:2 [a]Ac 14:8 [b]Lk 16:20 [c]Jn 9:8
3:6 [d]ver 16; Ac 4:10
3:8 [e]Ac 14:10
3:9 [f]Ac 4:16,21
3:10 [g]ver 2
3:11 [h]Lk 22:8 [i]Jn 10:23; Ac 5:12
3:13 [j]Ac 5:30

Peter Heals the Crippled Beggar

3 One day Peter and John[x] were going up to the temple[y] at the time of prayer—at three in the afternoon.[z] **2**Now a man crippled from birth[a] was being carried to the temple gate[b] called Beautiful, where he was put every day to beg[c] from those going into the temple courts. **3**When he saw Peter and John about to enter, he asked them for money. **4**Peter looked straight at him, as did John. Then Peter said, "Look at us!" **5**So the man gave them his attention, expecting to get something from them.

6Then Peter said, "Silver or gold I do not have, but what I have I give you. In the name of Jesus Christ of Nazareth,[d] walk." **7**Taking him by the right hand, he helped him up, and instantly the man's feet and ankles became strong. **8**He jumped to his feet and began to walk. Then he went with them into the temple courts, walking and jumping,[e] and praising God. **9**When all the people[f] saw him walking and praising God, **10**they recognized him as the same man who used to sit begging at the temple gate called Beautiful,[g] and they were filled with wonder and amazement at what had happened to him.

Peter Speaks to the Onlookers

11While the beggar held on to Peter and John,[h] all the people were astonished and came running to them in the place called Solomon's Colonnade.[i] **12**When Peter saw this, he said to them: "Men of Israel, why does this surprise you? Why do you stare at us as if by our own power or godliness we had made this man walk? **13**The God of Abraham, Isaac and Jacob, the God of our fathers,[j] has glorified his servant Jesus. You handed him over to be killed, and you disowned

[l]35 Psalm 110:1

him before Pilate,[a] though he had
decided to let him go.[b] **14**You disowned the Holy[c] and Righteous
One[d] and asked that a murderer
be released to you.[e] **15**You killed
the author of life, but God raised
him from the dead.[f] We are witnesses of this. **16**By faith in the
name of Jesus, this man whom you
see and know was made strong. It is
Jesus' name and the faith that
comes through him that has given
this complete healing to him, as
you can all see.

17"Now, brothers, I know that
you acted in ignorance,[g] as did
your leaders.[h] **18**But this is how
God fulfilled what he had foretold[i] through all the prophets,[j]
saying that his Christ[m] would suffer.[k] **19**Repent, then, and turn to
God, so that your sins may be
wiped out,[l] that times of refresh-
ing may come from the Lord, **20**and
that he may send the Christ, who
has been appointed for you—even
Jesus. **21**He must remain in heav-
en[m] until the time comes for God
to restore everything,[n] as he promised long ago through his holy
prophets.[o] **22**For Moses said, 'The
Lord your God will raise up for you
a prophet like me from among your
own people; you must listen to everything he tells you.[p] **23**Anyone
who does not listen to him will be
completely cut off from among his
people.'[n][q]

24"Indeed, all the prophets[r]
from Samuel on, as many as have
spoken, have foretold these days.
25And you are heirs[s] of the prophets and of the covenant[t] God
made with your fathers. He said to
Abraham, 'Through your offspring
all peoples on earth will be
blessed.'[o][u] **26**When God raised
up[v] his servant, he sent him first[w]
to you to bless you by turning each
of you from your wicked ways."

Peter and John Before the Sanhedrin

4 The priests and the captain of
the temple guard[x] and the
Sadducees[y] came up to Peter and
John while they were speaking to
the people. **2**They were greatly disturbed because the apostles were
teaching the people and proclaiming in Jesus the resurrection of the
dead.[z] **3**They seized Peter and
John, and because it was evening,
they put them in jail[a] until the
next day. **4**But many who heard the
message believed, and the number
of men grew[b] to about five thousand.

5The next day the rulers,[c] elders
and teachers of the law met in Jerusalem. **6**Annas the high priest
was there, and so were Caiaphas,[d]
John, Alexander and the other men
of the high priest's family. **7**They
had Peter and John brought before
them and began to question them:
"By what power or what name did
you do this?"

8Then Peter, filled with the Holy
Spirit, said to them: "Rulers and elders of the people![e] **9**If we are being called to account today for an
act of kindness shown to a cripple[f]
and are asked how he was healed,
10then know this, you and all the
people of Israel: It is by the name of
Jesus Christ of Nazareth, whom
you crucified but whom God raised
from the dead,[g] that this man
stands before you healed. **11**He is

" 'the stone you builders
rejected,
which has become the
capstone.[p]'[q][h]

12Salvation is found in no one else,
for there is no other name under
heaven given to men by which we
must be saved."[i]

13When they saw the courage of
Peter and John[j] and realized that
they were unschooled, ordinary
men,[k] they were astonished and
they took note that these men had
been with Jesus. **14**But since they
could see the man who had been
healed standing there with them,
there was nothing they could say.
15So they ordered them to with-

3:13 [a]Mt 27:2 [b]Lk 23:4
3:14 [c]Mk 1:24; Ac 4:27 [d]Ac 7:52 [e]Mk 15:11; Lk 23:18-25
3:15 [f]Ac 2:24
3:17 [g]Lk 23:34 [h]Ac 13:27
3:18 [i]Ac 2:23 [j]Lk 24:27 [k]Ac 17:2,3; 26:22,23
3:19 [l]Ac 2:38
3:21 [m]Ac 1:11 [n]Mt 17:11 [o]Lk 1:70
3:22 [p]Dt 18:15,18; Ac 7:37
3:23 [q]Dt 18:19
3:24 [r]Lk 24:27
3:25 [s]Ac 2:39 [t]Ro 9:4,5 [u]Ge 12:3; 22:18; 26:4; 28:14
3:26 [v]ver 22; Ac 2:24 [w]Ac 13:46; Ro 1:16
4:1 [x]Lk 22:4 [y]Mt 3:7
4:2 [z]Ac 17:18
4:3 [a]Ac 5:18
4:4 [b]Ac 2:41
4:5 [c]Lk 23:13
4:6 [d]Mt 26:3; Lk 3:2
4:8 [e]ver 5; Lk 23:13
4:9 [f]Ac 3:6
4:10 [g]Ac 2:24
4:11 [h]Ps 118:22; Isa 28:16; Mt 21:42
4:12 [i]Mt 1:21; Ac 10:43; 1Ti 2:5
4:13 [j]Lk 22:8 [k]Mt 11:25

[m]*18* Or *Messiah;* also in verse 20
[n]*23* Deut. 18:15,18,19 [o]*25* Gen. 22:18; 26:4 [p]*11* Or *cornerstone* [q]*11* Psalm 118:22

draw from the Sanhedrin[a] and then conferred together. **16**"What are we going to do with these men?"[b] they asked. "Everybody living in Jerusalem knows they have done an outstanding miracle,[c] and we cannot deny it. **17**But to stop this thing from spreading any further among the people, we must warn these men to speak no longer to anyone in this name."

18Then they called them in again and commanded them not to speak or teach at all in the name of Jesus.[d] **19**But Peter and John replied, "Judge for yourselves whether it is right in God's sight to obey you rather than God.[e] **20**For we cannot help speaking about what we have seen and heard."

21After further threats they let them go. They could not decide how to punish them, because all the people[f] were praising God[g] for what had happened. **22**For the man who was miraculously healed was over forty years old.

The Believers' Prayer

23On their release, Peter and John went back to their own people and reported all that the chief priests and elders had said to them. **24**When they heard this, they raised their voices together in prayer to God. "Sovereign Lord," they said, "you made the heaven and the earth and the sea, and everything in them. **25**You spoke by the Holy Spirit through the mouth of your servant, our father David:[h]

" 'Why do the nations rage
and the peoples plot in vain?
26The kings of the earth take their stand
and the rulers gather together
against the Lord
and against his Anointed One.[r]'[s][i]

27Indeed Herod[j] and Pontius Pilate[k] met together with the Gentiles and the people[t] of Israel in this city to conspire against your holy servant Jesus,[l] whom you anointed. **28**They did what your power and will had decided beforehand should happen.[m] **29**Now, Lord, consider their threats and enable your servants to speak your word with great boldness.[n] **30**Stretch out your hand to heal and perform miraculous signs and wonders[o] through the name of your holy servant Jesus."[p]

31After they prayed, the place where they were meeting was shaken.[q] And they were all filled with the Holy Spirit and spoke the word of God boldly.[r]

The Believers Share Their Possessions

32All the believers were one in heart and mind. No one claimed that any of his possessions was his own, but they shared everything they had.[s] **33**With great power the apostles continued to testify[t] to the resurrection[u] of the Lord Jesus, and much grace was upon them all. **34**There were no needy persons among them. For from time to time those who owned lands or houses sold them,[v] brought the money from the sales **35**and put it at the apostles' feet,[w] and it was distributed to anyone as he had need.[x]

36Joseph, a Levite from Cyprus, whom the apostles called Barnabas[y] (which means Son of Encouragement), **37**sold a field he owned and brought the money and put it at the apostles' feet.[z]

Ananias and Sapphira

5 Now a man named Ananias, together with his wife Sapphira, also sold a piece of property. **2**With his wife's full knowledge he kept back part of the money for himself, but brought the rest and put it at the apostles' feet.[a]

3Then Peter said, "Ananias, how is it that Satan[b] has so filled your heart[c] that you have lied to the Holy Spirit[d] and have kept for yourself some of the money you received for the land? **4**Didn't it be-

4:15 [a]Mt 5:22
4:16 [b]Jn 11:47 [c]Ac 3:6-10
4:18 [d]Ac 5:40
4:19 [e]Ac 5:29
4:21 [f]Ac 5:26 [g]Mt 9:8
4:25 [h]Ac 1:16
4:26 [i]Ps 2:1,2; Da 9:25; Lk 4:18; Ac 10:38; Heb 1:9
4:27 [j]Mt 14:1 [k]Mt 27:2; Lk 23:12 [l]ver 30
4:28 [m]Ac 2:23
4:29 [n]ver 13,31; Ac 9:27; 14:3; Php 1:14
4:30 [o]Jn 4:48 [p]ver 27
4:31 [q]Ac 2:2 [r]ver 29
4:32 [s]Ac 2:44
4:33 [t]Lk 24:48 [u]Ac 1:22
4:34 [v]Mt 19:21; Ac 2:45
4:35 [w]ver 37; Ac 5:2 [x]Ac 2:45; 6:1
4:36 [y]Ac 9:27; 1Co 9:6
4:37 [z]ver 35; Ac 5:2
5:2 [a]Ac 4:35,37
5:3 [b]Mt 4:10 [c]Jn 13:2,27 [d]ver 9

[r]*26* That is, Christ or Messiah [s]*26* Psalm 2:1,2 [t]*27* The Greek is plural.

long to you before it was sold? And
after it was sold, wasn't the money
at your disposal? What made you
think of doing such a thing? You
have not lied to men but to God."
5When Ananias heard this, he
fell down and died.[a] And great
fear[b] seized all who heard what
had happened. **6**Then the young
men came forward, wrapped up his
body,[c] and carried him out and
buried him.
7About three hours later his wife
came in, not knowing what had
happened. **8**Peter asked her, "Tell
me, is this the price you and Ananias got for the land?"
"Yes," she said, "that is the
price."[d]
9Peter said to her, "How could
you agree to test the Spirit of the
Lord?[e] Look! The feet of the men
who buried your husband are at the
door, and they will carry you out
also."
10At that moment she fell down
at his feet and died.[f] Then the
young men came in and, finding
her dead, carried her out and buried her beside her husband.
11Great fear[g] seized the whole
church and all who heard about
these events.

The Apostles Heal Many

12The apostles performed many
miraculous signs and wonders[h]
among the people. And all the believers used to meet together[i] in
Solomon's Colonnade.[j] **13**No one
else dared join them, even though
they were highly regarded by the
people.[k] **14**Nevertheless, more
and more men and women believed in the Lord and were added
to their number. **15**As a result, people brought the sick into the streets
and laid them on beds and mats so
that at least Peter's shadow might
fall on some of them as he passed
by.[l] **16**Crowds gathered also from
the towns around Jerusalem,
bringing their sick and those tormented by evil[u] spirits, and all of
them were healed.[m]

The Apostles Persecuted

17Then the high priest and all his
associates, who were members of
the party[n] of the Sadducees,[o]
were filled with jealousy. **18**They
arrested the apostles and put them
in the public jail.[p] **19**But during
the night an angel[q] of the Lord
opened the doors of the jail[r] and
brought them out. **20**"Go, stand in
the temple courts," he said, "and
tell the people the full message of
this new life."[s]
21At daybreak they entered the
temple courts, as they had been
told, and began to teach the people.
When the high priest and his associates[t] arrived, they called together the Sanhedrin[u]—the full
assembly of the elders of Israel—
and sent to the jail for the apostles.
22But on arriving at the jail, the officers did not find them there. So
they went back and reported,
23"We found the jail securely
locked, with the guards standing at
the doors; but when we opened
them, we found no one inside."
24On hearing this report, the captain of the temple guard and the
chief priests[v] were puzzled, wondering what would come of this.
25Then someone came and said,
"Look! The men you put in jail are
standing in the temple courts
teaching the people." **26**At that,
the captain went with his officers
and brought the apostles. They did
not use force, because they feared
that the people[w] would stone
them.
27Having brought the apostles,
they made them appear before the
Sanhedrin[x] to be questioned by
the high priest. **28**"We gave you
strict orders not to teach in this
name,"[y] he said. "Yet you have
filled Jerusalem with your teaching
and are determined to make us
guilty of this man's blood."[z]
29Peter and the other apostles
replied: "We must obey God rather
than men![a] **30**The God of our fathers[b] raised Jesus from the

5:5 [a]ver 10 [b]ver 11
5:6 [c]Jn 19:40
5:8 [d]ver 2
5:9 [e]ver 3
5:10 [f]ver 5
5:11 [g]ver 5; Ac 19:17
5:12 [h]Ac 2:43 [i]Ac 4:32 [j]Ac 3:11
5:13 [k]Ac 2:47; 4:21
5:15 [l]Ac 19:12
5:16 [m]Mk 16:17
5:17 [n]Ac 15:5 [o]Ac 4:1
5:18 [p]Ac 4:3
5:19 [q]Mt 1:20; Lk 1:11; Ac 8:26; 27:23 [r]Ac 16:26
5:20 [s]Jn 6:63,68
5:21 [t]Ac 4:5,6 [u]ver 27,34,41; Mt 5:22
5:24 [v]Ac 4:1
5:26 [w]Ac 4:21
5:27 [x]Mt 5:22
5:28 [y]Ac 4:18 [z]Mt 23:35; 27:25; Ac 2:23,36; 3:14,15; 7:52
5:29 [a]Ac 4:19
5:30 [b]Ac 3:13

[u]16 Greek *unclean*

dead[a]—whom you had killed by
hanging him on a tree.[b] 31God exalted him to his own right hand[c] as
Prince and Savior[d] that he might
give repentance and forgiveness of
sins to Israel.[e] 32We are witnesses
of these things,[f] and so is the Holy
Spirit,[g] whom God has given to
those who obey him."

33When they heard this, they
were furious[h] and wanted to put
them to death. 34But a Pharisee
named Gamaliel,[i] a teacher of the
law,[j] who was honored by all the
people, stood up in the Sanhedrin
and ordered that the men be put
outside for a little while. 35Then he
addressed them: "Men of Israel,
consider carefully what you intend
to do to these men. 36Some time
ago Theudas appeared, claiming to
be somebody, and about four hundred men rallied to him. He was
killed, all his followers were dispersed, and it all came to nothing.
37After him, Judas the Galilean appeared in the days of the census[k]
and led a band of people in revolt.
He too was killed, and all his followers were scattered. 38Therefore,
in the present case I advise you:
Leave these men alone! Let them
go! For if their purpose or activity is
of human origin, it will fail.[l] 39But
if it is from God, you will not be
able to stop these men; you will
only find yourselves fighting
against God."[m]

40His speech persuaded them.
They called the apostles in and had
them flogged.[n] Then they ordered
them not to speak in the name of
Jesus, and let them go.

41The apostles left the Sanhedrin, rejoicing[o] because they had
been counted worthy of suffering
disgrace for the Name.[p] 42Day after day, in the temple courts[q] and
from house to house, they never
stopped teaching and proclaiming
the good news that Jesus is the
Christ.[v]

The Choosing of the Seven

6 In those days when the number of disciples was increasing,[r] the Grecian Jews[s] among
them complained against the He-
braic Jews because their widows[t]
were being overlooked in the daily
distribution of food.[u] 2So the
Twelve gathered all the disciples
together and said, "It would not be
right for us to neglect the ministry
of the word of God in order to wait
on tables. 3Brothers,[v] choose sev-
en men from among you who are
known to be full of the Spirit and
wisdom. We will turn this responsibility over to them 4and will give
our attention to prayer[w] and the
ministry of the word."

5This proposal pleased the
whole group. They chose Stephen,[x] a man full of faith and of
the Holy Spirit;[y] also Philip,[z]
Procorus, Nicanor, Timon, Parme-
nas, and Nicolas from Antioch, a
convert to Judaism. 6They presented these men to the apostles, who
prayed[a] and laid their hands on
them.[b]

7So the word of God spread.[c]
The number of disciples in Jerusalem increased rapidly, and a large
number of priests became obedient to the faith.

Stephen Seized

8Now Stephen, a man full of
God's grace and power, did great
wonders and miraculous signs[d]
among the people. 9Opposition
arose, however, from members of
the Synagogue of the Freedmen (as
it was called)—Jews of Cyrene[e]
and Alexandria as well as the provinces of Cilicia[f] and Asia.[g] These
men began to argue with Stephen,
10but they could not stand up
against his wisdom or the Spirit by
whom he spoke.[h]

11Then they secretly[i] persuaded some men to say, "We have
heard Stephen speak words of blasphemy against Moses and against
God."[j]

12So they stirred up the people
and the elders and the teachers of
the law. They seized Stephen and
brought him before the Sanhedrin.[k] 13They produced false wit-

5:30 [a] Ac 2:24 [b] Ac 10:39; 13:29; Gal 3:13; 1Pe 2:24
5:31 [c] Ac 2:33 [d] Lk 2:11 [e] Mt 1:21; Lk 24:47; Ac 2:38
5:32 [f] Lk 24:48 [g] Jn 15:26
5:33 [h] Ac 2:37; 7:54
5:34 [i] Ac 22:3 [j] Lk 2:46
5:37 [k] Lk 2:1,2
5:38 [l] Mt 15:13
5:39 [m] Pr 21:30; Ac 7:51; 11:17
5:40 [n] Mt 10:17
5:41 [o] Mt 5:12 [p] Jn 15:21
5:42 [q] Ac 2:46
6:1 [r] Ac 2:41 [s] Ac 9:29 [t] Ac 9:39,41 [u] Ac 4:35
6:3 [v] Ac 1:16
6:4 [w] Ac 1:14
6:5 [x] ver 8; Ac 11:19 [y] Ac 11:24 [z] Ac 8:5-40; 21:8
6:6 [a] Ac 1:24; 8:17; 13:3; 2Ti 1:6 [b] Nu 8:10; Ac 9:17; 1Ti 4:14
6:7 [c] Ac 12:24; 19:20
6:8 [d] Jn 4:48
6:9 [e] Mt 27:32 [f] Ac 15:23,41; 22:3; 23:34 [g] Ac 2:9
6:10 [h] Lk 21:15
6:11 [i] 1Ki 21:10 [j] Mt 26:59-61
6:12 [k] Mt 5:22

[v] 42 Or *Messiah*

nesses, who testified, "This fellow never stops speaking against this holy place[a] and against the law. **14**For we have heard him say that this Jesus of Nazareth will destroy this place and change the customs Moses handed down to us."[b]

15All who were sitting in the Sanhedrin[c] looked intently at Stephen, and they saw that his face was like the face of an angel.

Stephen's Speech to the Sanhedrin

7 Then the high priest asked him, "Are these charges true?"

2To this he replied: "Brothers and fathers,[d] listen to me! The God of glory[e] appeared to our father Abraham while he was still in Mesopotamia, before he lived in Haran.[f] **3**'Leave your country and your people,' God said, 'and go to the land I will show you.'[w][g]

4"So he left the land of the Chaldeans and settled in Haran. After the death of his father, God sent him to this land where you are now living.[h] **5**He gave him no inheritance here, not even a foot of ground. But God promised him that he and his descendants after him would possess the land,[i] even though at that time Abraham had no child. **6**God spoke to him in this way: 'Your descendants will be strangers in a country not their own, and they will be enslaved and mistreated four hundred years.[j] **7**But I will punish the nation they serve as slaves,' God said, 'and afterward they will come out of that country and worship me in this place.'[x][k] **8**Then he gave Abraham the covenant of circumcision.[l] And Abraham became the father of Isaac and circumcised him eight days after his birth.[m] Later Isaac became the father of Jacob,[n] and Jacob became the father of the twelve patriarchs.[o]

9"Because the patriarchs were jealous of Joseph,[p] they sold him as a slave into Egypt.[q] But God was with him[r] **10**and rescued him from all his troubles. He gave Joseph wisdom and enabled him to gain the goodwill of Pharaoh king of Egypt; so he made him ruler over Egypt and all his palace.[s]

11"Then a famine struck all Egypt and Canaan, bringing great suffering, and our fathers could not find food.[t] **12**When Jacob heard that there was grain in Egypt, he sent our fathers on their first visit.[u] **13**On their second visit, Joseph told his brothers who he was,[v] and Pharaoh learned about Joseph's family. **14**After this, Joseph sent for his father Jacob and his whole family,[w] seventy-five in all.[x] **15**Then Jacob went down to Egypt, where he and our fathers died.[y] **16**Their bodies were brought back to Shechem and placed in the tomb that Abraham had bought from the sons of Hamor at Shechem for a certain sum of money.[z]

17"As the time drew near for God to fulfill his promise to Abraham, the number of our people in Egypt greatly increased.[a] **18**Then another king, who knew nothing about Joseph, became ruler of Egypt.[b] **19**He dealt treacherously with our people and oppressed our forefathers by forcing them to throw out their newborn babies so that they would die.[c]

20"At that time Moses was born, and he was no ordinary child.[y] For three months he was cared for in his father's house.[d] **21**When he was placed outside, Pharaoh's daughter took him and brought him up as her own son.[e] **22**Moses was educated in all the wisdom of the Egyptians[f] and was powerful in speech and action.

23"When Moses was forty years old, he decided to visit his fellow Israelites. **24**He saw one of them being mistreated by an Egyptian, so he went to his defense and avenged him by killing the Egyptian. **25**Moses thought that his own people would realize that God was using him to rescue them, but they did not. **26**The next day Moses

6:13 [a]Ac 21:28
6:14 [b]Ac 15:1; 21:21; 26:3; 28:17
6:15 [c]Mt 5:22
7:2 [d]Ac 22:1 [e]Ps 29:3 [f]Ge 11:31; 15:7
7:3 [g]Ge 12:1
7:4 [h]Ge 12:5
7:5 [i]Ge 12:7; 17:8; 26:3
7:6 [j]Ex 12:40
7:7 [k]Ex 3:12
7:8 [l]Ge 17:9-14 [m]Ge 21:2-4 [n]Ge 25:26 [o]Ge 29:31-35; 30:5-13, 17-24; 35:16-18, 22-26
7:9 [p]Ge 37:4,11 [q]Ge 37:28; Ps 105:17 [r]Ge 39:2,21, 23
7:10 [s]Ge 41:37-43
7:11 [t]Ge 41:54
7:12 [u]Ge 42:1,2
7:13 [v]Ge 45:1-4
7:14 [w]Ge 45:9,10 [x]Ge 46:26,27; Ex 1:5; Dt 10:22
7:15 [y]Ge 46:5-7; 49:33; Ex 1:6
7:16 [z]Ge 23:16-20; 33:18,19; 50:13; Jos 24:32
7:17 [a]Ex 1:7; Ps 105:24
7:18 [b]Ex 1:8
7:19 [c]Ex 1:10-22
7:20 [d]Ex 2:2; Heb 11:23
7:21 [e]Ex 2:3-10
7:22 [f]1Ki 4:30; Isa 19:11

[w]3 Gen. 12:1 [x]7 Gen. 15:13,14 [y]20 Or *was fair in the sight of God*

came upon two Israelites who were
fighting. He tried to reconcile them
by saying, 'Men, you are brothers;
why do you want to hurt each
other?'
27"But the man who was mis-
treating the other pushed Moses
aside and said, 'Who made you ruler and judge over us? 28Do you
want to kill me as you killed the
Egyptian yesterday?'[z] 29When Moses heard this, he fled to Midian,
where he settled as a foreigner and
had two sons.[a]
30"After forty years had passed,
an angel appeared to Moses in the
flames of a burning bush in the
desert near Mount Sinai. 31When
he saw this, he was amazed at the
sight. As he went over to look more
closely, he heard the Lord's
voice:[b] 32'I am the God of your fathers, the God of Abraham, Isaac
and Jacob.'[a] Moses trembled with
fear and did not dare to look.[c]
33"Then the Lord said to him,
'Take off your sandals; the place
where you are standing is holy
ground.[d] 34I have indeed seen the
oppression of my people in Egypt.
I have heard their groaning and
have come down to set them free.
Now come, I will send you back to
Egypt.'[b][e]
35"This is the same Moses whom
they had rejected with the words,
'Who made you ruler and judge?'[f]
He was sent to be their ruler and
deliverer by God himself, through
the angel who appeared to him in
the bush. 36He led them out of
Egypt[g] and did wonders and miraculous signs in Egypt, at the Red
Sea[c][h] and for forty years in the
desert.
37"This is that Moses who told
the Israelites, 'God will send you a
prophet like me from your own
people.'[d][i] 38He was in the assembly in the desert, with the angel[j]
who spoke to him on Mount Sinai,
and with our fathers;[k] and he received living words[l] to pass on to
us.[m]
39"But our fathers refused to
obey him. Instead, they rejected
him and in their hearts turned back
to Egypt.[n] 40They told Aaron,
'Make us gods who will go before
us. As for this fellow Moses who led
us out of Egypt—we don't know
what has happened to him!'[e][o]
41That was the time they made an
idol in the form of a calf. They
brought sacrifices to it and held a
celebration in honor of what their
hands had made.[p] 42But God
turned away[q] and gave them over
to the worship of the heavenly bodies.[r] This agrees with what is written in the book of the prophets:

" 'Did you bring me sacrifices
and offerings
forty years in the desert,
O house of Israel?
43You have lifted up the shrine of
Molech
and the star of your god
Rephan,
the idols you made to
worship.
Therefore I will send you into
exile'[f][s] beyond
Babylon.

44"Our forefathers had the tabernacle of the Testimony[t] with them
in the desert. It had been made as
God directed Moses, according to
the pattern he had seen.[u] 45Hav-
ing received the tabernacle, our fathers under Joshua brought it with
them when they took the land from
the nations God drove out before
them.[v] It remained in the land until the time of David, 46who enjoyed God's favor and asked that he
might provide a dwelling place for
the God of Jacob.[g][w] 47But it was
Solomon who built the house for
him.
48"However, the Most High does
not live in houses made by men.[x]
As the prophet says:

49" 'Heaven is my throne,
and the earth is my
footstool.[y]
What kind of house will you

7:29 [a]Ex 2:11-15
7:31 [b]Ex 3:1-4
7:32 [c]Ex 3:6
7:33 [d]Ex 3:5; Jos 5:15
7:34 [e]Ex 3:7-10
7:35 [f]ver 27
7:36 [g]Ex 12:41; 33:1 [h]Ex 14:21
7:37 [i]Dt 18:15,18; Ac 3:22
7:38 [j]ver 53 [k]Ex 19:17 [l]Dt 32:45-47; Heb 4:12 [m]Ro 3:2
7:39 [n]Nu 14:3,4
7:40 [o]Ex 32:1,23
7:41 [p]Ex 32:4-6; Ps 106:19,20; Rev 9:20
7:42 [q]Jos 24:20; Isa 63:10 [r]Jer 19:13
7:43 [s]Am 5:25-27
7:44 [t]Ex 38:21 [u]Ex 25:8,9,40
7:45 [v]Jos 3:14-17; 18:1; 23:9; 24:18; Ps 44:2
7:46 [w]2Sa 7:8-16; Ps 132:1-5
7:48 [x]1Ki 8:27; 2Ch 2:6
7:49 [y]Mt 5:34,35

[z]*28* Exodus 2:14 [a]*32* Exodus 3:6 [b]*34* Exodus 3:5,7,8,10 [c]*36* That is, Sea of Reeds [d]*37* Deut. 18:15 [e]*40* Exodus 32:1 [f]*43* Amos 5:25-27 [g]*46* Some early manuscripts *the house of Jacob*

build for me?
says the Lord.
Or where will my resting
place be?
50Has not my hand made all
these things?'[h][a]

51"You stiff-necked people,[b]
with uncircumcised hearts[c] and
ears! You are just like your fathers:
You always resist the Holy Spirit!
52Was there ever a prophet your fathers did not persecute?[d] They
even killed those who predicted
the coming of the Righteous One.
And now you have betrayed and
murdered him[e]— **53**you who have
received the law that was put into
effect through angels[f] but have
not obeyed it."

The Stoning of Stephen

54When they heard this, they
were furious[g] and gnashed their
teeth at him. **55**But Stephen, full of
the Holy Spirit, looked up to heav-
en and saw the glory of God, and
Jesus standing at the right hand of
God.[h] **56**"Look," he said, "I see
heaven open[i] and the Son of
Man[j] standing at the right hand of
God."
57At this they covered their ears
and, yelling at the top of their
voices, they all rushed at him,
58dragged him out of the city[k] and
began to stone him.[l] Meanwhile,
the witnesses laid their clothes[m] at
the feet of a young man named
Saul.[n]
59While they were stoning him,
Stephen prayed, "Lord Jesus, receive my spirit."[o] **60**Then he fell on
his knees[p] and cried out, "Lord, do
not hold this sin against them."[q]
When he had said this, he fell
asleep.

8 And Saul[r] was there, giving
approval to his death.

The Church Persecuted and Scattered

On that day a great persecution
broke out against the church at Jerusalem, and all except the apostles were scattered[s] throughout
Judea and Samaria.[t] **2**Godly men

7:50 [a]Isa 66:1,2
7:51 [b]Ex 32:9; 33:3,5 [c]Lev 26:41; Dt 10:16; Jer 4:4; 9:26
7:52 [d]2Ch 36:16; Mt 5:12 [e]Ac 3:14; 1Th 2:15
7:53 [f]ver 38; Gal 3:19; Heb 2:2
7:54 [g]Ac 5:33
7:55 [h]Mk 16:19
7:56 [i]Mt 3:16 [j]Mt 8:20
7:58 [k]Lk 4:29 [l]Lev 24:14,16; Dt 13:9 [m]Ac 22:20 [n]Ac 8:1
7:59 [o]Ps 31:5; Lk 23:46
7:60 [p]Ac 9:40 [q]Mt 5:44
8:1 [r]Ac 7:58 [s]Ac 11:19 [t]Ac 9:31
8:3 [u]Ac 7:58 [v]Ac 22:4,19; 26:10,11; 1Co 15:9; Gal 1:13,23; Php 3:6; 1Ti 1:13
8:4 [w]ver 1 [x]Ac 15:35
8:5 [y]Ac 6:5
8:7 [z]Mk 16:17 [a]Mt 4:24
8:9 [b]Ac 13:6 [c]Ac 5:36
8:10 [d]Ac 14:11; 28:6
8:12 [e]Ac 1:3 [f]Ac 2:38
8:13 [g]ver 6; Ac 19:11
8:14 [h]ver 1 [i]Lk 22:8
8:15 [j]Ac 2:38
8:16 [k]Ac 19:2 [l]Mt 28:19; Ac 2:38

buried Stephen and mourned
deeply for him. **3**But Saul[u] began
to destroy the church.[v] Going from
house to house, he dragged off
men and women and put them in
prison.

Philip in Samaria

4Those who had been scattered[w]
preached the word wherever they
went.[x] **5**Philip[y] went down to a
city in Samaria and proclaimed the
Christ[i] there. **6**When the crowds
heard Philip and saw the miraculous signs he did, they all paid
close attention to what he said.
7With shrieks, evil[j] spirits came
out of many,[z] and many paralytics
and cripples were healed.[a] **8**So
there was great joy in that city.

Simon the Sorcerer

9Now for some time a man
named Simon had practiced sorcery[b] in the city and amazed all
the people of Samaria. He boasted
that he was someone great,[c] **10**and
all the people, both high and low,
gave him their attention and exclaimed, "This man is the divine
power known as the Great Pow-
er."[d] **11**They followed him because
he had amazed them for a long
time with his magic. **12**But when
they believed Philip as he preached
the good news of the kingdom of
God[e] and the name of Jesus
Christ, they were baptized,[f] both
men and women. **13**Simon himself
believed and was baptized. And he
followed Philip everywhere, astonished by the great signs and miracles[g] he saw.
14When the apostles in Jerusalem heard that Samaria[h] had accepted the word of God, they sent
Peter and John[i] to them. **15**When
they arrived, they prayed for them
that they might receive the Holy
Spirit,[j] **16**because the Holy Spirit
had not yet come upon any of
them;[k] they had simply been baptized into[k] the name of the Lord
Jesus.[l] **17**Then Peter and John

[h]*50* Isaiah 66:1,2 [i]*5* Or *Messiah*
[j]*7* Greek *unclean* [k]*16* Or *in*

placed their hands on them,[a] and they received the Holy Spirit.

18When Simon saw that the Spirit was given at the laying on of the apostles' hands, he offered them money **19**and said, "Give me also this ability so that everyone on whom I lay my hands may receive the Holy Spirit."

20Peter answered: "May your money perish with you, because you thought you could buy the gift of God with money![b] **21**You have no part or share in this ministry, because your heart is not right[c] before God. **22**Repent of this wickedness and pray to the Lord. Perhaps he will forgive you for having such a thought in your heart. **23**For I see that you are full of bitterness and captive to sin."

24Then Simon answered, "Pray to the Lord for me[d] so that nothing you have said may happen to me."

25When they had testified and proclaimed the word of the Lord, Peter and John returned to Jerusalem, preaching the gospel in many Samaritan villages.[e]

Philip and the Ethiopian

26Now an angel[f] of the Lord said to Philip, "Go south to the road—the desert road—that goes down from Jerusalem to Gaza." **27**So he started out, and on his way he met an Ethiopian[l][g] eunuch,[h] an important official in charge of all the treasury of Candace, queen of the Ethiopians. This man had gone to Jerusalem to worship,[i] **28**and on his way home was sitting in his chariot reading the book of Isaiah the prophet. **29**The Spirit told[j] Philip, "Go to that chariot and stay near it."

30Then Philip ran up to the chariot and heard the man reading Isaiah the prophet. "Do you understand what you are reading?" Philip asked.

31"How can I," he said, "unless someone explains it to me?" So he invited Philip to come up and sit with him.

32The eunuch was reading this passage of Scripture:

8:17 [a]Ac 6:6
8:20 [b]2Ki 5:16; Da 5:17; Mt 10:8; Ac 2:38
8:21 [c]Ps 78:37
8:24 [d]Ex 8:8; Nu 21:7; 1Ki 13:6
8:25 [e]ver 40
8:26 [f]Ac 5:19
8:27 [g]Ps 68:31; 87:4; Zep 3:10 [h]Isa 56:3-5 [i]1Ki 8:41-43; Jn 12:20
8:29 [j]Ac 10:19; 11:12; 13:2; 20:23; 21:11
8:33 [k]Isa 53:7,8
8:35 [l]Mt 5:2 [m]Lk 24:27; Ac 17:2; 18:28; 28:23
8:36 [n]Ac 10:47
8:39 [o]1Ki 18:12; 2Ki 2:16; Eze 3:12,14; 8:3; 11:1,24; 43:5; 2Co 12:2
8:40 [p]ver 25 [q]Ac 10:1,24; 12:19; 21:8, 16; 23:23,33; 25:1,4,6,13
9:1 [r]Ac 8:3
9:2 [s]Ac 19:9,23; 22:4; 24:14, 22

"He was led like a sheep to the
slaughter,
and as a lamb before the
shearer is silent,
so he did not open his
mouth.
33In his humiliation he was
deprived of justice.
Who can speak of his
descendants?
For his life was taken from
the earth."[m][k]

34The eunuch asked Philip, "Tell me, please, who is the prophet talking about, himself or someone else?" **35**Then Philip began[l] with that very passage of Scripture[m] and told him the good news about Jesus.

36As they traveled along the road, they came to some water and the eunuch said, "Look, here is water. Why shouldn't I be baptized?"[n][n] **38**And he gave orders to stop the chariot. Then both Philip and the eunuch went down into the water and Philip baptized him. **39**When they came up out of the water, the Spirit of the Lord suddenly took Philip away,[o] and the eunuch did not see him again, but went on his way rejoicing. **40**Philip, however, appeared at Azotus and traveled about, preaching the gospel in all the towns[p] until he reached Caesarea.[q]

Saul's Conversion

9:1–19pp — Ac 22:3–16; 26:9–18

9 Meanwhile, Saul was still breathing out murderous threats against the Lord's disciples.[r] He went to the high priest **2**and asked him for letters to the synagogues in Damascus, so that if he found any there who belonged to the Way,[s] whether men or women, he might take them as prisoners to Jerusalem. **3**As he neared Damascus on his journey, suddenly a light from heaven flashed around

[l]27 That is, from the upper Nile region [m]33 Isaiah 53:7,8 [n]36 Some late manuscripts *baptized?"* [37]*Philip said, "If you believe with all your heart, you may." The eunuch answered, "I believe that Jesus Christ is the Son of God."*

him.[a] 4He fell to the ground and heard a voice say to him, "Saul, Saul, why do you persecute me?"

5"Who are you, Lord?" Saul asked.

"I am Jesus, whom you are persecuting," he replied. 6"Now get up and go into the city, and you will be told what you must do."[b]

7The men traveling with Saul stood there speechless; they heard the sound[c] but did not see anyone.[d] 8Saul got up from the ground, but when he opened his eyes he could see nothing. So they led him by the hand into Damascus. 9For three days he was blind, and did not eat or drink anything.

10In Damascus there was a disciple named Ananias. The Lord called to him in a vision,[e] "Ananias!"

"Yes, Lord," he answered.

11The Lord told him, "Go to the house of Judas on Straight Street and ask for a man from Tarsus[f] named Saul, for he is praying. 12In a vision he has seen a man named Ananias come and place his hands on[g] him to restore his sight."

13"Lord," Ananias answered, "I have heard many reports about this man and all the harm he has done to your saints[h] in Jerusalem.[i] 14And he has come here with authority from the chief priests[j] to arrest all who call on your name."

15But the Lord said to Ananias, "Go! This man is my chosen instrument[k] to carry my name before the Gentiles[l] and their kings[m] and before the people of Israel. 16I will show him how much he must suffer for my name."[n]

17Then Ananias went to the house and entered it. Placing his hands on[o] Saul, he said, "Brother Saul, the Lord—Jesus, who appeared to you on the road as you were coming here—has sent me so that you may see again and be filled with the Holy Spirit." 18Immediately, something like scales fell from Saul's eyes, and he could see again. He got up and was baptized, 19and after taking some food, he regained his strength.

Saul in Damascus and Jerusalem

Saul spent several days with the disciples[p] in Damascus.[q] 20At once he began to preach in the synagogues[r] that Jesus is the Son of God.[s] 21All those who heard him were astonished and asked, "Isn't he the man who raised havoc in Jerusalem among those who call on this name?[t] And hasn't he come here to take them as prisoners to the chief priests?"[u] 22Yet Saul grew more and more powerful and baffled the Jews living in Damascus by proving that Jesus is the Christ.[o][v]

23After many days had gone by, the Jews conspired to kill him, 24but Saul learned of their plan.[w] Day and night they kept close watch on the city gates in order to kill him. 25But his followers took him by night and lowered him in a basket through an opening in the wall.[x]

26When he came to Jerusalem,[y] he tried to join the disciples, but they were all afraid of him, not believing that he really was a disciple. 27But Barnabas[z] took him and brought him to the apostles. He told them how Saul on his journey had seen the Lord and that the Lord had spoken to him,[a] and how in Damascus he had preached fearlessly in the name of Jesus.[b] 28So Saul stayed with them and moved about freely in Jerusalem, speaking boldly in the name of the Lord. 29He talked and debated with the Grecian Jews,[c] but they tried to kill him.[d] 30When the brothers[e] learned of this, they took him down to Caesarea[f] and sent him off to Tarsus.[g]

31Then the church throughout Judea, Galilee and Samaria[h] enjoyed a time of peace. It was strengthened; and encouraged by the Holy Spirit, it grew in numbers, living in the fear of the Lord.

[o]22 Or *Messiah*

9:3 [a] 1Co 15:8
9:6 [b] ver 16
9:7 [c] Jn 12:29 [d] Da 10:7; Ac 22:9
9:10 [e] Ac 10:3,17, 19
9:11 [f] ver 30; Ac 21:39; 22:3
9:12 [g] Mk 5:23
9:13 [h] ver 32; Ro 1:7; 16:2, 15 [i] Ac 8:3
9:14 [j] ver 2,21
9:15 [k] Ac 13:2; Ro 1:1; Gal 1:15 [l] Ro 11:13; 15:15,16; Gal 2:7,8; Eph 3:7,8 [m] Ac 25:22,23; 26:1
9:16 [n] Ac 20:23; 21:11; 2Co 11:23-27
9:17 [o] Ac 6:6
9:19 [p] Ac 11:26 [q] Ac 26:20
9:20 [r] Ac 13:5,14 [s] Mt 4:3
9:21 [t] Ac 8:3 [u] Gal 1:13,23
9:22 [v] Ac 18:5,28
9:24 [w] Ac 20:3,19
9:25 [x] 1Sa 19:12; 2Co 11:32,33
9:26 [y] Ac 22:17; 26:20; Gal 1:17,18
9:27 [z] Ac 4:36 [a] ver 3-6 [b] ver 20,22
9:29 [c] Ac 6:1 [d] 2Co 11:26
9:30 [e] Ac 1:16 [f] Ac 8:40 [g] ver 11
9:31 [h] Ac 8:1

Aeneas and Dorcas

32As Peter traveled about the
country, he went to visit the
saints[a] in Lydda. 33There he found
a man named Aeneas, a paralytic
who had been bedridden for eight
years. 34"Aeneas," Peter said to
him, "Jesus Christ heals you.[b] Get
up and take care of your mat." Immediately Aeneas got up. 35All
those who lived in Lydda and Sharon[c] saw him and turned to the
Lord.[d]
36In Joppa[e] there was a disciple
named Tabitha (which, when
translated, is Dorcas[p]), who was
always doing good[f] and helping
the poor. 37About that time she became sick and died, and her body
was washed and placed in an upstairs room.[g] 38Lydda was near
Joppa; so when the disciples[h]
heard that Peter was in Lydda, they
sent two men to him and urged
him, "Please come at once!"
39Peter went with them, and
when he arrived he was taken upstairs to the room. All the widows[i]
stood around him, crying and
showing him the robes and other
clothing that Dorcas had made
while she was still with them.
40Peter sent them all out of the
room;[j] then he got down on his
knees[k] and prayed. Turning toward the dead woman, he said,
"Tabitha, get up." She opened her
eyes, and seeing Peter she sat up.
41He took her by the hand and
helped her to her feet. Then he
called the believers and the widows
and presented her to them alive.
42This became known all over Joppa, and many people believed in
the Lord. 43Peter stayed in Joppa
for some time with a tanner named
Simon.[l]

Cornelius Calls for Peter

10 At Caesarea[m] there was a
man named Cornelius, a
centurion in what was known as
the Italian Regiment. 2He and all
his family were devout and God-
fearing;[n] he gave generously to
those in need and prayed to God
regularly. 3One day at about three
in the afternoon[o] he had a vision.[p]
He distinctly saw an angel[q] of
God, who came to him and said,
"Cornelius!"
4Cornelius stared at him in fear.
"What is it, Lord?" he asked.
The angel answered, "Your
prayers and gifts to the poor have
come up as a memorial offering[r]
before God.[s] 5Now send men to
Joppa[t] to bring back a man named
Simon who is called Peter. 6He is
staying with Simon the tanner,[u]
whose house is by the sea."
7When the angel who spoke to
him had gone, Cornelius called two
of his servants and a devout soldier
who was one of his attendants. 8He
told them everything that had happened and sent them to Joppa.[v]

Peter's Vision

10:9–32Ref — Ac 11:5–14

9About noon the following day
as they were on their journey and
approaching the city, Peter went
up on the roof[w] to pray. 10He became hungry and wanted something to eat, and while the meal
was being prepared, he fell into a
trance.[x] 11He saw heaven opened
and something like a large sheet
being let down to earth by its four
corners. 12It contained all kinds of
four-footed animals, as well as reptiles of the earth and birds of the
air. 13Then a voice told him, "Get
up, Peter. Kill and eat."
14"Surely not, Lord!"[y] Peter replied. "I have never eaten anything
impure or unclean."[z]
15The voice spoke to him a second time, "Do not call anything impure that God has made clean."[a]
16This happened three times,
and immediately the sheet was tak-
en back to heaven.
17While Peter was wondering
about the meaning of the vision,
the men sent by Cornelius[b] found
out where Simon's house was and
stopped at the gate. 18They called
out, asking if Simon who was

9:32 [a]ver 13
9:34 [b]Ac 3:6,16; 4:10
9:35 [c]1Ch 5:16; 27:29; Isa 33:9; 35:2; 65:10 [d]Ac 11:21
9:36 [e]Jos 19:46; 2Ch 2:16; Ezr 3:7; Jnh 1:3; Ac 10:5 [f]1Ti 2:10; Tit 3:8
9:37 [g]Ac 1:13
9:38 [h]Ac 11:26
9:39 [i]Ac 6:1
9:40 [j]Mt 9:25 [k]Lk 22:41; Ac 7:60
9:43 [l]Ac 10:6
10:1 [m]Ac 8:40
10:2 [n]ver 22,35; Ac 13:16,26
10:3 [o]Ac 3:1 [p]Ac 9:10 [q]Ac 5:19
10:4 [r]Mt 26:13 [s]Rev 8:4
10:5 [t]Ac 9:36
10:6 [u]Ac 9:43
10:8 [v]Ac 9:36
10:9 [w]Mt 24:17
10:10 [x]Ac 22:17
10:14 [y]Ac 9:5 [z]Lev 11:4-8, 13-20; 20:25; Dt 14:3-20; Eze 4:14
10:15 [a]Mt 15:11; Ro 14:14,17, 20; 1Co 10:25; 1Ti 4:3,4; Tit 1:15
10:17 [b]ver 7,8

p36 Both *Tabitha* (Aramaic) and *Dorcas* (Greek) mean *gazelle*.

known as Peter was staying there.
19While Peter was still thinking
about the vision, the Spirit said[a] to
him, "Simon, three[q] men are looking for you. 20So get up and go
downstairs. Do not hesitate to go
with them, for I have sent them."[b]
21Peter went down and said to
the men, "I'm the one you're looking for. Why have you come?"
22The men replied, "We have
come from Cornelius the centurion. He is a righteous and God-fearing man,[c] who is respected by all
the Jewish people. A holy angel
told him to have you come to his
house so that he could hear what
you have to say."[d] 23Then Peter invited the men into the house to be
his guests.

Peter at Cornelius' House

The next day Peter started out
with them, and some of the brothers[e] from Joppa went along.[f]
24The following day he arrived in
Caesarea.[g] Cornelius was expecting them and had called together
his relatives and close friends. 25As
Peter entered the house, Cornelius
met him and fell at his feet in reverence. 26But Peter made him get up.
"Stand up," he said, "I am only a
man myself."[h]
27Talking with him, Peter went
inside and found a large gathering
of people. 28He said to them: "You
are well aware that it is against our
law for a Jew to associate with a
Gentile or visit him.[i] But God has
shown me that I should not call any
man impure or unclean.[j] 29So
when I was sent for, I came without
raising any objection. May I ask
why you sent for me?"
30Cornelius answered: "Four
days ago I was in my house praying
at this hour, at three in the afternoon. Suddenly a man in shining
clothes stood before me 31and
said, 'Cornelius, God has heard
your prayer and remembered your
gifts to the poor. 32Send to Joppa
for Simon who is called Peter. He is
a guest in the home of Simon the
tanner, who lives by the sea.' 33So
I sent for you immediately, and it
was good of you to come. Now we
are all here in the presence of God
to listen to everything the Lord has
commanded you to tell us."
34Then Peter began to speak: "I
now realize how true it is that God
does not show favoritism[k] 35but
accepts men from every nation who
fear him and do what is right.[l]
36You know the message God sent
to the people of Israel, telling the
good news[m] of peace[n] through
Jesus Christ, who is Lord of all.[o]
37You know what has happened
throughout Judea, beginning in
Galilee after the baptism that John
preached— 38how God anointed[p]
Jesus of Nazareth with the Holy
Spirit and power, and how he went
around doing good and healing[q]
all who were under the power of
the devil, because God was with
him.[r]
39"We are witnesses[s] of everything he did in the country of the
Jews and in Jerusalem. They killed
him by hanging him on a tree,[t]
40but God raised him from the
dead[u] on the third day and caused
him to be seen. 41He was not seen
by all the people,[v] but by witnesses whom God had already chosen—by us who ate[w] and drank
with him after he rose from the
dead. 42He commanded us to
preach to the people[x] and to testify that he is the one whom God appointed as judge of the living and
the dead.[y] 43All the prophets testify about him[z] that everyone[a] who
believes in him receives forgiveness of sins through his name."
44While Peter was still speaking
these words, the Holy Spirit came
on[b] all who heard the message.
45The circumcised believers who
had come with Peter[c] were astonished that the gift of the Holy Spirit
had been poured out[d] even on the
Gentiles.[e] 46For they heard them
speaking in tongues[r][f] and praising God.
Then Peter said, 47"Can anyone

10:19 [a]Ac 8:29
10:20 [b]Ac 15:7-9
10:22 [c]ver 2 [d]Ac 11:14
10:23 [e]Ac 1:16 [f]ver 45; Ac 11:12
10:24 [g]Ac 8:40
10:26 [h]Ac 14:15; Rev 19:10
10:28 [i]Jn 4:9; 18:28; Ac 11:3 [j]Ac 15:8,9
10:34 [k]Dt 10:17; 2Ch 19:7; Job 34:19; Ro 2:11; Gal 2:6; Eph 6:9; Col 3:25; 1Pe 1:17
10:35 [l]Ac 15:9
10:36 [m]Ac 13:32 [n]Lk 2:14 [o]Mt 28:18; Ro 10:12
10:38 [p]Ac 4:26 [q]Mt 4:23 [r]Jn 3:2
10:39 [s]Lk 24:48 [t]Ac 5:30
10:40 [u]Ac 2:24
10:41 [v]Jn 14:17,22 [w]Lk 24:43; Jn 21:13
10:42 [x]Mt 28:19,20 [y]Jn 5:22; Ac 17:31; Ro 14:9; 2Co 5:10; 2Ti 4:1; 1Pe 4:5
10:43 [z]Isa 53:11 [a]Ac 15:9
10:44 [b]Ac 8:15,16; 11:15; 15:8
10:45 [c]ver 23 [d]Ac 2:33,38 [e]Ac 11:18
10:46 [f]Mk 16:17

[q]19 One early manuscript *two*; other manuscripts do not have the number.
[r]46 Or *other languages*

keep these people from being baptized with water?[a] They have received the Holy Spirit just as we
have."[b] 48So he ordered that they
be baptized in the name of Jesus
Christ.[c] Then they asked Peter to
stay with them for a few days.

Peter Explains His Actions

11 The apostles and the brothers[d] throughout Judea
heard that the Gentiles also had received the word of God. 2So when
Peter went up to Jerusalem, the
circumcised believers[e] criticized
him 3and said, "You went into the
house of uncircumcised men and
ate with them."[f]
4Peter began and explained everything to them precisely as it had
happened: 5"I was in the city of
Joppa praying, and in a trance I saw
a vision.[g] I saw something like a
large sheet being let down from
heaven by its four corners, and it
came down to where I was. 6I
looked into it and saw four-footed
animals of the earth, wild beasts,
reptiles, and birds of the air. 7Then
I heard a voice telling me, 'Get up,
Peter. Kill and eat.'
8"I replied, 'Surely not, Lord!
Nothing impure or unclean has
ever entered my mouth.'
9"The voice spoke from heaven a
second time, 'Do not call anything
impure that God has made
clean.'[h] 10This happened three
times, and then it was all pulled up
to heaven again.
11"Right then three men who
had been sent to me from Caesarea
stopped at the house where I was
staying. 12The Spirit told[i] me to
have no hesitation about going
with them.[j] These six brothers
also went with me, and we entered
the man's house. 13He told us how
he had seen an angel appear in his
house and say, 'Send to Joppa for
Simon who is called Peter. 14He
will bring you a message through
which you and all your household[k]
will be saved.'
15"As I began to speak, the Holy
Spirit came on[l] them as he had
come on us at the beginning.[m]
16Then I remembered what the
Lord had said: 'John baptized
with[s] water, but you will be baptized with the Holy Spirit.'[n] 17So if
God gave them the same gift as he
gave us,[o] who believed in the Lord
Jesus Christ, who was I to think
that I could oppose God?"
18When they heard this, they had
no further objections and praised
God, saying, "So then, God has
granted even the Gentiles repentance unto life."[p]

The Church in Antioch

19Now those who had been scattered by the persecution in connection with Stephen[q] traveled as far
as Phoenicia, Cyprus and Antioch,[r] telling the message only to
Jews. 20Some of them, however,
men from Cyprus[s] and Cyrene,[t]
went to Antioch and began to
speak to Greeks also, telling them
the good news about the Lord
Jesus. 21The Lord's hand was with
them,[u] and a great number of people believed and turned to the
Lord.[v]
22News of this reached the ears
of the church at Jerusalem, and
they sent Barnabas[w] to Antioch.
23When he arrived and saw the evidence of the grace of God,[x] he was
glad and encouraged them all to remain true to the Lord with all their
hearts.[y] 24He was a good man, full
of the Holy Spirit and faith, and a
great number of people were
brought to the Lord.[z]
25Then Barnabas went to Tarsus[a] to look for Saul, 26and when
he found him, he brought him to
Antioch. So for a whole year Barnabas and Saul met with the church
and taught great numbers of people. The disciples[b] were called
Christians first[c] at Antioch.
27During this time some prophets[d] came down from Jerusalem to
Antioch. 28One of them, named
Agabus,[e] stood up and through the
Spirit predicted that a severe famine would spread over the entire
Roman world.[f] (This happened

10:47 [a]Ac 8:36 [b]Ac 11:17
10:48 [c]Ac 2:38; 8:16
11:1 [d]Ac 1:16
11:2 [e]Ac 10:45
11:3 [f]Ac 10:25,28; Gal 2:12
11:5 [g]Ac 10:9-32; 9:10
11:9 [h]Ac 10:15
11:12 [i]Ac 8:29 [j]Ac 15:9; Ro 3:22
11:14 [k]Jn 4:53; Ac 16:15, 31-34; 1Co 1:11,16
11:15 [l]Ac 10:44 [m]Ac 2:4
11:16 [n]Mk 1:8; Ac 1:5
11:17 [o]Ac 10:45,47
11:18 [p]Ro 10:12,13; 2Co 7:10
11:19 [q]Ac 8:1,4 [r]ver 26,27; Ac 13:1; 18:22; Gal 2:11
11:20 [s]Ac 4:36 [t]Mt 27:32
11:21 [u]Lk 1:66 [v]Ac 2:47
11:22 [w]Ac 4:36
11:23 [x]Ac 13:43; 14:26; 20:24 [y]Ac 14:22
11:24 [z]ver 21; Ac 5:14
11:25 [a]Ac 9:11
11:26 [b]Ac 6:1,2; 13:52 [c]Ac 26:28; 1Pe 4:16
11:27 [d]Ac 13:1; 15:32; 1Co 12:28,29; Eph 4:11
11:28 [e]Ac 21:10 [f]Mt 24:14

[s]16 Or *in*

during the reign of Claudius.)[a]
29The disciples,[b] each according
to his ability, decided to provide
help[c] for the brothers[d] living in
Judea. **30**This they did, sending
their gift to the elders[e] by Barnabas and Saul.[f]

Peter's Miraculous Escape From Prison

12 It was about this time that
King Herod arrested some
who belonged to the church, intending to persecute them. **2**He
had James, the brother of John,[g]
put to death with the sword. **3**When
he saw that this pleased the Jews,[h]
he proceeded to seize Peter also.
This happened during the Feast of
Unleavened Bread.[i] **4**After arresting him, he put him in prison,
handing him over to be guarded by
four squads of four soldiers each.
Herod intended to bring him out
for public trial after the Passover.
5So Peter was kept in prison, but
the church was earnestly praying to
God for him.[j]
6The night before Herod was to
bring him to trial, Peter was sleeping between two soldiers, bound
with two chains,[k] and sentries
stood guard at the entrance. **7**Suddenly an angel[l] of the Lord appeared and a light shone in the cell.
He struck Peter on the side and
woke him up. "Quick, get up!" he
said, and the chains fell off Peter's
wrists.[m]
8Then the angel said to him,
"Put on your clothes and sandals."
And Peter did so. "Wrap your cloak
around you and follow me," the angel told him. **9**Peter followed him
out of the prison, but he had no
idea that what the angel was doing
was really happening; he thought
he was seeing a vision.[n] **10**They
passed the first and second guards
and came to the iron gate leading
to the city. It opened for them by
itself,[o] and they went through it.
When they had walked the length
of one street, suddenly the angel
left him.
11Then Peter came to himself[p]
and said, "Now I know without a
doubt that the Lord sent his angel
and rescued me[q] from Herod's
clutches and from everything the
Jewish people were anticipating."
12When this had dawned on him,
he went to the house of Mary the
mother of John, also called Mark,[r]
where many people had gathered
and were praying.[s] **13**Peter
knocked at the outer entrance, and
a servant girl named Rhoda came
to answer the door.[t] **14**When she
recognized Peter's voice, she was
so overjoyed[u] she ran back without opening it and exclaimed, "Peter is at the door!"
15"You're out of your mind,"
they told her. When she kept insist-
ing that it was so, they said, "It
must be his angel."[v]
16But Peter kept on knocking,
and when they opened the door
and saw him, they were astonished.
17Peter motioned with his hand[w]
for them to be quiet and described
how the Lord had brought him out
of prison. "Tell James[x] and the
brothers[y] about this," he said, and
then he left for another place.
18In the morning, there was no
small commotion among the soldiers as to what had become of Peter. **19**After Herod had a thorough
search made for him and did not
find him, he cross-examined the
guards and ordered that they be executed.[z]

Herod's Death

Then Herod went from Judea to
Caesarea[a] and stayed there a
while. **20**He had been quarreling
with the people of Tyre and Sidon;[b] they now joined together
and sought an audience with him.
Having secured the support of
Blastus, a trusted personal servant
of the king, they asked for peace,
because they depended on the
king's country for their food supply.[c]
21On the appointed day Herod,
wearing his royal robes, sat on his
throne and delivered a public address to the people. **22**They shouted, "This is the voice of a god, not

11:28 [a]Ac 18:2
11:29 [b]ver 26 [c]Ro 15:26; 2Co 9:2 [d]Ac 1:16
11:30 [e]Ac 14:23 [f]Ac 12:25
12:2 [g]Mt 4:21
12:3 [h]Ac 24:27 [i]Ex 12:15; 23:15
12:5 [j]Eph 6:18
12:6 [k]Ac 21:33
12:7 [l]Ac 5:19 [m]Ac 16:26
12:9 [n]Ac 9:10
12:10 [o]Ac 5:19; 16:26
12:11 [p]Lk 15:17 [q]Ps 34:7; Da 3:28; 6:22; 2Co 1:10; 2Pe 2:9
12:12 [r]ver 25; Ac 15:37,39; Col 4:10; Phm 24; 1Pe 5:13 [s]ver 5
12:13 [t]Jn 18:16,17
12:14 [u]Lk 24:41
12:15 [v]Mt 18:10
12:17 [w]Ac 13:16; 19:33; 21:40 [x]Ac 15:13 [y]Ac 1:16
12:19 [z]Ac 16:27 [a]Ac 8:40
12:20 [b]Mt 11:21 [c]1Ki 5:9,11; Eze 27:17

of a man." **23**Immediately, because Herod did not give praise to God, an angel of the Lord struck him down,[a] and he was eaten by worms and died.

24But the word of God continued to increase and spread.[b]

25When Barnabas[c] and Saul had finished their mission,[d] they returned from[t] Jerusalem, taking with them John, also called Mark.[e]

Barnabas and Saul Sent Off

13 In the church at Antioch[f] there were prophets[g] and teachers: Barnabas,[h] Simeon called Niger, Lucius of Cyrene, Manaen (who had been brought up with Herod[i] the tetrarch) and Saul. **2**While they were worshiping the Lord and fasting, the Holy Spirit said,[j] "Set apart for me Barnabas and Saul for the work[k] to which I have called them."[l] **3**So after they had fasted and prayed, they placed their hands on them[m] and sent them off.[n]

On Cyprus

4The two of them, sent on their way by the Holy Spirit,[o] went down to Seleucia and sailed from there to Cyprus.[p] **5**When they arrived at Salamis, they proclaimed the word of God in the Jewish synagogues.[q] John[r] was with them as their helper.

6They traveled through the whole island until they came to Paphos. There they met a Jewish sorcerer[s] and false prophet[t] named Bar-Jesus, **7**who was an attendant of the proconsul,[u] Sergius Paulus. The proconsul, an intelligent man, sent for Barnabas and Saul because he wanted to hear the word of God. **8**But Elymas the sorcerer[v] (for that is what his name means) opposed them and tried to turn the proconsul[w] from the faith.[x] **9**Then Saul, who was also called Paul, filled with the Holy Spirit,[y] looked straight at Elymas and said, **10**"You are a child of the devil[z] and an enemy of everything that is right! You are full of all kinds of deceit and trickery. Will you never stop perverting the right ways of the Lord?[a] **11**Now the hand of the Lord is against you.[b] You are going to be blind, and for a time you will be unable to see the light of the sun."

Immediately mist and darkness came over him, and he groped about, seeking someone to lead him by the hand. **12**When the proconsul[c] saw what had happened, he believed, for he was amazed at the teaching about the Lord.

In Pisidian Antioch

13From Paphos,[d] Paul and his companions sailed to Perga in Pamphylia, where John[e] left them to return to Jerusalem. **14**From Perga they went on to Pisidian Antioch.[f] On the Sabbath[g] they entered the synagogue[h] and sat down. **15**After the reading from the Law[i] and the Prophets, the synagogue rulers sent word to them, saying, "Brothers, if you have a message of encouragement for the people, please speak."

16Standing up, Paul motioned with his hand[j] and said: "Men of Israel and you Gentiles who worship God, listen to me! **17**The God of the people of Israel chose our fathers; he made the people prosper during their stay in Egypt, with mighty power he led them out of that country,[k] **18**he endured their conduct[u][l] for about forty years in the desert,[m] **19**he overthrew seven nations in Canaan[n] and gave their land to his people[o] as their inheritance. **20**All this took about 450 years.

"After this, God gave them judges[p] until the time of Samuel the prophet.[q] **21**Then the people asked for a king,[r] and he gave them Saul[s] son of Kish, of the tribe of Benjamin,[t] who ruled forty years. **22**After removing Saul,[u] he made David their king.[v] He testified concerning him: 'I have

12:23 [a] 1Sa 25:38; 2Sa 24:16,17
12:24 [b] Ac 6:7; 19:20
12:25 [c] Ac 4:36 [d] Ac 11:30 [e] ver 12
13:1 [f] Ac 11:19 [g] Ac 11:27 [h] Ac 4:36; 11:22-26 [i] Mt 14:1
13:2 [j] Ac 8:29 [k] Ac 14:26 [l] Ac 22:21
13:3 [m] Ac 6:6 [n] Ac 14:26
13:4 [o] ver 2,3 [p] Ac 4:36
13:5 [q] Ac 9:20 [r] Ac 12:12
13:6 [s] Ac 8:9 [t] Mt 7:15
13:7 [u] ver 8,12; Ac 19:38
13:8 [v] Ac 8:9 [w] ver 7 [x] Ac 6:7
13:9 [y] Ac 4:8
13:10 [z] Mt 13:38; Jn 8:44 [a] Hos 14:9
13:11 [b] Ex 9:3; 1Sa 5:6,7; Ps 32:4
13:12 [c] ver 7
13:13 [d] ver 6 [e] Ac 12:12
13:14 [f] Ac 14:19,21 [g] Ac 16:13 [h] Ac 9:20
13:15 [i] Ac 15:21
13:16 [j] Ac 12:17
13:17 [k] Ex 6:6,7; Dt 7:6-8
13:18 [l] Dt 1:31 [m] Ac 7:36
13:19 [n] Dt 7:1 [o] Jos 19:51
13:20 [p] Jdg 2:16 [q] 1Sa 3:19,20
13:21 [r] 1Sa 8:5,19 [s] 1Sa 10:1 [t] 1Sa 9:1,2
13:22 [u] 1Sa 15:23,26 [v] 1Sa 16:13; Ps 89:20

[t]*25* Some manuscripts *to* [u]*18* Some manuscripts *and cared for them*

found David son of Jesse a man after my own heart;[a] he will do everything I want him to do.'

23"From this man's descendants[b] God has brought to Israel the Savior[c] Jesus,[d] as he promised.[e] 24Before the coming of Jesus, John preached repentance and baptism to all the people of Israel.[f] 25As John was completing his work,[g] he said: 'Who do you think I am? I am not that one.[h] No, but he is coming after me, whose sandals I am not worthy to untie.'[i]

26"Brothers, children of Abraham, and you God-fearing Gentiles, it is to us that this message of salvation[j] has been sent. 27The people of Jerusalem and their rulers did not recognize Jesus,[k] yet in condemning him they fulfilled the words of the prophets[l] that are read every Sabbath. 28Though they found no proper ground for a death sentence, they asked Pilate to have him executed.[m] 29When they had carried out all that was written about him,[n] they took him down from the tree[o] and laid him in a tomb.[p] 30But God raised him from the dead,[q] 31and for many days he was seen by those who had traveled with him from Galilee to Jerusalem.[r] They are now his witnesses[s] to our people.

32"We tell you the good news:[t] What God promised our fathers[u] 33he has fulfilled for us, their children, by raising up Jesus. As it is written in the second Psalm:

" 'You are my Son;
today I have become your
Father.'[v][w][v]

34The fact that God raised him from the dead, never to decay, is stated in these words:

" 'I will give you the holy and
sure blessings promised
to David.'[x][w]

35So it is stated elsewhere:

" 'You will not let your Holy
One see decay.'[y][x]

36"For when David had served God's purpose in his own generation, he fell asleep; he was buried with his fathers[y] and his body decayed. 37But the one whom God raised from the dead did not see decay.

38"Therefore, my brothers, I want you to know that through Jesus the forgiveness of sins is proclaimed to you.[z] 39Through him everyone who believes is justified from everything you could not be justified from by the law of Moses.[a] 40Take care that what the prophets have said does not happen to you:

41" 'Look, you scoffers,
wonder and perish,
for I am going to do something
in your days
that you would never believe,
even if someone told
you.'[z]"[b]

42As Paul and Barnabas were leaving the synagogue,[c] the people invited them to speak further about these things on the next Sabbath. 43When the congregation was dismissed, many of the Jews and devout converts to Judaism followed Paul and Barnabas, who talked with them and urged them to continue in the grace of God.[d]

44On the next Sabbath almost the whole city gathered to hear the word of the Lord. 45When the Jews saw the crowds, they were filled with jealousy and talked abusively[e] against what Paul was saying.[f]

46Then Paul and Barnabas answered them boldly: "We had to speak the word of God to you first.[g] Since you reject it and do not consider yourselves worthy of eternal life, we now turn to the Gentiles.[h] 47For this is what the Lord has commanded us:

" 'I have made you[a] a light for
the Gentiles,[i]
that you[a] may bring
salvation to the ends of
the earth.'[b]"[j]

13:22 [a] 1Sa 13:14
13:23 [b] Mt 1:1 [c] Lk 2:11 [d] Mt 1:21 [e] ver 32
13:24 [f] Mk 1:4
13:25 [g] Ac 20:24 [h] Jn 1:20 [i] Mt 3:11; Jn 1:27
13:26 [j] Ac 4:12
13:27 [k] Ac 3:17 [l] Lk 24:27
13:28 [m] Mt 27:20-25; Ac 3:14
13:29 [n] Lk 18:31 [o] Ac 5:30 [p] Lk 23:53
13:30 [q] Mt 28:6; Ac 2:24
13:31 [r] Mt 28:16 [s] Lk 24:48
13:32 [t] Ac 5:42 [u] Ac 26:6; Ro 4:13
13:33 [v] Ps 2:7
13:34 [w] Isa 55:3
13:35 [x] Ps 16:10; Ac 2:27
13:36 [y] 1Ki 2:10; Ac 2:29
13:38 [z] Lk 24:47; Ac 2:38
13:39 [a] Ro 3:28
13:41 [b] Hab 1:5
13:42 [c] ver 14
13:43 [d] Ac 11:23; 14:22
13:45 [e] Ac 18:6; 1Pe 4:4; Jude 10 [f] 1Th 2:16
13:46 [g] ver 26; Ac 3:26 [h] Ac 18:6; 22:21; 28:28
13:47 [i] Lk 2:32 [j] Isa 49:6

[v]33 Or *have begotten you* [w]33 Psalm 2:7
[x]34 Isaiah 55:3 [y]35 Psalm 16:10
[z]41 Hab. 1:5 [a]47 The Greek is singular.
[b]47 Isaiah 49:6

48When the Gentiles heard this, they were glad and honored the word of the Lord; and all who were appointed for eternal life believed.

49The word of the Lord spread through the whole region. **50**But the Jews incited the God-fearing women of high standing and the leading men of the city. They stirred up persecution against Paul and Barnabas, and expelled them from their region.[a] **51**So they shook the dust from their feet[b] in protest against them and went to Iconium.[c] **52**And the disciples were filled with joy and with the Holy Spirit.

In Iconium

14 At Iconium[d] Paul and Barnabas went as usual into the Jewish synagogue. There they spoke so effectively that a great number of Jews and Gentiles believed. **2**But the Jews who refused to believe stirred up the Gentiles and poisoned their minds against the brothers. **3**So Paul and Barnabas spent considerable time there, speaking boldly[e] for the Lord, who confirmed the message of his grace by enabling them to do miraculous signs and wonders.[f] **4**The people of the city were divided; some sided with the Jews, others with the apostles.[g] **5**There was a plot afoot among the Gentiles and Jews, together with their leaders, to mistreat them and stone them.[h] **6**But they found out about it and fled[i] to the Lycaonian cities of Lystra and Derbe and to the surrounding country, **7**where they continued to preach[j] the good news.[k]

In Lystra and Derbe

8In Lystra there sat a man crippled in his feet, who was lame from birth[l] and had never walked. **9**He listened to Paul as he was speaking. Paul looked directly at him, saw that he had faith to be healed[m] **10**and called out, "Stand up on your feet!" At that, the man jumped up and began to walk.[n]

11When the crowd saw what Paul had done, they shouted in the Lycaonian language, "The gods have come down to us in human form!"[o] **12**Barnabas they called Zeus, and Paul they called Hermes because he was the chief speaker. **13**The priest of Zeus, whose temple was just outside the city, brought bulls and wreaths to the city gates because he and the crowd wanted to offer sacrifices to them.

14But when the apostles Barnabas and Paul heard of this, they tore their clothes[p] and rushed out into the crowd, shouting: **15**"Men, why are you doing this? We too are only men,[q] human like you. We are bringing you good news,[r] telling you to turn from these worthless things[s] to the living God,[t] who made heaven and earth[u] and sea and everything in them.[v] **16**In the past, he let[w] all nations go their own way.[x] **17**Yet he has not left himself without testimony:[y] He has shown kindness by giving you rain from heaven and crops in their seasons;[z] he provides you with plenty of food and fills your hearts with joy." **18**Even with these words, they had difficulty keeping the crowd from sacrificing to them.

19Then some Jews[a] came from Antioch and Iconium[b] and won the crowd over. They stoned Paul[c] and dragged him outside the city, thinking he was dead. **20**But after the disciples[d] had gathered around him, he got up and went back into the city. The next day he and Barnabas left for Derbe.

The Return to Antioch in Syria

21They preached the good news in that city and won a large number of disciples. Then they returned to Lystra, Iconium[e] and Antioch, **22**strengthening the disciples and encouraging them to remain true to the faith.[f] "We must go through many hardships[g] to enter the kingdom of God," they said. **23**Paul and Barnabas appointed elders[c][h] for them in each church and, with prayer and fasting,[i] committed

13:50 [a] 1Th 2:16
13:51 [b] Mt 10:14; Ac 18:6 [c] Ac 14:1,19, 21; 2Ti 3:11
14:1 [d] Ac 13:51
14:3 [e] Ac 4:29 [f] Jn 4:48; Heb 2:4
14:4 [g] Ac 17:4,5
14:5 [h] ver 19
14:6 [i] Mt 10:23
14:7 [j] Ac 16:10 [k] ver 15,21
14:8 [l] Ac 3:2
14:9 [m] Mt 9:28,29
14:10 [n] Ac 3:8
14:11 [o] Ac 8:10; 28:6
14:14 [p] Mk 14:63
14:15 [q] Ac 10:26; Jas 5:17 [r] ver 7,21; Ac 13:32 [s] 1Sa 12:21; 1Co 8:4; 1Th 1:9 [t] Mt 16:16 [u] Ge 1:1; Jer 14:22 [v] Ps 146:6; Rev 14:7
14:16 [w] Ac 17:30 [x] Ps 81:12; Mic 4:5
14:17 [y] Ac 17:27; Ro 1:20 [z] Dt 11:14; Job 5:10; Ps 65:10
14:19 [a] Ac 13:45 [b] Ac 13:51 [c] 2Co 11:25; 2Ti 3:11
14:20 [d] ver 22,28; Ac 11:26
14:21 [e] Ac 13:51
14:22 [f] Ac 11:23; 13:43 [g] Jn 16:33; 1Th 3:3; 2Ti 3:12
14:23 [h] Ac 11:30; Tit 1:5 [i] Ac 13:3

c23 Or *Barnabas ordained elders*; or *Barnabas had elders elected*

them to the Lord,[a] in whom they
had put their trust. 24After going
through Pisidia, they came into
Pamphylia, 25and when they had
preached the word in Perga, they
went down to Attalia.
26From Attalia they sailed back
to Antioch,[b] where they had been
committed to the grace of God[c] for
the work they had now completed.[d] 27On arriving there, they
gathered the church together and
reported all that God had done
through them[e] and how he had
opened the door[f] of faith to the
Gentiles. 28And they stayed there a
long time with the disciples.

The Council at Jerusalem

15 Some men[g] came down
from Judea to Antioch and
were teaching the brothers: "Unless you are circumcised,[h] according to the custom taught by Moses,[i] you cannot be saved." 2This
brought Paul and Barnabas into
sharp dispute and debate with
them. So Paul and Barnabas were
appointed, along with some other
believers, to go up to Jerusalem[j]
to see the apostles and elders[k]
about this question. 3The church
sent them on their way, and as they
traveled through Phoenicia and Samaria, they told how the Gentiles
had been converted.[l] This news
made all the brothers very glad.
4When they came to Jerusalem,
they were welcomed by the church
and the apostles and elders, to
whom they reported everything
God had done through them.[m]
5Then some of the believers who
belonged to the party of the Pharisees stood up and said, "The Gentiles must be circumcised and required to obey the law of Moses."
6The apostles and elders met to
consider this question. 7After
much discussion, Peter got up and
addressed them: "Brothers, you
know that some time ago God
made a choice among you that the
Gentiles might hear from my lips
the message of the gospel and believe. 8God, who knows the heart,[n]
showed that he accepted them by
giving the Holy Spirit to them,[o]
just as he did to us. 9He made no
distinction between us and them,[p]
for he purified their hearts by
faith.[q] 10Now then, why do you try
to test God by putting on the necks
of the disciples a yoke[r] that neither we nor our fathers have been
able to bear? 11No! We believe it is
through the grace[s] of our Lord
Jesus that we are saved, just as
they are."
12The whole assembly became
silent as they listened to Barnabas
and Paul telling about the miraculous signs and wonders[t] God had
done among the Gentiles through
them.[u] 13When they finished,
James[v] spoke up: "Brothers, listen
to me. 14Simon[d] has described to
us how God at first showed his concern by taking from the Gentiles a
people for himself. 15The words of
the prophets are in agreement with
this, as it is written:

16" 'After this I will return
and rebuild David's fallen
tent.
Its ruins I will rebuild,
and I will restore it,
17that the remnant of men may
seek the Lord,
and all the Gentiles who bear
my name,
says the Lord, who does these
things'[e][w]
18 that have been known for
ages.[f]

19"It is my judgment, therefore,
that we should not make it difficult
for the Gentiles who are turning to
God. 20Instead we should write to
them, telling them to abstain from
food polluted by idols,[x] from sexual immorality,[y] from the meat of
strangled animals and from
blood.[z] 21For Moses has been
preached in every city from the earliest times and is read in the synagogues on every Sabbath."[a]

14:23 [a]Ac 20:32
14:26 [b]Ac 11:19 [c]Ac 15:40 [d]Ac 13:1,3
14:27 [e]Ac 15:4,12; 21:19 [f]1Co 16:9; 2Co 2:12; Col 4:3; Rev 3:8
15:1 [g]ver 24; Gal 2:12 [h]ver 5; Gal 5:2,3 [i]Ac 6:14
15:2 [j]Gal 2:2 [k]Ac 11:30
15:3 [l]Ac 14:27
15:4 [m]ver 12; Ac 14:27
15:8 [n]Ac 1:24 [o]Ac 10:44,47
15:9 [p]Ac 10:28,34; 11:12 [q]Ac 10:43
15:10 [r]Mt 23:4; Gal 5:1
15:11 [s]Ro 3:24; Eph 2:5-8
15:12 [t]Jn 4:48 [u]Ac 14:27
15:13 [v]Ac 12:17
15:17 [w]Am 9:11,12
15:20 [x]1Co 8:7-13; 10:14-28; Rev 2:14,20 [y]1Co 10:7,8 [z]ver 29; Ge 9:4; Lev 3:17; Dt 12:16,23
15:21 [a]Ac 13:15; 2Co 3:14,15

[d]*14* Greek *Simeon,* a variant of *Simon;* that is, Peter [e]*17* Amos 9:11,12 [f]*17,18* Some manuscripts *things'— / [18]known to the Lord for ages is his work*

The Council's Letter to Gentile Believers

22Then the apostles and elders, with the whole church, decided to choose some of their own men and send them to Antioch with Paul and Barnabas. They chose Judas (called Barsabbas) and Silas,[a] two men who were leaders among the brothers. **23**With them they sent the following letter:

> The apostles and elders, your brothers,
>
> To the Gentile believers in Antioch,[b] Syria and Cilicia:[c]
>
> Greetings.[d]
>
> **24**We have heard that some went out from us without our authorization and disturbed you, troubling your minds by what they said.[e] **25**So we all agreed to choose some men and send them to you with our dear friends Barnabas and Paul— **26**men who have risked their lives[f] for the name of our Lord Jesus Christ. **27**Therefore we are sending Judas and Silas to confirm by word of mouth what we are writing. **28**It seemed good to the Holy Spirit[g] and to us not to burden you with anything beyond the following requirements: **29**You are to abstain from food sacrificed to idols, from blood, from the meat of strangled animals and from sexual immorality.[h] You will do well to avoid these things.
>
> Farewell.

30The men were sent off and went down to Antioch, where they gathered the church together and delivered the letter. **31**The people read it and were glad for its encouraging message. **32**Judas and Silas, who themselves were prophets, said much to encourage and strengthen the brothers. **33**After spending some time there, they were sent off by the brothers with the blessing of peace[i] to return to those who had sent them.[g] **35**But Paul and Barnabas remained in Antioch, where they and many others taught and preached[j] the word of the Lord.

Disagreement Between Paul and Barnabas

36Some time later Paul said to Barnabas, "Let us go back and visit the brothers in all the towns[k] where we preached the word of the Lord and see how they are doing." **37**Barnabas wanted to take John, also called Mark,[l] with them, **38**but Paul did not think it wise to take him, because he had deserted them[m] in Pamphylia and had not continued with them in the work. **39**They had such a sharp disagreement that they parted company. Barnabas took Mark and sailed for Cyprus, **40**but Paul chose Silas[n] and left, commended by the brothers to the grace of the Lord.[o] **41**He went through Syria[p] and Cilicia,[q] strengthening the churches.[r]

Timothy Joins Paul and Silas

16 He came to Derbe and then to Lystra,[s] where a disciple named Timothy[t] lived, whose mother was a Jewess and a believer, but whose father was a Greek. **2**The brothers[u] at Lystra and Iconium[v] spoke well of him. **3**Paul wanted to take him along on the journey, so he circumcised him because of the Jews who lived in that area, for they all knew that his father was a Greek.[w] **4**As they traveled from town to town, they delivered the decisions reached by the apostles and elders[x] in Jerusalem[y] for the people to obey.[z] **5**So the churches were strengthened[a] in the faith and grew daily in numbers.

Paul's Vision of the Man of Macedonia

6Paul and his companions traveled throughout the region of

15:22 [a]ver 27,32,40
15:23 [b]ver 1 [c]ver 41 [d]Ac 23:25,26; Jas 1:1
15:24 [e]ver 1; Gal 1:7; 5:10
15:26 [f]Ac 9:23-25; 14:19
15:28 [g]Ac 5:32
15:29 [h]ver 20; Ac 21:25
15:33 [i]Mk 5:34; Ac 16:36; 1Co 16:11
15:35 [j]Ac 8:4
15:36 [k]Ac 13:4,13, 14,51; 14:1,6, 24,25
15:37 [l]Ac 12:12
15:38 [m]Ac 13:13
15:40 [n]ver 22 [o]Ac 11:23
15:41 [p]ver 23 [q]Ac 6:9 [r]Ac 16:5
16:1 [s]Ac 14:6 [t]Ac 17:14; 18:5; 19:22; Ro 16:21; 1Co 4:17; 2Co 1:1,19; 1Th 3:2,6; 1Ti 1:2,18; 2Ti 1:2,5,6
16:2 [u]ver 40 [v]Ac 13:51
16:3 [w]Gal 2:3
16:4 [x]Ac 11:30 [y]Ac 15:2 [z]Ac 15:28,29
16:5 [a]Ac 9:31; 15:41

[g]33 Some manuscripts *them,* [34]*but Silas decided to remain there*

Phrygia[a] and Galatia,[b] having
been kept by the Holy Spirit from
preaching the word in the province
of Asia.[c] 7When they came to the
border of Mysia, they tried to enter
Bithynia, but the Spirit of Jesus[d]
would not allow them to. 8So they
passed by Mysia and went down to
Troas.[e] 9During the night Paul had
a vision[f] of a man of Macedonia[g]
standing and begging him, "Come
over to Macedonia and help us."
10After Paul had seen the vision,
we[h] got ready at once to leave for
Macedonia, concluding that God
had called us to preach the gospel[i] to them.

Lydia's Conversion in Philippi

11From Troas[j] we put out to sea
and sailed straight for Samothrace,
and the next day on to Neapolis.
12From there we traveled to Philippi,[k] a Roman colony and the leading city of that district of Macedonia.[l] And we stayed there several
days.
13On the Sabbath[m] we went outside the city gate to the river, where
we expected to find a place of
prayer. We sat down and began to
speak to the women who had gathered there. 14One of those listening
was a woman named Lydia, a deal-
er in purple cloth from the city of
Thyatira,[n] who was a worshiper of
God. The Lord opened her heart[o]
to respond to Paul's message.
15When she and the members of
her household[p] were baptized, she
invited us to her home. "If you consider me a believer in the Lord,"
she said, "come and stay at my
house." And she persuaded us.

Paul and Silas in Prison

16Once when we were going to
the place of prayer,[q] we were met
by a slave girl who had a spirit[r] by
which she predicted the future.
She earned a great deal of money
for her owners by fortune-telling.
17This girl followed Paul and the
rest of us, shouting, "These men
are servants of the Most High
God,[s] who are telling you the way
to be saved." 18She kept this up for
many days. Finally Paul became so
troubled that he turned around and
said to the spirit, "In the name of
Jesus Christ I command you to
come out of her!" At that moment
the spirit left her.[t]
19When the owners of the slave
girl realized that their hope of making money[u] was gone, they seized
Paul and Silas[v] and dragged[w]
them into the marketplace to face
the authorities. 20They brought
them before the magistrates and
said, "These men are Jews, and are
throwing our city into an uproar[x]
21by advocating customs unlawful
for us Romans[y] to accept or practice."[z]
22The crowd joined in the attack
against Paul and Silas, and the
magistrates ordered them to be
stripped and beaten.[a] 23After they
had been severely flogged, they
were thrown into prison, and the
jailer[b] was commanded to guard
them carefully. 24Upon receiving
such orders, he put them in the inner cell and fastened their feet in
the stocks.[c]
25About midnight Paul and Silas
were praying and singing hymns[d]
to God, and the other prisoners
were listening to them. 26Suddenly
there was such a violent earthquake that the foundations of the
prison were shaken.[e] At once all
the prison doors flew open,[f] and
everybody's chains came loose.[g]
27The jailer woke up, and when he
saw the prison doors open, he drew
his sword and was about to kill
himself because he thought the
prisoners had escaped.[h] 28But
Paul shouted, "Don't harm yourself! We are all here!"
29The jailer called for lights,
rushed in and fell trembling before
Paul and Silas. 30He then brought
them out and asked, "Sirs, what
must I do to be saved?"[i]
31They replied, "Believe in the
Lord Jesus, and you will be saved
—you and your household."[j]
32Then they spoke the word of the
Lord to him and to all the others in
his house. 33At that hour of the
night[k] the jailer took them and

16:6 [a]Ac 18:23 [b]Ac 18:23; Gal 1:2; 3:1 [c]Ac 2:9
16:7 [d]Ro 8:9; Gal 4:6
16:8 [e]ver 11; 2Co 2:12; 2Ti 4:13
16:9 [f]Ac 9:10 [g]Ac 20:1,3
16:10 [h]ver 10-17 [i]Ac 14:7
16:11 [j]ver 8
16:12 [k]Ac 20:6; Php 1:1; 1Th 2:2 [l]ver 9
16:13 [m]Ac 13:14
16:14 [n]Rev 1:11 [o]Lk 24:45
16:15 [p]Ac 11:14
16:16 [q]ver 13 [r]Dt 18:11; 1Sa 28:3,7
16:17 [s]Mk 5:7
16:18 [t]Mk 16:17
16:19 [u]ver 16; Ac 19:25,26 [v]Ac 15:22 [w]Ac 8:3; 17:6; 21:30; Jas 2:6
16:20 [x]Ac 17:6
16:21 [y]ver 12 [z]Est 3:8
16:22 [a]2Co 11:25; 1Th 2:2
16:23 [b]ver 27,36
16:24 [c]Job 13:27; 33:11; Jer 20:2,3; 29:26
16:25 [d]Eph 5:19
16:26 [e]Ac 4:31 [f]Ac 12:10 [g]Ac 12:7
16:27 [h]Ac 12:19
16:30 [i]Ac 2:37
16:31 [j]Ac 11:14
16:33 [k]ver 25

washed their wounds; then immediately he and all his family were
baptized. **34**The jailer brought
them into his house and set a meal
before them; he[a] was filled with
joy because he had come to believe
in God—he and his whole family.
35When it was daylight, the magistrates sent their officers to the
jailer with the order: "Release
those men." **36**The jailer[b] told
Paul, "The magistrates have ordered that you and Silas be released. Now you can leave. Go in
peace."[c]
37But Paul said to the officers:
"They beat us publicly without a
trial, even though we are Roman
citizens,[d] and threw us into prison. And now do they want to get rid
of us quietly? No! Let them come
themselves and escort us out."
38The officers reported this to
the magistrates, and when they
heard that Paul and Silas were Roman citizens, they were alarmed.[e]
39They came to appease them and
escorted them from the prison, re-
questing them to leave the city.[f]
40After Paul and Silas came out of
the prison, they went to Lydia's
house,[g] where they met with the
brothers[h] and encouraged them.
Then they left.

In Thessalonica

17 When they had passed
through Amphipolis and
Apollonia, they came to Thessalonica,[i] where there was a Jewish
synagogue. **2**As his custom was,
Paul went into the synagogue,[j]
and on three Sabbath[k] days he reasoned with them from the Scriptures,[l] **3**explaining and proving
that the Christ[h] had to suffer[m] and
rise from the dead.[n] "This Jesus I
am proclaiming to you is the
Christ,[h]"[o] he said. **4**Some of the
Jews were persuaded and joined
Paul and Silas,[p] as did a large
number of God-fearing Greeks and
not a few prominent women.
5But the Jews were jealous; so
they rounded up some bad characters from the marketplace, formed
a mob and started a riot in the
city.[q] They rushed to Jason's[r]
house in search of Paul and Silas in
order to bring them out to the
crowd.[i] **6**But when they did not
find them, they dragged[s] Jason
and some other brothers before the
city officials, shouting: "These
men who have caused trouble all
over the world[t] have now come
here,[u] **7**and Jason has welcomed
them into his house. They are all
defying Caesar's decrees, saying
that there is another king, one
called Jesus."[v] **8**When they heard
this, the crowd and the city officials were thrown into turmoil.
9Then they made Jason[w] and the
others post bond and let them go.

In Berea

10As soon as it was night, the
brothers sent Paul and Silas away
to Berea.[x] On arriving there, they
went to the Jewish synagogue.
11Now the Bereans were of more
noble character than the Thessalonians,[y] for they received the message with great eagerness and examined the Scriptures[z] every day
to see if what Paul said was true.
12Many of the Jews believed, as did
also a number of prominent Greek
women and many Greek men.
13When the Jews in Thessalonica learned that Paul was preaching
the word of God at Berea, they
went there too, agitating the
crowds and stirring them up. **14**The
brothers immediately sent Paul to
the coast, but Silas[a] and Timothy[b] stayed at Berea. **15**The men
who escorted Paul brought him to
Athens[c] and then left with instructions for Silas and Timothy to join
him as soon as possible.[d]

In Athens

16While Paul was waiting for
them in Athens, he was greatly distressed to see that the city was full
of idols. **17**So he reasoned in the
synagogue[e] with the Jews and the
God-fearing Greeks, as well as in
the marketplace day by day with

16:34 [a]Ac 11:14
16:36 [b]ver 23,27 [c]Ac 15:33
16:37 [d]Ac 22:25-29
16:38 [e]Ac 22:29
16:39 [f]Mt 8:34
16:40 [g]ver 14 [h]ver 2; Ac 1:16
17:1 [i]ver 11,13; Php 4:16; 1Th 1:1; 2Th 1:1; 2Ti 4:10
17:2 [j]Ac 9:20 [k]Ac 13:14 [l]Ac 8:35
17:3 [m]Lk 24:26; Ac 3:18 [n]Lk 24:46 [o]Ac 9:22; 18:28
17:4 [p]Ac 15:22
17:5 [q]ver 13; 1Th 2:16 [r]Ro 16:21
17:6 [s]Ac 16:19 [t]Mt 24:14 [u]Ac 16:20
17:7 [v]Lk 23:2; Jn 19:12
17:9 [w]ver 5
17:10 [x]ver 13; Ac 20:4
17:11 [y]ver 1 [z]Lk 16:29; Jn 5:39
17:14 [a]Ac 15:22 [b]Ac 16:1
17:15 [c]ver 16,21,22; Ac 18:1; 1Th 3:1 [d]Ac 18:5
17:17 [e]Ac 9:20

[h]3 Or *Messiah* [i]5 Or *the assembly of the people*

those who happened to be there. **18**A group of Epicurean and Stoic philosophers began to dispute with him. Some of them asked, "What is this babbler trying to say?" Others remarked, "He seems to be advocating foreign gods." They said this because Paul was preaching the good news about Jesus and the resurrection.[a] **19**Then they took him and brought him to a meeting of the Areopagus,[b] where they said to him, "May we know what this new teaching[c] is that you are presenting? **20**You are bringing some strange ideas to our ears, and we want to know what they mean." **21**(All the Athenians and the foreigners who lived there spent their time doing nothing but talking about and listening to the latest ideas.)

22Paul then stood up in the meeting of the Areopagus and said: "Men of Athens! I see that in every way you are very religious. **23**For as I walked around and looked carefully at your objects of worship, I even found an altar with this inscription: TO AN UNKNOWN GOD. Now what you worship as something unknown[d] I am going to proclaim to you.

24"The God who made the world and everything in it[e] is the Lord of heaven and earth[f] and does not live in temples built by hands.[g] **25**And he is not served by human hands, as if he needed anything, because he himself gives all men life and breath and everything else.[h] **26**From one man he made every nation of men, that they should inhabit the whole earth; and he determined the times set for them and the exact places where they should live.[i] **27**God did this so that men would seek him and perhaps reach out for him and find him, though he is not far from each one of us.[j] **28**'For in him we live and move and have our being.'[k] As some of your own poets have said, 'We are his offspring.'

29"Therefore since we are God's offspring, we should not think that the divine being is like gold or silver or stone—an image made by man's design and skill.[l] **30**In the past God overlooked[m] such ignorance,[n] but now he commands all people everywhere to repent.[o] **31**For he has set a day when he will judge[p] the world with justice[q] by the man he has appointed.[r] He has given proof of this to all men by raising him from the dead."[s]

32When they heard about the resurrection of the dead,[t] some of them sneered, but others said, "We want to hear you again on this subject." **33**At that, Paul left the Council. **34**A few men became followers of Paul and believed. Among them was Dionysius, a member of the Areopagus,[u] also a woman named Damaris, and a number of others.

17:18 [a]ver 31,32; Ac 4:2 **17:19** [b]ver 22 [c]Mk 1:27 **17:23** [d]Jn 4:22 **17:24** [e]Isa 42:5; Ac 14:15 [f]Dt 10:14; Mt 11:25 [g]Ac 7:48 **17:25** [h]Ps 50:10-12; Isa 42:5 **17:26** [i]Dt 32:8; Job 12:23 **17:27** [j]Dt 4:7; Jer 23:23,24; Ac 14:17 **17:28** [k]Job 12:10; Da 5:23 **17:29** [l]Isa 40:18-20; Ro 1:23 **17:30** [m]Ac 14:16; Ro 3:25 [n]ver 23; 1Pe 1:14 [o]Lk 24:47; Tit 2:11,12 **17:31** [p]Mt 10:15 [q]Ps 9:8; 96:13; 98:9 [r]Ac 10:42 [s]Ac 2:24 **17:32** [t]ver 18,31 **17:34** [u]ver 19,22 **18:1** [v]Ac 17:15 [w]Ac 19:1; 1Co 1:2; 2Co 1:1,23; 2Ti 4:20 **18:2** [x]Ro 16:3; 1Co 16:19; 2Ti 4:19 [y]Ac 11:28 **18:3** [z]Ac 20:34; 1Co 4:12; 1Th 2:9; 2Th 3:8 **18:4** [a]Ac 13:14 **18:5** [b]Ac 15:22 [c]Ac 16:1 [d]Ac 16:9; 17:14,15 [e]ver 28; Ac 17:3 **18:6** [f]Ac 13:45 [g]2Sa 1:16; Eze 18:13; 33:4

In Corinth

18 After this, Paul left Athens[v] and went to Corinth.[w] **2**There he met a Jew named Aquila, a native of Pontus, who had recently come from Italy with his wife Priscilla,[x] because Claudius[y] had ordered all the Jews to leave Rome. Paul went to see them, **3**and because he was a tentmaker as they were, he stayed and worked with them.[z] **4**Every Sabbath[a] he reasoned in the synagogue, trying to persuade Jews and Greeks.

5When Silas[b] and Timothy[c] came from Macedonia,[d] Paul devoted himself exclusively to preaching, testifying to the Jews that Jesus was the Christ.[i][e] **6**But when the Jews opposed Paul and became abusive,[f] he shook out his clothes in protest and said to them, "Your blood be on your own heads![g] I am clear of my responsibility.[h] From now on I will go to the Gentiles."[i]

7Then Paul left the synagogue and went next door to the house of Titius Justus, a worshiper of God.[j] **8**Crispus,[k] the synagogue ruler,[l] and his entire household[m] believed in the Lord; and many of the

[h]Ac 20:26 [i]Ac 13:46 **18:7** [j]Ac 16:14 **18:8** [k]1Co 1:14 [l]Mk 5:22 [m]Ac 11:14

[i]5 Or *Messiah;* also in verse 28

Corinthians who heard him believed and were baptized.
9One night the Lord spoke to
Paul in a vision: "Do not be afraid;
keep on speaking, do not be silent.
10For I am with you,[a] and no one
is going to attack and harm you, because I have many people in this
city." **11**So Paul stayed for a year
and a half, teaching them the word
of God.
12While Gallio was proconsul of
Achaia,[b] the Jews made a united
attack on Paul and brought him
into court. **13**"This man," they
charged, "is persuading the people
to worship God in ways contrary to
the law."
14Just as Paul was about to
speak, Gallio said to the Jews, "If
you Jews were making a complaint
about some misdemeanor or serious crime, it would be reasonable
for me to listen to you. **15**But since
it involves questions about words
and names and your own law[c]—
settle the matter yourselves. I will
not be a judge of such things." **16**So
he had them ejected from the
court. **17**Then they all turned on
Sosthenes[d] the synagogue ruler
and beat him in front of the court.
But Gallio showed no concern
whatever.

Priscilla, Aquila and Apollos

18Paul stayed on in Corinth for
some time. Then he left the brothers[e] and sailed for Syria, accompanied by Priscilla and Aquila. Before
he sailed, he had his hair cut off at
Cenchrea[f] because of a vow he
had taken.[g] **19**They arrived at Ephesus,[h] where Paul left Priscilla and
Aquila. He himself went into the
synagogue and reasoned with the
Jews. **20**When they asked him to
spend more time with them, he declined. **21**But as he left, he promised, "I will come back if it is God's
will."[i] Then he set sail from Ephesus. **22**When he landed at Caesarea,[j] he went up and greeted the
church and then went down to Antioch.[k]
23After spending some time in
Antioch, Paul set out from there
and traveled from place to place
throughout the region of Galatia[l]
and Phrygia, strengthening all the
disciples.[m]
24Meanwhile a Jew named Apollos,[n] a native of Alexandria, came
to Ephesus. He was a learned man,
with a thorough knowledge of the
Scriptures. **25**He had been instructed in the way of the Lord, and he
spoke with great fervor[k][o] and
taught about Jesus accurately,
though he knew only the baptism
of John.[p] **26**He began to speak
boldly in the synagogue. When
Priscilla and Aquila heard him,
they invited him to their home and
explained to him the way of God
more adequately.
27When Apollos wanted to go to
Achaia,[q] the brothers[r] encouraged him and wrote to the disciples
there to welcome him. On arriving,
he was a great help to those who by
grace had believed. **28**For he vigorously refuted the Jews in public debate, proving from the Scriptures[s]
that Jesus was the Christ.[t]

Paul in Ephesus

19 While Apollos was at Corinth,[u] Paul took the road
through the interior and arrived at
Ephesus.[v] There he found some
disciples **2**and asked them, "Did
you receive the Holy Spirit when[1]
you believed?"
They answered, "No, we have
not even heard that there is a Holy
Spirit."
3So Paul asked, "Then what baptism did you receive?"
"John's baptism," they replied.
4Paul said, "John's baptism was
a baptism of repentance. He told
the people to believe in the one
coming after him, that is, in
Jesus."[w] **5**On hearing this, they
were baptized into[m] the name of
the Lord Jesus. **6**When Paul placed
his hands on them,[x] the Holy Spirit came on them,[y] and they spoke
in tongues[n][z] and prophesied.

[k]25 Or *with fervor in the Spirit* [l]2 Or *after* [m]5 Or *in* [n]6 Or *other languages*

18:10 [a]Mt 28:20
18:12 [b]ver 27
18:15 [c]Ac 23:29; 25:11,19
18:17 [d]1Co 1:1
18:18 [e]Ac 1:16 [f]Ro 16:1 [g]Nu 6:2,5,18; Ac 21:24
18:19 [h]ver 21,24; 1Co 15:32
18:21 [i]Ro 1:10; 1Co 4:19; Jas 4:15
18:22 [j]Ac 8:40 [k]Ac 11:19
18:23 [l]Ac 16:6 [m]Ac 14:22; 15:32,41
18:24 [n]Ac 19:1; 1Co 1:12; 3:5, 6,22; 4:6; 16:12; Tit 3:13
18:25 [o]Ro 12:11 [p]Ac 19:3
18:27 [q]ver 12 [r]ver 18
18:28 [s]Ac 17:2 [t]ver 5; Ac 9:22
19:1 [u]Ac 18:1 [v]Ac 18:19
19:4 [w]Jn 1:7; Ac 13:24,25
19:6 [x]Ac 6:6; 8:17 [y]Ac 2:4 [z]Mk 16:17; Ac 10:46

7There were about twelve men in
all.
8Paul entered the synagogue[a]
and spoke boldly there for three
months, arguing persuasively
about the kingdom of God.[b] 9But
some of them[c] became obstinate;
they refused to believe and publicly maligned the Way.[d] So Paul left
them. He took the disciples[e] with
him and had discussions daily in
the lecture hall of Tyrannus. 10This
went on for two years,[f] so that all
the Jews and Greeks who lived in
the province of Asia[g] heard the
word of the Lord.
11God did extraordinary miracles[h] through Paul, 12so that even
handkerchiefs and aprons that had
touched him were taken to the
sick, and their illnesses were
cured[i] and the evil spirits left
them.
13Some Jews who went around
driving out evil spirits[j] tried to invoke the name of the Lord Jesus
over those who were demon-possessed. They would say, "In the
name of Jesus,[k] whom Paul
preaches, I command you to come
out." 14Seven sons of Sceva, a Jewish chief priest, were doing this.
15⌊One day⌋ the evil spirit answered
them, "Jesus I know, and I know
about Paul, but who are you?"
16Then the man who had the evil
spirit jumped on them and overpowered them all. He gave them
such a beating that they ran out of
the house naked and bleeding.
17When this became known to
the Jews and Greeks living in Ephesus,[l] they were all seized with
fear,[m] and the name of the Lord
Jesus was held in high honor.
18Many of those who believed now
came and openly confessed their
evil deeds. 19A number who had
practiced sorcery brought their
scrolls together and burned them
publicly. When they calculated the
value of the scrolls, the total came
to fifty thousand drachmas.[o] 20In
this way the word of the Lord
spread widely and grew in power.[n]
21After all this had happened,
Paul decided to go to Jerusalem,[o]
passing through Macedonia[p] and
Achaia.[q] "After I have been there,"
he said, "I must visit Rome also."[r]
22He sent two of his helpers,[s] Timothy[t] and Erastus,[u] to Macedonia, while he stayed in the province
of Asia[v] a little longer.

The Riot in Ephesus

23About that time there arose a
great disturbance about the Way.[w]
24A silversmith named Demetrius,
who made silver shrines of Artemis, brought in no little business
for the craftsmen. 25He called
them together, along with the
workmen in related trades, and
said: "Men, you know we receive a
good income from this business.[x]
26And you see and hear how this
fellow Paul has convinced and led
astray large numbers of people
here in Ephesus[y] and in practical-
ly the whole province of Asia. He
says that man-made gods are no
gods at all.[z] 27There is danger not
only that our trade will lose its
good name, but also that the temple of the great goddess Artemis
will be discredited, and the goddess herself, who is worshiped
throughout the province of Asia
and the world, will be robbed of her
divine majesty."
28When they heard this, they
were furious and began shouting:
"Great is Artemis of the Ephesians!"[a] 29Soon the whole city was
in an uproar. The people seized Gaius[b] and Aristarchus,[c] Paul's traveling companions from Macedo-
nia,[d] and rushed as one man into
the theater. 30Paul wanted to appear before the crowd, but the disciples would not let him. 31Even
some of the officials of the province, friends of Paul, sent him a
message begging him not to venture into the theater.
32The assembly was in confusion: Some were shouting one
thing, some another.[e] Most of the
people did not even know why they
were there. 33The Jews pushed Al-

19:8 [a]Ac 9:20 [b]Ac 1:3; 28:23
19:9 [c]Ac 14:4 [d]ver 23; Ac 9:2 [e]ver 30; Ac 11:26
19:10 [f]Ac 20:31 [g]ver 22,26,27
19:11 [h]Ac 8:13
19:12 [i]Ac 5:15
19:13 [j]Mt 12:27 [k]Mk 9:38
19:17 [l]Ac 18:19 [m]Ac 5:5,11
19:20 [n]Ac 6:7; 12:24
19:21 [o]Ac 20:16,22; Ro 15:25 [p]Ac 16:9 [q]Ac 18:12 [r]Ro 15:24,28
19:22 [s]Ac 13:5 [t]Ac 16:1 [u]Ro 16:23; 2Ti 4:20 [v]ver 10,26,27
19:23 [w]Ac 9:2
19:25 [x]Ac 16:16,19, 20
19:26 [y]Ac 18:19 [z]Dt 4:28; Ps 115:4; Isa 44:10-20; Jer 10:3-5; Ac 17:29; 1Co 8:4; Rev 9:20
19:28 [a]Ac 18:19
19:29 [b]Ac 20:4; Ro 16:23; 1Co 1:14 [c]Ac 20:4; 27:2; Col 4:10; Phm 24 [d]Ac 16:9
19:32 [e]Ac 21:34

[o]*19* A drachma was a silver coin worth about a day's wages.

exander to the front, and some of
the crowd shouted instructions to
him. He motioned[a] for silence in
order to make a defense before the
people. 34But when they realized
he was a Jew, they all shouted in
unison for about two hours: "Great
is Artemis of the Ephesians!"
35The city clerk quieted the
crowd and said: "Men of Ephesus,[b] doesn't all the world know
that the city of Ephesus is the
guardian of the temple of the great
Artemis and of her image, which
fell from heaven? 36Therefore,
since these facts are undeniable,
you ought to be quiet and not do
anything rash. 37You have brought
these men here, though they have
neither robbed temples[c] nor blasphemed our goddess. 38If, then,
Demetrius and his fellow craftsmen have a grievance against anybody, the courts are open and there
are proconsuls.[d] They can press
charges. 39If there is anything further you want to bring up, it must
be settled in a legal assembly. 40As
it is, we are in danger of being
charged with rioting because of today's events. In that case we would
not be able to account for this commotion, since there is no reason for
it." 41After he had said this, he dismissed the assembly.

Through Macedonia and Greece

20 When the uproar had ended, Paul sent for the disciples[e] and, after encouraging them,
said good-by and set out for Macedonia.[f] 2He traveled through that
area, speaking many words of encouragement to the people, and finally arrived in Greece, 3where he
stayed three months. Because the
Jews made a plot against him[g] just
as he was about to sail for Syria, he
decided to go back through Macedonia.[h] 4He was accompanied by
Sopater son of Pyrrhus from Berea,
Aristarchus[i] and Secundus from
Thessalonica,[j] Gaius[k] from Derbe, Timothy[l] also, and Tychicus[m]
and Trophimus[n] from the province
of Asia. 5These men went on ahead
and waited for us[o] at Troas.[p] 6But
we sailed from Philippi[q] after the
Feast of Unleavened Bread, and
five days later joined the others at
Troas,[r] where we stayed seven
days.

Eutychus Raised From the Dead at Troas

7On the first day of the week[s]
we came together to break bread.
Paul spoke to the people and, because he intended to leave the next
day, kept on talking until midnight. 8There were many lamps in
the upstairs room[t] where we were
meeting. 9Seated in a window was
a young man named Eutychus, who
was sinking into a deep sleep as
Paul talked on and on. When he
was sound asleep, he fell to the
ground from the third story and
was picked up dead. 10Paul went
down, threw himself on the young
man[u] and put his arms around
him. "Don't be alarmed," he said.
"He's alive!"[v] 11Then he went upstairs again and broke bread[w] and
ate. After talking until daylight, he
left. 12The people took the young
man home alive and were greatly
comforted.

Paul's Farewell to the Ephesian Elders

13We went on ahead to the ship
and sailed for Assos, where we were
going to take Paul aboard. He had
made this arrangement because he
was going there on foot. 14When he
met us at Assos, we took him
aboard and went on to Mitylene.
15The next day we set sail from
there and arrived off Kios. The day
after that we crossed over to Sa-
mos, and on the following day arrived at Miletus.[x] 16Paul had decided to sail past Ephesus[y] to
avoid spending time in the province of Asia, for he was in a hurry to
reach Jerusalem,[z] if possible, by
the day of Pentecost.[a]
17From Miletus, Paul sent to
Ephesus for the elders[b] of the
church. 18When they arrived, he

19:33 [a] Ac 12:17
19:35 [b] Ac 18:19
19:37 [c] Ro 2:22
19:38 [d] Ac 13:7,8,12
20:1 [e] Ac 11:26 [f] Ac 16:9
20:3 [g] ver 19; Ac 9:23,24; 23:12,15,30; 25:3; 2Co 11:26 [h] Ac 16:9
20:4 [i] Ac 19:29 [j] Ac 17:1 [k] Ac 19:29 [l] Ac 16:1 [m] Eph 6:21; Col 4:7; 2Ti 4:12; Tit 3:12 [n] Ac 21:29; 2Ti 4:20
20:5 [o] Ac 16:10 [p] Ac 16:8
20:6 [q] Ac 16:12 [r] Ac 16:8
20:7 [s] 1Co 16:2; Rev 1:10
20:8 [t] Ac 1:13
20:10 [u] 1Ki 17:21; 2Ki 4:34 [v] Mt 9:23,24
20:11 [w] ver 7
20:15 [x] ver 17; 2Ti 4:20
20:16 [y] Ac 18:19 [z] Ac 19:21 [a] Ac 2:1; 1Co 16:8
20:17 [b] Ac 11:30

said to them: "You know how I
lived the whole time I was with
you,[a] from the first day I came into
the province of Asia. **19**I served the
Lord with great humility and with
tears, although I was severely tested by the plots of the Jews.[b] **20**You
know that I have not hesitated to
preach anything[c] that would be
helpful to you but have taught you
publicly and from house to house.
21I have declared to both Jews[d]
and Greeks that they must turn to
God in repentance[e] and have faith
in our Lord Jesus.[f]
22"And now, compelled by the
Spirit, I am going to Jerusalem,[g]
not knowing what will happen to
me there. **23**I only know that in every city the Holy Spirit warns me[h]
that prison and hardships are facing me.[i] **24**However, I consider my
life worth nothing to me,[j] if only I
may finish the race and complete
the task[k] the Lord Jesus has given
me[l]—the task of testifying to the
gospel of God's grace.
25"Now I know that none of you
among whom I have gone about
preaching the kingdom will ever
see me again.[m] **26**Therefore, I declare to you today that I am innocent of the blood of all men.[n]
27For I have not hesitated to proclaim to you the whole will of
God.[o] **28**Keep watch over yourselves and all the flock of which the
Holy Spirit has made you overseers.[p][p] Be shepherds of the
church of God,[q] which he bought
with his own blood. **29**I know that
after I leave, savage wolves[q] will
come in among you and will not
spare the flock.[r] **30**Even from your
own number men will arise and
distort the truth in order to draw
away disciples[s] after them. **31**So
be on your guard! Remember that
for three years[t] I never stopped
warning each of you night and day
with tears.[u]
32"Now I commit you to God[v]
and to the word of his grace, which
can build you up and give you an
inheritance[w] among all those who
are sanctified.[x] **33**I have not coveted anyone's silver or gold or clothing.[y] **34**You yourselves know that
these hands of mine have supplied
my own needs and the needs of my
companions.[z] **35**In everything I
did, I showed you that by this kind
of hard work we must help the
weak, remembering the words the
Lord Jesus himself said: 'It is more
blessed to give than to receive.' "
36When he had said this, he
knelt down with all of them and
prayed.[a] **37**They all wept as they
embraced him and kissed him.[b]
38What grieved them most was his
statement that they would never
see his face again.[c] Then they accompanied him to the ship.

On to Jerusalem

21 After we[d] had torn ourselves away from them, we
put out to sea and sailed straight to
Cos. The next day we went to
Rhodes and from there to Patara.
2We found a ship crossing over to
Phoenicia,[e] went on board and set
sail. **3**After sighting Cyprus and
passing to the south of it, we sailed
on to Syria. We landed at Tyre,
where our ship was to unload its
cargo. **4**Finding the disciples[f]
there, we stayed with them seven
days. Through the Spirit[g] they
urged Paul not to go on to Jerusalem. **5**But when our time was up,
we left and continued on our way.
All the disciples and their wives
and children accompanied us out
of the city, and there on the beach
we knelt to pray.[h] **6**After saying
good-by to each other, we went
aboard the ship, and they returned
home.
7We continued our voyage from
Tyre[i] and landed at Ptolemais,
where we greeted the brothers[j]
and stayed with them for a day.
8Leaving the next day, we reached
Caesarea[k] and stayed at the house
of Philip[l] the evangelist,[m] one of
the Seven. **9**He had four unmarried
daughters who prophesied.[n]

20:18 [a]Ac 18:19-21; 19:1-41 **20:19** [b]ver 3 **20:20** [c]ver 27 **20:21** [d]Ac 18:5 [e]Ac 2:38 [f]Ac 24:24; 26:18; Eph 1:15; Col 2:5; Phm 5 **20:22** [g]ver 16 **20:23** [h]Ac 21:4 [i]Ac 9:16 **20:24** [j]Ac 21:13 [k]2Co 4:1 [l]Gal 1:1; Tit 1:3 **20:25** [m]ver 38 **20:26** [n]Ac 18:6 **20:27** [o]ver 20 **20:28** [p]1Pe 5:2 **20:29** [q]Mt 7:15 [r]ver 28 **20:30** [s]Ac 11:26 **20:31** [t]Ac 19:10 [u]ver 19 **20:32** [v]Ac 14:23 [w]Eph 1:14; Col 1:12; 3:24; Heb 9:15; 1Pe 1:4 [x]Ac 26:18 **20:33** [y]1Sa 12:3; 1Co 9:12; 2Co 7:2; 11:9; 12:14-17 **20:34** [z]Ac 18:3 **20:36** [a]Lk 22:41; Ac 21:5 **20:37** [b]Lk 15:20 **20:38** [c]ver 25 **21:1** [d]Ac 16:10 **21:2** [e]Ac 11:19 **21:4** [f]Ac 11:26 [g]ver 11; Ac 20:23 **21:5** [h]Ac 20:36 **21:7** [i]Ac 12:20 [j]Ac 1:16 **21:8** [k]Ac 8:40 [l]Ac 6:5; 8:5-40 [m]Eph 4:11; 2Ti 4:5 **21:9** [n]Lk 2:36; Ac 2:17

[p]28 Traditionally *bishops* [q]28 Many manuscripts *of the Lord*

10After we had been there a
number of days, a prophet named
Agabus[a] came down from Judea.
11Coming over to us, he took Paul's
belt, tied his own hands and feet
with it and said, "The Holy Spirit
says, 'In this way the Jews of Jerusalem will bind[b] the owner of this
belt and will hand him over to the
Gentiles.' "[c]
12When we heard this, we and
the people there pleaded with Paul
not to go up to Jerusalem. **13**Then
Paul answered, "Why are you
weeping and breaking my heart? I
am ready not only to be bound, but
also to die[d] in Jerusalem for the
name of the Lord Jesus."[e] **14**When
he would not be dissuaded, we
gave up and said, "The Lord's will
be done."
15After this, we got ready and
went up to Jerusalem. **16**Some of
the disciples from Caesarea[f] accompanied us and brought us to
the home of Mnason, where we
were to stay. He was a man from
Cyprus[g] and one of the early disciples.

Paul's Arrival at Jerusalem

17When we arrived at Jerusalem,
the brothers received us warmly.[h]
18The next day Paul and the rest of
us went to see James,[i] and all the
elders[j] were present. **19**Paul greeted them and reported in detail
what God had done among the
Gentiles[k] through his ministry.[l]
20When they heard this, they
praised God. Then they said to
Paul: "You see, brother, how many
thousands of Jews have believed,
and all of them are zealous[m] for the
law.[n] **21**They have been informed
that you teach all the Jews who live
among the Gentiles to turn away
from Moses,[o] telling them not to
circumcise their children[p] or live
according to our customs.[q]
22What shall we do? They will certainly hear that you have come,
23so do what we tell you. There are
four men with us who have made a
vow.[r] **24**Take these men, join in
their purification rites[s] and pay
their expenses, so that they can
have their heads shaved.[t] Then everybody will know there is no truth
in these reports about you, but that
you yourself are living in obedience
to the law. **25**As for the Gentile believers, we have written to them
our decision that they should abstain from food sacrificed to idols,
from blood, from the meat of strangled animals and from sexual immorality."[u]
26The next day Paul took the
men and purified himself along
with them. Then he went to the
temple to give notice of the date
when the days of purification
would end and the offering would
be made for each of them.[v]

Paul Arrested

27When the seven days were
nearly over, some Jews from the
province of Asia saw Paul at the
temple. They stirred up the whole
crowd and seized him,[w] **28**shouting, "Men of Israel, help us! This is
the man who teaches all men everywhere against our people and
our law and this place. And besides, he has brought Greeks into
the temple area and defiled this
holy place."[x] **29**(They had previously seen Trophimus[y] the Ephesian[z] in the city with Paul and assumed that Paul had brought him
into the temple area.)
30The whole city was aroused,
and the people came running from
all directions. Seizing Paul,[a] they
dragged him[b] from the temple,
and immediately the gates were
shut. **31**While they were trying to
kill him, news reached the commander of the Roman troops that
the whole city of Jerusalem was in
an uproar. **32**He at once took some
officers and soldiers and ran down
to the crowd. When the rioters saw
the commander and his soldiers,
they stopped beating Paul.[c]
33The commander came up and
arrested him and ordered him to be
bound[d] with two[e] chains.[f] Then
he asked who he was and what he
had done. **34**Some in the crowd
shouted one thing and some another,[g] and since the commander

21:10 [a] Ac 11:28
21:11 [b] ver 33 [c] 1Ki 22:11
21:13 [d] Ac 20:24 [e] Ac 9:16
21:16 [f] Ac 8:40 [g] ver 3,4
21:17 [h] Ac 15:4
21:18 [i] Ac 15:13 [j] Ac 11:30
21:19 [k] Ac 14:27 [l] Ac 1:17
21:20 [m] Ac 22:3; Ro 10:2; Gal 1:14 [n] Ac 15:1,5
21:21 [o] ver 28 [p] Ac 15:19-21; 1Co 7:18,19 [q] Ac 6:14
21:23 [r] Ac 18:18
21:24 [s] ver 26; Ac 24:18 [t] Ac 18:18
21:25 [u] Ac 15:20,29
21:26 [v] Nu 6:13-20; Ac 24:18
21:27 [w] Ac 24:18; 26:21
21:28 [x] Mt 24:15; Ac 24:5,6
21:29 [y] Ac 20:4 [z] Ac 18:19
21:30 [a] Ac 26:21 [b] Ac 16:19
21:32 [c] Ac 23:27
21:33 [d] ver 11 [e] Ac 12:6 [f] Ac 20:23; Eph 6:20; 2Ti 2:9
21:34 [g] Ac 19:32

could not get at the truth because of the uproar, he ordered that Paul be taken into the barracks.[a] **35**When Paul reached the steps,[b] the violence of the mob was so great he had to be carried by the soldiers. **36**The crowd that followed kept shouting, "Away with him!"[c]

Paul Speaks to the Crowd

22:3–16pp — Ac 9:1–22; 26:9–18

37As the soldiers were about to take Paul into the barracks,[d] he asked the commander, "May I say something to you?"

"Do you speak Greek?" he replied. **38**"Aren't you the Egyptian who started a revolt and led four thousand terrorists out into the desert[e] some time ago?"[f]

39Paul answered, "I am a Jew, from Tarsus[g] in Cilicia,[h] a citizen of no ordinary city. Please let me speak to the people."

40Having received the commander's permission, Paul stood on the steps and motioned[i] to the crowd. When they were all silent, he said to them in Aramaic[r]:[j]

22 **1**"Brothers and fathers,[k] listen now to my defense."

2When they heard him speak to them in Aramaic,[l] they became very quiet.

Then Paul said: **3**"I am a Jew,[m] born in Tarsus[n] of Cilicia, but brought up in this city. Under[o] Gamaliel[p] I was thoroughly trained in the law of our fathers[q] and was just as zealous[r] for God as any of you are today. **4**I persecuted[s] the followers of this Way to their death, arresting both men and women and throwing them into prison,[t] **5**as also the high priest and all the Council[u] can testify. I even obtained letters from them to their brothers[v] in Damascus,[w] and went there to bring these people as prisoners to Jerusalem to be punished.

6"About noon as I came near Damascus, suddenly a bright light from heaven flashed around me.[x] **7**I fell to the ground and heard a voice say to me, 'Saul! Saul! Why do you persecute me?'

8" 'Who are you, Lord?' I asked.

" 'I am Jesus of Nazareth, whom you are persecuting,' he replied. **9**My companions saw the light,[y] but they did not understand the voice[z] of him who was speaking to me.

10" 'What shall I do, Lord?' I asked.

" 'Get up,' the Lord said, 'and go into Damascus. There you will be told all that you have been assigned to do.'[a] **11**My companions led me by the hand into Damascus, because the brilliance of the light had blinded me.[b]

12"A man named Ananias came to see me.[c] He was a devout observer of the law and highly respected by all the Jews living there.[d] **13**He stood beside me and said, 'Brother Saul, receive your sight!' And at that very moment I was able to see him.

14"Then he said: 'The God of our fathers[e] has chosen you to know his will and to see[f] the Righteous One[g] and to hear words from his mouth. **15**You will be his witness[h] to all men of what you have seen and heard. **16**And now what are you waiting for? Get up, be baptized[i] and wash your sins away,[j] calling on his name.'[k]

17"When I returned to Jerusalem[l] and was praying at the temple, I fell into a trance[m] **18**and saw the Lord speaking. 'Quick!' he said to me. 'Leave Jerusalem immediately, because they will not accept your testimony about me.'

19" 'Lord,' I replied, 'these men know that I went from one synagogue to another to imprison[n] and beat[o] those who believe in you. **20**And when the blood of your martyr[s] Stephen was shed, I stood there giving my approval and guarding the clothes of those who were killing him.'[p]

21"Then the Lord said to me,

[r]40 Or possibly *Hebrew*; also in 22:2
[s]20 Or *witness*

21:34 [a]ver 37; Ac 23:10,16, 32
21:35 [b]ver 40
21:36 [c]Lk 23:18; Jn 19:15; Ac 22:22
21:37 [d]ver 34
21:38 [e]Mt 24:26 [f]Ac 5:36
21:39 [g]Ac 9:11 [h]Ac 22:3
21:40 [i]Ac 12:17 [j]Jn 5:2
22:1 [k]Ac 7:2
22:2 [l]Ac 21:40
22:3 [m]Ac 21:39 [n]Ac 9:11 [o]Lk 10:39 [p]Ac 5:34 [q]Ac 26:5 [r]Ac 21:20
22:4 [s]Ac 8:3 [t]ver 19,20
22:5 [u]Lk 22:66 [v]Ac 13:26 [w]Ac 9:2
22:6 [x]Ac 9:3
22:9 [y]Ac 26:13 [z]Ac 9:7
22:10 [a]Ac 16:30
22:11 [b]Ac 9:8
22:12 [c]Ac 9:17 [d]Ac 10:22
22:14 [e]Ac 3:13 [f]1Co 9:1; 15:8 [g]Ac 7:52
22:15 [h]Ac 23:11; 26:16
22:16 [i]Ac 2:38 [j]Heb 10:22 [k]Ro 10:13
22:17 [l]Ac 9:26 [m]Ac 10:10
22:19 [n]ver 4; Ac 8:3 [o]Mt 10:17
22:20 [p]Ac 7:57-60; 8:1

'Go; I will send you far away to the Gentiles.' "[a]

Paul the Roman Citizen

22 The crowd listened to Paul until he said this. Then they raised their voices and shouted, "Rid the earth of him![b] He's not fit to live!"[c]

23 As they were shouting and throwing off their cloaks[d] and flinging dust into the air,[e] 24 the commander ordered Paul to be taken into the barracks.[f] He directed[g] that he be flogged and questioned in order to find out why the people were shouting at him like this. 25 As they stretched him out to flog him, Paul said to the centurion standing there, "Is it legal for you to flog a Roman citizen who hasn't even been found guilty?"[h]

26 When the centurion heard this, he went to the commander and reported it. "What are you going to do?" he asked. "This man is a Roman citizen."

27 The commander went to Paul and asked, "Tell me, are you a Roman citizen?"

"Yes, I am," he answered.

28 Then the commander said, "I had to pay a big price for my citizenship."

"But I was born a citizen," Paul replied.

29 Those who were about to question him withdrew immediately. The commander himself was alarmed when he realized that he had put Paul, a Roman citizen,[i] in chains.

Before the Sanhedrin

30 The next day, since the commander wanted to find out exactly why Paul was being accused by the Jews,[j] he released him[k] and ordered the chief priests and all the Sanhedrin[l] to assemble. Then he brought Paul and had him stand before them.

23 Paul looked straight at the Sanhedrin[m] and said, "My brothers,[n] I have fulfilled my duty to God in all good conscience[o] to this day." 2 At this the high priest Ananias[p] ordered those standing near Paul to strike him on the mouth.[q] 3 Then Paul said to him, "God will strike you, you whitewashed wall![r] You sit there to judge me according to the law, yet you yourself violate the law by commanding that I be struck!"[s]

4 Those who were standing near Paul said, "You dare to insult God's high priest?"

5 Paul replied, "Brothers, I did not realize that he was the high priest; for it is written: 'Do not speak evil about the ruler of your people.'[t]"[t]

6 Then Paul, knowing that some of them were Sadducees and the others Pharisees, called out in the Sanhedrin, "My brothers,[u] I am a Pharisee,[v] the son of a Pharisee. I stand on trial because of my hope in the resurrection of the dead."[w] 7 When he said this, a dispute broke out between the Pharisees and the Sadducees, and the assembly was divided. 8 (The Sadducees say that there is no resurrection,[x] and that there are neither angels nor spirits, but the Pharisees acknowledge them all.)

9 There was a great uproar, and some of the teachers of the law who were Pharisees[y] stood up and argued vigorously. "We find nothing wrong with this man,"[z] they said. "What if a spirit or an angel has spoken to him?"[a] 10 The dispute became so violent that the commander was afraid Paul would be torn to pieces by them. He ordered the troops to go down and take him away from them by force and bring him into the barracks.[b]

11 The following night the Lord stood near Paul and said, "Take courage![c] As you have testified about me in Jerusalem, so you must also testify in Rome."[d]

The Plot to Kill Paul

12 The next morning the Jews formed a conspiracy and bound themselves with an oath not to eat or drink until they had killed

22:21 [a] Ac 9:15; 13:46
22:22 [b] Ac 21:36 [c] Ac 25:24
22:23 [d] Ac 7:58 [e] 2Sa 16:13
22:24 [f] Ac 21:34 [g] ver 29
22:25 [h] Ac 16:37
22:29 [i] ver 24,25; Ac 16:38
22:30 [j] Ac 23:28 [k] Ac 21:33 [l] Mt 5:22
23:1 [m] Ac 22:30 [n] Ac 22:5 [o] Ac 24:16; 1Co 4:4; 2Co 1:12; 2Ti 1:3; Heb 13:18
23:2 [p] Ac 24:1 [q] Jn 18:22
23:3 [r] Mt 23:27 [s] Lev 19:15; Dt 25:1,2; Jn 7:51
23:5 [t] Ex 22:28
23:6 [u] Ac 22:5 [v] Ac 26:5; Php 3:5 [w] Ac 24:15,21; 26:8
23:8 [x] Mt 22:23
23:9 [y] Mk 2:16 [z] ver 29; Ac 25:25; 26:31 [a] Ac 22:7,17, 18
23:10 [b] Ac 21:34
23:11 [c] Ac 18:9 [d] Ac 19:21; 28:23

t5 Exodus 22:28

Paul.[a] **13**More than forty men were
involved in this plot. **14**They went
to the chief priests and elders and
said, "We have taken a solemn oath
not to eat anything until we have
killed Paul.[b] **15**Now then, you and
the Sanhedrin[c] petition the commander to bring him before you on
the pretext of wanting more accurate information about his case.
We are ready to kill him before he
gets here."
16But when the son of Paul's sister heard of this plot, he went into
the barracks[d] and told Paul.
17Then Paul called one of the
centurions and said, "Take this
young man to the commander; he
has something to tell him." **18**So he
took him to the commander.
The centurion said, "Paul, the
prisoner,[e] sent for me and asked
me to bring this young man to you
because he has something to tell
you."
19The commander took the
young man by the hand, drew him
aside and asked, "What is it you
want to tell me?"
20He said: "The Jews have
agreed to ask you to bring Paul before the Sanhedrin[f] tomorrow on
the pretext of wanting more accurate information about him.[g]
21Don't give in to them, because
more than forty[h] of them are waiting in ambush for him. They have
taken an oath not to eat or drink
until they have killed him.[i] They
are ready now, waiting for your
consent to their request."
22The commander dismissed the
young man and cautioned him,
"Don't tell anyone that you have
reported this to me."

Paul Transferred to Caesarea

23Then he called two of his centurions and ordered them, "Get
ready a detachment of two hundred soldiers, seventy horsemen
and two hundred spearmen[u] to go
to Caesarea[j] at nine tonight.[k]
24Provide mounts for Paul so that
he may be taken safely to Governor
Felix."[l]
25He wrote a letter as follows:

26Claudius Lysias,

To His Excellency,[m] Governor Felix:

Greetings.[n]

27This man was seized by
the Jews and they were about
to kill him,[o] but I came with
my troops and rescued him,[p]
for I had learned that he is a
Roman citizen.[q] **28**I wanted to
know why they were accusing
him, so I brought him to their
Sanhedrin.[r] **29**I found that
the accusation had to do with
questions about their law,[s]
but there was no charge
against him[t] that deserved
death or imprisonment.
30When I was informed[u] of a
plot[v] to be carried out against
the man, I sent him to you at
once. I also ordered his accusers[w] to present to you their
case against him.

31So the soldiers, carrying out
their orders, took Paul with them
during the night and brought him
as far as Antipatris. **32**The next day
they let the cavalry[x] go on with
him, while they returned to the
barracks.[y] **33**When the cavalry[z]
arrived in Caesarea,[a] they delivered the letter to the governor[b]
and handed Paul over to him.
34The governor read the letter and
asked what province he was from.
Learning that he was from Cilicia,[c]
35he said, "I will hear your case
when your accusers[d] get here."
Then he ordered that Paul be kept
under guard[e] in Herod's palace.

The Trial Before Felix

24 Five days later the high
priest Ananias[f] went down
to Caesarea with some of the elders
and a lawyer named Tertullus, and
they brought their charges[g]
against Paul before the governor.[h]
2When Paul was called in, Tertullus presented his case before Felix:

[u]23 The meaning of the Greek for this word is uncertain.

23:12 [a]ver 14,21,30; Ac 25:3
23:14 [b]ver 12
23:15 [c]ver 1; Ac 22:30
23:16 [d]ver 10; Ac 21:34
23:18 [e]Eph 3:1
23:20 [f]ver 1 [g]ver 14, 15
23:21 [h]ver 13 [i]ver 12,14
23:23 [j]Ac 8:40 [k]ver 33
23:24 [l]ver 26,33; Ac 24:1-3,10; 25:14
23:26 [m]Lk 1:3; Ac 24:3; 26:25 [n]Ac 15:23
23:27 [o]Ac 21:32 [p]Ac 21:33 [q]Ac 22:25-29
23:28 [r]Ac 22:30
23:29 [s]Ac 18:15; 25:19 [t]ver 9; Ac 26:31
23:30 [u]ver 20,21 [v]Ac 20:3 [w]ver 35; Ac 24:19; 25:16
23:32 [x]ver 23 [y]Ac 21:34
23:33 [z]ver 23,24 [a]Ac 8:40 [b]ver 26
23:34 [c]Ac 6:9; 21:39
23:35 [d]ver 30; Ac 24:19; 25:16 [e]Ac 24:27
24:1 [f]Ac 23:2 [g]Ac 23:30,35 [h]Ac 23:24

"We have enjoyed a long period of
peace under you, and your fore-
sight has brought about reforms in
this nation. **3**Everywhere and in every way, most excellent[a] Felix, we
acknowledge this with profound
gratitude. **4**But in order not to weary you further, I would request that
you be kind enough to hear us
briefly.

5"We have found this man to be
a troublemaker, stirring up riots[b]
among the Jews[c] all over the
world. He is a ringleader of the
Nazarene[d] sect[e] **6**and even tried
to desecrate the temple;[f] so we
seized him. **8**By[v] examining him
yourself you will be able to learn
the truth about all these charges
we are bringing against him."

9The Jews joined in the accusation,[g] asserting that these things
were true.

10When the governor[h] motioned
for him to speak, Paul replied: "I
know that for a number of years
you have been a judge over this nation; so I gladly make my defense.
11You can easily verify that no
more than twelve days[i] ago I went
up to Jerusalem to worship. **12**My
accusers did not find me arguing
with anyone at the temple,[j] or
stirring up a crowd[k] in the synagogues or anywhere else in the city.
13And they cannot prove to you the
charges they are now making
against me.[l] **14**However, I admit
that I worship the God of our fathers[m] as a follower of the Way,[n]
which they call a sect.[o] I believe
everything that agrees with the Law
and that is written in the Prophets,[p] **15**and I have the same hope
in God as these men, that there will
be a resurrection[q] of both the righteous and the wicked.[r] **16**So I
strive always to keep my conscience clear[s] before God and
man.

17"After an absence of several
years, I came to Jerusalem to bring
my people gifts for the poor[t] and
to present offerings. **18**I was ceremonially clean[u] when they found
me in the temple courts doing this.
There was no crowd with me, nor
was I involved in any disturbance.[v]
19But there are some Jews from the
province of Asia, who ought to be
here before you and bring charges
if they have anything against me.[w]
20Or these who are here should
state what crime they found in me
when I stood before the Sanhedrin— **21**unless it was this one
thing I shouted as I stood in their
presence: 'It is concerning the resurrection of the dead that I am on
trial before you today.' "[x]

22Then Felix, who was well acquainted with the Way, adjourned
the proceedings. "When Lysias the
commander comes," he said, "I
will decide your case." **23**He ordered the centurion to keep Paul
under guard[y] but to give him some
freedom[z] and permit his friends to
take care of his needs.[a]

24Several days later Felix came
with his wife Drusilla, who was a
Jewess. He sent for Paul and listened to him as he spoke about
faith in Christ Jesus.[b] **25**As Paul
discoursed on righteousness, self-
control[c] and the judgment[d] to
come, Felix was afraid and said,
"That's enough for now! You may
leave. When I find it convenient, I
will send for you." **26**At the same
time he was hoping that Paul
would offer him a bribe, so he sent
for him frequently and talked with
him.

27When two years had passed,
Felix was succeeded by Porcius
Festus,[e] but because Felix wanted
to grant a favor to the Jews,[f] he
left Paul in prison.[g]

The Trial Before Festus

25 Three days after arriving in
the province, Festus went
up from Caesarea[h] to Jerusalem,
2where the chief priests and Jewish
leaders appeared before him and
presented the charges against
Paul.[i] **3**They urgently requested
Festus, as a favor to them, to have

24:3 [a]Lk 1:3; Ac 23:26; 26:25
24:5 [b]Ac 16:20; 17:6 [c]Ac 21:28 [d]Mk 1:24 [e]ver 14; Ac 26:5; 28:22
24:6 [f]Ac 21:28
24:9 [g]1Th 2:16
24:10 [h]Ac 23:24
24:11 [i]Ac 21:27; ver 1
24:12 [j]Ac 25:8; 28:17 [k]ver 18
24:13 [l]Ac 25:7
24:14 [m]Ac 3:13 [n]Ac 9:2 [o]ver 5 [p]Ac 26:6,22; 28:23
24:15 [q]Ac 23:6; 28:20 [r]Da 12:2; Jn 5:28,29
24:16 [s]Ac 23:1
24:17 [t]Ac 11:29,30; Ro 15:25-28, 31; 1Co 16:1-4, 15; 2Co 8:1-4; Gal 2:10
24:18 [u]Ac 21:26 [v]ver 12
24:19 [w]Ac 23:30
24:21 [x]Ac 23:6
24:23 [y]Ac 23:35 [z]Ac 28:16 [a]Ac 23:16; 27:3
24:24 [b]Ac 20:21
24:25 [c]Gal 5:23; 2Pe 1:6 [d]Ac 10:42
24:27 [e]Ac 25:1,4,9, 14 [f]Ac 12:3; 25:9 [g]Ac 23:35; 25:14
25:1 [h]Ac 8:40
25:2 [i]ver 15; Ac 24:1

[v]6-8 Some manuscripts *him and wanted to judge him according to our law.* [7]*But the commander, Lysias, came and with the use of much force snatched him from our hands* [8]*and ordered his accusers to come before you. By*

Paul transferred to Jerusalem, for they were preparing an ambush to kill him along the way. **4**Festus answered, "Paul is being held[a] at Caesarea, and I myself am going there soon. **5**Let some of your leaders come with me and press charges against the man there, if he has done anything wrong."

6After spending eight or ten days with them, he went down to Caesarea, and the next day he convened the court[b] and ordered that Paul be brought before him. **7**When Paul appeared, the Jews who had come down from Jerusalem stood around him, bringing many serious charges against him,[c] which they could not prove.[d]

8Then Paul made his defense: "I have done nothing wrong against the law of the Jews or against the temple[e] or against Caesar."

9Festus, wishing to do the Jews a favor,[f] said to Paul, "Are you willing to go up to Jerusalem and stand trial before me there on these charges?"[g]

10Paul answered: "I am now standing before Caesar's court, where I ought to be tried. I have not done any wrong to the Jews, as you yourself know very well. **11**If, however, I am guilty of doing anything deserving death, I do not refuse to die. But if the charges brought against me by these Jews are not true, no one has the right to hand me over to them. I appeal to Caesar!"[h]

12After Festus had conferred with his council, he declared: "You have appealed to Caesar. To Caesar you will go!"

Festus Consults King Agrippa

13A few days later King Agrippa and Bernice arrived at Caesarea[i] to pay their respects to Festus. **14**Since they were spending many days there, Festus discussed Paul's case with the king. He said: "There is a man here whom Felix left as a prisoner.[j] **15**When I went to Jerusalem, the chief priests and elders of the Jews brought charges against him[k] and asked that he be condemned.

16"I told them that it is not the Roman custom to hand over any man before he has faced his accusers and has had an opportunity to defend himself against their charges.[l] **17**When they came here with me, I did not delay the case, but convened the court the next day and ordered the man to be brought in.[m] **18**When his accusers got up to speak, they did not charge him with any of the crimes I had expected. **19**Instead, they had some points of dispute[n] with him about their own religion[o] and about a dead man named Jesus who Paul claimed was alive. **20**I was at a loss how to investigate such matters; so I asked if he would be willing to go to Jerusalem and stand trial there on these charges.[p] **21**When Paul made his appeal to be held over for the Emperor's decision, I ordered him held until I could send him to Caesar."[q]

22Then Agrippa said to Festus, "I would like to hear this man myself."

He replied, "Tomorrow you will hear him."[r]

Paul Before Agrippa

26:12–18pp — Ac 9:3–8; 22:6–11

23The next day Agrippa and Bernice[s] came with great pomp and entered the audience room with the high ranking officers and the leading men of the city. At the command of Festus, Paul was brought in. **24**Festus said: "King Agrippa, and all who are present with us, you see this man! The whole Jewish community[t] has petitioned me about him in Jerusalem and here in Caesarea, shouting that he ought not to live any longer.[u] **25**I found he had done nothing deserving of death,[v] but because he made his appeal to the Emperor[w] I decided to send him to Rome. **26**But I have nothing definite to write to His Majesty about him. Therefore I have brought him be-

25:4 [a]Ac 24:23
25:6 [b]ver 17
25:7 [c]Mk 15:3; Lk 23:2,10; Ac 24:5,6 [d]Ac 24:13
25:8 [e]Ac 6:13; 24:12; 28:17
25:9 [f]Ac 24:27 [g]ver 20
25:11 [h]ver 21,25; Ac 26:32; 28:19
25:13 [i]Ac 8:40
25:14 [j]Ac 24:27
25:15 [k]ver 2; Ac 24:1
25:16 [l]ver 4,5; Ac 23:30
25:17 [m]ver 6,10
25:19 [n]Ac 18:15; 23:29 [o]Ac 17:22
25:20 [p]ver 9
25:21 [q]ver 11,12
25:22 [r]Ac 9:15
25:23 [s]ver 13; Ac 26:30
25:24 [t]ver 2,3,7 [u]Ac 22:22
25:25 [v]Ac 23:9 [w]ver 11

fore all of you, and especially before you, King Agrippa, so that as a
result of this investigation I may
have something to write. 27For I
think it is unreasonable to send on
a prisoner without specifying the
charges against him."

26

Then Agrippa said to Paul,
"You have permission to
speak for yourself."[a]
So Paul motioned with his hand
and began his defense: 2"King
Agrippa, I consider myself fortu-
nate to stand before you today as I
make my defense against all the accusations of the Jews, 3and especially so because you are well acquainted with all the Jewish customs[b] and controversies.[c]
Therefore, I beg you to listen to me
patiently.
4"The Jews all know the way I
have lived ever since I was a child,[d]
from the beginning of my life in my
own country, and also in Jerusalem. 5They have known me for a
long time[e] and can testify, if they
are willing, that according to the
strictest sect of our religion, I lived
as a Pharisee.[f] 6And now it is because of my hope[g] in what God has
promised our fathers[h] that I am on
trial today. 7This is the promise our
twelve tribes[i] are hoping to see
fulfilled as they earnestly serve
God day and night.[j] O king, it is
because of this hope that the Jews
are accusing me.[k] 8Why should
any of you consider it incredible
that God raises the dead?[l]
9"I too was convinced[m] that I
ought to do all that was possible to
oppose[n] the name of Jesus of Nazareth.[o] 10And that is just what I
did in Jerusalem. On the authority
of the chief priests I put many of
the saints[p] in prison,[q] and when
they were put to death, I cast my
vote against them.[r] 11Many a time
I went from one synagogue to another to have them punished,[s] and
I tried to force them to blaspheme.
In my obsession against them, I
even went to foreign cities to persecute them.
12"On one of these journeys I
was going to Damascus with the
authority and commission of the
chief priests. 13About noon, O
king, as I was on the road, I saw a
light from heaven, brighter than
the sun, blazing around me and my
companions. 14We all fell to the
ground, and I heard a voice[t] saying
to me in Aramaic,[w] 'Saul, Saul,
why do you persecute me? It is hard
for you to kick against the goads.'
15"Then I asked, 'Who are you,
Lord?'
" 'I am Jesus, whom you are persecuting,' the Lord replied. 16'Now
get up and stand on your feet.[u] I
have appeared to you to appoint
you as a servant and as a witness of
what you have seen of me and what
I will show you.[v] 17I will rescue
you[w] from your own people and
from the Gentiles.[x] I am sending
you to them 18to open their eyes[y]
and turn them from darkness to
light,[z] and from the power of Satan to God, so that they may receive forgiveness of sins[a] and a
place among those who are sanctified by faith in me.'[b]
19"So then, King Agrippa, I was
not disobedient to the vision from
heaven. 20First to those in Damascus,[c] then to those in Jerusalem[d]
and in all Judea, and to the Gentiles[e] also, I preached that they
should repent[f] and turn to God
and prove their repentance by their
deeds.[g] 21That is why the Jews
seized me[h] in the temple courts
and tried to kill me.[i] 22But I have
had God's help to this very day, and
so I stand here and testify to small
and great alike. I am saying nothing
beyond what the prophets and Moses said would happen[j]— 23that
the Christ[x] would suffer and, as
the first to rise from the dead,[k]
would proclaim light to his own
people and to the Gentiles."[l]
24At this point Festus interrupt-
ed Paul's defense. "You are out of
your mind,[m] Paul!" he shouted.
"Your great learning[n] is driving
you insane."

26:1 [a]Ac 9:15; 25:22
26:3 [b]ver 7; Ac 6:14 [c]Ac 25:19
26:4 [d]Gal 1:13,14; Php 3:5
26:5 [e]Ac 22:3 [f]Ac 23:6; Php 3:5
26:6 [g]Ac 23:6; 24:15; 28:20 [h]Ac 13:32; Ro 15:8
26:7 [i]Jas 1:1 [j]1Th 3:10; 1Ti 5:5 [k]ver 2
26:8 [l]Ac 23:6
26:9 [m]1Ti 1:13 [n]Jn 16:2 [o]Jn 15:21
26:10 [p]Ac 9:13 [q]Ac 8:3; 9:2, 14,21 [r]Ac 22:20
26:11 [s]Mt 10:17
26:14 [t]Ac 9:7
26:16 [u]Eze 2:1; Da 10:11 [v]Ac 22:14,15
26:17 [w]Jer 1:8,19 [x]Ac 9:15
26:18 [y]Isa 35:5 [z]Isa 42:7,16; Eph 5:8; Col 1:13; 1Pe 2:9 [a]Lk 24:47; Ac 2:38 [b]Ac 20:21,32
26:20 [c]Ac 9:19-25 [d]Ac 9:26-29; 22:17-20 [e]Ac 9:15; 13:46 [f]Ac 3:19 [g]Mt 3:8; Lk 3:8
26:21 [h]Ac 21:27,30 [i]Ac 21:31
26:22 [j]Lk 24:27,44; Ac 10:43; 24:14
26:23 [k]1Co 15:20, 23; Col 1:18; Rev 1:5 [l]Lk 2:32
26:24 [m]Jn 10:20; 1Co 4:10 [n]Jn 7:15

[w]14 Or *Hebrew* [x]23 Or *Messiah*

25"I am not insane, most excellent[a] Festus," Paul replied. "What
I am saying is true and reasonable.
26The king is familiar with these
things,[b] and I can speak freely to
him. I am convinced that none of
this has escaped his notice, because it was not done in a corner.
27King Agrippa, do you believe the
prophets? I know you do."
28Then Agrippa said to Paul, "Do
you think that in such a short time
you can persuade me to be a Christian?"[c]
29Paul replied, "Short time or
long—I pray God that not only you
but all who are listening to me today may become what I am, except
for these chains."[d]
30The king rose, and with him
the governor and Bernice[e] and
those sitting with them. 31They left
the room, and while talking with
one another, they said, "This man
is not doing anything that deserves
death or imprisonment."[f]
32Agrippa said to Festus, "This
man could have been set free[g] if
he had not appealed to Caesar."[h]

Paul Sails for Rome

27 When it was decided that
we[i] would sail for Italy,[j]
Paul and some other prisoners
were handed over to a centurion
named Julius, who belonged to the
Imperial Regiment.[k] 2We boarded
a ship from Adramyttium about to
sail for ports along the coast of the
province of Asia,[l] and we put out
to sea. Aristarchus,[m] a Macedoni-
an[n] from Thessalonica,[o] was with
us.
3The next day we landed at Sidon;[p] and Julius, in kindness to
Paul,[q] allowed him to go to his
friends so they might provide for
his needs.[r] 4From there we put
out to sea again and passed to the
lee of Cyprus because the winds
were against us.[s] 5When we had
sailed across the open sea off the
coast of Cilicia[t] and Pamphylia,
we landed at Myra in Lycia. 6There
the centurion found an Alexandrian ship[u] sailing for Italy[v] and
put us on board. 7We made slow
headway for many days and had
difficulty arriving off Cnidus. When
the wind did not allow us to hold
our course,[w] we sailed to the lee of
Crete,[x] opposite Salmone. 8We
moved along the coast with difficulty and came to a place called
Fair Havens, near the town of La-
sea.
9Much time had been lost, and
sailing had already become danger-
ous because by now it was after the
Fast.[y][y] So Paul warned them,
10"Men, I can see that our voyage is
going to be disastrous and bring
great loss to ship and cargo, and to
our own lives also."[z] 11But the
centurion, instead of listening to
what Paul said, followed the advice
of the pilot and of the owner of the
ship. 12Since the harbor was un-
suitable to winter in, the majority
decided that we should sail on,
hoping to reach Phoenix and winter there. This was a harbor in
Crete, facing both southwest and
northwest.

The Storm

13When a gentle south wind began to blow, they thought they had
obtained what they wanted; so they
weighed anchor and sailed along
the shore of Crete. 14Before very
long, a wind of hurricane force,[a]
called the "northeaster," swept
down from the island. 15The ship
was caught by the storm and could
not head into the wind; so we gave
way to it and were driven along.
16As we passed to the lee of a small
island called Cauda, we were hardly able to make the lifeboat secure.
17When the men had hoisted it
aboard, they passed ropes under
the ship itself to hold it together.
Fearing that they would run
aground[b] on the sandbars of Syr-
tis, they lowered the sea anchor
and let the ship be driven along.
18We took such a violent battering
from the storm that the next day
they began to throw the cargo overboard.[c] 19On the third day, they

y9 That is, the Day of Atonement (Yom Kippur)

26:25 [a]Ac 23:26
26:26 [b]ver 3
26:28 [c]Ac 11:26
26:29 [d]Ac 21:33
26:30 [e]Ac 25:23
26:31 [f]Ac 23:9
26:32 [g]Ac 28:18 [h]Ac 25:11
27:1 [i]Ac 16:10 [j]Ac 18:2; 25:12,25 [k]Ac 10:1
27:2 [l]Ac 2:9 [m]Ac 19:29 [n]Ac 16:9 [o]Ac 17:1
27:3 [p]Mt 11:21 [q]ver 43 [r]Ac 24:23; 28:16
27:4 [s]ver 7
27:5 [t]Ac 6:9
27:6 [u]Ac 28:11 [v]ver 1
27:7 [w]ver 4 [x]ver 12,13,21
27:9 [y]Lev 16:29-31; 23:27-29; Nu 29:7
27:10 [z]ver 21
27:14 [a]Mk 4:37
27:17 [b]ver 26,39
27:18 [c]ver 19,38; Jnh 1:5

threw the ship's tackle overboard
with their own hands. 20When neither sun nor stars appeared for
many days and the storm continued raging, we finally gave up all
hope of being saved.
21After the men had gone a long
time without food, Paul stood up
before them and said: "Men, you
should have taken my advice[a] not
to sail from Crete;[b] then you
would have spared yourselves this
damage and loss. 22But now I urge
you to keep up your courage,[c] because not one of you will be lost;
only the ship will be destroyed.
23Last night an angel[d] of the God
whose I am and whom I serve[e]
stood beside me[f] 24and said, 'Do
not be afraid, Paul. You must stand
trial before Caesar;[g] and God has
graciously given you the lives of all
who sail with you.'[h] 25So keep up
your courage,[i] men, for I have
faith in God that it will happen just
as he told me.[j] 26Nevertheless, we
must run aground[k] on some island."[l]

The Shipwreck

27On the fourteenth night we
were still being driven across the
Adriatic[z] Sea, when about midnight the sailors sensed they were
approaching land. 28They took
soundings and found that the water was a hundred and twenty feet[a]
deep. A short time later they took
soundings again and found it was
ninety feet[b] deep. 29Fearing that
we would be dashed against the
rocks, they dropped four anchors
from the stern and prayed for daylight. 30In an attempt to escape
from the ship, the sailors let the
lifeboat[m] down into the sea, pretending they were going to lower
some anchors from the bow.
31Then Paul said to the centurion
and the soldiers, "Unless these
men stay with the ship, you cannot
be saved."[n] 32So the soldiers cut
the ropes that held the lifeboat and
let it fall away.
33Just before dawn Paul urged
them all to eat. "For the last fourteen days," he said, "you have been
in constant suspense and have
gone without food—you haven't
eaten anything. 34Now I urge you
to take some food. You need it to
survive. Not one of you will lose a
single hair from his head."[o] 35Af-
ter he said this, he took some bread
and gave thanks to God in front of
them all. Then he broke it[p] and began to eat. 36They were all encouraged[q] and ate some food themselves. 37Altogether there were 276
of us on board. 38When they had
eaten as much as they wanted, they
lightened the ship by throwing the
grain into the sea.[r]
39When daylight came, they did
not recognize the land, but they
saw a bay with a sandy beach,[s]
where they decided to run the ship
aground if they could. 40Cutting
loose the anchors,[t] they left them
in the sea and at the same time untied the ropes that held the rud-
ders. Then they hoisted the foresail
to the wind and made for the
beach. 41But the ship struck a
sandbar and ran aground. The bow
stuck fast and would not move, and
the stern was broken to pieces by
the pounding of the surf.[u]
42The soldiers planned to kill
the prisoners to prevent any of
them from swimming away and escaping. 43But the centurion wanted to spare Paul's life[v] and kept
them from carrying out their plan.
He ordered those who could swim
to jump overboard first and get to
land. 44The rest were to get there
on planks or on pieces of the ship.
In this way everyone reached land
in safety.[w]

Ashore on Malta

28 Once safely on shore, we[x]
found out that the island[y]
was called Malta. 2The islanders
showed us unusual kindness. They
built a fire and welcomed us all because it was raining and cold. 3Paul
gathered a pile of brushwood and,

27:21 [a]ver 10 [b]ver 7
27:22 [c]ver 25,36
27:23 [d]Ac 5:19 [e]Ro 1:9 [f]Ac 18:9; 23:11; 2Ti 4:17
27:24 [g]Ac 23:11 [h]ver 44
27:25 [i]ver 22,36 [j]Ro 4:20,21
27:26 [k]ver 17,39 [l]Ac 28:1
27:30 [m]ver 16
27:31 [n]ver 24
27:34 [o]Mt 10:30
27:35 [p]Mt 14:19
27:36 [q]ver 22,25
27:38 [r]ver 18; Jnh 1:5
27:39 [s]Ac 28:1
27:40 [t]ver 29
27:41 [u]2Co 11:25
27:43 [v]ver 3
27:44 [w]ver 22,31
28:1 [x]Ac 16:10 [y]Ac 27:26,39

[z]*27* In ancient times the name referred to an area extending well south of Italy.
[a]*28* Greek *twenty orguias* (about 37 meters)
[b]*28* Greek *fifteen orguias* (about 27 meters)

as he put it on the fire, a viper, driv-
en out by the heat, fastened itself
on his hand. 4When the islanders
saw the snake hanging from his
hand,[a] they said to each other,
"This man must be a murderer; for
though he escaped from the sea,
Justice has not allowed him to
live."[b] 5But Paul shook the snake
off into the fire and suffered no ill
effects.[c] 6The people expected
him to swell up or suddenly fall
dead, but after waiting a long time
and seeing nothing unusual happen to him, they changed their
minds and said he was a god.[d]

7There was an estate nearby that
belonged to Publius, the chief official of the island. He welcomed us
to his home and for three days en-
tertained us hospitably. 8His father
was sick in bed, suffering from fever and dysentery. Paul went in to
see him and, after prayer,[e] placed
his hands on him and healed him.[f]
9When this had happened, the rest
of the sick on the island came and
were cured. 10They honored us in
many ways and when we were
ready to sail, they furnished us with
the supplies we needed.

Arrival at Rome

11After three months we put out
to sea in a ship that had wintered in
the island. It was an Alexandrian
ship[g] with the figurehead of the
twin gods Castor and Pollux. 12We
put in at Syracuse and stayed there
three days. 13From there we set sail
and arrived at Rhegium. The next
day the south wind came up, and
on the following day we reached
Puteoli. 14There we found some
brothers[h] who invited us to spend
a week with them. And so we came
to Rome. 15The brothers[i] there
had heard that we were coming,
and they traveled as far as the Fo-
rum of Appius and the Three Tav-
erns to meet us. At the sight of
these men Paul thanked God and
was encouraged. 16When we got to
Rome, Paul was allowed to live by
himself, with a soldier to guard
him.[j]

Paul Preaches at Rome Under Guard

17Three days later he called together the leaders of the Jews.[k]
When they had assembled, Paul
said to them: "My brothers,[l] although I have done nothing against
our people[m] or against the customs
of our ancestors,[n] I was arrested in
Jerusalem and handed over to the
Romans. 18They examined me[o]
and wanted to release me,[p] because I was not guilty of any crime
deserving death.[q] 19But when the
Jews objected, I was compelled to
appeal to Caesar[r]—not that I had
any charge to bring against my own
people. 20For this reason I have
asked to see you and talk with you.
It is because of the hope of Israel[s]
that I am bound with this chain."[t]

21They replied, "We have not received any letters from Judea concerning you, and none of the brothers[u] who have come from there has
reported or said anything bad
about you. 22But we want to hear
what your views are, for we know
that people everywhere are talking
against this sect."[v]

23They arranged to meet Paul on
a certain day, and came in even
larger numbers to the place where
he was staying. From morning till
evening he explained and declared
to them the kingdom of God[w] and
tried to convince them about
Jesus[x] from the Law of Moses and
from the Prophets.[y] 24Some were
convinced by what he said, but others would not believe.[z] 25They dis-
agreed among themselves and began to leave after Paul had made
this final statement: "The Holy
Spirit spoke the truth to your forefathers when he said through Isaiah the prophet:

26" 'Go to this people and say,
"You will be ever hearing but
never understanding;
you will be ever seeing but
never perceiving."
27For this people's heart has
become calloused;[a]
they hardly hear with their
ears,

28:4 [a] Mk 16:18 [b] Lk 13:2,4
28:5 [c] Lk 10:19
28:6 [d] Ac 14:11
28:8 [e] Jas 5:14,15 [f] Ac 9:40
28:11 [g] Ac 27:6
28:14 [h] Ac 1:16
28:15 [i] Ac 1:16
28:16 [j] Ac 24:23; 27:3
28:17 [k] Ac 25:2 [l] Ac 22:5 [m] Ac 25:8 [n] Ac 6:14
28:18 [o] Ac 22:24 [p] Ac 26:31,32 [q] Ac 23:9
28:19 [r] Ac 25:11
28:20 [s] Ac 26:6,7 [t] Ac 21:33
28:21 [u] Ac 22:5
28:22 [v] Ac 24:5,14
28:23 [w] Ac 19:8 [x] Ac 17:3 [y] Ac 8:35
28:24 [z] Ac 14:4
28:27 [a] Ps 119:70

and they have closed their
eyes.
Otherwise they might see with
their eyes,
hear with their ears,
understand with their
hearts
and turn, and I would heal
them.'[c][a]

28"Therefore I want you to know
that God's salvation[b] has been
sent to the Gentiles,[c] and they will
listen!"[d]
30For two whole years Paul
stayed there in his own rented
house and welcomed all who came
to see him. 31Boldly and without
hindrance he preached the kingdom of God[d] and taught about the
Lord Jesus Christ.

28:27 [a]Isa 6:9,10
28:28 [b]Lk 2:30 [c]Ac 13:46
28:31 [d]ver 23; Mt 4:23

[c]*27* Isaiah 6:9,10 [d]*28* Some manuscripts *listen!" 29After he said this, the Jews left, arguing vigorously among themselves.*

Romans

Title and Background

When Paul wrote this letter, he was probably in Corinth on his third missionary journey. His work in the eastern Mediterranean was almost finished, and he greatly desired to visit the Roman church. At this time, however, he could not go to Rome, so he sent a letter there, intending to visit Rome while en route on a mission to Spain. This letter served as a theological introduction to that hoped-for personal ministry.

Author and Date of Writing

The writer of this letter was the apostle Paul, and it was probably written in the early spring of A.D. 57.

Theme and Message

Paul's primary theme in Romans is the basic gospel, God's plan of salvation and righteousness for all mankind, Jew and Gentile alike. "The gospel of God" (1:1) includes justification by faith, but it also embraces such related ideas as guilt, sanctification and security. Romans is the most comprehensive and systematic statement of the Christian faith in the Bible.

Outline

I. Introduction (1:1-15)
II. Theme: Righteousness from God (1:16-17)
III. The Unrighteousness of all Mankind (1:18-3:20)
IV. Righteousness Imputed: Justification (3:21-5:21)
V. Righteousness Imparted: Sanctification (6:1-8:39)
VI. God's Righteousness Vindicated: The Problem of Israel's Rejection (9:1-11:36)
VII. Righteousness Practiced (12:1-15:13)
VIII. Conclusion (15:14-33)
IX. Commendation and Greetings (16:1-27)

---

1 Paul, a servant of Christ Jesus,
called to be an apostle[a] and
set apart[b] for the gospel of
God[c]— **2**the gospel he promised
beforehand through his prophets
in the Holy Scriptures[d] **3**regarding
his Son, who as to his human nature[e] was a descendant of David,
4and who through the Spirit[a] of
holiness was declared with power
to be the Son of God[b] by his resurrection from the dead: Jesus Christ
our Lord. **5**Through him and for his
name's sake, we received grace and
apostleship to call people from
among all the Gentiles[f] to the
obedience that comes from faith.[g]
6And you also are among those
who are called to belong to Jesus
Christ.[h]

7To all in Rome who are loved by
God[i] and called to be saints:

Grace and peace to you from
God our Father and from the Lord
Jesus Christ.[j]

Paul's Longing to Visit Rome

8First, I thank my God through
Jesus Christ for all of you,[k] be-

1:1 [a] 1Co 1:1 [b] Ac 9:15 [c] 2Co 11:7
1:2 [d] Gal 3:8
1:3 [e] Jn 1:14
1:5 [f] Ac 9:15 [g] Ac 6:7
1:6 [h] Rev 17:14
1:7 [i] Ro 8:39 [j] 1Co 1:3
1:8 [k] 1Co 1:4

[a]4 *Or who as to his spirit* [b]4 *Or was appointed to be the Son of God with power*

cause your faith is being reported all over the world.[a] 9God, whom I serve[b] with my whole heart in preaching the gospel of his Son, is my witness[c] how constantly I remember you 10in my prayers at all times; and I pray that now at last by God's will the way may be opened for me to come to you.[d]

11I long to see you[e] so that I may impart to you some spiritual gift to make you strong— 12that is, that you and I may be mutually encouraged by each other's faith. 13I do not want you to be unaware, brothers, that I planned many times to come to you (but have been prevented from doing so until now)[f] in order that I might have a harvest among you, just as I have had among the other Gentiles.

14I am obligated[g] both to Greeks and non-Greeks, both to the wise and the foolish. 15That is why I am so eager to preach the gospel also to you who are at Rome.[h]

16I am not ashamed of the gospel,[i] because it is the power of God[j] for the salvation of everyone who believes: first for the Jew,[k] then for the Gentile.[l] 17For in the gospel a righteousness from God is revealed,[m] a righteousness that is by faith from first to last,[c] just as it is written: "The righteous will live by faith."[d][n]

God's Wrath Against Mankind

18The wrath of God[o] is being revealed from heaven against all the godlessness and wickedness of men who suppress the truth by their wickedness, 19since what may be known about God is plain to them, because God has made it plain to them.[p] 20For since the creation of the world God's invisible qualities—his eternal power and divine nature—have been clearly seen, being understood from what has been made,[q] so that men are without excuse.

21For although they knew God, they neither glorified him as God nor gave thanks to him, but their thinking became futile and their foolish hearts were darkened.[r] 22Although they claimed to be wise, they became fools[s] 23and exchanged the glory of the immortal God for images[t] made to look like mortal man and birds and animals and reptiles.

24Therefore God gave them over[u] in the sinful desires of their hearts to sexual impurity for the degrading of their bodies with one another.[v] 25They exchanged the truth of God for a lie,[w] and worshiped and served created things[x] rather than the Creator—who is forever praised.[y] Amen.

26Because of this, God gave them over[z] to shameful lusts.[a] Even their women exchanged natural relations for unnatural ones.[b] 27In the same way the men also abandoned natural relations with women and were inflamed with lust for one another. Men committed indecent acts with other men, and received in themselves the due penalty for their perversion.[c]

28Furthermore, since they did not think it worthwhile to retain the knowledge of God, he gave them over[d] to a depraved mind, to do what ought not to be done. 29They have become filled with every kind of wickedness, evil, greed and depravity. They are full of envy, murder, strife, deceit and malice. They are gossips,[e] 30slanderers, God-haters, insolent, arrogant and boastful; they invent ways of doing evil; they disobey their parents;[f] 31they are senseless, faithless, heartless,[g] ruthless. 32Although they know God's righteous decree that those who do such things deserve death,[h] they not only continue to do these very things but also approve[i] of those who practice them.

God's Righteous Judgment

2 You, therefore, have no excuse,[j] you who pass judgment on someone else, for at whatever point you judge the other, you are

1:8 [a] Ro 16:19
1:9 [b] 2Ti 1:3
[c] Php 1:8
1:10 [d] Ro 15:32
1:11 [e] Ro 15:23
1:13 [f] Ro 15:22,23
1:14 [g] 1Co 9:16
1:15 [h] Ro 15:20
1:16 [i] 2Ti 1:8
[j] 1Co 1:18
[k] Ac 3:26
[l] Ro 2:9,10
1:17 [m] Ro 3:21
[n] Hab 2:4; Gal 3:11; Heb 10:38
1:18 [o] Eph 5:6; Col 3:6
1:19 [p] Ac 14:17
1:20 [q] Ps 19:1-6
1:21 [r] Jer 2:5; Eph 4:17,18
1:22 [s] 1Co 1:20,27
1:23 [t] Ps 106:20; Jer 2:11; Ac 17:29
1:24 [u] Eph 4:19
[v] 1Pe 4:3
1:25 [w] Isa 44:20
[x] Jer 10:14
[y] Ro 9:5
1:26 [z] ver 24,28
[a] 1Th 4:5
[b] Lev 18:22,23
1:27 [c] Lev 18:22; 20:13
1:28 [d] ver 24,26
1:29 [e] 2Co 12:20
1:30 [f] 2Ti 3:2
1:31 [g] 2Ti 3:3
1:32 [h] Ro 6:23
[i] Ps 50:18; Lk 11:48; Ac 8:1; 22:20
2:1 [j] Ro 1:20

[c] 17 Or is *from faith to faith* [d] 17 Hab. 2:4

condemning yourself, because you who pass judgment do the same things.[a] **2**Now we know that God's judgment against those who do such things is based on truth. **3**So when you, a mere man, pass judgment on them and yet do the same things, do you think you will escape God's judgment? **4**Or do you show contempt for the riches[b] of his kindness,[c] tolerance[d] and patience,[e] not realizing that God's kindness leads you toward repentance?[f]

5But because of your stubbornness and your unrepentant heart, you are storing up wrath against yourself for the day of God's wrath, when his righteous judgment[g] will be revealed. **6**God "will give to each person according to what he has done."[e][h] **7**To those who by persistence in doing good seek glory, honor[i] and immortality,[j] he will give eternal life. **8**But for those who are self-seeking and who reject the truth and follow evil,[k] there will be wrath and anger. **9**There will be trouble and distress for every human being who does evil: first for the Jew, then for the Gentile;[l] **10**but glory, honor and peace for everyone who does good: first for the Jew, then for the Gentile.[m] **11**For God does not show favoritism.[n]

12All who sin apart from the law will also perish apart from the law, and all who sin under the law[o] will be judged by the law. **13**For it is not those who hear the law who are righteous in God's sight, but it is those who obey[p] the law who will be declared righteous. **14**(Indeed, when Gentiles, who do not have the law, do by nature things required by the law,[q] they are a law for themselves, even though they do not have the law, **15***since they* show that the requirements of the law are written on their hearts, their consciences also bearing witness, and their thoughts now accusing, now even defending them.) **16**This will take place on the day when God will judge men's secrets[r] through Jesus Christ,[s] as my gospel[t] declares.

2:1 [a]2Sa 12:5-7; Mt 7:1,2
2:4 [b]Ro 9:23; Eph 1:7,18; 2:7 [c]Ro 11:22 [d]Ro 3:25 [e]Ex 34:6 [f]2Pe 3:9
2:5 [g]Jude 6
2:6 [h]Ps 62:12; Mt 16:27
2:7 [i]ver 10 [j]1Co 15:53,54
2:8 [k]2Th 2:12
2:9 [l]1Pe 4:17
2:10 [m]ver 9
2:11 [n]Ac 10:34
2:12 [o]Ro 3:19; 1Co 9:20,21
2:13 [p]Jas 1:22,23, 25
2:14 [q]Ac 10:35
2:16 [r]Ecc 12:14 [s]Ac 10:42 [t]Ro 16:25
2:17 [u]ver 23; Mic 3:11; Ro 9:4
2:21 [v]Mt 23:3,4
2:22 [w]Ac 19:37
2:23 [x]ver 17
2:24 [y]Isa 52:5; Eze 36:22
2:25 [z]Gal 5:3 [a]Jer 4:4
2:26 [b]Ro 8:4 [c]1Co 7:19
2:27 [d]Mt 12:41,42
2:28 [e]Mt 3:9; Jn 8:39; Ro 9:6,7 [f]Gal 6:15
2:29 [g]Php 3:3; Col 2:11 [h]Ro 7:6 [i]Jn 5:44; 1Co 4:5; 2Co 10:18; 1Th 2:4; 1Pe 3:4

The Jews and the Law

17Now you, if you call yourself a Jew; if you rely on the law and brag about your relationship to God;[u] **18**if you know his will and approve of what is superior because you are instructed by the law; **19**if you are convinced that you are a guide for the blind, a light for those who are in the dark, **20**an instructor of the foolish, a teacher of infants, because you have in the law the embodiment of knowledge and truth— **21**you, then, who teach others, do you not teach yourself? You who preach against stealing, do you steal?[v] **22**You who say that people should not commit adultery, do you commit adultery? You who abhor idols, do you rob temples?[w] **23**You who brag about the law,[x] do you dishonor God by breaking the law? **24**As it is written: "God's name is blasphemed among the Gentiles because of you."[f][y]

25Circumcision has value if you observe the law,[z] but if you break the law, you have become as though you had not been circumcised.[a] **26**If those who are not circumcised keep the law's requirements,[b] will they not be regarded as though they were circumcised?[c] **27**The one who is not circumcised physically and yet obeys the law will condemn you[d] who, even though you have the[g] written code and circumcision, are a lawbreaker.

28A man is not a Jew if he is only one outwardly,[e] nor is circumcision merely outward and physical.[f] **29**No, a man is a Jew if he is one inwardly; and circumcision is circumcision of the heart, by the Spirit,[g] not by the written code.[h] Such a man's praise is not from men, but from God.[i]

God's Faithfulness

3 What advantage, then, is there in being a Jew, or what value is there in circumcision? **2**Much in

[e]6 Psalm 62:12; Prov. 24:12
[f]24 Isaiah 52:5; Ezek. 36:22 [g]27 Or *who, by means of a*

every way! First of all, they have
been entrusted with the very words
of God.[a]
[3]What if some did not have
faith?[b] Will their lack of faith nullify God's faithfulness?[c] [4]Not at
all! Let God be true,[d] and every
man a liar.[e] As it is written:

"So that you may be proved
right when you speak
and prevail when you
judge."[h][f]

[5]But if our unrighteousness
brings out God's righteousness
more clearly, what shall we say?
That God is unjust in bringing his
wrath on us? (I am using a human
argument.)[g] [6]Certainly not! If that
were so, how could God judge the
world?[h] [7]Someone might argue,
"If my falsehood enhances God's
truthfulness and so increases his
glory,[i] why am I still condemned
as a sinner?" [8]Why not say—as we
are being slanderously reported as
saying and as some claim that we
say—"Let us do evil that good may
result"?[j] Their condemnation is
deserved.

No One Is Righteous

[9]What shall we conclude then?
Are we any better[i]? Not at all! We
have already made the charge that
Jews and Gentiles alike are all under sin.[k] [10]As it is written:

"There is no one righteous, not
even one;
[11] there is no one who
understands,
no one who seeks God.
[12]All have turned away,
they have together become
worthless;
there is no one who does good,
not even one."[j][l]
[13]"Their throats are open graves;
their tongues practice
deceit."[k][m]
"The poison of vipers is on
their lips."[l][n]
[14] "Their mouths are full of
cursing and
bitterness."[m][o]

3:2 [a]Dt 4:8; Ps 147:19
3:3 [b]Heb 4:2 [c]2Ti 2:13
3:4 [d]Jn 3:33 [e]Ps 116:11 [f]Ps 51:4
3:5 [g]Ro 6:19; Gal 3:15
3:6 [h]Ge 18:25
3:7 [i]ver 4
3:8 [j]Ro 6:1
3:9 [k]ver 19,23; Gal 3:22
3:12 [l]Ps 14:1-3
3:13 [m]Ps 5:9 [n]Ps 140:3
3:14 [o]Ps 10:7
3:18 [p]Ps 36:1
3:19 [q]Jn 10:34 [r]Ro 2:12
3:20 [s]Ac 13:39; Gal 2:16 [t]Ro 7:7
3:21 [u]Ro 1:17; 9:30 [v]Ac 10:43
3:22 [w]Ro 9:30 [x]Ro 10:12; Gal 3:28; Col 3:11
3:24 [y]Ro 4:16; Eph 2:8 [z]Eph 1:7,14; Col 1:14; Heb 9:12
3:25 [a]1Jn 4:10 [b]Heb 9:12,14 [c]Ac 17:30
3:27 [d]Ro 2:17,23; 4:2; 1Co 1:29-31; Eph 2:9
3:28 [e]ver 20,21; Ac 13:39; Eph 2:9
3:29 [f]Ro 9:24

[15]"Their feet are swift to shed
blood;
[16] ruin and misery mark their
ways,
[17]and the way of peace they do
not know."[n]
[18] "There is no fear of God
before their eyes."[o][p]

[19]Now we know that whatever
the law says,[q] it says to those who
are under the law,[r] so that every
mouth may be silenced and the
whole world held accountable to
God. [20]Therefore no one will be declared righteous in his sight by observing the law;[s] rather, through
the law we become conscious of
sin.[t]

Righteousness Through Faith

[21]But now a righteousness from
God,[u] apart from law, has been
made known, to which the Law and
the Prophets testify.[v] [22]This righteousness from God comes
through faith[w] in Jesus Christ to
all who believe. There is no difference,[x] [23]for all have sinned and
fall short of the glory of God, [24]and
are justified freely by his grace[y]
through the redemption[z] that
came by Christ Jesus. [25]God presented him as a sacrifice of atonement,[p][a] through faith in his
blood.[b] He did this to demonstrate
his justice, because in his forbearance he had left the sins committed beforehand unpunished[c]—
[26]he did it to demonstrate his justice at the present time, so as to be
just and the one who justifies those
who have faith in Jesus.
[27]Where, then, is boasting?[d] It
is excluded. On what principle? On
that of observing the law? No, but
on that of faith. [28]For we maintain
that a man is justified by faith apart
from observing the law.[e] [29]Is God
the God of Jews only? Is he not the
God of Gentiles too? Yes, of Gentiles too,[f] [30]since there is only one

[h]*4* Psalm 51:4 [i]*9* Or *worse* [j]*12* Psalms 14:1-3; 53:1-3; Eccles. 7:20 [k]*13* Psalm 5:9 [l]*13* Psalm 140:3 [m]*14* Psalm 10:7 [n]*17* Isaiah 59:7,8 [o]*18* Psalm 36:1 [p]*25* *Or as the one who would turn aside his wrath, taking away sin*

God, who will justify the circumcised by faith and the uncircumcised through that same faith.[a]
31Do we, then, nullify the law by
this faith? Not at all! Rather, we
uphold the law.

Abraham Justified by Faith

4 What then shall we say that
Abraham, our forefather, discovered in this matter? **2**If, in fact,
Abraham was justified by works, he
had something to boast about—
but not before God.[b] **3**What does
the Scripture say? "Abraham believed God, and it was credited to
him as righteousness."[q][c]

4Now when a man works, his
wages are not credited to him as a
gift,[d] but as an obligation. **5**However, to the man who does not work
but trusts God who justifies the
wicked, his faith is credited as righteousness. **6**David says the same
thing when he speaks of the
blessedness of the man to whom
God credits righteousness apart
from works:

7"Blessed are they
whose transgressions are
forgiven,
whose sins are covered.
8Blessed is the man
whose sin the Lord will never
count against him."[r][e]

9Is this blessedness only for the
circumcised, or also for the uncircumcised?[f] We have been saying
that Abraham's faith was credited
to him as righteousness.[g] **10**Under
what circumstances was it credited? Was it after he was circumcised, or before? It was not after,
but before! **11**And he received the
sign of circumcision, a seal of the
righteousness that he had by faith
while he was still uncircumcised.[h]
So then, he is the father[i] of all who
believe[j] but have not been circumcised, in order that righteousness might be credited to them.
12And he is also the father of the
circumcised who not only are circumcised but who also walk in the
footsteps of the faith that our father Abraham had before he was
circumcised.

13It was not through law that
Abraham and his offspring received
the promise[k] that he would be heir
of the world,[l] but through the
righteousness that comes by faith.
14For if those who live by law are
heirs, faith has no value and the
promise is worthless,[m] **15**because
law brings wrath.[n] And where
there is no law there is no transgression.[o]

16Therefore, the promise comes
by faith, so that it may be by grace[p]
and may be guaranteed[q] to all
Abraham's offspring—not only to
those who are of the law but also to
those who are of the faith of Abraham. He is the father of us all. **17**As
it is written: "I have made you a father of many nations."[s][r] He is
our father in the sight of God, in
whom he believed—the God who
gives life[s] to the dead and calls[t]
things that are not[u] as though they
were.

18Against all hope, Abraham in
hope believed and so became the
father of many nations,[v] just as it
had been said to him, "So shall
your offspring be."[t][w] **19**Without
weakening in his faith, he faced the
fact that his body was as good as
dead[x]—since he was about a hundred years old[y]—and that Sarah's
womb was also dead.[z] **20**Yet he did
not waver through unbelief regarding the promise of God, but was
strengthened in his faith and gave
glory to God,[a] **21**being fully persuaded that God had power to do
what he had promised.[b] **22**This is
why "it was credited to him as righteousness."[c] **23**The words "it was
credited to him" were written not
for him alone, **24**but also for us,[d] to
whom God will credit righteous-
ness—for us who believe in him[e]
who raised Jesus our Lord from the
dead.[f] **25**He was delivered over to
death for our sins[g] and was raised
to life for our justification.

3:30 [a]Gal 3:8
4:2 [b]1Co 1:31
4:3 [c]ver 5,9,22; Ge 15:6; Gal 3:6; Jas 2:23
4:4 [d]Ro 11:6
4:8 [e]Ps 32:1,2; 2Co 5:19
4:9 [f]Ro 3:30 [g]ver 3
4:11 [h]Ge 17:10,11 [i]ver 16,17; Lk 19:9 [j]Ro 3:22
4:13 [k]Gal 3:16,29 [l]Ge 17:4-6
4:14 [m]Gal 3:18
4:15 [n]Ro 7:7-25; 1Co 15:56; 2Co 3:7; Gal 3:10; Ro 7:12 [o]Ro 3:20; 7:7
4:16 [p]Ro 3:24 [q]Ro 15:8
4:17 [r]Ge 17:5 [s]Jn 5:21 [t]Isa 48:13 [u]1Co 1:28
4:18 [v]ver 17 [w]Ge 15:5
4:19 [x]Heb 11:11,12 [y]Ge 17:17 [z]Ge 18:11
4:20 [a]Mt 9:8
4:21 [b]Ge 18:14; Heb 11:19
4:22 [c]ver 3
4:24 [d]Ro 15:4; 1Co 9:10; 10:11 [e]Ro 10:9 [f]Ac 2:24
4:25 [g]Isa 53:5,6; Ro 5:6,8

[q]3 Gen. 15:6; also in verse 22
[r]*8* Psalm 32:1,2 [s]*17* Gen. 17:5
[t]*18* Gen. 15:5

Peace and Joy

5 Therefore, since we have been justified through faith,[a] we[u] have peace with God through our Lord Jesus Christ, **2**through whom we have gained access[b] by faith into this grace in which we now stand.[c] And we[u] rejoice in the hope[d] of the glory of God. **3**Not only so, but we[u] also rejoice in our sufferings,[e] because we know that suffering produces perseverance;[f] **4**perseverance, character; and character, hope. **5**And hope[g] does not disappoint us, because God has poured out his love into our hearts by the Holy Spirit,[h] whom he has given us.

6You see, at just the right time,[i] when we were still powerless, Christ died for the ungodly.[j] **7**Very rarely will anyone die for a righteous man, though for a good man someone might possibly dare to die. **8**But God demonstrates his own love for us in this: While we were still sinners, Christ died for us.[k]

9Since we have now been justified by his blood,[l] how much more shall we be saved from God's wrath[m] through him! **10**For if, when we were God's enemies,[n] we were reconciled[o] to him through the death of his Son, how much more, having been reconciled, shall we be saved through his life![p] **11**Not only is this so, but we also rejoice in God through our Lord Jesus Christ, through whom we have now received reconciliation.

Death Through Adam, Life Through Christ

12Therefore, just as sin entered the world through one man,[q] and death through sin,[r] and in this way death came to all men, because all sinned— **13**for before the law was given, sin was in the world. But sin is not taken into account when there is no law.[s] **14**Nevertheless, death reigned from the time of Adam to the time of Moses, even over those who did not sin by breaking a command, as did Adam, who was a pattern of the one to come.[t]

15But the gift is not like the trespass. For if the many died by the trespass of the one man,[u] how much more did God's grace and the gift that came by the grace of the one man, Jesus Christ,[v] overflow to the many! **16**Again, the gift of God is not like the result of the one man's sin: The judgment followed one sin and brought condemnation, but the gift followed many trespasses and brought justification. **17**For if, by the trespass of the one man, death[w] reigned through that one man, how much more will those who receive God's abundant provision of grace and of the gift of righteousness reign in life through the one man, Jesus Christ.

18Consequently, just as the result of one trespass was condemnation for all men,[x] so also the result of one act of righteousness was justification[y] that brings life for all men. **19**For just as through the disobedience of the one man[z] the many were made sinners, so also through the obedience[a] of the one man the many will be made righteous.

20The law was added so that the trespass might increase.[b] But where sin increased, grace increased all the more,[c] **21**so that, just as sin reigned in death,[d] so also grace might reign through righteousness to bring eternal life through Jesus Christ our Lord.

Dead to Sin, Alive in Christ

6 What shall we say, then? Shall we go on sinning so that grace may increase?[e] **2**By no means! We died to sin;[f] how can we live in it any longer? **3**Or don't you know that all of us who were baptized[g] into Christ Jesus were baptized into his death? **4**We were therefore buried with him through baptism into death in order that, just as Christ was raised from the dead[h] through the glory of the Father, we too may live a new life.[i]

[u]*1,2,3* Or *let us*

5:1 [a]Ro 3:28
5:2 [b]Eph 2:18 [c]1Co 15:1 [d]Heb 3:6
5:3 [e]Mt 5:12 [f]Jas 1:2,3
5:5 [g]Php 1:20 [h]Ac 2:33
5:6 [i]Gal 4:4 [j]Ro 4:25
5:8 [k]Jn 15:13; 1Pe 3:18
5:9 [l]Ro 3:25 [m]Ro 1:18
5:10 [n]Ro 11:28; Col 1:21 [o]2Co 5:18,19; Col 1:20,22 [p]Ro 8:34
5:12 [q]ver 15,16,17; 1Co 15:21,22 [r]Ge 2:17; 3:19; Ro 6:23
5:13 [s]Ro 4:15
5:14 [t]1Co 15:22,45
5:15 [u]ver 12,18,19 [v]Ac 15:11
5:17 [w]ver 12
5:18 [x]ver 12 [y]Ro 4:25
5:19 [z]ver 12 [a]Php 2:8
5:20 [b]Ro 7:7,8; Gal 3:19 [c]1Ti 1:13,14
5:21 [d]ver 12,14
6:1 [e]ver 15; Ro 3:5,8
6:2 [f]Col 3:3,5; 1Pe 2:24
6:3 [g]Mt 28:19
6:4 [h]Col 2:12 [i]Ro 7:6; Gal 6:15; Eph 4:22-24; Col 3:10

5If we have been united with him
like this in his death, we will certainly also be united with him in
his resurrection.[a] 6For we know
that our old self[b] was crucified
with him[c] so that the body of sin[d]
might be done away with,[v] that we
should no longer be slaves to sin—
7because anyone who has died has
been freed from sin.
8Now if we died with Christ, we
believe that we will also live with
him. 9For we know that since
Christ was raised from the dead,[e]
he cannot die again; death no longer has mastery over him.[f] 10The
death he died, he died to sin[g] once
for all; but the life he lives, he lives
to God.
11In the same way, count yourselves dead to sin[h] but alive to God
in Christ Jesus. 12Therefore do not
let sin reign in your mortal body so
that you obey its evil desires. 13Do
not offer the parts of your body to
sin, as instruments of wickedness,[i] but rather offer yourselves
to God, as those who have been
brought from death to life; and offer the parts of your body to him as
instruments of righteousness.[j]
14For sin shall not be your master,
because you are not under law,[k]
but under grace.[l]

Slaves to Righteousness

15What then? Shall we sin because we are not under law but under grace? By no means! 16Don't
you know that when you offer yourselves to someone to obey him as
slaves, you are slaves to the one
whom you obey—whether you are
slaves to sin,[m] which leads to
death,[n] or to obedience, which
leads to righteousness? 17But
thanks be to God[o] that, though
you used to be slaves to sin, you
wholeheartedly obeyed the form of
teaching[p] to which you were entrusted. 18You have been set free
from sin[q] and have become slaves
to righteousness.
19I put this in human terms[r] because you are weak in your natural
selves. Just as you used to offer the
parts of your body in slavery to impurity and to ever-increasing wickedness, so now offer them in slavery to righteousness[s] leading to
holiness. 20When you were slaves
to sin,[t] you were free from the
control of righteousness. 21What
benefit did you reap at that time
from the things you are now
ashamed of? Those things result in
death![u] 22But now that you have
been set free from sin[v] and have
become slaves to God,[w] the benefit you reap leads to holiness, and
the result is eternal life. 23For the
wages of sin is death,[x] but the gift
of God is eternal life[y] in[w] Christ
Jesus our Lord.

An Illustration From Marriage

7 Do you not know, brothers[z]
—for I am speaking to men
who know the law—that the law
has authority over a man only as
long as he lives? 2For example, by
law a married woman is bound to
her husband as long as he is alive,
but if her husband dies, she is released from the law of marriage.[a]
3So then, if she marries another
man while her husband is still
alive, she is called an adulteress.
But if her husband dies, she is released from that law and is not an
adulteress, even though she marries another man.
4So, my brothers, you also died
to the law[b] through the body of
Christ,[c] that you might belong to
another, to him who was raised
from the dead, in order that we
might bear fruit to God. 5For when
we were controlled by the sinful
nature,[x] the sinful passions
aroused by the law[d] were at work
in our bodies,[e] so that we bore
fruit for death. 6But now, by dying
to what once bound us, we have
been released from the law so that
we serve in the new way of the Spirit, and not in the old way of the
written code.[f]

Struggling With Sin

7What shall we say, then? Is the

6:5 [a] 2Co 4:10; Php 3:10,11
6:6 [b] Eph 4:22; Col 3:9 [c] Gal 2:20; Col 2:12,20 [d] Ro 7:24
6:9 [e] Ac 2:24 [f] Rev 1:18
6:10 [g] ver 2
6:11 [h] ver 2
6:13 [i] ver 16,19; Ro 7:5 [j] Ro 12:1; 1Pe 2:24
6:14 [k] Gal 5:18 [l] Ro 3:24
6:16 [m] Jn 8:34; 2Pe 2:19 [n] ver 23
6:17 [o] Ro 1:8; 2Co 2:14 [p] 2Ti 1:13
6:18 [q] ver 7,22; Ro 8:2
6:19 [r] Ro 3:5 [s] ver 13
6:20 [t] ver 16
6:21 [u] ver 23
6:22 [v] ver 18 [w] 1Co 7:22; 1Pe 2:16
6:23 [x] Ge 2:17; Ro 5:12; Gal 6:7,8; Jas 1:15 [y] Mt 25:46
7:1 [z] Ro 1:13
7:2 [a] 1Co 7:39
7:4 [b] Ro 8:2; Gal 2:19 [c] Col 1:22
7:5 [d] Ro 7:7-11 [e] Ro 6:13
7:6 [f] Ro 2:29; 2Co 3:6

v6 Or *be rendered powerless* w23 Or *through* x5 Or *the flesh*; also in verse 25

law sin? Certainly not! Indeed I
would not have known what sin
was except through the law.[a] For I
would not have known what covet-
ing really was if the law had not
said, "Do not covet."[y][b] **8**But sin,
seizing the opportunity afforded by
the commandment,[c] produced in
me every kind of covetous desire.
For apart from law, sin is dead.[d]
9Once I was alive apart from law;
but when the commandment
came, sin sprang to life and I died.
10I found that the very commandment that was intended to bring
life[e] actually brought death. **11**For
sin, seizing the opportunity afforded by the commandment, deceived
me,[f] and through the commandment put me to death. **12**So then,
the law is holy, and the commandment is holy, righteous and good.[g]

13Did that which is good, then,
become death to me? By no means!
But in order that sin might be recognized as sin, it produced death in
me through what was good, so that
through the commandment sin
might become utterly sinful.

14We know that the law is spiritual; but I am unspiritual,[h] sold[i]
as a slave to sin. **15**I do not understand what I do. For what I want to
do I do not do, but what I hate I
do.[j] **16**And if I do what I do not
want to do, I agree that the law is
good.[k] **17**As it is, it is no longer I
myself who do it, but it is sin living
in me.[l] **18**I know that nothing
good lives in me, that is, in my sinful nature.[z][m] For I have the desire
to do what is good, but I cannot
carry it out. **19**For what I do is not
the good I want to do; no, the evil
I do not want to do—this I keep on
doing.[n] **20**Now if I do what I do not
want to do, it is no longer I who do
it, but it is sin living in me that does
it.[o]

21So I find this law at work:[p]
When I want to do good, evil is right
there with me. **22**For in my inner
being[q] I delight in God's law;[r]
23but I see another law at work in
the members of my body, waging
war[s] against the law of my mind
and making me a prisoner of the
law of sin at work within my members. **24**What a wretched man I am!
Who will rescue me from this body
of death?[t] **25**Thanks be to God—
through Jesus Christ our Lord!

So then, I myself in my mind am
a slave to God's law, but in the sinful nature a slave to the law of sin.

Life Through the Spirit

8 Therefore, there is now no condemnation[u] for those who are
in Christ Jesus,[a][v] **2**because
through Christ Jesus the law of the
Spirit of life[w] set me free[x] from
the law of sin[y] and death. **3**For
what the law was powerless[z] to do
in that it was weakened by the sinful nature,[b] God did by sending his
own Son in the likeness of sinful
man[a] to be a sin offering.[c][b] And
so he condemned sin in sinful
man,[d] **4**in order that the righteous
requirements of the law might be
fully met in us, who do not live according to the sinful nature but according to the Spirit.[c]

5Those who live according to the
sinful nature have their minds set
on what that nature desires;[d] but
those who live in accordance with
the Spirit have their minds set on
what the Spirit desires.[e] **6**The
mind of sinful man[e] is death, but
the mind controlled by the Spirit is
life[f] and peace; **7**the sinful mind[f]
is hostile to God.[g] It does not submit to God's law, nor can it do so.
8Those controlled by the sinful nature cannot please God.

9You, however, are controlled
not by the sinful nature but by the
Spirit, if the Spirit of God lives in
you.[h] And if anyone does not have
the Spirit of Christ,[i] he does not
belong to Christ. **10**But if Christ is
in you,[j] your body is dead because
of sin, yet your spirit is alive because of righteousness. **11**And if
the Spirit of him who raised Jesus

7:7 [a] Ro 3:20; 4:15 [b] Ex 20:17; Dt 5:21
7:8 [c] ver 11 [d] Ro 4:15; 1Co 15:56
7:10 [e] Lev 18:5; Lk 10:26-28; Ro 10:5; Gal 3:12
7:11 [f] Ge 3:13
7:12 [g] 1Ti 1:8
7:14 [h] 1Co 3:1 [i] 1Ki 21:20,25; 2Ki 17:17
7:15 [j] ver 19; Gal 5:17
7:16 [k] ver 12
7:17 [l] ver 20
7:18 [m] ver 25
7:19 [n] ver 15
7:20 [o] ver 17
7:21 [p] ver 23,25
7:22 [q] Eph 3:16 [r] Ps 1:2
7:23 [s] Gal 5:17; Jas 4:1; 1Pe 2:11
7:24 [t] Ro 6:6; 8:2
8:1 [u] ver 34 [v] ver 39; Ro 16:3
8:2 [w] 1Co 15:45 [x] Ro 6:18 [y] Ro 7:4
8:3 [z] Ac 13:39; Heb 7:18 [a] Php 2:7 [b] Heb 2:14,17
8:4 [c] Gal 5:16
8:5 [d] Gal 5:19-21 [e] Gal 5:22-25
8:6 [f] Gal 6:8
8:7 [g] Jas 4:4
8:9 [h] 1Co 6:19; Gal 4:6 [i] Jn 14:17; 1Jn 4:13
8:10 [j] Gal 2:20; Eph 3:17; Col 1:27

[y]7 Exodus 20:17; Deut. 5:21 [z]18 Or *my flesh* [a]1 Some later manuscripts *Jesus, who do not live according to the sinful nature but according to the Spirit,* [b]3 Or *the flesh*; also in verses 4, 5, 8, 9, 12 and 13 [c]3 Or *man, for sin* [d]3 Or *in the flesh* [e]6 Or *mind set on the flesh* [f]7 Or *the mind set on the flesh*

from the dead[a] is living in you, he
who raised Christ from the dead
will also give life to your mortal
bodies[b] through his Spirit, who
lives in you.

12Therefore, brothers, we have
an obligation—but it is not to the
sinful nature, to live according to
it. **13**For if you live according to the
sinful nature, you will die; but if by
the Spirit you put to death the misdeeds of the body, you will live,[c]
14because those who are led by the
Spirit of God[d] are sons of God.[e]
15For you did not receive a spirit
that makes you a slave again to
fear,[f] but you received the Spirit of
sonship.[g] And by him we cry,
"Abba,[h] Father."[g] **16**The Spirit
himself testifies with our spirit[h]
that we are God's children. **17**Now
if we are children, then we are
heirs[i]—heirs of God and co-heirs
with Christ, if indeed we share in
his sufferings in order that we may
also share in his glory.[j]

Future Glory

18I consider that our present sufferings are not worth comparing
with the glory that will be revealed
in us.[k] **19**The creation waits in eager expectation for the sons of God
to be revealed. **20**For the creation
was subjected to frustration, not by
its own choice, but by the will of
the one who subjected it,[l] in hope
21that[i] the creation itself will be
liberated from its bondage to decay[m] and brought into the glorious
freedom of the children of God.

22We know that the whole creation has been groaning[n] as in the
pains of childbirth right up to the
present time. **23**Not only so, but we
ourselves, who have the firstfruits
of the Spirit,[o] groan[p] inwardly as
we wait eagerly[q] for our adoption
as sons, the redemption of our bodies. **24**For in this hope we were
saved.[r] But hope that is seen is no
hope at all. Who hopes for what he
already has? **25**But if we hope for
what we do not yet have, we wait
for it patiently.

26In the same way, the Spirit
helps us in our weakness. We do
not know what we ought to pray
for, but the Spirit himself intercedes for us[s] with groans that
words cannot express. **27**And he
who searches our hearts[t] knows
the mind of the Spirit, because the
Spirit intercedes for the saints in
accordance with God's will.

More Than Conquerors

28And we know that in all things
God works for the good of those
who love him,[j] who[k] have been
called[u] according to his purpose.
29For those God foreknew[v] he also
predestined[w] to be conformed to
the likeness of his Son,[x] that he
might be the firstborn among many
brothers. **30**And those he predestined,[y] he also called; those he
called, he also justified;[z] those he
justified, he also glorified.[a]

31What, then, shall we say in response to this?[b] If God is for us,
who can be against us?[c] **32**He who
did not spare his own Son,[d] but
gave him up for us all—how will he
not also, along with him, graciously
give us all things? **33**Who will bring
any charge[e] against those whom
God has chosen? It is God who justifies. **34**Who is he that condemns?
Christ Jesus, who died[f]—more
than that, who was raised to life
—is at the right hand of God[g] and
is also interceding for us.[h] **35**Who
shall separate us from the love of
Christ? Shall trouble or hardship or
persecution or famine or nakedness or danger or sword?[i] **36**As it is
written:

"For your sake we face death
all day long;
we are considered as sheep
to be slaughtered."[l][j]

37No, in all these things we are
more than conquerors[k] through
him who loved us.[l] **38**For I am
convinced that neither death nor

8:11 [a]Ac 2:24 [b]Jn 5:21
8:13 [c]Gal 6:8
8:14 [d]Gal 5:18 [e]Jn 1:12; Rev 21:7
8:15 [f]2Ti 1:7; Heb 2:15 [g]Mk 14:36; Gal 4:5,6
8:16 [h]Eph 1:13
8:17 [i]Ac 20:32; Gal 4:7 [j]1Pe 4:13
8:18 [k]2Co 4:17; 1Pe 4:13
8:20 [l]Ge 3:17-19
8:21 [m]Ac 3:21; 2Pe 3:13; Rev 21:1
8:22 [n]Jer 12:4
8:23 [o]2Co 5:5 [p]2Co 5:2,4 [q]Gal 5:5
8:24 [r]1Th 5:8
8:26 [s]Eph 6:18
8:27 [t]Rev 2:23
8:28 [u]1Co 1:9; 2Ti 1:9
8:29 [v]Ro 11:2 [w]Eph 1:5,11 [x]1Co 15:49; 2Co 3:18; Php 3:21; 1Jn 3:2
8:30 [y]Eph 1:5,11 [z]1Co 6:11 [a]Ro 9:23
8:31 [b]Ro 4:1 [c]Ps 118:6
8:32 [d]Jn 3:16; Ro 4:25; 5:8
8:33 [e]Isa 50:8,9
8:34 [f]Ro 5:6-8 [g]Mk 16:19 [h]Heb 7:25; 9:24; 1Jn 2:1
8:35 [i]1Co 4:11
8:36 [j]Ps 44:22; 2Co 4:11
8:37 [k]1Co 15:57 [l]Gal 2:20; Rev 1:5; 3:9

[g]15 Or *adoption* [h]15 Aramaic for *Father* [i]20,21 Or *subjected it in hope.* [21]*For* [j]28 Some manuscripts *And we know that all things work together for good to those who love God* [k]28 Or *works together with those who love him to bring about what is good—with those who* [l]36 Psalm 44:22

life, neither angels nor demons,[m]
neither the present nor the future,
nor any powers,[a] **39**neither height
nor depth, nor anything else in all
creation, will be able to separate us
from the love of God[b] that is in
Christ Jesus our Lord.

God's Sovereign Choice

9 I speak the truth in Christ—I
am not lying,[c] my conscience
confirms[d] it in the Holy Spirit— **2**I
have great sorrow and unceasing
anguish in my heart. **3**For I could
wish that I myself[e] were cursed[f]
and cut off from Christ for the sake
of my brothers, those of my own
race,[g] **4**the people of Israel. Theirs
is the adoption as sons;[h] theirs the
divine glory, the covenants,[i] the
receiving of the law,[j] the temple
worship[k] and the promises.[l]
5Theirs are the patriarchs, and
from them is traced the human ancestry of Christ,[m] who is God over
all,[n] forever praised![n][o] Amen.
6It is not as though God's word
had failed. For not all who are descended from Israel are Israel.[p]
7Nor because they are his descendants are they all Abraham's children. On the contrary, "It is
through Isaac that your offspring
will be reckoned."[o][q] **8**In other
words, it is not the natural children
who are God's children,[r] but it is
the children of the promise who are
regarded as Abraham's offspring.
9For this was how the promise was
stated: "At the appointed time I
will return, and Sarah will have a
son."[p][s]
10Not only that, but Rebekah's
children had one and the same father, our father Isaac.[t] **11**Yet, before the twins were born or had
done anything good or bad—in order that God's purpose[u] in election might stand: **12**not by works
but by him who calls—she was
told, "The older will serve the
younger."[q][v] **13**Just as it is written:
"Jacob I loved, but Esau I hat-
ed."[r][w]
14What then shall we say? Is God
unjust? Not at all![x] **15**For he says
to Moses,

"I will have mercy on whom I
have mercy,
and I will have compassion
on whom I have
compassion."[s][y]

16It does not, therefore, depend on
man's desire or effort, but on God's
mercy.[z] **17**For the Scripture says to
Pharaoh: "I raised you up for this
very purpose, that I might display
my power in you and that my name
might be proclaimed in all the
earth."[t][a] **18**Therefore God has
mercy on whom he wants to have
mercy, and he hardens whom he
wants to harden.[b]
19One of you will say to me:[c]
"Then why does God still blame
us? For who resists his will?"[d]
20But who are you, O man, to talk
back to God? "Shall what is formed
say to him who formed it,[e] 'Why
did you make me like this?' "[u][f]
21Does not the potter have the
right to make out of the same lump
of clay some pottery for noble purposes and some for common use?[g]
22What if God, choosing to show
his wrath and make his power
known, bore with great patience[h]
the objects of his wrath—prepared
for destruction? **23**What if he did
this to make the riches of his glory[i] known to the objects of his
mercy, whom he prepared in advance for glory[j]— **24**even us,
whom he also called,[k] not only
from the Jews but also from the
Gentiles?[l] **25**As he says in Hosea:

"I will call them 'my people'
who are not my people;
and I will call her 'my loved
one' who is not my loved
one,"[v][m]

26and,

"It will happen that in the very
place where it was said
to them,
'You are not my people,'

8:38 [a]Eph 1:21; 1Pe 3:22
8:39 [b]Ro 5:8
9:1 [c]2Co 11:10; Gal 1:20; 1Ti 2:7 [d]Ro 1:9
9:3 [e]Ex 32:32 [f]1Co 12:3; 16:22 [g]Ro 11:14
9:4 [h]Ex 4:22 [i]Ge 17:2; Ac 3:25; Eph 2:12 [j]Ps 147:19 [k]Heb 9:1 [l]Ac 13:32
9:5 [m]Mt 1:1-16 [n]Jn 1:1 [o]Ro 1:25
9:6 [p]Ro 2:28,29; Gal 6:16
9:7 [q]Ge 21:12; Heb 11:18
9:8 [r]Ro 8:14
9:9 [s]Ge 18:10,14
9:10 [t]Ge 25:21
9:11 [u]Ro 8:28
9:12 [v]Ge 25:23
9:13 [w]Mal 1:2,3
9:14 [x]2Ch 19:7
9:15 [y]Ex 33:19
9:16 [z]Eph 2:8
9:17 [a]Ex 9:16
9:18 [b]Ex 4:21
9:19 [c]Ro 11:19 [d]2Ch 20:6; Da 4:35
9:20 [e]Isa 64:8 [f]Isa 29:16
9:21 [g]2Ti 2:20
9:22 [h]Ro 2:4
9:23 [i]Ro 2:4 [j]Ro 8:30
9:24 [k]Ro 8:28 [l]Ro 3:29
9:25 [m]Hos 2:23; 1Pe 2:10

[m]*38* Or *nor heavenly rulers* [n]*5* Or *Christ, who is over all. God be forever praised!* Or *Christ. God who is over all be forever praised!* [o]*7* Gen. 21:12 [p]*9* Gen. 18:10,14 [q]*12* Gen. 25:23 [r]*13* Mal. 1:2,3 [s]*15* Exodus 33:19 [t]*17* Exodus 9:16 [u]*20* Isaiah 29:16; 45:9 [v]*25* Hosea 2:23

they will be called 'sons of the
living God.' "[w][a]

27Isaiah cries out concerning Israel:

"Though the number of the
Israelites be like the
sand by the sea,[b]
only the remnant will be
saved.[c]
28For the Lord will carry out
his sentence on earth with
speed and finality."[x][d]

29It is just as Isaiah said previously:

"Unless the Lord Almighty[e]
had left us descendants,
we would have become like
Sodom,
we would have been like
Gomorrah."[y][f]

Israel's Unbelief

30What then shall we say? That
the Gentiles, who did not pursue
righteousness, have obtained it, a
righteousness that is by faith;[g]
31but Israel, who pursued a law of
righteousness,[h] has not attained
it.[i] **32**Why not? Because they pursued it not by faith but as if it were
by works. They stumbled over the
"stumbling stone."[j] **33**As it is written:

"See, I lay in Zion a stone that
causes men to stumble
and a rock that makes them
fall,
and the one who trusts in him
will never be put to
shame."[z][k]

10 Brothers, my heart's desire
and prayer to God for the Israelites is that they may be saved.
2For I can testify about them that
they are zealous[l] for God, but
their zeal is not based on knowledge. **3**Since they did not know the
righteousness that comes from
God and sought to establish their
own, they did not submit to God's
righteousness.[m] **4**Christ is the end
of the law[n] so that there may be
righteousness for everyone who believes.[o]

9:26 [a]Hos 1:10
9:27 [b]Ge 22:17; Hos 1:10 [c]Ro 11:5
9:28 [d]Isa 10:22,23
9:29 [e]Jas 5:4 [f]Isa 1:9; Dt 29:23; Isa 13:19; Jer 50:40
9:30 [g]Ro 1:17; 10:6; Gal 2:16; Php 3:9; Heb 11:7
9:31 [h]Isa 51:1; Ro 10:2,3 [i]Gal 5:4
9:32 [j]1Pe 2:8
9:33 [k]Isa 28:16; Ro 10:11
10:2 [l]Ac 21:20
10:3 [m]Ro 1:17
10:4 [n]Gal 3:24; Ro 7:1-4 [o]Ro 3:22
10:5 [p]Lev 18:5; Ne 9:29; Eze 20:11,13, 21; Ro 7:10
10:6 [q]Ro 9:30 [r]Dt 30:12
10:8 [s]Dt 30:14
10:9 [t]Mt 10:32; Lk 12:8 [u]Ac 2:24
10:11 [v]Isa 28:16; Ro 9:33
10:12 [w]Ro 3:22,29 [x]Ac 10:36
10:13 [y]Ac 2:21 [z]Joel 2:32
10:15 [a]Isa 52:7; Na 1:15
10:16 [b]Isa 53:1; Jn 12:38
10:17 [c]Gal 3:2,5 [d]Col 3:16

5Moses describes in this way the
righteousness that is by the law:
"The man who does these things
will live by them."[a][p] **6**But the righteousness that is by faith[q] says:
"Do not say in your heart, 'Who will
ascend into heaven?'[b]"[r] (that is,
to bring Christ down) **7**"or 'Who
will descend into the deep?'[c]"
(that is, to bring Christ up from the
dead). **8**But what does it say? "The
word is near you; it is in your
mouth and in your heart,"[d][s] that
is, the word of faith we are proclaiming: **9**That if you confess[t]
with your mouth, "Jesus is Lord,"
and believe in your heart that God
raised him from the dead,[u] you
will be saved. **10**For it is with your
heart that you believe and are justified, and it is with your mouth that
you confess and are saved. **11**As the
Scripture says, "Anyone who trusts
in him will never be put to
shame."[e][v] **12**For there is no difference between Jew and Gentile[w]
—the same Lord is Lord of all[x] and
richly blesses all who call on him,
13for, "Everyone who calls on the
name of the Lord[y] will be
saved."[f][z]

14How, then, can they call on the
one they have not believed in? And
how can they believe in the one of
whom they have not heard? And
how can they hear without someone preaching to them? **15**And how
can they preach unless they are
sent? As it is written, "How beautiful are the feet of those who bring
good news!"[g][a]

16But not all the Israelites accepted the good news. For Isaiah
says, "Lord, who has believed
our message?"[h][b] **17**Consequently,
faith comes from hearing the message,[c] and the message is heard
through the word of Christ.[d] **18**But
I ask: Did they not hear? Of course
they did:

[w]*26* Hosea 1:10 [x]*28* Isaiah 10:22,23
[y]*29* Isaiah 1:9 [z]*33* Isaiah 8:14; 28:16
[a]*5* Lev. 18:5 [b]*6* Deut. 30:12
[c]*7* Deut. 30:13 [d]*8* Deut. 30:14
[e]*11* Isaiah 28:16 [f]*13* Joel 2:32
[g]*15* Isaiah 52:7 [h]*16* Isaiah 53:1

"Their voice has gone out into
all the earth,
their words to the ends of
the world."[i][a]

19Again I ask: Did Israel not understand? First, Moses says,

"I will make you envious[b] by
those who are not a
nation;
I will make you angry by a
nation that has no
understanding."[j][c]

20And Isaiah boldly says,

"I was found by those who did
not seek me;
I revealed myself to those
who did not ask for
me."[k][d]

21But concerning Israel he says,

"All day long I have held out
my hands
to a disobedient and
obstinate people."[l][e]

The Remnant of Israel

11 I ask then: Did God reject
his people? By no means![f]
I am an Israelite myself, a descendant of Abraham,[g] from the tribe
of Benjamin.[h] 2God did not reject
his people, whom he foreknew.[i]
Don't you know what the Scripture
says in the passage about Elijah
—how he appealed to God against
Israel: 3"Lord, they have killed your
prophets and torn down your altars; I am the only one left, and
they are trying to kill me"[m]?[j] 4And
what was God's answer to him? "I
have reserved for myself seven
thousand who have not bowed the
knee to Baal."[n][k] 5So too, at the
present time there is a remnant[l]
chosen by grace. 6And if by grace,
then it is no longer by works;[m] if it
were, grace would no longer be
grace.[o]
7What then? What Israel sought
so earnestly it did not obtain,[n] but
the elect did. The others were hardened,[o] 8as it is written:

"God gave them a spirit of
stupor,
eyes so that they could not
see
and ears so that they could
not hear,[p]
to this very day."[p][q]

9And David says:

"May their table become a
snare and a trap,
a stumbling block and a
retribution for them.
10May their eyes be darkened so
they cannot see,
and their backs be bent
forever."[q][r]

Ingrafted Branches

11Again I ask: Did they stumble
so as to fall beyond recovery? Not
at all![s] Rather, because of their
transgression, salvation has come
to the Gentiles[t] to make Israel envious.[u] 12But if their transgression
means riches for the world, and
their loss means riches for the Gentiles,[v] how much greater riches
will their fullness bring!
13I am talking to you Gentiles.
Inasmuch as I am the apostle to the
Gentiles,[w] I make much of my
ministry 14in the hope that I may
somehow arouse my own people to
envy[x] and save[y] some of them.
15For if their rejection is the reconciliation[z] of the world, what will
their acceptance be but life from
the dead?[a] 16If the part of the
dough offered as firstfruits[b] is
holy, then the whole batch is holy;
if the root is holy, so are the
branches.
17If some of the branches have
been broken off,[c] and you, though
a wild olive shoot, have been grafted in among the others[d] and now
share in the nourishing sap from
the olive root, 18do not boast over
those branches. If you do, consider
this: You do not support the root,
but the root supports you.[e] 19You

10:18 [a]Ps 19:4; Mt 24:14; Col 1:6,23; 1Th 1:8
10:19 [b]Ro 11:11,14 [c]Dt 32:21
10:20 [d]Isa 65:1; Ro 9:30
10:21 [e]Isa 65:2
11:1 [f]1Sa 12:22; Jer 31:37 [g]2Co 11:22 [h]Php 3:5
11:2 [i]Ro 8:29
11:3 [j]1Ki 19:10,14
11:4 [k]1Ki 19:18
11:5 [l]Ro 9:27
11:6 [m]Ro 4:4
11:7 [n]Ro 9:31 [o]ver 25; Ro 9:18
11:8 [p]Mt 13:13-15 [q]Dt 29:4; Isa 29:10
11:10 [r]Ps 69:22,23
11:11 [s]ver 1 [t]Ac 13:46 [u]Ro 10:19
11:12 [v]ver 25
11:13 [w]Ac 9:15
11:14 [x]ver 11; Ro 10:19 [y]1Co 1:21; 1Ti 2:4; Tit 3:5
11:15 [z]Ro 5:10 [a]Lk 15:24,32
11:16 [b]Lev 23:10, 17; Nu 15:18-21
11:17 [c]Jer 11:16; Jn 15:2 [d]Ac 2:39; Eph 2:11-13
11:18 [e]Jn 4:22

[i]*18* Psalm 19:4 [j]*19* Deut. 32:21
[k]*20* Isaiah 65:1 [l]*21* Isaiah 65:2
[m]*3* 1 Kings 19:10,14 [n]*4* 1 Kings 19:18
[o]*6* Some manuscripts *by grace. But if by works, then it is no longer grace; if it were, work would no longer be work.*
[p]*8* Deut. 29:4; Isaiah 29:10
[q]*10* Psalm 69:22,23

will say then, "Branches were broken off so that I could be grafted
in." **20**Granted. But they were broken off because of unbelief, and
you stand by faith.[a] Do not be arrogant,[b] but be afraid.[c] **21**For if
God did not spare the natural
branches, he will not spare you either.
22Consider therefore the kindness[d] and sternness of God: sternness to those who fell, but kindness to you, provided that you continue[e] in his kindness. Otherwise,
you also will be cut off.[f] **23**And if
they do not persist in unbelief, they
will be grafted in, for God is able to
graft them in again.[g] **24**After all, if
you were cut out of an olive tree
that is wild by nature, and contrary
to nature were grafted into a cultivated olive tree, how much more
readily will these, the natural
branches, be grafted into their own
olive tree!

All Israel Will Be Saved

25I do not want you to be ignorant[h] of this mystery,[i] brothers,
so that you may not be conceited:[j]
Israel has experienced a hardening[k] in part until the full number
of the Gentiles has come in.[l]
26And so all Israel will be saved, as
it is written:

"The deliverer will come from
Zion;
he will turn godlessness away
from Jacob.
27And this is[r] my covenant with
them
when I take away their
sins."[s][m]

28As far as the gospel is concerned, they are enemies[n] on your
account; but as far as election is
concerned, they are loved on account of the patriarchs,[o] **29**for
God's gifts and his call[p] are irrevocable.[q] **30**Just as you who were at
one time disobedient[r] to God have
now received mercy as a result of
their disobedience, **31**so they too
have now become disobedient in
order that they too may now[t] receive mercy as a result of God's
mercy to you. **32**For God has bound
all men over to disobedience[s] so
that he may have mercy on them
all.

Doxology

33Oh, the depth of the riches[t] of
the wisdom and[u]
knowledge of God![u]
How unsearchable his
judgments,
and his paths beyond tracing
out![v]
34"Who has known the mind of
the Lord?
Or who has been his
counselor?"[v][w]
35"Who has ever given to God,
that God should repay
him?"[w][x]
36For from him and through him
and to him are all
things.[y]
To him be the glory forever!
Amen.[z]

Living Sacrifices

12 Therefore, I urge you,[a]
brothers, in view of God's
mercy, to offer your bodies as living
sacrifices,[b] holy and pleasing to
God—this is your spiritual[x] act of
worship. **2**Do not conform[c] any
longer to the pattern of this
world,[d] but be transformed by the
renewing of your mind.[e] Then you
will be able to test and approve
what God's will is[f]—his good,
pleasing and perfect will.
3For by the grace given me[g] I say
to every one of you: Do not think of
yourself more highly than you
ought, but rather think of yourself
with sober judgment, in accordance with the measure of faith
God has given you. **4**Just as each of
us has one body with many members, and these members do not all
have the same function,[h] **5**so in
Christ we who are many form one
body,[i] and each member belongs
to all the others. **6**We have different

11:20 [a]1Co 10:12; 2Co 1:24 [b]Ro 12:16; 1Ti 6:17 [c]1Pe 1:17
11:22 [d]Ro 2:4 [e]1Co 15:2; Heb 3:6 [f]Jn 15:2
11:23 [g]2Co 3:16
11:25 [h]Ro 1:13 [i]Ro 16:25 [j]Ro 12:16 [k]ver 7; Ro 9:18 [l]Lk 21:24
11:27 [m]Isa 27:9; Heb 8:10,12
11:28 [n]Ro 5:10 [o]Dt 7:8; 10:15; Ro 9:5
11:29 [p]Ro 8:28 [q]Heb 7:21
11:30 [r]Eph 2:2
11:32 [s]Ro 3:9
11:33 [t]Ro 2:4 [u]Ps 92:5 [v]Job 11:7
11:34 [w]Isa 40:13, 14; Job 15:8; 36:22; 1Co 2:16
11:35 [x]Job 35:7
11:36 [y]1Co 8:6; Col 1:16; Heb 2:10 [z]Ro 16:27
12:1 [a]Eph 4:1 [b]Ro 6:13,16, 19; 1Pe 2:5
12:2 [c]1Pe 1:14 [d]1Jn 2:15 [e]Eph 4:23 [f]Eph 5:17
12:3 [g]Ro 15:15; Gal 2:9; Eph 4:7
12:4 [h]1Co 12:12-14 Eph 4:16
12:5 [i]1Co 10:17

[r]27 Or *will be* [s]27 Isaiah 59:20,21; 27:9; Jer. 31:33,34 [t]31 Some manuscripts do not have *now.* [u]33 Or *riches and the wisdom and the* [v]34 Isaiah 40:13 [w]35 Job 41:11 [x]1 Or *reasonable*

gifts,[a] according to the grace given us. If a man's gift is prophesying, let him use it in proportion to his[y] faith.[b] **7**If it is serving, let him serve; if it is teaching, let him teach;[c] **8**if it is encouraging, let him encourage;[d] if it is contributing to the needs of others, let him give generously;[e] if it is leadership, let him govern diligently; if it is showing mercy, let him do it cheerfully.

Love

9Love must be sincere.[f] Hate what is evil; cling to what is good. **10**Be devoted to one another in brotherly love.[g] Honor one another above yourselves.[h] **11**Never be lacking in zeal, but keep your spiritual fervor,[i] serving the Lord. **12**Be joyful in hope,[j] patient in affliction,[k] faithful in prayer. **13**Share with God's people who are in need. Practice hospitality.[l]

14Bless those who persecute you;[m] bless and do not curse. **15**Rejoice with those who rejoice; mourn with those who mourn.[n] **16**Live in harmony with one another.[o] Do not be proud, but be willing to associate with people of low position.[z] Do not be conceited.[p]

17Do not repay anyone evil for evil.[q] Be careful to do what is right in the eyes of everybody.[r] **18**If it is possible, as far as it depends on you, live at peace with everyone.[s] **19**Do not take revenge,[t] my friends, but leave room for God's wrath, for it is written: "It is mine to avenge; I will repay,"[a][u] says the Lord. **20**On the contrary:

"If your enemy is hungry, feed
    him;
  if he is thirsty, give him
    something to drink.
In doing this, you will heap
    burning coals on his
    head."[b][v]

21Do not be overcome by evil, but overcome evil with good.

Submission to the Authorities

13 Everyone must submit himself to the governing authorities,[w] for there is no authority except that which God has established.[x] The authorities that exist have been established by God. **2**Consequently, he who rebels against the authority is rebelling against what God has instituted, and those who do so will bring judgment on themselves. **3**For rulers hold no terror for those who do right, but for those who do wrong. Do you want to be free from fear of the one in authority? Then do what is right and he will commend you.[y] **4**For he is God's servant to do you good. But if you do wrong, be afraid, for he does not bear the sword for nothing. He is God's servant, an agent of wrath to bring punishment on the wrongdoer.[z] **5**Therefore, it is necessary to submit to the authorities, not only because of possible punishment but also because of conscience.

6This is also why you pay taxes, for the authorities are God's servants, who give their full time to governing. **7**Give everyone what you owe him: If you owe taxes, pay taxes;[a] if revenue, then revenue; if respect, then respect; if honor, then honor.

Love, for the Day Is Near

8Let no debt remain outstanding, except the continuing debt to love one another, for he who loves his fellowman has fulfilled the law.[b] **9**The commandments, "Do not commit adultery," "Do not murder," "Do not steal," "Do not covet,"[c][c] and whatever other commandment there may be, are summed up in this one rule: "Love your neighbor as yourself."[d][d] **10**Love does no harm to its neighbor. Therefore love is the fulfillment of the law.[e]

11And do this, understanding the present time. The hour has come[f] for you to wake up from your slumber,[g] because our salva-

12:6 [a]1Co 7:7; 12:4,8-10 [b]1Pe 4:10,11
12:7 [c]Eph 4:11
12:8 [d]Ac 15:32 [e]2Co 9:5-13
12:9 [f]1Ti 1:5
12:10 [g]Heb 13:1 [h]Php 2:3
12:11 [i]Ac 18:25
12:12 [j]Ro 5:2 [k]Heb 10:32, 36
12:13 [l]1Ti 3:2
12:14 [m]Mt 5:44
12:15 [n]Job 30:25
12:16 [o]Ro 15:5 [p]Jer 45:5; Ro 11:25
12:17 [q]Pr 20:22 [r]2Co 8:21
12:18 [s]Mk 9:50; Ro 14:19
12:19 [t]Lev 19:18; Pr 20:22; 24:29 [u]Dt 32:35
12:20 [v]Pr 25:21,22; Mt 5:44; Lk 6:27
13:1 [w]Tit 3:1; 1Pe 2:13,14 [x]Da 2:21; Jn 19:11
13:3 [y]1Pe 2:14
13:4 [z]1Th 4:6
13:7 [a]Mt 17:25; 22:17,21; Lk 23:2
13:8 [b]ver 10; Jn 13:34; Gal 5:14; Col 3:14
13:9 [c]Ex 20:13-15, 17; Dt 5:17-19,21 [d]Lev 19:18; Mt 19:19
13:10 [e]ver 8; Mt 22:39,40
13:11 [f]1Co 7:29-31; 10:11 [g]Eph 5:14; 1Th 5:5,6

[y]*6* Or *in agreement with the* [z]*16* Or *willing to do menial work* [a]*19* Deut. 32:35 [b]*20* Prov. 25:21,22 [c]*9* Exodus 20:13-15,17; Deut. 5:17-19,21 [d]*9* Lev. 19:18

tion is nearer now than when we first believed. 12The night is nearly over; the day is almost here.[a] So let us put aside the deeds of darkness[b] and put on the armor[c] of light. 13Let us behave decently, as in the daytime, not in orgies and drunkenness, not in sexual immorality and debauchery, not in dissension and jealousy.[d] 14Rather, clothe yourselves with the Lord Jesus Christ,[e] and do not think about how to gratify the desires of the sinful nature.[e]

The Weak and the Strong

14 Accept him whose faith is weak,[f] without passing judgment on disputable matters. 2One man's faith allows him to eat everything, but another man, whose faith is weak, eats only vegetables. 3The man who eats everything must not look down on[g] him who does not, and the man who does not eat everything must not condemn[h] the man who does, for God has accepted him. 4Who are you to judge someone else's servant?[i] To his own master he stands or falls. And he will stand, for the Lord is able to make him stand.

5One man considers one day more sacred than another;[j] another man considers every day alike. Each one should be fully convinced in his own mind. 6He who regards one day as special, does so to the Lord. He who eats meat, eats to the Lord, for he gives thanks to God;[k] and he who abstains, does so to the Lord and gives thanks to God. 7For none of us lives to himself alone[l] and none of us dies to himself alone. 8If we live, we live to the Lord; and if we die, we die to the Lord. So, whether we live or die, we belong to the Lord.[m]

9For this very reason, Christ died and returned to life[n] so that he might be the Lord of both the dead and the living.[o] 10You, then, why do you judge your brother? Or why do you look down on your brother? For we will all stand before God's judgment seat.[p] 11It is written:

> " 'As surely as I live,' says the Lord,
> 'every knee will bow before me;
> every tongue will confess to God.' "[f][q]

12So then, each of us will give an account of himself to God.[r]

13Therefore let us stop passing judgment[s] on one another. Instead, make up your mind not to put any stumbling block or obstacle in your brother's way. 14As one who is in the Lord Jesus, I am fully convinced that no food[g] is unclean in itself.[t] But if anyone regards something as unclean, then for him it is unclean.[u] 15If your brother is distressed because of what you eat, you are no longer acting in love.[v] Do not by your eating destroy your brother for whom Christ died.[w] 16Do not allow what you consider good to be spoken of as evil.[x] 17For the kingdom of God is not a matter of eating and drinking,[y] but of righteousness, peace and joy in the Holy Spirit,[z] 18because anyone who serves Christ in this way is pleasing to God and approved by men.[a]

19Let us therefore make every effort to do what leads to peace[b] and to mutual edification.[c] 20Do not destroy the work of God for the sake of food.[d] All food is clean, but it is wrong for a man to eat anything that causes someone else to stumble.[e] 21It is better not to eat meat or drink wine or to do anything else that will cause your brother to fall.[f]

22So whatever you believe about these things keep between yourself and God. Blessed is the man who does not condemn[g] himself by what he approves. 23But the man who has doubts[h] is condemned if he eats, because his eating is not from faith; and everything that does not come from faith is sin.

15 We who are strong ought to bear with the failings of the weak[i] and not to please ourselves. 2Each of us should please his

13:12 [a] 1Jn 2:8 [b] Eph 5:11 [c] Eph 6:11,13
13:13 [d] Gal 5:20,21
13:14 [e] Gal 3:27; 5:16; Eph 4:24
14:1 [f] Ro 15:1; 1Co 8:9-12
14:3 [g] Lk 18:9 [h] Col 2:16
14:4 [i] Jas 4:12
14:5 [j] Gal 4:10
14:6 [k] Mt 14:19; 1Co 10:30,31; 1Ti 4:3,4
14:7 [l] 2Co 5:15; Gal 2:20
14:8 [m] Php 1:20
14:9 [n] Rev 1:18 [o] 2Co 5:15
14:10 [p] 2Co 5:10
14:11 [q] Isa 45:23; Php 2:10,11
14:12 [r] Mt 12:36; 1Pe 4:5
14:13 [s] Mt 7:1
14:14 [t] Ac 10:15 [u] 1Co 8:7
14:15 [v] Eph 5:2 [w] 1Co 8:11
14:16 [x] 1Co 10:30
14:17 [y] 1Co 8:8 [z] Ro 15:13
14:18 [a] 2Co 8:21
14:19 [b] Ps 34:14; Ro 12:18; Heb 12:14 [c] Ro 15:2; 2Co 12:19
14:20 [d] ver 15 [e] 1Co 8:9-12
14:21 [f] 1Co 8:13
14:22 [g] 1Jn 3:21
14:23 [h] ver 5
15:1 [i] Ro 14:1; Gal 6:1,2; 1Th 5:14

[e]14 Or *the flesh* [f]11 Isaiah 45:23
[g]14 Or *that nothing*

neighbor for his good,[a] to build
him up.[b] 3For even Christ did not
please himself[c] but, as it is written: "The insults of those who insult you have fallen on me."[h][d]
4For everything that was written in
the past was written to teach us,[e]
so that through endurance and the
encouragement of the Scriptures
we might have hope.

5May the God who gives endurance and encouragement give you
a spirit of unity[f] among yourselves
as you follow Christ Jesus, 6so that
with one heart and mouth you may
glorify the God and Father[g] of our
Lord Jesus Christ.

7Accept one another,[h] then, just
as Christ accepted you, in order to
bring praise to God. 8For I tell you
that Christ has become a servant of
the Jews[i][i] on behalf of God's
truth, to confirm the promises[j]
made to the patriarchs 9so that the
Gentiles[k] may glorify God[l] for his
mercy, as it is written:

"Therefore I will praise you
among the Gentiles;
I will sing hymns to your
name."[j][m]

10Again, it says,

"Rejoice, O Gentiles, with his
people."[k][n]

11And again,

"Praise the Lord, all you
Gentiles,
and sing praises to him, all
you peoples."[l][o]

12And again, Isaiah says,

"The Root of Jesse[p] will spring
up,
one who will arise to rule
over the nations;
the Gentiles will hope in
him."[m][q]

13May the God of hope fill you
with all joy and peace[r] as you trust
in him, so that you may overflow
with hope by the power of the Holy
Spirit.[s]

15:2 [a]1Co 10:33 [b]Ro 14:19
15:3 [c]2Co 8:9 [d]Ps 69:9
15:4 [e]Ro 4:23,24
15:5 [f]Ro 12:16; 1Co 1:10
15:6 [g]Rev 1:6
15:7 [h]Ro 14:1
15:8 [i]Mt 15:24; Ac 3:25,26 [j]2Co 1:20
15:9 [k]Ro 3:29 [l]Mt 9:8 [m]2Sa 22:50; Ps 18:49
15:10 [n]Dt 32:43
15:11 [o]Ps 117:1
15:12 [p]Rev 5:5 [q]Isa 11:10; Mt 12:21
15:13 [r]Ro 14:17 [s]ver 19; 1Co 2:4; 1Th 1:5
15:14 [t]Eph 5:9 [u]2Pe 1:12
15:15 [v]Ro 12:3
15:16 [w]Ac 9:15; Ro 11:13 [x]Ro 1:1 [y]Isa 66:20
15:17 [z]Php 3:3 [a]Heb 2:17
15:18 [b]Ac 15:12; 21:19; Ro 1:5 [c]Ro 16:26
15:19 [d]Jn 4:48; Ac 19:11 [e]ver 13 [f]Ac 22:17-21
15:20 [g]2Co 10:15, 16
15:21 [h]Isa 52:15
15:22 [i]Ro 1:13
15:23 [j]Ac 19:21; Ro 1:10,11
15:24 [k]ver 28

Paul the Minister to the Gentiles

14I myself am convinced, my
brothers, that you yourselves are
full of goodness,[t] complete in
knowledge[u] and competent to instruct one another. 15I have written
you quite boldly on some points, as
if to remind you of them again, because of the grace God gave me[v]
16to be a minister of Christ Jesus to
the Gentiles[w] with the priestly
duty of proclaiming the gospel of
God,[x] so that the Gentiles might
become an offering[y] acceptable to
God, sanctified by the Holy Spirit.

17Therefore I glory in Christ
Jesus[z] in my service to God.[a] 18I
will not venture to speak of anything except what Christ has accomplished through me in leading
the Gentiles[b] to obey God[c] by
what I have said and done— 19by
the power of signs and miracles,[d]
through the power of the Spirit.[e]
So from Jerusalem[f] all the way
around to Illyricum, I have fully
proclaimed the gospel of Christ.
20It has always been my ambition
to preach the gospel where Christ
was not known, so that I would not
be building on someone else's
foundation.[g] 21Rather, as it is
written:

"Those who were not told
about him will see,
and those who have not
heard will
understand."[n][h]

22This is why I have often been hindered from coming to you.[i]

Paul's Plan to Visit Rome

23But now that there is no more
place for me to work in these regions, and since I have been longing for many years to see you,[j] 24I
plan to do so when I go to Spain.[k]
I hope to visit you while passing
through and to have you assist me
on my journey there, after I have

[h]3 Psalm 69:9 [i]8 Greek *circumcision*
[j]9 2 Samuel 22:50; Psalm 18:49
[k]10 Deut. 32:43 [l]11 Psalm 117:1
[m]12 Isaiah 11:10 [n]21 Isaiah 52:15

enjoyed your company for a while.
25Now, however, I am on my way to
Jerusalem[a] in the service[b] of the
saints there. 26For Macedonia[c]
and Achaia[d] were pleased to make
a contribution for the poor among
the saints in Jerusalem. 27They
were pleased to do it, and indeed
they owe it to them. For if the Gentiles have shared in the Jews' spiritual blessings, they owe it to the
Jews to share with them their material blessings.[e] 28So after I have
completed this task and have made
sure that they have received this
fruit, I will go to Spain and visit you
on the way. 29I know that when I
come to you,[f] I will come in the
full measure of the blessing of
Christ.

30I urge you, brothers, by our
Lord Jesus Christ and by the love of
the Spirit,[g] to join me in my struggle by praying to God for me.[h]
31Pray that I may be rescued[i] from
the unbelievers in Judea and that
my service in Jerusalem may be acceptable to the saints there, 32so
that by God's will[j] I may come to
you[k] with joy and together with
you be refreshed.[l] 33The God of
peace[m] be with you all. Amen.

Personal Greetings

16 I commend[n] to you our sister Phoebe, a servant[o] of
the church in Cenchrea.[o] 2I ask
you to receive her in the Lord[p] in
a way worthy of the saints and to
give her any help she may need
from you, for she has been a great
help to many people, including me.

3Greet Priscilla[p] and Aquila,[q] my
fellow workers in Christ
Jesus.[r] 4They risked their
lives for me. Not only I but all
the churches of the Gentiles
are grateful to them.
5Greet also the church that meets
at their house.[s]
Greet my dear friend Epenetus,
who was the first convert[t] to
Christ in the province of Asia.
6Greet Mary, who worked very
hard for you.
7Greet Andronicus and Junias,
my relatives[u] who have been
in prison with me. They are
outstanding among the apostles, and they were in Christ
before I was.
8Greet Ampliatus, whom I love in
the Lord.
9Greet Urbanus, our fellow worker in Christ,[v] and my dear
friend Stachys.
10Greet Apelles, tested and approved in Christ.
Greet those who belong to the
household of Aristobulus.
11Greet Herodion, my relative.[w]
Greet those in the household of
Narcissus who are in the
Lord.
12Greet Tryphena and Tryphosa,
those women who work hard
in the Lord.
Greet my dear friend Persis, another woman who has worked
very hard in the Lord.
13Greet Rufus, chosen in the Lord,
and his mother, who has been
a mother to me, too.
14Greet Asyncritus, Phlegon, Hermes, Patrobas, Hermas and
the brothers with them.
15Greet Philologus, Julia, Nereus
and his sister, and Olympas
and all the saints[x] with
them.[y]
16Greet one another with a holy
kiss.[z]
All the churches of Christ send
greetings.

17I urge you, brothers, to watch
out for those who cause divisions
and put obstacles in your way that
are contrary to the teaching you
have learned.[a] Keep away from
them.[b] 18For such people are not
serving our Lord Christ, but their
own appetites.[c] By smooth talk
and flattery they deceive[d] the
minds of naive people. 19Everyone
has heard[e] about your obedience,
so I am full of joy over you; but I
want you to be wise about what is
good, and innocent about what is
evil.[f]

15:25 [a]Ac 19:21 [b]Ac 24:17
15:26 [c]Ac 16:9; 2Co 8:1 [d]Ac 18:12
15:27 [e]1Co 9:11
15:29 [f]Ro 1:10,11
15:30 [g]Gal 5:22 [h]2Co 1:11; Col 4:12
15:31 [i]2Th 3:2
15:32 [j]Ac 18:21 [k]Ro 1:10,13 [l]1Co 16:18
15:33 [m]Ro 16:20; 2Co 13:11; Php 4:9; 1Th 5:23; Heb 13:20
16:1 [n]2Co 3:1 [o]Ac 18:18
16:2 [p]Php 2:29
16:3 [q]Ac 18:2 [r]ver 7,9,10
16:5 [s]1Co 16:19; Col 4:15; Phm 2 [t]1Co 16:15
16:7 [u]ver 11,21
16:9 [v]ver 3
16:11 [w]ver 7,21
16:15 [x]ver 2 [y]ver 14
16:16 [z]1Co 16:20; 2Co 13:12; 1Th 5:26
16:17 [a]Gal 1:8,9; 1Ti 1:3; 6:3 [b]2Th 3:6,14; 2Jn 10
16:18 [c]Php 3:19 [d]Col 2:4
16:19 [e]Ro 1:8 [f]Mt 10:16; 1Co 14:20

[o]*1* Or *deaconess* [p]*3* Greek *Prisca,* a variant of *Priscilla*

[20]The God of peace[a] will soon
crush[b] Satan under your feet.

The grace of our Lord Jesus be
with you.[c]

[21]Timothy,[d] my fellow worker,
sends his greetings to you, as do
Lucius,[e] Jason[f] and Sosipater,
my relatives.[g]

[22]I, Tertius, who wrote down this
letter, greet you in the Lord.

[23]Gaius, whose hospitality I and
the whole church here enjoy, sends
you his greetings.

Erastus,[h] who is the city's director of public works, and our brother Quartus send you their greetings.[q]

[25]Now to him who is able[i] to establish you by my gospel[j] and the
proclamation of Jesus Christ, according to the revelation of the
mystery[k] hidden for long ages
past, [26]but now revealed and made
known through the prophetic writings by the command of the eternal
God, so that all nations might believe and obey him— [27]to the only
wise God be glory forever through
Jesus Christ! Amen.[l]

16:20 [a]Ro 15:33 [b]Ge 3:15 [c]1Th 5:28
16:21 [d]Ac 16:1 [e]Ac 13:1 [f]Ac 17:5 [g]ver 7,11
16:23 [h]Ac 19:22
16:25 [i]Eph 3:20 [j]Ro 2:16 [k]Eph 1:9; Col 1:26,27
16:27 [l]Ro 11:36

q23 Some manuscripts *their greetings.* [24]*May the grace of our Lord Jesus Christ be with all of you. Amen.*

1 Corinthians

Title and Background

Located between the Corinthian Gulf and the Saronic Gulf, the city of Corinth was a wealthy trading center. It was also a wicked city and was known for that throughout the Roman world. Because the church in Corinth was new, it was hard for the Christians there not to act like their neighbors; consequently the church was having some problems.

Author and Date of Writing

Paul is acknowledged as the author both in the letter itself and by the early church fathers. This book was written about A.D. 55, toward the close of Paul's three-year residency in Ephesus.

Theme and Message

The letter revolves around the theme of problems in Christian conduct. It thus has to do with progressive sanctification, the continuing development of holiness of character. Obviously Paul was personally concerned with the Corinthians' problems, revealing a true pastor's (shepherd's) heart. In spite of the concentration on problems, the book contains some of the most familiar and beloved chapters in the entire Bible—for example, chapter 13 (on love) and chapter 15 (on resurrection).

Outline

I. Introduction: Greetings and Thanksgiving (1:1-9)
II. Divisions in the Church (1:10-4:21)
III. Moral and Ethical Disorders (5:1-6:20)
IV. Instruction on Marriage (7:1-40)
V. Instruction on Questionable Practices (8:1-11:1)
VI. Instruction on Public Worship (11:2-14:40)
 A. Propriety in Worship (11:2-16)
 B. The Lord's Supper (11:17-34)
 C. Spiritual Gifts (12:1-14:40)
VII. Instruction on the Resurrection (15:1-58)
VIII. Conclusion: Practical and Personal Matters (16:1-24)

---

1 Paul, called to be an apostle[a]
of Christ Jesus by the will of
God,[b] and our brother Sosthenes,[c]

2To the church of God in Corinth,[d] to those sanctified in Christ
Jesus and called[e] to be holy, together with all those everywhere
who call on the name of our Lord
Jesus Christ—their Lord and ours:

3Grace and peace to you from
God our Father and the Lord Jesus
Christ.[f]

Thanksgiving

4I always thank God for you[g] because of his grace given you in
Christ Jesus. 5For in him you have
been enriched[h] in every way—in
all your speaking and in all your
knowledge[i]— 6because our testimony[j] about Christ was confirmed
in you. 7Therefore you do not lack
any spiritual gift as you eagerly
wait for our Lord Jesus Christ to be
revealed.[k] 8He will keep you

1:1 [a] Ro 1:1; Eph 1:1 [b] 2Co 1:1 [c] Ac 18:17
1:2 [d] Ac 18:1 [e] Ro 1:7
1:3 [f] Ro 1:7
1:4 [g] Ro 1:8
1:5 [h] 2Co 9:11 [i] 2Co 8:7
1:6 [j] Rev 1:2
1:7 [k] Php 3:20; Tit 2:13; 2Pe 3:12

strong to the end, so that you will
be blameless[a] on the day of our
Lord Jesus Christ. 9God, who has
called you into fellowship with his
Son Jesus Christ our Lord,[b] is
faithful.[c]

Divisions in the Church

10I appeal to you, brothers, in
the name of our Lord Jesus Christ,
that all of you agree with one another so that there may be no divisions among you and that you may
be perfectly united in mind and
thought. 11My brothers, some from
Chloe's household have informed
me that there are quarrels among
you. 12What I mean is this: One of
you says, "I follow Paul";[d] another, "I follow Apollos";[e] another, "I
follow Cephas[a]";[f] still another, "I
follow Christ."

13Is Christ divided? Was Paul
crucified for you? Were you baptized into[b] the name of Paul?[g] 14I
am thankful that I did not baptize
any of you except Crispus[h] and
Gaius,[i] 15so no one can say that
you were baptized into my name.
16(Yes, I also baptized the household of Stephanas;[j] beyond that, I
don't remember if I baptized anyone else.) 17For Christ did not send
me to baptize,[k] but to preach the
gospel—not with words of human
wisdom,[l] lest the cross of Christ
be emptied of its power.

Christ the Wisdom and Power of God

18For the message of the cross is
foolishness to those who are perishing,[m] but to us who are being
saved it is the power of God.[n]
19For it is written:

> "I will destroy the wisdom of
> the wise;
> the intelligence of the
> intelligent I will
> frustrate."[c][o]

20Where is the wise man?[p]
Where is the scholar? Where is the
philosopher of this age? Has not
God made foolish[q] the wisdom of
the world? 21For since in the wisdom of God the world through its
wisdom did not know him, God was
pleased through the foolishness of
what was preached to save those
who believe. 22Jews demand miraculous signs[r] and Greeks look
for wisdom, 23but we preach Christ
crucified: a stumbling block[s] to
Jews and foolishness[t] to Gentiles,
24but to those whom God has
called,[u] both Jews and Greeks,
Christ the power of God and the
wisdom of God.[v] 25For the foolishness[w] of God is wiser than man's
wisdom, and the weakness[x] of
God is stronger than man's
strength.

26Brothers, think of what you
were when you were called. Not
many of you were wise by human
standards; not many were influential; not many were of noble birth.
27But God chose[y] the foolish[z]
things of the world to shame the
wise; God chose the weak things of
the world to shame the strong.
28He chose the lowly things of this
world and the despised things—
and the things that are not[a]—to
nullify the things that are, 29so that
no one may boast before him.[b] 30It
is because of him that you are in
Christ Jesus, who has become for
us wisdom from God—that is, our
righteousness,[c] holiness and redemption.[d] 31Therefore, as it is
written: "Let him who boasts boast
in the Lord."[d][e]

2 When I came to you, brothers,
I did not come with eloquence
or superior wisdom[f] as I proclaimed to you the testimony
about God.[e] 2For I resolved to
know nothing while I was with you
except Jesus Christ and him crucified.[g] 3I came to you[h] in weakness
and fear, and with much trembling.
4My message and my preaching
were not with wise and persuasive
words, but with a demonstration of
the Spirit's power,[i] 5so that your
faith might not rest on men's wisdom, but on God's power.[j]

1:8 [a] 1Th 3:13
1:9 [b] 1Jn 1:3 [c] Isa 49:7; 1Th 5:24
1:12 [d] 1Co 3:4,22 [e] Ac 18:24 [f] Jn 1:42
1:13 [g] Mt 28:19
1:14 [h] Ac 18:8; Ro 16:23 [i] Ac 19:29
1:16 [j] 1Co 16:15
1:17 [k] Jn 4:2 [l] 1Co 2:1,4,13
1:18 [m] 2Co 2:15 [n] Ro 1:16
1:19 [o] Isa 29:14
1:20 [p] Isa 19:11,12 [q] Job 12:17; Ro 1:22
1:22 [r] Mt 12:38
1:23 [s] Lk 2:34; Gal 5:11 [t] 1Co 2:14
1:24 [u] Ro 8:28 [v] ver 30; Col 2:3
1:25 [w] ver 18 [x] 2Co 13:4
1:27 [y] Jas 2:5 [z] ver 20
1:28 [a] Ro 4:17
1:29 [b] Eph 2:9
1:30 [c] Jer 23:5,6; 2Co 5:21 [d] Ro 3:24; Eph 1:7,14
1:31 [e] Jer 9:23,24; 2Co 10:17
2:1 [f] 1Co 1:17
2:2 [g] Gal 6:14; 1Co 1:23
2:3 [h] Ac 18:1-18
2:4 [i] Ro 15:19
2:5 [j] 2Co 4:7; 6:7

[a] *12* That is, Peter [b] *13* Or *in*; also in verse 15 [c] *19* Isaiah 29:14 [d] *31* Jer. 9:24
[e] *1* Some manuscripts *as I proclaimed to you God's mystery*

Wisdom From the Spirit

6We do, however, speak a message of wisdom among the mature,[a] but not the wisdom of this
age[b] or of the rulers of this age,
who are coming to nothing. 7No,
we speak of God's secret wisdom, a
wisdom that has been hidden and
that God destined for our glory before time began. 8None of the rulers of this age understood it, for if
they had, they would not have crucified the Lord of glory.[c] 9Howev-
er, as it is written:

"No eye has seen,
no ear has heard,
no mind has conceived
what God has prepared for
those who love
him"[f][d]—

10but God has revealed[e] it to us by
his Spirit.[f]

The Spirit searches all things,
even the deep things of God. 11For
who among men knows the
thoughts of a man[g] except the
man's spirit[h] within him? In the
same way no one knows the
thoughts of God except the Spirit
of God. 12We have not received the
spirit[i] of the world[j] but the Spirit
who is from God, that we may understand what God has freely given
us. 13This is what we speak, not in
words taught us by human wisdom[k] but in words taught by the
Spirit, expressing spiritual truths
in spiritual words.[g] 14The man
without the Spirit does not accept
the things that come from the Spirit of God, for they are foolishness[l]
to him, and he cannot understand
them, because they are spiritually
discerned. 15The spiritual man
makes judgments about all things,
but he himself is not subject to any
man's judgment:

16"For who has known the mind
of the Lord
that he may instruct
him?"[h][m]

But we have the mind of Christ.[n]

On Divisions in the Church

3 Brothers, I could not address
you as spiritual[o] but as worldly[p]—mere infants[q] in Christ. 2I
gave you milk, not solid food,[r] for
you were not yet ready for it.[s] Indeed, you are still not ready. 3You
are still worldly. For since there is
jealousy and quarreling[t] among
you, are you not worldly? Are you
not acting like mere men? 4For
when one says, "I follow Paul," and
another, "I follow Apollos,"[u] are
you not mere men?

5What, after all, is Apollos? And
what is Paul? Only servants,
through whom you came to believe—as the Lord has assigned to
each his task. 6I planted the seed,[v]
Apollos watered it, but God made it
grow. 7So neither he who plants
nor he who waters is anything, but
only God, who makes things grow.
8The man who plants and the man
who waters have one purpose, and
each will be rewarded according to
his own labor.[w] 9For we are God's
fellow workers;[x] you are God's
field,[y] God's building.[z]

10By the grace God has given
me,[a] I laid a foundation[b] as an expert builder, and someone else is
building on it. But each one should
be careful how he builds. 11For no
one can lay any foundation other
than the one already laid, which is
Jesus Christ.[c] 12If any man builds
on this foundation using gold, silver, costly stones, wood, hay or
straw, 13his work will be shown for
what it is,[d] because the Day[e] will
bring it to light. It will be revealed
with fire, and the fire will test the
quality of each man's work. 14If
what he has built survives, he will
receive his reward. 15If it is burned
up, he will suffer loss; he himself
will be saved, but only as one escaping through the flames.[f]

16Don't you know that you yourselves are God's temple[g] and that
God's Spirit lives in you? 17If anyone destroys God's temple, God

2:6 [a] Eph 4:13; Php 3:15; Heb 5:14 [b] 1Co 1:20
2:8 [c] Ac 7:2; Jas 2:1
2:9 [d] Isa 64:4; 65:17
2:10 [e] Mt 13:11; Eph 3:3,5 [f] Jn 14:26
2:11 [g] Jer 17:9 [h] Pr 20:27
2:12 [i] Ro 8:15 [j] 1Co 1:20,27
2:13 [k] 1Co 1:17
2:14 [l] 1Co 1:18
2:16 [m] Isa 40:13 [n] Jn 15:15
3:1 [o] 1Co 2:15 [p] Ro 7:14; 1Co 2:14 [q] Heb 5:13
3:2 [r] Heb 5:12-14; 1Pe 2:2 [s] Jn 16:12
3:3 [t] 1Co 1:11; Gal 5:20
3:4 [u] 1Co 1:12
3:6 [v] Ac 18:4-11
3:8 [w] Ps 62:12
3:9 [x] 2Co 6:1 [y] Isa 61:3 [z] Eph 2:20-22; 1Pe 2:5
3:10 [a] Ro 12:3 [b] Ro 15:20
3:11 [c] Isa 28:16; Eph 2:20
3:13 [d] 1Co 4:5 [e] 2Th 1:7-10
3:15 [f] Jude 23
3:16 [g] 1Co 6:19; 2Co 6:16

[f] 9 Isaiah 64:4 [g] *13* Or *Spirit, interpreting spiritual truths to spiritual men*
[h] *16* Isaiah 40:13

will destroy him; for God's temple
is sacred, and you are that temple.
18Do not deceive yourselves. If
any one of you thinks he is wise[a]
by the standards of this age, he
should become a "fool" so that he
may become wise. 19For the wisdom of this world is foolishness[b]
in God's sight. As it is written: "He
catches the wise in their craftiness"[i];[c] 20and again, "The Lord
knows that the thoughts of the
wise are futile."[j][d] 21So then, no
more boasting about men![e] All
things are yours,[f] 22whether Paul
or Apollos or Cephas[k][g] or the
world or life or death or the present
or the future[h]—all are yours,
23and you are of Christ,[i] and
Christ is of God.

Apostles of Christ

4 So then, men ought to regard
us as servants of Christ and as
those entrusted[j] with the secret
things[k] of God. 2Now it is required
that those who have been given a
trust must prove faithful. 3I care
very little if I am judged by you or
by any human court; indeed, I do
not even judge myself. 4My conscience is clear, but that does not
make me innocent.[l] It is the Lord
who judges me. 5Therefore judge
nothing[m] before the appointed
time; wait till the Lord comes. He
will bring to light what is hidden in
darkness and will expose the motives of men's hearts. At that time
each will receive his praise from
God.[n]
6Now, brothers, I have applied
these things to myself and Apollos
for your benefit, so that you may
learn from us the meaning of the
saying, "Do not go beyond what is
written."[o] Then you will not take
pride in one man over against another.[p] 7For who makes you different from anyone else? What do you
have that you did not receive?[q]
And if you did receive it, why do
you boast as though you did not?
8Already you have all you want!
Already you have become rich![r]
You have become kings—and that
without us! How I wish that you
really had become kings so that we
might be kings with you! 9For it
seems to me that God has put us
apostles on display at the end of
the procession, like men condemned to die[s] in the arena. We
have been made a spectacle[t] to
the whole universe, to angels as
well as to men. 10We are fools for
Christ,[u] but you are so wise in
Christ![v] We are weak, but you are
strong![w] You are honored, we are
dishonored! 11To this very hour we
go hungry and thirsty, we are in
rags, we are brutally treated, we are
homeless.[x] 12We work hard with
our own hands.[y] When we are
cursed, we bless;[z] when we are
persecuted, we endure it; 13when
we are slandered, we answer kindly. Up to this moment we have become the scum of the earth, the refuse[a] of the world.
14I am not writing this to shame
you, but to warn you, as my dear
children.[b] 15Even though you have
ten thousand guardians in Christ,
you do not have many fathers, for
in Christ Jesus I became your father through the gospel.[c] 16There-
fore I urge you to imitate me.[d]
17For this reason I am sending to
you Timothy, my son[e] whom I
love, who is faithful in the Lord. He
will remind you of my way of life in
Christ Jesus, which agrees with
what I teach everywhere in every
church.[f]
18Some of you have become arrogant, as if I were not coming to
you. 19But I will come to you very
soon,[g] if the Lord is willing,[h] and
then I will find out not only how
these arrogant people are talking,
but what power they have. 20For
the kingdom of God is not a matter
of talk but of power. 21What do you
prefer? Shall I come to you with a
whip,[i] or in love and with a gentle
spirit?

Expel the Immoral Brother!

5 It is actually reported that
there is sexual immorality

3:18 [a]Isa 5:21; 1Co 8:2
3:19 [b]1Co 1:20,27 [c]Job 5:13
3:20 [d]Ps 94:11
3:21 [e]1Co 4:6 [f]Ro 8:32
3:22 [g]1Co 1:12 [h]Ro 8:38
3:23 [i]1Co 15:23; 2Co 10:7; Gal 3:29
4:1 [j]1Co 9:17; Tit 1:7 [k]Ro 16:25
4:4 [l]Ro 2:13
4:5 [m]Mt 7:1,2; Ro 2:1 [n]Ro 2:29
4:6 [o]1Co 1:19,31; 3:19,20 [p]1Co 1:12
4:7 [q]Jn 3:27; Ro 12:3,6
4:8 [r]Rev 3:17,18
4:9 [s]Ro 8:36 [t]Heb 10:33
4:10 [u]1Co 1:18; Ac 17:18 [v]1Co 3:18 [w]1Co 2:3
4:11 [x]Ro 8:35; 2Co 11:23-27
4:12 [y]Ac 18:3 [z]1Pe 3:9
4:13 [a]La 3:45
4:14 [b]1Th 2:11
4:15 [c]1Co 9:12,14,18,23
4:16 [d]1Co 11:1; Php 3:17; 1Th 1:6; 2Th 3:7,9
4:17 [e]1Ti 1:2 [f]1Co 7:17
4:19 [g]2Co 1:15,16 [h]Ac 18:21
4:21 [i]2Co 1:23; 13:2,10

[i]*19* Job 5:13 [j]*20* Psalm 94:11 [k]*22* That is, Peter

among you, and of a kind that does not occur even among pagans: A man has his father's wife.[a] 2And you are proud! Shouldn't you rather have been filled with grief[b] and have put out of your fellowship the man who did this? 3Even though I am not physically present, I am with you in spirit.[c] And I have already passed judgment on the one who did this, just as if I were present. 4When you are assembled in the name of our Lord Jesus[d] and I am with you in spirit, and the power of our Lord Jesus is present, 5hand this man over[e] to Satan, so that the sinful nature[l] may be destroyed and his spirit saved on the day of the Lord.

6Your boasting is not good.[f] Don't you know that a little yeast[g] works through the whole batch of dough?[h] 7Get rid of the old yeast that you may be a new batch without yeast—as you really are. For Christ, our Passover lamb, has been sacrificed.[i] 8Therefore let us keep the Festival, not with the old yeast, the yeast of malice and wickedness, but with bread without yeast,[j] the bread of sincerity and truth.

9I have written you in my letter not to associate[k] with sexually immoral people— 10not at all meaning the people of this world[l] who are immoral, or the greedy and swindlers, or idolaters. In that case you would have to leave this world. 11But now I am writing you that you must not associate with anyone who calls himself a brother but is sexually immoral or greedy, an idolater[m] or a slanderer, a drunkard or a swindler. With such a man do not even eat.

12What business is it of mine to judge those outside[n] the church? Are you not to judge those inside?[o] 13God will judge those outside. "Expel the wicked man from among you."[m][p]

Lawsuits Among Believers

6 If any of you has a dispute with another, dare he take it before the ungodly for judgment instead of before the saints?[q] 2Do you not know that the saints will judge the world?[r] And if you are to judge the world, are you not competent to judge trivial cases? 3Do you not know that we will judge angels? How much more the things of this life! 4Therefore, if you have disputes about such matters, appoint as judges even men of little account in the church![n] 5I say this to shame you.[s] Is it possible that there is nobody among you wise enough to judge a dispute between believers?[t] 6But instead, one brother goes to law against another—and this in front of unbelievers![u]

7The very fact that you have lawsuits among you means you have been completely defeated already. Why not rather be wronged? Why not rather be cheated?[v] 8Instead, you yourselves cheat and do wrong, and you do this to your brothers.[w]

9Do you not know that the wicked will not inherit the kingdom of God?[x] Do not be deceived:[y] Neither the sexually immoral nor idolaters nor adulterers nor male prostitutes nor homosexual offenders 10nor thieves nor the greedy nor drunkards nor slanderers nor swindlers will inherit the kingdom of God. 11And that is what some of you were.[z] But you were washed,[a] you were sanctified,[b] you were justified in the name of the Lord Jesus Christ and by the Spirit of our God.

Sexual Immorality

12"Everything is permissible for me"—but not everything is beneficial.[c] "Everything is permissible for me"—but I will not be mastered by anything. 13"Food for the stomach and the stomach for food"—but God will destroy them both.[d] The body is not meant for sexual immorality, but for the Lord, and the Lord for the body. 14By his power God raised the Lord from the dead, and he will raise us also.[e]

5:1 [a]Lev 18:8; Dt 22:30
5:2 [b]2Co 7:7-11
5:3 [c]Col 2:5
5:4 [d]2Th 3:6
5:5 [e]1Ti 1:20
5:6 [f]Jas 4:16 [g]Mt 16:6,12 [h]Gal 5:9
5:7 [i]Mk 14:12; 1Pe 1:19
5:8 [j]Ex 12:14,15; Dt 16:3
5:9 [k]Eph 5:11; 2Th 3:6,14
5:10 [l]1Co 10:27
5:11 [m]1Co 10:7,14
5:12 [n]Mk 4:11 [o]ver 3-5; 1Co 6:1-4
5:13 [p]Dt 13:5
6:1 [q]Mt 18:17
6:2 [r]Mt 19:28; Lk 22:30
6:5 [s]1Co 4:14 [t]Ac 1:15
6:6 [u]2Co 6:14,15
6:7 [v]Mt 5:39,40
6:8 [w]1Th 4:6
6:9 [x]Gal 5:21 [y]1Co 15:33; Jas 1:16
6:11 [z]Eph 2:2 [a]Ac 22:16 [b]1Co 1:2
6:12 [c]1Co 10:23
6:13 [d]Col 2:22
6:14 [e]Ro 6:5; Eph 1:19,20

l5 Or *that his body;* or *that the flesh*
m13 Deut. 17:7; 19:19; 21:21; 22:21,24; 24:7
n4 Or *matters, do you appoint as judges men of little account in the church?*

15Do you not know that your bodies are members of Christ himself?[a] Shall I then take the members of Christ and unite them with
a prostitute? Never! 16Do you not
know that he who unites himself
with a prostitute is one with her in
body? For it is said, "The two will
become one flesh."[o][b] 17But he
who unites himself with the Lord is
one with him in spirit.[c]
18Flee from sexual immorality.[d]
All other sins a man commits are
outside his body, but he who sins
sexually sins against his own
body.[e] 19Do you not know that
your body is a temple[f] of the Holy
Spirit, who is in you, whom you
have received from God? You are
not your own;[g] 20you were bought
at a price.[h] Therefore honor God
with your body.

Marriage

7 Now for the matters you wrote
about: It is good for a man not
to marry.[p][i] 2But since there is so
much immorality, each man
should have his own wife, and each
woman her own husband. 3The
husband should fulfill his marital
duty to his wife,[j] and likewise the
wife to her husband. 4The wife's
body does not belong to her alone
but also to her husband. In the
same way, the husband's body
does not belong to him alone but
also to his wife. 5Do not deprive
each other except by mutual consent and for a time,[k] so that you
may devote yourselves to prayer.
Then come together again so that
Satan[l] will not tempt you[m] because of your lack of self-control. 6I
say this as a concession, not as a
command.[n] 7I wish that all men
were as I am.[o] But each man has
his own gift from God; one has this
gift, another has that.[p]
8Now to the unmarried and the
widows I say: It is good for them to
stay unmarried, as I am.[q] 9But if
they cannot control themselves,
they should marry,[r] for it is better
to marry than to burn with passion.
10To the married I give this command (not I, but the Lord): A wife
must not separate from her husband.[s] 11But if she does, she must
remain unmarried or else be reconciled to her husband. And a husband must not divorce his wife.
12To the rest I say this (I, not the
Lord):[t] If any brother has a wife
who is not a believer and she is
willing to live with him, he must
not divorce her. 13And if a woman
has a husband who is not a believer
and he is willing to live with her,
she must not divorce him. 14For
the unbelieving husband has been
sanctified through his wife, and the
unbelieving wife has been sanctified through her believing husband. Otherwise your children
would be unclean, but as it is, they
are holy.[u]
15But if the unbeliever leaves, let
him do so. A believing man or
woman is not bound in such circumstances; God has called us to
live in peace.[v] 16How do you
know, wife, whether you will save[w]
your husband?[x] Or, how do you
know, husband, whether you will
save your wife?
17Nevertheless, each one should
retain the place in life that the Lord
assigned to him and to which God
has called him.[y] This is the rule I
lay down in all the churches.[z]
18Was a man already circumcised
when he was called? He should not
become uncircumcised. Was a man
uncircumcised when he was
called? He should not be circumcised.[a] 19Circumcision is nothing
and uncircumcision is nothing.[b]
Keeping God's commands is what
counts. 20Each one should remain
in the situation which he was in
when God called him.[c] 21Were you
a slave when you were called?
Don't let it trouble you—although
if you can gain your freedom, do so.
22For he who was a slave when he
was called by the Lord is the Lord's
freedman;[d] similarly, he who was a
free man when he was called is
Christ's slave.[e] 23You were bought

6:15 [a] Ro 12:5 **6:16** [b] Ge 2:24; Mt 19:5; Eph 5:31 **6:17** [c] Jn 17:21-23; Gal 2:20 **6:18** [d] 2Co 12:21; 1Th 4:3,4; Heb 13:4 [e] Ro 6:12 **6:19** [f] Jn 2:21 [g] Ro 14:7,8 **6:20** [h] Ac 20:28; 1Co 7:23; 1Pe 1:18,19; Rev 5:9 **7:1** [i] ver 8,26 **7:3** [j] Ex 21:10; 1Pe 3:7 **7:5** [k] Ex 19:15; 1Sa 21:4,5 [l] Mt 4:10 [m] 1Th 3:5 **7:6** [n] 2Co 8:8 **7:7** [o] ver 8; 1Co 9:5 [p] Mt 19:11,12; Ro 12:6; 1Co 12:4,11 **7:8** [q] ver 1,26 **7:9** [r] 1Ti 5:14 **7:10** [s] Mal 2:14-16; Mt 5:32; 19:3-9; Mk 10:11; Lk 16:18 **7:12** [t] ver 6,10; 2Co 11:17 **7:14** [u] Mal 2:15 **7:15** [v] Ro 14:19; 1Co 14:33 **7:16** [w] Ro 11:14 [x] 1Pe 3:1 **7:17** [y] Ro 12:3 [z] 1Co 4:17; 14:33; 2Co 8:18; 11:28 **7:18** [a] Ac 15:1,2 **7:19** [b] Ro 2:25-27; Gal 5:6; 6:15; Col 3:11 **7:20** [c] ver 24 **7:22** [d] Jn 8:32,36; Phm 16 [e] Eph 6:6

[o] *16* Gen. 2:24 [p] *1* Or *"It is good for a man not to have sexual relations with a woman."*

at a price;[a] do not become slaves of men. **24**Brothers, each man, as responsible to God, should remain in the situation God called him to.[b]

25Now about virgins: I have no command from the Lord,[c] but I give a judgment as one who by the Lord's mercy[d] is trustworthy. **26**Because of the present crisis, I think that it is good for you to remain as you are.[e] **27**Are you married? Do not seek a divorce. Are you unmarried? Do not look for a wife. **28**But if you do marry, you have not sinned; and if a virgin marries, she has not sinned. But those who marry will face many troubles in this life, and I want to spare you this.

29What I mean, brothers, is that the time is short.[f] From now on those who have wives should live as if they had none; **30**those who mourn, as if they did not; those who are happy, as if they were not; those who buy something, as if it were not theirs to keep; **31**those who use the things of the world, as if not engrossed in them. For this world in its present form is passing away.[g]

32I would like you to be free from concern. An unmarried man is concerned about the Lord's affairs[h]—how he can please the Lord. **33**But a married man is concerned about the affairs of this world—how he can please his wife—**34**and his interests are divided. An unmarried woman or virgin is concerned about the Lord's affairs: Her aim is to be devoted to the Lord in both body and spirit.[i] But a married woman is concerned about the affairs of this world—how she can please her husband. **35**I am saying this for your own good, not to restrict you, but that you may live in a right way in undivided[j] devotion to the Lord.

36If anyone thinks he is acting improperly toward the virgin he is engaged to, and if she is getting along in years and he feels he ought to marry, he should do as he wants. He is not sinning.[k] They should get married. **37**But the man who has settled the matter in his own mind, who is under no compulsion but has control over his own will, and who has made up his mind not to marry the virgin—this man also does the right thing. **38**So then, he who marries the virgin does right,[l] but he who does not marry her does even better.[q]

39A woman is bound to her husband as long as he lives.[m] But if her husband dies, she is free to marry anyone she wishes, but he must belong to the Lord.[n] **40**In my judgment,[o] she is happier if she stays as she is—and I think that I too have the Spirit of God.

Food Sacrificed to Idols

8 Now about food sacrificed to idols:[p] We know that we all possess knowledge.[r][q] Knowledge puffs up, but love builds up. **2**The man who thinks he knows something[r] does not yet know as he ought to know.[s] **3**But the man who loves God is known by God.[t]

4So then, about eating food sacrificed to idols:[u] We know that an idol is nothing at all in the world[v] and that there is no God but one.[w] **5**For even if there are so-called gods,[x] whether in heaven or on earth (as indeed there are many "gods" and many "lords"), **6**yet for us there is but one God, the Father,[y] from whom all things came[z] and for whom we live; and there is but one Lord,[a] Jesus Christ, through whom all things came[b] and through whom we live.

7But not everyone knows this. Some people are still so accustomed to idols that when they eat such food they think of it as having been sacrificed to an idol, and

7:23 [a] 1Co 6:20
7:24 [b] ver 20
7:25 [c] ver 6; 2Co 8:8 [d] 2Co 4:1; 1Ti 1:13,16
7:26 [e] ver 1,8
7:29 [f] ver 31; Ro 13:11,12
7:31 [g] 1Jn 2:17
7:32 [h] 1Ti 5:5
7:34 [i] Lk 2:37
7:35 [j] Ps 86:11
7:36 [k] ver 28
7:38 [l] Heb 13:4
7:39 [m] Ro 7:2,3 [n] 2Co 6:14
7:40 [o] ver 25
8:1 [p] Ac 15:20 [q] Ro 15:14
8:2 [r] 1Co 3:18 [s] 1Co 13:8,9, 12; 1Ti 6:4
8:3 [t] Ro 8:29; Gal 4:9
8:4 [u] ver 1,7,10 [v] 1Co 10:19 [w] Dt 6:4; Eph 4:6
8:5 [x] 2Th 2:4
8:6 [y] Mal 2:10 [z] Ro 11:36 [a] Eph 4:5 [b] Jn 1:3

[q]36-38 Or [36]*If anyone thinks he is not treating his daughter properly, and if she is getting along in years, and he feels she ought to marry, he should do as he wants. He is not sinning. He should let her get married.* [37]*But the man who has settled the matter in his own mind, who is under no compulsion but has control over his own will, and who has made up his mind to keep the virgin unmarried—this man also does the right thing.* [38]*So then, he who gives his virgin in marriage does right, but he who does not give her in marriage does even better.*
[r]1 Or *"We all possess knowledge," as you say*

since their conscience is weak,[a] it
is defiled. **8**But food does not bring
us near to God;[b] we are no worse if
we do not eat, and no better if we
do.

9Be careful, however, that the
exercise of your freedom does not
become a stumbling block[c] to the
weak.[d] **10**For if anyone with a
weak conscience sees you who
have this knowledge eating in an
idol's temple, won't he be embold-
ened to eat what has been sacrificed to idols? **11**So this weak
brother, for whom Christ died, is
destroyed[e] by your knowledge.
12When you sin against your brothers[f] in this way and wound their
weak conscience, you sin against
Christ. **13**Therefore, if what I eat
causes my brother to fall into sin, I
will never eat meat again, so that I
will not cause him to fall.[g]

The Rights of an Apostle

9 Am I not free? Am I not an
apostle?[h] Have I not seen
Jesus our Lord?[i] Are you not the
result of my work in the Lord?[j]
2Even though I may not be an apostle to others, surely I am to you! For
you are the seal[k] of my apostleship
in the Lord.

3This is my defense to those who
sit in judgment on me. **4**Don't we
have the right to food and drink?[l]
5Don't we have the right to take a
believing wife[m] along with us, as
do the other apostles and the
Lord's brothers[n] and Cephas[s]?
6Or is it only I and Barnabas[o] who
must work for a living?

7Who serves as a soldier at his
own expense? Who plants a vineyard[p] and does not eat of its
grapes? Who tends a flock and does
not drink of the milk? **8**Do I say this
merely from a human point of
view? Doesn't the Law say the
same thing? **9**For it is written in the
Law of Moses: "Do not muzzle an
ox while it is treading out the
grain."[t][q] Is it about oxen that God
is concerned?[r] **10**Surely he says
this for us, doesn't he? Yes, this
was written for us,[s] because when
the plowman plows and the thresh-
er threshes, they ought to do so in
the hope of sharing in the harvest.[t] **11**If we have sown spiritual
seed among you, is it too much if
we reap a material harvest from
you?[u] **12**If others have this right of
support from you, shouldn't we
have it all the more?

But we did not use this right.[v]
On the contrary, we put up with
anything rather than hinder[w] the
gospel of Christ. **13**Don't you know
that those who work in the temple
get their food from the temple, and
those who serve at the altar share
in what is offered on the altar?[x]
14In the same way, the Lord has
commanded that those who preach
the gospel should receive their living from the gospel.[y]

15But I have not used any of
these rights.[z] And I am not writing
this in the hope that you will do
such things for me. I would rather
die than have anyone deprive me of
this boast.[a] **16**Yet when I preach
the gospel, I cannot boast, for I am
compelled to preach.[b] Woe to me
if I do not preach the gospel! **17**If I
preach voluntarily, I have a reward;[c] if not voluntarily, I am simply discharging the trust committed to me.[d] **18**What then is my reward? Just this: that in preaching
the gospel I may offer it free of
charge,[e] and so not make use of
my rights in preaching it.

19Though I am free[f] and belong
to no man, I make myself a slave to
everyone,[g] to win as many as possible.[h] **20**To the Jews I became like
a Jew, to win the Jews.[i] To those
under the law I became like one
under the law (though I myself am
not under the law), so as to win
those under the law. **21**To those not
having the law I became like one
not having the law[j] (though I am
not free from God's law but am under Christ's law), so as to win those
not having the law. **22**To the weak
I became weak, to win the weak. I
have become all things to all men[k]
so that by all possible means I
might save some.[l] **23**I do all this

8:7 [a]Ro 14:14; 1Co 10:28
8:8 [b]Ro 14:17
8:9 [c]Gal 5:13 [d]Ro 14:1
8:11 [e]Ro 14:15,20
8:12 [f]Mt 18:6
8:13 [g]Ro 14:21
9:1 [h]2Co 12:12 [i]1Co 15:8 [j]1Co 3:6; 4:15
9:2 [k]2Co 3:2,3
9:4 [l]1Th 2:6
9:5 [m]1Co 7:7,8 [n]Mt 12:46
9:6 [o]Ac 4:36
9:7 [p]Dt 20:6; Pr 27:18
9:9 [q]Dt 25:4; 1Ti 5:18 [r]Dt 22:1-4
9:10 [s]Ro 4:23,24 [t]2Ti 2:6
9:11 [u]Ro 15:27
9:12 [v]Ac 18:3 [w]2Co 11:7-12
9:13 [x]Lev 6:16,26; Dt 18:1
9:14 [y]Mt 10:10; 1Ti 5:18
9:15 [z]Ac 18:3 [a]2Co 11:9,10
9:16 [b]Ro 1:14; Ac 9:15
9:17 [c]1Co 3:8,14 [d]Gal 2:7; Col 1:25
9:18 [e]2Co 11:7; 12:13
9:19 [f]ver 1 [g]Gal 5:13 [h]Mt 18:15; 1Pe 3:1
9:20 [i]Ac 16:3; 21:20-26; Ro 11:14
9:21 [j]Ro 2:12,14
9:22 [k]1Co 10:33 [l]Ro 11:14

[s]5 That is, Peter [t]9 Deut. 25:4

for the sake of the gospel, that I may share in its blessings.

24Do you not know that in a race all the runners run, but only one gets the prize? Run[a] in such a way as to get the prize. **25**Everyone who competes in the games goes into strict training. They do it to get a crown that will not last; but we do it to get a crown that will last forever.[b] **26**Therefore I do not run like a man running aimlessly; I do not fight like a man beating the air. **27**No, I beat my body[c] and make it my slave so that after I have preached to others, I myself will not be disqualified for the prize.

Warnings From Israel's History

10 For I do not want you to be ignorant of the fact, brothers, that our forefathers were all under the cloud[d] and that they all passed through the sea.[e] **2**They were all baptized into Moses in the cloud and in the sea. **3**They all ate the same spiritual food **4**and drank the same spiritual drink; for they drank from the spiritual rock[f] that accompanied them, and that rock was Christ. **5**Nevertheless, God was not pleased with most of them; their bodies were scattered over the desert.[g]

6Now these things occurred as examples[u] to keep us from setting our hearts on evil things as they did. **7**Do not be idolaters,[h] as some of them were; as it is written: "The people sat down to eat and drink and got up to indulge in pagan revelry."[v][i] **8**We should not commit sexual immorality, as some of them did—and in one day twenty-three thousand of them died.[j] **9**We should not test the Lord, as some of them did—and were killed by snakes.[k] **10**And do not grumble, as some of them did[l]—and were killed[m] by the destroying angel.[n]

11These things happened to them as examples and were written down as warnings for us, on whom the fulfillment of the ages has come.[o] **12**So, if you think you are standing firm,[p] be careful that you don't fall! **13**No temptation has seized you except what is common to man. And God is faithful;[q] he will not let you be tempted beyond what you can bear.[r] But when you are tempted, he will also provide a way out so that you can stand up under it.

Idol Feasts and the Lord's Supper

14Therefore, my dear friends, flee from idolatry. **15**I speak to sensible people; judge for yourselves what I say. **16**Is not the cup of thanksgiving for which we give thanks a participation in the blood of Christ? And is not the bread that we break a participation in the body of Christ?[s] **17**Because there is one loaf, we, who are many, are one body,[t] for we all partake of the one loaf.

18Consider the people of Israel: Do not those who eat the sacrifices[u] participate in the altar? **19**Do I mean then that a sacrifice offered to an idol is anything, or that an idol is anything?[v] **20**No, but the sacrifices of pagans are offered to demons,[w] not to God, and I do not want you to be participants with demons. **21**You cannot drink the cup of the Lord and the cup of demons too; you cannot have a part in both the Lord's table and the table of demons.[x] **22**Are we trying to arouse the Lord's jealousy?[y] Are we stronger than he?[z]

The Believer's Freedom

23"Everything is permissible"—but not everything is beneficial.[a] "Everything is permissible"—but not everything is constructive. **24**Nobody should seek his own good, but the good of others.[b]

25Eat anything sold in the meat market without raising questions of conscience,[c] **26**for, "The earth is the Lord's, and everything in it."[w][d]

27If some unbeliever invites you to a meal and you want to go, eat whatever is put before you[e] with-

9:24 [a]Gal 2:2; 2Ti 4:7; Heb 12:1
9:25 [b]Jas 1:12; Rev 2:10
9:27 [c]Ro 8:13
10:1 [d]Ex 13:21 [e]Ex 14:22,29
10:4 [f]Ex 17:6; Nu 20:11; Ps 78:15
10:5 [g]Nu 14:29; Heb 3:17
10:7 [h]ver 14 [i]Ex 32:4,6,19
10:8 [j]Nu 25:1-9
10:9 [k]Nu 21:5,6
10:10 [l]Nu 16:41 [m]Nu 16:49 [n]Ex 12:23
10:11 [o]Ro 13:11
10:12 [p]Ro 11:20
10:13 [q]1Co 1:9 [r]2Pe 2:9
10:16 [s]Mt 26:26-28
10:17 [t]Ro 12:5; 1Co 12:27
10:18 [u]Lev 7:6,14,15
10:19 [v]1Co 8:4
10:20 [w]Dt 32:17; Ps 106:37; Rev 9:20
10:21 [x]2Co 6:15,16
10:22 [y]Dt 32:16,21 [z]Ecc 6:10; Isa 45:9
10:23 [a]1Co 6:12
10:24 [b]ver 33; Ro 15:1,2; 1Co 13:5; Php 2:4,21
10:25 [c]Ac 10:15; 1Co 8:7
10:26 [d]Ps 24:1
10:27 [e]Lk 10:7

[u]6 Or *types*; also in verse 11 [v]7 Exodus 32:6 [w]26 Psalm 24:1

out raising questions of conscience. 28But if anyone says to you, "This has been offered in sacrifice," then do not eat it, both for the sake of the man who told you and for conscience' sake[x][a]— 29the other man's conscience, I mean, not yours. For why should my freedom[b] be judged by another's conscience? 30If I take part in the meal with thankfulness, why am I denounced because of something I thank God for?[c]

31So whether you eat or drink or whatever you do, do it all for the glory of God.[d] 32Do not cause anyone to stumble,[e] whether Jews, Greeks or the church of God[f]— 33even as I try to please everybody in every way.[g] For I am not seeking my own good but the good of many, so that they may be saved.[h]

11 1Follow my example,[i] as I follow the example of Christ.

Propriety in Worship

2I praise you[j] for remembering me in everything[k] and for holding to the teachings,[y] just as I passed them on to you.[l]

3Now I want you to realize that the head of every man is Christ,[m] and the head of the woman is man,[n] and the head of Christ is God.[o] 4Every man who prays or prophesies with his head covered dishonors his head. 5And every woman who prays or prophesies[p] with her head uncovered dishonors her head—it is just as though her head were shaved.[q] 6If a woman does not cover her head, she should have her hair cut off; and if it is a disgrace for a woman to have her hair cut or shaved off, she should cover her head. 7A man ought not to cover his head,[z] since he is the image[r] and glory of God; but the woman is the glory of man. 8For man did not come from woman, but woman from man;[s] 9neither was man created for woman, but woman for man.[t] 10For this reason, and because of the angels, the woman ought to have a sign of authority on her head.

11In the Lord, however, woman is not independent of man, nor is man independent of woman. 12For as woman came from man, so also man is born of woman. But everything comes from God.[u] 13Judge for yourselves: Is it proper for a woman to pray to God with her head uncovered? 14Does not the very nature of things teach you that if a man has long hair, it is a disgrace to him, 15but that if a woman has long hair, it is her glory? For long hair is given to her as a covering. 16If anyone wants to be contentious about this, we have no other practice—nor do the churches of God.[v]

The Lord's Supper

11:23–25pp — Mt 26:26–28; Mk 14:22–24; Lk 22:17–20

17In the following directives I have no praise for you,[w] for your meetings do more harm than good. 18In the first place, I hear that when you come together as a church, there are divisions[x] among you, and to some extent I believe it. 19No doubt there have to be differences among you to show which of you have God's approval.[y] 20When you come together, it is not the Lord's Supper you eat, 21for as you eat, each of you goes ahead without waiting for anybody else.[z] One remains hungry, another gets drunk. 22Don't you have homes to eat and drink in? Or do you despise the church of God[a] and humiliate those who have nothing?[b] What shall I say to you? Shall I praise you[c] for this? Certainly not!

23For I received from the Lord[d] what I also passed on to you:[e] The Lord Jesus, on the night he was be-

10:28 [a] 1Co 8:7, 10-12
10:29 [b] Ro 14:16; 1Co 9:1,19
10:30 [c] Ro 14:6
10:31 [d] Col 3:17; 1Pe 4:11
10:32 [e] Ac 24:16 [f] Ac 20:28
10:33 [g] Ro 15:2; 1Co 9:22 [h] Ro 11:14
11:1 [i] 1Co 4:16
11:2 [j] ver 17,22 [k] 1Co 4:17 [l] 1Co 15:2,3; 2Th 2:15
11:3 [m] Eph 1:22 [n] Ge 3:16; Eph 5:23 [o] 1Co 3:23
11:5 [p] Ac 21:9 [q] Dt 21:12
11:7 [r] Ge 1:26; Jas 3:9
11:8 [s] Ge 2:21-23; 1Ti 2:13
11:9 [t] Ge 2:18
11:12 [u] Ro 11:36
11:16 [v] 1Co 7:17
11:17 [w] ver 2,22
11:18 [x] 1Co 1:10-12; 3:3
11:19 [y] 1Jn 2:19
11:21 [z] 2Pe 2:13; Jude 12
11:22 [a] 1Co 10:32 [b] Jas 2:6 [c] ver 2,17
11:23 [d] Gal 1:12 [e] 1Co 15:3

[x]28 Some manuscripts *conscience' sake, for "the earth is the Lord's and everything in it"*
[y]2 Or *traditions*
[z]4-7 Or *4Every man who prays or prophesies with long hair dishonors his head. 5And every woman who prays or prophesies with no covering of hair on her head dishonors her head—she is just like one of the "shorn women." 6If a woman has no covering, let her be for now with short hair, but since it is a disgrace for a woman to have her hair shorn or shaved, she should grow it again. 7A man ought not to have long hair*

trayed, took bread, **24**and when he
had given thanks, he broke it and
said, "This is my body, which is for
you; do this in remembrance of
me." **25**In the same way, after supper he took the cup, saying, "This
cup is the new covenant[a] in my
blood;[b] do this, whenever you
drink it, in remembrance of me."
26For whenever you eat this bread
and drink this cup, you proclaim
the Lord's death until he comes.
27Therefore, whoever eats the
bread or drinks the cup of the Lord
in an unworthy manner will be
guilty of sinning against the body
and blood of the Lord.[c] **28**A man
ought to examine himself[d] before
he eats of the bread and drinks of
the cup. **29**For anyone who eats
and drinks without recognizing the
body of the Lord eats and drinks
judgment on himself. **30**That is why
many among you are weak and
sick, and a number of you have fall-
en asleep. **31**But if we judged ourselves, we would not come under
judgment.[e] **32**When we are judged
by the Lord, we are being disciplined[f] so that we will not be condemned with the world.
33So then, my brothers, when
you come together to eat, wait for
each other. **34**If anyone is hungry,[g]
he should eat at home,[h] so that
when you meet together it may not
result in judgment.
And when I come[i] I will give further directions.

Spiritual Gifts

12 Now about spiritual gifts,[j]
brothers, I do not want you
to be ignorant. **2**You know that
when you were pagans,[k] somehow
or other you were influenced and
led astray to mute idols.[l] **3**Therefore I tell you that no one who is
speaking by the Spirit of God says,
"Jesus be cursed,"[m] and no one
can say, "Jesus is Lord,"[n] except
by the Holy Spirit.[o]
4There are different kinds of
gifts, but the same Spirit.[p] **5**There
are different kinds of service, but
the same Lord. **6**There are different
kinds of working, but the same
God[q] works all of them in all men.
7Now to each one the manifesta-
tion of the Spirit is given for the
common good.[r] **8**To one there is
given through the Spirit the message of wisdom,[s] to another the
message of knowledge[t] by means
of the same Spirit, **9**to another
faith[u] by the same Spirit, to another gifts of healing[v] by that one
Spirit, **10**to another miraculous
powers,[w] to another prophecy, to
another distinguishing between
spirits,[x] to another speaking in different kinds of tongues,[a][y] and to
still another the interpretation of
tongues.[a] **11**All these are the work
of one and the same Spirit,[z] and
he gives them to each one, just as
he determines.

One Body, Many Parts

12The body is a unit, though it is
made up of many parts; and though
all its parts are many, they form
one body.[a] So it is with Christ.[b]
13For we were all baptized by[b] one
Spirit[c] into one body—whether
Jews or Greeks, slave or free[d]—
and we were all given the one Spirit
to drink.[e]
14Now the body is not made up
of one part but of many. **15**If the
foot should say, "Because I am not
a hand, I do not belong to the
body," it would not for that reason
cease to be part of the body. **16**And
if the ear should say, "Because I am
not an eye, I do not belong to the
body," it would not for that reason
cease to be part of the body. **17**If
the whole body were an eye, where
would the sense of hearing be? If
the whole body were an ear, where
would the sense of smell be? **18**But
in fact God has arranged[f] the parts
in the body, every one of them, just
as he wanted them to be.[g] **19**If they
were all one part, where would the
body be? **20**As it is, there are many
parts, but one body.[h]
21The eye cannot say to the
hand, "I don't need you!" And the
head cannot say to the feet, "I

11:25 [a]Lk 22:20 [b]1Co 10:16
11:27 [c]Heb 10:29
11:28 [d]2Co 13:5
11:31 [e]Ps 32:5; 1Jn 1:9
11:32 [f]Ps 94:12; Heb 12:7-10; Rev 3:19
11:34 [g]ver 21 [h]ver 22 [i]1Co 4:19
12:1 [j]Ro 1:11; 1Co 14:1,37
12:2 [k]Eph 2:11,12; 1Pe 4:3 [l]Ps 115:5; Jer 10:5; Hab 2:18,19; 1Th 1:9
12:3 [m]Ro 9:3 [n]Jn 13:13 [o]1Jn 4:2,3
12:4 [p]Ro 12:4-8; Eph 4:11; Heb 2:4
12:6 [q]Eph 4:6
12:7 [r]Eph 4:12
12:8 [s]1Co 2:6 [t]2Co 8:7
12:9 [u]Mt 17:19,20; 2Co 4:13 [v]ver 28,30
12:10 [w]Gal 3:5 [x]1Jn 4:1 [y]Mk 16:17
12:11 [z]ver 4
12:12 [a]Ro 12:5 [b]ver 27
12:13 [c]Eph 2:18 [d]Gal 3:28; Col 3:11 [e]Jn 7:37-39
12:18 [f]ver 28 [g]ver 11
12:20 [h]ver 12,14

[a]*10* Or *languages;* also in verse 28 [b]*13* Or *with;* or *in*

don't need you!" **22**On the contrary, those parts of the body that seem to be weaker are indispensable, **23**and the parts that we think are less honorable we treat with special honor. And the parts that are unpresentable are treated with special modesty, **24**while our presentable parts need no special treatment. But God has combined the members of the body and has given greater honor to the parts that lacked it, **25**so that there should be no division in the body, but that its parts should have equal concern for each other. **26**If one part suffers, every part suffers with it; if one part is honored, every part rejoices with it.

27Now you are the body of Christ,[a] and each one of you is a part of it.[b] **28**And in the church[c] God has appointed first of all apostles,[d] second prophets, third teachers, then workers of miracles, also those having gifts of healing,[e] those able to help others, those with gifts of administration,[f] and those speaking in different kinds of tongues.[g] **29**Are all apostles? Are all prophets? Are all teachers? Do all work miracles? **30**Do all have gifts of healing? Do all speak in tongues[c]?[h] Do all interpret? **31**But eagerly desire[d][i] the greater gifts.

Love

And now I will show you the most excellent way.

13 If I speak in the tongues[e][j] of men and of angels, but have not love, I am only a resounding gong or a clanging cymbal. **2**If I have the gift of prophecy and can fathom all mysteries[k] and all knowledge, and if I have a faith[l] that can move mountains,[m] but have not love, I am nothing. **3**If I give all I possess to the poor[n] and surrender my body to the flames,[f][o] but have not love, I gain nothing.

4Love is patient,[p] love is kind. It does not envy, it does not boast, it is not proud. **5**It is not rude, it is not self-seeking,[q] it is not easily angered, it keeps no record of wrongs. **6**Love does not delight in evil[r] but rejoices with the truth.[s] **7**It always protects, always trusts, always hopes, always perseveres.

8Love never fails. But where there are prophecies,[t] they will cease; where there are tongues,[u] they will be stilled; where there is knowledge, it will pass away. **9**For we know in part[v] and we prophesy in part, **10**but when perfection comes,[w] the imperfect disappears. **11**When I was a child, I talked like a child, I thought like a child, I reasoned like a child. When I became a man, I put childish ways behind me. **12**Now we see but a poor reflection as in a mirror; then we shall see face to face.[x] Now I know in part; then I shall know fully, even as I am fully known.[y]

13And now these three remain: faith, hope and love.[z] But the greatest of these is love.[a]

Gifts of Prophecy and Tongues

14 Follow the way of love[b] and eagerly desire[c] spiritual gifts,[d] especially the gift of prophecy. **2**For anyone who speaks in a tongue[g][e] does not speak to men but to God. Indeed, no one understands him; he utters mysteries[f] with his spirit.[h] **3**But everyone who prophesies speaks to men for their strengthening,[g] encouragement and comfort. **4**He who speaks in a tongue[h] edifies himself, but he who prophesies[i] edifies the church. **5**I would like every one of you to speak in tongues,[i] but I would rather have you prophesy.[j] He who prophesies is greater than one who speaks in tongues,[i] unless he interprets, so that the church may be edified.

6Now, brothers, if I come to you and speak in tongues, what good will I be to you, unless I bring you some revelation[k] or knowledge or prophecy or word of instruction?[l]

12:27 [a] Eph 1:23; 4:12; Col 1:18,24 [b] Ro 12:5
12:28 [c] 1Co 10:32 [d] Eph 4:11 [e] ver 9 [f] Ro 12:6-8 [g] ver 10
12:30 [h] ver 10
12:31 [i] 1Co 14:1,39
13:1 [j] ver 8
13:2 [k] 1Co 14:2 [l] 1Co 12:9 [m] Mt 17:20; 21:21
13:3 [n] Mt 6:2 [o] Da 3:28
13:4 [p] 1Th 5:14
13:5 [q] 1Co 10:24
13:6 [r] 2Th 2:12 [s] 2Jn 4; 3Jn 3, 4
13:8 [t] ver 2 [u] ver 1
13:9 [v] ver 12; 1Co 8:2
13:10 [w] Php 3:12
13:12 [x] Ge 32:30; 2Co 5:7; 1Jn 3:2 [y] 1Co 8:3
13:13 [z] Gal 5:5,6 [a] 1Co 16:14
14:1 [b] 1Co 16:14 [c] ver 39; 1Co 12:31 [d] 1Co 12:1
14:2 [e] Mk 16:17 [f] 1Co 13:2
14:3 [g] ver 4,5,12, 17,26; Ro 14:19
14:4 [h] Mk 16:17 [i] 1Co 13:2
14:5 [j] Nu 11:29
14:6 [k] ver 26; Eph 1:17 [l] Ro 6:17

[c]30 Or *other languages* [d]31 Or *But you are eagerly desiring* [e]1 Or *languages* [f]3 Some early manuscripts *body that I may boast* [g]2 Or *another language*; also in verses 4, 13, 14, 19, 26 and 27 [h]2 Or *by the Spirit* [i]5 Or *other languages*; also in verses 6, 18, 22, 23 and 39

7Even in the case of lifeless things
that make sounds, such as the flute
or harp, how will anyone know
what tune is being played unless
there is a distinction in the notes?
8Again, if the trumpet does not
sound a clear call, who will get
ready for battle?[a] 9So it is with
you. Unless you speak intelligible
words with your tongue, how will
anyone know what you are saying?
You will just be speaking into the
air. 10Undoubtedly there are all
sorts of languages in the world, yet
none of them is without meaning.
11If then I do not grasp the meaning of what someone is saying, I am
a foreigner to the speaker, and he is
a foreigner to me. 12So it is with
you. Since you are eager to have
spiritual gifts, try to excel in gifts
that build up the church.

13For this reason anyone who
speaks in a tongue should pray that
he may interpret what he says.
14For if I pray in a tongue, my spirit
prays, but my mind is unfruitful.
15So what shall I do? I will pray
with my spirit, but I will also pray
with my mind; I will sing[b] with my
spirit, but I will also sing with my
mind. 16If you are praising God
with your spirit, how can one who
finds himself among those who do
not understand[i] say "Amen"[c] to
your thanksgiving,[d] since he does
not know what you are saying?
17You may be giving thanks well
enough, but the other man is not
edified.

18I thank God that I speak in
tongues more than all of you. 19But
in the church I would rather speak
five intelligible words to instruct
others than ten thousand words in
a tongue.

20Brothers, stop thinking like
children.[e] In regard to evil be infants,[f] but in your thinking be
adults. 21In the Law[g] it is written:

"Through men of strange
tongues
and through the lips of
foreigners
I will speak to this people,
but even then they will not
listen to me,"[k][h]
says the Lord.

22Tongues, then, are a sign, not
for believers but for unbelievers;
prophecy,[i] however, is for believers, not for unbelievers. 23So if the
whole church comes together and
everyone speaks in tongues, and
some who do not understand[l] or
some unbelievers come in, will
they not say that you are out of
your mind?[j] 24But if an unbeliever
or someone who does not understand[m] comes in while everybody is
prophesying, he will be convinced
by all that he is a sinner and will be
judged by all, 25and the secrets of
his heart will be laid bare. So he
will fall down and worship God, ex-
claiming, "God is really among
you!"[k]

Orderly Worship

26What then shall we say, brothers? When you come together, everyone[l] has a hymn,[m] or a word of
instruction,[n] a revelation, a
tongue or an interpretation. All of
these must be done for the
strengthening[o] of the church. 27If
anyone speaks in a tongue, two—
or at the most three—should
speak, one at a time, and someone
must interpret. 28If there is no in-
terpreter, the speaker should keep
quiet in the church and speak to
himself and God.

29Two or three prophets should
speak, and the others should weigh
carefully what is said.[p] 30And if a
revelation comes to someone who
is sitting down, the first speaker
should stop. 31For you can all
prophesy in turn so that everyone
may be instructed and encouraged.
32The spirits of prophets are subject to the control of prophets.[q]
33For God is not a God of disorder[r]
but of peace.

As in all the congregations of the
saints,[s] 34women should remain
silent in the churches. They are not

14:8 [a] Nu 10:9; Jer 4:19
14:15 [b] Eph 5:19; Col 3:16
14:16 [c] Dt 27:15-26; 1Ch 16:36; Ne 8:6; Ps 106:48; Rev 5:14; 7:12 [d] 1Co 11:24
14:20 [e] Eph 4:14; Heb 5:12,13; 1Pe 2:2 [f] Ro 16:19
14:21 [g] Jn 10:34 [h] Isa 28:11,12
14:22 [i] ver 1
14:23 [j] Ac 2:13
14:25 [k] Isa 45:14; Zec 8:23
14:26 [l] 1Co 12:7-10 [m] Eph 5:19 [n] ver 6 [o] Ro 14:19
14:29 [p] 1Co 12:10
14:32 [q] 1Jn 4:1
14:33 [r] ver 40 [s] Ac 9:13

[i]16 Or *among the inquirers*
[k]21 Isaiah 28:11,12 [l]23 Or *some inquirers*
[m]24 Or *or some inquirer*

allowed to speak, but must be in
submission,[a] as the Law[b] says.
35If they want to inquire about
something, they should ask their
own husbands at home; for it is disgraceful for a woman to speak in
the church.
36Did the word of God originate
with you? Or are you the only people it has reached? **37**If anybody
thinks he is a prophet[c] or spiritually gifted, let him acknowledge
that what I am writing to you is the
Lord's command.[d] **38**If he ignores
this, he himself will be ignored.[n]
39Therefore, my brothers, be eager[e] to prophesy, and do not forbid
speaking in tongues. **40**But everything should be done in a fitting
and orderly[f] way.

The Resurrection of Christ

15 Now, brothers, I want to remind you of the gospel[g] I
preached to you, which you received and on which you have tak-
en your stand. **2**By this gospel you
are saved,[h] if you hold firmly[i] to
the word I preached to you. Otherwise, you have believed in vain.
3For what I received[j] I passed
on to you[k] as of first importance[o]:
that Christ died for our sins[l] according to the Scriptures,[m] **4**that
he was buried, that he was raised[n]
on the third day[o] according to the
Scriptures,[p] **5**and that he appeared
to Peter,[p][q] and then to the
Twelve.[r] **6**After that, he appeared
to more than five hundred of the
brothers at the same time, most of
whom are still living, though some
have fallen asleep. **7**Then he appeared to James, then to all the
apostles,[s] **8**and last of all he appeared to me also,[t] as to one ab-
normally born.
9For I am the least of the apostles[u] and do not even deserve to be
called an apostle, because I persecuted[v] the church of God. **10**But
by the grace of God I am what I am,
and his grace to me[w] was not without effect. No, I worked harder
than all of them[x]—yet not I, but
the grace of God that was with
me.[y] **11**Whether, then, it was I or
they, this is what we preach, and
this is what you believed.

The Resurrection of the Dead

12But if it is preached that Christ
has been raised from the dead, how
can some of you say that there is no
resurrection of the dead?[z] **13**If
there is no resurrection of the
dead, then not even Christ has
been raised. **14**And if Christ has not
been raised,[a] our preaching is useless and so is your faith. **15**More
than that, we are then found to be
false witnesses about God, for we
have testified about God that he
raised Christ from the dead.[b] But
he did not raise him if in fact the
dead are not raised. **16**For if the
dead are not raised, then Christ has
not been raised either. **17**And if
Christ has not been raised, your
faith is futile; you are still in your
sins.[c] **18**Then those also who have
fallen asleep in Christ are lost. **19**If
only for this life we have hope in
Christ, we are to be pitied more
than all men.[d]
20But Christ has indeed been
raised from the dead,[e] the firstfruits[f] of those who have fallen
asleep.[g] **21**For since death came
through a man,[h] the resurrection
of the dead comes also through a
man. **22**For as in Adam all die, so in
Christ all will be made alive.[i]
23But each in his own turn: Christ,
the firstfruits;[j] then, when he
comes,[k] those who belong to him.
24Then the end will come, when he
hands over the kingdom[l] to God
the Father after he has destroyed
all dominion, authority and power.[m] **25**For he must reign until he
has put all his enemies under his
feet.[n] **26**The last enemy to be destroyed is death.[o] **27**For he "has
put everything under his feet."[q][p]
Now when it says that "everything"
has been put under him, it is clear
that this does not include God
himself, who put everything under

14:34 [a]1Ti 2:11,12 [b]Ge 3:16
14:37 [c]2Co 10:7 [d]1Jn 4:6
14:39 [e]1Co 12:31
14:40 [f]ver 33
15:1 [g]Ro 2:16
15:2 [h]Ro 1:16 [i]Ro 11:22
15:3 [j]Gal 1:12 [k]1Co 11:23 [l]Isa 53:5; 1Pe 2:24 [m]Lk 24:27; Ac 26:22,23
15:4 [n]Ac 2:24 [o]Mt 16:21 [p]Ac 2:25,30, 31
15:5 [q]Lk 24:34 [r]Mk 16:14
15:7 [s]Lk 24:33,36, 37; Ac 1:3,4
15:8 [t]Ac 9:3-6,17; 1Co 9:1
15:9 [u]Eph 3:8; 1Ti 1:15 [v]Ac 8:3
15:10 [w]Ro 12:3 [x]2Co 11:23 [y]Php 2:13
15:12 [z]Ac 17:32; 23:8; 2Ti 2:18
15:14 [a]1Th 4:14
15:15 [b]Ac 2:24
15:17 [c]Ro 4:25
15:19 [d]1Co 4:9
15:20 [e]1Pe 1:3 [f]ver 23; Ac 26:23; Rev 1:5 [g]ver 6,18
15:21 [h]Ro 5:12
15:22 [i]Ro 5:14-18
15:23 [j]ver 20 [k]ver 52
15:24 [l]Da 7:14,27 [m]Ro 8:38
15:25 [n]Ps 110:1; Mt 22:44
15:26 [o]2Ti 1:10; Rev 20:14; 21:4
15:27 [p]Ps 8:6

[n]38 Some manuscripts *If he is ignorant of this, let him be ignorant*
[o]3 Or *you at the first*
[p]5 Greek *Cephas*
[q]27 Psalm 8:6

Christ.[a] 28When he has done this, then the Son himself will be made subject to him who put everything under him,[b] so that God may be all in all.[c]

29Now if there is no resurrection, what will those do who are baptized for the dead? If the dead are not raised at all, why are people baptized for them? 30And as for us, why do we endanger ourselves every hour?[d] 31I die every day[e]—I mean that, brothers—just as surely as I glory over you in Christ Jesus our Lord. 32If I fought wild beasts[f] in Ephesus[g] for merely human reasons, what have I gained? If the dead are not raised,

"Let us eat and drink,
  for tomorrow we die."[r][h]

33Do not be misled: "Bad company corrupts good character." 34Come back to your senses as you ought, and stop sinning; for there are some who are ignorant of God—I say this to your shame.

The Resurrection Body

35But someone may ask,[i] "How are the dead raised? With what kind of body will they come?"[j] 36How foolish![k] What you sow does not come to life unless it dies.[l] 37When you sow, you do not plant the body that will be, but just a seed, perhaps of wheat or of something else. 38But God gives it a body as he has determined, and to each kind of seed he gives its own body.[m] 39All flesh is not the same: Men have one kind of flesh, animals have another, birds another and fish another. 40There are also heavenly bodies and there are earthly bodies; but the splendor of the heavenly bodies is one kind, and the splendor of the earthly bodies is another. 41The sun has one kind of splendor, the moon another and the stars another; and star differs from star in splendor.

42So will it be[n] with the resurrection of the dead. The body that is sown is perishable, it is raised imperishable; 43it is sown in dishonor, it is raised in glory;[o] it is sown in weakness, it is raised in power; 44it is sown a natural body, it is raised a spiritual body.[p]

If there is a natural body, there is also a spiritual body. 45So it is written: "The first man Adam became a living being"[s];[q] the last Adam,[r] a life-giving spirit.[s] 46The spiritual did not come first, but the natural, and after that the spiritual. 47The first man was of the dust of the earth,[t] the second man from heaven.[u] 48As was the earthly man, so are those who are of the earth; and as is the man from heaven, so also are those who are of heaven.[v] 49And just as we have borne the likeness of the earthly man,[w] so shall we[t] bear the likeness of the man from heaven.[x]

50I declare to you, brothers, that flesh and blood[y] cannot inherit the kingdom of God, nor does the perishable inherit the imperishable. 51Listen, I tell you a mystery:[z] We will not all sleep, but we will all be changed[a]— 52in a flash, in the twinkling of an eye, at the last trumpet. For the trumpet will sound,[b] the dead[c] will be raised imperishable, and we will be changed. 53For the perishable must clothe itself with the imperishable,[d] and the mortal with immortality. 54When the perishable has been clothed with the imperishable, and the mortal with immortality, then the saying that is written will come true: "Death has been swallowed up in victory."[u][e]

55"Where, O death, is your
  victory?
 Where, O death, is your
  sting?"[v][f]

56The sting of death is sin,[g] and the power of sin is the law.[h] 57But thanks be to God![i] He gives us the victory through our Lord Jesus Christ.[j]

58Therefore, my dear brothers, stand firm. Let nothing move you. Always give yourselves fully to the work of the Lord,[k] because you

15:27 [a]Mt 28:18
15:28 [b]Php 3:21 [c]1Co 3:23
15:30 [d]2Co 11:26
15:31 [e]Ro 8:36
15:32 [f]2Co 1:8 [g]Ac 18:19 [h]Isa 22:13; Lk 12:19
15:35 [i]Ro 9:19 [j]Eze 37:3
15:36 [k]Lk 11:40 [l]Jn 12:24
15:38 [m]Ge 1:11
15:42 [n]Da 12:3; Mt 13:43
15:43 [o]Php 3:21; Col 3:4
15:44 [p]ver 50
15:45 [q]Ge 2:7 [r]Ro 5:14 [s]Jn 5:21; Ro 8:2
15:47 [t]Ge 2:7; 3:19 [u]Jn 3:13,31
15:48 [v]Php 3:20,21
15:49 [w]Ge 5:3 [x]Ro 8:29
15:50 [y]Jn 3:3,5
15:51 [z]1Co 13:2 [a]Php 3:21
15:52 [b]Mt 24:31 [c]Jn 5:25
15:53 [d]2Co 5:2,4
15:54 [e]Isa 25:8; Rev 20:14
15:55 [f]Hos 13:14
15:56 [g]Ro 5:12 [h]Ro 4:15
15:57 [i]2Co 2:14 [j]Ro 8:37
15:58 [k]1Co 16:10

[r]*32* Isaiah 22:13 [s]*45* Gen. 2:7
[t]*49* Some early manuscripts *so let us*
[u]*54* Isaiah 25:8 [v]*55* Hosea 13:14

know that your labor in the Lord is
not in vain.

The Collection for God's People

16 Now about the collection[a]
for God's people:[b] Do what
I told the Galatian[c] churches to
do. 2On the first day of every
week,[d] each one of you should set
aside a sum of money in keeping
with his income, saving it up, so
that when I come no collections
will have to be made.[e] 3Then,
when I arrive, I will give letters of
introduction to the men you approve[f] and send them with your
gift to Jerusalem. 4If it seems ad-
visable for me to go also, they will
accompany me.

Personal Requests

5After I go through Macedonia, I
will come to you[g]—for I will be going through Macedonia.[h] 6Perhaps
I will stay with you awhile, or even
spend the winter, so that you can
help me on my journey,[i] wherever
I go. 7I do not want to see you now
and make only a passing visit; I
hope to spend some time with you,
if the Lord permits.[j] 8But I will
stay on at Ephesus[k] until Pentecost,[l] 9because a great door for ef-
fective work has opened to me,[m]
and there are many who oppose
me.

10If Timothy[n] comes, see to it
that he has nothing to fear while he
is with you, for he is carrying on the
work of the Lord,[o] just as I am.
11No one, then, should refuse to
accept him.[p] Send him on his way
in peace[q] so that he may return to
me. I am expecting him along with
the brothers.

12Now about our brother Apollos:[r] I strongly urged him to go to
you with the brothers. He was quite
unwilling to go now, but he will go
when he has the opportunity.

13Be on your guard; stand firm[s]
in the faith; be men of courage; be
strong.[t] 14Do everything in love.[u]

15You know that the household
of Stephanas[v] were the first converts[w] in Achaia,[x] and they have
devoted themselves to the service
of the saints. I urge you, brothers,
16to submit[y] to such as these and
to everyone who joins in the work,
and labors at it. 17I was glad when
Stephanas, Fortunatus and Achai-
cus arrived, because they have supplied what was lacking from you.[z]
18For they refreshed[a] my spirit
and yours also. Such men deserve
recognition.[b]

Final Greetings

19The churches in the province
of Asia send you greetings. Aquila
and Priscilla[w][c] greet you warmly
in the Lord, and so does the church
that meets at their house.[d] 20All
the brothers here send you greetings. Greet one another with a holy
kiss.[e]

21I, Paul, write this greeting in
my own hand.[f]

22If anyone does not love the
Lord[g]—a curse[h] be on him.
Come, O Lord[x]![i]

23The grace of the Lord Jesus be
with you.[j]

24My love to all of you in Christ
Jesus. Amen.[y]

16:1 [a]Ac 24:17 [b]Ac 9:13 [c]Ac 16:6
16:2 [d]Ac 20:7 [e]2Co 9:4,5
16:3 [f]2Co 8:18,19
16:5 [g]1Co 4:19 [h]Ac 19:21
16:6 [i]Ro 15:24
16:7 [j]Ac 18:21
16:8 [k]Ac 18:19 [l]Ac 2:1
16:9 [m]Ac 14:27
16:10 [n]Ac 16:1 [o]1Co 15:58
16:11 [p]1Ti 4:12 [q]Ac 15:33
16:12 [r]Ac 18:24; 1Co 1:12
16:13 [s]Gal 5:1; Php 1:27; 1Th 3:8; 2Th 2:15 [t]Eph 6:10
16:14 [u]1Co 14:1
16:15 [v]1Co 1:16 [w]Ro 16:5 [x]Ac 18:12
16:16 [y]Heb 13:17
16:17 [z]2Co 11:9; Php 2:30
16:18 [a]Phm 7 [b]Php 2:29
16:19 [c]Ac 18:2 [d]Ro 16:5
16:20 [e]Ro 16:16
16:21 [f]Gal 6:11; Col 4:18
16:22 [g]Eph 6:24 [h]Ro 9:3 [i]Rev 22:20
16:23 [j]Ro 16:20

[w]*19* Greek *Prisca,* a variant of *Priscilla*
[x]*22* In Aramaic the expression *Come, O Lord* is *Marana tha.*
[y]*24* Some manuscripts do not have *Amen.*

2 Corinthians

Title and Background

This letter seems to have been written a few months after the first letter. The divisions and problems spoken of in 1 Corinthians were still present in the church at Corinth. False teachers were challenging both Paul's personal integrity and his authority as an apostle. They were saying that he was not a genuine apostle and that he was putting into his own pocket the money they had collected for the poverty-stricken believers in Jerusalem.

Author and Date of Writing

Paul was the author of this letter. It is stamped with his style and contains more autobiographical material than any of his other writings. The available evidence indicates that 1 Corinthians was written in the spring of A.D. 55 and that 2 Corinthians was written in the fall of that same year.

Theme and Message

Paul shows his feelings in this letter more than in any other. He goes from despair to ecstatic joy. The letter falls naturally into three sections: (1) Paul explains the reasons for the change of his itinerary (chapters 1-7); (2) he encourages the Corinthians to complete the collection in preparation for his arrival (chapters 8-9); (3) he stresses the certainty of his coming, his authenticity as an apostle and his readiness as an apostle to exercise discipline if necessary (chapters 10-13).

Outline

I. Introduction: Greetings and Thanksgiving (1:1-11)
II. Paul's Explanation of His Conduct and Apostolic Ministry (1:12-7:16)
III. The Collection for the Christians at Jerusalem (8:1-9:15)
IV. Paul's Vindication of His Apostolic Authority (10:1-13:10)
V. Conclusion (13:11-14)

---

1 Paul, an apostle of Christ Jesus by the will of God,[a] and Timothy our brother,

To the church of God[b] in Corinth, together with all the saints throughout Achaia:[c]

2Grace and peace to you from God our Father and the Lord Jesus Christ.[d]

The God of All Comfort

3Praise be to the God and Father of our Lord Jesus Christ,[e] the Father of compassion and the God of all comfort, **4**who comforts us[f] in all our troubles, so that we can comfort those in any trouble with the comfort we ourselves have received from God. **5**For just as the sufferings of Christ flow over into our lives,[g] so also through Christ our comfort overflows. **6**If we are distressed, it is for your comfort and salvation;[h] if we are comforted, it is for your comfort, which produces in you patient endurance of the same sufferings we suffer. **7**And our hope for you is firm, because we know that just as you share in our sufferings,[i] so also you share in our comfort.

8We do not want you to be uninformed, brothers, about the hardships we suffered[j] in the province of Asia. We were under great pres-

1:1 [a] 1Co 1:1; Eph 1:1; Col 1:1; 2Ti 1:1 [b] 1Co 10:32 [c] Ac 18:12
1:2 [d] Ro 1:7
1:3 [e] Eph 1:3; 1Pe 1:3
1:4 [f] 2Co 7:6,7,13
1:5 [g] 2Co 4:10; Col 1:24
1:6 [h] 2Co 4:15
1:7 [i] Ro 8:17
1:8 [j] 1Co 15:32

sure, far beyond our ability to endure, so that we despaired even of
life. **9**Indeed, in our hearts we felt
the sentence of death. But this
happened that we might not rely on
ourselves but on God,[a] who raises
the dead. **10**He has delivered us
from such a deadly peril,[b] and he
will deliver us. On him we have set
our hope that he will continue to
deliver us, **11**as you help us by your
prayers.[c] Then many will give
thanks[d] on our[a] behalf for the gracious favor granted us in answer to
the prayers of many.

Paul's Change of Plans

12Now this is our boast: Our conscience[e] testifies that we have
conducted ourselves in the world,
and especially in our relations with
you, in the holiness and sincerity[f]
that are from God. We have done so
not according to worldly wisdom[g]
but according to God's grace. **13**For
we do not write you anything you
cannot read or understand. And I
hope that, **14**as you have understood us in part, you will come to
understand fully that you can boast
of us just as we will boast of you in
the day of the Lord Jesus.[h]
15Because I was confident of
this, I planned to visit you[i] first so
that you might benefit twice.[j] **16**I
planned to visit you on my way[k] to
Macedonia and to come back to
you from Macedonia, and then to
have you send me on my way to Judea. **17**When I planned this, did I
do it lightly? Or do I make my plans
in a worldly manner[l] so that in the
same breath I say, "Yes, yes" and
"No, no"?
18But as surely as God is faithful,[m] our message to you is not
"Yes" and "No." **19**For the Son of
God, Jesus Christ, who was
preached among you by me and Silas[b] and Timothy, was not "Yes"
and "No," but in him it has always[n] been "Yes." **20**For no matter
how many promises[o] God has
made, they are "Yes" in Christ. And
so through him the "Amen"[p] is
spoken by us to the glory of God.
21Now it is God who makes both us

1:9 [a]Jer 17:5,7
1:10 [b]Ro 15:31
1:11 [c]Ro 15:30; Php 1:19 [d]2Co 4:15
1:12 [e]Ac 23:1 [f]2Co 2:17 [g]1Co 2:1,4,13
1:14 [h]1Co 1:8
1:15 [i]1Co 4:19 [j]Ro 1:11,13; 15:29
1:16 [k]1Co 16:5-7
1:17 [l]2Co 10:2,3
1:18 [m]1Co 1:9
1:19 [n]Heb 13:8
1:20 [o]Ro 15:8 [p]1Co 14:16
1:21 [q]1Jn 2:20,27
1:22 [r]2Co 5:5
1:23 [s]Ro 1:9; Gal 1:20 [t]1Co 4:21; 2Co 2:1,3; 13:2,10
1:24 [u]1Pe 5:3 [v]Ro 11:20; 1Co 15:1
2:1 [w]2Co 1:23
2:2 [x]2Co 7:8
2:3 [y]2Co 7:8,12 [z]2Co 12:21 [a]2Co 8:22; Gal 5:10
2:4 [b]2Co 7:8,12
2:5 [c]1Co 5:1,2
2:6 [d]1Co 5:4,5
2:7 [e]Gal 6:1; Eph 4:32
2:9 [f]2Co 10:6
2:11 [g]Mt 4:10 [h]Lk 22:31; 2Co 4:4; 1Pe 5:8,9
2:12 [i]Ac 16:8 [j]Ro 1:1

and you stand firm in Christ. He
anointed[q] us, **22**set his seal of
ownership on us, and put his Spirit
in our hearts as a deposit, guaranteeing what is to come.[r]
23I call God as my witness[s] that
it was in order to spare you[t] that I
did not return to Corinth. **24**Not
that we lord it over[u] your faith, but
we work with you for your joy, because it is by faith you stand firm.[v]
2 **1**So I made up my mind that I
would not make another pain-
ful visit to you.[w] **2**For if I grieve
you,[x] who is left to make me glad
but you whom I have grieved? **3**I
wrote as I did[y] so that when I came
I should not be distressed[z] by
those who ought to make me rejoice. I had confidence[a] in all of
you, that you would all share my
joy. **4**For I wrote you[b] out of great
distress and anguish of heart and
with many tears, not to grieve you
but to let you know the depth of my
love for you.

Forgiveness for the Sinner

5If anyone has caused grief,[c] he
has not so much grieved me as he
has grieved all of you, to some extent—not to put it too severely.
6The punishment[d] inflicted on
him by the majority is sufficient for
him. **7**Now instead, you ought to
forgive and comfort him,[e] so that
he will not be overwhelmed by excessive sorrow. **8**I urge you, therefore, to reaffirm your love for him.
9The reason I wrote you was to see
if you would stand the test and be
obedient in everything.[f] **10**If you
forgive anyone, I also forgive him.
And what I have forgiven—if there
was anything to forgive—I have forgiven in the sight of Christ for your
sake, **11**in order that Satan[g] might
not outwit us. For we are not unaware of his schemes.[h]

Ministers of the New Covenant

12Now when I went to Troas[i] to
preach the gospel of Christ[j] and
found that the Lord had opened a

[a]*11* Many manuscripts *your* [b]*19* Greek *Silvanus*, a variant of *Silas*

door[a] for me, 13I still had no peace of mind,[b] because I did not find my brother Titus[c] there. So I said good-by to them and went on to Macedonia.

14But thanks be to God,[d] who always leads us in triumphal procession in Christ and through us spreads everywhere the fragrance[e] of the knowledge of him. 15For we are to God the aroma of Christ among those who are being saved and those who are perishing.[f] 16To the one we are the smell of death;[g] to the other, the fragrance of life. And who is equal to such a task?[h] 17Unlike so many, we do not peddle the word of God for profit.[i] On the contrary, in Christ we speak before God with sincerity,[j] like men sent from God.[k]

3 Are we beginning to commend ourselves[l] again? Or do we need, like some people, letters of recommendation[m] to you or from you? 2You yourselves are our letter, written on our hearts, known and read by everybody.[n] 3You show that you are a letter from Christ, the result of our ministry, written not with ink but with the Spirit of the living God, not on tablets of stone[o] but on tablets of human hearts.[p]

4Such confidence[q] as this is ours through Christ before God. 5Not that we are competent in ourselves to claim anything for ourselves, but our competence comes from God.[r] 6He has made us competent as ministers of a new covenant[s]—not of the letter but of the Spirit; for the letter kills, but the Spirit gives life.[t]

The Glory of the New Covenant

7Now if the ministry that brought death, which was engraved in letters on stone, came with glory, so that the Israelites could not look steadily at the face of Moses because of its glory,[u] fading though it was, 8will not the ministry of the Spirit be even more glorious? 9If the ministry that condemns men[v] is glorious, how much more glorious is the ministry that brings righteousness![w] 10For what was glorious has no glory now in comparison with the surpassing glory. 11And if what was fading away came with glory, how much greater is the glory of that which lasts!

12Therefore, since we have such a hope, we are very bold.[x] 13We are not like Moses, who would put a veil over his face[y] to keep the Israelites from gazing at it while the radiance was fading away. 14But their minds were made dull,[z] for to this day the same veil remains when the old covenant[a] is read.[b] It has not been removed, because only in Christ is it taken away. 15Even to this day when Moses is read, a veil covers their hearts. 16But whenever anyone turns to the Lord,[c] the veil is taken away.[d] 17Now the Lord is the Spirit,[e] and where the Spirit of the Lord is, there is freedom.[f] 18And we, who with unveiled faces all reflect[c][g] the Lord's glory,[h] are being transformed into his likeness[i] with ever-increasing glory, which comes from the Lord, who is the Spirit.

Treasures in Jars of Clay

4 Therefore, since through God's mercy[j] we have this ministry, we do not lose heart. 2Rather, we have renounced secret and shameful ways;[k] we do not use deception, nor do we distort the word of God.[l] On the contrary, by setting forth the truth plainly we commend ourselves to every man's conscience[m] in the sight of God. 3And even if our gospel[n] is veiled,[o] it is veiled to those who are perishing.[p] 4The god[q] of this age has blinded[r] the minds of unbelievers, so that they cannot see the light of the gospel of the glory of Christ, who is the image of God. 5For we do not preach ourselves,[s] but Jesus Christ as Lord, and our-

2:12 [a] Ac 14:27
2:13 [b] 2Co 7:5 [c] 2Co 7:6,13; 12:18
2:14 [d] Ro 6:17 [e] Eph 5:2; Php 4:18
2:15 [f] 1Co 1:18
2:16 [g] Lk 2:34 [h] 2Co 3:5,6
2:17 [i] 2Co 4:2 [j] 1Co 5:8 [k] 2Co 1:12
3:1 [l] 2Co 5:12; 12:11 [m] Ac 18:27
3:2 [n] 1Co 9:2
3:3 [o] Ex 24:12 [p] Pr 3:3; Jer 31:33; Eze 11:19
3:4 [q] Eph 3:12
3:5 [r] 1Co 15:10
3:6 [s] Lk 22:20 [t] Jn 6:63
3:7 [u] Ex 34:29-35
3:9 [v] ver 7 [w] Ro 1:17; 3:21,22
3:12 [x] Eph 6:19
3:13 [y] ver 7; Ex 34:33
3:14 [z] Ro 11:7,8 [a] Ac 13:15 [b] ver 6
3:16 [c] Ro 11:23 [d] Ex 34:34
3:17 [e] Isa 61:1,2 [f] Jn 8:32
3:18 [g] 1Co 13:12 [h] 2Co 4:4,6 [i] Ro 8:29
4:1 [j] 1Co 7:25
4:2 [k] 1Co 4:5 [l] 2Co 2:17 [m] 2Co 5:11
4:3 [n] 2Co 2:12 [o] 2Co 3:14 [p] 1Co 1:18
4:4 [q] Jn 12:31 [r] 2Co 3:14
4:5 [s] 1Co 1:13

[c] 18 Or *contemplate*

selves as your servants[a] for Jesus' sake. **6**For God, who said, "Let light shine out of darkness,"[d][b] made his light shine in our hearts[c] to give us the light of the knowledge of the glory of God in the face of Christ.

7But we have this treasure in jars of clay[d] to show that this all-surpassing power is from God[e] and not from us. **8**We are hard pressed on every side,[f] but not crushed; perplexed, but not in despair; **9**persecuted,[g] but not abandoned;[h] struck down, but not destroyed.[i] **10**We always carry around in our body the death of Jesus, so that the life of Jesus may also be revealed in our body.[j] **11**For we who are alive are always being given over to death for Jesus' sake,[k] so that his life may be revealed in our mortal body. **12**So then, death is at work in us, but life is at work in you.[l]

13It is written: "I believed; therefore I have spoken."[e][m] With that same spirit of faith we also believe and therefore speak, **14**because we know that the one who raised the Lord Jesus from the dead will also raise us with Jesus[n] and present us with you in his presence.[o] **15**All this is for your benefit, so that the grace that is reaching more and more people may cause thanksgiving[p] to overflow to the glory of God.

16Therefore we do not lose heart. Though outwardly we are wasting away, yet inwardly[q] we are being renewed[r] day by day. **17**For our light and momentary troubles are achieving for us an eternal glory that far outweighs them all.[s] **18**So we fix our eyes not on what is seen, but on what is unseen.[t] For what is seen is temporary, but what is unseen is eternal.

Our Heavenly Dwelling

5 Now we know that if the earthly[u] tent[v] we live in is destroyed, we have a building from God, an eternal house in heaven, not built by human hands. **2**Meanwhile we groan,[w] longing to be clothed with our heavenly dwelling,[x] **3**because when we are clothed, we will not be found naked. **4**For while we are in this tent, we groan and are burdened, because we do not wish to be unclothed but to be clothed with our heavenly dwelling,[y] so that what is mortal may be swallowed up by life. **5**Now it is God who has made us for this very purpose and has given us the Spirit as a deposit, guaranteeing what is to come.[z]

6Therefore we are always confident and know that as long as we are at home in the body we are away from the Lord. **7**We live by faith, not by sight.[a] **8**We are confident, I say, and would prefer to be away from the body and at home with the Lord.[b] **9**So we make it our goal to please him,[c] whether we are at home in the body or away from it. **10**For we must all appear before the judgment seat of Christ, that each one may receive what is due him[d] for the things done while in the body, whether good or bad.

The Ministry of Reconciliation

11Since, then, we know what it is to fear the Lord,[e] we try to persuade men. What we are is plain to God, and I hope it is also plain to your conscience.[f] **12**We are not trying to commend ourselves to you again,[g] but are giving you an opportunity to take pride in us,[h] so that you can answer those who take pride in what is seen rather than in what is in the heart. **13**If we are out of our mind,[i] it is for the sake of God; if we are in our right mind, it is for you. **14**For Christ's love compels us, because we are convinced that one died for all, and therefore all died.[j] **15**And he died for all, that those who live should no longer live for themselves[k] but for him who died for them and was raised again.

16So from now on we regard no one from a worldly[l] point of view. Though we once regarded Christ in this way, we do so no longer. **17**Therefore, if anyone is in Christ,

4:5 [a] 1Co 9:19
4:6 [b] Ge 1:3 [c] 2Pe 1:19
4:7 [d] Job 4:19; 2Co 5:1 [e] 1Co 2:5
4:8 [f] 2Co 7:5
4:9 [g] Jn 15:20 [h] Heb 13:5 [i] Ps 37:24
4:10 [j] Ro 6:5
4:11 [k] Ro 8:36
4:12 [l] 2Co 13:9
4:13 [m] Ps 116:10
4:14 [n] 1Th 4:14 [o] Eph 5:27
4:15 [p] 2Co 1:11
4:16 [q] Ro 7:22 [r] Col 3:10
4:17 [s] Ro 8:18; 1Pe 1:6,7
4:18 [t] Ro 8:24; Heb 11:1
5:1 [u] 1Co 15:47 [v] 2Pe 1:13,14
5:2 [w] ver 4; Ro 8:23 [x] 1Co 15:53, 54
5:4 [y] 1Co 15:53, 54
5:5 [z] Ro 8:23; 2Co 1:22
5:7 [a] 1Co 13:12
5:8 [b] Php 1:23
5:9 [c] Ro 14:18
5:10 [d] Mt 16:27; Ro 14:10; Eph 6:8
5:11 [e] Heb 10:31; Jude 23 [f] 2Co 4:2
5:12 [g] 2Co 3:1 [h] 2Co 1:14
5:13 [i] 2Co 11:1,16, 17
5:14 [j] Gal 2:20
5:15 [k] Ro 14:7-9
5:16 [l] 2Co 11:18

[d]6 Gen. 1:3 [e]13 Psalm 116:10

he is a new creation;[a] the old has
gone, the new has come![b] **18**All
this is from God, who reconciled us
to himself through Christ[c] and
gave us the ministry of reconciliation: **19**that God was reconciling
the world to himself in Christ, not
counting men's sins against
them.[d] And he has committed to
us the message of reconciliation.
20We are therefore Christ's ambassadors,[e] as though God were making his appeal through us. We implore you on Christ's behalf: Be
reconciled to God. **21**God made
him who had no sin[f] to be sin[f] for
us, so that in him we might become
the righteousness of God.[g]
6 As God's fellow workers[h] we
urge you not to receive God's
grace in vain. **2**For he says,

> "In the time of my favor I heard
> you,
> and in the day of salvation I
> helped you."[g][i]

I tell you, now is the time of God's
favor, now is the day of salvation.

Paul's Hardships

3We put no stumbling block in
anyone's path,[j] so that our ministry will not be discredited. **4**Rather,
as servants of God we commend
ourselves in every way: in great endurance; in troubles, hardships
and distresses; **5**in beatings, im-
prisonments[k] and riots; in hard
work, sleepless nights and hunger;[l] **6**in purity, understanding,
patience and kindness; in the Holy
Spirit[m] and in sincere love; **7**in
truthful speech[n] and in the power
of God; with weapons of righteousness[o] in the right hand and in the
left; **8**through glory and dishonor,[p]
bad report and good report; genuine, yet regarded as impostors;[q]
9known, yet regarded as unknown;
dying,[r] and yet we live on;[s] beat-
en, and yet not killed; **10**sorrowful,
yet always rejoicing;[t] poor, yet
making many rich;[u] having nothing, and yet possessing everything.[v]
11We have spoken freely to you,
Corinthians, and opened wide our

5:17 [a]Gal 6:15 [b]Isa 65:17; Rev 21:4,5
5:18 [c]Ro 5:10; Col 1:20
5:19 [d]Ro 4:8
5:20 [e]2Co 6:1; Eph 6:20
5:21 [f]Heb 4:15; 1Pe 2:22,24; 1Jn 3:5 [g]Ro 1:17
6:1 [h]1Co 3:9; 2Co 5:20
6:2 [i]Isa 49:8
6:3 [j]Ro 14:13,20; 1Co 9:12; 10:32
6:5 [k]2Co 11:23-25 [l]1Co 4:11
6:6 [m]1Th 1:5
6:7 [n]2Co 4:2 [o]2Co 10:4; Eph 6:10-18
6:8 [p]1Co 4:10 [q]Mt 27:63
6:9 [r]Ro 8:36 [s]2Co 1:8-10; 4:10,11
6:10 [t]2Co 7:4 [u]2Co 8:9 [v]Ro 8:32; 1Co 3:21
6:11 [w]2Co 7:3
6:13 [x]1Co 4:14
6:14 [y]1Co 5:9,10 [z]Eph 5:7,11; 1Jn 1:6
6:15 [a]Ac 5:14
6:16 [b]1Co 3:16 [c]Lev 26:12; Jer 32:38; Eze 37:27
6:17 [d]Rev 18:4 [e]Isa 52:11
6:18 [f]Isa 43:6
7:1 [g]2Co 6:17,18
7:2 [h]2Co 6:12,13
7:3 [i]2Co 6:11,12

hearts to you.[w] **12**We are not withholding our affection from you, but
you are withholding yours from us.
13As a fair exchange—I speak as to
my children[x]—open wide your
hearts also.

Do Not Be Yoked With Unbelievers

14Do not be yoked together[y]
with unbelievers. For what do righteousness and wickedness have in
common? Or what fellowship can
light have with darkness?[z] **15**What
harmony is there between Christ
and Belial[h]? What does a believer[a] have in common with an unbeliever? **16**What agreement is there
between the temple of God and
idols? For we are the temple[b] of
the living God. As God has said: "I
will live with them and walk among
them, and I will be their God, and
they will be my people."[i][c]

> **17**"Therefore come out from
> them[d]
> and be separate,
> says the Lord.
> Touch no unclean thing,
> and I will receive you."[j][e]
> **18**"I will be a Father to you,
> and you will be my sons and
> daughters,[f]
> says the Lord
> Almighty."[k]

7 Since we have these promises,[g] dear friends, let us purify ourselves from everything that
contaminates body and spirit, per-
fecting holiness out of reverence
for God.

Paul's Joy

2Make room for us in your
hearts.[h] We have wronged no one,
we have corrupted no one, we have
exploited no one. **3**I do not say this
to condemn you; I have said before
that you have such a place in our
hearts[i] that we would live or die
with you. **4**I have great confidence

[f]*21* Or *be a sin offering* [g]*2* Isaiah 49:8
[h]*15* Greek *Beliar*, a variant of *Belial*
[i]*16* Lev. 26:12; Jer. 32:38; Ezek. 37:27
[j]*17* Isaiah 52:11; Ezek. 20:34,41
[k]*18* 2 Samuel 7:14; 7:8

in you; I take great pride in you. I
am greatly encouraged; in all our
troubles my joy knows no
bounds.[a]
5For when we came into Macedonia,[b] this body of ours had no
rest, but we were harassed at every
turn[c]—conflicts on the outside,
fears within.[d] 6But God, who comforts the downcast,[e] comforted us
by the coming of Titus,[f] 7and not
only by his coming but also by the
comfort you had given him. He told
us about your longing for me, your
deep sorrow, your ardent concern
for me, so that my joy was greater
than ever.
8Even if I caused you sorrow by
my letter,[g] I do not regret it.
Though I did regret it—I see that
my letter hurt you, but only for a
little while— 9yet now I am happy,
not because you were made sorry,
but because your sorrow led you to
repentance. For you became sorrowful as God intended and so
were not harmed in any way by us.
10Godly sorrow brings repentance
that leads to salvation[h] and leaves
no regret, but worldly sorrow brings
death. 11See what this godly sorrow
has produced in you: what earnestness, what eagerness to clear yourselves, what indignation, what
alarm, what longing, what concern,[i] what readiness to see justice done. At every point you have
proved yourselves to be innocent in
this matter. 12So even though I
wrote to you,[j] it was not on account of the one who did the
wrong[k] or of the injured party, but
rather that before God you could
see for yourselves how devoted to
us you are. 13By all this we are encouraged.
In addition to our own encouragement, we were especially delighted to see how happy Titus[l]
was, because his spirit has been refreshed by all of you. 14I had boasted to him about you,[m] and you
have not embarrassed me. But just
as everything we said to you was
true, so our boasting about you to
Titus[n] has proved to be true as
well. 15And his affection for you is

7:4 [a] 2Co 6:10
7:5 [b] 2Co 2:13 [c] 2Co 4:8 [d] Dt 32:25
7:6 [e] 2Co 1:3,4 [f] ver 13; 2Co 2:13
7:8 [g] 2Co 2:2,4
7:10 [h] Ac 11:18
7:11 [i] ver 7
7:12 [j] ver 8; 2Co 2:3,9 [k] 1Co 5:1,2
7:13 [l] ver 6; 2Co 2:13
7:14 [m] ver 4 [n] ver 6
7:15 [o] 2Co 2:9 [p] Php 2:12
7:16 [q] 2Co 2:3
8:1 [r] Ac 16:9
8:3 [s] 1Co 16:2
8:4 [t] Ac 24:17 [u] Ro 15:25; 2Co 9:1
8:6 [v] ver 17; 2Co 12:18 [w] ver 16,23 [x] ver 10,11
8:7 [y] 2Co 9:8 [z] 1Co 1:5
8:8 [a] 1Co 7:6
8:9 [b] 2Co 13:14 [c] Mt 20:28; Php 2:6-8
8:10 [d] 1Co 7:25,40 [e] 1Co 16:2,3; 2Co 9:2
8:11 [f] 2Co 9:2
8:12 [g] Mk 12:43,44; Lk 21:3

all the greater when he remembers
that you were all obedient,[o] receiving him with fear and trembling.[p] 16I am glad I can have complete confidence in you.[q]

Generosity Encouraged

8 And now, brothers, we want
you to know about the grace
that God has given the Macedoni-
an[r] churches. 2Out of the most severe trial, their overflowing joy and
their extreme poverty welled up in
rich generosity. 3For I testify that
they gave as much as they were
able,[s] and even beyond their ability. Entirely on their own, 4they urgently pleaded with us for the privi-
lege of sharing in this service[t] to
the saints.[u] 5And they did not do
as we expected, but they gave
themselves first to the Lord and
then to us in keeping with God's
will. 6So we urged[v] Titus,[w] since
he had earlier made a beginning, to
bring also to completion[x] this act
of grace on your part. 7But just as
you excel in everything[y]—in faith,
in speech, in knowledge,[z] in complete earnestness and in your love
for us[1]—see that you also excel in
this grace of giving.
8I am not commanding you,[a]
but I want to test the sincerity of
your love by comparing it with the
earnestness of others. 9For you
know the grace of our Lord Jesus
Christ,[b] that though he was rich,
yet for your sakes he became
poor,[c] so that you through his poverty might become rich.
10And here is my advice[d] about
what is best for you in this matter:
Last year you were the first not only
to give but also to have the desire
to do so.[e] 11Now finish the work,
so that your eager willingness[f] to
do it may be matched by your completion of it, according to your
means. 12For if the willingness is
there, the gift is acceptable according to what one has,[g] not according to what he does not have.
13Our desire is not that others
might be relieved while you are

[1]7 Some manuscripts *in our love for you*

hard pressed, but that there might be equality. **14**At the present time your plenty will supply what they need,[a] so that in turn their plenty will supply what you need. Then there will be equality, **15**as it is written: "He who gathered much did not have too much, and he who gathered little did not have too little."[m][b]

Titus Sent to Corinth

16I thank God,[c] who put into the heart[d] of Titus[e] the same concern I have for you. **17**For Titus not only welcomed our appeal, but he is coming to you with much enthusiasm and on his own initiative.[f] **18**And we are sending along with him the brother[g] who is praised by all the churches[h] for his service to the gospel.[i] **19**What is more, he was chosen by the churches to accompany us[j] as we carry the offering, which we administer in order to honor the Lord himself and to show our eagerness to help.[k] **20**We want to avoid any criticism of the way we administer this liberal gift. **21**For we are taking pains to do what is right, not only in the eyes of the Lord but also in the eyes of men.[l]

22In addition, we are sending with them our brother who has often proved to us in many ways that he is zealous, and now even more so because of his great confidence in you. **23**As for Titus, he is my partner[m] and fellow worker[n] among you; as for our brothers,[o] they are representatives of the churches and an honor to Christ. **24**Therefore show these men the proof of your love and the reason for our pride in you,[p] so that the churches can see it.

9 There is no need[q] for me to write to you about this service to the saints.[r] **2**For I know your eagerness to help, and I have been boasting[s] about it to the Macedonians, telling them that since last year[t] you in Achaia[u] were ready to give; and your enthusiasm has stirred most of them to action. **3**But I am sending the brothers in order that our boasting about you in this matter should not prove hollow, but that you may be ready, as I said you would be.[v] **4**For if any Macedonians[w] come with me and find you unprepared, we—not to say anything about you—would be ashamed of having been so confident. **5**So I thought it necessary to urge the brothers to visit you in advance and finish the arrangements for the generous gift you had promised. Then it will be ready as a generous gift,[x] not as one grudgingly given.[y]

Sowing Generously

6Remember this: Whoever sows sparingly will also reap sparingly, and whoever sows generously will also reap generously.[z] **7**Each man should give what he has decided in his heart to give,[a] not reluctantly or under compulsion,[b] for God loves a cheerful giver.[c] **8**And God is able[d] to make all grace abound to you, so that in all things at all times, having all that you need,[e] you will abound in every good work. **9**As it is written:

"He has scattered abroad his
gifts to the poor;
his righteousness endures
forever."[n][f]

10Now he who supplies seed to the sower and bread for food[g] will also supply and increase your store of seed and will enlarge the harvest of your righteousness.[h] **11**You will be made rich[i] in every way so that you can be generous on every occasion, and through us your generosity will result in thanksgiving to God.[j]

12This service that you perform is not only supplying the needs[k] of God's people but is also overflowing in many expressions of thanks to God.[l] **13**Because of the service[m] by which you have proved yourselves, men will praise God[n] for the obedience that accompanies your confession of the gospel of Christ,[o] and for your generosity in

8:14 [a]2Co 9:12
8:15 [b]Ex 16:18
8:16 [c]2Co 2:14 [d]Rev 17:17 [e]2Co 2:13
8:17 [f]ver 6
8:18 [g]2Co 12:18 [h]1Co 7:17 [i]2Co 2:12
8:19 [j]1Co 16:3,4 [k]ver 11,12
8:21 [l]Ro 12:17; 14:18
8:23 [m]Phm 17 [n]Php 2:25 [o]ver 18,22
8:24 [p]2Co 7:4,14; 9:2
9:1 [q]1Th 4:9 [r]2Co 8:4
9:2 [s]2Co 7:4,14 [t]2Co 8:10 [u]Ac 18:12
9:3 [v]1Co 16:2
9:4 [w]Ro 15:26
9:5 [x]Php 4:17 [y]2Co 12:17, 18
9:6 [z]Pr 11:24,25; 22:9; Gal 6:7, 9
9:7 [a]Ex 25:2; 2Co 8:12 [b]Dt 15:10 [c]Ro 12:8
9:8 [d]Eph 3:20 [e]Php 4:19
9:9 [f]Ps 112:9
9:10 [g]Isa 55:10 [h]Hos 10:12
9:11 [i]1Co 1:5 [j]2Co 1:11
9:12 [k]2Co 8:14 [l]2Co 1:11
9:13 [m]2Co 8:4 [n]Mt 9:8 [o]2Co 2:12

[m]15 Exodus 16:18 [n]9 Psalm 112:9

sharing with them and with everyone else. 14And in their prayers for you their hearts will go out to you, because of the surpassing grace God has given you. 15Thanks be to God[a] for his indescribable gift![b]

Paul's Defense of His Ministry

10 By the meekness and gentleness[c] of Christ, I appeal to you—I, Paul,[d] who am "timid" when face to face with you, but "bold" when away! 2I beg you that when I come I may not have to be as bold[e] as I expect to be toward some people who think that we live by the standards of this world. 3For though we live in the world, we do not wage war as the world does. 4The weapons we fight with[f] are not the weapons of the world. On the contrary, they have divine power[g] to demolish strongholds.[h] 5We demolish arguments and every pretension that sets itself up against the knowledge of God,[i] and we take captive every thought to make it obedient[j] to Christ. 6And we will be ready to punish every act of disobedience, once your obedience is complete.[k]

7You are looking only on the surface of things.[o][l] If anyone is confident that he belongs to Christ,[m] he should consider again that we belong to Christ just as much as he.[n] 8For even if I boast somewhat freely about the authority the Lord gave us for building you up rather than pulling you down,[o] I will not be ashamed of it. 9I do not want to seem to be trying to frighten you with my letters. 10For some say, "His letters are weighty and forceful, but in person he is unimpressive[p] and his speaking amounts to nothing."[q] 11Such people should realize that what we are in our letters when we are absent, we will be in our actions when we are present.

12We do not dare to classify or compare ourselves with some who commend themselves.[r] When they measure themselves by themselves and compare themselves with themselves, they are not wise. 13We, however, will not boast beyond proper limits, but will confine our boasting to the field God has assigned to us,[s] a field that reaches even to you. 14We are not going too far in our boasting, as would be the case if we had not come to you, for we did get as far as you[t] with the gospel of Christ.[u] 15Neither do we go beyond our limits by boasting of work done by others.[p][v] Our hope is that, as your faith continues to grow,[w] our area of activity among you will greatly expand, 16so that we can preach the gospel in the regions beyond you.[x] For we do not want to boast about work already done in another man's territory. 17But, "Let him who boasts boast in the Lord."[q][y] 18For it is not the one who commends himself[z] who is approved, but the one whom the Lord commends.[a]

Paul and the False Apostles

11 I hope you will put up with[b] a little of my foolishness;[c] but you are already doing that. 2I am jealous for you with a godly jealousy. I promised you to one husband,[d] to Christ, so that I might present you[e] as a pure virgin to him. 3But I am afraid that just as Eve was deceived by the serpent's cunning,[f] your minds may somehow be led astray from your sincere and pure devotion to Christ. 4For if someone comes to you and preaches a Jesus other than the Jesus we preached,[g] or if you receive a different spirit[h] from the one you received, or a different gospel[i] from the one you accepted, you put up with it easily enough. 5But I do not think I am in the least inferior to those "super-apostles."[j] 6I may not be a trained speaker,[k] but I do have knowl-

9:15 [a] 2Co 2:14 [b] Ro 5:15,16
10:1 [c] Mt 11:29 [d] Gal 5:2
10:2 [e] 1Co 4:21; 2Co 13:2,10
10:4 [f] 2Co 6:7 [g] 1Co 2:5 [h] Jer 1:10; 2Co 13:10
10:5 [i] Isa 2:11,12; 1Co 1:19 [j] 2Co 9:13
10:6 [k] 2Co 2:9; 7:15
10:7 [l] Jn 7:24 [m] 1Co 1:12; 3:23; 14:37 [n] 2Co 11:23
10:8 [o] 2Co 13:10
10:10 [p] 1Co 2:3; Gal 4:13,14 [q] 1Co 1:17
10:12 [r] 2Co 3:1
10:13 [s] ver 15,16
10:14 [t] 1Co 3:6 [u] 2Co 2:12
10:15 [v] Ro 15:20 [w] 2Th 1:3
10:16 [x] Ac 19:21
10:17 [y] Jer 9:24; 1Co 1:31
10:18 [z] ver 12 [a] Ro 2:29; 1Co 4:5
11:1 [b] ver 4,19,20; Mt 17:17 [c] ver 16,17,21; 2Co 5:13
11:2 [d] Hos 2:19; Eph 5:26,27 [e] 2Co 4:14
11:3 [f] Ge 3:1-6,13; Jn 8:44; 1Ti 2:14; Rev 12:9
11:4 [g] 1Co 3:11 [h] Ro 8:15 [i] Gal 1:6-9
11:5 [j] 2Co 12:11; Gal 2:6
11:6 [k] 1Co 1:17

o7 Or *Look at the obvious facts* p13-15 Or *13We, however, will not boast about things that cannot be measured, but we will boast according to the standard of measurement that the God of measure has assigned us—a measurement that relates even to you. 14 . . . . 15Neither do we boast about things that cannot be measured in regard to the work done by others.* q17 Jer. 9:24

edge.[a] We have made this perfectly clear to you in every way.
7Was it a sin[b] for me to lower
myself in order to elevate you by
preaching the gospel of God to you
free of charge?[c] **8**I robbed other
churches by receiving support from
them[d] so as to serve you. **9**And
when I was with you and needed
something, I was not a burden to
anyone, for the brothers who came
from Macedonia supplied what I
needed. I have kept myself from
being a burden to you[e] in any way,
and will continue to do so. **10**As
surely as the truth of Christ is in
me,[f] nobody in the regions of
Achaia[g] will stop this boasting[h] of
mine. **11**Why? Because I do not love
you? God knows I do![i] **12**And I will
keep on doing what I am doing in
order to cut the ground from under
those who want an opportunity to
be considered equal with us in the
things they boast about.
13For such men are false apostles,[j] deceitful[k] workmen, mas-
querading as apostles of Christ.[l]
14And no wonder, for Satan himself
masquerades as an angel of light.
15It is not surprising, then, if his
servants masquerade as servants of
righteousness. Their end will be
what their actions deserve.[m]

Paul Boasts About His Sufferings

16I repeat: Let no one take me
for a fool.[n] But if you do, then receive me just as you would a fool,
so that I may do a little boasting.
17In this self-confident boasting I
am not talking as the Lord would,[o]
but as a fool. **18**Since many are
boasting in the way the world does,
I too will boast.[p] **19**You gladly put
up with fools since you are so
wise![q] **20**In fact, you even put up
with anyone who enslaves you[r] or
exploits you or takes advantage of
you or pushes himself forward or
slaps you in the face. **21**To my
shame I admit that we were too
weak[s] for that!
What anyone else dares to boast
about—I am speaking as a fool—I
also dare to boast about.[t] **22**Are
they Hebrews? So am I.[u] Are they
Israelites? So am I.[v] Are they Abraham's descendants? So am I. **23**Are
they servants of Christ? (I am out of
my mind to talk like this.) I am
more. I have worked much harder,[w] been in prison more frequently,[x] been flogged more severely,
and been exposed to death again
and again. **24**Five times I received
from the Jews the forty lashes[y] mi-
nus one. **25**Three times I was beat-
en with rods,[z] once I was stoned,[a]
three times I was shipwrecked, I
spent a night and a day in the open
sea, **26**I have been constantly on
the move. I have been in danger
from rivers, in danger from bandits,
in danger from my own countrymen,[b] in danger from Gentiles; in
danger in the city,[c] in danger in
the country, in danger at sea; and
in danger from false brothers.[d] **27**I
have labored and toiled and have
often gone without sleep; I have
known hunger and thirst and have
often gone without food;[e] I have
been cold and naked. **28**Besides everything else, I face daily the pressure of my concern for all the
churches. **29**Who is weak, and I do
not feel weak? Who is led into sin,
and I do not inwardly burn?
30If I must boast, I will boast of
the things that show my weakness.[f] **31**The God and Father of
the Lord Jesus, who is to be praised
forever,[g] knows that I am not lying. **32**In Damascus the governor
under King Aretas had the city of
the Damascenes guarded in order
to arrest me.[h] **33**But I was lowered
in a basket from a window in the
wall and slipped through his
hands.[i]

Paul's Vision and His Thorn

12 I must go on boasting.[j] Although there is nothing to
be gained, I will go on to visions
and revelations[k] from the Lord. **2**I
know a man in Christ who fourteen
years ago was caught up[l] to the
third heaven.[m] Whether it was in
the body or out of the body I do not
know—God knows.[n] **3**And I know

11:6 [a]Eph 3:4
11:7 [b]2Co 12:13 [c]1Co 9:18
11:8 [d]Php 4:15,18
11:9 [e]2Co 12:13, 14,16
11:10 [f]Ro 9:1 [g]Ac 18:12 [h]1Co 9:15
11:11 [i]2Co 12:15
11:13 [j]2Pe 2:1 [k]Tit 1:10 [l]Rev 2:2
11:15 [m]Php 3:19
11:16 [n]ver 1
11:17 [o]1Co 7:12,25
11:18 [p]Php 3:3,4
11:19 [q]1Co 4:10
11:20 [r]Gal 2:4
11:21 [s]2Co 10:1,10 [t]Php 3:4
11:22 [u]Php 3:5 [v]Ro 9:4
11:23 [w]1Co 15:10 [x]Ac 16:23; 2Co 6:4,5
11:24 [y]Dt 25:3
11:25 [z]Ac 16:22 [a]Ac 14:19
11:26 [b]Ac 9:23; 14:5 [c]Ac 21:31 [d]Gal 2:4
11:27 [e]1Co 4:11,12; 2Co 6:5
11:30 [f]1Co 2:3
11:31 [g]Ro 9:5
11:32 [h]Ac 9:24
11:33 [i]Ac 9:25
12:1 [j]2Co 11:16,30 [k]ver 7
12:2 [l]Ac 8:39 [m]Eph 4:10 [n]2Co 11:11

that this man—whether in the body or apart from the body I do not know, but God knows— **4**was caught up to paradise.[a] He heard inexpressible things, things that man is not permitted to tell. **5**I will boast about a man like that, but I will not boast about myself, except about my weaknesses. **6**Even if I should choose to boast, I would not be a fool,[b] because I would be speaking the truth. But I refrain, so no one will think more of me than is warranted by what I do or say.

7To keep me from becoming conceited because of these surpassingly great revelations, there was given me a thorn in my flesh,[c] a messenger of Satan, to torment me. **8**Three times I pleaded with the Lord to take it away from me.[d] **9**But he said to me, "My grace is sufficient for you, for my power[e] is made perfect in weakness." Therefore I will boast all the more gladly about my weaknesses, so that Christ's power may rest on me. **10**That is why, for Christ's sake, I delight in weaknesses, in insults, in hardships,[f] in persecutions,[g] in difficulties. For when I am weak, then I am strong.[h]

Paul's Concern for the Corinthians

11I have made a fool of myself,[i] but you drove me to it. I ought to have been commended by you, for I am not in the least inferior to the "super-apostles,"[j] even though I am nothing.[k] **12**The things that mark an apostle—signs, wonders and miracles[l]—were done among you with great perseverance. **13**How were you inferior to the other churches, except that I was never a burden to you?[m] Forgive me this wrong![n]

14Now I am ready to visit you for the third time,[o] and I will not be a burden to you, because what I want is not your possessions but you. After all, children should not have to save up for their parents,[p] but parents for their children.[q] **15**So I will very gladly spend for you everything I have and expend myself as well.[r] If I love you more, will you love me less? **16**Be that as it may, I have not been a burden to you.[s] Yet, crafty fellow that I am, I caught you by trickery! **17**Did I exploit you through any of the men I sent you? **18**I urged[t] Titus to go to you and I sent our brother[u] with him. Titus did not exploit you, did he? Did we not act in the same spirit and follow the same course?

19Have you been thinking all along that we have been defending ourselves to you? We have been speaking in the sight of God[v] as those in Christ; and everything we do, dear friends, is for your strengthening.[w] **20**For I am afraid that when I come[x] I may not find you as I want you to be, and you may not find me as you want me to be.[y] I fear that there may be quarreling,[z] jealousy, outbursts of anger, factions,[a] slander, gossip,[b] arrogance and disorder.[c] **21**I am afraid that when I come again my God will humble me before you, and I will be grieved[d] over many who have sinned earlier[e] and have not repented of the impurity, sexual sin and debauchery in which they have indulged.

Final Warnings

13 This will be my third visit to you.[f] "Every matter must be established by the testimony of two or three witnesses."[r][g] **2**I already gave you a warning when I was with you the second time. I now repeat it while absent: On my return I will not spare[h] those who sinned earlier[i] or any of the others, **3**since you are demanding proof that Christ is speaking through me.[j] He is not weak in dealing with you, but is powerful among you. **4**For to be sure, he was crucified in weakness,[k] yet he lives by God's power.[l] Likewise, we are weak[m] in him, yet by God's power we will live with him to serve you.

5Examine yourselves[n] to see

12:4 [a]Lk 23:43; Rev 2:7
12:6 [b]2Co 11:16
12:7 [c]Nu 33:55
12:8 [d]Mt 26:39,44
12:9 [e]Php 4:13
12:10 [f]2Co 6:4 [g]Ro 5:3; 2Th 1:4 [h]2Co 13:4
12:11 [i]2Co 11:1 [j]2Co 11:5 [k]1Co 15:9,10
12:12 [l]Jn 4:48
12:13 [m]1Co 9:12,18 [n]2Co 11:7
12:14 [o]2Co 13:1 [p]1Co 4:14,15 [q]Pr 19:14
12:15 [r]Php 2:17; 1Th 2:8
12:16 [s]2Co 11:9
12:18 [t]2Co 8:6,16 [u]2Co 8:18
12:19 [v]Ro 9:1 [w]2Co 10:8
12:20 [x]2Co 2:1-4 [y]1Co 4:21 [z]1Co 1:11; 3:3 [a]Gal 5:20 [b]Ro 1:29 [c]1Co 14:33
12:21 [d]2Co 2:1,4 [e]2Co 13:2
13:1 [f]2Co 12:14 [g]Dt 19:15; Mt 18:16
13:2 [h]2Co 1:23 [i]2Co 12:21
13:3 [j]Mt 10:20; 1Co 5:4
13:4 [k]Php 2:7,8; 1Pe 3:18 [l]Ro 1:4; 6:4 [m]ver 9
13:5 [n]1Co 11:28

[r]*1* Deut. 19:15

whether you are in the faith; test
yourselves.[a] Do you not realize
that Christ Jesus is in you[b]—unless, of course, you fail the test?
6And I trust that you will discover
that we have not failed the test.
7Now we pray to God that you will
not do anything wrong. Not that
people will see that we have stood
the test but that you will do what is
right even though we may seem to
have failed. 8For we cannot do anything against the truth, but only for
the truth. 9We are glad whenever
we are weak but you are strong; and
our prayer is for your perfection.[c]
10This is why I write these things
when I am absent, that when I
come I may not have to be harsh in
my use of authority—the authority
the Lord gave me for building you
up, not for tearing you down.[d]

Final Greetings

11Finally, brothers,[e] good-by.
Aim for perfection, listen to my appeal, be of one mind, live in
peace.[f] And the God of love and
peace[g] will be with you.
12Greet one another with a holy
kiss.[h] 13All the saints send their
greetings.[i]
14May the grace of the Lord
Jesus Christ,[j] and the love of
God,[k] and the fellowship of the
Holy Spirit[l] be with you all.

13:5 [a] Jn 6:6 [b] Ro 8:10
13:9 [c] ver 11
13:10 [d] 2Co 10:8
13:11 [e] 1Th 4:1; 2Th 3:1 [f] Mk 9:50 [g] Ro 15:33; Eph 6:23
13:12 [h] Ro 16:16
13:13 [i] Php 4:22
13:14 [j] Ro 16:20; 2Co 8:9 [k] Ro 5:5; Jude 21 [l] Php 2:1

Galatians

Title and Background

Judaizers were Jewish Christians who believed, among other things, that a number of the ceremonial practices of the Old Testament were still binding on the New Testament church. Following Paul's successful campaign in Galatia, they insisted that Gentile converts to Christianity abide by certain Old Testament rites, especially circumcision. The Judaizers argued that Paul was not an authentic apostle and that out of a desire to make the message more appealing to Gentiles he had removed from the gospel certain legal requirements. Paul responds by writing this letter.

Author and Date of Writing

The opening verse identifies the author as the apostle Paul. Various dates have been given for the writing of this letter, but it was probably written around A.D. 50.

Theme and Message

Galatians stands as an eloquent and vigorous defense for the essential New Testament truth that we are justified by faith in Jesus Christ—by nothing less and nothing more—and that we are sanctified by the obedience that comes from faith in God's work for us, in us and through us by the grace and power of Christ and the Holy Spirit. Some have called the letter the *Magna Charta* of Christian liberty.

Outline

I. Introduction: Greetings and Denunciation (1:1-9)
II. Authentication of the Apostle of Liberty and Faith (1:10-2:21)
III. Justification of the Doctrine of Liberty and Faith (3:1-4:31)
IV. Practice of the Life of Liberty and Faith (5:1-6:10)
V. Conclusion (6:11-18)

---

1 Paul, an apostle—sent not
from men nor by man, but by
Jesus Christ[a] *and God the Father,*
who raised him from the dead[b]—
2and all the brothers with me,[c]

To the churches in Galatia:[d]

3Grace and peace to you from
God our Father and the Lord Jesus
Christ,[e] **4**who gave himself for our
sins[f] to rescue us from the present
evil age, according to the will of our
God and Father,[g] **5**to whom be glory for ever and ever. Amen.[h]

No Other Gospel

6I am astonished that you are so
quickly deserting the one who
called[i] you by the grace of Christ
and are turning to a different gospel[j]— **7**which is really no gospel
at all. Evidently some people are
throwing you into confusion[k] and
are trying to pervert the gospel of
Christ. **8**But even if we or an angel
from heaven should preach a gospel other than the one we preached
to you,[l] let him be eternally condemned![m] **9**As we have already
said, so now I say again: If anybody
is preaching to you a gospel other
than what you accepted,[n] let him
be eternally condemned!

10Am I now trying to win the approval of men, or of God? Or am I
trying to please men?[o] If I were
still trying to please men, I would
not be a servant of Christ.

1:1 [a]Ac 9:15 [b]Ac 2:24
1:2 [c]Php 4:21 [d]Ac 16:6; 1Co 16:1
1:3 [e]Ro 1:7
1:4 [f]Mt 20:28; Ro 4:25; Gal 2:20 [g]Php 4:20
1:5 [h]Ro 11:36
1:6 [i]Gal 5:8 [j]2Co 11:4
1:7 [k]Ac 15:24; Gal 5:10
1:8 [l]2Co 11:4 [m]Ro 9:3
1:9 [n]Ro 16:17
1:10 [o]Ro 2:29; 1Th 2:4

Paul Called by God

11 I want you to know, brothers,[a] that the gospel I preached is not something that man made up. 12 I did not receive it from any man,[b] nor was I taught it; rather, I received it by revelation[c] from Jesus Christ.

13 For you have heard of my previous way of life in Judaism,[d] how intensely I persecuted the church of God and tried to destroy it.[e] 14 I was advancing in Judaism beyond many Jews of my own age and was extremely zealous for the traditions of my fathers.[f] 15 But when God, who set me apart from birth[a][g] and called me[h] by his grace, was pleased 16 to reveal his Son in me so that I might preach him among the Gentiles,[i] I did not consult any man,[j] 17 nor did I go up to Jerusalem to see those who were apostles before I was, but I went immediately into Arabia and later returned to Damascus.

18 Then after three years,[k] I went up to Jerusalem[l] to get acquainted with Peter[b] and stayed with him fifteen days. 19 I saw none of the other apostles—only James,[m] the Lord's brother. 20 I assure you before God that what I am writing you is no lie.[n] 21 Later I went to Syria and Cilicia.[o] 22 I was personally unknown to the churches of Judea[p] that are in Christ. 23 They only heard the report: "The man who formerly persecuted us is now preaching the faith[q] he once tried to destroy." 24 And they praised God[r] because of me.

Paul Accepted by the Apostles

2 Fourteen years later I went up again to Jerusalem,[s] this time with Barnabas. I took Titus along also. 2 I went in response to a revelation and set before them the gospel that I preach among the Gentiles.[t] But I did this privately to those who seemed to be leaders, for fear that I was running or had run my race[u] in vain. 3 Yet not even Titus,[v] who was with me, was compelled to be circumcised, even though he was a Greek.[w] 4 This matter arose, because some false brothers[x] had infiltrated our ranks to spy on[y] the freedom[z] we have in Christ Jesus and to make us slaves. 5 We did not give in to them for a moment, so that the truth of the gospel[a] might remain with you.

6 As for those who seemed to be important[b]—whatever they were makes no difference to me; God does not judge by external appearance[c]—those men added nothing to my message. 7 On the contrary, they saw that I had been entrusted with the task[d] of preaching the gospel to the Gentiles,[c][e] just as Peter[f] had been to the Jews.[d] 8 For God, who was at work in the ministry of Peter as an apostle[g] to the Jews, was also at work in my ministry as an apostle to the Gentiles. 9 James, Peter[e][h] and John, those reputed to be pillars,[i] gave me and Barnabas[j] the right hand of fellowship when they recognized the grace given to me.[k] They agreed that we should go to the Gentiles, and they to the Jews. 10 All they asked was that we should continue to remember the poor,[l] the very thing I was eager to do.

Paul Opposes Peter

11 When Peter[m] came to Antioch,[n] I opposed him to his face, because he was clearly in the wrong. 12 Before certain men came from James, he used to eat with the Gentiles.[o] But when they arrived, he began to draw back and separate himself from the Gentiles because he was afraid of those who belonged to the circumcision group.[p] 13 The other Jews joined him in his hypocrisy, so that by their hypocrisy even Barnabas[q] was led astray.

14 When I saw that they were not acting in line with the truth of the gospel,[r] I said to Peter[s] in front of

1:11 [a] 1Co 15:1
1:12 [b] ver 1 [c] ver 16
1:13 [d] Ac 26:4,5 [e] Ac 8:3
1:14 [f] Mt 15:2
1:15 [g] Isa 49:1,5; Jer 1:5 [h] Ac 9:15
1:16 [i] Gal 2:9 [j] Mt 16:17
1:18 [k] Ac 9:22,23 [l] Ac 9:26,27
1:19 [m] Mt 13:55
1:20 [n] Ro 9:1
1:21 [o] Ac 6:9
1:22 [p] 1Th 2:14
1:23 [q] Ac 6:7
1:24 [r] Mt 9:8
2:1 [s] Ac 15:2
2:2 [t] Ac 15:4,12 [u] 1Co 9:24; Php 2:16
2:3 [v] 2Co 2:13 [w] Ac 16:3; 1Co 9:21
2:4 [x] 2Co 11:26 [y] Jude 4 [z] Ac 15:1; Gal 5:1,13
2:5 [a] ver 14
2:6 [b] Gal 6:3 [c] Ac 10:34
2:7 [d] 1Th 2:4; 1Ti 1:11 [e] Ac 9:15 [f] ver 9,11,14
2:8 [g] Ac 1:25
2:9 [h] ver 7,11,14 [i] 1Ti 3:15 [j] Ac 4:36 [k] Ro 12:3
2:10 [l] Ac 24:17
2:11 [m] ver 7,9,14 [n] Ac 11:19
2:12 [o] Ac 11:3 [p] Ac 11:2
2:13 [q] ver 1; Ac 4:36
2:14 [r] ver 5 [s] ver 7, 9,11

[a] 15 Or *from my mother's womb* [b] 18 Greek *Cephas* [c] 7 Greek *uncircumcised* [d] 7 Greek *circumcised*; also in verses 8 and 9 [e] 9 Greek *Cephas*; also in verses 11 and 14

them all, "You are a Jew, yet you live like a Gentile and not like a Jew.[a] How is it, then, that you force Gentiles to follow Jewish customs?

15"We who are Jews by birth[b] and not 'Gentile sinners'[c] **16**know that a man is not justified by observing the law, but by faith in Jesus Christ.[d] So we, too, have put our faith in Christ Jesus that we may be justified by faith in Christ and not by observing the law, because by observing the law no one will be justified.

17"If, while we seek to be justified in Christ, it becomes evident that we ourselves are sinners,[e] does that mean that Christ promotes sin? Absolutely not![f] **18**If I rebuild what I destroyed, I prove that I am a lawbreaker. **19**For through the law I died to the law[g] so that I might live for God.[h] **20**I have been crucified with Christ[i] and I no longer live, but Christ lives in me.[j] The life I live in the body, I live by faith in the Son of God,[k] who loved me[l] and gave himself for me.[m] **21**I do not set aside the grace of God, for if righteousness could be gained through the law,[n] Christ died for nothing!"[f]

Faith or Observance of the Law

3 You foolish Galatians! Who has bewitched you?[o] Before your very eyes Jesus Christ was clearly portrayed as crucified.[p] **2**I would like to learn just one thing from you: Did you receive the Spirit by observing the law, or by believing what you heard?[q] **3**Are you so foolish? After beginning with the Spirit, are you now trying to attain your goal by human effort? **4**Have you suffered so much for nothing—if it really was for nothing? **5**Does God give you his Spirit and work miracles[r] among you because you observe the law, or because you believe what you heard?

6Consider Abraham: "He believed God, and it was credited to him as righteousness."[g][s] **7**Understand, then, that those who believe[t] are children of Abraham. **8**The Scripture foresaw that God would justify the Gentiles by faith, and announced the gospel in advance to Abraham: "All nations will be blessed through you."[h][u] **9**So those who have faith[v] are blessed along with Abraham, the man of faith.

10All who rely on observing the law are under a curse, for it is written: "Cursed is everyone who does not continue to do everything written in the Book of the Law."[i][w] **11**Clearly no one is justified before God by the law, because, "The righteous will live by faith."[j][x] **12**The law is not based on faith; on the contrary, "The man who does these things will live by them."[k][y] **13**Christ redeemed us from the curse of the law[z] by becoming a curse for us, for it is written: "Cursed is everyone who is hung on a tree."[l][a] **14**He redeemed us in order that the blessing given to Abraham might come to the Gentiles through Christ Jesus,[b] so that by faith we might receive the promise of the Spirit.[c]

The Law and the Promise

15Brothers, let me take an example from everyday life. Just as no one can set aside or add to a human covenant that has been duly established, so it is in this case. **16**The promises were spoken to Abraham and to his seed.[d] The Scripture does not say "and to seeds," meaning many people, but "and to your seed,"[m] meaning one person, who is Christ. **17**What I mean is this: The law, introduced 430 years[e] later, does not set aside the covenant previously established by God and thus do away with the promise. **18**For if the inheritance depends on the law, then it no longer depends on a prom-

2:14 [a] Ac 10:28
2:15 [b] Php 3:4,5 [c] 1Sa 15:18
2:16 [d] Ac 13:39; Ro 9:30
2:17 [e] ver 15 [f] Gal 3:21
2:19 [g] Ro 7:4 [h] Ro 6:10,11, 14; 2Co 5:15
2:20 [i] Ro 6:6 [j] 1Pe 4:2 [k] Mt 4:3 [l] Ro 8:37 [m] Gal 1:4
2:21 [n] Gal 3:21
3:1 [o] Gal 5:7 [p] 1Co 1:23
3:2 [q] Ro 10:17
3:5 [r] 1Co 12:10
3:6 [s] Ge 15:6; Ro 4:3
3:7 [t] ver 9
3:8 [u] Ge 12:3; Ac 3:25
3:9 [v] ver 7; Ro 4:16
3:10 [w] Dt 27:26; Jer 11:3
3:11 [x] Hab 2:4; Gal 2:16; Heb 10:38
3:12 [y] Lev 18:5; Ro 10:5
3:13 [z] Gal 4:5 [a] Dt 21:23; Ac 5:30
3:14 [b] Ro 4:9,16 [c] ver 2; Joel 2:28; Ac 2:33
3:16 [d] Lk 1:55; Ro 4:13,16
3:17 [e] Ge 15:13,14; Ex 12:40

[f] *21* Some interpreters end the quotation after verse 14. [g] *6* Gen. 15:6 [h] *8* Gen. 12:3; 18:18; 22:18 [i] *10* Deut. 27:26 [j] *11* Hab. 2:4 [k] *12* Lev. 18:5 [l] *13* Deut. 21:23 [m] *16* Gen. 12:7; 13:15; 24:7

ise;[a] but God in his grace gave it to Abraham through a promise.

[19]What, then, was the purpose of the law? It was added because of transgressions[b] until the Seed[c] to whom the promise referred had come. The law was put into effect through angels[d] by a mediator.[e] [20]A mediator,[f] however, does not represent just one party; but God is one.

[21]Is the law, therefore, opposed to the promises of God? Absolutely not![g] For if a law had been given that could impart life, then righteousness would certainly have come by the law.[h] [22]But the Scripture declares that the whole world is a prisoner of sin,[i] so that what was promised, being given through faith in Jesus Christ, might be given to those who believe.

[23]Before this faith came, we were held prisoners[j] by the law, locked up until faith should be revealed. [24]So the law was put in charge to lead us to Christ[n][k] that we might be justified by faith.[l] [25]Now that faith has come, we are no longer under the supervision of the law.

Sons of God

[26]You are all sons of God[m] through faith in Christ Jesus, [27]for all of you who were baptized into Christ[n] have clothed yourselves with Christ.[o] [28]There is neither Jew nor Greek, slave nor free,[p] male nor female, for you are all one in Christ Jesus.[q] [29]If you belong to Christ,[r] then you are Abraham's seed, and heirs according to the promise.[s]

4 What I am saying is that as long as the heir is a child, he is no different from a slave, although he owns the whole estate. [2]He is subject to guardians and trustees until the time set by his father. [3]So also, when we were children, we were in slavery[t] under the basic principles of the world.[u] [4]But when the time had fully come,[v] God sent his Son, born of a woman,[w] born under law,[x] [5]to redeem those under law, that we might receive the full rights[y] of sons. [6]Because you are sons, God sent the Spirit of his Son into our hearts,[z] the Spirit who calls out, *"Abba,*[o] Father."[a] [7]So you are no longer a slave, but a son; and since you are a son, God has made you also an heir.[b]

Paul's Concern for the Galatians

[8]Formerly, when you did not know God,[c] you were slaves to those who by nature are not gods.[d] [9]But now that you know God—or rather are known by God[e]—how is it that you are turning back to those weak and miserable principles? Do you wish to be enslaved[f] by them all over again?[g] [10]You are observing special days and months and seasons and years![h] [11]I fear for you, that somehow I have wasted my efforts on you.[i]

[12]I plead with you, brothers,[j] become like me, for I became like you. You have done me no wrong. [13]As you know, it was because of an illness[k] that I first preached the gospel to you. [14]Even though my illness was a trial to you, you did not treat me with contempt or scorn. Instead, you welcomed me as if I were an angel of God, as if I were Christ Jesus himself.[l] [15]What has happened to all your joy? I can testify that, if you could have done so, you would have torn out your eyes and given them to me. [16]Have I now become your enemy by telling you the truth?[m]

[17]Those people are zealous to win you over, but for no good. What they want is to alienate you ⌊from us⌋, so that you may be zealous for them. [18]It is fine to be zealous, provided the purpose is good, and to be so always and not just when I am with you.[n] [19]My dear children,[o] for whom I am again in the pains of childbirth until Christ is formed in you,[p] [20]how I wish I could be with you now and change my tone, because I am perplexed about you!

[n]24 Or *charge until Christ came*
[o]6 Aramaic for *Father*

3:18 [a]Ro 4:14
3:19 [b]Ro 5:20 [c]ver 16 [d]Ac 7:53 [e]Ex 20:19
3:20 [f]Heb 8:6; 9:15; 12:24
3:21 [g]Gal 2:17 [h]Gal 2:21
3:22 [i]Ro 3:9-19; 11:32
3:23 [j]Ro 11:32
3:24 [k]Ro 10:4 [l]Gal 2:16
3:26 [m]Ro 8:14
3:27 [n]Mt 28:19; Ro 6:3 [o]Ro 13:14
3:28 [p]Col 3:11 [q]Jn 10:16; 17:11; Eph 2:14,15
3:29 [r]1Co 3:23 [s]ver 16
4:3 [t]Gal 2:4 [u]Col 2:8,20
4:4 [v]Mk 1:15; Eph 1:10 [w]Jn 1:14 [x]Lk 2:27
4:5 [y]Jn 1:12
4:6 [z]Ro 5:5 [a]Ro 8:15,16
4:7 [b]Ro 8:17
4:8 [c]1Co 1:21; Eph 2:12; 1Th 4:5 [d]2Ch 13:9; Isa 37:19
4:9 [e]1Co 8:3 [f]ver 3 [g]Col 2:20
4:10 [h]Ro 14:5
4:11 [i]1Th 3:5
4:12 [j]Gal 6:18
4:13 [k]1Co 2:3
4:14 [l]Mt 10:40
4:16 [m]Am 5:10
4:18 [n]ver 13,14
4:19 [o]1Co 4:15 [p]Eph 4:13

Hagar and Sarah

21Tell me, you who want to be
under the law, are you not aware of
what the law says? **22**For it is written that Abraham had two sons,
one by the slave woman[a] and the
other by the free woman.[b] **23**His
son by the slave woman was born in
the ordinary way;[c] but his son by
the free woman was born as the result of a promise.[d]

24These things may be taken figuratively, for the women represent
two covenants. One covenant is
from Mount Sinai and bears children who are to be slaves: This is
Hagar. **25**Now Hagar stands for
Mount Sinai in Arabia and corre-
sponds to the present city of Jerusalem, because she is in slavery
with her children. **26**But the Jerusalem that is above[e] is free, and
she is our mother. **27**For it is written:

"Be glad, O barren woman,
who bears no children;
break forth and cry aloud,
you who have no labor pains;
because more are the children
of the desolate woman
than of her who has a
husband."[p][f]

28Now you, brothers, like Isaac,
are children of promise. **29**At that
time the son born in the ordinary
way[g] persecuted the son born by
the power of the Spirit.[h] It is the
same now. **30**But what does the
Scripture say? "Get rid of the slave
woman and her son, for the slave
woman's son will never share in the
inheritance with the free woman's
son."[q][i] **31**Therefore, brothers, we
are not children of the slave woman, but of the free woman.

Freedom in Christ

5 It is for freedom that Christ has
set us free.[j] Stand firm,[k]
then, and do not let yourselves be
burdened again by a yoke of slavery.[l]

2Mark my words! I, Paul, tell you
that if you let yourselves be circumcised,[m] Christ will be of no value to you at all. **3**Again I declare to
every man who lets himself be circumcised that he is obligated to
obey the whole law.[n] **4**You who are
trying to be justified by law have
been alienated from Christ; you
have fallen away from grace.[o] **5**But
by faith we eagerly await through
the Spirit the righteousness for
which we hope.[p] **6**For in Christ
Jesus neither circumcision nor uncircumcision has any value.[q] The
only thing that counts is faith expressing itself through love.[r]

7You were running a good race.[s]
Who cut in on you[t] and kept you
from obeying the truth? **8**That kind
of persuasion does not come from
the one who calls you.[u] **9**"A little
yeast works through the whole
batch of dough."[v] **10**I am confident[w] in the Lord that you will
take no other view.[x] The one who
is throwing you into confusion[y]
will pay the penalty, whoever he
may be. **11**Brothers, if I am still
preaching circumcision, why am I
still being persecuted?[z] In that
case the offense[a] of the cross has
been abolished. **12**As for those agi-
tators,[b] I wish they would go the
whole way and emasculate themselves!

13You, my brothers, were called
to be free. But do not use your freedom to indulge the sinful nature[r];[c] rather, serve one another[d]
in love. **14**The entire law is
summed up in a single command:
"Love your neighbor as your-
self."[s][e] **15**If you keep on biting
and devouring each other, watch
out or you will be destroyed by
each other.

Life by the Spirit

16So I say, live by the Spirit,[f]
and you will not gratify the desires
of the sinful nature.[g] **17**For the
sinful nature desires what is contrary to the Spirit, and the Spirit
what is contrary to the sinful nature.[h] They are in conflict with

4:22 [a]Ge 16:15 [b]Ge 21:2
4:23 [c]Ro 9:7,8 [d]Ge 18:10-14; Heb 11:11
4:26 [e]Heb 12:22; Rev 3:12
4:27 [f]Isa 54:1
4:29 [g]ver 23 [h]Ge 21:9
4:30 [i]Ge 21:10
5:1 [j]Jn 8:32 [k]1Co 16:13 [l]Ac 15:10; Gal 2:4
5:2 [m]Ac 15:1
5:3 [n]Gal 3:10
5:4 [o]Heb 12:15; 2Pe 3:17
5:5 [p]Ro 8:23,24
5:6 [q]1Co 7:19 [r]1Th 1:3
5:7 [s]1Co 9:24 [t]Gal 3:1
5:8 [u]Ro 8:28; Gal 1:6
5:9 [v]1Co 5:6
5:10 [w]2Co 2:3 [x]Php 3:15 [y]Gal 1:7
5:11 [z]Gal 4:29; 6:12 [a]1Co 1:23
5:12 [b]ver 10
5:13 [c]1Co 8:9; 1Pe 2:16 [d]1Co 9:19; Eph 5:21
5:14 [e]Lev 19:18; Mt 22:39
5:16 [f]Ro 8:2,4-6,9,14 [g]ver 24
5:17 [h]Ro 8:5-8

[p]*27* Isaiah 54:1 [q]*30* Gen. 21:10 [r]*13* Or *the flesh*; also in verses 16, 17, 19 and 24
[s]*14* Lev. 19:18

each other, so that you do not do what you want.[a] **18**But if you are led by the Spirit, you are not under law.[b]

19The acts of the sinful nature are obvious: sexual immorality,[c] impurity and debauchery; **20**idolatry and witchcraft; hatred, discord, jealousy, fits of rage, selfish ambition, dissensions, factions **21**and envy; drunkenness, orgies, and the like.[d] I warn you, as I did before, that those who live like this will not inherit the kingdom of God.

22But the fruit[e] of the Spirit is love,[f] joy, peace, patience, kindness, goodness, faithfulness, **23**gentleness and self-control.[g] Against such things there is no law. **24**Those who belong to Christ Jesus have crucified the sinful nature[h] with its passions and desires.[i] **25**Since we live by the Spirit, let us keep in step with the Spirit. **26**Let us not become conceited,[j] provoking and envying each other.

Doing Good to All

6 Brothers, if someone is caught in a sin, you who are spiritual[k] should restore him gently. But watch yourself, or you also may be tempted. **2**Carry each other's burdens, and in this way you will fulfill the law of Christ.[l] **3**If anyone thinks he is something[m] when he is nothing, he deceives himself. **4**Each one should test his own actions. Then he can take pride in himself, without comparing himself to somebody else, **5**for each one should carry his own load.

6Anyone who receives instruction in the word must share all good things with his instructor.[n]

7Do not be deceived:[o] God cannot be mocked. A man reaps what he sows.[p] **8**The one who sows to please his sinful nature, from that nature[t] will reap destruction;[q] the one who sows to please the Spirit, from the Spirit will reap eternal life.[r] **9**Let us not become weary in doing good,[s] for at the proper time we will reap a harvest if we do not give up.[t] **10**Therefore, as we have opportunity, let us do good[u] to all people, especially to those who belong to the family[v] of believers.

Not Circumcision but a New Creation

11See what large letters I use as I write to you with my own hand![w]

12Those who want to make a good impression outwardly are trying to compel you to be circumcised.[x] The only reason they do this is to avoid being persecuted[y] for the cross of Christ. **13**Not even those who are circumcised obey the law,[z] yet they want you to be circumcised that they may boast about your flesh.[a] **14**May I never boast except in the cross of our Lord Jesus Christ, through which[u] the world has been crucified to me, and I to the world.[b] **15**Neither circumcision nor uncircumcision means anything;[c] what counts is a new creation.[d] **16**Peace and mercy to all who follow this rule, even to the Israel of God.

17Finally, let no one cause me trouble, for I bear on my body the marks[e] of Jesus.

18The grace of our Lord Jesus Christ[f] be with your spirit,[g] brothers. Amen.

[t]8 *Or his flesh, from the flesh* [u]14 *Or whom*

5:17 [a]Ro 7:15-23
5:18 [b]Ro 6:14; 1Ti 1:9
5:19 [c]1Co 6:18
5:21 [d]Ro 13:13
5:22 [e]Mt 7:16-20; Eph 5:9 [f]Col 3:12-15
5:23 [g]Ac 24:25
5:24 [h]Ro 6:6 [i]ver 16,17
5:26 [j]Php 2:3
6:1 [k]1Co 2:15
6:2 [l]Ro 15:1; Jas 2:8
6:3 [m]Ro 12:3; 1Co 8:2
6:6 [n]1Co 9:11,14
6:7 [o]1Co 6:9 [p]2Co 9:6
6:8 [q]Job 4:8; Hos 8:7 [r]Jas 3:18
6:9 [s]1Co 15:58 [t]Rev 2:10
6:10 [u]Pr 3:27 [v]Eph 2:19
6:11 [w]1Co 16:21
6:12 [x]Ac 15:1 [y]Gal 5:11
6:13 [z]Ro 2:25 [a]Php 3:3
6:14 [b]Ro 6:2,6
6:15 [c]1Co 7:19 [d]2Co 5:17
6:17 [e]Isa 44:5; 2Co 1:5
6:18 [f]Ro 16:20 [g]2Ti 4:22

Ephesians

Title and Background

Ephesus was the most important city in western Asia Minor (now Turkey). Because it was at an intersection of major trade routes, it became a commercial center. It also boasted a pagan temple dedicated to the Roman goddess Diana (Greek *Artemis*). Paul made Ephesus a center for evangelism for about three years. This letter was probably not sent merely to the church at Ephesus but also to the various churches in the province of Asia, where Paul conducted his third missionary journey.

Author and Date of Writing

The more widely held position is that Paul wrote this letter about A.D. 60, during his two-year imprisonment in Rome.

Theme and Message

Unlike several of Paul's other letters, Ephesians does not address any particular error or heresy. Paul wrote to help his readers better understand the dimensions of God's eternal purpose and grace and come to appreciate the high goals God has for the church. One of Paul's themes is that of unity—all Christians are one family in Jesus, and they should act with love toward each other. He also writes about the church—not a church building, but the church that is made up of all Christians through all the ages.

Outline

I. Greetings (1:1-2)
II. The Glory and Headship of Christ (1:3-14)
III. Prayer That Christians May Realize God's Purpose and Power (1:15-23)
IV. Steps Toward the Fulfillment of God's Purpose (2:1-3:21)
V. Ways to Fulfill God's Purpose in the Church (4:1-6:20)
VI. Conclusion (6:21-24)

---

1 Paul, an apostle[a] of Christ
Jesus by the will of God,[b]

To the saints in Ephesus,[a] the
faithful[b] [c] in Christ Jesus:

2Grace and peace to you from
God our Father and the Lord Jesus
Christ.[d]

Spiritual Blessings in Christ

3Praise be to the God and Father
of our Lord Jesus Christ,[e] who has
blessed us in the heavenly realms[f]
with every spiritual blessing in
Christ. 4For he chose us in him before the creation of the world to be
holy and blameless[g] in his sight.
In love[h] 5he[c] predestined[i] us to
be adopted as his sons through
Jesus Christ, in accordance with
his pleasure[j] and will— 6to the
praise of his glorious grace, which
he has freely given us in the One he
loves.[k] 7In him we have redemption[l] through his blood, the forgiveness of sins, in accordance
with the riches of God's grace 8that
he lavished on us with all wisdom
and understanding. 9And he[d]

1:1 [a] 1Co 1:1 [b] 2Co 1:1 [c] Col 1:2
1:2 [d] Ro 1:7
1:3 [e] 2Co 1:3 [f] Eph 2:6; 3:10; 6:12
1:4 [g] Eph 5:27; Col 1:22 [h] Eph 4:2,15, 16
1:5 [i] Ro 8:29,30 [j] 1Co 1:21
1:6 [k] Mt 3:17
1:7 [l] Ro 3:24

[a] *1* Some early manuscripts do not have *in Ephesus.* [b] *1* Or *believers who are* [c] *4,5* Or *sight in love.* [5]*He* [d] *8,9* Or *us. With all wisdom and understanding,* [9]*he*

made known to us the mystery[a] of
his will according to his good pleasure, which he purposed in Christ,
10to be put into effect when the
times will have reached their fulfillment[b]—to bring all things in
heaven and on earth together under one head, even Christ.[c]
11In him we were also chosen,[e]
having been predestined according
to the plan of him who works out
everything in conformity with the
purpose[d] of his will, **12**in order
that we, who were the first to hope
in Christ, might be for the praise of
his glory.[e] **13**And you also were included in Christ when you heard
the word of truth,[f] the gospel of
your salvation. Having believed,
you were marked in him with a
seal,[g] the promised Holy Spirit,
14who is a deposit guaranteeing
our inheritance[h] until the redemption of those who are God's possession—to the praise of his glory.

Thanksgiving and Prayer

15For this reason, ever since I
heard about your faith in the Lord
Jesus and your love for all the
saints,[i] **16**I have not stopped giving thanks for you,[j] remembering
you in my prayers. **17**I keep asking
that the God of our Lord Jesus
Christ, the glorious Father,[k] may
give you the Spirit[f] of wisdom[l]
and revelation, so that you may
know him better. **18**I pray also that
the eyes of your heart may be enlightened[m] in order that you may
know the hope to which he has
called you, the riches of his glorious inheritance in the saints, **19**and
his incomparably great power for
us who believe. That power[n] is like
the working of his mighty
strength,[o] **20**which he exerted in
Christ when he raised him from the
dead[p] and seated him at his right
hand in the heavenly realms, **21**far
above all rule and authority, power
and dominion, and every title[q]
that can be given, not only in the
present age but also in the one to
come. **22**And God placed all things
under his feet[r] and appointed him
to be head[s] over everything for the
church, **23**which is his body, the
fullness of him who fills everything
in every way.

Made Alive in Christ

2 As for you, you were dead in
your transgressions and sins,[t]
2in which you used to live[u] when
you followed the ways of this world
and of the ruler of the kingdom of
the air,[v] the spirit who is now at
work in those who are disobedient.[w] **3**All of us also lived among
them at one time, gratifying the
cravings of our sinful nature[g][x] and
following its desires and thoughts.
Like the rest, we were by nature objects of wrath. **4**But because of his
great love for us, God, who is rich in
mercy, **5**made us alive with Christ
even when we were dead in transgressions[y]—it is by grace you have
been saved.[z] **6**And God raised us
up with Christ and seated us with
him[a] in the heavenly realms[b] in
Christ Jesus, **7**in order that in the
coming ages he might show the in-
comparable riches of his grace, expressed in his kindness[c] to us in
Christ Jesus. **8**For it is by grace you
have been saved,[d] through faith
—and this not from yourselves, it is
the gift of God— **9**not by works,[e]
so that no one can boast.[f] **10**For
we are God's workmanship, created[g] in Christ Jesus to do good
works,[h] which God prepared in advance for us to do.

One in Christ

11Therefore, remember that formerly you who are Gentiles by birth
and called "uncircumcised" by
those who call themselves "the circumcision" (that done in the body
by the hands of men)[i]— **12**remember that at that time you were
separate from Christ, excluded
from citizenship in Israel and foreigners to the covenants of the
promise,[j] without hope[k] and
without God in the world. **13**But
now in Christ Jesus you who once

1:9 [a]Ro 16:25
1:10 [b]Gal 4:4 [c]Col 1:20
1:11 [d]Eph 3:11; Heb 6:17
1:12 [e]ver 6,14
1:13 [f]Col 1:5 [g]Eph 4:30
1:14 [h]Ac 20:32
1:15 [i]Col 1:4
1:16 [j]Ro 1:8
1:17 [k]Jn 20:17 [l]Col 1:9
1:18 [m]Ac 26:18; 2Co 4:6
1:19 [n]Col 1:29 [o]Eph 6:10
1:20 [p]Ac 2:24
1:21 [q]Php 2:9,10
1:22 [r]Mt 28:18 [s]Eph 4:15; 5:23
2:1 [t]ver 5; Col 2:13
2:2 [u]Col 3:7 [v]Jn 12:31; Eph 6:12 [w]Eph 5:6
2:3 [x]Gal 5:16
2:5 [y]ver 1 [z]ver 8; Ac 15:11
2:6 [a]Eph 1:20 [b]Eph 1:3
2:7 [c]Tit 3:4
2:8 [d]ver 5
2:9 [e]2Ti 1:9 [f]1Co 1:29
2:10 [g]Eph 4:24 [h]Tit 2:14
2:11 [i]Col 2:11
2:12 [j]Gal 3:17 [k]1Th 4:13

[e]11 Or *were made heirs* [f]17 Or *a spirit*
[g]3 Or *our flesh*

were far away have been brought near[a] through the blood of Christ.[b]

14For he himself is our peace, who has made the two one[c] and has destroyed the barrier, the dividing wall of hostility, 15by abolishing in his flesh[d] the law with its commandments and regulations.[e] His purpose was to create in himself one[f] new man out of the two, thus making peace, 16and in this one body to reconcile both of them to God through the cross,[g] by which he put to death their hostility. 17He came and preached peace to you who were far away and peace to those who were near.[h] 18For through him we both have access[i] to the Father[j] by one Spirit.[k]

19Consequently, you are no longer foreigners and aliens,[l] but fellow citizens[m] with God's people and members of God's household,[n] 20built on the foundation[o] of the apostles and prophets, with Christ Jesus himself as the chief cornerstone.[p] 21In him the whole building is joined together and rises to become a holy temple[q] in the Lord. 22And in him you too are being built together to become a dwelling in which God lives by his Spirit.

Paul the Preacher to the Gentiles

3 For this reason I, Paul, the *prisoner*[r] *of Christ Jesus* for the sake of you Gentiles—

2Surely you have heard about the administration of God's grace that was given to me[s] for you, 3that is, the mystery[t] made known to me by revelation,[u] as I have already written briefly. 4In reading this, then, you will be able to understand my insight[v] into the mystery of Christ, 5which was not made known to men in other generations as it has now been revealed by the Spirit to God's holy apostles and prophets.[w] 6This mystery is that through the gospel the Gentiles are heirs[x] together with Israel, members together of one body,[y] and sharers together in the promise in Christ Jesus.

7I became a servant of this gospel[z] by the gift of God's grace given me through the working of his power.[a] 8Although I am less than the least of all God's people,[b] this grace was given me: to preach to the Gentiles the unsearchable riches of Christ, 9and to make plain to everyone the administration of this mystery,[c] which for ages past was kept hidden in God, who created all things. 10His intent was that now, through the church, the manifold wisdom of God[d] should be made known[e] to the rulers and authorities[f] in the heavenly realms, 11according to his eternal purpose which he accomplished in Christ Jesus our Lord. 12In him and through faith in him we may approach God[g] with freedom and confidence.[h] 13I ask you, therefore, not to be discouraged because of my sufferings for you, which are your glory.

A Prayer for the Ephesians

14For this reason I kneel[i] before the Father, 15from whom his whole family[h] in heaven and on earth derives its name. 16I pray that out of his glorious riches he may strengthen you with power[j] through his Spirit in your inner being,[k] 17so that Christ may dwell in your hearts[l] through faith. And I pray that you, being rooted[m] and established in love, 18may have power, together with all the saints, to grasp how wide and long and high and deep[n] is the love of Christ, 19and to know this love that surpasses knowledge—that you may be filled[o] to the measure of all the fullness of God.[p]

20Now to him who is able[q] to do immeasurably more than all we ask or imagine, according to his power that is at work within us, 21to him be glory in the church and in Christ Jesus throughout all generations, for ever and ever! Amen.[r]

2:13 [a] ver 17; Ac 2:39 [b] Col 1:20
2:14 [c] 1Co 12:13
2:15 [d] Col 1:21,22 [e] Col 2:14 [f] Gal 3:28
2:16 [g] Col 1:20,22
2:17 [h] Ps 148:14; Isa 57:19
2:18 [i] Eph 3:12 [j] Col 1:12 [k] 1Co 12:13
2:19 [l] ver 12 [m] Php 3:20 [n] Gal 6:10
2:20 [o] Mt 16:18; Rev 21:14 [p] 1Pe 2:4-8
2:21 [q] 1Co 3:16,17
3:1 [r] Ac 23:18; Eph 4:1
3:2 [s] Col 1:25
3:3 [t] Ro 16:25 [u] 1Co 2:10
3:4 [v] 2Co 11:6
3:5 [w] Ro 16:26
3:6 [x] Gal 3:29 [y] Eph 2:15,16
3:7 [z] 1Co 3:5 [a] Eph 1:19
3:8 [b] 1Co 15:9
3:9 [c] Ro 16:25
3:10 [d] 1Co 2:7 [e] 1Pe 1:12 [f] Eph 1:21
3:12 [g] Eph 2:18 [h] Heb 4:16
3:14 [i] Php 2:10
3:16 [j] Col 1:11 [k] Ro 7:22
3:17 [l] Jn 14:23 [m] Col 1:23
3:18 [n] Job 11:8,9
3:19 [o] Col 2:10 [p] Eph 1:23
3:20 [q] Ro 16:25
3:21 [r] Ro 11:36

[h]15 Or *whom all fatherhood*

Unity in the Body of Christ

4 As a prisoner[a] for the Lord, then, I urge you to live a life worthy[b] of the calling you have received. **2**Be completely humble and gentle; be patient, bearing with one another[c] in love.[d] **3**Make every effort to keep the unity[e] of the Spirit through the bond of peace. **4**There is one body and one Spirit[f]— just as you were called to one hope when you were called— **5**one Lord, one faith, one baptism; **6**one God and Father of all, who is over all and through all and in all.[g]

7But to each one of us[h] grace has been given[i] as Christ apportioned it. **8**This is why it[i] says:

"When he ascended on high,
he led captives[j] in his train
and gave gifts to men."[j][k]

9(What does "he ascended" mean except that he also descended to the lower, earthly regions[k]? **10**He who descended is the very one who ascended higher than all the heavens, in order to fill the whole universe.) **11**It was he who gave some to be apostles,[l] some to be prophets, some to be evangelists,[m] and some to be pastors and teachers, **12**to prepare God's people for works of service, so that the body of Christ[n] may be built up **13**until we all reach unity[o] in the faith and in the knowledge of the Son of God and become mature,[p] attaining to the whole measure of the fullness of Christ.

14Then we will no longer be infants,[q] tossed back and forth by the waves,[r] and blown here and there by every wind of teaching and by the cunning and craftiness of men in their deceitful scheming.[s] **15**Instead, speaking the truth in love, we will in all things grow up into him who is the Head,[t] that is, Christ. **16**From him the whole body, joined and held together by every supporting ligament, grows[u] and builds itself up in love, as each part does its work.

Living as Children of Light

17So I tell you this, and insist on it in the Lord, that you must no longer live as the Gentiles do, in the futility of their thinking.[v] **18**They are darkened in their understanding[w] and separated from the life of God[x] because of the ignorance that is in them due to the hardening of their hearts.[y] **19**Having lost all sensitivity,[z] they have given themselves over[a] to sensuality[b] so as to indulge in every kind of impurity, with a continual lust for more.

20You, however, did not come to know Christ that way. **21**Surely you heard of him and were taught in him in accordance with the truth that is in Jesus. **22**You were taught, with regard to your former way of life, to put off[c] your old self,[d] which is being corrupted by its deceitful desires; **23**to be made new in the attitude of your minds;[e] **24**and to put on the new self,[f] created to be like God in true righteousness and holiness.[g]

25Therefore each of you must put off falsehood and speak truthfully[h] to his neighbor, for we are all members of one body.[i] **26**"In your anger do not sin"[l]: Do not let the sun go down while you are still angry, **27**and do not give the devil a foothold. **28**He who has been stealing must steal no longer, but must work,[j] doing something useful with his own hands,[k] that he may have something to share with those in need.[l]

29Do not let any unwholesome talk come out of your mouths,[m] but only what is helpful for building others up according to their needs, that it may benefit those who listen. **30**And do not grieve the Holy Spirit of God,[n] with whom you were sealed for the day of redemption.[o] **31**Get rid of all bitterness, rage and anger, brawling and slander, along with every form of malice.[p] **32**Be kind and compassionate to one another, forgiving

4:1 [a]Eph 3:1 [b]Php 1:27; Col 1:10
4:2 [c]Col 3:12,13 [d]Eph 1:4
4:3 [e]Col 3:14
4:4 [f]1Co 12:13
4:6 [g]Ro 11:36
4:7 [h]1Co 12:7,11 [i]Ro 12:3
4:8 [j]Col 2:15 [k]Ps 68:18
4:11 [l]1Co 12:28 [m]Ac 21:8
4:12 [n]1Co 12:27
4:13 [o]ver 3,5 [p]Col 1:28
4:14 [q]1Co 14:20 [r]Jas 1:6 [s]Eph 6:11
4:15 [t]Eph 1:22
4:16 [u]Col 2:19
4:17 [v]Ro 1:21
4:18 [w]Ro 1:21 [x]Eph 2:12 [y]2Co 3:14
4:19 [z]1Ti 4:2 [a]Ro 1:24 [b]Col 3:5
4:22 [c]1Pe 2:1 [d]Ro 6:6
4:23 [e]Col 3:10
4:24 [f]Ro 6:4 [g]Eph 2:10
4:25 [h]Zec 8:16 [i]Ro 12:5
4:28 [j]Ac 20:35 [k]1Th 4:11 [l]Lk 3:11
4:29 [m]Col 3:8
4:30 [n]1Th 5:19 [o]Ro 8:23
4:31 [p]Col 3:8

[i]8 Or *God* [j]8 Psalm 68:18 [k]9 Or *the depths of the earth* [l]26 Psalm 4:4

each other, just as in Christ God
forgave you.[a]

5 Be imitators of God,[b] therefore, as dearly loved children
2and live a life of love, just as Christ
loved us and gave himself up for
us[c] as a fragrant offering and sacrifice to God.[d]

3But among you there must not
be even a hint of sexual immorality, or of any kind of impurity, or of
greed,[e] because these are improp-
er for God's holy people. **4**Nor
should there be obscenity, foolish
talk or coarse joking, which are out
of place, but rather thanksgiving.[f]
5For of this you can be sure: No immoral, impure or greedy person—
such a man is an idolater[g]—has
any inheritance in the kingdom of
Christ and of God.[m][h] **6**Let no one
deceive you with empty words, for
because of such things God's
wrath[i] comes on those who are
disobedient. **7**Therefore do not be
partners with them.

8For you were once[j] darkness,
but now you are light in the Lord.
Live as children of light[k] **9**(for the
fruit[l] of the light consists in all
goodness, righteousness and truth)
10and find out what pleases the
Lord. **11**Have nothing to do with
the fruitless deeds of darkness, but
rather expose them. **12**For it is
shameful even to mention what the
disobedient do in secret. **13**But everything exposed by the light[m] becomes visible, **14**for it is light that
makes everything visible. This is
why it is said:

"Wake up, O sleeper,[n]
  rise from the dead,[o]
and Christ will shine on you."[p]

15Be very careful, then, how you
live—not as unwise but as wise,
16making the most of every opportunity,[q] because the days are
evil.[r] **17**Therefore do not be foolish, but understand what the
Lord's will is.[s] **18**Do not get drunk
on wine,[t] which leads to debauchery. Instead, be filled with the Spirit.[u] **19**Speak to one another with
psalms, hymns and spiritual
songs.[v] Sing and make music in
your heart to the Lord, **20**always
giving thanks[w] to God the Father
for everything, in the name of our
Lord Jesus Christ.

21Submit to one another[x] out of
reverence for Christ.

Wives and Husbands

5:22–6:9pp — Col 3:18–4:1

22Wives, submit to your husbands[y] as to the Lord.[z] **23**For the
husband is the head of the wife as
Christ is the head of the church,[a]
his body, of which he is the Savior.
24Now as the church submits to
Christ, so also wives should submit
to their husbands in everything.

25Husbands, love your wives,[b]
just as Christ loved the church and
gave himself up for her[c] **26**to make
her holy, cleansing[n] her by the
washing[d] with water through the
word, **27**and to present her to himself as a radiant church, without
stain or wrinkle or any other blemish, but holy and blameless.[e] **28**In
this same way, husbands ought to
love their wives[f] as their own bodies. He who loves his wife loves
himself. **29**After all, no one ever
hated his own body, but he feeds
and cares for it, just as Christ does
the church— **30**for we are members
of his body.[g] **31**"For this reason a
man will leave his father and mother and be united to his wife, and
the two will become one flesh."[o][h]
32This is a profound mystery—but
I am talking about Christ and the
church. **33**However, each one of
you also must love his wife[i] as he
loves himself, and the wife must respect her husband.

Children and Parents

6 Children, obey your parents in
the Lord, for this is right.[j]
2"Honor your father and mother"
—which is the first commandment
with a promise— **3**"that it may go
well with you and that you may enjoy long life on the earth."[p][k]

4Fathers, do not exasperate your

4:32 [a]Mt 6:14,15
5:1 [b]Lk 6:36
5:2 [c]Gal 1:4 [d]2Co 2:15; Heb 7:27
5:3 [e]Col 3:5
5:4 [f]ver 20
5:5 [g]Col 3:5 [h]1Co 6:9
5:6 [i]Ro 1:18
5:8 [j]Eph 2:2 [k]Lk 16:8
5:9 [l]Gal 5:22
5:13 [m]Jn 3:20,21
5:14 [n]Ro 13:11 [o]Jn 5:25 [p]Isa 60:1
5:16 [q]Col 4:5 [r]Eph 6:13
5:17 [s]Ro 12:2; 1Th 4:3
5:18 [t]Pr 20:1 [u]Lk 1:15
5:19 [v]Ac 16:25; Col 3:16
5:20 [w]Ps 34:1
5:21 [x]Gal 5:13
5:22 [y]Ge 3:16; 1Pe 3:1,5,6 [z]Eph 6:5
5:23 [a]1Co 11:3; Eph 1:22
5:25 [b]Col 3:19 [c]ver 2
5:26 [d]Ac 22:16
5:27 [e]Eph 1:4; Col 1:22
5:28 [f]ver 25
5:30 [g]1Co 12:27
5:31 [h]Ge 2:24; Mt 19:5; 1Co 6:16
5:33 [i]ver 25
6:1 [j]Col 3:20
6:3 [k]Ex 20:12

[m]5 Or *kingdom of the Christ and God*
[n]26 Or *having cleansed*
[o]31 Gen. 2:24
[p]3 Deut. 5:16

children;[a] instead, bring them up in the training and instruction of the Lord.[b]

Slaves and Masters

5Slaves, obey your earthly masters with respect[c] and fear, and with sincerity of heart,[d] just as you would obey Christ.[e] **6**Obey them not only to win their favor when their eye is on you, but like slaves of Christ, doing the will of God from your heart. **7**Serve wholeheartedly, as if you were serving the Lord, not men,[f] **8**because you know that the Lord will reward everyone for whatever good he does,[g] whether he is slave or free.

9And masters, treat your slaves in the same way. Do not threaten them, since you know that he who is both their Master and yours[h] is in heaven, and there is no favoritism with him.

The Armor of God

10Finally, be strong in the Lord[i] and in his mighty power.[j] **11**Put on the full armor of God[k] so that you can take your stand against the devil's schemes. **12**For our struggle is not against flesh and blood, but against the rulers, against the authorities,[l] against the powers[m] of this dark world and against the spiritual forces of evil in the heavenly realms.[n] **13**Therefore put on the full armor of God, so that when the day of evil comes, you may be able to stand your ground, and after you have done everything, to stand. **14**Stand firm then, with the belt of truth buckled around your waist,[o] with the breastplate of righteousness in place,[p] **15**and with your feet fitted with the readiness that comes from the gospel of peace.[q] **16**In addition to all this, take up the shield of faith,[r] with which you can extinguish all the flaming arrows of the evil one. **17**Take the helmet of salvation[s] and the sword of the Spirit, which is the word of God.[t] **18**And pray in the Spirit on all occasions[u] with all kinds of prayers and requests.[v] With this in mind, be alert and always keep on praying for all the saints.

19Pray also for me,[w] that whenever I open my mouth, words may be given me so that I will fearlessly[x] make known the mystery of the gospel, **20**for which I am an ambassador[y] in chains.[z] Pray that I may declare it fearlessly, as I should.

Final Greetings

21Tychicus,[a] the dear brother and faithful servant in the Lord, will tell you everything, so that you also may know how I am and what I am doing. **22**I am sending him to you for this very purpose, that you may know how we are,[b] and that he may encourage you.

23Peace[c] to the brothers, and love with faith from God the Father and the Lord Jesus Christ. **24**Grace to all who love our Lord Jesus Christ with an undying love.

6:4 [a]Col 3:21 [b]Ge 18:19; Dt 6:7
6:5 [c]1Ti 6:1 [d]Col 3:22 [e]Eph 5:22
6:7 [f]Col 3:23
6:8 [g]Col 3:24
6:9 [h]Job 31:13,14
6:10 [i]1Co 16:13 [j]Eph 1:19
6:11 [k]Ro 13:12
6:12 [l]Eph 1:21 [m]Ro 8:38 [n]Eph 1:3
6:14 [o]Isa 11:5 [p]Isa 59:17
6:15 [q]Isa 52:7
6:16 [r]1Jn 5:4
6:17 [s]Isa 59:17 [t]Heb 4:12
6:18 [u]Lk 18:1 [v]Mt 26:41; Php 1:4
6:19 [w]1Th 5:25 [x]Ac 4:29; 2Co 3:12
6:20 [y]2Co 5:20 [z]Ac 21:33
6:21 [a]Ac 20:4
6:22 [b]Col 4:7-9
6:23 [c]Gal 6:16; 1Pe 5:14

firming the gospel, all of you share
in God's grace with me. **8**God can
testify[a] how I long for all of you
with the affection of Christ Jesus.

9And this is my prayer: that your
love[b] may abound more and more
in knowledge and depth of insight,
10so that you may be able to discern what is best and may be pure
and blameless until the day of
Christ,[c] **11**filled with the fruit of
righteousness[d] that comes
through Jesus Christ—to the glory
and praise of God.

Paul's Chains Advance the Gospel

12Now I want you to know,
brothers, that what has happened
to me has really served to advance
the gospel. **13**As a result, it has become clear throughout the whole
palace guard[b] and to everyone else
that I am in chains[e] for Christ.
14Because of my chains,[f] most of
the brothers in the Lord have been
encouraged to speak the word of
God more courageously and fearlessly.

15It is true that some preach
Christ out of envy and rivalry, but
others out of goodwill. **16**The latter
do so in love, knowing that I am put
here for the defense of the gospel.[g]
17The former preach Christ out of
selfish ambition,[h] not sincerely,
supposing that they can stir up
trouble for me while I am in
chains.[c i] **18**But what does it matter? The important thing is that in
every way, whether from false motives or true, Christ is preached.
And because of this I rejoice.

Yes, and I will continue to rejoice, **19**for I know that through
your prayers[j] and the help given
by the Spirit of Jesus Christ,[k] what
has happened to me will turn out
for my deliverance.[d] **20**I eagerly expect[l] and hope that I will in no
way be ashamed, but will have sufficient courage[m] so that now as always Christ will be exalted in my
body,[n] whether by life or by
death.[o] **21**For to me, to live is
Christ[p] and to die is gain. **22**If I am
to go on living in the body, this will
mean fruitful labor for me. Yet
what shall I choose? I do not know!
23I am torn between the two: I desire to depart[q] and be with
Christ,[r] which is better by far;
24but it is more necessary for you
that I remain in the body. **25**Convinced of this, I know that I will remain, and I will continue with all of
you for your progress and joy in the
faith, **26**so that through my being
with you again your joy in Christ
Jesus will overflow on account of
me.

27Whatever happens, conduct
yourselves in a manner worthy[s] of
the gospel of Christ. Then, whether
I come and see you or only hear
about you in my absence, I will
know that you stand firm[t] in one
spirit, contending[u] as one man for
the faith of the gospel **28**without
being frightened in any way by
those who oppose you. This is a
sign to them that they will be destroyed, but that you will be
saved—and that by God. **29**For it
has been granted to you[v] on behalf
of Christ not only to believe on
him, but also to suffer[w] for him,
30since you are going through the
same struggle[x] you saw[y] I had,
and now hear[z] that I still have.

Imitating Christ's Humility

2 If you have any encouragement
from being united with Christ,
if any comfort from his love, if any
fellowship with the Spirit,[a] if any
tenderness and compassion,[b]
2then make my joy complete[c] by
being like-minded,[d] having the
same love, being one[e] in spirit and
purpose. **3**Do nothing out of selfish
ambition or vain conceit,[f] but in
humility consider others better
than yourselves.[g] **4**Each of you
should look not only to your own
interests, but also to the interests
of others.

5Your attitude should be the
same as that of Christ Jesus:[h]

[b]*13* Or *whole palace* [c]*16,17* Some late manuscripts have verses 16 and 17 in reverse order. [d]*19* Or *salvation*

1:8 [a]Ro 1:9
1:9 [b]1Th 3:12
1:10 [c]ver 6; 1Co 1:8
1:11 [d]Jas 3:18
1:13 [e]ver 7,14,17
1:14 [f]ver 7,13,17
1:16 [g]ver 7,12
1:17 [h]Php 2:3 [i]ver 7,13,14
1:19 [j]2Co 1:11 [k]Ac 16:7
1:20 [l]Ro 8:19 [m]ver 14 [n]1Co 6:20 [o]Ro 14:8
1:21 [p]Gal 2:20
1:23 [q]2Ti 4:6 [r]Jn 12:26; 2Co 5:8
1:27 [s]Eph 4:1 [t]1Co 16:13 [u]Jude 3
1:29 [v]Mt 5:11,12 [w]Ac 14:22
1:30 [x]Col 2:1; 1Th 2:2 [y]Ac 16:19-40 [z]ver 13
2:1 [a]2Co 13:14 [b]Col 3:12
2:2 [c]Jn 3:29 [d]Php 4:2 [e]Ro 12:16
2:3 [f]Gal 5:26 [g]Ro 12:10; 1Pe 5:5
2:5 [h]Mt 11:29

Philippians

Title and Background

Philippians was written during Paul's first Roman imprisonment and is known as a "Prison Letter" (along with Ephesians, Colossians and Philemon). The church at Philippi had sent Paul a gift by way of Epaphroditus, their messenger. Epaphroditus had become sick in Rome, and the Philippian Christians were concerned about him. This made Epaphroditus all the more eager to return home. Paul therefore wrote this letter to his Christian friends in Philippi, expressing his gratitude for their love and help.

Author and Date of Writing

The first verse of Philippians tells us Paul wrote the letter, and the writing itself reveals the stamp of genuineness. The many personal references of the author fit what we know of Paul from other New Testament books. The most widely accepted date for the writing of the letter is about A.D. 61.

Theme and Message

The theme of the book is "joy," or "rejoicing in the Lord." The word "joy" in its various forms occurs sixteen times. There were also perils to watch for, because there were enemies of the church, both inside and outside. Paul warns the Philippians of the present dangers of a self-seeking attitude and an attitude of pride, both of which could lead to harmful divisions. The book of Philippians also contains the most profound statement of the meaning of the incarnation (2:5-11).

Outline

I. Greetings, Thanksgiving and Prayer (1:1-11)
II. Paul's Personal Circumstances (1:12-26)
III. Exhortations (1:27-2:18)
  A. Live a Life Worthy of the Gospel (1:27-30)
  B. Follow the Servant Attitude of Christ (2:1-18)
IV. Paul's Associates in the Gospel (2:19-30)
V. Warnings Against Judaizers and Libertines (3:1-4:1)
VI. Final Exhortations, Thanks and Conclusion (4:2-23)

---

1 Paul and Timothy,[a] servants
of Christ Jesus,

To all the saints[b] in Christ Jesus
at Philippi,[c] together with the
overseers[a][d] *and deacons:*[e]

2Grace and peace to you from
God our Father and the Lord Jesus
Christ.[f]

Thanksgiving and Prayer

3I thank my God every time I remember you.[g] **4**In all my prayers
for all of you, I always pray[h] with
joy **5**because of your partnership[i]
in the gospel from the first day[j]
until now, **6**being confident of this,
that he who began a good work in
you will carry it on to completion
until the day of Christ Jesus.[k]

7It is right[l] for me to feel this
way about all of you, since I have
you in my heart;[m] for whether I am
in chains[n] or defending[o] and con-

1:1 [a]Ac 16:1; 2Co 1:1 [b]Ac 9:13 [c]Ac 16:12 [d]1Ti 3:1 [e]1Ti 3:8 **1:2** [f]Ro 1:7 **1:3** [g]Ro 1:8 **1:4** [h]Ro 1:10 **1:5** [i]Ac 2:42; Php 4:15 [j]Ac 16:12-40 **1:6** [k]ver 10; 1Co 1:8 **1:7** [l]2Pe 1:13 [m]2Co 7:3 [n]ver 13,14,17; Ac 21:33 [o]ver 16

[a]*1* Traditionally *bishops*

6Who, being in very nature[e]
God,[a]
did not consider equality
with God[b] something to
be grasped,
7but made himself nothing,
taking the very nature[f] of a
servant,[c]
being made in human
likeness.[d]
8And being found in appearance
as a man,
he humbled himself
and became obedient to
death[e]—
even death on a cross!
9Therefore God exalted him[f] to
the highest place
and gave him the name that
is above every name,[g]
10that at the name of Jesus every
knee should bow,[h]
in heaven and on earth and
under the earth,[i]
11and every tongue confess that
Jesus Christ is Lord,[j]
to the glory of God the
Father.

Shining as Stars

12Therefore, my dear friends, as
you have always obeyed—not only
in my presence, but now much
more in my absence—continue to
work out your salvation with fear
and trembling,[k] **13**for it is God who
works in you[l] to will and to act according to his good purpose.
14Do everything without complaining[m] or arguing, **15**so that you
may become blameless and pure,
children of God[n] without fault in a
crooked and depraved generation,[o] in which you shine like stars
in the universe **16**as you hold out[g]
the word of life—in order that I
may boast on the day of Christ that
I did not run or labor for nothing.[p]
17But even if I am being poured out
like a drink offering[q] on the sacrifice[r] and service coming from your
faith, I am glad and rejoice with all
of you. **18**So you too should be glad
and rejoice with me.

Timothy and Epaphroditus

19I hope in the Lord Jesus to
send Timothy to you soon,[s] that I
also may be cheered when I receive
news about you. **20**I have no one
else like him,[t] who takes a genuine interest in your welfare. **21**For
everyone looks out for his own interests,[u] not those of Jesus Christ.
22But you know that Timothy has
proved himself, because as a son
with his father[v] he has served with
me in the work of the gospel. **23**I
hope, therefore, to send him as
soon as I see how things go with
me.[w] **24**And I am confident[x] in the
Lord that I myself will come soon.
25But I think it is necessary to
send back to you Epaphroditus, my
brother, fellow worker[y] and fellow
soldier,[z] who is also your messenger, whom you sent to take care of
my needs.[a] **26**For he longs for all of
you[b] and is distressed because you
heard he was ill. **27**Indeed he was
ill, and almost died. But God had
mercy on him, and not on him only
but also on me, to spare me sorrow
upon sorrow. **28**Therefore I am all
the more eager to send him, so that
when you see him again you may
be glad and I may have less anxiety.
29Welcome him in the Lord with
great joy, and honor men like
him,[c] **30**because he almost died
for the work of Christ, risking his
life to make up for the help you
could not give me.[d]

No Confidence in the Flesh

3 Finally, my brothers, rejoice in
the Lord! It is no trouble for me
to write the same things to you
again, and it is a safeguard for you.
2Watch out for those dogs,[e]
those men who do evil, those muti-
lators of the flesh. **3**For it is we who
are the circumcision,[f] we who
worship by the Spirit of God, who
glory in Christ Jesus, and who put
no confidence in the flesh—
4though I myself have reasons for
such confidence.
If anyone else thinks he has reasons to put confidence in the flesh,
I have more: **5**circumcised[g] on the

2:6 [a]Jn 1:1 [b]Jn 5:18
2:7 [c]Mt 20:28 [d]Jn 1:14; Heb 2:17
2:8 [e]Mt 26:39; Jn 10:18; Heb 5:8
2:9 [f]Ac 2:33; Heb 2:9 [g]Eph 1:20,21
2:10 [h]Ro 14:11 [i]Mt 28:18
2:11 [j]Jn 13:13
2:12 [k]2Co 7:15
2:13 [l]Ezr 1:5
2:14 [m]1Co 10:10; 1Pe 4:9
2:15 [n]Mt 5:45,48; Eph 5:1 [o]Ac 2:40
2:16 [p]1Th 2:19
2:17 [q]2Ti 4:6 [r]Ro 15:16
2:19 [s]ver 23
2:20 [t]1Co 16:10
2:21 [u]1Co 10:24; 13:5
2:22 [v]1Co 4:17; 1Ti 1:2
2:23 [w]ver 19
2:24 [x]Php 1:25
2:25 [y]Php 4:3 [z]Phm 2 [a]Php 4:18
2:26 [b]Php 1:8
2:29 [c]1Co 16:18; 1Ti 5:17
2:30 [d]1Co 16:17
3:2 [e]Ps 22:16,20
3:3 [f]Ro 2:28,29; Gal 6:15; Col 2:11
3:5 [g]Lk 1:59

[e]6 Or *in the form of* [f]7 Or *the form*
[g]16 Or *hold on to*

eighth day, of the people of Israel,[a] of the tribe of Benjamin,[b] a
Hebrew of Hebrews; in regard to
the law, a Pharisee;[c] **6**as for zeal,
persecuting the church;[d] as for le-
galistic righteousness,[e] faultless.
7But whatever was to my profit I
now consider loss[f] for the sake of
Christ. **8**What is more, I consider
everything a loss compared to the
surpassing greatness of knowing[g]
Christ Jesus my Lord, for whose
sake I have lost all things. I consider them rubbish, that I may gain
Christ **9**and be found in him, not
having a righteousness of my own
that comes from the law,[h] but that
which is through faith in Christ—
the righteousness that comes from
God and is by faith.[i] **10**I want to
know Christ and the power of his
resurrection and the fellowship of
sharing in his sufferings,[j] becoming like him in his death,[k] **11**and
so, somehow, to attain to the resurrection[l] from the dead.

Pressing on Toward the Goal

12Not that I have already obtained all this, or have already been
made perfect,[m] but I press on to
take hold[n] of that for which Christ
Jesus took hold of me.[o] **13**Brothers, I do not consider myself yet to
have taken hold of it. But one thing
I do: Forgetting what is behind[p]
and straining toward what is
ahead, **14**I press on[q] toward the
goal to win the prize for which God
has called[r] me heavenward in
Christ Jesus.
15All of us who are mature[s]
should take such a view of things.[t]
And if on some point you think differently, that too God will make
clear to you. **16**Only let us live up to
what we have already attained.
17Join with others in following
my example,[u] brothers, and take
note of those who live according to
the pattern we gave you. **18**For, as
I have often told you before and
now say again even with tears,[v]
many live as enemies of the cross of
Christ.[w] **19**Their destiny is destruction, their god is their stomach,[x]
and their glory is in their shame.[y]
Their mind is on earthly things.[z]
20But our citizenship[a] is in heav-
en.[b] And we eagerly await a Savior
from there, the Lord Jesus Christ,[c]
21who, by the power[d] that enables
him to bring everything under his
control, will transform our lowly
bodies[e] so that they will be like his
glorious body.[f]

4 Therefore, my brothers, you
whom I love and long for,[g] my
joy and crown, that is how you
should stand firm[h] in the Lord,
dear friends!

Exhortations

2I plead with Euodia and I plead
with Syntyche to agree with each
other[i] in the Lord. **3**Yes, and I ask
you, loyal yokefellow,[h3] help these
women who have contended at my
side in the cause of the gospel,
along with Clement and the rest of
my fellow workers, whose names
are in the book of life.
4Rejoice in the Lord always. I
will say it again: Rejoice![j] **5**Let
your gentleness be evident to all.
The Lord is near.[k] **6**Do not be anxious about anything,[l] but in everything, by prayer and petition, with
thanksgiving, present your requests to God.[m] **7**And the peace of
God,[n] which transcends all understanding, will guard your hearts
and your minds in Christ Jesus.
8Finally, brothers, whatever is
true, whatever is noble, whatever is
right, whatever is pure, whatever is
lovely, whatever is admirable—if
anything is excellent or praiseworthy—think about such things.
9Whatever you have learned or received or heard from me, or seen in
me—put it into practice.[o] And the
God of peace[p] will be with you.

Thanks for Their Gifts

10I rejoice greatly in the Lord
that at last you have renewed your
concern for me.[q] Indeed, you have
been concerned, but you had no
opportunity to show it. **11**I am not
saying this because I am in need,
for I have learned to be content[r]

h3 Or *loyal Syzygus*

3:5 [a] 2Co 11:22 [b] Ro 11:1 [c] Ac 23:6
3:6 [d] Ac 8:3 [e] Ro 10:5
3:7 [f] Mt 13:44; Lk 14:33
3:8 [g] Eph 4:13; 2Pe 1:2
3:9 [h] Ro 10:5 [i] Ro 9:30
3:10 [j] Ro 8:17 [k] Ro 6:3-5
3:11 [l] Rev 20:5,6
3:12 [m] 1Co 13:10 [n] 1Ti 6:12 [o] Ac 9:5,6
3:13 [p] Lk 9:62
3:14 [q] Heb 6:1 [r] Ro 8:28
3:15 [s] 1Co 2:6 [t] Gal 5:10
3:17 [u] 1Co 4:16; 1Pe 5:3
3:18 [v] Ac 20:31 [w] Gal 6:12
3:19 [x] Ro 16:18 [y] Ro 6:21 [z] Ro 8:5,6
3:20 [a] Eph 2:19 [b] Col 3:1 [c] 1Co 1:7
3:21 [d] Eph 1:19 [e] 1Co 15:43-53 [f] Col 3:4
4:1 [g] Php 1:8 [h] 1Co 16:13; Php 1:27
4:2 [i] Php 2:2
4:4 [j] Ro 12:12; Php 3:1
4:5 [k] Heb 10:37; Jas 5:8,9
4:6 [l] Mt 6:25-34 [m] Eph 6:18
4:7 [n] Isa 26:3; Jn 14:27; Col 3:15
4:9 [o] Php 3:17 [p] Ro 15:33
4:10 [q] 2Co 11:9
4:11 [r] 1Ti 6:6,8

whatever the circumstances. **12**I
know what it is to be in need, and
I know what it is to have plenty. I
have learned the secret of being
content in any and every situation,
whether well fed or hungry,[a]
whether living in plenty or in
want.[b] **13**I can do everything
through him who gives me
strength.[c]
14Yet it was good of you to
share[d] in my troubles. **15**Moreover,
as you Philippians know, in the
early days[e] of your acquaintance
with the gospel, when I set out
from Macedonia, not one church
shared with me in the matter of giving and receiving, except you
only;[f] **16**for even when I was in
Thessalonica,[g] you sent me aid
again and again when I was in
need.[h] **17**Not that I am looking for
a gift, but I am looking for what
may be credited to your account.[i]
18I have received full payment and

4:12 [a] 1Co 4:11 [b] 2Co 11:9
4:13 [c] 2Co 12:9
4:14 [d] Php 1:7
4:15 [e] Php 1:5 [f] 2Co 11:8,9
4:16 [g] Ac 17:1 [h] 1Th 2:9
4:17 [i] 1Co 9:11,12
4:18 [j] Php 2:25 [k] 2Co 2:14
4:19 [l] Ps 23:1; 2Co 9:8 [m] Ro 2:4
4:20 [n] Gal 1:4 [o] Ro 11:36
4:21 [p] Gal 1:2
4:22 [q] Ac 9:13
4:23 [r] Ro 16:20

even more; I am amply supplied,
now that I have received from
Epaphroditus[j] the gifts you sent.
They are a fragrant[k] offering, an
acceptable sacrifice, pleasing to
God. **19**And my God will meet all
your needs[l] according to his glorious riches[m] in Christ Jesus.
20To our God and Father[n] be
glory for ever and ever. Amen.[o]

Final Greetings

21Greet all the saints in Christ
Jesus. The brothers who are with
me[p] send greetings. **22**All the
saints[q] send you greetings, especially those who belong to Caesar's
household.
23The grace of the Lord Jesus
Christ[r] be with your spirit.
Amen.[i]

[i]23 Some manuscripts do not have *Amen.*

Colossians

Title and Background

During Paul's three-year ministry in Ephesus, Epaphras had been converted and had carried the gospel to Colosse. The young church that resulted then became the target of heretical attack (the Colossian heresy), which led to Epaphras's visit to Paul in Rome and ultimately to the penning of this letter.

Author and Date of Writing

Some have argued that Paul wrote Colossians from Ephesus or Caesarea, but most of the evidence favors Rome as the place. It should be dated about A.D. 60, during Paul's first Roman imprisonment.

Theme and Message

Paul's purpose is to refute the Colossian heresy. To accomplish this goal, he exalts Christ and states that Christ is completely adequate. The theme is the complete adequacy of Christ as contrasted with the emptiness of mere human philosophy. We "have been given fullness in Christ" (2:10).

Outline

I. Greetings, Thanksgiving and Prayer (1:1-14)
II. The Supremacy of Christ (1:15-23)
III. Paul's Labor for the Church (1:24-2:7)
IV. Freedom from Human Regulations through Life with Christ (2:8-23)
V. Rules for Holy Living (3:1-4:6)
VI. Final Greetings and Conclusion (4:7-18)

---

1 Paul, an apostle[a] of Christ
Jesus by the will of God,[b] and
Timothy our brother,

2To the holy and faithful[a] brothers in Christ at Colosse:

Grace[c] and peace to you from
God our Father.[b][d]

Thanksgiving and Prayer

3We always thank God,[e] the Father of our Lord Jesus Christ, when
we pray for you, 4because we have
heard of your faith in Christ Jesus
and of the love[f] you have for all
the saints[g]— 5the faith and love
that spring from the hope[h] that is
stored up for you in heaven[i] and
that you have already heard about
in the word of truth, the gospel
6that has come to you. All over the
world[j] this gospel is bearing fruit[k]
and growing, just as it has been doing among you since the day you
heard it and understood God's
grace in all its truth. 7You learned
it from Epaphras,[l] our dear fellow
servant, who is a faithful minister[m]
of Christ on our[c] behalf, 8and who
also told us of your love in the Spirit.[n]

9For this reason, since the day
we heard about you,[o] we have not
stopped praying for you and asking
God to fill you with the knowledge
of his will[p] through all spiritual
wisdom and understanding.[q]
10And we pray this in order that
you may live a life worthy[r] of the
Lord and may please him in every

1:1 [a] 1Co 1:1 [b] 2Co 1:1
1:2 [c] Col 4:18 [d] Ro 1:7
1:3 [e] Ro 1:8
1:4 [f] Gal 5:6 [g] Eph 1:15
1:5 [h] 1Th 5:8; Tit 1:2 [i] 1Pe 1:4
1:6 [j] Ro 10:18 [k] Jn 15:16
1:7 [l] Phm 23 [m] Col 4:7
1:8 [n] Ro 15:30
1:9 [o] Eph 1:15 [p] Eph 5:17 [q] Eph 1:17
1:10 [r] Eph 4:1

a2 Or *believing* b2 Some manuscripts *Father and the Lord Jesus Christ* c7 Some manuscripts *your*

way: bearing fruit in every good work, growing in the knowledge of God, 11being strengthened with all power[a] according to his glorious might so that you may have great endurance and patience,[b] and joyfully 12giving thanks to the Father,[c] who has qualified you[d] to share in the inheritance[d] of the saints in the kingdom of light. 13For he has rescued us from the dominion of darkness[e] and brought us into the kingdom[f] of the Son he loves,[g] 14in whom we have redemption,[e][h] the forgiveness of sins.[i]

The Supremacy of Christ

15He is the image[j] of the invisible God,[k] the firstborn over all creation. 16For by him all things were created:[l] things in heaven and on earth, visible and invisible, whether thrones or powers or rulers or authorities;[m] all things were created by him and for him.[n] 17He is before all things,[o] and in him all things hold together. 18And he is the head[p] of the body, the church; he is the beginning and the firstborn from among the dead,[q] so that in everything he might have the supremacy. 19For God was pleased[r] to have all his fullness[s] dwell in him, 20and through him to reconcile[t] to himself all things, whether things on earth or things in heaven,[u] by making peace through his blood,[v] shed on the cross.

21Once you were alienated from God and were enemies[w] in your minds[x] because of[f] your evil behavior. 22But now he has reconciled you by Christ's physical body[y] through death to present you holy in his sight, without blemish and free from accusation[z]— 23if you continue in your faith, established[a] and firm, not moved from the hope[b] held out in the gospel. This is the gospel that you heard and that has been proclaimed to every creature under heaven,[c] and of which I, Paul, have become a servant.[d]

1:11 [a]Eph 3:16 [b]Eph 4:2 **1:12** [c]Eph 5:20 [d]Ac 20:32 **1:13** [e]Ac 26:18 [f]Eph 6:12; 2Pe 1:11 [g]Mt 3:17 **1:14** [h]Ro 3:24 [i]Eph 1:7 **1:15** [j]2Co 4:4 [k]Jn 1:18 **1:16** [l]Jn 1:3 [m]Eph 1:20,21 [n]Ro 11:36 **1:17** [o]Jn 1:2 **1:18** [p]Eph 1:22 [q]Ac 26:23; Rev 1:5 **1:19** [r]Eph 1:5 [s]Jn 1:16 **1:20** [t]2Co 5:18 [u]Eph 1:10 [v]Eph 2:13 **1:21** [w]Ro 5:10 [x]Eph 2:3 **1:22** [y]Ro 7:4 [z]Eph 5:27 **1:23** [a]Eph 3:17 [b]ver 5 [c]Ro 10:18 [d]ver 25; 1Co 3:5 **1:24** [e]2Co 1:5 **1:25** [f]ver 23 [g]Eph 3:2 **1:26** [h]Ro 16:25 **1:27** [i]Mt 13:11 **1:28** [j]Col 3:16 [k]1Co 2:6,7 [l]Eph 5:27 **1:29** [m]1Co 15:10 [n]Col 2:1 [o]Eph 1:19 **2:1** [p]Col 1:29; 4:12 [q]Rev 1:11 **2:2** [r]Col 4:8 **2:3** [s]Ro 11:33; 1Co 1:24,30 **2:4** [t]Ro 16:18 **2:5** [u]1Th 2:17 [v]1Co 14:40

Paul's Labor for the Church

24Now I rejoice in what was suffered for you, and I fill up in my flesh what is still lacking in regard to Christ's afflictions,[e] for the sake of his body, which is the church. 25I have become its servant[f] by the commission God gave me[g] to present to you the word of God in its fullness— 26the mystery[h] that has been kept hidden for ages and generations, but is now disclosed to the saints. 27To them God has chosen to make known[i] among the Gentiles the glorious riches of this mystery, which is Christ in you, the hope of glory.

28We proclaim him, admonishing[j] and teaching everyone with all wisdom,[k] so that we may present everyone perfect[l] in Christ. 29To this end I labor,[m] struggling[n] with all his energy, which so powerfully works in me.[o]

2 I want you to know how much I am struggling[p] for you and for those at Laodicea,[q] and for all who have not met me personally. 2My purpose is that they may be encouraged in heart[r] and united in love, so that they may have the full riches of complete understanding, in order that they may know the mystery of God, namely, Christ, 3in whom are hidden all the treasures of wisdom and knowledge.[s] 4I tell you this so that no one may deceive you by fine-sounding arguments.[t] 5For though I am absent from you in body, I am present with you in spirit[u] and delight to see how orderly[v] you are and how firm[w] your faith in Christ is.

Freedom From Human Regulations Through Life With Christ

6So then, just as you received Christ Jesus as Lord,[x] continue to live in him, 7rooted[y] and built up in him, strengthened in the faith as

[w]1Pe 5:9 **2:6** [x]Col 1:10 **2:7** [y]Eph 3:17

[d]*12* Some manuscripts *us* [e]*14* A few late manuscripts *redemption through his blood* [f]*21* Or *minds, as shown by*

you were taught, and overflowing
with thankfulness.
8See to it that no one takes you
captive through hollow and deceptive philosophy,[a] which depends
on human tradition and the basic
principles of this world[b] rather
than on Christ.
9For in Christ all the fullness of
the Deity lives in bodily form,
10and you have been given fullness
in Christ, who is the head[c] over every power and authority. **11**In him
you were also circumcised,[d] in the
putting off of the sinful nature,[g][e]
not with a circumcision done by
the hands of men but with the circumcision done by Christ, **12**having
been buried with him in baptism
and raised with him[f] through your
faith in the power of God, who
raised him from the dead.[g]
13When you were dead in your
sins[h] and in the uncircumcision of
your sinful nature,[h] God made
you[i] alive with Christ. He forgave
us all our sins, **14**having canceled
the written code, with its regulations,[i] that was against us and
that stood opposed to us; he took it
away, nailing it to the cross.[j]
15And having disarmed the powers
and authorities,[k] he made a public
spectacle of them, triumphing over
them[l] by the cross.[j]
16Therefore do not let anyone
judge you[m] by what you eat or
drink,[n] or with regard to a religious
festival,[o] a New Moon celebration[p] or a Sabbath day.[q] **17**These
are a shadow of the things that
were to come;[r] the reality, however, is found in Christ. **18**Do not let
anyone who delights in false humility[s] and the worship of angels
disqualify you for the prize.[t] Such
a person goes into great detail
about what he has seen, and his
unspiritual mind puffs him up with
idle notions. **19**He has lost connection with the Head,[u] from whom
the whole body, supported and
held together by its ligaments and
sinews, grows as God causes it to
grow.[v]
20Since you died with Christ to
the basic principles of this world,[w]
why, as though you still belonged
to it, do you submit to its rules:[x]
21"Do not handle! Do not taste! Do
not touch!"? **22**These are all destined to perish[y] with use, because
they are based on human commands and teachings.[z] **23**Such
regulations indeed have an appearance of wisdom, with their self-im-
posed worship, their false humility
and their harsh treatment of the
body, but they lack any value in restraining sensual indulgence.

Rules for Holy Living

3 Since, then, you have been
raised with Christ, set your
hearts on things above, where
Christ is seated at the right hand of
God. **2**Set your minds on things
above, not on earthly things.[a] **3**For
you died,[b] and your life is now hidden with Christ in God. **4**When
Christ, who is your[k] life, appears,[c]
then you also will appear with him
in glory.[d]
5Put to death, therefore, whatever belongs to your earthly nature:
sexual immorality, impurity, lust,
evil desires and greed,[e] which is
idolatry.[f] **6**Because of these, the
wrath of God[g] is coming.[l] **7**You
used to walk in these ways, in the
life you once lived.[h] **8**But now you
must rid yourselves[i] of all such
things as these: anger, rage, malice, slander,[j] and filthy language
from your lips.[k] **9**Do not lie to each
other,[l] since you have taken off
your old self with its practices
10and have put on the new self,
which is being renewed[m] in knowledge in the image of its Creator.[n]
11Here there is no Greek or Jew,[o]
circumcised or uncircumcised,[p]
barbarian, Scythian, slave or free,[q]
but Christ is all,[r] and is in all.
12Therefore, as God's chosen
people, holy and dearly loved,
clothe yourselves with compassion, kindness, humility,[s] gentleness and patience.[t] **13**Bear with

2:8 [a] 1Ti 6:20 [b] Gal 4:3
2:10 [c] Eph 1:22
2:11 [d] Ro 2:29; Php 3:3 [e] Gal 5:24
2:12 [f] Ro 6:5 [g] Ac 2:24
2:13 [h] Eph 2:1,5
2:14 [i] Eph 2:15 [j] 1Pe 2:24
2:15 [k] Eph 6:12 [l] Lk 10:18
2:16 [m] Ro 14:3,4 [n] Ro 14:17 [o] Ro 14:5 [p] 1Ch 23:31 [q] Gal 4:10
2:17 [r] Heb 8:5
2:18 [s] ver 23 [t] Php 3:14
2:19 [u] Eph 1:22 [v] Eph 4:16
2:20 [w] Gal 4:3,9 [x] ver 14,16
2:22 [y] 1Co 6:13 [z] Isa 29:13; Mt 15:9; Tit 1:14
3:2 [a] Php 3:19,20
3:3 [b] Ro 6:2; 2Co 5:14
3:4 [c] 1Co 1:7 [d] 1Pe 1:13; 1Jn 3:2
3:5 [e] Eph 5:3 [f] Eph 5:5
3:6 [g] Ro 1:18
3:7 [h] Eph 2:2
3:8 [i] Eph 4:22 [j] Eph 4:31 [k] Eph 4:29
3:9 [l] Eph 4:22,25
3:10 [m] Ro 12:2; Eph 4:23 [n] Eph 2:10
3:11 [o] Ro 10:12 [p] 1Co 7:19 [q] Gal 3:28 [r] Eph 1:23
3:12 [s] Php 2:3 [t] 2Co 6:6; Gal 5:22,23

[g] *11* Or *the flesh* [h] *13* Or *your flesh* [i] *13* Some manuscripts *us* [j] *15* Or *them in him* [k] *4* Some manuscripts *our* [l] *6* Some early manuscripts *coming on those who are disobedient*

each other[a] and forgive whatever
grievances you may have against
one another. Forgive as the Lord
forgave you.[b] **14**And over all these
virtues put on love,[c] which binds
them all together in perfect
unity.[d]

15Let the peace of Christ[e] rule
in your hearts, since as members of
one body you were called to peace.
And be thankful. **16**Let the word of
Christ[f] dwell in you richly as you
teach and admonish one another
with all wisdom,[g] and as you sing
psalms, hymns and spiritual songs
with gratitude in your hearts to
God.[h] **17**And whatever you do,[i]
whether in word or deed, do it all in
the name of the Lord Jesus, giving
thanks[j] to God the Father through
him.

Rules for Christian Households

3:18–4:1pp — Eph 5:22–6:9

18Wives, submit to your husbands,[k] as is fitting in the Lord.

19Husbands, love your wives and
do not be harsh with them.

20Children, obey your parents in
everything, for this pleases the
Lord.

21Fathers, do not embitter your
children, or they will become discouraged.

22Slaves, obey your earthly masters in everything; and do it, not
only when their eye is on you and
to win their favor, but with sincerity of heart and reverence for the
Lord. **23**Whatever you do, work at it
with all your heart, as working for
the Lord, not for men, **24**since you
know that you will receive an inheritance[l] from the Lord as a reward. It is the Lord Christ you are
serving. **25**Anyone who does wrong
will be repaid for his wrong, and
there is no favoritism.[m]

4 Masters, provide your slaves
with what is right and fair, because you know that you also have
a Master in heaven.

Further Instructions

2Devote yourselves to prayer,[n]
being watchful and thankful. **3**And
pray for us, too, that God may open
a door[o] for our message, so that we
may proclaim the mystery of
Christ, for which I am in chains.[p]
4Pray that I may proclaim it clearly,
as I should. **5**Be wise[q] in the way
you act toward outsiders;[r] make
the most of every opportunity.[s]
6Let your conversation be always
full of grace,[t] seasoned with salt,[u]
so that you may know how to answer everyone.[v]

Final Greetings

7Tychicus[w] will tell you all the
news about me. He is a dear brother, a faithful minister and fellow
servant[x] in the Lord. **8**I am sending
him to you for the express purpose
that you may know about our[m] circumstances and that he may encourage your hearts.[y] **9**He is coming with Onesimus,[z] our faithful
and dear brother, who is one of
you. They will tell you everything
that is happening here.

10My fellow prisoner Aristarchus[a] sends you his greetings, as
does Mark, the cousin of Barnabas.[b] (You have received instructions about him; if he comes to
you, welcome him.) **11**Jesus, who is
called Justus, also sends greetings.
These are the only Jews among my
fellow workers for the kingdom of
God, and they have proved a comfort to me. **12**Epaphras,[c] who is
one of you and a servant of Christ
Jesus, sends greetings. He is always wrestling in prayer for you,[d]
that you may stand firm in all the
will of God, mature[e] and fully assured. **13**I vouch for him that he is
working hard for you and for those
at Laodicea[f] and Hierapolis.
14Our dear friend Luke,[g] the doctor, and Demas[h] send greetings.
15Give my greetings to the brothers
at Laodicea, and to Nympha and
the church in her house.[i]

16After this letter has been read
to you, see that it is also read[j] in
the church of the Laodiceans and

3:13 [a] Eph 4:2 [b] Eph 4:32
3:14 [c] 1Co 13:1-13 [d] Eph 4:3
3:15 [e] Jn 14:27
3:16 [f] Ro 10:17 [g] Col 1:28 [h] Eph 5:19
3:17 [i] 1Co 10:31 [j] Eph 5:20
3:18 [k] Eph 5:22
3:24 [l] Ac 20:32
3:25 [m] Ac 10:34
4:2 [n] Lk 18:1
4:3 [o] Ac 14:27 [p] Eph 6:19,20
4:5 [q] Eph 5:15 [r] Mk 4:11 [s] Eph 5:16
4:6 [t] Eph 4:29 [u] Mk 9:50 [v] 1Pe 3:15
4:7 [w] Ac 20:4 [x] Eph 6:21,22
4:8 [y] Eph 6:21,22
4:9 [z] Phm 10
4:10 [a] Ac 19:29 [b] Ac 4:36
4:12 [c] Col 1:7; Phm 23 [d] Ro 15:30 [e] 1Co 2:6
4:13 [f] Col 2:1
4:14 [g] 2Ti 4:11; Phm 24 [h] 2Ti 4:10
4:15 [i] Ro 16:5
4:16 [j] 2Th 3:14

[m] 8 Some manuscripts *that he may know about your*

that you in turn read the letter from
Laodicea.
17Tell Archippus:[a] "See to it
that you complete the work you
have received in the Lord."[b]

4:17
[a] Phm 2
[b] 2Ti 4:5

4:18
[c] 1Co 16:21
[d] Heb 13:3

18I, Paul, write this greeting in
my own hand.[c] Remember[d] my
chains. Grace be with you.[e]

[e] 1Ti 6:21; 2Ti 4:22; Tit 3:15; Heb 13:25

1 Thessalonians

Title and Background

Paul founded the church at Thessalonica during his second missionary journey. He had taught there just three weeks when he had to leave suddenly because of the opposition of the Jews. Recent converts from paganism were thus left with little external support in the midst of persecution. Paul wrote to give encouragement to them.

Author and Date of Writing

Both external and internal evidence support the view that Paul wrote 1 Thessalonians. It is generally dated about A.D. 51. Except for the possibility of an early date for Galatians (48-49), 1 Thessalonians is Paul's earliest canonical letter.

Theme and Message

Although the thrust of the letter is varied, the subject of eschatology seems to be predominant in both Thessalonian letters. Every chapter of 1 Thessalonians ends with a reference to the second coming of Christ, with chapter 4 giving it major consideration. Thus, the second coming seems to permeate the letter and may be viewed in some sense as its theme.

Outline

I. Greetings and Thanksgiving (1:1-10)
II. Paul's Defense of His Actions and Absence (2:1-3:13)
III. Exhortations (4:1-5:22)
   A. About Personal Life (4:1-12)
   B. About Christ's Coming (4:13-5:11)
   C. About Church Life (5:12-22)
IV. Concluding Prayer, Greetings and Benediction (5:23-28)

---

1 Paul, Silas[a] and Timothy,[a]
To the church of the Thessalo-
nians[b] *in God the Father and the*
Lord Jesus Christ:

Grace and peace to you.[b][c]

Thanksgiving for the Thessalonians' Faith

2We always thank God for all of
you,[d] mentioning you in our
prayers. 3We continually remember before our God and Father your
work produced by faith,[e] your labor prompted by love, and your endurance inspired by hope in our
Lord Jesus Christ.
4For we know, brothers loved by
God, that he has chosen you, 5be-
cause our gospel[f] came to you not
simply with words, but also with
power, with the Holy Spirit and
with deep conviction. You know
how we lived among you for your
sake. 6You became imitators of
us[g] and of the Lord; in spite of severe suffering,[h] you welcomed the
message with the joy given by the
Holy Spirit.[i] 7And so you became
a model to all the believers in Macedonia and Achaia. 8The Lord's
message rang out from you not only
in Macedonia and Achaia—your
faith in God has become known everywhere.[j] Therefore we do not

1:1 [a]Ac 16:1; 2Th 1:1 [b]Ac 17:1 [c]Ro 1:7
1:2 [d]Ro 1:8
1:3 [e]2Th 1:11
1:5 [f]2Th 2:14
1:6 [g]1Co 4:16 [h]Ac 17:5-10 [i]Ac 13:52
1:8 [j]Ro 1:8; 10:18

[a]*1* Greek *Silvanus*, a variant of *Silas*
[b]*1* Some early manuscripts *you from God our Father and the Lord Jesus Christ*

need to say anything about it, **9**for
they themselves report what kind
of reception you gave us. They tell
how you turned to God from idols[a]
to serve the living and true God,
10and to wait for his Son from heav-
en, whom he raised from the
dead[b]—Jesus, who rescues us
from the coming wrath.[c]

Paul's Ministry in Thessalonica

2 You know, brothers, that our
visit to you[d] was not a failure.
2We had previously suffered[e] and
been insulted in Philippi, as you
know, but with the help of our God
we dared to tell you his gospel in
spite of strong opposition. **3**For the
appeal we make does not spring
from error or impure motives,[f] nor
are we trying to trick you. **4**On the
contrary, we speak as men approved by God to be entrusted with
the gospel.[g] We are not trying to
please men[h] but God, who tests
our hearts. **5**You know we never
used flattery, nor did we put on a
mask to cover up greed[i]—God is
our witness.[j] **6**We were not looking for praise from men, not from
you or anyone else.

As apostles[k] of Christ we could
have been a burden to you, **7**but we
were gentle among you, like a
mother caring for her little children.[l] **8**We loved you so much that
we were delighted to share with
you not only the gospel of God but
our lives as well,[m] because you had
become so dear to us. **9**Surely you
remember, brothers, our toil and
hardship; we worked[n] night and
day in order not to be a burden to
anyone[o] while we preached the
gospel of God to you.

10You are witnesses,[p] and so is
God, of how holy,[q] righteous and
blameless we were among you who
believed. **11**For you know that we
dealt with each of you as a father
deals with his own children,[r]
12encouraging, comforting and
urging you to live lives worthy[s] of
God, who calls you into his kingdom and glory.

13And we also thank God continually[t] because, when you received
the word of God,[u] which you heard
from us, you accepted it not as the
word of men, but as it actually is,
the word of God, which is at work
in you who believe. **14**For you,
brothers, became imitators of
God's churches in Judea,[v] which
are in Christ Jesus: You suffered
from your own countrymen[w] the
same things those churches suffered from the Jews, **15**who killed
the Lord Jesus[x] and the prophets[y]
and also drove us out. They displease God and are hostile to all
men **16**in their effort to keep us
from speaking to the Gentiles[z] so
that they may be saved. In this way
they always heap up their sins to
the limit.[a] The wrath of God has
come upon them at last.[c]

Paul's Longing to See the Thessalonians

17But, brothers, when we were
torn away from you for a short time
(in person, not in thought),[b] out of
our intense longing we made every
effort to see you.[c] **18**For we wanted
to come to you—certainly I, Paul,
did, again and again—but Satan[d]
stopped us.[e] **19**For what is our
hope, our joy, or the crown[f] in
which we will glory[g] in the presence of our Lord Jesus when he
comes?[h] Is it not you? **20**Indeed,
you are our glory[i] and joy.

3 So when we could stand it no
longer,[j] we thought it best to
be left by ourselves in Athens.[k]
2We sent Timothy, who is our
brother and God's fellow worker[d]
in spreading the gospel of Christ, to
strengthen and encourage you in
your faith, **3**so that no one would
be unsettled by these trials. You
know quite well that we were destined for them.[l] **4**In fact, when we
were with you, we kept telling you
that we would be persecuted. And
it turned out that way, as you well
know.[m] **5**For this reason, when I
could stand it no longer,[n] I sent to
find out about your faith. I was

1:9 [a] 1Co 12:2; Gal 4:8
1:10 [b] Ac 2:24 [c] Ro 5:9
2:1 [d] 1Th 1:5,9
2:2 [e] Ac 16:22; Php 1:30
2:3 [f] 2Co 2:17
2:4 [g] Gal 2:7 [h] Gal 1:10
2:5 [i] Ac 20:33 [j] Ro 1:9
2:6 [k] 1Co 9:1,2
2:7 [l] ver 11
2:8 [m] 2Co 12:15; 1Jn 3:16
2:9 [n] Ac 18:3 [o] 2Th 3:8
2:10 [p] 1Th 1:5 [q] 2Co 1:12
2:11 [r] ver 7; 1Co 4:14
2:12 [s] Eph 4:1
2:13 [t] 1Th 1:2 [u] Heb 4:12
2:14 [v] Gal 1:22 [w] Ac 17:5; 2Th 1:4
2:15 [x] Ac 2:23 [y] Mt 5:12
2:16 [z] Ac 13:45,50 [a] Mt 23:32
2:17 [b] 1Co 5:3; Col 2:5 [c] 1Th 3:10
2:18 [d] Mt 4:10 [e] Ro 1:13; 15:22
2:19 [f] Php 4:1 [g] 2Co 1:14 [h] Mt 16:27; 1Th 3:13
2:20 [i] 2Co 1:14
3:1 [j] ver 5 [k] Ac 17:15
3:3 [l] Ac 9:16; 14:22
3:4 [m] 1Th 2:14
3:5 [n] ver 1

c16 Or *them fully* d2 Some manuscripts *brother and fellow worker;* other manuscripts *brother and God's servant*

afraid that in some way the tempter[a] might have tempted you and
our efforts might have been useless.[b]

Timothy's Encouraging Report

6But Timothy has just now come
to us from you[c] and has brought
good news about your faith and
love.[d] He has told us that you always have pleasant memories of us
and that you long to see us, just as
we also long to see you. 7Therefore,
brothers, in all our distress and
persecution we were encouraged
about you because of your faith.
8For now we really live, since you
are standing firm[e] in the Lord.
9How can we thank God enough for
you[f] in return for all the joy we
have in the presence of our God because of you? 10Night and day we
pray[g] most earnestly that we may
see you again[h] and supply what is
lacking in your faith.
11Now may our God and Father
himself and our Lord Jesus clear
the way for us to come to you.
12May the Lord make your love increase and overflow for each other[i] and for everyone else, just as
ours does for you. 13May he
strengthen your hearts so that you
will be blameless[j] and holy in the
presence of our God and Father
when our Lord Jesus comes[k] with
all his holy ones.

Living to Please God

4 Finally, brothers,[l] we instructed you how to live in order to please God,[m] as in fact you
are living. Now we ask you and urge
you in the Lord Jesus to do this
more and more. 2For you know
what instructions we gave you by
the authority of the Lord Jesus.
3It is God's will that you should
be sanctified: that you should
avoid sexual immorality;[n] 4that
each of you should learn to control
his own body[e][o] in a way that is
holy and honorable, 5not in passionate lust[p] like the heathen,[q]
who do not know God; 6and that in
this matter no one should wrong
his brother or take advantage of
him.[r] The Lord will punish men
for all such sins,[s] as we have already told you and warned you.
7For God did not call us to be impure, but to live a holy life.[t]
8Therefore, he who rejects this instruction does not reject man but
God, who gives you his Holy Spirit.[u]
9Now about brotherly love[v] we
do not need to write to you,[w] for
you yourselves have been taught by
God to love each other.[x] 10And in
fact, you do love all the brothers
throughout Macedonia.[y] Yet we
urge you, brothers, to do so more
and more.[z]
11Make it your ambition to lead
a quiet life, to mind your own business and to work with your
hands,[a] just as we told you, 12so
that your daily life may win the respect of outsiders[b] and so that you
will not be dependent on anybody.

The Coming of the Lord

13Brothers, we do not want you
to be ignorant about those who fall
asleep, or to grieve like the rest of
men, who have no hope.[c] 14We believe that Jesus died and rose again
and so we believe that God will
bring with Jesus those who have
fallen asleep in him.[d] 15According
to the Lord's own word, we tell you
that we who are still alive, who are
left till the coming of the Lord, will
certainly not precede those who
have fallen asleep.[e] 16For the Lord
himself will come down from heav-
en, with a loud command, with the
voice of the archangel and with the
trumpet call of God,[f] and the dead
in Christ will rise first.[g] 17After
that, we who are still alive and are
left[h] will be caught up together
with them in the clouds[i] to meet
the Lord in the air. And so we will
be with the Lord[j] forever. 18There-
fore encourage each other with
these words.

5 Now, brothers, about times
and dates[k] we do not need to
write to you,[l] 2for you know very

[e]4 Or *learn to live with his own wife;* or *learn to acquire a wife*

3:5 [a]Mt 4:3 [b]Gal 2:2; Php 2:16
3:6 [c]Ac 18:5 [d]1Th 1:3
3:8 [e]1Co 16:13
3:9 [f]1Th 1:2
3:10 [g]2Ti 1:3 [h]1Th 2:17
3:12 [i]1Th 4:9,10
3:13 [j]1Co 1:8 [k]1Th 2:19
4:1 [l]2Co 13:11 [m]2Co 5:9
4:3 [n]1Co 6:18
4:4 [o]1Co 7:2,9
4:5 [p]Ro 1:26 [q]Eph 4:17
4:6 [r]1Co 6:8 [s]Heb 13:4
4:7 [t]Lev 11:44; 1Pe 1:15
4:8 [u]Ro 5:5; Gal 4:6
4:9 [v]Ro 12:10 [w]1Th 5:1 [x]Jn 13:34
4:10 [y]1Th 1:7 [z]1Th 3:12
4:11 [a]Eph 4:28; 2Th 3:10-12
4:12 [b]Mk 4:11
4:13 [c]Eph 2:12
4:14 [d]1Co 15:18
4:15 [e]1Co 15:52
4:16 [f]Mt 24:31 [g]1Co 15:23; 2Th 2:1
4:17 [h]1Co 15:52 [i]Ac 1:9; Rev 11:12 [j]Jn 12:26
5:1 [k]Ac 1:7 [l]1Th 4:9

well that the day of the Lord[a] will come like a thief in the night.[b] 3While people are saying, "Peace and safety," destruction will come on them suddenly, as labor pains on a pregnant woman, and they will not escape.

4But you, brothers, are not in darkness[c] so that this day should surprise you like a thief. 5You are all sons of the light and sons of the day. We do not belong to the night or to the darkness. 6So then, let us not be like others, who are asleep,[d] but let us be alert and self-controlled. 7For those who sleep, sleep at night, and those who get drunk, get drunk at night.[e] 8But since we belong to the day, let us be self-controlled, putting on faith and love as a breastplate,[f] and the hope of salvation[g] as a helmet.[h] 9For God did not appoint us to suffer wrath but to receive salvation through our Lord Jesus Christ.[i] 10He died for us so that, whether we are awake or asleep, we may live together with him.[j] 11Therefore encourage one another and build each other up, just as in fact you are doing.

Final Instructions

12Now we ask you, brothers, to respect those who work hard among you, who are over you in the Lord[k] and who admonish you. 13Hold them in the highest regard in love because of their work. Live in peace with each other.[l] 14And we urge you, brothers, warn those who are idle,[m] encourage the timid, help the weak,[n] be patient with everyone. 15Make sure that nobody pays back wrong for wrong,[o] but always try to be kind to each other[p] and to everyone else.

16Be joyful always;[q] 17pray continually; 18give thanks in all circumstances, for this is God's will for you in Christ Jesus.

19Do not put out the Spirit's fire;[r] 20do not treat prophecies[s] with contempt. 21Test everything.[t] Hold on to the good. 22Avoid every kind of evil.

23May God himself, the God of peace,[u] sanctify you through and through. May your whole spirit, soul and body be kept blameless at the coming of our Lord Jesus Christ. 24The one who calls you is faithful[v] and he will do it.

25Brothers, pray for us.[w] 26Greet all the brothers with a holy kiss.[x] 27I charge you before the Lord to have this letter read to all the brothers.[y]

28The grace of our Lord Jesus Christ be with you.[z]

5:2 [a] 1Co 1:8 [b] 2Pe 3:10
5:4 [c] Ac 26:18; 1Jn 2:8
5:6 [d] Ro 13:11
5:7 [e] Ac 2:15; 2Pe 2:13
5:8 [f] Eph 6:14 [g] Ro 8:24 [h] Eph 6:17
5:9 [i] 2Th 2:13,14
5:10 [j] 2Co 5:15
5:12 [k] 1Ti 5:17; Heb 13:17
5:13 [l] Mk 9:50
5:14 [m] 2Th 3:6,7, 11 [n] Ro 14:1
5:15 [o] 1Pe 3:9 [p] Gal 6:10; Eph 4:32
5:16 [q] Php 4:4
5:19 [r] Eph 4:30
5:20 [s] 1Co 14:1-40
5:21 [t] 1Co 14:29; 1Jn 4:1
5:23 [u] Ro 15:33
5:24 [v] 1Co 1:9
5:25 [w] Eph 6:19
5:26 [x] Ro 16:16
5:27 [y] Col 4:16

5:28 [z] Ro 16:20

2 Thessalonians

Title and Background

See Introduction to 1 Thessalonians.

Author and Date of Writing

Because of its similarity to 1 Thessalonians, it must have been written not long after the first letter, about A.D. 51 or 52.

Theme and Message

Like 1 Thessalonians, this letter deals extensively with eschatology. In fact, in 2 Thessalonians eighteen of the forty-seven verses deal with this subject. Some people had misunderstood Paul and were sure Jesus was coming very soon. In fact, they had stopped working and were just waiting for Jesus to return. Paul writes to correct this misunderstanding.

Outline

I. Greetings, Thanksgiving and Prayer (1:1-12)
II. Instruction on Christ's Coming and Christian Conduct (2:1-17)
III. Request for Prayer and Warning against Idleness (3:1-15)
IV. Final Greetings and Benediction (3:16-18)

---

1 Paul, Silas[a] and Timothy,[a]
To the church of the Thessalo-
nians in God our Father and the
Lord Jesus Christ:

2Grace and peace to you from
God the Father and the Lord Jesus
Christ.[b]

Thanksgiving and Prayer

3We ought always to thank God
for you, brothers, and rightly so,
because your faith is growing more
and more, and the love every one of
you has for each other is increasing.[c] **4**Therefore, among God's
churches we boast[d] about your
perseverance and faith[e] in all the
persecutions and trials you are enduring.[f]
5All this is evidence[g] that God's
judgment is right, and as a result
you will be counted worthy of the
kingdom of God, for which you are
suffering. **6**God is just: He will pay
back trouble to those who trouble
you[h] **7**and give relief to you who
are troubled, and to us as well. This
will happen when the Lord Jesus is
revealed from heaven in blazing
fire with his powerful angels.[i] **8**He
will punish those who do not know
God[j] and do not obey the gospel of
our Lord Jesus.[k] **9**They will be
punished with everlasting destruction[l] and shut out from the presence of the Lord and from the majesty of his power[m] **10**on the day[n]
he comes to be glorified[o] in his
holy people and to be marveled at
among all those who have believed.
This includes you, because you believed our testimony to you.[p]
11With this in mind, we constantly pray for you, that our God
may count you worthy[q] of his calling, and that by his power he may
fulfill every good purpose of yours
and every act prompted by your
faith.[r] **12**We pray this so that the
name of our Lord Jesus may be glorified in you,[s] and you in him, ac-

1:1 [a]Ac 16:1; 1Th 1:1
1:2 [b]Ro 1:7
1:3 [c]1Th 3:12
1:4 [d]2Co 7:14 [e]1Th 1:3 [f]1Th 2:14
1:5 [g]Php 1:28
1:6 [h]Col 3:25; Rev 6:10
1:7 [i]1Th 4:16; Jude 14
1:8 [j]Gal 4:8 [k]Ro 2:8
1:9 [l]Php 3:19; 2Pe 3:7 [m]2Th 2:8
1:10 [n]1Co 3:13 [o]Jn 17:10 [p]1Co 1:6
1:11 [q]ver 5 [r]1Th 1:3
1:12 [s]Php 2:9-11

[a]*1* Greek *Silvanus*, a variant of *Silas*

cording to the grace of our God and
the Lord Jesus Christ.[b]

The Man of Lawlessness

2 Concerning the coming of our
Lord Jesus Christ and our being gathered to him,[a] we ask you,
brothers, **2**not to become easily unsettled or alarmed by some prophecy, report or letter[b] supposed to
have come from us, saying that the
day of the Lord[c] has already come.
3Don't let anyone deceive you[d] in
any way, for ⌊that day will not come⌋
until the rebellion occurs and the
man of lawlessness[c] is revealed,[e]
the man doomed to destruction.
4He will oppose and will exalt himself over everything that is called
God[f] or is worshiped, so that he
sets himself up in God's temple,
proclaiming himself to be God.[g]
5Don't you remember that when
I was with you I used to tell you
these things? **6**And now you know
what is holding him back, so that
he may be revealed at the proper
time. **7**For the secret power of lawlessness is already at work; but the
one who now holds it back will
continue to do so till he is taken
out of the way. **8**And then the lawless one will be revealed, whom the
Lord Jesus will overthrow with the
breath of his mouth[h] and destroy
by the splendor of his coming. **9**The
coming of the lawless one will be in
accordance with the work of Satan
displayed in all kinds of counterfeit
miracles, signs and wonders,[i]
10and in every sort of evil that deceives those who are perishing.[j]
They perish because they refused
to love the truth and so be saved.
11For this reason God sends them[k]
a powerful delusion so that they
will believe the lie **12**and so that all
will be condemned who have not
believed the truth but have delighted in wickedness.[l]

Stand Firm

13But we ought always to thank
God for you, brothers loved by the
Lord, because from the beginning
God chose you[d][m] to be saved[n]
through the sanctifying work of the
Spirit[o] and through belief in the
truth. **14**He called you to this
through our gospel, that you might
share in the glory of our Lord Jesus
Christ. **15**So then, brothers, stand
firm[p] and hold to the teachings[e]
we passed on to you,[q] whether by
word of mouth or by letter.
16May our Lord Jesus Christ
himself and God our Father, who
loved us[r] and by his grace gave us
eternal encouragement and good
hope, **17**encourage[s] your hearts
and strengthen[t] you in every good
deed and word.

Request for Prayer

3 Finally, brothers,[u] pray for
us[v] that the message of the
Lord[w] may spread rapidly and be
honored, just as it was with you.
2And pray that we may be delivered
from wicked and evil men,[x] for not
everyone has faith. **3**But the Lord is
faithful,[y] and he will strengthen
and protect you from the evil one.[z]
4We have confidence[a] in the Lord
that you are doing and will continue to do the things we command.
5May the Lord direct your hearts[b]
into God's love and Christ's perseverance.

Warning Against Idleness

6In the name of the Lord Jesus
Christ,[c] we command you, brothers, to keep away from[d] every
brother who is idle[e] and does not
live according to the teaching[f] you
received from us.[f] **7**For you yourselves know how you ought to follow our example.[g] We were not
idle when we were with you, **8**nor
did we eat anyone's food without
paying for it. On the contrary, we
worked[h] night and day, laboring
and toiling so that we would not be
a burden to any of you. **9**We did
this, not because we do not have
the right to such help,[i] but in order to make ourselves a model for
you to follow.[j] **10**For even when

2:1 [a]Mk 13:27; 1Th 4:15-17
2:2 [b]2Th 3:17 [c]1Co 1:8
2:3 [d]Eph 5:6-8 [e]Da 7:25; 8:25; 11:36; Rev 13:5,6
2:4 [f]1Co 8:5 [g]Isa 14:13,14; Eze 28:2
2:8 [h]Isa 11:4; Rev 19:15
2:9 [i]Mt 24:24; Jn 4:48
2:10 [j]1Co 1:18
2:11 [k]Ro 1:28
2:12 [l]Ro 1:32
2:13 [m]Eph 1:4 [n]1Th 5:9 [o]1Pe 1:2
2:15 [p]1Co 16:13 [q]1Co 11:2
2:16 [r]Jn 3:16
2:17 [s]1Th 3:2 [t]2Th 3:3
3:1 [u]1Th 4:1 [v]1Th 5:25 [w]1Th 1:8
3:2 [x]Ro 15:31
3:3 [y]1Co 1:9 [z]Mt 5:37
3:4 [a]2Co 2:3
3:5 [b]1Ch 29:18
3:6 [c]1Co 5:4 [d]Ro 16:17 [e]ver 7,11 [f]1Co 11:2
3:7 [g]1Co 4:16
3:8 [h]Ac 18:3; Eph 4:28
3:9 [i]1Co 9:4-14 [j]ver 7

b12 Or *God and Lord, Jesus Christ*
c3 Some manuscripts *sin*
d13 Some manuscripts *because God chose you as his firstfruits*
e15 Or *traditions*
f6 Or *tradition*

we were with you,[a] we gave you
this rule: "If a man will not work,[b]
he shall not eat."
11We hear that some among you
are idle. They are not busy; they are
busybodies.[c] **12**Such people we
command and urge in the Lord
Jesus Christ[d] to settle down and
earn the bread they eat.[e] **13**And as
for you, brothers, never tire of doing what is right.[f]
14If anyone does not obey our instruction in this letter, take special
note of him. Do not associate with
him,[g] in order that he may feel
ashamed. **15**Yet do not regard him
as an enemy, but warn him as a
brother.[h]

Final Greetings

16Now may the Lord of peace[i]
himself give you peace at all times
and in every way. The Lord be with
all of you.[j]
17I, Paul, write this greeting in
my own hand,[k] which is the distinguishing mark in all my letters.
This is how I write.
18The grace of our Lord Jesus
Christ be with you all.[l]

3:10 [a] 1Th 3:4 [b] 1Th 4:11
3:11 [c] ver 6,7; 1Ti 5:13
3:12 [d] 1Th 4:1 [e] 1Th 4:11; Eph 4:28
3:13 [f] Gal 6:9
3:14 [g] ver 6
3:15 [h] Gal 6:1; 1Th 5:14
3:16 [i] Ro 15:33 [j] Ru 2:4
3:17 [k] 1Co 16:21 **3:18** [l] Ro 16:20

1 Timothy

Title and Background

During his fourth missionary journey, Paul had instructed Timothy to care for the church at Ephesus while he went on to Macedonia. When Paul realized he might not return to Ephesus in the near future, he wrote this first letter to Timothy. He repeatedly states his desire and determination to visit Timothy, which shows he was not in prison when he wrote the letter.

Author and Date of Writing

Both early church tradition and the salutations of the Pastoral Letters (1, 2 Timothy, Titus) themselves confirm Paul as the author of this letter. 1 Timothy was written about A.D. 64, at least eight years after Paul's three-year stay in Ephesus.

Theme and Message

The letter was written to Timothy to give him instructions regarding the church. Paul wrote to develop the charge he had given his young assistant: to refute false teachings and to supervise the affairs of the growing Ephesian church. A major problem in this church was a heresy that combined Gnosticism (whose central teaching was that spirit is entirely good and matter is entirely evil), decadent Judaism (which taught that a number of the ceremonial practices of the Old Testament were still binding on the New Testament church) and false asceticism (with its belief that the body should be treated harshly).

Outline

I. Warning Against False Teachers (1:1-11)
II. The Lord's Grace to Paul (1:12-17)
III. The Purpose of Paul's Instructions (1:18-20)
IV. Instructions for the Church (2:1-3:16)
V. Dealing With False Teachers (4:1-16)
VI. Dealing With Different Groups (5:1-6:2)
VII. Miscellaneous Matters (6:3-21)

---

1 Paul, an apostle of Christ Jesus
by the command of God[a] our
Savior and of Christ Jesus our
hope,[b]

2To Timothy[c] my true son[d] in
the faith:

Grace, mercy and peace from
God the Father and Christ Jesus
our Lord.

Warning Against False Teachers of the Law

3As I urged you when I went into
Macedonia, stay there in Ephesus[e] so that you may command
certain men not to teach false doctrines[f] any longer 4nor to devote
themselves to myths[g] and endless
genealogies. These promote controversies[h] rather than God's
work—which is by faith. 5The goal
of this command is love, which
comes from a pure heart[i] and a
good conscience and a sincere
faith.[j] 6Some have wandered away
from these and turned to meaningless talk. 7They want to be teachers
of the law, but they do not know

1:1 [a] Tit 1:3 [b] Col 1:27
1:2 [c] Ac 16:1 [d] 2Ti 1:2; Tit 1:4
1:3 [e] Ac 18:19 [f] Gal 1:6,7
1:4 [g] 1Ti 4:7; Tit 1:14 [h] 1Ti 6:4
1:5 [i] 2Ti 2:22 [j] 2Ti 1:5

what they are talking about or what they so confidently affirm.

8We know that the law is good if one uses it properly. **9**We also know that law[a] is made not for the righteous but for lawbreakers and rebels,[a] the ungodly and sinful, the unholy and irreligious; for those who kill their fathers or mothers, for murderers, **10**for adulterers and perverts, for slave traders and liars and perjurers—and for whatever else is contrary to the sound doctrine[b] **11**that conforms to the glorious gospel of the blessed God, which he entrusted to me.[c]

The Lord's Grace to Paul

12I thank Christ Jesus our Lord, who has given me strength,[d] that he considered me faithful, appointing me to his service. **13**Even though I was once a blasphemer and a persecutor[e] and a violent man, I was shown mercy because I acted in ignorance and unbelief.[f] **14**The grace of our Lord was poured out on me abundantly,[g] along with the faith and love that are in Christ Jesus.[h]

15Here is a trustworthy saying[i] that deserves full acceptance: Christ Jesus came into the world to save sinners—of whom I am the worst. **16**But for that very reason I was shown mercy[j] so that in me, the worst of sinners, Christ Jesus might display his unlimited patience as an example for those who would believe on him and receive eternal life. **17**Now to the King[k] eternal, immortal, invisible,[l] the only God, be honor and glory for ever and ever. Amen.[m]

18Timothy, my son, I give you this instruction in keeping with the prophecies once made about you,[n] so that by following them you may fight the good fight,[o] **19**holding on to faith and a good conscience. Some have rejected these and so have shipwrecked their faith.[p] **20**Among them are Hymenaeus[q] and Alexander,[r] whom I have handed over to Satan[s] to be taught not to blaspheme.

Instructions on Worship

2 I urge, then, first of all, that requests, prayers, intercession and thanksgiving be made for everyone—**2**for kings and all those in authority,[t] that we may live peaceful and quiet lives in all godliness and holiness. **3**This is good, and pleases God our Savior, **4**who wants[u] all men[v] to be saved and to come to a knowledge of the truth.[w] **5**For there is one God[x] and one mediator[y] between God and men, the man Christ Jesus, **6**who gave himself as a ransom for all men—the testimony[z] given in its proper time.[a] **7**And for this purpose I was appointed a herald and an apostle—I am telling the truth, I am not lying—and a teacher[b] of the true faith to the Gentiles.[c]

8I want men everywhere to lift up holy hands[d] in prayer, without anger or disputing.

9I also want women to dress modestly, with decency and propriety, not with braided hair or gold or pearls or expensive clothes,[e] **10**but with good deeds, appropriate for women who profess to worship God.

11A woman should learn in quietness and full submission.[f] **12**I do not permit a woman to teach or to have authority over a man; she must be silent. **13**For Adam was formed first, then Eve.[g] **14**And Adam was not the one deceived; it was the woman who was deceived and became a sinner.[h] **15**But women[b] will be saved[c] through childbearing—if they continue in faith, love[i] and holiness with propriety.

Overseers and Deacons

3 Here is a trustworthy saying:[j] If anyone sets his heart on being an overseer,[d][k] he desires a noble task. **2**Now the overseer must be above reproach,[l] the husband of but one wife, temperate, self-controlled, respectable, hospitable,[m] able to teach,[n] **3**not given to

1:9 [a]Gal 3:19
1:10 [b]2Ti 4:3; Tit 1:9
1:11 [c]Gal 2:7
1:12 [d]Php 4:13
1:13 [e]Ac 8:3 [f]Ac 26:9
1:14 [g]Ro 5:20 [h]2Ti 1:13
1:15 [i]1Ti 3:1; 2Ti 2:11; Tit 3:8
1:16 [j]ver 13
1:17 [k]Rev 15:3 [l]Col 1:15 [m]Ro 11:36
1:18 [n]1Ti 4:14 [o]2Ti 2:3
1:19 [p]1Ti 6:21
1:20 [q]2Ti 2:17 [r]2Ti 4:14 [s]1Co 5:5
2:2 [t]Ezr 6:10; Ro 13:1
2:4 [u]Eze 18:23,32 [v]Tit 2:11 [w]2Ti 2:25
2:5 [x]Ro 3:29,30 [y]Gal 3:20
2:6 [z]1Co 1:6 [a]1Ti 6:15
2:7 [b]2Ti 1:11 [c]Ac 9:15; Eph 3:7,8
2:8 [d]Ps 134:2; Lk 24:50
2:9 [e]1Pe 3:3
2:11 [f]1Co 14:34
2:13 [g]Ge 2:7,22; 1Co 11:8
2:14 [h]Ge 3:1-6,13; 2Co 11:3
2:15 [i]1Ti 1:14
3:1 [j]1Ti 1:15 [k]Ac 20:28
3:2 [l]Tit 1:6-8 [m]Ro 12:13 [n]2Ti 2:24

a9 Or *that the law* b15 Greek *she* c15 Or *restored* d1 Traditionally *bishop*; also in verse 2

drunkenness, not violent but gentle, not quarrelsome,[a] not a lover
of money.[b] **4**He must manage his
own family well and see that his
children obey him with proper respect.[c] **5**(If anyone does not know
how to manage his own family, how
can he take care of God's
church?)[d] **6**He must not be a recent convert, or he may become
conceited[e] and fall under the
same judgment as the devil. **7**He
must also have a good reputation
with outsiders, so that he will not
fall into disgrace and into the devil's trap.[f]

8Deacons,[g] likewise, are to be
men worthy of respect, sincere, not
indulging in much wine,[h] and not
pursuing dishonest gain. **9**They
must keep hold of the deep truths
of the faith with a clear conscience.[i] **10**They must first be
tested; and then if there is nothing
against them, let them serve as
deacons.

11In the same way, their wives[e]
are to be women worthy of respect,
not malicious talkers[j] but temperate and trustworthy in everything.

12A deacon must be the husband
of but one wife and must manage
his children and his household
well.[k] **13**Those who have served
well gain an excellent standing and
great assurance in their faith in
Christ Jesus.

14Although I hope to come to
you soon, I am writing you these
instructions so that, **15**if I am delayed, you will know how people
ought to conduct themselves in
God's household, which is the
church[l] of the living God, the pillar and foundation of the truth.
16Beyond all question, the mystery[m] of godliness is great:

He[f] appeared in a body,[g][n]
  was vindicated by the Spirit,
was seen by angels,
  was preached among the
    nations,[o]
was believed on in the world,
  was taken up in glory.[p]

3:3 [a] 2Ti 2:24 [b] Heb 13:5; 1Pe 5:2
3:4 [c] Tit 1:6
3:5 [d] 1Co 10:32
3:6 [e] 1Ti 6:4
3:7 [f] 2Ti 2:26
3:8 [g] Php 1:1 [h] Tit 2:3
3:9 [i] 1Ti 1:19
3:11 [j] 2Ti 3:3; Tit 2:3
3:12 [k] ver 4
3:15 [l] ver 5; Eph 2:21
3:16 [m] Ro 16:25 [n] Jn 1:14 [o] Col 1:23 [p] Mk 16:19
4:1 [q] Jn 16:13 [r] 2Ti 3:1 [s] 2Th 2:3
4:2 [t] Eph 4:19
4:3 [u] Heb 13:4 [v] Col 2:16 [w] Ge 1:29 [x] Ro 14:6
4:4 [y] Ro 14:14-18
4:6 [z] 1Ti 1:10
4:7 [a] 2Ti 2:16
4:8 [b] 1Ti 6:6 [c] Ps 37:9,11; Mk 10:29,30
4:9 [d] 1Ti 1:15
4:11 [e] 1Ti 5:7; 6:2
4:12 [f] Tit 2:7; 1Pe 5:3 [g] 1Ti 1:14
4:14 [h] 1Ti 1:18 [i] Ac 6:6; 2Ti 1:6

Instructions to Timothy

4 The Spirit[q] clearly says that in
later times[r] some will abandon the faith and follow deceiving
spirits[s] and things taught by demons. **2**Such teachings come
through hypocritical liars, whose
consciences have been seared as
with a hot iron.[t] **3**They forbid people to marry[u] and order them to
abstain from certain foods,[v] which
God created[w] to be received with
thanksgiving[x] by those who believe and who know the truth. **4**For
everything God created is good,[y]
and nothing is to be rejected if it is
received with thanksgiving, **5**because it is consecrated by the word
of God and prayer.

6If you point these things out to
the brothers, you will be a good
minister of Christ Jesus, brought
up in the truths of the faith[z] and of
the good teaching that you have
followed. **7**Have nothing to do with
godless myths and old wives'
tales;[a] rather, train yourself to be
godly. **8**For physical training is of
some value, but godliness has value for all things,[b] holding promise
for both the present life[c] and the
life to come.

9This is a trustworthy saying[d]
that deserves full acceptance
10(and for this we labor and strive),
that we have put our hope in the
living God, who is the Savior of all
men, and especially of those who
believe.

11Command and teach these
things.[e] **12**Don't let anyone look
down on you because you are
young, but set an example[f] for the
believers in speech, in life, in love,
in faith[g] and in purity. **13**Until I
come, devote yourself to the public
reading of Scripture, to preaching
and to teaching. **14**Do not neglect
your gift, which was given you
through a prophetic message[h]
when the body of elders laid their
hands on you.[i]

15Be diligent in these matters;
give yourself wholly to them, so

[e] 11 Or *way, deaconesses* [f] 16 Some manuscripts *God* [g] 16 Or *in the flesh*

that everyone may see your progress. 16Watch your life and doctrine closely. Persevere in them,
because if you do, you will save
both yourself and your hearers.

Advice About Widows, Elders and Slaves

5 Do not rebuke an older man[a]
harshly,[b] but exhort him as if
he were your father. Treat younger
men[c] as brothers, 2older women
as mothers, and younger women as
sisters, with absolute purity.
3Give proper recognition to
those widows who are really in
need.[d] 4But if a widow has children or grandchildren, these
should learn first of all to put their
religion into practice by caring for
their own family and so repaying
their parents and grandparents,[e]
for this is pleasing to God.[f] 5The
widow who is really in need[g] and
left all alone puts her hope in
God[h] and continues night and day
to pray[i] and to ask God for help.
6But the widow who lives for pleasure is dead even while she lives.[j]
7Give the people these instructions,[k] too, so that no one may be
open to blame. 8If anyone does not
provide for his relatives, and especially for his immediate family, he
has denied[l] the faith and is worse
than an unbeliever.
9No widow may be put on the list
of widows unless she is over sixty,
has been faithful to her husband,[h]
10and is well known for her good
deeds,[m] such as bringing up children, showing hospitality, washing
the feet[n] of the saints, helping
those in trouble[o] and devoting
herself to all kinds of good deeds.
11As for younger widows, do not
put them on such a list. For when
their sensual desires overcome
their dedication to Christ, they
want to marry. 12Thus they bring
judgment on themselves, because
they have broken their first pledge.
13Besides, they get into the habit
of being idle and going about from
house to house. And not only do
they become idlers, but also gossips and busybodies,[p] saying
things they ought not to. 14So I
counsel younger widows to marry,[q] to have children, to manage
their homes and to give the enemy
no opportunity for slander.[r]
15Some have in fact already turned
away to follow Satan.[s]
16If any woman who is a believer
has widows in her family, she
should help them and not let the
church be burdened with them, so
that the church can help those widows who are really in need.[t]
17The elders[u] who direct the affairs of the church well are worthy
of double honor,[v] especially those
whose work is preaching and
teaching. 18For the Scripture says,
"Do not muzzle the ox while it is
treading out the grain,"[i][w] and
"The worker deserves his
wages."[j][x] 19Do not entertain an
accusation against an elder[y] unless it is brought by two or three
witnesses.[z] 20Those who sin are to
be rebuked[a] publicly, so that the
others may take warning.[b]
21I charge you, in the sight of
God and Christ Jesus[c] and the
elect angels, to keep these instructions without partiality, and to do
nothing out of favoritism.
22Do not be hasty in the laying
on of hands,[d] and do not share in
the sins of others.[e] Keep yourself
pure.
23Stop drinking only water, and
use a little wine[f] because of your
stomach and your frequent illnesses.
24The sins of some men are obvious, reaching the place of judgment ahead of them; the sins of
others trail behind them. 25In the
same way, good deeds are obvious,
and even those that are not cannot
be hidden.
6 All who are under the yoke of
slavery should consider their
masters worthy of full respect,[g] so
that God's name and our teaching
may not be slandered.[h] 2Those
who have believing masters are not

h9 Or *has had but one husband* i18 Deut. 25:4 j18 Luke 10:7

5:1 [a]Tit 2:2 [b]Lev 19:32 [c]Tit 2:6
5:3 [d]ver 5,16
5:4 [e]Eph 6:1,2 [f]1Ti 2:3
5:5 [g]ver 3,16 [h]1Co 7:34; 1Pe 3:5 [i]Lk 2:37
5:6 [j]Lk 15:24
5:7 [k]1Ti 4:11
5:8 [l]2Pe 2:1; Jude 4; Tit 1:16
5:10 [m]Ac 9:36; 1Ti 6:18; 1Pe 2:12 [n]Lk 7:44 [o]ver 16
5:13 [p]2Th 3:11
5:14 [q]1Co 7:9 [r]1Ti 6:1
5:15 [s]Mt 4:10
5:16 [t]ver 3-5
5:17 [u]Ac 11:30 [v]Php 2:29; 1Th 5:12
5:18 [w]Dt 25:4; 1Co 9:7-9 [x]Lk 10:7; Lev 19:13; Dt 24:14,15; Mt 10:10; 1Co 9:14
5:19 [y]Ac 11:30 [z]Mt 18:16
5:20 [a]2Ti 4:2; Tit 1:13 [b]Dt 13:11
5:21 [c]1Ti 6:13; 2Ti 4:1
5:22 [d]Ac 6:6 [e]Eph 5:11
5:23 [f]1Ti 3:8
6:1 [g]Eph 6:5; Tit 2:9; 1Pe 2:18 [h]Tit 2:5,8

to show less respect for them because they are brothers.[a] Instead, they are to serve them even better, because those who benefit from their service are believers, and dear to them. These are the things you are to teach and urge on them.[b]

Love of Money

3If anyone teaches false doctrines[c] and does not agree to the sound instruction[d] of our Lord Jesus Christ and to godly teaching, **4**he is conceited and understands nothing. He has an unhealthy interest in controversies and quarrels about words[e] that result in envy, strife, malicious talk, evil suspicions **5**and constant friction between men of corrupt mind, who have been robbed of the truth[f] and who think that godliness is a means to financial gain.

6But godliness with contentment[g] is great gain.[h] **7**For we brought nothing into the world, and we can take nothing out of it.[i] **8**But if we have food and clothing, we will be content with that.[j] **9**People who want to get rich[k] fall into temptation and a trap[l] and into many foolish and harmful desires that plunge men into ruin and destruction. **10**For the love of money[m] is a root of all kinds of evil. Some people, eager for money, have wandered from the faith[n] and pierced themselves with many griefs.

Paul's Charge to Timothy

11But you, man of God,[o] flee from all this, and pursue righteousness, godliness, faith, love,[p] endurance and gentleness. **12**Fight the good fight[q] of the faith. Take hold of[r] the eternal life to which you were called when you made your good confession in the presence of many witnesses. **13**In the sight of God, who gives life to everything, and of Christ Jesus, who while testifying before Pontius Pilate[s] made the good confession, I charge you[t] **14**to keep this command without spot or blame until the appearing of our Lord Jesus Christ, **15**which God will bring about in his own time—God, the blessed[u] and only Ruler,[v] the King of kings and Lord of lords,[w] **16**who alone is immortal[x] and who lives in unapproachable light, whom no one has seen or can see.[y] To him be honor and might forever. Amen.

17Command those who are rich in this present world not to be arrogant nor to put their hope in wealth,[z] which is so uncertain, but to put their hope in God,[a] who richly provides us with everything for our enjoyment.[b] **18**Command them to do good, to be rich in good deeds,[c] and to be generous and willing to share.[d] **19**In this way they will lay up treasure for themselves[e] as a firm foundation for the coming age, so that they may take hold of the life that is truly life.

20Timothy, guard what has been entrusted[f] to your care. Turn away from godless chatter[g] and the opposing ideas of what is falsely called knowledge, **21**which some have professed and in so doing have wandered from the faith.[h]

Grace be with you.[i]

6:2 [a] Phm 16 [b] 1Ti 4:11
6:3 [c] 1Ti 1:3 [d] 1Ti 1:10
6:4 [e] 2Ti 2:14
6:5 [f] Tit 1:15
6:6 [g] Php 4:11; Heb 13:5 [h] 1Ti 4:8
6:7 [i] Job 1:21; Ecc 5:15
6:8 [j] Heb 13:5
6:9 [k] Pr 15:27 [l] 1Ti 3:7
6:10 [m] 1Ti 3:3 [n] Jas 5:19
6:11 [o] 2Ti 3:17 [p] 2Ti 2:22
6:12 [q] 1Co 9:25,26; 1Ti 1:18 [r] Php 3:12
6:13 [s] Jn 18:33-37 [t] 1Ti 5:21
6:15 [u] 1Ti 1:11 [v] 1Ti 1:17 [w] Rev 17:14; 19:16
6:16 [x] 1Ti 1:17 [y] Jn 1:18
6:17 [z] Lk 12:20,21 [a] 1Ti 4:10 [b] Ac 14:17
6:18 [c] 1Ti 5:10 [d] Ro 12:8,13
6:19 [e] Mt 6:20
6:20 [f] 2Ti 1:12,14 [g] 2Ti 2:16
6:21 [h] 2Ti 2:18 [i] Col 4:18

2 Timothy

Title and Background

After Paul's release from prison in Rome in A.D. 62-63 and after his fourth missionary journey, during which he wrote 1 Timothy and Titus, he was again imprisoned in Rome under Emperor Nero about 66-67. He was languishing in a cold dungeon, chained like a common criminal. Paul knew that his work was done and that his life was nearly at an end.

Author and Date of Writing

The first verse states that the author is Paul, and numerous references in the letter confirm this. 2 Timothy was written about A.D. 66.

Theme and Message

Paul had three reasons for writing to Timothy at this time: (1) Paul was lonely because many of his friends had deserted him. Paul wanted very much for Timothy to join him; (2) he was concerned about the welfare of the churches during this time of persecution under Nero, and he admonishes Timothy to guard the gospel and, if necessary, to suffer for it; (3) he wanted to write to the Ephesian church through Timothy.

Outline

I. Paul's Concern for Timothy (1:1-14)
II. Paul's Situation (1:15-18)
III. Instructions to Timothy (2:1-26)
IV. Warning About the Last Days (3:1-17)
V. Paul's Charge, Requests and Greetings (4:1-22)

---

1 Paul, an apostle of Christ Jesus
by the will of God,[a] according
to the promise of life that is in
Christ Jesus,[b]

2To Timothy,[c] my dear son:[d]

Grace, mercy and peace from
God the Father and Christ Jesus
our Lord.

Encouragement to Be Faithful

3I thank God,[e] whom I serve, as
my forefathers did, with a clear
conscience, as night and day I constantly remember you in my
prayers.[f] **4**Recalling your tears,[g] I
long to see you,[h] so that I may be
filled with joy. **5**I have been reminded of your sincere faith,[i]
which first lived in your grandmother Lois and in your mother
Eunice[j] and, I am persuaded, now
lives in you also. **6**For this reason I
remind you to fan into flame the
gift of God, which is in you through
the laying on of my hands.[k] **7**For
God did not give us a spirit of ti-
midity,[l] but a spirit of power, of
love and of self-discipline.

8So do not be ashamed[m] to testify about our Lord, or ashamed of
me his prisoner.[n] But join with me
in suffering for the gospel,[o] by the
power of God, **9**who has saved us
and called[p] us to a holy life—not
because of anything we have done
but because of his own purpose
and grace. This grace was given us
in Christ Jesus before the beginning of time, **10**but it has now been

1:1 [a] 2Co 1:1 [b] Eph 3:6; 1Ti 6:19
1:2 [c] Ac 16:1 [d] 1Ti 1:2
1:3 [e] Ro 1:8 [f] Ro 1:10
1:4 [g] Ac 20:37 [h] 2Ti 4:9
1:5 [i] 1Ti 1:5 [j] Ac 16:1
1:6 [k] 1Ti 4:14
1:7 [l] Ro 8:15
1:8 [m] Mk 8:38; Ro 1:16 [n] Eph 3:1 [o] 2Ti 2:3,9; 4:5
1:9 [p] Ro 8:28

revealed[a] through the appearing of
our Savior, Christ Jesus, who has
destroyed death[b] and has brought
life and immortality to light
through the gospel. **11**And of this
gospel I was appointed a herald
and an apostle and a teacher.[c]
12That is why I am suffering as I
am. Yet I am not ashamed, because
I know whom I have believed, and
am convinced that he is able to
guard[d] what I have entrusted to
him for that day.[e]

13What you heard from me,
keep[f] as the pattern of sound
teaching, with faith and love in
Christ Jesus.[g] **14**Guard the good
deposit that was entrusted to you
—guard it with the help of the Holy
Spirit who lives in us.[h]

15You know that everyone in the
province of Asia has deserted me,[i]
including Phygelus and Hermoge-
nes.

16May the Lord show mercy to
the household of Onesiphorus,[j]
because he often refreshed me and
was not ashamed of my chains.
17On the contrary, when he was in
Rome, he searched hard for me until he found me. **18**May the Lord
grant that he will find mercy from
the Lord on that day! You know
very well in how many ways he
helped me[k] in Ephesus.

2 You then, my son, be strong[l]
in the grace that is in Christ
Jesus. **2**And the things you have
heard me say[m] in the presence of
many witnesses[n] entrust to reliable men who will also be qualified
to teach others. **3**Endure hardship
with us like a good soldier[o] of
Christ Jesus. **4**No one serving as a
soldier gets involved in civilian affairs—he wants to please his commanding officer. **5**Similarly, if anyone competes as an athlete, he
does not receive the victor's
crown[p] unless he competes according to the rules. **6**The hard-
working farmer should be the first
to receive a share of the crops. **7**Reflect on what I am saying, for the
Lord will give you insight into all
this.

8Remember Jesus Christ, raised
from the dead,[q] descended from
David.[r] This is my gospel,[s] **9**for
which I am suffering[t] even to the
point of being chained like a criminal. But God's word is not chained.
10Therefore I endure everything[u]
for the sake of the elect, that they
too may obtain the salvation that
is in Christ Jesus, with eternal
glory.[v]

11Here is a trustworthy saying:

If we died with him,
  we will also live with him;[w]
12if we endure,
  we will also reign with him.[x]
If we disown him,
  he will also disown us;[y]
13if we are faithless,
  he will remain faithful,[z]
  for he cannot disown himself.

A Workman Approved by God

14Keep reminding them of these
things. Warn them before God
against quarreling about words;[a] it
is of no value, and only ruins those
who listen. **15**Do your best to
present yourself to God as one approved, a workman who does not
need to be ashamed and who correctly handles the word of truth.[b]
16Avoid godless chatter,[c] because
those who indulge in it will become
more and more ungodly. **17**Their
teaching will spread like gangrene.
Among them are Hymenaeus[d] and
Philetus, **18**who have wandered
away from the truth. They say that
the resurrection has already taken
place, and they destroy the faith of
some.[e] **19**Nevertheless, God's solid foundation stands firm,[f] sealed
with this inscription: "The Lord
knows those who are his,"[a][g] and,
"Everyone who confesses the name
of the Lord[h] must turn away from
wickedness."

20In a large house there are articles not only of gold and silver, but
also of wood and clay; some are for
noble purposes and some for igno-
ble.[i] **21**If a man cleanses himself
from the latter, he will be an instrument for noble purposes, made

1:10 [a] Eph 1:9 [b] 1Co 15:26, 54
1:11 [c] 1Ti 2:7
1:12 [d] 1Ti 6:20 [e] ver 18
1:13 [f] Tit 1:9 [g] 1Ti 1:14
1:14 [h] Ro 8:9
1:15 [i] 2Ti 4:10,11, 16
1:16 [j] 2Ti 4:19
1:18 [k] Heb 6:10
2:1 [l] Eph 6:10
2:2 [m] 2Ti 1:13 [n] 1Ti 6:12
2:3 [o] 1Ti 1:18
2:5 [p] 1Co 9:25
2:8 [q] Ac 2:24 [r] Mt 1:1 [s] Ro 2:16
2:9 [t] Ac 9:16
2:10 [u] Col 1:24 [v] 2Co 4:17
2:11 [w] Ro 6:2-11
2:12 [x] Ro 8:17; 1Pe 4:13 [y] Mt 10:33
2:13 [z] Nu 23:19; Ro 3:3
2:14 [a] 1Ti 6:4
2:15 [b] Eph 1:13; Jas 1:18
2:16 [c] Tit 3:9
2:17 [d] 1Ti 1:20
2:18 [e] 1Ti 1:19
2:19 [f] Isa 28:16 [g] Jn 10:14 [h] 1Co 1:2
2:20 [i] Ro 9:21

[a] *19* Num. 16:5 (see Septuagint)

holy, useful to the Master and prepared to do any good work.[a]

22Flee the evil desires of youth, and pursue righteousness, faith, love[b] and peace, along with those who call on the Lord out of a pure heart.[c] **23**Don't have anything to do with foolish and stupid arguments, because you know they produce quarrels. **24**And the Lord's servant must not quarrel; instead, he must be kind to everyone, able to teach, not resentful.[d] **25**Those who oppose him he must gently instruct, in the hope that God will grant them repentance leading them to a knowledge of the truth,[e] **26**and that they will come to their senses and escape from the trap of the devil,[f] who has taken them captive to do his will.

Godlessness in the Last Days

3 But mark this: There will be terrible times in the last days.[g] **2**People will be lovers of themselves, lovers of money,[h] boastful, proud,[i] abusive, disobedient to their parents,[j] ungrateful, unholy, **3**without love, unforgiving, slanderous, without self-control, brutal, not lovers of the good, **4**treacherous, rash, conceited,[k] lovers of pleasure rather than lovers of God— **5**having a form of godliness but denying its power. Have nothing to do with them.

6They are the kind who worm their way[l] into homes and gain control over weak-willed women, who are loaded down with sins and are swayed by all kinds of evil desires, **7**always learning but never able to acknowledge the truth. **8**Just as Jannes and Jambres opposed Moses,[m] so also these men oppose[n] the truth—men of depraved minds,[o] who, as far as the faith is concerned, are rejected. **9**But they will not get very far because, as in the case of those men,[p] their folly will be clear to everyone.

Paul's Charge to Timothy

10You, however, know all about my teaching,[q] my way of life, my purpose, faith, patience, love, endurance, **11**persecutions, sufferings—what kinds of things happened to me in Antioch,[r] Iconium and Lystra, the persecutions I endured.[s] Yet the Lord rescued me from all of them.[t] **12**In fact, everyone who wants to live a godly life in Christ Jesus will be persecuted,[u] **13**while evil men and impostors will go from bad to worse,[v] deceiving and being deceived. **14**But as for you, continue in what you have learned and have become convinced of, because you know those from whom you learned it,[w] **15**and how from infancy[x] you have known the holy Scriptures,[y] which are able to make you wise[z] for salvation through faith in Christ Jesus. **16**All Scripture is God-breathed[a] and is useful for teaching,[b] rebuking, correcting and training in righteousness, **17**so that the man of God[c] may be thoroughly equipped for every good work.[d]

4 In the presence of God and of Christ Jesus, who will judge the living and the dead,[e] and in view of his appearing and his kingdom, I give you this charge:[f] **2**Preach[g] the Word;[h] be prepared in season and out of season; correct, rebuke[i] and encourage—with great patience and careful instruction. **3**For the time will come when men will not put up with sound doctrine.[j] Instead, to suit their own desires, they will gather around them a great number of teachers to say what their itching ears want to hear. **4**They will turn their ears away from the truth and turn aside to myths.[k] **5**But you, keep your head in all situations, endure hardship,[l] do the work of an evangelist,[m] discharge all the duties of your ministry.

6For I am already being poured out like a drink offering,[n] and the time has come for my departure.[o] **7**I have fought the good fight,[p] I have finished the race,[q] I have kept the faith. **8**Now there is in store for me[r] the crown of righteousness, which the Lord, the righteous Judge, will award to me

2:21 [a] 2Ti 3:17
2:22 [b] 1Ti 1:14; 6:11 [c] 1Ti 1:5
2:24 [d] 1Ti 3:2,3
2:25 [e] 1Ti 2:4
2:26 [f] 1Ti 3:7
3:1 [g] 1Ti 4:1
3:2 [h] 1Ti 3:3 [i] Ro 1:30 [j] Ro 1:30
3:4 [k] 1Ti 3:6
3:6 [l] Jude 4
3:8 [m] Ex 7:11 [n] Ac 13:8 [o] 1Ti 6:5
3:9 [p] Ex 7:12
3:10 [q] 1Ti 4:6
3:11 [r] Ac 13:14,50 [s] 2Co 11:23-27 [t] Ps 34:19
3:12 [u] Ac 14:22
3:13 [v] 2Ti 2:16
3:14 [w] 2Ti 1:13
3:15 [x] 2Ti 1:5 [y] Jn 5:39 [z] Ps 119:98,99
3:16 [a] 2Pe 1:20,21 [b] Ro 4:23,24
3:17 [c] 1Ti 6:11 [d] 2Ti 2:21
4:1 [e] Ac 10:42 [f] 1Ti 5:21
4:2 [g] 1Ti 4:13 [h] Gal 6:6 [i] 1Ti 5:20; Tit 1:13; 2:15
4:3 [j] 1Ti 1:10
4:4 [k] 1Ti 1:4
4:5 [l] 2Ti 1:8 [m] Ac 21:8
4:6 [n] Php 2:17 [o] Php 1:23
4:7 [p] 1Ti 1:18 [q] 1Co 9:24
4:8 [r] Col 1:5

on that day[a]—and not only to me,
but also to all who have longed for
his appearing.

Personal Remarks

9Do your best to come to me
quickly, **10**for Demas,[b] because he
loved this world,[c] has deserted me
and has gone to Thessalonica.
Crescens has gone to Galatia,[d] and
Titus to Dalmatia. **11**Only Luke[e] is
with me.[f] Get Mark[g] and bring
him with you, because he is helpful
to me in my ministry. **12**I sent Tychicus[h] to Ephesus. **13**When you
come, bring the cloak that I left
with Carpus at Troas, and my
scrolls, especially the parchments.
14Alexander[i] the metalworker
did me a great deal of harm. The
Lord will repay him for what he has
done.[j] **15**You too should be on
your guard against him, because he
strongly opposed our message.
16At my first defense, no one
came to my support, but everyone
deserted me. May it not be held
against them.[k] **17**But the Lord
stood at my side[l] and gave me
strength, so that through me the
message might be fully proclaimed
and all the Gentiles might hear it.[m]
And I was delivered from the lion's
mouth. **18**The Lord will rescue me
from every evil attack[n] and will
bring me safely to his heavenly
kingdom. To him be glory for ever
and ever. Amen.[o]

Final Greetings

19Greet Priscilla[b] and Aquila[p]
and the household of Onesiphorus.
20Erastus[q] stayed in Corinth, and I
left Trophimus[r] sick in Miletus.
21Do your best to get here before
winter.[s] Eubulus greets you, and
so do Pudens, Linus, Claudia and
all the brothers.
22The Lord be with your spirit.[t]
Grace be with you.[u]

4:8 [a] 2Ti 1:12
4:10 [b] Col 4:14 [c] 1Jn 2:15 [d] Ac 16:6
4:11 [e] Col 4:14 [f] 2Ti 1:15 [g] Ac 12:12
4:12 [h] Ac 20:4
4:14 [i] Ac 19:33 [j] Ro 12:19
4:16 [k] Ac 7:60
4:17 [l] Ac 23:11 [m] Ac 9:15
4:18 [n] Ps 121:7 [o] Ro 11:36
4:19 [p] Ac 18:2
4:20 [q] Ac 19:22 [r] Ac 20:4
4:21 [s] ver 9
4:22 [t] Gal 6:18; Phm 25 [u] Col 4:18

[b]19 Greek *Prisca*, a variant of *Priscilla*

Titus

Title and Background

When Paul left Antioch to discuss "his" gospel with the Jerusalem leaders, he took Titus with him. Presumably Titus, who is not referred to in Acts, worked with Paul at Ephesus during the third missionary journey. From there the apostle sent him to Corinth to help that church with its work. Following Paul's release from his first Roman imprisonment, he and Titus worked briefly in Crete, after which he commissioned Titus to remain there as his representative and complete some needed work.

Author and Date of Writing

Paul probably wrote this letter to Titus from Corinth about A.D. 64.

Theme and Message

Paul wrote Titus to give him personal authorization and guidance in meeting opposition, instructions about faith and conduct, and warnings about false teachers. He also informed Titus of his future plans for him.

Outline

I. Concerning Elders (1:1-9)
II. Concerning False Teachers (1:10-16)
III. Concerning Various Groups (2:1-15)
IV. Concerning Believers in General (3:1-8)
V. Concerning Response to Spiritual Error (3:9-15)

---

1 Paul, a servant of God[a] and an
apostle of Jesus Christ for the
faith of God's elect and the knowledge of the truth[b] that leads to
godliness— **2**a faith and knowledge resting on the hope of eternal
life,[c] which God, who does not lie,
promised before the beginning of
time,[d] **3**and at his appointed season[e] he brought his word to light[f]
through the preaching entrusted to
me[g] by the command of God our
Savior,[h]

4To Titus,[i] my true son in our
common faith:

Grace and peace from God the
Father and Christ Jesus our Savior.

Titus' Task on Crete

1:6–8Ref – 1Ti 3:2–4

5The reason I left you in Crete[j]
was that you might straighten out
what was left unfinished and appoint[a] elders[k] in every town, as I
directed you. **6**An elder must be
blameless,[l] the husband of but
one wife, a man whose children believe and are not open to the charge
of being wild and disobedient.
7Since an overseer[b][m] is entrusted
with God's work,[n] he must be
blameless—not overbearing, not
quick-tempered, not given to
drunkenness, not violent, not pursuing dishonest gain.[o] **8**Rather he
must be hospitable,[p] one who
loves what is good,[q] who is self-
controlled, upright, holy and disciplined. **9**He must hold firmly[r] to
the trustworthy message as it has
been taught, so that he can encourage others by sound doctrine[s] and
refute those who oppose it.

1:1 [a]Ro 1:1 [b]1Ti 2:4
1:2 [c]2Ti 1:1 [d]2Ti 1:9
1:3 [e]1Ti 2:6 [f]2Ti 1:10 [g]1Ti 1:11 [h]Lk 1:47
1:4 [i]2Co 2:13
1:5 [j]Ac 27:7 [k]Ac 11:30
1:6 [l]1Ti 3:2
1:7 [m]1Ti 3:1 [n]1Co 4:1 [o]1Ti 3:3,8
1:8 [p]1Ti 3:2 [q]2Ti 3:3
1:9 [r]1Ti 1:19 [s]1Ti 1:10

[a]5 Or *ordain* [b]7 Traditionally *bishop*

[10]For there are many rebellious people, mere talkers[a] and deceivers, especially those of the circumcision group.[b] [11]They must be silenced, because they are ruining whole households[c] by teaching things they ought not to teach—and that for the sake of dishonest gain. [12]Even one of their own prophets[d] has said, "Cretans[e] are always liars, evil brutes, lazy gluttons." [13]This testimony is true. Therefore, rebuke[f] them sharply, so that they will be sound in the faith[g] [14]and will pay no attention to Jewish myths[h] or to the commands[i] of those who reject the truth. [15]To the pure, all things are pure, but to those who are corrupted and do not believe, nothing is pure.[j] In fact, both their minds and consciences are corrupted. [16]They claim to know God, but by their actions they deny him.[k] They are detestable, disobedient and unfit for doing anything good.

What Must Be Taught to Various Groups

2 You must teach what is in accord with sound doctrine.[l] [2]Teach the older men to be temperate, worthy of respect, self-controlled, and sound in faith,[m] in love and in endurance.

[3]Likewise, teach the older women to be reverent in the way they live, not to be slanderers or addicted to much wine,[n] but to teach what is good. [4]Then they can train the younger women to love their husbands and children, [5]to be self-controlled and pure, to be busy at home, to be kind, and to be subject to their husbands,[o] so that no one will malign the word of God.[p]

[6]*Similarly, encourage the young* men[q] to be self-controlled. [7]In everything set them an example[r] by doing what is good. In your teaching show integrity, seriousness [8]and soundness of speech that cannot be condemned, so that those who oppose you may be ashamed because they have nothing bad to say about us.[s]

[9]Teach slaves to be subject to their masters in everything,[t] to try to please them, not to talk back to them, [10]and not to steal from them, but to show that they can be fully trusted, so that in every way they will make the teaching about God our Savior attractive.[u]

[11]For the grace of God that brings salvation has appeared to all men.[v] [12]It teaches us to say "No" to ungodliness and worldly passions,[w] and to live self-controlled, upright and godly lives[x] in this present age, [13]while we wait for the blessed hope—the glorious appearing of our great God and Savior, Jesus Christ,[y] [14]who gave himself for us to redeem us from all wickedness and to purify for himself a people that are his very own,[z] eager to do what is good.[a]

[15]These, then, are the things you should teach. Encourage and rebuke with all authority. Do not let anyone despise you.

Doing What Is Good

3 Remind the people to be subject to rulers and authorities,[b] to be obedient, to be ready to do whatever is good,[c] [2]to slander no one,[d] to be peaceable and considerate, and to show true humility toward all men.

[3]At one time we too were foolish, disobedient, deceived and enslaved by all kinds of passions and pleasures. We lived in malice and envy, being hated and hating one another. [4]But when the kindness[e] and love of God our Savior appeared,[f] [5]he saved us, not because of righteous things we had done,[g] but because of his mercy. He saved us through the washing of rebirth and renewal[h] by the Holy Spirit, [6]whom he poured out on us[i] generously through Jesus Christ our Savior, [7]so that, having been justified by his grace,[j] we might become heirs[k] having the hope[l] of eternal life.[m] [8]This is a trustworthy saying.[n] And I want you to stress these things, so that those who have trusted in God may be careful to devote themselves to doing what

1:10 [a] 1Ti 1:6 [b] 11:2
1:11 [c] 2Ti 3:6
1:12 [d] Ac 17:28 [e] Ac 2:11
1:13 [f] 2Co 13:10 [g] Tit 2:2
1:14 [h] 1Ti 1:4 [i] Col 2:22
1:15 [j] Ro 14:14,23
1:16 [k] 1Jn 2:4
2:1 [l] 1Ti 1:10
2:2 [m] Tit 1:13
2:3 [n] 1Ti 3:8
2:5 [o] Eph 5:22 [p] 1Ti 6:1
2:6 [q] 1Ti 5:1
2:7 [r] 1Ti 4:12
2:8 [s] 1Pe 2:12
2:9 [t] Eph 6:5
2:10 [u] Mt 5:16
2:11 [v] 1Ti 2:4
2:12 [w] Tit 3:3 [x] 2Ti 3:12
2:13 [y] 2Pe 1:1
2:14 [z] Ex 19:5 [a] Eph 2:10
3:1 [b] Ro 13:1 [c] 2Ti 2:21
3:2 [d] Eph 4:31; 2Ti 2:24
3:4 [e] Eph 2:7 [f] Tit 2:11
3:5 [g] Eph 2:9 [h] Ro 12:2
3:6 [i] Ro 5:5
3:7 [j] Ro 3:24 [k] Ro 8:17 [l] Ro 8:24 [m] Tit 1:2
3:8 [n] 1Ti 1:15

is good.[a] These things are excellent and profitable for everyone.
9But avoid foolish controversies
and genealogies and arguments
and quarrels[b] about the law, because these are unprofitable and
useless. **10**Warn a divisive person
once, and then warn him a second
time. After that, have nothing to do
with him.[c] **11**You may be sure that
such a man is warped and sinful; he
is self-condemned.

Final Remarks

12As soon as I send Artemas or
Tychicus[d] to you, do your best to
come to me at Nicopolis, because I
have decided to winter there.[e]
13Do everything you can to help Ze-
nas the lawyer and Apollos[f] on
their way and see that they have everything they need. **14**Our people
must learn to devote themselves to
doing what is good,[g] in order that
they may provide for daily necessi-
ties and not live unproductive
lives.
15Everyone with me sends you
greetings. Greet those who love us
in the faith.[h]

Grace be with you all.[i]

3:8 [a] Tit 2:14
3:9 [b] 1Ti 1:4; 2Ti 2:14
3:10 [c] Ro 16:17
3:12 [d] Ac 20:4 [e] 2Ti 4:9,21
3:13 [f] Ac 18:24
3:14 [g] ver 8
3:15 [h] 1Ti 1:2 [i] Col 4:18

Philemon

Title and Background

Philemon was a believer in Colosse who, along with other Christians, was a slave owner. One of his slaves, Onesimus, had apparently stolen from him and then run away, which under Roman law was punishable by death. But Onesimus met Paul and through his ministry became a Christian. Now he was willing to return to his master.

Author and Date of Writing

Paul wrote this short letter about A.D. 60 from prison and sent it to Colosse with Onesimus and Tychicus.

Theme and Message

Paul writes this personal appeal to ask Philemon to accept Onesimus as a Christian brother, not as a slave. Now that Onesimus (whose name means useful) was a believer, he was really useful (see verses 10 and 11 and the footnote on verse 10).

Outline

I. Greetings (1-3)
II. Thanksgiving and Prayer (4-7)
III. Paul's Plea for Onesimus (8-21)
IV. Conclusion (22-25)

1Paul, a prisoner[a] of Christ
Jesus, and Timothy our brother,[b]

To Philemon our dear friend and
fellow worker,[c] **2**to Apphia our sister, to Archippus[d] our fellow soldier[e] and to the church that meets
in your home:[f]

3Grace to you and peace from
God our Father and the Lord Jesus
Christ.

Thanksgiving and Prayer

4*I always thank my God*[g] as I remember you in my prayers, **5**because I hear about your faith in the
Lord Jesus and your love for all the
saints.[h] **6**I pray that you may be active in sharing your faith, so that
you will have a full understanding
of every good thing we have in
Christ. **7**Your love has given me
great joy and encouragement,[i] because you, brother, have refreshed[j] the hearts of the saints.

Paul's Plea for Onesimus

8Therefore, although in Christ I
could be bold and order you to do
what you ought to do, **9**yet I appeal
to you on the basis of love. I then,
as Paul—an old man and now also
a prisoner[k] of Christ Jesus— **10**I
appeal to you for my son[l] Onesimus,[a][m] who became my son while
I was in chains. **11**Formerly he was
useless to you, but now he has become useful both to you and to
me.

12I am sending him—who is my
very heart—back to you. **13**I would
have liked to keep him with me so
that he could take your place in
helping me while I am in chains for
the gospel. **14**But I did not want to
do anything without your consent,

1:1 [a]ver 9,23; Eph 3:1 [b]2Co 1:1 [c]Php 2:25
1:2 [d]Col 4:17 [e]Php 2:25 [f]Ro 16:5
1:4 [g]Ro 1:8
1:5 [h]Eph 1:15; Col 1:4
1:7 [i]2Co 7:4,13 [j]ver 20
1:9 [k]ver 1,23
1:10 [l]1Co 4:15 [m]Col 4:9

[a]10 *Onesimus* means *useful.*

so that any favor you do will be
spontaneous and not forced.[a]
15Perhaps the reason he was separated from you for a little while was
that you might have him back for
good— **16**no longer as a slave, but
better than a slave, as a dear brother.[b] He is very dear to me but even
dearer to you, both as a man and as
a brother in the Lord.

17So if you consider me a partner,[c] welcome him as you would
welcome me. **18**If he has done you
any wrong or owes you anything,
charge it to me. **19**I, Paul, am writing this with my own hand. I will
pay it back—not to mention that
you owe me your very self. **20**I do
wish, brother, that I may have some
benefit from you in the Lord; refresh[d] my heart in Christ. **21**Confident[e] of your obedience, I write to
you, knowing that you will do even
more than I ask.

22And one thing more: Prepare a
guest room for me, because I hope
to be[f] restored to you in answer to
your prayers.[g]

23Epaphras,[h] my fellow prisoner
in Christ Jesus, sends you greetings. **24**And so do Mark,[i] Aristarchus,[j] Demas[k] and Luke, my fellow workers.

25The grace of the Lord Jesus
Christ be with your spirit.[l]

1:14 [a] 2Co 9:7; 1Pe 5:2
1:16 [b] Mt 23:8; 1Ti 6:2
1:17 [c] 2Co 8:23
1:20 [d] ver 7
1:21 [e] 2Co 2:3
1:22 [f] Php 1:25; 2:24 [g] 2Co 1:11
1:23 [h] Col 1:7
1:24 [i] Ac 12:12 [j] Ac 19:29 [k] Col 4:14
1:25 [l] 2Ti 4:22

Hebrews

Title and Background

The first-century church underwent much persecution, and this letter was written in that setting. The persecution had not yet resulted in martyrdom, but it was severe. The intended readers seem to have been Jewish Christians who were thinking of abandoning their faith and of lapsing back into Judaism. So the author exhorts them to hold fast to their confession of Christ as Savior and Lord.

Author and Date of Writing

The author of this letter does not identify himself, but he was obviously well known to the original recipients. For many years Paul was considered to be the author, but since the Reformation it has been widely recognized that Paul could not have been the author. Apollos and Barnabas are those most often suggested. The book was written prior to the fall of Jerusalem in A.D. 70.

Theme and Message

The theme of Hebrews is the absolute supremacy and sufficiency of Jesus Christ as revealer and as mediator of God's grace. The prologue presents Christ as God's full and final revelation. Hebrews could be called "the book of better things," since the two Greek words for "better" and "superior" occur 15 times in the letter. Practical applications of this theme are given throughout the book.

Outline

I. Christ's Superior Revelation (1:1-4)
II. Christ's Superiority Over Angels (1:5-2:18)
III. Christ's Superiority Over Moses (3:1-4:13)
IV. Christ's Superiority Over Aaronic Priests (4:14-7:28)
V. Christ's Superior Sacrifice (8:1-10:39)
VI. Plea for Persevering Faith (11:1-12:29)
VII. Conclusion (13:1-25)

The Son Superior to Angels

1 In the past God spoke[a] to our
forefathers through the prophets[b] at many times and in various
ways,[c] **2**but in these last days he
has spoken to us by his Son, whom
he appointed heir[d] of all things,
and through whom[e] *he* made the
universe. **3**The Son is the radiance
of God's glory[f] and the exact rep-
resentation of his being, sustaining
all things[g] by his powerful word.
After he had provided purification
for sins,[h] he sat down at the right
hand of the Majesty in heaven.[i]
4So he became as much superior to
the angels as the name he has inherited is superior to theirs.[j]
5For to which of the angels did
God ever say,

"You are my Son;
today I have become your
Father[a]"[b]?[k]

Or again,

"I will be his Father,
and he will be my Son"[c]?[l]

6And again, when God brings his
firstborn into the world,[m] he says,

1:1 [a]Jn 9:29; Heb 2:2,3 [b]Ac 2:30 [c]Nu 12:6,8
1:2 [d]Ps 2:8 [e]Jn 1:3
1:3 [f]Jn 1:14 [g]Col 1:17 [h]Heb 7:27 [i]Mk 16:19
1:4 [j]Eph 1:21; Php 2:9,10
1:5 [k]Ps 2:7 [l]2Sa 7:14
1:6 [m]Heb 10:5

[a]5 Or *have begotten you* [b]5 Psalm 2:7
[c]5 2 Samuel 7:14; 1 Chron. 17:13

"Let all God's angels worship
him."[d][a]

7In speaking of the angels he says,

"He makes his angels winds,
his servants flames of
fire."[e][b]

8But about the Son he says,

"Your throne, O God, will last
for ever and ever,
and righteousness will be the
scepter of your kingdom.
9You have loved righteousness
and hated wickedness;
therefore God, your God, has
set you above your
companions[c]
by anointing you with the
oil[d] of joy."[f]

10He also says,

"In the beginning, O Lord, you
laid the foundations of
the earth,
and the heavens are the work
of your hands.
11They will perish, but you
remain;
they will all wear out like a
garment.[e]
12You will roll them up like a
robe;
like a garment they will be
changed.
But you remain the same,[f]
and your years will never
end."[g][g]

13To which of the angels did God
ever say,

"Sit at my right hand
until I make your enemies
a footstool[h] for your
feet"[h]?[i]

14Are not all angels ministering
spirits[j] sent to serve those who
will inherit salvation?[k]

Warning to Pay Attention

2 We must pay more careful attention, therefore, to what we
have heard, so that we do not drift
away. 2For if the message spoken[l]
by angels[m] was binding, and every
violation and disobedience received its just punishment,[n] 3how
shall we escape if we ignore such a
great salvation?[o] This salvation,
which was first announced by the
Lord,[p] was confirmed to us by
those who heard him.[q] 4God also
testified to it by signs, wonders and
various miracles,[r] and gifts of the
Holy Spirit[s] distributed according
to his will.[t]

Jesus Made Like His Brothers

5It is not to angels that he has
subjected the world to come, about
which we are speaking. 6But there
is a place where someone has testified:

"What is man that you are
mindful of him,
the son of man that you care
for him?[u]
7You made him a little[i] lower
than the angels;
you crowned him with glory
and honor
8 and put everything under his
feet."[j][v]

In putting everything under him,
God left nothing that is not subject
to him. Yet at present we do not see
everything subject to him. 9But we
see Jesus, who was made a little
lower than the angels, now
crowned with glory and honor[w] because he suffered death,[x] so that
by the grace of God he might taste
death for everyone.[y]

10In bringing many sons to glory,
it was fitting that God, for whom
and through whom everything exists,[z] should make the author of
their salvation perfect through suffering.[a] 11Both the one who makes
men holy and those who are made
holy[b] are of the same family. So
Jesus is not ashamed to call them
brothers.[c] 12He says,

"I will declare your name to my
brothers;
in the presence of the

1:6 [a]Dt 32:43 (LXX and DSS) Ps 97:7
1:7 [b]Ps 104:4
1:9 [c]Php 2:9 [d]Isa 61:1,3
1:11 [e]Isa 34:4
1:12 [f]Heb 13:8 [g]Ps 102:25-27
1:13 [h]Jos 10:24; Heb 10:13 [i]Ps 110:1
1:14 [j]Ps 103:20 [k]Heb 5:9
2:2 [l]Heb 1:1 [m]Dt 33:2; Ac 7:53 [n]Heb 10:28
2:3 [o]Heb 10:29 [p]Heb 1:2 [q]Lk 1:2
2:4 [r]Jn 4:48 [s]1Co 12:4 [t]Eph 1:5
2:6 [u]Job 7:17
2:8 [v]Ps 8:4-6; 1Co 15:25
2:9 [w]Ac 2:33; 3:13; Php 2:9 [x]Php 2:7-9 [y]Jn 3:16; 2Co 5:15
2:10 [z]Ro 11:36 [a]Lk 24:26; Heb 7:28
2:11 [b]Heb 10:10 [c]Mt 28:10; Jn 20:17

[d]6 Deut. 32:43 (see Dead Sea Scrolls and Septuagint) [e]7 Psalm 104:4 [f]9 Psalm 45:6,7 [g]12 Psalm 102:25-27 [h]13 Psalm 110:1 [i]7 Or *him for a little while*; also in verse 9 [j]8 Psalm 8:4-6

congregation I will sing
your praises."[k][a]

13 And again,

"I will put my trust in him."[l][b]

And again he says,

"Here am I, and the children
God has given me."[m][c]

14 Since the children have flesh
and blood, he too shared in their
humanity[d] so that by his death he
might destroy[e] him who holds the
power of death—that is, the devil[f]— 15 and free those who all their
lives were held in slavery by their
fear[g] of death. 16 For surely it is not
angels he helps, but Abraham's
descendants. 17 For this reason he
had to be made like his brothers[h]
in every way, in order that he might
become a merciful[i] and faithful
high priest[j] in service to God,[k]
and that he might make atonement
for[n] the sins of the people. 18 Because he himself suffered when he
was tempted, he is able to help
those who are being tempted.[l]

Jesus Greater Than Moses

3 Therefore, holy brothers,[m]
who share in the heavenly calling, fix your thoughts on Jesus, the
apostle and high priest[n] whom we
confess.[o] 2 He was faithful to the
one who appointed him, just as
Moses was faithful in all God's
house.[p] 3 Jesus has been found
worthy of greater honor than Moses, just as the builder of a house
has greater honor than the house
itself. 4 For every house is built by
someone, but God is the builder of
everything. 5 Moses was faithful as
a servant[q] in all God's house,[r]
testifying to what would be said in
the future. 6 But Christ is faithful as
a son[s] over God's house. And we
are his house,[t] if we hold on[u] to
our courage and the hope[v] of
which we boast.

Warning Against Unbelief

7 So, as the Holy Spirit says:[w]

"Today, if you hear his voice,
8 do not harden your hearts
as you did in the rebellion,
during the time of testing in
the desert,
9 where your fathers tested and
tried me
and for forty years saw what I
did.[x]
10 That is why I was angry with
that generation,
and I said, 'Their hearts are
always going astray,
and they have not known my
ways.'
11 So I declared on oath in my
anger,
'They shall never enter my
rest.'"[y][o][z]

12 See to it, brothers, that none of
you has a sinful, unbelieving heart
that turns away from the living
God. 13 But encourage one another
daily,[a] as long as it is called Today,
so that none of you may be hardened by sin's deceitfulness.[b] 14 We
have come to share in Christ if we
hold firmly[c] till the end the confidence we had at first. 15 As has just
been said:

"Today, if you hear his voice,
do not harden your hearts
as you did in the rebellion."[p][d]

16 Who were they who heard and
rebelled? Were they not all those
Moses led out of Egypt?[e] 17 And
with whom was he angry for forty
years? Was it not with those who
sinned, whose bodies fell in the
desert?[f] 18 And to whom did God
swear that they would never enter
his rest[g] if not to those who disobeyed[q]?[h] 19 So we see that they
were not able to enter, because of
their unbelief.[i]

A Sabbath-Rest for the People of God

4 Therefore, since the promise of
entering his rest still stands,
let us be careful that none of you be
found to have fallen short of it.[j]

2:12 [a] Ps 22:22
2:13 [b] Isa 8:17 [c] Isa 8:18; Jn 10:29
2:14 [d] Jn 1:14 [e] 1Co 15:54-57; 2Ti 1:10 [f] 1Jn 3:8
2:15 [g] 2Ti 1:7
2:17 [h] Php 2:7 [i] Heb 5:2 [j] Heb 4:14,15; 7:26,28 [k] Heb 5:1
2:18 [l] Heb 4:15
3:1 [m] Heb 2:11 [n] Heb 2:17 [o] Heb 4:14
3:2 [p] Nu 12:7
3:5 [q] Ex 14:31 [r] ver 2; Nu 12:7
3:6 [s] Heb 1:2 [t] 1Co 3:16 [u] Ro 11:22 [v] Ro 5:2
3:7 [w] Heb 9:8
3:9 [x] Ac 7:36
3:11 [y] Heb 4:3,5 [z] Ps 95:7-11
3:13 [a] Heb 10:24,25 [b] Eph 4:22
3:14 [c] ver 6
3:15 [d] ver 7,8; Ps 95:7,8
3:16 [e] Nu 14:2
3:17 [f] Nu 14:29; Ps 106:26
3:18 [g] Nu 14:20-23 [h] Heb 4:6
3:19 [i] Jn 3:36
4:1 [j] Heb 12:15

k *12* Psalm 22:22
l *13* Isaiah 8:17
m *13* Isaiah 8:18
n *17* Or *and that he might turn aside God's wrath, taking away*
o *11* Psalm 95:7-11
p *15* Psalm 95:7,8
q *18* Or *disbelieved*

2 For we also have had the gospel
preached to us, just as they did; but
the message they heard was of no
value to them, because those who
heard did not combine it with
faith.[r][a] 3 Now we who have believed enter that rest, just as God
has said,

"So I declared on oath in my
anger,
'They shall never enter my
rest.' "[s][b]

And yet his work has been finished
since the creation of the world.
4 For somewhere he has spoken
about the seventh day in these
words: "And on the seventh day
God rested from all his work."[t][c]
5 And again in the passage above he
says, "They shall never enter my
rest."[d]

6 It still remains that some will
enter that rest, and those who formerly had the gospel preached to
them did not go in, because of their
disobedience.[e] 7 Therefore God
again set a certain day, calling it
Today, when a long time later he
spoke through David, as was said
before:

"Today, if you hear his voice,
do not harden your
hearts."[u][f]

8 For if Joshua had given them
rest,[g] God would not have spoken[h] later about another day.
9 There remains, then, a Sabbath-
rest for the people of God; 10 for
anyone who enters God's rest also
rests from his own work, just as
God did from his.[i] 11 Let us, therefore, make every effort to enter that
rest, so that no one will fall by following their example of disobedience.[j]

12 For the word of God[k] is living
and active.[l] Sharper than any double-edged sword,[m] it penetrates
even to dividing soul and spirit,
joints and marrow; it judges the
thoughts and attitudes of the
heart.[n] 13 Nothing in all creation is
hidden from God's sight.[o] Everything is uncovered and laid bare
before the eyes of him to whom we
must give account.

Jesus the Great High Priest

14 Therefore, since we have a
great high priest who has gone
through the heavens,[v][p] Jesus the
Son of God, let us hold firmly to the
faith we profess.[q] 15 For we do not
have a high priest who is unable to
sympathize with our weaknesses,
but we have one who has been
tempted in every way, just as we
are[r]—yet was without sin.[s] 16 Let
us then approach the throne of
grace with confidence, so that we
may receive mercy and find grace
to help us in our time of need.

5 Every high priest is selected
from among men and is ap-
pointed to represent them in matters related to God, to offer gifts
and sacrifices[t] for sins.[u] 2 He is
able to deal gently with those who
are ignorant and are going astray,[v]
since he himself is subject to weakness.[w] 3 This is why he has to offer
sacrifices for his own sins, as well
as for the sins of the people.[x]

4 No one takes this honor upon
himself; he must be called by God,
just as Aaron was.[y] 5 So Christ also
did not take upon himself the glory[z] of becoming a high priest. But
God said[a] to him,

"You are my Son;
today I have become your
Father.[w]"[x][b]

6 And he says in another place,

"You are a priest forever,
in the order of
Melchizedek."[y][c]

7 During the days of Jesus' life on
earth, he offered up prayers and petitions with loud cries and tears[d]
to the one who could save him from
death, and he was heard because of
his reverent submission.[e] 8 Although he was a son, he learned

4:2 [a] 1Th 2:13
4:3 [b] Ps 95:11; Heb 3:11
4:4 [c] Ge 2:2,3; Ex 20:11
4:5 [d] Ps 95:11
4:6 [e] Heb 3:18
4:7 [f] Ps 95:7,8; Heb 3:7,8,15
4:8 [g] Jos 22:4 [h] Heb 1:1
4:10 [i] ver 4
4:11 [j] Heb 3:18
4:12 [k] 1Pe 1:23 [l] Jer 23:29 [m] Eph 6:17; Rev 1:16 [n] 1Co 14:24, 25
4:13 [o] Ps 33:13-15
4:14 [p] Heb 6:20 [q] Heb 3:1
4:15 [r] Heb 2:18 [s] 2Co 5:21
5:1 [t] Heb 8:3 [u] Heb 7:27
5:2 [v] Heb 2:18 [w] Heb 7:28
5:3 [x] Heb 7:27; 9:7
5:4 [y] Ex 28:1
5:5 [z] Jn 8:54 [a] Heb 1:1 [b] Ps 2:7
5:6 [c] Ps 110:4; Heb 7:17,21
5:7 [d] Mt 27:46,50 [e] Mk 14:36

[r] 2 Many manuscripts *because they did not share in the faith of those who obeyed*
[s] 3 Psalm 95:11; also in verse 5 [t] 4 Gen. 2:2
[u] 7 Psalm 95:7,8 [v] *14* Or *gone into heaven*
[w] *5* Or *have begotten you* [x] *5* Psalm 2:7
[y] 6 Psalm 110:4

obedience from what he suffered[a]
9and, once made perfect,[b] he became the source of eternal salvation for all who obey him 10and was
designated by God to be high
priest[c] in the order of Melchizedek.[d]

Warning Against Falling Away

6:4–6Ref — Heb 10:26–31

11We have much to say about
this, but it is hard to explain because you are slow to learn. 12In
fact, though by this time you ought
to be teachers, you need someone
to teach you the elementary
truths[e] of God's word all over
again. You need milk, not solid
food![f] 13Anyone who lives on
milk, being still an infant,[g] is not
acquainted with the teaching
about righteousness. 14But solid
food is for the mature,[h] who by
constant use have trained themselves to distinguish good from
evil.[i]

6 Therefore let us leave[j] the elementary teachings[k] about
Christ and go on to maturity, not
laying again the foundation of repentance from acts that lead to
death,[z][l] and of faith in God, 2in-
struction about baptisms,[m] the
laying on of hands,[n] the resurrection of the dead,[o] and eternal
judgment. 3And God permitting,[p]
we will do so.

4It is impossible for those who
have once been enlightened,[q] who
have tasted the heavenly gift,[r]
who have shared in the Holy Spirit,[s] 5who have tasted the goodness
of the word of God and the powers
of the coming age, 6if they fall
away, to be brought back to repentance,[t] because[a] to their loss they
are crucifying the Son of God all
over again and subjecting him to
public disgrace.

7Land that drinks in the rain often falling on it and that produces
a crop useful to those for whom it
is farmed receives the blessing of
God. 8But land that produces
thorns and thistles is worthless and
is in danger of being cursed.[u] In
the end it will be burned.

9Even though we speak like this,
dear friends,[v] we are confident of
better things in your case—things
that accompany salvation. 10God is
not unjust; he will not forget your
work and the love you have shown
him as you have helped his people
and continue to help them.[w] 11We
want each of you to show this same
diligence to the very end, in order
to make your hope[x] sure. 12We do
not want you to become lazy, but to
imitate[y] those who through faith
and patience[z] inherit what has
been promised.[a]

The Certainty of God's Promise

13When God made his promise
to Abraham, since there was no
one greater for him to swear by, he
swore by himself,[b] 14saying, "I will
surely bless you and give you many
descendants."[b][c] 15And so after
waiting patiently, Abraham received what was promised.[d]

16Men swear by someone greater
than themselves, and the oath confirms what is said and puts an end
to all argument.[e] 17Because God
wanted to make the unchanging[f]
nature of his purpose very clear to
the heirs of what was promised,[g]
he confirmed it with an oath.
18God did this so that, by two un-
changeable things in which it is impossible for God to lie,[h] we who
have fled to take hold of the hope[i]
offered to us may be greatly encouraged. 19We have this hope as
an anchor for the soul, firm and secure. It enters the inner sanctuary
behind the curtain,[j] 20where
Jesus, who went before us, has entered on our behalf.[k] He has become a high priest[l] forever, in the
order of Melchizedek.[m]

Melchizedek the Priest

7 This Melchizedek was king of
Salem and priest of God Most
High.[n] He met Abraham returning
from the defeat of the kings and

[z]*1* Or *from useless rituals* [a]*6* Or *repentance while* [b]*14* Gen. 22:17

5:8 [a]Php 2:8
5:9 [b]Heb 2:10
5:10 [c]ver 5 [d]ver 6
5:12 [e]Heb 6:1 [f]1Co 3:2; 1Pe 2:2
5:13 [g]1Co 14:20
5:14 [h]1Co 2:6 [i]Isa 7:15
6:1 [j]Php 3:12-14 [k]Heb 5:12 [l]Heb 9:14
6:2 [m]Jn 3:25 [n]Ac 6:6 [o]Ac 17:18,32
6:3 [p]Ac 18:21
6:4 [q]Heb 10:32 [r]Eph 2:8 [s]Gal 3:2
6:6 [t]2Pe 2:21; 1Jn 5:16
6:8 [u]Ge 3:17,18; Isa 5:6
6:9 [v]1Co 10:14
6:10 [w]Mt 10:40, 42; 25:40; 1Th 1:3
6:11 [x]Heb 3:6
6:12 [y]Heb 13:7 [z]2Th 1:4; Jas 1:3; Rev 13:10 [a]Heb 10:36
6:13 [b]Ge 22:16; Lk 1:73
6:14 [c]Ge 22:17
6:15 [d]Ge 21:5
6:16 [e]Ex 22:11
6:17 [f]Ps 110:4 [g]Heb 11:9
6:18 [h]Nu 23:19; Tit 1:2 [i]Heb 3:6
6:19 [j]Lev 16:2; Heb 9:2,3,7
6:20 [k]Heb 4:14 [l]Heb 2:17 [m]Heb 5:6
7:1 [n]Mk 5:7

blessed him,[a] **2**and Abraham gave
him a tenth of everything. First, his
name means "king of righteousness"; then also, "king of Salem"
means "king of peace." **3**Without
father or mother, without genealogy,[b] without beginning of days or
end of life, like the Son of God[c] he
remains a priest forever.

4Just think how great he was:
Even the patriarch[d] Abraham gave
him a tenth of the plunder![e] **5**Now
the law requires the descendants of
Levi who become priests to collect
a tenth from the people[f]—that is,
their brothers—even though their
brothers are descended from Abraham. **6**This man, however, did not
trace his descent from Levi, yet he
collected a tenth from Abraham
and blessed[g] him who had the
promises.[h] **7**And without doubt
the lesser person is blessed by the
greater. **8**In the one case, the tenth
is collected by men who die; but in
the other case, by him who is declared to be living.[i] **9**One might
even say that Levi, who collects the
tenth, paid the tenth through Abraham, **10**because when Melchizedek
met Abraham, Levi was still in the
body of his ancestor.

Jesus Like Melchizedek

11If perfection could have been
attained through the Levitical
priesthood (for on the basis of it
the law was given to the people),[j]
why was there still need for another
priest to come[k]—one in the order
of Melchizedek,[l] not in the order
of Aaron? **12**For when there is a
change of the priesthood, there
must also be a change of the law.
13He of whom these things are said
belonged to a different tribe,[m] and
no one from that tribe has ever
served at the altar.[n] **14**For it is
clear that our Lord descended from
Judah,[o] and in regard to that tribe
Moses said nothing about priests.
15And what we have said is even
more clear if another priest like
Melchizedek appears, **16**one who
has become a priest not on the basis of a regulation as to his ancestry
but on the basis of the power of an

7:1 [a]Ge 14:18-20
7:3 [b]ver 6 [c]Mt 4:3
7:4 [d]Ac 2:29 [e]Ge 14:20
7:5 [f]Nu 18:21,26
7:6 [g]Ge 14:19,20 [h]Ro 4:13
7:8 [i]Heb 5:6; 6:20
7:11 [j]ver 18,19; Heb 8:7 [k]Heb 10:1 [l]ver 17
7:13 [m]ver 11 [n]ver 14
7:14 [o]Isa 11:1; Mt 1:3; Lk 3:33
7:17 [p]Ps 110:4; ver 21; Heb 5:6
7:18 [q]Ro 8:3
7:19 [r]Ac 13:39; Ro 3:20; Heb 9:9 [s]Heb 4:16
7:21 [t]1Sa 15:29 [u]Ps 110:4
7:22 [v]Heb 8:6
7:24 [w]ver 28
7:25 [x]ver 19 [y]Ro 8:34
7:26 [z]2Co 5:21 [a]Heb 4:14
7:27 [b]Heb 5:1 [c]Heb 5:3 [d]Heb 9:12,26,28 [e]Eph 5:2; Heb 9:14,28
7:28 [f]Heb 5:2 [g]Heb 1:2 [h]Heb 2:10
8:1 [i]Heb 2:17

indestructible life. **17**For it is declared:

> "You are a priest forever,
> in the order of
> Melchizedek."[c][p]

18The former regulation is set
aside because it was weak and useless[q] **19**(for the law made nothing
perfect),[r] and a better hope is introduced, by which we draw near to
God.[s]

20And it was not without an
oath! Others became priests without any oath, **21**but he became a
priest with an oath when God said
to him:

> "The Lord has sworn
> and will not change his
> mind:[t]
> 'You are a priest forever.' "[c][u]

22Because of this oath, Jesus has
become the guarantee of a better
covenant.[v]

23Now there have been many of
those priests, since death prevented them from continuing in office;
24but because Jesus lives forever,
he has a permanent priesthood.[w]
25Therefore he is able to save completely[d] those who come to God[x]
through him, because he always
lives to intercede for them.[y]

26Such a high priest meets our
need—one who is holy, blameless,
pure, set apart from sinners,[z] exalted above the heavens.[a] **27**Unlike the other high priests, he does
not need to offer sacrifices[b] day after day, first for his own sins,[c] and
then for the sins of the people. He
sacrificed for their sins once for
all[d] when he offered himself.[e]
28For the law appoints as high
priests men who are weak;[f] but
the oath, which came after the law,
appointed the Son,[g] who has been
made perfect[h] forever.

The High Priest of a New Covenant

8 The point of what we are saying is this: We do have such a
high priest,[i] who sat down at the

[c] *17,21* Psalm 110:4 [d] *25* Or *forever*

right hand of the throne of the Majesty in heaven, **2**and who serves in the sanctuary, the true tabernacle[a] set up by the Lord, not by man.

3Every high priest is appointed to offer both gifts and sacrifices,[b] and so it was necessary for this one also to have something to offer.[c] **4**If he were on earth, he would not be a priest, for there are already men who offer the gifts prescribed by the law.[d] **5**They serve at a sanctuary that is a copy[e] and shadow[f] of what is in heaven. This is why Moses was warned[g] when he was about to build the tabernacle: "See to it that you make everything according to the pattern shown you on the mountain."[e][h] **6**But the ministry Jesus has received is as superior to theirs as the covenant[i] of which he is mediator[j] is superior to the old one, and it is founded on better promises.

7For if there had been nothing wrong with that first covenant, no place would have been sought for another.[k] **8**But God found fault with the people and said[f]:

"The time is coming, declares
the Lord,
when I will make a new
covenant[l]
with the house of Israel
and with the house of Judah.
9It will not be like the covenant
I made with their
forefathers[m]
when I took them by the hand
to lead them out of Egypt,
because they did not remain
faithful to my covenant,
and I turned away from
them,
declares the Lord.
10This is the covenant I will
make with the house of
Israel
after that time, declares the
Lord.
I will put my laws in their
minds
and write them on their
hearts.[n]
I will be their God,
and they will be my people.[o]
11No longer will a man teach his
neighbor,
or a man his brother, saying,
'Know the Lord,'
because they will all know
me,[p]
from the least of them to the
greatest.
12For I will forgive their
wickedness
and will remember their sins
no more."[q][g][r]

13By calling this covenant "new," he has made the first one obsolete;[s] and what is obsolete and aging will soon disappear.

Worship in the Earthly Tabernacle

9 Now the first covenant had regulations for worship and also an earthly sanctuary.[t] **2**A tabernacle[u] was set up. In its first room were the lampstand,[v] the table[w] and the consecrated bread;[x] this was called the Holy Place. **3**Behind the second curtain was a room called the Most Holy Place,[y] **4**which had the golden altar of incense[z] and the gold-covered ark of the covenant.[a] This ark contained the gold jar of manna,[b] Aaron's staff that had budded,[c] and the stone tablets of the covenant. **5**Above the ark were the cherubim of the Glory,[d] overshadowing the atonement cover.[h] But we cannot discuss these things in detail now.

6When everything had been arranged like this, the priests entered regularly[e] into the outer room to carry on their ministry. **7**But only the high priest entered[f] the inner room, and that only once a year,[g] and never without blood, which he offered for himself[h] and for the sins the people had committed in ignorance. **8**The Holy Spirit was showing[i] by this that the way[j] into the Most Holy Place had not yet been disclosed as long as the

8:2 [a]Heb 9:11,24
8:3 [b]Heb 5:1 [c]Heb 9:14
8:4 [d]Heb 5:1
8:5 [e]Heb 9:23 [f]Col 2:17; Heb 10:1 [g]Heb 11:7; 12:25 [h]Ex 25:40
8:6 [i]Lk 22:20 [j]Heb 7:22
8:7 [k]Heb 7:11,18
8:8 [l]Jer 31:31
8:9 [m]Ex 19:5,6
8:10 [n]2Co 3:3; Heb 10:16 [o]Zec 8:8
8:11 [p]Isa 54:13; Jn 6:45
8:12 [q]Heb 10:17 [r]Jer 31:31-34
8:13 [s]2Co 5:17
9:1 [t]Ex 25:8
9:2 [u]Ex 25:8,9 [v]Ex 25:31-39 [w]Ex 25:23-29 [x]Lev 24:5-8
9:3 [y]Ex 26:31-33
9:4 [z]Ex 30:1-5 [a]Ex 25:10-22 [b]Ex 16:32,33 [c]Nu 17:10
9:5 [d]Ex 25:17-19
9:6 [e]Nu 28:3
9:7 [f]Lev 16:11-19 [g]Lev 16:34 [h]Heb 5:2,3
9:8 [i]Heb 3:7 [j]Jn 14:6; Heb 10:19,20

[e]*5* Exodus 25:40 [f]*8* Some manuscripts may be translated *fault and said to the people.* [g]*12* Jer. 31:31-34 [h]*5* Traditionally *the mercy seat*

first tabernacle was still standing. **9**This is an illustration for the present time, indicating that the gifts and sacrifices being offered[a] were not able to clear the conscience of the worshiper. **10**They are only a matter of food[b] and drink[c] and various ceremonial washings—external regulations[d] applying until the time of the new order.

The Blood of Christ

11When Christ came as high priest[e] of the good things that are already here,[i][f] he went through the greater and more perfect tabernacle[g] that is not man-made, that is to say, not a part of this creation. **12**He did not enter by means of the blood of goats and calves;[h] but he entered the Most Holy Place[i] once for all[j] by his own blood, having obtained eternal redemption. **13**The blood of goats and bulls and the ashes of a heifer[k] sprinkled on those who are ceremonially unclean sanctify them so that they are outwardly clean. **14**How much more, then, will the blood of Christ, who through the eternal Spirit[l] offered himself unblemished to God, cleanse our consciences[m] from acts that lead to death,[j][n] so that we may serve the living God!

15For this reason Christ is the mediator[o] of a new covenant, that those who are called may receive the promised eternal inheritance—now that he has died as a ransom to set them free from the sins committed under the first covenant.[p]

16In the case of a will,[k] it is necessary to prove the death of the one who made it, **17**because a will is in force only when somebody has died; it never takes effect while the one who made it is living. **18**This is why even the first covenant was not put into effect without blood.[q] **19**When Moses had proclaimed every commandment of the law to all the people, he took the blood of calves, together with water, scarlet wool and branches of hyssop, and sprinkled the scroll and all the people.[r] **20**He said, "This is the blood of the covenant, which God has commanded you to keep."[l][s] **21**In the same way, he sprinkled with the blood both the tabernacle and everything used in its ceremonies. **22**In fact, the law requires that nearly everything be cleansed with blood,[t] and without the shedding of blood there is no forgiveness.[u]

23It was necessary, then, for the copies[v] of the heavenly things to be purified with these sacrifices, but the heavenly things themselves with better sacrifices than these. **24**For Christ did not enter a man-made sanctuary that was only a copy of the true one;[w] he entered heaven itself, now to appear for us in God's presence. **25**Nor did he enter heaven to offer himself again and again, the way the high priest enters the Most Holy Place[x] every year with blood that is not his own.[y] **26**Then Christ would have had to suffer many times since the creation of the world.[z] But now he has appeared once for all[a] at the end of the ages to do away with sin by the sacrifice of himself. **27**Just as man is destined to die once,[b] and after that to face judgment,[c] **28**so Christ was sacrificed once to take away the sins of many people; and he will appear a second time,[d] not to bear sin,[e] but to bring salvation to those who are waiting for him.[f]

Christ's Sacrifice Once for All

10 The law is only a shadow[g] of the good things[h] that are coming—not the realities themselves.[i] For this reason it can never, by the same sacrifices repeated endlessly year after year, make perfect[j] those who draw near to worship. **2**If it could, would they not have stopped being offered? For the worshipers would have been cleansed once for all, and would no longer have felt guilty for their sins. **3**But those sacrifices are an annual

9:9 [a]Heb 5:1
9:10 [b]Lev 11:2-23 [c]Col 2:16 [d]Heb 7:16
9:11 [e]Heb 2:17 [f]Heb 10:1 [g]Heb 8:2
9:12 [h]Heb 10:4 [i]ver 24 [j]Heb 7:27
9:13 [k]Nu 19:9,17,18
9:14 [l]1Pe 3:18 [m]Tit 2:14; Heb 10:2,22 [n]Heb 6:1
9:15 [o]1Ti 2:5 [p]Heb 7:22
9:18 [q]Ex 24:6-8
9:19 [r]Ex 24:6-8
9:20 [s]Ex 24:8; Mt 26:28
9:22 [t]Lev 8:15 [u]Lev 17:11
9:23 [v]Heb 8:5
9:24 [w]Heb 8:2
9:25 [x]Heb 10:19 [y]ver 7,8
9:26 [z]Heb 4:3 [a]Heb 7:27
9:27 [b]Ge 3:19 [c]2Co 5:10
9:28 [d]Tit 2:13 [e]1Pe 2:24 [f]1Co 1:7
10:1 [g]Heb 8:5 [h]Heb 9:11 [i]Heb 9:23 [j]Heb 7:19

[i]*11* Some early manuscripts *are to come*
[j]*14* Or *from useless rituals*
[k]*16* Same Greek word as *covenant*; also in verse 17
[l]*20* Exodus 24:8

reminder of sins,[a] 4because it is
impossible for the blood of bulls
and goats[b] to take away sins.
5Therefore, when Christ came
into the world,[c] he said:

"Sacrifice and offering you did
not desire,
but a body you prepared for
me;[d]
6with burnt offerings and sin
offerings
you were not pleased.
7Then I said, 'Here I am—it is
written about me in the
scroll[e]—
I have come to do your will,
O God.' "[m][f]

8First he said, "Sacrifices and offerings, burnt offerings and sin offerings you did not desire, nor were
you pleased with them"[g] (although the law required them to be
made). 9Then he said, "Here I am,
I have come to do your will."[h] He
sets aside the first to establish the
second. 10And by that will, we have
been made holy[i] through the sacrifice of the body[j] of Jesus Christ
once for all.[k]
11Day after day every priest
stands and performs his religious
duties; again and again he offers
the same sacrifices,[l] which can
never take away sins.[m] 12But when
this priest had offered for all time
one sacrifice for sins, he sat down
at the right hand of God. 13Since
that time he waits for his enemies
to be made his footstool,[n] 14be-
cause by one sacrifice he has made
perfect[o] forever those who are being made holy.
15The Holy Spirit also testifies[p]
to us about this. First he says:

16"This is the covenant I will
make with them
after that time, says the
Lord.
I will put my laws in their
hearts,
and I will write them on their
minds."[n][q]

17Then he adds:

"Their sins and lawless acts
I will remember no more."[o][r]

18And where these have been forgiven, there is no longer any sacrifice for sin.

A Call to Persevere

19Therefore, brothers, since we
have confidence to enter the Most
Holy Place[s] by the blood of Jesus,
20by a new and living way[t] opened
for us through the curtain,[u] that is,
his body, 21and since we have a
great priest[v] over the house of
God, 22let us draw near to God[w]
with a sincere heart in full assurance of faith, having our hearts
sprinkled to cleanse us from a
guilty conscience[x] and having our
bodies washed with pure water.
23Let us hold unswervingly to the
hope[y] we profess, for he who
promised is faithful.[z] 24And let us
consider how we may spur one another on toward love and good
deeds. 25Let us not give up meeting
together,[a] as some are in the habit
of doing, but let us encourage one
another[b]—and all the more as you
see the Day approaching.
26If we deliberately keep on sinning[c] after we have received the
knowledge of the truth, no sacrifice
for sins is left, 27but only a fearful
expectation of judgment and of
raging fire[d] that will consume the
enemies of God. 28Anyone who rejected the law of Moses died without mercy on the testimony of two
or three witnesses.[e] 29How much
more severely do you think a man
deserves to be punished who has
trampled the Son of God under
foot,[f] who has treated as an unholy thing the blood of the covenant[g]
that sanctified him, and who has
insulted the Spirit[h] of grace?[i]
30For we know him who said, "It is
mine to avenge; I will repay,"[p][j]
and again, "The Lord will judge his
people."[q][k] 31It is a dreadful thing
to fall into the hands of the living
God.[l]
32Remember those earlier days

10:3 [a]Heb 9:7
10:4 [b]Heb 9:12,13
10:5 [c]Heb 1:6 [d]1Pe 2:24
10:7 [e]Jer 36:2 [f]Ps 40:6-8
10:8 [g]ver 5,6; Mk 12:33
10:9 [h]ver 7
10:10 [i]Jn 17:19 [j]Heb 2:14; 1Pe 2:24 [k]Heb 7:27
10:11 [l]Heb 5:1 [m]ver 1,4
10:13 [n]Heb 1:13
10:14 [o]ver 1
10:15 [p]Heb 3:7
10:16 [q]Jer 31:33; Heb 8:10
10:17 [r]Heb 8:12
10:19 [s]Eph 2:18; Heb 9:8,12,25
10:20 [t]Heb 9:8 [u]Heb 9:3
10:21 [v]Heb 2:17
10:22 [w]Heb 7:19 [x]Eze 36:25; Heb 9:14
10:23 [y]Heb 3:6 [z]1Co 1:9
10:25 [a]Ac 2:42 [b]Heb 3:13
10:26 [c]Nu 15:30; 2Pe 2:20
10:27 [d]Isa 26:11; 2Th 1:7; Heb 9:27
10:28 [e]Dt 17:6,7; Heb 2:2
10:29 [f]Heb 6:6 [g]Mt 26:28 [h]Eph 4:30; Heb 6:4 [i]Heb 2:3
10:30 [j]Dt 32:35; Ro 12:19 [k]Dt 32:36
10:31 [l]Mt 16:16

m7 Psalm 40:6-8 (see Septuagint) n*16* Jer. 31:33 o*17* Jer. 31:34 p*30* Deut. 32:35 q*30* Deut. 32:36; Psalm 135:14

after you had received the light,[a] when you stood your ground in a great contest in the face of suffering.[b] **33**Sometimes you were publicly exposed to insult and persecution;[c] at other times you stood side by side with those who were so treated.[d] **34**You sympathized with those in prison[e] and joyfully accepted the confiscation of your property, because you knew that you yourselves had better and lasting possessions.[f]

35So do not throw away your confidence; it will be richly rewarded. **36**You need to persevere[g] so that when you have done the will of God, you will receive what he has promised. **37**For in just a very little while,

"He who is coming[h] will come
and will not delay.[i]
38 But my righteous one[r] will
live by faith.[j]
And if he shrinks back,
I will not be pleased with
him."[s]

39But we are not of those who shrink back and are destroyed, but of those who believe and are saved.

By Faith

11 Now faith is being sure of what we hope for and certain of what we do not see.[k] **2**This is what the ancients were commended for.[l]

3By faith we understand that the universe was formed at God's command,[m] so that what is seen was not made out of what was visible.

4By faith Abel offered God a better sacrifice than Cain did. By faith he was commended as a righteous man, when God spoke well of his offerings.[n] And by faith he still speaks, even though he is dead.[o]

5By faith Enoch was taken from this life, so that he did not experience death; he could not be found, because God had taken him away.[p] For before he was taken, he was commended as one who pleased God. **6**And without faith it is impossible to please God, because anyone who comes to him[q] must believe that he exists and that he rewards those who earnestly seek him.

7By faith Noah, when warned about things not yet seen, in holy fear built an ark[r] to save his family.[s] By his faith he condemned the world and became heir of the righteousness that comes by faith.

8By faith Abraham, when called to go to a place he would later receive as his inheritance,[t] obeyed and went,[u] even though he did not know where he was going. **9**By faith he made his home in the promised land[v] like a stranger in a foreign country; he lived in tents,[w] as did Isaac and Jacob, who were heirs with him of the same promise.[x] **10**For he was looking forward to the city[y] with foundations,[z] whose architect and builder is God.

11By faith Abraham, even though he was past age—and Sarah herself was barren[a]—was enabled to become a father[b] because he[t] considered him faithful who had made the promise. **12**And so from this one man, and he as good as dead,[c] came descendants as numerous as the stars in the sky and as countless as the sand on the seashore.[d]

13All these people were still living by faith when they died. They did not receive the things promised;[e] they only saw them and welcomed them from a distance.[f] And they admitted that they were aliens and strangers on earth.[g] **14**People who say such things show that they are looking for a country of their own. **15**If they had been thinking of the country they had left, they would have had opportunity to return.[h] **16**Instead, they were longing for a better country—a heavenly one.[i] Therefore God is not ashamed[j] to be called their God,[k] for he has prepared a city[l] for them.

17By faith Abraham, when God tested him, offered Isaac as a sacrifice.[m] He who had received the

[r]*38* One early manuscript *But the righteous*
[s]*38* Hab. 2:3,4
[t]*11* Or *By faith even Sarah, who was past age, was enabled to bear children because she*

10:32 [a]Heb 6:4 [b]Php 1:29,30
10:33 [c]1Co 4:9 [d]Php 4:14; 1Th 2:14
10:34 [e]Heb 13:3 [f]Heb 11:16
10:36 [g]Lk 21:19; Heb 12:1
10:37 [h]Mt 11:3 [i]Rev 22:20
10:38 [j]Ro 1:17; Gal 3:11
11:1 [k]Ro 8:24; 2Co 4:18
11:2 [l]ver 4,39
11:3 [m]Ge 1; Jn 1:3; 2Pe 3:5
11:4 [n]Ge 4:4; 1Jn 3:12 [o]Heb 12:24
11:5 [p]Ge 5:21-24
11:6 [q]Heb 7:19
11:7 [r]Ge 6:13-22 [s]1Pe 3:20
11:8 [t]Ge 12:7 [u]Ge 12:1-4; Ac 7:2-4
11:9 [v]Ac 7:5 [w]Ge 12:8; 18:1,9 [x]Heb 6:17
11:10 [y]Heb 12:22; 13:14 [z]Rev 21:2,14
11:11 [a]Ge 17:17-19; 18:11-14 [b]Ge 21:2
11:12 [c]Ro 4:19 [d]Ge 22:17
11:13 [e]ver 39 [f]Mt 13:17 [g]Ge 23:4; Ps 39:12; 1Pe 1:17
11:15 [h]Ge 24:6-8
11:16 [i]2Ti 4:18 [j]Mk 8:38 [k]Ex 3:6,15 [l]Heb 13:14
11:17 [m]Ge 22:1-10; Jas 2:21

promises was about to sacrifice his
one and only son, 18even though
God had said to him, "It is through
Isaac that your offspring[u] will be
reckoned."[v][a] 19Abraham reasoned that God could raise the
dead,[b] and figuratively speaking,
he did receive Isaac back from
death.
20By faith Isaac blessed Jacob
and Esau in regard to their future.[c]
21By faith Jacob, when he was
dying, blessed each of Joseph's
sons,[d] and worshiped as he leaned
on the top of his staff.
22By faith Joseph, when his end
was near, spoke about the exodus
of the Israelites from Egypt and
gave instructions about his
bones.[e]
23By faith Moses' parents hid
him for three months after he was
born,[f] because they saw he was no
ordinary child, and they were not
afraid of the king's edict.[g]
24By faith Moses, when he had
grown up, refused to be known as
the son of Pharaoh's daughter.[h]
25He chose to be mistreated[i]
along with the people of God rather
than to enjoy the pleasures of sin
for a short time. 26He regarded disgrace[j] for the sake of Christ as of
greater value than the treasures of
Egypt, because he was looking
ahead to his reward.[k] 27By faith he
left Egypt,[l] not fearing the king's
anger; he persevered because he
saw him who is invisible. 28By faith
he kept the Passover and the sprinkling of blood, so that the destroyer
of the firstborn would not touch
the firstborn of Israel.[m]
29By faith the people passed
through the Red Sea[w] as on dry
land; but when the Egyptians tried
to do so, they were drowned.[n]
30By faith the walls of Jericho
fell, after the people had marched
around them for seven days.[o]
31By faith the prostitute Rahab,
because she welcomed the spies,
was not killed with those who were
disobedient.[x][p]
32And what more shall I say? I do
not have time to tell about Gideon,
Barak,[q] Samson, Jephthah, David,[r] Samuel[s] and the prophets,
33who through faith conquered
kingdoms,[t] administered justice,
and gained what was promised;
who shut the mouths of lions,[u]
34quenched the fury of the flames,
and escaped the edge of the sword;
whose weakness was turned to
strength;[v] and who became powerful in battle and routed foreign
armies.[w] 35Women received back
their dead, raised to life again.[x]
Others were tortured and refused
to be released, so that they might
gain a better resurrection. 36Some
faced jeers and flogging,[y] while
still others were chained and put in
prison.[z] 37They were stoned[y];[a]
they were sawed in two; they were
put to death by the sword.[b] They
went about in sheepskins and goatskins,[c] destitute, persecuted and
mistreated— 38the world was not
worthy of them. They wandered in
deserts and mountains, and in
caves[d] and holes in the ground.
39These were all commended[e]
for their faith, yet none of them received what had been promised.[f]
40God had planned something better for us so that only together with
us would they be made perfect.

God Disciplines His Sons

12 Therefore, since we are surrounded by such a great
cloud of witnesses, let us throw off
everything that hinders and the sin
that so easily entangles, and let us
run[g] with perseverance[h] the race
marked out for us. 2Let us fix our
eyes on Jesus, the author and perfecter of our faith, who for the joy
set before him endured the cross,[i]
scorning its shame,[j] and sat down
at the right hand of the throne of
God. 3Consider him who endured
such opposition from sinful men,
so that you will not grow weary[k]
and lose heart.
4In your struggle against sin, you
have not yet resisted to the point of
shedding your blood.[l] 5And you

11:18 [a]Ge 21:12; Ro 9:7
11:19 [b]Ro 4:21
11:20 [c]Ge 27:27-29, 39,40
11:21 [d]Ge 48:1,8-22
11:22 [e]Ge 50:24,25; Ex 13:19
11:23 [f]Ex 2:2 [g]Ex 1:16,22
11:24 [h]Ex 2:10,11
11:25 [i]ver 37
11:26 [j]Heb 13:13 [k]Heb 10:35
11:27 [l]Ex 12:50,51
11:28 [m]Ex 12:21-23
11:29 [n]Ex 14:21-31
11:30 [o]Jos 6:12-20
11:31 [p]Jos 2:1,9-14; 6:22-25; Jas 2:25
11:32 [q]Jdg 4-5 [r]1Sa 16:1,13 [s]1Sa 1:20
11:33 [t]2Sa 7:11; 8:1-3 [u]Da 6:22
11:34 [v]2Ki 20:7 [w]Jdg 15:8
11:35 [x]1Ki 17:22,23
11:36 [y]Jer 20:2 [z]Ge 39:20
11:37 [a]2Ch 24:21 [b]1Ki 19:10 [c]2Ki 1:8
11:38 [d]1Ki 18:4
11:39 [e]ver 2,4 [f]ver 13
12:1 [g]1Co 9:24 [h]Heb 10:36
12:2 [i]Php 2:8,9 [j]Heb 13:13
12:3 [k]Gal 6:9
12:4 [l]Heb 10:32-34

[u]*18* Greek *seed* [v]*18* Gen. 21:12
[w]*29* That is, Sea of Reeds [x]*31* Or *unbelieving* [y]*37* Some early manuscripts *stoned; they were put to the test;*

have forgotten that word of encouragement that addresses you as
sons:

"My son, do not make light of
the Lord's discipline,
and do not lose heart when
he rebukes you,
6because the Lord disciplines
those he loves,[a]
and he punishes everyone he
accepts as a son."[zb]

7Endure hardship as discipline;
God is treating you as sons.[c] For
what son is not disciplined by his
father? **8**If you are not disciplined
(and everyone undergoes discipline),[d] then you are illegitimate
children and not true sons. **9**Moreover, we have all had human fathers who disciplined us and we respected them for it. How much
more should we submit to the Father of our spirits[e] and live![f]
10Our fathers disciplined us for a
little while as they thought best;
but God disciplines us for our
good, that we may share in his holiness.[g] **11**No discipline seems
pleasant at the time, but painful.
Later on, however, it produces a
harvest of righteousness and
peace[h] for those who have been
trained by it.
12Therefore, strengthen your
feeble arms and weak knees.[i]
13"Make level paths for your
feet,"[aj] so that the lame may not
be disabled, but rather healed.[k]

Warning Against Refusing God

14Make every effort to live in
peace with all men[l] and to be
holy;[m] without holiness no one will
see the Lord.[n] **15**See to it that no
one misses the grace of God[o] and
that no bitter root grows up to
cause trouble and defile many.
16See that no one is sexually immoral, or is godless like Esau, who
for a single meal sold his inheritance rights as the oldest son.[p]
17Afterward, as you know, when he
wanted to inherit this blessing, he
was rejected. He could bring about
no change of mind, though he
sought the blessing with tears.[q]

12:6 [a]Ps 94:12; Rev 3:19 [b]Pr 3:11,12
12:7 [c]Dt 8:5
12:8 [d]1Pe 5:9
12:9 [e]Nu 16:22 [f]Isa 38:16
12:10 [g]2Pe 1:4
12:11 [h]Isa 32:17; Jas 3:17,18
12:12 [i]Isa 35:3
12:13 [j]Pr 4:26 [k]Gal 6:1
12:14 [l]Ro 14:19 [m]Ro 6:22 [n]Mt 5:8
12:15 [o]Gal 5:4; Heb 3:12
12:16 [p]Ge 25:29-34
12:17 [q]Ge 27:30-40
12:18 [r]Ex 19:12-22; Dt 4:11
12:19 [s]Ex 20:18 [t]Ex 20:19; Dt 5:5,25
12:20 [u]Ex 19:12,13
12:22 [v]Gal 4:26 [w]Heb 11:10
12:23 [x]Lk 10:20 [y]Ps 94:2 [z]Php 3:12
12:24 [a]Ge 4:10; Heb 11:4
12:25 [b]Heb 8:5; 11:7 [c]Heb 2:2,3
12:26 [d]Ex 19:18 [e]Hag 2:6
12:27 [f]1Co 7:31; 2Pe 3:10
12:28 [g]Da 2:44 [h]Heb 13:15
12:29 [i]Dt 4:24
13:1 [j]Ro 12:10; 1Pe 1:22

18You have not come to a mountain that can be touched and that is
burning with fire; to darkness,
gloom and storm;[r] **19**to a trumpet
blast[s] or to such a voice speaking
words that those who heard it
begged that no further word be spoken to them,[t] **20**because they
could not bear what was commanded: "If even an animal
touches the mountain, it must be
stoned."[bu] **21**The sight was so terrifying that Moses said, "I am trembling with fear."[c]
22But you have come to Mount
Zion, to the heavenly Jerusalem,[v]
the city[w] of the living God. You
have come to thousands upon
thousands of angels in joyful assembly, **23**to the church of the firstborn, whose names are written in
heaven.[x] You have come to God,
the judge of all men,[y] to the spirits
of righteous men made perfect,[z]
24to Jesus the mediator of a new
covenant, and to the sprinkled
blood that speaks a better word
than the blood of Abel.[a]
25See to it that you do not refuse
him who speaks. If they did not escape when they refused him who
warned[b] them on earth, how much
less will we, if we turn away from
him who warns us from heaven?[c]
26At that time his voice shook the
earth,[d] but now he has promised,
"Once more I will shake not only
the earth but also the heavens."[de]
27The words "once more" indicate
the removing of what can be shak-
en[f]—that is, created things—so
that what cannot be shaken may
remain.
28Therefore, since we are receiving a kingdom that cannot be shak-
en,[g] let us be thankful, and so worship God acceptably with reverence and awe,[h] **29**for our "God is a
consuming fire."[ei]

Concluding Exhortations

13 Keep on loving each other
as brothers.[j] **2**Do not for-

[z]*6* Prov. 3:11,12 [a]*13* Prov. 4:26
[b]*20* Exodus 19:12,13 [c]*21* Deut. 9:19
[d]*26* Haggai 2:6 [e]*29* Deut. 4:24

get to entertain strangers,[a] for by
so doing some people have enter-
tained angels without knowing it.[b]
3Remember those in prison[c] as if
you were their fellow prisoners,
and those who are mistreated as if
you yourselves were suffering.
4Marriage should be honored by
all, and the marriage bed kept
pure, for God will judge the adulterer and all the sexually immoral.[d] **5**Keep your lives free from the
love of money and be content with
what you have,[e] because God has
said,

"Never will I leave you;
never will I forsake you."[f][f]

6So we say with confidence,

"The Lord is my helper; I will
not be afraid.
What can man do to me?"[g]

7Remember your leaders,[g] who
spoke the word of God to you. Consider the outcome of their way of
life and imitate[h] their faith. **8**Jesus
Christ is the same yesterday and today and forever.[i]
9Do not be carried away by all
kinds of strange teachings.[j] It is
good for our hearts to be strengthened[k] by grace, not by ceremonial
foods,[l] which are of no value to
those who eat them. **10**We have an
altar from which those who minister at the tabernacle have no right
to eat.[m]
11The high priest carries the
blood of animals into the Most
Holy Place as a sin offering, but the
bodies are burned outside the
camp.[n] **12**And so Jesus also suffered outside the city gate[o] to
make the people holy through his
own blood. **13**Let us, then, go to
him outside the camp, bearing the
disgrace he bore.[p] **14**For here we
do not have an enduring city, but
we are looking for the city that is to
come.[q]
15Through Jesus, therefore, let
us continually offer to God a sacrifice[r] of praise—the fruit of lips[s]
that confess his name. **16**And do
not forget to do good and to share
with others,[t] for with such sacrifices[u] God is pleased.
17Obey your leaders and submit
to their authority. They keep watch
over you[v] as men who must give an
account. Obey them so that their
work will be a joy, not a burden, for
that would be of no advantage to
you.
18Pray for us.[w] We are sure that
we have a clear conscience[x] and
desire to live honorably in every
way. **19**I particularly urge you to
pray so that I may be restored to
you soon.[y]
20May the God of peace,[z] who
through the blood of the eternal
covenant[a] brought back from the
dead[b] our Lord Jesus, that great
Shepherd of the sheep,[c] **21**equip
you with everything good for doing
his will, and may he work in us[d]
what is pleasing to him,[e] through
Jesus Christ, to whom be glory for
ever and ever. Amen.[f]

22Brothers, I urge you to bear
with my word of exhortation, for I
have written you only a short letter.[g]
23I want you to know that our
brother Timothy[h] has been released. If he arrives soon, I will
come with him to see you.
24Greet all your leaders[i] and all
God's people. Those from Italy[j]
send you their greetings.
25Grace be with you all.[k]

13:2 [a]Mt 25:35 [b]Ge 18:1-33
13:3 [c]Mt 25:36; Col 4:18
13:4 [d]1Co 6:9
13:5 [e]Php 4:11 [f]Dt 31:6,8; Jos 1:5
13:7 [g]ver 17,24 [h]Heb 6:12
13:8 [i]Heb 1:12
13:9 [j]Eph 4:14 [k]Col 2:7 [l]Col 2:16
13:10 [m]1Co 9:13; 10:18
13:11 [n]Ex 29:14; Lev 16:27
13:12 [o]Jn 19:17
13:13 [p]Heb 11:26
13:14 [q]Php 3:20; Heb 12:22
13:15 [r]1Pe 2:5 [s]Hos 14:2
13:16 [t]Ro 12:13 [u]Php 4:18
13:17 [v]Isa 62:6; Ac 20:28
13:18 [w]1Th 5:25 [x]Ac 23:1
13:19 [y]Phm 22
13:20 [z]Ro 15:33 [a]Isa 55:3; Eze 37:26; Zec 9:11 [b]Ac 2:24 [c]Jn 10:11
13:21 [d]Php 2:13 [e]1Jn 3:22 [f]Ro 11:36
13:22 [g]1Pe 5:12
13:23 [h]Ac 16:1
13:24 [i]ver 7,17 [j]Ac 18:2
13:25 [k]Col 4:18

[f]5 Deut. 31:6 [g]6 Psalm 118:6,7

he who said, "Do not commit adultery,"[b][a] also said, "Do not murder."[c][b] If you do not commit adultery but do commit murder, you have become a lawbreaker.

[12]Speak and act as those who are going to be judged by the law that gives freedom,[c] [13]because judgment without mercy will be shown to anyone who has not been merciful.[d] Mercy triumphs over judgment!

Faith and Deeds

[14]What good is it, my brothers, if a man claims to have faith but has no deeds?[e] Can such faith save him? [15]Suppose a brother or sister is without clothes and daily food.[f] [16]If one of you says to him, "Go, I wish you well; keep warm and well fed," but does nothing about his physical needs, what good is it?[g] [17]In the same way, faith by itself, if it is not accompanied by action, is dead.

[18]But someone will say, "You have faith; I have deeds."

Show me your faith without deeds,[h] and I will show you my faith by what I do.[i] [19]You believe that there is one God.[j] Good! Even the demons believe that[k]—and shudder.

[20]You foolish man, do you want evidence that faith without deeds is useless[d]?[l] [21]Was not our ancestor Abraham considered righteous for what he did when he offered his son Isaac on the altar?[m] [22]You see that his faith and his actions were working together,[n] and his faith was made complete by what he did.[o] [23]And the scripture was fulfilled that says, "Abraham believed God, and it was credited to him as righteousness,"[e][p] and he was called God's friend.[q] [24]You see that a person is justified by what he does and not by faith alone.

[25]In the same way, was not even Rahab the prostitute considered righteous for what she did when she gave lodging to the spies and sent them off in a different direction?[r] [26]As the body without the spirit is dead, so faith without deeds is dead.[s]

Taming the Tongue

3 Not many of you should presume to be teachers, my brothers, because you know that we who teach will be judged more strictly. [2]We all stumble[t] in many ways. If anyone is never at fault in what he says,[u] he is a perfect man,[v] able to keep his whole body in check.[w]

[3]When we put bits into the mouths of horses to make them obey us, we can turn the whole animal.[x] [4]Or take ships as an example. Although they are so large and are driven by strong winds, they are steered by a very small rudder wherever the pilot wants to go. [5]Likewise the tongue is a small part of the body, but it makes great boasts.[y] Consider what a great forest is set on fire by a small spark. [6]The tongue also is a fire,[z] a world of evil among the parts of the body. It corrupts the whole person,[a] sets the whole course of his life on fire, and is itself set on fire by hell.

[7]All kinds of animals, birds, reptiles and creatures of the sea are being tamed and have been tamed by man, [8]but no man can tame the tongue. It is a restless evil, full of deadly poison.[b]

[9]With the tongue we praise our Lord and Father, and with it we curse men, who have been made in God's likeness.[c] [10]Out of the same mouth come praise and cursing. My brothers, this should not be. [11]Can both fresh water and salt[f] water flow from the same spring? [12]My brothers, can a fig tree bear olives, or a grapevine bear figs?[d] Neither can a salt spring produce fresh water.

Two Kinds of Wisdom

[13]Who is wise and understanding among you? Let him show it[e] by his good life, by deeds done in the humility that comes from wis-

2:11 [a]Ex 20:14; Dt 5:18 [b]Ex 20:13; Dt 5:17
2:12 [c]Jas 1:25
2:13 [d]Mt 5:7; 18:32-35
2:14 [e]Mt 7:26; Jas 1:22-25
2:15 [f]Mt 25:35,36
2:16 [g]1Jn 3:17,18
2:18 [h]Ro 3:28 [i]Jas 3:13
2:19 [j]Dt 6:4 [k]Mt 8:29; Lk 4:34
2:20 [l]ver 17,26
2:21 [m]Ge 22:9,12
2:22 [n]Heb 11:17 [o]1Th 1:3
2:23 [p]Ge 15:6; Ro 4:3 [q]2Ch 20:7; Isa 41:8
2:25 [r]Heb 11:31
2:26 [s]ver 17,20
3:2 [t]1Ki 8:46; Jas 2:10 [u]1Pe 3:10 [v]Mt 12:37 [w]Jas 1:26
3:3 [x]Ps 32:9
3:5 [y]Ps 12:3,4
3:6 [z]Pr 16:27 [a]Mt 15:11,18,19
3:8 [b]Ps 140:3; Ro 3:13
3:9 [c]Ge 1:26,27; 1Co 11:7
3:12 [d]Mt 7:16
3:13 [e]Jas 2:18

[b]*11* Exodus 20:14; Deut. 5:18 [c]*11* Exodus 20:13; Deut. 5:17 [d]*20* Some early manuscripts *dead* [e]*23* Gen. 15:6 [f]*11* Greek *bitter* (see also verse 14)

dom. 14But if you harbor bitter envy and selfish ambition[a] in your hearts, do not boast about it or deny the truth.[b] 15Such "wisdom" does not come down from heaven[c] but is earthly, unspiritual, of the devil.[d] 16For where you have envy and selfish ambition, there you find disorder and every evil practice.

17But the wisdom that comes from heaven[e] is first of all pure; then peace-loving, considerate, submissive, full of mercy[f] and good fruit, impartial and sincere.[g] 18Peacemakers who sow in peace raise a harvest of righteousness.[h]

Submit Yourselves to God

4 What causes fights and quarrels[i] among you? Don't they come from your desires that battle[j] within you? 2You want something but don't get it. You kill and covet, but you cannot have what you want. You quarrel and fight. You do not have, because you do not ask God. 3When you ask, you do not receive,[k] because you ask with wrong motives,[l] that you may spend what you get on your pleasures.

4You adulterous people, don't you know that friendship with the world[m] is hatred toward God?[n] Anyone who chooses to be a friend of the world becomes an enemy of God.[o] 5Or do you think Scripture says without reason that the spirit he caused to live in us envies intensely?[g] 6But he gives us more grace. That is why Scripture says:

"God opposes the proud
but gives grace to the
humble."[h][p]

7Submit yourselves, then, to God. Resist the devil,[q] and he will flee from you. 8Come near to God and he will come near to you.[r] Wash your hands,[s] you sinners, and purify your hearts, you double-minded.[t] 9Grieve, mourn and wail. Change your laughter to mourning and your joy to gloom.[u] 10Humble yourselves before the Lord, and he will lift you up.

11Brothers, do not slander one another.[v] Anyone who speaks against his brother or judges him[w] speaks against the law and judges it. When you judge the law, you are not keeping it,[x] but sitting in judgment on it. 12There is only one Lawgiver and Judge, the one who is able to save and destroy.[y] But you—who are you to judge your neighbor?[z]

Boasting About Tomorrow

13Now listen, you who say, "Today or tomorrow we will go to this or that city, spend a year there, carry on business and make money."[a] 14Why, you do not even know what will happen tomorrow. What is your life? You are a mist that appears for a little while and then vanishes.[b] 15Instead, you ought to say, "If it is the Lord's will,[c] we will live and do this or that." 16As it is, you boast and brag. All such boasting is evil.[d] 17Anyone, then, who knows the good he ought to do and doesn't do it, sins.[e]

Warning to Rich Oppressors

5 Now listen, you rich people,[f] weep and wail because of the misery that is coming upon you. 2Your wealth has rotted, and moths have eaten your clothes.[g] 3Your gold and silver are corroded. Their corrosion will testify against you and eat your flesh like fire. You have hoarded wealth in the last days.[h] 4Look! The wages you failed to pay the workmen[i] who mowed your fields are crying out against you. The cries[j] of the harvesters have reached the ears of the Lord Almighty.[k] 5You have lived on earth in luxury and self-indulgence. You have fattened yourselves[l] in the day of slaughter.[i][m] 6You have condemned and murdered innocent men,[n] who were not opposing you.

g5 Or *that God jealously longs for the spirit that he made to live in us*; or *that the Spirit he caused to live in us longs jealously* h6 Prov. 3:34 i5 Or *yourselves as in a day of feasting*

3:14 [a]ver 16 [b]Jas 5:19
3:15 [c]Jas 1:17 [d]1Ti 4:1
3:17 [e]1Co 2:6 [f]Lk 6:36 [g]Ro 12:9
3:18 [h]Pr 11:18; Isa 32:17
4:1 [i]Tit 3:9 [j]Ro 7:23
4:3 [k]Ps 18:41 [l]1Jn 3:22; 5:14
4:4 [m]Jas 1:27 [n]1Jn 2:15 [o]Jn 15:19
4:6 [p]Ps 138:6; Pr 3:34; Mt 23:12
4:7 [q]Eph 4:27; 1Pe 5:6-9
4:8 [r]2Ch 15:2 [s]Isa 1:16 [t]Jas 1:8
4:9 [u]Lk 6:25
4:11 [v]1Pe 2:1 [w]Mt 7:1 [x]Jas 1:22
4:12 [y]Mt 10:28 [z]Ro 14:4
4:13 [a]Pr 27:1
4:14 [b]Job 7:7; Ps 102:3
4:15 [c]Ac 18:21
4:16 [d]1Co 5:6
4:17 [e]Lk 12:47; Jn 9:41
5:1 [f]Lk 6:24
5:2 [g]Job 13:28; Mt 6:19,20
5:3 [h]ver 7,8
5:4 [i]Lev 19:13 [j]Dt 24:15 [k]Ro 9:29
5:5 [l]Am 6:1 [m]Jer 12:3; 25:34
5:6 [n]Heb 10:38

ce in Suffering

tient, then, brothers, until
's coming. See how the
ts for the land to yield its
op and how patient he is
mn and spring rains.[a]
oe patient and stand
, because the Lord's coming is
near.[b] **9**Don't grumble against
each other, brothers,[c] or you will
be judged. The Judge[d] is standing
at the door![e]

10Brothers, as an example of patience in the face of suffering, take
the prophets[f] who spoke in the
name of the Lord. **11**As you know,
we consider blessed[g] those who
have persevered. You have heard of
Job's perseverance[h] and have seen
what the Lord finally brought
about.[i] The Lord is full of compassion and mercy.[j]

12Above all, my brothers, do not
swear—not by heaven or by earth
or by anything else. Let your "Yes"
be yes, and your "No," no, or you
will be condemned.[k]

The Prayer of Faith

13Is any one of you in trouble?
He should pray.[l] Is anyone happy?
Let him sing songs of praise.[m] **14**Is
any one of you sick? He should call
the elders of the church to pray
over him and anoint him with oil[n]
in the name of the Lord. **15**And the
prayer offered in faith will make
the sick person well; the Lord will
raise him up. If he has sinned, he
will be forgiven. **16**Therefore confess your sins[o] to each other and
pray for each other so that you may
be healed.[p] The prayer of a righteous man is powerful and effec-
tive.[q]

17Elijah was a man just like us.[r]
He prayed earnestly that it would
not rain, and it did not rain on the
land for three and a half years.[s]
18Again he prayed, and the heavens gave rain, and the earth produced its crops.[t]

19My brothers, if one of you
should wander from the truth[u] and
someone should bring him back,[v]
20remember this: Whoever turns a
sinner from the error of his way will
save[w] him from death and cover
over a multitude of sins.[x]

5:7 [a] Dt 11:14; Jer 5:24 **5:8** [b] Ro 13:11; 1Pe 4:7 **5:9** [c] Jas 4:11 [d] 1Co 4:5; 1Pe 4:5 [e] Mt 24:33 **5:10** [f] Mt 5:12 **5:11** [g] Mt 5:10 [h] Job 1:21,22; 2:10 [i] Job 42:10, 12-17 [j] Nu 14:18 **5:12** [k] Mt 5:34-37 **5:13** [l] Ps 50:15 [m] Col 3:16 **5:14** [n] Mk 6:13 **5:16** [o] Mt 3:6 [p] 1Pe 2:24 [q] Jn 9:31 **5:17** [r] Ac 14:15 [s] 1Ki 17:1; Lk 4:25 **5:18** [t] 1Ki 18:41-45 **5:19** [u] Jas 3:14 [v] Mt 18:15 **5:20** [w] Ro 11:14 [x] 1Pe 4:8

1 Peter

Title and Background

The recipients of this letter had been suffering various trials and afflictions, and the possibility of greater and more severe difficulties was very real. This letter is addressed to Christians who were scattered throughout the Roman world. In fact, the readers were called "strangers in the world."

Author and Date of Writing

The author identifies himself as the apostle Peter, and the contents and character of the letter support his authorship. Moreover, the letter reflects the history and terminology of the Gospels and Acts, notably Peter's speeches. The book was written about A.D. 64.

Theme and Message

1 Peter touches on various doctrines and has much to say about Christian life and duties. It has been characterized as a letter of separation, of suffering and persecution, of suffering and glory, of hope, of pilgrimage, of courage, and as a letter dealing with the true grace of God. The letter is composed also of a series of exhortations focusing on the call to holy living, especially in anticipation of the end times.

Outline

I. Greetings (1:1-2)
II. Praise for God's Grace and Salvation (1:3-12)
III. Holy Living (1:13-5:11)
IV. The Purpose of the Letter (5:12)
V. Closing Greetings (5:13-14)

---

1 Peter, an apostle of Jesus
Christ,[a]

To God's elect,[b] strangers in the
world, scattered throughout Pontus, Galatia, Cappadocia, Asia and
Bithynia,[c] 2who have been chosen
according to the foreknowledge[d]
of God the Father, through the
sanctifying work of the Spirit,[e] for
obedience to Jesus Christ and
sprinkling by his blood:[f]

Grace and peace be yours in
abundance.

Praise to God for a Living Hope

3Praise be to the God and Father
of our Lord Jesus Christ![g] In his
great mercy[h] he has given us new
birth into a living hope through the
resurrection of Jesus Christ from
the dead,[i] 4and into an inheritance that can never perish, spoil
or fade—kept in heaven for you,[j]
5who through faith are shielded by
God's power[k] until the coming of
the salvation that is ready to be revealed in the last time. 6In this you
greatly rejoice,[l] though now for a
little while[m] you may have had to
suffer grief in all kinds of trials.[n]
7These have come so that your
faith—of greater worth than gold,
which perishes even though refined by fire[o]—may be proved genuine[p] and may result in praise, glory and honor when Jesus Christ is

1:1 [a] 2Pe 1:1 [b] Mt 24:22 [c] Ac 16:7 **1:2** [d] Ro 8:29 [e] 2Th 2:13 [f] Heb 10:22; 12:24 **1:3** [g] 2Co 1:3; Eph 1:3 [h] Tit 3:5; Jas 1:18 [i] 1Co 15:20 **1:4** [j] Col 1:5 **1:5** [k] Jn 10:28 **1:6** [l] Ro 5:2 [m] 1Pe 5:10 [n] Jas 1:2 **1:7** [o] Job 23:10; Ps 66:10; Pr 17:3 [p] Jas 1:3

revealed.[a] **8**Though you have not seen him, you love him; and even though you do not see him now, you believe in him[b] and are filled with an inexpressible and glorious joy, **9**for you are receiving the goal of your faith, the salvation of your souls.[c]

10Concerning this salvation, the prophets, who spoke[d] of the grace that was to come to you, searched intently and with the greatest care,[e] **11**trying to find out the time and circumstances to which the Spirit of Christ[f] in them was pointing when he predicted the sufferings of Christ and the glories that would follow. **12**It was revealed to them that they were not serving themselves but you, when they spoke of the things that have now been told you by those who have preached the gospel to you[g] by the Holy Spirit sent from heaven. Even angels long to look into these things.

Be Holy

13Therefore, prepare your minds for action; be self-controlled; set your hope fully on the grace to be given you when Jesus Christ is revealed. **14**As obedient children, do not conform[h] to the evil desires you had when you lived in ignorance.[i] **15**But just as he who called you is holy, so be holy in all you do;[j] **16**for it is written: "Be holy, because I am holy."[a][k]

17Since you call on a Father who judges each man's work impartially,[l] live your lives as strangers here in reverent fear.[m] **18**For you know that it was not with perishable things such as silver or gold that you were redeemed[n] from the empty way of life handed down to you from your forefathers, **19**but with the precious blood of Christ, a lamb[o] without blemish or defect.[p] **20**He was chosen before the creation of the world,[q] but was revealed in these last times[r] for your sake. **21**Through him you believe in God,[s] who raised him from the dead and glorified him, and so your faith and hope are in God.

22Now that you have purified[t] yourselves by obeying the truth so that you have sincere love for your brothers, love one another deeply,[u] from the heart.[b] **23**For you have been born again,[v] not of perishable seed, but of imperishable, through the living and enduring word of God.[w] **24**For,

"All men are like grass,
and all their glory is like the
flowers of the field;
the grass withers and the
flowers fall,
25 but the word of the Lord
stands forever."[c][x]

And this is the word that was preached to you.

2 Therefore, rid yourselves[y] of all malice and all deceit, hypocrisy, envy, and slander[z] of every kind. **2**Like newborn babies, crave pure spiritual milk,[a] so that by it you may grow up[b] in your salvation, **3**now that you have tasted that the Lord is good.[c]

The Living Stone and a Chosen People

4As you come to him, the living Stone[d]—rejected by men but chosen by God and precious to him—**5**you also, like living stones, are being built[e] into a spiritual house[f] to be a holy priesthood,[g] offering spiritual sacrifices acceptable to God through Jesus Christ.[h] **6**For in Scripture it says:

"See, I lay a stone in Zion,
a chosen and precious
cornerstone,[i]
and the one who trusts in him
will never be put to
shame."[d][j]

7Now to you who believe, this stone is precious. But to those who do not believe,[k]

"The stone the builders
rejected

1:7 [a]Ro 2:7
1:8 [b]Jn 20:29
1:9 [c]Ro 6:22
1:10 [d]Mt 26:24 [e]Mt 13:17
1:11 [f]2Pe 1:21
1:12 [g]ver 25
1:14 [h]Ro 12:2 [i]Eph 4:18
1:15 [j]2Co 7:1; 1Th 4:7
1:16 [k]Lev 11:44,45
1:17 [l]Ac 10:34 [m]Heb 12:28
1:18 [n]Mt 20:28; 1Co 6:20
1:19 [o]Jn 1:29 [p]Ex 12:5
1:20 [q]Eph 1:4 [r]Heb 9:26
1:21 [s]Ro 4:24
1:22 [t]Jas 4:8 [u]Jn 13:34; Heb 13:1
1:23 [v]Jn 1:13 [w]Heb 4:12
1:25 [x]Isa 40:6-8
2:1 [y]Eph 4:22 [z]Jas 4:11
2:2 [a]1Co 3:2 [b]Eph 4:15,16
2:3 [c]Heb 6:5
2:4 [d]ver 7
2:5 [e]1Co 3:9 [f]1Ti 3:15 [g]Isa 61:6 [h]Php 4:18; Heb 13:15
2:6 [i]Eph 2:20 [j]Isa 28:16
2:7 [k]2Co 2:16

[a]*16* Lev. 11:44,45; 19:2; 20:7 [b]*22* Some early manuscripts *from a pure heart*
[c]*25* Isaiah 40:6-8 [d]*6* Isaiah 28:16

has become the
capstone,[e]"[f][a]

8and,

"A stone that causes men to
stumble
and a rock that makes them
fall."[g][b]

They stumble because they disobey the message—which is also
what they were destined for.[c]
9But you are a chosen people,[d] a
royal priesthood, a holy nation,[e] a
people belonging to God, that you
may declare the praises of him who
called you out of darkness into his
wonderful light.[f] 10Once you were
not a people, but now you are the
people of God;[g] once you had not
received mercy, but now you have
received mercy.
11Dear friends, I urge you, as
aliens and strangers in the world,
to abstain from sinful desires,[h]
which war against your soul.[i]
12Live such good lives among the
pagans that, though they accuse
you of doing wrong, they may see
your good deeds[j] and glorify God[k]
on the day he visits us.

Submission to Rulers and Masters

13Submit yourselves for the
Lord's sake to every authority[l] instituted among men: whether to
the king, as the supreme authority,
14or to governors, who are sent by
him to punish those who do
wrong[m] and to commend those
who do right.[n] 15For it is God's
will[o] that by doing good you
should silence the ignorant talk of
foolish men.[p] 16Live as free men,[q]
but do not use your freedom as a
cover-up for evil; live as servants of
God.[r] 17Show proper respect to
everyone: Love the brotherhood of
believers,[s] fear God, honor the
king.[t]
18Slaves, submit yourselves to
your masters with all respect,[u] not
only to those who are good and
considerate,[v] but also to those
who are harsh. 19For it is commendable if a man bears up under
the pain of unjust suffering because he is conscious of God.[w]
20But how is it to your credit if you
receive a beating for doing wrong
and endure it? But if you suffer for
doing good and you endure it, this
is commendable before God.[x]
21To this[y] you were called, because Christ suffered for you, leaving you an example,[z] that you
should follow in his steps.

22"He committed no sin,
and no deceit was found in
his mouth."[h][a]

23When they hurled their insults at
him, he did not retaliate; when he
suffered, he made no threats.[b] Instead, he entrusted himself[c] to
him who judges justly. 24He himself bore our sins[d] in his body on
the tree, so that we might die to
sins[e] and live for righteousness; by
his wounds you have been
healed.[f] 25For you were like sheep
going astray,[g] but now you have returned to the Shepherd[h] and Overseer of your souls.

Wives and Husbands

3 Wives, in the same way be submissive[i] to your husbands[j]
so that, if any of them do not believe the word, they may be won
over[k] without words by the behavior of their wives, 2when they see
the purity and reverence of your
lives. 3Your beauty should not
come from outward adornment,
such as braided hair and the wearing of gold jewelry and fine
clothes.[l] 4Instead, it should be
that of your inner self,[m] the unfad-
ing beauty of a gentle and quiet
spirit, which is of great worth in
God's sight. 5For this is the way the
holy women of the past who put
their hope in God[n] used to make
themselves beautiful. They were
submissive to their own husbands,
6like Sarah, who obeyed Abraham
and called him her master.[o] You
are her daughters if you do what is
right and do not give way to fear.

2:7 [a]Ps 118:22
2:8 [b]Isa 8:14; 1Co 1:23 [c]Ro 9:22
2:9 [d]Dt 10:15 [e]Isa 62:12 [f]Ac 26:18
2:10 [g]Hos 1:9,10
2:11 [h]Gal 5:16 [i]Jas 4:1
2:12 [j]Php 2:15; 1Pe 3:16 [k]Mt 5:16; 9:8
2:13 [l]Ro 13:1
2:14 [m]Ro 13:4 [n]Ro 13:3
2:15 [o]1Pe 3:17 [p]ver 12
2:16 [q]Jn 8:32 [r]Ro 6:22
2:17 [s]Ro 12:10 [t]Ro 13:7
2:18 [u]Eph 6:5 [v]Jas 3:17
2:19 [w]1Pe 3:14,17
2:20 [x]1Pe 3:17
2:21 [y]Ac 14:22 [z]Mt 16:24
2:22 [a]Isa 53:9
2:23 [b]Isa 53:7 [c]Lk 23:46
2:24 [d]Heb 9:28 [e]Ro 6:2 [f]Isa 53:5; Heb 12:13; Jas 5:16
2:25 [g]Isa 53:6 [h]Jn 10:11
3:1 [i]1Pe 2:18 [j]Eph 5:22 [k]1Co 7:16; 9:19
3:3 [l]Isa 3:18-23; 1Ti 2:9
3:4 [m]Ro 7:22
3:5 [n]1Ti 5:5
3:6 [o]Ge 18:12

[e]7 Or *cornerstone* [f]7 Psalm 118:22
[g]8 Isaiah 8:14 [h]22 Isaiah 53:9

7Husbands,[a] in the same way be considerate as you live with your wives, and treat them with respect as the weaker partner and as heirs with you of the gracious gift of life, so that nothing will hinder your prayers.

Suffering for Doing Good

8Finally, all of you, live in harmony with one another; be sympathetic, love as brothers,[b] be compassionate and humble.[c] 9Do not repay evil with evil[d] or insult with insult,[e] but with blessing, because to this[f] you were called so that you may inherit a blessing.[g] 10For,

"Whoever would love life
and see good days
must keep his tongue from evil
and his lips from deceitful
speech.
11He must turn from evil and do
good;
he must seek peace and
pursue it.
12For the eyes of the Lord are on
the righteous
and his ears are attentive to
their prayer,
but the face of the Lord is
against those who do
evil."[i][h]

13Who is going to harm you if you are eager to do good?[i] 14But even if you should suffer for what is right, you are blessed.[j] "Do not fear what they fear[j]; do not be *frightened*."[k][k] 15But in your hearts set apart Christ as Lord. Always be prepared to give an answer[l] to everyone who asks you to give the reason for the hope that you have. But do this with gentleness and respect, 16keeping a clear conscience,[m] so that those who speak maliciously against your good behavior in Christ may be ashamed of their slander.[n] 17It is better, if it is God's will,[o] to suffer for doing good[p] than for doing evil. 18For Christ died for sins[q] once for all, the righteous for the unrighteous, to bring you to God. He was put to death in the body[r] but made alive by the Spirit,[s]

3:7 [a]Eph 5:25-33
3:8 [b]Ro 12:10 [c]1Pe 5:5
3:9 [d]Ro 12:17 [e]1Pe 2:23 [f]1Pe 2:21 [g]Heb 6:14
3:12 [h]Ps 34:12-16
3:13 [i]Pr 16:7
3:14 [j]1Pe 2:19,20; 4:15,16 [k]Isa 8:12,13
3:15 [l]Col 4:6
3:16 [m]Heb 13:18 [n]1Pe 2:12,15
3:17 [o]1Pe 2:15 [p]1Pe 2:20
3:18 [q]1Pe 2:21 [r]Col 1:22; 1Pe 4:1 [s]1Pe 4:6
3:19 [t]1Pe 4:6
3:20 [u]Ge 6:3,5,13,14 [v]Heb 11:7
3:21 [w]Tit 3:5 [x]1Pe 1:3
3:22 [y]Mk 16:19 [z]Ro 8:38
4:2 [a]Ro 6:2
4:3 [b]Eph 2:2
4:4 [c]1Pe 3:16
4:5 [d]Ac 10:42; 2Ti 4:1
4:6 [e]1Pe 3:19
4:7 [f]Ro 13:11
4:8 [g]1Pe 1:22 [h]Pr 10:12
4:9 [i]Php 2:14

19through whom[l] also he went and preached to the spirits in prison[t] 20who disobeyed long ago when God waited patiently in the days of Noah while the ark was being built.[u] In it only a few people, eight in all, were saved[v] through water, 21and this water symbolizes baptism that now saves you[w] also—not the removal of dirt from the body but the pledge[m] of a good conscience toward God. It saves you by the resurrection of Jesus Christ,[x] 22who has gone into heaven and is at God's right hand[y]—with angels, authorities and powers in submission to him.[z]

Living for God

4 Therefore, since Christ suffered in his body, arm yourselves also with the same attitude, because he who has suffered in his body is done with sin. 2As a result, he does not live the rest of his earthly life for evil human desires,[a] but rather for the will of God. 3For you have spent enough time in the past[b] doing what pagans choose to do—living in debauchery, lust, drunkenness, orgies, carousing and detestable idolatry. 4They think it strange that you do not plunge with them into the same flood of dissipation, and they heap abuse on you.[c] 5But they will have to give account to him who is ready to judge the living and the dead.[d] 6For this is the reason the gospel was preached even to those who are now dead,[e] so that they might be judged according to men in regard to the body, but live according to God in regard to the spirit.

7The end of all things is near.[f] Therefore be clear minded and self-controlled so that you can pray. 8Above all, love each other deeply,[g] because love covers over a multitude of sins.[h] 9Offer hospitality to one another without grumbling.[i] 10Each one should use

[i]*12* Psalm 34:12-16 [j]*14* Or *not fear their threats* [k]*14* Isaiah 8:12 [l]*18,19* Or *alive in the spirit, 19through which* [m]*21* Or *response*

whatever gift he has received to serve others,[a] faithfully[b] administering God's grace in its various forms. **11**If anyone speaks, he should do it as one speaking the very words of God. If anyone serves, he should do it with the strength God provides,[c] so that in all things God may be praised[d] through Jesus Christ. To him be the glory and the power for ever and ever. Amen.

Suffering for Being a Christian

12Dear friends, do not be surprised at the painful trial you are suffering,[e] as though something strange were happening to you. **13**But rejoice that you participate in the sufferings of Christ, so that you may be overjoyed when his glory is revealed.[f] **14**If you are insulted because of the name of Christ, you are blessed,[g] for the Spirit of glory and of God rests on you. **15**If you suffer, it should not be as a murderer or thief or any other kind of criminal, or even as a meddler. **16**However, if you suffer as a Christian, do not be ashamed, but praise God that you bear that name.[h] **17**For it is time for judgment to begin with the family of God;[i] and if it begins with us, what will the outcome be for those who do not obey the gospel of God?[j] **18**And,

"If it is hard for the righteous
to be saved,
what will become of the
ungodly and the
sinner?"[n][k]

19So then, those who suffer according to God's will should commit themselves to their faithful Creator and continue to do good.

To Elders and Young Men

5 To the elders among you, I appeal as a fellow elder,[l] a witness[m] of Christ's sufferings and one who also will share in the glory to be revealed:[n] **2**Be shepherds of God's flock[o] that is under your care, serving as overseers—not because you must, but because you are willing, as God wants you to be; not greedy for money,[p] but eager to serve; **3**not lording it over[q] those entrusted to you, but being examples[r] to the flock. **4**And when the Chief Shepherd appears, you will receive the crown of glory[s] that will never fade away.

5Young men, in the same way be submissive[t] to those who are older. All of you, clothe yourselves with humility toward one another, because,

"God opposes the proud
but gives grace to the
humble."[o][u]

6Humble yourselves, therefore, under God's mighty hand, that he may lift you up in due time.[v] **7**Cast all your anxiety on him[w] because he cares for you.[x]

8Be self-controlled and alert. Your enemy the devil prowls around[y] like a roaring lion looking for someone to devour. **9**Resist him,[z] standing firm in the faith,[a] because you know that your brothers throughout the world are undergoing the same kind of sufferings.[b]

10And the God of all grace, who called you to his eternal glory[c] in Christ, after you have suffered a little while, will himself restore you and make you strong,[d] firm and steadfast. **11**To him be the power for ever and ever. Amen.[e]

Final Greetings

12With the help of Silas,[p][f] whom I regard as a faithful brother, I have written to you briefly,[g] encouraging you and testifying that this is the true grace of God. Stand fast in it.

13She who is in Babylon, chosen together with you, sends you her greetings, and so does my son Mark.[h] **14**Greet one another with a kiss of love.[i]

Peace[j] to all of you who are in Christ.

4:10 [a] Ro 12:6,7 [b] 1Co 4:2
4:11 [c] Eph 6:10 [d] 1Co 10:31
4:12 [e] 1Pe 1:6,7
4:13 [f] Ro 8:17
4:14 [g] Mt 5:11
4:16 [h] Ac 5:41
4:17 [i] Jer 25:29 [j] 2Th 1:8
4:18 [k] Pr 11:31; Lk 23:31
5:1 [l] Ac 11:30 [m] Lk 24:48 [n] 1Pe 1:5,7; Rev 1:9
5:2 [o] Jn 21:16 [p] 1Ti 3:3
5:3 [q] Eze 34:4 [r] Php 3:17
5:4 [s] 1Co 9:25
5:5 [t] Eph 5:21 [u] Pr 3:34; Jas 4:6
5:6 [v] Jas 4:10
5:7 [w] Ps 37:5; Mt 6:25 [x] Heb 13:5
5:8 [y] Job 1:7
5:9 [z] Jas 4:7 [a] Col 2:5 [b] Ac 14:22
5:10 [c] 2Co 4:17 [d] 2Th 2:17
5:11 [e] Ro 11:36
5:12 [f] 2Co 1:19 [g] Heb 13:22
5:13 [h] Ac 12:12
5:14 [i] Ro 16:16 [j] Eph 6:23

[n] *18* Prov. 11:31 [o] *5* Prov. 3:34
[p] *12* Greek *Silvanus,* a variant of *Silas*

2 Peter

Title and Background

The recipients of this letter were the same group of Christians addressed in Peter's first letter. They were in danger of being confused by false teachers.

Author and Date of Writing

The author identifies himself as Simon Peter. He asserts that this is his second letter to the readers (3:1) and refers to Paul as "our dear brother" (3:15). The character of the letter is compatible with the claim that it was written by Peter. It was written about A.D. 66.

Theme and Message

Peter as a "shepherd" of Christ's sheep is particularly concerned about the false teachers and evildoers who have come into the church. He teaches the church how to deal with these false teachers but also seeks to commend to his readers a wholesome combination of Christian faith and practice. The Lord is certain to return, so the believers are to be watchful.

Outline

I. Introduction (1:1-2)
II. Growth in Christian Virtues (1:3-11)
III. Peter's Message (1:12-21)
IV. Warning Against False Teachers (2:1-22)
V. Christ's Return (3:1-16)
VI. Conclusion (3:17-18)

---

1 Simon Peter, a servant[a] and
apostle of Jesus Christ,[b]
To those who through the righteousness[c] of our God and Savior
Jesus Christ[d] have received a faith
as precious as ours:

2Grace and peace be yours in
abundance through the knowledge
of God and of Jesus our Lord.[e]

Making One's Calling and Election Sure

3His divine power[f] has given us
everything we need for life and godliness through our knowledge of
him who called us[g] by his own glory and goodness. **4**Through these
he has given us his very great and
precious promises,[h] so that
through them you may participate
in the divine nature[i] and escape
the corruption in the world caused
by evil desires.[j]

5For this very reason, make every
effort to add to your faith goodness;
and to goodness, knowledge;[k]
6and to knowledge, self-control;[l]
and to self-control, perseverance;
and to perseverance, godliness;[m]
7and to godliness, brotherly kindness; and to brotherly kindness,
love.[n] **8**For if you possess these
qualities in increasing measure,
they will keep you from being inef-
fective and unproductive[o] in your
knowledge of our Lord Jesus
Christ. **9**But if anyone does not
have them, he is nearsighted and
blind,[p] and has forgotten that he
has been cleansed from his past
sins.[q]

10Therefore, my brothers, be all
the more eager to make your call-

1:1 [a] Ro 1:1 [b] 1Pe 1:1 [c] Ro 3:21-26 [d] Tit 2:13
1:2 [e] Php 3:8
1:3 [f] 1Pe 1:5 [g] 1Th 2:12
1:4 [h] 2Co 7:1 [i] Eph 4:24; Heb 12:10; 1Jn 3:2 [j] 2Pe 2:18-20
1:5 [k] Col 2:3
1:6 [l] Ac 24:25 [m] ver 3
1:7 [n] 1Th 3:12
1:8 [o] Jn 15:2; Tit 3:14
1:9 [p] 1Jn 2:11 [q] Eph 5:26

ing and election sure. For if you do these things, you will never fall,[a] **11**and you will receive a rich welcome into the eternal kingdom of our Lord and Savior Jesus Christ.

Prophecy of Scripture

12So I will always remind you of these things,[b] even though you know them and are firmly established in the truth you now have. **13**I think it is right to refresh your memory as long as I live in the tent of this body,[c] **14**because I know that I will soon put it aside,[d] as our Lord Jesus Christ has made clear to me.[e] **15**And I will make every effort to see that after my departure[f] you will always be able to remember these things.

16We did not follow cleverly invented stories when we told you about the power and coming of our Lord Jesus Christ, but we were eyewitnesses of his majesty.[g] **17**For he received honor and glory from God the Father when the voice came to him from the Majestic Glory, saying, "This is my Son, whom I love; with him I am well pleased."[a][h] **18**We ourselves heard this voice that came from heaven when we were with him on the sacred mountain.[i]

19And we have the word of the prophets made more certain, and you will do well to pay attention to it, as to a light[j] shining in a dark place, until the day dawns and the morning star[k] rises in your hearts. **20**Above all, you must understand that no prophecy of Scripture came about by the prophet's own interpretation. **21**For prophecy never had its origin in the will of man, but men spoke from God[l] as they were carried along by the Holy Spirit.[m]

False Teachers and Their Destruction

2 But there were also false prophets[n] among the people, just as there will be false teachers among you.[o] They will secretly introduce destructive heresies, even denying the sovereign Lord[p] who bought them[q]—bringing swift destruction on themselves. **2**Many will follow their shameful ways and will bring the way of truth into disrepute. **3**In their greed these teachers will exploit you[r] with stories they have made up. Their condemnation has long been hanging over them, and their destruction has not been sleeping.

4For if God did not spare angels when they sinned, but sent them to hell,[b] putting them into gloomy dungeons[c] to be held for judgment;[s] **5**if he did not spare the ancient world[t] when he brought the flood on its ungodly people, but protected Noah, a preacher of righteousness, and seven others;[u] **6**if he condemned the cities of Sodom and Gomorrah by burning them to ashes,[v] and made them an example[w] of what is going to happen to the ungodly; **7**and if he rescued Lot,[x] a righteous man, who was distressed by the filthy lives of lawless men[y] **8**(for that righteous man, living among them day after day, was tormented in his righteous soul by the lawless deeds he saw and heard)— **9**if this is so, then the Lord knows how to rescue godly men from trials[z] and to hold the unrighteous for the day of judgment, while continuing their punishment.[d] **10**This is especially true of those who follow the corrupt desire[a] of the sinful nature[e] and despise authority.

Bold and arrogant, these men are not afraid to slander celestial beings;[b] **11**yet even angels, although they are stronger and more powerful, do not bring slanderous accusations against such beings in the presence of the Lord.[c] **12**But these men blaspheme in matters they do not understand. They are like brute beasts, creatures of instinct, born only to be caught and destroyed, and like beasts they too will perish.[d]

1:10 [a] 2Pe 3:17
1:12 [b] Php 3:1; 1Jn 2:21
1:13 [c] 2Co 5:1,4
1:14 [d] 2Ti 4:6 [e] Jn 21:18,19
1:15 [f] Lk 9:31
1:16 [g] Mt 17:1-8
1:17 [h] Mt 3:17
1:18 [i] Mt 17:6
1:19 [j] Ps 119:105 [k] Rev 22:16
1:21 [l] 2Ti 3:16 [m] 2Sa 23:2; Ac 1:16; 1Pe 1:11
2:1 [n] Dt 13:1-3 [o] 1Ti 4:1 [p] Jude 4 [q] 1Co 6:20
2:3 [r] 2Co 2:17; 1Th 2:5
2:4 [s] Jude 6; Rev 20:1,2
2:5 [t] 2Pe 3:6 [u] Heb 11:7; 1Pe 3:20
2:6 [v] Ge 19:24,25 [w] Nu 26:10; Jude 7
2:7 [x] Ge 19:16 [y] 2Pe 3:17
2:9 [z] 1Co 10:13
2:10 [a] 2Pe 3:3 [b] Jude 8
2:11 [c] Jude 9
2:12 [d] Jude 10

[a]*17* Matt. 17:5; Mark 9:7; Luke 9:35
[b]*4* Greek *Tartarus* [c]*4* Some manuscripts *into chains of darkness* [d]*9* Or *unrighteous for punishment until the day of judgment*
[e]*10* Or *the flesh*

13They will be paid back with harm for the harm they have done. Their idea of pleasure is to carouse in broad daylight.[a] They are blots and blemishes, reveling in their pleasures while they feast with you.[f][b] **14**With eyes full of adultery, they never stop sinning; they seduce[c] the unstable; they are experts in greed[d]—an accursed brood![e] **15**They have left the straight way and wandered off to follow the way of Balaam[f] son of Beor, who loved the wages of wickedness. **16**But he was rebuked for his wrongdoing by a donkey—a beast without speech—who spoke with a man's voice and restrained the prophet's madness.[g]

17These men are springs without water[h] and mists driven by a storm. Blackest darkness is reserved for them.[i] **18**For they mouth empty, boastful words[j] and, by appealing to the lustful desires of sinful human nature, they entice people who are just escaping from those who live in error. **19**They promise them freedom, while they themselves are slaves of depravity—for a man is a slave to whatever has mastered him.[k] **20**If they have escaped the corruption of the world by knowing[l] our Lord and Savior Jesus Christ and are again entangled in it and overcome, they are worse off at the end than they were at the beginning.[m] **21**It would have been better for them *not to have known the* way of righteousness, than to have known it and then to turn their backs on the sacred command that was passed on to them.[n] **22**Of them the proverbs are true: "A dog returns to its vomit,"[g][o] and, "A sow that is washed goes back to her wallowing in the mud."

The Day of the Lord

3 Dear friends, this is now my second letter to you. I have written both of them as reminders[p] to stimulate you to wholesome thinking. **2**I want you to recall the words spoken in the past by the holy prophets and the command given by our Lord and Savior through your apostles.

3First of all, you must understand that in the last days[q] scoffers will come, scoffing and following their own evil desires.[r] **4**They will say, "Where is this 'coming' he promised?[s] Ever since our fathers died, everything goes on as it has since the beginning of creation."[t] **5**But they deliberately forget that long ago by God's word[u] the heavens existed and the earth was formed out of water and by water.[v] **6**By these waters also the world of that time was deluged and destroyed.[w] **7**By the same word the present heavens and earth are reserved for fire,[x] being kept for the day of judgment and destruction of ungodly men.

8But do not forget this one thing, dear friends: With the Lord a day is like a thousand years, and a thousand years are like a day.[y] **9**The Lord is not slow in keeping his promise,[z] as some understand slowness. He is patient[a] with you, not wanting anyone to perish, but everyone to come to repentance.[b]

10But the day of the Lord will come like a thief.[c] The heavens will disappear with a roar; the elements will be destroyed by fire, and the earth and everything in it will be laid bare.[h][d]

11Since everything will be destroyed in this way, what kind of people ought you to be? You ought to live holy and godly lives **12**as you look forward[e] to the day of God and speed its coming.[i][f] That day will bring about the destruction of the heavens by fire, and the elements will melt in the heat.[g] **13**But in keeping with his promise we are looking forward to a new heaven and a new earth,[h] the home of righteousness.

14So then, dear friends, since you are looking forward to this, make every effort to be found spot-

2:13 [a]Ro 13:13 [b]1Co 11:20, 21; Jude 12
2:14 [c]ver 18 [d]ver 3 [e]Eph 2:3
2:15 [f]Nu 22:4-20; Jude 11
2:16 [g]Nu 22:21-30
2:17 [h]Jude 12 [i]Jude 13
2:18 [j]Jude 16
2:19 [k]Jn 8:34; Ro 6:16
2:20 [l]2Pe 1:2 [m]Mt 12:45
2:21 [n]Heb 6:4-6
2:22 [o]Pr 26:11
3:1 [p]2Pe 1:13
3:3 [q]1Ti 4:1 [r]2Pe 2:10; Jude 18
3:4 [s]Isa 5:19; Eze 12:22; Mt 24:48 [t]Mk 10:6
3:5 [u]Ge 1:6,9; Heb 11:3 [v]Ps 24:2
3:6 [w]Ge 7:21,22
3:7 [x]ver 10,12; 2Th 1:7
3:8 [y]Ps 90:4
3:9 [z]Hab 2:3; Heb 10:37 [a]Ro 2:4 [b]1Ti 2:4
3:10 [c]Lk 12:39; 1Th 5:2 [d]Mt 24:35; Rev 21:1
3:12 [e]1Co 1:7 [f]Ps 50:3 [g]ver 10
3:13 [h]Isa 65:17; 66:22; Rev 21:1

[f]13 Some manuscripts *in their love feasts*
[g]22 Prov. 26:11
[h]10 Some manuscripts *be burned up*
[i]12 Or *as you wait eagerly for the day of God to come*

less, blameless and at peace with
him. **15**Bear in mind that our Lord's
patience[a] means salvation,[b] just
as our dear brother Paul also wrote
you with the wisdom that God gave
him.[c] **16**He writes the same way in
all his letters, speaking in them of
these matters. His letters contain
some things that are hard to understand, which ignorant and unstable[d] people distort, as they do the
other Scriptures,[e] to their own destruction.
17Therefore, dear friends, since
you already know this, be on your
guard[f] so that you may not be carried away by the error[g] of lawless
men and fall from your secure position.[h] **18**But grow in the grace and
knowledge of our Lord and Savior
Jesus Christ.[i] To him be glory
both now and forever! Amen.

3:15 [a] Ro 2:4 [b] ver 9 [c] Eph 3:3
3:16 [d] 2Pe 2:14 [e] ver 2
3:17 [f] 1Co 10:12 [g] 2Pe 2:18 [h] Rev 2:5
3:18 [i] 2Pe 1:11

1 John

Title and Background

False teachers were trying to mislead first-century Christians by denying, among other things, the true humanity of Christ. This view was incorporated within the system called Gnosticism and is the background of much of 1 John.

Author and Date of Writing

The author is John son of Zebedee—the apostle and the author of the Gospel of John and the book of Revelation. He was a first cousin of Jesus. The letter is difficult to date with precision, but many factors indicate that it was written near the end of the first century, probably around A.D. 90.

Theme and Message

John had two basic purposes in mind in this letter: (1) to expose false teachers, and (2) to give believers assurance of salvation. In keeping with his intention to combat Gnostic teachers, who taught that the spirit is entirely good and matter is entirely evil, John specifically struck at their total lack of morality; and by giving eyewitness testimony to the incarnation, he sought to confirm his readers' belief in the incarnate Christ. He tells his readers that if he is successful in doing this, it would give him great joy.

Outline

I. The Reality of the Incarnation (1:1-4)
II. Fellowship With the Father and the Son (1:5-2:28)
III. Divine Sonship (2:29-4:6)
IV. Ethics and Christ (4:7-5:12)
V. Great Christian Certainties (5:13-21)

The Word of Life

1 That which was from the beginning,[a] which we have
heard, which we have seen with our
eyes,[b] which we have looked at
and our hands have touched[c]—
this we proclaim concerning the
Word of life. 2The life appeared;[d]
we have seen it and testify to it, and
we proclaim to you the eternal life,
which was with the Father and has
appeared to us. 3We proclaim to
you what we have seen and heard,
so that you also may have fellowship with us. And our fellowship is
with the Father and with his Son,
Jesus Christ.[e] 4We write this[f] to
make our[a] joy complete.[g]

1:1 [a]Jn 1:2 [b]Jn 1:14 [c]Jn 20:27
1:2 [d]Jn 1:1-4; 1Ti 3:16
1:3 [e]1Co 1:9
1:4 [f]1Jn 2:1 [g]Jn 3:29
1:5 [h]1Jn 3:11
1:6 [i]2Co 6:14 [j]Jn 3:19-21
1:7 [k]Heb 9:14
1:8 [l]Pr 20:9 [m]1Jn 2:4
1:9 [n]Ps 32:5; 51:2

Walking in the Light

5This is the message we have
heard[h] from him and declare to
you: God is light; in him there is no
darkness at all. 6If we claim to have
fellowship with him yet walk in the
darkness,[i] we lie and do not live
by the truth.[j] 7But if we walk in
the light, as he is in the light, we
have fellowship with one another,
and the blood of Jesus, his Son, purifies us from all[b] sin.[k]

8If we claim to be without sin,[l]
we deceive ourselves and the truth
is not in us.[m] 9If we confess our
sins, he is faithful and just and will
forgive us our sins[n] and purify us

[a]4 Some manuscripts *your* [b]7 Or *every*

from all unrighteousness. **10**If we
claim we have not sinned, we make
him out to be a liar[a] and his word
has no place in our lives.[b]

2 My dear children,[c] I write this
to you so that you will not sin.
But if anybody does sin, we have
one who speaks to the Father in
our defense[d]—Jesus Christ, the
Righteous One. **2**He is the atoning
sacrifice for our sins,[e] and not only
for ours but also for[c] the sins of the
whole world.

3We know that we have come to
know him if we obey his commands.[f] **4**The man who says, "I
know him," but does not do what
he commands is a liar, and the
truth is not in him.[g] **5**But if anyone
obeys his word,[h] God's love[d] is
truly made complete in him.[i] This
is how we know we are in him:
6Whoever claims to live in him
must walk as Jesus did.[j]

7Dear friends, I am not writing
you a new command but an old
one, which you have had since the
beginning.[k] This old command is
the message you have heard. **8**Yet I
am writing you a new command;[l]
its truth is seen in him and you, because the darkness is passing[m] and
the true light[n] is already shining.[o]

9Anyone who claims to be in the
light but hates his brother is still in
the darkness. **10**Whoever loves his
brother lives in the light,[p] and
there is nothing in him[e] to make
him stumble. **11**But whoever hates
his brother is in the darkness and
walks around in the darkness; he
does not know where he is going,
because the darkness has blinded
him.[q]

12I write to you, dear children,
because your sins have been
forgiven on account of
his name.
13I write to you, fathers,
because you have known him
who is from the
beginning.
I write to you, young men,
because you have overcome
the evil one.[r]
I write to you, dear children,
because you have known the
Father.
14I write to you, fathers,
because you have known him
who is from the
beginning.
I write to you, young men,
because you are strong,[s]
and the word of God lives in
you,[t]
and you have overcome the
evil one.[u]

Do Not Love the World

15Do not love the world or anything in the world.[v] If anyone loves
the world, the love of the Father is
not in him.[w] **16**For everything in
the world—the cravings of sinful
man,[x] the lust of his eyes[y] and the
boasting of what he has and does
—comes not from the Father but
from the world. **17**The world and its
desires pass away,[z] but the man
who does the will of God lives forever.

Warning Against Antichrists

18Dear children, this is the last
hour; and as you have heard that
the antichrist is coming,[a] even
now many antichrists have come.[b]
This is how we know it is the last
hour. **19**They went out from us,[c]
but they did not really belong to us.
For if they had belonged to us, they
would have remained with us; but
their going showed that none of
them belonged to us.[d]

20But you have an anointing[e]
from the Holy One,[f] and all of you
know the truth.[f g] **21**I do not write
to you because you do not know
the truth, but because you do know
it[h] and because no lie comes from
the truth. **22**Who is the liar? It is the
man who denies that Jesus is the
Christ. Such a man is the antichrist—he denies the Father and
the Son.[i] **23**No one who denies the
Son has the Father; whoever ac-

1:10 [a] 1Jn 5:10 [b] 1Jn 2:14
2:1 [c] ver 12,13,28 [d] Ro 8:34; Heb 7:25
2:2 [e] Ro 3:25
2:3 [f] Jn 14:15
2:4 [g] 1Jn 1:6,8
2:5 [h] Jn 14:21,23 [i] 1Jn 4:12
2:6 [j] Mt 11:29; 1Pe 2:21
2:7 [k] 1Jn 3:11,23; 2Jn 5,6
2:8 [l] Jn 13:34 [m] Ro 13:12 [n] Jn 1:9 [o] Eph 5:8; 1Th 5:5
2:10 [p] 1Jn 3:14
2:11 [q] Jn 12:35
2:13 [r] ver 14
2:14 [s] Eph 6:10 [t] Jn 5:38; 1Jn 1:10 [u] ver 13
2:15 [v] Ro 12:2 [w] Jas 4:4
2:16 [x] Ro 13:14 [y] Pr 27:20
2:17 [z] 1Co 7:31
2:18 [a] ver 22; 1Jn 4:3; 2Jn 7 [b] 1Jn 4:1
2:19 [c] Ac 20:30 [d] 1Co 11:19
2:20 [e] 2Co 1:21 [f] Mk 1:24 [g] Jn 14:26
2:21 [h] 2Pe 1:12; Jude 5
2:22 [i] 2Jn 7

c2 Or *He is the one who turns aside God's wrath, taking away our sins, and not only ours but also* d5 Or *word, love for God* e10 Or *it* f20 Some manuscripts *and you know all things*

knowledges the Son has the Father also.[a]

24See that what you have heard from the beginning remains in you. If it does, you also will remain in the Son and in the Father.[b] **25**And this is what he promised us—even eternal life.

26I am writing these things to you about those who are trying to lead you astray.[c] **27**As for you, the anointing[d] you received from him remains in you, and you do not need anyone to teach you. But as his anointing teaches you about all things and as that anointing is real, not counterfeit—just as it has taught you, remain in him.

Children of God

28And now, dear children,[e] continue in him, so that when he appears[f] we may be confident[g] and unashamed before him at his coming.[h]

29If you know that he is righteous,[i] you know that everyone who does what is right has been born of him.

3 How great is the love[j] the Father has lavished on us, that we should be called children of God![k] And that is what we are! The reason the world does not know us is that it did not know him.[l] **2**Dear friends, now we are children of God, and what we will be has not yet been made known. But we know that when he appears,[g] we *shall be like him,*[m] *for we shall* see him as he is.[n] **3**Everyone who has this hope in him purifies himself,[o] just as he is pure.

4Everyone who sins breaks the law; in fact, sin is lawlessness.[p] **5**But you know that he appeared so that he might take away our sins. And in him is no sin.[q] **6**No one who lives in him keeps on sinning.[r] No one who continues to sin has either seen him[s] or known him.[t]

7Dear children,[u] do not let anyone lead you astray.[v] He who does what is right is righteous, just as he is righteous.[w] **8**He who does what is sinful is of the devil,[x] because the devil has been sinning from the beginning. The reason the Son of God appeared was to destroy the devil's work. **9**No one who is born of God[y] will continue to sin,[z] because God's seed[a] remains in him; he cannot go on sinning, because he has been born of God. **10**This is how we know who the children of God are and who the children of the devil are: Anyone who does not do what is right is not a child of God; nor is anyone who does not love[b] his brother.

Love One Another

11This is the message you heard[c] from the beginning: We should love one another.[d] **12**Do not be like Cain, who belonged to the evil one and murdered his brother.[e] And why did he murder him? Because his own actions were evil and his brother's were righteous. **13**Do not be surprised, my brothers, if the world hates you.[f] **14**We know that we have passed from death to life,[g] because we love our brothers. Anyone who does not love remains in death.[h] **15**Anyone who hates his brother is a murderer,[i] and you know that no murderer has eternal life in him.[j]

16This is how we know what love is: Jesus Christ laid down his life for us. And we ought to lay down our lives for our brothers.[k] **17**If anyone has material possessions and sees his brother in need but has no pity on him,[l] how can the love of God be in him?[m] **18**Dear children,[n] let us not love with words or tongue but with actions and in truth.[o] **19**This then is how we know that we belong to the truth, and how we set our hearts at rest in his presence **20**whenever our hearts condemn us. For God is greater than our hearts, and he knows everything.

21Dear friends, if our hearts do not condemn us, we have confidence before God[p] **22**and receive from him anything we ask,[q] because we obey his commands and do what pleases him.[r] **23**And this

2:23 [a] Jn 8:19; 1Jn 4:15
2:24 [b] Jn 14:23
2:26 [c] 2Jn 7
2:27 [d] ver 20
2:28 [e] ver 1 [f] 1Jn 3:2 [g] 1Jn 4:17 [h] 1Th 2:19
2:29 [i] 1Jn 3:7
3:1 [j] Jn 3:16 [k] Jn 1:12 [l] Jn 16:3
3:2 [m] Ro 8:29; 2Pe 1:4 [n] 2Co 3:18
3:3 [o] 2Co 7:1; 2Pe 3:13,14
3:4 [p] 1Jn 5:17
3:5 [q] 2Co 5:21
3:6 [r] ver 9 [s] 3Jn 11 [t] 1Jn 2:4
3:7 [u] 1Jn 2:1 [v] 1Jn 2:26 [w] 1Jn 2:29
3:8 [x] Jn 8:44
3:9 [y] Jn 1:13 [z] 1Jn 5:18 [a] 1Pe 1:23
3:10 [b] 1Jn 4:8
3:11 [c] 1Jn 1:5 [d] Jn 13:34,35; 2Jn 5
3:12 [e] Ge 4:8
3:13 [f] Jn 15:18,19; 17:14
3:14 [g] Jn 5:24 [h] 1Jn 2:9
3:15 [i] Mt 5:21,22; Jn 8:44 [j] Gal 5:20,21
3:16 [k] Jn 15:13
3:17 [l] Dt 15:7,8 [m] 1Jn 4:20
3:18 [n] 1Jn 2:1 [o] Eze 33:31; Ro 12:9
3:21 [p] 1Jn 5:14
3:22 [q] Mt 7:7 [r] Jn 8:29

g2 Or *when it is made known*

is his command: to believe[a] in the name of his Son, Jesus Christ, and to love one another as he commanded us.[b] **24**Those who obey his commands live in him,[c] and he in them. And this is how we know that he lives in us: We know it by the Spirit he gave us.[d]

Test the Spirits

4 Dear friends, do not believe every spirit, but test the spirits to see whether they are from God, because many false prophets have gone out into the world.[e] **2**This is how you can recognize the Spirit of God: Every spirit that acknowledges that Jesus Christ has come in the flesh[f] is from God,[g] **3**but every spirit that does not acknowledge Jesus is not from God. This is the spirit of the antichrist,[h] which you have heard is coming and even now is already in the world.

4You, dear children, are from God and have overcome them, because the one who is in you[i] is greater than the one who is in the world.[j] **5**They are from the world[k] and therefore speak from the viewpoint of the world, and the world listens to them. **6**We are from God, and whoever knows God listens to us; but whoever is not from God does not listen to us.[l] This is how we recognize the Spirit[h] of truth[m] and the spirit of falsehood.

God's Love and Ours

7Dear friends, let us love one another,[n] for love comes from God. Everyone who loves has been born of God and knows God.[o] **8**Whoever does not love does not know God, because God is love.[p] **9**This is how God showed his love among us: He sent his one and only Son[i] into the world that we might live through him.[q] **10**This is love: not that we loved God, but that he loved us[r] and sent his Son as an atoning sacrifice for[j] our sins.[s] **11**Dear friends, since God so loved us,[t] we also ought to love one another. **12**No one has ever seen God;[u] but if we love one another, God lives in us and his love is made complete in us.[v]

13We know that we live in him and he in us, because he has given us of his Spirit.[w] **14**And we have seen and testify[x] that the Father has sent his Son to be the Savior of the world.[y] **15**If anyone acknowledges that Jesus is the Son of God,[z] God lives in him and he in God. **16**And so we know and rely on the love God has for us.

God is love.[a] Whoever lives in love lives in God, and God in him.[b] **17**In this way, love is made complete[c] among us so that we will have confidence on the day of judgment, because in this world we are like him. **18**There is no fear in love. But perfect love drives out fear,[d] because fear has to do with punishment. The one who fears is not made perfect in love.

19We love because he first loved us.[e] **20**If anyone says, "I love God," yet hates his brother,[f] he is a liar.[g] For anyone who does not love his brother, whom he has seen,[h] cannot love God, whom he has not seen.[i] **21**And he has given us this command: Whoever loves God must also love his brother.[j]

Faith in the Son of God

5 Everyone who believes that Jesus is the Christ[k] is born of God,[l] and everyone who loves the father loves his child as well.[m] **2**This is how we know that we love the children of God: by loving God and carrying out his commands. **3**This is love for God: to obey his commands.[n] And his commands are not burdensome,[o] **4**for everyone born of God overcomes[p] the world. This is the victory that has overcome the world, even our faith. **5**Who is it that overcomes the world? Only he who believes that Jesus is the Son of God.

6This is the one who came by water and blood[q]—Jesus Christ. He did not come by water only, but by

3:23 [a] Jn 6:29 [b] Jn 13:34
3:24 [c] 1Jn 2:6 [d] 1Jn 4:13
4:1 [e] 2Pe 2:1; 1Jn 2:18
4:2 [f] Jn 1:14; 1Jn 2:23 [g] 1Co 12:3
4:3 [h] 1Jn 2:22; 2Jn 7
4:4 [i] Ro 8:31 [j] Jn 12:31
4:5 [k] Jn 15:19
4:6 [l] Jn 8:47 [m] Jn 14:17
4:7 [n] 1Jn 3:11 [o] 1Jn 2:4
4:8 [p] ver 7,16
4:9 [q] Jn 3:16,17; 1Jn 5:11
4:10 [r] Ro 5:8,10 [s] 1Jn 2:2
4:11 [t] Jn 3:16
4:12 [u] Jn 1:18; 1Ti 6:16 [v] 1Jn 2:5
4:13 [w] 1Jn 3:24
4:14 [x] Jn 15:27 [y] Jn 3:17
4:15 [z] Ro 10:9
4:16 [a] ver 8 [b] 1Jn 3:24
4:17 [c] 1Jn 2:5
4:18 [d] Ro 8:15
4:19 [e] ver 10
4:20 [f] 1Jn 2:9 [g] 1Jn 2:4 [h] 1Jn 3:17 [i] ver 12
4:21 [j] Mt 5:43
5:1 [k] 1Jn 2:22 [l] Jn 1:13; 1Jn 2:23 [m] Jn 8:42
5:3 [n] Jn 14:15; 2Jn 6 [o] Mt 11:30
5:4 [p] Jn 16:33
5:6 [q] Jn 19:34

h6 Or *spirit* i9 Or *his only begotten Son*
j10 Or *as the one who would turn aside his wrath, taking away*

water and blood. And it is the Spirit
who testifies, because the Spirit is
the truth.[a] **7**For there are three[b]
that testify: **8**the[k] Spirit, the water
and the blood; and the three are in
agreement. **9**We accept man's testimony,[c] but God's testimony is
greater because it is the testimony
of God,[d] which he has given about
his Son. **10**Anyone who believes in
the Son of God has this testimony
in his heart.[e] Anyone who does not
believe God has made him out to
be a liar,[f] because he has not believed the testimony God has given
about his Son. **11**And this is the testimony: God has given us eternal
life, and this life is in his Son.[g]
12He who has the Son has life; he
who does not have the Son of God
does not have life.[h]

Concluding Remarks

13I write these things to you who
believe in the name of the Son of
God[i] so that you may know that
you have eternal life.[j] **14**This is the
confidence[k] we have in approaching God: that if we ask anything according to his will, he hears us.[l]
15And if we know that he hears
us—whatever we ask—we know[m]
that we have what we asked of him.

16If anyone sees his brother
commit a sin that does not lead to
death, he should pray and God will
give him life.[n] I refer to those
whose sin does not lead to death.
There is a sin that leads to death.[o]
I am not saying that he should pray
about that.[p] **17**All wrongdoing is
sin,[q] and there is sin that does not
lead to death.[r]

18We know that anyone born of
God does not continue to sin; the
one who was born of God keeps
him safe, and the evil one cannot
harm him.[s] **19**We know that we are
children of God,[t] and that the
whole world is under the control of
the evil one.[u] **20**We know also that
the Son of God has come and has
given us understanding,[v] so that
we may know him who is true.[w]
And we are in him who is true—
even in his Son Jesus Christ. He is
the true God and eternal life.[x]

21Dear children, keep yourselves
from idols.[y]

5:6 [a]Jn 14:17
5:7 [b]Mt 18:16
5:9 [c]Jn 5:34 [d]Mt 3:16,17; Jn 8:17,18
5:10 [e]Ro 8:16; Gal 4:6 [f]Jn 3:33
5:11 [g]Jn 1:4; 1Jn 2:25
5:12 [h]Jn 3:15,16, 36
5:13 [i]1Jn 3:23 [j]Jn 20:31; 1Jn 1:1,2
5:14 [k]1Jn 3:21 [l]Mt 7:7
5:15 [m]ver 18,19,20
5:16 [n]Jas 5:15 [o]Heb 6:4-6; 10:26 [p]Jer 7:16
5:17 [q]1Jn 3:4 [r]1Jn 2:1
5:18 [s]Jn 14:30
5:19 [t]1Jn 4:6 [u]Gal 1:4
5:20 [v]Lk 24:45 [w]Jn 17:3 [x]ver 11
5:21 [y]1Co 10:14; 1Th 1:9

[k]*7,8* Late manuscripts of the Vulgate *testify in heaven: the Father, the Word and the Holy Spirit, and these three are one. 8And there are three that testify on earth: the* (not found in any Greek manuscript before the sixteenth century)

2 John

Title and Background

During the first two centuries A.D. the gospel was taken from place to place by traveling evangelists and teachers. Believers customarily took these missionaries into their homes and gave them provisions for their journey when they left. Since Gnostic teachers also relied on this practice, 2 John was written to urge discernment in supporting traveling teachers.

Author and Date of Writing

The apostle John is the author of this letter. He most likely wrote the book at about the same time as 1 John, about A.D. 90. Note these obvious similarities between 1 and 2 John: 2 John 5 and 1 John 2:7; 2 John 6 and 1 John 5:3; 2 John 7 and 1 John 4:2–3; 2 John 12 and 1 John 1:4.

Theme and Message

John writes of how important it is for Christians to love one another. To love means to obey God's commandments, and God's commandments in turn tell us to live lives of love. John again emphasizes the importance of the doctrine that Jesus is God's Son—both God and man. Christians should separate themselves from those who teach that Jesus is not God's Son.

Outline

I. Greeting (1-3)
II. Commendation (4)
III. Exhortation and Warning (5-11)
IV. Conclusion (12-13)

1The elder,[a]

To the chosen[b] lady and her
children, whom I love in the
truth—and not I only, but also all
who know the truth[c]— **2**because
of the truth,[d] which lives in us[e]
and will be with us forever:

3Grace, mercy and peace from
God the Father and from Jesus
Christ,[f] the Father's Son, will be
with us in truth and love.

4It has given me great joy to find
some of your children walking in
the truth,[g] just as the Father commanded us. **5**And now, dear lady, I
am not writing you a new command but one we have had from
the beginning.[h] I ask that we love
one another. **6**And this is love:[i]
that we walk in obedience to his
commands. As you have heard
from the beginning, his command
is that you walk in love.

7Many deceivers, who do not acknowledge Jesus Christ[j] as coming in the flesh, have gone out into
the world.[k] Any such person is the
deceiver and the antichrist.[l]
8Watch out that you do not lose
what you have worked for, but that
you may be rewarded fully.[m] **9**Anyone who runs ahead and does not
continue in the teaching of Christ
does not have God; whoever continues in the teaching has both the
Father and the Son.[n] **10**If anyone
comes to you and does not bring
this teaching, do not take him into
your house or welcome him.
11Anyone who welcomes him

1:1 [a]3Jn 1 [b]Ro 16:13 [c]Jn 8:32
1:2 [d]2Pe 1:12 [e]1Jn 1:8
1:3 [f]Ro 1:7
1:4 [g]3Jn 3,4
1:5 [h]1Jn 2:7; 3:11
1:6 [i]1Jn 2:5
1:7 [j]1Jn 2:22; 4:2,3 [k]1Jn 4:1 [l]1Jn 2:18
1:8 [m]1Co 3:8
1:9 [n]1Jn 2:23

shares in his wicked work.
12 I have much to write to you,
but I do not want to use paper and
ink. Instead, I hope to visit you and
talk with you face to face,[a] so that
our joy may be complete.
13 The children of your chosen[b]
sister send their greetings.

1:12 [a] 3Jn 13,14
1:13 [b] ver 1

3 John

Title and Background

Itinerant teachers sent out by John were rejected in one of the churches in the province of Asia by a dictatorial leader, Diotrephes. This man had gone so far as to excommunicate members who showed hospitality to John's messengers.

Author and Date of Writing

This letter was probably written about the same time as 1 and 2 John, around A.D. 90. A comparison of 2 and 3 John suggests that the apostle John was the author of both letters. John functioned as an elder in his later years, and he begins both 2 and 3 John with that designation. John uses identical phrases in both books: "love in the truth" (2 John 1 and 3 John 1) and "walking in the truth" (2 John 4 and 3 John 4). The conclusions to both letters are similar as well.

Theme and Message

John wrote to Gaius, his friend and a leader in the church. He writes to praise and thank Gaius for his help and to give him encouragement. He also reproves Diotrephes for not cooperating and for rebelling against John's leadership. In a later visit John will deal with him personally.

Outline

I. Greeting (1-2)
II. Commendation of Gaius (3-8)
III. Condemnation of Diotrephes (9-10)
IV. Exhortation to Gaius (11)
V. Example of Demetrius (12)
VI. Conclusion (13-14)

1The elder,[a]

To my dear friend Gaius, whom I
love in the truth.

2Dear friend, I pray that you may
enjoy good health and that all may
go well with you, even as your soul
is getting along well. 3It gave me
great joy to have some brothers[b]
come and tell about your faithfulness to the truth and how you continue to walk in the truth.[c] 4I have
no greater joy than to hear that my
children[d] are walking in the truth.
5Dear friend, you are faithful in
what you are doing for the brothers, even though they are strangers
to you.[e] 6They have told the
church about your love. You will do
well to send them on their way in a
manner worthy of God. 7It was for
the sake of the Name[f] that they
went out, receiving no help from
the pagans.[g] 8We ought therefore
to show hospitality to such men so
that we may work together for the
truth.

9I wrote to the church, but Diotrephes, who loves to be first, will
have nothing to do with us. 10So if
I come,[h] I will call attention to
what he is doing, gossiping maliciously about us. Not satisfied with
that, he refuses to welcome the
brothers.[i] He also stops those who
want to do so and puts them out of
the church.[j]

11Dear friend, do not imitate
what is evil but what is good.[k] Anyone who does what is good is from
God.[l] Anyone who does what is
evil has not seen God.[m] 12Demetri-
us is well spoken of by everyone[n]
—and even by the truth itself.

1:1 [a] 2Jn 1
1:3 [b] ver 5,10 [c] 2Jn 4
1:4 [d] 1Co 4:15; 1Jn 2:1
1:5 [e] Ro 12:13; Heb 13:2
1:7 [f] Jn 15:21 [g] Ac 20:33,35
1:10 [h] 2Jn 12 [i] ver 5 [j] Jn 9:22,34
1:11 [k] Ps 37:27 [l] 1Jn 2:29 [m] 1Jn 3:6,9,10

We also speak well of him, and
you know that our testimony is
true.[a]
13I have much to write you, but I
do not want to do so with pen and
ink. 14I hope to see you soon, and
we will talk face to face.[b]
Peace to you. The friends here
send their greetings. Greet the
friends there by name.[c]

1:12 [a]Jn 21:24
1:14 [b]2Jn 12 [c]Jn 10:3

Jude

Title and Background

Jude originated as a personal letter from a leader in the apostolic church to one or more of the congregations dispersed throughout the Roman empire. The dangers facing the church at this time were not those of outright persecution and extinction but of heretics and distorters of the faith.

Author and Date of Writing

The author identifies himself as Jude, another form of the Hebrew name Judah. He was most likely Judas the brother of our Lord. The letter was probably written about A.D. 65.

Theme and Message

Although Jude was eager to write to his readers about salvation, he thought he must instead warn them about certain immoral men circulating among them who were perverting the grace of God. Apparently these false teachers were trying to convince believers that being saved by grace gave them license to sin since their sins would no longer be held against them. It has been thought that these false teachers were Gnostics, who believed that the spirit is entirely good and matter is entirely evil, probably forerunners of second-century, fully developed Gnosticism.

Outline

I. Introduction (1-2)
II. Occasion for the Letter (3-4)
III. Warning Against False Teachers (5-16)
IV. Exhortation to Believers (17-23)
V. Concluding Doxology (24-25)

---

1 Jude,[a] a servant of Jesus Christ
and a brother of James,

To those who have been called,[b]
who are loved by God the Father
and kept by[a] Jesus Christ:[c]

2 Mercy, peace and love be yours
in abundance.[d]

The Sin and Doom of Godless Men

3 Dear friends, although I was
very eager to write to you about the
salvation we share,[e] I felt I had to
write and urge you to contend[f] for
the faith that was once for all entrusted to the saints. **4** For certain
men whose condemnation was
written about[b] long ago have secretly slipped in among you.[g] They
are godless men, who change the
grace of our God into a license for
immorality and deny Jesus Christ
our only Sovereign and Lord.[h]
5 Though you already know all
this, I want to remind you that the
Lord[c] delivered his people out of
Egypt, but later destroyed those
who did not believe.[i] **6** And the angels who did not keep their positions of authority but abandoned
their own home—these he has
kept in darkness, bound with everlasting chains for judgment on the
great Day.[j] **7** In a similar way, Sodom and Gomorrah and the surrounding towns[k] gave themselves

1:1 [a] Mt 13:55; Ac 1:13 [b] Ro 1:6,7 [c] Jn 17:12
1:2 [d] 2Pe 1:2
1:3 [e] Tit 1:4 [f] 1Ti 6:12
1:4 [g] Gal 2:4 [h] Tit 1:16; 2Pe 2:1
1:5 [i] Nu 14:29; Ps 106:26
1:6 [j] 2Pe 2:4,9
1:7 [k] Dt 29:23

[a] *1* Or *for;* or *in* [b] *4* Or *men who were marked out for condemnation* [c] *5* Some early manuscripts *Jesus*

up to sexual immorality and perversion. They serve as an example
of those who suffer the punishment of eternal fire.[a]
8In the very same way, these
dreamers pollute their own bodies,
reject authority and slander celestial beings.[b] 9But even the archangel Michael,[c] when he was disputing with the devil about the body of
Moses, did not dare to bring a slanderous accusation against him, but
said, "The Lord rebuke you!"[d]
10Yet these men speak abusively
against whatever they do not understand; and what things they do
understand by instinct, like unrea-
soning animals—these are the very
things that destroy them.[e]
11Woe to them! They have taken
the way of Cain;[f] they have rushed
for profit into Balaam's error;[g]
they have been destroyed in Korah's rebellion.[h]
12These men are blemishes at
your love feasts,[i] eating with you
without the slightest qualm—
shepherds who feed only themselves. They are clouds without
rain,[j] blown along by the wind;[k]
autumn trees, without fruit and uprooted[l]—twice dead. 13They are
wild waves of the sea,[m] foaming up
their shame;[n] wandering stars, for
whom blackest darkness has been
reserved forever.[o]
14Enoch,[p] the seventh from
Adam, prophesied about these
men: "See, the Lord is coming with
thousands upon thousands of his
holy ones[q] 15to judge[r] everyone,
and to convict all the ungodly of all
the ungodly acts they have done in
the ungodly way, and of all the
harsh words ungodly sinners have
spoken against him."[s] 16These
men are grumblers and faultfind-
ers; they follow their own evil desires; they boast[t] about themselves and flatter others for their
own advantage.

A Call to Persevere

17But, dear friends, remember
what the apostles of our Lord Jesus
Christ foretold.[u] 18They said to
you, "In the last times[v] there will
be scoffers who will follow their
own ungodly desires."[w] 19These
are the men who divide you, who
follow mere natural instincts and
do not have the Spirit.[x]
20But you, dear friends, build
yourselves up[y] in your most holy
faith and pray in the Holy Spirit.[z]
21Keep yourselves in God's love as
you wait[a] for the mercy of our Lord
Jesus Christ to bring you to eternal
life.
22Be merciful to those who
doubt; 23snatch others from the
fire and save them;[b] to others
show mercy, mixed with fear—hating even the clothing stained by
corrupted flesh.[c]

Doxology

24To him who is able[d] to keep
you from falling and to present you
before his glorious presence[e]
without fault[f] and with great joy—
25to the only God[g] our Savior be
glory, majesty, power and authority, through Jesus Christ our Lord,
before all ages, now and forevermore![h] Amen.[i]

1:7 [a] 2Pe 2:6
1:8 [b] 2Pe 2:10
1:9 [c] Da 10:13,21 [d] Zec 3:2
1:10 [e] 2Pe 2:12
1:11 [f] Ge 4:3-8; 1Jn 3:12 [g] 2Pe 2:15 [h] Nu 16:1-3, 31-35
1:12 [i] 2Pe 2:13; 1Co 11:20-22 [j] Pr 25:14; 2Pe 2:17 [k] Eph 4:14 [l] Mt 15:13
1:13 [m] Isa 57:20 [n] Php 3:19 [o] 2Pe 2:17
1:14 [p] Ge 5:18, 21-24 [q] Dt 33:2; Da 7:10
1:15 [r] 2Pe 2:6-9 [s] 1Ti 1:9
1:16 [t] 2Pe 2:18
1:17 [u] 2Pe 3:2
1:18 [v] 1Ti 4:1 [w] 2Pe 2:1
1:19 [x] 1Co 2:14,15
1:20 [y] Col 2:7 [z] Eph 6:18
1:21 [a] Tit 2:13; 2Pe 3:12
1:23 [b] Am 4:11; Zec 3:2-5 [c] Rev 3:4
1:24 [d] Ro 16:25 [e] 2Co 4:14 [f] Col 1:22
1:25 [g] Jn 5:44; 1Ti 1:17 [h] Heb 13:8 [i] Ro 11:36

Revelation

Title and Background

Since Roman authorities at this time were beginning to enforce the cult of emperor worship, Christians—who held that Christ, not Caesar, was Lord—were facing increasing hostility. Some in the church were advocating a policy of compromise; this had to be corrected before its subtle influence could undermine believers' determination to stand fast in the perilous days that lay ahead.

Author and Date of Writing

Four times the author identifies himself as John, and John was held to be the author from as early as the second century. Most scholars hold that the book was written about A.D. 95.

Theme and Message

John writes to encourage the faithful to resist staunchly the demands that they worship the emperor. He informs his readers that the final showdown between God and Satan is imminent. Satan will increase his persecution of believers, but they must stand fast, even to death. They are sealed against any spiritual harm and will soon be vindicated when Christ returns, when the wicked are forever destroyed, and when God's people enter an eternity of glory and blessedness.

Outline

I. Jesus Among the Seven Churches (1:1-20)
II. Letters to the Seven Churches (2:1-3:22)
III. The Throne, the Scroll and the Lamb (4:1-5:14)
IV. The Seven Seals (6:1-8:1)
V. The Seven Trumpets (8:2-11:19)
VI. Various Personages and Events (12:1-14:20)
VII. The Seven Bowls (15:1-16:21)
VIII. Babylon: The Great Prostitute (17:1-19:5)
IX. The Wedding of the Lamb (19:6-10)
X. The Return of Christ (19:11-21)
XI. The Thousand Years (20:1-6)
XII. Satan's Doom (20:7-10)
XIII. Great White Throne Judgment (20:11-15)
XIV. New Heaven, New Earth, New Jerusalem (21:1-22:5)
XV. Conclusion (22:6-21)

Prologue

1 The revelation of Jesus Christ,
which God gave him to show
his servants what must soon take
place. He made it known by sending his angel[a] to his servant John,
2who testifies to everything he
saw—that is, the word of God and
the testimony of Jesus Christ.[b]
3Blessed is the one who reads the
words of this prophecy, and
blessed are those who hear it and
take to heart what is written in it,[c]
because the time is near.

Greetings and Doxology

4John,

To the seven churches in the
province of Asia:

1:1 [a] Rev 22:16
1:2 [b] 1Co 1:6; Rev 12:17
1:3 [c] Lk 11:28

Grace and peace to you from him who is, and who was, and who is to come, and from the seven spirits[a][a] before his throne, 5 and from Jesus Christ, who is the faithful witness,[b] the firstborn from the dead,[c] and the ruler of the kings of the earth.[d]

To him who loves us and has freed us from our sins by his blood, 6 and has made us to be a kingdom and priests[e] to serve his God and Father—to him be glory and power for ever and ever! Amen.[f]

7 Look, he is coming with the
 clouds,[g]
and every eye will see him,
even those who pierced him;
and all the peoples of the
 earth will mourn[h]
 because of him.
So shall it be! Amen.

8 "I am the Alpha and the Omega,"[i] says the Lord God, "who is, and who was, and who is to come, the Almighty."[j]

One Like a Son of Man

9 I, John, your brother and companion in the suffering[k] and kingdom and patient endurance[l] that are ours in Jesus, was on the island of Patmos because of the word of God and the testimony of Jesus. 10 On the Lord's Day I was in the Spirit,[m] and I heard behind me a loud voice like a trumpet,[n] 11 which said: "Write on a scroll what you see and send it to the seven churches:[o] to Ephesus, Smyrna, Pergamum, Thyatira, Sardis,[p] Philadelphia and Laodicea."

12 I turned around to see the voice that was speaking to me. And when I turned I saw seven golden lampstands,[q] 13 and among the lampstands was someone "like a son of man,"[b][r] dressed in a robe reaching down to his feet and with a golden sash around his chest.[s] 14 His head and hair were white like wool, as white as snow, and his eyes were like blazing fire.[t] 15 His feet were like bronze glowing in a furnace,[u] and his voice was like the sound of rushing waters.[v] 16 In his right hand he held seven stars,[w] and out of his mouth came a sharp double-edged sword.[x] His face was like the sun shining in all its brilliance.

17 When I saw him, I fell at his feet[y] as though dead. Then he placed his right hand on me and said: "Do not be afraid. I am the First and the Last.[z] 18 I am the Living One; I was dead,[a] and behold I am alive for ever and ever![b] And I hold the keys of death and Hades.[c]

19 "Write, therefore, what you have seen, what is now and what will take place later. 20 The mystery of the seven stars that you saw in my right hand and of the seven golden lampstands[d] is this: The seven stars are the angels[c] of the seven churches,[e] and the seven lampstands are the seven churches.[f]

To the Church in Ephesus

2 "To the angel[d] of the church in Ephesus write:

These are the words of him who holds the seven stars in his right hand[g] and walks among the seven golden lampstands:[h] 2 I know your deeds,[i] your hard work and your perseverance. I know that you cannot tolerate wicked men, that you have tested[j] those who claim to be apostles but are not, and have found them false.[k] 3 You have persevered and have endured hardships for my name,[l] and have not grown weary.

4 Yet I hold this against you: You have forsaken your first love.[m] 5 Remember the height from which you have fallen! Repent[n] and do the things you did at first. If you do not repent, I will come to you and remove your lampstand[o] from its place. 6 But you have this in

1:4 [a] Rev 3:1; 4:5
1:5 [b] Rev 3:14 [c] Col 1:18 [d] Rev 17:14
1:6 [e] 1Pe 2:5 [f] Ro 11:36
1:7 [g] Da 7:13 [h] Zec 12:10
1:8 [i] Rev 21:6 [j] Rev 4:8
1:9 [k] Php 4:14 [l] 2Ti 2:12
1:10 [m] Rev 4:2 [n] Rev 4:1
1:11 [o] ver 4,20 [p] Rev 3:1
1:12 [q] Ex 25:31-40; Zec 4:2
1:13 [r] Eze 1:26; Da 7:13; 10:16 [s] Da 10:5; Rev 15:6
1:14 [t] Da 7:9; 10:6; Rev 19:12
1:15 [u] Da 10:6 [v] Eze 43:2; Rev 14:2
1:16 [w] Rev 2:1; 3:1 [x] Isa 49:2; Heb 4:12; Rev 2:12,16
1:17 [y] Eze 1:28; Da 8:17,18 [z] Isa 41:4; 44:6; 48:12; Rev 22:13
1:18 [a] Ro 6:9 [b] Rev 4:9,10 [c] Rev 20:1
1:20 [d] Zec 4:2 [e] ver 4,11 [f] Mt 5:14,15
2:1 [g] Rev 1:16 [h] Rev 1:12,13
2:2 [i] Rev 3:1,8,15 [j] 1Jn 4:1 [k] 2Co 11:13
2:3 [l] Jn 15:21
2:4 [m] Mt 24:12
2:5 [n] ver 16,22 [o] Rev 1:20

[a]4 Or *the sevenfold Spirit* [b]13 Daniel 7:13 [c]20 Or *messengers* [d]1 Or *messenger*; also in verses 8, 12 and 18

your favor: You hate the practices of the Nicolaitans,[a]
which I also hate.
7He who has an ear, let him
hear[b] what the Spirit says to
the churches. To him who
overcomes, I will give the right
to eat from the tree of life,[c]
which is in the paradise[d] of
God.

To the Church in Smyrna

8"To the angel of the church in
Smyrna[e] write:

These are the words of him
who is the First and the Last,[f]
who died and came to life
again.[g] 9I know your afflictions and your poverty—yet
you are rich![h] I know the slander of those who say they are
Jews and are not,[i] but are a
synagogue of Satan.[j] 10Do
not be afraid of what you are
about to suffer. I tell you, the
devil will put some of you in
prison to test you,[k] and you
will suffer persecution for ten
days.[l] Be faithful,[m] even to
the point of death, and I will
give you the crown of life.
11He who has an ear, let him
hear what the Spirit says to the
churches. He who overcomes
will not be hurt at all by the
second death.[n]

To the Church in Pergamum

12"To the angel of the church in
Pergamum[o] write:

These are the words of him
who has the sharp, double-
edged sword.[p] 13I know where
you live—where Satan has his
throne. Yet you remain true to
my name. You did not re-
nounce your faith in me,[q]
even in the days of Antipas,
my faithful witness, who was
put to death in your city—
where Satan lives.[r]
14Nevertheless, I have a few
things against you:[s] You have
people there who hold to the
teaching of Balaam,[t] who
taught Balak to entice the Israelites to sin by eating food
sacrificed to idols and by committing sexual immorality.[u]
15Likewise you also have
those who hold to the teaching of the Nicolaitans.[v] 16Re-
pent therefore! Otherwise, I
will soon come to you and will
fight against them with the
sword of my mouth.[w]
17He who has an ear, let him
hear what the Spirit says to the
churches. To him who overcomes, I will give some of the
hidden manna.[x] I will also
give him a white stone with a
new name[y] written on it,
known only to him who re-
ceives it.[z]

To the Church in Thyatira

18"To the angel of the church in
Thyatira[a] write:

These are the words of the
Son of God, whose eyes are
like blazing fire and whose
feet are like burnished
bronze.[b] 19I know your
deeds,[c] your love and faith,
your service and perseverance,
and that you are now doing
more than you did at first.
20Nevertheless, I have this
against you: You tolerate that
woman Jezebel,[d] who calls
herself a prophetess. By her
teaching she misleads my servants into sexual immorality
and the eating of food sacrificed to idols. 21I have given
her time[e] to repent of her immorality, but she is unwilling.[f] 22So I will cast her on a
bed of suffering, and I will
make those who commit adultery[g] with her suffer intensely, unless they repent of her
ways. 23I will strike her children dead. Then all the
churches will know that I am
he who searches hearts and
minds,[h] and I will repay each
of you according to your
deeds. 24Now I say to the rest
of you in Thyatira, to you who
do not hold to her teaching

2:6 [a]ver 15
2:7 [b]Mt 11:15; Rev 3:6,13,22 [c]Ge 2:9; Rev 22:2,14, 19 [d]Lk 23:43
2:8 [e]Rev 1:11 [f]Rev 1:17 [g]Rev 1:18
2:9 [h]Jas 2:5 [i]Rev 3:9 [j]Mt 4:10
2:10 [k]Rev 3:10 [l]Da 1:12,14 [m]ver 13
2:11 [n]Rev 20:6,14; 21:8
2:12 [o]Rev 1:11 [p]Rev 1:16
2:13 [q]Rev 14:12 [r]ver 9,24
2:14 [s]ver 20 [t]2Pe 2:15 [u]1Co 6:13
2:15 [v]ver 6
2:16 [w]2Th 2:8; Rev 1:16
2:17 [x]Jn 6:49,50 [y]Isa 62:2 [z]Rev 19:12
2:18 [a]Rev 1:11 [b]Rev 1:14,15
2:19 [c]ver 2
2:20 [d]1Ki 16:31; 21:25; 2Ki 9:7
2:21 [e]Ro 2:4 [f]Rev 9:20
2:22 [g]Rev 17:2; 18:9
2:23 [h]1Sa 16:7; Jer 11:20; Ac 1:24; Ro 8:27

and have not learned Satan's
so-called deep secrets (I will
not impose any other burden
on you):[a] **25**Only hold on to
what you have[b] until I come.
26To him who overcomes
and does my will to the end, I
will give authority over the nations[c]—

27'He will rule them with an
iron scepter;[d]
he will dash them to
pieces like
pottery'[e][e]—

just as I have received authority from my Father. **28**I will also
give him the morning star.[f]
29He who has an ear, let him
hear[g] what the Spirit says to
the churches.

To the Church in Sardis

3 "To the angel[f] of the church
in Sardis write:

These are the words of him
who holds the seven spirits[g][h]
of God and the seven stars.[i] I
know your deeds;[j] you have a
reputation of being alive, but
you are dead.[k] **2**Wake up!
Strengthen what remains and
is about to die, for I have not
found your deeds complete in
the sight of my God. **3**Remember, therefore, what you have
received and heard; obey it,
and repent.[l] But if you do not
wake up, I will come like a
thief,[m] and you will not know
at what time I will come to
you.
4Yet you have a few people
in Sardis who have not soiled
their clothes.[n] They will walk
with me, dressed in white,[o]
for they are worthy. **5**He who
overcomes will, like them, be
dressed in white. I will never
blot out his name from the
book of life,[p] but will acknowledge his name before
my Father[q] and his angels.
6He who has an ear, let him
hear[r] what the Spirit says to
the churches.

2:24 [a]Ac 15:28
2:25 [b]Rev 3:11
2:26 [c]Ps 2:8; Rev 3:21
2:27 [d]Rev 12:5 [e]Isa 30:14; Jer 19:11
2:28 [f]Rev 22:16
2:29 [g]ver 7
3:1 [h]Rev 1:4 [i]Rev 1:16 [j]Rev 2:2 [k]1Ti 5:6
3:3 [l]Rev 2:5 [m]2Pe 3:10
3:4 [n]Jude 23 [o]Rev 4:4; 6:11; 7:9,13,14
3:5 [p]Rev 20:12 [q]Mt 10:32
3:6 [r]Rev 2:7
3:7 [s]Rev 1:11 [t]1Jn 5:20 [u]Isa 22:22; Mt 16:19
3:8 [v]Ac 14:27 [w]Rev 2:13
3:9 [x]Rev 2:9 [y]Isa 49:23 [z]Isa 43:4
3:10 [a]2Pe 2:9 [b]Rev 2:10 [c]Rev 6:10; 17:8
3:11 [d]Rev 2:25 [e]Rev 2:10
3:12 [f]Gal 2:9 [g]Rev 14:1; 22:4 [h]Rev 21:2,10
3:14 [i]Col 1:16,18

To the Church in Philadelphia

7"To the angel of the church in
Philadelphia[s] write:

These are the words of him
who is holy and true,[t] who
holds the key of David.[u] What
he opens no one can shut, and
what he shuts no one can
open. **8**I know your deeds. See,
I have placed before you an
open door[v] that no one can
shut. I know that you have little strength, yet you have kept
my word and have not denied
my name.[w] **9**I will make those
who are of the synagogue of
Satan,[x] who claim to be Jews
though they are not, but are liars—I will make them come
and fall down at your feet[y]
and acknowledge that I have
loved you.[z] **10**Since you have
kept my command to endure
patiently, I will also keep
you[a] from the hour of trial
that is going to come upon the
whole world to test[b] those
who live on the earth.[c]
11I am coming soon. Hold
on to what you have,[d] so that
no one will take your crown.[e]
12Him who overcomes I will
make a pillar[f] in the temple
of my God. Never again will he
leave it. I will write on him the
name of my God[g] and the
name of the city of my God,
the new Jerusalem,[h] which is
coming down out of heaven
from my God; and I will also
write on him my new name.
13He who has an ear, let him
hear what the Spirit says to the
churches.

To the Church in Laodicea

14"To the angel of the church in
Laodicea write:

These are the words of the
Amen, the faithful and true
witness, the ruler of God's creation.[i] **15**I know your deeds,
that you are neither cold nor

[e]27 Psalm 2:9 [f]1 Or *messenger;* also in verses 7 and 14 [g]1 Or *the sevenfold Spirit*

hot.[a] I wish you were either one or the other! **16**So, because you are lukewarm—neither hot nor cold—I am about to spit you out of my mouth. **17**You say, 'I am rich; I have acquired wealth and do not need a thing.'[b] But you do not realize that you are wretched, pitiful, poor, blind and naked. **18**I counsel you to buy from me gold refined in the fire, so you can become rich; and white clothes to wear, so you can cover your shameful nakedness;[c] and salve to put on your eyes, so you can see.

19Those whom I love I rebuke and discipline.[d] So be earnest, and repent.[e] **20**Here I am! I stand at the door[f] and knock. If anyone hears my voice and opens the door,[g] I will come in[h] and eat with him, and he with me.

21To him who overcomes, I will give the right to sit with me on my throne,[i] just as I overcame[j] and sat down with my Father on his throne. **22**He who has an ear, let him hear[k] what the Spirit says to the churches."

The Throne in Heaven

4 After this I looked, and there before me was a door standing open in heaven. And the voice I had first heard speaking to me like a trumpet[l] said, "Come up here,[m] and I will show you what must take place after this."[n] **2**At once I was in the Spirit,[o] and there before me was a throne in heaven[p] with someone sitting on it. **3**And the one who sat there had the appearance of jasper and carnelian. A rainbow,[q] resembling an emerald, encircled the throne. **4**Surrounding the throne were twenty-four other thrones, and seated on them were twenty-four elders.[r] They were dressed in white[s] and had crowns of gold on their heads. **5**From the throne came flashes of lightning, rumblings and peals of thunder.[t] Before the throne, seven lamps[u] were blazing. These are the seven spirits[h][v] of God. **6**Also before the throne there was what looked like a sea of glass,[w] clear as crystal.

In the center, around the throne, were four living creatures,[x] and they were covered with eyes, in front and in back. **7**The first living creature was like a lion, the second was like an ox, the third had a face like a man, the fourth was like a flying eagle.[y] **8**Each of the four living creatures had six wings[z] and was covered with eyes all around, even under his wings. Day and night they never stop saying:

"Holy, holy, holy
is the Lord God Almighty,[a]
who was, and is, and is to
come."[b]

9Whenever the living creatures give glory, honor and thanks to him who sits on the throne[c] and who lives for ever and ever, **10**the twenty-four elders[d] fall down before him[e] who sits on the throne,[f] and worship him who lives for ever and ever. They lay their crowns before the throne and say:

11"You are worthy, our Lord and
God,
to receive glory and honor
and power,[g]
for you created all things,
and by your will they were
created
and have their being."[h]

The Scroll and the Lamb

5 Then I saw in the right hand of him who sat on the throne[i] a scroll with writing on both sides[j] and sealed[k] with seven seals. **2**And I saw a mighty angel proclaiming in a loud voice, "Who is worthy to break the seals and open the scroll?" **3**But no one in heaven or on earth or under the earth could open the scroll or even look inside it. **4**I wept and wept because no one was found who was worthy to open the scroll or look inside. **5**Then one

3:15 [a]Ro 12:11
3:17 [b]Hos 12:8; 1Co 4:8
3:18 [c]Rev 16:15
3:19 [d]Pr 3:12; Heb 12:5,6 [e]Rev 2:5
3:20 [f]Mt 24:33 [g]Lk 12:36 [h]Jn 14:23
3:21 [i]Mt 19:28 [j]Rev 5:5
3:22 [k]Rev 2:7
4:1 [l]Rev 1:10 [m]Rev 11:12 [n]Rev 1:19
4:2 [o]Rev 1:10 [p]Isa 6:1; Eze 1:26-28; Da 7:9
4:3 [q]Eze 1:28
4:4 [r]Rev 11:16 [s]Rev 3:4,5
4:5 [t]Rev 8:5; 16:18 [u]Zec 4:2 [v]Rev 1:4
4:6 [w]Rev 15:2 [x]Eze 1:5
4:7 [y]Eze 1:10; 10:14
4:8 [z]Isa 6:2 [a]Isa 6:3; Rev 1:8 [b]Rev 1:4
4:9 [c]Ps 47:8
4:10 [d]ver 4 [e]Rev 5:8,14 [f]ver 2
4:11 [g]Rev 5:12 [h]Rev 10:6
5:1 [i]ver 7,13 [j]Eze 2:9,10 [k]Isa 29:11; Da 12:4

[h]5 Or *the sevenfold Spirit*

of the elders said to me, "Do not
weep! See, the Lion[a] of the tribe of
Judah, the Root of David,[b] has triumphed. He is able to open the
scroll and its seven seals."
6Then I saw a Lamb,[c] looking as
if it had been slain, standing in the
center of the throne, encircled by
the four living creatures and the elders. He had seven horns and seven
eyes,[d] which are the seven spirits[i]
of God sent out into all the earth.
7He came and took the scroll from
the right hand of him who sat on
the throne.[e] 8And when he had
taken it, the four living creatures
and the twenty-four elders fell
down before the Lamb. Each one
had a harp[f] and they were holding
golden bowls full of incense, which
are the prayers[g] of the saints. 9And
they sang a new song:[h]

"You are worthy[i] to take the
scroll
and to open its seals,
because you were slain,
and with your blood[j] you
purchased[k] men for God
from every tribe and language
and people and nation.
10You have made them to be a
kingdom and priests[l] to
serve our God,
and they will reign on the
earth."

11Then I looked and heard the
voice of many angels, numbering
thousands upon thousands, and
*ten thousand times ten thou-
sand.*[m] They encircled the throne
and the living creatures and the elders. 12In a loud voice they sang:

"Worthy is the Lamb, who was
slain,
to receive power and wealth
and wisdom and strength
and honor and glory and
praise!"[n]

13Then I heard every creature in
heaven and on earth and under the
earth[o] and on the sea, and all that
is in them, singing:

"To him who sits on the throne
and to the Lamb[p]
be praise and honor and glory
and power,
for ever and ever!"[q]

14The four living creatures said,
"Amen,"[r] and the elders fell down
and worshiped.[s]

The Seals

6 I watched as the Lamb[t]
opened the first of the seven
seals.[u] Then I heard one of the
four living creatures[v] say in a voice
like thunder,[w] "Come!" 2I looked,
and there before me was a white
horse![x] Its rider held a bow, and he
was given a crown,[y] and he rode
out as a conqueror bent on conquest.[z]
3When the Lamb opened the
second seal, I heard the second living creature[a] say, "Come!" 4Then
another horse came out, a fiery red
one.[b] Its rider was given power to
take peace from the earth[c] and to
make men slay each other. To him
was given a large sword.
5When the Lamb opened the
third seal, I heard the third living
creature[d] say, "Come!" I looked,
and there before me was a black
horse![e] Its rider was holding a pair
of scales in his hand. 6Then I heard
what sounded like a voice among
the four living creatures,[f] saying,
"A quart[j] of wheat for a day's
wages,[k] and three quarts of barley
for a day's wages,[k] and do not
damage[g] the oil and the wine!"
7When the Lamb opened the
fourth seal, I heard the voice of the
fourth living creature[h] say,
"Come!" 8I looked, and there before me was a pale horse![i] Its rider
was named Death, and Hades[j]
was following close behind him.
They were given power over a
fourth of the earth to kill by sword,
famine and plague, and by the wild
beasts of the earth.[k]
9When he opened the fifth seal,
I saw under the altar[l] the souls of
those who had been slain[m] because of the word of God and the

i6 Or *the sevenfold Spirit* j6 Greek *a choinix* (probably about a liter) k6 Greek *a denarius*

5:5 [a]Ge 49:9 [b]Isa 11:1,10; Ro 15:12; Rev 22:16
5:6 [c]Jn 1:29 [d]Zec 4:10
5:7 [e]ver 1
5:8 [f]Rev 14:2 [g]Ps 141:2
5:9 [h]Ps 40:3 [i]Rev 4:11 [j]Heb 9:12 [k]1Co 6:20
5:10 [l]1Pe 2:5
5:11 [m]Da 7:10; Heb 12:22
5:12 [n]Rev 4:11
5:13 [o]ver 3; Php 2:10 [p]Rev 6:16 [q]1Ch 29:11
5:14 [r]Rev 4:9 [s]Rev 4:10; 19:4
6:1 [t]Rev 5:6 [u]Rev 5:1 [v]Rev 4:6,7 [w]Rev 14:2; 19:6
6:2 [x]Zec 6:3; Rev 19:11 [y]Zec 6:11; Rev 14:14 [z]Ps 45:4
6:3 [a]Rev 4:7
6:4 [b]Zec 6:2 [c]Mt 10:34
6:5 [d]Rev 4:7 [e]Zec 6:2
6:6 [f]Rev 4:6,7 [g]Rev 9:4
6:7 [h]Rev 4:7
6:8 [i]Zec 6:3 [j]Hos 13:14 [k]Jer 15:2,3; Eze 5:12,17
6:9 [l]Rev 14:18; 16:7 [m]Rev 20:4

testimony they had maintained. 10They called out in a loud voice, "How long,[a] Sovereign Lord, holy and true,[b] until you judge the inhabitants of the earth and avenge our blood?"[c] 11Then each of them was given a white robe,[d] and they were told to wait a little longer, until the number of their fellow servants and brothers who were to be killed as they had been was completed.[e]

12I watched as he opened the sixth seal. There was a great earthquake.[f] The sun turned black[g] like sackcloth made of goat hair, the whole moon turned blood red, 13and the stars in the sky fell to earth,[h] as late figs drop from a fig tree[i] when shaken by a strong wind. 14The sky receded like a scroll, rolling up, and every mountain and island was removed from its place.[j]

15Then the kings of the earth, the princes, the generals, the rich, the mighty, and every slave and every free man hid in caves and among the rocks of the mountains.[k] 16They called to the mountains and the rocks, "Fall on us[l] and hide us from the face of him who sits on the throne and from the wrath of the Lamb! 17For the great day[m] of their wrath has come, and who can stand?"[n]

144,000 Sealed

7 After this I saw four angels standing at the four corners of the earth, holding back the four winds[o] of the earth to prevent any wind from blowing on the land or on the sea or on any tree. 2Then I saw another angel coming up from the east, having the seal of the living God. He called out in a loud voice to the four angels who had been given power to harm the land and the sea: 3"Do not harm[p] the land or the sea or the trees until we put a seal on the foreheads[q] of the servants of our God." 4Then I heard the number[r] of those who were sealed: 144,000[s] from all the tribes of Israel.

5From the tribe of Judah
12,000 were sealed,
from the tribe of Reuben
12,000,
from the tribe of Gad 12,000,
6from the tribe of Asher 12,000,
from the tribe of Naphtali
12,000,
from the tribe of Manasseh
12,000,
7from the tribe of Simeon
12,000,
from the tribe of Levi 12,000,
from the tribe of Issachar
12,000,
8from the tribe of Zebulun
12,000,
from the tribe of Joseph
12,000,
from the tribe of Benjamin
12,000.

The Great Multitude in White Robes

9After this I looked and there before me was a great multitude that no one could count, from every nation, tribe, people and language,[t] standing before the throne[u] and in front of the Lamb. They were wearing white robes and were holding palm branches in their hands. 10And they cried out in a loud voice:

"Salvation belongs to our
God,[v]
who sits on the throne,
and to the Lamb."

11All the angels were standing around the throne and around the elders[w] and the four living creatures.[x] They fell down on their faces[y] before the throne and worshiped God, 12saying:

"Amen!
Praise and glory
and wisdom and thanks and
honor
and power and strength
be to our God for ever and ever.
Amen!"[z]

13Then one of the elders asked me, "These in white robes—who are they, and where did they come from?"

6:10 [a]Zec 1:12 [b]Rev 3:7 [c]Rev 19:2
6:11 [d]Rev 3:4 [e]Heb 11:40
6:12 [f]Rev 16:18 [g]Mt 24:29
6:13 [h]Mt 24:29; Rev 8:10; 9:1 [i]Isa 34:4
6:14 [j]Jer 4:24; Rev 16:20
6:15 [k]Isa 2:10,19, 21
6:16 [l]Hos 10:8; Lk 23:30
6:17 [m]Zep 1:14,15; Rev 16:14 [n]Ps 76:7
7:1 [o]Da 7:2
7:3 [p]Rev 6:6 [q]Eze 9:4; Rev 22:4
7:4 [r]Rev 9:16 [s]Rev 14:1,3
7:9 [t]Rev 5:9 [u]ver 15
7:10 [v]Ps 3:8; Rev 12:10; 19:1
7:11 [w]Rev 4:4 [x]Rev 4:6 [y]Rev 4:10
7:12 [z]Rev 5:12-14

14I answered, "Sir, you know."
And he said, "These are they who
have come out of the great tribula-
tion; they have washed their
robes[a] and made them white in
the blood of the Lamb.[b] **15**Therefore,

"they are before the throne of
God[c]
and serve him[d] day and
night in his temple;[e]
and he who sits on the throne
will spread his tent over
them.[f]
16Never again will they hunger;
never again will they thirst.
The sun will not beat upon
them,
nor any scorching heat.[g]
17For the Lamb at the center of
the throne will be their
shepherd;[h]
he will lead them to springs
of living water.
And God will wipe away every
tear from their eyes."[i]

The Seventh Seal and the Golden Censer

8 When he opened the seventh
seal,[j] there was silence in
heaven for about half an hour.
2And I saw the seven angels[k]
who stand before God, and to them
were given seven trumpets.
3Another angel,[l] who had a
golden censer, came and stood at
the altar. He was given much incense to offer, with the prayers of
all the saints,[m] on the golden altar[n] before the throne. **4**The
smoke of the incense, together
with the prayers of the saints, went
up before God[o] from the angel's
hand. **5**Then the angel took the
censer, filled it with fire from the
altar,[p] and hurled it on the earth;
and there came peals of thunder,[q]
rumblings, flashes of lightning and
an earthquake.[r]

The Trumpets

6Then the seven angels who had
the seven trumpets[s] prepared to
sound them.
7The first angel sounded his
trumpet, and there came hail and
fire[t] mixed with blood, and it was
hurled down upon the earth. A
third[u] of the earth was burned up,
a third of the trees were burned up,
and all the green grass was burned
up.[v]
8The second angel sounded his
trumpet, and something like a
huge mountain,[w] all ablaze, was
thrown into the sea. A third[x] of the
sea turned into blood,[y] **9**a third[z]
of the living creatures in the sea
died, and a third of the ships were
destroyed.
10The third angel sounded his
trumpet, and a great star, blazing
like a torch, fell from the sky[a] on
a third of the rivers and on the
springs of water[b]— **11**the name of
the star is Wormwood.[1] A third[c] of
the waters turned bitter, and many
people died from the waters that
had become bitter.[d]
12The fourth angel sounded his
trumpet, and a third of the sun was
struck, a third of the moon, and a
third of the stars, so that a third[e]
of them turned dark.[f] A third of
the day was without light, and also
a third of the night.
13As I watched, I heard an eagle
that was flying in midair[g] call out
in a loud voice: "Woe! Woe! Woe[h]
to the inhabitants of the earth, because of the trumpet blasts about
to be sounded by the other three
angels!"
9 The fifth angel sounded his
trumpet, and I saw a star that
had fallen from the sky to the
earth.[i] The star was given the key
to the shaft of the Abyss.[j] **2**When
he opened the Abyss, smoke rose
from it like the smoke from a gigan-
tic furnace.[k] The sun and sky were
darkened[l] by the smoke from the
Abyss. **3**And out of the smoke locusts[m] came down upon the earth
and were given power like that of
scorpions[n] of the earth. **4**They
were told not to harm[o] the grass of
the earth or any plant or tree,[p] but

7:14 [a]Rev 22:14 [b]Heb 9:14; 1Jn 1:7
7:15 [c]ver 9 [d]Rev 22:3 [e]Rev 11:19 [f]Isa 4:5,6; Rev 21:3
7:16 [g]Isa 49:10
7:17 [h]Ps 23:1; Jn 10:11 [i]Isa 25:8; Rev 21:4
8:1 [j]Rev 6:1
8:2 [k]ver 6-13; Rev 9:1,13; 11:15
8:3 [l]Rev 7:2 [m]Rev 5:8 [n]Ex 30:1-6; Heb 9:4; Rev 9:13
8:4 [o]Ps 141:2
8:5 [p]Lev 16:12,13 [q]Rev 4:5 [r]Rev 6:12
8:6 [s]ver 2
8:7 [t]Eze 38:22 [u]ver 7-12; Rev 9:15,18; 12:4 [v]Rev 9:4
8:8 [w]Jer 51:25 [x]ver 7 [y]Rev 16:3
8:9 [z]ver 7
8:10 [a]Isa 14:12; Rev 6:13; 9:1 [b]Rev 14:7; 16:4
8:11 [c]ver 7 [d]Jer 9:15; 23:15
8:12 [e]ver 7 [f]Ex 10:21-23; Rev 6:12,13
8:13 [g]Rev 14:6; 19:17 [h]Rev 9:12; 11:14
9:1 [i]Rev 8:10 [j]ver 2,11; Lk 8:31
9:2 [k]Ge 19:28; Ex 19:18 [l]Joel 2:2,10
9:3 [m]Ex 10:12-15 [n]ver 5,10
9:4 [o]Rev 6:6 [p]Rev 8:7

[1]*11* That is, Bitterness

only those people who did not have the seal of God on their foreheads.[a] **5**They were not given power to kill them, but only to torture them for five months.[b] And the agony they suffered was like that of the sting of a scorpion[c] when it strikes a man. **6**During those days men will seek death, but will not find it; they will long to die, but death will elude them.[d]

7The locusts looked like horses prepared for battle.[e] On their heads they wore something like crowns of gold, and their faces resembled human faces.[f] **8**Their hair was like women's hair, and their teeth were like lions' teeth.[g] **9**They had breastplates like breastplates of iron, and the sound of their wings was like the thundering of many horses and chariots rushing into battle.[h] **10**They had tails and stings like scorpions, and in their tails they had power to torment people for five months.[i] **11**They had as king over them the angel of the Abyss,[j] whose name in Hebrew is Abaddon, and in Greek, Apollyon.[m]

12The first woe is past; two other woes are yet to come.[k]

13The sixth angel sounded his trumpet, and I heard a voice coming from the horns[n][l] of the golden altar that is before God.[m] **14**It said to the sixth angel who had the trumpet, "Release the four angels who are bound at the great river Euphrates."[n] **15**And the four angels who had been kept ready for this very hour and day and month and year were released to kill a third of mankind.[o] **16**The number of the mounted troops was two hundred million. I heard their number.[p]

17The horses and riders I saw in my vision looked like this: Their breastplates were fiery red, dark blue, and yellow as sulfur. The heads of the horses resembled the heads of lions, and out of their mouths[q] came fire, smoke and sulfur.[r] **18**A third of mankind was killed[s] by the three plagues of fire, smoke and sulfur[t] that came out of their mouths. **19**The power of the horses was in their mouths and in their tails; for their tails were like snakes, having heads with which they inflict injury.

20The rest of mankind that were not killed by these plagues still did not repent of the work of their hands;[u] they did not stop worshiping demons,[v] and idols of gold, silver, bronze, stone and wood—idols that cannot see or hear or walk.[w] **21**Nor did they repent[x] of their murders, their magic arts,[y] their sexual immorality[z] or their thefts.

The Angel and the Little Scroll

10 Then I saw another mighty angel[a] coming down from heaven. He was robed in a cloud, with a rainbow above his head; his face was like the sun,[b] and his legs were like fiery pillars.[c] **2**He was holding a little scroll, which lay open in his hand. He planted his right foot on the sea and his left foot on the land, **3**and he gave a loud shout like the roar of a lion. When he shouted, the voices of the seven thunders[d] spoke. **4**And when the seven thunders spoke, I was about to write; but I heard a voice from heaven say, "Seal up what the seven thunders have said and do not write it down."[e]

5Then the angel I had seen standing on the sea and on the land raised his right hand to heaven.[f] **6**And he swore by him who lives for ever and ever, who created the heavens and all that is in them, the earth and all that is in it, and the sea and all that is in it,[g] and said, "There will be no more delay![h] **7**But in the days when the seventh angel is about to sound his trumpet, the mystery[i] of God will be accomplished, just as he announced to his servants the prophets."

8Then the voice that I had heard from heaven[j] spoke to me once more: "Go, take the scroll that lies open in the hand of the angel who

9:4 [a]Rev 7:2,3
9:5 [b]ver 10 [c]ver 3
9:6 [d]Job 3:21; Jer 8:3; Rev 6:16
9:7 [e]Joel 2:4 [f]Da 7:8
9:8 [g]Joel 1:6
9:9 [h]Joel 2:5
9:10 [i]ver 3,5,19
9:11 [j]ver 1,2
9:12 [k]Rev 8:13
9:13 [l]Ex 30:1-3 [m]Rev 8:3
9:14 [n]Rev 16:12
9:15 [o]ver 18
9:16 [p]Rev 5:11; 7:4
9:17 [q]Rev 11:5 [r]ver 18
9:18 [s]ver 15 [t]ver 17
9:20 [u]Dt 31:29 [v]1Co 10:20 [w]Ps 115:4-7; 135:15-17; Da 5:23
9:21 [x]Rev 2:21 [y]Rev 18:23 [z]Rev 17:2,5
10:1 [a]Rev 5:2 [b]Mt 17:2; Rev 1:16 [c]Rev 1:15
10:3 [d]Rev 4:5
10:4 [e]Da 8:26; 12:4,9; Rev 22:10
10:5 [f]Da 12:7
10:6 [g]Rev 4:11; 14:7 [h]Rev 16:17
10:7 [i]Ro 16:25
10:8 [j]ver 4

[m]*11* *Abaddon* and *Apollyon* mean *Destroyer.*
[n]*13* That is, projections

is standing on the sea and on the
land."
⁹So I went to the angel and asked
him to give me the little scroll. He
said to me, "Take it and eat it. It
will turn your stomach sour, but in
your mouth it will be as sweet as
honey."[a] ¹⁰I took the little scroll
from the angel's hand and ate it. It
tasted as sweet as honey in my
mouth, but when I had eaten it, my
stomach turned sour. ¹¹Then I was
told, "You must prophesy[b] again
about many peoples, nations, languages and kings."

The Two Witnesses

11 I was given a reed like a
measuring rod[c] and was
told, "Go and measure the temple
of God and the altar, and count the
worshipers there. ²But exclude the
outer court;[d] do not measure it,
because it has been given to the
Gentiles.[e] They will trample on
the holy city[f] for 42 months.[g]
³And I will give power to my two
witnesses,[h] and they will prophesy
for 1,260 days, clothed in sackcloth."[i] ⁴These are the two olive
trees[j] and the two lampstands
that stand before the Lord of the
earth.[k] ⁵If anyone tries to harm
them, fire comes from their
mouths and devours their enemies.[l] This is how anyone who
wants to harm them must die.[m]
⁶These men have power to shut up
the sky so that it will not rain dur-
ing the time they are prophesying;
and they have power to turn the
waters into blood[n] and to strike
the earth with every kind of plague
as often as they want.
⁷Now when they have finished
their testimony, the beast[o] that
comes up from the Abyss will attack them,[p] and overpower and
kill them. ⁸Their bodies will lie in
the street of the great city, which is
figuratively called Sodom[q] and
Egypt, where also their Lord was
crucified.[r] ⁹For three and a half
days men from every people, tribe,
language and nation will gaze on
their bodies and refuse them burial.[s] ¹⁰The inhabitants of the
earth[t] will gloat over them and
will celebrate by sending each other gifts,[u] because these two prophets had tormented those who live
on the earth.
¹¹But after the three and a half
days a breath of life from God entered them,[v] and they stood on
their feet, and terror struck those
who saw them. ¹²Then they heard
a loud voice from heaven saying to
them, "Come up here."[w] And they
went up to heaven in a cloud,[x]
while their enemies looked on.
¹³At that very hour there was a
severe earthquake[y] and a tenth of
the city collapsed. Seven thousand
people were killed in the earthquake, and the survivors were terrified and gave glory[z] to the God of
heaven.[a]
¹⁴The second woe has passed;
the third woe is coming soon.[b]

The Seventh Trumpet

¹⁵The seventh angel sounded his
trumpet,[c] and there were loud
voices[d] in heaven, which said:

"The kingdom of the world has
 become the kingdom of
 our Lord and of his
 Christ,[e]
and he will reign for ever and
 ever."[f]

¹⁶And the twenty-four elders,[g]
who were seated on their thrones
before God, fell on their faces and
worshiped God, ¹⁷saying:

"We give thanks to you, Lord
 God Almighty,[h]
the One who is and who was,
because you have taken your
 great power
and have begun to reign.[i]
¹⁸The nations were angry;[j]
and your wrath has come.
The time has come for judging
 the dead,
and for rewarding your
 servants the prophets[k]
and your saints and those who
 reverence your name,
both small and great[l]—
and for destroying those who
 destroy the earth."

10:9 [a]Jer 15:16; Eze 2:8-3:3
10:11 [b]Eze 37:4,9
11:1 [c]Eze 40:3; Rev 21:15
11:2 [d]Eze 40:17,20 [e]Lk 21:24 [f]Rev 21:2 [g]Da 7:25; Rev 13:5
11:3 [h]Rev 1:5 [i]Ge 37:34
11:4 [j]Ps 52:8; Jer 11:16; Zec 4:3,11 [k]Zec 4:14
11:5 [l]2Ki 1:10; Jer 5:14 [m]Nu 16:29,35
11:6 [n]Ex 7:17,19
11:7 [o]Rev 13:1-4 [p]Da 7:21
11:8 [q]Isa 1:9 [r]Heb 13:12
11:9 [s]Ps 79:2,3
11:10 [t]Rev 3:10 [u]Est 9:19,22
11:11 [v]Eze 37:5,9,10,14
11:12 [w]Rev 4:1 [x]2Ki 2:11; Ac 1:9
11:13 [y]Rev 6:12 [z]Rev 14:7 [a]Rev 16:11
11:14 [b]Rev 8:13
11:15 [c]Rev 10:7 [d]Rev 16:17; 19:1 [e]Rev 12:10 [f]Da 2:44; 7:14,27
11:16 [g]Rev 4:4
11:17 [h]Rev 1:8 [i]Rev 19:6
11:18 [j]Ps 2:1 [k]Rev 10:7 [l]Rev 19:5

19Then God's temple[a] in heaven
was opened, and within his temple
was seen the ark of his covenant.
And there came flashes of lightning, rumblings, peals of thunder,
an earthquake and a great hailstorm.[b]

The Woman and the Dragon

12 A great and wondrous sign
appeared in heaven: a woman clothed with the sun, with the
moon under her feet and a crown of
twelve stars on her head. **2**She was
pregnant and cried out in pain[c] as
she was about to give birth. **3**Then
another sign appeared in heaven:
an enormous red dragon with seven
heads and ten horns[d] and seven
crowns[e] on his heads. **4**His tail
swept a third[f] of the stars out of
the sky and flung them to the
earth.[g] The dragon stood in front
of the woman who was about to
give birth, so that he might devour
her child[h] the moment it was born.
5She gave birth to a son, a male
child, who will rule all the nations
with an iron scepter.[i] And her
child was snatched up to God and
to his throne. **6**The woman fled
into the desert to a place prepared
for her by God, where she might be
taken care of for 1,260 days.[j]

7And there was war in heaven.
Michael and his angels fought
against the dragon,[k] and the dragon and his angels fought back. **8**But
he was not strong enough, and they
lost their place in heaven. **9**The
great dragon was hurled down—
that ancient serpent[l] called the
devil,[m] or Satan, who leads the
whole world astray.[n] He was
hurled to the earth,[o] and his angels with him.

10Then I heard a loud voice in
heaven[p] say:

"Now have come the salvation
and the power and the
kingdom of our God,
and the authority of his
Christ.
For the accuser of our
brothers,[q]
who accuses them before our
God day and night,
has been hurled down.
11They overcame him
by the blood of the Lamb[r]
and by the word of their
testimony;[s]
they did not love their lives so
much
as to shrink from death.[t]
12Therefore rejoice, you
heavens[u]
and you who dwell in them!
But woe[v] to the earth and the
sea,[w]
because the devil has gone
down to you!
He is filled with fury,
because he knows that his
time is short."

13When the dragon[x] saw that he
had been hurled to the earth, he
pursued the woman who had given
birth to the male child.[y] **14**The
woman was given the two wings of
a great eagle,[z] so that she might fly
to the place prepared for her in the
desert, where she would be taken
care of for a time, times and half a
time,[a] out of the serpent's reach.
15Then from his mouth the serpent
spewed water like a river, to overtake the woman and sweep her
away with the torrent. **16**But the
earth helped the woman by opening its mouth and swallowing the
river that the dragon had spewed
out of his mouth. **17**Then the dragon was enraged at the woman and
went off to make war[b] against the
rest of her offspring[c]—those who
obey God's commandments[d] and
hold to the testimony of Jesus.[e]

13 **1**And the dragon[o] stood on
the shore of the sea.

The Beast out of the Sea

And I saw a beast coming out of
the sea.[f] He had ten horns and
seven heads,[g] with ten crowns on
his horns, and on each head a blasphemous name.[h] **2**The beast I saw
resembled a leopard,[i] but had feet
like those of a bear[j] and a mouth

11:19 [a] Rev 15:5,8 [b] Rev 16:21
12:2 [c] Gal 4:19
12:3 [d] Da 7:7,20; Rev 13:1 [e] Rev 19:12
12:4 [f] Rev 8:7 [g] Da 8:10 [h] Mt 2:16
12:5 [i] Ps 2:9; Rev 2:27
12:6 [j] Rev 11:2
12:7 [k] ver 3
12:9 [l] Ge 3:1-7 [m] Mt 25:41 [n] Rev 20:3,8, 10 [o] Lk 10:18; Jn 12:31
12:10 [p] Rev 11:15 [q] Job 1:9-11; Zec 3:1
12:11 [r] Rev 7:14 [s] Rev 6:9 [t] Lk 14:26
12:12 [u] Ps 96:11; Isa 49:13; Rev 18:20 [v] Rev 8:13 [w] Rev 10:6
12:13 [x] ver 3 [y] ver 5
12:14 [z] Ex 19:4 [a] Da 7:25
12:17 [b] Rev 11:7 [c] Ge 3:15 [d] Rev 14:12 [e] Rev 1:2
13:1 [f] Da 7:1-6; Rev 15:2 [g] Rev 12:3 [h] Da 11:36; Rev 17:3
13:2 [i] Da 7:6 [j] Da 7:5

[o] *1* Some late manuscripts *And I*

5After this I looked and in heav-
en the temple,[a] that is, the tabernacle of the Testimony,[b] was
opened. **6**Out of the temple[c] came
the seven angels with the seven
plagues.[d] They were dressed in
clean, shining linen and wore gold-
en sashes around their chests.[e]
7Then one of the four living creatures[f] gave to the seven angels
seven golden bowls filled with the
wrath of God, who lives for ever and
ever. **8**And the temple was filled
with smoke[g] from the glory of God
and from his power, and no one
could enter the temple[h] until the
seven plagues of the seven angels
were completed.

The Seven Bowls of God's Wrath

16 Then I heard a loud voice
from the temple saying to
the seven angels,[i] "Go, pour out
the seven bowls of God's wrath on
the earth."

2The first angel went and poured
out his bowl on the land,[j] and ugly
and painful sores[k] broke out on
the people who had the mark of the
beast and worshiped his image.[l]

3The second angel poured out
his bowl on the sea, and it turned
into blood like that of a dead man,
and every living thing in the sea
died.[m]

4The third angel poured out his
bowl on the rivers and springs of
water,[n] and they became blood.[o]
5Then I heard the angel in charge
of the waters say:

"You are just in these
judgments,[p]
you who are and who were,[q]
the Holy One,[r]
because you have so judged;
6for they have shed the blood of
your saints and prophets,
and you have given them
blood to drink[s] as they
deserve."

7And I heard the altar[t] respond:

"Yes, Lord God Almighty,
true and just are your
judgments."[u]

8The fourth angel[v] poured out
his bowl on the sun, and the sun
was given power to scorch people
with fire.[w] **9**They were seared by
the intense heat and they cursed
the name of God,[x] who had control over these plagues, but they refused to repent[y] and glorify him.[z]

10The fifth angel poured out his
bowl on the throne of the beast,[a]
and his kingdom was plunged into
darkness.[b] Men gnawed their
tongues in agony **11**and cursed[c]
the God of heaven[d] because of
their pains and their sores,[e] but
they refused to repent of what they
had done.[f]

12The sixth angel poured out his
bowl on the great river Euphrates,[g] and its water was dried up to
prepare the way for the kings from
the East.[h] **13**Then I saw three evil[t]
spirits that looked like frogs; they
came out of the mouth of the dragon,[i] out of the mouth of the
beast[j] and out of the mouth of the
false prophet.[k] **14**They are spirits
of demons[l] performing miraculous signs, and they go out to the
kings of the whole world, to gather
them for the battle[m] on the great
day of God Almighty.

15"Behold, I come like a thief!
Blessed is he who stays awake[n]
and keeps his clothes with him, so
that he may not go naked and be
shamefully exposed."

16Then they gathered the kings
together to the place that in Hebrew[o] is called Armageddon.[p]

17The seventh angel poured out
his bowl into the air,[q] and out of
the temple[r] came a loud voice[s]
from the throne, saying, "It is
done!"[t] **18**Then there came
flashes of lightning, rumblings,
peals of thunder[u] and a severe
earthquake.[v] No earthquake like
it has ever occurred since man has
been on earth,[w] so tremendous
was the quake. **19**The great city[x]
split into three parts, and the cities
of the nations collapsed. God re-

15:5 [a]Rev 11:19 [b]Nu 1:50
15:6 [c]Rev 14:15 [d]ver 1 [e]Rev 1:13
15:7 [f]Rev 4:6
15:8 [g]Isa 6:4 [h]Ex 40:34,35; 1Ki 8:10,11; 2Ch 5:13,14
16:1 [i]Rev 15:1
16:2 [j]Rev 8:7 [k]Ex 9:9-11 [l]Rev 13:15-17
16:3 [m]Ex 7:17-21; Rev 8:8,9
16:4 [n]Rev 8:10 [o]Ex 7:17-21
16:5 [p]Rev 15:3 [q]Rev 1:4 [r]Rev 15:4
16:6 [s]Isa 49:26; Rev 17:6
16:7 [t]Rev 6:9 [u]Rev 15:3; 19:2
16:8 [v]Rev 8:12 [w]Rev 14:18
16:9 [x]ver 11,21 [y]Rev 2:21 [z]Rev 11:13
16:10 [a]Rev 13:2 [b]Rev 9:2
16:11 [c]ver 9,21 [d]Rev 11:13 [e]ver 2 [f]Rev 2:21
16:12 [g]Rev 9:14 [h]Isa 41:2
16:13 [i]Rev 12:3 [j]Rev 13:1 [k]Rev 19:20
16:14 [l]1Ti 4:1 [m]Rev 17:14
16:15 [n]Lk 12:37
16:16 [o]Rev 9:11 [p]2Ki 23:29,30
16:17 [q]Eph 2:2 [r]Rev 14:15 [s]Rev 11:15 [t]Rev 21:6
16:18 [u]Rev 4:5 [v]Rev 6:12 [w]Da 12:1
16:19 [x]Rev 17:18

[t]*13* Greek *unclean*

membered[a] Babylon the Great[b] and gave her the cup filled with the wine of the fury of his wrath.[c] **20**Every island fled away and the mountains could not be found.[d] **21**From the sky huge hailstones[e] of about a hundred pounds each fell upon men. And they cursed God on account of the plague of hail,[f] because the plague was so terrible.

The Woman on the Beast

17 One of the seven angels[g] who had the seven bowls[h] came and said to me, "Come, I will show you the punishment[i] of the great prostitute,[j] who sits on many waters.[k] **2**With her the kings of the earth committed adultery and the inhabitants of the earth were intoxicated with the wine of her adulteries."[l]

3Then the angel carried me away in the Spirit into a desert.[m] There I saw a woman sitting on a scarlet beast that was covered with blasphemous names[n] and had seven heads and ten horns.[o] **4**The woman was dressed in purple and scarlet, and was glittering with gold, precious stones and pearls.[p] She held a golden cup[q] in her hand, filled with abominable things and the filth of her adulteries. **5**This title was written on her forehead:

MYSTERY
BABYLON THE GREAT[r]
THE MOTHER OF PROSTITUTES
AND OF THE ABOMINATIONS OF THE
EARTH.

6I saw that the woman was drunk with the blood of the saints,[s] the blood of those who bore testimony to Jesus.

When I saw her, I was greatly astonished. **7**Then the angel said to me: "Why are you astonished? I will explain to you the mystery[t] of the woman and of the beast she rides, which has the seven heads and ten horns.[u] **8**The beast, which you saw, once was, now is not, and will [illegible]ne up out of the Abyss and go to [illegible]destruction.[v] The inhabitants [illegible] earth[w] whose names have not been written in the book of life[x] from the creation of the world will be astonished[y] when they see the beast, because he once was, now is not, and yet will come.

9"This calls for a mind with wisdom.[z] The seven heads are seven hills on which the woman sits. **10**They are also seven kings. Five have fallen, one is, the other has not yet come; but when he does come, he must remain for a little while. **11**The beast who once was, and now is not,[a] is an eighth king. He belongs to the seven and is going to his destruction.

12"The ten horns[b] you saw are ten kings who have not yet received a kingdom, but who for one hour[c] will receive authority as kings along with the beast. **13**They have one purpose and will give their power and authority to the beast.[d] **14**They will make war[e] against the Lamb, but the Lamb will overcome them because he is Lord of lords and King of kings[f]—and with him will be his called, chosen[g] and faithful followers."

15Then the angel said to me, "The waters[h] you saw, where the prostitute sits, are peoples, multitudes, nations and languages.[i] **16**The beast and the ten horns you saw will hate the prostitute. They will bring her to ruin[j] and leave her naked;[k] they will eat her flesh[l] and burn her with fire.[m] **17**For God has put it into their hearts to accomplish his purpose by agreeing to give the beast their power to rule, until God's words are fulfilled.[n] **18**The woman you saw is the great city[o] that rules over the kings of the earth."

The Fall of Babylon

18 After this I saw another angel[p] coming down from heaven.[q] He had great authority, and the earth was illuminated by his splendor.[r] **2**With a mighty voice he shouted:

"Fallen! Fallen is Babylon the
Great![s]

16:19 [a]Rev 18:5 [b]Rev 14:8 [c]Rev 14:10
16:20 [d]Rev 6:14
16:21 [e]Rev 11:19 [f]Ex 9:23-25
17:1 [g]Rev 15:1 [h]Rev 21:9 [i]Rev 16:19 [j]Rev 19:2 [k]Jer 51:13
17:2 [l]Rev 14:8; 18:3
17:3 [m]Rev 12:6,14 [n]Rev 13:1 [o]Rev 12:3
17:4 [p]Rev 18:16 [q]Jer 51:7; Rev 18:6
17:5 [r]Rev 14:8
17:6 [s]Rev 18:24
17:7 [t]ver 5 [u]ver 3
17:8 [v]Rev 13:10 [w]Rev 3:10 [x]Rev 13:8 [y]Rev 13:3
17:9 [z]Rev 13:18
17:11 [a]ver 8
17:12 [b]Rev 12:3 [c]Rev 18:10, 17,19
17:13 [d]ver 17
17:14 [e]Rev 16:14 [f]1Ti 6:15; Rev 19:16 [g]Mt 22:14
17:15 [h]Isa 8:7 [i]Rev 13:7
17:16 [j]Rev 18:17,19 [k]Eze 16:37,39 [l]Rev 19:18 [m]Rev 18:8
17:17 [n]Rev 10:7
17:18 [o]Rev 16:19
18:1 [p]Rev 17:1 [q]Rev 10:1 [r]Eze 43:2
18:2 [s]Rev 14:8

She has become a home for
demons
and a haunt for every evil[u]
spirit,
a haunt for every unclean
and detestable bird.[a]
3For all the nations have drunk
the maddening wine of her
adulteries.[b]
The kings of the earth
committed adultery with
her,[c]
and the merchants of the
earth grew rich[d] from
her excessive luxuries."[e]

4Then I heard another voice from
heaven say:

"Come out of her, my people,[f]
so that you will not share in
her sins,
so that you will not receive
any of her plagues;
5for her sins are piled up to
heaven,[g]
and God has remembered[h]
her crimes.
6Give back to her as she has
given;
pay her back[i] double for
what she has done.
Mix her a double portion
from her own cup.[j]
7Give her as much torture and
grief
as the glory and luxury she
gave herself.[k]
In her heart she boasts,
'I sit as queen; I am not a
widow,
and I will never mourn.'[l]
8Therefore in one day[m] her
plagues will overtake
her:
death, mourning and famine.
She will be consumed by fire,[n]
for mighty is the Lord God
who judges her.

9"When the kings of the earth
who committed adultery with her[o]
and shared her luxury see the
smoke of her burning,[p] they will
weep and mourn over her.[q] **10**Terrified at her torment, they will
stand far off[r] and cry:

" 'Woe! Woe, O great city,[s]
O Babylon, city of power!
In one hour[t] your doom has
come!'

11"The merchants[u] of the earth
will weep and mourn over her because no one buys their cargoes
any more[v]— **12**cargoes of gold, silver, precious stones and pearls;
fine linen, purple, silk and scarlet
cloth; every sort of citron wood,
and articles of every kind made of
ivory, costly wood, bronze, iron and
marble;[w] **13**cargoes of cinnamon
and spice, of incense, myrrh and
frankincense, of wine and olive oil,
of fine flour and wheat; cattle and
sheep; horses and carriages; and
bodies and souls of men.[x]

14"They will say, 'The fruit you
longed for is gone from you. All
your riches and splendor have vanished, never to be recovered.'
15The merchants who sold these
things and gained their wealth
from her[y] will stand far off, terrified at her torment. They will weep
and mourn[z] **16**and cry out:

" 'Woe! Woe, O great city,
dressed in fine linen, purple
and scarlet,
and glittering with gold,
precious stones and
pearls![a]
17In one hour[b] such great wealth
has been brought to
ruin!'[c]

"Every sea captain, and all who
travel by ship, the sailors, and all
who earn their living from the
sea,[d] will stand far off. **18**When
they see the smoke of her burning,
they will exclaim, 'Was there ever a
city like this great city?'[e] **19**They
will throw dust on their heads,[f]
and with weeping and mourning
cry out:

" 'Woe! Woe, O great city,
where all who had ships on
the sea
became rich through her
wealth!
In one hour she has been
brought to ruin![g]

18:2 [a]Isa 13:21,22; Jer 50:39
18:3 [b]Rev 14:8 [c]Rev 17:2 [d]Eze 27:9-25 [e]ver 7,9
18:4 [f]Isa 48:20; Jer 50:8; 2Co 6:17
18:5 [g]Jer 51:9 [h]Rev 16:19
18:6 [i]Ps 137:8; Jer 50:15,29 [j]Rev 14:10; 16:19
18:7 [k]Eze 28:2-8 [l]Isa 47:7,8; Zep 2:15
18:8 [m]ver 10; Isa 47:9; Jer 50:31,32 [n]Rev 17:16
18:9 [o]Rev 17:2,4 [p]ver 18; Rev 19:3 [q]Eze 26:17,18
18:10 [r]ver 15,17 [s]ver 16,19 [t]Rev 17:12
18:11 [u]Eze 27:27 [v]ver 3
18:12 [w]Rev 17:4
18:13 [x]Eze 27:13; 1Ti 1:10
18:15 [y]ver 3 [z]Eze 27:31
18:16 [a]Rev 17:4
18:17 [b]ver 10 [c]Rev 17:16 [d]Eze 27:28-30
18:18 [e]Eze 27:32; Rev 13:4
18:19 [f]Jos 7:6; Eze 27:30 [g]Rev 17:16

[u]2 Greek *unclean*

20Rejoice over her, O heaven![a]
Rejoice, saints and apostles
and prophets!
God has judged her for the way
she treated you.' "[b]

21Then a mighty angel[c] picked
up a boulder the size of a large millstone and threw it into the sea,[d]
and said:

"With such violence
the great city of Babylon will
be thrown down,
never to be found again.
22The music of harpists and
musicians, flute players
and trumpeters,
will never be heard in you
again.[e]
No workman of any trade
will ever be found in you
again.
The sound of a millstone
will never be heard in you
again.[f]
23The light of a lamp
will never shine in you again.
The voice of bridegroom and
bride
will never be heard in you
again.[g]
Your merchants were the
world's great men.[h]
By your magic spell[i] all the
nations were led astray.
24In her was found the blood of
prophets and of the
saints,[j]
and of all who have been
killed on the earth."[k]

Hallelujah!

19 After this I heard what
sounded like the roar of a
great multitude[l] in heaven shouting:

"Hallelujah!
Salvation[m] and glory and
power[n] belong to our
God,
2 for true and just are his
judgments.
He has condemned the great
prostitute
who corrupted the earth by
her adulteries.

18:20 [a]Jer 51:48; Rev 12:12 [b]Rev 19:2
18:21 [c]Rev 5:2 [d]Jer 51:63
18:22 [e]Isa 24:8; Eze 26:13 [f]Jer 25:10
18:23 [g]Jer 7:34; 16:9; 25:10 [h]Isa 23:8 [i]Na 3:4
18:24 [j]Rev 16:6; 17:6 [k]Jer 51:49
19:1 [l]Rev 11:15 [m]Rev 7:10 [n]Rev 4:11
19:2 [o]Dt 32:43; Rev 6:10
19:3 [p]Isa 34:10; Rev 14:11
19:4 [q]Rev 4:4 [r]Rev 4:6 [s]Rev 5:14
19:5 [t]Ps 134:1 [u]Rev 11:18; 20:12
19:6 [v]Rev 11:15
19:7 [w]Mt 22:2; 25:10; Eph 5:32 [x]Rev 21:2,9
19:8 [y]Rev 15:4
19:9 [z]ver 10 [a]Rev 1:19 [b]Lk 14:15 [c]Rev 21:5; 22:6
19:10 [d]Rev 22:8 [e]Ac 10:25,26; Rev 22:9 [f]Rev 12:17

He has avenged on her the
blood of his servants."[o]

3And again they shouted:

"Hallelujah!
The smoke from her goes up
for ever and ever."[p]

4The twenty-four elders[q] and
the four living creatures[r] fell
down[s] and worshiped God, who
was seated on the throne. And they
cried:

"Amen, Hallelujah!"

5Then a voice came from the
throne, saying:

"Praise our God,
all you his servants,[t]
you who fear him,
both small and great!"[u]

6Then I heard what sounded like
a great multitude,[v] like the roar of
rushing waters and like loud peals
of thunder, shouting:

"Hallelujah!
For our Lord God Almighty
reigns.
7Let us rejoice and be glad
and give him glory!
For the wedding of the Lamb[w]
has come,
and his bride[x] has made
herself ready.
8Fine linen, bright and clean,
was given her to wear."
(Fine linen stands for the righteous
acts[y] of the saints.)

9Then the angel said to me,[z]
"Write:[a] 'Blessed are those who
are invited to the wedding supper
of the Lamb!' "[b] And he added,
"These are the true words of
God."[c]
10At this I fell at his feet to worship him.[d] But he said to me, "Do
not do it! I am a fellow servant with
you and with your brothers who
hold to the testimony of Jesus.
Worship God![e] For the testimony
of Jesus[f] is the spirit of prophecy."

The Rider on the White Horse

11I saw heaven standing open

and there before me was a white horse, whose rider[a] is called Faithful and True.[b] With justice he judges and makes war.[c] **12**His eyes are like blazing fire,[d] and on his head are many crowns.[e] He has a name written on him that no one knows but he himself.[f] **13**He is dressed in a robe dipped in blood,[g] and his name is the Word of God.[h] **14**The armies of heaven were following him, riding on white horses and dressed in fine linen,[i] white and clean. **15**Out of his mouth comes a sharp sword[j] with which to strike down[k] the nations. "He will rule them with an iron scepter."[v][l] He treads the winepress[m] of the fury of the wrath of God Almighty. **16**On his robe and on his thigh he has this name written:[n]

KING OF KINGS AND LORD OF LORDS.[o]

17And I saw an angel standing in the sun, who cried in a loud voice to all the birds[p] flying in midair,[q] "Come,[r] gather together for the great supper of God, **18**so that you may eat the flesh of kings, generals, and mighty men, of horses and their riders, and the flesh of all people,[s] free and slave, small and great."

19Then I saw the beast and the kings of the earth[t] and their armies gathered together to make war against the rider on the horse and his army. **20**But the beast was captured, and with him the false prophet[u] who had performed the miraculous signs on his behalf.[v] With these signs he had deluded those who had received the mark of the beast and worshiped his image. The two of them were thrown alive into the fiery lake[w] of burning sulfur.[x] **21**The rest of them were killed with the sword[y] that came out of the mouth of the rider on the horse,[z] and all the birds[a] gorged themselves on their flesh.

The Thousand Years

20 And I saw an angel coming down out of heaven,[b] having the key[c] to the Abyss and holding in his hand a great chain. **2**He seized the dragon, that ancient serpent, who is the devil, or Satan,[d] and bound him for a thousand years.[e] **3**He threw him into the Abyss, and locked and sealed[f] it over him, to keep him from deceiving the nations[g] anymore until the thousand years were ended. After that, he must be set free for a short time.

4I saw thrones[h] on which were seated those who had been given authority to judge. And I saw the souls of those who had been beheaded[i] because of their testimony for Jesus and because of the word of God. They had not worshiped the beast[j] or his image and had not received his mark on their foreheads or their hands.[k] They came to life and reigned with Christ a thousand years. **5**(The rest of the dead did not come to life until the thousand years were ended.) This is the first resurrection.[l] **6**Blessed[m] and holy are those who have part in the first resurrection. The second death[n] has no power over them, but they will be priests[o] of God and of Christ and will reign with him[p] for a thousand years.

Satan's Doom

7When the thousand years are over,[q] Satan will be released from his prison **8**and will go out to deceive the nations[r] in the four corners of the earth—Gog and Magog[s]—to gather them for battle.[t] In number they are like the sand on the seashore.[u] **9**They marched across the breadth of the earth and surrounded[v] the camp of God's people, the city he loves. But fire came down from heaven[w] and devoured them. **10**And the devil, who deceived them,[x] was thrown into the lake of burning sulfur, where the beast and the false prophet had been thrown. They will be tormented day and night for ever and ever.[y]

19:11 [a]Rev 6:2 [b]Rev 3:14 [c]Isa 11:4
19:12 [d]Rev 1:14 [e]Rev 6:2 [f]Rev 2:17
19:13 [g]Isa 63:2,3 [h]Jn 1:1
19:14 [i]ver 8
19:15 [j]Rev 1:16 [k]Isa 11:4; 2Th 2:8 [l]Ps 2:9; Rev 2:27 [m]Rev 14:20
19:16 [n]ver 12 [o]Rev 17:14
19:17 [p]ver 21 [q]Rev 8:13 [r]Eze 39:17
19:18 [s]Eze 39:18-20
19:19 [t]Rev 16:14,16
19:20 [u]Rev 16:13 [v]Rev 13:12 [w]Da 7:11; Rev 20:10,14,15; 21:8 [x]Rev 14:10
19:21 [y]ver 15 [z]ver 11,19 [a]ver 17
20:1 [b]Rev 10:1 [c]Rev 1:18
20:2 [d]Rev 12:9 [e]2Pe 2:4
20:3 [f]Da 6:17 [g]Rev 12:9
20:4 [h]Da 7:9 [i]Rev 6:9 [j]Rev 13:12 [k]Rev 13:16
20:5 [l]Lk 14:14; Php 3:11
20:6 [m]Rev 14:13 [n]Rev 2:11 [o]Rev 1:6 [p]ver 4
20:7 [q]ver 2
20:8 [r]ver 3,10 [s]Eze 38:2; 39:1 [t]Rev 16:14 [u]Heb 11:12
20:9 [v]Eze 38:9,16 [w]Eze 38:22; 39:6
20:10 [x]Rev 19:20 [y]Rev 14:10,11

[v]*15* Psalm 2:9

The Dead Are Judged

11Then I saw a great white throne[a] and him who was seated on it. Earth and sky fled from his presence, and there was no place for them. 12And I saw the dead, great and small, standing before the throne, and books were opened.[b] Another book was opened, which is the book of life.[c] The dead were judged according to what they had done[d] as recorded in the books. 13The sea gave up the dead that were in it, and death and Hades[e] gave up the dead[f] that were in them, and each person was judged according to what he had done. 14Then death[g] and Hades were thrown into the lake of fire. The lake of fire is the second death. 15If anyone's name was not found written in the book of life,[h] he was thrown into the lake of fire.

The New Jerusalem

21 Then I saw a new heaven and a new earth,[i] for the first heaven and the first earth had passed away, and there was no longer any sea. 2I saw the Holy City, the new Jerusalem, coming down out of heaven from God,[j] prepared as a bride beautifully dressed for her husband. 3And I heard a loud voice from the throne saying, "Now the dwelling of God is with men, and he will live with them. They will be his people, and God himself will be with them and be their God.[k] 4He will wipe every tear from their eyes.[l] There will be no more death[m] or mourning or crying or pain,[n] for the old order of things has passed away."

5He who was seated on the throne[o] said, "I am making everything new!" Then he said, "Write this down, for *these words are trustworthy and true.*"[p]

6He said to me: "It is done.[q] I am the Alpha and the Omega,[r] the Beginning and the End. To him who is thirsty I will give to drink [illegible]hout cost from the spring of the [illegible] of life.[s] 7He who overcomes [illegible]herit all this, and I will be his God and he will be my son. 8But the cowardly, the unbelieving, the vile, the murderers, the sexually immoral, those who practice magic arts, the idolaters and all liars[t]—their place will be in the fiery lake of burning sulfur. This is the second death."[u]

9One of the seven angels who had the seven bowls full of the seven last plagues[v] came and said to me, "Come, I will show you the bride,[w] the wife of the Lamb." 10And he carried me away[x] in the Spirit[y] to a mountain great and high, and showed me the Holy City, Jerusalem, coming down out of heaven from God. 11It shone with the glory of God,[z] and its brilliance was like that of a very precious jewel, like a jasper, clear as crystal.[a] 12It had a great, high wall with twelve gates, and with twelve angels at the gates. On the gates were written the names of the twelve tribes of Israel.[b] 13There were three gates on the east, three on the north, three on the south and three on the west. 14The wall of the city had twelve foundations, and on them were the names of the twelve apostles of the Lamb.

15The angel who talked with me had a measuring rod[c] of gold to measure the city, its gates and its walls. 16The city was laid out like a square, as long as it was wide. He measured the city with the rod and found it to be 12,000 stadia[w] in length, and as wide and high as it is long. 17He measured its wall and it was 144 cubits[x] thick,[y] by man's measurement, which the angel was using. 18The wall was made of jasper,[d] and the city of pure gold, as pure as glass.[e] 19The foundations of the city walls were decorated with every kind of precious stone.[f] The first foundation was jasper, the second sapphire, the third chalcedony, the fourth emerald, 20the fifth sardonyx, the sixth carnelian,[g] the seventh chrysolite, the

[w]16 That is, about 1,400 miles (about 2,200 kilometers) [x]17 That is, about 200 feet (about 65 meters) [y]17 Or *high*

20:11 [a]Rev 4:2
20:12 [b]Da 7:10 [c]Rev 3:5 [d]Jer 17:10; Mt 16:27; Rev 2:23
20:13 [e]Rev 6:8 [f]Isa 26:19
20:14 [g]1Co 15:26
20:15 [h]ver 12
21:1 [i]Isa 65:17; 2Pe 3:13
21:2 [j]Heb 11:10; 12:22; Rev 3:12
21:3 [k]2Co 6:16
21:4 [l]Rev 7:17 [m]1Co 15:26; Rev 20:14 [n]Isa 35:10; 65:19
21:5 [o]Rev 4:9; 20:11 [p]Rev 19:9
21:6 [q]Rev 16:17 [r]Rev 1:8; 22:13 [s]Jn 4:10
21:8 [t]1Co 6:9 [u]Rev 2:11
21:9 [v]Rev 15:1,6,7 [w]Rev 19:7
21:10 [x]Rev 17:3 [y]Rev 1:10
21:11 [z]Rev 15:8; 22:5 [a]Rev 4:6
21:12 [b]Eze 48:30-34
21:15 [c]Rev 11:1
21:18 [d]ver 11 [e]ver 21
21:19 [f]Isa 54:11,12
21:20 [g]Rev 4:3

Table of Weights and Measures

BIBLICAL UNIT		APPROXIMATE AMERICAN EQUIVALENT	APPROXIMATE METRIC EQUIVALENT
		WEIGHTS	
talent	*(60 minas)*	75 pounds	34 kilograms
mina	*(50 shekels)*	1 1/4 pounds	0.6 kilogram
shekel	*(2 bekas)*	2/5 ounce	11.5 grams
pim	*(2/3 shekel)*	1/3 ounce	7.6 grams
beka	*(10 gerahs)*	1/5 ounce	5.5 grams
gerah		1/50 ounce	0.6 gram
		LENGTH	
cubit		18 inches	0.5 meter
span		9 inches	23 centimeters
handbreadth		3 inches	8 centimeters
		CAPACITY	
		Dry Measure	
cor [homer]	*(10 ephahs)*	6 bushels	220 liters
lethek	*(5 ephahs)*	3 bushels	110 liters
ephah	*(10 omers)*	3/5 bushel	22 liters
seah	*(1/3 ephah)*	7 quarts	7.3 liters
omer	*(1/10 ephah)*	2 quarts	2 liters
cab	*(1/18 ephah)*	1 quart	1 liter
		Liquid Measure	
bath	*(1 ephah)*	6 gallons	22 liters
hin	*(1/6 bath)*	4 quarts	4 liters
log	*(1/72 bath)*	1/3 quart	0.3 liter

The figures of the table are calculated on the basis of a shekel equaling 11.5 grams, a cubit equaling 18 inches and an ephah equaling 22 liters. The quart referred to is either a dry quart (slightly larger than a liter) or a liquid quart (slightly smaller than a liter), whichever is applicable. The ton referred to in the footnotes is the American ton of 2,000 pounds.

This table is based upon the best available information, but it is not intended to be mathematically precise; like the measurement equivalents in the footnotes, it merely gives approximate amounts and distances. Weights and measures differed somewhat at various times and places in the ancient world. There is uncertainty particularly about the ephah and the bath; further discoveries may give more light on these units of capacity.

Bible Verses for Daily Life

"Your word," writes the psalmist, "is a lamp to my feet and a light for my path" (Ps. 119:105). Throughout history God has continued to direct and illumine humankind through his written Word, the Bible. It presents a lifelong challenge: to learn to know God, to love him, to obey him.

The following selected verses help to highlight the Biblical message. If you find a particular topic or verse helpful, you may wish to locate the reference in the Bible and read its context. As you incorporate the Word of God into your life, he will bless you with direction and meaning.

Our Relationship to God

Guilt (Sin)

Isaiah 64:6 All of us have become like one who is unclean, and all our righteous acts are like filthy rags.

Jeremiah 17:9 The heart is deceitful above all things and beyond cure. Who can understand it?

Romans 3:10 There is no one righteous, not even one.

Forgiveness (Repentance)

Psalm 32:5 Then I acknowledged my sin to you and did not cover up my iniquity. I said, "I will confess my transgressions to the LORD"—and you forgave the guilt of my sin.

1 John 1:9 If we confess our sins, he is faithful and just and will forgive us our sins and purify us from all unrighteousness.

God's Love

1 John 4:9 This is how God showed his love among us: He sent his one and only Son into the world that we might live through him.

John 3:16 For God so loved the world that he gave his one and only Son, that whoever believes in him shall not perish but have eternal life.

Salvation

Romans 10:9 If you confess with your mouth, "Jesus is Lord," and believe in your heart that God raised him from the dead, you will be saved.

Acts 4:12 Salvation is found in no one else, for there is no other name under heaven given to men by which we must be saved.

Ephesians 2:8,9 It is by grace you have been saved, through faith—and this not from yourselves, it is the gift of God—not by works, so that no one can boast.

Worship (Praise)

Hebrews 13:15 Through Jesus let us continually offer to God a sacrifice of praise—the fruit of lips that confess his name.

Psalm 29:2 Ascribe to the LORD the glory due his name; worship the LORD in the splendor of his holiness.

John 4:23,24 . . . true worshipers will worship the Father in spirit and truth, for they are the kind of worshipers the Father seeks. God is spirit, and his worshipers must worship in spirit and in truth.

Guidance

Psalm 143:10 Teach me to do your will, for you are my God; may your good Spirit lead me on level ground.

John 16:13 When he, the Spirit of truth, comes, he will guide you into all truth.

Obedience

Matthew 12:50 Whoever does the will of my Father in heaven is my brother and sister and mother.

Luke 11:28 Blessed are those who hear the word of God and obey it.

John 14:15 If you love me, you will obey what I command.

Our Relationships With Others

Love

John 13:34,35 Love one another. As I have loved you, so you must love one another. All men will know that you are my disciples if you love one another.

John 15:13 Greater love has no one than this, that he lay down his life for his friends.

Ephesians 5:1,2 Be imitators of God as dearly loved children and live a life of love, just as Christ loved us and gave himself up for us . . .

1 Peter 4:8 Above all, love each other deeply, because love covers over a multitude of sins.

1 John 3:18 Dear children, let us not love with words or tongue but with actions and in truth.

Compassion (Kindness)

Colossians 3:12 Clothe yourselves with compassion, kindness, humility, gentleness and patience.

Philippians 2:4 Each of you should look not only to your own interests, but also to the interests of others.

Romans 12:15 Rejoice with those who rejoice; mourn with those who mourn.

Matthew 25:40 The King will reply, "I tell you the truth, whatever you did for one of the least of these brothers of mine, you did for me."

Galatians 6:2 Carry each other's burdens, and in this way you will fulfill the law of Christ.

Ephesians 4:32 Be kind and compassionate to one another, forgiving each other, just as in Christ God forgave you.

Forgiveness

Colossians 3:13 Bear with each other and forgive whatever grievances you may have against one another. Forgive as the Lord forgave you.

Mark 11:25 And when you stand praying, if you hold anything against anyone, forgive him, so that your Father in heaven may forgive you your sins.

Proverbs 19:11 A man's wisdom gives him patience; it is to his glory to overlook an offense.

Proverbs 24:17 Do not gloat when your enemy falls; when he stumbles, do not let your heart rejoice.

Revenge

Romans 12:19–21 Do not take revenge, my friends, but leave room for God's wrath, for it is written: "It is mine to avenge; I will repay," says the Lord. On the contrary: "If your enemy is hungry, feed him; if he is thirsty, give him something to drink. In doing this, you will heap burning coals on his head." Do not be overcome by evil, but overcome evil with good.

Romans 12:14 Bless those who persecute you; bless and do not curse.

Matthew 5:43,44 You have heard that it was said, "Love your neighbor and hate your enemy." But I tell you: Love your enemies and pray for those who persecute you.

Luke 6:31 Do to others as you would have them do to you.

Anger

1 Timothy 2:8 I want men everywhere to lift up holy hands in prayer, without anger or disputing.

James 1:19,20 My dear brothers, take note of this: Everyone should be quick to listen, slow to speak and slow to become angry, for man's anger does not bring about the righteous life that God desires.

Psalm 37:8 Refrain from anger and turn from wrath; do not fret—it leads only to evil.

Proverbs 15:1 A gentle answer turns away wrath, but a harsh word stirs up anger.

Ephesians 4:26 Do not let the sun go down while you are still angry.

Galatians 5:19,20 The acts of the sinful nature are . . . hatred, discord, jealousy, fits of rage . . .

Hatred (Strife)

1 John 4:20 If anyone says, "I love God," yet hates his brother, he is a liar. For anyone who does not love his brother, whom he has seen, cannot love God, whom he has not seen.

Proverbs 10:12 Hatred stirs up dissension, but love covers over all wrongs.

Peace

Romans 12:18 If it is possible, as far as it depends on you, live at peace with everyone.

Romans 14:19 Let us therefore make every effort to do what leads to peace and to mutual edification.

The Church

Romans 12:5 In Christ we who are many form one body, and each member belongs to all the others.

Ephesians 4:4–6 There is one body and one Spirit—just as you were called to one hope when you were called—one Lord, one faith, one baptism; one God and Father of all, who is over all and through all and in all.

1 Peter 4:10 Each one should use whatever gift he has received to serve others, faithfully administering God's grace in its various forms.

Ephesians 4:11–13 It was [Christ] who gave [gifts], to prepare God's people for works of service, so that the body of Christ may be built up until we all reach unity in the faith and in the knowledge of the Son of God.

Unity

Romans 15:5,6 May the God who gives endurance and encouragement give you a spirit of unity among yourselves as you follow Christ Jesus, so that with one heart and mouth you may glorify the God and Father of our Lord Jesus Christ.

Ephesians 4:2,3 Be completely humble and gentle; be patient, bearing with one another in love. Make every effort to keep the unity of the Spirit through the bond of peace.

Psalm 133:1 How good and pleasant it is when brothers live together in unity!

Honesty (Truthfulness)

Ephesians 4:25 Each of you must put off falsehood and speak truthfully to his neighbor, for we are all members of one body.

Psalm 15:1–3 Lord, who may dwell in your sanctuary? Who may live on your holy hill? He whose walk is blameless and who does what is righteous, who speaks the truth from his heart and has no slander on his tongue, who does his neighbor no wrong and casts no slur on his fellow man.

Acceptance (Judging)

Romans 15:7 Accept one another, then, just as Christ accepted you, in order to bring praise to God.

Matthew 7:1,2 Do not judge, or you too will be judged. For in the same way you judge others, you will be judged, and with the measure you use, it will be measured to you.

Ephesians 5:21 Submit to one another out of reverence for Christ.

The Family

Ephesians 5:22 Wives, submit to your husbands as to the Lord.

Ephesians 5:25 Husbands, love your wives, just as Christ loved the church and gave himself up for her.

Hebrews 13:4 Marriage should be honored by all, and the marriage bed kept pure, for God will judge the adulterer and all the sexually immoral.

Matthew 5:32 Anyone who divorces his wife, except for marital unfaithfulness, causes her to commit adultery, and anyone who marries a woman so divorced commits adultery.

Ephesians 6:1 Children, obey your parents in the Lord, for this is right.

Proverbs 22:6 Train a child in the way he should go, and when he is old he will not turn from it.

Deuteronomy 11:19 Teach [God's commandments] to your children, talking about them when you sit at home and when you walk along the road, when you lie down and when you get up.

Society

1 Peter 2:11,12 Dear friends, I urge you, as aliens and strangers in the world, to abstain from sinful desires, which war against your soul. Live such good lives among the pagans that, though they accuse you of doing wrong, they may see your good deeds and glorify God on the day he visits us.

Romans 13:7 Give everyone what you owe him: If you owe taxes, pay taxes; if revenue, then revenue; if respect, then respect; if honor, then honor.

1 Peter 2:17 Show proper respect to everyone:

Love the brotherhood of believers, fear God, honor the king.

Personal Guidelines

Correct Values

Philippians 4:8 Finally, brothers, whatever is true, whatever is noble, whatever is right, whatever is pure, whatever is lovely, whatever is admirable—if anything is excellent or praiseworthy—think about such things.

Jeremiah 9:23,24 This is what the LORD says: "Let not the wise man boast of his wisdom or the strong man boast of his strength or the rich man boast of his riches, but let him who boasts boast about this: that he understands and knows me, that I am the LORD, who exercises kindness, justice and righteousness on earth, for in these I delight," declares the LORD.

Proverbs 4:7 Wisdom is supreme; therefore get wisdom. Though it cost all you have, get understanding.

Matthew 22:37–40 Jesus replied: " 'Love the Lord your God with all your heart and with all your soul and with all your mind.' This is the first and greatest commandment. And the second is like it: 'Love your neighbor as yourself.' All the Law and the Prophets hang on these two commandments."

Humility (Pride)

Micah 6:8 He has showed you, O man, what is good. And what does the LORD require of you? To act justly and to love mercy and to walk humbly with your God.

Psalm 25:9 He guides the humble in what is right and teaches them his way.

1 Peter 5:5,6 Clothe yourselves with humility toward one another, because, "God opposes the proud but gives grace to the humble." Humble yourselves, therefore, under God's mighty hand, that he may lift you up in due time.

Luke 18:14 Everyone who exalts himself will be humbled, and he who humbles himself will be exalted.

Worldliness

1 John 2:15,16 Do not love the world or anything in the world. If anyone loves the world, the love of the Father is not in him. For everything in the world—the cravings of sinful man, the lust of his eyes and the boasting of what he has and does—comes not from the Father but from the world.

Colossians 3:5,8,9 Put to death whatever belongs to your earthly nature: sexual immorality, impurity, lust, evil desires and greed, which is idolatry. . . . Rid yourselves of all such things as these: anger, rage, malice, slander, and filthy language from your lips. Do not lie to each other, since you *have taken off your old self with its* practices.

Galatians 5:24 Those who belong to Christ Jesus have crucified the sinful nature with its passions and desires.

Godliness (Righteousness)

Galatians 5:22,23 But the fruit of the Spirit is love, joy, peace, patience, kindness, goodness, faithfulness, gentleness and self-control.

Ephesians 4:22–24 You were taught . . . to be made new in the attitude of your minds; and to put on the new self, created to be like God in true righteousness and holiness.

1 Peter 1:15 But just as he who called you is holy, so be holy in all you do.

Contentment (Greed)

1 Timothy 6:6,10 Godliness with contentment is great gain. . . . For the love of money is a root of all kinds of evil.

Hebrews 13:5 Keep your lives free from the love of money and be content with what you have.

Luke 12:15 Watch out! Be on your guard against all kinds of greed; a man's life does not consist in the abundance of his possessions.

Matthew 6:19–21 Do not store up for yourselves treasures on earth, where moth and rust destroy, and where thieves break in and steal. But store up for yourselves treasures in heaven, where moth and rust do not destroy, and where thieves do not break in and steal. For where your treasure is, there your heart will be also.

Peace

Proverbs 14:30 A heart at peace gives life to the body, but envy rots the bones.

Philippians 4:7 And the peace of God, which transcends all understanding, will guard your hearts and your minds in Christ Jesus.

Isaiah 26:3 You will keep in perfect peace him whose mind is steadfast, because he trusts in you.

John 14:27 Peace I leave with you; my peace I give you. I do not give to you as the world gives. Do not let your hearts be troubled and do not be afraid.

Fear

Psalm 27:1 The LORD is my light and my salvation—whom shall I fear? The LORD is the stronghold of my life—of whom shall I be afraid?

Hebrews 13:5,6 God has said, "Never will I leave you; never will I forsake you." So we say with confidence, "The Lord is my helper; I will not be afraid. What can man do to me?"

Anxiety (Worry)

Psalm 55:22 Cast your cares on the LORD and he will sustain you; he will never let the righteous fall.

Matthew 6:25 Do not worry about your life, what you will eat or drink; or about your body, what you will wear. Is not life more important than food, and the body more important than clothes?

Philippians 4:6 Do not be anxious about anything, but in everything, by prayer and petition, with thanksgiving, present your requests to God.

Depression

Psalm 42:5,6 Why are you downcast, O my soul? Why so disturbed within me? Put your hope in God, for I will yet praise him, my Savior and my God.

Suffering (Trials)

Matthew 11:28 Come to me, all you who are weary and burdened, and I will give you rest.

2 Corinthians 12:9 My grace is sufficient for you, for my power is made perfect in weakness.

Hebrews 12:2,3 Let us fix our eyes on Jesus, the author and perfecter of our faith, who for the joy set before him endured the cross, scorning its shame, and sat down at the right hand of the throne of God. Consider him who endured such opposition from sinful men, so that you will not grow weary and lose heart.

John 16:33 In this world you will have trouble. But take heart! I have overcome the world.

2 Corinthians 4:8,9 We are hard pressed on every side, but not crushed; perplexed, but not in despair; persecuted, but not abandoned; struck down, but not destroyed.

Hebrews 4:16 Let us approach the throne of grace with confidence, so that we may receive mercy and find grace to help us in our time of need.

Faith (Doubt)

John 20:29 Jesus told him, "Because you have seen me, you have believed; blessed are those who have not seen and yet have believed."

Hebrews 11:1,6 Now faith is being sure of what we hope for and certain of what we do not see. . . . And without faith it is impossible to please God, because anyone who comes to him must believe that he exists and that he rewards those who earnestly seek him.

Matthew 21:22 If you believe, you will receive whatever you ask for in prayer.

James 1:6,7 When he asks, he must believe and not doubt, because he who doubts is like a wave of the sea, blown and tossed by the wind. That man should not think he will receive anything from the Lord.

Prayer

Matthew 7:7,8 Ask and it will be given to you; seek and you will find; knock and the door will be opened to you. For everyone who asks receives; he who seeks finds; and to him who knocks, the door will be opened.

Psalm 37:7 Be still before the LORD and wait patiently for him.

James 4:8 Come near to God and he will come near to you.

Psalm 61:1,2 Hear my cry, O God; listen to my prayer. From the ends of the earth I call to you, I call as my heart grows faint; lead me to the rock that is higher than I.

Luke 18:1 [Disciples] should always pray and not give up.

Perseverance

2 Thessalonians 3:13 And as for you, brothers, never tire of doing what is right.

Galatians 6:9 Let us not become weary in doing good, for at the proper time we will reap a harvest if we do not give up.

Hebrews 10:36 You need to persevere so that when you have done the will of God, you will receive what he has promised.

Happiness (Joy)

Psalm 16:11 You have made known to me the path of life; you will fill me with joy in your presence, with eternal pleasures at your right hand.

1 Peter 1:8 Though you have not seen him, you love him; and even though you do not see him now, you believe in him and are filled with an inexpressible and glorious joy.

Psalm 37:4 Delight yourself in the LORD and he will give you the desires of your heart.

Psalm 97:1 The LORD reigns, let the earth be glad; let the distant shores rejoice.

Philippians 4:4 Rejoice in the Lord always. I will say it again: Rejoice!

Psalm 28:7 The LORD is my strength and my shield; my heart trusts in him, and I am helped. My heart leaps for joy and I will give thanks to him in song.

Thankfulness (Gratitude)

Psalm 136:1 Give thanks to the LORD, for he is good.

Isaiah 63:7 I will tell of the kindnesses of the LORD, the deeds for which he is to be praised, according to all the LORD has done for us—yes, the many good things he has done for the house of Israel, according to his compassion and many kindnesses.

Ephesians 5:20 Always [give] thanks to God the Father for everything, in the name of our Lord Jesus Christ.

Psalm 68:19 Praise be to the Lord, to God our Savior, who daily bears our burdens.

Temptation

2 Thessalonians 3:3 The Lord is faithful, and he will strengthen and protect you from the evil one.

Hebrews 2:18 Because he himself suffered when he was tempted, he is able to help those who are being tempted.

1 Corinthians 10:13 No temptation has seized you except what is common to man. And God is faithful; he will not let you be tempted beyond what you can bear. But when you are tempted, he will also provide a way out so that you can stand up under it.

Grief (Loss)

Matthew 5:4 Blessed are those who mourn, for they will be comforted.

John 11:25,26 Jesus said to her, "I am the resurrection and the life. He who believes in me will live, even though he dies; and whoever lives and believes in me will never die."

John 16:22 Now is your time of grief, but I will see you again and you will rejoice, and no one will take away your joy.

Psalm 23:1 The LORD is my shepherd, I shall lack nothing.

Loneliness

Psalm 25:1,16 To you, O LORD, I lift up my soul. . . . Turn to me and be gracious to me, for I am lonely and afflicted.

Matthew 28:20 [Jesus said,] "Surely I will be with you always, to the very end of the age."

Dictionary-Concordance

Aaron—the brother of Moses; he served as Moses' spokesman before Pharaoh (Ex 4:14-16,27-31; 7:1-2); Israel's first high priest (Ex 28:1; Nu 17; Heb 5:1-4).

Abba—the word for *father* in Aramaic, one of the three languages Jesus spoke.
Ro 8:15 And by him we cry "*A*, Father."
Gal 4:6 the Spirit who calls out, "*A*, Father"

Abel—the second son of Adam (Ge 4:2); he offered the proper sacrifice to God (Ge 4:4; Heb 11:4), but was murdered by his brother Cain (Ge 4:8; Mt 23:35; 1Jn 3:12).

abhor—to hate or to turn away from.

Abigail—the wife of Nabal; she helped save David's life (1Sa 25:14-35) and later became his wife (1Sa 25:36-42).

abolish—to destroy completely; to put an end to.

abomination—a thing to be hated.

abound—to be more than enough; to overflow.

Abraham—the father of the Jewish nation. God established a covenant with him in which God promised that he would make a mighty nation of Abraham's children and would give them the land of Canaan (Ge 15; 17; 22; Ro 4; Heb 6:13-15). A son, Isaac, was born to Sarah and Abraham in their old age (Ge 17:16; 18:9-15; 21:1-7; Heb 11:11-12). Later, as a test, God told him to offer Isaac as a sacrifice (Ge 22; Heb 11:17-19) but withdrew this command when Abraham showed that he would trust the Lord even in this matter.

Absalom—a son of David (2Sa 3:3); he fled from Israel after murdering his half-brother Amnon (2Sa 13). Upon his return, he plotted to take David's throne. He met death when his long hair became entangled in an oak tree and Joab, David's commander, thrust javelins into his heart (2Sa 14-18).

abstain—to keep yourself from doing something.

accordance—agreement.

accredited—officially approved.

accursed—to be condemned or doomed by a curse.

Achan—an Israelite who kept spoil from the conquest of Jericho for himself; as a result of Achan's stealing what belonged to God, the Israelites were defeated at Ai and he and his family were stoned to death (Jos 7; 22:20).

acknowledge—to know and to say that something is true.

acquit—to free from punishment or blame.

acts—deeds.
Ps 150:2 Praise him for his *a* of power
Isa 64:6 all our righteous *a* are like filthy

Adam—the first man God created (Ge 1:26-2:25); he sinned by disobeying God (Ge 3) thereby bringing all people under the curse of sin (Ro 5:12-21).

admonish—to give warning or advice in a caring way.

adorn—to make more beautiful.

adultery—having sexual relations with someone other than one's husband or wife.
Ex 20:14 You shall not commit *a*
Mt 5:28 lustfully has already committed *a*

adversary—enemy; opponent.

advocate—1. *(v.)* to speak in favor of. 2. *(n.)* someone who speaks in another person's defense. Jesus is our advocate.

affliction—trouble or pain that lasts a long time.
Ro 12:12 patient in *a*, faithful in prayer.

aforethought—thought about or planned ahead of time.

Ahab—a wicked king of Israel; the husband of Jezebel (1Ki 16:31). He caused Israel to worship Baal rather than God (1Ki 16:31-33) and was opposed by God's prophet Elijah (1Ki 17:1; 18; 21).

alabaster—a hard marblelike material that can be made into jars, vases or sculptures.

alien—a foreigner or stranger.
Ex 22:21 "Do not mistreat an *a*
Eph 2:19 no longer foreigners and *a*, but fellow citizens
1Pe 2:11 as *a* and strangers in the world

alienate—to make unfriendly; to turn a person's interest or affection away from another person or thing.

allot—to divide and give away in parts. In Old Testament times the land of Canaan was allotted to the twelve tribes of Israel.

Almighty—a name used to show how strong and powerful God is.
Ge 17:1 "I am God *A*; walk before me
Isa 6:3 "Holy, holy, holy is the LORD *A*

altar—a raised platform, made of stones, metal, dirt or wood, on which sacrifices were made.

Amen—So be it; Let it become true.

Ananias—1. the husband of Sapphira; he was struck dead for lying to God (Ac 5:1-11); 2. the disciple who baptized Saul (Ac 9:10-19); 3. the high priest before whom Paul was tried in Jerusalem (Ac 22:30-24:1).

Ancient of Days—a name for God that was often used to tell of his wisdom and dignity.

Andrew—one of the twelve apostles; the brother of Peter (Mt 4:18; 10:2; Ac 1:13).

angel—a heavenly being.
Ps 34:7 The *a* of the LORD encamps
Heb 1:14 Are not all *a* ministering spirits
Heb 2:7 made him a little lower than the *a*
1Pe 1:12 Even *a* long to look

annals—historical writings.

annihilate—to destroy completely.

anoint—to pour oil on a person's head.

antichrist—a person who is against Christ.
1Jn 2:18 have heard that the *a* is coming
1Jn 2:22 a man is the *a*—he denies

anxiety—worry.
1Pe 5:7 Cast all your *a* on him

Apollos—a Christian from Alexandria who knew the Scriptures well (Ac 18:24-28) and helped Paul to minister in Corinth (Ac 19:1; 1Co 1:12).

apostle—1. the twelve men Jesus chose to work with him during his earthly ministry; after being equipped by the Holy Spirit, they were sent out to preach about Jesus; The twelve are: Andrew, James the son of Alphaeus, James the son of Zebedee, John, Judas Iscariot, Matthew, Nathanael (Bartholomew), Peter, Philip, Simon, Thaddaeus (Judas), and Thomas. 2. later, someone who had been with Jesus, had seen his miracles and then taught others about him.
Mk 3:14 twelve—designating them *a*—
1Co 12:28 God has appointed first of all *a*
1Co 15:9 For I am the least of the *a*

aqueduct—a channel for bringing water from one place to another.

Aquila—the husband of Priscilla; Aquila and Priscilla were co-workers with Paul in Corinth (Ac 18; Ro 16:3).

Aramaic—the main language used in the countries east of the Mediterranean Sea during Jesus' earthly ministry.

archangel—an angel of high rank; a leader of other angels.

archives—the official records of a government.

ark of the Testimony—a large gold-covered box housed in the Tabernacle, with two gold cherubim on its lid. It contained the Ten Commandments (Tablets of Testimony), a jar of manna and Aaron's staff, and was kept inside the Most Holy Place in the Tent of Meeting. It was a sign to the Israelites ofGod's presence with them, and was also the place where God revealed to his people, through the priests, what was his will for them.

Armageddon—the site of the final battle between God and Satan.
Rev 16:16 that in Hebrew is called *A*.

armor—protective clothing worn in battle, usually made of metal
Eph 6:11 Put on the full *a* of God.

arrogant—proud; conceited.

ascend—to go up. Jesus ascended to heaven to return to God the Father.

ascribe—to think of as caused by, coming from or belonging to.
1Ch 16:28 *a* to the LORD glory and strength

assert—to say positively.

astray—mistaken; not on the right path; lost.

atone—to make right, by paying the penalty, the relationship between God and humans that we broke through sin. In the Old Testament people atoned symbolically for their sins by offering sacrifices to God. In the New Testament Jesus corrected the relationship between God and people once and for all by dying for our sins.

atonement—the payment that corrects the relationship between God and humans that we broke through sin.
Lev 17:11 it is the blood that makes *a*
Lev 23:27 this seventh month is the Day of *A*.
Ro 3:25 presented him as a sacrifice of *a*,
Heb 2:17 that he might make *a* for the sins

authority—the right and power to give orders.
Mt 9:6 the Son of Man has *a* on earth
Mt 28:18 "All *a* in heaven and on earth has
Ro 13:1 for there is no *a* except that which
Heb 13:17 your leaders and submit to their *a*.

avenge—to get back at or punish someone who has done wrong.
Dt 32:35 It is mine to *a*; I will repay.

awe—respect and wonder; a holy fear of God because of his great power.
Ecc 5:7 Therefore stand in *a* of God.
Ac 2:43 Everyone was filled with *a*
Heb 12:28 acceptably with reverence and *a*

Baal—the name of many false gods in Canaan. Each section of Canaan had its own Baal, for example, Baal of Peor, Baal of Hermon, Baal-Berith.
1Ki 18:25 Elijah said to the prophets of *B*

Babylon—the beautiful capital of Babylonia; it was a powerful and influential city in the Near East from the eighteenth to the sixth centuries B.C. The Babylonians destroyed Jerusalem in 602 B.C. and took many Israelites, such as Daniel and his friends, to Babylon. These captives lived there for about seventy years. In the New Testament, Babylon represents the godless city.
Ps 137:1 By the rivers of *B* we sat and wept

Balaam—a seer who tried to curse Israel during their journey to the promised land, but God would not allow it (Nu 22-24).

balm—a skin cream used to heal sores and relieve pain.

banish—to force a person away from a place.

baptize—a religious ceremony in which water is used as a symbol of cleansing from sin. Some churches today baptize by sprinkling or pouring water over a person. Baptism is a sign that our sins are washed away and that Jesus has taken us to be his own.
Mk 1:9 and was *b* by John in the Jordan.
Mk 16:16 believes and is *b* will be saved.
Ac 1:5 but in a few days you will be *b*
Ac 2:38 Repent and be *b*, every one of you.
Ac 16:33 he and all his family were *b*.
Ac 18:8 heard him believed and were *b*.

Barabbas—the Jews chose this criminal, rather than Jesus, to be released by Pilate (Mt 27:26).

Barnabas—an apostle; he was a co-worker with Paul on his first missionary journey (Ac 9:27; chs 13-15).

barren—1. unable to have children. 2. unable to produce crops.

Bartholomew—one of the twelve apostles (Mt 10:3; Ac 1:13). He was also probably known as Nathanael (Jn 1:45-49; 21:2).

Bathsheba—the wife of Uriah; she committed adultery with David and later became his wife (2Sa 11); the mother of Solomon (2Sa 12:24).

Beelzebub—the prince of demons; Satan.
Lk 11:15,"By *B*, the prince of demons,

believe—to accept as true; to trust; to have faith.
Mk 1:15 Repent and *b* the good news!"
Mk 9:24 "I do *b*; help me overcome my
Jn 1:7 that through him all men might *b*.
Jn 3:18 does not *b* stands condemned
Jn 20:27 Stop doubting and *b*."
Ac 16:31 They replied,"*B* in the Lord Jesus,
Ro 3:22 faith in Jesus Christ to all who *b*.
1Th 4:14 We *b* that Jesus died and rose again

Benjamin—the twelfth son of Jacob. Rachel was his mother and he was the younger brother of Joseph (Ge 35:16-24; chs. 42-45).

bereaved—left alone, especially because of the death of a close friend or relative.

besiege—to surround a city or town completely with an army, so that nothing can go in or out.

bestow—to give.

Bethlehem—the city in Judea where Jesus was born (Mt 2:1).

betray—to turn a friend over to his or her enemies; to be unfaithful to.

betroth—to promise to marry.

bewildered—confused; puzzled.

bier—a platform on which a coffin or dead body is carried.

birthright—the special rights of the firstborn son. In the Old Testament, after the father died the oldest son received the father's power and right to make decisions for the entire family. He also got twice as much money and property as each of his brothers.
Ge 25:34 So Esau despised his *b*.

blameless—without fault.
Ge 17:1 walk before me and be *b*.
1Co 1:8 so that you will be *b* on the day
Php 2:15 so that you may become *b* and pure

blaspheme—to speak carelessly, falsely or insultingly about God or holy things.
Mk 3:29 whoever *b* against the Holy Spirit

blemish—a spot or mark that makes something imperfect.

bless—1. to make holy; 2. to show favor to; 3. to ask God to show favor to.
Ge 2:3 And God *b* the seventh day
Ge 12:3 I will *b* those who *b* you,
Mt 5:3 saying "*B* are the poor in spirit
Ro 12:14 *b* those who persecute you; *b*

blight—a disease in plants that makes them shrivel up and die.

blood—
Ex 12:13 and when I see the *b*, I will pass
Mt 26:28 This is my *b* of the covenant
Ro 5:9 have now been justified by his *b*
Eph 1:7 we have redemption through his *b*
Heb 9:12 once for all by his own *b*
Rev 5:9 with your *b* you purchased men
Rev 7:14 white in the *b* of the Lamb.

boast—to brag.
Ps 34:2 My soul will *b* in the LORD
Gal 6:14 May I never *b* except in the cross

Boaz—a wealthy man who lived in Bethlehem in the days of the judges; he married Ruth (Ru 2; 4).

body—
Ro 6:13 Do not offer the parts of your *b*
Ro 12:1 to offer your *b* as living sacrifices,
1Co 6:19 not know that your *b* is a temple
1Co 12:12 The *b* is a unit, though it is made up
Eph 5:30 for we are members of his *b*.

bondage—slavery.
Ezr 9:9 God has not deserted us in our *b*.

booty—valuables taken from a conquered people.

branch—
Isa 4:2 In that day the *B* of the LORD will
Jer 33:15 I will make a righteous *B* sprout
Jn 15:5 "I am the vine; you are the *b*.

bread—
Dt 8:3 that man does not live on *b* alone
Pr 30:8 but give me only my daily *b*.
Isa 55:2 Why spend money on what is not *b*
Mt 6:11 Give us today our daily *b*.
Jn 6:35 Jesus declared, "I am the *b* of life.

breastpiece—a decorated square of linen cloth worn by the high priest when he

entered the Holy Place. The breastpiece was worn chest-high and over a robe. On it were twelve gems, one for each of the twelve tribes of Israel.
Ex 28:15 "Fashion a *b* for making decisions

breastplate—a chest-covering made of metal or leather, worn by soldiers for protection.

brother—
Ge 4:9 "Am I my *b* keeper?"
Ps 133:1 is when *b* live together in unity!
Mt 18:15 'If your *b* sins against you

burden—a heavy load.
Mt 11:30 my yoke is easy and my *b* is light.
Gal 6:2 Carry each other's *b*

Caesar—the title of many Roman emperors.
Lk 2:1 In those days *C* Augustus
Mt 22:21 "Give to *C* what is Caesar's

Cain—Adam and Eve's firstborn son; he murdered his brother Abel (Ge 4:1-16).

calamity—a disaster, usually causing great loss and suffering.

caldron—a large clay or metal pot.

Caleb—one of the twelve men who spied out Canaan. He came back with a positive report and encouraged the Israelites to take possession of Canaan. His faith allowed him to enter Canaan (Nu 13:6-14:38; Dt 1:36) whereas those Israelites who believed the report of the other ten spies died during Israel's forty years of wandering in the wilderness.

call (*v.*)—
2Ch 7:14 if my people, who are *c*
Ps 145:18 near to all who *c* on him
Isa 65:24 Before they *c* I will answer
Mt 9:13 come to *c* the righteous
Jn 10:3 He *c* his own sheep by name
Ro 8:30 And those he predestined, he also *c*
Ro 10:12 and richly blesses all who *c* on him
1Pe 2:9 of him who *c* you out of darkness

call, calling (*n.*)—
Ro 11:29 gifts and his *c* are irrevocable
Eph 4:1 worthy of the *c* you have received
2Pe 1:10 all the more eager to make your *c*

Canaan—1. the land God promised to the nation of Israel; 2. the promised land.
1Ch 16:18 "To you I will give the land of *C*

capstone—the stone that holds two walls together; the stone that finishes a wall.
1Pe 2:7 has become the *c*,

censer—a bowl or dish used for carrying hot coals or for burning incense.

centurion—a Roman army officer in charge of one hundred soldiers.

chaff—the seed covering of a grain such as wheat. In Bible times the grain and chaff were separated by tossing the grain into the air so the wind could blow the chaff away.
Ps 1:4 they are like *c*
Mt 3:12 up the *c* with unquenchable fire

chariot—a two-wheeled vehicle pulled by horses.
2Ki 6:17 and *c* of fire all around Elisha

chasten—to correct or improve by punishment or suffering.

cheerful—
Pr 15:13 A happy heart makes the face *c*
2Co 9:7 for God loves a *c* giver.

cherub—an angel, with an appearance something like a human being. The word for more than one cherub is *cherubim*.

children—
Ps 8:2 from the lips of *c* and infants
Pr 17:6 Children's *c* are a crown
Mt 19:14 "Let the little *c* come to me
Ro 8:16 with our spirit that we are God's *c*.
Eph 6:1 *C*, obey your parents in the Lord,
Eph 6:4 do not exasperate your *c*; instead
1Jn 3:1 that we should be called *c* of God

choose—
Jos 24:15 then *c* for yourselves this day
Jn 15:16 You did not *c* me,
Jn 15:16 But I *c* you to go and bear fruit
Eph 1:4 he *c* us in him before the creation
2Th 2:13 from the beginning God *c* you

chosen—
Mt 22:14 For many are invited, but few are *c*
Jn 15:19 but I have *c* you out of the world
1Pe 2:9 But you are a *c* people, a royal

Christ—the official title of Jesus, meaning "the Anointed One." It is a Greek word, and it means the same as the Hebrew word *Messiah*.
Mt 1:16 was born Jesus, who is called *C*.
Mt 16:16 Peter answered, "You are the *C*
Jn 1:41 found the Messiah" (that is, the *C*).
Jn 20:31 you may believe that Jesus is the *C*
Ro 5:8 While we were still sinners, *C* died
1Co 1:23 but we preached *C* crucified
1Co 12:27 Now you are the body of *C*
Eph 5:2 as *C* loved us and gave himself up
Eph 5:23 as *C* is the head of the church
Php 1:21 to live is *C* and to die is gain.
2Th 2:1 the coming of our Lord Jesus *C*

Christian—a believer in or follower of Christ.
Ac 11:26 The disciples were first called *C*
1Pe 4:16 as a *C*, do not be ashamed,

chronicles—a history of events in the order in which they took place.

church—
Mt 16:18 and on this rock I will build my *c*
Eph 5:23 as Christ is the head of the *c*
Col 1:24 the sake of his body, which is the *c*.

circumcise—to cut off the loose fold of skin at the end of the penis.
Ge 17:10 Every male among you shall be *c*.

cistern—a pit dug into the ground for storing rainwater.

citadel—a tower or building equipped for war, especially one in a city.

city of refuge—one of six cities set aside by Moses and Joshua for those who had accidentally killed someone. Such people would be safe there until a fair trial could be held.

clean animals—animals God allowed the Israelites to sacrifice and eat.

cleanse—to make clean; to wash.

cloak—a loose-fitting coat without sleeves.

co-heir—one of two persons who receive an inheritance. Because of Christ's death and resurrection, we are co-heirs with him of our inheritance in God.

Ro 8:17 heirs of God and *c* with Christ

comfort—

Ps 23:4 rod and your staff, they *c* me.
Zec 1:17 and the LORD will again *c* Zion
2Co 1:4 so that we can *c* those

commandment—an order given by God. God gave the Ten Commandments to the Israelites while they were encamped in the area of Mount Sinai.

Ex 20:6 who love me and keep my *c*.
Mt 22:38 This is the first and greatest *c*.
Jn 13:34 "A new *c* I give you: Love one

commemorate—to remember an event with a special celebration or ceremony.

commend—1. to praise; 2. to hand over to someone for safekeeping.

compassion—sympathy; pity.

Ps 103:4 and crowns me with love and *c*.
Mt 9:36 When he saw the crowds, he had *c*
Ro 9:15 and I will have *c* on whom I have *c*.
Col 3:12 clothe yourselves with *c*, kindness,

compassionate—

Ne 9:17 gracious and *c*, slow to anger

complacent—contented; unconcerned.

conceive—1. to become pregnant; 2. to think up or imagine.

Mt 1:20 what is *c* in her is from the Holy
1Co 2:9 no mind has *c*

concubine—in Bible times, a woman who belonged to a man but did not have the rights of a wife. She was often one of the spoils of war, and her primary purpose was to bear children for the man.

condemn—to give out punishment to; to pronounce guilty.

Jn 3:17 Son into the world to *c* the world,
Ro 8:34 Who is he that *c*? Christ Jesus

condemnation—

Ro 8:1 there is now no *c* for those who are

confess—1. to say what you believe; 2. to tell your sins to someone.

Lev 26:40 "But if they will *c* their sins
Ro 10:9 That if you *c* with your mouth
Php 2:11 every tongue *c* that Jesus Christ is
1Jn 1:9 If we *c* our sins, he is faithful

conform—to agree with and try to be like someone; to do what others say to do.

Ro 8:29 predestined to be *c* to the likeness
1Pe 1:14 do not *c* to the evil desires you had

conscience—the sense of knowing if something is good or bad; a sense of right and wrong.

Ro 2:15 their *c* also bearing witness
Tit 1:15 their minds and *c* are corrupted.
Heb 9:14 cleanse our *c* from acts that lead

conscript—1. to take for government use; 2. to force to serve in an army.

consecrate—to set aside or dedicate for God's use.

Ex 13:2 "*C* to me every firstborn male
Lev 20:7 "*C* yourselves and be holy

console—to comfort.

conspire—to plan together to do evil.

consume—1. to use up or eat up; 2 to destroy completely.

Jn 2:17 "Zeal for your house will *c* me."
Heb 12:29 for our God is a *c* fire.

contempt—lack of respect; looking down on someone or something as being worthless.

Pr 14:31 He who oppresses the poor shows *c*
1Th 5:20 do not treat prophecies with *c*.

content—

Php 4:11 to be *c* whatever the circumstances,
Heb 13:5 and be *c* with what you have

contrite—to feel sorry for one's sins; to feel repentant.

Ps 51:17 a broken and *c* heart
Isa 66:2 he who is humble and *c* in spirit

convert—a person who has changed from one belief to another.

1Ti 3:6 He must not be a recent *c*

convict—1. to prove one wrong; 2. to make a person feel sorrow.

Jn 16:8 he will *c* the world of guilt in regard

convulsion—a wild shaking of the body; violent contraction and expansion of one's muscles.

Cornelius—a Roman to whom Peter preached the gospel; he became the first Gentile Christian (Ac 10).

cornerstone—the first or most important stone laid when constructing a building.

Eph 2:20 with Christ Jesus himself as the chief *c*.

corrupt—1. (*v.*) to change from good to bad; 2. (*adj.*) wicked.

Ge 6:11 Now the earth was *c* in God's sight

1Co 15:33 "Bad company *c* good character."

counsel—to give advice to.

Counselor—another name for the Holy Spirit.
Jn 14:26 But the *C*, the Holy Spirit,
Jn 15:26 "When the *C* comes, whom I will

covenant—1. an agreement between two people or two groups of people, in which usually both make specific promises. 2. the promises of God for salvation.
Ge 9:9 "I now establish my *c* with you
Ge 17:2 I will confirm my *c* between me
Ex 19:5 if you obey me fully and keep my *c*
Jer 31:31 "when I will make a new *c*
Eze 37:26 I will make a *c* of peace with them
1Co 11:25 "This cup is the new *c* in my blood
Heb 9:15 Christ is the mediator of a new *c*

covet—to want for yourself something that belongs to another person.
Ex 20:17 You shall not *c* your neighbor's

create—to make; to bring into being. God created the world; the world is God's creation; God is the Creator.
Ge 1:1 In the beginning God *c* the heavens
Ps 51:10 *C* in me a pure heart, O God
Col 1:16 For by him all things were *c*
Rev 10:6 who *c* the heavens and all that is

cross—
Mt 10:38 and anyone who does not take his *c*
Gal 6:14 in the *c* of our Lord Jesus Christ
Php 2:8 even death on a *c*!
Col 2:14 he took it away, nailing it to the *c*
Heb 12:2 set before him endured the *c*

crown—
Pr 4:9 present you with a *c* of splendor."
Isa 61:3 to bestow on them a *c* of beauty
1Co 9:25 it to get a *c* that will last forever.
2Ti 4:8 store for me the *c* of righteousness
Rev 2:10 and I will give you the *c* of life.

crucify—to put to death by nailing or tying a person's body to a cross.
Mt 27:22 They all answered, "*C* him!"
Jn 19:18 Here they *c* him, and with him two
1Co 1:23 but we preach Christ *c*: a stumbling
Gal 2:20 I have been *c* with Christ

curse—(*v.*) to ask God to bring evil or injury to; (*n.*) a prayer or desire that evil or injury come upon someone.
Lev 20:9 "If anyone *c* his father or mother
Dt 21:23 hung on a tree is under God's *c*.
Lk 6:28 bless those who *c* you, pray
Gal 3:13 *C* is everyone who is hung on a tree
Jas 3:9 with it we *c* men, who have been

Daniel—a young Jewish exile; he lived in Babylon during the reign of several kings, including Nebuchadnezzar. He was found praying to God, contrary to an edict prohibiting for thirty days subjects from praying to anyone except the king. For this he was thrown into a lion's den (Da 1-6).

David—the son of Jesse; in early life: anointed by Samuel to become king of Israel (1Sa 16:1-13); killed the giant Goliath (1Sa 17); and was pursued by Saul. After Saul's death (2Sa 1) he was made king (2Sa 5:1-4), and it was during his reign that Israel's place in the land of Canaan was made secure.

day—
Ge 1:5 God called the light "*d* "
Ps 118:24 This is the *d* the Lord has made;
Ecc 12:1 Creator in the *d* of your youth,
Joel 2:31 and dreadful *d* of the LORD.
Mic 4:1 in the last *d*
Lk 11:3 Give us each *d* our daily bread.
Heb 1:2 in these last *d* he has spoken to us
2Pe 3:8 With the Lord a *d* is like

deacon—a church leader chosen to take care of money matters and to give money to the widows and the poor.
1Ti 3:8 *D*, likewise, are to be men worthy

death—
Ps 23:4 the valley of the shadow of *d*,
Ecc 7:2 for *d* is the destiny of every man;
Isa 25:8 he will swallow up *d* forever.
Ro 6:23 For the wages of sin is *d*,
1Co 15:21 For since *d* came through a man,
1Co 15:55 Where, O *d*, is your sting?"
Rev 1:18 And I hold the keys of *d* and Hades
Rev 21:4 There will be no more *d*

debauchery—living an immoral life or a life without religion; living to please only yourself.

Deborah—a prophetess who led Israel to victory over the Canaanites (Jdg 4-5).

debt—something that one person owes another. (Also, debtor.)
Mt 6:12 Forgive us our *d*,

deceive—(*v.*) to fool or trick; to lie (*n.* deceit, deception; *adj.* deceitful).
Ge 3:13 "The serpent *d* me, and I ate."
1Co 3:18 Do not *d* yourselves.
Gal 6:7 Do not be *d*: God cannot be
1Jn 1:8 we *d* ourselves and the truth is not

decree—an order or law given by someone with power and authority.

dedicate—to set apart for a special purpose, often for God's use.

defect—imperfection; fault.

defile—to make something that is good and pure impure or unclean.

defraud—to cheat someone by trickery.

Deity—God.
Col 2:9 of the *D* lives in bodily form,

deliver—to rescue; to set free.

demon—evil spirit. A demon-possessed person is one who is controlled by evil spirits.
Mk 5:15 possessed by the legion of *d*
Ro 8:38 neither angels not *d*, neither
1Co 10:20 of pagans are offered to *d*,
1Ti 4:1 spirits and things taught by *d*.
Jas 2:19 Good! Even the *d* believe that
Rev 16:14 of *d* performing miraculous signs

denarius—a small Roman coin made of silver. During Jesus' earthly ministry, one denarius was the payment for about one day's work.

denounce—to say a person or thing is evil.

depraved—evil or sinful.
Php 2:15 fault in a crooked and *d* generation

depravity—
Ro 1:29 of wickedness, evil, greed and *d*.
2Pe 2:19 they themselves are slaves of *d*

desecrate—to treat without respect or reverence.

desolate—not lived in; lonely; deserted.

destine—(*v.*) to decide ahead of time (*n.* destiny).

destitute—not having necessary things such as money and food.

detest—to hate.

devil—
Lk 4:2 forty days he was tempted by the *d*.
Eph 4:27 and do not give the *d* a foothold.
Eph 6:11 stand against the *d* schemes.
2Ti 2:26 and escape from the trap of the *d*,
Jas 4:7 Resist the *d*, and he will flee
1Pe 5:8 Your enemy the *d* prowls
1Jn 3:8 was to destroy the *d* work.
Rev 12:9 that ancient serpent called the *d*

devote—to set apart for a special person or for a special reason; to set apart for God's use.

devout—religious; giving much time to prayer and worship.

die—
Ge 2:17 when you eat of it you will surely *d*
2Ki 14:6 each is to *d* for his own sins."
Ecc 3:2 a time to be born and a time to *d*
Eze 3:18 that wicked man will *d* for his sin
Eze 18:4 soul who sins is the one who will *d*.
Jn 11:26 and believes in me will never *d*.
Ro 14:8 and if we d, we d to the Lord.
1Co 15:22 in Adam all *d*, so in Christ all will
Php 1:21 to live is Christ and to *d* is gain.
Rev 14:13 Blessed are the dead who *d*

dirge—a song of deep sadness, usually sung at funerals.

discern—to understand; to come to know the difference between two or more things.
Php 1:10 you may be able to *d* what is best

disciple—a follower or student, especially one who believes what the leader teaches. Anyone who believes in Jesus is his disciple.
Lk 14:27 and follow me cannot be my *d*.
Jn 13:35 men will know that you are my *d*

discipline—(*v.*) to correct; to teach what is right; (*n.*) training that corrects, molds or perfects moral character.
Ps 39:11 You rebuke and *d* men for their sin
Pr 15:5 A fool spurns his father's *d*
Pr 29:17 *D* your son, and he will give you
Heb 12:6 the Lord *d* those he loves
Rev 3:19 Those whom I love I rebuke and *d*.

disclose—to show or reveal.

discourse—1. (*v.*) to talk together; 2. (*n.*) a conversation or speech.

discriminate—to make a difference where no such difference should or does exist; to treat two persons or things differently because one seems better than the other.
Jas 2:4 have you not *d* among yourselves

disgrace—to bring shame to.

disown—to reject someone or something so completely that it no longer belongs to you.
Mt 26:35 to die with you, I will never *d* you."
2Ti 2:12 if we *d* him,

disperse—to scatter; to spread around.

dissension—disagreement; quarreling.

dissipation—living only for your own pleasure; wasting your life on foolish or evil pleasures.

divination—seeing into the future by magic.
Lev 19:26 " 'Do not practice *d* or sorcery.

divine—given by God; belonging to God.
Ro 1:20 his eternal power and *d* nature
2Co 10:4 they have *d* power

divorce—
Mal 2:16 "I hate *d*," says the LORD God
Mt 19:3 for a man to *d* his wife for any
1Co 7:11 And a husband must not *d* his wife.

doctrine—teachings or beliefs about God.
1Ti 4:16 Watch your life and *d* closely.
Tit 2:1 is in accord with sound *d*.

dominion—power; rule.
Ps 22:28 for *d* belongs to the LORD
Eph 1:21 far above all rule and authority, power and *d*

doom—1. (*v.*) to make certain something will fail or be destroyed; 2. (*n.*) fate; condemnation; ruin.

door—
Mt 7:7 and the *d* will be opened to you.
Rev 3:20 I stand at the *d* and knock.

doubt—
Mt 21:21 if you have faith and do not *d*

Mk 11:23 and does not *d* in his heart
Jas 1:6 he must believe and not *d*

dropsy—puffiness or swelling of the body caused by a disease of the kidneys, liver or heart.

earth—
Ge 1:1 God created the heavens and the *e*.
Ps 24:1 *e* is the LORD's and everything
Mt 6:10 done on *e* as it is in heaven.
Mt 24:35 Heaven and *e* will pass away
Lk 2:14 on *e* peace to men
Php 2:10 in heaven and on *e* and under the *e*
2Pe 3:13 to a new heaven and a new *e*

edict—an order or law made by a person who has the power to enforce it.

edify—to teach someone to live a godly life, or to help someone to live in such a way.
1Co 14:4 but he who prophesies *e* the church

elders—1. the older men of a town or nation. They were the leaders of their community and made all the important decisions. Each town had its own groups of elders. After the Jews returned from exile in Babylon, the elders made up the Sanhedrin, the ruling council of the Jews. 2. the leaders of the church.
1Ti 5:17 The *e* who direct the affairs
Tit 1:5 and appoint *e* in every town

election—
Ro 9:11 God's purpose in *e* might stand
2Pe 1:10 to make your calling and *e* sure.

Eli—the high priest with whom Samuel spent the early years of his life (1Sa 2:11-26).

Elijah—a prophet of the Lord during the reign of Ahab. He predicted a famine in Israel (1Ki 17:1), and defeated the prophets of Baal at Carmel in the test of whose God would set fire to the altar (1Ki 18:16-46). He was taken to heaven in a whirlwind (2Ki 2:11-12) and later appeared with Moses at the transfiguration of Jesus (Mk 9:1-8).

Elisha—the prophet who succeeded Elijah. He was present when God took Elijah to heaven, and he took his place as prophet to Israel (2Ki 2:1-18).

Elizabeth—the mother of John the Baptist. She became pregnant when she was very old; Mary went to visit her when she found out she, too, was pregnant (Lk 1:5-58).

enchanter—a magician or snake charmer.

endure—to continue; to keep on going; to bear something that is difficult or painful.
Ps 136:1 His love *e* forever.
Mal 3:2 who can *e* the day of his coming
2Ti 2:3 *E* hardship with us like a good

enmity—hatred or bad feelings that make two people or two groups enemies.
Ge 3:15 And I will put *e*

Enoch—a man who "walked with God." Later in life, God "took him away" (Ge 5:18-24).

envy—to want for yourself something that belongs to another person.
1Co 13:4 It does not *e*, it does not boast

ephod—a linen apron worn by a priest over his robe. It was decorated with gold, blue, purple and scarlet yarns.

Ephraim—1. one of Joseph's sons; 2. one of the tribes of Israel. Its members were descendants of Ephraim. 3. a name for the northern kingdom of Israel after the ten tribes of Israel and the two tribes of Judah separated from each other.
Ge 41:52 The second son he named *E*
Isa 7:17 unlike any since *E* broke away from Judah

epileptic—a person afflicted with a disorder of the brain that makes one lose control of his or her muscles and sometimes causes unconsciousness. In Bible times epilepsy was a dreaded disease; but today it can be controlled by medicine.

equity—fairness.

Esau—the firstborn son of Isaac and twin of Jacob (Ge 25:21-26). He sold his birthright to Jacob for a pot of stew (Ge 25:29-34) and was tricked out of his blessing by this same brother (Ge 27). Later in his life he and Jacob met and were reconciled (Ge 33).

esteem—1. (*v.*) to value; to consider important; 2. (*n.*) high regard or respect.

Esther—a Jewish woman who lived in Persia (Est 2:7). Xerxes chose her to be queen (Est 2:8-18). Upon being told of a plot by Haman to kill the Jews, she went to the king and pleaded for the Jewish people and thus saved them (Est 3-4; 7-9).

eternal—without beginning or end; forever; timeless. God is eternal.
Dt 33:27 The *e* God is your refuge,
Jn 3:16 him shall not perish but have *e* life.
Ro 6:23 but the gift of God is *e* life
1Jn 5:13 you may know that you have *e* life.

eunuch—1. the most important official after the king or queen; 2. a man whose sex organs have been removed so that he cannot produce children.

evangelist—a person who preaches the good news about Jesus.
Ac 21:8 stayed at the house of Philip the *e*
Eph 4:11 some to be prophets, some to be *e*

Eve—the first woman God created (Ge 2:20-24). Her name means, Mother of all the living (Ge 3:20).

everlasting—forever; without end.
Ps 90:2 from *e* to *e* you are God.
Isa 9:6 *E* Father, Prince of Peace
Isa 55:3 I will make an *e* covenant with you

Jn 6:47 the truth, he who believes has *e* life.
2Th 1:9 punished with *e* destruction

evil—wicked; doing things against God's will.
Ge 2:9 of the knowledge of good and *e*
Ps 23:4 I will fear no *e*
Isa 13:11 I will punish the world for its *e*
Isa 55:7 and the *e* man his thoughts.
Mt 6:13 but deliver us from the *e* one."
Ro 12:9 Hate what is *e;* cling
Ro 12:17 Do not repay anyone *e* for *e*.
Eph 6:16 all the flaming arrows of the *e* one.
Jas 1:13 For God cannot be tempted by *e*

exalt—to praise; to raise to an important position.
Ps 118:28 you are my God, and I will *e* you.
Ps 148:13 for his name alone is *e*
Pr 14:34 Righteousness *e* a nation
Mt 23:12 For whoever *e* himself will be

exile—(*v.*) to force someone to leave his or her country or home; (*n.*) forced removal from one's country or home.
2Ch 36:20 He carried into *e* to Babylon

exodus—the departure of a large group of people from one place to go to another. The book of Exodus is the story of the Israelites' journey from Egypt to Canaan.

exploit—to take unfair advantage of.

extol—to praise.
Ps 34:1 I will *e* the LORD at all times
Ps 95:2 and *e* him with music and song.

extortion—something gotten from a person by force or by using other illegal means.

Ezekiel—a priest who was called to be a prophet to the Jewish people when they were in exile in Babylon (Eze 1-3). He had many visions from the Lord (Eze 37; 40).

Ezra—a priest and teacher of the Law; he led a group of Jewish exiles back to Israel and helped them reestablish the temple of God and restore proper worship (Ezr 7-8).

faction—a group of people trying to get its own way or promote its own interests.

faith—belief and trust in God; knowing that God is real, even though we can't see him.
Hab 2:4 but the righteous will live by his *f*
Mt 17:20 if you have *f* as small as a mustard
Lk 7:9 I have not found such great *f*
Ro 1:17 "The righteous will live by *f*."
Ro 3:22 *comes through f in Jesus Christ*
1Co 13:2 and if I have a *f* that can move
2Co 5:7 We live by *f*, not by sight.
Eph 6:16 to all this, take up the shield of *f*.
1Ti 6:12 Fight the good fight of the *f*.
Heb 11:1 *f* is being sure of what we hope for
Heb 11:8 By *f* Abraham, when called to go
Heb 12:2 the author and perfecter of our *f*
Jas 2:26 so *f* without deeds is dead.

faithful—trustworthy; loyal. God is faithful.
Ps 145:13 the LORD is *f* to all his promises
Mt 25:21 "Well done, good and *f* servant!
Ro 12:12 patient in affliction, *f* in prayer.
1Co 10:13 And God is *f;* he will not let you be
1Jn 1:9 he is *f* and just and will forgive us
Rev 1:5 who is the *f* witness, the firstborn

faithfulness—
Ps 86:15 to anger, abounding in love and *f*.
La 3:23 great is your *f*.
Gal 5:22 patience, kindness, goodness, *f*

falsehood—a lie.

family—
Ps 68:6 God sets the lonely in *f*
Lk 9:61 go back and say good-by to my *f*."
Lk 12:52 in one *f* divided against each other
1Ti 3:4 He must manage his own *f* well
1Ti 5:4 practice by caring for their own *f*

father—
Ge 2:24 this reason a man will leave his *f*
Ge 17:4 You will be the *f* of many nations.
Ex 20:12 "Honor your *f* and your mother
Pr 23:22 Listen to your *f*, who gave you life
Mt 6:9 "Our *F* in heaven
Lk 11:11 "Which of you *f*, if your son asks
Lk 23:34 Jesus said, "*F*, forgive them
Jn 10:30 I and the *F* are one."
Jn 14:2 In my *F* house are many rooms
Jn 14:6 No one comes to the *F*

fear—(*v.*) 1. to respect highly; to feel reverence and awe for; 2. to be afraid of. (n.) profound reverence toward God; anticipation or awareness of danger.
Dt 6:13 *F* the LORD your God, serve him
Job 1:8 a man who *f* God and shuns evil."
Ps 91:5 You will not *f* the terror of night
Ps 111:10 *f* of the LORD is the beginning
Isa 41:10 So do not *f*, for I am with you
Php 2:12 to work out your salvation with *f*

fellowship—companionship or friendship.
1Jn 1:6 claim to have *f* with him yet walk
1Jn 1:7 we have *f* with one another,

fig—1. a brownish pear-shaped fruit that grows in countries near the Mediterranean Sea; 2. the tree that grows this fruit.

firstborn—a family's first male child. The firstborn son became the head of the family when his father died. He also received twice as much money and property as each of his brothers.
Ex 11:5 Every *f* son in Eygpt will die

firstfruits—the first vegetables, fruits and grains harvested from the field.
Ex 23:19 "Bring the best of the *f* of your soil

flawless—without fault or defect; perfect.

flog—to beat with a stick or a whip.

forbearance—patience; tolerance.

forefather—a male ancestor.

foreknow—to know ahead of time.
Ro 8:29 For those God *f* he
Ro 11:2 not reject his people, whom he *f*

forgive—to pardon or excuse; no longer to blame or be angry with someone who had done you wrong.
Mt 6:14 For if you *f* men when they sin
Lk 23:34 Jesus said, "Father, *f* them
Col 3:13 *F* as the Lord forgave you.
1Jn 1:9 and just and will *f* us our sins

forsake—to leave another completely alone, with no hope that you will ever return.
Jos 1:5 I will never leave you or *f* you.
Isa 55:7 Let the wicked *f* his way
Mt 27:46 my God, why have you *f* me?

frankincense—an incense burned for its sweet smell.

free—
Jn 8:32 and the truth will set you *f*."
Ro 6:18 You have been set *f* from sin

freedom—
2Co 3:17 the Spirit of the Lord is, there is *f*.
Gal 5:13 But do not use your *f* to indulge

friend—
Pr 18:24 there is a *f* who sticks closer
Jn 15:13 that one lay down his life for his *f*.
Jas 4:4 Anyone who chooses to be a *f*

fruitful—productive; yielding much fruit.
Ge 1:22 "Be *f* and increase in number
Jn 15:2 clean so that it will be even more *f*.

fulfill—to complete a promise or project.
Ps 116:14 I will *f* my vows to the LORD
Mk 14:49 But the Scriptures must be *f*."
Lk 24:44 Everything must be *f* that is

fulfillment—
Ro 13:10 Therefore love is the *f* of the law.

Gabriel—the angel who announced the births of John the Baptist and Jesus (Lk 1:11-20, 26-38).

Galilee—the northern part of Palestine. Palestine had three main parts: Galilee, Samaria and Judea. Jesus grew up, preached and did most of his miracles in Galilee. Today this area is in northern Israel.

gall—1. a plant with an extremely bitter-tasting fruit; 2. the liquid made by the liver.
Mt 27:34 mixed with *g*; but after tasting it

genealogy—a list of a person's ancestors or descendants; a family tree.

generation—the entire number of people born and living at about the same time. Grandparents, parents and children are three different generations.
Ps 102:12 your renown endures through all *g*.
Lk 1:48 now on all *g* will call me blessed

Gentile—anyone who is not a Jew.
Ro 3:9 and *G* alike are all under sin.
Ro 11:13 as I am the apostle to the *G*
Eph 3:6 the gospel the *G* are heirs together

Gideon—a judge who freed Israel from the rule and terror of the Midianites (Jdg 6-8). He asked for a sign from God, and God showed him his will by means of dew and a fleece (Jdg 6:36-40).

gift—
Ro 6:23 but the *g* of God is eternal life
1Co 12:4 There are different kinds of *g*,
2Co 9:15 be to God for his indescribable *g*!

gleanings—the grain or fruit left behind after harvesting. Poor people were allowed to pick up and use these leftovers.

glory—1. honor; praise; 2. a source of pride or worthiness.
Ps 8:5 and crowned him with *g* and honor.
Ps 19:1 The heavens declare the *g* of God
Lk 2:14 saying, "*G* to God in the highest
Jn 1:14 We have seen his *g*, the *g* of the one
1Co 10:31 whatever you do, do it all for the *g*
Rev 4:11 to receive *g* and honor and power

glutton—a person who eats too much.

gnash—to grind (one's teeth) together.

God—
Ge 1:1 In the beginning *G* created
Ge 17:1 "I am *G* Almighty; walk before me
Ge 50:20 but *G* intended it for good
Ex 8:10 is no one like the LORD our *G*.
Ex 20:5 the LORD your *G*, am a jealous *G*
Nu 23:19 *G* is not a man, that he should lie
Dt 4:31 the LORD your *G* is a merciful *G*
Dt 6:4 LORD our *G*, the LORD is one.
Dt 6:5 Love the LORD your *G*
Dt 32:4 A faithful *G* who does no wrong
Ne 9:17 But you are a forgiving *G*
Ps 46:1 *G* is our refuge and strength
Ps 71:22 harp for your faithfulness, O my *G*
Jn 1:18 ever seen *G*, but *G* the only Son
Jn 3:16 "For *G* so loved the world that he
Jn 4:24 *G* is spirit, and his worshipers must
1Co 10:13 *G* is faithful; he will not let you be
1Co 14:33 For *G* is not a *G* of disorder
Heb 12:10 but *G* disciplines us for our good
Jas 1:13 For *G* cannot be tempted by evil
1Jn 4:16 *G* is love.
Rev 4:8 holy is the Lord *G* Almighty

Golgotha—the hill outside Jerusalem where Jesus was hung on a cross.
Jn 19:17 (which in Aramaic is called *G*).

Goliath—the Philistine giant who was killed by David (1Sa 17; 21:9).

gospel—1. the good news that Jesus died for our sins and rose again; 2. Gospel, any of the first four books of the New Testament.
Ro 1:16 I am not ashamed of the *g*
Ro 15:16 duty of proclaiming the *g* of God
1Co 9:16 Woe to me if I do not preach the *g*!

1Co 15:2 By this *g* you are saved
2Co 9:13 your confession of the *g*
1Th 2:4 by God to be entrusted with the *g*

grace—an undeserved favor or gift; the undeserved forgiveness, kindness and mercy that God gives us.
Ro 3:24 and are justified freely by his *g*
Ro 5:20 where sin increased, *g* increased all
2Co 12:9 "My *g* is sufficient for you
Eph 2:5 it is by *g* you have been saved.
Tit 3:7 having been justified by his *g*

guilty—having broken a law or commandment; deserving punishment.
Ex 34:7 does not leave the *g* unpunished
1Co 11:27 in an unworthy manner will be *g*
Heb 10:22 to cleanse us from a *g* conscience
Jas 2:10 at just one point is *g* of breaking all

Hades—hell; the place where the spirits of the dead live.
Mt 16:18 the gates of *H* will not overcome it.

Hagar—a servant of Sarah and one of Abraham's wives; the mother of Ishmael (Ge 16:1-6; 25:12). After giving birth to Isaac, Sarah drove Hagar away (Ge 21:9-21).

Haggai—a prophet who encouraged the Israelites who returned from exile in Babylon to rebuild the temple (Ezr 5:1; Hag 1-2).

hallelujah—praise the Lord; a song of praise.
Rev 19:1 "*H!* Salvation and glory and power

hallow—to make holy; to set apart as special.

Hannah—the wife of Elkanah; she prayed for a son and God gave her Samuel. She dedicated him to God and he lived in the temple as a boy and became a prophet and judge (1Sa 1-2).

harlot—a woman who lets a man use her body for sex in exchange for money.

haughty—proud.
Pr 16:18 a *h* spirit before a fall.

heart—
Dt 6:5 LORD your God with all your *h*
1Sa 16:7 but the LORD looks at the *h*."
1Ch 28:9 for the LORD searches every *h*
Ps 51:10 Create in me a pure *h*, O God
Ps 119:11 I have hidden your word in my *h*
Ps 139:23 Search me, O God, and know my *h*
Jer 29:13 when you seek me with all your *h*.
Eze 36:26 I will give you a new *h*
Mt 5:8 Blessed are the pure in *h*
Mt 22:37 the Lord your God with all your *h*
Ro 10:10 is with your *h* that you believe

heaven—
Ge 14:19 Creator of *h* and earth.
Mt 19:23 man to enter the kingdom of *h*.
Mk 16:19 he was taken up into *h*
Php 3:20 But our citizenship is in *h*.
Rev 21:1 Then I saw a new *h* and a new earth

Hebrew—1. another name for an Israelite; a descendant of Abraham; 2. the language spoken by the Jews. The Old Testament was written in Hebrew.

heir—someone who receives the property or blessings of a person who has died. In Bible times an heir was usually male.
Ro 8:17 then we are *h*—*h* of God
Eph 3:6 gospel the Gentiles are *h* together

heresy—false teaching about God.

Herod—the family name of five kings who ruled Palestine under the Roman emperor: Herod the Great (Mt 2:16); Herod Antipas (Mk 6:14-29); Herod Philip (Mt 14:3; Mk 6:17); Herod Agrippa I (Ac 12:1-4,19-23); Herod Agrippa II (Ac 23:35; 25:13-26:32).

Herodias—the wife of Herod Antipas; she persuaded her daughter to ask Antipas for the head of John the Baptist (Mk 6:17).

Hezekiah—a king of Judah; he restored the temple, reinstituted proper worship and sought the Lord's help against the Assyrians. He showed his faith when, suffering from a serious illness, he prayed to God and was healed; yet he also showed the Babylonians his treasures and God punished him and the Israelites for this (2Ch 29-31; 2Ki 18-20).

high priest—the chief religious official in the Jewish religion. In the Old Testament he offered the most important sacrifices to God in behalf of the people. In Jesus' time he was also the head of the Sanhedrin (the highest Jewish court), and a powerful political leader—even having a small army.

hinder—to hold back; to prevent; to delay.

holy—(*v.*) set apart for God; (*adj.*) belonging to God; pure; godly.
Ex 20:8 the Sabbath day by keeping it *h*.
Lev 11:44 and be *h*, because I am *h*.
Isa 6:3 "*H*, *h*, *h* is the Lord Almighty;
Ro 12:1 as living sacrifices, *h* and pleasing
Rev 4:8 "*H*, *h*, *h* is the LORD Almighty

Holy Spirit—the third person of the Trinity; the Spirit lives and works in our hearts and minds. Jesus promised his disciples that he would send his Spirit (Jn 14:16-26), and it came at Pentecost in a powerful way (Ac 2). Other names are: the Spirit, Counselor and *Comforter*.

Homage—honor; respect.

homosexual—someone who has sexual relations with a person of the same sex.
1Co 6:9 male prostitutes nor *h* offenders

hope (*v.*; *n.*)—
Ps 42:5 Put your *h* in God
Isa 40:31 but those who *h* in the LORD
Ro 8:24 But *h* that is seen is no *h* at all.
1Co 15:19 for this life we have *h* in Christ

Heb 11:1 faith is being sure of what we *h* for

hosanna—a Hebrew word of praise meaning "save."
Mt 21:9 "*H* in the highest!"

hospitality—welcoming people into one's home; sharing one's home and food with others.
Ro 12:13 Practice *h*.
1Pe 4:9 Offer *h* to one another

humble—(*v.*) to make humble in spirit or manner; (*adj.*) not proud; not pretending to be important.
Ps 147:6 The LORD sustains the *h*
Mt 23:12 whoever exalts himself will be *h*
Jas 4:10 *H* yourselves before the Lord

humiliate—to make humble; to reduce to a lower position; to make ashamed.
1Co 11:22 and *h* those who have nothing?

hymn—a song of praise to God.

hypocrite—a person who pretends to love God.
Mt 6:5 when you pray, do not be like the *h*
Mt 7:5 you *h*, first take the plank out

hyssop—a plant used to sprinkle water or blood for religious cleansing.
Ps 51:7 with *h*, and I will be clean

idol—a statue made by people and worshiped as if it had the power of a god; anything that takes the place of God in a person's life. Worshiping idols is called idolatry.
1Co 8:4 We know that an *i* is nothing at all
Col 3:5 evil desires and greed, which is *i*.

Immanuel—a name for Jesus meaning "God with us."
Isa 7:14 birth to a son, and will call him *I*.
Mt 1:23 and they will call him *I*"

immortal—free from death; not able to die.
1Ti 1:17 Now to the King eternal, *i*

immortality—
1Co 15:53 and the mortal with *i*.

imperishable—not able to die or to be destroyed.
1Pe 1:23 not of perishable seed, but of *i*

impure—not pure; not clean.
1Th 4:7 For God did not call us to be *i*

incense—1. spices burned to make a sweet-smelling smoke, as a way of worshiping God; 2. the sweet smell or the smoke of burning spices.
Ps 141:2 my prayer be set before you like *i*
Mt 2:11 him with gifts of gold and of *i*

incensed—very angry; filled with rage.

indignation—anger.

infirmity—physical weakness; disease.
Isa 53:4 Surely he took up our *i*

inherit—to receive money, property or keepsakes from a person after his or her death.
Mt 5:5 for they will *i* the earth.
Mk 10:17 "what must I do to *i* eternal life?"

inheritance—money, property or keepsakes received from a person after his or her death.
Dt 4:20 to be the people of his *i*
1Pe 1:4 and into an *i* that can never perish

iniquity—sin; wickedness.
Ps 51:2 Wash away all my *i*
Ps 103:10 or repay us according to our *i*.
Isa 53:6 the *i* of us all.
Mic 7:19 and hurl all our *i* into the depths.

injustice—unfairness.

inscription—1. the writing on a coin; 2. a written title or message.

insolent—proud, in an insulting way.

institute—to establish; to begin.

insurrection—revolt or rebellion against a government.

integrity—complete honesty.

intercede—to beg or plead for another person.
Ro 8:26 but the Spirit himself *i* for us

intercession—
Isa 53:12 and made *i* for the transgressors.

intermarry—to marry someone from a different race or religion.
Dt 7:3 Do not *i* with them.

irrevocable—not able to be taken back or changed.

Isaac—the promised son of Abraham and Sarah (Ge 17:19; 21:1-7); offered as a sacrifice by Abraham (Ge 22); married Rebekah (Ge 24) and was the father of Esau and Jacob (Ge 25). Rebekah and Jacob plotted together to trick Isaac into blessing Jacob instead of Esau (Ge 27).

Isaiah—prophet called by God (Isa 6) to prophesy to Judah (Isa 1:1). Some of his prophesies are about the coming Messiah (Isa 53).

Ishmael—the son of Abraham and Hagar (Ge 16); he was not to be the son of the covenant (Ge 17:18-21). Sarah and Abraham sent both Hagar and Ishmael away from them (Ge 21:8-21).

Israel—1. the nation made up of descendants of the twelve sons of Jacob. Israel became a nation when God took his people out of Egypt (Ex 1-14); 2. the new name God gave to Jacob (Ge 32:28); 3. the northern ten tribes after they separated from Judah and Benjamin.
Dt 6:4 Hear, O *I*: The LORD our God
Eze 39:23 of *I* went into exile for their sin
Lk 22:30 judging the twelve tribes of *I*.
Eph 3:6 Gentiles are heirs together with *I*

Israelites—the people of Israel.
Ex 14:22 and the *I* went through the sea
Ro 9:27 the number of the *I* be like the sand

Jacob—the second son of Isaac and Rebekah; he was the twin brother of Esau (Ge 25:21-26). He bought Esau's birthright for a pot of stew (Ge 25:29-34) and later tricked Isaac into giving him the blessing that belonged to Esau (Ge 27:1-37). After running away from Esau, he wrestled with God, and his name was changed to Israel (Ge 32:22-32). He had twelve sons and all of them eventually went to Egypt during a famine (Ge 42-43). He settled in Egypt, but was buried by his son Joseph in Canaan, the promised land (Ge 46; 50).

James—1. one of the twelve apostles; the brother of John (Mt 4:21-22). He was present at the transfiguration (Mt 17:1-13); he was later killed by Herod (Ac 12:2); 2. one of the twelve apostles; the son of Alphaeus (Mt 10:3); 3. the brother of Jesus (Mk 6:30); he waited with the believers for the promised Holy Spirit after Christ's ascension (Ac 2:1-3); became a leader in the church in Jerusalem (Ac 12:17; 15; 21:18; Gal 2:9); author of the epistle of James (Jas 1:1).

Japheth—one of the sons of Noah (Ge 5:32); he was blessed because he covered his father's nakedness (Ge 9:18-28).

jealous—1. afraid of losing someone's love or affection; 2. angry or unhappy because of what someone else has; 3. careful to guard or keep what one has.

Joel 2:18 the LORD will be *j* for his land
2Co 11:2 I am *j* for you with a godly jealousy

jealousy—
Gal 5:20 hatred, discord, *j*, fits of rage

Jeremiah—a prophet called by God (Jer 1) to prophesy to Judah (Jer 1:1-3). His life was in danger because of what he prophesied (Jer 11:18-23:26), and he was subsequently put in stocks (Jer 20:1-2), imprisoned (Jer 37), and thrown in a cistern (Jer 38). He was forced to flee to Egypt from the Babylonians (Jer 43). He is often referred to as the prophet of gloom, because he prophesied about the destruction of Judah.

Jeroboam—an official in Solomon's court; he rebelled and became the first king of Israel (the northern ten tribes) (1Ki 11:26-40; 12:1-20).

Jerusalem—the political and religious center of Judah.

2Ki 23:27 and I will reject *J*, the city I chose
Ne 2:17 *Come, let us rebuild the* wall of *J*
Ps 137:5 If I forget you, O *J*
Jn 4:20 where we must worship is in *J*."
Rev 21:2 I saw the Holy City, the new *J*

Jeshua—see Joshua (2).

Jew—an Israelite; one of the chosen people of God; a descendant of Abraham through Jacob.

Mt 2:2 who has been born king of the *J* ?
Ro 3:29 Is God the God of *J* only?
Gal 3:28 There is neither *J* nor Greek

Jezebel—the Sidonian wife of King Ahab (1Ki 16:31). She promoted Baal worship in Israel (1Ki 16:32-33); had many prophets of God killed (1Ki 18:4,13); and opposed the prophet Elijah (1Ki 19:1-2). Elijah prophesied her death (1Ki 21:17-24).

Joash—the boy-king of Judah; he repaired the temple (2Ki 12).

Job—a wealthy man from the land of Uz who feared God (Job 1:1-5). His righteousness was tested by disaster (Job 1:6-22) and personal affliction (Job 2), but, in the end, God restored wealth and honor to him (Job 42).

John—1. John the Baptist (Mk 1:2-8); the son of Zechariah and Elizabeth (Lk 1). He preached in the desert, preparing the people for Jesus (Mt 3:11-12); baptized Jesus in the Jordan River (Mt 3:13-17); was arrested (Mk 1:14) and executed by Herod (Mk 6:14-29); 2. one of the twelve apostles; brother of the apostle James (Lk 5:1-10). He was present at Jesus' transfiguration (Lk 9:28-36); became one of the leaders of the church at Jerusalem (Ac 4:1-3); wrote the Gospel of John, the letters of John (2Jn 1; 3Jn 1) and the book of Revelation (Rev 1:1; 22:8).

John, Mark (see Mark, John).

Jonah—a prophet in the days of Jeroboam II of Israel (2Ki 14:25). He was called to preach to Nineveh but instead fled to Tarshish (Jnh 1:1-3). While at sea a great storm arose because of his disobedience; he was thrown into the sea and was swallowed by a large fish (Jnh 1:4-17). He then repented and went to Nineveh and preached, telling the people to repent (Jnh 3).

Jonathan—a son of King Saul (1Sa 13:16). He had a special friendship with David (1Sa 18:1-4); 19-20; 23:16-18). When he was killed

(1Sa 31) David mourned greatly for him **Jordan**—a river in Palestine that flows between the Sea of Galilee and the Dead Sea.

Jos 4:22 Israel crossed the *J* on dry ground."
Mt 3:6 baptized by him in the *J* River.

Joseph—1. the son of Jacob and Rachel (Ge 30:24). He was favored by his father, but hated by his brothers (Ge 37:3-4). He was sold into slavery by his brothers (Ge 37:12-36), taken to Egypt and there served Potiphar *until put in prison* on a false charge (Ge 39). While in prison he interpreted the dreams of Pharaoh's servants (Ge 40), and then interpreted Pharaoh's dreams (Ge 41:4-40). For this, he was given a high position under Pharaoh (Ge 41:41-57). During a famine his brothers came to Egypt to buy grain, and so Joseph was reunited with his aged father and with his brothers (Ge 42-47); 2. the husband of Mary and childhood father of Jesus (Mt 1:16-24; 2:13-19); 3. a disciple of Jesus from Arimathea; he gave his tomb for Jesus' burial

(Mt 27:57-61); 4. the original name of Barnabas (Ac 4:36).

Joshua—1. the son of Nun (Nu 13:8); Moses' aide on Mount Sinai, when God revealed how Israel was to live as his chosen people (Ex 24:13); spied out the land of Canaan (Nu 13); and he and Caleb, though members of the generation of Israelites who had showed a lack of faith forty years earlier, were allowed to enter the promised land (Nu 14:6,30). As the successor of Moses (Dt 31:1-18), he led the Israelites across the Jordan River into Canaan (Jos 3-4); was the commander in the conquest of Jericho (Jos 6), Ai (Jos 7-8), and a large part of Canaan (Jos 10-12); oversaw the dividing up of the promised land among the twelve tribes of Israel (Jos 13-22); 2. the high priest in Israel during the rebuilding of both the temple (Hag 1-2) and the altar (Ezr 3:2,8); also called Jeshua.

Judah—1. Jacob's fourth son; 2. the tribe of Israel whose members were descendants of Judah; 3. a name for the southern kingdom after Judah and Benjamin separated from the northern ten tribes.

Ge 29:35 So she named him *J*.
Jer 13:19 All *J* will be carried into exile.
Zec 10:4 From *J* will come the cornerstone

Judaism—the teachings of the Jewish religion.

Judas—1. one of the twelve apostles (Lk 6:16; Ac 1:13); was probably also called Thaddaeus (Mt 10:3); 2. one of the brothers of Jesus (Mt 13:55); author of the last letter in the New Testament (Jude 1); 3. one of the twelve apostles, also called Iscariot; he betrayed Jesus (Mk 3:19; 14:10-50) and then hung himself (Mt 27:3-5).

judge—to decide if something is good or bad; to condemn.

Ps 9:8 He will *j* the world in righteousness
Mt 7:1 Do not *j*, or you too will be judged.
2Ti 4:1 who will *j* the living and the dead.

judgment—1. a decision or opinion; 2. a decision of guilt or innocence made by a judge in a court of law; punishment decided on by a court; 3. a decision from God, especially the final judgment when God will reward those who believe in him and condemn all others to hell.

Dt 1:17 of any man, for *j* belongs to God.
Ps 119:66 Teach me knowledge and good *j*
Isa 66:16 the Lord will execute *j*
Mt 5:21 who murders will be subject to *j*.
Mt 12:36 have to give account on the day of *j*
Jn 5:22 but has entrusted all *j* to the Son
Ro 14:10 stand before God's *j* seat.
2Co 5:10 appear before the *j* seat of Christ

jurisdiction—one's power and right to rule.

justice—fairness.

Isa 30:18 For the LORD is a God of *j*.
Isa 61:8 "For I, the LORD, love *j*
Zec 7:9 'Administer true *j*; show mercy
Lk 11:42 you neglect *j* and the love of God.

justification—God's action in treating us as if we had never sinned.

Ro 4:25 and was raised to life for our *j*.
Ro 5:18 of righteousness was *j* that brings

justify—to erase someone's sins; to declare righteous.

Ac 13:39 him everyone who believes is *j*
Ro 3:24 and are *j* freely by his grace
Ro 5:1 since we have been *j* through faith
Gal 3:24 to Christ that we might be *j* by faith

kingdom—

Ex 19:6 you will be for me a *k* of priests
Mt 6:33 But seek first his *k* and his
Mt 16:19 the keys of the *k* of heaven
Jn 18:36 "My *k* is not of this world.
1Co 15:24 hand over the *k* to God the Father
Rev 11:15 of the world has become the *k*

kingdom of heaven (also called, kingdom of God)—God's rule in the lives of his chosen people and in his creation. Anyone who is born again by believing in Jesus enters this kingdom.

Mt 3:2 "Repent, for the *k* of heaven is near,"
Mt 5:3 for theirs is the *k* of heaven.

kinsman-redeemer—a close male relative who had the right to marry a widow and buy ("redeem") her husband's property.

Ruth 3:9 over me, since you are a *k*."

Laban—the brother of Rebekah (Ge 24:29-51) and father of Rachel and Leah (Ge 29-31).

lamb—

Isa 53:7 he was led like a *l* to the slaughter
1Co 5:7 our Passover *l*, has been sacrificed.
Rev 5:6 Then I saw a *L*, looking

Lamb of God—a name for Jesus that reminds us that he is like the lambs offered for sacrifice in the Old Testament.

Jn 1:29 *L* of God, who takes away the sin

lament—a cry of grief. (Also, lamentation)

law—1. God's rules, which help his people know what is right and wrong. The Ten Commandments are part of God's law; 2. Law, the first five books of the Bible, written by Moses.

Ne 8:8 from the Book of the *L* of God
Ps 1:2 and on his *l* he meditates day
Ps 19:7 the *l* of the LORD is perfect
Ps 119:97 Oh, how I love your *l* !
Mt 22:40 All the *L* and the Prophets hang
Ro 8:3 For what the *l* was powerless to do
Ro 13:10 love is the fulfillment of the *l*
Gal 3:24 So the *l* was put in charge to lead us

Lazarus—1. the poor man in one of Jesus' parables (Lk 16:19-31); 2. the brother of Mary and Martha; Jesus raised him from the dead (Jn 11:1-12:19).

Leah—the wife of Jacob; she had six sons and one daughter (Ge 29:16-30:21).

legion—1. a group of 6,000 soldiers in the Roman army; 2. any very large group of people or things.

leprosy—a word used in the Bible for many different skin diseases and infections.

Levite—a member of the tribe of Levi. The Levites took care of the temple. Only Levites could become priests, but not all Levites were priests.
Nu 1:53 The *L* are to be responsible

lewd—indecent; wicked.

life—
physical life
Ge 2:7 into his nostrils the breath of *l*
Ps 23:6 all the days of my *l*
Jer 10:23 that a man's *l* is not his own
Mk 10:45 to give his *l* as a ransom for many."
Jn 15:13 lay down his *l* for his friends.
Eph 4:1 I urge you to live a *l* worthy
Col 1:10 order that you may live a *l* worthy
spiritual life
Mt 6:25 Is not *l* more important than food
Mt 10:39 Whoever finds his *l* will lose it
Jn 1:4 In him was *l*, and that *l* was
Jn 3:15 believes in him may have eternal *l*.
Jn 3:36 believes in the Son has eternal *l*
Jn 11:25 "I am the resurrection and the *l*.
Jn 14:6 am the way and the truth and the *l*.
Jn 20:31 that by believing you may have *l*
Ro 6:13 have been brought from death to *l*
Ro 6:23 but the gift of God is eternal *l*
1Jn 3:14 we have passed from death to *l*

light—
Ge 1:3 "Let there be *l*," and there was *l*
2Sa 22:29 LORD turns my darkness into *l*.
Ps 27:1 LORD is my *l* and my salvation
Ps 119:105 and a *l* for my path.
Isa 9:2 have seen a great *l*
Mt 5:16 let your *l* shine before men
Jn 8:12 he said, "I am the *l* of the world.
2Co 4:6 made his *l* shine in our hearts
1Jn 1:5 God is *l*; in him there is no

live—
Ex 20:12 so that you may *l* long
Ro 1:17 "The righteous will *l* by faith."
2Co 5:7 We *l* by faith, not by sight.
Php 1:21 to *l* is Christ and to die is gain.

locusts—a type of grasshopper. When they would settle in a grain field, orchard or other cultivated area in Bible times, they could devastate the crop.

Lord—
Mt 3:3 'Prepare the way for the *L*
Mt 22:37 " 'Love the *L* your God
Lk 2:9 glory of the *L* shone around them
Ac 16:31 replied, "Believe in the *L* Jesus
Ro 10:13 on the name of the *L* will be saved
Php 2:11 confess that Jesus Christ is *L*
Heb 13:6 *L* is my helper
2Pe 1:16 and coming of our *L* Jesus Christ
Rev 17:14 he is *L* of lords and King of kings
Rev 22:20 Come, *L* Jesus

LORD (Yahweh)—
Ge 2:4 When the *L* God made the earth
Ex 20:2 "I am the *L* your God, who
Ps 23:1 The *L* is my shepherd, I shall lack
Ps 103:1 Praise the *L*, O my soul
Pr 1:7 The fear of the *L* is the beginning
Isa 6:3 Holy, holy, holy is the *L* Almighty
Isa 55:6 Seek the *L* while he may be found

Lot—the nephew of Abraham (Ge 12:5). He chose to live in Sodom (Ge 13). At one point Abraham rescued him from four kings (Ge 14), and later he pleaded with God for Lot's life when God was about to destroy Sodom (Ge 19:1-29).

lot—one of the ways used in Bible times to find out God's will about a matter. It is something like drawing straws.
Mt 27:35 divided up his clothes by casting *l*.
Ac 1:26 Then they drew *l*, and the *l* fell

love (*v.*; *n.*)—
Ex 20:6 showing *l* to thousands who *l* me
Ps 23:6 Surely goodness and *l* will follow
Ps 136:1-26 His *l* endures forever.
Isa 61:8 "For I, the LORD, *l* justice
Mt 3:17 "This is my Son, whom I *l*
Mt 5:44 *L* your enemies and pray
Mt 19:19 and '*l* your neighbor as yourself.' "
Jn 13:34 I give you: *L* one another.
Jn 15:13 Greater *l* has no one than this
Ro 13:10 Therefore *l* is the fulfillment
Gal 5:22 But the fruit of the Spirit is *l*, joy
Eph 1:4 in *l* he predestined us
1Jn 3:10 anyone who does not *l* his brother
1Jn 3:16 This is how we know what *l* is
1Jn 4:7 for *l* comes from God.
1Jn 4:10 This is *l*; not that we loved God
1Jn 4:16 God is *l*.

Luke—a co-worker with Paul; he wrote the books of Luke and Acts (Col 4:14).

lust—a strong desire for something wrong.
Pr 6:25 Do not *l* in your heart
Ro 1:26 God gave them over to shameful *l*.

lute—a stringed musical instrument, with a pear-shaped body and neck. It is played in the same way as a guitar.

lyre—a small lap harp with three to twelve strings.

Magi—men of Arabia and Persia who studied the stars. People thought they had the power to tell the meaning of dreams.
Mt 2:1 *M* from the east came to Jerusalem

maimed—crippled; having lost a part of one's body, such as an arm or leg.

majestic—great and powerful.
Ex 15:6 was *m* in power.
Ps 8:1 how *m* is your name in all the earth!
Ps 111:3 Glorious and *m* are his deeds

malice—hatred; wishing harm on someone else.

manger—a feedbox for cows or other animals.
Lk 2:7 in strips of cloth and lying in a *m*."

manna—the special food God gave daily to the Israelites until they reached the promised land.
Ex 16:31 people of Israel called the bread *m*.
Jn 6:49 Your forefathers ate the *m*

Mark, John—the cousin of Barnabas (Col 4:10); a helper to Paul and Barnabas (Ac 13:5); later a co-worker with Barnabas (Ac 15:39) and then Paul (Phm 24); author of the second Gospel, according to early church tradition.

marriage—
Mt 22:30 neither marry nor be given in *m*
Ro 7:2 she is released from the law of *m*.
Heb 13:4 by all, and the *m* bed kept pure

Martha—the sister of Mary and Lazarus, the man whom Jesus raised from the dead (Jn 11; 12:2).

martyr—a person who suffers greatly or dies for what he or she believes in.

marvel—to be surprised; to be filled with wonder.

Mary—1. the mother of Jesus (Mt 1:16-25; Mk 3:31; Jn 19:25-27; Ac 1:14); 2. Mary Magdalene—a woman whom Jesus freed from demons (Lk 8:2); became a supporter of Jesus' ministry (Lk 8:1-3); was present at the cross (Mk 15:40); and was one of the women who came on Easter morning to the tomb (Mt 27:61), where she saw the angel (Lk 24:1-12) and the resurrected Jesus (Jn 20:1-18); 3. the sister of Martha and Lazarus, the man whom Jesus raised from the dead (Jn 11); she washed Jesus' feet with expensive perfume (Jn 12:1-8).

Matthew—a tax collector who became one of the twelve apostles (Mt 9:9-13); also called Levi (Mk 2:14-17).

mediator—one who makes peace between two people or two groups who are displeased and/or angry with each other. Jesus is the mediator between us and God.
1Ti 2:5 and one *m* between God and men
Heb 9:15 For this reason Christ is the *m*

meditate—to think seriously and carefully.
Ps 1:2 and on his law he *m* day and night.
Ps 119:15 I *m* on your precepts

medium—a person who can supposedly talk with the spirits of people who have died.

meek—patient; mild; gentle.
Mt 5:5 Blessed are the *m*

mercy—kindness and forgiveness, especially when given to a person who doesn't deserve it.
Mic 6:8 To act justly and to love *m*
Ro 9:15 "I will have *m* on whom I have *m*
1Pe 1:3 In his great *m* he has given us new

Messiah—the "Anointed One"; Christ; the one the Jews expected to come and be their king.
Jn 1:41 "We have found the *M*" (that is

Methuselah—a man in early Bible times who lived 969 years (Ge 5:27).

midwife—a woman who helped with the birth of a baby.

millstone—one of a pair of stones used to crush grain for flour.
Lk 17:2 sea with a *m* tied around his neck

minister—(*v.*) to serve; to give care or attention to; (*n.*) one who serves; one who gives care or attention to.
1Sa 3:1 The boy Samuel *m*
2Co 3:6 as *m* of a new covenant
1Ti 4:6 you will be a good *m*

miracle—an unusual happening, one that goes against the normal laws of nature. Miracles are done by the power of God.
Ps 77:14 You are the God who performs *m*
Jn 14:11 the evidence of the *m* themselves.
Ac 2:22 accredited by God to you by *m*
Heb 2:4 it by signs, wonders and various *m*

Miriam—the sister of Moses and Aaron (Nu 26:59); led the Israelites in praising God in dance and song after he had parted the waters of the Red Sea (Ex 15:20-21); later temporarily struck with leprosy because she criticized Moses (Nu 12).

money—
Ecc 5:10 Whoever loves *m* never has *m*
Mt 6:24 You cannot serve both God and *M*.
1Co 16:2 set aside a sum of *m* in keeping
1Ti 6:10 For the love of *m* is a root

mortal—human; able to die.
1Co 15:53 and the *m* with immortality.

Moses—the leader of Israel from the flight out of Egypt to their arrival outside the promised land. As a baby, his mother and sister placed him in a basket in the Nile River to save his life; he was discovered here by Pharaoh's daughter (Ex 2:1-10), who raised him at the royal court. After killing an Egyptian he fled to Midian (Ex 2:11-15), where he was called by the Lord to deliver Israel (Ex 3-4). Pharaoh refused to listen to God's warnings (Ex 5), and God punished him and his people with ten plagues (Ex 7-11). Moses instructed the people in their initial observance of the Passover and led them in the exodus out of Egypt, culminating in their passing through the Red Sea (Ex 12-14). He received the law of God at Sinai (Ex 19-23) and gave it to the people of Israel. He supervised the building of the tabernacle (Ex 36-40), set apart Aaron and priests to lead the Israelites in worshiping God (Ex 8-9), and, under his supervision, twelve spies were sent into Canaan (Nu 13). When ten of the spies returned with a pessimistic report, the Israelites believed this account, thereby showing a lack of faith in

God. God in turn punished them with forty years of wandering outside the promised land (Nu 14). Moses was allowed to view the land of Canaan from the top of Mount Nebo, but died without entering it (Nu 20:1-13; Dt 34:5-12).

muster—to gather together, especially to gather soldiers for war.

mute—unable to speak.

myrrh—the sweet-smelling sap of the myrrh bush. It was used to make the sacred anointing oil.
Mt 2:11 of gold and of incense and of *m*.

Naomi—the mother-in-law of Ruth (Ru 1); she advised Ruth to seek marriage with Boaz (Ru 2-4).

nard—a pleasant-smelling oil from the spikenard, a plant that grew in India. Since this oil had to be brought from India to Israel, it was very expensive.

Nathanael—one of the twelve apostles (Jn 1:45-49); was probably also called Bartholomew (Mt 10:3).

Nazarene—1. a person who lived in or came from the town of Nazareth in Galilee. 2. a member of an early sect of Jewish converts to Christianity who retained the Mosaic ritual.
Mk 16:6 looking for Jesus the *N*

Nazirite—a person who separated himself or herself by taking a vow to do special work for God. This included a promise not to cut one's hair and not to drink wine.
Jdg 13:5 because the boy is to be a *N*

Nehemiah—the Jewish "cupbearer" of King Artaxerxes of Persia (Ne 2:1); a trusted and highly placed official in the court of Artaxerxes; temporarily appointed governor of Judah; while in Jerusalem rebuilt the walls of the city (Ne 2-6) and with Ezra reestablished the worship of God there after the Babylonian exile (Ne 8).

Nicodemus—a Pharisee who visited Jesus at night (Jn 3) and learned about being born again. With Joseph of Arimathea, he prepared Jesus' body for burial (Jn 19:38-42).

Noah—"a righteous man" in early Bible times; he built an ark, as God commanded him (Ge 6-8). God made a covenant with him never again to cover the entire earth with a flood (Ge 9).

nullify—to make of *no value; to make unimportant.*

oath—a promise in which one asks God to witness that something is true.

obey—to do as asked; to yield to someone's commands or wishes.
Dt 6:3 careful to *o* so that it may go well
Dt 13:4 Keep his commands and *o* him
1Sa 15:22 To *o* is better than sacrifice
Jn 14:23 loves me, he will *o* my teaching.
Ac 5:29 "We must *o* God rather than men!
Eph 6:1 *o* your parents in the Lord

offend—to make someone angry by what you do.

offering—1. something given to God as an act of worship; 2. the killing of an animal to make the relationship between God and man right again. In the Old Testament, animals and grains were regularly used as offerings, in an attempt to bring the people closer to God.
Ge 22:8 provide the lamb for the burnt *o*
Isa 53:10 the LORD makes his life a guilt *o*
Mk 12:33 is more important than all burnt *o*
Eph 5:2 as a fragrant *o* and sacrifice to God.

offshoot—a branch off the main stem of a tree or plant.

offspring—children.
Ge 3:15 and between your *o* and hers
Ge 12:7 "To your *o* I will give this land."

omen—an event or sign believed to foretell the future.

oppress—to control people unfairly and cruelly by the use of one's power.
Isa 53:7 He was *o* and afflicted
Zec 7:10 Do not *o* the widow

oracle—1. a saying or answer; 2. the word of the Lord.

ordain—1. to set apart for a specific office or duty; 2. to order or command.

ordinance—1. an official law; 2. a law made or commanded by God.

overseer—a person who watches over and takes care of others. *Overseer* was one of the terms used for leaders in the early church.
Ac 20:28 the Holy Spirit has made you *o*.
1Ti 3:2 Now the *o* must be above reproach

pagan—a person who does not worship God, especially someone who worships idols.
1Pe 2:12 such good lives among the *p* that

papyrus—1. a large water plant, similar to the reed, that grows in marshes and lakes. Moses' mother put him in a basket made from papyrus (Ex 2:3); 2. a paper made from this plant.

parable—a story that tells a special lesson or truth. Jesus told many parables.

paradise—a perfect place; heaven.
Lk 23:43 today you will be with me in *p*."

paralytic—a person who is unable to move certain parts of his or her body.
Mk 2:3 bringing to him a *p*, carried by four

parents—
Pr 17:6 and *p* are the pride of their children.
Eph 6:1 Children, obey your *p* in the Lord
Col 3:20 obey your *p* in everything

Passover—an annual Jewish holiday that yet today reminds the Jewish people of how God

freed them from slavery in Egypt. At the Passover feast, the Jews eat bread made without yeast (unleavened bread), bitter herbs and lamb. With the unleavened bread they remember that they left Egypt hastily. There was no time to wait for yeast bread to rise. Bitter herbs remind them of their suffering in Egypt. The lamb reminds them of the lamb they killed at the first Passover and how they put its blood on their doorframes. The Lord "passed over" the homes so marked, but he killed all the other firstborn in Egypt.
Ex 12:11 Eat it in haste; it is the LORD's *P*.

Passover Lamb—the lamb killed on the Passover as a sacrifice. Jesus is our Passover Lamb. He was sacrificed for our deliverance from sin, in the same way a lamb was sacrificed to show deliverance from Egypt.
1Co 5:7 our *P* lamb, has been sacrificed.

patience—
Gal 5:22 joy, peace, *p*, kindness, goodness

patient—able to put up with problems or pain without complaining or becoming angry.
Ro 12:12 Be joyful in hope, *p* in affliction
1Co 13:4 Love is *p*, love is kind.

patriarch—the father and ruler of a family; the head of a tribe.

Paul—a Pharisee from Tarsus (Ac 9:11); named Saul at birth (Ac 13:9). Jesus appeared to him on the road to Damascus, and in this way God turned one of the fiercest persecutors of the Christian church into one of its mightiest servants (Ac 9:4-9; 26:12-18). Paul became an apostle (Gal 1), and preached the Good News to the Gentiles. His first missionary journey was to Cyprus and Galatia (Ac 13-14); his second journey, with Silas, took him to Macedonia (Ac 16:6-10). After his return to Jerusalem, he was arrested (Ac 21), but continued to preach (Ac 23:1-11). He was then transferred to Caesarea (Ac 23:12-35), where he was tried before Felix (Ac 24). After being imprisoned for two years Paul was tried further, first before Festus and then before King Agrippa (Ac 25; 26). Despite shipwreck on the voyage to Rome (Ac 27), he arrived safely and was put under house arrest (Ac 28). It seems evident from Paul's writings that he was released from this first Roman imprisonment and that he ministered further to the growing Christian church. He died, perhaps beheaded, in Rome. Paul's writings make up a significant portion of the New Testament, and range from intricate theology to passionate letters to struggling churches.

peace—freedom from disturbance; calm.
Isa 9:6 Everlasting Father, Prince of *P*
Lk 2:14 on earth *p* to men on whom his
Jn 14:27 *P* I leave with you; my *p*
Ro 5:1 we have *p* with God
Gal 5:22 joy, *p*, patience, kindness
1Pe 3:11 he must seek *p* and pursue it.

Pentecost—a Jewish feast celebrated fifty days after the Passover. Today the Christian church celebrates Pentecost because it was the day the Holy Spirit came to dwell with Christ's followers.
Ac 2:1-4

people—
Jer 24:7 They will be my *p*
Ac 15:14 from the Gentiles a *p*
2Co 6:16 and they will be my *p*."
1Pe 2:9 you are a chosen *p*

perishable—able to spoil; able to be destroyed.
1Co 15:42 the body that is sown is *p*

perjurer—a person who lies under oath.

persecute—to continually treat someone cruelly and unfairly, even though that person has done nothing wrong. The early Christians were persecuted for believing in Jesus as the Son of God.
Jn 15:20 they *p* me, they will *p* you
Ro 12:14 Bless those who *p* you; bless

persecution—
Ro 8:35 or hardship or *p* or famine

perseverance—
Ro 5:3 we know that suffering produces *p*
Ro 5:4 *p*, character; and character, hope.
Heb 12:1 run with *p* the race marked out

persevere—to refuse to give up; to keep on trying; to continue in one's actions or beliefs in spite of problems.
Heb 10:36 You need to *p* so that

pervert—to use wrongly; to turn from what is right.

pestilence—a plague; a disease that spreads quickly and kills many people.

Peter—one of the twelve apostles; the brother of Andrew, also called Simon (Lk 6:14) and Cephas (Jn 1:42). Although Jesus predicted that Peter would deny him (Mk 14:27-31), and though he did deny Jesus three times (Mk 14:66-72), after his resurrection Jesus commissioned Peter to shepherd his flock (Jn 21:15-23). At Pentecost he becomes bold and preaches a sermon (Ac 2), and he continues to heal (Ac 3:1-10) and preach (Ac 3:11-26), even though challenged by the Sanhedrin (Ac 4:1-22). Later God speaks to him in a vision and Peter goes to the Gentile Cornelius to tell him about Jesus (Ac 10).

Pharisees—a group of Jews who obeyed very strictly both God's laws and all their own rules about God's laws.
Mt 5:20 surpasses that of the *P*

Philip—1. one of the twelve apostles (Mt 10:3); 2. a deacon (Ac 6:1-7) and evangelist in Samaria; he witnessed to an Ethiopian (Ac 8:4-40).

phylactery—a small leather box containing verses from the Old Testament; male Jews

wore these boxes on their foreheads and left arms when they prayed.
Mt 23:5 They make their *p* wide

piety—love and reverence for God; devotion to God.

Pilate—the governor of Judea who questioned Jesus (Lk 22:66-23:25) and then sent him to Herod (Lk 23:6-12). Pilate finally consented to Jesus' crucifixion when the crowds chose Barabbas rather than Jesus to be released (Lk 23:13-25).

plague—1. a disease that kills many people, such as the plague of boils; 2. an event that causes much suffering or loss, especially a trouble in which there is a great number of offending agents, such as the plague of locusts.

plowshare—the pointed part of the plow; it cuts into the soil to make rows.
Isa 2:4 They will beat their swords into *p*

plunder—1. (*v.*) to loot or rob during a war; 2. (*n.*) property taken by plundering.

pomegranate—a reddish fruit about the size of an orange. It has many seeds and a juicy pulp.

poor—
Dt 15:4 there should be no *p* among you
Ps 82:3 maintain the rights of the *p*
Pr 14:31 oppresses the *p* shows contempt
Isa 61:1 me to preach good news to the *p*.
Mt 5:3 "Blessed are the *p* in spirit
Mt 26:11 the *p* you will always have
1Co 13:3 If I give all I possess to the *p*
2Co 8:9 yet for your sakes he became *p*

praise—(*v.*) to glorify; to say good things about someone or something; (*n.*) approval; worship.
Ex 15:2 He is my God, and I will *p* him
Ps 119:175 Let me live that I may *p* you
Eph 1:12 might be for the *p* of his glory

pray—
2Ch 7:14 will humble themselves and *p*
Mt 6:5 "But when you *p*, do not be like
Ro 8:26 do not know what we ought to *p*.
1Th 5:16,17 Be joyful always; *p* continually

precept—command; law; rule.
Ps 19:8 the *p* of the LORD are right
Ps 119:69 I keep your *p* with all my heart.

predestine—to decide or decree ahead of time.
Ro 8:30 And those he *p*, he also called
Eph 1:5 In love he *p* us to be adopted

prevail—to triumph or succeed.

pride—
Pr 8:13 I hate *p* and arrogance
Pr 16:18 *P* goes before destruction
Gal 6:4 Then he can take *p* in himself

priest—a Levite who offered sacrifices and prayers to God for the people.
Heb 4:14 have a great high *p* who has gone
Heb 7:26 Such a high *p* meets our need

proclaim—to announce or declare.
1Ch 16:23 *p* his salvation day after day
Ps 19:1 the skies *p* the work of his hands.
1Co 11:26 you *p* the Lord's death

profane—to make a holy thing impure by treating it with disrespect or irreverence.
Lev 22:32 Do no *p* my holy name.

prone—naturally inclined; having a tendency toward or liking for.

prophecy—a message from God that a prophet brings to the people.
1Co 13:8 where there are *p*, they will cease
2Pe 1:20 you must understand that no *p*

prophesy—to give the message of God to the people.
Joel 2:28 Your sons and daughters will *p*
1Co 14:39 my brothers, be eager to *p*

prophet—a person who receives messages from God to tell to his people. A prophet is called by God to speak for him.
Dt 18:18 up for them a *p* like you
Lk 24:25 believe all that the *p* have spoken!
Ac 10:43 All the *p* testify about him that
2Pe 1:19 word of the *p* made more certain

prostitute—a person who lets someone use his or her body for sexual relations, in exchange for money.
Lk 15:30 property with *p* comes home
1Co 6:9 male *p* nor homosexual offenders

prostrate—lying facedown on the ground.

provoke—to make angry; to cause trouble.

psalm—poetry written to praise God.
Eph 5:19 Speak to one another with *p*

purify—to make pure or clean.
1Jn 1:7 of Jesus, his Son, *p* us from all sin.
1Jn 1:9 and *p* us from all unrighteousness

Purim—an annual Jewish holiday for celebrating Queen Esther's rescue of the Jews when Haman plotted to destroy them.

Rachel—the daughter of Laban (Ge 29:16); she became Jacob's wife (Ge 29:28) and bore him two sons, Joseph and Benjamin (Ge 30:22-24; 35:16-24).

ransom—the price paid to get back a person who is held as a slave. Because we were slaves of sin, a ransom had to be paid for us. That ransom was the death of a sinless person. Jesus, the perfect one, paid our ransom when he died on the cross for us.
Mt 20:28 and to give his life as a *r* for many."
Heb 9:15 as a *r* to set them free

reap—1. to cut down grain at harvest time; to gather a crop together; 2. to get as a result or reward.
Gal 6:7 A man *r* what he sows.

Rebekah—the sister of Laban and Isaac's wife (Ge 24); the mother of Esau and Jacob (Ge 25:19-26). With her encouragement Jacob tricked his father into giving him the blessing that belonged to Esau (Ge 27:1-17).

rebel—1. (*v.*) to disobey and turn against

those in authority; 2. (*n.*) a person who disobeys and flaunts authority.

rebuke—to scold sharply.
2Ti 4:2 correct, *r* and encourage
Rev 3:19 Those whom I love I *r*

recompense—to pay or repay; to make up for.

reconcile—to return to friendship after a quarrel.
Mt 5:24 First go and be *r* to your brother
Ro 5:10 we were *r* to him through death

reconciliation—
Ro 5:11 whom we have now received *r*.
2Co 5:18 and gave us the ministry of *r*
2Co 5:19 committed to us the message of *r*

redeem—1. to free from evil by paying a price (Gal 3:13); 2. to buy back.
Ex 6:6 slaves to them and will *r* you
Gal 3:13 Christ *r* us from the curse

redemption—the act of being bought back.
Eph 1:7 In him we have *r* through his blood
Col 1:14 in whom we have *r*, the forgiveness

Rehoboam—the son of Solomon; he became king after his father's death (1Ki 11:43). Because of his harsh treatment of the people, Israel was divided into two kingdoms (1Ki 12:1-24; 14:21-31).

rejoice—to express joy or gladness.
Ps 118:24 let us *r* and be glad in it.
Lk 1:47 and my spirit *r* in God my Savior
Php 4:4 *R* in the Lord always.

repent—to turn away from sin; to be sorry for what you have done and to promise not to do it again.
Mt 4:17 "*R*, for the kingdom of heaven is
Lk 13:3 unless you *r*, you too will all perish.
Ac 2:38 Peter replied, "*R* and be baptized,

repentance—
Lk 3:8 Produce fruit in keeping with *r*.
2Co 7:10 Godly sorrow brings *r* that leads

reproach—1. (*v.*) to blame or accuse; 2. (*n.*) something for which one can be blamed or criticized; blame, criticism.

restore—to bring back; to return something to its former condition.
Ps 23:3 he *r* my soul.
Ps 51:12 *R* to me the joy of your salvation

resurrection—the act of coming back to life after being dead.
Jn 11:25 Jesus said to her, "I am the *r*
Ro 1:4 Son of God by his *r* from the dead
1Co 15:12 some of you say that there is no *r*

retribution—punishment for doing wrong.
Jer 51:56 For the LORD is a God of *r*

revelation—the act of making known or telling about.
Gal 1:12 I received it by *r* from Jesus Christ.
Rev 1:1 *r* of Jesus Christ, which God gave

revenge—to hurt or punish a person who has wronged you; to get back at someone who has hurt you.
Lev 19:18 "Do not seek *r* or bear a grudge
Ro 12:19 Do not take *r*, my friends

revere—to feel respect for.

reverence—a feeling of respect and honor.
Ps 5:7 in *r* will I bow down
Col 3:22 of heart and *r* for the Lord.

revile—to call someone a bad name; to scold in an insulting way.

reward (*v.*; *n.*)—
Ps 127:3 children a *r* from him.
Jer 17:10 to *r* a man according to his conduct
Mt 5:12 because great is your *r* in heaven
Mt 6:5 they have received their *r* in full.
Rev 22:12 I am coming soon! My *r* is with me

righteous—without sin; doing what is right.
Isa 64:6 and all our *r* acts are like filthy rags
Mt 13:49 and separate the wicked from the *r*
Ro 1:17 as it is written: "The *r* will live
Ro 3:10 "There is no one *r*, not even one
1Jn 3:7 does what is right is *r*, just as he is *r*.

righteousness—
Ge 15:6 and he credited it to him as *r*.
Ps 23:3 He guides me in paths of *r*
Mt 5:6 those who hunger and thirst for *r*
Mt 6:33 But seek first his kingdom and his *r*
Ro 4:3 and it was credited to him as *r*."
2Ti 3:16 correcting and training in *r*

Ruth—a Moabite widow who went with her mother-in-law Naomi to Bethlehem (Ru 1). There she gathered the gleanings from the field of Boaz (Ru 2), whom she later married (Ru 3-4:12). She was an ancestor of David (Ru 4:13-22) and of Jesus (Mt 1:5).

Sabbath—the seventh day of the week; the Jewish day of rest and worship. It extended from Friday sunset until Saturday sunset.
Ex 20:8 "remember the *S* day

sackcloth—a rough cloth, usually woven from goats' hair. Clothing made of sackcloth was worn as a sign of mourning for the dead or as a sign that a person was sorry for his or her sins.

sacred—holy; set apart for God in a special way.

sacrifice—(*v.*) to offer as a sacrifice, (*n.*) an offering given to God for the sins of the people. In the Old Testament God commanded the people to pay for their sins by sacrificing cattle, lambs, goats, doves or pigeons. The animals were killed, their blood splattered against the altar and their bodies burned on the altar. People who were very poor could bring flour to be burned on the altar. These sacrifices were pictures of Jesus' coming as a once-for-all sacrifice for sinners.

Ge 22:2 *S* him there as a burnt offering
Ex 12:27 "It is the Passover *s* to the LORD
1Sa 15:22 To obey is better than *s*
Ro 12:1 to offer your bodies as living *s*
Heb 9:28 so Christ was *s* once
1Jn 2:2 He is the atoning *s* for our sins

Sadducees—a group of Jewish leaders, many of them priests, who accepted only the written law of God. They opposed the Pharisees, who had many additional laws that had been passed down to them by their religious teachers. Unlike the Pharisees, the Sadducees did not believe in a resurrection of the dead, but they agreed with the Pharisees in their hatred of Jesus.

Mk 12:18 *S*, who say there is no resurrection

saints—Christians; people whom God has made holy. A saint can be either a Christian who is alive on earth or one who is already in heaven.

Ro 8:27 intercedes for the *s* in accordance
Eph 1:1 To the *s* in Ephesus,

salvation—deliverance from the guilt and power of sin. By his death and resurrection, Jesus brings salvation to people who believe in him.

Ps 27:1 The LORD is my light and my *s*
Lk 2:30 For my eyes have seen your *s*
Ac 4:12 *S* is found in no one else,
2Co 7:10 brings repentance that leads to *s*
Php 2:12 to work out your *s* with fear
Heb 2:3 escape if we ignore such a great *s*?

Samaritan—a person of late Old Testament or New Testament times who lived in or came from Samaria. The Samaritans were only partly Jewish, and they worshiped God differently than Jews in Israel. Jews from Judea and Galilee hated the Samaritans. They would go out of their way to travel around Samaria (Lk 10:30-37).

Samson—an Israelite judge whose birth was foretold by an angel (Jdg 13). He married a Philistine woman (Jdg 14) and later took vengeance on the Philistines for forcing his wife to tell the answer to the riddle with which he had challenged them (Jdg 15). He was again betrayed by a woman, Delilah, but in the end became obedient to God and was used by God to punish the Philistines (Jdg 16).

Samuel—*often called* the last of Israel's judges and the first of her prophets (see also Heb 11:32). His birth was earnestly prayed for by his mother Hannah (1Sa 1:10-18), and when he was old enough she brought him to the temple and he was dedicated to the Lord (1Sa 1:21-28). There he was raised by Eli (1Sa 2:11; 18-26) and was called to be a prophet (1Sa 3). He anointed Saul as king (1Sa 9-10), but later announced God's rejection of Saul (1Sa 15). He anointed David as king (1Sa 16) and protected him from Saul (1Sa 19:18-24).

sanctify—to make holy. Our sanctification begins when we become Christians. It is continued by the ongoing work of the Holy Spirit in our hearts.

Ro 15:16 to God, *s* by the Holy Spirit.
1Th 5:23 *s* you through and through.
2Th 2:13 through the *s* work of the Spirit

sanctuary—a place where God is worshiped; a holy place.

Sanhedrin—the ruling council of the Jews in Jesus' time. It was made up of seventy men, and the leader was the high priest. Even though the Romans had conquered Palestine and a Roman governor ruled the country, the Jews were allowed to judge many of their own matters. The Sanhedrin could decide whether someone was innocent or guilty of breaking a Jewish law, but it could not put anyone to death without the permission of the Roman governor.

Mk 14:55 and the whole *S* were looking for evidence

Sarah—the wife of Abraham and mother of Isaac; first called Sarai (Ge 11:29-31). God promised her that, though she had been barren throughout her life, she would give birth to a son in her old age (Ge 17:15-21; 18:10-15).

Satan—the devil; the leader of the fallen spirits; the most powerful enemy of God and humans.

Mk 4:15 *S* comes and takes away the word
2Co 11:14 for *S* himself masquerades
Rev 12:9 serpent called the devil or *S*

Saul—1. the first king of Israel (1Sa 9-10). He was anointed by Samuel but was later rejected by God because he failed to destroy all of the Amalekites (1Sa 15). When David killed Goliath (1Sa 17), Saul attempted to kill him (1Sa 18; 19). Although pursued by Saul, David spared the king's life twice (1Sa 24; 26). Saul was wounded by the Philistines in battle and took his own life (1Sa 31). 2. See Paul.

Savior—a name for Jesus that means he saves his people from sin.

Isa 43:11 and apart from me there is no *s*.
Lk 1:47 and my spirit rejoices in God my *S*
1Ti 4:10 who is the *S* of all men
1Jn 4:14 Son to be the *S* of the world

scabbard—the case that a knife, dagger or sword is carried in.

scepter—a rod or stick held by a king or queen as a sign of royal power and authority.

scorpion—a spider-like animal with a poisonous stinger at the end of its tail.

scribe—a person with the important task of copying letters, books and legal papers.

Scripture—all or part of the Bible. When the Bible uses this word it means the Old

Testament, since the New Testament had not yet been written. Today we call the Old and New Testaments the Bible or Scripture.
Jn 10:35 and the *S* cannot be broken
2Ti 3:16 All *S* is God-breathed
2Pe 1:20 that no prophecy of *S* came about

scroll—a book made of a long piece of leather or paper that was rolled around a stick at both ends.
Eze 3:1 eat what is before you, eat this *s*

seal—1. a tool with a design raised on it or cut into it; 2. the mark made by pressing this tool onto wax, paper or other soft material. A seal was used to close a letter or legal paper or to prove the authority of the paper.
2Co 1:22 set his *s* of ownership on us
Rev 5:2 "Who is worthy to break the *s*

sect—a group of people who hold one or more beliefs in common; especially, a small religious group that has separated from a larger group.

seer—a prophet; a person who, with God's help, can see what will happen in the future.
1Sa 9:9 of today used to be called a *s*.

self-control—the ability to control your own actions and feelings.
Gal 5:23 faithfulness, gentleness and *s*.
2Pe 1:6 and to knowledge, *s*; and to *s*

self-indulgence—doing whatever you feel like doing. Self-indulgence is the opposite of self-control.

sensual—appealing to the body's senses; caring too much for physical pleasures.

sexual immorality—using sex in ways God says are wrong.
1Co 6:13 body is not meant for *s* immorality
1Th 4:3 that you should avoid *s* immorality

shekel—a specific weight of silver, used as money.

Shem—one of the three sons of Noah (Ge 5:32). He, along with his brother Japheth, covered his father when he was naked (Ge 9:21-31). Abraham was one of his descendants (Ge 11:10-32).

shepherd—
Ps 23:1 LORD is my *s*, I shall lack nothing.
Jer 31:10 will watch over his flock like a *s*.'
Jn 10:11 The good *s* lays down his life
Ac 20:28 Be *s* of the church of God

sickle—a tool with a long, curved blade and a short handle, used for cutting grain.

signet—a ring with a design on it. The design was stamped in wax to seal a letter or legal paper. Signet rings were usually worn by people in authority.

Simon—1. see Peter; 2. one of the twelve apostles; also called the Zealot (Mt 10:4; Ac 1:13); 3. a sorcerer in Samaria who had great influence on the Samaritan people during the early days of the church; he was severely rebuked by Peter (Ac 8:9-24) for attempting to buy the power of the Holy Spirit.

sin—(*v.*) to break the law of God; (*n.*) the act of not doing what God wants.
Nu 32:23 be sure that your *s* will find you
1Ki 8:46 for there is no one who does not *s*
Ps 51:2 and cleanse me from my *s*.
Ps 119:11 that I might not *s* against you.
Jn 1:29 who takes away the *s* of the world!
Ro 3:23 for all have *s* and fall short
Ro 6:23 For the wages of *s* is death
2Co 5:21 God made him who had no *s* to be *s*
1Jn 3:6 No one who lives in him keeps on *s*

sinner—
Ps 1:1 or stand in the way of *s*
Ps 51:5 Surely I have been a *s* from birth
Mt 9:13 come to call the righteous, but *s*."
Lk 15:7 in heaven over one *s* who repents
Lk 18:13 'God, have mercy on me, a *s*.'
Ro 5:8 While we were still *s*, Christ died

sins—
Isa 1:18 "Though your *s* are like scarlet
Mt 1:21 he will save his people from their *s*."
Mt 18:15 "If your brother *s* against you
Lk 11:4 Forgive us our *s*
Ac 22:16 be baptized and wash your *s* away
Eph 2:1 dead in your transgressions and *s*
Heb 7:27 He sacrificed for their *s* once for all
1Pe 2:24 He himself bore our *s* in his body
1Jn 1:9 If we confess our *s*, he is faithful
Rev 1:5 has freed us from our *s* by his blood

slander—(*v.*) saying untrue things about another person in order to hurt him or her; (*n.*) false charges or misrepresentations about another person.
Lev 19:16 " 'Do not go about spreading *s*
Tit 3:2 to *s* no one, to be peaceable

Sodom and Gomorrah—the two cities destroyed by God because the people were so wicked.
Ge 19:24 rained down burning sulfur on *S*

Solomon—the son of David and Bathsheba (2Sa 12:24). He became king of Israel after David died (1Ki 1). He asked God for wisdom and was given it (1Ki 3), and he built the temple (1Ki 5-7) and dedicated it to God with prayer (1Ki 8). His many foreign wives turned his heart away from God (1Ki 11:1-13). Jeroboam, one of his officials, rebelled against him (1Ki 11:26-40).

son—
Pr 10:1 A wise *s* brings joy to his father
Joel 2:28 Your *s* and daughters will prophesy
Jn 12:36 so that you may become *s* of light."
Ro 8:14 by the Spirit of God are *s* of God
1Jn 4:9 only *S* into the world that we might

Son of Man—a name for Jesus. Jesus used

this name to show he was the Messiah prophesied about in Daniel 7:13.
Mt 20:18 and the *S* of Man will be betrayed
Mk 14:62 you will see the *S* of Man sitting
Lk 19:10 For the *S* of Man came to seek
Jn 3:14 so the *S* of Man must be lifted up

soothsayer—a person who could foretell the future.

sorcerer—a magician.

soul—the spiritual part of a person; the part of a person that does not die.
Dt 6:5 with all your *s* and with all your
Ps 23:3 he restores my *s*.
Mt 10:28 kill the body but cannot kill the *s*.
Mt 11:29 and you will find rest for your *s*.
Mt 16:26 yet forfeits his *s*? Or what can
Mt 22:37 with all your *s* and with all your

sovereign—having authority over everything.

sow—to plant seeds. In Jesus' time seeds were sown by scattering them by hand over the ground.
Job 4:8 and those who *s* trouble reap it
Gal 6:7 A man reaps what he *s*.

spirit—1. the part of a person that is not the body; the soul; 2. beings who do not have bodies; 3. another name for Holy Spirit.
1. spirit
Ps 31:5 Into your hands I commit my *s*
Eze 36:26 you a new heart and put a new *s*
Mt 5:3 saying: "Blessed are the poor in *s*
Mt 26:41 *s* is willing, but the body is weak."
2. spirit
1Jn 4:1 Dear friends, do not believe every *s*
3. Spirit
Ge 1:2 and the *S* of God was hovering
Ps 51:11 or take your Holy *S* from me.
Mt 1:18 to be with child through the Holy *S*.
Mt 3:11 will baptize you with the Holy *S*
Mt 3:16 he saw the *S* of God descending
Mt 28:19 and of the Son and of the Holy *S*
Jn 14:26 But the Counselor, the Holy *S*
Jn 20:22 and said, "Receive the Holy *S*.
Ac 1:5 will be baptized with the Holy *S*."
Ac 2:4 of them were filled with the Holy *S*
Ac 2:38 will receive the gift of the Holy *S*.
Ro 8:26 the *S* helps us in our weakness.
1Co 2:10 God has revealed it to us by his *S*.
1Co 6:19 body is a temple of the Holy *S*,
Gal 5:22 But the fruit of the *S* is love, joy,
Eph 5:18 Instead, be filled with the *S*.

squall—a sudden, strong wind often accompanied by rain or snow.

staff—a stick used to lean on; a rod used by a shepherd.
Ps 23:4 your rod and your *s*

stature—height; normal growth or development.
Lk 2:52 And Jesus grew in wisdom and *s*

stiff-necked—stubborn.

stone—to kill or to try to kill someone by throwing rocks or stones at him or her.

strength—
Ex 15:2 The LORD is my *s* and my song
Dt 6:5 all your soul and with all your *s*.
Ps 46:1 God is our refuge and *s*
Isa 40:31 will renew their *s*.
Php 4:13 through him who gives me *s*

subdue—to bring under control; to conquer.

submission—humbleness; obedience.
1Co 14:34 but must be in *s*, as the Law says.
1Ti 2:11 learn in quietness and full *s*.

submit—
Ro 13:1 Everyone must *s* himself
Eph 5:21 *S* to one another out of reverence
Col 3:18 Wives, *s* to your husbands
Jas 4:7 *S* yourselves, then, to God.

suffer—
Mk 8:31 the Son of Man must *s* many things
Lk 24:26 the Christ have to *s* these things
1Co 12:26 If one part *s*, every part *s* with it

suffering—
Isa 53:3 of sorrows, and familiar with *s*.
Ac 5:41 worthy of *s* disgrace for the Name.
Ro 8:17 share in his *s* in order that we may
2Ti 1:8 But join with me in *s* for the gospel

supplication—a humble prayer to God; pleading or begging.

sustain—to give support; to help; to comfort.
Ps 18:35 and your right hand *s* me;
Ps 146:9 and *s* the fatherless and the widow,

symbol—an object or action that stands for or suggests something else. The cross is a symbol of Jesus' death.

synagogue—the Jewish place of worship and religious teaching.
Lk 4:16 the Sabbath day he went into the *s*
Ac 17:2 custom was, Paul went into the *s*

tabernacle—the tent used by the Israelites for meeting with God; the place where God chose to show his presence. The tabernacle was made by God's command and according to his plans. It is described in detail in Exodus 26.
Ex 40:34 the glory of the LORD filled the *t*.

talent—a large amount of silver or gold, worth very much money.
Mt 25:15 to another one *t*, each according

teach—
Ex 33:13 *t* me your ways so I may know you
Ps 90:12 *T* us to number our days aright
Lk 11:1 said to him, "Lord, *t* us to pray
Jn 14:26 will *t* you all things and will remind

temperate—moderate; having self-control.

tempest—a violent storm.

temple—1. the place where the Jewish people worshiped and sacrificed in Jerusalem. The first temple was built by King Solomon as a house for God. 2. the human body.
1Ki 8:27 How much less this *t* I have built!
Ac 17:24 does not live in *t* built by hands.
1Co 6:19 you not know that your body is a *t*
2Co 6:16 For we are the *t* of the living God.

tempt—to try to get someone to do wrong.
Mt 4:1 into the desert to be *t* by the devil.
1Co 7:5 again so that Satan will not *t* you.

temptation—
Mt 6:13 And lead us not into *t*
1Co 10:13 No *t* has seized you except what is

testimony—a statement made by a witness to prove that something is true.
Lk 18:20 not give false *t*, honor your father

tetrarch—a ruler over one-fourth of a kingdom.

Thaddaeus—one of the twelve apostles (Mk 3:18); son of James and probably also known as Judas (Lk 6:16; Ac 1:13).

thanks—
1Ch 16:8 give *t* to the LORD, call
Ps 100:4 give *t* to him and praise his name.
1Co 15:57 *t* be to God! He gives us the victory
2Co 9:15 *T* be to God for his indescribable
1Th 5:18 give *t* in all circumstances

thanksgiving—
Ps 100:4 Enter his gates with *t*
Php 4:6 by prayer and petition, with *t*

Thomas—one of the twelve apostles (Lk 6:15; Ac 1:13); he doubted Jesus' resurrection but upon seeing Jesus believed (Jn 20:24-28).

threshing floor—the place where grain was trampled by oxen or beaten with a stick to separate it from the stalk.

Timothy—fellow-traveler and official representative of the apostle Paul. He and his mother and grandmother were led by Paul to see Christ as the fulfillment of the Old Testament law (2Ti 1:5). He joined Paul on his second missionary journey (Ac 16-20), and at one point in this journey Paul sent him to minister to the church at Corinth (1Co 4:17; 16:10). He was the leader of the church at Ephesus (1Ti 1:3) and a co-writer with Paul (1Th 1:1; 2Th 1:1; Phm 1).

tithe—the giving to God of one-tenth of what you earn.
Lev 27:30 " 'A *t* of everything from the land
Mal 3:8 the whole *t* into the storehouse

Titus—a Gentile co-worker with Paul (Gal 2:1-3; 2Ti 4:10). Paul sent him to Corinth to aid in solving some of the problems there (2Co 2:13; 7-8; 12:18).

tomb—a burial place. In Bible times, tombs often were either caves or were dug into stone cliffs.
Mt 27:65 make the *t* as secure as you know
Lk 24:2 the stone rolled away from the *t*

tongue—
Ps 39:1 and keep my *t* from sin
Ac 2:4 and began to speak in other *t*
Php 2:11 every *t* confess that Jesus Christ is
Jas 1:26 does not keep a tight rein on his *t*

tradition of the elders—the rules that the Jewish religious leaders gave to the people and which they in turn passed on to their children; laws added to the Old Testament by the Jewish leaders.
Mt 15:2 break the *t* of the elders?

trance—a condition of being partly awake and partly in a dream-like state.

transfigure—to change the appearance of; to make bright and glorious.
Mt 17:2 There he was *t* before them.

transgression—sin; disobeying the law of God.
Ps 32:1 whose *t* are forgiven,
Isa 53:5 But he was pierced for our *t*
Eph 2:1 you were dead in your *t* and sins

treaty—an agreement between two people or groups or nations.

trespass—sin; wrongdoing.
Ro 5:17 For if, by the *t* of the one man

true—
Ps 119:160 All your words are *t*
Jn 17:3 the only *t* God, and Jesus Christ
Ro 3:4 Let God be *t*, and every man a liar.
Php 4:8 whatever is *t*, whatever is noble

trust (*v.*); (*n.*)—
Ps 37:3 *T* in the LORD and do good
Pr 3:5 *T* in the LORD with all your heart
Isa 30:15 in quietness and *t* is your strength
Jn 14:1 *T* in God; *t* also in me.
1Co 4:2 been given a *t* must prove faithful.

truth—
Ps 51:6 Surely you desire *t*
Zec 8:16 are to do: Speak the *t* to each other
Jn 8:32 Then you will know the *t*
Jn 8:32 and the *t* will set you free."
Jn 14:6 I am the way and the *t* and the life.
Ro 1:25 They exchanged the *t* of God.
1Co 13:6 in evil but rejoices with the *t*.
Eph 4:15 Instead, speaking the *t* in love
Heb 10:26 received the knowledge of the *t*
1Jn 1:6 we lie and do not live by the *t*.
1Jn 1:8 deceive ourselves and the *t* is not

tunic—a long shirt worn by men in Bible times.
Lk 6:29 do not stop him from taking your *t*.

turban—a head-covering made by winding a cloth around the head.

unbelief—doubt.
Mk 9:24 help me overcome my *u*!

unbeliever—one who does not believe in Jesus.
2Co 6:14 Do not be yoked together with *u*.

unclean animals—animals the Israelites were not allowed to sacrifice or to eat.

unity—being one.
Ps 133:1 when brothers live together in *u*!
Col 3:14 them all together in perfect *u*.

unleavened bread—bread made without yeast. It is usually flat, like a pancake or cracker.
Ex 12:17 "Celebrate the Feast of *U* Bread

unrepentant—not sorry for one's sins.

upright—honest; doing what is right and good.

usury—very high and unfair interest charged on a loan.
Ne 5:10 But let the exacting of *u* stop!

vain—worthless; unsuccessful; foolish. "In vain" means without success or result.

vassal—1. a servant or slave; 2. someone who is under another person's protection. The vassal received land and protection from a lord. In return, he owed the lord his loyalty and obedience, part of his crops, and, in case of war, help in fighting.

vengeance—hurt or punishment done to another person who has done something wrong to you.
Isa 34:8 For the LORD has a day of *v*,

vile—disgusting, evil.

vindicate—to defend; to provide justice for; to set free.

violate—1. to rape; 2. to make something unholy; 3. to fail to obey.

virgin—a woman or girl who has never had sexual intercourse.
Isa 7:14 The *v* will be with child
Mt 1:23 "The *v* will be with child

vision—a dream from God.
Nu 12:6 I reveal myself to him in *v*
Joel 2:28 your young men will see *v*.
Ac 26:19 disobedient to the *v* from heaven.

vow—a solemn promise made before God or to God.
Jdg 11:30 Jephthah made a *v* to the LORD
Ps 116:14 I will fulfill my *v* to the LORD

wail—to cry loudly.

walk—
Ps *1:1 who does not w in the counsel*
Isa *2:5 let us w in the* light of the LORD.
Mic 6:8 and to *w* humbly with your God.
2Jn 6 his command is that you *w* in love.

wash—
Ps 51:7 *w* me and I will be whiter
Ac 22:16 be baptized and *w* your sins away

watch—
Jer 31:10 will *w* over his flock like a shepherd.'
Mt 26:41 "*W* and pray so that you will not fall

way—
2Sa 22:31 "As for God, his *w* is perfect
Ps 1:1 or stand in the *w* of sinners
Ps 37:5 Commit your *w* to the LORD
Isa 53:6 each of us has turned to his own *w*
Jn 14:6 "I am the *w* and the truth
2Co 12:31 will show you the most excellent *w*.

wicked—sinful.
Ps 1:1 walk in the counsel of the *w*
Isa 55:7 Let the *w* forsake his way

will (*v.*; *n.*)—
Ps 143:10 Teach me to do your *w*
Isa 53:10 Yet it was the LORD's *w*
Mt 6:10 your *w* be done
Mt 26:39 Yet not as I *w*, but as you *w*."
Ro 12:2 and approve what God's *w* is
Eph 5:17 understand what the Lord's *w* is.
1Jn 5:14 we ask anything according to his *w*
Rev 4:11 and by your *w* they were created

work—(*v.*; *n.*)—
Ex 23:12 "Six days do your *w*
Jn 9:4 we must do the *w* of him who sent
Php 2:12 continue to *w* out your salvation
2Ti 3:17 equipped for every good *w*.

world—
Mt 5:14 "You are the light of the *w*.
Mk 16:15 into all the *w* and preach the good
Jn 1:29 who takes away the sin of the *w*!
Jn 3:16 so loved the *w* that he gave his one
Jn 8:12 he said, "I am the light of the *w*.
1Jn 2:15 not love the *w* or anything in the *w*.

worldly—loving the things of the world more than the things of God.
Tit 2:12 to ungodliness and *w* passions

worship—(*v.*) to give praise, honor and respect to God; (*n.*) reverence given to God.
Ps 95:6 Come, let us bow down in *w*
Jn 4:24 and his worshipers must *w* in spirit

worthy—having value; honorable; deserving.
1Ch 16:25 For great is the LORD and most *w*
Eph 4:1 to live a life *w* of the calling you
Rev 5:2 "Who is *w* to break the seals

wrath—great anger; the strong anger of God.
Pr 15:1 A gentle answer turns away *w*
Ro 5:9 saved from God's *w* through him!

wretch—1. a very unhappy person; someone who has had many bad or difficult things happen to him or her; 2. an evil person.

yearn—to long for; to want very much.

yoke—1. (*v.*) to join together; 2. (*n.*) a wooden bar that goes over the necks of two animals, usually oxen. The yoke holds the animals together as they pull an object, such as a plow or a cart.
Mt 11:29 Take my *y* upon you and learn
2Co 6:14 Do not be *y* together

zeal—eagerness; strong desire.
Ro 12:11 Never be lacking in *z*

Zealot—a member of the Jewish group that wanted to fight against and overthrow the Roman government.

Zechariah—a prophet and priest who returned to Jerusalem from the Babylonian captivity; he encouraged the Jews to rebuild the temple (Ezr 5:1; 6:14; Zec 1:1).

Zerubbabel—a descendant of David (1Ch 3:19) and heir to the throne of Judah (1Ch 3:17-19); he led the return from the Babylonian captivity and was appointed governor of Judah by Cyrus, king of Persia (Ezr 1-3; Ne 7:7; Hag 1-2; Zec 4).

Zion—1. the hill on which the city of Jerusalem first stood; David's royal palace and the temple were both built on Mount Zion; 2. the entire city of Jerusalem.
Jer 50:5 They will ask the way to *Z*
Ro 11:26 "The deliverer will come from *Z*